PUBLIC PAPERS OF THE PRESIDENTS
OF THE
UNITED STATES

PUBLIC PAPERS OF THE PRESIDENTS
OF THE
UNITED STATES

William J. Clinton

1998

(IN TWO BOOKS)

BOOK II—JULY 1 TO DECEMBER 31, 1998

UNITED STATES GOVERNMENT PRINTING OFFICE
WASHINGTON : 2000

Published by the
Office of the Federal Register
National Archives and Records Administration

Foreword

The last half of 1998 was a time of great challenge in Washington, but of even greater prosperity and progress for our Nation. Rising personal incomes, the lowest unemployment in 28 years, and the first Federal budget surplus in 29 years, all served to validate the success of our 6-year-old economic strategy of fiscal discipline, expanded trade, and greater investent in our people. In October, I signed a budget reaffirming that strategy with vital new investments, including a down payment to hire 100,000 new, highly trained teachers to bring class sizes down to an average of 18 in the early grades. To maintain fiscal discipline, I rejected proposals from the congressional majority to spend the surplus before we had a plan in place to save Social Security. To build a bipartisan consensus for such a plan, I hosted the first-ever White House conference on the future of Social Security. To advance my goal of reinventing the Federal Government to better serve the American people, I signed landmark bills reforming the Internal Revenue Service and Federal job training programs.

During this period, challenges to peace and prosperity arose around the world, testing the mettle of American leadership. When terrorists associated with Osama bin Laden bombed U.S. embassies in Kenya and Tanzania, America struck back at his terrorist network. When Saddam Hussein refused to cooperate with U.N. weapons inspectors, American and British forces struck hard at Iraq's capacity to build weapons of mass destruction and threaten its neighbors militarily. When financial turmoil in Asia spread to Russia and Brazil, dampening U.S. exports and putting the entire global financial system at risk, America led efforts that stemmed the threat. We helped strengthen the International Monetary Fund's ability to combat financial contagion, and in October, I set out a six-point plan to dampen the cycle of boom and bust in world financial markets.

And when the Middle East peace process was in danger of collapsing, I invited Prime Minister Netanyahu of Israel and Chairman Arafat of the Palestine Liberation Organization to join me at the Wye River Plantation in Maryland. For 9 exhausting days we helped these two leaders make difficult decisions for peace, aided by the appearance of my friend, the late King Hussein of Jordan.

The agreement they signed not only put this holy and tortured land back on a path toward peace, but also reaffirmed my belief that it is often at the moment of greatest challenge that we are capable of making the greatest progress.

Preface

This book contains the papers and speeches of the 42d President of the United States that were issued by the Office of the Press Secretary during the period July 1–December 31, 1998. The material has been compiled and published by the Office of the Federal Register, National Archives and Records Administration.

The material is presented in chronological order, and the dates shown in the headings are the dates of the documents or events. In instances when the release date differs from the date of the document itself, that fact is shown in the textnote. Every effort has been made to ensure accuracy: Remarks are checked against a tape recording, and signed documents are checked against the original. Textnotes and cross references have been provided by the editors for purposes of identification or clarity. Speeches were delivered in Washington, DC, unless indicated. The times noted are local times. All materials that are printed full-text in the book have been indexed in the subject and name indexes, and listed in the document categories list.

The Public Papers of the Presidents series was begun in 1957 in response to a recommendation of the National Historical Publications Commission. An extensive compilation of messages and papers of the Presidents covering the period 1789 to 1897 was assembled by James D. Richardson and published under congressional authority between 1896 and 1899. Since then, various private compilations have been issued, but there was no uniform publication comparable to the Congressional Record or the United States Supreme Court Reports. Many Presidential papers could be found only in the form of mimeographed White House releases or as reported in the press. The Commission therefore recommended the establishment of an official series in which Presidential writings, addresses, and remarks of a public nature could be made available.

The Commission's recommendation was incorporated in regulations of the Administrative Committee of the Federal Register, issued under section 6 of the Federal Register Act (44 U.S.C. 1506), which may be found in title 1, part 10, of the Code of Federal Regulations.

A companion publication to the Public Papers series, the Weekly Compilation of Presidential Documents, was begun in 1965 to provide a broader range of Presidential materials on a more timely basis to meet the needs of the contemporary reader. Beginning with the administration of Jimmy Carter, the Public Papers series expanded its coverage to include additional material as printed in the Weekly Compilation. That coverage provides a listing of the President's daily schedule and meetings, when announced, and other items of general interest issued by the Office of the Press Secretary. Also included are lists of the President's nominations submitted to the Senate, materials released by the Office of the Press Secretary that are not printed full-text in the book, and proclamations, Executive orders, and other Presidential documents released by the Office of the Press Secretary and published in the *Federal Register*. This information appears in the appendixes at the end of the book.

Volumes covering the administrations of Presidents Hoover, Truman, Eisenhower, Kennedy, Johnson, Nixon, Ford, Carter, Reagan, and Bush are also included in the Public Papers series.

The Public Papers of the Presidents publication program is under the direction of Frances D. McDonald, Managing Editor, Office of the Federal Register. The series is produced by the Presidential and Legislative Publications Unit, Gwen H. Estep, Chief. The Chief Editor of this book was Karen Howard Ashlin, assisted by Brad Brooks, Anna Glover, Margaret A. Hemmig, Maxine Hill, Michael Hoover, Alfred Jones, Jennifer S. Mangum, Melanie L. Marcec, Michael J. Sullivan, and Karen A. Thornton.

The frontispiece and photographs used in the portfolio were supplied by the White House Photo Office. The typography and design of the book were developed by the Government Printing Office under the direction of Michael F. DiMario, Public Printer.

Raymond A. Mosley
Director of the Federal Register

John W. Carlin
Archivist of the United States

Contents

Cabinet

Secretary of State	Madeleine K. Albright
Secretary of the Treasury	Robert E. Rubin
Secretary of Defense	William S. Cohen
Attorney General	Janet Reno
Secretary of the Interior	Bruce Babbitt
Secretary of Agriculture	Dan Glickman
Secretary of Commerce	William M. Daley
Secretary of Labor	Alexis M. Herman
Secretary of Health and Human Services	Donna E. Shalala
Secretary of Housing and Urban Development	Andrew M. Cuomo
Secretary of Transportation	Rodney E. Slater
Secretary of Energy	Elizabeth A. Moler, Acting Bill Richardson (effective September 11)
Secretary of Education	Richard W. Riley
Secretary of Veterans Affairs	Togo D. West, Jr.
United States Representative to the United Nations	Bill Richardson
Administrator of the Environmental Protection Agency	Carol M. Browner
United States Trade Representative	Charlene Barshefsky

Director of the Office of Management
and Budget .... Jacob J. Lew

Chief of Staff .... Erskine B. Bowles
                                                      John D. Podesta
                                                      (effective November 1)

Chair of the Council of Economic Advisers ..... Janet Yellen

Director of National Drug Control Policy .... Barry R. McCaffrey

Administrator of the Small Business
Administration .... Aida Alvarez

Director of Central Intelligence .... George J. Tenet

Director of the Federal Emergency
Management Agency .... James Lee Witt

Administration of William J. Clinton

1998

Remarks to Business Leaders in Shanghai, China
July 1, 1998

Thank you very much. Thank you. Ladies and gentlemen, thank you for your warm welcome, and let me begin by thanking Charles Wu for inviting me here today. I am honored to be joined not only by Secretary Daley but by Secretary Albright and Ambassador Barshefsky, from whom you have already heard, and the distinguished congressional delegation and our fine Ambassador, Jim Sasser.

It is fitting that the American Chamber of Commerce here in Shanghai is the fastest growing one in Asia. Over the past 24 hours or so, I've had the chance to see examples of the kind of ingenuity and energy of those who live and work here, from the magnificent examples of architecture and culture to the people. Yesterday I hosted a discussion with a range of Chinese leaders in academia, in law, in the media, in culture and nongovernmental organizations, all working to create a more responsive, open, decentralized society.

And also yesterday some of you may have heard the radio call-in show that I had, where the mayor joined me. It was very much like call-in shows in America. People were concerned about quite immediate issues, by and large. My favorite caller said he did not want to talk to the President; he wanted to talk to the mayor about traffic issues. [*Laughter*] One of the greatest American politicians in the last 50 years, the late Speaker Tip O'Neill, once told all of our Democrats in the House that all politics was local. That's the most extreme expression I've seen in a long time, and I liked it very much.

Later today I will have the opportunity to speak with several new entrepreneurs and to families who have recently moved into their own home for the first time. All of this to me has been very, very encouraging. Many of you have helped to nurture Shanghai's success and, in so doing, have helped to nurture China's ongoing evolution to a more open, stable, and prosperous society. Your presence in Shanghai is

vitally important for the future of China and the United States and the larger world.

China has, of course, been one of our largest trading partners. They bring more jobs, better pay, more growth, greater prosperity back home to the American people. In the 21st century more than ever, our ability to compete in foreign markets will be a critical source of our strength and prosperity at home. We have, after all, in the United States just 4 percent of the world's population, but we produce 20 percent of its wealth. Clearly, we must do something with the other 96 percent of the people on this small planet in order to maintain our standard of living and our ability to stand up for our values around the world. We especially must reach out to the developing world, whose economies are projected to grow at 3 times the rate of the developed economies over the next 20 years, including, of course, the largest country, China.

America, as Secretary Daley has said, has been very blessed these last 5½ years. I am grateful to have had the chance to serve, and I'm very grateful for the support I have received from the Members of Congress here in this audience and, even more importantly, for the work the American people have done to bring our country back, bring our country together, and move our country forward.

But it is very important to note that a big part of all those numbers that Secretary Daley read off was the expanding, vigorous American presence in foreign markets. About 30 percent of the growth that produced those 16 million new jobs and the revenues necessary to balance the budget for the first time since 1969 and run a surplus came from expanded trade. And it is a cause we must keep at.

I also want to say that in addition to the positive impacts you have on the United States, your work here has a very positive impact in China. China's 20-year track record of unprecedented growth has been fueled in part by foreign products, know-how, investment, trade, and energy. These ties also have more subtle and perhaps more profound, long-lasting effects. They strengthen the rule of law, openness, and accountability. They expose China to fair labor practices and stronger environmental standards. They spread powerful agents of change, fax machines and photocopiers, computers and modems.

Over time, the more China enters the world community and the global economy, the more the world will strengthen freedom and openness in China. You are in the vanguard, therefore, of an historic process.

Our commercial relationship has also helped to strengthen and in turn has been strengthened by expanding diplomatic cooperation between our nations. I will do everything I can to encourage stronger trade ties between the United States and China. Just before my departure, the House Ways and Means Committee voted overwhelmingly in favor of normal trade treatment for China, MFN. I hope the rest of Congress soon will follow suit. Failure to renew that would sever our economic ties, denying us the benefits of China's growth, endangering our strategic partnership, turning our back on the world's largest nation at a time when cooperation for peace and stability is more important and more productive than ever.

China and, indeed, Shanghai face major challenges in advancing economic progress beyond the present point—we all know that: more restructuring of state-owned enterprises, developing a transparent legal and regulatory system, preserving the environment as the economy grows, building a strong financial system, opening markets, playing a responsible role in sustaining the international financial system. The United States is prepared to work with China in meeting these challenges because the success of China will affect not only the Chinese people and Chinese prosperity but America's well-being and global stability as well.

First, restructuring state enterprise is critical to building a modern economy, but it also is disrupting settled patterns of life and work, cracking the "iron rice bowl." In the short term, dismantling state enterprises puts people out of jobs—lots of them—and into competition for employment for private jobs. Those who lack the right education, skills, and support risk being left behind here, as they do, I might add, in the United States and other countries under-going changes because of the global economy and the information age.

China will have to devise new systems of training workers and providing social benefits and social security. We have asked our Council of Economic Advisers, the Treasury, Commerce, and Labor Departments to share their expertise and experiences with Chinese to help them navigate this transition.

Second, China is working to put in place a more transparent and predictable legal and regulatory system, with enforceable rights, clear procedures, and strong efforts to combat corruption. I am pleased that American businesses have pledged financial support for the rule of law initiative President Jiang and I have launched. It is terribly important. It will improve legal education and judicial training in China, streamline the regulatory system, and improve legal aid for the poor. Just as important, it can be the basis for strengthening the protection of personal rights and constraining arbitrary government. We've also initiated a dialog between our labor ministers that will address worker rights. I challenge you to set a good example here to show that respect for core labor standards goes hand in hand with good and successful business practices.

Third, as we go forward we must ensure that economic development does not lead to environmental catastrophe. Respiratory illness from air pollution is now China's number one health problem. Every major body of water is polluted. The water table is dropping all over the country. China is about to assume the unfortunate distinction of replacing the United States as the largest emitter of greenhouse gases that are dangerously warming our planet.

Increasingly, pollution at home, whether in China or the United States or elsewhere, becomes a worldwide environmental problem, as well as a health, environmental, and economic problem for people in their home countries. Climate change is a real and growing issue. The 5 hottest years recorded on the planet since 1400 have all occurred in the 1990's. If present trends continue, 1998 will be the hottest year ever recorded.

Now, unfortunately, it is still the dominant opinion in virtually all developing countries—and I might add, in many sectors of the United States, including among many in the Congress—that there is an iron, unbreakable link between economic growth and industrial age energy practices. If that is the link, we can hardly expect decisionmakers in countries with a lot of poor people trying to come to grips with the enormous changes of the global economy to do anything other than either deny the environmental problems or say that their children will have to fix them. Happily, it is not true. It is simply not true.

We have example after example after example of countries whose economies are doing well as they adopt more sensible environmental and energy practices, and companies in the United States who are making a significant share of their profits through conservation and the implementation of new technologies, everything from simple initiatives like using more natural gas, using better lighting and insulation material, use of waste heat from power generation facilities to provide heating, cooling, and lighting, and about to be widely available, fuel-injection engines which will cut pollution from automobiles by 80 percent.

All these things are available. Shanghai could be the center of an energy revolution in China which would actually lead to faster economic growth, less resources invested in cleaning up the mess later, and less resources invested in taking care of sick people who won't get sick if more is done to preserve the environment.

But we have to do something to break the idea in people's minds that the only way to grow the economy of a developing country is to adopt industrial age energy use patterns. It is not true; it is a huge problem. It is still a problem in the United States, and I ask you to lead the way.

All the evidence is, if you look at the record of our country going back to 1970, every time the United States has adopted higher environmental standards, businesses have created new technologies to meet them, and we have actually had faster economic growth with better and better paying jobs as a result. This is something we will have to do together.

I am pleased that the energy and environment initiative we launched last October has begun already to yield concrete clean energy and clean air projects, which I'll have an opportunity to talk about more tomorrow in Guilin. But I wanted to take this opportunity to ask all of you to try to change the thinking, because I have no right as President of the United States to ask China to slow its economic growth. I don't

have a right to do that. But as a citizen of the world and the leader of my country, I have a responsibility to ask us all to work together for a planet that our grandchildren can still enjoy living on. And so do you.

Fourth, you know better than I that China faces significant challenges in strengthening its financial and its banking systems. America learned some hard lessons from our savings and loan crisis in the 1980's. The Asian financial crisis today demonstrates the havoc a weak and inadequately supervised banking system can create. We want to help China avoid similar errors by improving regulations, opening to foreign competition, training bank supervisors and employees, and in the process, I might add, developing the capacity to fund more private entrepreneurs in small businesses.

Fifth, as you are well aware, China's economy still is burdened with complicated and overlapping barriers. More open markets are important to the United States, which buys today about a third of China's exports and, in turn, should have a fair shot at China's markets. It is important to China as it builds an economy that must compete globally. In America, as in China, rapid change and the disruptions it brings make it tempting to turn inward and to slow down. But for China, as for America, the promise for the future lies in helping our citizens to master the challenges of the global economy, not to deny them or run away from them.

President Jiang and I agree on the importance of China's entry into the World Trade Organization. But that can only happen on strong terms, the same terms that other nations of the world abide by to benefit from WTO membership. Of course, there will have to be an individual agreement that recognizes the transitions China must undertake, but the terms have to be clear and unambiguous.

I'm disappointed that we didn't make more progress on this issue, but we'll keep working at it until we reach a commercially viable agreement. I also want to emphasize something I'm sure every Member of Congress here would agree with, which is that we cannot build support for permanent MFN for China in the Congress on the basis of anything less.

Finally, China must help to meet the challenge of an international financial system with no respect for borders. I must say that I appreciate the very constructive role China has played in promoting financial stability in the region, through direct assistance, multilateral cooperation, participation in the international financial institutions. Premier Zhu and President Jiang told me China is determined to play its part in avoiding another round of competitive devaluations, which I believe would also be damaging to China, as well as to the region.

Both our countries have important responsibilities to counter the threat to the international financial system, and I am confident that working together, we can do so. Of course, we have work to do to meet all these challenges, but you can help, as I'm sure you know, explaining to Chinese colleagues the important and tangible benefits in the information age of increasing individual freedom, and limiting arbitrary governmental decisions.

It isn't simply a philosophical matter that no one has a monopoly on the truth. If you look at what is driving the information age, it is ideas. The Chairman of the Federal Reserve, Alan Greenspan, was having a conversation with me several weeks ago, and he told me something that I didn't know—he usually tells me something that I don't know when I visit with him— [*laughter*]—but he said that, actually, economists had measured the physical size of national output and compared changes in GNP or GDP with changes in physical size. He says that in the last 15 years, while America's income has gone way up, the bulk of what we've produced has hardly increased at all. Why? Because wealth is being generated by ideas.

That will become increasingly true everywhere. In that kind of world we must all value the ability of people to think and speak and explore and debate, not only because it is, we believe in America, morally right but because it is the only thing in the end that will actually work to maximize the potential of the people of China. And they deserve a chance, after so much struggle and so much hard work, to live up to their potential and to see their nation live up to its potential.

I also believe it is important to explain to American colleagues and friends back home the importance of our engagement with China. There are some people who actually question whether I ought to have come on this trip and who had, I thought, prescriptive advice which would have completely undermined the effectiveness of the trip.

It is important for Americans to remember, as we go around the world telling people that no one has a monopoly on the truth, that we don't either and that we live in a world where the unique position of the United States as the world's remaining military superpower, with all of our economic strength, is such that we can maximize our influence only by reaching out a hand of cooperation as well as standing strong when the moment requires it. We have to make most of our progress with most people by working with them, and that requires us to seek to understand and communicate and reciprocate and to live by the values we espouse.

So I hope you will do both these things. I hope you will bring energy and commitment to these tasks. I hope you will be immensely successful at what we call your day job as well, because we have a lot to do to help America and China reach their full potential in the 21st century. But a great deal is riding on our success, and I believe we will succeed.

Thank you. Thank you very much.

NOTE: The President spoke at 9:37 a.m. in the Atrium of the Portman Ritz Carlton hotel. In his remarks, he referred to Charles Wu, president, American Chamber of Commerce; and Premier Zhu Rongji and President Jiang Zemin of China.

Interview With Central China Television in Shanghai
July 1, 1998

President's Visit to China

Q. Mr. President, we are very honored to have this opportunity to talk to you, now that your trip in China is almost halfway. And I guess you have gained a clearer picture of to-day's China and what it is all about. So we noticed that when you visit China, you chose Xi'an as the first stop. Can you tell us why you decided to visit Xi'an first, in your first trip ever to China?

The President. I wanted to start with a place that embodied the history of China, the culture of China, the permanent character, if you will, for the Chinese people. And I did it for personal reasons, because I think it's always helpful for me to understand where people are and where they're going—if you understand where they come from.

But I also did it because I knew the American people would see this. And one big goal of this trip for me was to have the American people learn more about China and the Chinese people learn more about America. So that's why I went to Xi'an first.

Eastern and Western Philosophies

Q. Now, Mr. President, speaking of Xi'an, I remember at your speech at the Xi'an airport you quoted "Li Shi," which is an ancient Chinese philosophy book. Now, in your opinion, based on the several days of observation you've had in China, do you think there's still a difference between Eastern and Western philosophy? And if so, how can these two philosophies cohabitate with each other in the world today?

The President. Oh, I think there are some differences. Western philosophy is probably somewhat more explicitly individualistic. And much Western philosophy is rooted either in the religious tradition of Judaism and Christianity, or in kind of the materialist tradition. But still, I think, at bottom the best of Western and Eastern philosophy attempt to get at the truth of human life and human nature and attempt to find a way for people to live more fully up to that human truth. And so I think if you strip it away, we have a lot to learn from Eastern philosophy and perhaps China can learn some things from Western philosophy, because they help us to look at the world in a different way and acquire a fuller view of what the truth is.

President's Introduction to China

Q. And you do mention that it's a very good way to learn the history and culture of a nation in order to understand more about the nation. So, Mr. President, in your memory can you recall the first time you ever learned or heard about China? I mean, for instance, is it by a book or a movie or some other means?

The President. Oh, no, no. I remember—it's when I was a young boy, and I was reading— my mother and father, they got me a set of encyclopedias when I was a boy, where you go—it's world topics, A through Z—no computers, you know?

Q. And China is C. *[Laughter]*

The President. And I remember looking at the maps of the world and reading about China. I was probably, I don't know, 8 or 9 years old. And I was fascinated by what I read. I always wanted to come here from that time on.

Q. Now, Mr. President, now that you're in China—this is your 7th day in China, and during the last 7 days you've talked to people from all walks of life; you've discussed issues on a wide range with many various people. Is the China in your impression now different from when your mother first gave you that map when you were 8 or 9 years old?

The President. Oh, yes.

Q. And what's the most impressive difference?

The President. Well, for one thing, at that time I had very little understanding. It's still the most populous country in the world, but I think one is immediately struck by the dramatic economic growth and by the opening of China to the rest of the world, in terms of learning, the quest for information. You know, I went to that Internet cafe this morning. And watching the Chinese young people get on the Internet and go all over the world looking for information, this is, I think, a very important development.

I also believe there is a genuine increase in people's control over their own lives. Incomes are going up; people have more choices in education, more choice in jobs, the freedom to travel. The state-run industries are going down in relative importance, and cooperatives and private businesses are coming up. And there's more say at the grassroots level now over who the local leaders are and what their policies are. So I think there's a genuine movement toward openness and freedom in China, which obviously, as an American and as an American President, I hope will continue and increase and which I believe is right—morally right, but I also think it's good for China.

Q. Do you have any surprises, except for this?

The President. Well, I don't know about surprises. I think I was—I was a little surprised— yes, I have two. First, I did not expect when I came here that my entire press conference with President Jiang would be played live on television, and then my speech at Beijing University. And then, of course, yesterday I had the call-in radio show here in Shanghai. So I did not anticipate being able to have that sort of open, sweeping communication with the Chinese people. And I'm very pleased, and I appreciate President Jiang's decision to let the press conference be aired and all the other decisions that were made. That, I think, was very good. I think it was also good for the Chinese leaders. I mean, the mayor of Shanghai and I had a wonderful time on the radio yesterday.

So I think bringing the people into the process of making these decisions and having these discussions I think is very, very important, because if you think about a lot of the problems that we face—we could take American issues; we could take Chinese issues—how are you going to guarantee that all these people who work for state-owned industries get good jobs? How are you going to deal with the housing problems if people no longer have a housing guarantee connected to their job, but there are vacant apartments in Shanghai, but you can't seem to put the two together? How do you solve these problems?

Very often there's not any simple answer. And people feel better just to know that their views are heard, their concerns are heard, and that there can be a discussion where people work together toward the answers. So I think this whole democratic process, in my view, is very, very important to make society work when things are changing as quickly as they are now.

Comparison to President Jiang

Q. Now, Mr. President, you've obviously made very indepth observations of China today. You mentioned a lot of the problems that this society is dealing with today, for instance, state-owned enterprise reforms and so on and so forth. So whose job do you think is tougher, if you have to make a comparison, yours or President Jiang Zemin's?

The President. Oh, I don't know. I think that he faces enormous challenges here at home, of a scope that Americans have a hard time imagining. Probably the only element of my job which is more difficult right now is that since the cold war is over and America has this role which is temporary—it won't last forever—as the only superpower in the world, I have a lot of work to do to deal with America's challenges and problems at home and then to try to get the American people to support our Nation

doing what we should do as a force for peace and prosperity and stability around the world.

So our people have normally been rather like the Chinese people, you know—we want to attend to our own affairs and not be so involved in the rest of the world unless we just had to be, throughout the last 200 years. But in the last 50 years, we've learned that we can only succeed at home if we have positive relationships around the world, which is the main reason I wanted to come to China.

U.S. Leadership in the World

Q. Now, allow me to follow up on that, Mr. President. You mentioned America is the only superpower left for now in the world. And America's leadership role in the world has often been talked about in domestic politics, if not sometimes in international occasions, too. Now, in your opinion, does the world today need a leader, and, if so, how should the United States assume the responsibility and why?

The President. Well, I think the short answer to your question is, yes, the world needs a leader, but not in the sense of one country telling everyone else what to do. That is—let's take something that didn't happen in Asia. If you look at the problem, the civil war in Bosnia, the terrible problem in Bosnia, we had the military resources to work with NATO our military allies in Europe, to move in and stop the war. Because we were the largest party to NATO, if we hadn't been willing to take the initiative, it wouldn't have happened. On the other hand, we couldn't have done it alone. We had to have people work with us.

I'll give you another example. We want to do everything we can to end the stalemate between North and South Korea. But if China had not been willing to work with us, I don't think we could have started these four-party talks again or we would be very effective in urging North Korea and South Korea to talk directly. But because we can work with China, we can have more influence.

Here, I come to China, and I say, we want to be your friends; we share the security interest, and we're working together with India and Pakistan on the nuclear tests; we're working to stop the transfer of dangerous weapons; we're working to cooperate in environmental projects; and we know we have differences, and I want to tell you why I believe in religious freedom or political freedom. If you think about it, that's a leadership issue for the United States. But the success of the leadership depends upon having a partnership with China.

So it's a different sort of world leadership than in the past where it's just a question of who has the biggest army gets to send a list of instructions to another country, and you think it will be done. That's not the way the world works now. You have to have—sometimes you have to stand strong for what you believe in, in terms of sending the soldiers into Bosnia or imposing economic sanctions on South Africa, as both China and the U.S. did in the time of apartheid. But most days you get more done by finding a way to engage countries and work with them and persuade them that you're doing the right thing. It's important to have allies in the world we live in, to be more cooperative; even from a leader's point of view, you have to have allies and people that will work with you.

Q. According to my understanding, Mr. President, the role of America in the world, I mean, the United States in the world, in international affairs is not, as some people believe or argue, the role of world cop according to your understanding?

The President. No. We're not the world's policeman. But sometimes we have to be prepared to do things that other countries can't or won't do. For example, I think we did absolutely the right thing these last several years to insist that we keep economic sanction on Iraq until they give up their weapons of mass destruction program. I think we did the right thing to go into Bosnia. I think we did the right thing to restore democracy in Haiti.

But most times the problems cannot be solved by military means. And most times, even if we take initiative, we should be trying to create a world in the 21st century where there is a structure where peace and prosperity and the ability to solve new problems—like the environmental problems—where that kind of structure works and where you minimize weapons of mass destruction, drug trafficking, ethnic wars like we had from Rwanda to the Middle East to Northern Ireland.

And so the United States role, I think, is to try to create a structure where, more likely than not, the right things will be done when problems arise—not to just do it all ourselves or tell other people what to do.

Achievements of the China Visit

Q. Okay, Mr. President, let's come back to your trip in China. Now you have already finished, let's say, already you have been in China for almost one week. What do you think are the major achievements through your trip here?

The President. I think there are several. First of all, in the whole area of nonproliferation, the fact that we have agreed not to target nuclear weapons at each other is very important. It's important for, I think, three reasons. One is, it eliminates the prospect that there will ever be a mistaken launch of a nuclear weapon. Second, it's a great confidence-building measure. It's a symbol, if you will, of the growing friendship of the two countries, and it should make other countries in the Asia-Pacific region relax a little. And third, since India and Pakistan did these nuclear tests, it reaffirms that we believe that's not the right way to go. We should be moving away from nuclear weapons, not toward them. So that's the first thing.

The second thing is, China has agreed to work with us to stop the transfer of technologies to countries that might misuse it, to not assist unsafeguarded nuclear facilities like Pakistan's, and to consider joining the worldwide system that prevents the exportation of dangerous technologies. So that's important.

We announced more efforts on our energy and environmental initiative. This is very important, you know. You have long-related problems with the number one health problem in China because of air pollution. Your major waterways have pollution; the water table is down. We have to find a way to grow the economy and replenish the environment. So this—I predict to you, 10 years from now people will look back and say, "That's one of the biggest things they did; they agreed to work more there." We agreed to deepen our cooperation in science and technology, where we've already achieved a lot together. So I think in all these areas this is important.

There is a huge potential benefit to the Chinese people and, therefore, to the American people in the rule of law project we're doing, where we're working with Chinese people to set up the right kind of legal procedures to deal with all the questions that are going to come up as you privatize the economy. For example, my wife met the other day, I think in Beijing——

Q. Beijing University.

The President. ——yes, and she was telling me about a case that was raised where a woman was divorced from her husband because there had been problems in the home. And they had one child, but they couldn't move out of the home, even though they had a divorce, because the house came to the husband through his job.

So as you change the society, there will have to be all kinds of legal changes made. And I think if we work together on that, I think we can find a way to enhance freedom and stability. So all these things are important.

But finally, I think that in the end it may be that the biggest achievement was the increased understanding and the sense of a shared future. I mean, I think the press conference that President Jiang and I did will be viewed as historic for a long time to come. And the fact that he wanted to do it, he enjoyed it, and it was on national television, I think, was very important.

Q. And I think Chinese people and American people enjoyed that.

The President. I think so. So I think it's a very productive trip.

China-U.S. Relations

Q. Now, Mr. President, you mentioned the achievements in the last several areas, for instance, detargeting of nuclear missiles at each other and cooperation in scientific and environmental areas, and increased understanding. In your joint statements with President Jiang Zemin, you both also acknowledged that China and the United States have areas of disagreement. In one word, you have agreed to agree and you have agreed to disagree.

Now, in your opinion, in the world today, China is now the largest developing nation and the United States is the largest developed nation. For these two nations to have areas of agreements and disagreements, how should they develop their relationship? Is the world too small for two large nations?

The President. No. No. For one thing, in every relationship, in every business partnership, in every family, in every enterprise, you have agreements and disagreements. I'll bet you at your station you have agreements and disagreements. So what you have to do is, you identify your agreements, and then you identify your disagreements. And then you say, here's how

we're going to deal with these, and you keep working to try to bridge the gap.

Our major differences are in trade, over some terms of trade issues, and in the human rights area, how we define it, how China defines it, where we should go from here. But if you back up 3 years ago, we've made significant progress in both those areas. And if you back up 5 years ago, we had a lot of difference in the proliferation area, most of which have been eliminated.

So there's been a lot of progress in this relationship in the last 5½ years. And I would say to the people of China and the people of the United States, the world is not too small for two big countries. It is a small world, and we should all act that way. That should make us both more responsible, with a greater sense of responsibility for our own people, for our partnership with each other, and for the rest of the world, as well.

Q. Now, Mr. President, you mentioned the areas of differences between China and the United States. However, do you think that this trip to China has helped you understand why China is the way China is?

The President. Oh, absolutely. There's no question about that. And I hope that this trip to China has helped the Chinese people understand why Americans are the way we are.

Chelsea Clinton and China's Youth

Q. Mr. President, we have noticed that your daughter, Chelsea, accompanied you to Beijing and to all of the China trip, and also particularly to the Beijing University when you made the speech.

The President. Yes.

Q. And in your speech, high hope was placed on the young generation of both China and the United States. And we wondered whether Chelsea—did Chelsea ever mention to you her impression of the Chinese youth in her interaction with the Chinese college students?

The President. Oh, yes, she very much wanted to come here. She wanted to make this trip, and her university work was concluded in time for her to be able to come. But she has very much enjoyed getting out, meeting young Chinese people, and seeing what's going on. She said to me just yesterday how incredibly exciting she thought Shanghai was and how she wished she could stay here a while when we leave and go back, just to see more of it.

And I think any young person in the world coming here would be excited by it and would be excited to see how eager the young Chinese people are to build good lives for themselves, to learn more about the rest of the world. The hunger for knowledge and for the improvement of one's capacity to do things among these young people is truly amazing. The energy they generate is astonishing, and it makes me feel very hopeful about the future.

Relationship With President Jiang

Q. One last question, Mr. President. Do you think that your conversation with President Jiang face to face in such a summit is easier than the hotline, which has to go over the Pacific?

The President. Oh, yes, always better. I think face-to-face is always better. But I also believe that once you get to know someone and you feel comfortable with them—you know, President Jiang and I have a very friendly relationship, and it permits us to deal with all these issues so that the hotline then becomes very useful.

If we were strangers, for example, the hotline would not be so helpful because it would be awkward. But when there's a problem, as there was with the nuclear tests—and I didn't want to wait until I got to China to talk to President Jiang about how we should respond to the India and Pakistani nuclear tests, so I called him on the hotline. And because we had already met several times and we felt—and he had had this very successful state visit to the United States, the hotline was very, very important, very helpful. So I think the telephone is important. The Internet is important. All communications can be good, but none of it can take the place of face-to-face communications.

Q. Thank you very much for giving us this opportunity to sit together with you, face to face. Thank you very much.

The President. Thank you.

NOTE: The interview began at approximately 3:30 p.m. at the Shanghai Stock Exchange, but the transcript was embargoed for release until 7:30 p.m. In his remarks, the President referred to Mayor Xu Kuangdi of Shanghai. A tape was not available for verification of the content of this interview.

Remarks to the Building Construction and Finance Community in Shanghai
July 1, 1998

Thank you very much, Vice Mayor Zhou; Deputy Magistrate Wang; to developer Gu Cai Xin; to the Tang family, whose home the Members of the U.S. Congress visited; and to Ms. Yu and her family, who were very kind to take me into their home; and to all of you. It's a pleasure to be here today.

I would like to begin by thanking the folk music band for the wonderful music. Thank you very much. And I would like to say to all of you who are moving into new homes, *Gong xi, gong xi.* Congratulations.

More than 20 years ago, I bought my first home. I actually bought it because my girlfriend liked the house. [*Laughter*] We were driving by the house one day—it was a very small house—and she said, "I like that house very much." So I found out the house did not cost too much money, and I bought it. And then I said to my girlfriend, "I bought that house you like; now you'll have to marry me." [*Laughter*] And she did. So I hope that your homes bring you as much joy as mine did 23 years ago.

I came here with your local officials and Ambassador Sasser and Ambassador Li and the Members of Congress to emphasize the importance of homeownership to the future of the people of China and to the prosperity of your country. As you could see from what Ms. Yu said, owning a home is a source of pride to a family and a tribute to its industry and hard work. But all China benefits from more homeowners because that means more jobs, a stronger economy, stronger families. And of course, when people own their own homes, they are free to take new jobs without worrying about losing housing benefits. We also see around the world that homeowners take more responsibility for the communities in which they live.

In America, we have worked hard to expand the dream of homeownership, and today, 65 percent of all Americans—an all-time record—live in homes that they own. This has made our country stronger, and I know greater homeownership will also strengthen China.

Because we want to support greater homeownership, I am proud to announce today that we are creating a U.S.-China residential building council to promote new technologies and energy-efficient materials to build sturdy homes that are affordable to live in. Our Department of Commerce will also bring Americans to China to discuss how to build a stronger system of financing homes, from strengthening property rights to developing stronger mortgage markets. This will help to make more homes available to more Chinese families.

I am determined to build a strong partnership and a good friendship between the United States and China that will actually make a positive difference in people's lives.

Congratulations to all of you on your new homes and on the bright futures you are building for your families.

Thank you very much, and we thank the weather for holding off until after the event is over. [*Laughter*]

Thank you.

NOTE: The President spoke at 3:47 p.m. in the Jin Hui Gardens. In his remarks, he referred to Vice Mayor Zhou Muyao of Shanghai; Wang Zuchao, deputy magistrate for urban construction affairs, Minhang District of Shanghai; Gu Cai Xin, Jin Hui Gardens developer; homeowner Yu Jianyuan; and Chinese Ambassador to the U.S. Li Xhaoxing.

Statement on New Medicare Benefits
July 1, 1998

I am pleased to announce that starting today Medicare will cover two new preventive benefits to help detect osteoporosis and manage diabetes. These important benefits were part of the Balanced Budget Act I signed into law last year, which contained the most significant reforms in Medicare since the program's enactment in 1965.

Medicare's new prevention benefits will provide older Americans the tools they need to fight some of our most devastating chronic diseases. While one out of two women over the age of 50 will have an osteoporosis-related fracture during her lifetime, many women are not aware that they have this disease until they have a broken bone or fracture. I am extremely pleased that the First Lady, Mrs. Gore, and

Secretary Shalala will be helping to publicize this new benefit to help women detect this disease early. Also, the new diabetes benefit is critical to the over 7 million Medicare beneficiaries who suffer from this disease. This benefit is part of our diabetes initiative that the American Diabetes Association believes is "as important to people with diabetes as the discovery of insulin in 1921."

This month marks the 33d anniversary of the Medicare program—one of our Nation's most important commitments to older Americans and people with disabilities. I am extremely pleased that we can strengthen this important program and help some of our most vulnerable Americans stay healthier and stronger.

Message on the Observance of Independence Day, 1998
July 1, 1998

I am delighted to join my fellow Americans across the nation and around the world in celebrating Independence Day.

Throughout the year, we set aside special times to remember and celebrate our different ethnic roots. But on Independence Day, we rejoice in our common heritage as Americans and in the values and history we share.

We have all benefited from the wisdom of our nation's founders, who crafted a blueprint for democracy that has served us well for more than 200 years and continues to inspire newly independent nations around the world. We are all heirs to the rights articulated in our Constitution and reaffirmed by courageous men and women of every generation who have struggled to secure justice and equality for all. We are all forever indebted to the millions of Americans in uniform who have shed their blood to defend our freedom and preserve our values across America and around the globe.

But we Americans are bound together not only by a shared past, but also by a common future. Blessed with peace and prosperity, we have an unprecedented opportunity to prepare for the challenges of the next century: to keep America free and secure, to improve health care and education, to bring the opportunities of the Information Age into every home and classroom, and to strengthen the bonds of our national community as we grow more racially and ethnically diverse.

On this Independence Day, as we celebrate our rights and freedoms and look forward to a new century of limitless possibilities, Hillary joins me in wishing you a wonderful Fourth of July.

BILL CLINTON

Letter to Congressional Leaders Transmitting a Report on the Conventional Armed Forces in Europe Treaty
July 1, 1998

Dear _____:

In accordance with Condition (14)(B) of the resolution of advice and consent to ratification of the Document Agreed Among the States Parties to the Treaty on Conventional Armed Forces in Europe (CFE) of November 19, 1990, adopted by the Senate of the United States on May 14, 1997, enclosed is the Report on CFE Treaty Designated Permanent Storage Sites (DPSS).

The Report is provided in both a classified and unclassified form.

Sincerely,

WILLIAM J. CLINTON

NOTE: Identical letters were sent to Newt Gingrich, Speaker of the House of Representatives; Richard A. Gephardt, House minority leader; and Jesse Helms, chairman, and Joseph R. Biden, Jr., ranking member, Senate Committee on Foreign Relations.

Letter to Congressional Leaders Transmitting a Report on the Emigration Policies and Trade Status of Mongolia
July 1, 1998

Dear Mr. Speaker: (*Dear Mr. President:*)

On September 4, 1996, I determined and reported to the Congress that Mongolia was "not in violation of" the freedom of emigration criteria of sections 402 and 409 of the Trade Act of 1974. This action allowed for the continuation of most-favored-nation status for Mongolia and certain other activities without the requirement of an annual waiver.

As required by law, I am submitting an updated report to Congress concerning the emigration laws and policies of Mongolia. You will find that the report indicates continued Mongolian compliance with U.S. and international standards in the area of emigration.

Sincerely,

WILLIAM J. CLINTON

NOTE: Identical letters were sent to Newt Gingrich, Speaker of the House of Representatives, and Albert Gore, Jr., President of the Senate. This letter was released by the Office of the Press Secretary on July 2.

Remarks in a Roundtable Discussion With Environmental Specialists in Guilin, China
July 2, 1998

[*The discussion is joined in progress.*]

Participant. ——the local government to stop the logging. But the local government is so poor, they ask for compensation. And then finally, the central Government agreed to give them 11 million RMB per year to stop the logging.

The President. Good.

Participant. So now, well, for the time being, the monkeys are safe. This is one thing we have done. And I brought with me a picture of the monkeys and will give it to you as a gift.

The President. Oh, thank you.

Participant. So this is the only red-lipped primate besides human beings. And the total number of it is less than 12——

The President. My cousins. [*Laughter*] How many total number?

Participant. Less than 1,200. Less than 1,200.

The President. You know, in our country we have exactly the same issue. We have, in the Pacific Northwest and the West, California, Oregon, Washington—the U.S., we have—about 90 percent of our old-growth forest is gone. So now we have a law, a national law on endangered species, and it also protects the forest.

And we still have some logging in the forest, but you can't go in and just cut all the trees down. You have to be very careful, tree by tree, as the aging process goes, because I don't know how old the trees are, but these trees in the U.S. sometimes take 200 years for full growth. When our native tribes were there—Native American tribes—they would only cut the trees after seven generations of growth. And, of course, that's not enough for an industrial society. So now, we have pine forests; we just grow them faster. In 20 to 30 years, they can be harvested. And we try to get people to stay away from the old growth.

So, in this case, as I understand it, the provincial government has the first say, but the National Government can come in and stop it.

Participant. Yes. And actually, the county government, they own—they run the state timber companies there.

The President. What about tree planting projects, who does that? At what level is that done?

Participant. Well, at different levels. The central Government, local government, and also NGO's are all involved in this tree planting. But tree planting is so slow that all these older forests—they may have some trees over 400 years old, and all these newly planted trees are so small, there's no comparison with the forest.

The President. I agree with that. Interestingly enough, we now believe that tree planting may be most important in cities. We just had a study done in the U.S. which shows that a tree planted in a city will take in 10 times as much carbon dioxide as a tree planted in the countryside. Now, you say, well, of course, because that's where the smog is. But the important thing is we did not know until this study was done that the tree could take in 10 times as much and still process it.

I noticed in Shanghai yesterday—I say this because Shanghai, you know, is growing very fast, and they have all these wonderful new buildings—but when I drove to one of the building complexes yesterday to meet a family in their new home, and I drove past a lot of the old residential areas, and in all the old areas there were lots of trees, not only trees down the street but trees up against the buildings.

So we're looking at whether in our country we should be supporting more of these tree planting operations in the cities because they do much more to clean the air than we had thought they did.

[*The discussion continued.*]

The President. Well, one of the things I think will really help is, your government is moving to ban lead in the gasoline, going to unleaded gasoline. And that will help a great deal. And that's a very forward step.

But also children's lungs, they get polluted with all the things in the atmosphere. And you're right, that will make—smoking will become, interestingly enough, even more dangerous, more difficult because of all the pollution in the atmosphere.

So one of the things that I hope we can do in our partnership with the Chinese Government is to work on the technologies that will clean up the air in ways that we have been able to do without hurting the economy. We think there are ways to do that.

In fact, one of the things that I hope—I'm glad we have one business person here because one of the things we have seen is that we have actually created a lot of new businesses for cleaning the environment, and it creates a lot of jobs, provides a lot of opportunity for people to get an education and do this work.

[*The discussion continued.*]

The President. I believe that China has a unique opportunity, because you're developing rapidly but later in time than other countries, to avoid some of the terrible mistakes we made. And if I could just mention, in the conservation area, our traditional energy use that causes pollution is about one-third in vehicles, transportation; about one-third in buildings, both housing and office buildings; and about one-third in factories and in powerplants. And I think that if you—again, in China, it's probably more in factories and powerplants—a bigger percentage—probably now, but it will come toward these numbers. If you just take them each in turn, in the vehicles, you have opportunities that, I think, that will come to you because of the development of fuel-injection engines, which will take 80 percent of the pollution away, or natural gas-powered vehicles, which, I think, are worth looking at.

In the residential areas—yesterday in Shanghai, I spoke to the American Chamber of Commerce in Shanghai, and there on a visit was the businessman who is the head of our homebuilders association in the whole U.S. Just a few weeks ago, we went to California, which has a warm climate like much of China, and we started—we announced a low-cost housing project for people with modest incomes. And in these houses, they have solar panels that now look like ordinary shingles on the roof and can be produced and sold for very little money, but they save huge amounts of money—energy; you know, then the powerplant can be used to power the country's industry if you use it. They have windows which let in more light but keep out more heat and cold. Now, they cost a little more, but over a 10-year period, they save huge amounts of energy.

All these things could be jobs for Chinese people coming out of the state-owned enterprises. Someone could come in and start making these solar panels that go on the roof; someone should start making these windows. They have light bulbs that cost—in our country, they cost twice as much, but they last 4 or 5 times longer, and they don't emit the same amount of pollution.

And then, finally, in the manufacturing industries, there are whole businesses in America—like you said, they make money going into these plants and saying, here are 100 things you can do and you will cut your energy use by 20 percent and increase your profits by 20 percent.

And in powerplants, in our old powerplants, as much as 70 percent of the energy that goes in them, as you know, is lost in waste heat. So now we have huge facilities in America being heated and cooled with the waste heat.

I was in a cafe yesterday in Shanghai that had a picture of a famous American basketball player, Michael Jordan. Everybody knows who he is. Almost no one knows that the United Center where he plays basketball is completely heated and powered by waste heat, recovered from the normal electric generating capacity.

So these are things that we would like to work with you on, because these are all mistakes Americans made that we had to go back and undo. But since China is now building new factories, building new powerplants, building new homes, selling new cars, if you can do these things in the proper way the first time, you will have undreamed-of efficiencies. And it will help the economy, not hurt it.

So I thank you for what you're doing.

[*A participant noted the improvement of water and air quality in Guilin since the 1970's, discussed the city's current environmental problems and the impact of tourism on energy, and expressed the hope that China-U.S. cooperation on environmental issues would improve because of the President's visit.*]

The President. One of the things we find—I'd like to ask Mr. Kong to talk next and then come back to Mr. Zhou, because I want to pursue this. I think it's a very good thing if one business does the right thing here, but if you don't have legislation, sometimes it can be unfair to one business. Because if one business does the right thing and the others don't, then the business that's the most responsible could have a hard time making a profit. But if everyone in the province or country has to do it, then everyone is in the same footing.

I would like to ask two questions. One is, if you were to adopt legislation, say, limiting the discharge of factories into the water and requiring that it be treated, would it be done at the provincial level or the national level? And two, are there funds available from the National Government to help communities like Guilin finance sewage treatment centers for the tourists or for the people who live here?

Because 20 years ago in the U.S., this was a horrible problem. And I grew up in a little town—a town not so little, about 35,000—that

had 3 lakes. And the lake with the largest number of people living on it and the largest number of tourists was totally polluted, but we could not afford to fix it. But the National Government said—they gave us, over time, about 65 percent of the cost of it, and we came up with the rest, and we cleaned up the lake. So now the children can swim there. People don't get sick if they ingest the water. But we had to have some help.

Where would the laws come from, provincial or national level? And is there now a fund which helps you with the sewage treatment?

[*A participant responded that China had national legislation governing water and air pollution, noise control, marine environment, and wildlife protection, in addition to provincial level legislation. The participant said that all factories had to comply with the same standards and that funding from the National Government was supplemented by some local taxation and factory fees.*]

The President. It can be more stringent?

Participant. Can be more stringent. It only can be more stringent.

The President. But not weaker? That's good, yes.

Participant. But funds from the central Government, basically—the investment for the environment basically is the responsibility for the local government, including fees. The central Government gave them a little money. It basically is not a common case. The reason is that—so in this case the central Government gave them some money. But basically it was provided by themselves, locally.

The President. You actually—you're a lawyer, and you helped to write these laws, right? [*Laughter*] So what do you think the next step should be? What is the next most important thing to be done?

Participant. I think the central Government should provide some additional funding to local government—is my personal will. And—[*inaudible*]—people, they share the same idea. But we have some different ideas from the economic people, from—[*inaudible*]—people. So we still have different views and positions on this issue.

The President. Let me say, in our country there is still a big fight over every new step, because there are always people who are afraid that if we take a new step, it will hurt the economy. But in the end—he talked about the tourists—if you want the tourists to come to Guilin, you have to have a clean environment. If you want a stronger economy, you have to produce healthy children. So at some point we have to see these things together.

Participant. The problem right now is the fee or the penalty is too light.

The President. Too light?

Participant. So a lot of our experts suggest to raise the penalty for the polluters.

[*A participant noted the difference on the emphasis placed on enforcement of environmental laws in the U.S. and China.*]

The President. Do you believe—let me ask you this, do you believe that most ordinary Chinese people believe that the environmental standards should be raised, that they basically support a strong environmental policy?

Participant. I think this public awareness is still not so strong, so public should be educated, make them know they have a right to that.

The President. That goes back to what Mr. Liang said about educating the public.

Mr. Kong, why did you clean up your factory if you didn't have to do it?

[*Kong Fanjian, founder and president, Liquan Brewery, said that modern entrepreneurs had the responsibility not only to create wealth but also to protect the environment. He stated that his company's shareholders had deferred their dividends to set up a waste treatment facility to clean up the river. Noting that his company invested in many environmental projects that had yet to turn a profit, Mr. Kong expressed the need for more public awareness and assistance from the National Government.*]

The President. I know we have to go out to the program, but I wanted to give every one of you a chance to say—is there any specific thing that you believe that I could do or the United States could do in partnership with China that would be most helpful to you in what you're trying to achieve? If you were to ask us to go back and work with the Chinese Government on one thing that we could do, or with our business people on one thing to be helpful, what would it be?

[*A participant suggested more direct communication between American and Chinese environmentalists, rather than merely in government circles. The participant said the Chinese could benefit from the maturity of the American envi-*

ronmental movement and suggested an educational television program be produced.]

The President. So you think, for example, if we could arrange to have some of our leaders of our environmental groups come here and meet with citizens like you, you think that would be helpful?

[*The participant responded that it would be helpful and again suggested that an American-produced television program on environmental protection could be used on Chinese national television to broaden public awareness about environmentally hazardous materials, such as one-time-use products.*]

The President. One-time-use, yes. Yes, I agree with that.

[*The participant then described efforts to attract a nongovernmental organization training center that might provide training for the enforcement of environmental law. The participant then noted that the U.S. lagged far behind Europe and Japan in providing assistance to China on environmental issues.*]

The President. I agree with that. Give that speech to the Congress. Unfortunately, all the people here from my Congress agree with you, but we believe that the U.S. Congress does not give enough aid in these areas. And I think it is a huge mistake, and I'm always trying to get more. So I will take what you said and publish it widely when we get home.

You raised another issue that I think is important. We have this rule of law project with China, and my wife met with some people earlier in the week about this. But what happens when you have these environmental laws and the government has to enforce them is, you will always have some honest disputes. And so there has to be some way of resolving them. When our environmental agencies impose regulations, if the companies think they're wrong or unfair or they made a mistake or they think they have a cheaper way to do the same thing, well, they have a way to go into the courts, and we examine that. So there has to be—I agree with you, that will be a part of it.

What else? Anybody else want to say what you think of that? Yes, Mr. Zhou.

[*A participant suggested the President could support Chinese environmentalists in achieving an* alliance with American business leaders to promote energy efficiency in China.

At this point, there was a break in the transcript. It resumed with a participant who discussed facing the problem of balancing economic development and environmental protection.]

The President. It's an honest problem, too. And in the rural areas in all developed countries, people tend to be poorer. And they have to make their living, they believe, from natural resources. I told you, we had the same problem with the old-growth forests, and we had never handled this very well. So, in 1993 and '94, the Congress adopted a plan that I asked them to adopt to provide extra funds to these communities which were making the money from the logging to try to change the basis of their economy.

To be honest, no one knew whether we could do it or not. We didn't know. We thought we could, but we didn't know. But I can tell you now, 5 years later, the unemployment rate in all those communities is now lower than it was before we started to protect the trees. So over a 5-year period, we were able to do this. And I think it requires a lot of effort and some money and a lot of thought and very good, vigorous local leaders. You have to have local leaders who have confidence and then people who can change, you know. But I think this can be done.

[*Liao Xiaoyi, founder, Global Village Cultural Center, described her women's nongovernmental organization's focus on sustainable consumption and children's education, noting that the organization used a U.S. Environmental Protection Agency grant to publish a children's environmental guide.*]

The President. Really?

[*Ms. Liao said that women were an important force in the environmental movement because as mothers they care for their children's future. She described her organization's annual forum on women in journalism and the environment; noted that as consumer decisionmakers, women were receptive to ideas such as recycling; and expressed hope that the President's visit would promote more cooperation between the two nations.*]

The President. I agree with that. But interestingly enough, as a result of what you're saying—and that goes back to what Mr. Liang was saying—I think the more awareness the children have about this, and the more this is taught in school, the better. Because in our country now, I believe that the children are the strongest environmentalists.

You know, when I visit a community in America, suppose I—next week I have to go to Atlanta, Georgia, when I get back—very often a group of children will meet me at the airport, and they will bring me letters that the children have written. Sometimes they're 6 years old, these children, very young. And I always look over these letters to see what they're writing me about. They ask me questions, and sometimes they're "How do you like being President?" or something. But there are more letters from children age 12 and under on the environment than any other subject now, for the last several years.

So when the children begin to ask their parents about this, when they begin to talk about this at dinner, when it becomes a concern for the children, and then when the mothers are concerned about their health, I think it can change a country. No American official can talk to any group of schoolchildren for 10 minutes without being asked about the environment. It's an amazing thing. The children are sort of out there.

Well, I suppose we better go do the program, but this is very helpful. And we have taken careful note of what you have all said, and we will try to follow up. And I admire you all very much, and I thank you for what you're doing. It will help not only the Chinese people but all the rest of us as well.

Thank you.

NOTE: The discussion began at approximately 11 a.m. at Seven Star Park. In his remarks, the President referred to Liang Congjie, founder, Friends of Nature; Don Martin, president, National Association of Home Builders; and Zhou Dadi, director, Beijing Energy Conservation Center. The transcript released by the Office of the Press Secretary did not include the opening portion of the discussion.

Remarks to the People of Guilin
July 2, 1998

Thank you very much. Thank you very much, Mr. Mayor. Thank you for welcoming us to your community and for your fine remarks. And Senator Baucus, thank you for what you said. I want to thank you and all the Members of the United States Congress who are here with you; our American Ambassador to China and the Chinese Ambassador to the United States and the other members of the Chinese Government who are here, and especially I'd like to thank Chairman Ding for being here; and our Secretary of State, Madeleine Albright, and others from the White House. We are all delighted to be among you in Guilin today.

I would also like to express my appreciation to the seven Chinese citizens with whom I have just met because they are taking an active role in helping to clean up the environment, either of this area or the entire country, and I thank them for that. And they're all right there; I'd like to ask them to stand up because they spoke for all of China to me today. Please stand. [*Applause*]

And since we're here to talk about saving the environment, I want to thank Ambassador Li for giving me this energy-efficient air conditioner. [*Laughter*]

Since Chinese civilization first began to express itself thousands of years ago, its poems and paintings have sung of the beauty of the land, the air, the water. No place in China is more evocative of the beauty of your country than Guilin. The stunning mountains along the Li River are instantly familiar to millions and millions of Americans. When we see them, the landscapes of Guilin remind us of China's past, but we know they are alive, and we are grateful for their preservation.

A new sense of cooperation is building between the people of China and the people of the United States, based on our shared ties of commerce and culture, our common security interests, and our common enthusiasm for the future. But a big part of that cooperation must rest on our common understanding that we live on the same planet, sharing the same oceans and breathing the same air.

Not so many years ago in the United States, one of our rivers was so polluted it actually caught on fire. Foul air blanketed our cities; acid rain blighted our landscape. Over the last generation, we have worked hard to restore our natural treasures and to find a way to conduct our economy that is more in harmony with the environment.

China's extraordinary growth has put the same kind of pressures on your environment, and the costs of growth are rising right along with your prosperity. You know better than I that polluted air and water are threatening your remarkable progress. Smog has caused entire Chinese cities to disappear from satellite photographs. And respiratory illness is China's number one health problem.

We also know that more and more environmental problems in the United States, in China, and elsewhere are not just national problems, they are global problems. We must work together to protect the environment, and there is a great deal that we can do together.

China has the world's longest meteorological records, going back over 500 years. They help us clearly to understand the problem of global warming. The 5 warmest years since the 15th century have all been in the 1990's; 1997 was the warmest year ever recorded. And if present trends continue, 1998 will break the record. We know that if this trend continues, it will bring more and more severe weather events, and it will disrupt the lives of hundreds of millions of people in the world during the coming century.

China is already taking impressive steps to protect its future. Leaded gasoline is being banned. Inefficient stoves have been upgraded. People can find out about air quality from newspapers. Communities and provinces and the National Government are doing more to clean up rivers. Chinese scientists are fighting deforestation and soil erosion. And citizens are doing more to promote public education about the environment among families and especially among children.

The United States is determined to strengthen our cooperation with you. Last year our Vice President, Al Gore, and the Chinese Government launched a forum to coordinate sustainable development and environmental protection. In

October at our summit, President Jiang and I oversaw the beginning of a joint initiative on clean energy.

This week we have made important new progress. We will provide China assistance to monitor air quality. We will increase our support for programs that support renewable energy sources to decrease China's dependence on coal. We are helping China develop its coal gasification and working with the Chinese to make financing available for clean energy projects through the Export-Import Bank. Because the United States and China are the world's two largest emitters of greenhouse gases that are dangerously warming our planet, we must do more to avoid increasing severe droughts and floods and the other kinds of destructive things that will occur.

Let me say, Mr. Mayor, I want to extend my sympathies to you on behalf of the American people for the families who suffered losses in the recent flooding here. It occurred just a few days ago, and some of our young Americans were already here working on the trip. They were honored to be able to work with you in some of the sandbagging and other things that were done. But we grieve with you in the losses that were sustained.

We cannot completely eliminate floods and fires and other natural disasters, but we know they will get worse if we do not do something about global warming. There are many people who simply don't believe that anything can be done about it because they don't believe that you can grow an economy unless you use energy in the same way America and Europe have used it for the last 50 years—more and more energy, more and more pollution to get more and more growth. That's what they believe. But I disagree.

Without any loss of economic opportunity, we can conserve energy much more than we do; we can use clean, as opposed to dirty, energy sources much more than we do; and we can adopt new technologies to make the energy we have go further much more than we do.

Now is the time to join our citizens and our governments, our businesses and our industries in the fight against pollution and global warming, even as we fight for a brighter economic future for the people of China and the people of the entire world.

As we move forward together, let us, Chinese and Americans, preserve what we have inherited from the past, and in so doing, preserve the future we are working so hard to build for our children.

Thank you very much.

NOTE: The President spoke at 12:22 p.m. on the Camel Hill Lawn in Seven Star Park. In his remarks, he referred to Mayor Cai Yong Lin of Guilin; U.S. Ambassador to China James M. Sasser; Chinese Ambassador to the U.S. Li Xhaoxing; Ding Zongyi, chairman, Chinese Children's Medical Society; and President Jiang Zemin of China.

Remarks at a Dinner Hosted by Chief Executive C.H. Tung in Hong Kong Special Administrative Region, China
July 2, 1998

Chief Executive Tung. President Clinton, Mrs. Clinton, distinguished guests, ladies and gentlemen. First of all, Mr. President, may I, on behalf of all the Hong Kong people, extend our sincerest and warmest welcome to you and to Mrs. Clinton. It is indeed a great pleasure and a unique honor to see you here in Hong Kong, the first serving U.S. President to make such a visit. And although your time here is very short, I hope you and Mrs. Clinton will leave with memories to last you a lifetime.

Mr. President, as you know, your visit comes at an especially significant time in Hong Kong's history. We are celebrating our first anniversary as a Special Administrative Region of the People's Republic of China. Like the reunification itself just a year and one day ago, our first anniversary was a day of great pride—pride in that, after 156 years of separation, we are at last reunited with our own country.

We are Chinese, and like you Americans, our patriotic feeling is something very natural to us. We were saddened by China's past humiliation, and rejoice and take pride in her improving fortune today. As we welcome the 21st century, we are confident China will be more open and more prosperous and will play an increasingly important and responsible role in world affairs in the interdependent global community.

Yesterday was our first anniversary, and like all birthdays it was time for some reflection, to contemplate the challenges that lie ahead and how to achieve a brighter future for our community. Strengthening our ties with the United States is an important element in this quest.

Your landmark visit to our country over this past week and your summit with President Jiang Zemin bring with it the prospect of a new era of stability, prosperity, and peace in the Asia-Pacific region and indeed in the whole world. As you yourself noted earlier this month, and here I quote: "A stable, open, prosperous China that assumes its responsibilities for building a more peaceful world is clearly and profoundly in our interest. On that point, all Americans agree," end of quote. We in Hong Kong also agree.

We're immensely pleased to see a deepening of the U.S.-Sino relationship. I'm certain that your visit heralds the beginning of a new chapter of cooperation between the two great countries.

For obvious reasons, stable and cordial Sino-U.S. relations are of enormous benefit and importance to us here in Hong Kong. At the same time, the excellent relationship between Hong Kong and the United States I believe can help to engender a deeper mutual understanding and respect between Chinese and American people.

The fact is, we are Chinese and have been brought up in Chinese tradition and values. We are proud of our heritage and our culture. But at the same time, many of us have received the benefit of education in the United States, and we respect the long-held beliefs and traditions of the American people.

Mr. President, almost 10 months ago, I had the pleasure of meeting you and your top advisers in the Oval Office of the White House. I was deeply touched by your very warm welcome that you afforded me and my colleagues, and impressed by your genuine interest in the knowledge of China and of Hong Kong. I assured you then, as I assure you now, and as I hope you will see for yourself on this visit, that the unique concept of "one country, two systems" is working and working well.

This past year has been tremendous and historic for Hong Kong and for our 6½ million people. The eyes of the world have not averted their gaze since our national and SAR regional flag were hoisted on the stroke of midnight on June 30th last year. But they have been transfixed by events we did not see coming, rather than those so confidently predicted by skeptics before reunification.

Were we simply to content ourselves with making a success of "one country, two systems," then I deeply believe we would have few, if any, detractors. Indeed, the central Government leaders are determined to ensure the successful implementation of the Basic Law. And just yesterday, at our first anniversary celebration, both President Jiang Zemin and Vice Premier Qian have reaffirmed such determination. We in Hong Kong, too, are determined to ensure the concept of "one country, two systems," which is enshrined in the Basic Law, be fully implemented. We will also gradually evolve our political structure, with universal suffrage our ultimate objective, in full accordance with the timetable laid down by the Basic Law and what is in the best interest of the people of Hong Kong.

This past year has brought to the region unprecedented financial turmoil, which is still sending waves of uncertainty across the world. In Hong Kong, our economy has also been severely damaged by this turmoil. Indeed, Hong Kong is presently undergoing a painful adjustment, which is essential if we are to continue to be competitive. However, with the entrepreneurial spirit of the Hong Kong people, expanding economy of the mainland, together with traditional prudent financial management, sound banking system, huge foreign exchange reserve that supports a stable exchange rate, we continue to look forward to our future with confidence.

Mr. President, what started as a regional crisis has taken on global significance which needs a global solution. Furthermore, a stable yen exchange rate and a healthy Japanese economy is essential not only for the financial stability of Asia but also for the world as a whole. In these aspects, we are looking towards you for your continued strong leadership, which you alone can provide.

While Asia remains in economic doldrums, the United States is enjoying tremendous economic success. Inflationary pressure has vanished, unemployment is at historical low level, and much-talked-about budget deficit has been erased. The American multinational today is lean, efficient, and competitive. The United States is truly playing a world leadership role in the financial and economic arena. Much of this has been achieved, sir, under your leadership and during your Presidency.

On the world stage, despite mounting interest group pressures and ongoing differences between China and the United States, you have courageously stepped forward to lay the foundation for a strategic partnership between the two countries. A long-term relationship between U.S. and China, based on mutual trust, respect, and benefit, is undoubtedly in the interests of China, the United States, and indeed the whole world.

The continued economic vitality of the United States and the constructive relationship between our sovereign and the United States are both matters of great importance to us in Hong Kong. Mr. President, you were recently quoted by a publication here in Asia as saying, and here I quote: "If the choice was between making a symbolic point and a real difference, I choose to make a real difference," end of quote. Mr. President, you have made such difference on these important issues, and in Hong Kong we appreciate very much what you have done.

Mr. President, Americans have commercial, cultural, and family ties in Hong Kong, stretching back over a century and a half. The American community in Hong Kong, the largest expatriate business group in the SAR, underlines the fact that Hong Kong is America's closest business partner here in Asia. I extend to you and to all Americans an open invitation to visit our home, to experience our hospitality, and to join hands with us across the Pacific to forge an even greater friendship than that which we already know and we cherish.

Mr. President, thank you very much.

President Clinton. Thank you very much, Chief Executive Tung, Mrs. Tung, members of your government, and citizens of Hong Kong. Hillary and I and our delegation, including several Members of the United States Congress and members of our Cabinet and other Americans, are all delighted to be here tonight.

Hong Kong is a world symbol of trade, enterprise, freedom, and global interdependence.

Visitors come here for fashion and food. The world consumes your electronics products and your movies. And every American who has ever wanted to travel anywhere has wanted to come to Hong Kong.

This is, it is true, the first visit to Hong Kong of a President, and it's a fortuitous one for me that I can come and wish all of you a happy anniversary, but it is not my first trip to Hong Kong. My wife and I have both been here in our previous lives—or, as we say when we're back home, back when we had a life—[laughter]—and were free people and could travel, we came to Hong Kong.

Much has changed since we were last here, more than 10 years ago now. I'm told that a 7-year-old girl back then was asked what she thought of Hong Kong, and she said, "It will be a great city once they finish it." [Laughter] Of course, a great city is never finished. And this great city has always given me the feeling that it is always becoming something more and new and different.

Indeed, I was privileged, I suppose, to be one of the first people to land at your new airport tonight coming in. I have to say it was a mixed blessing because for those of us who have ever sat in a cockpit and landed at your old airport, it was one of the most exciting and uncertain experiences of my lifetime. [Laughter]

But I saw your brilliant new airport, and I was reminded that, indeed, in spite of the present difficulties in Asia, Hong Kong is still very much a city that is becoming. That is also true of America. President Franklin Roosevelt once said that our freedom was a never-ending seeking for better things. Hong Kong shows that that is what you are doing as well.

I must say too that I am profoundly appreciative to President Jiang and to all others who have helped make this trip to China a remarkably successful attempt to continue to build our partnership for the future. The open press conference we had that was televised to the Chinese people; the opportunity I had to speak to the students at Beijing University and to answer their questions, which were quite pointed and good, I thought, and then to meet with several thousand students outside; the television and radio interviews; the opportunities that Hillary and I had to meet with citizens from all walks of life in China—all this was encouraging and made me believe that we can build together a future that is more stable, more prosperous, and free.

And so I thank you all for giving me the best possible place to end my trip to China. I think that all that Hong Kong is to Americans and to the rest of the world is somehow embodied in your Chief Executive. He was born in Shanghai, raised in Hong Kong, educated in England, worked in New York and Boston. His children all have U.S. citizenship because they were born there. He's a fan of the Liverpool soccer club and the San Francisco 49ers. [*Laughter*] The world's city should have a citizen of the world as its Chief Executive.

I want you to know that the United States considers Hong Kong vital to the future not only of China and Asia but of the United States and the world as well. Our ties must grow stronger, and they will. And this present financial crisis too will pass, if we work together with discipline and vision to lift the fortunes of our neighbors. Believe me, there is no one in America who is not eagerly awaiting the resumption of real growth and stability in the Asian economy, and we are prepared to do whatever we can to support it. We also appreciate what China and Hong Kong have done and the price that has been paid to stabilize the situation.

So let us look forward to the future with all its vitality and all of its unpredictable events. Some will be difficult, but most will be very good, if, as I said to President Jiang, we stay on the right side of history.

Thank you very much.

Chief Executive Tung. Mr. President, I'd like to propose a toast to your health, to Hillary's health, and to the people of the United States of America.

[*At this point, a toast was offered.*]

President Clinton. And I, sir, would like to propose a toast to you and Mrs. Tung, to the people of Hong Kong, and to the future of our rich friendship.

NOTE: The remarks began at 10:05 p.m. in the Grand Ballroom at the Government House. In his remarks, the President referred to Betty Tung, wife of Hong Kong Chief Executive Tung. Mr. Tung referred to Vice Premier Qian Qichen of China.

Remarks to the Business Community in Hong Kong Special Administrative Region
July 3, 1998

Thank you very much. To Jeff Muir and Victor Fong, thank you both for your fine remarks and for hosting me. I thank all the members of the Hong Kong Trade Development Council and the American Chamber of Commerce for making this forum available, and so many of you for coming out on this morning for what will be my last public speech, except for my press conference, which the members of the press won't permit to become a speech, before I go home.

It has been a remarkable trip for my wife and family and for the Senate delegation and members of our Cabinet and White House. And we are pleased to be ending it here.

I want to say a special word of appreciation to Secretary Albright and Secretary Daley, to Senator Rockefeller, Senator Baucus, Senator Akaka, Congressman Dingell, Congressman Hamilton, Congressman Markey, and the other members of the administration and citizens who have accompanied me on this very long and sometimes exhausting but ultimately, I believe, very productive trip for the people of the United States and the people of China.

I'm glad to be back in Hong Kong. As I told Chief Executive Tung and the members of the dinner party last night, I actually—I may be the first sitting President to come to Hong Kong, but this is my fourth trip here. I was able to come three times before, once with Hillary, in the period which we now refer to as back when we had a life—[*laughter*]—before I became President. And I look forward to coming again in the future.

I think it's quite appropriate for our trip to end in Hong Kong, because, for us Americans, Hong Kong is China's window on the world.

I have seen remarkable changes taking place in China and sense the possibilities of its future, much of which clearly is and for some time has been visible here in Hong Kong, with its free and open markets and its vibrant entrepreneurial atmosphere. Devoid of natural resources, Hong Kong always has had to fall back on the most important resource of all, its people. The entrepreneurs, the artists, the visionaries, the hardworking everyday people have accomplished things that have made the whole world marvel. Hong Kong people have dreamed, designed, and built some of the world's tallest buildings and longest bridges. When Hong Kong ran out of land, the people simply went to the sea and got more. To the average person from a landlocked place, that seems quite stunning.

I thank you for giving me a chance to come here today to talk about the relationship between the United States and all of Asia. I have had a great deal of time to emphasize the importance of our future ties with China, and I would like to reiterate them today and mention some of the points that the two previous speakers made. But I would like to put it in the context of the entire region. And after all, it is the entire region that has been critical to the success of Hong Kong.

We have a fundamental interest in promoting stability and prosperity in Asia. Our future is tied to Asia's. A large and growing percentage of our exports, our imports, and our investments involve Asian nations. As President, besides this trip to China, I have been to Japan, Korea, Indonesia, the Philippines, Australia, and Thailand, with more to come. I have worked with the region's leaders on economic, political, and security issues. The recent events in South Asia, in Indonesia, in financial markets all across the region remind the American people just how very closely our future is tied to Asia's.

Over the course of two centuries, the United States and Asian nations have built a vast, rich, complex, dynamic relationship, forged in the beginning by trade, strained on occasion by misunderstanding, tempered by three wars in living memory, enriched by the free flow of ideas, ideals, and culture. Now, clearly, at the dawn of the 21st century, our futures are inextricably bound together, bound by a mutual interest in seeking to free future generations from the specter of war. As I said, Americans can remember three wars we have fought in Asia. We must make it our mission to avoid another.

The cornerstone of our security in Asia remains our relationship of longstanding with five key democratic allies: Japan, South Korea, Australia, Thailand, the Philippines. Our military presence in Asia is essential to that stability, in no small measure because everyone knows we have no territorial ambitions of any kind.

Nowhere is this more evident than on the Korean Peninsula, where still every day, after 40 years, 40,000 American troops patrol a border that has known war and could know war again. We clearly have an interest in trying to get a peace on the Korean Peninsula. We will continue to work with China to advance our efforts in the four-party talks, to encourage direct and open dialog between North and South Korea, to faithfully implement the agreement with North Korea to end their nuclear weapons program, and to insist that North Korea do the same.

I am encouraged by the openness and the energy of South Korea's new leader, Kim Daejung. Last month, in an address to our Congress, he said, "It is easier to get a passerby to take off his coat with sunshine than with a strong wind."

Of course, our security is also enormously enhanced by a positive partnership with a prosperous, stable, increasingly open China, working with us, as we are, on the challenges of South Asian nuclear issues, the financial crisis in the region, the Korean peace effort, and others.

Our oldest ties to Asia are those of trade and commerce, and now they've evolved into some of our strongest. The fur pelts and cottons our first traders bought here more than 200 years ago have given way to software and medical instruments. Hong Kong is now America's top consumer for cell phones. Today, roughly a third of our exports and 4 million jobs depend on our trade to Asia. As was earlier said, over 1,000 American companies have operations in Hong Kong alone. And as we've seen in recent months, when markets tremble in Tokyo or Hong Kong, they cause tremors around the world.

That is why I have not only sought to ease the Asian economic difficulties but to institutionalize a regional economic partnership through the Asian Pacific Economic Council leaders meetings that we started in Seattle, Washington, in 1993, and which, in every year since, has advanced the cause of economic integration and growth in the region. That is why

I'm also working to broaden and deepen our economic partnership with China and China's integration into the world economic framework.

It clearly is evident to anyone who knows about our relationship that the United States supports China's economic growth through trade. We, after all, purchase 30 percent of the exports of China, far more than any other country in the world, far more than our percentage of the world's GDP.

We very much want China to be a member of the World Trade Organization. We understand the enormous challenges that the Chinese Government faces in privatizing the state industries and doing so at a rate and in a way which will permit people who lose their jobs in the state industries to be reintegrated into a changing economy and have jobs and be able to educate their children, find a place to live, and succeed in a stable society.

So the real question with this WTO accession is not whether the United States wants China in the WTO. Of course, we do. And the real question, in fairness to China, is not whether China is willing to be a responsible international partner in the international financial system. I believe they are. The question is, how do you resolve the tension between the openness requirements for investment and for trade through market access of the WTO with the strains that are going to be imposed on China anyway as it undertakes to speed up the economic transition and the change of employment base within its own country?

We are trying to work these things out. We believe that there must be an end agreement that contains strong terms that are commercially reasonable. We understand that China has to have some transitional consideration because of the challenges at home. I think we'll work this out. But I want you to understand that we in the United States very much want China to be a member of the WTO. We would like it to happen sooner, rather than later, but we understand that we have not only American but global interests to consider in making sure that when the whole process is over that the terms are fair and open and further the objectives of more open trade and investment across the world.

I also would say in that connection, I am strongly supporting the extension of normal trading status, or MFN, to China. I was encouraged by the vote in the House Ways and Means Committee shortly before we left. I hope we will

be successful there. I think anything any of you can do to support the integrity of the existing obligations that all of us have, including and especially in the area of intellectual property, will be very helpful in that regard in helping us to move forward.

In addition to trade and security ties, the United States and Asia are bound by family ties, perhaps our most vital ones. Seven million Americans today trace their roots to Asia, and the percentage of our citizens who are Asian-Americans is growing quite rapidly. These roots are roots they are eager to renew or rebuild or to keep. Just last year 3.4 million Americans traveled to Asia; 7.8 million Asians traveled to the United States. Thousands of young people are crossing the Pacific to study, and in so doing, building friendships that will form the foundations of cooperation and peace for the 21st century. All across the region, we see evidence that the values of freedom and democracy are also burning in the hearts of the people in the East as well as the West. From Japan to the Philippines, South Korea to Mongolia, democracy has found a permanent home in Asia.

As the world becomes smaller, the ties between Asia and the United States—the political ties, the family ties, the trade ties, the security ties—they will only become stronger. Consider this one little statistic: In 1975 there were 33 million minutes of telephone traffic between the U.S. and Asia; in 1996 there were 4.2 billion minutes of such traffic, a 127-fold increase. That doesn't count the Internet growth that is about to occur that will be truly staggering.

Now, the result of all this is that you and I in our time have been given a remarkable opportunity to expand and share the storehouse of human knowledge, to share the building of wealth, to share the fights against disease and poverty, to share efforts to protect the environment and bridge age-old gaps of history and culture that have caused too much friction and misunderstanding.

This may be the greatest moment of actual possibility in human history. At the same time, the greater openness, the pace of change, the nature of the global economy, all these things have brought with them disruption. They create the risk of greater gaps between rich and poor, between those equipped for the information age and those who aren't. It means that problems, whether they are economic problems or environmental problems, that begin in one country can quickly spread beyond that country's borders. It means that we're all more vulnerable, in a more open atmosphere, to security threats that cross national borders, to terrorism, to drug smuggling, to organized crime, to people who would use weapons of mass destruction.

Now, how are we going to deepen this relationship between the U.S. and Asia, since all of us recognize that it is in our interest and it will further our values? I believe there are three basic lessons that we can learn from the immediate past that should guide our path to the future.

First, building economies and people, not weapons of mass destruction, is every nation's best path to greatness. The vast majority of nations are moving away from not toward nuclear weapons, and away from the notion that their influence in the future will be defined by the size of their military rather than the size of their GDP and the percentage of their citizens who know a great deal about the world.

India and Pakistan's recent nuclear test, therefore, buck the tide of history. This is all the more regrettable because of the enormous potential of both countries. The United States has been deeply enriched by citizens from both India and Pakistan who have done so very well in America. They and their relatives could be doing very well at home, and therefore, could be advancing their nations' cause around the world. Both these countries could achieve real, different, fundamental greatness in the 21st century, but it will never happen if they divert precious resources from their people to develop nuclear and huge military arsenals.

We have worked hard with China and other leading nations to forge an international consensus to prevent an intensifying arms race on the Indian subcontinent. We don't seek to isolate India and Pakistan, but we do seek to divert them from a self-defeating, dangerous, and costly course. We encourage both nations to stop testing, to sign the Comprehensive Test Ban Treaty, to settle their differences through peaceful dialog.

The second lesson that we should take into the future is that nations will only enjoy true and lasting prosperity when governments are open, honest, and fair in their practices, and when they regulate and supervise financial markets rather than direct them.

Too many booming economies, too many new skyscrapers now vacant and in default were built on shaky foundations of cronyism, corruption, and overextended credit, undermining the confidence of investors with sudden, swift, and severe consequences. The financial crisis, as all of you know far better than I, has touched nearly all the nations and households of Asia. Restoring economic stability and growth will not be easy. The steps required will be politically unpopular and will take courage. But the United States will do all we can to help any Asian government willing to work itself back to financial health. We have a big interest in the restoration of growth, starting the flows of investment back into Asia.

There is a very limited time period in which we can absorb all the exports to try to do our part to keep the Asian economy going. And while we may enjoy a brief period of surging extra investment, over the long run, stable growth everywhere in the world is the best prescription for stable growth in America.

We are seeing some positive steps. Yesterday Japan announced the details of its new and potentially quite significant banking reform proposals. We welcome them. Thailand and Korea are taking decisive action to implement the IMF-supported economic reform programs of their countries. Indonesia has a fresh opportunity to deepen democratic roots and to address the economic challenges before it. Thanks to the leadership of President Jiang and Premier Zhu, China has followed a disciplined, wise policy of resisting competitive devaluations that could threaten the Chinese economy, the region's, and the world's.

Even as your own economy, so closely tied to those of Asia, inevitably feels the impact of these times, Hong Kong continues to serve as a force for stability. With strong policies to address the crisis, a healthy respect for the rule of law, a strong system of financial regulation and supervision, a commitment to working with all nations, Hong Kong can help to lead Asia out of turbulent times as it contributes to China's astonishing transformation by providing investment capital and expertise in privatizing state enterprises and sharing legal and regulatory experience.

The final lesson I believe is this: Political freedom, respect for human rights, and support for representative governments are both morally right and ultimately the best guarantors of stability in the world of the 21st century. This spring the whole world looked on with deep interest as courageous citizens in Indonesia raised their voices in protest against corruption and government practices that have brought their nation's economy to its knees. They demonstrated for change, for the right to elect leaders fully accountable to them. And in just 2 weeks the universal longing for democratic, responsive, accountable government succeeded in altering their political future.

America will stand by the people of Indonesia and others as they strive to become part of the rising tide of freedom around the world. Some worry that widespread political participation and loud voices of dissent can pull a nation apart. Some nations have a right to worry about instability because of the pain of their own past. But nonetheless, I fundamentally disagree, especially given the dynamics of the 21st century global society.

Why? Democracy is rooted in the propositions that all people are entitled to equal treatment and an equal voice in choosing their leaders and that no individual or group is so wise or so all-knowing to make all the decisions that involve unfettered power over other people. The information age has brought us yet another argument for democracy. It has given us a global economy that is based on, more than anything else, ideas. A torrent of new ideas are generating untold growth and opportunity, not only for individuals and firms, but for nations. As I saw again in Shanghai when I met with a dozen incredibly impressive Chinese entrepreneurs, ideas are creating wealth in this economy.

Now, it seems to me, therefore, inevitable that societies with the freest flow of ideas are most likely to be both successful and stable in the new century. When difficulties come, as they do to every country and in all ages—there is never a time that is free of difficulties—it seems to me that open debate and unconventional views are most likely to help countries most quickly overcome the difficulties of unforeseen developments.

Let me ask you this: A year ago, when you celebrated the turnover from Great Britain to China of Hong Kong, what was everybody buzzing about after the speeches were over? "Will this really work? Will this two-system thing work? Will we be able to keep elections? Will this work?" How many people were off in a corner saying, "You know, this is a pretty tough time to be doing this, because a year from now the whole Asian economy is going to be in collapse, and how in the world will we deal with this?" When you cannot foresee the future and when problems coming on you have to bring forth totally new thinking, the more open the environment, the quicker countries will respond. I believe this is profoundly important.

I also believe that, by providing a constructive outlet for the discontent that will always exist in every society—because there is no perfect place, and because people have different views and experience reality differently—and by finding a way to give everybody some sense of empowerment and role in a society, that freedom breeds the responsibility without which the open, highly changing societies of the 21st century simply cannot succeed.

For all these reasons, I think the forces of history will move all visionary people, including Asians, with their legendary assets of hard work, intelligence, and education, toward freer, more democratic societies and ways of ordering their affairs.

For me, these lessons we must carry forward into the new century. And in this time of transition and change, as we deepen America's partnership with Asia, success will come to those who invest in the positive potential of their people, not weapons to destroy others. Open governments and the rule of law are essential to lasting prosperity. Freedom and democracy are the birthrights of all people and the best guarantors of national stability and progress.

Now, as I said, a little over a year ago, no one could have predicted what you would have to endure today in the form of this crisis. But I am confident Hong Kong will get through this and will help to lead the region out of it, because of the lessons that I have just mentioned, and because they have been a part of the fabric of your life here for a very long time.

For years, Hong Kong people have enjoyed the right to organize public demonstrations, due process under law, 43 newspapers and 700 periodicals, giving life to the principle of government accountability, debate, free and open. All this must continue. The world was impressed by the record turnout for your May elections. The results were a mandate for more democracy, not less, and faster, not slower strides toward political freedom. I look forward to the day when all of the people of Hong Kong realize the rights and responsibilities of full democracy.

I think we should all pledge, each in our own way, to build that kind of future, a future where we build people up, not tear our neighbors down; a future where we order our affairs in a legal, predictable, open way; a future where we try to tap the potential and recognize the authority of each individual.

I'm told that this magnificent convention center was built in the shape of a soaring bird on a patch of land reclaimed from the sea. It's an inspiring symbol of the possibilities of Hong Kong, of all of Asia, and of our relationship with Asia. Just a couple of days ago, Hong Kong celebrated its first anniversary of reversion to China. I am going home for America's 222d anniversary tomorrow.

May the future of this special place, of China, of the relationship between the United States and China and Asia, soar like the bird that gave life to this building.

Thank you very much.

NOTE: The President spoke at 10:42 a.m. in the Hong Kong Convention Center. In his remarks, he referred to Jeff Muir, chairman, American Chamber of Commerce in Hong Kong; Victor Fong, chairman, Hong Kong Trade Development Council; Chief Executive C.H. Tung of Hong Kong; and President Jiang Zemin and Premier Zhu Rongji of China.

The President's News Conference in Hong Kong Special Administrative Region
July 3, 1998

The President. Good afternoon. I know most of the American journalists here are looking forward, as I am, to returning home for the Fourth of July. But I didn't want to leave China without first reflecting on the trip and giving you a chance to ask some questions.

Let me begin, however, by thanking the people who came with me, who worked so hard on this trip: Secretary Albright, Secretary Rubin, Charlene Barshefsky, Secretary Daley, Secretary Glickman, Janet Yellen, Mark Gearan. I'd like to say a special word of thanks to all the members of the White House staff who worked so hard to prepare me for this trip, along with the Cabinet Secretaries. I want to thank the congressional delegation: Senator Akaka, Senator Rockefeller, Senator Baucus, Congressman Hamilton, Congressman Dingell, and Congressman Markey, and also the staff of the Embassy and the consulates.

Over the past week, we have seen the glory of China's past in Xi'an, the vibrancy of its present in Beijing, the promise of its future in Shanghai and Hong Kong. I don't think anyone who was on this trip could fail to appreciate the remarkable transformation that is underway in China as well as the distance still to be traveled.

I visited a village that chooses its own leaders in free elections. I saw cell phones and computers carrying ideas, information, and images around the world. I had the opportunity to talk directly to the Chinese people through national television about why we value human rights and individual freedom so highly. I joined more than 2,000 people in worship in a Beijing church. I spoke to the next generation of China's leaders at Beijing University; to people working for change in law, academia, business, and the arts; to average Chinese during a radio call-in show. I saw the explosion of skyscrapers and one of the world's most modern stock exchanges in Shanghai. I met with environmentalists in Guilin to talk about the challenge China faces in developing its economy while improving its environment. And here in Hong Kong, we end the trip where I hope China's future begins, a place where free expression and free markets flourish under the rule of law.

Clearly, China is changing, but there remain powerful forces resisting change, as evidenced by continuing governmental restrictions on free speech, assembly, and freedom of worship. One of the questions I have tried to frame, on this trip, for the future is how do we deal with these issues in a way most likely to promote progress? The answer I think is clear: dealing directly, forcefully, but respectfully with the Chinese about our values.

Over the past week, I have engaged not only the leadership but the Chinese people about our experience and about the fact that democracy is a universal aspiration, about my conviction that in the 21st century democracy also will be the right course practically as well as morally, yielding more stability and more progress.

At the same time, expanding our areas of cooperation with China advances our interests: stability in Asia, nonproliferation, the rule of law, science and technology, fighting international crime and drugs, and protecting the environment. The relationship between our two countries is terribly important. The hard work we've accomplished has put that relationship on a much more positive and productive footing. That is good for America, good for China, good for Asia, good for the world.

Now I look forward to returning home and pressing for progress on a number of fronts: passing a balanced budget that makes the investments in education and research we need for the 21st century; expanding health care and providing a Patients' Bill of Rights; pursuing campaign finance reform; protecting our children from the dangers of tobacco.

Now I'd be happy to take your questions, and I'd like to begin with Mr. Bazinet [Kenneth Bazinet, United Press International].

President's Trip to China

Q. Mr. President, from your staff to President Jiang Zemin, this trip has been hailed as a success. But we are leaving here with one symbolic agreement. I wonder if you could explain to us what exactly or how exactly you will show your critics back in Congress that you did meet your expectations on this trip. Thank you.

The President. Well, on the substance, I think we have reinforced our common commitment to regional security, which is terribly important given the progress I believe can be made in the next several months, in the next couple of years in Korea, and the job we have to do in South Asia with India and Pakistan. We made substantial progress in nonproliferation, not only in detargeting but in other areas as well. We got a significant commitment from the Chinese to take another step toward full participation in the Missile Technology Control Regime. We had an agreement on the rule of law which I believe practically—these rule of law issues I think will practically do an enormous amount to change the lives of ordinary Chinese citizens, not only in regularizing commercial dealings but

in helping them with other daily problems that impinge on freedom if they're not fairly and fully resolved.

I'm pleased by the science and technology initiative that we signed, which has already produced significant benefits for both our people. I'm very pleased that we now have a Peace Corps agreement with China. And I think we have really broken some ground in cooperation on the environment. And again I say that I think China and the United States will both have heavy responsibilities to our own people and to the rest of the world in this area.

I believe that the fact that we debated openly these matters, at the press conference, of our disagreements is quite important, as well. And I might say that a lot of the democracy activists from Hong Kong said that they felt that in some ways the fact that we had this public discussion, the President of China and I, in the press conference might have a bigger impact over the long run on the human rights picture than anything else that happened here.

I have acknowledged in candor that we have not made as much progress on some of the trade issues as I had hoped, but I also now have a much clearer understanding of the Chinese perspective. I think they want to be in the WTO; I think they want to assume the responsibilities of opening their markets and taking down barriers and allowing more investment. But I think, understandably, since they are also committed to privatizing state-owned industries, they have big chunks of unemployment for which they have to create big chunks of employment. And they want to have a timing for WTO membership that will permit them to continue to absorb into the work force people that are displaced from the state industries.

So I have an idea now about how we may be able to go back home, put our heads together, and come up with another proposal or two that will enable us to push forward our trade agenda with the Chinese. So in all those areas, I think that we made substantial, substantive progress.

Mr. Hunt [Terence Hunt, Associated Press].

Strategic Partnership With China

Q. Mr. President, have you and President Jiang Zemin achieved the constructive strategic partnership that you've talked about? What do you mean by that term, and how can you have that kind of a relationship with a country that you say unfairly restricts American businesses?

The President. For one thing, I don't think it's the only country in the world where we don't have complete fair access to the markets. We still have trade differences with Japan, which is a very close ally of ours, and a number of other countries. So we don't have—we can have a strategic partnership with a country with whom we do not have a perfect relationship.

I think that—first of all, let me remind you about what our interests are. We have a profound interest in a stable Asia that is progressing. We have a profound interest in a partnership with the world's largest country in areas where we can't solve problems without that kind of partnership, and I cite Korea, the Indian subcontinent, the Asian financial crisis, and the environmental challenges we face as examples of that. So I think that our interests are clear, and I think we're well on the way toward expanding areas of cooperation and defining and honestly and openly dealing with areas of differences that are the essential elements of that kind of partnership.

Mr. McQuillan [Larry McQuillan, Reuters].

Alleged Chinese Involvement in 1996 Campaign Fundraising

Q. Mr. President, during your news conference with President Jiang, he mentioned that you raised campaign fundraising with him. And I wonder if you could share with us just what ideas you expressed to him. And also, since he said that the Chinese conducted an investigation and that they found the charges were totally absurd, did you suggest that he might want to cooperate with Justice Department and also congressional investigations?

The President. Let me say, he is interested in a very—in what I might call a narrow question here, but a very important one, and in my mind, the most important one of all. The question here—the question that was raised that was most troubling was whether people at high levels in the Government of China had either sanctioned or participated in the channeling of funds in violation of American law not only into the Presidential campaign but into a number of congressional campaigns. That charge has been made. He said they looked into that, and he was, obviously, certain, and I do believe him, that he had not ordered or authorized or approved such a thing, and that he could find

no evidence that anybody in governmental authority had done that.

He said that he could not speak to whether any people pursuing their own business interests had done that. He didn't say that it happened or he knew that it happened. I want to make it clear. He just said that his concern was on the governmental side.

And I told him that that was the thing that we had to have an answer to, and that I appreciated that, and that if he were—if the Government of China were contacted by any people doing their appropriate work, I would appreciate their telling them whatever they could tell them to help them to resolve that to their satisfaction, because I do think that is the really important issue.

Mr. Pelley [Scott Pelley, CBS News].

Human Rights and Democracy in China

Q. Thank you, Mr. President. Many democracy advocates were encouraged by your trip to China and, in fact, Bao Tong granted an interview to test the limits of Chinese tolerance. But sir, why did you find it impossible to meet with the democracy advocates in Beijing, where it would have had the most impact? And would you feel compelled to intervene personally if Bao Tong is arrested after you leave?

The President. Well, I have continued—first, let me answer the second question first. I have continued to raise individual cases and will continue to do so with the Chinese Government and with the President. I would very much like to see China reassess its position on categories of arrestees as well. And let me just mention, for example, they're probably 150 people who are still incarcerated as a result of the events in Tiananmen Square who were convicted of nonviolent offenses. There are also several people still incarcerated for a crime that is no longer a crime, that the Chinese themselves have said, "We no longer want to, in effect, pursue people who have committed certain offenses against the state under—which were basically a rubric for political dissidents." I suggested that they look at that. So in all that, I will continue to be active.

On your first question, I did my best to meet with people who represented all elements of Chinese society and to do whatever I could to encourage democratic change. The decisions I made on this trip—as I remind you, the first trip by an American President in a decade—

about with whom to meet and how to handle it were basically designed—were based on my best judgment about what would be most effective in expanding human rights. And we'll have to—I think, at this moment, it looks like the decisions I made were correct, and we'll have to see over the course of time whether that is accurate or not.

Mr. Blitzer [Wolf Blitzer, Cable News Network].

Forced Abortions in China

Q. Mr. President, in the days leading up to your visit there was very dramatic testimony in the U.S. Congress about forced abortions—allegations, reports that there were forced abortions still continuing in China. Did you specifically raise the issue of forced abortions with President Jiang Zemin? And if you did, what did he say to you about this allegation?

The President. Well, they all say the same thing. They say that is not Chinese policy, that it violates Chinese policy. My view is that if these reports are accurate, there may be insufficient monitoring of what's being done beyond the Capital and beyond the place where the orders are being handed out to the place where the policy is being implemented.

And so I hope by our presence here and our concern about this, which I might add was—this issue was first raised most forcefully a couple of years ago by the First Lady when she came to Beijing to speak at the Women's Conference—I'm very hopeful that we will see some progress on this and that those who are making such reports will be able to tell us over the coming weeks and months that there has been some real progress.

Q. But did you raise it with President Jiang?

The President. We talked about it briefly. But they all say the same thing, Mr. Blitzer. They all say that this is not policy, that they've tried to make it clear. And I have tried to make it clear that it's something that we feel very, very strongly about. But as I said, I believe that, if in fact the policy is being implemented in a way that is different from what is the stated policy in Beijing, we may get some reports of improvements in the weeks and months ahead, and I hope we will.

Mr. Donaldson [Sam Donaldson, ABC News].

Kosovo

Q. Mr. President, while you've been in China, the ethnic cleansing in Kosovo appears to be continuing. You and the Secretary of State have both talked very firmly to President Milosevic about stopping, and it is not stopping. Is there a point at which you're going to move, or is, in fact, this a bluff which he's successfully calling?

The President. No, I don't think that's accurate. But the situation—let me say, first of all, I still believe the situation is serious. I still believe, as a practical matter, the only way it will ultimately be resolved is if the parties get together and resolve it through some negotiation and dialog. I think that the Serb—excuse me, the—I think that Belgrade is primarily responsible here. But I think that others, when they're having a good day or a good week on the military front, may also be reluctant to actually engage in dialog. So I think this is something that all parties are going to have to deal with.

Now, I have, since I have been on this trip, checked in almost daily on the Kosovo situation and continue to support strongly, with our allies, continuing NATO planning and a clear and unambiguous statement that we have not, nor should we, rule out any options. And I hope that is still the position of our European allies.

Q. While NATO is planning, people are dying every day.

The President. They are, Mr. Donaldson, but there is—the conflict is going on; both sides are involved in it. There is some uncertainty about who is willing and who is not willing to even negotiate about it. And we're working on it as best we can.

Mr. Bloom [David Bloom, NBC News].

Human Rights and Democracy in China

Q. Mr. President, if this trip is followed in the days or weeks to come by the piecemeal release of a few Chinese dissidents, would you consider that a success? And why not set a deadline for China to release all of its political prisoners? And, if I may, sir, you spoke a minute ago about the powerful forces resisting change in China. Do you believe there could ever be democracy here?

The President. Oh, yes. The answer to the second question is yes. I believe there can be, and I believe there will be. And what I would like to see is the present Government, headed by this President and this Premier, who are clearly committed to reform, ride the wave of change and take China fully into the 21st century and basically dismantle the resistance to it. I believe there—not only do I believe there can be, I believe there will be.

Now, I believe that, again—on your first question, I think I have to do what I think is most effective. And obviously, I hope there will be further releases. As I said, I would like to see not only targeted, selected high-profile individual releases, which are very important, but I think that the next big step would be for China to look at whether there could be some expedited process to review the sentences of whole categories of people, because that would tend to show a change in policy rather than just the product of negotiation with the Americans.

In all fairness, while I very much value the role that I and our country have been able to play here, the best thing for China will be when no outside country is needed to advance the cause of human rights and democracy.

Go ahead.

Taiwan and President's Previous Views on China

Q. Mr. President, the U.S. policy pushed for a negotiated reconciliation between the People's Republic and Taiwan. But some in Taiwan believe that, by endorsing the "three no's," your administration has taken away some of the bargaining power that they would need in a negotiation. Did that concern you? And can you tell us why you thought it was important to publicly articulate the "three no's" policy, when people in Taiwan were saying this would make it more difficult?

And also, if you'll forgive me just a quick two-parter, as you look back at the ups and downs of your China policy over the past 6 years, have you ever had occasion to regret the very tough and sometimes personal words you had on the subject for George Bush in 1992?

The President. Let me answer the Taiwan question first. First, I think there may be difference of opinion in Taiwan. Yesterday the Taiwanese leader, Mr. Li, said that the United States had kept its commitments not to damage Taiwan or its interests in any way here. I publicly stated that, because I was asked questions in public about Taiwan, and I thought it was an appropriate thing to do under the circumstances. But I did not announce any change

in policy. In fact, the question of independence for Taiwan, for example, has been American policy for a very long time and has been a policy that has been embraced by the Government in Taiwan, itself.

So I believe that I did the right thing there to simply clarify to both sides that there had been no change in our policy. The substance of the policy is obviously something that the Chinese Government agrees with. I think what the Taiwan Government wants to hear is that we favor the cross-strait dialog, and we think it has to be done peacefully and in orderly fashion. That is, I believe, still the intention and the commitment of the Chinese Government.

So I didn't intend, and I don't believe I did, change the substance of our position in any way by anything that I said. I certainly didn't try to do that.

Mr. Maer [Peter Maer, NBC Mutual Radio].

Q. And about what you said——

The President. Oh, I'm sorry, I forgot. Well, let me go back and try to retrace the steps there. I think that at the time—you may have a better record of exactly what was said and what wasn't—I felt very strongly that the United States should be clear and unambiguous in our condemnation about what happened 9 years ago, at the time. And that then we needed to have a clear road going forward which would attempt to—not to isolate the Chinese but would attempt to be very strong about how we felt about what happened and would, in essence, broaden the nature of our policy.

What I felt was that in a genuine concern to maintain a constructive relationship with China, for security reasons and for economic reasons, that we didn't have high enough visibility for the human rights issue. I believed that then; I still believe that. I think any President would say that, once you've served in this job, you understand a little bit more the nuances of all policies than you did before you get it. But I believe, on balance, that we have a stronger human rights component to our engagement strategy than was the case before, and I think that is quite important.

Mr. Maer.

Human Rights in China

Q. Mr. President, during your trip, at least in the first cities you visited, we saw a sort of "catch and release" program of human rights dissidents. And of course, thousands of others are still in prison, in labor camps. Since you did not meet with them, sir, what would your message be to those who wanted to meet with you? And to follow up on your response to an earlier question, why is it that you feel that it would not help their cause to have sat down and met with some of them?

The President. Because I believe over the long run what you want is a change in the policy and the attitude of the Chinese Government on whole, not just on this, that, or the other specific imprisoned dissident or threatened dissident, although those things are very important. I don't want to minimize that. I'm glad Wei Jingsheng is out of jail. I'm glad the bishop is out of jail. I'm glad Wang Dan is out of jail. I think these things are important.

But what I am trying to do is to argue to the Chinese Government that, not because we're pressuring them publicly but because it is the right thing to do—the right thing to do—that the whole policy should be changed. And after all, our relationships have been characterized, I think, by significant misunderstanding, including the misunderstanding of the Chinese of our motive in raising these issues.

And so I felt that by going directly to engage the Chinese, starting with the President, and especially taking advantage of the opportunity to have this free and open debate before all the Chinese people, I could do more in the short and in the long run to advance the cause of human rights.

Q. The other part of the question is, is there some message to these individuals that you'd like to send them?

The President. My message is that the United States is on your side, and we did our best. We're on the side of free speech. We're on the side of not putting people who dissent in prison. We're on the side of letting people who only dissented and exercised their free speech out of prison, and that we believe that this new, heretofore unprecedented open debate about this matter will lead to advances. We think that it's going to take a lot of discipline and a lot of effort, but we believe that this strategy is the one most likely to advance the cause of free speech and free association and free expression of religious conviction, as well.

Northern Ireland Peace Process

Q. A question from the Irish Times. I understand, Mr. President, that you have been fol-lowing events in Northern Ireland very closely during your trip and that you telephoned party leaders from Air Force One yesterday, and you spoke to them about the prospect of serious violence this weekend—*[inaudible]*. Could I ask you, what would you say to those on the opposite side of the dispute at this time, and also about the burning of 10 Catholic churches in Northern Ireland? And could I ask you, too, is there any prospect of you visiting Ireland this year, now that the Northern Ireland elections are behind us?

The President. Well, yes, I did call Mr. Trimble and Mr. Hume to congratulate them on the respective performances of their parties, and the leadership position that—this was right before the elections—I mean, the election for leadership—but that we had assumed Mr. Trimble would be elected and that either Mr. Hume or the nominee of his party, which turned out to be Mr. Mallon, would be selected as the First Deputy. And I wanted to talk to them about what the United States could do to continue to support this process and, in particular, whether there was anything that could be done to diffuse the tension surrounding the marching season and, especially, the Drumcree march.

And we had very good, long talks. They said they needed to get the leadership elections out of the way. They wanted to consult with Prime Minister Blair, who's been up there, and with Prime Minister Ahern, and that we would agree to be in, more or less, daily contact in the days running up to the marching date in the hope that that could be done.

I think it's very important that the people of Ireland give this new Assembly a chance to work—people of Northern Ireland. And I think it would be tragic indeed if either side felt so aggrieved by the ultimate resolution of the marching issue that they lost the bigger picture in the moment. I think that is something that must not happen.

Obviously, I feel personally horrible about what has happened to the churches. In our country, we had this round of church burnings in the last few years. And during the civil rights days, we had a number of bombings of black churches, which really reflected the darkest impulses of some of our people at their worst moments. And I would just plead to whoever was responsible for this for whatever reason, you need to take the churches off the list, and you need to take violence off the list.

Japanese Economy

Q. Mr. President, this morning you mentioned the new package of Japanese banking reforms and said you welcomed them. Do you believe that those reforms and other domestic financial measures will be sufficient to stem the slide of the yen and prevent the Japanese economy from going deeper into recession, perhaps spreading fear in China and elsewhere in the region and to the United States?

The President. Well, the Japanese economy has been at a period of slow to no growth for a period of years now. And if you look at the dislocation here in Hong Kong, for example, you see what regional ramifications that has as Japan slows down; then you have the problems in Indonesia and Korea and Thailand and elsewhere.

I will reiterate: I think that the Chinese have done a good thing by maintaining the stability of their currency and not engaging in competitive devaluations. I hope they will continue to do that. But I don't think anyone seriously believes that the financial situation in Asia can get better and that, therefore, we can resume global growth in a way that won't have a destructive impact on the United States and other countries unless Japan can grow again. We all have a vested interest in that, as well as our best wishes for the people of Japan.

Now, I'm encouraged by the fact that the Prime Minister announced this program and announced it several days before he had originally intended to. And I think what the markets are waiting for now is some action and a sense that, if it turns out that the implementation of this program is not enough, that more will be done.

It is not rational, in my view, to believe that the Japanese economy is meant to contract further. This is an enormously powerful, free country, full of brilliant people and successful businesses and staggering potential. And this is almost like a historical anomaly. Now, we know generally what the elements of the program are. But what I hope very much is that as soon as these elections are over, there will be a strong sense of determination and confidence not only on the part of the Japanese Government but the Japanese people, and that the rest of us will do whatever it is we have to do to support their doing whatever they have to do to get this turned around. But we have a huge stake in getting Japanese growth going, and I think

that it can be done because of the fundamental strengths of the Japanese people and their economy. But I think that it's going to take some real concerted action. And if the first steps don't work, then you just have to keep doing more. You just have to keep working through this until it's turned around.

It's not a situation like the Depression in the United States in the thirties, which took, literally, years and years and years to work out of, because we had fallen so much below anything that they're facing now. And we didn't have anything like the sophisticated understanding or the sophisticated economy or capacity in the thirties that they have now.

So I think we can get through this in a reasonable amount of time, but the rest of us, including the United States and China, need to have both good wishes and determination for Japan and just understand that, however, there's a limit to what we can do until they do the things that they have to do. But I think after this election, you may see a little more moment there.

Mr. Walsh [Ken Walsh, U.S. News & World Report].

President Jiang Zemin of China

Q. Mr. President, you spent considerable time with President Jiang Zemin this week both in public and in private. I wonder if you could give us your assessment of him not only as a strategic partner but as a leader and as an agent for change in China.

The President. Well, first of all, I have a very high regard for his abilities. I remember not so many years ago, there was a—the conventional wisdom was that he might be a transitional figure. And after I met with him the first time, I felt very strongly that his chances of becoming the leader of China for a sustained period were quite good, because he's a man of extraordinary intellect, very high energy, a lot of vigor for his age or indeed for any age. And I think he has a quality that is profoundly important at this moment in our history when there's so much change going on: He has a good imagination. He has vision; he can visualize; he can imagine a future that is different from the present.

And he has, I think, a very able partner in Premier Zhu Rongji, who has enormous technical competence and almost legendary distaste for stalling and bureaucracy and just staying in the same path the way—even if it's not working. So my view is that the potential we have for a strategic partnership is quite strong.

However, I think that like everyone else, he has constituencies with which he must work. And I hope that more of them are now more convinced that we can build a good, positive partnership as a result of this trip. I hope more of them understand that America wishes China well, that we are not bent on containing China, and that our human rights policy is not an excuse for some larger strategic motive. It's what we really believe. We believe it's morally right, and we believe it's best for them, as a practical matter, over the long run.

So I believe that there's a very good chance that China has the right leadership at the right time, and that they understand the daunting, massive nature of the challenges they face. They want us to understand that there is much more personal freedom now, in a practical sense, for most Chinese than there was when President Nixon came here or 10 years ago. But I think they understand that this is an unfolding process, and they have to keep going. And I hope that we can be a positive force there.

Yes, go ahead.

Q. Following up on that, do you consider that the three televised appearances were, in part, a personal expression of gratitude from President Jiang to you?

The President. I don't know about that. I think that it might have been—I think it was a personal expression of confidence in the good will that we have established to build the right kind of relationship. But more importantly, I think it was a personal expression of confidence that he could stand there and answer questions before the people of China that might come not only from Chinese press but from ours as well.

So I wouldn't say gratitude; I think confidence is the right answer. But I can tell you, every place I went after that, you know, when I came down to Shanghai or when I flew over to Hong Kong, lots and lots of people I met with mentioned it to me, that it really meant something, that it changed the whole texture of what had happened. And I think that we did the right thing. And I'm certain that he did the right thing.

Go ahead.

Democracy in China

Q. Ambassador Sasser said earlier this week that he believes that communism in China will end. You just said now that democracy will come to China. What is the timeframe for that? Will it happen in your lifetime?

The President. I certainly hope so. [*Laughter*] That's like saying—I don't mean to trivialize the question, but let me give you—do I believe a woman will be elected President of the United States? I do. Do I think it will be a good thing? I do. Do I know when it will happen? I don't. Who will make the decision? The American people.

As I said, I believe that leaders of vision and imagination and courage will find a way to put China on the right side of history and keep it there. And I believe that even as—when people are going through changes, they may not believe that this is as morally right as we do. But I think they will also be able to see that it is in their interest to do this, that their country will be stronger, that when people have—if you look at just the last 50 years of history in China, and if you look at the swings back and forth, when Mao Tse-tung was alive and you were letting a thousand flowers bloom, and all of a sudden there was a reaction, you know; and there was the Cultural Revolution, and then there was the reaction, and we liked the reaction of that; then there was Tiananmen Square.

If you want to avoid these wild swings where society is like a pressure cooker that blows the top off, then there has to be some institutional way in which people who have honest grievances, even if they're not right—not all the critics will always be right all the time, just like the government, the officials won't always be right all the time—but if there is a normalized way in which people can express their dissent, that gives you a process that then has the integrity to carry you on more of a straight line to the future, instead of swinging back and forth all the time. The very ability to speak your mind, even if you think you can't prevail, is in itself empowering.

And so, one of the things that I hope is that— the Chinese leaders, I've always been impressed, have an enormous sense of history, and they're always looking for parallels and for differences. It's a wise thing. Our people need to understand more of our own history and how it may or may not relate to the moment and to the future.

And if you think about—one of the things that, if I were trying to manage this huge transition—and I'll just give you, parenthetically, one thing,—the Mayor of Shanghai told me that in just the last couple of years 1.2 million people had been displaced from state industries in Shanghai and over one million had already found other jobs. That's just in one area of the country. If you're trying to manage that sort of transition, one of the things that I would be looking for is how I could keep this thing going down the track in the right direction and not have wild swings and not be confronted with a situation which would then be unmanageable.

So that's what I hope has happened and where I hope we'll go.

Mr. Knoller [Mark Knoller, CBS Radio], I'll take your question and then I'll go. You guys may want to shop some more. [*Laughter*]

Policy of Constructive Engagement

Q. Mr. President, if constructive engagement is the right policy in your view for dealing with China, why isn't it an appropriate policy for dealing with other countries, say, Cuba?

The President. That's not the question I thought you were going to ask—[*laughter*]—I mean, the example I thought you were going to give. I think each of these has to be taken on its own facts. In the case of Cuba, we actually have tried—I would remind you, we have tried in good faith on more than one occasion to engage Cuba in a way that would develop the kind of reciprocal movement that we see in China.

Under the Cuban Democracy Act, which was passed by the Congress in 1992 and signed by President Bush, but which I strongly supported during the election season, we were given a clear roadmap of balanced actions that we could take and that Cuba could take. And we were, I thought, making progress with that map until the people, including American citizens, were unlawfully shot out of the sky and killed. That led to the passage of the Helms-Burton law.

And even after that, after the Pope went to Cuba, I took some further actions, just about everything I'm empowered to take under the Helms-Burton law, to again increase people-to-people contacts in Cuba, to empower the church more with our support as an instrument of civil society, and to send a signal that I did not want the United States to be estranged from the people of Cuba forever.

I do believe that we have some more options, and I think Cuba is a case where, because it's close to home and because of the position we occupy in the region, our policy has a greater chance of success. But even there, you see, whatever policy you pursue, you have to be prepared to have a little patience and work with it and hope that it will work out in the long run.

But nothing would please me more than to get some clear signal that Cuba was willing to be more open and more free and more democratic and work toward a common future and join the whole rest of the hemisphere. You know, in our hemisphere, every country but Cuba is a democracy, and I would like the see—nothing would please me more than to see some rapprochement between the people of our two countries, especially because of the strong Cuban-American population in our Nation.

Thank you very much.

NOTE: The President's 162d news conference began at 5:23 p.m. in the Grand Ballroom of the Grand Hyatt Hotel. In his remarks, he referred to President Jiang Zemin and Premier Zhu Rongji of China; President Li Teng-hui of Taiwan; freed Chinese dissidents Wei Jingsheng, Bishop Zeng Jingmu, and Wang Dan; David Trimble of the Ulster Unionist Party and John Hume and Seamus Mallon of the Social Democratic and Labor Party of Ireland; Prime Minister Tony Blair of the United Kingdom; Prime Minister Bertie Ahern of Ireland; Prime Minister Ryutaro Hashimoto of Japan; Mayor Xu Kuangdi of Shanghai, China; and Pope John Paul II. Reporters referred to freed Chinese dissident Bao Tong; President Slobodan Milosevic of the Federal Republic of Yugoslavia (Serbia and Montenegro); and former President George Bush.

Memorandum on the Joint Institute for Food Safety Research
July 3, 1998

Memorandum for the Secretary of Health and Human Services and the Secretary of Agriculture

Subject: Joint Institute for Food Safety Research

Americans enjoy the most bountiful and safe food supply in the world. My Administration has made substantial improvements in the food safety system, from modernizing meat, seafood, and poultry inspections to creating a high-tech early warning system to detect and control outbreaks of foodborne illness.

Our success has been built on two guiding principles: (1) engaging all concerned parties including consumers, farmers, industry, and academia, in an open and far-ranging dialogue about improving food safety; and (2) grounding our efforts in the best science available. We have made progress, but more can be done to prevent the many foodborne illnesses that still occur in our country.

As we look to the future of food safety, science and technology will play an increasingly central role. An expanded food safety research agenda is essential to continued improvements in the safety of America's food. We need new tools to detect more quickly dangerous pathogens, like E. coli O157:H7 and campylobacter, and we need better interventions that reduce the risk of contamination during food production.

Food safety research is a critical piece of my Fiscal Year 1999 food safety initiative; and I have urged the Congress to revise the appropriations bills it currently is considering to provide full funding for this initiative. I also have urged the Congress to pass two critical pieces of legislation to bring our food safety system into the 21st century: (1) legislation ensuring that the Food and Drug Administration halts imports of fruits, vegetables, and other food products that come from countries that do not meet U.S. food safety requirements or that do not provide the same level of protection as is required for U.S. products; and (2) legislation giving the Department of Agriculture the authority to impose civil penalties for violations of meat and poultry regulations and to issue mandatory recalls to remove unsafe meat and poultry from the marketplace.

At the same time, we need to make every effort to maximize our current resources and authorities. One very important way to achieve this objective is to improve and coordinate food safety research activities across the Federal Government, with State and local governments, and the private sector. Solid research can and will help us to identify foodborne hazards more rapidly and accurately, and to develop more effective intervention mechanisms to prevent food contamination.

I therefore direct you to report back to me within 90 days on the creation of a Joint Institute for Food Safety Research that will: (1) develop a strategic plan for conducting food safety research activities consistent with my Food Safety Initiative; and (2) efficiently coordinate all Federal food safety research, including with the private sector and academia. This Institute, which will operate under your joint leadership, should cooperate and consult with all interested parties, including other Federal agencies and offices—particularly, the Environmental Protection Agency, the National Partnership for Reinventing Government, and the Office of Science and Technology Policy—State and local agencies focusing on research and public health, and on consumers, producers, industry, and academia. The Institute should make special efforts to build on efforts of the private sector, through the use of public-private partnerships or other appropriate mechanisms.

These steps, taken together and in coordination with our pending legislation, will ensure to the fullest extent possible the safety of food for all of America's families.

WILLIAM J. CLINTON

NOTE: This memorandum was made available by the Office of the Press Secretary on July 3 but was embargoed for release until 10:06 a.m. on July 4.

The President's Radio Address
July 4, 1998

Good morning, I've just returned from my trip to China, a great and ancient nation that is undergoing historic change, change I could see in new private businesses that are helping China's economy to grow, in people free for the first time to work in jobs of their own choosing, and in Chinese villages in the first free elections of local leaders.

I was able to speak directly not only to President Jiang and the leaders of the Chinese Government but to the Chinese people themselves about the partnership we hope to build with China for peace and prosperity and about the importance of freedom and what it means to us in America. At this particular moment in history, when for the first time a majority of the world's people live under governments of their own choosing, and when in China the positive impacts of greater openness and personal liberties are already apparent, I'm especially glad to be home for Independence Day, the day we celebrate the freedom our Founders declared 222 years ago this Fourth of July.

And this Fourth of July, even as we celebrate, we should be not only grateful for the freedom we enjoy; we should rededicate ourselves to the work of responsible citizenship. For example, on the Fourth of July, families and friends come together all over America at backyard barbecues and parks for picnics. As they enjoy their meals, I want to report to you about what I'm doing to make sure the food and drinks we serve our families this Independence Day and every day are safe.

Our food supply is the most bountiful and the safest in the world, but we know we can do better. For nearly 6 years, I've worked hard to put in place a modern food safety system for the 21st century. I signed into law legislation to keep harmful pesticides off our fruits and vegetables. We put in place strong protections to ensure that seafood is safe, and we're modernizing our meat and poultry safety system.

Last year we launched a nationwide early warning system to catch outbreaks of food-borne illnesses sooner and prevent them from happening in the first place. But as much as we've done, we know we have to do more to keep our families safe and strong. We know older people and children are especially vulnerable to contaminated food. That lesson was driven home tragically last year, when apple juice contaminated with a deadly strain of *E. coli* caused the death of a 16-month-old child in Washington State and led to the hospitalization of more than a dozen other children.

Today we're taking two important steps to ensure that our food supply is as safe as we can make it. First, I am pleased to announce a new rule that requires warning labels on all packaged juice that has not been pasteurized or processed to kill harmful bacteria. These warnings will help families make better decisions about the juice they buy, and they will help us to prevent thousands of Americans from becoming ill every year.

Second, I'm directing the Department of Health and Human Services and the Department of Agriculture to report back to me within 90 days with a plan to create a new national institute for food safety research. This institute will join the resources of the public and private sectors and bring together the talents of the most esteemed scientists in the government, in universities, and in businesses to develop cutting edge techniques to keep our food safe.

I'm doing what I can to protect our families from contaminated food. Congress must also do its part to ensure the safety of America's food supply. First and most important, it should fully fund my comprehensive $101 million food safety initiative. Among other important programs, this initiative will pay for 225 new food and drug administrators, inspectors, and employees: people who can keep unsafe food away from our borders, out of our stores, and off our dining room tables.

Congress should also give the FDA greater authority to halt imports of fruits, vegetables, and other food products that are produced under safety conditions that simply do not match our own strict standards. It should give the U.S. Department of Agriculture new authority to impose tough fines on businesses who violate those standards and to issue mandatory recalls of unsafe meat and poultry before they reach our table; and it should confirm a respected, experienced scientist, Dr. Jane Henney, to lead our food safety efforts as Commissioner of FDA.

Food can never be made entirely safe. Therefore, every parent also has a responsibility: a responsibility to handle food carefully, especially during the summer. Meanwhile, we must do everything we can to protect the food Americans eat and to give our families the peace of mind they deserve. That's one important way, on this Fourth of July, we can resolve to keep our Nation strong as we move into the 21st century.

Happy Independence Day, Americans, and thanks for listening.

NOTE: The address was recorded at 7:18 a.m. on July 3 in the Grand Hyatt Hotel, Hong Kong SAR, China, for broadcast at 10:06 a.m., e.d.t., on July 4. The transcript was made available by the Office of the Press Secretary on July 3 but was embargoed for release until the broadcast. In his address, the President referred to President Jiang Zemin of China, and Jane E. Henney, Food and Drug Administration Commissioner-designate.

Remarks on Medicare and the Legislative Agenda and an Exchange With Reporters
July 6, 1998

The President. Good morning. I'm delighted to be here with Secretary Shalala, Mr. Apfel, and Ron Pollack to make an announcement today. Let me first, by way of introduction, say, as all of you know, the First Lady and I just returned this weekend from our trip to China. It was a trip that advanced America's interests and values in a secure, stable, and increasingly open China by achieving solid progress in a number of areas and an honest, unprecedentedly open discussion with both Chinese leaders and the Chinese people.

We've come back to America at a critical time. We're exactly halfway through the Major League Baseball season, but we're already in the ninth inning of this congressional session. We have to use wisely the remaining 38 working days to make a season of progress.

With an economy the strongest in a generation and our social fabric strengthening, it is, as I have said repeatedly, extremely tempting for all of us to kick back and soak in the good times. But that would be wrong. There are still enormous challenges and opportunities facing the United States on the edge of the 21st century. We must make this a moment of opportunity, not missed opportunity.

First, we have to advance the economic strategy that has brought so much opportunity to so many Americans. In the coming weeks, I will insist that the House join me and the Senate in reserving the surplus until we save Social Security first. We should fulfill our obligation

to America's children, with smaller class sizes, modernized schools, higher standards, more Head Start opportunities, more reading help for third graders, more access to college.

We should strengthen the International Monetary Fund because our prosperity depends upon the stability of our trading partners in Asia and around the world. We should press forward with our reform of Government by passing IRS reform to guard against abuses and extend taxpayers' rights, and through bipartisan campaign finance reform.

And we must further strengthen families and communities across our country with a juvenile crime bill that uses prosecutors and probation officers to crack down on gangs, guns, and drugs, and bars violent juveniles from buying guns for life; with comprehensive tobacco legislation; and with the Patients' Bill of Rights that says critical medical decisions can only be made by doctors, not insurance company accountants.

There is much to do in these remaining 38 days. Congress has a choice to make in writing this chapter of our history. It can choose partisanship, or it can choose progress. Congress must decide.

I stand ready to work with lawmakers of good faith in both parties, as I have for 5½ years, to move our Nation forward. And I have a continuing obligation to act, to use the authority of the presidency and the persuasive power of the podium to advance America's interest at home and abroad. Nowhere is that need greater than our mission to provide quality health care for every American, especially the elderly.

Last year's bipartisan balanced budget agreement gave seniors and people with disabilities new help to pay their Medicare premiums. This was the right thing to do. Yet a new study released today by Mr. Pollack's Families USA shows that over 3 million of the hardest-pressed Medicare beneficiaries still do not receive the help to which they are due.

I want to thank Ron Pollack for his continuing excellent work for accessible and quality care for all Americans, and for continuing to point out the problems in achieving that goal.

Today I am launching a national effort to educate every single Medicare recipient about this opportunity, using the mail, Medicare and Social Security notices, case workers, field offices, working with State governments, and using the Internet. Through this effort, hundreds of thousands of older and disabled low-income Americans will receive more affordable health care without any new congressional action. This is a duty we owe our parents and our fellow citizens, and we should honor it. It's the right thing to do.

I want to thank Secretary Shalala and Mr. Apfel for working out the details of this outreach. We look forward to signing up people and getting them on the Medicare rolls as quickly as possible.

This is a moment of opportunity. We have to use it decisively. We can do so, and if we do we will strengthen our Nation. Again I say, we have to choose progress over partisanship.

Thank you.

Fast-Track Trading Authority

Q. Speaker Gingrich said that he may bring up fast-track legislation again this fall. Are you planning an aggressive push for fast track this year?

The President. Well, I don't know that anything has changed in terms of the votes. I would like to see the Africa trade bill, which did pass the House, and the Caribbean Basin Initiative, which I understand has been modified in the Senate so it may pass, pass. You know I'm strongly for fast track, but if there is no reason to believe we can pass it, it would be a mistake

to keep the other initiatives from passing which would do a great deal of good for the United States and for the countries in our neighborhood and in Africa.

Health Maintenance Organizations

Q. Mr. President, in 12 States big HMO's have dropped Medicaid coverage altogether. In at least 12 States, major HMO's have dropped Medicaid——

The President. Yes, I read that story in the morning paper, and I was very concerned about it. And before I came out here, I talked to Secretary Shalala about it. She says that in some States, there is contrary evidence, so I have asked her to look at all 50 States, get all the facts, report back to me as soon as possible, and then we'll let you know what we find out as quickly as we can. It was a very disturbing story, but we want to get all the facts, and then we'll make them available to you.

Thank you.

Death of Roy Rogers

Q. Your thoughts on Roy Rogers?

The President. I would like to say something about Roy Rogers because he was, as you know, most prominent in my childhood. I think it was from the midforties to the midfifties when he was the number one Western star. And like most people my age, I grew up on Roy Rogers, Dale Evans, and Trigger, and Gabby Hayes. I really appreciate what he stood for, the movies he made, and the kind of values they embodied, and the good-natured spirit that he exhibited all the way up until his last interviews, not so very long ago.

And my thoughts are with his family and his many friends, but today there will be a lot of sad and grateful Americans, especially of my generation, because of his career.

Thank you.

NOTE: The President spoke at 10:45 a.m. in the Rose Garden at the White House. In his remarks, he referred to Ronald F. Pollack, vice president and executive director, Families USA; Roy Rogers' wife, actress Dale Evans, and his horse, Trigger; and the late actor George (Gabby) Hayes.

Letter to Congressional Leaders Reporting on the National Emergency With Respect to Libya
July 6, 1998

Dear Mr. Speaker: *(Dear Mr. President:)*

I hereby report to the Congress on the developments since my last report of January 13, 1998, concerning the national emergency with respect to Libya that was declared in Executive Order 12543 of January 7, 1986. This report is submitted pursuant to section 401(c) of the National Emergencies Act, 50 U.S.C. 1641(c); section 204(c) of the International Emergency Economic Powers Act (IEEPA), 50 U.S.C. 1703(c); and section 505(c) of the International Security and Development Cooperation Act of 1985, 22 U.S.C. 2349aa–9(c).

1. On January 2, 1998, I renewed for another year the national emergency with respect to Libya pursuant to IEEPA. This renewal extended the current comprehensive financial and trade embargo against Libya in effect since 1986. Under these sanctions, virtually all trade with Libya is prohibited, and all assets owned or controlled by the Libyan government in the United States or in the possession or control of U.S. persons are blocked.

2. There have been no amendments to the Libyan Sanctions Regulations, 31 C.F.R. Part 550 (the "Regulations"), administered by the Office of Foreign Assets Control (OFAC) of the Department of the Treasury, since my last report of January 13, 1998.

3. During the reporting period, OFAC reviewed numerous applications for licenses to authorize transactions under the Regulations. Consistent with OFAC's ongoing scrutiny of banking transactions, the largest category of license approvals (34) concerned requests by non-Libyan persons or entities to unblock certain interdicted funds transfers. Three licenses authorized receipt of payment for the provision of legal services to the Government of Libya in connection with actions in U.S. courts in which the Government of Libya was named as defendant and for other legal services. One license authorizing certain travel transactions was issued. A total of 38 licenses were issued during the reporting period.

4. During the current 6-month period, OFAC continued to emphasize to the international banking community in the United States the importance of identifying and blocking payments made by or on behalf of Libya. OFAC worked closely with the banks to assure the effectiveness of interdiction software systems used to identify such payments. During the reporting period, more than 140 transactions potentially involving Libya, totaling more than $8.9 million, were interdicted.

5. Since my last report, OFAC has collected 15 civil monetary penalties totaling nearly $280,000 for violations of the U.S. sanctions against Libya. Fourteen of the violations involved the failure of banks and U.S. corporations to block payments or letters of credit transactions relating to Libyan-owned or -controlled financial institutions. One U.S. individual paid an OFAC penalty for commercial exports to Libya.

Various enforcement actions carried over from previous reporting periods have continued to be pursued aggressively. Numerous investigations are ongoing and new reports of violations are being scrutinized.

6. The expenses incurred by the Federal Government in the 6-month period from January 7 through July 6, 1998, that are directly attributable to the exercise of powers and authorities conferred by the declaration of the Libyan national emergency are estimated at approximately $960,000. Personnel costs were largely centered in the Department of the Treasury (particularly in the Office of Foreign Assets Control, the Office of the General Counsel, and the U.S. Customs Service), the Department of State, and the Department of Commerce.

7. The policies and actions of the Government of Libya continue to pose an unusual and extraordinary threat to the national security and foreign policy of the United States. In adopting UNSCR 883 in November 1993, the United Nations Security Council determined that the continued failure of the Government of Libya to demonstrate by concrete actions its renunciation of terrorism, and in particular its continued failure to respond fully and effectively to the requests and decisions of the Security Council in Resolutions 731 and 748, concerning the bombing of the Pan Am 103 and UTA 772 flights,

constituted a threat to international peace and security. The United States will continue to coordinate its comprehensive sanctions enforcement efforts with those of other U.N. member states. We remain determined to ensure that the perpetrators of the terrorist acts against Pan Am 103 and UTA 772 are brought to justice. The families of the victims in the murderous Lockerbie bombing and other acts of Libyan terrorism deserve nothing less. I shall continue to exercise the powers at my disposal to apply economic sanctions against Libya fully and effectively, so long as those measures are appropriate, and will continue to report periodically to the Congress on significant developments as required by law.

Sincerely,

WILLIAM J. CLINTON

NOTE: Identical letters were sent to Newt Gingrich, Speaker of the House of Representatives, and Albert Gore, Jr., President of the Senate. This letter was released by the Office of the Press Secretary on July 7.

Remarks on Signing the Memorandum on Ensuring Compliance With the Health Insurance Portability and Accountability Act
July 7, 1998

Thank you. Mr. Pomeroy, we're delighted to have you here, along with your colleagues, and we appreciate the work you do every day. I want to thank all of those who are here with me on this platform who are responsible for the action we're taking today and the work we've done on health care. And, like the Vice President, I'd like to say a special word of appreciation to Senator Kennedy.

I honestly believe that when the history of the United States Congress in the 20th century is written, there will be very few people who have exercised as much positive influence to benefit the American people, whether they were in the majority or the minority, as Senator Kennedy. And this is one of the crowning achievements of his career, and I'm very grateful to him for what he's done.

I have done everything I knew to do to help our country move forward to expand health care access and improve health care quality. Yesterday I announced an important initiative to help more than 3 million senior citizens get assistance in paying their Medicare bills. I have called upon Congress to rise above partisanship and join me in ensuring that the well-being of the patient will always be our health care system's bottom line, whether or not the patient is in a managed care plan or in traditional fee-for-service medicine. And in a few moments, I intend to take action to strengthen the vital health care protections of the Kennedy-Kassebaum law.

It was nearly 2 years ago that I stood with many of the people in this room on the South Lawn to proudly sign that bill into law. It was a remarkable achievement, the product of extraordinary dedication by Senators Kassebaum Baker and Senator Kennedy and others. It's given millions of Americans the chance to change jobs without losing health insurance even if they or someone in their family has a so-called pre-existing condition.

Unfortunately, reports have shown that some health plans are paying no more than lip service to the requirements of the law, delaying or denying coverage to eligible Americans. That is unacceptable. It is wrong.

I will sign an Executive order, at the conclusion of this event, to give new teeth to the Kassebaum-Kennedy law and new peace of mind to Americans with pre-existing conditions. As the single largest buyer of private health insurance, the Federal Government speaks with a very loud voice. With that voice, we now put health plans on notice. This administration has zero tolerance for actions that undermine these vital health care protections. If you violate the letter or the spirit of the Kassebaum-Kennedy law, we will, if necessary, terminate your contract to provide health insurance to Federal employees. If you say no to people with pre-existing conditions, the Federal Government will say no to you.

I am very pleased that the National Association of Insurance Commissioners will join the

Department of Health and Human Services and the Office of Personnel Management in these efforts. As the primary enforcers of the Kassebaum-Kennedy law, the State commissioners play a crucial role, and I thank them for their help.

Now it's Congress' turn also to get involved. We must work together in the same spirit of bipartisanship that produced the Kassebaum-Kennedy law to enact an enforceable Patients' Bill of Rights. All Americans deserve to know that the medical decisions they depend upon are being made by medical doctors and not insurance company accountants. All Americans have the right to know all their medical options and not just the cheapest. All Americans should have the right to choose the specialists they want for the care they need. All Americans should have the right to emergency room care whenever and wherever they need it. Traditional care or managed care, all Americans deserve quality care.

In February I took executive action to extend this Patients' Bill of Rights to all the 85 million Americans who get their health insurance through the Federal Government. Now Congress must do so for every American.

Today there are only 37 working days left in this session of Congress, but that's no excuse for failing to act, and millions of Americans are looking to us for the right kind of action. They want us to pass a strong, bipartisan Patients' Bill of Rights. They want us to put progress over partisanship. They want us to leave our country stronger for the century just ahead. I believe this action today helps to achieve that goal, and I thank all of you for your role in it.

Thank you very much.

NOTE: The President spoke at 2:20 p.m. in the Grand Foyer at the White House. In his remarks, he referred to Glenn Pomeroy, president, National Association of Insurance Commissioners. The President also referred to the Health Insurance Portability and Accountability Act of 1996, Public Law 104–191; and his memorandum of February 20 on Federal agency compliance with the Patient Bill of Rights (*Public Papers of the Presidents: William J. Clinton, 1998 Book I* (Washington: U.S. Government Printing Office, 1999), p. 260).

Memorandum on Ensuring Compliance With the Health Insurance Portability and Accountability Act
July 7, 1998

Memorandum for the Secretary of Labor, the Secretary of Health and Human Services, the Director of the Office of Personnel Management

Subject: Ensuring Compliance with the Health Insurance Portability and Accountability Act of 1996

Earlier this year, my Administration received a number of troubling reports that health insurers were circumventing insurance protections under the Health Insurance Portability and Accountability Act of 1996 (HIPAA) by giving financial incentives to agents to avoid enrolling Americans with pre-existing conditions. In addition, we learned that some agents were delaying the processing of applications submitted by qualified individuals in order to ensure that the applicant had a sufficient break in coverage to lose eligibility for HIPAA protections. Such actions clearly were and are inconsistent with the letter and spirit of HIPAA.

In February, I directed the Department of Health and Human Services (HHS) to take appropriate actions to encourage health insurers and their agents to stop all such harmful practices. The Health Care Financing Administration (HCFA) responded by immediately releasing a strong guidance bulletin on March 18 to every insurance commissioner in the Nation, advising them of our strong commitment to ensure compliance with HIPAA.

Today, I am taking additional actions to ensure that health plans comply with this law. I direct the Office of Personnel Management (OPM) to use its contractual relationship with health plans to improve HIPAA compliance. The

OPM oversees the Federal Employees Health Benefit Program (FEHBP), the Nation's largest employer-sponsored health benefits program with 9 million enrollees and 350 participating health plans.

Specifically, I direct the OPM to take all appropriate action—up to and including termination of a participating health plan from the FEHBP—if the OPM determines, consistent with HIPAA and implementing regulations, that a plan is engaging in insurance practices that are inconsistent with the letter and spirit of HIPAA. In order to be eligible to participate in the FEHBP, carriers subject to HIPAA will have to certify to the OPM that they are providing access to health insurance in compliance with HIPAA. Such action by the OPM will provide another enforcement tool to the Federal Government without in any way altering or hindering any other enforcement action by the HCFA or State insurance commissioners.

To help ensure that the OPM can take these important enforcement actions, I direct the HCFA to immediately send to the OPM reports of violations by insurers or their representatives that preclude or inhibit access to the insurance protections provided under HIPAA. Any such referral to the OPM would not alter the responsibility of States or the HCFA to utilize any and all enforcement tools at their disposal to ensure HIPAA compliance.

Finally, I direct that the HHS and the Department of Labor report to me, through the Vice President, within 6 months on the successes and shortcomings of HIPAA. This report should be produced after consultation with the States and the National Association of Insurance Commissioners and should include specific legislative or regulatory recommendations to further strengthen this law.

My Administration has zero tolerance for any actions that hinder vulnerable Americans from accessing insurance, consistent with HIPAA's protections. This directive is intended to ensure that health plans come into compliance with this important statute so that Americans are assured these insurance protections.

WILLIAM J. CLINTON

Statement on the Death of M.K.O. Abiola of Nigeria
July 7, 1998

I was deeply saddened to learn of the sudden and untimely death of M.K.O. Abiola, a distinguished citizen and patriot of Nigeria. I extend my heartfelt condolences to his family and to all of the people of Nigeria.

Members of a U.S. delegation, led by Under Secretary of State Thomas Pickering, and Nigerian officials were with Chief Abiola when he fell ill. They accompanied him to the hospital with a physician and Government officials and witnessed physicians at the State House clinic work to try to save Chief Abiola.

I have been encouraged by the efforts of the new head of state, General Abdulsalam Abubakar, to restore public confidence in the Government of Nigeria and to take crucial initial steps to embark on a credible transition to civilian democratic rule. I urge the Government of Nigeria to continue and to expedite this transition and call upon all the people of Nigeria to contribute peacefully and constructively to build a brighter future for their country.

In this time of tragedy, I wish to reaffirm the longstanding friendship of the people of the United States for the people of Nigeria.

Remarks on Efforts to Promote Gun Safety and Responsibility
July 8, 1998

I would like to begin by thanking Suzann Wilson for making the long trip up here from Arkansas with her sister to be with us today, so soon after that terrible tragedy. Most people wouldn't feel like going out of the house, much less coming all the way to Washington, and I think it is a real credit to her and to her devotion to her daughter that she is here today.

I want to thank Colonel Mitchell and Lieutenant Governor Kathleen Kennedy Townsend and, in his absence, Governor Glendening, for the pathbreaking work being done in Maryland on this important issue. I thank Secretary Rubin and Mr. Johnson and Mr. Magaw for being here and the work the Treasury Department is doing. Thank you, Secretary Riley, for the work you've done to have zero tolerance for guns in schools. Thank you, Attorney General Reno, for the steady work now we have done for 6 years to try to bring this issue to the American people.

I thank Senator Durbin, Senator Chafee, and Senator Kohl, and a special word of thanks to Representative Carolyn McCarthy. And to all the advocates out here, I welcome you here, and I thank you, and especially to the law enforcement officers.

I think that this recent series of killings in our schools has seared the heart of America about as much as anything I can remember in a long, long time. I will always personally remember receiving the news from Jonesboro because it's a town I know well. I know the local officials; I know the school officials. I've spent large numbers of days there. I've been in all the schools and answered the children's questions. And once you know a place like that, you can't possibly imagine something like this occurring.

But it's happened all over the country. I was in Springfield, Oregon, as you know, in the last couple of weeks, meeting with the families there. I think every American has sent out prayers to Suzann and the other parents and the other spouses and people who were so wounded by this. But in a fundamental way, our entire Nation has been wounded by these troubled children with their guns.

As has already been said, these events have been even more difficult for us to understand because they're occurring at a time when we've had the lowest crime rate in America in 25 years and for the first time in a decade, a steady drop in the juvenile crime rate. So we struggle for answers. We say, "Well, does the popular culture have anything to do with this? Does good parenting have anything to do with this?" And we know that probably everything we consider has something to do with this. But no matter how you analyze this, it is clear that the combination of children and firearms is deadly. As parents, public officials, citizens, we simply cannot allow easy access to weapons that kill.

For 5 years now, our administration has worked to protect our children, and we are making progress, as has been said. A great deal of the credit goes to farsighted leaders at the city level and at the State level, people like Lieutenant Governor Kathleen Kennedy Townsend and Superintendent Mitchell and Governor Glendening.

We're well on our way toward putting 100,000 police on the street. About a quarter of a million people have not been able to buy guns in the first place because of the Brady law, because of their criminal background or their mental health history. We have banned several types of assault weapons and have struggled to preserve the integrity of that law against a commercial assault from importers.

School security is tighter; antigang prevention is better; penalties are stronger. We promoted discipline in schools with antitruancy and curfew and school uniform policies, and in various ways, they have worked marvelously in many communities. And we have a national policy now, in all our schools, of zero tolerance for guns in schools. Over 6,000 students with guns were disarmed and sent home last year, doubtless preventing even more terrible acts of violence.

But it is not enough if children have access to guns. In Springfield, Oregon, the young man in custody was sent home the day before because he had a gun in the school.

So, yes, our laws must be strong, our enforcement resolute. At home, parents must teach their children the difference between right and wrong and lead them away from violence. But recent events remind us that even if all this is done, it is still too easy for deadly weapons to wind up in the hands of children, by intent or by accident, and then to lead to tragedy, by intent or by accident.

We can't shrug our shoulders and say, "Well, accidents will happen," or "Some kids are just beyond hope." That is a copout. Instead, every one of us must step up to our responsibility. That certainly includes gun owners, gun purchasers, and gun dealers. Today we say to them, protecting children is your responsibility too, and there are penalties for the failure to fulfill it.

In response to the directive I issued to Secretary Rubin in June of last year, all Federal gun dealers will now be required to issue written warnings and post signs like that one over there. The sign makes it plain for all to see, in simple, direct language, that it's illegal to sell, deliver, or transfer a handgun to a minor, period. From now on, no customer or employee can avoid personal responsibility by pleading ignorance of the law.

Responsibility at gun shops, of course, must be matched by responsibility at home. Suzann talked movingly about that. Guns are kept in the home for many purposes, from hunting to self-defense. That is every family's right, and as she said more eloquently than I, that is not in question. The real question is every parent's responsibility, every adult's responsibility to make sure that unsupervised children cannot get a hold of the guns. When guns are stored carelessly, children can find them, pick them up, court danger. Most will put them back where they found them. Others, as we know now from hard experience, will touch the trigger by accident. A troubled few will take guns to school with violence in mind.

Too many guns wielded in rage by troubled adolescents can be traced back to an irresponsible adult. As has been previously said, in Maryland now, and now in 14 other States, parents have a legal responsibility to keep guns locked and out of reach of young hands. That should be the law in all 50 States. There are 35 more that ought to follow Maryland's lead. It should be the practice in every home.

There is also a proper Federal role in preventing children's access to firearms, and Congress should pass a tough, targeted child access prevention law with new penalties to punish the most egregious offenders.

I applaud Senators Chafee and Durbin for their legislation starting us down the road toward making this the law of the land. I thank Senator Kohl and Representative McCarthy for their strong support. They are doing the right thing. And during the last days of this legislative session, this is how we should move forward, again I say, with progress, not partisanship.

There is much we must do in public life to fulfill our obligation to our children. More than a year ago, we directed all Federal law enforcement agencies to issue child safety locks to Federal officers so that their guns could not be misused. A majority of our gun manufacturers have joined us voluntarily in this effort, and that has been successful. I hope all other gun manufacturers will follow suit.

The real work, of course, must still be done in our homes, beyond law and policy, to the most basic values of respect, right and wrong, conscience and community, and violence rejected in favor of nonviolence and communication. Only parents can remedy what ails children in their heart of hearts. But the rest of us must do our part to help and must do our part to contain the potential for destructive violence when things fail at home.

So I say again, this is an issue that has wounded every American in one way or the other. Of the four women standing to my right, three have lost members of their immediate family because of gun violence. All of us have grieved with them. We can do better. This is one big first step.

Thank you very much.

NOTE: The President spoke at 12:03 p.m. in Room 450 of the Old Executive Office Building. In his remarks, he referred to Suzann Wilson, whose daughter Britthney Varner was killed in the Westside Middle School shooting in Jonesboro, AR; Maryland Superintendent of Police Col. David B. Mitchell; Lt. Gov. Kathleen Kennedy Townsend and Gov. Parris N. Glendening of Maryland; and Kipland P. Kinkel, who was charged with the May 21 shooting at Thurston High School in Springfield, OR, in which 2 students were killed and 22 wounded.

Remarks in the PBS "Presidential Dialogue on Race"
July 8, 1998

Moderator Jim Lehrer. Good evening. I'm Jim Lehrer. Welcome to an hour of conversation with President Clinton about race in America. And welcome to you, Mr. President.

The President. Thank you, Jim.

Mr. Lehrer. The President's conversation will be with eight Americans: four NewsHour regulars: essayist Richard Rodriguez of the Pacific News Service, Roger Rosenblatt and Clarence Page of the Chicago Tribune, and regional commentator Cynthia Tucker of the Atlanta Constitution; plus, four others: Roberto Suro of the Washington Post, author of a recent book on Hispanic-Americans; Kay James, dean of Regent University's School of Government; Elaine Chao, former head of United Way of America, now at the Heritage Foundation; and Sherman Alexie, novelist, poet, and screenwriter.

Keep in mind, please, that whatever their affiliation and, most importantly, their race, each is here as an individual speaking only for him or herself.

Richard Rodriguez, what do you think is the single most important thing the President could do to improve race relations in this country?

[*Mr. Rodriguez asserted his belief that although race issues in the country had become more complicated, the national discussion initiated under "One America: The President's Initiative on Race" and its Chair, John Hope Franklin, had not kept pace with that complexity.*]

The President. Well, I basically agree with you about that. As a Southerner, like Dr. Franklin, I think that there are unique and still-unresolved issues between black and white Americans, and there are some conditions in America which disproportionately involve African-Americans. Some of them are not old. Today there was just this Journal of American Medical Association story saying that African-Americans metabolize nicotine in a different way than other races, as far as we know, and therefore, even though blacks smoke fewer cigarettes, they're more likely to get lung cancer—interesting thing.

But to get back to your main point, I have tried to emphasize that America is becoming a multiracial, multiethnic, multireligious society, and therefore it would be more important both to understand the differences and to identify the common values that hold us together as a country.

And I often cite, since we're in northern Virginia where this program is being filmed, I often cite the Fairfax County School District, which is now the most diverse school district in the country, with people from over 100 different racial and ethnic groups with over 100 different languages, actually, in this school district. And I think that's a pattern of where we're going. I've got a friend who is a Southern Baptist minister here; he used to be a minister in Arkansas. He's got a Korean ministry in his church. That's just one tiny example of the kind of things you're going to see more and more of in the country.

Mr. Lehrer. Cynthia, is the unfinished business still black and white?

[*Ms. Tucker suggested that what many considered racial differences were actually class differences, that disproportionately poor blacks resented whites, and that working-class whites with stagnant or declining incomes blamed blacks and immigrants. She voiced the opinion that the wealth gap was, in part, responsible for the continuing racial problems.*]

The President. There's no doubt about that. And I think that whenever possible, if you think that there is a class-related or income-related element in the difficulties we have with race, we ought to have income-based solutions to it.

A lot of things that I've asked the Congress to do over the last 5½ years, a lot of things that are in this budget now are designed to address that, with grater incentives for people to invest in inner cities and Native American reservations and other poor areas; tax systems, which would disproportionately benefit working people on the lower income of the scale. I think those things are very important because—and there is, by the way, some evidence that, in the last couple of years, the income inequality has begun to abate some.

But I think it's very important not to confuse the two. I mean, I believe the primary reason for income inequality—increasing inequality in America is that we have changed the nature of the economy. That is, if you go back to 100 years ago, and you see when we moved from an agricultural to an industrial economy, we also had a big influx of immigrants. There was a hug increase in inequality, not so much because of the immigrants, but because the way people made money changed. The whole basis of wealth changed. That's what's happened in this computer-based information economy, and the premium on education these days is so much greater than it's ever been, that there's a lot of stagnant incomes out there from people who have worked hard all of their lives but aren't part of the modern economy. And I think that we need strategies to identify the people that aren't winning and turn them into winners. And at the very least, turn their children into winners.

Mr. Lehrer. Kay James, class or race?

[*Ms. James responded that no matter how middle class a person became, if that person was black, he or she still experienced discrimination. She suggested that issues of poverty and class, although worthy topics, should not take precedence over the discussion of racism in America.*]

The President. Well, obviously, I agree with that, or I wouldn't have set up this initiative. I think that the point I wanted to make is to whatever extent you can have an economic approach that embraces people of all races, if it elevates disproportionately—racial groups that have been disproportionately depressed, you'll help to deal with the race problem.

But there is—no one could look around the world—if you forget about America, just look at the rest of the world; no one could doubt the absence of a deep, inbred predisposition of people to fear, look down on, separate themselves from, and, when possible, discriminate against people who are of different racial and ethnic groups than themselves. I mean, this is the primary factor in the world's politics today at the end of the cold war.

Mr. Lehrer. Sherman, does a poor Native American starting out face more hurdles than a poor white American starting out?

Mr. Alexie. A poor Native American faces more hurdles than a poor anybody.

Mr. Lehrer. Anybody?

[*Mr. Alexie described conditions in Native American reservations and noted the lack of role models.*]

The President. Let me ask you something. I'd like to start, because I think this will help us to get to the race issue you talked about. Let's just talk about the Native American population. When I was running for President in 1992, I didn't know much about the American Indian condition, except that we had a significant but very small population of Indians in my home State and that my grandmother was one-quarter Cherokee; that's all I knew. And I spent a lot of time going around to the reservations and to meet with leaders and to learn about the sort of nation-to-nation legal relationship that's supposed to exist between the U.S. Government and the Native American tribes.

I concluded that the American Indians had gotten the worst of both worlds, that they had not been given enough empowerment or responsibility or tools to make the most of their own lives, and the sort of paternalistic relationship the U.S. Government had kept them in was pathetic and inadequate. So they literally got the worst of both worlds. They weren't given enough help, and they certainly didn't have enough responsibility and power, in my view, to build the future.

So what do you think the most important thing is for Americans to know about American Indians? And what do you think the most important thing American Indians should be doing for themselves or should ask us to do to change the future?

[*Mr. Alexie answered that people needed to understand that Native Americans are separate, as sovereign nations, politically and economically. He then said that Native Americans themselves had to recognize the value of education.*]

Mr. Lehrer. Elaine Chao, where do the Asian-Americans—what kinds of obstacles do they start out with compared to white Americans or Native Americans or black Americans, whatever?

[*Ms. Chao noted the increased strain in relations between races due to feelings of unequal treatment and the Asian-American community's underrepresentation in the minority figures.*]

The President. Give us an example.

[*Ms. Chao related the story of an Asian-American single mother in San Francisco whose son had been denied admission into a school, despite high test scores, because it already had "too many Chinese-Americans."*]

The President. Let's go back to what Kay said. What do you think the roots of racism are?

[*Ms. James suggested that the root of racism was a problem of character and integrity and asserted that it could only be overcome if people interacted and dispelled preconceived notions, prejudices, and stereotypes.*]

The President. Do you think young people— and you're a dean of a school of government— do you think young people are less racially prejudiced than their parents on the whole?

[*Ms. James related her own experience as a youth and part of a group that integrated schools in the South and how over time, relationships were established that broke the barrier of race and friendships flourished.*]

Mr. Lehrer. Roger Rosenblatt, how would you answer the President's question? Where do we get our attitudes about race? Where do they come from?

[*Mr. Rosenblatt suggested that racial attitudes stemmed from fear, ignorance, and a sense of otherness, a perceived difference that caused hatred in some and a shy retreat in others. He noted that the focus was too often placed on blame rather than solutions and suggested reaffirming the goal of integration.*]

The President. What about what Elaine said, though? Let me give you a little background, although I don't know about the facts of this case. California—I give them a lot of credit— California is trying to have within the public school system a much higher performing school by, among other things, going to charter schools, which are—which seek to have the benefits of public education with the strengths of private, standard-spaced education. And San Francisco has a number of schools—this is probably a part of their school choice program—where they basically create schools. They get out from under the rules and regulations of central administration, and they hold the kids to high standards.

But apparently, they've made a decision also that they think they ought to have some diversity within their student body. And so, is it fair for a Chinese student who may be the fifth best Chinese student, but also the fifth best overall student who has to get in a class, to be deprived of the chance to get in the class? And if it's not fair, if this child was unfairly treated, what do you do with the kids who didn't do very

well, and what school should they go to, and how can you guarantee them the same standards?

Mr. Lehrer. How would you answer that, Roberto?

[*Mr. Suro remarked on the expansion of the racism problem from the long-established black/white paradigm and the lack of language and mechanisms to deal with the increasing diversity of racism. He asked the President how he applied his own experiences to a more complicated Nation.*]

The President. Well, the short answer is that I try to do now what I tried to do when I was a kid, when I realized what was going on, because I had an unusual background for a lower middle class white guy in the South because I had grandparents who believed in integration, and my grandfather ran a little store, and most of his customers were black. So I had an atypical background. But I was sort of hungering for contact with people who were different from me. And my theory, going back to what Kay said, is that basically, if you would ask me what's the most important thing we could do, I think it is the more people work and learn and worship, if they have faith, and serve together, the more likely you are to strike the right balance between celebrating our differences instead of being afraid of them and still identifying common values.

Now, you still have—you have a separate problem for Native Americans, who literally— many of whom still live on reservations. But there has to be a way—you cannot overcome what you do not know. And if I could just say one other thing. One of the complicating— believe me, there are lots of hard questions. I don't think—one of the hard questions is the education question, whether it's affirmative action in college admissions or what Elaine said, for the simple reason that I believe there is an independent value to having young people have—learn in an environment where they're with people of many different racial and ethnic backgrounds. And the question is, how can you balance that with our devotion to merit and then not discriminating against people because of their race, in effect, when they would otherwise, on grounds of academic merit, get a certain situation? That's one of the hardest questions we face.

But I still think, the more we are together—I was quite impressed, for example, when our daughter was trying to select a college. And one of the things that she did, she went around and actually got the composition and makeup of every school to which she applied, because she wanted—and then she actually went there to see whether those people were actually—[*laughter*]—not just admitted but actually really getting—relating to each other.

But a lot of the young people in her generation that I spend time talking to understand that this is something they need to do. I mean, they figured out that their life is going to be real different from ours, and they better figure out how to live together.

Mr. Lehrer. Clarence, does that make sense to you?

[*Mr. Page explained that people needed to realize that if they wanted diversity, they had to accept sacrifice. He noted that establishing diversity and maintaining it necessitated curbing equal opportunity to some extent, and that achieving dialog and desegregation required work.*]

Mr. Lehrer. Somebody has to get hurt in order for other people to be helped?

[*Mr. Page noted the difficulties of affirmative action, the most divisive issue in race relations, and suggested the President was reluctant to deal with that. He posed the question of defining, as a nation, affirmative action and said that until it was dealt with effectively, it would continue to be a political tool.*]

The President. See, I believe—I frankly—I believe that the real reason it's a problem—it's more a problem in education now than in economics because the unemployment rate is so low and because the jobs are opening up, so most gifted people feel that if they're willing to work hard, they can find a job. We don't have the anxiety about affirmative action we used to have when the police departments and the fire departments were being integrated and promotions were being given. Every now and then you hear something about that, but most of the controversy now is about education. Why? Because people know education is really important, and if parents and children make a decision about where they want to go to school—in the case of Elaine, a public school—that they believe is good, or a college, they're afraid if they don't get in where they want to get in, they'll get a substandard education.

I have a different view. The reason I've supported affirmative action, as long as you don't just let people in who are blatantly unqualified to anything, is that I think, number one, test scores and all these so-called objective measures are somewhat ambiguous and they're not perfect measures of people's capacity to grow. But secondly and even more importantly, I think our society has a vested interest in having people from diverse backgrounds.

When I went to college in the "dark ages," one of the reasons I applied to Georgetown was they had foreign students there, and they had a policy of having a kid from every State there. Maybe I got in because there weren't so many people from Arkansas who applied, for all I know. I think that there are independent educational virtues to a diverse student body, and young people learn different things in different ways. And I don't think objective measurements are perfect. So I don't have a problem with it.

But I think the most important thing is that we have to understand that this is one of the hard questions. And it is best worked out, in my view, by people sitting around a table trying to work out the specifics, like in San Francisco. And when people feel like they have no voice, then they feel robbed. But there will never be a perfect resolution of this.

Mr. Lehrer. Richard, do you agree? No perfect resolutions to this?

[*Mr. Rodriguez agreed and related his experiences with affirmative action in college and the job market, saying he was offered opportunities solely because of his Hispanic heritage rather than personal merit. He suggested that the lack of a basic understanding of the issues involved would trouble race discussions.*]

The President. Let me ask you—let me ask everybody—first of all, I'm glad you said that, because we're in the business of defining stereotypes tonight, so that's good. I think all of us who have worked hard to get where we are are sort of proud of that. I mean, when I was a young man, I was the only person on my law school faculty that voted against our tenure policy because I never wanted anybody to guarantee me a job. I told them they could tell me to leave tomorrow, and I'd go. I mean, I really identify with what you've done. I'm proud of that.

Suppose you're the president of the university. Would you like, other things being equal, to have a faculty that were not—that were reasonably racially diverse? And even more importantly, would you like, other things being equal, to have a student body that reflected the America these young people are going to live in once they've graduated? And if you believe that, and you didn't want to infuriate people like you've been infuriated and make them feel like you've felt, how would you go about achieving that?

I think this is tough stuff. I don't pretend that my position is easy or totally defensible. How would you do it?

[*Mr. Rodriguez answered that matters should be addressed early on, in the first grade as opposed to graduate school. Mr. Rosenblatt agreed and suggested that setting goals was better than setting quotas.*]

The President. Let's go back to this. I want to ask you, too, to come in, because I want you to go in here. [*Laughter*] What exactly was it did you resent? Did you resent the fact they were going to guarantee you a job whether you were any good or not? Or did you resent the fact that they were looking for Hispanic faculty members?

[*Mr. Rodriguez said he resented being entitled to an opportunity because he was a needed minority in a quota system and getting opportunity because his skin was darker than another's. Mr. Suro related his experiences, recalling that there were times when he consciously did not want to be regarded as a Hispanic journalist. He also remarked on the diversity of groups that did not share common histories yet were lumped together in one group.*]

Mr. Lehrer. Cynthia, the differences—in other words, dealing with people differently.

[*Ms. Tucker stated that the black experience in America was distinct. She recounted her own experience living under Jim Crow laws in southern Alabama, and she said that affirmative action was useful and not synonymous with "unqualified." Ms. Chao then stated that the history of America regarding race relations was very tragic, and that it was still not a perfect world, but it was incumbent on people to maintain the ideal of equal opportunity for all. She also stressed the importance of equal standards for all.*]

Mr. Page. Well, how do you define merit? Does—should there be an equal opportunity to get into Berkeley and UCLA? But how do you define merit? Is it SAT's or ACT's or other criteria?

Ms. Chao. No, I think clearly, merit.

Mr. Lehrer. Let me ask Sherman, where do Native Americans fit into the affirmative action debate?

[*Mr. Alexie asserted the illusionary nature of the debate over affirmative action and stated that national policy was being made based on isolated and anecdotal examples. Ms. Chao remarked on the reality of differential standards for different groups.*]

The President. Do you want to answer Clarence?

[*Ms. Chao stressed the importance of education and suggested that the real goal for the country was to eliminate crime and create economic opportunity for all.*]

The President. What were you going to say about this?

Ms. James. I was just going to say, Mr. President, I think the operative phrase was, in your question, "all things being equal," wouldn't we like a diverse community, particularly in the academic arena? And I was looking around the table and thinking, gee whiz, I bet I'm the only one here at the table that has to make admissions decisions.

The President. You're going to make these decisions. [*Laughter*]

[*Ms. James stated that most Americans had a high esteem for the idea of diversity, but they felt there was unfair preferential treatment bestowed on some to achieve it. She suggested focusing on the income-based programs and preferential treatment for reasons other that race.*]

The President. Let me go back to something Clarence said at the beginning. You pointed out—we talked about prejudice, discrimination, then we started talking about diversity and all that. I think you need—if I could go back to the very first thing that all of you started talking about—we need a vocabulary that embraces America's future, and we need a vocabulary that embraces America's present and past on this race issue. And we need to know when we're making distinctions. And then we need to fess up to the fact, at least when it comes to Native Americans, that, if we don't do something fairly dramatic, the future is going to be like the past for too many people.

For example, I think most Americans, whether they're conservatives or liberals or Republicans or Democrats, would support, for example, my budget proposal to give more resources to the EEOC to get rid of the backlog. Because all of the surveys show that 85 percent of the American people, or 90 percent, or something, believe that actual discrimination against an individual person in the workplace is wrong, based on race.

Now, the real problem is that affirmative action, I think now, since there are a lot of middle-class blacks, middle-class Hispanics, that it's almost—people are not so sure in the workplace and the schoolplace whether it is furthering the goal of getting rid of the lingering effects of discrimination, which is Cynthia's experience, and mine as a Southerner—ours—you know, or whether it is now being used to create a more diverse environment which people feel is a good thing, but not a good thing if it is sticking it to this hard-working Chinese mother in San Francisco and her children, who is raising her kids under adverse circumstances.

And I guess one of the things that bothers me is that a lot—we need to make these kinds of discussions practical and institution- or community-based, because, I'll say again, I think that we want our children to grow up to learn to live in the world that they will in fact live in. Therefore, if you forget about discrimination for a minute—you can't ever do that, but let's just assume there is no discrimination—America has a wonderful system of higher education. There are hundreds of schools, I think, you can get a world-class undergraduate education in. And I believe that, therefore, it's worth having some policy to try to diversify the student body.

It's interesting to see what Texas did when the *Hopwood* decision came down. They said, "Well, we don't want to have a totally segregated set of colleges and universities in Texas, so we'll just say the top 10 percent of every high school can automatically go to any Texas institution of higher education." That looks like a merit-based decision, but, of course, it's not any more merit-based than the other decision, because there

are segregated high schools, and there are differences in test scores, and all that.

So we need to kind of—we need 10 hours to discuss this, and I'd like to listen to you. But the only thing I want to point out is, the American people have got to decide. Do they want a housing project in Chicago—in this case, only the people from Chicago have to decide—that's integrated? If so, the people who don't get in there, do they have reasonable alternatives? That's one realistic thing. If a child doesn't get into a good school that he or she wants to get into, do they have an equivalent alternative? If they don't, you maybe have hurt them for life. Is it worth it to get—the discrimination?

Or in the case—look at Kay's problem. She runs a government department, makes these admission decisions in a school that has a certain religious and value-based approach to life. So if a child gets deprived of going into there, even if the kid goes to Harvard, it may not be the cultural environment——

Ms. James. They couldn't get near the education they get at Regent. [*Laughter*]

The President. But let's assume it's equivalent. The child may lose something noneducational. So all these things are—I just want the American people to start talking about this in a way that's real here.

[*Mr. Rodriguez remarked on the increasing numbers of young people who did not want to be defined as belonging to a particular race. He recalled an encounter with a woman in San Francisco whose father was African-American, whose mother was Mexican, and who described herself as a "Blaxican." Mr. Rodriguez said youth would redefine the look of America.*]

The President. That's good.

Mr. Lehrer. Cynthia, and then to Roger—on this question that the President raised, the new dialog—and to Richard—what are the new words we use? What do we talk about in this new world?

[*Ms. Tucker suggested the importance of acknowledging how much the world had changed and the need for a stronger sense of history. Mr. Rosenblatt questioned the similarity of racism today and when he was growing up. He also questioned the importance of affirmative action as an issue for debate.*]

Mr. Lehrer. Roberto, how would you define the new vocabulary?

Mr. Suro. We've talked a lot about how—trying to describe the population and how it's changed. Roger touches on an important point. We have to have a new vocabulary to describe our attitudes. Discrimination is a different thing in this country than it was 20 years ago.

Mr. Lehrer. In what way?

[*Mr. Suro explained that discrimination was based on more factors than solely race, requiring more complicated vocabulary to describe attitudes and more complicated remedies. Mr. Page noted that, even in suburban neighborhoods, some groups tended to be as widely discriminated against as their counterparts in inner-city neighborhoods.*]

Mr. Lehrer. What do you tell your son? What do you tell your son about why this is happening?

[*Mr. Page responded that he answered any of his son's questions and that the child was aware of racial differences but did not consider any race better than others. He then noted that segregation still existed. Mr. Rodriguez recalled being stopped by black police officers while jogging before dawn and remarked on the complexity of American society.*]

Mr. Page. Who said blacks couldn't be prejudiced? Of course.

The President. I agree with that. You know, I'm very sympathetic with what you say. And I want it to be as you say. And I agreed that we have all kinds of overlapping stereotypes that we haven't even talked about. One of the things that came up after Los Angeles riots, you know, the attitudes of the African-Americans to the Korean grocers and the Arab grocers and the Hispanic customers and all of that—it's a lot more complicated than it used to be.

But as a factual matter, if you just look at the prison population—you wanted to bring that up—if you look at all the unemployment rate among young, single African-American males without an education, if you look at the physical isolation of people in these inner-city neighborhoods—we have the lowest unemployment rate in 28 years; there are still New York City neighborhoods where the unemployment rate is 15 percent—if you look at these things, if I could just come back to sort of what I think is practical here, I think it is imperative that we somehow develop a bipartisan consensus in this country that we will do those things which we know will stop another generation of these kids from getting in that kind of trouble.

My best model now, I guess, is what they're trying to do in Chicago in the school system and what they've done in Boston with the juvenile justice system. In Boston, they went for 2 years without one kid under 18 being killed with a gun. Unheard of in a city that size. And if you look at what they did in Houston, we need to at least adopt those strategies that will invest money in keeping these kids out of trouble in the first place and try to keep them out of jail and give them the chance to have a good life. And if there's disproportionate manifestation of race, then so be it. Then we ought to have an affirmative action program, if you will, that invests in those kids' futures and gives them a chance to stay out of trouble.

To me, it's the kids that are being lost altogether and the disproportionate presence of racial minorities among those kids that is still the most disturbing thing in the world. Because if you get these kids up there, 18 or 19, heck, they'll figure out things. Our kids will figure out things we weren't smart enough to figure out. That's how society goes on. That's what progress is all about. But I think we have to recognize that's still a big race problem in this country, especially for African-Americans.

Mr. Lehrer. Clarence raised the point, Sherman, about race talk in his family, and the President—Mr. President, you have said you had trouble getting people to talk bluntly and honestly about race.

The President. Yes. We're all too polite about it.

Mr. Lehrer. How do you get people to talk about race?

[*Mr. Alexie remarked that people were always talking about race, though the language sometimes was coded.*]

Mr. Lehrer. But do Indians talk about race?

Mr. Alexie. Oh, yeah, we're actually probably a lot more conservative and racist than any other single group of people. We're much more reactionary. It's funny; politically, we give our money to Democrats, but we vote for Republicans. [*Laughter*] I'm going to leave that one alone. [*Laughter*]

Mr. Lehrer. How do you get honest talk? Do you think there is honest talk about race?

[*Ms. James responded that people were most likely to talk about race by relating personal experiences.*]

Ms. Chao. I think the bottom line is, I think there has to be not allocation of programs based on preferential treatment but that there is equal opportunity. And going back to Clarence's issue about merit——

Mr. Lehrer. We're talking about talking bluntly about race.

Ms. Chao. Right. I think this is part of it. And I think the President wanted me to answer Clarence's comments, Clarence's question about merit.

Mr. Lehrer. Okay, but we have to—I have to interrupt you all now to say, thank you, Mr. President, and thanks to all the rest of——

The President. We're just getting warmed up.

Mr. Lehrer. I know, I know, I know.

Ms. Chao. It's got to be the same standards for everybody, however merit is defined.

Mr. Lehrer. Okay. But from Washington this has been a conversation with President Clinton about race. I'm Jim Lehrer. Thank you, and good night. And as you see, may the conversation continue.

NOTE: The program was recorded at 2 p.m. in the WETA–TV studios in Arlington, VA, for broadcast on PBS at 8 p.m. on July 9.

Remarks on Launching the National Youth Antidrug Media Campaign in Atlanta, Georgia
July 9, 1998

Thank you very much. Thank you. First of all, let's begin by giving Kim and James another hand. Didn't they do a good job? [*Applause*] They spoke well for you.

Mr. Speaker, Governor Miller, Mr. Mayor, General McCaffrey, General Reno, Secretary Shalala, I thank you all for your superb efforts in this endeavor. I'd like to say a special word of appreciation to Jim Burke, the president of the Partnership for a Drug-Free America. He's not as well-known to most American children as the President or the Speaker or the Governor, but no American has done more to save the children of this country from the horror of drug abuse than Jim Burke. And we all owe him a very great debt of gratitude. Thank you.

I'd also like to thank the Ad Council, the Community Anti-Drug Coalition, the athletic teams and sports figures that are represented here today, the business groups, the Georgia attorney general and agriculture commissioner, and the other State and municipal and county officials. And Congressman Peter Deutsch from Florida is here with us today. I thank all of them for being here. And there are many others who aren't here who are supporting what we are doing together as Americans.

I was interested, when we just watched the ads, to see what the young people's reaction was to the various ads. I was wondering to myself whether the ads that were most effective with me were also the ones that were most effective to you, or whether they were different. I say that to make the point that the Speaker made so eloquently. In the end, this is about you, what touches you, what you believe, what your convictions are.

We know from the stories that we just heard from James and from Kim, we know from all the available scientific research, that what Governor Miller said is right: Attitudes drive actions. There are lots of other factors. There are some places where kids are subject to more temptation than others; there are some blocks where there are more drug dealers than others. All of us have to deal with that. But we know that the more young people fear drugs, the more they disapprove of them, the less likely they are to use them. Therefore, kicking America's drug habit requires a dramatic change in attitudes, accompanied and reinforced by a dramatic increase in personal responsibility by all Americans.

Parents have the greatest power. That's what one of the ads showed us. The ads we saw today are not meant to replace parents' voices but to reinforce them. Ultimately, the best drug enforcement program, the best drug prevention program is an effective, caring, loving parent sitting down with a child and talking seriously about drugs early.

Parents have already told us that these ads help to break the ice with their children. So I ask the parents of America today, don't wait until your children are using drugs to talk to them about drugs. Watch the ads together and discuss them, beginning tonight.

Every one of the rest of us can and must help parents to teach their children to turn away from drugs. The entertainment industry can shape attitudes, as anyone who has a teenager can tell you. The media should never glamorize drugs. I'm pleased that, across the entertainment industry, a real effort is now being made to help, with the antidrug messages on the Wonderful World of Disney, antidrug chat groups on America Online, even training sessions about youth drug use for screenwriters and producers at Fox—something I hope we will see for all people who prepare television programs on all networks.

Professional athletes can shape attitudes. I thank Major League Soccer, the Florida Marlins, the New York Mets, Atlanta's own Braves for agreeing to air the ads during their home games. And while one of government's primary responsibilities is to enforce the law—and we should— we can also support this change in attitudes.

As General McCaffrey said, with the help of the Speaker and people from across the political spectrum, we have aggressively pursued a comprehensive antidrug strategy. We've put more police on our streets. We've strengthened our border patrols. We've toughened penalties. We do more drug testing of prisoners and parolees to break the link between crime and drugs. We work more with countries where drugs are grown and processed to try to stop the drugs from coming into the United States in the first place.

But with this ad campaign, in which the public's investment is matched, dollar for dollar, by private partners, America is mounting a new and sweeping effort to change the attitude of an entire generation of young people.

Already, we've seen an impact in the 12 cities where the ads have run as a pilot project. Calls—listen to this—in just those 12 cities, calls to local antidrug coalition hotlines have increased by up to 500 percent. Calls to our national antidrug helpline have nearly tripled. Young people here in Atlanta say that the ads

make them realize the serious consequences of using drugs. In Denver, middle school students think the ads could "scare kids out of using drugs," to quote one of them. In Washington, DC, young people say, to quote one, "the ads make them stop and think about what illegal drugs can do."

Tonight, when these ads run on every national television network, they will reach more than 40 million Americans, including millions and millions of children. That is just the beginning. Over the next 5 years, we'll help to make sure that when young people turn on the television, listen to the radio, read the newspaper, or surf the Web, they get the powerful message that drugs are wrong, illegal, and can kill.

I'm proud to say, as has already been said by General McCaffrey, that this national media campaign was a part of the historic bipartisan balanced budget agreement reached last year with Speaker Gingrich and the other leaders of Congress. And I thank you, Mr. Speaker, for including this in our budget agreement. It shows what we can accomplish when we put progress ahead of partisanship. I will work with the Congress to fund other important programs in our drug control strategy.

All of us—parents, the media, athletes, business, government—have an opportunity and an obligation to make a real difference in the fight against drugs. But nothing we do will succeed, as the Speaker said, unless young people also take responsibility for themselves.

We've heard some personal stories; I'd like to close with two: one from my family and one from the job the American people have so generously given me these 6 years. Let me begin with the job.

I spent a lot of time haranguing, cajoling, trying to persuade, sometimes putting brutal pressure on countries where drugs are grown or processed, or through which drugs pass, trying to get people to stop doing things that send drugs to us. And we've had some success. We supported remarkable efforts by the Coast Guard, for example, to cut off drugs before they get to this country. But we can never cut off the whole flow. And every time I'd do this, some leader of a country where drugs are grown will say, "You know, Mr. President, you're right. We have a lot of poor farmers in our country, and I wish they'd grow something else. But America has 4 percent of the world's people, and you're buying almost 50 percent of the world's drugs. Nobody is making you buy those drugs. So you can say whatever you want to us. If you just said tomorrow—everybody in America said, we're not going to buy any more drugs, all our farmers would immediately start to grow something legal and good." And that's true.

Now, that doesn't let them off the hook; it doesn't excuse the inexcusable behavior of the Colombian drug cartels or any other groups in any part of the world. But it is true. It is true. It doesn't mean we should stop trying to kill the drugs at the border and stop the imports and break the drug gangs. But it's true. If every American young person tomorrow said, "No, thank you," they would grow something else. The laboratories would make other chemicals that are legal and not harmful.

I'll tell you another story that's fairly well-known, but I want you to think about what it means for families. This young man was brave enough to say that his mother used drugs and talk about what—the pain it caused the family. My brother nearly died from a cocaine habit. And I've asked myself a thousand times, what kind of fool was I that I did not know this was going on? You know, I got myself elected President; I'm supposed to know what people are thinking, what's going on in their minds. How did this happen that I didn't see this coming and didn't stop it?

And when it all happened he said—I said, "When did this start?" He said, "Well, in high school; I started using marijuana and drinking beer." I said, "How often?" He said, "Every day." And I thought to myself, what kind of family member was I?

And these things make you do really bad things. They make you abuse other people. Most of the people selling drugs on the street are out there supporting their own habits. So you take other people, people who are basically good people, and you turn them into animals, because they don't care what they do to anybody else because they've got to get the money, if they have to destroy somebody else, so they can keep feeding their own habits. They destroy families. Mothers who love their sons wind up neglecting them, abusing them, walking away, weakening the family. Everybody gets hurt. Nobody in America is free of this. Not the President; not

any community, any school, any church, any neighborhood.

So the hardest thing in the world to do is to get people to change their habits, especially if what you're doing feels good in the moment. But it's very important. Nothing is so important, not the laws, not the investments, not anything. Nothing is so important as what the American people get up and do every day just because they think it's the right thing to do. Nothing comes close to it.

So we're here today because we took a little bit of the money the American people gave the National Government—a billion dollars over the next 5 years—put it with at least that much and maybe more coming from private sources, to send a message to all these kids. I look at all these little girls out here in their Girl Scouts or their Brownie uniforms; the message seems simple today. When they're 14 or 15 or 16 or 17 or 18, and life gets more complicated, it's real important that they carry with them the message that they have today deep in their heart.

I look at all these kids with these America's Pride T-shirts on, and what I want them to do is to go back and somehow reach all those kids that are in their schools that don't wear those T-shirts. There's somebody like my brother back at your school who is a good kid, just a little lost. Somebody told him something is all right that wasn't. And the family members were just a little out of it and couldn't believe it was going on. You can save them. That's what these ads are all about.

These ads are designed to knock America upside the head and get America's attention and to empower all of you who are trying to do the right thing. Please do it.

Thank you, and God bless you.

NOTE: The President spoke at 10:40 a.m. in the Sidney Marcus Auditorium in the Georgia World Congress Center. In his remarks, he referred to student antidrug organization leaders Kim Willis of Erie, PA, and James Miller III, of Portland, OR; Gov. Zell Miller, Attorney General Thurbert E. Baker, and Agriculture Commissioner Tommy Irvin of Georgia; Mayor Bill Campbell of Atlanta; and James E. Burke, chairman, Partnership for a Drug-Free America.

Remarks at a Democratic Senatorial Campaign Committee Luncheon in Atlanta
July 9, 1998

Thank you very much, and welcome. Michael, I would say, with family like this and support like this, you have an excellent chance to win.

I want to thank all of you for coming today in support of Michael Coles and his wonderful family. I want to especially thank the mayor and the Governor and all of the State and local officials who are here, and my good friends, the mayor's predecessors, Maynard Jackson and Andrew Young, for coming.

I feel a great deal of gratitude to Georgia for many things. In 1992, when I started running for President, Zell Miller was about the only person besides my mother and my wife who thought I could win. [*Laughter*] And then, I didn't win in New Hampshire, where I had one or two minor obstacles—[*laughter*]—and an opponent who lived 5 miles from the State line, and they said, "You know, if Bill Clinton doesn't get 40 percent in Georgia, he'll have to withdraw; he's toast; he's history." And I said, "Now, Zell, I don't want to put any pressure on you." [*Laughter*] So we got 57 percent in the Georgia primary in 1992. And there have been a lot of wonderful experiences since, and I am very grateful for this State.

I'm grateful for people like Maynard and Andy, who have been friends of mine and my wife's for many, many years. I'm grateful for Bill Campbell's leadership. I can honestly say that I know quite a bit about being a Governor. I was a Governor for 12 years. One of the great honors of my life was when my colleagues once voted me the most effective Governor in the country. I'm saying that not to brag on myself but to establish my bona fide for what I am about to say.

In my experience, I believe that what Zell Miller has done as Governor of Georgia has affected more people more personally, positively, than the work of any other Governor with whom I have worked in the last 20 years.

I also want to say, when I'm a very old man, if the Lord lets me live that long, and I'm thinking about—over the high points of my wonderful career for which I'm very grateful, in the late of the night, one of the things I will always remember is Zell Miller's voice at the New York convention in 1992. I can give that speech about the house his mama built better than he can. [*Laughter*] But it captured the heart of America and the heart of what we're all about.

When we were sitting here at lunch, I went around the table before I came up, and I said, "Can you folks—how are we going to win this race? What do you want me to say? How is this going to work?" And they all gave me their ideas. And I don't know if I can add anything to what's already been said. Very often, since I became President, I always get to speak last. That's a great honor. But very often, it's that sort of situation where everything that needs to be said has already been said, but not everyone said it.

I think maybe there is something I can say. What do you need to win a race like this? To convince voters in what is clearly an American battleground State for the future, where Atlanta now is home to more foreign companies than any other city in America, where you have in this city really everything that you can imagine the future being about in America, but where in the State the parties are pretty evenly divided and the philosophies are pretty evenly divided, and the races have a way of being agonizingly close, as I have found in my joy and disappointment. What can I say?

Well, you have a good candidate who has demonstrated his character. Through overcoming adversity, he's demonstrated that he understands the American economic system through triumphing in it. He has built a great family, which is the most important thing for anyone to have in life. He has the guts to challenge incumbents who are going to have tons of money, which is evidence of courage in public life.

But what I would like to say to you is that we have to convince moderate Republicans and independent voters that what happened in America in the last 6 years and what happened in Georgia in Zell Miller's tenure was not an accident and was directly related—not that I am responsible for every good thing that's happened in this country or not that he's responsible for every good thing that's happened in

Georgia—but there is a connection between the ideas that leaders have and the policies that are pursued and the consequences in the lives of people.

It's not just that Zell Miller is a good man with a lot of energy and a lot of courage, and he was brave in the Marine Corps, and he gives a great speech; the HOPE scholarship was, in fact, the right thing to do. It was the right thing to do. And what I can tell you from my experience is—I was a Southern Governor; I listened to the Republicans bad-mouth the Democratic Party from can till can't, from dawn until dark, year-in and year-out, forever and a day. And that time I ran for President, I had umpty-dump people in Arkansas who had voted for me repeatedly for Governor who never thought they would vote for a Democrat for President. Some of them didn't vote for a Democrat even when it was me—[*laughter*]—after voting for me repeatedly, because Republicans had done a great job of sort of doing reverse plastic surgery on the Democrats. You know, they'd say, "You can't vote for them; they can't handle the budget; they can't handle this; they're weak on foreign policy." You know that whole litany. "They want to take your money and give it to people on welfare; don't believe in work." I can give that speech better than they can give it, too. I've heard it so many times. [*Laughter*] And they still milk that old cow every chance they get.

And when 1992—I wanted to take the Democratic Party in a new direction based on its oldest values. I believed that we could unite the country and move it forward, that we could build that bridge to the 21st century based on opportunity and responsibility and a sense of community. And we set about doing things that really were different. We had new ideas on the economy. We said we believe it's possible to cut the deficit and balance the budget and still have money to invest in education and in science and technology and building the future. We believe it's possible to expand American trade and still care about preserving the environment and the standards of our working people.

We believe it's possible to be tough on crime but to be smart, too, and to find ways to keep more kids out of trouble in the first place. We believe it is possible to move people from welfare to work but not to ask them to hurt their children; to empower people to move from welfare to work by saying, "Yes, if you're able-

bodied, you have to do it. But by the way, there's got to be a job there and there ought to be child care and you ought not to have to neglect your role as a parent to do your role as a worker in this society."

We believed that America could be a force for good in the world and still help the economic interests of our country. We believed we could have a smaller Government that was more effective, that worked on empowering people to make the most of their own lives. And we believed that we could build one America, across all the lines that divide us, because what unites us is more important than what divides us. And if we could ever learn to appreciate our differences instead of be afraid of them, we would be a very great country, indeed.

Now, that's what we believe. Now, after 6 years—and again, I say I do not believe that I, my party, or Washington, DC, is responsible for every good thing that's happened in America; most of the good things that happen in a free country happen by the billions and billions and billions of decisions that ordinary people make every day on their own. But what the President does and the policies that are pursued are not unrelated to what happens in the country. They have an impact.

And I am profoundly grateful that you gave me the chance to do this job, and I am very grateful that, after 6 years, we have the lowest crime rate in 25 years, the lowest unemployment rate in 28 years, the lowest inflation rate in 29 years, the lowest welfare rolls in 29 years, the first balanced budget and surplus in 29 years, and the highest rate of homeownership in the history of the country. I'm proud of that, and you should be, too.

Now, that's not a reason to let Michael Coles—and I can't run for reelection. And if I could, it wouldn't be a reason to reelect me. I remember once I was about to run for reelection after I had been in 10 years, and I asked a guy at the State Fair once—we were having Governor's Day—and this guy came up in overalls and said, "Are you going to run for reelection?" And I said, "Yes, I might. Will you vote for me if I do?" He said, "I will; I always have." And I said, "Well, aren't you sick of me after 10 years?" He said, "No, but most of my friends are." [*Laughter*] And I said, "Well," I said, "Don't they think I've done a good job?" He said, "Yes, but you drew a check every two weeks, didn't you?" [*Laughter*] He said, "That's what we hired you to do."

So what's that got to do with this race, where we are now? I'll tell you what it's got to do with it. Number one, it's some indication that, if the ideas we had in the past were right, that the ideas we're advocating for the future may be right as well, and what we are trying to do in education with smaller classes and modernized schools and computers in all the schools and higher standards, that these things are important. Because no one in the world believes we have the best system of public education in the world. And everyone knows we have the best system of college education in the world. And we will never be what we ought to be for every American child until our elementary and secondary education system is also the best in the world.

You take health care. We're having this big debate over the Patients' Bill of Rights. I pleaded with the Congress to pass it, and I thought for sure they would. Now, the health insurance companies, a lot of them are against it—but not all of them, I might add. Most people are in managed care plans today. I have never been one of those that attacked managed care.

When I became President, health care costs were inflating at 3 times the rate of inflation. It was unsustainable. It was going to break every business in the country that tried to provide health insurance for their kids. It was going to consume the whole economy. We had to do something to slow down the rate of inflation. On the other hand, any system taken to extremes is subject to abuse. I don't care what system it is.

The genius of the American Constitution is the limits it places on all of us in power. And whenever we forget that, we do so at our peril. That is the problem with managed care today. People still ought to be able to get an emergency room when they need to go. They need to be able to see a specialist when they need to see a specialist. They need to be able to appeal these decisions when they need to be able to appeal them. And that's what the Patients' Bill of Rights is all about. So that's an important issue.

We have all these exciting ideas about how we can grow the economy while doing a better job at preserving the environment. Look at these wildfires that your neighbor down in Florida has been suffering. I'm going down to Daytona,

when I leave you, to thank the firefighters down there. Florida had the wettest few months in history in the fall and winter; then they had the driest few months they had ever had; then June was the hottest month they had ever had; hotter than any July or August they had ever had.

The 5 hottest years on record since 1400 have all occurred in the 1990's. And 1998 is going to be the hottest of all if trends continue. Now, we have two choices. We can do what my— as my leaders of the other party do in Washington, which is to deny that this climate change is going on, deny this is a problem, and say we're going to go right on and do everything just like we've been doing it. If it rips the sheet, we're going to do it, and everybody else is just, you know, like Chicken Little. Or, we can face the evidence and say: Do we have to give up economic growth to change our energy use patterns, try to cool the climate, try to be more responsible? And when you look at the evidence, the evidence is plainly, no, you can grow the economy, at least as rapidly as we've been growing, with a different energy strategy and without having the heavy hand of government regulation do it if you just give business and citizens the incentive to do what is plainly there before them to do.

These are huge decisions. What I want to tell you is, if you like those statistics I just read off, the ideas we've had in the past are an indication that the ideas we have in the future may be right.

The third point I want to make is this: I do not expect this man, if he gets elected to Senate, to vote with me on every issue. I want him to only do so when it is consistent with his conscience and when he believes it's the right thing for the people of Georgia. But I believe he thinks enough, like all of you do and like we do, to know that we will be building a future based on progress not partisanship. And that's the last point I want to make. Look at the record of the alternative.

I am grateful that the Republicans worked with me to sign the Balanced Budget Act last year. But don't you ever forget that 93 percent of that deficit was reduced—it was 93 percent gone on the day I signed the Balanced Budget Act because of a bill that every single one of them voted against in 1993 to get it started. Don't forget that. They said we were going to wreck the economy.

When we said, "You know, it seems to me that if somebody's got a criminal record or a serious mental health history, they ought not just to be able to walk in and buy a handgun," even in Arkansas, where nearly everybody's got a gun, why, they accused me of the awfullest things you ever heard. They said, "Oh, the world was going to come to an end." And one of the reasons they won the Congress in 1994 is because I disagreed with the NRA over the Brady bill and the assault weapons ban. And it wasn't just in the South; they took out a Congressman in New Hampshire, too. In 1996 I went back to New Hampshire where I started, and I got a bunch of those hunters together. And I said, "Do you remember what they told you in '94?" I said, "Well, as of today, there have been 80,000 felons, fugitives, and stalkers who couldn't buy handguns because of the Brady law." I said, "Now, if there's a single one of you who lost your hunting rifle because of what I did, I want you to vote against me for reelection. But if you didn't, then they lied to you, and you need to get even." [*Laughter*] And in Republican New Hampshire, they got even, and I'm grateful. [*Laughter*]

I say that because we actually view the world in different ways. You've got to understand. Somehow—I talked to Zell on the way in here—those of you who are in this room, we have to be able to reach out to the voters who don't follow politics as closely as you do, and say, look, there are consequences to these ideas. This is not just about whether the President can give a good speech or Michael Coles made a lot of money or—even though I admire him enormously, it's not even about whether he overcame all that adversity from his terrible accident. It's also about whether we're doing the right thing for America's future.

And you know, when times are good like this, most people tend to relax, and you want to say, "Gosh, I just want to go out and sit in the Sun. I went through the seventies; I went through the eighties; I lived through all this tumult. I'm making money; the stock market's up. Leave me alone; I don't want to have to think about this. [*Laughter*] I'm going to vote for the person that looks nicest on television, makes me feel good—[*laughter*]—promises me to keep taxes down. And just don't bother me." [*Laughter*]

I had a great-uncle one time, who just died at 91, who had about a fourth grade education.

He said, "All I want you to do is keep the brooks clean so I can fish and make sure there's plenty of birds in the air and animals in the woods in hunting season. And otherwise, just leave me alone." [*Laughter*]

There's a lot of people who feel that way. But let me tell you, any person living in Atlanta knows that this is a very dynamic world. You see what they're going through in Asia now economically. You know about all the ethnic and racial and religious tensions all over the world. If you've looked at the demographics and you know what happens when the baby boomers—and I'm the oldest of the baby boomers—when we retire, what we're going to do, the pressures we're going to put on the Social Security system and the Medicare system—we have big, long-term challenges in this country that we have to face. It is easier to take the long-term challenges on when you're doing well. We have the confidence in this country to do well.

And Georgia ought to have the confidence to vote for somebody like Michael Coles for the Senate. We ought to say, "Look, we've got the confidence to do that. Here's a guy who has done all these other things right in his life, and he's a doer. You know, get out and do things, and it will be for progress, not partisanship. I think I'll take a chance and do it, because this is a time when we have the opportunity to deal with these long-term challenges." And I want you to go out and tell people that.

I'm telling you, I've been in Washington 6 years, and I only have 2½ years to go. Then I can go be a real person again just like the rest of you. But what we need is progress over partisanship. What we need is people who are willing to take a chance to deal with the long-term challenges of the country. What we need is people who understand that we cannot lead the world to a better place unless we are becoming a better country at home, that we can always do better.

Our Founders left us a charge that is a permanent mission—it's never finished: to form a more perfect Union. I think that any one of the Founding Fathers, here today, could read about this man, his family, his work, his values, and say, "That's the kind of person we had in mind."

Thank you very much.

NOTE: The President spoke at 1:10 p.m. in the Marquis Ballroom at the Marriott Marquis Hotel.

In his remarks, he referred to Georgia Senatorial candidate Michael J. Coles; Mayor Bill Campbell and former mayors Maynard Jackson and Andrew Young of Atlanta; and Gov. Zell Miller of Georgia.

Remarks to Firefighters and Relief Workers in Daytona Beach, Florida
July 9, 1998

Thank you so much. Well, ladies and gentlemen, first of all, I'd like to thank Karen Terry and Randy Holmes for their remarks and the introduction and for giving me and all of you and all of America, thanks to the media folks who are here, one vivid picture of what these last couple of weeks have been all about.

I want to thank my good friend Governor Chiles for the work that he has done. I thank Lieutenant Governor MacKay and all the other State officials who are here. I thank Mayor Asher and Mr. Rosevear, the chair of the county council. The mayor asked me to say in front of national television what Lawton has already said, that Daytona Beach is open for tourists. People all over America are calling the White House on the comment line. They want to know, what can we do to help the people of Florida? Well, one thing you can do is, if you haven't taken your vacation yet and you were trying to decide whether to come, give these people an economic boost down here. They've got the fires under control, and they need some help and support. It would be a good thing to do.

I want to thank the Members of Congress who are here—Corrine Brown, Peter Deutsch, and Allen Boyd—for representing you well and for supporting strongly the emergency appropriations that make it possible for FEMA and the other agencies to do its work. I thank our Agriculture Secretary, Dan Glickman, and our wonderful FEMA Director, James Lee Witt, for the work they have done.

I want to thank all the firefighters who are here. I know we have people from Palm Coast Fire Department, from the National Guard, from the U.S. Forest Service, from the Division of Florida Forestry, the Florida Emergency Management Division, and a lot of State and local emergency workers; Mr. Myers, your emergency management director here; and I'm glad to see Mr. Barbera from the International Association of Fire Fighters here.

There's so many people I want to thank, but I'd like to say a special word of thanks, too, to Bill Franz for making Daytona available as a headquarters for the firefighters and for the effort here. I really appreciate that.

They had to postpone the race this year because there was a more important race going on, and you just heard them talk about it, a race that was fought house by house and family by family. There are 150,000 fans that normally show up here, and even though the race was delayed, I hope they'll show up later to show their loyalty and support not only to Daytona but to all of you for what you did here.

I'm here because I think it's important that every American knows that this summer, notwithstanding the great movies, the real American heroes are not up in space fighting asteroids, they're in Florida fighting fires. And I thank you for it.

You might be interested to know, those of you who are firefighters, that on the several occasions when I would call—and I want to thank our great Vice President, Al Gore, for coming down here on my behalf, because I was in China when much of this occurred, and I would call back and get my daily reports, and every day, people said, "You would not believe what the firefighters are doing. The only real worry we have is, none of them will sleep; none of them will rest."

As you know, there are almost 100 injuries and no telling how much exhaustion here. And I guess I'm cutting into your rest time now, so I've now become part of the problem. [*Laughter*] But I think it's important that America know that, too. Every single report I got on the progress of these fires, someone said, our real concern is the people who are fighting the fires will not sleep; they will not rest; they are obsessed with saving every home. And I thank you for that.

I'd also like to thank the people who came from all corners of our country and from Canada and even some came from as far away as Russia to help, showing that this was a human challenge that touched the hearts of people the world over. When I was in China, and we were in the midst of tough discussions and arguing over things that are profoundly important over the long run, my Chinese host asked me how the people of Florida were doing with the fires. You really reached the hearts of people throughout the world.

I also want to thank the people with the public works departments across the State for the work they did in cutting fire lines and clearing the fields. And I want to thank again—no telling how many of you did things that I don't know about, but I want to echo something Governor Chiles said. Maybe it shouldn't require a disaster like this, but you did show our country at its best. You showed people at its best. You showed people what the meaning of community is and why we all really do depend on each other. And as we go back to our daily lives and, I hope, a much more ordinary routine, I hope it's something we never forget, that we are all in this together; we need each other; and we're all at our best when we're giving not only to our families but to our neighbors. It's something I will never forget, and I hope all of you can help the rest of the people of Florida and the United States remember it in good times and rainy times.

There were children who gave up their Fourth of July picnics and trips to Disney World—I met a couple of them earlier, Katie and Megan Hendren—to help out and donate food and money; hotel managers giving free rooms; churches helping people cook food for all the empty pots; laundromat owners cleaning soot and ash from uniforms. I even heard about the truckload of bananas that were mistakenly donated to Volusia County when you put out the word that bandannas were needed for the firefighters. [*Laughter*] Well, the older I get and the more muscle cramps I get doing my exercises, the more I appreciate bananas. So the firefighters may need the bananas as well as the bandannas. And I thank all the people who made them available.

Our Government has tried to be a good partner. I just met with several people who have been victimized by this fire, and I want to thank the families that took the time to talk to me. A lot of them are still hurting. Some of them don't have their children living with the parents

yet; they're all spread out all over. And a lot of them are still uncertain about what their future living conditions are going to be. And a couple of them gave me some very specific suggestions about what we still might do to serve people here better. And I thank them for that.

Today I want to say that there are some new things we're going to do, and I'd like to mention them just briefly. First of all, I've directed our Agriculture Secretary, who is here with me, Dan Glickman, to declare all of our Florida counties eligible for farmers emergency loans if they've been affected by the drought, which is directly connected to this fire. Second, the Labor Department will pay for hundreds of jobs to expedite the recovery process, which is important. Third, FEMA will develop a long-term recovery plan with the State and work with our economic development administration to analyze the economic impact of the fires and see what else we can do to help. And finally, FEMA will be giving individual assistance to 29 more counties, providing temporary housing, crisis counseling, repairing homes, replacing essential items. We're going to do everything we can until the full recovery is completed.

Let me just say one other thing. You all probably know this, but this fire was made worse because you had, first, the wettest few months you'd ever had, followed by the driest few months you'd ever had, and then June was the hottest month ever recorded, even hotter than any July or August ever recorded in Florida.

No one entirely understands what is bringing about this extreme weather. But I can tell you this—and I've got it on my mind since I just got back from China, and they've been keeping weather records there for 500 years and more. Since the 1400's, the 5 hottest years ever recorded all occurred in the 1990's; 1997 was the hottest year ever recorded. If present temperature trends continue, 1998 will be warmer than 1997 was.

Now, you'll hear a lot of political debate, and the Vice President and I believe that the climate is warming and that we ought to take steps to cool it off and that we can do it without hurting economic growth. Others may disagree. The point I want to make today is I'm going to go back to Washington determined to try to do whatever I can to make sure that you and people like you all over America can be even better prepared, because if we are going to have hotter and hotter and drier and drier years—and even if we move aggressively to try to combat this climate change, we'll have that for a while—then, when you or other people like you have to face this again, we need to learn from what you've gone through; we need your best advice.

So that's the last thing I want to ask you. I want to ask you for one last shred of citizen service. When this is all over, you need to get together with the groups of people that fought this fire; you need to put your heads together; you need to ask yourself, what specific things could have been done to provide even better preparedness? What do you do when you're fighting three fires in three places at once? What do you do when you have to make choices about what you're going to do? Is there any way to avoid making those kind of choices? What else can we do?

Because we have to believe, based on the evidence of the last decade, that if we get hotter and hotter, and we have periods of more extreme wet followed by periods of more extreme drought, we're going to have more things like this happen. You can help America to deal with this.

And so, when you get some sleep, when you get some rest, when you're absolutely confident this crisis is past, if you've got some ideas, get them to the State, or get them to our FEMA people, because we want to build on what you've done. This has been heroic, but if we

can do anything to prevent these things or to be better prepared the next time because of your experience and your knowledge, I implore you to share it with us, because we have to believe we're facing things like this in the near future.

Finally, let me say, I found, with the help of some of our people who know I'm interested in Scripture, a verse from Isaiah that I think captures what you've all been through. And I'd like to read it to you in closing. Isaiah 57:10: "You were wearied with the length of your way, but you did not say it is hopeless. You find new life for your strength."

And because you did, our country is stronger. Thank you, and God bless you.

NOTE: The President spoke at 4:15 p.m. at Daytona International Speedway. In his remarks, he referred to Karen Terry, a Palm Coast, FL, resident whose house was saved by firefighters of the Palm Coast Fire Department, one of whom was Randy Holmes, who introduced the President; Gov. Lawton Chiles and Lt. Gov. Buddy MacKay of Florida; Mayor Baron H. Asher of Daytona Beach; R. Stanley Rosevear, chairman, Volusia County Council; Joseph F. Myers, director, Florida Division of Emergency Management; Dominick F. Barbera, vice president, 12th District, International Association of Fire Fighters; Bill Franz, owner, Daytona International Speedway; and President Jiang Zemin of China.

Statement on Senate Action on Internal Revenue Service Reform Legislation
July 9, 1998

I am pleased that the Senate has finally passed bipartisan legislation to reform the IRS and strengthen taxpayer rights. This reform will help my effort to create an IRS that respects American taxpayers and respects their values. I look forward to signing it into law.

Statement on Senate Action on Legislation on Sanctions Against India and Pakistan
July 9, 1998

I am pleased that the Senate has passed legislation today that is consistent with my view that U.S. food exports should not become an unintended victim of an important nonproliferation law. Food should not be used as a weapon, and I will resist any action that would lead to a de facto grain embargo.

I look forward to working with Congress to make sure this legislation or separate legislation gives us the broadest possible flexibility to further our nonproliferation policy without putting American businesses and farmers at an unfair disadvantage.

Letter to Congressional Leaders on the Emigration Policies and Trade Status of Certain Former Eastern Bloc States
July 9, 1998

Dear Mr. Speaker: (Dear Mr. President:)
On September 21, 1994, I determined and reported to the Congress that the Russian Federation was in "full compliance" with the freedom of emigration criteria of sections 402 and 409 of the Trade Act of 1974. On June 3, 1997, I determined and reported to the Congress that Armenia, Azerbaijan, Georgia, Moldova, and Ukraine were in "full compliance" with these same criteria, and I made an identical determination on December 5, 1997, with respect to Kazakhstan, Kyrgyzstan, Tajikistan, Turkmenistan, and Uzbekistan. These actions allowed for the continuation of most-favored-nation (MFN) status for these countries and certain other activities without the requirement of an annual waiver.

As required by law, I am submitting an updated report to the Congress concerning the emigration laws and policies of Armenia, Azerbaijan, Georgia, Kazakhstan, Kyrgyzstan, Moldova, the Russian Federation, Tajikistan, Turkmenistan, Ukraine, and Uzbekistan. The report indicates continued compliance of these countries with international standards concerning freedom of emigration.

Sincerely,

WILLIAM J. CLINTON

NOTE: Identical letters were sent to Newt Gingrich, Speaker of the House of Representatives, and Albert Gore, Jr., President of the Senate.

Remarks at a Democratic Congressional Campaign Committee Dinner in Miami, Florida
July 9, 1998

Thank you very much. First let me thank my friend Dick Gephardt for his leadership of our party in the House of Representatives, for his wonderful remarks tonight. I thank Martin Frost. We were together in Texas, Martin's home State, a couple of weeks ago, and I was trying to be helpful and funny at the same time when I said that I named my dog Buddy, but I had considered naming him after Martin Frost because Martin Frost is like a dog with a bone; when he asks you to do something, you might as well just go on and say yes, because it's the only way to get him to let your leg go. [*Laughter*] And he has had a very thankless job, which he has performed magnificently for our people, and I thank him for that.

I thank all the Members of Congress who are here tonight from Florida and from around the country, and the leaders of Florida in our Democratic Party here, including Buddy MacKay and his newly announced running mate, Senator Dantzler. I'm delighted that they're here, and I'm for them, strongly.

Mayor Penelas, Attorney General Butterworth, Commissioner Crawford; and we also have here the mayor of Akron, Ohio, Don Plusquellic. I don't know what he's doing here, but I'm glad to see him. [*Laughter*] He's a good friend of mine, and I'm delighted that he and his wife are here. He may be running for Congress in Florida for all I know. But I'm glad he's here.

I'd like to thank the Paxsons and all the other major sponsors of this event tonight. And Sylvester Stallone, thank you for having us at your home and for giving me those boxing gloves. I can use them. [*Laughter*] I think I have established that I can take a punch; now the time has come for me to deliver a few. And I would like to have a few.

Let me say to all of you in this magnificent home tonight that I always love coming here, and I feel so deeply indebted to the people of Florida and especially to my fellow Democrats, because it was in December of 1991, at the Florida Democratic Convention, that I won the first victory of any kind when I was out trying to become the nominee of my party. And in 1996, you brought Florida back to a Democratic candidate for the first time in two decades, when your State voted for me and for Al Gore. And I'm very grateful to you for that, and I thank you.

I want to make a brief case tonight. It's late, and all of you know that my family and many members of our administration just got back from China. And they say if there's a 12-hour time difference, it takes you 12 days to get over it. I don't know about that, but for the last four nights, sometime between 9 and 10 o'clock, I hit the skids. And I'll be all right; so if I fall asleep up here in this speech, if you'll just wait about 5 minutes, I'll be fine, and I may go on to 3 in the morning after that. [*Laughter*]

But I've given a lot of thought to what I might say tonight. You know, a lot of you come to a lot of these dinners, and you wonder— I wonder, what could I say that would really

animate all the people that were here, that would make them say, "Boy, I made a good investment tonight, and I want to go out and talk to my friends and neighbors about this tomorrow, and I'm still going to feel good about this in October, and I want to talk about it some more"?

You know, when I was in China, I thought it was so fitting that, after I was given this incredible opportunity on your behalf to speak for the American people in China and to try to listen to the Chinese people and their leaders, that I was coming home for the Fourth of July. It was a wonderful feeling to think about, being on Air Force One, having worked as hard as I could to press America's cause, our interests, our values, our desire to have a genuine, constructive friendship with the Chinese in the 21st century, and that I was coming home for the Fourth of July; that Hillary and Chelsea and I would be able to see the fireworks on The Mall from the White House and celebrate with a lot of people who work hard all year for us.

So I was thinking, what is this election about? You know, I'm not on the ballot, and I can't run anymore. I'm here for others and for things in which I believe.

In 1992, when I started running for President, I believed that our country was in trouble and that Washington was paralyzed by partisan politics and old ideas. I wanted to try to modernize our party and come up with some new ideas without violating our most deeply held principles. And I've tried to do that. I tried to stick with the things that made us a great party and the things that made us a great country: opportunity for all, responsibility from all, an American community of all people. And I said to the American people, if you will elect me, here are the policies I will pursue in the economy and welfare and education and crime, health care, foreign policy.

As Dick said, I would never say that I, as President, or our party were completely responsible for a lot of the good things, all the good things that have happened in this country in the last 5½ years. I appreciate very much what Bud said about the telecommunications bill, because we worked very hard to create opportunities there. But I will tell you this: There is a connection between the decisions made by the leaders in this country and the consequences that flow from them and the options that are available to Americans. And there are profound differences between the two parties in the House of Representatives about whether we've been right and what we should do going forward.

And when I was coming home and I made a list of all the things I'm grateful for for America—I mean, I'm very grateful for all of us that we have the lowest crime rate in 25 years, the lowest unemployment rate in 28 years, the lowest welfare rolls in 29 years. We're having the first balanced budget and surplus in 29 years. We have the lowest inflation in 32 years, the smallest Federal Government in 35 years, and the highest homeownership in the history of the United States. I am grateful for that.

I am grateful that we're giving 5 million children, who couldn't afford it otherwise, health insurance; that we have the highest rate of childhood immunization in our country's history; that we've proved you can clean the environment and grow the economy. The air is cleaner; the water is cleaner; the food is safer; there are more toxic wastes cleaned up. We've made a big step toward helping to save the Everglades and protect Yellowstone Park from a gold mine and done a lot of other things to try to prove that we can have a healthy economy in America and honor our responsibilities to the environment.

And you should know, when you're asking yourself, "What am I doing here?" number one, that I think the evidence is we were right on the economy. And Dick Gephardt and these other Members here supported us, and the other party said that if my economic policy were implemented, it would lead to a recession in America. Well, we now have some evidence; we know they were wrong.

I think we were right on crime, to try to put 100,000 police on the street and to stop selling handguns to people with criminal records and mental health histories. And they went out there and told everybody we were trying to take guns away, but I think they are wrong.

I think we were right to say, okay, we're going to require able-bodied people to go to work if they're on welfare, but we're not going to punish them in their most important job, which is taking care of their children. So we're going to give them money for child care, and we're going to support their kids with health care. I think we were right. And I think that's one of the reasons we've got the lowest welfare rolls

now in 29 years. And there was a difference of opinion on this between the two parties.

I think we were right to say we're a nation of immigrants, and we ought not to discriminate against immigrants who are here legally. We're proud of that. And we had a difference of opinion on that.

When I was up at Daytona Beach today, I saw a lot of young AmeriCorps volunteers from all over America who had come here to help fight these fires, young people who were giving up a year or two of their lives to serve their country in local communities and earning credit for college. I did AmeriCorps because I thought it would help us to make one America in the 21st century if we got more young people serving in their communities, dealing with people that were different from them in terms of income and background and race and religion, and proving that people who worked together and learned together and served together can live together, because we then appreciate each other's differences instead of being afraid of them. And we know that we've got more in common than we have dividing us.

I think we were right to set up that AmeriCorps program. I saw those kids today, happy, proud after fighting those fires, and I realized we had a big difference between the two parties on that. They thought it was a waste of money. Well, I think we were right, and they were wrong.

And I think that—I say that not to be partisan, because I'm grateful for the handful of Republicans that supported us on the crime bill, that supported us on our immigration position, that support our education position, but because I think it's important that you understand this is not just another dinner where you pick your politician and take your choice and listen to a speech. There are real differences and ideas with real consequences for the life and future of America. And you can see it in the last 5½ years.

And if you look up the road, which is more important, you can see more. And again, I'm not here telling you that we deserve credit for every good thing that's happened in the country. But it's not an accident, and we had something to do with it. And I'm proud of what we did, and I think our ideas were right.

But every election—as I learned when I was a Governor, every election is about the future. I'll never forget, after I had been Governor 10 years, I was thinking about running again for another term, and every year in Arkansas we had this great State fair. And I would go out to the fairgrounds and have Governor's Day at the fair. And I'd sit in a little booth, and anybody in the State could come up and talk to me about anything they wanted.

And this guy came up to me one day in overalls, and he said, "Bill, you going to run for Governor again?" And I said, "Well, I might. If I do, will you vote for me?" He said, "Yeah, I guess I will. I always have." And I said, "Well, aren't you sick of me after 10 years?" He said, "No, but nearly all my friends are." [*Laughter*] And I said, "Well, don't you think I've done a good job?" He said, "Yeah, I do, but you drew a paycheck every 2 weeks, too, didn't you?" [*Laughter*] He said, "That's what we hired you to do. Why do you want credit for that?"

So I say to you—I mentioned all these things about the record only to point out that there are differences between the parties. But if you look ahead, there's first a question of attitude. You know, when times are good after they haven't been so good for a while, we're tempted to just relax, especially in a place like Florida, and kind of sit in the sun. But this is a very dynamic time in which we live. There are lots of changes going on. And if you think about the confidence the American people have now, it seems to me self-evident that, as Mr. Gephardt said, this is a time when we ought to be saying, "Hey, what are the remaining challenges facing this country as we move into the 21st century, and what should we be doing about them now?" And that, I would argue, is the most important reason to support the candidates who are here and our congressional committee.

And let me just give you a couple of examples about the future. Number one, in the House of Representatives, only our party is clear and unambiguous that we don't want to go around spending this surplus until we have saved Social Security for the 21st century and fixed it so the baby boomers don't bankrupt our children and our grandchildren.

You know, sometimes I think I'm lost in a funhouse in Washington; people start talking about spending a surplus that hasn't materialized yet, after we have punished ourselves for 29 years of profligate spending. We have a Social Security challenge out there because the baby boomers are a very big group—and I'm the old-

est one of them, so I know. And none of us, people I grew up with in my hometown, most of whom who are middle class people, none of them want to think they're hurting their children or their children's ability to raise their grandchildren by having Social Security become unbearably expensive. We have to reform it in a way that keeps the country together and moves the country forward.

The second thing we have to do is to give America the best system of elementary and secondary education in the world. No one doubts that we have the best college education system in the world, and no one doubts that we do not have the best elementary and secondary education system in the world. We have some money to do something about it now. And we have a program in Washington: smaller class sizes, modernize schools, 5,000 new and improved schools—big deal in Florida, where you've got school district after school district after school district, with people—kids going to school in trailers because they've grown so much—connecting all the classrooms to the Internet, higher standards, reading programs for children so they can all read independently in English by the end of the third grade.

We have an agenda there. If you look at how the Republican majority in the House has voted in their committees on the budget, they have consistently voted against our education agenda. They don't want to do any of it, and they want to undo some of the things we've done. It's a choice you have to make.

If you look at the environment, which is very important to me—look at these wildfires in Florida. You know what the background of it is; most of you know. In the fall and winter, you had 4 of the wettest months—the 4 wettest months consecutively in the history of Florida, followed by 3 or 4 of the driest months in the history of Florida, followed by June, the hottest month in the history of Florida—ever—hotter than any July or August ever in Florida's history.

When I was in China, I was reminded that one of the reasons we have weather records going back hundreds of years is that the Chinese weather people, what we now call the meteorologists, have literally been keeping detailed records since the 15th century. And we now know that the 5 hottest years recorded since the 1400's all have occurred in the 1990's—every one of them. Last year was the hottest year ever recorded. This year is going to be hotter if present temperature trends are maintained through December.

Now, the overwhelming opinion of scientists is that the climate is getting warmer at a rate that is unsustainable. The overwhelming evidence is that we can slow it down without slowing down the growth of the economy. Why? Well, greenhouse gas emissions, CO_2 basically warm up the climate. A third of it comes from automobiles and trains and trucks and other travel. A third of it comes from buildings, residential and commercial. A third of it comes from factories and powerplants.

In every case, there is presently available technology—or in the case of automobiles, now-being-developed technology—that will dramatically cut these emissions, slow the rate of climate change, and move our children and grandchildren's Earth away from potential disaster without hurting the economy.

So I presented a program to the Congress of tax incentives and investment, nothing in the way of regulation to slow down economic growth; every bit of it rejected by the Republican majority. And they're now trying to pass a bill to stop me from even doing what is now legal to do to try to protect the economy for our children and grandchildren, in spite of the overwhelming majority opinion of scientists all over the world that this is happening and the commonsense experience of people like those firefighters in Florida.

The first time I met Mr. Stallone was last summer up in Massachusetts at a party for a friend of mine, and he said—I'd never met him before—and he said, "You know, I think I have seen the climate change, just because I'm outside every year—every day for the last 10 years."

Now, you have to decide. They act like it's an act of faith to destroy everything I'm trying to do to raise the awareness of the American people about this major environmental issue.

When I was in Shanghai speaking to the American Chamber of Commerce—this is hardly a liberal Democratic group, the American Chamber of Commerce in Shanghai—I got two rounds of spontaneous applause, and one of them was when I asked them to work with the people of China so that they could take a different route into the future in terms of their energy use, so we could save the planet, and that we did not have to pollute the environment of China by seeing them make the same mis-

takes we'd made to grow economically. And the business people starting applauding. Why? Because they knew I was telling the truth, and because they've seen it with their own eyes in China, because the number one health problem of the children there are lung problems, bronchial problems, because of air pollution.

If you look at something that's closer to home in Florida, I'm really proud of the fact that we had what I thought was a bipartisan commitment to invest lots of Federal money in the Everglades to help to save the Everglades. It was part of our bipartisan balanced budget agreement.

But in this year, as the present Republican majority prepares their budget for next year, they have so far rejected my call for more investments in the Everglades, and they have cast some votes which imply that they're going to walk away from the commitment made last year to save the Everglades. Marjorie Stoneman Douglas once said, "The Everglades is a test; if we pass, we get to keep the planet." So far, Dick Gephardt and the Democrats pass the Everglades test. And the members of the other party, this year, have so far flunked it. It's not too late, and I hope this dinner will send them a message to shape up and do their part on the Everglades.

But these—I say this to you because I wasn't a particularly partisan person when I went to Washington. I was a Governor. I was used to working with Republicans and Democrats. I was a Democrat by heritage, instinct, and conviction, but I wanted people to work together. And I thought I could learn something from everybody. The atmosphere in Washington is too partisan, and we have blinders on—some of the decisionmakers not doing what is plainly in the long-term best interest of this country.

So I'm here today for these people because they will choose progress over partisanship, not because they all agree with me all the time. Every Member of the Democratic caucus in the House here tonight, every single one of them has disagreed with me about something that I felt fairly strongly about. I don't ask them all to be rubber stamps for me. All I ask them to do is to be builders, not wreckers; unifiers, not dividers.

And so I want—when you leave here tonight, I want you to leave with some of these issues that I have raised in your mind. If you want a health care bill of rights and you want us to be able to have managed care but still protect the quality of health care, if you want high-class education and you want the National Government to do its part, if you don't want us to squander this balanced budget until we have fixed Social Security, in short, if you want us to build the country for the 21st century and put progress ahead of partisanship, then you have made a very good investment here tonight.

And when people ask you tomorrow morning or a month from now or 2 months from now, why you did it, tell them you did it because you wanted the schools to be better, because you wanted health care to be better, because you wanted the environment to be protected, because you wanted to build your country for the 21st century. And if you prevail, and if they

prevail, I promise you this country will be a better, stronger place.

Thank you, and God bless you all.

NOTE: The President spoke at 10:30 p.m. at a private residence. In his remarks, he referred to Lt. Gov. Buddy MacKay, candidate for Governor of Florida, and former State Senator Rick Dantzler, candidate for Lieutenant Governor; Mayor Alex Penelas of Metro-Dade County; State Attorney General Bob Butterworth; State Agriculture Commissioner Bob Crawford; Mayor Donald L. Plusquellic of Akron, OH, and his wife, Mary; and dinner cohosts Lowell (Bud) Paxson, chairman, Paxson Communications Corp., his wife, Marla, and actor Sylvester Stallone.

Remarks on Presenting the Congressional Medal of Honor to Hospital Corpsman Third Class Robert R. Ingram, USN
July 10, 1998

Welcome. Thank you, Admiral, for your invocation. Ladies and gentlemen, welcome to the White House. I thank Secretary Cohen and Secretary West, Secretary Gober, Deputy Secretary Hamre, Secretary Dalton, Secretary Caldera, Acting Air Force Secretary Peters, General Shelton, and other members of the Joint Chiefs, and general officers here present today. I thank the Members of the Congress from the Florida delegation who are here, and other Members of Congress, including Senator Thurmond, Senator Graham, Senator Mack, Senator Glenn, Senator Cleland, Representative Brown, Representative McHale, and all those in Congress whose action helped to make this day possible.

Today we present the Medal of Honor, our Nation's highest military honor, to Robert R. Ingram for extraordinary heroism above and beyond the call of duty on March 28, 1966, in Quang Ngai Province, South Vietnam.

Today, more than 30 years later, Bob Ingram is manager of a medical service practice in Jacksonville, a registered nurse, a man who loves to work on cars. His wife, Doris, his children, and his close friends are here with us today, and we welcome them.

His story spans decades and continents, but across these divides, friendship and loyalty have

endured and have brought us to this moment. Mr. Ingram enlisted in the Navy in 1963 and joined the Hospital Corps. He went to Vietnam with Company C, 1st Battalion, 7th Marines, in July 1965.

One day in February of 1966, the company came under heavy fire, and Petty Officer Ingram rushed forward to treat the wounded. Enemy bullets punctured both his canteens. When the unit's machine gunner was hit, he manned the gun. And for his bravery on that day, he received the Silver Star.

On March 28, 1966, Petty Officer Ingram accompanied the point platoon of his company as it was suddenly attacked by 100 North Vietnamese in a hail of automatic rifle fire. In moments, the platoon was decimated. Oblivious to the danger, he crawled across the terrain to reach a wounded marine. While administering aid, a bullet went through his hand. After administering aid there, he heard more calls for a corpsman. Still bleeding, he edged across the fire-swept landscape, collecting ammunition from the dead and attending to the wounded, receiving two additional wounds from rifle fire.

Though severely wounded, he continued administering aid to the wounded and the dying marines while gathering ammunition and encouraging others capable of doing so to return fire. While dressing the head wound of another corpsman, he sustained his fourth wound. Enduring extreme pain from his own wounds and disregarding the probability of his own death, Petty Officer Ingram pushed, pulled, cajoled, and doctored his marines for hours more. Losing strength and almost unrecognizable from his injuries, finally he was pulled to safety, where he tried to refuse evacuation, saying that others should go first. His vital signs dropped to the point that he was tagged "killed in action" and placed in a dead pile.

But, as you can see, he did not die. Eleven members of Charlie Company, however, were killed that day, and 53 more were wounded. Some are alive today because of the extraordinary selflessness and bravery of Robert Ingram.

Harvey Kappeler, a corporal in the lead platoon, wrote last year, "I observed Robert Ingram perform acts of heroism I have never seen before, during, or after my tour of Vietnam." Mr. Ingram later recalled, "I was just doing my job; my job was to take care of the men."

Three weeks after the attack, he wrote his platoon from his hospital bed: "I've got a tube in my throat, leg elevated, arm elevated, can't move, but I wanted you all to know I'm still alive." After 8 months recovering, he went back to sea on another deployment.

Other members of the company were honored for their bravery on that day in March of 1966, but no one doubted that Robert Ingram deserved the highest honor. We don't know how his citation got lost all those years ago, but we do know why he is here today: Because his friends never forgot what he did for them.

Jim Fulkerson commanded the 3d Platoon of Charlie Company. In 1995 he organized a reunion of members of the battalion, including Bob Ingram. They remembered the war, the endless cold soaking rains, the terrible firefights. And Ingram's friends resolved to do everything possible to ensure that America finally gave him appropriate recognition.

Charlie Company's commander, Ben Goodwyn, wrote to General Krulak, "I saw my fair share of combat in Vietnam. Of all the men I brought with me, Doc Ingram was undoubtedly the most courageous."

Mr. Ingram is the 22d Navy corpsman to receive the Medal of Honor, and his reward comes appropriately as we celebrate the 100th anniversary of the Navy Hospital Corps. Through all our conflicts, they have been there on ships at sea, on the front lines, performing foxhole surgery, saving thousands of lives while risking and sometimes sacrificing their own. I salute their courageous service to our Nation.

The last troops left Vietnam almost 25 years ago now. But we do not and we must not forget their sacrifices and bravery. As Mr. Kappeler recently wrote of the firefight in Quang Ngai that day, "As I grow old, I look back to that day and the heroism of the marines and our Navy corpsman, and I understand what is meant by the highest traditions of service. I am extremely proud to call Robert Ingram a friend."

On that battlefield so many years ago, Robert Ingram performed truly heroic deeds and asked for nothing in return. At long last, it is time to honor him.

Mr. Ingram, on behalf of all Americans, we thank you for your service, for your courage, for your determination, for your loyalty to comrades and country. We are all proud to call you an American. Hillary and I are proud that you are in the White House with us today, and I am very proud to award you the Medal of Honor.

Major Everhart, read the citation.

[At this point, Maj. Carlton Everhart, USAF, Air Force Aide to the President, read the citation, and Lt. Comdr. Wesley Huey, USN, Naval Aide to the President, assisted the President in presenting the medal.]

NOTE: The President spoke at 3:18 p.m. in the State Dining Room at the White House. In his remarks, he referred to Rear Adm. A. Byron Holderby, USN, Chief of Chaplains, U.S. Navy, who offered the invocation.

Remarks Celebrating the 200th Anniversary of the United States Marine Corps Band
July 10, 1998

Thank you, ladies and gentlemen. Please be seated. Thank you so much, General Krulak. Colonel Foley, to the officials of the Pentagon, the leaders of our military services, Members of Congress, the Medal of Honor winners, and especially to the Ingram family—all of you who are here today—it's a great honor for Hillary and I to welcome you to the White House on what is not only a very important occasion for our Nation but which, as you have heard from my wife and others, is one of the most important occasions for me personally since I've been President. We're also delighted to have a number of distinguished composers in the audience, of music which has been played by our Marine Band.

And I can't let the moment go by without noticing that this is also the birthday of the wife of the Commandant of the Marine Corps. Mrs. Krulak, happy birthday to you. We hope you have a great day.

On July 11, 1798, my predecessor and the first President to live in the house just behind me, John Adams, approved the bill establishing this band. As a footnote, I might also add it established the Marine Corps itself. Of course, the Marines had already been proudly serving our people, starting back in 1775.

Since its founding, the Marine Band's history has been in large measure the history of America. The band played at Thomas Jefferson's Inauguration in 1801 and hasn't missed a single one since. Jefferson was a violin player who loved music almost as much as he loved freedom. He named the band "The President's Own," and it has stuck ever since.

The Marine Band was there to play "The Marseillaise" when President John Quincy Adams, in 1825, gave the first White House toast ever, in honor of General Lafayette and his services to the American Revolution. The Marine Band was by President Abraham Lincoln's side when he delivered the Gettysburg Address.

The Marine Band were among the first musicians ever to be captured for posterity on Thomas Edison's revolutionary phonograph. The Marine Band's broadcasts were a highlight of radio's first years. The Marine Band was at MIT in 1949 to accompany Winston Churchill as he proudly sang every single word of "The Marines' Hymn." And the Marine Band led us in mourning in the funeral procession for President Kennedy.

You have played for kings and prime ministers in great halls overseas, for people in parks and theaters across our country, nearly every day, in so many different musical styles, which you've shared with us on this day. You've accompanied great artists, from Sinatra to Baryshnikov. It is entirely fitting that our Marine Band was among the very first class of inductees into the American Classical Music Hall of Fame. Through long summers you play in oppressive heat, as you have today. And you're always ready to go on Inauguration Day, no matter how bitter the cold.

As time has marched on, you have commemorated changes in band leadership by the passing of a cherished symbol, a gold-tipped baton owned by your most famous conductor. John Philip Sousa was born just two blocks from the band's home at the Marine Barracks here. He was a determined young man who joined the band as an apprentice musician at the age of 13, after his father, one of the band's trombonists, had foiled his plot to run away with the circus. Thank goodness Dad succeeded.

At age 25, after 5 years of touring with orchestras and vaudeville shows, Sousa returned to become the Marine Band's director, and he served there for 12 years. But until his dying day, he never stopped conducting or promoting music education or fighting for composers' rights. Just weeks before his death, at the age of 77, Sousa rose at a gathering here in Washington to lead this band in his greatest march, "The Stars and Stripes Forever."

John Philip Sousa's drive, his love of innovation, his desire to thrill the crowd while taking musical excellence to new heights, that legacy still guides the United States Marine Band. That spirit still keeps your music soaring on the edge of a new century and a new millennium. No President could fail to be proud to say you are "The President's Own."

Happy birthday. Congratulations to all of you. God bless you, and God bless America.

NOTE: The President spoke at 4:34 p.m. on the South Lawn at the White House. In his remarks, he referred to Gen. Charles C. Krulak, USMC, Commandant, U.S. Marine Corps, and his wife, Zandra; Lt. Col. Timothy W. Foley, USMC, Director, United States Marine Band; and Congressional Medal of Honor recipient Robert R. Ingram.

Statement on Senate Action on Higher Education Reauthorization Legislation
July 10, 1998

The bill passed last night by the Senate will help my effort to usher more Americans through the doors of higher education, doors we have opened wide since 1993. There are still serious fiscal and policy issues that need to be resolved, and I am committed to working with Congress to do that. But I am pleased that the Senate bill endorses the new low interest rate for student loans that I proposed to save students $11 billion; improves teacher recruitment and training provided by our colleges; takes important steps in response to my call for colleges to help children at high-poverty schools prepare for and attend college; expands access to quality distance learning technologies; and creates what would be the Government's first performance-based organization, an innovation recommended by our reinventing Government effort.

Joint Statement on United States-Polish Relations
July 10, 1998

President Bill Clinton and Prime Minister Jerzy Buzek of Poland met today at the White House to discuss Poland's anticipated entry into NATO, common efforts to advance regional cooperation in Central and Eastern Europe and steps to deepen the close bilateral relations between the United States and Poland. Vice President Gore met separately with the Prime Minister earlier today and hosted a luncheon for the Prime Minister, his delegation and members of the Polish-American community.

The President and Prime Minister Buzek stressed the paramount importance of the U.S. Senate vote on NATO enlargement. They welcomed Poland's entry into the Alliance. Prime Minister Buzek declared that this step will fulfill the aspirations of the Polish people to belong to the Transatlantic community, guaranteeing the security of a sovereign and democratic Poland. President Clinton responded that Poland's membership in the Atlantic Alliance will advance the interests of the American people in a secure, undivided Europe. Both leaders agreed that NATO is the essential foundation of transatlantic security and reaffirmed their support for NATO's "open door" policy for aspiring new members, as an indispensable instrument to strengthening stability and eliminating the old dividing lines in Europe.

President Clinton expressed strong support for Poland's strides in building ties with its neighbors and efforts to promote stability, democracy, and free market economics throughout Central and Eastern Europe. The two leaders discussed efforts already under way to establish trilateral economic cooperation among the United States, Poland and Ukraine, as well as Poland's efforts to establish peacekeeping battalions with Ukraine and Lithuania. They resolved that, as allies, they should expand such common efforts to strengthen democracy and regional stability.

The President applauded Poland's active role as Chairman-in-Office of the Organization for Security and Cooperation in Europe (OSCE) and thanked Prime Minister Buzek for Poland's strong contribution to the international effort to create stability in the Former Yugoslavia. He particularly praised Poland's participation in both IFOR and SFOR in Bosnia-Herzegovina.

President Clinton praised Poland for the bold, free-market reforms it has pioneered since 1989 as proof that the legacies of communism can be overcome. Prime Minister Buzek expressed profound gratitude for the American assistance provided during the difficult early years of its free market transformation. The leaders noted that Polish effort and sacrifice combined with United States assistance has produced several important successes in the transformation of the Polish economy. They noted particularly that:

Poland's progress in banking reform enabled the 10 contributing governments to authorize release to Poland in April of the $450 million ($221 million U.S.) they had contributed to the Polish Bank Privatization Fund, set up in 1992.

The Polish-American Enterprise Fund (PAEF) has used $257 million provided by the U.S. government for capital and technical assistance to great effect in supporting the emergence of Poland's vibrant, free market economy. The two leaders discussed the future of the PAEF. They agreed that final disposition of the PAEF's assets can be achieved in ways that further enhance Polish-American relations and advance our mutual interests in building a prosperous and democratic Europe.

The remaining U.S. government assistance is now being used to help the Polish government to continue this transformation in a number of critical areas, including local government and pension reform.

Given Poland's remarkable progress and integration into the competitive global economy, both governments took note of the new phase in our economic relationship based on investment, trade and other forms of cooperation, with private sectors in the lead. Both governments pledged to take steps to help bolster mutually beneficial trade and investment, noting that the U.S. is already the leading foreign investor in Poland. The U.S. Under Secretary of State for Economic, Business and Agricultural Affairs will visit Warsaw soon to develop this bilateral consultative mechanism on economic issues in Polish-American relations.

Poland and the United States welcomed their intense and regular bilateral dialogue in other areas as well. They noted the accomplishments of our Bilateral Working Group on Defense Matters and agreed to continue to use this as a key mechanism to prepare Poland for full integration into NATO's military structures. They also agreed to hold regular consultations on regional and global issues.

Both governments will work to increase cooperation on law enforcement. As part of this effort, the United States will work with Poland to conduct cooperative prosecutor and police training in Poland and regionally to strengthen our ability to combat transnational crime. The United States applauds Poland's efforts to develop a Polish International Training Center for Specialist Police Forces which will serve an important role in regional efforts to combat crime.

The United States and Poland welcome the enlargement of the European Union as an essential step in completing construction of a Europe that is truly whole and free. The United States supports timely accession of Poland to the EU and looks forward to Poland's early and active participation in the Transatlantic Dialogues. Both governments pledge their support for the further development of transatlantic cooperation beneficial for all countries involved.

The President also recognized Poland's considerable contributions to multilateral peacekeeping efforts around the world and announced the U.S. Government's readiness to use the Enhanced International Peacekeeping Capabilities Initiative (EIPC) to further develop Poland's already strong capabilities in this area. The President expressed appreciation for Poland's participation in the international coalition which pressed the Iraqi government to comply with UNSC resolutions, as well as day-to-day representation of U.S. interests in Baghdad. The two leaders expressed their determination to work together with other interested parties to promote diplomatic resolution to this continuing challenge to stability in the Persian Gulf.

NOTE: An original was not available for verification of the content of this joint statement.

The President's Radio Address
July 11, 1998

Good morning. This week General Barry McCaffrey, Attorney General Reno, and I were in Atlanta to launch an unprecedented antidrug campaign to ensure that when young people watch television, listen to the radio, read the newspaper, or surf the Web, they will get the powerful message that drugs are wrong, illegal, and can kill. They're both with me here today. This morning I'd like to talk to you about how we are working to sever the dangerous link between illegal drugs and violent crime.

There is no greater threat to our families and communities than the abuse of illegal drugs. For the last 5½ years, we've worked hard to fight drugs on every front: on our streets, in our schools, at our borders, in our homes. We've made real progress. Today there are 50 percent fewer Americans using drugs than just 15 years ago.

This morning the Justice Department will release a study that highlights several areas where we have more work to do. On the positive side, it shows that crack cocaine, which once ravaged whole neighborhoods, is now on the decline. In Manhattan, for example, the number of young criminals testing positive for crack cocaine dropped from 77 percent in 1988 to just 21 percent last year.

However, abuse of methamphetamine—after falling for 2 years—is now rising in the West and Southwest. Clearly, we have more to do. In six cities where methamphetamine is prevalent, we will help local governments attack this outbreak with the same community policing strategies that are allowing us to get crack cocaine off the streets.

The Justice Department study also shows that we must do more to make criminals make a clean break from illegal drugs. The study reports that between one-half and three-quarters of the people charged with crimes have drugs in their system at the time of their arrest. We already know that many of these offenders will commit more crimes if they are released with their drug habits intact. Now, if we want to continue to make our communities safer, we simply must get more crime-committing addicts to kick the habit.

In 1989 Attorney General Reno helped to pioneer one of the most successful ways of getting criminals to give up drugs. Her innovation, known as a drug court, gives nonviolent offenders a simple deal: If you submit to regular drug testing, enroll in court-supervised drug treatment, and keep yourself clean, you can stay out of jail; but if you fail tests or fail to show up, you'll be punished to the full extent of the law.

In 1994, through our historic crime bill, we helped to expand drug courts from a mere handful back then to more than 400 today. The results have been remarkable. In some cities, drug court participants have recidivism, or repeater rates, as low as 4 percent. So today we'll take another step to break the cycle of drugs and crime by awarding grants to build and enhance drug courts in more than 150 communities across our Nation. To stop the revolving door of crime and narcotics, we must make offenders stop abusing drugs.

Now Congress must get involved. I've asked Congress to fund an $85 million testing and treatment initiative like the ones passed just this year in Connecticut and Maryland, initiatives that will help to support even more drug courts, as well as mandatory drug treatment and testing programs for probationers, prisoners, and parolees. So far, Congress has taken no action on this request, despite the indisputable evidence that mandatory drug testing and treatment works for probationers, prisoners, and parolees, and that drug courts clearly work.

I know all Members of Congress, regardless of party, want drug use and crime in America to keep going down. On Thursday Speaker Gingrich stood with us in Atlanta and pledged to attack the Nation's drug problem in a nonpartisan manner. The best way to do that is for Congress to work with me in the remaining days of this legislative session to create even more drug courts and to expand mandatory testing and treatment of those who commit crimes.

By putting progress ahead of partisanship, we can enhance responsibility, fight drugs, cut crime, and strengthen our Nation for the 21st century.

Thank you for listening.

NOTE: The President spoke at 10:06 a.m. from the Oval Office at the White House.

Remarks at the National Treasures Tour Kickoff
July 13, 1998

Thank you very much. Is this a great way to start the week, or what? [*Laughter*] Thank you, Secretary Heyman, Ms. Rimel, Mr. Mayor and members of the city council, Mr. Moe. Thank you, Denyce, as always, for being so wonderful. Thank you, Ralph Lauren, for this incredible act of generosity and, I think, foresight. And I want to thank the First Lady for once again creating something of enduring value to our country in this Millennium Project.

You know, Hillary mentioned this, but 1814 was not a particularly good year for America, and the British did burn the White House. And we've just finished a 15-year renovation of the White House, and we left two of the great stones unpainted to remind people that it only became the White House after the British burned it. And when the burn marks couldn't be scrubbed off, the beautiful stone had to be painted white to cover the memory of what had happened. It's rather nice, actually, to have a couple of the stones unpainted so that we don't completely forget.

Not since that time has the United States been invaded. And so the confidence of all the people who were involved was well-founded. Francis Scott Key wrote "The Star-Spangled Banner" in the midst of a very fierce battle. He was standing on the deck of a ship, behind enemy lines, looking into darkness, searching for the fate of the flag. The poem he wrote about it became our national anthem. If you remember the words and then you look at this massive flag, you can imagine what it must have been like in 1814, waving gallantly during the fight, standing unconquered in the dawn's early light. Think how you would have felt if you had seen it then.

This Star-Spangled Banner and all its successors have come to embody our country, what we think of as America. It may not be quite the same for every one of us who looks at it, but in the end, we all pretty much come out where the framers did. We know we have a country founded on the then-revolutionary idea that all of us are created equal and equally entitled to life, liberty, and the pursuit of happiness; that this whole country was put together out of an understanding that no individual can maximize the pursuit of life, liberty, and the pursuit of happiness alone, and so we had to join together to reinforce each other's efforts.

And then there was another great insight, which is that in the joining we couldn't repeat the mistakes of the monarchies from which we fled and give anyone absolute power over anyone else. And so we created this written Constitution to say that, okay, we've got to join together, and some people have to be our representatives and they should be given authority to make certain decisions, but never unlimited and never forever.

And I'd say that system has worked pretty well over the last 220-plus years. And that's what that flag embodies—at a moment when we could have lost it all, when the White House itself was burned, when a lot of people didn't think that we had such a good idea. And so now it's standing there, a little worse for the wear, but quite ready to be restored. And in that sense, it is a metaphor for our country, which is always ready to be restored.

When Hillary and I were talking about what we should do to commemorate the millennium and she came up with this phrase, "Honoring the past, and imagining the future," I loved it because it seems to me to be so much two sides of the same coin. You heard her only slightly making fun of me there about my obsession with the history of the United States and the White House and this great city. When I became President, I was often made fun of for my obsession about the future and trying to modernize the country. And to me, the two things are not inconsistent at all, because America is a country that has always been in the act of becoming.

You heard—if you listened carefully to the remarkable statement by Secretary Heyman, he mentioned the phrase of the Founders, "to form a more perfect Union." If you think about it, that is the enduring mission of America. They were very smart people, and they understood that any great nation is always a work in progress. They understood that they could never imagine the far reaches of America's future. They understood that these ideals they set up would never be perfectly realized. And so they gave us a mission that will be just as good for our grandchildren as it is for us, just as good as it was for George Washington and Abraham Lincoln, "to form a more perfect Union," because there will always be something there to do better, always a new challenge. And I agree that if you look at where we are today, we have both the traditional responsibilities of every generation of Americans, to deepen the meaning of our freedom and to widen the circle of opportunity, and all these new challenges.

One of them is to deal with our phenomenally increasing diversity. Didn't you get a kick out of seeing all those kids standing there doing the Pledge of Allegiance, from all their backgrounds? Who were their grandparents? Who were their great-great-grandparents? Where did they come from? What was their story? It doesn't matter, because they now have a chance to live the dream that was promised to all of us so long ago. That's what that flag embodies.

We have all kinds of responsibilities now to the rest of the world we didn't have before, because now the world is yearning for freedom, and there is no cold war, and we must summon ourselves to understand that in the 21st century, preserving everything good about America at home requires us to be more involved with our neighbors around the world than ever before.

We have new challenges when it comes to our natural environment, to prove that we can continue to enjoy the fruits of material prosperity while replenishing the Earth, not destroying it.

There will be new and different challenges, but we can meet them best if we remember what got us here. That's why saving the Star-Spangled Banner is important. That's why I asked the American people to do it in the State of the Union. That's why I'm very grateful to Ralph Lauren today for stepping forward. You know, most of us have—well, maybe not most of us, but a lot of us, including Hillary and me—have those great Polo sweaters with the American flag on it. I wish I had one with the Star-Spangled Banner on it because that's the gift that he's given America today.

Now, I want to echo what Hillary said. There is more to do. President Lincoln and his family and many other Presidents' families used to stay in a little cabin up with the Old Soldiers' Home here in Washington, DC, in the summertime because the Potomac was so hot. That ought to be preserved for all time to come. And this committee has identified dozens of other sites.

But I also want to emphasize something else Hillary said, as she begins this tour over the next 4 days to identify nationally significant treasures. Every community in this country has got some piece of itself that needs to endure. And I hope that the public airing that this event receives today will make people in every community across our country once again say, "What have we got here that we should preserve for our grandchildren and for all time to come?" Americans need to know the stories of their country, their States, their communities, their families.

Let me especially thank the History Channel for doing its part to share the story of the Star-Spangled Banner by producing its own TV documentary and providing teachers with educational packets about it.

Again let me say to all of you, too, we must continue to imagine the future. I asked the Congress to pass the Save America's Treasures program, as well as the biggest research program for the future in history, and to put them together so that our people could see that the story of America is a seamless one.

I hope all of you in this room and all of the people who are involved in this endeavor, every time you see the Star-Spangled Banner for the rest of your life, will think about preserving our past, honoring it, but also will think about imagining the future. What an imagination it took in 1814 to believe that America had a boundless future. The Continental Congress said when it authorized the first flag of 13 stars that they were "a new constellation." They were right.

When I looked at all those children today saying the Pledge of Allegiance, I thought, now we are a newer constellation—different than they could have imagined—racially, religiously. We have no longer a small country on the eastern seaboard but a continental nation, with the greatest influence for good the world has ever seen and an enormous responsibility for the future.

And that is the last point I would like to make today. You can neither honor the past, nor imagine the future, nor achieve it without the kind of citizenship embodied by all of our memories of the flag. So as you see this flag and leave this place, promise yourself that when your great-grandchildren are here, they'll not only be able to see the Star-Spangled Banner, it will mean just as much to them then as it does to you today.

Thank you, and God bless you.

NOTE: The President spoke at 8:48 a.m. at the National Museum of American History. In his remarks, he referred to I. Michael Heyman, Secretary, Smithsonian Institution; Rebecca W. Rimel, president, The Pew Charitable Trusts; Mayor Marion S. Barry, Jr., of Washington, DC; Richard Moe, president, National Trust for Historic Preservation; mezzo-soprano Denyce Graves; and Ralph Lauren, chairman and chief executive officer, Polo Ralph Lauren Corp.

Statement on the Proposed International Monetary Fund Financing Program for Russia
July 13, 1998

I welcome the announcement this morning by Michel Camdessus, managing director of the International Monetary Fund, that he will recommend a new financing program for Russia to the Fund's Executive Board. This new program of Russian policy commitments and international financial support can provide a sound basis for increased stability and confidence. Strong implementation by the Russian Government of these important reform measures is essential. I continue to believe that a partnership with a stable, democratic, and prosperous Russia is a vital U.S. national interest.

Statement on Brazil's Ratification of the Comprehensive Nuclear Test Ban and Nuclear Non-Proliferation Treaties
July 13, 1998

Today Brazil ratified the Comprehensive Test Ban Treaty (CTBT) and acceded to the Nuclear Non-Proliferation Treaty (NPT). I want to congratulate President Cardoso and the Government of Brazil for taking this historic step.

Brazil's decision renews momentum for the international effort to halt the spread of nuclear weapons and promote disarmament around the world. At a time when actions by India and Pakistan threaten a nuclear competition in South Asia, Brazil has chosen a different course—to invest in its people, not in a costly arms race.

Brazil's action today to ratify the CTBT makes it all the more important for the U.S. to do the same. I call on our Senate to act expeditiously to approve the CTBT—already signed by 149 nations and supported by the Joint Chiefs of Staff—so that the United States can lead in this vital endeavor.

Remarks at a New Democratic Network Dinner
July 13, 1998

Thank you very much. Well, Joe, I agree with Hadassah; this is pretty impressive. I would like to thank all the members who are here, all the candidates who are here, the sponsors of this event, and those of you who have contributed, because this group is going to give the American people a chance to finally and fully ratify the ideas that we have been pursuing the last 6 years.

I want to thank Simon. I did tell Senator Lieberman I thought Simon had given a good talk. One of the things that I always think that all of us should be doing is trying to recruit good young people and lift them up. Simon self-selected; we didn't have to recruit him at all. [*Laughter*] After surviving the War Room in '92, he understands that all you have to do is just sort of stand there and keep going, and it will be all right.

I'm delighted to see so many of you here, so many old friends and some people who are getting involved in this. And I will be a little brief tonight. I rewrote my talk; here it is. Even I can't read it, so it will be less.

Well, I'd like to just kind of recap how this all began. I'll never forget the first time or two I talked to Al From and the first encounter I had with many of you through the DLC, and how strongly we felt that our party, which we had no intention of leaving, was being rendered irrelevant in national elections, partly by being caricatured successfully by the very adroit tactics of our friends in the Republican Party and partly because we seemed unable to break out of the conventional wisdom which had worked for us in the past but which seemed inadequate to the dynamic present. And that had been the case for some years.

If you look around the world today—and I don't want to make any untoward foreign policy comments—but if you look around the world today, you see that there is always quite a high price to pay if you stay with a strategy that once worked for you, or with ideas and policies that once worked for you, when circumstances change and they no longer fit. We find that in business; we find that in our personal lives, in virtually every form of human endeavor.

And so more than a decade ago, those of us that loved and believed in the Democratic Party as the instrument of progressive government, lifting people up, giving them a chance, building the American community, and expecting responsibility from every citizen, started, through the Democratic Leadership Council, to try to come up with the ideas that would carry America forward.

It is true that we built it on the old bedrock values of our party—and, I think, of our country—of opportunity, responsibility, and community. It's also true that we said some things which made everybody angry and often confused our friends in the press. And they sometimes said, "Well, if you don't fit into these old categories, you must not have any principles."

I mean, whoever—it's obviously stupid to believe you could reduce the deficit and balance the budget and still keep investing more in education and science and technology, for example; hard to believe that, on crime, the only thing that would ever work would be to be tough on people who should be properly punished, but to do smart things to prevent crime in the first place; on welfare, to say that if you're able-bodied you ought to go to work, but we don't expect you to give up your most important job, which is raising your child; or on the environment, to say that it's crazy to believe that we can ever have long-term economic growth without preserving the environment, but we think we can do it and still grow the economy.

And when we said these things, for years people said, "Well, those people, they don't have any principles, because, after all, we know what a principle is; a principle is an old liberal idea or a new conservative idea. That's what a principle is. And that way we don't have to think anymore. We were relieved of all the burden of thinking about the complexities of the modern world if we just put you in some box. And if you guys don't fit, it must mean that there is no core there."

But we sort of pressed ahead. And when I started running in '92, a lot of you helped me, even though you honestly didn't believe I had a chance to win. [*Laughter*] Only my mother thought I could win. That's not true; Hillary did. And the American people gave us a chance. And we set about the business of doing this.

And along the way, we found that, as all people do, it wasn't always easy to take your general principles and turn them into specific bills and specific policies. From time to time, we had disagreements, but it's clear the path we have followed. And it was clear to us very often even when it wasn't clear to people who were commenting on it.

I remember when we had the debate on welfare reform, for example, and I vetoed the first two bills and I signed the third one, so people said, "Well, obviously, the President just didn't want the Democrats to be exposed to another veto in an election year." I never read a single article which analyzed the difference in the bill I signed and the two I vetoed. The two I vetoed said, "We're going to make you go to work if you're able-bodied, and if you have to give up being a good parent, that's fine with us. We're not going to give your kids Medicaid. We're not going to give your kids food stamps. We're not going to provide adequate child care for you. The most important thing is work, and if you can't be a good parent, that's tough." I still believe that's the most important job in America. So when they fixed the bill, I signed it.

So fast-forward to the present. If you look back on the last 6 years, if somebody told you on the day of Inauguration in 1993 that after 6 years we'd have the lowest crime rate in 25 years, the lowest unemployment rate in 28 years and 16 million new jobs, the lowest welfare rolls in 29 years, the first balanced budget in 29 years, the lowest inflation in 32 years, the smallest Federal Government in 35 years, the highest rate of homeownership in history, a quarter of a million people who couldn't buy guns because they had mental health histories or criminal records, cleaner air, cleaner water, safer food, fewer toxic waste dumps, 90 percent of our kids immunized, and a foreign policy that's helped to advance the cause of freedom from Bosnia to the Middle East to Northern Ireland to Haiti, that's expanded trade and stood up for human rights in places like China and other places around the world—you would have said, "Never happen in 5½ years."

The American people did it. We had something to do with it because we gave them the ability to do it, because we said the role of Government should be to give people the power, the tools to make the most of their own lives and then to provide the conditions within which they can accomplish that, but always to remind people that one of the big differences between ourselves and the other party historically, and still, is that we believe that we are fundamentally interdependent and that our personal independence can only really be manifested when we're working together for the greater good. And those who say that's a flaky idea and inappropriate to the moment need only go back and read our founding documents.

Our Founders pledged their lives and fortunes and sacred honor to the proposition that we should all be able to pursue life, liberty, and happiness within the context of a free government of limited power but unlimited potential and that our eternal mission as a country was to form a more perfect Union, not to form a more perfect collection of swarming individuals but to form a more perfect Union.

And I'm very grateful that I was given the chance to serve. And it's a good thing we got that constitutional amendment, or I'd try to get another chance. [*Laughter*]

But I want to tell you, I am absolutely convinced that we have not finished the job of convincing the American people that the prospects for the future depend upon the continued embrace and development of the ideas which have produced the results of the last 6 years. That's what this election is all about. They say, "Oh well, you know,"—I hear a lot of my Republican friends say, "Well, you know, you go all the way back to the Civil War, and the party of the President always loses seats in the midterm election, especially in the second term of the President." And I said, "Well, that's because they think they're sort of retiring." I'm not sitting in the sun here; we've got an agenda.

We don't believe America should be sitting on its laurels. We believe, first of all, that we hadn't had a balanced budget and a surplus for 29 years, and we don't want the majority in Congress to spend it before we save Social Security. We want to reform Medicare in a way that is relevant to the 21st century, that protects the health care of seniors. And we don't want Social Security and Medicare to bankrupt the children and grandchildren of the baby boomers. And we believe we can do both things. And we think, as Democrats, we're better suited to that path.

We want to continue to reform education, even as they try to eviscerate our agenda, as I speak, in the House of Representatives. We want to continue to advance the environmental agenda with market technology and research to prove that we can improve the environment while we grow the economy. We want to continue to prove that we can be one America, across all the lines that divide us, because what we have in common is more important.

We have a lot of big things to do. We want to prove that we can go into inner-city neighborhoods and isolated rural areas and Native American reservations and bring the principles of market economy and the right kind of support and prove that even in the poorest parts of America we can create a system of opportunity that will work for people and that they ought to have a chance to be a part of.

We have a lot to do. This country still has responsibilities in the world that we are not fully meeting. If we're going to create the kind of world trading system we want, if we're going to continue to be a force for human rights and democracy, if we're going to organize ourselves against the security threats of the 21st century—including biological and chemical warfare, small-scale nuclear warfare, terrorism, narcotrafficking—we have other things to do.

And if we keep these ideas up front, I think that the people we have seen here tonight, the Members of Congress and the candidates, have an excellent chance of winning. And I think we have an excellent chance to genuinely build a majority party not based on the success of one person from, as one of my adversaries once said, a small Southern State.

I am very grateful for the chance I had to serve and run. I'm grateful for the chance that I've had to win elections. I've loved every day, every month, every year of my life in politics. But the success America enjoys today is fundamentally due, first, to the character and effort and ingenuity of the American people and, secondly, to the fact that we have done the right thing. Ideas matter; there are consequences that flow from actions taken or forgone. And you know and I know—and I can tell you agree with me because you're quiet and you're listening—that two Presidential elections in good times—the second one in good times—do not necessarily ratify what we're doing.

We have worked like crazy to hammer these ideas into policies. And we've had honest debates and arguments, and sometimes we still disagree, but we know we're moving the country in a certain direction and we know it works. And we've got to go out there in this election season and tell the American people that, "Hey, you know, I like the President, too, but this is not a personality contest; this is the struggle for the ideas that should properly dominate the public policy of this country, that should guide this country where we're going, and should lift us up and give us a chance to do even better in the 21st century."

What you're doing is very, very important. And if you're undertaking one of these congressional races out there in an open seat—maybe it's held by a Republican; maybe it was held by a Republican—and it gets tough and you get discouraged, just remember, you know in the very marrow of your being that two-thirds of the American people, if they could get rid of all the cardboard, cut-out, superficial, negative images that our friends in the Republican Party have laid on us for 20 years relentlessly, cleverly, and often effectively, and strip all that away and just look at what they stand for and what we stand for, and have an honest choice of the ideas before them, they would say, "I think I like that New Democrat way; I think that's right."

So don't get discouraged when you're still shedding the shackles of history. Don't get discouraged when you're still scrubbing the barnacles off the tarnished image that we had for too long. Don't get discouraged when you're still moving against the preconceptions that people have embedded over 20 years. The hardest thing in the world to change is a mind. But ideas move people; they drive countries; they change destinies—in people's individual lives and family lives and work lives and in the course of a country's life. And this country has had a good 6 years because of the ideas that all of you worked hard on for years and years and years, before I had the extreme good fortune to serve as President in 1993.

So don't give up on that, and don't get discouraged. And don't think that just because every election since the Civil War in an off year has turned out a certain way, that this one will, because there's something different about now. The country is doing well. We've got the ideas, and we've got youth. And if you keep your spirits up and you understand the historic mission you're on and you think about what your country ought to look like when your children are your age, I think you'll be very pleased by how it turns out.

Thank you very much, and God bless you.

NOTE: The President spoke at approximately 8:05 p.m. in the Crystal Ballroom at the Sheraton Carlton Hotel. In his remarks, he referred to Senator Joseph I. Lieberman, cofounder, and Simon Rosenberg, executive director, New Democratic Network; Senator Lieberman's wife, Hadassah; and Al From, president, Democratic Leadership Council.

Remarks on the Year 2000 Conversion Computer Problem
July 14, 1998

Thank you very much, Mr. Vice President, Dr. Alberts, to all of our platform guests, Senator Bennett, Senator Dodd, Congressmen Horn, Kucinich, LaFalce, and Turner, and members of the administration who are here and all the rest of you who are committed to dealing with this challenge.

This is one of those days that I never thought would ever arrive, where Al Gore has to listen to me give a speech about computers. [*Laughter*] Being President has its moments. [*Laughter*]

International Monetary Fund Financing for Russia

I have to ask your indulgence because this is my only opportunity to appear before the press today, and I need to make a brief comment about something that is also of importance to all of you, and that is the agreement that was reached yesterday between Russia and the International Monetary Fund to stabilize the Russian economy.

I think all of us understand that a stable and democratic and prosperous Russia is critical to our long-term national interests. Ever since the fall of communism there, there has been a strong bipartisan consensus in our National Government and, I believe, in our country to working toward that end.

The commitments that Russia made in connection with yesterday's agreement will substantially advance economic reform and stability there. Now it is critical that those commitments be implemented to strengthen confidence in their economy.

It is clear, I think, to all of us now that our prosperity here at home in America is deeply affected by the economic conditions elsewhere in the world. About a third of our economic expansion that the Vice President referred to, which has given us 16 million new jobs and the lowest unemployment rate in 28 years with the lowest inflation rate in 32 years, has come from our exports and our economic relations with the rest of the world. We therefore have a clear interest in playing a leading role to advance freedom and prosperity and stability.

One of the most cost-effective ways of doing that is through the International Monetary Fund, the world's financial firefighter. For the first time in 20 years now, the IMF has had to draw on special emergency reserves to underwrite this Russian financial package, because its resources were stretched dangerously thin due to the financial difficulties throughout Asia, principally.

To protect our economic strength, therefore, it is imperative that Congress act now to promote global economic stability by paying in America's share to the IMF. Earlier this year, the Senate, in an overwhelming bipartisan vote, endorsed legislation to strengthen the IMF and to pay our fair share into it. Since then, the legislation has languished in the House. If we fail to act responsibly at a time when there is so much financial uncertainty in the world, we will be putting our farmers, our workers, and our businesses at risk. This is a time to put progress ahead of partisanship, and I ask Congress to proceed to do so. [*Applause*] Thank you.

Year 2000 Conversion

Let me also say at the outset, I want to say a special word of thanks, as the Vice President did, to John Koskinen and his whole team for the work they are doing and to all the people that are working with them. We have, just on this platform, representative people from utilities, from transportation, from finance, from telecommunications, and from small business. And this really is a joint effort we are all making.

But I thank you, John. You know, before I became President, John Koskinen was a personal friend of mine—I doubt if he still is now that I got him to do this. [*Laughter*] But what's a friendship to save the country's wires, so I thank him. [*Laughter*]

I asked Bruce Alberts this—I remembered that Richard Berks' magnificent statue of Albert Einstein is right outside here, and I wish we could bring him to life for this moment. But I think I'll drive by it on the way out for inspiration.

It seems unbelievable that it's only 535 days from now, at the stroke of midnight, when we will usher in a new year, a new century, a new millennium. It will be, to be sure, an astonishing age of possibility, of remarkable advances in science and technology, a time when information clearly will widen the circle of opportunity to more people in the world than ever before and when technology will continue to shrink our small planet and require us to deal with challenges together, including that climate change challenge that Dr. Alberts referred to.

It is fitting, if more than a little ironic, that this same stroke of midnight will pose a sharp and signal test of whether we have prepared ourselves for the challenges of the information age. The Vice President discussed the design flaw in millions of the world's computers that will mean they will be unable to recognize the year 2000. And if they can't, then we will see a series of shutdowns, inaccurate data, faulty calculations.

Because the difficulty is as far flung as the billions of microchips that run everything from farm equipment to VCR's, this is not a challenge that is susceptible to a single Government program or an easy fix. It is a complex test that requires us all to work together, every government agency, every university, every hospital, every business, large and small.

I came here today because I wanted to stress the urgency of the challenge to people who are not in this room. So often one of the wry and amusing aspects of the nature of my work is that when I give a speech like this, I am typically preaching to the choir, as we say back home. But hopefully the sermon is heard beyond the four walls of this room, because clearly we must set forth what the Government is doing, what business is doing, but also what all of us have yet to do to meet this challenge together. And there is still a pressing need for action.

The consequences of the millennium bug, if not addressed, could simply be a rash of annoyances, like being unable to use a credit card at the supermarket, or the video store losing track of the tape you have already returned. Has that ever happened to you? [*Laughter*] It really is aggravating. It could affect electric power—I just wanted to remind you that I used to have a life, and I know about things like that. [*Laughter*] It could affect electric power, phone service, air travel, major governmental service.

As the Vice President said, we're not just talking about computer networks but billions of embedded chips built into everyday products. And it's worth remembering that the typical family home today has more computer power in it than the entire MIT campus had 20 years ago. An oil drilling rig alone may include 10,000 separate chips.

The solution, unfortunately, is massive, painstaking, and labor intensive. It will take a lot of time to rewrite lines of computer code in existing systems, to buy new ones, to put in place backup plans so that essential business and government services are not interrupted.

With millions of hours needed to rewrite billions of lines of code and hundreds of thousands of interdependent organizations, this is clearly one of the most complex management challenges in history. Consider just one major bank, Chase Manhattan. It must work through 200 million lines of code, check 70,000 desktop computers, check 1,000 software packages from 600 separate software vendors.

The Government's Health Care Financing Administration, known affectionately by the Governors and others as HCFA, which runs Medicare, processes almost one billion transactions a year. Its computer vendors must painstakingly renovate 42 million lines of computer code.

All told, the worldwide cost will run into the tens, perhaps the hundreds of billions of dollars, and that's the cost of fixing the problem, not the cost if something actually goes wrong.

Already extraordinary efforts are underway by the people on the platform, many of you out here, and others, but more must be done. We know first we have to put our own house in order to make certain the Government will be able to continue to guard our borders, guide air traffic, send out Social Security and Medicare checks, and fulfill our other duties. We've worked hard to be ready. I set a government-wide goal of full compliance by March of 1999. John Koskinen is heading our council on the Y2K problem. I've met with the Cabinet and charged them personally to produce results and report quarterly to OMB on progress. We're working with State and local governments to do the same thing.

We have made progress. As has already been said, the Social Security Administration has more than 90 percent of its critical systems ready. Other agencies, like EPA, FEMA, and the VA, are well on their way to meeting our goal. But not every agency is as far along as it should be. I have made it clear to every member of my Cabinet that the American people have a right to expect uninterrupted service from Government, and I expect them to deliver.

I want to thank the thousands of individuals who are working to prepare our Government and to make sure we can stay open for business. I especially want to thank the Vice President and John Koskinen and the people who are working with them at OMB and elsewhere. And I very much appreciate these Members of Congress who are here and the extraordinary bipartisan interest and support meeting this challenge has engendered.

In my proposed balanced budget for 1999, I asked Congress to fund this initiative on a one-time basis, because it is literally a once-in-a-lifetime challenge. I urged the Congress to fully fund it and to provide contingency funding so that we can respond to unforeseen difficulties that are sure to arise as we near January of 2000. We have worked closely with Senators Bennett and Dodd and Congressman Horn and Congressman Kucinich and the other Members who are here, Congressmen LaFalce and Turner and others in the Congress. As I said, there has been a heartening amount of interest in this by people who actually know quite a lot about it in the Congress, and that's a very good thing.

I think we all understand that this is a case where we cannot allow, even in this election season, any shred of partisanship to impinge on the national interest. We, after all, only have 17 months to go.

I believe we also have a role to play in helping to meet this challenge around the world. Surely we can't be responsible for the preparedness of other countries, but I can make the same argument I just made about the IMF and Russia: If increasingly our prosperity is tied to the well-being of other nations, it would obviously have adverse consequences for us here at home if a number of our trading partners had major malfunctions.

When I was meeting with the world's major industrial organizations in Birmingham, England, a few months ago, I brought this up, and I found that we had become far more invested in this and involved in this than some other major nations. When I was in Santiago, Chile, at the Summit of the Americas, I brought it up in our private meeting, and a number of countries had literally only begun just to think about the problem.

So I think it is important that the United States recognize that the more we can do to help other countries meet this challenge in a timely fashion, the better off our own economy is going to be and the more smoothly our own businesses will be able to function as we pass over into the new millennium. The United States, to try to help, will provide $12 million to support the World Bank's Year 2000 Fund for developing countries.

I also want to say what we all know and what you can see from the platform, which is this is not a Government problem alone. By far, the most significant potential risks fall in the private sector. Large firms already have spent hundreds of millions of dollars to make sure their systems are ready. Many have spearheaded remarkable efforts to make sure their firms and their whole industries are ready. We're encouraged that dozens of firms and thousands of people on Wall Street last night began a simulation to test whether they are ready. And the telecommunication, banking, electric power, and airline industries all deserve praise for the seriousness with which they are taking the challenge.

I want to compliment one person back here in particular. Steve Wolf came all the way back from Africa, got here at 3 o'clock in the morning to show up to manifest his understanding of the importance of this challenge to the airline industry, and he is still breathing the rarefied air of Kilimanjaro, so we thank him especially for doing that.

But let me say, in spite of all this progress, in the business sector just as in the Government sector, there are still gaping holes. Far too many businesses, especially small and medium-sized firms, will not be ready unless they begin to act. A recent Wells Fargo Bank survey shows that of the small businesses that even know about the problem, roughly half intend to do nothing about it. Now, this is not one of the summer movies where you can close your eyes during the scary parts. Every business, of every size, with eyes wide open, must face the future and act.

So today I would issue three challenges to our business community. First, every business must take responsibility for making sure it is ready. Any business that approaches the new year armed only with a bottle of champagne and a noisemaker is likely to have a very big hangover on New Year's morning. [*Laughter*] Every business should assess its exposure, ask vendors and suppliers to be ready as well, and develop contingency plans, as we are, in case critical systems or systems of vendors fail as we move into the year 2000.

I want to especially thank Aida Alvarez and the Small Business Administration and its supporters in Congress. And I thank you, Mr. La-Falce, in particular, for the work that has been done to spread the message in the small business community.

And I'd like to salute one firm represented here, the Torrington Research Company, which makes fans for cars and computers. It has only 55 employees, but they've taken the time to check their systems and by the end of this year they will be ready—by the end of this year. I want every small business in America to follow their lead.

As the Vice President said, we need literally an army of programmers and information technology experts to finish the task. Many of the computers involved are decades old; some of them use programming language no longer used or even taught. There is a wealth of knowledge in America's tens of thousands of retirees who once worked in the computer industry or Government as programmers or information technology managers. I'm pleased to announce that the Department of Labor will expand its job bank and talent bank to help to meet this challenge. And I thank Secretary Herman and Deputy Secretary Higgins for that.

The AARP has also agreed to help out. And we're reaching out to civilian and military retirees who did this work for Government before. I will ask these older Americans to set aside their well-earned rest and help our Nation to meet this challenge.

Second, businesses should exchange and pool information among themselves. It makes no sense for every firm to have to reinvent the digital wheel. Businesses should be able to benefit from the experiences of other firms in the same situation that have found solutions or identified new obstacles.

Today, too many businesses are understandably reluctant to share information, fearing legal complications. We have to take prudent steps to clear away any legal barriers to effective action. Earlier this month, the Justice Department stated that competitors who merely share information on how to solve this problem are not in violation of the Nation's antitrust laws. We need to get that message out there loud and clear: No one should be afraid to help another company to deal with this challenge.

There is more we can do. This week I will propose good samaritan legislation to guarantee that businesses which share information about their readiness with the public or with each other, and do it honestly and carefully, cannot be held liable for the exchange of that information if it turns out to be inaccurate. And here, too, time is of the essence.

Our third challenge to business is that you should take responsibility to accurately and fully tell your customers how you're doing and what you're doing. By letting customers know they are on top of the problem, businesses can help to maintain confidence and avoid overreaction. This is very important. It is important that we act and not be in denial; it is also very important that we avoid overreaction from people who hear, "Oh my goodness, this problem is out there." And so we have to do both things.

The proposed good samaritan law will give companies the confidence they need to ensure that they keep their customers informed. If ordinary citizens believe they're being told the full story, they'll be far less likely to act in ways that could themselves hurt our economy.

We can do more to help businesses reach these goals. Later this month, our Council on the Year 2000 Conversion will launch a national campaign for year 2000 solutions, to promote partnerships between industry groups and Government agencies, with the goal of sharing information about what actually works and to prod organizations at every level to get ready, making certain Government services are not interrupted, minimizing disruption to commerce, encouraging businesses to share with each other and report honestly to customers, and above all, every business in America taking responsibility for being a part of the solution in the year 2000 conversion. These are the ways we, the American people, can be prepared to meet this challenge.

Now, no one will ever find every embedded microchip, every line of code that needs to be rewritten. But if companies, agencies, and organizations are ready, if they understand the threat and have backup plans, then we will meet this challenge.

The millennium bug is a vivid and powerful reminder of the ways that we are growing ever more interdependent° as we rise to the challenges of this new era. When our Founding Fathers urged us to form a more perfect Union, I don't think they had this in mind, but they might be quite pleased. The powerful forces of change that have created unimagined abundance also bear within them, as is consistent with human nature, the possibilities of new and unexpected challenges.

But if we act properly, we won't look back on this as a headache, sort of the last failed challenge of the 20th century. It will be the first challenge of the 21st century successfully met. That is the American way, and together we can do it.

Thank you very much.

NOTE: The President spoke at 11:13 a.m. at the National Academy of Sciences. In his remarks, he referred to Bruce Alberts, president, National Academy of Sciences; and Stephen M. Wolf, chairman and chief executive officer, US Airways Group, Inc.

Statement on the Departments of Labor and Health and Human Services Appropriations Legislation
July 14, 1998

Making strategic investments in our people, especially our children, has been a critical component of my economic strategy from the start. Last year we worked together on a bipartisan basis to open the doors of college, expanding Pell grants and creating $1,500 HOPE scholarships to advance the critical goal of making college universally available. This year I have proposed strategic investments to improve and reform K–12 education by putting standards, accountability, and choice back into our public schools. My agenda reduces class size, modernizes schools, invests in technology, and puts an end to social promotion. These initiatives would help ensure that every 8-year-old can read, every 14-year-old can sign on to the Internet, and every 18-year-old can be ready for college.

That is why I am deeply concerned with the Labor/HHS appropriations bill that Congress is considering today. This legislation denies essential educational opportunities to young people across the country and important training and job opportunities for all Americans.

On balance, this bill fails to provide young Americans with the schooling and training that will be essential to their success as working adults and to our success as a nation. The bill is fundamentally flawed. Overall, it cuts $2 billion from our request for education investment, short-changing initiatives on education reform, on raising educational achievement for our children, and on providing focused help for students who need it most. In addition, the bill fails to fund my childcare initiatives, eliminates current job training and other programs for low-income Americans, and has many other problems as well.

By turning their backs on America's young in this bill, the House Republicans are taking

---

° White House correction

a step backward. I urge the committee to provide the funds necessary for this bill to move America into the future, not backward. This bill shortchanges investments in education, and if it were sent to me in its current form, I would have no choice but to veto it.

Message to the Congress Transmitting a Report on Federal Advisory Committees
July 14, 1998

To the Congress of the United States:

As provided by the Federal Advisory Committee Act (FACA), as amended (Public Law 92–463; 5 U.S.C. App. 2, 6(c)), I am submitting the *Twenty-sixth Annual Report on Federal Advisory Committees*, covering fiscal year 1997.

Consistent with my commitment to create a more responsive government, the executive branch continues to implement my policy of maintaining the number of advisory committees within the ceiling of 534 required by Executive Order 12838 of February 10, 1993. As a result, the number of discretionary advisory committees (established under general congressional authorizations) was held to 467, or 42 percent fewer than those 801 committees in existence at the beginning of my Administration.

Through the advisory committee planning process required by Executive Order 12838, the total number of advisory committees specifically mandated by statute has declined. The 391 such groups supported at the end of fiscal year 1997 represents a 4 percent decrease over the 407 in existence at the end of fiscal year 1996. Compared to the 439 advisory committees mandated by statute at the beginning of my Administration, the net total for fiscal year 1997 reflects an 11 percent decrease since 1993.

Furthermore, my Administration will assure that the total estimated costs to fund these groups in fiscal year 1998, or $43.8 million, are dedicated to support the highest priority public involvement efforts. We will continue to work with the Congress to assure that all advisory committees that are required by statute are regularly reviewed through the congressional reauthorization process and that any such new committees proposed through legislation are closely linked to national interests.

Combined savings achieved through actions taken by the executive branch to eliminate unneeded advisory committees during fiscal year 1997 were $2.7 million, including $545,000 saved through the termination of five advisory committees established under Presidential authority.

During fiscal year 1997, my Administration successfully worked with the Congress to clarify further the applicability of FACA to committees sponsored by the National Academy of Sciences (NAS) and the National Academy of Public Administration (NAPA). This initiative resulted in the enactment of the Federal Advisory Committee Act Amendments of 1997 (Public Law 105–153), which I signed into law on December 17, 1997. The Act provides for new and important means for the public and other interested stakeholders to participate in activities undertaken by committees established by the Academies in support of executive branch decisionmaking processes.

As FACA enters its second quarter-century during fiscal year 1998, it is appropriate for both the Congress and my Administration to continue examining opportunities for strengthening the Act's role in encouraging and promoting public participation. Accordingly, I am asking the Administrator of General Services to prepare a legislative proposal for my consideration that addresses an overall policy framework for leveraging the public's role in Federal decisionmaking through a wide variety of mechanisms, including advisory committees.

By jointly pursuing this goal, we can fortify what has been a uniquely American approach toward collaboration. As so aptly noted by Alexis de Tocqueville in *Democracy in America* (1835), "In democratic countries knowledge of how to combine is the mother of all other forms of knowledge; on its progress depends that of all the others." This observation strongly resonates at this moment in our history as we seek to combine policy opportunities with advances in collaboration made possible by new technologies, and an increased desire of the Nation's citizens to make meaningful contributions to their individual communities and their country.

WILLIAM J. CLINTON

The White House,

July 14, 1998.

Message to the Congress Transmitting the Comprehensive National Energy Strategy
July 14, 1998

To the Congress of the United States:

I am pleased to transmit the Comprehensive National Energy Strategy (Strategy) to the Congress. This report required by section 801 of the Department of Energy Organization Act (Public Law 95–91; 42 U.S.C. 7321(b)), highlights our national energy policy. It contains specific objectives and plans for meeting five essential, common sense goals enumerated in the accompanying message from Secretary Peña.

Energy is a global commodity of strategic importance. It is also a key contributor to our economic performance, and its production and use affect the environment in many ways. Thus, affordable, adequate, and environmentally benign supplies of energy are critical to our Nation's economic, environmental, and national security.

The Strategy reflects the emergence and interconnection of three preeminent challenges in the late 1990s: how to maintain energy security in increasingly globalized energy markets; how to harness competition in energy markets both here and abroad; and how to respond to local and global environmental concerns, including the threat of climate change. The need for research and development underlies the Strat-

egy, which incorporates recommendations of my Committee of Advisors on Science and Technology (PCAST) for improvements in energy technologies that will enable the United States to address our energy-related challenges. Advances in energy technology can strengthen our economy, reduce our vulnerability to oil shocks, lower the cost of energy to consumers, and cut emissions of air pollutants as well as greenhouse gases.

This Strategy was developed over several months in an open process. Three public hearings were held earlier this year in California, Texas, and Washington, D.C., and more than 300 public comments were received. This Strategy is not a static document; its specifics can be modified to reflect evolving conditions, while the framework provides policy guidance into the 21st century. My Administration looks forward to working with the Congress to implement the Strategy and to achieve its goals in the most effective manner possible.

WILLIAM J. CLINTON

The White House,
July 14, 1998.

Remarks in a Roundtable Discussion on the Patients' Bill of Rights
July 15, 1998

The President. Hello, everybody. I'd like to make a very brief opening statement, beginning with expressing my thanks to whoever's about to turn that tape recorder off. [*Laughter*] I'd like to thank Dr. Dickey, Dr. Smoak, Dr. Ander-

son, and all the people at the AMA for having us. I thank the members of our roundtable for joining us, including Secretary Shalala, Secretary Herman, Secretary West, Dr. Kizer, the director of the health agency at the VA. And I want to say to the members of the press who are here, I am joined today by patients and their families, by doctors, nurses, and other health care providers who have widely different experiences and perspectives, but all agree that we very badly need a Patients' Bill of Rights.

More than 160 million Americans are in managed care today. At best, the system can drive health care costs down and make health care more affordable and accessible for more Americans. We should all be encouraged—representing that best—that a coalition of 25 progressive HMO's this week endorsed the Patients' Bill of Rights. But as we will hear in a few minutes, at its worst, managed care can also dehumanize health care, hamstringing doctors' decisions, alienating patients, even endangering lives.

In an increasingly complicated health care system, we need a simple standard. Traditional care or managed care, all Americans are entitled to quality care. That is why in my State of the Union Address I asked Congress to put progress ahead of partisanship and to pass a Patients' Bill of Rights.

To do our part to meet this challenge, I signed an Executive order back in February to extend the protections of the Patients' Bill of Rights to 85 million Americans in Federal health plans. Today we're taking further action. I am pleased to announce that the Department of Veterans Affairs, which provides health services to more than 3 million veterans, is putting in place a new procedure to help those veterans appeal health decisions, one of the most important protections in our Patients' Bill of Rights, and I thank Secretary West for that action.

To ensure, however, that every American is protected by a Patients' Bill of Rights, Congress has to act. In the remaining days left in this legislative session, once again I ask Congress to pass a strong and enforceable Patients' Bill of Rights that guarantees access to specialists so that people with cancer, heart disease, and other life-threatening illnesses can get the health care they need; that guarantees continuity of care, for example, so that pregnant women can have the same doctor throughout their pregnancy, even if a doctor is dropped from a health plan; a bill that makes these rights real by guaranteeing a remedy to people who have been injured or lost family members as a result of bad decisions; a bill that guarantees there will be no secret financial incentives for doctors to

limit care. That is the kind of comprehensive Patients' Bill of Rights America needs and deserves. We need, again I say, progress, not partisanship.

And now I would like to hear from all of you. I would just start—I have a few questions I want to ask, but I think it's important for you basically to make a brief opening statement and tell us what your experiences have been. And, Mary, if you don't mind, I'd like to begin with you.

[*Mary Kuhl related her experience with a health maintenance organization (HMO) after her husband's heart attack, when the HMO denied rehabilitation services and diagnostic procedures because the Kuhls were not certified. Ms. Kuhl described her frustration with HMO rules of procedure which limited her husband's ability to get the care he needed and would not allow the recommended time in a hospital.*]

The President. You mean the HMO would only let him stay 2 days?

Ms. Kuhl. Yes, they would only let him stay 2 days. We did all that, and he never got on the list, he just—on December 28, 1989, he dropped dead in our front yard and died in my arms. And I just don't think HMO's should have that right to make a decision whether you're going to live or die. I think it should be up to the doctors, because all the doctors agreed that he needed to be in St. Louis on July 6. So that's my story, Mr. President.

The President. Well, if we had this kind of legislation, you would have had that right.

Ms. Kuhl. Well, he did start a lawsuit against the insurance company and it went through all the courts. It went through the Federal court; it went to the court of appeals; and then finally it was in the Supreme Court, but they kicked it out, too, because of the bill, ERISA——

The President. But ours would take care of that; our legislation would take care of the legal bar to your remedy.

Ms. Kuhl. I would be very happy that nobody else had to go through this.

The President. Thank you.

Mr. Garvey.

[*David Garvey told the story of his wife, who was diagnosed with aplastic anemia while on vacation in Hawaii in 1994. Doctors in Hawaii recommended a bone marrow transplant and determined that Mrs. Garvey's condition made it* dangerous for her to travel home to Chicago for treatment. Her HMO physician in Chicago agreed with treating her in Hawaii, but was immediately taken off her case, and the new doctor, without examination or consultation with doctors on the case, insisted she return to Chicago for treatment or her bills would not be covered. Left without an immune system, Mrs. Garvey suffered a stroke on her flight home, developed a fungal infection which kept her too unstable for bone marrow transplants, and died 9 days later. Mr. Garvey described the devastation his wife's death had caused his family, saying that HMO's were more interested in money than human life.]

The President. If this legislation were to pass, one of the things that would happen—this would also have been relevant to your situation in St. Louis—is that people would be eligible for out-of-the-network—the so-called out-of-the-network treatment if it was indicated as being in the best interests of the patient, and also always held to the same services that are in the nature of an emergency.

We hear stories like this all the time. Thank goodness very few of them result in death. But someone who's not there on the scene, who's not a physician, should not be second-guessing a doctor who's there on the scene prescribing a certain treatment.

Mr. Garvey. Yes. It's a shame, but that's what happened.

The President. I don't think that's ever what anyone intended to happen from managed care. And I think that it's clear to me that just looking around the country, that even though a lot of States have passed these Patients' Bill of Rights, there's no real uniformity to it, and there ought to be a clear national rule that would cover both of the cases here that you have mentioned.

Dr. Evjy, do you want to comment on this? And if you could all speak up a little bit so they can hear you. I know we're getting it—this is feeding into the mult box, but we need to talk a little bit louder.

[Medical oncologist Jack Evjy said that when his daughter discovered a lump in her breast, she had to persuade her managed care provider to properly diagnose the problem with a biopsy, eventually had to change doctors to get anything done, and ultimately lost both breasts. Dr. Evjy also told the story of a patient who suffered from lymphedema, saying that when he recommended that the patient see specialists, the patient's health care provider took months to give permission for the treatment. Dr. Evjy then expressed his support for a Patients' Bill of Rights.]

The President. Did your daughter, when she had these tests, did she have to change doctors and medical plans?

Dr. Evjy. She did. She didn't change plans, but she changed doctors.

The President. Because one of the things that we hear a lot of complaints about, that is not totally unrelated to the story that Mary and David had in their lives but has more specific application to a person like you, is that a lot of people complain that basically there's not access to specialists and specialist care at the time they needed them in these plans. Your daughter deserves a lot of credit——

Dr. Evjy. She's feisty——

The President. That's what we really need, is aggressive health care providers urging people to get these tests, not flip them off. Because a lot of people go into denial, and they don't want to deal with these tests, and the responsible thing is for the physician to get them to do that.

Dr. Evjy. I mean, when you're sick, Mr. President, and you have the burden of worrying about your life and well-being, the last thing you need is to have to fight with a bunch of other people to get the care which is essential to well-being. It's just not right.

The President. Well, thank you for sticking up for your folks.

Dr. Evjy. Thank you.

The President. Beverly Malone is the president of the American Nurses Association, and maybe she would like to talk a little bit about this from her perspective.

[Ms. Malone told a similar story of a young woman who discovered lumps in her breast but was told by her provider that malignancy in someone her age was unlikely. By the time her symptoms required her to see a specialist, her condition had advanced significantly. Ms. Malone said as a nurse she saw this kind of unnecessary suffering all the time, and she expressed her support for a Patients' Bill of Rights and thanked the President for his work on the issue.]

The President. Thank you.

Mr. Fleming, tell us your story.

[*Mick Fleming told the story of his younger sister, who also discovered a lump in her breast. After a mastectomy, cancer was discovered in her lungs, and specialists explained that there was only a 2- to 3-month window for a procedure where high-dose chemotherapy and a bone marrow transplant could save her life. Mr. Fleming said preauthorization from her insurance carrier or $250,000 in cash was required before treatment could begin. Her insurance carrier did not preauthorize and, after a 4-month delay, ruled that the procedure was experimental and therefore denied. Her family hired attorneys to challenge the decision, and the insurance carrier then authorized the treatment. However, the cancer had by then spread to her brain, and she died 10 months later. Mr. Fleming said congressional action was necessary to change the system, and he expressed support for a Patients' Bill of Rights.*]

The President. Carol Anderson is a billing manager in an oncologist's office. You've heard all these stories; have you seen this happen a lot? I think it's important, since you do this, and that we've got the press coverage here, that you say whether or not you think we looked around and found all these people who are just needles in haystacks or if they're typical stories. That's what we have to convince the Congress of. This is not unusual. We haven't found the only three people in America who could tell these stories.

[*Ms. Anderson agreed, saying denials such as the ones in the participants' experiences were common and that appeals were not effective. She offered the example of a 12-year-old boy who developed a cancerous bone lesion on his leg. The doctor recommended a treatment which would have saved the boy's leg, but the insurance carrier would only authorize amputation. After a 4-month appeal of the treatment dispute, the leg had to be amputated. Ms. Anderson said most hospitals operated in debt and required money from patients up front, and that problems with getting authorization from carriers hindered proper care. She expressed her hope that political partisanship would not delay progress on resolving such problems.*]

The President. I honestly believe that—I don't see how—I don't think that this has anything to do with any kind of—it's not a political issue.

And I think everybody who's ever personally experienced it feels the same way.

And the only thing I would like to emphasize for the—especially for the public record here is that one of the things that we have proposed, that the insurers have been so resistant to in our bill, is an appeals process, some way of enforcing the substantive guarantees of the Patients' Bill of Rights. But you have—we just sat here now and heard all these examples of your tragedy, your tragedy, your tragedy—and your daughter slipped the noose so she saved her life—which demonstrates that medical care delayed might as well be denied. I mean, delayed medical care can be a death sentence, pure and simple. And maybe you save money that way if you're running the operation, but that's not what it is set up to do.

I just want to say, from my point of view, your very brave and moving statements today have made an utterly overwhelming case that, yes, we need very clear substantive rights and disclosure, as Mick said, in the law, but you've got to have some way of enforcing this because—look, I deal with this all the time in other less tragic contracts. We have trade disputes with other countries. They know that if we're right and they're wrong and they can drag it out until kingdom come, it doesn't matter if we win. And I can give you lots of other examples.

I'm a lawyer. From the time I was in law school, we were taught that justice delayed is justice denied. And we spend literally—the legal profession spends years and years and years of time trying to figure out how to expedite processes without doing injustice to either side. This is a clear case of that principle where the stakes are a heck of a lot higher than they are in virtually any other area of our national life. And so I think—I don't see how anybody could listen to all of you and walk away from the responsibility to pass this bill.

Nancy, would you like to say anything?

[*Dr. Nancy W. Dickey, president, American Medical Association, said the solution indeed appeared to be political. She stated that the health care delivery system was too often hampered by accountants and clerks affecting the decisionmaking, and State laws that attempted to strike a balance between proper care and delivery processes were instantly appealed in court. Dr. Dickey thanked the President for his leadership*] *on the issue, noting that the medical community had been waiting for legislative action since the 103d Congress, and said she supported the Patients' Bill of Rights.*]

The President. Secretary Shalala and Secretary Herman cochaired this quality health care commission for me, and we had representations from the nurses, the doctors, and consumer groups, from business groups and insurers. And they came up with the recommendation of passing a strong Patients' Bill of Rights. And I wondered if either one of them would like to say something or ask any of you a question and to comment about where we are.

[*Secretary of Labor Alexis M. Herman emphasized the need to strengthen the Employee Retirement Income Security Act of 1974 (ERISA) in three areas: the relationship between right and remedy, faster and fairer appeals, and protections for persons wrongly denied care. Secretary of Health and Human Services Donna E. Shalala noted that while there was a lot of discussion about Americans wanting less Government, this was an issue where they would like Government attention. She said a Patients' Bill of Rights was necessary for people to get the medical attention they deserve.*]

The President. I would like to just say, again, I think it's important to point out that there are a lot of good managed care operations. They are put at an unfair advantage when other people behave in an unscrupulous way. If you were running a managed care operation and you did everything you could do to make sure these decisions were made like this—[at this point, the President snapped his fingers]—so nobody ever died from delay, and you were willing to pay a little more to do it and risk a little more and invest a little more, why should you be put at a competitive disadvantage because somebody else is out there putting lives at risk?

So I think the industry itself, the good people in the industry, deserve this. And they would be better off if we had this bill, because the people who are out there doing the right thing anyway shouldn't ever be at any kind of financial disadvantage.

Alexis asked a question—I don't know, maybe Carol or some of the doctors, somebody else would like to answer it—but when you think about all the experiences that we heard about, the delays—how come his wife got put on a plane when she should have been taken care of in Hawaii; why didn't they get an answer in 30 days so this procedure could be performed; why didn't his sister get her answer quicker? How do you deal with what—even if this bill passes exactly as we proposed it, okay—even if the bill passes exactly as we've proposed it, there will be health care plans that have certain premiums in return for certain coverage, and somebody has to make a judgment about whether—what is covered. What's the right way?

Well, I was struck when Carol was describing this, about how long—how many times she had to keep calling back before she got to somebody that even knew as much as you do about it, much less as much as a doctor does. So, what is the right answer, practically, to the systems that the HMO's and the insurers should have for making these decisions in a timely fashion so we're not out there letting people die just by kicking the can down the road?

[*Ms. Anderson answered that if a clerk could not give authorization for a procedure, the request should be passed up to a more professional level immediately and addressed in a timely fashion rather than denied.*]

The President. Dr. Dickey, has the AMA spoken to this directly?

[*Dr. Dickey said the AMA recommended more straightforward processes with fewer stages to pass through, to let patients know their options sooner, and establishment of a timeline on authorization. She also noted the effectiveness of forcing providers to take responsibility by taking names for the possibility of future legal action.*]

The President. It looks to me like, too, there ought to be very, very clear rules whenever a doctor certifies that the condition is life-threatening. They ought to—I think they ought to be able to kick it right up to the—make a decision in 72 hours, then that gives—then they ought to have no more than a week for reconsideration, and then you ought to have your remedy kick in so you can get—the whole thing will be over. And I think the court should give whatever—however the remedies work—it depends on whether our bill passes as it is, but that ought to be resolved in a limited amount of time.

I mean, they are—when my mother got sick and was considered for various kinds of treatment, most of which she turned down because she thought she was too old and didn't want to bump anybody else out of it, but I really, just by sort of filling my head with all of this, I became much more sensitive about the time. I mean, to a lot of these people, the difference in 48 hours is an eternity about whether a given procedure will work or not—and you're just out there fiddling around. I mean, it's just—it's absolutely inexcusable.

And a lot of these people—like when you ask them for their name—a lot of these people are following the path of least resistance. They're doing what they think will please the people for whom they work. They're not out there trying to kill your patients. They're out there doing what they think is going to please the people that cut them a check every 2 weeks. And we've got to change that.

[*Secretary Shalala suggested that the Patients' Bill of Rights would actually save money because it would reduce the cases of wrongly denied coverage for symptoms of a disease at an early, perhaps curable, and less expensive stage. Dr. Evjy agreed, and noted that the insurance system had a responsibility to provide patients with accurate options, much the way doctors must explain conditions to their patients. Mr. Fleming noted that the ERISA laws governing the majority of health plans were outdated and out of pace with medical technology and that insurance carriers must also keep pace with modernity. Secretary of Veterans Affairs Togo D. West, Jr., endorsed Mr. Fleming's point and stressed the importance of definite timelines in providing care. Secretary Shalala said congressional action was necessary to give the public the rights the President gave to those in Federal plans. A participant noted that the Patients' Bill of Rights would be instrumental in ensuring information to empower patients and providers to work col-*lectively. *Dr. Dickey agreed and said she looked forward to working with the President to enact such legislation.*]

The President. I want to thank all of you. This has been very helpful to me and to members of our administration and I hope to the press and to the public. So thank you for hosting us. And I want to say a special word of thanks to Mary and to David and to Mick and Dr. Evjy and to Carol for relating some painful personal experiences.

And I would just leave you with this thought: For me, this is about even more than health care; this is about how people feel about America. I mean, for 6 years I've worked hard to make this country work again, to give people the sense that they can be really not only proud of America, but they can feel that it is a fair and decent place where everybody has a chance. And that obviously has to apply to decisions of life or death in the health care field, just as much as going to vote, getting a job, living in a safe neighborhood.

These stories are not the kind of stories any American of conscience would ever want to be told in the United States. And it's not the United States we want, as we stand on the verge of a new century. I know it's been painful for you, but you've done your country a great service today, and I thank you very much. Thank you.

NOTE: The President spoke at 2 p.m. at the American Medical Association. In his remarks, he referred to association officers Randolph D. Smoak, Jr., M.D., chairman, and E. Ratcliffe Anderson, Jr., M.D., executive vice president. The President also referred to his memorandum of February 20 on Federal agency compliance with the Patient Bill of Rights.

Statement on Signing the Agriculture Export Relief Act of 1998
July 15, 1998

Late last night, I was pleased to sign into law a bill that exempts agriculture credits from the nuclear sanctions imposed on Pakistan and India.

We need to make sure that our sanctions policy furthers our foreign policy goals without imposing undue burdens on our farmers. That's why I supported this legislation to ensure that U.S. wheat and other farm products will not be the unintended victims of an important nonproliferation law. When implementing sanctions, we must never forget their humanitarian impact.

This action allows us to send a strong message abroad without ignoring the real needs of those here at home. After Congress phased out Federal farm supports, it became more essential for American farmers to sell their grains, meats, fruits, and vegetables to markets around the world. And today, products from one of every three acres planted in America are sold abroad. Whenever we can, we should look for ways to expand our agricultural exports, not restrict them.

NOTE: S. 2282, approved July 14, was assigned Public Law No. 105–194.

Statement on the Report Entitled "America's Children: Key National Indicators of Well-Being"
July 15, 1998

Today my administration released an important report card on our Nation's children, "America's Children: Key National Indicators of Well-Being." Last year I called for this yearly report to provide the American people with a portrait of our children in critical areas such as health, education, and economic security.

In this second annual report, we find much to be grateful for—infant mortality is at an all-time low; the number of children with high blood lead levels, which can cause IQ or behavioral problems, has declined dramatically; more toddlers are up-to-date on their immunizations; more children are entering preschool, improving in math, and moving on to graduate from college; teen pregnancy has decreased; and a majority of parents are reporting that their children are in very good or excellent health. These strides reflect strategic investments in our Nation's children, which have always been central to my agenda to prepare America for the 21st century.

The report released today also demonstrates that we must now commit ourselves to making further progress for our children. Unfortunately, substance abuse and cigarette smoking among children are at unacceptable levels; reading scores are stagnant; and too many of our Nation's children live in poverty.

We have demonstrated that we can work on a bipartisan basis to address the challenges our children face. That's why, as I said yesterday, I am extremely disappointed that some in Congress have taken actions that threaten to undermine the important progress we have made by failing to provide critical investments for our young people. Our children deserve progress, not partisanship. As we pause to consider this report card on our children, I urge Members of Congress to work together to build a stronger future for our Nation's children.

Letter to Congressional Leaders on Financial Assistance for Farmers
July 15, 1998

Dear Mr. Leader:

I am very concerned about the financial stress facing farmers and ranchers in many regions of the country. Natural disasters, combined with a downturn in crop prices and farm income, expected by the Department of Agriculture (USDA) to remain weak for some time, cause me to question again the adequacy of the safety net provided by the 1996 farm bill. In some areas of the U.S., as many as five consecutive years of weather and disease-related disasters have demonstrated weaknesses in the risk protection available through crop insurance.

During the debate on the 1996 farm bill, I encouraged Congress to maintain a sufficient farm safety net, and since its enactment my Administration has repeated that call, proposing measures to buttress the safety net that are consistent with the market-oriented policy of the

1996 farm bill. The 1994 Crop Insurance Reform Act established a policy of improving the crop insurance program in order to remove the need for ad hoc disaster payments. This commitment to crop insurance as the preferred means of managing crop loss risks was reaffirmed in the 1996 farm bill. Farmers have responded to this policy by maintaining their enrollment in crop insurance at very high levels, especially in the Northern Plains states.

Therefore, I am instructing the Secretary of Agriculture to redouble his efforts to augment the current crop insurance program to more adequately meet farmers' needs to protect against farm income losses. In the interim, to respond to the current unusual situations, I urge the Congress to take emergency action to address specific stresses now afflicting sectors of the farm economy.

I agree with the intent of Senator Conrad's amendment and recommend that funding to address these problems be designated as emergency spending. A supplemental crop insurance program for farmers who experience repeated crop losses, a compensation program for farmers and ranchers whose productive land continues to be under water, and extended authority for the livestock disaster program are examples of the type of emergency actions that could help farmers and ranchers.

It is also crucial that the Congress provide the level of funding proposed in my FY 1999 budget in the regular appropriations bills and that the Congress pass the full IMF package to support the efforts of American farmers.

I am confident that you and your colleagues share my concern for American farmers and ranchers who are experiencing financial stress from natural disasters and low prices, exacerbated by the global downturn in agricultural trade, and I encourage the Congress to take emergency action quickly.

Sincerely,

WILLIAM J. CLINTON

NOTE: Identical letters were sent to Thomas A. Daschle, Senate minority leader, and Richard A. Gephardt, House minority leader. An original was not available for verification of the content of this letter.

Remarks at an Empowerment Zone Reception
July 15, 1998

Thank you so much. Welcome to the White House. Thank you for the good work you've been doing. I want to thank all the people who are responsible for this reception. I thank my Cabinet members and the Members of Congress for coming. I welcome all of you here, including the many, many elected officials, and especially Mayor Corradini. We wish her well as she assumes the helm of the U.S. Conference of Mayors. I'd like to thank the Marine Band for playing for you. They just celebrated their 200th birthday last weekend. As far as I know, there are no members of the original band still playing—[*laughter*]—but they have a magnificent sense of tradition.

I am so happy to have you here, to look out and see all of you, because you are the living embodiment of the political philosophy I have sought to bring alive in this country. You are the living embodiment of how I believe Washington, DC, should work: putting progress and people over partisanship, community over division, tomorrow's hopes over yesterday's fears.

I cannot thank the Vice President enough for shepherding this community empowerment process these last several years from what was just a gleam in our eyes over one of our weekly lunches to this vast array of Americans. And if you look around this crowd, if this isn't one America for the 21st century, I don't know what is. I thank you.

I want you to take away from here, in addition to all the practical things you've learned and the sense of enthusiasm and positive outlook you have, a couple of very brief points. So I want to repeat briefly some of the things the Vice President said, because we still need your help.

You know, when we came here, we had a philosophy of Government that we thought was appropriate to the 1990's and beyond. We wanted to get beyond what I thought was a completely sterile debate in Washington about whether Government could solve all the problems or Government was the source of all the problems. We thought our job was to empower people, to be a catalyst, to be a partner, to give people the tools to solve their own problems and make the most of their own lives and build strong personal lives, strong families, strong neighborhoods, strong communities. You have been the instrument of that, and many of you were just doing that anyway. We have tried to be good partners to you, and you have certainly been all we could ever have asked for.

If anybody had told me in 1993 when I took the oath of office as President and began to implement the ideas that we ran on, that in less than 6 years we'd have over 16 million jobs, the lowest unemployment rate in 28 years, the lowest crime rate in 25 years, the lowest percentage of our people on welfare at 29 years, the first balanced budget and surplus in 29 years, the lowest inflation rate in 32 years, the highest homeownership in history, millions of people taking advantage of the family leave law, getting pensions they couldn't get before, 5 million more kids getting health insurance, the highest immunization rates of children in our history, opening the doors of college to all Americans through the HOPE scholarship—and we do all that with the smallest Federal Government in 35 years—I would say, I'll take that, and be grateful for America.

But I have been urging the American people and urging this Congress to use these good times, not simply to enjoy them but to see them as the solemn responsibility to our children and grandchildren to take on the larger challenges that we face moving into the 21st century. And you know what they are as well as I do. You know we still have a lot of work to do to make the world a place of peace and freedom and prosperity. That's why I went to China to do my best to make a constructive partnership with the people of the world's most populous nation.

You know we still have work to do to give this country the world's best system of elementary and secondary education. We've got the best college system in the world, but everybody knows we can't stop until our children, from the first day of school, know that their schools are the best in the world.

You know we've still got work to do to prove that we can deal with these enormous environmental challenges we have, from brownfields in the cities to still work we need to do with clean water, to saving our oceans, to dealing with the challenge of climate change. And I take it, after having the 5 hottest years in the last 600 years in the 1990's, no one seriously quarrels with the idea that the Vice President was right years ago when he told us that global warming was real, and we have to find a way to grow the economy and preserve our environment.

And in spite of this great, wonderful crowd, we still have work to do to prove that we can all live together, across the lines of race and religion and other differences that divide us, because what we share in common is more important. That's what you live. You live that philosophy every day in your communities, and we need our political leaders to be as good as you are. And if America is going to lead the world to a better place, America has to always be striving to be better, to really, truly be one America where everybody has a chance and everybody has a role to play.

We have to save Social Security and Medicare for the 21st century so that when the baby boomers like me retire, we've got a decent retirement, but we don't bankrupt our children and our grandchildren. No person in the baby boom generation I have ever talked to—without regard to their income, their race, or what they did for a living—did not want desperately to make the changes now that have to be made so that when we retire, we do not impose an unconscionable burden on the future generations. We have to work on that. And we can do it if we do it together in a fair and decent and honorable way.

And I would say the last big challenge we face is the one that you're here working on. Yes, we have the best economy in a generation, maybe the best economy we have ever had. But there's still a lot of farming communities that don't know it. I got a letter from a farmer in North Dakota today who said that Arkansas is not the only town with a place called Hope. But there's not much of it left in Hope, North Dakota, because of the problems they face. And I saw the pictures of his little town, and it looked like so many towns in my home State back in the eighties.

There are a lot of Native American tribes represented here, and a lot of them still don't have the jobs they need, the education they need, the support they need. There are a lot of urban neighborhoods represented here, where the unemployment rate is still too high, the crime rate is still too high, and the children still don't have enough hope for the future.

And so I say to you, we want to be good partners. But to do it, you have to help us convince the Congress to put progress and people over partisanship.

We need another round of empowerment zones in this 1999 budget. Secretary Cuomo has got a budget that would provide for another 180,000 units of affordable housing, 50,000 housing vouchers for people moving from welfare to work, hundreds of millions of dollars for economic development in our most distressed communities.

We have an education empowerment zones initiative that deserves to pass so that we'll have more places like Chicago, which now has the sixth biggest school district in the country in summer school, which now is feeding tens of thousands of kids three square meals a day. We need to pass our initiative to help more communities provide after-school programs for kids to keep them out of trouble and to keep them learning. We have a lot to do.

We still have brownfields to clean up. We still have toxic waste dumps to clean up. We still have work to do. We want to expand the Community Development Financial Institution so we can make more of those microcredit loans. We made 2 million of those microcredit loans with American tax dollars in Africa and Latin America and Asia last year. If they work there, 2 million loans like that could revolutionize inner-city America, could revolutionize the Native American communities, could revolutionize a lot of small, rural communities in this country. We can do it, and we need your help to do it.

So I say to you, we need these things. And finally, all of you deserve a full and fair count of the American people in the 2000 census so you're not shortchanged just because you don't have the political power that money brings. You represent people in this country, and you're entitled to your fair share of our future. When you think about how far we've come and you know how far you could take your communities, when you think about how desperately America needs every child, every mind, every able-bodied adult at work, every person with a new idea with a chance to start a business—if you really believe in the American community, it must mean that every American should be part of a strong and growing and thriving and united community.

So I say to you, I'm happy you're here. I'm proud of your success. I am so grateful that I had a chance to be President during these last 6 years. But we need to bear down and do more so that when we are all done we can look back and say, we built our bridge; we prepared our country; we went into the 21st century with everybody making the trip.

Thank you, and God bless you.

NOTE: The President spoke at 7:27 p.m. on the South Lawn at the White House. In his remarks, he referred to Mayor Deedee Corradini of Salt Lake City, UT.

Remarks on Proposed Patients' Bill of Rights Legislation
July 16, 1998

Thank you very much, all of you, for your obvious passion and concern for this issue. I thank Senator Daschle and Congressman Gephardt. I thank Congressman Ganske for his very moving and highly illustrative argument. I don't think any of you will ever forget it. I thank Barbara Blakeney and Dr. Smoak for their strong representation of health care providers throughout our country. I thank all the health care advocates who are here today, all the Members of Congress, especially I thank also Senator Kennedy and Congressman Dingell, and Secretary Shalala and Secretary Herman who cochaired our quality health care commission that produced our recommendation for a health care bill of rights for patients.

Let me say, first of all, I hope that the presence of Congressman Ganske and Congressman

Forbes will be appreciated not just by Democrats on Capitol Hill but by Republicans out in America. I don't believe this is a partisan issue any place but Washington, DC. I've tried for years to talk them out of it, but I think most doctors are still Republican. [*Laughter*] I've tried for years to turn them around, but most voters in most parts of my country still vote Republican. But when you show up at a hospital in an emergency room, or you test positive on a biopsy, nobody asks you what political party you belong to.

You know, this period and the period in which we're about to enter in the 21st century will be looked at 100, 200 years from now—the last 50 years and the next 50 years—as one of the most remarkable times in human history for advances in health: average life expectancy going up, the quality of our lives improving, not only because we're learning to manage our own lives better but because of immunizations against dreaded childhood diseases, organ transplants, bioengineered drugs, promising new therapies for repairing human genes.

And it is indeed ironic that at this moment when medicine is becoming more and more successful and, I might add—we talk about the work of nurses and other medical professionals—when we're more and more knowledgeable about how to get the benefits of medicine to people everywhere and technology is making it possible to bring them to rural areas, for example, that this aspect of the medical system is so desperately in need of repair.

Now, I have always tried to say at every one of these events that managed care has not been an unmixed curse for America. There was a reason that we developed managed care systems. Health inflation was going up at 3 times the rate of inflation in our economy. It was simply unsustainable. And there were management economies which could be achieved just by running the system better. But what's happened is that the imperatives of managed care have overtaken the objective of the health system so often that often doctors are hamstrung, patients are alienated, and as you've heard, lives are endangered.

Our job, representing all the American people, is not to abolish managed care. Our job is to restore managed care to its proper role in American life, which is to give us the most efficient and cost-effective system possible consistent with our first goal, which is—managed

care or regular care—the first goal is quality health care for the American people. That is our job.

And I just want to—the previous speakers have talked very movingly about examples and about the specific provisions of the bill. There's no need in repeating all that, but I would like to make two points very briefly. Number one, the panel of people from whom we heard yesterday—Dr. Smoak referred to them—are not atypical. The woman who told me that she and her husband were celebrating their 25th anniversary and she realized he had a terrible heart problem, and the doctor recommended a certain procedure, and it was delayed and delayed and delayed until finally it was too late, and so when he was 45 years old he collapsed in his own yard and died in her arms—at 45. The man who talked about his wife having a serious medical condition; she had a difficulty when they were in Hawaii on vacation; the doctor pleaded to perform the necessary procedure in Hawaii. The HMO said, "No, put her on a plane"—make her fly 4,000 miles or however many miles it is back to the United States—and so she died on the way because her system couldn't stand the pressure of the transatlantic plane flight. The man who talked about how he lost his sister to cancer because the only thing that had a chance to save her life was denied until finally it was too late to do and, oh, then it got approved.

I think, in a way, the most moving witness we had yesterday was a woman who works in a doctor's office and handles the insurance claims and has to get the approval from the insurance companies for the procedures. She just broke down and started crying because she said, "You can't imagine how awful it is. I'm the one who has to look into the eyes of all those patients and tell them 'no' or 'not yet' or 'maybe' when my doctor is saying 'now, yes, immediately.'"

So the first point I want to make is, these stories are not examples that we've all seen in other areas—and everyone who's elected is guilty of using them—these are not isolated anecdotes. These are representative examples of systematic abuse. That's the first point. Don't let anybody kid you—[*applause*].

Now, second point I want to make is, we have to have comprehensive national legislation. That is one of the biggest problems with the bill offered by the Republican leadership: it covers too few people. It is not true that you can leave this issue up to the States. We have to have comprehensive, national legislation.

I've already signed an executive memorandum to extend the protection of the Patients' Bill of Rights to the 85 million Americans who are enrolled in Federal health plans or covered by Federally funded plans. But as all the doctors, the nurses, the benefit managers—25 progressive HMO's have endorsed this legislation. Why? Because they know we have to have national, comprehensive legislation.

Today we are going to have some more evidence of it. Families USA will release a report showing that most States that have acted have enacted only a few of the basic protections for patients, and not a single State in America has passed all the protections contained in the Patients' Bill of Rights. Americans deserve a bill that provides all the protections for all the people. It requires a national solution.

Now, the bill sponsored by Representatives Dingell and Ganske and Senators Kennedy and Daschle does that, and you've already heard what their provisions are. I want to make one last point because I expect, as we see the debate unfold in the few next weeks, this will be one of the major sticking points. Some people will come to us, and they say, "Okay, we'll be for all the substantive positions in your bill, or most of them, as long as you don't give the patients a right to sue or some other enforceable legal right." And that will be appealing when a lot of people hear it, because people say, "Gosh, I don't want—I can't imagine—I don't want any more lawyers; I don't want any more lawsuits; I don't want any more problems like that."

But let me say again, the thing that struck me yesterday at this hearing that we had at the AMA building was in three cases where people died, in all three cases, what the doctor told the patient the patient needed was ultimately approved. And in all three cases, it was approved so late that it was too late to do the procedure. So they died anyway. So you can write all the guarantees you want into the law here in Washington, and if nobody can enforce them, the delay in the system will still cause people to die. We have to do something about this.

Now again I say to you, we need to do this for America. We need to do everything we can to stop this from being a partisan political issue, because it isn't anywhere but Washington. It's a people issue. It's about the integrity of the health care system. It's about how people feel about our country.

We've got a lot of young people here, working here, probably some of them just for the summer, in Washington. I hope when they leave here and they go back to whatever else they're doing, they'll feel better about America than they did when they came here. And I hope they'll communicate that to other people all around their communities or their universities or wherever they are.

How do you think the people yesterday who were telling me their stories feel about America? This is not even about just health care; this is about how American citizens feel about our country. Are we a fair place? Are we a decent place? Are we a place where everybody counts? This is a huge issue. And we must do everything we can to make it a bipartisan issue or a nonpartisan issue, to put progress ahead of partisanship. That's how we achieved a balanced budget. That's how we achieved the Kennedy-Kassebaum bill. That's how we got the Senate to pass the Chemical Weapons Convention and the expansion of NATO.

In the end, all the really big, important things we do around here are when we behave here the way the American people behave every day wherever they live, doing whatever they're doing. And that's what we have to do on this issue. This is a huge thing for millions and millions and millions of Americans. But for all of us—for all of us—even if we live our entire lives and never get sick, we should always remember the picture that Dr. Ganske showed us and the story he told, because if you love America and you believe in the promise of America, every one of you, without regard to your party or your philosophy, has a personal, deep, vested interest in seeing every child like that treated with the dignity that we say in our Constitution and Bill of Rights is the God-given inherent right of every person on Earth.

Thank you, and God bless you.

NOTE: The President spoke at 12:45 p.m. in the Dirksen Senate Office Building. In his remarks, he referred to Barbara A. Blakeney, second vice president, American Nurses Association; and Randolph D. Smoak, Jr., M.D., chairman, American Medical Association.

Joint Statement on United States-Romanian Relations
July 16, 1998

President Clinton and President Emil Constantinescu met today at the White House to discuss ongoing efforts to strengthen bilateral relations through the U.S.-Romania Strategic Partnership, as well as common efforts to advance regional cooperation, security and stability in Southeast Europe. They also discussed NATO's open door policy and Romania's aspirations to join the Alliance.

The two Presidents expressed great satisfaction with the status of the bilateral relationship, which has expanded significantly over the past year. They noted in particular the deepening of relations through the development of the U.S.-Romania Strategic Partnership, announced during President Clinton's visit to Bucharest last July, and the key role it plays in the U.S. Action Plan for Southeastern Europe as well as for the overall stability of Central and Eastern Europe.

The Presidents reviewed the outcome of the latest round of Strategic Partnership talks, held July 15 at the Department of State. A wide variety of joint projects have been completed successfully in the first year of the Partnership. The two militaries collaborated on Partnership for Peace and bilateral exercises, exchanged students at military institutions, and agreed to establish a regional center for defense resources management in Romania. U.S. and Romanian law enforcement agencies are working closely together in the fight against global threats such as drug trafficking, money laundering, illegal migration and organized crime. The two sides also discussed plans to establish a center for regional cooperation in the fight against cross-border crime in Bucharest. Bilateral agreements on civil aviation, on scientific and technological cooperation, on customs cooperation, and on peaceful nuclear cooperation were signed during President Constantinescu's visit.

In the coming year, the two governments have agreed the Partnership will place greater emphasis on the economic sector, focusing on energy, information technology and on the development of small- and medium-size enterprises. President Clinton reiterated the U.S. commitment under the Strategic Partnership to help make Romania the strongest possible candidate for NATO membership and integration into other Western structures. Partnership activities aimed at increasing political cooperation, and coordinating efforts to combat non-traditional threats will also continue to progress.

The Presidents reviewed the pace of free market reforms in Romania as a part of Romania's efforts to consolidate its political transition, reinvigorate its economic transition, and hasten its full integration into Euroatlantic institutions. They emphasized the crucial need to accelerate privatization of large state enterprises and banks, to push forward restructuring of privatized companies, and to refocus reforms with the aim of negotiating a new IMF agreement. The Presidents agreed that these reforms, combined with a stable legal environment, will attract greater U.S. investment, which in turn will further Romania's overall development. President Constantinescu noted that Minister for Privatization Sorin Dimitriu has been named Trade and Investment Ombudsman, to help U.S. and other foreign investors expedite and streamline bureaucratic procedures to successfully do business in Romania.

President Clinton expressed appreciation for Romania's ongoing assistance on issues affecting the two countries' security, including participation in Dayton implementation efforts in Bosnia and offer to contribute to the post-UNPREDEP mission in FYR Macedonia as well as to other missions in the region. The two Presidents expressed their mutual concern over the situation in Kosovo and reiterated their determination to work together with other interested parties to promote a diplomatic resolution of this crisis.

NOTE: An original was not available for verification of the content of this joint statement.

Statement on Signing the Child Support Performance and Incentive Act of 1998
July 16, 1998

Today, I am pleased to sign into law H.R. 3130, the "Child Support Performance and Incentive Act of 1998." My Administration has conducted an unprecedented campaign to increase parental responsibility to ensure that parents support their children. We have had many successes. Through tougher enforcement, we have collected a record $13.4 billion in child support, an increase of 68 percent since 1992, with 1.4 million more families now receiving child support. In addition, we located one million delinquent parents during the first 9 months of using a new collection system that tracks parents across State lines—a system initiated as part of the 1996 welfare law, and first proposed by my Administration in 1994. On paternity establishment, which is often the crucial first step in child support cases, in 1997, a record 1.3 million paternities were established, two and a half times as many as in 1992. Last month, I signed the Deadbeat Parents Punishment Act of 1998, a law based on my Administration's 1996 proposal to crack down on egregious child support evaders by creating a new felony offense for those who flee across State lines to avoid supporting their children.

However, there is much more that we can and must do. H.R. 3130 will build on this progress and help ensure that parents give their children all the support they need and deserve. First, the new law puts in place additional tough penalties for States that fail to automate their child support computer systems on time. Under this new law, States that fail to establish these State-wide systems face automatic and escalating penalties, ranging from 4 percent of Federal child support enforcement funds for the first year to 30 percent for the fifth year in which a State fails to meet national certification standards. Second, H.R. 3130 incorporates a proposal that my Administration sent to the Congress last year to reward States for their performance on a wide range of key child support goals, such as the number of paternity establishments and child support orders, rather than only on cost-effectiveness, as current law provides. Third, the law will make it easier for States to secure medical support for children in cases in which the non-custodial parent has private health coverage, by facilitating the creation of a medical support notice that all health plans will recognize.

Many members of Congress, Administration officials, State officials, experts, and children's advocates worked together constructively in a bipartisan fashion to craft this valuable piece of legislation, and I wish to thank them for their efforts. In particular, I would like to thank Representatives Levin and Shaw, and Senators Moynihan, Roth, Rockefeller, and Baucus.

WILLIAM J. CLINTON

The White House,
July 16, 1998.

NOTE: H.R. 3130, approved July 16, was assigned Public Law No. 105–200.

Statement on Senate Action on Food Safety Legislation
July 16, 1998

I welcome today's 66–33 vote to restore much needed funds to our food safety programs. Food safety should not be about politics; instead it must be about protecting our families and children. Today, the Senate put Americans first and partisanship last. With this money we will be able to improve safety inspections of foods, better educate the public on how to handle food safely, improve research, and aid the effort to track food borne outbreaks such as salmonella and *E. coli*. We must continue to work together in the coming months on this issue and on the many other issues which the American people care about. The American people want action, not political wrangling.

Statement on Action on Title III of the Cuban Liberty and Democratic Solidarity (LIBERTAD) Act of 1996
July 16, 1998

Today I am notifying the Congress of my decision to suspend for an additional 6 months the provision of the Cuban Liberty and Democratic Solidarity Act (LIBERTAD Act) allowing U.S. nationals to file suit against foreign firms trafficking in confiscated properties in Cuba. I have made this decision because of my strong commitment to implementing the Act in a way that best advances U.S. national interests and hastens a peaceful transition to democracy in Cuba.

In January 1997 I said that I expected to continue suspending this provision of the Act so long as our friends and allies continue their stepped-up efforts to promote a democratic transition in Cuba. I made this decision to take advantage of the growing realization throughout the world, in Europe and Latin America especially, that Cuba must change. We and our allies agree on the importance of promoting democracy, human rights, and fundamental freedoms in Cuba, and over the past 2 years we have worked together to support concrete measures that promote peaceful change.

Events in the past 6 months reaffirm that international cooperation for Cuban democracy is increasing. The January visit of His Holiness John Paul II inspired the Cuban people and gave encouragement to the Cuban Catholic Church and Cuban advocates for democratic change. The Pope gave hope to the Cuban people when he called for greater freedom and respect for individual rights.

Building on the Pope's important visit, European Union (EU) member states have reiterated their commitment to democratic transition in Cuba and, in June, as a group reaffirmed their Common Position on Cuba, committing them to take concrete steps toward that end. The EU has continued to urge Cuba to release imprisoned dissidents and stop harassing people who seek peaceful democratic change. The EU Working Group on Human Rights, formed last year among embassies in Havana, has met with Cuban dissidents. These are positive steps, and we encourage the EU to be even more active in their efforts.

On May 18, we and our EU allies reached the Understanding with Respect to Disciplines on Expropriated Property, a major advance in our efforts to protect property rights worldwide, including in Cuba. By discouraging investment in illegally expropriated property, the Understanding sends a strong signal that Cuba must follow the rule of law and respect fundamental rights. Of particular importance, the EU nations expressly acknowledged that the Cuban Government's expropriation of property from U.S. citizens appears to have been contrary to international law. We will work with the Congress to bring this important U.S.–EU understanding into effect.

Nations of the Americas are also working for democracy in Cuba. In the last 6 months, the Presidents of Argentina, Brazil, El Salvador, and Nicaragua have restated calls for Cuba to begin a democratic transition. Brazil's Foreign Minister met with a leading dissident in Cuba and took the opportunity to voice strong support for human rights.

Government cooperation has been reinforced by the efforts of international nongovernmental organizations (NGO's), which have increased support for dissidents and helped focus attention on Cuban Government repression. The Dutch group Pax Christi has reported on political and religious repression. Amnesty International has maintained pressure on Cuba to release members of the Dissident Working Group who were arrested in July 1997, and issued a special report on new cases of imprisonment for political offenses. The international effort to promote "best business practices" in Cuba is also advancing, with several NGO's developing a working group to encourage businesses to support fundamental rights.

Thus, we see progress on many fronts in our effort to promote international cooperation to bring democracy and human rights to the Cuban people. There is still much to be done, and we will continue to work with our friends and allies on effective measures to bring a peaceful transition to a free Cuba.

Letter to Congressional Leaders on Action on Title III of the Cuban Liberty and Democratic Solidarity (LIBERTAD) Act of 1996
July 16, 1998

Dear _____:

Pursuant to subsection 306(c)(2) of the Cuban Liberty and Democratic Solidarity (LIBERTAD) Act of 1996 (Public Law 104–114), (the "Act"), I hereby determine and report to the Congress that suspension for 6 months beyond August 1, 1998, of the right to bring an action under title III of the Act is necessary to the national interests of the United States and will expedite a transition to democracy in Cuba.

Sincerely,

WILLIAM J. CLINTON

NOTE: Identical letters were sent to Robert L. Livingston, chairman, and David R. Obey, ranking member, House Committee on Appropriations; Benjamin A. Gilman, chairman, and Lee H. Hamilton, ranking member, House Committee on International Relations; Jesse Helms, chairman, and Joseph R. Biden, Jr., ranking member, Senate Committee on Foreign Relations; and Ted Stevens, chairman, and Robert C. Byrd, ranking member, Senate Committee on Appropriations.

Remarks at a Democratic National Committee Jefferson Trust Dinner in Chevy Chase, Maryland
July 16, 1998

The President. Thank you very much, Alan, for all the wonderful work you've done. And I thank all the members of the Jefferson Trust. I want to thank Steve Grossman and Carol Pensky and Len Barrack. I want to especially thank Cynthia Friedman for having us in her beautiful home and for—[*applause*]—and for giving us the opportunity to meet your family. Thank you very much.

I want to thank one of our distinguished former chairmen, Chuck Manatt, who also led this party in a very difficult time, for being here, and to say to all of you—I kept trying to think what could I say to all of you tonight who have had to endure so many of my speeches. [*Laughter*]

Audience member. We love them! [*Laughter*]

The President. I think alternative A is just to do it all over again. [*Laughter*] I once—when I was a younger man, or as Hillary and I refer to it, back when we had a life—[*laughter*]—Tina Turner gave a concert in Little Rock one night. And she—you know, Tina Turner went into a big decline and disappeared and then made this remarkable resurgence and is now still enormously popular around the world. But anyway, she came to Little Rock to the

place where we had our concerts. And I took about six people to the concert. And the guy that normally seated me when I was Governor, knowing that it was not prudent for the Governor to be on the front row at a rock concert, always put me back about 15 rows but gave me good seats. But he knew I was especially fond of Tina Turner, and so on this night he put me on the front row.

And I never will forget this concert. She sang all these new songs, and she had all of her new musicians. And then at the end, the band began to play "Proud Mary," which was her first hit. And every time she walked up to the microphone the crowd would scream. So she'd back off and walk up, back off and walk up. Finally she said, "You know, I have been singing this song for 25 years, but it gets better every time I do it." [*Laughter*] So I could do that. [*Laughter*]

Instead, I think I'd like to just make a couple points tonight about this. First, it's almost impossible to remember just what a miserable condition we were in as a party after we had won the first two Presidential elections back-to-back since Franklin Roosevelt. And there was an almost bitter determination to try to bring to an end our ability to function, notwithstanding the fact that we had been, as compared with others, far more open and up front, helpful and forthcoming in trying to deal with the campaign finance questions which were asked. And a number of lionhearted women and men decided that we would not die, and we did not. And you know what the announcement was about our debt being paid down to $3 million from a staggering sum less than 2 years ago.

So you have done a very great thing, and I hope you will always be proud of it. But I think it's important to remember that what you've done is basically to give America a chance to keep moving forward. You know, I've had a number of interesting experiences in the last few days that have really hammered home to me the incredible opportunity the American people, with your help, have given me to serve at this pivotal moment in our history.

I had quite a magnificent trip to China. But being given the opportunity to debate political liberty and human rights, the role of dissent in society, the role of religious freedom in a society, on Chinese television, directly to the people of China for the first time in history—and I'm not sure I was even aware of the magnitude of it until it was all over, because I was concentrating so hard on not messing up for you—[*laughter*]—but it was—when it was over, I thought to myself, this is what America can be for people in the 21st century. We can help lift people's material conditions but also to change the way they think about the nature of life, the nature of their relations with their neighbors, and the nature of their relations with the rest of the world.

Today the President of Romania came to see me, and he gave me this incredible picture. I was in Romania almost a year ago today—just a little more than a year ago—and there were somewhere between 150,000 and 200,000 people in the streets in Bucharest—this vast sea of people. They didn't come to see me. They came to see the United States, what they think we can represent to the world and to the future.

A couple of days ago, Hillary and I kicked off this Millennium Project she conceived and is executing—some of you are helping on—to save the Star-Spangled Banner. And I—we said the Pledge of Allegiance with a class of kids—just one class of about 20 school kids—and there were people from at least 8 different racial and

ethnic backgrounds there in this one little class, a real picture of our future.

Today Dick Gephardt and Tom Daschle spoke passionately in favor of the Patients' Bill of Rights at a big caucus meeting of the Democrats in the Congress, but we invited Republicans to come. And two were brave enough to show. [*Laughter*] One of them, Greg Ganske, is a Congressman from Iowa, and I wish he were a member of our caucus. But I want to tell you what happened.

We were talking about the—the Republicans have offered this alternative patients' bill of rights which, oh, by the way, doesn't cover about 100 million Americans and doesn't give anybody any of the substantive guarantees, and if you get shafted by your HMO, you don't have any right to appeal to anybody, so the bill doesn't do anything really.

But this doctor—this brave Republican doctor who is in the Congress, who's a cosponsor with John Dingell of the House version of the bill we're supporting, got up and said—he was introduced by Dick Gephardt—and said that when he wasn't an active Member of Congress, he gave of his free time to go to Central America, because he was a plastic surgeon, to deal with children with cleft palates.

So Dr.—Congressman Ganske got up there, in a crowd in which he was one of only two Republican Congressmen, and he had a staff person there—he said, "I want you to look at this picture." And the staff member held up this huge picture of this little boy with a horrible, unfixed cleft palate. And the crowd gasped. And he said, "This is not an Indian child from Central America; this is an American citizen. And this young boy was denied the surgery necessary to fix this cleft palate by a company that said it was 'cosmetic' and not covered by the insurance policy." And then he showed the next picture of a young boy with his face fixed anyway. And he was this beautiful, bright-eyed, young boy, smile—I mean, it was unbelievable. You could not breathe in that room.

And I say that to make the point that we invited all of the Republicans in Congress who wanted to come today because our party is trying to advance the cause of America. We belong to a party not so that we can beat up on the other party; we belong to a party because we think it offers us the best vehicle to do what we think is right for our country. And I was very proud to be there with just those two

House Members—the other was Congressman Forbes from Long Island. But we kept the door open to everybody, and more important, we tried to lift the sights of the country.

Hillary spoke at Saratoga Springs to 20,000 people today on the 150th anniversary of the dawn of the women's movement, in this remarkable tour they've had around the Northeast trying to save our national treasures. They went to George Washington's headquarters in the Revolutionary War, something which, unbelievably to me, has never been adequately protected. It was the first military shrine of America, arguably.

So I say all of this just to give you little pieces of the picture that my life is every day with the job that the American people have given me. And what I believe so strongly is that our party has always had a mission of being the instrument of progress.

Thomas Jefferson—this is the Jefferson Trust, so I got this little quote I thought you might be interested—Thomas Jefferson said, "The ground of liberty must be gained by inches, for it takes time to persuade men to do even what is in their own interest." And goodness knows we've had examples of that in the last 6 years. But what I want you to think about on the eve of this '98 election is, since the Civil War, it has been unfailingly true that the party of the President loses seats in the midterm election if the President is in his second term. In the first term it has only failed to happen two or three times. We are going to change that if we continue to put progress ahead of partisanship, people ahead of politics, unity ahead of division, and we have good ideas for America's future.

Because all over the world there are people who are looking to us, and in this country there are people looking to us to have a genuine sense of direction. People are smart enough to know that you'll never solve all the problems of any country at any time; that endemic to human nature is the prospect of failure; that times change. What people want to know is, what is the direction we are taking? And I'll just remind you that in 1992 we ran a campaign that was the most specific, detailed campaign, literally, in American history, where a candidate for President said, these are the ideas on which I am running; these are the policies I will implement. And a distinguished scholar of the Presidency said, as of 1995—and that was 3 years

ago—we had already kept more of our campaign promises than the last five Presidents. And now almost everything we've—almost everything— we've pledged to do in '92 has been done.

And what I want you to do now is to talk to your friends and neighbors and to help us to continue to get the message out that "Yes, we won two elections, and yes, I helped the President, but we represent a certain set of ideas." We believed that you could balance the budget and still invest in the people of this country. We believed you can protect the environment and still grow the economy. We believed you could require able-bodied people on welfare to go to work without hurting their children and taking food and medicine away from them, and without undermining the ability of people who move from welfare to work to be good parents. We believed that you could be tough on people who violate the law and should be punished, and still recognize that we'll never solve the problem until we keep more kids out of trouble in the first place.

Boston didn't go 2 years without a single kid being killed by a gun by jailing all the people who might have done it. They did it by having the most aggressive, systematic, people-oriented prevention strategy in the United States.

We had different ideas. We believed that we could pursue America's commercial interest in the world in a way that was consistent with both our national security and our advancement of human rights and freedom. In other words, we believed that a lot of the debates that had dominated Washington for the last 20 to 30 years were not relevant to the 21st century.

In education, we believed that you could be for preserving public education and putting more money into programs and still lifting standards and having more accountability. We thought all these dichotomies that tend to dominate the easy language of politics were essentially not relevant to the way people wanted to live and the America we wanted to build for the 21st century.

And the consequences have been indisputable. It was not just that we had the right people; we were doing the right things. That's what we have to convince the American people of now. If it takes time to persuade people to do what is in their own interests, if the ground of liberty has to be gained in inches, then it is not enough for my leadership to have been ratified in two national elections. We have to persuade people not just that we had the right people but that we did the right things; that there is a connection between what is happening in America and what was done in Washington; that it cannot be by accident that we have the lowest crime rate in 25 years and the lowest unemployment rate in 28 years and the lowest welfare rolls in 29 years and the first balanced budget in 29 years and the lowest inflation rate in 32 years and the highest homeownership in history and the fact that we've opened the doors to college to everybody now who's willing to work for a college education and added 5 million children to the ranks of those with health insurance and kept a quarter of a million people with criminal backgrounds from getting handguns. And we have cleaner water, cleaner air, safer food, and we set aside more land in national trust than any administration except those of the two Roosevelts. And we did it all while giving people the smallest Government we've had in 35 years.

Those things did not occur by accident. The ideas were right. And if we can get that message over here, and furthermore, if we can say, look, in spite of all this, all we've really done is make America work again; now it's time to face the big challenges of the 21st century—fixing Social Security and Medicare so the baby boomers have something to retire on without bankrupting our children and our grandchildren; proving we can meet the challenge of global warming, which now, I take almost nobody takes issue with— you look at the way Florida has—Florida had the wettest winter, the driest spring, in history. And then June in Florida was the hottest month in Florida's history, hotter than any July or August in history. The 5 hottest years since 1400 have all been in the 1990's; 1997 was the hottest year ever recorded; 1998 is going to be hotter unless it changes dramatically. We have to prove that we can come to grips with this responsibly, lead other countries to do so, and still grow our economy.

I spoke to the American Chamber of Commerce in Shanghai, not exactly a liberal Democratic stronghold, right? [*Laughter*] The American Chamber of Commerce in Shanghai—I got two rounds of applause, spontaneous—one of them was when I said, you have got to take a leadership role in convincing the Chinese to grow their economy with different energy patterns that we used; otherwise, they're going to choke off their future and destroy their environ-

ment and ruin the health of their people and make it impossible for us to meet the challenge of climate change. All these conservative business people started applauding. Why? Because they know it's true.

We have to prove that we can bring the spirit of enterprise to the urban communities, the rural communities, and the Native American reservations that still haven't felt this economic recovery. We've never done that, not really. And if we can't do it when we've got the lowest unemployment rate in 28 years, we'll never get around to it.

We have to prove that we're serious about health care reform and pass this Patients' Bill of Rights. We have to prove that we're serious about making our elementary and secondary education the world's best, just as our higher education is now. We have to prove we're serious about building one America. And we have to prove that we're serious about engaging the rest of the world to take it where we want to go. That's why—even though I got all those attacks about going to China, it never once crossed my mind to cancel the trip. I didn't care if I only had 10 percent support for it, because I knew it was the right thing to do for America.

So we can beat the odds in this congressional election, and we can do just fine in 2000— if we deserve it. And what we have to do is to sort of cut through all the continuous fog and incoming fire and all this partisan stuff that happens and say, "We didn't just have the right people; we did the right things. Our ideas are good"—point one. Point two: "We're not tired; we're just getting warmed up. We still have big challenges out there, and we want you to join us in facing those challenges."

We've got to make your investment good. You saved the Democratic Party. And our adversaries thought they were going to destroy it. They thought they had a moment in which they could absolutely try to reverse the results of the last election and, in the process, destroy the Democratic Party, and you said, "I don't think so."

It is a very great thing you have done, and you should be very proud of that. But you did not do it for the purpose—as much fun as we're having—of being here with me. [*Laughter*] You did it so we could continue to move this country forward.

So go out there and tell them that: We did the right things. We've got good ideas. You now have the evidence; come with us. Secondly, we have an agenda for the future: put people over politics, put progress over partisanship, put the unity of country over division, think about your grandchildren in the 21st century. That is the message of the Democratic Party. You've made it possible for us to take it out there. Now let's go out and do it.

Thank you. God bless you.

NOTE: The President spoke at 8:45 p.m. at a private residence. In his remarks, he referred to Alan D. Solomont, former national finance chair, Steve Grossman, national chair, Carol Pensky, treasurer, Leonard Barrack, national finance chair, and Charles T. Manatt, former national chair, Democratic National Committee; and Cynthia Friedman, national cochair, Women's Leadership Forum.

Message to the Congress on the Emigration Policies and Trade Status of Albania
July 16, 1998

To the Congress of the United States:

I am submitting an updated report to the Congress concerning the emigration laws and policies of Albania. The report indicates continued Albanian compliance with U.S. and international standards in the area of emigration. In fact, Albania has imposed no emigration restrictions, including exit visa requirements, on its population since 1991.

On December 5, 1997, I determined and reported to the Congress that Albania is not in violation of the freedom of emigration criteria of sections 402 and 409 of the Trade Act of 1974. That action allowed for the continuation of most-favored-nation (MFN) status for Albania and certain other activities without the requirement of an annual waiver. This semiannual report is submitted as required by law pursuant to the determination of December 5, 1997.

WILLIAM J. CLINTON

The White House,
July 16, 1998.

NOTE: This message was released by the Office of the Press Secretary on July 17.

Message to the Congress Reporting on the National Emergency With Respect to the Federal Republic of Yugoslavia (Serbia and Montenegro) and the Bosnian Serbs
July 16, 1998

To the Congress of the United States:

On May 30, 1992, by Executive Order 12808, President Bush declared a national emergency to deal with the unusual and extraordinary threat to the national security, foreign policy, and economy of the United States constituted by the actions and policies of the Governments of Serbia and Montenegro, blocking all property and interests in property of those Governments. President Bush took additional measures to prohibit trade and other transactions with the Federal Republic of Yugoslavia (Serbia and Montenegro) (the "FRY (S&M)"), by Executive Orders 12810 and 12831, issued on June 5, 1992, and January 15, 1993, respectively.

On April 25, 1993, I issued Executive Order 12846, blocking the property and interests in property of all commercial, industrial, or public utility undertakings or entities organized or located in the FRY (S&M), and prohibiting trade-related transactions by United States persons involving those areas of the Republic of Bosnia and Herzegovina controlled by the Bosnian Serb forces and the United Nations Protected Areas in the Republic of Croatia. On October 25, 1994, because of the actions and policies of the

Bosnian Serbs, I expanded the scope of the national emergency by issuance of Executive Order 12934 to block the property of the Bosnian Serb forces and the authorities in the territory that they controlled within the Republic of Bosnia and Herzegovina, as well as the property of any entity organized or located in, or controlled by any person in, or resident in, those areas.

On November 22, 1995, the United Nations Security Council passed Resolution 1022 ("Resolution 1022"), immediately and indefinitely suspending economic sanctions against the FRY (S&M). Sanctions were subsequently lifted by the United Nations Security Council pursuant to Resolution 1074 on October 1, 1996. Resolution 1022, however, continues to provide for the release of funds and assets previously blocked pursuant to sanctions against the FRY (S&M), provided that such funds and assets that are subject to claims and encumbrances, or that are the property of persons deemed insolvent, remain blocked until "released in accordance with applicable law." This provision was implemented in the United States on December 27, 1995, by Presidential Determination No. 96–7. The determination, in conformity with Resolution 1022, directed the Secretary of the Treasury, *inter alia*, to suspend the application of sanctions imposed on the FRY (S&M) pursuant to the above-referenced Executive Orders and to continue to block property previously blocked until provision is made to address claims or encumbrances, including the claims of the other successor states of the former Yugoslavia. This sanctions relief was an essential factor motivating Serbia and Montenegro's acceptance of the General Framework Agreement for Peace in Bosnia and Herzegovina initialed by the parties in Dayton on November 21, 1995 (the "Peace Agreement") and signed in Paris on December 14, 1995. The sanctions imposed on the FRY (S&M) and on the United Nations Protected Areas in the Republic of Croatia were accordingly suspended prospectively, effective January 16, 1996. Sanctions imposed on the Bosnian Serb forces and authorities and on the territory that they controlled within the Republic of Bosnia and Herzegovina were subsequently suspended prospectively, effective May 10, 1996, in conformity with Resolution 1022. On October 1, 1996, the United Nations passed Resolution 1074, terminating U.N. sanctions against the FRY (S&M) and the Bosnian Serbs in light of the elections that took place in Bosnia and Herzegovina on

September 14, 1996. Resolution 1074, however, reaffirms the provisions of Resolution 1022 with respect to the release of blocked assets, as set forth above.

The present report is submitted pursuant to 50 U.S.C. 1641(c) and 1703(c) and covers the period from November 30, 1997, through May 29, 1998. It discusses Administration actions and expense directly related to the exercise of powers and authorities conferred by the declaration of a national emergency in Executive Order 12808 as expanded with respect to the Bosnian Serbs in Executive Order 12934, and against the FRY (S&M) contained in Executive Orders 12810, 12831, and 12846.

1. The declaration of the national emergency on May 30, 1992, was made pursuant to the authority vested in the President by the Constitution and laws of the United States, including the International Emergency Economic Powers Act (50 U.S.C. 1701 *et seq.*), the National Emergencies Act (50 U.S.C. 1601 *et seq.*), and section 301 of title 3 of the United States Code. The emergency declaration was reported to the Congress on May 30, 1992, pursuant to section 204(b) of the International Emergency Economic Powers Act (50 U.S.C. 1703(b)) and the expansion of that national emergency under the same authorities was reported to the Congress on October 25, 1994. The additional sanctions set forth in related Executive orders were imposed pursuant to the authority vested in the President by the Constitution and laws of the United States, including the statutes cited above, section 1114 of the Federal Aviation Act (49 U.S.C. App. 1514), and section 5 of the United Nations Participation Act (22 U.S.C. 287c).

2. The Office of Foreign Assets Control (OFAC), acting under authority delegated by the Secretary of the Treasury, implemented the sanctions imposed under the foregoing statutes in the Federal Republic of Yugoslavia (Serbia and Montenegro) and Bosnian Serb-Controlled Areas of the Republic of Bosnia and Herzegovina Sanctions Regulations, 31 C.F.R. Part 585 (the "Regulations").

To implement Presidential Determination No. 96–7, the Regulations were amended to authorize prospectively all transactions with respect to the FRY (S&M) otherwise prohibited (61 *FR* 1282, January 19, 1996). Property and interests in property of the FRY (S&M) previously blocked within the jurisdiction of the United States remain blocked, in conformity with the

Peace Agreement and Resolution 1022, until provision is made to address claims or encumbrances, including the claims of the other successor states of the former Yugoslavia.

On May 10, 1996, OFAC amended the Regulations to authorize prospectively all transactions with respect to the Bosnian Serbs otherwise prohibited, except with respect to property previously blocked (61 *FR* 24696, May 16, 1996). On December 4, 1996, OFAC amended Appendices A and B to 31 chapter V, containing the names of entities and individuals in alphabetical order and by location that are subject to the various economic sanctions programs administered by OFAC, to remove the entries for individuals and entities that were determined to be acting for or on behalf of the Government of the Federal Republic of Yugoslavia (Serbia and Montenegro). These assets were blocked on the basis of these persons' activities in support of the FRY (S&M)—activities no longer prohibited—not because the Government of the FRY (S&M) or entities located in or controlled from the FRY (S&M) had any interest in those assets (61 *FR* 64289, December 4, 1996).

On April 18, 1997, the Regulations were amended by adding a new Section 585.528, authorizing all transactions after 30 days with respect to the following vessels that remained blocked pursuant to the Regulations, effective at 10:00 a.m. local time in the location of the vessel on May 19, 1997: the M/V MOSLAVINA, M/V ZETA, M/V LOVCEN, M/V DURMITOR and M/V BAR (a/k/a M/V INVIKEN) (62 *FR* 19672, April 23, 1997). During the 30-day period, United States persons were authorized to negotiate settlements of their outstanding claims with respect to the vessels with the vessels' owners or agents and were generally licensed to seek and obtain judicial warrants of maritime arrest. If claims remained unresolved 10 days prior to the vessels' unblocking (May 8, 1997), service of the warrants could be effected at that time through the United States Marshal's Office in the district where the vessel was located to ensure that U.S. creditors of a vessel had the opportunity to assert their claims. Appendix C to 31 CFR, chapter V, containing the names of vessels blocked pursuant to the various economic sanctions programs administered by OFAC (61 FR 32936, June 26, 1996), was also amended to remove these vessels from the list effective May 19, 1997. There have been no

amendments to the Regulations since my report of December 3, 1997.

3. Over the past 2 years, the Departments of State and the Treasury have worked closely with European Union member states and other U.N. member nations to implement the provisions of Resolution 1022. In the United States, retention of blocking authority pursuant to the extension of a national emergency provides a framework for administration of an orderly claims settlement. This accords with past policy and practice with respect to the suspension of sanctions regimes.

4. During this reporting period, OFAC issued two specific licenses regarding transactions pertaining to the FRY (S&M) or property in which it has an interest. Specific licenses were issued (1) to authorize U.S. creditors to exchange a portion of blocked unallocated FRY (S&M) debt obligations for the share of such obligations assumed by the obligors in the Republic of Bosnia and Herzegovina; and (2) to authorize certain financial transactions with respect to blocked funds located at a foreign branch of a U.S. bank.

During the past 6 months, OFAC has continued to oversee the maintenance of blocked FRY (S&M) accounts and records with respect to: (1) liquidated tangible assets and personalty of the 15 blocked U.S. subsidiaries of entities organized in the FRY (S&M); (2) the blocked personalty, files, and records of the two Serbian banking institutions in New York previously placed in secure storage; (3) remaining blocked FRY (S&M) tangible property, including real estate; and (4) the 5 Yugoslav-owned vessels recently unblocked in the United States.

On September 29, 1997, the United States filed Statements of Interest in cases being litigated in the Southern District of New York: *Beogradska Banka A.D. Belgrade v. Interenergo, Inc.*, 97 Civ. 2065 (JGK); and *Jugobanka A.D. Belgrade v. U.C.F. International Trading, Inc. et al.*, 97 Civ. 3912, 3913 and 6748 (LAK). These cases involve actions by blocked New York Serbian bank agencies and their parent offices in Belgrade, Serbia, to collect on defaulted loans made prior to the imposition of economic sanctions and dispensed, in one case, to the U.S. subsidiary of a Bosnian firm and, in the other cases, to various foreign subsidiaries of a Slovenian firm. Because these loan receivables are a form of property that was blocked prior to December 27, 1995, any funds collected as a consequence of these actions would remain blocked and subject to United States jurisdiction. Defendants asserted that the loans had been made from the currency reserves of the central bank of the former Yugoslavia to which all successor states had contributed, and that the loan funds represent assets of the former Yugoslavia and are therefore subject to claims by all five successor states. The Department of State, in consultation with the Department of the Treasury, concluded that the collection of blocked receivables through the actions by the bank and the placement of those collected funds into a blocked account did not prejudice the claims of successor states nor compromise outstanding claims on the part of any creditor of the bank, since any monies collected would remain in a blocked status and available to satisfy obligations to United States and foreign creditors and other claimants—including possible distribution to successor states under a settlement arising from the negotiations on the division of assets and liabilities of the former Yugoslavia. On March 31, 1998, however, the Court dismissed the claims as nonjustifiable. Another case, *D.C. Precision, Inc. v. United States, et al.*, 97 Civ. 9123 CRLC, was filed in the Southern District of New York on December 10, 1997, alleging that the Government had improperly blocked Precision's funds held at one of the closed Serbia banking agencies in New York.

5. Despite the prospective authorization of transactions with the FRY (S&M), OFAC has continued to work closely with the U.S. Customs Service and other cooperating agencies to investigate alleged violations that occurred while sanctions were in force. On February 13, 1997, a Federal grand jury in the Southern District of Florida, Miami, returned a 13-count indictment against one U.S. citizen and two nationals of the FRY (S&M). The indictment charges that the subjects participated and conspired to purchase three Cessna propeller aircraft, a Cessna jet aircraft, and various aircraft parts in the United States and to export them to the FRY (S&M) in violation of U.S. sanctions and the Regulations. Timely interdiction action prevented the aircraft from being exported from the United States.

Since my last report, OFAC has collected one civil monetary penalty totaling nearly $153,000 for violations of the sanctions. These violations involved prohibited payments to the Government of the FRY (S&M) by a U.S. company.

6. The expenses incurred by the Federal Government in the 6-month period from November 30, 1997, through May 29, 1998, that are directly attributable to the declaration of a national emergency with respect to the FRY (S&M) and the Bosnian Serb forces and authorities are estimated at approximately $360,000, most of which represents wage and salary costs for Federal personnel. Personnel costs were largely centered in the Department of the Treasury (particularly in OFAC and its Chief Counsel's Office, and the U.S. Customs Service), the Department of State, the National Security Council, and the Department of Commerce.

7. In the last 2 years, substantial progress has been achieved to bring about a settlement of the conflict in the former Yugoslavia acceptable to the parties. Resolution 1074 terminates sanctions in view of the first free and fair elections to occur in the Republic of Bosnia and Herzegovina, as provided for in the Peace Agreement. In reaffirming Resolution 1022, however, Resolution 1074 contemplates the continued blocking of assets potentially subject to conflicting claims and encumbrances until provision is made to address them under applicable law, including claims of the other successor states of the former Yugoslavia. The resolution of the crisis and conflict in the former Yugoslavia that has resulted from the actions and policies of the Government of the Federal Republic of Yugoslavia (Serbia and Montenegro), and of the Bosnian Serb forces and the authorities in the territory that they controlled, will not be complete until such time as the Peace Agreement is implemented and the terms of Resolution 1022 have been met. Therefore, I have continued for another year the national emergency declared on May 30, 1992, as expanded in scope on October 25, 1994, and will continue to enforce the measures adopted pursuant thereto.

I shall continue to exercise the powers at my disposal with respect to the measures against the Government of the Federal Republic of Yugoslavia (Serbia and Montenegro), and the Bosnian Serb forces, civil authorities, and entities, as long as these measures are appropriate, and will continue to report periodically to Congress on significant developments pursuant to 50 U.S.C. 1703(c).

WILLIAM J. CLINTON

The White House,
July 16, 1998.

NOTE: This message was released by the Office of the Press Secretary on July 17.

Remarks to the American Legion Girls Nation and an Exchange With Reporters
July 17, 1998

The President. Thank you very much. I think I should take Janet Murguia with me wherever I go to always introduce me. [*Laughter*] I think she's a great advertisement for Girls Nation. And someday before long, a number of you will have these opportunities as well.

I'd like to welcome your president, Alana Aldag, and your vice president, Jennifer Hall, and thank Diane Duscheck and Barbara Kranig and the other members of the American Legion Auxiliary for what they do for Girls Nation. I hope you've had a very good week in Washington. Some of you may know that this week, these 2 days here, the 35th reunion class of my Boys Nation group is also meeting here. I happened to turn on the television last night to see that Ted Koppel on "Nightline" was doing a 2-day review of it. And I thought to myself, it wasn't all that long ago, but all of us are aging rather gracefully. [*Laughter*]

Let me say to all of you, the people I met then, many of whom have been my friends over all these 35 years, made me believe that anything was possible. President Kennedy spoke to us and made me believe that together we could change the world. I think that is certainly no less true for you and your generation because you will live in the time of greatest possibility in all human history.

If you think of the revolutionary changes that have taken place just in the course of your still relatively short lifetimes: The cold war cast a shadow over my childhood; it has ended. Technology has advanced at a breathtaking pace, fundamentally altering the way all of us live and work and learn. A typical laptop computer today has more computer power in it than the world's largest supercomputer did in the year you were born.

Many of the barriers that kept women from making the most of their potential and contributing their talents to our society have fallen away. Yesterday the First Lady was up in New York commemorating the 150th anniversary of Elizabeth Cady Stanton and 68 other women and 32 brave men gathering in New York with their statement of sentiments, with their 18 objections against men in America, which included the fact that they did not have the right to own property—even the clothes married women had on their backs belonged to their husbands 150 years ago; they couldn't inherit; they didn't vote. And what a long way we have come in the last 150 years and in your lifetime.

I met my wife in law school when it was still a relatively unusual thing to find a law school with any significant number of women in it. Today, a lawyer in America is 12 times more likely to be a woman than a lawyer was in 1963, when I came to Boys Nation.

Women are earning more college degrees than men; they outnumber men in graduate school. Women-owned businesses are growing faster than the national economy. Forty-one percent of our administration's appointees, including the Secretary of State, the Secretary of Health and Human Services, the Attorney General, the Director of the Environmental Protection Agency, the Secretary of Labor, our Trade Ambassador, and many others, are women—by far the highest percentage of women in high positions in any administration in the history of the United States.

I look forward to the day when I read in the newspaper that America's new President has invited her own Girls Nation reunion class back to the White House to gather. In the meantime, we need to be working together to strengthen our country for this new century, because it is a time of dramatic change.

Five and half years ago, I came here to move America in a new direction based on our old values of opportunity for all, responsibility from all, in an American community of all citizens. We took a new direction in economic policy and education policy and environmental policy, in welfare policy, in health care policy, in crime policy, and foreign policy.

We also articulated a new role for Government. We tried to break through the debate that had then dominated Washington for nearly 20 years, some people saying Government could solve all our problems and others saying Government was the source of all of our problems. I had been a Governor for a dozen years, and I thought the argument was frankly ridiculous. I thought that neither extreme was true. And we have sought to create a Government whose primary role is to create the conditions and give people the tools to solve their own problems and make the most of their own lives and build good lives, good families, good communities, and a strong country.

The results have been, I think, quite good. America has the lowest crime rate in 25 years, the lowest unemployment rate in 28 years, the smallest percentage of people on welfare in 29 years. We're about to have our first balanced budget and surplus in 29 years, the lowest inflation rate in 32 years, and the highest home-ownership in the history of the country. We have also opened the doors of college to virtually every American through our HOPE scholarships and other tax credits for college education, through a better student loan program, through more work-study positions and more Pell grant scholarships.

We have added 5 million people who are children to the ranks of people with health insurance; we are in the process of doing that. We have the highest rates of childhood immunization in history. We have worked hard on the environment, and the water is cleaner; the air is cleaner; the food is safer. There are fewer toxic waste dumps, and we have put more land aside to preserve forever than any administration in the history except those of the two Roosevelts.

We started the AmeriCorps program and now have had almost 100,000 young people, like you, just a little older than you, serving in their communities, earning money for college, making America a better place. With our America Reads program alone, which is designed to get young college students to go in and help make sure all of our third graders can read independently by the end of the third grade, we now have 1,000 colleges participating.

While all this has happened, we've actually reduced the size of Government. The Federal Government is now the smallest it has been since I came here to meet President Kennedy 35 years ago. So I believe that this country is moving in the right direction.

Now, I think one of the great decisions facing the American people now is what to do about this. I like the fact that there is a good sense of well-being in America. I like the fact that, after over 20 years of downhill movement, public confidence in Government and the role of Government in our lives is going back up again. I like that very much. But I feel very strongly, and I predict that if you just read the paper, I think you can see, I think, support from my point of view that is a grave mistake to say, "Okay, things are going well in America, and we don't need to do much. We should relax now." Why? For two reasons. One is, you will see, the older you get, no condition lasts forever. The good times don't last forever—but neither do the bad ones, and that's the good news. [*Laughter*]

Secondly, we are living in a very dynamic time. We are enjoying the success that we are enjoying today partly because the American people have been very aggressive, because, you know, we live in a country where citizens deserve most of the credit. What we have done to get these impressive numbers again is to create the right conditions, the right environment, the right incentives for the American people then to take advantage of it and go forward. But we have to—this is a very dynamic time. And there are all kinds of difficulties and challenges out there.

So, for America to sit back now would be a great mistake. When times are good but dynamic, that's the time to bear down, to take on the big challenges, the long-term challenges, the things that will affect your lifetime when you begin to have children and you begin to do your work and you begin to take full responsibility for the welfare of the country. What are those things? Let me just mention a few of them.

Number one, I am the oldest of the baby boomers, the largest generation of young people ever in—to grow up, except the generation of which you are the oldest. That is, we—for the last year, for the first time since I was in high school, we had a bigger group of children in kindergarten through 12th grade than the baby boom generation. Now, what does that mean?

It means, among other things, that if we continue to retire at present trends and the birth rates continue as they are and the immigration rates continue as they are, by the time all of our baby boomers retire we'll only have about two people working for every one person eligible for Social Security. And that is unsustainable. Medicare would be unsustainable.

So what's the answer? The answer is to find a way to preserve these fundamental programs that have lifted the elderly out of poverty and given dignity and strength to our professed family values in a way that does not bankrupt our children and grandchildren. Everybody I know my age is obsessed with the idea that we must not have the cost of our retirement be lowering your standard of living, be undermining your ability to raise your own children.

Now, if we're going to have a surplus, we ought to make sure we've got a long-term plan to save Social Security before we squander that surplus on tax cuts, which may be very popular in the short run but which may leave us with a terrible problem that will cost us a lot more than you could ever get in a small tax cut by the time you have to be taking responsibility for your parents' retirements and your children's education. And we should do it now when times are good and we're projecting a surplus.

Number two, we should recognize that while we have the best system of higher education in the world, no one believes our schools are yet the best in the world. And we should take advantage of this moment to make sure all American young people have access to world-class education with higher standards, with technology that hooks up every American classroom to the Internet and all the riches that it holds by the year 2000, with smaller classes and with more access to more constructive choices through things like the charter school movement, which is very prominent in many of your States.

Number three, we should recognize that the environmental challenges we have are real and global. If there is anybody here from Florida—and I'm sure there is—if you—all the rest of us have been watching those fires. I went down and saw and flew over those areas that have been burned up. Florida had the wettest fall and winter than they had ever had. They had the driest spring they had ever had, and then the month of June in Florida was the hottest month in the history of the State, hotter than

any July or August; and in Florida, that's saying something.

There is ample evidence now that what my wonderful Vice President has been saying for years and years and years is true, that the climate of the globe is warming at a rate which is unsustainable, which will lead us to more extreme weather conditions. We now have records going back over 500 years which we can use to measure what the temperature was on this planet. The 5 hottest years ever recorded have been in the 1990's. Nineteen ninety-seven was the hottest year on record; 1998 is going to be hotter if it continues.

A big part of the problem is the way countries get rich with their use of energy. We have to prove—and by the way, we can prove—that we can grow the economy and improve the environment at the same time. The young people of this country, without regard to their other differences of region and political party and philosophy, by and large are much more committed to this proposition than older people are. Young people—I find even young people in grade school are just instinctive environmentalists. We are depending on you to provide the phalanx of brainpower and voting power to move America to the proposition that we can preserve our environment and grow the economy.

Next, we have to prove that we can bring the benefits of this new economy to people who don't have it yet. Believe it or not, there are still some urban neighborhoods that have unemployment rates above 10 percent, some above 15 percent, while the national unemployment rate is below 5 percent. If you talk to the delegates here from North Dakota where they're having a collapse of farm prices in the aftermath of a terrible, terrible set of natural disasters all through the high plains, it's hard—you could walk down the street in a lot of towns in North Dakota, and they'd have a hard time believing we've got the strongest economy in a generation. If any of you have ever been on a Native American reservation that doesn't have a lot of money from gaming enterprises, you know that there are still an awful lot of the first Americans who have received no tangible benefit from this economic growth. Now that the economy is strong, we should be working to implement strategies that will bring this growth to them to make sure that all Americans feel that they're a part of our future.

Just two more things, quickly. Over the long run, we have got to prove that we can be one America. I like it—I look around this room; I see all of you come from different racial and ethnic and religious backgrounds. That's a great, great advantage to America in a global society, a global economy.

Look around the world at all of the problems we have that are based on racial, ethnic, and religious differences. Why did those three little children have to die in that firebomb in Ireland a few days ago? Because somebody just cannot give up the idea that they ought to fight until the end of time over their religious differences. Why can we not achieve a lasting peace in the Middle East? What is at the root of the problem in Bosnia, in Kosovo? Why did hundreds of thousands of people die in Rwanda in a matter of days in 1994? All over the world you see this. If America wants to do good in a world like that, we must be good at home. We must be able to live in all of our communities like you're working and living together here. And you can lead the way on that.

It is very important that we continue, finally, to be engaged in the world. That's why I went to China, even though some people said I shouldn't: not because we agree with everything the Chinese do but because we respect the progress they have made in the last several years and because they are going to be the biggest country in the world. And it is much better if we work with them to try to build the kind of world we want than if we're forced into a situation of continuous conflict and estrangement. And I feel a moral obligation to you and your future and your children to try to create that kind of world. But first, the power of the American example is important, and you must never forget that.

Now, against that background, you need to evaluate everything we're doing here. How are we doing to keep America working today; are we dealing with the long-term challenges of the country? Every issue should be evaluated in that context.

One of the things that's most troubling to me is that we have the best health care in the world, but we don't have the best health care system in the world, and we don't have the healthiest people in the world, partly because of institutional problems. One we've been talking about is the necessity to pass the Patients' Bill of Rights so we get the benefit of managed care without the burden of having accountants make decisions doctors should make in the medical area.

Another big problem we have—it's probably the most prominent health problem your generation faces—is the problem of, epidemic of teen smoking, with 3,000 young people starting to smoke every day; 1,000 will have their lives shortened as a result of it. More people die from smoking than accidents and murders and AIDS and other unrelated maladies put together in this country. So it is a very, very serious problem.

I have been working very hard now for a long time to pass legislation that will raise the price of cigarettes, give the FDA the authority to regulate tobacco as a drug, stop the marketing of cigarettes to teenagers, launch new antismoking research and education drives, protect the tobacco farmers and their communities, and use the money to pay for health care and medical research, education, and child care, and any tax cuts that the Congress wanted to pass, so it didn't affect our surplus and our commitment to save Social Security.

Now, right now, our legislative drive has been stalled in the face of a $40 million advertising campaign by the tobacco companies that has been unanswered by the public health advocates because they don't have that kind of money. But the facts are clear, and if we keep working, I think we will prevail on the issue. Why? Well, the main reason is the evidence that the tobacco companies themselves have given us about the dangers of smoking and their strategy. We now have, as a result of all these lawsuits, internal tobacco company documents that show that even as they publicly denied that nicotine was addictive, they conducted secret research in their labs, devised secret marketing strategies in their boardrooms to addict children to smoking for life, and they knew exactly what they were doing.

How do we know it? Again, look at the documents that they, themselves, have produced in the court cases. These documents tell us in the tobacco companies' own words how children and minorities became the primary targets they saw as new customers. There are memos admitting in plain English, for example, quote, "The base of our business is the high school student." Memos saying, quote, "Creating a fad in the 14- to 20-year-old market can be a great bonanza." And even as they insisted that young people are off limits for advertising, one company document from 1984 recommended targeting younger adult smokers as the only source of replacement smokers in the future. Well, children are the future of America, not the future of the tobacco companies. And that future should not go up in smoke.

These documents contain a treasure trove of information that can be used to save lives. Public health experts can design more effective antismoking strategies by studying the marketing plans of the cigarette companies. Scientists can look to documents for findings that can aid their research into nicotine addiction and tobacco-related illnesses. And all Americans can understand the role the industry has played in hooking our children to the habit of smoking.

There are tens of millions of pages of these documents. While some of them are already on the Internet, most are stored in depositories all across our Nation and as far away as England. They aren't easy to find. So I've decided to use this moment with you to show you one thing that the President can do with executive authority that has nothing to do with legislative action in Congress. I am directing the Secretary of Health and Human Services to report back to me in 90 days with a plan to make these documents more accessible to all Americans, so anybody that can get on the Internet can get them all and can understand them all.

The plan should include a strategy for indexing them and for making that index widely available through both the Internet and other methods. It should also have a strategy for broad and rigorous analysis of the information contained in all these documents. I'm also pleased that the Attorney General will file a brief in support of the State of Minnesota's efforts to make the tobacco industry's own currently existing index to all of these millions of documents available to the general public.

We must lift the veil of secrecy on the tobacco industry so that all Americans understand that there is an epidemic of teen smoking and how it came about. Let us use the darkest secrets of the industry to save a new generation of children from this habit and to help us fight and win.

This administration and many of our Nation's leaders are working to make sure that this challenge, along with these larger, longer term challenges that I've mentioned—education, climate change, Social Security—do not become intrac-

table problems of your future. I don't want your generation of Americans to have to face a problem like the magnitude of the deficit that I faced here when we took office,

I can tell you that the tougher problems are, the harder the resolution is, and the more controversial the resolution is, and the more painful the price to pay is. We had to make a lot of tough decisions in 1993 to get that deficit under control, and a lot of brave Members of Congress lost their seats in Congress because they voted for an economic program in 1993, the benefits of which were not apparent in 1994 when they were up. But when we got ready to pass the Balanced Budget Act in 1997 on a bipartisan basis, guess what? Over 92 percent of the deficit had already disappeared because of what had been done in 1993.

The best thing for a smart country to do is to take these challenges when they come up and deal with them quickly, looking to the long run, not waiting for those things to fester and become infected and become a wound in the Nation's psyche. That is what we're trying to do here.

That's why I think programs like Girls Nation are so important, because they enlist people in the work of citizenship as a disciplined habit, not as something that you think about when an emergency comes along. I hope you will be able to do that to your friends and your neighbors and your family members when you go home. I hope you will always continue now to help raise awareness of the issues you care about and propose solutions to them. I hope you will always continue to lobby your elected leaders and to participate until you become one.

Our democracy is only as strong as its citizens. Think about this when you go home: Our Founders did a revolutionary thing. They created a whole country based on the idea, at the time totally unheard of, that God gave every person in equal portion—every person in equal portion—the right to life, liberty, and the pursuit of happiness. They said, "We've got to create this Government because there's no way we can individually protect and enhance these rights. That's why we're doing this."

And then they gave us—all of us, every American until time immemorial—a mission: They said, "We must work together to form a more perfect Union." They were really smart, those guys. [*Laughter*] They were really smart. They understood that every generation would have its own challenges. They understand the work of liberty would never be over—they understood all that. They understood it all, and they gave us a permanent mission.

And keep in mind, they created a limited Government, which means that in this country, the most important players will always be the citizens. As great as the leaders are, and all the monuments you've seen to our great leaders around this city since you've been here this week, none of them could have accomplished anything if the people hadn't said, "Okay, we agree; we'll do our part."

So again, I say, you've had a remarkable opportunity this week to learn more about how your country works. You have, yourselves, been good citizen servants by doing it. You've had a chance to manifest your love in America and your belief in America. For the rest of your life, I hope you'll do what you can to make our Union more perfect.

Good luck, and God bless you. [*Applause*] Thank you.

Now, I'm just going to go sign this order, and I'm going to ask your president and vice president to stand with me, and then I'm going to turn the microphone over to them. Come on.

[*At this point, the President signed the memorandum.*]

Q. Mr. President, do you think that the court ruling can——

The President. I'll answer questions, but let's do—let us finish the program, and then I'll answer a few questions. That'll be fun for them; they'll see a little press conference here. [*Laughter*]

Okay, you've got the floor.

[*At this point, Jennifer Hall, vice president, 1998 Girls Nation Session, made brief remarks and presented the President with a Girls Nation sweatshirt.*]

The President. That's wonderful. Thank you.

[*At this point, Alana Aldag, president, 1998 Girls Nation Session, made brief remarks and presented to the President legislation passed by the 1998 Girls Nation Senate.*]

The President. This is the largest legislative package that's passed in Washington so far this week. [*Laughter*] And I thank you very much.

Thank you. I will have our people review this for good ideas. [*Laughter*]

Now, go ahead. Helen [Helen Thomas, United Press International], first—we'll take two or three questions. Go ahead.

Court Rulings on Secret Service Agent Testimony

Q. Well, do you think that the court rulings are jeopardizing the duties of the Secret Service?

The President. Well, they believe—that is, the Treasury Department and the Secret Service, based on their experience not just with me but with all the Presidents, in the institutional memory of the Secret Service—they believe that. And so, they are determined to pursue it, and the Attorney General has agreed to represent them in that. But that is their professional judgment. I have decided that it would be inappropriate for me to express an opinion, and I have not done so. And I believe that I should stay out of it. But they have a very strong professional opinion about it, and they are pursuing it.

Q. But you have an opinion, surely.

The President. I do have an opinion. I have an opinion. I have a legal opinion, and I have a personal opinion, but I think that's not—I think it's important, and I think it would be completely inappropriate for me to be involved in this. I want the American people to understand that, notwithstanding what some have said and others have implied, this was a decision that came out of the Secret Service about which they feel very strongly. And these people risk their lives to protect me and other Presidents in a professional way, not a political way. They have strong convictions. They have manifested those convictions. The Attorney General has determined that there is sufficient legal merit in their position that they ought to be represented, and they are pursuing their case, which they have a right to do. I believe that they should speak for themselves, and I should not interject myself into it.

Q. Mr. President, I wonder if you could respond to the ruling yesterday by the Appeals Court, and specifically the opinion of one judge when he said that the White House had effectively declared war on the Independent Counsel——

The President. I think you have to consider the source of that comment. And that is simply not true. The judge should—can have a right to his legal opinion about what the Treasury Department and Justice Department said, but I have told you that this case is about their professional judgment about what's necessary to do their job. And I have not—neither I nor the White House has been involved in it in any way, shape, or form—nor will we, nor will I complicate it by commenting further on what he said.

Q. But in a larger sense, you don't believe that the White House is——

The President. Well, in a larger sense, I am spoken for on that by Mr. Kendall. I think the facts speak for themselves. I think—again, I say you've got to consider the source of that comment.

Press Secretary Mike McCurry. Last question.

U.S. Trade Deficit and Asian Economies

Q. Mr. President, the trade deficit in May was up around $15 billion. Are you willing to overlook that while the Asian financial crisis plays itself out?

The President. Well, I don't think—no, I don't think we should overlook it, I think it ought to prompt us to action. But let's understand why the trade deficit is so large. The trade deficit is large because we live in an integrated global economy, and our economy has been strong while the Asian economy has been in trouble. What does that mean? When their economy is in trouble, the value of their currency goes down. What does that mean? That means that compared to yesterday, if their currency goes down, their money is worth less than ours in the same amounts. That means it becomes—their goods that they sell to us become cheaper, and it means our goods that we would sell to them become more expensive.

Almost the entire increase in the trade deficit is due to the Asian economic trouble, which is why, since January, I have been saying we should make our proper contribution to the International Monetary Fund to promote economic reform and economic recovery in Asia. And the fact that we have not done so is endangering the livelihood of American farmers and American factory workers because we are not making the exports, especially to Asia, that we otherwise could be making if those economies were coming back. And a critical part of that is our contribution to the International Monetary Fund.

So, we should not ignore it, because, as I said in the State of the Union Address way back in January, our welfare is tied to the welfare of Asia. We've got 16 million new jobs in the last 5½ years; 30 percent of our economic growth is due to exports. A significant area of export growth has been Asia.

That's why I worked hard to—the other big area of real growth has been in Latin America. And what I've tried to do is to head these things off. You may remember a couple of years ago when we moved in aggressively to help Mexico when their economy was in trouble and a lot of people criticized that. But Mexico paid back their loan ahead of schedule and at profit to the United States. And they are now a functioning economic partner with us again. That's what we need in Asia.

So, the American people should be concerned about this, but we should know that there is a disciplined answer. We need to restore growth in Japan, restore growth in Asia, and our major goal here for our own action should be to pay our fair share to the International Monetary Fund so we can support economic recovery, so they can afford to buy our products, and so there's some greater parity in the prices of our products. Meanwhile, what you see is a product of the strength, not the weakness, of the American economy.

Tax Cuts

Q. What do you think of the Speaker's proposal to use this budget surplus for big tax cuts?

The President. I think, first of all, let's remember how we got where we are. We got the strength of our economy to the point where it is now by being determined to bring down the deficit until we balanced the budget, by expanding trade to sell more American products around the world, and by investing in education, in training, in technology, in scientific research. Those are the engines of our economic recovery.

Now, we have not had a balanced budget for 29 years. And now, before we've had the first year, the first year of a surplus, to be talking about spending hundreds of billions of dollars on a tax cut based on projected surpluses that may or may not materialize, before we have spent the first dollar to save Social Security so that you aren't going to have to support your parents in a way that diminishes your standard of living, I think is a mistake. So I'll go back to my position: I think we should save Social

Security first. Let's show the American people this balanced budget. Let's show the American people this surplus. Let's try to keep this economy going and get our growth going, and when we have passed a plan to save Social Security, let's see what it costs and then make a decision on the tax issue.

We don't want to count our chickens before they hatch. Now, the end of the fiscal year here is September 30th. And it's now projected that we'll have a $63 billion surplus, and I earnestly hope we do. But it wouldn't do any harm to rack one up before we start spending it. We had 29 years of deficits. Between 1981 and 1983—in 12 years alone, we increased by 4 times the total debt of the United States. We quadrupled the debt of the United States in 12 years that we had amassed in the previous 200. It won't do us any harm to take one year

and enjoy the fact that we've balanced our books, ran up a surplus, and planned to save Social Security. That will not do us any harm. It will keep our economy stronger, and it's better for America's future.

Thank you very much.

NOTE: The President spoke at 9:30 a.m. in Room 450 of the Old Executive Office Building. In his remarks, he referred to Diane Duscheck, director, 1998 Girls Nation Session; Barbara Kranig, national president, American Legion Auxiliary; ABC News anchor Ted Koppel; brothers Richard, Mark, and Jason Quinn, who died in a firebombing attack on their home in Ballymoney, Northern Ireland, on July 12; Judge Laurence H. Silberman of the U.S. Court of Appeals for the District of Columbia; and attorney David E. Kendall.

Memorandum on Public Availability of Tobacco Documents
July 17, 1998

Memorandum for the Secretary of Health and Human Services

Subject: Public Availability of Tobacco Documents

For decades, the tobacco industry sought to hide from the American people critically important information about the health hazards of tobacco and the industry's efforts to induce children to smoke. Recently, court cases and congressional subpoenas have forced the tobacco companies to make many of their documents public.

These documents confirm that for decades the tobacco companies did intensive research on the smoking habits of children, knew tobacco products were addictive and deadly, understood that a price increase would drive down the number of young people who smoke, and deliberately marketed their products to young people and minorities.

Because they provide new information about which types of advertising appeal to children, these documents can help public health experts design counter-advertising campaigns and other strategies to protect children. These documents also can assist scientists in understanding more

about the addictive nature of nicotine, the health consequences of tobacco use, and the effects of certain tobacco product designs and ingredients. It is therefore critical to the fight against youth smoking that the Nation's scientists and public health experts carefully examine and analyze these documents.

Although many tobacco industry documents are now public, most are not readily accessible. While many public health leaders have found and highlighted important documents, there is no comprehensive public index to help researchers locate information contained in the documents. Only a small percentage of the documents are posted on the Internet and it is difficult to search through them in their current format.

The State of Minnesota is currently involved in litigation to obtain the public release of a computerized index (the so-called 4–A Index), created by the tobacco industry for use during litigation. The tobacco industry has fought to prevent the release of this index. It is the industry's road map to its own documents and could improve significantly the ability of public health experts, scientists, State and Federal officials, and the public to search through industry documents. The bipartisan comprehensive tobacco legislation recently considered in the Senate contained strong provisions for public disclosure of tobacco industry documents. While I will continue to fight to enact comprehensive tobacco legislation, I am determined to move forward to protect America's children from tobacco.

Therefore, I hereby direct you, working with the Attorney General, the States, public health professionals, librarians, and other concerned Americans, to report back to me in 90 days with a plan to make the tobacco industry documents more readily accessible to the public health community, the scientific community, the States, and the public at large. This plan should:

(1) Propose a method for coordinating review of the documents and making available an easily searchable index and/or digest of the reviewed documents.

(2) Propose a plan to disseminate widely the index and/or digest as well as the documents themselves, including expanded use of the Internet.

(3) Provide a strategy for coordinating a broad public and private review and analysis of the documents to gain critical public health information. Issues to be considered as part of this analysis include: nicotine addiction and pharmacology; biomedical research, including ingredient safety; product design; and youth marketing strategies.

To help ensure greater access to these documents, the Department of Justice plans to file an amicus brief in the trial court in support of the State of Minnesota's motion to unseal the industry-created 4–A index.

I remain committed to using every power of my office to protect children from the dangers of tobacco. Through these actions, we can use the industry's darkest secrets to save a new generation of children from this deadly habit.

WILLIAM J. CLINTON

Remarks on Arrival at Little Rock Air Force Base in Jacksonville, Arkansas
July 17, 1998

Thank you very much. Thank you very much, General. First let me say I am delighted to be back home. I'm glad to be with your Congressman, Vic Snyder, and our Secretary of Transportation, Rodney Slater. They're doing a great job for you. Mr. Mayor, thank you for coming out to make me welcome, and thank all of you for coming out.

I want to spend most of my time just saying hello to people in the crowd, but let me just make a couple of points. First of all, I am so grateful to the people of Arkansas for all that you did to give me a chance to serve as President. And I hope you take a certain amount of personal pride in the role you played when you read every day the news of our country's progress.

I'm very grateful that I had a chance to serve in a time when, working together, we've got the lowest crime rate in 25 years, the lowest unemployment rate in 28 years, the first balanced budget in 29 years, the lowest welfare rolls in 29 years, the lowest inflation rate in 32 years, and the highest homeownership in the history of America. I'm proud of that. You should be proud of that.

I'm also very, very proud of the work that America is doing, and the role that the people who serve at this base have in it, in advancing peace and freedom and prosperity and security around the world. And I know you have some folks overseas right now doing important missions; we thank them for that.

I also want you to know that I consider the training mission of this base vital, and I'm very pleased with the Air Force report, which has been embraced by the Defense Department, to continue the important mission of the base here, and I will support that. I know you will too. Thank you for what you do every day.

Now let me say, one of the things that the President cannot do anything about, at least in the short run, is the heat. [*Laughter*] So I think it's time to stop the speeches and start the greeting, so you can get out of here before anything too bad happens.

But I'm glad to be back. Thank you. Thank you for everything. God bless you. Thank you.

NOTE: The President spoke at 2:10 p.m. on the Little Rock Air Force Base flight line. In his remarks, he referred to Brig. Gen. Jack R. Holbein, USAF, Commander, 314th Airlift Wing; and Mayor Tommy Swaim of Jacksonville, AR.

Remarks to the Arkansas State Democratic Committee in Little Rock, Arkansas
July 18, 1998

Thank you very much. It's good to see you. It's wonderful to be home. I always learn something new. When Bill Bristow was giving that speech, I said to myself, "I am sitting here watching before my very eyes the broadening of the base of the Democratic Party." He now has got every math teacher in Arkansas committed forever. [*Laughter*]

Thank you very much, Bill. I thought that was a terrific—didn't he do a great job? Let's give him another hand; I thought that was great, really great. [*Applause*]

I want to thank Blanche Lincoln, Bill Bristow, Judy Smith for being here and for their candidacies; Kurt Dilday, my longtime friend; Mark Pryor. I thank Congressman Vic Snyder for the wonderful job he does in Washington every day. And in his absence—I know he had to be away at a funeral today—I want to thank Marion Berry, too. He has done a wonderful job, especially for farmers.

I thank Jimmie Lou and Gus Wingfield and Charlie Daniels and all the people who have kept the light going in the Democratic Party and State office; Judge Corbin. I'm so pleased to see many people running for office. You know, I had mixed feelings about this term limit issue when it came along, but I felt a little better when Mary Anne Salmon decided to run for the legislature, and I'm glad to see her back there.

I want to say to all of you, too, I read that article in the paper today, and I want to comment a little more about it, ask you whether my Presidency had been good or bad for the State. And the one example on the negative side they had was what happened in a recent transportation bill where even the Transportation Secretary from Arkansas could not implement the plain recommendation of the study because our neighbor from Mississippi jerked away funding for I–69. No one pointed out in the Arkansas Democrat article that that would not have happened if we had a Democratic Congress—that would not have occurred. I say that because, what the heck, I never get to be partisan, and it's nice to be home—[*laughter*]—and also because it's true. [*Laughter*]

Let me say to all of you, I am profoundly grateful for everything you've done for me and for our family. Hillary just got back from a remarkably successful tour, the first of our millennium tours where we're trying to save the treasures of the United States as we approach the year 2000. She went—first of all, we began by trying to save the Star-Spangled Banner. And then she took a remarkable tour through a lot of our country's heritage: Thomas Edison's home, Harriet Tubman's home, George Washington's military headquarters, and then to Seneca Falls, New York, where the women's movement began 150 years ago, where the declaration of sentiments by 68 women and 32 men who had these radical ideas, like women ought to be able to vote—[*laughter*]—run for office, own the clothes on their back. We've come a long way. And she asked me to tell you hello.

And I just want all of you to know, too, that I think quite often of that day in October, nearly 7 years ago now, when I stood on the steps of the old State Capitol—many of you were there—and said that I wanted to build a better future for our children. And I want to quote— I wrote this down; usually when I come home I feel free to speak without notes, but I did want to write this down—nearly 7 years ago, this is really the test—"to restore the American dream, to fight for the forgotten middle class, to provide more opportunity, insist on more responsibility, and create a greater sense of community for our great country."

Now, there are some things, it seems to me, that are fairly clear and difficult to debate. And I think it's important, when we evaluate the coming campaigns of Blanche Lincoln, Vic Snyder, Judy Smith, Bill Bristow, Kurt Dilday, Mark Pryor, and others, to remember what America was like 7 years ago. We had high unemployment, rising crime and welfare rates, increasing social division, no clear vision driving the country at home or abroad preparing us for the 21st century. And Washington was doing what I thought it had done too much of before, and what I still hate to see: They were having increasingly harsh political debates in terms that didn't make a lick of sense to most of us who lived out here in the country.

There were the standard debates about "Well, the Government is the problem"; "the Government is the answer." No one I knew believed either thing. I couldn't figure out anybody who believed it until they got into Washington, DC. Everybody had to be a conservative or a liberal. And if you had a different position, somehow there was something wrong with you because it required the people interpreting you to America to think about it, and the people driving the politics of the Nation's Capital didn't like it.

But we came forward in that campaign in '91 and '92 with a set of new ideas. We had new approaches to the economy, to education, to crime, to welfare, to the environment, to foreign policy, to the whole idea of Government. It seemed to me that the answer was that we ought to look at Government as our partner in building the American future and that the rule of Government ought to be to give the tools to solve their own problems, to build strong communities and families, and to create the conditions in which that could be possible.

No one thought Government could solve all the problems, but to pretend that by getting out of the way, we'd all be better off would be to violate the very insight of the Founding Fathers, who said they formed a Government in the first place because we could not do alone some of the things that were necessary for America to pursue life, liberty, and happiness.

And now, we've had a few years to evaluate the results. So when people ask you, "Has it made a difference?"—let me ask you this: If on Inauguration Day in 1993, someone that had told you that within 5½ years America would have 16 million new jobs and the lowest unemployment rate in 28 years, the lowest crime rate in 25 years, the lowest welfare rolls in 29 years, the first balanced budget and surplus in 29

years, the lowest inflation rate in 32 years, the highest homeownership in history with the smallest Government in 35 years, would you have said, "I will accept that and be glad for the next 5 years for what's going on in America"? [*Applause*]

And along the way, with the HOPE scholarships, the tax credits for college, the reformed student loan program, 300,000 more work-study positions, we can literally say we've opened the doors to college to anybody who's willing to work for it.

We have the highest childhood immunization rates in history. We've added 5 million children to the ranks of the health insured—we're in the process of doing that. We protected the pensions of millions and millions of Americans and made it easier for people working for small business or for themselves to take out pensions and to get health insurance; 12½ or 13 million people have taken time off from their job without getting fired when a baby was born or a parent was sick because of the family and medical leave bill. We raised the minimum wage and are trying to do it again to try to help people on the lower end of the economic ladder who are working hard. And we gave a big tax cut in 1993, worth about $1,000 a year today, to working families with incomes under $30,000.

We have 1,000 colleges in America involved in sending their students into our schools to make sure all of our kids can read well by the time they get out of the third grade. We have 100,000 young people now—just at 100,000—who served in the AmeriCorps program, working all over America, including in Arkansas. And I see kids from Arkansas all over America when I travel around, helping to solve the problems of this country at the grassroots level and earning money for college. Our country is a better, stronger, more united place than it was in 1992. You helped to make it possible, and you ought to be proud of it.

But here's the main point I want to make today, in behalf of Blanche and Bill and all our other candidates up here, in behalf of the record that Vic Snyder has already begun to establish and the efforts that Marion Berry is making. You've been awful good to me, and you made me feel great as a person when I came in. And I appreciate being given some responsibility for the good things that have happened. And I think there is a connection between what we have done and what has occurred, even though, as always, the American people themselves deserve most of the credit, as is always true in a free society. But the changes we made, the decisions we made had consequences.

The point I want to make to you as Democrats in Arkansas, thinking about your State, these elections, and your country's future, is it's not just important to get the right people; it matters if you're doing the right things. If you say all that matters is that you have the right people, then every election is a new story, and people can say, "Oh well, Bill Clinton gave a speech," or this, that, or the other thing, or "He was a pretty good leader. He could take a lot of heat." You may have seen, by the way, the other day in Florida, Sylvester Stallone gave me the gloves, the boxing gloves he used in "Rocky"—[*laughter*]—and I said it was a good thing, because I proved I could take a punch for the last 6 years, and I was ready to deliver a few now. I thought it was a good idea. [*Laughter*]

What I want you to focus on today, because it really matters to the case you're going to make here between now and November, is two things are important: You have to get good people, but you have to do the right things. These things happen because we've done the right things, and there are honest, principled disagreements at home and in Washington about the right things.

We've got the lowest crime rate in 25 years. And they're still trying to stop my efforts to put 100,000 police on the street. I mean, it's unbelievable. We have proved what works in education, and yet, they're still saying no to smaller classes, no to better school buildings, no to so many of our efforts to improve the education of our children.

We have proved we can grow the economy and improve the environment. And they're still trying to weaken our efforts to protect the environment, even though, I might have said, while all this economic good news is occurring; the water is cleaner; the air is cleaner; the food is safer; we have more toxic waste dumps cleaned up in 4 years, our first 4 years, than they did in 12; and we set aside more land in perpetuity than any administrations except Franklin and Theodore Roosevelt. So we've

proved you could do that, but there's still an assault on the environment.

And all this rhetoric about how perfectly terrible Government is—well, when they had control of it, it was bigger than it is now but not as good.

This is real important. If you want to go out and make an argument for why Bill Bristow or any Democrat should be Governor, for what Attorney General Mark Pryor would do working with like-minded Democrats, for why it would make a difference if Judy Smith were in Congress, and for why one Republican from Arkansas is more than enough in the United States Senate, you've got to know what you're talking about. You have to understand that there are really consequences. I'm telling you, it makes a difference.

We're not in this old debate anymore. It's the real world now. People need to see things unfolding as they are, not all this "Are you anti-Government or pro-Government; are you liberal or conservative?" What do you stand for? Or what is your education policy? What is your health care policy? Are you for the health care bill of rights, or not? Do you believe that everybody in an HMO ought to have the right to an emergency room service if they need it, ought to have a right to a specialist if they need it?

You've been seeing all the press we're getting in Washington on that. We're bringing in all of these people; we're talking about the horror stories, all the doctors pleading and pleading and pleading with the insurance companies, do this procedure, that procedure, the other procedure. They take 90 days or 180 days; the time the procedure gets approved, it's too late, and the people die.

We had a woman who spends her life working in a medical office, calling, trying to get authorization for procedures. She broke down and cried at this hearing I had the other day, this meeting, saying, "I'm just so sick and tired of telling people that they can't have the health care my doctor is begging to give them."

We had a hearing in Washington last week. We had two brave Republicans show up with all the Democrats in the House and several in the Senate, saying, "We're for a Patients' Bill of Rights." And one of these Republicans was a doctor. And I said, "You know, we Democrats, now, what we're trying to do, we want to put progress over partisanship. We welcome anybody to come who agrees with our ideas." And this brave doctor from Iowa stood up there and said that—he had been introduced as a doctor who in his spare time would go to Central America and help children with cleft palates and fix them so they wouldn't be disfigured for life. And then he showed a picture of such a child, and the whole room gasps. And he said, "This child is not from Central America. This child is from the United States of America, and this child was denied coverage for fixing his cleft palate on the theory that it was cosmetic surgery." And then he showed another picture where the kid got fixed anyway and how good-looking the child was, and everybody cheered; we all felt good.

Now, the fact is that the Democrats up there are for a strong Patients' Bill of Rights, and the leadership of the other party are opposing it. The fact is the Democrats are for giving the States and the Governors and the legislatures and the teachers help for smaller classes, for better school buildings, for more charter schools, for greater investments of all kinds. And by and large, our whole agenda is being opposed by the leaders of the other party.

The fact is, our party is in Washington working hard to prove that we can grow the economy and preserve the environment. After this summer, don't you believe the climate is warming up? [*Laughter*] Don't you think Al Gore was right after all? [*Applause*] We now have ways of measuring temperature changes for over 500 years. The 5 hottest years in history, the 1990's—in over 500 years, the 5 hottest years in history—1997, the hottest year. This is going to be hotter.

I did my radio address today on things we're trying to do to help farmers. We have this bizarre situation in America now where worldwide bumper crops and financial weakness in Asia and, for many of our farmers, heat or flood or pestilence have created this crazy condition where prices are low because there are big supplies and fewer buyers, and they don't have much of a crop anyway—North Dakota farm income down 90 percent from last year—90 percent. And so we're doing what we can to, first of all, purchase a lot more food and give it to countries where people are hungry. Secondly, I presented to Congress a number of other ideas to immediately release hundreds of million of dollars that would raise farm income.

But anyway, we're having this big discussion up there. Now, we either are going to do these things, or we're not. But in a larger sense, I want to make the point that the climate is changing. When I was in China recently, I spoke to the American Chamber of Commerce—this is not the Democratic Party—the American Chamber of Commerce in Shanghai. [*Laughter*] And I got two spontaneous ovations. One was when I talked about climate change and how we had to work with the Chinese to see them grow their economy without using energy in the same way we did; otherwise, we could burn up the atmosphere, and it would be hard for us to breathe, which is already a big problem over there.

Now, I'm telling you, if you look at what's happening to the climate, if you look at what happened in Florida—you saw all those fires in Florida. Florida had the wettest winter, the driest spring in history. Then June in Florida was hotter than any July and August. And if you've ever been to Florida in July and August, that's saying something—the hottest month ever. Things are changing.

Now, we can put our heads in the sand, or we can say we're going to figure out how Americans solve this problem. The leaders of the other party, in one of their committees, they have voted to deny me the right to use any funds even to have seminars about this problem and talk to the American people about it.

You know, I never will forget the day some young person who worked for me said, "Denial is not just a river in Egypt." [*Laughter*] And there are lots of examples like this, in health care, in education, in the environment, in economic policy.

In economic policy—yes, we've got a good economy. There are still towns in the Delta that need help. There are still neighborhoods in our cities that need help. There are still Native American reservations out West that need help. We've got a whole agenda that says we ought to bring the benefits of this economic moment of golden prosperity to everybody in America and give everybody a chance to be a part of it. And so far it has not been embraced in Congress by the leaders of the other party. So I ask you about all this.

What is this, a nightclub? [*Laughter*] I will now sing "Danny Boy," and you will applaud at the right time. [*Laughter*] Somebody leaned against the wall there last night. Somebody was up too late last night over there by the wall, they just leaned against the wall and nodded out. [*Laughter*]

We're laughing; we're having a good time. But I want you to be serious between now and November. I have tried to put progress over partisanship. All of you know me. You know I work with anybody who wants to work with me. And you get it, what's going on, and I can tell by the way you clapped before at the appropriate moment. [*Laughter*]

But let me tell you, in the end, what matters is what happens in the lives of the American people. The Democrats will be rewarded if we do the right things, if we have the right consequences, and if we convince people that it's not just a matter of name-calling and labeling but whether you have the right ideas.

I want you to think about it. We've got new leadership in the party. I thank Vaughn McQuary and all the other folks that are coming in here and trying to get this thing up and going. And I like to see your enthusiasm; I'm glad you're here in such large numbers. But if somebody asks you why you're a Democrat, why you support the President, why we've succeeded in the last 5½ years, what we would do if given the Governor's office and the attorney general's office, you need to have answers. And you need to be able to tell people in ways that are not hateful or small or mean spirited. We don't need to respond to them in kind, as they have to us; we need to remember our scriptural lessons. We need instead to lift our visions and lift the vision of the people and talk to them about what we're going to do.

While I was listening to Bill Bristow talk—you know, we can do a lot in Washington to help education. But the constitution of almost every State in the Union makes it clear that education is the primary responsibility of the States and the communities and the schools.

Now, let me ask you something. No one here, I take it, would dispute the proposition that we have the finest system of higher education in the world in America. No one disputes that. Otherwise, why do people come here from all over the world every year to get into it? And no one would seriously assert that America's elementary and secondary schools are the finest in the world. But they could be, and in points they are, and from time to time they manifest that.

You look over the horizon and you ask yourself, what are the big challenges of the future? The first thing that comes to mind is we've got to prove we can have the finest elementary and secondary education for all our kids without regard to their income, their background, their race, or their region in the world.

Now, if you believe that, then every time you're in the coffee shop, every time you're on the street, every time you're talking to somebody, you have to say to them, "You cannot make these decisions in November—you cannot cast a vote for Governor; you cannot cast a vote for Congress; you cannot cast a vote for the Senate—you cannot make these decisions without asking yourself, 'Who's got the best ideas for education; who's best for my children or my grandchildren; what's Arkansas going to look like 50 years from now?'" You know this is true.

In the Congress—let me give you another example—a huge issue—I'm the oldest of the baby boomers, and if present rates of birth, immigration, and retirement continue, by the time all of us get retired, there will only be about two Americans working for every person drawing Social Security. Unless we make some changes and start to make them now, by the time this happens we will have an unsustainable situation in which we will either have to have a huge cut in the Social Security benefits of retirees or a huge increase in the taxes on our kids, thereby undermining their ability to raise our grandchildren.

Every baby boomer I know is determined to avoid both these consequences. Now, are there ways we can do it? You bet there are. But we have to start now, which is why I have said, "Let's don't spend any of this surplus, even on stuff Democrats like. Let's don't give any tax cuts, even tax cuts Democrats like, until we save Social Security for the 21st century." That's important.

Believe me, this is a huge issue. Some of their leaders are saying, "Well, now they estimate we'll have a $63 billion surplus this year, and that means the surpluses out in the years ahead are going to be even bigger than we thought. And we can't use all that money. We need a big tax cut now." And, oh, it just happens to be right here before the election.

Well, I know it's right here before the election, but let me remind you, man, we've been waiting for 29 years for a balanced budget.

[*Laughter*] It took me 5½ years to get it done because there was a $290 billion deficit when we got up there. And we won't have a balanced budget or a surplus officially until the new fiscal year starts on October 1st, after we close our books at midnight on September 30th. It looks to me like, after 29 years of being in the red, after the years of 1981 to 1993 when we quadrupled the debt of the country in 12 years, it looks to me like we could wait just one year until we figured out how to save Social Security and stop assuming that we were going to have a surplus that hadn't even materialized yet. I'd just like to see the bank account just for a day or two. Wouldn't you? [*Applause*]

Now, if you believe that, that's an important idea. You need to know if you believe that. And you need to tell your friends and neighbors who aren't as political as you are or maybe not even Democrats—and maybe they're independents, maybe they're Republicans, but they're thinking about this—"Look, you got to think about this. This is not just where you go in and vote the way you normally do. We're in a time of enormous change. We didn't just elect the right people in 1992; we began to do the right things. And it is profoundly important that we do the right things in the future: saving Social Security and Medicare for the 21st century; making education the best in the world; proving we can grow the economy and preserve the environment; taking care of our health care system so that we don't keep ferreting people out and we, instead, keep bringing people in."

And let me just mention one other thing, that Arkansas people I think understand more, partly because we have so many farmers here. One of the biggest problems we've got now, looming ahead, is our trade deficit's gotten real big. Now, why has our trade deficit gotten real big? Because of the economic crisis in Asia, primarily. What's happened? Well, when the people you're doing business with run out of money, one of the things that they do is mark down the things they're selling you so it's cheaper, and they hope you buy more of it. And they still don't have any money to buy what you've been selling them.

Now, I have been trying for 6 months—now, this is a hard one, except for people in agriculture who understand it—I've been trying for 6 months to get the Congress just to pay America's fair share to the International Monetary Fund. And there are a lot of politicians up there making those election year speeches, saying, "Oh, man, this is just a big bailout to the foreigners," and "Why should we be doing this?"

We contributed, along with other nations, to this fund to stabilize and reform economies when they get in trouble. Why should we do it? Well, 30 percent of the growth that you just applauded for, when I came in and I started reeling off all those statistics, came because we were selling more of our stuff to other countries. We have 4 percent of the world's people in America; we have 20 percent of the world's income. If we want to keep doing better, we've got to sell something to the other 96 percent. And we have to expect them to keep doing better, too; otherwise, they not only won't want to, they won't be able to buy more of our things.

That's what this International Monetary Fund issue is about in Washington, DC. If we want our neighbors to buy our products, they've got to have the money to do it. And when they get in trouble because they're developing their societies and their economic systems, this whole fund was set up not as a bailout, not as a gift, not as a welfare program but as an instrument to force reform and revitalization.

These are things worth debating. You know, there's a big debate here in Arkansas because of what some of the elected officials said about whether I should have gone to China. I take it there's not as much debate now as there was before I went. And I hope there's not. But let me ask you—so we've got to decide that. This matters.

You look all over the world. We've got people that differ with us. They have different religious systems, different political systems, different cultural values. We have to decide when we deal with them and when we don't. Now, if people do things we really think are terrible, should we have economic sanctions? I think we should. But look what happened when I put economic sanctions on India and Pakistan. We pointed out, "Well, we don't like it if it's on food." And we say, "Well, we don't like it if it's on food because you shouldn't punish people when they're eating. But we also don't like it because it hurts our farm income in a bad year." So we want a mixed approach, where we kept trying to reach out and work with people.

China has got 1.2 billion people. They're going to have a lot to do with how your children and grandchildren live. And we ought to try to get along with them and work with them and build a common future with them if we can. And we ought to have a way of expressing our honest disagreements when we have to. And you can only do both of those things if you're dealing with people. This is worth debating.

The last point I want to make is this: Something a long way from Arkansas usually is my foreign policy job, a lot of the challenges I face. But you just look around the world at the things I've dealt with since you sent me to Washington. Last week, three little Irish-Catholic boys killed in a firebomb in Northern Ireland, because they're still fighting over religious battles that have roots that are 600 years old. In Kosovo, a place a lot of Americans still have a little trouble finding on a map, we're worried about a new destabilizing war breaking out because the Albanians and the Serbs can't get along, the same thing that happened in Bosnia. In the Middle East, we still have trouble because we can't get people to take just one more step to bring the Arabs and the Jews, the Israelis, together. But we're working on it.

When Hillary and I went to Africa, we went to Rwanda, where two different tribal peoples that most Americans aren't even aware exist, in a country that has been coherent for hundreds of years, got in a fight, and 900,000 people or so died in a matter of 100 days. Why? Because as we know from our own painful civil rights history, getting people to be pitted against each other because of their differences is deeply ingrained in the human psyche and easy to bring up and very often profitable for people who seek power.

And if you contrast that with what we are trying to achieve in America today, where we're a more and more diverse country, from more and more different backgrounds, in a world that is getting smaller and smaller because of technology, this country's best days are clearly still ahead. But we have to do the right things as well as elect the right people. And it's time the American people and the people of our State actually had to think about that. What are the right things to do in education in Arkansas? What are the right things to do in health care? What are the right things to do in economic policy? What is the right policy in building one community, one State, and one Nation, across all the lines that divide us?

I have tried to give the Democratic Party new ideas based on old values. I have tried to persuade the American people that the con-

sequences that are good that are coming today are due to them, but also due to the fact that in Washington we have done the right things.

Now, this is a very important election. It's important for that little child there and all the kids in this State. And it's very important that the citizens of our State not do what people so often do when times are good, which is just relax and say, "Just leave everything more or less the way it is," because when times are good but changing rapidly, you have to use the good times and the confidence people have to deal with the underlying challenges, and because as all of us who are older here know, no conditions last forever. If we can't use these good times to deal with our long-term challenges, when will we ever do it?

So I ask you—I'm glad to see you; I've had a good time; I've enjoyed the jibes and the cheering and the yelling. But I want you to keep clearly in mind that we have a future to build for these children. You've got a State to build and a country to build. And the reason we're in the shape we're in today is because we had good ideas that we implemented that had good consequences. And the reason that I will be a member of this party until the day I die is that more often than not, we have been the instrument in this century and in my lifetime in fulfilling the vision that the Founding Fathers gave us to always deepen our freedom and always perfect our Union.

So I want you to help me. I want you to elect these people. I want you to work. And I want you to go out there and literally grab your friends and neighbors by the shoulder and say, "Let's talk about this. Don't go through this election in a fog. Don't say, 'Oh, everything is fine; let's just keep on going the way we're going.' Think about where we are as a State and Nation. And think about where we were in 1992." And I think you'll have quite a good case to make.

Thank you, and God bless you.

NOTE: The President spoke at 10:05 a.m. in the auditorium at the Embassy Suites Hotel. In his remarks, he referred to Arkansas gubernatorial candidate Bill Bristow; senatorial candidate Blanche Lambert Lincoln; Judy Smith, candidate for Arkansas' Fourth Congressional District; Kurt Dilday, candidate for Lieutenant Governor; Mark Pryor, candidate for State attorney general; Jimmie Lou Fisher, State treasurer; Gus

Wingfield, State auditor; Charlie Daniels, State land commissioner; Arkansas Supreme Court Associate Justice Donald L. Corbin; Mary Anne Salmon, executive director, Clinton Arkansas Office; and Vaughn McQuary, Arkansas Democratic Party chair.

The President's Radio Address
July 18, 1998

Good morning. I'm speaking to you from my home State of Arkansas, a State that, like many across our Nation, depends heavily on agriculture. America's farm communities are more than a critical part of our economy. They are places where American values have deep roots and flourish: faith and family, hard work and respect for neighbors, devotion to community. Every American has a stake in the strength of rural America.

With family incomes rising, the lowest unemployment in nearly 30 years, the highest home-ownership rate in history, most Americans today are enjoying the dividends of the strongest American economy in a generation. Unfortunately, life on the farm is not so easy today.

For 5½ years, I have worked to expand opportunity for our farm families. We've strengthened crop insurance, provided critical disaster assistance to ranchers who have lost livestock, doubled our use of export credits from last year, improved our school lunch programs by buying surplus commodities, and worked to diversify the sources of enterprise and income in rural America.

But with the economic crisis in Asia weakening some of our best customers for farm products, and with strong world crop production bringing prices down, and with farmers facing floods and fires and drought and crop disease, our farmers face a difficult and dangerous moment. Many farm families have been pushed off their land, and many more could suffer the same fate unless our Nation revives its commitment to helping farmers weather hard times.

When I signed the 1996 farm bill, at a time when farm prices were very strong, I made clear my concern that there was not an adequate safety net for farmers. The bill had to be signed to avoid putting our farmers in an even more difficult situation under the old 1949 farm bill. But sooner or later, prices were bound to fall so low that we would need that safety net. That day has come. With prices for many farm products plummeting, America's farm families face a crisis, and we have an obligation to help.

At the same time we see a very different crisis in some parts of the world, a crisis of hunger, where too many families face famine and starvation. For decades, American Presidents have addressed such crises. That's what I'm doing today.

Today I am acting within my full authority as President to take immediate steps to help our family farmers and to reduce crop surpluses at home. Within days, the United States Government will begin to purchase more than 80 million bushels of wheat, which could lift prices as much as 13 cents a bushel. With this wheat, I've instructed Secretary of Agriculture Dan Glickman to launch a new food aid initiative to press the world struggle against hunger.

Secretary Glickman, working with our Agency for International Development, will use the authority granted to him by Congress to oversee substantial donations of U.S. wheat to countries where the need is greatest, places such as Sudan and Indonesia. Donations will also be made to private humanitarian groups. All told, this is in the best humanitarian tradition, an action based on human need to help save lives as it opens new links of trade with these nations. It's good for American farmers, good for our economy, and it's the right thing to do.

This effort will provide a much needed boost to U.S. wheat farmers, but we can and must do more. I'm pleased that this week Congress took prompt bipartisan action to exempt agricultural trade from U.S. sanctions against India and Pakistan in the wake of their nuclear test. But more congressional action must follow. We should expand eligibility for direct and guaranteed loans, extend marketing loans when crop prices are low or transportation problems make marketing difficult, give farmers more flexibility to plant other crops when their primary crops fail. And above all, we must keep the market for our products growing by paying our dues to the International Monetary Fund so that we can stabilize and help to reform Asian economies that are such important customers for America's farmers and for our other exporters who are responsible for 30 percent of the remarkable growth we've enjoyed since 1993.

In my State of the Union Address, I urged Congress to do this for the sake of our own economy. Six months later, the need is greater than ever. We must pay our dues to the International Monetary Fund so that our people can sell their products abroad.

The steps I take today are in the best tradition of America. From our beginnings, we have recognized that the agricultural tradition strengthens the national community. In the depths of the Great Depression, President Franklin Roosevelt said, "No cracked Earth, no blistering Sun, no burning wind are a permanent match for the indomitable American farmers who inspire us with their self-reliance, their tenacity, and their courage." Today, at a moment of broad prosperity for our Nation, we have an obligation to expand opportunity for all Americans as we move strongly into the 21st century.

Thanks for listening.

NOTE: The address was recorded at 8:58 p.m. on July 17 in the Cabinet Room at the White House for broadcast at 10:06 a.m. on July 18. The transcript was made available by the Office of the Press Secretary on July 18 but was embargoed for release until the broadcast.

Remarks at an Arkansas Victory '98 Dinner in Little Rock
July 18, 1998

Thank you. Well, first of all, like all of you, I want to thank Maurice and Betty for once again being there for all of us and having us in their home, giving us a view of the river. I'm trying to get accustomed to it. In a couple of years, I'm going to have a library about a mile down the road there, and I'm going to be looking up this river, just like all the rest of you. I also want to thank Vaughn for being willing to come in here and go to work for our party and give us some energy and direction.

Today I had a great, great morning with the State Democratic Committee and a number of other people who came, and I tried to get them revved up and also remind them that the stakes in this election are quite high and we need to go to work on it. I feel very good about our candidates. I feel very good about the issues. I think the main thing we have to recognize is that in the non-Presidential years, voter turnout tends to go down, and that's not good for Democrats—number one. Number two, when times are good, the tendency of any people in any society is to sort of relax and think, "Well, why rock the boat?"

If you look at the newspaper, however, on any given day, if you analyze, among other things, the turmoil in Asia, you see, however, that we're living in a very dynamic time. Things can change overnight in a thousand ways. And my whole argument to the American people and the argument that I want to see brought home here in our State is that this is a time when we should be bearing down and moving forward and being even more committed to doing the things that need to be done to get our people ready for a new century and a completely different way of living and relating to the rest of the world. If you can't do it when times are good, then you're not going to do it. And we need to do that.

The other point I tried to make today, which I will make very briefly, is that thanks to the 22d amendment, I'm not going to be a candidate anymore. But I think it's very important that people understand—that the voters understand—and this election gives us an opportunity to—is it's not just a question of putting certain people in and having good things happen; it really matters what your ideas are, what your policies are. There is a connection between what we do in public office and what consequences flow in the country and in the world.

And that's the argument we've got to make. There are real, clear, unambiguous, powerful differences on State issues and national issues between Democrats and Republicans. And we are now no longer vulnerable to the kind of reversed plastic surgery they used to do on us at every election. That is, no one can say we're not responsible on the budget or the economy or welfare or crime or foreign policy or national defense or all those other things they used to say. So now people are free to take a clear-eyed view of the future. And it's very important that all of us use these funds you've given and use our personal contacts to say, "Listen, this wasn't just a matter of Bill Clinton getting elected President. The Democratic Party has a bunch of new ideas. We've put them into action, and they worked." And they are still relevant, these differences, to every race in the State and every race for Congress that's going to be held this fall.

If the American people believe that, we're going to have an historic upset of the patterns that normally prevail in these midterm elections. So that's what we're going to use these funds for. I believe that we can do quite well indeed, because there are people like you all over America that feel the same way you do. But just don't forget, we have succeeded in convincing people that America is successful, and we're moving in the right direction. And I've been the luckiest person in the world. The American people have continued to support me in the face of unprecedented attacks.

But that's not the most important thing for this election. The most important thing is people realize—is we actually had a plan; we had ideas; we had policies; we had a plan. We implemented them, and the results were good. That's why things are good in America. And that's why they should support all of these other Democrats that are running in all the State offices and the races for Congress.

It is logical, and it is clear, but in good times, sometimes people just don't think about it. That's the case we have to make. We've got all the way between now and November to make it, and we certainly have a very impressive array of candidates.

For all of you who are running and all those who were here who are now over at the other event, I want to say I appreciate the fact that you've been willing to offer yourselves. Sometimes I know it's hard to do, especially when you see what happens to people who are successful. [*Laughter*] But you did, and I'm grateful. And I think we're going to be very grateful on election night in November. And I thank you very much.

Thank you.

NOTE: The President spoke at 7:40 p.m. at a private residence. In his remarks, he referred to dinner hosts Maurice and Betty Mitchell; and Vaughn McQuary, Arkansas Democratic Party chair.

Remarks at a Democratic Senatorial Campaign Committee Dinner in Little Rock
July 18, 1998

Blanche, that was a great talk. And I can't believe you remember that, but it is a true story. After we walked on up the steps—that story you were telling—the Irish Ambassador looked at me kind of funny. I said, "Listen, those guys are from my home State, and I'm absolutely certain they're Irish." [*Laughter*] So he was fine. [*Laughter*] People have learned to make allowances for my Arkansas ways in Washington, you know.

I want to thank Senator Pryor for a lot of things, for being my friend—he and Barbara were in the snows of New Hampshire with Hillary and me and our campaign—for many years

of service in a stunning, wonderful, decent way, and for coming home and not only not losing interest but actually generating more interest and energy in the future of the children of Arkansas. And we are all very much in his debt that he is doing that, and I thank you, sir.

I want to thank all the officeholders and the candidates who are here. I thank especially Congressman Snyder and Congressman Berry who have been great friends to me and to our administration and to our cause. And I want to ask you all to do everything you can to help Vic Snyder win reelection. He is a truly exceptional human being, and we need more people like him in the Congress.

I ask for your support for Bill Bristow and his running mate, and Judy Smith, and of course, Mark Pryor. Every time I look at Mark Pryor I think, you know, the first time I saw that guy he wasn't old enough to vote. [*Laughter*] Actually, I'm not sure he knew what voting was the first time I saw him.

But it's wonderful to see all these new people coming in, all this new blood, all these young people coming in. I'm very grateful. But the most important thing of all—I'd like to acknowledge all the relatives of Blanche who are here and the other six people in the audience. [*Laughter*] You know, I thought I'd done pretty good; I had relatives in 15 counties. She makes me look like a piker. [*Laughter*]

Actually, it's great to see this election be a family affair, not only for her family members but for all the rest of you. And we've had a good time tonight. I've enjoyed visiting with everybody, and all of you have heard me speak a thousand times anyway, and you probably think that everything that needs to be said has already been said, but not everyone has had the chance to say it yet. But there are a couple of things I would like for you to know.

First of all, I would like for you to know that not everybody in the U.S. Senate is like Dale Bumpers and David Pryor. And I don't mean in terms of party or philosophy. And I see a couple of people nodding their head back there who have to come to Washington and lobby all the time.

I would like for you to know that maybe because we're from here, but for whatever reason, people like Blanche and me, we sort of had this apparently naive idea that if we went to Washington, we'd just sit down with everybody who's interested in solving a problem without regard to their party or where they were from, and we'd figure out how to do it just the way we do at home. We thought that people would always put progress over partisanship. And you can tell by the stories that were told that we believe that politics is about people not power.

We think the Founding Fathers believed that, too, by the way. If you go back and read the Constitution, power is given to people who are in politics temporarily and in limited fashion for the sole purpose of advancing the cause of the rest of the folks that live in this country.

And you know, I went to one of these events in Washington, DC, that the press puts on every year, and it was a kind of a toast and roast, and everyone makes fun of me, so I get to say a few wisecracky things. And I alluded to the fact that some people have criticized Hillary and me for traveling abroad from time to time. And I said that we always liked to go to a new country and that we particularly enjoyed the opportunity to get a visa to come to Washington, DC, and see how a completely different culture lives. [*Laughter*]

I say that to make a very serious point. There are two reasons you should send Blanche to the Senate: One is because the ideas and the direction that we and our party now represent are good for America; two is because we still believe politics is about people, not power. We still believe progress should be put over partisanship. And I'll say again, not everybody does.

I'll just give you a couple of examples. First of all, let me say, I'm really grateful to all of you for giving me the chance to serve, for giving me permission to run in '91. And I think that you must be pleased that our country is in the shape it's in, that we do have the lowest—every time you hear something about it, I hope you take some measure of personal pride and ownership when you hear that we have the lowest crime rate in 25 years, the lowest unemployment rate in 28 years, the lowest welfare rolls in 29 years, the first balanced budget and surplus in 29 years, the lowest inflation in 32 years, the highest homeownership in history, and, oh, by the way, the Federal Government is the smallest—under Democrats, not Republicans—the smallest it's been in 35 years. But we did not do it by posturing, by putting power over people and politics, by elevating partisanship over progress. We did it in just the reverse way. In other words, I have tried to work with like-minded people to get something done in Washington that would elevate the lives of the American people and the future of our children. And I'm telling you, you cannot possibly underestimate the enormous significance of every single seat in the United States Senate, not only for having the right ideas and doing the right things but for doing it in the right way.

And a lot of you have been kind enough to come up and say, "Well, gosh, Bill, you look like you're having a good time. You look pretty good." I mean, I don't know what you all expected. [*Laughter*] Did you think they'd wheel me in here in a gurney tonight? [*Laughter*] Listen, you prepared me well. This is no big deal. You know what the deal is; I know what the deal is. I'm working for the American people and their future, and we're all fine because we are determined to take this country into the 21st century in a way that befits our heritage and that honors our children.

I want you to think about this. There really are differences here. We don't see the world in the same way as many of the Washington Republicans. I make a big distinction between Republicans that I come across all over America in different walks of life.

I'll just give you one example. We had an incredible event a couple of days ago in Washington to endorse the passage of a very strong Patients' Bill of Rights, because there are more and more Americans who are insured by HMO's, and because they have cost pressures of all kinds, and because increasingly doctors' decisions are being overridden or disregarded when it comes to emergency room treatment or specialists or a whole range of other things.

So I appointed this quality medical care commission, had all different kinds of folks on it from all sectors of our health care society including insurers. And they recommended that we have this Patients' Bill of Rights so that people could have some enforceable way of making sure that when it came right down to it, especially in life-threatening conditions, that these health care decisions were made by doctors.

So we said we're going to have a big event about this. Democrats in the House came; Democrats in the Senate came. Two Republicans showed up. And I honor them. But their real problem is they don't act like they're from Washington, DC; they still act like they're, in one case, Long Island, in another case, Iowa.

One of them has a terrible problem: He's a doctor; he knows what the facts are. It's an enormous burden, you know. [*Laughter*] It's hard to live in that nether neverworld if you actually know what the facts are. So here's this Republican doctor up here with a bunch of Democratic Congressmen, and it had been pointed out that when he wasn't in Congress, because he was a physician, he would often go to Central America and help to fix the cleft palates of young children so that they could have normal lives. So this doctor holds up a picture of a young boy with a cleft palate. And

everybody gasped in the room because it was so awful. And he said, "The problem is this young man is not from Central America. This young man is from the United States of America, and he was denied the procedure to fix his face because it was deemed by an accountant to be cosmetic." Then he held up a picture of the boy with his face fixed, and everybody cheered.

Now, why am I here at this event talking to you about what a Republican Congressman from Iowa said? Because all of us who were Democrats were cheering. Why? Because our country comes first, and people come first, and progress and moving forward and meeting new challenges come first. But don't you forget, that happened at a caucus of our party because we're for that, and they're not.

We're for an education agenda that gives us the best elementary and secondary schools in the world because we already have the best colleges and universities in the world. We're for smaller classes and higher standards and more teachers in the early grades and hooking up every classroom to the Internet and a bunch of other things that they're not for. They think we're wrong. I think our ideas are right.

I don't see how we can ever make America everything it ought to be, I don't see how we can ever lift up every poor community in this State until we can say with a straight face, "Yes, we've had the best university system in the world for a long time. Now we have a system of elementary and secondary education that is second to none in the world." I think we're right about that.

I went all over the country when I was running for President—indeed, long before—and asked all these police officers, I said, "What's the most important thing you could do to drive the crime rate down?" And they said two things: Put more police on the street working in the neighborhoods, and give these kids something positive to do to keep them out of trouble in the first place.

Now, we had a few Republicans who voted with us to put 100,000 police on the street, but most of them didn't. And some of them are still trying to undo it and stop it, today, when we've got the lowest crime rate in 25 years. I thank those who are voting with us, but don't forget, it is our party that fought for this and stands for this, and it helped to give us the lowest crime rate in 25 years. And anybody here who's ever been a victim of a crime, there is no more issue—no issue more important.

So I just give you these examples. But to back off—you heard Blanche saying all that stuff about Arkansas values. You know, I used to be embarrassed to talk about that—I'll be honest with you—because my mother raised me not to be self-promotional in any way like that. But I'm telling you, it's real. There is a real and profound difference.

There are times when I wake up in our Nation's Capital, and I deal with people day-in and day-out, and they say one thing one day and then the next day they're trying to basically say that I'm the worst thing since Joe Stalin. The day before we were all working together, hunky-dory, and I said, "What happened here?" They said, "Oh, they got a different poll last night or something." [*Laughter*] And I said, "Hello!"

There is a difference in the parties in Washington, not only in what our ideas are—and I believe ours are better and right, and I think you've got evidence of that now, so you don't have to have a debate about that—but in how we believe people should be treated, what we think it is legitimate to do to try to defeat your enemies, and how we believe we should work with everybody when it comes right down to it, to put the interest of the country first.

I'll just give you one last example, because it meant a lot to me. Blanche wrote me a letter. When I said we hadn't had a surplus for 29 years, we quadrupled the debt of the country from 1981 to 1993, and now we're going to have one—the last thing in the world we need to do is start promising all this money to people in an election year in tax cuts or spending programs until we fix Social Security for the baby boom generation in a way that does not require either the baby boomers, because we're so large, to be poor when we're old, or require our children to be poor and our grandchildren to be worse off because they have to spend so much money to take care of us. And Blanche said, "I am for that."

Now, we see everybody—we see other people in the other party saying, "Oh, I don't know. We're going to have a $60 billion surplus this year. That means it's going to be a lot bigger over the next few years than I thought, so let's just go on and pass a big tax cut now"—oh, by the way, just before the election. Well, just because I'm not running again doesn't mean I don't remember what it's like to be just before an election.

But folks, we've been waiting for 29 years to get out of the red. It's not even going to happen officially until October 1st. Don't you think at least we ought to look at the bank balance for a week or two before we start spending it again? [*Applause*]

That's another important thing. She will come home and say, "Look, I know this isn't popular, but I think it's the right thing to do." And, believe me, there are a lot of those decisions that have to be made.

So when you leave here tonight, I want you to leave here with a happy heart and in good spirits. I want you to be proud that your country is in good shape. And I want you to be proud of your personal role in helping me to play the part in that, that I've had the chance to play. I want you to be committed to the proposition that now is not the time to relax and lay back and enjoy it but to bear down and deal with the large questions that are still before us on the edge of a new century.

And I want you to remember why you are here for Blanche Lambert, besides the fact that you either love her or are kin to her. [*Laughter*] There are differences in Washington more profound than the differences out here in the country on the issues, and we now have evidence. We've got a 5½-year record about who's right about these ideas.

And even more important, when the chips are down, there are profound differences in those Arkansas values. We believe in people over power, and progress over partisanship. And believe you me, we need a lot more of that in the United States Congress. Send her there, and she'll make you proud.

Thank you, and God bless you.

NOTE: The President spoke at 9:39 p.m. in the Robinson Auditorium at the Robinson Center Exhibition Hall. In his remarks, he referred to former Congresswoman Blanche Lincoln, candidate for U.S. Senate; Mark Pryor, candidate for State attorney general, and his parents, former Senator David H. and Barbara Pryor; Arkansas gubernatorial candidate Bill Bristow; Kurt Dilday, candidate for Lieutenant Governor; and Judy Smith, candidate for Arkansas' Fourth Congressional District.

Remarks to the 75th Annual Convention of the American Federation of Teachers in New Orleans, Louisiana
July 20, 1998

The President. Thank you very much, ladies and gentlemen of the AFT, Senator Landrieu, Congressman Jefferson, Secretary Slater. Mayor Morial, thank you for hosting this fine group of America's teachers in this wonderful city.

To President Sandy Feldman and Ed McElroy and your newly elected executive VP, Nat LaCour, and all the officers and people who are here. Let me say, when Sandy was up here giving her introduction, my mind was racing back over lots of events going back to early 1992 when we first went to a school in New York together.

Audience member. Cardozo.

The President. Cardozo, that's right; you were there, weren't you? [*Applause*] Now, anytime I'm talking, if I mention something that gives you an opportunity to flack for your school, you stand up and do it. [*Laughter*] I won't be offended. I think you ought to be proud of what you do and where you work and the children that you're trying to help to prepare for tomorrow.

And when you think about where we were then as a nation and where we are now, I was so concerned because not only was the economy in the doldrums, but our society was becoming more divided; the crime rates were going up; the welfare rolls were exploding; there were tensions among our people; people were looking for racial or ethnic or religious or political reasons to blame other people for the general problems and challenges we shared as Americans.

One of the things that I always admired most about the AFT was that I felt that you have always found the right balance between being passionately devoted to public education and to the welfare and working conditions of teachers and uncompromising—uncompromising—in your advocacy of high standards and accountability and educational excellence for every single American child.

Shortly before I came out here, your officers told me that Eadie Shanker had decided to give the Medal of Freedom that I awarded to Al to the AFT for safekeeping. I love that. For it was your legacy, your values that he worked so hard to serve. You take good care of it. He earned it, and so did you.

This is a remarkable time in our country's history, a time of prosperity and confidence and breathtaking change if you think about where we are now compared to where we were on the day that I was fortunate enough to be inaugurated President. I don't say that our administration is 100 percent responsible for all the good things that have happened. That would be foolish. In a free society, the people deserve the lion's share of any change that occurs.

But I will say this, we had new ideas and new policies. We said we would take this country in a new direction. And there were consequences to those decisions, just as there will be consequences to the decisions of those who disagree with us if they hold sway.

And I think every single one of you should feel a personal measure of pride if you helped Al Gore and me win those elections in '92 and '96 because of what has happened—every single one of you.

Because when you hear these statistics—I mean, think about this. Compared to 1992, we have 16 million new jobs and the lowest unemployment rate in 28 years, the lowest crime rate in 25 years, the lowest percentage of our people on welfare in 29 years, the first balanced budget and surplus in 29 years, the lowest inflation in 32 years, the highest homeownership in the history of the country, and the smallest National Government in 35 years, and the biggest investment in education in our Nation's history. I am proud of that, and you should be too.

Now, today I want to ask you to look ahead at where we are and what our challenges are. And I want to ask you to help me with a lesson plan for America's future. I know you're mildly acquainted with such things. [*Laughter*] I also know that this union represents people who help you in schools who are not teachers, and I thank all of them, all the support people here who are here. Thank you for your service.

We have to decide what to do with this moment. And I want to talk about education and the role of some other issues. But let me just back up and say, there are three things I want you to think about. First of all, all these numbers and statistics that I mentioned are very rewarding because they represent real positive changes in real peoples' lives: incomes for ordinary people are up; poverty is down, as Sandy said; 90 percent of our kids are immunized; we've virtually opened the doors of college to everyone who will work for it. I'm proud of all that.

But you know and I know that we face some big long-term challenges. And I'd just like to mention a couple of them, because I want you to talk to your students and to the parents and to the people that you work with about them, because people need to understand that just because times are good, it doesn't mean we should all be relaxing—except if you want to go out in the sun in New Orleans and relax, I'm for it. [*Laughter*] But I don't want it to be a permanent condition for the American people.

Because we have big challenges facing us if we're going to go into the 21st century with the American dream alive for everyone, with America coming together as a community across all of our differences, and with our country leading the world for peace and freedom and prosperity. What are they? Well, let me just mention a few of them.

Number one, we have to save Social Security and Medicare for the baby boom generation. And we have to do it in a way that recognizes that they lift millions and millions and millions of seniors out of poverty but that, as presently constructed, it is not sustainable because when—and I'm the oldest baby boomer, so I can say this—when we retire, at present birth rates and present immigration rates and present retirement rates, there will only be about two people working for every person drawing Social Security. So we have to make some changes. If we make modest changes now, we can avoid drastic changes later. We must do that, and every American must support it. And we must find an American, unified way to do it.

The second thing we have to do is to recognize, as you can see from this sweltering heat, that the Vice President is right: The climate of our country and our globe is changing. The globe is warming. And our principal contribution to it, human beings everywhere, is that we're putting too many greenhouse gases into the atmosphere, primarily because we insist on maintaining Industrial Age patterns of energy use

when all the technology available indicates that you don't have to do that to grow an economy.

So we have got to take advantage of the fact that our children are natural environmentalists, to use them, to empower them, to help us all to find a way to save our planet, to improve our environment, even as we grow the economy. I promise you it can be done, but we've got to get people to think differently. This is a huge education issue.

The third thing we have to do is to prove that we can bring the benefits of this great economic recovery to all Americans—not just to those who have it now—in our inner cities, in our rural areas, our farming areas, on our Native American reservations.

The fourth thing we have to do is to persuade the American people that if we're going to lead the world for peace and freedom and prosperity, we have to be farsighted. We have to pay our way in an interdependent world. That means we can't walk away from our investment in the United Nations. We can't walk away from our investment in the International Monetary Fund.

I was just home for the weekend, and I know what a lot of folks at home think. They think, "Why does Bill Clinton want to spend money on the International Monetary Fund? We've got needs here at home." I'll tell you why. Because unless we help to reform and restore growth in the Asian countries, for example, they won't be able to buy our products and 30 percent of our growth—if you like these 16 million new jobs, if you like this low unemployment, if you like the taxes that are flowing into local government for education because of the economy—somebody has got to buy our stuff around the world, and if they don't have any money, they can't buy it. And if they don't have any money, the value of their currency goes down, so their products they sell here are cheaper. So our trade deficit goes up.

If you want us to grow in America, we have to grow together with our friends and neighbors around the world. We have to be responsible partners, and we've got to teach people that.

Just two other quick points. We've got to be able to live together as one America across all the lines that divide us. Many of you teach in school districts where there are children from 20, 40, 60, 80, maybe even 100 different racial and ethnic groups, speaking dozens of different languages as their native tongues. This is a good thing for America in the 21st century, in a global economy, an information age.

If we can overcome the demons of racial and ethnic and religious hatred which are bedeviling the world in our time, from Bosnia and Kosovo to Rwanda, to Northern Ireland, to the Middle East, to the conflict between Greece and Turkey, to the difficulties between India and Pakistan, and if you want your country to lead the world away from all that, I can just say this: In order for America to do good throughout the world, we have to be good at home. We have to be one America.

Finally, the last big challenge that I think we face—big challenge for the 21st century—is providing every single child with world-class excellence in education—every child, every child. No one anywhere in the world questions that we offer more rich, quality opportunities for people to go on to college than any other country in the world. We've worked very hard to open the doors of college to everybody who will work for it. But no one who is honest would say we don't have serious challenges in our elementary and secondary education. There are all kinds of different arguments about, well, what caused it or what the problems are or what the solutions are.

You and I, by and large, agree on the solutions. But the main thing we've got to agree on is that this is one of the five or six challenges that will shape the America our children and grandchildren will live in, in the 21st century. If you do not want our country to continue to be divided along the lines of income, to continue to grow more unequal, if you don't want the 21st century to see an America where there are fabulously wealthy, successful people living alongside breathtakingly poor people, isolated in areas where opportunity never reaches, we have to realize that if this is an information age and if the economy is growing by ideas, then it is more important than ever before that educational excellence be universal. And we have to provide that.

Now, I also want to say a few words today about an issue that may seem somewhat mundane to people who've never been in the classroom and faced it, but America has been thinking about it because of all the tragedies in all the schools in the last year or so, and that is the whole issue of school safety and the critical role of a safe classroom and a safe school and

a safe schoolyard play in the work that teachers do.

Every day, you work hard to broaden young minds, to unlock their potential, to sharpen skills. You have faith in the possibilities of our children. If you didn't, you wouldn't be doing this, because just about every one of you could be making more money doing something else. If you weren't devoted to our children, you wouldn't be doing this. It keeps you in front of a chalkboard or a keyboard; it keeps you up late at night grading papers and making lesson plans.

We have tried to be a good partner with you, as Sandy said. I have loved working with you to raise standards, to increase accountability, to improve teaching, to give schools the tools and the flexibility they need to reach the national education goals, to try to help make sure all of our children can read and can log on to the Internet and can go on to college.

We now have, I think, a great challenge before us, because in spite of the fact that this agenda is clearly an integral part of America's economic success over the next few years, believe it or not, there are people who don't want to continue it in Washington and some who downright are committed to undoing it. But I have put before the Congress an agenda to modernize our schools, to reduce class size, to connect every classroom to the Internet, to end social promotion but provide more funding for after-school and summer school programs that work to give our children a chance, to give more schools who are in disadvantaged areas the funds and the support they need to adopt the kind of comprehensive approach that Chicago is pursuing with such success, to give more students in disadvantaged areas mentors and the certainty in junior high school or middle school that they can go on to college if they learn and become good citizens and succeed in school, to provide more funds to put teachers into underserved areas, to do everything I can to help to provide 100,000 more master teachers so that we can do what needs to be done in every school building in the country, and to support your efforts to improve teaching.

I salute Sandy Feldman's plan to improve teacher quality, and I want to support your efforts. I have always been impressed, I will say again, that the AFT was never afraid to say that before a teacher is certified, it is reasonable to have the demonstrated competence of the teacher. I have always respected that, and I thank you for that.

But I will also say that while I have strongly supported the testing of teachers before they're certified, I also have strongly supported paying them once they are certified and strongly supported having master teachers in every school building in America and doing the things that Sandy outlined in her proposal.

So, as teachers, you're stepping up to your responsibility. I have tried to preserve the gains of the last 5½ years and put forward an ambitious program for the future. And we've had a lot of success working with Congress in a bipartisan way for education. In the balanced budget bill, as Sandy said, we got this huge increase in funding for education, and we got the HOPE scholarship; we got more work-study positions; we got big increases in Pell grants.

We have, earlier than that, got a big improvement in the student loan program to open the doors of college. We've got 1,000 colleges now participating with their kids in the America Reads program, going into your schools. We've got AmeriCorps people; almost 100,000 young people have been in AmeriCorps. When I drove by a grade school this morning on the way here, there were the AmeriCorps volunteers out there with their kids, holding up signs, welcoming me to New Orleans. We have been able to do those things by working together.

Now is the time for Congress to turn away from some of these recent committee votes where they say no to smaller classes, no to modernized schools, no to AmeriCorps. They haven't yet said yes to America Reads. I am pleased that we seem to be making some bipartisan progress with the proposals to prepare teachers for the classroom.

But I ask Congress to support all these proposals. They are not my ideas. They are the ideas of educators. They are the ideas that we know work. All of them came from grassroots America. I was in Philadelphia the other day where the average age of a school building is 65 years. A lot of those buildings are beautiful, but they need rehabilitating.

I was in Florida in a little town where there were 17—count them, 17—trailers outside the major school building because the school population had grown so much. If you want smaller classes, they have to be held somewhere, and there have to be teachers to walk in the classroom. We have got to do this. This is important.

So I ask you to redouble your efforts, to reach out to all Members of Congress without regard to their party and say, "Look, if there's one thing in America, even in Washington, DC, we ought to be able to put beyond partisan politics, it should be education of our children." Now, if you want to fight about whether you believe in vouchers or not, fine, let's have an argument about it. I don't mind that. But while we're arguing about it, don't forget this: Over 90 percent of the people are out there in those public schools. And these ideas are good on their own merit, and they deserve to be implemented and passed without regard to party in Washington, DC. We have the money to do it, it is allocated, and we should do it.

Now, let me also say that you know, better than anybody, learning cannot occur unless our schools are safe and orderly places where teachers can teach and children can learn. Wherever there is chaos where there should be calm, wherever there is disorder where there should be discipline, make no mistake about it, it's not just a threat to our classrooms and to your mission; it is a threat to the strength and vitality of America.

In a recent study, 81 percent of teachers said the worst behaved students absorb the most attention in school, not the struggling students, not the striving students, the worst behaved. Seventy-one percent of all high school students said there were too many disruptive students in their own classes. And only 13 percent of public school students said their classmates were, quote, very respectful of teachers.

Now, teachers can't teach if they have to fight for respect or fear for their safety. Students can't study if there is disorder in a classroom. And the disruption won't change unless there are clear, strict standards for behavior. You know better than anyone that we either have discipline in a classroom or we have disorder and, too often, danger. Hard experience has taught us this lesson all too well. As a nation, therefore, we must recognize that giving you the tools to have a safe, orderly classroom is central to the mission of renewing America.

There is another lesson to be learned from all this. In this case, it is from the overall decline in crime. And let me back up and say one of the cruel ironies of these horrible killings in all these States over the last year or so has been that they have occurred against the backdrop of a dramatic drop in crime and the first drop in juvenile crime in years and years and years. Crime is dropping around the country because we're getting serious about community policing, effective punishment, and effective prevention. Crime is dropping because whole communities, like Boston, are taking responsibility for their streets and their neighborhoods and because government is giving them the support they need.

I mention Boston because they went 2 years and a few weeks without a single, solitary child under the age of 18 being killed with a gun. That's an amazing statistic.

Now, these things do not happen by accident. They happen by design at the grassroots level, but people must have the tools to do the job. That's the idea behind our efforts to put 100,000 police on the street. When I became President, violent crime had tripled in the last 30 years, and the number of police officers had only increased by 10 percent. You didn't have to be Einstein to figure out that was a mathematical equation for disaster. And the police officers told us we can prevent crime if you give us enough police to walk the streets, to be on the blocks, to know the kids, to know the parents, to know the store owners, to figure out what's going on. So that's what we did.

But if you look at what happened in community after community where the crime rate dropped, they first of all put in place a system that said, "We are going to have respect for the law, and here's the system we're going to have to maximize respect, hold people accountable who don't respect the law." And guess what? More and more people started to follow the law in the first place, to behave as responsible citizens, to walk away from the prospect of criminal conduct.

That's what we've tried to do with school safety. We've worked hard to tighten security, to give you the tools to do that, to strengthen prevention, to toughen penalties. We initiated this nationwide policy of zero tolerance for guns in schools. In the '96–'97 school year, this policy led to the expulsion of about 6,100 law-breaking students. It obviously prevented countless acts of violence. Yet, as we have seen from the recent acts of violence, we have to do more.

When I was in Springfield, Oregon, I was so moved by what the parents of injured children said, the parents in some cases of children who were killed. The teachers who were there talked about the necessity of doing more and

developing the right kinds of intervention strategies. This is terribly important.

And one of the things I came here today to do is to say that in the fall, I will host the first-ever White House conference on school safety, and I want you to be a part of that. We want to bring together educators and law enforcement officers and families whose lives have been touched by these terrible tragedies to find new solutions to this profound challenge.

Again, I ask Congress also to be our partner. And again I say, this should not be a partisan issue. I have proposed a juvenile crime bill to ban violent juveniles from buying guns for life and to take other important steps to give communities much needed support. I've asked that in our balanced budget, $95 million be allocated to the prevention of juvenile crime. I urge Congress to invest in prevention.

You know, when we talk, those of us who have run for office, we all like to talk about punishment because everybody has known someone who's been hurt, who's been a victim of crime, and because we are outraged when we see children have their lives cut short. And I would point out that in our '94 crime bill we did more to stiffen punishment for crimes under Federal law than had ever been done. But you know and I know that we cannot jail our way out of this problem; we've got to prevent more of these kids from getting in trouble in the first place.

Again I say, this is not a Democratic or a Republican issue. We should simply invest in prevention because the police officers tell us it works, because the teachers tell us it works, because the social workers tell us it works, because the religious leaders tell us it works, because the children themselves tell us it works. We should be investing in a summer jobs program, in the summer school program, in the after-school program because it works.

We also know, by way of lessons, that the small stuff matters, the basics matter. In most schools it's not the sensational acts of violence but smaller acts of aggression, threats, scuffles, constant backtalk that take a terrible toll on the atmosphere of learning, on the morale of teachers, on the attitudes of other students. And that's why setting strict standards and enforcing them can make a powerful difference all across America, as they are doing in many places.

And let me just give three or four examples. Our first effort has to be to get kids inside the schoolhouse doors and keep them there during school hours. Truancy is more than a warning sign; it is trouble, a gateway to drugs, alcohol, gangs, and violence. Our children will either sit in class or stand on the streets. They'll either learn from teachers or learn from the gang leaders on the streets. It used to be the rule that truancy laws were enforced, that local police knew kids and brought them back to school. But in too many places, that has long since ceased to be the case.

Thankfully, communities again are turning their attention to the old-fashioned remedy of enforcing the truancy laws. In Milwaukee, officers can now stop students on the street during school hours. In Boston, where more than a quarter of the public school students were absent 3 weeks or more this past school year, they now have a strict new promotion policy. If you don't attend, you don't advance.

Other cities are forming truancy task forces, a united front of schools, social services, community police to keep our children in school and out of trouble. This is important. A teacher's day must sometimes seem very long. But we know the school day lasts precious few hours, and there's no time to waste.

The other thing I—next thing I'd like to say is, when the kids are there, they need to feel free, and they need to feel free of danger going to and from school. That's one of the ideas behind this incredible wave of enthusiasm across the country for school uniforms. When I spoke about school uniforms in my 1996 State of the Union Address—besides making half the kids in America mad at me—[*laughter*]—it struck a lot of people as an idea long out of date. And it was just gathering steam in places like Long Beach, California.

But in the years since, I have been heartened by the flood of interest, from New York to Houston. From Dade County to Chicago, school districts are adopting school uniform policies, and they're finding ways to do it in ways that give the children and the parents and the teachers all a say in how they do it and that don't put poor kids at a disadvantage when they can't afford the uniforms.

But students have told me—I've talked to a lot of students about this in schools that have uniform policies—when one student is no longer obsessed by another student's sneakers or designer jackets and where students are focused not on appearances but on learning, crime and

violence go down; attendance and learning go up. And I am proud of the support we have given to those of you who have done this.

The next thing I'd like to say—and I know you believe this, because you applauded earlier when I mentioned it—is that the responsibility that we adults have for our kids doesn't end when the last school bell rings. After school, an awful lot of children's parents are still working, and there's nobody home to either supervise them there or know where they are or where they're going when they leave school. Well, a lot of kids get in trouble after school, and youth crime is at its peak during the unsupervised hours of 3 to 6. That's why I have said that our schools should remain open, to become community learning centers where children are safe and can learn and grow.

In this budget for 1999, for next year, I have proposed a significant expansion in our investments for before- and after-school programs. And for the later hours when streets become darker and more dangerous, I have often urged communities to install curfews, to follow the example of New Orleans, where Mayor Morial, who is here with us today, put in place community-based curfews with very impressive results, in no small measure because the children are also taken, if they violate curfew, to somebody who can help them if they've got a problem and support them and get them back on the right path. But these are the things that we have to do if we expect you to have a safe learning environment.

I should also say that I think that the character education programs that our Education Secretary, Dick Riley, has done so much to help implement across the country are a positive force for a more disciplined school environment where the little nagging, terrible problems don't occur.

So we're going to have this conference in the fall on school violence. I want the AFT involved. I want the teachers who know what the problems are to participate. But I want to encourage every place to adopt antitruancy efforts, to consider school uniforms, to look at the curfew issue, to look at character education programs, to look to a new approach to restoring discipline in our schools and order in our children's lives. We can do this. The three R's of the AFT: responsibility, respect, results—that's what school discipline is all about.

In closing, let me say I am always struck by how every challenge in American education has been solved by somebody somewhere. Therefore, I am always frustrated that we have not yet found a way to make sure when somebody somewhere solves a problem, we cannot model that and make sure it's solved by everybody everywhere. That is one of the things that the AFT has been devoted to: finding what works, developing a systematic approach, trying to get it done everywhere. And it's one thing America needs desperately in this area of school discipline, school order, and school safety.

Again, I say I am very proud to be your partner in building a 21st century America that is leading the world to peace and freedom and prosperity, an America in which every child is a responsible citizen with unparalleled opportunity, in a community that reveals in its diversity but is bound together in our wonderful ongoing effort to form a more perfect Union.

You, the educators of our Nation, are the architects of that 21st century America. Build well.

Thank you very much, and God bless you.

NOTE: The President spoke at 11:30 a.m. at the Ernest N. Morial Convention Center. In his remarks, he referred to Mayor Marc H. Morial of New Orleans; Edward J. McElroy, secretary-treasurer, American Federation of Teachers; and Edith Shanker, former AFT President Albert Shanker's widow.

Remarks at a Luncheon for Representative William J. Jefferson in New Orleans
July 20, 1998

Thank you so much, Congressman, Senator Landrieu, Mr. Mayor, Lieutenant Governor Blanco, members of the city council, the Jefferson Parish Council, and let me thank all of you for coming. If Al Gore were giving this speech, he would say thank you for the standing ovation. [*Laughter*] I think it's a pretty good joke, too, but I can never bear to give it without giving him some credit for it. [*Laughter*]

I want to say also to Andrea and to the Jefferson daughters and to their vast families over there, they could even elect Bill to Congress, they have so many in their families. [*Laughter*]

Let me thank all of you for coming. Let me once again not miss an opportunity to thank the people of Louisiana for supporting Hillary and me and the Vice President and our team twice, for dramatically increasing our margin in 1996, and for electing Mary Landrieu to the Senate. I thank you for all that.

I have so many rich and wonderful memories of this city. I first came here when I was about 4 years old, and I still remember at least one thing that happened then, when my mother was in nurse's training here—I maybe even was younger. I must have been younger; I must have been about 2½. But I still remember leaving on the train, and I still remember being on the top floor of the Jung Hotel. And I don't remember much else, but whatever happened, I was bit, and I've been coming back ever since.

I want to tell you that I am honored to be here for your Congressman. I remember when Bill and Andrea had me in their home early in 1992. I remember well the meeting that John Lewis and Mike Espy and he had with me and their early commitment, which meant a great deal. I remember in the Democratic primary in Louisiana, 69 percent of the voters voted for me against a rather wide array of choices that they had. You don't forget things like that, and I'll always be grateful.

But I also want you to know that Mr. Jefferson here, while we rag each other a lot and make a lot of fun of each other and have had an enormously good time knowing each other, is a truly gifted and extraordinary public servant. He has the necessary blend of education and intelligence and practical sense. He is a visionary who wants to get things done. He knows what to be serious about and not to take himself too seriously. And I can tell you that once he makes up his mind to do something, he is absolutely dogged.

I don't know how many people there are in this audience that he has personally talked to me about some issue or another that you were interested in and involved in, committed to. But I am especially grateful to him for his support for education and the education initiatives that we have put before the American people—his family is the living embodiment of that commitment—and for his support for economic expansion through trade. I think the people of New Orleans understand, without regard to party, that if we're going to keep growing our economy and lifting incomes and finding more for more people to do, since we're only 4 percent of the world's people and we enjoy 20 percent of the world's wealth, we have to sell some more to the other 96 percent of the world out there. And I am very grateful for his support on those issues.

I can also tell you he's done a great job with this Africa trade bill, which I think represents an enormous opportunity for America in the years ahead, both in economic opportunity and in opportunity to build friendships and partnerships in a part of the world that too many of our people have ignored for too long, which is very, very important to the future of the globe.

Hillary and I had a wonderful trip to Africa not very long ago, and Bill went on the trip, and he did you proud. You would have been very, very proud of that.

So for all those reasons, I am here for my old friend, for a gifted public servant, for a supporter of the things that I believe in are right for America in the 21st century. I'm glad you're taking good care of him, and I hope you always will, because he sure takes good care of you.

Thank you, and God bless you.

NOTE: The President spoke at 1:43 p.m. in the Imperial Ballroom at the Fairmont Hotel. In his remarks, he referred to Mayor Marc H. Morial of New Orleans; Lt. Gov. Kathleen Blanco of Louisiana; Representative Jefferson's wife, Andrea; and former Secretary of Agriculture Mike Espy.

Remarks at a Democratic National Committee Dinner in New Orleans
July 20, 1998

Thank you. Now you shamed me, and I can no longer make fun of you—[*laughter*]—Sheriff Lee. What he was afraid is I was going to say that he had offered to take me hunting and take you, and he said that he would provide the game. [*Laughter*] And I said, if you took me, you'd all be safe because I'd be blamed for it, no matter what happened. It would be great. [*Laughter*]

Let me say, I'd better get out of town because I'm really beginning to enjoy myself here and—[*laughter*]—and you know, it's just been wonderful.

First of all, let me thank a lot of the people who are here. I want to thank Len Barrack who came up here before me. I know most of you don't know him, but he is a Philadelphia lawyer and a gentleman and wonderful human being. Like Congressman and Mrs. Jefferson, he has five great children, and like Congressman Jefferson, he overmarried. You can't imagine— here's a guy with a busy life and a lot to do, and he could be home in Philadelphia. And every night he's somewhere else in America trying to help rebuild our party and make sure we're victorious in November. And I thank you. Thank you very much.

I never want to speak again in Louisiana without thanking the people of this State for voting for me twice for President and voting for me overwhelmingly in the primary in 1992 and giving me the chance to serve. And it is a real joy to me to see you doing so well and to see the young leaders coming in.

I can tell you would be very, very proud of the mark that Mary Landrieu is making, not only from what you know here in Louisiana, but if you were in Washington and you heard it the way I hear it from the Senators, they believe that she is a fine Senator with an unlimited future, and so do I.

And I can't say enough about your mayor. New Orleans is getting a national reputation for saving its children, for putting its economy back in order, for showing the right face to the world, for bringing people together, for being a genuinely progressive city in the best sense. And, Mr. Mayor, I thank you for what you're doing, and I'm always proud.

I want to thank your State party chair, Ben Jeffers, and all the other people who've been active in the Democratic Party. I can't say enough in terms of thanks to Ray Reggie and to Congressman Jefferson for doing this tonight. I also want to thank them for the people who are here. I know there are a lot of younger people here tonight that I have not met before. There are some former Republicans who are here tonight that I have not met before, and I thank you.

You know, I always tell my Republican friends in Washington that, being a Southern Baptist, I believe in deathbed conversions, but I hate to wait that long. [*Laughter*] So I feel somewhat encouraged that I won't have to wait that long for some of you.

I thank my longtime friend and our Transportation Secretary, Secretary Rodney Slater, for being here with me tonight—a great friend of the people of Louisiana.

And let me just recognize one other person. We're just 11 seats from winning a majority in the House of Representatives and being able once again to put progress over partisanship in America. And I believe that Marjorie McKeithen will be one of those 11 victories, and I thank her for being here today. Let's give her a hand. [*Applause*]

Jeff talked a little bit about how we tried to change the Democratic Party. I think it's worth all of us, because we're neighbors and friends, going back to where we were a few years ago and thinking about those circumstances. Most of my Republican friends in the late eighties and early nineties thought there would never be another Democratic President in their lifetime, because they thought we kept shooting ourselves in the foot, and because they thought they had developed a kind of a cardboard cookie image of us that they could always present to the American people, and because they thought that they could always sort of divide every issue into the liberal position and the conservative position, and the conservative position was always right, the liberal position was always wrong. And at a very high level of rhetoric with a lot of emotion and a lot of heat and as little light as possible, they could turn every election into one where the voters didn't think, and their emotions carried them to ratify their governance.

The thing that bothered me about that, as a Governor of a State that went through all the turmoil of the eighties, just like all of you did, that—I kept reading the newspaper every day, just like all of you, and I heard all those debates in Washington, just like all of you. And most of what I heard didn't make a lot of sense to me, because I didn't know anybody who talked that way or who thought that way. Most of the people that I knew, whether they were Republicans or Democrats, we all had fights over the issues, but we understood there was some core things we had to do in my home State, and we did it; we worked together.

And I thought, well, maybe it was just something in the water, maybe that Washington is so far away from the people that you have to communicate in more abstract terms. And I do think there's something to that. You have to elevate the debate and make it more general to some extent.

But the truth is this country was in trouble in 1992. And if it hadn't been, I would not have been elected; I think we all know that. I think we all know that I had the great good fortune to bring to the American people some new ideas and a new direction at a time when they were open to hearing it. And otherwise, the Governor of a small Southern State, as my distinguished opponent often dubbed me, would not have had a chance to become President.

But I'd like to review with you just for a moment what those ideas were, because I think it's worth pointing out what they were. We believed that, first of all, we had to ground our party in the values that made our country great and the values that our party embodied when we were the leading party in America; that we were for opportunity for everybody, we were for responsibility from everybody, and we thought we had to build an American community of everybody; and that this country wouldn't work if we couldn't do those three things; and that, basically, the debate which was going on in the early nineties in this country, I thought, was largely irrelevant to the real problems of real people when we had unemployment high, crime rising, welfare rising, incomes diverging, the country showing uncertainty around the world, and great difficulties.

On economic policy it seemed to me that we had a lot of people talking about how terrible

Government spending was, while they quadrupled the debt of the country, which I though was a pretty neat trick. It seemed to me that what we had to do was to close the gap between the two positions and say, "We can't stop investing in our people, we can't stop investing in education and science and technology and all this research, because that's the future of the country, but we've got to do it in a way that eliminates this deficit." And when I said, I think we ought to invest more and still cut the deficit, and that if we cut out unnecessary programs and reduce the size of Government, we could do that; if we eliminated unnecessary inflation in some of our programs, we could do that, a lot of people thought we were nuts. But actually, it turned out we were right.

On education, I said, I'm all for spending more money on education, but we also have to lift the standards of excellence and accountability. Today I came to New Orleans in part to speak to the American Federation of Teachers, and probably more than any other single educational organization over the last 15 years, they have constantly echoed that theme. And they deserve a lot of credit from the American people for always saying, "Hey, we want to be held accountable, and if we're not good at what we do, we shouldn't be in the classroom, and we're not afraid of accountability, but we expect you to invest in our children and our future."

On matters of the environment, it always seemed to me that if we got into a position where we had to choose between preserving our environment and growing our economy, we were going to be defeated before we started, because in the end, if we use up our environment, we won't have an economy, and if we have to ask people to give up their right to make a living, then there won't be any support for a clean environment. So we said our environmental policy is going to be designed to improve the environment as we grow the economy.

On crime, it seemed to me that the further away you got from the streets where crime occurred, the more politicians, despairing that they could do anything, talked tough but did nothing. So I said, yes, we ought to punish people more if they deserve it. But we also ought to give local law enforcement officials the tools they need to prevent crime in the first place and give these kids something they can do to stay out of trouble in the first place.

On welfare, the debate in Washington in 1992, before I showed up, seemed to be between those who said we ought to make every able-bodied person work, and if they can't take care of their kids, that's just tough; and those who said there's no way to do that, so we just have to keep the same old system, as bad as it is. I thought that was a foolish choice.

So we said, the position ought to be every able-bodied person should work, but we should never forget that everyone's job, most important job—everyone's most important job, even the President, if you have a child, is being a good parent. So we can't make people sacrifice their children. So we're going to make people work, but we're going to give them child care and the support their children need for medical care so you can be a good parent and a good worker. That's what all of us want to do. That's what we should want poor people to do as well.

I haven't won all my debates in the Democratic Party. Mr. Jefferson and I are still fighting the debate on trade, because some people still believe that if you expand trade, well, inevitably you will empower people who will despoil the global economy and weaken workers around the world. It seems to me that when countries get richer, they're more likely to lift the conditions of their workers, and wealthy countries do better by the environment than poor countries do. So my belief is we can expand trade and improve the conditions of people around the world.

And I want to thank Bill Jefferson for sticking up for that position. I know that's good for the Port of New Orleans. The truth is it's good for the rest of America, because we're only 4 percent of the world's population, we have 20 percent of the world's income; if we want to keep it—the developing world is growing at 3 times the rate of the already developed countries. You don't have to be a mathematical genius to figure out that if you want to keep your income, we 4 percent have to sell something to the other 96 percent. And we've got a real interest in their growing.

Therefore, Bill Jefferson's interest in Africa, his support of the Africa trade bill, his support of our outreach to the Caribbean and to Latin America, these things are very, very important. And the support that he and Mary and others have given to our attempt to get some funds into the revitalization of the Asian economies is profoundly important. If you want the American economy to keep growing, then please support our efforts to get growth back in Asia. That is the only way for us to continue to grow over the long run.

So anyway, we said, "These are our new ideas." And a lot of people said, "Oh, they don't believe in anything, because they're not completely liberal; they're not completely conservative." That's the last refuge of a scoundrel, you know, if you have to think, just accuse the other people of having no conscience, no convictions. And I say, yes, we have very strong convictions, but we have new ideas. Only foolish people stay with yesterday's ideas in today's circumstances facing a different tomorrow.

And so we have vigorously pursued those ideas in the Democratic Party, not abandoning our principles but building on our bedrock principles to meet the needs of America in the 21st century. And while the American people deserve most of the credit for any good thing that happens, there is definitely a connection between the policies we have followed and the results which have ensued.

We have the lowest crime rate in 25 years, the lowest unemployment rate in 28 years, the smallest percentage of people on welfare in 29 years. We're going to have the first balanced budget and surplus in 29 years. We've got the lowest inflation in 32 years, the highest home-ownership in history. And by the way, under a Democratic administration, the Federal Government is the smallest it's been in 35 years. This is working. This is working.

More to the point, one big reason that you ought to elect Marjorie and that what you're doing for the Democratic Party is important is because we are committed to making the tough decisions over the long run, to putting the progress of the country ahead of short-term partisan advantage. I'll just give you a few examples.

We've got to reform the Social Security and Medicare system so they'll be there for the baby boomers under circumstances that don't bankrupt our children and their ability to raise our grandchildren. We have to do it now. We are committed to doing that in a way that is fair and balanced to all generations.

We have got to continue working until we can say with a straight face, yes, we've had the best college education in the world for a long time; now we've got the best elementary and secondary education for all of our people.

We have got to continue to come to grips with the fact that we have more and more Americans in managed care. And that's a good thing if you're getting rid of waste in the system, but it's a terrible thing if people can't have emergency room care when they need it, can't have specialists when they need it, when you have literally disastrous, heart-breaking circumstances, which is why we have so many Republicans all across America and the American Medical Association and a lot of other people supporting the Democratic Party's position for a Patients' Bill of Rights that will protect the health care interests of all of our people.

Well, you get the idea. We're trying very hard to pass legislation to protect children from the dangers of tobacco. We don't want to bankrupt the tobacco companies; we want to get them out of the business of marketing tobacco to our children. And it's a profoundly important thing.

And we're prepared to make tough decisions, to make principled decisions, to put the progress of the country ahead of the partisan divide. We have to do this. And so I ask all of you to renew your dedication; I thank you. But remember, what makes a successful country in times like this is not all that different from what makes a successful company or community or family endeavor. If you look at the whole history of America, at all dynamic change eras, when things were really up in the air, as they are now, we have grown stronger and stronger and stronger, and we're now the longest lasting democracy in history, because we have done what the Founding Fathers told us to do.

They set up this very flexible system, rooted in bedrock values, that said, in every age and time, you must first of all deepen freedom and extend it to all law-abiding people. Secondly, you must seek to widen the circle of opportunity, what they called the pursuit of happiness. Thirdly, you must recognize that you cannot do this alone, and this is maybe the significant difference between the two parties today. And I say that, having eliminated more Government programs, more Government regulations, and reduced the size of the Government more than any Republican President in the last 50 years. Still, remember what the Founders said: We are forming this Government because alone, we cannot protect, pursue, and enhance life, liberty, and happiness. That's why we got together, because in the nature of things, we can't do all these things all by ourselves.

Maybe the most important thing we've done is to try to redefine the role of Government. The old debate was Government's the problem versus Government's the solution. Our position is Government is neither. Government is a glue that binds us together. And the job of Government on the edge of the 21st century is to create the conditions and give people the tools to make the most of their own lives; to solve their problems in their individual lives, their family lives, their community lives, their business lives; to be good for the American people as stewards; and to be a leading force in the world for peace and freedom and prosperity.

And so finally, I would say that the third mission is, after freedom and opportunity, is that we are constantly forced to redefine our National Union. And that is the difference, the critical difference between the two parties today. I do not believe that we can be what we need to be unless we still believe that our eternal mission is what they said it was 220 years ago: to form a more perfect Union. Nobody—you won't find anybody in America that likes our diversity anymore than I do. I love our racial diversity. I love our ethnic diversity. I love our religious diversity. I love our cultural diversity.

That's why I love to come to New Orleans, right?

But what is important is—and what makes it possible to enjoy all that is that underneath it all, at the bedrock, we are bound together by common values and a common understanding that we are going into tomorrow together. And the only way we can make the most of this phenomenal opportunity we have is to do it.

So I ask you to go and impart that message to your friends and neighbors. Help us to strengthen our party. Help us to continue to move forward. Help us to get the message to Washington, "The American people want progress over partisanship," and the Democratic Party—far more important, the American people—will go strong into that new century.

Thank you, and God bless you.

NOTE: The President spoke at 7:24 p.m. at Emeril's Restaurant. In his remarks, he referred to Sheriff Harry Lee of Jefferson Parish; Leonard Barrack, national finance chair, Democratic National Committee; Representative William Jefferson's wife, Andrea; Mayor Marc H. Morial of New Orleans; Ray Reggie, event coordinator; and Marjorie McKeithen, candidate for Louisiana's Sixth Congressional District.

Remarks Announcing New Nursing Home Regulations and an Exchange With Reporters
July 21, 1998

The President. Thank you, Secretary Shalala, and Nancy-Ann Min DeParle, and the advocates who are here. I wish your mother were here, Secretary Shalala. I have met her, and even a skeptical press corps would believe your account of her in full if they could see her.

The duty we owe to our parents is one of the most sacred duties we, as Americans, owe to each other. Nowhere is that duty more important than when a family makes the choice to move a parent into a nursing home. When that time comes, all of us need to know that all our parents will be well cared for.

Today, more than 1.6 million Americans live in more than 16,000 nursing homes nationwide. When the baby boom generation moves into retirement, the number will rise even higher.

By 2030, the number of Americans over the age of 85 will double, making compassionate quality nursing home care even more important.

At their best, nursing homes can be a Godsend for older Americans and their families, providing a safe haven in times of need. But at their worst, they can actually endanger their residents, subjecting them to the worst kinds of abuse and neglect. For nearly 6 years, as Secretary Shalala said, we've worked hard to give our most vulnerable citizens the security and health services they need to live in peace and safety.

I am committed to honoring the great social compact between the generations, first, let me say, by reserving every penny of the budget surplus until we save Social Security first. The historic balanced budget I signed last summer preserves the Medicare Trust Fund into the 21st century. We've taken action to root out Medicare fraud and abuse, saving taxpayers over $20 billion.

Finally, we're fighting to meet the challenge of our changing health system by enacting a Patients' Bill of Rights, to include access to specialists and the right to appeal health care decisions. I have extended those rights already to Medicare beneficiaries; they should be the rights of every American.

One of the most important ways we can help our senior citizens is by improving the quality of care in our nursing homes. In 1995, when Congress tried to eliminate Federal assurances of nursing home quality, I said no. It was the right thing to do. That same year, we put into place tough regulations to crack down on abuse and neglect in our nursing homes. Since then, we have made real progress, as Secretary Shalala said, stepping up onsite inspections and helping nursing homes to find and fix problems.

As the HCFA report Secretary Shalala talked about shows all too clearly, however, the job is far from over. When people living in nursing homes have as much fear from dehydration and poor nutrition as they do from the diseases of old age, when families must worry as much about a loved one in a nursing home as one living alone, then we are failing our parents, and we must do more.

Today I'm acting within my power as President to crack down on unsafe nursing homes. Effective immediately, HCFA will require States to step up investigations of nursing homes, making onsite inspections more frequent and less predictable, so there is no time to hide neglect and abuse. Whenever we find evidence that a nursing home is failing to provide its residents with proper care or even mistreating them, we will fine that facility on the spot. And if State enforcement agencies don't do enough to monitor nursing home quality, we will cut off their contracts and find someone else who will do the job right.

I'll continue to do everything I can to fight nursing home abuse and neglect and to give more options to elderly, disabled, and chronically ill Americans who choose to stay at home. But Congress also must act. This week I am proposing comprehensive legislation to protect older Americans with a national registry to track nursing home employees down known to abuse nursing home residents, and criminal background checks to keep potentially abusive employees from being hired in the first place. I ask the Congress to put progress ahead of partisanship on this issue and pass this legislation to improve our Nation's nursing homes this year.

Choosing to move a parent or a loved one into a nursing home is one of life's most difficult decisions. But with these steps we can at least give families a greater sense of security in knowing we are doing everything we possibly can to make our nursing homes safe and secure.

Thank you very much.

Q. Do you think the Congress would be against the registry, per se?

The President. No, I have no reason to believe they would be, and I hope they would pass it.

Q. What do you mean by putting partisanship aside?

The President. Well, we haven't had a lot of bills coming out of Congress this year, but I hope very much that they will pass this. I don't believe—not since 1995, when there was an attempt to strip the Federal authority standards, has there been a serious move on this issue. And I believe there are a lot of Republicans, as well as Democrats, in Congress who will support this. So I'm quite hopeful that it will pass.

Patients' Bill of Rights

Q. How about the Patients' Bill of Rights; do you think you're going to get that?

The President. Well, I don't know. That's up to them. We have to have some significant amount of Republican support to get a strong bill. We have to have 60 votes to break a filibuster in the Senate and, obviously, a majority in the House, sufficient to actually make sure the bill could come to a vote. But we're still working on it, and it's terribly important.

Everywhere I go in the country—you know, I was just home last weekend, and I was stunned at the number of people who came up to me and just started talking about it and talking about their own experiences and how important they thought it was. So I'm very hopeful we'll get it.

Q. How can you parlay that, then, into a real public response?

The President. Well, I'm working at it. We've had a lot of events on the Patients' Bill of Rights. I'm trying to get the public involved in this, trying to get them to express their opinions to their Members of Congress, and I will continue to do so.

Testimony of Secret Service Agents

Q. I wanted to ask you about another issue, sir. Now that the Secret Service agents have testified, are you concerned about what they might be saying, one; and, two, do you find yourself holding them more at arm's length, sir?

The President. The Secret Service has made its own decisions about what to say and how to do it, based on their professional sense of responsibility, and I'm not going to get into this. I've refused to comment on it so far, and I'm going to continue to refuse to comment.

Libya and the 1988 Bombing of Pan Am 103

Q. Mr. President, your administration is making a new push to end the standoff with Libya over the Lockerbie bombing, including possibly holding a trial in a neutral country, under U.S. or Scottish jurisdiction. Are you optimistic that this climate might help, and what has brought on this new push?

The President. Well, we have always said that our first goal was to bring the perpetrators of Pan Am 103 murders to justice. That's our first purpose. And since I got here, we've been looking for ways to do that. We have had conversations with representatives of the British Government as well. We've always said we thought that there had to be a trial under American or Scottish law. There may be some possibility of standing up a Scottish court in another country, but there are lots of difficulties with it as well, apparently.

All I can tell you is that it's one of the things that we have explored with a view toward accelerating the day—it's been a long time now; it's been a lot of years since that terrible day when Pan Am 103 crashed over Lockerbie. And we're looking at it, but I don't know that it can be done. Our people have spent a lot of time on it. We've talked to the British at great length about it. We're trying to find some way that

has real integrity, that will work. But there are all kinds of practical difficulties that I'm sure our folks can explain. I don't know if we can do it, but we're working on it.

Q. What brought it up now? I mean, what—all of a sudden, after so many years?

The President. I don't know why it is just now coming into the press. But it's not just being brought up now. We have literally been working for years; I have personally been engaged in this for years, trying to find a way to get the suspects out of Libya, into a court where we thought an honest and fair and adequate trial could occur.

And in a case like this, like every other case, as the years go by, you run more and more chances that something will happen to the evidence that is available, to any witnesses that might be available. So we've had a sense of urgency about this for some time. But my guess is that it has come to public light because a significant number of conversations have had to be held between the American and the British authorities and between others in potential third-party venues, like The Netherlands, and I know there's been some discussion of that. But it has not been resolved yet.

Thank you.

Q. Is there any indication that the Libyans might go along, sir?

Retracted CNN Report on Use of Nerve Gas in Vietnam

Q. Sir, can you comment on CNN's nerve gas report, that the Pentagon—[*inaudible*]—today?

The President. All I know is what Secretary Cohen has said to you, to the public, and to me, which is that their view is that it did not occur.

Thank you all very much.

NOTE: The President spoke at 3:16 p.m. in the Oval Office at the White House. In his remarks, he referred to Health and Human Services Secretary Donna E. Shalala's mother, Edna Shalala.

Statement on Signing Legislation on Funding for the Disposition of Depleted Uranium Hexafluoride
July 21, 1998

Today I have signed into law S. 2316, a bill designed to help ensure that certain funds of the United States Enrichment Corporation will be dedicated to the disposition of depleted uranium hexafluoride. I strongly support this bill, but note that by virtue of the Recommendations Clause of the Constitution, Article II, section 3, the Congress may not require the President to recommend legislation to the Congress. Therefore, to the extent the bill would infringe upon my discretion to determine whether to recommend legislation to the Congress, I must treat it as hortatory. In this case, however, I believe that the development of proposed legislation by the Secretary of Energy furthers important and valuable objectives, and I intend to instruct the Secretary to develop proposed legislation for inclusion in my budget request for fiscal year 2000.

WILLIAM J. CLINTON

The White House,
July 21, 1998.

NOTE: S. 2316, approved July 21, was assigned Public Law No. 105–204.

Message to the House of Representatives Returning Without Approval Education Savings Legislation
July 21, 1998

To the House of Representatives:

I am returning herewith without my approval H.R. 2646, the "Education Savings and School Excellence Act of 1998."

As I have said before, we must prepare our children for the 21st century by providing them with the best education in the world. To help meet this goal, I have sent the Congress a comprehensive agenda for strengthening our public schools, which enroll almost 90 percent of our students. My plan calls for raising standards, strengthening accountability, and promoting charter schools and other forms of public school choice. It calls for reducing class size in the early grades, so our students get a solid foundation in the basic skills, modernizing our schools for the 21st century, and linking them with the Internet. And we must strengthen teaching and provide students who need additional help with tutoring, mentoring, and after-school programs. We must take these steps now.

By sending me this bill, the Congress has instead chosen to weaken public education and shortchange our children. The modifications to the Education IRAs that the bill would authorize are bad education policy and bad tax policy. The bill would divert limited Federal resources away from public schools by spending more than $3 billion on tax benefits that would do virtually nothing for average families and would disproportionately benefit the most affluent families. More than 70 percent of the benefits would flow to families in the top 20 percent of income distribution, and families struggling to make ends meet would never see a penny of the benefits. Moreover, the bill would not create a meaningful incentive for families to increase their savings for educational purposes; it would instead reward families, particularly those with substantial incomes, for what they already do.

The way to improve education for all our children is to increase standards, accountability, and choice within the public schools. Just as we have an obligation to repair our Nation's roads and bridges and invest in the infrastructure of our transportation system, we also have an obligation to invest in the infrastructure needs of our public schools. I urge the Congress to meet that obligation and to send me instead the legislation I have proposed to reduce class size; improve the quality of teaching; modernize our schools; end social promotions; raise academic standards;

and hold school districts, schools, and staff accountable for results.

WILLIAM J. CLINTON

The White House,

July 21, 1998.

Message to the Congress Reporting on the National Emergency With Respect to Terrorists Who Threaten To Disrupt the Middle East Peace Process
July 21, 1998

To the Congress of the United States:

I hereby report to the Congress on the developments concerning the national emergency with respect to terrorists who threaten to disrupt the Middle East peace process that was declared in Executive Order 12947 of January 23, 1995. This report is submitted pursuant to section 401(c) of the National Emergencies Act, 50 U.S.C. 1641(c), and section 204(c) of the International Emergency Economic Powers Act (IEEPA), 50 U.S.C. 1703(c).

1. On January 23, 1995, I signed Executive Order 12947, "Prohibiting Transactions with Terrorists Who Threaten To Disrupt the Middle East Peace Process" (the "Order") (60 *Fed. Reg.* 5079, January 25, 1995). The Order blocks all property subject to U.S. jurisdiction in which there is any interest of 12 terrorist organizations that threaten the Middle East peace process as identified in an Annex to the Order. The Order also blocks the property and interests in property subject to U.S. jurisdiction of persons designated by the Secretary of State, in coordination with the Secretary of the Treasury and the Attorney General, who are found (1) to have committed, or to pose a significant risk of committing, acts of violence that have the purpose or effect of disrupting the Middle East peace process, or (2) to assist in, sponsor, or provide financial, material, or technological support for, or services in support of, such acts of violence. In addition, the Order blocks all property and interests in property subject to U.S. jurisdiction in which there is any interest of persons determined by the Secretary of the Treasury, in coordination with the Secretary of State and the Attorney General, to be owned or controlled by, or to act for or on behalf of, any other person designated pursuant to the Order (collec-

tively "Specially Designated Terrorists" or "SDTs").

The Order further prohibits any transaction or dealing by a United States person or within the United States in property or interests in property of SDTs, including the making or receiving of any contribution of funds, goods, or services to or for the benefit of such persons. This prohibition includes donations that are intended to relieve human suffering.

Designations of persons blocked pursuant to the Order are effective upon the date of determination by the Secretary of State or her delegate, or the Director of the Office of Foreign Assets Control (OFAC) acting under authority delegated by the Secretary of the Treasury. Public notice of blocking is effective upon the date of filing with the *Federal Register*, or upon prior actual notice.

Because terrorist activities continue to threaten the Middle East peace process and vital interests of the United States in the Middle East, on January 21, 1998, I continued for another year the national emergency declared on January 23, 1995, and the measures that took effect on January 24, 1995, to deal with that emergency. This action was taken in accordance with section 202(d) of the National Emergencies Act (50 U.S.C. 1622(d)).

2. On January 25, 1995, the Department of the Treasury issued a notice listing persons blocked pursuant to Executive Order 12947 who have been designated by the President as terrorist organizations threatening the Middle East peace process or who have been found to be owned or controlled by, or to be acting for or on behalf of, these terrorist organizations (60 *Fed. Reg.* 5084, January 25, 1995). The notice identified 31 entities that act for or on behalf of the 12 Middle East terrorist organizations

listed in the Annex to Executive Order 12947, as well as 18 individuals who are leaders or representatives of these groups. In addition, the notice provided 9 name variations or pseudonyms used by the 18 individuals identified. The list identifies blocked persons who have been found to have committed, or to pose a significant risk of committing acts of violence that have the purpose or effect of disrupting the Middle East peace process or to have assisted in, sponsored, or provided financial, material or technological support for, or services in support of, such acts of violence, or are owned or controlled by, or act for or on behalf of other blocked persons. The Department of the Treasury issued three additional notices adding the names of three individuals, as well as their pseudonyms, to the List of SDTs (60 *Fed. Reg.* 41152, August 11, 1995; 60 *Fed. Reg.* 44932, August 29, 1995; and 60 *Fed. Reg.* 58435, November 27, 1995).

3. On February 2, 1996, OFAC issued the Terrorism Sanctions Regulations (the "TSRs" or the "Regulations") (61 *Fed. Reg.* 3805, February 2, 1996). The TSRs implement the President's declaration of a national emergency and imposition of sanctions against certain persons whose acts of violence have the purpose or effect of disrupting the Middle East peace process. There have been no amendments to the TSRs, 31 C.F.R. Part 595, administered by the Office of Foreign Assets Control of the Department of the Treasury, since my report of January 28, 1998.

4. Since January 25, 1995, OFAC has issued six licenses pursuant to the Regulations. These licenses authorize payment of legal expenses and the disbursement of funds for normal expenditures for the maintenance of family members, the employment and payment of salary and educational expenses, payment for secure storage of tangible assets, and payment of certain administrative transactions, to or for individuals designated pursuant to Executive Order 12947.

5. The expenses incurred by the Federal Government in the 6-month period from January 23 through July 22, 1998, that are directly attributable to the exercise of powers and authorities conferred by the declaration of the national emergency with respect to organizations that disrupt the Middle East peace process, are estimated at approximately $165,000. These data do not reflect certain costs of operations by the intelligence and law enforcement communities.

6. Executive Order 12947 provides this Administration with a tool for combating fundraising in this country on behalf of organizations that use terror to undermine the Middle East peace process. The Order makes it harder for such groups to finance these criminal activities by cutting off their access to sources of support in the United States and to U.S. financial facilities. It is also intended to reach charitable contributions to designated organizations and individuals to preclude diversion of such donations to terrorist activities.

Executive Order 12947 demonstrates the determination of the United States to confront and combat those who would seek to destroy the Middle East peace process, and our commitment to the global fight against terrorism. I shall continue to exercise the powers at my disposal to apply economic sanctions against extremists seeking to destroy the hopes of peaceful coexistence between Arabs and Israelis as long as these measures are appropriate, and will continue to report periodically to the Congress on significant developments pursuant to 50 U.S.C. 1703(c).

WILLIAM J. CLINTON

The White House,
July 21, 1998.

Remarks on Crime Prevention Efforts
July 22, 1998

Thank you very much. If I had any sense at all, I would not say a word. [*Laughter*] I've got to tell you, before I came over here, my staff all gathered very solemnly in the Oval Office, and they said, "Now, you know, there's going to be a lot of preachers there today, and Reverend Anthony said he was going to be moved by the spirit. You stick to the text. We don't want you to get too moved by the spirit." [*Laughter*] I don't know if I can honor that.

Death of Alan B. Shepard, Jr.

Let me say, before I begin—I was just handed a note; I think it's appropriate since we have so many ministers here—that one of our greatest astronauts, Alan Shepard, has just passed away. Those of us who are old enough to remember the first space flights will always remember what an impression he made on us and on the world. And so I would like to express the gratitude of our Nation and to say that our thoughts and prayers are with his family.

Crime Prevention Efforts

Let me begin by thanking all the people who are here, Eric Holder and Ray Fisher , all the people at the Justice Department who have done such a good job. Commissioner Evans, it's good to see you again, and I never get tired of hearing the story of what Boston has done. Reverend Anthony, thank you for your wonderful statement and the power of your example. I thank Congressmen Cummings and Cardin, who are here from Maryland, and two Senators who have supported this program very strongly and were not able to come at the last minute: I want to acknowledge Senator Joe Biden and Senator Carol Moseley-Braun.

I thank Mayor Alan Styles from Salinas, California; Mayor James Garner from Hempstead, New York; Mayor Marion Barry from Washington; Mayor Kurt Schmoke from Baltimore; and Mayor and Reverend Emanuel Cleaver from Kansas City, Missouri, for being here. The chief of police of Washington, DC, Charles Ramsey, is here; Reuben Greenberg from Charleston, South Carolina; Michelle Mitchell from Richmond. There are children here from Brown Junior High School and from Baltimore and from Philadelphia. We welcome you all.

This is really about what we can do together to save our children and to strengthen our country's future. For all the good things that are happening in America—unemployment, inflation, crime, welfare the lowest in somewhere between 25 and 32 years, depending on the statistic—we have to understand that there are still too many of our children who are left out and left behind and that, in order to honor our solemn responsibilities as citizens and our fundamental moral duties as human beings, we have to do a better job.

I am gratified that crime is at a 25-year low. Surely, the improving economy had something

to do with it. But I am persuaded that the lion's share of credit goes to people—those nameless people Reverend Anthony spoke about, who wear uniforms and who work in churches and other religious institutions, who work in schools and work on streets, and who talk to their kids at home at night. What is working in America is a community-based, prevention-oriented, broad-based partnership to try to bring crime down and bring out kids back. And the faith community has an important role to play.

I noted—one of the things that I remembered about the first time I went to Boston and met with the mayor's youth council is it was being run by a Roman Catholic nun. Everybody showed up; they were on time—*[laughter]*—it ran like clockwork; it was great—*[laughter]*—including me. We all did our part.

And I think it is important to say that this community-based, prevention-oriented, broad-based partnership represented by the children and the adults here, including the members of the faith community, that it is working. And what we want to do today is to see it work everywhere in America.

You heard Commissioner Evans say that in Boston, police, prosecutors, principals, pastors, they all got together around the table. They called on everybody to take responsibility to stop gangs and guns and drugs and to change attitudes—above all, to change attitudes: how people look at themselves, how they look at other people, whether they treat them with respect. And they recognized that the only strategy that will work in the long run is one that keeps our children out of trouble in the first place.

I can't help noting that I've had the opportunity to spend quite a bit of time in the city of Chicago. You all clapped when the mention was made of our commitment to before- and after-school programs. There are now over 40,000 children, I believe, that get three square meals a day in the Chicago school system; they stay through supper. And the summer school is now the sixth largest school district in the United States, and a lot of the kids have to go because they don't make good enough grades during the year. But because it's a positive thing, the community groups, the parents groups, everybody supports it. It's a way of building a good future for our children.

So that's what we're here to celebrate and to emphasize that there is a critical, fundamental role for the faith community in teaching our children a sense of right and wrong and self-discipline and respect. Boston's pastors and faith communities took the lead. Often, they are the most stable institutions left in unstable neighborhoods. I think it is important that these mentors saw in each child a cause and not just a case file; a future, not just a present full of problems.

When young people learn to turn to values, then they turn away from gangs. That was the message of what Reverend Anthony said more eloquently than I could. When they learn the basic rules of right and wrong, then they can reject the rules of the street. If it's true in Boston, if it's true in Washington, if it's true anywhere, it can be true everywhere. And that is what we're here about. If something can happen somewhere, it is our duty to make sure it happens everywhere.

Indeed, that has been the whole philosophy behind this administration's anticrime efforts. When I was Governor, I worked a lot on these issues at home. Very often, I would work with religious leaders—Christian leaders, Jewish leaders; in my State, black Muslims were often quite active in community-based efforts to save our children. But the thing that struck me was that there was never a system. And the thing that Boston has done so well is that they have created a system within which everybody has a role to play where they can be most effective. And it has worked.

Last year researchers at Harvard found that urban neighborhoods with a strong sense of community and shared values had much, much lower crime rates than those without it—big surprise. But when you hear people in my position or elected officials talking about crime, how often do you hear them talk about that? You get more emotion on the meter readers if you give some rough, tough speech about jails and punishment. Well, we have to have jails, and people who do the wrong things have to be punished. But we will never jail our way out of America's problems, and you know that.

I want to thank exhibit A here for coming—if I could call him that—Reverend Eugene Rivers, who's sitting behind me. I thank him for being here. He has gotten to know some of Boston's most troubled children, welcoming them to his parish, Baker House; offering counseling, recreation, and an occasional pizza party; introducing children who have known nothing but chaos at home to the serenity of prayer.

He mediates fights, visits homes, shows up at school when they get in trouble. He has been there for his kids, making them understand that God cares about each and every one of them and he cares whether they do well. He cares whether they get an A or an F on a test, whether they get in a fight or get a citation for doing good at school. They will be praised when they succeed, disciplined when they fail.

Two of his children are with him today: Kenyatta Moon and Tony Barry. Growing up hasn't been easy for either of them. But with Reverend Rivers' help, they have stayed on track. Tony is taking college prep courses; Kenyatta will begin college this fall. And we congratulate you.

You know, we have worked very hard to open the doors of college to all Americans, to give scholarships and tax credits, and to make sure, in effect, we can make 2 years of college virtually free to nearly everyone in this country. But you still have to get in. And this is very, very important, what is being done. I know there are many more just like Reverend Rivers and just like these young people, doing good things across this country, more like our wonderful speaker, who gave me such a powerful introduction. What we have to do is to give all of them the tools they need to succeed.

That is what we're here to do today. Today I am glad and proud to announce that we will be making new value-based violence prevention grants to 16 communities across our country, to help law enforcement, schools, businesses, and faith communities, together, work to prevent truancy, mentor, teach values, and offer children positive alternatives to gangs and drugs.

Congress, too, must act because 16 is not enough. In the juvenile justice bill, which I modeled in large measure on the Boston success story, there are funds for more of these kinds of programs. We need these funds. We need more funds for before- and after-school programs, for the summer school programs, for the community-based programs. We need these funds. Our role here in Washington on this is to give people the tools and to clear away the obstacles necessary to have more success stories.

I can't thank the mayors and the police chiefs who are here enough for the examples that they have set in their own communities.

Carl Sandburg once said that a baby is God's opinion that the world should go on. Well, when we lose our children, we are thwarting the opinion of God. We are blessed with our children. They will be America in the 21st century. What America will be depends upon what we do to help them become all they can be. That depends upon us. It is our responsibility.

I can't tell you how moved I am by all the stories I have read, all the examples I have seen, all the work that has been done by the people that are in this room and the people they represent all across America. Some of them have been out there for years and years and years. But now, they have found a way to work together that will have dramatic, profound, and permanent success. We owe it to them to help them.

We're taking a big first step today, and if Congress will give me the funds, we'll put the welfare of the American people first. Even in an election year, let's not let partisanship get in the way of this critical mission. We will see these stories sweep across this country, and we'll have a lot more children to celebrate.

Thank you, and God bless you.

NOTE: The President spoke at 10:55 a.m. in Room 450 of the Old Executive Office Building. In his remarks, he referred to Rev. Lewis M. Anthony, senior pastor, Metropolitan Wesley AME Zion Church, Washington, DC, who introduced the President; Paul Evans, Boston police commissioner; Reuben Greenberg, police chief, Charleston, SC; Michelle B. Mitchell, sheriff, Richmond, VA; and Rev. Eugene F. Rivers III, codirector, National Ten Point Leadership Foundation.

Remarks on Signing the Internal Revenue Service Restructuring and Reform Act of 1998
July 22, 1998

Death of Alan B. Shepard, Jr.

Thank you very much. Ladies and gentlemen, before I make my statement, I would like to amplify a little bit on the remarks I made earlier this morning on the death of Alan Shepard.

He is one of the great heroes of modern America: our first astronaut; our first American in space. None of us who were alive then will ever forget him sitting so calmly in *Freedom 7*, atop a slender and sometimes unreliable Mercury Redstone rocket. As President Kennedy observed at the time, America chose to make this first risky launch in full view of the world, and our entire Nation, in his words, "which risked much, gained much."

Alan Shepard understood the odds. He faced them bravely, and he led our country and all humanity beyond the bounds of our planet, across a truly new frontier, into the new era of space exploration.

A decade later, in 1971, Commander Shepard fought his way back from a debilitating ear infection to become the commander of *Apollo 14* and the fifth person to walk on the Moon. On behalf of myself and Mr. Bowles, I can't help noting that there, on the Moon, he lived every golfer's dream—[*laughter*]—taking his six iron and hitting the ball, in his words, "for miles and miles." [*Laughter*]

Alan Shepard truly had the right stuff. His service will always loom large in America's history. I extend to his wife, Louise, his family, and his colleagues in the Navy and at NASA the thanks of a grateful Nation and our thoughts and prayers.

Internal Revenue Service

Now, I'd like to join Secretary Rubin in thanking Commissioner Rossotti, the Vice President, and you, Mr. Secretary, for what you have done. But I especially want to acknowledge the presence of all the Members of Congress here. And in particular, let me thank Senator Kerrey and Congressman Portman, Senator Roth, Senator Moynihan, Senator Grassley, Congressman Archer, Congressman Rangel, Congressman Cardin for their leading work that makes it possible for me to sign into law today the Internal Revenue Service Restructuring and Reform Act. The bill is a culmination of the commitment and hard work of many people but especially those whom I have just mentioned.

We've all worked hard to give the American people an IRS that reflects America's values and respects America's taxpayers. Two years ago I was proud to sign into law a Taxpayer Bill of Rights—again, passed by an overwhelming bipartisan majority of the Congress—that has helped to make the IRS fairer and more responsive. Under the leadership of the Vice President and Secretary Rubin, we've upgraded customer service at the IRS, appointing Charles Rossotti, a seasoned private sector CEO, to reshape the agency; expanding office hours and phone hours; making it easier to file taxes over the telephone or by computer. We've created problem-solving days where taxpayers can work face-to-face with IRS customer service representatives.

For the first time this year, IRS helplines were open for the full 24 hours preceding the final filing deadline, April 15th. And in 1999, they will be open 24 hours a day, 7 days a week, all year long. This year 40 million more callers heard a human voice, not a busy signal, when they called an IRS helpline. Nearly 25 million taxpayers took advantage of our new high-tech filing options. That's a 25 percent increase from the previous year.

Our streamlined IRS webpage had nearly half a billion hits this year. All this has meant quicker refunds, less paperwork, and fewer hassles for American taxpayers.

But clearly, there is more to do to build an IRS for the 21st century. This bill takes important steps in that direction. It will help the IRS to serve taxpayers as well as the best private companies serve their customers, building on efforts to offer simple high-tech options for filing taxes and making tax forms more easily available over the Internet.

As Secretary Rubin has said, it expands taxpayer rights, extending refund periods, protecting innocent spouses, cutting penalties in half for 2½ million taxpayers who are paying what they owe on installment plans. In all these ways, the bill will give the American people an IRS they deserve.

Again, let me thank the Congress for helping the IRS to meet the challenge of serving taxpayers by giving it the time it needs also to meet the challenge of the year 2000 computer conversion. I call on the Congress to fully fund our year 2000 effort to allow all Federal agencies to respond flexibly to unforeseen difficulties that are sure to arise.

This bill shows what we can do when we work together, when we put the progress of America ahead of our partisan concerns, when we put our people over politics. That is how we have balanced the budget for the first time in 30 years while cutting taxes, expanding trade, and investing in our people. It is how I believe we can continue to make the Tax Code fairer for our people.

I have asked Congress to provide targeted tax relief for American families for child care, to expand pensions, to spur school construction, to protect our environment. In the context of comprehensive legislation to protect our children from tobacco, I have supported the effort to address the marriage penalty by cutting taxes for American families.

Every one of these tax cuts is prudent, bipartisan, and fully paid for. For 29 years, our country ran up large deficits, quadrupling our debt in the 12 years before I became President. It caused us to fall behind in the global economy; it caused our incomes to stagnate. Now we're on the verge of achieving our first balanced budget and our first surplus in a generation, and our economy is the envy of the world.

Fiscal responsibility has driven this economic expansion. A return to irresponsibility would put that prosperity at risk. After 29 years, it seems to me, it's worth taking one year to address the challenge of fixing the Social Security system before we start spending the surplus on tax cuts or new spending programs, however worthy they might be.

The American people expect us to have the good sense to rack up the surplus before we spend it and to save Social Security first. I know there are many people who think we should spend the surplus now and spend hundreds of billions of dollars on tax cuts before we have the bipartisan plan to save Social Security. I think it's the wrong course for America, in no small measure because we haven't fixed the price tag for saving Social Security and because, as we all know, we can't really predict with any absolute certainty what will happen 10 or 15 years from now.

I believe we should tell our children and our grandchildren that we think enough of them and their future that we're going to resist spending a penny of the surplus on things that I would very much like to spend it on—or you would—until we have met our basic obligation to our future, passing a bipartisan plan to save Social Security, which I am convinced the Congress will do early next year. I do not intend to waver from my commitment to future generations, and I hope the rest of us will do the same.

Now it is my honor to sign into law the Internal Revenue Service Restructuring and Reform Act. I would like to ask all the Members of Congress to come up here and join me on the stage. Thank you very much.

NOTE: The President spoke at 1:40 p.m. in the East Room at the White House. H.R. 2676, approved July 22, was assigned Public Law No. 105–206.

Message to the Congress Designating Provisions of the Internal Revenue Service Restructuring and Reform Act of 1998 as an Emergency Requirement
July 22, 1998

To the Congress of the United States:

Pursuant to section 3309(c) of the Internal Revenue Service Restructuring and Reform Act of 1998, I hereby designate the provisions of subsections (a) and (b) of section 3309 of such Act as an emergency requirement pursuant to section 252(e) of the Balanced Budget and Emergency Deficit Control Act of 1985, as amended.

WILLIAM J. CLINTON

The White House,
July 22, 1998.

NOTE: The Internal Revenue Service Restructuring and Reform Act of 1998, approved July 22, was assigned Public Law No. 105–206.

Statement on House of Representatives Action To Extend Normal Trade Relations With China
July 22, 1998

I welcome the strong, bipartisan vote in the House today to extend normal trade relations with China.

This vote reflects my conviction that active engagement with China—expanding our areas of cooperation while dealing forthrightly with our differences—is the most effective way to advance our interests and our values. Over the past year and during my recent trip to China, engagement has produced tangible results and steady progress on vital issues: fostering political and economic stability in Asia, stopping the spread of weapons of mass destruction, combating international crime and drug trafficking, protecting the environment, promoting human rights and religious freedom.

Trade is a vital part of engagement, supporting jobs here at home, lowering product prices, and helping us to build ties to nearly one quarter of the world's people. Normal trade relations with China will help us strengthen those ties and continue our efforts to make China an increasingly open and productive partner for America.

Statement on Senate Armed Services Committee Action on the Nomination of Daryl Jones To Be Secretary of the Air Force
July 22, 1998

I am deeply disappointed that the Senate Armed Services Committee declined to send to the full Senate the nomination of Daryl Jones to be Secretary of the Air Force. Mr. Jones has a distinguished record of public service in Florida and a strong commitment to the Air Force. I know him to be a good, decent, able man. He was an outstanding candidate for this position, and he deserved the opportunity to be considered by the full Senate. I appreciate the support he received from Chairman Thurmond, Senator Levin, and many other Senators in both parties. I thank Mr. Jones for his willingness to serve his country. I am confident that he will continue to make vital contributions to Florida and to our Nation.

Remarks Announcing the White House Press Secretary Transition and an Exchange With Reporters
July 23, 1998

The President. I have not become the White House Press Secretary, yet. [*Laughter*] I have two announcements to make today; one involves the gentlemen on my—plural—right and left.

Heat Wave

But first, I'd like to make an announcement about the heat wave. All Americans have been deeply concerned and troubled by the human toll of the record heat wave that has spread across many parts of the United States. Already this summer in many Southern and Southwestern States, temperatures have been 20 percent higher than normal. This scorching heat shows no signs of abating. It has destroyed crops, led to widespread power outages, and worst of all, has resulted in the deaths of over 100 people. The most vulnerable—the very old, the very young, people with disabilities—are at greatest risk. Those who cannot afford air-conditioning are at real peril of further health risks as the heat wave goes on.

In times of human crisis we have an obligation to act, to strengthen the ties that bind us as one nation. When fire or flood or earthquakes strike, we step in. When blizzards and high energy costs put elderly and poor citizens at risk, we step in. When smothering heat threatens the lives of people, we can step in, and that is what I am doing today.

The Low Income Home Energy Assistance Program, LIHEAP, makes funds available for emergency use to help at-risk families in times of weather distress. Today I am directing the Department of Health and Human Services to release $100 million in emergency funds for the 11 hottest Southern and Western States, to help families pay for air-conditioners, fans, electric bills, and other ways to beat the heat.

This emergency relief was paid for in the bipartisan balanced budget agreement reached with Congress last year. It reflects the longstanding commitment by both parties to help citizens protect their families in severe weather conditions.

It is, I might say, in light of these terrible weather conditions—and I would point out, I believe—I saw one television program yesterday that pointed out that the 9 hottest years on record have occurred in the last 11 years; that 1997 was the hottest year on record; that in each and every month in 1998, it has beaten the previous record month. So this will be the hottest year on record if something doesn't happen.

Therefore, it is all the more disturbing that Republican leaders in the House of Representatives are attempting to entirely eliminate the LIHEAP program. If Congress proceeds to try and eliminate all funding for this vital emergency assistance, it would be an act of political irresponsibility. It would put partisanship ahead of the progress and the people of our country.

Now, only a few days remain in this session of Congress. We can still make it a time of progress. We can fund the LIHEAP program. We can enact a Patients' Bill of Rights. We can continue our policy of fiscal discipline by reserving the surplus until we fix the Social Security system. We can strengthen education. We can save our children from the dangers of tobacco. There is still time to choose people and progress over partisanship and division.

For my part, I am determined to take every action within my power to help our people, and I look forward to working with lawmakers of both parties to restore LIHEAP funding and to make further progress. Meanwhile, I hope these funds will be of help to people in those 11 States. I know there are many volunteer efforts going on, and I would encourage them.

This is an especially difficult time in a lot of these States. I was home in Arkansas last weekend, and the temperature was above 100 degrees on both days. There are an awful lot of people, especially elderly people living in rural areas without access to air-conditioning or people on limited incomes that can't pay their bills, that are at real risk. So I hope we can all band together and redouble our efforts.

White House Press Secretary Transition

Now, I now have the privilege of making the second most important personnel announcement in the news today. I have no information about the status of any of the Chicago Bulls. [*Laughter*] However, the long-awaited coup in the Press Office is finally taking place. [*Laughter*]

Much to my regret but with my full understanding and support, Mike McCurry will be leaving us in the fall. I have also determined to appoint Joe Lockhart as his successor.

Quite simply, Mike McCurry has set the standard by which future White House Press Secretaries will be judged. In an age where Washington has come to be governed by a 24-hour news cycle and endless cable channels with their special niche audiences, Mike has redefined the job of Press Secretary in a new and more challenging era.

Whatever the news, in good times and bad, he is trusted by the American people and trusted by our administration to provide accurate information about our policies and to be a forceful and effective advocate for them. His ability and his eagerness to fight the good fight on political or policy issues is well known. And few

could hope to match his intelligence and wit from the podium.

But the most difficult and sensitive part of being White House Press Secretary is explaining the foreign policy positions of the United States to the world. His mastery of foreign policy, his understanding not only of broader issues but of the nuances of them, his ability to respond to developments precisely—and when necessary, not so precisely—have made him a unique and instrumental element of our Nation's public diplomacy around the world.

Hillary and I have both enjoyed and deeply valued Mike's presence not only for his obvious skills but for his wonderful sense of humor and his genuine friendship. We've appreciated his hard work, his loyalty, and his ability. We will miss him a great deal, and we're glad he's going to be around a while longer.

I am also very fortunate to have in Joe Lockhart an outstanding successor for Mike. I've had an opportunity to work with him very closely, especially over the last several months, not only on important trips to Europe, to Africa, to Latin America but also on our work on economic and other domestic issues. He is smart; he knows our policies, foreign and domestic; and he has skillfully articulated them.

Mike and Joe were a great team in our 1996 campaign. Mike served as Press Secretary at the White House; Joe did a superb job for Vice President Gore and me during our reelection effort. You all know that the great teamwork has continued here at the White House, with Joe and Barry Toiv serving as Mike's deputies.

When Mike told me at the beginning of the summer that he would begin planning an orderly transition, I knew that Joe would be the ideal replacement, not only for me but I believe also for you. Joe knows you well, and you know him well, and that's probably half the battle. Joe knows that he can only serve my interests well if he takes care of yours also by being your advocate here at the White House. He does that well already, and I know he will continue to be sensitive to your requirements when Mike leaves later this year.

I'll have more to say about Joe and about Mike this fall when we actually make the change. But it's rare in this White House that I get to announce my own personnel decisions— [*laughter*]—especially involving the press. So I wanted you to be the first to know—after Mike's

Press Office staff, who were just told a few moments ago.

Joe has accepted my offer to be Assistant to the President and Press Secretary.

I also would like to say a word about two very special women who are here, Debra McCurry and Joe's wife, Laura Logan. While these guys have the pleasure of working until all hours here, it's their families, especially their spouses, who make very special sacrifices. We appreciate them and their willingness to lend Mike and Joe to the American people for a short while.

Now, I'm going to be with you later at a meeting for Congress, and I'll be able to answer your questions then. So I'd like to get back to our regularly scheduled programming, under the leadership of old what's-his-name over here. [*Laughter*]

Q. What does this say for Joe's credibility when I asked him yesterday if McCurry was leaving? [*Laughter*]

The President. Did he say no or not yet?

Q. He didn't say no—yes, he said no; he didn't say not yet.

The President. Well, the answer yesterday was no. [*Laughter*] The answer today is no. But at sometime in the near future, the answer will be yes.

Mike, thank you so much.

Heat Wave

Q. Other than the $100 million, sir, is there anything else you can do about the drought conditions, the heat wave? Is there other stuff we ought to be thinking about?

The President. Well, we're looking at it. I wish I could seed the clouds and make it rain.

But this is very disturbing. We're going to be looking at it. In all the States, I'm sure there are vigorous efforts going on through the State emergency offices, and my understanding is— I've asked for an update—I didn't get it before I came out here—of the volunteer efforts that are going on. This happened to me once when I was Governor, and we had to move a lot of seniors into our senior citizen centers, because they were air-conditioned, and just set up cots. And we were handing out, literally, hundreds and hundreds of fans to people who had no air-conditioning in their homes.

We can give the money out, and we're going to look and see what else we can do. We're going to look and see whether we can get some more help from other States, perhaps, that aren't so hard-hit. Actually, ironically, a few more than half of our States are having temperatures slightly below normal this year. But these 11—there are some more, above the 11, who are a little above average, but these are 20 percent above average in the hottest months. So we're looking at it. If I can determine anything else I can do, believe me, I will do it, because there are an awful lot of people that just cannot take this heat without some more help. And we'll do whatever we can.

Q. Mr. President, how serious is this Iranian missile test?

The President. I'll answer all the other questions when I—I'll be glad to answer the questions, but I just—I want to wait to let you do this thing with Mike, and then I'll see you about an hour or whenever.

NOTE: The President spoke at 1:15 p.m. in the Briefing Room at the White House.

Remarks Following a Meeting on Agricultural Assistance and an Exchange With Reporters
July 23, 1998

The President. After the clicking stops, here's what I want to do. [*Laughter*] As you can all see, I'm here with Senator Daschle, Senator Harkin, Senator Conrad, Senator Dorgan, and Secretary Glickman, Deputy Secretary Rominger; and these young people here are national officers of the FFA.

In a few moments, I'm going to do a national radio press conference with agricultural reporters from agricultural radio networks around the country. I've got a brief statement here that I would like to read, and then I'd like to give the Senators a chance to make whatever comments they would like to make, and then I will do what I said I'd do in the pressroom a while ago: I'll let you all ask some questions, if you have questions on other subjects, and then we'll go do the ag press conference.

We're here because all of us are profoundly concerned about the communities that are suffering from both low prices and all kinds of natural disasters around the country. In Texas, about three quarters of the cotton crop has been lost. Senator Dorgan said the other day that North Dakota retired auctioneers are being pressed into duty to handle all the families that are being forced to sell their farms.

For 5½ years, we've worked hard to help America's farm families with disaster assistance to ranchers who've lost livestock, surplus commodity purchases for school lunches, diversifying the sources of enterprise and income in rural America. We've increased our use of export credits by a third in the last year alone.

This year's farm crisis demands that we do more. On Saturday I directed Secretary Glickman to buy more than 80 million bushels of wheat to help lift prices for American farmers and ease hunger in the developing world. Today I'm announcing that we are providing disaster assistance for farmers in Texas—the entire State has been declared a disaster area—to help those whose crops and livestock have been ravaged by the drought. I believe today is the 18th day in a row that it's above 100 degrees in Dallas, Texas. Next week I will send Secretary Glickman to Texas and Oklahoma to assess what other help is needed.

As we head into the conference, I ask all of you young people who are here to go back home and help us to do whatever we can to pass the $500 million in emergency farmer and rancher assistance contained in the amendment sponsored by Senators Conrad and Dorgan and strongly supported by our ranking Democrat on the committee, Senator Harkin, and our leader, Senator Daschle.

We also have to help to revive the rural economy with exports. We have to give the International Monetary Fund the resources it needs to strengthen the Asian economies. Let me tell you how big a deal this is. About 40 to 50 percent of all American grain production is exported; 40 percent of all the exports go to Asia. We have a 30 percent decline in farm exports to Asian countries, excluding China and Japan— they're down about 13 percent in Japan; they're down about 6 percent in China—30 percent in the other countries this year because of the Asian financial crisis.

The International Monetary Fund is designed to reform those economies and boost them. They need money in order to buy our food. It is not a very complicated thing. But I have asked for this since January now. I was very disturbed to see in the morning press there's been another decision to delay a vote on this in the House of Representatives. I think it is a big mistake. I am doing what I can to continue to boost food exports. I don't believe that they should be subject to sanctions and our policies except under the most extreme circumstances. And I believe we have to do more.

Finally, I want to do whatever I can to strengthen the farm safety net. We should expand eligibility for direct and guaranteed loans; improve the crop insurance program, which simply is not working for too many farmers; and extend marketing loans when the prices are low. We have to give farmers more flexibility in planning when to receive Federal income support. They ought to be able to get these payments early. I proposed that last spring. I saw that there was some support for that in the House leadership last week, and I'm grateful for that, but I'd like to pass that and get it out and do it soon.

All these things I think will help. But we have to understand we've got a price crisis in America today because of high worldwide crop production, the decline of the Asian economies, and the decline in the currencies of so many countries relative to the dollar, which means they can't buy as much food. That's why the IMF is important. We also have a disaster problem because of the drought and other significant natural problems. And no farmer should go broke because of an act of God. So that's our policy, and we're going to try to implement it.

And I'd like to give the Senators a chance to make a few remarks, and then I'll answer your other questions.

Senator Daschle.

[Senator Thomas A. Daschle made brief remarks.]

The President. Senator Harkin.

[Senator Tom Harkin made brief remarks.]

The President. The North Dakota Senators— I think North Dakota, I should say for the benefit of the national press, I believe has had the largest drop in farm income in any State of the country by a good stretch.

[*Senators Kent Conrad and Byron L. Dorgan made brief remarks.*]

The President. Well, let me just make one more comment about this, and then I'll answer your questions.

When the freedom to farm bill was passed, those of us who came from farming areas knew that it had a lot of very good provisions. It got the Government out of micromanaging farming; it gave farmers more freedom to make their own planting decision; it had terrific conservation provisions; it had good rural development provisions. But it did not have an adequate safety net. We all knew it at the time, and there were those, and there still are some, who believe that we really don't need one.

But I just think that's wrong. To go back to what Senator Harkin said, I believe if you look at the trends in world population growth and agricultural production elsewhere, in most normal years, for the next 30 years, American farmers should do better and better and better. This would be a very good time for a whole generation of our farmers. But the average farmer is about 59 years old in America today. So what I'm worried about is that, you know, you get a bad year or two like this coming along without an adequate safety net in this bill, then you wind up changing the whole structure of agriculture in ways that I don't think are good for America.

So we're going to work on this. We're going to try to get it done. But I do say to the young people here, I agree with Senator Harkin. I think the future trends around the world look quite good for America's farmers if we can get through this rough spot.

Thank you.

Q. Why can't you lawmakers convince your fellows on the Hill? I mean, what is the holdup?

The President. Well, don't you think your bill will pass? I think it'll pass.

Senator Dorgan. It passed the Senate. We've got to get it through conference, and I think we'll get it——

The President. And the Senate passed the International Monetary Fund.

Senator Harkin. Yes. And we've got the indemnity fund in there.

Senator Conrad. We're about to——

The President. You're about to—but you're going to pass it.

Q. What's the problem?

The President. The problem is in the House, and we just have to hope that they will follow the lead of the Senate here.

Iran-U.S. Relations

Q. Mr. President, what impact do you see the missile test having on your efforts to try and warm relations with Iran?

The President. Well, we've been following this for some time. And we knew that Iran was attempting to develop this capability. It's just a test. But if they—obviously, if they were to develop an intermediate range missile, it could change the regional stability dynamics in the Middle East. And that's why we've worked so hard with North Korea and with others to try to get them not to transfer missiles and missile technology to Iran.

If we do continue to have an opening of relations, because the new President seems more open to it, obviously this is one of the things I would raise with him. We've been very concerned about this. And we believe that the future of the Middle East would be better if they'd invest more money, all those countries, in something other than military technology.

So we're very, very concerned about it, but not surprised by it.

Q. [*Inaudible*]

The President. One at a time. Obviously, it is an obstacle. But I don't think it's an argument for closing off all avenues of opportunity. The country is in a dynamic state now. There's some dynamism there, and there's some reason to believe that, it seems to me, that at least making it clear what our position is on that—on the Middle East peace process, on terrorism, support of terrorism, on all these issues with which we've had problems with Iran in the past—and still being glad that there's some movement toward greater popular government, more openness in the country argues for what we're doing—a cautious, deliberate approach.

Fast-Track Trade Legislation

Q. Mr. President, besides the IMF bill, high on the farm agenda is fast-track legislation. Why not go along with Speaker Gingrich and schedule a vote—a September vote on this?

The President. First of all, I strongly support fast track, as you know. I was bitterly disappointed that we couldn't pass it earlier, and he and I both worked very hard to pass it. There is no evidence that one single vote has changed. If anything, there's some evidence that we'd have more trouble passing it.

So if we bring it up in a bill that also has the International Monetary Fund or the Africa trade bill or the Caribbean Basin initiative—all of which I think are good for America—the impact would be, in all probability, to kill them all and to make it even harder to pass fast track early next year. I still believe we'll pass fast track next year when we get beyond this election year. I think it is so evidently in the best interest of the country. That's the first answer.

The second point is, the International Monetary Fund funding will do much more good in the short run because it puts money into the countries that want to buy our food today. Fast track gives the United States the power to open new markets in the future, to enter negotiations to open new markets in the future.

So it's not terribly significant whether we get the fast-track legislation in August, let's say, or September or January or February next year or March, because we still have to start the negotiations and open new markets. We're already going to negotiate in opening agricultural markets, for example within the World Trade Organization to try to deal with the European subsidy issue that was mentioned earlier.

So I'm strongly for fast track. I think we will pass it next year. I have no evidence that a single vote has changed since it was not passed earlier, and I don't want to kill all the rest of that. We ought to pass the Africa trade bill now, the modified Caribbean Basin bill now. But most important of all, dwarfing everything else, in the near term, for these farmers with their prices low, is the International Monetary Fund funding, because that will float cash into these countries as a condition for reform, and it will give the money to buy our food. That's more important.

Middle East Peace Process

Q. Why have you thrown in the towel on the Middle East?

The President. Well, we haven't. I saw that story. That's just not so.

Let me say first of all, if I thought the process were over, I would say it was over. We have continued intense negotiations to this day with both sides, based on the ideas we advanced earlier, which, as you know, were accepted in principle by Mr. Arafat and not by Mr. Netanyahu, but a negotiation ensued.

Secretary Albright has worked very, very hard on this. We have made a not inconsiderable amount of progress, but differences remain. We haven't thrown in the towel because I think it's a lot better to get an agreement, to get them into final status talks than it is to give up and let this thing drift dangerously toward conflict and dissolution.

So if we come to a time when I think it's hopeless, I'll say it's hopeless and that ideas weren't accepted. But right now, I'm not prepared to say that. I think there's still a chance we can get an agreement, and we're going to keep working for it.

NOTE: The President spoke at 2:45 p.m. in the Oval Office at the White House. In his remarks, he referred to Chairman Yasser Arafat of the Palestinian Authority; and Prime Minister Binyamin Netanyahu of Israel. The President also referred to the Future Farmers of America (FFA). A tape was not available for verification of the content of these remarks.

Remarks in a Teleconference With Rural Radio Stations on Agricultural Issues and Farming
July 23, 1998

[*Secretary of Agriculture Dan Glickman, acting as moderator of the teleconference, made brief opening remarks and introduced the President.*]

The President. Thank you very much, Secretary Glickman. And I want to thank you all for giving me a chance to speak to people in rural America.

Today, most of our fellow citizens are enjoying the dividends of the strongest American economy in a generation. We have the lowest unemployment rate in 28 years. We're about to have the first balanced budget and surplus in 29 years, with the highest homeownership in American history. But with the economic crisis in Asia hurting our farm exports, with crop prices squeezed by abundant world supplies, and with farms devastated by floods and fires and droughts, communities in parts of the South and Great Plains are withering; in Texas, almost three-quarters of the cotton crop is lost; and in North Dakota, retired auctioneers are being pressed into duty just to handle all the families who are being forced to sell their farms.

Secretary Glickman and I are joined in the Oval Office today by several young leaders of the FFA. They represent the future of American agriculture and they deserve a chance to have that future. As the former Governor of a State that depends heavily on farming, I know we must never turn our backs on farmers when Mother Nature or the world economy turns a callous eye.

Our farm communities feed our Nation and much of the world. They also nourish the values on which our country was born and which have led us now for over 220 years, hard work and faith and family, devotion to community and to the land. We simply can't flourish if we let our rural roots shrivel and decline.

For 5½ years, I've worked to expand opportunity for farm families, providing critical disaster assistance to ranchers who have lost livestock, purchasing surplus commodities for school lunches, working to diversify the sources of income in rural America, increasing our use of export credits by a third in the past year alone. But this year's farm crisis demands that we provide more help to farmers teetering on the edge.

Last Saturday I directed Secretary Glickman to buy more than 80 million bushels of wheat to help lift prices for American farmers while easing hunger in the developing world. Today, in addition to helping citizens in 11 Southern States beat by unrelenting heat, I'm announcing we will provide immediate disaster assistance for farmers throughout the State of Texas to help those whose crops and livestock have been ravaged by drought.

Next week, I'll send Secretary Glickman to Texas and Oklahoma to talk with drought-stricken farmers and assess what other help they require. And once again, I urge Congress: We must provide the $500 million in emergency assistance, sponsored by Senators Conrad, Dorgan, Daschle, and Harkin, for farmers and ranchers throughout the country who have been afflicted not only by drought but also by fires and floods and other disasters. They are our neighbors in need.

With these measures, we can help farmers weather the current crisis. But to strengthen rural America for the long run, we have to do more. First, we have to revive the rural economy with exports. Today, products from one of every three acres planted in America are sold abroad. We have to continue to open new foreign markets and enforce our existing trade agreements. We must give the International Monetary Fund the resources it needs to strengthen and reform the Asian economies so that they will have the money to buy our farm products.

Yesterday, unfortunately, the House of Representatives delayed this critical funding for the IMF. American farmers cannot afford to wait; they need help now. We should also be prepared to donate food generously to those around the world at risk of malnutrition or starvation. As a general principle, I believe commercial exports of food should not be used as a tool of foreign policy, except under the most compelling circumstances.

A week ago, I signed the Agricultural Export Relief Act, enabling U.S. farmers to sell 300,000 tons of wheat to Pakistan the next day. I urge Congress to provide me authority to waive sanctions on food when it is in the national interest and to work with me to incorporate flexibility in sanctions policy more broadly.

Second, we simply have to strengthen the farm safety net. We should expand eligibility for direct and guaranteed loans, improve crop insurance, which is not working for a lot of farmers today, and extend marketing loans when crop prices are too low.

And we should give farmers more flexibility in planning when to receive Federal income support payments and in planting new crops when their primary crops fail. I proposed allowing our farmers to receive Federal income support payments—early—last spring. There is now some support for it apparently in the Congress; I hope very much it will pass soon.

Third, we must improve the infrastructure in rural communities. We have to preserve universal service and defend the vital E-rate initiative so that all rural homes can count on affordable telephone rates and rural schools, libraries, and health centers can tap into the promise of the Internet. We have to modernize rural schools and transportation systems, improve the quality of rural health with advanced telemedicine, cleaner drinking water, and safer food.

These steps are in the best tradition of our Nation. Whenever disaster strikes, Americans join together to help see their neighbors through. That's what happened in Florida when brave men and women from across the country help put out the State's fires, and that's what we'll do throughout rural America to save our farmers from losing their homes and crops.

At this moment of broad prosperity for our Nation, we are certainly able to and we clearly must help our neighbors on the farm throughout this current crisis so that we can strengthen our rural communities for the 21st century. Now, I'll be happy to take your questions.

Secretary Glickman. Thank you, Mr. President. I get to be the role of moderator today, and our first question comes——

The President. You sound kind of like a deejay.

Secretary Glickman. That's right. You should hear me sing. But we won't do that here. Our first question comes from Shelly Beyer who is with the Brownfield Network out of Jefferson City, Missouri.

Shelly, are you on?

[Ms. Beyer asked the President if he favored Congress taking steps on fast-track trading authority.]

The President. Well, Shelly, fast track wouldn't actually help the farmers right now. I would support voting on fast track whenever we think we can pass it, but you know, we had a huge struggle to pass fast track earlier this year, and we failed. I believe it will pass early next year. I don't believe that any votes have changed.

And keep in mind what fast track does. Fast track simply gives me the authority that previous Presidents have had to negotiate new trade agreements, tearing down trade barriers to American products in other countries

By contrast, getting the funding for the International Monetary Fund will immediately create

markets for American products. Let me just give you an example. About 40 to 50 percent of our grains are exported. Forty percent of our export market is in Asia. If you take all the Asian countries except for Japan and China, our exports are down 30 percent because of their economic problems. They're down 13 percent in Japan; they're down 6 percent in China.

Now, if we could get the International Monetary Fund funding and those countries could get more money, then they'll immediately have more money to buy our food. So I think that the IMF funding will do more in the short run to boost American farm prices.

Now, over the next year, we've got to get the fast-track authority so that we can continue to open more markets. We will also begin negotiations in the World Trade Organization to try to get every country that signed on to that to lower their agricultural tariffs and other barriers so that we can sell in more markets.

So I agree that we need to do fast track. I am determined to get other countries to lower their agricultural barriers, but all that takes time. And if I had the fast-track authority tomorrow, it would still take time to open those markets and reach those agreements. We need to open the markets now. That's why the International Monetary Fund is more important, because it will flow cash into countries; they'll immediately have money, when they can immediately start to buy more food.

[Secretary Glickman introduced Gary Wergin of WHO Radio in Des Moines, IA, who asked the President why Democratic votes in Congress for fast-track trade authority had been difficult to obtain.]

The President. I believe that what happened was the Members got dug in before they saw the final bill, and I also think that there were more Republicans voting against it than the Speaker thought. This was one issue where, notwithstanding our well-publicized conflicts, Speaker Gingrich and I worked hand-in-glove, and we worked very, very hard.

But the truth is that, for reasons that I wasn't privy to, by the time the bill was actually brought up in the House, the people who were against fast track had been working against it so hard, they'd gotten so many commitments, that when—even though the bill, on its merits, I think, was very much deserving of passing and met a lot of the concerns for labor rights, for environmental concerns, and other things, we couldn't get the votes.

The only point I want to make is, to the best of my knowledge, we have not changed either 10 Democratic votes or 10 Republican votes from no to yes. If we don't have those votes, why would we kill the Africa trade bill, which is good for us, or the Caribbean trade bill or, even more important by far, the International Monetary Fund, by tying all this stuff together? Why not pass what we can pass now, get the immediate benefits, and then work on passing fast track when the election is behind us?

I think it's clear that it will pass early next year, because it's manifestly in the national interest, and because, frankly, then a lot of the Members of Congress who got committed against it early will be forced to look at what the actual details of the bill say and will feel freer to vote for it.

[Secretary Glickman introduced Stewart Doan of the Arkansas Radio Network, who spoke from KARN in Little Rock, AR.]

The President. Hello, Stewart. What's the temperature down there?

Mr. Doan. Right about 100, sir. About the same as it was Saturday when you were out at Chenal.

The President. I know. It was over 100 both days I was out there.

[Mr. Doan said that congressional leaders blamed much of the agriculture crisis on 1996 farm legislation. He asked if the President agreed and would support increasing the guaranteed minimum price for grain, soybeans, and cotton.]

The President. Well, first of all, I think I would partly agree with what they say. I think that fundamental cause of the crisis today is a price crisis. It's a market crisis caused by a combination of things. You've got adequate—and more than adequate—world supplies. You've got a significant decline in the economic capacity of Asia to buy our food products. You've got a big drop in the currency values in other countries relative to the American dollar, which makes our food, relatively speaking, more expensive, which makes it even harder. And that's a big problem. And then in America, you've also got a disaster crisis. You've got some places where they have no price and no crop. Usually when farmers have no crop, at least the no

crop they have has a high price, because the supply has dried up. But now, the worldwide supply is so big that they've got a double hit. So that's the fundamental problem.

When I signed the '96 freedom to farm bill, I pointed out that it had a lot of good provisions in it, but it didn't have a real safety net. Let's remember what the good provisions were. Number one, it got the Government out of micromanaging planning decisions. Number two, it had terrific conservation provisions. Number three, it had good rural development provisions. And I had no choice but to sign it because, if I hadn't, we would have been back on the '49 farm law, which would have been even worse for the farmers. But I said in '96, the crop prices are not going to be high forever, and when they drop, we're going to regret not having an adequate safety net. So the first thing we have to do is to develop an adequate safety net.

Now, let me just—you asked about the proposals by Senator Harkin and others; let me just run through some of the things that I have proposed, and then I'll answer your question about their proposal. First of all, Senators Dorgan and Conrad have a $500 million bill up there—it's passed the Senate and I hope and believe will pass the House—which would improve and expand crop insurance; it would compensate farmers whose crop and pasture land is flooded; it would provide emergency feed assistance to livestock producers who are suffering from drought and allow us to use export enhancement funds that are left over in future years for food aid and other purposes. These things I think will be quite helpful.

Now, in addition to that, I've asked the Congress to help strengthen the safety net by extending the term of marketing assistance loans, by allowing flexibility for farmers to receive advanced AMTA payments. I asked for that last April. The Speaker and other House Republicans are now saying, in the last week or so, they are open to that. That would have, I think, a lot of impact.

And I, finally, asked for a provision that would improve credit ability and modify the one-strike policy for farmers who have had a debt write-down, and I've also proposed to let USDA guaranteed operating loans be used to refinance. So if we were to do all these things, I think we'd strengthen the safety net.

Now, in principle, I think it's clear that the commodity loan cap is not working, and it needs to be modified. The question is, how should we modify it, and how are we going to pay for it within the context of the balanced budget? But in principle, I don't think there's any question that what Senator Harkin and Congressman Gephardt and others say is right, that the present cap is too low.

And there are some people who think this system is fine the way it works, but I don't. I think what it will do is inevitably reduce the number of family farmers, even if it doesn't reduce the acreage being farmed. And I don't think that's a good thing for America. So I would like to see a system where farmers don't fail because of acts of God.

[Secretary Glickman remarked that the Agriculture Department would continue to try to keep farm prices from dropping too low and allow farmers flexibility in marketing. He introduced Mike Hergert of the Red River Farm Network in Grand Forks, ND, who asked what farmers could expect regarding the crop insurance program.]

The President. Well, first of all, we've expanded the size of the program, which I thought was important; it was way too small in '93 when I took office. We've more than doubled it, and we've expanded farmers' choices by creating new varieties of crop insurance, and we've introduced the concept of revenue insurance in a large majority of the grain-producing parts of the country.

But I still think there are some other things that have to be done. I think that even though we've improved the program by offering coverage on preventive planning since '93 and increasingly based the coverage on farmers' individual yields, it's just not working for most farmers. And what we're trying to do now is to look at all the ways we can help our farmers get through tough times that we can pass in the Congress.

Maybe Secretary Glickman would like to talk about this, but I must say, I've been waiting for someone to ask this question, because when I was home last weekend talking to the farmers, that's the only thing they said. They said, "This crop insurance is a joke; it doesn't really help anybody." So maybe, Secretary Glickman, that's too blunt for me to say that our Government's crop insurance program is a joke, but maybe

you should talk a little more about some of the things we're looking at to improve it.

[Secretary Glickman explained that under the current crop insurance system, farmers experiencing repeated disasters found that their premiums paid could be much greater than their benefits received. He commended the legislation sponsored by Senators Dorgan and Conrad.]

The President. Mike, Senator Dorgan and Senator Conrad were just here with us in the Oval Office just a few minutes ago, and we were talking about this. I think the provision in their bill is going to pass. I believe it will. But I would just say to any of our listeners there, if you've got any ideas about what we can do with this program, this insurance program to make it fairer and more affordable and more functional or how it could be modified in some ways, I would urge you to directly contact Secretary Glickman or write to us here at the White House, because I am hearing from farmers all over the country that it's simply not working. And as Dan Glickman said, it's really not like buying car insurance or home insurance or something like that. It's almost like buying flood insurance in a 25-year flood plain where you just have no control over what's going to happen. But we have a national interest in seeing that land, which is highly productive, in North Dakota be planted.

So I think the whole concept behind the requirement that it be, quote, "actuarially sound" misperceives the facts there. And I don't believe the Congress meant to say we don't want anybody planting in North Dakota anymore because they've had floods and disease and pests and everything. I don't believe that was the intent of the act of Congress. So I think this is one where an honest error was made, and we would like to correct it and if you've got any ideas, for goodness sakes, give them to us.

[Secretary Glickman introduced Bart Walker from WGNS in Murfreesboro, TN, who said that economic success in his area had driven up population, resulting in family farms being turned into subdivisions; while at the same time, most students majoring in agriculture at Middle Tennessee State University went into related fields rather than farming. Mr. Walker asked if there were plans for low interest loans that would enable and encourage students to take up farming.]

The President. Yes. We actually have a program that provides low interest loans for first-time farmers, as well as a program in the Department of Agriculture that gives kind of technical support and assistance for new farmers. And one of the things that I've asked Secretary Glickman to do is to assess the adequacy of that program and to look at some of the things that we're doing in nonfarm communities, setting up community financial institutions that make extra loans and things of that kind to see if they might be relevant to first-time farmers.

As I said at the beginning of our interview here, I got the national officers of the FFA here with me. And these young farmers are the future of America. The average farmer is about 59 years old in America today, and I'm very concerned about that in places where, like in Murfreesboro where you're doing very well economically, if a farmer chooses to sell his or her land to a developer, and you subdivide it, well, there's nothing I can do about it and probably nothing you would want to do about it. You don't remove the right to do that if that's what the market is dictating. But I think where young people want to farm and are able to farm, if they can get the credit, they ought to be able to get the loans at affordable terms and at good repayment terms.

One of the things that we've done for college loans since I've been here, that I think might have some applicability to first-time farmer loans I want to look at, is to structure the repayment in a way that's tied directly to income. So for example, if a young person wants to go to college and then take a job as a schoolteacher, and another would go to college and take a job as a stockbroker, and they borrow the same exact amount of money to get out of college, but the stockbroker has an income of 3 times the schoolteacher's, under the new provisions of our college loan program, the schoolteacher can pay back the money with a ceiling on it as a percentage of his or her income. So if a young person wants to go into some sort of public service—to be a police officer, a nurse, a schoolteacher, a social worker, something like that—they can do that.

Well, if you think about the early years of farming and how meager the income might be, there may be something we can do to structure the same sort of loan program for first-time farmers. So we're looking at a lot of other op-tions. But we do have—to go back to your first question—we actually do have a program in the Department for first-time farmers to provide for loans and for technical assistance to help them get started.

[*Secretary Glickman noted that the Agriculture Department's outreach office provided technical assistance to first-time farmers. He then introduced Bill Ray of the Agrinet Farm Radio Network in Kill Devil Hills, NC, who welcomed listeners to the Outer Banks.*]

The President. That's near Kitty Hawk, isn't it?

Mr. Ray. That's exactly right.

The President. I went there once, about 26 years ago. It's beautiful.

Mr. Ray. Well, a lot of folks would like to have you back, Mr. President.

The President. Thank you.

[*Mr. Ray asked what long-range plans the President recommended to help food producers all across the country.*]

The President. Well, over the long haul, I believe that the provisions of the '96 bill—let me just say what I think we ought to keep. I've said what I think is wrong about it; let me say what I think we ought to keep. I think it would be better if we could avoid having the Government go back to micromanaging the farmers' planting decisions. I think letting the farmers make the decisions about what crops they're going to plant is the right thing to do; I think we ought to keep the strong conservation provisions of the farm bill of '96; and finally, I'd like to keep and even strengthen the rural development provisions of the farm bill.

One of the things that we haven't talked about is there are a lot of people who live in agricultural communities who farm, who—either they—either the farmer or the farmer's spouse gets a significant income from other kinds of work. And so what I would like to see is—I'd like to see us do more on rural development, because the more we can diversify the economies of these small towns, the more people can afford to farm, because they'll have a salaried income coming in, too, which will help them to deal with the problems of the bad years. So I think those are the good things to keep.

I think that we should redouble our efforts in agricultural research. Secretary Glickman mentioned this. I hope that we can get the actual dollar figure I recommended for ag research funded in this year's budget, because we get such a huge return from ag research.

The second thing I'd like to say is I think, if we can get an adequate farm safety net in this present structure and then we can continue to open farm markets and get fair treatment with the fast-track legislation, with the new agricultural negotiations we're going to have through the World Trade Organization, with the funding for the International Monetary Fund, then I think the future for our farmers actually looks quite good.

If you look at the all the new things that are coming out of agricultural research, if you look at all the new applications of farm products that are being developed, and if you look at the growth of world population and the projected agricultural production in other parts of the world, I would say that the next 30 years for our farmers will probably be very, very good if we can continue to invest in research and stay ahead of the curve, and if we can continue to open new markets, and if we're smart enough and honest enough to recognize that we're always going to have bad years, we're always going to have acts of God, we're always going to have things like this go wrong, especially when there's some evidence that there is a lot of change in our climate that's warming the Earth's climate and leading to more disruption. So let's put in an adequate safety net, pay for it, deal with it, and say it's an investment in America's future. I think if we just do those things, our farmers are going to do quite well.

[*Secretary Glickman introduced Tony Purcell from the Texas State News Network.*]

The President. What's the temperature down there?

Mr. Purcell. We're pushing 100 degrees right now for the 19th day in a row.

The President. Well, I'm surprised you're not shorted out. I'm glad we can hear each other.

[*Mr. Purcell thanked the President for providing emergency disaster funding for areas suffering losses from the heat wave and asked about relief for agricultural businesses affected.*]

The President. Depending on the dimensions, there are standards in the Federal law for my disaster declarations, but normally, when a disaster declaration affects an entire State in agricultural losses, then small businesses that are

affected by it and communities that are affected by it are also eligible for other kinds of assistance. And I'll tell you what I will do. I'll have our people do some research on it and get back to you directly on it.

But let me also just say, there's one thing in this bill that's coming up that I think could be quite helpful. I've mentioned this several times, the bill by Senators Conrad and Dorgan that's got $500 million more in emergency assistance. A lot of the problems in Texas are livestock problems, even though you've lost most of your cotton crop and had a lot of other problems.

We had a program which permitted the Federal Government, in times of disaster for people with their livestock, to buy up surplus feed and give it to the livestock farmers. That was suspended in 1996 in the farm bill until 2002. Under our provision, under this emergency provision, we'd get some of that back, and we could get some feed down there to those livestock folks that I think would be very, very helpful. So that's another thing we're trying to do for the farmers. But I believe that there is some community and small business assistance that can flow, too. If Secretary Glickman can answer the question now, fine; if not, I'll have somebody directly contact you later today.

[*Secretary Glickman mentioned various USDA and FEMA disaster assistance programs and said he would visit Texas and Oklahoma in the coming week to see the damage firsthand and determine what else could be done.*]

The President. But if I could, to go back to your question about the nonagricultural losses related to the agricultural crisis—as Secretary Glickman said, some of our emergency programs were funded through the Federal Emergency Management Agency. And we have—obviously, you have a Governor's emergency management person there who works with us on that.

Then, we also have some programs funded through the Small Business Administration, some programs funded through the Commerce Department, some programs funded through the Housing and Urban Development Department. We'll just have to do an inventory. And I would urge all of the people who are listening to us through your network there to make sure that their mayors or Members of Congress or State officials have access to Secretary Glickman when he comes down there and give him as complete a picture as you can of what the problems are. And, obviously, we'll do our best to bring to bear whatever resources we can legally provide to help you deal with the terrible difficulties you are in.

Today I announced that we were going to give $100 million to Texas and 10 other States just to help with utility bills, with air-conditioning, with fans, with other things, for all these people who don't have adequate cooling. We've had 100 deaths now between—basically between Dallas on the west and then across Arkansas and north Louisiana and then to Tennessee and north Alabama and Mississippi and all in through that 11-State area, all the way over to the East Coast, because of the record heat. And I'm hoping that we can help you with that as well and save some more lives.

[*Secretary Glickman noted the program was out of time and invited the President to make closing comments.*]

The President. Well, I would just like to say, first of all, that I'm very concerned about the problems that are being faced up and down and North and West and East and South in the farm belt. They're significant, and they're different from place to place in our country. We're doing our best to respond. I'm trying to listen to your elected representatives here.

I'm trying to move the system here as quickly as I can. I hope you will urge your representatives to vote for the Conrad-Dorgan bill to get some more emergency assistance out there. I hope you'll support us in building a more permanent, adequate farm safety net and in building new markets for our farm products.

But if you have any more ideas, I would urge you to get in touch with the Secretary of Agriculture or with me. We did this interview in part just to reach out and show our concern to farmers and to rural America and to ask for your ideas. If you have any ideas about anything else we can do, if there's something we're overlooking, we want to get on it; we want to be responsive. We know that it's not the best of times for a lot of our farmers, and we want to be there for you. America is doing very well as a whole, and we think you should be part of that.

Thank you, and God bless you all.

NOTE: The President spoke at 3:12 p.m. in the Oval Office at the White House. In his remarks, the President referred to the Future Farmers of America (FFA); and the Agricultural Market Transition Act (AMTA), part of the Federal Agriculture Improvement and Reform Act of 1996, Public Law 104–127.

Statement on House of Representatives Action on Environmental Legislation
July 23, 1998

I am pleased that the House of Representatives, in a bipartisan fashion, today rejected an unwise and unwarranted attempt to deny the American people the facts about global warming.

With much of the country suffering a stifling heat wave and with each month so far this year setting a new record for global temperature, the American people expect and deserve a fair, honest, and informed debate on the issue of climate change. Some in Congress would have stifled that debate by effectively imposing a gag order on Federal agencies. Thankfully, the House

voted to remove this language from the VA–HUD appropriations bill.

Unfortunately, the bill still contains other provisions that would restrict our ability to move forward with cost-effective steps to reduce the greenhouse gases that cause global warming. And appropriations bills moving through Congress would cut by nearly one half my proposed research and tax incentives for energy efficiency and clean energy technologies, measures that would reduce energy costs for American families while curbing greenhouse gases.

Americans have demonstrated time and again that we can protect our environment while growing our economy. We can and must meet the challenge of climate change in the same way. I urge Congress to join us in this critical endeavor.

Remarks at a Birthday Celebration for Jazz Musician Lionel Hampton
July 23, 1998

Thank you. I would say you gave a better speech for me than I played a song for you. [*Laughter*]

Let me say to Lionel Hampton and this wonderful orchestra, to all of you who are here who made this evening possible. LeVerne, thank you. Max Roach, thank you for coming. All of us who have been your fans for so long are honored to be in your presence. Thank you, Reverend Jackson. Thank you, all the Members of Congress who are here. A very, very special word of thanks to two perfectly wonderful men and fellow travelers along the road of jazz music and progressive politics—[*laughter*]—John Conyers and Charlie Rangel. Thank you for making this evening possible.

You know, Hillary and I have loved many things about the opportunity to serve here, but maybe none more than the opportunity to share with America the great gifts of our artists. And this is a special night. Lionel Hampton is 90 years old this year. You should know that he has played for every President since Harry Truman. I was minus one when Harry Truman became President—[*laughter*]—so he's been at this a day or two.

It's been a long time since he joined Louis Armstrong and gave him a hit song and revolu-tionized jazz music forever. I was telling Hillary, when Hamp was up there playing and singing, I said, "You know, my ears are going. I can't even hear the pitch anymore, and there he is, hitting the pitch." [*Laughter*] All of you who've ever played or tried to sing, the idea that he hit the pitch is something. And they played magnificently tonight. They lifted our spirits; they lifted our hearts.

I am personally indebted to Hillary and Charlie Rangel and John Conyers for cooking this night up, and I think all of us are. And I just want to say that even though your real birthday was a few months earlier, what the heck, you only turn 90 once—[*laughter*]—we think it ought to be a year-long celebration.

So I would like to ask the White House magnificent chef, who does these things for us, to bring Mr. Hampton a little gift in here, and I'd like to ask all of you to stand and join me in singing "Happy Birthday" to him.

NOTE: The President spoke at 8 p.m. in the East Room at the White House. In his remarks, he referred to LeBaron Taylor, senior vice president-corporate affairs, Sony Corporation; musician Max Roach; and civil rights activist Rev. Jesse Jackson.

Remarks to the American Legion Boys Nation
July 24, 1998

Thank you very much. Good morning, and thank you, "Sheriff" Riley, for that introduction and for your wonderful work for the education of our young people.

I'd like to welcome your Boys Nation director, Ron Engel; your legislative director, George Blume; your director of activities, Jack Mercier, celebrating 35 years with Boys Nation—he was here when I was here, back in the "dark ages"; your national chairman for the American Legion, Joseph Caouette President Sladek; Vice President Rogers.

We've got a good representation for former Boys Nation people here. I know Fred DuVal, my Deputy Assistant, who was in Boys Nation class of 1972, has already spoken to you. I'd also like to recognize Sean Stephenson, class of 1996, now an intern in Cabinet Affairs; thank you for what you're doing here. And I'd like to acknowledge someone who has worked with Boys Nation, year after year as long as I've been here, in facilitating this event, a long, long-time friend of mine, Dan Wexler, who is leaving the White House. This is his very last event. And thank you, Mr. Wexler, for a wonderful job for the United States.

As some of you may know, a few days ago we had a reunion here at the White House for our 35th anniversary of our Boys Nation summer, and "Nightline" ran 2 nights on our reunion. I asked your president if he'd seen either one of them; he said he saw the first one, the second one he was here on duty. But I had an opportunity to meet with about half the men who were with me 35 years ago, and we were reminiscing. It was exactly 35 years ago on this day, July 24, 1963, that President Kennedy spoke to us right here in the Rose Garden about our future. He made us believe that together we could change the world. I still believe that, and I think it is no less true for your generation. Indeed, I believe you will live in the time of greatest possibility in all human history.

Today I want to talk with you a little bit about what we have to do as a country to make the most of those possibilities, specifically about what we have to do to strengthen our education system.

When I was here, President Kennedy complimented us for supporting civil rights legislation which the Nation's Governors had declined to do. I was very proud of that because two delegates from Louisiana and I and one from Mississippi were four Southerners who broke from the pack and ensured that the legislation would pass. But I have to say that, looking back over the years, we knew then that our school systems were separate and unequal and that we never could make them what we ought to until we integrated our schools so that we could integrate our country. What we did not see then and what we know now is that equal access to public schools does not guarantee the educational excellence that should be the birthright of every American on the edge of the 21st century.

Today we enjoy a remarkable amount of peace and prosperity and security. We have the lowest unemployment rate in 28 years, lowest

percentage of our people on welfare in 29 years, lowest crime rate in 25 years. On October 1st we will realize the first balanced budget and surplus we have had in 29 years. We have the highest homeownership in history, and the Government has played an active role in this, but it is the smallest Government we have had in 35 years, since I was here where you are today.

Still, the world is changing fast, and it is full of challenges that we have to meet. We must build an alliance of nations, committed to freedom and human rights and to fighting against terrorism and organized crime and drug trafficking, against weapons of mass destruction, and racial, ethnic, and religious violence that bedevils so much of the world. We must build a global alliance against the global environmental and health challenges we face, including the degradation of our oceans and especially the problem of climate change.

Those of you who come from Texas and Arkansas and Oklahoma and the other places in the South that have been experiencing record heat know a little about this, but it's worth pointing out that the 9 hottest years on record have occurred in the last 11 years; 1997 was the hottest year ever recorded; each and every month of 1998 has broken a record. So unless something happens, notwithstanding this cool morning we're enjoying now, 1998 will be the hottest year on record. Unless we act now, by the time you're my age, you will have a much, much more severe problem to confront.

We have a lot of challenges here at home. We have to save Social Security and Medicare for the 21st century in a way that protects the retirement age of the baby boomers without bankrupting our children and our grandchildren. Until your generation—that is, you and all the people younger than you, starting the year before last—entered school, my generation—and I'm the oldest of the baby boomers—were the largest group of Americans ever. When our fathers came home to meet our mothers after World War II, there was a sense of enthusiasm and exuberance which manifested itself in unusually large families. [*Laughter*] And we all enjoyed being part of the baby boom generation, at least I think most of us did. But all of us now, I think without regard to our station in life, are quite concerned about the potential burdens we might impose on our children.

Not so long ago, I had to go home to Arkansas because we had some serious tornadoes.

After I toured the damage sites, I had dinner at the airport in Little Rock with about 20 people I grew up with. And I try to stay in touch with them, and we just went around the table, and most of them are just middle class working people. Every one of them was absolutely determined that we had to make the changes now to prepare ourselves to retire in ways that didn't impose undue burdens on our children. Because when we begin to retire, when all the baby boomers get into their retirement age—that is over 65—at present birth rates and immigration rates and retirement rates, there will only be about two people working for every person retired.

Now, this is a significant challenge. But it can be met. It is, in this way, like the problem of climate change. If we act now and take modest but disciplined steps now, well ahead of the time when we have to face the crisis, then we won't have to take big, dramatic, and maybe draconian steps later. So, especially saving Social Security is important.

And I'd like to say just a couple more words about it, because I want all of you to think about it; it's important. The idea behind Social Security is, number one, even though your retirement may be a long way off, you can know that it's going to be there for you. Number two, even though most Americans have something other than Social Security to retire on— and you should begin as soon as you get into the work force to save and plan for your own retirement, because if you save a little bit when you're young, you'll have a whole lot when you're older—Social Security actually is responsible for keeping about half of our senior citizens out of poverty. And beginning about 10 or 15 years ago, we achieved a remarkable thing for a society. We had a poverty rate among seniors that was lower than the poverty rate for the society as a whole. We want to continue that, and we can.

Thanks to our fiscal discipline, we're going to have the first budget surplus we've had, as I said, in 29 years. And this gives us some money to help to pay for the transition. I believe it is very important to set aside every penny of this surplus until we save Social Security. Now, that's a big challenge here in Washington, because after all, it's an election year, and it's more popular to give tax cuts or even to have big new spending programs than to say to people, "Okay, we've got this money, but we don't want to spend it right now. We may well be able to afford new spending programs; we may well be able to afford a tax cut, but we need to know how much it's going to cost to fix Social Security and how we can make it as small a burden as possible today and tomorrow."

That's why I have said save Social Security first. If it doesn't take all the money of the projected surplus, then we can figure out what else to do with it. I believe that is important. Some people here disagree with me; some want a tax cut before we fix Social Security. I am determined not to let that happen, because I think we should invest in your future, not squander it.

I do not believe that those of us who are adults should enjoy a limited small tax cut now and sacrifice your future tomorrow. And I'm going to do what I can to stop that. I think there is broad support for this position among both Democrats and Republicans in Washington, and I hope very much that, by the time you're out in the work force and having children of your own, that this will be yesterday's problem, and you will not have to confront it. And we're going to do our best to see that that happens.

Let me talk a little about, very briefly, some other challenges we face. We have to provide access to affordable quality health care to all Americans. More and more Americans, probably a lot of you here, are in managed care plans. Managed care has done a lot of good. It's cut a lot of inflation out of health care costs. But health care decisions ought to be made by doctors and patients, not by accountants and insurance company executives who are determined to save money whether or not it's the right thing to do for the patients. That's the idea behind the Patients' Bill of Rights we're trying to pass up here in this session of Congress.

I think it is very important that we recognize that, in spite of all this economic growth, there are still areas of our country which have not reaped the benefits of American enterprise. There are inner-city neighborhoods, there are Native-American communities, and as a lot of our farmers have been telling America lately, there are a lot of rural American communities that still have not felt the benefits of the economic recovery. If we can't find a way to expand opportunity to these areas now, when we're doing so well, we will not be able to do it the next time a recession comes along. So that, I think, is a very important challenge.

I think it is very important that we build an America, as Secretary Riley says, that crosses the boundaries of race and religion and culture; that respects, revels in our diversity; that enjoys our heated arguments; but that recognizes that underneath it all we are bound together by those things that the framers laid out so long ago. We all believe in life, liberty, and the pursuit of happiness. We all believe that we have constituted a free Government of willing citizens because there are things we have to do together that we can't do alone. We all believe that America will always be on a permanent mission to form a more perfect Union.

So I say to all of you, even though I think it's a great thing to have vigorous debates—I love them. I think it's a good thing that we have different opinions. I think it is a terrific thing that we have people in America who come from every other country on Earth. Just across the Potomac River here, in Fairfax County, there are students from 180 different national, racial, and ethnic groups in one school district, and they come from 100 different language groups. That is great for America in a global society. But we still have to find a way to be one America, to recognize that what we have in common as human beings, as children of God, is more important than what divides us.

And finally let me say, we have to build a world-class system of elementary and secondary education. You heard Secretary Riley say that we have done a lot of work to open the doors of college to everyone who is willing to work for it. And just about everyone in the world believes that America has the finest system of higher education in the world. Now we have the HOPE scholarship, a $1,500 tax credit for the first 2 years of college; tax credits for the junior and senior year, for graduate school, for adults who have to go back for continuing education; a direct student loan program that allows you to borrow money and then pay it back as a percentage of your income so you don't ever have to worry about borrowing money, making you go broke later, just to get an education; more work-study positions, more Pell grants. We have the AmeriCorps program for young people who want to do national service for a year or two and then earn credit for college. And this has been a very, very good thing.

But almost no one believes that every American has access to world-class elementary and secondary education. And if you think about all the other challenges I have mentioned, they all rely on a well-educated, responsible citizenry. You have to be well-educated, and you have to be a good citizen to say—take the Social Security challenge—"Don't give me a little bit of money now. Save me a huge headache later. Save my children; save my grandchildren. I'll give it up right now so we can do something good for tomorrow."

You have to be well-educated to imagine what the world would be like if this climate change continues and the polar ice caps melt and the water levels rise and the Everglades are buried or the Louisiana sugar plantations are underwater or Pacific island nations are buried, to understand what it means when the climate changes and mosquitoes bearing malaria go to higher and higher climates and infect more and more people, and then they get on airplanes and meet you in the airport, and now people in Norway come home with airport malaria. It sounds funny, but it's happening. You have to have an education to understand these things.

It helps to be well-educated to understand the importance of diversity and respect for diversity and still what we have in common. So every other challenge we face requires us to meet the challenge of educating all our citizens.

We've come a long way since 1963, when most of the schools in the South were segregated, and when I was here—listen to this—one quarter of our high school students dropped out of school before they graduated; less than half went on to college. Today, almost 90 percent of high school students do graduate, and nearly 70 percent will get some further education.

Many of you are here, as I was 35 years ago, in part because of a special teacher who's had a positive influence on your life. Our schools have always been the cornerstone of our democracy. At a time of increasing diversity through immigration, they are more important than ever. Ninety percent of our children are in our public schools, and in an age of information and ideas, a strong education system is now even more important to you than it was to me when I was your age. Now is the time to strengthen public education, not to drain precious resources from it. That is America's first priority, and it is our administration's first priority.

If our schools are to succeed in the next century, however, it will require more than money.

We have to raise standards for students and teachers. We have to heighten accountability. We should widen choices for parents and students. We have to expect more of everyone, of our students who must master the basics and more and behave responsibly; of our teachers who must inspire students to learn and to be good citizens; and of our schools which must be safe and state-of-the-art.

We've worked hard to strengthen our public schools, to promote higher standards and to measure student progress, to do what we can to improve teaching and to certify more master teachers throughout the country, to give schools the means to meet our national education goals and to help students not going to 4-year colleges make the transition from school to work, to get more aid to students in schools with special challenges and to hook all the classrooms and libraries in our country up to the Internet by the year 2000, and to have more public school choice.

But we clearly have to do more. I have called for smaller classes in our early grades and 100,000 new teachers to fill them, teachers that pass rigorous competency tests before they set foot in the classroom. I've called for an end to social promotion so that no child is passed from grade to grade, year after year, without mastering the materials and for extra help for those who don't pass, like the summer school program in Chicago.

Chicago now has mandatory—mandatory—summer school for children who don't make the social promotion hurdle. And the summer school there is now the sixth biggest school district in the entire United States of America. I don't think I have to tell you that more children are learning and the juvenile crime rate is way down. We need more of that in America.

These are important investments. We have to also do more. We need to build more schools and modernize more schools. I was in Philadelphia the other day where the average school building is 65 years old. They are magnificent old buildings. They're very well built, but they need to be modernized. A child that goes to school every day in a school where a whole floor is closed off or the roof leaks or the rooms are dark or the windows are cracked gets a signal, a clear signal that he or she is not as important as we all say they are day in and day out.

I have been to school districts in Florida where there were more than a dozen trailers outside the main school building because the schools are so overcrowded and the districts don't have the funds to keep building schools to deal with the new students. We have to do that.

We have to finish our effort to connect all our classrooms to the Internet. We have got to, in other words, make these investments that will make our country strong.

President Kennedy said our progress as a Nation can be no swifter than our progress in education. That is more true now than ever before, and I hope in the remaining few days of this congressional session, our Congress will put progress above partisanship, leave politics at the schoolhouse door, and make the education of our children America's top priority.

We know our schools are strengthened also by innovation and competition brought about increasingly in our country by more choice in the public schools children attend. Public school choice gets parents and communities more involved in education, not just in helping with homework or attending parent-teacher conferences but actually in shaping the schools.

Some of you, having gone to public schools of choice, may know this from experience. David Haller, for example, from Arkansas, attends a school that's very close to my heart, in the town I grew up in, the Arkansas School of Math and Science in Hot Springs, which I help to found as Governor.

Across our Nation, public school choice and, in particular, charter schools are renewing public education with new energy and new ideas. Charter schools are creative schools, innovative schools, public with open enrollment, strengthened by the commitment of parents and educators in the communities they serve. They can be models of accountability for all public schools, because they are chartered only when they meet rigorous standards of quality, and they should remain open only as long as they meet those standards.

According to new data from Secretary Riley's Department of Education, parents are choosing charter schools more and more often because they're small, safe, supportive, and committed to academic excellence. We can do more of this.

I am pleased to report some interesting progress. When I was elected President, campaigning on the idea that we should have more of these charter schools, there was only one such school in the country. It was in the State of Minnesota. I am pleased to tell you that this fall there will be 1,000 of them, serving more than 200,000 children. We're well on our way to meeting my goal of creating 3,000 such schools by the beginning of the next century, and again, I ask Congress to help us meet the goal and finish its work on the bipartisan charter school legislation that is now making its way through Congress.

The Department of Education has released a guidebook to help communities learn from each other's successes. I commend it to you. Charter schools do very well in general, but they face a lot of challenges, including finding the funding to get started and keep going. Lack of access to startup funding, as the report I release today shows, is the biggest obstacle facing more rapid development of these schools. To make it easier for parents and educators to innovate, I have proposed to increase the $80 million for startup funds this year to 100 million next year. That's up from 6 million when we started in 1994.

Now, let me just say one other thing. A lot of you are going back for your senior years. You'll be leaving your hometown school. Some of you will be going a long way away to college. I urge you to go wherever your dreams take you. But in the years to come, I hope you won't forget about your schools. I am very impressed by all the resolutions and the legislation that you have passed, and I have been given a review of it this morning before I came out here. But I'm also impressed by the commitment that so many of you have expressed to citizen service. I hope you will always take part of your time to be servants to young people who are younger than you are.

Some of you may become teachers or professors, but most of you won't. Wherever your life's travels take you, every one of you can find some enduring connection to education. I hope some of you will consider, some time during your next few years, joining our national service program, AmeriCorps, and serving young people in your community and building up some more scholarship money.

But whatever you do when you get out of school, I hope you will maintain a connection to young people and to their schools. You can volunteer your time, you can mentor someone who needs guidance. You can remember that only a very few young people ever have the experience you're having now, but hundreds and thousands more can hear about it from you and be inspired by it, to believe in our country and to believe in themselves and their capacity to learn and live out their dreams.

As I get older and older, I think more and more, as is natural I suppose, about people who are coming along behind me. It's hard to get used to—most of us will tell you that we consider anyone who is a year younger than we are to be young, however old we are. I never will forget, once I was talking to Senator Mike Mansfield, who was our Ambassador to Japan, and Senator Mansfield must be about 96 now. He still walks about 5 miles a day. And he was having lunch with another former Senator, J. William Fulbright—who was a mentor of mine and for whom I worked when I was in college—when Senator Mansfield was 91, and Senator Fulbright was 87. He looked at him, and he said, "Bill, how old are you now?" And he said, "I'm 87." And Mansfield said, "Oh, to be 87 again." [*Laughter*] So we all get our perspective from our own age.

And for you, your future is all ahead of you. But just think about how many Americans there already are who are younger than you are, and think about how many there are who would never have a chance like the one you've had this past week. And just remember, never, never, never underestimate your ability to teach, to inspire, to guide, to help them to love this country the way you do, to embrace concepts of good citizenship the way you have, and frankly, to live a good, constructive, ambitious life the way you will. All of us—all of us—sometimes underestimate the enormous power that we have to influence other people one-on-one.

Alexis de Tocqueville said a long time ago that America is great because America is good. America cannot be good except through her people. To say America is good is to say the American people are good. We have all these big challenges. I'm convinced we will meet them, as we have all our other challenges for over 200 years, because America is good.

I ask your support in meeting those challenges, and I ask for your commitment never to forget all those young people who are coming along behind.

Good luck, and God bless you. Thank you very much.

NOTE: The President spoke at 9:25 a.m. in the Rose Garden at the White House. In his remarks, he referred to Secretary of Education Richard W. Riley, who, as a boy, was elected sheriff of Boys State, South Carolina; and Kevin Sladek, president, and Jeffrey Rogers, vice president, 1998 Boys Nation Session.

Statement on House of Representatives Action on Patients' Bill of Rights Legislation
July 24, 1998

The Patients' Bill of Rights should not be designed for the political needs of any party; it should be designed to meet the health needs of all Americans. Unfortunately, the House Republicans passed legislation today that simply does not meet this test. This bill leaves out millions of Americans; it leaves out critical patient protections; and it adds in "poison pill" provisions which undermine the possibility of passing a strong bipartisan Patients' Bill of Rights this year.

The Republican leadership's legislation does not apply to the individual insurance market and therefore excludes millions of Americans. It does not include many important protections such as ensuring direct access to specialists so that patients can see the cancer doctors or heart specialists that they need, or ensuring that care will not abruptly change if a patient's provider is unexpectedly dropped or an employer changes health plans. Moreover, the enforcement mechanism in this legislation is insufficient as it gives little recourse to patients who are injured or who die because of a health plan's actions. Finally, this legislation is undermined by provisions that have nothing to do with patients' rights.

Americans want a Patients' Bill of Rights that gives them the protections they need in a rapidly changing health care system. The legislation passed by the House Republicans today falls far short of ensuring Americans the quality care they need and deserve. It is my strongest hope that the Senate will move quickly to have a fair and open debate that can produce a strong, enforceable, and bipartisan Patients' Bill of Rights this year.

Message to the Congress Reporting a Budget Rescission
July 24, 1998

To the Congress of the United States:
In accordance with the Congressional Budget and Impoundment Control Act of 1974, I herewith report one proposed rescission of budgetary resources, totaling $5.2 million.

The proposed rescission affects programs of the Department of the Interior.

WILLIAM J. CLINTON

The White House,

July 24, 1998.

NOTE: The report detailing the proposed rescission was published in the *Federal Register* on August 3.

Statement on the Shootings at the Capitol
July 24, 1998

Hillary and I were deeply disturbed to hear of the shootings this afternoon at the United States Capitol. Like all Americans, we extend our thoughts and prayers to the families of the slain officers, Jacob Chestnut and John Gibson, as well as to the injured victim and her family. The Capitol is the people's house, a place where visitors and workers should not have to fear violence. Every American appreciates the bravery of the Capitol Police who prevented further injury through their courageous actions.

NOTE: The statement referred to Angela Dickerson, who was injured during the incident.

Remarks at Andrews Air Force Base, Maryland, on the Shootings at the Capitol
July 25, 1998

Good morning. The shooting at the United States Capitol yesterday was a moment of savagery at the front door of American civilization. Federal law enforcement agencies and the United States Attorney's Office are working closely with the DC police and the Capitol Police to ensure that justice is pursued.

Meanwhile, I would ask all Americans to reflect for a moment on the human elements of yesterday's tragedy. The Scripture says, "Greater love hath no man than this: that he lay down his life for his friends." Officer Jacob "J.J." Chestnut and Detective John Gibson laid down their lives for their friends, their coworkers, and their fellow citizens, those whom they were sworn to protect. In so doing, they saved many others from exposure to lethal violence.

Every day, a special breed of men and women pin on their badges, put on their uniforms, kiss their families goodbye, knowing full well they may be called on to lay down their lives. This year alone, 79 other law enforcement officers have made the ultimate sacrifice. Every American should be grateful to them for the freedom and the security they guard with their lives, and every American should stand up for them and stand against violence.

Officer Chestnut was a Vietnam veteran, a member of the Capitol Police for 18 years, just months away from retirement. Detective Gibson was a deeply religious man, beloved by his coworkers and, being from Massachusetts, devoted to the Red Sox and the Bruins. Both leave behind loving wives and children, the affection of neighbors, friends, and coworkers, and the deep gratitude of those who are alive today because of their bravery.

In this one heartless act, there were many acts of heroism: by strangers who shielded children with their bodies, by officers who fanned across the Capitol, by Dr. Bill Frist, a renowned heart surgeon before his election to the Senate from Tennessee, who had just put down his gavel when he rushed to tend the injured. To all these and others who stood for our common humanity, we extend the thanks of our Nation.

To the families of Officer Chestnut and Detective Gibson, nothing we say can bring them back. But all Americans pray that the power of a loving God and the comfort of family and friends will, with time, ease your sorrow and swell your pride for loved ones and the sacrifice they made for their fellow citizens.

To Angela Dickerson, the young woman who was injured in the shooting, we extend our prayers and hope for your speedy recovery.

To every American who has been shaken by this violent act, to the millions of parents who have taken your children through those very same doors, I ask you to think about what our Capitol means. All around the world, that majestic marble building is the symbol of our democracy and the embodiment of our Nation. We must keep it a place where people can freely and proudly walk the halls of their Government. And we must never, ever take for granted the values for which it stands or the price of preserving them.

Thank you very much.

NOTE: The President spoke at 9:10 a.m. at Air Force One, prior to his departure for Norfolk, VA.

The President's Radio Address
July 25, 1998

Good morning. This year we've seen a disturbing string of weather-related emergencies all around our country, from flash floods in Tennessee to wildfires in Florida to ice storms last winter in New England. This summer record heat and drought are taking a terrible human toll, destroying crops, causing power outages, worst of all, taking lives. Just since June, more than 130 people have died because of the heat.

Certainly, the latest El Niño is partly to blame for the severe weather conditions that have besieged so many communities. But growing evidence suggests that the extreme and erratic weather we're seeing in America and around the world is being intensified by global warming.

Consider this: 1997 was the warmest year on record, and 1998 is on track to break that record. Five of the hottest years in history— the 5 hottest years—have all occurred in the 1990's. Scientists predict that July may be the hottest month since mankind began recording temperatures. The world's leading climate experts predict even more extreme weather unless we reverse this dangerous warming trend.

We're doing everything we can in the short term to help communities cope with this devastating heat wave. This week I released $100 million in emergency funds to the 11 hottest States. On Monday Agriculture Secretary Glickman and FEMA Director James Lee Witt will travel to Texas and Oklahoma to see what more we can do to help there. Today I'm pleased to announce that the Department of Energy will begin providing new crisis assistance to low-income families, repairing and replacing air-conditioners and fans, installing insulation, and giving advice on the best way to keep homes cool in this extreme heat.

But to meet the long-term challenge of global warming, we must do more. Vice President Gore and I have launched a comprehensive, cost-effective strategy to protect our environment while creating new opportunities for economic growth. I've proposed $6.3 billion in research and tax incentives over the next 5 years to encourage the private sector to work with us to improve our energy efficiency, generate clean power, and reduce the greenhouse gases that contribute so much to global warming.

We must all do our part to protect the environment, and as the Nation's largest energy consumer, the Federal Government must lead. At my direction, we're undertaking a multipart initiative to put our own house in order. Today I'm pleased to announce the first four parts of this plan, aimed at increasing the efficiency of Federal buildings.

First, I'm directing Federal agencies to work more closely with private contractors to retrofit Federal buildings and other facilities with the best energy-saving technology, at no cost to taxpayers. Second, we'll replace hundreds of thousands of conventional light bulbs and fixtures with more efficient fluorescents, which will pay back in energy savings nearly 5 times what they cost to install. Third, I'm directing all agencies to work toward bringing their existing buildings up to EPA's Energy Star standard of energy efficiency. And fourth, the Defense Department and six other Federal agencies will adopt "sustainable design" guidelines for all new Federal buildings to reduce their energy use.

Now, together these measures will save taxpayers as much as a billion dollars a year in energy costs. They'll help to jumpstart markets for new technologies, and they'll protect our environment by reducing greenhouse gas emissions.

We are facing squarely the problem of global warming, but there are still some in Congress who would rather pretend it doesn't exist. Despite mounting evidence, they would deny the science and ignore the warning signs. Rather than invest in a commonsense strategy to reduce greenhouse gas emissions, they want to cut programs for energy efficiency and renewable energy, programs that long have enjoyed bipartisan support.

Worst of all, some have even tried to keep the public from learning the facts about global warming by barring Federal agencies from even talking about the issue. Thankfully, this gag order was defeated in the House of Representatives just this week. Global warming is real. The risks it poses are real, and the American people have a right to know it and a responsibility to do something about it. The sooner Congress understands that, the sooner we can protect our Nation and our planet from increased flood, fire, drought, and deadly heat waves.

To protect our environment, we must put progress ahead of partisanship. For nearly 30 years now, we've had a bipartisan commitment to preserving the environment. We have to bring it to this new challenge.

As sweltering as this summer has been, if we don't act now, our children may look back on the summer of 1998 as one that was relatively mild and cool. There's no excuse for delay. We have the tools; we have the ingenuity to head off this threat. We have the opportunity and the deepest of obligations to leave our children and our grandchildren a healthy, thriving planet, God's great gift to us all.

Thanks for listening.

NOTE: The address was recorded at 12:23 p.m. on July 24 in the Cabinet Room at the White House for broadcast at 10:06 a.m. on July 25. The transcript was made available by the Office of the Press Secretary on July 24 but was embargoed for release until the broadcast.

Memorandum on Cutting Greenhouse Gases Through Energy Savings Performance Contracts
July 25, 1998

Memorandum for the Heads of Executive Departments and Agencies

Subject: Cutting Greenhouse Gases through Energy Savings Performance Contracts

My Administration has made addressing the threat of global climate change one of our top environmental priorities. As the Nation's largest consumer of the fossil fuels that scientists believe are driving global warming, the Federal Government has a special responsibility to lead in developing clean energy solutions and in reducing Federal energy consumption. While Government-wide energy saving activities over the last several years have resulted in significant achievements, we can and should do more.

On March 9, 1994, I issued Executive Order 12902, Energy Efficiency and Water Conservation at Federal Facilities, which directed all executive agencies to reduce energy consumption 30 percent below 1985 levels by the year 2005. We have made significant strides, but in order to achieve this goal we must make better use of a critical energy management tool. Energy Saving Performance Contracts (ESPCs), which are authorized under the National Energy Conservation Policy Act, as modified by the Energy Policy Act of 1992, provide significant opportu-

nities for making Federal buildings more energy efficient at little or no cost to taxpayers. Under ESPC authority, agencies can contract with private energy service companies to retrofit Federal buildings with no up-front payments by the Government. These companies recover their costs from a negotiated share of the energy cost savings, with the remaining savings being returned to the contracting agency and to taxpayers. The Federal Government must make more use of these highly cost-effective contracts.

I therefore direct all Federal agencies to maximize use of this authority by the year 2000, when the authority expires. I also direct the Department of Energy (DOE) to lead an interagency effort to develop a legislative proposal extending ESPC authority past the year 2000. As part of this effort, I direct all agencies to identify and propose areas for expansion of ESPC authority—for instance, as appropriate, to some leased buildings, mobility, and other Federal assets. In addition, I direct agencies to propose ways to procure electricity produced using cost-effective renewable sources.

While ESPC authority has existed for some time, I have encouraged significant steps to streamline and promote greater use of this tool. To this end, the DOE and the Department of

Defense (DOD) have negotiated contracts with energy service companies over most regions of the country. These ESPCs currently allow up to $5 billion worth of projects at Federal facilities within these regions. The DOE and the DOD anticipate that by the end of this year they will negotiate contracts allowing an additional $2.7 billion worth of such work in specific regions. The combined $7.7 billion provides, in effect, the total dollar amount of retrofit projects that Federal agencies can complete at their facilities using ESPCs. In addition, the DOE anticipates negotiating over $1 billion for ESPCs to finance the installation of renewable energy and other efficient technology systems in the near future.

To further compliance with this directive, I have asked the Office of Management and Budget to provide new guidance to agencies that will help remove barriers and provide more incentives for using ESPCs. This guidance will change the budgetary treatment of these contracts to be consistent with the unique statutory authority for ESPCs. Specifically, the full amount of budget authority for the contract will no longer be needed up front, but can be made available over a number of years. In addition, this guidance will encourage agencies to permit up to 50 percent of the energy savings from ESPCs to remain at the facility or site where they occur. Both of these policies will help motivate Federal energy managers to make greater use of ESPCs and reduce agency operating costs.

To make use of this authority, Federal facilities need to contact the DOE or the DOD to engage contractors already pre-approved to complete ESPC work. Agencies can also consider using direct appropriations or contract with their local utilities. I also direct Federal agencies

to maximize efforts to earn an ENERGY STAR label, demonstrating to the public that they rank in the top 25 percent for building energy efficiency. Combining energy savings contracting authority with utility programs and agency funded efforts can save taxpayers as much as one billion dollars a year in energy costs over the next 15 years, and can reduce greenhouse gas emissions by up to 3 million metric tons of carbon annually.

To ensure the full use and benefits of ESPC authority, I further direct each executive agency to submit to me, in the next 90 days, a memorandum detailing:

1. Your agency's accomplishments in reducing energy consumption since 1985, and your plans to reduce energy consumption 30 percent below 1985 levels by 2005, in compliance with Executive Order 12902;

2. Your agency's plan to use ESPCs and other tools, as well as your plans to achieve ENERGY STAR labels for your facilities, as part of your increased attention to saving money through energy efficiency and renewable energy;

3. Your proposals on how to expand the Federal Government's use of these tools, for inclusion in our request to the Congress for extending ESPC authority beyond the year 2000; and

4. Your strategy for encouraging use of ESPCs and other financing mechanisms to install renewable energy production systems—such as those called for in the Million Solar Roofs Initiative.

WILLIAM J. CLINTON

NOTE: This memorandum was embargoed for release until 10:06 a.m.

Remarks at the Commissioning of the U.S.S. *Harry S. Truman* in Norfolk, Virginia
July 25, 1998

Thank you very much. Secretary Cohen, Mrs. Cohen; Secretary Riley; Secretary and Mrs. Dalton; Senator Robb; Governor Carnahan; Representative Skelton; Congressman Pickett and other Members of Congress; Admiral

Johnson and Admirals Bowman and Reason and Gehman, and the other distinguished leaders of the Navy who are here; Captain Otterbein; men and women of the Navy; veterans; Mr. Fricks and others who had a role in building this magnificent vessel; my fellow Americans:

Good morning, and what a beautiful morning it is. Let me begin this day by saying that we are all thinking of someone who should be here but cannot be, Margaret Truman Daniel. She has been a great friend to Hillary and our daughter and to me—a great American citizen. And Harry Truman was very proud of her, justifiably. I wish she could be here.

I'd also like to thank especially a man who will speak after me, one who knew President Truman well and stands in his tradition, and who did so much to make this day happen, Representative Ike Skelton of Missouri.

In 1913 Harry Truman was a young Missouri farmer experiencing some business difficulties, as he did from time to time. But as always, he didn't give up easily. He wrote to his sweetheart and future wife, Bess, these words: "My ship's going to come in yet." Now, we all know that Harry Truman was a man of his word. It took 85 years, but here on July 25, 1998, Harry Truman's ship has come in.

Of course, President Truman's hometown of Independence, Missouri, is not exactly a center of naval operations. Coming from the State just south of Missouri, you know, we're completely landlocked. And Harry Truman was an Army man. But in 1944, as a United States Senator, he spoke at the christening of the battleship *Missouri*, on whose decks Japan surrendered just a year later. He felt a life-long affection for the ship known as the "Mighty Mo." And as President, he came to rely, as all Presidents do, on the world's greatest Navy.

The American people still feel a strong affection for Harry Truman. He seemed to some an ordinary man, but he became an extraordinary President. He represented the best in us, and he gave us the best in himself. He never failed to live up to the words of his fellow Missourian Mark Twain, which he kept on his desk at the Oval Office: "Always do right. This will gratify some people and astonish the rest."

Fifty years ago, when Harry Truman became our President, America faced a mountain of crises: Europe lay shattered; a cold war bred danger around the world; terrible new weapons made every false step a potential catastrophe; and angry voices were being raised here at home by Americans against other Americans. At such a time, and after the rigors of World War II, some wanted to turn away from the world, to

relinquish the leadership that had rescued freedom from tyranny. But Harry Truman said no. He made courageous decisions, focused always on doing right, making sure everyone knew the buck stopped with him.

He approved massive aid to Europe, including our former enemy, in one of the most farsighted instances of enlightened self-interest in history. In 1948 he became the first world leader to recognize the new state of Israel, over the bitter protest of his advisers. That same year, when Stalin closed off Western access to Berlin, he ordered the heroic airlift to relieve the beleaguered city.

And 50 years ago tomorrow, as Secretary Cohen has noted, Harry Truman made one of the best decisions any Commander in Chief ever made. He was sickened by stories of African-American veterans fighting heroically for America in war, only to return to violence and hatred. He wrote, "As President, I know this is bad. I shall fight to end evils like this." And despite the extraordinary political pressures against him, despite growing up himself in a segregated community, on July 26, 1948, Harry Truman ordered the Armed Forces to integrate with Executive Order 9981. From that day forward our men and women in uniform have truly been a force for freedom and a shining example to all humanity.

President Truman's decisive acts made crystal clear that America would not stand by while the world unraveled, that our ideals were not just words on parchment but guideposts for coming together as Americans. As Truman said in the first address by any American President to the NAACP, "When I say all Americans, I mean all Americans." When we scan the landscape of the new century ahead, the future Harry Truman defined is the promise we now enjoy.

Think of what has happened, growing out of the decisions he made 50 years ago: The cold war is over; Europe is thriving; Berlin is united; Greece and Turkey are vital NATO allies working with us to promote peace in the Balkans; Israel, Japan, South Korea are among our strong, democratic partners; international organizations like NATO, the United Nations, the International Monetary Fund are essential components of the architecture of peace and prosperity. These are not accidents of history. They reflect the vision of the leader we celebrate here today.

Harry Truman knew that a President's ability to persuade others in the world is greatly enhanced when commanding the world's strongest military. That is still true. When we aimed to restore hope in Haiti 4 years ago, the Navy was there to make it happen. When violence tore apart Bosnia, naval operations in the Adriatic helped to create the conditions of peace. When we needed a quick action in the Persian Gulf last winter, the Navy was there again to put steel behind our diplomacy.

And on this day, our persuasiveness has been enhanced considerably. This carrier occupies 4½ acres, stands 20 stories tall; it will be home to up to 6,000 personnel, about the population of Harry Truman's hometown. From aviators in their ready rooms to the engineers in their spaces, from catapult officers who can launch four aircraft in just one minute to the cooks who prepare 18,000 meals a day, the men and women of the *Harry S. Truman* will do America proud.

And let me say to the families of those crewmen here today, we appreciate your commitment, too. Your loved ones on the *Harry S. Truman* will never be sent into harm's way without clear purpose and superior preparation. As Secretary Cohen has made clear, the readiness of our military will remain a top priority. Today and for the future, our forces will be fully capable of meeting our commitments around the world.

We have done much to meet these readiness goals, but we must do more. As the Members of Congress here keenly appreciate, Congress is the vital partner in this effort. This year, with bipartisan congressional support, we provide emergency funding for our military operations in Bosnia and southwest Asia and, thus, are able to meet critical readiness needs. But Congress as yet has not approved the funding we need on the same terms for the crucial operations in fiscal year 1999, which begins only 9 weeks from now. If we are to remain fully prepared, it is imperative that Congress act.

A month ago the Defense Department sent to Congress a request to transfer $1 billion from lower priority programs to important training, maintenance, and readiness requirements to sustain our readiness. Again, I ask Congress to approve this request before the summer recess.

This ship, the *Harry Truman,* is a monument to strength of character—to the character of a President and the character of those who serve aboard her, to the character of the shipyard workers who built her in Newport News. The motto you have adopted says it all: "The buck stops here."

Over the next 50 years, America must continue to be responsible, to say the buck stops with the United States, to ask the questions that the President we honor here today asked. What do the decisions we make today mean for our children and grandchildren? Is what we are doing good for all our people? Will it deepen our freedom, expand opportunity, strengthen our Union, advance the cause of freedom and peace and security in the world? Will it bring hope to the oppressed and fear to the oppressors?

The very sight of the *Harry S. Truman* will summon our best ideals and recall the will and vision of a man who arrived when we needed him most. Some will look at this carrier and see only her massive physical dimensions. I hope most of us will see something even bigger, the living spirit of America and the indomitable courage of one of the greatest leaders our still young Nation has yet produced.

To the men and women who will serve on the *Harry S. Truman,* remember, the buck stops with the United States. Godspeed, and if he were here he would say, "Give 'em hell." God bless you, and thank you very much.

NOTE: The President spoke at 11:40 a.m. on the ceremonial quarterdeck of the U.S.S. *Harry S. Truman* at Norfolk Naval Base. In his remarks, he referred to Janet Langhart, wife of Secretary of Defense William S. Cohen; Margaret Dalton, wife of Secretary of the Navy John H. Dalton; Gov. Mel Carnahan of Missouri; Adm. Jay L. Johnson, USN, Chief of Naval Operations; Adm. Frank L. Bowman, USN, Director, Naval Nuclear Propulsion; Adm. J. Paul Reason, USN, Commander in Chief, U.S. Atlantic Fleet; Adm. Harold W. Gehman, Jr., USN, Commander in Chief, U.S. Atlantic Command; Capt. Thomas G. Otterbein, USN, commanding officer, U.S.S. *Harry S. Truman*; and W.P. (Bill) Fricks, chairman and chief executive officer, Newport News Shipbuilding.

Remarks at a Democratic National Committee Dinner in Aspen, Colorado
July 25, 1998

Thank you very much. Thank you, Beth. Thank you, Steve. Like others, I want to thank Christy and Sheldon for having us in this magnificent home tonight with the wonderful natural surroundings. I haven't been to Aspen for a long time, and for the last 3 or 4 hours I've been kicking myself for how many years it's been since I was here last. But in the eighties, Hillary and I had some wonderful trips up here, and just looking around has been very—it's a wonderful opportunity. And again I say that this has been a particularly unique opportunity for me to see many of you and to see you in these magnificent settings. So, thank you, Sheldon; thank you, Christy. We're very grateful.

I'd like to thank many people here. I thank Secretary Riley and Secretary Slater for coming out here and being a part of this. Once I had a meeting of Presidential scholars at a time when things were not so rosy for our administration as they are now—after the '94 elections, I don't know, it was early '95, and my obituary once again had been written several times by several people. [*Laughter*] And this fellow who is a professor at Harvard in Presidential studies, he said, " I think you're probably going to be reelected." And I said, "Why?" And he said, "Well, for one thing, you have the most loyal Cabinet since Thomas Jefferson's second administration," which was very touching to me because they're also very good.

Rodney Slater has worked with me for more than 15 years now, and I'm very proud of the work he has done. And Secretary Riley and I have been friends for more than 20 years now, and colleagues. We are so creaky; we were actually Governors in the 1970's. [*Laughter*] So I thank them for being here and for their ardent support of our political objectives.

I thank Senator Feinstein and Congresswoman DeGette. I'd also like to thank my wonderful friend Governor Roy Romer. He and Bea are here tonight, and he has done a great job being a spokesperson from our party, going around the country trying to do his job as Governor of Colorado and give us as much time as he can. I thank Steve Grossman and Barbara, and Lynn and Len Barrack, who are here, and all the weekend hosts.

I thought I would tell you, I was asking myself—although some of you are actually new to this, most people have heard me give too many speeches, and I was feeling very badly for all of you tonight. [*Laughter*] So I was thinking what I could tell you, and I thought maybe I ought to start with where I started this day.

Hillary and Chelsea and I had a wonderful weekend. Last night—or yesterday afternoon we all went out to Camp David, and we managed to fool my brother into believing that we had to have this high-powered family conference. And I think he honestly thought I was going to tell him that I had a life-threatening illness or something. [*Laughter*] And we had gathered his 20 best friends from all around America, and we threw a surprise birthday party for him last night, and he never did figure out what it was about until we hit him with it. So I didn't think I was capable of such sleight of hand, and I felt very good about myself afterwards. [*Laughter*]

And then, this morning I got up and I flew to Newport News, Virginia, to commission our newest aircraft carrier, the United States Ship *Harry Truman*. Margaret Truman, Harry Truman's daughter, is a good friend of Hillary's and mine, and she was, unfortunately, unable to be there. But all President Truman's grandchildren and great-grandchildren were there, and it was quite an extraordinary day.

I say that because if you think about what Harry Truman did 50 years ago, entering as he was, and as America was, into a new and very different time after World War II, it gives you some guidance in terms of what we ought to be doing today. And let me just mention three things.

Number one, at the end of World War II, he understood that America could not be isolated from the rest of the world, as we had been after World War I and historically, throughout our country's history before. So he was the first world leader to recognize the state of Israel, 50 years ago this year, against the advice of most of his advisers.

Number two, he understood that America was fundamentally at that time still quite a hypocritical society in that there was such a huge gap between what was written on paper in the Declaration of Independence, the Constitution, and the Bill of Rights, and how we were living. Fifty years ago tomorrow, Harry Truman issued the Executive order to integrate the Armed Forces. Fifty years later, we have the most diverse and the most successful military anywhere in the world.

Number three, Harry Truman understood that you could not go into a new and different time with just the right ideas; there also had to be some institutional mechanisms through which people could work to achieve their common objectives, just as—the same way that if you have an idea to make money in the free enterprise system, you still have to organize a business to do it. And that's what the United Nations was all about; that's what the International Monetary Fund was all about; that's what NATO was all about.

So Harry Truman committed us to the world, committed us to being one America, and committed America to building and supporting the institutions necessary to make it possible for the American people to make the most of their own lives and to advance the cause of peace and freedom and prosperity around the world.

Now, if you fast-forward to the present moment, on the edge of a new century and a new millennium, we have some of the same challenges and some very different ones. But the thing I want to say to you is, the world is moving quickly and changing profoundly, and we need that level of vision as a people to decide where we want to go. And I believe that our party best embodies that in America today.

And I'd like to just give you just a few examples. First of all, when I came to office in 1993 I was determined to reflect at least as best I could what I thought the real experience of Americans was out in the country and not just to get into this Washington sort of hyperpolitical rhetoric and shouting that is the staple of everyday life in Washington, DC.

I had the privilege to serve as a Governor with two of the Coloradans here present, Roy Romer and Dick Lamm. And when we argued about things, we almost always were arguing about what would work or not, based on what kind of country we wanted to build, what kind of future we wanted to have for our children, what kind of legacy we wanted to leave them.

So we started with a different economic policy, a different welfare policy, a different education policy, a different crime policy, and very often what I tried to do was misunderstood at least by the political writers who were quite angry that they could no longer put it into a little neat box of whether it was old-fashioned liberal or old-fashioned conservative. I concede that I caused them the discomfort of having to think about it, but I thought that's what we should be doing. We had gone on too long on automatic in American politics, and the time had come to lower the rhetoric and open our ears and our eyes and think about it.

I often used to quote Benjamin Franklin's famous saying that our critics are our friends, for they show us our faults. And then I found so many friends in Washington, I stopped saying it. [*Laughter*] But nonetheless, there's some truth to it.

So if you look at where are we today, today we have the lowest unemployment rate in 28 years, the lowest crime rate in 25 years, the lowest percentage of people on welfare in 29 years, the first balanced budget and surplus in 29 years, with the lowest inflation in 32 years, the highest homeownership in history, the smallest Federal Government in 35 years; with scholarships and loans that have opened the doors of college to all Americans; with cleaner air, cleaner water, safer food, fewer toxic waste dumps, more land set aside in national trust than any administration except the two Roosevelts; 5 million children with health insurance; and a real ethic of national service among citizens out there, with things like AmeriCorps, which is now at 100,000 young people serving in communities across America, and 1,000 different colleges which have had their students working in our grade schools, teaching our kids to read.

So this is a better country, stronger, more well prepared for the future. But I would say to you we still have a lot of huge, big institutional challenges. I believe that where we are now, compared to where we were 6 years ago, is that America is working again. And we should come to the point where we expect that—not that there won't always be ups and downs in the economy, but we should expect ourselves to have a functioning society.

And we should take this moment of prosperity and instead of doing what our friends in the Republican Party hope will happen—which is that the status quo will prevail and they will hold on to power by doing the things they've done to kill campaign finance reform and to kill the tobacco reform legislation and so far to kill the Patients' Bill of Rights and a lot of other things that I think should be passed—we ought to be saying, no, no, no, no. When things are changing and the challenges are big, we should use the prosperity and the confidence it gives us to ask ourselves, what are the big long-term challenges this country faces, and how are we going to meet them? And that's what I want the Democrats to do.

Because as long as our party is seen as the party of constructive change and inclusive change, where we're embracing new ideas but we're rooted in traditional values, we're going to do better and better and better, because we have broken out of the paralysis of the past. And I think it's obvious to anyone just following the news that the members of the other party can't really say that today.

So let me just give you a few examples of what I think we ought to be doing. First of all, if we're looking to the future, we have to look at how we can build one America generationally, which means that we cannot permit the baby boom generation to retire with the present systems of Social Security and Medicare unaltered, because when you have two people working for every one person retired—which is what's going to happen when all the baby boomers retire, at present rates of birth, retirement, and immigration—the present systems, as they're constructed, are unsustainable.

Now, Monday I'm going down to New Mexico to hold the second of our national forums on Social Security. But there's got to be—Social Security has done a lot of good; 48 percent of the seniors in this country who are above the poverty line would be below it if there were no Social Security. It's done a lot of good. But the people that I know in my generation are obsessed with the thought—and I'm not just talking about well-off people; I mean the middle-class working people I grew up with in Arkansas—are obsessed with the thought that when we retire we will impose unfair burdens on our children and their ability to raise our grandchildren. We are determined not to see it happen. Therefore, our party, which created Social Security and created Medicare, has the responsibility to take the lead in a constructive reform of them if we want to honor the compact

in America between the generations. That's a first big issue. I hope it will be done in early 1999.

Second, we have an obligation to prove that we can grow the economy and finally make it reach people in places that it hasn't reached: in inner-city neighborhoods; in rural areas—you know, if you've been following the farm crisis, you know there's been a 90 percent drop in farm income in North Dakota in one year; in Native American communities, where the ones that don't have casino gambling have hardly had any advance in their economic well-being at all in the last 6 years. If we can't improve the economic circumstances, not by giving money but by creating enterprise, in these communities when we're doing well, we'll never be able to do it.

The third thing we have to do—and I cannot say how important I think is—a lot of you were kind enough to mention the China trip. And let me just make a little timeout here. Jiang Zemin once asked me if I was trying to contain China, if I were scared of China and I thought America had to keep it in. And I said, "No, I'm not worried about that. Historically, your country has not been particularly aggressive towards its neighbors, and you suffered from more invasion than you've done invading." I said, "But you do present a threat to our security." And he looked at me and he said, "What is it?" I said, "I'm afraid you're going to insist on getting rich the same way we did." [*Laughter*] "And I want you to get rich, but if you get rich the same way we did, nobody on the planet will be able to breathe."

And we have to prove that we do not have to maintain industrial age energy use patterns to have a successful, sustainable economy in which our children have unparalleled opportunities. And if you look at the technology now available, I predict to you that in the 21st century, energy will go the way of electronics in the last 50 years, you know, everything getting smaller and smaller and smaller. The only reason we got this year 2000 computer problem is that those of us like Americans who computerized early did it when the chips wouldn't hold much memory. And so all the dates were just put in with two numbers instead of four because memory was a precious commodity. That will never be a problem again because smaller chips hold unbelievable memory. The average home computer now has more power than the average supercomputer did when my daughter was born, for example.

So we have to do this. This is a huge deal. Nine of the hottest years in history, since temperatures have been measured, have been in the last 11 years. Florida had the wettest winter, the driest spring in history, and June was the hottest month in the history of Florida, hotter than any July or August in Florida history. Ninety-seven was the hottest year in the history of the world; '98, every single month has set a new record. So unless something happens, in spite of the wonderful cool evening we're enjoying in Aspen, this will be the hottest year on record.

Now, I am not advocating a policy of no growth or low growth. I am advocating a policy of putting our brains and our market enterprise to the task of growing the economy while reducing the per unit energy use required to do it and changing the nature of energy.

The Sterns from Chicago are here; their son, Todd, runs this program for me, my climate change program. And he's a brilliant young man, and he's doing a wonderful job. But we have got to somehow convince the American people and the Chinese people that we can grow the economy and improve the environment. And if we don't—unfortunately, while I was joking with Jiang Zemin, I told him the truth. If you go to China today, what's the number one health problem they've got? Bronchial problems, breathing problems, children with asthma—terrible problems. And we can do better. But it's our solemn obligation to do it.

Let me just mention one or two other things. First of all, I want to talk about education just briefly. This is area where there's the biggest difference between the Republicans and the Democrats in Congress in this session. Everybody knows America has the best system of higher education in the world. That's why people from all over the world come here to go to college and to graduate school. And we welcome them. I love it. It's like our major exchange program. It saves the Government a lot of money that people want to come here anyway to go to college and graduate school. And it helps us to become even more tied into the rest of the world.

No serious person who knows a lot about education believes that we have the best system of elementary and secondary education in the world. And yet, in a world where the economy is based on ideas, where even those of you in agriculture who are here are benefiting from and have to embrace newer and newer technologies every year, we need more universal education than ever before. So I have put before the American people and before the Congress an agenda that would support higher standards and greater accountability and better teaching and smaller classes in the early grades and hooking all the classes up to the Internet and more choice within the public schools.

And the main thing I want to say to you is that this is not a time for what I take to be the Republican response, which is, make possible for more people to go to private school and everything will be fine. When 90 percent of our kids are in public school, that's just not accurate. What we need is universal excellence of opportunity. And so that's something the Democrats have to be on the forefront of.

The last thing I'd like to say is that we've got to be interested in creating one America in a time that's far more complicated than Harry Truman's time, and in having that America lead the world in a time when the issues are more complicated than they were in his time. The cold war may be over, but believe you me, in the lifetime of people in this room, we will be confronting serious challenges—of terrorists, drug runners, organized criminals, having access to chemical and biological weapons, other high-tech weapons—I hope not—but they would try to get small-scale nuclear weapons.

In the lifetime of the people in this room, in this modern age, the ancient racial and religious and ethnic hatreds, which have killed hundreds of thousands of people in Rwanda, bedeviled Northern Ireland, continue to paralyze the Middle East, caused the Bosnian war, now have all the problems in Kosovo—the possibility that those things might be mixed with weapons of mass destruction is enormous.

And all of you that are involved in finance know what this problem in Asia—these Asian financial problems and the challenges of Russia have done to the international markets there and the prospect of supporting peace and prosperity and freedom in those countries in that region. Our own economy has slowed considerably because of the Asian financial crisis. So that the last thing I want to tell you.

We have got to reaffirm—we've got to tell people, who cares that the cold war is over?

It's more important than ever before that America be in there leading the way to create an international economy that works, that works for people abroad, and works for the American people as well.

Now, I think if the Democratic Party stands for that kind of constructive future for America and comes forward with those kinds of ideas and is uncompromising, and if we get enough help to get our message out—and Steve Grossman didn't say this, but we picked up some seats in 1996. In the last 10 days, our candidates in the 20 closest House races were outspent 4½ to one. We're not talking about peanuts here. We're talking about—and the stakes could hardly be larger.

Now, you pick up the paper every day; you watch the news every day. Do you hear debates at the level that I've just been talking to you about on these issues? Is this what you think they're talking about in Washington? You put us in, and that's what we'll be talking about, and your children will enjoy the fruits of it. That's why you're here, and we're very grateful.

Thank you, and God bless you.

NOTE: The President spoke at 9:30 p.m. at a private residence. In his remarks, he referred to Beth Dozoretz, senior vice president, FHC Health Systems, who introduced the President; dinner hosts Christy and Sheldon Gordon; former Gov. Richard Lamm of Colorado; President Jiang Zemin of China; and the following Democratic National Committee personnel: Steve Grossman, national chair, and his wife, Barbara; Gov. Roy Romer of Colorado, general chair, and his wife, Bea; and Leonard Barrack, national finance chair, and his wife, Lynn. A tape was not available for verification of the content of these remarks.

Remarks and a Question-and-Answer Session at a Democratic National Committee Reception in Aspen
July 25, 1998

The President. Thank you. That was better than I can do, Michael. Thank you very much. Thank you and thank you, Ana, for welcoming all of us into your home. And I want to thank my long, longtime friend Roy Romer for being willing to keep his day job and take on another job as well for our party.

Since you mentioned the Brady bill, I think what I'd like to do is maybe just talk just for a few minutes and then, probably to the chagrin of all the people who came here with me, take a few minutes, if any of you have any questions or comments or you want to give a speech to me, I'll listen to that. But if—you think about it, if you've got any questions you want to ask.

But you heard the example Michael gave you of the Brady bill, and if you ask me about what I have tried to do through and with our Democratic Party and as President that makes it worthy of the support of thoughtful Americans, many of whom might have even been Republicans before, I would say two things.

First of all, I've tried to move our party and to move our country and, hardest of all, to move Washington, DC, away from sort of yesterday's categorical, partisan name calling toward a genuine debate over new ideas, because we are living in a new and different time that, coincidentally, is at the turn of the century and the turn of the millennium, but is indisputably different. It is different because the way we work and live and relate to each other and the rest of the world is different. It is different because the nature of the challenges we face, among other things, in relating to the natural environment are profoundly different than any previous generation. So that's the first thing; it is different.

The second thing I would say is that I have tried to redefine what it means for Americans to be engaged in what our Founding Fathers said would be our permanent mission, forming a more perfect Union. And the Brady bill is about as good an example as any I can think of for what the difference is today, in Washington at least—not so much out in the country maybe but certainly in Washington—between the two parties.

If you go back to the beginning of the Republic, the people who got us started were very smart people; they understood that they weren't perfect. Thomas Jefferson said when he thought of slavery, he trembled to think that God was just and might judge him justly. So they knew they weren't perfect even then. And then they knew there would be new and uncharted challenges in the future. But they essentially—if you go back and read the Declaration of Independence and the Constitution and the Bill of Rights, it all comes down to the fact that they believe that God gave everybody the inherent right to life, liberty, and the pursuit—not the guarantee but the pursuit—of happiness, and that in those shared rights we were created equal, not with equal abilities, not with equal tastes, not all the same, but equal in a fundamental human sense.

And then the second thing that distinguishes the Democrats from the Republicans even today, I think—even more today than in the last 50 years—the Founding Fathers said, "Look, we can't pursue these objectives completely by ourselves. We can't protect or enhance the right to life, liberty, and the pursuit of happiness unless we band together and form a government. But governments ought to be limited. They ought to be limited in scope, limited in power, limited in reach, but they should do those things that we cannot do alone." And sometimes, in order to advance our collective life, liberty, and happiness, individually we have to make a few sacrifices. That's really what the Brady bill is all about.

You know, in a country with 200 million guns, where last year, with our zero tolerance for guns, we sent home—6,100 kids got sent home from school because they brought guns to school, and you've seen in the series of murders in the schools the consequences of failure when that policy either doesn't work or isn't enough, the Brady bill, by requiring a background check and making people wait 5 days between the time they order and get a handgun, has kept a quarter of a million people with criminal records, stalking records, or records of mental health instability from getting handguns. That's one of the reasons that crime is at a 25-year low, and murder has dropped even more.

Now, did it inconvenience some people to wait 5 days? Doubtless so; maybe some people that were mad at other people who cooled down after they waited 5 days. Is it an unconstitutional abridgement of the right to keep and bear arms? Not on your life.

In 1996 one of the most moving encounters I had in the campaign was when I went back to New Hampshire, the State that basically allowed me to go on when the first, we now know, Republican-inspired assault was waged against me in 1991 and '92 in New Hampshire. And they gave me a good vote, and I got to go on, so I went back there. Then they voted for me in 1992 for President. And in 1996 they voted for me again, which is unheard of because it's an overwhelmingly Republican State in elections.

But I went into an area of people who are big sportsmen, and they had defeated a Congressman who supported our crime bill with the ban on assault weapons and the Brady bill. And I had all these hunters there, and I'd been going to see them a long time. And I said, "I'll tell you what, remember back in '94 when you beat that Congressman because the NRA told you that the President was trying to take your guns away with the assault weapons ban, and the NRA?" I said, "Well, you beat him last time." I said, "Now, every one of you who lost your hunting rifle, I expect you to vote against me this time. But," I said, "if you didn't, they lied to you, and you ought to get even." [*Laughter*] And you could have heard a pin drop there, because they realized all of a sudden that this sort of radical individualism, meaning you have no responsibilities to collective citizenship, was wrong. And they could perfectly well pursue their heritage that's deeply a part of New Hampshire, where people could hunt and fish and do whatever they want, and still have sufficient restraints to try to keep our children alive. And that's just one example. And I could give you countless others.

But as you look ahead in a world where we have done our best to promote global markets, to promote efficient enterprise, we still have to recognize that there are some obligations we have to each other we have to fulfill together. And as you look ahead, let me just mention two or three—and I won't mention them all, but two or three.

One is, as presently structured, both the Social Security system and the Medicare system are unsustainable once all the baby boomers retire. And I look at all these young people who are working here and young enough, most of them, to be, for most of us, to be our children. Not very long ago I went home to Arkansas because we had a terrible tornado. And after

I toured the damaged area, I got a bunch of people I went to high school with to come out and have dinner with me. We ate barbecue from a place we've been eating at 40 years and sat around and talked. Now, most of my high school classmates had never been to Aspen. Most of my high school classmates are just middle class people with modest incomes, doing the best they can to raise their kids. But every one of them said to me, "You've got to do something to modify the Social Security system. Make it as strong for us as you can; do the best you can; but we are obsessed with not bankrupting our children and their ability to raise our grandchildren because the baby boom generation is so big that by the time we're all in it, there will be only two people working for every one person drawing."

Now, I personally believe, since the Democratic Party created Social Security and Medicare and since they, I believe, they've been great for America, that we should take the responsibility of constructively reforming them rather than going into denial and pretending that it doesn't have to be done. That's one example.

Example number two: We've got the best system of college education in the world, but nobody thinks we have the best elementary and secondary education system in the world. Ninety percent of the kids in this country are in public schools. We have got to modernize these schools, raise the standards, and do a thousand things that are necessary that Governor Romer and I have been working on for 20 years now if we expect America to grow together in the 21st century.

Example number three—and then I'll quit after this, although there are more, but I think it's important here in Colorado, especially in Aspen—we've got to prove that we can grow the economy and improve the environment, not just preserve it the way it is but actually make it better. We have to make energy use like electricity and other things in the next 50 years the way electronics has been in the last 50, where everything gets smaller and smaller and smaller, with more and more power.

I mentioned this at the previous dinner, but I'll say it again: The main reason we have a year 2000 problem with all these computers, you know, where everybody is afraid that we'll flip into—at the stroke of midnight, December 31st, January 1st, 1999, 2000, we'll all go back to 1900 and everything will stop, is because we computerized early in America. And when we computerized, these chips that hold memory were rudimentary by today's standards. And so they had all the numbers they did on dates, they just had the last 2 years; they didn't have 4 years. So they're not capable of making this transition. Today, it's a no-brainer. If you were building something today, the power of these chips is so great, nobody would even think about making it possible to have four digits on there and you could go right on until the year 9999.

So we've got to deal with this education challenge, and we've got to prove that we can do it. And then the second thing we have to do on this is to prove that we can do with energy what we have done with electronics and the computer chip.

The best example of that, that all of you will be able to access within 3 or 4 years, is a fuel-injection engine. Where today about 70 percent of the heat value of gasoline is lost as it works its way through a regular engine, when the fuel can be directly injected into the process of turning the engine over you will cut greenhouse gas emissions by 75 to 80 percent and triple mileage. And that's just one example. I was in a low-income housing development in California a couple weeks ago where the windows let in twice as much light and kept out twice as much heat and cold. All of this is designed to do in energy what we have already done in electronics and so many other things. This is a huge challenge.

I was pleased to wake up just the other morning and look at CNN; the first story was on climate change because of all the scorching heat in the South and the fires in Florida, pointing out that the 9 hottest years ever recorded have occurred in the last 11 years; the 5 hottest years ever recorded have all occurred in the 1990's; 1997 was the hottest year ever recorded; and each and every month of 1998 has broken that month's record for 1997.

This is not a game. We cannot afford to go into denial about this. We have to find a way to reduce the emission of greenhouse gases into the atmosphere and still keep growing the economy, not just for America but for China, for India, for all the people that are looking for their future. These are just three examples.

Last point: 50 years ago tomorrow—I had this on my mind because I dedicated the aircraft carrier, the *Harry Truman*, today; some of you may have seen it on TV tonight—50 years ago tomorrow Harry Truman signed the Executive order ending segregation in the United States military. And 50 years later—there are a lot of people who whined and squalled about it and said it was the end of the world and how awful it would be—50 years later we have the finest military in the world, in no small measure because it is the most racially diverse military in the world, where everybody meets uniform standards of excellence.

Today we have one school district in Washington—across the river from Washington, DC, with children from 180 different national and ethnic groups, speaking over 100 different native languages—one school district.

So that's the last point I will make. It is particularly important that we figure out how to live together and work together, to relish our differences but understand that what binds us together is more important. When you look at Kosovo and Bosnia, when you look at Northern Ireland and the Middle East, when you look at the tribal warfare in Rwanda and elsewhere, you look at the way the whole world is bedeviled by not being able to get along because of their racial, ethnic, and religious differences, if you want America to do a good job in the rest of the world, we have to be good at home.

Those are some of the things I think we should be thinking about. And I believe politics should be about this. So if when you turn on the television at night and you hear reports about what's being discussed in Washington, the tone in which it's being discussed, and the alternatives that are being presented, you hardly ever hear this, do you? You ought to ask yourself why. I can tell you this: You help more of our guys get in—what you're doing by your presence here—you'll have more of this kind of discussion, and I think America will be better in the 21st century.

Thank you very much.

National Economy

Q. As you know, I'm a Houstonian, but I have a house down the street from my friends the Goldbergs. I want to say that in your last trimester of your stewardship, I remember sitting on a bus with Senator John Breaux, my boyhood friend, and you talked about your plans for America. And I haven't seen this in the paper lately, but I guess I want to tell you that we recognize low unemployment; we recog-

nize low interest rates; we recognize low inflation and, I think, a booming economy. And I think with that track record, that I should be reading that in the paper more. But I want to tell you that I thank you, and I think all these people here thank you.

The President. Thank you. If I could just say one thing about it—as you well know, because you work all over the world, the economy is a constantly moving target. And I am very grateful we have the lowest unemployment rate in 28 years and the lowest percentage of people on welfare in 29 years and the lowest inflation in 32 years and the highest homeownership ever. That's the good news.

About a third of our economic growth has come from exports. About a third to 40 percent of our export growth—40 percent—has gone in Asia. If Asia goes down, our export growth goes down; our economic growth goes down. That is already happening. So one of the things that I think is very important to do is that we impress upon the Members of Congress, both Republican and Democratic, that we have to do those things which are designed to keep the rest of the world growing. Otherwise, we can't grow.

We are 4 percent of the world's population; we have 20 percent of the world's income. It does not require much mathematical computation to realize that if we want to sustain our income, we have to sell more to the other 96 percent of the people in the world.

And that's why I've been in such a big fight in Washington to fund America's dues to the International Monetary Fund to modernize and strengthen and restore growth in these economies, why I want to see us continue to be engaged with Japan, why I went to China: because a strong economy will cure a lot of social problems. And very few social problems can be cured in a democracy in the absence of a strong economy because the middle class becomes preoccupied with its own problems. But in this day and age, we can't sustain a strong economy without a strong foreign policy that commits us to be constructively involved with the rest of the world.

And one of the things that I worry most about in Washington is, in various ways, there are elements that are still—some in our party but more in the other party—still pulling away from our constructive engagement in the rest of the world. We cannot become what we ought to become unless we continue to get more deeply involved, not less involved, with the rest of the world. But I thank you for what you said.

Go ahead.

Republican Congress

Q. You mentioned Harry Truman, and I still remember those headlines, "Dewey Wins," right? And in fact it was Harry that won. And my question is, I believe—I am not smart enough to know exactly why, but I believe that one of the reasons he won is he said, "That do-nothing 80th Congress"—is that the right number, 80, I hope?—"and we're going to really show them." When are we going to—when do your advisers say it's time to start talking in the parts of matter, instead of more that sort of global thing where we are all going to be together and be all a happy family?

The President. Well, I have been hitting them pretty hard over the way they killed the tobacco bill, the way they are so far killing the Patients' Bill of Rights, the way they killed campaign finance reform, the way they are endangering our future economic prosperity by walking away from our dues to the International Monetary Fund. You know I haven't attacked them personally in the way they have attacked me, but I've tried to make it clear that I think there are serious risks being played with America's future there.

But I frankly believe that we have to wait until—see what happens in the first 2 weeks after the August recess. They're about to go out. Then they'll come back, and they'll have to make a final decision whether they are going to work with us to get something done for America or whether they're just going to play politics. And I believe the American people will have an extremely negative reaction if they walk away as a do-nothing Congress.

So far—one of the major papers called them a "done-nothing" Congress. They said, so far, they're a "done-nothing" Congress. They're not yet a do-nothing Congress because they still have a few days left. But they're not meeting very much this year and so far—I just think that they believe that conventional wisdom is that when times are good, incumbents all win, so what they really have to do is to keep their base happy. And in this case, the base is the most ideologically conservative people in the country. And I think they think they can keep them happy just by banging on me and doing a few other things.

And I basically disagree with that because I do not think, as good as times are, I don't think this is an inherently stable time—I mean, stable is wrong—I think it's stable but not status quo. I think all you have to look—5 years ago, Japan thought they had a permanent formula for prosperity. Now they've had 5 years of no growth, and their stock market has lost half its value.

But one of the reasons that our country is working so well is that the private sector, the entrepreneurs in this country, can stay in constant motion. There are opportunities out there. They can see things that are changing, and they can move and everything. And we've got to equip more people to do that.

But I guess I'm having a vigorous agreement with you, but I think the Republican political analysis is that they can get by this election by doing nothing because times are so good that all incumbents will benefit, even if the President is more benefited than others.

My belief is that the good times impose on us a special responsibility to bear down and take on these long-term challenges because good times never last forever and because things inherently change more rapidly now than they ever have before. So I think they're making probably a political miscalculation and certainly a miscalculation in terms of what's best for our country. And I think you'll hear more of it in the last 6 weeks before the election.

Yes?

1998 Elections

Q. The Republican Party has clearly been captured by the conservative ideologues. The Christian right, the religious right, knows what they're doing; they know what they believe; they're well organized; and I think they are probably the most—[*inaudible*]—that we have. On the other hand, Democrats, we have a—all of us have a tradition of understanding and of tolerance for the discrepancies and the differences in opinions across the party; we're not so well organized. How do we face this——

The President. Well, first of all——

Q. ——election against people who are as determined, as well organized, and as well funded as the conservative right is?

The President. Well, we are working hard to get better organized. And I think we are going to be better organized than we ever have been.

We were quite well organized in '96, and we did well. We would have won the House in '96, but for the fact that in the last 10 days of the election, in the 20 closest races they outspent us 4½ to one—in the last 10 days. Over and above that, you had all these third party groups like the Christian Coalition groups doing mass mailings into these districts, basically talking about what heathens our candidates were. And I think the Democrats are just going to have to decide whether they're going to be tough enough to handle that. I mean, we don't—but I think we will be better organized. I think we will be better funded this time. They did their best to bankrupt us the last 2 years, and it didn't work.

So I think if we're better organized and better funded and we train our candidates better, then what we have to do is be ready for that last 10-day onslaught where the Christian Coalition and the other far right groups do these heavy, heavy mailings basically trying to convince the people they're mailing to that we're cultural aliens and that we don't have good values and we don't support families and the country will come apart at the seams if we become the majority again. And if we're tough enough to handle that, I think we've got a chance to do pretty well.

We were doing fine in '96; we just didn't have enough ammunition at the end. We were so far down in '95 that we had to spend a lot of our party money to get back up, and then the last 10 days they just blew us away. But you've helped a lot by being here, and I think we know now that you don't have to descend to the level of personal meanness that your attackers do, but you do have to show a similar level of vigor, with a strategy that will work.

My own view is that we've got a strategy that will work; we've got a message that will play. And you asked about the partisanship thing—the most effective partisan attack, and a truthful one, is to say that they are being partisan in preventing us from making progress. It's not just to say Democrats are better than Republicans. It's to say they're being partisan; they're preventing us from making progress. Here are our ideas. Now, what are their ideas; measure them up. Two-thirds of the American people will pick ours.

So if they don't stampede us with fear and money, we'll do fine. And that's the ultimate answer to the question you asked.

Go ahead.

International Environmental Issues

Q. Mr. President, first of all, I think it's really wonderful—you've had a long day, and you're answering our questions. That's really the American way. Thank you.

The President. It's 1:15 a.m. our time.

Q. [*Inaudible*]—you're doing incredible things worldwide. I read the newspapers where you even got those two suspected terrorists, and they may end up getting tried in The Hague. And that's wonderful. And NAFTA was the greatest thing. I know you have to give and take, Mr. President, but during NAFTA I know one of the things you had to kind of give on a bit was to let the Mexican fishermen take up to 10,000 dolphins and kill them. Is there any way in the last year and a half we could take a couple of these ecological issues and maybe readdress them again to help make the world a better place to live?

The President. Well, we've got a lot of—one of the reasons we did that is that we finally got the Mexicans to agree to at least end some of the unsanitary conditions under which people were living along the border. And we tried to build up a border commission that would allow us to invest in the environment and elevate the public health of the people in the Maquilladora areas along the border.

I think that you will see, I predict, a number of areas where there will be advances in wildlife protection and the environment in the last 2 years. We're doing our best to get a much broader agreement, for example, on all kinds of efforts to restore the oceans generally. There's been a significant and alarming deterioration in the oceans, not unrelated to climate change and global warming but caused by forces in addition to that. There is a dead spot the size of the State of New Jersey in the Gulf of Mexico outside the mouth of the Mississippi, for example. And we're trying to address all those.

I believe the American people—I think within a decade you'll see an overwhelming majority of the American people for operational environmentalism. Today we have 70 percent of our people are environmentalists. And almost all little children are—it's something they have to be taught to abandon—their instincts are to preserve the planet. But I think that people still believe something I don't anymore, which is that you have to give up all this if you want to grow the economy. I just don't believe that. And I think that you will see a steady movement toward more aggressive environmental policies which will come to dominate both parties, I believe, in the next 10 years. And I hope before I leave office I can do more.

I even had somebody from Utah come up to me tonight and thank me for saving the Red Rocks, the Grand Staircase Escalante, you know, who said they didn't think it was right when I did it before.

Moderator. Mr. President, I know your schedule. Would you mind taking just a couple more?

The President. Go ahead.

Nuclear Proliferation in South Asia

Q. Mr. President, I've got a question about foreign policy. Do you have any concern about India and Pakistan, South Asia, what's happening over there and what kind of leadership role you can take to bring peace over there or even float the idea of creating an independent country of Kashmir, because that's the biggest problem there? What can you do about it?

The President. Well, one of the problems we've had—I thought—I actually feel bad about this because I had a trip set up for the fall to India and Pakistan. And in 1993, when I took office, I got all of our people—actually, before I took office—and I said, "Let's look at the major foreign policy challenges this country faces and figure out how we're going to deal with them and in what order." And as you might imagine, we went through the Middle East and Bosnia, and then we had Haiti on the list. We went through the idea that we had to build a trade alliance with Latin America, that we needed a systematic outreach to Africa, that the big issues were how were Russia and China going to define their future greatness and could we avoid a destructive future. And we worked hard on that.

But I told everybody at the time, I said, one of the things that never gets in the newspapers in America is the relationship between India and Pakistan and what happens on the Indian subcontinent, where they already—India already has a population of over 900 million; in 30 years it will be more populous than China; it already has the world's biggest middle class. And Paki-

stan has well over 100 million people, and so does Bangladesh. So it's an amazing place.

So I had planned to go there with plans to try to help resolve the conflicts between the two countries. One big problem is India steadfastly resists having any third party, whether it's the United States or the United Nations or anybody else, try to mediate on Kashmir. It's not surprising. India is bigger than Pakistan, but there are more Muslims than Hindus in Kashmir. I mean, it's not—the same reason that Pakistan, on the flipside, is dying to have international mediation because of the way the numbers work.

What I think we have to do is go back to find a series of confidence-building measure which will enable these two nations to work together and trust each other more and to move back from the brink of military confrontation and from nuclear confrontation. And we have to find a way to involve the Russians and the Chinese, because the Indians always say they're building nuclear power because of China being a nuclear power and the border disputes they've had with China—and oh, by the way, we happen to have this Pakistani problem.

So I have spent a lot of time on that, even though it hasn't achieved a lot of notoriety in the press. And I'm still hopeful that before the year is over, we'll be able to put them back on the right path toward more constructive relations.

I mean, India, interestingly enough, is a democracy just as diverse, if not more diverse, than America. Almost no one knows this. But most—most, but not all—the various minority groups in India live along the borders of India in the north. And it's just—it would be, I think, a terrible tragedy if Hindu nationalism led to both estrangement with the Muslim countries on the border and the minorities—Muslim and otherwise—within the borders of India, when Gandhi basically set the country up as a model of what we would all like to be, and when India's democracy has survived for 50 years under the most adverse circumstances conceivable and is now, I believe, in a position to really build a level of prosperity that has not been possible before.

I feel the same thing with the Pakistanis. I think if they could somehow—they're much more vulnerable to these economic sanctions than the Indians are. If they could somehow ease their concerns which are leading to such enormous military expenditures and put it into people expenditures, we could build a different future there. I don't know if I can do any good with it, but I certainly intend to try because I think, whether we like it or not, I think that the one good thing that the nuclear tests have done is that they have awakened the West, and Americans in particular, to the idea that a lot of our children's future will depend on what happens in the Indian subcontinent.

Q. How about if you called their Prime Ministers here?

The President. Well, I can't force a settlement on them, but I can—that's why I say because of their relationships with India and China, we need their help as well. And so far—excuse me—with Russia and China. And so far, the Russians and the Chinese have been very helpful to me in trying to work out a policy that we can pursue. But I'm working on it. Believe me, if I thought it would work, I would do it tomorrow, and I will continue to explore every conceivable option.

Q. That's great. Thank you very much.

The President. Thanks. One last question. Go ahead.

Intellectual Property Rights

Q. I'm an intellectual property owner. I represent a lot of entrepreneurial and independent—[*inaudible*]—interests against a lot of the large multinational companies. I know what it's like to be on the nose cone of a missile pretty much. And these interests can tell us that basically that black is white in Congress and try to weaken the patent system and protection of intellectual property. But Governor Romer's son is one of the most vocal spokesmen for—the thing that differentiates us from the rest of the world is intellectual property, and I'd be interested in your views on this.

The President. Well, it's interesting that you'd say that. First of all, I don't think we should weaken the system. And secondly, I think we should continue to aggressively pursue those protections in our trade relations. I have spent an enormous amount of time with the Chinese, for example, trying to protect against pirated CD's of all kinds and other technology.

And the consequences are far greater than they used to be. And we always had a lot of this in Asia. We had Gucci handbags and the Rolex watches and then when I first went to Taiwan 20 years ago, you could buy all the latest

hardcover books for $1.50; that was something that was done. But the volume and level of trade and the interconnections and the sophistication of what was being copied were nowhere near what they are today, where you're talking about billions and billions and billions of dollars that can literally undermine the creative enterprise of whole sectors of our economy.

So I think it's important, first, to keep the legal protections there, but secondly, it's important that the United States make this a big part of our foreign policy and all of our trade policy. And we try to do it. I spent a huge amount of time on it myself.

Education

Q. Mr. President, recently Massachusetts had some ugly test scores from its teachers; they couldn't pass 10th grade equivalency. And there's a problem, I guess, in other States, as well. Is there any way that the education of the kids won't take another generation to upgrade the teaching in the public schools?

The President. Well, first of all, yes, I think—I advocate—I think what Massachusetts did was a good thing, not a bad thing. Most people, every time they read bad news think this is a bad thing. Sometimes when you read bad news, it's a good thing, because otherwise how are you going to make it better if you don't know what the facts are? So the first thing I'd like to say is we ought to give Massachusetts a pat on the back for having the guts to have the teacher testing, get the facts out, and deal with them.

Now, what I think should happen is, I think every State should do this for first-time teachers just the way they do it for lawyers and doctors. Then I believe there should be a much more vigorous system for trying to support and improve teaching as we go along, trying to bring like retired people with degrees in science and mathematics and other things into the teacher corps, which is very uneven across the country.

And there's also something called the National Board for Professional Teacher Standards, which certifies master teachers every year, people who have great academic knowledge, could knock the socks off that test, and people who have proven ability in the classroom. And one of the things that I've got in my budget is enough money to fund 100,000 of those master teachers, which would be enough to put one master teacher in every school building in the country. And if you look at—I don't want to embarrass him, but Tony Robbins standing here, if you ever listen to his tapes or look at him on television, you know he's a teacher. He's teaching people to change how they behave.

Well, it just stands to reason that if you could get one really great teacher in every class, in every school building in America, you would change the culture of that school building if they had mentoring as part of their responsibility. So I think this is a huge deal.

But let me say, there's a lot more to do. You have to recognize, too, that we have to do more to get young people into teaching, even if they only stay a few years—really bright young people. One of the proposals I've got before the Congress today would fund several thousand young people going into inner-city schools and other underserved areas to teach just for a couple of years and they would, in turn, get a lot of their college costs knocked off for doing it. Congress hasn't adopted it yet, but I think that's another important avenue to consider. You've got to—the quality of teaching matters.

Now, I won't go through my whole education agenda with you, but the other thing that you have to remember, whether you're in Colorado or anyplace else, is that when most of us who are my age at least were children, the smartest women were teaching because they couldn't do anything else for a living. And they weren't making much for doing it, but it was all they could do.

And now, a smart woman can run a big company, can create a company and then take it public and be worth several hundred million

dollars, can be elected to the United States Senate and, before you know it, will be President of the United States. So that means if you want good young people to be teachers, we're going to have to pay them more. And that's—everybody nods their head and then nobody wants to come up with the bread to do it, but you've got to do it. I mean, there's no question about it. If you really want to maintain quality over a long period of time, you have to do—you have to pay people; you have to improve the pay scales.

The best short-run fix is to get really smart people who did other things and now have good retirement income to come in because they don't need the salary as much, or to get really smart young people to do it for a few years as soon as they get out of college by helping them cover their college costs.

Moderator. Mr. President, Michael Goldberg promised me he would show me some reruns of his brother, the wrestler, on winning his championship after you were done speaking.

The President. I'm really impressed by that.

Moderator. You're running me out of my time on watching that wrestling. [*Laughter*]

The President. Thank you very much.

NOTE: The President spoke at 10:58 p.m. at a private residence. In his remarks, he referred to dinner hosts Michael and Ana Goldberg; Gov. Roy Romer of Colorado, general chair, Democratic National Committee; and motivational speaker Anthony Robbins. The transcript was released by the Office of the Press Secretary on July 26.

Remarks at a Democratic National Committee Brunch in Aspen
July 26, 1998

Thank you, Fred. First I'd like to thank Fred and Lisa for welcoming us into their modest little home. [*Laughter*] I live in public housing, myself. [*Laughter*] I want to thank Roy Romer for the wonderful job he's done as the general chair of our party and also as the Governor of this magnificent State. I thank all the members of the Democratic Party's hierarchy here today, Len Barrack and others who are here.

But I want to especially thank all of you who have been part of this weekend.

Most of you have already heard me give two talks, and at least I've had a night's sleep now, but I don't want to make you go through it all again. I would like to make a couple of points very briefly.

First of all, I want to make explicit what Fred said. You should all feel some sense of personal responsibility for the buoyant economy, for the lessening social problems of our country, for the role that the United States has been able to play in advancing the cause of peace and freedom and security in the world.

So many of you said something nice to me yesterday about our trip to China, which would not have been possible had I not been elected and reelected. And I think we have the right policy there, where we're trying to advance both our security partnership and our economic interests and still stick up for democracy and freedom that we all believe in. You are responsible for that.

The second point I want to make, very briefly—it looks like the rain is coming again—is that in these elections, we're going to try to elect more Democrats to the House, to the Senate, and to the Governor's office. We're going to try to defend the incumbents that are up for reelection. I honestly believe, and any major national survey will show, that nearly two-thirds of the American people agree with us on virtually every significant question. And the attacks that Republicans have raised against Democrats—that we were weak on the economy; we couldn't be trusted on the deficit; we never met

a tax we didn't like; we were weak on welfare and crime; we couldn't be trusted with foreign policy—all that has no salience anymore.

So, if we can convince the American people that by electing more Members to the House and Senate, they can have more of the progress they like instead of the partisanship they deplore in Washington day-in and day-out—instead of letting them get carried away by the kind of emotional, negative, but unfortunately very powerful tactics that our adversaries used in the last 2 or 3 weeks of every election—you can take pride that the next 2 years can produce even more progress than the last 6 have. That's what I want you to think about. That's what you've been here for. And I am profoundly grateful. Thank you very much.

Now show everybody the Democrats have enough sense to get in out of the rain. [*Laughter*]

NOTE: The President spoke at 12:10 p.m. at a private residence. In his remarks, he referred to Fred and Lisa Baron, dinner hosts; and Leonard Barrack, national finance chair, Democratic National Committee.

Statement on the Death of David J. McCloud
July 26, 1998

Hillary and I were greatly saddened to learn of the death in a plane crash of Lieutenant General David J. McCloud, Commander, Alaskan Command. He hosted us several weeks ago at Elmendorf Air Force Base on our way to China and proudly described for us the mission his command carries out in furtherance of our national security interests. General McCloud was a superb airman and an exemplary leader. He

helped ensure that our forces from all of the military services were prepared to meet the challenges of the post-cold-war environment. His impact was felt throughout the United States Air Force and the Department of Defense. On behalf of all Americans, we extend our condolences to his family and the men and women of the Alaskan Command that he led so well.

Remarks in a National Forum on Social Security in Albuquerque, New Mexico
July 27, 1998

Shootings at the Capitol

Thank you very much. Ladies and gentlemen, before you sit down, if I might, I want to do something quite serious but, I think, important here at the beginning. I would like to ask Senator Domenici and Senator Bingaman and Congressmen Kolbe and Becerra to come up and stand with me, and I'd like to ask all of us to offer a moment of silent prayer for the memory and the families of the two police officers who were slain at our Nation's Capitol.

[*At this point, a moment of silence was observed.*]

Amen. Thank you very much.

Social Security

Let me, now on a somewhat lighter note, say that Mayor Baca was reeling off all of his relatives on Social Security—I'm glad to see one person here who I believe is now eligible for Social Security, former Governor Bruce King, and his wife, Alice, over there. I point them out for a special purpose. One of the demographic realities we have to confront is that women are living longer than men. Governor King is in a wheelchair because of a fright he received from a rattlesnake, which his wife killed. [*Laughter*] So we congratulate both of them.

Let me also say, I'm glad to see this great and diverse group of Americans here in Albuquerque. You can always depend upon getting an audience that genuinely does look like America if you come to Albuquerque. I thank all the Native Americans here who are in the audience. Thank you very much for coming. I see our friends from the Sikh community over there. I know there are a lot of Hispanic-Americans here. I know there are African-Americans, Asian-Americans, and others. We thank you for coming here. And I also thank all the young people that are in the audience, because this is an issue for all ages of Americans to deal with together.

I would like to acknowledge our Social Security Commissioner, Ken Apfel; thank Bill Gordon, the provost of the University of New Mexico, and all the university family for making us welcome here today. I thank Horace Deets of the AARP for being here, and Harvey Meyerhoff of the Concord Coalition, and Carolyn Lukensmeyer of Americans Discuss Social Security. I want to say a special word of thanks to the AARP and the Concord Coalition for hosting this forum. And of course, I thank the Members of Congress who are here and the leaders of the Congress for nominating the Members who are on this program.

We are very blessed at this moment to have a strong economy in America. The question for us is whether we will do what societies often do when times are good and sit back and enjoy it, or whether we will face the larger challenges that our present prosperity and confidence permit us to face. They are significant and formidable. If you think about the next 50 years, how are we going to build the world's best elementary and secondary education system? How are we going to bring economic opportunity to the people who don't enjoy this prosperity, whether they're in inner-city neighborhoods or rural communities where agriculture is in trouble or Native American communities? How are we going to deal with the challenge of growing the economy and preserving our natural environment? Big, significant challenges.

One of those challenges, clearly, that we must face together is saving Social Security—and I might add, with it, Medicare—for the 21st century. One of our biggest challenges is what I call a high-class problem: We are an aging society. We are living longer and better and healthier, and that imposes costs. The older I get, the more I like that problem; that's a high-class problem. It wouldn't have been too many years ago that it would have been rather unusual to find a mayor who could stand up and cite 3 of his family members who are over 75 years of age. That's not so unusual anymore. But we know now that because of the demographic challenges facing us, we have to make some adjustments in the Social Security system to strengthen and preserve it in a new century.

As all of you know, I have said since my State of the Union Address that we should set aside every penny of any surplus until we save Social Security first. At the very moment when we have switched from deficits as far as the eye can see to surpluses as far as the eye can see, it's tempting to offer a large tax cut or perhaps a new spending program paid for by the projected surplus. Some have advocated this course, but we must not squander the hard-won legacy of fiscal responsibility that has brought us our present moment of prosperity. Instead, we should use it to tackle the long-term challenges of the United States.

Any new tax cut or spending program done before we save the Social Security system would commit funds that may be needed to honor our commitment to our parents and our commitment to our children. I think those of us who are part of the so-called baby boom generation feel that most acutely because it is in the years when all of us, that is—and I'm the oldest of the baby boomers—those who are between the ages of roughly 52 and 34, when we all get into the retirement system. It is then when the greatest stresses will be placed upon it at present levels of retirement, projected birth rates, and projected immigration rates.

So I am very grateful for the bipartisan spirit in which we have been pursuing this. I'm grateful for the people who are here. I appreciate Senator Domenici's strong leadership and his strong support for taking the responsible course. In an election year, asking politicians to hold off on a tax cut is almost defying human nature, but Senator Domenici and many Republicans have joined our Democrats in saying together, "Let's deal with this problem. The American people waited 29 years to get out of the red ink and look at the black; we can take a year to enjoy the black and deal with the long-term problems of the country before we decide everything we have to do with the surplus. Let's deal with first things first."

Also I want to thank, as I said, Senator Bingaman, Congressman Kolbe, and Congressman Becerra. We have to reach across the lines of party, philosophy, and generation. This will require open minds and generous spirits. We all have to be willing to listen and learn. In preparation for this forum today, I had three different sessions with my staff members briefing me on all the various reforms that have been advocated by the extraordinarily distinguished panel of experts from whom you will hear in a few moments. And I've been doing

my best to be open to new ideas and to listen and to learn.

I have asked every Member of Congress not only to support the forums we're having here today but to hold town meetings in every district in America. And we will have a White House Conference on Social Security at the end of this year. Next year I will convene the bipartisan leadership of Congress to craft a solution.

The stakes are very high. Those of you who are older or who have had family members dependent on Social Security know that for 60 years Social Security has been far more than an ID number on a tax form, even more than a monthly check in the mail. It reflects the duties we owe to our parents and to each other, and this kind of society we are trying to build.

Today, 44 million Americans depend on Social Security, and for two-thirds of seniors it's the main source of income. Today, nearly one in three of the beneficiaries, however, is not a retiree. Social Security is also a life insurance policy and a disability policy.

Since its enactment over 60 years ago, it has changed the face of America. When President Roosevelt signed Social Security into law, most seniors were poor. A typical elderly person sent a letter to FDR begging him to terminate the "stark terror of penniless old age." Now, in 1996, the elderly poverty rate was below 11 percent. Without Social Security, today nearly half of all seniors would still live in poverty.

Today, the system is sound, but we all know a demographic crisis is looming. There are 76 million of us baby boomers now looking ahead to retirement age and longer life expectancies. By 2030, there will be twice as many elderly as there are today, with only two people working for every one person drawing Social Security. After 2032, contributions from payroll taxes to the Social Security Trust Fund will be only enough to cover about 75 cents on the dollar of current benefits.

We know the problem. We know that if we act now, it will be easier and less painful than if we wait until later. I don't think any of you want to see America in a situation where we have to cut benefits 25 percent or raise inherently regressive payroll taxes 25 percent to deal with the challenge of the future and our obligations to our seniors.

I can tell you, I've spent a lot of time talking to the people I grew up with. Most of them are middle class people with very modest incomes, and they are appalled at the thought that their retirement might lower the standard of living of their children or undermine their children's ability to raise their grandchildren. So let's do something now in a prudent, disciplined way that will avoid our having to make much more dramatic and distasteful decisions down the road.

Now, today we're going to discuss one of the most interesting and important issues that will affect how much it will cost to stabilize the Social Security Trust Fund and what the nature of it will be, and that is, whether and how there should be Social Security investments not just in low-risk government bonds, as the investments are made today, but also in the stock market. I think we have to be openminded about these proposals, and we also have to ask the hard questions.

One I'll start with is, in the 6 years I've been President, the value of the stock market has nearly tripled. I'm grateful for that. Can we look forward to having that happen every 6 years from now on? If not, what are the risks? What will it cost to administer such a program? If you don't have individual accounts where administration costs may be higher, what would be the dangers of having the Government, either itself or through some third party independent agency, make such investments?

I think that we just have to look at this and listen, and I hope all of you today will leave with a better understanding of both the appeal as well as the questions in each and every proposal that has been raised. As I said, I have spent a lot of time studying them. I have tried to set out the five principles by which I think we should judge any proposed reforms. And let me just briefly state them again.

First of all, I think we should reform Social Security in a way that protects the guarantee for the 21st century. We shouldn't abandon a program that has lifted our seniors out of poverty and that is reliable.

Second, I think whatever we do, we should maintain universality and fairness in the program. For a half century, this has been a progressive guarantee for citizens.

Third, Social Security must provide a benefit that people can count on so they can plan for their future. Regardless of the gyrations of the markets, there must be at least a dependable foundation of retirement security.

Third, Social Security must continue to provide financial security for disabled and low-income beneficiaries. Remember, one in three Social Security recipients is not a retiree, something that is often lost on people when they comment on the relatively low rate of return of the retirement program.

Now, finally, we must maintain our hard-won fiscal discipline in anything that we do. That means, from my point of view, that any change we adopt must not lead to greater long-term projected deficits. We worked awful hard for a generation to get our country out of the deficit mode. It's resulted in a lot of prosperity for our country. I can tell you, as I deal with other nations around the world—with the Asian financial crisis, with all the challenges other countries face—money moves around the world today in the flash of an eye. Investment is important. America will continue to be successful because of our great free enterprise system as long as we have a responsible economic policy in this country. So we should not abandon that.

Now, those are the principles that I will use when I try to evaluate all these proposals. But they don't answer the questions. These are hard questions. And every person who's on this panel of experts has worked hard to answer them. You'll see they have very different answers, but they all deserve a respectful listen from you. And you need to start, as I always try to start, by saying, "What's good about this idea? What are the positives about it? What are the inherent questions that are raised?" Try to work them through for yourself and go back and discuss them with your friends and neighbors. And most of all, let's try to keep an open, positive, old-fashioned American attitude toward this.

We dare not let this disintegrate into a partisan rhetorical battle. Senior citizens are going to be Republicans and Democrats and independents. They're going to come from all walks of life, from all income backgrounds, from every region of this country, and therefore, so will their children and their grandchildren. This is an American challenge, and we have to meet it together.

Thank you very much.

NOTE: The President spoke at 10:30 a.m. in the Johnson Center Gymnasium at the University of New Mexico. In his remarks, he referred to Mayor Jim Baca of Albuquerque; Horace B. Deets, executive director, American Association of Retired

Persons (AARP); Harvey M. Meyerhoff, member, board of directors, Concord Coalition; and Carolyn J. Lukensmeyer, executive director, Americans Discuss Social Security.

Teleconference Remarks From Albuquerque to Regional Social Security Forums
July 27, 1998

The President. Thank you, Ken. First of all, let me say I'd like to thank the Older Women's League, who are watching in Chicago; Congressman Mike Castle of Delaware and his group; Congressman Earl Pomeroy of North Dakota, who's had such a leading role in this effort, and his group; and Congressman David Price of North Carolina. I thank you all for hosting this forum.

Our economy is the strongest it's been in a generation. We have the lowest unemployment rate in 28 years, the lowest crime rate in 25 years, the lowest percentage of our people on welfare in 29 years, the first balanced budget and surplus in 29 years, the lowest inflation rate in 32 years, the highest homeownership in history, and the smallest National Government in 35 years. But this sunlit moment is not a time to rest. Instead, it offers us a rare opportunity to prepare our Nation for the challenges ahead. And one of our greatest challenges is to strengthen Social Security for the 21st century.

As you know, I believe strongly that we must set aside every penny of any budget surplus until we have saved Social Security first. Fiscal responsibility gave us our strong economy. Fiscal irresponsibility would put it at risk. On whether we save Social Security first, I will not be moved. But on how we save Social Security, that will require us to have open minds and generous spirits. It will require listening and learning and looking for the best ideas wherever they may be. We simply must put progress ahead of partisanship.

The stakes couldn't be higher. For 60 years, Social Security has reflected our deepest values, the duties we owe to our parents, to each other, and to our children. Today, 44 million Americans depend upon Social Security. For two-thirds of our seniors, it is the main source of income. And nearly one in three beneficiaries are not retirees, for Social Security is also a life insurance policy and a disability policy, along with being a rock-solid guarantee of support in old age.

Today, Social Security is sound, but a demographic crisis is looming. By 2030, there will be twice as many elderly as there are today, with only two people working for every person drawing Social Security. After 2032, contributions from payroll taxes will only cover 75 cents on the dollar of current benefits. So we must act and act now to save Social Security.

How should we judge any comprehensive proposals to do this? I will judge them by five principles.

First, I believe we must reform Social Security in a way that strengthens and protects a guarantee for the 21st century. We shouldn't abandon a basic program that has been one of America's greatest successes.

Second, we should maintain universality and fairness. For a half century, this has been a progressive guarantee for our citizens. We have to keep it that way.

Third, Social Security must provide a benefit people can count on. Regardless of the ups and downs of the economy or the gyrations of the financial markets, we have to provide a solid and dependable foundation for retirement security.

Fourth, Social Security must continue to provide financial security for disabled and low-income beneficiaries. We can never forget that one in three Social Security beneficiaries are not retirees.

And fifth, anything we do to strengthen Social Security now must maintain our hard-won fiscal discipline. It is the source of much of the prosperity we enjoy today.

Now, all this will require us to plan for the future, to consider new ideas, to engage in what President Roosevelt called "bold, persistent experimentation." I thank you for doing your part and for participating in this important national effort to save Social Security.

Now I'd like to hear from all of you. I guess we should start with Betty Lee Ongley of the Older Women's League in Chicago. Then we'll go on to Representative Mike Castle in Wilmington, Delaware; then to Representative Earl Pomeroy in Bismarck, North Dakota; and then to Representative David Price in Raleigh, North Carolina. So let's begin.

[At this point, the regional discussion proceeded.]

The President. Thank you. I'll be glad to comment on that. Let's go now to Congressman Pomeroy in North Dakota. And again let me thank you all for the leading role you've played in this right from the beginning and for your efforts to increase retirement benefits generally for seniors.

[The regional discussion continued.]

The President. Well, first of all, let me say that we're having this forum today in Albuquerque, New Mexico, with a number of experts whose opinions range across the spectrum, from believing that we should have a large portion—some believe almost half of the present payroll tax—converted over a period of 20 or 25 years into individual investment accounts, to those who believe maybe you should have a small percentage of payroll tax or a small annual payment to people for individual investment accounts, to those who believe that the Social Security Trust Fund itself should invest, beginning with a modest amount, a limited amount of its funds to increase the rate of return. So let me try to answer all these questions.

Let me begin by going back to Betty Lee Ongley's question about the impact on women. First of all, I think it's quite important that we maintain in the Social Security system the life insurance benefits. Because so many women are the primary home raisers of their children, even if they're in the work force, I think maintaining this life insurance benefit for the children when the wage earner is killed or disabled is terribly important. And that is, I think, a very important thing.

Now, the second thing I would say is, I personally believe we're going to have to do some things beyond the Social Security system to help women to deal with the fact that they live longer and that today their earnings base is not as great because they're out of the work force for an average of 11 years.

On the question of getting pay up, I think that there is legislation in Congress that would deal with the equal pay issue, which would solve some of the other problems. And I would like to see more aggressive work done on that, to do even more work to enforce the equal pay requirements of our law for women. So, if I could just leave that there.

Now, let me move into the questions raised by the other people who called. And I want to give Ken Apfel a chance to talk, especially if I make a technical mistake.

In various ways, you all asked the same questions about the private accounts. First of all, let's back up and realize why we're dealing with this. By 2030, there will be only two people working for every one person drawing Social Security. The average rate of return on the investment any worker makes on Social Security will go down as more people live longer and more people are in the retirement fund, because Government securities, while they're 100 percent certain, don't have a particularly high rate of return, like any kind of 100 percent certain investment.

So the question is then raised, well, if—over any 30- or 40-year period, an investment portfolio that, let's say, was 60 percent in stocks and 40 percent in government bonds, or 40 and 60 the other way, would have an average rate of return far higher. And even after you take account of the stock market going down and maybe staying down for a few years, shouldn't we consider investing some of this money, because otherwise we'll have to either cut benefits or raise taxes to cover them, if we can't raise the rate of return. So—and I think those are the three main options.

And younger people especially, many of whom are used to doing things on their own, accessing information over the Internet, and also have only experienced a growing stock market, which has been growing since 1980 and which since 1993 has virtually tripled, have been especially interested in these individual accounts. So let me just try to deal with these issues.

First of all, what about individual accounts, and how could we set them up? There are, I think, basically two basic options that have been advanced. One is, should we take a one percent or 2 percent, or some percentage of the payroll tax and, instead of putting that into Social Security, put it into a mandatory savings account for workers, and then they can invest it in stocks if they like? What's the downside of that? The downside of that is twofold. Basically, your investments might lose money, and you might not be so well off with them when you retire, so that the combination of your investment fund plus your guaranteed Social Security fund might be smaller than would have otherwise been the case.

The second issue that's related to that is that if individuals are investing like this, the administrative costs of managing it can be quite high, much, much higher than Social Security, so that even though you might earn a higher rate of return, a lot of it would be taken right back from the people who are handling your account. So we have to work through that.

What about having the Government do it? What about having everybody have an account, a number, in effect, attached to their name for this money but having some public source invest this money? Congressman Castle asked a question, as well as Congressman Price, and I think Mr. Weber in North Dakota asked this question.

Now, the virtue of that is that if the Government were making these investments, you could do two things. Number one, you'd have much lower administrative costs. Number two, you could protect people who retire in the bad years, because you would average the benefits. And as I said, as we know, over any 30- or 40-year period—and the average person will work 40 years—the average rate of returns are higher. So you could always reap the average rate of return.

Now, if you were a particularly brilliant investor, you'd get less than you would have if you'd done it on your own. But on the other hand, you wouldn't get burned. And if you happen to be among unfortunate people who retired in a long period where the market wasn't doing well, like it was in between 1966 and 1982, you'd still be held harmless for that because of the overall performance of the market.

People worry about having the Government invest that much money. There may be a way to set up an independent board immunized from political pressure to do it, but still, that would be a whole lot of money coming from, in effect, one source, going into the stock market. So we're looking at the experience of Canada and some other countries to see what we can learn about that. And we're also looking at the experience of Chile, as a place where they've used

individual accounts, to see what the pluses and minuses are.

I think—what I would like to say is, if we go down this road, we need to make sure that behind this there's still a rock-solid guarantee of a threshold retirement that people will be able to survive on. And then we can debate the relative merits of these individual accounts versus individual guarantees within these bigger units. But I think I've given you the main arguments, pro and con, of both the individual accounts and the Government units—Government investment—I'm sorry.

Let me just add one thing, if I might, because I think it was Mr. Weber who talked about a lot of—either that or Congressman Pomeroy talked about a lot of the people in North Dakota that depend upon Social Security have very modest incomes from the farm or from other sources. One kind of modified proposal that has been debated is the question of whether, instead of dedicating a percentage of payroll to an individual account, we should use the surpluses over the next several years to guarantee workers, let's say, $500 a year.

If you did that, obviously, as a percentage of income—and that would amount to quite a bit after a few years of getting that $500 check in an investment account—obviously, as a percentage of income, the impact on lower wage workers would be far greater than the impact on higher income workers, because the $500, and then the 1,000 and then the 1,500 and 2,000 and so on, would be a much bigger percentage of a lower wage worker's income than just giving everybody one percent of payroll so the dollars would be much bigger if your payroll was bigger.

So that's another thing we've been asked to consider by various people, whether or not the fairest way to do it would be to just give a cash grant into the account of each Social Security-covered person who is paying in. And that's also being debated. And you all may have an opinion about that you want to forward to us.

[The regional discussion continued.]

The President. I would also emphasize—and again, I don't want to further complicate this discussion, but I believe we have to do two things. I think we have to reform Social Security in a way that makes it viable and available for the baby boom generation when all of us get into retirement age, and it doesn't bankrupt our children or our children's ability to raise our grandchildren.

But over and above that, we have to do some other things, which a number of the Members of Congress who are here in New Mexico and out there at these forums have been interested in, to increase the options for retirement savings beyond Social Security. Right now, Social Security is responsible for lifting about half the American senior population out of poverty who would be in poverty without it.

But most seniors do not rely solely on Social Security. And more and more seniors, as we live longer, will need other sources of income, as well. So we're going to work hard on this, but we're also working on legislation to provide other avenues of retirement savings over and above this.

Thank you very much, all of you, for joining us. Commissioner Apfel and I are going to go back to work here in Albuquerque, and we're going to try to listen to the arguments of these experts on the questions you've asked: Should the Government invest in private securities, in the stock market, or should Social Security funds be invested in the stock market? And if so, should it be done by a public entity, or should it be done by individuals with individual accounts? And we'll try to get the pros and cons out and make sure they're widely publicized, and we welcome your views, as well.

Thank you.

NOTE: The President spoke at 11:35 a.m. by satellite from Room 124 of the Johnson Center Gymnasium, University of New Mexico, to regional forums meeting in Chicago, IL; Wilmington, DE; Bismarck, ND; and Raleigh, NC. In his remarks, he referred to Commissioner of Social Security Kenneth S. Apfel; Betty Lee Ongley, president, Older Women's League; and Richard Weber, vice president of administrative services, Basin Electric Power Cooperative.

Remarks in a National Social Security Forum Townhall Meeting in Albuquerque
July 27, 1998

[*Moderator Gloria Borger, U.S. News and World Report, explained that she would take questions from the audience but first wanted the President to comment on a USA Today poll in which two-thirds of the voters liked the idea of private investment accounts, but most also did not want the Government investing their money for them.*]

The President. Well, I think there are a couple of explanations. First of all, we live in a time where people are using technology to become more and more self-sufficient and to get more and more information directly. I mean, the Internet is the fastest growing communications organism in human history. So I think that. Secondly, I think there's always been a healthy skepticism of Government. And thirdly, the Government hasn't been in very great favor over the last 17 or 18 years, although it's doing better now than it was a few years ago. Now, I think—in public esteem—all the surveys also show that.

I think the real question is, from my point of view, we ought to get down to the merits of this. The first question you have to ask yourself is, should a portion of the Social Security tax funds go into securities, into stocks? And if they should go into stocks or into corporate bonds, should that decision be made according to individual accounts, or should they be invested en masse either by the Government or by some sort of nonprofit, nonpolitical corporation set up to handle this?

And I think there are genuine concerns. For example, if the Government did it and they invested the money in stocks, would private retirement funds just have to make up the difference by buying Government bonds, or would there be no aggregate increase in saving or investment in the country? Would it give the Government too much influence over any company or any sector of our economy?

But I think most people just think, "If there is going to be a risk taken, I'd rather take it than have the Government take it for me." I don't think it's very complicated, so I think that those who believe that it's safer and better for people to have the public do the investing—

or the Government do the investment—have to bear that burden. Those who favor, by the way, having individual accounts, have to ask what happens to people who happen to retire after the market has gone down for 5 years. So there are problems with both approaches, and benefits.

[*An audience member asked if the Government would guarantee current benefits if individual accounts were exhausted by old age, bad investments, or market downturns; if doing so would create another problem; or if not doing so would inevitably plunge old people into poverty.*]

The President. Well, why don't we let—I think those are good questions, but I think there are answers to them. And maybe I should let either Dr. Weaver or Professor Boskin answer, and then if I want to add anything, or any of the Members do, we can.

[*Carolyn Weaver, American Enterprise Institute, suggested that at least a portion of personal account accumulations should be converted into some type of annuity or withdrawal on a phased basis so that the individual could not exhaust those funds. Michael Boskin, Hoover Institution, agreed, explaining that paying benefits for current and future retirees plus the individual accounts would create trillions of dollars of debt. Peter Diamond, Massachusetts Institute of Technology, noted the extra cost of annuities to insurance companies and voiced concern that, when people want early access to their money upon retirement, requiring everyone to buy annuities might be a major political question for future Congresses. Senator Pete Domenici suggested to avoid a risk of a downturn at the end, investment firms would be required to invest in less risky accounts for a person in the last 5 to 7 years prior to retirement. Mr. Boskin noted that, historically, long term investment in the stock market has accumulated vastly more than investing in Government bonds. An audience member asked about the experience in Chile and Australia in terms of the costs and the benefits and the risks of setting up private accounts.*]

The President. I would invite everybody to comment on Chile and Australia and maybe on the UK and now on Canada, since Canada is investing the money directly. And maybe if you all could give us whatever information you have about that—in whatever order.

Jim, do you want to start?

[*Representative Jim Kolbe said that Chile had been successful over the last 18 years in going to total privatization, despite a bad economy. He also said that Britain, Australia, Mexico, and most of Latin America were pleased with their systems of individual accounts. Mr. Diamond said that the administrative costs were high in Chile; in Britain, with a voluntary opt-out system, the costs were even higher; and in Australia, where the employer must set up the system, the employees sometimes did not get any choices, and account spending was not regulated, which often left survivors with nothing but poverty support from the Government. Representative Xavier Becerra cautioned that because the United States is very different from other countries, its solution must be unique. Ms. Weaver agreed but pointed out that under the Chilean system, people could always know precisely what they had accumulated and how to adjust their savings and retirement date. An audience member then asked if it would be possible to rely on watchdog organizations to either cap fees associated with the privatization and individual accounts or allow a limited amount of profit per transaction.*]

The President. Well, I think maybe Mr. Boskin, haven't you commented on that before? I think Michael has—at least I believe, in the preparation I did running up to this, that the most forceful advocates of individual accounts have recognized that it might be necessary to have some kind of limit on the individual administrative costs.

One of the problems in Chile has been that they've got all these different people competing for your account. And if they're competing to give you higher return for lower costs, that's good. They offer people vacation trips and then when the market is down maybe they offer them toasters, I don't know. But there are a lot of built-in costs, and you might be able to get the best of both worlds at least on the costs, that is, to have the individuals do the investments, make the investment decisions. I think there would be ways to put caps on the aggregate costs.

[*Mr. Boskin agreed that fees should be uniform to avoid hurting low income people with small accounts and suggested that competition would keep costs down. Mr. Diamond pointed out that regulating fees could be tricky.*]

The President. In fairness now—I should say, I'm very grateful for a lot of the work that Professor Diamond has done, and I'm very sympathetic with a lot of it. But I don't think that's a very good argument. I mean, we have a Securities and Exchange Commission to regulate the stock market. We have more than one Federal agency that overlooks various aspects of what our banks do. And one of the reasons that our market economy works so well is that we have basic Government intermediary institutions that set rules and regulations and parameters. And that's how we get the benefit of the market without having to bear all the downsides.

So I would think that nearly everybody would want some sort of Government regulation if we were to get into this. But that doesn't necessarily mean that direct investment by the Government would be better than the individual investment. It doesn't answer the question one way or the other. I don't mean that it—but I think that, to me, that's not a reason to attack this. I think we should all—that's what we do in almost every major area of our national life.

[*Mr. Diamond responded that additional regulation would be needed but that he was concerned about regulation of prices, not regulation about safety and soundness of financial institutions.*]

The President. You all may want to ask some more questions; I don't want to interrupt anymore. But I think it's important. We're not just talking about price here. One of the major issues is—sometimes I think we get into one little thing, and we forget how it fits into the big picture. So let me just back up.

Suppose you took—I'll take the simplest case—suppose you said we're going to give everybody one percent of payroll to invest in an individual account, okay—and we're going to take all the rest of the payroll and keep on paying Social Security, but we're going to reduce the basic guaranteed benefit, both because we can't afford it because of what's happening to population and life expectancy, and because we just took a percent out of payroll. That's the bad news. The good news is we think you'll get a bigger benefit out of the one percent. Right? That's the argument here.

Now, on the administrative costs, what you have to figure out is, it will be more expensive administratively—I don't care what we do—than having the Social Security Administration or the Government run it all. Why? Because of just

economies of scale. But if you get a much bigger rate of return, then you're still ahead.

So what you have to do is calculate all these things. And all these folks in Congress here are going to have to figure it out, too. So I just ask you, don't forget what the framework here is. And one big thing we haven't discussed is—although our panelists did while I was out of the room, because I watched them—it's not just the administrative costs, it's what are the range of investment decisions that will be available to American citizens for their payroll tax in their individual account? Are there any investment decisions they won't be able to make? And then, how will they get the information necessary, the advice necessary to make good decisions, and how is that figured into the costs? I think you have to look at it like that. What you want to know is, where are you going to come out on the other end of this deal, in all probability.

[*Robert Reischauer, Brookings Institute, discussed with Representative Kolbe and Professor Boskin what might happen if Social Security benefits were reduced and people invested unwisely or unluckily in their private accounts. An audience member then asked who would pay for the transition to privatization and suggested that the program follow the lead of the Federal Employees Retirement System, incorporating a traditional pension, Social Security, and a private investment plan. Representative Kolbe agreed that the Thrift Savings Plan was a possible solution.*]

The President. Go ahead, Michael.

[*Mr. Boskin said that a plan that compounded at a higher rate would offer benefits exceeding the transition costs, as well as addressing unfunded liabilities under the current system.*]

The President. Maybe I could say this at a little—I keep trying to get back to the basic thing. If we don't do anything, sometime in about 35 years, we're going to have to—Senator Domenici said 50 percent; I think it comes a little later than that, 50 percent. But let's say in 2030, we run out of money. We're going to have to do one of three things: We're either going to have to raise the payroll tax by quite a lot; we're going to have to cut benefits by quite a lot; or we're going to have to have the Government stop doing a huge percentage of everything else it's doing, most of which are things that you believe we should be doing, and just put the money into Social Security.

So we really got into this whole discussion—both if you take Professor Reischauer's view that the Government should invest more in equities to get a higher rate of return, or the view expressed by Dr. Weaver that individual accounts should do it—we got into this discussion to figure out whether we could have, at acceptable risk, a higher rate of return on the money that's already there so we wouldn't have to raise taxes, cut benefits dramatically, or shut down a whole lot of the rest of the Government. So there's going to be a transition cost regardless.

Now, one of the things that I want to compliment all these Members of Congress here for doing, we want to avoid having to have a big tax increase for the transition, which is why we're trying to hold on to this surplus we've got for the first time in 29 years, because whatever we decide to do with this, we're going to have to commit a substantial part of the money that has been accumulated or will be accumulated to fund that.

And I want to ask you one question. Are you saying that you would support some portion of the payroll tax being made available for individual accounts if retirees, or future retirees—savers, workers—also had the option to opt into a system like the one we've got, so you could choose the one we have or you could choose one with a smaller guaranteed benefit and more investment? Is that what you're saying? I just want to make sure because I think that's something we need to know.

[*Mr. Reischauer said that the Federal employee system would not solve the problem if Social Security were cut. Senator Bingaman voiced concern that if money were taken out of the payroll tax to finance individual retirement accounts, then benefits would have to be cut and the retirement age would have to be raised. Audience members then discussed how to invest the budget surplus.*]

The President. The point is, though—I agree that we have a surplus because, basically, we're still getting more money every year in from Social Security taxes than we're paying out in retirement on a current basis. And the money, therefore, is invested in bonds, and when it pays back, the Government has it to pay retirement later.

But—so that's fine. But the real question is, can we get a higher rate of return in the future for a fixed amount of money that's going to be invested by the American people in their retirement through the taxes of their employers and themselves than we have gotten in the past? Because if we can get a higher rate of return, then even though there will be fewer people working compared to the people retired, people can have a comfortable, decent retirement; we'll be earning more for the money we've got. That's really the question. Is there a safer way to do that?

Now, I'd like to ask Mr. Reischauer a question; then we'll go back to the audience. You make a very compelling argument that economically there's no difference in having individuals do it and having the Government do it, or having the Government set up somebody to do it, except that there's far less risk on the individual, you can average the benefits, and if somebody retires in a bad year or if there's 5 bad years in a row—like in Japan, which 8 years ago, everybody would say we should do everything they do; now for 5 years, their stock market has lost half its value—if somebody has 5 of those bad years, if the Government is doing it in the aggregate, it is true that over any 40-year period the return will still be greater—even in Japan I think that's true, even now—but you protect people from those bad years, as well as from their own mistakes.

How will you ever convince the American people of that, since they always believe the Government would mess up a two-car parade? [*Laughter*] I mean, even if you're right, politically, how do we ever—how do you make that sale to the American people?

Mr. Reischauer. Well, Mr. President, it's not in my job description to defend the Federal Government. [*Laughter*]

The President. Well, you tell me how to do it then.

[*Mr. Reischauer suggested setting up an institution that would be protected from interference of politicians and, by law, would be required to invest passively, by selecting a little of all available stocks and bonds. An audience member asked who would make the final decision if there were no bipartisan agreement.*]

The President. Well, I think what we're—let me just say what the good news is about this panel. You may leave here more confused than you came in about the details of these options. And if so, I would tell you that's a good thing, not a bad thing. I've been working very seriously on this for a couple of years; these are complex problems. But I think that there is the good news here, which is that most of us have been on opposite sides of a bunch of issues over the last 20 years, and we all believe that we have to act now rather than later.

Keep in mind, every year we let go by, all options become less attractive and require greater risk and more exertion. So, as compared with 10 years from now, anything we would do today is quite modest in scope and has the opportunity to build in more protections. And because you're 32, I think I should also emphasize that under all these options, nearly everybody believes we have to guarantee the system as it is for people, let's say, at 55 and up, and then some period of transition, and ultimate protections built into the system over the long run.

So I think that you don't have any guarantee. If nobody ever makes this decision, then 35 years from now the system will run out of money and the market will make the decision. I mean, people will stop getting checks, or there will be a big tax increase, or we'll shut down a whole bunch of the Government to pay the difference.

So that's why I think that you should feel good. There is a big bipartisan consensus, I think, in the Congress that we have to reach agreement, and we have to act, and we have to do it soon.

[*An audience member asked what the President would do if it were entirely up to him and a decision had to be made today.*]

The President. If I answered that question today, it would make it less likely the decision would be made. That's the truth. You have to understand—let me just say—and I'm not dodging this. I honestly don't know what I would do today, because I have—and I've spent hours and hours just getting ready for this meeting, trying to master all the details of the various plans that the people at this table have proposed.

I don't know what I would do. But I am open to the idea that if we can get a higher rate of return in some fashion than we have been getting in the past, while being fair to everybody, and guaranteeing that we'll still be lifting the same percentage of people out of poverty, we ought to be open to those options. Because I think that's better than raising the payroll tax a lot more—because it's a regressive tax and, for example, more and more people work for small business, and if you're a small-business person you've got to pay a payroll tax whether you make any money or not. Seventy percent of the people pay more payroll tax than they do income tax today, working people. And I'd hate to do that.

I don't want to cut benefits substantially, because most people have something besides Social Security, but Social Security alone lifts half our seniors out of poverty—48 percent, literally. And we've got the smallest Government we've had in 35 years, and I don't want to close down the National Park Service or stop supporting education or stop running our environmental protection programs. And we've cut the national defense about all we can, given our present responsibilities in the world and our need to modernize it.

So the reason I'm here with you is I think all these people deserve to be heard, because if there's any way we can get a higher rate of return in a market economy while minimizing the risk, whether it's in either one of these approaches, we ought to go for it, because the other alternatives are much less pleasant already. And if we wait around for 5 or 10 years, they're going to get a whole lot worse than they are today.

[*Senator Bingaman asked if a privatized retirement system would maintain the insurance, disability benefits, and survivors benefits of the present Social Security system. Mr. Boskin, Representative Kolbe, Mr. Diamond, Senator Domenici, and Representative Becerra discussed how the disability and survivors benefits could be maintained.*]

The President. Can I ask a question here? I would like to ask the Social Security Commissioner or someone else here who's in the audience or with our staff to come up and give me the answer to the question the gentleman asked about disability—the exact answer. About a third of the people who draw Social Security checks are either dependents of people who were killed or disabled on the work force or disabled people themselves. So I want somebody to come bring me that information and how much it's grown, and I'll give it to you precisely.

[*Ms. Weaver voiced concern about the growing number of people drawing disability benefits.*]

The President. Commissioner Apfel just said that the number of people drawing disability has grown dramatically from more or less equally from two sources: One is the addition of mental impairments to physical ones; the other is the aging of the baby boom generation because the rate of disability increases as you approach age 50. So for people like from their late forties until retirement age not drawing Social Security, there's significantly increased number of people because there are just more baby boomers in that age group now.

[*An audience member suggested raising the ceiling for incomes subject to Social Security tax.*]

The President. Let me say, first of all, the incomes of American people have grown to the point now that there is a larger percentage of people who get the benefit of the cap than there used to be. That is, a higher percentage of our people—I forget what it is, maybe one of you know—but most Americans are under the cap. That is, most Americans have income under the tax cap.

People at higher income levels pay higher tax rates on their Social Security incomes than people at lower income levels. And I think that's—one of the reasons that the cap has not been raised at least a dramatic amount more is to avoid having it be an actual negative investment for the people involved, where you're just taxing people's payroll far more than they'll ever get back, and they're just subsidizing the system. The way it is now, it happens a little bit, but not much. And people at higher incomes, once they start to draw that Social Security, do pay a higher rate of tax on it than people at lower incomes.

Michael, you wanted—anybody else want to say anything?

[*Mr. Boskin, Ms. Weaver, Representative Becerra, Senator Kolbe, and Senator Domenici discussed taking both the tax side and benefit side need into careful consideration so that all Americans would still feel that Social Security is a good investment.*]

Ms. Borger. Mr. President, we only have a few minutes left in this forum, and I just wanted to give you the opportunity to give us your final thoughts about what's occurred here today and what's coming in the future.

The President. Well, I'd like to go back to the question the gentleman asked me when he said, "If this were up to you, and you had to decide today, what would you do if you were all by yourself?" There may come a time when I wish that we have so many headaches working this out, I wish it were just my decision to make, all by myself.

I think it's important for me and for the others in the Congress who care about this to maintain—but especially for the President—to maintain an open mind as much as possible now, because I don't want a particular proposal just because it's been endorsed by me to have to be supported or opposed by other people because of their political position. I'm doing my best to keep this a matter of people and progress over partisan politics.

But I also want to make it clear to you that I honestly, myself, have not made up my mind exactly what I think we ought to do on this because, as you can hear from this debate, there are arguments on both sides of all proposals, and it's a rather complicated matter.

I can tell you this: I want a guaranteed benefit. I want it to be fair and progressive and universal. I want to have the best earnings we possibly can within that framework. And I don't want to come to a point down the road where we have to wreck the financial responsibility we worked so hard to bring into this country to give us our present prosperity to pay for the retirement of my generation because we didn't have the responsibility to take action now, when we should.

And I think if we can stay with these general principles and continue to learn and explore all these debates and learn as much as we can from the experiences of other countries—we didn't have a chance to get into this today, but you all laughed when I was kidding Mr. Reischauer about the popular skepticism of Government making these investments. But Canada is starting to do it, and we'll have a chance to watch them and see how they do it and see how they deal with some of the objections that have been raised.

So I think that what I would urge you to do is to continue to learn about this. If you know what you think, make your voices heard. And support your Senators and your Congressmen in saying that we have to act on this, and we have to do it next year because we can't afford to wait. We're taking this year, studying, raising public awareness, presenting all the alternatives to people. By next year we'll be ready to act and we should do it.

And if we have the support of the people in this room, that vary across age and income groups and all kinds of other ways, then we'll be able to do what's right for America because we will be doing the work of democracy.

Thank you very much.

NOTE: The discussion began at 12:48 p.m. in the Johnson Center Gymnasium at the University of New Mexico. In his remarks, the President referred to Commissioner of Social Security Kenneth S. Apfel. The panel included Carolyn L. Weaver, resident scholar, American Enterprise Institute; Fernando Torres-Gil, director, Center for Policy Research on Aging, University of California Los Angeles; Robert D. Reischauer, senior fellow, Brookings Institute; Michael J. Boskin, senior fellow, Hoover Institution; and Peter A. Diamond, institute professor, Massachusetts Institute of Technology. Moderator Gloria Borger was assisted by Matt Miller and Susan Dantzler. Vice President Al Gore participated in a panel discussion at a National Social Security Forum, also sponsored by the American Association of Retired Persons and the Concord Coalition, in Cranston, Rhode Island, on July 1.

Remarks at a Reception for Gubernatorial Candidate Martin J. Chavez in Albuquerque
July 27, 1998

The President. Thank you. Thank you very much. Thank you for your muted welcome. [*Laughter*] I am delighted to be here.

Audience members. We love for you to be here. [*Laughter*]

The President. Thank you. I'm glad to be here for Marty and Margaret, and Diane and Herb, and all the Democratic ticket. I'm honored to be on the platform with Senator Bingaman. And I am very grateful that a man I first met and began to admire almost 30 years ago, Fred Harris, is now the chairman of the Democratic Party in New Mexico. Thank you.

I want to thank all the State officials who are here and the mayor and the speaker and the former State chairs, who are my friends, and all the candidates. But I have to say a special word. You have been so good to me and to Hillary and to the Vice President. New Mexico has voted twice for our ticket and has played a major role in a lot of the policies we have implemented. I almost feel embarrassed to ask you to do anything else just for us, but if you really wanted to do me a favor, you'd send Shirley Baca and Tom Udall and Phil Maloof to Congress and give me a Congress we can work with.

And I want to make one specific comment, and that is, I would ask that people in New Mexico who have voted in the past, for whatever reason, for the Green Party, but who honestly care about that environment, to take another look at the consequences of their votes. And I would like to just mention one thing, just for example, that affects New Mexico.

I've worked hard with Tom Udall and with Jeff Bingaman, who has worn me out about this—[*laughter*]—to try to get the Baca Ranch preserved. It is the largest volcanic crater in the United States. It's home to one of our biggest wild elk herds. It's an investment not just in the environment but in the long-term economic well-being of New Mexico. I believe the preservation of your natural resources is the key to the new economy of the entire Southwest.

It's one of several places in New Mexico that I have proposed to preserve, on a list of 100 I have sent to Congress. I sent the list to Congress in February. Let me just tell you how it works. We get money approved for these projects, but then under the law I have to send them to Congress, and they have to approve the release of money for the projects.

I sent the list up in February. In April, on Earth Day, I asked again for the money to be released. It's now nearly August, and there's still been no action. Now, it seems to me that that's one more example, here in New Mexico, where the Democratic Party is on the side of responsible, constructive environmentalism. And I would hope that all people would look at that before going to the polls again in November and voting in these congressional races.

In a larger sense, let me say that I have been trying since I first came to New Mexico as a candidate to try to prepare this great country of ours for a new century which is very different than the times in which most of us grew up, the times in which our parents lived. Think about what the characteristics of tomorrow will be, not just for someone in Los Angeles or Silicon Valley or New York City or Boston but for someone in Albuquerque or Little Rock or the smallest town in New Mexico or my home State of Arkansas.

No matter how small, we live in a global economy that is basically growing by ideas. The fastest growing thing in the world today is the Internet—by far—fastest growing organism in history—social organism in history. And it is a metaphor, a symbol of how this economy is both going global and rooted in new ideas.

I met a young man yesterday in Colorado who was telling me his story about how he was just a middle class young guy that had an idea, and he's about to take his company public, and he's worth more than he knew existed in the world just 10 years ago because America gave him a chance, but also because he understood where tomorrow will be.

Now, in that kind of economy, the second thing we know is that education for everybody will be more important than ever before. It's always been a personal advantage to have a good education. Now we know our whole country depends upon building the finest opportunities in elementary and secondary education for every child in this country, without regard to their income, their race, their background, or whether they live on a reservation or in a rural community or in an inner-city neighborhood.

The third thing we know is that the economy depends upon having an environment that is not only preserved, but it is to some extent improved. You know, I've just been—you've been seeing all these fires in Florida. We've had 20 days of 100 degree temperature or higher, or above, from Dallas east across the whole wide swath of America. The 9 hottest years ever recorded in the history have occurred in the last 11 years; 1997 was the hottest year ever recorded. Every month of 1998 has broken the 1997 record. Now, my daughter's friends used to say, "Denial is not just a river in Egypt."

[*Laughter*] We can grow the economy and have a responsible environmental policy. We can do that, but we have to make a decision to do it. And we have to understand it's one of the big issues out there.

What are the other big issues? I'll just—we can't forget the human element in a global economy. We can't let people get left behind. That's why I'm fighting so hard for this Patients' Bill of Rights. In an economy that is increasingly based on ideas and information and organization, the human element can get left behind. One of the things our party has always done is to remind people of the human element. I'm proud of that. And I think that we have proved in the last 6 years you can take care of the human element; you can take care of the environment; and you can still grow the economy if you do it right.

And the last point I want to make is—and if you look around this room today, you see it illustrated—the world we're living in will reward nations that can reflect that world in the best sense. How much of your time as President have I had to spend dealing with other people's religious, racial, and ethnic conflicts? As America grows ever more diverse, if you want us to do good in a world like that, we have to be good at home. We have to reflect the best of America.

And what's all that got to do with Marty and Diane? I'll tell you what. In this economy that we've produced, I've tried to actually reduce the role of the Federal Government in inessential areas, delegate more to the States where I thought it was appropriate. We now have the smallest Federal Government we've had in 35 years. What does that mean? That means it matters a whole lot more who the Governor is. It matters what the education policy of the State is. It matters what the policy is of moving people from welfare to work and whether you're helping people raise their kids as well as expecting them to work if they're able-bodied. It matters what the environmental policy of the State is. These things matter.

It matters. We passed, in the balanced budget bill, we passed funds to give the States the ability to insure another 5 million kids who don't have any health insurance. But the Federal Government is not doing it; the State is doing it with money we gave them. Therefore, it really matters whether a Governor wakes up every morning worrying about whether some kid somewhere in New Mexico who might get sick, whose family doesn't have any health insurance.

So it is not enough, as important as it is, for you to make the right decisions for Senator and Congress and for President in the year 2000. It really matters to the shape of your children's future who the Governor of this State is. It matters who the Lieutenant Governor is. It matters if they have an approach that is consistent with your values and if they really care about how you're going to live in this great new 21st century.

So I'm proud to be here because New Mexico has done a lot for me and for my family and for our administration. But New Mexico should now do itself a favor and elect this great ticket.

Thank you, and God bless you.

NOTE: The President spoke at approximately 2:35 p.m. in the Regal and Registry Room at the Sheraton Uptown Hotel. In his remarks, he referred to Mr. Chavez's wife, Margaret; Diane Denish, candidate for Lieutenant Governor, and her husband, Herb; Mayor Jim Baca of Albuquerque; Raymond G. Sanchez, speaker, New Mexico House of Representatives; and Shirley Baca, Tom Udall, and Phillip Maloof, candidates for New Mexico's Second, Third, and First Congressional Districts, respectively.

Remarks at the Congressional Tribute Honoring Officer Jacob J. Chestnut and Detective John M. Gibson
July 28, 1998

To the Chestnut and Gibson families and my fellow Americans:

The Bible defines a good life thusly: "To love justice, to do mercy, and to walk humbly with thy God." Officer J.J. Chestnut and Detective John Gibson loved justice. The story of what they did here on Friday in the line of duty is already a legend. It is fitting that we gather here to honor these two American heroes, here in this hallowed chamber that has known so many heroes, in this Capitol they gave their lives to defend.

And we thank their families for enduring the pain and extra burden of joining us here today. For they remind us that what makes our democracy strong is not only what Congress may enact or a President may achieve; even more, it is the countless individual citizens who live our ideals out every day, the innumerable acts of heroism that go unnoticed, and especially, it is the quiet courage and uncommon bravery of Americans like J.J. Chestnut and John Gibson and, indeed, every one of the 81 police officers who just this year have given their lives to ensure our domestic tranquility.

John Gibson and J.J. Chestnut also did mercy in giving their lives to save the lives of their fellow citizens. We honor them today, and in so doing, we honor also the hundreds of thousands of other officers, including all of their comrades, who stand ready every day to do the same. They make it seem so ordinary, so expected, asking for no awards or acknowledgment, that most of us do not always appreciate—indeed, most of the time we do not even see—their daily sacrifice. Until crisis reveals their courage, we do not see how truly special they are. And so they walked humbly.

To the Gibsons, to Lyn, Kristen, Jack, and Danny; to the Chestnuts, Wenling, Joseph, Janece, Janet, Karen, and William; to the parents, the brothers, the siblings, the friends here, you always knew that John and J.J. were special. Now the whole world knows as well.

Today we mourn their loss, and we celebrate their lives. Our words are such poor replacements for the joys of family and friends, the turning of the seasons, the rhythms of normal life that should rightfully have been theirs. But we offer them to you from a grateful Nation, profoundly grateful that in doing their duty, they saved lives; they consecrated this house of freedom; and they fulfilled our Lord's definition of a good life. They loved justice. They did mercy. Now and forever, they walk humbly with their God.

NOTE: The President spoke at 3:30 p.m. in the United States Capitol Rotunda. The transcript released by the Office of the Press Secretary also included the remarks of Vice President Al Gore. Officer Chestnut and Detective Gibson died as a result of gunshot wounds suffered during an attack at the Capitol on July 24.

Statement on the Resolution of the United Auto Workers Strike at General Motors
July 28, 1998

I am pleased that the United Auto Workers and General Motors have resolved their differences today. Getting GM back to work is a win-win solution—a victory for the company and its employees and a victory for all Americans. It also shows that the collective bargaining process works. American companies can remain competitive in the world economy while providing good jobs and good benefits for their employees.

I would like to thank Secretary of Labor Alexis Herman, who worked night and day behind the scenes to keep both parties working toward a resolution. She and her team deserve a great deal of credit for their patience and determination in the effort to help bring this dispute to a close.

Statement on Expanding the Executive Order on Proliferation of Weapons of Mass Destruction
July 28, 1998

Today I am expanding existing Executive order authority to enhance America's ability to deal with one of the toughest security challenges we face: the spread of weapons of mass destruction and missiles to deliver such weapons.

Two weeks ago, the Russian Government announced it was investigating a number of Russian entities suspected of violating weapons of mass destruction export control provisions.

Today's Executive order amendment will allow us to respond more effectively to evidence that foreign entities around the world, such as these Russian entities, have assisted in the transfer of dangerous weapons and weapons technologies. The United States will use the amended Executive order, along with other existing authorities, to bar assistance to seven of the entities identified by Russia, as well as to bar exports to and imports from these entities.

The new Executive order amends Executive Order 12938, issued in 1994, in key respects:

—The amended E.O. addresses not only transfers of chemical and biological weapons, as provided in the original E.O., but also nuclear weapons and missiles capable of delivering weapons of mass destruction;

—The amended E.O. imposes penalties not only where a transfer has been carried out, as provided in the original E.O., but also in the event of an attempt to transfer;

—The amended E.O. expressly expands the range of potential penalties on entities that have contributed to proliferation. Penalties include prohibition of U.S. Government assistance to the entity and prohibition of imports into the U.S., or U.S. Government procurement of goods, technology, and services.

The amended E.O. ensures that our Government has the necessary flexibility in deciding when and to what extent to impose penalties. In the fight to stem the spread of dangerous weaponry, we must be resourceful and focus on doing what works. Being able to offer both incentives and disincentives enhances our capacity to deal with these threats. I will continue to work with Congress to ensure that America's policy provides tough penalties—and also sufficient flexibility to give us the best chance to achieve positive results.

My administration is working actively with our friends and allies around the world to prevent the proliferation of weapons of mass destruction. We are encouraged by recent commitments by Russia, by our European allies, and others to increase their efforts, and we will continue to press for even stronger commitments.

NOTE: Executive Order 12938 of November 14, 1994, was published in the *Federal Register* at 59 FR 59099. The Executive order amending it is listed in Appendix D at the end of this volume.

Message to the Congress on Expanding the Executive Order on Proliferation of Weapons of Mass Destruction
July 28, 1998

To the Congress of the United States:

On November 14, 1994, in light of the danger of the proliferation of nuclear, biological, and chemical weapons (weapons of mass destruction) and of the means of delivering such weapons, using my authority under the International Emergency Economic Powers Act (50 U.S.C. 1701 *et seq.*), I declared a national emergency and issued Executive Order 12938. Because the proliferation of weapons of mass destruction continues to pose an unusual and extraordinary threat to the national security, foreign policy, and economy of the United States, I have renewed the national emergency declared in Executive Order 12938 annually, most recently on November 14, 1997. Pursuant to section 204(b) of the International Emergency Economic Powers Act (50 U.S.C. 1703(b)), I hereby report to the Congress that I have exercised my statutory authority to issue an Executive order to amend Executive Order 12938 in order to more effectively to respond to the worldwide threat of weapons of mass destruction proliferation activities.

The amendment of section 4 of Executive Order 12938 strengthens the original Executive order in several significant ways.

First, the amendment broadens the type of proliferation activity that is subject to potential penalties. Executive Order 12938 covers contributions to the efforts of any foreign country, project, or entity to use, acquire, design, produce, or stockpile chemical or biological weapons (CBW). This amendment adds potential penalties for contributions to foreign programs for nuclear weapons and missiles capable of delivering weapons of mass destruction. For example, the new amendment authorizes the imposition of measures against foreign entities that materially assist Iran's missile program.

Second, the amendment lowers the requirements for imposing penalties. Executive Order 12938 required a finding that a foreign person "knowingly and materially" contributed to a foreign CBW program. The amendment removes the "knowing" requirement as a basis for determining potential penalties. Therefore, the Secretary of State need only determine that the foreign person made a "material" contribution to a weapons of mass destruction or missile program to apply the specified sanctions. At the same time, the Secretary of State will have discretion regarding the scope of sanctions so that a truly unwitting party will not be unfairly punished.

Third, the amendment expands the original Executive order to include "attempts" to contribute to foreign proliferation activities, as well as actual contributions. This will allow imposition of penalties even in cases where foreign persons make an unsuccessful effort to contribute to weapons of mass destruction and missile programs or where authorities block a transaction before it is consummated.

Fourth, the amendment expressly expands the range of potential penalties to include the prohibition of United States Government assistance to the foreign person, as well as United States Government procurement and imports into the United States, which were specified by the original Executive order. Moreover, section 4(b) broadens the scope of the United States Government procurement limitations to include a bar on the procurement of technology, as well as goods or services from any foreign person described in section 4(a). Section 4(d) broadens the scope of import limitations to include a bar on imports of any technology or services produced or provided by any foreign person described in section 4(a).

Finally, this amendment gives the United States Government greater flexibility and discretion in deciding how and to what extent to impose penalties against foreign persons that assist proliferation programs. This provision authorizes the Secretary of State, who will act in consultation with the heads of other interested agencies, to determine the extent to which these measures should be imposed against entities contributing to foreign weapons of mass destruction or missile programs. The Secretary of State will act to further the national security and foreign policy interests of the United States, including principally our nonproliferation objectives. Prior to imposing measures pursuant to this provision, the Secretary of State will take into account

the likely effectiveness of such measures in furthering the interests of the United States and the costs and benefits of such measures. This approach provides the necessary flexibility to tailor our responses to specific situations.

I have authorized these actions in view of the danger posed to the national security and foreign policy of the United States by the continuing proliferation of weapons of mass destruction and their means of delivery. I am enclosing a copy of the Executive order that I have issued exercising these authorities.

WILLIAM J. CLINTON

The White House,
July 28, 1998.

NOTE: Executive Order 12938 of November 14, 1994, was published in the *Federal Register* at 59 FR 59099. The Executive order amending it is listed in Appendix D at the end of this volume.

Remarks to the National Council of Senior Citizens
July 28, 1998

Thank you very much. Well, I don't know what all the young folks in Washington are doing tonight, but whatever it is, they don't have half the energy you do. [*Laughter*]

I can't thank you enough for that wonderful welcome. I want to thank you, Tom, for your introduction. I also want to tell you—we were standing outside when Tom was talking and he said that I was looking for an interpreter to explain these—[*laughter*]—I mean, you know, folks, this is America. Where else do you get to talk to a Greek from Uruguay? I mean, come on. [*Laughter*] I can't decide whether I want him to solve all the South American border wars or go fix the Cyprus problem—[*laughter*]—but, meanwhile, he's doing a fine job for you, and we love working with him.

I thank you for honoring Dorothy Height and Bob Georgine, two good friends of mine. I wish your president, George Kourpias, well in his trip to Greece. And let me join the applause you gave to this young lady, Paula Postell, who sang the national anthem. I think she's got a great future. [Applause]

It's become commonplace to say that Americans over 85 are the fastest growing group in the country, but I'd also like to acknowledge that you have two members here who are entering that extremely select group of centenarians, Cliff Holliday and Genevieve Mother Johnson. Congratulations to you. Thank you, Cliff, Genevieve. Congratulations to both of you. We'd all like to join your group. I must say, there are plenty of days around here when I feel like I'm 100. [*Laughter*] But I'm still working at it.

Before I begin, I think I'd like to just make a few remarks to say how very pleased I am on behalf of all the American people and the prospects of our growing economy that the United Auto Workers and General Motors resolved their differences earlier today. This is truly a win-win-win situation. It's a victory for the company, a victory for the employees and a victory for all Americans, who understand, I think, now more clearly than ever after the last 60 days, what a great stake all of us in the United States have in the success of General

Motors and our auto industry in general and those jobs and those workers, the cars they produce, and the contributions they make to our general welfare.

It also shows that the collective bargaining process works. And I'm glad that I have been able to defend it for the last 6 years. I believe that one of many things the United States has proved over the last 6 years, nearly 6 years I've been privileged to be your President, is that it is possible for us to be competitive in a global economy and still have good jobs with good benefits for productive employees.

I have spoken with President Steve Yokich of the UAW, and Jack Smith, the CEO of GM. And again, I want to publicly thank them for their role in this. And as a matter of personal privilege, I also want you to know that our terrific Secretary of Labor, Alexis Herman, worked day and night behind the scenes to keep the parties in the room together, keep the temperatures down and the lines of communication open. And I appreciate that.

I am profoundly honored to be here tonight. The NCSC has stood by me and our administration in all the fights we have waged from 1992 forward. You know, just before I left the house—normally, when I have to go out at night like this, Hillary says something like, "This is the time when I'm glad you've got the job. You go give the speech." Tonight she said, "I kind of resent the fact that you're going and I'm staying home. I love those people; they have been so good to me."

We will never forget the fight that you helped us wage for better health care for all Americans. And it was not a fight in vain. I will say more about it, but you know, we helped to increase the awareness of the American people about the problems. And we told them that unless we did something, more and more people would lose their insurance at work. Our attackers said, "Oh, the President is trying to have the Government take over the health care system." I said, "No, I'm not. I'm trying to have the Government guarantee that every American family has access to affordable, quality health care that they don't lose."

Well, since then we've done a lot of, I think, quite important things. We strengthened the Medicare program. We're doing more now to help prevent breast cancer with mammographies. We're doing more to deal with osteoporosis. We're doing more in research and treatment for both breast cancer and prostate cancer. We're doing a great deal more with diabetes. Last year I signed legislation that the American Diabetes Association said represented the greatest step forward in the treatment of diabetes since the discovery of insulin 70 years ago. We are adding 5 million children to the ranks of those with health insurance. And so while we haven't solved the whole problem, we have come a long way, thanks in no small measure to your advocacy and your work and your conscience.

I should also tell you that—you remember when our attackers said we were trying to have the Government take over the health care system, and we pointed out that we weren't. When they made that charge, 40 percent of all dollars going into the health care system in America— 40 cents on the dollar—came from the public. Today, because so many private employers have dropped their employees from health insurance since the cost goes up, 47 cents on the dollar comes from public sources in health care.

So we have to keep working on this. But don't forget, you stood up for a good cause, and we have advanced the cause. And there are millions of children who are now going to get health care as a result of that provision in the balanced budget amendment that I am absolutely convinced would not have happened had it not been for your advocacy. I do not believe we would have passed the Kennedy-Kassebaum bill, saying people can't lose their health insurance when someone in their family is sick or when they change jobs, had it not been for your advocacy. So you should be proud of what you accomplished, as well as the fight you fought that you didn't win. I'm proud of you, and I thank you for that.

I thank you for sticking up for retirees and for working families. I thank you, too, for your commitment to helping us meet the challenge of the year 2000 computer problem by reaching out to senior citizens to enlist their help. And I know other people have talked to you about this—this is a big deal. America computerized more extensively earlier than any other country. When we first did that, memory in these computer chips was a precious commodity, so a lot of these little chips only had two slots for year numbers, instead of four. Well now, of course, it's an entirely different thing. You can get hundreds of millions of bits of information out of these little computer chips.

And we now have a whole generation of people out there working that don't even know how to go in and speak the language that will fix these problems. So we've got to have retirees come back and help us. I think it's interesting: You have all these 25-year-old kids worth $200 million or $300 million in Silicon Valley, but they need you to come back and help them fix this Y2K computer problem so they don't lose their investment. We still need more help, so I thank you.

Let me say also that I'm very grateful for the general support you have given me. If I told you on the day I was inaugurated President that I would come back in 5½ years and that we would be able to say, in the last 5½ years this is what America has accomplished: We have the lowest unemployment rate in 28 years, 16 million new jobs, the lowest crime rate in 25 years, the smallest percentage of our people on welfare in 29 years, the first balanced budget and surplus in 29 years, the lowest inflation rate in 32 years, the highest homeownership in American history, with the smallest Federal Government in 35 years—I think you would say that's a pretty good record for 5½ years. And I thank you for your role in that.

Now, I think our obligation is to use this moment. And I think that the senior citizens of our country have a special role in making sure that our people, in general, and our political system, in particular, has the right response. Because normally when people work hard and their life is full of hassles and they deal with one crisis after another, when they hit a good patch, they just want to sit back, relax, and enjoy it. And countries are like people and families. But the world is changing so fast and there are so many challenges all around the world that I submit to you we cannot afford to do that; that, instead, we have to use the prosperity we now enjoy and the confidence we now have to face the large, long-term challenges of America. Now, what are they? I'll just mention a few.

One is to give America the best elementary and secondary school system in the world. We have done a good job with our university system, and now, in the last 5½ years, we've also virtually opened the doors of college to everybody who will work for it, with the HOPE scholarship and more work-study funds and AmeriCorps national service scholarships and more Pell grants and all of these things. We've really worked hard. But we've got to have the best elementary and secondary system in the world for all of our kids.

The second thing we've got to do is bring the benefits of this prosperity to the places that haven't felt them yet: to the inner-city neighborhoods, where the unemployment rate is still in double digits; to the small, rural communities that lost the factory or where the farm income is down; to the Native American communities, where there has been no spark of enterprise. We have to prove that America can work for all Americans who are willing to work.

The third thing we have to do is to recognize that we have a huge obligation to our children to begin a process, that I believe will continue well into the 21st century, of proving that a country can both grow rich and improve, rather than destroy the environment. Folks, I'm telling you, this climate change/global warming issue is real. You see the fires in Florida. They had the wettest winter, the driest spring and the hottest month in their history in June, and then they got the fires. Nine hottest years on record—the 9 hottest years on record have all occurred in the last 11 years; 1997 was the hottest year ever recorded; every single month of 1998 has topped the preceding month in 1997.

Now, do we have to give up good jobs to do it? No, we don't. Thankfully, what we now know and what is about to happen in energy use enables us to cool the planet, reduce greenhouse gas emissions, and grow more jobs that are good jobs with good wages. But we have to make a decision to do it. It's a big, long-term challenge for America.

We have to continue to move forward on health care, and I'll say a little more about that in a moment because there are still great challenges out there. I remember when Hillary said in 1994, "Look, there's going to be a big growth in managed care. The question is whether we'll have managed care that's also quality care for all Americans." And then people said, "Well, why is she trying to promote that?" That was one of the attacks. So now you see we have more people than ever before in managed care, 160 million. But the issue now is there aren't enough guarantees of quality care, which is what we all want. That's a huge challenge for the American people and we have to meet it.

Not especially popular to say, but we have to remain engaged with the rest of the world. I'm trying to get Congress to pay our fair share to something called the International Monetary Fund. And nearly any Congressman could come here and give you a speech and convince you it was a bad idea, saying, "Why are we giving money to all those other countries?" Well, the reason is that if we help to reform and restore growth in Asia, they'll buy our products. One-third of our economic growth has come from international trade. About half our grain that our farmers grow is sold abroad; 40 percent of it is sold in Asia. They can't buy it if they don't have any money. Today, they don't have much money; therefore, the price of grain is down. Farm income has dropped 90 percent in one year in North Dakota.

So we have to stay involved in a constructive way in the rest of the world as a force for peace and freedom and prosperity. The next thing we have to do is—I made a joke about my Uruguayan-Greek friend here, or my Greek-Uruguayan friend or whatever it is—[laughter]—but the truth is—the truth is that this is a country where we have people from everywhere. And in a global society, a global economy, that is a great economic boom if we prove that we really can be one America, that we celebrate our differences, that we respect our differences, and that we're bound together by a set of shared values. If we want to do good around the world, we have to first be good here at home and set a good example for the rest of the world.

So those are the big challenges. But there's one other big challenge. Those of us in the baby boom—and I'm the oldest of the baby boomers at just nearly 52—the generation now aged 34 to 52, the biggest group of Americans ever, until last year's school class got in. When we retire, when we're all in the retirement pool, in about 2030 or a little before—actually a little before that—there will only be about two people working for every one person drawing Social Security. We have to protect and save and reform Social Security so that it will be there for the baby boom generation on terms that won't bankrupt our children and their ability to raise our grandchildren. And we have to do it in a way that gives absolute security to all the people now on Social Security and those who will go on it in the next few years.

So I want to talk to you about that tonight, because we need your support and involvement. You know, for 60 years Social Security has meant more than an ID number or even that monthly check. It really has become the symbol of the responsibility we feel to one another across the generations.

You know, in 1985, our country passed a watershed and I always think of it—1985 was the first year in the history of America when people over 65 had a poverty rate below that of the general population. Today, it's under 12 percent. And 48 percent, almost half of all senior citizens, are lifted out of poverty because of Social Security. It is very important.

Now, we know we're going to have a budget surplus this year. We don't know exactly how much, but it's going to be quite sizable. And it's going to be the first one since 1969. We project that we will have one for years to come. And even when the country has recessions now and then, we think over a long period of time, if we stay with the same framework of budget discipline we've got now, we will run surpluses. So we've tried to move from deficits as far as the eye can see and a quadrupling of the Nation's debt in the 12 years before I took office, to surpluses as far as the eye can see.

Now, I know you heard me say in the State of the Union, and I've said it 100 times since, we shouldn't spend a penny of that surplus until we save Social Security first. I'm happy that there are both Republican and Democratic Members of Congress who agree with me. Some do not. And I know it is terribly tempting in an election year to offer people a tax cut or to offer people a new spending program that I might love. Even if I could design the tax cut—and there are some we badly need—or design the spending program, I would say we should not take it out of the surplus.

You know, we've waited 29 years to see the red ink go away. It looks to me like we should wait just a year until we fix Social Security before we run the risk of getting into it again. And I say that to you because you have something America needs now: memory. It is very important to look to the future. You know, my campaign theme song in 1992 was "Don't Stop Thinking About Tomorrow." My campaign slogan in 1996 was "building a bridge to the 21st century." But the First Lady's slogan for honoring the year 2000 and our millennium may have more relevance today: "Honoring the past, imagining the future." To be successful you have to do both. And I'm here to tell you the only way we can really imagine the future and come up with all these new ideas and actualize them is if we remember our roots, our basic values, and we don't always take the easy way out.

You have memory. We have waited a long time for this balanced budget. We have waited a long time for this surplus. There are a lot of things that you would like to do with this surplus, and we may be able to do some of them if it doesn't take all the money that we project to be in the surplus to fix the Social Security system. But first you've got to know it's going to be there.

As I said—let me say again—by the year 2030, there will be twice as many seniors as there are today, with only two people working for every one person drawing, at present rates of birth, immigration, and retirement. Around that time, 2030, if we just leave the system the way it is and we do not do anything, there will only be enough money coming in to fund 75 cents on the dollar current benefit.

Today Social Security is sound. Let me say this again: Today Social Security is sound. We're talking about 2030 and beyond. For today's seniors, Social Security is as strong as it's ever been. For those tomorrow, it's as strong as it's ever been. But here's the issue: If we wait until 2025 to start fooling with it, it will require breathtaking, dramatic changes that will either require huge tax increases or huge benefit cuts or the virtual abolition of the rest of domestic Government, our investments in education, in scientific research and the environment, and maybe even some of our defense programs, just to pay the difference.

But if we start now and make modest, disciplined changes that will take effect over the long run, then we can say Social Security is not only there for all the seniors now, Social Security is not only there for all those that are going to be there in the next few years; it will be there for the baby boomers, and it will be there for the baby boomers in a way that will be good for their children and their grandchildren. That's what this is about and that's what I ask your support on.

I want to thank your officers for consulting with us. We've consulted before, all of the three forums we've had around the country, bipartisan forums to raise the issues here in the debate. The Vice President and I have been to three of them. In December I'm going to host a White House Conference on Social Security. I want you involved. And then in January I'm going to try to get all the leaders of Congress

together to fashion a bipartisan resolution the way it was done back in 1983. This is only going to work if we can find a way to reach across the lines of party, philosophy, and generation, because Republicans and Democrats get old together. [*Laughter*] Sometimes I think they forget it, but we do. All of them get old but Senator Thurmond. He never does, but everybody else does. [*Laughter*] And we've got to do this together. We're going to have to have open minds and generous spirits. We've all got to be willing to listen and learn.

There are going to be a lot of proposals out there, and some of them will be good, and some of them I think will be quite unwise. But I wanted to share with you how I think we should all judge these proposals for dealing with tomorrow's challenge in Social Security. And you need to decide whether you agree with these five principles, and if you don't, how you would judge them.

First, we have to strengthen and protect the guarantee of Social Security for the 21st century. People have to know it's there. There has to be a certainty about it.

Secondly, we must maintain universality and fairness. It must be available to all and fair to all. It's been a progressive guarantee. All of you understand that well. There's a lot of people who work all their lives for very modest wages that would not have enough to live on if Social Security were not a progressive program, and we have to keep it that way.

Third, it must provide a benefit people can count on, regardless of the ups or downs of the economy or the financial market. It has to be a program that has a foundation of financial security in good economic times and bad. Not every 6 years will be as good as the last 6 years have been on Wall Street or Main Street. But people will retire every year. People will continue to age every year.

Fourth, Social Security must continue to provide financial security for disabled and low-income beneficiaries. We can't forget that one in three people on Social Security is not a retiree. One in three people is a disabled person or a family where the wage earner has been killed or disabled or died young. It's a life insurance program and a disability program and a retirement program. And I believe, when we get done with reforming it, it should still be all three, because those one in three people need that help as well.

And finally, I believe anything we do to strengthen Social Security now must be done within the framework of the hard-won fiscal discipline we have seen since 1993. When we voted in 1993 to drive that deficit down—and a lot of members in our party took the heat for doing it; some of them laid down their seats in Congress for doing it—it drove down interest rates; it increased investment; it caused the economy to explode. The American people were out there waiting to work, to create jobs, to start new businesses, to prove they could compete in the world, and they have done it in stunning order.

If you look around the world today at the problems a lot of our friends and neighbors are having, our trading partners are having, they begin to have these problems when there is a sense that they don't have their financial house in order. Because whether we like it or not, this money moves around the world at the speed of light and people can move money in and out at breathtaking speed. So no matter what we try to do to help anyone else, they first have to help themselves. But we can't forget that lesson ourselves. We cannot allow ourselves to get in another situation where we quadruple the debt in 10 years. The consequences would be far more serious if we did that again. So we can reform Social Security, but we have to do it consistent with what's growing our economy today.

Now, those are the things that I believe we should be doing. You and I have worked together to preserve and strengthen Medicare, as Steve said. We've worked to secure the Medicare Trust Fund for a decade. And we've made, as I said, mammographies and diabetes screening more available. We've increased health plan choices while making beneficiaries know they can choose to keep their current plans. Next year we'll also have to act to strengthen Medicare for the long-term, and once again as with Social Security, I'll ask for your help, because the answer is to strengthen the program, not to dismantle it. So I ask you to think about that and to be involved in it.

And one last health issue that I think is important that's before the Congress today is this Patients' Bill of Rights. It includes the guarantee of access to specialists, access to emergency rooms, the right to appeal health care decisions. Basically, it includes the right to say, "Okay, we want the benefits of managed care, but we don't want someone who is an accountant telling a doctor and a patient that they can't have a life-saving procedure." It's very important.

Now, if you're on Medicare, I have, by Executive order, extended those rights to everybody on Medicare. But most Americans are not on Medicare or Medicaid. And they're entitled to the same protection. We should manage the system as efficiently as we can. We should do everything we can to get the cost down, except risk someone's life or deny them the quality health care they deserve. That's what we're paying for. So we shouldn't put the cart before the horse, here, or let the tail wag the dog. That's what the Patients' Bill of Rights is all about.

We've also, as you know, fought together against proposals to block-grant the Medicaid program, to eliminate Federal nursing home standards, to get rid of the health care guarantee for people on welfare and their children. Last week I launched a major legislative and administrative initiative to improve our nursing homes, with more frequent inspections, immediate fines for nursing homes that provide inadequate or abusive care, a national registry for nursing home workers known to be abusive, and unprecedented efforts to prevent poor nutrition and other health concerns from threatening people in nursing homes. And I thank you for your support of that.

Before I go, there are two other things that I'd ask you to help me with. I want you to keep working with me until we actually succeed in reauthorizing the Older Americans Act. It's funded Meals on Wheels and many other programs. [*Applause*] Thank you.

I also ask you to work with me again and to continue to oppose the public housing bill that recently passed the House of Representatives. It could be devastating to our Nation's hardest pressed seniors, unnecessarily denying them housing assistance when they need it the most.

We've got a big agenda out there, and you've got to be involved in it: Social Security reform, Medicare reform, the Older Americans Act, all these other issues. I have done my best as President to bring this country together when others sought to divide it, to put progress ahead of partisanship and people ahead of politics, to build a stronger world for our children and grandchildren and a decent world for all of you.

I've been thinking a lot about this country today, because I'm sure all of you know we had a very emotional service today in the United States Capitol for the two brave police officers who were killed last Friday. And I told their families that I realize that any words of mine were poor substitutes for the time they should have been given with their family and friends. It is unnatural for people to have their days terminated before they see the seasons turn enough, before they get their fill of the rhythms of daily life, before they see their grandchildren wandering around their feet.

But those people put on that uniform and went to work that day, like every other day, because they knew that somebody had to do that so that the rest of us could enjoy all that normal life. I tried to tell the families that their fathers and husbands, in laying down their lives, had not only saved the lives of many of their fellow citizens, which clearly they did, but they had really consecrated our Capitol as the house of freedom.

So I think today we can put aside a lot of our normal conflicts and just think about what America is at its best. If you go all the way back to the beginning, if you go—and I do this on a regular basis—and reread the Declaration of Independence, it's very interesting to see that the guidance they gave then is the guidance we ought to have today. We believe everybody is created equal, endowed by God with the right to life, liberty, and the pursuit of happiness. And we put this Government together because we can't protect and enhance those rights alone; there are some things we have to do together, as one people. The Government should be limited in power and scope but should have enough authority to do what we all need to do together that we can't do alone.

And for over 200 years now we've worked together within that framework to widen the circle of opportunity for more people—that's what Social Security did; to deepen the meaning of American freedom—that's what the civil rights law did; and to strengthen the bonds of our Union, our common home.

Every time we stand up for a decent cause— every time we stand up for something, even though it may help some other group of people more than it helps us, because we know that we're better off and we're stronger if everybody in America has a decent life and a fair chance— we honor the sacrifice those men made last Friday. I think you do that every week, every month, every year. And I thank you from the bottom of my heart.

Thank you.

NOTE: The President spoke at 8:30 p.m. in the Regency Ballroom at the Hyatt Regency Hotel. In his remarks, he referred to R. Thomas Buffenbarger, president, International Association of Machinists and Aerospace Workers, and national vice president, National Council of Senior Citizens (NCSC); Dorothy Height, chair and president emerita, National Council of Negro Women; Robert Georgine, president, Building and Construction Trade Development, AFL–CIO; Cliff Holliday, committee chair, Gerdena Valley Democratic Club; NCSC officers George Kourpias, president, Genevieve Johnson, general vice president, and Steve Protulis, executive director; and Officer Jacob J. Chestnut and Detective John M. Gibson, who died as a result of gunshot wounds suffered during an attack at the Capitol on July 24.

Message to the Congress on Continuation of the National Emergency With Respect to Iraq
July 28, 1998

To the Congress of the United States:

Section 202(d) of the National Emergencies Act (50 U.S.C. 1622(d)) provides for the automatic termination of a national emergency unless, prior to the anniversary date of its declaration, the President publishes in the *Federal Register* and transmits to the Congress a notice stat-

ing that the emergency is to continue in effect beyond the anniversary date. In accordance with this provision, I have sent the enclosed notice, stating that the Iraqi emergency is to continue in effect beyond August 2, 1998, to the *Federal Register* for publication.

The crisis between the United States and Iraq that led to the declaration on August 2, 1990, of a national emergency has not been resolved. The Government of Iraq continues to engage in activities inimical to stability in the Middle East and hostile to United States interests in the region. Such Iraqi actions pose a continuing unusual and extraordinary threat to the national security and vital foreign policy interests of the United States. For these reasons, I have determined that it is necessary to maintain in force the broad authorities necessary to apply economic pressure on the Government of Iraq.

WILLIAM J. CLINTON

The White House,
July 28, 1998.

NOTE: This message was released by the Office of the Press Secretary on July 29. The notice of July 28 is listed in Appendix D at the end of this volume.

Message to the Congress Reporting on Efforts To Achieve a Sustainable Peace in Bosnia and Herzegovina
July 28, 1998

To the Congress of the United States:

Pursuant to section 7 of Public Law 105–174, I am providing this report to inform the Congress of ongoing efforts to meet the goals set forth therein.

With my certification to the Congress of March 3, 1998, I outlined ten conditions—or benchmarks—under which Dayton implementation can continue without the support of a major NATO-led military force. Section 7 of Public Law 105–174 urges that we seek concurrence among NATO allies on: (1) the benchmarks set forth with the March 3 certification; (2) estimated target dates for achieving those benchmarks; and (3) a process for NATO to review progress toward achieving those benchmarks. NATO has agreed to move ahead in all these areas.

First, NATO agreed to benchmarks parallel to ours on May 28 as part of its approval of the Stabilization Force (SFOR) military plan (OPLAN 10407). Furthermore, the OPLAN requires SFOR to develop detailed criteria for each of these benchmarks, to be approved by the North Atlantic Council, which will provide a more specific basis to evaluate progress. SFOR will develop the benchmark criteria in coordination with appropriate international civilian agencies.

Second, with regard to timelines, the United States proposed that NATO military authorities provide an estimate of the time likely to be required for implementation of the military and civilian aspects of the Dayton Agreement based on the benchmark criteria. Allies agreed to this approach on June 10. As SACEUR General Wes Clark testified before the Senate Armed Services Committee June 4, the development and approval of the criteria and estimated target dates should take 2 to 3 months.

Third, with regard to a review process, NATO will continue the 6-month review process that began with the deployment of the Implementation Force (IFOR) in December 1995, incorporating the benchmarks and detailed criteria. The reviews will include an assessment of the security situation, an assessment of compliance by the parties with the Dayton Agreement, an assessment of progress against the benchmark criteria being developed by SFOR, recommendations on any changes in the level of support to civilian agencies, and recommendations on any other changes to the mission and tasks of the force.

While not required under Public Law 105–174, we have sought to further utilize this framework of benchmarks and criteria for Dayton implementation among civilian implementation agencies. The Steering Board of the Peace Implementation Council (PIC) adopted the same framework in its Luxembourg declaration of June 9, 1998. The declaration, which serves as the civilian implementation agenda for the next 6 months, now includes language that corresponds to the benchmarks in the March 3 certification to the Congress and in the SFOR OPLAN. In addition, the PIC Steering Board called on the High Representative to submit a report on the progress made in meeting these goals by mid-September, which will be considered in the NATO 6-month review process.

The benchmark framework, now approved by military and civilian implementers, is clearly a better approach than setting a fixed, arbitrary end date to the mission. This process will produce a clear picture of where intensive efforts will be required to achieve our goal: a self-sustaining peace process in Bosnia and Herzegovina for which a major international military force will no longer be necessary. Experience demonstrates that arbitrary deadlines can prove impossible to meet and tend to encourage those who would wait us out or undermine our credibility. Realistic target dates, combined with concerted use of incentives, leverage and pressure with all the parties, should maintain the sense of urgency necessary to move steadily toward an enduring peace. While the benchmark process will be useful as a tool both to promote and review the pace of Dayton implementation,

the estimated target dates established will be notional, and their attainment dependent upon a complex set of interdependent factors.

We will provide a supplemental report once NATO has agreed upon detailed criteria and estimated target dates. The continuing 6-month reviews of the status of implementation will provide a useful opportunity to continue to consult with Congress. These reviews, and any updates to the estimated timelines for implementation, will be provided in subsequent reports submitted pursuant to Public Law 105–174. I look forward to continuing to work with the Congress in pursuing U.S. foreign policy goals in Bosnia and Herzegovina.

WILLIAM J. CLINTON

The White House,
July 28, 1998.

NOTE: This message was released by the Office of the Press Secretary on July 29.

Message to the Congress Transmitting the District of Columbia Budget Request
July 28, 1998

To the Congress of the United States:

In accordance with section 202(c) of the District of Columbia Financial Responsibility and Management Assistance Act of 1995, I am transmitting the District of Columbia's Fiscal Year 1999 Budget Request Act.

This proposed Fiscal Year 1999 Budget represents the major programmatic objectives of the Mayor, the Council of the District of Columbia, and the District of Columbia Financial Responsibility and Management Assistance Authority. It also meets the financial stability and management improvement objectives of the National Capital Revitalization and Self-Government Im-

provement Act of 1997. For Fiscal Year 1999, the District estimates revenues of $5.230 billion and total expenditures of $5.189 billion resulting in a $41 million budget surplus.

My transmittal of the District of Columbia's budget, as required by law, does not represent an endorsement of its contents.

WILLIAM J. CLINTON

The White House,
July 28, 1998.

NOTE: This message was released by the Office of the Press Secretary on July 29.

Remarks to the Education International World Congress
July 29, 1998

Thank you. First of all, let me thank my long-time friend Mary Hatwood Futrell for that won-

derful introduction. And thank you for your

warm welcome. I thank the leaders of our education organizations, Bob Chase and Sandy Feldman, for their work, and welcome all of the members of EI here to the United States. I am delighted to join in your second congress, on your final day in Washington. I hope you've had a successful meeting; even more, I hope you will be going home with new energy for your lifetime commitment to your children and the future of your nations.

It is always an honor for me to meet with educators. As President, I have had the privilege of visiting schools around our Nation and around the world. And wherever I have been, whether in a small village in Uganda or a poor neighborhood in Rio de Janeiro, a town in California or an inner-city school in Chicago or Philadelphia, I always meet teachers whose dedication to their students is nothing short of heroic, men and women for whom kindling the spark of possibility in every child, from that once-in-a-lifetime mathematics prodigy to a young girl who dreams of being the very first in her family just to finish school and go on to college—for those people, teaching is not a job but a mission. I know that, for you, it is such a mission. So let me thank you and your 23 million colleagues across the world for making the education of our world's children your life's work.

We are living in an era of unprecedented hope and possibility, but profound challenge. A technological revolution is sweeping across the globe. It is changing the way we live and work and relate to each other. It is binding our economies closer together, whether we like it or not. It is making our world smaller. Today, 100 million people are logging onto the Internet. In just 3 years, that number will be about 700 million.

With all these changes come new challenges. We know that new democracies must be very carefully tended if they are to take root and thrive. We know that with technology advancing at rapid speed, the best jobs and the best opportunities will be available only to those with the knowledge to take advantage of them. We know that if we do not take action, dangerous opportunity gaps between those people and those nations who have these skills and those who do not have them will grow and deepen.

The best way, therefore, to strengthen democracy, to strengthen our Nation, to make the most of the possibilities, and to do the best job of meeting the challenges of the 21st century is to guarantee universal, excellent education for every child on our planet.

Where once we focused our development efforts on the construction of factories and powerplants, today we must invest more in the power of the human mind, in the potential of every single one of our children. A world-class education for all children is essential to combating the fear, the ignorance, the prejudice that undermine freedom all across the globe today in the form of ethnic, religious, and racial hatreds. It is essential to creating a worldwide middle class. It is essential to global prosperity. It is essential to fulfilling the most basic needs of the human body and the human spirit. That is why the 21st century must be the century of education and the century of the teacher.

As Mary said, throughout my career, first as the Governor of one of our States and now as President, I have worked to make education my top priority. Today I want to share with you what we are doing to provide every American at every stage in life a world-class education. And I want to recommit the United States to working with other nations to advance education as our common cause.

We are working very hard with nations all across the world through our AID programs, our Agency for International Development, and in other ways. At the recent Summit of the Americas in Santiago, Chile, we reaffirmed the commitment of the Americas to work in common on the training of teachers and the development and dissemination of not only technology but educational software, so that we could learn more everywhere we live, so that children in small villages in South America could have access to things which today are only dreams.

When I was in Africa, I reaffirmed the focus of many of our AID programs to be on education. We announced in South Africa a project with our Discovery Channel to try to bring technology and the benefits of it to small African villages. We are working in Bosnia and Croatia to help the students there learn about democracy so that they can preserve what so many have given so much to create, a real sustainable peace in a multi-ethnic democracy.

All across the world, America has an interest in seeing education improve. One-third of the adults in the world are illiterate today; two-thirds of them live in the poorest countries. We are doing better. The literacy rate was only

43 percent in 1970. The percentage of our children going to school in 1970 across the world was only 48 percent. Today, it's 77 percent, at least in the primary school years.

And something that's very important to my wife and to me, in 1970, only 38 percent of all schoolchildren were girls; today, the percentage is 68 percent—all girls in school. But think about it, that means 32 percent of the girls who should be in school are not. And I still visit countries where basic primary education for girls is still a dream in some places. That must not be. If we want to see these societies elevated, if we want to see the economies grow, if we want to see families made whole and able to plan their futures, we must educate all our children, the boys and the girls alike.

Here in America, we have recognized the increasing importance of a college education to our position in the global economy. In our last census, it became clear that young people who had less than 2 years of post-high-school education were likely to get jobs where their incomes never grew and were far more likely to become unemployed.

And so we have done everything we can to open the doors of college to all Americans who will work for it. We have made the first 2 years of college virtually free, with a tax credit we call the HOPE scholarship. Through expanded low-cost student loans and more student work positions, through tax credit and deductions for all college postgraduate and continuing education work by older workers, through giving our young people the opportunity to earn scholarship money by doing community service, we are making all forms of higher education more affordable to all kinds of Americans.

Second, we are working to establish high national standards to ensure that our children, from the earliest years, master the basics. Many of your countries already have national standards. Because in America we have a history of education being the responsibility of State governments and being within the span of control of local school boards, we don't have such national standards.

I believe, in a global economy, every nation should have national standards that meet international norms. I believe that so many students from around the world did better than their American counterparts in the Third International Math and Science Study because their country had set high standards, challenged their

students to master rigorous and advanced material, and used national tests to make sure that they did. I want to do the same in America, beginning with high standards in fourth grade reading and eighth grade mathematics, to give teachers and parents the tools they need to secure our children's future.

Third, we know that good teachers are the key to good schools. We are working to reward the most innovative and successful teachers in our classrooms, to help those who fail to perform to move on or improve, and to recruit more of our best and brightest to enter the teaching profession, especially in areas where there are a lot of poor children in desperate need of more help.

Fourth, we are working to create better learning environments by modernizing our schools and reducing class size, especially in the early grades, where research has shown it makes a positive and permanent difference in learning in our country.

Fifth, we are working hard to prepare our children for the demands of the information age by connecting every classroom and library to the Internet by the year 2000 and by training teachers in these new technologies.

Sixth, we are working to deal with one of America's most painful problems, the presence of violence in our schools. We have a zero-tolerance policy for guns in our schools. Later this year, we will be having our first-ever conference—White House conference in Washington on school safety. I hope and pray this is not a problem in any of the countries here represented, but if it is, we would be glad to have your ideas and to share ours with you. Teaching cannot succeed and learning cannot occur unless classrooms are safe, disciplined, and drug-free. And we are working are on it, and we welcome your support and help.

Next, we are working to end one of the most harmful practices of a public school system that is too often overwhelmed by the challenges it faces and the lack of resources to meet them, the so-called practice of social promotion, where children are passed from grade to grade even when they don't learn the material first. But we believe that along with ending the practice, we must follow the examples set in our city of Chicago, where there is extra help for the children after school and in the summer, so that we don't just identify children as failures but instead say, "We're going to give you more help until you succeed." I think that is profoundly important.

Finally, we are working to establish mentoring programs for children in our poorest and most underserved areas, along with guarantees of access to college that they get in their middle school years if they continue to learn and perform, so that when these children are 11 or 12 or 13 they can be told, "If you stay in school and learn and you want to go on to a college or university, we can tell you right now you will have the help you need to do it." I think it is a powerful incentive, and in areas where children have been so used to being ignored for so long and feel that they will always be trapped in poverty, I think it is profoundly important.

Today, there is a vigorous debate going on in our Congress over the nature and extent of our responsibilities as a nation to our children's education. There are some in the other party who don't see eye-to-eye with me on what we should be doing for our public schools. Even as we recognize the importance of raising academic standards and challenging our students to meet them, there are those who would actually prohibit the development of national tests for our schools, even if it's voluntary to participate. Even as more studies confirm what we have already suspected about the importance of early childhood development, some would deny Head Start opportunities to as many as 25,000 of our disadvantaged children.

Even as the greatest number of children since the baby boom are enrolling in our schools, some would weaken our efforts to recruit new, highly qualified teachers. Even as hundreds of thousands of high-paying, high-tech jobs all across America go begging for workers, some would cut our investments in education technology and technology training for teachers. Even as the evidence is overwhelming that smaller classes, especially in areas where children have difficulties learning, can make a permanent, positive difference in what children learn and what they continue to learn throughout their lifetime in the early grades, there are those who say we have no business investing national tax dollars in such endeavors.

Believe it or not, there are even some who are trying to kill one of our most successful efforts to provide on-the-job training to our young people and to give them something positive to do and ensure that they stay out of trouble in their free time. For a generation in our country, legislators from both our major political parties have supported the summer jobs program that has helped millions of our most disadvantaged young people appreciate the responsibility of a regular job and the reward of a regular paycheck. Eliminating summer jobs would mock the very values we Americans cherish most, hard work, responsibility, opportunity. If we truly believe in these things, then we should help to expose all our young people, especially those who need it, to the world of work. If we insist upon responsibility from all our people, then those of us in power must take responsibility for giving our teenagers the jobs that will help them succeed in the future and keep them on a good path today. If we believe in opportunity for all, then we must not deny our young people this vital springboard to opportunity.

I say this to point out to all of you that if you don't get your way on education every day in your own countries, don't be surprised if we don't get to do everything we want to do, either. What seems so self-evident to you and me is still not entirely clear to all decisionmakers. But I want to encourage you to keep up the fight.

In all my visits at home and abroad, I have found out that you can learn a lot about a country's future by visiting its public schools. Does every child—boy and girl, rich and poor—have the same opportunity to learn? Are they engaged by patient, well-trained, and inspiring teachers? Do they have access to the materials they need to learn? Are they learning what they need to know to succeed in the country they will live in and in the future that they will create? Do they have opportunities to go on to university if they do well and deserve the chance to do so? Are the schools themselves safe, positive, good places to learn? We have to build a future together where the answer to all these questions is "yes" in every community, in every nation.

I believe we can build a future where every child in every corner of the world, because of the explosion of technology and because of the dedication of teachers, will have the skills, the opportunity, the education to fulfill his or her God-given potential. I know this will happen if teachers lead the way.

I know that there will be political fights to be fought and won. I know one of your honorees at this conference is being honored for taking huge numbers of children out of bondage and putting them back in school. Some people still view children as little more than a material asset. They are us, as children, and they are our future and the future of the world.

When he came to the White House to be honored as our National Teacher of the Year, Philip Bigler said, "To be a teacher is to be forever an optimist." I thank you for your unshakeable optimism. I ask you not only to be vigorous in the classroom but vigorous as citizens. You must not stop until every political leader with any political influence, in any political party, in any nation, knows that this is something that has to be lifted above political partisanship. This is something that ought to be beyond all debate.

If you understand how the world is going to work tomorrow and you have any concern about the integrity and the richness of the human spirit in every child, then all of us must join hands to help you succeed in giving all those children the tomorrows they deserve.

Thank you, and God bless you.

NOTE: The President spoke at 11:31 a.m. at the Washington Hilton. In his remarks, he referred to Mary Hatwood Futrell, president, Education International; Robert Chase, president, National Education Association; Sandra Feldman, president, American Federation of Teachers; and Albert Shanker Education Award recipient Dr. Shantha Sinha, secretary trustee, M. Venkatarangaiya Foundation, Andhra Pradesh, India.

Statement on Signing the National Science Foundation Authorization Act of 1998
July 29, 1998

Today I am pleased to sign into law H.R. 1273, the "National Science Foundation Authorization Act of 1998."

Science, engineering, and technology are potent forces for progress and achievement. Over the past century, advances in science and technology have driven much of our economic growth and shaped the lives of every generation of Americans in previously unimaginable ways. As we approach the 21st Century, many of our society's expectations for a better future are dependent upon advances in science and technology.

The science and engineering investments made by the National Science Foundation (NSF) will create new knowledge, spur innovations, foster future breakthroughs, and provide cutting-edge research facilities to help power our Nation in the next century. These investments will help secure the continued prosperity of our economy, improvements in health care and our standards of living, and better education and training for America's students and workers.

This Act will enable the NSF to continue to play an important leadership role in sustaining scientific and technological progress. I am pleased to note that the appropriation authoriza-

tion levels in H.R. 1273 are the same as proposed in my FY 1999 Budget, and I urge that these amounts be appropriated. The proposed funding for the NSF is part of my Administration's broader, aggressive agenda for science and technology investments throughout the Federal Government, which includes the NSF's participation in the Global Observations to Benefit the Environment Initiative, the Partnership for a New Generation of Vehicles Program, and the Education and Training Technology Initiative. I especially commend the Congress for authorizing the NSF's participation in the Next Generation Internet Program. This multi-agency program will push the frontiers of computation and communications and help fuel the revolution in information technology.

I want to acknowledge the bipartisan efforts in the House and the Senate that produced this important legislation and, in particular, remember the contributions of the late Steve Schiff of New Mexico, Chairman of the House Basic Research Subcommittee. Throughout his life and career, Steve Schiff dedicated his time and talents to make life better for the people of New Mexico and for this fellow Americans. Even as he waged his final courageous battle against cancer, he continued his efforts to make life better for families across this country. This Act is just one piece of his legacy and demonstrates how the Congress and the Administration can work together to help continue U.S. leadership in science and technology. I am pleased to sign it into law.

WILLIAM J. CLINTON

The White House,

July 29, 1998.

NOTE: H.R. 1273, approved July 29, was assigned Public Law No. 105–207.

Statement on Signing the Homeowners Protection Act of 1998
July 29, 1998

Today I am pleased to sign into law S. 318, the Homeowners Protection Act, which will save many American families thousands of dollars over the lifetime of their home mortgages. This bill will enable homeowners to cancel private mortgage insurance ("PMI") that they no longer need and make sure they receive full disclosure of their right to cancel.

Mortgage insurance has helped expand homeownership by allowing homeowners to make lower downpayments. But far too many homeowners continue to pay for mortgage insurance long after they have built enough equity so that the lender has little risk of loss. This bill would address that problem by making sure that homeowners have the right to cancel PMI, or by making that cancellation automatic, when home-

owners build up enough equity in their homes. For a family that buys a $160,000 home, this bill would ensure savings of $1,600 if they do not move or refinance for 15 years.

Since I took office, homeownership has climbed to its highest rate in American history. But now is not a time to rest. I have set a national goal of helping 8 million new families move into homes of their own by the year 2000. Lowering the cost of homeownership is one more way we are helping America's working families. That is why I am pleased to sign this homeowner- and consumer-friendly legislation.

NOTE: S. 318, approved July 29, was assigned Public Law No. 105–216.

Statement on the Death of Jerome Robbins
July 29, 1998

Hillary and I are deeply saddened to learn of the death of Jerome Robbins. Like so many Americans, our lives were enriched immeasurably by his artistic genius. Through his brilliant choreography, he brought the joy and passion of the human experience to millions, lifting

American theater and dance to new heights. And in the treasury of timeless masterpieces he leaves behind—from "Fancy Free" and "On the Town" to "West Side Story" and "Fiddler on the Roof"—his creative spirit will live forever.

Memorandum on Outreach Actions To Increase Employment of Adults With Disabilities

July 29, 1998

Memorandum for the Attorney General, the Secretary of Health and Human Services, the Chair of the Equal Opportunity Commission, the Administrator of the Small Business Administration

Subject: Outreach Actions to Increase Employment of Adults with Disabilities

As we commemorate the eighth anniversary of the Americans with Disabilities Act of 1990 (ADA), we have much to celebrate. This landmark civil rights law is making it possible for millions of Americans to participate more fully in society—through employment, access to public facilities, and participation in community and leisure activities—and to do their part to make us a stronger and better country. At the same time, we are reminded that significant challenges remain. Far too many of the 30 million working-age adults with disabilities are still unemployed, especially those with significant disabilities.

To address employment barriers for people with disabilities, I issued Executive Order 13078 on March 13, 1998, establishing the National Task Force on Employment of Adults with Disabilities. The Task Force will issue in November the first in a series of reports on what the Federal Government can do to help bring the employment rate of adults with disabilities into line with that of the general population. The Task Force already has identified important ways to reduce barriers to work for people with disabilities, and I hereby direct you to act on these findings.

First, although awareness of the ADA is increasing among persons with disabilities, employers, and the general public, too many people still are not aware of their rights and responsibilities under the ADA. There is a particular need to educate the small business community, which employs most of the private work force and includes the vast majority of employers.

I therefore direct the Attorney General, the Chair of the Equal Employment Opportunity Commission, and the Administrator of the Small Business Administration to expand public education regarding the requirements of the ADA to employers, employees, and others whose rights may be affected, with special attention to small businesses and underserved communities, such as racial and language minorities that may not have ready access to information that is already available.

Second, lack of adequate private health insurance options is a disincentive to leave Social Security programs for work. Few private health plans cover the personal assistance and other types of services that make work possible for many people with disabilities. Recognizing this problem, I proposed and the Congress passed a new Medicaid option last year that allows people with disabilities to buy into Medicaid without having to receive cash assistance. A number of States have expressed an interest in offering this new option and the Secretary of Health and Human Services has been working with them to do so. Much more, however, needs to be done to increase the public outreach and education activities about these important laws and options.

I therefore direct the Secretary of Health and Human Services to continue to take all necessary actions to inform Governors, State legislators, State Medicaid directors, consumer organizations, employers, providers, and other interested parties about section 4733 of the Balanced Budget Act of 1997. Section 4733 allows States to provide Medicaid coverage for working individuals with disabilities who, because of their earnings, would not qualify for Medicaid under current law. Additional guidance, letters, technical assistance, and other efforts by the Department of Health and Human Services about the enormous benefits of this option can go a long way in encouraging States to adopt and use this Medicaid buy-in.

This memorandum is for the internal management of the executive branch and does not create any right or benefit, substantive or procedural, enforceable by a party against the United States, its agencies or instrumentalities, its officers or employees, or any other person.

WILLIAM J. CLINTON

Message to the Congress Transmitting the Report of the Corporation for Public Broadcasting
July 29, 1998

To the Congress of the United States:

In accordance with the Public Broadcasting Act of 1967, as amended (47 U.S.C. 396(i)), I transmit herewith the Annual Report of the Corporation for Public Broadcasting (CPB) for Fiscal Year 1997 and the Inventory of the Federal Funds Distributed to Public Telecommunications Entities by Federal Departments and Agencies: Fiscal Year 1997.

Thirty years following the establishment of the Corporation for Public Broadcasting, the Congress can take great pride in its creation. During these 30 years, the American public has been educated, inspired, and enriched by the programs and services made possible by this investment.

The need for and the accomplishments of this national network of knowledge have never been more apparent, and as the attached 1997 annual CPB report indicates, by "Going Digital," public broadcasting will have an ever greater capacity for fulfilling its mission.

WILLIAM J. CLINTON

The White House,
July 29, 1998.

Remarks at the American Heritage Rivers Designation Signing Ceremony in Ashe County, North Carolina
July 30, 1998

The President. Thank you. Thank you so much. Thank you for the warm welcome. Thank you for being here. Thank you, Sheila Morgan. Didn't she do a good job? [*Applause*]

I want to——

Audience member. We love you, Mr. President!

The President. Thank you, ma'am. [*Laughter*]

I want to thank all of you. I want to especially thank my good friend Governor Hunt, America's premier and senior Governor on so many issues and especially the education of our children. He's done a wonderful job for you.

I want to thank Congressman Burr for his statement, his commitment, his support of this project, and proving once again that at its best, America's commitment to our natural environment and our children's future is a bipartisan effort. I want to thank Congressman Rahall, my good friend from West Virginia, for reminding us that Virginia and West Virginia are also a part of the New River designation and very proud of it.

I thank Chair of the Federal Advisory Commission, Dayton Duncan, and the other members who are here today; the chair of the American Heritage River Alliance, Peter Stroh. I think the North Carolina poet laureate, Fred Chappell, is here, and I thank him for coming; I hope he'll write a poem about this. I want to say to Chairman Yeats and Mayors Baldwin, Brown, and Hightower, we're glad to be here in your neighborhood.

I would like to say a special word of thanks to the Vice President, for the magnificent record he has established in protecting our environment and in so many other areas of our national life, and to my great good friend Erskine Bowles, perhaps the most effective Chief of Staff any President ever had, and a relentless promoter of North Carolina and the New River. I think the Vice President would agree with me when I say, on October 1st we will close our books on the old budget year and open our books on the new one, and for the first time in 29 long years America is going to have a balanced budget and a surplus, thanks in no small measure to Erskine Bowles' leadership.

I want to thank all the people who made this day possible, the young people, the River Builders; I thank the young AmeriCorps volunteers who are here. I thank all the older people who also worked hard. I don't know how in the world you all got this place outfitted for this many people in no more time than you had to work on it, but I hope we could all join one more time in thanking Bill and Lula Severt and their family. The Severts have been great to make us at home in their home. Thank you, bless you.

Can you imagine how he felt—they said, "How would you like to just take out a minute or two in a couple of weeks, Bill, to entertain the President, the Vice President, the Governor, two Congressmen, and 6,500 of their closest friends." [*Laughter*] Just another day on the farm. [*Laughter*]

In just a few moments I will sign a proclamation making all this official, awarding our Nation's first American Heritage Rivers designations to the New River, the Blackstone and Woonasquatucket, the Connecticut, the Cuyahoga, the Detroit, the Hanalei, the Hudson, the Upper and Lower Mississippi, the Potomac, the Rio Grande, the St. Johns, the Upper Susquehanna and Lackawanna, and the Willamette. Those places tell you an awful lot about America. They span our history. They span our country. They capture our imagination.

I want to congratulate the communities that participated in all these—all these—designations, and also those who worked so hard who didn't quite make it this time. It was an amazing process.

You know, for 5½ years the Vice President and I have worked hard to honor one of our Nation's oldest, most enduring values, to preserve for future generations the Earth God gave us. That's really what this river initiative is all about.

The First Lady has headed up our coming celebration, moving toward the year 2000, of the millennium, starting a new century and a new 1,000 years. And she came up with this theme that we should honor the past and imagine the future. You may have seen a few days ago she went out to Fort McHenry, where the Star-Spangled Banner flew, to celebrate the restoration of the Star-Spangled Banner; then on to the home of Thomas Edison; Harriet Tubman; and then to George Washington's Revolutionary War headquarters—the thing that got North Carolina into this country in the first place and put it in a position to give up Tennessee. [*Laughter*]

So I think——

[*At this point, the President looked at Vice President Gore.*]

The President. He's laughing. [*Laughter*] I'll hear about that later.

What we do today is an important part of honoring our past, and it's far more distant, and it also will stretch far, far into the future. Like the rings of a stately old oak, the currents of our rivers carry remarkable stories.

The New River tells stories of a region, the southern Appalachian region, where tight-knit communities remain true to tradition, where neighbors share a vision of wise stewardship of water and land. It tells the stories of our emerging Nation, for Colonel Peter Jefferson, Thomas Jefferson's father, surveyed this river, and Daniel Boone trapped here for beaver and bear. It tells stories of earlier settlements through tools left by the Canaway, Cherokee, and Creek. It tells the story of our planet, for scientists can tell by the river's location and direction of flow that it is not only the oldest river in North America but the second oldest river on the face of the Earth.

The other American Heritage Rivers all have compelling stories of their own, but there is one story all these rivers share, the story of communities rallying around their rivers the way neighbors rally around each other in time of need or to get something done in the community.

Sheila talked about what you did here. In each and every community that won this designation—and, I add, those who came close, and there were dozens of them—we were simply overwhelmed by the cooperation between interests who often disagree and by the creative but practical plans forged by communities for protecting natural resources, spurring revitalization of the economy, and preserving cultural heritage.

Now we intend to work with you to realize our plans. This is the beginning, not the end, of this celebration. First, let me say, there will be no Federal mandates, no restrictions on property holders' rights. Our goal instead is to help local groups enhance historic rivers and make them attractive and commercially vibrant even as we preserve their environmental characteristics.

Here, for example, we'll start working with the New River Heritage Task Force to help family farmers increase their incomes with alternative crops and innovative techniques, while cutting the flow of pollutants into the river. On the Detroit River we'll help to revitalize an urban waterfront to bring new opportunity to downtown Detroit. On the St. Johns River we will help to control future floods and enhance environmental protection for rare species like the manatee. On each and every one of these rivers, we will help to unite our communities to further our country's river renaissance.

For nearly three decades now, as the Congressman said earlier and as the Vice President echoed, our Nation has made strong, visible, bipartisan progress in cleaning up our environment, while enhancing our economy at the same time. Today, our economy is the strongest in a generation, but we also have cleaner air, cleaner water, fewer toxic waste dumps, safer food, the cleanest environment in a generation. And we should be proud of that. The two go hand in hand.

I want to talk a little politics, but not partisan politics, with you. Jim Hunt and I were riding out here, and I looked at all those folks waving to me with their American flags. And I said, "Jim, is this a Democrat area or a Republican area?" [*Laughter*] He said, "It's about 50–50." He said, "It comes and goes." [*Laughter*] I said, "Kind of like America."

Well, I want to ask you to manifest the bipartisan or nonpartisan commitment I see in this crowd today to the environment in your voices in Washington, because some folks in Congress are no longer committed to bipartisan progress on the environment. They really do see, I believe honestly, polluted streams and fields or noxious air as overstated problems that can be put off for another day.

We can only deal with this if we have progress, not partisanship, because here are the facts: Today, 40 percent of our waters are still too polluted for fishing and swimming. That's why I launched the Clean Water Action Plan to help communities finish the job that the Vice President mentioned. So far, Congress has refused to fully fund this initiative. I ask them to reconsider. I think every child in America ought to have the same chance your children do to fish or swim or float on a river that's clean and pure.

We need progress, not partisanship, to protect our land. Last February, several months ago, I submitted a list of 100 new sites we can add to our Nation's endowment of protected lands, including a beautiful site here in the southern Appalachians along the trout-rich Thompson River. While Congress has appropriated the money to preserve these natural and historic treasures, under the law the leadership must approve the release of the funds. And so far they haven't done it. So today I ask again, let's work together to protect these wonders. The money is in the bank. The sites have been identified. They're not going anywhere, but we need to preserve them for everyone for all time.

We also need to work together to meet the challenge of climate change, which has already been mentioned by the Governor and others. Let me tell you, folks, the first time I had a long talk with Al Gore, he showed me this book he wrote, "Earth in the Balance," which I had already read and understood about half of. [*Laughter*] And he whipped out this chart showing how much more elements we were putting in the air in the form of greenhouse gases that were heating the planet.

And I listened, and it made a lot of sense to me, but I didn't know anybody who believed it, or at least not enough to actually come up with a plan. Well, now we know that the 9 hottest years in history have occurred in the last 11 years, that the 5 hottest years in history have occurred in the 1990's, that 1997 was the hottest year ever recorded on Earth, and every month of 1998 has broken the 1997 record in America. And I'm glad the clouds came up and made me cool while I'm saying that.

But there is a way, just like there has always been a way. Since we started doing this in 1970, there has always been a way for us to preserve the environment and grow the economy. There is a way for us to meet the challenge of climate change and global warming and continue to grow the economy. We just have to be innovative, and we have to be willing to change.

And again, I have not proposed a lot of big, burdensome new regulations; I have proposed tax incentives and investments in new technologies and partnerships so we can reduce the harmful fumes we put into the atmosphere from transportation, from construction, from utilities, from all the work we do. We can do this. This is not going to be that hard once we make up our mind.

But I can tell you, we can never do it unless there are Democrats and Republicans for it. We never make any real progress on any great challenge unless we go forward together. And I ask you to ask our country to go forward as you have gone forward together here. We need these programs for energy efficiency, renewable energy, and tax incentives. They've long enjoyed the support of business and environmentalists; they should enjoy the support of Congress.

And we also need to stop using legislative gimmicks in Washington to weaken environmental protection. In the Senate, for example, lawmakers have attached to bills that are totally unrelated devices called riders that would cripple our wildlife protection efforts, deny taxpayers a fair return on oil leasing on public lands, allow a $30 million road through a wildlife refuge in Alaska, the first road ever through a Federal wilderness. We don't need to do this. We need to keep going forward.

Look out at that river and just imagine, just try to imagine what it would be like to be 300 million years old. I'm grateful for our economic prosperity. I'm grateful for the fact that the crime rate is down, and we have the smallest percentage of our people on welfare in 29 years. I'm grateful for these things. But you know and I know that the world is still changing fast, that there are many challenges out there that we're trying to meet right now—the challenge of the problems that our friends in Asia have which could affect the whole world economy, just for example. We're trying to deal with wars of racial and religious and ethnic hatred that could spill into other countries and engage our young people again.

We know that we will have future challenges because in the nature of things, once you solve one set of problems there's always a new set of challenges coming along. That's one of the gifts that God has given us. So we'll always have new challenges, but you'll always have the New River, too.

For those of us who are old enough to be parents or grandparents, we know when our children and grandchildren are our age the facts of their lives might be a little different. It's kind of heartening to know, isn't it, that the New River will be the same because of what you are doing here today.

This ancient river has flowed through the heart of this land for millions of years—hundreds of millions of years longer than blood has flowed through any human heart. The Cherokee even say that this was the very first river created by the Great Spirit's hand. Who are we, such brief visitors on this Earth, to disturb it? But when we cherish it and save it and hand it on to our children, we have done what we were charged to do, not only in our own Constitution and history but by our Maker.

You should be very, very proud of yourselves today. I thank you for what you have done. God bless you.

NOTE: The President spoke at 1:08 p.m. at the Severt family farm. In his remarks, he referred to Sheila Morgan, co-owner of the Todd General Store on the New River, who introduced the President; Gov. James B. Hunt, Jr., of North Carolina; George Yeats, chairman, Ashe County Commission; Mayor Dale Baldwin of West Jefferson, NC; Mayor Dayna Brown of Lansing, NC; Mayor D.E. Hightower of Jefferson, NC; and Bill and Lula Severt, who hosted the event. The proclamation is listed in Appendix D at the end of this volume.

Letter to Congressional Leaders Transmitting a Report on Cyprus
July 30, 1998

Dear Mr. Speaker: (*Dear Mr. Chairman:*)

In accordance with Public Law 95–384 (22 U.S.C. 2373(c)), I submit to you this report on progress toward a negotiated settlement of the Cyprus question covering the period April 1 to May 31, 1998. The previous submission covered events during February and March 1998.

My Special Presidential Emissary for Cyprus, Ambassador Richard C. Holbrooke, accompanied by Special Cyprus Coordinator Ambassador Thomas J. Miller, traveled to Cyprus in early April and held a series of intensive talks with the leaders of both communities. In early May, they returned to the island at the request of both leaders and encouraged them to begin serious negotiations toward a bizonal, bicommunal federation. Unfortunately, the Turkish side took the position that talks could not begin unless certain preconditions were satisfied, including recognition of the "Turkish Republic of Northern Cyprus" and the withdrawal of Cyprus' application to the European Union.

Although progress was not possible during Ambassador Holbrooke's May visit, he assured both parties that the United States would remain engaged in the search for a solution.

Sincerely,

WILLIAM J. CLINTON

NOTE: Identical letters were sent to Newt Gingrich, Speaker of the House of Representatives, and Jesse Helms, chairman, Senate Committee on Foreign Relations.

Remarks at a Reception for Senatorial Candidate John Edwards in Raleigh, North Carolina
July 30, 1998

Thank you very much. Thank you for being here. Thank you for waiting. Thank you for enduring the heat. I'll tell the Vice President 100 percent of the people in this crowd believe there is global warming now. [*Laughter*] Thank you so much.

I'd like to thank all the young people who provided our music over there. [*Inaudible*]— thank you very much. I'd like to thank the Lieutenant Governor, your Education Commissioner, and the other officials who are here; my old friend Dan Blue; my former Ambassador Jeanette Hyde and Wallace are here. Barbara Allen, your State chair, thank you very much. I saw Sheriff Baker here. I thank him for being here. I think every county ought to have a sheriff that's 9 feet tall. I wish I could find one everywhere.

I want to thank my good friend Erskine Bowles for coming home to North Carolina with me. You should know that on October 1st, when we have that balanced budget and surplus for the first time in so many years, there is no single person in America more responsible for the first balanced budget in a generation than Erskine Bowles. And it's a good thing for this country, and I appreciate it.

I thank my great friend Jim Hunt. We've been friends for 20 years now, a long time before some of you were born. And we've been out here working to try to improve education and move our country forward, move our States forward.

I want to thank Margaret Rose Sanford, Mrs. Terry Sanford, for being here tonight. Thank you for coming. But most of all, I want to thank John Edwards and his wife and his children for this race for the Senate.

You know, it's just a commonplace today that you can't beat a Republican incumbent running for the Senate because they have all the money—and that's why campaign finance reform never passes, I might add. [*Laughter*] And so times are good; people are happy; your opponent has money, he's already in; therefore, you can't win.

And John Edwards said, "I don't think so. I think we can do better." And I appreciate and respect that. I also want to thank them for giving up their anniversary dinner to come here and be with us. [*Laughter*] I'm not going to talk that long. It will still be open when we finish tonight. [*Laughter*]

I want to make a couple of brief points. It's hot, and you've heard it all. I feel like the guy that got up to the banquet and said, "Everything that needs to be said has already been said, but not everyone has said it yet, so you all sit tight." [*Laughter*] I'll be very brief.

First, I bring you greetings from the Vice President and the First Lady, who wish they could be here tonight. We want to thank the people in North Carolina who have been our friends since 1992, who stayed with us every step of the way, who believed in us when we were often under attack.

Here are the points I want to make, and they all bear on this race for the Senate. Number one: We came to office in 1992 carried by people who believed our country could do better if we had not only new leadership but new ideas. We not only had the right people,

I believe we did the right things. We said, "We want a Democratic Party based on the old virtues of opportunity, responsibility, and community, but with new ideas for the 21st century."

Five and a half years later, we have the lowest unemployment rate in 28 years, the lowest crime rate in 25 years, the lowest welfare rolls in 29 years, the first balanced budget in 29 years, the lowest inflation in 32 years, the highest home-ownership in American history, with the smallest Federal Government in 35 years, since John Kennedy was the President of the United States.

There were fights over these ideas. When we passed the budget in 1993 that reduced the deficit by over 90 percent, not a single member of the other party was with us. When we passed the crime bill to put 100,000 police officers on the street, which officers had been begging for—I just left Bristol, Tennessee, the airport, all these law enforcement officers standing there in east Tennessee, saying, "Thank you very much for still helping us to keep our community safe"—very few members of the other party were there. When we passed the family and medical leave bill that's allowed 12½ million people to get a little time off from work when they've got a new baby or a sick parent, most of the people in the other party opposed us.

It was the Democratic Party that said, "Yes, balance the budget, but give 5 million poor children health insurance. Give a HOPE scholarship to make the first 2 years of college free for virtually all Americans; increase those Pell grants; increase those work-study funds; give tax deductibility for the interest rates on student loans. Let's make college universal for everybody who is willing to work for it." That was our party's legacy.

It was the Democratic Party that said, "We can grow the economy and improve the environment; we can't afford to do the reverse." And against often relentless odds, I can tell you today, compared to 6 years ago, we not only have more new jobs, we have cleaner air, cleaner water, safer food, fewer toxic waste dumps, the most land set aside for eternal preservation since the administration of Franklin Roosevelt. We are moving this country in the right direction.

I love John Edwards' idea for the way to conduct a Senate campaign. I'm convinced that one of the few reasons that I am President today is that when I went to New Hampshire in 1992, a State with fewer than a million people, with the first election, I just started having open townhall meetings—said, "Folks, come on in here. We're going to talk." And I'd talk 5 or 6 minutes, and they would ask questions for an hour or two. And pretty soon the word got around. This is a little State, keep in mind. So I went to a place, and they said, "Bill, if you get 50 people it's an acceptable crowd. If you get 150 people, it's a huge crowd." There were 400 people who showed up. Why? Because they wanted to participate in their democracy. John Edwards is trying to give this Senate race and this Senate seat back to you, and I hope that his opponent will accept his offer.

Here's the second point I want to make. Here's why you ought to be for him: Most people, when times are good, especially if times have been bad, want to take a breather. They want to say, "Oh, everything is fine in America today"—it's in my self-interest to say that. So people say, "Oh, everything is fine. Let's just relax and kick back and kick off our shoes," and "It's a hot summer. We'll drink lemonade and leave them all in."

But let me tell you, those of you who study what's going on know that the world is changing very fast still, every day. The way we work, the way we live, the way we learn, the way we relate to the rest of the world, it's changing. We cannot afford to sit back. We have to bear down. Pretty soon us baby boomers will retire, and we don't want to bankrupt our kids and our grandkids. That's why I say—and John Edwards says—don't you dare spend that surplus until we save the Social Security system for the next generation.

We have already 160 million Americans in HMO's and other managed care plans. We say, "Okay, manage the care; save the money. But don't turn people away from an emergency room. Don't turn people away from a specialist. Don't have an accountant making a decision a doctor should make with a patient to save lives and guarantee quality health care." That's what the Patients' Bill of Rights is all about.

We say America has the finest system of college education in the world, and most of our public schools are doing a good job. But nobody believes every American child has the finest elementary and secondary education in the world. So let's keep working until they do, with smaller classes in the early grades; hooking up all the schools, even the poorest, to the Internet; giving kids the chance to have opportunities in the summer and after school if they need it to learn more. In other words, let's make a commitment that our elementary and high school education will be world-class for everybody, just like college education is. That's my commitment, and that's his.

And so, I have never given a speech in a cool room in North Carolina. [*Laughter*] And I tell you, you got my blood running strong. You make me feel good. I can't wait to go home and tell about it. But don't you forget, this good man and his family, here before you on their 21st anniversary, defied all the conventional wisdom along with the good people that ran in the primary with him, and they said, "We can do better. Just because America's doing well, just because North Carolina's doing well, we have to think about the long-term challenges."

Folks, when times are good, that's the time to repair the house; that's the time to prepare for the future; that's the time to build on the confidence you have. You stay with him and bring him home to the United States Senate, and we'll build a stronger America together for the 21st century.

Thank you, and God bless you.

NOTE: The President spoke at 7:35 p.m. in the Governor W. Kerr Scott Building at the North Carolina State Fairgrounds. In his remarks, he referred to Lt. Gov. Dennis Wicker of North Carolina; Lynda McCulloch, State education commissioner; State Representative Dan Blue; Jeanette Hyde, former Ambassador to Barbados, and her husband, Wallace; Barbara Allen, State Democratic Party chair; Sheriff John Baker of Wake County; Gov. James B. Hunt, Jr., of North Carolina; Margaret Rose Sanford, wife of former Gov. Terry Sanford; and Elizabeth Edwards, wife of candidate John Edwards.

Remarks to an Overflow Crowd in Raleigh
July 30, 1998

Thank you. We wanted to come by and thank you. I know that you had to come here; you didn't get in the other room. You had to listen; you couldn't see. But if it's any consolation, you are much, much cooler than anybody in that other room is right now.

And I just want to thank you all from the bottom of my heart for being so good to me and the First Lady and the Vice President over the last 5½ years, for the support that I've gotten from people from North Carolina, especially from my number one North Carolinian, Erskine Bowles, who has been a wonderful Chief of Staff.

I want to thank you for your commitment to John Edwards. And I want to ask you—you know, you heard us talking in the speeches about his proposal today to Senator Faircloth that they give up the ads and just spend all their money paying for honest conversations with the people of North Carolina. I think that's a good idea.

You just think about how it would change politics in America forever if North Carolina had an election in which there were no 30-second attack ads and the two candidates sat down around a table or maybe had 20 or 30 or 50 citizens sitting with them and honestly discussed the issues on television where everybody could be a part of it, write them, tell them what they thought, decide what they agree with, what they disagree with. Think about it. It would recreate old-fashioned citizenship again.

Now, if you like that, don't let it be one letter in one statement in one day. Go out tomorrow and talk about it and the next day and talk to your friends and neighbors about it and get a little ground swell built up about it, because I can tell you that I think that this candidate will be much more eager to do this than his opponent. But it's the right thing to do for the folks.

So stay with us; keep working. We're going to keep moving this country forward. Remember the last thing I said in there: Times are good now, and I'm grateful for that. But that's not a time to sit on your laurels and sit back and congratulate yourself. When America is going into a new century and things are changing as they are, we should use the confidence of these good times to take on those big long-term challenges. And that's what you have to think about with these elections coming up.

Who do you really want to be dealing with the challenges of saving Social Security and Medicare for the 21st century? Who do you really trust to do more to build the best public schools in America for all of our children, without regard to their income, their race, or their region of the country? Who do you believe is more likely to get quality, affordable health care for all Americans and say to the HMO's and

to the managed care people, "We want managed care, but we don't want accountants making decisions doctors should make. We want people to get in the emergency room, to see the specialists, to have quality health care when they need it"? The answer is John Edwards. And I'm honored to be in North Carolina with him tonight.

Thank you, and God bless you all. Thank you.

NOTE: The President spoke at 8:15 p.m. in Dorton Arena at the North Carolina State Fairgrounds.

Message to the Congress Transmitting a Report on Efforts To End the Arab League Boycott of Israel
July 30, 1998

To the Congress of the United States:

In accordance with the request contained in section 540 of Public Law 105–118, Foreign Operations, Export Financing, and Related Programs Appropriations Act, 1998, I submit to you the attached report providing information on steps taken by the United States Government to bring about an end to the Arab League boycott of Israel and to expand the process of nor-

malizing ties between Israel and the Arab League countries.

WILLIAM J. CLINTON

The White House,
July 30, 1998.

NOTE: This message was released by the Office of the Press Secretary on July 31.

Remarks on the National Economy and an Exchange With Reporters
July 31, 1998

The President. Good morning. I want to thank the Vice President, Mr. Bowles, and our economic team for joining us today to talk about the continuing strength of our economy and what we have to do to make it stronger as we move toward a new century.

Five and a half years ago, we set a new strategy for the new economy, founded on fiscal discipline, expanded trade, and investment in our people. Today our economy is the strongest in a generation. While the latest economic report shows that growth in the second quarter of 1998 was more moderate than the truly remarkable first quarter, it shows that our economy continues to enjoy steady growth. So far this year, economic growth has averaged 3.5 per-

cent. This is growth the right way, led by business investment and built on a firm foundation of fiscal discipline.

We've also learned today that since I took office the private sector of our economy has grown by nearly 4 percent, while we have reduced the Federal Government to its smallest size in 35 years. Wages are rising. Investment and consumer confidence remain high. Unemployment and inflation remain low. Prosperity and opportunity abound for the American people.

In the long run, we can keep our economy on its strong and prosperous course. Our economic foundation is solid. Our strategy is sound. Still, we know from events that, more than ever, the challenges of the global marketplace demand that we press forward with the comprehensive strategy we began 6 years ago.

First, we have to maintain our fiscal discipline. This week marks the fifth anniversary of the 1993 economic plan that charted our course to a balanced budget and reduced the deficit by over 90 percent by the time we signed the Balanced Budget Act in 1997. This fiscal discipline has had a powerful, positive impact, driving interest rates down, pushing investment to historic levels, creating a virtuous cycle of economic activity that has helped cut the deficit even further. We must hold a steady course, and we should not spend a penny of the surplus until we have saved Social Security first. Fiscal discipline helped to build this strong economy; fiscal recklessness could undermine it dramatically. We must use these good times to honor our parents and the next generation by saving Social Security first.

Second, we must continue to invest in the American people. Five years ago I said we had to close two gaps, one in the budget and the other in the skills of our people. Now, as we hear of a shortage of highly skilled workers all across our country, we have more confirmation that America simply must do more in education and training. To fill those high-wage jobs, we must have a training system that works.

In 1995 I put forward a comprehensive proposal to modernize, overhaul, and streamline our job training programs. I called it a "GI bill" for America's workers. With bipartisan support, Congress is now poised to finish the job. I was so pleased by the bipartisan overwhelming vote in the Senate last night for the "GI bill." And I look forward to prompt House action and to signing the bill into law soon. Congress must continue this path to progress without partisanship. They should abandon plans to make drastic cuts in our Nation's education budget. An investment in education is clearly the most important long-term economic investment we can make in our future.

The third thing we have to do is to lead the world in this age of economic interdependence, and we have to do more there. More than a quarter of our economic growth during the past 5 years has come from exports. One of the reasons that growth moderated in the second quarter is because we are feeling the direct, discernible effects of the Asian economic downturn. Simply put, the health of the Asian economy affects the health of our own.

Just with our grain crops, about half of that crop is exported, and about 40 percent of the exports go to Asia. We have seen, therefore, this impact already in our rural communities. And I've talked about that quite a bit in the last couple of weeks. The Asian financial crisis has literally led to a 30 percent decline in farm exports to Asia.

The International Monetary Fund is designed to support necessary reforms in those economies, to help them help themselves, and to restore growth and confidence in their economies.

Now, I also want to say something that you all know. It is especially important for Asia and for our economy that the new Japanese Government move forward quickly and effectively to strengthen its financial system and stimulate and open its economy. It is going to be very, very difficult for Asia to recover unless its leading economy, Japan, leads the way. I welcome the election of the new Prime Minister, as well as a former Prime Minister with whom I have worked, Mr. Miyazawa, as the new Finance Minister. I am looking forward to talking with the new Prime Minister tomorrow.

And again, I remind the American people of our long friendship and partnership in so many ways—political, security, and economics—with Japan. We want to work with them, and we hope that this new government can find the keys to restore to the Japanese people, who have a great economy and a great society, the growth that they deserve.

Finally, let me say, we must do our part. That is why a commitment to the International Monetary Fund is an investment not simply in other countries, in their reform but in our own economy. We have to grow this economy by selling things to other people. They need the money to buy our products. That is why Congress should step up to its responsibility, put, again, progress ahead of partisanship, and renew our commitment and pay our fair share to the IMF. I urge Congress to do this quickly and not to put at risk our prosperity.

Open and fair trade, a balanced budget, saving Social Security, better education, and higher skills—the strategy that has boosted our economy for 5½ years will boost it further as we boldly move into a new century. I will continue to do everything in my power and to work as hard as I can with Congress to strengthen an economy that offers opportunity to all, a society rooted in responsibility, and a nation that lives as a community with each other and with the rest of the world.

Again, I want to say to all the economic team how much I appreciate the special and the difficult work we have done these last 3 months as our country has coped with the General Motors strike, which, thank goodness, has now concluded on successful terms, and with the problems in Asia and elsewhere.

Thank you very much.

President's Testimony

Q. Mr. President——

Q. Mr. President——

The President. Wait, wait, wait. Everybody has got a question. Let me give you the answer to all of them.

Q. You didn't hear——

The President. I know—yes, I did. I heard all of you shouting about it.

No one wants to get this matter behind us more than I do—except maybe all the rest of the American people. I am looking forward to the opportunity in the next few days of testifying. I will do so completely and truthfully. I am anxious to do it. But I hope you can understand why, in the interim, I can and should have no further comment on these matters.

Thank you very much.

NOTE: The President spoke at 11:57 a.m. in the Rose Garden at the White House. In his remarks, he referred to Prime Minister Keizo Obuchi and Finance Minister Kiichi Miyazawa of Japan.

Statement on Senate Action on Job Training Reform Legislation
July 31, 1998

For years now, I have been fighting for a "GI bill" for America's workers to modernize job training for the economy of the next century. I appreciate the bipartisan effort in the Senate that led to passage of legislation to do just that last night. This bill will make sure that job training in America helps our people meet the demands of a rapidly changing economy. I hope the House will continue this bipartisan effort to give Americans new training opportunities designed for the cutting-edge jobs of the future.

This legislation will fundamentally reform job training by empowering individuals to learn new skills with a simple skill grant. It also consolidates the tangle of training programs; creates a network of One-Stop Career Centers; increases accountability to ensure results; allows States and communities to tailor programs to locally determined needs; and ensures that business, labor, and community organizations are full partners in system design and quality assurance. It targets vocational and adult education funds to educational agencies and institutions with the greatest need, and to activities that promote program quality. It improves the vocational rehabilitation program by streamlining eligibility determination, improving State planning, and strengthening program accountability. And it includes the youth opportunity areas initiative—which was funded in last year's appropriations process—that will create jobs and opportunity for out-of-school youth in high-poverty areas.

Statement on Congressional Action on Job Training Reform Legislation
July 31, 1998

I am pleased that both Houses of Congress have now passed a comprehensive bill to give Americans new opportunities and choices to train for the jobs of the future. This bill will modernize job training to fit the needs of today's economy, and I appreciate the bipartisan spirit that prevailed in getting that done. Modeled on my "GI bill" for America's workers, this new training bill streamlines the vast array of existing job programs and empowers individuals to learn new skills with a simple grant. It makes sure that job training helps Americans meet the demand of a rapidly changing economy, and I look forward to signing it into law.

Statement on Senate Confirmation of Bill Richardson To Be Secretary of Energy
July 31, 1998

I am very pleased that the Senate today voted unanimously to confirm Ambassador Bill Richardson as Secretary of Energy.

Ambassador Richardson brings extraordinary experience and expertise to this vital post. As a Member of the U.S. Congress representing New Mexico, an energy-rich State that is home to two Department of Energy national laboratories, he has extensive firsthand experience on issues ranging from oil and gas deregulation to alternative energy to ensuring strong environmental standards in energy development. As U.S. Ambassador to the United Nations, he has been a vigorous and articulate proponent of U.S. engagement and has successfully tackled tough negotiating challenges around the world.

I am confident that Ambassador Richardson's tremendous energy, creativity, and leadership will help secure our Nation's energy future so that America continues to prosper.

Remarks at a Democratic National Committee Dinner in East Hampton, New York
July 31, 1998

First of all, I thank Bruce and Claude for their wonderful hospitality in this magnificent home and the terrific dinner. Our compliments to all the—the chef and the people in the kitchen. I thank Alan and Susan for dreaming up this weekend and all of you who have come to be a part of it.

We've had a great time tonight. Since Bruce asked me if I would go in there, when we're having coffee in the other room, and answer questions, I will spare you any extended remarks. I want to ask you to think about something. I am—we're here for the Democratic Committee, and I'm very grateful to Steve Grossman and to Len Barrack and to Fran Katz and all the other people. But I was born a Democrat because I was a Depression era— my parents were and my grandparents. My grandfather, who raised me until I was 4, thought he was going to Franklin Roosevelt when he died.

But I was determined in 1991 and 1992 to be faithful to the traditional values of our country and our party, but to modernize our party and to bring a new set of ideas to the debate in Washington, which I thought, frankly, was stale and divisive and dominated by the people in the other party who thought they had an entitlement to the White House. Some days, I think they still do. [*Laughter*] And I thought the White House belonged to all the rest of you and everybody else in the country and was the instrument of ideas consistent with our democracy to keep our country moving forward.

Now, Hillary is leading this Millennium Project, which was referred to earlier. And you probably saw that they started—Hillary and Ralph Lauren started by saving the Star-Spangled Banner the other day. And then she went to Fort McHenry, and then to Thomas Edison's home, and then to Harriet Tubman's home, and then to George Washington's Revolutionary War headquarters in New York.

But the theme of the Millennium Project is honoring the past and imagining the future. So I think about that all the time. Tom said that McKinley was the last President to come here, for example; it must be true. [*Laughter*] Now,

McKinley was an interesting fellow, but I'll tell you the interesting—McKinley was elected President in 1896 and reelected in 1900. Now, between 1868, Ulysses Grant, Rutherford Hayes, Benjamin Harrison, and William McKinley were elected President. You know what they had in common? They were all generals in the Union Army from Ohio.

If you got to be a general in the Union Army, and you were from Ohio, you had about a 50 percent chance of being President in that period of time. [*Laughter*] That's a rather interesting bit of our history. [*Laughter*] So tell that tomorrow when they tell you McKinley was the last President. I care a lot about this country's history. I've spent a lot of time reading it, studying it, trying to feel it in the White House, in every room, in the life of every predecessor I have had and their families. And I think it's very important when you imagine the future that we do it in a way that is consistent with the history of this country.

So I will say that I think the most important things about American history can be found in the ideas of the Declaration of Independence and the Constitution, which—and manifest in every changing time, this country has always been about at least three things: widening the circle of opportunity for responsible citizens, deepening the meaning of freedom in each succeeding generation, and strengthening the bonds of our Union.

The reason I'm a Democrat in 1998, apart from the fact that I was born and raised one and believed in the civil rights movement and the things that were dominant in my childhood, is that I think we more clearly represent the last of those ideas. I think we believe that Union is very important. I think we believe that part of the Declaration of Independence, that we are dedicated to the permanent mission of forming a more perfect Union, because there are some things that we want to achieve for ourselves, our families, and our future that we cannot achieve alone or in isolated groups.

And I say that because I think that we've, for the last couple of decades, seen a real assault on government and on the idea that we do have sort of mutual ties and bonds and responsibilities to one another that enhance our own lives. And I believe that very strongly.

So as we look ahead, I think—I will just tell you what I think some of the great challenges of tomorrow are. I think, first of all, it will

be the period of greatest possibility in all human history, and we ought to be ashamed of ourselves if we mess it up. It will be an age of breathtaking biological advances. It will be an age of breathtaking technological advances. It will be an age where we will be able to relate to people around the world through the device of the Internet—the fastest growing social organism in history, I might add—in ways that our parents could never imagine, probably in ways that most of us could never imagine.

But we have some big challenges at home and abroad. And I will just mention them and stop, and you ask yourself: If you're trying to imagine the future, what do you think the big challenges are? Now, let me just mention what I think they are.

At home, I think, first of all, the baby boomers have got to retire in a way that preserves the dignity of American society for the elderly without bankrupting our kids and undermining their ability to raise our grandchildren, which means we have to reform Social Security and Medicare in a way that keeps them there functioning for people who need them to the extent that they're needed and brings our country together, but does it in a way that does not dramatically undermine the standard of living of our children and their ability to raise our grandchildren.

Secondly, we have to recognize that in an information society we have to do a much better job of elementary and secondary education and preschool education, and not just for some or most but for all of our children. And we have to maximize everything we know about child psychology, about support for kids who come from troubled families and live in troubled neighborhoods, about the access to technology. But no one in the world who really knows anything about it would seriously question the proposition that American has the finest system of higher education in the world. No one believes that America has the finest system of elementary and secondary education in the world for all its children. And I think that's a big challenge.

Number three, I think we have a whole new attitude about the environment. We have basically, for 30 years, done great things as a country on the environment since the passage of the Clean Air Act and setting up the EPA, and we concluded that, if we take these things one at a time, we can afford to clean up the environment and keep our economy still growing. I think now we have to understand that we cannot maintain or sustain our economy unless we make the preservation and even the improvement of the environment an integral part of our economic policy.

In other words, I believe global warming is real. I do not think it is an accident that 9 hottest years on record have all occurred in the last 11 years. I don't think that's an accident. I don't think it's an accident that '97 was the hottest year on record, and every month in '98 has been hotter than every month in '97. And I think there are at hand the means to continue to grow the economy and improve the environment in ways that will make sure it's all here a hundred years from now for our great-great-grandchildren.

Let me just mention a couple of other things. I believe that, with regard to the economy—I think it's obvious—and around our table I had a fascinating conversation talking about the global economy, in particular, as you might imagine, Japan and Asia, China, and we talked about Russia. We have a lot of challenges in the global economy; we have a lot of challenges in the area of world peace, the proliferation of weapons of mass destruction, dealing with terrorism, and trying to stop people from killing each other because of their ethnic, racial, and religious differences.

There will be plenty to do in the post-cold-war world to create a trade-centered, people-centered, peaceful network of national cooperation and institutions to help deal with those who won't be part of that framework.

We also have to recognize, I think, that we have an incredible opportunity and an obligation here—and those of you from New York, I'd say, should feel it especially—to prove that we can bring free enterprise to the areas of America which haven't received it yet. There are still neighborhoods in New York City that have double-digit unemployment rates, largely because of underinvestment and low skill levels, not because most people aren't responsible; most people in most neighborhoods get up and go to work every day, pay taxes, and try to be good citizens. So we're never going to have a better time than the next couple of years to try to help.

And the last thing I'd like to say is I think that this theme, that Hillary and I have worked on, of one America means something to me. It means one America across all the lines that divide us. It means an America in which citizens commit themselves to serve their fellow human beings, which is why I'm so proud of our AmeriCorps program, our national service program. It also means that we understand that the unity we have is a precious gift, and we should manage our differences with dignity and decency and always strive for unity over division; always put people over politics; always put progress over partisanship. That's what I believe.

And if we do those things, I think we're going to do just great in the 21st century. And I'm going to do everything I can for the next 2½ years to make sure that that is exactly what we do.

Thank you very much.

NOTE: The President spoke at 9:40 p.m. at a private residence. In his remarks, he referred to dinner hosts Bruce and Claude Wasserstein; event cochairs Alan and Susan Patricof; Steve Grossman, national chair, Leonard Barrack, national finance chair, and Fran Katz, national finance director, Democratic National Committee; and fashion designer Ralph Lauren.

The President's Radio Address
August 1, 1998

Good morning. Today Hillary and I are at the fire station in Amagansett, Long Island, New York, one of many beautiful communities on Long Island, where we're joined today by doctors, nurses, breast cancer patients, and public health advocates to talk about something that concerns all Americans, making a Patients' Bill of Rights the law of the land.

I'm also very proud to be joined by Congressman Michael Forbes and his family. Congressman Forbes is a Republican who is cosponsoring bipartisan legislation to achieve a genuine Patients' Bill of Rights.

We all know that our health care system is rapidly changing. Since 1990 the number of Americans in managed care has nearly doubled. Today, most Americans, 160 million of us, are in managed care plans. I think that, on balance, managed care has been good for America because it's made health care more affordable and more accessible for more Americans. But sometimes cost cutting can lead to lower standards. That's when the bottomline becomes more important than patients' lives. And when families have nowhere to turn when their loved ones are harmed by health care plans' bad decisions, when there's a denial of specialist care or emergency care when they're plainly needed and recommended by physicians, when those kinds of things happen, we know we have to take action.

Whether in managed care or traditional care, every single American deserves quality care. I'm doing everything I can as President to help to meet that challenge. For 9 months I have worked in good faith with lawmakers of both parties to pass a strong, enforceable, bipartisan Patients' Bill of Rights, a bill that covers individual and group plans, a bill that guarantees access to specialists and emergency room care, a bill that guarantees doctors are not receiving secret financial incentives to limit care, a bill that guarantees a remedy to families who have suffered harm because of bad decisions by their health plans. And for 9 months the American people have waited.

Finally, the Republican leadership has proposed a partisan bill that does not provide these guarantees. Now they've left town without taking action, leaving millions of Americans without the health care protections they need. Any bill that doesn't guarantee these protections is a Patients' Bill of Rights in name only.

Today the American Medical Association, the American Nurses Association, the National Breast Cancer Coalition, the American College of Emergency Room Physicians, the American Small Business Alliance, and the National Partnership for Women and Families have all come

forward to say the plan of the Republican leadership is an empty promise; it simply will not protect the American public or ensure the quality health care they deserve. Now Congress should rise to its responsibilities and guarantee a Patients' Bill of Rights, and they should reject proposals that are more loopholes than law.

Until Congress acts, I will continue to do everything I can to ensure that more Americans are protected by a Patients' Bill of Rights. In February I signed an executive memorandum that extends those protections to 85 million Americans in Federal health plans. Last month the Department of Veterans Affairs put in place a new health care appeals procedure for 3 million veterans.

Today we're building on our efforts. I'm pleased to announce that the Defense Department is issuing a directive to make the protections of the Patients' Bill of Rights real for more than 8 million servicemen and women, their families, and Defense Department employees. These men and women stand ready every day to keep our Nation safe. They should not have to worry about the heath care they or their families receive.

This action brings us one step closer to a Patients' Bill of Rights for all Americans, but Congress must act. And so once again, I ask Congress to do its part. There are just a few weeks left in this legislative session, only a few weeks left to improve health care and strengthen our families. Let's put progress ahead of partnership. I ask all Members of Congress to join Congressman Forbes, me, and the other Democrats and Republicans who want a real Patients' Bill of Rights.

Thanks for listening.

NOTE: The President spoke at 10:06 a.m. from the Amagansett Fire Station in Long Island, NY. In his address, he referred to his memorandum of February 20 on Federal agency compliance with the Patient Bill of Rights (*Public Papers of the Presidents: William J. Clinton, 1998 Book I* (Washington: U.S. Government Printing Office, 1999), p. 260).

Remarks at a Democratic National Committee Reception in East Hampton
August 1, 1998

Thank you. This is one clever man. I want you to watch this. You see this? He took the watch again. [*Laughter*] Thank you, Jonathan. Thank you, Christopher. I want to thank Andy and Jeff and Elizabeth and all the others who were cochairs tonight. I want to thank Sandy Thurman and Richard Socarides and Marsha Scott, who've done a lot of great work for me and on my behalf with so many of you.

And I want to thank Brian Rich for serving as a White House volunteer. The whole place runs on volunteers, believe it or not, to an astonishing extent. I want to thank Steve and Len and all fine people here from the DNC, and all of you for being here.

Last night we were with some people, and a person who's lived here for many years said, "You know, the last sitting President to visit Long Island was William McKinley—the eastern end of Long Island—William McKinley." And everybody laughed. They didn't exactly see me as a natural successor to William McKinley. We don't think of him in the same terms that I'm frequently painted these days.

But I'll tell you an interesting thing about William McKinley. He was the last of a line of either four or five generals, Union generals from Ohio, to be elected President between 1868 and 1896, that included Ulysses Grant; his successor, Rutherford Hayes; James Garfield, who, unfortunately, was assassinated and lived only a few months; Mr. McKinley—Mr. Harrison might have been from Ohio; I'm not sure. But the point is, if you were a Union general from Ohio, you had about a 50 percent chance of being elected President between the end of the Civil War and 1900.

Now, what has that got to do with all this today? There's a reason they won. They won because Ohio was the heartland of America at the time and because they embodied the idea of the Nation for which Abraham Lincoln gave his life, that slavery was wrong, that discrimination based on race was wrong, and that we needed a strong, united country for America and for all Americans to fulfill their God-given capacity.

Throughout American history, one of our two parties has always been essentially the party of the Nation. And even though the Democrats, I regret to say, after the Civil War, were just kind of coming to that—they were the party of immigrants, and that was good, and they stood against discrimination against immigrants—but for all kinds of reasons, we didn't become the party of the Nation until the election of Woodrow Wilson. And then, our fate was sealed when Franklin Roosevelt was elected and Harry Truman succeeded him.

We haven't always been right on every issue in the 20th century, but I think it's clear that we have been on the right side of history. And I think that's why you're here today. And a lot of you said a lot of very kind things to me as I worked my way through the crowd, and I appreciate them more than you know. When I ran for President in 1992, I did it because I thought our country was divided, that we hadn't taken care of the business before us, and we certainly weren't planning for the future very well. It seemed to me that we needed to be trying to create an America in which there was genuine opportunity for every responsible citizen, in which we were continuing to lead the world toward peace and freedom and prosperity, and in which we were coming closer together as one community.

Or, if you put it in another way—if you go back and read the Declaration of Independence, it basically lays out the things that our country has been for all along. We just never perfectly lived up to them. We've always been for deepening the meaning of freedom. Keep in mind, when all those people said all people are created equal, if you weren't a white male property owner, you couldn't even vote. But Jefferson said, "When I think of slavery, I tremble to think that God is just."

So we set out an ideal, and then we knew we'd have to be working toward it for a long time, constantly redefining it, deepening the meaning of freedom. We've always tried to widen the circle of opportunity, and we have been on a permanent mission, in the Founders' words, to "form a more perfect Union."

Now, on all fronts, I believe our party is on the right side of history on the edge of this new millennium. Hillary is running this great

Millennial Project called imagining the past and envisioning the future—imagine the future—excuse me, "Honor the past; imagine the future." It's been a long day. [*Laughter*] Anyway, the thing I like about it is, I don't think you can imagine the future unless you do it in terms of the values and the history of the past, and I don't think you can just live in the past. So everything I've done the last 6 years, I've tried to make America, first of all, work again. I've tried to develop a working definition of what the role of the Federal Government in our national life should be. And I've tried to get out of the old debate about Government is the problem, Government is the solution, toward seeing Government as an empowering agent to enable the rest of us to live our lives and to create the conditions and give people the tools to do what needs to be done.

And I think that the ideas we brought to the economic and social debate, to the foreign policy debate have contributed measurably to the remarkable conditions in our country today. Most of you know that we have the lowest unemployment rate in 28 years and the lowest crime rate in 25 years and the lowest percentage of people on welfare in 29 years. We're about to have the first balanced budget and surplus in 29 years, the highest homeownership in history, with the smallest Government in 35 years.

But we also have advanced the cause of peace and freedom around the world, advanced the cause of interdependence around the world through economic cooperation, and advanced the cause of unity at home with things like citizen service and the opportunities I've had to work with many of you to remind the American people that we're all one country and that everybody is entitled to be treated with dignity and respect and equality.

And I would just like to say, if you look ahead at the big challenges facing the country—how are we are going to prepare for the retirement of the baby boom generation? We have to reform Social Security and Medicare so that it will do what it needs to do to hold our society together and provide for dignity in old age, without bankrupting our children and grandchildren, those of us who are baby boomers.

We have to provide, for the first time in history, a genuine world-class elementary and secondary education for all of our kids, not just those who are middle class or better. We have to prove that we can grow the economy and improve the environment—not just preserve it, but improve it—because I believe that the global warming phenomenon is real. I know the oceans are being slowly undermined. And we had a fabulous conference on that recently in California.

We have to prove that America can still be a force for peace and freedom and security around the world, standing up against all this racial and ethnic and religious hatred around the world and the spread of dangerous weapons and taking advantage of the opportunities that are there.

And finally, I don't think we can do good around the world unless we are good at home. And that's why I have always said I belong to a party that puts progress over partisanship, that puts people over politics, that puts unity over division.

And you know, sometimes when you try to affect that kind of transformation, you know you're going to provoke a reaction. I didn't dream it would be quite as profound as it has been, this reaction. But I must say, if I had it to do over again, I would gladly assume the challenge because it's been a wonderful thing. And if it weren't for the 22d amendment, I'd give the people one more chance to elect or defeat me—[*laughter*]—because I believe in what we're doing. And I've been blessed to have not only a wife but also a wonderful Vice President who believes in what we're doing.

And I just want to say to all of you, what Hillary said is right. We can do very well in this election. If you go all the way back to the Civil War, the party of the President, when the President's in his second term, always has lost seats at midterm. It may not happen this time, which is one reason the heat, the incoming fire is so intense now, because they know it may not happen this time. Why? Because we have an agenda out there: We have a Patients' Bill of Rights. We've got an education agenda. We've got an environmental agenda. We've got a foreign policy agenda. We've got an economic agenda for the inner cities. The debate, the substantive debate is out there.

And I still believe that the biggest problem with the American people not feeling the sense of unity and mutual harmony and respect that affects among other things—among others, people in the gay community all the time, is a lack of genuine, open, unthreatening contact, debate, discussion.

And so, I just want to say to you, I thank you for your contributions; I thank you for being here. We'll try to make good use of the investments you've given us. But I hope between now and November, you will go out and tell people that it's not an accident that America is better off today than it was 6 years ago, that there are ideas behind the changes that took place in this country, and they're good ideas. And the ideas we have for the future are good ideas. And the American people ought to go out there in this election and be heard on those ideas. And if they are, I think that our Democrats will do very well indeed, because we know that given a reasoned chance to make a judgment, we win two-to-one on almost every critical issue facing the country.

But given organized and well-financed disinformation campaigns, we sometimes have trouble, as we did recently when, much to Andy's grief, we lost the fight with the big tobacco interests in Congress. I'm not done with that, and we're going to come back to it.

But you can help us prevail. And the last thing I'd like to say is—the other thing Hillary said is right—a part of this strategy that we're up against is designed to depress the vote. In 1994 we had a very depressed vote. Now, I personally don't think it's going to work this time, because the country is in better shape and the consequences of the policies of the administration are more evident, and the strategy against us is a little more bald, I'd say. I think that's a delicate way of saying it. And so I don't think it will work.

But you've got to think about that. Go out there and tell people that you're doing this because, throughout history, America was always at its best by trying to perfect what we started with in the Declaration of Independence, to widen the circle of opportunity, deepen the meaning of freedom, strengthen the bonds of our Union, and because we're on the edge of a whole new millennium, a whole new way of thinking and living and working and relating to each other and the rest of the world; and the party of the future is the party that's on the right side of history and that you're proud to be a part of it.

Thank you, and God bless you.

NOTE: The President spoke at 6:30 p.m. at a private residence. In his remarks, he referred to reception hosts Jonathan Sheffer and Christopher Barley; event cochairs Andy Tobias and Jeff Soref; Elizabeth Birch, executive director, Human Rights Campaign; and Steve Grossman, national chair, and Leonard Barrack, national finance chair, Democratic National Committee.

Remarks at a Saxophone Club Reception in East Hampton
August 1, 1998

Thank you very much. Wow! [*Laughter*] First, I want to thank you for being so laid back and quiet and restrained. Aren't you proud you're here and proud of what we're trying to do for our country? [*Applause*]

Let me begin by thanking Alec and Kim for opening their home tonight to this intimate little gathering, giving up their privacy for this high public purpose, and making us all feel like we're very welcome at their beautiful home. Thank you very much.

I want to thank Judith Hope and Tom Twomey, Alan and Susan Patricof, Liz Robbins, all the cochairs of the event tonight. Thank you, Chairman Grossman, and all the people from the DNC. And thank you, Hootie and the Blowfish. Thank you. I told some people coming in even an old guy like me likes them. I love them. I thank Congressman Meeks, Congresswoman McCarthy, Lieutenant Governor Ross, Mark Green, all the other office holders who are here.

Ladies and gentlemen, I am so thrilled to see you. I'm thrilled that you're here for this purpose, and I want you to take this enthusiasm out from under this tent back to your daily lives. And I want you to infect every person you meet with it between now and November.

You know, in—a young girl came through the line earlier tonight, shook my hand, and had her picture taken with me, a little girl. And she said, "Why did you want to be President?"

She must have been about 8 years old, maybe 7. I said, "Well, I wanted you to have a better future; I wanted your country to do better; and I wanted you to live in a safe world." And she said, "That sounds pretty good to me." [*Laughter*]

When I ran for President in 1992, I wanted this country to move in a different direction. And here we are, on the edge of a new millennium, just 2 years away from a new century, a new 1,000 years, an amazing time. Hillary was in Seneca Falls and at George Washington's Revolutionary War headquarters and other places in New York, sort of promoting our idea of how we should mark this sea change in history by honoring our past and imaging our future, a future where things are changing faster and more profoundly in the way we live, the way we work, the way we related to each other and the rest of the world.

We've been working on this for 6 years, thanks to New York in 1992 and the magnificent victory the people here gave us in 1996. And I thank you. And you ought to tell the doubters that there is a connection between the economic and social policies and foreign policies this country has pursued for the last 6 years and the fact that we have the lowest unemployment rate in 28 years, the lowest crime rate in 25 years, the smallest percentage of people on welfare in 29 years, the first balanced budget and surplus in 29 years, the highest homeownership in history, with the lowest, smallest Federal Government in 35 years. And I am proud of that.

We also made the first 2 years of college virtually free to most Americans; opened the doors of college to everyone; immunized over 90 percent of our children; kept 250,000 people with a bad criminal or mental health history

from buying handguns, with the Brady bill; banned the assault weapons over the opposition of the other party. The water is cleaner; the air is cleaner; the food is safer; there are fewer toxic waste dumps. We are moving in the right direction, my fellow Americans.

And our party right now is working in Congress, not just to pass a Patients' Bill of Rights, but also to put 100,000 more teachers in the early grades, to build new schools and repair old ones, to bring economic opportunity to urban neighborhoods and rural areas that haven't gotten it yet, to have a genuine environmental policy that will deal with the problem of climate change and continue to grow the economy, that will have record amounts of money going into medical research and other scientific research, in short, that will prepare our path for the 21st century.

And in almost every area, we are being opposed by the leadership of the other party. The choice is clear. The record is clear. The results are in. You're here—go out of here and tell the American people you're proud to be part of the direction we're taking to tomorrow.

Thank you, and God bless you all.

NOTE: The President spoke at 8:24 p.m. at a private residence. In his remarks, he referred to actors Alec Baldwin and Kim Basinger, reception hosts; New York State Democratic Chair Judith Hope; Tom Twomey, Alan and Susan Patricof, and Liz Robbins, event cochairs; Steve Grossman, national chair, Democratic National Committee; the music group Hootie and the Blowfish; Assemblyman Gregory W. Meeks, 31st New York District; Lt. Gov. Betsy McCaughey Ross of New York; and Mark Green, New York City public advocate.

Remarks on Summer Jobs Program Funding in Cheverly, Maryland
August 3, 1998

Thank you very much. Let's give Terence another hand. Wasn't he good? [*Applause*] Well, I would say Terence has gotten quite a lot out of his job opportunity here. And he made quite a good speech. Maybe he needs a summer job with Wayne Curry or Congressman Wynn or

Lieutenant Governor Kathleen Kennedy Townsend or the President or something. He's very good, I think.

I'd like to thank my friend, Wayne Curry, for that wonderful welcome. I thank Lieutenant Governor Kathleen Kennedy Townsend for her sentiments and her passionate work for our children. And I thank, in his absence, Governor Glendening for his support for so many good causes, but especially the one we have come here to advance today.

I thank Al Wynn. He didn't even come close to breaking the Barbara Mikulski step up here. [*Laughter*] But every day he comes close to the ideal of what I think a Congressman should be.

I thank the State and the local officials who are here, and I thank this hospital. As Wayne said, it's quite an accommodation to take in a Presidential visit, and I thank them for making me and Secretary Herman and our party feel so welcome.

I, too, want to say my personal thanks to Secretary Herman for her role in settling the General Motors strike. We want to keep the economy going, and we don't do very well in America unless all of our autoworkers are out there working hard and making cars. And I know we're all grateful for that.

Let me say to all the young people here in this audience on the summer job program, both those behind me and on the stage and those out here in the audience, I am very proud of what you're doing here, and I hope you are as well, because whether you're serving lunch in a cafeteria or escorting patients in the hallways, you're not only helping this hospital to help others, you're helping to build a better future for yourselves, proving that, given the opportunity to work and to learn, there is no limit to what our young people can do.

I want to talk to you today about what we are doing to make sure more young people have the chance to continue to participate in summer jobs and to continue to improve their education. One of the principal reasons I ran for President in 1992 was to make sure that, as we move into the 21st century, every young person in this country, without regard to their income, their race, their background, or where they live, would have the opportunity to make the most of his or her life.

I wanted to create a 21st century America where the American dream is alive for all our people and where our people are coming together, across all lines that divide us, into one American community and where that gives us the strength to continue to lead the world to greater peace and freedom and prosperity. None of that can occur unless we make sure that every American has a first-class education, and then, that we have an economy that functions so every American can make the most of that education.

Right now in Washington we are preparing the budget that will determine how we continue to reform, renew, and advance education next year. This isn't just a normal budget. Because of 5 years of strict budget discipline in our Nation, this will be the first balanced budget in most of your lifetimes, the first one in 29 years. It is also a validation of our economic strategy that you can cut the deficit and continue to invest money in people, in science and technology, in education, in the environment, in building the right kind of future. We have to do both.

To do our part, I have proposed in this balanced budget a comprehensive education agenda with high national standards; more accountability; more school choice in charter schools; more well-qualified teachers; smaller classrooms; modernized schools equipped with computers and hooked up to the Internet; reading tutors for children who are falling behind; before- and after-school programs and summer school programs to keep young people learning in the classroom, not lost on the streets; and summer jobs programs, like this one, to give young people the skills they need to succeed when they leave school and to give them something to do and a way to earn money during the summer.

I believe all these things are necessary to help all of you and people like you all across this country live up to their God-given potential. I believe they're necessary to make the America we all want in the 21st century.

I am very proud of the fact that today we are enjoying the lowest unemployment in 28 years, the lowest crime rate in 25 years; we have the smallest percentage of people on welfare in 29 years; and as I've said, we're about to have the first balanced budget and surplus in 29 years, the highest homeownership in history. I'm proud of that.

But this a rare moment in American history when we have a lot of confidence about our ability to make things work in this country. And we have to use it as an opportunity to act, to give everyone—everyone—a chance. We can't let this moment pass us by. And we have to make progress, both parties together, especially when it comes to the interest of children, education, employment, and the future.

There are, as you have already heard from previous speakers, those in Congress who disagree with this agenda. They have proposed a narrow and much more partisan plan that, in my view, is not a step into the future but a step backward. At a time when we should be increasing our investments in education and training, their plan actually cuts more than $3 billion from the plan I proposed. At a time when we should be raising standards and challenging our students to meet them and helping school districts with a lot of poor children to do just that, their plan would prohibit the development of national tests for our schools. At at time when more children enter school now than anytime since my generation, the baby boomers, were in school, I have proposed to expand Head Start. Their plan would deny 25,000 children the opportunity to participate in that important early learning program when compared with my budget.

My America Reads initiative, which already involves volunteer students from 1,000 colleges and universities around America and many churches and other organizations going into the schools, working with children one-on-one to make sure they can read independently by the time they finish the third grade, it would give thousands more students a chance to have a tutor and to help them learn. Their plan would cut that program off without a penny.

At a time when we should be helping young people learn the skills they need to succeed in the jobs of tomorrow, their plan would make it harder for 400 of our school districts across America to buy computers. It would cut $140 million from my proposal to expand after-school programs that keep young people learning in the classroom, not lost on the streets, in the hours of prime activity for juvenile crime. And believe it or not, the House Republican budget plan would even kill summer jobs programs like this one next year.

I'm sure when you started this program some of you didn't know how rewarding it would be. I was quite amused to hear what Terence said about his experience and the dress code. [*Laughter*] But now that you know how rewarding these programs can be, now that you know that there is no limit to what you can achieve if you continue to work hard and be responsible citizens, you must surely know that other young people like you deserve the same chance next

year and that you may need this chance next year.

Today, because of the budget we passed last year, there are half a million young people just like you in summer jobs programs. And if my budget passes this year, there will be half a million next year. But if the House Republican budget passes, most of those children would not have a job next year.

And that's not all the Republicans plan to do away with. At a time when more families have both parents working, their plan would cut nearly $180 million from my proposal to make child care centers better, safer places for our children. At a time when we are struggling so hard around the world to protect children from being abused in other countries to send cheap products here, it undercuts our ability to fight the exploitative practice of child labor. At a time when our Nation is experiencing extremely severe weather, from crippling cold in the winter to record heat waves that have killed more than 100 people already this summer, the House Republicans want to eliminate the program called LIHEAP that today helps millions and millions of families, millions of families with low incomes, a lot of them very vulnerable older people, pay for home heating and, this summer, for cooling cost. If this budget were to pass, those folks would be on their own.

This is a time when we ought to be putting progress ahead of partisanship. We've got all the evidence in the world that when we do that, it works. Look at how America is doing. The House Republican plan puts politics ahead of people and puts your future in the backseat. That is wrong. And if a bill like the one that is proposed by the House Republicans passes, I will veto it.

I have sent Congress a balanced budget that proves we can maintain our budget responsibility and still invest in our people. So far, Congress hasn't passed that budget or one of its own. Within less than 2 months, they'll have to act because our new budget year will start. Because of the delay, they may decide to send me a barebones budget that fails to expand the critical investments we need to make, from education to summer jobs to school modernization to child care. But the last budget of the 20th century should be preparing our Nation for the challenges of the next. I will not accept a budget that fails to do this.

There are those in both parties who understand this. It was mentioned earlier that the Congress, just last Friday night, passed the Senate bid, the "GI bill" for America's workers, that consolidates scores and scores of disparate training programs into one program that will give skills grants to people in their working years, to adults who have to go back to school and learn new skills. It was one of the major commitments I made when I ran for President in '92. I have worked for 4 years on this. So there is the capacity there to forge this kind of bipartisan relationship. We have to do it for summer jobs and for education.

Let me just close with this—it's not in my notes, but I was looking at Terence up there talking, and I thought you might like to know that, over 30 years ago, I was involved in two federally funded summer jobs programs. I didn't get to wear a shirt and tie to work; I was working at our National Park in my hometown doing basic maintenance and clearing work. And then I worked in a summer camp for disadvantaged young people where I was a counselor, after

my first year in college. I loved that work, and I loved those kids. And I was very grateful that my country gave me an opportunity to do something productive, to learn something, and to make a little money.

I hope when the history books are written, it will look like a pretty good investment that was made in a young man from a modest family in a small town a long time ago.

You, too, will do great things. And, in part, it will be because your country has believed in you and invested in you. And I don't want us to stop. I want us to do more.

Thank you, and God bless you.

NOTE: The President spoke at 11:36 a.m. in the Deitz Memorial Auditorium at Prince Georges Hospital Center. In his remarks, he referred to Terence Newton, who introduced the President; Prince Georges County Executive Wayne K. Curry; and Gov. Parris N. Glendening of Maryland. The President also referred to the Low Income Home Energy Assistance Program (LIHEAP).

Statement on Congressional Action on Campaign Finance Reform Legislation
August 3, 1998

Tonight's vote for the Shays-Meehan bill is a breakthrough in the fight for bipartisan campaign finance reform. The breadth of its support, from Members of both parties, showed that reform is an idea whose time has come, even in the face of persistent obstruction by the Republican leaders of Congress. It is time to ban soft money, improve disclosure, and curb backdoor campaign spending. Now, a majority of both the House and the Senate have gone

on record for this legislation. I urge the House to move this legislation to final passage before they adjourn for the August recess. And I urge the Republican leaders of the Senate, who are using procedural tactics to block this measure, to listen to the will of the majority and the loud voice of the American people. I congratulate Representatives Chris Shays, Martin Meehan, and their colleagues for their courage and their persistence.

Remarks on the Anniversary of the Personal Responsibility and Work Opportunity Reconciliation Act of 1996
August 4, 1998

Thank you. Thank you very much, Vesta Kimble, for that fine statement and for the good

work you do. And I welcome your colleagues and co-workers from Maryland here. I thank

Congressman Levin and Congressman Roemer for coming. There was a vote in the House of Representatives which was concluded literally 2 minutes before we started this ceremony, and they got here as quick as they could. We welcome you and thank you for your role in welfare reform.

I'd like to thank Secretary Herman and Secretary Shalala for the terrific job they have done and welcome all of you in the audience, including my good friend, Eli Segal, who founded our partnership with the business community, about which I'll say more later. The First Lady was recently—just a few moments ago meeting with members and, I think, maybe some former members of the DC control board. I know that some of them are here, and I welcome them as well.

Two years ago, I stood with many of you in the Rose Garden and made the following statement: "From now on, our Nation's answer to the problems of poverty will no longer be a never-ending cycle of welfare; it will be the dignity, the power, and the ethic of work. . . . We are taking an historic chance to make welfare what it was meant to be: a second chance, not a way of life."

As those of us who have been working for years and years to change the system know all too well, welfare had, in too many ways, failed our society and, more important, failed the millions of families it was designed to help. So in the Rose Garden, we came together 2 years ago to restore our basic bargain of providing opportunity to all those willing to exercise responsibility in turn. We ended welfare as we knew it and made way for a system based on the dignity of independence and the value of work.

But I would also like to reiterate something Secretary Shalala said. We did not want to put poor people moving from welfare to work in the exact same position too many people who've always been in the work force find themselves, of having to choose between being a good worker and a good parent. So we said, "Okay, we will require people who have to move from welfare to work, if they're able-bodied, to go to work. But we will leave their children with food assistance and guaranteed medical coverage, and we will invest more in child care and other family supports."

Today we come here not only to observe this anniversary but to lay to rest the last vestige of the old system, an antiwork, antifamily provision that has deprived some two-parent families of their Medicaid coverage when a parent secures a full-time job.

But first, on this important anniversary, I think it's important to recognize that this new strategy, this great new experiment that we launched 2 years ago, has already shown remarkable signs of success. Two years ago we said welfare reform would spark a race to independence, not a race to the bottom, and this prediction is coming true.

According to the National Governors' Association, State investments in helping former welfare parents succeed at work have gone up by one-third, and spending on child care has increased by one-half. And let me remind you, I believe this has happened partly because the Congress in the balanced budget amendment appropriated $3 billion for child care, but partly because there was a little-noticed provision in the welfare reform law which lets States keep the amount of money they were receiving for the welfare caseload in February of '94, when it had reached an all-time high. So as the caseloads go down, they can keep the money as long as they reinvest it in the potential of the families involved. And I think that was a very good thing to do.

We also said back then that work should pay more than welfare. Last week the Urban Institute reported that family income goes up more than 50 percent, on average, when parents move form welfare to part-time entry-level jobs and significantly more when they move up to full-time work. And I must say, I was especially pleased to note how helpful the earned-income tax credit is for families making this transition. In several States, it accounts for almost half the income gains.

For those of you who may not know it, the earned-income tax credit is a tax cut to lower income working people that is especially generous to working families with children. We doubled it in 1993. And because of that provision, today it's worth a tax cut of approximately $1,000 a year to a family of four with an income of under $30,000 a year. Obviously, for people working for more modest wages than that, it means a very great deal.

Today we have more good news. In a few moments, I will release our first annual report to Congress on welfare reform, precisely the kind of report we had hoped for 2 years ago. It shows that the number of welfare recipients entering the work force rose by nearly 30 percent in a single year. It reports that States are spending more per person on welfare-to-work efforts than they did 2 years ago, including health care, job training, job placement, child care, and job retention.

Come in, Congressman Shaw, you're welcome. [*Laughter*] Thank you for the role you've played in welfare reform legislation. We're glad to see you.

It shows that more single parents are moving into the work force, a very significant statistic. And it confirms that the percentage of Americans now on welfare is at its lowest level since 1969, 29 years. There are other, more powerful signs of success that, of course, a report can't show. Too often we take for granted what it really means for a family to reconnect to the world of work. Work is more than a punchcard, more than a paycheck. It provides structure to a day, link to a society, dignity for a family. It can build self-confidence and self-esteem. There is nothing like the pride in a child's eyes when he or she goes to school and can answer, often for the first time, what their parents do for a living.

One of the most important ways we can now build on these everyday triumphs is to make absolutely sure that parents who do enter the work force can go to bed at night without worrying that they will lose health coverage for their families. That is why I'm proud to announce that the Department of Health and Human Services will revise its regulations to allow all States to continue to provide Medicaid coverage to two-parent families after a parent takes a full-time job. Believe it or not, under the old rules, adults in two-parent families who worked more than 100 hours per month could actually be cut off Medicaid in many States.

Perhaps no aspect of the old welfare system did more to defy common sense and insult our common values than this so-called 100-hour rule. Just think of the message it sent. It took away health care from people who secured a full-time job just as we were imploring everybody to move from welfare to work. Instead of rewarding stable families, it actually punished couples that work and work hard to stay together. Instead of demanding responsibility, it basically said a father could do more for his children's health by sitting at home or walking away than earning a living.

The 100-hour rule was wrong. Now, it and every other strand of the old welfare system are history. The remaining challenges are ones we all have to accept. All of us, the public, private, religious, nonprofit sectors, have an obligation to continue helping all former welfare recipients not only find but stay in those jobs.

First, we must continue to offer States and communities the tools they need to promote work. Today we will release $60 million more in welfare-to-work grants to States to help mothers and fathers facing the most significant employment hurdles. And I also want to call on Congress to fully fund my plan to provide housing vouchers for welfare recipients who need to move closer to their place of work.

Some recent studies, including some coming out of New York, show that the effects of welfare reform in terms of people being able to move into the workplace have been quite uneven, depending upon the level of preparation of the people on welfare for the work force and their level of isolation from available jobs. So these are important next steps.

Second, the private sector, the true engine of job creation in our country, must continue to do its part. Listen to this: Last year our welfare-to-work partners, who were mobilized by Eli Segal, as I said earlier, hired more than 135,000 former welfare recipients. I have asked them to hire another 270,000 by the end of this year. Thank you, Eli, but you have to do more. [*Laughter*]

Third, we must continue to welcome former welfare recipients into the Federal family work force. Today we released new data showing that the Federal Government has hired more than 5,700 former welfare recipients in just the past year. That means we're well over half the way toward our goal of hiring 10,000 by the year 2000.

Fourth, let me say again, I think it's important that we do more to bring the benefits of this economic revival our country is enjoying into isolated urban and rural areas where free enterprise has not yet reached. A lot of the people who are still stuck on welfare are physically separate from the job availability. And I have asked the Congress to approve a second round of empowerment zones, to approve a whole range of initiatives, and Secretary Herman and Secretary Cuomo's budget designed to create jobs principally in the private sector in isolated inner-city and rural neighborhoods. So I hope that will be a part of the work we conclude in the days remaining in this congressional session.

Welfare reform itself was a bipartisan effort. It became an American issue. Now, providing jobs and opportunity and new businesses and new free enterprise in these neighborhoods that still have not felt the economy should also be an American issue.

We have now the lowest unemployment in 28 years, the lowest inflation in 32 years, the highest homeownership in history. Wages are on the rise for our families after 20 years of stagnation. This is our window of maximum opportunity to make sure every poor person in America stuck on welfare has a chance to be a part of America's future and to share in the American dream. If we can't do it now, when our economy and our prospects and our confidence are so strong, then when?

Now we have jobs waiting to be filled in almost every community. I've been working with people here in Washington, DC—there are hundreds of thousands of jobs in information technology-related fields open today, everywhere from Silicon Valley to the suburban areas of the Nation's Capital. If we make the best use of this time, we can change the whole culture of poverty and long neglected neighborhoods. We can help millions more people ensure that their children will be raised in homes full of hope and pride based on dignity and work.

To all of you who have made this day come to pass, who have played a role in the progress of the last 2 years, and to all of you who are committed to keeping on until the job is done, I extend the thanks of our Nation. Great job. Let's do better.

Thank you very much, and God bless you.

NOTE: The President spoke at 3:15 p.m. in the East Room at the White House. In his remarks, he referred to Vesta Kimble, deputy director, Anne Arundel County Department of Social Services, MD; and Eli Segal, president and chief executive officer, Welfare to Work Partnership. The Personal Responsibility and Work Opportunity Reconciliation Act of 1996, Public Law 104–193, was approved August 22, 1996.

Statement on the Death of Arthur Barbieri
August 4, 1998

Hillary and I are deeply saddened by the death of Arthur Barbieri. New Haven has lost a great political leader; I have lost a mentor and a friend.

When I was a law student, I was lucky enough to work by Arthur's side and learn grassroots politics at its absolute best. I'm forever grateful for all that he taught me. Our thoughts and prayers are with his loved ones.

Statement on House Action on Credit Union Legislation
August 4, 1998

I am pleased that the House has passed the "Credit Union Membership Access Act" to protect and strengthen credit unions for the 71 million Americans who own, use, and rely upon them. This bill resolves uncertainty about the future of credit unions, created by a recent Supreme Court decision, by protecting existing credit union members and making it easier for credit unions to expand where appropriate. It also helps put credit unions on sounder footing by making important reforms that could pay enormous dividends in more difficult times. This bill ensures that consumers continue to have a broad array of choices in financial services, and, when Congress sends me this bill, I will sign it.

Remarks at a Democratic Congressional Campaign Committee Dinner
August 4, 1998

Thank you very much. Maxine, you have neither been a fair-weather nor a faint-hearted friend. [*Laughter*] And you have always let me know exactly what you think, whether I wanted to hear it or not—[*laughter*]—in good times and bad. And I thank you.

I thank all of you for coming. Sidney, thank you for being here and for the service you've rendered our country as an Ambassador. I thank the Members of the Democratic congressional caucus who are here: Congressman Ford; Congressman Frost, the head of the DCCC; Congressman Hoyer; Congresswoman Lee; Congressman Rush; and Congressman Lewis, who, like Maxine, started out with me in 1991; and Congressman Stokes, we're going to miss you, and we thank you for your service.

I would like to thank two former members of your group who are here, also my longtime friends, Harold Ford, Sr., and Andrew Young. Thank you both for being here tonight. I also note your high degree of judgment, about how the Federal Government works, in bringing Secretary Slater. You probably know he got the first budget out this year. He has all the money. [*Laughter*] He may have the only money in the Federal Government. He's doing a wonderful job, and I thank you for bringing him tonight.

Let me say very briefly, we've already had a chance to visit individually and in groups. More than anything else, I would like to thank you. I'd like to thank you for supporting our congressional candidates and the genuine prospect we have to reverse 150-plus years of history in making historic gains in this election. And I would like to thank you for the example you have set for Americans—for all Americans—the work you have done, the barriers you have broken, the hurdles you have overcome, the Americans you have helped, and the reaffirmation you give in your daily lives that the American dream can be made real in the lives of all kinds of people.

I also thank you for the specific ideas you gave me tonight to move forward. I would just like to make a couple of observations. I'm very grateful to have had the chance to serve as President at a time of remarkable change and to try to make sure that this period of change

works for all Americans and that, when we get to the 21st century, the American dream is alive and well for everybody who is responsible enough to work for it, that our country is strong and visionary enough to continue to lead the world toward prosperity and peace and freedom, and that we can do that because we have enough sense to come together, across all the lines that divide us, into one America. That is what I have worked for.

Now, we all know that we are facing a new time of economic challenge because of the difficulties in Asia, which I have spent an enormous amount of time on, as you might imagine actually, since last November. For quite a long while now, we've been working on that, and every day we work on it, because Asia is a big part of our economic growth. Thirty percent of our growth in the last 6 years has come from exports and expanding our position in foreign countries.

But I want to ask you to think about where we go now. The temptation for a great, free country when you have the lowest unemployment rate in 28 years and the lowest crime rate in 25 years and the lowest percentage of people on welfare in 29 years and the first balanced budget and surplus in 29 years and the highest homeownership in history, is to say that's pretty good; let's take a break; I've been working myself to death; let's just take a break. [*Laughter*]

But the truth is, as all of you who deal in international economics know especially, that things are changing so fast, we can't afford to take a break, number one; and number two, we now have the confidence and the resources to deal with the long-term challenges of the country. And I would like to just offer a couple of observations.

We are working with our friends in Asia to try to restore economic growth, and we will do everything we can to help those who are prepared to take the necessary steps to help themselves. But we have to look also at what other opportunities are there to continue to grow the American economy. And I would just like to offer a couple of observations.

Number one, there are still places in this country that have not fully absorbed this economic recovery. The unemployment rate in New York City is 9 percent; the unemployment rate in many neighborhoods is considerably higher. And yet in all those neighborhoods, over 80 percent of the people are working. There's opportunity for investment that will create jobs for the others and bring a very high rate of return, with no risk of inflation to the aggregate economy because those are underutilized human resources. And it's true in every city in this country; it's true in a lot of smaller towns; it's true in a lot of Native American communities. We're going to have a Native American economic conference in the next few days, first one ever held. And I think it is very important that we focus on the fact that people who are out of work or communities where the unemployment rate is too high and the investment rate is too low are enormous opportunities for us at a time when there is some turmoil around the world.

The second thing I'd like to do is make a plug again for Africa. We have an Africa trade bill before the Congress. I took a great trip to Africa; a number of you went on it. American investors earned a 30 percent return on their investment in Africa last year—30 percent. Now, you may say, "Well, yes, Mr. President, but those were the easiest investments, and they picked the low-hanging fruit." But you could go a ways down from 30 percent and still make pretty good money.

And so I say again, I think that is an important thing. Tomorrow Deputy President Mbeki of South Africa is coming back to the United States for another one of his meetings with the Vice President and the Gore-Mbeki Commission, and I intend to see him. Secretary Daley is going to Africa in September. Secretary Slater and Secretary Rubin were there last month. So we have followed up on the trip that Hillary and I took to Africa with, as I said, a number of you in this room, and we want to continue to work on that. It is of enormous importance.

I would also note that Latin America is doing very well. Our neighbors in Latin America and in the Caribbean are doing relatively well and continuing to prosper in this difficult time. And there are opportunities in the Caribbean, where there was a relative disinvestment for several years, that I think need to be looked at by Americans. And we have a lot of cultural ties to a lot of the island nations of the Caribbean as well as to Latin America that I think would bear fruit.

And so I think it very important that in America, while we do everything we can to focus on the Asian financial challenges, that we also know that there are opportunities here at home and opportunities in Africa and opportunities in Latin America and elsewhere to continue to grow the American economy.

Now, in connection with the issues here at home, the thing that I think is important to remember in this election is that, in order for the Democrats to buck the tide of a century and a half of history, we have to continue to do what we've been doing for the last 8 months. We have to continue to press our agenda and to be for something that will excite America and bring hope.

We have before the Congress now an opportunity agenda that would help a lot of you to make more investments in America's communities: a second round of empowerment zones, another round of community development financial institutions. One of you told me today you're involved with a community development bank in Los Angeles that this administration helped to set up. These things are going to make a huge difference around the country if we can reach a critical mass of capital in enough communities.

Secretary Cuomo at HUD has a number of initiatives, that are part of this, that will actually create significant numbers of jobs with investment—private sector jobs in communities where they're needed.

So I ask for your support in publicizing of the community empowerment agenda that we have been pushing now ever since my State of the Union Address in Congress and that the Democratic caucus, as far as I know, unanimously supports.

We need to stand up for the educational empowerment zones that we have been pushing. In Chicago now, the summer school in Chicago, since it's summer, I can say is the sixth largest school district in America. That's how many children are in summer school. Guess what? The juvenile crime rate is way down in Chicago, and the learning is way up.

Over 40,000 children during a regular school year now get 3 square meals a day at their school in that city. We have an educational community empowerment initiative before the Congress that would enable us to support other communities in doing that, giving children a chance to stay out of trouble and in school, after school, giving children a chance to go to summer programs like this, giving us a chance to give educational opportunities to all different kinds of people. And I ask for your support for that, but I ask you to talk to your friends and neighbors about it. There are big issues in this election season that deserve to be debated.

What we really need to do is to make sure that every child, of whatever race and of whatever station, in whatever neighborhood they're born in, has the chance to live the success stories that you have lived. What we really need to do is to make sure that we are still working hard to create one America. What we really need to do is to make sure that we're not sitting on our laurels and being distracted but instead bearing down and looking forward and lifting up and pulling together this country.

All over the world people still look to the United States for leadership, for peace, for freedom, for security. But in order for us to do good in the 21st century around the world, we first must be good here at home on those things that we know matter most.

You've helped us a lot, and I can tell you that Maxine is grateful; I am grateful. You're going to make Congressman Frost look better tomorrow with what he's done for the Democratic Congressional Campaign Committee. But the most important thing is, by being here tonight, you have helped us to work with your constituents to make 21st century America the greatest period in our Nation's history, and I thank you for it.

Thank you, and God bless you.

NOTE: The President spoke at 8:24 p.m., in Ballroom Two at the Washington Court Hotel. In his remarks, he referred to Representative Maxine Waters; Sidney Williams, former Ambassador to the Bahamas; and Deputy President Thabo Mbeki of South Africa.

Statement on the Fifth Anniversary of the Family and Medical Leave Act
August 5, 1998

Five years ago today, the Family and Medical Leave Act went into effect, giving tens of millions of Americans the peace of mind that they would never have to choose between the jobs they need and the families they love. I am very proud that the Family and Medical Leave Act was the very first piece of legislation I signed into law.

Millions of Americans have benefited from this historic legislation by taking time off—without fear of losing their jobs—to care for a newborn or adopted child, to attend to their own serious health needs, or to care for a seriously ill parent, child, or spouse. In addition, a report issued today by the Department of Labor shows the relative ease with which the law has been

implemented; the overwhelming majority of employers have found the FMLA easy to administer, and 9 out of 10 complaints have been successfully resolved, often with a simple phone call.

I have always believed that we can help our workers fulfill their family responsibilities and strengthen the economy and America's businesses. For 5 years, the Family and Medical Leave Act has helped us to fulfill both of those critical goals.

NOTE: The Family and Medical Leave Act of 1993, Public Law 103–3, was approved February 5, 1993.

Statement on House Action on the Census Amendment
August 5, 1998

I am very disappointed that the House failed to adopt an amendment to the FY '99 Commerce-Justice-State appropriations bill that would have removed onerous restrictions on the Census Bureau's plan for the decennial census. By failing to adopt this amendment, the House is undermining the Census Bureau's ability to plan and conduct an accurate decennial census.

To ensure a fair and accurate count, my administration has supported the 2000 census plan, developed by the experts at the Census Bureau, that was based upon recommendations by the National Academy of Sciences. It is a plan that will correct the inaccuracies of the 1990 census, which missed millions of Americans and disproportionately undercounted children, minorities, and residents in urban and rural communities. This is the first census of the 21st century, and we must ensure that the census, the single most important source of information about the American people, is accurate.

Congress must remove these restrictions. It is critically important that the Census Bureau have the funding it needs to implement its 2000 census plan, a plan that will produce the most accurate census in history using the best, most up-to-date scientific methods.

Remarks at a Unity '98 Dinner
August 5, 1998

Thank you. I know you need a stretch, but it's going on too long. [*Laughter*]

Let me just say the most important words I can say: Thank you. Thank you for your support for me and for our administration and for our candidates for Senate and Congress and for the whole concept of this Unity campaign. Thank you, Representative Pelosi and Leader Gephardt and Senator Torricelli and Steve Grossman, all dedicated Democrats, all dedicated Americans.

Thank you, Mr. Vice President, for the wonderful work that you have done in so many ways, and everything that we've done together in the last 5½ years.

In 1996, when the American people were good enough to give the Vice President and me another term and made me the first Democratic President in 60 years, since Franklin Roosevelt in 1936, to be reelected, we picked up some seats in the House. And if we had picked up a few more, we would have won the House. There was, I think, one overwhelming reason: In the last 10 days, even though we had the issues and the direction, we were outspent in the 20 closest districts 4½ to one.

But we did begin this Unity concept a little too late, but it still did very well. All of our contributors liked it because all three committees weren't asking at the same time to give money or raise it. But it was the right thing to do, because we could work on helping particular candidates, targeting particular States, going after particular constituencies, getting our turnout up.

This year we're trying to go sooner and do more. And I cannot say enough for what I believe is the vision of the leaders of the House, the Senate, and the Democratic Committee for doing this early and doing it together and in good faith with a good heart. The Vice President and I and the First Lady and Tipper, we're all committed to making this work.

The Vice President gave that wonderful portrait of what's happened the last 6 years through chapter 6. Chapter 7 is, we win if we do the right things; if we do the right things, we win.

Hillary came up with this great motto for the millennial celebration we're going to have on New Year's Eve 1999–2000 and between now and then: "Honor the past; imagine the future." And we started out a couple of weeks ago honoring the past by announcing grants by private citizens to help us save the Star-Spangled Banner. It's hard to think of anything that embodies our past more. And then Hillary went to Thomas Edison's° home in New Jersey to talk about saving that and then to Harriet Tubman's home, then to George Washington's revolutionary headquarters, then to New York to celebrate the 150th anniversary of the beginning of the women's movement, all honoring the past.

But we've also had a lot of interesting lectures at the White House imagining the future. Stephen Hawking, the great physicist from Cambridge, England, came and spoke in a very heroic way, because he suffers from Lou Gehrig's disease, about what we would learn about the larger world in the future. We had poets for the first time in a long time, a genuine poetry reading in the White House with our poet laureates and ordinary citizens, including children, thinking about their future.

Steve said that never, at least—I quit looking at the Civil War because I'm not sure before that political trends are indicative. But since the Civil War, the party of the President in the President's second term has always lost some seats at midterm. But there is a reason for that which we have determined to erase—and these records are made to be changed—and that is, that generally there is the sense that no matter how well liked the President might be, the term is three-quarters over, so what else is new?

Well, when I was reelected, the Vice President and I sat down one day, and I told our people, I said, "Look, I want us to drive the agenda of this country until the last hour of the last day of my term in January of 2001. That is what we signed on for. That is what we owe the American people. That is the right thing to do." And if you look at what is happening today, our party—I love what Dick Gephardt said about, when he was the majority leader, how he met with the minority leader and how we tried to work together. Because this election fundamentally is not about the Democratic Party. It's about the American people, and it's about our agenda, which puts progress over partisanship and people over power and unity over division.

We believe this country has big challenges. We believe, first, you don't sit on a lead in a global economy and society like the one we're living in. You know, the temptation is, after all the tough years we had, "Things are going so well now; why don't we just relax, kick back,

and enjoy it?" All you have to do is pick up the paper every day to know that it's a reasonably dynamic world we're living in.

If someone had told you 5 years ago that Japan would have 5 years of one percent growth a year during which time the stock market there would lose half its value, would you have believed that? Is there a person in this room that really thought that would happen? If there is, I'd like to clean out what little I've got left in my bank account and let you be my investment adviser from now on. [*Laughter*]

Now, they're a very great country, and they're going to come back. I don't mean that in a negative way. I'm trying to point out that nothing stays the same. The way people work and live and relate to each other and the rest of the world is changing at a breathtaking pace. Nobody is smart enough to understand it all and figure out all of its ramifications. But I know this: When people have the good fortune of good times, they should take their treasure and their confidence and think about tomorrow and deal with the long-term challenges of the country.

There are four big issues that I think will sweep across the country this year and carry us home if our party will advance them.

Number one, we waited 29 years to get out of the red. Let's don't run out and spend this surplus on a tax cut or a spending program until we save the Social Security system for the 21st century so that the baby boomers don't bankrupt their kids and their ability to raise their grandchildren when we retire.

Number two, managed care, on balance, has been a good thing for America because we couldn't sustain inflation in health care costs at 3 times the rate of inflation in the economy. That was an unsustainable trend that developed in the 1980's. But it is just a device, and it must not be allowed to block quality care. Therefore, we should have a Patients' Bill of Rights that puts quality care back at the center of the health care debate.

People should have access to the medical care they need; decisions should be made by doctors, not by accountants; people shouldn't be turned away from emergency rooms or specialists if they need them; and their privacy should not be violated in the medical arena. That's what this Patients' Bill of Rights is all about. It's a first step toward reconciling the imperative of having better management in the health care

---

° White House correction.

system with keeping health care uppermost in the health care system.

And a lot of you are in the health care business. One of the reasons we need legislation is, it is simply unfair to all the good people out there in health care today that are already complying with the requirements of the Patients' Bill of Rights because they think it is the morally right thing to do. It is unfair for them to be at an economic disadvantage with those who don't. So we need a Patients' Bill of Rights.

Number three, we have succeeded in the last 5½ years in opening the doors of college to just about everybody in America. The HOPE scholarship makes the first 2 years of college virtually free to most Americans. It certainly makes community college virtually free to most Americans. We now have tax credits for the junior and senior year and for graduate school. The interest deductibility on student loans is back. We've dramatically increased scholarships and work-study positions. We had 100,000 young people go through AmeriCorps. One of you told me you had a child going to California in the AmeriCorps program, and I thank you for that.

But no one believes that we still even after all this, we still can't say that we have the best elementary and secondary education in the world for all Americans. We have an agenda for smaller classes, more teachers, more well-trained teachers, modernized schools, hooking up all the classrooms to the Internet, more after-school programs, more summer school programs for kids in difficult areas with troubled lives—things that we know work—higher standards, greater accountability, more charter schools, more school choice. We've got an agenda, and we think it ought to be supported. So we have a better schools agenda.

Number four, after this summer, I take it no one seriously questions the fact that the climate is genuinely changing. The 9 hottest years on record have occurred in the last 11 years. The 5 hottest years in history have occurred in the 1990's. Last year was the hottest year on record; this year every month has been hotter than the same month last year. This is not a joke.

We still have 40 percent of our water that's not safe for swimming, in spite of all the work since the Clean Water Act passed. We still have problems with safe drinking water in some places. We still have too many toxic waste dumps in some places.

If there is one thing America has learned since 1970, it is that we improve the quality of life and the strength of the economy when we clean up the environment in the right way. So this old-fashioned, antienvironmental rhetoric doesn't hold much water. We've got to face the environmental challenges of today and tomorrow and do them in a way that promotes new markets, new technologies, new jobs, but a cleaner environment and a growing economy.

So those, I think, are the four great national issues: save Social Security, pass a Patients' Bill of Rights, improve the public schools, clean up the environment and improve the economy. There are lots of local issues. In a lot of places our farmers are in trouble. A lot of urban areas, where we have a good empowerment agenda, still haven't felt the economic recovery. But Social Security first, the Patients' Bill of Rights, the school agenda, the environmental agenda, those things will help us to move forward. And if we can get the Congress to face our clear international economic responsibilities, which take an awful lot of my time these days, then obviously that's something that the new Congress won't have to do. And I'm still hoping and praying that we'll face up to our responsibilities as Americans and do the International Monetary Fund and these other things we have to do.

But that is an agenda we can win on. You win elections with a message, with candidates, and with the means for the candidate to get the message to the people. That's what the Unity campaign is all about. I believe that I've gone to more of these events than any person in America in the last 6 years. [*Laughter*] Therefore, the happiest citizen in the United States was me when the Shays-Meehan campaign finance reform bill passed the House last week.

And we Democrats have been almost unanimous in support of real campaign finance reform. The other party's leadership has been unanimous against it, although we have had some of their great renegades. We got 51, I think, bolted and voted with us last week, and I applaud them. But until we get that done, we've got the candidates; we've got the message; you're giving us the means to get the message out; and you're going to have a lot to celebrate this November.

Thank you, and God bless you.

NOTE: The President spoke at 8:46 p.m. in the Crystal Ballroom at the Carlton Hotel. In his remarks, he referred to Steve Grossman, national chair, Democratic National Committee.

Remarks on the Proposed Extension of the Brady Handgun Violence Prevention Act
August 6, 1998

Thank you, Sarah and Jim. I think every American should be grateful that the power of your spirit was great enough to overcome the pain of your injury and disappointment, so that you could dedicate all these years to this great cause.

Thank you, Mr. Vice President, for being, as you said when you got such a laugh, a critical part of every good thing that happens and, even before we met, an early sponsor of the Brady bill. Coming from where we come from, the Vice President and I were not always popular with all of our constituents because we were always for the Brady bill, but just about every one of them knows now that it was the right thing to do.

I thank the Attorney General and the Secretary of the Treasury for all they have done. I thank all the law enforcement officials, the leaders of the Association of Chiefs of Police, the Sheriffs Association, the Brotherhood of Police Officers who are here. And Officer Flynn, I thought you were just downright terrific up here today, and I was very proud of you. Thank you.

I want to thank all the Members of Congress who are here. I think the Vice President attempted to introduce everyone. I think we inadvertently didn't mention Congressman Roemer from Indiana. We thank him for being there. And there are a number of you who have played large roles over the years. I hesitate to single out anyone, but I want to thank Senator Durbin, and I want to say a special word of appreciation to Congressman Schumer. Thank you, sir, and all the rest of you for what you have done.

As the Vice President said, more than 5 years ago we committed ourselves to a comprehensive strategy to lower the crime rate and to make America a safer place to live: community policing; antigang initiatives; targeted deterrence; tougher penalties; but most important of all, because of what law enforcement officers and community leaders told us, smarter, more comprehensive prevention.

The strategy from the Brady bill to the crime bill, from the assault weapons ban to the Violence Against Women Act has begun to show remarkable results, thanks to police officers and citizens all across America. We're ahead of schedule and under budget in meeting our goal of putting 100,000 police on the street. All across America, violent crime, property crime, murder are down. Crime rates overall are at 25-year low. Americans should take pride in that but should resolve to do better. No serious person believes that this country is as safe as it ought to be.

The Brady law, in particular, shows the progress we can make when we take responsibility for making our community safe. Since the law took effect, gun trafficking and gun-related crime are on the wane. And as has been said, according to a recent Justice Department report, background checks have put a stop to nearly a quarter of a million handgun purchases since the law took effect, 62 percent of them based on felony convictions or indictment.

Now, that sounds like a big number, and Officer Flynn mentioned those gripping, personal, tragic cases. But let me break it down for you: That number is 118 felons a day, every day, since the Brady law took effect, 118 a day going home empty-handed instead of well-armed. How many people are alive today because of that law? We will never know. But no one doubts the number is very, very large indeed.

As we near the fifth anniversary of the law and celebrate its progress, we have to continue to fight against crime and violence. We cannot retreat. Yet, as has already been noted, that is precisely what the gun lobby and its allies on Capitol Hill have asked us to do, to retreat from a law that is keeping guns out of the hands of criminals, retreat from the national interests, surrender our fight for safety to the special interests.

Now, before the Brady law even goes fully into effect, the gun lobby and its friends in Congress are trying to destroy it. They claim to support the national insta-check system but would deny the FBI the funds necessary to make the system work. They claim to support background checks but would have the FBI immediately destroy records vital to the process. In their official literature, the gun lobby is proudly calling this measure, and I quote, "an anti-Brady amendment."

Let me be clear. I will oppose any legislation that would gut the Brady law and put guns back into the hands of felons and fugitives when we can prevent it. Here again, this is a place we ought to put progress ahead of partisanship, public safety ahead of politics.

Years of experience now show that this law works, as the Vice President so clearly argued. Now we have to make it more effective, not less effective. I have asked Congress to extend Brady background checks to violent juveniles who should not be able to buy a gun on their 21st birthday. Congress should also enact the Brady waiting period as a permanent requirement before it expires in November.

Too many crimes are committed within hours of a handgun purchase. The waiting period gives tempers time to cool. It gives potential criminals the time to consider the consequences. It gives local law enforcement officials the time to check all relevant records, even those not computerized, and stop every last prohibited person, who can be found, from walking home with a gun in hand and violence in mind.

This is good law enforcement. It's smart. It works. That's why both the International Brotherhood of Police Officers and the International Association of Chiefs of Police are today supporting permanent extension of the Brady waiting period. The real measure of our progress, of course, is more than a decline in crime; it's a rise in responsibility and respect for the law and the feeling of security that is so intangible yet so profoundly important to the essence of American citizenship.

For those of us in public life, it is our obligation to strengthen that feeling of security, especially the laws that protect our families, save lives, and draw the line between right and wrong and against violence. At heart, this is

what the Brady law has accomplished, and this is the vision to which we must all remain true if we are to build a safer and stronger America for the 21st century.

There has been another development today that, because of this opportunity, I feel I have to comment on. One of the reasons that the crime rate has gone down, as everyone knows, is that the economy has gone up and the unemployment rate is at a 28-year low. I think it is important to keep the economy strong and for the long run and to honor our obligations across the generations. That's why I have said that I'm proud we're going to have the first balanced budget and surplus in 29 years, but I don't want us to run right out and spend it before we take care of the crisis in Social Security that is looming when the baby boomers retire.

Therefore, I was disappointed today when the Speaker proposed to drain $700 million from the surplus before we have even realized the surplus and before we take even the first steps to save Social Security. As I said in my State of the Union Address, we should reserve every penny of the surplus until we save Social Security for the 21st century.

You know, we waited 29 years for this, to get out of the red ink. It looks to me like we could at least wait a year and enjoy it and take care of future generations' challenges before we run right out and spend this money. This is about our budget, the health of our economy, keeping us strong and safer, about our fundamental values as a country. We worked a long time to get back on the path of responsibility, and we shouldn't abandon it before we've even achieved our real objectives.

Now, I think it would be wrong for us to end today without hearing from the person whose courage made this day possible, our friend Jim Brady.

NOTE: The President spoke at 11:06 a.m. in the Rose Garden at the White House. In his remarks, he referred to James Brady, former White House Press Secretary, who was wounded in the 1981 assassination attempt on President Ronald Reagan, and his wife Sarah Brady, chair, Handgun Control, Inc.; and Gerald Flynn, national vice president, International Brotherhood of Police

Officers. The transcript released by the Office of the Press Secretary also included the remarks of James Brady. The Brady Handgun Violence Pre-vention Act, title I of Public Law 103–159, was approved November 30, 1993.

Statement on House Action on the Executive Order on Prohibiting Discrimination Based on Sexual Orientation in the Federal Civilian Work Force
August 6, 1998

I am gratified that the House has defeated an attempt to overturn my Executive order providing a uniform policy to prohibit discrimination based on sexual orientation in the Federal civilian work force.

This vote reflected the values of our Nation. The American people believe in fairness, not discrimination, and the Hefley amendment would have legitimized Government-sponsored discrimination against its own citizens based on their sexual orientation.

It has always been the practice of this administration to prohibit employment discrimination in the Federal civilian work force based on sexual orientation. Most Federal agencies and departments have taken actions to memorialize that policy. The Executive order does no more than make that policy uniform across the Federal Government. It does not authorize affirmative action or preferences or special rights for anyone.

The Executive order reflects this administration's firm commitment that the Federal Government make employment-related decisions in the civilian work force based on individual ability and not on sexual orientation.

NOTE: Executive Order 13087 of May 28 on equal employment opportunity in the Federal Government was published in the *Federal Register* at 63 FR 30097.

Remarks to the White House Conference on Building Economic Self-Determination in Indian Communities
August 6, 1998

The President. Thank you. Thank you for the wonderful welcome. Thank you for the song. Thank you, Dominic, for giving us a picture of opportunity and hope for the future. I'm very glad that you're not only a good student but a good entrepreneur and a good promoter. Dominic was kind enough to give me one of his bracelets before I came out. [*Laughter*] So I'm his latest walking advertisement, and I'm glad to shill for him. [*Laughter*]

I would like to thank the members of the administration, the 15 agencies that have come together with the White House to sponsor this conference. I thank Secretary Daley, Secretary Riley, Secretary Glickman, Small Business Administrator Aida Alvarez, who are here. I'd like to thank Deputy Assistant Secretary Michael Anderson, Kevin Gover, Mark Van Norman, Angela Hammond, and two young people on our staff, Julie Fernandes and Mary Smith, who work with Mickey Ibarra and Lynn Cutler; all of them worked very hard on this conference. I thank them.

I'm proud to be here with Chief Marge Anderson, Governor Walter Dasheno, Chief Joyce Dugan, Chairman Frank Ettawageshik, Chairman Roland Harris, Chairwoman Kathryn Harrison, President Ivan Makil, Governor Mary Thomas, Chairman Brian Wallace, President John Yellow Bird Steele. I thank all of you.

I have looked forward to this day for quite a long time. The Iroquois teach us that every decision we make, every action we take, must be judged not only on the impact it makes today but on the impact it makes on the next seven generations. It is, therefore, fitting on the eve of a new century and a new millennium, that we come together today to determine what we must do to build a stronger future for our children, for our grandchildren, for future generations of Native Americans and, indeed, for all Americans.

For too many Americans, our understanding of Native Americans is frozen in time, in sepia-toned photography of legendary chieftains, in the ancient names of rivers, lakes, and mountain ranges, in the chapters of old history books. But as we have all seen at this conference, the more than 2 million members of tribal nations in the United States, from energetic, young entrepreneurs like Dominic to innovative leaders like the ones sitting here with me today, are a vital part of today's America and must be an even more vital part of tomorrow's America.

We are living in a time of great opportunity and hope, with our economy the strongest in a generation. Soon we will have the first balanced budget and surplus in 29 years, the lowest unemployment in 28 years, the highest homeownership in history. Social problems are finally beginning to bend to our efforts as a Nation: the crime rate, the lowest in 25 years; the welfare rolls, the smallest percentage of our people in 29 years. We are taking strong steps toward the America I dreamed of when I first ran for this office beginning in late 1991, an America where there is opportunity for all, responsibility from all, a community of all our people.

It is a time of unprecedented prosperity for some of our tribes as well. Gaming and a variety of innovative enterprises have enabled tribes to free their people from lives of poverty and dependence. The new wealth is sparking a cultural renaissance in parts of Indian country, as tribes build new community centers, museums, language schools, elder care centers.

But we also know the hard truth, that on far too many reservations across America such glowing statistics and reports mean very little indeed. While some tribes have found new success in our new economy, too many more remain caught in a cycle of poverty, unemployment, and disease. The facts are all too familiar. More than a third of all Native Americans still live in poverty. With unemployment at a 28-year low, still, on some reservations more than 70 percent of all adults do not have regular work. Diabetes in Indian country has reached epidemic proportions. Other preventable diseases and alcoholism continue to diminish the quality of life for hundreds of thousands.

At a time of such great prosperity, when we know we don't have a person to waste, this is an unacceptable condition. That's why we're here today, to find new ways to empower our people, especially our children, with the tools and the opportunity to build brighter futures for themselves and their families. Our Government alone cannot solve the problems of Indian country, nor can tribal governments be left to fend alone for themselves.

Everyone must do his or her part, tribal and Federal governments, along with the private sector. We all have to work together to empower our people with the tools they need to succeed. Most of all, every individual must take responsibility to seize the opportunities of this new time and to break the cycle of poverty.

As President, I have worked very hard to honor tribal sovereignty and to strengthen our government-to-government relationships. Long ago, many of your ancestors gave up land, water, and mineral rights in exchange for peace, security, health care, education from the Federal Government. It is a solemn pact. And while the United States Government did not live up to its side of the bargain in the past, we can and we must honor it today and into that new millennium.

Four years ago, when I became the first President since James Monroe in the 1820's to invite the leaders of every tribe to the White House, I issued a memorandum directing all Federal agencies to consult with the Indian tribes before making decisions on matters affecting your people. This spring I strengthened that directive so that decisions made by the Federal Government regarding Indian country are always made in cooperation with the tribes.

In the last 6 months, Jackie Johnson has joined the staff at HUD, Carrie Billy at Education, Rhonda Whiting at the Small Business Administration to help coordinate and promote Native American initiatives at these agencies. Raynell Morris will join the White House Office of Intergovernmental Affairs to help Mickey Ibarra and Lynn Cutler with Native American initiatives and outreach. I welcome all to my administration.

We also, as all of you know, have been working very hard for more than a year now on a race initiative designed to address the opportunity gaps for all Americans, and I thank those of you who have had a role in that. The most recent public event we did with the race initiative was an hour-long conversation on Jim Lehrer's Public Broadcasting System show. The Native American community was represented by a delightful, energetic young man named Sherman Alexie, whose new movie, "Smoke Signals," is receiving very good reviews around the country, and I had it brought to me at the White House and watched it. He's got a great talent, and I wish him well.

Today I want to talk about opportunity and about three tools of opportunity every American needs to thrive in the 21st century, how we can bring these tools to every person in very corner of Indian country, from Pine Ridge, South Dakota, to Window Rock, Arizona, to Cherokee, North Carolina.

[*At this point, an audience member cheered.*]

The President. That's okay. [*Laughter*]

The first and most important tool of opportunity, of course, is education. Throughout history, in the United States, education has been the key to a better life for generations of Americans. This will clearly be even more true in a global, knowledge-based economy that will reward children, but only children who have the skills to succeed and to keep learning for a lifetime.

Today fewer than two-thirds of our Native Americans over the age of 25 hold high school degrees. Fewer than 10 percent go on to college. If the trend continues, then the future for Native American children will become even bleaker. The opportunity gap between them and their peers will widen to a dangerous chasm. In a few moments, therefore, I will sign an Executive order directing our administration to work together with tribal and State governments to improve Native American achievement in math and reading, to raise high school and postsecondary graduation rates, to reduce the influence of poverty and substance abuse on student performance, to create safe drug-free schools, to expand the use of science and technology. I believe in this. I have done what I could to support Native American higher education and will continue to do so.

We have also tried to open the doors of college to all, with more Pell grants, tax credits which make the first 2 years of college now virtually free to all Americans, increased work-study slots, and AmeriCorps community service slots—other things we have tried to do to make college education more affordable. But we have to have more people who are able to take advantage of it.

The second tool is high-quality health care. Native American communities will never reach their full potential if people continue to be hobbled by disease, diseases often preventable, easily treatable. Native Americans are 3 times as likely to suffer from diabetes as white people. Therefore, they should get 3 times the benefit of the remarkable advances that we made in the last year in the diabetes prevention effort.

The American Diabetes Association said that what we did for diabetes not too long ago was the most important step forward since the discovery of insulin, in treatment, in prevention, in research. Every tribe should know what is in the law, what the benefits are, and should be in a position to take maximum advantage of it.

Last summer, as I said when I signed this legislation, I wanted to make sure that it helped all Americans with diabetes but especially those in our Native American communities. Earlier this year, I launched an initiative to help eliminate health disparities between racial and ethnic minority groups by the year 2010. I want you to make sure Congress fully funds this initiative as well.

Today I am pleased to announce that we're going to make an adjustment in our new children's health insurance program to ensure that Native American children get the health care they need. In the balanced budget bill which passed Congress last year, we had $24 billion over a 5-year period to extend health insurance to 5 million more children. The action I'm taking today makes sure that the money is fairly allocated so that Native American children who are disproportionately without health insurance will now have their fair chance to be covered.

I also want you to know that I am committed to working with Congress and Secretary Shalala to elevate the Director of the Indian Health Service, Dr. Michael Trujillo, who is here today, to the rank of Assistant Secretary for Health and Human Services. By elevating the head of the Indian Health Service, we can ensure that the health needs of our Native Americans get the full consideration they deserve when it comes to setting health policy in our country.

The third tool is economic opportunity, in the form of jobs, credit, small business. Very few grocery stores, gas stations, restaurants, and banks are doing business on reservations. As a result, money that could be used to build tribal economies and create jobs is spent too often off reservation.

I've issued a new directive to boost economic development in Indian country. The directive will do three things. It will ask the Department of Commerce to work with the Interior Department and with the tribal governments to study and develop a plan to meet the technology infrastructure needs of Indian country. No tribe will be able to attract new business if it doesn't have the phone, fax, Internet, and other technology capabilities essential to the 21st century.

The directive calls on several agencies to coordinate and strengthen our existing Native American economic development initiatives. And I might say in particular, I think microcredit institutions have a terrific potential to do even more than some of you have already done for the last several years in Indian country. The community development financial institutions that we have established in this country in the last few years have played an important role in providing credit to people who otherwise could not get it to start small businesses or to expand small businesses. I have asked the Congress for a significant expansion in the Community Development Financial Institutions Act. I believe in microlending.

The United States, last year, through our aid programs, financed 2 million small loans in developing nations around the world. Think how much good we could do if we could finance 2 million small loans in developing communities in the United States of America. We're also directing the Department of Treasury and HUD to work with tribal governments to create and improve one-stop mortgage shopping centers to help more Native Americans obtain loans more easily. And our first pilot will be in the Navajo nation.

Last, I am proud to announce the plan by the United States Department of Agriculture to help seven tribes to get a foothold in our high-tech economy. The Department will help these tribes establish small technology companies to

obtain Government contracts for software development and other services.

I have asked HUD Secretary Andrew Cuomo to visit several reservations to determine what more his department and our administration can do to boost economic development there. A few weeks ago he met with leaders of 60 Alaskan native villages; today he's visiting Pine Ridge and Lower Brule Indian reservations in South Dakota.

The next millennium must be a time of great progress and prosperity for our Native American communities, and we can make it so. Today, American Indian population is still very young. In the last census, 39 percent of all Native Americans were under the age of 20. I kind of wish I were one of them. [*Laughter*]

But this statistic is one that should bring us great hope, even as it poses your and my greatest challenge. We have a new large generation of young people who, if given the tools, the encouragement, and the opportunity, can work together to lead their families out of the stifling poverty and despair of the past.

So let us work to bring this generation and the next seven generations a world of abundant hope and opportunity, where all tribes have vanquished poverty and disease and all people have the tools to achieve their greatest potential.

I leave you with the words of the Lakota song we heard a few moments ago. "Beneath the President's flag, the people stand, that they may grow for generations to come." Let us stand together under America's flag to build that kind of future for generations to come.

Thank you, and God bless you.

NOTE: The President spoke at 1:55 p.m. in the Independence Ballroom at the Grand Hyatt Hotel. In his remarks, he referred to Dominic Ortiz, owner, Pottawatomie Traders; Mark Van Norman, Deputy Director, and Angela Hammond, Conference Coordinator, Office of Tribal Justice, Department of Justice; Mary Smith, Associate Director for Policy Planning, Domestic Policy Council; Marge Anderson, chief, Mille Lacs Reservation; Walter Dasheno, governor, Pueblo Santa Clara; Joyce Dugan, chief, Eastern Band of Cherokee; Frank Ettawageshik, president, Little Traverse Bay Band of Odawa; Roland Harris, chairman, Mohegan Indian Tribe; Kathryn Harrison, chairperson, Confederated Tribes of the Grand Ronde; Ivan Makil, president, Salt River

Maricopa Indian Community; Mary Thomas, governor, Gila River Indian Community; Brian Wallace, chairman, Washoe Tribal Council; and John Yellow Bird Steele, president, Oglala Sioux. The President also referred to his memorandum of April 29, 1994 (59 FR 22951); Executive Order 13084 of May 14 (63 FR 27655); Executive Order 13096 of Aug. 6 (63 FR 42681); and the Medicare, Medicaid, and Children's Health Provisions, title IV of the Balanced Budget Act of 1997, Public Law 105–33, approved August 5, 1997.

Memorandum on Economic Development in American Indian and Alaska Native Communities
August 6, 1998

Memorandum for the Secretary of Commerce, the Secretary of Housing and Urban Development, the Secretary of the Interior, the Secretary of the Treasury, Administrator of the Small Business Administration

Subject: Economic Development in American Indian and Alaska Native Communities

Across America, communities are recognizing that technology and information technologies are key to creating economic opportunities and increasing productivity. My Administration has made substantial gains in spurring the development of an advanced information infrastructure in order to bring the benefits of the Information Age to all Americans.

Looking to the future, we know that technology is critical to economic growth. We need to stimulate the growth of modern production facilities, small business incubators, capital access for start-up companies, and strategic planning to develop a vision for technologically competent communities. In particular, as telecommunications and information technologies continue to play a key role in providing new job and educational opportunities, we must ensure that all of our communities are able to participate fully in the new information economy.

Because of their often remote locations, American Indian and Alaska Native communities stand to benefit greatly from the Information Age, yet are in grave danger of being left behind. For example, a recent Department of Commerce study on Internet and computer usage in America shows that, although many more Americans now own computers, minority and low-income households are still far less likely than white and more affluent households to have personal computers or access to the Internet. Even more disturbing, this study reveals that this "digital divide" between households of different races and income levels is growing. We must act to ensure that American Indian and Alaska Native communities gain the new tools they need to battle high levels of unemployment and low per-capita income.

The ability to own a home and have access to capital are also very important for economic development. Residents of Indian reservations encounter several unique issues when seeking to obtain a mortgage. Trust land status, tribal sovereignty, and requirements to gain clear title from the Bureau of Indian Affairs are examples of issues that lenders and borrowers must grapple with during the mortgage lending process. Thus, individuals seeking to acquire a homesite lease or a residential mortgage are often required to obtain approval from several Federal, tribal, State, and local agencies as well as private providers.

I am proud that the Department of Commerce, particularly through the Economic Development Administration, has a 30-year history of investing over $730 million in economic development projects in American Indian and Alaska Native communities, working with its existing network of 65 tribal planning organizations. Additionally, the Commerce Department's National Telecommunications and Information Administration has funded demonstration projects that help show Native American communities how they can use technologies to improve the quality of life on reservations. And the Commerce Department's Minority Business Development Agency has funded eight Native American Business Development Centers that provide assistance with accounting, administration, business planning, construction, and marketing.

To continue our focus on infrastructure technology needs and business development in American Indian and Alaska Native communities, I direct the following actions.

First, I direct the Secretary of Commerce, in collaboration with the Department of the Interior and tribal governments, to report back to me within 9 months on the state of infrastructure technology needs in Indian communities, including distance learning facilities, telecommunications capabilities, and manufacturing facilities. This report should identify the infrastructure technology needs in Indian country and set forth proposals that would help address these needs.

Second, I direct the Secretary of the Interior, the Secretary of Commerce, and the Administrator of the Small Business Administration to report back to me within 90 days with a strategic plan for coordinating existing economic development initiatives for Native American and Alaska Native communities, including initiatives involving the private sector. In developing this strategic plan, the Secretaries and the Administrator should consult with all interested parties, including tribal governments and other Federal agencies and offices—particularly, the Departments of Housing and Urban Development, Transportation, and Agriculture. The plan should build upon current efforts in the agencies and detail future efforts such as providing technical assistance, enhancing infrastructure, and developing software.

Third, I direct the Secretaries of the Treasury and of Housing and Urban Development, in partnership with local tribal governments and in cooperation with other Federal agencies—particularly, the Departments of the Interior, Veterans Affairs, and Agriculture—to initiate a project to help streamline the mortgage lending process in Indian country in order to improve access to mortgage loans on Indian reservations. The Secretaries should initiate this effort through a year-long pilot program on the Navajo Nation and in at least one other location.

These steps, taken together, will help ensure the continued economic development of American Indian and Alaska Native communities and help them recognize the full benefits of the Information Age.

WILLIAM J. CLINTON

Statement on House Action on Campaign Finance Reform Legislation
August 6, 1998

The vote for final passage of the Shays-Meehan bipartisan campaign finance reform bill is a heartening sign for the health of our democracy. The House vote to ban soft money and improve disclosure, in defiance of the Republican leadership, is a rebuke to the cynical view that political reform can never happen. Now, only a minority of the United States Senate stands in the way of campaign finance reform becoming the law of the land. I call upon those few Senators who now block reform to heed the actions of the House and the will of the people and pass bipartisan campaign finance reform. I again congratulate Representatives Christopher Shays, Marty Meehan, and all their colleagues who set aside partisanship to make real progress today.

Statement on Iraq's Failure To Comply With United Nations Weapons Inspections
August 6, 1998

Iraq's latest refusal to cooperate with the international weapons inspectors is unacceptable. Far from hastening the day the international community lifts sanctions against Iraq, as Iraq intends, its failure to live up to its obligations will perpetuate those sanctions and keep the Iraqi economy under tight international control.

As a condition of the cease-fire in the Gulf war, the United Nations demanded and Iraq agreed to account for its nuclear, chemical, and biological weapons and the missiles to deliver them within 15 days and to destroy them. Last February Iraq reiterated that commitment in an agreement it signed with U.N. Secretary-General Annan. In short, Iraq has had it within its power to end the sanctions by meeting this affirmative obligation, letting the inspectors finish their job, and complying with the other relevant Security Council resolutions.

Instead of cooperating, Iraq has spent the better part of this decade avoiding its commitments to the international community. Recent discoveries by the weapons inspectors, including new documents on chemical munitions used in the Iran-Iraq war and nerve gas residue on Iraqi warheads, only underscore Iraq's failure to meet its obligations to the world.

Iraq's most recent refusal to cooperate with U.N. weapons inspectors is another misguided attempt to divide the international community in order to gain the lifting of the sanctions. These sanctions have denied Iraq over $120 billion in resources to rebuild its military and build more weapons of mass destruction. Its current tactics once again will backfire. Unless Iraq reverses course and cooperates fully with the international weapons inspectors, the United States will stop any and all efforts to alter the sanctions regime. This will deny the Iraqi leadership what it wants most: an end to sanctions. Because of the expanded oil-for-food arrangement we created last winter, the Iraqi people will continue to receive the food, medicine, and other essential supplies they need.

The burden has always been and remains on Iraq to disclose and dismantle its weapons of mass destruction capability. We remain determined to see that Iraq keeps that commitment.

Remarks on Signing the Workforce Investment Act of 1998
August 7, 1998

Thank you very much, and good morning. Thank you very much, Mr. Antosy, to Benny Hernandez, examples of what we come here to celebrate and enhance today. Thank you, Secretary Herman, for your leadership on this bill which was so essential to its passage. Chairman Goodling, Senator DeWine, Congressman Clay, Congressman McKeon, Congressman Kildee, many other Members of the House Representatives who are here. To Senator Jeffords and others who are not here, who, along with Senator DeWine, worked on the passage in the Senate.

I'd also like to thank the representatives of the National Association of Counties and other local groups who are here. And I will say more about all of you in a moment.

I hope you will understand why I feel the need to comment on the fact that early this morning bombs exploded outside two of our American Embassies in Africa. An explosion in Nairobi, Kenya, killed and wounded scores of people. We have reports that several Americans are among the dead. Another explosion in Dar es Salaam, Tanzania, also caused many casualties. At this time, there are no reports that any Americans were killed in that attack, although our Embassy appears to have been the target.

Both explosions caused large-scale damage to our Embassies and to surrounding buildings, as you may have already seen from the pictures coming in. Though the attacks appear to have been coordinated, no one has yet claimed responsibility for them.

As I speak, we have dispatched Defense Department and State Department-led emergency response teams to the region. The teams include medical personnel, disaster relief experts, criminal investigators, counter- terrorism specialists. We have taken appropriate security measures at our Embassies and military facilities throughout the region and around the world.

These acts of terrorist violence are abhorrent; they are inhuman. We will use all the means at our disposal to bring those responsible to justice, no matter what or how long it takes. Let me say to the thousands and thousands of hard-working men and women from the State Department and from our other Government agencies who serve us abroad in these Embassies, the work you do every day is vital to our security and prosperity. Your well-being is, therefore, vital to us, and we will do everything we can to assure that you can serve in safety.

To the families and loved ones of the American and African victims of these cowardly attacks, you are in our thoughts and prayers. Out of respect for those who lost their lives, I have ordered that the American flag be flown at half-staff at all Government buildings here at home and around the world. We are determined to get answers and justice.

Now, we are here to do something very important for America's long-term future today. I mentioned the Congressmen and Senators who played a leading role who are here. I'd like to also acknowledge those who are out there whose names I have, and if I make a mistake, stand up and be recognized. [*Laughter*] If I say you're here, and you're not, just let it go. [*Laughter*]

In addition to Senator DeWine and Chairman Goodling and Mr. Clay and Mr. McKeon, Mr. Kildee, we have here Congressman Barrett, Congressman Chaka Fattah, Representative Sheila Jackson Lee, Representative Dennis Kucinich, Representative Carrie Meek, Representative Dan Miller, Representative Patsy Mink, Representative Louis Stokes, Representative Steve LaTourette, Representative George Brown, Representative Paul Kanjorski, Congressman Bruce Vento, Congressman Donald Payne, and Congressman Tim Roemer with his own version of America's future in his lap. [*Laughter*]

I'd also like to thank, again, Alexis Herman and Erskine Bowles and all the people on my staff for their role in this. But one person above all who has been with me since 1991 and who shared my dream of consolidating this blizzard of Government programs into one grant that we could give a person who was unemployed or underemployed so that they could decide, as Mr. Antosy did, what to do with the help we were giving them on the theory that they would know their own best interest and be able to pursue it, and that is Gene Sperling, who has worked on this for years and years. This is—his heart is in this bill. And I want to thank him as well as all the staff people in Congress.

As Secretary Herman said, this bill fulfills principles for reform of our work force training program that I outlined in my first campaign for President over 6 years ago and that the Vice President set out in our National Performance Review. It is a model of what we should be doing, and also the way we did it is a model of how our Government ought to work. It was a truly bipartisan, American effort.

This morning we received some more good news about our economy. Even though the latest economic report shows the effects of the now settled GM strike, we still see that, over the past year, wages have risen at more than twice the rate of inflation, the fastest real wage growth for ordinary Americans in 20 years. This past month our unemployment rate held firm, in spite of the GM strike, at 4½ percent. For nearly a quarter century, not once had our Nation's unemployment rate gone below 5 percent. It's now been below 5 percent for 13 months in a row. We have low unemployment, low inflation, strong growth, and higher wages.

But to maintain this momentum, we must continue to change and move forward. Over the long run, in the face of daily new challenges in the global marketplace, we simply must press forward with the economic strategy outlined 5½ years ago: fiscal discipline, expanded trade, investment in our people and communities. To maintain fiscal discipline, we must save every penny of our surplus until we save the Social Security system. To maintain exports, we must immediately support the international efforts to stabilize our customers in Asia to reform and lift their economies. In recent weeks we have clearly seen that the crisis in Asia is having an impact on our economy. You can talk to any American grain farmer who will tell you that. For our economy to remain strong, therefore, we must pay our dues to the International Monetary Fund. To invest in our people we have to give all our people access to world-class education and training, beginning with our children before their school years and ending with people who have access to education throughout a lifetime.

The story Mr. Antosy told is a moving and heartening story. There are a lot of people in his position. In a dynamic global economy, more and more people, even if they stay with the same employer, will have to change the nature of their work several times over the course of a lifetime. It is, therefore, very important that every person who is willing to work hard to make the most of his or her own life should be able to become the success stories we celebrate with Benny Hernandez and James Antosy.

Therefore, we have to do more than we have been doing, even though we have been making progress. The vast majority of corporate managers say the number one prerequisite for continued prosperity is finding a way to fill all our high-skill jobs.

I'm telling you today, there are—even with the unemployment rate as low as it is, there are hundreds of thousands of jobs which are going begging that are high-wage, high-skill jobs, undermining the ability of our free enterprise economy to maximize its benefits to all our people to reach into all the urban neighborhoods and the rural communities and the places that it has not yet reached. Therefore, giving all Americans the tools they need to learn for a lifetime is critical to our ability to continue to grow.

We are making progress in building an America where every 8-year-old can read, every 12-year-old can log on to the Internet, every 18-year-old can go on to college. And today we celebrate a big step forward in making sure that every adult can keep on learning for a lifetime, where no disadvantaged child, no displaced worker, no welfare parent, no one willing to learn and work is left behind.

This is the crowning jewel of a lifetime learning agenda: the Work Force Investment Act to give all our workers opportunities for growth and advancement. It, as Mr. Goodling said and Mr. Clay said in specifying what was in the bill, has many things that will help millions of workers enhance our Nation's competitive age.

Let me just mention some of the things that are most important to me. It empowers workers, not Government programs, by offering training grants directly to them, so they can choose for

themselves what kind of training they want and where they want to get it. There was a time, decades ago, when Congress actually needed to pass specified training programs with specific purposes and mechanisms to implement them. But that time has long since passed. Almost every American is within driving distance of a community college or some other mechanism of advanced training. And almost every American has more than enough sense to decide what is in his or her best interest, given a little good helpful advice on the available alternatives.

The law streamlines and consolidates a tangle of training programs, therefore, into a single, commonsense system. And it also expands our successful model of one-stop career centers so people don't have to trot around to one different agency after another when they find themselves in the position that Mr. Antosy found himself in. It enhances accountability for tough performance standards for States and communities and training providers, even as it gives more flexibility to the States to develop innovative ways to serve our working people better.

It helps to create opportunities for disadvantaged youth. And I think that is terribly important. Everybody is concerned about the juvenile crime rate. We need to be concerned, therefore, about the number of juveniles that are out here on the street, out of school, not doing what could be done to give them a more constructive future.

And finally, it does two more things that I think are quite important. It has a real emphasis on helping people with disabilities prepare for employment, and it gives adults who need it literacy support to move ahead. You cannot train for a lot of these programs if you cannot read at an adequate level. And I think that is terribly important.

What all this amounts to is that we get to celebrate Labor Day a month early this year. At long last, we're giving our workers the tools they need to move quickly to 21st century jobs, higher incomes, and brighter futures. I thank all those on this stage, all those in this audience, and those who could not be here who have worked and waited for this day.

Let me also say that just a couple of minutes ago I had the chance to sign another bill that helps all Americans share in our prosperity, the Credit Union Membership Access Act. Credit unions serve a vital and unique purpose; they make sure financial services and credit are available to people of modest means. The law I signed strengthens them, helps them to withstand hard economic times, clarifies who can join, and ensures that those who are in credit unions now won't ever get locked out. It will help extend greater credit to those who need it most. It is also good for our economy.

Both these bills are bipartisan bills. They passed with overwhelming bipartisan majorities. They show what can happen when we can put our differences aside and put progress ahead of partisanship and people ahead of politics. That's a good thing because our plate is still full. In the few days remaining in this legislative session, we must still work together to save Social Security first; secure funding for the International Monetary Fund to stabilize our own economic growth; to pass a strong Patients' Bill of Rights, a very crowded education agenda built on excellence and opportunity, and an important

element of our environmental agenda to preserve our environment and grow the economy.

We can do all these things. And as we see today on this very happy occasion, when we do it, we strengthen our country and the future of the children over there with Congressman Roemer and all the others like them throughout America.

Thank you very much.

NOTE: The President spoke at 11:04 a.m. in the Rose Garden at the White House. In his remarks, he referred to job training beneficiary James Antosy, who introduced the President; and college student Benny Hernandez, a former gangmember. H.R. 1385, approved August 7, was assigned Public Law No. 105–220. H.R. 1151, the Credit Union Membership Access Act, also approved August 7, was assigned Public Law No. 105–219. The proclamation of August 7 on the victims of the bombing incidents in Africa is listed in Appendix D at the end of this volume.

Statement on Signing the Credit Union Membership Access Act
August 7, 1998

Today I am pleased to sign into law H.R. 1151, the "Credit Union Membership Access Act," which will ensure that millions of Americans have the choice of getting consumer financial services from a credit union.

Our credit unions are special institutions. Providing primarily consumer loans—for cars, education, home improvement and home purchases—and other financial services, like checking accounts and certificates of deposit, they are democratically controlled, member-owned cooperatives, with volunteer, unpaid directors. Because they are not-for-profit organizations, credit unions often can charge lower fees, require lower minimum deposits, and provide more personalized service.

Early this year, a decision by the Supreme Court created uncertainty about the future of credit unions in a case about how credit unions could draw their membership. This bill will re-

store membership flexibility to credit unions, allowing, for example, employees of a number of smaller companies or members of a number of churches to join together to form a credit union. The bill also provides important new safety and soundness reforms. Unfortunately, the bill does not include some important reforms to reaffirm the responsibility of credit unions to meet the needs of low- and moderate-income persons, and to assess their performance in meeting that goal. However, on balance, this bill will significantly strengthen credit unions, which provide so many benefits to consumers.

WILLIAM J. CLINTON

The White House,
August 7, 1998.

NOTE: H.R. 1151, approved August 7, was assigned Public Law No. 105–219.

Statement on Acquisition of the New World Mine
August 7, 1998

I am proud to announce completion today of a major initiative to preserve one of America's true crown jewels, Yellowstone National Park.

Two years ago, to protect the park from the potential ravages of mining, I announced an agreement to acquire the proposed New World Mine outside Yellowstone from its owner, Crown Butte Mines, Inc. Last year, with critical support from Senator Max Baucus, Congress appropriated $65 million for the acquisition. Over the past several months, the administration completed several intermediate steps, including an agreement with Crown Butte to ensure cleanup of contamination from nearly 100 years of mining near Yellowstone. Today, the New World Mine property was formally transferred to the U.S. Forest Service, completing this historic acquisition.

Yellowstone, America's first national park, is the heart of a magnificent landscape and ecosystem that we are working to restore and preserve for all time. Today's action culminates an extraordinary collaboration by the administration, the State of Montana, Crown Butte, and conservationists to protect both Yellowstone and the economy it sustains. Years from now, bison, wolves, and other wildlife will flourish, and visitors will enjoy Yellowstone in all its splendor.

Statement on House of Representatives Action on District of Columbia Appropriations Legislation
August 7, 1998

I am deeply disappointed that the District of Columbia appropriations bill passed by the House imposes unacceptable restrictions on our Nation's Capital City.

Early this morning, the House adopted a series of objectionable amendments. They include provisions to establish a school voucher program that would drain resources and attention from the hard work of reforming the District's public schools, to prohibit adoptions in the District by unmarried or unrelated couples, and to prohibit the use of Federal and local funds for needle exchange programs or to deny any funding in the bill to private agencies that operate such programs. These measures all undermine local control, are unacceptable, and should be dropped before Congress completes action on the bill.

I am concerned that other shortcomings in this bill undermine the District of Columbia's autonomy by imposing severe restrictions on local operations. For example, this bill would also bar the use of local District funds for abortions and strip local funds from the advisory neighborhood commissions, which are a foundation of local government.

I am also disappointed that the House fails to fund the much-needed economic revitalization plan for the District of Columbia. I urge Congress to provide appropriate resources for the economic development plan in order to capitalize the locally chartered National Capital Revitalization Corporation, which is key to the future economic growth of the Nation's Capital.

At a time when the District of Columbia has made enormous strides toward financial responsibility and the eventual return of self-government, it is wrong for Congress to turn the clock backward by imposing unwarranted restrictions on broad policymaking and on day-to-day decisionmaking at the local level.

The President's Radio Address
August 8, 1998

Good morning. I want to talk to you about the terrorist bombings yesterday that took the lives of Americans and Africans at our Embassies in Nairobi, Kenya, and Dar es Salaam, Tanzania; to tell you what we're doing and how we are combating the larger problem of terrorism that targets Americans.

Most of you have seen the horrible pictures of destruction on television. The bomb attack in Nairobi killed at least 11 Americans. In Dar es Salaam, no Americans lost their lives, but at least one was gravely wounded. In both places, many Africans were killed or wounded, and devastating damage was done to our Embassies and surrounding buildings.

To the families and friends of those who were killed, I know nothing I can say will make sense of your loss. I hope you will take some comfort in the knowledge that your loved ones gave their lives to the highest calling, serving our country, protecting our freedom, and seeking its blessings for others. May God bless their souls.

Late yesterday, emergency response teams, led by our Departments of State and Defense, arrived in Africa. The teams include doctors to tend to the injured, disaster relief experts to get our Embassies up and running again, a military unit to protect our personnel, and counterterrorism specialists to determine what happened and who was responsible.

Americans are targets of terrorism, in part, because we have unique leadership responsibilities in the world, because we act to advance peace and democracy, and because we stand united against terrorism. To change any of that—to pull back our diplomats and troops from the world's trouble spots, to turn our backs on those taking risks for peace, to weaken our opposition to terrorism—that would give terrorism a victory it must not and will not have.

Instead, we will continue to take the fight to terrorists. Over the past several years, I have intensified our effort on all fronts in this battle: apprehending terrorists wherever they are and bringing them to justice; disrupting terrorist operations; deepening counterterrorism cooperation with our allies and isolating nations that support terrorism; protecting our computer networks; improving transportation security; combating the threat of nuclear, chemical, and biological weapons; giving law enforcement the best counterterrorism tools available. This year I appointed a national coordinator to bring the full force of our resources to bear swiftly and effectively.

The most powerful weapon in our counterterrorism arsenal is our determination to never give up. In recent years, we have captured major terrorists in the far corners of the world and brought them to America to answer for their crimes, sometimes years after they were committed. They include the man who murdered two CIA employees outside its headquarters. Four years later we apprehended him halfway around the world, and a Virginia jury sentenced him to death. The mastermind of the World Trade Center bombing, who fled far from America, 2 years later we brought him back for trial in New York. And the terrorist responsible for bombing a Pan Am jet bound for Hawaii from Japan in 1982, we pursued him for 16 years. This June we caught him.

Some serious acts of terror remain unresolved, including the attack on our military personnel at Khobar Towers in Saudi Arabia; the bombing of Pan Am 103 over Lockerbie, Scotland; and now, these horrible bombings in Africa. No matter how long it takes or where it takes us, we will pursue terrorists until the cases are solved and justice is done.

The bombs that kill innocent Americans are aimed not only at them but at the very spirit of our country and the spirit of freedom. For terrorists are the enemies of everything we believe in and fight for: peace and democracy, tolerance and security.

As long as we continue to believe in those values and continue to fight for them, their enemies will not prevail. And our responsibility is great, but the opportunities it brings are even greater. Let us never fear to embrace them.

Thank you for listening.

NOTE: The President spoke at 10:06 a.m. from the Oval Office at the White House. The proclamation of August 7 on the victims of the bombing incidents in Africa is listed in Appendix D at the end of this volume.

Remarks on the Patients' Bill of Rights in Louisville, Kentucky
August 10, 1998

The President. Thank you. Thank you, Dr. Peeno. Thank you, Dr. Peters. I must say, after they have spoken there hardly needs to be much else said. I was profoundly moved, as I know all of you were, by what both these fine doctors said, and I thank them for giving their time and their lives to the work that they have discussed with us today. Yes, let's give them another hand. I thought they were great. [*Applause*] Thank you.

Thank you, Mr. Mayor, for your warm welcome and your leadership. Thank you, my good friend, Senator Ford, for all the years of wise counsel and advice, for your work for Kentucky, for its communities, its farmers, its people. Thank you, Governor Patton, for your friendship and for working for the education and health of your children. Thank you, Congressman Baesler, for voting with us and supporting the Patients' Bill of Rights, along with Senator Ford, for both of them.

I'd like to thank your Lieutenant Governor, and doctor, Stephen Henry, for being here today; and State Auditor Edward Hatchett; Secretary of State John Brown; my good friend Judge Dave Armstrong from the same little patch of ground that I'm from in Arkansas. I'd like to thank our Director of Personnel Management, Janice Lachance, for coming down with me here today. And I'd like to thank all of the health care professionals who are here.

Embassy Bombings in Kenya and Tanzania

Ladies and gentlemen, before we begin, I would like to just ask you to permit me to say a few words about the terrible tragedy that occurred at our Embassies in Tanzania and Kenya. Our hearts are heavy with the news that now 12 Americans, brave people who were working to build a better world and represent all of us abroad, have lost their lives. Somewhere around 200 Africans have died in those bombs now. We mourn their loss. We extend our sympathies to their loved ones. To the nations of Kenya and Tanzania, we thank them for their friendship to us. We grieve for the loss of their citizens.

I would just like to ask all of you to take just a few seconds of silence in their honor.

[*A moment of silence was observed.*]

Amen.

We go forward now. You should all know that our teams are on the ground in Africa. They're tending to the wounded. They're providing security. They are searching and finding evidence. We will do whatever we can to bring the murderers to justice.

I must have said this 100 times or more since I've been President, but I want to say it again because it bears special meaning today. The world we are living in and the world we are moving toward will allow us to move around the world more rapidly and more freely than ever before and to move information, ideas, and money around the world more rapidly, more freely than ever before. It will be a global society that I am convinced will bring all Americans our Nation's best years. But there has never been a time in human history when we have been free of the organized forces of destruction. And the more open the world becomes, the more vulnerable people become to those who are organized and have weapons, information, technology, and the ability to move.

We must be strong in dealing with this. We must not be deterred by the threat of other actions. There is no way out if we start running away from this kind of conduct. We have to build a civilized, open world for the 21st century.

Now, back to the important business at hand. For 5½ years now, I have had the great honor of serving you and working with others to strengthen America for a new century, a global information age. We have tried to look ahead with new ideas relevant to the times, but based on our oldest values of opportunity for all citizens, responsibility from all citizens, and a community of all our citizens.

Thanks to the hard work, ingenuity, and civic spirit of the American people and to this new direction in policy, this is a time of great prosperity and profound national strength for America. We have a lowest unemployment in 28 years, the lowest crime rate in 25 years, the smallest percentage of our people on welfare in 29 years, the smallest Federal Government in 35 years, the highest homeownership rate in history. Wages are rising at twice the rate of inflation. We have, as the Governor said, provided for the opportunity for health insurance for 5 million uninsured children. We have provided HOPE scholarships, worth about $1,500 in tax credits a year for the first 2 years of college, tax credits for other years of college, interest deduction on—tax deductions on the interest on student loans, more Pell grants, more work-study positions to open the doors of college to everyone.

Compared to 5½ years ago, our air and water are clearer; our food is safer; there are fewer toxic waste dumps. And soon—soon—we will have the first balanced budget since Neil Armstrong walked on the Moon in 1969.

Now, here's the problem with that. Usually, in our personal lives, our family lives, our work lives, and a nation's life, after a series of difficult years, when times get good you want to say, "Thank goodness. I'm tired. I need a rest. I want to sit back and enjoy this. I've been working like crazy for years, and now things are good. Give me a break. Let me have a break." [*Applause*] And you agree, see?

That is the natural human tendency; that would be a mistake. Why? The world is changing very rapidly, as we see every day in the way we work and live and relate to each other and the rest of the world. If someone had told you 5 or 6 years ago that today Japan would be having the problems it's having, would you have believed that? I say that not critically; it is a great country full of brilliant people, and they will come back. But it is a reminder that things change in a hurry and we must always be ready.

I think you can overdo sports analogies, but I can't resist one since I'm in Kentucky. [*Laughter*] The way the world works today is like the last 10 minutes of a basketball game between two really talented teams. Now, you think about last season and what the Kentucky Wildcats did to people who sat on the lead. Now, think about it. How many games were you behind in that you won? You can't afford to do it. The world is changing, so we should take the confidence, the resources, the good fortune that we gratefully have now and use it to meet the big challenges still facing the country. That is very important.

We've got to continue to work on economic growth, to stay with the strategy of fiscal discipline and open trade and investment in our people that has brought us this far. And we have to prove we can extend the benefits of this recovery to people who haven't felt it yet, from the inner cities to Appalachia.

We have to continue to lead the world toward peace and freedom. We can't withdraw from the world. Witness the events of the last few days. We have to stand against the spread of chemical, biological, and nuclear weapons. We have to stand against the reach of international organizations of crime and terror and narcotrafficking. We have to stand against the destruction of racial and ethnic and religious hatred, against the threat of global environmental and health challenges.

Here at home we have to honor our obligations to future generations. And the most important thing we should do is to set aside every penny of the surplus we're going to have on October 1st until we have saved the Social Security system for the 21st century when the baby boomers require it.

We have to make sure all of our people have a chance in tomorrow's world by making our elementary and secondary schools the best in the world. We need smaller classes, more highly trained teachers. We need modernized schools connected to the Internet. We need schools where there is discipline and good behavior and no gangs, guns, and drugs.

We need high standards and accountability and great flexibility in meeting them. We need to prove we can protect our environment and still grow our economy. We have to continue to prove we can reach across the lines that divide us in this increasingly diverse country and be one America.

A good way to view this moment in history, I believe, is through the lens of the First Lady's theme that she came up with for our Millennium Project as we look toward how we will mark the changing of the centuries and the changing of 1,000 years: "Honor the past; imagine the future." That's what we should be doing.

We have come here today to talk about a very important part of one other big challenge we face: how we can put progress over partisanship, people over politics, to expand access to quality health care to every American. Nothing is more critical to the securities of our families, the strength of our communities. Health is something we take for granted until we or our loved ones don't have it anymore. But people like the two fine doctors who talked to us deal with folks like that every day. It isn't a partisan issue, and I appreciated the fact that they made that clear. You know, when someone gets sick and comes in to see one of these two doctors and fills out a form, there is no box that says, "Republican, Democrat, or independent."

Health care is being revolutionized in America. Most of the changes are good. Stunning biomedical breakthroughs pose the possibilities of vaccines or cures for our deadliest enemies, from diabetes to AIDS to Alzheimer's. Before you know it, this genome project will be finished, and we'll be able to decode the genetic structure of every person. Mothers will know when they bring their babies home from the hospital what the potential problems are that those babies have, and some of it will be troubling to know, but most of it will be good because they'll be able to avoid all kinds of problems that might otherwise have come to their children.

It will be unbelievable what's going to happen to health care in the 21st century. There have already been examples of nerve transplantations in laboratory animals where their spines have been severed and now their lower limbs are moving again. It will be an amazing time.

The trick is how to extend affordable coverage of all these miracles and basic preventive health care to all Americans. That's really how the managed care revolution began. You know, when I became President, for the last 10 years health care costs had been going up at 3 times the rate of inflation. We were spending approximately 4 percent more of our national income—and at the time, that was about $240 billion a year—than any other country on Earth on health care, even though we were one of the few industrialized countries that still have a significant percentage of our people without any health insurance. That was an unsustainable trend.

Since 1990 the number of people in managed care has nearly doubled. Today most Americans, 160 million of us, are in managed care plans. And as has already been said, I think, on balance, there have been a lot of good things to come out of managed care to make it more affordable, more accessible, to make the resources go further. But you've heard these doctors say that some very, very costly errors have been made by putting the dollar over the person.

I'll never forget the people that I have met and the stories they've told me. I met a woman named Mary Kuhl, from Kansas City, whose husband died. He needed specialized, urgent heart surgery. By the time he got the clearance to get it, it was too late. I met Mick Fleming, whose sister died of breast and lung cancer after she was denied treatment that she was later determined to have been entitled to. I met a billings manager that the doctor referred to, who herself bears the scars of having to turn away patients. I think in some ways, of all the people that have talked to me, she was the most moving of all, because she had to deliver the "no" face to face.

Now, when the bottom line is more important than patients' lives, when families have nowhere to turn, when their loved ones are harmed by bad decisions, when specialist care is denied, when emergency care is not covered, we have to act. That's why you heard, at the grassroots level in America, Republicans and Democrats, conservatives and liberals, even people who think normally the Government should not do anything that can fairly be done by the private sector, have developed this overwhelming grassroots consensus that we need a Patients' Bill of Rights in America.

I've done what I could administratively, and some of you are probably covered by decisions that I and my administration have made. I acted to extend the protections of the Patients' Bill of Rights to 85 million Americans who get health care through Federal plans. In June I extended it to 40 million people who receive Medicare. Last month we put in place new rapid appeals for the 3 million veterans who receive health care through the Department of Veterans Affairs. Last week the Department of Defense issued a directive to all military bases throughout the world, extending protections to 8 million service men and women and their families at nearly 600 hospitals and clinics all around the globe.

We are already extending many patient protections, such as the right to a specialist and continuity of care, to Federal workers. And that's why Janice Lachance is here with me today, because we are announcing that we are now requiring that 350 health plans that serve Federal employees to repeal the gag rules that keep doctors from telling patients all their health care options, not just the cheapest ones.

Now, a lot of States are acting in this area, too. Kentucky has a patients' bill of rights. But I can tell you because of the way the laws work, there is no substitute for a national law. We cannot provide protection for all Americans. We will leave many, many tens of millions behind unless we have strong, bipartisan legislation that covers every American.

Now, for 9 months, I've worked in good faith with lawmakers of both parties to pass a strong, enforceable, bipartisan bill of rights. We are fighting for a bill supported by both Democrats and Republicans, and again, I thank Wendell Ford and Scotty Baesler for their support.

Now, for 9 months, the leadership of the majority party in Congress has resisted taking any action at all. They have listened to those with an interest in preserving the status quo, rather than the clear call of the public interest we have heard echoing across this hall today. Now public demand is rising, and the Republican leadership has discovered the need to act. So the House passed a plan last month, and the Senate Republicans have offered a similar bill. But these bills would give patients and their families a false sense of security.

You've already heard some of the comments. But this is very important, that when everybody is calling for a Patients' Bill of Rights and both parties pushing proposals, how can the American people know what a real one is? Well, that's what this chart is about over here. And maybe— Jerry, would you hand me the chart? You don't have to bring the stand; just bring that chart up here. I'll hold it. He said he's the Vanna White of Louisville here. [*Laughter*] I'm not going to discuss that. [*Laughter*]

I want you to look at this, because that's what this is all about. A real Patients' Bill of Rights at least continues and should strengthen the medical privacy provisions in place today. In the age of computer databases and the Internet, we should strengthen the privacy of medical records. Don't you want yours private? Don't you? [*Applause*] I have a proposal that would do this.

The House Republican bill would dramatically increase the number of people who can see your medical records without your knowledge or consent. It overturns privacy protections already on the books in 20 States, including Kentucky. The bill would just wipe them from the books, and that is wrong. So here's the first test, protecting medical privacy laws: the Repub-

lican plan, no; our bipartisan proposal—and I should say we do have Republican support, including a fine doctor from Iowa, Dr. Ganske, in the Congress, for the bipartisan bill.

Second, a real Patients' Bill of Rights will guarantee the right to see specialists that you need. To reap the full rewards of modern medicine, you must have the ability to see, for example, a neurologist or a cardiologist if that is what is medically indicated. The congressional bills don't give you that right. Ours does. That's the second no-yes.

The third issue, a real Patients' Bill of Rights guarantees you won't lose your doctor in the middle of a medical treatment even if your employer switches health plans. This is a big deal! Now, the GOP leadership bills don't do that. An insurance company could switch obstetricians in the 6th month of pregnancy or drop your oncologist in the middle of chemotherapy just because your employer switches plans.

A real Patients' Bill of Rights makes sure that health plans don't secretly give incentives to doctors to limit medical care. Now, the Republican leadership plan would permit that. Ours would not.

A real Patients' Bill of Rights guarantees you the right to emergency room care when and where you need it. When you are wheeled into an emergency room, you shouldn't have to start negotiating with your health plan.

This is the financial incentive; this is keeping your doctor through critical treatments—no, yes; no, yes. Emergency room—theirs, no; ours, yes.

A real Patients' Bill of Rights holds health care plans accountable for the harm patients face if they are denied critical care. Now, that's important. If a doctor denies you the health care you need, you can get help to pay for lost wages or medical costs today. If an HMO denies you the care you need, under the congressional leadership bill, you won't get any help at all. Now, if you have rights with no remedies, are they rights? How would you feel—what would you say to me?

What they're saying is, "Oh, this bipartisan bill, they have all these remedies, and it's just going to be a mess with a bunch of lawyers. Isn't that awful?" And a lot of people say, "Well, I don't like lawyers. I don't like lawsuits. Who wants to be in court?" Sounds pretty good.

Let me ask you this: How would you react if I gave a speech tomorrow that said, "My fellow Americans, I love the Bill of Rights. I love the freedom of speech, the freedom of assembly, the freedom of religion, the right to travel. I love all those Bill of Rights. But I don't like all these lawsuits. We got too many of them in America. Therefore, I have proposed to amend the Constitution so that no one can ever sue to enforce the right to free speech, free assembly, free practice of religion, or any other of the rights that have kept our country strong for 220 years." You would say——

Audience members. No way! [*Laughter*]

The President. So when you talk about remedies, do you have rights without remedies? I think we've seen enough there. That's a big issue.

A real Patients' Bill of Rights should apply to every plan, every single one. The Republican plan leaves out—listen to this—as many as 100 million people, many of them working for small businesses; 100 million people would still be under the present system, 100 million people who need our help. It is wrong. If we're going to do this, I don't want to leave 100 million Americans behind, and I don't think you do either, even if you would be covered. That's not right.

So you need to remember here, it isn't the title, "Patients' Bill of Rights"; it is the specifics. What are the specifics? Medical privacy: yes on our bill, no on theirs. Access to specialists: yes on our bill, no on theirs. Assuring that accountants don't make arbitrary medical decisions: yes on our bill, no on theirs—a big deal to doctors, because they know what happens to patients. Providing real emergency room protections: yes on our bill, no on theirs. Holding health plans accountable if patients are harmed: yes on our bill, no on theirs. Protecting patients from secret financial incentives: yes on our bill, no on theirs. Keeping your doctor through critical treatments—huge issue—I saw a lot of you nodding your heads when I said that you'd lose your doctor in the middle of your treatment: yes on our bill, no on theirs. And then covering all health plans, that is, all Americans: yes on our bill, no on theirs.

That's what's at issue. This is not about politics. This is not about party. This is about a crying need for the American people, and it's time we did the right thing. We ought to do it now, in September, when Congress comes back.

I want to thank the American Medical Association, the American Nurses Association, the American College of Emergency Room Physicians, and so many others. I have to tell you, we need a bill of rights, not a bill of goods. We need a law, not another loophole. If I get that other bill of rights, I will be forced to veto it, and I will.

Now, I will say again, this is not a partisan issue any place in the country but Washington, DC. I believe Republicans and independents are just as much for this bill out here in the real world as Democrats are. Nothing should be less partisan than the quality of health care our people receive. We're a little more than 500 days from that new millennium, but there's only a handful of days left in this session of Congress. We cannot let this moment of opportunity be remembered as a time of missed opportunity.

Think of what I said about the basketball game. Think about how fast things are changing. Think about how fast things can change in your life, in your family's life, in your business' life, and in the life of our Nation. Now is the time to say, we thank God for the good fortune we have, but we are using it to look forward to the future, to make a better future, to meet the big challenges of this country. And we ought to begin next month, when Congress returns, with the Patients' Bill of Rights.

Thank you, and God bless you all.

NOTE: The President spoke at 11:35 a.m. at the Commonwealth Convention Center. In his remarks, he referred to Dr. Linda Peeno, cancer survivor, who introduced the President; Dr. Kenneth Peters, president, Kentucky Medical Association; Mayor Jerry E. Abramson of Louisville; Gov. Paul E. Patton and Lt. Gov. Stephen L. Henry of Kentucky; Kentucky State Auditor Edward B. Hatchett, Jr.; Kentucky Secretary of State John Y. Brown III; Judge/Executive David L. Armstrong, Jefferson County Commission; and Janice R. Lachance, Director, Office of Personnel Management.

Remarks at a Victory in Kentucky Luncheon in Louisville
August 10, 1998

Thank you. Thank you very much, ladies and gentlemen. You know, unfortunately, I don't get to run for office anymore. [*Laughter*] And therefore, I'm supposed to appear above the fray and unpolitical. But I have some experience in this area, and I would say, if I asked you—if I gave everybody here a piece of paper and a pencil and I said I want you to write down why Scotty Baesler believes he should be the Senator, I believe you could all write something down now, couldn't you? [*Laughter*] That is the definition of a good political speech. Let's give him a hand. [*Applause*] That was a great, great thing to do. Thank you.

You know, I love this State, and the mayor almost made fun of me—and the Governor—for coming here so much to Kentucky. I don't want to apologize, but I have been coming here a long time now and a lot of times since I've been President. And this State has been very good to the Vice President and to me, and I want to say a special word of thanks for that, for the support and the electoral votes we received from the people of Kentucky in both our runs. On behalf of the First Lady and Al and Tipper, all of us, we're very grateful to Kentucky for that.

I want to thank the Governor for being my friend and for doing such a wonderful job. I want to say to Steve Henry and Charlie Owen, I think you both have bright futures, and you've shown a lot of character by the way you've rallied behind Scotty Baesler and the idea of the Democratic Party and the principles for which you made your race. And I appreciate it very, very much.

I want to thank all the other officials who are here, including my longtime friend and fellow Arkansan, your county judge/executive, David Armstrong; your State party chair, Ron McCloud. And we've got a congressional candidate here, Chris Gorman. Chris, stand up there; good for you for running.

Where's Fred Cowen? Fred, stand up; stand up there. When I was a young man starting out in politics 20-plus years ago, Fred Cowen was then an Arkansan. And on October 3d, 1991, when I ran—announced my candidacy for President, there were only two elected officials

from outside Arkansas who were on the steps of the old statehouse with me, and one of them was Fred Cowen. So I want you to help him get elected here. It would mean a lot to me personally to do that.

Senator Ford, I'm going to miss you—and you do look good. [*Laughter*] We've all had that experience. I knew I was sort of on the other side of the divide when an 80-year-old woman came up to me that I'd known many years and looked up at me and said, "Bill, you look so good for a man your age." [*Laughter*]

I'd also like to thank one other person who is here. I was a Governor, you know, forever and a day. I was a Governor for 12 years. And then I got beat once, so I was out for 2 years. So over a 14-year span, I had the privilege of working with five Kentucky Governors. You know, you had that one-term deal then, so all I had to do was hold on to my job, and I'd always know somebody new from Kentucky if I'd just wait around. [*Laughter*] But one of them who was a particular friend of mine is John Y. Brown, and he's here today, and I thank him very much for coming. Thank you, Governor. Thank you.

Now, look, Scotty has given the speech, but let me tell you, the stakes are very high. The issue he mentioned, many others I could mention, they depend upon having people in the Congress who will do the right thing. Now, just ask yourself—just take the three things he mentioned that are in the past, and one in the future, and think about the issues we'll be facing. Think about the minimum wage, the family and medical leave law, the crime bill, and the Patients' Bill of Rights. What do all those things have in common? The real beneficiaries of that legislation are the ordinary folks in this country, the people who work here at this place, not those of us who are sitting here at these tables.

The real beneficiaries are the people who are not organized, who could never afford to come to a luncheon like this, but who are the heart and soul of this country, who get up every day and do the best they can at their job. They do the best they can to raise their children and take care of their parents. They pay their taxes. They fight our wars. They do all the work in this country. And all they want is a fair deal.

And when things change as much as they've been changing in how we work and live and relate to each other and the rest of the world, the job of the Government is to take our oldest values and hook them to new ideas so that we can move into the future and make it a better time than the past.

You go back through the whole history of this country, and you see that the country has always been about certain basic things. It's been about freedom for responsible citizens and widening the circle of freedom. We redefine it quite a lot. When we started out, you had to be a white male property owner to vote. We didn't even let all the white men vote when we started. We said, "All people are created equal," and then we said, "Oh, by the way, here's our definition." So we've had to do a lot of work on freedom.

It's about opportunity. I'm grateful for the fact that there are 16 million new jobs and that we have the lowest unemployment rate in 28 years. But as Congressman Baesler said, there are still a lot of people who are working hard and don't have enough to get by. There are still some places in this country—inner-city neighborhoods, places like Appalachia, and places in South Texas, Native American reservations—where they don't know there's been an economic recovery. It's about widening the circle of opportunity.

And it's about deepening the bonds of our community, the idea that we want to live in a country where not only we are treated fairly, but everyone else is, too; where not only we have a chance to raise our children and build our families and our communities, but everyone else does, too.

So you think about the crime bill. The crime bill is about freedom and community, because if you're scared to death when your child goes to school, if you don't feel secure on your own street, you're not really free.

You think about the minimum wage. It's about opportunity and community. And by the way, it's always turned out to be good economics, because if working people are making enough money, then they'll be spending it with other people who are in business.

If you take the Patients' Bill of Rights—and it's the most important thing now, because it's something we still have to do—160 million Americans are in managed care. Now, I don't think that's a bad thing, because before managed care, inflation in health care costs had gone up at 3 times the rate of inflation. That was unsustainable. It was going to bankrupt businesses; it was going to bankrupt families; it was going to take too much of our money away.

But any device for saving money should be hooked to the values of the mission. The mission of the health care system is to take care of people. And the problem with managed care is that there are no limits that express the values of the country.

Now, this Patients' Bill of Rights, here's what it does—let me just tell you what it does, because it says a lot. I could go through all these other issues, but I'm going to take my cue from the Congressman, because here's an issue—every single issue—keep in mind, every single issue, he's on one side, his opponent is on the other.

This Patients' Bill of Rights says you ought to have a right to a specialist if you've got a medical condition which requires a specialist. We had a lot of breast cancer survivors at our former event. Why? Well, one reason is, they know that it makes a big difference, if you're a woman with breast cancer and you have to have a mastectomy, whether you have a specialist or a general surgeon. Just one example. We say yes; they say no.

Two, you ought to have a right to emergency room care in emergency conditions where the nearest emergency room is. And you just think about it. If one of your kids gets in a car wreck, and they get hauled into a hospital, and your children are on life supports, do you want the doctors to have to wait to call an insurance company to get approval before they start taking care of them? I don't think so. Just ask yourself what you want. Most of us wouldn't have to worry about it. Millions of Americans do. Should we change that? We say yes; they say no.

Here's another thing that happens. Suppose you've got an HMO, and your employer, as he or she ought to have the right to do, has to change insurers at a certain time. Should they be able to make you change your doctor if you're in the middle of treatment? If you're a woman who is 7 months pregnant or 6 months pregnant and you've been going to the same doctor all the time, should they be able to force you to change obstetricians? What if you're in the process—what if you've got some sort of lymphoma or cancer, you're taking chemotherapy, and you're in the middle of treatment? Should they be able to make you change your oncologist, or should there be protections against that? We say, yes, there should be protections, and you ought to be able to complete your treatment before you can be required to change doctors. They say no.

Should you have real protections of privacy for your medical records that are even stricter than the ones we've got now, or should we make your records available to more people? They say, make them available to more people. We say, not without your permission. We think, in this computerized age where everything about us is on a computer, we need more privacy protections, not fewer.

See, all this is about the world we're moving into. And interestingly enough, there are 43 managed care firms supporting our bill. Why? Because they're out there doing the right thing already, and they're being subject to unfair competition because they're determined to take care of people. And they don't think it's right to have somebody else get a financial advantage with them just because they've got enough power to kill a bill in Congress.

So this is about the future. Man, I'm telling you, most of the medical stories you're going to be hearing in the next 10 years are going to be good medical stories, unbelievable advances in medical research. Last year—how many people do you know, how many friends or family members have you had in your life who were confined to wheelchairs because of spinal cord injuries? Last year, for the first time ever, a laboratory animal got movement back in its lower limbs, after its spine had been shattered, because of a nerve transplant.

How many people do you know whose child had some sort of predisposition to a medical condition that, if the parents had known when the baby went home from the hospital, they wouldn't have suffered as much as they did? Within 5 or 10 years every mother will get a genetic code map of their children's bodies, how it works, what the pluses and minuses are. Most of the medical stories are going to be good stories. And there's going to have to be business management brought to the medicine like everything else. But you have to put people first.

You know, Scotty is independent. We don't agree on everything. When he doesn't agree with me, he votes the other way. And most of the time, I imagine, his constituents agreed more with him than me. That's what Representatives are for. But I'll tell you something, I never had any doubt that he was the same person in Washington that he was in Kentucky and that he wasn't up there doing rhetoric to try to inflame people for no good reason. This election is about whether we're going to put the progress of the country over the partisanship of Washington, whether we're going to put the people's interest over the interest of politics, whether we're going to try to make America more unified as we go into the future or more divided.

And you really can see this Patients' Bill of Rights as a metaphor for every other issue. I could give you a speech about education, about how to preserve the environment and grow the economy, about how we're going to deal with the problems so horribly manifested in what we went through with our Embassies in Africa and all the losses of life. But every issue for the future—you just remember—the right answer is new ideas, old values. Take care of most people, and those of us that are doing pretty well are going to do fine anyway. We'll figure out how to do fine if we've got a system that takes care of most ordinary Americans.

That's what this guy will do. He'll be a great Senator for the 21st century. I hope you will help him. I hope you will help Chris Gorman. We need every person we can in the Congress who believes in what Scotty stood up here and talked about today. And I thank you for being here to help him.

God bless you. Thank you.

NOTE: The President spoke at 1:20 p.m. at the Seelbach Hotel. In his remarks, he referred to Representative Scotty Baesler, candidate for the U.S. Senate, and his primary election opponents, Lt. Gov. Stephen L. Henry and Charlie Owen; Mayor Jerry E. Abramson of Louisville; Gov. Paul E. Patton of Kentucky; Chris Gorman, candidate for Kentucky's Third Congressional District; Fred Cowen, candidate for Jefferson County judge/executive; and John Y. Brown, former Kentucky Governor.

Letter to President's Information Technology Advisory Committee Co-Chairmen Bill Joy and Ken Kennedy
August 10, 1998

Dear Bill and Ken:

Thank you for your Interim Report advising me of the President's Information Technology Advisory Committee's (PITAC) findings and recommendations on future directions for federal support of information technology research and development. The Vice President joins me in thanking you and the other PITAC members for your guidance on how best to preserve America's commanding lead in computing and communications technology.

Our nation's economic future and the welfare of our citizens depend on continued advances and innovations in the information technologies that have produced so many remarkable developments in science, engineering, medicine, business, and education. Sustained prosperity for America requires a steady stream of technological innovation. The knowledge-based society of the next century makes our participation in the front ranks of research essential if our nation is to capture the gains of scientific and technological advances. Half of our economic productivity in the last half century is attributable to science and technological innovation. One third of our economic growth since 1992 has been spurred by businesses in the computing and communications industries. Information technology sustains our global competitiveness, provides opportunities for lifelong learning, and expands our ability to solve critical problems affecting our environment, health care and national security.

Through my Administration's initiatives in computing and communications, such as the Next Generation Internet, the Defense Advanced Research Projects Agency's support for breakthrough technologies, the Department of Energy's high performance computing programs, and the National Science Foundation's Knowledge and Distributed Intelligence emphasis, we have laid the foundations for the technological advances that promise to profoundly transform the next millennium. Yet, to maintain this momentum, we must adequately fund critical federal investments in fundamental research. In my recent speech at the Massachusetts Institute of Technology, I proposed significant increases in computing and communications research. Your proposed research agenda will help guide Dr. Neal Lane, my Assistant for Science and Technology, in developing a detailed plan for my review.

For six years in a row, I have proposed budget increases to sustain American leadership across the frontiers of scientific knowledge. Most recently, I was pleased to sign into law the National Science Foundation Authorization Act of 1998, which will create new knowledge, spur innovations, foster future breakthroughs, and provide cutting-edge research facilities that will produce the finest American scientists and engineers for the 21st century. I am hopeful that the Congress and my Administration can work together to advance the leading edges of computational science to help us discover new technologies that can make this a better world. We have a duty—to ourselves, to our children, and to future generations—to make these and other farsighted investments in science and technology to take America into the next century well-equipped for the challenges and opportunities that lie ahead.

Sincerely,

WILLIAM J. CLINTON

NOTE: An original was not available for verification of the content of this letter.

Remarks at a Unity '98 Dinner in Chicago, Illinois
August 10, 1998

Thank you very much. First of all, I want to thank all the previous speakers for saying everything that needs to be said; I am free to say whatever I like. I am deeply indebted, as all of you know, to this city and this State for many things, the most important of which is clearly the First Lady, who asked me to be remembered to all of you tonight.

I have a picture on my wall in my office of Hillary and me on St. Patrick's Day in 1992 in Chicago—that was the night of the primaries in Illinois and Michigan, the night we knew that unless the wheel completely ran off, I would probably become the nominee of our party. And from that day and before to this, no place has been better to us and to the Vice President and to our whole team than the city of Chicago and the State of Illinois. And I am profoundly grateful to all of you, and I thank you for it.

I also want to say a word of appreciation to Steve Grossman, who has done a magnificent job. I thank Congressman Rangel, who has to put on his uniform every day. He's now in the most severe combat he's been in since the Korean war, I think, with the Republicans in the House, but he holds up his end right well. And I thank you, Charles. I'm proud of you in every way.

I want to thank Secretary Daley, who will soon get over being 50. [*Laughter*] Oh, to be 50 again. [*Laughter*] It's all a matter of perspective, you know. I want to thank Mayor Daley for his leadership here and his support and friendship. I thank Senator Durbin for many things and for being so courageous in his leadership to protect our children against the dangers of tobacco, to keep our streets and our communities safe, and many other things. I want to say a little more about Carol Moseley-Braun in a moment.

I want to thank Reverend Jesse Jackson for being a good friend of my family in personal as well as political ways, and for doing a superb job for our country as our Special Envoy to Africa, a very important part of America's future. Thank you, Reverend Jackson, for doing that.

Now, you heard all the politics. I would like to talk a little bit about—specifically about Illi-

nois and how if fits into the larger picture of America and our future. I ran for President because I honestly believed our country was not doing what was necessary to prepare for a new century, a new millennium, a completely new way of living and working and relating to each other and the rest of the world. And I think that what we have sought to do is best captured in the theme the First Lady picked for our Millennium Project, the things we are doing over the next 2½ years to celebrate the coming of a new century and a new millennium. The theme is "Honoring the past; imagining the future."

And that is what we have tried to do: to offer new ideas based on our oldest values; to deepen the meaning of our freedom; to widen the circle of opportunity; to build the bonds of our Union stronger; to help America be the strongest force for peace and freedom and prosperity in the world; to give our children—all our children—the best chance to live out their dreams any generation of children has ever known. That is what we have worked on doing.

Now, all those words sound good, and it is an important thing, words. They spark ideas. They spark the human spirit. They motivate people to act. But in the end, you have to turn the words into action. And I would like to just give you one example.

The lion's share of credit for the economic statistics the Vice President reeled off belongs to the American people, to their hard work, their ingenuity, their good citizenship. But the policies of this administration have plainly played a role in giving people the tools to do what has been done and creating the conditions for success.

If it hadn't been for Carol Moseley-Braun or Glenn Poshard or Charlie Rangel or Al Gore, the economic plan in 1993—which drove interest rates down, drove the deficit down, got investment up, expanded our commitment to promote economic opportunity in the inner cities, including in Chicago—would not have passed, because it passed by one vote in both Houses, because every single member of the other party voted against it. And I want to tell you that I am proud to be a member of my party and proud to be an ardent supporter of the reelection of Senator Carol Moseley-Braun and the election of Glenn Poshard.

There is—I was told today when I came into Chicago that Congressman Poshard's opponent has an ad on attacking him for voting for our 1993 economic plan, claiming it was a big tax increase, neglecting to point out that income taxes were raised on about two-tenths of a percent of the American people, that 5 times as many people in Illinois got a tax cut as got a tax increase—working families who need it the most—and that that bill lowered the deficit 92 percent before the bipartisan balanced budget agreement passed and, therefore, was the single most important vote to the economic recovery America enjoys today.

I think Glenn Poshard should thank his opponent for advertising for him. It's a good difference between Republicans and Democrats. They're still trying to mischaracterize the bill that brought America back. And I hope you will send a message on election day, by reelecting Carol Moseley-Braun and electing Glenn Poshard, that Illinois likes this economy and will support people who brought it about.

We have the lowest crime rate in 25 years. The crime bill of 1994 played a major role in that, with 100,000 police on the street and grants to communities like Chicago not just to punish people but to give our young people something to say yes to, so that more communities could have more programs like your after-school programs here and your summer school programs here. And most of the members, not all but most of the members of the other party voted against it. Carol Moseley-Braun and Glenn Poshard voted for it.

And so, if you like the fact that Chicago has all these new police officers under the crime bill and you like what has been done here to make the streets safer, I think you should show that you like it when words are turned into action by voting to reelect Carol Moseley-Braun and to elect Glenn Poshard. I think these are the kinds of things that you have to say to people.

Now, as the Vice President said, we have to decide what we're going to do with the good times we have. We are sobered and humbled when our friends in Asia, who once we thought would never have any economic problems again, have their own struggles. But we should be humbled because, when things change fast, the ground can move, and the world is changing very fast.

We are heartbroken at what has happened in Africa to our Embassies, the tragic loss of life of American public servants and the more than 200 Africans who have died now and thousands wounded because some terrorist criminal wanted to hurt America. But this reminds us that freedom is a precious thing, prosperity is a wonderful thing, but in a dynamic world they bring responsibilities.

And this election year should not be about negative 30-second ads, or all the mean things they've said about me or the rest of you, or any mean thing we can say back to them. It really ought to be about what do we do now. We have been given the gift of this moment of prosperity, which gives us confidence and energy. What do we do with it?

What have you done in the times in your life when you thought everything was hunky-dory? After things have been tough—and they were tough for America for a long time—the natural thing to do is to sort of say, "Man, I have been working like crazy. This is great. Leave me alone. Give me a break."

That was really, in fairness, the import behind the quote by the Speaker that the Vice President read, "We don't really have to do anything. We just have to avoid another shutdown and get out of town. And things are so good, and we've got more money than the Democrats do. We'll be fine in the election. We'll worry about all of this tomorrow."

And that is playing into what is often the dominant feeling in human nature. I suggest to you it would be a mistake for us to have that attitude today as a nation and that instead we ought to say, "Hey, we may not get a time this good again for a while. Let's take this time to think about the big, long-term challenges this country faced, and let's go on and face them and deal with them now. If not now, when? If we can't do it now, when will we ever have a better time?" And that's what we ought to be thinking about now.

So I'll tell you what I think they are, in no particular order—you may have different rank order. They've been alluded to already, but let me just tell you because this is why it's important to have people in the positions of Congressmen and Senators who will make good decisions about this.

One of the biggest challenges this country is going to face—every advanced country is going to face it—is when all the baby boomers retire. I know; I'm the oldest of the baby boomers. I'm the oldest man my age in America now. [*Laughter*] Think about that. Because we are the biggest group of Americans ever to live, until this group of kids that just started school last year, when we retire, at present rates of retirement, birth rates, and immigration rates, for the first time since Social Security came in there will only be about two people working for every one person eligible for Social Security.

The system we have, that has literally on its own lifted half of our elderly people out of poverty, is unsustainable as it is. But it has done a lot of good for the elderly, for the disabled, for children whose parents die when they're still children. So one of the things that we have to do—and we ought to do it early next year— we ought to stop fooling around with it. The longer we wait, the harder it will be. We are prosperous now. We are confident now. We should reform Social Security to preserve its best characteristics and make sure it will survive into the 21st century.

You have to decide, who do you think you want to do that? And don't you want somebody that will come in there and keep the very best of the system but have the courage to tell you what changes have to be made now?

The same thing is true of Medicare. We have to do that. It's a big challenge. That's why I have said, "Let's don't spend any of this surplus on a spending program or a tax cut that I like, even something I would dearly love to do. Let's don't do that until we know we have done what is necessary to save Social Security for the 21st century."

Now, it's election year. It's popular to say, "I want to give you a tax cut," or "I'm going to give you a new program, and we're going to have a surplus, and it's projected to be such and such." Well, let me tell you, we won't even have the surplus until October 1st. And we've been waiting for 29 years to get out of the red. I'd just kind of like to look at the black ink for just a few months—[*laughter*]—before we go squander this money that we don't even have yet.

And I think down deep inside you and every other responsible person in Illinois, Republican, Democrat, or independent, knows that's the right thing to do. So go out and say, we ought to save Social Security first, and you're for that.

I think everybody in America knows we've got the best system of higher education in the world. And one of my proudest achievements as President is that, working with the Congress, we've opened the doors wider than ever before with the HOPE scholarships, the Pell grants, the work-study grants, letting people deduct the interest on their student loans, all of the things that we've done.

No one believes we've got the best elementary and secondary education in the world for all our children yet. No one believes that, because it's not true. But we need it. And I have given this Congress an agenda for smaller classes in the early grades and more teachers and modernized schools, whether we're repairing old schools or building new ones, and connecting all the classrooms to the Internet and providing for better trained teachers and raising standards and trying to support things like the mayor's reforms here in Chicago, including more after-school programs and more summer school programs.

And that school construction and repair initiative would not be a part of my program if it weren't for Carol Moseley-Braun. And it ought to pass, and if you reelect her, you'll send a loud message to Washington that you believe it ought to. It's an important issue.

We just glanced over the Patients' Bill of Rights today. You know, there are 160 million Americans in managed care. And when Hillary and I told the American people we had to find a way, because managed care was growing, to allow people to be in managed care to control costs, but we ought to make health care affordable and available and quality for all Americans, we were attacked by our adversaries, saying we wanted to have the Government take over health care.

I'll tell you something interesting. When they attacked me for that, 40 cents on the dollar of health care dollars came from public sources. Do you know what it is today? Forty-seven cents, not 40. Do you know why? Because employers cannot afford to buy health insurance, so they don't cover their employees, and more and more people even in the work force are eligible for Government-funded programs today.

But 160 million Americans in Medicare—our Patients' Bill of Rights is the next big item on the health care agenda. Why? Because we think that it's a good thing to manage health care costs and control them, but you ought to be able to go to an emergency room if you get hurt, without having to lay there on the gurney. How would you feel if somebody in your family were in a car wreck, lying in an emergency room on a gurney, and you're trying to call the insurance company to get authorization? We believe if somebody needs a specialist, they ought to be able to get a specialist. And if the doctor believes that, he ought to be free to say so. That's what we believe.

We believe if a woman is 6 months pregnant and her employer changes insurance carriers, she ought not to have to give up her obstetrician before the baby's born. Or if somebody is taking chemotherapy and they are 80 percent of the way through and the same thing happens, they ought to be able to stay with their oncologist until the treatment is over. But it doesn't always happen today.

That's what this Patients' Bill of Rights is about. It's about common sense, balancing of the need to control costs on the one hand with the need never to forget that the health care of the American people comes first. We are for that. We have a few—a very few—Republicans who are helping, and God bless them, including the physician representing the State of Iowa in the House of Representatives, a brave man, Congressman Ganske. But the leadership of the other party is against this, and what they would do would make it weaker.

We believe, with all this stuff being computerized, you ought to have more privacy in your medical records, not less. And I think most of you think that. That's what the Patients' Bill of Rights is about. Carol Moseley-Braun is for it; the leadership of the other party is against it. On that ground alone you should make sure she gets reelected. This is a big battle for how you and your families and your children will live in the 21st century.

I could go right down the list with the environment; with the need for us to build one America working together; with the need to provide more economic opportunity in inner cities, isolated rural areas where there has been no opportunity; and with the need for America to fulfill its responsibilities. The Vice President made the remarks about the International Monetary Fund and the U.N.

You know, Reverend Jackson and I and the First Lady and a big delegation, we just went to Africa not very long ago. Believe it or not, several of those African economies are growing at 5, 6, 7, 8, 9 percent a year. They want to buy our products. They want to be our partners. An investment there today will pay our children many times over in return tomorrow.

All over the world, people still look to us to take the lead to stand against the kind of terrorism that we experienced just a few days ago; to stand against the kind of racial and ethnic and religious hatreds that we see in places like Bosnia, that are the part of the process of peace in the Middle East and Northern Ireland.

And if we want to be a source of peace and freedom and prosperity all around the world, then we have to have people who will say in Congress, "I realize it's not free. I'm prepared to invest in it and go home to my hometown in the heartland of America and say it's important."

You know why it's important in Illinois? How many people do you believe, if you went down to the central part of this State and said, "Do you know what the IMF is?" could give you an answer? Or, "It's the International Monetary Fund; do you know what it does?" They might not know, but here's why it matters. The International Monetary Fund provides funds to countries in economic trouble in return for their willingness to undertake disciplined steps to improve reform and grow their economies. Why does that matter to you? We export half of our wheat and our corn—half of it. Forty percent of all of that goes to Asia. Today, the exports to Asia are down 30 percent. It's costing the farmers of Illinois a pretty penny because there is a deep, profound economic crisis in Asia. And that will cost the people who do business with the farmers in Illinois a pretty penny.

But the United States is strong, and we should be leading. We shouldn't be looking for excuses not to assume our responsibility. We should be leading.

Now, those are the big things. So I ask you to think big, be big. But remember, with every high-flown idea, with every passionate phrase, in the end, as Governor Cuomo used to say, you have to turn the poetry of a campaign into the prose of daily work. We must turn these passionate ideas into action. That's what this administration has been about. That's what Carol Moseley-Braun has helped us to do. That's what

Charles Rangel has helped us to do. That's why I hope you are here.

And I would implore you to go out of here with a great deal of pride and energy and determination. And when somebody asks you, "Why did you go to that Democratic fundraiser?" you can say, "Because I'm for saving Social Security and Medicare for the 21st century; because I'm going to keep working until our schools are the best in the world; because I want American health care to be affordable and available and quality for all of our citizens; because I want to grow the economy and preserve the environment; because I want us to be one America, across all the lines that divide us; and because

I still believe our best days are ahead as long as we're willing to stand up against the terrorists and stand up for freedom."

Thank you, and God bless you.

NOTE: The President spoke at 8:35 p.m. in the Atrium at the Chicago Historical Society. In his remarks, he referred to Steve Grossman, national chair, Democratic National Committee; Mayor Richard M. Daley of Chicago; Representative Glenn Poshard, Democratic candidate for Governor of Illinois, and his Republican opponent, George H. Ryan, Illinois secretary of state; and Mario Cuomo, former Governor of New York.

Letter to Congressional Leaders Reporting on the Deployment of United States Forces in Response to the Embassy Bombings in Kenya and Tanzania
August 10, 1998

Dear Mr. Speaker: *(Dear Mr. President:)*

On August 7, 1998, two bombs exploded about five minutes apart at the U.S. Embassies in Nairobi, Kenya, and Dar es Salaam, Tanzania. A number of American citizens were killed or wounded, and the embassies suffered extensive damage. Department of State officials requested immediate medical, security, and disaster response assistance from the Department of Defense.

On August 7, 1998, a Joint Task Force of U.S. military personnel from U.S. Central Command deployed to Nairobi to coordinate the medical and disaster response assistance arriving in Kenya and Tanzania. In addition, on August 8, 1998, teams of approximately 50–100 security personnel each arrived in Nairobi and Dar es Salaam. These teams will enhance the ability of the United States to ensure the security of the American Embassies and American citizens in these countries.

The U.S. forces comprising the Joint Task Force and the medical and security assistance come primarily from elements of the U.S. Central and U.S. European Commands. Other elements are U.S.-based units. Each of the armed

services is represented. Although U.S. forces are equipped for combat, this movement is being undertaken solely for the purpose of enhancing embassy security and ensuring the security of American citizens. United States forces will redeploy as soon as the additional security support is determined to be unnecessary.

I have taken this action pursuant to my constitutional authority to conduct U.S. foreign relations and as Commander in Chief and Chief Executive.

I am providing this report as part of my efforts to keep the Congress fully informed, consistent with the War Powers Resolution. I appreciate the support of the Congress in this action to assist in embassy security and the security of American citizens overseas.

Sincerely,

WILLIAM J. CLINTON

NOTE: Identical letters were sent to Newt Gingrich, Speaker of the House of Representatives, and Strom Thurmond, President pro tempore of the Senate. This letter was released by the Office of the Press Secretary on August 11.

Remarks at the Harry Tracy Water Filtration Plant in San Bruno, California
August 11, 1998

Thank you very much. Good morning. I asked Lorraine if any of her children were here, and she said they were all here. I would like to ask the members of your family to stand. Everybody in Lorraine's family, stand. [*Applause*] Good for you. There are your children, your husband. Thank you all. I'd say they were worth fighting for.

Good morning, everyone. Thank you for braving this beautiful but rather warm California sunshine to participate in this event. Thank you, Mr. Mayor. Thank you, Ann Caen, for your service and the reference to Herb. Thank you, Lieutenant Governor Gray Davis, for your support for the environment. Thank you to Superintendent Paul Mazza and the members of the facility here, all of the people who work here. I'd like to thank them for what they do to help improve the lives of the people in this area. Thank you very much. I know we have members of the San Mateo board of supervisors and other—perhaps other officials here.

And I'd like to say a special word of appreciation to Congressman Tom Lantos and especially for the reference he made to the terrible events a few days ago in Kenya and Tanzania. We now have—as the Congressman mentioned, the American citizens who were killed there are coming home, and Hillary and I will go to Andrews Air Force Base to meet that sad homecoming plane on Thursday. In addition to that, you should know now, over 200—well over 200 African citizens have been killed and almost 5,000 injured. There are over 500 people still in the hospital in Nairobi in Kenya.

I think it's important for me to tell you that we have worked very closely with the Governments of Kenya and Tanzania in, first of all, determining and finding those who were killed and those who were injured and now in their treatment. And also they are working very closely with us in our attempts to find those who are responsible.

And I know this is terribly frightening to people when something like this happens, but in an ever more open world where people are traveling more and where more information and technology and, unfortunately, weaponry are available across national lines, and more and more information through the Internet, I think it is important that we all, as Americans, send a clear signal to the world that we are not going to back away from our involvement with other people, and we are not going to back away from our opposition to terrorism. It makes us more vulnerable as targets because we have taken the toughest stand around the world against terrorism. Now is the time to bear down, not back up, on that. And that is my determination. And I believe that's what the American people support, and I hope all of you will.

Let me say that today is a happy day because it marks another step forward in our attempt to bring the American people the kind of life I believe that all hard-working citizens deserve. It is tempting because our own country has enjoyed so much prosperity and a declining crime rate, declining welfare rolls, and declining other social problems, rising wages. Particularly in a place like California, where you had such a tough time for so many years, it's tempting at a good time like this for everybody to say, "Okay, we went through all those tough times. Now we've got good times. Mr. President, leave us alone. We want to relax. We want to enjoy this. We want to chill out." I think that's what some people say.

I think that would be a mistake. Why? Because all you have to do is pick up the newspaper any day or watch the news any night, and we see how fast the world continues to change—always changing—the way we work, the way we live, the challenges we face, the way we relate to each other and the rest of the world. At a time like this we should take our prosperity and the self-confidence it has given us as a country and say, "What are the challenges of the future? And how can we use this moment of opportunity, because we're doing well, to take care of the long-term challenges to our children's future and to make America what it ought to be?"

We have to, for example, save Social Security for the 21st century, before all the baby boomers retire and impose unbearable strains on the system as it's now constituted. We have to make our elementary and secondary schools the best in the world, just as our higher education system is now. We have to prove that we can provide affordable and quality health care to all people, which is why I've fought so hard for this Patients' Bill of Rights.

We have to expand opportunity into inner-city areas and rural areas and Native American reservations where there has been no recovery yet. We have to prove we can live together as one America as we get more diverse. We have to, as Tom Lantos said, fulfill our responsibilities in the world, because we cannot grow and prosper at home unless we are also strong abroad in pursuit of peace and freedom and prosperity.

But one thing we clearly have to do is to prove that we can grow our economy while we improve the environment and public health. The two things must never be seen in conflict. When they are, we pay a price that is terrible, first in the environment, second in public health, and eventually in the health of our economy.

And one example of that is what we're here to talk about today, the importance of our drinking water. It may have been gold that brought people to California 150 years ago, but water has enabled them to stay here and enabled this State to grow and expand to the point where now California comprises 13 percent of our entire Nation's population. It may be that the clear water that flows down the Sierra slopes and was miraculously, a long time ago, through pipes and channels, taken into a reservoir here to provide water for this area was an even greater discovery than the gold. I think clearly it was.

Few States are blessed with such a supply of fresh water, and none have done more to put it to productive use than California. Still, although there are problems, and I understand there are still disputes over water, I have seen in my own administration how, by working patiently together with different groups, cooperation can win out to protect this vital resource so there's enough for the farms, for the wildlife, and for the people.

Now, we also have to work to assure the quality as well as the supply. That's what we're here to talk about today. Mrs. Ross told you about what happened to her family and others in the Silicon Valley. Five years ago, the citizens of Milwaukee found themselves with 400,000 people sick, dozens of people dead because a microbe called cryptosporidium had contaminated their water supply.

The Vice President and I have worked hard to deal with this issue, to strengthen the Safe Drinking Water Act, to help communities upgrade treatment plants, and to zero in on contaminants posing the greatest threat. We required more industries to publicly disclose the chemicals they release into the air and water. The results of that have been quite remarkable. The factories required to provide this information—listen to this, just the community right-to-know—the factories required to provide the information about the chemicals they release into the air and water have reduced their toxic releases by almost half. That's what right-to-know can do.

Now, today we take another important step to empower communities with information. Beginning next year, under a new EPA community right-to-know rule I'm announcing today, water systems across our country must give their customers regular reports on the water flowing from their taps, to tell consumers where the water comes from, whether it meets Federal standards, as well as the likely source of any contaminants and their potential health effects.

Thanks to these reports, contamination in the water will no longer be invisible to the eye. Families will see at a glance whether their drinking water is safe. When it is not, utilities will have a crystal-clear incentive to clean it up, and citizens like Lorraine Ross will not have to fly blind. They will be able to come up all over America, and they will know what they have to work with and what they must work toward.

Safe water for our children is something all Americans agree on. This should not be a partisan issue. We've improved the quality of drinking water so much over the years, in fact, because of a bipartisan effort. And yet, there is in Congress today a disturbing trend to break up what has historically, at least for the last 30 years, been a bipartisan consensus on the environment. If there is ever an area where we need progress, not partisanship, it is to ensure the purity and safety of our environment. But there is a question about that. So far, Congress has refused to fund my clean water action plan that would help to restore the—listen to this—the 40 percent of our waters that are still too polluted for fishing and swimming.

In February, I proposed to add 100 national and historic sites across our country to our endowment of protected areas. One of the things I'm proudest of that our administration has done is that we have protected more land in perpetuity than any administration in history except those of the two Roosevelts. And now we have 100 more sites, places like Bair Island, a haven for endangered wildlife in San Francisco Bay, and the gravesite of John Muir, perhaps the greatest preservationist of all time. Believe it or not, the money has been appropriated for all these sites, but under the law, once they're selected, the congressional leaders must approve its release. So far, that approval has not been forthcoming for months and months. Today, for the sites in California and throughout the country, again I ask Congress to release the funds already approved so we can preserve these precious places.

We need progress and not partisanship in our efforts to avoid the degradation of our ocean waters. We had a big ocean conference out here on the Monterey Peninsula not very long ago. And we need it in our efforts to combat climate change and to do America's part.

Just yesterday the Vice President announced new data showing that the month of July was the hottest month ever recorded since climate records have been kept on Earth. This is not some fly-by-night phenomenon. The 9 hottest years ever recorded have occurred in the last 11 years; '97 was the hottest year ever measured; every month in '98 has been hotter than the preceding month in '97. And we need to work together.

Yet many in Congress want to cut the common-sense technology, market-oriented initiatives I have proposed to reduce our greenhouse gas emissions and to do America's part. We can grow this economy, reduce greenhouse gas emissions, improve the environment. If we do not do so at some point in the not-too-distant future, our children will be living in an economy that is much reduced, because we didn't do right by the environment. And we should never forget that.

Let me finally say that one of the things that I have found most frustrating in trying to create a bipartisan consensus on the environment is that I keep finding in all these bills that are sent to me legislative gimmicks called riders, which have nothing to do with the bills that pass, where the little rider is designed to weaken some environmental protection the United States has. Lawmakers have attached language to unrelated bills to cripple wildlife protection and cut through an Alaskan wildlife refuge with a $30-million road. These back-door assaults must also stop. We shouldn't squander our bounty for short-term gain.

Now, the people of California know this. From Monterey Bay to Lake Tahoe, people who haven't always seen eye to eye on any political issue are working together to preserve their water and land. We are rebuilding at the grassroots level a consensus for preserving our environment, advancing the public health as we grow our economy.

That message needs to get back to Washington, because every American has to come to grips with this fundamental challenge. We can never create the 21st century America we want for our children until we do not think of economic growth as divorced from the preservation of the environment and the public health. They must be seen as absolutely part of one indivisible effort to create the good life for the American people. If we do that and if we fulfill our responsibilities, then I'm convinced that for the children here in this audience, America's best days are still ahead.

Thank you, and God bless you.

NOTE: The President spoke at 10:22 a.m. outside the plant. In his remarks, he referred to community activist Lorraine Ross; Mayor Edward Simon of San Bruno; Ann Moller Caen, president, San Francisco Public Utilities Commission, and her late husband, Herb Caen; gubernatorial candidate Lt. Gov. Gray Davis; and Paul Mazza, superintendent, East Bay Water Treatment Facilities.

Remarks at a Luncheon for Lieutenant Governor Gray Davis of California in San Francisco
August 11, 1998

Thank you. Well, thank you, Governor Davis. That sounds pretty good, doesn't it? [*Applause*] That sounds pretty good. You know, Gray was up here making all those sort of funny, self-deprecating remarks about being dull, and I thought, well, as long as we carry Willie Brown around with us, all the rest of us will look dull. [*Laughter*]

Mr. Mayor, it's nice to be back in your city. I'd like to thank all the Members of Congress who are here: Representatives Harman and Tauscher and Lantos and Sanchez and, I believe, visiting Representatives Reyes and McCarthy.

Senator Cranston, thank you for coming. It's good to see you looking so young and fit. When I was a young Governor, I used to go to Washington, DC, and every morning I'd get up very early and go running along The Mall in Washington. And I would end down there around—there's a pool right in front of the Capitol, and I'd run around that three or four times. The only person I ever saw up that early running was Alan Cranston. And I've never forgotten it, and I am delighted to see him.

I want to compliment the Democrats in California on putting together such an impressive ticket, with Cruz Bustamante and my longtime friend Phil Angelides and Senator Lockyer and Michela Alioto, who used to work with us in the administration; Delaine Eastin and Kathleen Connell—all of these people are very, very impressive, and they'll be a good team with Gray Davis. And I want to compliment you on that.

I'd also like to say to Gray and Sharon, I thank you for offering yourselves to California and to its future. I am deeply indebted, and I promised myself I would never come out here again without just saying thank you to the people of California for making it possible for Hillary and me and for Al and Tipper Gore to serve our country, to help to move America forward, to help to bring America back. And of course, now I have a little extra debt to California for the educational opportunity you're giving to our daughter. And I thank you for that.

I want to make a few brief points. Everything that needs to be said has been said; not everyone has said it yet. But I would like to make a couple of points that I'd ask you to keep in mind between now and the November election as events heat up and unfold. I am very glad and grateful that you have come here to this fundraiser, that you have contributed to this good man's worthy campaign, and I thank you for that. But one of the things we really need in America and in California at this moment of renewed prosperity and opportunity is for people to take more interest in the daily work of citizenship and to understand that there really is a connection between the decisions elected officials make and the consequences we feel in our daily lives.

That is so important. It may sound so self-evident to you. But do you ever ask yourself why an otherwise responsible person who has to get up and work every day and is forced to pay taxes, and if times are bad, suffers for it, and if times are good, benefits from it—a normal American that doesn't vote—millions of them don't? It is, I think, because they don't understand the connection between the decisions made by people in public life and the conditions they face, and they don't believe they can make a difference. But they can make all the difference.

Now, if you look at where we are as a country today compared to where we were—Gray said some of this—we have the lowest unemployment rate in 28 years and the lowest crime rate in 25 years and the lowest percentage of people on welfare in 29 years; we're about to have the first balanced budget and surplus in 29 years, with the lowest inflation in 32 years, the highest homeownership in history; and the Federal Government is the smallest it's been in 35 years. That's pretty good. That's pretty good.

The American people deserve the lion's share of credit for this because of their hard work, their ingenuity, getting over some of the economic problems of the eighties. But the policies of the Government are not unrelated to what has happened. They have created the conditions and given people the tools to make these good things happen.

And I say that because I think—if you think of the changes that have been made in the last 6 years and then the things you're facing here in this State over the next 6 years, I think you can make a compelling argument that it is more important than ever before who is the Governor of California. What is his philosophy—in this case, since you have two male candidates—what is the dominant philosophy? How is the job defined? How will their positions on issues and the actions they take affect the lives that you and your children and the people you care about live? Will it be something that fits in with what we have tried to do in Washington to bring America back? Will it be an administration that makes the most of every opportunity that we could provide in the next 2 years and, hopefully, beyond?

This is an important election. This is a huge deal. If we've had the smallest Federal Government in 35 years, it means that we have, among other things, given more flexibility to the States in how they pursue education reform. One thing the legislature has done—thank you, Senator Lockyer—that I approve of strongly is to support the charter school movement out here, which are public schools, but they're created under new rules without so much hassle from central administration, and they have high standards, and they only stay in existence as long as they meet them. It is a great reform. California is now leading the way there.

Now, we have all kinds of programs to support those charter schools. When I became President, there was one charter school in America. And I was out there talking about—in 1992 it wasn't one of the more widely applauded parts of my campaign speech, because most people didn't know what they were. There are now 1,000—1,000—and I want there to be at least 3,000 by the year 2000. It's very important. In California, you've got all these different kinds of folks with all these different challenges and ideas and opportunities; this is the ideal place in America to have a real generation of this. It'll matter a lot what the policy of the administration is on this.

We are ahead of schedule and under budget in putting 100,000 police officers on the street. That has contributed to the decline in the crime rate. And I just want to say it's important to remember that it matters whether the mayors

and whether the Governor really believe in what we're trying to do and are really trying to help grassroots law enforcement officials drive the crime rate down to make sure California gets its fair share of those remaining officers.

In the Balanced Budget Act, we passed a bill, as a part of the Balanced Budget Act, to provide for health insurance for 5 million children—mostly the children of the working poor who do not have health insurance. But the system by which they will be insured must be developed State by State. Now, from the day I became President, even before, I was besieged by appeals from representatives from California about the unfair cost California bore of health care, because the Federal Government didn't pick up its legitimate share of what should be the health care burdens of the State of California. Now, California's about 13 percent of America's population, but more—I'll bet you anything—more of the percentage of uninsured children who are eligible for this program.

You need somebody who believes in the potential of government to alleviate problems and strengthen our common life to be the Governor, to make sure that we do this right. I worked very hard to get that $24 billion in that Balanced Budget Act. I want 5 million kids to know and I want their parents to have the peace of mind to know that they can have health care if they need it. But it's got to be implemented by the Governors. So, anyway, you get the point.

Gray and I were out here the other day; we were talking about—we had this oceans conference on the Monterey Peninsula. We had to face the fact that the ocean quality in this country is deteriorating. The global warming, among other things, is changing the whole biostructure along the coastline, and we need to help meet this challenge. Now, some of this is a national challenge, but some of it is a State challenge. You can't think of an area of our common life where it won't make a difference who the Governor is.

I spent a lot of time talking about our big challenges as a nation: education; growing the economy while preserving the environment; extending economic opportunity to people who haven't felt it, even in the recovery; quality health care for everybody; passing a Patients' Bill of Rights to guarantee people the right, even in an HMO, to emergency room care and appropriate specialists, privacy for their records.

These kinds of challenges are important—proving that we can be one America across all the racial and ethnic and religious and other lines that divide us. And by the way, I'm getting sick and tired of coming to San Francisco and saying, as I must say one more time, Jim Hormel should have a hearing. Anyway, these are big issues.

Now, in almost everything—there is one thing I have to do in the next year that I don't believe the Governors can help or hurt on, and that is that Congress should not spend any of this surplus until we have saved Social Security for the 21st century and alleviated the questions that are there. And we have some national security matters, as we've been painfully reminded of in the last few days, that are national. Every other single challenge I'm trying to get our country to face will be better met if there is a strong person in the Governor's office who has your values and cares about the future of your children.

I have to put in a plug, too, for Senator Boxer and for the Members of our House delegation that are up. You know, everybody is going around celebrating the new economy. But I just want to remind you that way back in 1993, 5 years ago this month, when all the chips were on the line and America finally had to decide whether we were going to unhook ourselves from this addictive deficit spending we had been doing, and I presented a plan to the Congress to reduce the deficit by hundreds of billions of dollars, there was not a single member of the other party that voted for it, and it passed by one vote in both Houses. So I would say to the people of California, if you like where the California economy is today, remember, if Barbara Boxer had voted the other way, we wouldn't be here today. And she deserves to be reelected to the Senate this November.

So here's the last point I want to make. I thank you for being here. I thank you for contributing to Gray Davis. I thank you for your good citizenship. I thank you for the support of the initiatives of the administration, for the friendship you have given to the First Lady, to me, to the Vice President, to our families. And I will always be grateful to California. But the thing that I don't want to see happen is this: The most natural thing in the world when times are good, after they've been tough, is for people to relax when times are good. Isn't it? It's natural in your personal life, your family life, your business life. People say to me all the time, "Man, it was tough out here before the last 4 or 5 years; we worked hard to get California back." My advice to you is to go out and tell your friends and neighbors that this is a time too dynamic to rest in. You can enjoy it, but you can't take it for granted, and you can't kick back.

I think the only thing that could keep this good man from becoming Governor is a low voter turnout caused by people who think that things have been made all right, therefore there is nothing for them to do, and the consequences are not so great. Nothing could be further from the truth. When things are changing as fast as they are changing now, good times are not to be relaxed in; they are to be seized, used, made the most of. We have the confidence, the resources to face the long-term challenges of the country, to think about the future. That's what you've got to go out and tell people.

So you give him the contributions; that makes it possible for his voice to be heard across a bigger microphone. But you have a voice every day. You come in contact with people every day. And you have to convey your sense of confidence and pride in the people you support and where we are now, but also a sense of urgency that we have big challenges to face, that the world is changing, and that our best days are before us, but only if we remember our fundamental responsibilities, as citizens, to the future.

California has always been about the future. This is not a time to relax in that pursuit. We've worked too hard to get this far. We have to take advantage of it. And the best way to do it is to elect Gray Davis Governor.

Thank you very much, and God bless you.

NOTE: The President spoke at 1:05 p.m. in the Grand Ballroom at the Westin Saint Francis Hotel. In his remarks, he referred to Mayor Willie L. Brown, Jr., of San Francisco; Representative Karen McCarthy; former Senator Alan Cranston; State Assembly Speaker Cruz Bustamante, candidate for Lieutenant Governor; Phil Angelides, candidate for State treasurer; State Senator Bill Lockyer; Michela Alioto, candidate for California secretary of state; Delaine Eastin, State superintendent of public instruction; Kathleen Connell, State controller; and James C. Hormel, nominee for Ambassador to Luxembourg.

Remarks at a Reception for Lieutenant Governor Gray Davis of California in Los Angeles
August 11, 1998

Thank you very much. First of all, I think we should tell Gray Davis that he's going to have to stop getting so many laughs and having so many good lines in his speeches. He's going to completely destroy his reputation. [*Laughter*]

I want to thank Bruce and Janet for having us in their magnificent home, and especially out here in this beautiful open-air area. I want to thank them for putting those trees up so I can't look down on Riviera and be distracted while I speak tonight. [*Laughter*]

I'd like to say a special word of appreciation to Janet for being involved in the Los Angeles Conservation Corps. That corps and a remarkable project that began in Boston called City Year were the two inspirations for me for the proposal I made in the 1992 campaign to have a national community service program, AmeriCorps. And when it was created, it was one of the proudest moments of my life. We've now given about 100,000 young people a chance to work in communities in all kinds of work all across America, some of them with the L.A. Conservation Corps and, in so doing, to earn some money for college as well. And it's very, very important. I think that the more we can get people when they're young to do community service and to do it with people who are different than them—different in terms of race, in income, in background—the more likely we are to succeed in building one America.

I also promised myself a long time ago that I'd never come to California again without saying a profound word of thanks to the people of this State for giving Hillary and me and Al and Tipper Gore and our administration a chance to serve, a chance to do the work we have done this last 5½ years. And no matter what you read, every day has been a joy for me, and I have loved it.

I have tried to be a good President for California, and I could mention 10 or 11 things. But a lot of you thanked me for spending all day with Gray Davis. But I can tell you, I can't think of a better gift I could give the people of California than playing some role in the election of this good man to the governorship. It will be great for your future.

I was just sitting up there listening to Gray talk, and I—he mentioned the education issues and the difference between himself and his opponent—the crime issues. Last week I had Jim and Sarah Brady with me in the White House; you may have seen it. We celebrated the fifth anniversary of the Brady bill, another piece of legislation that most of the leaders in the other party opposed. Since the Brady bill became law, about a quarter of a million people with criminal and mental health histories that were destructive have not been able to buy handguns. Let me break it down just on the felons. Since I signed that bill into law and it took effect, 118 felons an hour—every hour of the day—have been denied the ability to buy a handgun.

Now, I feel very strongly about the assault weapons ban that Gray has tried—as he talked about the enforcement of the California law. As most of you know, Senator Feinstein was the leading sponsor of the bill in the Senate that we incorporated into the crime bill to ban assault weapons there. I have tried to strengthen that. I've tried to stop foreign manufacturers from getting around it.

These kinds of issues tell you a lot not just about the issues but about the general attitude of people who would be in public service and, therefore, are a pretty good predictor of the kind of decisions they might make on hundreds of other issues. And the request I want to make of you tonight is that you do more than you've done here, because, keep in mind, the truth is that most of you will do all right whether Gray wins or not. But the people that are serving our food here tonight, the people that are parking cars, the people that work in every place of business that I pass on the way up here tonight, it makes a whole lot of difference to them and their children. And in the end, how your children and your grandchildren do will be determined more than anything else by how everybody else does. And it is profoundly important. So I just want you to think about that.

I also have to put in a good word here tonight for someone who is not here. I thank Congresswoman Jane Harman and Sidney for being here and Congresswoman Ellen Tauscher. They do a wonderful job for the State of California in the Congress. And I did get to go to Jane and Sidney's, to their event for Gray, and having lost two elections myself, I can say two things. Number one, it's not fatal; and number two, you know what the right thing to do is, but it's not always easy. And she has done the right thing and then some, and I respect her for it immensely. And I thank her. Thank you very much.

I'd also like to say a word for Barbara Boxer, who isn't here. That young man at the water treatment facility today, he did say to me, "Mr. President, my life is better since you've been in. The California economy has come back; things are better here." I want you to just remember one thing. I want to give a speech for Gray, so I don't want to get off on Barbara too much, and besides, most of you know that I'm related to her by marriage, so you have to discount some of what I say. [*Laughter*]

But in 1993, 5 years ago this month, when the whole future of the economic ideas that I wanted to bring the American people was on the line in the economic plan I presented to Congress, when I said it would reduce the deficit by at least $500 billion and probably more, that it would bring interest rates down, get investments up, that it would also provide tax cuts to lower income working families and provide real incentives to invest in our cities, which had been neglected, and put more money into education, not a single Republican voted for that bill—not one—not one. The bill passed by one vote in the House, by one vote in the Senate. If Barbara Boxer had not voted for it—and keep in mind, she was elected in 1992 with only 47 percent of the vote, and she could not possibly have known for sure what the outcome would be. And all the Republicans were saying, "This will be a disaster; it will bring on a recession. We will attack the Democrats." And she didn't blink. She went right down the aisle and cast her vote, "Aye."

So when you look at the fact that we have the lowest unemployment in 28 years, the smallest percentage of people on welfare in 29 years, the first balanced budget and surplus in 29 years, with the lowest inflation in 32 years and the smallest Federal Government in 35 years, that vote alone, in my judgment, plus the fact that she has worn me out, just like Gray has, on offshore oil drilling and every other California issue I can possibly think of—[*laughter*]—

no family dinner with my extended family and all my wife's family is ever free from an interruption of lobbying on your behalf—that deserves your support for reelection, and I hope you'll give it to her.

Now, I'll be brief. Gray gave you his campaign speech, and I won't give it to you again. I want to make a point that only I understand. Before I became President, I was a Governor for 12 years. Unlike Gray, I did get to live in public housing, and I rather enjoyed it. [*Laughter*] I don't even know what it costs to rent a place; what am I going to do when I get out in a couple years? [*Laughter*] Anyway— and I think by experience more understanding than anyone here could possibly have about the relationship of the National Government to the State government, how it's changed in the last 8 years, and why I have tried to make the Governor's job more important.

But let me take one step back. One crusade I've been on all across America—everywhere I go I make this point. I say I am grateful for the good times we now enjoy. I think the lion's share of the credit goes to the American people for their hard work and ingenuity and good citizenship. But I think the policies of this administration have made a lot of it possible by creating the conditions and giving people the tools to make the most of their own lives.

Now, after all California went through in the late eighties and early nineties, it is tempting for a State or for a nation to do what every individual or family or business is tempted to do after you've been through tough times and all of the sudden you're in the pink and things are going well. You want to just take a deep breath, relax, put your feet up on the couch, and forget about it for a while. Speaker Gingrich said the other day the only thing they had to do to hold the Congress was pass the continuing resolution, not shut the Government down, and just go home—don't do anything, because times are good, people are happy, and they'll just vote for the status quo.

My argument is that that would be the exact wrong thing to do for America at this time. And I'll just give you an example that I think makes the point. If I had come here in 1992 and said to you, "Vote for me because I have a crystal ball, and I can see the future, and in 5, 6 years, not only will we have the strongest economy in the world, but the value of the Japanese stock market will be one-half of what it is today, and they will have no growth for 5 years," you would think I had a screw loose, wouldn't you? There's not a soul in this place that would have believed me if I'd said that 5 years ago—maybe a few of you who understood the real estate issues and all of that, but most people would have said no.

Now, I say that not to be critical of the Japanese. They are a very great people with enormous intelligence, enormous wealth, enormous potential, and they will be back. I say it to make this point: The world is changing more rapidly and more profoundly than almost any of us can understand—the way we work, the way we live, the way we relate to each other and the rest of the world, the nature of the foreign policy challenges we face. So when you have good times like this, but you know times are changing, if you want them to continue, the only responsible thing to do is to say, okay, we've got money; we've got confidence; we've got breathing space; we don't have to worry about where our next nickel or meal is coming from; let's look at the big long-term challenges and face them.

Now, I believe this country has seven big long-term challenges, and I'll just mention them to you, and you'll see what relevance it has to the Governor's race, because the last four depend on what is done at the State level as well as what's done at the national level.

Number one, we have got to stop playing with whether we're an isolationist power or whether we're going to lead the world for peace and freedom and prosperity. We have got to stop it. We've got to pay our debts to the U.N. We've got to pay our debts to the International Monetary Fund. We've got to be proud and aggressive of what we did in Bosnia, what we did in Haiti, what we've done in Northern Ireland, what we're trying to do in the Middle East, what I hope we can do by stopping another horrible ethnic cleansing in Kosovo. We've got to be tough in standing up against terrorism from whatever source and the spread of weapons of mass destruction. We've got to be willing to invest the money to do it, and we've got to realize that if we're going to trade all around the world, we have to have a world where commerce is possible because freedom is possible. We have got to do that.

Now, number two, we've got to understand if we want to do good abroad in a world totally awash in racial and ethnic and religious hatred,

we have to be good at home. We have got to build one America across the lines that divide us.

Number three, we have got to look out for the next generation and the implications of the retirement of the baby boomers. I can say that; I'm the oldest baby boomer. I don't know how you call anyone who is almost 52 baby anything. [*Laughter*] But when we all retire, all of us baby boomers, people who are this year turning between 34 and 52 years of age, at present rates of work force participation, retirement, birth rates, and immigration rates, there will only be about two people working for every person drawing Social Security. That will put untenable strains on both the Social Security and the Medicare program as they presently operate.

That is why I am so diametrically opposed to these suggestions that some in the other party have made that we're going to have a huge surplus, therefore we ought to spend hundreds of billions of dollars right now on a permanent tax cut. If the surplus doesn't materialize, do you think we'd repeal the tax cut?

Look, it's election year; I'd like to give you a tax cut as much as anybody else. Even though I'm not running, I want everybody else to win—that I'm for, that is. [*Laughter*] But that would not be responsible. We don't know how much it's going to cost to preserve what is essential about Social Security as we reform it to make it sustainable. And the same is true of the Medicare program. So I say, we've been waiting for 29 years to get out of the red; wouldn't you like to spend just a few months looking at the black ink before we squander it all again? Isn't that the right thing to do? [*Applause*]

You see all these young people around here. The baby boomers I know, we are plagued with the thought that we will lower the standard of living of our children and undermine their ability to raise our grandchildren because it will cost so much to take care of us when we're old, and we don't want it to happen. And we'll find a right balance, but we can't do it overnight.

Now, those are three big challenges that the State doesn't have anything to do with. We have to do that nationally. But what are the others? And Gray talked about a couple of them.

Number one, we have the best system of higher education in the world. No serious person believes we have the best system of elementary and secondary education in the world for all our kids. Until we can say we do, we will never be what we ought to be. And we can help. I've got a good program for smaller classes, higher standards, better training of teachers, hooking up all the classrooms to the Internet. But in the end, it's fundamentally a State responsibility, carried out by local people ultimately in the schools, the principals, the teachers, the parents, and the students. It matters who the Governor is.

Next, we've got to prove that we can grow the economy and improve the environment. A lot of it has to be done at the national level. The challenge of climate change primarily has to be done, I'm convinced, by a sensible program at the national level. The challenge of cleaning up our oceans has to be done primarily at the national level. But so much can and must be done here.

I'm telling you, I was driving across Los Angeles today thinking, thank God the people of California stood up for clean air and cleaned up the air here. How many children are free of bronchial diseases in this State because you believed in the environment and because you understood you could do it and still have a strong economy? You don't need someone in the Governor's chair who does not believe that passionately. It is very important—very important.

Just two other issues, very quickly. Economic policy: We've got a great economic recovery, but there are places—cities, rural areas, Indian reservations—where there is no free enterprise economic recovery. We can do something nationally; some of it has to be done at the State level.

And finally, health care. You know, when Hillary and I tried to reform the health care system and the Republicans and the insurance companies beat us and said we were trying to have the Government take over health care, they said, "Oh, they're going to have the Government take over health care." Of course, that wasn't true, but that's what they said. And they spent a lot of money, and they convinced a lot of people it was right.

Let me give you an interesting statistic. When they beat our health care program, 40 percent of all health care dollars came from public sources. What do you think it is today? Forty-seven percent. Why? Because private employers don't insure as many of their employees any more, and even lower income working people are now more eligible for Medicaid.

Now, what I've tried to do is to find a way step by step to deal with that, to have the benefits of managed care without the burdens. That's what the Patients' Bill of Rights is all about. And I think it's very important.

But let me give you one example. We passed in the Balanced Budget Act of 1997 a bill—part of that—to provide $24 billion to give health insurance to 5 million children who don't have it, most of them in low income working families. Thirteen percent of the country lives in California, but a lot more than 13 percent of the eligible kids live in California—working people who can get their kids insured now because we put that money into the balanced budget. But the whole program has to be developed by the States. They have to come up with a system to do it. That's one of the biggest responsibilities of a Governor today—figure out how his State or her State can get their fair share of money to get these children in working families so they can see a doctor on a regular basis and get preventive care so they don't get sick, so their parents aren't torn up with worry.

Now, you tell me—you know who the two candidates for Governor are—if you thought that was one of the most important responsibilities, and also you wanted less drain on your State tax dollars from people getting real sick and showing up at public hospitals and public health centers, which one do you think is more likely to spend more time designing an aggressive, appropriate plan to protect the working families of this State and their health care? The answer is Gray Davis. It's clear.

You can see I don't feel very strongly about this. [*Laughter*] If you think about it, there are seven big challenges this country is facing for the 21st century. Four of them, no matter what I do as President or whether I can prevail in Congress, depend upon having the right kind of visionary leadership at the State level. This is a big deal. And I want you to go out and talk to your friends and neighbors between now and November and tell them the only way this guy can lose this race is if a lot of people who care and know better don't vote because they really don't think it matters, because they can relax because things are going so well.

Things are going so well because of all the hard work we have all done together. And they will continue to go well as long as—but only as long as—we continue to face the challenges of today and tomorrow. That is the major case for Gray Davis. You've given him a chance tonight to have a bigger bullhorn, to get his message out. Tomorrow you can give him a chance to have a lot more apostles, one on one, and in the end, that can be even more important.

Thank you, and God bless you.

NOTE: The President spoke at 7:38 p.m. at a private residence. In his remarks, he referred to reception hosts Bruce and Janet Karatz; former White House Press Secretary James Brady and his wife, Sarah, chair, Handgun Control, Inc.; and Sidney Harman, chief executive officer, Harman International Industries, Inc.

Remarks at a Dinner for Lieutenant Governor Gray Davis of California in Los Angeles
August 11, 1998

Thank you. First of all, thank you for coming tonight. Thank you for making me feel so welcome. Many of you said especially kind things to me when I was going around and visiting with you, and I thank you for that.

I thank Jeffrey and Marilyn for now—now I have visited in all their residences. [*Laughter*] I'm three for three; I get to start on my second round now. And I thank them for having all of us in here in this beautiful and, for this sort of political event, rather cozy setting. I've enjoyed it very much.

We've been working all day, as Gray said, and you've probably heard about all the speeches you want to hear. I would just like to tell you a couple of things that are very much on my mind. First, I want to thank you and the people of California for giving me and Hillary and Al and Tipper Gore the chance to serve these last 5½ years and to play our role in this country's renaissance. I'm grateful for that. Second, I thank you for helping Gray Davis. I think he is a good man. I think he will be elected Governor if the people of California show up at the polls in November.

Thirdly, I want to ask you to just think about one thing briefly and seriously, and that is, okay, California is back, America is moving forward— Gray reeled off the statistics, you heard them— we're in the best shape we've been in a generation. Our economy is growing; our social problems are declining. What are we to do with this moment? And what does the race for Governor have to do with it? What does Senator Boxer's race have to do with it? Is it really

a good thing that a guy like Rob Reiner has put his neck on the line to put a proposition on the ballot to try to provide a better early beginning for our children? What does all this matter?

And it may seem self-evident, but it's not really. I mean, if you think about your own life, just go back over periods of your life, and you go through a really tough time—and just about all of us in this crowd have lived long enough to have had a few tough times—and then things get really good; what is the temptation? You want to say, "I had all these tough times and now things are going well for me, and I want to enjoy it. I want to kick back, relax, enjoy it, smell the roses." That's what people want to do, families want to do, businesses are inclined to do.

And the point I would like to make, that I think is so urgent when it comes to the decisions the voters will make here in California this November, is that we can't afford to do that now. We have to resist the temptation of saying these good times can let us be a little bit lazy, and say instead: The world is changing too fast; the challenges are still too profound; and we have an obligation to use these good times and the confidence they've given us to meet the long-term challenges of the future.

For me, it means we have to solve the problems of Social Security and Medicare before the baby boomers retire, so we can do it in a way that will provide dignity to my old age and our generation in a way that does not bankrupt our children and their ability to raise our grandchildren. So even though it's election year, I'm against the Republican House proposal for a tax cut. We've had a deficit for 29 years; now we're going to have a surplus—I'd like to look at the black ink for a few months and take care of our kids' future before we squander it for political purposes. A good reason to vote to reelect Barbara Boxer—a good reason.

We have got to resolve this ambivalent feeling that—or these messages that America has sent out because of the votes, or lack of them, in Congress about whether we're prepared to continue to lead the world for peace and freedom and prosperity. We've got to pay our dues to the U.N., our debt to the International Monetary Fund; we've got to say we're proud of what we've done for peace in Northern Ireland, in Bosnia, in Haiti, what we're working on in the Middle East, the humanitarian disaster we want to avoid in Kosovo. We've got to say we're not going to let the terrorists back us down or get away with it in the wake of these horrible Embassy bombings in Africa. We have got to stand up for our leadership role in the world.

We have got to face big challenges here at home. Let me just reel some of them off; Gray talked about some of them. We've got the best system of college in the world. One of the major achievements of our administration is we've opened the door to college wider than ever before with tax credits and more scholarships and more work-study positions and the national service program, AmeriCorps, to let people earn college scholarship money. But nobody thinks we've got the best elementary and secondary system in the world. And it's too late to have a debate about what to do about it. But I'll tell you this: Every problem in American education has been solved by somebody somewhere, and there is no excuse for us not doing it everywhere. Now, that has to be done partly by the National Government, but largely at the State and local level. Which candidate for Governor do you really believe is more likely to make a contribution to that?

We've got to continue the fight to provide health care to all of our people. At the national level we need to pass a Patients' Bill of Rights to balance managed care with patient care and get the balance right. But when we passed the balanced budget bill, we made it possible for 5 million American kids to get health care, but we said the States had to figure out how to do it, here's the money. Which candidate for Governor is more likely to see that more of California's children get decent health care?

We have to figure out a way to grow the economy while we preserve the environment. I hope all of you in this crowd believe that the phenomenon of global warming is real. It is. When I was out on the Monterey Peninsula a few weeks ago, I went out with some young marine biologists from Stanford, and we stood in the bay there and we looked at marine life there that just 20 years ago was no further north than 50 miles south of there. That's a phenomenal change in marine life because of the warming of the planet. But a lot of the environmental challenges of this State have to be met here in California. What candidate for Governor is more likely to help you meet the environmental challenges of the future and grow California's economy? I could go on and on and on.

The last thing I'd like to say is that one of the things that's made me proudest to be a Democrat in the last few years is that we have continued to stand for the proposition that this has to be one America; that all the lines that divide us, the lines of race and religion and income, all the other things that divide people in this society that have been used by people in political campaigns to drive wedges between us, that we have to overcome those things because what we have in common is more important than what divides us.

And I believe that California sends a signal to America because this State is so diverse. And the decision you make in the Governor's race here will have a lot to say about whether State politics continues to be a source of constant social division or whether you've got a Governor up there leading people to aspire to their better selves. And I don't think there's any question in your mind about which candidate is more likely to do that.

And let me say one last thing on an issue. When I come to California, it makes my heart leap with joy to see so much prosperity where once there was so many problems. And I'm very proud of the role that we have played in it. But I just want to remind you that politics is more than speeches at events like this. After the poetry of the campaign, as Governor Cuomo used to say, there is the prose of making decisions—and a lot of them hard and controversial, with tough choices and trade-offs.

Five years ago this month I presented to the Congress the economic plan that began the recovery of this country by driving the deficit down, driving interest rates down, driving investment up. The Republicans attacked it, characterized it unfairly as a tax increase on the whole American people, said it would be a disaster. And not a single, solitary Republican—after they have quadrupled the debt in 4 years—would step forward to vote for that plan. It passed by one vote in the House, one vote in the Senate. If one person had failed to be there, then the thing that set this whole recovery in motion would not have occurred.

Barbara Boxer won by about 47 percent of the vote in 1992. She could have taken a powder because she didn't have a majority going in. And she stood 7 feet tall and walked down the aisle and voted for the economic plan that we are now celebrating the consequences of in California and all over America. For that vote alone, I believe she deserves to be reelected in November, and I hope you will help her.

So let me ask you to go out here and talk about these things, talk about the issues that are on the ballot, talk about these candidates. You've given a much bigger bullhorn to Gray Davis by your contributions tonight, and that's very important. But it's important that the people you come in contact with, many of whom influence a lot of other people, understand that this is not a time for sitting around, because the world is changing too fast.

Let me just ask you this. If somebody told you 5 years ago when I became President—5½ years ago—that over the next 5½ years America will become the strongest economy in the world with the strongest economy in a generation here, and meanwhile the Japanese stock market will lose one-half of its value and Japan will not grow for 5 years, you would not have believed that, I bet. But that happened. I say that not to criticize the Japanese—they're a very

great people; they're brilliant; they're rich; they're strong; they're smart; and they'll be back—but to show you that you can never afford just to relax and stay with the established order of things. We have to keep doing what got us here.

When Hillary agreed to take over this celebration of the Millennium Project, she came up with this theme, "Honoring the past, and imagining the future." In a dynamic time, that's what we all have to do. Gray talked about honoring the past by doing the right things for the future. And that's what we represent.

If you look at the whole history of the country—Gray talked about "Saving Private Ryan." I told him one of my favorite parts of that movie was George Marshall reading Abraham Lincoln's letter to Mrs. Bixby, which I used to read every Memorial Day, because it captures what America is all about.

But I believe that the party I'm a part of and the candidates I'm supporting and the work we're trying to do embody the best of our past and the best hope for the future. Because what are we trying to do? We're trying to widen the circle of opportunity, deepen the reach of our freedom, strengthen the bonds of our community.

You've helped us to do that tonight. I hope tomorrow when you wake up you'll be proud you were here tonight. And I hope you'll want to talk to others about why we should not relax, we should thank God for the blessings we enjoy and do our best to preserve and spread them.

Thank you, and God bless you.

NOTE: The President spoke at 10:10 p.m. at a private residence. In his remarks, he referred to dinner hosts Jeffrey and Marilyn Katzenberg; film director Rob Reiner, founder, I Am Your Child campaign; and Mario Cuomo, former New York Governor.

Statement on Signing the Emergency Farm Financial Relief Act
August 12, 1998

Today I am signing into law S. 2344, the "Emergency Farm Financial Relief Act," which will allow farmers to receive their market transi-

tion payments earlier than usual. This legislation is necessary in a year marked by low crop prices, a series of natural disasters, and other financial strains in agricultural markets. By speeding up these payments, this law will help many rural American communities and farm families, particularly those facing financial pressures through no fault of their own. Secretary of Agriculture Glickman proposed this idea earlier this year, and I am pleased that the Congress has moved forward on it. However, this legislation fails to provide any additional direct Federal income support payments; it simply accelerates them. We must take further action to provide a proper safety net for family farmers during this difficult year.

There is more we can do. Earlier this month, the Department of Agriculture purchased 535,000 tons of wheat for donation to hungry people overseas, the first step in the plan I announced in July to purchase more than 80 million bushels of American wheat and wheat flour. This will help strengthen crop prices and meet humanitarian· needs abroad. I have also urged the Congress to move forward on the proposal of Senators Dorgan and Conrad to provide at least $500 million in emergency assistance to farmers who have been hit hard by natural disasters and low prices. Such emergency legislation would provide a supplemental crop insurance benefit to producers with multiple-year losses, compensate farmers whose crop and pasture land has been flooded, and provide emergency feed assistance to livestock producers suffering from drought. The Dorgan/Conrad proposal has already passed the Senate, and I

urge the full Congress to approve their amendment and send it to me for signature so we can give hard-pressed farmers the relief they deserve as soon as possible.

Moreover, Secretary Glickman and I have challenged the Congress to improve the farm safety net in a number of very specific ways. Our proposals would extend the term of marketing assistance loans; give farmers real flexibility in planting by allowing them to insure new and different crops; make credit more widely available and modify the "one strike" policy for farmers who had a debt write-down; use leftover Export Enhancement Program funds in future years for food aid and other purposes; let farmers use USDA-guaranteed operating loans to refinance; and expand and improve crop insurance. Finally, the Congress must also end its delay on funding for the International Monetary Fund so that we can help stabilize the markets in Asia that are such important customers for our farm exports.

These are tough times for many American farmers. We must continue to look for ways to help our farm communities get through them.

WILLIAM J. CLINTON

The White House,
August 12, 1998.

NOTE: S. 2344, approved August 12, was assigned Public Law No. 105–228.

Memorandum on Assistance for Federal Employees Affected by the Embassy Bombings in Kenya and Tanzania
August 12, 1998

Memorandum for the Heads of Executive Departments and Agencies

Subject: Assistance for Federal Employees Affected by the Bombings at U.S. Embassies in Kenya and Tanzania

I am deeply saddened by the loss of life and suffering caused by the bombings of the U.S. embassies in Nairobi, Kenya, and Dar es Salaam, Tanzania. I convey my deepest sympathy and heartfelt sorrow to those affected by these senseless acts of violence. The Federal Govern-

ment is committed to assist employees and their families in responding to this tragedy.

As part of this effort, I ask the heads of executive departments and agencies having Federal civilian employees affected by the bombings (including Foreign Service National employees) to excuse from duty, without charge to leave or loss of pay, any such employee who is prevented from reporting to work or faced with a personal emergency because of the bombings and who can be spared from his or her usual responsibilities. This policy should also be applied to any employee who is needed for security, relief, or recovery efforts as authorized by the chief of mission at each embassy.

I am also directing the Office of Personnel Management to establish an emergency leave transfer program under which employees in any executive agency may donate unused annual leave for transfer to employees of the same or other agencies who were adversely affected by the bombings and who need additional time off for recovery. Workers' compensation benefits are available in the case of Federal employees who were injured or killed in the bombing, as are certain other benefits. I am further directing the Office of Personnel Management and the Department of Labor to provide additional information and assistance as appropriate.

WILLIAM J. CLINTON

Remarks at a Memorial Service at Andrews Air Force Base, Maryland, for the Victims of the Embassy Bombings in Kenya and Tanzania
August 13, 1998

To the members of the families here, Secretary Albright, Secretary Cohen, members of the Cabinet, Members of Congress, leaders of the Armed Forces, members of the diplomatic corps, friends, and we say a special appreciation to the representatives here from Kenya and Tanzania.

Every person here today would pray not to be here. But we could not be anywhere else, for we come to honor 12 proud sons and daughters who perished half a world away but never left America behind, who carried with them the love of their families, the respect of their countrymen, and above all, the ideals for which America stands. They perished in the service of the country for which they gave so much in life.

To their families and friends, the rest of your fellow Americans have learned a little bit about your loved ones in the past few days. Of course, we will never know them as you did or remember them as you will, as a new baby, a proud graduate, a beaming bride or groom, a reassuring voice on the phone from across the ocean, a tired but happy traveler at an airport, bags stuffed with gifts, arms outstretched. Nothing can bring them back, but nothing can erase the lives they led, the difference they made, the joy they brought.

We can only hope that even in grief you can take pride and solace in the gratitude all the rest of us have for the service they gave.

The men and women who serve in our Embassies all around this world do hard work that is not always fully appreciated and not even understood by many of their fellow Americans.

They protect our interests and promote our values abroad. They are diplomats and doctors and drivers, bookkeepers and technicians and military guards. Far from home, they endure hardships, often at great risk.

These 12 Americans came from diverse backgrounds. If you see their pictures, you know they are a portrait of America today and of America's tomorrow. But as different as they were, each of them had an adventurous spirit, a generous soul. Each relished the chance to see the world and to make it better.

They were: a senior diplomat I had the honor to meet twice, and his son, who proudly worked alongside him this summer; a budget officer, a wife and mother who had just spent her vacation caring for her aged parents; a State Department worker who looked forward to being back home with her new grandson; a Foreign Service officer born in India who became an American citizen and traveled the world with her family for her new country; a Marine sergeant, the son of very proud parents; an Air Force sergeant who followed in her own father's footsteps; an epidemiologist who loved her own children and worked to save Africa's children from disease and death; an Embassy administrator who married a Kenyan and stayed in close touch with her children back in America; a Foreign Service officer and mother of three children, including a baby girl; a Foreign Service member who was an extraordinarily accomplished jazz musician and devoted husband; an Army sergeant, a veteran of the Gulf war, a husband, a father, who told his own father that if anything ever happened to him, he wanted his ashes scattered in the Pacific off Big Sur because that was where he had met his beloved wife.

What one classmate said to me of his friend today we can say of all of them: They were what America is all about.

We also remember today the Kenyans and Tanzanians who have suffered great loss. We are grateful for your loved ones who worked alongside us in our Embassies. And we are grateful for your extraordinary efforts in great pain in the wake of this tragedy. We pray for the speedy recovery of all the injured, Americans and Africans alike.

No matter what it takes, we must find those responsible for these evil acts and see that justice is done. There may be more hard road ahead, for terrorists target America because we act and stand for peace and democracy, because the spirit of our country is the very spirit of freedom. It is the burden of our history and the bright hope of the world's future.

We must honor the memory of those we mourn today by pressing the cause of freedom and justice for which they lived. We must continue to stand strong for freedom on every continent. America will not retreat from the world and all its promise, nor shrink from our responsibility to stand against terror and with the

friends of freedom everywhere. We owe it to those we honor today.

As it is written: "Their righteous deeds have not been forgotten. Their glory will not be blotted out. Their bodies were buried in peace, but their names shall live forever."

Sergeant Jesse Nathan Aliganga.
Julian Bartley, Sr.
Julian Bartley, Jr.
Jean Dalizu.
Molly Huckaby Hardy.
Sergeant Kenneth Hobson.
Prabhi Guptara Kavaler.
Arlene Kirk.
Dr. Mary Louise Martin.
Ann Michelle O'Connor.
Senior Master Sergeant Sherry Lynn Olds.
Uttamlal "Tom" Shah.

May they find peace in the warm embrace of God. And may God give peace to those who loved them, and bless their beloved country.

NOTE: The President spoke at 11:20 a.m. at Hangar 3. The transcript released by the Office of the Press Secretary also included the remarks of Secretary of Defense William S. Cohen and Secretary of State Madeleine K. Albright.

Statement on Signing the Biomaterials Access Assurance Act of 1998
August 13, 1998

I am pleased to sign today the Biomaterials Access Assurance Act of 1998, which should help to ensure the continued availability of life-saving and life-enhancing medical devices. The bill protects certain raw materials and parts suppliers from liability for harm caused by a medical implant. Congress heard evidence that these biomaterials suppliers are increasingly unwilling to sell their goods to implant manufacturers. Although these suppliers have never been found liable, they fear that their costs to defend themselves, if dragged into litigation over the medical device, would far outweigh the profits they would earn from supplying the raw materials. But without those materials, Americans would

have to live without the heart valves, jaw implants, artificial hips, and other medical devices (including many not yet imagined) that can help the victims of disease and injury stay alive or improve the quality of their lives.

This bill addresses concerns that I raised, when I vetoed the product liability bill in 1996, about that bill's biomaterials provision. This bill is very narrowly crafted to accomplish its specific objective—maintaining the supply of biomaterials.

NOTE: H.R. 872, approved August 13, was assigned Public Law No. 105–230.

Statement on the Settlement of Holocaust Assets Lawsuits
August 13, 1998

I am pleased that Holocaust survivors and private Swiss banks reached a settlement of several pending lawsuits. Both sides demonstrated understanding, flexibility, and determination in reaching a settlement that, once approved by the district court, will bring long-delayed justice to Holocaust victims and their families.

I applaud the work of the World Jewish Congress and key Members of the U.S. Congress for their roles in focusing attention on this important issue and for their strong advocacy on behalf of the claimants.

I also commend the active role played by Under Secretary Stuart Eizenstat and his team at the State Department, whose work with the parties earlier this year laid the groundwork for a settlement.

Letter to Congressional Leaders on Continuation of the National Emergency With Respect to the Lapse of the Export Administration Act of 1979
August 13, 1998

Dear Mr. Speaker: (Dear Mr. President:)

On August 19, 1994, in light of the expiration of the Export Administration Act of 1979, as amended (50 U.S.C. App. 2401 *et seq.*), I issued Executive Order 12924, declaring a national emergency and continuing the system of export regulation under the International Emergency Economic Powers Act (50 U.S.C. 1701 *et seq.*). Under section 202(d) of the National Emergencies Act (50 U.S.C. 1622(d)), the national emergency terminates on the anniversary date of its declaration unless the President publishes in the *Federal Register* and transmits to the Congress a notice of its continuation.

I am hereby advising the Congress that I have extended the national emergency declared in Executive Order 12924. Enclosed is a copy of the notice of extension.

Sincerely,

WILLIAM J. CLINTON

NOTE: Identical letters were sent to Newt Gingrich, Speaker of the House of Representatives, and Albert Gore, Jr., President of the Senate. This letter was released by the Office of the Press Secretary on August 14. The notice of August 13 is listed in Appendix D at the end of this volume.

Letter to Congressional Leaders Reporting on the National Emergency With Respect to Iraq
August 13, 1998

Dear Mr. Speaker: (Dear Mr. President:)

I hereby report to the Congress on the developments since my last report of February 3, 1998, concerning the national emergency with respect to Iraq that was declared in Executive Order 12722 of August 2, 1990. This report is submitted pursuant to section 401(c) of the National Emergencies Act, 50 U.S.C. 1641(c), and section 204(c) of the International Emergency Economic Powers Act (IEEPA), 50 U.S.C. 1703(c).

Executive Order 12722 ordered the immediate blocking of all property and interests in property of the Government of Iraq (including the Central Bank of Iraq) then or thereafter located in the United States or within the possession or control of a United States person. That order also prohibited the importation into the United States of goods and services of Iraqi origin, as well as the exportation of goods, services, and technology from the United States to Iraq. The order prohibited travel-related transactions to or from Iraq and the performance of any contract in support of any industrial, commercial, or governmental project in Iraq. United States persons were also prohibited from granting or extending credit or loans to the Government of Iraq.

The foregoing prohibitions (as well as the blocking of Government of Iraq property) were continued and augmented on August 9, 1990, by Executive Order 12724, which was issued in order to align the sanctions imposed by the United States with United Nations Security Council Resolution (UNSCR) 661 of August 6, 1990.

This report discusses only matters concerning the national emergency with respect to Iraq that was declared in Executive Order 12722 and matters relating to Executive Orders 12724 and 12817 (the "Executive Orders"). The report covers events from February 2 through August 1, 1998.

1. In April 1995, the U.N. Security Council adopted UNSCR 986 authorizing Iraq to export up to $1 billion in petroleum and petroleum products every 90 days for a total of 180 days under U.N. supervision in order to finance the purchase of food, medicine, and other humanitarian supplies. UNSCR 986 includes arrangements to ensure equitable distribution of humanitarian goods purchased with UNSCR 986 oil revenues to all the people of Iraq. The resolution also provides for the payment of compensation to victims of Iraqi aggression and for the funding of other U.N. activities with respect to Iraq. On May 20, 1996, a memorandum of understanding was concluded between the Secretariat of the United Nations and the Government of Iraq agreeing on terms for implementing UNSCR 986. On August 8, 1996, the UNSC committee established pursuant to UNSCR 661 ("the 661 Committee") adopted procedures to be employed in implementation of UNSCR 986. On December 9, 1996, the President of the Security Council received the report prepared by the Secretary General as requested by paragraph 13 of UNSCR 986, making UNSCR 986 effective as of 12:01 a.m. December 10, 1996.

On June 4, 1997, the U.N. Security Council adopted UNSCR 1111, renewing for another 180 days the authorization for Iraqi petroleum sales and purchases of humanitarian aid contained in UNSCR 986 of April 14, 1995. The Resolution became effective on June 8, 1997. On September 12, 1997, the Security Council, noting Iraq's decision not to export petroleum and petroleum products pursuant to UNSCR 1111 during the period June 8 to August 13, 1997, and deeply concerned about the resulting humanitarian consequences for the Iraqi people, adopted UNSCR 1129. This resolution replaced the two 90-day quotas with one 120-day quota and one 60-day quota in order to enable Iraq to export its full $2 billion quota of oil within the original 180 days of UNSCR 1111. On December 4, 1997, the U.N. Security Council adopted UNSCR 1143, renewing for another 180 days, beginning December 5, 1997, the authorization for Iraqi petroleum sales and humanitarian aid purchases contained in UNSCR 986.

On February 20, 1998, the U.N. Security Council adopted UNSCR 1153, authorizing the sale of Iraqi petroleum and petroleum products and the purchase of humanitarian aid for a 180-day period beginning with the date of notification by the President of the Security Council to the members thereof of receipt of the report requested in UNSCR 1153. UNSCR 1153 authorized the sale of $5.256 billion worth of Iraqi petroleum and petroleum products. On March 25, 1998, the Security Council, noting the shortfall in revenue from Iraq's sale of petroleum and petroleum products during the first 90-day period of implementation of UNSCR 1143, due to the delayed resumption in sales and a serious decrease in prices, and concerned about the resulting humanitarian consequences for the Iraqi people, adopted UNSCR 1158. This Resolution reaffirmed the authorization for Iraqi petroleum sales and purchases of humanitarian aid contained in UNSCR 1143 for the remainder of the second 90-day period and set the authorized value during that time frame to $1.4 billion pending implementation of UNSCR 1153. The 180-day period authorized in UNSCR 1153 began on May 30, 1998. On June 19, 1998, the Security Council adopted UNSCR 1175, authorizing the expenditure of up to $300 million on Iraqi oil infrastructure repairs in order to help Iraq reach the higher export ceiling permitted under UNSCR 1153. UNSCR 1175 also reaffirmed the Security Council's endorsement of the Secretary General's recommendation that the "oil-for-food" distribution plan be ongoing and project-based. During the period covered by this report, imports into the United States under the program totaled about 14.2 million barrels, bringing total imports since December 10, 1996, to approximately 51.5 million barrels.

2. There have been no amendments to the Iraqi Sanctions Regulations, 31 C.F.R. Part 575 (the "ISR" or the "Regulations") administered by the Office of Foreign Assets Control (OFAC) of the Department of the Treasury during the reporting period.

As previously reported, the Regulations were amended on December 10, 1996, to provide a statement of licensing policy regarding specific licensing of United States persons seeking to purchase Iraqi-origin petroleum and petroleum products from Iraq (61 *Fed. Reg.* 65312, December 11, 1996). Statements of licensing policy were also provided regarding sales of essential parts and equipment for the Kirkuk-Yumurtalik pipeline system, and sales of humanitarian goods to Iraq, pursuant to United Nations approval. A general license was also added to authorize dealings in Iraqi-origin petroleum and petroleum products that have been exported from Iraq with United Nations and United States Government approval.

All executory contracts must contain terms requiring that all proceeds of oil purchases from the Government of Iraq, including the State Oil Marketing Organization, must be placed in the U.N. escrow account at Banque Nationale de Paris, New York (the "986 escrow account"), and all Iraqi payments for authorized sales of pipeline parts and equipment, humanitarian goods, and incidental transaction costs borne by Iraq will, upon approval by the 661 Committee and satisfaction of other conditions established by the United Nations, be paid or payable out of the 986 escrow account.

3. Investigations of possible violations of the Iraqi sanctions continue to be pursued and appropriate enforcement actions taken. Several cases from prior reporting periods are continuing, and recent additional allegations have been referred by OFAC to the U.S. Customs Service for investigation.

Investigation also continues into the roles played by various individuals and firms outside Iraq in the Iraqi government procurement network. These investigations may lead to additions to OFAC's listing of individuals and organizations determined to be Specially Designated Nationals (SDNs) of the Government of Iraq.

Since my last report, OFAC has collected two civil monetary penalties totaling $9,000 from one company and one individual for violations of IEEPA and ISR prohibitions against transactions with Iraq.

4. The Office of Foreign Assets Control has issued hundreds of licensing determinations regarding transactions pertaining to Iraq or Iraqi assets since August 1990. Specific licenses have been issued for transactions such as the filing of legal actions against Iraqi governmental entities, legal representation of Iraq, and the exportation to Iraq of donated medicine, medical supplies, and food intended for humanitarian relief purposes, sales of humanitarian supplies to Iraq under UNSCRs 986, 1111, 1143, and 1153, diplomatic transactions, the execution of powers of attorney relating to the administration of personal assets and decedents' estates in Iraq, and the protection of preexistent intellectual property rights in Iraq. Since my last report, 75 specific licenses have been issued, most with respect to sales of humanitarian goods.

Since December 10, 1996, OFAC has issued specific licenses authorizing commercial sales of humanitarian goods funded by Iraqi oil sales pursuant to UNSCRs 986, 1111, 1143, and 1153 valued at more than $324 million. Of that amount, approximately $298 million represents sales of basic foodstuffs, $14 million for medicines and medical supplies, $9.2 million for water testing and treatment equipment, and nearly $3 million to fund a variety of United Nations activities in Iraq. International humanitarian relief in Iraq is coordinated under the direction of the United Nations Office of the Humanitarian Coordinator of Iraq. Assisting U.N. agencies include the World Food Program, the U.N. Population Fund, the U.N. Food and Agriculture Organization, the World Health Organization, and UNICEF. As of June 29, 1998, OFAC had authorized sales valued at more than $85 million worth of humanitarian goods during the current reporting period.

5. The expenses incurred by the Federal Government in the 6-month period from February 2 through August 1, 1998, that are directly attributable to the exercise of powers and authorities conferred by the declaration of a national

emergency with respect to Iraq, are reported to be about $1.1 million, most of which represents wage and salary costs for Federal personnel. Personnel costs were largely centered in the Department of the Treasury (particularly in the Office of Foreign Assets Control, the U.S. Customs Service, the Office of the Under Secretary for Enforcement, and the Office of the General Counsel), the Department of State (particularly the Bureau of Economic and Business Affairs, the Bureau of Near Eastern Affairs, the Bureau of International Organization Affairs, the Bureau of Political-Military Affairs, the Bureau of Intelligence and Research, the U.S. Mission to the United Nations, and the Office of the Legal Adviser), and the Department of Transportation (particularly the U.S. Coast Guard).

6. The United States imposed economic sanctions on Iraq in response to Iraq's illegal invasion and occupation of Kuwait, a clear act of brutal aggression. The United States, together with the international community, is maintaining economic sanctions against Iraq because the Iraqi regime has failed to comply fully with relevant United Nations Security Council resolutions. Iraqi compliance with these resolutions is necessary before the United States will consider lifting economic sanctions. Security Council resolutions on Iraq call for the elimination of Iraqi weapons of mass destruction, Iraqi recognition of Kuwait and the inviolability of the Iraq-Kuwait boundary, the release of Kuwaiti and other third-country nationals, compensation for victims of Iraqi aggression, long-term monitoring of weapons of mass destruction capabilities, the return of Kuwaiti assets stolen during Iraq's illegal occupation of Kuwait, renunciation of terrorism, an end to internal Iraqi repression of its own civilian population, and the facilitation of access by international relief organizations to all those in need in all parts of Iraq. Eight years after the invasion, a pattern of defiance persists: a refusal to account for missing Kuwaiti detainees; failure to return Kuwaiti property worth millions of dollars, including military equipment that was used by Iraq in its move-

ment of troops to the Kuwaiti border in October 1994; sponsorship of assassinations in Lebanon and in northern Iraq; incomplete declarations to weapons inspectors and refusal to provide immediate, unconditional, and unrestricted access to sites by these inspectors; and ongoing widespread human rights violations. As a result, the U.N. sanctions remain in place; the United States will continue to enforce those sanctions under domestic authority.

The Baghdad government continues to violate basic human rights of its own citizens through systematic repression of all forms of political expression, oppression of minorities, and denial of humanitarian assistance. The Government of Iraq has repeatedly said it will not comply with UNSCR 688 of April 5, 1991. The Iraqi military routinely harasses residents of the north, and has attempted to "Arabize" the Kurdish, Turkomen, and Assyrian areas in the north. Iraq has not relented in its artillery attacks against civilian population centers in the south, or in its burning and draining operations in the southern marshes, which have forced thousands to flee to neighboring states.

The policies and actions of the Saddam Hussein regime continue to pose an unusual and extraordinary threat to the national security and foreign policy of the United States, as well as to regional peace and security. The U.N. resolutions affirm that the Security Council be assured of Iraq's peaceful intentions in judging its compliance with sanctions. Because of Iraq's failure to comply fully with these resolutions, the United States will continue to apply economic sanctions to deter it from threatening peace and stability in the region.

Sincerely,

WILLIAM J. CLINTON

NOTE: Identical letters were sent to Newt Gingrich, Speaker of the House of Representatives, and Albert Gore, Jr., President of the Senate. This letter was released by the Office of the Press Secretary on August 14.

Remarks at a Democratic National Committee Labor Luncheon
August 14, 1998

Thank you, John, for the wonderful introduction and, even more, for your friendship and your leadership. I thank all the officers of the AFL–CIO and our friends from the National Education Association who are here.

I'd like to say a special word of appreciation to my good friend Gerry McEntee, the chair of your political committee; and I'd like to congratulate Morty Bahr on settling the CWA/Bell Atlantic strike. I gave him his reward today; I have ordered him to be on a plane for the Middle East by 9 o'clock tonight. [*Laughter*]

I want to thank Governor Romer and Steve Grossman and Len Barrack and all the DNC staff and the White House staff and all who have done so much work with you in substance and on politics over the last few years. We've been a good team; we've gotten a lot done; America's a better place. But we've got a lot still to do.

Before I begin, I'd like to make a brief announcement about help to our hardest pressed communities during what is now officially the hottest summer ever recorded. For 17 years now, the LIHEAP program—that's the Low Income Home Energy Assistance Program—has helped the neediest Americans to protect their families in times of extreme weather conditions, helping pay for air-conditioners and electric bills and fans during the hot summer months, for heating in times of extreme cold. It has literally been a lifesaver for many, many Americans in my personal experience in times of very difficult weather.

As you know, we are experiencing the hottest summer on record. In many States in the mid-South, including my home State of Arkansas, we had for the first time ever 3 weeks or more of straight 100 degree-plus days. Earlier this week the Vice President announced that last month was the hottest record ever recorded on the planet Earth, beating out July 1997 by half a degree. July was the seventh month in a row where 1998 was hotter than 1997, and 1997 was the hottest year ever recorded.

This heat wave has destroyed crops, caused power outages, led to the deaths of more than 100 Americans. It threatens mostly our most vulnerable people, young children, the disabled, the elderly. And for those who don't have air-conditioning, the high temperatures for those in physically difficult positions will continue to be life threatening.

We've been able to make this heat wave safer because of the LIHEAP program. It's a good program. Last month I directed the Department of Health and Human Services to release $100 million in emergency funds for the 11 hottest Southern States. Today, because the heat wave has continued and families continue to struggle, I have ordered the release of another $50 million to these States.

One of the difficult issues we are fighting out in the Congress this year is that the House committee with jurisdiction over these matters has recommended the elimination of this program. I think, based on the experience of ordinary people this summer, that would be a mistake. I can understand that it might be beyond the experience of some people, because they live in moderate climates or they've never dealt with this. But I'll never forget one summer when I was in Arkansas, and it was so hot the elderly people—and there were thousands and thousands of them that lived in homes without air-conditioning—we had to bring them into the senior citizen centers and put up cots. We had to buy thousands and thousands of fans for people who were in their homes.

You know, most of us, we're pretty comfortable. We're sitting here in this beautiful hotel; we've got this nice air-conditioning going. We take some things for granted. There are a lot of our fellow Americans out there that are literally in danger this summer.

So we'll do what we can, but I hate to put anything else on your legislative plate, but I need you to help me get this LIHEAP program continued. It looks like extreme weather will intensify, not abate, and America needs to be there to help our most vulnerable citizens.

I want to talk to you today about the important choice facing the American people, including the members of your organizations, all of them, in this election season. I have said before and I will say again that we have to decide to move forward with the same approach that has brought our Nation to its present strength and prosperity, an approach that puts progress over partisanship and people over politics and unity over division. That is the choice.

Five and a half years ago, when you helped Al Gore and me to get elected, we said we would bring the country a new direction with new leadership and new ideas based on old values. You've fought alongside us to help us to bring these changes to not just your members but all the American people. And now the results can be seen.

Thanks to the hard work, the ingenuity, the good citizenship of our fellow Americans, but supported by the policies of this administration, we now have the lowest unemployment rate in 28 years and 16 million new jobs; the lowest crime rate in 25 years; the smallest percentage of the people on welfare in 29 years. We're about to have the first balanced budget and surplus since Neil Armstrong walked on the Moon 29 years ago; inflation, the lowest in 35 years; homeownership, the highest in history. Last year wages went up at twice the rate of inflation after having been stagnant for so very long.

Millions of Americans have taken advantage of the family and medical leave law. Because of the Brady law, 118 felons an hour have been unable to get a handgun. We will never know how many lives that has saved. Millions more children are getting health care; the doors to college are open wider than ever before; the environment is cleaner even as the economy has grown. And you can take a lot of responsibility for that.

I would like to say a special word of appreciation to the Federal employees, the members of our Federal work force, for they have produced more while reducing the size of Government by approximately 350,000 people to its smallest point since John Kennedy was President 35 years ago. None of this would have been possible had it not been for their ingenuity and continued dramatic increases in productivity. And I am profoundly grateful for that.

Now, this is a golden moment for our country, and the big question is what to do with it. I'm proud of the things that have been accomplished so far, but every election is about the future.

Some of you have heard me tell this story, but when I had been Governor 10 years and was trying to decide whether to run for another 4-year term, I went out to the State fair. And a guy came up to me in overalls and said, "Bill, are you going to run again?" And I said, "Well, if I do, will you vote for me?" He said, "Sure, I always have." And I said, "Well, aren't you sick of me after all these years?" He said, "No, but about everybody else I know is." [*Laughter*] And I said, "Well, don't they think I've done a good job?" He said, "Sure, but that's what we paid you for. You drew a check every 2 weeks, didn't you?" [*Laughter*] It was a very interesting, insightful conversation with him. Elections are and properly should be about the future.

Now, the conventional wisdom is, whenever unemployment is low and inflation is low and job growth is high and things are good, that countries will be like people and families and businesses. You just want to say, "Gosh, man, we had years when things were a real hassle, and I just want to take a break. I want to be left alone."

I think, under these circumstances, it would be a serious mistake to take that approach. Why? Because, as every one of you knows—and you heard John Sweeney talk about the speech I gave to the World Trade Organization—we were over there talking about the impact of the Asian financial crisis on the American economy. Every one of you knows the world is changing very rapidly in ways that affect how we work, how we live, how we relate to each other, how we relate to our friends beyond our Nation's borders.

If we sit still and say, "Gosh, isn't this great," we won't be able to maintain these great conditions. The only way to do it is to stay ahead of the changes, to keep our energy level up, to keep our focus up, to keep looking at the long-term challenges facing America. So I would like to respectfully suggest that this election ought to be what's right for the country and that good policy would be good politics.

What are the long-term challenges of America? First and foremost, we've got to stick with the economic strategy that got us here and refine it and improve it: fiscal discipline, expanding our exports, investing in the skills and education of our people. We can't depart from this path. I would like to see an expansion of our efforts to bring the benefits of the economic recovery to urban neighborhoods, small rural towns, and Indian reservations which haven't felt the benefit of it yet. And it is an inflation-free way to grow the economy. I keep arguing to my friends in the business community that the biggest untapped market for American goods and services is here in America. It's in the neighborhoods, the small towns, the Native American communities which have not yet felt the lift of this recovery.

Second, related to our economy, we have to honor our parents and future generations, and we, those of us in the baby boom generation, have to do our duty by our children and grandchildren by saving Social Security for the 21st century. And we shouldn't spend a penny of this surplus until we know we have provided for a Social Security system that is decent, comprehensive, and adequate, but we've done it in a way that will not lower the standard of living of the children of the baby boomers.

Now, we were very fortunate to have an economic estimate come out a few weeks ago, estimating that the projected surplus over the next 10 years was going to be about double what we had previously thought. And that's good; I'm glad to have an estimate like that. But we'll get another estimate next year and another estimate the year after and another estimate the year after that.

In an election year, it is tempting to offer and provide a great big tax cut or a great big new program, but you know and I know, if you pass a tax cut, you're never going to repeal it, whether or not that projected surplus materializes.

Now, I'm not against tax cuts; I've got a targeted tax cut before the Congress right now to help working families with child care, to help meet some of the energy challenges we face, to help deal with some of the other personal family challenges that people face. I'm not against that. What I am against is promising something to the American people and giving it to them that sounds good today but that will give us a royal headache in the future.

The biggest challenge we've got out there is when I retire—I'm the oldest of the baby boomers—and then all the ones that are down to 18 years younger than me get in, at present birth rates, work force participation rates, immigration rates, and retirement rates—when all that happens, there will only be two people working for every person drawing Social Security. Therefore, the system, as presently constituted, is unsustainable. And if we do not act now to reform it, including having available whatever money the American people have pro-

duced through this surplus, we will regret it for a long time. Because I don't think—I can tell you that every person I know in my generation, including middle-class, middle-income people living on very modest incomes, nobody wants us to retire in ways that say to our kids, "Okay, let's raise your payroll tax 2½ percent. I want to lower your standard of living to take care of mine. I want to undermine your ability to raise and educate my grandchildren so I can live just like my parents did in retirement." We don't want that.

Now, since that's a few years off, small changes today can make a big impact tomorrow. I know you have supported us on this, but this is profoundly important. It's also very important to our economic stability. Suppose we were to do this with this surplus, and then it didn't materialize. Then where would we be? Do you want to go back to the economic policies of the eighties where we quadrupled the debt in 12 years? I don't think so. So it's very important.

The third thing I want to say is, we have to protect our families in the health care area with a strong Patients' Bill of Rights. We've got 160 million people in managed care plans. They do a lot of good, managed care plans, in some areas. They can make health care more affordable and more available. But medical decisions ought to be made by doctors and patients, not accountants. That means, among other things, access to specialists; access to the emergency room; continuity of care, even if your employer changes health care providers while you're pregnant, while you're in the middle of chemotherapy, while you're in the middle of something else. Every American deserves quality care. Every American deserves privacy of medical records as well. And I want to thank you for the very effective grassroots campaign you're waging for the Patients' Bill of Rights.

The differences between the bipartisan bill that the Democrats support and that of the Republican leadership in Congress are breathtaking. You may have seen this little chart I showed in Louisville, Kentucky, a couple of days ago. I wish you could mail it to every member of every organization here present. Protecting medical privacy—big deal to most families: Our proposal does; theirs doesn't. Guaranteeing direct access to specialists: Our proposal does; theirs doesn't. Assuring that accountants don't make arbitrary medical decisions: Our proposal does; theirs doesn't. Providing real emergency room protection: Ours, yes; theirs, no. Holding health plans accountable if they harm patients: Ours, yes; theirs, no. Protecting patients from secret financial incentives to doctors to deny care: Ours, yes; theirs, no. Keeping your same doctor through critical treatment periods: Ours, yes; theirs, no. Maybe most important of all, covering all health plans: Ours, yes; theirs leaves 100 million Americans out.

So when Congress comes back, everybody is going to be for a Patients' Bill of Rights. It's going to be like motherhood and apple pie and the Fourth of July. So you've got to look beyond the label, and the American people are very sophisticated about this because they have to navigate through their health care plans. You need to help them and help us get this information out.

The fourth thing we have to do is to make sure our kids have the best education in the world. We've done a great deal to open the doors of college to all Americans. We've made community college virtually free to most American families. And everybody believes we've got the best system of higher education in the world. But nobody believes every child in this country—every child—has a chance to get an elementary and secondary education that's the best in the world.

Now, I have given Congress a plan to support reform effort to the grassroots level: high but voluntary national standards; hiring more highly trained teachers; having smaller classes in the early grades; building new schools and modernizing old ones; hooking up classrooms to the Internet; creating charter schools; and providing more opportunities for more kids to go to summer school and after-school programs so they learn more and get in less trouble. That's our agenda.

We have the money to do it, and we should debate that in this election because the Congress disagrees with me on it, at least the Republican majority does. On September 8th all across America, our teachers will shine a spotlight on one of these issues, the need to modernize our school buildings. I thank them for doing that; you can't build the children up in school buildings that are falling down.

Fifth, we have to pass on to future generations the Earth God gave us. We have to prove that we can grow the economy and improve the environment. For all the advances in clean water, 40 percent of our lakes and streams and rivers are still too polluted for fishing and swimming. And a lot of your members, the only vacation they ever get is when they go to a State park or a national park or to some fishing resort or someplace to a lake where they can take their kids skiing. So our clean water initiative is just one example of what we can do and must do to grow the economy and to preserve the environment.

The last thing I want to say is this, because the AFL–CIO has a very important responsibility, in my view, that you have always fulfilled, to try to educate your own members and the country generally about the importance of America's leadership in the world for peace and freedom and prosperity. And as these awful events in Africa have reminded us, as the Asian financial turmoil has reminded us—where 40 percent of our farm exports go, and they're down 30 percent this year, just for one example—our fate is increasingly bound up with the rest of the world, and we cannot retreat from America's responsibility to stand up for peace and freedom and prosperity. Our own peace, freedom, and prosperity depends upon our willingness to stand for it around the world.

In the last few days, I've spent more time on these two challenges, by far, than anything else, and we have more to do. I had a good talk with President Yeltsin today. A few days ago, I talked with the new Japanese Prime Minister. I'm soon going to Russia and then over to Ireland to keep doing what we can to support the peace process there. We're pushing ahead to try to bring peace to the Middle East and to stop the very difficult situation in Kosovo. Most Americans don't think about a lot of this a lot of the time. A lot of Americans might not know what the International Monetary Fund is, but having the right kind of international posture is critical to our own prosperity and critical to our own security. And I have always respected the support the AFL–CIO has given to Republican and Democratic Presidents alike for the proposition that we have to stand strong for freedom in the world.

America has got a good agenda in the coming months. We can be for saving Social Security first, better schools, a cleaner environment, and a Patients' Bill of Rights, and we can sell that in every place in America. They are real choices real Americans face in this election. We don't have to be excessively partisan. We can say we're for the progress of this country. We want to build on what brung us, if you'll forgive me an Arkansas phrase. And we're going to do it.

And you'll be critical to that. Without your help, we never would have had the minimum wage; we wouldn't have protected Medicare and Medicaid; we wouldn't have had family and medical leave; we wouldn't have had the economic plan of 1993, which reduced the deficit by 92 percent before we ever passed the balanced budget plan. Without your help, none of that could have happened.

When I visited California and campaigned against Proposition 226 out there, all the smart prognosticators said there was no way you could win that fight. But when I saw your dedication and skill, the level and intensity of your commitment, I thought, I'm not so sure. Besides, you were right on the issue, and your message prevailed.

So I will say again: This election is about the future, and it should be. It is about ideas, and it should be. We have good candidates; I've seen a lot of them out there. We've got a good Democratic National Committee that's worked its heart out to restore its health and direction and energy. And if you will help us, we can go out there and tell everybody in America, "Let's stay with what brought us to this point, but be active. Let's save Social Security first before we spend that surplus. Let's give our kids the best elementary and secondary schools in the world. Let's have a Patients' Bill of Rights. Let's prove we can continue to grow

the economy and improve the environment. Let's keep standing up for peace and freedom and prosperity. We're going to be just fine."

You know, the First Lady, in this Millennial Project of ours, has a theme: "Honor the past; imagine the future." That pretty well captures where organized labor is today. You've got an enormous sense of your own roots, your own accomplishments, the deeply held values that have never changed. But there is more imagination, more willingness to think new thoughts, come up with new ideas, work out creative relationships with management so that everybody can win than I have ever seen in my lifetime. If America will honor the past and imagine the future and vote on that basis, we're going to have a good November.

Thank you, and God bless you. [*Applause*] Thank you.

NOTE: The President spoke at 1:30 p.m. in the John Hay Room at the Hay Adams Hotel. In his remarks, he referred to John J. Sweeney, president, AFL–CIO; Gerald W. McEntee, president, American Federation of State, County, and Municipal Employees; Morton Bahr, president, Communications Workers of America (CWA); Gov. Roy Romer of Colorado, general chair, Steve Grossman, national chair, and Leonard Barrack, national finance chair, Democratic National Committee; President Boris Yeltsin of Russia; and Prime Minister Keizo Obuchi of Japan.

Statement on Announcing Assistance to Heat-Stricken Areas in the South and Southwest
August 14, 1998

Today I am pleased to announce that additional relief is on the way to thousands directly impacted by the heat wave in the South and Southwest.

On July 23, I announced the release of $100 million in emergency Low Income Home Energy Assistance Program (LIHEAP) funds to the 11 Southern and Southwestern States that were hit hardest by the heat wave. Since this time, the heat wave has continued, so today I am directing the Department of Health and Human

Services to release an additional $50 million in LIHEAP assistance to those 11 States.

Funds will be released to 11 Southern and Southwestern States: Texas, Arkansas, Louisiana, South Carolina, Oklahoma, Georgia, Florida, Alabama, Tennessee, North Carolina, and Mississippi.

This scorching heat wave has destroyed crops, caused widespread power outages, and worst of all, led to the deaths of more than 100 Americans. The heat poses the greatest threat to our most vulnerable citizens—children, the disabled, and the elderly. And for all those who cannot afford air-conditioning, the high temperatures will continue to be life threatening.

The release of these emergency LIHEAP funds will help eligible families and individuals pay for costs associated with home cooling, in-

cluding the purchase of air-conditioners and payment of electricity bills.

This emergency relief was paid for in last year's bipartisan balanced budget agreement. And thanks to our bipartisan commitment, thousands of Americans will be better able to protect their children and families this summer.

Statement on the Petition to the Court of Appeals on Regulation of Tobacco Products
August 14, 1998

The Solicitor General has today authorized the filing of a petition in the Court of Appeals for the Fourth Circuit seeking rehearing en banc of the three-judge panel's decision regarding FDA regulation of tobacco products. I am firmly committed to the FDA's rule and its role in protecting our children from tobacco. Confirming the FDA's authority over tobacco products is necessary to help stop young people from

smoking before they start by stopping advertising targeted at children and curbing minors' access to tobacco products. Almost 3,000 young people become regular smokers each day, and 1,000 of them will die prematurely as a result. If the leadership in Congress would act responsibly, it would enact bipartisan comprehensive tobacco legislation to confirm the FDA's authority and take this matter out of the courtroom.

Videotaped Address to the People of Kenya and Tanzania
August 14, 1998

I am honored to address you, the people of Kenya and Tanzania. On behalf of all the American people, I extend our deepest condolences to the families and the friends of those Kenyans and Tanzanians who perished in the tragic attacks in Nairobi and Dar es Salaam.

Some of them worked alongside Americans at our Embassies, making vital contributions to our common efforts, and we are very grateful for their service. Others were nearby, working hard, as they did every day. All of these men and women were important to America, because we cherish our friendship with your peoples. We have long admired the achievements of your citizens and the beauty of your lands. All three of our nations have lost beloved sons and daughters, and so many, many more were injured. We pray, too, for their speedy recovery.

Let me express America's profound gratitude for your extraordinary efforts, with Americans

and others, to respond to this shared tragedy, pulling people from the wreckage, aiding the wounded, searching for evidence as to who committed these terrible acts.

Violent extremists try to use bullets and bombs to derail our united efforts to bring peace to every part of this Earth. We grieve together, but I am proud that our nations have also renewed our commitment to stand together, to bring the offenders swiftly to justice, to combat terrorism in all its forms and to create a more tolerant and more peaceful world for our children.

NOTE: The address was videotaped at 10:10 a.m. in the Cabinet Room at the White House for later broadcast on the U.S. Information Agency WORLDNET, and the transcript was embargoed for release until 11:30 p.m. A tape was not available for verification of the content of this address.

The President's Radio Address
August 15, 1998

Good morning. Two days ago, at Andrews Air Force Base, we welcomed them home: America's brave sons and daughters, carried under Stars and Stripes, flanked by the silent sentries of the honor guard. They had perished in Nairobi, cruelly and without warning, in an act of terror at the American Embassy. It was not the sort of homecoming any of us would have wished. But it was a tribute that befit their service to our Nation.

Hillary and I had the honor to meet with their families on the morning of the ceremony. They shared stories with us, stories and memories, showing us photographs. Their shoulders were heavy with sadness; their voices sometimes shook. But anyone could tell that their hearts were full of pride for the brave service of their loved ones and pride in the Nation they so ably and faithfully represented around the world. Collectively, over the course of their careers, these 12 men and women represented the United States in more than 20 countries across the globe, from Brazil to Botswana, from France to the Philippines, from South Korea to their final post, Kenya.

They represented America not simply by their deeds but by their character: by the quiet labors of a medical doctor, the careful diplomacy of a Foreign Service officer, the iron discipline of men and women in uniform. Their dedication to America was matched by their dedication to their families. In all these ways, they represented the best of our country. They showed the world our very best face and shared with its people our most cherished values.

As a nation, we have lost much. These families have lost even more. Words cannot describe and tributes cannot begin to fill the cruel vacancy left by evil acts of terror. But in the example of the proud and grieving families I met on Thursday, we find an embodiment of American resolve. They made it clear to me they did not want us to give in to terror or to turn inward or retreat, for the world is full of promise, and they do not want us to try to stop resolving the misunderstandings that can deteriorate into the rot of hatred. Instead, they urged us to stand strong, as ever, for freedom and democracy in all countries and for all people.

And our administration will remain committed to the fight against terror. Over the last few years, working with Congress, we have passed tough new criminal penalties, tightened security at airports, strengthened protection of our troops overseas. We have created an international coalition to help us combat terrorism and have apprehended or helped to capture more than 40 terrorists abroad, including those involved in attacks on Pan Am Flight 830 and the World Trade Center and in the murder of two CIA employees in Virginia.

We must continue to lead the world toward peace, freedom, and prosperity. That is why our diplomats are on the job today around the world, working to ensure our national security, working to strengthen the global economy, working to bring peace to troubled regions, working often at risk to themselves. And that is why we now must work to rebuild our Embassies in Nairobi and Dar es Salaam, to secure our Embassies and outposts around the world, to support our friends in Tanzania and Kenya as they rebuild. This week I have spoken with leaders in Congress, Republicans and Democrats alike. In the finest American tradition, they have pledged to join me in protecting America's presence throughout the world.

Today we think especially of those serving in our diplomatic posts. I ask all our citizens to say a prayer for them and to express gratitude for their service. The spirit of the patriots who have dedicated or lost their lives to service is the spirit of America. They help to keep our Nation strong and free, peaceful and proud, a powerful beacon of hope for the world.

Thank you for listening.

NOTE: The President spoke at 10:06 a.m. from the Oval Office at the White House.

Statement on the Terrorist Bombing in Omagh, Northern Ireland
August 15, 1998

Today's terrorist bombing in Omagh was a barbaric act intended to wreck Northern Ireland's aspirations for peace and reconciliation. On behalf of every American, I condemn this butchery and hope that the culprits will be brought to justice quickly. I extend our deep sympathy to those affected by this tragedy. I renew my pledge to stand with the people of Northern Ireland against the perpetrators of violence; they will find no friends here.

Now is the time for the parties of peace in Northern Ireland to redouble their efforts.

Address to the Nation on Testimony Before the Independent Counsel's Grand Jury
August 17, 1998

Good evening. This afternoon in this room, from this chair, I testified before the Office of Independent Counsel and the grand jury. I answered their questions truthfully, including questions about my private life, questions no American citizen would ever want to answer.

Still, I must take complete responsibility for all my actions, both public and private. And that is why I am speaking to you tonight.

As you know, in a deposition in January I was asked questions about my relationship with Monica Lewinsky. While my answers were legally accurate, I did not volunteer information. Indeed, I did have a relationship with Ms. Lewinsky that was not appropriate. In fact, it was wrong. It constituted a critical lapse in judgment and a personal failure on my part for which I am solely and completely responsible.

But I told the grand jury today, and I say to you now, that at no time did I ask anyone to lie, to hide or destroy evidence, or to take any other unlawful action.

I know that my public comments and my silence about this matter gave a false impression. I misled people, including even my wife. I deeply regret that. I can only tell you I was motivated by many factors: first, by a desire to protect myself from the embarrassment of my own conduct. I was also very concerned about protecting my family. The fact that these questions were being asked in a politically inspired lawsuit which has since been dismissed was a consideration, too.

In addition, I had real and serious concerns about an Independent Counsel investigation that began with private business dealings 20 years ago—dealings, I might add, about which an independent Federal agency found no evidence of any wrongdoing by me or my wife over 2 years ago. The Independent Counsel investigation moved on to my staff and friends, then into my private life. And now the investigation itself is under investigation. This has gone on too long, cost too much, and hurt too many innocent people.

Now this matter is between me, the two people I love most, my wife and our daughter, and our God. I must put it right, and I am prepared to do whatever it takes to do so. Nothing is more important to me personally. But it is private. And I intend to reclaim my family life for my family. It's nobody's business but ours. Even Presidents have private lives.

It is time to stop the pursuit of personal destruction and the prying into private lives and get on with our national life. Our country has been distracted by this matter for too long. And I take my responsibility for my part in all of this; this is all I can do. Now it is time—in fact, it is past time—to move on. We have important work to do, real opportunities to seize, real problems to solve, real security matters to face.

And so, tonight I ask you to turn away from the spectacle of the past 7 months, to repair the fabric of our national discourse, and to return our attention to all the challenges and all the promise of the next American century.

Thank you for watching, and good night.

NOTE: The President spoke at 10:02 p.m. from the Map Room at the White House. In his remarks, he referred to former White House intern Monica S. Lewinsky, subject of Independent Counsel Kenneth Starr's expanded investigation.

Letter to Congressional Leaders Reporting on the Deployment of United States Forces To Protect the United States Embassy in Albania
August 18, 1998

Dear Mr. Speaker: *(Dear Mr. President:)*

After receiving credible information of a possible attack against the U.S. embassy in Tirana, Albania, similar to the attacks against our missions in Nairobi and Dar es Salaam, the Department of State authorized the draw-down of embassy personnel. Embassy business is currently conducted from the Rilindja Ridge Housing Complex in Tirana, as a new embassy building with improved security features is currently undergoing construction. The Marine Security Guard detachment at the embassy consists of six Marines.

Consequently, to enhance security at the present site of embassy operations, on Sunday, August 16, 1998, at about 12:00 p.m. eastern daylight time, a combat-equipped unit consisting of about 200 Marines from the 22nd Marine Expeditionary Unit and 10 Navy SEALS was deployed to Albania to provide security to the embassy compound at the Rilindja Ridge site. These personnel were deployed from ships that were already in the Adriatic Sea region preparing for an amphibious NATO military exercise, which was scheduled for August 17–22,

1998. As of August 17, 1998, all personnel from this unit except for 50 Marines have returned to their ships to participate in the previously scheduled NATO exercise. United States Armed Forces personnel will continue to augment security at the Rilindja Ridge compound until it is determined that the additional security support is unnecessary.

I have taken this action pursuant to my constitutional authority to conduct U.S. foreign relations and as Commander in Chief and Chief Executive.

I am providing this report as part of my efforts to keep the Congress fully informed, consistent with the War Powers Resolution. I appreciate the support of the Congress in this action to assist in embassy security and the security of American citizens overseas.

Sincerely,

WILLIAM J. CLINTON

NOTE: Identical letters were sent to Newt Gingrich, Speaker of the House of Representatives, and Strom Thurmond, President pro tempore of the Senate.

Letter to Congressional Leaders on Additional Sanctions Under the National Emergency With Respect to Angola (UNITA)
August 18, 1998

Dear Mr. Speaker: *(Dear Mr. President:)*

Pursuant to section 204(b) of the International Emergency Economic Powers Act, 50 U.S.C. 1703(b), I hereby report to the Congress that I have exercised my statutory authority to take additional steps with respect to the actions and policies of the National Union for the Total Independence of Angola (UNITA) and the na-

tional emergency declared in Executive Order 12865.

The circumstances that led to the declaration on September 26, 1993, of a national emergency have not been resolved. The actions and policies of UNITA continue to pose an unusual and extraordinary threat to the foreign policy of the United States. United Nations Security Council

Resolution 864 (1993) imposed prohibitions against the sale of weapons, military materiel, and petroleum products to UNITA. United Nations Security Council Resolutions 1127 of August 28, 1997, and 1130 of September 29, 1997, imposed additional sanctions against UNITA due to the serious difficulties in the Angolan peace process resulting from delays by UNITA in the implementation of its essential obligations as established by the Lusaka Peace Protocol of November 20, 1994.

Recently, the United Nations Security Council acted to impose additional sanctions in response to UNITA's failure to comply with its obligations under the Lusaka Peace Protocol, which has jeopardized the return of peace to Angola. United Nations Security Council Resolutions 1173 of June 12, 1998, and 1176 of June 24, 1998, responded in particular to UNITA's continued refusal to allow the Government of Angola to establish state administration over four towns that remain under UNITA's control. These resolutions demand UNITA's compliance with its obligations under the Lusaka Peace Protocol, including demilitarization of all its forces, and full cooperation in the process of allowing the Government of Angola to extend its authority throughout Angola.

Accordingly, and pursuant to the requirements of United Nations Security Council Resolutions 1173 and 1176, I have exercised my statutory authority and issued an Executive order which: (1) blocks property and property interests (within the United States or within the possession or control of United States persons) of UNITA, and of designated senior officials of UNITA and adult members of their immediate families; (2) prohibits the importation into the United States of all diamonds exported from Angola that are not controlled by a Certificate of Origin regime of the Government of Angola; (3) prohibits the sale or supply to Angola from the United States or by United States persons, except through designated points of entry, of motorized vehicles, watercraft, and spare parts for the foregoing, and equipment used in mining, regardless of origin; and (4) prohibits the sale or supply to Angola from the United States or by United States persons of mining services or of ground or waterborne transportation services, regardless of origin, to persons in UNITA-held territory. The order also prohibits any transaction by a United States person, or within the United States, that evades or avoids, or has the purpose of evading or avoiding, or attempts to violate, any of the prohibitions set forth in the order.

In furtherance of the goals of United Nations Security Council Resolutions 1173 and 1176, and of the foreign policy interests of the United States, the order makes explicit that exemptions from the prohibitions that it imposes may be authorized for medical and humanitarian purposes.

The order defines UNITA to include: (1) the National Union for the Total Independence of Angola; (2) the Armed Forces for the Liberation of Angola (FALA); and (3) any person acting or purporting to act for or on behalf of the foregoing, including the Center for Democracy in Angola (CEDA).

The measures taken in the order will immediately demonstrate to UNITA the seriousness of our concern over its delays in implementing the peace process. The blocking of UNITA's property and the other prohibitions imposed under this Executive order will further limit UNITA's capacity to pay for its military build-up and to undermine the peace process. It is particularly important for the United States and the international community to demonstrate to UNITA the necessity of completing the peace process in Angola.

When UNITA fully complies with its obligations and completes its transition from an armed movement to an unarmed political party, the United States will support measures lifting these sanctions.

I am enclosing a copy of the Executive order I have issued. The order is effective at 12:01 a.m., eastern daylight time on August 19, 1998.

Sincerely,

WILLIAM J. CLINTON

NOTE: Identical letters were sent to Newt Gingrich, Speaker of the House of Representatives, and Albert Gore, Jr., President of the Senate. This letter was released by the Office of the Press Secretary on August 19. The Executive order of August 18 is listed in Appendix D at the end of this volume.

Remarks in Martha's Vineyard, Massachusetts, on Military Action Against Terrorist Sites in Afghanistan and Sudan
August 20, 1998

Good afternoon. Today I ordered our Armed Forces to strike at terrorist-related facilities in Afghanistan and Sudan because of the threat they present to our national security.

I have said many times that terrorism is one of the greatest dangers we face in this new global era. We saw its twisted mentality at work last week in the Embassy bombings in Nairobi and Dar es Salaam, which took the lives of innocent Americans and Africans and injured thousands more. Today we have struck back.

The United States launched an attack this morning on one of the most active terrorist bases in the world. It is located in Afghanistan and operated by groups affiliated with Usama bin Ladin, a network not sponsored by any state but as dangerous as any we face. We also struck a chemical weapons-related facility in Sudan. Our target was the terrorists' base of operation and infrastructure. Our objective was to damage their capacity to strike at Americans and other innocent people.

I ordered this action for four reasons: first, because we have convincing evidence these groups played the key role in the Embassy bombings in Kenya and Tanzania; second, because these groups have executed terrorist attacks against Americans in the past; third, because we have compelling information that they were planning additional terrorist attacks against our citizens and others with the inevitable collateral casualties we saw so tragically in Africa; and fourth, because they are seeking to acquire chemical weapons and other dangerous weapons.

Terrorists must have no doubt that, in the face of their threats, America will protect its citizens and will continue to lead the world's fight for peace, freedom, and security.

Now I am returning to Washington to be briefed by my national security team on the latest information. I will provide you with a more detailed statement later this afternoon from the White House.

Thank you very much.

NOTE: The President spoke at 1:55 p.m. in the gymnasium at Edgartown Elementary School, prior to his departure for Washington, DC.

Address to the Nation on Military Action Against Terrorist Sites in Afghanistan and Sudan
August 20, 1998

Good afternoon. Today I ordered our Armed Forces to strike at terrorist-related facilities in Afghanistan and Sudan because of the imminent threat they presented to our national security.

I want to speak with you about the objective of this action and why it was necessary. Our target was terror; our mission was clear: to strike at the network of radical groups affiliated with and funded by Usama bin Ladin, perhaps the preeminent organizer and financier of international terrorism in the world today.

The groups associated with him come from diverse places but share a hatred for democracy, a fanatical glorification of violence, and a horrible distortion of their religion to justify the murder of innocents. They have made the United States their adversary precisely because of what we stand for and what we stand against.

A few months ago, and again this week, bin Ladin publicly vowed to wage a terrorist war against America, saying, and I quote, "We do not differentiate between those dressed in military uniforms and civilians. They're all targets."

Their mission is murder and their history is bloody. In recent years, they killed American, Belgian, and Pakistani peacekeepers in Somalia. They plotted to assassinate the President of Egypt and the Pope. They planned to bomb six United States 747's over the Pacific. They bombed the Egyptian Embassy in Pakistan. They gunned down German tourists in Egypt.

The most recent terrorist events are fresh in our memory. Two weeks ago, 12 Americans and nearly 300 Kenyans and Tanzanians lost their lives, and another 5,000 were wounded, when our Embassies in Nairobi and Dar es Salaam were bombed. There is convincing information from our intelligence community that the bin Ladin terrorist network was responsible for these bombings. Based on this information, we have high confidence that these bombings were planned, financed, and carried out by the organization bin Ladin leads.

America has battled terrorism for many years. Where possible, we've used law enforcement and diplomatic tools to wage the fight. The long arm of American law has reached out around the world and brought to trial those guilty of attacks in New York and Virginia and in the Pacific. We have quietly disrupted terrorist groups and foiled their plots. We have isolated countries that practice terrorism. We've worked to build an international coalition against terror. But there have been and will be times when law enforcement and diplomatic tools are simply not enough, when our very national security is challenged, and when we must take extraordinary steps to protect the safety of our citizens.

With compelling evidence that the bin Ladin network of terrorist groups was planning to mount further attacks against Americans and other freedom-loving people, I decided America must act. And so this morning, based on the unanimous recommendation of my national security team, I ordered our Armed Forces to take action to counter an immediate threat from the bin Ladin network.

Earlier today the United States carried out simultaneous strikes against terrorist facilities and infrastructure in Afghanistan. Our forces targeted one of the most active terrorist bases in the world. It contained key elements of the bin Ladin network's infrastructure and has served as a training camp for literally thousands of terrorists from around the globe. We have reason to believe that a gathering of key terrorist leaders was to take place there today, thus underscoring the urgency of our actions.

Our forces also attacked a factory in Sudan associated with the bin Ladin network. The factory was involved in the production of materials for chemical weapons.

The United States does not take this action lightly. Afghanistan and Sudan have been warned for years to stop harboring and supporting these terrorist groups. But countries that persistently host terrorists have no right to be safe havens.

Let me express my gratitude to our intelligence and law enforcement agencies for their hard, good work. And let me express my pride in our Armed Forces who carried out this mission while making every possible effort to minimize the loss of innocent life.

I want you to understand, I want the world to understand that our actions today were not aimed against Islam, the faith of hundreds of millions of good, peace-loving people all around the world, including the United States. No religion condones the murder of innocent men, women, and children. But our actions were aimed at fanatics and killers who wrap murder in the cloak of righteousness and in so doing profane the great religion in whose name they claim to act.

My fellow Americans, our battle against terrorism did not begin with the bombing of our Embassies in Africa, nor will it end with today's strike. It will require strength, courage, and endurance. We will not yield to this threat; we will meet it, no matter how long it may take. This will be a long, ongoing struggle between freedom and fanaticism, between the rule of law and terrorism. We must be prepared to do all that we can for as long as we must.

America is and will remain a target of terrorists precisely because we are leaders; because we act to advance peace, democracy, and basic human values; because we're the most open society on Earth; and because, as we have shown yet again, we take an uncompromising stand against terrorism.

But of this I am also sure: The risks from inaction, to America and the world, would be far greater than action, for that would embolden our enemies, leaving their ability and their willingness to strike us intact. In this case, we knew before our attack that these groups already had planned further actions against us and others.

I want to reiterate: The United States wants peace, not conflict. We want to lift lives around the world, not take them. We have worked for peace in Bosnia, in Northern Ireland, in Haiti, in the Middle East, and elsewhere. But in this day, no campaign for peace can succeed without a determination to fight terrorism.

Let our actions today send this message loud and clear: There are no expendable American targets; there will be no sanctuary for terrorists; we will defend our people, our interests, and our values; we will help people of all faiths, in all parts of the world, who want to live free of fear and violence. We will persist, and we will prevail.

Thank you. God bless you, and may God bless our country.

NOTE: The President spoke at 5:32 p.m. from the Oval Office at the White House.

Statement on the 1999 Federal Pay Raise
August 20, 1998

I am announcing today my support for a 3.6 percent pay raise in 1999 for Federal civilian employees and military personnel. This increase is consistent with preliminary appropriations and authorizing actions already taken in Congress. I urge the Congress to enact legislation providing for such an increase, and if Congress fails to act, I will use my executive authority to guarantee that a 3.6 increase takes effect.

An increase of 3.6 percent for Federal employees would essentially allow Federal pay to match the growth in private sector wages. Given the high level of productivity of Federal employees and the continuing trend of solid real income gains in the private sector, I believe that Federal employees deserve the recognition and compensation that this increase provides. I will continue to work with Congress and labor to review the means by which we ensure fair and equitable pay.

Since the first days of this administration, the Vice President and I have worked to streamline the Federal Government. Today, the Government operates more efficiently and better serves the American people. This success would not have been possible without Government employees who have been called upon to work harder and to do more with less. Our Federal employees have risen to that mission, and with this action, we recognize their efforts.

Statement on the 1997 National Household Survey on Drug Abuse
August 21, 1998

Today's 1997 National Household Survey on Drug Abuse shows that while overall drug use remains flat, teen drug use continues to represent a serious and growing problem. That is why, last month, I launched a 5-year, $2 billion youth antidrug media campaign to use the full force of the media to make sure that our children get the message that drugs are dangerous, wrong, and can kill you. That is also why I have asked Congress to pass a comprehensive drug strategy that aims to cut youth drug use in half through better prevention, more effective treatment, tougher law enforcement, and improved interdiction. And finally, that is a powerful reason why I have tried to do as much as possible to curb youth use of tobacco because, as today's survey also shows, teen smokers are about 12 times as likely to use illegal drugs as those who don't smoke.

But our efforts depend on all Americans—parents, teachers, coaches, and clergy—taking responsibility and talking to our children about the dangers of drugs, alcohol, and tobacco. If we all take this first and important step, we can finally reverse this longstanding trend and help keep our Nation's children drug-free.

Letter to Congressional Leaders on Terrorists Who Threaten To Disrupt the Middle East Peace Process
August 20, 1998

Dear Mr. Speaker: (Dear Mr. President:)

On January 23, 1995, in light of the threat posed by grave acts of violence committed by foreign terrorists that disrupt the Middle East peace process, using my authority under, *inter alia*, the International Emergency Economic Powers Act (50 U.S.C. 1701 *et seq.*), I declared a national emergency and issued Executive Order 12947. Because such terrorist activities continue to pose an unusual and extraordinary threat to the national security, foreign policy, and economy of the United States, I have renewed the national emergency declared in Executive Order 12947 annually, most recently on January 21, 1998. Pursuant to section 204(b) of the International Emergency Economic Powers Act (50 U.S.C. 1703(b)) and section 201 of the National Emergencies Act (50 U.S.C. 1631), I hereby report to the Congress that I have exercised my statutory authority to issue an Executive Order that amends Executive Order 12947 in order more effectively to respond to the worldwide threat posed by foreign terrorists.

The amendment to the Annex of Executive Order 12947 adds Usama bin Muhammad bin Awad bin Ladin (a.k.a. Usama bin Ladin), Islamic Army, Abu Hafs al-Masri, and Rifa'i Ahmad Taha Musa to the list of terrorists that are subject to the prohibitions contained in the Executive Order. These prohibitions include the blocking of all property and interests in the property of the terrorists listed in the Annex, the prohibition of any transaction or dealing by United States persons or within the United States in property or interests in property of the persons designated, and the prohibition of

any transaction by any United States persons or within the United States that evades or avoids, or has the purpose of evading or avoiding, any of the prohibitions set forth in the Executive Order.

Usama bin Ladin and his organizations and associates have repeatedly called upon their supporters to perform acts of violence. Bin Ladin has declared that killing Americans and their allies "is an individual duty for every Muslim . . . in order to liberate the Al-Aqsa Mosque and the Holy Mosque." These threats are clearly intended to violently disrupt the Middle East peace process.

This Executive Order does not limit or otherwise affect the other provisions of Executive Order 12947.

I have authorized these actions in view of the danger posed to the national security, foreign policy, and economy of the United States by the activities of Usama bin Muhammad bin Awad bin Ladin (a.k.a. Usama bin Ladin), Islamic Army, Abu Hafs al-Masri, and Rifa'i Ahmad Taha Musa that disrupt the Middle East peace process. I am enclosing a copy of the Executive Order that I have issued exercising my emergency authorities.

Sincerely,

BILL CLINTON

NOTE: Identical letters were sent to Newt Gingrich, Speaker of the House of Representatives, and Albert Gore, Jr., President of the Senate. This letter was released by the Office of the Press Secretary on August 22. The Executive order of August 20 is listed in Appendix D at the end of this volume.

Letter to Congressional Leaders Reporting on Military Action Against Terrorist Sites in Afghanistan and Sudan
August 21, 1998

Dear Mr. Speaker: (*Dear Mr. President:*)

At approximately 1:30 p.m. eastern daylight time, on August 20, 1998, at my direction, U.S. forces conducted strikes in Afghanistan against a series of camps and installations used by the Usama bin Ladin organization, and in Sudan where the bin Ladin organization has facilities and extensive ties to the government. I ordered these actions based on convincing information from a variety of reliable sources that the bin Ladin organization is responsible for the devastating bombings on August 7, 1998, of the U.S. Embassies in Nairobi, Kenya, and Dar es Salaam, Tanzania, that killed over 250 persons. United States forces struck a facility in Sudan being used to produce materials for chemical weapons. They also struck facilities in Afghanistan that are being used for terrorist training and as basing and supply camps for staging terrorist activities.

The United States acted in exercise of our inherent right of self-defense consistent with Article 51 of the United Nations Charter. These strikes were a necessary and proportionate response to the imminent threat of further terrorist attacks against U.S. personnel and facilities. These strikes were intended to prevent and deter additional attacks by a clearly identified terrorist threat. The targets were selected because they served to facilitate directly the efforts of terrorists specifically identified with attacks on U.S. personnel and facilities and posed a continuing threat to U.S. lives.

The U.S. forces involved in these strikes have completed their mission. No U.S. personnel were injured or killed in connection with this action.

I directed these actions pursuant to my constitutional authority to conduct U.S. foreign relations and as Commander in Chief and Chief Executive.

I am providing this report as part of my efforts to keep the Congress fully informed, consistent with the War Powers Resolution. I appreciate the support of the Congress as we continue to take all necessary steps to protect U.S. citizens at home and abroad.

Sincerely,

WILLIAM J. CLINTON

NOTE: Identical letters were sent to Newt Gingrich, Speaker of the House of Representatives, and Strom Thurmond, President pro tempore of the Senate. This letter was released by the Office of the Press Secretary on August 22.

The President's Radio Address
August 22, 1998

Good morning. I want to talk to you about our strike against terrorism last Thursday. Two weeks ago, a savage attack was carried out against our Embassies in Kenya and Tanzania. Almost 300 innocent people were killed; thousands were injured. The bombs were aimed at us, but they claimed anyone who happened to be near the Embassies that morning. They killed both Africans and Americans indiscriminately, cruelty beyond comprehension.

From the moment we learned of the bombings, our mission was clear: Identify those responsible; bring them to justice; protect our citizens from future attacks.

The information now in our possession is convincing. Behind these attacks were the same hands that killed American and Pakistani peacekeepers in Somalia, the same hands that targeted U.S. airlines, and the same hands that plotted the assassinations of the Pope and President Mubarak of Egypt. I'm referring to the bin Ladin network of radical groups, probably the most dangerous non-state terrorist actor in the world today.

We also had compelling evidence that the bin Ladin network was poised to strike at us again, and soon. We know he has said all Americans—not just those in uniform—all Americans are targets. And we know he wants to acquire chemical weapons.

With that information and evidence, we simply could not stand idly by. That is why I ordered our military strikes last Thursday. Our goals were to disrupt bin Ladin's terrorist network and destroy elements of its infrastructure in Afghanistan and Sudan. And our goal was to destroy, in Sudan, the factory with which bin Ladin's network is associated, which was producing an ingredient essential for nerve gas.

I am proud of the men and women of our Armed Forces who carried out this mission and proud of the superb work of our intelligence and law enforcement communities. I thank the congressional leadership for their bipartisan support. And I'm grateful to America's friends around the world who have expressed their solidarity. For this is not just America's fight; it's a universal one, between those who want to build a world of peace and partnership and prosperity and those who would tear everything down through death and destruction; a fight that joins people from Northern Ireland and Africa and the Middle East; a fight not directed at any particular nation or any particular faith but at a callous criminal organization whose policies of violence violate the teachings of every religion.

In particular, it is very important that Americans understand that the threat we face is not part of the Islamic faith. Hundreds of millions of Muslims all over the world, including millions right here in the United States, oppose terrorism and deplore the twisting of their religious teachings into justification of inhumane, indeed ungodly acts.

Our efforts against terrorism cannot and will not end with this strike. We should have realistic expectations about what a single action can achieve, and we must be prepared for a long battle. But it's high time that those who traffic in terror learn they, too, are vulnerable.

I'm determined to use all the tools at our disposal. That is why I have just signed an Executive order directing the Treasury to block all financial transactions between the bin Ladin terrorist group and American persons and companies. We'll urge other governments to do the same. We must not allow sanctuary for terrorism, not for terrorists or for their money. It takes money, lots of it, to build the network bin Ladin has. We'll do our best to see that he has less of it.

Finally, as we close ranks against international threats, we must remember this: America will never give up the openness, the freedom, and the tolerance that define us. For the ultimate target of these terrorist attacks is our ideals, and they must be defended at any cost.

Thanks for listening.

NOTE: The address was recorded at 11:55 a.m. on August 21 in the Oval Office at the White House for broadcast at 10:06 a.m. on August 22. The transcript was made available by the Office of the Press Secretary on August 21 but was embargoed for release until the broadcast. In his address, the President referred to Pope John Paul II; President Hosni Mubarak of Egypt; and Usama bin Ladin, who allegedly sponsored terrorist attacks on the U.S. Embassies in Kenya and Tanzania. The Executive order of August 20 is listed in Appendix D at the end of this volume.

Statement on Progress Against Drunk Driving
August 24, 1998

The data released today by the Department of Transportation shows that we are making real progress in protecting Americans from drunk drivers. Last year, the number of people killed in alcohol-related crashes dropped to an all-time low, representing a decline of over a third since 1982. For the first time since we started keeping these statistics in 1975, drunk driving deaths accounted for less than 40 percent of all traffic deaths. And alcohol-related fatalities among 16- to 20-year-olds dropped by 5 percent last year alone.

Our progress is the result of stronger laws, tougher enforcement, and increased public awareness. In particular, today's statistics show the importance of the legislation I fought for and signed 3 years ago to ensure zero tolerance for underage drinking and driving. But there is more we must do. We could save even more lives by passing a tough national standard of impaired driving at .08 blood alcohol content (BAC)—and I continue to challenge the Congress to enact this life-saving measure. If we work together, we can spare thousands of families from the grief and anger of losing a loved one to a preventable drunk driving crash, and make our roads, highways, and communities safer for all Americans.

NOTE: The statement referred to the National Highway System Designation Act of 1995, Public Law 104–59, approved November 28, 1995.

Statement on the Death of Lewis F. Powell, Jr.
August 25, 1998

Hillary and I are deeply saddened by the death of Justice Lewis F. Powell, Jr., one of our most thoughtful and conscientious Justices. For over 15 years on the Supreme Court, he approached each case without an ideological agenda, carefully applying the Constitution, the law, and Supreme Court precedent regardless of his own personal views about the case. His opinions were a model of balance and judiciousness. As a result, he was the decisive voice on the Court in addressing some of the most important issues of our day.

Justice Powell was an admirable public servant. Our thoughts and prayers are with his loved ones.

NOTE: The related proclamation of August 25 is listed in Appendix D at the end of this volume.

Memorandum on the National Academy of Sciences Report on Food Safety
August 25, 1998

Memorandum for the President's Council on Food Safety

Subject: National Academy of Sciences Report

My Administration is committed to ensuring that the American people enjoy the safest food possible. We have made great progress by implementing science-based prevention control systems for seafood, meat, and poultry; developing a comprehensive initiative to ensure the safety of domestic and imported fruits and vegetables; and launching an interagency food safety initiative that focuses on key food safety issues from the farm to the table. We can and must continue to build upon these efforts.

Under our current food safety system, several different Federal agencies have responsibility for improving food safety. Within the framework of our interagency initiative, we have taken a number of steps to improve the coordination of our food safety efforts. Most recently, we established a Joint Institute for Food Safety Research to develop a strategic plan for conducting food safety research activities and to coordinate all Federal food safety research, including with the private sector and academia.

Today, I signed an Executive Order establishing the President's Council on Food Safety. To strengthen and focus our efforts to coordinate food safety policy and resources and improve food safety for American consumers, the Council will develop a comprehensive strategic plan for Federal food safety activities, ensure the most effective use of Federal resources through the development and submission of coordinated food safety budgets, and oversee the Joint Institute for Food Safety Research.

The National Academy of Sciences (NAS) recently issued a thoughtful and highly informative report on food safety issues, entitled "Ensuring Safe Food from Production to Consumption."

This report recommends additional ways to enhance coordination and improve effectiveness in the food safety system, including through reform of current food safety legislation.

I hereby direct the Council to review and respond to this report as one of its first orders of business. After providing opportunity for public comment, including public meetings, the Council shall report back to me within 180 days with its views on the NAS's recommendations. In developing this report, the Council should take into account the comprehensive strategic Federal food safety plan that it will be developing.

I thank the Council for its efforts to improve food safety, and I look forward to the continued leadership of the President's Council on Food Safety.

WILLIAM J. CLINTON

NOTE: The Executive order is listed in Appendix D at the end of this volume.

Statement on the Bombings in South Africa and Uganda
August 26, 1998

Hillary and I join the American people in extending our deepest sympathies to the victims of bomb attacks in South Africa and Uganda on August 25, and to their families and friends. We reaffirm our unshakeable friendship and support for them and for all of the people of South Africa and Uganda.

The United States condemns, in the strongest possible terms, these senseless attacks on innocent civilians that have taken the lives of at least 29 Ugandans and 2 South Africans.

Earlier this month, South Africa provided immediate and invaluable assistance to the United States, Kenya, and Tanzania in the wake of the bombings of the U.S. Embassies in those countries. We are grateful for the generous response and will do what we can to assist South Africa and Uganda in the wake of these senseless acts.

Remarks Announcing Safe Schools and Police Corps Initiatives in Worcester, Massachusetts
August 27, 1998

Thank you. Ladies and gentlemen, first let me thank you for your remarkable and warm welcome. I'm glad to be here in Worcester, the heartbeat of Massachusetts for 150 years now, and in this grand hall where so many great Americans have spoken, from Frederick Douglas to Susan B. Anthony to Henry David Thoreau. I'm honored to share this stage with Kathleen Bisson, and I thank her for her commitment to teaching our children and for keeping them safe, and with Officer Michael Jones, who moved us all with how he responded to his personal tragedy.

Mr. Mayor, I thought you gave a great talk. When he was up here kind of moving around, doing his shtick, I said—I was amazed. Kathleen said, "You know, he ought to be in Hollywood. You should see the rap act he does for the school kids." [*Laughter*] So I thank you.

Chief Gardella, I cannot thank you enough for what you said, and I appreciate more than you will ever know the impact that we have had the opportunity to have through the community policing and the other law enforcement programs.

I thank Scott Harshbarger, who has been a friend of mine for a long time and who has, I can tell you from my personal experience not only as President but even before when I was Governor, always been on the forefront of law enforcement reforms that would give our children a safer future.

I thank Congressman McGovern who has worked in both the areas we celebrate today and in so many other ways. It's interesting to see a man who both knows what he's doing down to the tiniest detail about how Congress works and how the committees work and how the procedures work. And I think Congressman Moakley's tutelage had something to do with that before he showed up. But it's interesting to see someone who has that feel for the mechanics and also is plainly so connected at an emotional, human level to the people in his district and so passionately cares about it and was able to convey that to all of us today through the wonderful metaphor of his wife and young child—and if you want to cry, go right ahead. [Laughter]

Let me also thank Congressman Markey, who is here, and Congressman Neal for coming out to the airport to meet me. I thank Senator Kerry, who has long been one of the leaders in law enforcement issues in the Congress, for his involvement in both these issues. And I thank Senator Kennedy for making sure that even though this is the end of a long program, none of us could possibly go to sleep. [Laughter] I always marvel at his continuing energy and commitment and dedication. And some days, when I get tired and weary, I think, he's been doing this longer than I have, and he never gets tired or weary. And that's a good thing.

Let me say—I have a few brief things to add to what has been said about the two issues we came here to discuss today. But because this is my only opportunity to speak with you and, through you, to the American people, I want to say a couple of things about Hurricane Bonnie and the havoc it's wreaked in North Carolina over the last day, and the flooding caused in Texas by Tropical Storm Charley.

I know that all of our hearts go out to the families affected by these storms. Yesterday I declared a disaster in Texas because of the flooding, and today there's a disaster declaration that has just been issued for North Carolina. That makes Federal funds available immediately to people who have been harmed in both places.

Thankfully, the winds are dying down in North Carolina. Hopefully, the floods soon will recede in Texas. In both cases, FEMA, our Federal Emergency Management Agency, is working with State and local agencies to assess the damage and to stay there for as long as it takes to help the people rebuild.

While we're here today, Vice President and Mrs. Gore and Secretary of Education Dick Riley are in California talking about the same things, our common commitment to make our streets and our schools safe for families and children.

This is, as Senator Kennedy noted, a time of great prosperity for our people. We have the lowest unemployment in 28 years, the smallest percentage of people on welfare in 29 years, about to realize the first balanced budget and surplus in 29 years, and we learned not very long ago that homeownership is at its highest rate in American history. And this has occurred at a time when we have reduced the Government to the smallest size it is at since John Kennedy was the President of the United States.

I come here, as I have gone across this country, to say to my fellow Americans, this is not a time to celebrate but to be grateful. It is not a time to rest on our laurels but to use the confidence, the resources, and the understanding we have acquired for the last 6 years to face the long-term challenges of this country, for the world is changing very quickly, full of new challenges.

Senator Kennedy mentioned one of them, the problem of terrorism, which has become a bigger problem for us as we become more open and as information and money and technology can move around the world so quickly, as people themselves can move across borders so quickly. These multinational problems like terrorism or even the global spread of disease or shared environmental problems are things that visionaries must think about and take steps now to prepare for.

The world will never be free of problems. And we know that the world is changing fast, which means that if we wish to maintain our present level of success, we must keep up. We cannot afford to relax. We must become more rigorous. And we must—I say again— use the newfound confidence of America to think more boldly, not less boldly, and to act more boldly, not less boldly, for our children's future.

There is critical business ahead of us, business that we will take up as soon as Congress comes back to work. One of the Members who spoke before me mentioned it, but we want to make sure—I think Congressman McGovern did—we want to make sure that we have saved the Social Security system for the 21st century before a penny of that surplus is touched. We think it is important.

We want to help the teachers like Kate Bisson, not only with school violence but with the tools necessary to move our children forward. I have an education agenda before the Congress that would provide funds in the balanced budget for school construction, to help repair and rebuild and build new buildings so that children aren't in substandard conditions. We have children going to school, in some cities in America today, in buildings that are 65, 70, 80 years old, where the windows are broken, where they go in—where whole floors are closed down. What kind of signal does that send to children about their importance?

In other parts of our country we have children going to school in housetrailers because the school districts are growing so fast and there's no way the people can afford to keep up with it. I was in a small school district in Florida recently where there were 17 trailers outside the main school building. This is important.

We have a program to help our school districts hire 100,000 teachers in the early grades so we can get down to an average class size of 18. It is the single most significant thing that the research shows, over more than a decade now, that will guarantee that children will get off to a good start in school.

We're trying to hook up all our classrooms to the Internet. We're trying to support the establishment of voluntary national standards. We are trying, in short, to make sure we can say to our children: No matter where you grow up or what your racial or ethnic or income background is, you have access to the finest system of elementary and secondary education in the world. That's a big part of our agenda.

We have a huge health care agenda, and it begins with the Patients' Bill of Rights. With 160 million people in managed care operations, people ought to have a right, whatever their health care plan, to see a specialist if their doctor recommends it, to have emergency room care where it's needed if they have an accident, to have their medical records kept private, to be able to appeal adverse decisions. These things are important. And so I say to you, we need your help.

There's going to be a big debate on campaign finance reform when we get back, and the Shays-Meehan—[*inaudible*]—bill, that is cosponsored by Congressman Meehan from Massachusetts, is going to be in a version before the United States Senate. And our people are going to work hard to pass it. There will be major environmental debates when we get back. And these things are important.

So I say to you, the energy that brought you here today, the concern you have for these issues, you need to bring it back to every single major challenge this country faces. If I had told you 6 years ago that in 6 years we would have 16 million new jobs and all these other things, you would have said, "There's another politician running for office." It happened not by accident but because of the hard work and the vision and the citizen spirit of the American people and the disciplined efforts that we have all made. And we must not forget that now that times are good.

We also can't forget that, unless we make our communities, our schools, and our children safe, prosperity doesn't mean very much. That is why this is at the core of what we have tried to do.

I told this story many times, but I want you to let me share it one more time. Right before the New Hampshire primary in 1992, a period when I was dropping like a rock in the polls— I have some experience with that—I was going through a kitchen in New York City. And I was walking to one of these banquets, one of these fundraising banquets. I didn't have any idea whether it would be three people or 300 or 700 when I got out the door. I was just walking through the kitchen to get there.

And a waiter came up to me, in this nice hotel in New York. And I wasn't very well-known then. I was the Governor of Arkansas. I just started running in New Hampshire. And this man came up to me and stopped me, and he said, "Mr. Governor, I want to talk to you." He said, "My 10-year-old boy here in New York," he said, "he studies these elections, and he reads up on the candidates, and he says I should vote for you." He said, "Now, if I vote for you, I want you to do something for me." I said, "Well, what is it?" I couldn't imagine what this man who was a waiter in a hotel in New York wanted me to do for him. He said, "Well, the place where we came from in the old country, we were much poorer, but at least we were free." He said, "Here I make more money, but we're not free. When my boy goes across our apartment house, across the street to play in the city park, I have to go with him because I'm afraid for his safety. Our school is only a couple of blocks from our apartment, but I have to walk him because I'm afraid for his safety. So if I do what my boy wants and I vote for you, would you make my boy free?" I will never forget that as long as I live.

The comprehensive approach we followed on crime is basically what, as Senator Kerry said, and he certainly supported it very strongly, is just what the local law enforcement people and the local community leaders taught us to do: Be smart about prevention; be smart about giving kids something to say yes to; be smart about law enforcement patterns; be smart about punishment. Crime rates are now at a 25-year low, juvenile crime is finally coming down. People do think, I think, that they are more free.

We have worked hard especially in the schools with the Safe and Drug-Free Schools program. We've supported communities in schools that offer antitruancy, curfew, school uniforms, and dress code policies. We have strictly enforced zero tolerance for guns. Last year alone, over 6,000 students with guns were disarmed and sent home. This year, recently, a new report showed that the overwhelming majority of our schools are, in fact, safe. But it's not enough, as we know from the recent rash of killings in our schools all over the country.

When children in inner-city schools have to walk through metal detectors, when high schools in small towns like Jonesboro, Arkansas, in my home State, or Springfield, Oregon, are torn apart by disturbed children with deadly weapons, when gang violence still ravages communities large and small, we have to do more.

This fall, we are going to hold the first-ever White House Conference on School Safety, and today we're taking two steps that I think will make our schools safer and our communities stronger. First, offering a guide to help prevent school violence before it starts and, second, expanding the remarkable Police Corps program to Massachusetts and elsewhere.

Let me show you what this early warning guide is all about. Earlier this year, in the aftermath of the tragedy of Springfield, Oregon, I actually went there to Springfield, and I spent an extended period of time in the school library, going from table to table to table, meeting with the families of the victims, children who had been killed, and a much larger number of children who had been wounded. I talked to the school officials. I asked them what they knew about the young man who was apparently in-

volved in this incident. I asked them how they dealt with kids who were in trouble; how did they know when children were in trouble. And we began to ask other people, and we concluded that not everybody knew everything they needed to know in clear, practical terms about how to spot the danger signals early and then what to do about them.

So I asked Secretary Riley and Attorney General Reno to develop the safe school guides for educators, for parents, for fellow students to help them recognize and then respond to early warning signs. This is the guide. It says, "Early Warning Timely Response: A Guide to Safe Schools." Now, over the next few weeks, every single school in America will get a copy of this in time for the start of the new school year. It will help schools to recognize a troubled or potentially violent young person. It outlines steps to intervene early before it's too late.

As Secretary Riley and General Reno say in their introduction, the guide should never be used to stigmatize or label young people in distress. Instead, it should be used as a vital part of overall school violence prevention efforts that have to include, as others have said before and as your mayor said about Worcester, every teacher, every parent, and every young person. This guide can make a difference in the lives of our children.

The Police Corps can also make a difference. It embodies the same commitment to every person and the commitment to public service that was embodied in the life service of John and Robert Kennedy.

I first heard about the Police Corps from Adam Wolinsky, who has previously been eulogized by Senators Kerry and Kennedy, when I was the Governor of Arkansas. I was so impressed by this program and by Adam's commitment to it, that I became a charter member of the National Committee for the Police Corps on the spot. Adam and his wife, Jane, are here, and I know they've already been introduced, but I want you to know that we would not be here talking about this today were it not for this one American citizen and his harboring a dream for years and years and years until it became real in the lives of people. And I thank him for it.

When I was Governor, I signed a bill to create a Police Corps scholarship program in our home State. And when I became President, thanks to the efforts of Senator Kennedy, Senator Kerry, and others, especially of Lieutenant Governor Kathleen Kennedy Townsend of Maryland and Adam, we put the Police Corps in the 1994 crime bill.

We've already heard that, much in the way that ROTC functions, this remarkable program gives talented young people college scholarships in return for their commitment to serve as police officers in their communities. I should mention, as was pointed out to me here today before I came here, that a preference is given to one group only, the children of police officers killed in the line of duty. And I understand that the State police here has already identified several young people who are the children of police officers who have died in the line of service in Massachusetts who, themselves, want to go into law enforcement and would be eligible to get these scholarships.

In 17 States around the country, that's what the Police Corps is already doing, creating a new generation of police officers trained to stand on the front lines and listen on the front porches, to work in distressed communities and be role models for young people.

Now, the young members of the Police Corps who are here with us today—and I think there are some, aren't there? Are there any Police Corps members here today? What? Stand up. We have invested in their honor, their courage, their commitment to community and country. We need more like them. That is why the announcement we make today expanding the Police Corps to 6 more States, including Massachusetts, awarding scholarships to more than 300 dedicated young people, is a good thing for the United States.

This Police Corps is an incredible example of what we can do when we put progress ahead of partisanship, people ahead of politics, the future of our children ahead of all else. As the mayor said, in referring to the First Lady, it does take a village. But both of us note, as we travel around the country—and Hillary mentioned to me just about a week ago when she came back from another stop—it is astonishing—it is astonishing how many places we go will there be somebody in the receiving line who will thank us for the community police officers in their community, large and small.

Robert Kennedy once said, "The fight against crime is, in the last analysis, a fight to preserve that quality of community which is at the root of our greatness, a fight to preserve confidence in ourselves and in our fellow citizens, a battle for the quality of our lives." With these actions, we move a step closer to winning that battle for all our people and to building that bridge toward a strong America in the 21st century.

Thank you, and God bless you all.

NOTE: The President spoke at 12 p.m. at Mechanics Hall. In his remarks, he referred to Kathleen Bisson, teacher, Burncoat Middle School, who introduced the President; Officer Michael D. Jones, Baltimore City, MD, police department; Mayor Raymond V. Mariano of Worcester; Worcester Chief of Police Edward P. Gardella; Massachusetts Attorney General Scott Harshbarger; Greek immigrant Dimitrious Theofanis and his son, Nick; Kipland P. Kinkel, who was charged with the May 21 shooting at Thurston High School in Springfield, OR, in which 2 students were killed and 22 wounded; and Adam Wolinsky, founder, Police Corps. He also referred to the Violent Crime Control and Law Enforcement Act of 1994, Public Law 103–322.

Statement on the Arrest of Mohammad Rashid for the Terrorist Attack on the United States Embassy in Kenya
August 27, 1998

Late last night, American law enforcement authorities brought to the United States Mohammad Rashid, a suspect in the bombing attack on the United States Embassy in Nairobi, Kenya. The suspect's involvement in the bombing was established as the result of a joint investigation by the Kenyan police and an FBI team. He is associated with Usama bin Ladin, the preeminent organizer and financier of international terrorism whose network we struck in Afghanistan and Sudan last week.

This arrest does not close this case. We will continue to pursue all those who helped plan, finance, and carry out the attacks on our Embassies in Kenya and Tanzania, which took the lives of 12 Americans and hundreds of Africans.

Let me express my gratitude to our law enforcement and intelligence agencies for a job very well done and to the Kenyan and Tanzanian authorities for their hard work and close cooperation with the FBI.

This is an important step forward in our struggle against terrorism, but there is a long road ahead. The enemies of peace and freedom undoubtedly will strike again. Our resolve must be for the long run. We have and we will continue to use all the tools at our disposal—law enforcement, diplomacy, and when necessary, America's military might. No matter what it takes, how long it takes, or where it takes us, we will bring to justice those responsible for the murder and maiming of American citizens. We will defend our interests, our people, and our values.

Statement on Vice President Al Gore's 1996 Campaign Financing Activities
August 27, 1998

I am confident that all of the Vice President's actions were legal and proper and that any review will conclude that.

Remarks on the 35th Anniversary of the March on Washington in Oak Bluffs, Massachusetts
August 28, 1998

Thank you very much. First of all, hasn't this day made you proud to be an American? [*Applause*] I want to thank Dr. Ogletree and the entire committee, Skip Gates, Anita Hill, Judge Higginbotham. I want to thank Sebastian for doing a superb job of reminding us of the important facts of Martin Luther King's life. Marianne, thank you for your work and your words today. I thank Sabrina and Elza for leading us in the singing, and Giles, Olivia, and Mia for reading from the "I Have A Dream" speech. Rebecca, thank you for the books. Mr. Bryan, thank you for making us welcome in your congregation.

And should I say, Reverend Lewis? John, I would not be a bit surprised if, when we walk out these doors today, every chicken on this island will be standing out there—[*laughter*]—in the street waiting for their leader. [*Laughter*]

John Lewis has been my friend for a long time—a long time—a long time before he could have ever known that I would be here. And he stood with me in 1991 when only my mother and my wife thought I had any chance of being elected. So you have to make allowances and discount some of what he says. [*Laughter*] But I treasure the years of friendship we have shared. I have boundless admiration for him. He and Lillian have been an incredible source of strength and support for Hillary and me, and our country is a much, much better place because of the road John Lewis has walked.

The summer of 1963 was a very eventful one for me, the summer I turned 17. What most people know about it now is the famous picture of me shaking hands with President Kennedy in July. It was a great moment. But I think the moment we commemorate today—a moment I experienced all alone—had a more profound impact on my life.

Most of us who are old enough remember exactly where we were on August 28, 1963. I was in my living room in Hot Springs, Arkansas.

I remember the chair I was sitting in. I remember exactly where it was in the room. I remember exactly the position of the chair when I sat and watched on national television the great March on Washington unfold. I remember weeping uncontrollably during Martin Luther King's speech, and I remember thinking, when it was over, my country would never be the same, and neither would I.

There are people all across this country who made a more intense commitment to the idea of racial equality and justice that day than they had ever made before. And so, in very personal ways, all of us became better and bigger because of the work of those who brought that great day about. There are millions of people, who John Lewis will never meet, who are better and bigger because of what that day meant.

And the words continue to echo down to the present day, spoken to us today by children who were not even alive then. And God willing, their grandchildren will also be inspired and moved and become better and bigger because of what happened on that increasingly distant summer day.

What I'd like to ask you to think about a little today and to share with you—and I'll try to do it without taking my spectacles out, but I don't write very well, and I don't read too well as I get older—is what I think this means for us today. I was trying to think about what John and Dr. King and others did, and how they did it, and how it informs what I do and how I think about other things today. And I would ask you only to think about three things— the hour is late and it's warm in here, and I can't bring the chickens home to roost. [*Laughter*]

But I think of these three things. Number one, Dr. King used to speak about how we were all bound together in a web of mutuality, which was an elegant way of saying, whether we like it or not, we're all in this life together. We are interdependent. Well, what does that mean? Well, let me give you a specific example.

We had some good news today: Incomes in America went up 5 percent last year. That's a big bump in a year. We've got the best economy in a generation. That's the good news. But we are mutually interdependent with people far beyond our borders. Yesterday there was some more news that was troubling out of Russia— some rumor, some fact—about the decline in the economy. Our stock market dropped over

350 points. And in Latin America, our most fast-growing market for American exports, all the markets went down, even though, as far as we know, most of those countries are doing everything right. Why? Because we're in a tighter and tighter and tighter web of mutuality.

Asia has these economic troubles. So even though we've got the best economy in a generation, our farm exports to Asia are down 30 percent from last year, and we have States in this country where farmers, the hardest working people in this country, can't make their mortgage payments because of things that happened half a world away they didn't have any direct influence on at all. This world is being bound together more closely.

So what is the lesson from that? Well, I should go to Russia, because, as John said, anybody can come see you when you're doing well. I should go there and we should tell them that, if they'll be strong and do the disciplined, hard things they have to do to reform their country, their economy, and get through this dark night, that we'll stick with them. And we ought to meet our responsibilities to the International Monetary Fund and these other international groups, because we can't solve the world's problems alone. We can't even solve our problems alone, because we're in this web of mutuality. But I learned that from the civil rights movement, not from an economics textbook.

The second thing, even if you're not a pacifist, whenever possible, peace and nonviolence is always the right thing to do. I remember so vividly in 1994—John writes about this in the book—I was trying to pass this crime bill, and all the opposition to the crime bill that was in the newspapers, all the intense opposition was coming from the NRA and the others that did not want us to ban assault weapons, didn't believe that we ought to have more community policemen walking the streets, and conservatives who thought we should just punish people more and not spend more money trying to keep kids out of trouble in the first place. And it was a huge fight.

And so they came to see me, and they said, "Well, John Lewis is not going to vote for this bill." And I said, "Why?" And they said, "Because it increases the number of crimes subject to the Federal death penalty, and he's not for it. And he's not in bed with all those other people, he thinks they're wrong, but he can't vote for it." And I said, "Well, let him alone.

There's no point in calling him, because he's lived a lifetime dedicated to an idea." And while I may not be a pacifist, whenever possible it's always the right thing to do, to try to be peaceable and nonviolent.

What does that mean for today? Well, there's a lot of good news. It's like the economy. The crime rate is at a 25-year low; juvenile crime is finally coming down. Yesterday we put out a handbook to send to every school in the country to try to increase the ability of teachers and others to identify kids in trouble, to try to stop these horrible, although isolated, examples when young people wreak violence on others. We've got, all over the country now, these exciting community-based programs that are dramatically reducing violence among young people—the school uniforms and curfew programs, and summer school in Chicago now is the sixth biggest school district in America—the summer school. Over 40,000 kids are now getting three square meals a day in the schools of that city. There's a lot of great things going on. But it is still a pretty violent world.

A black man was murdered recently in Texas in the most horrible way, because people not representative of that community but people living in that community were driven crazy through their demonic images of a man of a different race.

We have more diversity than ever before. It's wonderful, but there are still—we now see different minority groups at each other's throat from time to time, not understanding their racial or their cultural or their religious differences. And again, there is this web of mutuality.

Half a world away, terrorists trying to hurt Americans blow up two Embassies in Africa, and they kill some of our people, some of our best people, of, I might add, very many different racial and ethnic backgrounds, American citizens, including a distinguished career African-American diplomat and his son. But they also killed almost 300 Africans and wounded 5,000 others.

We see their pictures in the morning paper; two of them who did that, we're bringing them home. And they look like active, confident young people. What happened inside them that made them feel so much hatred toward us that they could justify not only an act of violence against innocent diplomats and other public servants but the collateral consequences to Africans whom they would never know? They had children, too.

So it is always best to remember that we have to try to work for peace in the Middle East, for peace in Northern Ireland, for an end to terrorism, for protections against biological and chemical weapons being used in the first place.

The night before we took action against the terrorist operations in Afghanistan and Sudan, I was here on this island, up until 2:30 in the morning, trying to make absolutely sure that at that chemical plant there was no night shift. I believed I had to take the action I did, but I didn't want some person, who was a nobody to me but who may have a family to feed and a life to live and probably had no earthly idea what else was going on there, to die needlessly.

It's another reason we ought to pay our debt to the United Nations, because if we can work together, together we can find more peaceful solutions. Now, I didn't learn that when I became President. I learned it from John Lewis and the civil rights movement a long time ago.

And the last thing I learned from them on which all these other things depend, without which we cannot build a world of peace or one America in an increasingly peaceful world bound together in this web of mutuality, is that you can't get there unless you're willing to forgive your enemies.

I never will forget one of the most—I don't think I've ever spoken about this in public before, but I—one of the most meaningful, personal moments I've had as President was a conversation I had with Nelson Mandela. And I said to him, I said, "You know, I've read your book, and I've heard you speak, and you spent time with my wife and daughter, and you've talked about inviting your jailers to your Inauguration." And I said, "It's very moving." And I said, "You're a shrewd as well as a great man. But come on, now, how did you really do that? You can't make me believe you didn't hate those people who did that to you for 27 years."

He said, "I did hate them for quite a long time. After all, they abused me physically and emotionally. They separated me from my wife, and it eventually broke my family up. They kept me from seeing my children grow up." He said, "For quite a long time I hated them." And then he said, "I realized one day, breaking rocks, that they could take everything away from me— everything—but my mind and my heart. Now, those things I would have to give away. And I simply decided I would not give them away."

So, as you look around the world you see, how do you explain these three children who were killed in Ireland, or all the people who were killed in the square when the people were told to leave the city hall, there was a bomb there, and then they walked out toward the bomb? What about all those families in Africa? I don't know; I can't pick up the telephone and call them and say, "I'm so sorry this happened." How do we find that spirit?

All of you know, I'm having to become quite an expert in this business of asking for forgiveness. It gets a little easier the more you do it. And if you have a family, an administration, a Congress, and a whole country to ask, you're going to get a lot of practice. [*Laughter*]

But I have to tell you that, in these last days, it has come home to me, again, something I first learned as President, but it wasn't burned in my bones, and that is that in order to get it, you have to be willing to give it.

And all of us—the anger, the resentment, the bitterness, the desire for recrimination against people you believe have wronged you, they harden the heart and deaden the spirit and lead to self-inflicted wounds. And so it is important that we are able to forgive those we believe have wronged us, even as we ask for forgiveness from people we have wronged. And I heard that first—first—in the civil rights movement: "Love thy neighbor as thyself."

What does it all mean and where do we take it from here? I'm so glad John told you the story of the little kids, of whom he was one, holding the house down. I want to close with what else he said about it, because it's where I think we have to go in order for the civil rights movement to have a lasting legacy.

In the prolog of John's book, he tells the story about the kids holding the house down. And then he says the following: "More than half a century has passed since that day. And it has struck me more than once over those many years that our society is not unlike the children in that house, rocked again and again by the winds of one storm or another, the walls around us seeming at times as if they might fly apart. It seemed that way in the 1960's when America felt itself bursting at the seams; so many storms.

"But the people of conscience never left the house. They never ran away. They stayed. They came together. They did the best they could, clasping hands and moving toward the corner of the house that was weakest. And then another corner would lift, and we would go there. And eventually, inevitably, the storm would settle, and the house would still stand. But we knew another storm would come, and we would have to do it all over again. And we did. And we still do, all of us, you and I. Children holding hands, walking with the wind. That is America to me. Not just the movement for civil rights, but the endless struggle to respond with decency, dignity, and a sense of brotherhood to all the challenges that face us as a nation as a whole."

And then he says this: "That is a story, in essence, of my life, of the path to which I've been committed since I turned from a boy to a man and to which I remain committed today, a path that extends beyond the issue of race alone, beyond class as well, and gender and age and every other distinction that tends to separate us as human beings rather than bring us together. The path involves nothing less than the pursuit of the most precious and pure concept I have ever known, an ideal I discovered as a young man that has guided me like a beacon ever since, a concept called 'the beloved community.'"

That is the America we are trying to create. That is the America John Lewis and his comrades, on this day 35 years ago, gave us the chance to build for our children.

Thank you, and God bless you.

NOTE: The President spoke at 2:54 p.m. in the Union Chapel. In his remarks, he referred to event host committee chairman Charles J. Ogletree, Jr., professor, Harvard University Law School, and members Henry Louis (Skip) Gates, Jr., director, W.E.B. DuBois Institute for Afro-American Research, Harvard University, author Anita Hill, visiting professor, University of California at Berkeley, and A. Leon Higginbotham, Jr., former Chief Justice, Third Circuit, U.S. Court of Appeals; students Sebastian Corwin, Giles Welch, Olivia Lew, Mia Gonsalves, and Rebecca Chastang; author Marianne Larned; singers Sabrina Luening and Elza Minor; James H. Bryan, president, Union Chapel; Representative John Lewis and his wife, Lillian; murder victim James Byrd, Jr.; U.S. Embassy bombing suspects Mohammed Saddiq Odeh and Mohammad Rashid; and State President Nelson Mandela of South Africa.

The President's Radio Address
August 29, 1998

Good morning. I'm speaking to you today from the Edgartown Elementary School in Martha's Vineyard, Massachusetts. I'd like to talk to you about how we can put progress over partisanship in efforts to expand access to quality health care for every American.

Years from now, when we look back on the greatest accomplishments of this century, miraculous advances in medical care surely will be at the top of the list. But for all the successes of medicine, for all the wonders of its quality, parts of our rapidly changing medical system that deal with access to medical care are in desperate need of repair.

Like many of you, I've been appalled by tragic and repeated stories of men and women fighting for their lives and, at the same time, forced to fight insurance companies focused not on getting them the medical care they need but on cutting costs even if it denies that medical care.

Recently, I met Mary Kuhl, the wife of a 45-year-old man who died after his insurance company canceled his emergency heart surgery, against his doctor's urgent warnings. I met Mick Fleming, whose sister died of breast and lung cancer after she was unfairly denied the treatment her doctor recommended, treatment for which she was eligible and desperately needed. These stories and these practices are callous and unacceptable. We must do everything in our power to give our families greater protection at this time of great change in medical science.

These things happen when, against doctors' recommendations, managed care plans deny procedures or treatment. Now, nobody wants to waste money, and the managed care movement has done a lot of good in slowing down unnecessary inflation. But none of us wants to see medical decisions affecting our families made by insurance company employees who are trained and paid to think like cost-cutting accountants, not care-giving doctors.

That's why I've worked so hard to pass a Patients' Bill of Rights, available to all Americans in all plans, a Patients' Bill of Rights that would say medical decisions should be made by doctors, not accountants; emergency room procedures should be made available whenever and wherever they're needed; no one should

be denied access to a specialist when it's needed; no one should be forced to change doctors in the middle of treatment just because an employer changes medical plans; there ought to be an appeal of a medical decision made by an accountant all the way up the chain in the company, quickly, until it gets to a doctor; people who are hurt ought to have redress; and medical records should be kept private.

We've worked very hard to make these protections available to everyone we could. We've extended the protections of a Patients' Bill of Rights to 85 million Americans who get their health care through Federal plans, Medicare, Medicaid, the Federal Employee Plan, the Veterans' Administration. Today we'll take executive action once again.

More than 120 million Americans are in workplace health plans that are protected under Federal law. The Secretary of Labor has now been instructed to ensure that all these people can quickly appeal, through an internal review process, any coverage decision that denies the care their doctors said was needed and appropriate. That means 120 million more people will no longer have to take an HMO accountant's "no" for an answer. This will bring a lot greater peace of mind.

In many of these stories we hear about, the HMO actually, ultimately, approves the treatment the doctor recommended but only after it goes through layer after layer after layer of appeal. And sometimes there's no appeal at all. What we're doing today is trying to give quick and prompt appeals through an internal review process to the insurance companies and plans that are within our jurisdiction. It will help 120 million Americans. But it's not enough. It is simply not enough.

We do not have the authority to extend all the critical patients' rights protections I mentioned to all the American people, and we won't have it until Congress acts. That's why I've worked, since last November, with doctors, nurses, consumers, lawmakers of both parties to get a strong, enforceable, and bipartisan bill of rights—again, one that says you have the right to emergency room care whenever and wherever you need it; the right to see that medical decisions are made by medical doctors, not insurance company accountants; the right to know you can't be forced to switch doctors abruptly; the right to see a specialist when you need it; the right to hold your health care plan accountable if it causes harm; and the right to privacy in medical records.

These protections could have spared the Kuhls, the Flemings, and large numbers of other families across our country needless tragedies. They are protections all Americans deserve. Unfortunately, not a single one of these vital protections is assured in the Republican leadership bills now in the House and Senate. Both leave millions and millions of Americans without any protections at all. The Republican leadership of both Houses has not allowed full and open debate on the issue. The Senate hasn't even held a single vote.

But remember, this is not a partisan issue. Nobody asks your party affiliation when you visit your doctor. No one wants to see unfeeling practices by insurance companies add to the pain of injury and disease. So when the Senate returns from recess next week, I urge lawmakers of both parties to make patient protections their first order of business.

Last year, we worked together in a bipartisan spirit to pass a balanced budget which included historic Medicare reforms and the largest investment in children's health in more than 30 years. This year, Congress must act like that again. It must put progress ahead of partisanship and join me in giving Americans a Patients' Bill of Rights strong enough, enforceable enough to make quality health care every insurance company's bottom line.

Thanks for listening.

NOTE: The President spoke at 10:06 a.m. from the Edgartown Elementary School on Martha's Vineyard, MA.

Opening Remarks at a Roundtable Discussion on Education in Herndon, Virginia
August 31, 1998

Thank you. First of all, let me thank all of you for that warm welcome, and Michele Freeman, thank you for welcoming me to Herndon Elementary School. All of you know, better than I, that this is the beginning of a new school year where parents and children are meeting their teachers for the first time, and there is excitement and anticipation of what everyone hopes will be a very successful year for the children, and insofar as it is, it's a good year for America.

I have done everything I knew to do, for the last 6 years, to try to focus the attention of the American people on the whole question of education, because I think it is one of the big questions which will determine the shape of our children's future and the world in the 21st century.

If you think about the other major challenges we face as Americans—reforming Social Security and Medicare so that we baby boomers don't bankrupt the country when we retire—[*laughter*]—providing quality affordable health care for all of our people; proving we can preserve and improve the environment and grow the economy; building one America across all the racial and religious and other lines that separate us, something I've been very involved in, in the last several weeks, as all of you know; trying to construct a world free of terrorism and more full of peace and prosperity and security and freedom—every single one of those challenges depends upon our ability to have educated citizens, not just educated Presidents, not just educated Secretaries of Education, but citizens who can absorb complicated information and all these things that are flying at them all the time and evaluate it and measure it, who can develop reasoned principles, passionate responses, to keep the idea of America going into this new century.

That's why I wanted to come here today. Many of you know that I am leaving. When I go back from you, I go back to Washington and then the First Lady and I are going to

Russia and then to Ireland with a team of people to deal with the issues there, and I'd like to just say one word about it, because it's my only real opportunity to talk with you and through you, thanks to our friends in the press here, to the American people. Because this trip is an example of one of the most important lessons every child needs to learn in America from a very early age. And that is, we are living in a smaller and smaller world.

This global economy, the global society, it is real. Information, ideas, technology, money, people can travel around the world at speeds unheard of not very long ago. Our economies are increasingly interconnected. Our securities are increasingly interconnected. I'm sure all of you have followed the events in the aftermath of the tragic bombing at our Embassies in Africa, and you know that there were far more Africans killed than Americans, even though America was the target. And you know that the person responsible did not belong to any government but had an independent terrorist network capable of hitting people and countries all around the world.

So there's been a lot of good. We've benefited a lot from this global society of ours. We have over 16 million new jobs in the last 6 years, and we're about to have our first balanced budget and surplus in 29 years. We have benefited from the world of the 21st century. But we have a lot of responsibilities. And the reason I'm going to Russia is because we have learned the hard way that problems that develop beyond our borders sooner or later find their way to our doorstep unless we help our friends and our neighbors to deal with them as quickly and promptly as possible.

Now, the Russian people are to be commended for embracing democracy and getting rid of the old Communist system. But they're having some troubles today making the transition from communism to a free market economy and from communism to a democratic society that has supports for people who are in trouble.

What I want to do is to go there and tell them that the easy thing to do is not the right thing to do. The easy thing to do would be to try to go back to the way they did it before, and it's not possible, but that if they will stay on the path of reform, to stabilize their society and to strengthen their economy and to get growth back, then I believe America and the rest of the Western nations with strong econo-mies should help them and, indeed, have an obligation to help them and that it's in our interest to help them.

If you say "Why?" let me just give you a couple of reasons. First of all, Russia and the United States still have the biggest nuclear arsenals in the world. And at a time when India and Pakistan have tested nuclear weapons, we need to be moving the world away from nuclear war, not toward it. We have to have the cooperation and the partnership with the Russians to do that.

We don't want terrorists to get a hold of weapons of mass destruction. A weakened Russia, a weakened Russian economy would put enormous pressure on people, who have those technologies and understandings, to sell them. We don't want that to happen. We know we need Russia's partnership to solve problems in that part of the world. If it hadn't been for Russia's partnership, we could not have ended the war in Bosnia, which all of you remember, a couple of years ago, was threatening the entire stability of Europe. Next door, in Kosovo, there is a similar problem today; we've got to have Russia's partnership to solve that. So if Russia will stay on the path of reform, I believe America and the rest of the West must help them.

I'm also going to Ireland, which is the homeland of over 40 million Americans. We trace our ancestry there. And they've been working a long time on a peace process in which we've been intimately involved, and I'm going to do my best to advance that. I think we have a good chance to do so. But I want you to understand that I do these things because I think they are in America's interest. They're not just the right things to do, they're not just nice things to have happen.

But every child—you look around this room and see how many children are here who come from different cultures themselves, whose ancestors come from different countries themselves. There is no nation in the world better positioned than the United States to do well in the 21st century, because we're a people from everywhere. If our values and our ideals can spread around the world, then we can create a peaceful, secure world. So that's what I'm trying to do.

But to get back to the main point, the ultimate national security of any country rests in the strength of its own citizens. And for us, that means we have got to prove that no matter how diverse we are, we can still offer a world-class education to every single American child.

I'm sure all of you know this, but virtually everyone in the world believes that America has the finest system of higher education anywhere. We are flooded every year with students and graduate students coming from every other country in the world to our colleges and universities because they think they're the best in the world, and they have made us very strong. But we now know that, in the world we're living in, it's not enough just to educate half the people very well through university; you must educate 100 percent of the people very well in elementary and secondary school.

We know we've got a lot of challenges. Our kids come from different places. A lot of them have different cultures. They have different learning patterns. They speak different languages as their native language. A lot of them are poor. A lot of them live in neighborhoods that are difficult. And so this is a great challenge for us. But it is a worthy challenge. It's a worthy challenge for a great country to prove that we can take all this diversity, not just racial and ethnic and religious diversity but diversity of life circumstance, and still give every single child a shot at living his or her dream. That is what this is all about, and that's why I'm here today.

This is just as much a part of our national security as that trip I'm taking to Russia, and I want you to understand that I believe that. So when we finish the roundtable, I want to say a little about what we can do to help and what's going on in Congress and what will happen in Congress over the next month, because it's very important. But the most important thing, as the Secretary said, is what's happening here. So I'd like to stop talking and start listening now, and we'll do the roundtable. And I think we should start with Michele Freeman and let her talk about this school and her experiences and her challenges and what she's doing about it.

NOTE: The President spoke at 11:40 a.m. in the gymnasium at Herndon Elementary School. In his remarks, he referred to Michele J. Freeman, principal, Herndon Elementary School; and suspected terrorist leader Usama bin Ladin.

Remarks During a Roundtable Discussion on Education in Herndon
August 31, 1998

The President. Let me just say very briefly before I move on, you probably know this because you talked about how your school was growing. But I believe, Secretary Riley, I think it was last year was the first year that we actually had a school class from kindergarten through high school bigger than the baby boom generation. And this explosion of children into our schools has created enormous strains on school districts all across America.

I was in a school in Florida. I believe it had 17 trailers outside.

Fairfax County Superintendent of Schools Daniel A. Domenech. We have that beat, Mr. President. [*Laughter*]

The President. This was just one school, not a school district, and it was amazing. But there was an article in The Washington Post and in other newspapers over the weekend about the teacher shortage in America, and I'm very concerned about it. We have two proposals. One is to put 35,000 teachers in the most difficult and underserved areas in the country—it's part of our budget—the other would put 100,000 teachers out there across the country in the first 3 grades, to try to keep class size down below 20. And I think those things are very, very important.

One of the things I'm hoping I can do is to persuade the Congress in the next month to embrace the idea that we clearly have a national obligation now to support what is a national phenomenon, the explosion of the number of schoolchildren in our schools. So when you say what you did, it made me want to think about that.

I'd like to go on now to JoAnn Shackelford, because it seems to be a logical followup to what you said about the diversity of your student body and teaching people to read and this Saturday program, which I'm very interested in. It sounds to me like something everybody ought to be doing.

Ms. Shackelford. Thank you. First of all, I wanted to tell you, welcome to our school. We're so excited you're here. Miss Freeman is a hard act to follow, so I won't try. But I do have a few things to ask for. [*Laughter*]

The President. Who picked this questioner? [*Laughter*]

[*At this point, Ms. Shackelford, a reading specialist, expressed the faculty's conviction that students could learn to read by the end of the third grade. She described the Reading Recovery program, focusing on building on the strengths of the weakest first grade students, and the Excel Saturday program, consisting of high school student and teacher volunteers tutoring elementary school children on Saturdays. Ms. Shackelford then said more funding was needed to expand the outreach of the programs and suggested scholarships for high school tutors.*]

The President. I'd just like to make a couple of observations. First of all, I'll think about this high school scholarship thing. The only high school scholarships directly for service, community service we have are the ones that I announced at Penn State a couple of years ago, where we give a modest scholarship that's matched in the local community to one person for outstanding community service in high school.

So we now have 1,000 colleges and universities providing reading volunteers through the America Reads program to go into schools to help young children learn to read, and most of them are work-study students. But a lot of them are not eligible for work-study, and they just do it anyway. There may be something we can do on that, and I'll think about it.

The other thing I'd say is that I'm a big fan of the Reading Recovery program. And if you look at the research, it has about the best long-term results of any strategy. But there is a reason for it. It's very expensive, because it's so labor intensive. And it's something that maybe Secretary Riley wants to talk about this a little bit.

We've discussed before that whether the generalized assistance we give to school districts for supportive programs like this, or the States, which then the school districts get, should be more focused. And we've tried not to sort of pick and choose among the various reading strat-

egies because of the limited amount of money and the large number of programs underway in the country.

But there's no question that the Reading Recovery strategy, particularly when you've got a lot of young people whose first language is not English, has had, I believe, the best long-term results, but it's because it's so labor intensive and is quite expensive, and it's something we need to look at.

Dick, you want to say anything about this?

[*Secretary of Education Richard W. Riley praised the Reading Recovery program's contribution to national education goals.*]

The President. Maybe we should go on now to, since we're talking about this subject, to Maria Gorski, who is a parent liaison. And you talked about involving the parents, so talk a little about that for us, Maria.

[*Ms. Gorski, liaison to parents of Spanish-speaking immigrant students, noted the difficulty some parents had in helping their children with homework because of language barriers and lack of time. She asked for the President's support of the United Neighborhood program, run by the Herndon Police Department, in which volunteers tutored students in the evenings.*]

The President. Thank you. How many parents volunteer in this school? Do you know how many?

[*Herndon Elementary School Principal Michele J. Freeman said there were about 500 volunteers a year, in addition to volunteers who worked from home, sending in materials for use at the school.*]

The President. What about the children who have both parents work and maybe have two jobs? How do you work out time for them to meet with the teachers?

[*Ms. Gorski said that due to parents' schedules, such meetings usually occurred on Saturdays.*]

The President. What about—how does the school work? What does the assistant principal do to make sure that there are no fires started and everybody sort of shows up more or less on time and all of that? [*Laughter*]

[*Herndon Elementary School Assistant Principal Jude Isaacson noted the staff's dedication to educating and nurturing every child, using discipline with dignity, and getting to know the* students' families through extracurricular activities. She said the school's counselors aided in peer mediation and conflict resolution and offered classes on parenting skills. Ms. Isaacson noted the visible and proactive presence of the school administration among the students and described the Adopt-a-Cop program, which allowed local police to have lunch with students and discuss safety awareness. She expressed pride in the school staff and their interaction with the community to foster discipline and safety.]

The President. Last week, I went up to Worcester, Massachusetts, and released there this handbook that Secretary Riley and Attorney General Reno did for all the schools on trying to identify children that have problems and trying to prevent things from happening before they go too far. But I tried to emphasize to them that the schools—still, schools are basically the safest places in the country for our kids. But when something goes wrong, it can be terribly tragic.

But I think it's important that the American people know that most schools have people like you in them and other people who are really working hard to do their part to help the children grow up in a safe, secure environment so they can learn. And I know Secretary Riley—he mentioned the character education program; he's been promoting that and worked hard for it ever since we've been here, and I thank him.

What about the teachers? It's about time we heard—[*inaudible*].

[*First grade teacher Martha Bell noted that teachers looked at the challenges of each individual student and tried to learn how best to communicate with the parents. She stressed the need to convince middle school and high school students of the rewards of a career in teaching and urged more funding for higher education.*]

The President. What's the most challenging thing that new teachers face—first-year teachers?

[*Ms. Bell replied that it was a teacher's first conference or phone call with parents, and she stressed the importance of establishing a rapport with them.*]

The President. I could use her in any number of positions—[*laughter*]—in the Federal Government. We've got an airplane strike in the Mid-

west I think you could settle—[*laughter*]—by tonight, and I'd appreciate it.

Principal Freeman. Mr. President, she's taken. [*Laughter*]

The President. But one of those parents who is sitting to your left—Mr. Lewis, you're the PTA president. First of all, I know this is not what you are going to say, but what do you do when you're not the PTA president, and why did you decide to do this?

[*E. Tracey Lewis commended the President on his education policies. He remarked on his work with Bill Milliken in the Communities in Schools program, the largest stay-in-school program in the Nation. Mr. Lewis stressed a citizen's obligation to the community and likened the Herndon Elementary School PTA to the President's theme of building bridges to the 21st century. He noted the PTA's emphasis on building a community context around the school and its students. He then outlined 10 guiding principles that directed the PTA's decisionmaking.*]

The President. I would just like to say a couple of things and ask you one question. First of all, I want to thank you for your work with the Cities in Schools program. I brought it to Arkansas with Bill Milliken probably 15 years ago, and that's a long time ago. Secondly, I want to thank you for your work in the PTA, and as a father who used to be an active participant in all our school events, I think it's a good thing to have men as well as women be present. And I think that's good.

How many members does your PTA have? How many parent members?

Mr. Lewis. Last year, 47 percent of the parent population of Herndon Elementary School were members of the PTA. This year, under the able leadership of Mary Mann, who is our vice president for membership, we expect to go to scale, 100 percent. [*Laughter*]

The President. I'd say that's pretty good.

Ms. Mann. We think big here.

The President. Well, Mr. Superintendent, are all your schools like this? [*Laughter*]

[*Superintendent Domenech noted that the county had the Nation's 12th largest and best school system. He attributed its success to dedicated staff and community and to the diversity of the county's overall student body. He remarked on the challenges that confronted the county in providing more facilities for handling overcrowding*] and obtaining better technology for the class-room. He described the Success by Eight program, whereby all students were expected to be able to read by the time they were 8 years old, and stressed the need for smaller class sizes to achieve that goal.]

The President. Well, let me say, I think this is a truly extraordinary school district. And I have done my part to promote you, you know, around the country. [Laughter] I always talk about what an amazing school district this is. Some of your schools, particular schools are as diverse as any in America and a stunning array of people coming from different places. So I'm very impressed, and I thank you for what you're doing.

I wonder if—Secretary Riley, would you like to say anything before I talk a little bit about the congressional agenda?

[Secretary Riley announced the availability within days of guidebooks on early warning signals to help detect school violence before it happened. He then commended the members of the round-table for their participation in the discussion.]

The President. Didn't they do a great job? [Applause]

[Secretary Riley then introduced the President.]

The President. The way I was prepared for this, I was supposed to go up there to the po-dium and give a little talk, and it's way too past that. [Laughter] We've had too much fun.

But what I would like to do is to outline to you—there are six things that the Congress should pass that are in my budget that don't break the balanced budget, that are in our bal-anced budget, that they can pass or not pass in the next few days, that I think would really help our children a lot. Five of them bear di-rectly on our schools, one indirectly. But I'd like to just mention them so you would know, because I would like to see them get broad bipartisan support. I don't really believe we're best served when education is a partisan issue. I think we're best served when it's an American issue that crosses party lines.

First of all, I have given Congress a plan for smaller classes, better-trained teachers, and more modern schools. Let's begin with the teacher shortage. You know what's acute here; it is profound in many places. Now, let me say one other word of introduction. There has been what I consider to be a legitimate question

raised of me by many Members of Congress who say, "Well, now, look Mr. President, you're trying to get the Federal Government into fi-nancing things that the Federal Government has never before financed. We've never been into building or repairing schools, for example—there are many States in this country where the States don't even do that, where it all has to be done at the local level—or putting 100,000 teachers out there for smaller classes in the early grades."

My answer is as follows: Number one, it's hard to think of a more important national issue. Number two, I'm not doing anything to interfere with the local direction of the schools or the States' constitutional responsibility to set the framework of public education. And number three, in some places, like this district, the level of growth and, in other places, the level of pov-erty make it simply inconceivable that they can achieve these objectives otherwise.

So I think, if we have the money, this is what we ought to do. But I want to prepare you in case any of you feel moved by the spirit to call or write your Congressman or Senator. [Laughter] There is a legitimate historic pattern here where they'll say, "Well, you know, Presi-dent Clinton's got a lot of energy, but he may have gone too far this time because the Federal Government's never done this." There is a rea-son we're doing it now. There's a reason we're doing it now. We have to prove that our ele-mentary and secondary schools can be uniformly as excellent as our colleges and universities are and give all of our kids world-class education. And unless we do this, I am convinced there won't be the resources out there to get the job done.

So let me say first of all, the teacher short-age—I've asked Congress to pass a plan to help school districts hire 100,000 new teachers, all trained, tested, and certified by State education authorities, targeted to smaller classes in the early grades. Again, where all the research shows, there are permanent gains if kids get the kind of individual attention they need in the early grades.

I've also asked them to help me support bet-ter teacher training programs not directed by Washington, those things that all of you know work, all educators know work. There is not today, in my opinion, a sufficient commitment to helping teachers continue to improve their skills, upgrade their skills, work with other teachers, to have the time necessary to try to continue to improve, to avoid burnout under all the pressures that they're under. When I go out and talk to educators, there's really a lot of support for increased investment in teacher training. So I hope that Congress will fully fund this class size reduction program. It would get us down to an average of 18 children per class once we do it.

The second problem is, it's hard to have a small class without a classroom. [*Laughter*] What did you call them, learning cottages? Learning cottages. That sounds like someplace you're sent when you misbehave—[*laughter*]—learning cottages. Anyway, so I have also presented a plan to help to modernize or build new, 5,000 schools. Next Tuesday, when I get back from my trip, the Secretary and I and others are going to hold school modernization days all across America to highlight our proposal which would provide tax credit to build or modernize or rebuild 5,000 public schools.

I have been to schools in this country where whole floors were closed because they were so old. But they're wonderful buildings. Structurally, no one could afford to build such buildings today because of the cost of construction. But if you go to an inner-city school, for example, think of what message it gives a 7-year-old child to walk up the steps of a school where the paint's peeling off and the windows are broken. Think of the message you're sending your child. You want to say, "Oh, every child is a treasure," all these things that your PTA president said; I believe every one of them. But sometimes, the actions speak louder than words. You can tell those children that, but if they have to keep walking up steps into broken-down buildings, do they really think we believe it?

The other day, I was in Philadelphia in a school—the average school building—the average age of school buildings in Philadelphia is 65 years. That's the average age. Now, the good news is those structures, by and large, are magnificent. The bad news is a whole lot of them are in terrible shape, and I think it's a worthy investment. I think it's a worthy investment of our money.

So, we want to give fast-growing districts like this one and districts with good structures but old, run-down buildings the chance they need to go forward. So that's the first: more teachers for smaller classes and more classes.

Second, we want to fully fund my plan to equip our Nation's classrooms with computers and cutting-edge educational software and to train teachers to be there to make sure that the technology is properly used. I want to hook up every classroom and library in the entire country to the Internet by the year 2000 and make sure that the software is good and that the teachers are trained to make the most of it. And we have to help you do that. You shouldn't have to fully fund that.

Third, I want to strengthen the charter school movement. There are some school districts that have been greatly advanced by letting teachers and others get together and start new schools within the framework of the school district where the whole district's not reforming, but they want to try something new. We've got now about almost 1,000 of those schools out there. When I became President, there was only one in the whole country. When I was talking about it in 1992, I might have been trying to explain the theory of relativity. Everybody thought I was nuts. [*Laughter*] But now, first we had one, now we've got nearly 1,000, and if my budget passes, we'll have 3,000 funded by the year 2000.

Fourth, I want to continue to open the doors of college to all Americans who will work for it by reauthorizing the Higher Education Act. Now, that doesn't mean anything, so let me tell you what that means, that reauthorization. [*Laughter*]

This legislation will help more children reach their potential by improving teacher education. It will help struggling communities to hire 35,000 well-qualified teachers. It will expand mentoring programs, something that you've already said is important to you. It will reduce interest rates on student loans. It will extend Pell grants and the Federal work-study program. We've taken it from 700,000 work-study positions to a million in 3 years. So these things are very important.

You know, we have provided for lower interest rates on student loans, better repayment, 300,000 more work-study slots, and now tax credits worth about $1,500 a year for the first 2 years of college, and then for junior and senior year and graduate school. I am determined that when I leave office, no American will ever, ever walk away from college because of the cost. We can open the doors of college to everybody who is qualified, and it's important.

Fifth, let's go back to what we were talking about on reading. We want to pass a bipartisan early literacy bill to help to train teachers and mobilize an army of volunteer tutors, because as I said, we already have 1,000 colleges participating in this program. And I think it's very, very important.

Sixth, we have a general program to strengthen our schools that would expand Head Start, strengthen after-school programs for hundreds of thousands of children. This is a huge deal in areas with a lot of juvenile crime, with a lot of dangerous streets, with a lot of gangs. These after-school programs and summer school programs have dramatically reduced student problems while increasing student achievement, and I think that's very, very important.

We have a special initiative aimed at Hispanic young people because the school dropout rate is still much higher for Hispanics than for any other group, largely because of language barriers and economic problems. And we also have, in this package program I just mentioned, our Safe and Drug-Free Schools program. We've tried to take the initiatives that we know work in schools like this one and make sure they are in every single school in America.

Now, the bill that the House Republican majority has proposed falls short of these goals in every single one of these areas. But it's not too late. The bill has to be considered in the Senate; then both the Senate and the House must vote on it. So I would implore you, without regard to your political party, just to contact your Members of Congress, your Senators and ask them to support this agenda. We have the money.

We have worked hard to balance the budget. We've worked hard to show fiscal discipline, to get the economy going again. There is no more important area in which to spend the money now that we have it, and so I hope you will help us to do that.

Let me just say one final thing. The Senate tomorrow takes up the summer jobs program. Now, that's not for this summer, but—the one we just passed—but for the summer about to come. It provides more than 500,000 young people a chance to work. It is a godsend to this country. And because of the funding—Federal-funded summer jobs program, we have a lot of places which we are able then to go out and get other people to put up money to expand the program. For reasons I do not understand, the House committee wants to disband it, and I think it would be a disastrous error.

It comes up in the Senate tomorrow, and again, this is fundamentally an education issue, because if kids get in trouble over the summer or they have problems and they don't have something to do or if they need the money and they can't earn it, it increases the chances that they'll drop out. So I hope that you will also support the summer jobs program. The Senate is taking it up quite soon. I believe the Senate, across party lines, will vote to extend it, but we need help.

So I just wanted to close by trying to close this circle here. We started, in this roundtable, talking about what you are doing to give to children in your charge the future they deserve and a future America desperately needs for them to have. But we think we have a role here if we're going to build those bridges to the 21st century. And I've done my best to define that role based on 20 years now of working with people in education. I think it's a good agenda. Secretary Riley and I, ourselves, started working together almost 20 years ago on public education. I guess next year will be our 20th anniversary of working together on these things when we were young Governors.

I know that you know that there are things we should do, and I believe if we don't be harsh and political in our rhetoric, we talk about our children and what we know to be true of education, we can get a listening ear among enough thoughtful Republicans to join our Democrats to build a bipartisan coalition to do what the National Government should do to help make possible more stories like the ones we've heard around this table today. That is my whole goal. And I know that we won't have all the stories we need unless we also do our part. So I ask you: Whatever you can do to contact your Representatives and Senators, whatever you can do to make it clear that these are not partisan issues, these are people issues, and that our future is riding on it, if you can do that, I would be very grateful. And thank you for what you do here every day.

Thank you.

NOTE: The President spoke at 12:45 p.m. in the gymnasium at Herndon Elementary School. In his remarks, he referred to William E. Milliken, president, Communities in Schools, Inc. (formerly, Cities in Schools, Inc.).

Statement on the Northwest Airlines Pilots Strike
August 31, 1998

I have asked Northwest Airlines and its pilots to redouble their efforts to resolve their differences. Senior members of my administration continue to be in contact with the parties, but it is up to the negotiating parties to reach an agreement. Specifically, I have asked Secretary of Transportation Rodney Slater to meet with the parties' leadership. I hope that an agreement will be concluded soon in their interests and the interest of the American people.

Message to the Senate Transmitting the Guatemala-United States Treaty on Stolen Vehicles and Aircraft
August 31, 1998

To the Senate of the United States:

With a view to receiving the advice and consent of the Senate to ratification, I transmit herewith the Treaty Between the Government of the United States of America and the Government of the Republic of Guatemala for the Return of Stolen, Robbed, Embezzled or Appropriated Vehicles and Aircraft, with Annexes and a related exchange of notes, signed at Guatemala City on October 6, 1997. I transmit also, for the information of the Senate, the report of the Department of State with respect to the Treaty.

The Treaty is one of a series of stolen vehicle treaties being negotiated by the United States in order to eliminate the difficulties faced by owners of vehicles that have been stolen and transported across international borders. It is the first of these newly negotiated treaties to provide for the return of stolen aircraft as well as vehicles. When it enters into force, it will be an effective tool to facilitate the return of U.S. vehicles and aircraft that have been stolen, robbed, embezzled, or appropriated and taken to Guatemala.

I recommend that the Senate give early and favorable consideration to the Treaty, with Annexes and a related exchange of notes, and give its advice and consent to ratification.

WILLIAM J. CLINTON

The White House,
August 31, 1998.

NOTE: This message was released by the Office of the Press Secretary on September 1.

Remarks at First Day of School Festivities in Moscow, Russia
September 1, 1998

Thank you all very much. I am delighted to be here not only with my wife, who has worked for better education in our country for many years, but with the Secretary of State, the Secretary of Commerce, our American Ambassador here, and five Members of our Congress. I thank all of them for being here. We are delighted to join you on this day.

I would also like to thank Vice Mayor Schantsev and Mr. Muzikantskiy from the Moscow City School Board for joining us. I would like to thank your principal; Ms. Garashkova; and most of all, I want to thank these fine students, Konstantine Sokolov and Valentina Smirnova. I think they did a fine job, and you should give them applause. You should be very proud of them. [*Applause*]

Now, in the spirit of the day, even though Konstantine's English is very good, I thought I should try to say something in Russian, like *privet* [hello]. How's that? Is that good? [*Applause*] Or *S novym uchebnym godom* [Happy New School Year]. Is that good? [*Applause*]

In America this is also the first day of school for many students. I understand that some of you have studied in America. I hope more of you will do so in the future, and I hope more Americans will come here to study. And in the meantime, perhaps more and more of you can meet on the Internet.

I know that Russian students love to read and are proud of your country's great writers. A teacher here in Moscow asked her first-grade class why they thought reading was important. One girl stood up and answered, "You can read any book. You can read Pushkin." No one in the first grade in my country is reading Pushkin. [*Laughter*] Now, another student answered the same question in a different way. He said, "If you can read, you can read a fax." [*Laughter*]

So whether you want to be a business person reading a fax, a writer, or a teacher, or pursue any other career in the modern world, a good school will help you get there. In a world where people are working closer and closer together, a good school, with its languages and its learning about other countries, is very important. Because more and more of our jobs and lives depend on computers and technology, more and more of us have to read well, do mathematics, and know other subjects good schools teach.

In the past, America and Russia too often used our knowledge in opposition to each other. But things are very different now. Today, we use what we know to work together for new jobs, better health care, a cleaner environment, the exploration of space, the exchange of ideas, art, music, videos. Our countries are becoming partners, and more and more of our people are becoming friends.

Your country is going through some difficult changes right now, and I know things aren't always easy for a lot of people. But I also know that in times of crisis the Russian people have always risen to the occasion with courage and determination.

The challenges of this new global economy and society are great, but so are the rewards. For those who have good schools, like this one, with teachers and parents who work hard to help children learn, and with that learning and the new freedom you have in Russia, all of you will be ready for that future, and you will do very well.

So I say to all the students here, learn as much as you can about as many subjects as you can and about other people. And imagine what you would like to see happen in the future, for yourselves, your nation, and the world. And always keep those dreams with you, for in the new century, you will be able to live those dreams.

Thank you. *Spasibo.*

NOTE: The President spoke at 3:25 p.m. in the auditorium at the 19th Elementary School. In his remarks, he referred to Deputy Mayor Valeriy Schantsev of Moscow; Aleksandr Muzikantskiy, chairman, Moscow City School Board; Galina Bezrodnaya, principal, and Natalya Garashkova, assistant principal for English language programs, 19th Elementary School; and students Konstantine Sokolov and Valentina Smirnova, who spoke at the festivities and presented gifts to the President and Mrs. Clinton.

Remarks to Future Russian Leaders in Moscow
September 1, 1998

Thank you very much. First I'd like to thank Maxim Safonov for that fine introduction and for his very encouraging remarks. Rector Torkunov, Minister Primakov, to all the members of the American delegation. We have Secretary of State Albright; Secretary of Commerce Daley; Secretary of Energy Richardson; National Security Adviser Berger; our Ambassador, Jim Collins; and five distinguished Members of the United States Congress here, Senator Domenici, Senator Bingaman, Representatives Hoyer, King, and Deutsch.

I think their presence here should speak louder than any words I could say that America considers our relationship with Russia to be important. It is a relationship of friendship, of mutual responsibility, and of commitment to the future. We are all honored to be here today, and we thank you for your welcome.

On this first day of school across both our countries, students are resuming their studies, including their study of history. At this critical, surely historic, moment, let me start with a few words about what I believe the past can teach us as we and, especially, as the Russian people face the challenges of the present and the future.

Two hundred and twenty-two years ago, we Americans declared our freedom from the tyranny of King George of England. We set out to govern ourselves. The road has not often or certainly not always been easy. First, we fought a very long war for independence. Then it took more than 10 years to devise a Constitution that worked. Then in 1814, we went to war with England again. They invaded our Capital City and burned the President's house, the White House. Then in 1861, we began our bloodiest war ever, a civil war, fought over the conflicts of slavery. It almost divided our country forever, but instead we were reunited, and we abolished slavery.

In the 1930's, before World War II, our country sank into an enormous depression with 25 percent of our people unemployed and more than one-third of our people living in poverty. Well, you know the rest. We were allies in World War II, and after World War II we were adversaries. But it was a time of great prosperity for the American people, even though there were tense and difficult moments in the last 50 years.

The larger point I want to make, as Russia goes through this time of extreme difficulty, is that over the life of our democracy we have had many intense, even bitter debates about what are the proper relations between people of different races or religions or backgrounds, over the gap between rich and poor, over crime and punishment, even over war and peace. We Americans have fought and argued with each other, as we do even today, but we have preserved our freedom by remembering the fundamental values enshrined in our Constitution and our Declaration of Independence, by continuing to respect the dignity of every man, woman, and child, to tolerate those with different ideas and beliefs than our own, to demand equality

of opportunity, to give everyone a chance to make the most of his or her life.

Russia's great ally in World War II, our President, Franklin Roosevelt, said that democracy is a never-ending seeking for better things. For Americans, that means, in good times and bad, we seek to widen the circle of opportunity, to deepen the meaning of our freedom, to build a stronger national community.

Now, what does all that got to do with Russia in 1998? Your history is much longer than ours and so rich with accomplishment, from military victories over Napoleon and Hitler to the literary achievements of Pushkin, Tolstoy, Chekhov, Pasternak, and so many others to great achievements in art, music, dance, medicine, science, space flight. Yet for all your rich, long history, it was just 7 years ago that Russia embarked on its own quest for democracy, liberty, and free markets—just 7 years ago—a journey that is uniquely your own and must be guided by your own vision of Russia's democratic destiny.

Now you are at a critical point on your journey. There are severe economic pressures and serious hardships which I discussed in my meetings with your leaders this morning. The stakes are enormous. Every choice Russia makes today may have consequences for years and years to come. Given the facts before you, I have to tell you that I do not believe there are any painless solutions, and indeed, an attempt to avoid difficult solutions may only prolong and worsen the present challenges.

First, let me make a couple of points. The experience of our country over the last several years, and especially in the last 6 years, proves that the challenges of the global economy are very great, but so are its rewards. The Russian people have met tremendous challenges in the past. You can do it here. You can build a prosperous future. You can build opportunity and jobs for all the people of this land who are willing to work for them if you stand strong and complete, not run from but complete the transformation you began 7 years ago.

The second point I want to make is the rest of the world has a very large stake in your success. Today, about a quarter of the world's people are struggling with economic challenges that are profound, the people of your country, the people in Japan, who have had no economic growth for 5 years—it's still a very wealthy country, but when they don't have any growth, it's harder for all other countries that trade with them who aren't so wealthy, to grow—other countries in Asia. And now we see, when there are problems in Russia or in Japan or questions about the economy of China, you see all across the world, the stock market in Latin America drops, you see the last 2 days, we've had big drops in the American stock market.

What does that say? Well, among other things, it says, whether we like it or not, we must build the future together, because, whether we like it or not, we are going to be affected by what we do. We will be affected by what you do; you will be affected by what we do. We might as well do it together and make the most of it.

Now, in terms of what has happened in America, obviously it's always more enjoyable when our stock market goes up than when it goes down. But I have talked to our Secretary of the Treasury about this several times since yesterday. I want to reiterate the point that I think is important for Russia, for America, for every country: We believe our fundamental economic policy is sound; we believe our people are working at record rates; and we are determined to stay on a path of fiscal discipline that brought us to where we are. I think that, wherever there are markets, there will always be changes in those markets. But we must attempt to move in the right direction.

And that's what I want to talk to you about today: How can we move in the right direction? When I look at all the young people here today—and I have read about you and your background—young people from all over Russia, seizing the possibilities of freedom to chart new courses for yourselves and your nation, making a difference by building businesses from modest loans and innovative ideas, by taking technologies created for weapons and applying them to human needs, by finding creative government solutions to complex problems, by improving medical care and fighting disease, by publishing courageous journalism, exposing abuses of power, producing literature and art and scholarship, changing the way people see their own lives, organizing citizens to fight for justice and human rights and a cleaner environment, reaching out to the world—in this room today, there are young people doing all those things. That should give you great reason to hope.

You are at the forefront of building a modern Russia. You are a new generation. You do represent the future of your dreams. Your efforts today will not only ensure better lives for yourselves but for your children and generations that follow.

I think it is important to point out, too, that when Russia chose freedom, it was not supposed to benefit only the young and well educated, the rich and well connected; it was also supposed to benefit the men and women who worked in factories and farms and fought the wars of the Soviet era, those who survive today on pensions and Government assistance. It was also supposed to benefit the laborers and teachers and soldiers who work every day but wait now for a paycheck.

The challenge is to create a new Russia that benefits all responsible citizens of this country. How do you get there? I do not believe it is by reverting to the failed policies of the past. I do not believe it is by stopping the reform process in midstream, with a few Russians doing very well but far more struggling to provide for their families. I believe you will create the conditions of growth if, but only if, you continue to move decisively along the path of democratic, market-oriented, constructive revolution.

The Russian people have made extraordinary progress in the last 7 years. You have gone to the polls to elect your leaders. Some 65 to 70 percent of you freely turn out in every election. People across Russia are rebuilding diverse religious traditions, launching a wide range of private organizations. Seventy percent of the economy now is in private hands. Not bureaucrats but consumers determine what goods get to stores and where people live. You have reached out to the world with trade and investment, exchanges of every kind, and leadership in meeting security challenges around the globe.

Now you face a critical moment. Today's financial crisis does not require you to abandon your march toward freedom and free markets. Russians will define Russia's future, but there are clear lessons, I would argue, from international experience. Here's what I think they are.

First, in tough times governments need stable revenues to pay their bills, support salaries, pensions, and health care. That requires decisive action to ensure that everyone pays their fair share of taxes. Otherwise, a few pay too much, many pay too little, the government is in the hole and can never get out, and you will never be able to have a stable economic policy. It is tempting for everyone to avoid wanting to pay any taxes. But if everyone will pay their fair share, the share will be modest and their incomes will be larger over the long run because of the stability and growth it will bring to this Russian economic system.

Second, printing money to pay the bills and bail out the banks does not help. It causes inflation and ultimately will make the pain worse.

Third, special bailouts for a privileged few come at the expense of the whole nation.

Fourth, fair, equitable treatment of creditors today will determine their involvement in a nation tomorrow. The people who loan money into this nation must be treated fairly if you want them to be loaning money into this nation 4 years, 5 years, 10 years hence.

These are not radical theories, they are simply facts proven by experience. How Russia reacts to them will fundamentally affect your future. Surviving today's crisis, however difficult that may be, is just the beginning. To create jobs, growth, and higher income, a nation must convince its own citizens and foreigners that they can safely invest. Again, experience teaches what works: fair tax laws and fair enforcement; easier transferability of land; strong intellectual property rights to encourage innovation; independent courts enforcing the law consistently and upholding contract rights; strong banks that safeguard savings; securities markets that protect investors; social spending that promotes hope and opportunity and a safety net for those who, in any given time in an open market economy, will be dislocated; and vigilance against hidden ties between government and business interests that are inappropriate.

Now, this is not an American agenda. I will say it again: This is not an American agenda. These are the imperatives of the global marketplace, and you can see them repeated over and over and over again. You can also see the cost of ignoring them in nation after nation after nation.

Increasingly, no nation, rich or poor, democratic or authoritarian, can escape the fundamental economic imperatives of the global market. Investors and entrepreneurs have a very wide and growing range of choices about where they put their money. They move in the direction of openness, fairness, and freedom. Here, Russia has an opportunity. At the dawn of a new century, there is a remarkable convergence. Increasingly, the very policies that are needed

to thrive in the new economy are also those which deepen democratic liberty for individual citizens.

This is a wealthy country. It is rich in resources. It is richer still in people. It has done a remarkable job of providing quality education to large numbers of people. You have proven over and over and over again, in ways large and small, that the people of this country have a sense of courage and spirit, an unwillingness to be beat down and to give up. The future can be very, very bright.

But we can't ignore the rules of the game, because if there is a system of freedom, you cannot take away, and no country, not even the United States with the size of our economy, no country is strong enough to control what millions and millions and millions of people decide freely to do with their money. But every country will keep a large share of its own citizens' money and get a lot of money from worldwide investors if it can put in place systems that abide by the rules of international commerce. And all Russia needs is its fair share of this investment. You have the natural wealth. You have the people power. You have the education. All you need is just to get your fair share of the investment.

Now, 21st century economic power will rest on creativity and innovation. I believe the young people in this room think they can be as creative or innovative as anyone in the world. It will rest on the free flow of information. It will rest on ideas. Consider this, those of you who are beginning your careers: America's three largest computer and software companies are now worth more than all the American companies in our steel, automotive, aerospace, chemical, and plastics industries combined—combined— our three biggest computer companies.

The future is a future of ideas. No nation will ever have a monopoly on ideas. No people will ever control all the creative juices that flow in the human spirit more or less evenly across the world. You will do very well if you just get your fair share of investment. To get your fair share of investment, you have to play by the rules that everyone else has to play by. That's what this whole crisis is about. No one could ever have expected your country to be able to make this transition without pain. You've only been at this 7 years.

Look at any European country that has had an open market society for decades and decades and decades. They have hundreds, indeed thousands of little organizations; they have major national institutions that all tend to reinforce these rules that I talked about earlier. Don't be discouraged, but don't be deterred. Just keep working until you get it in place. Once you get it in place, Russia will take off like a rocket, because you have both natural resources and people resources.

Now, I think it's important to point out, however, that economic strength—let's go back to the rules—it depends on the rule of law. If somebody from outside a country intends to put money into a foreign country, they want to know what the rules are. What are the terms on which my money is being invested? How will my investment be protected? If I lose money, I want to know it's because I made a bad decision, not because the law didn't protect my money. It is very important. Investors, therefore, seek honest government, fair systems, fair for corporations and consumers, where there are strong checks on corruption and abuse of authority, and openness in what the rules are on how investment capital is handled.

Economic strength depends on equality of opportunity. There must be strong schools and good health care and everyone must have a chance to share in the nation's bounty. And economic power must lie with people who vote their consciences, use new technologies to spread ideas, start organizations to work for change, and build enterprises of all kinds.

Now, some seek to exploit this power shift that's going on in the world to take advantage of their fellow citizens. When this nation went from the old Communist command and control system to an open free system, without all the intermediate institutions and private organizations that it takes years to build up, vacuums were created. And into those vacuums, some moved with an intent to exploit their fellow citizens, to enrich themselves without regard to fairness or safety or the future. The challenges for any citizen—this is not Russia specific; this would have happened and has happened in every single country that has had to make this transition. There's nothing inherently negative about this development. It is as predictable as the Sun coming up in the morning. Every country has had to face this. But you must overcome it.

You must have a state that is strong enough to control abuses: violence, theft, fraud, bribery,

monopolism. But it must not be so strong that it can limit the legitimate rights and dreams and creativity of the people. That is the tension of creating the right kind of democratic market society.

The bottom line is that the American people very much want Russia to succeed. We value your friendship. We honor your struggle. We want to offer support as long as you take the steps needed for stability and progress. We will benefit greatly if you strengthen your democracy and increase your prosperity.

Look what our partnership has already produced. We reversed the dangerous buildup of nuclear weapons. We're 2 years ahead of schedule in cutting nuclear arsenals under START I. START II, which still awaits ratification in the Duma, will reduce our nuclear forces by two-thirds from cold-war levels. President Yeltsin and I already have agreed on a framework for START III to cut our nuclear arsenals even further.

For you young people, at a time when India and Pakistan have started testing nuclear weapons, America and Russia must resume the direction the world should take, away from nuclear weapons, not toward them. This is a very important thing.

We are working to halt the spread of weapons of mass destruction. We signed the Comprehensive Nuclear Test Ban Treaty with 147 other countries. We're working to contain the arms race between India and Pakistan, to strengthen controls on transfers of weapons technologies, to combat terrorism everywhere.

Our bonds are growing stronger, and as they do we will move closer to our goal of a Europe undivided, democratic, and at peace. We reached agreement for greater cooperation between NATO and Russia. And our soldiers serve side by side, making peace possible in Bosnia.

We don't always agree, and our interests aren't always identical. But we work together more often than not, and the world is a better place as a result. Building peace is our paramount responsibility, but there is more we must do together. One thing we need to do more together is prove that you can grow the economy without destroying the environment.

A great man, looking at the condition of the environment, charged that humanity was a destroyer. He wrote, "Forests keep disappearing. Rivers dry up. Wildlife has become extinct. The climate is ruined. The land grows poorer and uglier every day." Chekhov wrote those words 100 years ago. Just imagine his reaction to the present environmental conditions, with toxic pollution ruining our air and water, and global warming threatening to aggravate flooding and drought and disease.

Together, we can create cleaner technologies to grow our economies without destroying the world's environment and imperiling future generations. Together, we can harness the genius of our citizens not for making weapons but for building better communications, curing disease, combating hunger, exploring the heavens. Together, we can reconcile societies of different people with different religions and races and viewpoints, and stand against the wars of ethnic, religious, and racial hatred that have dominated recent history.

If we stand together and if we do the right things, we can build that kind of world. If the people of Russia stand for economic reform that benefits all the people of this country, America will stand with you. As the people of Russia work for education and scientific discovery, as they stand against corruption and for honest government, against the criminals and terrorists and for the safety of ordinary citizens, against aggression and for peace, America will proudly stand with you. It is the right thing to do, but it is also very much in the interest of the American people to do so.

I was amazed there were some doubters back in America who said perhaps I shouldn't come here because these are uncertain times politically and economically. And there are questions being raised in the American press about the commitment of Russia to the course of reform and democracy. It seems to me that anybody can get on an airplane and take a trip in good times and that friends come to visit each other in challenging and difficult times.

I come here as a friend, because I believe in the future of Russia. I come here also because I believe someone has to tell the truth to the people, so that you're not skeptical when your political leaders tell you things that are hard to hear. There is no way out of playing by the rules of the international economy if you wish to be a part of it. We cannot abandon the rules of the international economy. No one can.

There is a way to preserve the social safety net and the social contract and to help the people who are too weak to succeed. There is a way to do that. And there are people who will help to do that. But it has to be done. So I come here as a friend. I come here because I know that the future of our children and the future of Russia's young people are going to be entwined, and I want it to be a good future. And I believe it can be.

Recently, a woman from Petrozavodsk—I hope I pronounced that right, Petrozavodsk—wrote these words about your people who won World War II and rebuilt from the rubble. Listen to this. She said, "We survived the ruins, the devastation, the hunger, and the cold. It is not possible that our people can do this again? If people raise themselves, they can move mountains. Toward what end? Pushkin once said that so long as we burn with freedom, we can fulfill the noble urges of our souls."

In all this dry and sometimes dour talk about economics and finance, never forget that, whatever your human endeavor, the ultimate purpose of it is to fulfill the noble urges of your soul. That is the ultimate victory the Russian people will reap if you will see this process through to the end. I hope you will do that, and I hope we will be able to be your partners every step of the way.

Thank you very much.

NOTE: The President spoke at 4:50 p.m. in the auditorium at Moscow State University. In his remarks, he referred to Maxim Safonov, student, and Anatoliy V. Torkunov, rector, Moscow State University for International Relations; and Minister of Foreign Affairs Yevgeniy Primakov and President Boris Yeltsin of Russia. A portion of these remarks could not be verified because the tape was incomplete.

Statement on the Northern Ireland Peace Process
September 1, 1998

I join Prime Ministers Blair and Ahern in welcoming today's statement by Sinn Fein President Gerry Adams committing to exclusively democratic and peaceful means in the political process in Northern Ireland. Sinn Fein joins its voice to the vast majority of Northern Ireland's people who are determined to see, in Mr. Adams' words, that "violence is a thing of the past, over, done with, and gone." This statement is an important contribution to building the trust and confidence necessary to make the Good Friday accord a reality.

I am looking forward to meeting personally with all the party leaders in Northern Ireland. I will urge them to work for full and speedy implementation of the Good Friday accord— the best way to put an end to conflict and ensure peace in Northern Ireland.

Statement on Harold Ickes' 1996 Campaign Financing Activities
September 1, 1998

Harold Ickes has been an important part of this administration's efforts to move our country forward and has devoted much of his life to improving the lives of all Americans. He has been a trusted adviser and a dedicated public servant. I am confident that investigators will find he acted lawfully and appropriately.

NOTE: Mr. Ickes was formerly Assistant to the President and Deputy Chief of Staff for Policy and Political Affairs.

Statement on Senate Action on Appropriations Legislation
September 1, 1998

For the past month, I have criticized the House Republican education and training budget because it shortchanges America's future. Today I am pleased that a bipartisan group of Senators voted to reject parts of the extreme House Republican education and training budget and make many—but not all—of the critical investments in our future that I believe are necessary for America to succeed in the 21st century. This afternoon the Senate Labor-HHS appropriations subcommittee voted to restore full funding for home heating and cooling assistance for low-income families and summer jobs for disadvantaged youth. Unlike the House Republican budget, they voted to make many of the essential investments in our children for which I have been fighting.

The Senate subcommittee, however, did not adequately fund several education and training investments that I believe are vitally important to our Nation's future. For example, they did not provide the resources necessary for us to move forward to ensure that every 8-year-old can read on his or her own and every 12-year-old can log on to the information superhighway. The Senate bill is a good first step, but there is still more work to do.

I look forward to working with the Senate on this bill to expand educational opportunity, improve child care, set voluntary national academic standards, protect continuity in critical health programs, and help young people in high-poverty areas. Finally, as I have said before, Congress must take action to modernize our schools and help provide smaller classes with well-qualified teachers.

Letter to the Majority Leader of the Senate on the Patients' Bill of Rights
September 1, 1998

Dear Senator Lott:

Thank you for your letter regarding the patients' bill of rights. I am pleased to reiterate my commitment to working with you—and all Republicans and Democrats in the Congress—to pass long overdue legislation this year.

Since last November, I have called on the Congress to pass a strong, enforceable, and bipartisan patients' bill of rights. During this time, I signed an Executive Memorandum to ensure that the 85 million Americans in federal health plans receive the patient protections they need, and I have indicated my support for bipartisan legislation that would extend these protections to all Americans. With precious few weeks remaining before the Congress adjourns, we must work together to respond to the nation's call for us to improve the quality of health care Americans are receiving.

As I mentioned in my radio address this past Saturday, ensuring basic patient protections is not and should not be a political issue. I was therefore disappointed by the partisan manner in which the Senate Republican Leadership bill was developed. The lack of consultation with the White House or any Democrats during the drafting of your legislation contributed to its serious shortcomings and the fact it has failed to receive the support of either patients or doctors. The bill leaves millions of Americans without critical patient protections, contains provisions that are more rhetorical than substantive, completely omits patient protections that virtually every expert in the field believes are basic and essential, and includes "poison pill" provisions that have nothing to do with a patients' bill of rights. More specifically, the bill:

Does not cover all health plans and leaves more than 100 million Americans completely unprotected. The provisions in the Senate Republican Leadership bill apply only to self-insured plans. As a consequence, the bill leaves out more than 100 million Americans, including millions of workers in small businesses. This approach contrasts with the bipartisan Kassebaum-Kennedy insurance reform law, which provided a set of basic protections for all Americans.

Lets HMOs, not health professionals, define medical necessity. The external appeals process provision in the Senate Republican Leadership bill makes the appeals process meaningless by allowing the HMOs themselves, rather than informed health professionals, to define what services are medically necessary. This loophole will make it very difficult for patients to prevail on appeals to get the treatment doctors believe they need.

Fails to guarantee direct access to specialists. The Senate Republican Leadership proposal fails to ensure that patients with serious health problems have direct access to the specialists they need. We believe that patients with conditions like cancer or heart disease should not be denied access to the doctors they need to treat their conditions.

Fails to protect patients from abrupt changes in care in the middle of treatment. The Senate Republican Leadership bill fails to assure continuity-of-care protections when an employer changes health plans. This deficiency means that, for example, pregnant women or individuals undergoing care for a chronic illness may have their care suddenly altered mid course, potentially causing serious health consequences.

Reverses course on emergency room protections. The Senate Republican Leadership bill backs away from the emergency room protections that Congress implemented in a bipartisan manner for Medicare and Medicaid beneficiaries in the Balanced Budget Act of 1997. The bill includes a watered-down provision that does not require health plans to cover patients who go to an emergency room outside their network and does not ensure coverage for any treatment beyond an initial screening. These provisions put patients at risk for the huge costs associated with critical emergency treatment.

Allows financial incentives to threaten critical patient care. The Senate Republican Leadership bill fails to prohibit secret financial incentives to providers. This would leave patients vulnerable to financial incentives that limit patient care.

Fails to hold health plans accountable when their actions cause patients serious harm. The proposed per-day penalties in the Senate Republican Leadership bill fail to hold health plans accountable when patients suffer serious harm or even death because of a plan's wrongful action. For example, if a health plan improperly denies a lifesaving cancer treatment to a child, it will incur a penalty only for the number of days it takes to reverse its decision; it will not have to pay the family for all the damages the family will suffer as the result of having a child with a now untreatable disease. And because the plan will not have to pay for all the harm it causes, it will have insufficient incentive to change its health care practices in the future.

Includes "poison pill" provisions that have nothing to do with a patients' bill of rights. For example, expanding Medical Savings Accounts (MSAs) before studying the current demonstration is premature, at best, and could undermine an already unstable insurance market. As I have said before, I would veto a bill that does not address these serious flaws. I could not sanction presenting a bill to the American people that is nothing more than an empty promise. At the same time, as I have repeatedly made clear, I remain fully committed to working with you, as well as the Democratic Leadership, to pass a meaningful patients' bill of rights before the Congress adjourns. We can make progress in this area if, and only if, we work together to provide needed health care protections to ensure Americans have much needed confidence in their health care system.

Producing a patients' bill of rights that can attract bipartisan support and receive my signature will require a full and open debate on the Senate floor. There must be adequate time and a sufficient number of amendments to ensure that the bill gives patients the basic protections they need and deserve. I am confident that you and Senator Daschle can work out a process that accommodates the scheduling needs of the Senate and allows you to address fully the health care needs of the American public.

Last year, we worked together in a bipartisan manner to pass a balanced budget including historic Medicare reforms and the largest investment in children's health care since the enactment of Medicaid. This year, we have another opportunity to work together to improve health care for millions of Americans.

I urge you to make the patients' bill of rights the first order of business for the Senate. Further delay threatens the ability of the Congress to pass a bill that I can sign into law this year. I stand ready to work with you and Senator Daschle to ensure that patients—not politics—are our first priority.

Sincerely,

WILLIAM J. CLINTON

NOTE: The letter referred to the President's memorandum of February 20 on Federal agency compliance with the Patient Bill of Rights (*Public Papers of the Presidents: William J. Clinton, 1998 Book I* (Washington: U.S. Government Printing Office, 1999), p. 260). An original was not available for verification of the content of this letter.

The President's News Conference With President Boris Yeltsin of Russia in Moscow
September 2, 1998

President Yeltsin. Distinguished ladies and gentlemen, the official visit of the President of the United States, Bill Clinton, to Russia is coming to an end. We have had intensive, productive negotiations. We have managed to discuss a wide range of topical issues. I would like to emphasize the exchanges were sincere and keen. The dialog was marked by the spirit of mutual understanding.

Responsibility of our two countries for maintaining and strengthening peace and stability is obvious. That is why we have paid special attention to the discussion of the entire spectrum of security issues in the world.

The discussion has included the implementation of international and bilateral treaties and agreements concerning the weapons of mass destruction, as well as the elaboration of common approaches to dealing with the threat of nuclear weapons proliferation and their delivery means.

Unfortunately, this is not the only major task the humanity struggles to resolve. That is why President Clinton and I have discussed global threats and challenges. Our positions on this issue have coincided, and this closeness of approaches is reflected in the joint statement on common security changes on the threshold of the 21st century. I consider this document to be a significant step towards strengthening strategic partnership between Russia and the United States.

We have also had substantial talks on the most topical international issues. And there are quite a few such issues. I'll put it frankly: Here our approaches have not always completely coincided. Russia rejects the use of power methods as a matter of principle. Conflicts of today have no military solutions, be it in Kosovo or around Iraq or Afghanistan or others. Also we do not accept the NATO centrism idea for the new European security architecture. Nevertheless, our talks have been conducive to greater mutual understanding on these issues.

Of course, we could not do without discussing economy problems. Current dimensions of our economic relations should be brought up to a qualitatively new level. We shall have to suffer through much blood, sweat, and tears before new forms of business cooperation, worthy of our two great powers, are found, the forms that would be able to withstand volatile circumstances. There exist quite a few opportunities for this. These are mentioned in our joint statement on economic issues.

In conclusion, I would like to say—and I hope Bill will agree with me—the summit was a success. This meeting, the 15th in a row, confirmed once again, when Presidents of Russia and the United States join their efforts, no issue is too big for them.

Thank you for your kind attention.

President Clinton. Thank you very much, Mr. President, for your hospitality and for giving Hillary and me and our team the chance to come to Moscow again.

Over the past 5 years, I have been in this great, historic city in times of bright hope and times of uncertainty. But throughout, I have witnessed the remarkable transformation of this nation to democracy and to a more open economy. We all know that this meeting comes at a challenging time for the Russian people. But I don't believe anyone could ever have doubted that there would be obstacles on Russia's road to a vibrant economy and a strong democracy. I don't also believe that anyone can seriously doubt the determination of the Russian people to build a brighter, better, stronger future.

Russia is important to America. Our economies are connected. We share values, interests, and friendship. We share security interests and heavy security responsibilities. In our discussions, President Yeltsin and I spoke about Russia's options for stabilizing its economy and restoring confidence. I reaffirmed America's strong view that Russia can move beyond today's crisis and create growth and good jobs but only if it carries forward with its transformation, with a strong and fair tax system, greater rule of law, dealing forthrightly with financial institutions, having regulation that protects against abuses, and yes, developing an appropriate safety net for people who are hurt during times of change.

President Yeltsin reaffirmed his commitment to reform, and I believe that is the right commitment. The answer to the present difficulties is to finish the job that has been begun, not to stop it in midstream or to reverse course. This is a view I will reaffirm when I meet today with leaders of the Duma and the Federation Council. America and the international community are, I am convinced, ready to offer further assistance if Russia stays with the path of reform.

We discussed also at length common security concerns. We've reached an important agreement to increase the safety of all our people, an arrangement under which our countries will give each other continuous information on worldwide launches of ballistic missiles or space-launch vehicles detected by our respective early warning systems. This will reduce the possibility of nuclear war by mistake or accident and give us information about missile activity by other countries.

We've also agreed to remove from each of our nuclear weapons programs approximately 50 tons of plutonium, enough to make literally thousands of nuclear devices. Once converted, this plutonium can never again be used to make weapons that become lethal in the wrong hands. Our experts will begin meeting right away to finalize an implementation plan by the end of this year.

I'd like to say in passing, I'm very grateful for the support this initiative received in our Congress. We have four Members of Congress here with us today, and I especially thank Senator Domenici for his interest in this issue.

Next let me say I look forward to and hope very much that the Russian Duma will approve

START II, so that we can negotiate a START III agreement that would cut our levels of arsenals down to one-fifth of cold war levels. I think that would be good for our mutual security and good for the Russian economy.

In recent months Russia has taken important steps to tighten its export controls on weapons of mass destruction and the missiles to deliver them, and to penalize offenders. This week Russia barred three companies from transactions with Iran. Today we agreed to intensify our cooperation by creating seven working groups on export controls to further strengthen Russia's ability to halt the spread of dangerous weapons. Also, we renewed our commitment to persuade India and Pakistan to reverse their arms race. And we pledged to accelerate international negotiations to establish a tough inspection regime for the Biological Weapons Convention. I don't believe it's possible to overstate the importance of this initiative for the next 20 years.

Russia and the United States share a commitment to combat terrorism. We agree that there is no possible justification for terrorism. It is murder, plain and simple. Today we instructed our Foreign Ministers to develop a plan to deepen our cooperation against this danger to our own people and to innocent people around the world.

We agree on the importance of further strengthening the partnership between NATO and Russia through practical cooperation. We plan to accelerate talks on adapting the treaty that limits conventional military forces in Europe, the CFE, to reflect changes in Europe since the treaty was signed in 1990, with an aim to complete an adapted treaty by the 1999 summit of the OSCE.

Finally, we discussed our common foreign policy agenda, including, first and foremost, the need to continue to strengthen the peace in Bosnia and to look for a peaceful solution in Kosovo, where the humanitarian situation is now quite grave. We agreed that the Serbian Government must stop all repressive actions against civilian populations, allow relief organizations immediate and full access to those in need, and pursue an interim settlement.

President Yeltsin and I also agree that Iraq must comply fully with all relevant U.N. Security Council resolutions imposed after the gulf war and, in particular, must agree to allow the international weapons inspectors to again pursue their mission without obstruction or delay. Far from advancing the day sanctions are lifted, Iraq's most recent efforts to undermine the inspectors will perpetuate sanctions, prevent Iraq from acquiring the resources it needs to rebuild its military, and keep Iraq's economy under tight international control.

On energy and the environment, we reiterated our commitment to the emissions reductions targets and the market-based mechanisms established at Kyoto to slow the dangerous process of global warming. We agreed that multiple pipeline routes were essential to bring energy from the Caspian to international markets and to advance our common security and commercial interests.

This has been a full agenda, a productive summit. Again, let me say that I have great confidence that the people of this great nation can move through this present difficult moment to continue and complete the astonishing process of democratization and modernization that I have been privileged to witness at close hand over the last 5½ years.

Again, Mr. President, thank you for your hospitality. And I suppose we should answer a few questions.

Russian official. Now we will have a Q-and-A session, so the work will proceed in the way that the U.S. and Russian press corps could ask questions in turn. Using the privilege of the host, I will give the floor to the representatives of ORT television.

Summit Goals/Russia-U.S. Relations

Q. A question to both Presidents. Prior to meeting, many experts, politicians, and public at large believed that your meeting is futile, nobody needs it, no results will be produced due to the known difficulties both in Russia and America. I understand now you're trying to make the case it's the other way around, the situation is different. So what was the psychological atmosphere to your talks, bearing in mind this disbelief in the success, this skeptical approach?

And second, are we, Russia and U.S., partners right now or still contenders? And today, bidding farewell, Boris Yeltsin and Bill Clinton, are they still friends?

Thank you.

President Yeltsin. I will start with your last question. Yes, we stay friends and the atmosphere, since the beginning of the talks until the end, was a friendly one. I would say it was very considerate, and there were no discontents during the talks that we had.

And this brings my conclusion that since we did not have any differences, in my opinion, there will be no differences also in our activities, in what we do bilaterally. Of course, that goes without saying. This is very logical.

Now, in response to those skeptical observers who alleged, and continue to do so, that they don't believe, I've been always saying no, on the contrary, we need to repeat it: we do believe we do that in order to remove the tension. And each time, having those meetings, we've been able to do something to alleviate the tension. This is what really matters. We've been doing that, removing that tension. And this time, again, we have removed part of the tension one more time.

President Clinton. Well, first of all, I think it's important to answer your question of what happened from the point of view of the Russian people and then from the point of view of the American people.

You ask if we're still friends. The answer to that is yes. You ask if Russia and the United States have a partnership. I think the plain answer to that is yes, even though we don't always agree on every issue. I can tell you from my point of view this was a successful meeting on the national security issues, because I think establishing this early warning information sharing is important, and I know that the destruction of this huge volume of plutonium is important. And it also might be important to the Russian economy. It can be an economic plus as well as a national security plus.

Now, on the domestic economic issues, from the point of view of America, it was important to me to come here just to say to the President and to his team and to the Duma leaders I will see later and the Federation Council leaders that I know this is a difficult time, but there is no shortcut to developing a system that will have the confidence of investors around the world. These are not American rules or anybody else's rules. These are—in a global economy, you have to be able to get money in from outside your country and keep the money in your country invested in your country.

And if the reform process can be completed, then I for one would be strongly supportive of greater assistance to Russia from the United States and the other big economic powers, because I think we have a very strong vested interest in seeing an economically successful Russia that is a full partner across the whole range of issues in the world. I also think it's good for preserving Russia's democracy and freedom.

So, from my point of view, saying that we support reform and saying we will support those who continue it was in itself a reason to come.

From Russia's point of view, I think knowing that the United States and others want to back this process and will do so and at least having someone else say, "There is a light at the end of this tunnel; there is an end to this process; and it could come quickly if these laws are passed in the Duma and the things that the President has asked for already are done and the decisions are made well," I think that is worth something apart from the specific agreements that we have made.

But my answer to you is that, in foreign policy and security, this meeting produced something. Whether it produces real economic benefits for the people of Russia depends upon what happens now in Russia. But at least everyone knows that we're prepared to do our part and to support this process.

President Yeltsin. I would like to add just for one second, please, just two words here. We have put it on paper. We have decided to set up, on the territory of Russia, a joint center of control over the missile launches. For the first time, this has been done. This is exceptionally important.

President Clinton. I agree with that.

Press Secretary Mike McCurry. Our tradition—questions from our wire services. Terence Hunt of the Associated Press.

Russian and American Economies

Q. President Yeltsin, yesterday President Clinton spoke of the painful steps that Russia will have to take and the need to play by the rules of international economics. What difficult steps are you prepared to take? And are you committed to play by these rules of international economics?

And to President Clinton, the world stock market seems very fragile right now. How can the United States withstand all these outside pressures?

President Clinton. Do you want me to go first?

I think the answer to your question about what we can do that's best for our economy is really twofold. The first thing we have to do is to do our very best to make the right decisions at home. You know, we have to stay with the path of discipline that has brought us this far in the last 5½ years, and we have to make the investments and decisions that we know will produce growth, over the long run, for the American economy. Whether it's in education or science and technology, we have to do the things that send the signal that we understand how the world economy works and we intend to do well in it. But the most important thing is sticking with sound economic policy.

Now, in addition to that, it is important that more and more Americans, without regard to party, understand that we are in a global economy, and it's been very good to the United States over the last 5½ years—about 30 percent of our growth has come from exports—but that we, at this particular moment in history, because of our relative economic strength, have an extra obligation to try to build a system for the 21st century where every person in every country who is willing to work hard has a chance to get a just reward for it.

And that means that we have to—in my opinion, that means that we have to continue to contribute our fair share to the International Monetary Fund. It means that we have to do everything we can to support our friends in Russia who believe that we should continue to reform. It means that Secretary Rubin's upcoming meeting with the Finance Minister of Japan, former Prime Minister Miyazawa, is profoundly important. Unless Japan begins to grow again, it's going to be difficult for Russia and other countries to do what they need to do. It means, in short, that America must maintain a leadership role of active involvement in trying to build an economic system that rewards people who do the right thing. And that's in our best interest.

So I think this is a terribly important thing. The volatility in the world markets, including in our stock market, I think is to be expected under these circumstances. The right thing to do is to try to restore growth in the economies of the world where there isn't enough growth now and to continually examine whether the institutions we have for dealing with problems are adequate to meet the challenges of today and tomorrow. And we are aggressively involved in both those activities.

President Yeltsin. Naturally, we face problems basically of our own. We have not been able to do many things over the past time when we started our reforms. And still we need to conclude our reforms, to bring them to completion, and consequently to get results.

We are not saying that we count solely on the support from outside. No. One more time, I will reiterate this: No. So let your mass media not spread the word to the effect that allegedly we would count solely on the support from the West, and to this end we have gathered together here—by no means. What we need from the United States is political support to the effect that the United States is in favor of reforms in Russia. This is what we really need, and then all the investors who would like to come to the Russian reformed market will do so, will come with their investments. And this is what we really need now. This is what is lacking, investments. This is first and foremost.

Certainly, we ought to fight our expenditures pattern and mismanagement. This is the second issue which, to us, is one of the most important issues. And we have been adopting, accordingly, the measures which need to be taken, like we have adopted the program of stabilization measures; in other words, those measures which will result in stabilization of our reforms. Stabilization—I believe that such measures and such a program will work, promptly; over the coming 2 years, it will produce results.

Russia-U.S. Relations

Q. I'd like to pose a question to the President of the United States, Mr. Clinton. One gets the impression that some politicians in the United States right now like to somehow frighten the people with Russia. On the other hand, we are aware of the fact that you are never afraid of Russia, yourself, and you did everything possible so that people in the U.S. would not be afraid of Russia. Now, on the results of these talks, tell us please your belief—what is the basis of your belief that our country will get back to its feet and that Russian-U.S. relations have promising prospects?

Thank you.

President Clinton. Well, my belief that Russian-U.S. relations have promising prospects has been supported by the agreements we have made in the security and foreign policy areas. My belief that Russia will get back on its feet is based on my observation that, in Russian history, every time outsiders counted the Russian people out, they turned out to be wrong. And this is a very big challenge, but, I mean, a country that rebuffed Napoleon and Hitler can surely adjust to the realities of the global marketplace.

Now, what has to be done? The reason I wanted to come here—and, to be fair, let me back up and say, I don't think there are many people in America who are afraid of Russia anymore. I think there are some people in America who question whether I should come at this moment of great economic and political tension for the country, but I don't think it's because they want something bad to happen to Russia. I think, by and large, the American people wish Russia well and want things to go well for Russia and like the fact that we are partners in Bosnia and that we've reduced our nuclear arsenals so much and that we've reduced our defense establishment and that we've found other ways to cooperate, in space for example. I think most Americans like this very, very much.

So let me go back to the economic question. I believe whether you succeed and how long it takes you to succeed in restoring real growth to the Russian economy depends upon President Yeltsin's ability to persuade the Duma to support his formation of a Government which will pursue a path of reform with a genuine sensitivity to the personal dislocation of the people who have been hurt. And here's where I think the World Bank and other institutions can come in and perhaps help deal with some of the fallout, if you will, of the reform process.

But I think, if other political forces in Russia try to force the President to abandon reform in midstream or even reverse it, what I think will happen is even less money will come into Russia and even more economic hardship will result. I believe that because that is, it seems to me, the unwavering experience of every other country.

That does not mean you should not have a social safety net. It does not mean you have to make the same domestic decisions that the United States or Great Britain or France or Sweden or any other country has made. You have to form your own relationship with this new economic reality. But I still believe that unless there is a manifest commitment to reform, the economy will not get better.

So I support President Yeltsin's commitment in that regard. And I think—my conviction that it will get better is based on my reading of your history. How long it will take to get better

depends a lot more on you and what happens here than anything else we outsiders can do, although if there is a clear movement toward reform, I'll do everything I can to accelerate outside support of all kinds.

Press Secretary McCurry. Lori Santos, United Press International.

President's Effectiveness

Q. Sir, you were just speaking of the challenges that we face as a nation. And what has the reaction since your admission of a relationship with Ms. Lewinsky caused you any—given you any cause for concern that you may not be as effective as you should be in leading the country?

President Clinton. No, I've actually been quite heartened by the reaction of the American people and leaders throughout the world about it. I have acknowledged that I made a mistake, said that I regretted it, asked to be forgiven, spent a lot of very valuable time with my family in the last couple of weeks, and said I was going back to work. I believe that's what the American people want me to do. And based on my conversations with leaders around the world, I think that's what they want me to do, and that is what I intend to do.

As you can see from what we're discussing here, there are very large issues that will affect the future of the American people in the short run and over the long run. There are large issues that have to be dealt with now in the world and at home. And so I have been quite encouraged by what I think the message from the American people has been and what I know the message from leaders around the world has been. And I'm going to do my best to continue to go through this personal process in an appropriate way but to do my job, to do the job I was hired to do. And I think it very much needs to be done right now.

Russia and NATO Expansion

Q. Boris Nikolayevich, this question has to do with the relationship between Russia and NATO. I understand you had time to discuss this issue with the U.S. President. It's known that the next NATO summit will take place in Washington, where important decisions will be taken regarding the European security architecture. How do you think this relation should evolve in the future?

President Yeltsin. Yes, we have discussed with President Clinton the question concerning the relationship between Russia and NATO. We're not running away from the position which has been that we are against NATO expanding eastward. We believe this is a blunder, a big mistake, and one day, this will be a historic error.

Therefore, at this point in time, what we necessarily would like to do is to improve relations so that there be no confrontation. Therefore, we have signed an agreement between Russia and NATO. And in accordance with that agreement we want to do our job. However, no way shall we allow anybody to transgress that agreement, bypass that agreement, or generally speaking, put it aside. No, this will not happen.

And naturally, we shall participate in the Warsaw meeting, and there we shall very closely follow the vector of NATO and what they intend to do in regards to, so to say, deploying their forces and their power.

We still are in favor of being cautious with regards to NATO. We don't have any intentions to move towards the west, ourselves. We don't intend to create additional forces. We're not doing that, and we're not planning to do that. This is what really matters.

President Clinton. I would like to say one word about that. We obviously, President Yeltsin and I, have a disagreement about whether it was appropriate for NATO to take on new members or not. But I think there is a larger reality here where we are in agreement, and I would like to emphasize it.

Russia has made historic commitments in the last few years to essentially redefine its greatness, not in terms of the territorial dominance of its neighbors but, instead, of constructive leadership in the region and in the world. The expansion of NATO, therefore, should be seen primarily as nations interested in working together to deal with common security problems, not to be ready to repel expected invasions.

And if you look at what the NATO members will be discussing next year, they're talking about how they can deal with regional security challenges, like in Bosnia and Kosovo, both of which—one of which we would never—we would not have solved the Bosnia war, or ended it, had it not been for the leadership of Russia and the partnership between NATO and Russia. It simply would not have happened in the way it did, in a way that reinforced harmony in the region. Similarly, we have got to work together

in Kosovo to prevent another Bosnia from occurring.

If we have problems with terrorism or with the spread of chemical or biological weapons, they will be problems we all have in common. That's why you have two dozen nations, that are not NATO members, a part of our Partnership For Peace, because they know that nation-states in the future are going to have common security problems and they will be stronger if they work together.

And that's why I was especially proud of the charter that Russia and NATO signed. I intend to honor it. I intend to build on it. And I hope that within a few years we'll see that this partnership is a good thing and continues to be a good thing and brings us closer together rather than driving us apart.

Press Secretary McCurry. Larry McQuillan, Reuters.

Russia's Political Situation/President's August 17 Address

Q. President Yeltsin, do you see any circumstance in which you could accept someone other than Mr. Chernomyrdin to be your Prime Minister? And if you can't accept that, does that mean you're prepared to dissolve the Duma if they refuse to confirm him?

And Mr. President, another Lewinsky question. You know, there have been some who have expressed disappointment that you didn't offer a formal apology the other night when you spoke to the American people. Are you—do you feel you need to offer an apology? And in retrospect now, with some distance, do you have any feeling that perhaps the tone of your speech was something that didn't quite convey the feelings that you had, particularly your comments in regard to Mr. Starr?

President Yeltsin. Well, I must say, we will witness quite a few events for us to be able to achieve all those results. That's all. [*Laughter*]

President Clinton. That ought to be my answer, too. That was pretty good. [*Laughter*]

Well, to your second question, I think I can almost reiterate what I said in response to the first question. I think the question of the tone of the speech and people's reaction to it is really a function of—I can't comment on that. I read it the other day again, and I thought it was clear that I was expressing my profound regret to all who were hurt and to all who were involved, and my desire not to see any more people hurt by this process and caught up in it. And I was commenting that it seemed to be something that most reasonable people would think had consumed a disproportionate amount of America's time, money, and resources and attention, and was now—continued to involve more and more people. And that's what I tried to say.

And all I wanted to say was I believe it's time for us to now go back to the work of the country and give the people their Government back and talk about and think about and work on things that will affect the American people today and in the future. That's all I

meant to say, and that's what I believe, and that's what I intend to do.

NOTE: The President's 163d news conference began at 1:17 p.m. in the Catherine Hall at the Kremlin. President Yeltsin spoke in Russian, and his remarks were translated by an interpreter. In their remarks, the two Presidents referred to Finance Minister Kiichi Miyazawa of Japan; Prime Minister-designate Viktor Chernomyrdin of Russia; the Conventional Armed Forces in Europe (CFE) Treaty; and the Organization for Security and Cooperation in Europe (OSCE). Reporters referred to former White House intern Monica S. Lewinsky and Independent Counsel Kenneth Starr. The tape did not include a complete translation of President Yeltsin's remarks.

Joint Statement on the Situation in Kosovo
September 2, 1998

The Presidents of the United States and the Russian Federation noted with concern that the situation in Kosovo continues to deteriorate, causing growing alarm among the world public about the growing negative consequences for regional stability. Despite extensive attempts of the Contact Group, OSCE, and other international institutions, there has not yet been success in achieving an end to the armed clashes and senseless bloodshed and in initiating serious and meaningful negotiations between the authorities in Belgrade and leaders of Kosovo Albanians that would make it possible to agree promptly on measures to build confidence and security in the province as an interim step on the way to a final settlement of the Kosovo problem including the definition of the status of enhanced Kosovo self-government with strict respect for the territorial integrity of the FRY.

The escalation of tension in Kosovo inflicts heavy suffering on innocent civilians. Over 200,000 people were forced to leave their homes as the result of armed clashes. The situation is aggravated by large-scale destruction of houses, food shortages, and the risk of epidemic disease. The threat of humanitarian catastrophe is becoming ever more real.

Slobodan Milošević, as President of the FRY, must order a halt to all repressive actions against the civilian population in Kosovo. All violence by all Kosovo Albanian armed groups must cease immediately. President Milošević and the Kosovo Albanian leadership must intensify the negotiating process.

Urgent measures should be taken promptly to prevent humanitarian catastrophe in Kosovo. Necessary conditions should be created without delay for the refugees and displaced persons to return freely to the places of their permanent residence before the advent of winter. The scope and acuteness of the problem call for urgent joint actions of the authorities in Belgrade, the Kosovo Albanians, and international humanitarian organizations. Constant international monitoring in the field, accompanied both by progressive withdrawal of Serb security forces to their permanent locations, and the cessation of armed actions by the Kosovo Albanians, are needed to inspire confidence among people in their safety and prospects for restoring normal life. A mechanism for creating favorable conditions in the most heavily affected locations in the province—a series of "pilot projects"—should be set in motion immediately. The Serb authorities should implement in practice unimpeded access to all areas of the province for humanitarian organizations and diplomatic observers.

The cessation of violence and amelioration of the humanitarian situation would facilitate the creation of a favorable environment for progress in the negotiating process over the entire range of issues. President Milošević and all Kosovo Albanian leaders should engage actively in the negotiating process, with a view toward achieving a political solution to the crisis and a framework for durable peace in Kosovo.

Moscow
September 2, 1998

NOTE: An original was not available for verification of the content of this joint statement.

Joint Statement on a Protocol to the Convention on the Prohibition of Biological Weapons
September 2, 1998

The Presidents of the United States and the Russian Federation, recognizing the threat posed by biological weapons, express strong support for the aims and tasks of the Ad Hoc Group of States Parties to establish a regime to enhance the effective implementation of the 1972 Convention on the Prohibition of the Development, Production, and Stockpiling of Bacteriological (Biological) and Toxin Weapons and on their Destruction. We urge the further intensification and successful conclusion of those negotiations to strengthen the Convention by adoption of a legally binding Protocol at the earliest possible date.

We have agreed to contribute to accomplishing these tasks. Consequently, the United States of America and the Russian Federation will make additional efforts in the Ad Hoc Group to promote decisive progress in negotiations on the Protocol to the Convention, to ensure its universality and enable the Group to fulfill its mandate.

We agree that the Protocol to the Convention must be economical to implement, must adequately guarantee the protection of national security information, and must provide confidentiality for sensitive commercial information. We also consider it extremely important to create a mechanism for implementation that will be consistent with the scope of the measures provided for in the Protocol.

We recognize the necessity for the Protocol to include those measures that would do the most to strengthen the Convention.

We express our firm commitment to global prohibition of biological weapons and for full and effective compliance by all States Parties with the Convention prohibiting such weapons.

We support the language in the Final Declaration of the Fourth Review Conference of the States Parties to the Convention (1996) that the Convention forbids the use of bacteriological (biological) and toxin weapons under any circumstances.

Moscow
September 2, 1998

NOTE: An original was not available for verification of the content of this joint statement.

Joint Statement on the Exchange of Information on Missile Launches and Early Warning
September 2, 1998

Taking into account the continuing worldwide proliferation of ballistic missiles and of missile technologies, the need to minimize even further the consequences of a false missile attack warning and above all, to prevent the possibility of a missile launch caused by such false warning, the President of the United States and the President of the Russian Federation have reached agreement on a cooperative initiative between the United States and Russia regarding the exchange of information on missile launches and early warning.

The objective of the initiative is the continuous exchange of information on the launches of ballistic missiles and space launch vehicles derived from each side's missile launch warning system, including the possible establishment of a center for the exchange of missile launch data operated by the United States and Russia and separate from their respective national centers. As part of this initiative, the United States and Russia will also examine the possibility of establishing a multilateral ballistic missile and space launch vehicle pre-launch notification regime in which other states could voluntarily participate.

The Presidents have directed their experts to develop as quickly as possible for approval in their respective countries a plan for advancing this initiative toward implementation as soon as practicable.

Russia, proceeding from its international obligations relating to information derived from missile attack warning systems, will reach agreement regarding necessary issues relating to the implementation of this initiative.

The President of the United States of America:	The President of the Russian Federation:
William J. Clinton	*Boris Yeltsin*

Moscow

September 2, 1998

NOTE: An original was not available for verification of the content of this joint statement.

Joint Statement on Trade, Investment, Technology, and Non-Governmental Cooperation
September 2, 1998

We, the Presidents of the United States of America and the Russian Federation, set priorities to deepen our trade, investment, technological and non-governmental cooperation. We reviewed the key role the U.S.-Russian Commission on Economic and Technological Cooperation has played in strengthening the bilateral relations between our two countries. We agreed to take the following actions, which help build investor and consumer confidence, and have charged the co-chairmen of the Commission to oversee their implementation:

- Promote, under the auspices of the U.S.-Russian Business Development Committee, the further strengthening of bilateral trade and investment flows by working together to support cooperative projects between U.S. and Russian business, to reduce remaining barriers to market access, to strengthen the rule of law in business, and to increase the dialog on commercial taxation, standards, and customs matters.
- Extend technical exchanges between the U.S. Federal Reserve System and the Bank of Russia, and arrange for technical exchanges with the Comptroller of the Currency and Federal Deposit Insurance Corporation.
- Extend cooperation between the U.S. Securities and Exchange Commission and the Russian Federal Commission for the Securities Markets in order to develop and implement sound, effective regulatory policies.
- Intensify technical cooperation between the U.S. Treasury Department and the Russian Ministry of Finance and the Bank of Russia on issues pertaining to strengthening the financial sector.
- Facilitate the development of the small and medium business sector, including through U.S. and Russian experts working at the regional and local levels to develop business management skills, to increase the access of small and medium business to finance, and to support exchanges of U.S. and Russian entrepreneurs.

We discussed Russia's current trade and investment priorities. In this regard, we discussed Russia's desire to be designated as a "market economy" for purposes of U.S. trade laws. The Russian side will submit a memorandum of justification to the U.S. Department of Commerce to initiate a review process.

Space-related industries in both countries are poised for rapid growth and can revolutionize communications and high-technology industries across the globe. U.S.-Russian commercial space ventures are already generating thousands of high-tech jobs in the U.S. and Russia, with projected revenues in the billions of dollars. We reaffirmed the need to meet our respective commitments to the International Space Station to continue advance in space that benefit our people. We recognized the importance of protecting U.S. and Russian sensitive technologies in our commercial and governmental joint space efforts and instructed our experts to continue to work together in this area.

Cooperation in the energy field has unprecedented possibilities for attracting investment and creating jobs, and ensuring sustained growth in Russia. Such cooperation will be enhanced as legislation on production sharing is implemented fully, harmonized with the tax code, and applied to the development of new oil and gas fields. We recognize the importance of commercially viable and environmentally sound multiple pipeline system for the transportation of energy resources of the Caspian Basin to international markets. We encourage U.S. and Russian companies to expand their work together on these and other energy projects.

U.S.-Russian cooperation in the field of civil aviation can lead to a change in the character of global transportation in the 21st Century. We note the progress that has been achieved on a bilateral agreement to enhance air transportation between our two countries, and underline the importance of additional efforts to conclude negotiations. We recognize the great value of the new bilateral agreements on enhancing flight safety signed today. We welcome the cooperation among the United States, Russia, and the International Civil Aviation Organization in developing safe, efficient, and cost-effective access to air traffic control services, recognizing the importance of this endeavor for global aviation.

Our countries are aware of our important role in helping to protect the global environment. We agreed to continue working together on the problem of greenhouse gas emissions. The United States and Russia reiterate their commitments to achieving the emissions targets agreed to at Kyoto. We will cooperate on efforts to establish a broad-based, unrestricted emissions trading system that is both environmentally and economically successful. The United States and Russia intend to use the Kyoto protocol's flexible, market-based mechanisms, particularly emissions trading.

We note with satisfaction the progress achieved in integrating Russia into international economic and financial structures, especially in regard to the G–8, the Paris club and APEC. We tasked our experts with intensifying their work on Russia's accession to the World Trade Organization and the Organization for Economic Cooperation and Development.

We support the strong non-governmental ties that have developed between our citizens. Cooperation between U.S. and Russian hospitals, universities, community, human rights and other organizations is rapidly expanding. Thousands of U.S. and Russian citizens and communities, throughout all 89 Russian regions and each of the 50 United States, are now involved in these contacts. From science and business to the arts and religion, we are committed to sustaining, expanding, and developing these contacts in all their diversity. In this spirit, we announced a new joint fellowship program for young Americans and Russians committed to public service, providing an opportunity for future leaders from our two countries to learn about our societies during university-level academic study and professional internships. These new, non-governmental, people-to-people relationships are the foundations for ensuring prosperity and a better understanding between our countries that will take us into the next century.

Moscow
September 2, 1998

NOTE: An original was not available for verification of the content of this joint statement.

Joint Statement on Common Security Challenges at the Threshold of the Twenty-First Century
September 2, 1998

We, the Presidents of the United States of America and of the Russian Federation, declare that cooperation between the U.S. and Russia will be of the greatest import in the twenty-first century for promoting prosperity and strengthening security throughout the world. In this connection, we reaffirm that the United States of America and the Russian Federation are natural partners in advancing international peace and stability. We have devoted particular attention to intensifying joint efforts to eliminate threats inherited from the Cold War and to meet common security challenges at the threshold of the twenty-first century.

We understand that the most serious and pressing danger is the proliferation of nuclear, biological, chemical, and other types of weapons of mass destruction, the technologies for their production, and their means of delivery. Given the increasing interdependence of the modern world, these threats are becoming transnational and global in scope; they affect not only the national security of the United States and the Russian Federation, but also international stability. We reaffirm the determination of the U.S. and Russia to cooperate actively and closely with each other, as well as with all other interested countries, to avert and reduce this threat by taking new steps, seeking new forms of collaboration, and strengthening generally recognized international norms.

We recognize that more must be done and today we have taken a number of steps to enhance not only our security, but global security as well. We are declaring our firm commitment to intensifying negotiations toward early completion of the Biological Weapons Convention Protocol. We are embarking on new and important cooperation to further lessen the risks of false warnings of missile attacks. And, we have agreed on principles to guide our cooperation in the management and disposition of plutonium from nuclear weapons programs so that it can never again be used in a nuclear weapon.

Common commitments have made the U.S. and Russia partners in developing the foundations of an international non-proliferation regime, including the Treaty on the Non-Prolifera-tion of Nuclear Weapons, IAEA safeguards, the Convention on Biological and Toxin Weapons, and the Comprehensive Test Ban Treaty. Russia and the U.S. reaffirm their commitment to the goal of having all countries accede to the Treaty on the Non-Proliferation of Nuclear Weapons in its present form, without amendments. They are also committed to the strengthened guidelines of the Nuclear Suppliers Group. As participants in the Conference on Disarmament, they jointly achieved success in the negotiations of the Chemical Weapons Convention and of the Comprehensive Test Ban Treaty, and call upon all countries to accede to these treaties. Guided by these obligations, they have taken substantial practical steps to reduce the global nuclear threat and control transfers of sensitive technology. They remain deeply concerned about the nuclear tests in South Asia and reaffirm U.S. and Russian commitments to coordinate closely support for all steps set forth in the Joint Communiqué of the "P-5", as endorsed by the G-8 and the UN Security Council.

The START Treaty and Presidents' nuclear arms reduction initiatives in 1991–92 will help to ensure the ultimate goal of nuclear disarmament and enhance international security. We have together eliminated more than 1,700 heavy bombers and missile launchers, including more than 700 launch silos, 45 submarines capable of launching nuclear missiles, and deactivated or eliminated more than 18,000 strategic and tactical nuclear warheads. Reaffirming our commitment to strict compliance with our obligations under the START I and ABM Treaties, we declare our resolve to collaborate in expediting the entry into force of the START II Treaty. Immediately after Russian ratification of START II, the U.S. and Russia will begin negotiations regarding lower levels within the framework of a START III Treaty.

As a result of significant reductions in their nuclear forces, the United States and Russia have large stockpiles of nuclear materials that are no longer needed for defense purposes. They remain committed to providing the maximum degree of security and accountability for these and other stockpiles of weapons-grade fissile materials and reaffirm the importance of implementing the U.S. Vice President's and Russian Prime Minister's July 1998 Agreement on Scientific and Technical Cooperation in the Management of Plutonium that has been Withdrawn from Nuclear Military Programs.

We reaffirm our commitment to further cooperation on export controls as an essential part of ensuring non-proliferation. Our governments recently created an additional mechanism for cooperation in the field of exports of sensitive technology. To this end, at our meeting today we agreed to establish expert groups on nuclear matters, missile and space technology, catch-all and internal compliance, conventional weapons transfers controls, as well as law enforcement, customs matters, and licensing in order to enhance cooperation and to implement specific bilateral assistance and cooperative projects. These groups will be formed within the next month and begin practical activities without delay. A protected communications channel between senior officials of both countries has also been established, which will ensure the rapid and confidential exchange of information on non-proliferation matters.

We reaffirmed the importance of the Conventional Armed Forces in Europe (CFE) Treaty and its fundamental contribution to stability, predictability and cooperation in Europe. As we work together to build a more integrated and secure Europe, we are committed to accelerating the negotiations to adapt the Treaty to changing circumstances. We consider it necessary to complete work on adapting the Treaty in the nearest future. We reaffirm our commitment to comply with the Treaty's provisions during the process of its adaptation.

The U.S. and Russia remain committed to jointly building an enduring peace based upon the principles of democracy and the indivisibility of security. They reaffirm the common objective of strengthening security and stability in the interest of all countries, and combating aggressive nationalism and preventing abuses of human rights. They will consult with each other and strive to cooperate in averting and settling conflicts and in crisis management. In this regard, we attach great importance to operational military cooperation, in both bilateral and multilateral settings, between the armed forces of the U.S. and Russia. We are pleased to note that definite progress has been achieved in the area of defense cooperation, particularly in strengthening nuclear security and in implementation of the Cooperative Threat Reduction Program.

We recognize that the soundness of an increasingly interdependent world financial and economic system affects the well-being of people in all countries. We agree on the importance to the international community of the success of economic and structural reform in Russia.

Strengthening environmental protection in the 21st century is imperative in order to protect natural systems on which humanity depends. Russia and the U.S. will work together to resolve the global climate problem, to preserve the ozone layer, to conserve biodiversity, and to ensure the sustainable management of forests and other natural resources. We underscored the necessity of deepening broad based international and bilateral cooperation in this area.

We declare that terrorism in all its forms and manifestations, irrespective of its motives, is utterly unacceptable. The U.S. and Russia harshly condemn the recent terrorist bombings in Kenya and Tanzania. At our meeting today we agreed on a series of actions that respond to this growing scourge.

We agreed to intensify joint efforts to counteract the transnational threats to our economies and security, including those posed by organized crime, the narcotics trade, the illegal arms trade, computer and other high-technology crime, and money laundering. We agreed to establish a bilateral law enforcement working group that will meet on a regular basis, and we agreed to step up law enforcement efforts and improve the public information system to eradicate trafficking in women and children. We agreed that the United States and Russia will take an active part in working out an effective UN convention to combat transnational organised crime. We welcome Russia's hosting of a G–8 transnational crime conference at the ministerial level in Moscow in 1999.

We recognize the importance of promoting the positive aspects and mitigating the negative aspects of the information technology revolution now taking place, which is a serious challenge to ensuring the future strategic security interests of our two countries. As part of the efforts to resolve these problems the U.S. and Russia have already held productive discussions within the framework of the Defense Consultative Group on resolving the potential Year 2000 computer problem. The U.S. and Russia are committed to continuing consultations and to studying the wider consequences of this computer problem in order to resolve issues of mutual interest and concern.

We declare that the common security challenges on the threshold of the twenty-first century can be met only by consistently mobilizing the efforts of the entire international community. All available resources must be utilized to do so. In the event that it is necessary, the world community must promptly take effective measures to counter such threats. The U.S. and Russia will continue to play a leadership role bilaterally and multilaterally to advance common objectives in the area of security.

The President of the   The President of the
United States of America: Russian Federation:

William J. Clinton   *Boris Yeltsin*

Moscow
September 2, 1998

NOTE: An original was not available for verification of the content of this joint statement.

Memorandum of Understanding Between the United States of America and Russian Federation on Cooperation in the Field of Civil Aircraft Accident/Incident Investigation and Prevention
September 2, 1998

The Government of the United States of America and the Government of the Russian Federation, hereinafter referred to as the Parties,

Desiring to promote civil aviation safety and accident prevention,

Recognizing the mutual benefit of improved procedures for the investigation and reporting of the facts, conditions, and circumstances of civil aviation accidents/incidents,

Recognizing the many mutual aviation safety benefits that have been realized through cooperation in accident/incident investigation and prevention under the auspices of the Working Group on Accident Investigation, pursuant to cooperative agreements between the United States and Russia; and,

Recognizing the February 5, 1997, joint statement of the U.S.-Russian Commission on Economic and Technological Cooperation indicating that the Parties intend to develop bilateral cooperation in the field of civil aviation,

Have agreed as follows:

1. The Parties shall take measures to strengthen cooperation on civil aircraft accident/incident investigation and prevention. Cooperation may include, but is not limited to:

  a. Assistance and exchange of techniques for the investigation and prevention of civil aircraft accidents and incidents.

  b. Exchange of accident/incident investigation and prevention data.

  c. Assistance and exchange of information on issues related to accident/incident investigation and prevention within the competence of the International Civil Aviation Organization.

2. Competent Authorities responsible for implementation of this Memorandum of Understanding (MOU) are:

For the Government of the United States of America—The National Transportation Safety Board (NTSB), with support and participation of the Federal Aviation Administration.

For the Government of the Russian Federation:

The Interstate Aviation Committee (IAC), a specially authorized body in the area of aircraft accident investigation that shall act on behalf of and on instructions of the Government of the Russian Federation;

The Federal Aviation authority of Russia (FAAR), a specially authorized body in the area of prevention of aircraft accidents and investigation of incidents with civil aircraft that shall act on behalf of and on instructions of the Government of the Russian Federation.

3. Aircraft accident and incident investigations shall be carried out in accordance with the Convention on International Civil Aviation (Chicago Convention of 1944) and Annex 13 to the Chicago Convention of 1944. Pursuant to Annex 13, the following authorities shall be responsible

for instituting and conducting the accident/incident investigation under the following circumstances:

The NTSB shall have primary responsibility in the event of any aircraft accident/incident occurring on the territory of the U.S. involving a Russian-operated or -registered aircraft or an accident/incident occurring in the U.S. involving an aircraft or aircraft engine of Russian design or manufacture. The FAA shall participate in the NTSB investigation. The NTSB shall also have responsibility for providing the U.S.-accredited representative to investigations of accidents/incidents occurring on the territory of the Russian Federation involving a U.S.-operated or -registered aircraft or an accident/incident occurring in the Russian Federation involving an aircraft or aircraft engine of U.S. design or manufacture. The FAA shall participate as an advisor to the NTSB accredited representative.

The IAC shall have primary responsibility in the event of any aircraft accident occurring on the territory of the Russian Federation involving a U.S.-operated or -registered aircraft or an accident occurring in the Russian Federation involving an aircraft or aircraft engine of U.S. design or manufacture. The IAC shall also have responsibility for providing the Russia-accredited representative to investigations of accidents occurring on the territory of U.S. involving a Russia-operated or -registered aircraft or an accident/incident occurring in U.S. involving an aircraft or aircraft engine of Russian design or manufacture.

The FAAR shall have primary responsibility in the event of any aircraft incident occurring on the territory of the Russian Federation involving a U.S.-operated or -registered aircraft or an incident occurring in the Russian Federation involving an aircraft or aircraft engine of U.S. design or manufacture. The FAAR shall

also have responsibility for providing the Russia-accredited representative to investigations of incidents occurring on the territory of U.S. involving a Russia-operated or -registered aircraft.

4. The Parties shall take steps to establish mutual confidence in each other's civil aircraft accident/incident investigation and prevention system, and shall cooperate to improve those systems.

5. The Parties shall implement this MOU in accordance with their respective national laws and regulations and in accordance with the rules and principles of international law. Security and confidentiality of data, especially proprietary documents, are subject to the respective national laws and regulations of both Parties.

6. The Competent Authorities shall continue participation in the Working Group on Accident Investigation, and prepare recommendations in the optimum working relationship among the Competent Authorities of the Parties.

7. This MOU shall enter into force upon signature and shall remain in force until terminated by six (6) months' written notice from one Party to the other Party.

In Witness Whereof, the undersigned, being duly authorized by their respective Governments, have signed the Memorandum of Understanding.

Done at Moscow, this second day of September, 1998, in duplicate, in the English and Russian languages, each text being equally authentic.

For the Government of the United States of America:	For the Government of the Russian Federation:
William J. Clinton	*Boris Yeltsin*

NOTE: An original was not available for verification of the content of this memorandum.

Memorandum of Understanding Between the United States of America and Russian Federation on the Principles of Cooperation in the Fields of Culture, the Humanities, the Social Sciences, Education, and the Mass Media
September 2, 1998

The Government of the United States of America and the Government of the Russian Federation (hereinafter referred to as "the Participants");

Desiring to enhance mutual understanding and strengthen the friendly relations between the peoples of the United States of America and the Russian Federation;

Believing that further development of cooperation on the basis of equality and mutual benefit will facilitate attainment of these objectives;

Reaffirming the enduring validity of the principle of compliance with the international norms governing rights to intellectual property;

Guided By the provisions of the Charter for American-Russian Partnership and Friendship signed at Washington on June 17, 1992; and

Declaring their intent to encourage direct ties between the citizens and appropriate institutions of the United States of America and the Russian Federation, as well as between the U.S. and Russian non-governmental institutions, in the fields of culture the humanities, the social sciences, education, and the mass media;

Have reached mutual understanding that:

1. The Participants intend to promote the strengthening of mutual cooperation in the fields of culture, the humanities, the social sciences, education, archival science, and the mass media.

2. The Participants intend to encourage the development of cultural exchanges in order to promote better understanding of each other's culture, particularly through:

- organization of theatrical performances and art exhibitions;
- dissemination of instructional materials, books, periodicals, scholarly publications, radio and television programs, films, and other audiovisual materials;
- organization of lectures, seminars, and joint scholarly research; and

- participation in other activities in the fields of culture and art carried out in the United States of America and the Russian Federation.

3. The Participants intend to facilitate the establishment of contacts between interested governmental and non-governmental organizations in order to develop programs and joint projects in fields of mutual interest that help strengthen bilateral ties.

4. The Participants plan to encourage scholarly research in the fields of culture, the humanities, and education conducted by appropriate academic institutions in the two countries.

5. The Participants intend to provide assistance in the study of the Russian and English languages in the United States of America and the Russian Federation, respectively.

6. The Participants intend to facilitate the reciprocal sending of pupils, undergraduate and graduate students, faculty, and scholars for instruction and scholarly research, as well as high school teachers to work as interns and give lectures.

7. The Participants intend to encourage the development of contacts between libraries and archives in order to provide wider access to the information available in them.

8. The Participants intend to facilitate exchanges and contacts between journalists, publishers, and mass media associations.

9. The Participants intend to encourage contacts and cooperation between youth, women's, and other non-governmental organizations in the two countries.

10. The activities set forth in this Memorandum may be carried out in the form of joint projects or individual programs of appropriate governmental or non-governmental organizations in the United States of America and the Russian Federation.

11. The Participants plan for their representatives to meet as necessary or at the request of either Participant to exchange views and also

to formulate recommendations on specific aspects of the development of cultural cooperation. Matters relating to this will be coordinated through diplomatic channels.

12. In matters pertaining to cooperation in the fields of culture, the humanities, the social sciences, education, and the mass media, the Participants intend to be guided by this Memorandum in accordance with the laws and regulations of the United States of America and the Russian Federation and in accordance with the principles and norms of international law, beginning on the date of its signature and until such time as either Participant informs the other in writing to the contrary.

The provisions of this Memorandum do not affect other active projects or programs.

Signed at Moscow, this second day of September, 1998, in duplicate, each in the English and Russian languages.

For the Government of the United States of America:

William J. Clinton

For the Government of the Russian Federation:

Boris Yeltsin

NOTE: An original was not available for verification of the content of this memorandum.

Agreement Between the United States of America and the Russian Federation for Promotion of Aviation Safety
September 2, 1998

The Government of the United States of America and the Government of the Russian Federation, hereinafter referred to as the Contracting Parties,

Desiring to promote civil aviation safety and environmental quality,

Noting common concerns for the safe operation of civil aircraft,

Recognizing the emerging trend toward multinational design, production, and interchange of civil aeronautical products,

Desiring to enhance cooperation and increase efficiency in matters relating to civil aviation safety,

Considering the possible reduction of the economic burden imposed on the aviation industry and operators by redundant technical inspections, evaluations, and testing,

Recognizing the mutual benefit of improved procedures for the reciprocal acceptance of airworthiness approvals, environmental testing, and development of reciprocal recognition procedures for approval and monitoring of flight simulators, aircraft maintenance facilities, maintenance personnel, airmen, and flight operations,

Have agreed as follows:

Article I

A. To facilitate acceptance by each Contracting Party of the other Contracting Party's

(a) airworthiness approvals and environmental testing and approval of civil aeronautical products, and (b) qualification evaluations of flight simulators.

B. To facilitate acceptance by each Contracting Party of the approvals and monitoring of maintenance facilities and alteration or modification facilities, maintenance personnel, airmen, aviation training establishments, and flight operations of the other Contracting Party.

C. To provide for cooperation in sustaining an equivalent level of safety and environmental objectives with respect to aviation safety.

D. Each Contracting Party shall designate the appropriate authorities as its executive agent(s) to implement this Agreement.

For the Government of the United States of America, the executive agent shall be the Federal Aviation Administration (FAA) of the Department of Transportation.

For the Government of the Russian Federation, the executive agent shall be the Interstate Aviation Committee (IAC) for type design approval, initial airworthiness approvals, environmental approval, and environmental testing of civil aeronautical products; and the Federal Aviation Authority of Russia (FAAR) for approval of maintenance facilities, maintenance personnel, and airmen; approval of flight operations; qualification evaluation of flight simulators; approval of aviation training establishments; and continuing in-service airworthiness issues related to civil aeronautical products. For the purpose of carrying out the provisions of this Agreement, the IAC shall act under the authority and on behalf of the Government of the Russian Federation.

Article II

For the purposes of this Agreement, the terms below have the following meaning:

A. "Airworthiness approval" means a finding that the type design or change to a type design of a civil aeronautical product meets standards agreed between the Contracting Parties or that a product conforms to a type design that has been found to meet those standards, and is in a condition for safe operation.

B. "Alterations or modifications" means making a change to the construction, configuration, performance, environmental characteristics, or operating limitations of the affected civil aeronautical product.

C. "Approval of flight operations" means the technical inspections and evaluations conducted by a Contracting Party, using standards agreed between the Contracting Parties, of an entity providing commercial air transportation of passengers or cargo, or the finding that the entity complies with those standards.

D. "Civil aeronautical product" means any civil aircraft, aircraft engine, or propeller or sub-assembly, appliance, material, part, or component to be installed thereon.

E. "Environmental approval" means a finding that a civil aeronautical product complies with standards agreed between the Contracting Parties concerning noise and/or exhaust emissions. "Environmental testing" means a process by which a civil aeronautical product is evaluated for compliance with those standards, using procedures agreed between the Contracting Parties.

F. "Flight simulator qualification evaluations" means the process by which a flight simulator is assessed by comparison to the aircraft it simulates, in accordance with standards agreed between the Contracting Parties, or the finding that it complies with those standards.

G. "Maintenance" means the performance of inspection, overhaul, repair, preservation, and the replacement of parts, materials, appliances, or components of a product to assure the continued airworthiness of that product, but excludes alterations of modifications.

H. "Monitoring" means the periodic surveillance by a Contracting Party's appropriate executive agent to determine continuing compliance with the appropriate standards.

Article III

A. The Contracting Parties' appropriate executive agents shall conduct technical assessments and work cooperatively to develop an understanding of each other's standards and systems in the following areas:

1. Airworthiness approvals of civil aeronautical products;
2. Environmental approval and environmental testing;
3. Approval of maintenance facilities, alteration or modification facilities, maintenance personnel, and airmen;
4. Approval of flight operations;
5. Qualification evaluation of flight simulators; and
6. Approval of aviation training establishments.

B. When the appropriate executive agents of the Contracting Parties agree that the standards, rules, practices, procedures, and systems of both Contracting Parties in one of the technical specialties listed above are sufficiently equivalent or compatible to permit acceptance of findings of compliance made by one Contracting Party for the other Contracting Party to the agreed-upon standards, the appropriate executive agents shall execute written Implementation Procedures describing the methods by which such reciprocal acceptance shall be made with respect to that technical specialty.

C. The Implementation Procedures shall include at a minimum:

1. Definitions;
2. A description of the particular area of civil aviation to be addressed;
3. Provisions for reciprocal acceptance of appropriate executive agent actions such as test witnessing, inspections, qualifications, approvals, and certifications;
4. Accountability of executive agents;
5. Provisions for mutual cooperation and technical assistance;
6. Provisions for periodic evaluations; and
7. Provisions for amendments to or termination of the Implementation Procedures.

Article IV

Any disagreement regarding the interpretation or application of this Agreement or its Implementation Procedures shall be resolved by consultation between the Contracting Parties or their appropriate executive agents, respectively.

Article V

This Agreement shall enter into force upon signature and shall remain in force until terminated by sixty (60) days' written notice from one Contracting Party to the other Contracting Party. Such termination shall also act to terminate all existing Implementation Procedures executed in accordance with this Agreement. This Agreement may be amended by the written agreement of the Contracting Parties. Individual Implementation Procedures may be terminated or amended by the appropriate executive agents.

In Witness Whereof, the undersigned, being duly authorized by their respective Governments, have signed this Agreement.

Done at Moscow, this second day of September, 1998, in duplicate, in the English and Russian languages, each text being equally authentic.

For the Government of the
United States of America:

William J. Clinton

For the Government of the
Russian Federation:

Boris Yeltsin

NOTE: An original was not available for verification of the content of this agreement.

Remarks at a Meeting With Duma and Regional Leaders in Moscow
September 2, 1998

Thank you very much, Mr. Ambassador. I'd like to thank all of you who have come here today to Spaso House. I have met with several of you before here, and as always, I attempt to come to Russia with the view of listening to a wide variety of views and meeting everyone I can who is involved in the activities of the day.

I am pleased to be joined by the Secretary of State, Madeleine Albright; our Secretary of Commerce, Bill Daley; and the Secretary of Energy, Bill Richardson; and with some distinguished Members of Congress. I see Senator Bingaman and Congressman King. I don't know if Senator Domenici and Congressman Hoyer are here or not. But we all want to get to know all of you.

I am proud of what America and Russia have achieved together in reducing the threat of nuclear war and in cooperating in areas like Bosnia. Today we announced two other steps to cooperate: First, in the sharing of early warning information on missile firings; and second, in a commitment to dramatically reduce our stocks of plutonium, a move that might also be of benefit to the Russian economy.

I'd like to, before I go out and start to visit with you individually, make just a couple of observations about the economic challenges facing Russia today. First of all, I recognize that around this room there are many different points of view represented, and I think that is a good thing for the strength of Russian democracy. Second, I think it's important to point out that all over the world there are many countries that have democratically-elected leaders and successful economies and rather dramatically different social systems, different approaches to achieving success economically with elected leadership. So Russia must have its own approaches that keep the nation strong, that care for the people who are in need, that prepare for the future of your children. And no other country can define that approach, and no other country's approach would be exactly right for Russia. But I do not believe you can find one country in the world that is economically successful that has completely ignored the ground rules of the global economy.

For all their differences, all the countries that are succeeding have some things in common. They have tax systems that are fair and bring in revenues adequate to meet their spending requirements. They have marketing systems that regulate and provide for effective banking and trading in the country. They have a rule of law which permits commerce to succeed and to proceed on predictable terms in which individual interests are properly protected.

Now, when countries have this, whether they're large or small, whether they're in Latin America, Asia, or Africa, wherever they are, they see that money flows into the country instead of flowing out of it.

I come here as someone who considers himself a friend of your country and someone who deeply believes that in the century just ahead of us, America and Russia must be partners. I hope you will be able to bridge your differences to agree on, first, a program to stabilize the current situation, and then, a path to finish the framework of basic things that every successful economy has; then, within your democratic system, whatever decisions you make about how to organize your society are your decisions to make, and we will support you and find a way to work together.

But if the basic framework is not in place, as a friend I say, I do not believe that you can defy the rules of the road in today's global economy anymore than I could defy the laws of gravity by stepping off the top floor of Spaso House. It has nothing to do with politics and everything to do with the way the world is working today. But if you can find a way to work together and work through this crisis, the United States will stand with you and will not presume to judge on the specific social systems you decide to put in place within a democratic system with a strong economy that has integrity of its fundamental elements.

Thank you again for coming.

NOTE: The President spoke at 3:20 p.m. in Spaso House. In his remarks, the President referred to James F. Collins, U.S. Ambassador to Russia, who introduced the President.

Remarks to the Northern Ireland Assembly in Belfast
September 3, 1998

Thank you. Lord Mayor Alderdice, First Minister Trimble, Deputy First Minister Mallon, Mr. Prime Minister; to the members of the Northern Ireland Assembly, the citizens of Belfast and Northern Ireland, it is an honor for me to be back here with the First Lady, our delegation, including two members of our Cabinet, distinguished Members of Congress, our Ambassador, and Consul General, and of course, the best investment we ever made in Northern Ireland, Senator Mitchell.

I want to begin very briefly by thanking Prime Minister Blair and echoing his comments about the thoughts and prayers we have with the passengers and families of the Swissair flight that crashed this morning near Nova Scotia, Canada. The flight was en route to Geneva from New York, and as I speak, Canadians are conducting an extensive search operation. We hope for the best, and we are deeply grieved that this has occurred.

I would like to also begin just by simply saying thank you to the leaders who have spoken before me, to David Trimble and Seamus Mallon; to the party leaders and the other members of the Assembly whom I met earlier today; to Tony Blair and, in his absence, to Prime Minister Ahern; and to their predecessors with whom I have worked, Prime Ministers Bruton and Reynolds and Major.

This has been a magic thing to see unfold, this developing will for peace among the people of Northern Ireland. Three years ago, when Hillary and I were here, I could see it in the eyes of the people in Belfast and Derry. We saw, as Seamus Mallon said, the morning light begin to dawn after Ireland's long darkness on Good Friday with the leaders' commitment to solve your problems with words, not weapons. It lit the whole sky a month later when you voted so overwhelmingly for the peace agreement. Now this Assembly is the living embodiment of the promise of that covenant.

Together, people and leaders are moving Northern Ireland from the deep freeze of despair to the warm sunlight of peace. For 30 long years the Troubles took a terrible toll: Too many died; too many families grieved. Every family was denied the quiet blessings of a normal life, in the constant fear that a simple trip to the store could be devastated by bombs and bullets, in the daily disruptions of roadblocks and searches, in the ominous presence of armed soldiers always on patrol, in neighborhoods demarcated by barbed wire, guarded gates, and 20-foot fences.

No wonder this question was painted on a Belfast wall: Is there life before death? Now, at last, your answer is yes.

From here on, the destiny of Northern Ireland is in the hands of its people and its representatives. From farming to finance, education to health care, this new Assembly has the opportunity and the obligation to forge the future. The new structures of cooperation you have approved can strengthen the quality of your ties to both London and Dublin, based on the benefits of interdependence, not the burdens of division or dominance. In peace you can find new prosperity, and I heard your leaders seeking it.

Since the 1994 cease-fire, the number of passengers coming to and from your international airport and ferryport has increased more than 15 percent. The number of hotel rooms under construction has doubled. And in the wake of the Good Friday agreement, you are projected to receive record levels of investment, foreign and domestic, bringing new jobs, opportunity, and hope.

The United States has supported our quest for peace, starting with Irish-Americans, whose commitment to this cause is passionate, profound, and enduring. It has been one of the great privileges of my Presidency to work with the peacemakers, Protestant and Catholic leaders here in the North, Prime Minister Blair, and Prime Minister Ahern. Our Congress, as you can see if you had visited with our delegation, has reached across its own partisan divide for the sake of peace in Northern Ireland. I hope some of it will infect their consciousness as they go back home. [*Laughter*]

They have voted extraordinary support for the International Fund for Ireland, the $100 million over the past 5 years. I am delighted that there are both Republican and Democratic Members with me today, as well as Jim Lyons, my Special Adviser for Economic Initiatives in Northern Ireland, and Senator Mitchell, whom you welcomed so warmly and justly a few moments ago.

In the months and years ahead, America will continue to walk the road of renewal with you. We will help to train your Assembly members,

support NGO's that are building civil societies from the grassroots, invest in our common future through education, promote cross-border and cross-community understanding, create with you microcredit facilities to help small businesses get off the ground, support the trade and investment that will benefit both our people.

I thank the Secretary of Education for being with us today, and the Secretary of Commerce who led a trade mission here in June, already showing results. Chancellor Brown takes the next important step with his mission to 10 American cities next month. As you work to change the face and future of Northern Ireland, you can count on America.

Of course, for all we can and will do, the future still is up to you. You have agreed to bury the violence of the past; now you have to build a peaceful and prosperous future. To the members of the Assembly, you owe it to your country to nurture the best in your people by showing them the best in yourselves. Difficult, sometimes wrenching decisions lie ahead, but they must be made. And because you have agreed to share responsibilities, whenever possible you must try to act in concert, not conflict; to overcome obstacles, not create them; to rise above petty disputes, not fuel them.

The Latin word for assembly, "concilium," is the root of the word "reconciliation." The spirit of reconciliation must be rooted in all you do.

There is another quality you will need, too. Our only Irish-Catholic President, John Kennedy, loved to quote a certain British Protestant Prime Minister. "Courage," Winston Churchill said, "is rightly esteemed as the first of all human qualities because it is the quality that guarantees all the others."

Courage and reconciliation were the heart of your commitment to peace. Now, as you go forward, courage and reconciliation must drive this Assembly in very specific ways: to decommission the weapons of war that are obsolete in Northern Ireland at peace; to move forward with the formation of an executive council; to adapt your police force so that it earns the confidence, respect, and support of all the people; to end street justice, because defining crime, applying punishment, and enforcing the law must be left to the people's elected representatives, the courts, and the police; to pursue early release for prisoners whose organizations have truly abandoned violence and to help them find a productive, constructive place in society; to build a more just society where human rights are birthrights and where every citizen receives equal protection and equal treatment under the law. These must be the benchmarks of the new Northern Ireland.

I must say, the words and the actions of your leaders, this week, and their willingness to meet are hopeful reflections of the spirit of courage and reconciliation that must embrace all the citizens. Also hopeful are the activities of the community leaders here today, the nongovernmental organizations, those in business, law, and academia. And especially I salute the women who have been such a powerful force for peace. Hillary had a wonderful day yesterday at your Vital Voices conference. And as she said, we are pledged to follow up on the partnerships established there.

All your voices are vital. The example you set among your neighbors, the work you do in your communities, the standards you demand from your elected officials: All these will have a very, very large impact on your future. And to the people of Northern Ireland I say it is your will for peace, after all, that has brought your country to this moment of hope. Do not let it slip away. It will not come again in our lifetime. Give your leaders the support they need to make the hard, but necessary decisions. With apologies to Mr. Yeats, help them to prove that things can come together, that the center can hold.

You voted for a future different from the past. Now you must prove that the passion for reason and moderation can trump the power of extremes. There will be hard roads ahead. The terror in Omagh was not the last bomb of the Troubles; it was the opening shot of a vicious attack on the peace. The question is not whether there will be more bombs and more attempts to undo with violence the verdict of the ballot box. There well may be. The question is not whether tempers will flare and debates will be divisive. They certainly will be. The question is: How will you react to it all, to the violence? How will you deal with your differences? Can the bad habits and brute forces of yesterday break your will for tomorrow's peace? That is the question.

In our so-called modern world, from Bosnia to the Middle East, from Rwanda to Kosovo, from the Indian subcontinent to the Aegean, people still hate each other over their differences of race, tribe, and religion, in a fruitless struggle to find meaning in life in who we are not, rather than asking God to help us become what we ought to be. From here on, in Northern Ireland, you have said only one dividing line matters, the line between those who embrace peace and those who would destroy it, between those energized by hope and those paralyzed by hatred, between those who choose to build up and those who want to keep on tearing down.

So much more unites you than divides you: the values of faith and family, work and community, the same land and heritage, the same love of laughter and language. You aspire to the same things: to live in peace and security, to provide for your loved ones, to build a better life and pass on brighter possibilities to your children. These are not Catholic or Protestant dreams, these are human dreams, to be realized best together.

The American people, as the Lord Mayor noted, know from our own experience about bigotry and violence rooted in race and religion. Still today, we struggle with the challenge of building one nation out of our increasing diversity. But it is worth the effort. We know we are wiser, stronger, and happier when we stand on common ground. And we know you will be, too.

And so, members of the Assembly, citizens of Belfast, people of Northern Ireland, remember that in the early days of the American Republic, the Gaelic term for America was *Inis Fa'il*, Island of Destiny. Today, Americans see you as *Inis Fa'il*, and your destiny is peace. America is with you. The entire world is with you. May God be with you and give you strength for the good work ahead.

Thank you very much.

NOTE: The President spoke at 12:40 p.m. in the main auditorium at Waterfront Hall. In his remarks, he referred to Lord Mayor David Alderdice of Belfast; First Minister David Trimble and Deputy First Minister Seamus Mallon of the Northern Ireland Assembly; Prime Minister Tony Blair, former Prime Minister John Major, and Chancellor of the Exchequer Gordon Brown of the United Kingdom; Philip Lader, U.S. Ambassador to the United Kingdom; Ki Fort, U.S. Consul General, Belfast; former Senator George J. Mitchell, independent chairman of the multiparty talks in Northern Ireland; and Prime Minister

Bertie Ahern and former Prime Ministers John
Bruton and Albert Reynolds of Ireland.

Remarks at a Groundbreaking Ceremony for Springvale Educational Village in Belfast
September 3, 1998

Thank you very much, Margaret. Margaret and Gerard said everything that needs to be said. I feel sort of like a fifth wheel now. They, just standing here and speaking as they did, embodied everything I would like to say to you and everything you would like to say to each other and everything your better selves calls on all of you to do. And I thank them for being here.

Thank you, Mr. Prime Minister, for your leadership in so many ways, large and small. Hillary and I are delighted to be back in Northern Ireland and to be here with you and Cherie. And I thank all those who were responsible for the Vital Voices conference at which Hillary spoke yesterday. I also would like to thank Secretary Mo Mowlam, who is one of the most remarkable people I ever met.

I thank others who have made this possible. Mo mentioned the First Lady. I also would like to thank Willie McCarter, the Chairman of the International Fund for Ireland; Lord Smith of Clifton, Vice Chancellor of the University; Professor Patrick Murphy, the Director of the Belfast Institute. I thank the members of the new Assembly with us today, the Deputy First Minister Seamus Mallon, David Ervine, Joe Hendron, and of course, Gerry Adams. We're glad to be in your constituency, and I echo the words of the Prime Minister.

I thank the Americans who are here: the distinguished congressional delegation; the Secretary of Education, Dick Riley; the Secretary of Commerce, Bill Daley. You will notice, if you get a list of the Congress Members and the list of the people in the delegation, that— Assistant Secretary of Labor Kitty Higgins— there will be an enormous preponderance of Irish names in the American delegation here. And I thank them all. I thank especially Jim Lyons, my Special Adviser for Economic Initiatives, and Senator George Mitchell. I also would like to remember today our late Commerce Secretary, Ron Brown, who did so much to bring opportunity here and who envisioned this day that we celebrate.

I want to say that, above all, the people who deserve recognition today are people on both sides of the peace line who need the work that will be done here. Here there is a site; there is a design; there are resources. But more than that, there is a glimpse of the future, that people so long torn apart will create something together that will benefit all.

Of course, there remain those who oppose the vision all of you share for reconciliation and tolerance. Thank God they live in the past and their support dwindles. With courage, determination, and palpable pride, which we saw all up and down the streets today driving from the Waterfront Hall to here, it is clear that people have chosen peace and the chance for prosperity.

These neighborhoods are your home, and you have taken them back. Now you are ready to move forward into a new century of hope, or, in the words of that great son of Belfast, Van Morrison, to "walk down the avenues again" because "the healing has begun."

Indeed, the future has begun. And clearly the best path to a future that involves every citizen of every circumstance in every neighborhood is a strong education. Springvale Educational Village will help you get there. It will be a living, breathing monument to the triumph of peace. It will turn barren ground into fertile fields cultivating the world's most important resource, the minds of your people, providing opportunity not just for the young but for those long denied the chance for higher learning, creating jobs in neighborhoods where too many have gone without work for too long, bringing more technology and skill so that Northern Ireland at last can reap the full benefits of this new economy, creating unity from division, transforming a barbed wire boundary that kept communities apart into common ground of learning and going forward together.

Again, let me thank Gerry Adams, who has worked hard to bring justice and a better life to the people of this constituency. There is more to be done by people on all sides. But his words this week, and I quote, "Violence must be a thing of the past, over, done with, gone"—those words were music to ears all across the world, and they pave the way for the progress still to come. Thank you, sir.

I am grateful that America was able to support Springvale working through the International Fund for Ireland, together with generous funding provided by the United Kingdom, the University of Ulster, and the Belfast Institute. All these allow us to break ground today.

I also want to acknowledge the support of Gateway 2000, an American company which has such a strong presence in the Republic and which has announced plans to donate a state-of-the-art computer system when Springvale opens. And I'm proud of the people here in Northern Ireland who, once again, have moved beyond pain to accomplishment.

Now you have, in the words of Seamus Heaney, a "chance to know the incomparable and dive to a future." You have dared to dream of a better tomorrow. Now you dare to build one. That is even better. On this site and across this isle, what once seemed impossible is now becoming real. Don't stop.

Thank you very much.

NOTE: The President spoke at 1:57 p.m. in a tent at the construction site. In his remarks, he referred to students Margaret Gibney, who introduced the President, and Gerard Quinn, who introduced Prime Minister Tony Blair of the United Kingdom; Prime Minister Blair's wife, Cherie Blair; United Kingdom Secretary of State for Northern Ireland Marjorie (Mo) Mowlam; William T. McCarter, chairman, International Fund for Ireland; Lord Trevor Smith, vice chancellor, University of Ulster; Professor Patrick Murphy, chairman, Belfast Institute of Further and Higher Education; Deputy First Minister Seamus Mallon, and members David Ervine, Joseph Hendron, and Sinn Fein leader Gerry Adams, Northern Ireland Assembly; former Senator George J. Mitchell, independent chairman of the multiparty talks in Northern Ireland; musician Van Morrison; and poet Seamus Heaney.

Remarks to Victims of the Bombing in Omagh, Northern Ireland
September 3, 1998

Thank you very much. Mr. Prime Minister, Mrs. Blair, Secretary Mowlam, Ambassador Lader, Senator Mitchell; to the people of Omagh. Hillary and I are honored to be in your presence. We come to tell you that, a long way away, the American people have mourned the loss of 28 innocents and all those who were injured. For those victims and family members who have come here today to say a word to us, we thank you for your presence.

To all of you, we thank you for standing up in the face of such a soul-searing loss and restating your determination to walk the road of peace.

We came here, knowing, as the Prime Minister said, that words are not very good at a time like this, simply to express our sympathy with the good people of this community, especially with the victims and their families, and again to support your determined refusal to let a cowardly crime rob you of the future you have chosen.

What happened here on August 15th was so incredibly unreasonable, so shocking to the conscience of every decent person in this land, that it has perversely had exactly the reverse impact that the people who perpetrated this act intended. By killing Catholics and Protestants, young and old, men, women, and children, even those about to be born, people from Northern Ireland, the Irish Republic, and abroad—by doing all that in an aftermath of what the people have voted for in Northern Ireland, it galvanized, strengthened, and humanized the impulse to peace.

Even more than when we were here 3 years ago, people are saying to me: "It's high time that the few stop ruining the lives of the many;

high time that those who hate stop bullying those who hope; high time to stop the lilt of laughter and language being drowned out by bombs and guns and sirens; high time to stop yesterday's nightmares from killing tomorrow's dreams."

All I wanted to say today is that nothing any of us can say will erase the pain that those of you who have experienced loss know now. Just a few days ago, we had to—Hillary and I did—go to the airport to meet the plane bringing home the bodies of the Americans who were killed in the Embassy bombing in Africa, and to go from table to table to meet their families. There is no word to explain a mindless act of terror that grabs the life of an innocent. But I think the only way to truly redeem such a terrible loss is to make the memories of the innocents monuments to peace. We cannot brook a descent into terror. Northern Ireland is walking away from it. Life will never be the same here, but it will go on.

Since the bombings, one of the victims, Nicola Emory, has given birth to a healthy baby. I pray that baby will never know an act of terror and will live a long, full life in the 21st century, proud of a hometown that learned, through tragedy, the meaning of community.

I'd like to close my remarks by reading to you from a letter that our Ambassador in Dublin received from a young man named Michael Gallagher from County Mayo after this happened. He wrote to the American Ambassador: "You don't know me. You may not even get this letter. But after yesterday's tragedy, I just wanted to do something. I am 29 years old, an Irishman to the very core of my being. But throughout my life, there has never been peace on this island. I never realized how precious peace could be until my wife, Martina, gave birth to our daughter, Ashleen, 20 months ago. We don't want her to grow up in a society that is constantly waiting for the next atrocity, the next bunch of young lives snuffed out in a sea of hatred and fear. Ashleen's name means 'vision' or 'dream,' and we have a dream of what Ireland might be like when she grows up. It could be a place where dreams come true, where people would achieve things never imagined before, where people would not be afraid of their neighbors. Hopefully, this can happen. But after yesterday, one has to wonder. We know America has done much for Ireland. All we ask is that you keep trying, even when times are hard. Please keep Ireland in mind because Ashleen and all Irish children need to be able to dream."

So we came here today to say we grieve for your loss, but to pledge to that little Ashleen in Mayo and Nicola's newborn here in Omagh that we will work to build this peace, to make it a place where children can dream, to redeem the loss of innocence from the madness of people who must fail so that your life can go on.

Thank you for letting us come here, and God bless you.

NOTE: The President spoke at 4:05 p.m. at the Leisure Center. In his remarks, he referred to Prime Minister Tony Blair of the United Kingdom and his wife, Cherie; United Kingdom Secretary of State for Northern Ireland Marjorie (Mo) Mowlam; Philip Lader, U.S. Ambassador to the United Kingdom; and former Senator George J. Mitchell, independent chairman of the multiparty talks in Northern Ireland.

Statement on the Northern Ireland Peace Process
September 3, 1998

Yesterday's announcement that Martin McGuinness will oversee decommissioning issues for Sinn Fein is an important step. I welcome it as the kind of action essential not only to fulfill the Good Friday commitments, but to deepen public confidence in the overall process of making peace a reality in Northern Ireland.

NOTE: The statement referred to Martin McGuinness, Sinn Fein chief negotiator.

Statement on the Crash of Swissair Flight 111
September 3, 1998

Hillary and I were deeply saddened to learn of the fatal crash of Swissair Flight 111 off Halifax, Nova Scotia, last night. We join the American people in extending our deepest sympathies to the families of the passengers and crewmembers aboard the aircraft.

I want to thank the Canadian Government and people for the extraordinary way in which they responded to this tragedy. Hundreds of people, including many volunteers, searched through the night. The United States will continue to do everything we can to assist the Canadian and Swiss authorities in the search for survivors and to determine the cause of the accident. Members of the National Transportation Safety Board are on the scene of the crash, and we have offered support from our Navy, the Coast Guard, and other Federal agencies.

I ask that the American people remember in their prayers the families who lost loved ones on that flight.

Letter to Congressional Leaders Reporting on Iraq's Compliance With United Nations Security Council Resolutions
September 3, 1998

Dear Mr. Speaker: *(Dear Mr. President:)*

Consistent with the Authorization for Use of Military Force Against Iraq Resolution (Public Law 102–1) and as part of my effort to keep the Congress fully informed, I am reporting on the status of efforts to obtain Iraq's compliance with the resolutions adopted by the United Nations Security Council (UNSC). This report covers the period from June 24 to the present.

Introduction

From June 24 until August 5, Iraq had provided site access to U.N. weapons inspectors, as required under UNSC resolutions and reaffirmed under the terms of the February 23 Secretary General/Tariq Aziz MOU and UNSC Resolution 1154. In June, UNSCOM inspectors presented a work plan to Iraq to delineate areas of concern and elements that Iraq needed to disclose. However, in June, UNSCOM revealed that it had found evidence of Iraqi weaponization of VX nerve agent and in July, Iraq refused to turn over a document accounting for use of CW during the Iran-Iraq war. On August 3–4 when Chairman Butler was in Iraq to discuss phase two of the work plan, the Iraqi Deputy Prime Minister claimed that Iraq was fully "disarmed" and demanded that this be reported to the Council; Butler refused, and subsequently departed Baghdad.

On August 5, Iraq declared that it was suspending all cooperation with UNSCOM and the IAEA, except some limited monitoring activities. On August 6, the Security Council President issued a press statement which noted that Iraq's action contravenes the February 23 MOU and relevant Security Council resolutions. On August 11/12, the IAEA and UNSCOM sent letters to the Security Council that noted that Iraq's decision to suspend cooperation with them halted "all of the disarmament activities" of UNSCOM and placed limitations on the inspection and monitoring activities of both organizations. On August 18, the Council President replied in writing to UNSCOM and IAEA on the Council's behalf reiterating full support for the full implementation of their mandates and underscoring Iraq's obligation to cooperate in the conduct of their activities, including inspections. Chairman Butler wrote to the Iraqi regime August 19 expressing his willingness to resume activity, but that offer was rebuffed.

On August 20, the Security Council met to conduct the periodic review of Iraq's compliance with relevant Security Council resolutions. It stated that "the necessary conditions do not exist for the modification of the regime established" in relevant resolutions. Moreover, the Security Council "reiterates that the decision by Iraq to suspend cooperation with UNSCOM and the

IAEA (on August 5) is totally unacceptable" and that it "views with extreme concern the continuing refusal by the Government of Iraq to rescind its decision." The United States is working with other Security Council members to suspend subsequent periodic reviews until Iraq reverses course and resumes cooperation with UNSCOM and the IAEA.

The cornerstone of U.S. policy is to contain Iraq and prevent it from threatening regional peace and security. To that end, the United States has supported UNSCOM since its inception and continues to do so, as an integral part of our policy to contain Iraq and disarm it of its WMD. We have consistently worked to uphold the principle that UNSCOM must be able to do its job, free of Iraqi restrictions and impediments. That includes inspections wherever, whenever, and however the Executive Chairman of UNSCOM directs. There have been allegations recently that the United States impeded some kinds of inspections since last fall. In fact, the international effort to secure full access for UNSCOM and the IAEA last fall and winter was lead by the United States. Since early August, the United States has again lead the effort to reverse Iraq's decision blocking UNSCOM activities. Decisions on how UNSCOM does its job, including timing, locations and modalities for inspections, are the Chairman's to make. As Chairman Butler stated on August 14, "Consultations on policy matters take place regularly between the Executive Chairman and Council members, but all operational decisions are taken by the Executive Chairman (of UNSCOM) who has not been given and would find it invidious were any attempt made to direct his operational decisions or to micro-manage the day-to-day work of the Special Commission."

Iraq's refusal to cooperate with UNSCOM and the IAEA is totally unacceptable; Iraq must meet its international obligations. In the first instance, the Council and the Secretary General must respond effectively to Iraq's flagrant challenge to their authority. We are working with Council members to ensure that there is a clear, united and forceful U.N. response to Iraq's actions. If the Council fails to persuade the Iraqi regime to resume cooperation, all other options are on the table.

We continue to support the international community's efforts to provide for the humanitarian needs of the Iraqi people through the "oil-for-food" program and other humanitarian efforts.

On May 27, 1998, Iraq presented a distribution plan for the implementation of Resolution 1153, which had been adopted on February 20. Under phase three of the "oil-for-food" program, which ran from December 3, 1997, through June 2, 1998, $1.1 billion worth of humanitarian goods were approved for export to Iraq. Under the current phase, phase four, which began in June, the U.N. Sanctions Committee has approved the purchase of over $562 million worth of humanitarian goods. United States companies can participate in the "oil-for-food" program, and over $165 million worth of contracts for U.S. firms have been approved since the program began.

On June 26, the Secretary of State reported to the Congress on plans to establish a program to support the democratic opposition in Iraq, as required by section 10008 of the 1998 Supplemental Appropriations and Rescissions Act (Public Law 105–174). Opposition leaders and their representatives have been generally receptive to the focus on the central themes of building a consensus on the transition from dictatorship to pluralism, conveying to the U.N. opposition views on Iraqi noncompliance with U.N. resolutions and compiling information to support the indictment of Iraqi officials for war crimes. The new Radio Free Iraq service, also funded by that Act, is preparing to broadcast directly to the Iraqi people under the direction of Radio Free Europe/Radio Liberty. These new programs will help us encourage the Iraqi people to build a pluralistic, peaceful Iraq that observes the international rule of law and respects basic human rights. Such an Iraq would have little trouble regaining its rightful place in the region and in the international community.

The United States maintains a significant military presence in the region in order to provide the full range of military options necessary to deter Iraqi aggression, to ensure that UNSC resolutions are enforced, and to deal with other contingencies that may arise.

U.S. and Coalition Force Levels in the Gulf Region

In view of Saddam's record of aggressive behavior, it is prudent to retain a significant force presence in the region to deter Iraq and deal with any threat it might pose to its neighbors. The U.S. and allied forces now in the region are prepared to deal with all contingencies. We have the capability to respond rapidly to possible Iraqi aggression. We have restructured our in-theater force levels since my last report. We will continue to maintain a robust force posture, and moreover, have established a rapid reinforcement capability to supplement our forces in the Gulf when needed. Our cruise missile force is twice the pre-October 1997 level, a number that can be augmented significantly within days. Our contingency plans allow us the capability for a swift, powerful strike.

The aircraft carrier USS ABRAHAM LINCOLN and accompanying combatant ships and aircraft are on station in the Gulf today. Our forces in the region include land and carrier-based aircraft, surface warships, a Marine expeditionary unit, a Patriot missile battalion, a mechanized battalion task force and a mix of special operations forces deployed in support of USCINCCENT operations. To enhance force protection throughout the region, additional military security personnel are also deployed.

Operation Northern Watch and Operation Southern Watch

The United States and coalition partners continue to enforce the no-fly zones over Iraq under Operation Northern Watch and Operation Southern Watch. There have been no observed no-fly zone violations. However, on June 30, U.S. forces responded to an Iraqi "threat radar" and subsequently defended the coalition forces by firing an anti-radiation (HARM) missile. We have made clear to Iraq and to all other relevant parties that the United States and coalition partners will continue to enforce both no-fly zones. The no-fly zones remain in effect.

The Maritime Interception Force

The Maritime Interception Force (MIF), operating under the authority of UNSC Resolution 665, vigorously enforces U.N. sanctions in the Gulf. The U.S. Navy is the single largest component of this multinational force, but it is frequently augmented by ships and aircraft from Australia, Canada, Belgium, The Netherlands, New Zealand, and the United Kingdom. Today in the Gulf, ships and aircraft from Canada and the United Kingdom are operating with us in maritime patrols. Member states of the Gulf Cooperation Council support the MIF by providing logistical support and shipriders and by accepting vessels diverted for violating U.N. sanctions against Iraq.

The MIF continues to intercept vessels involved in illegal smuggling from Iraq. In late

August, we conducted stepped-up operations in the far northern Gulf in the shallow waters near the major Iraqi waterways. These operations severely disrupted smuggling operations in the region. Since the beginning of the year, over thirty vessels have been detained for violations of the embargo and sent to ports in the Gulf for enforcement actions by the GCC. Kuwait and the UAE, two countries adjacent to the smuggling routes, have also stepped up their enforcement efforts and have recently intercepted and detained vessels involved in sanctions violations. Although petroleum products comprise most of the prohibited traffic, the MIF has recently diverted vessels engaged in date smuggling as well. Smuggling into Iraq is also a target for MIF patrols. One additional difficulty remains in our effort to enforce U.N. sanctions. Ships involved in smuggling have often utilized the territorial seas of Iran to avoid MIF inspections. We have recently provided detailed reports of these illegal activities to the U.N. sanctions Committee in New York.

Chemical Weapons

Despite major progress reported by UNSCOM in accounting for SCUD CBW warheads during this period, the Iraqis have taken a giant step backward by continuing to deny the weaponization of VX nerve agent. This denial is in direct contravention of the finding for UNSCOM by the U.S. Army Edgewood Arsenal of stabilized VX nerve agent in SCUD missile warhead fragments recovered by UNSCOM in Iraq. France and Switzerland are now examining further samples taken in Iraq. They may not report results to UNSCOM until late September.

However, we, UNSCOM Executive Chairman Butler, and a team of international experts gathered by Butler are unanimously confident of the scientific accuracy of the Edgewood results—which Butler has declared publicly. Iraq is lying today about VX.

While the Iraqis provided new documents to help account for R–400 aerial bombs used for chemical weapons, they have failed to provide the needed accounting for missing 155mm mustard-filled shells.

On July 22, 1998, UNSCOM reported in a letter to the President of the Security Council that Iraq had refused to allow an UNSCOM chief inspector to take, or even copy, a document found in Iraqi air force headquarters that gave an accounting of chemical munitions used during the Iran-Iraq war. This document would be of great value in helping UNSCOM establish a true material balance for Iraqi chemical munitions—a mandatory task for UNSCOM. During Butler's aborted visit to Iraq August 3–4, the Iraqi Deputy Prime Minister told Ambassador Butler that Iraq would never give it to the Commission. This evidence directly contradicts the Iraqi claim that it has given UNSCOM all the information it has.

Biological Weapons

In July 1998, UNSCOM assembled yet another group of international experts to meet with Iraqi counterparts for review of Iraqi declarations on the biological weapons program. And again, the Iraqis presented no new material. The experts thus found, again, that Iraq's declarations are not adequate for credible verification. This conclusion covered weapons (SCUD missile BW warheads, R–400 BW bombs, drop-tanks to be filled with BW, and spray devices for BW), production of BW agents (botulinum toxin, anthrax, aflatoxin, and wheat cover smut), and BW agent growth media.

The report of this UNSCOM–250 mission of international experts recommended to the UNSCOM Executive Chairman that no further verification of Iraq's declarations be conducted until Iraq commits itself to provide new and substantive information, stating that any other approach would be counter-productive.

Long-Range Missiles

UNSCOM Executive Chairman Richard Butler reported to the Security Council on August 5 that UNSCOM and Iraq had made significant progress in the accounting of both CBW and conventional SCUD warheads, as well as the material balance of major components for SCUD engine production. However, no progress was reported in accounting for the unique SCUD propellant possessed by Iraq, and the Iraqi Deputy Prime Minister refuses to allow further discussion of Iraq's concealment program, including the hiding of SCUD warheads.

Nuclear Weapons

In an interim report to the UNSC July 29, the IAEA said that Iraq had provided no new information regarding outstanding issues and concerns. The IAEA said while it has a "technically coherent picture" of Iraq's nuclear program, Iraq has never been fully transparent and its lack of transparency compounds remaining uncertainties. The IAEA noted Iraq claims to have no further documentation on such issues as weapons design engineering drawings, experimental data, and drawings received from foreign sources in connection with Iraq's centrifuge enrichment program. The IAEA also reported that Iraq said it was "unsuccessful" in its efforts to locate verifiable documentation of the abandonment of the nuclear program. Iraq has failed to pass the measures required under UNSC Resolution 715 to implement UNSC Resolutions 687, 707 and other relevant resolutions, including the penal laws required to enforce them.

Dual-Use Imports

Resolution 1051 established a joint UNSCOM/IAEA unit to monitor Iraq's imports of allowed dual-use items. Iraq must notify the unit before it imports specific items which can be used in both weapons of mass destruction and civilian applications. Similarly, U.N. members must provide timely notification of exports to Iraq of such dual-use items.

We continue to be concerned that Iraq's land borders are extremely porous. Iraq continues substantial trade with its neighbors. There is significant potential for evasion of sanctions by land routes, giving additional weight to our position that UNSCOM must have full unconditional access to all locations, and be allowed to inspect and monitor Iraqi compliance over time.

Iraq's Concealment Mechanisms

In June, UNSCOM Chairman Butler presented Iraq with a proposed work plan which, had Iraq cooperated, could have moved the process of verifying the disarmament forward. However, when Butler made a return visit August 3–4, the Iraqi Deputy Prime Minister denounced UNSCOM and demanded that UNSCOM report to the Council that Iraq was "disarmed in all areas." On August 5, Iraq announced it was suspending cooperation with UNSCOM and the IAEA. The following day, the Security Council President issued a press statement declaring the Iraqi decision "totally unacceptable," noting that it "contravened" relevant Security Council resolutions.

On August 11, 1998, IAEA Director-General El Baradei wrote to the President of the Security Council that Iraq's August 5 decision to suspend its cooperation with UNSCOM and the

IAEA "makes it impossible for the IAEA . . . to investigate . . . remaining questions and concerns . . .," and that Iraq's decision will allow only "limited implementation" of monitoring that will "fall short of full implementation of the OMV plan and result in a significantly reduced level of assurance" that Iraq is not renewing its programs for weapons of mass destruction.

On August 12, 1998, UNSCOM Executive Chairman Butler sent the President of the Security Council a letter similar to the August 11 letter of the IAEA noted above, saying that "Iraq's actions bring to a halt all of the disarmament activities of the Commission and place limitations on the rights of the Commission to conduct its monitoring operations."

On August 18, the Council President replied to UNSCOM and the IAEA on behalf of the Council, reiterating the full support of the Council for IAEA and UNSCOM to fully implement their mandates and noting that Iraq is obliged to cooperate with them in their activities, including inspections. On August 19, Chairman Butler wrote to the Iraqi government seeking a resumption of the dialogue between UNSCOM and the regime and of all substantive UNSCOM work. That request was immediately rebuffed.

On August 20, the Security Council conducted its periodic review of Iraq's compliance with relevant Security Council resolutions. The Council stated that "the Sanctions Review showed that the necessary conditions do not exist for the modification of the regime" and reiterated that "the decision by Iraq to suspend cooperation with UNSCOM and the IAEA is totally unacceptable." Further, "they view with extreme concern the continuing refusal by the Government of Iraq to rescind its decision."

We continue to work with the Council in its effort to bring about full Iraqi cooperation with UNSCOM and the IAEA. We are now seeking a Council resolution that would suspend further periodic reviews until Iraq reverses course and resumes cooperation with UNSCOM and the IAEA. Iraq's refusal to cooperate is a challenge to the authority of the Security Council and to the credibility of all international weapons nonproliferation efforts, since UNSCOM and the IAEA are responsible to the Security Council for the most thorough arms control regime on earth.

The U.N.'s "Oil-for-Food" Program

We continue to support the international community's efforts to provide for the humanitarian needs of the Iraqi people through the "oil-for-food" program and other humanitarian efforts. Under the last phase of the "oil-for-food" program, which ran from December 3, 1997, through June 2, 1998, $1.1 billion worth of humanitarian goods were approved for export to Iraq. United States companies can participate in "oil-for-food" and over $165 million worth of contracts for U.S. firms have been approved.

Under the current phase of "oil-for-food" Iraq is authorized to sell up to $5.2 billion worth of oil every 180 days, up from $2.0 billion in previous phases. Although the UNSC resolution outlining this program, Resolution 1153, was adopted on February 20, Iraq did not present an acceptable distribution plan for the implementation of Resolution 1153 until May 27, 1998; it was accepted by the U.N. Secretary General on May 29.

Under the current phase of the "oil-for-food" program, 235 contracts for the purchase of humanitarian goods for the Iraqi people have been presented for approval; of these, 162 contracts worth over $562 million have been approved and 13 are on hold pending clarification of questions about the proposed contracts. With regard to oil sales, 50 contracts with a total value of $955 million have been approved so far during this phase.

The United States has supported the repair of the Iraqi oil infrastructure in order to allow sufficient oil to be exported to fund the level of humanitarian purchases the Security Council approved in UNSC Resolution 1153. Treasury is in the process of amending its regulations to allow U.S. companies to bid on oil infrastructure repair contracts just as they are permitted both to purchase Iraqi oil and sell humanitarian goods under the U.N. "oil-for-food" program.

Resolution 1153 maintains the separate program for northern Iraq, administered directly by the U.N. in consultation with the local population. This program, which the United States strongly supports, receives 13 to 15 percent of the funds generated under the "oil-for-food" program. The separate northern program was established because of the Baghdad regime's proven disregard for the humanitarian condition of the Kurdish, Assyrian, and Turkomen minorities of northern Iraq and its readiness to apply the most brutal forms of repression against them. The well-documented series of chemical weapons attacks a decade ago by the government against civilians in the north is only one example of this brutality. In northern Iraq, where Baghdad does not exercise control, the "oil-for-food" program has been able to operate relatively effectively. The Kurdish factions are seeking to set aside their differences to work together so that the UNSC Resolution 1153 is implemented as efficiently as possible.

The U.N. must carefully monitor implementation of Resolution 1153. As the current phase anticipates a doubling of goods flowing into Iraq, including equipment for infrastructure repairs in areas such as oil export capacity, generation of electricity, and water purification, the U.N. faces increasing challenges in monitoring. The Iraqi government continues to insist on the need for rapid lifting of the sanctions regime, despite its clear record of non-compliance with its obligations under relevant U.N. resolutions—a record which was unanimously acknowledged during the Security Council's 39th sanctions review on June 24. We will continue to work with the U.N. Secretariat, the Security Council, and others in the international community to ensure that the humanitarian needs of the Iraqi people are met while denying any political or economic benefits to the Baghdad regime.

The Human Rights Situation in Iraq

The human rights situation throughout Iraq continues to be a cause for grave concern. Particularly troubling are the assassinations of two distinguished Shia clerics—Ayatollah Borujerdi on April 22 and Grand Ayatollah Mirza Ali Gharavi on June 18. These killings have been widely attributed to the Baghdad regime and were followed by an increased security presence in the predominantly Shia cities of south and central Iraq, such as Najaf and Karbala. These events expose a callous disregard for human life and the free exercise of religion. Summary, arbitrary, and extra-judicial executions also remain a primary concern. Baghdad still refuses to allow independent inspections of Iraqi prisons despite the conclusion of U.N. Special Rapporteur for Iraq, Max Van der Stoel, that "there is strong evidence that hundreds of prisoners (were) executed in Abu Graraib and Radwaniyah prisons" late last year. As noted in my last report, based on these reports of summary executions and other ongoing humans rights violations, the U.N.

Human Rights Commission in April issued a strong condemnation of the "all-pervasive repression and oppression" of the Iraqi government. Nevertheless, sources inside Iraq report another wave of executions in June, with about sixty people summarily killed.

In southern Iraq, the government continues to repress the Shia population, destroying the Marsh Arabs' way of life and the unique ecology of the southern marshes. In the north, outside the Kurdish-controlled areas, the government continues the forced expulsion of tens of thousands of ethnic Kurds and Turkomen from Kirkuk and other cities. The government continues to stall and obfuscate attempts to account for more than 600 Kuwaitis and third-country nationals who disappeared at the hands of Iraqi authorities during or after the occupation of Kuwait. The Government of Iraq shows no sign of complying with UNSC Resolution 688, which demands that Iraq cease the repression of its own people.

Northern Iraq: Deepening Engagement

In northern Iraq, the cease-fire between the Kurdish parties, established in November 1997 as the result of U.S. efforts, continues to hold. It is strengthened by growing and effective cooperation between the parties on humanitarian matters, particularly those related to the U.N.'s "oil-for-food" program. Working with the U.N., the Kurds have been able to resolve nutrition and medical problems and look forward to rebuilding their infrastructure as U.N. programs expand. David Welch, Principal Deputy Assistant Secretary of State for Near Eastern Affairs, led a U.S. delegation to the north, July 17–20. He encouraged the Kurds' efforts towards peace; underscored U.S. support for their human rights, physical welfare and safety; and renewed our decades-long engagement with them. During the visit, Massoud Barzani, leader of the Kurdistan Democratic Party (KDP), and Jalal Talabani, leader of the Patriotic Union of Kurdistan (PUK), made positive, forward-looking statements on political reconciliation, and they accepted separate invitations to visit the United States later this year.

The United States firmly supports the territorial integrity of Iraq. Supporting the rights and welfare of Iraqi Kurds within Iraq in no way contradicts that support. The United States is committed to ensuring that international aid continues to get through to the north, that the human rights of the Kurds and northern Iraq minority groups, such as the Turkomen, Assyrians, Yezedis and others are respected, and that the no-fly zone enforced by Operation Northern Watch is observed.

We will continue our efforts to reach a permanent reconciliation through mediation in order to help the people of northern Iraq find the permanent, stable settlement they deserve, and to minimize the influence of either Baghdad or Tehran. Baghdad continues to pressure the two groups to enter into negotiations.

The Iraqi Opposition

It is the policy of the U.S. Government to support the Iraqi opposition by establishing unifying programs on which all of the opposition can agree. Section 10008 of the 1998 Supplemental Appropriations and Rescissions Act (P.L. 105–174), earmarks $5 million in FY 98 Economic Support Funds for these programs. These programs are designed to encourage and assist political opposition groups, nonpartisan opposition groups, and unaffiliated Iraqis concerned about their nation's future in peacefully espousing democracy, pluralism, human rights, and the rule of law for their country. Based on extensive consultations with opposition leaders and representatives, we have found a deep resonance on several central themes. These are: building a consensus on the transition from dictatorship to pluralism, conveying to the U.N. opposition views on Iraqi noncompliance with U.N. resolutions and compiling information to support indictment of Iraqi officials for war crimes.

Iraq is a diverse country—ethnically, religiously, and culturally. The Iraqi opposition reflects this diversity. We emphasize themes and programs, rather than individuals and groups, in order to encourage unity and discourage the rivalries which have divided the opposition in the past. Many opposition political groups that formerly coordinated their efforts decided several years ago to work independently. We are interested in working with them towards greater unity on their own terms, not enforcing the issue by declaring that any one group must take the lead. We firmly believe they can succeed in this effort.

We anticipate that there will be a need for additional funding for these programs as the opposition becomes more active and as it grows. The funds will be administered by the Department of State working through established NGOs, Federal institutions, and comparable private organizations. To ensure transparency and accountability and to avoid creating potential rivalries among opposition groups, none of these funds will go directly to any opposition group.

The United Nations Compensation Commission

The United Nations Compensation Commission (UNCC), established pursuant to UNSC Resolutions 687 and 692, continues to resolve claims against Iraq arising from Iraq's unlawful invasion and occupation of Kuwait. The UNCC has issued over 1.3 million awards worth approximately $7 billion. Thirty percent of the proceeds from the oil sales permitted by UNSC Resolution 986, 1111, 1143, and 1153 have been allocated to the Compensation Fund to pay awards and to finance operations of the UNCC. To the extent that money is available in the Compensation Fund, initial payments to each claimant are authorized for awards in the order in which the UNCC has approved them, in installments of $2,500. To date, 809 U.S. claimants have received an initial installment payment, and payment is still in process for another 25 U.S. claimants.

Conclusion

Iraq remains a serious threat to international peace and security. I remain determined to see Iraq comply fully with all of its obligations under UNSC resolutions. The United States looks forward to the day when Iraq rejoins the family of nations as a responsible and law-abiding member.

I appreciate the support of the Congress for our efforts and shall continue to keep the Congress informed about this important issue.

Sincerely,

WILLIAM J. CLINTON

NOTE: Identical letters were sent to Newt Gingrich, Speaker of the House of Representatives, and Strom Thurmond, President pro tempore of the Senate.

Remarks to a Gathering for Peace in Armagh, Northern Ireland
September 3, 1998

Thank you. Thank you for the wonderful welcome. I am very, very proud to be the first American President to visit Armagh. Thank you for making Hillary and me feel so welcome tonight.

I thank Mayor Turner; my good friend Prime Minister Blair, who will speak in a moment. I thank First Minister Trimble and First Deputy Minister Seamus Mallon for their remarks and their leadership, the role-modeling they are doing by working together for a peace for all the people of Northern Ireland. I think we should give them both a big hand for that. [*Applause*] I thank them.

There are other members of the Assembly here tonight who represent surrounding areas, Paul Berry, Danny Kennedy, Pat McNamee, Conor Murphy, John Fee. We thank them for their service in Northern Ireland's new Assembly, the hope for its peaceful future.

I also would like to say a special word of appreciation to the remarkable young woman who introduced me, Sharon Haughey. I'll never forget the letter she wrote me in 1995. A 14-year-old girl, in the midst of all this violence, said "Both sides have been hurt. Both sides will have to forgive." It was so simple, so profound, that I quoted it when I came here 3 years ago. Well, she's grown up to be quite an impressive young 17-year-old, and I was very honored to have her here tonight as the symbol of what Northern Ireland can become if you put away war and take up peace forever. Thank you, Sharon.

I'd like to thank the wonderful choir who sang for us a few moments ago. I would like to thank the members of our delegation, the Secretaries of Education and Commerce, and 12 Members of the United States Congress from both parties, for coming here.

You know, many United States Presidents' ancestors actually came to America from Northern Ireland. Andrew Jackson's father was from Cerrick Fergis in County Antrim. Woodrow Wilson's grandfather left Dergalt in County Tyrone. My ancestors were so humble, everyone knows they came from somewhere in Northern Ireland, and no one is quite sure where. [*Laughter*] Most believe the 18th century Cassadys, my mother's people, were from County Fermanagh. Most believe that those people were my forebears, and I have a painted watercolor of an 18th century farmhouse on our wall at the White House to prove it. The truth is, I can't be sure, so I'll save all the genealogists a lot of trouble by saying, wherever I am tonight, it is good to be home in Northern Ireland.

I am especially proud to be here with my wife at this important time. Yesterday she spoke to the Vital Voices conference, hundreds of women from Northern Ireland, working across all the lines that divide you, for a better future. Tonight we are proud to be in a place that is a spiritual home to Irish people of both religious traditions and to millions of Irish-Americans as well.

Armagh is a city on a hill in every sense. Your faith and tolerance are making a new era of peace possible. For yourselves and all the world, in every act of genuine reconciliation, you renew confidence that decency can triumph over hatred. You have inspired the rest of us to aim a little higher. I thank you, and America thanks you for the precious gift you give us all, a gift of hope redeemed and faith restored.

Indeed, I am tempted in this city of saints and cathedrals to call the peace of 1998 a miracle. After all, it was delivered through the agency of that good American angel, Senator George Mitchell, who is here. It was delivered on Good Friday.

Nonetheless, I think you would all agree that, at least in the normal sense in which we use the word, the peace of Good Friday was not a miracle. You did it yourselves. It rose from the public's passionate demand to take a different course. It came about from the hard work of leaders like those who are on this stage, from David Trimble and Seamus Mallon, from the leaders of the other parties, from Tony Blair and the Irish Prime Minister, as well. It came from honest debate. And again, it came loud and clear from an overwhelming vote of the people for peace. It is you who have told your leaders that you long for peace as never before. You gave them the confidence to move forward, to give up the past, and speak the language of the future.

Armagh has stood for these better aspirations throughout its long history. If there is a recurring theme to this seat of learning and religion, it is the largeness of the human spirit. Here, a Briton, Saint Patrick, devoted himself to the cause of Ireland and left a legacy of faith and compassion. Here, the Book of Armagh preserved his gentle message and the power of the gospels.

Today, the two cathedrals that dominate the landscape stand for the idea that communion is better than destructive competition. Two proud traditions can exist side by side, bringing people closer to God and closer to each other. I salute the leadership of Dr. Sean Brady and Dr. Robin Eames, the Archbishops of the Catholic and the Church of Ireland dioceses, respectively. For years they have walked together when it counted. I salute the Presbyterians and the Methodists who have worked hard for peace, indeed, the men and women of all denominations.

Here, there have been difficulties, as elsewhere, but the historic streets of this old town remind us of a fundamental fact about your community: Armagh literally encircles its many traditions in a single community. That is what Northern Ireland must do if you want the future of peace and prosperity that belongs to the children in this crowd tonight.

As you look ahead, to be sure, in this peace process, there will be false steps and disappointments. The question is not if the peace will be challenged; you know it will. The question is, how will you respond when it is challenged? You don't have to look too far. The bomb that tore at the heart of Omagh was a blatant attack on all of Northern Ireland's people who support peace.

The Prime Minister and Mrs. Blair and Hillary and I just came from Omagh. We met with the families whose innocents were slaughtered. We met with those who were terribly wounded. We saw children scarred, some of them for life, because of the madness that, if someone could just set off a big enough bomb and kill enough Protestants and Catholics, kill enough men, women, and children, including two pregnant women, kill enough people from Northern Ireland, Ireland, and foreign countries, that maybe everybody would walk away from peace.

But it backfired. Out of the unimaginably horrible agony of Omagh, the people said, "It is high time somebody told these people that we are through with hate, through with war, through with destruction. It will not work anymore."

Think of what it will be like when everyone forever can simply walk freely through Armagh with no anxiety about what street you walk down or with whom you talk. Think how beautiful this city can be without any barbed wire and never a thought of a burned church. Peace brings peace of mind and prosperity and new friends eager to see this historic and compelling land for the first time. People once were afraid to come to Armagh and Northern Ireland. Now they will be hard pressed to stay away.

We wanted to come here in person to thank you, to thank you for the peace, to thank you for strengthening the hand of everyone, everyone anywhere who is working to make the world a little better.

When I go now to other troubled places, I point to you as proof that peace is not an idle daydream, for your peace is real, and it resonates around the world. It echoes in the ears of people hungry for the end of strife in their own country. Now, when I meet Palestinians and Israelis, I can say, "Don't tell me it's impossible. Look at Northern Ireland." When I meet Albanians and Serbs in Kosovo, I can say, "Don't tell me it's impossible. Look at Northern Ireland." When I hear what the Indians and Pakistanis say about each other over their religious differences, I say, "Don't tell me you can't work this out. Look at Northern Ireland." Centuries were put to bed, and a new day has dawned. Thank you for that gift to the world.

And never underestimate the impact you can have on the world. The great English poet and clergyman, John Donne, wrote those famous lines: "No man is an island. We are all a piece of the continent, a part of the main." Tonight we might even say, in this interconnected world, not even an island, not even a very unique island, not even Ireland is fully an island.

On this island, Northern Ireland obviously is connected in ways to the Republic, as well as to England, Scotland, and Wales, and in ways, the Republic of Ireland is connected to them also. All of you on this island increasingly are connected to Europe and to the rest of the world, as ideas and information and people fly across the globe at record speeds. We are tied ever closer together, and we have obligations now that we cannot shirk, to stand for the cause of human dignity everywhere.

To continue John Donne's beautiful metaphor, when the bells of Armagh toll, they ring out not just to the Irish of Protestant and Catholic traditions. They ring out to people everywhere in the world who long for peace and freedom and dignity. That is your gift.

We Americans will do what we can to support the peace, to support economic projects, to support education projects. Tomorrow the Secretary of Education will announce a cooperative effort here to help children bring peace by doing cross-community civic projects. We know we have an obligation to you because your ancestors were such a source of strength in America's early history. Because their descendants are building America's future today, because of all that, we have not forgotten our debt to Ulster. But we really owe an obligation to you because none of us are islands; we are all now a part of the main.

Three years ago I pledged that if you chose peace, America would walk with you. You made the choice, and America will honor its pledge.

Thank you for the springtime of hope you have given the world. Thank you for reminding us of one of life's most important lessons, that it is never too late for a new beginning. And remember, you will be tested again and again, but a God of grace has given you a new beginning. Now you must make the most of it, mindful of President Kennedy's adage that "Here on Earth, God's work must truly be our own."

Your work is the world's work. And everywhere, in every corner, there are people who long to believe in our better selves, who want to be able to say for the rest of their lives, in the face of any act of madness born of hatred over religious, or racial, or ethnic or tribal differences, they want to be able to shake their fists in defiance and say, "Do not tell me it has to be this way. Look at Northern Ireland."

Thank you, and God bless you.

NOTE: The President spoke at 8 p.m. at the Mall of Armagh. In his remarks, he referred to Mayor Robert Turner; Prime Minister Tony Blair of the United Kingdom and his wife, Cherie; First Minister David Trimble and Deputy First Minister Seamus Mallon of the Northern Ireland Assembly; former Senator George J. Mitchell, independent chairman of the multiparty talks in Northern Ireland; and Prime Minister Bertie Ahern of Ireland.

Exchange With Reporters Prior to Discussions With Prime Minister Bertie Ahern of Ireland in Dublin
September 4, 1998

Senator Joseph I. Lieberman's Remarks

Q. Mr. President, do you have any comments on Senator Lieberman's remarks?

The President. I've been briefed on them, and basically I agree with what he said. I've already said that I made a bad mistake, it was indefensible, and I'm sorry about it. So I have nothing else to say except that I can't disagree with anyone else who wants to be critical of what I have already acknowledged was indefensible.

Q. Do you think the Senate is the right format for——

The President. That's not for me to say. That's not for me to say. I don't—I've known Senator Lieberman a long time. We've worked together on a lot of things. And I'm not going to get into commenting on that, one way or the other.

That's not—it wouldn't be an appropriate thing for me to do.

Q. But do you think it's helpful for him to make that kind of——

The President. It's not for me to say. But there's nothing that he or anyone else could say in a personally critical way that I—that I don't imagine that I would disagree with, since I have already said it myself, to myself. And I'm very sorry about it. There's nothing else I could say.

Q. Mr. President, do you think an official censure by the Senate would be inappropriate?

The President. I just don't want to comment on that. I shouldn't be commenting on that while I'm on this trip, and I don't think that—my understanding is that was not a decision that was made or advocated clearly yesterday.

So I don't want to get into that. If that's not an issue, I don't want to make it, one way or the other. I don't think that's appropriate right now.

Northern Ireland Peace Process

Q. Mr. President, it usually seems to take a visit from you to give the peace process a boost. Will we need to see you again?

The President. Well, for the sake of the peace process, I hope not. For my own sake, I hope so. But I hope the next time I come it won't be in aid of the peace process, because I hope it will be institutionalized and off and going.

I do think that a lot of progress has been made. I give the *Taoiseach* a lot of credit, Prime Minister Blair, and the party leaders. I think the statements in the last few days by Gerry Adams and Mr. Trimble's response make me quite hopeful about next week. And then, after that, we'll just have to see where we go from there.

Q. Mr. President, do you believe that from what you've heard from political leaders yesterday that David Trimble is now ready to sit down with Gerry Adams in government in Northern Ireland?

The President. Well, first of all, they talked about meeting, and I think they need—I expect that at some point there will be a meeting, and I think that's a good thing. And then, we'll have to take the next steps. I think that what you want is—what we all want is for the agreement to be fully implemented so that all parts of it—the decommissioning, the participation in government by everyone who qualifies by vote of the people—all parts of it will be fully implemented. And I think that eventually it will get there, and I hope it's sooner rather than later.

Q. Mr. President, what were your views of Omagh yesterday? It was a very emotional day. You seemed to work the crowd so well; you spent a lot of time meeting those people there yesterday. What were your feelings?

The President. Well, first of all, like everyone in the world that knew about it, I was just overwhelmed by the dimension of the tragedy and the random, cruel nature of the violence. And my experience has been, dealing with the families who have suffered a similar fate, is that they know there's nothing you can do to bring their loved ones back or bring their limbs back or give them sight or whatever else the problem may be. But sometimes just listening to people's

story and letting them say what they hope will happen next, in many cases yesterday letting them reaffirm their belief in the peace, sometimes that helps.

And what I was hoping to do yesterday was to bring the support of the people of the United States as well as my own and Hillary's to the families there and just give them a chance to continue the healing process.

I must say I was very, very impressed with the people of the community, who turned out, on the street where the bomb had exploded, in large numbers to say hello to us and to encourage us. And I'm grateful for that. But it was an amazing experience talking to those families in the building there and just listening to them.

Q. You were clearly moved by it.

The President. Anyone would have been.

Q. Mr. President, where do you rank the Northern Ireland peace process among the policy initiatives you've pursued in office?

The President. Oh, I don't know about ranking. It was important to me. Once I realized that there was something the United States could do, which probably happened somewhere in late 1991, long before I was elected, I decided I would try. And I just hope it succeeds.

I believe that—at the end of the cold war, I think the United States has a particular responsibility, that goes beyond my personal passion for the Irish question, to do two things. One is to do whatever we can, wherever we can, to try to minimize the impact of ethnic and religious and tribal and racial conflicts. And we're in this position of responsibility there because of where we find ourselves at the end of the cold war.

In addition to that, I think we have a particular responsibility to try to organize the world against the new security threats of the 21st century, the terrorism and narcotraffickers, the potential for the spread of weapons of mass destruction. And I have tried to do that.

I don't suspect that either of those jobs will be completely done in 2001 when I leave office, but at least the world will be on the way to having a framework to deal with both the opportunities for peace and the challenges to security. And I think you have to see the Irish question in that context, apart from my personal feelings about it. Because if you, all of you—the Prime Minister of Great Britain and the *Taoiseach* and the Irish party leaders—if you're able to make this peace go, as I said in Armagh yesterday, then we can say to the places—to the Middle East, we can say in the Aegean, we can say in the Indian subcontinent, we can say in the tribal strife of Africa, "Look at this thing that happened in Northern Ireland. There's the Troubles for 30 years, but there were conflicts for hundreds of years. This can be done."

And so the potential impact of resolving this could wash over many more people than just those that live on this island.

Military Action Against Terrorist Sites

Q. Mr. President, how do you reconcile the peaceful strides you've made in the Northern process with your foreign policy and your reaction to the threat of Islamic militants and the airstrikes on Afghanistan and Sudan?

The President. Well, I think you have to, first of all, look at what happened in the Middle East and here. In the Middle East and here, I have worked hard to get people to turn away from terror toward a peace process, not just the Irish parties that had once participated in violence, but in the Middle East it's the same. The PLO has moved away from violence towards the peace process.

The problem with the bombings in our Embassies in Africa is that they were carried out by an operation which does not belong to a nation and does not have a claim or a grievance against the particular nation that it wants to resolve so that it can be part of a normal civic life. It is an organization without that kind of political agenda. Its agenda is basically to strike out against the United States, against the West, against the people in the Middle East it doesn't like. And it is funded entirely from private funds under the control of Usama bin Ladin, without the kind of objectives that we see that, even on the darkest days, the Irish parties that were violent had, the PLO had.

So it's an entirely different thing. And I think it's quite important that people see it as different, because one of the things that we have to fight against is having the world's narcotraffickers tie up with these multinational or non-national global terrorist groups in a way that will provide a threat to every country in the world. It's just an entirely different situation.

Northern Ireland Peace Process

Q. Taoiseach, how important was the President to the developments that took place earlier

this week which seemed to have injected a new momentum into the peace process?

Prime Minister Ahern. They were immensely important, because even if Omagh never happened and the terrible tragedy that it was, in early September we had to focus back, preparing for the next meeting of the Assembly, for heading on to preparations for the executive North-South Council and all of the other aspects of the agreement. And we needed to focus very clearly on those. And what the President's visit has done is, it has got the parties to, I think, move what might have taken weeks and months over a very short period, because they looked at the agenda that was set before us, and they've made the moves.

Now, there are clearly more moves to be made. And I think what the President said in Armagh last night, we would totally agree with in the Irish Government, because I think he's laying down for us and for all of us that there is a path to follow. If we are sensible, if we're brave, and then we follow that path, the reward is peace and stability and confidence. If we don't, well, then the future is as gloomy as the past.

And I just believe that this visit at this time, it has been immensely important. It's given confidence to us all, I think, to move on. It's given confidence, I think, to the Unionist Party and Sinn Fein to make moves that are brave and efficient to the process. And we're very grateful not only for this visit, not only for the last visit, but the fact that this President of the United States has given us an enormous amount of time, a huge amount of support, and an enormous amount of encouragement to move forward. And we're very grateful for that.

Q. How will history judge his role, President Clinton's role in the Northern Ireland peace process?

Prime Minister Ahern. Well, I always say, President Carter and U.S. Presidents—and successive Presidents and administrations have taken an interest in affairs, and a supportive interest. But the facts are, never before have we had such intense and sustained contact from the United States President, and that in a period when we desperately need it to be able to move forward. I said, I think, in Washington last March that maybe it was the luck of the Irish, but we don't take it for granted, and we're very grateful for it.

NOTE: The exchange began at 11:12 a.m. in the Office of the *Taoiseach*. In his remarks, the President referred to Sinn Fein leader Gerry Adams; First Minister David Trimble of the Northern Ireland Assembly; Prime Minister Tony Blair of the United Kingdom; and Usama bin Ladin, who allegedly sponsored terrorist attacks on the U.S. Embassies in Kenya and Tanzania. A tape was not available for verification of the content of this exchange.

Remarks at a Reception With Community Leaders in Dublin
September 4, 1998

Thank you. Thank you, *Taoiseach*, Celia, ladies and gentlemen. Hillary and I and all of our American delegation are delighted to be here. I've been looking out in the crowd, and I see some Americans who have swelled the ranks even since I arrived in Ireland. Anytime we can pad your crowd, *Taoiseach*, we want to do that. [*Laughter*]

I'd like to thank the Royal College of Surgeons for making it possible for us to be here and for setting a standard for international excellence. I know there are now students from over 40 nations here at this distinguished institution.

If you would permit, before I get into my prepared remarks, I think that, for the benefit of the Americans here and because it's my only chance to talk to the press, I would like to make just a couple of comments on the terrible tragedy of the crashing of Swissair Flight 111.

The victims, their families, their friends are very much in our thoughts and prayers. A very large number of those victims were American citizens, but also a large number were Europeans. And if you've been reading about it, you know that. It now appears that there were no survivors in what is the worst tragedy in the history of Swissair, with its very fine record. I have been fully briefed on the extensive efforts under way to recover the victims and to uncover what happened. And we will continue to do whatever we can to support the truly extraordinary efforts of the Canadian authorities. And I want to thank them for what they have done.

Just for right now, I would like to ask all of you in your own way, if we could, just to take a moment to reflect in silence on this tragedy and on any senseless loss of life and ask that the families of the people who were killed be strengthened at this moment. Thank you very much.

[*At this point, a moment of silence was observed.*]

Amen. Thank you.

Let me say to all of you, it's great to be back in Dublin. Even though there is a little rain in the air today, it's always bright and sunny for me here. The day that we were in College Green, in 1995, will go down for me as one of the great days of my Presidency and, indeed, one of the great days of my life.

But these days have been good as well, working to cement the peace process. And I can't say enough about the role of the *Taoiseach* in making this Irish peace process come to fruition. I want to say a little more about it later in specific terms as we look ahead, but I just want to say to all you, you can be very proud of his leadership, as well as your own overwhelming vote for peace a few months ago.

I'd also like to thank Ireland for setting a good example by building bridges to other nations by being such an open economy, by encouraging business ventures from around the world, and by working together here at home.

We were talking, before we came in, about this whole concept of social partners and how all the elements of Irish society have worked together to give you what is, I believe, the highest growth rate in Europe now, of any country of Europe, because you have worked together to draw out the strengths of every element of this society and to minimize conflict.

And all I can say is, I hope there will be more of this in the years ahead. I hope that success will whet your appetite for working together instead of causing, as success sometimes does, people to forget what brought them to the point of success. Because the Irish story is a truly astonishing, astonishing thing that I believe can be a model for nations large and small throughout the world.

There has literally never been a better time, I don't suppose, to be Irish because of the economic success; because of the renaissance in writing, filmmaking; because of what so many people are doing in so many ways to advance the cause of peace. Of course, for me, your overwhelming vote for peace and your constant leadership for the peace process over the last several years are the most important things. And I would like to thank you, on behalf of the American people, for what you have done.

I can also say that—to Prime Minister Ahern, that peace literally would not have happened, in my judgment, if it hadn't been for him. He led a campaign sometimes under great personal duress. His pleas for peace began early in his service. He has been fair and open. He has been terrifically effective in working with Prime Minister Blair and all the parties in both communities. There are many people from many backgrounds who deserve a lot of credit for this peace, including George Mitchell, whose name was mentioned earlier, but none more than Bertie Ahern. And I thank him for that.

The last time I saw the *Taoiseach* I believe was on St. Patrick's Day in Washington. He always comes there and gives me my shamrocks and puts me in a good frame of mind. [*Laughter*] And then we always have a celebration at the White House in the evening, and everybody is in a good frame of mind. [*Laughter*] But we were especially happy this St. Patrick's Day because the sense of peace was in the air. We thought there was a real possibility for all that has happened to occur.

We now know, from the tragedy of Omagh and from those three small boys that were killed, that there will be those who test the peace, who do not want to move into tomorrow, who are literally trapped in the patterns, the hatreds, the mindset of yesterday. I think the most important thing that Hillary and I saw in Omagh yesterday was that even the people who have suffered the most from the testers of the peace don't want to give in to them.

They don't want to give in. They don't want to go back. They want to summon their strength and courage and lean on their friends and neighbors and go forward.

So the most important thing I can say to you here today is, I hope you will continue to be a model for the world in responsible citizenship. Ireland—there hasn't been a day in the last 40 years that some citizen of this great country has not been abroad in another land working for the cause of peace. I hope you will continue to be a model of an open economy, where people work together, instead of fight with each other, to increase wealth, employment, opportunity, and social harmony. And I hope you will continue to labor for peace here because, if we can complete this peace process, as I said to the citizens of Armagh yesterday, you can't imagine what it will enable the United States to do in trying to stand up for peace in other parts of the world where people have fought over their religious, their racial, their ethnic, their tribal differences. I can always then say, "No, no, no, look at Ireland," when they tell me it can't be done.

So please know that the rest of the world has an enormous stake in the way your society conducts itself, in your economic success, in your social harmony, and in your passion for peace. So far, you are doing much better than any of the rest of us could ever have dreamed or hoped for, and the world is in your debt.

The United States is proud of our Irish ties, and I am personally extremely grateful for what has been done here in these last few years.

Thank you very, very much.

NOTE: The President spoke at 1:05 p.m. at the Royal College of Surgeons. In his remarks, he referred to Prime Minister Bertie Ahern of Ireland; Celia Larkin, who accompanied Prime Minister Ahern; Prime Minister Tony Blair of the United Kingdom; and former Senator George J. Mitchell, independent chairman of the multiparty talks in Northern Ireland.

Remarks to Employees at Gateway, Inc., in Santry, Ireland
September 4, 1998

Thank you for the wonderful welcome, the waving flag, the terrific shirts. I want one of those shirts before I leave. At least shirts have not become virtual; you can actually have one of them. [*Laughter*]

I want to say to the *Taoiseach* how very grateful I am for his leadership and friendship. But I must say that I was somewhat ambivalent when we were up here giving our virtual signatures. Do you have any idea how much time I spend every day signing my name? I'm going to feel utterly useless if I can't do that anymore. [*Laughter*] By the time you become the leader of a country, someone else makes all the decisions; you just sign your name. [*Laughter*] You may find you can get away with virtual Presidents, virtual Prime Ministers, virtual everything. Just stick a little card in and get the predictable response.

I want to congratulate Baltimore Technologies on making this possible, as well. And Ted Waitt, let me thank you for the tour of this wonderful facility. As an American, I have to do one little chauvinist thing. I asked Ted—I saw the Gateway—do you see the Gateway boxes over there and the Gateway logo, and I got a Gateway golf bag before I came in, and it was black and white like this. So I said, "Where did this logo come from?" And he said, "It's spots on a cow." He said, "We started in South Dakota and Iowa and people said, 'How can there be a computer company in the farmland of America?'" And now there is one in the farmland of America that happens to be in Ireland. [*Laughter*]

But it's a wonderful story that shows the point I want to make later, which is that there is no monopoly on brain power anywhere. There have always been intelligent people everywhere, in the most underinvested and poorest parts of the world. Today, on the streets of the poorest neighborhoods in the most crowded country in the world—which is probably India—in the cities, there are brilliant people who need a chance.

And technology, if we handle it right, will be one of the great liberating and equalizing forces in all of human history, because it proves that, unlike previous economic waves, you could be on a small farm in Iowa or South Dakota or you could be in a country like Ireland, long underinvested in by outsiders, and all of a sudden open the whole world up. And you can prove that people you can find on any street corner can master the skills of tomorrow. So this is a very happy day.

I want to thank the other officials from the Irish Government, Minister Harney and Minister O'Rourke and others. I thank my great Commerce Secretary, Bill Daley, for being here, and Jim Lyons, who heads my economic initiatives for Ireland, and Ambassador Jean Kennedy Smith, who has done a magnificent job for us and will soon be going home after having played a major role in getting the peace process started, and we thank her.

I thank you all personally for the warm reception you gave George Mitchell, because you have no idea how much grief he gave me for giving him this job. [*Laughter*] You all voted for the agreement now, and everything is basically going in the right direction, but it was like pulling fingernails for 3 years; everybody arguing over every word, every phrase, every semicolon, you know? In the middle of that, George Mitchell was not all that happy that I had asked him to undertake this duty.

But when you stood up and you clapped for him today, for the first time since I named him, he looked at me and said, "Thank you." So thank you again. You made my day.

I'd also like to thank your former Prime Minister and *Taoiseach*, John Bruton, who's here and who also worked with us on the peace process. Thank you, John, for coming; it's delightful to see you. And I would like for you to know that there are a dozen Members of the United States Congress here, from both parties, showing that we have reached across our own divide to support peace and prosperity in Ireland. And I thank all the Members of Congress, and I'd like to ask them to stand up, just so you'll see how many there are here. Thank you very much.

I know that none of the Irish here will be surprised when I tell you that a recent poll of American intellectuals decided that the best English language novel of the 20th century was a book set in Dublin, written by an Irishman, in Trieste and Zurich, and first published in New York and Paris, a metaphor of the world in which we now live. James Joyce's "Ulysses" was the product of many cultures, but it remains a deeply Irish work.

Some of you will remember that, near the beginning of the book, Joyce wrote, "History is a nightmare from which I am trying to awake." Much of Irish history, of course, is rich and warm and wonderful, but we all know it has its nightmarish aspects. They are the ones from which Ireland is now awakening, thanks to those who work for peace and thanks to those who bring prosperity.

Much of Ireland's new history, of course, will be shaped by the Good Friday peace agreement. You all, from your response to Senator Mitchell, are knowledgeable of it and proud of it, and I thank you for voting for it in such overwhelming numbers in the Republic.

I think it's important that you know it's a step forward not only for Irish people but for all people divided, everywhere, who are seeking new ways to think about old problems, who want to believe that they don't forever have to be at the throats of those with whom they share a certain land just because they are of a different faith or race or ethnic group or tribe. The leaders and the people of Ireland and Northern Ireland, therefore, are helping the world to awaken from history's nightmares.

Today, Ireland is quite an expansive place, with a positive outlook on the world. The 1990's have changed this country in profound and positive ways. Not too long ago, Ireland was a poor country by European standards, inward-looking, sometimes insular.

Today, as much as any country in Europe, Ireland is connected, in countless ways, to the rest of the world, as Ted showed me when we moved from desk to desk to desk downstairs with the people who were talking to France and the people who were talking to Germany and the people who were talking to Scandinavia and on and on and on.

This country has strong trade relations with Britain and the United States, with countries of the European Union and beyond. And Ireland, as we see here at this place, is fast becoming a technological capital of Europe. Innovative information companies are literally transforming the way the Irish interact and communicate with other countries. That is clear here, perhaps clearer here than anywhere else, at Gateway, a company speaking many languages and most of all the language of the future. Gateway and other companies, like Intel and Dell and Digital, are strengthening Ireland's historic links to the United States and reaching out beyond.

I think it is very interesting, and I was not aware of this before I prepared for this trip, that Dublin is literally becoming a major telecommunications center for all of Europe. More and more Europeans do business on more and more telephones, and more and more of their calls are routed through here. You connect people and businesses in every combination: a German housewife, a French computer company, a Czech businessman, a Swedish investor, people all around Europe learning to do business on the Internet.

At the hub of this virtual commerce is Ireland, a natural gateway for the future also of such commerce between Europe and the United States. In the 21st century, after years and years and years of being disadvantaged because of what was most important to the production of wealth, Ireland will have its day in the Sun because the most important thing in the 21st century is the capacity of people to imagine, to innovate, to create, to exchange ideas and information. By those standards, this is a very wealthy nation indeed.

Your growth has been phenomenal: last year, 7.7 percent; prices rising at only 1½ percent; unemployment at a 20-year low. Ireland is second only to the United States in exporting software. This year the Irish Government may post a surplus of $1.7 billion. The Celtic tiger is roaring, and you should be very proud of it.

It has been speculated, half seriously, that there are more foreigners here than at any time since the Vikings pillaged Ireland in the 9th century. [Laughter] I guess I ought to warn you—you know, whenever a delegation of Congressmen comes to Ireland they all claim to be Irish—and in a certain way they all are— but one of the Members of the delegation here, Congressman Hoyer, who has been a great friend of the peace process, is in fact of Viking heritage, descent. [Laughter] And he said— stand up, Steny. Now, all the rest of us come here and pander to you and tell you we love Ireland because there is so much Irish blood running in our veins. He comes here and says he loves Ireland because there is so much of his blood running in your veins. [Laughter]

Let me get back to what I was saying about the Internet because your position vis-a-vis telecommunication can be seen through that. When I came here just 3 years ago—had one of the great days of my life; there was so much hope about the peace process then—only 3 million people worldwide were connected to the Internet, 3 years ago. Today, there are over 120 million people, a 40-fold increase in 3 years. In the next decade sometime, it will be over a billion. Already, if you travel, you can see the impact of this in Russia or in China or other far-flung places around the globe.

I had an incredible experience in one of these Internet cafes in Shanghai, where I met with young high school students in China working the Internet. Even if they didn't have computers at home, they could come to the cafe, buy a cup of coffee, rent a little time, and access the Internet. This is going to change dramatically the way we work and live. It is going to democratize opportunity in the world in a way that has never been the case in all of human history. And if we are wise and decent about it, we can not only generate more wealth, we can reduce future wars and conflicts.

The agreement that we signed today does some important things. It commits us to reduce unnecessary regulatory barriers, to refrain from imposing customs duties, to keep taxes to a minimum, to create a stable and predictable environment for doing business electronically. It helps us, in other words, to create an architecture for one of the most important areas of business activity in the century ahead.

There are already 470 companies in Ireland that are American, and many of them are in the information sector. The number is growing quickly. So I say to you that I think this agreement we have signed today and the way we have signed it will not only be helpful in and of themselves but will stand for what I hope will be the future direction of your economy and America's, the future direction of our relationship, and will open a massive amount of opportunity to ordinary people who never would have had it before.

A strong modern economy thrives on education, innovation, respect for the interests of workers and customers, and a respect for the Earth's environment. An enlightened population is our best investment in a good future. Prosperity reinforces peace as well. The Irish have long championed prosperity, peace, and human decency, and for all that, I am very grateful.

I would like to just say, because I can't leave Ireland without acknowledging this, that there are few nations that have contributed more than Ireland, even in times which were difficult for this country, to the cause of peace and human rights around the world. You have given us now Mary Robinson to serve internationally in that cause. But since peacekeeping began for the United Nations 40 years ago, 75 Irish soldiers have given their lives. Today, we work shoulder-to-shoulder in Bosnia and the Middle East. But I think you should know that, as nearly as I can determine, in the 40 years in which the world has been working together on peacekeeping, the only country in the world which has never taken a single, solitary day off from the cause of world peace to the United Nations peacekeeping operations is Ireland. And I thank you.

In 1914, on the verge of the First World War, which would change Europe and Ireland forever, William Butler Yeats wrote his famous line, "In dreams begins responsibility." Ireland has moved from nightmares to dreams. Ireland has assumed great responsibility. As a result, you are moving toward permanent peace, remarkable prosperity, unparalleled influence, and a brighter tomorrow for your children. May the nightmares stay gone, the dreams stay bright, and the responsibilities wear easily on your shoulder, because the future is yours.

Thank you, and God bless you.

NOTE: The President spoke at 4:12 p.m. on the factory floor. In his remarks, he referred to Ted Waitt, chief executive officer, Gateway, Inc.; Deputy Prime Minister Mary Harney and Minister for Public Enterprise Mary O'Rourke of Ireland; former Senator George J. Mitchell, independent chairman of the multiparty talks in Northern Ireland; and U.N. High Commissioner for Human Rights Mary Robinson, former President of Ireland.

Message on the Observance of Labor Day, 1998
September 4, 1998

For more than a century, we have set aside this time each year to pay tribute to America's working men and women. We honor the heroes of our past, who built our great cities, bridges, and railways; who cleared the fields and plowed the farms to feed our nation and the world; who climbed down mine shafts and up the skeletons of skyscrapers to keep America growing. We honor those men and women of conscience who fought for fair wages, decent working conditions, and equal opportunity for all.

And we honor workers across America today, who are the heart of our nation and the engine of our dynamic economy. In large part because of their efforts, productivity, and commitment to excellence, our nation is enjoying unprecedented growth and prosperity. Our economy is the best it has been in a generation. Inflation and unemployment are at their lowest levels in nearly 30 years, while real wages are growing at the fastest rate in a quarter-century.

Yet, in the spirit of those who came before us, we must not become self-satisfied or complacent. As we celebrate Labor Day, let us recommit ourselves to raising the minimum wage, to promoting training and continuing education for workers, to providing affordable health care to every family, and to building a stronger national community of people who believe in the value of work and who recognize the importance of maintaining dignity and justice for those who perform it. By doing so, we can make the American Dream a reality for all our people and build a brighter future for our children.

Best wishes to all for a memorable holiday.

BILL CLINTON

The President's Radio Address
September 5, 1998

Good morning. On this Labor Day weekend, when we celebrate the dignity of work and enjoy the fruits of our labor, I want to talk to you about the continuing strength of America's economy and what we must do to continue our progress in the face of increasing uncertainty in the global economy.

As you know, I am just completing a trip to Russia, which has had a great deal of difficulty as a result of the loss of investment from overseas, and to Ireland, which has done much, much better because of its commitment to open trade and its ability to attract investment from all around the world.

At home, yesterday we learned that the unemployment rate remained at 4.5 percent, more evidence of the continued health of the American economy, at the same time as financial turmoil has struck several countries, particularly in Asia and in Russia, and is now being felt in our own stock market.

This proves the point I have made again and again since taking office: We are in a global economy, and we are affected by events beyond our shores. We cannot ignore them. And when we do things to help others meet their economic challenges, we are helping ourselves.

Earlier this week I asked the Chair of my Economic Council of Advisers, Dr. Janet Yellen, to report to me on the overall state of the American economy today. What I heard from Dr. Yellen should be reassuring to America's families. While the Asian crisis has dampened exports, especially for our farmers, and caused losses for some financial institutions, the pillars of our prosperity stands solid: Inflation and unemployment are still at their lowest levels and consumer confidence near its highest level in 30 years; we still have an historic boom in business investment; and we're still creating jobs, 365,000 last month alone.

Perhaps most important, standards of living continue to rise. Wages are growing at twice the rate of inflation, the strongest real wage growth in over 20 years. After decades in which incomes stagnated in our country, a growing economy means real opportunity for millions of families, the opportunity to buy a home, take a vacation, know your children will be educated, save for your retirement, live out the American dream.

The bottom line is, for all the quicksilver volatility in the world's financial markets, the American economy is on the right track. From autos to computers, from biotech to construction, our industries continue to lead the world. But we have an obligation to keep America on the right track and a duty to press forward with the strategy that has helped turn our economy around.

First, in this time of financial uncertainty, we must maintain America's hard-won fiscal discipline. Our economic expansion is built not on the illusion of Government debt but on the solid foundation of private sector growth spurred by low interest rates. Now we must use these good times to build a secure retirement for the baby boomers and a secure future for our children. Again, I will insist that we set aside every penny of any budget surplus until we save the Social Security system first. I'll resist any tax cut or any new spending plan that squanders the surplus before we've even had one year of black ink after 29 years of deficits.

Second, we must invest in the skills of our people. That's the key to long-term prosperity. I'll work with the Congress in coming weeks to enact our agenda to make American education the best in the world, for more teachers and smaller classes in the early grades, to extra help with early reading, modernizing our schools, connecting all of our classrooms and libraries to the Internet by the year 2000.

Third, we must master the complex realities of the new global economy. It can be a source of tremendous strength for America. Indeed, about 30 percent of the remarkable growth we've enjoyed in the last 5½ years has come as a result of our expanding trade. I've said to Russia and our Asian trading partners, "If you take the tough steps to reform yourselves and restore economic confidence, America will work with the international community to help you get back on your feet."

I ask Congress to step up to its responsibility for growth at home and financial stability abroad by meeting our obligation to the International Monetary Fund. There is no substitute for action and no reason for delay. The International Monetary Fund is a critical device to get countries to reform and do the right things and return to growth. Without it, they won't be able to buy America's exports, and we won't be able to do as well as we otherwise could do.

Markets rise and fall. But our economy is the strongest it's been in a generation, and its fundamentals are sound. Let's stay on the right track and take strong steps to steer our Nation through the new global economy so that we can continue to widen the circle of opportunity as we approach the 21st century.

Thanks for listening.

NOTE: The address was recorded at approximately 6:05 p.m. on September 4 at the U.S. Ambassador's residence in Dublin, Ireland, for broadcast at 10:06 a.m. on September 5. The transcript was made available by the Office of the Press Secretary on September 4 but was embargoed for release until the broadcast.

Remarks in Limerick, Ireland
September 5, 1998

Audience member. Welcome, Mr. Clinton!

The President. Thank you. I feel welcome. Thank you. Mayor Harrington, City Manager Murray, *Taoiseach,* Celia, to the university rectors, to the officials of the Irish and American Governments and the distinguished Members of our Congress who have accompanied me here. Let me say on behalf of my wife and myself and all of us who have come from America, you have made us feel very much at home in Limerick, and we thank you.

I would like to thank the Irish Chamber Orchestra, and Michael O'Suilleabhain, who performed before I came. I would like to thank everyone who did anything to make this possible. I especially thank you for the Freedom of the City. I told the mayor that I was relieved to have the Freedom of the City here. It means when I'm no longer President and I come back to Ireland, I won't have to stay in Dublin alone; I can come to Limerick, too. And I thank you.

I thank the universities for the rectors' award. The work of peace is always a community effort. I am pleased that the United States could play a role. But for all your generosity today, make no mistake about it, the major credit for the peace process belongs to the Irish—to the people, to the people who voted for the Good Friday agreement, to the leaders of the various groups in Northern Ireland who supported it, to the Prime Minister of Great Britain, and to your extraordinary *Taoiseach*, Bertie Ahern, who has been brilliant in his leadership in this endeavor.

Let me also echo something the mayor said. We have this wonderful delegation from the United States Congress here who have loved Ireland and worked and longed for peace here for many years. But one of them actually has his roots and some of his relatives here in Ireland, Congressman Peter King, who is here with his relatives today. So thank you, Peter. And I think you have—[*applause*]—thank you.

Ladies and gentlemen, 35 years ago, in June of 1963, President Kennedy came to Limerick and promised he would return in the springtime. He was not able to fulfill that promise. But I appreciate the opportunity to renew it, and to thank you for the springtime of hope the Irish people have given the entire world in 1998.

You see, a great deal of my time as President is spent dealing with the troubles people cause themselves around the world when they hate their neighbors because of their religious, their racial, their ethnic, their tribal differences. I saw hundreds of thousands of people die in a matter of months over tribal differences. We see the continuing heartbreak in the Middle East, the trouble in the Balkans spread from now Bosnia to Kosovo. We see trouble in the Aegean, trouble on the Indian subcontinent, trouble the world over, because people cannot understand that underneath whatever differences their neighbors have with them, there lurks the common humanity in the soul of us all.

Because of what you have done in Ireland in 1998, you have made it possible for me, on behalf of the United States and the cause of peace in the world, to tell every warring, feuding, hating group of people trapped in the prison of their past conflicts to look at Ireland and know there can be a better day. Thank you for that.

I came here, too, to Limerick and to western Ireland to see this historic point of embarkation for the New World, where the Shannon approaches the Atlantic and so many faces turned in hope to America over the years. I wanted to remember our common pasts and to imagine for a few moments with you the future we can build together. For the last decade is only a tiny portion of Irish history, though it has witnessed a sea change in the life of the Irish people. The demons of the past are losing their power to divide you, and a new and better and more prosperous history is unfolding before you.

You mentioned the McCourt brothers from Limerick who did grace the White House last St. Patrick's Day. Now I'll have to go home and tell Frank McCourt, "You know, Frank, you made a lot of money writing about the old Limerick, but I like the new one better, and I think you would, too."

Here in this city, wars were fought and treaties were signed, families struggled to make ends meet, and when those efforts failed, many left to cast their lot with our young Nation laying beyond the ocean. Here, when famine struck, Irish men and women boarded coffin ships for the hope of a better life, and many perished before they could fulfill their dreams.

But from Ireland's tragedy arose triumph, for the Irish who survived the crossing were strong, and they lent their strength to America. They never forgot the island where they came from, either. And today we celebrate, therefore, a double gift: Ireland's pride in America and America's immense pride in her Irish roots. Each has always made the other a better place. Our relationship has always been generous and giving and growing, but never before have we given so much good to one another.

The best moment of all, of course, was the Good Friday agreement—the leadership, as I said, of Prime Minister Ahern and Prime Minister Blair, the leaders of the Northern Ireland parties, those who agreed that words—words, not weapons—should be used to write the future.

I also thank, as the *Taoiseach* did, George Mitchell and Ambassador Jean Kennedy Smith and all the Americans who worked for that. But again I tell you, this peace is yours—yours and no one else's. All the leaders in the world, all the speeches in the world would not amount to a hill of beans if you hadn't gone out and voted "yes" and meant it loud and clear with every fiber of your being.

And as we mourn the losses of Omagh and the three little boys who were killed and taken from their parents' arms, remember there will be still efforts by the enemies of peace to break your will, to get you to turn back, to get you to lose faith. Don't do it. Don't do it. Remember what it was like when you were here on this day. No matter what happens by the enemies of peace from now until the whole thing is done and right, the way it's supposed to be, and every provision of that agreement is real in the life of Ireland, no matter what happens between now and then, remember what it was like on this day: Looking up this street, looking up that street, this is you at your best. Do not let them break your will.

Now, free of the demons of the past, you can look to the future. In less time than has elapsed since my last visit to Ireland in 1995, we all will be, like it or not, in a new century, in a new millennium. Nowhere on Earth does that new era hold more promise than here in Ireland. Nowhere does the change of the calendar correspond better to profound changes in the life of a people.

You know, George Bernard Shaw once quipped that he hoped to be in Ireland on the day the world ended, because the Irish were always 50 years behind the times. [*Laughter*] Well, Ireland has turned the tables on poor old Mr. Shaw, for today you are in the forefront of every change sweeping the world. This island is being redefined by new ideas, bringing prosperity and an increasingly international world view. You are connected to Europe and the rest of the world in countless ways: computers, the Internet, faxes, trade, all growing by leaps and bounds every year. Perhaps most important, your young people have a strong voice in determining Ireland's future, and they are making the future in a way that will change Ireland forever and for the better.

I also want to thank you for being more than newly prosperous. I want to thank you for not forgetting where you came from and your ties to the less fortunate. For the Irish people, who once knew hunger, today spare no effort to aid the afflicted in other places. The Irish people, who knew strife at home, now send peacekeepers every single day to troubled regions around the world. I wish that every country

could be as good and generous and caring to those who have been left out, left behind, downtrodden as the Irish people have been. And I thank you for that. Don't ever lose that. No matter what good things come to you, don't ever lose that.

The rest of the world has a lot to learn from an Ireland that is a place of inclusion, a place where labor and business and government work together, where the young are encouraged to dream and the elderly are respected, where human rights are protected at home and defended abroad. And I suppose I would be remiss and I don't want to leave this platform without thanking Ireland for our admiration for the work of your former President, now the United Nations High Commissioner for Human Rights, Mary Robinson. We appreciate her very much.

We believe that 21st century Ireland will be an inspiration to the rest of the world, and you can see it taking shape right here in Limerick. The university here, built in our lifetime, has become a magnet for your brightest young men and women. Here, new jobs are being created, entire industries being built on knowledge alone.

I am very proud that an American company, Dell Computers, has been able to play such a strong role in this progress. And I thank the *Taoiseach* and Dell for their announcement today. I also thank Dell for generously donating 100 computers to the schools at Omagh after last month's tragedy.

Now that you have given me the Freedom of the City, I can say, "my fellow citizens." Standing here on these streets on this fine late-summer day, we cannot possibly know all the changes the new millennium will bring. But I believe at the end of another thousand years, Limerick and western Ireland will still face out toward and reach out toward America. And I know America will never turn away. Three years ago in Dublin I promised the people of Ireland that as long as Ireland walks the road of peace, America will walk with you. You have more than kept your part of the deal, and we will keep ours.

When I was preparing for this trip, I got to thinking that when my own ancestors left for America from Ireland, they were longing for a new world of possibilities. They were longing for the chance to begin again. Ireland's great glory today is that you had the courage to begin again. And in so doing, you have opened limitless tomorrows for your children. You have redeemed the beauty of the Irish countryside. You have redeemed the power of Irish poetry. You have redeemed the loving faith of Saint Patrick. This island is coming home to itself.

In an old Irish tale, Finn MacCumhal says, "The best music in the world is the music of what happens." What happens here today is quite wonderful. Never let the music die in your heart, and it will always play out in your lives. And America will be there every step of the way.

Thank you, and God bless you. Thank you.

NOTE: The President spoke at 11:55 a.m. at the intersection of O'Connell Street and Bedford Row. In his remarks, he referred to Mayor Joe Harrington of Limerick; City Manager Con Murray; Prime Minister Bertie Ahern of Ireland; Celia Larkin, who accompanied Prime Minister Ahern; composer/pianist Michael O'Suilleabhain; Prime Minister Tony Blair of the United Kingdom; author Frank McCourt; former Senator George J. Mitchell, independent chairman of the multiparty talks in Northern Ireland; and U.S. Ambassador to Ireland Jean Kennedy Smith.

Remarks on National School Modernization Day in Silver Spring, Maryland
September 8, 1998

Thank you very much. I want to thank Carla for her introduction and her devotion to teaching. And I thought she did quite a good job of introducing her student. He's now sort of her boss, I guess, indirectly. [*Laughter*] And young man, you did a terrific job. You look great, and you stood up twice, and I think you ought to run for office some day. [*Laughter*] You really did a good job. I was very proud of you. I thought you were great.

I'd like to thank the State Superintendent, Nancy Grasmick, and Superintendent Vance and the other officials of this school district. And Board Chair Nancy King, thank you for being with me again. She said if I came to this school district one more time I would be charged my appropriate tax assessment—[*laughter*]—to help alleviate the overcrowding problem I came to talk about today.

I'd like to thank the members of the Maryland Legislature who are here, Senator Ruben and others, and County Council Chair Leggett and the other local officials who are here. I'd like to also thank the representatives of the education associations that are with us, including the NEA and the AFT. And I'd like to say a special word of appreciation to our wonderful Secretary of Education, Dick Riley; to Congressman Wynn, who has been a heroic champion of education; and to my good friend Kathleen Kennedy Townsend for everything she has done, especially for making Maryland the first State

in the country to require community service as a condition of public education. It is a very important thing. And I hope State after State, community after community will emulate it.

We are about to have our 100,000th young person in the AmeriCorps national service program. Creating an ethic of community service, I think, is one of the most important things we can do as America grows ever more diverse and still has a series of common challenges, common problems, and common opportunities. And no one in America has done more to promote it than Kathleen Kennedy Townsend. I thank her for that.

I also want to tell you that Congressman Wynn committed the truth up here when he said that the first time we talked, he was hitting on me for more Federal funds for education. And I told him if we could just complete the recovery of the economy, balance the budget, we'd have some money, and that I, for one, would be in favor of investing that money disproportionately in the education of our children and the future of our country. And together we're trying to achieve that.

I think you should know today that this event in which you are participating is one of 84 going on today in communities in 37 States. This is National School Modernization Day for us. The First Lady, the Vice President, Governors, about 40 Members of Congress, and the Cabinet—not just Secretary Riley but a lot of our other Cabinet members are out all across the country at gatherings like this. We are here to say that there is no more important long-term objective for America than world-class education for all our children, and that the children deserve schools that are as modern as the world in which they will live.

All of you know this is a time of great change and transition, and meeting the challenges of this time is daunting work. You have to follow any week, any month, the headlines about what is going on in the world and here at home, with the economy, in international political events, and you can imagine that, even on its worst day, this is a very interesting job the American people have given me. But it is daunting work dealing with the complex and dynamic world we're living in.

I have just seen it in Northern Ireland, where I visited with families, including those who were victims of the horrible bombing in Omagh, who are determined to abandon the hatred of the past and claim a different future for the children of Ireland. I have seen it in Russia, where people are working to lift their country out of economic crisis, even as they stay on a road to democracy and open economy.

And as Kathleen said, I had a good talk this morning with Senator Mikulski about Russia, and the Secretary of the Treasury is now, as we're here, in the Senate meeting with our Senate caucus to talk about the situation in Russia and generally what's going on in the global economy and how we can continue to push it forward.

At this moment I think all of us would admit that America, always a blessed nation, has particular blessings. We have the strongest economy in a generation. We have a dropping crime rate. We have the lowest welfare rolls in 29 years. We have the highest homeownership in history. Our country has had a remarkable run of economic and social progress, and we have been able to promote peace and security and freedom and human rights around the world.

But people with this many blessings also have significant responsibilities. We have significant responsibilities around the world not to continue to be—in the words of our Federal Reserve Chairman, Alan Greenspan, the other day—an island of prosperity in a sea of difficulty in the rest of the world. We owe it to the world to exercise our responsibilities to try to advance the cause of prosperity and peace. And it's also

in our interest, since our destiny is so inextricably bound up with the rest of the world.

And we have unique responsibilities here at home. I've talked about this a lot, but I would like to reemphasize it. Sometimes when things are going really, really well for people, they get a little self-indulgent, easily distracted, and basically just want to kick back and relax. It's a natural tendency for individuals. You go through a tough time, and you work and you work and work, and things get really good; you say, "Thank goodness things are not so bad as they used to be. I'm going to relax." There are people that have this whole theory that since we have the lowest unemployment in nearly 30 years and the lowest inflation in over 30 years, and the economy is as strong as it's been, we're about to have the first balanced budget and surplus in 29 years, we can all just sort of pat ourselves on the back.

I believe that would be a serious error—a serious error—because I think, again, at times when you have many blessings, your responsibilities are greater. And our responsibility is to say, what should we do? What should we do with the money that the American people have produced through their hard work and industry and through bringing this deficit down? What should we do with our prosperity? What should we do with our confidence?

I think there is no more important thing to do than to get in our minds what the big, long-term challenges facing this country are and to say, we'll never have a better chance to make a big down payment on meeting the huge challenges of the country than we do right now because we're in good shape, because we don't have to worry about where our next dollar is coming from, because most Americans don't have to worry about where their next meal is coming from, because we have confidence that we're doing well. Now is the time. If we can't do that now, if we can't look at the big challenges facing the country now, when can we ever do it?

Therefore, I think we ought to be asking ourselves, what do we have to do to keep this economic recovery going? What do we have to do to meet our responsibilities in the world? What do we have to do to save the Social Security and Medicare systems and make them work for the baby boomers when they retire without bankrupting our kids? One thing we ought not to do is go out and spend this surplus 60 days before an election on a tax cut when we haven't even manifested the surplus and won't have it until October the 1st. We waited 30 years for a surplus; we ought to at least look at the ink turn from red to black for a year before we start throwing it away.

I've been waiting—I've been counting the days until October 1st so I can say, "Whew, we actually have the surplus." And now nobody even wants us to get there before they start spending it again. And more importantly, spending it on a tax cut estimates what the surplus will be in years ahead. Now, we've been very good on estimating. I've been on the right side of that. Every year I've been President I've said, "Well, here's what I think the deficit is going to be," and it's always been lower. And we've always been fortunate because we haven't made a lot of false claims here. But we need to save the Social Security system before we start giving away the surplus that, in fact, has not even materialized yet. That's a big challenge.

The second thing we need to do is prove that we cannot just preserve but improve the environment as we grow the economy. We know we can do that, but you'd be amazed how many people don't believe we can do that still—you'd be utterly amazed—not just in America but all around the world, who still believe there's this sort of iron law of environmental degradation and economic growth, and that no scientific discovery, no technological advance, nothing will ever enable us to do it. I think it's a big challenge we need to face.

We've got over 160 million Americans in managed care plans. I think it's a big challenge to protect the rights of people in managed care so you can control costs as much as possible without sacrificing quality or peace of mind for families. I think people ought to be able to go to an emergency room when they need to, or see a specialist when they need to, and shouldn't have the doctor taken away in the middle of treatment. I think these are big issues, not little issues—big things for the country.

But there is no bigger issue—and there are lots of others—the Senate is going to get another chance to do the right thing on campaign finance reform. I wish they would. I'd like to see all my successors be able to spend less time raising money and more time helping you raise your kids. I hope that can happen. But let's not kid ourselves. Nothing we do will have a greater effect on the future of this country than guaranteeing every child, without regard to race or station in life or region in this country, a world-class education—nothing.

But first things first. You are all—I mean, this is sort of what's called preaching to the saved, because you all agree with all this on education. [*Laughter*] But even before the education issue, you must first decide, what should our attitude be about our present moment of good fortune? I think our attitude should be: It is not just a time to enjoy it, to indulge ourselves, to be diverted; it is a time to recognize the very serious questions before us and realize the unique opportunity we have to fulfill our responsibility to the future. And it always begins with our children.

As Secretary Riley said many times this month, we had a record number of schoolchildren start school—52.7 million—half a million more than last year, more than at the height of the baby boom, more than at any time. And all the indications are that this will continue, this so-called baby boom echo will continue to reverberate for years and years to come.

Now, there are a lot of things that we should be doing in education. I came to emphasize one today, but I think it's worth repeating that we have advocated high standards, high expectations, high levels of accountability, and high levels of support to achieve those objectives. We've got a program to expand charter schools; to end social promotion, but to provide after-school and summer school programs to people who need it; to reward our most committed teachers; to train more and certify more master teachers; to do more to help our children master the basics; and to pass voluntary national tests for fourth grade reading and eighth grade math. We've called for more efforts to make our schools safe and disciplined and drug-free. But it's important to point out that with the biggest group of schoolchildren in history enrolled, one of the biggest problems is the adequacy and the quality of the physical space itself and its capacity to hook into the information revolution.

The Vice President and I, for nearly 4 years now, have been working to hook all of our classrooms and libraries up to the Internet by the year 2000. There are a lot of these classrooms that aren't hookable. [*Laughter*] And basically we have two different kinds of problems.

First of all, too many schools are overcrowded: classes in hallways, gyms, portables on campuses—like here, outside. I was in a little town in Florida where one school had, as I remember, 12 different trailers out there behind it, maybe more. Then, not very long after that, I went to Philadelphia, where the average school building is 65 years old. And they're magnificent buildings. You couldn't afford to build buildings like that today. But they haven't been maintained.

And I always ask people, what kind of signal do you send to an inner-city child, whose one chance to make it in life is a decent education, if every day the child has to walk up the stairs and go into a school where the windows are broken, the paint is peeling, there's graffiti on the walls, maybe a whole floor is shut down because it is simply physically incapable of being occupied? And then the child will turn on the television and hear every politician like me saying, "Children are the most important things to our future. Education is the most important issue." The actions that the child sees walking up the steps to school every day are louder than all the words to the contrary of the politicians. This is a big issue.

So what we have done within the balanced budget—I want to emphasize this. It's true. Congressman Wynn will tell you I've disappointed some of my friends because I don't think we can vary from what got us to the dance of prosperity. And what got us to the dance of prosperity is being ruthless about balancing this budget, keeping the interest rates down, getting the investment up, and giving Americans a job so they can pay taxes to the local school district so you can do the lion's share of the work.

Consistent with that and within that framework, we have proposed the first-ever initiative at the national level to help communities build and repair and modernize more than 5,000 schools so that we can meet this huge need out there. It's a school construction tax cut that is completely and fully paid for in the balanced budget. It doesn't touch a penny of the surplus, and it is the right way to cut taxes. It respects discipline; it targets investments to the future where they're needed most.

And what I would like to ask all of you to do is to help Congressman Wynn reach the other Members of Congress and say this ought not to be a Republican or a Democratic issue. It ought not to be an issue that pits the rapidly growing suburbs against inner cities with old buildings that anybody would love to have if they were just properly modernized and wired. This ought to be an issue where we can all say that it's a national priority. And you can talk all you want to about education, but we don't need a crowded or a crumbling classroom or permanent reliance on housetrailers as the symbol of America's commitment to education. Now, that's important.

I also want to point out that we have paid for, within the balanced budget, in addition to the school construction, enough funds to help school districts hire another 100,000 teachers to lower the class size, average class size, to 18 in the early grades. And I think that's important.

All the research shows it makes a permanent difference if early in the educational experience teachers have the chance to give personal attention to students, and they have a chance to relate to each other in a class that is small enough to embed permanently not only learning skills but habits of relating and learning in the future. All the research shows that.

Finally, let me say, we have a proposal to provide scholarships to 35,000 young people who will agree to go out and teach in educationally underserved areas, based on the old idea of the National Health Service Corps. You know, I used to be Governor, as one of my opponents once said, of a small rural State—[*laughter*]— and we had all these places in the country that could never get a doctor. And the National Health Service Corps came along, and they gave these young people scholarships to medical schools and covered the enormous cost of going. And all they had to do was to be willing to go out either to an inner-city area or out in the rural area where they couldn't get a doctor and serve for a few years and work off the cost of medical school.

That's what we want to do with education. We want to say, "We will pay your way to school. We'll help you get an education. After a couple of years, you can do whatever you want to with your life, but we ask you in return for our investment in your education to go to an inner-city school or a rural school or a Native American school, go someplace where they won't have a good teacher if it weren't for you." I think it is a great idea. It is fully funded.

Now, the last thing I want to say—and this goes back to the school modernization—we've got to ask Congress to pass the budget to give us the funds to hook all the classrooms and the libraries up to the Internet by the year 2000.

This is a huge deal, and it is a major, major educational issue.

You may remember that last spring the First Lady and I and a large delegation of Members of Congress and others went to Africa. And it was the first time a sitting American President had ever taken an extensive trip to several countries in sub-Saharan Africa. It had never happened before. We visited a school in Uganda that will soon be linked to Pine Crest by the Internet. We were actually there.

When you see that school, if you have the visual link through the Internet, you want to give those kids some new maps, you'll want to send them some books, you'll want to do a lot of things, but you'll also know that they are beautiful, good, highly intelligent, and immensely, immensely eager to be connected to the rest of the world and to share a common future with our children.

So this is very important. Unfortunately, nearly half of our schools don't have the wiring necessary to support basic computer systems. We're doing a great job, and it's not just the Government—private sector, local districts, everybody—a fabulous job of getting these computers out into the classrooms. More and more, there is good educational software. But what we are going to do when the actual wiring is not there? We have to do this.

So again, I ask Congress to pass the funds—in the balanced budget—for the connection for the Internet. It's a huge thing. And it has more potential to dramatically revolutionize and equalize education, if the teachers are properly trained, than anything else. And in our plan,

we have funds for teacher training as well. Otherwise, you'll wind up having the kids know more about it. [*Laughter*] We can't afford to have that. [*Laughter*]

So that's what I'm here to say. Number one, let's get people out of the housetrailers and get them out of the falling-down buildings and give our kids something to be proud of and send them the right signal and have the physical facilities we need. We've got a plan to do it, with the right kind of tax cut; it's in the balanced budget. Number two, let's fund 100,000 teachers and take average class size down to 18 in the early grades. Number three, let's fund the money necessary to enable all of our classes and all of our libraries in all of our schools to be hooked up to the Internet by the year 2000. If we do that we're going to be very, very proud of how our kids turn out in the years ahead.

Thank you, and God bless you.

NOTE: The President spoke at 2:45 p.m. at Pine Crest Elementary School. In his remarks, he referred to Pine Crest teacher Carla McEachern, who introduced the President; Paul L. Vance, superintendent, Nancy J. King, president, and Geonard Butler, student member, Montgomery County Board of Education; Nancy S. Grasmick, State superintendent of schools; State Senator Ida G. Ruben; Isiah Leggett, president, Montgomery County Council; and Lt. Gov. Kathleen Kennedy Townsend of Maryland. The President also referred to the National Education Association (NEA) and the American Federation of Teachers (AFT).

Remarks at Hillcrest Elementary School in Orlando, Florida
September 9, 1998

Thank you very much. When President Waldrip—[*laughter*]—was up here speaking, I had two overwhelming thoughts: One is that even though I had been made a member of the PTA, she was one incumbent president I could never defeat in an election. [*Laughter*] My second thought was, I wish I could take her to Washington for about a month. It might change the entire atmosphere up there. [*Laughter*] It was great. She was unbelievable.

Let me say how delighted I am to be here at Hillcrest. I want to thank Principal Scharr for making me feel so welcome. And Clair Hoey, thank you for what you said about the education of our children. And thank you both for the comments you made about the First Lady and the work we have done over the years for children and for education.

I'd like to thank the Governor of Puerto Rico, Pedro Rossello, my longtime friend, for being here. It's quite fitting that you would be here at this school, which is committed to bilingualism and to a multicultural future for America.

I'd like to thank three Members of the United States Congress who came with me today, Representatives Corrine Brown, Robert Wexler, and Peter Deutsch. They're all here in the front row, and thank you for coming. Thank you, Anne MacKay, for being here. And I'd like to thank the State representatives who are here, Shirley Brown, Lars Hafner, and Orange County Chair Linda Chapin, and the superintendent of the schools, Dennis Smith.

Let me say to all of you, I was so excited when I heard about this school because it really does embody what I think we should be doing in education and, in a larger sense, what I think we should be trying to do with our country. And I'd like to begin by just saying a few words about it.

First of all, the principal has already outlined it better than I could, along with what your teacher and your PTA president said, but this is a school that has a lot of different kids in it, not only different ethnic groups, they have different religions; they have different cultural heritages; their parents have different financial circumstances—I would imagine breathtakingly different—and yet, if you look at them all together, they're all a part of our future.

And we say in our Constitution, we say in our laws, that every one of them is equal not only in the eyes of God but in the eyes of their fellow Americans. This school is trying to make that promise real for all of them. And in creating a community in which they all count and all have a chance to live up to the fullest of their God-given abilities, they're doing what we in America ought to be doing.

I also think some of the strategies are very good. I think the school uniform policy is a good one. I've tried to promote it because I think it promotes learning and discipline and order and gives kids a sense of solidarity and takes a lot of heat off parents without regard to their income and sort of reinforces the major mission of the school. I think that's a good thing. I think having a school-based academic strategy is important. I think the literacy programs are profoundly important. And I'm very glad you are involved in reading recovery.

So there are so many things that I think are quite good about this school, and I thank you

for giving me and Lieutenant Governor MacKay the chance to come by here today.

I want to talk about what we're trying to do in Washington for education and to support not only this school but the truly extraordinary effort that Governor Chiles and Lieutenant Governor MacKay have made here over the last few years to support Florida's schools. And let me begin by backing up a step.

I'm very grateful as an American to have had the chance to serve and to be a part of what our people have accomplished in the last 6 years: to have the lowest unemployment rate in a generation; to have in just a few more days the first balanced budget and surplus in 29 years; to have the lowest crime rate in 25 years; and the smallest percentage of our people on welfare in 29 years; and the lowest inflation rate in 32 years; and the highest homeownership in American history. And we did it while downsizing the National Government to its smallest size in 35 years and investing more in States and localities and schools. I'm grateful for what all of the American people have done together.

But my focus today is on what we should do with that. What should we do with that? Because normally, if people have been through some very trying times and very challenging times and they reach a kind of plateau, the easiest thing to do is to sort of say, "Whew, now let's just sort of sit back, relax, and enjoy it." I think that would be a mistake, because the world is changing very fast. You see that, don't you, if you pick up and see what's happened in the stock market—you know? We had a great big day, yesterday; we had not such a good week or so before that. And when you read and you say, "Well, why is all this happening? Are a bunch of companies going broke or are a bunch of new companies making a lot of money?" And you read between the lines and see, no, no, it's a lot of things that are happening around the world. What does that mean?

The more we become a part of the world in America, with the diversity of our population, the more America becomes a part of the world beyond our borders in our economic and other partnerships. And the world is changing so fast that I believe what we should do with these good times is not to pat ourselves on the back but to say, "Hey, thank goodness. We finally have the security and the resources to face the long-term challenges of this country. And that is what we intend to do with our good times."

That is what I have asked the American people, in this season when as citizens we think about voting, to think about: What are we going to do to deal with the long-term challenges of the country? When these children get out of high school, all the baby boomers will start retiring. I know that; I'm the oldest of the baby boomers. [*Laughter*] The baby boom generation are roughly Americans between the ages of 52 and 34. And until this group of schoolchildren that came into school the last 2 years, we were the biggest group of Americans ever.

Now, if we retire without making some changes in the Social Security system and reforming the Medicare system so it takes care of seniors but does it in a way that doesn't put unconscionable burdens on younger people—if we don't do that, then by the time we retire, one of two things is going to happen: Either the baby boomers are not going to have a very good retirement, or we're going to have it at the expense of lowering their standard of living, because there will be, for a period of time, two people working—only two people working for every one person retired. No one wants that.

We're in good shape now. That's why I say we shouldn't spend any of this surplus that, hopefully, we will have for several years, that we'll begin to realize on October 1st. We shouldn't spend it all in a tax cut or a spending program until first we know we've taken care of Social Security and Medicare, because I don't know anybody in my generation that wants to undermine their future to take care of our retirement. That's a big issue.

We have to prove in this global economy with, as you know in Florida, with a lot of global warming—you had all those fires this year; you had the hottest year in history, the hottest month you ever had in June—you know about that. We've got to prove we can deal with environmental challenges and grow the economy. Believe it or not, there are a lot of people that don't believe that. There are still a lot of people who think that it is impossible to have an economic growth in any advanced society unless you are deteriorating the environment. I don't believe that, I don't think the evidence supports that. We've got to prove that. We have to prove that.

We have to prove that we can give both quality and affordable health care to all our people, the 160 million people in managed care plans. People still want to know if they get hurt, they can go to an emergency room; if they need a specialist, they can see it; and their medical records are going to be protected. We have to prove we can have the most cost-effective health system and still maintain quality.

So we've got these big challenges, and we've got to deal with all these challenges in the global economy you've been dealing with, reading about. But let me say to you there is no more important challenge than giving every one of these children, especially if they start out in life without all the advantages that a lot of other children have, a chance to get a world-class education. There is no more important long-term challenge for America.

That is what will make us one America, whole, together, respecting each other's differences, when everybody's got a chance to sort of live out their dreams.

You know, we've all got this on our mind. I don't know if you all know this, but when I got off the plane today, the young man that caught Mark McGwire's home run last night was there waiting for me because he was flown down to Disney World today, which I thought was a real hoot—[*laughter*]—with his family. And last night, late last night, I talked to Mark McGwire and his wonderful young son, who's in uniform and always out there. And I got to thinking about what's Mark McGwire going to do with the rest of his life? What's he going to do with the rest of his season?

And I'll tell you what I think he'll do. I think he'll hit more home runs and play more baseball and do more things. But that's what you've got to think about America. How would you feel if Mark McGwire announced, "Well, I've been working real hard to do this all my life, and if it's all the same to you, I think I'll skip the last 18 games." [*Laughter*] Right? Or, "If it's all the same to you, I think I'll just stand up there and see how many times I could walk." You would be puzzled, at least, wouldn't you?

Well, that's the kind of decision we have to make as Americans. What are we going to do with our good economy? What are we going to do with our improving social fabric? I'd like to see our country become modeled on what you're trying to do here at Hillcrest.

And in specific terms, I want to say there are some things before the Congress today, some specific education bills that I think respond to the needs of the American people. And no matter how well you're doing, you know there are still some needs out there. I was especially impressed by what you said you were doing with new mothers and newborn children and trying to get kids off to a good start. Hillary and I had a conference on early childhood and the brain not very long ago, and I think we have all underestimated how much good can be done in those first couple of years of life. And that's very good.

Let me tell you—sort of set the scene here. The Department of Education today is releasing a report that shows that while we're making progress, students that live in high-poverty areas continue to lag behind other students in fourth grade reading and math scores. Fewer than half of all the fourth graders in the high-poverty areas are scoring at basic levels of performance in math.

Now, I will say again, you rebuke that whole idea that there has to be a difference in people based on the income of their parents or the nature of their neighborhood. That's what you're trying to prove does not have to be. And I believe that as well.

So let me just briefly review the agenda that these Members of Congress—these three here—are supporting, that we're going to try to pass in what is just a very few weeks left in this legislative session.

I want smaller classes in the early grades all across America. You've got that here. We have a program that would hire 100,000 teachers in the early grades. If we hired the 100,000 teachers—it's in our balanced budget—we could lower class size to an average of 18 in the early grades all across America.

I want Congress to help me create safer schools, to continue to build partnerships with local law enforcement and schools. Just this morning, the Justice Department has released over $16 million to 155 law enforcement agencies across the country to make sure we have community-based organizations to prevent crime in the first place.

This school—I understand you do a lot of work and loan out some computers so families can learn about computers. I think it's important that we hook up every classroom and every library and every school in America by the year

2000. We have a bill to do that in Congress, and we want to pass that bill.

We also have responses specifically to that education report I mentioned, a bill in Congress to create what we call education opportunity zones, as well as expanding funding for Title I. It would give extra help to the classrooms—the schools that are prepared to end social promotion but not tag kids as failures, that want to have after-school programs, that want to have summer school programs, that want to have extra help for kids who need it, that need more resources to do the kind of intensive effort that this reading recovery program here, for example, requires. Everybody knows it's one of the best programs in the world. Unfortunately, too many schools don't do it because it costs money to do it, because you really have to give intensive help to these children at an early age.

So I think that's important. A part of that would be paying the college expenses of 35,000 young people who agree when they get out of college to go out and teach off their college loans by going into underserved areas, in urban and rural areas in America. I think that's worth doing. I want to—[*applause*]—thank you.

And finally, we're trying to fully fund our America Reads program, which will make sure that we give enough reading tutors and trained volunteers to enough schools to make sure every 8-year-old in this country—every one—can read a book independently by the time they're in the third grade.

Now, this is very important stuff. And so far I can't tell you how it's going to come out in Washington. But remember, I'm not increasing the deficit. This is in the balanced budget that I presented to Congress. The money is there. So the issue is not whether the money is there; the issue is what are our priorities and what are we going to do with the money. Now, notwithstanding what Representatives Wexler, Deutsch, and Brown want to do, the House of Representatives voted to actually cut $2 billion off these programs. The Senate has not done so yet. They've been a little more encouraging. I don't want this to be a partisan issue; education should be an American issue. When I go to a school and walk up and down and shake hands with kids, I don't look for a political label on their uniforms. This is an American issue. But it is a big issue.

So I would just ask all of you to make it as clear as you can that you'd like for us in

Washington to put the same priority on education that the parents and the teachers and the kids do at Hillcrest, that you would like for us to try to create an American community like the one that you are trying to create with your children here at this school, and that there are very specific opportunities Congress is going to have in the next 3 weeks where a "yes" vote or a "no" vote is required, and you'd like to see us vote "yes" for our children and our future.

Thank you very much. Thank you.

NOTE: The President spoke at 1:10 p.m. in the cafeteria. In his remarks, he referred to Susan Waldrip, president, Parent-Teacher Association, Aliette Scharr, principal, and Clair Hoey, teacher, Hillcrest Elementary School; State Representatives Shirley Brown and Lars Hafner; Linda W. Chapin, chair, Orange County Board of Commissioners; Dennis M. Smith, superintendent, Orange County Public Schools; Gov. Lawton Chiles of Florida; gubernatorial candidate Lt. Gov. Buddy MacKay of Florida, and his wife, Anne; and St. Louis Cardinals first baseman Mark McGwire, who broke Major League Baseball's single-season home run record, his son Matt, and Tim Forneris, the Busch Stadium groundskeeper who retrieved the record-breaking ball. The President also referred to Title I of the Improving America's Schools Act of 1994 (Public Law 103–382), which amended Title I of the Elementary and Secondary Education Act of 1965 (Public Law 89–10).

Remarks at a Florida Democratic Party Luncheon in Orlando
September 9, 1998

The President. Thank you so much. Thank you, Jim Pugh, for all the work you've done on this dinner and lunch and for helping Buddy through this long campaign. And thank you, Governor Rossello, for everything you've said and for your leadership of our Democratic Governors' Association.

I'd like to thank the Members of Congress who are here, Peter Deutsch, Rob Wexler, Corrine Brown, and your State party chair, Mitch Ceasar. And especially I want to thank Buddy and Anne MacKay for years and years and years of devoted service to the people of Florida and for taking on this campaign and seeing it through to what I predict will be a victory that will surprise some but not me. And I thank them.

I came here today to talk to you about what we've done together in the last 6 years and what's at stake in this election. I think the people of this country have a serious choice to make in November between progress or partisanship, between people or politics, between unity or division.

You have been very good to me here in Florida—to me and to Hillary and to the Vice President and our administration——

Audience member. We love you, Bill!

The President. ——and I'm very grateful to you. You have been astonishingly kind and generous to me today. And I will never forget it. If God lets me live to be an old man, I will never forget what Buddy MacKay said today from this platform when he could have said nothing. And so I hope you will just indulge me for a minute while I say that I thank you for that.

I have been your friend. I've done my best to be your friend, but I also let you down. And I let my family down, and I let this country down. But I'm trying to make it right. And I'm determined never to let anything like that happen again. And I'm determined—[applause]—wait a minute, wait a minute. I'm determined to redeem the trust of people like Buddy and Anne, who were with me in 1991— a lot of the rest of you were, too—when nobody but my mother and my wife thought I had a chance to be elected.

When I was over at the Hillcrest School— Buddy and I were over there a few minutes ago, and I was shaking hands with all these little kids out there. And this kid that reminded me a lot of myself when I was that young— he was bigger than the other students and kind of husky—he said, "Mr. President, I want to grow up to be President. I want to be a President like you." And I said—I thought, I want to be able to conduct my life and my Presidency so that all the parents of the country could feel good if their children were able to say that again. I'll never forget that little boy, and it's a big guide for me.

So I ask you for your understanding, for your forgiveness on this journey we're on. I hope this will be a time of reconciliation and healing, and I hope that millions of families all over America are in a way growing stronger because of this. But I'll tell you one thing that I hope you won't let happen. There are a whole lot of people, in Washington especially, or who write about this, who would like for this—once again would like for something going on in Washington to be the subject of an election in November, instead of what's going on in the lives of the American people. And I want to be open with you; I want you to understand these have been the toughest days of my life. But they may turn out to be the most valuable, for me and my family. And I have no one to blame but myself for my self-inflicted wounds. But that's not what America is about. And it doesn't take away from whether we're right or wrong on the issues or what we've done for the last 6 years or what this election is about.

So what I want to say to you is, you've been kind and understanding to me today. I hope you'll tell your friends and neighbors that I'm grateful and that I'm determined to redeem the trust of all the American people. But don't be fooled, not for a minute, not for a day. Elections are about you and your children and your communities and your future. And I was looking at Buddy up here today, thinking, you know, how many people in how many places in this country would be well served to have somebody as profoundly decent and committed to doing the right thing as he is in any office in the land.

This is a big issue for Florida. What really matters is what decisions would the Governor of Florida make that would affect you. You take this HMO bill of rights—we're trying to pass one in Washington. Suppose we don't pass one. There is still a huge percentage of people in Florida that are in HMO's. Forty-three HMO's in this country have endorsed our plan. Why? Because they're out there treating people right already, and they think you ought to be able to go to an emergency room if you're hurt,

the one nearest to you and be reimbursed, not be taken across town. They think if you need a specialist, you ought to be able to get one. They believe if you have medical records, they ought to be private. They believe if your employer changes HMO's in the middle of your pregnancy or your cancer treatment, you ought not to have to switch doctors. And they believe if these rights are there, you ought to have some way to enforce them. Now, that's what this is about. Now, the vote for Governor of Florida could determine whether people in this State get those protections. That's what the election is about.

We heard Buddy talking about education. We've got an education opportunity in this country with the diversity of our kids, but we also have an obligation. The States have constitutional responsibility for education. The vote for Governor of Florida will determine what kind of education our children get.

You heard him talking about the gun issue. I was, I guess, the first President ever to get into a public squabble with the NRA over the Brady bill and then the assault weapons ban. I was sort of sad about it; actually, I had worked with them from time to time when I was Governor of Arkansas. But we were in the business of letting politics and rhetoric get in the way of children's lives. This is a better country because we passed the Brady bill and the assault weapons ban. And you've got this loophole in Florida—and this is about politics as opposed to principle. No one possibly could believe that if you need a check on the background, the criminal or mental health history of somebody who can go into a gun store and buy a gun, that you shouldn't have that on any gun purchase. It doesn't take that long.

Now, these are big issues. A quarter of a million people have not been able to buy guns because of their criminal history since the Brady bill passed. How many people do you think are alive because of that? So your decision in the Governor's race in Florida will have an effect on that.

And we're all here because we know all this, and I guess in a way I'm preaching to the choir again. But I wanted to say, as much as I have been touched by the wonderful reception you've given me today, as much as I hope you'll share what I said to you today with your friends and neighbors, never forget you come here as citizens, with the responsibilities of citizens. And we go forward from this room because we know that our individual lives and our family lives cannot be all they want to be unless our communities, our State, and our Nation is all it can be.

I go back to Washington to work on—with only a very few weeks left in this congressional session—an enormously important agenda for this country. And let me just give you three or four examples of what really the election ought to be about, because it will chart the future of the country for years ahead.

On October 1st—and I am counting the days—we are going to have the first balanced budget and surplus we've had in 29 years, and it's going to be amazing. Now, there are already people who say, "Well, it's election year. Let's give people a tax cut." Well, let me remind you, we have 16 million new jobs, the lowest unemployment rate in nearly 30 years, the lowest percentage of people on welfare in 29 years, and the first balanced budget in 29 years, and the highest homeownership in history, and the lowest inflation rate in 32 years because we didn't squander money. We kept at it until we eliminated the deficit. That got interest rates down; that led to huge investment and an explosion in the markets and the country going forward.

Now, if we spend this money because we estimate that we'll have surpluses for years ahead, what happens to our other obligations? You know, pretty soon the baby boomers will start to retire—I say, pretty soon, starting in about 13 years, 10, if you take early Social Security. I'm the oldest of the baby boomers. We're the biggest group of Americans, the people between 34 and 52, in the history of the country until the kids that started school last year. We finally have a bigger group of kids in school, which every Florida school district with a bunch of trailers out back of the regular building knows. [*Laughter*]

But before that, there was us, the baby boomers, the children of the World War II generation. Now, when we retire, at present rates of work force participation and birth rates and immigration rates, there will only be about two people working for every one person drawing Social Security. We'll all be eligible for Medicare. And I'm telling you, it is a mistake for us to go out and have an election year gimmick to please people, no matter how pleasing it would be with a tax cut, until we know we

have saved Social Security for the 21st century in a way that does not require us to maintain our retirement by lowering the standard of living of our children and grandchildren. It is important, and we ought to be tough about it.

And by the way, it's also good in the global economy for America to be strong and set an example. You see with all the gyrations in the stock market last week, a lot of you probably said, "Well, I hadn't noticed any companies going broke, and I haven't noticed any companies making windfall amounts of money. It looks like the economy is just growing steady. Why is the market jumping up and down?" And then when you read the articles they say, "Well, it's because of what's going on in the global economy."

So I say to you, the United States, as Alan Greenspan said the other day, cannot be an island of prosperity in a sea of distress. Thirty percent of our growth has come because of global growth, our expanding trade. In Florida, you know that. Buddy and I, we've done export events here in Florida with very impressive businesses here selling all over the world.

Now, the United States has an obligation to try to keep global economic growth going, to help the countries when they get in trouble, if they'll help themselves—if they'll help themselves—and to create an environment in which growth can occur. One of the things we have to do is at least pay our dues to the institutions like the International Monetary Fund that can put money into these countries that are reforming. And it's in our interest.

You know, we've got a lot of farmers in the Midwest and the high plains who are really going to have a hard time this year because in Asia, where the countries have had difficult economic problems, they can't afford to buy our food anymore. And it's led to big drops in farm income.

So I ask you to support, number one, an economic program that saves Social Security first, and don't fool with this balanced budget until we actually achieve it—we ought to look at the black ink just for a day or two before we start to give it away—[*laughter*]—and number two, fulfills our responsibilities to the global economy; and number three, recognizes that over the long run we can't grow this economy and become what we ought to be and be one country with all this diversity you have in Florida and throughout the country unless we have a commitment to have a world-class education that's available to every single child.

Now, we have a national plan that will help Florida, for the first time, to help to build or expand or remodel 5,000 schools, to have smaller classes in the early grades, to have safer schools, to have better reading programs, to hook up all of our schools to the Internet. But in the end, I will say again, it matters who is Governor. And if you think about Florida's long-term history, if you look at the record that Lawton and Buddy have made for the last 8 years, I hope you'll encourage everybody in this congressional delegation to put partisanship aside and vote for our education agenda, but even if it all passes, in order to have the maximum impact it matters who the Governor is.

And unless we can prove that America can be one out of all these many cultures—to echo what Governor Rossello said—we're not going to have the America we want. And we won't be able to do that unless we achieve in education.

So, balance the budget; save Social Security before you spend the surplus; meet our obligations to stabilize the international economy, because it's the right thing to do morally and it happens to be in our interest; give us a world-class education; pass the Patients' Bill of Rights on the national level and at the State level; prove that we can—big issue in Florida—prove that we can grow the economy while improving the environment. Forty percent of our lakes and rivers are still not safe to swim in. We still have places with safe drinking water needs. As you have seen in Florida, climate change and the warming of the planet is real. We have to prove we can deal with these things and grow the economy. I'm so grateful for the chance that we've had to be involved together in recovering the Everglades. There are ways

to do these things that will promote economic opportunity and still improve the environment.

There are lots of other issues coming up in Washington. We're finally going to get a chance to give the Senate one more chance to pass campaign finance reform. And I hope we do that. You know, you've done it in Florida. Every single member of our caucus in the Senate supports it. They are determined to kill the bill through a filibuster. But we finally passed a good campaign finance reform bill through the House. I thank the House Members here from Florida for supporting it. We've got a real chance in the Senate.

And all this ought to be dealt with in the next 3 weeks. And if it's not, the voters ought to deal with it in November—choices, choices, choices. Elections should be about you and your children and your future, not what somebody else tells you they ought to be about.

Again, let me thank you from the bottom of my heart for the support you've given to all of us. Let me thank you for your kindness to me today. Let me thank you most of all for supporting Buddy. But let me challenge you: This is a big, fast-growing State that is a model of the future of America; don't you let a single, solitary soul you know get away without voting in November, because the future of America is riding on it.

Thank you, and God bless you.

NOTE: The President spoke at 2:52 p.m. in the Lake Ivanhoe Room at the Orlando Marriott Downtown. In his remarks, he referred to Jim Pugh, event chair; gubernatorial candidate Lt. Gov. Buddy MacKay of Florida and his wife, Anne; Gov. Pedro Rossello of Puerto Rico; Hillcrest Elementary School student Marcos Encinias; and Gov. Lawton Chiles of Florida.

Statement on the United Nations Security Council Vote on Iraq
September 9, 1998

I applaud the decisive and unanimous vote by the United Nations Security Council to suspend the review of sanctions against Iraq until Baghdad resumes full cooperation with the international weapons inspectors. Far from has-

tening the day sanctions are lifted, Iraq's failure to honor its obligations will prolong the sanctions, constrain Iraq from acquiring resources to rebuild its military, and keep the Iraqi economy under tight international control. The

Security Council has made crystal clear that the burden remains on Iraq to declare and destroy all its nuclear, chemical, and biological weapons and the missiles to deliver them.

Remarks at a Florida Democratic Party Dinner in Coral Gables, Florida
September 9, 1998

Thank you very much. My good friend Buddy MacKay—I've had a wonderful time with Buddy and Anne today, and I think we did a little good in Orlando. And I certainly hope we're doing some good tonight. I want to thank Daryl Jones for being here and for what he said, for being my friend, for being willing to serve this country and go through a highly political process. It's a long road that doesn't turn, and yours is going to turn in the right direction, friend, for a long time to come.

I want to thank all the legislators and others who are here. I'd like to say a special word of thanks to Congressman Peter Deutsch, who came down with me from Washington and is going home tonight, so he's not going to get a lot of sleep. Thank you for being here.

I want to thank Mitch Ceasar for being with me today, and all the Democratic officials. And I would like to recognize our nominee for State comptroller, Newall Daughtrey. Thank you for being here, Newall, and good luck to you.

You know, I was sitting here listening to Daryl speak and then listening to Buddy speak, and I thought of that old saw: The last speaker at the banquet said, "Everything that needs to be said has been said, but not everyone has yet said it." [*Laughter*] And I thought of just standing up and saying, "Amen," and sitting down. [*Laughter*]

This has been a very moving day for me because of what Buddy MacKay said here and in Orlando, because of the children we saw today in Orlando and many of the things they said to me as I was greeting them. All of you know that I've been on a rather painful journey these last few weeks. And I've had to ask for things that I was more in the habit of giving in my life than asking for, in terms of understanding and forgiveness. But it's also given me the chance to try to ask, as all of us do: What do you really care about? What do you want to think about in your last hours on this Earth? What really matters?

I've tried to do a good job taking care of this country, even when I hadn't taken such good care of myself and my family, my obligations. I hope that you and others I have injured will forgive me for the mistakes I've made. But the most important thing is, you must not let it deter you from meeting your responsibilities as citizens.

There is always, at a moment like this, those who seek not to deal with the substance of whatever is at issue but those who seek some advantage and hope that the attention of the public will be diverted from the public's business. And these next 8 weeks ought to be devoted to you and your children and your grandchildren and the future of this country and the future of this State.

I've known Buddy MacKay for nearly 20 years, and I know he's got a tough race. I know he's been at a financial disadvantage. Now that he's stuck up for me, he may be at some sort of a political disadvantage, although I'm kind of an old-school guy, I think. They asked me why I went to Russia the other day, and I said, "Well, heck, anybody can go to Russia when times are good. I want them to be our friends, and I think we ought to build a future together."

And I'm proud to be here with him. I can tell you this—I'll tell you something that I don't believe there is a person in this room that would dispute. You may not know for sure how this Governor's race is going to turn out, but there is not a person here who doesn't believe that if he wins the governorship, even people who don't vote for him will be proud of the fact that he's the Governor of Florida and that he'd get reelected in a walk. Now, you all know that, don't you? You all know that, don't you? [*Applause*] If you believe that—and you did or you wouldn't have stood up—then you owe it not to Buddy and Anne but to yourselves, not to wake up on the morning after the election thinking about what might have been. He is a good man and a good leader.

And you know, one of the things that I always get a big hand at when I go through the litany of all the things that have changed in America, and I say we've got the lowest unemployment rate in 27 years, and the lowest crime rate in 25 years, and the smallest percentage of people on welfare in 29 years, and we're about to have the first balanced budget and surplus in 29 years, and we did it with the smallest Federal Government in 35 years, and people say, "Yeah, yeah."

You know what that means? That means that it's more important who's Governor now than it was the day I became President. That's what that means. It means that experience, which is easily dismissed by people who don't understand exactly what State government does in good economic times—I used to tell people—because most of the time when I was Governor, we were going through that terrible recession of the eighties in the middle of the country, so sometimes I'd feel a little bit of self-pity, and I'd say, "Shoot, if I had a good economy, I could have a lobotomy and be successful as Governor." [*Laughter*] And that was sort of a way of saying that maybe people didn't know exactly what was going on.

But it's not true. If you care about the education of your children, there's no single elected official that can have a bigger positive impact than the Governor. If you want to see Florida continue to prosper economically but you really care about preserving the environment in a way that's fair to everybody, it matters that the Federal Government can help save the Everglades and do some other things—sure, it matters—but it really matters who is the Governor.

If you're not sure that the Congress will ever do the right thing and pass the Patients' Bill of Rights, with 160 million people already in HMO's and millions more coming; and you like the fact that health costs ought to be managed and kept within inflation just as long as people aren't losing quality care; but you don't think somebody who is in an accident ought to be hauled halfway across town to an emergency room if there is one four blocks down the way and they might die on the way; and you don't believe that people ought to be told they can't have a specialist if they have to have surgery that could leave them marked for life if they don't have a specialist; and you don't think that an employee of a small business who happens to be pregnant should lose her obstetrician half-way through the pregnancy because the small business changes health care plans; and you don't believe that anybody ought to have access to your medical records, because you think you ought to have some rights to privacy—then it really does matter who the Governor is.

And none of those rights can be written into law and mean anything unless somebody has a way of enforcing them. It matters whether he wins the Governor's race for the health care and the peace of mind of working families in this State. So these stakes are high. This is not some casual deal here.

You clapped when he talked about the gun show loophole for background checks. Let me just tell you, since we passed the Brady bill, 250,000 people—250,000 people—since 1993 have been denied the right to get a handgun, because they had a criminal record. That's hundreds a day. I can't really—you know, you could work out the math, but anyway, it's a whole bunch of people every day. How many people—I'm trying to get out of being too—they say I'm too much of a wonk; I'm trying to forget the numbers and all that. [*Laughter*] How many people are living today because that thing was passed? How many lives might be saved? It might be worth it to elect him Governor just to save one child's life. It matters who's the Governor.

Now, the same thing is true about these elections coming up in 2 months for Congress. What is the subject? What's it going to be about? What do you think it ought to be about? Do you believe that because America is doing real well now, it really doesn't matter what it's about? Do you think—most of us in this room, I guess, are pretty ardent Democrats—do you think it really matters that in all off-year elections the electorate is smaller, and the people that tend to drop off are good, hard-working people who are struggling to keep body and soul together? And I'm not sure that it matters as much when there's not a Presidential election whether they go vote—the kind of people we try to represent, the kind of people like the people that put this food on our tables tonight—and if it does matter, what are you going to do to get them there? I think it really matters.

You know, on October 1st—I am counting the days—on October 1st, we're going to have the first balanced budget and surplus in 29 years. And already—I'm kind of like a kid waiting for Christmas; it's like a present—and already I've got people who want to spend the money. They're going to say, "Well, we're going to have this estimated surplus for now to kingdom come, so let's have a tax cut right now."

And I'm not against the right kind of tax cut. We have tax cuts in our budget for child care, for education, for environmental investment in our budget right now. But they're all paid for, and they don't get into the surplus for a very good reason. We know right now that we cannot sustain two of the most important programs in America—and very important to Florida—Social Security and Medicare, when the baby boomers retire, unless we make some changes in it. Because when all of us baby boomers retire—and I'm the oldest of the baby boomers; the people between 34 and 52 are the baby boom generation—when we all retire, at present birth rates, immigration rates, and work force participation rates, there will only be about two people working for every person drawing Social Security. And that's never happened before. And it will be that way for about 20 years, until all the kids that are now in school get out and they start working, because they're the first group that's bigger than we are. Then the numbers will start getting better again.

Now, during that period, if we don't make some changes now, one of two things is going to happen: We'll have to have a huge slash in the way the programs are run, thus imperiling the stability of old age for people who, unlike me, won't have a good pension and a decent income; or we will just come up with the money at that time to keep the same program going in exactly the same way, which will lower the standard of living of our children and their ability to raise our grandchildren. And no baby boomer I know wants that to happen.

Now we finally have the money to deal with that. And even though it's election season, I think the right thing to say to the American people is, "We're not against tax cuts. We need new spending programs. We need to spend more on education than I have proposed. We need to do a lot of things, and a lot of people could use a tax cut. But it is wrong to do this until we have saved Social Security and lifted that burden off our children, and made sure that elderly people 20 years from now are going to have the same level of security they do

today." Let's look at the big, long-term problems of America. That's what this ought to be doing.

But you see—let me give you another issue that directly affects not only those of you in this room who could pay to come to this fundraiser tonight but the people who put the food on our table. It may seem esoteric. And that is whether we continue to lead the world toward global prosperity and deal with all these international economic problems.

Ninety-one percent of the American people, I saw in a poll today in something I read today, know that the stock market dropped a lot last week—and I hope they know it came up a lot yesterday. But when you read—if you're somebody out there and you pick up the paper and you read why the stock market dropped so much in 2 or 3 days, and you say, "I don't know that there are a lot of businesses going broke," and everybody says it's because of events elsewhere in the world—we can't be just an island of prosperity; we have to want others in the world to do well if we want America to keep doing well. We have responsibilities. And a part of my budget involves paying our fair share to these international institutions to restore growth to places that are trying to take care of themselves and doing the right thing and trying to be responsible. And it's important to the economy of Florida and the United States.

The third thing we've got to do is try to prevail upon the Congress to follow the lead that Buddy's trying to take in passing a national bill for patients' rights.

The fourth thing we have to do is to help you with your education program. How many schools in Florida have kids going to class in housetrailers? That's why I have proposed, for the first time ever, that the National Government have a program to help build or remodel 5,000 schools in the fast-growing areas or in the areas where the schools are too dilapidated to really do the right thing by the children. That's why I proposed in our balanced budget providing funds for the States to hire 100,000 teachers to make sure we get the class sizes down to 18 in the early grades all across America.

These are big issues. In our balanced budget we also have money to continue to clean up the lakes and rivers of this country. Forty percent of the lakes and rivers in this country are still too polluted to swim in almost 30 years after the passage of the Clean Air Act—the Clean Water Act in the EPA.

And that's why I'm hoping this week we will finally get the Senate to stop filibustering and actually pass campaign finance reform, so we can follow Florida's lead, and we can have the right kind of system where everybody has a chance to run. Now, these are big issues.

A lot of people say, "Well, why go vote? America is in good shape." The world is changing very fast, and we are very blessed. But to be worthy of our blessings, we have to use them in the proper way. And when these good times are here, we need to use our money; we need to use the emotional space we've got; we need to use the confidence we've got to deal with the big issues.

So I say to you, I'm glad you're here. I appreciate the money that you've spent to contribute to the party. It will be well used to get votes out on election day. But every one of you as a citizen can go out and talk to your friends and neighbors and coworkers and people you see in every building you go in of any kind and tell them what the stakes are, why they should vote for Buddy MacKay, for Congress, why they should vote at all—for Governor— why they should vote at all.

I'm so sick and tired of—all the experts say, well, they know the vote will be down. The vote won't be down if people think it's in their interest to show up—if they think it's in their interest to show up.

And I'm telling you, our country has never had a better opportunity to build a world for the 21st century that's safer and more prosperous for our children. But it will only happen if we don't snooze away these good times, if we plan and act for the future.

The last thing I want to say is, when you go home tonight, think about the children that are the face and future of Florida and our country, increasingly diverse, from different racial and ethnic and religious and cultural backgrounds, all coming here because they believe there's some fabulous, unique promise and hope in our country. Before you go to bed tonight just ask yourself: Who do you really believe is more likely to go to bed every night as Governor thinking about those kids? Who do you think is more likely to wake up every day thinking about those kids? And who do you think is more likely to make decisions, the popular decisions and the unpopular decisions, that will give those kids a chance to grow up in one America?

That's why people ought to vote in November. That's why they ought to vote for Buddy MacKay. And that's why they ought to support our agenda for America's future. You can make sure it happens, and I hope you will.

Thank you, and God bless you.

NOTE: The President spoke at 9:40 p.m. in the Granada Ballroom at the Biltmore Hotel. In his remarks, he referred to Gubernatorial candidate Lt. Gov. Buddy MacKay of Florida, and his wife, Anne; Daryl L. Jones, State senator; and Mitch Ceasar, Florida Democratic Party chair.

Remarks on Presentation of the Presidential Awards for Excellence in Science, Math, and Engineering Mentoring
September 10, 1998

Thank you very much. I saw Representative Brown take my speech off the podium—[laughter]—and I thought that that was a rather extreme measure to take to demonstrate that he still knows much more about this subject than I do. [Laughter]

Let me thank all of you for coming and congratulate the awardees. I thank Secretary Slater and Secretary Riley for their support of this endeavor. I want to thank Neal Lane for agreeing to become the President's Science Adviser; and Dr. Rita Colwell for heading the NSF. When they were clapping for her, I didn't realize that she was sort of the poster woman of achievement for women in science. [Laughter] But I couldn't think of a better one.

I would like to say one very serious thing about George Brown. Many jokes have been made over the years about my affinity for issues that don't exactly grip the public consciousness from morning until night every day, but I think the public is more interested in science and technology than ever before and understands more clearly its role than ever before. And I believe it's important to acknowledge that in the last generation, the Member of Congress most responsible for our doing everything we've done right has been George Brown of California. And I thank you for that.

Let me say, I'm quite well aware that we're starting a little late today, and I regret that, but I was in an extended meeting with Senators from my own party, part of this process I'm going through of talking to people with whom I work and with whom I must work in your behalf to ask for their understanding, their forgiveness, and their commitment, not to let the events of the moment in Washington deter us from doing the people's work here and building the future of this country. And I can't think of a better moment really or subject for us to make that larger point.

All of you know how rapidly the world is changing. Now, everyday citizens see it when they watch the gyrations of the stock market up and down. I've been in Maryland and Florida the last couple of days, mostly in schools and with teachers and PTA leaders, and then at a couple of political events where regular business people would come up to me and say it truly is amazing to them how much events here are affected by events beyond our borders and how much people want us here to be strong, to be leading, to have a genuine and deep commitment to preparing for the future. There is no better example of that than the work that you do.

So the primary purpose of this event is for all of us, and especially me, to congratulate the President's Awardees for Excellence in Science, Mathematics, and Engineering Mentoring and to thank you for doing this, because not only those whom you mentor but those whom they touch will have a broader and more accurate worldview for the future. That will make our country a better place.

We are living in a truly remarkable time, driven in no small measure by the revolutions in science and technology. Our economy depends on it more and more, and the maintenance of our leadership depends upon our deepening commitment to it more and more. Yet statistics show that in science, engineering, and mathematics, minorities, women, and people with dis-

abilities are still grossly under-represented, even though we are becoming an ever more diverse society.

I've just really got this on my mind because I've been in a grade school in Maryland and a grade school in Orlando, Florida, this week, and I was looking at those kids. And it is hard to imagine an American future that works without those kids properly represented in the ranks of science and technology, without those kids making a profound commitment to mathematics, without those young people believing that if they have an interest there, they can pursue it to the nth degree.

And the truth is—you know, Rita talked about being discouraged just having people say they shouldn't waste scholarships on women; you hear similar stories from our first women astronauts. You hear similar stories from the first pioneers who broke racial and other barriers. But the truth is, even though we need our heroes and our trailblazers, that's no way to run a society. And people sooner or later just have to get over it. They have to get over it and open—[*applause*].

Now, look at this. Let me just read you this. The American Association for the Advancement of Sciences shows that between 1996 and 1997, 20 percent fewer African-Americans and 18.2 percent fewer Hispanic-American young people enrolled in graduate programs in science and engineering.

Judy Winston is here, who has done such a marvelous job of carrying our President's Initiative on Race. One of the things that I launched that initiative on race to do was to highlight developments like this, to talk about these disparities, to talk about what we could do about them. If we're serious about giving every American the chance to reach his or her dreams and building a work force for the global economy that reflects our national diversity and our global ties, if we're serious about having the finest scientists, mathematicians, and engineers in the world, we can't leave anybody behind.

Now, I've been working very hard to make sure that we have more uniform, high-quality, world-class public education in every school in America, that the children, without regard to their race or their income or the region of the country in which they live or the income of the neighborhood in which they live, will all have access to the kind of preparatory education they need.

And we work very hard—we've opened the doors of college wider than ever before in history with the HOPE scholarships, with the tax credits for all 4 years of college and graduate schools, with dramatic increases in Pell grants and work-study programs, with the improvements in the student loan programs. But we have to do more if we are going to address this problem. All that's been done, and the problem you're here to celebrate your contribution to solving is in many places and in many ways getting worse. And we have to face that, because it is not good for America.

We started an initiative that I hope will be funded in this Congress that I think could really help, called the High Hopes initiative, to provide mentors for disadvantaged middle school students and be able to tell these kids when they're in middle school, "You will be able to go on to college if you do well, and here's how much money you can get and here's what you can do with it."

But still, once these young people get to college, if they come from backgrounds where there is almost no record of achievement in the areas you represent, they need mentors. They need people who can guide them through all these decisions that have to be made about what you're going to major in and what else you take. I'm becoming an expert in that. [*Laughter*] They need people who can guide them into the right kinds of graduate programs. They need people who can support them through graduate work and help them to find a successful career.

Now, when we started these awards in 1996, we did it to encourage more scientists, engineers, and mathematicians to become mentors, and to encourage more minorities, women, and young people with disabilities to seek careers in science and math and technological fields. Today I want to announce a new step in this area. The Federal Government supports the work, literally, of tens of thousands of scientists and engineers at national labs and universities all across the country. If it were up to George and me, we'd support the work of many more. But these are tens of thousands of potential mentors working for our country through your tax dollar investments.

Today I'm directing the National Science and Technology Council to report back to me in 6 months with comprehensive recommendations about how we can use this fabulous resource to generate more mentors, to touch more kids, in a way that will have a huge positive impact on this problem we're trying to attack.

If every scientist and engineer who is doing something as a direct result of Federal investment were to become a committed, dedicated mentor, think what it would mean: a teenager from rural Tennessee reaching for the stars as a NASA technician; an inner-city child joining a clinical team that discovers a cure for cancer at the nearest teaching hospital; a first-generation American helping to build the next generation of the Internet.

Henry Adams once said that teachers affect eternity because they can never tell where their influence stops. I believe the same can be said about mentors. And I thank you, each and every one of you, for what you have done to help our country reach its full potential.

Thank you very much.

NOTE: The President spoke at 1:52 p.m. in the Roosevelt Room at the White House. In his remarks, he referred to Judith A. Winston, Executive Director, President's Initiative on Race.

Memorandum on Diversity in the Scientific and Technical Work Force
September 10, 1998

Memorandum for the National Science and Technology Council

Subject: Achieving Greater Diversity Throughout the U.S. Scientific and Technical Work Force

The world admires the American higher education system for its excellence in advanced training in science and engineering. Maintaining leadership across the frontiers of science and producing the finest scientists and engineers for the 21st century are principal goals of my Administration's science and technology policies. The work of individuals and organizations to inspire and mentor young people and offer role models is crucial to achieving these goals. To recognize this, I established the Presidential Award for Excellence in Science, Mathematics, and Engineering Mentoring in 1996. This annual award honors individuals and organizations for outstanding mentoring efforts that have encouraged significant numbers of individuals from groups under-represented in science, mathematics, and engineering to succeed in these fields.

As we work to develop the finest scientists and engineers for the 21st century, our human resources policies must address the composition of our science and engineering work force. Achieving diversity throughout the ranks of the scientific and technical work force presents a formidable challenge. The number of women, minorities, and persons with disabilities who have careers in science and engineering remains low. In every year of this decade, there have been far too few minorities awarded degrees in science or engineering, and the trend in minority admissions and degree awards is not encouraging. We need to draw upon the Nation's full talent pool. We cannot afford to overlook anyone.

Today, the science and engineering work force does not reflect the changing face of America. By 2010, approximately half of America's school-age population will be from minority groups. Minority participation in science and engineering careers should keep pace with this growing diversity. Expanding such participation will require drawing on and developing talent at all stages of educational preparation leading to advanced study. For example, only a small fraction, perhaps one-eighth, of all high school graduates have the mathematics and science preparation that would permit advanced study in a technical field; for under-represented minorities, that fraction is only half as much.

The Federal Government, working in partnership with the private sector and State governments, can be an effective agent of change; we can promote fuller participation of women, minorities, and people with disabilities in scientific and technical careers. With your help, my Administration has promoted quality education in the crucial early years by improving the quality of our schools and teachers, expanding access to the Internet and other technology-based learning tools, and basing all our efforts on rigorous standards through Goals 2000. We have expanded access to higher education by making it more affordable.

Existing Federal programs provide the means to achieve, but what are also needed in many cases are the mentors or role models that can help point the way to success. My High Hopes initiative will provide mentoring for middle and high school students to encourage larger numbers of low-income young people to enroll in colleges and universities. However, we must continue to assist under-represented minorities as they make their way through the myriad options available to them once they enter into our Nation's system of higher education. This is especially true for important technical career paths.

Therefore, I direct the National Science and Technology Council (NSTC) to develop recommendations within 180 days on how to achieve greater diversity throughout our scientific and technical work force. The NSTC recommendations will detail ways for the Federal Government to bolster mentoring in science and technology fields and to work with the private sector and academia to strengthen mentoring in higher education.

WILLIAM J. CLINTON

Statement on Senate Inaction on Campaign Finance Reform
September 10, 1998

I am very disappointed that a minority of the Senate, led by the Republican leadership, has once again voted to preserve the status quo of campaign finance by blocking tough bipartisan campaign finance reform. This comprehensive legislation has been passed by the House, is supported by the majority of the Senate, and is demanded by the American people.

If this minority of Senators continue to block this bill, they must take responsibility for the current campaign finance system, with its soft money and its inadequate disclosure requirements. And by doing so, they would deny the American people the best opportunity in a generation to pass meaningful, bipartisan campaign finance reform.

In the days to come, I urge the Senate to consider this issue again and give the American people the kind of campaign finance law they deserve.

Remarks on the Negotiated Agreement To End the Northwest Airlines Pilots' Strike
September 10, 1998

Good evening. I wanted to take this opportunity to say how delighted I am that Northwest Airlines and its pilots have reached the terms that form the basis of an agreement. The parties are now working on the specific time of getting back to work. The agreement, of course, will have to be approved, but I think this strike is over.

Earlier today, I spoke over the phone to the leaders of both parties: Randy Babbitt of the Air Line Pilots Association; and John Dasburg, the CEO of Northwest Airlines. I told them how important this negotiated agreement is to our country and to our economy, particularly at this time.

I'm pleased that they have worked so hard to make this happen. Getting Northwest planes and pilots back into the air is a victory for the company and for the employees and a victory for all Americans who rely on the airline.

I'd like to say a special word of appreciation to those here in the administration who were involved in this effort: to Secretary Slater; to my Deputy White House Counsel, Bruce Lindsey, who has developed quite an expertise in this whole area. They both went to Minnesota this week at my request to help to resolve the matter. I'd also like to say a special word of thanks to my labor adviser here in the White House, Karen Tramontano, for her work. All of them helped to spur these talks along. They deserve credit for their determination.

Again, let me say that this is good news for the American people. This is an indication that the collective bargaining process, if entered into in good faith, can actually work in a way that benefits everyone. I know there are a lot of people that depend upon Northwest who are relieved tonight, and again, I just want to thank all the parties, including you, Mr. Secretary.

Thank you very much.

NOTE: The President spoke at 6:53 p.m. on the South Lawn at the White House, prior to his departure for the Mayflower Hotel. In his remarks, he referred to Randall J. Babbitt, president, Air Line Pilots Association International, and John H. Dasburg, president and chief executive officer, Northwest Airlines.

Remarks at a Democratic Business Council Reception
September 10, 1998

Thank you. It's rare for me to feel that I am at a loss for words. I can only hope you know what I'm feeling, for you and for my wife and for my country. I think you do, and I thank you more than you can possibly know.

Hillary has mentioned all the people who are responsible for this evening. I would just echo my strong note of gratitude to all of you. Congressman Markey was here—there he is. Thank you very much for being here and for your support.

There are many distinguished citizens here, but I would like to acknowledge one because he embodies to me everything that is best about America. I think he is one of the bravest human beings I've ever known, and without him, Americans with disabilities would not be where they are today: a man I had the great honor to award the Presidential Medal of Freedom, Mr. Justin Dart. Thank you for being here, and God bless you, sir.

In addition to Roy and Len and Carol and all the DNC officers who are here, and Tom and Mike and John and Chris, who did this weekend—you know, Steve Grossman is not here tonight, but I just want to acknowledge how hard he has worked for all of us, to make our party strong.

There is one other person I want to mention. I'm glad Steve Grossman is not here tonight, because he went home to Massachusetts to Kirk O'Donnell's funeral. And a lot of you in this room knew Kirk O'Donnell. He was a magnificent human being, a great Democrat, a proud Irish-American, a passionate citizen and patriot. And this town is much the poorer for his passing.

When I called his wife the other night, I said, "You know, I'm not really a Washington insider. I think we've established that beyond any doubt." [*Laughter*] I said, "But Washington has a lot of great qualities, and maybe some that aren't so great. More than anybody I ever knew around here, I think Kirk O'Donnell had all the good and none of the bad." I'm proud he was a member of my party, and I just want to say to his wife and his two wonderful children, on behalf of a grateful nation, I thank them for his life, and I thank God for his life,

and I thank Steve Grossman for representing all of us at his funeral today in Massachusetts. Thank you.

Yesterday I was in Florida, and I went to this school in Orlando. And I wish all of you had been with me. It was an elementary school that was basically a multilingual international school, where all the kids that were there had to take at least two languages, English and something else. And there were a lot of Hispanic kids there; there were a lot of Asian kids there; there were kids from South Asia; there were African-American kids there; there was every conceivable ethnic group in this little grade school in Florida. And there was a wonderful Hispanic principal—American—whose mother, the principal's mother, spoke to me in Spanish and had to have it translated because I'm not as fluent as I should be—and hardly in English. [*Laughter*]

But anyway, these kids, they had a school uniform policy, which I love. They had a PTA president who was more charismatic than 90 percent of the politicians I've met in my life. They had a sense of community that required them to go out to every mother of a newborn in the jurisdiction of the elementary school and give the mothers classical music and other support for the newborns as a part of the elementary school's mission. And they had the genuine commitment that everybody that was within their embrace mattered, that every child could learn, that every child mattered, and that they were creating not just a school but a community in which they were prepared to accept responsibility for all these children's well-being.

And I'm telling you, it was an overwhelming experience being there. I say that because that school is a metaphor for what I have tried to do with America. And tonight all of you in this Business Council, you're pretty sophisticated about what's going on in this economy, and you understand that for all of our great good fortune today, this is an uncertain world, a lot of changes in it. The stock market goes up and down in no small measure because of perceived risk in America as a result of events far from our shores in economies much smaller than ours, reminding us that if we want the benefits of this global society, we must be able and willing to assume its responsibilities of leadership.

And so I want to just say two things that aren't particularly sophisticated. First of all, I am profoundly grateful for every single day, even the worst day, I have had to serve as your President because of where we are today. Secondly, when I was a young man—I don't believe I've ever said this in public except at my daughter's high school graduation—but when I was a young man I was complaining about something once, some perceived unfairness. And a much older man who sort of mentored me looked at me, and he said, "Let me tell you something, Bill." He said, "What you're saying is probably right, but just remember this: Most of us get out of this world ahead of where we would be if we only got what we deserved." [*Laughter*] He said, "No matter what happens, most of us get out of this world ahead." And we need to develop what Hillary later taught me is the discipline of gratitude. So that's the first thing I want you to know. I am grateful that we have had this chance to do these things.

The second thing I want to say is, usually when I come to a group like this, I say, isn't it wonderful that we have the lowest unemployment in 27 years, the lowest crime rate in 25 years, and the first balanced budget in 29 years, and the lowest percentage of people on welfare in 29 years, and you know the whole rest of it. And it is great.

But you understand a simple truth: This is a dynamic world. What really matters is not so much what we've had but what we intend to do with what we have. And a lot of times when things are going well, people think that they can indulge themselves in either idleness or things that are irrelevant to the mission at hand. I believe that in a dynamic world, our blessings confer special responsibilities to deal with the long-term challenges of the country.

We've got to really think about what we have learned about this global economy in the last 2 years. We learned a lot, you know. We learned a lot with NAFTA, with GATT, with our trade rules, with all the things we benefited—30 percent of our growth coming from trade. We learned a lot. What have we learned from the problems of the countries of Asia? What have we learned from the difficulties of the Russians? What have we learned from the difficulties of a great, vast, powerful country like Japan going 5 years without any real economic growth? And what should we as Americans do to inject stability and growth into this system? Because if we don't—as Chairman Greenspan said last week—we can't be an island of prosperity in a sea of distress. Big issue. We've got to start by paying our way to the International Monetary Fund.

But there is more, and it's big. We know that we have to prepare for the retirement of the baby boomers. Therefore, I say, let's don't spend this surplus until we save Social Security. Let's don't do that.

Maybe the Democrats feel more strongly about it because there were only Democrats voting for that economic plan in '93; we lost seats in the Congress on account of it. People bled over that plan. But when we passed the Balanced Budget Act, 92 percent of the deficit was already gone because of what our party did.

Now, we've been waiting 29 years—29 years. You know, I like tax cuts and spending programs as well as the next person. We've got both in our balanced budget, both targeted tax cuts for child care and education and the environment, and new investments in education and health care and other things. But I would like to see that ink change from red to black and just sort of savor it for a minute or two before we throw it all away again. [*Laughter*] And I think you would, too.

Now, everybody in this room who is between the ages of 34 and 52 in the baby boom generation, you've got to face the fact that if we do not meet our responsibilities to reform Social Security in a way that preserves its essential characteristics to give stability in old age to people who need it without imposing undue financial burdens—if we don't do it and do it now when it's least painful, then one of two things is going to happen: Either we'll all get to retirement, and we'll have to take a much lower standard of living; or we'll try to maintain the same system, which will cost our kids and grandkids so much money that they will have a lower standard of living. And that is a very foolish thing to do. We don't need to do it. So let's fix Social Security and then see how much money is left, and we can decide what to do with it then. That's what I think we ought to do.

We have just a few weeks left in this legislative session. I think it's important to make the right decisions. Look at the education bills we've got up there: 100,000 teachers in the early grades to lower average class size to 18; a program that will enable us to build or rehabilitate 5,000 schools to deal with school overcrowding and substandard condition; programs for safe schools; programs to hook all our classrooms and libraries up to the Internet by the year 2000; programs to create education opportunity zones, summer school, and after-school programs and mentoring programs and guaranteed scholarship programs for schools that aren't doing well that will agree to end social promotion but only if they help the kid, not stigmatize him. All of that's there.

The America Reads program: We had 1,000 colleges last year sending young people into schools to make sure that every 8-year old could read by the end of the third grade. It's all out there riding on what Congress does. You won't read anything about it, but it may be the most important set of decisions still to be made in this Congress. Will they embrace an education agenda that we never asked to be a partisan agenda? We never asked for it to be a partisan agenda. It is an agenda for America's children.

Or the health care bill of rights: 43 HMO's have now endorsed our health care bill of rights that says, in an accident you ought not have to drive across town to get to an emergency room, you ought to go to the nearest one; if you need a specialist, you ought to be able to get one; if you're getting care and your employer changes HMO's during the time of your pregnancy or your chemotherapy, they ought not to be able to change your doctor in the middle of the stream; and if you have privacy concerns, you ought to know your records will be kept private. Those are just some of the things in our bill. I think that's a big deal.

There are 160 million Americans in managed care, and I have never been an opponent of it, because I don't think we could be where we are today with the economy where it is unless we had broken the inflation in health care costs. But quality comes first. Now 43 HMO's have supported our bill. Why? Because they're doing the right thing anyway, and they're at an unconscionable disadvantage by treating their people right unless everybody else follows the same rules. This is a big deal for America. It's going to be decided between now and the next 3 weeks.

The same thing is true on the environment: 40 percent of our lakes and streams still not fit to swim in; even though the air and the water are cleaner and the food is safer, and we've cleaned up more toxic waste dumps, and we've also set aside more land than any administration except the two Roosevelts, we've still got 40 percent of the rivers and lakes in this country not fit to swim in.

We've got a lot of challenges to face. And man, I'm telling you, you ought to be attuned to this—there is a device in Washington—I had to learn about this; we didn't have these where I used to be involved in lawmaking—called a rider. That is not a person in a cowboy hat with spurs on. [*Laughter*] A rider is something you put on a bill that doesn't have much to do with the bill. And normally you put it on the bill because it couldn't stand on its own two feet so it's got to ride along on something that's got feet and legs and independence. And if you stick the rider on it, you know that the rider wouldn't be standing, so it's got to ride to get across the finish line of the law. And my job is to stop as many of those riders as I can. It's a big deal.

So I say to you, all of you, if you go back to the beginning, we are blessed. I am grateful. It imposes responsibilities. And the first and foremost of those is to say, what are the big challenges facing us on the brink of a new century and a new millennium? How are we going to be one America across all the lines that divide us? How are we going to keep growing? How are we going to fight the security threats like terrorism and weapons of mass destruction and seize the opportunities of this new world? I'll tell you, if we do what we're trying to do, we'll be doing our job.

So I say to you, we need more business support. We've got a lot more business Democrats than we had 6 years ago because we believe you can grow the economy and let people make good profits and still do right by the ordinary citizens of this country and lift the people up who deserve a fair chance. That's what we believe—that's what we believe.

So again I say, thank you for tonight, but remember those two things: We should be grateful, but we should be determined not to let America, her children, and her future down.

Thank you, and God bless you.

NOTE: The President spoke at 7:45 p.m. in the East Room at the Mayflower Hotel. In his remarks, he referred to Gov. Roy Romer of Colorado, general chair, Leonard Barrack, national finance chair, Carol Pensky, treasurer, and Steve Grossman, national chair, Democratic National Committee; C. Thomas Hendrickson, chair, and Mike Cherry, John Merrigan, and Chris Korge, cochairs, Democratic Business Council; and Kathryn O'Donnell, widow of attorney Kirk O'Donnell.

Remarks at a Democratic National Committee Dinner
September 10, 1998

Thank you so much. I want to thank Jim and Carol and Senator and Mrs. Pell, and all the others who had anything to do with this event tonight. This has been a particularly meaningful event. It wasn't just Jill who wanted Senator Pell's autograph; I got him to give me what he said about me, and I had him autograph it. [*Laughter*] I'll take it home, make sure my family believes me when I tell them he said it. [*Laughter*]

Thirty-four years ago I moved in across the street from this house, and I lived on the second floor of Loyola Hall as a freshman at Georgetown. And I looked out my window every morning into Senator Pell's garden—I don't want to you to think I was a peeping tom—[*laughter*]—I couldn't avoid it; I mean, if I looked out the window, I could see it. And I remember sometimes they would have garden parties in the springtime when the weather was warm, or I would see people come and go—famous people come and go. And it never occurred to me 34 years ago that someday I might be here with them, as President.

And I am very honored because, Senator, I thank you for the Pell grants. I thank you for your commitment to America's involvement in the world, for your belief in the United Nations and a world system of peace and prosperity. I wish you had another 35 years in the Senate. We need you there today more than ever. And I thank you.

So anyway, I'm feeling very, very nostalgic tonight. If anybody had told me when I was 18 I'd be in this backyard, I never would have believed it. I'd also like to thank all of you for your support, your personal support to me in this difficult time, in what I have tried to do to express apologies and seek forgiveness from the American people, but more important-

ly for your continuing commitment for what it is we're trying to do.

I saw a survey—I read something in the paper the other day that said that 91 percent of the American people were aware that the stock market had dropped 500 points, the day it dropped. Well, you know, 91 percent of the people—it's amazing that that many people would agree that the Sun comes up in the morning. I mean, that's a pretty high level. [*Laughter*]

And it's very interesting to me that—I now talk to all kinds of people. I was at a school in Florida yesterday, and the day before, a school in Maryland. And I would talk about this, and I'd say, "You all read about that, didn't you?" And they would say, "yes." And I said, "You read that the drop was generally attributed to developments beyond our borders that had no direct impact on the American economy." That is, no one could conclude from the momentary difficulties—or the difficulties, anyway, in Asia or Russia or whatever—that there was a direct impact on the economy today that was very severe. But we had this big drop.

And it's been very interesting, because these events and what people are learning about them and their apparent connection to the gyrations of the stock market have done more than anything—all the speeches I have given for 6 long years—to hammer home one point that I tried to hammer home when I ran for President in 1991 and 1992, which is: There is no longer an artificial dividing line between domestic and foreign policy, between economic and security policy; that we have to see a world in which we are growing closer together and an America in which we are growing ever more interconnected; and we have to look at the world in ways that enable us to fulfill our responsibilities toward peace and prosperity and freedom and human rights if we want America to do well at home.

And conversely, if we want America to be strong and be able to lead the world, we have to prove that we can develop the capacities of all of our people, that we can run a good, strong economy, and, very important over the long run, that in an increasingly interconnected world, that we have people from everywhere in America, but they all have a chance as long as they follow the rules. And I think that's important.

And our administration has really been devoted to giving everyone a chance to making America work again, and then to preparing us for the future, and to assume—to make sure we're doing what we can to lead the world toward peace and freedom and prosperity. I am grateful for what we've been able to do, but I will say this: I think the most important thing today is that Americans not take the blessings of the moment for granted, either to be idle or to pretend that we can indulge ourselves in self-defeating conduct as a nation.

When you get a moment like this when things seem to be going well, especially if there is a lot of churning dynamism elsewhere in the world, it is a time for an extra sense of responsibility to deal with the big challenges.

What have we learned about the world economy in the last 2 years that we didn't know? Have we learned anything we didn't know when we passed GATT, when we passed NAFTA, when we committed ourselves to an open trading system and to elevating other countries? What have we learned? What do we do about it?

Well, the first thing we've got to do is pay our way to the International Monetary Fund. If we want to have influence, we certainly have to pay our way. We need to pay our way to the United Nations. We need to do the things that a great country does.

But there is more we need to do. What are we going to do to make sure the baby boomers can retire, have the Social Security they need, the medical care they need, without bankrupting their children and grandchildren? What are we going to do to make sure, now that we have Pell grants, HOPE scholarships, record numbers of work-study positions, the most access to higher education in history, that we have the best elementary and secondary education in the world? What are we going to do to prove to other countries, by the power of our example,

that you can grow the economy and improve the environment at the same time? What are we going to do to reconcile our goals of having affordable health care with quality health care, through the Patients' Bill of Rights? What are we going to do, now that the House finally passed it, to stop the Senate Republican filibuster of campaign finance reform, killing it again? How can we raise this feeling that people have that their campaigns are properly run? There are a lot of big questions out there. Maybe most importantly of all, over the long run, what are we going to do to prove that we can be one America, no matter how diverse we get in terms of race, religion, culture? What are we going to do?

Because if we are—if we want to do good things in the rest of the world—some of you were so kind in what you said around the table tonight about the role the United States has been able to play in the last few years in the Irish peace process. We're working very, very hard this night in the Middle East peace process. We're working hard to reconcile people to one another. If we want to do good things around the world, we have to be good at home. We have to be able to set an example of reconciliation among ourselves, instead of destructive, divisive conduct.

So that's the only thing I would like for you to think about tonight. When you leave here, I hope, if somebody asks you why you came here, you will say, "I'm proud to be here because what we've done in the last 6 years made America work again. I'm proud to be here because we've got a vision of the world in the 21st century. And I'm proud to be here because we know that we dare not squander the blessings of the moment. Instead, we have to look at the big challenges that lie before us and seize them now when we have the resources and the confidence and the sheer emotional breathing room to do it." We don't want to let this pass us by. We want to seize it. And if we do, in a couple of years when we start that new century and that new millennium, America will give our children the future that we owe them.

Thank you very much, and God bless you.

NOTE: The President spoke at 9:38 p.m. at a private residence. In his remarks, he referred to dinner hosts Jim and Carol Lewin and their daughter Jill; and former Senator Claiborne Pell and his wife, Nualla.

Remarks at a Breakfast With Religious Leaders
September 11, 1998

Thank you very much, ladies and gentlemen. Welcome to the White House and to this day to which Hillary and the Vice President and I look forward so much every year.

This is always an important day for our country, for the reasons that the Vice President said. It is an unusual and, I think, unusually important day today. I may not be quite as easy with my words today as I have been in years past, and I was up rather late last night thinking about and praying about what I ought to say today. And rather unusually for me, I actually tried to write it down. So if you will forgive me, I will do my best to say what it is I want to say to you, and I may have to take my glasses out to read my own writing.

First, I want to say to all of you that, as you might imagine, I have been on quite a journey these last few weeks to get to the end of this, to the rockbottom truth of where I am and where we all are. I agree with those who have said that in my first statement after I testified, I was not contrite enough. I don't think there is a fancy way to say that I have sinned.

It is important to me that everybody who has been hurt know that the sorrow I feel is genuine: first and most important, my family; also my friends, my staff, my Cabinet, Monica Lewinsky and her family, and the American people. I have asked all for their forgiveness.

But I believe that to be forgiven, more than sorrow is required—at least two more things: first, genuine repentance, a determination to change and to repair breaches of my own making—I have repented; second, what my Bible calls a "broken spirit," an understanding that I must have God's help to be the person that I want to be, a willingness to give the very forgiveness I seek, a renunciation of the pride and the anger which cloud judgment, lead people to excuse and compare and to blame and complain.

Now, what does all this mean for me and for us? First, I will instruct my lawyers to mount a vigorous defense, using all available appropriate arguments. But legal language must not obscure the fact that I have done wrong.

Second, I will continue on the path of repentance, seeking pastoral support and that of other caring people so that they can hold me accountable for my own commitment.

Third, I will intensify my efforts to lead our country and the world toward peace and freedom, prosperity and harmony, in the hope that with a broken spirit and a still strong heart I can be used for greater good, for we have many blessings and many challenges and so much work to do.

In this, I ask for your prayers and for your help in healing our Nation. And though I cannot move beyond or forget this—indeed, I must always keep it as a caution light in my life—it is very important that our Nation move forward.

I am very grateful for the many, many people, clergy and ordinary citizens alike, who have written me with wise counsel. I am profoundly grateful for the support of so many Americans who somehow, through it all, seem to still know that I care about them a great deal, that I care about their problems and their dreams. I am grateful for those who have stood by me and who say that in this case and many others, the bounds of privacy have been excessively and unwisely invaded. That may be. Nevertheless, in this case, it may be a blessing, because I still sinned. And if my repentance is genuine and sustained, and if I can maintain both a broken spirit and a strong heart, then good can come of this for our country as well as for me and my family.

The children of this country can learn in a profound way that integrity is important and selfishness is wrong, but God can change us and make us strong at the broken places. I want to embody those lessons for the children of this country, for that little boy in Florida who came up to me and said that he wanted to grow up and be President and to be just like me. I want the parents of all the children in America to be able to say that to their children.

A couple of days ago when I was in Florida, a Jewish friend of mine gave me this liturgy book called "Gates of Repentance." And there was this incredible passage from the Yom Kippur liturgy. I would like to read it to you: "Now is the time for turning. The leaves are beginning to turn from green to red to orange.

The birds are beginning to turn and are heading once more toward the south. The animals are beginning to turn to storing their food for the winter. For leaves, birds, and animals, turning comes instinctively. But for us, turning does not come so easily. It takes an act of will for us to make a turn. It means breaking old habits. It means admitting that we have been wrong, and this is never easy. It means losing face. It means starting all over again. And this is always painful. It means saying I am sorry. It means recognizing that we have the ability to change. These things are terribly hard to do. But unless we turn, we will be trapped forever in yesterday's ways. Lord, help us to turn, from callousness to sensitivity, from hostility to love, from pettiness to purpose, from envy to contentment, from carelessness to discipline, from fear to faith. Turn us around, O Lord, and bring us back toward you. Revive our lives as at the beginning, and turn us toward each other, Lord, for in isolation there is no life."

I thank my friend for that. I thank you for being here. I ask you to share my prayer that God will search me and know my heart, try me and know my anxious thoughts, see if there is any hurtfulness in me, and lead me toward the life everlasting. I ask that God give me a clean heart, let me walk by faith and not sight.

I ask once again to be able to love my neighbor—all my neighbors—as myself; to be an instrument of God's peace; to let the words of my mouth and the meditations of my heart and, in the end, the work of my hands, be pleasing. This is what I wanted to say to you today.

Thank you. God bless you.

NOTE: The President spoke at 9:40 a.m. in the East Room at the White House. In his remarks, he referred to former White House intern Monica S. Lewinsky.

Remarks at a Memorial Service for the Victims of the Embassy Bombings in Kenya and Tanzania
September 11, 1998

Bishop Haines, Dean Baxter, Reverend Jackson, clergy; Vice President and Mrs. Gore, Secretary Albright, Secretary Cohen, Janet, Secretary Shalala; to the Members of Congress; our military service; distinguished members of the diplomatic corps, especially those from Kenya and Tanzania. Most of all, to the members of the families, friends, and colleagues of the deceased; the survivors of the attacks; Ambassador Bushnell and Chargé Lange; my fellow Americans.

Today we are gathered in a truly sacred and historic place to honor and to celebrate the lives of 12 Americans who perished in service to our Nation—their goodness, their warmth, their humanity, and their sacrifice. The two sides of their lives—who they were in their labors and who they were as husbands and wives, sons and daughters, friends and colleagues—came together. For as they showed every day in their devotion to family and friends, their work was about bringing better lives to all.

They worked to create opportunity and hope, to fight poverty and disease, to bridge divides between peoples and nations, to promote tolerance and peace. They expressed both their patriotism and their humanity, as Adlai Stevenson so well put it, "in the tranquil and steady dedication of a lifetime."

In the book of Isaiah it is written that the Lord called out, "Whom shall I send, and who will go for us?" And Isaiah, the prophet, answered, "Here am I, Lord; send me." These Americans, generous, adventurous, brave souls, said, "Send me. Send me in service. Send me to build a better tomorrow." And on their journey they perished, together with proud sons and daughters of Kenya and Tanzania.

Some of the Kenyans and Tanzanians worked alongside our Americans at our Embassies, making vital contributions. Others were simply, unfortunately, nearby, working or studying, providing for their loved ones, doing what they do and did every day. For those people, too, we mourn, we honor, we thank God for their lives.

All of them were taken too soon, leaving behind families, many including young children, and devoted friends and colleagues. No tribute from us can rouse them from a long night of mourning. That takes time and the mysterious workings of the heart. But surely some comfort comes with the memory of the happiness they brought, the difference they made, the goodness they left inside those whom they loved and touched.

Last month at Andrews Air Force Base, Hillary and I walked out into the hangar that day to meet the families and share with them the homecoming of their loved ones for the last time. There we saw a larger family, many standing and pressed together, people from the State and Defense Departments, from our military, from AID and the CDC. They, too, lost brothers and sisters. They, too, must be immensely proud of their friends, the traditions, the accomplishments, the life they shared.

All of us must stand together with our friends from Kenya and Tanzania and other peaceloving nations—yes, in grief, but also in common commitment to carry on the cause of peace and freedom, to find those responsible and bring them to justice, not to rest as long as terrorists plot to take more innocent lives, and in the end, to convince people the world over that there is a better way of living than killing others for what you cannot have today. For our larger struggle, for hope over hatred and unity over division, is a just one. And with God's help, it will prevail. We owe to those who have given their lives in the service of America and its ideal to continue that struggle most of all.

In their honor, let us commit to open our hearts with generosity and understanding; to treat others who are different with respect and kindness; to hold fast to our loved ones; and always to work for justice, tolerance, freedom, and peace.

May God be with their souls.

NOTE: The President spoke at 12:12 p.m. at the Washington National Cathedral. In his remarks, he referred to Bishop Ronald H. Haines and Dean Nathan Baxter, Washington National Cathedral; civil rights activist Rev. Jesse Jackson; Janet Langhart, wife of Secretary of Defense William S. Cohen; Prudence Bushnell, U.S. Ambassador to Kenya; and John E. Lange, U.S. Chargé d'Affaires, Tanzania.

Statement on the Nomination of Richard Holbrooke as United States Ambassador to the United Nations
September 11, 1998

On June 18, I announced my intent to nominate Richard Holbrooke as U.S. Ambassador to the United Nations because of my confidence that he will make an outstanding U.N. Ambassador. Ambassador Holbrooke has made remarkable contributions to our Nation's security in this administration and in previous administrations: working to bring lasting peace to Bosnia, helping to diffuse tensions and find workable solutions in Kosovo and Cyprus, serving as our Ambassador to Germany, promoting peace in regions of Asia.

Ambassador Holbrooke has stated that he is cooperating with a review by the Departments of State and Justice of his financial disclosure reports and contacts with State Department officials during the year following his departure from government service in February 1996. I look forward to a prompt resolution of this review and submission of his nomination to the Senate.

Remarks on Receiving the Paul O'Dwyer Peace and Justice Award
September 11, 1998

Thank you very much. Thank you. Well, I have loved this, but you must be exhausted. [*Laughter*] I want to say, Hillary and I have been over there just lapping this up. We don't want this to ever end. [*Laughter*] But I'm afraid you're going to get dizzy if you keep getting up and down.

Let me say to Brian O'Dwyer and the O'Dwyer family, I am profoundly grateful. Senator Kennedy, thank you so much for what you said and for more, what you have done. When the history of this century is written, I doubt very seriously that there will be a single other United States Senator who will have done so much for so long for the American people as Edward Kennedy of Massachusetts. I also like to borrow a lot of Senator Kennedy's lines when I can get away with it, and I might say, I will never let "St. George" live it down.

I want to thank all of you who are here: the members of my Cabinet, Secretary Daley and Administrator Aida Alvarez, and Kitty Higgins and others who are here in the administration. Thank you, John Sweeney, for your championing Irish-American and every American worker's rights, for what you have done.

I thank the Members of Congress who are here who have supported our policy, both Republicans and Democrats who have stood up for the initiative the United States has made and made it possible for me to continue to do whatever it is that we have been able to do to advance the cause of peace.

This is an honor that really belongs to all of you and many who are not even here today. But mostly, whenever I look at it, I will think of Paul O'Dwyer, for his devotion to civil rights and human rights and social justice and the cause of the Irish people and peace in the Irish heart. He was beloved by many people, including me. I will never forget when I first met him in 1991. I will never forget all that happened from that day to this, and the wonderful journey that that began with Irish-Americans and the people of Ireland.

There are many people that I would like to thank—and I'd like to save Senator Mitchell until last. I want to thank Tony Blair, who called me this afternoon again to continue to push

the Irish peace process. And the great Prime Minister of Ireland, the *Taoiseach*, Bertie Ahern. And thank you, Mr. Ambassador, for being here as well and for your service. I want to thank their predecessors. I want to thank all the Members of Congress, those that are here and those who aren't. I, too, want to say a good word for Jean Kennedy Smith, who from time to time rivaled her brother in their pushy insistence that I should do more—[*laughter*]—and more and more.

There are some people in the White House I'd like to thank. I want you to know the Vice President—first of all, he had his priorities in order, going to Parents Night, and that ought to speak volumes. But he only has one more to go, you know, so he doesn't want to miss another Parents Night. But I want you to know, all those things that he litanized there in his little speech, more than any other Vice President in the history of this country, he was involved in every difficult, controversial, and bold decision this administration has made, always pushing for it, including the work we did in the Irish peace process. And I'm grateful to him very much for that.

I want to thank Sandy Berger and Jim Steinberg with the National Security Council, and their predecessors in my first term—Tony Lake, and I thank Nancy Soderberg, now at the United Nations—for what they did for the Irish peace process.

I want to thank Hillary for reaching out to the women of Ireland, for going to the Vital Voices conference there last week, and building real, genuine partnerships with people who are reaching across the lines that have divided people for so long, to raise children and start businesses and build peace block by block. I personally believe that it was a sort of an unprecedented effort by an American public figure to deal at a human level that I can only wish I had had the opportunity to do. But I thank her for that because I think it's been very important.

There's one other person I'd like to thank who's not here, but I was sitting here thinking when I saw Congressman Manton out there, and I remembered the first time I came to the Queens Democratic Committee, and he was chairing the committee. And I was thinking about that first meeting we had in New York with Paul O'Dwyer; and I think my good friend Bruce Morrison, a former Congressman from Connecticut, was there, who Hillary and I have known for 30 years. But I would like to thank the person who introduced me to them, who started this whole journey, the man who ran my campaign in New York in 1991 and '92, Harold Ickes. Without him, none of this might not have happened, because he brought me to them.

Now, George Mitchell was unconscionable in the praise that he heaped on me tonight, but when I was in Northern Ireland with him, I felt like Ray Lankford. Anybody here know who Ray Lankford is? [*Applause*] He's the guy that bats behind Mark McGwire. [*Laughter*] And he's a good baseball player, by the way. I was standing up there and I had the feeling half of the crowd was saying, "Who's that big fellow up there with George Mitchell?" [*Laughter*] .

He can say whatever he wants about my phone calls and my meetings and my endless— somebody had to run that deal. When he started running that peace process, the people on opposite sides literally did not sit in the same room and listen to each other while the other one was talking. George's first big deal was to make sure that people stayed in the same room while their counterparts were talking, and actually listened. That's how far we have come. That was the distance that was traveled between the beginning and the Good Friday Agreement.

I cannot imagine another person who could have done it. I would never have had the patience to sit there and do it. I cannot imagine. And for years, George would hardly speak to me. [*Laughter*] He said, "I got out of public life; I left the Senate; I wanted to have a private life; I wanted to have a family. And then you stuck me with this." [*Laughter*]

I told him one time—he mentioned this in Ireland—I said, "George, you know the title of that old country song about the guy that makes a bad divorce settlement, 'She Got the Gold Mine and I Got the Shaft'? You got the shaft." [*Laughter*] We'd go everywhere, people would clap for me, and George would have to go back and sit in the meeting where people didn't talk to each other, you know. [*Laughter*] He'd have to wait for days on end to see if people would

sneeze in the right way. It was unbelievable. [*Laughter*]

Finally, on this last trip to Ireland, George Mitchell finally said, "Thank you. I'm glad I got to do it"—after 3 years. And I appreciate it.

I tell you that to make a serious and large point. All over the world there are people who ought to get along together who can't stand each other. All over the world there are people that have a great deal in common, but they will never find out because they won't even sit down and talk to each other and listen respectfully. All over the world there are people who spend day after day after day after day in abject misery because they are in the grip of a destructive obsession where they define the merit of their life by their ability to—[*inaudible*]—hopefully, in their minds, repress somebody who is of a different racial, religious, ethnic, or tribal group.

Piercing through to the human heart and engaging the human mind and opening human ears, and getting it all done at once, and then going through a rigorous system of work through complex, real issues where real interests are at stake is about the most difficult, exhausting, demanding work. And I personally hope I'll live to see George Mitchell get a Nobel Prize for what he did for the people of Ireland. [*Applause*] Thank you. Thank you.

I know it will grieve you, but I'm not going to give this speech that my wonderful staff wrote for me, because we've been here too long. But I want to make a couple of points. This is not a done deal, number one. It's wonderful, and even on our last trip it was great—Secretary Daley was there, and people were actually talking about business instead of fighting. We went to Stormont, and I got to meet—at least all the different parties stood in the same room together. Even Mr. Paisley's crowd was in the same room with everybody else—[*laughter*]— and we had a visit. It was kind of nice. I liked it.

And then I went to Waterfront Hall and tried to be as honest as I could be about what still has to be done. We've got to constitute a government over there, consistent with the agreement. We have to continue with the decommissioning. We have to complete every last step of this process.

But the good news is, the people really want it. You know, we went to Armagh, to this beautiful, beautiful city. We had thousands of people there, young and old, in the seat of St. Patrick's mission to Ireland—the last popular Englishman in Ireland until Tony Blair came along, I think. [*Laughter*] But it was so wonderful to see all those young people there. And then I can't add anything to what Hillary told you about Omagh, except that through all their heartbreak they wanted us to go on, and they wanted this to go on.

And in the Republic—we had 50,000 people in the streets in Limerick—50,000 people—including Congressman King and his mother and half of his relatives. [*Laughter*] And then every little Irish village I went through in the west of Ireland on the way to Ballybunion, where everybody was in the streets, and the stores had all been repainted, and it was just unbelievable—they weren't there for me so much as they were there for the United States and for the idea that the United States is a genuine friend to the Irish people and to the reconciliation of the Irish people.

And so I say to you, when you leave here today—we've had a great time, and Hillary and I will never forget what you've done for us today, and I suspect you know. But we've got a lot of work to do over there. We cannot have come all this way not to finish the job. And we must commit to that.

It's also very much in our interest. Ireland's got the fastest growing economy in Europe—about 500 American companies there already. We visited one, Gateway 2000, had an amazing experience there—the congressional delegation here that was with us. Our partnership means a lot to the world. No nation has done as much, as long, as consistently for peacekeeping as Ireland has. Over the last 40 years, I don't believe there's been a single day there hasn't been an Irish peacekeeper somewhere in the world. Seventy-five have perished. But today, they're still there, from Africa to the Middle East to Bosnia, shoulder-to-shoulder with American troops. So we have a common agenda in terms of our economic interests but a common agenda in terms of our deep commitment to peace.

All of this is important. But maybe the most important thing from my point of view is this: If after 30 years of the Troubles, and roughly 800 as nearly as I can figure going back and forth and fighting, the Irish can be reconciled to themselves, and Ireland can come home to itself, then the United States can look every other warring faction in the world dead in the eye and say, don't tell me this can't be done.

From the Middle East to Kosovo to Kashmir to the tribal conflicts in Africa, I would like to tell them the story of the hundreds of years of Irish history. I would like to tell them about the potato famine and the civil war and the conflicts with the British and the deeply embedded hatreds, and how in our time it all went away—because one of the problems we have in so many places is that people literally cannot imagine a future different from the present and the past. And if we finish this job, then we can go anywhere in the world and say, "Look, I know you've got a lot of problems and I know you can't stand your neighbor over there, but let me tell you about Northern Ireland." And every one of you knows—every one of you knows—that you have played a role in that.

A hundred years ago this year, William Butler Yeats gave a speech evaluating Ireland's past and predicting a new day. It's quite a deal for him to be optimistic, you know. He said, "We are building up a nation which shall be moved by noble purposes to noble ends." Well, it's taken some time to realize that vision. Almost 20 years after he wrote that, he was saying that things fall apart; the center cannot hold. I think he would be greatly pleased to know that things have come together, and the center seems to be holding very well, thank you.

So again let me say, I thank you all. This award belongs to all of you. But we have work to do. And when we do, when Ireland finally does completely come home to itself, it will be a gift not only to the Irish and not only to those of us who are Irish-Americans; it will be a gift for the whole world, a gift the world sorely needs. And all of you will have played a role in giving it.

God bless you, and thank you very much.

NOTE: The President spoke at 7 p.m. on the South Lawn at the White House. In his remarks, he referred to Brian O'Dwyer, chairman, Emerald Isle Immigration Center, and son of the late activist attorney Paul O'Dwyer; John J. Sweeney, president, AFL–CIO; former Senator George J. Mitchell, independent chairman of the multiparty talks in Northern Ireland; Prime Minister Tony Blair of the United Kingdom; Prime Minister Bertie Ahern and Ambassador to the U.S. Sean O'hUiginn of Ireland; U.S. Ambassador to Ireland

Jean Kennedy Smith; Anthony Lake, former Assistant to the President for National Security Affairs; Nancy E. Soderberg, former Deputy Assistant to the President for National Security Affairs; and Rev. Ian Paisley, leader of Northern Ireland's Democratic Unionist Party.

The President's Radio Address
September 12, 1998

Good morning. It's been an exhausting and difficult week in the Capital, not only for me but for many others. But as I told my Cabinet on Thursday, we cannot lose sight of our primary mission, which is to work for the American people and especially for the future of our children. The most important thing to do now is to stay focused on the issues the American people sent us here to deal with, from health care to the economy to terrorism.

Today that's exactly what we're doing. I want to tell you about the latest steps we're taking to combat a truly alarming trend, the growing use of drugs among our young people. The good news is that overall drug use has dropped by half since 1979. But among our children, the problem is getting worse. In fact, if present trends continue, half of all high school seniors will have smoked marijuana by the time they graduate. That's a frightening development. When we know that drugs lead to crime, to failure in school, to the fraying of families and neighborhoods, we know we must do better.

We can reverse this terrible trend if we attack it in the way we did the crime problem, by working together at the community level, neighborhood by neighborhood, block by block, person by person.

Crime overall has dropped to a 25-year low now, because whole communities are taking responsibility for their own streets and neighborhoods, and because here in Washington we're giving them the tools they need, such as support for community policing programs. When we assumed responsibility for bringing down crime, something remarkable happens: crime does go down.

We can have a similarly dramatic effect in curbing the use of drugs among our young people. But all of us have a responsibility to send our young people the same simple message: Drugs are wrong; drugs are illegal; and drugs can kill you.

This summer my administration launched an unprecedented media campaign to ensure that the message comes across when young people watch television, listen to radio, or read the newspaper. But media is not enough. We also must enlist the efforts of parents, teachers, ministers and clergy, coaches, principals from the community of adults around them. That's why, with the support of both Democrats and Republicans in Congress, and under the direction of General Barry McCaffrey, we're extending new help to community-based groups all over our Nation. Representatives of some of those groups are here with me in the Oval Office today. Already they are working to curb drug use by reclaiming drug houses, reaching out to at-risk foster kids, teaching parents to deliver the anti-drug message.

Today I'm delighted to announce the first round of high-impact, low-redtape grants to 93 communities. Their dollar amounts are not large, but if these grants empower communities to do more of what works to keep young people away from the scourge of drugs, their effect will be enormous.

Now, we also need the support of Congress on other serious issues facing our country. We are committed, in a bipartisan way, to fight against drug use among our young people. We must similarly be committed in a bipartisan way to continue our economic growth by staying with our economic strategy that has made our country the envy of the world, by maintaining our fiscal discipline, setting aside the surplus—every penny of it—until we save Social Security first.

We have to restore strength and growth to the world economy by investing our proportionate share in the International Monetary Fund. All of you know that the world economy has been going up and down and changing quite a bit lately. Treasury Secretary Rubin and I will go to New York on Monday, where I will discuss the current challenges of the global economy and the risks to our prosperity unless we act on the IMF request and take some other steps designed to make sure that America does not become a sea of prosperity in an ocean of distress.

We also have to continue to invest in the education of our people. We have to have smaller classes, more teachers, modernized schools, all the classrooms hooked up to the Internet, and higher standards.

We need a real Patients' Bill of Rights. We need to protect the environment. We need to protect our democracy by passing bipartisan campaign finance reform. All these items, also, are before Congress now.

It is truly encouraging to me how we have put aside partisan differences to save our children and their future from drugs. We have to do that on other issues critical to our future now—and even in the weeks before the election in November. We must stay focused on your business.

Thanks for listening.

NOTE: The President spoke at 10:06 a.m. from the Oval Office at the White House.

Remarks to the Council on Foreign Relations in New York City
September 14, 1998

Thank you very much, Pete. Hillary and I are delighted to be here with you and Joan, and I'm glad to be joined by Secretary Rubin and Jim Harmon, Gene Sperling, other members of our team. I'm glad to see Dick Holbrooke over here; I hope, if we can overcome the inertia of Congress, he will soon be a member of the team again. And I thank David Rockefeller and Les Gelb and others who welcomed us here today.

The subject that I want to discuss—let me just say one thing in advance—I'm going to give you my best thoughts. We have been working on this for 3 years at some level of intensity or another, going back to the Naples G–7 meeting in the aftermath of the Mexican financial crisis. I have done everything I could do personally to reach out across the country, and indeed across the world, for any new ideas from any source. I'm going to give you my best thinking today about what we can do, but I want you to know that I'm here, and if I had my druthers, this would be about a 3-hour session where I'd give this talk and then I would listen for the rest of the time.

So I want to encourage you, if you think we're right, to support us. But if you have any ideas, for goodness sake, share them, because I agree with what Pete said. This is the biggest financial challenge facing the world in a half century. And the United States has an absolutely inescapable obligation to lead, and to lead in a way that's consistent with our values and our obligation to see that what we're doing helps lift the lives of ordinary people here at home and all around the world.

The Council on Foreign Relations has always stood for political and economic freedom, since right after World War I. And I think one of the things that has impacted all of us, and it was implicit in what Pete said, is that for the last decade the growth of freedom around the world—with more than half the people in the world living under governments of their own choosing; more than half the villages, the one million villages, in China now even electing their own governments; and this sweeping replacement of command and control economies by market economies—I think it seems to have happened so easily, so effortlessly, so inexorably that I think we think the trend is inevitable and irreversible. But if you consider today's economic difficulties, disruptions, and the plain old deep, personal disappointments of now tens of millions of people around the world, it is clear to me that there is now a stark challenge not only to economic freedom, but, if unaddressed, a challenge that could stem the rising tide of political liberty as well.

Obviously, we have profound interests here. It is a great irony that we are at a moment of unsurpassed economic strength at a time of such turmoil in the world economy. We, I think, all of us in this room, know that our future prosperity depends upon whether we can work with others to restore confidence, manage change, stabilize the financial system, and spur robust global growth.

For most of the last 30 years, the United States and the rest of the world has been preoccupied by inflation, for reasons that all of you here know all too well. And it was a good thing to be preoccupied with. Today, the low and stable inflation we enjoy has been critical to our economic health, and low inflation has also contributed to that of many other nations as well. But clearly, the balance of risks has now shifted, with a full quarter of the world's population living in countries with declining economic growth or negative economic growth.

Therefore, I believe the industrial world's chief priority today, plainly, is to spur growth. It seems to me there are six immediate steps we should take to help contain the current financial turmoil around the world, and then two longer term projects in which we must be involved.

To take the immediate first, we must work with Japan, Europe, and other nations to spur growth. Second, we will expand our efforts to enable viable businesses in Asia to emerge from crippling debt burdens so they can once again contribute to growth and job creation. Third, we've asked the World Bank to double its support for the social safety net in Asia to help people who are innocent victims of financial turmoil. Fourth, we'll urge the major industrial economies to stand ready to use the $15 billion in IMF emergency funds to help stop the financial contagion from spreading to Latin America and elsewhere. Fifth, our Ex-Im Bank, under the leadership of Jim Harmon, will intensify its efforts to generate economic activity in the developing world immediately, in the next 3 months. And sixth, Congress must live up to its responsibility for continued prosperity by meeting our obligations to the International Monetary Fund.

Secretary Rubin has been working with his counterparts in the G–7 to get cooperative support for several of these measures. I understand Chairman Greenspan is also consulting with his counterparts on these items as well.

As we take these immediate steps, we also must intensify our efforts to reform our trade and financial institutions so that they can respond better to the challenges we now face and those we are likely to face in the future. We must build a stronger and more accountable global trading system, pressing forward with market-opening initiatives, but also advancing the protection of labor and environmental interests and doing more to ensure that trade helps the lives of ordinary citizens across the globe.

Above all, we must accelerate our efforts to reform the international financial system. Today I have asked Secretary Rubin and Federal Reserve Board Chairman Greenspan to convene a major meeting of their counterparts within the next 30 days to recommend ways to adapt the international financial architecture to the 21st century.

Over the past 6 years, our strategy at home of fiscal discipline, investment in the skills of our people, and open trade has worked for all Americans: unemployment at a 28-year low, inflation a 32-year low, wages rising at twice the rate of inflation after decades of stagnation. And on October 1st we'll have the first balanced budget in 29 years.

But the global economy brought a lot of that prosperity to us, and now fast-moving currents have brought or aggravated problems in Russia and Asia. They threaten emerging economies from Latin America to South Africa. With a quarter of the world's population in declining growth, we must recognize what Chairman Greenspan said the other day: We cannot forever be an oasis of prosperity. Growth at home depends upon growth abroad. A full 30 percent of our growth, just since I became President, has been due to our expanding positive involvement in the global economy.

That's why ordinary Americans should care if Asia or Russia or South America is on solid economic footing. These people are our customers. With one-third of the growth of our economy coming from exports, much of it from emerging markets, we know that those markets will falter as their economies flatten. When the problem is widespread and perceived to be moving in the wrong direction, we have seen that our stock market can react, having a direct and immediate impact on the wealth of the American people.

These nations are also our competitors. And under conditions of decent equilibrium, that is a very good thing, indeed. But when their currencies drop precipitously, the prices of their goods fall; they could undercut the sales of our own goods here at home that are otherwise profitable, dramatically increasing our trade deficit under circumstances that could cause the American people to turn away from open trade toward protectionism in a way that has terrific negative consequences long-term for our global growth objectives.

Finally, these nations are our friends, our allies, and our security partners. Where economic turmoil plunges millions into sudden poverty and disrupts and disorients the lives of ordinary people, the risks of political and social instability and of a turn from democracy clearly rise. Just look at Russia. Russia is facing an economic crisis that threatens the extraordinary progress the Russian people have made in just 7 years, building a new society from the ground up. The ruble and the stock market have plummeted; banks are weak; tax collections have slowed; the government has trouble paying its debts and its salaries. Some Russians have become wealthy, but many, many more are struggling to provide for their families. I talked to some of them when I was in Russia just a few days ago.

Amid such political uncertainty and economic difficulty, some now talk of abandoning the path of reform and returning to policies of the past, even policies that have already failed. At worst, adversity in Russia could affect not only the Russian economy and prospects for our economic cooperation—at worst, it could have an impact on our cooperation with Russia on nuclear disarmament, on fighting terrorism and the spread of weapons of mass destruction, on standing together for peace, from the Balkans to the Middle East.

Now Russia has a new Prime Minister, Mr. Primakov, who's been in office a grand total of 4 days. He and President Yeltsin face one of the great challenges of their time. Never has there been a more important moment to set a clear direction for the future, to affirm the commitment of Russia to democracy and to free markets, and to take decisive steps to stabilize the economy and restore investor confidence.

But if Russia is willing to take these steps, we must do everything we can to provide support to them. Because again I say, as long as ordinary people don't feel any benefits from this, in the end it's going to be difficult to sustain the direction we think the world should take.

On the other hand, we need to be honest with Russia and everyone else. No nation, rich or poor, democratic or authoritarian, can escape the fundamental economic imperatives of the global market. No nation can escape its dis-

cipline. No nation can avoid its responsibility to do its part.

But since all economies are increasingly interdependent, fear and uncertainty about the economy of one country can prompt investors to pull money out of other countries thousands of miles away. Markets work best when they are driven neither by excessive inflows or outflows of capital based on indiscriminate optimism or pessimism.

Regardless of what changes in policies or institutions may be warranted, we have to say we'll only be able to help those countries who are willing to help themselves. If a nation chooses to print money indiscriminately, to wink at cronyism or corruption, to hide bad loans and protect corrupt or inefficient banks, then investors, foreign and domestic, sooner or later will withdraw their investments, with consequences both swift and severe.

That is why we support the fundamental approach of the International Monetary Fund to extend assistance only when nations have taken responsibility, strengthening their banking systems, introducing honest accounting and open markets, awarding credit on merit instead of connections.

Still, what has been done is clearly not enough to reverse the decline in particular countries, to douse the flames of the international financial crisis, to support steady and sustainable growth in the future. In the face of this new challenge, America can and must continue to act and to lead to take the urgent steps needed today to calm the financial crisis, restart the engine of growth in Asia, and minimize the impact of financial turmoil on other nations, and to make certain that for tomorrow the institutions and rules of international finance and international trade are prepared to support steady and sustainable growth over the long term.

First and foremost, the leading economic nations must act together to spur global growth. Our strong and growing economy here has made a major contribution to global growth, just as our weak economy was holding the world back 6 years ago when I attended my first G–7 meeting in Tokyo and every other country said the first thing they needed was for America to put its economic house in order. We did that.

Now, I believe strongly we must maintain our fiscal discipline. It has led to lower interest rates and a huge investment and job growth. Maintaining economic growth is the best thing we can do right now, not only for the United States but for the global economy.

I would also remember that back in 1993 we had a general agreement that what was needed was America should get rid of its deficit, Europe should lower its interest rates, and Japan should open its markets. There was this general agreement that if we did all those things, we would have a remarkable resumption of growth.

Europe did moderate its interest rates. And the then Prime Minister, now the Finance Minister, Mr. Miyazawa, oversaw a significant market-opening trade agreement between the United States and Japan, which also benefited others, not just us. And of course, we got rid of our deficit. The results were quite satisfactory for several years for us.

Now Europe has to continue to pursue policies that will spur growth and keep their markets open because they, too, must be able to provide markets for Asian goods as those nations seek to find their footing. But the key here is Japan, for the second largest economy in the world, by far the biggest economy in Asia, has now gone several years without any economic growth. Thank goodness, a lot of their ordinary citizens have been able to maintain a decent life because of the wealth of their country and probably because of the enormous personal savings rate they have enjoyed for many, many years now.

But it is difficult to see how any actions of the world community can be successful in restoring growth in Asia in the absence of the restoration of growth in Japan, which would enable Japan to lead the region out of its present condition. Therefore, we must support Japan and do everything we can to help create the conditions in which together we can all lead again, just as we did in 1993.

Their challenges are quite formidable. They have to spur domestic demand, revive a banking system, restore confidence, deregulate the economy, and open markets. And we all know all the forces that seem to be working against these developments in Japan. But I would remind you that this is a very strong, sophisticated nation full of people of knowledge and enormous achievement. It is fully capable of playing its world leadership role. I believe its business leaders right now know what needs to be done and would support it.

Next week I'm going to meet with Prime Minister Obuchi here in New York to discuss how America can support Japan's efforts to restore economic growth and investor confidence. And I will do everything I can to try to make sure that, as we go forward, we have America, Europe, and Japan all doing our part to get beyond this present moment, just as we did back in 1993.

The second step we should take is to intensify our efforts to speed economic recovery in Asia. When countries like South Korea and Thailand have taken strong and responsible steps, the freefall has ended; progress is being made. But the human cost of Asia's collapse is only now being fully felt. Recent press reports have described an entire generation working its way into the middle class over 25 years, then being plummeted into poverty within a matter of months. The stories are heartbreaking: doctors and nurses forced to live in the lobby of a closed hospital; middle class families who owned their own homes, sent their children to college, traveled abroad, now living by selling their possessions.

It is in our interest to help these nations and these people recover. They will become once again our great markets and our great partners. It is also the right thing to do. We've worked with international lenders, like the IMF, to help these nations to adopt pro-growth budget, tax, and monetary policies, but clearly we're going to have to do more to restore Asian growth. We must work to lift the weight of private sector debt that has frozen the Asian economies.

Today I'm asking Secretary Rubin to work with other financial authorities and international economic institutions to enhance efforts to explore comprehensive plans to help Asian corporations emerge from massive debt where individual firms have been swept under by systemic national economic problems, rather than their own errors. We need to get credit flowing again. We need to get business back to making products, producing services, creating jobs.

Third, Asian businesses need assistance, but so do millions of Asian families. We must do more to establish an adequate social safety net in recovering nations. Wrenching economic transition without an adequate social safety net can sacrifice lives in the name of economic theory and, I might add, can generate thereby so much resistance that reform grinds to a halt. If we want these countries to do tough things, we have to protect the most defenseless people in the society, and we have to protect people who get hurt when they didn't do anything wrong. I think that is terribly important.

With our support, the World Bank and the Asian Development Bank have started to deal with these challenges, but they have to expand their efforts. There is simply not enough being done. I asked them to double their aid through an expanded social compact initiative focusing on job assistance, basic needs, and economic transition; on children and the elderly; on groups most vulnerable to economic change. And I want to commend Jim Wolfensohn for his efforts and his willingness to lead this expanded initiative.

Fourth, we have to be ready to respond immediately, and with financial force if necessary, to the currency crisis, if it spreads, especially if it threatens the economies of Latin America, where nations have struggled to make progress to do the right thing only to find themselves buffeted by economic storms outside their control. Therefore, the major economies should stand ready to activate the $15 billion now in the emergency funds of the IMF, the general agreement to borrow, to ensure that the IMF continues to support reform and fight economic contagion.

Fifth, our Export-Import Bank will increase its commitments to specific economic development projects over the next 3 years—3 months—projects which will have concrete benefits for ordinary citizens in other countries, projects which will increase our own exports and thereby help our economy, and ones which can help to restore confidence in countries that they are not alone and that actual, specific, positive developments can occur.

Sixth, for the effort of the international community to succeed, America simply must meet its own obligations to the International Monetary Fund. After a year of financial firefighting, the IMF's resources are badly strained. Every day we don't act, we undermine the confidence the world badly needs that we are trying to restore. Congress simply must assume its responsibility for our leadership in the economy.

In my State of the Union Address, I said it was better to prepare for a storm when the skies were clear than when the clouds were overhead. Well, 8 months later, the clouds are closer, and you can nearly hear the thunder.

Now, the Senate, by an overwhelming bipartisan majority, has, thankfully, approved our obligation to fund our part of the International Monetary Fund. But with only 5 weeks left in this congressional session, there is still no action from the House of Representatives.

Let me put this as plainly as I can. Failure by this Congress to pay our dues to the IMF will put our own prosperity at risk. Failure to act will send a sharp signal that at a time of economic challenge, our lawmakers were unwilling to protect our workers, our businesses, our farmers from the risk of global economic change and unwilling to maintain our leadership in building a global economic system that has benefited us more than any other nation.

Concerted action to spur growth, helping Asia through private sector debt restructuring, and a strengthened social safety net, helping to protect the rest of the world through the use of the IMF's emergency fund, increasing the activity of the Ex-Im Bank, and meeting our own obligations to the IMF: these are the six immediate steps we want to take.

But we must also be willing to take action for the long run to modify the financial and trading institutions of the world to match the realities of the new economy they serve. By creating the WTO, the World Trade Organization, in 1994, we began to build a modern trading system. We must redouble our efforts to tear down barriers around the world. But as I said in Geneva last May, we must do more to ensure that spirited economic competition among nations never becomes a race to the bottom in environmental protection, consumer protection, or labor standards.

We are working to open the procedures of the WTO to participation by the public and the full range of affected interests so that people will know and see and be able to do for themselves things which will ensure that the trading system makes the world better for all the people in all the countries.

We've already completed 260 trade agreements, opening markets in areas from autos to telecommunications. Next year we will host the meeting of the world's trade ministers to set the agenda for expanded trade in the first decade in the new century.

History teaches us that at a time of worldwide difficulty, it would be folly to retreat into a protectionist shell. We must keep trade flowing among nations. But I will say again, if we want to do that, we have got to give ordinary citizens and the groups that represent them in countries all over the world the sense that it is going to be done in a fair way, consistent with nations' obligations to advance the interests of their working people and protect not only their national but the global environment.

This November, when I meet with the leaders of the Asian economies at the APEC meeting, we will move forward to further open markets in Asia. And when Congress returns next year, I will work to pass legislation to open markets further, from trade negotiating powers to the African trade initiative. I will do so in a way that I believe will win broad support from a majority of both parties.

From the G–7 meeting in Halifax in 1995, in the wake of the Mexican financial crisis, to the Birmingham meeting this year, we have been working, also, with our major economic partners to plan for new financial architecture for the 21st century.

For the first time, this year we included key emerging markets in the process in a new Group of 22, recognizing their important stake in the global economy. This group has been working together for nearly a year now to improve the global financial assistance with a special focus on improving financial sectors, on transparency, and on private sector burden sharing.

I just want to emphasize again that even as we respond to the urgent alarms of the moment, we must speed the pace of this systemic work as well. That is why I have asked Secretary Rubin and Chairman Greenspan to convene the finance ministers and central bankers of the G–7 and key emerging economies in Washington within 30 days to develop a preliminary report to the heads of state by the beginning of next year on strengthening the world financial system.

We must develop policies so that countries can reap the benefits of free-flowing capital in a way that is safe and sustainable. We must adapt the IMF so that it can more effectively confront the new types of financial crises, minimizing their frequency, severity, and human cost. We need to consider ways to extend emergency financing when countries are battling crises of confidence due to world financial distress as distinct from their own errors in policy. We must find ways to tap the energy of global markets without sentencing the world to a cycle of continued extreme crises.

For half a century now in our national economy, we have learned not to eliminate but to tame and limit the swings of boom and bust. In the 21st century, we have to find a way to do that in the global economy as well.

I've discussed this in recent days with Prime Minister Blair of Great Britain, who is now the Chair of the G–7. He shares my belief that this is an urgent task. It is critical to the mission that he and I and Prime Minister Prodi of Italy will be discussing next week at the New York University Law School in a very interesting meeting that the First Lady and others in our administration helped to organize on how to extend the benefits of the world economy to all and how to strengthen democracy in a time of such sweeping economic change.

Now, let me just say it all again very briefly. In short, we must improve our ability to address the current financial emergency, and we must build a system to prevent such future emergencies, whenever possible, and to blunt their impact when they do occur. There is no mission more critical to our own strength and security.

And let me say this again, what is at stake is more than the spread of free markets and their integration into the global economy. The forces behind the global economy are also those that deepen democratic liberties: the free flow of ideas and information, open borders and easy travel, the rule of law, fair and evenhanded enforcement, protection for consumers, a skilled and educated work force. Each of these things matters not only to the wealth of nations but to the health of freedom. If citizens tire of waiting for democracy and free markets to deliver a better life for them, there is a real risk that democracy and free markets, instead of continuing to thrive together, will begin to shrivel together. This would pose great risks not only for our economic interests but for our security.

We see around the world the international aggressors, the harborers of terrorists, the druglords. Who are these countries? They're authoritarian nations without democracy and without open markets. Nations that give their people freedom are good neighbors. When nations turn away from freedom, they turn inward toward tension, hatred, and hostility.

We now have a chance to create opportunity on a worldwide scale. The difficulties of the moment should not obscure us to the advances of the last several years. We clearly have it within our means, if we do the right things, to lift billions and billions of people around the world into a global middle class and into participation in global democracy and genuine efforts toward peace and reconciliation. That is a possibility, but recent events show it is not a certainty. At this moment, therefore, the United States is called upon once again to lead, to organize the forces of a committed world, to channel the unruly energies of the global economy into positive avenues, to advance our interests, reinforce our values, enhance our security.

In this room, I think it is not too simple to say we know what to do. The World War II generation did it for us 50 years ago. Now it is time for us to rise to our responsibility, as America has been called upon to do so often so many times in the past. We can, if we do that, redeem the promise of the global economy and strengthen our own Nation for a new century.

Thank you very much.

NOTE: The President spoke at 12 p.m. in the David Rockefeller Room at the Council on Foreign Relations Building. In his remarks, he referred to Peter G. Peterson, chairman of the board, Council on Foreign Relations, and his wife, Joan Ganz Cooney; Richard C. Holbrooke, U.S. Ambassador-designate to the United Nations; David Rockefeller, honorary chairman, and Leslie H. Gelb, president, Council on Foreign Relations; Prime Minister Yevgeniy Primakov and President Boris Yeltsin of Russia; Minister of Finance Kiichi Miyazawa and Prime Minister Keizo Obuchi of Japan; James D. Wolfensohn, president, World Bank; Prime Minister Tony Blair of the United Kingdom; and Prime Minister Romano Prodi of Italy.

Remarks at a Unity '98 Luncheon in New York City
September 14, 1998

Thank you very much, all of you, for your warm welcome. Thank you, Denise, for having us here today and for sticking up for our party and for doing the work you have done in your daughter's memory and for being a true friend to Hillary and me. We are so grateful to you.

I want to thank Patti and Natalie for that unusual and perfectly wonderful version of "Over the Rainbow." One of the best things about being President is just being able to meet people that you've listened to sing or perform all your life, and then all of a sudden you get to know them, and then they do things like that, which are great gifts.

I'd like to thank Steve Grossman, who has been heroic in his work for our party. He is indefatigable, and he's effective, and he's a good man. And I'm very grateful to him for his leadership.

I want to thank the Members of Congress who are here—I look forward to saying to Mr. Rangel, "Chairman Rangel"—to Nancy Pelosi, to Carolyn Kilpatrick. Dick Gephardt just had to leave and has done a terrific job of holding our caucus together and working on things together. I thank Tom Daschle and Bob Torricelli

and Senator Kerrey, who just had to leave. He said he was going back to cast an agriculture vote. And I said, "How are you going to vote?" He said, "I'm from Nebraska." He said, "Whatever it is, I'm going back to vote for the farmers." [*Laughter*] And I appreciate his being here, and I appreciate Bob Torricelli's unbelievable work to help in this project. And I am very grateful for Tom Daschle's leadership in the Senate.

You know, last Friday Hillary and I had a lot of people down to the White House from New York—they weren't all from New York, but a lot of them were—when we had a celebration for Irish-Americans, for the progress that's been made in the Irish peace process. And I was thinking about what it was that our involvement there had to do with what we've tried to do at home. I was thinking about all the times that Hillary has been to Northern Ireland on her own to help women's groups who, predictably, even when the men's were still acting like fools, were out there working across religious lines to create a peace climate.

And I was thinking that there's something about the roots that we feel to Ireland—just as the roots we feel in the Middle East, the roots we feel in the Aegean, the roots we feel every place there are troubles in the world—that bring home to the heart both the cause of peace abroad and the cause of prosperity at home.

I was looking at the Vice President talking today and thinking, I don't know if every American knows this, but every American should know that whether you agree with what we have done or not, there is no question that far and away, beyond anyone who has ever served in that position before, Al Gore has had more influence over more issues and done more good than any Vice President in the history of the country, by light-years, for ordinary people. And I think that is important. And I am very grateful to him and to Tipper for her work on behalf of mental health, for all the things that we've been able to do together.

And let me say to all of you, I'm also—I know that I speak for Hillary when I say we thank you for your personal friendship and your support. It means more now than ever, and we'll never forget it.

I was trying to think—you know, everybody has gone through the issues here and the record—I was trying to think of some way to say in a sentence what our administration has tried to be about and why there are all those people out there on the street today, when a lot of other people have told them they shouldn't be there. And we were turning around the corner and Hillary said, "Look, look, look at that person there." And there was a guy standing there holding the book that Al Gore and I wrote for the '92 campaign. Remember what the title was? "Putting People First."

This is a season when we will ask ourselves, what is the purpose of our public life, what is the role of citizenship in the electoral process, and when we'll decide whether we're going to put progress over partisanship and people over politics. And I don't think there is any question what most Americans want to do.

What I want you to know is, the importance of your being here today is that you have given us a chance to do certain very important, specific things, which I will mention before I let you go, but in a larger sense to reaffirm the fact that the special thing about our party is when we gather in a fundraising event like this, we want to do a lot of things that will benefit people who could never afford to come here. And I think that's very, very important.

For so many people, politics is about power. For me, the power of politics is that it gives you a chance to use the authority that comes from the people in a democracy to help the people that were on the street out here clapping when I was driving to this place. And in the end, no country does well—no country does well—unless those folks do well. It never happens.

Let me just say, I also believe that we have one message we have to take to all the folks on the street that obviously didn't deter our fundraising event here—the adversity of the moment, I think, has led us to this record turnout. Why? Because people made a decision, and they thought they were needed and they stood up. That's not the real danger to the Democrats this November. The real danger to the Democrats this November is that history will repeat itself, complicated by good times.

What am I talking about? If you go back to the Civil War, there has never been an election for midterm—congressional election—since the Civil War when the party of the President in power, if the President was in his second term, didn't lose seats—not a single time. I think we're going to beat history.

But what is the real danger? The real danger is, the folks on the street will think, "Well, we've got the lowest unemployment rate in 28 years and the lowest inflation rate in 32 years and the first balanced budget in 29 years, the lowest percentage of people on welfare in 29 years; things are peachy-keen. I think I'll go to the movie on Tuesday. Or I'll take my kid to the day-care center, and I don't have time to go vote." That is the real danger.

The real danger is that people will think, as they typically do, our voters, who have to make a bigger effort to go vote because they have more family responsibilities, more work responsibilities, on average, lower incomes and more hassles in life, that things are going well and they don't need to go vote. That is the danger; don't misunderstand.

Once people understand there's an issue, they show up. That's what the success of this incredible day is testimony to, where the people that sponsor this event wound up turning people away, and we raised 25 percent more than we expected to. Once people know what's at stake, they will show up. The real danger is that people will say, "Things are going well; there's no need for my voting. I don't really know that anything too bad is going to happen one way or the other, or anything too good is going to happen one way or the other. But things are going well, and I'm satisfied."

It is our job to go out and tell people what is still at issue; not to take credit for what has happened—people already know what our role has been, I think, in all the things that the Vice President talked about—but to say, hey, yes, things are going well, but read the paper; look at all the things that are going on around the world; look at how things are changing every day. Remember, when things are at trouble around the world, it can affect us here at home. So we have to look at these big issues.

And because the balanced budget is here and because we have a strong economy and because we have confidence in ourselves again, we have an obligation to deal with the big issues: to give every kid in this country a world-class education; to prove we can grow the economy and preserve our environment; to not squander this surplus until we have dealt with the fact that when the baby boomers retire, there will only be two people working for every one person retired. And it is wrong for my generation to retire and undermine the standard of living of our children and grandchildren to pay for our retirement.

That's why we've got to save Social Security before we start spending this surplus in a politically popular election-year tax cut. That is wrong. We should not be doing that until we—first of all, it hasn't materialized yet. I'm just sitting around here like a—I haven't felt like this since the week before Chelsea was born. On October 1st, for the first time in 29 years, the ink will turn from red to black, and there are already people who don't want us to get to look at it. I'd say, let's just take a deep breath, realize the surplus, and say we're not going to spend it even if it's popular to do so, until we've saved Social Security and relieved our children and grandchildren from the burden of our retirement. I think it's important.

These are big issues. Today I spoke here in New York at the Council on Foreign Relations about the present crisis in the global economy. One quarter of the world is having negative economic growth. Thirty percent of our growth as Americans in the last 5 years has come from

our expanding trade. We cannot forever be an island of prosperity if the rest of the world gets in trouble. That's why people in every State and every community in this country ought to care about how folks in other countries are doing and whether we are working together with them.

So I went to the Council on Foreign Relations to say, look, here's what I want to do to try to deal with the challenges of the global economy. Let me say very briefly, we have to, first of all, restore growth. That's what got us a balanced budget and 16 million new jobs; we had a growing economy. That's what we need in the world.

The second thing we've got to do is to try to develop a system that limits these violent swings in how these countries are doing. You know, after the Great Depression in America, we learned how to limit the swings of the economy, and we haven't had another depression. And it stabilized things. We have to do that in the world.

The third thing we've got to do is to make the global economy more humane. We have to make it work for ordinary people. And when times are tough and countries have to go through difficult times, we've got to help the innocent and make sure they don't get punished too badly. Otherwise, the support for free markets and democracy will erode.

So I talked about that today, and I gave out a big plan that I really have worked hard on. And I pointed out that the Secretary of Treasury, Bob Rubin, and the head of our central bank, Alan Greenspan, our Federal Reserve, within the next 30 days are going to convene 22 countries, their counterparts in 22 countries, and make recommendations to us about what to do over the long run to fix the global financial system.

Today in London, the heads of the big industrial powers just issued a statement at 1:30 saying they essentially supported what we were trying to do and would be a part of it. This is a big deal. This is what the politics of America ought to be about now. If we can't keep the economy growing globally, it's going to be very hard to keep it impacting Main Street in a positive way. So that's what this is about.

Just one or two other issues. This health care issue is a huge deal. We've got 160 million Americans, more than half the people in this country, in managed care plans. They have a right to know that if they get hit down here walking across the street, they can go to the nearest emergency room; they won't have to be dragged to another borough to an emergency room because their plan says that. They have a right to know that if they get cancer or they're horribly scarred and they need a specialist to help them, they can get a specialist to deal with their problem. They have a right to know that if their employer changes health insurance carriers in the middle of a treatment—during a pregnancy, during a chemotherapy treatment, or whatever—they won't be required to change doctors. They have a right to know that their records will be private.

This is 160 million people. And we and our Republican friends in Washington are at direct loggerheads over this, something that affects 160 million people. That's the kind of thing this election is all about.

So what I want you to do is to know, number one, you have done a very good thing making this weekend possible, this event possible, because you are going to give us a chance to tell the people what putting people first means

in terms of 1998. But number two, I ask you to go back to your homes, go back to your friends and neighbors, and keep talking until you're blue in the face. Remember, our problem is not adversity; we will rise in adversity. Our problem is complacence. Our problem is the burden of history. Our problem is people thinking, "Things are good now; I don't have to move." We do have to move.

And if we talk about these big things and we remember these elections are never about us, they're always about those folks out on the street; they're always about what putting people first means; they're always about freedom and opportunity and reconciling Americans to each other across all the lines that divide us—if we do that, we're going to do just fine.

Thank you, and God bless you.

NOTE: The President spoke at 3:03 p.m. at a private residence. In his remarks, he referred to luncheon host Denise Rich; singers Patti LaBelle and Natalie Cole; and Steve Grossman, national chair, Democratic National Committee.

Statement on the Death of George C. Wallace
September 14, 1998

Hillary and I offer our condolences to the family and friends of George Wallace. I remember working with him at the Governors' conference in 1983. Governor Wallace was wheelchair-bound and often in great pain, but he rolled into the committee room to provide the crucial vote that enabled the Governors to help save Federal support for disabled Americans unable to work.

Like the State he served as Governor and the region he represented as a candidate for President, George Wallace made a painful—but essential—journey, abandoning, in the end, the politics of division and embracing the politics of inclusion and reconciliation. For that, all Americans can be grateful.

Statement on Government Use of Recycled Products
September 14, 1998

Today I am pleased to sign an Executive order strengthening Federal efforts to protect the environment and promote economic growth through the purchase of recycled and other environmentally preferable products.

As the Nation's largest paper purchaser, the Federal Government has a special responsibility to lead the way in building markets for recycled goods. Since 1993, when I signed an earlier Executive order to promote recycling, we have quadrupled our purchase of recycled-content paper. Today we are going the next step. I am directing agencies to ensure that as of January 1 they purchase only recycled paper. Through this single action, we will save up to half a million trees a year, reduce air and water pollution, and curb emissions that contribute to global warming. We will also harness our tremendous purchasing power to spur the growing market for recycled products.

To further promote the use of environmentally preferable products, this "Greening the Government" Executive order also directs agencies to establish recycling targets, encourages them to purchase biobased and other "green" products, and creates a White House task force to oversee Federal recycling efforts.

Recycling is one of America's great environmental success stories. Across the country, families and businesses each day demonstrate their commitment to our environment through the simple act of recycling. By redoubling our efforts to "green the Government," we are demonstrating once again that the environment and the economy go hand in hand, and helping to promote a more sustainable future for America.

NOTE: The Executive order is listed in Appendix D at the end of this volume.

Message to the Congress Transmitting a Report on Aeronautics and Space Activities
September 14, 1998

To the Congress of the United States:

I am pleased to transmit this report on the Nation's achievements in aeronautics and space during fiscal year (FY) 1997, as required under section 206 of the National Aeronautics and Space Act of 1958, as amended (42 U.S.C. 2476). Aeronautics and space activities involved 13 contributing departments and agencies of the Federal Government, and the results of their ongoing research and development affect the Nation in many ways.

A wide variety of aeronautics and space developments took place during FY 1997. The National Aeronautics and Space Administration (NASA) successfully completed eight Space Shuttle flights. There were 23 successful U.S. Expendable Launch Vehicle (ELV) launches in FY 1997. Of those, 4 were NASA-managed missions, 2 were NASA-funded/Federal Aviation Administration (FAA)-licensed missions, 5 were Department of Defense-managed missions, and 12 were FAA-licensed commercial launches. The Mars Pathfinder spacecraft and Sojourner rover captured the public's attention with a very successful mission. Scientists also made some dramatic new discoveries in various space-related fields such as space science, Earth science and remote sensing, and life and microgravity science. In aeronautics, activities included work on high-speed research, advanced subsonic technology, and technologies designed to improve the safety and efficiency of our commercial airlines and air traffic control system.

Close international cooperation with Russia occurred on the Shuttle-*Mir* docking missions and on the International Space Station program. The United States also entered into new forms of cooperation with its partners in Europe, South America, and Asia.

Thus, FY 1997 was a very successful one for U.S. aeronautics and space program. Efforts in these areas have contributed significantly to the Nation's scientific and technical knowledge, international cooperation, a healthier environment, and a more competitive economy.

WILLIAM J. CLINTON

The White House,
September 14, 1998.

Message to the Congress Transmitting a Report on United States Activities in the United Nations
September 14, 1998

To the Congress of the United States:

I am pleased to transmit herewith a report of the activities of the United States Government in the United Nations and its affiliated agencies during the calendar year 1997. The re-port is required by the United Nations Participation Act (Public Law 79–264; 22 U.S.C. 287b).

WILLIAM J. CLINTON

The White House,
September 14, 1998.

Remarks at a Unity '98 Dinner in New York City
September 14, 1998

Thank you very much. Let me begin by saying, for Hillary and for me, just your presence here, your enthusiasm, and your personal support mean more than you can possibly know. I'd like to thank Senator Torricelli and Representative Pelosi for doing a magnificent job. I thank Congresswoman Nita Lowey and Congressman Rangel for being here.

I thank—all three of the candidates for the United States Senate in New York tomorrow on our ticket have come here tonight. I don't know if they're all still here, but I know Congressman Schumer and Mark Green and Geraldine Ferraro were all here. And however that race comes out tomorrow, we have a lot of work to do, and won't it be fun. I know that we can depend on all of you to help make this night a part of a springboard to doing well in the Senate and the congressional elections beginning here in New York.

Since I'm in New York and you've been so wonderful to me since 1992, I'd like to tell you that there is no more effective member of our Cabinet than Andrew Cuomo, the Secretary of Housing and Urban Development. I'm very, very grateful to him for his support.

I'd also like to say again how very grateful I am to Tipper for all the work she's done for families, for children, for those who need mental health care, and the advances we've made that would not have occurred if it hadn't been for her.

I would like to say what I said at lunch today: All of you just need to remember that every single hard decision I had to make in the last 6 years that turned out right, that everybody said was wrong—whether it was bringing the deficit down, standing for the Brady bill and the assault weapons ban, doing the things that really hurt our people in Congress but helped America, taking the steps necessary to bring peace in Bosnia, and helping to end the Mexican financial crisis so the world could go on and grow and we could benefit—every single hard decision that was unpopular, Al Gore was there every step of the way, and you should never forget that.

Whether it's in technology policy or the environment or dealing with Russia or South Africa or giving us the smallest Federal Government in 35 years with the best output—I could go through issue after issue after issue, and I think it's very important that you understand—you may argue about many things about this administration, but one thing is absolutely unarguable: He has had more influence over more decisions and done more good by far than any Vice President in the history of the United States of America.

I'd also like to thank Hillary for a lot of things, but I just had one thing in particular on my mind. We just got back from Russia and Ireland, and when I was in Ireland, I went to the new Parliament at Stormont where all the parties are represented. We've got a chance to keep the peace process going in Ireland. And it's a big deal in New York; there are a lot of Irish people in New York, so I can talk about this with some confidence. They've had these

30 years of trouble, but they've been really fighting, the Catholics and Protestants, for 800 years. And my heart just swelled with pride when I was going through there. And every woman member came up to me and said, "Your wife was the first person that took us seriously, that believed we could make peace, and basically said—when the men were still out there fighting with each other and acting like children—knew we could make peace in Ireland. And we thank her for what she's done." And I thank her for representing the best of America all over the world and giving people hope that the world can be full of peace and opportunity.

We've got to go to "The Lion King." I want you to think about three things. Number one, we're trying to beat history here. Since the Civil War, in every midterm election when the President was in his second term, the party of the President has lost seats in the Congress—since the Civil War. Now, I believe we're going to beat history here, for one simple reason: We have a vision of the future, and our ideas are supported by more Americans than our adversaries' are.

You are here to make sure that we can get our message out, and you have succeeded magnificently. We've exceeded our goal tonight by more than 25 percent, and I'm very grateful to you for that. But I want you to leave here with a clear understanding that what we have to do is to go out to the American people and say, look, most elections in times like this are sort of stand-pat elections, where the electorate is rather complacent, the turnout is rather low. That always benefits the Republicans, because people who are older and wealthier and more likely to be Republicans vote.

But basically, they're stand-pat elections because we've got the lowest unemployment rate in 28 years and the smallest percentage of people on welfare in 29 years and the highest homeownership in history, and things are doing pretty well. October 1st we'll have the first balanced budget in 29 years. Now, that's good, but that is not the message of the election. If the message is we have done a good job, people will relax and stay home. That is not the message.

The message is, we're grateful for the chance to serve; we're grateful that America is better off; but this country has huge challenges. I just spoke this morning, as Hillary said, to the Council on Foreign Relations about all of this global,

economic, and financial turmoil, and what things America must do right now to try to turn it around and limit it, and what long-term steps we have to take.

So I think you need to go out and say to your friends and neighbors, "Look, we're glad things are doing well. We're on the edge of a new century and a new time, and things are changing; we have big challenges. And because we're doing well, we have the obligation to our children to think big, to think about the people of this country who aren't doing so well, and to think how we can bring this whole country together as one community in the 21st century."

That means we have to do our part to straighten the global economy out, because we can never be an island of prosperity in a sea of misery.

It means we have to do the big things like saving Social Security before we do the popular things like spending this surplus—it's only now beginning to materialize—for a tax cut. We've been waiting 29 years to see the red ink turn black, and before we've seen it even a day, some people want to spend it. I know it's election year, but I'm telling you, what I want is for the baby boomers like me, when we retire—I don't want us to bankrupt our children so they can't raise our grandchildren. I say, save Social Security first before you do anything else with the surplus. It's a big issue.

As Senator Torricelli said, we've still got to extend health opportunities to people, but there's 160 million people in managed care plans. I think they ought to have a right to an emergency room, to a specialist, to the protection of privacy of their records. That's what the health care bill of rights is all about—the Patients' Bill of Rights. We're for it; they're not. That's a big issue. The American people need to know that. It will shape the way millions of families live.

The environment's a big issue. We believe you can grow the economy and improve the environment; they disagree. That's a huge issue; it will shape the way millions of people live.

We're for campaign finance reform, and they aren't. It's a big issue.

So I ask you, go out there and talk about the big issues, talk about the people issues. And remember, in the end, the reason we're Democrats is because we believe, on the edge of a new century, that what we're doing will help to expand opportunity and deepen freedom and bring us closer together and promote peace and harmony in the world. That's what we believe.

Go talk big. Go tell people not to be complacent. Tell them not to worry about the adversity. Adversity makes people come out and show up—witness your presence here tonight.

What we've got to worry about is that people know what this election is about. Go out and tell them and make sure your investment tonight has a big, big payoff on election night in November.

Thank you, and God bless you all.

NOTE: The President spoke at 7:10 p.m. in the Dinner Room at the Supper Club.

Remarks at a Performance of "The Lion King" in New York City
September 14, 1998

Thank you so much. I will be very brief tonight. For one thing, you need to know that I have to be brief tonight because if we're not out of here, with all the pictures taken, by 11:30, we kick into overtime—[*laughter*]—and we dilute the impact of your contributions in November. [*Laughter*] And I don't want to do that.

But I do want to say to Peter, to Tom, to the incredible cast and the musicians, I found myself looking back and forth—I have a cricked neck from looking at these two percussionists here who were so magnificent tonight. Thank you very much.

And I just want to thank you all for giving us a night we'll never forget in this magnificent theater. I also want to thank all of you for being here, for being here for Hillary and me and Al and Tipper, for what we have done for the last 6 years and what we can do in the next 2 and what we should do in November.

This is a very, very important time. The stakes are high; the issues are clear. I knew Al Gore was going to stand up here and say that Scar was the embodiment of the other guys. [*Laughter*] That's what happens when you think you

can destroy the environment while you grow the economy. I knew he was thinking that. I knew he was thinking that.

Hillary said the same thing. Hillary said, "That's what happens if those Republicans that have the House get the whole thing. Look at that." [*Laughter*]

Well, we do believe in the balance of forces and the balance of people and in bringing everybody into our big tent. We believe that all the animals in the jungles can live together if they have peace in their heart.

So I want you to leave here determined to make your investment good, remembering why you came, proud of it, and touching everyone you can now about what is still at issue in this great, great cause.

Thank you, God bless you, and good night.

NOTE: The President spoke at 11:08 p.m. at the New Amsterdam Theater. In his remarks, he referred to Peter Schneider, president, and Tom Schumacher, executive vice president, Walt Disney Feature Animation and Theatrical Productions.

Remarks to the National Farmers Union
September 15, 1998

Thank you very much. Ladies and gentlemen, good afternoon; welcome to the White House. Lee, thank you for the award. Thank you for your comments. Thank you for your strength. Thank you for your leadership for our farmers. I've known him for years; I don't think I'd ever

focused on what a good speaker he was before. [*Laughter*] He could have been a politician or a preacher in addition to a farmer. It was great.

I want to thank Secretary Glickman for his truly outstanding work, along with Rich Rominger, Carl Whillock, and the others here from the Department of Agriculture, who really try to be your advocates every day. We have at least three NFU members who work at USDA, Mike Dunn, Larry Mitchell, and John Stencel, and I thank them in particular.

I want to thank Senator Dorgan and Congressman Pomeroy for coming and for being your vociferous advocates. I talked to Senator Harkin right before I came over here today, and he has also been your great friend, along with Senator Conrad and Senator Daschle and Congressman Boswell from Iowa, who couldn't come this morning. But all these people have been up here working hard for you, and I wanted you to know that.

I also would like to say that the National Farmers Union has done a lot of good for this administration and for our efforts here in Washington, from helping to keep our food supply safe, to working to expand health care, to giving us the first balanced budget in 29 years in just a couple of weeks now. You have been with me every step of the way, and I am very grateful for that.

When I was a boy growing up in Arkansas, I knew a lot about agriculture, but I didn't know much about the intersection of agriculture and politics. When I became a Governor and served for a dozen years, many of them very, very hard years in the 1980's on the farms in my State, I came to appreciate what it was like when the National Government had good policy, what it was like when it had bad policy, and what it was like when it had no policy.

I remember there were a couple of years when I was doing everything I could to be creative. And I think when you were head of the South Dakota Farmers Union, the State of South Dakota actually came to me—the Governor then—and asked me for a copy of the banking laws that I had changed in Arkansas, because I changed our State banking laws to try to help the bankers keep more farmers on the farm. And when we had that terrible situation when the price of land collapsed, all the collateral on the loans was no good. There was no way for people to finance their farms, and they were losing them, and we were able to give some help to our farmers then. But through the whole thing, I always felt so helpless that there wasn't an appropriate national response.

Now I feel especially bad for the farmers because it's been such a good time for the rest of the country. We've got nearly 17 million new

jobs now, and the lowest unemployment rate in 28 years, and the lowest inflation in 32 years, the highest homeownership in history, the lowest crime rate in 25 years, the smallest percentage of our people on welfare in 29 years. To somebody living in a city, to tell them that we have a farm crisis more extensive than we've had in decades, it's very hard for them to believe and understand.

You may note that in the local paper today I was criticized for supporting a farm relief initiative in Congress. And Secretary Glickman said, "Don't be upset. This is good news because they have noticed that the farmers are out there." [*Laughter*]

Yesterday I had a chance to go to New York and speak with some of the leaders in the United States in international finance, from our Nation's point of view, to talk to them about what I think we need to do to try to keep the global economy from further destabilizing, to try to help some of these countries help themselves that are in terrible trouble, to try to keep the global financial crisis from spreading to other countries, and to try to build an adequate trade and financial system for the 21st century that will benefit all Americans.

One—but not the only—but one element of the farm crisis today is that the farmers have felt first the crisis going on in the rest of the world. Because with roughly a quarter of the world's people in recession with declining economic growth, representing roughly a third of the world's economy, our agriculture, which depends so much on exports, have felt that quicker than the rest of the economy. But it's an important thing for Americans to be aware of what's going on on the farm today and to be aware that since the farmers, in effect, are the foot soldiers in the frontlines of America's march into the global economy of the 21st century, if we don't do something to help our farmers, eventually all other Americans will feel it as well.

And so I am delighted that you're here, and I thank you for coming. Let me also once again say, I thank you for making available the opportunity for all these young people to be here. I want them to see their country in action. I want them to learn—much earlier than I ever did—the relationship between the work that's done every day on the farm and the work that's done up here. I think it's very important. It will make them more effective citizens and more effective in farming in the years ahead.

Now, what's really going on here? I wanted to give this speech today—I realize to some extent I'm preaching to the saved today. [*Laughter*] But what I hope will happen by your coming here and by this event unfolding is that maybe, finally, we will break through the national consciousness and the consciousness of the Congress and our friends in the press corps not to panic, not to think that America's not doing well but to say that at a time when our country is doing well, surely at a time when the rest of us are doing well, we can be more attentive to the genuine needs and the conditions on the farm in America.

Events in the past year have strained many family farms to the breaking point. You know what they are: Flood, drought, crop disease have wiped out entire harvests; plummeting prices at home, collapsing markets in Asia—where our exports are down 30 percent in one year because of the economic crisis in Asia—these have threatened the livelihood of entire communities. Many farmers this year will see their net incomes drop by more than 40 percent below what they've earned on average for the last 5 years. And of course, in some places, like North Dakota, the drop is much, much steeper. If we don't do something and do it now—I want America to hear this; this is not a false alarm—if we don't do something and do it now, we could literally lose thousands and thousands of family farmers this year.

I want to come back to this and why it's not just about who's competitive in the market. The results are plain to see and painful to watch. Foreclosures and farm auctions are the order of the day already in many communities. I met a farmer named Deb Lungren not long ago who told me that in 1957 her grandfather made $11,000 on their family farm. And in 1997 she made $10,000 on the same land. The banks are ready to foreclose on the Lungren home. They don't see how they can possibly make it another year. I'll bet everybody here could tell me somewhere between one and a dozen stories just like that.

Now, again I say, I think every American has got a stake in rural America. Our farms feed the world and us at very low real costs, at very high quality. They also feed our sense of ourselves. They reinforce our values of hard work and faith and family and devotion to community and the land.

When I signed that farm bill, as Secretary Glickman said, in 1996, at a time when crop prices were strong—and I would remind you, the alternative was far worse; we would have been in even worse shape if I had vetoed it and we'd gone back to that decades-old law— I tried to make it clear that sooner or later we would have to do more to provide a safety net for hard times, that all the good things in that farm bill could not possibly wipe away the fact that if we have a family farm structure in America with widely varying prices because of market developments around the world, and the inevitable march of nature and disease, that sooner or later there would come a time when we see that if you really wanted a strong market, you had to do more for the family farmers. Well, that time has arrived.

I want to thank Secretary Glickman for all that he's done. And in July we announced that 80 million bushels of wheat, worth a quarter of billion dollars, would be purchased to help hungry people around the world and to help our farmers here at home. I strongly supported Senator Dorgan and Senator Conrad's proposal to provide farmers with emergency assistance. Last month I signed into law new legislation to speed up farm program payments to help farmers who need the money now.

And Secretary Glickman is doing everything else he possibly can to help. I know him well enough to know that from his years in Congress representing Kansas and his years as Secretary of Agriculture, if there is one single thing buried in the laws and regulations of the Department of Agriculture that he can do that he has not yet done to try to help farm income, he will find it and do it. But with crop and livestock prices still in danger of dropping, with foreign markets still in danger of collapse, and with thousands of farms in jeopardy, we simply have to do more.

The first and most important thing to do is to help the farmers in greatest need, those who have suffered significant losses of crop and livestock. I'll continue to press Congress to enact emergency assistance to do that—critical assistance to help thousands of farmers in keeping with the traditional budget rules that recognize the necessity of providing citizens help in times of crisis. We pass emergency bills for floods, for earthquakes, and we ought to do it for farm failure.

The next thing I think we ought to do—indeed, we have to do—is to do what we talked about back in 1996: We've got to reinforce the safety net for farmers and ranchers. That's why last Thursday I announced my support for Senator Harkin and Daschle's proposal to lift the cap on marketing loan rates for a year.

Yesterday our proposal was defeated in the United States Senate. Today, apparently, it is going to be voted on in its discrete elements. Whatever happens, we must find some way to provide emergency assistance to farmers facing dire circumstances so they have the resources now to plan for next year's crops.

And finally, let me say, we have to revive the rural economy through exports. The speech that I gave in New York yesterday outlining steps we need to take to try to limit and then resolve the global financial crisis, and then plan a better financial and trade system for the 21st century over the long term, will have more immediate impact on farmers if we can implement all these steps than any other group in America.

Farm products from one of every 3 acres is sold abroad. We must continue to open new markets. We must continue to enforce our existing trade agreements. And we must give the International Monetary Fund the resources it needs to strengthen and reform the economies of our customers in Asia and to try to protect the contagion from spreading to our friends in Latin America, so that others can continue to buy all of our goods and services and especially our farm products.

For 9 months now, since I called on Congress to do this in the State of the Union, there has been no action. The Senate has passed the funding for the International Monetary Fund, but with just a few weeks left, the House has still not acted. Our farmers and ranchers have a bigger stake in the short run in the passage of this than any other group in America. So I ask you to support that as well and tell the Congress we have to do it and do it now.

Now, these are the steps that I think we have to take. I'd just like to take one step back before I close and say that there has been a debate in America for decades that underlies the skepticism of those who don't support what I propose, who say, "Well, farmers ought to be subject to the market like everybody else. A guy running a dry cleaner, nobody brings the clothes in to be cleaned, he goes out of business." The people who basically believe that, in the face of all the evidence that we have the most productive agriculture in the world, don't understand the intersection between global impacts on farm prices, the financing challenges that family farmers, as opposed to big corporate farmers, face, and what can happen to you just by getting up in the morning if it happens to be a bad day.

I know a lot of you feel like Job, you know? "Test my faith, Lord. I didn't mean it that seriously." [Laughter] But we have an opportunity here; we have an opportunity to break through a kind of a euphoria that's out there about the condition of our economy and let people know what's going on on the farm. We have an opportunity to tie the global financial crisis to what's going on on the farm. We have an opportunity to convince Congressmen who come from suburban and urban areas that the welfare, the health, the strength of their citizens'—their citizens'—economy rests in lifting the whole American economy and doing the right thing beyond our borders. And they can see it in your stories, in your lives, in your experience, nothing more fully embodying the best of America than you do.

So let me say—I don't know how else to say this—there is suffering on the farm. There is agony on the farm. This is a horrible affront to everything we have worked so hard to achieve, to lift the economy for all Americans. And we cannot afford to walk away from this session of Congress—I don't care if there is an election; I don't care what else is happening—we can't afford to walk away until we do something to stave off the failure of thousands of productive family farms in America. We cannot do it.

Now, let me leave you with one beautiful quote. Franklin Roosevelt once said that American farmers, and I quote, "are the source from which the reservoirs of our Nation's strength are constantly renewed." For 6 years I have worked to renew America. We're a lot better off in virtually every way than we were 6 years ago. But we cannot walk across that bridge into the 21st century, we cannot truly renew our country, if we leave our family farmers behind. So let's go up to the Hill and tell everybody that we all want to saddle up and go together.

Thank you, and God bless you.

NOTE: The President spoke at 1 p.m. in Room 450 of the Old Executive Office Building. In his remarks, he referred to Leland Swenson, president, National Farmers Union, who presented the President with the organization's 1998 Golden Triangle Award for outstanding leadership on issues affecting rural America.

Remarks to the Military Readiness Conference
September 15, 1998

I'm pleased to have the second opportunity of this year to meet with Secretary Cohen, the Joint Chiefs of Staff, the senior operational commanders of our Armed Forces. Today we're going to focus on the steps necessary to preserve and provide for the readiness of our Armed Forces to defend our interests and security.

Readiness must be our number one priority. It is being monitored and addressed every day at every level of command. Our forward deployed and first-to-fight units are highly ready, and our overall force is fully capable of carrying out our national military strategy. But I'm determined that we don't relax our vigilance, to keep our forces ready to protect our security today and well into the 21st century.

In recent months, we've taken some important steps to strengthen our military readiness. This fiscal year we were able to protect important readiness accounts, such as spare parts and flying hours for our pilots, with the help of Congress' support for emergency funding for our peacekeeping mission in Bosnia and its approval of the request I made to reprogram $1 billion of our defense budget for readiness.

We struck a prudent balance between short-term readiness and longer term modernization, so that our fighting forces will have the cutting edge technology they need to avoid long-term readiness problems and to dominate the battlefields of the future.

The service chiefs and the commanders in chief have worked tirelessly also to improve the quality of life for our men and women in uniform and to recruit and retain a new generation of Americans for our all-volunteer forces. I want to thank them for that and say that I am well aware that we're going to have to do more in this area as well.

For example, the services have established standards to reduce the burden on our troops of the high tempo of operations and deployments. We've reduced the number and the duration of some deployments overseas, putting units on standby status in the United States instead.

Again, I want to call on Congress to support our ongoing engagement for peace in Bosnia in a way that does not force us to take money away from readiness and training. We will continue to monitor readiness, to deal quickly and effectively with any problems that do arise.

And now I want to hear directly from Secretary Cohen and from our senior military leaders on this critical issue to our security. Thank you very much.

NOTE: The President spoke at 2:17 p.m. at the National Defense University at Fort McNair.

Statement on the Appointment of the Assistant to the President and Special Counsel and Two Senior Advisors to the President
September 15, 1998

Today I have asked Gregory Craig to join the White House staff as Assistant to the President and Special Counsel, reporting to me in connection with matters arising from the Referral submitted by the Office of Independent Counsel to Congress. Joining Deputy Chief of Staff John Podesta, the Counsel to the President, Charles Ruff, and my personal attorney, David Kendall, in their representation before House Judiciary Committee, Mr. Craig will quarterback the response to the Referral. Mr. Craig currently serves as Director of Policy and Planning at the Department of State. I have known him for many years and have great confidence in his judgment and ability.

The White House has also added former Chief Senate Liaison and executive director of the Senate Campaign Committee Steve Ricchetti and former White House Deputy Director of Legislative Affairs Susan Brophy to work as Senior Advisors to the President.

Message on the Observance of Rosh Hashana, 1998
September 15, 1998

Warmest greetings to all who are celebrating Rosh Hashana.

Each year during this season of promise and renewal, the stirring sound of the shofar resonates in the air—a sacred summons calling Jews across America and around the world to celebrate the anniversary of God's creation of the world and the birth of a new year. Jews welcome this time of spiritual reawakening as a means to reaffirm their relationship with God and to prepare them for the joys and challenges of the coming year.

As the beginning of the High Holy Days, Rosh Hashana is a time of intense prayer and serious reflection; but it is also a time of rejoicing in the promises of the future and of renewed commitment to God and loved ones.

Hillary joins me in extending best wishes to all for a joyous celebration and for a year sweet with happiness and peace.

BILL CLINTON

Remarks at the Welcoming Ceremony for President Václav Havel of the Czech Republic
September 16, 1998

President Havel, Mrs. Havlova, members of the Czech delegation, my fellow Americans. Mr. President, it is a joy to welcome you to the United States and to the White House. Your remarkable life embodies a great lesson, that people who love their country can change it, even against tremendous odds; that words can be powerful instruments of change; and that, together, words and deeds can be the pillars of freedom.

Ten years ago, the world was a very different place. Like half of Europe, Czechoslovakia lay shrouded beneath a failed ideology. Human hopes were suppressed. Debate was stifled. And you spent years in jail for standing up and speaking out for liberty and human rights.

Today we celebrate the dramatic movement out of that very different, darker world, toward freedom and self-determination. We celebrate ideas, not ideologies. From South Africa to South Korea to South America, societies are redefining themselves, removing barriers to the imagination, struggling to find a new balance in a new world, cultivating the limitless resources of their people. This is a universal phenomenon, neither American nor European but, instead, universal. Nonetheless, it owes a very great deal in our time to the inspiration provided by a single man, Václav Havel, who for years spoke when it mattered and often at enormous personal cost.

Now we are poised to build a world of the new century. More people than ever are free to pursue their own destiny. And we are grateful for the unprecedented achievement of this century we are about to leave. We are also aware, however, that far too much of the 20th century saw division and dislocation and destruction, and nowhere more so than in the heart of Europe.

In the last decade, Europeans have gone far toward repairing the damage wrought by a century of war—rebuilding old relationships, unifying the hopes and dreams of people who were arbitrarily separated for far too long. No President, no person, has done better work toward this end than President Havel.

Since assuming office, Mr. President, you have provided a voice of dazzling eloquence to the debate over Europe's future and the future of the world, a voice of both humility and great power. You have addressed issues large and small, regional and global, material and spiritual, but always in the most human way. You have articulated a politics of hope, reminding us that all nations form a community on our small planet. You have spoken forcefully about our collective obligation to the future. And for our children's sake, we must do all we can to back up your vision with real deeds.

Since 1989 the Czech people have taken enormous strides to build that better world. You have made concrete contributions to the search for peace in Bosnia and Kosovo. In Bosnia, your soldiers stand shoulder-to-shoulder with ours. You have strengthened cooperation with your neighbors. You have taken steps to heal past wounds with Germany and Russia. You are providing humanitarian assistance to Chernobyl victims in Ukraine and sharing with other states the lessons you have learned in building a vibrant free-market democracy. You have stood with the community of nations against military aggression in the Gulf, sent peacekeepers to Africa and the former Soviet Union, and promoted efforts to control the proliferation of weapons of mass destruction. Soon you will be members of the most successful military alliance in history, NATO.

Of course, many challenges remain. Economic and political reform is a bumpy road; it does not happen overnight. And there are many new challenges to this new century we are about to enter. But together, we are building a stronger foundation for peace and prosperity.

I want to especially commend you now for looking toward the new millennium, for taking some time in each of these years leading up to the millennium to think about the future and plan for it in your Forum 2000 program, which you have invited the First Lady to participate in in the next couple of weeks.

Mr. President, at the end of your historic speech to Congress in 1990, you remembered that the people who founded America were bold in word and deed. Today there is not a leader on Earth whose words and deeds have meant more to the cause of freedom than your own. They will live forever in the hearts and minds of people who care about human dignity and the power of the imagination to shape the soul and the future.

On behalf of all Americans, I am deeply honored to welcome you back to the White House. Thank you very much.

NOTE: President Clinton spoke at 9:52 a.m. on the South Lawn at the White House, where President Havel was accorded a formal welcome with full military honors. In his remarks, President Clinton referred to President Havel's wife, Dagmar Havlova. The transcript released by the Office of the Press Secretary also included the remarks of President Havel.

The President's News Conference With President Václav Havel of the Czech Republic
September 16, 1998

President Clinton. Thank you very much. Please be seated.

Ladies and gentlemen, last June in Washington, I had the opportunity to speak of a remarkable trio of leaders, each a champion of freedom, each imprisoned by authoritarian rulers, each now, after decades of struggle, the President of his nation. Last June, I was hosting President Kim Dae-jung of Korea. Next week, President Nelson Mandela of South Africa will be here. And of course, today, I am very proud to stand with President Václav Havel of the Czech Republic.

In the Prague Spring of 1968, a celebrated young playwright boldly called for an end to one-party rule before Soviet tanks crushed the people's hopes. Václav Havel's plays were banned. He lost his job, but he carried on. In 1977, he spearheaded the Charter 77 human rights movement; and for his activism then, he faced more than a decade of harassment, interrogation, and incarceration. Still, he carried on. And in 1989, he was at the forefront of the Velvet Revolution that at last brought freedom to the Czech and to the Slovak peoples. There was exhilaration all around the world when he spoke as President on the first day of January 1990 and declared, "People, your Government has returned to you." I was proud to visit President Havel in Prague in 1994, to see the great energy, creativity, joy of the Czech people unleashed.

When we celebrate freedom today, we know that many challenges still lie ahead. President Havel recently put it very well. "Something is being born," he said. "One age is succeeding another. We live in a world where everything is possible and almost nothing is certain." Today our meetings focused on seizing those possibilities and minimizing those uncertainties. I'm delighted that Foreign Minister Kavan and Defense Minister Vetchy, representatives of the new government headed by Prime Minister Zeman, as well as Mr. Tosovsky, the governor of the Czech National Bank, were able to participate in our discussions.

We talked about the true partnership for security our nations have forged, our desire to build a world with greater tolerance, greater respect for human rights, to build a united, democratic, peaceful Europe. We talked about next year's NATO Summit here and the Czech Republic's preparations for integration into the NATO alliance. I thanked President Havel for beginning to talk with me a long time ago, even before I became President, about the importance of the expansion of NATO and the Czech Republic's role in it.

Already, Czech troops are working side by side with us in Bosnia, where we've just seen further evidence that the Bosnian people are on the path to lasting peace: a free election with a strong turnout. Czech soldiers served as peacekeepers and military observers in Macedonia, in Georgia, in Angola, in Mozambique and Liberia.

Today we spoke about the urgent need to bring stability to Kosovo to prevent suffering there, and the current tensions in Albania. We discussed ways to strengthen our cooperation against the terrible scourge of terrorism, and I had the chance to thank the President for the support we got from the Czech Republic for our actions against terrorism in the wake of the bombings of the American Embassies in Africa.

We talked about the situation in Russia, the economic crisis there, the new government. I underscored America's continuing support for Czech reforms, greater openness in economic institutions, and greater investment in their increasingly competitive economy. And I expressed our strong support for the Czech Republic's accession to the European Union and for the fair treatment of American businesses that would be affected.

We are making progress as friends and partners. That is possible only because of the courage President Havel and the Czech people have shown and continue to show today. We will continue to do the hard work together so that our children can reap the full benefits of it in the new century.

Thank you for coming, Mr. President. The floor is yours.

President Havel. Mr. President, I thank you for the floor and for these nice words. Ladies and gentlemen, thank you for coming. With your permission, I'll try to speak in your nice language.

The situation of the contemporary world is very complicated. We feel it especially in Europe, especially in Central Europe, especially in Czech Republic. And I think that in this situation, it's extremely important, the responsibility of the United States, as the biggest, most powerful country all around the world. And I'm extremely grateful or thankful to Mr. President and his leadership, because it was in his time when we received the chance to build a new Europe. And to build a new Europe—it means to build the new world, peaceful world, because in modern time, as you know, Europe was the main exporter of world wars, and now it has a completely different chance. And it was during his leadership when these chances were open, with support of your big country.

I would like to thank for all this to your President and to thank to all your Nation.

Thank you.

Kosovo/President's Moral Authority

Q. Mr. President, what can the U.S. and NATO do to stop the killing in Kosovo? And what do you say to people who have said that you have lost all the moral authority to lead this Nation or to conduct foreign affairs?

President Clinton. Let me answer the second question first, and then I will talk about Kosovo, because it's very important.

I have never stopped leading this country in foreign affairs in this entire year, and I never will. The issues are too important and they affect the way Americans live at home.

Just in the last several days, of course, we have taken action against those who killed our people and killed the Kenyans and Tanzanians. We have—I and my administration have been working for peace in Northern Ireland, for stability in Russia. I have been personally involved in the peace process in the Middle East again, as it reaches another critical phase.

I gave a speech Monday which I think is about the most important subject now facing the world community, how to limit this financial crisis, keep it from spreading, how to develop long-term institutions that will help to promote growth and opportunity for ordinary people around the world in a way that permits America's economic recovery to go on. After that, my objectives were embraced by the leaders, the financial leaders of the largest industrial countries in the world. Yesterday, as it happens, I got calls from the Presidents of Mexico, Brazil, and the Prime Minister of Canada, all thanking me for what I said on Monday and saying they wanted to be a part of it.

So I feel very good about where I am—in relations—to the rest of the world. I had a good talk with President Chirac of France, who called me a couple of days ago to talk about some of our common concerns and the U.N. inspection system in Iraq and other things. So I feel good about that.

Now, on Kosovo, the American people should know that we have looming there, right next door to Bosnia, a significant humanitarian problem. There are many, many tens of thousands of people who have been dislocated from their homes. But somewhere between 50,000 and 100,000—it's hard for us to know for sure— are above—not, I want to say, above the tree line—at least at very high levels in the mountains, which means it will get colder there much more quickly than in the rest of the country. Winter is coming on; you could have a major humanitarian disaster.

What are we doing about it? We're doing three things. First of all, we're doing everything we can to avert the humanitarian disaster. Secondly, we're pursuing negotiated settlement options through Ambassador Chris Hill. Thirdly, we're doing NATO planning and consulting with our allies, because I still believe the big problem here is Mr. Milosevic is determined to get a military solution if he can, instead of pursuing a diplomatic solution which would give the Kosovars the autonomy they're supposed to have under the Serbian system that they once had.

Now, I discussed this with President Havel; he may want to comment on it since it's in his neighborhood. But while the political and legal situation is not identical to what we had in Bosnia, the humanitarian issue is similar. And we don't want a repeat of Bosnia. We don't want another round of instability there. And I think it is imperative that we move forthrightly, with our allies, as firmly as possible, to avert the humanitarian tragedy and then to get a political solution.

Q. So you think you do have the moral authority to lead this Nation?

President Clinton. Well, you might—in my view, that is something that you have to demonstrate every day. My opinion is not as important as the opinion of others. What is important is that I do my job.

I said last Friday, and I'd like to say again, I am seized on two things: I'm trying to do the still quite painful work that I need to do with my family in our own life, and I'm determined to lead this country and to focus on the issues that are before us. It is not an option. There is no option; we have got to deal with these things. And I'm very, very heartened by what world leaders have said to me in the last 2 weeks about what they want us to do. And there was an enormous positive reaction here in America and around the world to the steps that I outlined on Monday. It was very, very heartening to me.

Czech-U.S. Shared Values

Q. I'm sorry, I will ask the question in Czech because I need a Czech answer.

[*A question was asked in Czech, and a translation was not provided.*]

President Havel. I have never said that we believe in different values. We believe in the same values like the United States. And the

United States and especially the American Nation is fantastic, big body with many very different faces. I love most of these faces. There are some which I don't understand. I don't like to speak about things which I don't understand. [*Laughter*]

President's Regrets and Goals

Q. Mr. President, from your understanding of events, is Monica Lewinsky's account of your relationship accurate and truthful? And do you still maintain that you did not lie under oath in your testimony?

President Clinton. Mr. Hunt [Terence Hunt, Associated Press], I have said for a month now that I did something that was wrong. On last Friday at the prayer breakfast, I laid out as carefully and as brutally honestly as I could what I believe the essential truth to be. I also said then, and I will say again, that I think that the right thing for our country and the right thing for all people concerned is not to get mired in all the details here but to focus—for me to focus on what I did, to acknowledge it, to atone for it; and then to work on my family, where I still have a lot of work to do, difficult work; and to lead this country, to deal with the agenda before us, these huge issues that I was just talking about internationally, plus, with only 2 weeks left to go in this budget year, a very, very large range of items before the American people here at home: doing our part to deal with this financial crisis, with funding the International Monetary Fund, saving the Social Security system before we spend the surplus, doing the important work that we can do to help educate our children, dealing with the Patients' Bill of Rights for these people, 160 million of them, in HMO's.

These are the things, to me, that I should be talking about as President, without in any way ever trying to obscure my own personal acknowledgment and chagrin about what I did wrong and my determination to put it right.

Friendship With President Clinton/ Mark McGwire and Sammy Sosa

Q. Mr. President Havel, you said today that President Clinton is your great friend. I wonder if the discovered misdeeds of President Clinton have anyhow influenced your approach to him, your relations with him.

President Havel. I didn't recognize any change.

I was speaking some minutes ago about these faces of America which I don't understand. There are some faces which we understand very well. In this connection, permit me to congratulate Mr. Mark McGwire and to wish the success to Mr. Sammy Sosa. [*Laughter*]

Press Secretary Mike McCurry. Larry McQuillan from Reuters.

Russia/Testimony Before Grand Jury

Q. Mr. President, as the Lewinsky matter continues to unfold, can you foresee any circumstance where you might consider resignation, either because of the personal toll on you or the toll on the country? And do you think it's fair if the House should release these videotapes?

And sir, if I could ask President Havel a question. With the current developments going on in Russia, are you concerned that there's a return to some degree of some former Soviet officials who are running the country? And do you have a fear that perhaps an old threat may return?

President Havel. I don't think that contemporary or current development in Russia is such a danger like old Soviet Union. It is a country in a very complicated situation, and it will be a country in complicated situation I think 50 or 100 years. But we understand this complication because we have the same. But for us, it is question of years; for them, it is question of decades. I don't see anything very dangerous in it. It's a natural process, and I think it is much more better to have ill Russia than healthy Soviet Union. [*Laughter*]

President Clinton. Let me, first of all, say that the personal toll on me is of no concern except insofar as it affects my personal life. I think the—and I feel the pain better now because I'm working on what I should be working on. I believe the right thing for the country—and what I believe the people of the country want is, now that they know what happened, they want to put it behind them, and they want to go on. And they want me to go on and do my job, and that's what I intend to do. That is the right thing to do.

In terms of the question you asked about the House, they have to decide that. That's not for me to decide. They have to do their job, and I have to do mine. There are some things, though, we need to do together. And again I would say, it's been quite a long time during this session, and there's still only one appropriation bill passed and a lot of other things still out there. So I hope we can work together to do some things for the American people. I think that the time has come to think about the American people and their interests and their future. And that's what I'm going to focus on, and that's what I would hope the Congress would focus on.

Q. When you gave the deposition, sir, were you fully aware that it might be released, the videotape?

President Clinton. Mr. McQuillan, I'm trying to remember. I think that—I knew that the rules were against it, but I thought it would happen. I think that's where I was on that. But it's not of so much concern to me. I mean, you know that I acknowledged an improper relationship and that I declined to discuss the details, and that's what happened. So I'll leave it for others to judge and evaluate; that's not for me to say. I want to work on my family and lead this country, and others will have to make all those judgments. They're not within my range of authority anyway, so it's pointless for me to comment on it.

Friendship With President Clinton

Q. Mr. President, you have mentioned in your speech that you appreciate the personal contribution of President Clinton to the NATO enlargement, and you see him also as a personal friend. I'd like to know, how do you think that an eventual resignation or impeachment of President Clinton would influence the American foreign policy and the Czech-American relations?

President Havel. Excuse me, I am a little bit tired. I prefer to speak in my language.

I believe that this is a matter for the United States and for the American people, who will be their President. When I have made a friendship with someone, I remain that person's friend, no matter which office he or she holds or doesn't hold.

Mr. McCurry. Thank you, ladies and gentlemen.

President Clinton. Do you want to take one more? April [April Ryan, American Urban Radio Networks], go ahead.

President's Initiative on Race

Q. Mr. President, your initiative on race finishes this month, and your Press Secretary yesterday agreed that the race initiative isn't flying because of your current problems and it was bogged down in the muck and mire. Do you regret that your personal problems affected your potential legacy on race and that it may just, at best, be a Band-Aid approach to racism in America?

President Clinton. First of all——

Mr. McCurry. That's not exactly what I said.

President Clinton. I don't know if he said that, but if he did, I strongly disagree with him. I don't think it's affected it at all. As a matter of fact, I think in the response you've seen from some sectors of the American community have reinforced and acknowledged the centrality of this issue to the work of the last 6 years, not just the work of the last year.

And let me also say that what is coming to an end here is this phase of it. And there will be a report—the board will give me a set of recommendations. Then we expect to produce a document. But the main thing is we have to keep making progress for the American people. I would remind you that we have before the Congress right now—just two things that I'd like to emphasize: number one, legislation, fully funded, within the balanced budget bill, to get rid of the backlog in the Equal Employment Opportunity Commission and otherwise enforce the antidiscrimination laws of the country; I think that is very important. Number two, we have an empowerment agenda put together by the Vice President and Secretary Cuomo and an education component put together by Secretary Riley to create affirmative economic and educational opportunities in distressed inner-city and isolated rural areas that are predominantly minority.

Both those are not particularly costly. Both those could be passed by this Congress in the next 2 weeks. Both those would actually do something for the American people that live beyond the borders of the Federal establishment here, and I very much hope they will pass.

But I expect this to be a central part of the work I do in the next 2 years. I expect this to be a central part of the work I do for the rest of my life. I think in the 21st century—when you go back to World War II, and you think about the part of the Nazi experience that was directed against the Jews, and you look all the way through the ensuing years, all the way to the end of this century, down to what we've seen in Rwanda, the Middle East, Northern Ireland, Bosnia, Kosovo—you name it—it will be incumbent upon the United States to be a force for tolerance and racial reconciliation for the foreseeable future.

So this is just simply a phase of this work that is coming to an end, and I think you should see it as a springboard, both in the recommendations the advisory commission will make and in the document that I will put out after that.

Q. So could there be a council on race?

President Clinton. I understand they may recommend that, and if they do, of course, I will take it very seriously.

President Havel. One of my whole life personal ideals is ideal of a civic society. I must tell you that America—and America especially in time of President Clinton, because this is the America I know the best—is for my work, for my support of civic society, a big inspiration.

Thank you.

President Clinton. Thank you very much.

NOTE: The President's 164th news conference began at 3:13 p.m. in the Dean Acheson Auditorium at the State Department. During the later portion of the news conference, President Havel spoke in Czech, and his remarks were translated by an interpreter. In his remarks, President Clinton referred to Minister of Foreign Affairs Jan Kavan, Minister of Defense Vladimir Vetchy, and Prime Minister Milos Zeman of the Czech Republic; Josef Tosovsky, Chairman, Czech National Bank; President Ernesto Zedillo of Mexico; President Fernando Henrique Cardoso of Brazil; Prime Minister Jean Chretien of Canada; President Jacques Chirac of France; Christopher R. Hill, U.S. Ambassador to the Former Yugoslav Republic of Macedonia; and President Slobodan Milosevic of the Federal Republic of Yugoslavia (Serbia and Montenegro). President Havel referred to St. Louis Cardinals first baseman Mark McGwire and Chicago Cubs outfielder Sammy Sosa, who broke Major League Baseball's single-season home run record. Reporters referred to former White House intern Monica S. Lewinsky.

Message to the Congress Transmitting the Report of the Commodity Credit Corporation
September 16, 1998

To the Congress of the United States:

As required by the provisions of section 13, Public Law 806, 80th Congress (15 U.S.C. 714k), I transmit herewith the report of the Commodity Credit Corporation for fiscal year 1996.

WILLIAM J. CLINTON

The White House,
September 16, 1998.

Remarks at the State Dinner Honoring President Václav Havel of the Czech Republic
September 16, 1998

The President. Good evening, ladies and gentlemen, President Havel, Mrs. Havlova, friends from the Czech Republic, my fellow Americans. Welcome to the White House, Mr. President.

As a playwright, you could hardly have written a more dramatic scenario than the one you have in fact lived over the last 10 years. Your Presidency has reminded people around the world that words do matter, that creativity has a place in politics, that a nation's strength is measured not by its ability to control people but rather by the opposite: its success in moving and empowering them.

As you showed us in the press conference today, you have never lost the honesty, spontaneity, the contagious friendliness of your writing. I feel quite certain no other head of state would have appointed Frank Zappa as a cultural ambassador—[*laughter*]—or taken our favorite Czech-American, Madeleine Albright, out on the town in New York to hear some good music; or given the President of the United States a personally inscribed tenor saxophone and forced him to play it. [*Laughter*]

Since you became President, you have brought back democracy and civil society. You have led the Czech Republic to a place of prominence in the new Europe, and we look forward to your becoming a member of NATO.

Together we have been partners in Bosnia and in other Balkan trouble spots, working to repair the ravages of intolerance and injustice. And together we will be partners to build a peaceful, prosperous, and free Europe in the 21st century.

We value our ties to the Czech people. The first Czechs arrived in the New World in the 17th century, and many more came in the wake of the revolution of 1848. Dvorak composed his magnificent, "New World Symphony," borrowing the rhythms he heard during his travels across the United States, especially from African-American folk music. The flag of the Czech Republic was designed and first flown in New York to honor a visit by the great patriot Tomas Masaryk. From athletes to artists, from actors to astronauts, from secretaries to Secretaries of State, Czech-Americans, many of whom are here tonight, have lent their gifts to our grateful Nation.

We shared the world's sadness when Czechoslovakia lost its freedom 50 years ago. We felt a similar sense of loss when the Prague Spring was followed by Soviet invasion in 1968. But you and your comrades, Mr. President, taught us again that all seasons are cyclical, that spring always returns. In 1989, your Velvet Revolution rejuvenated the entire world.

There is an old Czech-American saying that too much wisdom does not produce courage. That's a nice way of saying, I think, that too much time spent in books may keep people too much away from the active world. Mr. President, you have lived a life of the mind and a life of action. You have shown us wisdom and courage. You have made us believe that we can not only dream our dreams but redeem them.

Ladies and gentlemen, I ask you to join me in a toast to the President of the Czech Republic, Mrs. Havlova, and to the people of the Czech Republic.

[*At this point, President Havel made brief remarks, offered a toast, and then presented President Clinton with the Order of the White Lion.*]

The President. If I put all this on—[*laughter*]—I may feel like royalty.

Mr. President, I first saw Prague in the second week of January in 1970. I was a young student of no visible means and fairly poor prospects. I remember that I went to Prague with a pair of rawhide boots and a Navy pea jacket I bought in the Army-Navy surplus store. But I learned something there that is as vivid to me today as it was then.

When all of you were at a moment of despair, I saw in the young students I met there a love for freedom that you gave life to again. And whenever I look at this award, I will know that it's too grand for me to wear, but I will be very glad that we could do something in the United States, through NATO, to help ensure that that freedom will never, ever be lost again.

Thank you, sir.

NOTE: The President spoke at 8:53 p.m. in the East Room at the White House. In his remarks, he referred to Dagmar Havlova, wife of President Havel. The transcript released by the Office of the Press Secretary also included the remarks of President Havel.

Message to the Congress Reporting on the National Emergency With Respect to Iran
September 16, 1998

To the Congress of the United States:

I hereby report to the Congress on developments concerning the national emergency with respect to Iran that was declared in Executive Order 12957 of March 15, 1995, and matters relating to the measures in that order and in Executive Order 12959 of May 6, 1995, and in Executive Order 13059 of August 19, 1997. This report is submitted pursuant to section 204(c) of the International Emergency Economic Powers Act, 50 U.S.C. 1703(c) (IEEPA), section 401(c) of the National Emergencies Act, 50 U.S.C. 1641(c), and section 505(c) of the International Security and Development Cooperation Act of 1985, 22 U.S.C. 2349aa–9(c). This report discusses only matters concerning the national emergency with respect to Iran that was declared in Executive Order 12957 and does not deal with those relating to the emergency declared on November 14, 1979, in connection with the hostage crisis.

1. On March 15, 1995, I issued Executive Order 12957 (60 *Fed. Reg.* 14615, March 17, 1995) to declare a national emergency with respect to Iran pursuant to IEEPA, and to prohibit the financing, management, or supervision by United States persons of the development of Iranian petroleum resources. This action was in response to actions and policies of the Government of Iran, including support for international terrorism, efforts to undermine the Middle East peace process, and the acquisition of weapons of mass destruction and the means to deliver them. A copy of the Order was provided to the Speaker of the House and the President of the Senate by letter dated March 15, 1995.

Following the imposition of these restrictions with regard to the development of Iranian petroleum resources, Iran continued to engage in activities that represent a threat to the peace and security of all nations, including Iran's continuing support for international terrorism, its support for acts that undermine the Middle East peace process, and its intensified efforts to acquire weapons of mass destruction. On May 6, 1995, I issued Executive Order 12959 (60 *Fed. Reg.* 24757, May 9, 1995) to further respond

to the Iranian threat to the national security, foreign policy, and economy of the United States. The terms of that order and an earlier order imposing an import ban on Iranian-origin goods and services (Executive Order 12613 of October 29, 1987) were consolidated and clarified in Executive Order 13059 of August 19, 1997.

At the time of signing Executive Order 12959, I directed the Secretary of the Treasury to authorize through specific licensing certain transactions, including transactions by United States persons related to the Iran-United States Claims Tribunal in The Hague, established pursuant to the Algiers Accords, and related to other international obligations and U.S. Government functions, and transactions related to the export of agricultural commodities pursuant to preexisting contracts consistent with section 5712(c) of title 7, United States Code. I also directed the Secretary of the Treasury, in consultation with the Secretary of State, to consider authorizing United States persons through specific licensing to participate in market-based swaps of crude oil from the Caspian Sea area for Iranian crude oil in support of energy projects in Azerbaijan, Kazakhstan, and Turkmenistan.

Executive Order 12959 revoked sections 1 and 2 of Executive Order 12613 of October 29, 1987, and sections 1 and 2 of Executive Order 12957 of March 15, 1995, to the extent they are inconsistent with it. A copy of Executive Order 12959 was transmitted to the Congressional leadership by letter dated May 6, 1995.

On August 19, 1997, I issued Executive Order 13059 in order to clarify the steps taken in Executive Order 12957 and Executive Order 12959, to confirm that the embargo on Iran prohibits all trade and investment activities by United States persons, wherever located, and to consolidate in one order the various prohibitions previously imposed to deal with the national emergency declared on March 15, 1995. A copy of the Order was transmitted to the Speaker of the House and the President of the Senate by letter dated August 19, 1997.

The Order prohibits (1) the importation into the United States of any goods or services of

Iranian origin or owned or controlled by the Government of Iran except information or informational material; (2) the exportation, reexportation, sale, or supply from the United States or by a United States person, wherever located, of goods, technology, or services to Iran or the Government of Iran, including knowing transfers to a third country for direct or indirect supply, transshipment, or reexportation to Iran or the Government of Iran, or specifically for use in the production, commingling with, or incorporation into goods, technology, or services to be supplied, transshipped, or reexported exclusively or predominantly to Iran or the Government of Iran; (3) knowing reexportation from a third country to Iran or the Government of Iran of certain controlled U.S.-origin goods, technology, or services by a person other than a United States person; (4) the purchase, sale, transport, swap, brokerage, approval, financing, facilitation, guarantee, or other transactions or dealings by United States persons, wherever located, related to goods, technology, or services for exportation, reexportation, sale or supply, directly or indirectly, to Iran or the Government of Iran, or to goods or services of Iranian origin or owned or controlled by the Government of Iran; (5) new investment by United States persons in Iran or in property or entities owned or controlled by the Government of Iran; (6) approval, financing, facilitation, or guarantee by a United States person of any transaction by a foreign person that a United States person would be prohibited from performing under the terms of the Order; and (7) any transaction that evades, avoids, or attempts to violate a prohibition under the Order.

Executive Order 13059 became effective at 12:01 a.m., eastern daylight time on August 20, 1997. Because the order consolidated and clarified the provisions of prior orders, Executive Order 12613 and paragraphs (a), (b), (c), (d) and (f) of section 1 of Executive Order 12959 were revoked by Executive Order 13059. The revocation of corresponding provisions in the prior Executive orders did not affect the applicability of those provisions, or of regulations, licenses or other administrative actions taken pursuant to those provisions, with respect to any transaction or violation occurring before the effective date of Executive Order 13059. Specific licenses issued pursuant to prior Executive orders continue in effect, unless revoked or amended by the Secretary of the Treasury. General licenses, regulations, orders, and directives issued pursuant to prior orders continue in effect, except to the extent inconsistent with Executive Order 13059 or otherwise revoked or modified by the Secretary of the Treasury.

The declaration of national emergency made by Executive Order 12957, and renewed each year since, remains in effect and is not affected by the Order.

3. On March 4, 1998, I renewed for another year the national emergency with respect to Iran pursuant to IEEPA. This renewal extended the authority for the current comprehensive trade embargo against Iran in effect since May 1995. Under these sanctions, virtually all trade with Iran is prohibited except for trade in information and informational materials and certain other limited exceptions.

4. There have been no amendments to the Iranian Transactions Regulations, 31 CFR Part 560 (the "ITR"), since my report of March 16, 1998.

5. During the current 6-month period, the Department of the Treasury's Office of Foreign Assets Control (OFAC) made numerous decisions with respect to applications for licenses to engage in transactions under the ITR, and issued 12 licenses.

The majority of denials were in response to requests to authorize commercial exports to Iran—particularly of machinery and equipment for various industries—and the importation of Iranian-origin goods. The licenses that were issued authorized certain financial transactions and transactions relating to air safety policy. Pursuant to sections 3 and 4 of Executive Order 12959, Executive Order 13059, and consistent with statutory restrictions concerning certain goods and technology, including those involved in air safety cases, the Department of the Treasury continues to consult with the Departments of State and Commerce on these matters.

Since the issuance of Executive Order 13059, more than 1,500 transactions involving Iran initially have been "rejected" by U.S. financial institutions under IEEPA and the ITR. United States banks declined to process these transactions in the absence of OFAC authorization. Twenty percent of the 1,500 transactions scrutinized by OFAC resulted in investigations by OFAC to assure compliance with IEEPA and ITR by United States persons.

Such investigations resulted in 15 referrals for civil penalty action, issuance of 5 warning letters, and an additional 52 cases still under compliance or legal review prior to final agency action.

Since my last report, OFAC has collected 20 civil monetary penalties totaling more than $110,000 for violations of IEEPA and the ITR related to the import or export to Iran of goods and services. Five U.S. financial institutions, twelve companies, and three individuals paid penalties for these prohibited transactions. Civil penalty action is pending against another 45 United States persons for violations of the ITR.

6. On January 22, 1997, an Iranian national resident in Oregon and a U.S. citizen were indicted on charges related to the attempted exportation to Iran of spare parts for gas turbines and precursor agents utilized in the production of nerve gas. The 5-week trial of the American citizen defendant, which began in early February 1998, resulted in his conviction on all counts. That defendant is awaiting sentencing. The other defendant pleaded guilty to one count of criminal conspiracy and was sentenced to 21 months in prison.

On March 24, 1998, a Federal grand jury in Newark, New Jersey, returned an indictment against a U.S. national and an Iranian-born resident of Singapore for violation of IEEPA and the ITR relating to exportation of munitions, helicopters, and weapons systems components to Iran. Among the merchandise the defendants conspired to export were parts for Phoenix air-to-air missiles used on F–14A fighter jets in Iran. Trial is scheduled to begin on October 6, 1998.

The U.S. Customs Service has continued to effect numerous seizures of Iranian-origin merchandise, primarily carpets, for violation of the import prohibitions of the ITR. Various enforcement actions carried over from previous reporting periods are continuing and new reports of violations are being aggressively pursued.

7. The expenses incurred by the Federal Government in the 6-month period from March 15 through September 14, 1998, that are directly attributable to the exercise of powers and authorities conferred by the declaration of a national emergency with respect to Iran are reported to be approximately $1.7 million, most of which represent wage and salary costs for Federal personnel. Personnel costs were largely centered in the Department of the Treasury (particularly in the Office of Foreign Assets Control, the U.S. Customs Service, the Office of the Under Secretary for Enforcement, and the Office of the General Counsel); the Department of State (particularly the Bureau of Economic and Business Affairs, the Bureau of Near Eastern Affairs, the Bureau of Intelligence and Research, and the Office of the Legal Adviser); and the Department of Commerce (the Bureau of Export Administration and the General Counsel's Office).

8. The situation reviewed above continues to present an extraordinary and unusual threat to the national security, foreign policy, and economy of the United States. The declaration of the national emergency with respect to Iran contained in Executive Order 12957 and the comprehensive economic sanctions imposed by Executive Order 12959 underscore the Government's opposition to the actions and policies of the Government of Iran, particularly its support of international terrorism and its efforts to acquire weapons of mass destruction and the means to deliver them. The Iranian Transactions Regulations issued pursuant to Executive Orders 12957, 12959, and 13059 continue to advance important objectives in promoting the nonproliferation and anti-terrorism policies of the United States. I shall exercise the powers at my disposal to deal with these problems and will report periodically to the Congress on significant developments.

WILLIAM J. CLINTON

The White House,
September 16, 1998.

NOTE: This message was released by the Office of the Press Secretary on September 17.

Remarks to the International Brotherhood of Electrical Workers Convention
September 17, 1998

Thank you very much. Thank you for the wonderful welcome. You know, when I was walking out the door this morning to come over here, Hillary said, "Where are you going this morning?" I said, "I'm going to speak to the IBEW." She said, "Boy, I like those folks."

I cannot thank you enough for your warm welcome and for the purpose which brings you to Washington. I would like to thank John Sweeney for many things, but I would especially like to thank him for the introduction he gave Carol Hooper, not only because he told us about her life but because he told us about the life of America at its best: people taking care of their families, being good citizens, doing what they can to improve their own lives and the lives of their fellow citizens. It was a very impressive account, and I thank you, Carol Hooper, for your introduction, for your support of this legislation, and for the work you have done for a lifetime in the IBEW. Thank you, ma'am.

I am delighted to be here with Jack Barry and Ed Hill and Rick Diegel. I am especially delighted, always, to be on the platform with John Sweeney. He has given new energy, new direction, real life, real power in the best sense to the labor movement here in Washington and throughout this country.

I was talking with our friends in Congress on the way out here this morning. It is wonderful to see the labor movement back, not only back in Washington but back in the heart of America. Average citizens who do not belong to unions know you are on their side, too, and it means a lot. And our country is better because of what has happened in the last 4 or 5 years.

I would like to say a special word of thanks to Senators Daschle and Kennedy and Harkin and Rockefeller and to Congressmen McDermott, Filner, Pascrell, and Meeks for being here with me today and for fighting for you every day. We need more people like them in the Congress. In a few weeks, you'll have a chance to send a few more like them to the Congress. I hope you will.

I also want to thank our Labor Secretary, Alexis Herman, our HHS Secretary, Donna Shalala, and my labor adviser in the White House, Karen Tramontano, for not only coming here with me today but for working for you every day. They have really, really worked hard to change the daily life of the Government so that everybody is more oriented toward making decisions that have a positive impact on the ability of families to do their work and raise their children and live in strong and safe communities.

You've fought by our side for 6 years now, and we've got some pretty good results to show for it: the lowest unemployment rate in 28 years; nearly 17 million new jobs; the lowest crime rate in 25 years; the smallest percentage of Americans on welfare in 29 years; the lowest inflation in 32 years; the highest homeownership in history; and in just a couple of weeks, for the first time in 29 years, all that red ink on the Government's budget will turn to black, thanks to the people here, and I thank them for that.

We've also done a lot of good things to help the American people live their lives better. We raised the minimum wage, and I might say, we're going to be given a chance to do it again. Today Senator Kennedy's bill is coming up in the Senate, and he reminded me again before we came out here—you hear all these arguments about how the minimum wage will raise unemployment, all that sort of stuff they say. The minimum wage has been raised five times since World War II, since 1948; four of those times the unemployment rate was higher than it is now; and all five times, the inflation rate was higher than it is now. Twelve million people are out there working just like you, and nobody who works for a living—nobody—should have to wonder whether, no matter how hard they work, they still won't be able to provide for their children, educate their children, and have a decent life. It is time to raise the minimum wage again, and I think we ought to do it.

Together we doubled the tax credit for low-income working families, worth about $1,000 in lower taxes today to a family of four with an income of under $30,000. Together we've made college loans more affordable; we've given a tax credit for the first 2 years of college of $1,500 and tax credits for the rest of college and for adults to go back to school. Together we passed the family and medical leave bill, and millions and millions of families are better off as a result of it.

Together we have fought against efforts, constant efforts in the Congress, to undercut worker rights. And I remember last May, particularly, the pride I felt in being given the opportunity by John Sweeney to work with you in California to get the message out that it is simply wrong to pass a ballot initiative to silence the voice of workers in the political process, and you prevailed, and good for you. I, too, want to join John in thanking our friends in the Senate for making sure that people know that at least on our side, we think it's wrong to pass a salting bill to erode the rights of workers to organize.

So these are good times for the country, and that's good news for America, and it's good news for American labor. But the question is, what are we going to do with the good times we have? All you have to do is watch the evening news or pick up the paper to know that these are turbulent times around the world, that things are still changing at a very rapid rate, and that the American people have a very stark decision to make, which is whether to sit back and relax, maybe even pass up a chance to vote on election day, or seize on these good times and say, "We thank the good Lord and our good fortune and your hard efforts for the good times we've got, but we know we can't sit on them. We know we can't relax."

When you have good times, you need to take the confidence they give you, the resources they give you, and look at the real challenges facing the country and meet them. We need to make this a season of doing things for you, not idleness and not indulgence but doing things for you.

The children in this audience are going to live in a very different world than we grew up in. We know right now many of the things we should be doing to make sure that world is a better, safer, stronger world for ordinary people in this country, and it's time we acted on it. That is the choice: partisanship over progress, people over politics. In every issue facing the Congress and the country, that is the choice. And the people need to make their voices heard.

Let me just mention a few of them. First of all, we need to dance with what brought us to this prosperity. When I took office, we had a budget deficit of $290 billion, high interest rates, low investment, and high unemployment. Now, we have worked hard to get rid of that. The members of my party, I am proud to say—and only the members of my party—in 1993 voted for an economic plan that reduced the deficit by 92 percent before the bipartisan balanced budget bill passed.

Now we're going to have a balanced budget and a surplus this year, and it is projected that we will have a surplus in the out years because of what we have done. That is a good thing. Now, what should we do? Some of our friends in the other party say that, "Well, we're projecting a surplus, and it's close to the election, so let's give everybody a tax cut," or "Let's give some people a tax cut," and as you might imagine, some more than others. [*Laughter*]

So, in just a few moments the House Ways and Means Committee will begin to mark up an $85 billion tax cut to drain the surplus before it even shows up in the Treasury account. I've had a lot of interesting conversations about this. I have asked some of our Republican friends, I've said, "You know, we've been waiting 29 years for this. Couldn't we at least see the ink turn from red to black and then watch it dry for a minute or two before we get carried away?" [*Laughter*]

But it's election year, and it's popular. But it isn't right, and it isn't right for a couple of reasons. First of all, the world is in a lot of financial turmoil, and we need to set a standard for the world of solid, strong economic policy to try to get the world turned around, to make sure America's recovery is protected. And secondly, we've got something else that has to be done with that money first: We have to reform and save Social Security for the 21st century. That's what we've got to do. I have said over and over again that if Congress sends me a bill that squanders the surplus on tax cuts before we save Social Security, I'll veto it. [*Applause*]

Now, your clapping is an act of good citizenship. Why? Because some of you would get something out of that. But it's wrong. Why? Because when these children are in the work force and the baby boomers like me are retired, at present rates of participation in the work force, birthrates, immigration rates, there will only be two people working for every one person drawing Social Security.

Now, we have three choices. We can give the money away and fool around with it—or, we actually have four choices. We can do nothing, in which case we'll have two of our choices one of these days before long. We'll either have to lower the standard of living of our seniors rather dramatically, or we'll have to raise taxes so much to keep the system as it presently is that we will undermine the standard of living of our children and their ability to raise our grandchildren. And it's just wrong. I don't care how close it is to the election. It is wrong to do that until we have solved this problem.

Now, the other alternatives are, we can pass the tax cut and then just dismantle the Social Security system, and there are some who would like to do that. Or we can do the responsible thing even though it's election season: We can modify the Social Security system; and if we start now, because it's going to be several years before all the baby boomers get in the Social Security system—if we start now, we can make modest changes that will enable us to protect the retirement of the baby boom generation and protect the living standards of our children and their ability to raise our grandchildren. That is the right thing to do. It seems to me to be a no-brainer.

Now, it may not be popular within a few weeks of the election, but it is the right thing to do. And I ask you to say, "We don't care how close it is to the election. We care more about our children and our grandchildren and the dignity of life that Social Security has brought to so many. Half the seniors in the country today would be in poverty if it weren't for the Social Security system. We want to reform it in a sensible way and do it in a way that protects our children and our grandchildren. That's our position, and we're going to stick with it."

Now, the second thing we have to do is to do our part to try to stem and limit this global financial crisis you've been reading so much about that's affected Japan and Asia, that is running rampant through Russia today, that is threatening our best trading partners in Latin America who have good economic policy. I gave a talk about it in New York on Monday. Many people came up to me afterward, both Democrats and Republicans, saying, "America has to lead in this." We cannot be, to quote the words of the Federal Reserve Chairman, Alan Greenspan, "an island of prosperity."

About a third of our growth has come from selling things to other countries. Senator Daschle, who is as good a friend as working people have in the Congress, represents a State of farmers who are in terrible trouble today in part because the people in Asia cannot afford to buy the crops grown in South Dakota.

Now, that's what this bill funding the International Monetary Fund is all about. It doesn't throw money at people who won't help themselves. It says, "If you'll do the responsible thing to restore economic growth in your country, we'll be better off, and we'll help you, not out all by ourselves but working with others." It is very important. If we want America to grow, we have to be out there saying to our friends and neighbors, "We want you to grow, too. We don't think it would be a good thing for America to have a good economy and everybody else to have a bad economy," number one, because we don't feel that way and, number two, because eventually it will come back and bite America's economy. How many times have you seen that happen in the last 20 years? It's more true now than ever before.

Now, in this case the Senate has passed this bill for the International Monetary Fund. We're just a couple of weeks away from Congress going home to campaign, and we're still waiting after 8 months. And it needs to be done.

The third thing we need to do is to remember what the most important priority over the long run for America is, and that's the education of our people. We've opened the doors to college wider than ever before. If you look at all the things that have been done by this administration, working with our friends in Congress, it is literally true today that anyone who will work for it and deserves it can get a college education without going into so much debt they'll never be able to pay it off.

But nobody thinks that we yet can say that every child in America has access to the finest elementary and secondary education in the world. We've got a program within the balanced budget for smaller classes in the early grades, funds for States to hire 100,000 teachers to take the class size down to an average of 18, funds to help build or repair 5,000 schools, funds to hook up every classroom to the Internet by the year 2000. That's what we ought to be talking about in Washington, DC, something that will affect the lives of the children in this country.

The education budget needs to pass and needs to pass now.

Now let's talk about the subject that you're here to talk about, the subject that Carol spoke so eloquently about. We have come here to talk about health care. In 1996 you fought for and I signed the Kennedy-Kassebaum law so Americans can keep their health coverage when they change jobs or someone in their family gets sick.

Last year I signed a balanced budget bill that helps to make sure that 5 million uninsured children, virtually all of them in lower-income working families, can get the medical coverage they need and deserve—the biggest increase in coverage since Medicaid passed in 1965.

This year, we are fighting for the Patients' Bill of Rights. Why? You heard Carol's story; 160 million Americans are in managed care. These plans can save money and improve care. When I became President, health care costs were going up at 3 times the rate of inflation. That was totally unsustainable. It was destroying your ability to get a raise. It was undermining the fabric of the country. We had to do something about it. But like every other system, if the system becomes an end in itself and you lose sight of the purpose of health care, you get in trouble.

That is what has happened. I have seen too many people who have had medical procedures delayed or denied, not by their physicians but by health care bureaucrats because of the way these HMO's work. I've spoken to too many doctors and nurses who aren't able to give the kind of care they're trained to give. I've heard too many stories about parents rushing children to emergency rooms and wondering whether their health care plans will cover them in that emergency room.

I asked a bipartisan panel to develop a comprehensive set of rights for patients. I thank Bob Georgine of the Building Trades Council of the AFL–CIO for serving on that commission. They did a fine job. They were all different kinds of people from all parts of the health care sectors and all parts of the economy. They came up with a simple bottom line: the bottom line of health care must be to value patients. Medical decisions should be made by informed medical doctors, not insurance company accountants. Now, to do that, we've got to pass a Patients' Bill of Rights.

Let me just point out that there are 43 HMO's supporting this Patients' Bill of Rights. Why? Because they are doing the right thing anyway, or they want to do the right thing, and they know they're going to get the shaft when it comes to the bottom line unless everybody has to do it. But there are people in this business who know this is right.

Yesterday, as I'm sure you've already talked about, Senator Lott stopped the business of the Senate entirely, shut it all down, silenced all debate, just to stop Senator Daschle and Senator Kennedy with their allies here from bringing up this issue for a vote. Now, can you believe that? Why is that? Why would they shut the Senate down? Because when you go to an emergency room or an operating room or a doctor's office, nobody asks you whether you're a Republican or a Democrat. We all get sick. We all get in car wrecks. We all have kids that need help. So rather than get everybody on record, and put everybody on the bottom line, see who's standing up for the HMO's or the people, they just silenced the debate, because nobody wants to be recorded on the wrong side. So this is death by stealth. [*Laughter*]

Now, this is something that affects you and everybody you work with, everybody you see at your place of worship, everybody you see in all your recreational activities, everybody in your family. This affects you. This is a big deal.

Now, obviously, the real answer—we need more Senator Daschles and Senator Kennedys. We need more of these Congressmen here; we need more Senators like Senator Rockefeller and Senator Harkin. You'll have a chance in November to do something about that.

But this ought to be done now. This should not be a partisan issue. This is a case where Washington ought to work more like the emergency rooms and the operating rooms and the doctor's office. We could have had a Republican stand up here and give the same speech Carol did. This is not a partisan issue in America. It is only a partisan issue in Washington, and it is a practical issue in the country.

Now, I have done all I could here, and I'm going to do a little more today. We have extended the protections of the Patients' Bill of Rights to people in most Federal plans, in Medicare, in the Federal employees' plan. The Department of Health and Human Services has now completed all the work on proposed regulations that will extend the protections of the Patients' Bill of Rights to 20 million Americans in Medicaid managed care programs, vulnerable children, people with disabilities, pregnant women that have no other way to get health care. That's a good thing to do.

With this action, we have now extended the protections of the Patients' Bill of Rights to health plans serving tens of millions of Americans. That's good. But what about the 160 million Americans out there whom I can't reach with unilateral action? That's why we have to have Federal legislation.

Even with all the State bills that have passed, because of Federal laws there are a lot of people they can't protect. If every State in the country passed bills, there would be 100 million people they couldn't protect. There is no solution to this but a comprehensive piece of Federal legislation.

For 9 months we have worked in good faith with people in both parties, and there are some Republicans—there are a few Republicans who are really supporting this. But they can't get by the kind of tactics we saw yesterday.

In July, under pressure from the public, the House of Representatives finally passed something they called the Patients' Bill of Rights, but it is hollow. It gives only a false sense of security. But at least they passed a bill. The Senate, they don't want to be recorded on this. They want death by stealth.

I want you to know the difference between our bill and the Republican bill that passed in the House and that has the support of the leadership in the Senate.

I've got a chart here and I think you can see it. You may not be able to read it, but you get the noes and the yeses, and I'll tell you what they say. [*Laughter*]

Our bill says that managed care accountants can't make arbitrary medical decisions that doctors ought to make, and theirs doesn't.

Our bill says you ought to have a right to see a specialist if you have a medical condition that requires one, and theirs doesn't.

Our bill says that in an emergency you ought to have the right to the nearest emergency room. If you walk out here and you walk across the street and you get hit by a car, do you want to have to go halfway across town if there's a hospital around the block? Let's deal with this in very practical terms; we're talking about

how you live now. Our bill says if you get hurt, you ought to be able to go to the nearest emergency room without worrying whether your health care plan is going to cover it, and their bill doesn't.

Our bill says if your employer changes health plans, you shouldn't be forced to change your doctor if you're pregnant, if you're in the middle of chemotherapy treatment. Now, you ever had anybody in your family treated for chemotherapy? You know how long it takes; you know how you go through the sickness; you know how you wonder if your hair's going to fall out; you know all those things. How much worse is it if, in the middle of the treatment, they say, "I'm sorry. We've changed plans. You've got to change doctors"?

Remember what it was like when your family had the first child? How would you have felt if you were 6 months pregnant or your wife was 6 months pregnant, and they say, "I'm sorry. You've got to leave your doctor now and go see somebody else. I hope you'll like him or her"?

This is real stuff. This is where people live. Our bill says that can't happen. That has happened in America. Our bill says no more. Our bill gives you that right to stay with your doctor through the prescribed period of treatment, and their bill doesn't.

Our bill makes sure health care plans don't give doctors secret incentives to limit care, and theirs doesn't.

Our bill protects the privacy and confidentiality of your medical records. Theirs actually makes it easier for other people to look at your medical records. You think about that. I don't think that's right.

Our bill says you ought to be able to hold your health care plan accountable if it causes harm, and theirs doesn't. And let me just talk a little about that. I've heard all this talk about how the last thing we need is another provision and another bill in Washington that gives anybody the right to bring any legal action. But you just think about it: How would you feel if I said, "You've got a constitutional right to worship God as you please. You've got a constitutional right to freedom of speech. You've got a constitutional right to associate with whomever you want. You've got a constitutional right to travel. But I really think there's too many lawsuits in America, so we're going to repeal your right to defend those rights. You can't protect them. It'll be on the books all right, but if somebody throws you in jail for saying something they don't like, I'm sorry, you can't have any recourse"? There'd be a riot in this country, wouldn't there?

Look, in a lot of these cases where people really get hurt—I've sat here, and I've listened to all these stories; all of us have—believe it or not, finally the right medical decision is made by the HMO, but often it's too late. Why? Because they go up three layers or four, and the first two or three layers, the people there making those decisions—I've got a lot of sympathy with them—they're not doctors, and they know one thing: They are never going to get fired, demoted, or denied a raise for saying no.

You just think about it. When those files come in, they're never going to get in trouble for saying no. They're just like you; they want to keep their job; they want to take care of their kids. Nobody's ever going to burn them for saying no. But if they say yes, uh oh.

And what do they know; how do they sleep at night? Well, they know up the line somewhere eventually there's a doctor who's going to make a decision, and if the right answer is yes, he'll say yes—"so I better say no so I can keep my job and get my bonus, and I'll be all right." Now, that's the way this system works. That's fine if you've got something that somebody can diddle around with for 6 or 9 months. But what if you need a decision now or in 15 days or in 30 days? What if it's your family? That's what all this is about.

I'll say again, our bill covers every American. Their bill leaves out 100 million Americans. That's what this is about.

Now, I want to thank the AFL–CIO for the grassroots efforts you've made here. But I want to ask you to intensify your effort. I want you to think about how this could affect your family. Even if you've got a plan that takes care of all this, just think about what it's like for 150 or 60 million Americans who have to live with these uncertainties every single day—to think you've got health care coverage, but maybe you don't, and it just depends on what happens to you.

The IBEW knows better. You have made a major contribution to the prosperity and recovery of America, and I am very grateful. Nobody could blame you if, after all the fights you've had to fight, you wanted to take a deep breath and relax. But you remember the issues I gave you today. There are decisions being made or not made here which will affect your lives in the near term and have a huge impact on your children's lives, none more immediate than this Patients' Bill of Rights.

So go out and fight for it. And tell America, tell all your friends and neighbors: This is not a labor issue; this is not a Democratic Party issue; this is about what kind of country we are and what kind of country we're going to be. I think you know they will stand with you.

Thank you, and God bless you.

NOTE: The President spoke at 10:25 a.m. in the Regency Ballroom at the Hyatt Regency. In his remarks, he referred to John J. Sweeney, president, AFL–CIO, and the following International Brotherhood of Electrical Workers officers: Carol Hooper, Local 1690 president, who introduced the President; John J. Barry, international president; Edwin Hill, international secretary-treasurer; and Rick Diegel, political/legislative director.

Remarks at a Democratic Congressional Campaign Committee Luncheon in Cincinnati, Ohio
September 17, 1998

Thank you very much. Maybe I ought to read Stan's talking points again. [*Laughter*] The only thing I didn't like about what he said was all that bragging he did on Bruce Lindsey. I'll have to live with that for the next year or two. [*Laughter*]

Let me say, first of all, I'm delighted to be back here in this magnificent home with a person who has been a true friend of mine and Hillary's. I want to thank Mayor Qualls and Chris Gorman for being here and for running for Congress at a time when public service is not the easiest it's ever been. And I want to thank Lieutenant Governor Steve Henry—he's been a great friend of mine—for coming over from Kentucky. And David Leland, thank you; Tim Burke, thank you. And I want to thank Stan and Dick Lawrence for cochairing this dinner—this lunch.

I don't know if I'm going to be able to give a speech. It's not that I'm so emotionally choked up, but I never eat this much for lunch, and I'm actually sort of sleepy. [*Laughter*]

Let me say, I was deeply moved by what you said, but what I would like for you to think about, all of you, in terms of what Stan said, is not me. Hillary and I, we're doing fine. We're working on what we need to be working on, and we're doing fine. What I'm concerned about is the rest of the people that live in this country, and one more time having Washington obsessed with itself instead of America. Harry Truman once made that famous statement: "If you can't stand the heat, get out of the kitchen." So I think about that every morning, and go to the kitchen. [*Laughter*]

But all over the country—there is a country out there. This is a democracy. We're all hired hands. We showed up because we pledged to help the rest of the country and to do things the rest of the country needs. And I'm here today to help these people running for Congress, because the choice really is between partisanship and progress, between people and old-fashioned politics—or maybe even newfangled politics.

I think that's what I would like for you to focus on. By coming here today, you have helped these two candidates, and others that we're trying to advance, get their message out. And if America understands—we're 2 weeks away. When I gave the State of the Union Address, I said—and I'd like to say again, because it's an important lesson I try to remind myself of every day—when things are going well for a country, for a business, for a family, for a career, the temptation is to relax and say, "Gosh, I've been working hard. I've worked through all these tough times, and I think I'll just sort of sit in the sun for a while." For politicians, it's tempting to say, "I think I'll do nothing, because I'll get reelected because things are going well."

Do you know what we talked about around our table today? We talked about the financial crisis in Asia. We talked about what was going on in Russia. We talked about whether it could

spread to Latin America. We talked about the challenges of terrorism and weapons of mass destruction. We talked about how Americans are going to go on in an international environment that has a lot of big challenges out there.

What's that got to do with these races for Congress? The American people, whether they know it or not, are going to be making a decision about whether they really want to ratify— here we are 2 weeks before a new budget year. There is no budget resolution in the Congress; that is, that says what our budget is going to be. One of the 13 appropriations bills has passed. They've killed the tobacco legislation and campaign finance reform. And last night the Senate Republican leader literally shut the Senate down for 4 hours to keep them from casting a vote on the Patients' Bill of Rights, because they knew if they voted for the bill that the House passed, which does nothing, it would be harmful; and if they voted against our bill, it would really be harmful. So they started—they just decided to kill it by stealth. They just literally had to shut the Senate down to keep from doing the people's business.

So the choice before us is whether the American people will embrace a strategy of politics or a strategy of people, a strategy of partisanship or a strategy of progress; whether they will reward a strategy of not doing anything or embrace our agenda.

You know, I know it's popular to talk about a tax cut in an election year. We've got no business cutting taxes. We had a deficit for 29 years. We have no business cutting taxes until we save the Social Security system, because otherwise the baby boomers are going to—[*applause*].

I'm not against tax cuts; mine are paid for. We have tax cuts for child care, for education, and for the environment in this budget, but they're all paid for. But to spend this surplus that won't even materialize for 2 weeks, after 29 years without one—you know, I'd just kind of like to watch the ink turn from red to black and see it dry—[*laughter*]—before we start shoveling it out the door again. And I think that's very important.

It's important to our present economic health in a world of uncertainty. And it's important to our responsibilities long term. I've been waiting since January for the Congress to fund America's portion of the International Monetary

Fund. That's the fund that enables us to stabilize our trading partners and friends around the world so they can keep buying our products. Cincinnati, I think, is doing pretty well, from the look of things. But in the high plains of America, the farmers are having the worst year they've had in decades. And one big reason is, nobody in Asia can buy our farm products because they don't have any money.

So that's two big issues: Are we going to save Social Security first or play politics? Are we going to meet our international responsibilities that help us to grow economically, or are we just going to make speeches about it?

If you look at the issues here at home—the Lieutenant Governor of Kentucky rode in with Roxanne and Chris and me, and he's a doctor. A lot of you know that. We got to talking about this health care bill of rights. This is a very specific bill. This basically says there's 160 million Americans in managed care plans and other Americans in other kinds of plans, and without regard to their health care plan, if they get in a car accident, they ought to be able to go the closest emergency room, not one that's 10 miles down the road that happens to be covered in the plan. If they need a specialist, they ought to be able to get one; they shouldn't be able to be told by a business organization that a general surgeon will do as well or a general practitioner should do as well, particularly if the doctor is begging them to go to a specialist in the first place. If their employer changes health plans at some point during the year and the employee or someone in their family is pregnant, they ought not to have to change their obstetrician until the baby is born. If somebody in the family has got cancer, is getting chemotherapy, they ought not to have to stop in the middle of the treatment and go get another doctor. We believe medical records ought to be private. They want to make them more subject to invasion by other people.

So this is a big deal. This affects—you know, their bill leaves 100 million people out and doesn't do much for the people it covers. We're talking about a majority of the people in the United States of America who will be personally affected by how this election comes out.

And this is not a partisan issue. When somebody hauls you in on a stretcher to an emergency room and they start filling out those forms, as maddening as it can be, at least they

don't ask you what your party affiliation is. [*Laughter*]

This is an American issue. It's a huge issue. We're for the Patients' Bill of Rights, and they're not. And the choice the American people make in the election will determine whether they get one.

If you look at the education issue, I'm gratified that we've been able to open the doors of college wider than ever before. But our public schools are not the best in the world for all our students yet, and until they are, we can't stop.

In the balanced budget bill, paid for in the budget I sent them, there are funds to hire 100,000 teachers to take average class size down to 18 in the early grades. All the research shows that it has a dramatic, permanent effect on the ability of children to learn, especially kids that come from poor backgrounds and limited circumstances, where they may not be read to at home and get all the help they need there—paid for in the balanced budget.

We have a proposal that will help to build or remodel 5,000 schools. I cannot tell you how many schools I've visited that are surrounded by housetrailers because there are so many kids that have outstripped the ability of school districts to build a school.

I was in Philadelphia the other day, where the average age of the schools is 65 years. We tell these kids, "Oh, you're the most important thing in the world to us." Tell that to a kid that has to walk up the steps every day to a school where the windows are broken, where there's a whole floor closed down, where they don't function. These old buildings are priceless. We could never afford to build them today. But we can afford to repair them and make them what they ought to be, and it's in the plan.

In our plan there's enough money to hook up all the classrooms and libraries in the country to the Internet by the year 2000, especially important to kids that don't have a computer in their home. It's an education agenda worth fighting for.

If you just take those four issues—keeping our economy going by doing our part for the global economy; saving Social Security first, before we squander this surplus we're about to build up; doing something to really advance the cause of education; passing the Patients' Bill of Rights—if you don't remember anything but those four issues—and look, they've had 8 months—we've got one appropriation bill; they killed campaign finance reform, and they killed the tobacco legislation. Near as I can tell, that's the record of the last 8 months.

Now, that is what this is about. It is not about me; it is about the people of this country. It is about their children, their future, and our common efforts. I am going to do everything I can to fight for these things and to fight to help people who believe in them get elected. That's what you're doing here.

And what I want to say to you is, when you leave here, I don't want you to let a day go by that you don't talk to somebody about what our common responsibilities as citizens are and what is really at stake here, in very specific terms.

We're not particularly cynical, we Democrats. We believe we can always do better; we believe we have a responsibility to do better; and I think that it would be a very good thing if a few more of us were in the United States Congress now. The voters who used to worry about us who said that we couldn't be trusted with the budget, now they know that we can, and they can't. The voters that used to worry and say we couldn't be trusted to manage the economy know that that's not true; that we were weak on crime, know that's not true—all those things they used to say about us.

So now we're free to look to the future, and you have to tell voters our enemy is not adversity here; our enemy is complacence. We have to say to people, "Look at what's going on down there in Washington. This is about us and our future. Washington always thinks everything's about Washington. It's not about Washington; it's about America. And it's about these issues."

It's about our ability to lead the world toward peace and freedom and prosperity. And it's about our ability to do what needs to be done

to strengthen this country at home for a new century. If you just remember those 4 issues—there's 40 more—but those 4 will carry us a long way. Go out and hammer and hammer and hammer and hammer and tell people to show up.

Basically, the strategy of the other side is, it's a midterm election and our group doesn't vote as often as their group does. And so if everybody is sort of generally happy and there's a lot of static in the atmosphere and our base of voters don't go vote, then they win—and if they have more money. They always have more money.

So what you're saying is, you don't want them to have so much more money that we can't get our message out. And I thank you for that. But you must also be messengers. You must really talk to people about it. You've got to look your friends and neighbors dead in the eye and tell them this is a big election for this country. This is a huge choice about the direction of America in what is the last election of the 20th century. And if you will give them the specific examples of the Patients' Bill of Rights, the education issue, the saving Social Security, and exercising our leadership in the world economy to protect the American economy's growth at home, I think you'll be quite pleased with the results. And it will have been worth all of this to all of us.

Thank you very much.

NOTE: The President spoke at 3:05 p.m. at a private residence. In his remarks, he referred to luncheon hosts Stanley M. Chesley and Richard D. Lawrence; Mayor Roxanne Qualls of Cincinnati; Chris Gorman, candidate for Kentucky's Third Congressional District; Lt. Gov. Stephen L. Henry of Kentucky; David J. Leland, chairman, Ohio Democratic Party; and Timothy M. Burke, chairman, Hamilton County Democratic Party.

Letter to Congressional Leaders Transmitting a Report on Implementation of the Partnership For Peace
September 17, 1998

Dear _____:

In accordance with section 514(a) of Public Law 103–236 (22 U.S.C. 1928(a)), I am submitting to you this report on implementation of the Partnership for Peace (PFP).

As noted in last year's report to the Congress, the PFP has been a critical tool in helping all the Partners, regardless of their desire to join NATO, to build stronger ties with the Alliance and develop closer cooperative relationships with all their neighbors. As you will see from the attached report, NATO Allies and Partners have managed to create a fundamentally different Partnership through the Euro-Atlantic Partnership Council (EAPC) and PFP enhancements.

The EAPC and the PFP have provided means for incorporating partners into NATO's operation in Bosnia, assisting Macedonia in developing its armed forces, and by building cooperation and confidence among Partners in Southeastern Europe, which has both insulated them from the Kosovo crisis and enabled them to help NATO deal with Kosovo's destabilizing effects. Enhancements to the PFP, which are nearly fully implemented, provide a solid foundation for closer NATO-Partner collaboration and a mechanism for Partners to develop the interoperability with NATO that will be necessary for future NATO-led Allied/Partners missions.

Sincerely,

WILLIAM J. CLINTON

NOTE: Identical letters were sent to Jesse Helms, chairman, and Joseph R. Biden, Jr., ranking member, Senate Committee on Foreign Relations, Benjamin A. Gilman, chairman, and Lee H. Hamilton, ranking member, House Committee on International Relations.

Remarks at a Unity '98 Dinner in Boston, Massachusetts
September 17, 1998

Thank you very much. Well, this has been good. [*Laughter*] I kept watching these guys come up here, just turning up the temperature one after the other. It's been really great.

Let me say to all of you, first of all, thank you for your wonderful, wonderful welcome to me and to the Vice President. I thank all the people responsible for this dinner. I thank the Schusters, the Solomonts; thank you, Jack and Lyle; all the people at the tables who did all the work—all of you, thank you so much.

I want to thank the Massachusetts Democratic Party. Joan, thank you and all of your cohorts for what you have done. I thank Steve Grossman for doing an absolutely magnificent job, and his wife, Barbara, and his family and his co-workers, for putting up with it and enduring it all these long months. It has meant more than I will ever be able to say.

I want to thank all the nominees who are here for all the offices in Massachusetts. It could be good to have "Congressman" Capuano here pretty soon down in Washington. And I want to thank especially your Attorney General, Scott Harshbarger, for making this race for Governor. And I want you to make it a good race, a winning race. It's important to America; it's important to Massachusetts; and I want you to help him.

I also want to say a special word of thanks to Tom Menino, not only for being a remarkable mayor of Boston but for being so incredibly generous with his time in showing the rest of the country, and in allowing our administration to showcase to the rest of the country, the good work that has been done in Boston, especially in trying to save the lives and build the lives of the most vulnerable children of this city. He deserves a great deal of gratitude from all of us.

I really wish I didn't have to say anything tonight because I have enjoyed so much what has already been said, and I'm afraid I'll just mess it up. But I would like to thank John Kerry for what he said and for the conviction with which he said it. He and Teresa have been very good friends to Hillary and to me. And I think that—the thing I always think about when I talk with John is, no matter what the subject is, I never finish a conversation with him that he doesn't ask whether what we're really doing is right for the children. Is it the right thing for the children? When he always points out there's something wrong with our country when the poverty rate of the children is twice the rate of poverty in the country as a whole. There is something wrong when we're not doing more to save our kids, and we're putting too many in jail and too few in college. And that's very, very important that you have a Senator who cares about that.

I want to thank Dick Gephardt for—first of all, for never losing his energy or devotion or conviction about his work, when he went from being the majority leader to the minority leader of the House. A lesser person would simply have quit, and he didn't quit. Instead, he steeled himself for the work of the country. He knew that in some fundamental ways our country needed his leadership and our caucus to do our job, first to stop the contract on America, then to keep the deficit coming down, then to invest in our children and their future, more than ever before. And I thank him for that.

Now, I want to tell you just one thing about Senator Kennedy—Vicki may never speak to me again. But I want you to understand one thing very clearly. If you reelect him twice more, he'll break Strom Thurmond's record and become the longest serving Senator in the history of the United States of America. [*Laughter*] And comparatively, he'll still be a young man. [*Laughter*]

Today we started the day off together, Ted and I did, with the IBEW convention, talking about the Patients' Bill of Rights, talking about his fight for the minimum wage. The thing that astonishes me about him is, when Ted Kennedy came to the United States Senate, I was 15 years old—or 16 or something like that. He's still got more energy than I do, and he is still fighting with the same enthusiasm he was on the first day he showed up. That's a person who loves America and loves our people.

And finally let me say, there's not much I can't say about the Vice President that—that I can say you don't already know, maybe, but I would like you to just reflect on something. There are partisan disagreements about whether I was right or wrong and maybe just principled disagreements about whether I was right or wrong with the budget of 1993—I think the results have borne us out—or when we took on the fight with the Brady bill and the assault weapons ban, or when we tried to change the welfare system but protect the most vulnerable among us, or when we took the hard decisions in Bosnia and Haiti and Mexico, and to work for peace in Northern Ireland. And people may disagree with how we've handled the peace process in the Middle East. You can disagree with a lot of things, but no one will ever be

able to dispute one clear fact about the 8 years I served as President, and that is that in those 8 years, Albert Gore of Tennessee did more good in more different areas than any Vice President in the history of the United States of America.

Now, all I've done so far is talk about political activists and politicians. I think it's a high calling. I still want children to want to grow up to be President, to be in the Senate, to be Governor, to come to fundraisers, to go to rallies, to pass out cards, to believe in the political system. But that brings me to the most important thing, because what we're really all doing here has more to do with those kids that sang to us at the beginning of this banquet tonight than it does about most of the rest of us. And the reason most of us belong to our party is that we believe that the real thrill of public service is not partisan triumph or political power but advancing the lives of people and helping them to make the most of their own lives.

So let me take just a couple of minutes; I won't take long. You know what the issues are. But I want you to ask yourself tonight, why am I here? And what shall we make of this movement? Let me give you just a little bit of a sober note here. Ever since the Civil War, in every midterm election, the party of the President has lost seats in the Congress if the President was in his second term. Now, why is that? That is usually because people perceive that the party's agenda has already been implemented to whatever extent it is, and they're beginning to get restless, whether the party was in the majority or the minority in Congress.

I'll tell you another thing that's reasonably sobering. The Republicans have an enormous advantage at midterm elections because their electorate is wealthier and older and normally more ideological and, therefore, usually more likely to turn out.

Now, what shall we make of this moment? I would argue to you we can't reverse that with a better, more ardent political speech. But we can reverse that if the American people realize that we're the only ones who want this election to be about them, that we really believe that the voters, the citizens, should be in the saddle, and that Washington should not be about politicians looking at each other and carving themselves up. It should be about people in public life looking at the American people and building them up. That is what this election should be about.

So I say to you, you have given a great gift tonight. This gift you have given will enable us to help our House candidates and our Senate candidates who have a good chance to win—and a lot of them do—to reverse over 100 years of history, to be able to get their message out. They will help Steve Grossman to help our State parties to get the vote out on election day.

But I ask something more of you. I ask you to look into your heart and ask, what does it mean to be an American, and what should we make of this moment? It's clear what's afoot on the other side. We're 2 weeks from the beginning of a new budget year and, praise the Lord, the first balanced budget and surplus in 29 years—2 weeks away. Now, our administration has had a very active year, especially in foreign policy and dealing with economic matters. I've been to China; Hillary and I have been to Africa; I have been to Russia; and we went to Northern Ireland. And you know all about that. We're working on peace, and we're working on restoring economic growth. We've done a lot here at home to advance our health care and our education agenda within the framework of the executive branch powers.

We're 2 weeks away from a new budget year. One of 13 appropriations bills as been passed. They killed campaign finance reform. They killed the tobacco reform legislation. Last night in the Senate, the leader of the Senate literally shut business down for 4 hours to keep them from being able to vote on the Patients' Bill of Rights.

And they say, "Well, you know, the country is pretty happy now. We've got the lowest unemployment, the lowest percentage of people on welfare, the lowest crime rate, the lowest everything in 25 or 30 years. Everybody is pretty happy. And we'll have a bunch of smoke up here, and we won't do much, and we won't get ourselves caught on the wrong side of the issues. But we won't pass anything that our interest groups don't want us to pass."

Now, in that mix of things, is it possible for not only us but for you, for all of us together as committed citizens, to pierce through the fog to the heart of the matter? To say that, yes, things are good, but we're living in a dynamic, fast changing world. There are a lot of big challenges out there. And the United States should use this moment—indeed, we are obligated to

use this moment to protect our own economic prosperity, as the Vice President said, by investing in the international institutions that will enable our neighbors to start growing again so they can buy what we're trying to sell; by investing in the integrity of our future by saving the Social Security system, even if it means resisting the temptation to pass a tax cut right before the election and spend a surplus that hasn't even materialized yet; by sticking up for a Patients' Bill of Rights.

That sounds good. Do you know what that means? It means very practical things to people. There are 160 million people in this country in managed care plans—160 million—and many others in other kinds of plans with limits. Our bill simply says that if you walk out of this hotel tonight and you walk across the street and you get hit by a car, no matter what your health plan is, you can go to the nearest emergency room. You don't have to drive all the way across town and risk your life doing it.

It says, if you go to your doctor and he says, "I'm sorry, you need to see a specialist," that you'll be able to see that specialist without somebody worrying about the bottom line, not a doctor, saying, "I'm sorry, you can't see the specialist."

It says, if you work for a small business and they change insurance carriers and you're pregnant or your spouse is pregnant, they can't come to you when you're 6 months pregnant and say, "I'm sorry, you've got to change your obstetrician." You get to see it all the way through until the baby is born. I want you to think—this is what I want you to talk to people about. We're talking about rules that govern 160 million of your fellow citizens.

Have you ever had anybody in your family take chemotherapy? I have. You know what it's like for a family? You sit around and wonder, well—and you make jokes about whether your hair is going to fall out and when, whether you're going to be too sick to your stomach to eat tonight, and you just wait until the end of the treatment, and you pray to God it works. What this bill says is, they can't get you two-thirds through your treatment—say, "I'm sorry, you've got to change doctors."

This bill says that at least citizens ought to have some privacy in this country in their medical records. That's important.

Now, we're for all those things, and they're not. And it affects 160 million Americans. And

43 HMO's are supporting us and say, "It's not right for us to be put out of business because we're doing the right thing."

We're for an education program. That sounds great. What does that mean? In our budget—balanced budget—we say we're going to give 100,000 teachers in this country to the school districts who need it to take the early-grade class size down to an average of 18. That will change the face of education in America. Every single study shows if you give kids, particularly kids from disadvantaged homes, the chance to have that kind of early learning, the gains are permanent.

Our plan says we're going to build or remodel 5,000 schools, so our kids will be in good, safe schools. It says we're going to have the funds to hook up all the classrooms to the Internet by the year 2000. That's what it says. It's not pie in the sky. This is not "Wouldn't it be nice if we had an education program?" We have an education program, and this election will determine whether it becomes real in the life of the American people or not.

So you don't have to remember all the other issues; you can just remember those four. Do you want to keep our economy growing by getting the world economy fixed so they can buy our stuff? Don't you want to protect the surplus and the integrity of our budget until we honor our parents and our children by saving Social Security so that when the baby boomers retire, we don't either have a substandard retirement or we put an unconscionable burden on our children and grandchildren? Wouldn't it be nice if the best medical care in the world were available to everybody with insurance instead of being at the whim of accountants' rules? And don't you really believe that when we say we're for a world-class education for everybody, now that we have the money to do it, we finally ought to start living up to what we say we believe in? That's what this is about.

Now, we can beat over 100 years of history if we are on the side of the future. Records are made to be broken. I got home last night from the state dinner with Václav Havel, and I turned on the—we were in the bottom of the seventh inning between San Diego and Chicago, and the eighth inning came along and there were three people on base and two out and Sammy Sosa hit his 63d home run. We can do that. Records are made to be broken. We can do that.

But make no mistake about it: We can only do that if the people who work at this hotel, who have to struggle to keep body and soul together, who work late at night and early in the morning, on election day believe it is worth it to them to show up, because we care about them, because we're fighting for them, because we have a vision for their children's future.

If they think that, you can throw all the history records out the window, you can throw everything else out the window. This country still belongs to the people. Our party wants to give it back to them, and we want to give them a future. Your contribution has helped to give it to them; now let your voice, let the look in your eye, let the determination in how you spend your time between now and election day communicate to all the people that we have a job to do for America and we are determined to do it.

Thank you, and God bless you.

NOTE: The President spoke at 9:50 p.m. in the Imperial Ballroom at the Boston Park Plaza Hotel. In his remarks, he referred to dinner hosts Gerald and Elaine Schuster, Alan D. and Susie Solomont, John P. Manning, and Lyle Howland; Joan Menard, State chair, Massachusetts Democratic Party; Steve Grossman, national chair, Democratic National Committee, and his wife, Barbara; Mayor Michael E. Capuano of Somerville; Teresa Kerry, wife of Senator John F. Kerry; Victoria Kennedy, wife of Senator Edward M. Kennedy; and President Václav Havel of the Czech Republic. The President also referred to the International Brotherhood of Electrical Workers (IBEW).

Remarks in a Meeting With the President's Advisory Board on Race
September 18, 1998

[*Chairman John Hope Franklin described some of his experiences during his 15 months on the Board, saying that the most gratifying thing was the response of the American people to the President's Initiative on Race. Board member William F. Winter, former Governor of Mississippi, noted that the Board's report recommended that the President establish a council to carry forward the initiative in a permanent way. He then gave the President a poster-size photograph of an Oxford, MS, elementary school class which the Board had visited.*]

The President. What a wonderful poster!

[*Governor Winter read a student's letter to the President and then presented the President with a book of letters from the entire class.*]

The President. Isn't that great? Maybe I ought to read that to people.
Governor Winter. And they want you to come visit their class. [*Laughter*]
The President. This is your grandson's class?
Governor Winter. That's my grandson's class. That's right.
Chairman Franklin. We went to the classroom.
Governor Winter. We had a great day down there.
Chairman Franklin. We did, indeed.
Board Member Linda Chavez-Thompson. And I have to follow that? [*Laughter*] I didn't bring a book.
The President. This is beautiful, too. Nice.

[*Ms. Chavez-Thompson and Board members Thomas H. Kean and Angela E. Oh each made brief remarks thanking the President for the opportunity to serve on the Board, recounting their experiences, and urging the President to continue his efforts for educational and economic opportunity and racial reconciliation.*]

Chairman Franklin. There's one thing Angela didn't do; she didn't tell you that she's going to write a book saying, "How Being a Member of the Advisory Board Changed My Life." [*Laughter*]
The President. It's here on the tape, the first chapter. [*Laughter*]

[*Board member Robert Thomas praised the contributions of President's Race Initiative Executive Director Judith A. Winston and Board consultants Christopher Edley and Laura Harris. Emphasizing the importance of education, he joked that without "something big, huge, tremendous, way beyond the norm, we'll just be perfuming the pig."*]

The President. We had a long discussion about where that came from. [*Laughter*] I thought I never heard it before you said it, but I like it. I'm going to use it shamelessly. [*Laughter*]

[*After Mr. Thomas concluded his remarks, Board member Suzan D. Johnson Cook, thanked the President for opening the door to a conversation on race. She then asked him to autograph a picture for her son and presented him with a book entitled "Too Blessed To Be Stressed."*]

The President I accept that. That's great.
Ms. Cook. And so we're praying for you, and we thank you so much for flying on Air Force One and eating ribs with you. Thank you. [*Laughter*]
The President. You need to tell me how you want me to sign that, and I've got a special pen, and we'll sign it, and I'll bring it over there.

[*Laura Harris, the Board's consultant on Native American issues, explained the diversity of her son's ethnic background and joked that since she began her work with the Board, her son said the family should no longer refer to his Scot-Irish-Oklahoman grandfather as a redneck.*]

The President. That's a real advance. [*Laughter*]

[*Ms. Harris closed by thanking the President for improving the relationship between the Federal Government and tribal governments, and Chairman Franklin concurred.*]

The President. You know, let me just say— I'll be very brief, because I know we're supposed to go over to this other deal, and I think Linda's got to go. But I just want to thank you for doing this and for being brave enough to do it.

I knew when we started that all of us would be subject to some criticism because, number one, we couldn't solve every problem in America overnight related to race; number two, you could almost relate every problem in America to race; and number three, in a cynical and weary world, it's easy to devalue the importance of people going in good faith to raise the consciousness and quicken the conscience and kind of lift the spirits of other people and encourage them to do the right thing, and then to figure out—it is a complex thing, figuring out how much of this is policy, how much of this is dialog, how much of this is community, how much of this is almost spiritual.

I think you have really made a heroic effort to come to grips with all of these elements and to make this a very important milestone on America's journey here, and I hope you'll always be proud of it. I really think—you know, it was a big risk. I knew a lot of people would say, well, we didn't do this; we didn't do that; we didn't do the other thing; or we said this, and it was wrong. And probably some of that

criticism is valid. But when you take it all and shake it up, I think there is no question that what we did at this moment, in the absence of a searing crisis, facing a future of incredible kaleidoscopic diversity, was a very good thing for our country. And I do think that we have to keep it going, and I will take all these recommendations seriously.

I hope you all meant what you said today. I hope it was a great gift for you, because for your country it was a great gift.

Chairman Franklin. We are deeply grateful to you, Mr. President.

The President. Thank you. Well, I'll see you over there—except Linda, who has an excused absence.

NOTE: The President spoke at 2:20 p.m. in the Oval Office at the White House. A tape was not available for verification of the content of these remarks.

Remarks on Receiving the Report of the President's Advisory Board on Race
September 18, 1998

Thank you so much. Dr. Franklin, the Advisory Board, to the Members of the Congress who are here: Congresswoman Eddie Bernice Johnson, Congressman Amo Houghton, Congressman Jay Dickey, Congressman Ed Pastor, Congressman Tom Sawyer, and Congressman John Lewis, whose life could be a whole chapter of this report. We thank you for coming. We thank Mayor Archer, Mayor Webb, Mayor Bush, Mayor Flores, Governor Thomas of the Gila River Tribe, and other distinguished Americans who are here today—business, religious, community leaders.

I thank the Attorney General; the Deputy Attorney General, Eric Holder; the Secretary of Education; the Secretary of Housing and Urban Development; the Secretary of Transportation; SBA Administrator Alvarez; Acting Assistant AG Bill Lann Lee—I hope I won't have to say that "acting" forever—[*laughter*]—our Deputy SBA Administrator, Fred Hochberg. Thank you all for being here.

I'm especially gratified by the presence of a large number of Cabinet members, Members of Congress, and local leaders here today. I thank the head of the Council of Economic Advisers, Janet Yellen, for being here. I'll have more to say about that in a moment. Thank you, Rosa Parks, for coming.

I want to say a special word of thanks to all the people who made this Board possible: to John Hope Franklin for his wise and patient, but insistent, leadership; Reverend Suzan Johnson Cook; Angela Oh; Bob Thomas; Linda Chavez-Thompson, who was with us in the White House just a moment ago but has what I called an excused absence—[*laughter*]—my long-time friends and colleagues, the former Governors of Mississippi and New Jersey, Bill Winter and Tom Kean. I thank Laura Harris, who has been a wonderful consultant for us on Native American issues. My good friend Chris Edley, thank you for what you have done. I thank Judy Winston and the staff of the President's Initiative on Race for the remarkable job they have done, and I'd like to thank the people in the White House who worked with them, but especially Minyon Moore, Maria Echaveste, and before her, Sylvia Mathews. Thank you all so much for what you have done.

Now, some time ago, John Hope Franklin said, "The task of trying to reshape our society to bring about a climate of racial healing is so enormous, it strains the imagination." Well, again I'd say, I'd like to thank John Hope Franklin, the rest of this Board, and the staff for straining their imaginations and finding the energy to take on this tremendous task of focusing the Nation's attention on building one America for the new century. Often, this has meant enduring criticism, some of it perhaps justified; some of it I have questioned because, as Dr. Franklin said, no one could solve this problem in 15 months since it has not been resolved in all of human history to anyone's complete satisfaction. But they have taken on the endeavor.

And it has been a magnificent journey. They have crossed this country, the length and breadth of America. They have seen all different kinds of people. For them, it has been a journey across our land, a journey across our culture, a journey across our history, and a journey, I imagine, for all of them across their own personal lives and experiences. They've gone from Silicon Valley to Oxford, Mississippi, to the Fairfax County school district across the river here, where there are students from more than 100 different national and ethnic groups, 150 different national and ethnic groups.

We knew that no effort could solve all the challenges before us, but I thank this board because they have helped America to take important steps forward. I also thank Americans—unbelievable numbers of Americans—from all across the country who have participated, all those who wanted to tell their stories and all those who were willing to listen.

They have brought us closer to our one America in the 21st century. Out in the country, they found a nation full of people with common sense, good will, a great hunger to move beyond division to community, to move from the absence of discrimination to the presence of opportunity to the spirit of genuine reconciliation. This Board has raised the consciousness and quickened the conscience of America. They have moved us closer to our ideal, but we have more to do.

I want to say, I am especially proud of the work that every member of our administration has tried to do. When I look out here at the Secretary of Labor, the Attorney General, Secretary Cuomo, Secretary Riley, Secretary Slater, Aida Alvarez, Janet Yellen, all these people who work for me, they know that we care about this, and they have really worked hard to do you proud, and I thank them, too. But we have more to do.

You know, for more than two centuries we have been committed to the ideas of freedom and equality, but much of our history has been defined by our struggle to overcome our steadfast denial of those ideals and, instead, start to live by them. It has been a hard road. It is rooted deeply in our own history, as John Hope Franklin said. Indeed, I believe it is rooted in the deeper impulses that trace their beginnings back to the dawn of human society: the mistrust, the fear, the hatred of those who are the other, those who are them, not us.

In the area of race, it has been a special burden because you can see people who are different from you. And with Native Americans, it's been a special burden because we took land that was once theirs. With African-Americans, it's been a special burden because we all have to confront the accumulated weight of history that comes from one people enslaving another.

But with every area of racial tension, if you strip it all away, you can go back to the dawn of time, when people first began to live in societies and learned they were supposed to mistrust and fear and hate people who were not in their crowd. We see it manifest around the world in our time. We've seen it between the Catholics and Protestants in Northern Ireland, going on for hundreds of years—thank God, I hope, about to end. We've seen it with the Hutus and the Tutsis in Rwanda. We've seen it with the Arabs and the Jews in the Middle East; with the Serbs, the Croats, the Muslims in Bosnia; today, the Serbs and the Albanians in Kosovo. In America we see it manifest, still, in racial differences but also in religious and political differences, as well.

In whatever manifestation, I think we have to begin with one clear understanding: When we approach others with discrimination and distrust, when we demean them from the beginning, when we believe our power can only come from their subjugation, their weakness, or their destruction, as human beings and as citizens, we pay a terrible price.

Our Founders were pretty smart people. They knew we weren't perfect, but we needed to strive for perfect ideals. And they built us a country based on a Constitution that was literally made for reconciliation, for the honorable and principled resolution of differences, rooted in a simple proposition that God created us all equal.

Now, because they created a freedom of religion, they couldn't write in the Constitution, therefore, "The first and most important commandment is this, to love your neighbor as yourself." But what they did write in that Constitution is, you are commanded to respect and treat your neighbor as yourself. That's still a pretty good guidepost for what we have to do.

On the eve of a new millennium, our country is more free and equal than ever before, but we have to keep going until everybody has a chance to live out his or her dreams according to his or her capacities and efforts; until everyone has a chance at a good job, a decent house on a safe street, health care and education for their children; and most of all, the chance to be treated with dignity and respect and to reap the full rewards of citizenship; to relish what is different about themselves but respect what is different about others.

We know that gaps still exist in all these areas between the races, and we must work to bridge them. We must bridge the opportunity gaps. We must build an America where discrimination is something you have to look in the history books to find. We have to do a lot of things to achieve that. Let me just try to say what my thoughts are, kind of following up on what Dr. Franklin said.

The first thing we have to do is keep the conversation going. A real gap in perceptions still exists among the American people. Some believe that this is no longer really an issue, or it's just something that occurs when something terribly outrageous happened, as did in Jasper, Texas. But it's not just that. It's an issue in the back of someone's mind every time a police officer of one race pulls over somebody else of another race. It's an issue in the back of everyone's mind every time a perfectly normal child is put in a remedial class because of the color of his or her skin or the income of their parents.

We should not underestimate the power of dialog and conversation to melt away misunderstanding and to change the human heart. I am proud to say today that the National Conference for Community and Justice, led by Sandy Cloud, who is here, will soon convene a group of religious leaders to continue this work of fostering racial reconciliation. And I thank Sandy for taking on this important job.

The second thing we have to do, again to echo what Dr. Franklin said, is to make sure we have the facts about race in America. A lot of us have strong opinions on the subject; not all of us have the facts to back them up. As a matter of fact, the more I stay in Washington, the more I realize that sometimes the very ability to hold strong opinions depends upon being able to be deaf to the facts. [*Laughter*] That's why I am very, very pleased that the Council of Economic Advisers, under the leadership of Janet Yellen and Rebecca Blank, has produced a book, "Changing America: Indicators of Social and Economic Well-Being by Race and Hispanic Origin." And I commend it to all of you. It's also not too big. [*Laughter*] You can digest it with some level of comfort. But it's a good piece of work. This book will help us to understand how far we have come and what we still need to do in our efforts to extend opportunity to all our people.

Finally, we here in Washington have to act. We have put forward in this administration and within our balanced budget a comprehensive agenda to expand opportunity for all Americans in economic development, education, health care, crime, credit, and civil rights enforcement. Again, I thank the Cabinet for their leadership on these fronts.

Just today Small Business Administrator Aida Alvarez launched two major initiatives to streamline the application process for loans guaranteed by the SBA for less than $150,000, to make this credit available on more flexible terms, the size and kind of financing many minority- and women-owned businesses so desperately need, as well as many other people in inner-city and rural areas where the unemployment rate is still high. Through these efforts, we estimate more than $1 billion in loans will be available to help businesses expand and create new jobs. We have to make this opportunity available for more Americans.

I also would like to say I am still hoping that in this budget fight in the next few weeks, we can pass the economic opportunity agenda put forward by Secretary Cuomo and the Vice President to provide more community development banks, more job-creating initiatives in the inner cities and the isolated rural areas where the economic recovery has not yet hit.

Every place we went, from north to south to east to west, all the people with whom we talked recognized that in the future education will be even more central to equality than it has been in the past. We have to do a great deal to set high standards and increase accountability, to eliminate the gaps and resources and achievement between the races, to give our children the opportunity to attend schools where diversity will help to prepare them for the world in which they will live. We know too many schools are not as good as they should be. We know too many students still are caught in a web of low expectations, low standards, poor teaching, crowded classrooms.

The budget that I have sent to Congress proposes new education opportunity zones to reward poor school districts that follow Chicago's lead and introduce sweeping reforms, to close down failing schools, promote public school choice, eliminate social promotion but make sure students get the summer school and after-school help they need. Today, the summer school in Chicago—the summer school—is the sixth biggest school district in the United States, and over 40,000 kids are getting 3 square meals a day there. So it's fine to say, no more social promotion, if you give children the chance to learn and grow and do to the best of their ability.

I am also committed to providing 35,000 new scholarships to young people who will agree to become certified teachers and then teach in our neediest areas.

Finally, I think it is very important to fund our initiative to provide 100,000 teachers to lower the average class size to 18 in the early grades. It is clear from all the research that children who come from the most disadvantaged backgrounds are most likely to have permanent learning gains when small classes are provided so they can get individualized instruction in the early grades. And I think it is very important.

Today the House rejected that idea and instead passed a block grant proposal that would eliminate accountability, reject the idea of national responsibility for helping communities to raise standards, improve teaching, or bring the benefits of technology to our students. I also believe we have to pass this proposal to connect every classroom and library to the Internet by the year 2000. Otherwise, the poor kids will be left further behind.

Now, I think we should be doing more in education, not less. Governor Kean said to me today, he said, "I like this proposal to build or repair 5,000 schools. The problem is it's way too small. You should be doing more." So that voice, coming from a distinguished Republican former Governor, I hope will echo loudly on Capitol Hill today. [*Laughter*]

We have a lot to do here. We have a lot to do in the country. We've got to keep the connection between what we do here and what we do in the country, and that is a lot of what this board has recommended. So even though the work of the board is over, they have given us a continuing mission.

I will say again, if you look at the life of Rosa Parks, if you read the book that John Lewis has just produced about his life, if you consider the sacrifice of two people who—one just came to visit me—Václav Havel, the President of the Czech Republic, and one will be with us in a few days, Nelson Mandela, if you look at all this, you see that a people's greatness only comes when everybody has a chance to be great. And it comes from, yes, opportunity. It comes from, yes, learning. It comes from, yes, the absence of discrimination. But it also has to come from the presence of reconciliation, from a turning away from the madness that life only matters if there is someone we can demean, destroy, or put down. That is the eternal lesson of America.

We are now given a future of incomparable, kaleidoscopic possibility and diversity. And somehow we have to implant in the soul of every child that age-old seed of learning so that the future can be ours.

Thank you all. God bless you.

NOTE: The President spoke at 3:40 p.m. in Room 450 of the Old Executive Office Building. In his remarks, he referred to Mayor Dennis W. Archer of Detroit, MI; Mayor Wellington E. Webb of Denver, CO; Mayor Gordon Bush of East St. Louis, IL; Mayor Elizabeth G. Flores of Laredo, TX; Gov. Mary Thomas of the Gila River Indian Community; Fred P. Hochberg, Acting Deputy Administrator, Small Business Administration;

and civil rights activist Rosa Parks. He also referred to President's Advisory Board on Race Chairman John Hope Franklin; members Suzan D. Johnson Cook, Angela E. Oh, Robert Thomas, Linda Chavez-Thompson, former Gov. William F. Winter of Minnesota, and former Gov. Thomas H. Kean of New Jersey; and consultants Laura Harris and Christopher Edley; and President's Race Initiative Executive Director Judith A. Winston. The Board's report was entitled "One America in the 21st Century: Forging a New Future."

Statement on British Petroleum's Plan To Reduce Greenhouse Gas Emissions
September 18, 1998

I applaud the leadership demonstrated today by British Petroleum with its plan to dramatically reduce emissions contributing to global warming.

By committing to reduce its greenhouse gas emissions 10 percent below 1990 levels by the year 2010, British Petroleum is setting a new standard in corporate responsibility. The company plans to meet its ambitious target through a cost-effective strategy that combines innovative market-based approaches with the latest in energy-efficiency technologies. British Petroleum's bold strategy is further proof that we need not choose between a healthy economy and a healthy environment.

I urge other businesses to follow British Petroleum's lead and help meet the challenge of global warming. And I again call on Congress to help speed this effort by funding my proposals for new tax incentives and research investment to spur energy efficiency and clean energy technologies.

Statement on Senate Action on Year 2000 Information and Readiness Disclosure Legislation
September 18, 1998

I am pleased that the Senate Judiciary Committee yesterday approved S. 2392, the "Year 2000 Information and Readiness Disclosure Act," which builds upon a proposal my administration submitted to Congress in July. I urge Congress to act quickly to approve this critical legislation before the end of this session so that I can sign it into law. If it is not enacted this session, we will miss an important opportunity to help our Nation prepare its computer systems for the new millennium.

Only 469 days remain until January 1, 2000. For the millions of small businesses and small government entities around the world that are just now beginning efforts to prepare their computer systems for the transition to the next century, having access to technical information on how to solve the year 2000 computer problem may mean the difference between success and failure.

This important bipartisan legislation would help businesses and Government agencies grapple with the Y2K problem. By limiting liability for good-faith information disclosures, the bill would encourage organizations to share year 2000 information, either directly or through republication. The increased flow of technical data on solutions will serve as an important jumpstart to public and private sector Y2K efforts in the United States and abroad.

Business and government organizations need to be candid about the progress of their year 2000 efforts. This bill creates an environment in which organizations can communicate more openly with the public and with each other about the status of work on critical systems, and thus provide their customers and business partners with useful information about their Y2K progress.

This bill's protections are limited to those that are necessary to encourage greater information sharing. It does not shield companies from liability claims based on actual failures of products or services. Moreover, the bill protects consumers from misleading advertising or other statements when purchasing products for their own use.

This legislation has received support from numerous industry groups and State and local government associations including the National Governors' Association and the National Association of Counties. It has also received broad bipartisan support in Congress. In particular, I would like to thank Senate Judiciary Committee Chairman Hatch, Ranking Member Leahy, and Senators Kyl, Bennett, and Dodd for their efforts in ensuring prompt consideration of this important issue. It is truly an example of how we can put aside our differences to create vital legislation that is in the public interest.

Remarks at the Fourth Millennium Evening at the White House
September 18, 1998

[*The opening remarks by the First Lady and the President were made in a video presentation to the audience.*]

The First Lady. Good evening and welcome to the White House. The theme we have chosen for the millennium is "Honor the past; imagine the future." This lecture continues a series of Millennium Evenings with scholars, scientists and other creative individuals which we are holding to commemorate and celebrate this milestone.

The President. With the millennium, we must now decide how to think about our commitment to the future. Thomas Paine said, a long time ago, "We have it in our power to begin the world over again." We have always believed that in this country, and we must now take it upon ourselves to take stock as we approach this new millennium to commit ourselves to begin the world over again for our children, our children's children, for people who will live in a new century.

It is to the people of that new century that we must all offer our very best gifts. It is for them that we will celebrate the millennium.

[*The video presentation concluded, and the First Lady then made brief remarks.*]

The President. Thank you very much. Ladies and gentlemen, I want to join Hillary in welcoming all our musicians here tonight and all the jazz fans. I thank, in particular, President Havel and Mrs. Havel for being here. When I was in Prague, the President took me to a jazz club, gave me a saxophone he had personally inscribed, and provided me with a band that covered my sins. [*Laughter*] And then he accompanied me on the tambourine, made a CD of it, and sent it to me, so I'm actually a recording artist—[*laughter*]—thanks only to Václav Havel. I also want to thank the First Lady for having the idea for these Millennium Evenings and for agreeing eagerly to my entreaty that at least one of them ought to be devoted to this unique American contribution to the creativity of the world.

A little more than a century ago, a famous composer arrived on our shores and was amazed by what he heard: African-American music, blues and spirituals, street songs and work songs. It was unlike anything he had heard in Europe or, in fact, anywhere else in the world. After hearing these new, uniquely American sounds, he wrote: "America can have her own music, a fine music, growing up from her soil and having its own special character. The natural voice of a free and great nation." Those words were written by the great Czech composer Antonin Dvorak in 1892. It is especially fitting, therefore, that we have a worthy successor of Czech greatness in the President of the Czech Republic here with us tonight.

In time, the music Dvorak heard became what we know today as jazz. And jazz became the soundtrack of this, the American century. Like America itself, it is inventive and bold, vital and free, respectful of its roots, yet always changing, always becoming, always reinventing itself. The great drummer and band leader Art Blakey once said, "No America, no jazz." This was no mere boast. Jazz could only have happened here because it is music born of the American experience, and it gives voice, eloquent, insistent voice, to our American spirit.

Like our country, jazz is a cultural crossroads where the rhythms of Africa meet the musical instruments of Europe, where black meets white and Latino, where New Orleans meets the South Side of Chicago and 52d Street. And like our democracy, jazz provides a framework for flowing dialog, a basis for brilliant improvisation, a point of reference and a point of departure. It poses challenges and seeks resolution, finding it in the coordinated efforts of the community as well as in the unique voice of the individual, syncopation and solo.

Like me, you're probably eager to hear some of the music, so please join me in welcoming two remarkable musicians who are our hosts for this evening.

Marian McPartland, as you all know, plays improvisational jazz piano and has now been playing it quite wonderfully for over seven decades. With just as much energy and enthusiasm—I should not have said that. [*Laughter*] I had the chart here, that's the point where I should have ad libbed, but I didn't. [*Laughter*] The thing that I really appreciate is that Marian has long been introducing young students to jazz, even introducing them to Duke Ellington himself a number of years ago.

And in the great tradition of Duke Ellington, Wynton Marsalis is a distinguished composer, big band leader, devoted advocate for the arts and education. It is no wonder that last year he became the first jazz artist to win the Pulitzer Prize for music. And he may be the only musician in our lifetime to be virtually universally acclaimed as the finest player of his instrument in either classical or jazz mediums.

Wynton, Marian, the stage is yours.

[*At this point, the program, entitled "Jazz: An Expression of Democracy," proceeded.*]

The President. Thank you, Dianne. Thank you, Billy. Thank all of our wonderful musicians. And I want to say a special word of thanks to Marian and to Wynton for showing us how much jazz can tell us about our country, our century, our deepest aspirations.

I did grow up loving jazz. I was inspired, moved by the agility of Charlie Parker and Sonny Rollins, by the inventiveness of Thelonious Monk, by the incredible inventive

genius of John Coltrane and the incomparable Miles Davis. They and many others opened my ears and opened the ears of millions of our fellow citizens to a music that was profoundly human and distinctly American.

But if jazz is an American invention, it certainly travels well—from club to concert hall, from coast to coast, across the oceans and back, returning with the imprint of other cultures and new influences. Music that began as American at the core truly has become now the music of the world.

Jazz is also, as it has long been, the international language of liberation, what a man named Willis Conover called the "Music of Freedom." For more than 40 years during the cold war, Willis Conover hosted the jazz program on the Voice of America. Dictators banned it and jammed his broadcasts because they understood the power of jazz to unleash the human spirit. But they could not stop the music. Six nights a week, as Conover started his show with the first bars of "Take the A Train," 30 million listeners in the Soviet bloc would join him for the ride. As far away as China and as recently as 1989, students at Tiananmen Square hummed the tunes they heard on the Voice of America, Charlie Parker, Dizzy Gillespie. It became sort of a not-so-secret code in the struggle for human rights.

Tonight we are honored by the presence of someone who has stood at the frontline of that struggle and who can tell us the meaning of jazz for those yearning to be free. A few years ago, as I said tonight, when we were in Prague, we even performed a few tunes together. Please join me in welcoming an artist and a leader whose work is a tribute to the human spirit, and who perhaps will tell us a little bit about the impact of jazz on his Velvet Revolution, President Václav Havel of the Czech Republic.

[*President Havel made brief remarks, and the program continued with a question-and-answer session with participants around the world linked by Internet to the performance.*]

The First Lady. This is from Sarah Miles in Havasu, Alberta, Canada. Subject: Influences of jazz. Question: Mr. President, how did jazz influence your choice of going into public service over private business? We love you in Alberta. Respectfully. [*Laughter*]

The President. Well, my first thought is that when I was younger in my teens, I used to do this a lot. And I was honest enough to know when I was doing it that while I was never happier doing anything else, I knew I'd never be as good as these guys, so I figured I had to get a day job. [*Laughter*]

That's a very good question. I had never thought about it before, but I think the answer is, my association with music and the discipline and long hours of preparation it took and the joy it brought, particularly when I got into jazz, had a lot in common with what I love about public service. It is about communication; it's about creativity but cooperation, as Wynton said earlier. And like jazz, I don't think you can be really, really good at it unless you care about other people and have a good heart, like these guys do. Thank you.

[*A final question was taken, and the President was asked to make closing remarks.*]

The President. Well, we should probably end with the question. You know, one of the things that I'd like to say, I'd like to compliment the recording companies who have put out CD's recently, of all of Ella Fitzgerald's recordings, for example. And I would like to encourage all the people who are involved in this business to think about, as a way of celebrating the millennium, to look at all the great jazz music that is still available in any condition over the last decades and think about packaging anything that is not yet now in mint condition—the best available condition—in making it widely available, because I think that is very, very important. A lot of young people will listen to this, will carry it on, will imagine it and play it—as Marian said—if they have access to it. So that's a great, great question and a great way to end.

We can't know everything that will happen in the new millennium, but I'll bet you one thing we know. When you hear American jazz coming back transformed as Brazilian music or African music, as Hillary and I have in our trips around the world, I think jazz will be a big part of it. And all of you who are part of this night tonight will know that all of your work will live well into this new century and into this new millennium. And the world will be a better place because of it.

Thank you very much.

NOTE: The White House Millennium Evening program began at approximately 7:30 p.m. in the East Room at the White House. In his remarks, the President referred to President Václav Havel of the Czech Republic and his wife, Dagmar Havlova; jazz vocalist Dianne Reeves; and jazz pianist and historian Billy Taylor.

The President's Radio Address
September 19, 1998

Good morning. I want to talk to you this morning about what I believe we must do to continue building a stronger America for our children and our grandchildren in the 21st century.

We're in a time of great prosperity and even greater promise. For nearly 6 years, I've done everything in my power to create the conditions for that prosperity and to make sure all Americans can share in it. Today, we have nearly 17 million new jobs, the lowest unemployment in 28 years, the lowest inflation in 32 years, the smallest percentage of our people on welfare in 29 years, the lowest crime rate in 25 years, and the highest homeownership in history.

All Americans have a right to be proud of what together we have achieved. But we can't let these good times lull us into a dangerous complacency. The turmoil we see today in economies all around the world reminds us that things are changing at a rapid rate. We can't afford to relax. Instead, we must use our new prosperity, the resources it produces, and the confidence it inspires to build a more prosperous future for all our people.

In just 12 days now we will have the first balanced budget and the first budget surplus since Neil Armstrong walked on the Moon in 1969. This remarkable achievement is the product of hard work by the American people, by lawmakers of both parties who put progress ahead of partisanship. We have waited 29 years for this moment. Now we must ask ourselves, what should we make of it?

Above all, I believe we must use this moment of prosperity to honor the duty across generations and strengthen Social Security for the 21st century. Seventy-five million baby boomers will be retiring over the next two decades. We must act now, across party lines, to make Social Security as strong for our children as it has been for our parents.

In my State of the Union Address, I said we should reserve every penny of that hard-won surplus until we had taken the steps to save Social Security first. At the same time, I did propose tax cuts for education, for the environment, to help families pay for child care. But not a penny of these cuts comes out of the surplus. Every one is fully paid for in my balanced budget.

My plan also provides tax relief to families while preserving the strength of the Social Security system. That is very important. When all the baby boomers retire, there will only be about two people working for every person drawing Social Security. We can make moderate changes now and make sure that those who retire will be able to retire in dignity, without imposing on, burdening, or lowering the standard of living of their children and grandchildren.

Unfortunately, the Republicans in Congress have a different idea. The black ink in the budget hasn't even had a chance to dry; indeed, it hasn't appeared yet. But they already want to drain the surplus to fund a tax plan before we make the most of our opportunity, our historic opportunity to save Social Security.

I've already made it clear that if Congress sends me a bill that squanders the surplus before we save Social Security, I will veto it. But Republicans in the House of Representatives are proceeding anyway and will try to pass their tax bill next week. I believe strongly that this is the wrong way to give American families the tax relief they deserve, the wrong way to prepare our Nation for the challenges of the future.

So today I say again to the Republican leadership: Go back to the drawing board. Look at the targeted tax cuts for working families I proposed, and we all passed last year: $500 per child; a HOPE scholarship for the first 2 years of college and college credits thereafter; IRA incentives to save for children. They all take effect this year. They'll all be on your tax forms in April, and all of them are fully paid for.

So I say to Congress: Send me a plan like that, a plan with targeted tax relief while preserving all the surplus until we have saved Social Security. Send me a plan that rebuilds our crumbling schools, that helps working families with child care, and supports small businesses in getting pension plans—and pay for it. Send me a tax cut that keeps us on the path of fiscal responsibility, that honors our obligations to our parents and our children. If Congress sends me a tax cut plan like that, I'll gladly sign it.

This is a time of great hope for our Nation, but a time where continued global economic growth demands continued American economic leadership. Fiscal responsibility has created our prosperity, and fiscal irresponsibility would put it at risk. Let's do the right thing to provide for the security of our parents and opportunity for our children into the 21st century.

Thanks for listening.

NOTE: The President spoke at 10:06 a.m. from the Oval Office at the White House.

Remarks to the Congressional Black Caucus Foundation
September 19, 1998

Thank you very much. Thank you. You know, Maxine Waters would be so much more effective as the chair of the Congressional Black Caucus if she weren't so shy and retiring—[laughter]—so reluctant to express her opinion. [Laughter]

Thank you, my friends, for years of friendship. Thank you for the work we began back in 1991.

To the chair of the dinner, Congressman Clyburn, and the chair of the Foundation, Congresswoman Clayton—and congratulations on your recent outstanding primary victory—to the dean of this caucus and a great fighter for the American way, John Conyers, thank you.

To two great lions of the century we are about to end, Rosa Parks and Dr. Dorothy Height;

to three great friends of mine who have left or are now leaving the Congress, Ron Dellums, Floyd Flake, and Louis Stokes, I echo everything the Vice President said about you.

And to the family of Congressman Charles Diggs, Jr., I thank you for giving the awards to Secretary Herman and Secretary Slater, to Frank Raines and Congressman Rush and the other winners who have given so much to our country.

I thank the members of our administration who are here tonight: Attorney General Reno, Secretary Cuomo, SBA Administrator Alvarez. To the marvelous White House staff members who are here: Minyon Moore, Goody Marshall, Maria Echaveste, Bob Nash, Janis Kearney, Ben Johnson, Al Maldon, Tracey Thornton, Cheryl Mills, Judith Winston, Betty Currie, Janet Murguia, and goodness knows who else is here—they hate to miss this dinner. To all the members of the administration who are here, along with all the members of the caucus, I thank you.

After the speeches which have been given, the outstanding remarks of the Vice President—and let me say one thing about him. I sometimes regret that one of the burdens of being Vice President is having to brag on the President and never getting to brag on himself. Many things will be said, good and perhaps some not so good, about this administration. One thing that will never be in question is that in the history of our Republic no person has ever held the office of Vice President who had more influence on more decisions and did more good in more areas for more people in this country than Vice President Al Gore.

I have a speech I want to give, but first I'd like to say something from the heart. I want to thank you for standing up for America with me. I want to thank you for standing up for me and understanding the true meaning of repentance and atonement. I want to thank you for standing up consistently for people over politics, for progress over partisanship, for principle over power, for unity over division. I want to thank you for standing up, beyond race, for the very best in America. I am very, very grateful.

I am grateful for what the Congressional Black Caucus has done for the past 28 years to expand and enhance the promise of America and to lead our country toward a single shining ideal, perhaps captured best in that wonderful phrase from John Lewis' autobiography, "the be-loved community," one that dwells not on difference but instead gains strength from expanding diversity, one rooted in humane laws and generous spirits, in which all children's talents are matched by their opportunities, in which all Americans join their hands and, in John's words, "courageously walk with the wind." God knows your journey has not been easy. The winds have often blown bitter and cold. But always this caucus has walked with the wind.

Today, because of the long road you have walked, the house we call America is safer and stronger than ever. As I think back on what we have done together in the last 5½ years, I think of these things. We cut taxes for 15 million hard-working families through the earned-income tax credit, and when the Republicans tried to slash it, we said no. We increased the minimum wage to give 10 million Americans a well-deserved raise. And now we're trying to increase it again in a way that would affect 12 million of our fellow citizens, to ensure that people who work full time can raise their children out of poverty and that all people share in the bounty of our present prosperity.

Together we fought for and won the biggest increase in children's health care in more than three decades. It can add insurance—health insurance—to 5 million children in working families across this country. We expanded the Head Start program to help our children get off on the right foot, and we're going to expand it some more. We made it possible for nearly 2 million more women and infants to get the nutritional care they need. With the Family and Medical Leave Act, we gave millions of people the chance to take time off from work to care for an ailing parent or bond with a newborn child.

We have opened the doors of higher education with the HOPE scholarship, with more Pell grants, with tax credits for all higher education, with the deductibility of student loans. We have done that for every single qualified American who's willing to work for it. Money can no longer be considered an insurmountable obstacle. And you did that. You should be very, very proud.

Together with the Vice President's leadership, we created more than 100 empowerment zones and enterprise communities, established community development banks, doubled small business loans to minorities and tripled them to women. When people wanted to scrap affirmative action we said, "Mend it. Don't end it," because we believe the best investment in America makes us all stronger.

Together we shaped and passed the historic crime bill, overcoming immense pressure, with the Brady bill, the assault weapons ban, more police on our streets and, yes, more prevention for our children to keep them out of trouble in the first place.

Now, look what you have done: nearly 17 million jobs, the lowest unemployment rate in 28 years, the lowest African-American and Hispanic unemployment rates in a generation, the lowest African-American poverty rate since statistics have been kept, the fastest real wage growth in 20 years, a record number of new small businesses every year, violent crime down 6 years in a row, and the lowest crime rate in 25 years. None of this could have happened without the leadership, the friendship, the ideas of the Congressional Black Caucus.

And I thank the Vice President for his litany of our African-American appointments and for pointing out—in a phrase I will steal the first chance I get—that we are not successful in spite of our diversity; we are successful because of it. We can never say that enough. That is the truth, and America is better because all Americans can feel a part of this administration.

Now, here's the real question: What are we to do with this treasured moment of prosperity and progress? What are we do to with our resources? What are we to do with the self-confidence it has generated in America? Some people think that now is the time to kick back and relax. Others seem to think they can play games with our future with some of the proposals now before the Congress. I say we can look back a long way to the book of Genesis to see what we should do.

Remember Joseph? What did he do in a time of plenty? He did not rest. When people thought he was too farsighted and too burdensome, he instructed them to stockpile rich bounties of grain like sand to the sea. He knew the times of plenty had to be the busiest, the most productive, the most determined times of all. Wisdom and history teaches us that in times of prosperity we need to be more visionary, more vigorous, more determined to deal with the long-term challenges before us, and that we will only pay a price if we indulge ourselves in idleness or distractions.

I say we cannot rest until we save Social Security for the 21st century. Remember what we are facing today. In 1993 it was projected that the deficit would be about $300 billion and rising. In just a few days, a little more than a week, we'll have the first balanced budget and surplus in 29 years. Ninety-two percent—ninety-two percent of the gap was closed by the votes of members of this caucus and our party without any help. Then we did have a bipartisan balanced budget bill that had, thanks to your efforts, the health care and education initiatives I mentioned.

So now we are going to have a surplus because of the hard work and productivity of the American people. Some say, "It's just a few weeks before the election; we ought to have a tax cut." I'm not against tax cuts. This year, in the balanced budget bill, the American people will get, most of them, a $500 tax credit for every child at home; the HOPE scholarship and other credits for college education; the right to withdraw from an IRA without penalty for education, for health care, for buying a first-time home. That's a good thing. But they're paid for in the balanced budget.

And in my budget there are more tax cuts. There are tax cuts for education, to build and repair old schools; tax cuts to help families with the cost of child care; tax cuts to help small businesses take out pensions for their employees who don't have them today. But every one of them is paid for in the balanced budget.

By the time the baby boomers like me—and I'm the oldest of them—that's hard to say. [*Laughter*] By the time we retire, all of us in the baby boom generation, 18 years of us, there will only be about two people working for every one person drawing Social Security if the predictions are right.

Now, we have three choices. Number one, we can do nothing and wait until the crash comes, because the present system is not sustainable, and then we can simply cut the living standards of our seniors. For people like me it will be fine; I'll have a good pension. But don't forget, half the people in this country over 65 today are out of poverty because of Social Security. Or we can wait until that day comes, and we can say, "We can't do that to our parents and grandparents, so we can just simply raise the taxes a lot on the working families of this country to maintain the system just exactly as it is." And in so doing, people like me will have to face the prospect that we've lowered the standard of living of our children and our children's ability to raise our grandchildren. Or we can say, "If we start now with a sensible, modest proposal, we can save Social Security and save the future for our children and grandchildren." I don't think it's even close, and I don't think you do either.

But that means we can't rest. We have to work. We can't rest until all the children in all the communities have a world-class education. We have a budget before the Congress to hire 100,000 more teachers; to take those class sizes in the early grades down to 18; to rebuild or modernize 5,000 schools; to hook all the classrooms in the poorest schools, too, up to the Internet by the year 2000; to reward the school districts that are trying to reform and help kids, like Chicago, where there are so many kids in summer school it's the sixth biggest school district in America and over 40,000 kids get three square meals a day there; to hire 35,000 more teachers by paying their way through college and saying you can pay your student loan off if you'll go into the inner city or into another underserved area and teach our kids who need it; by passing Congressman Fattah's High Hopes proposal so that we can have the ability to mentor kids in junior high school and tell them, "If you'll stay out of trouble, stay in school, learn your lessons, we will tell you right now you will be able to go on to college, and here's how much money you will get to make sure it gets done." That's what we have to do. We cannot rest. We have work to do.

We can't rest until we pass the Patients' Bill of Rights. Now, that sounds like a high-flown term. Here's what it means. It means that with 160 million Americans in managed care systems, we still don't think an accountant ought to be making a decision a doctor should make. We believe if somebody walks out of this dinner tonight and—God forbid—is in a car accident, they ought to be able to go to the nearest emergency room, not one 5 or 6 miles away because it happens to be covered by the plan. We believe if somebody needs a specialist and their doctor says they need a specialist, they ought to be able to get a specialist and not be told no. We believe if a woman is 6 months pregnant and her insurance plan changes carriers, her employer, they ought not to be able to tell her

to get a different obstetrician until after the baby is born. That's what we believe.

And we believe the other party's bill is wrong for America, because it doesn't guarantee any of these rights. It enables people to invade the privacy of your records even more, and it leaves 100 million Americans out. We cannot rest. We have work to do.

We cannot rest while HIV and AIDS is escalating in the African-American community. Secretary Shalala just announced the first installment of a comprehensive prevention, education, and care plan in the African-American community. Working with Maxine Waters, Lou Stokes, and others in the CBC, we can and we must do more. But we're only 2 weeks away from this budget year, and Congress has still not passed the health budget. We cannot rest. We have work to do.

We cannot rest until we eliminate the unacceptable disparities in health that racial and ethnic minorities experience in America today. We are not one nation when it comes to infant mortality, heart disease, and prostate cancer for African-Americans. It is nearly double the rate for white Americans. There are other problems that Hispanics and Asians and other minorities have. That is why I challenged the Nation to eliminate these disparities by 2010, and asked Congress to pass $400 million to achieve this goal. Almost time for the new budget year, it still hasn't passed yet. We cannot rest. We have work to do.

Let me say this. The unemployment rate, the poverty rates, all those rates you hear about the African-American population, they're true. But they disguise a fact that is unacceptable: There are still disparities. We cannot rest until every community, every neighborhood, every block, every family has the chance to reap the benefits of our economic growth. That is why we have to fund the empowerment initiatives that the Vice President and Secretary Cuomo have worked so hard for, to provide housing assistance for those leaving welfare and entering work, to expand funding for the community development banks, to step up enforcement of fair housing laws, to revitalize more urban brownfield areas, and to restore summer jobs for our young people. We're less than 2 weeks away from a new budget year, and that has not been passed yet. We cannot rest. We have work to do.

We cannot rest while any communities are thoroughly segregated by income or by race. The Federal Government should lead the way in word and deed. I have directed Secretary Cuomo to seek a major legislative overhaul in the admission policy for public housing, to deconcentrate poverty, mix incomes, and thereby mix racial balances for Americans.

Tonight I ask all of you to send a clear message to Congress with me: Don't send me a public housing bill that doesn't include our admission reforms, reforms that will make public housing a model of one America in the 21st century. And I might add, we're less than 2 weeks away from a new budget year, and I still don't have the increase I asked for in the budget of the Equal Employment Opportunity Commission. We cannot rest. We have work to do.

And let me say one or two more words about this census. We can't rest until we have a fair one. Listen to this: In 1990 about 4½ percent of African-Americans were not counted. In Los Angeles County alone, nearly 40,000 African-American children were left out. This has enormous consequences for how we distribute the bounty of America, for how we draw our political distinctions, for the policies that we follow. This is a fundamental issue. This is a civil rights issue. Why? Why would the Republican leadership in Congress refuse methods of counting that even—listen to this—that even Republican experts say is the best way to count all Americans. We must count every American for one simple reason: Every American counts. We cannot rest. We have work to do on this census issue.

We cannot rest until we act as leaders to contain the global financial and economic crisis that grips Russia and Asia. Why? Because a third of our own economic growth in these last years has come from our trade with other nations. We have to try to build an adequate trade and financial system for a new century that takes into legitimate account the interests of working people, the interest of the environment, the interest all countries have in avoiding depressions and unusual boom and bust cycles. Why? Because it is in our interest in a world growing ever smaller to keep people free and give them a chance to work their way to prosperity, and because we can't be an island of prosperity in a sea of failure, as Alan Greenspan said so elo-

quently the other day. That means we've got to help the International Monetary Fund put out these economic fires across the world by paying our fair dues. It's in our interest to help emerging countries in Africa, in Latin America, in Asia.

Hillary and I saw the African renaissance with many of you this past spring, a trip that changed me forever. Across the continent, I saw hope rising, business growing, democracy gaining strength. Yes, I saw profound, continuing problems and enormous challenges, but I saw in the bright eyes of children and the stern resolve of their parents the potential of a wonderful future.

We have to work together to see that Africa's children, like America's, have a democratic, peaceful, prosperous future; to expand trade and partnership by passing our Africa trade bill; to deal effectively with the violent conflicts that continue to plague Africa today and threaten its future; to ensure that Africa's hospitality is not used to perpetuate acts of terrorism, as it was so terribly in the bombings in Kenya and Tanzania. I have asked Dr. David Satcher, our Surgeon General, to go to east Africa this month with a team of medical experts to do what they can to help people who are still ailing there.

There is still no action in Congress, after all these months, on the Africa trade bill or on the International Monetary Fund. But world events are not waiting for Congress. My friends, if you believe we have responsibilities in the world and you believe ultimately those responsibilities affect the welfare of your families, your children, and the future of this country, I say we cannot rest. We have work to do.

We cannot rest until we solve the oldest, most stubborn, most painful challenge of our Nation, the continuing challenge of race. Yesterday, for the final time, I met with my Advisory Board on Race and received their report. I am proud of their work, the guidance they have given us for policy, for dialog, for specific practices in every community in this country. But we know we've only just begun a work that will take a lifetime, only just begun to find ways finally to lift the burden of race and redeem the full promise of America.

You know, our Founders knew we weren't perfect, but they always strived for perfect ideals. They built us a country based on a Constitution that was literally made for reconciliation, for the honorable and principled resolution of differences, rooted in the simple proposition that God created us all equal. Therefore, the implicit mandate of the Constitution is that each of us should respect and treat our neighbors as we, ourselves, would like to be treated. It is still our most sure guidepost today. We can build an America where discrimination is something you have to look in the history books to find. But we've still got work to do. If it takes until my last day on this Earth, I owe it to you, to the American people who have been so good to me for so long, to keep working on guiding our people across all the great divides into that one beloved community.

My friends, this is not a time to rest. It's a time to work. Just as God is not finished with any of us yet, we must not be finished with God's work. We must not be finished with seeking peace or justice or freedom, equality, human dignity, and reconciliation. "Foxes have holes; birds of the air have nests; but the Son of Man has no place to rest his head." There is never going to be an end to this work. And the present moment of promise imposes upon all of us a special responsibility. So let there be no end to your faith, your energy, your courage, and your commitment.

And let me say one other thing. You and I need some help. And this November we'll be given a chance to get it. We have worked hard to make America a better place, and it is. We have worked hard to empower our people, and we have. But now they must use that power to be heard, to say what we shall do and where we shall go. This is a moment of decision for us. Will it be progress or partisanship, people or politics, principle or power?

The Scripture says that we should mount up with wings as eagles; we should run and not grow tired; we should walk and not faint. We should not grow weary in doing good, for in due season we shall reap, if we do not lose heart. For all the many things I am grateful to the Black Caucus for, the most important thing is that I know you have never lost heart and that in your heart there is a longing for the best, not just for African-Americans but for all Americans. We can help them get there, and they can lead us home.

Thank you, and God bless you all. Thank you.

NOTE: The President spoke at 10:17 p.m. at the Washington Convention Center. In his remarks, he referred to civil rights activist Rosa Parks; Dorothy Height, chair and president emerita, National Council of Negro Women; and Franklin D. Raines, former Director, Office of Management and Budget.

Statement on Signing the Military Construction Appropriations Act, 1999
September 20, 1998

Today I have signed into law H.R. 4059, the "Military Construction Appropriations Act, FY 1999," which provides funding for military construction and family housing programs of the Department of Defense (DOD).

The Act funds the vast majority of my request for military construction projects, including the military family housing program, other quality-of-life projects for our military personnel and their families, and the DOD base closure and realignment program.

I do have several concerns with the bill. The Congress has chosen to add funds for projects that the DOD has not identified as priorities. In particular, $243 million is provided for 38

projects that are not in the DOD's Future Years Defense Program. The bill also includes a prohibition on the use of any funds appropriated in the Act for Partnership for Peace Programs or to provide support for non-NATO countries. This restriction could impede NATO activities and could adversely affect future NATO-led military operations.

In addition, the Congress has again included a provision that requires the Secretary of Defense to give 30 days advance notice to certain congressional committees of any proposed military exercise involving construction costs anticipated to exceed $100,000. In approving H.R.

4059, I wish to reiterate an understanding, expressed by Presidents Reagan and Bush when they signed Military Construction Appropriations Acts containing a similar provision, that this section encompasses only exercises for which providing 30 days advance notice is feasible and consistent with my constitutional authority and duty to protect the national security.

I urge the Congress to complete action on the remaining FY 1999 appropriations bills as quickly as possible, and to send them to me in acceptable form.

WILLIAM J. CLINTON

The White House,
September 20, 1998.

NOTE: H.R. 4059, approved September 20, was assigned Public Law No. 105–237.

Statement on Fiscal Year 1999 Appropriations Legislation
September 20, 1998

Today I signed the Military Construction Appropriations Act, an important step for the well-being of our men and women in uniform and their families.

This is an example of what we can achieve when we work together—Congress and the President, Republicans and Democrats—for the public good. Unfortunately, with less than 2 weeks to go before the beginning of the new fiscal year, Congress has yet to pass a budget. In fact, Congress has finished work on only one of 13 appropriations bills—bills that are necessary to keep the Government running and to advance the interests of the American people.

I am pleased that the Senate has taken steps to support the priorities laid out in my budget. But on key investments to improve education, provide affordable child care, expand health care coverage, protect our environment, and stabilize the international economy, the House of Representatives is moving in the wrong direction. For example, the House is preparing to deny funding for smaller classes, after-school programs, technology in the classroom, and summer job programs. At the same time, some lawmakers have attached controversial and unrelated provisions guaranteed to mire these bills in unnecessary delay.

The new fiscal year begins on October 1. It is time for Congress to put progress ahead of partisanship and focus on the urgent challenges facing the American people.

NOTE: H.R. 4059, the Military Construction Appropriations Act, 1999, approved September 20, was assigned Public Law No. 105–237.

Remarks to the 53d Session of the United Nations General Assembly in New York City
September 21, 1998

Thank you very much. Mr. President, Mr. Secretary-General, the delegates of this 53d session of the General Assembly, let me begin by thanking you for your very kind and generous welcome and by noting that at the opening of this General Assembly the world has much to celebrate.

Peace has come to Northern Ireland after 29 long years. Bosnia has just held its freest elections ever. The United Nations is actively mediating crises before they explode into war all around the world. And today, more people determine their own destiny than at any previous moment in history.

We celebrate the 50th anniversary of the Universal Declaration of Human Rights with those rights more widely embraced than ever before. On every continent, people are leading lives of integrity and self-respect, and a great deal of credit for that belongs to the United Nations.

Still, as every person in this room knows, the promise of our time is attended by perils. Global economic turmoil today threatens to undermine confidence in free markets and democracy. Those of us who benefit particularly from this economy have a special responsibility to do more to minimize the turmoil and extend the benefits of global markets to all citizens. And the United States is determined to do that.

We still are bedeviled by ethnic, racial, religious, and tribal hatreds; by the spread of weapons of mass destruction; by the almost frantic effort of too many states to acquire such weapons. And despite all efforts to contain it, terrorism is not fading away with the end of the 20th century. It is a continuing defiance of Article 3 of the Universal Declaration of Human Rights, which says, and I quote, "Everyone has the right to life, liberty, and security of person."

Here at the U.N., at international summits around the world, and on many occasions in the United States, I have had the opportunity to address this subject in detail, to describe what we have done, what we are doing, and what we must yet do to combat terror. Today I would like to talk to you about why all nations must put the fight against terrorism at the top of our agenda.

Obviously, this is a matter of profound concern to us. In the last 15 years, our citizens have been targeted over and over again: in Beirut; over Lockerbie; in Saudi Arabia; at home in Oklahoma City, by one of our own citizens, and even here in New York, in one of our most public buildings; and most recently on August 7th in Nairobi and Dar es Salaam, where Americans who devoted their lives to building bridges between nations, people very much like all of you, died in a campaign of hatred against the United States.

Because we are blessed to be a wealthy nation with a powerful military and worldwide presence active in promoting peace and security, we are often a target. We love our country for its dedication to political and religious freedom, to economic opportunity, to respect for the rights of the individual. But we know many people see us as a symbol of a system and values they reject, and often they find it expedient to blame us for problems with deep roots elsewhere.

But we are no threat to any peaceful nation, and we believe the best way to disprove these claims is to continue our work for peace and prosperity around the world. For us to pull back from the world's trouble spots, to turn our backs on those taking risks for peace, to weaken our own opposition to terrorism, would hand the enemies of peace a victory they must never have.

Still, it is a grave misconception to see terrorism as only, or even mostly, an American problem. Indeed, it is a clear and present danger to tolerant and open societies and innocent people everywhere. No one in this room, nor the people you represent, are immune.

Certainly not the people of Nairobi and Dar es Salaam; for every American killed there, roughly 20 Africans were murdered and 500 more injured, innocent people going about their business on a busy morning. Not the people of Omagh, in Northern Ireland, where the wounded and killed were Catholics and Protestants alike, mostly children and women—and two of them pregnant—people out shopping together, when their future was snuffed out by a fringe group clinging to the past. Not the people of Japan who were poisoned by sarin gas in the Tokyo subway. Not the people of Argentina who died when a car bomb decimated a Jewish community center in Buenos Aires. Not the people of Kashmir and Sri Lanka killed by ancient animosities that cry out for resolution. Not the Palestinians and Israelis who still die year after year, for all the progress toward peace. Not the people of Algeria, enduring the nightmare of unfathomable terror with still no end in sight. Not the people of Egypt, who nearly lost a second President to assassination. Not the people of Turkey, Colombia, Albania, Russia, Iran, Indonesia, and countless other nations where innocent people have been victimized by terror.

Now, none of these victims are American, but every one was a son or a daughter, a husband or wife, a father or mother, a human life extinguished by someone else's hatred, leaving a circle of people whose lives will never be the same. Terror has become the world's problem. Some argue, of course, that the problem is overblown, saying that the number of deaths from terrorism is comparatively small, sometimes less than the number of people killed by lightning in a single year. I believe that misses the point in several ways.

First, terrorism has a new face in the 1990's. Today, terrorists take advantage of greater openness and the explosion of information and weapons technology. The new technologies of terror and their increasing availability, along with the increasing mobility of terrorists, raise chilling prospects of vulnerability to chemical, biological, and other kinds of attacks, bringing each of us into the category of possible victim. This is a threat to all humankind.

Beyond the physical damage of each attack, there is an even greater residue of psychological damage, hard to measure but slow to heal. Every bomb, every bomb threat has an insidious effect on free and open institutions, the kinds of institutions all of you in this body are working so hard to build.

Each time an innocent man or woman or child is killed, it makes the future more hazardous for the rest of us, for each violent act saps the confidence that is so crucial to peace and prosperity. In every corner of the world, with the active support of U.N. agencies, people are struggling to build better futures, based on bonds of trust connecting them to their fellow citizens and with partners and investors from around the world.

The glimpse of growing prosperity in Northern Ireland was a crucial factor in the Good Friday Agreement. But that took confidence—confidence that cannot be bought in times of violence. We can measure each attack and the grisly statistics of dead and wounded, but what are the wounds we cannot measure?

In the Middle East, in Asia, in South America, how many agreements have been thwarted after bombs blew up? How many businesses will never be created in places crying out for investments of time and money? How many talented young people in countries represented here have turned their backs on public service? The question is not only how many lives have been lost in each attack but how many futures were lost in their aftermath.

There is no justification for killing innocents. Ideology, religion, and politics, even deprivation and righteous grievance, do not justify it. We must seek to understand the roiled waters in which terror occurs; of course, we must.

Often, in my own experience, I have seen where peace is making progress, terror is a desperate act to turn back the tide of history. The Omagh bombing came as peace was succeeding in Northern Ireland. In the Middle East, whenever we get close to another step toward peace, its enemies respond with terror. We must not let this stall our momentum. The bridging of ancient hatreds is, after all, a leap of faith, a break with the past, and thus a frightening threat to those who cannot let go of their own hatred. Because they fear the future, in these cases, terrorists seek to blow the peacemakers back into the past.

We must also acknowledge that there are economic sources of this rage as well. Poverty, inequality, masses of disenfranchised young people are fertile fields for the siren call of the terrorists and their claims of advancing social justice. But deprivation cannot justify destruction, nor can inequity ever atone for murder. The killing of innocents is not a social program.

Nevertheless, our resolute opposition to terrorism does not mean we can ever be indifferent to the conditions that foster it. The most recent U.N. human development report suggests the gulf is widening between the world's haves and have-nots. We must work harder to treat the sources of despair before they turn into the poison of hatred. Dr. Martin Luther King once wrote that the only revolutionary is a man who has nothing to lose. We must show people they have everything to gain by embracing cooperation and renouncing violence. This is not simply an American or a Western responsibility; it is the world's responsibility.

Developing nations have an obligation to spread new wealth fairly, to create new opportunities, to build new open economies. Developed nations have an obligation to help developing nations stay on the path of prosperity and—and—to spur global economic growth. A week ago I outlined ways we can build a stronger international economy to benefit not only all nations but all citizens within them.

Some people believe that terrorism's principal fault line centers on what they see as an inevitable clash of civilizations. It is an issue that deserves a lot of debate in this great hall. Specifically, many believe there is an inevitable clash between Western civilization and Western values, and Islamic civilizations and values. I believe this view is terribly wrong. False prophets may use and abuse any religion to justify whatever political objectives they have, even cold-blooded murder. Some may have the world believe that Almighty God himself, the Merciful, grants a license to kill. But that is not our understanding of Islam.

A quarter of the world's population is Muslim, from Africa to Middle East to Asia and to the United States, where Islam is one of our fastest growing faiths. There are over 1,200 mosques and Islamic centers in the United States, and the number is rapidly increasing. The 6 million Americans who worship there will tell you there is no inherent clash between Islam and America. Americans respect and honor Islam.

As I talk to Muslim leaders in my country and around the world, I see again that we share the same hopes and aspirations: to live in peace and security, to provide for our children, to follow the faith of our choosing, to build a better life than our parents knew, and pass on brighter possibilities to our own children. Of course, we are not identical. There are important differences that cross race and culture and religion which demand understanding and deserve respect.

But every river has a crossing place. Even as we struggle here in America, like the United Nations, to reconcile all Americans to each other and to find greater unity in our increasing diversity, we will remain on a course of friendship and respect for the Muslim world. We will continue to look for common values, common interests, and common endeavors. I agree very much with the spirit expressed by these words of Mohammed: "Rewards for prayers by people assembled together are twice those said at home."

When it comes to terrorism, there should be no dividing line between Muslims and Jews, Protestants and Catholics, Serbs and Albanians, developed societies and emerging countries. The only dividing line is between those who practice, support, or tolerate terror, and those who understand that it is murder, plain and simple.

If terrorism is at the top of the American agenda—and should be at the top of the world's agenda—what, then, are the concrete steps we can take together to protect our common destiny? What are our common obligations? At least, I believe, they are these: to give terrorists no support, no sanctuary, no financial assistance; to bring pressure on states that do; to act together to step up extradition and prosecution; to sign the global anti-terror conventions; to strengthen the biological weapons and chemical conventions; to enforce the Chemical Weapons Convention; to promote stronger domestic laws and control the manufacture and export of explosives; to raise international standards for airport security; to combat the conditions that spread violence and despair.

We are working to do our part. Our intelligence and law enforcement communities are tracking terrorist networks in cooperation with other governments. Some of those we believe responsible for the recent bombing of our Embassies have been brought to justice. Early this week I will ask our Congress to provide emergency funding to repair our Embassies, to improve security, to expand the worldwide fight against terrorism, to help our friends in Kenya and Tanzania with the wounds they have suffered.

But no matter how much each of us does alone, our progress will be limited without our common efforts. We also will do our part to address the sources of despair and alienation through the Agency for International Development in Africa, in Asia, in Latin America, in Eastern Europe, in Haiti, and elsewhere. We will continue our strong support for the U.N. Development Program, the U.N. High Commissioners for Human Rights and Refugees, UNICEF, the World Bank, the World Food Program. We also recognize the critical role these agencies play and the importance of all countries, including the United States, in paying their fair share.

In closing, let me urge all of us to think in new terms on terrorism, to see it not as a clash of cultures or political action by other means or a divine calling but a clash between the forces of the past and the forces of the future, between those who tear down and those who build up, between hope and fear, chaos and community.

The fight will not be easy. But every nation will be strengthened in joining it, in working to give real meaning to the words of the Universal Declaration on Human Rights we signed 50 years ago. It is very, very important that we do this together.

Eleanor Roosevelt was one of the authors of the Universal Declaration. She said in one of her many speeches in support of the United Nations, when it was just beginning, "All agreements and all peace are built on confidence. You cannot have peace and you cannot get on with other people in the world unless you have confidence in them."

It is not necessary that we solve all the world's problems to have confidence in one another. It is not necessary that we agree on all the world's issues to have confidence in one another. It is not even necessary that we understand every single difference among us to have confidence in one another. But it is necessary that we affirm our belief in the primacy of the Universal Declaration on Human Rights, and therefore, that together we say terror is not a way to tomorrow; it is only a throwback to yesterday. And together—together—we can meet it and overcome its threats, its injuries, and its fears with confidence.

Thank you very much.

NOTE: The President spoke at 11:13 a.m. in the Assembly Hall at the United Nations. In his remarks, he referred to U.N. General Assembly President Didier Opertti and U.N. Secretary-General Kofi Annan.

Remarks at a United Nations Luncheon in New York City
September 21, 1998

Mr. Secretary-General, members of the Secretariat, President Opertti, fellow leaders, first let me thank the Secretary-General for his remarks and for his leadership and echo his remarks.

Franklin Roosevelt coined the term "United Nations." I think we all agree that we are more and more united with every passing year. We are more and more against the same things, but even more important, we are more and more for the same things. The United States has been a great beneficiary of the United Nations, and we honor the location of the United Nations here and the chance to be partners with all of you.

I would like to say just one particular word about the Secretary-General. I believe he has truly been the right leader for this time. In the United States we are ending the baseball season in our country, and here in New York there was once a great baseball figure named Leo Durocher whose most famous saying was

"Nice guys finish last." Kofi Annan proves that Leo Durocher was wrong. He has proceeded with great kindness and decency. He has proved to all of us that change is possible and that, in his words, one can dare to make a difference. He has stood for human rights and peace. He has demonstrated both strength and courage and humility and infinite patience.

I thank him for embodying the best of what we all hope the world can become, for his leadership, for reform, for putting a good team in place, for lifting the morale of the people who work here on all our behalf. And I ask all of you to join me in a toast to the Secretary-General and the staff of the United Nations.

NOTE: The President spoke at 1:50 p.m. in the North Delegates Lounge. In his remarks, he referred to U.N. General Assembly President Didier Opertti.

Remarks at "Strengthening Democracy in the Global Economy: An Opening Dialogue" in New York City
September 21, 1998

President Clinton. Thank you very much, John. I would like to thank you and the NYU School of Law, the Progressive Policy Institute, the World Policy Institute, and the New School University—all of you—for your support of this endeavor. And especially, we want to thank NYU Law School for hosting this.

I'd like to thank Hillary and the people on her staff and others who worked with you to conceive and execute this remarkable meeting.

I want to thank all the participants here on the previous panels. I have gotten a report about what you've said, and I will try not to be repetitive. I would also like to thank Prime Minister Blair, Prime Minister Prodi, President Stoyanov for being here and sharing this couple of hours with me. I want you to have the maximum amount of time to hear from them.

If you listened to the people in the earlier panels today, you know kind of how this so-called Third Way movement evolved, beginning in the 1980's here, in Great Britain, and in other places. If you look around the world, there is an astonishing emergence in so many countries, and obviously in different contexts, of people who are trying to be modern and progressive. That is, they're trying to embrace change; they're trying to embrace free markets; they're trying to embrace engagement in the rest of the world. But they do not reject the notion that we have mutual responsibilities to each other, both within and beyond our national borders.

Most of us have very strong views about the role of government. We believe that the government should support a pro-growth policy but one that is consistent with advancing the environment. And that's the other thing I know you've heard before, but there are hard choices to be made in life and in politics. But not all choices posed are real.

One of the things that paralyzes a country is when the rhetoric governing the national civic and political debate is composed of false choices designed to divide people and win elections but not to advance the common good once the elections were over. I think that, more than anything else, that feeling that I had many years ago back in the eighties got me into trying to rethink this whole notion of what our national political principles ought to be, what our driving platform ought to be.

I think that we have found that, yes, there are some very hard choices to be made, but some of the mega-choices that people tell us we have to make really are false: that you can't have a growing economy by pitting working people against business people, you have to get them to work together; you can't have a successful economic policy over the long run unless you improve the environment, not destroy it.

It is impossible to, anymore, have a clear division between domestic and foreign policy, whether it is economic policy or security policy, and I would like to argue, also, social policy. That is, I believe we have a vested interest in the United States in advancing the welfare of ordinary citizens around the world as we pursue our economic and security interests. And of course, that brings us to the subject we came to discuss today, which is how to make the global economy work for ordinary citizens.

I would just say, I'd like to make two big points. Number one is, the rest of us, no matter how good our conscience or how big out pocketbooks, cannot make the global economy work for ordinary citizens in any country if the country itself is not doing the right things. And I think it's very important to point that out. Second, all the countries in the world trying to do the right things won't make sense unless we recognize that we have responsibilities, collective responsibilities that go beyond our borders, and I would just like to mention a couple of them.

First of all, we have to create a trading system for the 21st century that actually works to benefit ordinary people in countries throughout the globe. That's what all this labor and environmental conditions and letting all the interest groups be a part of the trade negotiations— all of that's just sort of shorthand for saying, "Look, we've got to figure out some way that if wealth increases everywhere, real people get the benefit of it, and it's fairly spread, and people that work hard are rewarded for it."

Second, I think we simply have to realize that while the IMF and the World Bank and these international institutions have proved remarkably flexible and expandable, if you will, over the last 50 years, we are living in a world that is really quite different now, with these global financial markets and the increasing integration of the economy. And while, again I say, in the absence of good domestic policies, there is nothing a global system can do to protect people from themselves and their own mismanagement, the world financial system today does not guard against that boom/bust cycle that all of our national economic policies guard against, that it does not reflect the lessons that we learned in the aftermath of the Great Depression of 1929 nationally—it does not reflect those lessons on an international scale.

And I believe that the most urgent thing we can do is to find a way to keep capital flowing freely so that the market system works around the world, but do it in a way that prevents these catastrophic developments we've seen in some countries and also may prevent an overindulgence of giddiness in some places, where too much money flows in in the beginning without any sort of proper risk premium at all on it.

We have to recognize that there's going to be a global financial system, and we have to think about how we can deal with it in the way each of us deal nationally to avoid depression and to moderate boom/bust cycles.

Now, in the short run, I think there are a lot of other things we have to do: Europe, the United States, Japan adopting aggressive growth strategies; working through some of the bad debts in Asian countries; dealing with Russia, especially; preventing the contagion from going to Latin America, especially to Brazil. There are lots of other things we can do.

Just one point, finally, I do believe that it is unavoidable that trauma will come to some of the countries in the world through the workout they have to go through. And therefore, I believe that the developed countries, either directly through the G–8 or indirectly through the World Bank, should do much, much, much more to build social safety nets in countries that we want to be free market democracies, so that people who through no fault of their own find themselves destitute have a chance to reconstruct their lives and live in dignity in the meantime. I think that is quite important that Jim Wolfensohn has committed to do that, and I think the rest of us should, as well.

So in summary, I'm grateful that the Third Way seems to be taking hold around the world. I think if you look at the record of the people on either side of me, the evidence is that the policies work for ordinary citizens and our countries. I think the challenges ahead of us are very, very profound. But I think if we meet them we will find that this whole approach will work in a global sense in the same way it's worked nationally in the nations here represented and in many others around the world.

Thank you very much.

[At this point, Prime Minister Tony Blair of the United Kingdom, Prime Minister Romano Prodi of Italy, and President Petar Stoyanov of Bulgaria made brief remarks.]

Philosophy of Government

President Clinton. I would like to start the conversation by asking you to think about your jobs, first from a domestic point of view, just totally within your country, and then we'll move to our global responsibilities.

Let's go back to what Prime Minister Blair said. Basically, the whole idea of this Third Way is that we believe in activist government, but highly disciplined. On the economic front, we want to create the conditions and give people

the tools to make the most of their own lives, the empowerment notion. On the social front, we want to provide rights to people, but they must assume certain duties. Philosophically, we support a concept of community in which everyone plays a role.

Now, arguably, that philosophy has led, in every one of the countries here present, to some very impressive gains in economic policy, in crime policy, in welfare policy, and all of that. But I would like to ask you instead to talk about what the—what is the hardest domestic problem you face? What do you have to deal with that the—this so-called Third Way philosophy we've developed either doesn't give you the answer to, or at least you haven't worked through it yet? And how would you analyze what still needs to be done?

I think it's very important that we understand—that we not stand up here and pretend that we have found a sort of magic wand to make all the world's problems go away, but instead we've found a working plan that sensible and compassionate people can ally themselves with and be a part of. But I think it's important that we, frankly, acknowledge what out there still needs to be done, what seems to be beyond the reach of at least what we're doing now.

Tony, want to go first?

[At this point, the discussion proceeded.]

President Clinton. Former Governor of New York Mario Cuomo used to say, people campaign in poetry, but they must govern in prose. *[Laughter]*

Prime Minister Blair. Yes, we're on the prose part. *[Laughter]*

President Clinton. That's one part of what you said. It's also true, as I used to say, that I never met anyone who did not support change in general—everybody's for it in general; hardly anyone is for it in particular. And I think that's another problem we face. But I agree with that.

I'd like to follow up, but I'd like to go— Romano, what's your biggest domestic challenge?

Prime Minister Prodi. My prose, my prose. *[Laughter]* My problem is that——

President Clinton. Italians never have to speak in prose. *[Laughter]*

[The discussion continued.]

President Clinton. I might say one of the interesting things to me as an American about this consultative process in European governments is the extent to which it really does seem to work very well when practiced in good faith. I was just in Ireland, and Ireland has had the fastest growing growth rate in Europe, I think, for the last several years. Of course, it was starting from a lower base. But they have an intensive system like the one you describe.

And I have been particularly interested in the practice in The Netherlands, and they have sort of a Third Way government. I wish that Prime Minister Wim Kok were here, but he couldn't come. But they actually have an unemployment rate more or less comparable to what—to Great Britain and the United States, and a more—certainly a more generous social safety net than we do, with a very, very high percentage of part-time workers showing a higher level of flexibility in the work force than virtually any country with which I'm familiar. So I think there is something to be said for this.

One of the things that I think will be interesting is to see whether or not this whole model can produce both a good macroeconomic policy, which gives you growth, and lower unemployment in a way that still saves enough of a safety net for people to believe they're in a just society. I mean, it's a very tough thing.

In France—France has had significant growth in several years and still not lowered the unemployment rate. So this, I think, is a big challenge. But I think the point you made is very good.

What's your biggest domestic problem?

[*The discussion continued.*]

Problem-Solving in Advance

President Clinton. I would like to make a brief comment and then go into the second question, and then after we all do that, then maybe Dean Sexton will come up, and we'll go through the questions. I think one big problem that prosperous countries have is, even if you have the right sort of theory of government, even if you have a strong majority support, is dealing with the huge problems that won't have their major impact until a good time down the road.

For example, almost all developed economies are going to have a serious intergenerational problem when all the so-called baby boomers retire. And we are hoping that sometime early next year, that we'll be able to get our big national consensus in America to reform Social Security system, the retirement system, and our Medicare system, our medical program for elderly people, in a way that will meet the social objectives the program has met, in Social Security's case, for the last 60 years, and in the case of Medicare, for the last 30-plus years.

And we know if we start now, we can make minor changes that will have huge impacts. If we wait until it's a major crisis, then we'll either have to raise taxes and lower the standard of living of working people and their children to take care of the elderly, or we'll have to lower the standard of living of the elderly to protect the working people and their children.

So clearly this is something that it's really worth beginning now on, because by doing modest amounts now, you can avoid those dire consequences. And to be fair, I think the whole success of our kind of politics consists in our being able to hold people together, to give people a sense that there really is a genuine sense of community out there.

Ironically, in Japan, they have just the reverse problem: everybody is so panicked about it because their society is even older than Great Britain and the United States and Italy that they're almost oversaving, and it's hard to get growth going there. But for us, the other problem is the bigger one.

Now, having said that, I'd like to segue into the international arena. It seems to me that all of us who are internationalists are pretty good at solving problems when they're hitting us in the face, but not very good in convincing our parliaments to give us the investment to build progress over a long period of time that will avoid those problems in the first place.

For example, we all got together and stopped the war in Bosnia after too many people have died and had been on television for too long, and there was too much blood in the streets. And it was quite expensive, but we're all glad we did it. Now, for a pittance of what that cost, we could all send him a check, and we'd never have a problem like that in his country. I mean, that's just one example. [*Laughter*] I don't mean just give the money, I mean investment. You know, I don't mean—you know what I mean. But this is a big problem.

Hillary and I were in Africa a few months ago in a little village in Uganda, looking at all these microcredit loans that have gone to women in this small African village and watching them put together the infrastructure of a civil society. Now, the United States funded, with our aid programs, 2 million such loans last year. In a world with 6 billion people, with whom several billion are quite poor, we could fund for a modest amount of money 100 million such loans a year and create the core of a civil society in many places where we would never have to worry about terrorism, where we would never have to worry about huge public health outbreaks, where we'd never have to worry about these massive environmental problems.

So I put that out because I do believe that somehow, the investment systems of the global economy, through the World Bank, the IMF, and other things, are not—nor are the aid systems of various countries or in the aggregate, the EU—adequate to deal with what I think is the plain self-interest of the developed world in helping prove this global system will work for ordinary people, not because it's the morally right thing to do—it is the morally right thing to do—but because it would be good for ordinary Americans 10 years from now not to have to worry about other Bosnias, not to have to worry about the Ebola virus going crazy, not have to worry about the horrible problems of global warming and malaria reaching higher and higher climates. All these things, these are things that require disciplined commitments over a lifetime.

Maybe I've had it on my mind because I've been at the U.N. today, but if you think about what we spend on that as compared to what we happily spend to solve a problem—I mean, for example, if—God forbid—things really went bad in Albania and Kosovo at the same time, and you called me on the phone and rang the bell, you know, we would all show up. Whatever you tell me to do there, I'm going to try to help you, no matter how much it costs, right? But for a pittance, over a period of years, we could maybe move so many more people toward the future we seek.

And that goes back to the point Tony made. How do you have a genuinely internationalist outlook that resonates with the people that we have to represent, the kind of people that are out there on the street waving to us when we came in today, people who have worked for very modest salaries, and the kind of people that keep NYU Law School going—how do we make the argument that some of the money

they give us in taxes every year should be invested in the common future of humankind?

[The discussion continued.]

Human Rights Issues

President Clinton. Well, I think it does limit it, but I think that the answer to that is to keep pushing for more democracy and for more gender equality and more concern for all children, especially young girls. A lot of the most perverse manifestation of gender inequality that I have learned from Hillary's experiences has to do with the treatment of young girls and whether they get schooling and other kinds of things that are regularly offered to young boys in some developing societies. So I think that's very important.

But if you go back to your question, we're just celebrating the 50th anniversary of the Universal Declaration of Human Rights, something I talked about over at the U.N. today. Well, those human rights are not universal, but they're more widely embraced than ever before. I think we should push all these things simultaneously. I don't think you can possibly say, "Well, we won't do this until we've got these other nine things done." If we took that approach toward any endeavor in life, no business would ever be started, no marriage would ever be undertaken, no human endeavor would ever be undertaken.

I do think the accurate part of Professor Dworkin's implication is that if there is no prospect of achieving any advances on these fronts, then it's going to be hard to have a truly democratic market society. I do believe that. But I think that we just have to face the fact that some cultures are going to be different from others, and if they have democratic governments, we should keep pushing them on these other fronts. That's my view, anyway.

[The discussion continued.]

President Clinton. At the risk of getting myself in trouble, let me give a very specific example of—Professor Dworkin asked about women's rights. I think there is a very great difference in the question of what our policy should be, let's say, toward the Taliban—if they take Muslim women who are doctors and say, "You can't practice medicine anymore," in ways that really put the health system of the country at risk, because it violates their religious convictions—and how should we approach them, and how should we approach a country, let's say, in Africa or Latin America, which historically has had gross disparities in the education rates of young girls and young boys. I would argue that if you go into those countries and you start putting money into education, you start putting money into education technology, and you start putting money into these villages and microenterprise loans for village women, giving them power, independent power to the economy, that you will get the objective you want by making sure women get treated more equally with men, and their children are much more likely to be treated more equally.

So I think you have to look at it on the facts. Whereas, with another kind of society you might say, "Well, we need to approach a different strategy," But to go back to what Mr. Prodi said, 9 times out of 10 or more, it doesn't make any sense to isolate them. It's still better to try to find some way to engage these countries and work with them if they're willing to deal with us on peaceful and honorable terms.

Education

[*Referring to the First Lady's description of the government, the economy, and society as three legs of a stool, moderator John Sexton, dean, New York University School of Law, read a question concerning the role and goals of education, and the discussion continued.*]

President Clinton. I think the issue in education—I think the first question was, should it primarily teach good citizenship. I agree with Tony; you can't be a good citizen if you can't function. I think what you want is an education system that teaches knowledge, citizenship, and learning skills. You basically have to teach people how to keep learning for a lifetime. And I think that every country is different, but you have to disaggregate what the challenges are.

For example, if the system itself is of good quality but insufficiently accessed, or if there is no system, then what you have to do is just fix something that people can access. If the system is all there, but encrusted to some extent and not performing, then you have to go after the system, and that's much harder. That's what Tony was saying.

In our country, we have now dramatically increased access to higher education. Really, if you look at all the tax benefits, the scholarships, and the work-study programs and all this, there's

almost no reason that anybody in America who can otherwise qualify shouldn't go to college now. We need to do the same sort of thing, I think, with preschool programs, starting with very young children. We need to build that infrastructure out there. Now, in the schools, we need to do better, and part of it is influence. We need more good physical facilities. We need more teachers in the early grades. We need more teachers in the underserved areas.

But a lot of it is—are quality things. We need more competition. That's why I'm for the charter school movements and public school choice. We need more standards and accountability. That's why I'm for the master teacher movement and for—we need an end to social promotion. But if you do that in the inner-city schools and you have the kind of standards, as Tony is talking about, and you actually hold people, schools, teachers, and students, accountable for student performance, then I would argue, ethically as well as educationally, we are obliged to do what has been done in Chicago and give every child who is not performing well the chance to go to summer school and the chance to be in an after-school program. Chicago now has—the summer school in Chicago is now the sixth biggest school district in America—the summer school—and it's a great thing. And guess what happened to juvenile crime? So I just would point that out.

I think that each society needs an analysis of what it takes to take this three-legged school up—some of it is going to be more, some of it is going to be better. And it's very important not to confuse more with better in either direction, because better won't make more, but neither will more make better. By and large, most of us need to be doing some mix of both.

Mr. Sexton. Mr. President, I would be wrong to leave the topic of education without noting something narrowly self-interested, but important to many of the students, many of the students in this room.

President Clinton. It's the American way; do it. [*Laughter*]

[*Mr. Sexton thanked President Clinton for his efforts to eliminate the taxability of loan repayment assistance for law school tuition for former students who choose to forgo higher pay to enter public service.*]

President Clinton. I think that's very important. If that were the definition of narrow self-interest that most citizens embraced, this would be a better country today. That's great. [*Laughter*]

[*The discussion continued.*]

Environmental Issues

President Clinton. First of all, let me go back to the basic question as I remember the basic question was: Will environmental security be like a military security issue in the 21st century? The answer is, I think it's very likely that it will be. And the more irresponsible we are for a longer period of time, the more likely that is to happen.

I think it's useful in looking at environmental problems to break them down into two categories, although there's always some overlap. One is, there is one truly global environmental problem, and that's climate change, because the climate of the Earth is changing in ways that already is disrupting life throughout the Earth.

I mentioned one example earlier. You have mosquitoes at higher and higher levels now giving people malaria who never got it before. And there's no resistance to it so they're getting sicker, and they're getting on airplanes and flying. And now they're bumping into people at airports, and there's now a phenomenon called airport malaria in the world, where technology and global warming are bumping into each other. That's a global problem. You can see it in weather, in disease, and a little bit in air pollution.

Then there are national problems which have global impacts because they're so big, and they prevent countries from becoming what they ought to: air pollution, water pollution, soil erosion, food supply pollution, those kinds of things. Then there's a huge problem we've got that's sort of in the middle. It's partly the result of global warming and partly the results of national pollution, and that is the degradation of the oceans, which is a breathtaking environmental problem that, if unaddressed, we will pay a huge price for.

Now, from my point of view, there are two big issues here. One is—and I agree with Tony—I think Kyoto is a big step forward. So I go to my Congress that's supposed to be Republican, free market oriented, and I say, "Okay, guys, no regulations and no taxes, tax cuts and increases for research and development." And they say, "It's a Communist plot," and they hold

hearings—[*laughter*]—about how, you know, this is just some deep, dark conspiracy to undermine the strength of the United States. Now, wait a minute. You're laughing about this, but actually behind this, as opposed to some other things, there is the core of an idea they have. [*Laughter*]

This idea, widely shared in the developing world and held onto in America more than any other developed country, is—it goes right against what Tony said is—this is a very serious comment. We're having fun, but this is a serious conversation. Their idea is that there is an inevitable iron connection between the production of greenhouse gases through the burning of fossil fuel and economic growth, and if you reduce greenhouse gases going into the atmosphere, there is no way on Earth that you will not reduce economic growth. There's all this business about technology and conservation and it's all a big plot designed to bring down the growth machine of America. Now, you laugh—we've had hearings on it. We've spent hundreds of thousands of dollars complying with subpoena requests and document requests and sending witnesses up to the Hill to basically say, "This is not a conspiracy to destroy the future of America."

But the serious idea here is, if you want something done about climate change, you must prevail in every developing country with evidence—evidence that there is no longer an iron connection between the burning of fossil fuels and economic growth.

The second point I want to make goes to the second question they asked, about how come we spend so little on foreign aid on the poor now? Because they don't have any votes in our country and because we don't think enough about it. I mean, every year my foreign aid budget is cut back.

But one thing we can do is to participate jointly with other countries in environmental projects in developing countries in ways that help reduce climate global warming and create lots of jobs in areas where there are lots of poor people. I believe if there is a serious global effort to deal with these environmental challenges, we would be investing all over the world the way the United States did, for example, in a massive reforestation project in Haiti. And when you do that kind of work—a lot of this work is very basic work that needs to be done—

you can create huge numbers of jobs for poor people who would otherwise not have them.

So I would say to all of you, I think this is a big opportunity—I tried to say some provocative things to make you laugh so you'd listen, because it's late in the day and you're all tired. But I'm telling you, the biggest environmental—the obstacle to our having responsible environmental policy in the whole world, including in the United States, is the belief of too many policymakers in 1998 that there is still an iron law between how much junk you put in the atmosphere and how much your economy grows.

And until we break that in the minds of decisionmakers, we will not do what we should do on the climate change challenge. And until we do it, we are playing Russian roulette with our children's future and running an increased risk that this will be the national security issue of the 21st century.

[*The discussion continued.*]

Closing Remarks

President Clinton. John, I would like to thank you, the law school, and NYU and the other sponsors of the event. Again, let me thank all of you who participated. And I want to thank Hillary and Sid Blumenthal and the others who conceived of this, and Mr. Blair's folks in Great Britain who worked so closely with us on this.

I would like to close with—ask for just a brief reprise of two things we talked about. One is, can this whole Third Way approach be ap-plied successfully to long-term problems that have big consequences before they have them, i.e., in American terms, Social Security, Medicare, climate change. Two is, can we not only develop a global consciousness and global policies within our respective country but actually band together to deal with this present global financial challenge in a way that gives us a trading system, a labor rights system, an environmental system, and a financial system that, in effect, recreates what works on the national level globally, that in effect takes these great 50-year-old institutions and does whatever has to be done to make sure that they see us through for the next 50 years.

Will the ideas that we've developed and the approach that we have developed work in those two great areas of challenge? Because if they do work in those two great areas of challenge, then I think that the 21st century is in very good hands.

Thank you very much.

NOTE: The President spoke at 4:42 p.m. in Greenberg Lounge at the New York University School of Law. In his remarks, he referred to James D. Wolfensohn, President, World Bank; Prime Minister Wim Kok of The Netherlands; and Ronald Dworkin, professor, New York University School of Law. The transcript released by the Office of the Press Secretary also included the opening remarks of Prime Minister Blair.

Statement on the Death of Florence Griffith-Joyner
September 21, 1998

Hillary and I are shocked and saddened by the sudden death of Florence Griffith-Joyner. America—and the world—has lost one of our greatest Olympians. Ten years ago, in a blazing 10.49 seconds, Flo-Jo sprinted to Olympic gold and earned the right to be called the "World's Fastest Woman." We were dazzled by her speed, humbled by her talent, and captivated by her style. Though she rose to the pinnacle of the world of sports, she never forgot where she came from, devoting time and resources to helping children—especially those growing up in our most disadvantaged neighborhoods—make the most of their own talents. I was very proud to have her serve as cochair of the President's Council on Physical Fitness and Sports. Our thoughts and prayers go to her husband, Al, her daughter, Mary, and her entire family.

Remarks During Discussions With Prime Minister Keizo Obuchi of Japan and an Exchange With Reporters in New York City
September 22, 1998

President Clinton. Let me say that I'm very sorry that the weather didn't permit us to go up to Tarrytown today, but I'm pleased to welcome Prime Minister Obuchi and his entire team here. I have also invited the Prime Minister to come back for an official visit early next year so that we can work very closely together on the challenges we face. The United States has no more important relationship in the world than our relationship with Japan, for common security concerns, to advance democracy and peace, and in our common economic endeavors.

So we just had a good hour-long meeting, and we're going to have a couple of other sessions today, and then early next year we'll have another meeting.

Prime Minister Obuchi. I am very pleased to have this opportunity of having a discussion with President Clinton extensively on my first visit to the United States since I became the Prime Minister of Japan.

This meeting of mine with the President I had earlier today brought home to me the importance of Japan and the United States working closely together. And although I am only 2 months in office and the President has experience—a wealth of experience of over 5½ years as President of the United States, we spoke in a very candid manner as if we knew from before. I think although this was the first time that we met in this kind of setting, we had a very substantive and important meeting.

Let me take this opportunity to thank President Clinton for, as he mentioned earlier, extending to me the invitation to visit the United States early next year. I think that visit of mine will provide a good opportunity to continue our discussion further. And I do hope to make it realized. Details, I will instruct our officials to work out with U.S. counterparts.

As we moved from the prior room to this room, we talked about the Third Way, but the path that we had in between two rooms were not enough to complete the subject. [*Laughter*] So I do hope to elaborate on that subject later on.

Response to Independent Counsel's Referral

Q. Mr. President, would you consider an appearance before the House Judiciary Committee in person, as some in Congress have suggested?

President Clinton. Mr. Plante [Bill Plante, CBS News], I don't have anything to add to whatever the White House is saying about all this today. I'm here working on a very important thing for the American people and for the Japanese people. We have to work together to restore growth to the world and to help our friends.

Yesterday I was here working on terrorism and how to make the global economy work for ordinary citizens. That's what I'm doing, and I don't have any contribution to make to that discussion beyond whatever the White House has said.

Q. Do you pay any attention to what's going on other than this? Do you pay any attention to what happened yesterday, to what the lawyers are doing, to any aspect of this?

President Clinton. Not much. Believe it or not, I haven't read the report or my lawyers' replies. I think it's important that I focus on what I'm doing for the American people, and that's what I intend to do.

Japanese Financial Reform

Q. Mr. President, are you encouraged from what you heard today that Japan will be able to deal with its fiscal problems in a swift way and adequately?

President Clinton. Well, I think, first of all, let's look at the facts here. Japan is a very great country with a strong, sophisticated economy and immensely talented people and, as in America now, an increasingly complicated political situation. That is, we have a Democratic President and a Republican majority in the Congress. They have their government, and in one house of their Diet an opposition with more members. So they have to work out what is politically possible.

I think there is virtually unanimous support in the world for the kind of financial reforms that would restore economic growth in Japan. The rest of us want to be encouraging. We want to do what we can to be supportive to help do whatever we can to create the climate which would permit a quick restoration of economic growth in Japan and therefore in Asia. That's what our objective is, is to understand that they have unique challenges but enormous strengths and to help find a way to get this done.

Q. Mr. Prime Minister, how optimistic or pessimistic are you about the prospects of getting reforms passed through your parliament?

Prime Minister Obuchi. I'm neither optimistic or pessimistic on this, but I think, as much as I do realize, many in Japan would realize, that this is not only an issue for Japan but something that has major implications on economies of Asia as well as the whole world.

I think steps we take in Japan to address the issue of financial system has very large implications worldwide. So I think with this understanding, I intend to make my very best effort at addressing this issue. I am convinced that we will be able to do something.

NOTE: The President spoke at 12:10 p.m. at the Waldorf Astoria Hotel. A tape was not available for verification of the content of these remarks.

Remarks During Discussions With Prime Minister Keizo Obuchi of Japan and an Exchange With Reporters in New York City
September 22, 1998

President Clinton. Thank you. I'd like to say to the members of the Japanese press, I'm sorry that you had to go all the way to Tarrytown and then come back. But at least you have seen it—we didn't even get to see it. [*Laughter*]

I want to welcome Prime Minister Obuchi and his team here. We have had very good meetings already today. The United States has no more important relationship in the world than our relationship with Japan. We are very interested in deepening our partnership in the security area, in the political area, and in doing what we can economically together to restore growth in the world and to stabilize the world financial situation. All these matters we have discussed today in a friendly and constructive atmosphere.

I just wanted to say one other thing. I invited Prime Minister Obuchi to come back to Washington early next year for an official visit, and he accepted, and I thank him for that.

Prime Minister Obuchi. All the strong and solid partnership between Japan and the United States could not lift this fog, and it is unfortunate that some of you had to go to Tarrytown and come back, and I'm sorry about that. But as the President said just now, I've been invited, and I've accepted his invitation to visit the United States in the early part of next year. And I look forward to meeting him again in Washington.

Legislative Agenda

Q. Mr. President, you've said how busy you are, but I just wonder if you haven't found some time to check with Congress about how things are going?

President Clinton. Well, we're just a few days away from the new budget year, and I'd say things need to go a little faster. We need an education bill; we need a health bill. We desperately need the IMF funding. They need to pass a good Patients' Bill of Rights. There's a lot left to be done. Things are not going fast enough to suit me on the people's business.

NOTE: The President spoke at 1:02 p.m. at the Waldorf Astoria Hotel. A tape was not available for verification of the content of these remarks.

Common Agenda: Illustration of the New United States-Japan Cooperation
September 22, 1998

Five years after the creation of the U.S.-Japan Common Agenda for Cooperation in Global Perspective, President Clinton and Prime Minister Obuchi recognized the valuable work accomplished by dedicated Japanese and American scientists, researchers and aid workers to fight diseases, preserve natural resources and exchange scientific data on various natural disasters and global climate change.

The participation of U.S. and Japanese private citizens, foundations and other nongovernmental organizations in projects of the Common Agenda will enhance the impacts of these projects. Their participation is also expected to generate grassroots public support. On September 23, 1998, U.S. and Japanese representatives of private-sector organizations (in Japan, the Common Agenda Roundtable) that support the Common Agenda will meet in Honolulu to discuss how they can assist in promoting the objectives of the Common Agenda.

The President and the Prime Minister welcome the first meeting of private sector representatives and made special mention of three projects:

1) The United States and Japan will work with the Government of Panama and nongovernmental partners to preserve the Panama Canal watershed by developing a program to focus on environmental education and the training of local nongovernmental organizations.

2) In light of the recent forest fires which affected Southeast Asia, The United States and Japan will support efforts to address the underlying causes of the fires and assist local governments to promote sustainable agriculture, forestry and land use.

3) The United States and Japan have been playing key roles in the success of efforts to eradicate polio worldwide. *However, significant challenges remain.* The two countries will strengthen their commitment to end the scourge of this disease through, among other steps, expanding cooperative eradication efforts by U.S. Peace Corps Volunteers and the Japan Overseas Cooperation Volunteers especially in African *countries, keeping in mind the importance of U.S.-Japan collaboration through TICADII (The Second Tokyo International Conference of African Development) to be held in October in Tokyo.*

NOTE: An original was not available for verification of the content of this joint statement.

Japan-United States Joint Statement on Cooperation in the Use of the Global Positioning System
September 22, 1998

On the basis of a series of discussions between representatives and experts of the Government of the United States and the Government of Japan, U.S. President William Clinton and Japanese Prime Minister Keizo Obuchi have issued this Joint Statement regarding cooperation in the use of the Global Positioning System (GPS) Standard Positioning Service for global positioning and other applications.

Background

GPS is a constellation of orbiting satellites operated by the United States, which provides signals to aid position-location, navigation, and precision timing for civil and military purposes. GPS, as an evolving system, is becoming more important for a wide variety of civilian, commercial, and scientific applications such as car navigation, mapping and land surveying, maritime shipping, and international air traffic management.

The United States Government is operating a maritime Differential Global Positioning System (DGPS), and the Government of Japan is operating a similar system. Both Governments are developing augmentation systems to support air navigation—the United States is developing the Wide Area Augmentation System (WAAS), and Japan is developing the Multi-functional Transport Satellite (MTSAT)-based Satellite Augmentation System (MSAS).

The commercial GPS equipment and services industries of the United States and Japan lead the world, and augmentation systems to enhance the use of the GPS Standard Positioning Service Could further expand civil, commercial, and scientific markets.

Building a Cooperative Relationship

The United States Government intends to continue to provide the GPS Standard Positioning Service for peaceful civil, commercial, and scientific use on a continuous, worldwide basis, free of direct user fees.

The Government of Japan intends to work closely with the United States to promote broad and effective use of the GPS Standard Positioning Service as a worldwide positioning, navigation, and timing standard. Both Governments are convinced of the need to prevent the misuse of GPS and its augmentation systems without unduly disrupting or degrading civilian uses, as well as of the need to prepare for emergency situations. Both Governments intend to cooperate to promote and facilitate civilian uses of GPS. It is anticipated that cooperation will:

- promote compatibility of operating standards for GPS technologies, equipment, and services;
- help develop effective approaches toward providing adequate radio frequency allocations for GPS and other radio navigation systems;
- identify potential barriers to the growth of commercial applications of GPS and appropriate preventative measures;
- encourage trade and investment in GPS equipment and services as a means of enhancing the information infrastructure of the Asia-Pacific region; and

- facilitate exchange of information on GPS-related matters of interest to both countries, such as enhancement of global positioning, navigation, and timing technologies and capabilities.

The two Governments intend to work together as appropriate on GPS-related issues that arise in the International Civil Aviation Organization, the International Maritime Organization, the International Telecommunication Union, and Asia Pacific Economic Cooperation, or in other international organizations or meetings.

Cooperative Mechanism

The Government of the United States and the Government of Japan have decided to establish a mechanism for bilateral cooperation relating to the use of the GPS Standard Positioning Service, as follows:

- A plenary meeting will be held annually to review and discuss matters of importance regarding the use of the GPS Standard Positioning Service.
- Working groups will be set up under the plenary meeting to discuss issues of mutual interest. Discussions will focus initially on commercial and scientific use and transportation safety, including measures to identify and report intentional and unintentional interference, the use of the GPS Standard Positioning Service in emergency situations, and an emergency notification system. Each working group will annually report to the plenary meeting the outcome of its work.

The two Governments share the expectation that this mechanism will help the two Governments identify ways to deal with GPS-related issues that may arise as civilian use of GPS increases, and take actions as appropriate.

NOTE: An original was not available for verification of the content of this joint statement.

Statement on Senate Action on Minimum Wage Legislation
September 22, 1998

I am disappointed that the Senate today voted not to raise the minimum wage. This increase, one dollar over the next 2 years, would have raised the wages of 12 million Americans and helped ensure that parents who work hard and play by the rules do not have to raise their children in poverty.

The last time we raised the minimum wage, we said it would help working families and not cost jobs. We have been proven correct. Since I signed that law, wages for all Americans are rising again. Our economy is the strongest in a generation, with more than 16.7 million new jobs since the beginning of this administration. Inflation is down, and unemployment has dropped to its lowest level in 28 years.

We value working families, and that is why we should raise the value of the minimum wage. I will continue the fight in Congress to do just that.

Letter to Congressional Leaders on Cyprus
September 22, 1998

Dear Mr. Speaker: (Dear Mr. Chairman:)

In accordance with Public Law 95–384 (22 U.S.C. 2373(c)), I submit to you this report on progress toward a negotiated settlement of the Cyprus question covering the period June 1 to July 31, 1998. The previous submission covered events during April to May 1998.

Landings of combat aircraft on Cyprus by Greece and Turkey in mid-July escalated tensions in the region and complicated efforts to reach a bizonal, bicommunal settlement on the island. Despite this, we intensified our efforts to restart the negotiating process. United States representatives underscored my concern with the leaders of both Cypriot communities as well as Greek and Turkish officials and urged all parties to concentrate on ways to take those steps that will lead to solving the Cyprus problem.

United Nations Secretary-General Kofi Annan issued two reports on the U.N. Peacekeeping Forces in Cyprus (UNFICYP) and the U.N. Mission of Good Offices in Cyprus (copies enclosed). Thereafter, the U.N. Security Council adopted two resolutions, one renewing the UNFICYP mandate for a 6-month period and another endorsing the Secretary-General's Good Offices Mission (copies enclosed).

Sincerely,

WILLIAM J. CLINTON

NOTE: Identical letters were sent to Newt Gingrich, Speaker of the House of Representatives, and Jesse Helms, chairman, Senate Committee on Foreign Relations.

Remarks at a Reception for African-American Religious Leaders
September 22, 1998

The President. Thank you very much. The Scripture says it's more blessed to give than to receive. I was sitting here thinking, in this case, I wish I were on the giving rather than the receiving end. It is difficult to absorb the depth and breadth of what I have heard and what you have given to me through the words of Reverend King and through your expression, and I thank you.

I thank you also for what you have given to our country. I thank the Members of Congress and the administration, the educators, the ministers, the Ambassadors, all of you who are here, and our friends from South Africa.

Hillary and I are delighted to have President Mandela and Graca here. We thank you, Graca, for your concern for the children who have been made victims of war by being impressed into combat as children and the scars they bear from it. And we thank you, Mr. President, for being the person we'd all like to be on our best day.

I would like you all to think for a few moments, before I bring President Mandela on, not about the terrible unjust sacrifice of his 27 years in prison but about what he's done with the years since he got out of prison, not about how he purged his heart of bitterness and anger while still a prisoner but how he resists every day the temptation to take it up again in the pettiness and meanness of human events. In some ways, that is all the more remarkable.

There have been many blessings for Hillary and for me, far outweighing all the trials, of being given the opportunity by the American people to serve in this position and live in this house. But certainly one of the greatest ones has been the friendship of this good man.

And I want to tell you one little story—I try never to betray any private conversations I have with anybody, but I want to tell you this. [*Laughter*] When President Mandela—once I was talking to him, and I said to him, "You know, I have listened carefully to everything you have said, to how you laid your anger and your bitterness down. But on the day you got out of prison, Hillary and I were living in Arkansas, in the Governor's Mansion; our daughter was a very young girl. I got her up early on a Sunday morning, and I sat her down on the counter in our kitchen, because we had an elevated television. And I said, 'Chelsea, I want you to watch this. This is one of the great events of your lifetime, and I want you to watch this.' "

And she watched President Mandela walk down that last road toward freedom, after all those years in prison. So I said to him one day, I said, "Now, tell me this. I know you invited your jailers to the inauguration, and I know how hard you've worked on this. But weren't you angry one more time when you were walking down that road?" He said, "Yes, briefly, I was." I don't know if he remembers this. He said, "Yes, briefly, I was. And then I remembered, I have waited so long for freedom. And if my anger goes with me out of this place, I will still be their prisoner, and I want to be free. I want to be free."

I say that to set the stage for what is now happening in Nelson Mandela's life. Yesterday we were at the United Nations, and he and I spoke back-to-back, and then we had this luncheon. And we were talking about the troubles in the Congo; we were talking about the continuing, almost compulsive destructiveness of the people there and all the countries outside trying to get into the act to make sure that whoever they don't like doesn't get a leg up. And we were lamenting the colossal waste of

human potential in that phenomenally rich country.

And I thought to myself, apartheid is gone in the law in South Africa, but it is still alive in the heart of nearly everybody on Earth in some way or another. And here is this man still giving of himself to try to take the apartheid out of the heart of the people of his continent and, indeed, the people of the world.

We were talking just before we came down about a mutual friend of ours who is the leader of a country, and how he had called and admonished him to try to work through a problem that he has had for too long. And so, I say—I have to say one thing that is slightly amusing about this. Now, President Mandela will probably get up here and make some crack about being an old man and how his time is running out and all that. The truth is he's leaving office because he feels like he's about 25 years old again. [*Laughter*] And he's so happily married he can't be troubled with all these boring affairs of politics. [*Laughter*] But I must say, it's the only time I've ever known him to misrepresent the facts, but that is, I'm sure, what is going on here.

But I ask you to think about that. Every time Nelson Mandela walks into a room we all feel a little bigger; we all want to stand up; we all want to cheer, because we'd like to be him on our best day. But what I would say to you is, there is a little bit of apartheid in everybody's heart. And in every gnarly, knotted, distorted situation in the world where people are kept from becoming the best they can be, there is an apartheid of the heart. And if we really honor this stunning sacrifice of 27 years, if we really rejoice in the infinite justice of seeing this man happily married in the autumn of his life, if we really are seeking some driven wisdom from the power of his example, it will be to do whatever we can, however we can, wherever we are, to take the apartheid out of our own and others' hearts.

Ladies and gentlemen, the President of South Africa.

[*At this point, President Nelson Mandela of South Africa made brief remarks.*]

President Clinton. I want to leave you on a high note here. [*Laughter*] I want to tell you a story that I never told the President. I have a friend who is a minister—a white minister who was in South Africa recently. And he was given the chance to meet the President, but he was told, "You'll have to go to the airport if you want to meet the President." He said, "I'll go anywhere to shake his hand." So he said, "I was standing off here waiting for him to come, and here comes the President across the lobby of the airport." And he said, "President Mandela walked up to this gorgeous little blond-haired, blue-eyed girl, about 6 years old." And my friend went up to hear the conversation.

And he said to the little girl, "Do you know who I am?" She said, "Yes, you're President Mandela." And he looked at her, and he said,

"If you study hard and learn a lot, you can grow up to be President of South Africa some day."

That's a lot to say after this life. Remember the point. God bless you all. Thank you.

NOTE: The President spoke at 6:30 p.m. in the East Room at the White House. In his remarks, he referred to President Mandela's wife, Graca Machel. The transcript released by the Office of the Press Secretary also included the remarks of President Mandela.

Remarks on Presenting the Congressional Gold Medal to President Nelson Mandela of South Africa
September 23, 1998

Thank you. Mr. Speaker, Senator Thurmond, Senator Daschle, Congressman Gephardt. Representative Houghton, thank you for what you have done to make this day come to pass. We are all in your debt. Congresswoman Waters, Senator Moseley-Braun, Senator D'Amato. Congressman Dellums, thank you. To the Members of Congress here present, in both parties; members of the Cabinet, administration; to Graca Machel and all our friends from South Africa who are here.

To my friend President Mandela, Americans as one today, across all the lines that divide us, pay tribute to your struggle, to your achievement, and to the inspiration you have given us to do better.

Others have said with profound conviction and eloquence what it is that we love and admire. Today we offer a man who has received the Nobel Prize the highest honor within the gift of this country. But if this day is to be more than a day in which we bask in his reflected glory, we should ask ourselves, what gift can we really give Nelson Mandela in return for 10,000 long days in jail? How can we truly redeem the life of Amy Biehl? How can we honor all of those who marched and worked with Nelson Mandela, who are no longer standing by his side?

After the President was released and began his public career, he said, and I quote, "The true test of our devotion to freedom is just

beginning." Whenever we are together, he always talks about unfinished business. He thanked me again yesterday for saying something that, to be honest, I didn't even think about consciously. He said that the United States had now said not what can we do for South Africa, but what can we do with South Africa to build a common future. So I ask all of you to think about just two or three things.

The work of our common struggle with people with whom we share a common past and with whom we must build a common future in South Africa and throughout the African Continent has only begun. President Mandela says that he has now gotten old and is leaving the scene. The truth is, he has gotten married, and he feels young, and he is tired of his public responsibilities, and he wants to go forward into a brighter life.

Those of us who share his vision and lift him up in honor today owe it to him to build a permanent partnership between Americans and Africans, for the education of our children, for the solution of our problems, for the resolution of our differences, for the elevation of what is best about us all. That is what we owe to Nelson Mandela, to Amy Biehl and her family, and to all of those who have sacrificed.

We also owe—for those 10,000 long days and the shining example since—the clear understanding that a man who has given up so much of his life can give us that even more important than the sacrifice yesterday is what you are doing with today and what you will do with tomorrow. For that is the thing that always humbles me when I am with Nelson Mandela, the sense of serenity and peace and engagement in the moment. And so I say to all of you, we should not waste our days; we should make more of our days. Mr. Mandela waited a very long time to actually do something for his people, rather than just to be something to keep their hearts and hopes alive. And every day I watch him, that is what he does. So should we.

And finally, in forgiving those who imprisoned him, he reminded us of the most fundamental lesson of all, that in the end apartheid was a defeat of the heart, the mind, the spirit. It was not just a structure outside and jailhouses within which people were kept; it was a division of the mind and soul against itself. We owe it to Nelson Mandela not simply to give him this award but to live by the lesson he taught us

and to tear down every last vestige of apartheid in our own hearts, everything that divides us, one from another.

For those of us who have been privileged to know this remarkable man, no medal, no award, no fortune, nothing we could give him could possibly compare to the gift he has given to us and to the world. The only gift that is true recompense is to continue his mission and to live by the power of his profound and wonderful example.

Now, as prescribed by the law, it is my privilege to present the Congressional Gold Medal to President Nelson Mandela.

Mr. President.

NOTE: The President spoke at 11:10 a.m. in the Rotunda at the Capitol. In his remarks, he referred to President Mandela's wife, Graca Machel. The transcript released by the Office of the Press Secretary also included the remarks of President Mandela.

Statement on the United Nations Security Council Resolution on Kosovo
September 23, 1998

Today's U.N. Security Council resolution makes absolutely clear that the international community is determined to see an end to the violence and repression in Kosovo. The resolution places responsibility squarely on President Milosevic to take the concrete steps necessary to prevent a major humanitarian disaster and restore peace in the region.

I am particularly encouraged that the resolution, adopted under Chapter VII of the U.N. Charter, makes clear that the deterioration of

the situation in Kosovo constitutes a threat to regional peace and security.

The United States and its allies are moving NATO activities from the planning stage to readiness to act. With more than 250,000 Kosovars displaced from their homes and cold weather coming, Milosevic must act immediately to heed the will of the international community.

NOTE: The statement referred to President Slobodan Milosevic of the Federal Republic of Yugoslavia (Serbia and Montenegro).

Message to the Congress on Continuation of the National Emergency With Respect to UNITA
September 23, 1998

To the Congress of the United States:

Section 202(d) of the National Emergencies Act (50 U.S.C. 1622(d)) provides for the automatic termination of a national emergency un-

less, prior to the anniversary date of its declaration, the President publishes in the *Federal Register* and transmits to the Congress a notice stating that the emergency is to continue in effect beyond the anniversary date. In accordance with this provision, I have sent the enclosed notice, stating that the emergency declared with respect to the National Union for the Total Independence of Angola ("UNITA") is to continue in effect beyond September 26, 1998, to the *Federal Register* for publication.

The circumstances that led to the declaration on September 26, 1993, of a national emergency have not been resolved. The actions and policies of UNITA pose a continuing unusual and extraordinary threat to the foreign policy of the United States. United Nations Security Council Resolutions 864 (1993), 1127 (1997), 1173 (1998), and 1176 (1998) continue to oblige all member states to maintain sanctions. Discontinuation of the sanctions would have a prejudicial effect on the Angolan peace process. For these reasons, I have determined that it is necessary to maintain in force the broad authorities necessary to apply economic pressure to UNITA to reduce its ability to pursue its aggressive policies of territorial acquisition.

WILLIAM J. CLINTON

The White House,
September 23, 1998.

NOTE: The notice is listed in Appendix D at the end of this volume.

Memorandum on the Presidential Design Awards Program
September 23, 1998

Memorandum for the Heads of Executive Departments and Agencies

Subject: Presidential Design Awards Program

The strength of our economy and quality of life in America owe much to the genius and creativity of designers. From using simple brick and mortar to developing sophisticated computers, designers have turned the dreams of the Nation into reality.

As the single largest purchaser of design services, the Federal Government has been a leader in fostering design excellence. Begun in 1983, the quadrennial Presidential Design Awards Program recognizes successful achievements in Federal design and promotes standards of excellence throughout the Federal Government. By this memorandum, I am pleased to announce the call for entries for the next round of awards. This round will include special Presidential Design Excellence Millennium Awards in recognition of Federal design projects that have made a significant contribution to the environment and quality of life of the Nation during this century.

The National Endowment for the Arts and the General Services Administration will implement the Presidential Design Awards Program. Please designate an individual with an appropriate background and position to serve as your liaison to ensure the success of this important program. Good design combines problem solving with cost-effectiveness and performance with beauty, and I urge all agencies to integrate good design into their programs.

WILLIAM J. CLINTON

Remarks at the Congressional Hispanic Caucus Institute Dinner
September 23, 1998

Audience members. Viva Clinton!
The President. Thank you.
Audience member. Twelve more years! [*Laughter*]
The President. That's for the guy that just left. [*Laughter*] Thank you.

Congressman Becerra, thank you so much for your remarks and for your truly outstanding leadership of the Hispanic Caucus. Thank you, Carmen Delgado Votaw, for your welcome. I thank all the Members of Congress and our administration and staff who are here for their service to our country. I thank you for that warm welcome, for being my friends, for standing with me on sunny days and in strong winds. But most of all, I thank you for being willing to fight for the America we want for our children in a new century.

Hurricane Georges

Before we begin, as the Vice President indicated, I would like to say just a word about Hurricane Georges. In Puerto Rico, the U.S. Virgin Islands, in Haiti, in the Dominican Republic, businesses and homes have been swept away and lives have been lost. Tonight our thoughts and prayers are with the victims of this terrible storm. Our FEMA Director, James Lee Witt, has told me that we are already assisting in the cleanup effort, and we are providing humanitarian aid in Haiti and the Dominican Republic. We are also helping the people of Florida to prepare for the hurricane, and Secretary Cuomo is leading a delegation to Puerto Rico. I thank him for that. We will be there every step of the way to help these communities and these people to rebuild.

Congressional Hispanic Caucus

I also want to join the Vice President in paying tribute to Henry B. Gonzalez and Esteban Torres. They are both friends of mine.

I first met Henry Gonzalez in 1972. I never will forget an evening I spent with him in the Menger Hotel in San Antonio, Texas, the weekend before the Presidential election, and about the only thing we had to enjoy was the mango ice cream they had served there for over 100 years. [Laughter] On the night before my election as President in 1992, we had a late-night rally in San Antonio; and thinking of that night so long ago—20 years ago then—I got $400 worth of mango ice cream for our campaign plane so that we could eat it with two reasons to be happy. And let me say that Henry B. Gonzalez has been a pioneer and a conscience for the Congress and the country. He has the heart of a lion, and we'll always be grateful to him.

From his days as a UAW shop steward to his days as chair of this caucus, Esteban Torres has fought tirelessly to make certain that economic growth benefits all working people and not only the people of this country but of Mexico as well. He has been a lion in the fight for a decent and better America. I will miss

him, very, very much. And I thank you, sir, for your service.

If I could just continue the appreciation for a minute, I want to thank the members of this caucus and their supporters for what has been done for America and what we have done together. Together we expanded the earned-income tax credit and cut taxes for 15 million hard-working families, including more than one million Hispanic families. And when the majority in Congress tried to slash it, together we said no.

Together we increased the minimum wage for 10 million Americans, including nearly 2 million Hispanics. And we are trying to increase it again for 12 million Americans. I'm very disappointed that yesterday over 95 percent of the Senate Republicans voted against it, but I haven't stopped fighting, and I don't think you have either. It is time to raise the minimum wage for people who need and deserve it.

Together we fought for and won the biggest increase in children's health care in more than 3 decades to insure up to 5 million uninsured children, almost all of them in low-income working families in America. We expanded the Head Start program and passed the family and medical leave law, to give millions of people a chance to take time off from work when a baby is born or a parent is sick.

Together we have opened the doors of higher education with the HOPE scholarship, more Pell grants, tax credits for all higher education, deductible student loans. Because of your efforts, everyone who is willing to work hard can now go to college without being afraid of being crushed by the burden of debt, and I thank you for that.

Together, under the leadership of the Vice President, we created more than 100 empowerment zones and enterprise communities, community development banks; we doubled small business loans to minorities, tripled them to women. Administrator Aida Alvarez is here, and she would want me to say that businesses owned and operated by Hispanic women are the fastest growing category of small business in America today.

Together we shaped and passed an historic crime bill to take guns off our streets, put police back on our streets, and provide more prevention to keep our children out of trouble in the first place.

Together we have built an America that has the lowest unemployment rate in 28 years, the lowest Hispanic unemployment rate in a generation, the fastest real wage growth in 20 years, a record number of new small businesses every year, the lowest crime rate in 25 years, the highest homeownership in the history of our country—and you did it. None of this could have been done without the Congressional Hispanic Caucus.

I thank the Vice President for mentioning those who serve and who have served in the Cabinet, in high administration positions, and in the White House. I thank you for all you have done as well.

Now, having said that, the real question before us this evening is, what shall we do with this moment of prosperity? What shall we do with this moment of opportunity? You know, a lot of people, when times get really good, tend to do one of two things, and I would argue both of them are wrong: one, just say, "Well, I've worked really hard. Times have been tough. I think I'll just relax for a few years"; or, two is to say, "Well, things are so good, nobody can mess it up. So I think I will just indulge myself in some diversion." As a country, we cannot do that.

I tell you tonight, my friends, that the challenge before us is, what do we do with this prosperity; what do we do with this confidence; what do we do with these good times? I feel very strongly that we need to say loud and clear that we believe that the time has come to thank God for our blessings and then to say we intend to use these blessings to meet the big challenges facing America that will shape the future of our children, and to go back and pick up those folks who have not participated in the benefits of the last 6 years and give them a chance to do it as well.

There was an old Mexican proverb that says, *"El que no siembra, no levanta"; "*he who does not sow, doesn't get a crop." It is time to sow the seeds of the future, to build the America we want for our children. We cannot afford to rest; we have work to do.

And what is that work? First, we cannot rest until we save Social Security for the 21st century. Now, what do I mean by that? Every person in this audience thrills whenever anyone refers to *mi familia.* Our family, our national family, is getting older; I ought to know. I am. I'm the oldest 52-year-old man in America.

[*Laughter*] I am the oldest of the baby boomers, all of you who are my age. When all of us are retired, there will only be about two people working in America for every one person drawing Social Security.

Now, we have three choices. We can do something now, modest but disciplined, to preserve this system into the future, with all of its benefits. Or we can do nothing until the crisis occurs, and we'll have two choices. Those of us who are older can expect our children to hike their taxes a lot and lower the standard of living of their children. Or we can just do without a lot of the benefits that have lifted half the seniors in America out of poverty today. I don't think either one of those is a very good choice.

In just a few days we will have the first balanced budget and surplus in 29 years. Now, I believe if we really care about our national family, we ought to stand up and say, "Look, we know it's just a few weeks before the election. We know there are those on the other side who say that we ought to have a tax cut right now based on projected surpluses into the future. And we know that's widely popular at election time. But we didn't get the lowest unemployment rate in 28 years and the first balanced budget and surplus in 29 years by doing what was popular today. We did it by doing what was right for the long run. And we'd like to at least see the ink turn from red to black, then dry a little bit, and save Social Security before we squander this surplus." That is what I believe we should do.

Second, we can't rest until all our kids in all our communities have a world-class education. Our budget, our balanced budget, provides for hiring 100,000 more teachers to lower average class size to 18 in the early grades. All the research shows that does more to help children learn and have permanent learning gains than anything else we can do.

It provides funds to build or repair 5,000 schools with kids—the largest they've ever been in our classroom—the largest number of students. It provides funds to hook up all of our classrooms to the Internet, not just those of the wealthiest school districts.

It provides funds to reward school districts who undertake sweeping reforms like Chicago has. In Chicago today, the summer school—the summer school—is the sixth biggest school district in America. Over 40,000 children every day during the school year get three square meals at school. Yes, have high standards; yes, end social promotion; but for goodness sakes, do something for those kids that deserve a better shot and need more help to succeed in life.

And our budget provides funds to hire 35,000 teachers to go into troubled inner-city and other isolated neighborhoods by saying to the brightest young people, we'll pay your way to college if you'll teach off the cost by going into those tough neighborhoods and giving those kids a world-class education.

No community in America has a bigger stake in this than the Hispanic community. That's why I established an advisory commission on educational excellence for Hispanics, and why I have proposed a special $600 million Hispanic education action plan to transform schools with high dropout rates, to support Hispanic colleges, to help adults who want to learn English or get a high school diploma, to help all Latinos, young and old, to reach their dreams.

And you and I know, yes, our children must master English. That's why I fought for a 35 percent increase in bilingual education, to help 1,000 school districts improve teacher training and add extra classes for students who haven't yet mastered English. You know, when people go around and tell me all about the failures of bilingual education, I say, "Well, look at the number of school districts who have so many more children whose first language is not English that don't have any teachers who have been certified to teach them English." Let's solve the problem instead of making it a political issue. The Hispanic action education plan would help to train 20,000 teachers to help children with limited English.

This is not just a Hispanic problem anymore. Just across the river here in Fairfax County, there are children from 150 different national and ethnic groups. Being able to speak more than one language is a gift that more of us need. But in America, unless one of those languages is English, our children can never reach their full potential. This is not the subject of a divisive political battle. Let's look at the facts, put our children before our politics, and do what's right for the country, and actually give people the chance to speak this language.

Let me also say we can't rest, with 160 million Americans in managed care plans, until we pass a strong, enforceable Patients' Bill of Rights that says doctors ought to make medical decisions, not accountants.

Think of this. Don't you believe whatever your health plan is that you ought to have the right to see a specialist if you need it? If you walk out of this banquet tonight and—God forbid—you get hit by a car, don't you think they ought to take you to the closest emergency room, not one halfway across town that happens to be covered by your plan?

Those of you who are older, remember what it was like when a child was first born into your family? How would you feel if, because the mother or the father is in a plan covered by a small business, if the small business changes health plans and you're 6 months pregnant, or your wife is 6 months pregnant? I think you ought to be able to keep the same doctor until the baby is born. But that's not what plans provide today. I think that ought to be a right.

If you've ever had anybody in your family in chemotherapy treatment, it's pretty tough. I've been there; a lot of you have. You try to make jokes about whether your hair is going to fall out. You try to deal with people when they get sick to their stomach and they can't eat. Nobody ought to have to worry, in addition to that, about whether in the middle of the chemotherapy treatment somebody is going to send you a letter in the mail and say, "I'm sorry, you've got to change doctors. You've got to do it all over again. You've got to start all over again." That is wrong. That is wrong, and we ought to stop it. That's—we ought not to rest until we do.

We ought not to rest while any of our communities are still segregated by income or race. The Government should lead the way in word and deed. I've asked Secretary Cuomo to crack down on unfair housing practices, to double the number of housing discrimination cases, to work with you to undertake a major legislative overhaul so public housing will help to deconcentrate poverty, mix incomes, and thereby mix people of all races and ethnicities. We can't live together as one nation unless we're able to live together in our own communities. And I ask you to help me work together on this.

We can't rest until every neighborhood can reap the benefits of our economic growth. That's why we should fund the empowerment initiatives the Vice President and Secretary Cuomo

have worked so hard for, to get more investment, more jobs, and more opportunity into the
neighborhoods which still have unemployment
rates that are too high and incomes that are
too low. We can do it now. If we can't do
it now, with unemployment rates so low, when
will we ever be able to do it? We should not
walk away from this session of Congress without
that empowerment agenda.

We should be proud that we have the lowest
welfare rolls in 29 years, that we made good
on our promise to restore some benefits to legal
immigrants. But there is much more to be done.
The pressures to move from welfare to work
are intense, and the transition can be especially
difficult for Hispanic women who lack language
or job skills. I want to make sure every individual has the tools to succeed in this transition.
That's why we fought for a welfare-to-work fund
in the balanced budget, to help people make
it; for $50 million more for transportation for
people who don't have cars. And that's why I
have proposed in my balanced budget a $21
billion child care initiative to add to what we
fought for in the welfare bill. Nobody should
have to give up being a good parent to succeed
in the workplace.

And we cannot rest until we do have an accurate census count. I just want to make sure
everybody in this room understands the importance of that. Some in Congress would have
us ignore the best scientific methods for ensuring the most accurate count—that is, methods
that Republican as well as Democratic experts
say is the best way to make sure everybody
gets counted. I don't know why some people
are afraid of having all Americans counted—
counted in the drawing of congressional districts,
counted in the delivery of Federal aid funds.
In 1990, 5 percent of our Hispanic citizens were
not counted. Nearly 70—listen to this—nearly
70,000 Hispanic children in Los Angeles County
alone were left out. Now, we can do better
than that. This is a fundamental issue. This is
a civil rights issue. If you believe every American counts, don't you also believe we have to
count every American?

And while we're at it, once again I call upon
the Congress to give the 4 million people of
Puerto Rico the right to choose their own status.
It is important. Now, in December the Puerto
Rican people go to the polls. The Republican
leaders of the Senate say, and I quote, they
will "consider" the results of the referendum.

I say, I will respect the results of the referendum.

Now, we cannot rest until we keep economic
growth going throughout the world, until we
contain all this trouble our friends in Russia
and Asia are experiencing, until we do everything we can to keep it from spreading to Latin
America, which has been threatened by global
financial events that they had nothing to do with
creating. This is in our interests. The Latin markets are our fastest growing ones. They are the
people that are doing more every year to buy
American products as we build closer ties.

I have spent a lot of time on Latin America.
Hillary has gone to Latin America several times
and is about to go again. We always believed
that in the future of America, not only would
Hispanic-Americans become our largest minority
but Latin America would become our closest
partners for democracy as well as for prosperity.

Now, when you see all this debate in the
paper about the IMF, that's really what that's
about. The International Monetary Fund is a
way that we work with other people to help
countries that are doing the right thing get back
on their feet and to try to stem and limit this
economic turmoil. I ask your help in that. We
need to do it for the benefit of our own people,
as well as for our obligation.

Finally, let me say we cannot rest until we
continue to work to bring America together
across racial and ethnic lines. Last week, for
the final time, I met with my Advisory Board
on Race and received their report. Again, I say
to you this is not a black/white issue; this is
not even a black/white/brown issue. America is
becoming ever more diverse, and it is our great,
great asset as we move toward a new century
in what is not only a global economy but increasingly a global society, where we face the
same opportunities and the same dangers. We
have got to learn to stop using our racial and
ethnic differences as wedge issues in political
campaigns and start lifting them up as money
in the bank for 21st century America.

I see General McCaffrey out there, our drug
czar. You know, we had a meeting the other
day with the new Colombian President, a man
who has actually had his own life imperiled for
standing up against narcotrafficking. No children
anywhere have an interest in anything other
than doing everything we can to keep them
away from the dangers of drugs. No children,

without regard to race or income, have an interest in anything other than an America which educates all our children. No people anywhere in this country have an interest in anything other than an America which guarantees quality health care to all of our kids and gives every working family the dignity of knowing that if they work hard and obey the law, at least they should not live in poverty. That is the kind of America we have to build.

And let me say that immigration has been and will be an important part of that process. It is not only good for America; it is America. And I say to you, we must continue to welcome new immigrants, to encourage them to become a full part of American society, and to help them become citizens and voting citizens, not stand in their way when they seek to do it.

So I say to you, you have been very kind to me tonight. You were enthusiastic. You cheered. You were happy. I had a temptation to throw this speech away and give you an old whoop-de-do—[*laughter*]—even though I'm not running anymore for anything. But I decided it was the wrong thing to do because you need to know what is really at stake, what is really going on, what really should bring you here.

In a few weeks, all of you and all our fellow citizens will be given a chance to go to the polls in November and choose what to do with this moment. Will it be partisanship or progress? Will it be about people or politics? Will we squander the moment or seize it? That is the decision before us. And as happy as I am and grateful for the reception you gave me, that's not what this is about. It's about you and your children and all the people out there all over this country. That's what this is about.

Thirty years ago, Robert Kennedy traveled to California to see a prostrate Cesar Chavez, who was fasting in penance, bedridden, for the violence caused by the struggle for farm workers' rights. That night they broke bread together in a Thanksgiving mass, and someone read the words Chavez was too weak to speak, words

I would like to share with you tonight as I leave. Here is what he said: "Our lives are all that really belong to us, so it is how we use our lives that determines what kind of people we are." He said later that that night was the night Robert Kennedy made up his mind to run for President and, ultimately, to give his life for many of the causes for which we struggle today.

My friends, you and I are bound by a commitment to fulfill the legacy of this country's history, to deepen the meaning of our freedom, to widen the circle of opportunity, to strengthen the bonds of our community, and to stand against all those and all the forces that would divide us, demean us, or hold us back. Most everybody here has a magnificent American story. Most everybody here can look back on parents and grandparents and great-grandparents of whom you are immensely proud but who overcame unimaginable odds and braved great sacrifices so that one day their children or their children's children could put on the clothes we wear tonight and come to a banquet like this tonight and be grateful to them for what they did for us.

Once in a generation, a country is in the position we find ourselves in tonight. With this kind of success, this kind of prosperity, this kind of confidence, this kind of opportunity to lead in the world, we cannot rest; we cannot indulge ourselves. We have work to do. We have work to do so that when our children and our children's children reach their maturity, they will know that we did what was right in this time, and we listened to the words of Cesar Chavez.

God bless you, and thank you so much.

NOTE: The President spoke at 7:59 p.m. in the International Ballroom at the Washington Hilton. In his remarks, he referred to Carmen Delgado Votaw, vice chair, Congressional Hispanic Caucus Institute; and President Andres Pastrana of Colombia.

Remarks on the Census Bureau Report on Income and Poverty and an Exchange With Reporters
September 24, 1998

The President. Thank you very much. She was terrific, wasn't she? Let's give her another hand. I thought she was great. [*Applause*]

Congressman Cardin, welcome. I know you're proud of your constituent here. Jessica, welcome. We're glad to see you. I think Congressman Blagojevich is here. We welcome him, along with Senator Efrain Gonzalez, who is the president of National Hispanic Caucus of State Legislators, and Councilman Robert Cantana of Buffalo. Let me once again thank Monique for her remarkable statement and her even more remarkable life.

I'm delighted to be joined here by our economic team—by Erskine Bowles and Secretary Rubin, Secretary Herman, Gene Sperling, Jack Lew, Janet Yellen, Larry Summers. Their tireless, often literally sleepless work has been very instrumental in sparking and maintaining what soon will be the longest peacetime boom in American history.

Officials of the Census Bureau who are here today, I want to thank all of you. We're going to be talking a little bit about some Census Bureau statistics. Sometimes we take your hard work and statistics for granted. The fact is that you ensure that our democracy is truly representative. And let me say in that connection once again, Congress must not hamstring the Census Bureau's efforts to maintain the most up-to-date, accurate scientific methods to produce the year 2000 census. They deserve the chance to succeed. Monique Miskimon has shown us today once again that every American counts. That means every American deserves to be counted.

Hurricane Georges

Now, before I get into the details of the very positive economic report which Monique and her daughter so vividly represent, I think we all want to say just a few words and reflect on the powerful impact of Hurricane Georges. In the Caribbean islands, businesses and homes have been swept away; tragically, many lives have been lost. Meanwhile, the projected track of the storm places the hurricane center over or near the Florida Keys late tonight or early tomorrow morning. As we speak, we're helping the people of Florida prepare for the hurricane. We've already sent assistance to Haiti and the Dominican Republic. Obviously, we're working with the officials in Puerto Rico and the Virgin Islands.

James Lee Witt, the Director of the Federal Emergency Management Agency, has informed me that FEMA's Region VI emergency response team arrived in Tallahassee, Florida, at 10 o'clock this morning. Here in Washington, the FEMA emergency support team is operating at level one, its highest level, on a 24-hour basis.

Our support teams and our prayers are with those in the Caribbean as they begin to rebuild and those in the Florida Keys as they brace for the impact of the storm.

Income and Poverty Report

Now, as President, from my first day here, I have done my best to fulfill a commitment I made to the American people: first of all, to restore the reality of the American dream, of opportunity for all responsible citizens, of a community in which we all count and work together; and secondly, to reclaim the future for our children, to strengthen our country for the century ahead.

To accomplish that mission, we began first with an economic strategy to shrink the deficit and balance the budget, to invest in the education and skills of our people, and to expand the export of American goods. The census report released this morning represents one more year's worth of compelling evidence that this economic strategy is working and that there are lots more people out there like Monique Miskimon.

The report shows that last year the income of the typical American household grew at nearly twice the rate of inflation. Since we launched our economic plan in 1993, the typical family's real income has risen by more than $3,500. That's an extra $3,500 that hardworking families can put toward their children's education or a downpayment on a first home. Income for typical African-American and Hispanic families increased by more than $1,000 last year alone.

This report also shows that our growing economy is giving more and more families a chance to work their way out of poverty. The poverty rate fell to 13.3 percent, and while we still have plenty of room for improvement, the African-American poverty rate fell to another record low. Hispanic poverty saw the largest one-year drop in two decades. Child poverty has dropped in the past 4 years, more than in any 4-year period in the last three decades. And the earned- income tax credit, which Monique spoke of a moment ago, has raised more than 4 million people out of poverty in the last year alone.

The report this morning shows that economic growth continues to raise incomes, lift millions out of poverty, and extend opportunity. It also shows that we have more to do. Since 1993, every income group has benefited from our Nation's economic growth, and the lowest 20 percent of our people in terms of income have had the highest percentage increases. That's the good news, after over 20 years of increasing inequality.

But that inequality is still too high, and it simply means there are too many American families out there working hard, doing everything we could possibly ask of them, and still having a hard time getting ahead. We have to use our prosperity and the confidence that it inspires to help our hardest pressed families and our hardest pressed communities to ensure economic growth for all Americans.

The most important thing we have to do, of course, is to maintain the economic strategy that got us here in the first place, above all, the strict fiscal discipline that has given us low interest rates, low inflation, big investments, and more jobs.

Exactly a week from today, we will have the first balanced budget and surplus since Neil Armstrong walked on the Moon in 1969. Unfortunately, this week in the House of Representatives, the Republicans are moving forward with a proposal that drains the new surplus to pay for their tax plan. We can cut taxes. Indeed, my balanced budget includes targeted tax cuts for child care, for education, for environmental cleanup. But tax cuts must be paid for in full if we are to expand opportunity in the years to come.

I say again, we have been waiting for 29 years to see the red ink turn to black. We have a huge baby boom challenge coming when all the baby boomers retire. Social Security, as presently constituted, cannot sustain that retirement. We have to reform Social Security if we want to have it for our parents—that's me, when the baby boomers retire—without undermining the standard of living of our children and grandchildren.

So I say again, let us not get into this surplus we have worked for 29 years for—or we've waited for 29 years for and worked for 6 years for. Let's don't get into that and spend it in an election year tax cut until we have saved Social Security for the 21st century, for the sake of our children and our grandchildren.

Second, we have to continue to invest in our people and lift them all up. I was deeply disappointed this week when 95 percent of the Republicans in the Senate voted not to raise the minimum wage. To reject an increase in the minimum wage when there are still so many people working full-time and raising children in poverty, when the unemployment rate and the inflation rate is so low, I believe is a mistake and sends the wrong signal to the American people.

I thank the 95 percent of the Democratic caucus in the Senate who voted for the increase in the minimum wage. Working Americans deserve it. I'm disappointed, with only a week left in the fiscal year, we rejected this, and I haven't quit fighting for it. I think eventually we will get it in the next several months. If we have to wait until next year, we will get it.

But I'm also disappointed—as I said, a week from today we end the fiscal year, and we start a new one. And there's still been no action in the Congress on our vital education investments. Indeed, what action there has been in the House of Representatives has been negative, has been a setback for education.

Congress should work with us to enact my plan, paid for in the balanced budget, to reduce class size to an average of 18 in the early grades; to hire 100,000 teachers to teach those children in smaller classes; to rebuild or to construct or repair 5,000 schools so our kids will have good, adequate, safe schools to attend; to hook up all of our classrooms—all of them, even in the poorest neighborhoods—to the Internet by the year 2000; to improve early literacy by funding the program to send volunteers in to make sure that every 8-year-old can read; to lift our children's sights with voluntary national standards and clear means of measuring them.

Now, if we hope to maintain our economic growth well into the next generation, we have to give every American child a world-class elementary and secondary education. So I say again: We've been here for months and months; there's just a week left in the budget year; let's finally have action to improve our public schools and give all of our kids a world-class education.

The third thing I'd like to say is we have to continue to lead in the global economy if we want the American economy to continue to grow. We're enjoying unsurpassed economic prosperity, but all of you read the papers every day. You see the news at night. You know there are troubles elsewhere in the world. You know our friends in Asia and Russia are facing great turmoil. You know we're trying to keep our big trading partners and friends in Latin America from having the negative effect of that turmoil reach them, even though they are pursuing good policies. That's why it's important for Congress to fund our America's share of the International Monetary Fund, because the International Monetary Fund helps the countries that are helping themselves to return to growth and serves as an insurance policy against having the financial crisis spread to the countries that are doing the right thing and keeping Americans at work by buying our products.

Again I say, there is no reason not to do this. We've only got a week left in the budget year. We've been talking about it all year long. The problem has only gotten worse. It is time now to say, we're doing this because it's what America owes as the world leader, and more importantly, we're doing it because it is absolutely necessary to keep American economic growth going.

Finally, let me say that with just a week left in this budget year, I'd still like to see the Congress pass a decent Patients' Bill of Rights, one that covers—[*applause*]. Our bill would provide protections to all Americans, simple ones: If you get in an accident, you can go to the nearest emergency room, not be hauled to one halfway across town. If your doctor tells you you need to see a specialist, you can see one. If it comes down to a dispute about whether a medical procedure should or should not be applied, the decision should be made by a doctor, not an accountant. Your medical records ought to be protected in privacy. If your employer changes health care providers, it shouldn't affect you if you happen to be in the middle of a pregnancy or a chemotherapy treatment or some other thing that would be entirely disruptive and dangerous and damaging to your health care if you had to change doctors in the middle of the procedure.

Now, we do that for everyone. The House passed a bill on a partisan vote, completely party-line vote, that doesn't protect 100 million people and doesn't provide any of those protections to the people that are covered. The Senate majority leader actually shut down business in the Senate a few days ago to keep them from voting for it, so they wouldn't be recorded—they wouldn't be recorded as killing the Patients' Bill of Rights—but they could kill it and still satisfy the insurance companies that are doing their best to do it.

There's still time. We haven't broken for the election yet. We can still do the right thing by the American people. But we have to think about it. We have to focus on it, and we have to put our priorities where they ought to be. I think it's worth fighting for the Patients' Bill of Rights in the closing days of this congressional session.

Again, I want to thank the economic team here and our supporters in the Congress, including those who are here today, for giving more Americans a chance to live the story that Monique has told us about. I want to thank her for coming today and bringing her beautiful daughter. I know we all wish them well.

Our prayers are with the people who are about to be affected and those who have been affected by the hurricane. And I ask that all of us focus on using these last days of this congressional session to think about the American people, to think about our responsibilities, to think about what got us here over the last 6 years, and instead of departing from it, to bear down and build on it. That is my goal, and that's what we ought to do.

Thank you very much. Thank you.

Possibility of Impeachment Inquiry

Q. Mr. President, do you see any way out of an impeachment inquiry?

The President. Well, let me answer you this way: The right thing to do is for us all to focus on what's best for the American people. And the right thing for me to do is what I'm doing. I'm working on leading our country, and I'm working on healing my family.

And if you look at what we announced today, what does it tell you? It proves, number one, that the course we have followed has been the right course for America. That's what it proves. After 6 years, it can't be an accident anymore.

But the second thing it proves is that it is utterly foolish for people to be diverted or distracted from the urgent challenges still before us. I told you that we had a record—a record low in African-American unemployment and poverty; a record low in the poverty rate for children, of African-American children. Do you know what that record low is? It's about 39 percent. In other words, it's breathtakingly high. That's just one statistic.

So what does that tell me? It tells me that the right thing to do is, if we all put progress over partisanship, put people over politics, put the American people first—what would we do? Well, we would keep the budget balanced. We would save Social Security before we squandered the surplus. We would improve our schools. We would clean up our environment. We would pass the Patients' Bill of Rights. And we would keep the economy going. That's what we would be focused on. That's what I am focused on. That's the way out.

The way out here—and the only way out is for people in Washington to do what the folks in America want them to do, which is to take care of their concerns, their children, and their future. That's what I mean to do, and I'm going to do my best.

NOTE: The President spoke at 12:20 p.m. in the Rose Garden at the White House. In his remarks, he referred to Monique Miskimon, administrative assistant, Maryland Committee for Children, Inc., who introduced the President, and her daughter, Jessica; and State Senator Efrain Gonzalez, Jr., of New York, president, National Hispanic Caucus of State Legislators.

Statement on the Census Bureau Report on Income and Poverty
September 24, 1998

This morning the Census Bureau released its annual report on income and poverty. The report shows that our growing economy continues to raise incomes, lift millions out of poverty, and extend opportunity. It represents further evidence that we must maintain fiscal responsibility, investments in our people, and our global leadership on matters of finance and trade.

Last year the income of the typical American household grew by nearly twice the rate of inflation. Since we launched our economic plan in 1993, the typical family's income has risen by more than $3,500. The overall poverty rate fell to 13.3 percent. And while there is clearly more to be done, the African-American poverty rate fell to another record low; Hispanic poverty saw the largest one-year drop in two decades. Child poverty has dropped more in the past 4 years than any 4-year period in nearly 30 years; and the earned-income tax credit, which we have dramatically expanded and fought hard to preserve, raised more than 4 million people out of poverty last year.

All Americans have a right to be proud of these gains. But we can't let these good times lull us into complacency. We must work even harder to make sure that as our Nation races forward, we give everyone a chance to come along.

Statement on the Anniversaries of the Comprehensive Test Ban Treaty and the Limited Test Ban Treaty
September 24, 1998

Two years ago today, I was proud to be the first world leader to sign the Comprehensive Test Ban Treaty—first proposed by President Eisenhower over 40 years ago. Since then, 150 states have signed this historic treaty, including all of our NATO Allies, Russia, China, Israel, Japan, and South Korea. Twenty states already have ratified the CTBT, including Britain, France, Germany, Australia, and Brazil. It is my strong hope that India and Pakistan will join the list and thereby reduce nuclear tensions in South Asia. I discussed this with Prime Minister Sharif on Monday, and I welcome his commitment yesterday to adhere to the treaty by next fall. I look forward to further discussion with the leaders of Pakistan and India as we emphasize our common obligation to build peace and stability.

Today also marks the 35th anniversary of the Senate bipartisan vote, 80–19, to approve the Limited Test Ban Treaty, which President Kennedy considered his greatest accomplishment as President. In 1963, Senate approval of the LTBT took place less than 2 months after it was signed and within 7 weeks of its submission to the Senate. Contrast that with the CTBT. A year after it was submitted, the Senate has yet to take any action toward ratification.

The CTBT will ban all nuclear weapons explosions. As a result, it will constrain the development of more sophisticated and powerful nuclear weapons and give us a powerful new tool in the fight against the proliferation of weapons of mass destruction. The American people understand that Senate approval of the CTBT is the right thing to do. I strongly urge the Senate to give its advice and consent as early as possible next year.

NOTE: The statement referred to Prime Minister Nawaz Sharif of Pakistan.

Statement on House Action on Temporary Visas for Highly Skilled Immigrants
September 24, 1998

I am pleased that the House of Representatives has moved quickly to pass a bipartisan compromise to address a shortage of skilled workers, while providing new training and protections for U.S. workers. To address that shortage and maintain America's competitive edge, we must give U.S. workers new opportunities to train and to learn new skills. This legislation helps us meet that challenge by providing up to $250 million over 3 years in new funding to educate and train Americans for the jobs of the future.

This compromise institutes new reforms to ensure that employers do not replace U.S. workers with temporary foreign workers and requires employers to recruit U.S. workers. In short, it contains new investments in training, tougher enforcement, and new protections for U.S. workers. I look forward to Congress sending me a bill that is consistent with our bipartisan agreement.

Remarks at a Democratic National Committee Reception
September 24, 1998

Thank you very much. Ladies and gentlemen, first of all, I don't know if you can feel it, but I'm even happier to see you than you are to be here. [*Laughter*] I want to say—you remember that famous quote attributed to Harry Truman, "If you want a friend in Washington, get a dog"? [*Laughter*] Well, I got a dog, and I love him very much, but I'm glad to have you in the White House here tonight. I feel that I have friends here.

I want to thank all the previous speakers. I thank Maria Echaveste and John Podesta for the magnificent work they do for you and the American people every day. I thank Steve Grossman and Roy Romer for taking over our party at what was a financially perilous time, bringing us back to health, and helping to set up the organization, the structure, and the effort that has led to this incredibly talented and diverse array of people being here tonight representing the Democratic Party from every corner of our land.

I want to thank the Vice President. I've said this many times—the historians may argue about whether they agree with what I have done or not—there is one fact about our administration that is absolutely beyond any historical argument. The Vice President of the United States has had more influence over more decisions in more areas of our life and done more good by far than any person who has ever held that position in the history of the United States.

I want to thank Congresswoman Sheila Jackson Lee from Houston for being here and for being a stalwart supporter of our programs and initiatives. She's a great leader. I, too, join in thanking John Sweeney and all the members of the labor movement who are here for the incredible energy and direction and drive they have given to their movement and to our country.

I know we have a number of mayors here. I think Mayor Hammer from San Jose and Mayor Pastrick from East Chicago are here. If there are any other mayors who are here, I'm sorry I didn't call your name, but I love you anyway. [*Laughter*]

Let me say, you all know why we're here, but I would like to set the stage here. I, too, thank you for your role in what we have been able to do. Next week will mark the seventh anniversary—I can't believe this—the seventh anniversary of the day I announced my candidacy for President, October 3, 1991. Now, I said then that I was running because I wanted America to have a mission and a vision for the 21st century, to preserve the American dream, to restore the hopes of the forgotten middle class, to reclaim the future for our children. Even then I did not know that 7 years later, through two long elections and various trials and tribulations, I would be able to say that we have the lowest unemployment rate in 28 years, the lowest crime rate in 25 years, the smallest percentage of our people on welfare in 29 years, next week the first balanced budget and surplus in 29 years; that we would, with the HOPE scholarship, tax credits for all higher education, deductibility of student loans, more Pell grants, we would have opened the doors of college education to all Americans; that we would have protected the environment, passed the Brady bill, almost finished putting our 100,000 police on the street, the family and medical leave law, the Kennedy-Kassebaum bill; that we'd have cleaner water, cleaner air, safer food, fewer toxic waste dumps. That's all to the good, and I am very, very grateful for the chance to have served, for the chance that Hillary and I have had to live here and work. And by the way, she's out on the trail tonight and wishes she could be here, as has already been said.

But I want to say to you also, you're here to look to the future, because the real question is, what are we going to do with this moment we have; what shall we do with this moment of prosperity and confidence?

The people in the other party believe they're going to whip us with M&M's in this election. [*Laughter*] That stands for money. They've got a lot of it. If you kill the legislation designed to protect our kids from the dangers of tobacco and you kill campaign finance reform, you can get yourself a good chunk of change. And they'll have more money than we do, even though we're working hard to close the gap.

The other thing they'll have is midterms. Why should midterms matter? Because they think, "Well, our people will feel good, but they'll be complacent." And our people don't make as much money, don't have as much free time, have to go to more trouble to vote. And normally, we Democrats get a much bigger vote during Presidential elections than we do in these off-year elections.

Now, our enemy is not adversity. Adversity is our friend. Our enemy is complacency. And so I say to you: I'm glad you're here; I'm glad you cheered me; I'm glad you're having a good time. But I want you to be serious just for a minute. You've heard what they've all said. What have we done since January, when I have pleaded for the chance to work with the Republicans to build this country for the 21st century, when I have said, "Why should education be a partisan issue; why should the Patients' Bill of Rights be a partisan issue?" People show up in the emergency room—you don't have to show your party registration.

How can the environment be a partisan issue? We all breathe the same air and drink the same water. How can keeping our economic growth going by preventing this financial contagion that's engulfing so much of the rest of the world from hitting any more countries that are our trading partners, or from eventually biting us—how can that possibly be a partisan issue? Shoot, I bet Republicans have made even more money than Democrats have out of me being President. [*Laughter*] How can that be a partisan issue?

How can saving Social Security before we just go out and start spending the surplus to make votes with a tax cut in an election year be a partisan issue? We've been waiting for 29 years; I've been working for 6 years on this. I told you we'd get rid of it. And now, before the red ink turns to black and dries, they want to start spending the money again. And you know and I know when the baby boomers retire, there will only be two people working for every one person drawing Social Security, if all the present trends continue.

Now, this is a big deal. Half the people on Social Security today have been lifted out of poverty because of Social Security. Now, we don't have to do anything about it, we can go ahead and run it in the ditch if you want to. And when we do, we'll have two choices: We can either tax our children to pay for our retirement and undermine their ability to raise our grandchildren; or we can decide we can't possibly do that, and we can slash benefits hugely and have a lot of elderly people living in poverty again. Or we can say, "I don't care if it's just a few weeks before the election; I've been waiting 29 years for a balanced budget. We're going to have a surplus now, and before we spend it on indulgences or even things we need for ourselves, we ought to save Social Security and avoid those bad alternatives."

Now, that's what this is about. So—I'm just telling you: They've got money; they've got midterms. But we have the issues. And you need to go home and ask people a simple question: "Do you like where we are? Are we better off than we were 6 years ago?" And they'll say yes. "Do you really believe we've met the long-term challenges of the country? Do you think there's nothing left to be done?" And they'll say no. And then you can say, "You can choose partisanship, or you can choose progress. You can choose power, or you can choose people. You can choose politics, or you can choose principle. But if you stay home, you're choosing all the wrong things. You can't stay home." We need to go out and say, "Look, we stand for saving Social Security for the 21st century. We're not against tax cuts in the President's

budget. There are tax cuts for child care, for education, for the environment. But they're all paid for."

We stand for taking average class sizes down to 18, and putting—in the early grades—and putting 100,000 teachers out there. We stand for higher standards, and we stand for stopping social promotion. But we don't want to hurt kids, so we want every child who needs it to be able to have an after-school program and a summer school program. And we want to pay the college expenses of 35,000 bright young people and let them pay off all that money by going into the inner cities and teaching and helping our children and lifting them up. That's what we stand for. We stand for building or repairing 5,000 schools. We stand for hooking every classroom in the country, not just the wealthiest ones, up to the Internet. That's what we stand for.

And we stand for a Patients' Bill of Rights that affects everybody, without regard to their partisan affiliation. If you walked out of here tonight and you got hit by a car, wouldn't you like to go to the nearest emergency room instead of being carried 5 or 6 miles because your plan required it? If you go to the doctor next month and he said, "I'm sorry, you've got a condition I can't treat. I want to send you to a specialist," wouldn't you like the doctor be able to do that and not have an accountant be able to stop that doctor? If you work for a small business and your employer changes health care providers when you're 6 months pregnant, wouldn't you like to keep your obstetrician until your baby is born? If somebody in your family is having chemotherapy, don't you think they ought to be able to finish the treatment before they have to change doctors?

This is not idle—we're talking about real stuff here. There are 160 million Americans in managed care plans and millions more who could be affected by this. I've been through this, and I bet a lot of you have. You have somebody in your family who is taking chemotherapy, and you sit around trying to laugh about it. You try to make jokes about whether you're going to lose your hair or not or when you're going to get sick. How in goodness name could we ever justify letting any system prevail where you could say, "I'm sorry, you're midway through your treatment. Now go see Dr. Jones."

And don't you think your medical records ought to be private?

Now, let me just tell you what this is about. That's what this election is about. We had a bill that did that. In the House the Republicans passed a bill that didn't guarantee the emergency room, didn't guarantee the specialist, didn't guarantee your treatment couldn't be interrupted, didn't guarantee your privacy, and left 100 million Americans out of what little bit it did do. And in the Senate, when they tried to bring up our bill, the Senate was so concerned that they would have to vote against our bill to stay with the insurance companies that the leader of the Senate shut the Senate down for 4 hours in a panic, so it could die by stealth.

Now, that's what this election is about: real people, somebody making a minimum wage. That's worth going out to vote for—killing the minimum wage at a time when we have low unemployment and low inflation, when we all believe in the principle that everyone should participate in this prosperity—12 million people who are working hard, not on welfare, trying to do their part, paying their taxes.

We've got an economic program up there that the Vice President and Secretary Cuomo developed to put more investment, more free enterprise jobs in inner-city areas and rural areas and on Indian reservations where people haven't felt this recovery. If we can't give them a chance to be part of the American dream now, with the lowest unemployment rate in 28 years, when in the world will we ever get around to doing it? When will we ever do it?

Look, this is serious. You need to go back home and say, every time you see one of their ads on television, you say to yourself, "Well, why did you kill the education program? Why did you kill the Patients' Bill of Rights? Why did you kill the environmental initiatives? Why did you kill campaign finance reform? Why did you kill the tobacco legislation? Why did you kill minimum wage? What are we doing here anyway?"

This is a better country today because we have worked on the people's needs. And whenever we could, we have reached out to the Republicans and invited them to join us. They made all these decisions this year, not me. They have been in the majority.

With all this financial turmoil going on around the world, I have asked for 8 long months to simply pay our contribution to the International Monetary Fund, just so we could grow and keep growing and keep creating American jobs.

So I say to you, I want you to go home, and I want you to tell everybody the country is doing well, we're better off than we were 6 years ago because we followed the right policies. But we've got a lot to do. We've got to save Social Security first. We've got to give our kids the best schools in the world. We've got to pass the Patients' Bill of Rights. We've got to keep improving the environment. We've got to keep this economic growth going.

Now, if you want progress, vote for us; if you want partisanship, vote for them. If you want to vote for people, vote for us; if you want to vote for politics, vote for them. We'll prove M&M's doesn't amount to anything compared to the principle, the power, and the passion of the American people and the people's party.

Thank you, and God bless you.

NOTE: The President spoke at 7:35 p.m. in the East Room at the White House. In his remarks, he referred to Steve Grossman, national chair, and Gov. Roy Romer of Colorado, general chair, Democratic National Committee; John J. Sweeney, president, AFL–CIO; Mayor Susan Hammer of San Jose, CA; and Mayor Robert Pastrick of East Chicago, IN.

Remarks on Legislative Priorities and an Exchange With Reporters
September 25, 1998

Hurricane Georges

The President. Good morning. For the past several days Hurricane Georges has torn through the Caribbean, costing many lives. Now, as we speak, the hurricane is bearing down on south Florida. I have spoken several times with FEMA director, James Lee Witt. For the past day, an emergency response team has been on the ground working with the government and the people of Florida to prepare for the storm. We are as ready as we can be, and we pray that the human and material costs will be limited. In the coming days, we will work as closely as possible with the State of Florida to provide whatever assistance will do the most good.

Continuing Resolution

A few moments ago I signed stop-gap legislation to keep the Government open and running at the start of the new fiscal year. The legislation is a regrettable sign that the Republican majority in Congress has failed to address the urgent priorities of the American people. There is only one week left in this fiscal year, yet the Congress has passed and sent me only one of the 13 appropriations bills to fund the operation of the United States Government. And the Congress is 5 months past the legal deadline for passing a budget resolution.

By failing to meet its most basic governing responsibility, the Republican majority in Congress has its priorities wrong: partisanship over progress, politics over people. Moreover, on key national goals—improving education, providing affordable child care, expanding health coverage, protecting our environment, stabilizing the international economy—the House of Representatives, in fact, is moving in the wrong direction. For example, at a time when opportunity depends on education more than ever before, neither Chamber has even brought the education funding bill to a vote. And the House is preparing to deny funding for smaller classes, to cut after-school programs, to cut technology in the classroom, to eliminate summer jobs. At the same time, some lawmakers have attached con-troversial and unrelated provisions guaranteed to mire these bills in unnecessary delay.

For 6 years, our economic strategy of fiscal responsibility, investing in people, expanding America's exports has spurred lower interest rates and created conditions for the strongest economy in a generation. If we hold fast to fiscal discipline, we will enter a new and promising era of budget surpluses. We must keep our economy growing and use this time to meet the challenges facing our people.

I have laid out a concrete plan of how we can continue on that course to make smart investments, to maintain fiscal discipline, and to set aside the surplus until we have saved Social Security first. I have reached out to Members of Congress in both parties to work toward these ends. It isn't too late. But Congress cannot simply keep passing patchwork spending plans, putting off choices about national priorities until next year, or at least until after the election.

It is time now for Congress to buckle down, to send me the measures to keep the Government open and to invest in education, in health care, in other needs of the American people. It is time to put progress over partisanship. We should do the job the people sent us here to do and strengthen America for the new century.

Thank you very much.

Q. How do you think the Democrats are going to do in the election?

The President. I have nothing to add to what I said.

NOTE: The President spoke at 9:06 a.m. on the South Lawn at the White House, prior to his departure for Chicago, IL. H.J. Res. 128, approved September 25, was assigned Public Law No. 105–240.

Remarks at Jenner Elementary School in Chicago, Illinois
September 25, 1998

Thank you very much. There aren't all that many sixth graders that could do that and be less nervous than she was. She did a great job, didn't she? Thank you, Gina, thank you.

Ladies and gentlemen, I am so glad to be here today. I thank the mayor for his extraordinary work. And I want to thank Secretary Daley, too, for being a truly remarkable Secretary of Commerce. My old friend John Stroger, thank you for being here. I'd like to thank the board members of the Chicago School Reform Board, Gery Chico and the other members who are here. I thank Paul Vallas, your CEO. I thank your principal; thank you for your good work here. It's been my experience that all good schools have a good principal.

I want to thank Gina again. I'm sure the first time she was asked to do this, this was just one step above going to the dentist, you know. [*Laughter*] And I thought she did a superb job.

I'd like to thank Joanne Alter and all the people who are involved in the WITS program here in Chicago. I believe in this so strongly. Last year we arranged to have students from 1,000 colleges and universities go into our elementary schools to help to tutor, to try to follow the sterling example you have set here.

To all the parents, the teachers, the educators, the tutors, the students, thank you. I'd also like to thank Mary Lou Kearns for being here, for her work in health care, and for presenting herself as a candidate for Lieutenant Governor. And I'd like to thank Glenn Poshard—who wanted to be here, but I wouldn't have him anywhere else—he's back in Washington voting a tough vote so close to an election, voting not to give an election year tax cut before we make sure we've got the budget balanced and we save Social Security for the 21st century. It is the right thing to do, and I thank him for that. And we're glad to have Glenn's wife, Jo Poshard, here with us. Thank you, Jo, for coming. We're glad to see you.

Ladies and gentlemen, I told the mayor on the way in that he ought to put me on the payroll because I've become such a shameless advocate for the Chicago public schools. But I want to tell you why. First of all, I am deeply gratified by the success of our country. Most of the credit belongs to the American people. But I think our policies have had something to do with the fact that we have the lowest unemployment rate in 28 years, almost 17 million new jobs; the lowest crime rate in 25 years; the smallest percentage of people on welfare in 29 years; the lowest African-American poverty rate since statistics have been collected; the lowest inflation in 32 years; the highest real wage growth in more than 20 years; the highest homeownership in history; and in just 6 days, the first balanced budget and surplus in 29 long years.

I have been particularly grateful to the people of Illinois and the city of Chicago, without whom it is doubtful that I could have become President. I brought some of them with me here today, Secretary Daley and Rahm Emanuel. I was met at the airport by Kevin O'Keefe, who worked in the White House for several years. And I see my good friend Avis Lavelle out there, who was a part of our administration. And of course, the most important person from Chicago to this administration is the First Lady, who asked me to tell all of you hello. She's out on the West Coast today, and I'm going to meet her tonight so we can see our daughter tomorrow. But you've had a lot to do with it.

But I would like to especially thank Senator Carol Moseley-Braun and Congressman Glenn Poshard and the other members of the Democratic delegation in Illinois, without whom—without any one of whom we would not have passed the economic plan in 1993, which led to this big decline in the deficit, big decline in interest rates, big takeoff in the economy.

One of the things that very few people know about that economic plan was that it also doubled something called the earned-income tax credit, the EITC, which lowers taxes to working people on modest incomes with children. Today, for a family of four with an income of under $30,000, that amounts to about $1,000 a year going back to families. Last year alone, thanks to Glenn Poshard and Carol Moseley-Braun and these other folks—and remember, if one of them had fallen off, none of it would have passed—last year alone, 4 million working Americans, including 1.1 million African-Americans, were lifted out of poverty because of this tax cut. And that has made a major contribution to broadening economic growth. And the people of Illinois should be very grateful to them for making that historic vote in 1993 when it was hard to do. And I thank them.

Now, the mayor once said when he was talking that not so many years ago people were kind of defeatist about the American economy. There is still a great debate going on in Washington, DC, about public education. Everybody knows—everybody knows that we have the finest system of higher education in the world, and we have now opened the doors of college to everybody who is willing to work for it with the HOPE scholarship, the $1,500 tax credit for the first 2 years of college; with tax credits for all higher education; the deductibility of student loans; huge increase in Pell grants; 300,000 more work-study positions. We've done that. But all of us know that we can't stop until we can look each other straight in the eye and say with absolute conviction, every child in this country, without regard to their race, their income, their neighborhood, their family circumstances—every single child—has access to a world-class education. That is our national mission, and we cannot stop until we achieve it.

Now, back to what I was saying before, there really is an honest debate in Washington. Some people who haven't been to places like Jenner School have given up on the public schools. Chicago didn't give up. Chicago said, if we give the schools back to the parents, if we hold the students and teachers accountable, and if we help those who need help, we can make our schools work again.

As I was saying before, I go all over the country, and people's mouths drop open when I say, "They've ended social promotion in Chicago, but everybody gets to go to summer school; they have after-school programs." People's eyes pop out when I say Chicago's summer school is the sixth biggest school district in America; when I say over 40,000 kids are getting three square meals a day here. I say to you, if we can do this here, we can do it anywhere.

If these students—and look at them, their bright eyes and their whole life before them—but you know as well as I do—when I was in this little class beforehand—I want to thank the two young men who were in the tutoring class with me and the tutor who sat around the table and all the other young people that were in there—and by the way, one of the little lessons today was on Washington, DC, and one of the test questions was, "How many words can you make from the letters in 'Washington'?" One of the students got more words than I did. I liked that. [*Laughter*]

But one of the questions in the little forum they had today was, "If you were President, what would you do?" And one of the students said, "Well, if I were President, I'd do something to end the violence." Another said, "If I were President, I wouldn't sell guns to anybody but police officers." Another said, "If I were President, I would have more homes for the homeless and more clothes for them."

So I want these children to know—I know a lot of you have got it pretty tough. I know that life's not so easy for you when you're out of school. I know that you've seen a lot of things in your life already that children should never see. But I want you to know something else: If you make the most of your education, you can still live out your dreams. You can do what you want to do with your lives. You can be happy. You can be fulfilled. You can succeed. And that's what we owe you, an education that gives you a chance to be fully free to live out your own dreams. And we are determined to do it.

Now, if the principal, the students, the parents, the volunteers, and the students here can double reading scores and triple math scores—and according to what I saw, last year alone, reading scores in percentile terms increased by 50 percent—if you can do that, if you can do it here, then no one else in America has an excuse. They can do it, too. But if you can do it here, then the decisionmakers in Springfield and in Washington, DC, don't have an excuse either. We owe it to you to give you the tools and the support you need so that every child can be a part of a successful school. We don't have an excuse either.

Jenner proves, Chicago proves that the public schools can work. Now the rest of us have to go to work and give you the tools you need to succeed. I have given Congress a plan that would make a big dent in that. And I have worked as hard as I could now for 6 years to make education a bipartisan issue. America cannot be strong unless we give all of our children a world-class education. This should not be a partisan issue. But the fact is that the majority of the Congress is in the hands of the other party. And earlier this year I gave them an education plan that for both partisan and ideological reasons they refused to act on, and we know it could dramatically improve our schools.

Let me tell you what it does. It says, first of all, everybody's got to take responsibility for high standards and learning. But secondly, if there are going to be high standards, we have to give students the opportunity to reach those standards. That's the formula that's worked here, and it's the formula that will work throughout the country.

So I said, let's develop voluntary national standards; let's give exams to our kids to see if they're meeting it; but let's don't designate children failures before they ever have a chance. Give these kind of summer school and after-school opportunities to all the children of the United States, and you'll see what they'll do with them.

I said we ought to have smaller classes in the early grades and gave a budget plan to the Congress that would lower class size to an average of 18 in the first three grades and hire another 100,000 teachers. I said we ought to do even more for the really poor areas of America, and I gave Congress a plan to educate 35,000 bright young people and then let them pay off all their student loans by going into our hardest pressed areas and teaching for a few years. These are good ideas. They'll make America stronger.

I embrace Senator Carol Moseley-Braun's idea that we ought to have more places doing what Chicago's doing and building new schools and repairing old ones. So I gave the Congress a bill that says, let's tear down and rebuild or repair or build 5,000 schools. And here's a plan to do it, paid for in the balanced budget act.

All of these things are in this education bill. I gave them a plan for safer schools through more partnerships with local law enforcement. I gave them a plan to hook up every classroom to the Internet by the year 2000 so that every child can have access to the world of learning now on the Internet, and every child can have access to the wonders of computer technology. So far, Congress has not responded.

I gave them a plan for most charter schools, for better rewards for our more committed teachers, to do more to train teachers, to make sure we have certified master teachers in all the schools of America. Without touching a dime of the surplus, we did all that. So far, Congress has not responded.

So I say to you here in Chicago, you are doing your part, and it's time Washington, DC, did its part to help you succeed. That is our commitment to you.

There are a few days left in the congressional session. It's not too late. It's not too late for Congress to put aside the lure of election year and save Social Security before we spend the surplus; not too late to give all the patients in this country the protection of a Patients' Bill of Rights; not too late to keep our economy growing by protecting us against the troubles in the global economy and doing what we can to turn it back; not too late to reaffirm our commitment to a clean environment; and most important, not too late—not too late—to pass this education agenda so that every child has a chance to be part of the miracle of his or her own learning. That will be the surest way to America's greatest years in the 21st century.

Good luck, young people. Make the most of it.

Thank you, and God bless you.

NOTE: The President spoke at 12:05 p.m. in the gymnasium. In his remarks, he referred to sixth grade student Gina Borner, who introduced the President; John Stroger, president, Cook County Board of Commissioners; Gery J. Chico, president, Chicago School Reform Board of Trustees; Paul Vallas, chief executive officer, Chicago Public Schools; Sandra Satinover, school principal; Joanne Alter, chairman of the board, Working in the Schools (WITS); and gubernatorial candidate Representative Glenn Poshard and his wife, Jo.

Remarks at a Luncheon for Gubernatorial Candidate Glenn Poshard in Chicago
September 25, 1998

Thank you. I don't think Glenn can hear us, but I want to say that if I were a school principal today, I would happily give him an excused absence from this lunch—[*laughter*]—because I, too, wanted him to be in Washington. Finally, after almost 9 months now, 8 months, of virtual complete inaction, some votes are being cast in Congress. And I think this decision that is before the Congress today is terribly important.

We're quite close to an election. In a week we'll have the first balanced budget and surplus we've had in 29 years. And the majority party wants to make everybody happy close to an election by passing a tax cut. And believe me, I'd like to make everybody happy close to an election, too. Even though I'm not running, I've got a lot of friends on the ballot. But it's not the right thing to do.

We have a tax cut in our balanced budget for child care, for education, for the environment, but it's paid for. But you know, we have waited 29 years, and we have worked hard for 6 years to get this country a balanced budget. It has been instrumental, pivotal in bringing the country back economically. And before the red ink turns to black and it dries a little bit, people now want to turn around and spend it again before we do what I think must be our first priority, which is to save Social Security.

There are a lot of younger people here, and I thank you for being here. But if you've looked at the demographics, you know that when all the baby boomers retire—that's me and everybody 18 years younger, people between the ages of 34 and 52—when we retire, we'll be the biggest group of retirees ever to pack it in at one time in America. And at present rates of work force participation, immigration, and birth, there will only be about two people working for every one person drawing Social Security.

Now, we know that right now. We also know right now the Social Security system alone accounts for taking half the seniors in this country out of poverty and giving them a dignified life, and also relieving their children and their grandchildren of the enormous financial burden of supporting them.

If we act now, we can make modest changes in the Social Security system, using the surpluses—maybe not all of them but some of them—and we can avoid a train wreck. If we don't act now and we just wait for something bad to happen, we'll have one of two choices a few years down the road as a nation. Number one is we can decide we're going to keep the same system in the same way, in which case people like me will be sick because what that will mean is, in order to maintain the standard of living of the elderly, we will reduce the standard of living of our children and their ability to raise our grandchildren. Or we can say, no, we're not going to do that, and let the elderly poverty rate go way up again because we'll have to slash Social Security by a huge amount.

There is no reason to do that. If we start now, we can make a sensible, modest reform which will reflect the changing composition of our population. That's what Glenn Poshard is up there doing.

Now, I know a little bit about being Governor; I was a Governor for 12 years. Somebody said I could never get a promotion. I was a

Governor forever, it seemed like. I loved it. But I can tell you that if you're sitting there every day, making decisions that no one else can make, you have to do some things that don't please everyone in the short run because you know that they are right for the long-run interest of your State.

Here he is, just a few weeks from the election—Glenn Poshard went back to Washington, DC, to vote for the security of our country 20 years down the road, in the teeth of an election, by saying "We have waited 29 long years; we have worked for 6 years; we've got this balanced budget; and we're not going to squander this surplus until we save Social Security first." On that alone, he deserves to be elected Governor.

I want to thank Mike and Jim and Glenn and all the others who were responsible for selling tickets today. I told Mike Cherry he's been to so many of my fundraisers, he's the only guy I can think of that, if we get a Republican administration in and the stock market goes down, his income will go up just being free of the fundraisers. [*Laughter*]

I want to thank all of you from the bottom of my heart for coming. I want to thank Mayor Daley for his leadership and friendship. And Mike Madigan, thank you for being here and for your leadership. And Minority Leader Senator Jones and all the members of the legislature, I thank you. Mary Lou, thank you for running with Glenn and for your background in health care, which will be, I think, an enormous asset to this ticket, after the election, serving, because more and more, we're going to have to deal with all kinds of complicated health care questions.

Again I say, as a Governor, we can do a lot nationally on health care, but there are a lot of questions which will have to be made at the local level. I'll just give you one. When we passed the Balanced Budget Act in 1997, we put funds aside to provide aid to the States to provide health insurance for 5 million children in the families of lower-income working people. That is, children who are on welfare already get covered by Federal health care, and people who have good, solid jobs usually have health insurance with the job. But increasingly, more and more people have jobs that don't have any health insurance for their family. We put in the balanced budget funds that will give these working families the ability to insure their children, 5 million of them throughout America. But the programs have to be designed at the State level and implemented at the State level. It's another good reason to vote for Glenn and Mary Lou, because I know Glenn Poshard voted for it and I know he's committed to it, and he'll do a good job.

I want to thank Jo and all of her family for coming. Running for Governor is a family endeavor, and believe me, serving is a family endeavor. And I thank you for doing it.

You know, I'm deeply indebted to the State of Illinois and the City of Chicago. I might well not be President if it hadn't been for Illinois and the stunning vote that we received here on St. Patrick's Day in 1992. If you ever come to visit me in the White House, I'll take you back to my private office, and up there's a picture of Hillary and me in Chicago on St. Patrick's Day in 1992, with all the confetti coming down.

And I would just like to say to all of you who had anything to do with this administration, but especially to our terrific Secretary of Commerce, Bill Daley, to my friend Kevin O'Keefe, who worked with me for many years, and to all the others from Chicago who participated in our endeavors, I am very grateful.

I also want you to know that I'll have a hard time holding on to this Cubs shirt—[*laughter*]—when I get out to California tonight and Hillary sees it. [*Laughter*] She's in Oregon today campaigning for some of our candidates that we're going to meet tonight in California and spend a day with our daughter tomorrow. But we're thrilled with the success of the Cubs this year and, obviously, with Sammy Sosa. You know, this home run race has been good for America, and it's been great for baseball. But it makes us—now, we're sitting there—it's interesting, there is a little psychological lesson here, though—we're all sitting there saying, "Now, why haven't they hit another home run?" [*Laughter*] They just hit 65! Nobody else ever did it. Now we wake up every day, and we expect them to hit a home run. But I want to ask you to think about that in terms of this election season.

If either Mark McGwire or Sammy Sosa announced that even though there were 3 games left in the season, 65 was enough and get off their back and they were just going to sit out the games, we would think they had lost it, wouldn't we? We would be disappointed. We would be a little angry. And we would think they were downright foolish.

But if you think about where we are today as a country and you think about the pattern of democracies when times are good, essentially some people are betting on the fact that a lot of Americans will sit out the election on the argument that things are doing well and the country is going in the right direction. I've told many people—I thank you—so many of you said wonderful things to me and, through me to Hillary, today when we visited. But the enemy of the forces of progress in this election is not adversity. Adversity is our friend. Our enemy is complacency.

If I told you 6 years ago that in 6 years we would have the lowest unemployment rate in 28 years and 17 million new jobs—just under—that we would have the lowest crime rate in 25 years, that we would have the smallest percentage of people on welfare in 29 years, that we would have the first balanced budget and surplus in 29 years, the lowest inflation rate in 32 years, the highest homeownership in history, the lowest African-American poverty rate ever recorded, the biggest drop in Hispanic poverty in 20 years, with the smallest Government in 35 years—if I told you that, you would have said, "What planet is he from?"

But the American people have achieved that. And our policies have supported that. It all began—I'd just like to remind you again, one more time—with one vote in 1993 for an economic program that did not have a single, solitary vote from the other party, that drove down interest rates and reduced the deficit by 92 percent before the balanced budget bill passed with bipartisan support last year.

That bill also contained something called the earned-income tax credit—we doubled it. It's a tax cut for working people who have modest incomes. Single workers get a little bit of money out of it, but most of the money goes to people who have modest incomes who have children in their homes. And their taxes now—if your income is $27,000 a year or less and you have a couple of kids at home, your taxes are about $1,000 lower than they would otherwise be now because of that. We learned yesterday from the Census Bureau that 4 million working Americans were lifted out of poverty last year—4 million.

So we have proved that you can grow the economy, have record numbers of billionaires, have record numbers of new businesses, but that the people who are out there struggling to make ends meet can do well at the same time. And I'm very proud of that. I believe in that.

And as I said, along the way we passed the family and medical leave law, gave health insurance to 5 million people, gave a $1,500 tax credit for the first 2 years of college and other tax credits for other college education, made student loans deductible, created more Pell grants, put 100,000 police on the street, cleaned up toxic waste dumps, made the food safer, the air cleaner, and the water purer. That's good news.

It would be a great mistake to say, "We have hit 65 home runs; we think we'll sit out the next few weeks." Why? First of all, because the country still has serious challenges. This Social Security challenge is a big challenge. Another big challenge is to keep the economic recovery going in the midst of all this global financial turmoil.

When you read in the newspapers or see on the evening news about this debate we're having about the International Monetary Fund and you never thought about the International Monetary Fund before, just know that that's what we contribute to to help countries that are trying to get on their feet and to help prevent countries that are doing well from getting the financial flu that's sweeping the world, so that they in turn can buy our products and keep our people working. It's a big issue.

We just came from the Jenner School, as the mayor said. Education is a big issue. If there were no other reason to vote for the Democrats this year, it would be on education. We have a program sponsored and conceived by Carol Moseley-Braun to modernize, repair, or build 5,000 schools—no action on it yet in the Congress. We have a program to reduce class size to 18 in the first 3 grades, put 100,000 teachers out there—no action. We have a program to educate 35,000 bright young people and then let them pay their college loans off by going into the inner cities and teaching—no action. We have a program to hook up every single classroom to the Internet by the year 2000, so that all kids, without regard to their backgrounds or their family's incomes, have a chance to be a part of the emerging information economy—

no action. But Glenn Poshard supports it, just like he supported all my education bills. And it's a big issue.

So I say to you, the country has got a huge choice to make. One is, will we be apathetic or intense about building our future and building on what we've got? The second is, when we make these choices, what's going to dominate our thinking? Are we going to be for partisanship or progress? Are we going to be for politics or for people?

You know, when I go around the country and I speak for people that I believe in, almost none of them agree with me on every single issue. I never ask anybody to agree with me on everything. I couldn't possibly be right about everything. Neither could you, and neither could they. But I do think that we want people in office who wake up every day thinking about what it's like to struggle to make ends meet.

Look at the record of the Congress. We're a week from a new budget year. They pass one of the 13 bills it takes to keep the Government going—one. They're 5 months late on a budget resolution. But they've killed a lot of things. They killed campaign finance reform. They killed the tobacco legislation designed to protect our children from the dangers of tobacco. They killed a Patients' Bill of Rights designed to make sure our medical decisions are made by doctors and not by insurance company accountants. And last week, with the unemployment at a 28-year low and no inflation, they killed an increase in the minimum wage for 12 million workers.

Now, I don't believe we should be embracing those policies. I believe we ought to say, we want everybody to be a part of this. We're for saving Social Security, passing the Patients' Bill of Rights, passing the education agenda, protecting the environment even as we grow the economy, and we are for doing what it takes to keep this economic growth going and making sure everybody gets to participate—everybody gets to participate.

So I ask you to think about all that. And when I talked to Glenn on the phone this morning before I came out here, he reminded me of some time we spent together way back in 1986. That seems like—I still remember 1986, but vaguely now. [*Laughter*] And he and I, as you heard him say, were on something called the Lower Mississippi Delta Development Commission. Why? Because the Lower Mississippi is the poorest area of America.

And we started in Illinois, in southern Illinois, and went all the way to the mouth of the Mississippi, past New Orleans. And we went up and down the length of that great river, into little towns and to rural areas, talking to people about what we needed to do so that they could lift themselves out of poverty, so they could educate their children. Now, 12 years later, a lot of the things that were nightmares to us then are problems that are being solved.

This is a better country than it was 6 years ago. And if we bear down and choose progress over partisanship in this election, it will be better 2 years from now. But I want you to understand that it requires you to be vigilant. It requires you to say, "We are going to build on what we have done, not rest on it." And I will say again, I served as a Governor for 12 years. We've got the smallest Federal Government we've had in 35 years. I'm proud of that. But as a result of our policy, it is now more important who the State Governors are, not less, because it's education, it's health care, it's the environment, it's the economy. It matters.

So I ask you to go out here in the remaining days of this election—we've got several weeks—and first of all, send a message to Congress that you're tired of the partisan politics and you'd like to be considered first; you'd like for people to think about everybody outside of Washington, not everybody inside of Washington. You'd like to think about our future and our children.

And secondly, go out here and talk to your friends and neighbors and tell them that we've got a good ticket for Governor and Lieutenant Governor, and they deserve their consideration. They deserve their vote. They deserve their support, and there's a lot riding on it for the future of your children.

Thank you, and God bless you.

NOTE: The President spoke at 2:04 p.m. in the auditorium of the Mercantile Club. In his remarks, he referred to Mike Cherry, cochair, Democratic Business Council; Jim Levin, event cochair; Mayor Richard M. Daley of Chicago; Michael Madigan, speaker of the house, and Emil Jones, senate minority leader, Illinois State Legislature; Mary Lou Kearns, candidate for Lieutenant Governor; and Representative Poshard's wife, Jo.

Statement on Hurricane Georges
September 25, 1998

Hurricane Georges, which is bearing down on south Florida, has already cost many American citizens their lives in Puerto Rico, as well as caused huge human and material harm throughout the Caribbean. As we prepare for the impact of the storm on the mainland, we are working to bring relief to those already affected by the storm and to help them to begin rebuilding.

Yesterday I declared Puerto Rico and the U.S. Virgin Islands to be disaster areas. Already, the Federal Emergency Management Agency has sent over 200 emergency relief workers to assess the damage. I have sent Secretary of Housing and Urban Development Andrew Cuomo and Small Business Administrator Aida Alvarez to Puerto Rico to report to me on what further

steps need to be taken. We are gravely concerned about the loss of life and property in Puerto Rico and the U.S. Virgin Islands and will continue to work at the highest levels to bring the islands and their people back.

We are also working to help those affected outside our borders. Yesterday I sent an emergency response team from the Office of Foreign Disaster Assistance, together with relief workers and supplies. I have asked Hugh Palmer, the head of Humanitarian Response Programs at the Agency for International Development, to go to the Dominican Republic this weekend to assess the damage, supervise our efforts, and report to me on what further should be done.

Our thoughts and prayers are with those who have felt the force of this storm.

Statement on the National Economy
September 25, 1998

Today we received more proof that our economic strategy is working to deepen America's prosperity and widen the circle of opportunity to more American families. Over the past year, personal incomes have increased 5.0 percent—much faster than the rate of inflation. While our economic progress is strong, now is not a time to rest; it is a time to build.

To keep our economy on the right track, we must maintain our three-part economic strategy:

We must maintain our fiscal discipline by reserving every penny of the budget surplus until we have strengthened Social Security; we must continue to invest in our people through education, health care, and research and development; and we have to continue to lead the global economy and meet our obligation to the International Monetary Fund.

Statement on House of Representatives Action on Reciprocal Trade Agreement Authorities Legislation
September 25, 1998

At a time of global financial turmoil, we should be working together to build a new bipartisan international economic policy that strengthens America's competitive edge. Renewing traditional authority is the right thing to do, but now was clearly the wrong time to vote on it.

The House of Representatives should focus its energies on making sure that the International Monetary Fund is strong enough to confront the financial crisis that threatens our economy today. That legislation has strong bipartisan support in the Senate but has become entangled in politics in the House. Strengthening the IMF is the single most important thing we can do now to protect American farmers, ranch-

ers, and workers who depend on exports to make a living.

At a time when we need to forge a new consensus on trade, Congress has chosen partisanship over progress. To move our trade policy forward this year, Congress still has time to enact important legislation, from the Africa trade legislation to the global shipbuilding treaty and the Caribbean Basin Initiative. And when Congress returns next year, we should do the hard work of building a bipartisan coalition for traditional negotiating authority so that we can build on our successful record of expanding markets for American goods, services, and agricultural exports.

Joint Statement on United States-Saudi Relations
September 25, 1998

His Royal Highness Crown Prince Abdullah Bin Abdulaziz, First Deputy Prime Minister and Head of the Saudi Arabian National Guard, visited Washington, D.C. September 23–25, 1998 at the invitation of Vice President Al Gore.

The visit is in the framework of the close, strong and historic relations between the Kingdom of Saudi Arabia and the United States of

America stretching back more than a half century to President Roosevelt and King Abdul Aziz. It reflects the desire of both governments to have periodic high-level consultations to assure coordination of policies that affect mutual interests. Crown Prince Abdullah was received by President Clinton and Vice President Gore, as well as Secretary of State Albright. In addition, he received calls from Secretary of the Treasury Rubin, Secretary of Energy Richardson and Deputy Secretary of Defense Hamre.

The two sides discussed topics of mutual interest and concern. Both sides pledged to cooperate fully in the search for comprehensive, just and lasting peace in the Middle East based on Security Council Resolutions 242 and 338 and the principle of land for peace. The United States updated the Crown Prince on America's efforts to put the peace process back on track. President Clinton explained the progress made in narrowing the gaps during Ambassador Dennis Ross's recent visit to the region. Secretary Albright is meeting with Israeli Prime Minister Netanyahu and Chairman Arafat in New York this week to continue this process in an effort to achieve agreement on the basis of President Clinton's ideas. In this context, the United States expressed concern about unilateral acts taken by either side that undermine confidence in the negotiations.

Saudi Arabia expressed its full support for the peace efforts exerted by the United States and Saudi Arabia's willingness to support whatever the Palestinian side agrees to in the service of peace. Saudi Arabia expressed its deep concern about Israeli unilateral actions, including in Jerusalem, which could prejudge the outcome of the final status negotiations, and also called on Israel to fully implement the Oslo and Washington accords and to cooperate with the United States' initiative to reinvigorate the process. The United States and Saudi Arabia expect the two sides to strictly abide by their obligations. At the same time, the two sides underscored the importance of resuming negotiations on the Syrian and Lebanese tracks of the peace process as soon as possible in an effort to facilitate a comprehensive peace. Both countries expressed their support for the implementation of Resolutions 425 and 426.

During their discussion on Iraq, the two sides expressed their serious concern at the Iraqi government's decision to suspend cooperation with the UN Special Commission (UNSCOM) and the International Atomic Energy Agency (IAEA). They called upon the Iraqi government to comply with the recent UN Resolution which states that Iraq's action is totally unacceptable, and which demands that Iraq resume cooperation with UNSCOM and the IAEA. They agreed that the only way to alleviate the suffering of the Iraqi people lies in strict adherence to all Security Council Resolutions. They expressed their sympathy with the Iraqi people and satisfaction with UN resolution 1153 which addresses humanitarian needs.

Both countries welcome Iran's stated policy to improve relations with the states of the region and its renunciation of terrorism, and hope that these statements will translate into practice.

They discussed the situation in Afghanistan, and expressed support for the efforts of the United Nations and the Organization of Islam Conference aiming at a peaceful resolution and an end to the fighting. They called upon Iran and Afghanistan to resolve their differences by peaceful means. Also, both sides reaffirmed the danger and threat that terrorism constitutes for international security and stability. They called on all countries to prevent terrorists from operating from their soil and assist in bringing known terrorists to justice. They considered that concerted international action is an effective way to combat terrorism.

Both sides were united in the view that the current situation in Kosovo is unacceptable and condemned the harsh measures taken by the Yugoslav government causing displacement of large segments of the population of Kosovo. They also noted with concern the recent nuclear testing in India and Pakistan and called on all states to sign and ratify the CTBT at the earliest possible date.

They reviewed the current state of the international economy. Both sides agreed on the need to continue to consult closely on these issues and to continue cooperation to enhance trade and investment between the two countries. The United States expressed its support for Saudi Arabia's accession to the World Trade Organization, and both sides look forward to the increasing trade opportunities and further integration into the global economy which will flow from Saudi Arabia's membership in that organization. Both sides agreed to continue their efforts to complete these important economic negotiations as soon as possible. The American side welcomed continued Saudi efforts to enforce measures for protecting intellectual property rights and looked forward to further progress. The two sides renewed their intentions to fully consult and cooperate on the issues related to global climate change and will continue to assure that measures taken in this regard are based on the state of scientific evidence and data. They stressed the need to encourage technical cooperation and scientific research in the fields of water; agricultural standards, regulations and policies; and specification and measurements.

The two sides stressed the importance of the Kingdom of Saudi Arabia in the world oil market, and the United States reiterated its recognition of the Kingdom of Saudi Arabia as a secure and reliable supplier of energy resources, especially to the United States.

NOTE: An original was not available for verification of the content of this joint statement.

Remarks at a Democratic National Committee Dinner in San Jose, California
September 25, 1998

Thank you. Thank you, John. I sort of hate to speak after that. [*Laughter*] He made a better case than I could have made for myself. I thank you. And I want to thank Mayor Susan Hammer for her friendship and her leadership of this great city.

I'm delighted to be back here again—or in the new Tech, and I do hope that because of this event tonight, you'll receive even wider publicity and you'll have throngs of children coming here, learning all the things that they need to see about their own future. [*Applause*] Thank you very much.

I want to thank all of you for being here tonight. Some of you are probably in danger of overexposure. There are several people here who were with Hillary last night in Seattle. [*Laughter*] And you've already heard the better of the two speeches, I can tell you that. [*Laughter*]

We've been working—I was in Chicago today, and she was in Portland and Seattle last night, and we're going to, as you know, spend the night with our daughter tonight. And then I'm going on to San Diego tomorrow and then to Texas and then back to Washington. But I can't thank you enough, all of you, for the many kind things that you said, as I was going around before the dinner, about my family and what we're dealing with. And I just want to thank you on a very personal basis. Even Presidents have to be people from time to time, and you made me feel like one tonight, and I thank you very much.

I also want to thank you for giving me a way to work with this community. When I came out here with Al Gore and we were working in 1992, I felt that it was imperative that we establish a strong relationship with the people and the companies of this area for what we could do together to rebuild the American economy and then to build an American future that is worthy of our people. And you mentioned a few of those issues, but it's just the last list of issues. We've worked on a lot of things over the last 6 years, things that I never would have known very much about, and that most Presidents probably wouldn't, had it not been for your input and your consistent involvement and even sometimes your stimulating argument. And I thank you for that.

I don't know that that was the greatest endorsement my Vice President could ever get, what John said. [*Laughter*] But it's not all bad. I do want to say something about him. I thank you for working with him. As you all know, one of the reasons I asked him to become my Vice Presidential partner is that he had a background in technology issues far superior to mine and a consuming interest in it. And all of you have fed it and broadened it, and I'm very grateful to you.

I think that when the historians write about this administration, they may differ on whether our economic or social policies were right or wrong, but one thing is absolutely beyond question, and that is that the Vice President has had more influence on more important issues in more areas than any person in the history of this country that ever held that job. And he's made it possible for us to do a lot of the things that we've done, and I'm very grateful to him.

Now, if I could just run over—you mentioned a couple of things. We have worked out the so-called H–1B visa issue. It will be coming to my desk soon. And it was done in a way that's really good for everybody in America, because in addition to permitting more visas of high-skilled people to come into our country and strengthen us, it also provides a lot more funds to train our own people, to upgrade their skills. So it's a good, good bill. It has the best of both worlds.

The securities reform legislation is now in conference, and they're arguing only over some legislative intent language that those of you who are working the issue are very familiar with. But I think we'll be successful there. I think we've reached a broad agreement on encryption policy, and now you just have to make sure you work with us on the implementation of it so that the rules don't contradict the policy but instead reinforce them. And I think we can do that.

There's legislation to implement the world intellectual property agreements to which we are a part, and there's some problems there, but I think that on balance it does a lot of good. And I hope you'll help us get it right and get it through. The bill which keeps the Internet from being interrupted for a period of time by various kind of local taxes is making its way through the Senate, and there are some extraneous issues that are having an impact on it, but those of you who are working it understand that, and I remain committed to it. And I think we can be successful there. And I think it's very, very important.

One other thing I'd like to just say to you is, a lot of you are very concerned, as you should be, for your own markets, with the situation in Asia. And I am working very, very hard to help those countries regroup, to restore growth, and to limit the reach of the contagion. I believe we're doing about all we can do at this time, but we need some support, and I'll say more about that in a minute.

Now, I mention these issues partly to make a specific point to Silicon Valley, but partly to make a more general point. Today I was at Moffett Air Force Base, and we had an open arrival. And typically, when we do this, a couple hundred people will show up that are associated some way or another with the base facility. There were about 600 people there today, and they were all different kinds of people talking about very specific things about their lives, things that had changed—the schools their kids were in, the family and medical leave law, or other things that we had all been involved in together.

I entered public life because I thought it would give me an opportunity to work with people to help them make the most of their lives. I believe that Washington would serve America better if we worried more about the people that lived outside Washington than where people stood on the totem pole inside Washington. And I think you believe that, too. And that's what I ask you to think about tonight.

I'll be very brief. I want to mention to you what I think are the central questions facing the country in this election season which is unfolding rapidly now, and then what I think are some of the central questions facing this country over the next 20 years, because I ask you to begin thinking about it. We were talking about it at one of the tables tonight. And this community has got to continue to be involved in America to help us raise our imaginations and raise our visions toward these long-term issues as well.

I tell all my fellow Democrats that, contrary to what you might think, the great enemy of our cause in this election is not adversity; it is, instead, complacency. Because oftentimes, when people are doing well and things are doing well and they have a high level of comfort and confidence, particularly if they come through a very wrenching time—and our country came through a pretty wrenching time in the late eighties and early nineties, indeed throughout the decade of the eighties—the tendency is to say, "We'd like to relax a little bit. We're tired. Things are good for us now. We just want to not think about this." In this case, "this" is politics right now.

You live in a world that never permits that, because it's changing so fast. One thing I'd like to ask you to do is to think about how you can communicate that sense of urgency to the rest of your fellow Americans. And that's what I hope to do here tonight, because even though people may not understand it in the way you do if you're struggling to develop a new product, a new service, keep up with some new discovery, the truth is that everyone else's life is more dynamic than most people realize as well.

And while I am profoundly grateful that we have the lowest unemployment rate in 28 years and the lowest crime rate in 25 years and the smallest percentage of people on welfare in 29 years, and next week the first balanced budget and surplus in 29 years, and the highest home-ownership in history, and we just learned yesterday the lowest African-American poverty rate ever recorded, the biggest increase in wages in 20 years—I'm grateful for all that—the truth is that this is a dynamic world. And so the right thing to do is not to rest on that but to build on it, to ask ourselves, "Okay, what else needs to be done?"

Now, in this election season, I think there are the following major issues that, to me, are very important. We had a big vote on one in the House today. There are some who say, "Well, we're going to have a surplus for the first time in 29 years, and it's just a few weeks from the election, so let's have a tax cut." And even though I'm not a candidate anymore and won't be running for anything anymore, I understand the appeal of that, but I think it's dead wrong. For one thing, I'd just like to see the red ink turn to black and dry before we start spending again. [*Laughter*] I've been working for this for 6 years. I'd just like to see it dry, you know? [*Laughter*]

And in a more serious way, in this world financial situation we have been a pillar of stability and strength and responsibility, and we need to communicate that to people. And I know it's popular to offer a tax cut right here before an election, but in this case it would be wrong.

And there's another reason it's wrong. It's wrong because we finally have, I believe, a bipartisan consensus for making modifications in the Social Security system that will enable us to preserve it when the baby boomers retire and, at present rates, at least, there will only be two people working for every one person drawing. And I can just tell you the baby boomers are—and a lot of you are too young to be one—[*laughter*]—but, basically, the baby boom generation is everybody between the ages of 52 and 34. And when that group—only the present group in school is bigger than the baby boom generation. And when that group retires, unless we act now in a modest, measured, disciplined way—and if we don't do anything until the time comes to face it, and with every year it will become a more severe decision because you'll be closer in time to it—we'll have the decision of either cutting benefits for seniors so much that we'll erode the safety net, which today accounts for 48 percent of the people on Social Security being lifted out of poverty—

that is, they would be in poverty were it not for Social Security.

Or, in the alternative, we'll decide we can't bear that, and we'll raise taxes dramatically to maintain the old system, in which case we will undermine the standard of living of our children and grandchildren, which would be equally wrong. And that's not necessary. But in order to avoid it, we have to make an election-year decision and tell the American people the truth, that we ought to do something for the next 30 years and not for the next 30 days, and save Social Security before we entertain a tax cut out of this surplus. I think it is very important.

The second issue: If we want to continue to lead the world economy, we at least have to pay our way. For 8 months now, I've been trying to get the Congress to approve our contribution to the International Monetary Fund. Now, it's not perfect, and the IMF is having to make adjustments, too, to recognize the new realities of the global economy. But it is the most important instrument for helping countries, first of all, reform as they should, and then if they do, get back on their feet; and, secondly, for helping us limit the contagion that is now gripping so many Asian economies from bleeding over into Latin America, for example, our fastest growing market as a country, and into countries that have done a good job in managing their own economies. I think it is absolutely imperative.

And it's pretty hard to make an issue this, normally, esoteric, an issue in an election year. But I'm telling you, if we don't exercise our responsibility to try to stabilize the global economy, as Alan Greenspan said the other day, we cannot forever be an island of prosperity in a sea of dislocation. We have got to do this, and I feel very strongly about it.

The third thing that I think is very important is that the education agenda be continually pushed forward. Eight months ago I put before the Congress an education program based on the best research about what is working in our schools. Among other things in the balanced budget, not spending the surplus, it would provide funds for another 100,000 teachers to be hired to take average class size down to 18 in the early grades. It would provide a tax incentive program to rebuild, remodel, or build 5,000 schools at a time when it's a big problem. It has the funds to continue our part of hooking up all the classrooms to the Internet by the year 2000. It has funds for another, over a several year period, 3,000 charter schools—and thank you, Reed Hastings, for all the work you've done here in California. California is leading the way, thank you very much.

And a lot of other things that are very, very important, including paying the college expenses of 35,000 young people who can then pay their college expenses off by going into inner-city areas and other areas of teacher shortage and teaching for a few years to pay their expenses off. It contains the best examples of the most reform-oriented, big-city school system in the country, which I visited again today, I think for the sixth time, in Chicago, where they have ended social promotion. And underperforming students in what used to be thought of as the worst big-city school system in the country— I went to a school district today where 100 percent of the kids live in Cabrini-Green, one of the most economically challenged housing projects in America. They have doubled their reading scores and tripled their math scores in 4 years.

And there is no social promotion, but they don't just throw the kids out. Every child that doesn't perform has to go to summer school. And they have after-school tutoring programs, so that now the summer school program in Chicago is the sixth biggest school district in America—the summer school. Over 40,000 children get 3 square meals a day there. But learning is beginning to occur because they have standards and accountability, but support. They don't treat children who don't perform as failures; they treat them as people who need more support and more help. And I think that's important.

So we need to save Social Security. We need to fund the IMF. We need to pass the education program. Two other things I want to mention. I have worked very hard for the last 6 years, along with the Vice President, to persuade the American people that we can improve the environment and grow the economy. And compared to 6 years ago, the air is cleaner; the water is cleaner; the food is safer; lots of toxic waste dumps have been cleaned up. But there are still people who just don't believe it. And we're having a huge environmental fight up there, and protecting these environmental initiatives is very important.

Finally, I strongly believe that Congress ought to pass a uniform Patients' Bill of Rights for the country. And there may even be some disagreement about that in this audience, but I'd just like to tell you what my experience is here. There are 160 million Americans in managed care plans. Forty-three big managed care companies are supporting this legislation. Why? Because they provide these protections, and they know that they're being punished in the marketplace for doing what they believe is right.

Now, a lot of you are employers, and you're concerned about controlling costs, but let me just tell you some of the things that are actually happening in America today. In big cities, if somebody walks outside a hotel and gets hit by a car, depending on what the coverage of the plan is, they might drive past three hospitals to get to an emergency room covered by the plan, instead of going to the nearest emergency room. There are places where, even if your doctor recommends you see a specialist and says, "I'm sorry. I can't do this," they still can't get to see a specialist until they go through three or four layers of approval.

Many times all these horror stories you hear about people being denied care are not quite accurate. Actually, almost always, or more than half the time, the managed care company does approve the procedure, but the delays are so great that it's too late to do the right thing.

Another big problem for small businesses is, when the employer changes providers, very often immediately all the employees are affected by it. Now, that sounds reasonable. Except if you're pregnant, and you're 6 months pregnant, you shouldn't have to give up your obstetrician for months 7, 8, and 9. If you're in the middle of a chemotherapy treatment, you shouldn't have to give it up in the middle of the treatment. That's what this bill does. And it also protects the privacy of medical records, which I think is very, very important.

So I think this Patients' Bill of Rights is the right thing to do for the country, and I hope it will pass. Those are the big issues, to me, that we ought to be fighting for.

Now, in the election, the voters will have a clear choice. Do they want this kind of progress, or do they want partisanship? Do they want this to focus on people, or do they want this to focus on politics? And you can help us.

Now, if you look at the long run—let me just mention something very briefly, just a few things that I wish you'd begin to think about. How are we going to change Social Security and Medicare so that we legitimately care for the elderly without bankrupting their children and grandchildren? What are we going to do? We'll be making those decisions—I hope and pray—in the first 6 months of next year. How are we going to do this? The Medicare Commission will complete its report, and we will complete our year-long work on Social Security in December.

The second question: What else do we need to do in education, to really provide world-class education, K through 12, in America? Everybody knows we've got the best system of higher education in the world; how are we going to give every child, without regard to their circumstances in life, that opportunity?

Third question: How can we convince people that the problem of climate change is real and the biggest long-term environmental challenge—closely related, especially in California, to the problem of ocean degradation, which is fast becoming a global problem? And how can you here, who know it to be true, convince people that there is no longer an iron link between old-fashioned, industrial-era energy usage and economic growth? Because, make no mistake about it, that, in the end, is what is holding back our advances in the environment. Most people who are in decisionmaking capacities honestly believe you can't grow an economy unless you use energy in the way we've been using it for the last 50 years, and unless you use more of the same kind. You can help; you can make a huge difference there.

Fourthly, what are we going to do over the long run—and it has to be done fairly soon—to modify the world financial system and the world trading system so it works for ordinary people and it limits these huge boom/bust cycles without interrupting the free flow of capital? I am very worried that in country after country after country, if you have year after year after year of falling living standards, that people will fall out of love with free markets and free governments. It's only been the last 3 or 4 or 5 years that, for the first time in all human history, more people are living under governments that they chose themselves than dictatorships of one kind or another. This is a precious gift, this gift of freedom, but we have to prove that it will work for ordinary people. And the United States has to take the lead in that.

And all of you have a huge stake in it—a huge stake in it. Everything you want to do with the Internet rests on the premise that people will get freer and freer and freer, and that it is a very good thing. And you know I believe that. So we have got to deal with that.

And finally, I just ask you to help me—I got the last report of the President's Initiative on Race last week, and I've got this on my mind, too. If you think about what I do in foreign policy as your representative—we're worried about Kosovo today. What is Kosovo? It's an ethnic conflict between Serbs and Albanian Muslims. What is going on in the Middle East? It's an ethnic and religious conflict. I'm going to do a lot of work on that next week. What is the conflict—that we're celebrating, I hope, the final end of—in Northern Ireland? It's a religious conflict.

You may have been reading—a few years ago we had this horrible war in Rwanda, where over three-quarters of a million people were killed in a tribal conflict. And now in the Congo there are five different countries intervening in their conflict there, and part of it is the settling of old scores among tribal conflicts.

Now, here in Silicon Valley, you see people from all over the world, from all different racial and ethnic groups and religious and cultural backgrounds, finding a way to work together to make common cause. And over the long run it may be our ability to prove that we can preserve and advance the American system and give deeper meaning to the Constitution of the United States as we grow more diverse, than anything else, that will permit us to be a powerful force for good in the 21st century.

And so I say to you, I hope you'll keep working on that, and I hope you'll keep lifting that up, because I see deep in the heart of people all over the world this almost compulsive drive to define themselves in negative terms, in the fact that their life has meaning because they are not the "other," whatever the "other" is. And just the way you do things here is a constant, daily rebuke to that. And that's what America has to do. We have to prove that we are bringing out the best in each other if we hope to be a positive force in bringing out the best in people throughout the world.

Finally, let me just say, I believe that the best days of this country are still ahead of us. And I believe that we have been given a precious gift, but an enormous responsibility. The real question before us is, now that we have all this prosperity, now that we have all this confidence, now that we have this dominant position in the world, what are we going to make of this moment? Are we going to relax? Are we going to feed on each other? Are we going to care for each other and build a better tomorrow? I think I know what your answer is, and

I want you to help me make that America's answer.

Thank you, and God bless you.

NOTE: The President spoke at 9:55 p.m. at the Tech Museum of Innovation. In his remarks, he referred to dinner host John Doerr; Mayor Susan Hammer of San Jose; and Reed Hastings, chief executive officer, Technology Network.

The President's Radio Address
September 26, 1998

Good morning. As everyone knows, cancer can be the cruelest of fates—it strikes nearly every family. It struck mine; I lost my mother to cancer.

Losses like these are the reasons why tens of thousands of Americans are coming together today on the National Mall in Washington, DC, with one common purpose: to focus our entire Nation's attention on cancer. Gathering today are patients and survivors, families and friends, doctors, and Americans from all walks of life. The Vice President, who's been a real leader in our administration's struggle against cancer, will join their ranks and will speak about the specific steps we're taking to win the fight.

This morning I want to talk to you about our overall vision of cancer care and research as we approach the 21st century. This is a time of striking progress, stunning breakthroughs. With unyielding speed, scientists are mapping the very blueprint of human life, and expectations of the human genome project are being exceeded by the day. We are closing in on the genetic causes of breast cancer, colon cancer, and prostate cancer. New tools for screening and diagnosis are returning to many patients the promise of a long and healthy life. It's no wonder scientists say we are turning the corner in the fight against cancer.

For 6 years now, our administration has made a top priority of conquering this terrible disease. We've helped cancer patients to keep health coverage when they changed jobs. We've accelerated the approval of cancer drugs while maintaining safe standards. We've increased funding for cancer research and, as part of our balanced budget, strengthened Medicare to make the

screening, prevention, and detection of cancer more available and more affordable.

Still, we know that we must never stop searching for the best means of prevention, the most accurate diagnostic tools, the most effective and humane treatments, and someday soon, a cure. To that end, there are several steps we must take.

First, to build on our remarkable progress, I proposed an unprecedented, multiyear increase in funding for cancer research. As studies proceed, we must remember that patients, as much as scientists, have a critical perspective to add to any research program. That's why I'm announcing that all Federal cancer research programs will, by next year, fully integrate patients and advocates into the process of setting research priorities.

Next, as we continue to unravel the genetic secrets of cancer, we must apply that knowledge to the detection of the disease. I am therefore issuing a challenge to the scientific community to develop, by the year 2000, new diagnostic techniques for every major kind of cancer so we catch it at its earliest and often most treatable stage.

Also, we should give more patients access to cutting-edge clinical trials so they and researchers can get faster results. That's why I'm directing the National Cancer Institute to speed development of national clinical trials systems—a simple, accessible resource for health care providers and patients across our Nation. I'm also urging Congress to pass my proposal to cover the cost of those trials for Medicare beneficiaries who need them most.

Finally, we are fighting against the leading cause of preventable cancer by doing everything we can to stop children from smoking. America needs a Congress with the courage to finish the job and pass comprehensive tobacco legislation.

New technological tools, new networks of information, new research priorities—all are part of our overall approach to health care that puts the patient first. On this day, as Americans from all walks of life and all parts of our Nation renew our national fight against cancer, we do well to remember that we are doing more than curing a disease. We are curing the ills that disease may cause: the stigmas, the myths, the barriers to quality care. The concerned citizens on The Mall today show that we are overcoming those barriers, one by one, and at the same time building a stronger and healthier America.

Thank you for listening.

NOTE: The address was recorded at approximately 7:30 p.m. on September 25 at the Fairmont Hotel in San Jose, CA, for broadcast at 10:06 a.m. on September 26. The transcript was made available by the Office of the Press Secretary on September 25 but was embargoed for release until the broadcast.

Remarks at a Democratic National Committee Luncheon in Rancho Santa Fe, California
September 26, 1998

Thank you very much. Well, if I had any sense, I wouldn't say anything. [*Laughter*] Thank you, Bill. Thank you, Star. Thank you, Len. And all of you, I can't tell you how much I appreciate you being here. I'm delighted to see Lynn Schenk, and I'm delighted to see Christine Kehoe. And we are determined to see her prevail. If you want to do something for what you just stood up for, send her to Congress. Send her to Congress.

I'd also like to thank all of you who have been my friends over the years, and some of you whom I have just met today, I am very grateful to see you here. I'd like to thank all the people who are responsible for our wonderful meal and the terrific musicians. Let's give them a hand. Didn't they do a great job? Thank you. [*Applause*] The Wayne Foster Group. Thank you so much. Bless you.

It's nice to be here in this humble little house. [*Laughter*] This is the first place I've ever been where the fish are worth more than I make in a year. [*Laughter*] Listen, I want to say, this is really a magnificent home. It's a real tribute to the work that Bill has done over the years and to the feeling that they have for all of us that they open their home to us. And I'm very grateful to be here.

I will be brief. I've had a remarkable couple of days. I was in Chicago yesterday, which most of you know is my wife's hometown. And I got my Sammy Sosa Chicago Cubs baseball shirt, which was promptly taken away from me last night when I met up with Hillary and Chelsea in northern California.

Hillary has been up in Washington and Oregon and San Francisco campaigning, made an appearance last night for Barbara Boxer up there. And I'm here, and I'll be in Los Angeles tonight and tomorrow. I'm going on to El Paso and San Antonio, Texas, and then I'm going back to Washington on Sunday night to try to bring to a closure this session of Congress with some productive action. But I cannot tell you how much it means to me, not only as your President but as a person, what you have said here and what I have seen all across this country. And I'm grateful, and my family is grateful, and I thank you.

But there is something far bigger than all of us at stake here, and that is our country, our system, and where we're going. And I tell everybody who comes up to me worrying about this, that the real enemy of our party and our principles and our programs and the direction of the country is not adversity. Adversity is our friend. It inspires us to action. It gives energy. It gives us steel and determination. Our real enemy is complacency, or cynicism.

You know, things are going pretty well for our country now, and I'm very grateful that I had a chance to be President, to implement the policies that I ran on, that I talked about 6 years ago, I think, this month, when I was here with Bill and Star at their previous home. I'm grateful that we've got the lowest unemployment rate in 28 years and the lowest crime rate in 25 years and the smallest percentage of people on welfare in 29 years. And in just a few days, less than a week now, we'll have the first balanced budget and surplus in 29 years. I'm grateful for that. But the question is, what are we going to do with it?

I'm grateful that we've opened the doors of college to virtually anybody now who will work for it, with tax credits and the deductibility of student loans and more scholarships and work-study positions; and that we added 5 million kids to the ranks of those with health insurance, passed the Brady bill and the family medical leave act. I'm grateful for all that. But what are we going to do with it? What are we going to do with it? That's really what's at issue here.

Our friends in the Republican Party believe they're going to win in the midterms, first of all, because they wanted me——

[At this point, birds began chirping in the background.]

I don't mind the birds; it's just background music. [*Laughter*] Believe me, I've had worse background music lately. [*Laughter*]

The Republicans believe they're going to do well in these elections, first of all, because in every single election since the Civil War, with the President in his second term, the President's party has always lost seats at midterm. The second thing they're banking on is money. Even though you've been very generous and you've come here, they always have more money than we do, especially now that they're in the majority. But we have something that money can't buy and that history can't overcome: We are on the right side of the issues for America's future.

The history we want to make tomorrow and the next day and the next 10 or 20 years is the right history for America. And all we have to do is to get enough of our people to understand that, to get enough energy out there, to get enough people to show up on election day, and all the history in the world won't make a difference, and all the money in the world they have won't turn the tide. Because people now know that when it came to the budget vote in 1993, which reduced the deficit by 93

percent before we had the bipartisan Balanced Budget Act, we didn't have a single Republican vote. They know we barely had any votes for the crime bill when we banned assault weapons and put 100,000 police on the street, or for the Brady bill. They know that we had almost all and only Democratic votes—barely any Republican votes—for the family and medical leave law.

And if you look at the last year, when this country has had lots of challenges, and we had the resources to meet them, what has happened in this Congress in the last year? They've killed the tobacco legislation, to which Bill alluded. They've killed campaign finance reform. They have taken no action on my education program. The other night, in a breathtaking move, the Republican leader of the United States Senate actually had to shut the Senate down and make people go away for 4 hours because it was the only way to keep them from voting on the Patients' Bill of Rights. And he knew if we ever got a vote, one of two things was going to happen: it was either going to pass, or they were going to be punished for killing it for the insurance companies that wanted to kill it. So what did they do? They shut the place down. Unprecedented!

Now, what this is really about, this election, is not what's going on in Washington, DC; it's what's going to go on in the lives of the people in San Diego and El Paso and Racine, Wisconsin, and the Northeast Kingdom in Vermont and all the places in the country where the people live who send people to Washington, DC. That's what really matters.

And there is a very clear choice about what to do with this moment, and I think—if you just think about the things we need to do right now to prepare for America's future—I'll just mention five very quickly. Number one, we're going to have a balanced budget and a surplus on October 1st, for the first time in 29 years. They voted in the House and may vote in the Senate for a tax cut to start spending the surplus right away.

Now, I remind you, we quadrupled the debt of the country between 1981 and 1993, when I took office. These surpluses in the years ahead—they say, "Oh well, we know we're going to have them, so we can spend some now, and it's 4 or 5 weeks before the election, and won't that be popular to just dish out a tax cut right here before the election." And it's the Democratic Party that's standing up for fiscal responsibility and saying no, and I'm saying no. And I'll tell you why.

First of all, we have waited for 29 years. We have worked for 6 years to get out of this terrible hole. I would just like to see the red ink turn to black and watch the ink dry for a minute or two before we run another deficit. Wouldn't you like to see that? Wouldn't you just like to see the ink dry? [*Applause*] You know, they didn't want to wait a day just to enjoy this incredible achievement. Now, why is that important? Because we've got a lot of trouble in the world today, in the world economy.

I was up in Silicon Valley last night, where they understand how dynamic things are. They live in a perpetual state of change there. But so do we all, and we dare not forget it. We forget it at our peril. We have to set a standard if we want to keep growing this economy, that America, of all the countries in the world, is the most solid, the most sensible, the strongest country in the world.

The second reason we shouldn't spend that surplus right now is that, before you know it, the baby boomers will begin to retire, starting in about 10 years. I'm the oldest of the baby boomers. People between the ages of 34 and 52, when we all retire, there will only be about two Americans working for every American drawing Social Security. Unless something totally unforeseen happens to the birth rate or the immigration rate, it will be about two to one.

The Social Security system today alone keeps half of the seniors in this country out of poverty; that is, without it, 50 percent of the seniors in this country would be in poverty, even with their other sources of income. Now, if we begin today and make modest changes, we can preserve the universal character of Social Security in the sense that it's a bottom line safety net for people that don't fall into poverty. But we can increase the returns, make some other changes, and avoid putting an unconscionable burden on our children and grandchildren.

I'm telling you, everybody I know my age is worried about this. I was home a few months ago, and I had a barbecue about 6 o'clock in the evening with about 20 people I grew up with. Most of them are just middle class Americans, don't make much money. Every one of them said they were plagued with the thought that their retirement would be a burden to their children and their grandchildren. They're not wealthy people. They know they're not going to have enough. But they are plagued with the thought that they will have to take money away from their children and grandchildren.

Now, we have worked for 29 years for this. It's the right thing to do, anyway, right now, because of all the instability in the world, for us to stay strong and have this strong economy and have this little surplus. But secondly, it's the right thing to do before we—I'm not against tax cuts. We have some tax cuts in our budget, but they're all paid for. But before we get into that surplus for tax cuts, before we spend a penny of it for new programs, we ought to save the Social Security system for the 21st century, so that we do not either run a lot of seniors into poverty or undermine the welfare of their children and grandchildren. It is terribly important.

That's a big issue that affects people that live outside Washington, DC. The second big issue—it's very important, again related to the economy—is I'm doing everything I can to limit the financial turmoil in Asia now, to begin to reverse it, and to keep it from spreading to Latin America, which are our biggest markets, our fastest growing markets for American goods and services—everything I possibly can to sort of right this instability in the international financial system that you see most pronounced in Asia and Russia now, but could affect our welfare. Alan Greenspan said the other day, more eloquently than I could, America could not forever be an island of prosperity. For us to grow over the long run, our friends and neighbors all across the world, on every continent, who are doing the right thing and working hard need to be doing better as well. That's what this International Monetary Fund issue is all about.

For 8 months I have been pleading with Congress just to pay our fair share of the International Monetary Fund so we'll have the money to stop the financial virus before it spreads across the globe and begins to bite us. That's a big issue, and it hasn't been done yet.

The third thing I want to say is, we will never be permanently secure in this kind of economy until we can say not only that we have the best system of higher education in the world, but that every one of our children, without regard to race or income or neighborhood, has access to a world-class elementary and secondary education.

And for 8 months I have had before the Congress, fully paid for in the balanced budget, a bill that would lower class sizes to an average of 18 in the early grades and put another 100,000 teachers out there to teach them; that would build or repair another 5,000 schools because the schools are overcrowded; that would hook all the classrooms in the country up to the Internet by the year 2000; that would build 3,000 more charter schools—an issue that California has been on the forefront of—that would, in short, keep us on the forefront of education. It would also reward school districts that have poor performance and a lot of kids in trouble, if they adopted high standards, accountability, no social promotion, but actually helped the kids and didn't denominate them as failures when they're young and they are no such thing.

I was in Chicago the other day. Chicago used to be the poster child of a bad, failing urban school district. I went to the Jenner Elementary School, where every single child lives in Cabrini-Green, one of the toughest public housing projects in all of America. In the last 3 years, their reading scores have doubled and their math scores have tripled. Chicago has a "no social promotion" policy, but if you fail, they don't just say you're a failure. They say you didn't pass the test, and you have to go to summer school. The Chicago summer school now is the sixth biggest school district in America. [*Laughter*] Guess what's happened to juvenile crime in Chicago. There are now 40,000 kids in that city that get 3 square meals a day in the school. So that's also in our plan, funds for other troubled districts to follow that model.

We also have funds for 35,000 young people to pay for their college education, and then they can go out and work it off by teaching in underserved areas. This is a good program. That's an issue in this election. It matters to you and to your future and to your children's future and to your grandchildren's future whether we can rescue, revive, and make excellent the public educational opportunities of every child in this country.

So those are three things: saving Social Security, stabilizing the global economy, putting education first.

I'll just mention two others. Number one, one of the biggest fights I have all the time, convincing people on both sides, is that America has to find a way to protect the environment and grow the economy, and that if we have

to choose one or the other, we're in deep trouble. We have spent hundreds of thousands of dollars complying with subpoenas from a congressional committee that doesn't want me to give tax incentives and spend research and development dollars to figure out how to grow the economy and reduce CO_2 emissions. And that's out of step with the rest of the world.

I was in San Bernardino County not very long ago with the head of the National Association of Home Builders at a low-income housing project, where they had solar reflectors on the roof that are so thin now they look like ordinary shingles, and glass that keeps out 40 percent of the heat and cold and dramatically reduces the power cost. And it improves economic growth. It creates jobs and improves the environment—big issue.

But believe me, the budget I'm about to get, unless they change their tune, is going to be riddled with things designed to deny that and to weaken our environment.

And finally, to me the thing that embodies as much as anything else the great philosophical difference that's at stake now in Washington is the debate over the Patients' Bill of Rights. Now, let me set the stage. There are 160 million Americans in managed care plans. I have been a supporter of managed care. Why? Because when I became President, health care costs were going up at 3 times the rate of inflation. It was unsustainable. We were going to bankrupt the country. There wouldn't be enough money left to spend on anything else.

But it's like anything else: if the bottom line is just whether you save money, rather than the bottom line of saving as much money as you can consistent with the health of the people that are being treated, you get in trouble. And now many, many managed care plans have health care decisions made by insurance company accountants, and you have to appeal to two levels up or more until you finally get to a doctor.

Our bill, which has the support of 43 managed care companies who are doing this anyway and are being punished for it, says this—it says simply, if you get in an accident, you ought to be able to go to the nearest emergency room, not one that's 5 or 10 miles away because that's the only one that happens to be covered by your plan. Number two, if your doctor says that he or she can no longer treat your condition and you need to see a specialist, you ought to be able to see one. Number three, if you work for a small business who changes providers, health care providers, at a given time during the year, you still shouldn't have to change your doctor if you're in the middle of a critical treatment.

Now, let me just graphically demonstrate what that means. This happens; these things happen. You remember when you had your first child. How would you feel if you were 7 months pregnant and your employer says, "I'm sorry, go get another obstetrician"? If anybody in your family has ever had chemotherapy—I've been through that—if your family member needs chemotherapy, you sit around thinking; you try to figure out ways to make jokes about it. My mother stood there thinking, "Well, maybe I won't lose my hair, or when I do, maybe I will finally get a wig." I never had to—you think—you try to be funny about it. And then you wonder whether you're going to be too sick to eat, right? In the middle of a chemotherapy treatment, do you think somebody would say, "I'm sorry, go get another doctor"? That's what this is about—basic things.

Our bill also protects the privacy of your medical records, which I think is very, very important and will become more important in the years ahead.

Now, the House of Representatives, the Republican majority passed a bill that guarantees none of these rights and leaves 100 million Americans out of what little it does cover. The Senate wouldn't even vote on the bill because they didn't want to be recorded, so they shut down business.

That's what this election is about. Don't be fooled about a smokescreen. This election is: Are we going to have a Patients' Bill of Rights? Is our policy going to be to grow the economy and preserve the environment? Are we going to put education first? Are we going to stabilize the global economy, so we can continue to grow? Are we going to save Social Security first? That's what it's about.

And if we go out and say, we are Democrats, this is what we're running for; we believe elections should be about the people that live outside Washington, not about who's crawling on whom in Washington, DC—everything is going to be fine. So I ask you, go out there and make sure that's what it's about.

Thank you very much.

NOTE: The President spoke at 3:35 p.m. at a private residence. In his remarks, he referred to luncheon hosts William S. and Star Lerach; Leonard Barrack, national finance chair, Democratic National Committee; Lynn Schenk, candidate for State attorney general; and San Diego City Council member Christine Kehoe, candidate for California's 49th Congressional District.

Statement on Strengthening Social Security
September 26, 1998

The Republican tax plan drains billions of dollars from the surplus before we have done the hard work of strengthening Social Security. First things first. I will insist that we reserve the entire surplus until we have seized this historic opportunity to save Social Security, and veto any bill that doesn't meet that principle. While it is regrettable that this plan survived today, I am heartened by the strong commitment to fiscal discipline and Social Security shown by those who opposed it.

Remarks at a Unity '98 Dinner in Los Angeles, California
September 26, 1998

Thank you very much. I hate to begin with a request, but if there was any way to turn down some of these lights, I would like it. I can't see any of you out there. Can you turn these lights down? It's not a nightclub act. But I'd just like to know that you're out there, you know? [*Laughter*] Thank you.

Let me begin by telling you how very grateful I am for the warm welcome you have given me tonight, to those of you whom I saw earlier. I thank you especially for the personal messages you had for me and for Hillary. You know, even Presidents and their families have to be people, too, and that means a very great deal to us. And I thank you more than you will ever know.

I want to thank Haim and Cheryl for having me back in their home and having all of you here in this beautiful, beautiful setting. I'd like to thank Michael McDonald for that wonderful song. We were all up there singing, but not as well as you. I want to thank the staff of our Unity events, the people who catered this wonderful dinner, and the people who served it. I thank them all. They did a wonderful job for us. Thank you.

I want to thank Gray and Sharon Davis for being such good friends to Hillary and me and such good friends to the people of California. You have to make sure that on election night they're victorious, and I believe they will be. I thank you so much for being here. I thank my friend Phil Angelides for being here and for running for office.

Let me say to all the Members of Congress here, I'm very proud of this Unity event. We began to do this in 1996, to work together through the Democratic committee and the Senate campaign committee and the House campaign committee. We found that our contributors were relieved because they were only being hit once, instead of three times. But we also found that when we pooled our efforts, as is always true in life, when we work together, we do better. And Nancy Pelosi and Bob Torricelli have done a wonderful, wonderful job and a great thing for our country.

I'd like to thank the other Members who are here. You may have heard through the applause what Nancy said about Brad Sherman, that he was on Speaker Gingrich's top 10 hit list. Well, for whatever it's worth, he's on my top 10 protect list, and I think he's going to win in November, thanks in no small measure to your help. And I thank you for that.

I have a lot of things to be grateful to Henry Waxman for, but one thing stands out above all: He has put the public health of the children of this country over the interests of the tobacco

industry that has done so much to undermine it and to stop us from passing comprehensive tobacco legislation. He fought that battle a long time before it was popular and before we in our administration got into it. And Henry, we're going to win sooner or later, sure as the world, and when we do, it will be in no small measure because of you. And I thank you for what you've done for our children.

I want to say, too, that I'm very glad Barbara Boxer is here tonight. You know she's in a tough race. She's always been in a tough race. She was in '92; she is now; she has been since the spring. But I think she's tougher than her race is. And I can say this about, to some extent, every Member of Congress who's here. But I want you to remember that many of the things for which the American people very generously give our administration credit, which flow from the economic prosperity we have, on one August night in 1993 hung by the thread of a single vote, first in the House and then in the Senate. And we did not have a vote to spare when we passed the economic plan that brought the deficit down 92 percent, before we passed the bipartisan Balanced Budget Act. That plan cut taxes for 15 million working families on modest incomes. I invested dramatic new monies in health research, as Nancy said, and education. It gave real incentives for people to invest in inner cities that had been left behind in the development we had enjoyed. And it hung by a single vote.

And Barbara Boxer, who had been elected in a narrow race in California in 1992, never blinked. She just went up there and did the right thing for America. And now the voters of California should never blink. They should go to the polls and do the right thing for California and for America and reelect her, because we need her in Washington, DC, very, very badly.

I would also like to thank Dick Gephardt and Tom Daschle for their sterling leadership of our caucus in the Senate and the House through some very, very difficult days and tough decisions. Again I say to you, many of the things for which the administration is credited required the support of Democrats. Even in the bipartisan legislation, we never would have gotten the money to insure 5,000 children who don't have health insurance—5 million children. We never would have gotten the funds to give a $1,500 tax credit to virtually every family in the country for the first 2 years of college and tax breaks for the other costs of higher education, and to expand dramatically the student loan program and the scholarship programs, if it hadn't been for the leadership of Tom Daschle and Dick Gephardt.

So every time you think about the good things that I have been able to achieve, if a law was required and a change was required, I can tell you that if it hadn't been for those two men sharing the same values, the same hopes, the same dreams, and being willing to pay the same heat, it would not have happened. And I want to see them and their counterparts rewarded in this election because they have consistently, in the majority and the minority, done the right thing for the United States. They are builders, not wreckers; they are uniters, not dividers; and they ought to be the leaders of the United States Congress.

Let me just say one final thing of appreciation for the Democratic Party. I want to thank the chairs of this event nationally and the chairs in California. I want to thank Steve Grossman, who did the right thing to go back home to his child; and Len Barrack, our finance chair.

We've had a wonderful couple of days. Hillary just got back from Washington and Oregon, campaigning for our House candidates. She was in northern California with Barbara last night, and we got to spend the evening with Chelsea, and the morning until noon. And I was in Illinois yesterday and in San Jose last night, in Silicon Valley. I went to San Diego earlier today, and I'm here, and I'm going on to Texas in the morning.

America knows that it has a decision to make. And I want to talk to you pretty seriously about that just for a moment. The kind reception you gave me is an indication of a deep feeling that you and millions of other Americans have about what's going on in Washington. But what I desperately want this election to be about is what's going on outside of Washington, in the lives of the American people.

You know, I ran for this job because I did not believe the country was moving in the right direction, and I didn't think we had a vision to get to the new century. And I believe that we had some ideas—I and the people who were working with me—that would, first of all, make America work for ordinary people again; and secondly would bring us together in a spirit of reconciliation and community across this incred-

ible diversity that we have in our country. Indeed, one of the things that I regret the most about so much of the rancor of Washington is that it undermines what we so desperately need in this country now, which is a deepening spirit of unity and what we have in common with our neighbors and friends, no matter what the differences are. And I wanted America to be a force for peace and prosperity and freedom throughout the world.

And in the last 6 years, because of what we were able to do together, I'm very proud of the fact that we have the lowest unemployment rate in 28 years and the lowest crime rate in 25 years and the smallest percentage of people on welfare in 29 years, and we're about to have the first balanced budget and surplus in 29 years. I'm proud of the fact that we have advanced the cause of peace and freedom around the world and that we banned assault weapons at home and passed the Brady bill and passed the family and medical leave law and did a lot of other things to change life for people who could never afford to come to an event like this. I'm proud of all that.

But the real issue is, what are we going to do with this moment of prosperity and confidence? And you showed me once again tonight that adversity is not our enemy. Adversity is our friend. It's a harsh teacher sometimes, and I think we've all experienced that in one way or another in our lives. But it animates us to action and it forces us to get to the bottom of ourselves and ask what we really believe in and what we really care about and what we're prepared to work for and to sacrifice for. No, adversity is not our enemy in this election season, but complacency and cynicism are enemies.

Our opponents in the other party believe that they're going to pick up seats in this midterm election and because of what I call the M&M syndrome: midterms and money. Even though you're here tonight, they'll still have more money than we do for the next few weeks— quite a bit more. And usually at midterm elections, the electorate is older and wealthier and more likely to be Republican. In order for us to win, which I clearly believe we can, the American people have to understand what the real choice is and have to believe that just because times are good doesn't mean we can sit on our lead, because we can't.

All you have to do is look around the world today. Ron Burkle and I were talking tonight before I came over here about the troubles in Asia, the troubles in Japan, the terrible challenges the people of Russia are facing; the fear that many of us have that it could spread to our friends in Latin America who are actually doing a pretty good job running their economies; and what Alan Greenspan said the other night, that America could never remain—or at least not forever remain—an island of prosperity in a sea of economic distress.

The world is changing very fast. That's why I have said that we ought to be using this time to look at the big problems facing our country and to take action. Let me just mention a couple very quickly that I think are important and then give you the real comparison of what's going on.

Number one, we're going to have this surplus on October 1st. We've been waiting for it for 29 years; and every Member of Congress and I in this room, we've been working on it for 6 years. Now, I would like to see the red ink turn to black and dry a little. I'm just waiting for October 1st, just to take a deep breath and say that's another thing we did that was good for America.

The leaders of the other party, they want to give an election-year tax cut. Just a few weeks before the election, it would be popular; it would be great politics. But it's wrong. It is the wrong thing to do. It's wrong for two reasons.

One is, we need to show stability and discipline. We quadrupled the debt of this country in the 12 years before I became President. And now, with so much of the rest of the world in trouble, we need to show people we have got our head on straight and we are not going to knee-jerk in the management of our economy; we're going to be a force of strength and stability for the whole world.

The second and really the more important issue is that everybody knows the Social Security system we have now is not sustainable when the baby boomers retire. It's fine now, and it will be fine for several years in the future. But we know right now we cannot maintain the present Social Security system and take care of the elderly—and I remind you that half of the elderly people in this country are lifted out of poverty today because of Social Security. They would be in poverty were it not for Social Security, even those that have other sources of income.

Now, I have not said I'm against tax cuts. We have tax cuts in my budget, in the balanced budget, for child care, for education, for the environment. All I said is we shouldn't spend the surplus on tax cuts until we save Social Security for the 21st century. And that's very important. Everybody I know—there are some baby boomers here tonight—everybody between 34 and 52 is a baby boomer. I'm the oldest of them, though it grieves me to say so. [Laughter]

But I can tell you—not very long ago I was home in Arkansas eating barbecue with 20 people I grew up with, and very few of them would classify as upper middle class. Most of them have very modest incomes; they're just good, hard-working Americans doing the best they can to raise their kids. But every one of them was plagued with the notion that when they got ready to retire and there were only two people working for every one person on Social Security, if we don't do something about this now, we would have to take lots more money from our children and undermine their ability to raise our grandchildren just to sustain our retirement.

Now, you heard Bob Torricelli quoting de Tocqueville—we're going to see, because it's a clear choice in this election. They're offering everybody a quick-fix tax cut that won't amount to a lot of money to most people, but it sounds great before an election. And we're going into the teeth of the election and we say, "We would like to tell you this, but we're not going to do it; we're going to tell you truth: America needs to set a financial example, and we need to save Social Security first before we use any of that surplus for spending or for tax cuts. That's our position." It's a big issue, and it's the right thing for America.

The second big issue—I never thought I'd ever be giving a speech about this within 6 weeks of an election—is whether we're going to fund the International Monetary Fund. Most Americans probably don't know what it is. But I can tell you this, if you like the fact that your country has almost 17 million new jobs, and you want us to continue to lead the world, and you understand that 30 percent of our growth has come from what we sell to our friends around the world and a quarter of the world today is in a serious recession—in Asia, where so much of California's wealth has come from in the growth of our trading with Asian

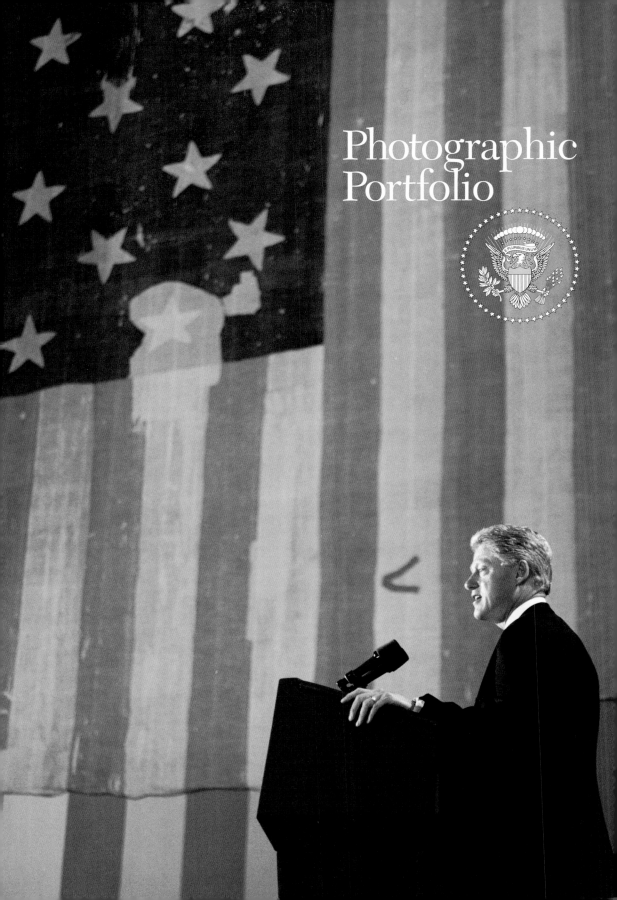

Photographic
Portfolio

Overleaf: Overleaf: Announcing a pledge of private funding for restoration of the Star-Spangled Banner at the National Museum of American History, July 13.
Above: At a discussion with environmental specialists in Guilin, China, July 2.
Above right: Participating in the White House Conference on School Safety in the East Room, October 15.
Left: With Secretary of State Madeleine Albright at the Wye River Conference on the Middle East in Queenstown, MD, October 15.
Right: Signing the Wye River Memorandum with Chairman Yasser Arafat of the Palestinian Authority, King Hussein I of Jordan, and Prime Minister Binyamin Netanyahu of Israel in the East Room, October 23.

WORKING TO PROTECT
SCHOOLS AND CHILDREN

Left: Decorating a Christmas tree at the Church of the Nativity in Bethlehem, Israel, December 15.
Below left: Greeting the people of Omagh, Northern Ireland, September 3.
Below: Addressing the people of Limerick, Ireland, September 5.
Right: Receiving a copy of the Koran presented by Chairman Yasser Arafat of the Palestinian Authority in Gaza City, Gaza, December 14.

Left: Working with a student at Jenner Elementary School in Chicago, IL, September 25.
Below: Participating in a demonstration of the food-service job training program at D.C. Central Kitchen, December 21.
Right: Greeting participants at a Veterans Day ceremony in Arlington, VA, November 11.
Overleaf: At the Pan Am Flight 103 bombing 10th anniversary observance in Arlington, VA, December 21.

markets—then you know that America has to do something to lead the way.

I'm doing my best to get all the other wealthy countries in the world to focus on this, to try to help Asia recover, to try to get Japan restored to growth, to try to help Russia, not only because it's the morally right thing to do for them but because it's in our interest. We can't grow and continue to prosper unless our friends and neighbors grow.

And for 8 months, I've been asking this Congress to fund our contribution to the International Monetary Fund. They need the money, and I can't do the job without it. And we can't possibly be expected to lead if we're the biggest piker on the block and we won't pay our fair share. So that's a big issue in this election.

The third thing I'd like to talk to you about is education. Eight months ago, in the State of the Union, I gave the United States Congress an education agenda to try to make sure that all of our children have access to world-class elementary and secondary education. It was based on the best research available of what we know works. The plan, paid for in the balanced budget, would put 100,000 teachers out there to lower average class size to 18 in the early grades. It would build or repair 5,000 schools, because a lot of schools are over-crowded or breaking down. It would hook up all the classrooms in the country to the Internet by the year 2000. It would provide for the development of voluntary national standards, exams to measure whether the kids were meeting them; and would reward school districts that are in trouble if they end social promotion and adopt tutoring, after-school and summer school programs for the kids who need it, so we don't tell them they're failures because they're in a system that's failed. It would provide college scholarships to 35,000 young people that they could pay off by going out into our most troubled school districts and giving a few years of their lives to teach. It would provide for 3,000 charter schools over the next few years, something that California is leading the way in.

It is a good program. It ought to be passed. And I can promise you it will not be passed by this election, and it won't be passed in toto unless we have a Democratic Congress. And that's a good reason to fight for the people who are here and all the people they represent throughout this country.

Finally, let me just give you one other issue, because to me it is sort of the crystal representation of the differences in our parties now. For 8 months, I have been trying to pass a Patients' Bill of Rights. It sounds good, but let me tell you what it really means—160 million of us Americans are in managed care plans now. I have supported managed care because when I became President, inflation costs in health care were going up at 3 times the rate of inflation, and it was going to absolutely bankrupt the country if we didn't do something about it.

On the other hand, I want to manage the health care system as best as possible, consistent with the main goal, which is keeping people healthy or making them well if they get sick. That's the goal; it's not managing the system. You manage the system so you can use your forces to advance the health of Americans. But in too many cases, health care decisions are being made by accountants, not by doctors. And in too many cases—cruel individual cases—the interest of ordinary people are being washed away.

So let me tell you what our bill does. It says that if—God forbid—you get hit by a car leaving this party tonight, and you're in a managed care plan, you should be taken to the nearest emergency room, not one 10 or 15 miles away just because it's covered by your plan. It says if your physician tells you that he or she can't treat you and you need to see a specialist, you have a right to see one. It says that if you're in the middle of a treatment of some kind, and your employer changes health care providers, you can stay with your doctor until you finish your treatment.

Just imagine—this actually happens in America now. Most of us—some of you have young children here; some of us have children that are grown or children who think they are grown. [*Laughter*] But just remember when your first child was born. How would you have felt 6 months into the pregnancy if somebody had said, "I hope you're all right, but you've got to change obstetricians"? It happens.

Have you ever had anybody in your family in chemotherapy? I have. And if you have, you'll identify with what I'm about to tell you. You know it happens, and you try to find a way to put on a happy face and be brave and even try to find a way to make jokes about whether your loved one is going to lose their hair or not. And then you wonder when you're going to be so sick you can't eat anymore. It's tough enough. If you're in the middle of a chemotherapy treatment, how would you feel to be told that you have to change doctors?

This is serious business. That's all our bill does. It gives you these basic, human protections. And it says your medical records ought to be kept private.

Now, for 8 months there's been no action on our bill. But let me tell you what the majority in the other party has done. In the House of Representatives, they passed a bill which they called the Patients' Bill of Rights which did not guarantee a single, solitary thing I just described to you, and left 100 million Americans out of what little it did provide.

In the Senate, when Senator Daschle and his friends attempted to bring up the Patients' Bill of Rights, the Senate Republican leader was so frightened of it, was so afraid to have his Members recorded voting against it that he actually shut down the Senate for 4 hours—unheard of. He called off business. They turned out the lights. They ran away and hid under their desk to kill it by stealth because they did not want to be caught voting for the insurance companies instead of for the people of this country.

Forty-three managed care plans are endorsing our bill. Why? Because they take good care of their people, and they're being punished for it.

Now, I want you to think about this. What do we stand for? We stand for saving Social Security first, for putting the education of our children before any other investment priority. We stand for America's continued leadership to keep our own growth going and to help the world economy. We stand for a Patients' Bill of Rights.

What have they done this year with their year in the Congress? They have killed the tobacco legislation that would have helped our children. They killed campaign finance reform. They are killing the Patients' Bill of Rights. They've taken no action on the International Monetary Fund, no action on the education program. And insofar as they have taken action, they've moved backwards on saving Social Security first, and they're still continuing their stealth attack on the environment.

Now, that's what this is about. It's about what kind of country America is going to be. So we have a choice to make. It in some ways grieves

me to make these speeches. I had hoped by the time I'd been here 6 years, trying to bring people together, that we would have a greater sense of bipartisanship in America; that there would be a greater sense of harmony here, just as I believe there is a greater sense of understanding across racial and ethnic and religious lines in this country than there was 6 years ago. But you know the truth. You knew the truth when you stood up and cheered. I wanted you to hear it tonight not in a political, rah-rah speech, but in calm, direct, but very blunt terms.

This is a very great country. We are blessed to be in this moment. But we have a solemn responsibility to our children, to our legacy, and to the world to make this election about the American people, not about the squabbles in Washington, DC. And if you will go out and do that, I promise you we'll spend every red cent you have given us tonight to do that.

But you have friends; you have neighbors; you have means of communication. You need to talk to people about what's really at stake here. And you tell them, "You know what the other guys are for. The Democrats are for keeping the economy strong, saving Social Security first, putting the education of our children above all other investment priorities, and passing that Patients' Bill of Rights. They're for an America coming together. They're for progress, not partisanship. They're for people, not politics." °

If you do that, we're going to have a stunning victory in November, against all the tide of history and against all the money and all the midterm arguments they can make, because it's the right thing for our country, for our children, and for our future.

Thank you, and God bless you.

NOTE: The President, spoke at 9:42 p.m. at a private residence. In his remarks, he referred to dinner hosts Haim and Cheryl Saban; musician Michael McDonald; California gubernatorial candidate Lt. Gov. Gray Davis and his wife, Sharon; Phil Angelides, candidate for State treasurer; Leonard Barrack, national finance chair, and Steve Grossman, national chair, Democratic National Committee; and Ron Burkle, chairman, Yucaipa Companies. A portion of these remarks could not be verified because the tape was incomplete.

° White House correction.

Remarks at a Reception for Gubernatorial Candidate Garry Mauro in San Antonio, Texas
September 27, 1998

The President. Thank you very much.

Audience member. Don't give up!

The President. Well, ladies and gentlemen—you don't have to worry about me giving up. [*Applause*] Thank you. Garry Mauro promised me that if I came to Texas in the wake of all this controversy, I would get a warm welcome. And he nearly overdid it today. [*Laughter*]

It's great to be back here. I want to thank Frank Herrera and his whole family for making us feel so welcome at their humble little homestead here. We ought to give him a hand. Thank you. [*Applause*]

I want to thank all the people who provided our music and catered our food and made this such an enjoyable occasion. I want to thank the candidates who are here who are running for office—Jim Mattox, Charlie Gonzalez—Richard Raymond is not here—Joe Henderson. I want to thank Molly Beth Malcolm, your State chair, and all the members of the Texas House and Senate who are here.

I want to say a special word of appreciation for the life and career of a man who has been my friend for more than 25 years, Henry B. Gonzalez. You can be really proud of what he has done.

And I want to thank my friend Ann Richards for finding ways to say things no one else can say that make a point no one could misunderstand. [*Laughter*] She's unbelievable.

I want to tell you why I wanted to come here today, for reasons other than the fact that Garry Mauro has been my friend since 1972.

Audience member. Mango ice cream!

The President. And the mango ice cream. [*Laughter*]

First of all, many of you whom I've already met have said some wonderful personal things to me about my family, and I thank you for that. You know, it's easy to forget in Washington, but Presidents and their families are still people. And it meant more to me than you'll ever know, and I thank you for that.

But I also want to tell you that I desperately want this election year, all across America and in Texas, not to be about what's going on in Washington, DC, but what's going on in San Antonio, in El Paso, in Lufkin, and towns like them all over America. You know, this is still a democracy; you're still in the driver's seat, but you have to get behind it and drive if you want to be heard.

Now, I ran for President—I started almost 7 years ago—in just about a week it will be the 7th anniversary of my declaration for President. When I started, nobody but my wife and my mother thought I could win. I had a lot of good friends in Texas and got two-thirds of the vote in the Democratic primary here on Super Tuesday, and it catapulted me on.

Now, I ran for President because I wanted to make this country work for ordinary citizens again; because I wanted us to be a leader for peace and prosperity and freedom in the rest of the world, to which we're closer and closer tied; and because I wanted to bring this country together in a spirit of harmony and unity across all the lines that divide us.

And in the last 6 years—Garry mentioned it, but I just want to reel it off to you—we tested the ideas that we brought to Washington. They're no longer the subject of debate. If you believe elections are about ideas, ideals, and the impact they have on ordinary people, in every election in this country and in every election in Texas, you ought to tell people we have the lowest unemployment rate in 28 years, the lowest crime rate in 25 years, the smallest percentage of people on welfare in 29 years. And Wednesday we'll have the first balanced budget and surplus in 29 years.

But the real question is, what will we do with it? I want you to remember what Garry said today. Our enemy is not adversity. Look at this crowd. Feel your own enthusiasm. Remember what many of you said to me today. Adversity is our friend. It forces us to dig deep, to ask ourselves what we believe in, what kind of people we are, what kind of people we want to be, where we want to go, and what we want to do with our lives. Adversity is our friend. Our enemies are complacency and cynicism. Those are our enemies, and don't misunderstand it.

The biggest problem Garry Mauro has got in this election is if people think, "Well, things are going well. Why do anything?" A lot of people think, "I had a tough time in the eighties, and things are going well now, and why don't we just relax and let things rock along?" And I can tell you that's appealing, but it's wrong. In Washington people think, "Things are going well; why don't we fight with each other and see who we can hurt?" [*Laughter*] And it's tempting, but it's wrong. It's wrong because the world is changing very fast.

I just got back from Silicon Valley, where all those computer companies are born, you know? Those people change for a living every day at blinding speed. But they understand something a lot of our fellow Americans don't, which is the world is changing for everyone. You pick up the papers; you know that we've got economic problems in Japan and the rest of Asia. There's a real risk that it will spread to our friends in Mexico and throughout Latin America who are doing a pretty good job managing their economies. If that happens, it will hurt Texas very, very badly, and our economy.

You see terrorism throughout the world; you see people fighting with each other throughout the world because of their racial, their ethnic, religious differences. We have challenges, and we have challenges at home. And the real question in this election in America and in Texas is, what are we going to do with this moment of prosperity?

This is Sunday, so I'll just make one Biblical reference. One of the most successful leaders in the Bible was Joseph. And what did he do? When Egypt was fat and sassy, he saved the grain. He made all those people go out and work and do things they'd just as soon not do. And they said, "This Joseph, why doesn't he let up on us?" But when the famine came, the people of Egypt were all right because a true leader did something in good times, understanding change.

When people ask you about Garry Mauro, you tell them about Joseph, and tell them what a mistake it would be for Texas to say, "We're just going to stand pat because things are good; who cares if anybody does anything? As long as I feel good, everything is all right."

Let me tell you what's going on in Washington. I believe as strongly as I can say that we have to use these good times as a responsibility to look to the future and deal with our challenges. Let me just mention four of them. Number one—and I'll compare the positions of the two parties.

Number one, Wednesday we're going to have the first balanced budget and surplus for 29 years. I've worked hard for it for the last 6 years. In 1993 we had a vote, without a single member of the other party—not a one—that passed by one vote in both Houses, that brought the deficit down over 90 percent before we passed the bipartisan balanced budget amendment. And that started this recovery. Now, the guys that didn't vote to balance the budget say, "Well, we're going to have a surplus for the first time in 29 years; let's give everybody an election-year tax cut 6 weeks before the election." Now, it's very popular. It's very popular, but it's dead wrong. And I'll tell you why.

Number one, it's wrong because the rest of the world is in economic trouble, and we have to set a standard of being strong economically and responsible. If we want to keep growing, we've got to help them get back on their feet, not make the same mistakes others are making.

Number two, the Social Security system is solid now, but it is not sustainable when the baby boomers retire. I ought to know; I'm the oldest of the baby boomers. [*Laughter*] And when we retire—you look at all the young people here today—when the baby boomers retire, there will only be two people working for every one person drawing Social Security. If we start now, well ahead of time, we can make modest changes that save Social Security that will not require us to make the horrible choice of either putting seniors back into poverty or taxing our children so that we undermine their ability to raise our grandchildren.

Now, people say no one thinks that far ahead. But you know that I'm telling the truth, don't you? [*Applause*] So I say, I want you to support us when the Republicans say, "Here's the goody; it's election time," and I say no. I'm not against tax cuts. We've got tax cuts for education, for child care, and for the environment in our balanced budget bill. But I'm against using that surplus for tax cuts or for spending programs until we save Social Security for our parents and our children.

Number two, I never thought this would be an election year issue, but you know now that 30 percent of our growth comes from our trading with other countries. Texas knows how important it is that we sell our goods and our products and our services to Latin America, to Asia, all over the world. We have got to lead the world back from the financial trouble they're in, or we will eventually get hurt. And it will be sooner rather than later.

In order for us to lead the world, we have to make our fair contribution to something called the International Monetary Fund. That's the fund we use to help the countries that are trying to help themselves and to keep the problems from spreading so we can keep selling our stuff. For 8 months I've been begging the Congress to do it, and they still haven't done it. So I say to you, if you like this economy and you want to keep it going, vote for us and our side because we will pay our fair share and lead the world back to prosperity.

Number three, in the balanced budget this year, I have given the Congress an education agenda. There has been no action for 8 months. Here's what it does: It puts 100,000 teachers in our classrooms to lower class size to 18 in the early grades; it repairs or builds 5,000 schools; it provides funds to hook up every classroom in the poorest schools in America to the Internet by the year 2000; it helps schools where the kids are poor and the neighborhoods are poor to adopt high standards, but to have after-school programs and summer school programs so the kids aren't deemed failures just because the system is failing them. It gives 35,000 young people college scholarships that they can pay off if they'll go out and teach in hard-pressed school districts for a few years after they get out of college. It is a good education program. It deserves to be passed. And our party is for it, and they're not.

Number four, Garry talked about the Patients' Bill of Rights. I want a national bill that says the following things: Number one, if you get hurt in an accident, they've got to take you to the nearest emergency room, not one halfway across town because it's covered by your plan. Number two, if your doctor tells you you need to see a specialist, you can. Number three, if you're in the middle of treatment and your company changes health insurance providers, they can't make you change doctors.

Now, let me tell you what's happening in America today. Pregnant women, 6, 7 months into their pregnancy—their employer changes coverage, they say, "Get another obstetrician." Have you ever had anybody in your family on chemotherapy? A lot of us have. I have, and it's pretty tough. And if somebody in your family—I bet you had the same experience we did when my mother had to do that. You sit around and you try to put on a brave face; you make a few jokes. You say, "Well, what are we going to do when you're running around bald?" And then you say, "Well, I'll finally get to wear that wig I've always wanted." You try to make fun of it to keep from the agony. And then you sit there and worry down deep inside, what's going to happen if you're so sick you can't eat anymore? Now, how would you feel in the middle of the chemotherapy treatment, if somebody said, "I'm sorry, your employer changed providers; you've got to get another doctor"? That happens.

And our bill would protect the privacy of your medical records, which is something people ought to care a lot more about today than ever before.

Now, in Congress, the Republicans passed a bill that didn't do any of that, and left 100 million Americans out of what little they did do. It is the symbol of the difference in the two parties in Washington and throughout the country today.

So I say to you, here's what we're for: We're for saving Social Security first; we're for keeping the economy going; we're for putting education first among all our investment priorities; and we're for a Patients' Bill of Rights. That's what we're for, and they're opposite us on all those issues. That is the choice nationally.

You want to know—Ann Richards asked if you could think of anything that Congress has done. Let me tell you what they've done this year, what our friends in the Republican Party have done with their majority. They killed campaign finance reform. They killed tobacco reform legislation to help us save our kids' health. They killed an increase in the minimum wage, with unemployment and inflation low, that would have helped 12 million hard-working Americans. They have gone backwards on saving Social Security first. They have gone backwards in protecting the environment. And they have done nothing on helping us to lead the international economy and nothing on the education agenda. That's what they have done less than a week before the end of this budget year. And that's the difference.

Well, what's that got to do with the Governor of Texas? I'll tell you what. For years and years and years, I heard the Republicans talk about how there ought to be more power given to the States, how the Federal Government did too much. They talked about it; we did something about it. We have the smallest Federal Government in 35 years. But what that means is it matters a lot more who the Governor is. We have given Governors more responsibility in education, more responsibility in health care, more responsibility in managing the environment, and more responsibility in growing the economy. It matters. If Garry Mauro were not my friend, I would be here saying he has a plan for Texas, and just because you're doing well doesn't mean you can stand pat. You need to bear down and think about your children and the future and stand up for what's right.

Now, our friends in the other party think they're going to do real well this year because of complacency and cynicism and what I call the M&M syndrome: money and midterms. They always have more money than we do. And at midterm elections our folks—who work hard, have a lot of hassles, and it's more trouble for them to vote—don't vote in the same numbers their folks do. But we can surprise them if the American people know what's really at stake.

If they understand this is a question about progress over partisanship, people over politics, unity over division.

And I'm telling you, you go out there and they ask you what it's about, tell them it's about the economy. Tell them it's about saving Social Security. Tell them it's about the integrity of your health care. Tell them it's about the education of your children. That's what we're for. And they know—every voter knows what they're for. Make a decision for your future and our country's future.

Thank you, and God bless you all.

NOTE: The President spoke at 3:09 p.m. at a private residence. In his remarks, he referred to reception host Frank Herrera; Jim Mattox, candidate for State attorney general; Charlie Gonzalez, candidate for Texas' 20th Congressional District; State Representative Richard Raymond, candidate for State land commissioner; Joe B. Henderson, candidate for State railroad commissioner; Molly Beth Malcolm, State Democratic chair; and Ann Richards, former Governor of Texas.

Statement on the Detention of Indicted War Criminal Stevan Todorovic in Bosnia
September 27, 1998

Early this morning in Bosnia, United States SFOR forces led a multinational effort to detain Stevan Todorovic, an indicted war criminal. The detention took place without incident, and Todorovic is now in the custody of the International War Crimes Tribunal in The Hague.

Todorovic, who served as chief of police for Bosanski Samac in 1992, is accused by the Tribunal of being personally responsible for some of the most heinous crimes that took place during the conflict in Bosnia.

This brings to 35 the number of indicted war criminals brought to justice. SFOR has assisted in well over half of these cases. This action by U.S. and other SFOR troops shows our continued determination to bring to justice those responsible for war crimes in Bosnia. This message should not be lost on those indicted war criminals still at large.

I wish to express my admiration for the SFOR troops who were involved in this operation and who continue to work daily to consolidate the peace in Bosnia and Herzegovina.

Statement on the Election of Gerhard Schroeder as Chancellor of Germany
September 27, 1998

Today the German people have once again exercised their democratic right to determine their national leadership. I extend my sincerest congratulations to Gerhard Schroeder. He and I had good discussions in Berlin this spring and in Washington this summer. I look forward to working closely with him. Germany is one of America's closest allies. As always, our two gov-

ernments will be fully engaged in a comprehensive policy agenda.

I also want to convey my gratitude and that of all Americans to Helmut Kohl. During his 16-year tenure, he has made historic contributions to the unity of his nation, the strength of our Euro-Atlantic community, and to peace throughout the world.

Remarks at a Dinner for Gubernatorial Candidate Garry Mauro in Houston, Texas
September 27, 1998

Thank you so much. I want to tell you that—I'll say a little more about this in a minute, but I'm very proud of Garry Mauro. I'm proud of him for having the courage to run. I'm proud of him for not listening to everybody, including me, who told him how terrible and difficult it would be. I'm proud of him because his commitment in the face of all the odds is the very kind of decision I now am trying to get the voters all over America to make in the coming election, and that is to discard what we normally do in good times—which is to just take a deep breath and kick our feet back and relax—and instead make a commitment to the future of our country.

He's coming out here against stiff odds because he thinks it's a mistake for Texas to sit back and relax and react to events but to take no initiative to prepare for tomorrow. It took a lot of courage. He made a very compelling presentation; and if you'll help him, if you'll get him enough help to get that message on television so that people can see what the real differences are, he'll make a very compelling presentation on election day in November as well.

I want to thank Lee and Sandra for having us in their unbelievably beautiful home and for doing so in a way that requires putting up a tent. I'd like to thank the people who prepared and served the meal. I'd like to thank the musicians; the piano player and the singer were wonderful, and the gospel group was amazing. And

I think I'm in the right frame of mind now to go back to Washington, DC, and deal with it for one more week. And I thank you for that.

I would like to thank Ambassador McLelland and Ambassador Schechter—boy, that sounds high-flown, doesn't it?—[*laughter*]—for being here tonight; my longtime friend Senator Rodney Ellis; Molly Beth Malcolm. Richard Raymond, thank you for running for office this year. And I'd like to say a special word of appreciation to Congresswoman Sheila Jackson Lee for her steadfast support of our agenda and work.

The temptation when you're with a bunch of old friends and some new ones, when you know you're basically preaching to the saved, especially on this day, is to kind of give a rah-rah speech. But if you'll forgive me, because of the present state of things and because I think this election is so profoundly important to the future of our country, I would like to take just a few moments to be serious with you.

I was looking at Garry today, thinking about how long ago it was I met him. And I saw Mark White tonight, and I thought about—it seemed like yesterday we were working as Governors together. It doesn't take long to live a life. It seems impossible to me, but next week it will have been 7 years next week since I first declared for President. The time has flown by. I want you to know, for all of you that have helped me make this journey, for all the slings and arrows, I wouldn't trade one single day of it for the opportunity it's given me to move this country in the right direction. And I want to thank you for it every day—every single day.

But the question for us as citizens is always, well, what now? You know, if I told you on the day I was inaugurated President, I'll come back here for the 1998 elections, and we will have had ample time to implement our program, and by then we'll have 16.7 million new jobs and the lowest unemployment rate in 28 years and the lowest crime rate in 25 years and the smallest percentage of people on welfare in 29 years and the lowest—the first balanced budget and surplus in 29 years and the highest real wage growth in 30 years and the lowest African-American poverty rate ever recorded and the biggest drop in Hispanic poverty in 20 years and the highest homeownership in history; and, oh, by the way, there will have been somewhere between 12 and 15 million people take advantage of the family and medical leave law; and a quarter of a million felons wouldn't have been able to buy handguns—and not a single hunter, in spite of what the NRA told them, has lost the ability to get a weapon and go hunting during hunting season, but a lot of innocent people's lives have been saved; and we'll be ahead of schedule and under budget in putting those 100,000 police on the street; and we've opened the doors of college to all Americans with a $1,500-a-year tax credit for the first 2 years and tax credits for the rest and deductibility of student loans and more scholarships and more work-study positions; and we've got 100,000 more young people in the AmeriCorps program working to make their communities better and earning money to go to college; we've got fewer toxic waste dumps, cleaner air, cleaner water, a safer food supply; and our country has been a force for peace all over the world and has tried to deal with the thorniest problems in the world in our time to make the world a safer place—now, if I had told you that on the day that I was inaugurated, you probably wouldn't have believed me.

But that's all true now. It turned out, because of the hard work of the American people and the wonderful people who were working with me and the loyalty of a Congress and the Democratic Party that had to fight bitter, bitter, bitter partisan opposition to nearly everything we did, we were able to implement the new ideas and

the new direction, and they turned out to be right. And I am grateful for how well America is doing today and for the support we have received.

And I'm grateful that Texas is doing well, and that every place I go in the country, people come up to me and say, "Mr. President, this is the best time I've had in a long time," or, "This is the best time I've had in my life." I am grateful for that. So what are we going to do about it? That's the question in the Governor's race. That's the question in these elections for Congress. What normally happens in good times is that people relax, and they're complacent.

A lot of you said some wonderful things to me tonight, gave me wonderful messages for Hillary tonight, proved once again what good people you are and what good friends you are. I thank you for all that. I'm very grateful. We've just had some great days, and we had one great night and a day with our daughter in California.

But I want to tell you, and I want you to hear me clearly, adversity is not our problem in this election. Adversity has energized our supporters. Adversity has clarified the choices. Adversity forces us to get to the bottom of ourselves and ask ourselves what we really believe in and what kind of people we want to be and what we're willing to put our necks on the line for.

Garry Mauro did something in presenting himself for Governor, near as I can tell, nobody else of his position, experience, and knowledge and ability was willing to do this year. Why? Because he believed it was time to make a difference.

Now, on the other side in Washington, as I've said many times, they believe that they'll do very well in these elections because of M&M—money and midterms—because they always have more money, and because traditionally at midterm elections the voter turnout goes down because our folks, the kind of folks that made it possible for us to have this good meal tonight, it's a bigger hassle for them to go vote than it is for most hardcore Republicans—who tend to be better off and older and find it easier to go to polls—and they tend not to be so interested. And then if you pile good times on top of it, there's a certain relaxation that says, "Well, let's just stay with the status quo and react to whatever comes along."

The enemies of our forces in this election are complacency and cynicism at what is going on in Washington, not adversity. Adversity is our friend. It's a harsh teacher sometimes, and I hate it. It's the kind of friend I could do without on some of the last several days. [*Laughter*] But it is, nonetheless, the truth. And what we have to decide as citizens is where we go from here.

Now, let me tell you what we're trying to do in Washington. What we're trying to tell the American people is, we're grateful that we're doing so well. But we did not get here by being casual, by reacting, by taking the easy path. We got here by making the big decisions and the tough ones in the right way. And the world is still changing very fast. All you have to do is pick up the paper any day and you see about the economic crises in Asia and the political turmoil in other parts of the world, and you realize that in this kind of dynamic world, as Alan Greenspan, the Chairman of the Federal Reserve, the other day said, America cannot simply be an island of prosperity in a sea of economic distress. So now that we have this balanced budget, this surplus, this success, we ought to use this moment to take on the big challenges facing America. That is the Democratic message. And let me give you four examples.

Number one, Wednesday we'll have the first balanced budget and surplus in a generation. The Republicans say, "Good, we finally got some money; let's spend it. Let's give everybody an election-year tax cut. It's only about 5½ weeks before the election, and we can make everybody so happy." It's great politics. And I say, it may be good politics, but it's the wrong thing to do. And it's wrong for two reasons.

First of all, this old world is in a lot of trouble. One-quarter of the world is in recession. Japan, the second biggest economy in the world, has had no growth for 5 years. Everybody looks to us to be strong and responsible and not to do the easy, quick thing but to do the right thing for our own growth and as a beacon of stability to the world. And I'm not going to give that up easily.

And even more important—even more important—everybody in America who has given it a minute's thought knows that while the Social Security system is very sound today and will be for anybody within shouting distance of needing it, that when the baby boomers retire—

that's me; I'm the oldest; it kills me to admit it. But people between the ages of 34 and 52 that were born after World War II are the biggest group of Americans ever, until the crowd of kids now in school. And when we retire, there will only be about two people working for every one person drawing Social Security. If we start now with this surplus to help us, we can make modest changes now that will enable us to secure the retirement of the baby boomers without imposing an unbearable burden on our children and their ability to raise our grandchildren.

Now, I know it's more popular to give an election-year tax cut. But I've been waiting for 29 years to get out of the red, and I've been working for 6 years to get out of the red. And when we voted in 1993 to get out of the red, for the economic program, we didn't have a single Republican vote. And the deficit was cut 92 percent before the bipartisan balanced budget bill passed in 1997. Now the same crowd that wouldn't help us cut the deficit wants to spend it before we even see the surplus. I would just like to see the red ink turn to black and dry at least for a day or two before we start spending it again, and I think that's right.

Now, this is a huge issue. Half the seniors in this country would be in poverty today if it were not for Social Security. We can make minor changes now, secure the retirement of the baby boom generation without undermining our children and grandchildren's future, and I am determined to do it. So that's the first issue. Do you believe in Social Security first, or do you want the election-year tax cut? Clear choice between the parties.

Issue number two: Do you believe that in order for us to grow economically, the rest of the world has to be growing so they can buy our products? Thirty percent of America's growth in the last 6 years has come from foreign trade. Now you've got a quarter of the world in recession, another quarter teetering. I have done my best to lay out a plan to try to help restore Asia, to try to help restore Russia if they will do what they can do for themselves; and more important for Texas, to try to keep what's going on there from spreading to Latin America and to Mexico, to our friends south of the border, our biggest trading partners in terms of growth. In order to do it, and for America to lead, we have at least got to pay our fair share to the International Monetary

Fund. That's where we get the money to do this stuff.

Ever since the State of the Union Address, I have been pleading with this Congress to fund our fair share of the International Monetary Fund, and they still haven't done it. They still haven't done it. And it's playing games with our own economic future and undermining our ability to lead. So that's the second issue. Do you want to keep the economic growth going in America, or do you want to take a powder?

The third issue is education. Garry spoke so movingly of that, but there are some things that we ought to do nationally to help. I have sent an education program to Congress in the balanced budget that does the following things: puts 100,000 teachers out there to lower class size to an average of 18 in the early grades all across America; it would build or repair 5,000 schools; it would provide funds to hook every classroom up to the Internet, including the poorest schools in south Texas or inner-city Houston or anywhere else in the country, by the year 2000; it would provide college scholarships to 35,000 young people and let them pay it off by going into our neediest areas and teaching off their college costs for 4 years. It would, in short, help move this country forward.

It would provide extra funds to the most troubled urban and rural school districts to have high standards, to stop social promotion, but not to tell the kids they're a failure when the system is failing them; instead, to give them after-school programs, summer school programs, mentoring programs to keep them off the street, out of trouble, and in learning. It is a good program, and it ought to pass. Now, for 8 months there has been no action, and the budget year begins on October 1st. We're for it, and they're not. It's a clear choice.

And the fourth issue is the Patients' Bill of Rights. You've had a little experience with that here. Our bill says, simply, you have a right to see a specialist if your doctor tells you you need it. If you get in an accident, you have a right to go to the nearest emergency room, not the nearest one your plan happens to cover that may be halfway across town. If you're in the middle of a treatment and your employer changes health plans, you can keep the doctor you've got until your treatment is over. In other words, they can't tell you when you're 7 months pregnant to get another obstetrician, or when you're 80 percent through a chemotherapy treat-

ment, you've got to stop and go see someone else; this happens today. It says if you have a question about whether a procedure is approved or not, you have a right to appeal it and get an answer, pronto, instead of months and months down the road when it's too late to do any good. It says you have a right to the privacy of your medical records. That's what we're for.

The response of the Republicans in Congress and the House was to pass a bill that didn't do any of the things I said, and left 100 million Americans out of what they did do. In the Senate, we tried to bring up the Patients' Bill of Rights, and the Republican majority was so afraid that the majority leader had to literally shut the Senate down for 4 hours the other night. I mean, they turned the lights out, and they got under their desks so they would not have to be recorded voting for the insurance companies against the people. I never saw anything like it in my life. It was death by stealth. [*Laughter*]

What else have they done with this last year, you might like to know. They have also killed campaign finance reform. They've killed the tobacco reform legislation to protect our kids from the dangers of tobacco. They killed the minimum wage legislation, and they're trying to continue their assault on the environment. I think we've proved you can improve the environment and grow the economy. That's the right policy, not to assault the environment.

So you've got a clear choice. In Washington, you've got a clear choice. Do you want to put Social Security first, make education our top investment priority, keep the economic growth going, and pass a Patients' Bill of Rights? Or do you want somebody that's against all that and wants to divert your attention to other things? It's a pretty clear choice. And if the American people understand it as that, I think they'll make the right decision.

In Texas, let me say one of the reasons I wanted to be here, apart from my friendship and admiration for Garry Mauro, is that I did something as President, with the help of the Democrats, that the Republicans talked about doing for years but never did. I don't know how many times Mark White and I went to the White House during the Governors' conference and listened to people intone about how, oh, the power in Washington should be devolved to the States. Near as I could tell, all they ever did was cut money and ask us to do more with less. But we never actually had any more flexibility, any more authority.

We actually did that. The Government today has over 300,000 fewer people in it than it did the day I was inaugurated—the Federal Government. It is the smallest in 35 years. The States have more responsibility—more responsibility for education, for the environment, for health care, for crime, for the economy. It matters more who the Governor is.

Now, come back to Texas—I did this Governor's job for 12 years, and I could still be doing it if I hadn't gotten diverted in 1991 and '92. [*Laughter*] I would never have gotten tired of it; I loved it. But I'm telling you, the time to act on the long-term problems of a State or a nation is the good time—not when times are bad, not when you don't have any money, not when people don't have any confidence, not when people are so worried about keeping body and soul together you couldn't even stand up and give a speech like the one I gave tonight; you would have to stand up and talk in slogans and deal with people's emotions. Now is the good time.

This is Sunday, so let me use one Biblical reference. We ought to behave like Joseph did in the Bible. Now, Joseph was a lot like Garry Mauro. He was not part of the elite of Egypt, and Garry Mauro is not part of the elite of Texas. Joseph was even a slave—at least Garry didn't have to go through that. [*Laughter*] And finally, Joseph got put in charge of Egypt, and times were very good. And he made a lot of people mad because he made all the people go out and work like crazy, as if their life depended on it, to gather up all the grain to guard against the days when things weren't so good. So when this famine came and swept over the land, Egypt kept right on chugging. Why? Because they had a leader who thought about tomorrow, who did not sit on the lead, bask in good times, and just react to whatever came up, but did what was right for the long term.

Our country needs to follow that example today. Respectfully, I believe this State should follow that example today. I applaud what Garry said. We don't want, we Democrats, we never want to get into responding in kind. One of the deepest disappointments of my Presidency is that I hoped that after 6 years of working to reconcile our people across the lines that divide us, things would be a little less acrimonious in Washington.

I think people are getting along better across racial and religious and ethnic lines out in the country, but there is still a big political divide in Washington. The only thing that can close it now is the vote of the people. The only thing that can elect Garry Mauro now is if you believe that it's better to have Joseph; that it's better to think in the good times you should take the big steps, not the baby steps; that in the good times you should be acting with confidence, not reacting to whatever happens to come along.

I promise you, I see it every day as your President in information you can read in the papers, in information that comes to me as classified: This is a dynamic changing world. We stand for progress over partisanship. We stand for people over politics. We stand for unity over division. And we stand for the future of our children over short-term advantage.

He deserves your support. And if you can get that message out, he's going to surprise a lot of people. And if you'll stay with that approach, we will win the congressional elections in November.

God bless you for being here, and thank you.

NOTE: The President spoke at 8:10 p.m. at a private residence. In his remarks, he referred to dinner hosts H. Lee and Sandra Godfrey; State Senator Rodney G. Ellis; Molly Beth Malcolm, State Democratic chair; State Representative Richard Raymond, candidate for State land commissioner; former U.S. Ambassador to Jamaica Stan McLelland; former U.S. Ambassador to Barbados Arthur L. Schechter; and Mark White, former Governor of Texas.

Remarks Following Discussions With Prime Minister Binyamin Netanyahu of Israel and Chairman Yasser Arafat of the Palestinian Authority and an Exchange With Reporters
September 28, 1998

President Clinton. First of all, I would like to publicly welcome Prime Minister Netanyahu and Chairman Arafat. We have had a very, very good meeting today, following the one-on-one meeting that the Prime Minister and the Chairman had last night, their first face-to-face meeting in a year.

I believe that we all agree that we have made progress on the path to peace. There has been a significant narrowing of the gaps between the two parties across a wide range of issues that were in the American initiative that we've been working on for months. I think also, to be candid, there's still a substantial amount of work to be done until a comprehensive agreement can be reached. And because I'm convinced that the two leaders and the people they represent want an agreement, I have asked them to come back to the United States in mid-October with their teams to do the intensive work necessary to see if we can conclude this.

Meanwhile, I've asked the Secretary of State and Ambassador Ross to go back to the region in early October to try to see how much preparatory work can be done to narrow the differences further and to agree on at least the modalities for what we will do here in mid-October.

So, all told, it was a good day. And again I want to thank both these men for the open, candid, respectful way in which they worked, and we worked, together. And we're going to work at this now to see if we can get it done.

Q. What are the major sticking——

Q. Mr. President, there was——

President Clinton. Wait, wait. One, two, three. We'll do them all.

Go ahead.

Palestinian State

Q. Mr. President, do you support the Palestinian state in principle, and do you think the Palestinians have the right to have a state made for—or in principle, and self-determination for them?

President Clinton. In the Oslo accords, that question was left for the final status negotiations.

Because of the heavy involvement of the United States in the peace process, I believe it would be in error for me to comment on that. I think the important thing is, that has to be resolved in the final status negotiations as provided for in the Oslo accords. As long as the peace process is going forward, whatever the United States says on that publicly will be unhelpful to the ultimate outcome.

Q. Mr. President, the First Lady commented on this in public——

Q. Mr. President, is it your assumption——

President Clinton. She did, but she's not the President, and she's not trying to manage this peace process. That's a different thing. But I'm telling you the—we gave our word, when we agreed to try to be an honest broker, to respect the Oslo process. And therefore—I have to tell you, when I'm in Israel or when I'm with American Jewish groups, they also try to get me to say things that I said before I was the President and the broker of the process, that I can no longer say. So it's a different—I gave my word that I would be faithful to the process that these two parties set out for the resolution of their agreement, and I have to try to do that.

Middle East Peace Process

Q. Mr. President, are you saying that the deadline is mid-October when you expect both Chairman Arafat and Prime Minister Netanyahu to come back to the United States for a settlement?

President Clinton. Well, let me say this. In the end, whether there will be this agreement depends upon how badly they want it, how much we can work together, how much trust can be built and sustained, what kind of process for ensuring the agreement can be agreed upon by the two parties. So I think what I'm telling you is that they have made a very unusual commitment; they have committed several days, and not only their own time but the time of their appropriate administration and staff people, to try to resolve the remaining gaps.

I can also tell you that I personally was very impressed by the way, the manner, and the substance of their conversation today with me. And so we all said we needed to continue to change the dynamics of the process to try to increase the likelihood of completion. We made significant progress on the path to peace, and I think we could finish it in mid-October, and I certainly hope we do.

Q. Mr. President——

Q. You promised me the question. Please. There was today—Mr. President——

Q. Could we hear from Chairman Arafat and Mr. Netanyahu——

Q. Mr. President, today there was a terror attack in Hebron, a shooting, and an Israeli woman was injured. The Israelis are saying that Arafat, Mr. President, Arafat is not fighting terrorism. Did you get any answers from Mr. Arafat concerning the implementation of the reciprocity principle? Is Mr. Arafat willing to stick to his commitments according to the Hebron accords and Oslo accords to fight terrorism?

President Clinton. Perhaps I should let him answer that. But he certainly affirmed that to us. And keep in mind, that's a part of the whole peace process, those kinds of agreements, and that's one of the things that the Prime Minister, representing the people of Israel, would raise, and something that has to be talked through.

But if either one of these gentlemen want to say——

Q. Chairman Arafat, what's your assessment of the talks today?

Chairman Arafat. What he has mentioned is covering everything—and instead of saying the same thing——

Q. ——Palestinian state today in——

Q. Mr. President, where has there been progress in the peace process——

Q. ——Mr. President.

Q. Chairman Arafat, are you convinced——

President Clinton. I believe there's been progress in all major areas. I think we're closer together on virtually—on every major issue that either Chairman Arafat has mentioned to me or that Prime Minister Netanyahu has mentioned to me than there was before. But we have an operating agreement here that we will all say that nothing has been agreed to until everything has been agreed to. I think that is a good operating agreement. If they ever decide to change it, then I will honor their decision. Otherwise, our position is that you cannot conclude that anything has been agreed to until everything has been agreed to.

Thank you.

NOTE: The President spoke at 12:45 p.m. in the Oval Office at the White House. A tape was not available for verification of the content of these remarks.

Message on the Observance of Yom Kippur, 1998
September 28, 1998

Warm greetings to all those observing Yom Kippur.

On the Day of Atonement, Jews across America and around the world fervently seek the blessing of forgiveness and reconciliation. The most solemn of Jewish holy days, Yom Kippur is a time of profound prayer, fasting, and self-examination.

Amid the clamor and distraction of everyday life, Yom Kippur is a call for silence and reflection, a summons for believers to remember and repair their fundamental relationships with God and with their fellow human beings. It is a challenge to Jews and a reminder to Americans of all faiths to live our lives according to our beliefs: to have faith in God's mercy and to have the humility and strength of spirit to begin again.

Best wishes for a blessed and meaningful Yom Kippur.

BILL CLINTON

Message to the Congress Transmitting the Report of the Railroad Retirement Board
September 28, 1998

To the Congress of the United States:

I transmit herewith the Annual Report of the Railroad Retirement Board for Fiscal Year 1997, pursuant to the provisions of section 7(b)(6) of the Railroad Retirement Act and section 12(1) of the Railroad Unemployment Insurance Act.

WILLIAM J. CLINTON

The White House,
September 28, 1998.

Remarks at a Democratic Senatorial Campaign Committee Dinner for Senator Barbara Boxer
September 28, 1998

First of all, I want to thank Smith and Elizabeth. I'm going to have to start paying a portion of the property tax on this home if I come here many more times this year. [*Laughter*] It's such a beautiful place; it's a happy place. The children are always around, which makes it more happy. It also reminds us what these elections are really all about.

The story Barbara told is true. I called her one night to see how she was doing and ask her about the campaign, make sure she had a theory of the case. [*Laughter*] And I offered to do something here in Washington.

Hillary was just in Washington and Oregon States and then came into northern California, where Barbara had a great event with Hillary's mom and Tony. Hillary said it was wonderful. Then we had a good night in Los Angeles on Saturday night.

I just got back from Chicago and making three stops in California and two in Texas. And I believe that we have an unusual opportunity in this election, and one that is unprecedented. But I want you to know why I'm glad you're here and why I'll be brief, because I want to go in there—you'd rather watch a movie than hear a speech, especially if the movie is only a minute long. [*Laughter*]

But I'd like to talk to you a little bit about this. In the—normally, the party of the President in Congress loses, not gains, seats at midterm. It is more than normal; it is virtually an unbroken record in the second term of the President. But we have things which are dif-

ferent now. For one thing, we have an agenda which is dominating the national debate, and our adversaries really don't have one. And insofar as they do, I think we get the better of the debate. A lot of people were worried about the adversity of the present moment for me and our family and our administration. But I have never believed, in political life, adversity was a big problem. I still believe the biggest problem for us is not adversity but complacency—and maybe cynicism, people saying, "I don't like this, so therefore, I won't participate." People should say, if they don't like it, "Therefore, I will participate."

But all over the country, now, I get these surveys showing our candidates and how they're doing. And it'll say, among registered voters, the Democrats have a healthy lead; among certain voters in a midterm election, the Democrat is a point or two behind. What does that tell you? Well, the kind of people that vote for us have to go to more trouble to vote. We have more low income working people, people that struggle with the burdens of child care and transportation and maybe ride to work on a bus everyday—you know, where it's a hassle. And when there's a Presidential election, they show up, because they know they're supposed to vote for President. And oftentimes in midterms, they don't show up, which puts us at a significant disadvantage.

Therefore, I will say again, adversity is our friend in the sense that at least everyone is now thinking about the political debate. I'd do nearly anything to help the Democrats get elected, but this is a little bit extreme. [*Laughter*] I want to say that people have been so uncommonly kind and generous to Hillary and to me and our family in the last few weeks, and I appreciate that. But we shouldn't be diverted from the fact that the public who sent Barbara Boxer here and who sent me here, what they really want us to do is to fight for them. And if they understand that the choice is a choice between saving Social Security and being financially responsible, before we give a popular election-year tax cut that won't amount to much for most ordinary people, but it sure sounds good—I mean, it's like—I always heard the Republicans were the party of fiscal responsibility; at least that's what they said all those years, although the deficit tripled—I mean, the debt tripled—quadrupled in the 12 years before I got here. But consider this—those of you—I see Ben Barnes back there and Marty Russo—those of us who have been involved in Democratic politics a long time, I never thought I'd live to see the day. I mean, the Republicans are saying, "It's just 5 weeks before the election; we've waited 29 years to balance the budget, but we're willing to give it up to give you an election-year tax cut, because it's just too good to be true." And you can say, "Well, we're not spending it all, or all the projected surplus."

And the Democrats are saying, "Hey, we worked for this for 6 years, and we appreciate the fact that you voted with us on the Balanced Budget Act, but, oh, by the way, the deficit was cut by 92 percent before we passed that bill. And we would just like to see the red ink turn to black, and dry, before we start spending it." [*Laughter*] You know, we'd just kind of like to see it dry.

And you know what? I may be dead wrong, but I believe the American people agree with us. I think they understand there is a lot of turmoil in the world and that the world looks to us to be strong, to do the responsible thing, to set a good example, to help get the economy going again, number one.

And even more important, nearly every American knows that when the baby boomers retire, the present Social Security system will be unsustainable, because there will only be two people working for every one person drawing.

Now, if our objective is what I think it is for 80-plus percent of all Americans, which is to find a way to modify the Social Security system that keeps its basic benefits—keep in mind one-half—one-half—the people over 65 in this country today would be in poverty were it not for Social Security. So we have to find a way to keep what's good about it, but to do it in a way that doesn't require us, when all us baby boomers retire, to sock our children and our grandchildren with a huge tax increase that undermines their standard of living.

And I go all across the country, and people my age, at least—at the end of the baby boom generation—are almost obsessed with this. I had barbecue with a bunch of my friends at home the other day. Half of them didn't have college degrees; none of them were wealthy; a lot of them lived on very modest incomes. Every single one of them was worried about this. They were tormented by the fact that when we retire, we will lower our children's standard of living to take care of us.

So it looks like we're going to have a surplus for a few years. I'm not against tax cuts. As Barbara said, we've got an education tax cut, a child care tax cut, an environmental tax cut in our balanced budget. If we can pay for them, fine. But I do not believe we should get into this surplus for tax cuts or for Democratic spending programs until we have saved the Social Security system for the 21st century and lifted that burden off our children and lifted the fear off our generation. I feel very strongly about it, and I think we can win that argument.

I think we ought to pass the Patients' Bill of Rights, because I'm for managed care, not against it. When I tried to change the health care system back in '93 and '94, I supported managed care. Look, we had to start managing the system better. In 1993, when I took office, health care costs were going up at 3 times the rate of inflation. It was unsustainable. It was going to bankrupt the country. But it's like any other—a management system—if you have a management system in your work, in your business, whatever it is, the purpose of the management system is to allow you to perform your primary mission in the best possible way at the lowest possible cost. The primary mission of the health care system is to help people when they're sick and keep people well. That's the primary mission of it. And the problem is that the management system has overtaken the mission because of the way the economics work.

I know I don't have to paint you all a lot of pictures, but imagine—suppose you were a

25-year-old accountant who dealt with entry-level reviews of requests from doctors' offices for certain procedures in Managed Care Company X. What do you know, every day when you go to work, about your job, how you're evaluated, and how you're going to be rewarded? You know one thing: You will never get in trouble for saying no. You will never—that is the system—you will never get in trouble for saying no.

These are good people, you know. They have children to feed. They have careers to make. They have lives to live. They have house payments to make. They will never get in trouble for saying no. Why? Because they're always told, "Well, two layers up in the managed care operation, there is a doctor. And if you make a mistake, and they appeal up, and the next person makes a mistake, and they appeal up, eventually a doctor will see it and correct it." And believe it or not, that often happens. But a lot of times it happens when it's too late to do any good for the people who were hurt in the first place, because they needed a procedure then or within 3 weeks or 6 weeks. Now, this is how it really works. That's what this whole thing is about.

So our little bill simply says, if you walk outside here—outside the Bagleys' home—and somebody races by and hits you in a car and they put you in an ambulance, you get to go the nearest emergency room, not one halfway across town because that's the one that happens to be covered by your plan. It says, if your doctor says he or she can't help you, you've got to have a specialist, you ought to be able to see one. It says, if your employer changes health care plans in the middle of your pregnancy or your chemotherapy treatment, you can't be required to stop and get another doctor or obstetrician. Now, this stuff happens. I'm not making this up; this happens in America. And it says the privacy of your medical records ought to be protected. That's the bill we're for.

The House passed a bill that didn't guarantee any of those rights, and left 100 million Americans out of what little it did do. When it was brought up in the Senate the other night—Barbara can tell you—I've never seen this happen. The Republican leader of the Senate was so terrified about having his people recorded voting no, but was determined not to let them vote yes because their supporters are all on the other side—the insurance companies that don't want

this—that they shut the Senate down for 4 hours to keep the vote from occurring. I've never seen anything like it.

They literally—they just called off—they were in a panic. They turned out the lights and got under their desks—[laughter]—killed it by stealth and waited for time to pass. I'm not exaggerating this. I've been astonished that there hasn't been more publicity on this. It was a breathtaking moment in American history.

And when they turned out the lights, I wondered if any of them had ever looked at some of the people I've looked at and heard some of the stories I've heard, looked at the woman who lost her husband at 45 after 25 years of marriage, who had a heart problem that could have been treated by proper surgery, but by the time they went through 9 months of hassling, the doctor had to say, "I'm sorry, it is too late. I can't do anything for you." And a few months later, he keeled over and died in their front yard. That's just one case.

So I don't know about you, I think we've got the better side of that argument. I'm happy to take into a midterm election an issue like this that touches people where they live. I think we've got the better side of that argument.

And I'll just mention two other things. A lot of you are atypical for Democrats, you know. Most people in your income groups, maybe in the business you do, maybe they're not Democrats. But I'm really proud of the fact that I proved that our administration could be pro-business as well as pro-labor, pro-growth as well as pro-environment, because I believe that. I think to have to make one of those choices puts you in a hole before you start.

And I've really tried to help put our country in the center of the emerging global economy. Oftentimes, I was at odds with some people in my own party for doing it. But look, now that we have these 16.7 million jobs; we need to be honest about where they came from. Thirty percent of our growth came from expanding exports. That means that what is morally right for us to do in terms of helping our neighbors around the world turns out to be in our economic best interest.

Now, you got all these problems in Asia—some of them, I think, were inevitable once the level of economic activity and movement of capital got to the point it did, but you have a quarter of the world in recession today and another quarter of the world teetering on the edge. You have—some of our biggest trading partners in Asia today are flat broke; so that, for example, in the State of North Dakota, which basically is a big wheat farming State, they're having a veritable depression today. And part of the reason is that we export half our wheat, and 40 percent of it goes to Asia, and they're buying 30 percent less this year than they did last year because they don't have any money to buy our food.

Now, the International Monetary Fund, I never thought—if you would have told me— a lot of things have happened to me that have surprised me since I've been here, I admit that, about the nature of politics. But if anybody had ever told me that the IMF would be a political issue in a congressional election, I would never have believed that because most people still don't know what the IMF is. [*Laughter*]

But they do know—they do know—that we've got to be able to sell what we make around the world. And when you explain to people that the International Monetary Fund helps our friends get back on their feet and helps prevent the spread of this financial crisis that everybody knows about to Latin America, our fastest growing markets, where countries have been shaken even though they're doing a good job managing their economy, and that the Democratic Party favors keeping our economic growth going and continuing to lead the world economically, and we've been waiting for 8 months and still can't get this passed, I think that's a major issue.

And I do not understand how in the world a person could say, "I want to be a Senator from California"—which is more closely tied to Asia than any place in the United States, not only economically but culturally—"but I do not want to do our fair share in helping to restore growth and opportunity in Asia, in markets for California products." So I'm happy to run on the issues. We've got the better side of that argument.

And let me just say one thing about the education issue. In the balanced budget, we have an education plan that I put together, based on the over 20 years that Hillary and I have worked in the schools and worked with educators and followed the research, and based on what education leaders say is needed now. And it's all paid for.

Here's what it does—keep in mind, they won't even give us a vote on this—put 100,000 teachers out there to lower class size to an average of 18 in the first 3 grades. It would build or repair 5,000 schools at a time when the kids are in housetrailers all over America and when school buildings in inner cities are being shut down. It would hook up all the classrooms to the Internet by the year 2000. It would give college scholarships to 35,000 young people that they could then pay off by going into the inner cities and other educationally underserved areas to teach. It would create 3,000 charter schools that are doing a lot, as Congresswoman Harman knows, in California and other places to reform public education.

And to go back to the point Barbara made, it provides unprecedented amounts of funds to school districts that will have high standards, not have social promotion, but won't finger children as failures just because the system they're in is failing. So if they will have tutorials, if they will have after-school programs, if they will have summer school programs, we help them to set those things up. That's our plan. It's all paid for in the budget, and we cannot get a vote on it.

So if the American people understand this is about saving Social Security for the 21st century, passing the Patients' Bill of Rights, putting education at the top of our investment priorities, and keeping economic growth going in America and throughout the world, and we're on the right side and our adversaries aren't, I think we've got a good chance to win that election. And I think we've got a good chance to convince people who otherwise would not show up, to come, and that's what concerns me.

I had hoped that by the time I had been here 6 years, we'd have some level of greater harmony and bipartisanship here, and that a lot of the divisions that I had seen from afar before I became President would get better. I do think in the country all the work we've done to bring people together across racial and religious and ethnic and cultural lines is really biting. I think that there is a greater sense of reaching out and unity in America. It isn't true in Washington, but I don't think anyone could fairly blame our party or our administration for that. And what we've got to do is to give the American people a chance to vote for that kind of country.

With their majority, this year, the leaders of the Republican Party have done a few things. They've killed campaign finance reform, which would have cut down on the number of these dinners you have to attend every year. [*Laughter*] They killed the tobacco legislation to protect our children from the dangers of tobacco. They killed the Patients' Bill of Rights. They killed an increase in the minimum wage for 12 million of the hardest working Americans at a time when unemployment is low and inflation is low. They took a step backwards on saving Social Security first by passing that tax bill in the House. They've taken a step backwards on the environment by continuing to litter every bill you can find with another environmental rider. And they've taken no action on the education agenda and no action on the International Monetary Fund.

And what I'd like to ask you to do when you go home—and there are a lot of people here from all over the country: Stick up for our people who are running, and stick up for the issues, and do what you can to make sure people understand—everybody that works for you, everybody you come in contact with—this is a very important election to vote in. Because what the other guys are gambling on is, it's a midterm election and people are doing well and they will be relaxing and they won't show up.

And what we have to say is, this is a magic moment all right, but the world is not free of difficulty. Things are changing, and we've got big challenges out there. And we're right on these issues, that the Democrats are for saving Social Security, keeping the economy going, putting education first, and passing the Patients' Bill of Rights. I think that's a pretty good program.

And I'd like to say one other thing just for the record, because I know it's not just us here, because this is being covered by the press. It is true that Barbara Boxer has been a conscience of the Senate. It is true that she stood up for principle. It's true that she is an independent voice; she certainly doesn't always vote the way I think she ought to. And that's good; that's what makes America work. But I think it's also important to point out for the record that she has been a very good Senator for California.

I have worked with Jane Harman on issues that affect her district. I have worked with many other Members. I've worked with Senator Feinstein on the Mojave Desert and other things. But California has a lot of people in the Congress; it's the biggest congressional delegation. So there's a lot of competition for this. The member of the California congressional delegation who has called me the largest number of times to do something very specific for the State of California is Barbara Boxer, and I want the voters to know that.

So you ought to be proud you were here. But when you go home, you ought to think about what I told you. You don't want to wake up on election day or the day after and think that all those polls of certain voters were the polls that counted instead of the polls of registered voters, which reflects how the people feel. What we have to do is to bring the public's feelings to the ballot box in November. You've helped Barbara tonight; let's keep working until we can help them all.

Thank you, and God bless you.

NOTE: The President spoke at 9:02 p.m. at a private residence. In his remarks, he referred to dinner hosts Smith and Elizabeth F. Bagley; Dorothy and Tony Rodham, the First Lady's mother and brother; Ben Barnes, owner, Entrecorp; and former Representative Marty Russo.

Statement on Senate Action on Higher Education Legislation
September 29, 1998

I am delighted that the Senate today passed the Higher Education Amendments of 1998. This legislation marks an important step forward in my effort to help more Americans enter the doors of college. In today's global economy, what you earn depends on what you learn. This bill will make it easier for millions of Americans to get the higher education they need to succeed in the global economy. It also demonstrates how we can make progress on education policy when we choose bipartisan cooperation over division.

By adopting the new low interest rate for student loans we proposed last winter, this bill will save American students and their families billions of dollars in interest payments. But this bill does much more to help all Americans go to college. It responds to the challenge I issued in the State of the Union to create a High Hopes initiative, where colleges reach down to middle school students in high-poverty areas to give them the support they need to be ready for higher education; incorporates our ideas on recruiting and training top-notch teachers for our public schools; builds on our efforts to de-ploy cutting-edge technology so that our students can learn anytime, anywhere; and modernizes the delivery of student aid by creating the Government's first-ever performance based organization, a recommendation made by the Vice President's National Performance Review.

I look forward to signing this bill into law, and I urge Congress to provide the accompanying funding for these new critical initiatives so that they can work effectively to give America's students the quality education they deserve.

Statement on the Death of Tom Bradley
September 29, 1998

Hillary and I were saddened to learn of the death of Mayor Tom Bradley. The son of a sharecropper who became a police lieutenant, he rose to lead our Nation's second largest city for two decades. He was a builder, bringing a remarkably successful Olympic Games to Los Angeles, encouraging a thriving downtown and improving mass transit. Just as important, he built bridges across the lines that divide us, uniting people of many races and backgrounds in the most diverse city in America. He was a pioneer and a leader. Our thoughts and prayers are with Ethel and their family.

Statement on Senate Action on Year 2000 Information and Readiness Legislation
September 29, 1998

I am pleased that the Senate last night passed the "Year 2000 Information and Readiness Disclosure Act," important bipartisan legislation to help our Nation prepare its computer systems for the new millennium.

This bill, which builds upon a proposal my administration submitted to Congress in July, will help businesses, State and local government, and Federal agencies better address the year 2000 (Y2K) problem by providing limited liability protections to encourage greater information sharing about solutions, while also protecting consumers from misleading advertising or other statements when purchasing products for their own use.

January 1, 2000, is one deadline we cannot push back. I urge the House to pass this critical legislation before the end of the legislative session. I look forward to signing it into law so that Y2K information sharing will enable the Nation to prepare for this global challenge.

Memorandum on Assistance for Federal Employees Affected by Hurricane Georges
September 29, 1998

Memorandum for the Heads of Executive Departments and Agencies

Subject: Assistance for Federal Employees Affected by Hurricane Georges

I am deeply concerned about the devastating losses suffered by many as a result of Hurricane Georges. Multiple parts of the Federal Government have been mobilized to respond to this disaster.

As part of this effort, I ask the heads of executive departments and agencies who have Federal civilian employees in designated disaster areas resulting from Hurricane Georges and its aftermath (including Puerto Rico and the U.S. Virgin Islands) to use their discretion to excuse from duty, without charge to leave or loss of pay, any such employee who is prevented from reporting to work or faced with a personal emergency because of this disaster and who can be spared from his or her usual responsibilities. This policy also should be applied to any em-

ployee who is needed for emergency law enforcement, relief, or clean-up efforts authorized by Federal, State, or other officials having jurisdiction.

I am also authorizing the Office of Personnel Management (OPM) to determine whether there is a need to establish an emergency leave transfer program to assist employees affected by this major disaster. An emergency leave transfer program would permit employees in an executive agency to donate their unused annual leave for transfer to employees of the same or other agencies who were adversely affected by the hurricane and who need additional time off for recovery. If the need for donated annual leave becomes evident, I direct OPM to establish the emergency leave transfer program and provide additional information to agencies on the programs's administration.

WILLIAM J. CLINTON

Letter to Congressional Leaders Reporting on the Deployment of United States Forces in Response to the Situation in Liberia
September 29, 1998

Dear Mr. Speaker: (Dear Mr. President:)

Liberia is just emerging from a 7-year civil war. Since democratic elections were held in July 1997 there have been moments of instability in that country. In the past 10 days, conflict erupted between Liberian security forces and supporters of another former faction leader, Roosevelt Johnson.

On the morning of September 19, Liberian government security forces fired on a small group of Liberians led by former Ulimo Krahn faction leader Roosevelt Johnson, who was speaking with U.S. Embassy officials outside the Embassy compound, after Johnson and his group were initially refused refuge. When Liberian government security forces opened fire on the group, the Embassy officials fled into the U.S. Embassy, and in the chaos were joined

by the Johnson party. Two Americans were wounded in the melee and four members of the Johnson party were killed. The U.S. personnel injured in the gunfire were a government contractor and an Embassy staff member.

Responding to a U.S. request for enhanced security, forces of the Economic Community of West Africa Observer Group (ECOMOG) subsequently positioned themselves in a defensive perimeter around the Embassy. Later, a group of 23 supporters of Mr. Johnson was discovered hiding on the Embassy grounds. After extensive negotiations between President Taylor and representatives of the U.S. Government and western African states, permission was obtained to airlift Mr. Johnson and his party to Freetown, Sierra Leone. This was accomplished without incident on September 25, 1998.

The situation in Monrovia continues to be uncertain and could deteriorate. Although ECOMOG forces remain in the vicinity of the Embassy compound, their numbers have been reduced. Our Embassy believes that security could deteriorate rapidly during President Taylor's absence for an official visit to France. The Embassy does, however, project that, barring further incidents, security should significantly improve over the course of the next several weeks as factional tensions ease in the wake of Mr. Johnson's departure. There are approximately 230 non-official American citizens in Liberia and 29 official Americans at the Embassy.

On September 27, 1998, due to the tenuous security situation and the potential threat to American citizens and the Embassy in Monrovia, a stand-by response and evacuation force of approximately 30 U.S. military personnel from the U.S. European Command deployed to Freetown, Sierra Leone. About half of this unit has moved onto the Navy's coastal patrol craft, USS CHINOOK (PC–9), which is operating in the waters off Monrovia. The U.S. military personnel are prepared, if needed, to augment the Embassy's security unit in Monrovia and to conduct an evacuation of American citizens, if required. Although the U.S. military personnel are equipped for combat, this action is being undertaken solely for the purpose of preparing to protect American citizens and property. The U.S. forces will redeploy as soon as it is determined that the threat to the Embassy compound has ended or, if an evacuation is necessary, it is completed.

I have taken this action pursuant to my constitutional authority to conduct U.S. foreign relations and as Commander in Chief and Chief Executive.

I am providing this report as part of my efforts to keep the Congress fully informed, consistent with the War Powers Resolution. I appreciate the support of the Congress in this action to assist in Embassy security and the security of American citizens overseas.

Sincerely,

WILLIAM J. CLINTON

NOTE: Identical letters were sent to Newt Gingrich, Speaker of the House of Representatives, and Strom Thurmond, President pro tempore of the Senate.

Remarks on Achieving a Budget Surplus
September 30, 1998

Thank you very much. Let me begin by saying to Kay McClure, we thank you for being here. All of us who have been a part of this effort to tame the deficit and to turn our economy around, we did it for people like you. And I think you made everybody here proud to be an American and everybody who was part of that project proud of that.

I'd like to thank the members of the Cabinet and administration who are here, and the former Cabinet members. I would also like to say that we invited Henry Fowler, who was President Johnson's Treasury Secretary the last time the budget was balanced, to come here, but he couldn't come because of hip surgery. Our thoughts are with him, and his thoughts are with us today.

I want to thank Senator Moynihan and Senator Robb, Senator Rockefeller, Senator Breaux, Senator Conrad, Senator Dorgan; Mr. Sabo, who was our chair, along with Senator Moynihan back in '93; and Congressmen Boyd, Brown, Edwards, Filner, Congresswoman Furse, Congressmen Hastings, Hinojosa, Markey, Vento, Wise, and Congresswoman Thurman for being here.

The Vice President also noted that there were several former Members of Congress here who voted for the budget in 1993. There are quite a number here, and since they—most of them who are here paid quite a high price for doing what makes it possible for us to be here today, I'd like to ask them to stand. Would every Member of Congress who is no longer a Member of Congress, who was here and voted for that budget in '93 please stand. Thank you very much. [*Applause*] Thank you.

Mark Twain once said that two things nobody should ever have to watch being made are laws and sausages. And the aftermath sometimes is not very pretty. They and many others had to endure being accused of raising taxes on people they didn't, being accused of not lowering taxes for people they did, and all manner of other perfidy to try to bring us to this moment, to break the spell that had gripped America and led to a quadrupling of the debt of this country in the previous 12 years. And a lot of the people who are still here took very significant risks, as well, and set the stage for what has been done since.

Let me ask you to begin by just thinking about what 29 years means. Twenty-nine years ago Neil Armstrong walked on the moon, "Bonanza" was one of our top-rated TV shows, and Sammy Sosa was one year old. [*Laughter*] We have waited a long time for this, not quite as long as we waited for Roger Maris' record to be broken, but nearly.

For 29 years, the last day of the fiscal year was not a day of celebration but a day we were handed a powerful reminder of our Government's inability to live within its means. In the 12 years before this administration took office the debt quadrupled, partisan gridlock intensified, and a crushing debt was being imposed upon our children. These deficits hobbled economic growth, spiked interest rates, robbed too many people of their chance at the American dream.

The end of this fiscal year, obviously, is different as the flashing sign behind me shows. Tonight at midnight, America puts an end to three decades of deficits and launches a new era of balanced budgets and surpluses. While the numbers will not be official until the end of the month, we expect the 1998 surplus to be about $70 billion. [*Applause*] Thank you.

This is the largest surplus on record and, as a percentage of our economy, the largest one since the 1950's. Our economy is the strongest in a generation. That's why we see the deficit clock has become a surplus clock. It will tally the growing opportunities of the 21st century. It is a landmark achievement not just for those in this room who have played a role in it but, indeed, for all the American people. And it will be a gift-giving achievement for generations to come.

I want you to think about what this means for our democracy and also what it means for our obligations now. First and foremost, as our previous speaker so eloquently noted, balancing the budget has brought tangible economic benefits to the American people.

In the 1980's, high interest rates kept entrepreneurs from starting new businesses. Tight money made it harder for people to buy a new home. When I came to Washington 6 years ago, nearly everybody felt our economy was drifting. College graduates were having a hard time finding jobs; factory workers were seeing their industries fall behind foreign competition. The deficit then was $290 billion and projected to be over $350 billion this year alone.

But even more than the economic problems, the deficit seemed to be exhibit A for those who claimed that America was in decline. The notion seems preposterous today. But it's worth remembering that just a decade ago the idea of America in decline was widely accepted in some circles, not only here but around the world. There were works of scholarship suggesting we were bound to go the way of other powers who had risen and then fallen. There was a little defeatism that became part of the conventional wisdom here in Washington, symbolized by this National Government that was inefficient, ineffectual, and insolvent. And therefore, the Government became the poster child for what people said was happening to America. The two political parties seemed inevitably locked in a series of false choices between old ideas competing in a very new time.

But a funny thing happened on the road to American decline. The American people stepped in. Just as we have at every critical juncture in our history, the people came together once again to become the captains of our fate, the commanders of our destiny. That is really what we celebrate here today.

The American people simply demanded a new direction. They demanded that our Government put its house in order. They demanded that America's greatness be reasserted, that opportunity be provided again to all who are willing to work for it. They demanded that we be able to say with confidence that the greatest days of this country still lie before us.

And so, in 1993, the members of our party in Congress, some at the cost of their careers, took the courageous action which began the road we celebrate today, a new economic strategy that reduced the deficit by more than 90 percent. Then 4 years later, Congress put progress over partisanship and passed a bipartisan balanced budget agreement that closed the rest of the deficit gap and will keep us in balance structurally for many years to come.

The deficit reduction has saved the American people more than a trillion dollars on the national debt. The new strategy has helped lead to lower interest rates, higher investments, unprecedented prosperity. We have already heard about that. The unemployment rate is the lowest in 28 years, the percentage of Americans on welfare the lowest in 29 years, the inflation rate the lowest in 33 years. More than 6 million American families have realized their dreams of owning a first home; another 10 million have refinanced their homes they had. Today, home-ownership is the highest in history. And for millions of Americans, these lower interest rates have amounted to an unofficial tax cut of tens of billions of dollars, making a college education, a new car, a family vacation more affordable.

Now, balancing the budget and increasing our investment in our people is the core of a new vision of Government, one that lives within its means; one that is the smallest in 35 years but, with the Vice President's leadership, has been redesigned to meet the challenges of this new era; one that cuts wasteful spending but also makes significant investments in education, health, and the environment. We have done a lot to make this new economy. But we now have to do more to see that all our people can participate in it fully.

Our success has helped to inspire confidence here and around the world. Six years ago, when I went to my first G–7 meeting in Tokyo, every leader told me that America was holding the rest of the world back and that, unless we were willing to get our deficit down, we would always be a drag on the world; we were taking money away; we were keeping interest rates high; that it was unfair.

Well, what we have done in the last 6 years has also helped to spark economic growth elsewhere. But now that there is so much turbulence for other reasons in other parts of the world, it is important to remember that our growing economy is today serving as a bulwark of stability in the rest of the world and that without it, the rest of the world would be in much worse shape, indeed.

Now, let me just ask you very briefly before we close in this celebration, what are we going to do with this moment of celebration of the balanced budget and unprecedented prosperity?

What exactly are we going to do with it? That really is before the American people today.

We see from troubled economies around the world, in my view, that this is not a time to simply celebrate and rest. It is not a time to be distracted from our mission of strengthening our country for the new century, of leading the world toward prosperity and peace and freedom, of bringing our people together.

For the sake of our children, now that we've balanced the budget, I think the first thing we ought to do is commit ourselves to save Social Security for the 21st century. The system is in very good shape now, but everyone knows in its present terms it is not sustainable when the baby boomers retire. And that if we do not act now, when the baby boomers do retire, we will be confronted with two very unpleasant choices: One is to lower the standard of living of the baby boomers so that their children can continue on with their business; the other is to lower the standard of living of their children and their ability to raise our grandchildren so that we can live in the same manner that seniors today are living. Neither choice need be made if we act now with discipline and use the fact that we're going to have this surplus to make a downpayment and to begin with deliberation to save Social Security. It is a huge issue.

Now, I am well aware that it is a popular thing, particularly right here, just 4 weeks and change before an election day, to serve up a tax cut, to say, "Well, we've got a surplus. We're going to give you some of your money back." But all of us know this surplus was run up over the years—or the deficit over the years was made smaller because we actually were taking in more money in Social Security taxes than we were paying out. And all of us know that this problem is looming out there and will need money to fix. And so I think the American people have waited 29 years, and I think most Americans would like to see the ink change from red to black and then just dry a little—[*laughter*]—before we put it at risk.

But if you think about this issue, there is hardly anything that goes to the core of what we are as a people more than our sense that we owe an obligation to both our parents and our children. And if we squander this surplus and start spending a little here, a little there, a little yonder on the tax cuts just because we're a few weeks before an election, before we take care of this, what are we going to do when times get tough and we still have to take care of it?

So I say to all of you again, I think that's the first thing that we ought to do. We are not against tax cuts. There are tax cuts in this budget, as has already been said, for education, for child care, to help small businesses provide pensions for their employees. There are tax cuts for environmental investments that help to cut energy bills. But we don't take any money out of the surplus. We adopted a disciplined framework for the future in 1997; we ought not to depart from it. We had a bipartisan commitment to that framework in 1997, and we ought not to depart from it.

The second thing we ought to do is to recognize that we have money set aside in the budget to invest in education, and we're still a long way from having the ability to say that every American child can get a world-class education. We ought to fund smaller classes. We ought to fund the initiative to revitalize, repair, or build 5,000 schools, to hook up all our classrooms to the Internet, to give kids in troubled communities mentoring programs, guarantees they can go on to college, after-school programs, summer schools programs, the kind of things that don't treat them as failures just because the system they've been in has failed.

We ought to pass the Patients' Bill of Rights for the 160 million Americans that are in managed care, to put health care first and make sure you're managing for a healthier America, not the other way around. We ought to keep the economy going and maintain our leadership in the global economy by funding our fair share of the International Monetary Fund because, as Alan Greenspan said the other day, we cannot forever maintain our position as an island of prosperity in a sea of distress.

Now, that's what we ought to be doing. So we're here to celebrate. But this country is here now, after 220 years, still again at the top of its game, having totally debunked all the defeatists who said we were in decline. But let's not forget why it happened. Don't you ever forget that these seven people back here stood up, and a lot like them, and laid their jobs on the line for America's future.

Now, when no one has that kind of risk, nobody is being asked to cut their throat and give up a job they love and work they believe in to do the right thing, no one is being asked to do that, how can we possibly walk away from this session of Congress, when there is no pain in doing the right thing—not the kind of pain they had to endure—without saying we're going to save Social Security first, put education as our first investment priority, pass a Patients' Bill of Rights, and keep America and the world's economy growing? How can we do that? We owe it to the people who made the sacrifice that brought us to this day to build for another day. We should not sit on or celebrate this balanced budget. We should build on it.

Thank you very much.

NOTE: The President spoke at 11:21 a.m. in Room 450 of the Old Executive Office Building. In his remarks, he referred to J. (Kay) McClure, president, Walhonde Tools, Inc., who introduced the President; and former Representative Martin Olav Sabo.

Remarks on the Legislative Agenda for Education
October 1, 1998

Thank you. Ladies and gentlemen, there really is nothing for me to say. I want to thank the previous speakers, each in their own way, for what they have given and what they will give to the children of our country. I believe that Secretary Riley is not only the longest serving but the most intensely committed and effective Secretary of Education this country has ever had.

I thank the Vice President for the vivid picture he painted for us of what is going on in these school buildings. We have been out there. We have been in these buildings. We have seen them. I believe the largest number of trailers or temporary classrooms, or whatever the politically correct term is, that I have seen at one school is a dozen in Florida. But they're everywhere. And there are a lot of magnificent old buildings in our cities that any person would be proud to go to school in if only they were fixed.

I'd like to thank Senator Daschle and Congressman Bonior and all the Members of Congress who are here whom they have represented today, for a genuine, consistent, passionate commitment to education that I have seen over my 6 years as President. It has never failed.

Thank you, Kathryn Scruggs, for giving your life to the education of our children. And from the look in your face and the lilt in your voice, I'd say it's been a good gift both ways. Thank you so much. Thank you.

I want to thank all the educators who are here, Arlene Ackerman, our friends from the AFT and the NEA and the other education associations. And I thank the young children for coming here today, for reminding us what this is all about. Welcome; we're glad you're all here from Stevens Elementary.

Let me begin where I meant to end: We can do this—we can do this. This is not an insurmountable problem. We have the resources; what we need is the will and the consensus. We need open minds and open hearts.

Yesterday I was privileged to announce to the American people that our Nation has triumphed over an enormous challenge. The red ink of the Federal budget deficits has been replaced by a surplus. We have brought order to our fiscal house. Now it is time to bring more learning to the schoolhouse.

In the end we needed a bipartisan consensus to pass a Balanced Budget Act that also had the biggest investment in the health care of our children in a generation and opened the doors of college wider than any act since the passage of the GI bill. That's what we need now.

Think of the challenges we have overcome as a people in the last 6 years. The crime rate has gone down to a 25-year low. The welfare rolls are at a 29-year low. It's the first time in 29 years we've had a balanced budget. The unemployment rate is at a 28-year low. The homeownership rate in this country is at an all-time high.

We are capable of overcoming challenges that people used to wring their hands about just a few years ago. But we have to put the progress of our people over partisanship and politics. So we all came here—let me join the chorus and say we came here not to ask for much from the majority in Congress, just one day—one day for our children and their future; one day between now and the end of this congressional session to strengthen our public schools, to provide those 100,000 teachers for the smaller classes, to build or repair those 5,000 schools, to provide those after-school and summer school programs to help our students meet higher academic standards.

In recent days Congress has given us a glimmer of hope by passing a higher education bill that includes our initiatives on higher education, that will help millions of Americans receive the college education they need to compete in the global economy the Vice President so vividly described. It reduces the cost of student loans and provides for mentors for middle school students who can get a guarantee that they will be able to finance their college education if they stay out of trouble, stay in school, and keep learning.

I applaud the Congress, members of both parties who did this, including many who are here today: Congressmen Goodling and Kildee and Clay; Senator Kennedy and his Republican colleague, Senator Jeffords.

But though we have the finest system of higher education in the world—and this is a good bill because it opened the doors to it even wider—we all know we have to have the finest K through 12 system of education in the world, and it has to be there for all of our kids as we grow increasingly more diverse. We know that nothing else we can do will more profoundly expand the circle of opportunity, more directly enhance our economic competitiveness, more clearly bridge the divisions of our society and bind us together as one nation.

And yet no issue has suffered more from misplaced priorities and partisan pursuits than America's public schools. Eight months ago I sent Congress the education agenda that has been described today. It demands accountability from everyone. It says to students, "We expect you to meet high standards of learning and discipline, but we want to give you the help you need to meet those standards." It should be bipartisan in its appeal.

There was a time when education was completely bipartisan because no one asked you to register by party when you sign up for school, because every American, even Americans that have no children in our schools, have a direct, immediate, and profound interest in the success of our children's education.

Now, it is not too late. There is still time before the end of this session of Congress to spend that one day so we can cast that one vote to transform public education—to reduce the class sizes by adding 100,000 teachers, goals Senator Patty Murray and Congressman Bill Clay have been fighting for; to build or modernize those 5,000 schools across our country, goals Congressman Charlie Rangel and Senator Carol Moseley-Braun have worked very hard for, for a long time now.

The plan also would connect all of our classrooms in these new or renovated buildings to the Internet by the year 2000 and train teachers to use the Internet properly and to train our children to do the same. Every school in this country should be as modern as the world our children will live in. One day, one vote, could make it happen.

The third thing we want to do on that one day is to help our students meet higher standards; and if they're in troubled neighborhoods or come from difficult families or have school systems that haven't been performing well, we know they could be helped immensely with summer school and after-school programs, programs that Senator Barbara Boxer and Congresswoman Nita Lowey have been spearheading our fight for.

I have seen the benefits of these programs all across America. Last week I visited a school in Chicago where all the students came from the, I think, now famous housing project of Cabrini-Green. Students in Chicago no longer advance to the next grade unless they can pass tests to demonstrate that they know what they were supposed to learn. But if they have trouble passing the tests, they are not branded failures, because the system has failed them. Instead, they are offered academically enriched summer school and after-school programs. Over 40,000 children now get 3 hot meals a day there. The summer school is now the sixth biggest school district in the United States. And guess what? In that school I visited in Cabrini-Green, the reading scores have doubled and the math scores have tripled in 3 years.

We only ask for one day for these initiatives— and, oh, by the way, one day for a decent appropriations bill. That's the job that Congress is supposed to do every year. And we are depending upon the leadership of Senator Tom Harkin and Congressman David Obey to see that we get that kind of appropriations bill. The one the House has passed does not meet that test.

Let me tell you a little about it. It shortchanges our youngest children in Head Start, our new initiatives in higher education for mentoring children, and preparing quality teachers. It shortchanges these after-school care programs. It shortchanges our major education program to help children learn the basics. It shortchanges my Hispanic education action plan. It shortchanges our efforts for school reform and high standards and our commitment to hook all those classrooms up to the Internet by 2000. It even shortchanges our efforts for safe, disciplined, drug-free schools. It shortchanges our young people in school-to-work efforts. It shortchanges workers who need retraining between jobs. It shortchanges our efforts to help disadvantaged youth get jobs. And in the House, unbelievably, it completely eliminates the summer job program for half a million young people. That is wrong. As your President, I will not stand for it.

The men and women who are up here with me stand ready to work with people in the other party, and they only ask them to do it for just one day, to strengthen our public schools for an entire new century, to affirm the bedrock American value that every child, regardless of race or neighborhood or income, deserves the chance to live up to his or her God-given abilities. Just one day to put in place a plan that will not only help those children but in so doing will make sure that America's greatest days lie ahead. I think it's worth one day, don't you?

Thank you very much, and God bless you.

NOTE: The President spoke at 3:40 p.m. on the South Lawn at the White House. In his remarks, he referred to Kathryn Scruggs, reading specialist, Ashlawn Elementary School, Arlington, VA, who introduced the President; and Arlene Ackerman, superintendent, District of Columbia Public Schools. The President also referred to the American Federation of Teachers (AFT) and the National Education Association (NEA). A portion of these remarks could not be verified because the tape was incomplete.

Statement on the Anniversary of the Children's Health Insurance Program
October 1, 1998

Today marks the one-year anniversary of the new Children's Health Insurance Program (CHIP). This historic effort—which I called for in my 1997 State of the Union and signed into law last summer as part of the historic bipartisan Balanced Budget Act—is the largest children's health coverage expansion since the enactment of Medicaid over 30 years ago. CHIP provides $24 billion to help States offer affordable health insurance to children in working families that make too much for Medicaid but too little to afford private coverage.

I am proud to announce that in its first year, nearly four out of five States are already participating in CHIP. A report released by the Department of Health and Human Services today finds that these State programs will provide health care coverage to over 2.3 million children when fully implemented. Many of these States have indicated they will expand their programs to even more children, and the remaining States have proposals that we expect to approve in the coming months.

However, much work remains to be done to improve the health of our Nation's children. We must work to ensure that every child eligible for CHIP gets enrolled. Equally important, over 4 million uninsured children are eligible but not signed up for Medicaid. Educating families, simplifying the enrollment process, and making health insurance a national priority requires a sustained commitment from the public and the private sector. This has been and will continue to be a top priority for my administration. I have directed 12 Federal agencies that serve children and families to reach out and enroll uninsured children and am extremely encouraged by our partnership with the States and the private sector to help meet this challenge.

We know that children with insurance are healthier—getting more regular checkups, more routine immunizations, and fewer ear infections. On the one-year birthday of CHIP, let us recommit ourselves to providing affordable health coverage to the millions of American children without insurance.

Statement on House Action on Year 2000 Information and Readiness Legislation
October 1, 1998

I am pleased that the House today joined the Senate in passing the "Year 2000 Information and Readiness Disclosure Act," a bill that will provide limited liability protections for sharing information while protecting consumers from misleading statements. This important bipartisan legislation, based on a proposal by my administration, will help our Nation prepare its computer systems for the new millennium.

By encouraging greater information sharing about Y2K solutions, this legislation will help businesses, State and local government, and Federal agencies in their efforts to address the year 2000 computer problem. I look forward to signing it into law.

Remarks at a Unity '98 Dinner
October 1, 1998

Thank you very much. I thought the Vice President was a nonviolent man. [*Laughter*] It's not our friends we're trying to unseat. [*Laughter*] It's just like practice; it's like a scrimmage, you know.

Well, first of all, thank you all for being here. This has been a very successful night. And I want to thank Nancy and Bob and Steve and everybody who worked on these Unity events; it's been a very good thing. Terry McAuliffe was laughing at me the other day. He said, "When we talk about these Unity events, everybody loves it because they think that they're not going to get hit from three different places as we move toward election. But then they get into it, and they find out they get hit three different times from the same committee." [*Laughter*] There's groaning in some places. But I thank you for supporting it. This is very, very important.

I thank you, Senator Breaux, for coming. Thank you, Mr. Vice President, for that great, great speech and reviewing the issues that are involved.

I want to just back up a minute, and I won't keep you long because the Vice President has clearly laid out what our case is about how the last year has been spent and what we believe the issues are. But I had the opportunity—I know Len—maybe some of the others, if you were there—Hillary has helped us put together a conference at New York University to coincide with the opening of the United Nations the other day. And the Prime Minister of Great Britain, Tony Blair, came. The Prime Minister of Italy, Romano Prodi, came. The President of Bulgaria came. And we talked about how many people around the world seemed to be voting for the approach that was embodied in the campaign that the Vice President and I ran in 1992 and 1996, based on some ideas that had been developed really in my own experience as a Governor nearly a decade before that. But I think it's important that we look at that, because this whole—this so-called Third Way—that's the new buzzword—basically struck me as nothing more than a commonsense application of old-fashioned Democratic and American values to the challenges of the moment.

It seemed to me, for example, that it was fruitless to have a Government in Washington that cursed the deficit and ran it up every year. I sort of came from a tradition that said we should talk less and do more. It seemed to me to be fruitless to talk about doing something about crime, and all that was ever done is more penalties were put on, but nobody ever did anything about prevention. No one ever listened to the police officers. No one ever did anything.

It seemed to me fruitless to have the same debate every time—Bob Torricelli mentioned this—between the environment and the economy. Obviously, the two have to be reconciled and both have to advance in lockstep; otherwise, we're sunk. And all you have to do is carry the argument that the other side always makes that there is an inevitable conflict always and forever between the environment and the economy to its logical extension, and we're sunk. Whichever rail you decide to ride, you run off the end of the mountain.

So we came up with this notion that there really was a way of going beyond the old fights that had dominated the 1980's, that we could reduce the deficit and ultimately balance the budget and still invest more in our children, in our health care system, in research, and in the future; that we could fight crime, and we could punish people who commit crime, but we could also do more with prevention; that we could improve the economy and improve the environment; that we could have a smaller Government that actually does more and works better and is more active—you know all the basic ideas we advanced—that we could respect individuality in this country and still say we ought to be coming together more across the lines that divide us, we ought to recognize what we have in common is more important.

And after 6 years, the truth is those ideas work pretty well. And now they're being embraced around the world, people trying to break out of the sort of ideological battlegrounds that gave high rhetorical content but low results. And it is deeply moving to me. And I think the fact that it works has been deeply frustrating to some of our political opponents.

But that's the first thing I'd like to say. I'm not up here to take credit for all that. I spent a lot of time—it was an advantage to me, frankly, during the 1980's to be working in public life outside Washington, because I got to see as an observer the shape of the political debate and to see how often our Democrats were unfairly treated by the voters because they didn't know what our people in Congress were doing because of the way the debate got beamed out to them.

For example, it might surprise you to know that every single year except one in the 12 years before I became President, the Democratic Congress that got all the credit from the other side for running the deficit up actually spent slightly less money than the Republican President asked them to spend—just one little fact that almost never got out there because we often lost the rhetorical war.

So what I tried to do is to lower the rhetoric, focus it on specific achievements, and find a way to bring people together. Now, one of the great failures of my administration is, I have not succeeded in reducing partisanship in Washington. But Lord knows I have tried—I have tried. And when we have been able to work together, the results have been pretty good. We had to have some Republicans to support our crime bill, although it was mostly a Democratic crime bill, and it's hard to quarrel with the results. We had a bipartisan balanced budget agreement. They got the tax cut they wanted; we supported the tax cut in the shape that it was in, but we also got the biggest increase in health care for children in 35 years and the biggest increase in aid to people going to college since the GI bill.

So we have tried to work together. And when we have done it, that's been good. When they haven't done it and we've been able to prevail, the results have been good. But I want to say to you today is, we cannot afford the luxury of thinking that just because we have the first balanced budget in 29 years and this $70 billion surplus and the lowest unemployment rate in 28 years and the lowest percentage of people on welfare in 29 years and the lowest inflation in 32 years and the smallest Government in 35 years and all the other statistics you know, we can't afford to say, "Isn't this wonderful. Now let's go back and have a mud fight again."

We have to keep at the business of building America's future. We have to make real all those ideas that Bob Torricelli talked about that were advanced early on by the Vice President. And all you've got to do is just watch, every day, watch the financial developments every day in the world and see how sometimes we react to them in America—sometimes the market drops; sometimes it goes up, but you see what's going on here—to realize this is a very dynamic time and that the peace of change has actually accelerated in the last 6 years, so that the approach that we had—forget about the specific issues—the approach we had was clearly the right one.

I got a letter from a friend of mine the other day who is a writer. He's a very eloquent man, and he wrote me this sort of blunt letter with no adjectives in it. He said, "Peace and pros-perity is not a bad legacy. I think one reason your administration has advanced is, it looks to me like all of you get up and go to work every day." Sort of a blunt letter, but there's something to be said for that.

One of the things I'm proudest of is that the people that work in our administration and the people we work with in the Congress, they do a phenomenal job of putting their egos aside and working as a team and really working through these things. A lot of this stuff is just hard work, and it takes a lot of time and a lot of concentration. And I'm here to tell you, if you like the results of the last 6 years, there needs to be a resounding message coming out of these congressional elections that that is what we think Washington should be about. Because, make no mistake about it, if you want to see these surpluses continue, if you want to see us deal with these big challenges, we have got to know the American people expect that of us. That has got to be what people see.

And it's hard for people, because we're so far away from them here, and there's so many layers between us and the people running all the small businesses in Spokane and Sacramento and Albuquerque and all the places in between, that it's easy to think that these word battles are what matter. But it's not. It's the results. It's the direction, the ideas, the implementation of the ideas, the constant, constant pressing to meet the challenges of the moment.

This international—let's start with that—this international financial crisis that we see gripping Asia, gripping Russia, echoing across in Latin America, being felt to some extent in our stock market here, this is a new but inevitable and thoroughly predictable phenomenon of the fact that, first, we built the global trading system in goods that got more and more integrated, then a global trading system in services; and the more goods and services you had to have, the more it was necessary that money roll around the world relatively unimpeded. And the institutions that we developed over the last 50 years were not fully sensitive and flexible enough to deal with all those challenges at once, plus whatever was going on or not going on within all these countries that are trying to move from either communist countries to free market countries or developing countries to a more developed status. Some of this stuff was bound to happen.

Now, what is the answer? No one has the whole answer, but I promise you this: It will not be solved by word games. It will be solved by work, by ideas, by real people thinking about real problems and working in a sustained way.

Four years ago—4 years ago—I got the leaders of the G–7 to begin working on this because I knew it was going to take years to figure out what modifications would be required to deal with this challenge. For one year, the finance ministers of 22 countries have been working on specific recommendations. They'll be here Monday, and we'll have thousands of people here Tuesday for the opening of the World Bank and the International Monetary Fund conference. Now, who'd have ever thought that would be an election and a congressional race in Nebraska? But it is. Whether we pay our fair share to the International Monetary Fund will determine, number one, whether they've got the money to deal with these crises which directly affect our economy; and number two, whether we can continue to lead the world in resolving them.

All the ideas in the world coming out of America won't amount to a hill of beans if America is not willing to carry its own load. Now, I said this in January. It is now October, and we still don't have it. And there are a lot of problems in the world. And if the American people like this economic recovery we have and they want it to go on, then we must recognize that 30 percent of it came from trade, and our ability to be strong and to lead the world depends upon our doing our part. That's a big issue in this election.

We believe—the Vice President and I ran on a platform that caused a lot of ripples. We said, "Look, we're for more global trade, and we're going to open more markets, but we believe we have to protect the working people of America and the working people of other countries. We believe we have to protect the environment of America and the environment of other countries. We believe we have to put a human face on the global trading system."

Now the financial challenges threaten to undermine the material benefits that people believe they get from it. If you believe in this, if you like the growth that America has had the last 6 years, if you believe that other people have a right to be rewarded for their labors around the world and you want us to continue to grow like this, this is a huge issue. And you know it's hard to turn it into a 5-second slogan and put it on a bumper sticker, but it has a lot to do with how your kids are going to live in the 21st century.

Same thing with this Social Security issue. I know it's popular to offer a tax cut 5 weeks before the election, say, "We finally got a surplus; we want to give you some of it." But it's dead wrong. After Social Security—I'm sorry Senator Breaux had to leave, because he's the chairman of our Medicare commission. No serious person believes that we can have a good society unless we take care of the elderly when it comes to baseline income and health care. And no serious person who has looked at it believes that the present system can do that when the baby boomers retire unless we make modifications. And if we start now and do things that are modest but disciplined, we can have a good society. That's what that surplus ought to be used for. We ought not to spend one red cent until we know we've taken care of Social Security for the 21st century. That's a huge issue, and it's more important than an election-year tax cut.

Those are big changes. And it may not be a bumper sticker, although "Social Security First" is pretty close. But if you're worried about how your kids are going to live in the 21st century and you're like me, you're a baby boomer that's plagued by the thought that we might reduce the standard of living of our children and our grandchildren because we didn't take care of this problem when we had the chance, then that's a big issue.

This education issue, you should have seen it; we must have had 60 Democratic Senators and Congressmen today on the South Lawn of the White House. The Vice President mentioned it. All we said was, "Look, for 8 months, 9 months now, we have had an education program up there, and you haven't let us bring it to the floor. Just give us one day. Don't you think our kids' education is worth one day?"

And in our balanced budget there is money for 100,000 teachers that takes average class size down to 18 in the first 3 grades in this country; there is a tax program that will help us to build or repair 5,000 schools. The Vice President and I could keep you here until dawn talking about the schools we have visited with all the housetrailers out back or the beautiful old buildings that have broken windows and whole floors closed down. We say our children are the most important things in the world to us. We're not acting like it.

Or our plan to pay for college education for 35,000 young people if they will go back and pay the education off by teaching in the most educationally underserved areas. Or our plan to make—Bob Torricelli said that the Vice President understood cyberspace before anybody else, coining the phrase "information superhighway." We want to hook every classroom in America up to it. We don't think—now that we know what it does, we think it is morally unacceptable to let the benefits of the information explosion be experienced by anything other than all of our children. Now, that's what's in there—that's what's in there.

And let me just say one other thing—we've got programs in there for after-school care, for summer school care. All these kids—we keep saying we want to end social promotion. We started that, our party did; we don't believe anybody should be promoted every year, year-in and year-out, whether they know anything or not. But we don't believe children should be dubbed failures because the system is failing them. And that's why we think these after-school programs, these summer school programs, these tutoring programs, are so important. This is a big deal. I don't know if you can put it on a bumper sticker or not, but I know this: It's going to have a lot more to do with how our kids live in the 21st century than a lot of what goes on around here.

The Patients' Bill of Rights symbolizes our continuing challenge to make health care affordable and quality for all Americans. It won't solve all the problems, but it will deal with the fact that 160 million Americans are in managed care. Forty-three managed care companies are supporting this bill because they're out there doing their best to take care of their patients, the people that subscribe to them, and they're at an economic disadvantage because others don't do it.

So these issues are big issues. And what I want to say to you is, if this were a normal election—that is, if this were a Presidential election year—we would be looking at a rout. Why? Because the American people agree with what we've done; they agree with the approach we've taken; they agree with us on these issues; and because in a Presidential year our candidates are guaranteed a national forum, and everybody hears everything through at least the megaphone of the debate in the Presidential race.

In an off-year the financial advantage that the other party always enjoys is dramatically magnified and normally reinforced by a lower turnout among baseline voters who normally vote with us, because our folks don't make as much money, have more child care problems, have more transportation problems, have more other hassles in their life. It's a bigger effort for them to vote.

That's why we did the Unity thing. That's why you're so important. The only thing I can tell you when you go out of here is that you cannot let this be your last effort. Every one of you has some network through which you can exercise your influence to try to get people to understand that this is a hugely important election and they must show up and be counted. If you believe in Social Security first, if you believe in America taking the lead in the international financial challenges, if you believe in education being our top investment priority, if you believe in the Patients' Bill of Rights, if you believe we should improve the environment, not weaken it, if you believe in these things, then you have got to help us for the next 5 weeks.

We can win a stunning, unprecedented, historically, literally unprecedented victory if only the people understand what the issues are, where the parties stand, where the candidates stand. But we have to push back the veil here and get people to think about their children and their future and understand that the people that have asked you to give this money are committed to it. If these ideas have worked for the last six years, they'll work just fine for the next 2 and for the next 20, if we're given the chance to implement them.

Thank you, and God bless you.

NOTE: The President spoke at 9:53 p.m. in the ballroom at the Sheraton Luxury Collection Hotel. In his remarks, he referred to Representative Nancy Pelosi; Senator Robert G. Torricelli; Terence McAuliffe, former national finance chair, Steve Grossman, national chair, and Leonard Barrack, national finance chair, Democratic National Committee; and President Petar Stoyanov of Bulgaria.

Remarks on Initiatives for the International Economy and an Exchange With Reporters
October 2, 1998

The President. Good morning. Today I would like to talk to you about the steps we are taking to keep our economy growing by keeping the world's economy growing. Less than 36 hours ago, America closed the books on an era of exploding deficits and diminished expectations by recording a budget surplus of $70 billion, the largest on record and the largest as a percentage of our economy since the 1950's. Every American should be proud of this.

Today we received more evidence that the economy remains solid. For 15 months in a row now, unemployment has stayed below 5 percent for the first time in 28 years. Over the last year, wages have risen at more than twice the rate of inflation, and now the economy has added more than 16.7 million new jobs since 1993.

Today, America enjoys a great moment of prosperity. But we cannot remain an oasis of prosperity in a world in which so much of our growth depends upon trade and in which so many of our trading partners are experiencing economic turmoil. We must hold to the economic strategy that has brought us to where we are today and move aggressively to deal with the challenges around the world. We must maintain our fiscal discipline. When I supported targeted tax cuts that we paid for in this budget, I made it clear, and I want to make it clear again: I will veto any tax plan that drains the new surplus. We simply have to set aside every penny of it, not only to set a good financial example around the world but to save Social Security first.

Second, we must continue to invest in education. The fiscal year has just ended. Yet, Congress still has not found time to send me an appropriations bill on education. Congress must put progress ahead of partisanship and send me an education bill that funds our investments in smaller classes; 100,000 new teachers, better trained; and safe, more modern schools, with every class able to be hooked to the Internet by the year 2000.

To ensure prosperity for the American economy, I say again, however, we must continue to lead, and we must move more aggressively to lead in the global economy. Today, the world faces the most serious financial challenge in 50 years. Our future prosperity depends upon whether we can work with others to restore confidence, to manage change, and to stabilize the financial system. Our chief priority is and must be economic growth, here and around the world.

Last month in New York, I outlined several steps we can take immediately to address the crisis. I asked Secretary Rubin and Federal Reserve Chairman Greenspan to convene a major meeting of their counterparts to recommend ways to adapt international financial institutions to the 21st century. Yesterday Secretary Rubin spoke about that, and I am pleased that, on short notice, Secretary Rubin and Chairman Greenspan have arranged the meeting of finance ministers and central bankers from the major industrialized nations and the key emerging markets for next Monday here in Washington. I will personally participate in their deliberations. The following day, I will address the World Bank and the International Monetary Fund to underscore the urgency of quick action and the need for long-term reform of the international financial system.

But we must do more to help the international community respond to the challenges posed by the current crisis. And today we are taking the following steps, steps that build on the approach I outlined a few weeks ago at the Council on Foreign Relations.

First, we must act to strengthen the international financial community's capacity to limit the contagion. This week, Secretary Rubin and Chairman Greenspan will explore with the International Monetary Fund and their G–7 colleagues whether best to design a new mechanism, anchored in the IMF, to provide contingent finance to help countries ward off global financial contagion. This step, combined with full funding for the IMF, would give the international community a powerful new tool to help reduce the risk posed by the current financial crisis.

Second, we must help the people who have been hurt by this crisis. As I said in New York, multilateral development banks like the World Bank, the Asian Development Bank, the Inter-American Development Bank have played a critical and positive role. Today I ask them to explore the following steps to develop a new emergency capacity to lend quickly so as to help other countries reform their financial sectors while also helping the most vulnerable citizens; to use loan guarantees and other innovative means to leverage private sector lending to emerging markets; and to expand their own lending as much as possible within their guidelines to countries now affected by the crisis who desperately need an infusion of new cash.

Finally, the United States will take new steps to encourage American businesses to continue exporting to and investing in emerging markets hurt by the crisis. Jim Harmon, the head of our Export-Import Bank, will travel to Brazil, Argentina, and Mexico over this month. I have asked him to establish new short-term credit facilities to make it easier for American businesses to continue exporting to critical Latin American markets. He will coordinate these efforts with his counterparts in other leading industrial nations to ensure that trade credit continues to flow during this period of financial stress. That is very, very important to our economy.

And the Overseas Private Investment Corporation, OPIC, has developed a new instrument to help emerging economies raise money from international capital markets. That also is very important.

Now, with these steps, we are acting to protect our own prosperity and to exercise responsible economic stewardship in the world. But we cannot act alone. Congress must take some responsibility as well. In the few working days it has left this year, the most important thing Congress can do to protect our farmers, our ranchers, our businesses, and our workers is to secure full funding for the International Monetary Fund. Congress cannot afford to delay approving IMF funding another day. Every day Congress delays increases our vulnerability to crisis, decreases confidence in global markets, and undermines our prospects.

Without giving the IMF the resources it needs, many vital efforts to strengthen the international financial institutions simply will fall short. We can have an honest debate about the best ways to put out economic fires abroad, but there should be no doubt about whether we give the fire department the resources to do the job. If America is to continue to grow, we must support the IMF. If America is to continue to grow, we must lead. We cannot lead if we won't even pay our fair share to the International Monetary Fund. I have been asking for this for nearly a year now. The crisis overseas has continued to intensify. This is inexcusable, and we need the money now for Americans and their interests and for the long-term stability of the world. This is terribly, terribly important.

We have done our best to manage this crisis, to mobilize other countries. We want other countries to do more. We are not going to be able to get them to do more if we won't even do what is plainly our responsibility. No other country in the world has benefited as much as we have in the last 6 years from the global economy. We can lead back away from this financial precipice, but we need the resources to do it.

Now, let me say to all of you: Remember where we were 6 years ago. There were some people who were saying America was in decline. Today, we have a new surplus. We have wages rising—the highest levels in over 20 years. We have the confidence in the country soaring. We have an unprecedented opportunity to build for the future. But with all this turmoil in the rest of the world, we also have a heavy responsibility to the future. We know that a lot of our growth has come because others were growing in the rest of the world and could buy American products and American services. We know we are going into an unprecedented time. This country has got to lead. We've got to be aggressive. We've got to stay on the balls of our feet. We've got to be aware that this thing is changing every day.

We can help a great deal to modify the difficulties, to move the world back toward growth, and to keep our own prosperity going. But if we're going to do that, we've got to lead. We've got to do our part. We can't talk about these things and not put up our share of the investment.

So again I say, we're going to do what we can. I'm looking very much forward to the IMF and the World Bank meeting. I'm looking forward to meeting with the finance leaders and the central bankers of these 22 countries. We're going to come up with some good ideas, but ideas have to be followed by action. And for us to take the action we need to take, the Congress has got to provide funds for the IMF.

Thank you very much.

Possibility of Worldwide Recession

Q. How close are we to a worldwide recession? Is there a danger of a recession in this world?

The President. Well, I think the proper answer to that, Sam [Sam Donaldson ABC News], is that about a quarter of the world is and has been in recession. About a quarter of the world is in a period of very low growth. The rest of us are growing. But in the nature of things, if you want growth to continue, you have to restore growth in that part of the world that's suffering now; and it cannot be done without aggressive action—as I said in New York a couple of weeks ago—aggressive action to restore the stability of the world financial system, to restore the confidence of investors, and to deal with the legitimate problems within each country that many of those countries have to deal with that we can't do anything about.

But there are three things we've got to do: We've got to do what we can to restore stability of the world financial system; we've got to restore the confidence of investors so they'll put their money back into markets everywhere; and we've got to work with these countries to solve the problems within the countries that only they can solve. But the answer to your question is, we don't have to have a worldwide recession if those of us that enjoy growth will take the initiative and move now.

But we cannot afford to dally around here. If we'd had this money 6 months ago, we could have done more than we have. So I think it's important that everybody recognize that we don't know—nobody can predict the future with great certainty, but I have a lot of confidence in the strength of the American economy and our ability to keep doing well, but it rests in large measure on our ability to do the right thing around the world.

But keep in mind, 30 percent of our growth in the last 6 years has come from our ability to sell our goods and services around the world. We have a personal, vested interest quite apart from our larger ethical responsibilities to lead the world that we've profited so much from; we've got a vested interest in averting a global financial slowdown by taking initiatives and doing it now. We've got to do it now.

Kosovo?

Kosovo

Q. On Kosovo, should the world be surprised that the Serbs believed that they could possibly get away with massive bloodletting once again in the region without fearing action from the United States and in particular its European allies?

The President. Well, that's the argument I've been making for months, that we have seen, we saw in Bosnia what works in dealing with Mr. Milosevic. And the Kosovo situation is somewhat different in that Kosovo is actually a part of Serbia, although by law it's supposed to be autonomous. But let me tell you what we're doing. Let's focus on what we're doing.

We have been working for months and months—I have personally been working for months, first of all, to get NATO and then to get the U.N. to send a message to Mr. Milosevic to stop the violence.

We have NATO working; we have the U.N. resolution. I believe that our allies in Europe are with us, and I think that we all understand and we hope he got the message. I think it is very important. We have to be very, very strong here. We need to stop the violence, get a negotiated settlement and work our way through this. We don't want thousands upon thousands of people to be caught up in a war or to starve or freeze this winter because they have been displaced. And we are working very, very hard on it, and we're briefing on the Hill as well.

I want to say a special word of appreciation to Senator Dole, who has been very outspoken about this, very supportive about an aggressive role for the United States, very understanding that we cannot allow this conflict to spread again and risk what we stopped in Bosnia, starting again in Kosovo. So we're working on it very hard, and I'm quite hopeful that we'll have a positive resolution of it. Thank you.

NOTE: The President spoke at 10 a.m. at the South Portico of the White House, prior to his departure for Cleveland, OH. In his remarks, he referred to President Slobodan Milosevic of the Federal Republic of Yugoslavia (Serbia and Montenegro).

Remarks at a Luncheon for Senatorial Candidate Mary Boyle in Cleveland, Ohio
October 2, 1998

The President. Well, let me begin by thanking you for the wonderful welcome, thanking you for being here for Mary. Tony and Kristine, I have now been in your home and Slam Jam's. [*Laughter*] And I like them both very much. Thank you so much for opening your home to a few of your friends today. It is a wonderful act of generosity.

I'd like to thank all the candidates who are here. They've all been introduced, but I thank them for coming. I thank Mayor Coyne and David Leland and Mayor Starr and—Mayor Coyne, thank you for being here. I would like to say also a special word of appreciation to David Leland and the work that he has done with the Ohio Democratic Party. I think it's one of the best State Democratic Parties in the entire United States, and I thank you. And I thank all of these legislators and others who are here who are a part of that.

I'd like to thank Tony and Kristine for having their family here; and I'd like to thank Mary for having her mother, her husband, her kids—her whole family here. This has turned out to be a family affair.

I'd also like to say a special word of thanks—I always try to do this when I come to Ohio. You know, the press said that I would be the nominee of the Democratic Party when I won the Ohio primary in 1992. And then at the Democratic Convention in New York, Ohio's votes put me over the top officially. And then on election night in 1992, all the experts didn't predict that I was a winner until Ohio flashed on the screen for the Clinton-Gore ticket. And I thank you for that. And then in 1996, our margin of victory here was more than tripled over 1992. And I thank you for that. It took a lot of heartache away from me on election day, so I thank you for all that.

As Tony has already said, I would like to say a special word of appreciation to the family of Tom Coury for continuing to sponsor and support this event, for the love they had for him. And I would like to say a special word of appreciation for the feeling he had for the First Lady. We talked about that a little tonight. She is down in Uruguay, having the second of

her Vital Voices conferences. That's a group that she's organized all over the world—starting, I might add for the Irish here, in Northern Ireland—to organize women committed to peace and to economic development and to good family-supportive policies. So I wish she could be here.

But I would like to thank Robert, Thomas, Traci, Teri, and Robert for being here and for what the Courys have meant in their support of me. And thank you for supporting Mary today. Yes, give them a hand again. That's good. [*Applause*]

I want you to know why I came here today. I am here to support Mary Boyle for the Senate. I'm here to support her because she's got an outstanding record in public service, because she has good values and good positions on the issues; you just heard them. I came here because I like her, I have confidence in her, and because if enough of you help her, she can win this election in November and make a big difference to the future of the United States.

Ohio in so many ways is so representative of America. And it's important that you understand that a Senator from Ohio, in a very profound sense, can represent America and the best in America and can have a profound impact on the future of this country, simply by doing what's best for you.

John Glenn called me night before last, just to tell me to hang in there and expressed his support and friendship. We've had a wonderful relationship. But he called me also one more time to thank me for letting him go up in that spaceship—[*laughter*]—because he was going down to Florida to complete his last training. First of all, he told me he was too old to be in the Senate, and then he asked me if he could go into space. [*Laughter*] When he said that, I didn't think we could get anybody to run for the Senate. I thought everybody would be mortally terrified. [*Laughter*]

But when I think about that—you should think about what kind of person you want to replace John Glenn, because he not only represented you, America looked to him—and not just because he went up in space early but because of what he represented after he came down. And I think you need to think about that.

You know, when I ran for President in 1992, except for President Carter's term, we hadn't had much success at electing Presidents since 1968. And I said to the American people and to the people of Ohio, "Look, I'd like to take a different approach to the country's problems. I'd like to put an end to a lot of this partisan bickering in Washington and the shouting back and forth." And I believe that a lot of what we're hearing about National Government is just flat wrong. I don't believe that you can help business by hurting labor. I think a good economic policy is pro-business and pro-labor. I don't believe you can grow the economy by destroying the environment. Over the long-run, that's a loser. I think we have to prove that we can improve the environment as we grow the economy. I don't believe that you can just jail your way out of the crime problem. Sure, people should be punished, but the best policy is to keep kids out of trouble in the first place with a sensible prevention policy.

I don't believe people on welfare who can work should be on welfare. I think they ought to have to work. But I don't think when they go to work their children ought to be punished by losing their nutrition and their health care benefits. If you took a totally nonpolitical poll of families and you asked them what they were really worried about—working people with children—most people would tell you, even in upper income levels, that what they really worry about is how to properly balance their job at work and their job at home, which is still the most important job in America, raising your kids. Most everybody would tell you that. So I said, "If you vote for me, I'll try to reform the welfare system to make people work who ought to work, but I'm not going to make them sacrifice their responsibilities to their kids. There's got to be a way to balance these two things." And that's what we've done.

I said there was a way to bring the deficit down and continue to invest in education, in health care, in research, in making this country strong. I felt that America could be more active than we had been in promoting peace and freedom and prosperity around the world. And the American people gave me and Al Gore and Hillary and our whole team a chance to see whether we were right or not.

And when we celebrated a couple of days ago the first balanced budget in 29 years, the biggest surplus in the history of the country, the biggest surplus as a percentage of our economy since the 1950's, it came at a time when we also had the lowest unemployment rate in 28 years, the lowest crime rate in 25 years, the smallest percentage of people on welfare in 29 years, the lowest inflation rate in 32 years, with the smallest Federal Government in 35 years, and the highest homeownership in the history of the country. I am proud that we were able to work together to achieve those results for the United States.

Now, let me tell you why this election is important. It's important for two reasons. First of all, we've got to decide what to do with this moment. That's the big issue. And let me say, I can't thank you enough, a lot of you who came by and said hello to me earlier, for the very kind, personal things you said to me and, through me, to my wife. But I want you to understand something very clearly. If I had to do it all over again, every day, I would do it in a heartbeat, to see America where it is today as compared to 6 years ago.

I want you to understand, too, that we all have to live with the consequences of our mistakes in life. Most of us don't have to live with it in quite such a public way. [Laughter] But nobody gets out of this life for free—nobody does. And so that's not the real point.

The other thing I want you to understand is that, in this election, all this adversity is not our enemy. The adversity is our friend. The mayor and Mary and I were just walking on the street not very long ago. We talked to a lot of people that couldn't afford to be here today, but they might vote now because they understand that there are big issues at stake. Adversity is not our enemy. Adversity is our friend. Complacency is our enemy.

If you listen to people talk on the other side about why they're going to do well in these congressional elections, they'll tell you—I mean, privately—they tell me, "Oh, we're going to do very well, Mr. President, in these midterms because we have so much more money than you do, than you Democrats, and because they're midterm elections and the people that came out and voted for you for President in 1996, a lot of them won't show up in 1998 because it's not a Presidential election."

The people that were good enough to serve you here at this event today, they've got a lot of hassles in their life. A lot of them have to worry about child care. A lot of them have to worry about transportation. They've got a lot of things on their mind. And the other guys say, just bluntly, you know, those people—working people on modest incomes, younger people with kids to deal with, along with their jobs, minorities who may live in inner cities that are too far away from the polling place to walk, and not have transportation—don't worry, they won't show up. Adversity is our friend, because it will focus us on what is at issue here.

And what is at issue here is, what are we going to do with this moment of prosperity? That's why this Senate seat is so important to Ohio and to the country. And I want you to think about it just a minute. Yes, we're doing well. I said all that; I just told you. We're doing very well. I'm grateful for that. I had some role in it, and so did you. When Mary Boyle said we produced the surplus, she was not wrong. You paid the money into the IRS. And you got up and went to work every day. And a lot of you created a lot of those new jobs. I didn't do that; we did that. My goal in Washington was to have the policies that would establish the conditions and give you the tools so that you could do the job. That's the way America works.

Now, I'm also gratified—and you just look around this crowd today, we have here at least Arab-Americans, Irish-Americans, African-Americans, and Lord knows what else—[*laughter*]—Ukrainians, Slovenians. [*Laughter*] What?

Audience member. One Ukrainian.

The President. And one Ukrainian. [*Laughter*] Probably some Jewish-Americans, probably some others. This is America. And this is what I try to do, not just for our party but for our country, just say, look, you know—you look around the world and people are so troubled because of their racial, their ethnic, their religious, their political differences. They're killing each other. If we want to be a good influence in the rest of the world, we have to be good at home. We have to prove that what we have in common is more important than our differences. And that's the only way we can celebrate our differences in a civil way.

And I'm proud of that, of the work we've done for peace in Bosnia and Northern Ireland and Haiti and the Middle East. A lot of you talked to me about the Middle East today. We had Mr. Arafat and Mr. Netanyahu here a few days ago. They talked alone for the first time in a year. We spent an hour and a half together, and they're coming back in a few days—little over a week. And we're going to work and work and work and try to take the next big step in the peace process. These things are important. But what you need to understand is, in large measure, it all rests on you.

Now, I have said that when things—we have two things going on. Number one, America is doing very well, right? Number one. Number two, America is doing very well in a very fast changing world, where events are changing every day. You see it. You see the financial crisis around the world. You see the troubles in Kosovo. When I was riding through the neighborhood, there was a young woman that had a sign that said, "Please help Kosovo."

Now, what are we going to do with this moment? I think we have to use it to deal with the big long-term challenges of the country. In this election it means, at a minimum, don't spend the surplus until we fix Social Security for the baby boom generation so that they can retire in dignity without hurting—so we, I'm one of them—[*laughter*]—so that we can retire in dignity without hurting our children and our grandchildren's standard of living. That is a huge issue.

Now, members of the other party are going to fan out all across America and say, "We're trying to give you an election year tax cut. I mean, it's just a few weeks before the election. We're trying to give it to you, and that mean old President and his party won't come across." But it's not very much money, and we waited 29 years and we worked hard for 6 years to see the red ink turn to black, and I'd kind of like to watch it dry for a day or two before we squander it.

People like Mary's mother, their Social Security is secure. You're 60 years old, now, your Social Security will be fine. But if we don't make some modest changes in the system, by the time all of us baby boomers retire and there are only two people working for every one person drawing, we will only have one of two bad alternatives. If you're between 34 and 52, you're in the baby boom generation. When you get into Social Security, if we don't make some changes, we'll have one of two alternatives: We'll either have to put a whopping tax increase on our kids so that we can continue to sustain the present system, undermining our children's ability to raise our grandchildren; or they'll have to put a whopping cut in Social Security benefits on us, undermining the security of our retirement. Not everybody is going to have as good a pension as I do, you know. [*Laughter*] And it's a serious thing. It's a serious thing. Half the senior citizens in this country today would be in poverty were it not for the Social Security system.

Now, people say, "Well, how can you do this, with the election 4½ weeks away and the tax cut something you get right away, and we're looking to the future?" America is around here after 220 years because when we needed to do it, we always looked to the future. And I trust the American people to say, "We prefer to put Social Security first and to save it." I think that's the right decision.

The second issue that's really big to me, that you can see if you see all this financial turmoil around the world: 30 percent of our growth comes from selling things to other countries, our products and our services. And when we can't, because they don't have any money, we suffer.

There are a bunch of farmers in North Dakota today, if you went up and told them these were America's best times, they would think that you needed a serious mental health examination. [*Laughter*] Why? Because they sell wheat. And we sell half our wheat overseas and 40 percent of it to Asia, and they don't have any money to buy their wheat. And farm income has dropped to nothing. We're going to lose this year, unless the Congress passes the emergency agricultural legislation I sent—we could lose 10,000 American farmers this year, family farmers.

So I say, we've got to take the lead in trying to do the following things. Number one, we've got to try to limit this financial crisis in Asia and Russia before it spreads to Latin America where our biggest markets are, our fastest growing ones. Number two, we've got to try to help them, our friends in Latin America and Russia, if they'll do the right things, get back on their feet so they can grow again and participate with us. And number three, we've got to make some

changes in the world financial and trade system so that it works for ordinary people.

Freedom and free enterprise will not be embraced forever around the world unless it works for ordinary people. The reason we've still got this system here is that most people, every time an election comes around, believe that freedom and free markets and free enterprise are good systems. And if they didn't, the voters would have changed them here a long time ago. Now, we've got to do that.

So I never thought in my life—if anybody ever told me when I came to Washington that funding for the International Monetary Fund would be an issue in an election, I never would have believed it. Most people, if you talk about the IMF, most people don't know what it means. But what the IMF means today is continued economic opportunity for the people of the United States of America. Now, I have been waiting 8 months for the Congress to fund what we owe to the IMF. The United States has got to lead the world out of this financial mess, and we've go to do it before it bites us and our friends in Europe, and even sooner, our friends in Latin America.

If you want—a lot of people here are concerned about the Middle East peace—one of the reasons we need to hurry up is the abject poverty in which too many people, not only Palestinians but others, Jordanians, others in the Middle East are living in. We can't help them unless there is a general climate of growth and investment in the world. This is a big deal. But it's become a partisan political issue in Washington, so after 8 months we still don't have it.

So if you want to send a message that you expect your country to protect your jobs and your businesses and your future, then you've got to support our program to keep America leading the way in the world economy. It's very important and very simple.

I'll just mention one other issue. I know I'm preaching to the saved here today, but when I leave, you're going to be here, and you've got to go talk to other people. The third issue is education. Now, I'm really proud of the fact that in the bipartisan balanced budget bill we opened the doors of college wider than ever before because our party's initiative, my administration's initiative, was embraced: tax credits for all 4 years of college, for graduate school; deductibility of interest on student loans; more scholarships through the Pell grant program; more work-study programs. That's great. Everybody knows now we've done that. But what we have not done is made our elementary and secondary schools the best in the world, no matter where children live, what their race is, what their income is, what their circumstances are. You know that.

Now, I gave the Congress 8 months ago an education program, fully paid for. Here's what it does. It would provide 100,000 teachers to take class size in the early grades down to an average of 18. All the research shows that's the most important thing you can do to give kids a good start in life and the benefits are permanent. That's the first thing it does.

The second thing it does is provide a tax incentive program to help rebuild and repair or build 5,000 schools. Why is that important? I visited a little school district—a little school district—in Florida the other day where one school had 12 trailers in the back for classrooms. It's the biggest group of kids ever in school, the first group bigger than the baby boomers. In Philadelphia, where I'm going when I leave you, the average school building is 65 years old. I visited a school where the whole floor is shut down.

We tell our kids they're the most important thing in the world; what do we say to them if they walk up the steps of the school and the windows are broken and the floors are closed and they can't even look out the window in a lot of these places? And they're not safe.

This program also would provide funds to school districts who would do like Chicago did and say, "We're not going to have any more social promotion; you've got to prove that you know what you're supposed to know to go to the next grade. But we will not tell you children that you are failures just because the system failed. So if you don't make the grade, we'll send you to after-school programs; we'll send you to summer school programs; we'll give you tutors." The Chicago school system's summer school is now the sixth biggest school district in the United States of America.

And I want to do that everywhere. I think every child deserves not to be defrauded in education. You're not doing them a favor if you promote them if they don't know anything, but you're sure not doing them a favor if you brand them a failure because the system failed them.

So give them the after-school programs and give them the summer school programs.

Now, this program expands our efforts for safe schools, a big issue now. It would hook up all the classrooms in the country, no matter how poor or rural they are, to the Internet by the year 2000. That's what it does—8 months, no action.

Now, what is the record of the other party? What have they done with their year in the majority? And keep in mind, I have done my best to work in a bipartisan way. We got a few Republicans—after no Republicans on our budget bill, we got a few for the Brady bill. We got a few for the crime bill to put 100,000 police on the street. We had a genuine bipartisan effort, big majorities in both parties, finally, for the welfare bill, after I vetoed the first two because it took the health and nutrition benefits away from the families. And now it's going in the other direction, in the wrong direction.

What have they done? They killed the minimum wage increase for 12 million Americans. They killed campaign finance reform. They killed the tobacco reform legislation that would have put in billions of dollars to protect our children from the danger of tobacco, still the number one public health problem in America today. They killed the Patients' Bill of Rights that says that you have a right to go to the nearest emergency room if you're in an accident, to see a specialist if you need one, to keep your doctor even if your health provider changes while you're pregnant or in chemotherapy or some other reason. They've actually gone backwards in protecting the environment; there are all kinds of assaults on the environment in their budget. They have gone backwards at protecting Social Security first with this House tax bill. And there's been no action on the International Monetary Fund and the education.

And this shows a larger set of different attitudes. I believe with all my heart that we're up there not to fight with each other about where we are on the totem pole but to fight for you to make sure you and your children have a better, safer, freer future. That's what I think we're there for.

If you want to send a message to Washington that you want your interests put first, that you want progress over partisanship, that you want people over politics, that you believe in Social Security first, education is our top investment priority, and keeping the economy going—if you want to send that message, the best way in the world you could ever send that message is to send Mary Boyle to the United States Senate.

Thank you, and God bless you.

NOTE: The President spoke at 2:35 p.m. at a private residence. In his remarks, he referred to luncheon hosts Tony and Kristine George; Mayor Thomas Coyne of Brook Park, OH; David J.

Leland, State Democratic Party chair; Mayor Gary Starr of Middleburg Heights, OH; Mary Boyle's husband, Jack, and her mother, Catherine O'Boyle; event cohost Thomas R. Coury, who died September 28, and his brother Robert Coury, Sr., son, Thomas J. Coury, granddaughters Traci A. Ade and Teri Coury Strimpel, and nephew Robert Coury, Jr.; Chairman Yasser Arafat of the Palestinian Authority; and Prime Minister Binyamin Netanyahu of Israel.

Statement on the Death of Gene Autry
October 2, 1998

Hillary and I are saddened to learn of the death of Gene Autry. An entire generation of Americans has lost a beloved old friend from childhood. Gene Autry's music and movies captured all that was good and inspiring about America's Old West. His characters taught children across America important lessons about

courage and freedom, justice and fairplay. And in leaving behind a treasure trove of recordings, from "Back in the Saddle Again" to "Rudolph the Red-Nosed Reindeer," America's First Singing Cowboy will sing forever. Our thoughts and prayers go out to the Autry family.

Remarks at a Democratic National Committee Reception in Philadelphia, Pennsylvania
October 2, 1998

Thank you. Thank you very much for the warm welcome. [*Laughter*] I've had a wonderful time in Philadelphia today, and I am deeply indebted to you for being here tonight, for supporting our party, our candidates, and what we stand for.

I, too, want to thank Congressman Chaka Fattah for the High Hopes program. He and the mayor met me today at the airport with a number of young children from Philadelphia who are in your school system, in your middle school system. And then later, we sat down and drank a soft drink together, and I visited with them. And Chaka asked how many of them wanted to go to college, and they all wanted to go. And now they and literally tens of thousands of children like them all across our country are going to be able to go because of the initiative that he brought to me, that I embraced, and that we have worked so hard to pass: the High Hopes scholarship program. And

we thank him. America is in your debt, Congressman. Thank you.

And I believe we have one of our candidates for Congress here, too, tonight, Roy Afflerbach. Let's give him a hand. He's somewhere—where are you, Roy? There you go. [*Applause*] Thank you. Thank you for running.

I want to thank Steve Grossman for doing a superb job as the chairman of the Democratic Party. And we will not tell his mayor that he bragged on Rendell shamelessly tonight. [*Laughter*] I also want to thank Len Barrack of Philadelphia for being our finance chair. He's doing a wonderful, wonderful, wonderful job.

And finally, let me say that the mayor was uncommonly generous tonight, but his administration is basically the embodiment of my philosophy of government. When we came before the American people, Al Gore and I, in 1992, we said we had a different idea, that we wanted everyone in America who was a responsible citizen to have opportunity. We wanted to come together as one community across all of our differences of race, religion, politics, income. We wanted to prove that you could be pro-business and pro-labor. We wanted to prove that you could be in favor of economic growth and still improve the environment. We wanted to end all these sort of false choices that had been imposed on us by the hot rhetoric of Washington for too many years. And we had a different theory of government, that we thought that the main role of government was to create the conditions and to give people the tools to make the most of their own lives.

And all the initiatives that the mayor mentioned, that he so generously gave me credit for, most all of them were available to a lot of other places, too. But Philadelphia made the most of its opportunities because, in no small measure, of the gifts, the dedication, and the downright aggression of its mayor. And I cannot tell you how much I admire him for that.

You know, I'm sure all of you have had an experience like this in your life in some context or another—by the time somebody calls you 15 times and asks you for something, you say yes just to stop them, you know. [*Laughter*] When Ed Rendell gets all over you like a wet blanket about something—[*laughter*]—you know you might as well just cry "uncle" and go on to something else. I say that because the achievements of this city have been truly phenomenal.

And I have always loved coming here. You know, the people of Philadelphia have been quite wonderful to me and Hillary and to Al and Tipper, voting for us in record numbers and by record margins in both elections and I'm very, very grateful.

Let me just take a few minutes to be a little serious with you tonight. I was so moved today by all the things that were said to me on the street—didn't even mind the protesters. That's the American way. But you like it even more when they're not in the majority—[*laughter*]—and that seemed to be the case today. But I want you to know that, on behalf of the First Lady and on my part, I'm very grateful for those personal expressions.

But I do not believe that adversity is the enemy of the Democratic Party in this election. Indeed, adversity can be our friend, because it's not only good for personal reformation; it's good for people to sort of dig down deep inside

and ask yourself what's really important and what's really fair. What do you really care about? What will you act for? What will you move for?

The real enemy the Democrats have in this election is complacency, because we are doing pretty well as a country. We've got the lowest unemployment rate in 28 years and the lowest percentage of people on welfare in 29 years and the first balanced budget and surplus in 29 years, and it's the biggest in history. We've got the best wage growth in way over 20 years. We've got, as Steve Grossman said, the biggest drop in Hispanic poverty in 30 years and the lowest unemployment rates and poverty rates among African-Americans since statistics have been kept, the highest homeownership in history. All that is very good. I'm grateful for that.

But the real question is, what will we do with this moment? Our friends in the other party know that in spite of your presence and generosity here tonight, they always have tons more money than we do. I'll tell you a little more about that in a minute. [*Laughter*] But they also know that oftentimes at these midterm elections, the people who always vote in presidential elections, a lot of them don't vote in midterm elections. And they tend to be our voters. Why? Well, they're young parents on modest incomes; they have to worry about how to juggle child care and work, and voting on a work day is another hassle. A lot of them live in cities and don't own cars and have transportation problems. And how are they going to get to work and to the polling place? And that extra effort is hard to make.

I tell you, my friends, our enemy is complacency. It is not adversity. Adversity is forcing us to focus on what is important and what we believe in and what we're prepared to fight for. And while I think it's a wonderful thing that all these good things are happening in our country, you know there are still some people in Philadelphia who have not felt the benefits of the things that have been done, and you know there's more to do.

I want you to know that a long way away from here, in the high plains of America, people that work hard to feed you on the farm don't know there's been a recovery because they have to export a lot of their products, and they've been flooded out or burned out or had diseases. They've had all kinds of problems. And now the Asian markets, where they sell their food, are closed to them because the folks don't have any money over there. We could lose 10,000 family farmers in America this year, at a time of greatest prosperity for the country as a whole in a generation.

So we have challenges at home. And I've always believed that when times are good, the worst thing you can do is kick back and relax. You have to see that as an obligation to look at the real challenges facing the country and take them on. That's what we've tried to do.

So we, the Democrats, have gone before the American people and we said, "Look, we have a program for this election, and we think it's worth your voting for. We know that the other side has tried to offer you—for most of you—a modest tax cut. Right here, before the election, they want to spend the surplus. And we've given you a harder message." We've said, "Look, we've waited for this for 29 years. We worked for it for 6 years. Shouldn't we let the red ink turn to black, and let's let it dry for a day or two before we squander it?"

At a time when there's so much financial turmoil throughout the world, shouldn't we set a good example to stabilize the global economy? And even more important, knowing as we all do—every person in this room knows that while Social Security is absolutely stable for the people who are now on it and the people who are about to go on it, when all the baby boomers get in, it is not sustainable under the present circumstances because there will only be two people working for every one person drawing Social Security.

Everybody in this room between the ages of 52 and 34 is a baby boomer. And everybody I know at least my age—and I'm the oldest of the baby boomers—we're all profoundly worried that if we don't do something about this now, when with modest changes now we can have huge impacts down the road, that the time will come when we'll retire and our country will be confronted with two terrible choices: Either we'll have to put a whopping tax increase on our kids to maintain the system as it is, undermining their ability to raise our grandchildren, which none of us want to do; or we'll have to take a whopping cut in Social Security benefits, which today keeps one-half of the senior citizens in America out of poverty.

So I say, tempting though it is before an election to shovel up a little tax cut, let's show a little restraint and a little knowledge of the

last 29 years and say, "No, no, we're going to save Social Security first before we spend it." I believe that's an issue worth voting on. And believe me, the elections will send a message to the Congress about which path you wish to take.

There is a second issue I think is important. I talked about it all day today, and I never thought I'd come to Philadelphia or go anyplace in America in a political election and say, "The big issue is, are we going to fund the IMF?" Most Americans don't know what the IMF is. Sounds like those people that make bowling equipment. [*Laughter*] The International Monetary Fund is a fund to which we and others contribute that helps countries that are poorer and developing, who have good policies, to try to grow their economy; or when they get in trouble, it tries to help them work out of trouble without just being absolutely destroyed.

For 8 months I've been trying to get America to make its fair share of contribution. Why? Because we can't lead the world—and you know the troubles that Asia has; you know the troubles in Russia; you see the impact, how it echoes in Latin America, our fastest growing market for American products. You see people say, when the stock market changes here, that that has something to do with this financial trouble overseas. We have an obligation not only to others throughout the world but to our own economy. Thirty percent of this growth we've enjoyed has come from selling things to people overseas who had enough money to buy them. And when they get in trouble, eventually we will suffer from that. And already, I've told you, our farmers are.

And so I say to you, if you want to keep the American economic recovery going, if you like the way it's gone the last 6 years, and you'd like to have a few more years of it, then America has to lead the world away from the brink of the worst financial crisis in decades. And that means we have to pay our fair share to the fund that will do it. And I think that's something worth voting for.

The third issue worth voting for is education. For 8 months I have had before the Congress an education program. We have succeeded in getting bipartisan agreement in the balanced budget for tax credits for all students to go to college, for the deductibility of interest on student loans, for more Pell grants. Our Democrats put that before the Republicans, and we were able to get bipartisan agreement—and now for Congressman Fattah's High Hopes program. That's great.

But you all know that we don't yet have a world-class elementary and secondary education system that will guarantee to every child, without regard to race or neighborhood or income, a chance to be able to take advantage of those college opportunities. And until we do, America will never be everything it ought to be.

And so I came before the Congress and I said, "Okay, we've listened to the educators. I, personally, and Hillary and I have been going into the schools for 20 years now listing and watching and learning, and here's our program. It's pretty straightforward." Number one, in the balanced budget—paid for—put up enough money for school districts across America to hire 100,000 teachers to take average class size down to 18 in the early grades. It will make a difference.

Number two, provide—provide a tax incentive that will help to build or repair 5,000 school buildings. I went to Jupiter, Florida, and saw a dozen housetrailers outside a school because the population is growing so fast. The mayor took me to a school building in Philadelphia that was over 65 years old. It was one of the most beautiful buildings I've ever seen, but it wasn't in good shape because there's not enough money to repair all those buildings. And all over America in the cities, I see people say, "Oh, our children are the most important things in the world to us." What does it say to them if they walk up the steps every day to a school where the windows are broken or a whole floor is closed down? Very often, people can't even look out the window in some of these places, because they can't afford to heat and cool them, so they just board them up. Five thousand school buildings—that's the second thing it does.

The third thing it does is to give funds to cities for after-school and summer school programs to help kids who are in trouble. I don't believe kids should be promoted endlessly if they don't learn what they're supposed to learn. But I don't think the children should be branded failures because the system fails them. So give them those after-school programs and the summer school programs and the mentors they need to learn what they need to learn. That's a part of our program as well.

The fourth thing it does is provide funds to hook every classroom in the country up to the Internet by the year 2000. Now, I think those are things that are worth voting for—I think they're worth voting for.

And finally, there's the Patients' Bill of Rights, the health care HMO bill of rights. Here's what it says: If you walk out of this room tonight and—God forbid—you get hit by a car, and you're covered by an HMO plan, a managed care plan, you ought to be able to go to the nearest emergency room, not one clear across town because that's the one that happens to be covered by your plan. It says if your doctors tells you that he or she can't help you and you need to see a specialist, you ought to be able to see one. It says if your employer changes HMO providers while you're going through a certain medical treatment, you ought to be able to finish with it.

Now, let me just tell you what that means. How would you feel if you were 7 months pregnant and somebody came to you and said, "I'm sorry, your employer changed providers; you've got to give up your obstetrician, and here's Dr. Jones"? How would you feel if someone in your family was undergoing chemotherapy—I've been through this, a lot of you have, and you know it's a pretty traumatic thing for families. I remember when my mother went through it, we sat around and tried to make jokes about whether she'd lose her hair and what kind of wig she'd buy. You get real nervous about whether your loved one is going to get so sick they can't eat. Now, this is serious; this happens. How would you feel if you were two-thirds of the way through a chemotherapy protocol and somebody said, "I'm sorry, you've got to change your doctor"? This is big stuff. And I think it's worth voting for—I think it's worth voting for.

The Congress—the House passed a bill that didn't guarantee any of those things and what little it did guarantee left out 100 million Americans. Then it went to the Senate, and our crowd had a right to bring our bill up in the Senate, and they couldn't keep it away. So you know what the leader of the Senate did? He shut the Senate down for 4 hours—I mean, turned out the lights; everybody got under the desks. Why? Because they didn't want to be recorded as voting against this, but they didn't want to make angry the insurance companies who oppose it. This is the symbol of the difference between the two parties today, make no mistake about it. And I think it's a big deal.

Now, what have they done with their year in the majority? Except for this higher education bill, I can't think of much. They killed the minimum wage. They killed campaign finance reform. They killed tobacco legislation reform that would have protected our children from the dangers of tobacco. They killed the Patients' Bill of Rights. They have continued their assault on the environment. They have gone backwards on paying for the International Monetary Fund; they've taken no action on it. And they've taken no action on the education bill, and they went backwards on saving Social Security first when the House passed their tax plan. It's over in the Senate now. There is this huge difference.

And what I want you to do—I thank you for coming here tonight. I thank you for these contributions. We need the money, and we'll spend it well. But you have to go out and tell people, there is this cynical idea that you won't vote and that good times makes you less likely to vote. And I know it's more trouble for a lot of people you know to vote. But if you

believe that America ought to be about not what goes on in Washington, DC, but what goes on in the neighborhoods of Philadelphia, in Boston, and in rural North Dakota and in rural Nebraska—if that's what you believe—if you believe in saving Social Security first, if you believe in the Patients' Bill of Rights, if you believe in education as our top investment priority, if you believe in keeping our economic recovery going, then you should support our party—not just tonight but on election day.

And I want every one of you to go out every day between now and then and stir it up among your friends, and make sure that we surprise the cynics on election day.

Thank you, and God bless you.

NOTE: The President spoke at 7:25 p.m. in Room 201 at Philadelphia City Hall. In his remarks, he referred to Mayor Edward Rendell of Philadelphia; and Roy C. Afflerbach, candidate for Pennsylvania's 15th Congressional District.

Remarks at a Democratic National Committee Dinner in Philadelphia
October 2, 1998

Thank you very much. I kind of hate to follow Rendell tonight. [*Laughter*] It's a true story, that story you heard about me asking if he modeled for these sculptures. [*Laughter*] You know, he did so well tonight, I think he sort of halfway talked himself into believing it. It was great. [*Laughter*]

I tell you, I would just like to say one serious thing about the mayor. I remember when we walked the street here in 1992, when he took me into a neighborhood where the gangs and the drugs had been cleared out. I remember when we shot baskets together. He won. [*Laughter*] I think I've demonstrated to the whole world that I'm not always very smart, but I was smart enough to know I shouldn't win that basketball game in '92. [*Laughter*] I knew the only score I was trying to win was in November and that it would help if I took a well-considered dive. [*Laughter*] No, he beat me fair and square, actually.

But I want you to know that to me it's just literally thrilling to come here to this city to

see what has been done, to see the whole sort of spirit of the place, to see the neighborhoods that have come back, to see the people that are working, to see the projects that are on line.

And when I became President, I believed that we needed in Washington to find a way to reduce the deficit until we balanced the budget, to reduce the size of Government, to reduce the burden of regulation, to reduce the plethora of programs in a lot of these areas, but to be more active in creating the conditions and giving people the tools to solve their problems at the grassroots level.

And every tool that we put out there, Ed Rendell used as well or better as anyone in America. And it is an awesome thing to see. And I just want to thank him for proving through this city that this great country can solve its problems, meet its challenges, and work in a stunning fashion. I am very grateful to him, not only for his friendship and support but for what he's done for you and for our country as mayor.

I would like to thank Congressman Bob Borski and Congressman Bob Brady and Congressman Chaka Fattah for being with me tonight and for being with me in Washington, where it really counts and where they have counted for you. I would like to thank our State party chair, Tina Tartaglione, a member of the legislature, I know; and Senator Fumo, thank you for coming, and all the other public officials who are here. I'd like to thank my good friend Marjorie Margolies-Mezvinsky for running for Lieutenant Governor and being my friend.

Tonight Hillary is finishing a trip to Uruguay, where they had one of a series of conferences that she's done around the world. The last one was in Northern Ireland. They're called Vital Voices conferences, where she goes to places and gets together women who are working for peace and reconciliation and development, and dealing with health and family related problems. And Marjorie has helped her a lot on that, and I'm very, very grateful to her, and for so much else.

Finally, let me say I want to thank Len Barrack for doing a fabulous job as the finance director of the DNC. The job has been good for him. He's even wearing three-button suits now—[*laughter*]—taken years off his life, looks so much younger.

Let me say very briefly, Ed talked about some of these issues tonight, but I would like to try to put this in some historical perspective. In 1992, when the citizens of this city gave Al Gore and me a great vote of endorsement and helped us to win the State of Pennsylvania, which was pivotal in our victory, we ran on a platform of change that said we didn't like very much what was going on in Washington and just the constant, endless, partisan bickering and rhetoric and setting up the American people against each other—business against labor, the economy against the environment, dividing the races, dividing present citizens against immigrants—all these things were going on as if there were no way out of these boxes that would build America, that would bring us together and move us forward.

And we said, among other things, if you vote for us we'll give you a Government that's smaller but more active. We'll reduce the deficit and balance the budget, but we'll invest more money in education and medical research and the envi-

ronment. We said we would try to deal with some of the challenges in the health care system and extend coverage to more people. We said that we thought we could improve the environment and grow the economy. We thought that we could be pro-business and pro-labor. We thought we could have a welfare system that required people who were able-bodied to work, without hurting them in their more important job, which is raising their children by doing what many in the other party wanted to do, which was to cut off their guarantee of nutrition and health care benefits to their children.

So we had a lot of ideas, and they were going to be tested. And after 6 years, most of those ideas have now been enacted into law and have been for some time part of the public policy of our country. I am very grateful for where America is tonight and grateful that you gave me the chance to do what I have done to contribute to that and grateful for your contributions. I'm grateful that we have the lowest unemployment rate in 28 years and the lowest crime in 25 years and the smallest percentage of people on welfare in 29 years and now the first balanced budget and surplus in 29 years. And we have record numbers of new businesses in each of the last 6 years, the fastest rising wages in over 20 years, the lowest poverty rate among African-Americans ever recorded, the biggest drop among Hispanics in 30 years. I'm grateful for all that.

The real question I want you to think about tonight when you leave here is why you came here—besides the fact that Ed made you—[*laughter*]—why you came here and what you're going to do when you leave. Because for all the kind and generous and wonderful things that the people of Philadelphia said to me today and the messages they gave, through me, to Hillary today, I have to tell you that I think that the biggest challenge we face in this election season is not adversity but complacency.

Painful though it is, I think adversity is our friend, not only for reasons of personal development and change but because when adversity affects any group of people, it forces you to dig down deep and ask yourself what you believe in, what you're doing, whatever you're doing it for, and what you intend to do tomorrow.

And usually when times are good like this, people relax. And with these elections coming up, our friends in the Republican Party, they believe they're going to be successful for two reasons: One, in spite of your presence here today, they always have tons more money than we do, which they spend very cleverly at the end. And secondly, they know that at midterm elections typically people who always vote in Presidential elections don't go vote. They don't go vote. And a lot of our folks—Ed talked about the child care issue—for a lot of the people that normally vote with our people, it's a lot more trouble for them to go vote. They have to balance children and work, and worry about child care. And election day is a work day, and it's a hassle.

And so I ask you, we have to decide, what is it that we should as a people do with this moment of prosperity, with this moment of confidence? And I would argue to you that we ought to think about the big challenges facing this country over the long run and the specific things we ought to be doing right now.

If you look at the big challenges over the long run facing America, what are they? Well, at home, when the baby boomers retire, we have got to modify Social Security and Medicare so it's there for the people that need it at a cost that doesn't bankrupt our children. It's a big challenge.

We've got to make sure that to go along with the finest higher education system in the world, we can offer world-class elementary and secondary education to every child without regard to race or income or neighborhood. We can't say that today, and we've got to be able to say that.

We've got to modify the international financial systems and trading systems so that we don't have the kind of instability you see today in Asia and Russia, and so that they work for ordinary people, so that we put a human face on the global economy, so that all these people in other countries that we depend upon to buy our products and services really believe that this system will work for them. If you want freedom and free enterprise to work around the world, it has to work for real people, just like it does in this country. Otherwise, it's not sustainable.

We have to prove all over the world that we can improve the environment and grow the economy, that there is not a connection between environmental destruction and economic growth anymore. And there isn't, by the way, on the evidence.

Now, we have to prove that we can get more and more and more diverse racially, religiously, culturally, politically, and still find a way to come together as one America. Those are just some of the really big challenges out there facing us.

What does that mean when you come down to the present day? Ed talked about a couple things. I think the biggest decisions facing us right now are: one, a decision to do the right thing for our children and our parents and not spend this surplus until we have overhauled the Social Security system in the 21st century.

Two, I think that we should make a clear commitment that we are going to continue to lead the world economically, that we recognize our own economy and our prosperity cannot be maintained if everybody else in the world gets in trouble, and there are too many people in trouble now in the world. And we have to lead the world. That means that Congress ought to give me the money—not for me, to our country—to contribute to the International Monetary Fund so we can keep this economy going. That's very important.

Three, Ed talked about education. Let me just—8 months ago in the State of the Union, I gave the Congress an education plan designed to make concrete my belief that we had to make sure every 8-year-old could read, every 12-year-old could log on to the Internet, every 18-year-old could go to college, and every adult could keep learning for a lifetime—to try to make real my belief that we've got to be able to say that all the kids in this country have access to a world-class elementary and secondary education.

And the program I put before the Congress was not a partisan program. It was based on the best ideas I could find around the country and the 20 years of experience that Hillary and I have had going into classrooms, going into schools, and looking at the research. So we did. We said, "Look, we'll put 100,000 teachers out there. They will all be well trained. And we'll put them in the early grades so we can lower average class size to 18, because all the research shows that small classes in the early grades guarantee more individual attention, higher levels of learning, and permanent learning benefits."

Then we will do what Ed talked about with the school facilities, because there are so many places where the school population is growing now, where there are these temporary classrooms. I was in one little town in Florida that had 12 of these behind one building, one school building. And then there are a lot of cities that have magnificent buildings, like Philadelphia, that simply can't be maintained and repaired given the present budget.

So we put a program forward that will allow us to build or repair 5,000 school buildings—be a good start on America's school challenge. We say our kids are the most important things in the world, but what kind of a message does it give a child to walk up the steps to a school building where the windows are broken out or a whole floor is closed down or all the windows have to be boarded up because nobody can afford the utility bills because they haven't been insulated properly? I see this kind of stuff all over America.

The third thing we wanted to do was to give districts the encouragement to impose high standards on kids and to stop just promoting them whether they were learning anything or not, but not to brand the children failures because the system is a failure. So we wanted to give districts the opportunity to have mentoring programs, after-school programs, summer school programs, so that kids could be held to higher standards, but would not be branded failures and instead would be helped, if they were prepared in school district after school district after school district to have those standards.

We wanted to give 35,000 bright young people college scholarships and pay all their expenses and say, "Now you can go out and pay all your college debt off by going into educationally underserved areas in the inner cities and rural areas and teaching for a few years and paying your expenses off." We wanted to provide the funds to hook up every classroom in the country to the Internet by the year 2000. And all that is paid for in the balanced budget.

And the fourth thing we wanted to do was to try to have some uniform rules for HMO's. And 43—43 HMO's have supported the Patients' Bill of Rights because they want to do this, and they don't think they can economically unless it's the same rules for everybody. And the rules are pretty simple: If you're in an accident and you have to get in an ambulance, you ought to be taken to the nearest emergency room, not one clear across town because it's the one that's covered. If your doctor says you need to see a specialist, you can see one. If

you're in the middle of treatment and your employer changes providers, they can't make you change doctors in the middle of a pregnancy or a chemotherapy treatment. And you get to have your records remain private.

Now, those are four specific examples of the big problems, of the things we can do right now to address these big problems.

Now, what's happened on the other side? Our friends in the other party with their majority this year, here's what they've done on those four things. Number one, on Social Security first, the House passed a tax cut because it's appealing 4 or 5 weeks before an election. And the Senate has it now, and I think they may have figured out that the people may be a little more broadminded and farsighted than they think, because I'm not sure they'll send it to me and let me veto it. [*Laughter*]

Number two, on the International Monetary Fund, most of the people who immediately know about this are Republicans, international business people. The Senate passed it overwhelmingly. We're still waiting for the House to vote for it, and every single day that goes by, we run the risk of increased instability in the world and increased risk to America. Now, I've been waiting for this for 8 months, and I'm telling you, this is a big American issue—still no action.

On education, no action. On the health care bill of rights, the House passed a bill that guarantees none of these rights—none that I mentioned—and cuts 100 million Americans out what little it did guarantee. And so it went to the Senate. Now, in the Senate the rules are different, and our guys can bring up our bill. So when we tried to bring up our bill, the majority leader of the Senate—I never thought I'd live to see this—they shut the Senate down the other night. They closed the house for 4 hours to keep the Patients' Bill of Rights from being considered. They just turned the lights out. People got under their desk, or did whatever they did. [*Laughter*] It was death by the stealth to the Patients' Bill of Rights. Why? Because they did not want to be recorded being against what they fully intended to kill.

Now, a few other things have happened this year. They killed the minimum wage increase. They killed campaign finance reform, which would have relieved you of some of the pain of being here tonight. [*Laughter*] They killed the tobacco reform legislation, which would have protected our children from what is still the number one public health problem in America today.

Now, that is what is happening. This stuff matters. And, oh, by the way, in the way of tax cuts, we had a targeted tax cut program, and it covered child care, as Ed Rendell said. It helped small businesses take out pension plans for their employees. And it was all paid for.

And on health care, we did have a provision so that 55- to 65-year-old people could buy into health care plans, because a huge number of them are forced into early retirement or their spouses go on Medicare, but they can't, so they lose their employer-based coverage, don't have any health insurance. And it doesn't cost much money. No action.

So I say to you, what is really at stake here is about whether this election is about Washington or about you; whether it's about power and politics or people; whether it's about partisanship or progress.

And when you leave here tonight, I want you to really think—go home and just talk. If you've got couples here tonight, talk among yourselves. What do you think the really big challenges facing this country are going to be in the next 25 or 30 years? What do you think the things are that we could do right now that would address them most? And if you believe we ought to save Social Security before we squander the first surplus we've had in a generation, if you believe we should pass this health care bill of rights, if you believe that we should put education first among our investment priorities, if you think—we ought to do what is necessary to keep America strong economically and in the leadership of the world economy and fighting for peace and freedom.

Our strength, economically, enables us to be a force for peace in Northern Ireland; enables us to continue to hold out hope of peace and work for it in the Middle East; enables us to do what we're trying to do now to avert a horrible incidence of the death of innocents in Kosovo this winter; enables us to try to work with other countries to bring down the threat of terrorism and nuclear weapons and chemical and biological weapons. It all rests on America's sense of strength and purpose.

Now, if you believe that we ought to be for those things, and if you believe this election ought to be about you and your children and your grandchildren and the other people that live in Philadelphia, then I would challenge you not to leave your citizenship responsibilities with the signing of the check that you wrote to get here tonight, because the direction of these issues will be determined not only by how people vote but whether they vote.

And so I say in closing, adversity is not our enemy—complacency is. This is the greatest country in history. For 220 years, against all the odds, no matter what happens, we always somehow figure out how to do the right thing to get a little closer to our ideals of a more perfect Union, of freedom and opportunity for everybody. And we can do it this time. But we need your voice. We need your efforts. We need you to talk like I'm talking to you, to everybody you see between now and November.

So when you go home tonight and you ask yourself, "Why did I go there?" I hope your answer will be, "Because I wanted to know exactly what I should do as a citizen in the next 5 weeks to do right by my country in the 21st century."

Thank you, and God bless you.

NOTE: The President spoke at 9:15 p.m. in Room 202 at Philadelphia City Hall. In his remarks, he referred to Mayor Edward Rendell of Philadelphia and State Senator Vincent Fumo.

The President's Radio Address
October 3, 1998

Good morning. This week I announced that we've closed the book on nearly three decades of deficits. Today I want to talk about another challenge we must face to keep our economy and our Nation growing strong: protecting America's farmers and ranchers.

For nearly 6 years now, strengthening our economy has been my top priority as President.

Today, because of the hard work of the American people, these are good times for our country, with nearly 17 million new jobs, wages rising, the lowest unemployment in nearly 30 years, the lowest inflation in more than 30 years. But for the farmers and ranchers whose hard work has helped to build our new prosperity, times are not as good. In fact, America's farms are facing the worst crisis in more than a decade.

This year, flood and drought and crop disease have wiped out entire harvests. Plummeting prices here at home and collapsing markets in Asia have threatened the livelihood of entire communities. Many farmers will see their net income this year drop by as much as 40 percent below a 5-year average. Farm failures have become so common that in some parts of our country trained farm auctioneers have been brought out of retirement. Families who have farmed the same land for generations are giving up and moving to town.

We've already taken steps to help farmers and ranchers weather the crisis. In August I signed new legislation to speed up farm program payments. Next week we'll purchase another allotment of the $250 million of wheat we pledged to buy to feed hungry people around the world and help our farmers here at home. And I've directed Secretary of Agriculture Dan Glickman to do everything within his authority to help farmers who have suffered significant losses and to give them the resources they need now to plan next spring's crops. But with crop and livestock prices still dropping, with foreign markets still in danger of collapse, with family farms still in jeopardy, we know we must do more.

As we near the end of the legislative session and finish our work on the budget, we have a real opportunity to protect our farmers. The strict budget rules permit special measures for one-time emergencies. And make no mistake, for America's farm families this is a real emergency, as harmful as a hurricane, a flood, or a riot.

So this summer, I sent a proposal to Congress for emergency aid for our farmers, and I backed a proposal by Senators Harkin and Daschle to lift the cap on marketing loan rates for one year. Since then, we've strengthened our proposal to help hundreds of thousands of farmers while honoring the budget rules.

Congress is now considering a package which, though it adopts many of the protections we've proposed, still does not do enough for farmers who are suffering from the lowest prices in decades. I call on Congress not to leave town before they've sent me a comprehensive plan that protects farmers by strengthening the safety net at this very difficult time.

With Congress in town for just a few more days, we must take another critical step to help our farmers and ranchers who rely on exports to make a living and support their families. Farm products from one of every three acres planted in America are sold abroad. And when those markets stumble, our farmers take a fall, too.

Just this week the New York Times ran a story that described the tons of wheat, apples, and other farm goods piling up on our docks because Asian customers can no longer afford them. That is why we must give the International Monetary Fund the resources it needs to help our customers in Asia so that they can continue to buy our farm products.

Congress has had months and months to create a stronger IMF, better able to deal with the most serious financial challenge the world has faced in 50 years. Now, each day Congress delays on IMF, our farmers, our ranchers, our economy, our future suffer.

It's way past time for Congress to act on the IMF and do the right thing for our farmers. Our farming families are the lifeblood of our land or, as President Franklin Roosevelt once called them, "the source from which the reservoirs of our Nation's strength are constantly renewed."

We cannot afford to let them fail. And with these steps, we will strengthen and support our farms and our farm families, just as they have sustained us throughout our history.

Thanks for listening.

NOTE: The address was recorded at 9:51 p.m. on October 2 at the Wyndham Hotel in Philadelphia, PA, for broadcast at 10:06 a.m. on October 3. The transcript was made available by the Office of the Press Secretary on October 2 but was embargoed for release until the broadcast.

Remarks at a Unity '98 Luncheon
October 5, 1998

Thank you very much. Let me begin by saying that we decided, Tom and Dick and I, after we found ourselves in the minority in 1995 and we were facing the Republican contract on America, that if we stayed together, that our policy positions could prevail and that what we wanted to do for the country would be much more difficult to do but that we could still get a lot of it done.

And we had that terrible experience of the Government shutdown in late '95 and '96. But after that, when the American people made their voices heard, we had a good election in '96. We had a balanced budget agreement, which closed the remaining 8 percent of the gap in balancing the budget, but importantly, should give us a balanced budget for years and years to come, with a lot of our priorities in it, including health care for 5 million kids and the widest opening of the doors of college since the GI bill. None of that would have happened if we hadn't worked together. And I could not have done any of it if it hadn't been for the Democrats in the House and the Senate. I think that's very important.

We are seeing the potential of a replay of that now, as we get closer and closer to the election and the feelings of the American people become apparent. In a few days I'll get a chance to sign a higher education bill which has a big drop in the interest rates on student loans and a program to provide mentors for inner-city kids in their junior high school years or middle school years that will include a guarantee of access to funds to go to college, if they stay out of trouble, stay in school, and learn.

These things would absolutely be impossible in the present array of Congress with the Republicans in the majority, if we weren't working together. So there is a substantive benefit to that.

Now, let me say, where we are now is a position that I think is virtually unprecedented in 150 years. In 150 years of American political history, the President's party in the midterm elections nearly always lose, and in the second term of the President, I don't think there's an exception. But we are on the verge of having

an exception, and I would like to tell you why, and why I think your investment is well made.

Normally, these midterm elections have a big fall-off in voter turnout. And that is the assumption and, indeed, what our opponents are literally working for and hoping for and praying for, because a lot of the people that vote for us would never be able to come into a home like this except to maybe serve lunch. And it's a big hassle for a lot of them to vote; you know, they have to worry about child care and the job and getting to vote and all that.

When I was in Philadelphia with Peter and others a couple of days ago, a friend of mine from New Jersey came over and brought me a survey that had just been done in New Jersey asking people if, in the current climate, they were more or less likely to vote in the midterm elections. Fifty percent said they were more likely; 10 percent said they were less likely. Fifty percent of the Republicans said they were more likely; 49 percent of the Democrats—I mean, 49 percent of the independents; 57 percent of the Democrats said they were more likely to go and vote.

So what is important for us is we don't have to run a negative campaign. All we have to do is say, you know, what their agenda is. Our agenda is, first of all, to see America lead in heading off this crisis in the global financial system, beginning with funding the International Monetary Fund contribution so we can keep the economy going at home. Secondly, don't spend the surplus now on a tax cut just before the election or right after the election; save the Social Security system first. Thirdly, continue education as our first investment priority. Fourthly, pass this HMO bill of rights, which, interestingly enough, has more than three-quarters support of the American people without regard to party—it's a uniform issue across the board—which they killed. And then, obviously, the other things that we believe in, including protecting the environment as we continue to grow the economy.

But if we run on the strength of the economy and our responsibility in the world economy to keep America's economy strong, on the education issue, on the saving Social Security first, these issues are very, very powerful, and they stand in stark contrast to the evident priorities of the majority in Congress.

So we actually have a chance to do something never before done here, but it will not happen unless, first of all, we stay together and, secondly, we have enough funds to get our message out. We don't have to have as much money as they do. We'll never have as much money as they do. But we have a chance to do something literally without precedent in 20th century American political history, just by doing the right thing. It's not even complicated. We just have to stand up there and fight for what is evidently in the interest of the American people.

And that is what your investment will be used to do. And they'll do it right. I've never seen the Democrats more well focused on how to do this business and how to be there in the last 10 days of the election when very often—and to give you an example, in 1996, when we picked up several House seats and lost two Senate seats in what was a very bad rotation for us—the next three rotations, by the way, are good for us in the Senate elections. We've had three that were terrible, in terms of we always had more seats up than they did; we had more people retiring than they did. But in '96, when we picked up a few House seats,

lost two Senate seats, we were outspent in the close races the last 10 days, near as I can tell, 4 to one, or more. That will give you an idea of the level of disadvantage here, and it also might explain why they killed campaign finance reform this year. But we can do this. And we can do it simply by doing what is right for America. It's not a complicated strategy. There's no twist and turn to it. It's very straightforward and, I think, self-evident.

So I feel good about where we are, good about where we're going, and very grateful to all of you, because the American people need stability and strength and a clear message on this economic issue, on the education issue, on the Social Security issue. And I think if we give it to them, we're going to be just fine, and it's going to be quite surprising to a lot of the pundits. But none of it would be possible if you weren't willing to come here today and do your part and then some, and we're very grateful.

Thank you very much.

NOTE: The President spoke at 1:20 p.m. at a private residence. In his remarks, he referred to Senator Thomas A. Daschle and Representative Richard A. Gephardt. A tape was not available for verification of the content of these remarks.

Remarks on the Legislative Agenda
October 5, 1998

Good afternoon. From the beginning of our efforts to create the economic renaissance America now enjoys, Congressman Gephardt and Senator Daschle have been tireless in working for that change. Especially in these last few weeks as the congressional session has entered its crucial final stage and the political season has intensified, these two leaders have stood above the crowd in their constant efforts to elevate progress over partisanship.

I realize that the calendar says the election is just a month away. The calendar also says it is now 8 months since I sent the Congress a budget, 5 months since the legal deadline for Congress to pass a budget resolution. And as all of you know, the fiscal year ended last week. Yet so far, Congress has sent me only 2 of

13 appropriations bills necessary to keep our Government running. On Friday the temporary spending measure I signed will run out. I want to work with Congress to get this important work done. There is still time for real achievement, still time for progress over partisanship.

That is why today I stand with Representative Gephardt and Senator Daschle to call on the congressional majority. Time is running short. Congress has important work left to do. Pass the necessary spending bills to keep the Government running; save Social Security for future generations; ensure a quality education for all our children; protect America from the global economic turmoil—these are the priorities of the American people, and they must be the priorities of Congress in these last days before the election.

First, we must save Social Security first. Last week I was privileged to announce the first budget surplus in a generation. Congress must not lose this spirit of fiscal discipline. I have proposed tax cuts, but they're fully paid for. If the Congress sends me a tax plan that drains billions from the surplus before saving Social Security, I will veto it. We've worked too hard for too long to abandon fiscal discipline and our economic strength and to weaken our commitment to Social Security just because it's election time.

Second, we must act to protect our prosperity in this turbulent international economy by meeting our obligations to the International Monetary Fund. The world is waiting—literally, the world is waiting—for Congress to step up to America's responsibility, provide funds to the IMF, and give us the tools we need to pull teetering economies back from the brink and to keep America's economic prosperity going. It would be unacceptable for Congress to leave Washington before acting.

Third, we must continue to invest in education. As the leaders here with me and about 50 other Members of Congress asked last week, we seek just one day for Congress to consider the education measures I have proposed, to pass a plan to provide our schools with the tools they need, with 100,000 teachers so we can have smaller classes in the early grades, with after-school and summer school programs to help students raise higher—achieve higher academic standards, with thousands of modernized schools for the 21st century.

And fourth, in these last few days, Congress must act to protect, not gut, the environment.

Republicans in Congress have sought to slip unacceptable provisions into unrelated bills that would cripple wildlife protection, force overcutting of our national forests, deny taxpayers a fair return on oil leasing, thwart commonsense efforts to address global warming. If they insist on sending these antienvironmental riders to my desk, again I will veto them.

Fifth, Congress must act to address a range of pressing emergencies that simply cannot wait for a new congressional session, emergencies including supporting our troops in Bosnia, maintaining our military readiness worldwide, providing assistance to our farmers who are in real crisis out there, protecting American citizens from terrorism, and providing resources to address the year 2000 computer problem.

For two administrations the budget rules under which both parties have operated have accommodated such emergencies. Troops in the field and citizens in crisis should never be subject to partisan wrangling. This is what we ought to do: We ought to save Social Security first, pass the education program, protect our own economy, and do what we should do to lead the world away from world financial crisis, pass the Patients' Bill of Rights, avoid these environmentally destructive riders. There is still time for us to put the people of our country ahead of politics, and I hope we'll do it.

Now I'd like to ask Senator Daschle and Congressman Gephardt to say a word.

NOTE: The President spoke at 3:17 p.m. on the South Lawn at the White House. The transcript released by the Office of the Press Secretary also included the remarks of Senator Thomas A. Daschle and Representative Richard A. Gephardt.

Remarks to Finance Ministers and Central Bank Governors
October 5, 1998

The President. First of all, let me welcome all of you here to the United States. It is a great honor for us to host this terribly important meeting.

Three weeks ago, at the Council on Foreign Relations in New York, I asked Secretary Rubin and Chairman Greenspan to call together their

counterparts from key emerging and industrial economies to discuss ways of building a new financial architecture for the 21st century and to also evaluate the specific measures that we should take together to deal with the current crisis. And I offered some ideas of my own on that day.

We began these discussions on reforming the international financial architecture at the G–7 meeting in Naples back in 1994. It seems like a century ago, when you think of how quickly the world has changed since then. In Halifax, in 1995, the G–7 followed up with the establishment of the special data dissemination standard, the IMF supplemental reserve facility, the new arrangements to borrow.

But clearly this is not just a task for the G–7 alone. This is an issue which, as we see, affects every nation in the world. That is why last year, when the APEC leaders met in Vancouver, we called for a process that permitted the world's leading economies and the world's emerging economies to work together. And this effort began in April of this year.

The expansion of international markets and the growth of the global economy over the past 50 years has helped to lift millions and millions of people out of poverty; it has raised living standards for millions more. But as we see, the fast-paced, high-volume global capital markets also can react swiftly and harshly when countries stray from sound policies. And the markets also can overreact, subjecting even countries following good policies to severe pressures.

When the tides of global finance turn against a country, the human costs can be great. This weekend you've held important talks on the immediate steps we can take to limit the present financial crisis. And I was pleased to hear that both the G–7 and the IMF interim committee have agreed to look at ways of strengthening our capacity for stability by establishing a new precautionary financial facility to help countries ward off financial contagion. Every leading industrial economy has a role to play, including the United States by securing full support for IMF funding, Japan by moving quickly to address its economic and financial challenges.

Tonight's meeting is an opportunity for us to look at not only the immediate crisis but to look further into the future. We must ensure that the international financial architecture is prepared for the new challenges of our time, especially the challenge of building a system that will lessen and manage the risks in the global market to allow countries to reap the benefits of free-flowing capital in a way that is safe and sustainable. I think this is imperative if we are to maintain global support among ordinary citizens for free markets and ultimately for free governments.

We must find ways that do not penalize those nations who follow strong economic policies in times of crisis that will minimize the frequency, severity, and human cost of the financial crisis, that will put in place social structures to protect the most defenseless, and that will promote broad democratic support, which is necessary for economic change.

You are doing important work, perhaps the most important work the world can be doing at this moment in history. The institutional reforms that flow from all this work will shape the global financial system for the next half-century. The way we move forward using our work here tonight will help to determine the course of our children's future. We must do whatever it takes to build them a future of stable and sustained progress and limitless opportunity.

I am convinced that, as formidable as the challenges may seem, it is well within our grasp if we determine to do what it takes.

Thank you very much.

[At this point, Treasury Secretary Robert Rubin invited the President to conduct the discussion.]

The President. Let me say, from my perspective, two things would be especially helpful to hear from all of you: First of all, briefly, what you think the causes of the present predicament are; and secondly, what you believe we should do, not only in the immediate present but over the long run with the architecture of the financial system. And insofar as there are new ideas to be advanced, I think we owe it to ourselves to say not only what the potential positive impacts are but whatever potential negative consequences might flow from the changes that we advocate.

And I would like to just suggest—if they're willing, I'd like to ask the head of the Mexican central bank, Mr. Ortiz, to begin; and perhaps Gordon Brown, the Chancellor of the Exchequer, would follow; and then, perhaps Minister of Finance Tharin from Thailand. And after those three talk, then we'll just open the floor and have a free-ranging discussion.

NOTE: The President spoke at 5:31 p.m. in the ballroom at the Sheraton Luxury Collection Hotel. In his remarks, he referred to Guillermo Ortiz, Governor of the Bank of Mexico; Chancellor of the Exchequer Gordon Brown of the United Kingdom; and Minister of Finance Tharin

Nimmanhemin of Thailand. The transcript released by the Office of the Press Secretary also included the opening remarks of Treasury Secretary Robert Rubin.

Remarks at a Unity '98 Reception
October 5, 1998

Thank you. Ladies and gentlemen, we have all been sitting up here on this stage listening to each other with a lot of echoes, wondering if you could hear us out here. Can you hear us all speaking? [*Applause*] We decided either you could hear us better than we could hear each other, or you were the most polite audience in human history. [*Laughter*]

Let me begin by thanking you personally for being here tonight, for your support for our party and our campaign in the Congress this year. I want to thank Steve Grossman for a magnificent job as head of our party and for the work he has done with Senator Torricelli and Representative Pelosi, who have been wonderful working together in unity to try to pool our resources and maximize our impact. I want to thank Dick Gephardt and Tom Daschle for truly extraordinary leadership.

You know, since the Republicans won the House of Representatives and the Senate in 1994, we have defeated their contract on America; we passed a balanced budget that had the biggest increase in health care for children and the biggest increase in college access since the GI bill. And every other progressive thing that has been done since I've been President, none of it would have been possible without the Democrats in Congress, and I am very grateful to them, but especially these last 4 long years when time after time after time, if they hadn't been with me, there would have been no one to say no to moving this country into an extreme position, no to moving this country away from the progressive path on which we put it, and yes to the initiatives we've taken. So we owe them a great debt of gratitude, and for that I am very grateful.

Let's talk about why you're here tonight, besides to hear Brian, who was fabulous. Was he great, or what? [*Applause*]

In a month we're going to have an election, a midterm election, an election in which our opponents believe they will do quite well because they're going to outspend us phenomenally, an election in which they believe they have an enormous advantage because a lot of Democratic voters normally don't vote when there's no Presidential election. They say, "Oh, well, our voters have to worry about child care and jobs and voting on the same day. That's a lot of trouble," or "Our voters are young. They just don't get into it in mid-term election." And all the things you've heard.

I want to tell you why you're here tonight. You're here to reverse 100 years of history, and you're here to make the next 100 years of America's history. You're here to make a decision. Most of you in this audience tonight are young, and I am not. So I can tell you one thing: It doesn't take long to live a life. It doesn't take long to move from your age tonight until you're the age of those of us on this platform. And the decisions you make in one point of your life for your country can shape everything that happens when you have your children and you raise them to be the age that you are now.

We have fought and fought and fought for 6 years to change the direction of America, to give you an economy that works for all the people, not just a few; to bring the crime rate down and to help more kids stay out of trouble in the first place; to move people from welfare to work in a way that was humane so they could still succeed in their most important jobs, raising children; to grow the economy and still preserve the environment; to be a force for world peace and humanity; and to be a force for bringing us together here at home across all the lines that divide us. Those are the issues at stake in this election.

If you look at the differences between the two parties, one that will affect you more than me is whether we are going to save this surplus until we save Social Security for the 21st century, instead of putting a big tax increase on you to take care of your parents. You know where they stand. They voted for a popular election-year tax cut to give people—a modest cut—to say, "Here's your little gift before the election."

And we stood up and said, "That may be appealing. Look at our tax cuts for child care, for education, for the environment. They're paid for in our balanced budget bill, and we're not going beyond them until we save Social Security because we don't want to burden our children and our grandchildren." It is the right thing to do.

We have asked for 8 long months—the other day the people here on this platform and I asked just for one day—just one day—to vote on matters that are critical to the education of our children. We are for 100,000 more teachers and smaller classes and 5,000 new or repaired schools and hooking up every classroom to the Internet and after-school and summer school programs for our kids. And they won't give us a vote on it. It's a clear choice, but it will affect the America you live in.

We have pleaded for 8 months for a vote on the Patients' Bill of Rights because almost all of you are going to be in managed care plans, and so are your parents and your children. And I think they can do a lot of good to hold down costs. But I think if—God forbid—you get hit by a car going out of this party tonight, you ought to go to the nearest emergency room, not one clear across town because it happens to be covered by your managed care plan. And if you have a serious medical condition and your doctor says you need to see a specialist, I think you ought to be able to see one. And if your employer changes health care providers while you're pregnant or getting chemotherapy or getting other serious treatment, I think you ought to be able to finish your treatment and not be told to get another doctor. That's a big issue. But you won't get that Patients' Bill of Rights unless we get the Congress, and you have it within your power to give the American people that gift for the 21st century.

I just left, before I came to be with you tonight, a meeting of 25 nations, finance ministers, and central bankers, the counterparts of Chairman Greenspan and Secretary Rubin, sitting around a big room with the heads of all the international financial institutions, talking about what we can do to stem this global financial crisis, because it's morally the right thing to do for people around the world who are struggling to lift themselves and their children up, and because it is practically essential if we want to keep America's economic prosperity going. And over and over and over again people said, "We appreciate the lead you're taking, Mr. President, but the Congress of the United States won't even fund America's participation in the International Monetary Fund." If you want to send a message, if you want America's economy to keep growing, you liked the last 6 years, you know then that we have to help the world to avoid this crisis and do our part. It's a big issue. It's a huge issue.

The young people in this audience should care about the environment—more than their parents and grandparents. You should care whether you're going to be able to raise your children with clean air, clean water, safe food, no toxic waste, and no global warming problem. You should care about that, and you should have an opinion about whether it is possible to grow the economy and improve the environment. With all my heart, I believe it is.

In this budget, it is littered up like a Christmas tree with what the Washington language dubs "riders, riders, riders." What they're doing is riding the environment down, and they try to put them all over all these bills in the hope that the President won't be able to even find them all, much less veto some of the bills.

You're going to be given a chance to say, "Our generation believes in protecting the environment and growing the economy, and we do not approve of the majority's approach to chipping away at our protections one by one." If you care about the environment and the economy, you have to vote for the Democrats in this race for Congress.

So I say to you, we have to prove to the people of the Washington establishment here, who say that midterm elections are always low-vote elections, that people like you know it's a big deal. You know your future in riding on it. You believe in what we've done in the last 6 years. You want everybody to have a chance to participate in our prosperity. You want this education program. You want us to lead in the global economy. You want the environment protected. You want the Patients' Bill of Rights, and you want to save Social Security before we squander a surplus that we worked 6 long years for. That's what you want.

And you understand what the choice is on the other side. And you want this election to be about you and your future. And you don't believe, contrary to all the conventional wisdom, that all the minorities are going to stay home, all the young women are going to stay home, all the young people are going to stay home, all the people that have the hassle of child care and work and still finding a way to go vote are going to stay home, because you're going to tell them what the stakes are. That's what we're going to use your money to do. I want you to leave here committed to using your voice

to do the same thing, and you will give America and your children a gift for the new millennium on election day.

Thank you, and God bless you. Thank you.

NOTE: The President spoke at 8:54 p.m. in the Great Hall at the National Building Museum. In his remarks, he referred to Steve Grossman, national chair, Democratic National Committee; and musician Brian McKnight.

Remarks at the International Monetary Fund/World Bank Annual Meeting
October 6, 1998

Kosovo

Thank you very much. Secretary Rubin, my friend President Menem, Minister Fernandez, Managing Director Camdessus, President Wolfensohn, Dr. Ruttenstorfer, ladies and gentlemen: Before I begin my remarks, I hope you will permit me to say a few words about another issue of real concern to the international community, about which I have been working already this morning, the subject of Kosovo.

I have been on the phone with many of my counterparts, and I just was speaking with Prime Minister Blair, who is in China. We all agree that Kosovo is a powder keg in the Balkans. If the violence continues, it could spill over and threaten the peace and stability of Bosnia, of Albania, of Macedonia, and other countries in the region. What is already a humanitarian crisis could turn into a catastrophe.

Some 250,000 people have been forced to flee their homes. Of that number, approximately 50,000 are actually homeless. As winter sets in, they risk freezing or starving to death. President Milosevic is primarily responsible for this crisis. The United Nations has made clear the steps we must take to end it: declare an immediate cease-fire, withdraw Serb security forces, give humanitarian relief groups full and immediate access to Kosovo, begin real negotiations with the Kosovar Albanians to find a peaceful and permanent solution to their rightful demand for autonomy.

As we meet here, my Special Envoy, Dick Holbrooke, is meeting with President Milosevic to reiterate what he must do and to make clear

that NATO is prepared to act if President Milosevic fails to honor the United Nations resolutions. The stakes are high. The time is now to end the violence in Kosovo. I hope all of you will do whatever you can to that end.

International Monetary Fund/World Bank

Now to the matter at hand. A half century ago, a visionary generation of leaders gathered at Bretton Woods to build a new economy to serve the citizens of every nation. In one of his last messages to Congress, President Franklin Roosevelt said that the creation of the International Monetary Fund and the World Bank, and I quote, "spelled the difference between a world caught again in the maelstrom of panic and economic warfare, or a world in which nations strive for a better life through mutual trust, cooperation, and assistance."

The Bretton Woods generation built a platform for prosperity that has lasted down to the present day. Economic freedom and political liberty has spread across the globe. Since 1945, global trade has grown fifteenfold. Since 1970 alone, infant mortality in the poorest countries is down by 40 percent; access to safe drinking water has tripled; life expectancy has increased dramatically. Even now, despite the difficulties of recent days, per capita incomes in Korea and Thailand are 60 percent higher than they were a decade ago. A truly global market economy has lifted the lives of billions of people.

But as we are all acutely aware, today the world faces perhaps its most serious financial crisis in half a century. The gains of global economic exchange have been real and dramatic.

But when tides of capital first flood emerging markets, then suddenly withdraw, when bank failures and bankruptcies grip entire economies, when millions in Asia who have worked their way into the middle class suddenly are plunged into poverty, when nations half a world apart face the same crisis at the same time, it is time for decisive action.

What has caused the current crisis? First, too many nations lack the financial, legal, and regulatory systems necessary to maintain investor confidence in adversity. Second, new technologies and greater global integration have led to vastly increased, often highly leveraged flows of capital, without accompanying mechanisms to limit the boom/bust cycle, mechanisms like those which are integral to the success of advanced economies.

I am confident that if we act together we can end the present crisis. We must take urgent steps to help those who have been hurt by it, to limit the reach of it, and to restore growth and confidence to the world economy. But even when the current crisis subsides, that will not be enough. The global economy simply cannot live with the kinds of vast and systemic disruptions that have occurred over the past year.

The IMF and the World Bank have been vital to the prosperity of the world for the past half century. We must keep them vital to the prosperity of the world for the next half century. Therefore, we must modernize and reform the international financial system to make it ready for the 21st century.

The central economic challenge we face is to harness the positive power of an open international economy while avoiding the cycle of boom and bust that diminishes hope and destroys wealth. And the central political challenge we face is to build a system that strengthens social protections and democratic institutions so that people everywhere can actually reap the rewards of growth.

We must put a human face on the global economy. An international market that fails to work for ordinary citizens will neither earn nor deserve their confidence and support. We need both an aggressive response to the immediate crisis and a thoughtful road map for the future. We must begin by meeting our most immediate challenges.

Two weeks ago, at the Council on Foreign Relations in New York, I outlined what we have done and what we must do. I am gratified that today the leading economies speak with one voice in saying the balance of risks have now shifted from inflation to slowdown. The principal goal of policymakers must be to promote growth. Every nation must take responsibility for growth.

The United States must do its part. The most important thing we can do is to keep our economy growing and open to others' products and services, by maintaining the fiscal responsibility that has led us to the first balanced budget and surplus in 29 years. Winning this discipline was not easy and was not always popular, but it was the right thing to do. That is why I have made it clear to our Congress that I will veto any tax plan that threatens that discipline.

Also, the United States must—must—meet our obligations to the IMF. I have told Congress we can debate how to reform the operations of the fire department, but there is no excuse for refusing to supply the fire department with water while the fire is burning.

Europe must continue to press forward with growth-oriented economic policies and keep its markets open. And Japan, the world's second largest economy and by far the largest in Asia, must do its part, as well. The United States values our strong partnership with Japan, our political, our security, our economic partnership. But now the health of Asia and, indeed, the world depends upon Japan. Just as the United States had to eliminate its deficits and high interest rates which were taking money away from the rest of the world over the last 6 years, now Japan must take strong steps to restart its economic growth by addressing problems in the banking system so that lending and investment can begin with renewed energy and by stimulating, deregulating, and opening its economy.

For all of us, there can be no substitute for action. And all of us must also act now to restart growth in the rest of Asia by helping to restructure firms paralyzed by crushing debt and replace debt with equity across entire economies. Through OPIC and the Export-Import Bank, we are providing short-term credit and investment insurance to keep capital flowing into emerging economies.

I welcome Japan's announcement that it will contribute to the reconstruction effort. And I am gratified that the World Bank has agreed to double its investment in the social safety net in Asia to help those who have been harmed by the economic crisis.

In all these ways, we can minimize the consequences of the current financial contagion. But the flash of this crisis throws new light on the need to do more, to renew the institutions of international finance so they reflect modern economic reality. The institutions built at Bretton Woods must be updated for 24-hour global markets if they are to continue to achieve the goals established by the Bretton Woods generation.

First, we must recognize that the free and open exchange of ideas and capital and goods across the globe is the surest route to prosperity for the largest number of people. But we must find a way to temper the volatile swings of the international marketplace, just as we have learned to do in our own domestic economies.

What is troubling today is how quickly discouraging news in one country can set off alarms in markets around the world. And all too often, investors move as a herd, with sweeping consequences for emerging economies with weak and strong policies alike. We've all read of families that worked hard for decades to become middle class, families that owned homes and cars, suddenly forced to sell off their possessions just to buy food. We've read of doctors and nurses forced to live in the lobby of a closed hospital. With fuel and food shortages in some countries, the onset of winter threatens mass misery. And in Asia, where the ethic of education is deeply ingrained and has led to the rise of tens of millions of people, and strong schools are the pride of nations, we now see too many children dropping out of school to help support their families.

Just as free nations found a way after the Great Depression to tame the cycles of boom and bust in domestic economies, we must now find ways to tame the cycles of boom and bust that today shake the world economy.

The most important step, of course, and the first step, is for governments to hold fast to policies that are sound and attuned to the realities of the international marketplace. No nation can avoid the necessity of an open, transparent, properly regulated financial system, an honest, effective tax system, and laws that protect investment. And no nation can for long purchase prosperity on the cheap, with policies that buy a few months of relief at the price of disaster over the long run.

That is why I support the fundamental approach of the IMF. The international community cannot save any nation unwilling to reform its own economy; to do so would be to pour good money after bad. But when nations are willing to act responsibly and take strong steps, the international community must help them to do so.

Too often, what has appeared to be a thriving market system, however, has masked an epidemic of corruption or cronyism. Investors and entrepreneurs, foreign and domestic, will not keep their money in economies where prosperity is a facade. Bank balance sheets should mean the same thing in one country as another. Contracts should be awarded on merit. Corruption cannot be tolerated.

To this end, I applaud the working group reports that call for the IMF to examine and publicize countries' adherence to strong international standards, as well as higher accounting and loan standards for private institutions. The United States will continue to press for new ways the private sector can implement sound practices, for example, through an accreditation system for national bank examiners.

But while strong policies and sound business practices within each nation are essential, at times they simply will not be enough. For even the best functioning markets can succumb to volatility, soaring in unrealistic expectations one minute, followed by a sudden crash when reality intervenes. Such miscalculations of risk are an inevitable fact of market psychology.

In our own domestic economies, we have learned to limit these swings in the business cycle. In the United States, for example, a strong Federal Reserve has ensured a stable money supply. The Securities and Exchange Commission promotes openness and makes the market work. Rigorous bank regulation and deposit insurance have helped to keep downturns in the business cycle from spinning out of control. Other nations have their own institutions performing these same functions.

Now, though we understand that the realities and the possibilities in the international marketplace are different, some of the same functions clearly need to be performed. We must address not only a run on a bank or a firm but also a run on nations. If global markets are to bring the benefits we believe they can, we simply must find a way to tame the pattern of boom/bust on an international scale. This task is one of the most complex we face. We must summon our most creative minds and carefully consider all options. In the end, we must fashion arrangements that serve the global economy as our domestic economies are served, enabling capital to flow freely without the crushing burdens the boom/bust cycle brings.

While we must not embrace false cures that will backfire and lead in the end to less liquidity and diminished confidence when we need more of both, we must—we must—keep working until we find the right answers. And we don't have a moment to waste.

Meanwhile, we must find creative ways to protect those countries that right now have strong economic policies, yet still face financial pressures not of their own making. This past weekend Secretary Rubin and Chairman Greenspan have worked with their G–7 counterparts to find new ways to strengthen our cooperation based on the IMF to make precautionary lines of credit available to nations committed to strong economic policies, so that action can be quick and decisive if needed. This is a critical way to prevent the present crisis from reaching Latin America and other regions, which are doing well. And I ask your support.

Strong government policies, sound business practices, new ways to limit the swings in the global market—all these steps are needed to ensure growth into the future. But let us also acknowledge that we face a political challenge. For the best designed international economic system will fail if it does not give a stake and a voice to ordinary citizens.

So I say again, today we see a profound political challenge to the global economic order. The financial crisis poses a stern test of whether democracies are capable of producing the broad public support necessary for difficult policies that entail sacrifice today for tomorrow's growth. I believe strong democracy, fair and honest regulation, sound social policy are not enemies of the market. I believe they are essential conditions for long-term success. Nations with freely elected governments, where the broad mass of people believe the government represents them and acts in their interests, have been willing and able to act to ward off crisis. Korea and Thailand, with elected leaders who have been willing to take very difficult steps, have succeeded in weathering the worst of the economic storm when so many others have not. Countries in central Europe have done remarkably well.

But even among the strongest nations, as we have found here in our own, broad change is often difficult. Unless the citizens of each nation feel they have a stake in their own economy, they will resist reforms necessary for recovery. Unless they feel empowered with the tools to master economic change, they will feel the strong temptation to turn inward, to close off their economies to the world.

Now, more than ever, that would be a grave mistake. At a moment of financial crisis, a natural inclination is to close borders and retreat behind walls of protectionism. But it is precisely at moments like this we need to increase trade to spur greater growth.

Again, we must never lose sight of what the fundamental problem is: We need more liquidity, more growth in this world today. Only by tearing down barriers and increasing trade will we be able to bring the nations of Asia, Latin America, and other parts of the world back onto the path of growth.

The world economy today needs more trade and more activity of all kinds, not less. That is why when the leaders of APEC meet next month, we must press forward to tear down barriers and liberalize trade among our countries; why next January when the United States Congress returns, we will seek a comprehensive effort to tear down barriers at home and around the world, including new negotiating authority and legislation to expand trade with Africa.

But unless we give working people a strong stake in the outcome, they will naturally and understandably erect obstacles to change. The answer to these difficulties is not to retreat. It is to advance and to make certain every nation has a strong safety net providing the security people need to embrace change.

At the very least, people who are suddenly without work must have access to food and shelter and medical care. And over time, all nations must develop effective unemployment and retirement systems. We must find ways to keep schools open and strong during times of economic downturn. We must make certain economic development does not come at the cost of new environmental degradation.

I am pleased that the World Bank will be redoubling its efforts to build this strong safety net, especially in Asia. And I urge all international financial institutions to do more to incorporate environmental issues into your operations and to significantly increase direct lending for environmental and natural resource projects. Every time we seek to protect the environment, shortsighted critics warn that it will hurt the economy. But over the last quarter century, we have seen time and again, in nation after nation, that protecting the environment actually strengthens, not weakens, our economies.

International institutions themselves must reinforce the values we honor in our own economies. In Geneva last May I asked the World Trade Organization to bring its operations into the sunlight of public scrutiny, to give all sectors of society a voice in building trade policies that will work for all people in the new century. We must do the same for other multilateral institutions.

When the IMF agrees with a member country on policy measures to restore stability, the people of that country and investors around the world should be told exactly what conditions have been set. Therefore, I urge the WTO, the World Bank, and the IMF, working with the ILO, to give greater consideration to labor and environmental protections as a part of your daily business. Only by advancing these protections will these organizations earn the confidence and support of the people they were created to serve.

Finally, though we are seized with the crisis of the moment, we must not neglect those whom the capital flows have passed by in the first place. That is why it is critical to continue our efforts to lighten debt burdens, to expand educational opportunities, to focus on basic human needs, as we work to bring the poorest countries in Africa and elsewhere into the international community of a thriving economy.

Creating a global financial architecture for the 21st century, promoting national economic reform, making certain that social protections are in place, encouraging democracy and democratic participation in international institutions—these are ambitious goals. But as the links among our nations grow ever tighter, we must act together to address problems that will otherwise set back all our aspirations. If we're going to have a truly global marketplace, with global flows of capital, we have no choice but to find ways to build a truly international financial architecture to support it, a system that is open, stable, and prosperous.

To meet these challenges I have asked the finance ministers and central bankers of the worlds' leading economies and the world's most important emerging economies to recommend the next steps. There is no task more urgent

for the future of our people. For at stake is more than the spread of free markets, more than the integration of the global economy. The forces behind the global economy are also those that deepen liberty, the free flow of ideas and information, open borders and easy travel, the rule of law, fair and evenhanded enforcement, protection for consumers, a skilled and educated work force. Each of these things matters not only to the wealth of nations but to the health of nations. If citizens tire of waiting for democracy and free markets to deliver a better life for themselves and their children, there is a risk that democracy and free markets, instead of continuing to thrive together, will shrivel together.

This century has taught us many lessons. It has taught us that when we act together we can lift people around the world and bind nations together in peace and reconciliation. It has also taught us the dangers of complacency, of protection, of withdrawal. This crisis poses a challenge not to any one nation but to every nation. None of us—none of us—will be unaffected if we fail to act.

On the day he died in 1945, as these institutions were taking shape, President Roosevelt wrote in the last line of his last speech: "The only limit to our realization of tomorrow will be our doubts of today. Let us move forward with a strong and active faith." At a time of testing, the generation that built the IMF and the World Bank moved forward with a strong and active faith.

Now we who have been blessed with so many advantages must ourselves act in the same manner. If we do, we will surmount the difficulty of this moment. We will build a stronger world for our children. We will honor our forebears by what we do to construct the first 50 years of the 21st century.

Thank you very much.

NOTE: The President spoke at 10:52 a.m. in the ballroom at the Marriott Wardman Park Hotel. In his remarks, he referred to President Carlos Menem and Minister of Economy, Public Works, and Services Roque Fernandez of Argentina; Michel Camdessus, Managing Director and Chairman of the Executive Board, International Monetary Fund (IMF); James D. Wolfensohn, President, International Bank for Reconstruction and Development (World Bank); State Secretary in the Austrian Finance Ministry Wolfgang

Ruttenstorfer, Chairman of the Board of Governors, IMF; Prime Minister Tony Blair of the United Kingdom; President Slobodan Milosevic of the Federal Republic of Yugoslavia (Serbia and Montenegro); and Special Envoy Richard C. Holbrooke, the President's nominee to be U.S. Ambassador to the United Nations. The President also referred to the International Labor Organization (ILO) and the Overseas Private Investment Corporation (OPIC).

Statement on Agriculture Legislation
October 6, 1998

I am disappointed that today's Senate vote on the agriculture bill failed to provide adequate emergency aid for farmers in this country who are suffering from the worst agricultural crisis in a decade. While this agriculture bill provides some help for farmers, it simply does not do enough.

This year flood, drought, and crop disease have wiped out entire harvests. Plummeting prices at home and collapsing markets in Asia have threatened the livelihoods of entire communities. Many farmers will see their net income this year drop by as much as 40 percent below a 5-year average.

It is time for us to take action that will make significant progress in alleviating the hardship in America's heartland. I continue to support Senator Daschle and Harkin's proposal to provide approximately $5 billion dollars in aid while establishing a system of payments that allows flexibility if commodity prices drop even further. I call on Congress to send me a comprehensive plan that protects farmers by strengthening the safety net at this difficult time. In addition, I urge Congress to support my own emergency aid proposal for $2.3 billion that originated with Senators Conrad and Dorgan to provide farmers with additional insurance and indemnity payments for crop loss.

This total package of aid would make a significant contribution to helping this Nation's farmers cope with the current agricultural crisis. I urge Congress to be fully responsive to their needs. If Congress insists on sending me an agricultural bill that fails to respond fully to the needs of America's farmers, then I will have no choice but to veto the bill.

Remarks Prior to Discussions With Prime Minister Viktor Orban of Hungary and an Exchange With Reporters
October 7, 1998

President Clinton. Let me say, first of all, I am delighted to welcome Prime Minister Orban and his representatives of his government to Washington. We are very, very excited about what is going on in Hungary, excited about his youthful and vigorous and progressive leadership.

Today we are going to talk about the date that's coming up that Hungary is joining NATO—it will be an historic date—and what we have to do between now and then. I want to talk about the importance of the stability of the region, about maintaining our commitments in Bosnia, where, I might say, we would not have been able to be successful had it not been for the Hungarians making available the base at Taszar for us to operate out of.

And thirdly, of course, we want to talk about Kosovo. And let me say again that I believe it is absolutely imperative that there be a cease-fire, a withdrawal of troops, that the humanitarian groups get access to these hundreds of thousands of people who have been displaced, and that negotiations resume. Those are the United Nations' conditions. I believe NATO must be prepared to take action if they are not met. But it will not be necessary if Mr. Milosevic does meet them.

So those are among the things we'll discuss today. I think it's very important. And Prime Minister, I am glad to have you here. If you'd like to make a brief statement, you can, and then I'll let them ask a question or two.

Prime Minister Orban. I'm very much delighted to be here. I'm very happy that I was invited to have this discussion with your President. I'm very happy to be here as probably the first time in the history of Hungary as Prime Minister of an ally to the United States, a future member of NATO. And I would express all of the Hungarian citizens' gratitude to the President that he was tough enough to convince all the Members of the Senate that enlargement of NATO and to involve Hungary into the process of enlargement is a step which is not just good for Hungary, but it is in the interest of NATO as well. And he was a tough fighter to convince everybody around the Western Hemisphere that NATO enlargement is in the interest of those countries living in central Europe who just got through the occupation of another empire.

So we consider your President as a person who brought his name into the history of Hungary, the Hungarian history, as a person who provided security and national independence to Hungary.

Just for a second, I have a letter to your President, anyway, which was sent by Mr. Pachinski, who was your tutor in Oxford and who was my tutor in Oxford as well. And I just met him a week ago in Budapest, and he asked me to give this letter to you. His best wishes probably you can find inside it.

We will discuss definitely about Kosovo, the Hungarian and foreign policies in the Middle East, that they should look for a peaceful solution. But if a decision would be taken by NATO, we are ready to contribute as an ally to do. Host nation support could be provided. Up until now, Hungary and foreign policy was not invited into this action, but we are ready to take part. And we will discuss many other points as well. It will be too long to explain just now, here.

Thank you very much.

Q. Good morning, Mr. President.

President Clinton. Good morning.

Impeachment Inquiry Vote

Q. When you talk to Members of Congress about impeachment, what do you tell them?

President Clinton. Well, first of all, I have received a large number of calls from House Members, and I have tried to return those calls. I haven't been able to return them all because we have other things to do, and I'll try to call the rest of them today. But I think the vote should be a vote of principle. It's up to others to decide what happens to me, and ultimately it's going to be up to the American people to make a clear statement there.

What I am more concerned about today by far is that they cast some votes necessary to advance the cause of our people. The most important votes they have to cast are the votes on funding the International Monetary Fund so we can continue our economic prosperity; on a budget which doesn't raid Social Security—raid the surplus until we fix Social Security. They still have a chance to do something for education.

This Congress has killed campaign finance reform, the minimum wage, tobacco reform legislation, even killed the Patients' Bill of Rights. But they can still do something on education; they can still help to save Social Security; they can still keep our economy going; they can still stop the war on the environment that is hidden in so many of these bills. It's not too late.

And that's got to be my focus in these closing days. What happens to me I think ultimately will be for the American people to decide. I owe them my best efforts to work for them, and that's what I'm going to do.

Q. Some Democrats, sir, have complained that they're being pressured by the White House on the subject of impeachment. Is that appropriate?

President Clinton. I think everybody should cast a vote on principle and conscience. But I doubt that—I doubt—keep in mind, the proposal advanced was developed entirely by Congressman Boucher from Virginia, a man who comes from a conservative rural district and who developed it on his own, fought for it in the Judiciary Committee, argued it, and said that the elemental principle of fairness was that we ought to define a standard of what conduct is being judged by.

So as far as I know, no one in the White House had anything to do with the development of the proposal. There have been conversations with Members—as I said yesterday, a large number called me. I'm attempting to call them all back, and I will try to do that. But I want them—more important than anything else to me is that they do the people's work and then let—the people will decide where we go from here.

Kosovo

Q. On Kosovo, how do you placate Russian concerns about NATO military strikes?

President Clinton. Well, I think the most important thing we can do is to try to work with the Russians to try to actually avoid military strikes by securing compliance with the U.N. resolutions by Milosevic. Now, we have done that. President Yeltsin sent a team of senior people to see Mr. Milosevic, and once again, as he did last June, he promised him that he would comply. He also said he would like some representatives from OSCE to come in and see if he was complying.

Now, if he does that, if he completely complies, he doesn't have to worry about military force. But I do not believe the United States can be in a position, and I do not believe NATO can be in the position of letting tens of thousands of people starve or freeze to death this winter because Mr. Milosevic didn't keep his word to the Russians and the world community one more time.

So the way to avoid NATO military action is for Mr. Milosevic to honor the U.N. resolutions. That's what should be done.

Middle East Peace Process

Q. How long do you expect next week's Middle East summit to last when they come to Washington?

President Clinton. I'd be happy if it were over in an hour, but I'm prepared to invest as much time as it takes.

Q. Do you foresee multiple days?

President Clinton. It might take more than a day, yes. I asked them to block out a couple of days to come back because I think it's very important that we try to get over these last humps and get into the last stage of negotiations. We need to get to final status talks, because, keep in mind, the whole thing is supposed to be wrapped up by May of next year. And the closer we get to that date without having been at least in the final status talks, where the parties have a relaxed opportunity, without being up against a timetable, to discuss these big issues of the future of the Middle East—the closer we get to that date without that happening, it's going to be more difficult. So it

is imperative that we move on and get this next big step done.

I'm encouraged that Secretary Albright is in the region today. She's going to have an announcement about it later today. I'm encouraged by the attitude and the sense of openness I felt from Prime Minister Netanyahu and Mr. Arafat the last time they were here. And if they can come back with that spirit, we're close enough now that we can get this done. And I just hope and pray that that will happen when they come back.

Q. Will you get personally involved throughout——

President Clinton. Well, I'll be involved quite a bit. I don't know what "throughout" will mean. I hope they'll be talking 12 hours a day or something. I don't know. We'll just have to see what happens. But I will be involved constantly throughout the process, yes.

[*At this point, one group of reporters left the room, and another group entered.*]

Discussions With Prime Minister Orban

President Clinton. Let me make a brief statement. First of all, I would like to welcome the Prime Minister and his team here to Washington. We are excited about having him here. We are excited about what we have heard about his leadership and the policies of his government.

I want to have a chance to discuss NATO's membership for Hungary, and it's coming up here very soon, next year. I want to have a chance to discuss the situation in Bosnia—and again I want to thank the Government and the people of Hungary for giving us the base at Taszar which made it possible for us to do our part in the Bosnian peace process.

And I want to discuss Kosovo, where I believe it is imperative that the international community enforce the United Nations resolutions requiring a cease-fire, a withdrawal of troops, access for the humanitarian agencies to the hundreds of thousands of people who have been displaced, and the beginning of negotiations. And I think the pressure of NATO is critical to achieving that goal.

So these are some of the things that I hope to discuss with the Prime Minister. Now, perhaps he would like to make a few opening remarks, and then we'll answer a couple of questions.

Prime Minister Orban. If you don't mind, I would like to do it in Hungarian.

President Clinton. Sure.

Prime Minister Orban. It is a pleasure to be here as almost an ally of the United States of America, as Hungary's impending membership of the NATO is very soon, indeed. We are planning to discuss various issues with the President of the United States of America, including NATO enlargement, the problems and matters in Kosovo, as well as the central European issues.

I would like to assure the President that Hungary is a factor and guarantor of stability in the central European region. And the Hungarian Government is making every effort to continue that role as a guarantor of stability and security in the central European region.

We would like to also assure the President that Hungary's membership in the NATO will be a benefit not only for Hungary but also for the NATO and the United States of America.

As far as Kosovo is concerned, Hungary has not yet received any official request to participate in that, and we hope that there is still a possibility for peaceful settlement. But if there is a request, of course, just because of our role as an ally in the NATO, we will do our best to help resolve the problem.

We will also discuss various issues concerning the world economic crisis, and I would like to—that there is no reason why the world should put Hungary in the same box with Russia and the crisis in the Russian Federation. And Hungary is not an emerging market. What I would like to call it is a converging market.

International Economic Situation

Q. Mr. President, what will be the impact of the global economic financial crisis on Hungary and the eastern European region? And what should the Hungarian Government do to avoid or minimize the impact?

President Clinton. Well, first, I think that—let me answer the second question first. I think the Hungarian Government is doing what it should do to minimize the impact by having a sound economic policy. And I'm very happy that so far the global economic crisis has not had much impact in central Europe.

Now, eventually, unless we can limit it and then beat it back, it will affect all of us because all of us depend upon each other for markets, for investments. So even if a country has a per-

fect economic policy, if its investors and the people who buy its products have their economies weakened, it will affect that country.

So what I would hope that Hungary would do, because it has a very aggressive and, I believe, progressive economic policy, is to support the efforts of the international community to—first of all, to beat the crisis back and to limit its reach and then to develop institutional responses for the future that will prevent such things for the future.

But I'm very impressed that central Europe has done so well; Hungary has done so well; Poland had done so well; other countries have done so well. You should be very happy about that. I think it's a great tribute to the confidence that the investment community around the world has in your people and your system, as well as to the policies that have been followed.

Kosovo

Q. When will the final decision be made on Kosovo, and what will the Hungarian role be?

President Clinton. Well, of course, what the Hungarian role could be is something that will have to be decided by Hungary, because until Hungary becomes a full-fledged NATO member, any other—if NATO has to act, any other participation would be voluntary. But at this point, I wouldn't think that Hungary would be involved in that, because what is contemplated is the prospect of airstrikes if President Milosevic refuses to comply with the U.N. resolutions. I still hope and pray that he will comply, so it will not be necessary.

Now, if he does comply, it may be necessary to have some verification group go in. Will that group be under the United Nations, under OSCE, or some other place? That's not resolved. Will Hungary be asked to participate or have an opportunity to? Not resolved. Then if there are negotiations which result in a settlement, there might be some request for an international presence to help the parties to honor a peace agreement on a third stage there. That's not resolved. So I guess the short answer to your question is, no one can know the answer to that yet.

Crime in Central Europe

Q. Mr. President, what do you think about the crime situation in central Europe and the cooperation?

President Clinton. Well, first, I think that your Government is very aware of it and very much determined to do something about it, because we have been engaged in talks to establish a joint strike force, to have an FBI presence, to work together. Frankly, I believe that international organized crime is going to be one of the great challenges all of us face, and it, I suppose, is an inevitable result of the new technologies available in the world, that these multinational syndicates now are much bigger than ever before. And I think that the only way to deal with them is to deal with them together. And I am committed to working with you to try to help to reduce the problem in Hungary. Thank you.

NOTE: The President spoke at 10:05 a.m. in the Oval Office at the White House. In his remarks, the President referred to President Slobodan Milosevic of the Federal Republic of Yugoslavia (Serbia and Montenegro); President Boris Yeltsin of Russia; Prime Minister Binyamin Netanyahu of Israel; and Chairman Yasser Arafat of the Palestinian Authority. The President also referred to the Organization for Security and Cooperation in Europe (OSCE). Prime Minister Orban spoke in Hungarian to the second group of reporters, and those remarks were translated by an interpreter. A tape was not available for verification of the content of these remarks.

Remarks on Signing the Higher Education Amendments of 1998
October 7, 1998

Thank you very much. Just so Harold doesn't mistake all that applause for me, let's give him another hand. I thought he was—[*applause*]. That's what this is all about today.

I want to thank all the previous speakers—Secretary Riley for being the most dedicated, complete, and productive Secretary of Education in the history of this country. I'm very grateful to him. [*Applause*] We always salt the crowd with employees of the Education Department. [*Laughter*] We are very, very grateful to you, sir.

I want to thank Senator Jeffords and Senator Kennedy, Chairman Goodling and Congressman Clay, and as was mentioned previously, Congressman McKeon and Congressman Kildee, all the members of the education committees of the House and the Senate and the staff.

I'd like to also point out that there are Members who care deeply about education who aren't on those committees, and some of them are here. We have over 30 Members of the Congress from both parties here. I'd like to ask the Members of the Congress who are here who aren't on the education committees and, therefore, have not yet stood up, to please stand up, all of you who are here.

I notice Senator Kennedy already acknowledged Senator Specter, understanding how the Appropriations Committee works. [*Laughter*]

But his presence here means he considers it to be an education committee, and we thank you for that.

I'd like to make one big point first. You've all heard about the details of this legislation. What I want us to all be very clear on is that the bill I will sign in a few moments will enhance the economic strength of America. It will strengthen the communities of America. It will improve the lives of the families of America. And it certainly will widen the circle of opportunity.

When I ran for President in 1992, one of the things I most wanted to do was to open the doors of college to all Americans who were willing to work for it. In the 1980's, the cost of a college education was the only really important thing to families that increased at a higher rate than the cost of health care.

And yet, in the world in which we live and certainly in the one in which Harold and his contemporaries will live, college is no longer a luxury for the well-to-do or even an opportunity for hard-working middle class kids whose parents save. It is an economic necessity for every American and for our country as a whole.

That is why we worked so hard in the bipartisan balanced budget agreement to create the $1,500 HOPE scholarships; the tax credits for the first 2 years of college; tax breaks for junior and senior years, for graduate school, for adults going back to school. That is why with bipartisan support we dramatically expanded the Pell grant program; created 300,000 more work-study positions; the education IRA's; the education grants for those serving in AmeriCorps now are nearly numbering 100,000 young Americans; student loans payable, or repayable, as a percentage of future incomes, so no one needed to fear borrowing the money and then being broke if they took a job that didn't pay a lot of money; the tax deductibility of the interest on student loans. And today, with this lowering of the interest rates, as has already been said, to the lowest rate in nearly two decades, we can really say that every high school graduate in America, regardless of income, can afford to go to college.

I asked the Congress to slash the interest rates on the student loans. As Chairman Goodling said, it was the lowest rate now in 17 years. Let me tell you what it means to a college student. It's a $700 tax cut to the average student borrowing for a college degree on the front end. And anybody who can remember what it was like back then knows that $700 to a college student is still real money.

I asked Congress to use technology to help all Americans, including those in the work force, to upgrade their skills any time, anywhere, and this bill does that. I asked them to help us recruit more and better trained teachers, to improve teacher training, direct our best teachers to schools with the greatest needs. This bill does that.

Finally, I asked Congress to create a nationwide mentoring program. You heard Harold talk about it, the one that affected his life. All of us have at some level come in contact with the pioneer program, Eugene Lang's "I Have a Dream" program in New York City. Many of us have been involved at the State level, as I was, in creating scholarships for all our young people who achieved a certain level of academic excellence. What this bill does is something more and, I think, profoundly important. And again, like others, I want to thank Senator Jim Jeffords, I want to thank Gene Sperling of my staff who worked on this, and I especially want to thank Congressman Chaka Fattah of Philadelphia who pushed this so hard. And we thank you, sir.

This bill seeks to make national what Harold talked about affecting his life. It essentially seeks, first of all, to provide mentors to kids in their middle school years who need it, and then to give the mentors weapons. At a minimum, the mentors will be able to say, "Look, here's who you are. Here's where you come from. Here's how much money you have. And if this is what your income looks like when you got out of high school and you stay in school and you learn your lessons, we can tell you right now, this is how much money you can get to go to college." Now, it's already there, but they don't know it. So we're not only trying to open the doors of college to all Americans but to make sure all Americans know the doors are open. And those are two very different things.

Secondly, this bill provides funds to enable partnerships to be established between universities and other groups and our middle schools so that they can have more programs, hopefully one for every school and every student in America, eventually, like the one that benefited Harold. So I can't tell you how important I think this is. So now we can say we've opened the doors to college to all Americans, and we have a system by which, if we really implement it, we can make sure all the Americans know the doors are open.

The other day I was in Philadelphia, and Chaka got a bunch of young kids, middle school kids together, and we took them down town and drank a Coke with them. Every one of them wanted to go to college. And we talked about this program, and every one of them was, I think, impressed by the fact that the Congress of the United States actually cared about them—and I might add, probably a little surprised—glad to know that somehow, somebody was trying to set up a system to really reach down into their lives, at one of the most challenging and difficult points in those lives, often under the most difficult circumstances under which they're living, and open the door to a different future.

I don't think anyone would question that when Harold talked about his friend who's now working as a scientist in Utah, that that young person is not only better off, the rest of us are better off as well. America is a better place as well.

I also want to say very briefly, I am personally grateful for the Congress in a bipartisan fashion responding to the problem of alcohol and drug abuse and the health threat it presents on our campuses—we all remember the tragic loss of five students last fall in Virginia—by changing the law to allow campuses to notify parents when children younger than 21 have alcohol and drug violations. We have no way of knowing, but we believe this will save lives. And I thank the Congress for giving us the chance to do that.

Let me also say something that I think it's important for me to say as President: I am proud not only of what is in this bill but of how this bill passed. This is the way America should work. This is the way Congress should work. Members of Congress, I assure you, brought their different convictions and their partisan views to the debate, and we had the debate. But in the end, we acted together; we put the progress of the country and the people of the country ahead of our partisan differences and reached a principled resolution of the matters in dispute. That's the way America is supposed to work, and that's the way the American people want us to work. And so I want to thank every one of you for making sure on this terribly important issue, that is exactly the way you worked. Thank you very much.

Finally let me just say, in the closing days of this congressional session I hope that there will be similar bipartisan action on the agenda for public school excellence that I offered 8 months ago, an agenda that demands high responsibility and high standards; offers choice and opportunity; calls for voluntary national standards and voluntary exams to measure their performance, supervised by a completely bipartisan committee; an end to social promotion, but help for the school districts that end social promotion, so that we don't brand children a failure when the system fails them but instead give

them access to the mentors, the after-school programs the summer school programs that they need; an effort to make our schools safer, more disciplined, more drug-free; a plan that would provide for 100,000 teachers, for smaller classes in the early grades; funds to modernize or build 5,000 schools at the time when we have the largest student population in history; a plan to connect all of our classrooms to the Internet by the year 2000.

Today we celebrate putting partisanship aside for a historic higher education law. We can do no less for our public schools. We have to pass the agenda, and we must pass, literally, the annual education investment bill which funds a lot of the programs, Head Start, technology, the summer school and after-school programs. So once again we have to put progress ahead of partisanship.

In this room, many Presidents have signed many pieces of legislation into law. Some of them were very momentous. But if, when you leave here today, you remember this life story of the young man who spoke before me and you imagine how many other people there are like him in America, and how many more stories there will be because of this bill, you can all feel very, very proud.

Thank you very much.

Can I ask the Members to come up, and we'll do this.

NOTE: The President spoke at 11:48 a.m. in the East Room at the White House. In his remarks, he referred to Harold Shields, a participant in the "Say Yes to Education" mentoring program. H.R. 6, approved October 7, was assigned Public Law No. 105–244.

Statement on Signing the Higher Education Amendments of 1998
October 7, 1998

Today I am pleased to sign into law H.R. 6, the "Higher Education Amendments of 1998." This legislation is the culmination of bipartisan efforts by the Congress and my Administration to increase access to college, make higher education more affordable, improve teacher quality, and modernize the delivery of student aid. I particularly want to thank Senators

Jeffords, Coats, Kennedy, and Dodd, and Representatives Goodling, McKeon, Clay, Kildee, Andrews, and Petri, as well as other Members of the Conference Committee, for their help in guiding this legislation through the Congress.

I also owe a particular debt of gratitude of Representative Fattah, whose consistent and tireless work resulted in a new effort that will turn the dream of college into a reality for many of the poorest families in America. The "GEAR UP" program, based in part on my High Hopes for College proposal, provides competitive grants to States and local partnerships to encourage colleges to work with middle schools in high-poverty areas to ensure that students receive and benefit from financial aid information, rigorous courses, tutoring, mentoring, and scholarships for college.

I am pleased to see a number of my other initiatives included in this bipartisan legislation. College students across the country will save hundreds or even thousands of dollars on their loan repayments with the extension of the low student loan interest rate on new loans that went into effect on July 1st of this year. In addition, the bill allows borrowers to refinance outstanding loans at a lower rate by extending for 4 months the current interest rate on Direct Consolidation Loans. The bill, however, is not perfect. It is unfortunate that the legislation permits continuation of the practice of providing excessive payments to lenders and guaranty agencies instead of reducing taxpayer costs by using competitive market forces. In addition, it is regrettable that the legislation does not allow more than 4 months for the millions of Americans who are paying high interest rates on their current student loans to get the new low consolidation rate, or make that rate available to all borrowers. I urge the Congress to revisit these issues in the future.

This bill builds upon the proposals I sent to the Congress to improve teacher quality, training, and recruitment as our Nation faces the need to hire more than two million teachers over the next 10 years. New partnerships between teacher education institutions and school districts, partnerships to improve teacher recruitment, Teacher Quality Enhancement State grants, and increased accountability will help improve teacher quality for all our children. I am also pleased that the Congress did not prohibit Federal funding for the National Board for Professional Teaching Standards.

This legislation will promote high-quality distance-learning opportunities to provide students, including non-traditional students, with increased educational opportunities. The Learning Anytime, Anywhere Partnership (LAAP) program, as I proposed, will award competitive grants to partnerships to create new distance-learning models, explore the efficiencies and

cost reductions that can be realized through institutional partnerships, and develop innovative measures of student achievement through distance learning.

I am also pleased that H.R. 6 reauthorizes and improves upon many programs in the current Higher Education Act designed to promote equal educational opportunity. In particular, I would like to commend Representative Hinojosa for his work to increase funding levels and improve programs for students attending Hispanic-serving institutions. I am also pleased that H.R. 6 reauthorizes the Education of the Deaf Act, which supports Gallaudet University and the National Technical Institute for the Deaf, and strengthens programs to support tribal and historically black colleges and universities.

The bill also revolutionizes the delivery of student aid by creating within the Government the first-ever Performance-Based Organization (PBO)—a concept promoted by Vice President Gore's National Partnership for Reinventing Government—to improve services to students and enhance administrative efficiency and accountability. I am delighted with this bipartisan effort to modernize student aid delivery in the Department of Education.

I do note some constitutional concerns regarding provisions in this bill relating to the appointment and reappointment of the Chief Operating Officer of the PBO, and the issuance of regulations regarding student loan repayment incentives that would have to be certified by the Congressional Budget Office. While I do not regard these provisions as binding, the Secretary of Education as a matter of policy will implement these provisions so far as possible in a manner consistent with the principles embodied in the legislation.

There are costs associated with H.R. 6 after fiscal year 1999 that are not fully offset under Administration budget scoring. Under the Budget Enforcement Act, a sequester of mandatory programs will be required in future years if savings to offset the costs of this Act are not enacted. My Administration will work with the Congress to offset these costs to avoid a potential sequester.

This bill represents a positive, bipartisan advancement for students, teachers, and the future of higher education. Now the Congress must take the critical next step, providing full funding for the new initiatives this legislation creates— GEAR UP, teacher preparation and recruitment, and LAAP—for fiscal year 1999. I look forward to working with the Congress to ensure this funding is made available.

WILLIAM J. CLINTON

The White House,
October 7, 1998.

NOTE: H.R. 6, approved October 7, was assigned Public Law No. 105–244.

Statement on Signing the Energy and Water Development Appropriations Act, 1999
October 7, 1998

Today I have signed into law H.R. 4060, the "Energy and Water Development Appropriations Act, 1999," which provides $20.8 billion in discretionary budget authority for the programs of the Department of Energy (DOE), the Department of the Interior's Bureau of Reclamation, the Army Corps of Engineers, and several smaller agencies.

The Act provides necessary funding to maintain my Administration's commitment to ensuring the safety and reliability of our Nation's nuclear weapons stockpile without nuclear testing. It also supports DOE's basic science programs, including funding for the Spallation Neutron Source Program. The Act also provides funding to develop and protect the Nation's water resources.

I am pleased that the Act includes authority to transfer funds to support the operation of the D.C. Courts.

However, I am disappointed that the Congress did not include my funding request for valuable research and development investments in renewable energy sources, and I will work with the Congress to explore options for funding these important investments. I am also dis-

appointed that the Congress provided no funding for the Next Generation Internet and for discretionary programs of the Tennessee Valley Authority, and inadequate funding for the Clean Water Initiative, including the Initiative's Everglades restoration activities and Columbia River salmon recovery efforts. I look forward to working with the Congress on options for financing and increasing support for these initiatives in the future.

Only 4 of the 13 FY 1999 appropriations bills have been sent to the White House. These 13 bills must be passed to fund the operation of the Government for the fiscal year that began on October 1. Time is growing short, and I urge the Congress not to delay, but to complete its work on the remaining bills by the end of this week, and to send them to me in an acceptable form.

WILLIAM J. CLINTON

The White House,
October 7, 1998.

NOTE: H.R. 4060, approved October 7, was assigned Public Law No. 105–245.

Remarks at the League of Conservation Voters Dinner
October 7, 1998

Thank you very much for that wonderful welcome. Let me say, first of all, I want to thank Deb Callahan for her opening remarks and her leadership. I thank your chairman, Mike Hayden. I'd like to thank my EPA Administrator, Carol Browner, for being here and for the good job she does. I'd like to say a special word

of appreciation to the three Members of Congress who are here tonight, without whom I could have accomplished very little over these last 6 years. Thank you, George Miller, Norm Dicks, Maurice Hinchey. Thank you for what you have done for our country.

And I'd also like to just express my appreciation to three people here—who aren't here, who have been a real inspiration to me and a constant source of support in a lot of these fights we have taken on: first and foremost, the Vice President; second, the First Lady; and third, Secretary Babbitt. They have all, in ways none of you will ever know, as well as all those you're aware of, had countless, countless conversations with me about a lot of the issues that I will mention tonight, and some I will forget.

But in an administration, the President often gets the credit when the inspiration, the ideas, the energy, and sometimes the constructive nagging comes from other people. Now, Carol Browner, for example, constructively nagged me—[*laughter*]—to make sure we stood up for clean air.

Congressman Boehlert, is that you back there? I didn't see you. Thank you, sir. [*Applause*] I'm glad to see you. Thank you very much.

But anyway, everybody said the sky was falling, and Carol said the kids need to breathe. And so we wound up doing it her way. [*Laughter*] And we're still rocking along pretty well.

And tonight I hope you'll permit me to say a very special word of appreciation to one of your honorees who is about to leave our administration, the Chair of the CEQ, Katie McGinty. Let's give her a hand. [*Applause*] Thank you.

I just was informed I missed another Member of Congress and another friend of the environment, Congresswoman Connie Morella. Where are you, Connie? There you are. Thank you very much. [*Applause*] Thank you.

We've had a lot of exceedingly complex, as well as difficult—politically difficult but also intellectually complex decisions we've had to make, working out our position on climate change, on how to deal with the northwest forest challenge, on whether we could figure out a way to save Yellowstone, on figuring out the genuine equities that lay underneath the big decision on Grand Staircase-Escalante. And in all of those cases, Katie McGinty has been there, working with all the various people affected and concerned, trying to make sure we did the right thing by the environment and to make sure we did it increasingly, I believe, in the right way. And I am very, very much indebted to her. I'll miss her, and we wish her well. Thank you. [*Applause*] She's actually going to India for awhile, and I told her I expect by the time I get there, there will be no longer any nuclear issues between the United States and India. [*Laughter*] If she can solve all these other problems, deal with all this other contention, this ought to be just another drop in the bucket.

Let me begin tonight where Deb Callahan left off. I agree that our job is not simply to convince people of the importance of environmental stewardship; the harder part is to convince people of the power they have not only to stand up for what they believe in but to change what they disagree with. We have seen that over and over and over again. For too many years, the champions of the environment have been in the clear majority in America but have been insufficiently organized across economic and regional and party lines to bring their force to bear with their friends in the Congress.

Now, we still have that task in the next 30 days, because the next 30 days will be critical to the future of the environment. Indeed, we have that task in the next few days, the last days of this congressional session before the election. And I'll have more to say about that in a moment.

One of the best illustrations of citizen power to change what is wrong is actually here under our noses. Just before America celebrated its first Earth Day, a wide-eyed but fairly low-level congressional staffer, recently out of college, had a great democratic idea, to create an environmental scorecard for Members of Congress and empower voters to make a more informed choice. With that idea, that young woman launched the League of Conservation Voters and had enormous influence ever since. Marion Edey, thank you very much. Where are you? Stand up. Where are you? [*Applause*] Thank you.

Over the past generation when we have faced clear common threats, our citizens often have joined together in common resolve. America came together to heed Rachel Carson's warnings by banning DDT and other poisons. America cleaned up rivers so filthy they were catching on fire. America phased out lead in gasoline and the chemicals that deplete our protective ozone layer. America achieved all these things in no small measure because of the broad bipartisan citizen power mobilized by groups like the LCV.

Over the past 6 years, we have worked together to build on these accomplishments, to preserve our national treasures like Florida's Everglades, California's ancient redwoods, the spectacular red-rock canyons of Utah. Just last month, Katie McGinty was out in Yellowstone commemorating our success in protecting the park from the New World Mine.

We are doing our best to lead the way on the global environment. We made sure the Kyoto agreement was strong and realistic, and we're determined that America must do its part to reverse global warming. We're protecting the health of our families and communities. We've accelerated Superfund cleanups, issued the toughest air quality standards ever, dramatically reduced toxic pollution, not through the heavy hand of regulation but by giving communities access to the information they deserve.

These efforts reflect not only our—yours and mine—our common commitment to protecting the environment but to doing it in the right way: innovative, commonsense solutions that achieve the greatest protection at the least cost. That means rejecting the false choice that pits the economy against the environment.

I want to say a little more about that in a moment. But I have to tell you that the largest obstacle we face in our Congress, in our country, and in the world in getting a united, serious approach to climate change is the deeply embedded, almost psychic dependence that so many decisionmakers in our country and all over the world have to the elemental notion that economic growth is still not possible without industrial era energy use patterns. People simply don't believe it, so that when I talk to people in developing countries and when I talk to people in the still-developing Congress—[*laughter*]—we have these—I say that in a—that's a compliment, as I will say more about it in a moment. [*Laughter*]

We still have the people that are literally obsessed with the notion that seriously addressing climate change is somehow a plot to wreck America's economic future and political sovereignty. I asked somebody today how much time we had spent complying—and most of you don't think I did enough on climate change, right? Is that right? Let's put it out here on the table. [*Laughter*] Most of you don't think I did enough on climate change. I proposed a series of very, I think, effective tax incentives to get people to do the right things and make them economically efficient and a major increase in research and development. And there is a

committee in the House of Representatives that acts like I'm right up there with the black helicopter crowd. [*Laughter*] It's true.

I asked today; we believe that we have spent 10,000 hours complying with subpoenas from a committee who believes we are subverting the future of America with these modest proposals on climate change—hundreds of thousands of dollars in compliance costs over and above the salaries of the people involved. Why is that? Are these bad people who don't love their country? Do they really want to destroy our environment? Do they believe their grandchildren don't need to deal with this? Absolutely not. They honestly still believe that economic growth is not possible without industrial age energy use patterns. "Don't show me those solar reflectors that go on roofs now that look just like ordinary shingles. Don't bother me with those windows that let in twice as much light and keep out twice as much heat and cold. I don't want to hear about the economics of insulation or the lights that will save themselves a ton of greenhouse emissions during the life of the lamp."

So I say to you, we have still a huge intellectual battle to fight, a way of looking at the world and the future that helps to bring us together instead of drive us apart. And one of the central ideas is the honest belief that you cannot only grow the economy and preserve the environment, you can actually grow the economy and improve the environment.

This country has the lowest unemployment rate in 28 years, the fastest wage growth in 20 years, the smallest percentage of the people on welfare in 29 years, the first surplus in 29 years, the highest homeownership ever. But compared to 6 years ago, the air is cleaner; the water is cleaner; the food is safer; there are fewer toxic waste dumps; and we have done quite a lot of other things to protect the environment. It is simply not true that you can't grow the economy and improve the environment. And vast, vast technological and conservation and alternative energy source opportunities have been completely untapped compared to their economically available potential in our country today.

So we have a lot more work to do, but I will say again, sometimes you have to win the battle of the big ideas, even if it's with simple, small examples, before you can really move our vast country in one direction without interruption.

So I would like to make here a point I have tried to make to our fellow citizens in every forum I could, since it became obvious that we were going to have a balanced budget and a surplus. The temptation is to be diverted or just relaxed in a good economic time. That would be an error. These times are, first of all, highly dynamic. We have enormous challenges of which you are well aware, the global financial challenge, the global environmental challenge. It would be a terrible mistake for us to squander this moment of opportunity, when so much good is happening for America and we have a level of confidence about our ability to meet challenges that we have not had in decades, by being either diverted or relaxed. We need to face the challenges we have and think about how we can best use this prosperity to build the kind of future we want.

Tonight I'll give you an example of one thing we're trying to do to use this time of prosperity, adding vital new protections for our Nation's wetlands. Earlier this year, as part of our clean water action plan, I set a goal of restoring 100,000 acres of wetlands a year by 2005. Today the Army Corps of Engineers is proposing changes to ensure that we think twice before building in our most sensitive wetlands. Twenty years ago, if you'd told me I'd see this day and this initiative from that august body, I never would have believed it. And I congratulate them on it and honor them for it.

From now on, we will require a full environmental review, with full public participation, of all projects in critical wetlands areas, particularly floodplains. In a typical year, 140 Americans die in floods, and $4 billion in property is destroyed. Just in this past week, nine people have died in floods in Missouri and Kansas. That's why FEMA Director James Lee Witt felt so strongly about strengthening protections for the floodplains. By thinking twice, we can prevent tragedy and save taxpayer dollars while protecting the environment.

And as we all know, if we are going to do this, make the most of this moment, we have to do it together. For years and years, protecting the environment was a matter of bipartisan concern. And frankly, for a lot of people it still is. You have three good Democrats and two fine Republicans here tonight, unless I missed someone else that I wasn't given. [Laughter] But in the last Congress it seemed not to be the case. There was a direct frontal assault on the environment, a rollback of—or an attempted rollback of 30 years on hard-won gains. As the LCV ably documented, more than a third of the Members of the 104th Congress scored a zero on the environment. The group tried to force me to sign a budget with unconscionable cuts in environmental protections. Twice the Government was shut down, in no small measure because of environmental controversies. But because together we decided not to give in and fought back, it came out all right.

Now a lot of the same folks are back with a different tactic, here in the waning days of the congressional session, a sneak attack. Not only are they refusing to fully fund environmental priorities—the clean water action plan to help clean up waterways too polluted for fishing and swimming, an extraordinary percentage of the waterways in America; the land and water conservation fund to protect precious lands in danger of development; the climate change technology initiative to take commonsense steps to reverse global warming—not only would they keep us from moving forward in these areas, but they're pushing once again in the opposite direction, as all of you know all too well, by loading appropriations bills up with a slew of antienvironmental riders.

Really, that "rider" word is really well chosen because it's sort of an unrelated passenger riding along on a piece of legislation that otherwise looks pretty good. These special interest riders, among other things, would carve roads through the Alaskan wilderness, force overcutting in our national forests, cripple wildlife protections, and sell the taxpayers short.

Now, the sponsors of these riders know that the proposals could not stand on their own. They know that, therefore, they have to resort to a stealth tactic to get this done. I personally believe this unrelated rider strategy, unless it's something that has broad bipartisan support necessary to preserve some immediate national need, is bad for the democratic process, as well as bad for the environment. So tonight let me say again, to you and to the Congress, I will veto any bill that will do unacceptable harm to our environment—[inaudible]. [Applause] Thank you.

Let me say to all of you, there is hope that we can do better. This afternoon—or this morning, I guess—time flies when you're having fun—[laughter]—anyway, sometime today we had a marvelous ceremony at the White House, with over 30 Members of Congress, signing a higher education bill that had enormous Republican and Democratic support, that among other things gave us the lowest interest rates on student loans in nearly 20 years, will save $11 billion to students with existing loans, about $700 a student, for college students.

Perhaps even more important over the long run, this bill, with an idea inspired by Congressman Chaka Fattah from Philadelphia, provides support to set up mentoring programs for middle-school children in tough inner-city and other poor school districts, and enables the mentors to tell the kids when they're 12 or 13, "If you stay in school and you keep learning, here is how much college aid you are going to be able to get, and I can tell you that right now." And it provides for partnerships so that universities and private donors can give more to the kids in those years and guarantee them. It was an extraordinary day.

And then this afternoon the House of Representatives rejected a parks bill that would have done a lot more harm than good—listen to this—by the bipartisan, overwhelming margin of 301 to 123. Thank you. Thank you. That is the kind of bipartisan spirit the modern environmental movement started with in 1970.

You know, I've never met anybody walking on a trail in a national park—never—that I knew when I saw them coming toward me what their party affiliation was, except on the rare occasions when I actually knew them. [*Laughter*] When you go into one of our wilderness areas, nobody asks you to declare your affiliation. We all assume that we drink the same water; we swim in the same lakes; we breathe the same air; we eat the same food; we love the same natural surroundings; we have the same common stake in preserving the same environment for our children and our grandchildren.

And I hope this vote today indicates that we have several more days, coming in time between now and when the Congress goes home at the end of the week, for this sort of spirit of coming together.

And then, in the next 30 days, during this election season, I hope that ordinary citizens who care deeply about these issues will bring their voices to bear in the election. Just think what would happen if people of both parties and independents simply said, "We're going to do better. We're going to change, at last and forever, the idea that we have to have old-fash-

ioned, destructive energy use patterns to grow the economy. We will not give in to those who want to put the sacred up for sale. The decisions we make today on climate change, water, wetlands, and air will have implications for decades, if not centuries to come. And we want a unifying vision that embraces people who may differ on many other things, to embrace our common home and our common future." I think the American people, for all kinds of reasons, are open to that sort of message in the next 30 days.

We are reminded by every event which occurs that we are living in a world in which we are ever more interdependent, not only with each other as Americans but with those who live beyond our borders and with the Earth we all share. We see it when there's a reverberation in our stock market because of what happens in Russia or Latin America or Asia. We see it when we understand some big chunk of Antarctica has broken off and is floating and indicates that the water level may be rising more rapidly because the climate is warming. We see it when we understand our common responsibility to try to stop people of different ethnic groups from killing each other in the Baltics and the Balkans and to try to get people of different racial and ethnic and religious groups to embrace what we have in common, even as we celebrate our differences at home.

The environmental movement and its leaders are probably better positioned, because of your general orientation of these issues, than virtually any other group in America to get the American people to rethink these big ideas; to think about how we can be reconciled to ourselves, to our environment, and committed to our future; to think about how we can appreciate not only our independence but our interdependence with one another and with our fellow human beings throughout the world.

On the edge of a new millennium, I really believe the development of that kind of approach, and whether we can do it and reconcile it, as I believe we can, in a very rich and wonderful way, with our own tradition of individual rights and individuality and autonomy—if we can do that, I believe that will do more to ensure that we make the right decisions as a people, across party and regional and income and other lines, on the most profound decisions of our future than anything else.

You—you are uniquely positioned to change our people's way of thinking about this. And you could hardly give a greater gift to your country at the end of one century and the dawn of another.

Thank you very much, and God bless you.

NOTE: The President spoke at 7:47 p.m. in the Grand Ballroom at the Mayflower Hotel. In his remarks, he referred to Deb Callahan, president, and John Michael Hayden, chairman of the board, League of Conservation Voters. The President also referred to the Kyoto Protocol on Climate Change and the Council on Environmental Quality (CEQ).

Remarks at a Democratic National Committee Dinner
October 7, 1998

Thank you very much. Ron, thank you for those words, and I thank Beth for them. Hillary and I were over here to dinner not very long ago. It was a smaller crowd; there were just four of us. And I think if we come back again, I should be assessed part of the contractor's fee. [*Laughter*] I'm afraid I'm overstaying my welcome, but I love this beautiful, beautiful home. I want to thank all of you for being here. I thank Steve Grossman for his tireless efforts and for bothering all of you so much.

And let me say to all of you, this is a very interesting time. You know that, of course. But I spent most of the last 2 weeks concerned about the developments in the international economy, what's going on in Asia, what's going on in Russia, will the financial contagion spread to Latin America. Today I talked to the President of Brazil twice about this and other matters. And yesterday I had a chance to go before the 4,000 delegates to the World Bank and International Monetary Fund annual meeting and say at least a general outline what I thought ought to be done to deal with the present crisis, limit its spread to—stop it from spreading to Latin America and other places, and deal with the problem over the long run.

We've been working on Kosovo. A lot of people don't know where Kosovo is. Once nobody knew where Bosnia was, either, and by the time we found out, a lot of people had died and the whole stability of that part of Europe was at stake. And Kosovo is next door, and 50,000 people are facing freezing or starvation this winter because the same person who caused the problems in Bosnia, Mr. Milosevic, refuses to abide by United Nations resolutions. So I'm trying to get the support not only of the leaders of both parties in our Congress but also of our Allies in NATO, to take aggressive action to protect those people's lives and restore peace there and stability, so that we won't have to do more there down the road and so that innocent lives can be saved.

I just went upstairs and took a call from Secretary Albright, who is in the Middle East working with Mr. Netanyahu and Mr. Arafat to get ready for their coming here next week. They're coming on the 15th and will be here for 3 or 4 days, and we're going to try to wrap up this phase of the Middle East peace talks. But with all the trouble and all the fighting in the world and all the squabbling in Washington, I thought you might like to know that today Binyamin Netanyahu became the first Israeli Prime Minister ever to go into Gaza, where he had lunch at Arafat's headquarters. And I dare say it must have made quite a statement to the people of the Middle East.

Today we had two great victories in Congress. I found this pattern is beginning to reassert itself; the Republican Congress starts voting like a Democratic one in the last week of every legislative session. [*Laughter*] It's quite flattering, although there's a definite political design behind it. But today the Congress voted 301 to 123 to kill Speaker Gingrich's parks bill because it has so many antienvironmental parts on it. So in the last week before the election or before breaking for the election, we got a great bipartisan vote there.

Today we celebrated the higher education act, a bill we've been trying to pass for a year. It passed with overwhelming bipartisan support, giving us the lowest interest rates on student loans in almost 20 years. It'll save $11 billion for students who are borrowing their way through college—$11 billion—and set up a mentoring program for kids in middle school in troubled inner-city and other districts, so that they not only will have mentors, but those children will be able to be told when they're 12 and 13 years old, "Look, if you stay in school and you make your grades, this is the economic benefit you will get in terms of aid to go to college." A very moving thing.

So I say all this to say that there are a lot of good things going on. And maybe the press of time and the imminence of the election and focusing people's minds, and maybe we'll have another good 3 or 4 days here in Washington before Congress goes home for the election. What has really bothered me about the last year is not the adversity I have been through but the almost casual way in which people in positions of responsibility have dealt with our new-found prosperity and success. Steve said I wanted to talk about that, and I do want to talk about that.

I mean, we worked for 6 years and waited for 29 years to get a balanced budget and a surplus. We have the smallest percentage of our people on welfare in 29 years, the fastest rising wages in over 20 years, the lowest unemployment rate in 28 years, the highest homeownership in history, the lowest African-American poverty rate ever recorded, the biggest drop in Hispanic poverty in 30 years, and things are beginning to work here—the lowest crime rate in 25 years. We proved that we can, if we get our act together, make America work.

We've been a force for peace and freedom throughout the world, from the Middle East to Northern Ireland to Bosnia to Haiti. And for the last year we've just seen, I think, a lot of indulgence with that good fortune. The United States needs to lead the world away from the brink of financial crisis. We need to restore growth in Asia and Russia and keep this thing from spreading to Latin America. We need to devise a new system for the international economy to keep things like this from happening in the future.

We can do all this but only if we have our heads on straight and if we're thinking about the American people and their interests and our responsibilities to the rest of the world. The United States needs to make a decision that we have no business spending this surplus until we make the changes necessary to secure Social Security when the baby boomers retire. Because if we don't and there are only two people working for every one person drawing Social Security, then we'll have two very unpleasant decisions if we don't make changes now.

We can, those of us who are baby boomers, be selfish and tax the living daylights out of our kids and lower the standard of living of our grandchildren so we can sustain the present system. Or we can take a huge cut in the present system and people like me with a good pension will be fine, but keep in mind, half the American senior citizens today are lifted out of poverty because of Social Security. So we have this surplus, and we ought to have the discipline to make little changes today that make a big difference in America tomorrow.

We need to keep working until our elementary and secondary schools are the best in the world. We need to keep working until we find a way to grow the economy while we improve the environment on a systematic basis. We need to deal with the fact that 160 million Americans are in managed care plans, but they're not all the same, and they don't all have the same policies. And people deserve certain uniform protections, like the right to go to the nearest emergency room, the right to see a specialist, the right to keep a doctor during a treatment, even if the employer changes providers, that these things are important to us as people, these values that bind us together.

We're even going to get, after 8 months of waiting, the International Monetary Fund contribution out of Congress that is critical to our leadership in the world, but we should have had it months ago. And so now we're leaving Washington at the end of the week and going back to the country, and the American people will have to decide how to vote. And our friends in the Republican Party believe they're going to win seats in the mid-term, and they believe it for reasons of history, money, and strategy. And you need to think about it, because that's why you're here.

We've just squandered this whole year—or they have. Basically with this Congress they killed an increase in the minimum wage; they killed campaign finance reform, which would have relieved you of the burden of coming to some of these dinners every year—[*laughter*]— they killed tobacco legislation to reform our laws there and protect our children from the dangers of tobacco; and they killed the Patients' Bill of Rights and took no action on my plan for the Patients' Bill of Rights, except to kill it. Then they didn't act on the IMF funding for months and months and months. They haven't acted on the education program I gave them 8 months ago.

Now what are they doing? They think they're going to win for reasons of history, money, and strategy. What's the history? The history is that since the Civil War when a President is in his second term, unfailingly his party has lost seats at midterm. Why? President Reagan in 1986 lost seats in the Congress midterm, even though he was quite popular. Why? Well, people thought, "Well, he'd done most of what he was hired to do," and the string was running out. That history doesn't hold this time. Why? Because our agenda is driving the national debate; because the ideas, the energy of the national debate on all the issues I just mentioned, whether it's the international economy, Social Security, education, health care, is what is coming out of the administration and the Democratic Party. So I don't think history is a very good argument.

Second, money. That's a problem. In spite of your presence here and in spite of the fact that some of you are getting sick of having dinner with me—[laughter]—they'll probably outspend us between the Republican Party, the candidates' treasure chest, and their so-called third-party, or whatever you call it, independent expenditure committees, probably 3 to one in all the close seats in the last 3 weeks of the election. In 1996, in the 20 closest House seats, they outspent us 4 to one or more—in the 20 closest House seats in the last 10 days. Now that will help them.

But my experience has been in politics if the other person has more money than you, it's devastating, unless you have enough. If you have enough for your message to be heard, for your voters to be contacted, to answer attacks, then if the other people have more money, you can still survive. And if you've got a better message and a better campaign and a better candidate, you can win. So your presence here is essential.

The third thing is strategy. What is their strategy? Normally, midterm elections are low turnout elections. Their electorate tends to be older, wealthier, more conservative, much more ideological, and therefore much more likely to vote than ours. That's essentially what happened in 1994, when in the published surveys they had about a 2 percent lead and they voted a 5 per-

cent lead or a 6 percent lead—won big in the Congress races. Now, I think they're wrong about that. You have to see everything that's happening now in terms of their strategy. Their strategy is to disappoint the Democratic base and inflame the Republican one. And I'm not talking out of school; this is what they say on the record.

You know what I think our strategy should be? The do-right rule, almost a nonpolitical strategy. Our strategy should be: If you want to play politics with what goes on in Washington, vote for them; if you want somebody who cares about what goes on in America, vote for us. Because we are the party committed to saving the surplus until we save Social Security, to maintaining America's leadership in the global economy so we can keep the American economy going, to smaller classes in the early grades, to building 5,000 more schools, to hooking our classrooms up to the Internet, to doing what is necessary to make excellence a way of life in American education, to passing that Patients' Bill of Rights, to protecting the environment as we grow the economy. That's what we're for. You know what they're for. You choose.

I believe we have enough spirit and strength and devotion and patriotism and energy in this country to overcome what I think is a rather cynical theory of history, money, and strategy. Your presence here gives us a chance to let America take a different course. And what I want you to think about is how all this business that we're debating now fits into the larger challenges facing America.

I have now been President 6 years. I spent a lot of time working on problems like the awful killings in Bosnia; dealing with the leaders of central Africa, where somewhere between 700,000 and a million people were hacked to death in the Rwandan civil war because they were of different tribes; working trying to end the old wars that date back 30 years in the modern era, and hundreds of years in history, in Ireland, the land of my forebears; working in the Middle East.

And the thing that strikes me about all these conflicts is how much they have in common with racial and religious and political hatreds that we see in America. You know, if you look at a lot of this politics, it's just downright hatred. And you almost want to say, hey, we should get a life. Things are going pretty good for us;

we should be grateful that we're Americans. And all these other people that share this country with us, they must not be so bad because we must be doing something right. And besides, our whole creed says that if we all show up and work hard and pay our taxes and do the right things, we should be able to share this land together.

What's the point I'm trying to make? If you look at every major conflict we face, it is essentially being driven by people who feel compelled to define themselves by what they are against, rather than by what they're for, and who seek conquest over reconciliation, and who see the future as a zero sum game where, "In order for me to win, somebody else has got to lose; in order for me to grow my economy, I've got to destroy the environment; there's no way that we can harmonize a common future." And I have to tell you, based on 6 years of hard, sometimes brutal, daily experience, I think that's wrong; and that I stand here tonight more idealistic about the prospect and, indeed, the necessity of bringing out the best in people than I was on the day I took the oath of office in January of 1993; and that in the end what really differentiates the two philosophies and certainly the strategies of the parties today is that.

I'm not trying to fight a win/lose game with the Republicans in Washington for who stands where on the totem pole in this town. It is a very greasy totem pole.

What I'm trying to do is to find a way in which we can work together with integrity, air our differences with integrity, and come to some resolution that will reconcile us, one to the other, so we can build a common home and a common future. In other words, if we want to be a good influence in the rest of the world, we have to do good here at home. And if we really want to live in a global economy in which we are all increasingly interdependent and we expect America to do well in that kind of economy, we have to do right here at home. I believe that. You may think it sounds naive and Pollyanna; I can tell you it is based on hour after hour after hour of hard, cold experience in the caldron that I have lived in for 6 years.

So I'm asking you not just to give your money. I'm asking you to be part of doing something that I think is pretty important. Our crowd is about to defy history. Our crowd is about to show that they don't want to be manipulated. Our crowd is about to say, "We've seen the last 6 years, and we like it, and we want an America that's coming together, not coming apart. We want an America that's committed to forward progress, not partisan fights, where politics is an instrument to advance people's lives, not to keep some people down to lift some up."

And I swear to you, what is right to do is what will work out best for America. We are moving into a world that is smaller and smaller and faster and faster. No one is smart enough to figure out how to solve every problem overnight. The only way we're going to survive and do well is if we never, ever, ever forget that we have to find a way for all of our partners on this little planet to win together.

That's what I tried to do with America. With all the successes I've had—I could stand up here and list all these statistics—the truth is, I have not yet succeeded in convincing the American people to vote—to vote—for reconciliation, for a common future, for a common home, for an end to Washington-centered destructive politics. And maybe it is the irony of this terribly painful moment, which I regret very much putting you all through, that we are being given yet one more chance to affirm our better selves. But I'm telling you, based on my experience, the right thing to do is the right thing to do.

Thank you, and God bless you.

NOTE: The President spoke at 10:17 p.m. at a private residence. In his remarks, he referred to dinner hosts Ronald and Beth Dozoretz; Steve Grossman, national chair, Democratic National Committee; President Fernando Henrique Cardoso of Brazil; President Slobodan Milosevic of the Federal Republic of Yugoslavia (Serbia and Montenegro); and Chairman Yasser Arafat of the Palestinian Authority. H.R. 6, the Higher Education Amendments of 1998, approved October 7, was assigned Public Law No. 105–244.

Message to the House of Representatives Returning Without Approval Agriculture Appropriations Legislation
October 7, 1998

To the House of Representatives:

I am returning herewith without my approval, H.R. 4101, the "Agriculture, Rural Development, Food and Drug Administration, and Related Agencies Appropriations Act, 1999." I am vetoing this bill because it fails to address adequately the crisis now gripping our Nation's farm community.

I firmly believe and have stated often that the Federal Government must play an important role in strengthening the farm safety net. This appropriations bill provides an opportunity each year for the Government to take steps to help hardworking farmers achieve a decent living, despite the misfortune of bad weather, crop disease, collapsing markets, or other forces that affect their livelihoods. It is especially necessary for the Government to act this year, with prices dropping precipitously, crops destroyed by flood, drought, and disease, and where many farmers will see their net income drop by as much as 40 percent below a 5-year average.

Two years ago, when I signed the "Freedom to Farm Bill," I made clear that it did not provide an adequate safety net for our Nation's farmers. There is no better proof of that bill's shortcomings than the hardship in America's farm country this year. Our farm families are facing their worst crisis in a decade.

My Administration has already taken steps to address this crisis. In July, we announced the purchase of $250 million of wheat to export to hungry people around the world. In August, I signed legislation to speed up farm program payments. But in the face of a growing emergency for our Nation's farmers, we must do more to ensure that American farmers can continue to provide, for years to come, the safest and least expensive food in the world. Last month, I sent to the Congress a request for $2.3 billion in emergency aid for our farmers, and I supported Senator Daschle's and Harkin's proposal to boost farm income by lifting the cap on marketing loan rates.

I am extremely disappointed that the Congress has reacted to this agriculture emergency situation by sending me a bill that fails to provide an adequate safety net for our farmers.

I have repeatedly stated that I would veto any emergency farm assistance bill if it did not adequately address our farmers' immediate needs, and this bill does not do enough.

The lack of sufficient emergency aid for farmers in this bill is particularly problematic in light of the bill's other provisions that affect farmers and their rural communities. Cutting edge agricultural research is absolutely essential to improve our farmers' productivity and to maintain their advantage over our competitors around the world. But this bill eliminates the $120 million in competitive research grants for this year that I strongly supported and signed into law just last June. It also blocks the $60 million from the Fund for Rural America provided through that same bill, preventing needed additional rural development funds that would help our Nation's rural communities to diversify their economies and improve their quality of life. The bill also cuts spending for our food safety initiative in half, denying funds for research, public education, and other food safety improvements.

Many of our most vulnerable farmers have also had to face an obstacle that no one in America ever should have to confront: racial discrimination. Over 1,000 minority farmers have filed claims of discrimination by USDA's farm loan programs in the 1980s and early 1990s that the statute of limitations bars from being addressed. While I am pleased that this legislation contains a provision waiving the statute of limitations, I am disappointed that it does not contain the language included in the Senate's version of this bill, which accelerates the resolution of the cases, provides claimants with a fair and full court review if they so choose, and covers claims stemming from USDA's housing loan programs.

Therefore, as I return this bill, I again call on the Congress to send me a comprehensive plan, before this session ends, that adequately responds to the very real needs of our farmers at this difficult time.

WILLIAM J. CLINTON

The White House,
October 7, 1998.

NOTE: This message was released by the Office of the Press Secretary on October 8.

Remarks on the Decision of Certain Health Maintenance Organizations To Opt Out of Some Medicare Markets
October 8, 1998

Thank you. I would like to begin by thanking Senator Rockefeller and Congressman Dingell for their steadfast support of Medicare and their participation in our Medicare Commission. Let me say just in advance, I would think that the very issue we discuss today offers further evidence that it is time to take a look at the challenges and the responsibilities of the Medicare program, long-term, and I'm glad we have Jay Rockefeller and John Dingell on that commission.

I'd like to thank Senator Kennedy and Senator Lieberman and Congressman Stark and Congressman Cardin also for being here today. I'd like to thank Secretary Shalala for her marvelous service, and Nancy-Ann Min DeParle who is here with her. I'd like to thank all the members of the seniors groups who are representing their constituents, standing to my right here. I thank them for joining us today.

Kosovo

Since this is the only time I'll have to talk to the press for the next several hours, I hope you will indulge me for a moment while I make a few comments about the present situation in Kosovo.

As a result of the unconscionable actions of President Milosevic, we face the danger of violence spreading to neighboring countries, threatening a wider war in Europe. We face a humanitarian crisis that could be a catastrophe in the making, as tens of thousands of homeless refugees risk freezing or starving to death as winter comes on.

Our goal is simple: It is full compliance with United Nations Security Council resolutions by President Milosevic. My Special Envoy, Richard Holbrooke, has just completed 3 days of talks with Mr. Milosevic, making absolutely clear that he must meet the demands of this Security Council resolution, end the violence, withdraw his forces, let the refugees return to their homes, give the humanitarian relief workers full and free access to the people who need them, and begin negotiations with the Kosovar Albanians on autonomy for their region, which is provided for under the law of their nation.

Yesterday I decided that the United States would vote to give NATO the authority to carry out military strikes against Serbia if President Milosevic continues to defy the international community. In the days ahead, my counterparts in Europe will be making similar decisions. We would prefer—we would far prefer—to secure President Milosevic's compliance with the will of the international community in a peaceful manner. But NATO must be prepared to act militarily to protect our interests, to prevent another humanitarian catastrophe in the Balkans.

HMO's and Medicare

Now, let me echo, first of all, the sentiments which have already been expressed here. Since John Dingell was in the chair when Medicare was passed, it has been more than a program; it has been a symbol of our intergenerational unity as a country, fulfilling our responsibilities to our grandparents and parents, protecting our families. Strengthening Medicare has been one of this administration's top priorities. Last year we took historic bipartisan action to improve benefits and extend the life of the Trust Fund for a decade. We expanded the number and types of health plans available to Medicare beneficiaries so that older Americans, like other Americans, would have more choices in their Medicare.

I think it ought to be said in defense of this decision and the enrollment of many seniors in managed care plans that one of the principal reasons that so many seniors wanted it is that there were managed care plans who thought, for the reimbursement then available, they could provide not only the required services under Medicare but also a prescription drug benefit, something that these Members and I tried to get done for all the seniors of the country at an earlier point in time.

Well, today there are 6½ million Medicare beneficiaries in HMO's. As we all know, in recent weeks the HMO industry announced that unless all Medicare HMO's could raise premiums and reduce benefits—all—some health plans would drop their Medicare patients by the end of the year.

We told them, no deal. That's what we should have done. We were not going to allow Medicare to be held hostage to unreasonable demands. So several HMO's decided to drop their patients. These decisions have brought uncertainty, fear, and disruption into the lives of tens of thousands of older Americans across the country. While the overwhelming majority of seniors affected will be able to join another HMO covering Medicare in their area, 50,000 of them will be left without a single managed care alternative.

Now, these HMO's say they are looking after the bottom line. All of you who understand the Medicare program know that the reimbursement rates are different across regions and in different areas. We have tried very hard to alleviate that, the problems with that system. And we recognize that there were problems. We have worked to alleviate them. But that wasn't what we were asked to do. We were asked just to give all HMO's permission to raise rates whether they needed to or not, without regard to how much money they were making or not. And I think that was wrong.

We have to do everything we can to protect Americans who have been dropped by their HMO's and to protect the health care options of all seniors in the future. So today we're taking three steps.

First, we'll do everything we can to encourage HMO's to enter the markets abandoned by managed care. Beginning immediately, the Health Care Financing Administration will give first priority in its review and approval process—first priority—to all new HMO's applying to serve seniors in deserted areas.

Second, I am asking Secretary Shalala to work with Congress, aging advocates, and health plans to develop new strategies to prevent another disruption in coverage like the one we are seeing now. I'm asking the Secretary to consider all possible legislative options that can be included in the next budget I send to Congress.

Finally, I am launching a comprehensive public information campaign to make sure all affected seniors understand the health coverage plans that are already available to them. We'll bring together a broad public and private coalition, from the AARP to the Older Women's League to the Social Security Administration to local offices on aging, to educate seniors about all their rights and options. We must say to them, losing HMO coverage does not mean losing Medicare coverage. You are still protected by Medicare. You are still eligible for the traditional fee-for-service program and for Medigap policies.

Let me just say one other thing. In the last few days before it adjourns, let me ask Congress again to put aside partisanship and embrace our common responsibilities by reauthorizing the Older Americans Act. For years, this law has improved the lives of millions of our senior citizens, providing everything from Meals on Wheels to counseling to legal services. Every day that goes by without passing the bipartisan legislation to reauthorize the act sends a troubling message to seniors that their needs are not a priority.

More than 30 years ago, Congress was able to put progress before partisanship when it created Medicare in the first place. As a result, millions of older Americans have been able to live healthier, happier, more stable lives. It is one of the signal achievements of this century.

So let me say again, we have to do that again—to work to strengthen Medicare, to reauthorize the Older Americans Act, to treat each other in the work of America as we want people out in America to treat each other and to work. The Members who are here have certainly done that. And for that, I am grateful.

Secretary Shalala and I hope very much that these steps we are taking today and the work we will do with these senior advocates will provide some peace of mind, some support, and some help to the seniors who have been so shaken by the events of the last few days here.

Thank you very much. Thank you.

I want to say one other thing. Senator Dodd came in late, but has actually offered legislation in this area, so I want to give him credit for that. Connecticut is the only State here with 100 percent representation. [*Laughter*] Thank you very much.

NOTE: The President spoke at 11:49 a.m. in the Roosevelt Room at the White House. In his remarks, he referred to President Slobodan Milosevic of the Federal Republic of Yugoslavia (Serbia and Montenegro).

Remarks on the Impeachment Inquiry Vote and an Exchange With Reporters
October 8, 1998

The President. We are about to start a meeting with the economic and budget team about the unfinished work in the budget that has to be done in the next few days. But before we start I'd like to make just a very brief comment on today's vote.

First of all, I hope that we can now move forward with this process in a way that is fair, that is constitutional, and that is timely. The American people have been through a lot on this, and I think that everyone deserves that. Beyond that, I have nothing to say. It is not in my hands; it is in the hands of Congress and the people of this country, ultimately in the hands of God. There is nothing I can do.

But there are things I can do something about. And the most important thing I can do now is to work in the next few days to work to cross party lines to do the work that we have to do here. We have got to pass a budget that protects the surplus and still to save Social Security, that keeps the American economy going amidst all this economic turmoil in the world, that protects, instead of damages, the environment, and that gives the kind of priority to our elementary and secondary education that it so clearly needs.

Those are my priorities. I think those are the priorities of the American people. It will require us to put progress ahead of partisanship, but it clearly will strengthen our country. And that's what we're going to work on, and I hope we can do it.

Q. Sir, you could speed the pace of this up if you were to volunteer to testify, decide whether or not now you would challenge Monica Lewinsky's account of your relationship. Have you made any decisions on that front?

The President. Let me say again, on that I will do what I can to help to ensure this is constitutional, fair, and timely. Ultimately, it is in the hands of the Congress. I don't think it's appropriate to comment further than that.

International Financial Situation

Q. Mr. President, what's your reaction to the Republican demands on the IMF funding bill, and how closely are you watching the decline of the dollar against the yen?

The President. Well, we're watching that very closely. Of course, the strengthening of the yen could be a good thing. The yen got too weak, and it led, for example, to breathtaking increases in imports of Japanese steel, which hurt a lot of our people, our industry, and our workers who were clearly competitive internationally. And if the Japanese yen were to come back because people believed Japan was serious about economic reform, then it would be a good thing. It would be a balancing of forces in the world economy. It would strengthen the American economy by strengthening our own domestic manufacturing sector and making our exports more competitive. It would make it possible for Japan to buy other countries' exports in Asia.

If it's a temporary phenomenon that evidences some sort of instability, then that's something we just have to try to sort out. But I don't think we can know for sure yet. The clear answer over the long run is for America to fund our responsibilities to the IMF, for Japan to get serious about its economic reform, for the Europeans to keep their markets open and continue growth, so that all of us can get more money back into the global economic system right now and then deal with the long-term problem. That's what I hope. I think it's very important not to be diverted by day-to-day developments here and think about what the larger problem is.

International Consultations/Impeachment Inquiry Vote

Q. Mr. President, have you talked to other world leaders today? And how are you feeling personally about the vote?

The President. Today I spoke with President Chirac of France. And I am meeting tomorrow with the man who will be the next German Chancellor, Mr. Schroeder. And we talked about Kosovo. And I have been working, as you know, all week long with people from all over the world on the international financial crisis.

Personally, I am fine. I have surrendered this. This is beyond my control. I have to work on what I can do. What I can do is to do my job for the American people. I trust the American people. They almost always get it right and have for 220 years. And I'm working in a way that I hope will restore their trust in me by working for the things that our country needs. These things we're going to discuss at this budget meeting, that's what I can have some impact on, and that's what I intend to do.

NOTE: The President spoke at 5 p.m. in the Cabinet Room at the White House. In his remarks, he referred to President Jacques Chirac of France and Chancellor-elect Gerhard Schroeder of Germany. A tape was not available for verification of the content of these remarks.

Statement on Senate Action on Internet Tax Freedom Legislation
October 8, 1998

I am pleased that the Senate has joined the House in passing the "Internet Tax Freedom Act." This bill will create a short-term moratorium on new and discriminatory taxes that would slow down the growth of the Internet and launch a search for long-term solutions to the tax issues raised by electronic commerce. As I said earlier this year in my speech on Internet policy, we cannot allow 30,000 State and local tax jurisdictions to stifle the Internet, nor can we allow the erosion of the revenue that State and local governments need to fight crime and invest in education. I look forward to signing this legislation into law so that America can continue to lead the world in the information age.

Letter to Senate Majority Leader Trent Lott Urging Reauthorization of the Older Americans Act
October 8, 1998

Dear Senator Lott:

I am writing to urge you to pass legislation to reauthorize the Older Americans Act (OAA) before the Congress adjourns this year. Failure to do so will call into question our nation's commitment to the Act and the vital services it provides to millions of older Americans. Legislation to reauthorize the OAA has gained an impressive degree of bipartisan support. In fact, the legislation proposed by Senator McCain and Senator Mikulski is cosponsored by more than 60 Senators.

The OAA is receiving broad support because it has played such an important role in responding to the diverse needs of our nation's seniors.

It provides more than 100 million meals to nearly one million vulnerable seniors each year through its meals-on-wheels program; it finances and supports an ombudsman program that helps resolve tens of thousands of problems, including abuse and neglect, affecting nursing home residents and other vulnerable populations; it provides job training for seniors who need or want to work; and, in many communities, it provides the type of adult day care that gives families a much needed respite from caregiving responsibilities.

These programs are essential to ensuring that our nation's seniors can maintain their independence. Sometimes a few basic services or programs, such as adult day care or adequate nutrition, are all that is necessary to allow seniors with limited resources to continue living in their homes and communities. Without the OAA, too many older Americans would have no choice but to turn to long-term care facilities to get the help they need. This harms those who would like to remain in their communities, significantly draining our nation's limited resources.

No political party gains—and all Americans lose—when we fail to work together to pass a bipartisan reauthorization of the OAA. I am committed to working with you to reauthorize this critically important legislation.

Sincerely,

WILLIAM J. CLINTON

NOTE: An original was not available for verification of the content of this letter.

Letter to House Speaker Newt Gingrich Urging Reauthorization of the Older Americans Act
October 8, 1998

Dear Mr. Speaker:

I am writing to urge you to pass legislation to reauthorize the Older Americans Act (OAA) before the Congress adjourns this year. Failure to do so will call into question our nation's commitment to the Act and the vital services it provides to millions of older Americans.

Legislation to reauthorize the OAA has gained an impressive degree of bipartisan support. In fact, the legislation introduced by Representative LoBiondo and Representative DeFazio has been cosponsored by more than 170 House Members.

The OAA is receiving broad support because it has played such an important role in responding to the diverse needs of our nation's seniors. It provides more than 100 million meals to nearly one million vulnerable seniors each year through its meals-on-wheels program; it finances and supports an ombudsman program that helps resolve tens of thousands of problems, including abuse and neglect, affecting nursing home residents and other vulnerable populations; it provides job training for seniors who need or want to work; and, in many communities, it provides the type of adult day care that gives families a much needed respite from caregiving responsibilities.

These programs are essential to ensuring that our nation's seniors can maintain their independence. Sometimes a few basic services or programs, such as adult day care or adequate nutrition, are all that is necessary to allow seniors with limited resources to continue living in their homes and communities. Without the OAA, too many older Americans would have no choice but to turn to long-term care facilities to get the help they need. This harms those who would like to remain in their communities, significantly draining our nation's limited resources.

No political party gains—and all Americans lose—when we fail to work together to pass a bipartisan reauthorization of the OAA. I am committed to working with you to reauthorize this critically important legislation.

Sincerely,

WILLIAM J. CLINTON

NOTE: An original was not available for verification of the content of this letter.

Message to the Congress Reporting on Telecommunications Services Payments to Cuba
October 8, 1998

To the Congress of the United States:

This report is submitted pursuant to 1705(e)(6) of the Cuban Democracy Act of 1992, 22 U.S.C. 6004(e)(6) (the "CDA"), as amended by section 102(g) of the Cuban Liberty and Democratic Solidarity (LIBERTAD) Act of 1996, Public Law 104–114 (March 12, 1996), 110 Stat. 785, 22 U.S.C. 6021–91 (the "LIBERTAD Act"), which requires that I report to the Congress on a semi-annual basis detailing payments made to Cuba by any United States person as a result of the provision of telecommunications services authorized by this subsection.

The CDA, which provides that telecommunications services are permitted between the United States and Cuba, specifically authorizes the President to provide for payments to Cuba by license. The CDA states that licenses may be issued for full or partial settlement of telecommunications services with Cuba, but may not require any withdrawal from a blocked account. Following enactment of the CDA on October 23, 1992, a number of U.S. telecommunications companies successfully negotiated agreements to provide telecommunications services between the United States and Cuba consistent with policy guidelines developed by the Department of State and the Federal Communications Commission.

Subsequent to enactment of the CDA, the Department of the Treasury's Office of Foreign Assets Control (OFAC) amended the Cuban Assets Control Regulations, 31 C.F.R. Part 515 (the "CACR"), to provide for specific licensing on a case-by-case basis for certain transactions incident to the receipt or transmission of telecommunications between the United States and Cuba, 31 C.F.R. 515.542(c), including settlement of charges under traffic agreements.

The OFAC has issued eight licenses authorizing transactions incident to the receipt or transmission of telecommunications between the United States and Cuba since the enactment of the CDA. None of these licenses permits payments to the Government of Cuba from a blocked account. For the period January 1 through June 30, 1998, OFAC-licensed U.S. carriers reported payments to the Government of Cuba in settlement of charges under telecommunications traffic agreements as follows:

AT&T Corporation (formerly, American Telephone and Telegraph Company)	$12,795,658
AT&T de Puerto Rico	292,229
Global One (formerly, Sprint Incorporated)	3,075,733
IDB WorldCom Services, Inc. (formerly, IDB Communications, Inc.)	4,402,634
MCI International, Inc. (formerly, MCI Communications Corporation)	8,468,743
Telefonica Larga Distancia de Puerto Rico, Inc	129,752
WilTel, Inc. (formerly, WilTel Underseas Cable, Inc.)	4,983,368
WorldCom, Inc. (formerly, LDDS Communications, Inc.)	5,371,531
Total	39,519,648

I shall continue to report semiannually on telecommunications payments to the Government of Cuba from United States persons.

WILLIAM J. CLINTON

The White House,

October 8, 1998.

NOTE: This message was released by the Office of the Press Secretary on October 9.

Remarks Honoring the National Association of Police Organizations' Top Cops
October 9, 1998

Tom, I accept the deal. [*Laughter*] Thank you for your work, on behalf of the law enforcement officers of our country. I want to thank Bob Scully as well, the executive director of NAPO. Thank you, Madam Attorney General, for all the support you have given to local law enforcement for 6 years now. I want to thank the Top Cops, their families, and their friends who are here. And I'd like to thank the Members of Congress who are here, supporters of law enforcement all: Senator Robb, Congresswoman Harman, Congresswoman McCarthy, Congressman Rogan, and Congressman Torres, who's here with some of his family. We're delighted to see all of you.

I'd like to say a special word of appreciation to those of you who brought your families and the children here as a clear reminder to us of what we've really come to honor today.

This July, just a mile from here in the Capitol Rotunda, I had the sad responsibility as President to honor the courage and the sacrifice of the two officers, J.J. Chestnut and Detective John Gibson, who were killed because they literally threw themselves between an assassin's bullets and innocent bystanders. They gave their lives to defend our freedom's house.

The men and women we honor here today put on their badges every day, prepared to make the same kind of sacrifice in their own communities. They are true American heroes. They have done astonishing acts of humanity and heroism, from crossing the line of fire to rescue wounded fellow officers to confronting criminals armed with assault weapons and body armor, to nursing a seriously injured neighbor back to health, to breaking in on a person with a bomb that was partially activated and—thank God—did not go up and blow them all away. And one of these officers, shot four times himself, including twice—once in the neck and once in the head, maintained his consciousness enough to save the life of a cab driver when the person who shot him had a gun at his head.

These stories of all these people are literally breathtaking. I hope that the members of the media who are here today who are covering this will find the time to read the specific cases of those whom we honor today and tell their stories across America. The story of the brave officer from New Hampshire who dealt with that terrible tragedy and the story of the officers from north Hollywood, because of the volume of fire that was involved in their incident, have been told beyond the borders of their States. But all these stories deserve to be told, and I hope they will be, because we honor here today, as I say again, both the heroism and the humanity that reflect the best of good, professional law enforcement.

We owe a great debt of gratitude to our Nation's police officers. And for 6 years we have worked, as Tom said and as the Attorney General noted, to give our law enforcement officers the tools they need to succeed at their jobs. We have worked to take back our streets from crime and violence with a comprehensive plan based on what law enforcement said we should be doing: new penalties on our books that were tough when they should be tough; efforts to help keep young people out of trouble in the first place; efforts to keep guns out of the hands of criminals; and most of all, efforts to put 100,000 more police on our streets.

Six years ago there were many Americans who believed that a rising crime rate was a problem that would be with us always. Today, because of efforts like those whom we honor, we have the lowest level of crime in 25 years. Respect for the law is on the rise. Our Nation's law enforcement officers are at the very center of this effort. They are cracking down on gun traffickers. They are working to keep guns out of the hands of criminals. They are working with local school authorities to keep our schools safe and drug-free. They are walking the beat and working with residents to prevent crime and to keep kids out of trouble in the first place.

But as all of them know, and as all of you know, this is not a problem we can afford to just congratulate ourselves on. Our country is still too violent. We still lose too many children. We still lose too many police officers. We have to take some more steps. And today I'd like to just mention a couple.

First, as Tom said so eloquently, all the cynics and the critics were wrong. These police are making a difference in our communities. We are well on our way; we're under a budget and ahead of schedule in our efforts to put 100,000 police on the street. Today we are awarding $30 million in new grant money to help communities hire more police. This will bring the total of police officers funded by the crime bill in 1994 and subsequent appropriations to more than 88,000. We are literally almost 90 percent of the way toward meeting our goal.

Second, we know what a difference the Brady background checks have made to keep illegal guns off our streets. I am pleased to say that we will give States $40 million to help them computerize the criminal history records they use to do those background checks, a simple procedure that has already stopped a quarter of a million fugitives and felons from purchasing guns, and saves who knows how many lives. These steps will help us to give law enforcement the tools they need.

Last night Congress passed a bill by a large bipartisan margin that will build on our progress, a bill I'll sign into law later today. It will provide States with more than a billion dollars over the next 5 years to modernize not only their criminal records systems but also to upgrade their communications and criminal identification systems. It will include legislation I proposed last year at the White House Conference on Child Care the First Lady and I sponsored, to help us build a new electronic information sharing partnership with State and local law enforcement to keep our child care and our elder care systems safe. I am pleased that Congress has taken this step to give law enforcement more tools to make a greater difference.

At the same time, I have to tell you there is one thing going on in Congress that I am very, very concerned about, an effort to undermine the very Brady law protections that have helped to make our streets and our police safer. The legislation would deny the FBI the full funds it needs to do the most effective background checks possible and would also impose undue administrative burdens on the FBI, threatening to bring this vitally important system to a halt. When we stood with America's police officers to pass the Brady law, it was a dramatic step forward. We cannot take an unacceptable step backward.

This law is working. And all the fears that were raised about it by people who said good sportsmen would lose their guns and people would be subject to unconscionable hassles, it all turned out to be a bunch of bull. All it has done is save lives. Why are we trying to mess with something that works, that saves lives, that makes law enforcement safer, that makes people safer? It is a terrible mistake. And I ask you all to help me stop it.

Now, this amendment was first proposed last summer, and I said then I would oppose it. So I will say again: I intend to oppose any effort to weaken the Brady law and to put guns back into the hands of felons and fugitives. We're going in the right direction. Let's don't make that mistake again.

Think of the stories here today. Every one of you out here represents or came with somebody who is up here today. Now, you just think about how many stories there would be like the ones we're celebrating today—and we're sitting here thanking the good Lord that at least these people are alive—you think how many more stories there would be, not only to honor but to mourn, if we were to turn our back on what we've been doing for the last 6 years.

So I say again, the Congress has made a lot of progress. It has increasingly been bipartisan on this law enforcement issue. Let's not take a step backward.

Now, before I close, let me once again thank the Top Cops for their remarkable achievements. And again let me say, I want to thank all of you who are members of their families. In so many ways, you make these achievements possible. You share the sacrifice, and you share the fear, and sometimes you have to share the loss. We know that. Therefore, you have to provide your own special brand of courage, and for that we are also profoundly grateful.

We honor all of you, your strength and your spirit, and from the bottom of our hearts, we thank you for what you have done to make America a better place.

Thank you very much, and God bless you.

NOTE: The President spoke at 10:57 a.m. in the Rose Garden at the White House. In his remarks, he referred to Thomas J. Scotto, president, and Robert T. Scully, executive director, National Association of Police Organizations.

Exchange With Reporters Prior to Discussions With Chancellor-Elect Gerhard Schroeder of Germany
October 9, 1998

Kosovo

Q. Mr. President, the Serbs are threatening to retaliate against aid workers if NATO uses force. Any second thoughts, sir?

President Clinton. I think they would regret that very much if they did it. I think they know better than to do that.

Q. What do you expect from the German side?

President Clinton. Perhaps the Chancellor-elect would like to make a statement about that.

Impeachment Inquiry

Q. Mr. President, is there anything you can do to speed up the impeachment inquiry on the Hill by agreeing not to challenge everything in the Starr report?

President Clinton. I don't have anything to add to what I said yesterday.

Q. Mr. President, have you had time——

Q. Are you in agreement on Kosovo?

Q. ——promises continuity. What do you expect——

President Clinton. He has something to say.

Kosovo

[*At this point, a question was asked and answered in German, and a translation was not provided.*]

President Clinton. Will somebody translate for the American press? I understood it, but I don't—[*laughter*].

Q. Well, then, you translate, sir.

Q. [*Inaudible*]—work on Kosovo?

President Clinton. Excuse me?

Q. Did you also agree with Mr. Fischer about Kosovo?

President Clinton. I don't know, I just——

Chancellor-Elect Schroeder. It's enough to agree with me.

President Clinton. That's right. [*Laughter*] I think—let me say—we had obviously spoken about Kosovo and that—we had agreed about the next steps to be taken, and you started to have them Monday in Germany. Is that right?

Chancellor-Elect Schroeder. Yes.

President Clinton. In other words, we believe the next step is that the NATO Allies must

approve the action order, and what Herr Schroeder said was he expected that to happen on Monday. And he has talked with Chancellor Kohl; they talk back and forth together about this.

Germany-U.S. Relations

Q. What would you say about the prospects of German-American relations with the new government?

President Clinton. Oh, I feel very good about it. The United States and Germany have had a unique and profoundly important relationship for decades, and I believe it will continue to be very strong. I am very—personally, very excited about a lot of the ideas that Mr. Schroeder advanced in the campaign, things that he wanted to try in Germany. They bear some similarity to some of the things that I have tried to do here, that Prime Minister Blair has tried to do in Great Britain.

I think we are all trying to adapt our countries to this global economy, a global society, to reap the benefits of it, but to keep a human face on it, to make sure that this world we're living in really works for ordinary citizens more effectively. And no one has all the magic answers, but I'm confident that we need bold experimentation. We need to be trying new things. And I hope we can work together on those things. I'm quite excited about the prospect of doing so.

Q. No worries about the Greens?

President Clinton. I have enough to do to worry about getting America to do what we need to do here. That's Germany's issue.

Chancellor-Elect Schroeder. That's my problem. [*Laughter*]

Kosovo

Q. Mr. President, what happens if the Germans do not pledge troops for Kosovo?

President Clinton. Excuse me?

Q. What would happen if the Germans would not pledge troops—ground troops or air troops from our contingent for NATO action on Kosovo?

President Clinton. Well, let me say, first of all—and it's important that all of you—there are two separate issues here, as I understand it, and if I make a mistake, Herr Schroeder can correct me. The first issue is whether Germany will support NATO issuing the action order to make sure that the plans are in place and authorized if military action should be needed. That is what he has said yes to today.

We all hope this will not happen. The President of Russia sent three high-ranking officials of his government to Mr. Milosevic, and he made a lot of specific commitments to honor the U.N. resolution. Those commitments are not being kept today. He can still keep the commitments that he made to President Yeltsin and keep the commitments inherent in the U.N. resolution, and none of this will happen. But I am convinced that it's important that we authorize NATO to act. So that's where the agreement is.

Now, as I understand it, the German Constitution requires the Bundestag to approve any out-of-Germany military action, and that is something that will have to await the Chancellor assuming office later this month, and then we will see. I don't think it's appropriate for me to comment on that. It's enough for me right now that we are in agreement on the action order. That's all that matters today.

And I think we—in fairness to him, he's putting together his government. He's working out the understandings of the coalition. He's preparing to assume office. He has to make a wide range of decisions about new domestic policies. I've been exactly where he is, and I don't think we ought to add to his burdens today.

Thank you.

NOTE: The exchange began at 12:30 p.m. in the Colonnade at the White House. In his remarks, he referred to Chancellor Helmut Kohl of Germany; Prime Minister Tony Blair of the United Kingdom; President Boris Yeltsin of Russia; and President Slobodan Milosevic of the Federal Republic of Yugoslavia (Serbia and Montenegro). A tape was not available for verification of the content of this exchange.

Remarks on Education Legislation
October 9, 1998

Let me begin my thanking Senator Daschle and Congressman Gephardt and all their colleagues who are here for their leadership and their commitment on the issue of education. Let me also ask you to listen to what they said. We are less than 4 weeks away from an election. All public officials would like to go home, but they said that they and their colleagues would put the American people before their political interests and would put progress before partisanship and would stay here until we finally address the issue of our children's education.

We had over 50 Members of Congress here just a few days ago to ask the Republican leadership to give us just one day, one day to pass a budget that honors our values and cares for our children's future in the area of education.

We have the first balanced budget in 29 years. Our economy is prosperous amid global turmoil. We have the confidence that we can solve our problems, and the space—the emotional and the intellectual space—to think about our future. Now, this budget is purely and simply a test of whether after 9 months of doing nothing, we are going to do the right thing about our children's future. Members of Congress should not go home until they pass a budget that will strengthen our public schools for the 21st century.

I am determined that this budget will make a strong downpayment on our drive to hire 100,000 new highly qualified teachers, to reduce class size in the early grades. Today there are a record number of children in our schools, and studies confirm what everyone knows: smaller classes and better trained teachers make all the difference. We have a duty to provide them.

Smaller classes and more teachers—well, you've got to have some place for the class to meet. All across America, children are being forced to learn in school buildings that are either too crowded or even crumbling or are not wired for the 21st century. I have asked the Republican majority repeatedly to act on an innovative plan to help communities modernize or build 5,000 schools. We can do this without a big new spending program; I thought they would like that. We can do it with targeted tax cuts, tax cuts that are paid for in the balanced budget that do not spend any of the surplus. I can't think of a better tax cut for our country's future than one that gives our children a modern, safe, adequately equipped place to learn.

This balanced budget should also meet our other educational priorities. It should fully fund the after-school programs to bring discipline and learning into the lives of our young people and to give them a change to keep on learning and not be branded failures because they may be in a system that is failing them. It should bring cutting-edge technology to the classroom. We ought to hook up all the classes of this country to the Internet by the year 2000. It should expand Head Start. It should provide funding for the childhood literacy programs so that every child can learn to read well and independently by the third grade. It should support our new monitoring drive to encourage young people to go to college. And finally, I believe it should move forward with voluntary national standards and voluntary national tests in the basics, administered by a bipartisan group.

We should not retreat from our commitments to our children's future. Unfortunately, that commitment was not reflected when the education bill was finally—finally—brought to the House floor yesterday, 8 days into the new budget year. It met none of these challenges. I have instructed my budget team to return to Capitol Hill to make the strongest possible case for the educational priorities that all of us standing here before you today share.

Now, what has happened in this Congress? What is the record to date of the majority? They have killed the bill to reform the way we treat tobacco and to protect our children from the dangers of tobacco. They killed campaign finance reform. They killed the minimum wage. Today, as Senator Daschle said, the Senate joined the House in putting an end to the Patients' Bill of Rights; that means no guarantees that people will go to the nearest emergency room when they're hurt, that they can see a specialist when they need to, that they won't lose their coverage in the middle of treatment, that their records will be kept private. They have tried to erode my commitment to saving Social Security first in the House of Representatives.

But still it is not too late for us to go forward together on our children's future. Politics should stop at the classroom door. It is not too late.

We are here not simply to state our strong conviction and our willingness—the willingness of these people who have to run—to defer their campaigns to take care of our children's future but to invite our Republican colleagues to join us and finally try to salvage some shred of positive accomplishment for the American people. I hope they'll do it. There is still time.

Thank you very much.

NOTE: The President spoke at 3:41 p.m. at the South Portico at the White House, following a meeting with congressional leaders.

Statement on Senate Action on Legislation To Promote International Religious Freedom
October 9, 1998

I welcome today's strong bipartisan Senate passage, and the anticipated passage in the House of Representatives, of the "International Religious Freedom Act of 1998."

I have made the promotion of religious freedom a priority of my Presidency and an integral part of our foreign policy through, among other efforts, the creation of the Advisory Committee on Religious Freedom Abroad and my appointment last June of our special representative on international religious freedom.

The "International Religious Freedom Act of 1998" is a welcome and responsible addition to our ongoing efforts. Its principled, measured approach rightly emphasizes effective remedies over broad, symbolic gestures.

I also wish to applaud the bipartisan, cooperative approach that helped achieve this legislation, in particular the leadership of Senators

Nickles, Lieberman, Hagel, Biden, Feinstein, and Specter and Representative Clement. I'd also like to pay tribute at this time to Representative Frank Wolf, whose longstanding and devoted advocacy for this issue has been an inspiration to those of us so determined to promote religious freedom abroad.

This legislation is not directed against any one country or religious faith. Indeed, this act will serve to promote the religious freedom of people of all backgrounds, whether Muslim, Christian, Jewish, Buddhist, Hindu, Taoist, or any other faith. I look forward to signing this act.

The President's Radio Address
October 10, 1998

Good morning. In the next few days, as it completes its work on the budget, Congress has the opportunity and the obligation to make enormous progress to renew and strengthen our schools. There is no more critical task before it.

Ten days ago we closed the books on our fiscal year, yet Congress still has not opened the books for the new fiscal year at hand. Last night, for the second time in 2 weeks, I signed stopgap legislation to keep our Government running. But I can't keep granting extensions indefinitely.

This week, unfortunately, we saw partisanship defeat progress, as 51 Republican Senators joined together to kill the HMO Patients' Bill of Rights. Rest assured, I will ask the next Congress to guarantee your right to see a specialist, to receive the nearest emergency care, to keep your doctor throughout your course of treatment, to keep your medical records private, and have other basic health care rights. I hope next year we'll have a Congress that agrees.

But I do not want to see this Congress walk away from America's schoolchildren as it has walked away from America's patients. We should be able to make real, bipartisan progress on education. After all, we've got the first balanced budget and surplus in 29 years; our economy continues to create jobs and broaden prosperity, despite the economic turmoil abroad. We must use this moment of good fortune to make an historic investment in the quality of our public schools, and we've still got a few days to do it.

Our Nation needs 100,000 new, highly qualified teachers to reduce class size in the early grades. All the studies confirm what every parent already knows: smaller classes and better trained teachers make a big difference—better academic performance, fewer discipline problems, more individualized attention. Of course, basic math tells us that smaller classes plus more teachers demand more classrooms, especially since we already have a record number of children in our schools. All across America, children are being forced to learn in school buildings that are overcrowded or even crumbling, or in temporary housing trailers.

So again today, I call on Congress to help communities build or modernize 5,000 schools with targeted tax credits. I can't think of a better tax cut for our country's future than one that gives our children a modern, safe, adequately equipped place to learn. And these tax credits are fully paid for in the balanced budget.

The budget should also bring cutting-edge technology to the classroom, continuing our efforts to connect all classrooms and libraries to the Internet by 2000, and make sure that the teachers are trained to use such technology. It should fund innovative charter schools so that parents and teachers can bring the benefits of choice and competition to our public schools. It should fully fund after-school programs, so young people learn their lessons in the classroom, not the streets. It should expand Head Start for the early years and insist on high standards in the basics, providing for voluntary national testing with a nonpartisan system to measure progress. It should fund our child literacy programs so that every child will be able to read well and independently by the end of the third grade. It should help bring out-of-school youth back into a learning environment. And it should support our new mentoring initiative to reach out to young people and encourage them early to stay in school, learn their lessons, and go on to college.

Small classes, trained teachers, modern schools, high standards, public school choice, and more—this is a plan that can revolutionize education in America. But the Republican majority in Congress hasn't even passed the annual education investment bill yet. When it comes to education, Congress simply must not settle for an incomplete. I ask the Republicans in Congress to join the Democrats to put progress over partisanship, and send me a full education investment bill.

Remember, the budget Congress must now finalize will be the last complete budget of the 20th century. We cannot pass up this golden opportunity to invest wisely now to help all our children seize the promise of the century to come.

Thanks for listening.

NOTE: The President spoke at 10:06 a.m. from the Oval Office at the White House.

Statement on the Attack on Matthew Shepard
October 10, 1998

I was deeply grieved by the act of violence perpetrated against Matthew Shepard of Wyoming.

The Justice Department has assured me that local law enforcement officials are proceeding diligently to bring those responsible to justice. And I am determined that we will do everything we can and offer whatever assistance is appropriate.

Hillary and I ask that your thoughts and your prayers be with Mr. Shepard and his family, and with the people of Laramie, Wyoming. In the face of this terrible act of violence, they are joining together to demonstrate that an act of evil like this is not what our country is all about. In fact, it strikes at the very heart of what it means to be an American and at the values that define us as a nation. We must all reaffirm that we will not tolerate this.

Just this year there have been a number of recent tragedies across our country that involve hate crimes. The vicious murder of James Byrd last June in Jasper, Texas, and the assault this week on Mr. Shepard are only among the most horrifying examples.

Almost one year ago I proposed that Congress enact the "Hate Crimes Prevention Act." Our Federal laws already punish some crimes committed against people on the basis of race or religion or national origin, but we should do more. This crucial legislation would strengthen and expand the ability of the Justice Department to prosecute hate crimes by removing needless jurisdictional requirements for existing crimes and by giving Federal prosecutors the power to prosecute hate crimes committed because of the victim's sexual orientation, gender, or disability. All Americans deserve protection from hate.

There is nothing more important to the future of this country than our standing together against intolerance, prejudice, and violent bigotry. It is not too late for Congress to take action before they adjourn and pass the "Hate Crimes Prevention Act." By doing so, they will help make all Americans more safe and secure.

Statement on the Death of Clark M. Clifford
October 10, 1998

Hillary and I were saddened to learn of the death of Clark Clifford, an American statesman who helped shape half a century's struggle for freedom. From his first days by President Truman's side as a young naval aide, to his wise counsel to President Carter, he was someone upon whom Presidents could rely for judicious and effective advice. When his wisdom and experience were needed, which was often, he offered it with charm, grace, and a certain humility. As Secretary of Defense at a critical time under President Johnson, he helped to begin the search for peace in Vietnam. His legacy of public service is notable in our history. Our thoughts and prayers go to his wife, Marny, and their three daughters.

Statement on Congressional Action on Charter School Expansion Legislation
October 10, 1998

I am very pleased that the Congress has approved the "Charter School Expansion Act of 1998." This law will ensure that the charter schools movement will give parents and students more choices, better schools, and greater accountability for results. When I was elected President, there was only one charter school in the Nation. With help from the charter school initiative I proposed in 1993 and signed into law in 1994, there are now more than 1,000 charter schools serving more than 200,000 students across the Nation. This new measure is an important step toward reaching my goal of creating 3,000 high-quality public charter schools that will educate more than half a million students.

There is more to do to create the renaissance in public education our Nation needs and our students deserve. Congress must put progress ahead of partisanship and strengthen our public schools by enacting legislation that will help communities hire 100,000 well-trained teachers to reduce class size in the early grades, modernize or build 5,000 schools, strengthen early literacy programs, provide quality after-school programs, and put in place high national standards and tests in the basic skills of reading and math.

Remarks During Education Budget Negotiations and an Exchange With Reporters
October 11, 1998

The President. In only 447 days, the 21st century begins, a century in which the education of our Nation's children will matter more than ever before. Yet, far too many of our schools are not ready for that new century. We've all seen the news stories about teachers teaching classes in subjects they didn't major in in college, about schools so overcrowded they have trailers out back to handle the overflow, about classrooms with 35 or more students all vying for a minute of attention from the teachers, about schools so old they can't be connected to the Internet.

This can be changed, but we cannot afford to wait. And we are waiting for the Republican majority in Congress to bring this year's education investment bill to the floor. The delay must end. On education, Congress must choose progress over partisanship. We need a strong bipartisan bill.

Just a few days ago, I had the honor of signing into law such a bill to open the doors wider to higher education. And in just the last 2 days, Republicans and Democrats have worked together to pass strong charter school and vocational education measures. And I'd like to thank Senator Jeffords, Senator Kennedy, Senator Coats, Congressmen Goodling and Clay and Roemer for that. Now it's time once again for Congress to cross party lines and send me an education budget that I can sign that is worthy of our children and their future.

This bill must make the right investments in our children's future. It must include a strong downpayment on my request for 100,000 teachers for smaller classes in the early grades. It must invest in academically enriched after-school and summer school programs to keep kids in school and out of trouble. It must invest in modernized schools for our children; we cannot raise students up in buildings that are falling down. Any budget that does not do anything to help modernize our schools to give our children safe and clean places to learn does not fully prepare them for the 21st century.

Tomorrow night the funding to keep the Government open expires again. Senator Daschle, Congressman Gephardt, their Democratic colleagues, and I will work with the Republican majority to do the right thing for our country. We must pass a budget that is fiscally responsible, that honors our values, that invests in the education of our children. That is the most important thing we can do in this long-running Congress.

Q. Mr. President, the Republican leaders were saying this morning that if you were serious about reaching this budget deal, that you would stay in Washington instead of going on to fundraisers tomorrow and the following day.

The President. Well, let me first of all say that in the State of the Union in January, I sent a program to Congress to save the surplus until Social Security is fixed, to invest in education as I just described, to pass a Patients' Bill of Rights, to keep our economy going amidst all this economic turmoil in the world. In February I sent them a balanced budget with the same education program in it.

This is the first Congress in 24 years that did not pass a budget—in 24 years. Now they have turned their attention to this, and we are making progress. And I worked on it yesterday; I am prepared to do whatever it takes to work with them, now that they have turned their attention to this, to get the job done. But in the end, it is their votes. We are aggressively working with them to resolve this, but they have to decide that they will agree with us after this whole year that it is a priority, that we are going to do it, and that we're going to do it now.

Continuing Resolution Legislation

Q. Mr. President, will you sign another continuing resolution if Congress passes one? Dick Armey said today that he felt one was needed.

The President. You mean for a couple days?

Q. That's right.

The President. Well, sure, we're not going to shut the Government down if we're working on this, of course. No one is interested in doing that. I just want to get this job done.

Representative Richard A. Gephardt. Mr. President, can I add an answer? This Congress has been here probably less than most Congresses, but what I'm worried about is not when they're not here. What I'm worried about is when they are here. They've killed campaign reform; they've killed the tobacco bill; they've killed all the education legislation the President has sent; they killed Patients' Bill of Rights; they tried to spend the surplus on a tax cut, rather than saving it for Social Security.

They shouldn't be worried about whether the President is here or not. The President is here; the President sent the bills. I'm worried about what they do when they are here. They kill everything that the American people want. And that's what they've got to get to work on, to do the things people want done.

1998 Congressional Elections

Q. Mr. President, you characterize this as a do-nothing Congress. Do you think, with the results of the upcoming election, will it be a referendum on your Presidency? You're going to run against this Congress. Do you think the election results will be a referendum on your Presidency?

The President. Well, first of all, I'm not running. But what I do intend to do is to bring the issues to the American people. The American people will have to decide if they believe that Social Security should be saved before this surplus is spent for other things. The American people will have to decide whether they really want a Patients' Bill of Rights that guarantees people in HMO's the right to see a specialist or go to the nearest emergency room or have their medical records private or finish a treatment for chemotherapy or pregnancy before they can be forced to change doctors.

These are the kinds of decisions the American people have to make about what they want for their future. What I'd like to see is this election to be about the American people and their future, not about Washington, DC—just as I think this last year could have been and should have been about the people in America and not about Washington, DC. That is the decision before them, and I trust them. I think they'll make the right decision.

NOTE: The President spoke at 1 p.m. in the Cabinet Room at the White House. A tape was not available for verification of the content of these remarks.

Remarks on the Budget Negotiations
October 12, 1998

Good afternoon. While Columbus Day is a day off for many Americans, here at the White House we have been working hard with the leaders of both parties on Capitol Hill to write a budget to strengthen our Nation for the 21st Century.

I have just spoken with my Chief of Staff, Erskine Bowles. He and our budget team report that they are making progress on important issues, but there are still quite a number of issues still to be resolved; the most critical one, perhaps, is education. Eight months ago, in my State of the Union Address, I asked the Congress to help local communities reduce class size in the early grades by hiring 100,000 new teachers. I also asked Congress to help local communities to build or repair thousands of schools so we would have the classrooms for the teachers to teach in.

A recent study from Congress' own General Accounting Office concluded that as many as one-third of our classrooms are in need of serious modernization and repair. With a third of our children in substandard classrooms, our future is at risk. I believe we can reach across the political divisions here in Washington to take the steps we must to reduce class size, to hire more teachers, to modernize our classrooms. Smaller classes, more teachers, modern classrooms can do for our public schools what 100,000 new police officers are doing to keep our communities safer. This should not be a partisan issue.

I know there's an election coming, but Members of Congress can return home to campaign knowing that they put progress ahead of partisanship on the important issue of education. We need 21st century schools where teachers can teach and students can learn.

Death of Matthew Shepard

Let me also take a moment here to offer my prayers and my condolences to the family of Matthew Shepard, as well as to the community of Laramie, Wyoming, and the university. While it wouldn't be proper for me to comment on the specifics of this case, I do want to say again, crimes of hate and crimes of violence cannot be tolerated in our country. In our shock and grief, one thing must remain clear: Hate and prejudice are not American values. The public outrage in Laramie and all across America today echoes what we heard at the White House Conference on Hate Crimes last year. There is something we can do about this. Congress needs to pass our tough hate crimes legislation. It can do so even before it adjourns, and it should do so.

I hope that in the grief of this moment for Matthew Shepard's family, and in the shared outrage across America, Americans will once again search their hearts and do what they can to reduce their own fear and anxiety and anger at people who are different. And I hope that Congress will pass the hate crimes legislation.

Thank you.

NOTE: The President spoke at 3:02 p.m. on the South Lawn at the White House, prior to his departure for New York City.

Remarks at a Reception for Gubernatorial Candidate Peter F. Vallone in New York City
October 12, 1998

The President. Thank you very much. First of all, let me thank Mayor Dinkins for his presence here tonight and his friendship and the many things he did for the people of New York and the many things that he's done for me over the years. And Peter, I want to tell you that I appreciate being invited to come by and be with your friends tonight and your supporters. I thank you and Tena for making this race, and I thank you for the personal support you have given me. I'm very grateful for that.

[At this point, a telephone rang.]

The President. Somebody answer that phone. *[Laughter]*

I'd also like to thank you for letting me— I've got one nonpaying guest here tonight, my senior Senator from Arkansas, Dale Bumpers, who's back there. He is universally considered to be the best speaker in the United States Senate, so if we were really being generous, I'd let him talk, and I'd sit down tonight. But I'll pull rank a little bit.

I want to make a couple of points, if I might. First of all, our country is in good shape. Compared to 6 years ago, we are in much better shape. We've got the first surplus in 29 years and the smallest percentage of people on welfare in 29 years and the lowest unemployment rate in 28 years, the lowest crime rate in 25 years, the highest homeownership in history. That's the good news.

But the important thing is that at this moment, we can't just sit around and enjoy that. We have to build on it. This is a record to build on, not to sit on, because we live—as everybody in New York City knows, here, the financial capital of our country, we are living in a very dynamic world. And there are a lot of things going on out there. Some of them are good, and some of them are quite challenging.

Not only that, there are a lot of challenges we haven't met here at home. And the reason that we're back in Washington working on this budget now, trying so hard—here we are just 3 weeks before an election—to get a budget passed, and this is the first time in 24 years

that the United States Congress has not passed a budget resolution with their own budget plan. But the reason we're doing it is because we know we still have big challenges out there.

We have got—just to take one example that's very important in New York—we have got to keep the economic growth going by maintaining our leadership in the global economy and stabilizing all these troubles elsewhere; otherwise, they'll come back here to hurt us. That's what this International Monetary Fund issue is all about.

We have got to expand economic opportunity into the poorest inner-city neighborhoods and rural areas in this country which haven't received them. Secretary Cuomo, from New York, the HUD Secretary, has got a great program up here that he and the Vice President put together to get more investment into those areas. And for the last 4 days, if you've been paying attention to the news, you know I've been involved in a pitched battle trying to pass the education plan that I sent to Washington— to Congress in January, for smaller classes in the early grades, for modernizing and building 5,000 schools, for hooking up all our classrooms to the Internet, for giving children after-school and summer school programs and mentoring programs for middle school kids from troubled neighborhoods so they can know they can go on to college if they settle down and do a good job in school.

We're fighting a huge battle that Senator Bumpers has really helped us on, on the environment, where every year now—every single year—we have to look at 10 or 15 bills having nothing to do, very often, with the environment, being littered with what they call riders in Washington, designed to undermine America's commitment to environmental protection at the very time when we know more than we ever have before about how to grow the economy and improve the environment.

We didn't succeed in passing the Patients' Bill of Rights, but we need to keep working until we do, because I think if someone gets hit—God forbid—going out of this hotel tonight, by a car, you shouldn't have to go all the way across town to an emergency room just because that's the only one covered by your HMO. If your doctor tells you you need a specialist, you ought to be able to get it. And you ought to know that your medical records are private. Those are just some of the things we're trying to do.

Now, what's that got to do with the Governor's race? A lot. The answer is a lot. There are some things that the President can do that will affect the country as a whole, independent of what is going on in the communities of America, the cities of America, or the States of America. You know, I have to get this International Monetary Fund funding passed. I have to come up with a plan to, in my judgment, reform the global financial system so that we avoid some sort of catastrophe here. That's my job. Tonight my Special Envoy for Kosovo, Dick Holbrooke, is briefing our NATO allies about what we're trying to do to make peace in Kosovo. Those are things that the President only can do.

But in education, in crime control—when we passed the crime bill to put 100,000 police on the street, that money went through the Governors and the mayors. If we pass a bill in the Congress to put 100,000 teachers in the classroom, that money will go through the Governors, and to some extent, the large local school districts.

But the Governors of this country have primary responsibility in so many areas—relating to education, relating to law enforcement, relating to the environment, relating to economic growth in a specific area. And if you look at Peter Vallone's record here in New York City, I defy you to find another city official anywhere else in America who has been as innovative in three things that all go together: improving education, fighting crime, and being responsible with the budget. You will not find a better record of reform from any big-city official anywhere in the United States. And I think that is very important.

Now, why is that important? Because whatever we do in Washington, it has to be made live on the streets of America, in the communities, and in the States. And I can tell you— I was a Governor for 12 years; I know a little about that job. And as we move into this next period of our Nation's history, we have given you the smallest Federal Government in 35 years. We have focused far more on empowering the American people to solve their own problems and less on setting up new bureaucracies. But we have also given big, big new responsibilities to the States. The Governors will have more to do than anybody else with whether we really succeed in adding 5 million children to the ranks of those with health insurance. The Governors will have a great deal to do with deciding whether all these funds we're trying to get in education actually lift the learning of our children all across America. And I could go on and on and on.

So I'm here not just because this man is my friend and he has stood up for me, but because, far more important, he has stood up for and led the people of New York City in an exemplary way, in a reformist way, building a better future for our children.

And let me just make one last point that's very much on my mind today. I'm sure that most of you saw in the press that the young man who was beaten so badly in Wyoming passed away today. We don't know the facts of the case, and none of us should comment on them or prejudge anyone. But the indications are that he was beaten so badly because he was gay, by people who were either full of hatred or full of fear or both. And yet if you think about it, the thing that's special about America is that we're supposed to create a place for every law-abiding citizen in this country, no matter how different we all are, one from another—by race, by religion, by circumstance, by neighborhood—no matter what.

One of the things I have tried hardest to do as President—I think with more success in the country than in Washington, DC—is to reconcile Americans to one another and to make us all understand that we don't have to be afraid of each other if we share the same values, follow the same rules, and are committed to building the same kind of future. That's another reason I'd like to see Peter Vallone have a chance to serve as Governor, because I think he's that kind of person.

Thank you very much.

NOTE: The President spoke at 5:25 p.m. in Conrad Salon E at the Waldorf Astoria Hotel. In his remarks, he referred to former Mayor David Dinkins of New York City; Mr. Vallone's wife, Tena; and murder victim Matthew Shepard.

Statement on Congressional Action on Digital Millennium Copyright Legislation
October 12, 1998

I am pleased that the Congress has passed the "Digital Millennium Copyright Act." This bill will implement the two new landmark World Intellectual Property Organization (WIPO) treaties that my administration negotiated. These treaties will provide clear international standards for intellectual property protection in the digital environment and protect U.S. copyrighted works, musical performances, and sound recordings from international piracy.

American copyright-based industries that produce and promote creative and high-technology products contribute more than $60 billion annually to the balance of U.S. trade. This bill will extend intellectual protection into the digital era while preserving fair use and limiting infringement liability for providers of basic communication services. I look forward to signing this legislation into law, and I urge the Senate to ratify these treaties so that America can continue to lead the world in the information age.

Remarks at a Reception for Senatorial Candidate Charles E. Schumer in New York City
October 12, 1998

Thank you very much. What a gift—thank you. Now you all have us in the right frame of mind. Let me say to all of you, I thank you for the warm welcome. I thank Iris and Jessica and Alison and all of Chuck's and Iris' family for being here. And I thank you for being part of Chuck's family at this important time.

I'm delighted to have the chance to be here with a number of distinguished New Yorkers, and I just want to mention a few. First I'd like to thank Gerry Ferraro and Mark Green for being here and showing their support. It means a great deal to me to see them put the profoundly important issue of this Senate seat first and their concern for the people of New York first. I'll never forget it, and I hope none of you do as well.

I'd like to welcome City Councilman Tony Weiner, the successor to Chuck Schumer in the United States Congress, for being here. And I don't want any of you to forget how terribly important it is to reelect our wonderful State comptroller, Carl McCall, who is also here. Thank you very much, Carl. Our candidate for attorney general, Eliot Spitzer, who's here; thank you, Eliot, for being here.

I told Eliot earlier tonight that's the best job I ever had. [*Laughter*] When I was attorney general, I didn't have to hire people or fire them, appoint people or disappoint them, raise taxes or cut spending, and if I did the first thing unpopular, I could always blame it on the Constitution. [*Laughter*] But it really matters who has the job, and I hope you'll help him. Thank you for being here, Eliot.

I'd like to welcome Manhattan Borough President Virginia Fields, Assemblyman Robert Ramirez, and City Councilmen Walter McCaffrey and Ken Fisher—all of them. Thank you all for being here. And I know our State party chair, Judith Hope, is here, and I want to thank her for the wonderful job she's done for New York.

Now, I told Chuck Schumer when he decided to take on this Herculean task that if he ever needed anybody to fill in for him, just to call me, and I'd try to do it. [*Laughter*] So here I am.

I want to say I've been a little bit amused by some of the things that have been said in this Senate race, including, apparently, the contention that Mr. Schumer doesn't have a good voting record in the Congress. And I don't see how any Republican could criticize any Democrat for not voting in Congress this year. I mean, this Congress has worked fewer days than any Congress I can remember. It's the first Congress in 24 years not to pass a budget resolution.

1783

And the reason they're still there so close to the election is, they blew the 9 months before. So nobody in the Republican Party should be blaming any of the Democrats for what they didn't do. And I hope you'll remember that when you see that ad.

Let me just say, they're showing some real progress now, and we're working with them in good faith. But if it weren't for these negotiations, now 11 days after the beginning of the new budget year, if it weren't for the fact that we're still there, finally looking at education and some of the other serious issues before us, this Congress would be known as the one that killed campaign finance reform, that killed the tobacco legislation designed to protect our children from the dangers of tobacco, that killed the Patients' Bill of Rights, that killed the minimum wage, that continued the assault on the environment, that attempted to divert the surplus before we could save Social Security first, and had taken no action to date on either education or the imperative nature of investing in the International Monetary Fund so that our country can continue to lead the world in this time of financial turmoil.

Now, if I were a part of their caucus, I don't believe I would be criticizing someone like Chuck Schumer for not showing up for duty. Let me tell you some of the things he did vote for. In 1993, when a single vote would have turned the tide the other way, Chuck Schumer voted for my economic plan that reduced the deficit 92 percent, before the Balanced Budget Act—the bipartisan Balanced Budget Act of 1997 passed—92 percent of the work done. If he had not voted that way, the whole thing would have failed because we didn't have a vote to spare. That's just one of the many issues on which he differed from his opponent, and I think Chuck Schumer was right. And I think you do, too. We now have the first balanced budget and surplus in 29 years as a direct result of that courageous vote.

Then in 1994, Chuck Schumer authored the Brady bill, now the Brady law. Now a quarter of a million felons and fugitives have been denied the ability to buy handguns—a quarter of a million—saving goodness only knows how many lives. He voted yes; his opponent voted no. So when there really was a vote that mattered, I believe Chuck Schumer was right, and I think the people of New York do, too.

When the vote in 1994 on the crime bill came up, and in the United States Senate there was this incredible effort—that I never shall forget as long as I live—by the leadership of the other party, then in the minority in the Senate, to prevent us from getting a vote to put 100,000 police officers on the street, to put the Violence Against Women Act into motion, to ban 19 kinds of assault weapons designed only to kill people, and in the Senate they were doing everything they could to keep it from even coming to a vote—the assault weapons ban, the 100,000 police, the programs to keep our children out of trouble in the first place, the Violence Against Women Act—Chuck Schumer was where he always is, out there leading the fight for public safety and civility and decency on our streets and in our neighborhoods and in our schools. And his opponent was on the other side.

So, if I had that kind of record, I don't believe I'd be criticizing Chuck Schumer for his voting record. Every time it counts, just like today, Chuck Schumer is there to vote for you, for New York, for your children, and for the future. And I hope you'll give him a bigger vote in the United States Senate.

You know, I have been increasingly concerned in the last few weeks about what the American people were going to say in this election about our future, about what they would say by not only how they voted but whether they vote—because, normally, when times are good—and to be sure, compared to 6 years ago, times are good, and I'm grateful for that and very grateful that the people of New York twice voted to give Al Gore and me a chance to serve our country and to implement our ideas and to work for you. But if you think about this, the lowest crime rate in 25 years—no person in America, I might add, more responsible, no Congressman in the country more responsible than Chuck Schumer—the lowest crime rate in 25 years, the lowest unemployment rate in 28 years, the smallest percentage of people on welfare in 29 years, the first balanced budget and surplus in 29 years, the highest homeownership in history, the lowest African-American poverty rate recorded, the biggest drop in Hispanic poverty in 30 years, the biggest rise in wages among average citizens in over 20 years—these are good things. But what are we going to do with them? What are we going to do with them?

I believe—notwithstanding the arguments that are being made in the television wars here that don't really have any underlying merit about the voting record of a Congressman, or even the contrast in their voting record that I just gave you, which is meaningful—the most important thing is who's going to do the most to make the most of this moment for our tomorrows. That overshadows everything else, because the thing that concerns me is, so often when times are good, people say, "Well, things are going fine and, therefore, we don't want to rock the boat, and maybe we don't even need to vote." But here in New York, the financial capital of our country and indeed the world, I think you know enough from seeing what all is going around in the world in terms of financial turmoil to know that in a dynamic world, the fact that things are good does not mean you can sit still. And I would argue that New York needs a visionary, an activist, a doer, someone who understands what needs to be done and has the courage to do it. And I would argue that our people—every one of them, without regard to party across this country—need to consider this a profoundly important election in which they want their voices to be heard, so that we send a clear message that we don't think this is just a time when we can fiddle around and not pay attention to the big issues.

And what are they? Number one, if we want to keep America's economic growth going, America must have the tools to lead the world away from the financial instability that has gripped so many other countries. That means funding the International Monetary Fund instead of running away from our obligations there.

Number two, if we want to be a symbol of stability in the world, it means not squandering this surplus until we have fixed Social Security for the 21st century. That is profoundly important.

Number three, it means not stopping until we know we have done everything we can to give all our kids, without regard to their income, their race, their background, access to a world-class education. The education program I sent to Congress in January that only now they are beginning to debate is a very simple, straightforward, but profoundly important one: 100,000 teachers to lower class size to an average of 18 in the early grades; funds to build or rehabilitate 5,000 schools; hooking up all the classrooms in the country to the Internet by the year 2000; after-school and summer school programs for

children so that we can end social promotion, but we don't dub the kids a failure if the system fails them; mentors for kids in their middle school years so that they can know they can go on to college if they stay in school and study and do well.

It is a good program. It is a matter of urgent national concern. And it should be beyond partisan politics, for every American—every American—has a vested interest in the success of our children.

Now, these are the big issues before us. To be sure, there are others. We should stay on the path of improving the environment as we grow the economy and not abandon that. We should, next year, pass this HMO Patients' Bill of Rights to guarantee people the right to see a specialist; the right to keep their medical records private; the right to keep a doctor during the course of treatment, even if the employer changes plans; the right to go to the nearest emergency room, not one halfway across town just because the nearest one is not covered by your plan. That's what this bill of rights does. These things are important to America's future.

And I'd like to say just one other thing. I know a lot of you were profoundly moved and saddened, as I was, with the news this morning that that young man from Wyoming, who was so badly beaten, passed away. It is inappropriate to speculate about the specifics of the case, but it does seem clear that he was beaten horribly because he was gay.

Now, New York is a place where we have gotten a lot of advantages as a country out of our remarkable diversity—our racial, our ethnic, our cultural diversity, our diverse skills, our language skills, our different connections with the rest of the world—and the idea that if you come here, no matter where you come from, if you're good at whatever it is you want to do, you'll have a chance to live out your dreams. All over the world, I see people held back because they can't find a way to look beyond the differences in people to what they share in common.

Today my Special Envoy for Kosovo, Dick Holbrooke, was working with our NATO allies in a feverish attempt to try to bring peace there without further violence. Today I talked to the Prime Minister of Israel and to Chairman Arafat about their coming to the United States in a few days in a determined effort to resolve this next big step on the road to peace in the Middle East. All over the world, I see people held back and heartbroken and lives crushed because there are those who are so animated by fear and their compulsive need to look down on others that whole nations are kept from becoming what they ought to be. And I say to you, in memory of that young man and his family, America cannot do good in the world unless America is good at home.

And another reason I would like to see a person like Chuck Schumer elevated to the Senate is that I believe that he and our party in this time have taken clear and unambiguous stands for the proposition that everybody who is a law-abiding citizen ought to have a home in America, ought to be treated with dignity and honor, that we do not countenance hate and discrimination and bigotry.

If you think about the way the world is changing, you could seriously argue that, as you look ahead, in terms of building a global society, we have three big challenges. One is to develop a financial system that doesn't go through a boom/bust cycle in the world in the way that we experienced, and others experienced here, many years ago. That's the threat—or the fear some people have out there. Two is to deal with global environmental challenges and still keep growing the economy. But three is to go to the heart—in country after country after country—of this dark compulsion people have to hate and fight and kill each other because of their religious, their racial, their cultural, or their other differences.

And I have done my best as President to try to get the American people to move beyond that. Today I asked the Congress once again to pass my anti-hate-crimes legislation. And as my staff never tires of telling me, I'm doing a better job of getting America to get over it than I am of getting the people in Washington to get over it.

But I ask you to think about that. Say a prayer when you go home tonight for that young man's family in Wyoming, and think about what kind of Senator New York ought to have. New York has been an integral part of America from the beginning. It has always been central to our conception of who we are as a country and where we're going.

Senator D'Amato has gotten some criticism that I never thought was fair, actually, for being called "Senator Pothole" and all that—you know that people make these funny little jokes. It's not funny if you've got a pothole in front of your house. [*Laughter*] It's not funny; it's important. It's hard to think about the higher things if you get a flat every morning. [*Laughter*]

So what I want to say to you, though, is—now, I want you to think about this—there is not a person here who would dispute what I am about to say. If Chuck Schumer is a Senator, given his level of energy, his intensity, his aggressiveness, he will make Senator D'Amato look laid back when it comes to filling potholes—[*laughter*]—or solving whatever other problems there are. But I don't think he should be criticized for that. That's an important part of this job.

But there are two other things that are very important. One is voting right, voting for the future, voting for the profound, deepest interests of the people of New York—and not just here 3 or 4 weeks before the election but every year, for 6 years, the entire term. And the other is being able to visualize the future we are tying to build, being able to represent and bring together this incredible diversity of New York and America, and giving voice to the tomorrow that is just over the horizon.

So I say to you—I started this speech by answering an ad against Chuck Schumer, and I think I did a pretty good job. [*Laughter*] I pointed out what I think is very important in his vote for the economic plan of '93 and the crime bill of '94 and his essential leadership. But the most important thing to me of all is, New York deserves a Senator who is both tied to the specific, concrete needs of individuals and their communities, and a Senator who will vote in the interest of the State and the Nation over the long run and finally give voice to what makes America a great nation. This is a time when we need people who are both practical and visionary, a time when we have business to attend to that is right before our eyes and dreams to dream and realize. And I am here proudly tonight because I believe Chuck Schumer can be that kind of Senator.

Thank you, and God bless you all.

NOTE: The President spoke at 7:40 p.m. in the Grand Ballroom at the New York Hilton and Towers. In his remarks, he referred to Mr. Schumer's wife, Iris Weinshall, and daughters, Jessica and Alison; Geraldine Ferraro and New York City

Public Advocate Mark Green, who both challenged Mr. Schumer in the Democratic primary; New York State Assemblyman Roberto Ramirez; murder victim Matthew Shepard; Prime Minister Binyamin Netanyahu of Israel; and Chairman Yasser Arafat of the Palestinian Authority.

Remarks in New York City on the Situation in Kosovo
October 12, 1998

Good evening. In recent weeks, faced with a deepening and dangerous crisis in Kosovo, the United States has worked to stop the violence and repression and put the people of Kosovo on the path to peace.

Last month the United Nations Security Council, through Resolution 1199, demanded that President Milosevic implement a cease-fire, withdraw the forces he has recently sent to Kosovo and garrison the rest, allow refugees to return to their villages, give immediate access to humanitarian relief agencies, and agree to a timetable for autonomy negotiations with the Kosovar Albanians.

President Milosevic has not yet complied with the international community's demands. Given his intransigence, the 16 members of NATO have just voted to give our military commanders the authority to carry out airstrikes against Serbia. This is only the second time in NATO's history that it has authorized the use of force—and the first time in the case of a country brutally repressing its own people.

The international community is now prepared to act. But as I have said from the beginning, we would prefer to resolve this crisis peacefully, rather than through military action. That is why I sent Ambassador Richard Holbrooke on a mission to make it clear to President Milosevic what the world expects him to do to avert the NATO airstrikes.

Ambassador Holbrooke has reported to me, and in the past few hours to NATO, that, faced with a solid international front, President Milosevic has made a series of commitments. If fully implemented—and that is a critical and very big "if"—these commitments could achieve the international community's objectives as stated in the United Nations resolution.

In light of President Milosevic's pledges and the independent verification system that will be established, NATO has agreed to delay action for 96 hours.

President Milosevic has agreed, first, to fully comply with U.N. Security Council Resolution 1199. Second, he has accepted an intrusive international inspection to verify compliance. Third, he has agreed to a timetable for completing interim autonomy arrangements with the Kosovar Albanians.

If these commitments are met, and the international community will be able to see for itself whether they are met, they could provide the basis for peace and progress.

All along our objectives have been clear: to end the violence in Kosovo which threatens to spill over into neighboring countries and to spark instability in the heart of Europe; to reverse a humanitarian catastrophe in the making as tens of thousands of homeless refugees risk freezing or starving to death in the winter; and to seek a negotiated peace.

But let me be very clear: Commitments are not compliance. Balkan graveyards are filled with President Milosevic's broken promises. In the days ahead, we will focus not only on what President Milosevic says but on what we see that he does, through a robust on-the-ground and in-the-air verification system.

I hope that the commitments President Milosevic has made can create a peaceful way forward. That has been our preference all along. But together with our NATO partners, we will determine whether President Milosevic follows words with deeds. And we will remain ready to take military action if Mr. Milosevic fails to make good on his commitments this time.

As we approach the next century, we must never forget one of the most indelible lessons of this one we're about to leave, that America has a direct stake in keeping the peace in Europe before isolated acts of violence turn into large-scale wars. Today determined diplomacy backed by force is creating the path to peace.

I want to thank Mr. Holbrooke; I want to thank Secretary General Solana and our NATO

Allies for all the contributions they have made. Now we must and we will do what is necessary to see that that path to peace is followed.

Thank you very much.

NOTE: The President spoke at 8:50 p.m. at the New York Hilton and Towers. In his remarks, he referred to President Slobodan Milosevic of the Federal Republic of Yugoslavia (Serbia and Montenegro); Special Envoy Richard C. Holbrooke, the President's nominee to be Ambassador to the U.N.; and NATO Secretary General Javier Solana.

Remarks at a G&P Charitable Foundation for Cancer Research Dinner in New York City
October 12, 1998

The President. Thank you. Well, when I told Denise I would do this for her and the memory of her daughter, I didn't know that an added bonus was I would be introduced by Bill Cosby, a man who—I mean, his net worth was 500 times mine before I met all those lawyers in Washington. [*Laughter*] But I thank you, Bill. I thank you and Camille for your friendship, the letters you sent me, the words of wisdom in the last several months, and for being here tonight.

I want to thank my wonderful friend Denise Rich for so many things, but for remembering her daughter in this magnificent and farsighted and humane way. Hillary would like to have been here with me tonight, but she is in Prague on a trip for our country. But we love you, Denise, and we thank you for what you're doing.

I want to thank Les Moonves for his work in making this evening a success. And I want to say I am delighted that you're honoring Milton Berle. Thank you. [*Applause*] Thank you.

You know, when you're President, you can speak off the cuff a little bit, but you have all these wonderful people who work for you, and they dig up interesting facts. Now, here are the facts they dug up for me to say about Milton Berle. [*Laughter*]

[*At this point, Mr. Berle stood up and pretended to depart.*]

The President. Oh, no, it gets better; sit down. He's been in show business for 85 years. He's performed in drag more than any other entertainer except the roadshow cast of "La Cage Aux Folles." [*Laughter*] And most important, he holds the Guinness Book of World Records for the most charity benefit performances of any entertainer in history. Thank you, Milton Berle.

I'd like to ask you to take just a couple of minutes to seriously consider the purpose for which you have come tonight. Twenty-five years ago, America declared war on cancer. Twenty-five years from now, I hope we will have won the war. I hope the war on cancer will have about as much meaning to schoolchildren as the War of 1812. Twenty-five years from now, I hope schoolchildren don't even know what the word "chemotherapy" means.

The progress now being made against cancer is stunning. We are closing in on the genetic causes of breast cancer, colon cancer, and prostate cancer; testing medicines actually to prevent these cancers. New tools for screening and diagnosis are returning to many patients the promise of a long and healthy life. From 1991 to 1995 cancer death rates actually dropped for the first time in history.

For the last 6 years, we have worked hard to fight this dreaded disease, helping cancer patients to keep their health coverage when they change jobs, accelerating the approval of cancer drugs while maintaining safe standards, continually every year increasing funding for cancer research.

In the last few weeks, four critical steps have been taken. First of all, in spite of all the fights we've been having in Washington, we did succeed in getting from Congress on a bipartisan basis the largest single increase in funding for cancer and other medical research in history, as part of our gift to the 21st century. Second, I directed the National Cancer Institute to expedite a new computer system to give tens of thousands of cancer patients across our country access to clinical trials on the kinds of new cancer treatments that can save their lives. Third, I have taken steps to ensure that by next year cancer patients and advocates will have a seat at the table when we set the medical research agenda in Government, because those who suffer from cancer know truths about these diseases that even the experts do not understand. And fourth, we've made $15 million available to study the long-term effects of cancer treatment and how to prevent cancer recurrence.

And I know, Denise, these grants have special significance to you because Gabrielle herself succumbed as a result of the treatment she received from Hodgkin's disease. So we give these grants with you and your family in mind.

Oh, we've still got a lot to do, all right, in this battle for victory over cancer. We have to convince the next Congress to finish the unfinished agenda of this one: to pass a Patients' Bill of Rights to ensure cancer patients high-quality care; to help Medicare beneficiaries with cancer be a part of these clinical trials; to convince the next Congress to confirm the first oncologist ever nominated to be head of the FDA, Dr. Jane Henney; and finally, to take strong action to protect our children against America's number one cancer threat, the sales of tobacco products illegally to our children.

But I came here to say to you two things. First of all, our country is moving in the right direction. And with all the partisanship in Washington, this is one area where we have pretty much moved together, hand in hand across party lines.

Secondly, I want you to know that there is so much to be done that in spite of increasing and unprecedented Government efforts, it's not enough. We need the kind of effort that you're making here tonight. You never know how many lives you'll save, how many children you'll give a future to. And it's really worth doing.

Let me just say one final thing. The fight against cancer is really a fight for life, a fight for the elemental proposition that all of us are bound to seek, not just for ourselves but for all others, the chance to live out our dreams for as long and as well as we can. And whenever

that chance is cut short, we are all diminished. I'm thinking about it in another context today because, like so many of you, I was heartbroken this morning to learn that young Matthew Shepard, who was beaten so viciously in Wyoming, succumbed to his injuries.

And I say that to remind you, when we come here tonight, you feel good about it; you feel good about yourselves. You're contributing money to help people you'll never know live lives you'll never be a part of, and that is in the best tradition of humanity. You do it because you know, in some profound and almost indescribable way, we share a common mission in these brief lives we live on Earth. And when someone else takes a life—as this young man was apparently beaten to death and apparently only because he was gay—and that taking is done out of blind hatred and maybe even fear, like cancer it violates every sense of how we think life ought to be.

So I say to you tonight, when you go home and you ask yourselves what happened tonight—besides the fact that you all look beautiful, and you saw a lot of interesting people, and you had to put up with a speech from the President, and you marveled at Milton Berle, and Bill Cosby made you laugh—you can say, "I stood for life, not my life but someone else's; not someone I know but someone I don't; not someone whose life I will share but someone whose life I hope will be wonderful."

And it is the recognition of how we are all bound together across all the lines that superficially divide us that make this a very great country. When we violate that, we diminish our own lives. When we honor it, we lift our lives. And I thank you for how you have honored it tonight.

God bless you.

NOTE: The President spoke at 9:15 p.m. in the Imperial Ballroom at the Sheraton New York Hotel and Towers. In his remarks, he referred to Denise Rich, president, G&P Charitable Foundation for Cancer Research; entertainer Bill Cosby and his wife, Camille; and Leslie Moonves, president, CBS Entertainment.

Remarks at a Dessert for Senatorial Candidate Charles E. Schumer in New York City
October 12, 1998

First of all, I want to thank Harvey for his wonderful words and for being a real friend to me and to Hillary and to our causes. And I want to thank Steve and Maureen for having us here tonight in their modest little home. [*Laughter*] I love this place. [*Laughter*] And you might be relieved to know that while Chuck Schumer was in here giving his speech to you, I was next door signing the budget bill so the Government won't shut down tomorrow morning. So they have—I was giving the Congress 4 more days to do right.

Let me say, first of all, I just talked to Hillary this morning. She's in Prague tonight, but she would like to be here. And when I tell her about it, she will be sorry that she wasn't. But she wanted me to say a special thank-you to all of you. New York has been especially wonderful to our family, to our administration, and especially supportive in these last several months, and I might say, no one more than Congressman Schumer. I also see Congressman Nadler over there, who was reminding people about the Constitution last week in a truly stunning way. Thank you, Congressman, for your great work.

And let me say, I went to a big fundraiser for Chuck Schumer earlier tonight at a hotel. There were hundreds of people there. And he wasn't there because he had been down voting, notwithstanding Mr. D'Amato's ads saying that he didn't show up. He was down there voting. So I told Chuck when he started running that I wasn't up this year, and if I could ever fill in for him, I'd be happy to. And so that's what I did earlier tonight. [*Laughter*]

And I'd like to just tell you a couple of the things that I said, because I—Harvey talked about standing by me. If you want to stand by me, the best thing you could do is stand up for him, for Congressman Schumer, and for the people who are basically supporting the vision we've all shared for moving this country forward.

I was amused to see this television ad saying that in this last year the Congressman had only voted—whatever—70-something percent of the time. You know, we don't, we the Democrats, we don't set the agenda for Congress, and we don't even determine how many days a week they work. But I think if you'll check, they worked fewer days this year than in any year in the last umpty-dump zillion; nobody can remember a time. And if I were a member of the Republican majority, I would not be criticizing Chuck Schumer for what he did in this Congress, because what they've done is to kill campaign finance reform, to kill the tobacco reform legislation, to kill the minimum wage increase, to kill the Patients' Bill of Rights, to try to stop us from saving the surplus for Social Security reform. So I don't believe I would be criticizing someone else.

I also, if I were this particular Republican from New York, I wouldn't be talking about Chuck Schumer's voting record, because we are enjoying the first surplus in 29 years in no small measure because in 1993, without a single Republican vote and without a vote to spare, Congressman Schumer, Congressman Nadler, and the Democratic caucus voted for an economic program that reduced the deficit by 92 percent, before we had the bipartisan balanced budget agreement of last year.

And then in 1994, if you want to really see the issues that divide these two candidates when they're a good ways away from an election, we had two issues that I can't help mentioning. One was the Brady bill, which Chuck Schumer wrote, which has now kept a quarter of a million felons and fugitives from getting handguns and saved Lord knows how many lives. Congressman Schumer was the sponsor of the bill; his opponent voted against it.

Then there was the crime bill. I remember well the crime bill of 1994, when the Democrats were in the majority in the Senate and the Republicans were in the minority, but they were trying to filibuster to keep us from actually even getting a vote on the crime bill—even bringing it to a vote. And therefore, Congressman Schumer was for putting 100,000 police on the street, for community policing; everybody that lives in New York City knows the crime rate has gone down because of community policing, people walking the streets. We have made that contribution all over the country, and we've got crime at a 25-year low. And Congressman Schumer was on one side, and his opponent was on another. The same thing with the assault weapons ban, same thing with the Violence Against Women Act; all those things were in that bill.

So if you're just going to look at this from a traditional point of view, the attacks and the parries and then the counterattacks, I think Schumer wins hands down.

There is another way to look at this. I probably shouldn't say this because Chuck's got an ad on this, but a lot of people, a lot of the Democrats, they make fun of Senator D'Amato for being called "Senator Pothole." And I'm kind of sympathetic with that. You can only make fun of that if you don't have a pothole in front of your house. If you have a pothole in front of your house, you would like it if someone filled it. And if you get a flat every time you get in your car, it's hard to think about the higher things. So there's something to be said for that.

But what I always say about Chuck Schumer is, having dealt with him now for years and years, he is the most intensely meticulous, detailed, constructively aggressive politician I ever dealt with. Therefore, no one will hold a candle to him when it comes to filling a pothole that needs to be filled. [*Laughter*]

But being a Senator is about more. So let me just take 2 minutes to ask you to think about what I think is really important. I mean, if you want to have people decide whether to vote on these ads, or whatever, I can give you all those answers. But what really matters is this: It's how people think we ought to be using our time today, and what that will mean tomorrow and next year and 5 and 10 years from now. That's what really matters.

I mean, if I told all of you that helped me in 1992, if I had told you—I said, okay, we'll meet in 6 years at Steve and Maureen's apartment, and when we meet we'll have nearly 17 million new jobs and the lowest unemployment rate in 28 years, and the first balanced budget in 29 years, and the smallest percentage of people on welfare in 29 years, and the lowest African-American poverty rate in history, and the highest homeownership in history, and the biggest real wage gains in 20 years, and finally, after 25 years, a reversal of wage inequality—

and, oh, by the way, we'll be making progress in making peace from Northern Ireland to the Middle East to Bosnia—tonight, thank God, to Kosovo—and you'd have said, "Well, it sounds good, but I don't believe you. It won't happen."

But it has happened. And I'm very grateful for having had the chance to serve. But what really matters in this Senate race, what really matters in all these Congress races, what really matters is, what in the world are we up to now? What are we about? What are we going to do with all this that we have? Are we going to just sort of sit back, relax, and enjoy it? Are we going to be preoccupied and distracted? Or are we going to recognize that it is a precious gift for a nation, a free nation, to have a moment like this? And it gives us the freedom to look beyond our nose and the daily concerns of life at the larger problems around us. That's what I hope and pray to goodness we'll do.

Now, everybody that lives in New York knows that in spite of the good times we're enjoying, this is a very turbulent time in the world. All of you know that because this is the home of the stock market, because you know what goes on in Asia and Russia and these other places. But there are lots of examples of that. And just because we're doing well doesn't mean that things are static and they're going to be that way a long time.

The real reason that I would like to see Chuck Schumer go to the Senate is that I think he has the unique capability of being both a practical, day-to-day person who will serve the immediate interests of the people of New York and of being a visionary who can make a contribution to the Nation's future.

And the thing that I have tried so hard to do since I became President is to get the people of this country to look down the road, beyond today, and to get the people to come together across the lines that divide them. Looking down the road, we've got to do something with the international financial systems. We've got to do something with Social Security and Medicare before all the baby boomers retire and bankrupt our kids. We've got to do something; we've got to keep doing things until we prove that we can have the best education system in the world for all of our children, who are increasingly minority, increasingly lower income, increasingly the children of single parents. We've got to prove we can grow the economy and improve the environment. And we have to prove that we can come together across the lines that divide us, and in so doing, we can lead the world to a better place.

It's amazing, isn't it, how much of your time I've had to spend as President dealing with people's primitive hatreds? You think about it. Rwanda, my people in Ireland—although we're doing real well right now; if the wheel doesn't run off, we're actually going to stay on the good path. In the Middle East, I talked to Prime Minister Netanyahu and Chairman Arafat today; they're coming on Thursday. We're going to work and try real hard to make that next big leap toward peace. But people have harbored ancient hatreds there.

Bosnia, Kosovo—today in Kosovo, NATO voted to give notice that we're prepared to conduct airstrikes to stop the slaughter of the innocents in Kosovo. And Mr. Milosevic said that he would fully comply with the U.N. resolutions and let us bring in an international set of observers to monitor it. So the NATO people said, "Okay, we'll take 4 days and watch and see." This is good news.

But this is amazing. This is the 21st century. We're talking about putting computers in every kid's classroom, and we're dealing with centuries-old ethnic, religious, and racial hatreds. And today, what was America's greatest sadness, that in Wyoming a young man who was brutally beaten died. And he was beaten up because he was gay.

So that's the last thing I'd like to say to you. I have tried to make our party and, hopefully, our country stand more for the proposition that we should not define ourselves in terms of what we aren't and who we can look down on, but we should instead define ourselves in terms of what we have in common and what we can together build. And I think it's fair to say that I've had more success out in the country and maybe out in the world than I have in Washington, DC, where old habits die hard.

But I can tell you, if you want your country to do good in the rest of the world, we must be good at home. And the sort of typical daily politics of give and take and cut a little here off of your opponent's hide and hit a little there, it's not worthy of a great country doing what we're doing now. We're doing very well in a world with a world of trouble. And a lot of the people in trouble helped us get rich the last 6 years. And we have higher obligations. We have responsibilities that no one else can

fulfill. And unless we fulfill them, the rest of the world won't do well, and eventually it will come back to haunt us and our children.

I can tell you now after 6 years as President, every single Senate seat—every one—is a matter of great import to the United States and to its future. New York—it's very hard to have a competitive Senate seat because once people get in, particularly if they're in the other party, they normally outspend us three or four to one. We now have a genuine debate going on here between two people who are, thanks to you, both going to be adequately funded, who will be able to discuss what the future ought to be like, and who have voting records which are indicative of how they will be in the future.

And I really believe that Chuck Schumer is an extraordinary human being. I believe he has the capacity to have a lot of the things that make Senator D'Amato popular with many New Yorkers: he'll be aggressive; he'll be persistent; and he'll fill the potholes. But he will vote a progressive tradition all 6 years of his term, not just as we get nearer to election. But far more important, he'll be thinking about these big issues.

So when you go home tonight, I want you to think about this. The outcome of these midterm elections will rest on whether people of a progressive bent, many of whom could never afford to come to an event like this, will take the trouble on election day to go and vote. If we were having a Presidential election, Mr. Schumer would be winning this race in a walk. You wouldn't have to worry about it. Why? Because there would be this huge turnout.

But normally, in the off years in the United States, a lot of people just don't go. And a lot of them are our people, the people that work and wear the uniforms at those three hotels I visited in New York before I got here. They're a lot of the people we're working for, and their children and the promise of their children. If they decide that they ought to show up, if they go through the hassle of figuring out how to vote while they're dealing with a job and the child care and everything else, then we have a chance to do something that has not been accomplished in 150 years in American politics.

But that's what your being here tonight will make possible. So, I want you to think about it. I think it's a very exciting time. It's not free from danger; this is not an easy time. This international financial situation is very, very important, and we have got to convince our allies to join with us, in my judgment, in taking strong action here, just like they did in taking strong action on Kosovo today.

But we can do these things. And again I want to say, New York has been a special part of this country from its inception. It is still a special part of our country. It carries all—when I got off the helicopter tonight down in lower Manhattan and I was fixing to get in my car, and it was kind of a warm fall night, and I looked out and I saw the Statue of Liberty down there, it just literally—still, after all these years—took my breath away.

This is a place that ought to be represented by a Senator who can make a major contribution to what America should become in the 21st century. That, more than anything else, is my case for Congressman Schumer.

Thank you very much.

NOTE: The President spoke at 10:05 p.m. at a private residence. In his remarks, he referred to dessert cohosts Harvey Weinstein, Steve Rattner, and Maureen White; and murder victim Matthew Shepard. H.J. Res. 134, making further continuing appropriations for the fiscal year 1999, approved October 12, was assigned Public Law No. 105–254.

Remarks on the Situation in Kosovo and an Exchange With Reporters
October 13, 1998

The President. Before I leave to visit a school in Maryland and talk more about our ongoing budget struggle to secure funding for education, I would like to say a few words about Kosovo.

Over the past few days, NATO has resolved to move President Milosevic from the battlefield to the bargaining table. The commitments he has made could lead—and I emphasize the word "could"—to the peaceful resolution of a crisis that threatens stability in the Balkans and the lives of tens of thousands of refugees, many of them homeless. But for that to happen, we must now see progress as President Milosevic turns his commitments into concrete realities.

First, the cessation of hostilities must continue. Second, the troops President Milosevic recently sent to Kosovo must begin to move out, and those already there must begin to come to garrison. Third, the international monitors must be allowed to enter and be given full freedom of movement. Fourth, humanitarian relief agencies must be able to bring help to the hundreds of thousands of displaced persons. And fifth, serious autonomy negotiations with the Kosovars must begin to go forward.

As I said last night, we will not rely on what President Milosevic says, but on what he does for the whole world to see. To that end, a key component of the commitments he has made is an intrusive, on-the-ground and in-the-air verification system. It will include about 2,000 international inspectors in Kosovo who will serve as watchdog to ensure that the cease-fire holds and the Serb forces withdraw, while building confidence among Kosovars to return to their homes. And it will involve unrestricted NATO aerial surveillance to monitor compliance and quickly detect violations.

The international community prefers compliance to conflict. But in voting to give our military commanders the authority to carry out airstrikes against Serbia, NATO sent a clear message to President Milosevic: NATO is ready to act. It is up now to the President of Serbia to follow through on his commitments.

Thank you.

Q. Mr. President, given your expressed distrust of Milosevic, how optimistic are you that he's going to be able to fulfill this long list of conditions by the deadline?

The President. Well, I'm neither optimistic, nor pessimistic because I have something better now. We have now a verification system, so we're not dependent upon our hopes. We have a verification system. There will be facts—facts on the ground which will tell us whether or not the compliance is there. And I certainly would hope that this NATO position will, in effect, be maintained until all the conditions are fully met. And I expect that it will be.

So I cannot—I would like to say again what I said last night—I'm very appreciative to Mr. Holbrooke, but also to Secretary General Solana and General Clark and all of our NATO Allies, as well as to the Secretary of State and Mr. Berger and our people who have worked for the better part of 3 months to try to bring about these developments. So I'm very pleased about where we are today, because we're not dependent on hope. We can just look at the facts and see what he does. It is a very good agreement. It is completely in accord with the United Nations resolution, and it gives us the chance to save an awful lot of innocent people from starvation or freezing this winter and to remove yet another very dangerous source of instability in Europe.

Q. Sir, if he doesn't comply, will he escape paying any price for what has happened so far?

The President. Well, I think he is going to pay the price of a defeat here for continued aggression by his government, and he's not going to succeed in his designs. I think the most important thing now is for us to save lives, return people to their homes, get them the humanitarian aid they need, and to remove completely and irrevocably the threat of aggression by the Serb military and other forces in Kosovo.

We've got to put first things first here. The most important thing is to right this situation, as we were able to do in Bosnia. And I think that today I'd say we have a pretty good chance of doing that. Again, we prefer compliance over conflict, and we hope that will be the case. But whether it is or not is entirely up to him now, and we have the verification system in place and so we'll know. And I'm very, very pleased with the work that all the people involved have done in these last several days. This is where the international community ought to be, what we ought to be doing, the position we ought to be taking. And I'm looking forward to events as they unfold.

Thank you.

NOTE: The President spoke at 11:22 a.m. on the South Lawn at the White House, prior to his departure for Silver Spring, MD. In his remarks, he referred to President Slobodan Milosevic of the Federal Republic of Yugoslavia (Serbia and Montenegro); Special Envoy Richard C. Holbrooke, the President's nominee to be Ambassador to the U.N.; NATO Secretary General Javier Solana; and Gen. Wesley K. Clark, Supreme Allied Commander, Europe.

Exchange With Reporters at Forest Knolls Elementary School in Silver Spring, Maryland
October 13, 1998

Classroom Space

Q. Mr. President, Ashley Lewis was telling us before you came in that she actually likes this classroom, that it's one of the biggest in the school——

The President. It is big.

Q. Why should—can you explain to her, maybe, why you feel the need to spend $1.1 billion to build new classrooms when the student population may not always be this size?

The President. Well, maybe I should let Secretary Riley answer that one, because it's going to be this size and bigger for a long time.

[*At this point, Secretary of Education Richard Riley made brief remarks explaining the need*

to replace temporary classrooms that were unsuitable for various reasons.]

The President. Accessibility.

Secretary Riley. Heat, cool, it's different kinds of problems in all the different temporary facilities. Some are better than others, as the Governor pointed out, but they're temporary, and it's not a permanent solution.

The President. Even if it is bigger. [*Laughter*]

NOTE: The President spoke at 1:05 p.m. in a portable trailer classroom. A reporter referred to sixth grade student Ashley Lewis, and Secretary Riley referred to Gov. Parris N. Glendening of Maryland. A tape was not available for verification of the content of this exchange.

Remarks at Forest Knolls Elementary School in Silver Spring
October 13, 1998

Thank you very, very much. Well, first of all, I'd like to thank Carolyne Starek for that marvelous statement. Didn't she do a good job? [*Applause*] And she talked about teachers using visual aids, and then pointed the press, helpfully, to the visual aid back here. [*Laughter*] I'm glad you're here, but if you'd ever like a job in communications at the White House, I think we might be able to arrange that. [*Laughter*]

Let me say to all of you how delighted I am to be here. I want to thank Nancy King for her devotion to education and her remarks, and Dr. Paul Vance, the other local officials who are here, Mr. Leggett and the delegates and the school board members. If I come out here to this school district one more time, I think you ought to devise a special assessment for me so I can contribute to the building fund of the schools—I have been here so much.

My great partner in our efforts to improve education is the Secretary of Education, Dick Riley, I believe, the best Secretary of Education America ever had, and I'd like to thank him for being here.

I want to thank Governor Parris Glendening and Lieutenant Governor Kathleen Kennedy Townsend for their extraordinary work and leadership. This is one of the most innovative State governments in America. Maryland is always at the forefront of whatever is happening in education and the environment and economic incentives. And as a person who served as Governor for 12 years, I believe I know a little something about that, and one of the things that I always love to do is to steal ideas from other Governors. You know, that's not a very delicate way of saying what the framers of our Constitution had in mind when they called the States the laboratories of democracy. That's what a laboratory is—you find a discovery, then no one else has to discover it; they can just borrow it. If I were a Governor today, I would be paying a lot of attention to what goes on in Maryland. And I thank them for what they have done.

I would also like to thank Senator Daschle and Congressman Gephardt. I think you could see the intensity, the passion they feel for our determination after nearly a year of trying to get education on the agenda of this Congress before it goes home. We cannot allow a budget to pass without a serious consideration of these issues. And their leadership and their passion and their commitment have made it possible.

A President—if the Congress is in the hands of the other party, and they passionately and genuinely, I think, disagree with us on whether we should put 100,000 teachers out there, or help build or repair thousands of schools—none of this would be possible if it weren't for their leadership. And I want you to understand that. I can give speeches until the cows come home, but until the majority party wanted to go home for the election, and our guys said no, my "no" was not enough. And so I thank them and all of their colleagues who are here today.

I want to introduce them just to show you the depth and the national sweep of our feeling about this. Senator Daschle is from South Dakota. He is joined by our leader in the Senate on education issues, Senator Ted Kennedy of Massachusetts, and Senator Byron Dorgan from North Dakota. You know Mr. Gephardt is from St. Louis; he said that. He's joined by David Bonior, from Michigan; Charles Rangel, from New York; Ted Strickland, from Ohio; Nita Lowey, from New York; Rubén Hinojosa, from South Texas; and two Congress Members from Maryland, Steny Hoyer and Albert Wynn.

I'd also like to acknowledge a longtime friend of mine who is a candidate for Congress. And as Ted Kennedy reminded me before I came up here, back in the great days when America was fighting for equal rights for all of these children, without regard to their race, Ralph Neas was known as the "101st United States Senator" for civil rights. And we're glad to have him here. Thank you.

When I ran for President 6 years ago, I had an absolute conviction—and a lot of people thought I was dead wrong—but I had an absolute conviction that we could reduce the deficit and eventually balance the budget and still invest more in our children and in our future. And we have been working to do that. The strategy has worked. We've got the strongest economy in a generation, the first balanced budget and surplus in 29 years, the lowest crime rate in 25 years, and the doors of college are more open than ever before.

I think it is literally possible to say now that because of the Pell grants, and the deductibility of student loan interest, and the fact that young people can pay back their college loans as a percentage of their incomes, and because of the widespread tax credits for $1,500 a year for the 2 years of college, and then tax credits for other years of college—that you—literally possible to say now that any young person that works for it will find the doors of college open to them and not barred by money. And I am very proud of that. I think we have done the right thing.

But we now have to decide as a people—not just because it's 3 weeks from an election, but because it's a very momentous time in our country's history—what we are going to do with this moment of prosperity, and whether we're going to fritter it away or build on it. Whether we're going to be divided and distracted, or focused on our children and our future.

This country still has a lot of challenges. If you've been following the news, you know there's a lot of turmoil in the international economy. And the United States has to take the lead in settling that down, because a lot of our growth comes from selling what we make here overseas. And eventually, if everybody else is in trouble, we'll be in trouble, too.

If you've been following the debates, you know that when the baby boomers retire, Social Security will be in trouble unless we move now to save it—which is why I don't want to spend this surplus until we save Social Security. If you've been following the national news, you know we still have big debates in Washington and in Congress over the environment. And I passionately believe that we can grow the economy and improve the environment. You know we've had big debates over whether the 160 million Americans in HMO's should be protected by a Patients' Bill of Rights.

But there is no bigger issue affecting our long-term security than education. And we cannot stop until this record number of children—whether or not they live in Maryland, or Utah, or someplace in between; whether they're rich or poor; whether they're African-Americans, Hispanic, Asian-Americans, Irish-Americans, or you have it; whether they are physically challenged or completely able-bodied; whether they're rich or poor; whether they live in an inner city or a rural area or a nice suburban community like

this one—until all of our children have access to a world-class elementary and secondary education. We owe that to them. And that is what this is all about.

Eight months ago in my State of the Union Address, I asked Congress to use this moment of confidence and prosperity and the money—that the fact that—that you've paid into the Treasury, because more of you are working than ever before—to make a critical downpayment on American excellence in education. I asked them to do a number of things, but I want to emphasize two.

First, I asked them to help local communities reduce class size in the early grades by hiring 100,000 new teachers. Study after study after study confirms what every parent and teachers know: smaller classes and better trained teachers make a huge, huge difference, especially in the early grades. They lead to permanent benefits from improved test scores to improved discipline.

Let me just tell you one story, just one. A few years ago when I was Governor, I used to spend a lot of time in classrooms—unfortunately, more time than I can now spend. And I enjoyed going into the classroom and meeting your students who were over there a few moments ago, but I can't do what Governor Glendening still does, go in and tutor and actually spend a lot of time and talk and listen. But there was a very poor rural school district in my State that had a visionary leader. And they came to me and said, "You know, Governor, we don't have much money, but if you could get the Federal Government to let us take our Title I money and some other money we're getting, some special education money, and put it all together, we'd like to try for a year or two to put all of our first graders in the same class." And the per capita income of this school district was way, way, way below even our State average, not to mention the national average.

Well anyway, to make a long story short, we were able to give permission to do that. We pooled all the money. We created four elementary school first grade classes of 15 kids each. Here's what happened. The overall performance of the children on the measured test increased by 60 percent. The performance in one year—the performance of the Title I kids doubled. Four children had been held back because they hadn't learned anything the first year. Their performance quadrupled.

And when Hillary and I were promoting education reform in Arkansas, one of the things we worked the hardest for was to bring average class size down to 20. If this 100,000 teachers proposal goes through, we can bring it down to an average of 18 in the early grades. It will make a huge difference—a huge difference.

In the wake of all the terrible school violence our country sustained in the last years—particularly in the last year or so—I asked Secretary Riley and Attorney General Reno to prepare a booklet that could be sent to every school in the country about how to identify kids that might be in trouble, how to stop bad things from happening in the first place. And so they went out across the country to listen to educators, and they came back and said, in place after place after place they were told, "Give us smaller classes in the early grades; we'll find the kids that are troubled, and we'll have a chance to help them lead good, productive lives."

I just want to echo what Mr. Gephardt said. Every time you see a State legislature having to build another prison—because the court will order you to build prisons that aren't overcrowded, but not schools that aren't overcrowded—every time you see that, you can bet your bottom dollar that 90 percent of the people going into that prison, if they had a little different childhood, could have been somewhere else. And we should never forget that.

The second thing I asked Congress to do was to give us the tools to help local communities modernize crowded and crumbling schools. We had a record number of schoolchildren start school this year—52.7 million, a half-million more than last year, more than at the height of the baby boom generation. In a recent study from the General Accounting Office, it concluded that as many as a third of our classrooms—a third—are in need of serious modernization or repair; one-third of our kids in substandard classrooms. I have seen old school buildings that are fine and strong—buildings, frankly, we couldn't afford to build today with the materials and the dimensions they have. But they have peeling paint and broken windows, bad wiring. They can't be hooked up to the Internet and the lights are too dim. And I have seen today, and in many other places, trailers that we call "temporary," but unless we do

something about it, they are anything but temporary. Now, we see stories of teachers holding classes in trailers and hallways and gyms. I don't believe a country that says it's okay for a huge number of its children to stay in trailers indefinitely is serious about preparing them all for the 21st century. And I believe we can do better. I believe you believe we can do better.

Now, this proposal, which has been championed in the Senate especially by Senator Carol Moseley-Braun from Illinois, and by Congressman Charles Rangel from New York and others in the House—Nita Lowey—I want to say to you, we want to come clean here; this has never been done before. And the members of the Republican majority are philosophically opposed to it. They say somehow it's an intrusion into local control—I frankly don't see—if we help the State provide more classrooms for this school. From what I just saw of her, I think your principal would still be in control. I do not believe that we would be running this school. [*Laughter*]

We want these classrooms to be more accessible to people with disabilities. We want these classrooms to be more accessible so they'll all be able to be hooked up to the Internet. We want them to be physically connected. You know, Senator Daschle and I were talking on the way out here. If you live in the Dakotas in the wintertime and you've got to walk just this far, you may be walking in 30-degree-below-zero temperatures.

And we believe that this proposal is good. It targets the investments where they're needed the most. It maintains our balanced budget. And it works in this way: There are targeted school construction tax cuts that are fully paid for; we don't take any money from the surplus. Yesterday, since Congress has not acted on this in 8 months, my budget team brought to Capitol Hill a detailed proposal to pay for these badly needed cuts, dollar for dollar, by closing various corporate loopholes.

Right here in Maryland, our plan would mean tax credits on more than $300 million of the bonds to build or modernize schools. That would save a ton of money for Maryland in building or modernizing schools. In Florida, where in the small community of Jupiter, I visited a school like this one and saw 12 facilities like this outside one small building—12—the

Vice President is visiting today. There, our proposal would help to build or modernize more than 300 schools.

As I said, there are a lot of other important elements in our plan: funds for after-school programs, before-school programs, summer school programs, money to connect all our classrooms to the Internet, money to promote the development of voluntary national standards into basics, and a nonpartisan, supervised exam to measure fourth grade reading and eighth grade math. But if you think about the most pressing big issues, the numbers of teachers and the conditions in crowded classrooms demand immediate national attention.

I wish I had time to win the philosophical debate with our friends on the other side, who somehow see helping more teachers teach and providing more school buildings as an intrusion into local affairs. It is not. Secretary Riley has dramatically reduced the regulations on local school districts and States' departments of education that were in place when we arrived here. What we are trying to do is to make sure people like you can give children like this the future they deserve. I think it's worth fighting for, and I don't think we should go home and pass a budget that doesn't take account of the educational needs of our children and the future of our country.

Let me remind you that in 1993 and '94, when I said we ought to put 100,000 more police officers on the street, I was told the same thing by the same people. They said, "Oh, this won't work; it won't help anything; it's an unwarranted intrusion into local government." It was weird—I had police departments begging me for the police, and I had Congressmen on the other side telling me, "Oh, these police chiefs don't know what they're talking about. You're really trying to run their business."

And anyway, we prevailed. And today, we've paid for 88,000 of those 100,000 police, and we have the lowest crime rate in 25 years. Wouldn't it be nice if we had 100,000 more teachers and we had the highest educational attainment in 25 years, or the highest educational attainment in history? [*Applause*]

Now, school is almost out of session on Capitol Hill. The Members are eager to return home for the election holiday. But we haven't finished our coursework yet, and the final exam has not been passed. And so I say to you— and let me say once again, I don't really relish education as a partisan debate because over the long run, that's not good for America. I don't have a clue whether these kids' parents are Democrats or Republicans or independents, and frankly, I could care less. I want them to have the best. I want America's future to be the best.

We are here fighting this fight because we have no other way, no other recourse to prevail on this important issue. We have worked quietly and earnestly for 8 months with no result. So now, for a few days, we are shouting loudly to the heavens; we have a moment of prosperity and a heavy responsibility to build these children the brightest possible future we can.

Thank you, and God bless you.

NOTE: The President spoke at 1:40 p.m. in the schoolyard. In his remarks, he referred to Carolyne Starek, principal, Forest Knolls Elementary School; Nancy J. King, president, Montgomery County School Board; Paul L. Vance, superintendent, Montgomery County Schools; Isiah Leggett, president, Montgomery County Council; Gov. Parris N. Glendening and Lt. Gov. Kathleen Kennedy Townsend of Maryland; and Ralph G. Neas, candidate for Maryland's Eighth Congressional District.

Message to the Congress Transmitting the Estonia-United States Fishery Agreement
October 14, 1998

To the Congress of the United States:

In accordance with the Magnuson Fishery Conservation and Management Act of 1976 (16 U.S.C. 1801 *et seq.*), I transmit herewith an Agreement between the Government of the United States of America and the Government of the Republic of Estonia extending the Agreement of June 1, 1992, Concerning Fisheries Off the Coasts of the United States, with annex, as extended ("the 1992 Agreement"). The present Agreement, which was effected by an exchange of notes in Tallinn on March 10 and June 11, 1998, extends the 1992 Agreement to June 30, 2000.

In light of the importance of our fisheries relationship with the Republic of Estonia, I urge that the Congress give favorable consideration to this Agreement at an early date.

WILLIAM J. CLINTON

The White House,

October 14, 1998.

Message to the Congress Transmitting the Lithuania-United States Fishery Agreement
October 14, 1998

To the Congress of the United States:

In accordance with the Magnuson Fishery Conservation and Management Act of 1976 (16 U.S.C. 1801 *et seq.*), I transmit herewith an Agreement between the Government of the United States of America and the Government of the Republic of Lithuania extending the Agreement of November 12, 1992, Concerning Fisheries Off the Coasts of the United States, with annex, as extended ("the 1992 Agreement"). The present Agreement, which was effected by an exchange of notes in Washington on April 20, September 16 and September 17, 1998, extends the 1992 Agreement to December 31, 2001.

In light of the importance of our fisheries relationship with the Republic of Lithuania, I urge that the Congress give favorable consideration to this Agreement at an early date.

WILLIAM J. CLINTON

The White House,

October 14, 1998.

Remarks Following Discussions With Israeli and Palestinian Leaders and an Exchange With Reporters
October 15, 1998

Middle East Peace Process

The President. Good morning. I am pleased to welcome Prime Minister Netanyahu, Chairman Arafat, and their delegations.

For 17 months, the Middle East peace process has been stalled, placing in jeopardy all that Israelis and Palestinians have achieved together since the Oslo accords. This week's talk at Wye River offered the chance for the parties to break the logjam and finally take the next essential steps for peace in the Middle East. We must remember as we come together again that in the end, peace is more than a process. It is, in the end, a destination. These two leaders have the power to lead their people to peace.

As I said to Prime Minister Netanyahu and Chairman Arafat only a few moments ago, I believe there are certain realities that underlie these negotiations. First, Israelis and Palestinians are neighbors, and what they must do, they must do together, or it will not be done at all. Second, mutual respect and understanding is required for any meaningful and enduring agreement. Otherwise, there can be no honorable, principled compromise.

As in any difficult problem, neither side can expect to win 100 percent of every point. But concessions that seem hard now will seem far less important in the light of an accord that moves Israelis and Palestinians closer to lasting peace, closer to a day when the people of Israel can have the safety and security they have been denied for too long, closer to the day when Palestinian people can realize their aspirations to be free and secure and able to shape their own political and economic destiny.

There remain enemies of this peace, extremists on both sides who feel threatened by the peace and will be tempted once again to kill it with violence. We can defeat that kind of threat by building a genuine Israeli-Palestinian partnership that will stand the test of time.

Too much time has already been lost. The issues on the table at Wye River are very important, and more difficult issues lie ahead in the implementation of any agreement the parties may reach and in the permanent status talks for a just and lasting peace in the region.

Secretary Albright and the Vice President and I and our entire team will do everything we can to make peace possible, at Wye River and beyond. But in the end, it is up to the leaders standing with me today, to their courage, their vision, their determination, and a shared understanding that the future has to be a shared in peace.

I hope you and my fellow Americans and the world will wish them, and all of us, well in these next few days.

Thank you very much.

Q. Mr. President, can a Palestinian state be achieved by 1999?

The President. Let me say—I know there are many questions—we have discussed this. There is so much work to be done, and all three of us have determined that we should not at this moment take questions but that we should get about the business at hand. And as we make progress, and if we've got something really good to say to you, then there'll be plenty of time for a lot of questions and answers. But for right now, we think it's time to go to work.

Thank you very much.

NOTE: The President spoke at 11:16 a.m. in the Rose Garden at the White House, following discussions with Prime Minister Binyamin Netanyahu of Israel and Chairman Yasser Arafat of the Palestinian Authority.

Remarks at the White House Conference on School Safety
October 15, 1998

The President. Thank you. Your kindness is interfering with my determination to stay on schedule. [*Laughter*] But thank you very much. I want to thank Secretary Riley and Attorney General Reno for their devotion and consistent work on this matter. I thank the Vice President. He and Hillary and I are delighted to have all of you here at the White House today, and the many, many people all across America who are joining us, thanks to the technological revolution.

I thank the Members of Congress who are here. And Governor, thank you for coming, and the mayors and the other members of the administration, and all the distinguished citizens who are here. Our good friend Edward James Olmos, thank you for being here.

I saw a survey, a public opinion survey, a few months ago that asked the American people what they thought the most important story of the first 6 months of 1998 was, and dwarfing everything else was the concern our people had

for the children who were killed in their schools. And I think that your presence here and the number of people who are involved all across America, the quality of the panelists and, indeed, the courage of many of them—the mother of one of the children killed at Jonesboro, Arkansas, in my home State, was on the morning panel with Hillary—this is truly a moving thing. And it's a very important thing for our country.

You know, when I leave here—and I hope I don't have to leave before this panel is over, but I think all of you know that we have been able to put together a conference for several days, a meeting between the Prime Minister of Israel and the Chairman of the PLO in our attempts to make the next big step toward peace in the Middle East. And I got to thinking about it on the way over here today, as I was walking over from the Oval Office, and all the things I'm trying to get these people to lay down and get over and give up, so they can go on with their children's future, so that we can stop innocent children from being killed in the place in the world that is the home of the world's three great monotheistic religions.

It's all a part of our attempt not to give up on anybody and not to permit hatred or anger to destroy even one child's life anywhere. And if we're going to do that elsewhere in the world, to try to be a force for good, then we have to be as good as we can here at home. And all of you are trying to help us achieve that, and I'm very, very grateful to you.

Because this is the only chance I'll have to do it today, and because all of you care so much about education, I'd like to just take a moment to talk about where these budget negotiations are on Capitol Hill. They're about to conclude, I hope. They've certainly gone on long enough. But we're not quite there yet. However, even though there are still points outstanding, I believe we'll succeed. And as the Vice President said, one thing we know already, we know that now this budget will reflect a major commitment to education and to the future of our children.

I am very pleased it will make the first installment on our plan to hire 100,000 new teachers. You heard the Vice President's catalog of the class size issue, but the Secretary of Education tells me that we haven't fully grasped it because, unlike the baby boom, we think that this increase in our children will go on more or less indefinitely, and we've got a lot of very fine teachers in the classroom who will be retiring in the next few years. So this is a huge challenge for us.

The United States has never before done anything like this. And there were a lot of people who honestly thought I was wrong to fight for this or they disagreed with me, but it seems to me that we had enough experience when we put 100,000 police on the street. I was told the United States had never done anything like that before. We didn't have anything to do with telling the cities where the police should go, but the results have been pretty satisfactory. And everywhere I go, someone mentions it to me.

If it worked there and we have crime at a 25-year low, how much more important is it to put the children in the classroom? And this will make a major downpayment toward our goal of an average class size of 18 in the early grades, very different from what has been reported.

And I should also say that when the Attorney General and the Secretary of Education went out across the country in the wake of all of these school shootings and they met with educators and they met with people talking about how we can prevent these things from happening in the first place, one of the things that they were told was, "Get us small classes in the early grades so that we can get to know these children, find out the ones who obviously have got some serious problems, and try to get them the help they need before their lives and others' are irrevocably changed." So this is a very, very good day for the United States.

There were some other very important educational initiatives that will be fully supported: our child literacy drive, to make sure every child can read independently by the end of the third grade; our college mentoring drive, to help lower-income students prepare for college and to be able to tell every one of them what kind of financial aid they'll get if they stay in school and learn their lessons and stay out of trouble. It increases support for Head Start, expands the number of innovative charter schools. There are now a thousand of those schools in America; there was one when I became President, and there will be 3,000 before we're done in 2000. We will provide for half a million summer jobs for our young people, a program that many had sought to eliminate. It will provide for after-school programs for a quarter million young people. And I think we all know how important that is.

I'm very, very grateful for the strong support I have received from the members of my party in the Congress to turn away attempts to actually cut funds from our public schools and instead to renew our historic commitment to them, to more and better-trained teachers, to smaller classes, to hooking up all those classrooms to the Internet by the year 2000, for extra support for children who need it, for accountability and choice. This is what I mean by putting partisanship behind progress, by putting people ahead of politics. And I am grateful to all those in both parties who are responsible for pulling this agreement together.

There's still a lot to be done. A lot of these teachers we'll hire will have to hold class in trailers or hallways or crowded or crumbling classrooms. I proposed in the State of the Union a targeted tax cut for school modernization that was fully paid for, wouldn't take a dime from the surplus, won't create a single new Federal bureaucracy, but it will lower the cost of building these buildings. It could mean as much as 300 new schools in Florida alone next year.

If our children are learning in trailers and schools with broken windows and where the wiring won't even permit them to be hooked up to computers, then we're not getting them ready for the 21st century. So I do want to say, while I am profoundly grateful for the 100,000 teachers, I am determined to see that we finish the job next year in the next Congress.

Now, I also want to thank the First Lady for her role in this conference. We've been at this a long time. In 1983, when I was Governor of our State, I asked Hillary to chair a commission on school standards, and one of the things that we fought hardest for, that was very controversial at the time, was to have a class size limit of 20 in the early grades. And 15 years ago, it was a hard fight, and we got it. And I haven't checked the numbers yet, but I bet, given the growth in population in our schools, they're being swamped and hard-pressed to meet it. And we really believe that making this a national goal and sticking with it will pay major, major benefits to our children all across the country.

Let me also say what I've already said a little bit of. The American people—if I had been polled, I would have been right there with them. I think that all of us were shocked by the violence we saw in Springfield and Paducah and Jonesboro and Edinboro and Pearl. I think we're still disturbed when we see the sights of metal detectors in school doorways or see gangs of young people who are on the streets when they ought to be in the halls of their schools.

We know that there are still some schools where children are afraid to go to school. And doing something about school violence, therefore, is very important, but also we have to understand the nature, the magnitude of the problem. Why do some teenagers from some troubled backgrounds pick up guns and open fire on their classmates? Why do some teenagers who don't appear to have trouble at home do the same thing? What is at the bottom of this, and what can we really do?

You know, I have to say this—and I'm not blaming anybody, because I've done it myself, so I will say I will posit the fact that I have done this—but when people are in elected office and they hear about a problem like this and they know the people they're doing their best to represent are afraid, the first impulse is always to say, "Well, if we just punish them a little harder and a little faster and kept them a little longer, everything would be all right." Now, the truth is that some people are so far gone and what they have done is so heinous that that is the appropriate thing to do. But I have never met a police officer in my life who believed that we could punish our way out of our social problems without other appropriate actions—not one time. And I think we're all here because we believe, in a good society, we would stop more bad things from happening in the first place.

The report that's being released today tells us that the vast majority of our schools are safe, that the majority of our children are learning in peace and security. But it also tells us that in too many schools students feel unsafe. Even if they're not, if they feel unsafe, it's going to have a huge detrimental impact on their ability to learn and grow and relate to their fellow students in an appropriate way.

In too many schools, there is still too much disrespect for authority and still too much intolerance of other students from different backgrounds. Our schools, all of them, must be sanctuaries of safety and civility and respect. Now, here are some things that I think we can do to help you meet the challenge.

First, in the schools with the biggest violence problems, security has to be the top priority. Today I am pleased to announce a new $65 million initiative to help schools hire and train 2,000 new community police and school resource officers to work closely with principals and teachers and parents and the students themselves to develop antiviolence and antidrug plans based on the actual needs of individual schools. Community policing has helped to make our streets safe. It can work for our schools, too.

I'm also very pleased that Congressman Jim Maloney of Connecticut has sponsored a bill to help schools use the funds available for hiring the community police officers to hire officers to work with the schools. This bill was passed by the House and Senate, and it will get up here to me in a day or two, and I'll look forward to signing it into law.

Second, we have to help schools recognize the early warning signs of violence and to respond to violence when it does strike. Today I want to tell you that soon I will be sending to Congress a plan to create a School Emergency Response to Violence, the SERV program, that will work just as FEMA does when it responds to natural disasters. Project SERV will travel to where the trouble is and help communities respond quickly to school violence, from helping schools to meet increased security needs, to providing emergency and longer-term mental health crisis counseling for students, faculty, and their families.

Now, let me just say a word here of appreciation to somebody who is not here, to Tipper Gore, who, once she became 50, fell victim to the Vice President and my propensity for leg injuries—[*laughter*]—but, you know, more than any other person in America, since we've been here in the White House, she has tried to elevate the importance of proper mental health care and the fundamental dignity of it. And I think that we have got to, all of us, keep working until we remove any last vestige of stigma that attaches to getting treatment for children who have troubling mental problems. We know that most of them, the vast majority of them, can be treated successfully. And we know that it is not a cause for shame or denial among families. And we have to keep working on that. And all of you, I ask you to join Tipper Gore and others who understand this and try to make that a part of our approach to this issue as well.

Third, we can't stop the prevention efforts at the schoolhouse door. As I said, the budget agreement we reached today will double or more the after-school programs that keep young people safe after the bell rings. But if young people leave the safe school and enter an unsafe community, they're in trouble.

Today we want to announce two new steps to help them met that challenge. Our safe schools/safe communities initiative will help 10 targeted communities develop plans to reduce youth violence and drug use in and out of school—not only more police but after-school programs, mentoring, counseling, conflict resolution, mental health services, and more. We wanted to put together, in at least 10 places that don't have it now, a truly comprehensive approach.

I'm also pleased to announce that in response to constructive criticism and suggestions from many Members of Congress and educators and community leaders across this country, we're going to overhaul our Safe and Drug-Free

Schools program, which we have dramatically increased in the last few years, to require schools who get the funds to establish tough but fair discipline rules; to put in place proven drug prevention strategies; to issue yearly school safety and drug use report cards to measure their own progress. These methods have worked so well in cities like Boston; they can work around the country. And it will guarantee that the money that's being spent will actually achieve the results that it's been appropriated to achieve.

Fourth, we have to expect more from young people themselves. Given the facts, the resources, the encouragement, almost all of them will do the right thing. This year we launched a huge media campaign to tell young people that drugs are wrong, illegal, and can kill you. Now we have to tell them they, too, have responsibilities to prevent youth violence, to help their fellow students who are violence prone, to report trouble signs they see, and try to help kids get the help they need.

I am pleased that MTV is going to work with us to launch a new campaign to encourage people to become mentors—young people—to help their peers resolve their conflicts peacefully. And again, I'm very grateful, and I'd like for all of you to join me in thanking MTV for their willingness to invest in this important endeavor. [*Applause*]

Lastly—I've spoken a little longer than I meant to, because I want to really hear the panelists, but I return to the theme on which I began and what I will do when I leave here in working for the peace process in the Middle East. We have got to do more to teach our young people to have tolerance and respect for one another, to understand the rich and only superficial dichotomy that the more we appreciate each other's diversity, the more we reaffirm the fundamental core values and existence we have in common.

The recent death of young Matthew Shepard in Wyoming makes it all too clear to us that violence still can be motivated by prejudice and hatred. Yes, we do need a new hate crimes law. And I have directed the Education Department Civil Rights Office to step up its enforcement to stop discrimination and harassment against students. But again, ultimately, we have to be reconciled to one another. We have to believe in one another's fundamental humanity and equal right to be here and to become whatever they can become.

And I hope that all of us—the young people of this country, because our school population is more diverse than ever before, and because to some extent they are unburdened by some of the problems that their parents and grandparents grew up with, can go either way with this issue. If they become the victims of a kind of a current climate of prejudice and bigotry and a sense of opposition and isolation because of our increasing diversity, it could wreak total havoc in this country in a way that we can't even imagine and even couldn't have imagined in the old days of the civil rights years. But if they do what they will do, left to their own better selves, then the increasing diversity of America is something that will guarantee us renewed strength, unparalleled opportunities in the 21st century world. So I don't think we should forget that, either. In the end, the human heart still counts for quite a great deal, and we ought to bring out the best in all the ones we can.

Now, I would like to start the program, and I'm going to sit down to do it. And I'd like to begin with Mr. Kent, Jamon Kent, who is the superintendent of the Springfield, Oregon, public schools, that I had the honor to visit after the terrible incident there. And because we're running a little late, I'm going to do something a little bit unconventional. I'm going to call on all the panelists to make their remarks and then open for questions, starting with Mr. Kent.

[*At this point, the discussion proceeded.*]

The President. I don't want to violate my own rule, so I won't ask a question, but I do want to highlight one thing he said, because if it resonates with your experience, then we need your feedback to the Attorney General and to the Secretary of Education, ultimately to the Congress.

We now have a national policy of zero tolerance for guns in schools. Last year I believe the number of—the Secretary of Education can correct me if I make a mistake—last year I believe there were 6,000 children who were found—students who were found with guns. Guns were taken, and they were sent home. This actually happened in Oregon to this young man right before he came back the next day and killed the kids.

So the question is, what is—we have to find a constitutional fix here; and then the schools have to have the resources so that you don't just take a gun and expel somebody, because there's obviously something going on inside the child that is just as important as the physical manifestation of having the gun. So that was the one thing that they've really done in Springfield, is to sort of spark a nationwide reassessment of what we ought to do with the children besides just send them home. And they've proposed a period of 72 hours or some sort of period of evaluation, and we're trying to work out the details of it. But if any of you have any thoughts about this, I would ask you to give it to us, because that's a very clear issue that was raised in the Springfield case, that I must confess, until I went and talked to them, had never occurred to me before.

I'd like to now call on Commissioner Paul Evans, the police commissioner from Boston, who led Boston's innovative Operation Ceasefire. I spent a half a day up there with the mayor and the commissioner and others several months ago. Any many of you know that Boston went for over 2 years without having a single child under 18 killed by a gun. That's an astonishing thing.

And so I would like for Commissioner Evans to make whatever remarks he'd like to make on this subject.

[*The discussion continued.*]

The President. I would like to make one brief observation about what the commissioner said, because I have spent a great deal of time in Boston, and I don't want to single them out in derogation of the astonishing efforts that have been made elsewhere, many of which have already been featured. But the thing that strikes me—it struck me when I spent a day up there and I met with—the mayor's got a nun who represents him, who has this youth council for the city. The city has its own youth council, like others have the city council. But the thing that struck me about Boston is, they do things that seem obvious when you hear about them, but a lot of people don't do it. The systematic contact that they have in a personal, one-to-one way, with a huge percentage of the young people in their cities is quite astonishing.

And if somebody asked me, in a sentence, why have they been so successful, I would say, they mobilize in a systematic way a consistent contact with a huge percentage of the young people. The idea of, you know, "Well, we hear we're going to have a gang problem in middle school. Why don't we go interview the customers?" You know, if you were running a business, that's exactly what you'd do. But I think they deserve a lot of appreciation, but also a lot of modeling, for that.

[The discussion continued.]

The President. I have two brief things to say. First of all, don't you feel better knowing that there are people like her in the classrooms of America? *[Applause]*

And second, I want to thank you for what you said about school uniforms. When Secretary Riley and I set out to promote school uniforms around the country, there were some here in Washington who derided this as one of those "little ideas" that we were constantly harping on. It may be a little idea, but I have never been to a school that had them that didn't think it made a huge difference in the lives of the children there. And so I thank you for giving a boost to that endeavor.

[The discussion continued.]

The President. Thank you very much. First of all, I want to apologize to all of you, and in particular to Mayor Corradini, who made a terrific presentation, according to the First Lady. I got a call. We just completed our agreement on the budget and the negotiations. In a half hour or so, for the members of the press, we'll have a statement about that.

But let me say, first, I think about Congressman Etheridge, it is—one of the things that we desperately—that we need so much in Congress—Congress works better when there are people in the Congress who have all kinds of different experiences that are relevant. It's an incredible gift that we have a Member of the House of Representatives that was actually a State superintendent of public instruction. And the influence he can have on other Members and the role he can play in the years ahead, I think, is virtually limitless just because of the life he lived before he came there. And I'm very grateful for what he said today and for what he's done.

I would also like to thank Mayor Corradini for the report, for the recommendations, and for the "Best Practices" booklet. I think that we need—every single challenge we've got in this country, we'd be a lot better off if everybody who was working on it issued a "Best Practices" book, because one of my pet theories is that everybody solved every problem somewhere, but we're not very good at playing copycat when we ought to. So I thank her for that.

The only other thing I want to say, and then I want to turn it over to the Vice President and let him ask a question, is that the mayors recommended new youth counselors, and Bob talked about other kinds of support personnel on security issues. One of the things that we had to fight hardest for in 1983, that Hillary convinced me we ought to do 15 years ago, was to require every elementary school to have a counselor. But 15 years later, it looks like a pretty good decision.

And I think we have to—with people who have to pay for these things, with the taxpayers and others who may not deal with it, we need to let them know that a well-trained counselor dealing with the kind of challenges these children face is a terrific investment. And I appreciate the recommendation of the mayors, and I look forward to following up on them.

[The discussion continued.]

The President. Well, it would depend on whether it was an elementary school or higher grades. If you start with an elementary school, I would have an elementary school that would have classes of between 15 and 20 in the early grades. I would have a maximum number of kids in the school of about 300. I would have—and about 1,000 for the high school. I would have the support personnel. I'd have all the teachers trained, and I'd have a parent coordinator that had huge numbers of the parents coming in and out of the schools all the time.

And then I'd try to figure out how to make young people like Liberty the rule rather than the exception. That is—I was sitting here when she was telling her story—I was thinking about—she got to the Boys and Girls Club, and that's a good thing, but there's a whole bunch of kids that live in the place where she does that didn't get there, and that's not a good thing. And so I think that would mean you'd either have comprehensive before- and after-school programs and summer school programs for the kids on site, or there would be some system by which the school, in effect, connected every child to responsible adult community groups of some kind that Professor Earls says works so well.

I think those are the things that I would— I basically believe you've got to have problem-solving mechanisms, but I think the prevention approach is by far the best approach. And I think almost all—so that's what I would do.

In the high schools, it's more complicated. I'd also have a uniform policy. I think they're very important. I'd be in a community that had a strong antitruancy policy. If I had a violence problem, I'd have a curfew. I'd be inter-connected with all of the churches and syna-gogues and other faith institutions. I would have the school bringing people in in a systematic way, and I would be connected with the police department that would do what the commissioner explained that they try to do in Boston.

But I think—in the high schools, I think that, as I said, I'd make sure that we had programs that would keep every child who needed it, give them all an opportunity to be in the school.

Let me just say one other thing that I think is worth saying. It may have been put on the table while I was out briefly. But twice—if you read what the mayors say here, twice, they say, they talk about the importance of the arts pro-grams, the music programs, the physical edu-cation programs, not the kids that are on the athletic teams, the other things. I have seen school after school after school all across this country, because of the financial burdens on the schools, have to abandon these programs. And I think it is terrible.

I think that—basically, all of these people are saying you've got to treat the whole child here, deal with the whole child, deal with the family situation, deal with the community situation. And I just wanted to put in a little plug for that. I think that there are a lot of ways to learn in this life, a lot of ways to communicate

in this life, and a lot of ways for people to find greater peace and connection. And I think it's been a terrible setback to American edu-cation that so many schools have had to abandon their art programs, their music programs, and their physical education programs for the nonteam athletes. Anything we can do to ad-vance that, I think, would also be positive.

[The discussion continued.]

The President. Let me say, I wish we could stay here another hour, but we have another panel. We don't want to deprive them of the opportunity to make their contributions and to be heard. Perhaps at the end of that, you could have a more free-flowing question and answer session.

But again, let me thank all of you. And let me ask you to join me in thanking all of our remarkable panelists for their contributions.

Thank you.

NOTE: The President spoke at 1:28 p.m. in the East Room at the White House. In his remarks, he referred to Gov. Paul E. Patton of Kentucky; actor Edward James Olmos; Suzann Wilson, mother of Jonesboro, AR, school shooting victim Britthney R. Varner; Kipland P. Kinkel, alleged gunman in the Springfield, OR, school shooting; and Mayor Thomas M. Menino of Boston, MA, and Sister Jean Gribaudo, the mayor's youth ad-viser. Participants in the conference were Jamon Kent, public schools superintendent, Springfield, OR; Paul Evans, police commissioner, Boston, MA; Liberty Franklin, Boys and Girls Club Youth of the Year; Joanna Quintana Barraso, teacher, Coral Way Elementary School, Miami, FL; Felton J. (Tony) Earls, professor, Harvard University, Cambridge, MA; Mayor Deedee Corradini of Salt Lake City, UT; and Representative Bob Etheridge.

Remarks on the Budget Agreement and an Exchange With Reporters
October 15, 1998

The President. Thank you very much. First of all, I would like to echo much of what has been said. I want to thank the members of our negotiating team. Erskine Bowles' swan song

turned out to be quite a show, and I thank him for everything he's done, for me and for our country, but especially for these last 8 days. I thank John Podesta and Maria Echaveste, Jack

Lew, Sylvia Mathews, the entire economic team that are back here.

I also want to make it clear that none of this could have been done, in my view, not a bit of it, if we hadn't had a strong, united front from the members of our party in both Houses, led by Tom Daschle and Dick Gephardt, who believe passionately in what we were fighting for for the American people.

And finally, let me say, I would like to thank the leaders of the Republican Party who made these agreements with us. And I ask you, as I make my remarks about what I think was most important about them, just think—we didn't even start this work until after the whole budget year was over. Just think what we could do for America if we had these priorities all year long instead of just for 8 days. And I just can't tell you how grateful I am for these achievements.

Let me give you my perspective. First of all, in terms of the priorities I set forth in the State of the Union Address last January, we did save the surplus for the hard work of Social Security reform early next year. Secondly, we made major strides in renewing our public schools, especially with the truly historic commitment of 100,000 new teachers to reduce class size in the early grades. And thirdly, we made a profound commitment to strengthening our own economy here by assuming our responsibility to stabilize the global economy on which so much of our prosperity depends. Now, without the perseverance of the people behind me and those whom they represent, none of that could have happened.

Let's look at the education issues. One hundred thousand new teachers will enable us to reduce class size in the early grades to an average of 18. Over here at this school violence conference that we sponsored all day, one of the things they kept hammering home, all these educators, was we can find the troubled children, we can prevent a lot of these problems, if we can have them in small enough classes in the early grades.

We achieved full funding for other important educational initiatives, from child literacy to college mentoring, from after-school programs to summer jobs. We did meet our obligations to the International Monetary Fund. And we honored our obligations to the next generation by strongly protecting the environment, and I'd just like to mention three things: One, we got rid of the most objectionable environmental riders; two, we had a full funding of our clean water initiative, which is very important—remember, 40 percent of our lakes and rivers are still not clean enough for our people to swim in them—and three, as the Vice President said, we received a substantial increase to meet our responsibilities in the area of global climate change. So that's very important.

But let me say that in many ways I am most proud of the decision that this budget reflects not to squander the surplus until we meet our responsibilities to reform Social Security for the 21st century.

Yes, there were some disappointments. I wished that we had passed the school rehabilitation and construction proposal. We have to have school facilities so that we can have those smaller classes. And yes, I wish we'd passed the Patients' Bill of Rights and campaign finance reform and the tobacco reform legislation and the minimum wage. But we can now go out and have a great national debate about that. The important thing that we have to recognize is that these hard-fought battles and major accomplishments represent, finally, in 8 days what we did not have for 8 months.

We were able to put the progress of the country ahead of partisanship. We were able to put people ahead of politics. And today every American can take a great deal of pride in knowing that we are going to save Social Security, that we are going to have 100,000 teachers, that we are going to continue to move forward on the environment, and that now we are free here in this administration to keep our economy going by meeting our responsibilities to deal with the global economic challenges.

This is a very, very good day for America. And I thank all the people behind me for everything they did to bring it about.

Thank you.

Legislative Agenda for Education

Q. Mr. President, you rattled off a list of many of your priorities which this Congress did not give you, priorities from your State of the Union Address. Why did you—and all of you, perhaps—specifically decide to hold the line on the education issue, on the idea of more funding for education, et cetera? Did you think that would have the most resonance with the voters?

The President. Well, no, it's what we believed in. We got the entire education program except for three things. First of all, the huge funding increases for education—but they were properly targeted. This 100,000 teachers, this is truly historic. The United States—this is the educational equivalent of what we did when we put 100,000 police on the street. And I will remind you that we now have the lowest crime rate in 25 years. We have never done that before. And we had the same partisan argument then. We were told that it wouldn't work, that it was interference in local government, even though all the police chiefs of the country were screaming, "Give it to us." Now we were told the same thing here.

This is an historic commitment by the United States to put 100,000 teachers out there for smaller classes in the early grades. That, plus the historic commitment we made to after-school and summer school programs, plus the continued funding to hook up all the classrooms to the Internet by the year 2000—these things are truly historic.

Now, I wish we had been able to persuade the Republican majority to give us the school construction and rehabilitation proposal, because we need modern facilities, and that proposal is a paid-for-tax cut in the balanced budget that would enable us to build or rehabilitate 5,000 schools. I think that's important. I still think we ought to be a nation which says we should

have high standards, and I wish we had had an explicit proposal on that. And I believe in the empowerment educational opportunity zones to reward schools that end social promotion and fund more after-school and summer school programs.

Now, those are three things that I would like to have. But we can debate those and work for those in the election. We have differences of opinions, and they have more Members than we do. They're against the Patients' Bill of Rights, and we're for it. They were against reforming—passing the tobacco reform legislation and against the campaign finance reform. But when you compare where we were for 8 months with where we are today, and how good this is for America, that the things that I talked about in the State of the Union in education, in the environment, in the international economy, and saving Social Security, these are huge victories for the American people.

We did the best we could, and I think the best we did by staying together was very good, indeed. And I think the American people will believe so, too.

Thank you.

NOTE: The President spoke at 3:30 p.m. in the South Lawn at the White House.

Remarks at the Plenary Session of the Wye River Conference on the Middle East in Queenstown, Maryland
October 15, 1998

I wish to welcome Prime Minister Netanyahu, Chairman Arafat, and the members of the Israeli and Palestinian delegations here. As I said earlier today at the White House, there is hard work ahead if we are to reach an agreement here and get the peace process moving again. Secretary Albright and I and our entire team are ready to do whatever we can.

As the press contingent prepares to leave, let me say that all of us are determined to keep our energies focused on the talks themselves. Therefore, we have agreed to confine our dealings with the media on this subject to periodic

briefings to be conducted by spokespersons. We have a lot of work to do, a limited amount of time to do it in, but we're ready to get to work.

Thank you very much.

NOTE: The President spoke at 5:07 p.m. in the Main Conference Room at the Aspen Institute Wye River Conference Center. In his remarks, he referred to Prime Minister Binyamin Netanyahu of Israel and Chairman Yasser Arafat of the Palestinian Authority.

Remarks on the Budget Agreement
October 16, 1998

Good morning. Please be seated. I am delighted to be here with the Vice President and Senator Daschle, Congressman Gephardt, Mr. Bowles, who's got a great closing act here— [*laughter*]—the terrific representation from Congress and the administration, especially our economic team, and all of you.

Northern Ireland Recipients of Nobel Peace Prize

Before I make some remarks on the budget, I'd like to first say how very pleased I was, personally and as President, that the Nobel Prize Committee has awarded the courage and the people of Northern Ireland by giving the Nobel Peace Prize to John Hume and to David Trimble today. I am very grateful for that.

For 30 years, John Hume has been committed to achieving peace through negotiations, not confrontation and violence. He has been an inspiration to the nationalist community, to all the people of Northern Ireland and, indeed, all around the world. David Trimble, as Unionist leader, took up the challenge of peace with rare courage, negotiating and beginning to implement the Good Friday accord. Both have earned this award.

But I believe there are others, too, who deserve credit for their indispensable roles, beginning with Gerry Adams, the Sinn Fein leader, without whom there would have been no peace; Prime Minister Ahern, Prime Minister Blair, Mo Mowlam, their predecessors, without whom there would have been no peace; other Irish leaders, like Seamus Mallon; and I would like to say a special word of thanks to Senator George Mitchell for his role in the peace talks. The American people appreciate the recognition the Nobel committee gave our Nation in the citation, and we thank all these people for their continuing work for peace.

Budget Agreement

Yesterday our administration and the Democrats in Congress reached agreement with the Republican leadership on a fiscally responsible balanced budget that seizes this moment of prosperity and wisely invests it in the future. By standing together, we were able to achieve historic victories for the American people.

We fought for and won vital new investments, especially for our children. By hiring 100,000 new teachers, we will reduce class size in the early grades to an average of 18. We will enhance individual attention, increase student learning and, as we learned yesterday at the school violence conference, find more kids who are in trouble and need help early, and prevent more bad things from happening while more good things happen. We're also making very important investments in child literacy, college mentoring, after-school programs, and summer jobs, all of them at risk until the people behind me stood firm and united.

We fought for and won emergency relief for our hard-pressed farmers and ranchers who are suffering not only from the collapse of world markets but from crop diseases and drought and floods. And we fought for and won an impressive package to deal with this emergency only because the people behind me were willing to sustain my veto of the first bill, and I thank them for that very much.

We fought for and won a substantial increase in funding for our clean water initiative to help restore the 40 percent of our lakes and rivers still too polluted for fishing and swimming. We won substantial increases in funding to head off the threat of global climate change which disruptive weather patterns in America have warned us about in the last couple of years. We fought for and won the ability to protect precious lands in America, and we struck down the worst of the antienvironmental provisions the Republicans had put into the budget bill, because of the people who are standing behind me.

And we worked and worked and worked for 8 long months until finally we were able to persuade the Republican majority to join with us in funding America's responsibility to the International Monetary Fund so that we can protect the American economy and fulfill our responsibility to stabilize the global economy. It is a critically important thing to our future; it could not have happened if the people behind us hadn't stood strong and united for months and months.

Let me say, I am especially proud of the way we fought and won the right to reserve every penny of the surplus until we save Social Security first. Despite the efforts of the majority, particularly in the House of Representatives, to squander the surplus on election-year tax plans, we are still now well positioned to save Social Security.

Although we can take justifiable pride in these accomplishments, let's not make any mistakes here. Eight days of progress cannot totally erase 8 months of partisanship. We all know that in those 8 months of partisanship, too many dreams of too many families were deferred. The Republican majority is now leaving town to campaign, but they're also leaving a lot of America's business unfinished.

Partisanship killed the Patients' Bill of Rights. Rest assured, as my first legislative priority, I will ask the next Congress to guarantee your right to see a specialist, to receive the nearest emergency care, to keep your doctor throughout your course of treatment, to keep your medical records private, to have medical decisions made by doctors, not insurance company accountants. That's unfinished business because of partisanship.

Partisanship killed our efforts to help students stuck in crumbled and overcrowded schoolrooms. We fought and fought and fought and won the right for the 100,000 teachers. Now we've got to fight to give the teachers someplace to teach and to give those smaller classes someplace to meet. This is a battle our children cannot afford to lose.

You know, I must say, of all the things that we disagreed with the Republicans on this year, this one mystified me the most. I would have thought they would like this program, not a Government spending program but a targeted tax cut, fully paid for in the balanced budget, that wouldn't take a dime from the surplus, wouldn't add an inch of redtape to the Government's rules but would build or repair 5,000 schools. We were right to fight for it, and we ought to take it to the American people and ask them to put progress over partisanship.

Republican partisanship killed an increase in the minimum wage. You can't really raise a family on $5.15 an hour anymore. If we value work and family, we ought to raise the minimum wage. You know, all those arguments against the minimum wage were wrong the last time we did it. We kept on growing, and unemploy-

ment now and inflation now are lower than they were the last time we raised it. Only partisanship killed it. I hope we can take that to the American people and come back here in January and raise the minimum wage.

And partisanship killed our best chance at bipartisan campaign finance reform. We had a handful of Republicans who did agree with us on this, but the majority was able to defeat us. Senator Daschle produced a unanimous vote from the Senate Democratic caucus—absolutely unanimous—but partisanship defeated us. It said yes to soft money, yes to the status quo, no to reform. The next Congress must strengthen our democracy and finally reform these outdated campaign finance laws, and people will do it who are here with me.

And finally, let me say that partisanship killed the comprehensive anti-tobacco legislation which would have saved millions of young Americans from painful and premature death. I still can't believe—I think about it every day—I still can't believe that the tobacco interests were able to persuade the Congress, with the majority in Congress, to walk away from this. It didn't have anything to do with the tobacco farmers; Senator Ford back there took care of that. [*Laughter*] This was about whether we were going to take appropriate action to save our children, and pure, old-fashioned partisanship killed it. The people behind me will save more of our children's lives when the voters give them a chance to do so next January. We're going to do that.

So let me say again, by way of thanks to all of them and to all of you who worked on this, we can be justifiably proud of the hard work and hard-won gains that this budget represents, of the 100,000 teachers, of the after-school programs, the saving the surplus for Social Security, of protecting the environment and advancing the cause of clean water, and a safer global environment, of keeping our economy going strong. But 8 days of progress cannot replace or make up for 8 months of partisanship, to protect our patients, to modernize our schools, to raise the minimum wage, to look out for the 21st century and reform Social Security and Medicare in the right way. We need a Congress that will put people before politics, progress ahead of partisanship.

I will always remember these last 8 days. I will always remember what our caucus, united, was able to achieve. And I will always be grateful to them for what they did for the American people. Thank you very much.

Now, I want to introduce the Vice President and the other leaders. Thank you very much.

[*At this point, Vice President Al Gore, Senator Thomas A. Daschle, and Representative Richard A. Gephardt made brief remarks.*]

The President. Let me say, as we close, how very grateful I am to all those who have spoken and those who have not spoken, those who are here and those who stood with us who are not here, for giving us a chance to, in the last 8 days, have some very important victories for the American people and, today, for giving us a chance to make it absolutely clear what is at stake in the next 2 years.

When we leave here, I am going to take a brief trip to Chicago to stand with Senator Carol Moseley-Braun. And I think it is worth pointing out today that she is the very first member of our caucus who stood up for the idea that the National Government had an opportunity and an obligation to do something to promote the building and the repair of school facilities for our children's future. I say that to make this point: Every one of us here, standing here, except Mr. Bowles, and he may be about to take the plunge—[*laughter*]—every one of us here is here because of the judgment of the American people. The jobs we hold are not our jobs in any fundamental sense; they belong to the American people.

And in 18 days, after a blizzard of advertisements—probably 2 or 3 times as much from the Republican side as from ours, maybe even more when you count the third-party committees and all that—they will make a decision. The first decision they'll have to make is whether to go and vote in a midterm election, which always, always seems to have lower turnout than the Presidential elections.

If we have accomplished nothing else here today, even when our voices reach those who disagree with us—who think we're making a mistake to put 100,000 teachers in the classroom, who think we're making a mistake to fight for a Patients' Bill of Rights or a rise in the minimum wage or better school facilities—if we have done nothing else, I hope we have reminded the American people that in the end, every one of us gets to raise our voice, to cast our vote, to wield our sign-or-veto pen because

of their judgments. And in 18 days, they will be given a chance to render another judgment.

Between now and then, they will have to sort their way through all the conflicting claims and the blizzard of advertisement. But I think that in the end, many will agree that it is worth going to vote to ratify those who fought for 100,000 teachers and a clean environment and a strong American economy and an America playing a responsible role in the world economy, and perhaps most important of all, people who voted to save the surplus until we save Social Security and honor the compact with generations and keep our country strong when the baby boomers retire.

In 18 days they'll have a chance not only to support those people but to say, "With my vote, I choose to go back and build world-class school facilities; I choose to say, yes, we're going to have managed care, but even people in managed care deserve the right to have medical decisions made by medical doctors, not accountants; to choose to give people the minimum wage; to choose to save Social Security in the right way; to choose these things."

That's the message. I hope the American people know that the people standing behind me earned their pay the last 8 or 9 days. They were worth every penny of tax dollars they got. And they did it the last 8 months because they fought and waited and stood in storm after storm until the time came when they could stand up and do something right for America. And in 18 days I hope the voters of this country, the citizens, will exercise their power to say, "This is the path I choose." Staying home is not a very good option when so much is riding on a trip to the ballot box.

Thank you, and God bless you.

NOTE: The President spoke at 10:36 a.m. in the Rose Garden at the White House. In his remarks, he referred to Presidential Chief of Staff Erskine B. Bowles; John Hume, leader, Social Democratic and Labor Party, and David Trimble, First Minister, Northern Ireland Assembly, Nobel Peace Prize Laureates; Sinn Fein leader and Northern Ireland Assembly member Gerry Adams; Prime Minister Bertie Ahern of Ireland; Prime Minister Tony Blair and Secretary of State for Northern Ireland Marjorie Mowlam of the United

Kingdom; Deputy First Minister Seamus Mallon of the Northern Ireland Assembly; and former Senator George J. Mitchell, independent chairman of the multiparty talks in Northern Ireland.

Remarks at a Luncheon for Senator Carol Moseley-Braun in Chicago, Illinois
October 16, 1998

The President. Thank you very much. I think the Senator has to go to a radio debate, so I'm going to let her off the hook. She's heard me speak a thousand times. You have an excused absence. Let's give her a hand. [*Applause*] You guys have got to stay with her now. Thank you. Goodbye.

I want to thank all of you who are responsible for this today. One of the things that Pat Arbor said to me—he said, "You know, the Union League Club took longer than America did to open up membership to women, but they elected a president quicker." Isn't that right? There's the president of the Union League Club. [*Applause*] Thank you. Hope the country does that before too long.

Let me say to Pat and to all of you who are responsible for this event, I thank you very much. I'd like to thank all the people who provided our meal, and I'd like to thank this wonderful pianist for all the great music he gave us during lunch. Thank you very much.

I will be pretty brief here, but I want to make a very important point to you. The election in less than 3 weeks now will be very important in defining what kind of country we decide to be well into the next century, whether we ratify the course that we have been taking for the last 6 years. Carol Moseley-Braun talked a lot about it; I'd like to give you some sense of what the last few days have looked like to me.

First of all, they've sort have been a blur because I haven't had a lot of sleep. Our country was able to persuade our NATO Allies to take a strong stand in Kosovo, and we have an agreement, which I think now will avoid mass starvation or freezing this winter and move that country on the path to peace.

We have been heavily involved in trying to stabilize the global financial system, which as all of you know has been very much in turmoil, and looking to the long-term need for reform, as well as what it takes to fix the short-term crisis.

Last night until well past midnight, I was talking with Prime Minister Netanyahu and Chairman Arafat, trying to make the next big agreement in the Middle East peace process. And I'm going to leave you after the lunch and one or two other things and go back to Washington to spend the weekend in intense efforts there. And I'm convinced they're both really trying to breach the gaps between them.

This morning I woke up to learn with a great deal of pride that John Hume and David Trimble had been awarded the Nobel Peace Prize for their role in bringing about the peace in Northern Ireland, something that my administration and our country have been heavily involved in.

And of course, we reached agreement on the balanced budget yesterday. Let me say, it's been a dizzying week but a wonderful week for our country. And I'd like to also say what I said just before I left Washington today: This budget would not have been possible unless the members of the Democratic caucus in Congress had been united behind me.

There is a reason that this budget looks like we wrote it and passed it, even though our party is in the minority. The Congress has to pass a budget; that's not an option. It's the first time in 24 years when there was no budget plan passed, but in the end, if you want to go home, you've got to pass a budget. And so by standing strong for the things we believed in and by having Carol Moseley-Braun and Glenn Poshard and other people in our party who agree with the course we're taking say so strongly, that's what made this possible. And I'd like to just reiterate a couple of the things that Carol said.

This budget, which will continue our balanced budget policy that produced the surplus this year, first of all, beat back an attempt to provide a popular—or maybe not so popular, come to think of it—tax cut just a few days before the election that would have eroded the surplus, which I'm totally opposed to, until we save the Social Security system.

We have to reform Social Security. We've got a bipartisan effort working on it. We're going to address it early next year. And we owe a lot to the fact that our Members of Congress, in tough races, Carol Moseley-Braun and Glenn Poshard—you just think about it. It would be easy to say, "Well, I've got a tough race back in Illinois, and I know it's wrong to squander the first surplus in 29 years on what would amount to a modest amount of money to most people in Illinois right before the election. I know that's the wrong thing to do. We've been in the red for 29 years. I know the right thing to do is to save this surplus until we reform Social Security. But, boy, I'm in a tough race." And both of them said, "No, I'm going to do what's right for the people of my State, the people of my country, for our children and our future." And on that issue alone, they deserve to be elected on election day in a couple of weeks.

And the second thing we did was to get not only 100,000 new teachers to bring average class size down to 18 in the early grades, which is a truly historic accomplishment—the National Government has never done anything like this before. And I might say, the people who opposed it in the other party are the same people that opposed me when I wanted to put 100,000 police on the street. A lot of them have come here to Chicago, and they said, "Oh, the Federal Government is going to try to take over State and local government." It was ridiculous. All we did was give people the means to put 100,000 more police on the street. We now have the lowest crime rate in 25 years. And Carol Moseley-Braun strongly supported the crime bill that put that 100,000 police on the street; so did Glenn.

And what we did with the teachers was the same thing. We said, "Look, we're just going to make this available, so we can have well-trained, properly educated and examined teachers out there in these early grades getting this class size down."

We also dramatically increased funding to make sure that we have a national reading program to ensure that all our 8-year-olds can read. We put in funds to continue our efforts to hook up every classroom to the Internet by the year 2000. And perhaps most important of all over the long run, after the 100,000 teachers, we have enough money to provide for after-school programs for a quarter of a million children who live in tough neighborhoods, who come from difficult home situations, and who need to be in school and not on the street after the bell rings in the afternoon. This is a terrific thing.

The third thing we did was to protect the environment. You heard Carol talking about it. We not only protected the environment, we passed the clean water initiative I gave to Congress, which is designed to clean up the 40 percent of the lakes and streams in America that are still too polluted to swim or fish in. We passed my anti-global-warming initiative, a program that is run by Dick Stern's son, Todd, in the White House, which was bitterly opposed by the entire leadership of the other party, but they know we're right. And in the end, we were able to fund it.

And finally, months and months late, but finally, we secured our own economic future by increasing our ability to take responsibility for the global economic crisis when the Congress funded America's contribution to the International Monetary Fund. All that happened in this budget. It is a great budget for the United States of America.

But I want you to understand, as President, even though I supported it strongly, I could not have done it, it would have not have happened, if Carol Moseley-Braun and Glenn Poshard, and the other members of our party in Congress hadn't stood foursquare with me and made it clear that was the condition of passing a budget and getting out of town. And we owe them all—every one of them—a great debt of gratitude. They have earned our support, and it's going to make a big difference for America.

Let me say, elections are always about tomorrow, and this one should be too. But yesterday is some indication of tomorrow. I'd just like to say I've been in Washington only as long as Carol Moseley-Braun has been in the Senate. And I hope earnestly that she'll be in the Senate longer than I'll be in Washington. But I have a different view of a lot of things than some people who live there. I tend to evaluate people based on what they do that affects the lives of people back home. And I'd just like to give you a few things that I think you ought to keep in mind, besides what I just told you about the budget.

The economic prosperity we enjoy today started in 1993, when my economic plan passed the Senate and the House by one vote. She could have said, "Well, you know, I had a tough race in 1992. I'm going to have a tough race in 1996. I don't believe I'll cast a tough vote." But she did cast the tough vote. In 1997, when we passed the bipartisan balanced budget agreement, the deficit had already been reduced by 93 percent because of Carol Moseley-Braun's vote. The people of Illinois should remember that on election day.

In 1994 we passed the Brady bill. She was a cosponsor of the Brady bill. It's kept a quarter of a million guns out of the hands of felons, fugitives, and stalkers, saving who knows who many thousands of lives. She supported the crime bill that's put all those community police on the streets of Chicago and little towns in Illinois, all across this State.

She supported the family and medical leave law, the first bill I signed. Twelve and a half million Americans have taken some time off from work without losing their jobs when a baby is born or a parent is sick.

So I believe she's been right on the issues all along. I know how important she was to this budget. One other thing I ought to mention about this budget is—it doesn't have much to do with Chicago, but there is a lot of agriculture in Illinois, and I vetoed the emergency farm legislation because I did not think it did enough for the farmers of this country that are in—many of them have been caught up in this global financial crisis and are in the worst shape they've been in in literally decades. And the support I received from Senator Moseley-Braun, from Congressman Poshard, and others, was essential in getting us a new farm bill, which is a big part of this final agreement.

Okay, that's my case for yesterday. Do you believe, if her opponent had been in the Senate, that he would have been there fighting with me for 100,000 teachers?

Audience members. No-o-o!

The President. Would he have voted for the Brady bill?

Audience members. No-o-o!

The President. Would he have voted for the crime bill?

Audience members. No-o-o!

The President. Would he have voted for the Family and Medical Leave Act?

Audience members. No-o-o!

The President. Would he have voted for my economic plan in 1993?

Audience members. No-o-o!

The President. Now, look to tomorrow. What's this election about?

Number one, we've got to come back in January and decide all over again if we're going to squander the surplus or save it and buckle down and fix Social Security.

Number two, the major education initiative that we did not adopt was to provide for 5,000 new or reconstructed schools so that we'll have thousands of classrooms for those 100,000 teachers to teach in. Carol Moseley-Braun was the first Member of the United States Congress to come out for that—the very first one. This has been her deal all along, and we are going to achieve that in January. We are going to pass the school construction program in January, because the American people are overwhelmingly for it, if they will just vote for it on election day.

Number three, among the many things we did not do in this session of Congress was to pass the patients' HMO bill of rights. That may not mean anything to some people. It basically means, if you're in an HMO, you have a right to see a specialist if your doctor says you need to see one; you have a right to go to nearest emergency room if you get hurt; you have a right to keep your doctor during a period of treatment, even if your employer changes health care providers; and you have a right to privacy in your medical records. The bottom line is that health care decisions will be made by medical professionals, not by accountants.

It is no mean thing. It is a big, big issue. Over 160 million of us are in managed care. Carol Moseley-Braun was for our bill. It was defeated in the House. It was defeated in the Senate by the members of the other party who did not support it.

The third thing we have to do is to finally pass campaign finance reform.

The fourth thing we have to do is to pass the bill—all year long we waited—to protect our children from the dangers of tobacco, the biggest public health problem in the country today.

And finally, we should pass a minimum wage increase. It's hard to support a family on $5.15

an hour. The only reason we didn't pass it this year is that the other party was completely against it, even though the unemployment rate is low, inflation is low, and we can do this and actually help the economy. The last time we raised the minimum wage a few years ago, they told me the unemployment rate would go up and job growth would go down. Well, job growth went up, and the unemployment rate went down.

So that's what this is about. This Senator has a good record. I just mentioned all these issues, and I asked you if you thought if her opponent had been there, would he have voted with me. You said no.

Now, who is going to vote to save Social Security first? Who is going to be more likely to give the American people and the people of Illinois, for the very first time in our history, this innovative program to build world-class schools for the 21st century? Who is going to be more likely to pass campaign finance reform, to stand up for the health interest of our children, to stand up for the interest of working families? I think you know the answer to that. I think you know the answer to that.

What I want to say to you is that I'm grateful for your presence here. I'm grateful for your contributions. I thank you for helping her in this way. But it is not enough, because it is not enough in this election to persuade people that you have the better side of the argument. You heard what Carol said. You also have to persuade them that the argument is worth their going to vote on election day. And every one of you, you have employees; you have friends who have employees; you have other people you know who have contact with large networks of people. This election will be determined not simply by who has the better side of the argument, or what people agree with in terms of what ought to be done, but who shows up.

And so I think here in Chicago—and this is what Hillary told me to say, by the way. She called me right before I got off the plane.

She said, here in Chicago you would understand that the only poll that counts is the poll that's manifest when people actually move away from their telephone and show up at the polling place.

So I ask every one of you to think about this. Believe me, we are shaping the future of 21st century America. Look at where we are now compared to where we were 6 years ago. Whatever anybody else tells you about the issues, on every single critical decision I have had to make for 6 years to affect the welfare and the future of America, that required a vote in Congress to support, Carol Moseley-Braun was there with me, standing with me, supporting me, trying to make this a better country with a better future.

She was the very first person in America, in the entire Congress, to say we ought to have a national school construction program for 21st century schools and smaller classes. She has supported all these other issues. She deserves—but more importantly, you deserve, your children deserve, this State deserves to be represented in the Senate by somebody who has that kind of vision and that kind of courage and that kind of willingness to put herself on the line.

So I ask you, don't give up. Bear down. We can win, if you do your part.

Thank you, and God bless you.

NOTE: The President spoke at 3:25 p.m. at the Union League Club. In his remarks, he referred to Patrick H. Arbor, chairman, Chicago Board of Trade; Laura J. Hagen, president, Union League Club of Chicago; pianist Hal Roche; Prime Minister Binyamin Netanyahu of Israel; Chairman Yasser Arafat of the Palestinian Authority; Nobel Peace Prize laureates John Hume, Social Democratic and Labor Party leader, and David Trimble, First Minister, Northern Ireland Assembly; Representative Glenn Poshard, Illinois Democratic gubernatorial candidate; and Republican senatorial candidate Peter Fitzgerald.

Statement Announcing the Award of the Presidential Medal of Freedom to Chancellor Helmut Kohl of Germany
October 16, 1998

I am very pleased to announce my intention to award the Presidential Medal of Freedom to Helmut Kohl, Chancellor of the Federal Republic of Germany. The Medal of Freedom is this Nation's highest civilian honor, and it is a fitting tribute to the extraordinary accomplishments of Chancellor Kohl.

Throughout his 16-year tenure as leader of Germany, Chancellor Kohl has made historic contributions to the cause of peace and freedom in Europe and around the world. With uncommon vision and unstinting courage, he led the reunification of Germany while pushing deeper European integration, bolstered transatlantic solidarity, and promoted the cause of democracy everywhere. Americans are grateful for the untiring efforts of this inspiring leader, who will rank among those who changed the course of history.

Helmut Kohl has been a lifelong friend of the United States and has personally committed himself to the enduring partnership of our two countries. On behalf of all Americans, it is my profound pleasure to honor him with this symbol of our Nation's high esteem and deep appreciation.

The President's Radio Address
October 17, 1998

Good morning. This week we reached an agreement on a balanced budget that invests in our people and our future. I'm proud of the results: 100,000 new teachers and funds for after-school programs for hundreds of thousands of children; new environmental protections and an advance in our clean water initiative to deal with the 40 percent of our lakes and rivers that aren't yet fit for swimming or drinking; aid for struggling farmers. We set aside the surplus until we save Social Security. This new budget will also help to strengthen our economy by meeting our commitment to the International Monetary Fund, a challenge I set for America in my State of the Union Address 9 months ago.

Although I'm pleased we've accomplished this, 8 days of progress cannot entirely make up for 8 months of partisanship. Let me tell you why this challenge has been so important.

Our economy is the strongest in a generation. We have a budget surplus and nearly 17 million new jobs. Unemployment has been below 5 percent for more than a year, at a 28-year low. Inflation is at historic lows. Wages are once again on the rise. More than ever, this economic strength rests upon the strength of an increasingly interdependent world. Our own recent growth depends heavily on expanded exports of American products and services.

But over the last year, the world's financial markets have been in turmoil. Countries all around the world are having a difficult time managing their own economies and, therefore, affording American goods, from wheat to apples, from computer chips to jumbo jets. We must act to promote our own prosperity and to protect our people at this critical moment by working to stabilize the global economy and helping our friends to restore growth. This week we did.

A month ago I said that the balance of risk in the world economy had shifted from inflation to slowdown and that all nations must work together to promote growth. Through the International Monetary Fund, nations can join forces to help countries in trouble help themselves. That's why I worked with Democratic and Republican Members of Congress to meet our commitment to the IMF, with a package of tough reforms to make the Fund more accountable, more focused on growth, better equipped to address the economic crisis of the 21st century. Our contribution will leverage a total of $90 billion in new funds for the IMF, expanding its reserves by 40 percent.

Now the IMF is stronger and ready to act. We must make certain that when it acts, it acts to promote global growth and to limit the reach of financial crisis. In turn, this will foster a stronger economy here at home and help our own workers, farmers, and ranchers. It is an insurance policy for our own economy.

By funding the IMF and keeping our economy sound and strong, the United States is doing its part in the world economy. But the world's other leading economies must also do theirs. Europe must continue to promote growth and keep its markets open. And Japan, the world's second largest economy and by far the largest in Asia, faces the most important task of all. I welcome the substantial assistance in Japan's legislation to repair its troubled banking system. Now it's critical to avoid further delay by moving quickly and using that money most effectively.

The United States values our strong relationship with Japan, our political, our security, and our economic partnership. But now the health of Asia's economy and, indeed, the world, depends upon Japan. That is why it must spur economic growth, open and deregulate its economy, and take these immediate steps to strengthen its financial system.

Working with our international partners, we must take further action to promote global growth and to strengthen the world financial system. It is particularly important to find new ways to keep this crisis from spreading. We stand ready to help countries that develop policies to keep their economy strong, and we must continue our work to modernize international financial institutions to meet the challenges of this changing world economy.

When he led the effort to create the International Monetary Fund, President Franklin Roosevelt said that it "spelled the difference between a world caught again in the maelstrom of panic and economic warfare, or a world in which nations strive for a better life through mutual trust, cooperation, and assistance." This week we have strengthened the IMF's ability to make that difference. When America acts and America leads, we can build a stronger, more prosperous economy, not only for our own people but also for the entire world.

Thanks for listening.

NOTE: The President spoke at 10:06 a.m. from the Oval Office at the White House.

Statement on Signing the Strom Thurmond National Defense Authorization Act for Fiscal Year 1999
October 17, 1998

I have today signed H.R. 3616, the "Strom Thurmond National Defense Authorization Act for Fiscal Year 1999." This Act authorizes Fiscal Year 1999 appropriations for military activities of the Department of Defense, military construction, and defense activities of the Department of Energy. Naming this Act in honor of Senator Thurmond is a well-deserved and appropriate tribute. Senator Thurmond served for 36 years in the U.S. Army Reserve. During his more than 40 years of Senate service, his primary legislative focus has been the national defense of this country and the well-being of our service members and veterans.

This Act provides for a strong national defense and supports our commitment to a better quality of life for our military personnel and

their families. Although I have reservations about some of the provisions of the Act, it authorizes funds for many defense readiness and modernization priorities. By providing the necessary support for our forces, it will ensure continued U.S. global leadership. I am especially pleased that the Act authorizes $1.9 billion in emergency funding for peacekeeping operations in Bosnia. Moreover, the conferees' revisions to the Act satisfactorily addressed several objectionable provisions that were included in earlier versions.

The Act supports my Administration's views on gender-integrated training by leaving intact our current system of gender-integrated flights, squadrons, and companies in basic training. The Act's provisions on gender-separate housing at basic training are fully consistent with Secretary of Defense Cohen's recent directives.

The Act contains a prudent and balanced approach on antipersonnel landmine issues. The 1-year moratorium on U.S. military use of such mines is repealed, providing the legislative relief that I had requested. Also, as requested, funds are authorized for research and development on alternatives to antipersonnel landmines and technologies to improve humanitarian demining efforts.

I am pleased with the Congress' continuing support for the important national security activities of the Department of Energy, including the Stockpile Stewardship Program, a program I directed the Department to develop 5 years ago. The success of this program is key to Senate ratification of the Comprehensive Test Ban Treaty, a building block for U.S. national security in the 21st century.

I also commend the Congress for authorizing virtually the entire amount requested for Cooperative Threat Reduction to assist in the elimination of weapons of mass destruction and prevention of their proliferation.

Finally, I am pleased the Act fully funds my request for the development of a national missile defense system.

Notwithstanding the important steps that we have taken to protect military readiness, we need to do more on this critical issue, as I stated in my September 22, 1998, letter to the congressional leadership. In this regard, I have instructed the Office of Management and Budget and the National Security Council to work with the Department of Defense to formulate a multi-year plan, which will detail the resources needed to preserve military readiness, support our troops, and modernize the equipment needed for the next century. I hope the Congress will support my efforts to implement better management practices, cut wasteful overhead, and reduce unnecessary base infrastructure and support services.

Although I believe that the majority of the provisions included in H.R. 3616 are beneficial and support our national defense program, a small number remain problematic. I am disappointed that funds were added to several unrequested research and development and procurement programs at the expense of more constructive programs. I am also dismayed that the Congress failed to enact cost-saving measures, such as additional base realignments and clo-

sures. This will upset the balanced financial plan in the Quadrennial Defense Review and delay our efforts to reduce costs by restructuring our defense establishment.

I am strongly opposed to a provision that, effective March 1999, will transfer the jurisdiction over satellite exports from the Department of Commerce to the Department of State. This change is not necessary to ensure effective control of U.S. exports of satellites and could hamper the U.S. satellite industry. The Congress repeatedly supported the transfer of satellite licensing jurisdiction to the Department of Commerce long before I ordered the transfer in 1996. I strongly urge the Congress to demonstrate its support for a strong domestic satellite industry by passing remedial legislation to halt this transfer of jurisdiction prior to its effective date.

In the meantime, I will take action to minimize the potential damage to U.S. interests that could arise from the Act's export control related requirements. I will direct the appropriate agencies to implement these provisions, subject to appropriate law and regulation, in a manner that supports legitimate commercial communications satellite exports while ensuring that the extensive safeguards needed to protect our national security remain in effect. I will also direct all concerned agencies, subject to appropriate law, regulation, and U.S. national security interests, to employ, to the extent appropriate, time-lines and transparent licensing practices for satellites and related items described in section 1513(a) of the Act in a manner consistent with current dual-use export license processing.

I note that H.R. 3616 also requires that I make certain certifications to the Congress in advance of any export of missile technology or equipment to the People's Republic of China (PRC). Specifically, I must certify that such exports will not be detrimental to the U.S. space launch industry and will not measurable improve the PRC's missile or space launch capabilities. In making this certification, I will be guided by the conference report that notes that "this certification is not, and is not intended to be, a prohibition on the export of U.S. satellites to be launched by the PRC, but is intended to ensure that U.S. national security would not be jeopardized by any such export." I agree with this objective. Further, I take note of the bill's legislative history with respect to the export of U.S.-made items in connection with emergency repair or replacement for commercial aircraft, and I will exercise the certification authority consistent with that view.

I am disappointed that the Congress, in a well-meaning effort to further protect nuclear weapons information, has included an overly broad provision that impedes my Administration's work to declassify historically valuable records. I am committed to submitting the plan required under this Act within 90 days. In the meantime, I will interpret this provision in a manner that will assure the maximum continuity of agency efforts, as directed by my Executive Order 12958, to declassify historically valuable records.

I am also concerned that several provisions of the Act could be interpreted to intrude unconstitutionally on the President's authority to conduct foreign affairs and to direct the military as Commander in Chief. These provisions could be read to regulate negotiations with foreign governments, direct how military operations are to be carried out, or require the disclosure of national security information. I will interpret these provisions in light of my constitutional responsibilities.

Finally, I strongly object to a provision that will impede the ability of the Department of Defense to assist small and disadvantaged businesses in obtaining contracts. My Administration recently announced new procurement policies to increase contracting opportunities for such businesses. This action was taken in order to help remedy discrimination and comply with constitutional requirements. It is unfortunate that this Act will undermine the effectiveness of our efforts and create difficulties in implementing these important policies in future years. My Administration will seek remedial legislation.

There are costs associated with this Act in FY 2002 that are not fully offset under Administration budget scoring. Under the Budget Enforcement Act, a sequester of mandatory programs will be required in the future if savings to offset the costs of this Act are not enacted. My Administration will work with the Congress to offset these costs to avoid a potential sequester.

Notwithstanding the concerns noted above, I believe that the Strom Thurmond National Defense Authorization Act for Fiscal Year 1999, as a whole, is beneficial to the national defense and will help us achieve our objectives in this important area.

WILLIAM J. CLINTON

The White House,
October 17, 1998.

NOTE: H.R. 3616, approved October 17, was assigned Public Law No. 105–261.

Statement on Signing the Department of Defense Appropriations Act, 1999
October 17, 1998

Today I have signed into law H.R. 4103, the "Department of Defense Appropriations Act, 1999."

Our military readiness must remain our top national security priority. This Act fully funds many of the Department's critical readiness programs and supports our commitments to a better quality of life for our military personnel and their families. I anticipate that the Congress shortly will act to include the emergency funds necessary for our ongoing participation in peacekeeping operations in Bosnia in a supplemental funding bill. I strongly urge them to do so. In addition, as I have said before, I believe we should examine near-term and long-term options to secure additional funds to address critical readiness shortfalls.

While the Act funds a number of modernization priorities, I have expressed my strong concerns that this legislation contains excessive funding for projects that are not currently needed for our Nation's defense at the expense of higher priority programs.

I am concerned about section 8115 of the Act, which forbids the obligation or expenditure of appropriated funds under this Act for any additional deployment of U.S. Armed Forces to the Federal Republic of Yugoslavia (Serbia and Montenegro), Albania, or Macedonia until after transmittal of a burdensome report to the Congress on the deployment. Consistent with the plain language of section 8115 and the intent of the Congress, I shall interpret it to apply only to the deployment of additional ground forces to one or more of the three countries. Further, I shall interpret and implement section 8115 consistent with my constitutional authority to conduct the foreign relations of the United States and as Commander in Chief and Chief Executive, and not in a manner that would encumber my constitutional authority.

I will continue to work with the Congress on the appropriate level of long-term funding for defense in order to adequately address the Nation's security needs.

WILLIAM J. CLINTON

The White House,
October 17, 1998.

NOTE: H.R. 4103, approved October 17, was assigned Public Law No. 105–262.

Remarks on Departure for the Wye River Middle East Peace Talks and an Exchange With Reporters
October 19, 1998

Terrorist Attack in Beersheba, Israel

The President. I want to begin by saying how much I deplore the grenade attack earlier today on a bus station in Beersheba, Israel. No cause, no grievance justifies terror. This is another attempt to murder, plain and simple.

Now, I am convinced that reaching a secure, just, and lasting peace between Israelis and Palestinians is the best way to ensure that terrorism has no future in the Middle East. I'm now returning to the Middle East peace talks to encourage the Israelis and the Palestinians to make the hard decisions necessary to move this peace process forward.

As I said when we launched the talks last week, the United States will do everything we can to help; but ultimately, only the parties themselves can bridge their differences and put their people on a more hopeful course. The issues are difficult. The distrust is deep. The going has been tough. But the parties must consider the consequences of failure and also the benefits of progress.

Flash Floods in Texas

Finally, let me say just a few words about the flash flooding that has wreaked havoc in southeast Texas. Reportedly, 18 people have lost their lives, 5,000 evacuated from their homes, 1,200 in refuge in emergency shelters. The storms themselves have not yet abated. We offer our thoughts, our prayers, our resolve to help to those who have lost family members, those who have been uprooted.

A short while ago, I spoke to our FEMA Director, James Lee Witt. He is already working with the Texas officials to assess the damage, and the budget I am about to sign contains nearly $1 billion in additional resources to FEMA so that this vital agency will be even stronger as it works to address this and future disasters. For now, the Nation stands ready to assist the people of Texas in their time of need.

Wye River Middle East Peace Talks

Q. Mr. President, will the Wye talks cancel your trip to California tomorrow in order to be available to continue the Middle East negotiations?

Q. Can they still succeed at Wye?

The President. I'm going back today to work on this. As you know, I got home at 3 o'clock last night. We're working hard through it. This incident in Israel is certainly a complicating factor. I have been briefed on the progress of events this morning, and we're going to work as hard as we can today and we'll have more to say about it as events unfold.

Thank you.

NOTE: The President spoke at 1:28 p.m. on the South Lawn at the White House.

Statement on Violence in the Republic of Georgia
October 19, 1998

I am deeply disturbed by reports of violence in the western part of the Republic of Georgia, where heavily armed opposition forces seized hostages and clashed with Government troops today.

The United States strongly supports the democratically elected Government of Georgia, headed by President Eduard Shevardnadze, and the stability, sovereignty, and territorial integrity of Georgia.

We are glad that the opposition forces decided late today to release their hostages, and we call on the opposition forces to resolve their differences with the Government through peaceful and democratic means rather than by armed confrontation.

Statement on Signing the Year 2000 Information and Readiness Disclosure Act
October 19, 1998

Today I am pleased to sign into law S. 2392, the "Year 2000 Information and Readiness Disclosure Act."

As our Nation prepares for the year 2000 (Y2K), we face an urgent need to address the Y2K problem, which may cause computers and embedded systems that run America's critical infrastructure to malfunction or even shut down. With little over a year until January 1, 2000, this is a serious global challenge that businesses and governments around the world must address.

Today, my Council on Year 2000 Conversion is launching "National Y2K Action Week," to urge small- and medium-sized businesses to take the necessary steps to ensure that the technologies they and their business partners depend upon are ready for the year 2000. Over the next 5 days, the Small Business Administration, the Department of Commerce, and several other Federal agencies will host Y2K educational events at their field offices across the Nation. As part of this week, we are also urging State, local, tribal governments, and community organizations to address this critical problem. More than 160 national organizations representing industries, professions, government, and the non-profit sector have joined the Council in promoting Y2K action during this week.

This legislation will help provide businesses, governments, and other organizations with the necessary informational tools to overcome the Y2K computer problem. This Act, which builds upon a proposal my Administration submitted to the Congress in July, is an important bipartisan accomplishment. I particularly want to thank those in the Congress whose hard work and support of this legislation made its passage possible. Representatives Horn, Kucinich, Morella, Barcia, Leach, LaFalce, Hyde, Conyers, Dreier, and Eshoo and Senators Bennett, Dodd, Hatch, Leahy, and Kyl were integral to getting this work done and done quickly.

Many organizations have been reluctant to share valuable information about their experiences in dealing with the Y2K problem or the status of their Y2K efforts for fear of lawsuits. The Act's limited liability protections will promote and encourage greater information sharing about both experiences and solutions, which will significantly enhance public and private sector efforts to prepare the Nation's computer systems for the new millennium. However, the bill will not affect liability that may arise from Y2K failures of systems or devices.

While I understand that companies have a wide range of concerns related to the Y2K transition and potential litigation, we must also protect the rights of consumers. Therefore, this legislation is focused exclusively on exposure related to information exchange and would not cover statements to individual consumers in marketing a product normally used for personal use.

Firms within an industry confront similar challenges as they work to ensure that their computer systems are Y2K compliant. Although the Department of Justice has already indicated that competitors in an industry who merely share information on Y2K solutions would not be in violation of the antitrust laws, this Act creates a specific exemption from the antitrust laws for these activities. The limited antitrust exemption created by S. 2392 will make it easier for firms to cooperate with one another to solve the Y2K problem while continuing to protect consumers from industry agreements to boycott, allocate a market, or fix prices or output.

Information sharing will be important not only to those who have already made progress addressing the Y2K problem, but also to the many small business and State, local, and tribal governments that are just beginning their Y2K work. I urge trade associations and umbrella organizations to collect such information from their members and provide it to others through websites and other means devoted to discussing Y2K experiences and solutions. My Council on Year 2000 Conversion looks forward to working with Federal agencies, other levels of government, and consumer and industry groups in expanding the website, *www.y2k.gov*, that already supports activities related to our Nation's efforts to address issues related to the Y2K transition.

The Y2K problem is an enormous challenge, and we must meet it. Enactment of this legislation is a significant achievement toward allowing all of us to take a successful step into the new millennium.

WILLIAM J. CLINTON

The White House,
October 19, 1998.

NOTE: S. 2392, approved October 19, was assigned Public Law No. 105–271.

Message to the Congress on Continuation of the National Emergency With Respect to Significant Narcotics Traffickers Centered in Colombia
October 19, 1998

To the Congress of the United States:

Section 202(d) of the National Emergencies Act (50 U.S.C. 1622(d)) provides for the automatic termination of a national emergency unless, prior to the anniversary date of its declaration, the President publishes in the *Federal Register* and transmits to the Congress a notice stating that the emergency is to continue in effect beyond the anniversary date. In accordance with this provision, I have sent the enclosed notice to the *Federal Register* for publication, stating that the emergency declared with respect to significant narcotics traffickers centered in Colombia is to continue in effect for 1 year beyond October 21, 1998.

The circumstances that led to the declaration on October 21, 1995, of a national emergency have not been resolved. The actions of significant narcotics traffickers centered in Colombia continue to pose an unusual and extraordinary threat to the national security, foreign policy, and economy of the United States and to cause unparalleled violence, corruption, and harm in the United States and abroad. For these reasons, I have determined that it is necessary to maintain in force the broad authorities necessary to maintain economic pressure on significant narcotics traffickers centered in Colombia by blocking their property subject to the jurisdiction of the United States and by depriving them of access to the United States market and financial system.

WILLIAM J. CLINTON

The White House,
October 19, 1998.

NOTE: The notice is listed in Appendix D at the end of this volume.

Remarks Announcing the White House Chief of Staff Transition
October 20, 1998

Thank you, and good morning. Thank you. Thank you very much for coming here for this important and happy announcement. For 6 years I have worked hard to prepare our Nation for the new century. We have changed America for the better. There is more opportunity, more citizen responsibility, a stronger American community. We are a stronger force for freedom and prosperity and for peace. In a few moments, I will return to the Wye Conference Center to continue our work on this Middle East peace process.

In all the work that has been done here in this house in the last 6 years, the White House staff has played a pivotal, indeed, irreplaceable role. For the past 2 years I have been blessed to have as my Chief of Staff a gifted manager and an inspiring leader, the world's best negotiator, and a great personal friend.

When Erskine took this position in 1996, I asked him to finish the job of balancing the budget. More than any other single individual, he was responsible for the agreement last year that just a few weeks ago wiped the red ink from the books here in Washington. He also cares passionately about education and led our negotiating team to impressive victories last week on behalf of our schools and our children. He fought hard to protect the surplus until we save Social Security. And as I said the other day, if you look at the last few days, he certainly knows how to stage an exit. [*Laughter*]

He also cares deeply about uniting the American people. He poured his heart into our race initiative. And throughout, he has worked hard to mold a streamlined White House staff into a genuine team.

Erskine has made it plain how much longer he has stayed here than he intended to or wanted to. [*Laughter*] At the end of the month he is going home to North Carolina. I'm only pleased that I was able to persuade him to stay this long. I know he still has a lot to give his State and his country, and I hope he has the opportunity to do so in the future.

To follow his leadership, I have chosen someone who is both a strong manager and a skilled policymaker, with a sharp mind, a strong, strong sense of courage, and a giving heart. John Podesta has those qualities, and I am honored to name him today as the next White House Chief of Staff.

We're delighted to have his family here and his many friends. I think it's important to point out for the record just how superbly qualified he is for this job. He used to be the chief counsel to the Senate Agriculture Committee—which is, in itself, unusual; that means that for the first time in years and years, there will actually be two people who work in the White House and know something about agriculture.

He has been a law professor. He has been an adviser to a generation of lawmakers. He has been at the heart of public policy and public life for a long time now. He has helped to guide our foreign, defense, and economic policy, served as a key liaison to Congress, most recently representing me as a leader in the budget negotiating team that delivered this balanced budget that invests so much in education.

Also, with the singular exception of the Vice President, he is the most technologically proficient of our administration, guiding our technology policy on many fronts. He has another great qualification for this job: He is a better hearts player than Erskine Bowles. [*Laughter*]

He knows how the White House works; this will be his third assignment here in the White House. But even more importantly, he knows why the White House ought to work and for whom every single one of us does work. He entered public service for the right reasons, and he has certainly stayed there for the right reasons.

As many of you know, he and his family have a taste for riding roller coasters. That will certainly serve him well here. [*Laughter*] He is brilliant. He has a tough hide, a dry wit, a lot of patience in dealing with the President, hard-won wisdom, and a genuine compassion for improving this Nation. He will lead a seasoned White House team, working with Deputy Chief of Staff Maria Echaveste and their colleagues, working every day for the American people.

They have a lot of work to do. I would remind you that while we have balanced the budget, set aside for the time being the record surplus, invested again in education, we know that if we do not act to save Social Security and do so soon, we will be running the risk that our retirement system will be in serious trouble as the baby boomers retire. We do have an opportunity to act to strengthen Social Security for the new century; the next Congress will be called upon to do just that.

There are other important challenges as well: Strengthening our economy at this time of global economic turmoil; passing the Patients' Bill of Rights; expanding opportunity through an increase in the minimum wage; passing our initiative to modernize our schools. None of this could be done without a strong and dedicated administration, and at the heart of our actions here, the White House staff.

So let me again say to my wonderful friend Erskine Bowles and to his successor, John Podesta, I thank you from the bottom of my heart. Mr. Bowles.

NOTE: The President spoke at 11:52 a.m. in the Rose Garden at the White House. The transcript released by the Office of the Press Secretary also included the remarks of Chief of Staff Erskine Bowles and Chief of Staff-designate John Podesta.

Statement on the Death of Chris Georges
October 20, 1998

Chris Georges was a reporter's reporter. Whether he was writing about the budget, Medicare, or welfare, Chris' journalistic integrity, attention to detail, and focus on the human side of policy earned him the respect of both his fellow reporters and those who work in the Congress and the White House. It was only fitting that his nomination for a Pulitzer Prize was for a story about welfare and HIV-positive children. Chris' friends and colleagues most remember his decency, integrity, wit, and sense of fairness. He will be deeply missed by his parents, sisters, and many friends.

Statement on Signing the Gallatin Land Consolidation Act of 1998
October 20, 1998

Yesterday I was pleased to sign into law H.R. 3381, the "Gallatin Land Consolidation Act of 1998." This law will direct the Secretaries of Agriculture and the Interior to transfer certain lands and other assets in Montana to the Big Sky Lumber Company in exchange for a significantly larger amount of land to be included in the Gallatin and Deer Lodge National Forests.

The Gallatin land exchange is consistent with my goal of restoring and protecting the greater Yellowstone ecosystem. It is complementary to my efforts to protect Yellowstone Park from the risks of mining, to secure to the public trust important tracts of land adjacent to Yellowstone, and to restore and ensure the well-being of Yellowstone wildlife.

I want to particularly thank Senator Max Baucus for his hard work and leadership on this matter over many years. Senator Baucus has long been a leader on the issue of preserving our Nation's natural heritage while remaining a tenacious advocate for the working families of Montana.

Although the Gallatin land exchange provides an opportunity to acquire environmentally sensitive lands that are essential to the conservation of wildlife habitat and improves public access to public lands, I do object to the language in this bill that declares that the studies undertaken over the last several years are "sufficient" for the purposes of compliance with environmental laws.

WILLIAM J. CLINTON

The White House,
October 20, 1998.

NOTE: H.R. 3381, approved October 19, was assigned Public Law No. 105–267.

Statement on Signing the Intelligence Authorization Act for Fiscal Year 1999
October 20, 1998

Today I have signed into law H.R. 3694, the "Intelligence Authorization Act for Fiscal Year 1999." The Act authorizes Fiscal Year 1999 appropriations for U.S. intelligence and intelligence-related activities.

The Act is the product of the dedication and effort of many people in Congress and my Administration. I believe that the Act will help our Nation maintain a strong intelligence capability and preserve the safety and security of our country.

I am pleased that the Act provides enhanced protective authority for CIA personnel and family members. This is extremely important given the continuing terrorist threat against U.S. citizens and interests. I also note that the Act names the CIA Headquarters Compound in Langley, Virginia, the "George Bush Center for Intelligence." This is an appropriate and well-deserved tribute to former President Bush.

Sections 601 and 602 of the Act enhance significantly our ability to conduct effective counterintelligence and international terrorism investigations. In addition, section 604 expands the Government's ability to conduct wiretaps when investigating a broad range of Federal felonies. The Attorney General will develop comprehensive guidelines and minimization procedures for the use of this expanded authority and will amend procedures currently contained in the manual for United States Attorneys to provide appropriate protection for the rights of Americans. Until such guidelines and procedures are finalized, the Government will conduct wiretaps in accordance with the standards provided under current law. The Department of Justice will include statistics on the use of the expanded authority in its annual wiretap report to the Congress.

Finally, I am satisfied that this Act contains an acceptable whistleblower protection provision, free of the constitutional infirmities evident in the Senate-passed version of this legislation. The Act does not constrain my constitutional authority to review and, if appropriate, control disclosure of certain classified information to the Congress. I note that the Act's legislative history makes clear that the Congress, although disagreeing with the executive branch regarding the operative constitutional principles, does not intend to foreclose the exercise of my constitutional authority in this area.

The Constitution vests the President with authority to control disclosure of information when necessary for the discharge of his constitutional responsibilities. Nothing in this Act purports to change this principle. I anticipate that this authority will be exercised only in exceptional circumstances and that when agency heads decide that they must defer, limit, or preclude the disclosure of sensitive information, they will contact the appropriate congressional committees promptly to begin the accommodation process that has traditionally been followed with respect to disclosure of sensitive information.

WILLIAM J. CLINTON

The White House,
October 20, 1998.

NOTE: H.R. 3694, approved October 20, was assigned Public Law No. 105–272.

Remarks on Funding for Breast Cancer Research
October 21, 1998

The President. Thank you very much. I'm delighted to be here with this distinguished panel of people, and I hope I can communicate a little bit of what we've tried to do in this area in just a few moments. As all of you know, I think, I have been spending most of the last week in the Middle East peace talks at Wye Plantation on the Eastern Shore. And when I conclude my remarks, I have to go take a call from Secretary Albright and see if I'm going back. So I hope you'll forgive me for leaving.

Let me say I'm delighted to be here with all of you. I thank all of you for your work. I am glad to see Senator Jeffords here. I used to refer to Senator Jeffords as my favorite Republican, and then I was informed that I had endangered his committee chairmanship and his physical well-being. [*Laughter*] So I never do that anymore, but I'm honored to have you back in the White House, Senator. And Mayor Beverly O'Neill from Long Beach, California, thank you for coming; and to all the rest of you.

Twenty-five years ago America declared war on cancer. Twenty-five years from now we have a good chance to have won the war. I hope the war on cancer 25 years from now will have about as much meaning to children in school as the War of 1812. I hope schoolchildren don't even know what chemotherapy means.

For nearly 6 years, we have worked hard to bring us closer to that day. We've helped cancer patients to keep their health coverage when they change jobs, accelerated the approval of cancer drugs while maintaining high standards of safety, continually increased funding for cancer research.

Recently, I named Dr. Jane Henney the first woman and the first oncologist to be the Commissioner of the Food and Drug Administration. And I am pleased to report that about 2 hours ago she was actually confirmed by the United States Senate.

Thanks to the work of a lot of you in this room, we have made genuine progress. We're closing in on the genetic causes of breast cancer, colon cancer, prostate cancer, and now testing medicines to actually prevent those cancers. New tools for screening and diagnosis are returning to many patients the promise of a long and healthy life. From 1991 to 1995, cancer death rates actually dropped for the first time in history.

I'm especially proud of the 5 years of progress we've made in prevention, detection, and treatment of breast cancer. Not one day goes by that I don't think about my mother and, through her, all the other women in this country who have had that dreaded disease. It requires more than courage to deal with it. We all owe it to ourselves and our future to make the sustained commitment to research that, once and for all, can win this war.

Without research, there would be no mammography. Without research, there would be no genetic testing for vulnerability to breast cancer. Without research, there would be no—how do you pronounce that——

Audience members. Tamoxifen.

The President. ——tamoxifen. I practiced this twice this morning. But since then, my chain of thought has been interrupted. [*Laughter*] Anyway, we wouldn't have it without research.

This afternoon, before I came over here, I signed the balanced budget that we fought so hard in the last days of this Congress. It has, among other things, breakthrough funding for cancer research and a general, large increase in research funding for our country's future, a part of the commitment that Hillary and I made when we asked Americans to honor the millennium by honoring our past and envisioning our future.

I'm pleased that the new budget includes a record increase of $400 million in new support for the National Cancer Institute. With nearly $3 billion in funding, NCI now will be able to fund critical new research, including a trial to expand the use of Herceptin to treat breast cancer earlier and 10 more new clinical trials for breast cancer treatment. This is an important victory for women's health. It reflects a balanced budget that honors our values. In this, as in so many other things, I also would like to thank the Vice President, who spearheaded our drive to get the research funding into the budget.

If you will, I'd like to mention just a couple of other ways that this budget strengthens our

Nation. First, it honors our duty of fiscal responsibility. It is a budget surplus that we now enjoy for the first time in nearly three decades, the largest in our history. And despite the temptations here just before an election to spend it on tax cuts and new spending programs, the budget actually meets my challenge to set aside the surplus until we save Social Security for the 21st century.

It also provides funding within the balanced budget to begin to hire 100,000 new teachers to reduce class size in the early grades, thousands of tutors to help children read, up to 100,000 mentors to help poor children prepare for college, after-school programs to give a quarter of a million children someplace to learn instead of the streets, a half a million summer jobs to teach young people the discipline and joy of work.

The budget strengthens our Nation in other ways as well. It will bolster our own prosperity and help us to meet our responsibilities to deal with the global economy turmoil by meeting our obligations to the International Monetary Fund. It actually strengthens the protection of the environment. It guarantees safer water, cleaner air, more pristine public lands. It will help struggling farmers who face natural disasters and dramatically declining markets as a result of the trouble in Asia.

We had to fight for each of these priorities, and the budget is not perfect. You know, I lost the line item veto in our court case, and there's a lot of little things tucked away there that I wish weren't in that budget. But on balance, it honors our values and strengthens our country and looks to the future.

Now, I believe that it's important to point out, too, that if we had the right sort of spirit throughout the year, we wouldn't have had to cram a year's worth of work into a 4,000-page, 40-pound document passed several days after the budget year had run out. There are still some elements of partisanship that I would like to note in the hope that they can be removed.

In the past few days, the Congress persisted in tying our United Nations dues to unrelated and controversial social provisions, which endanger the health of women and deny them even basic information about family planning, even though studies show that countries where women have access to strong family planning actually have fewer abortions. I've made it clear many times that I will veto such provisions. Con-

gress sent me the bill to fund our arrears to the United Nations, knowing full well I would do so. So today I did. I regret that.

I regret, too, that the 105th Congress leaves town with unfinished business, challenges that must be met in the coming months and years to strengthen our families and our Nation.

The next Congress must pass the Patients' Bill of Rights. I might say, there is bipartisan support for this, just not enough to get it by. Our plan says to cancer patients and all Americans: You should have the right to a specialist, such as an oncologist; you should not have to worry that you will have to change doctors in the middle of a cancer treatment if your employer changes health care providers; you should have a right to an independent appeals process if critical treatment is delayed or denied. Managed care or traditional care, every American should have quality care.

The next Congress should act in other ways to strengthen the health of women. This year I asked Congress to cover clinical trials for Medicare beneficiaries so they, too, can get cutting-edge treatment. [*Applause*] Thank you. And I asked Congress to outlaw discrimination based on the results of genetic screening. Both these measures failed to pass. The next Congress should pass them.

The next Congress should also meet our obligations to our children by modernizing our schools. And above all, the next Congress must be the Congress that acts to save Social Security.

This year we had a series of bipartisan forums around the country on how to reform Social Security to meet the burdens that will be there when the baby boomers retire, and we'll only have about two people working for every one person drawing Social Security. We're going to have a national conference in December. We were successful in saving the surplus until we could consider the cost in future years of reforming Social Security.

Social Security lifted a generation of elderly Americans from poverty. Today, even though most Americans have other sources of income who draw Social Security, fully one-half of our seniors would be in poverty without it. So here at the White House on Friday we will talk about the vital importance of Social Security, especially to women, who have fewer pensions and smaller savings.

If we want to keep this commitment as strong for our children as it was for our parents, and if we want to see the baby boomers retire in dignity without imposing unfair burdens on our children and their ability to raise our grand-children, we must act now.

I must say, I was disappointed a couple of days ago that the Senate majority leader said he may not now want to join me in reforming Social Security next year. If we don't, then there will be more pressure to squander this money on tax cuts or spending programs. I think that is unhelpful. We know that we can make modest changes now that have a huge impact down the road, in much the way that modest invest-ments in research now have a huge impact down the road on health care. And I believe this is an issue which really binds the American people, not only across generations but across political parties. None of us—none of us—wants to leave a legacy of burdening our children to support our retirement or risking that those of us who, unlike me, won't have a good pension, will face an undignified and impoverished old age just because the demographics are changing in America. So we need progress, not partisanship, on Social Security.

Now, there are 436 days left in this millen-nium. It can—it should be a time when we redouble our efforts to honor our parents, to strengthen our Nation, to prepare for our chil-dren's future, and to honor the tenacity and courage that those of you here have shown every day in dealing with this great challenge.

Again, let me say, I am very proud of what this budget did for cancer research. I'm very proud of what we are doing together to deal with the challenge of breast cancer. I want you to know that, that I believe that we are within reach of genuine cures and genuine prevention strategies of stunning impact. And we have to remember that on the things that really count, whether it's cancer research or saving Social Se-curity or educating our children, this country needs to be united. This country needs to be reconciled to one another, all of us, across all the lines that divide us. There are plenty of things to fight about. But on the fundamental things, we need to be one. That is, parentheti-cally, the argument I've been making for a week out at the Middle East peace talks.

The only way that life ever really works is when we understand that the only victories that have lasting impacts are not victories over other people but victories for our common humanity. And that's what I'm going to work for now. To me, that's what every day your struggle against breast cancer symbolizes. And I'm very grateful to all of you.

Thank you, and God bless you.

NOTE: The President spoke at 4:15 p.m. in the East Room at the White House. H.R. 4328, the Omnibus Consolidated and Emergency Supple-mental Appropriations Act, 1999, approved Octo-ber 21, was assigned Public Law No. 105–277.

Statement on Senate Action To Confirm Jane E. Henney as Commissioner of the Food and Drug Administration
October 21, 1998

I am extremely pleased that today the Senate, with strong bipartisan support, overwhelmingly voted to confirm Dr. Jane E. Henney to be the next Commissioner of the Food and Drug Administration. I am confident that as the first woman and first oncologist to be confirmed as FDA Commissioner, Dr. Henney will live up to the trust the Senate has placed in her.

The Nation now has an FDA Commissioner who is committed to assuring that Americans have safe food, safe and effective drugs and medical devices, and improved public health. Dr. Henney has blazed many trails, and no one

is more qualified to lead the FDA. She has served four Presidents and helped guide some of America's finest academic health centers. Her expertise in science and technology and lifelong dedication to individual patients will enable her to strike the important balance between the need for timely approval of prescription drugs and medical devices, while maintaining safety and quality.

I commend the Democrats and Republicans who worked to give Dr. Henney a full and fair hearing and help expedite this confirmation. I also want to thank representatives of consumers, physicians, nurses, and the industry for their steadfast and strong support for Dr. Henney. Their combined leadership made a vital contribution toward assuring we have the right person to lead the FDA into the 21st century.

Statement on Signing the Departments of Veterans Affairs and Housing and Urban Development, and Independent Agencies Appropriations Act, 1999
October 21, 1998

Today I have signed into law H.R. 4194, the "Departments of Veterans Affairs and Housing and Urban Development, and Independent Agencies Appropriations Act, 1999."

This Act will fund vital environmental, veterans, housing, community development, space, and science programs. Specifically, it provides funding for the Departments of Veterans Affairs (VA) and Housing and Urban Development (HUD), the Environmental Protection Agency (EPA), the National Aeronautics and Space Administration, the Federal Emergency Management Agency (FEMA), the National Science Foundation, and several other agencies.

The Act funds a number of my Administration's high priorities, including the Corporation for National and Community Service and the Community Development Financial Institutions (CDFI) fund. National Service gives young people the opportunity to obtain funding for a college education while serving the country in areas of great need, such as the environment, public safety, and human services. The CDFI fund is helping to create a network of community development banks across the country, thereby spurring the flow of capital to distressed neighborhoods and their currently underserved low-income residents and providing financing for neighborhood redevelopment and revitalization efforts. That is why I am pleased that the Congress agreed to a 19 percent increase in funding for CDFI.

The Act provides $7.56 billion for the EPA, which will enable the agency to enforce our environmental laws adequately. I am pleased that the Congress modified language in the Act concerning the Kyoto Protocol on global climate change and clarified what this language means in the Statement of Managers. In particular, the Congress made it clear that it does not intend to limit my Administration's ability to carry out

common-sense actions to reduce greenhouse gas emissions; its intent, rather, is only to limit funding that would implement actions called for solely under the Kyoto Protocol. As we have said on many occasions, my Administration will not seek to implement that Protocol prior to its ratification by the Senate. I am also pleased that H.R. 4194 fully funds my request for EPA's portion of the Clean Water Action Plan and the Drinking Water State Revolving Fund, and adequately funds the Clean Water State Revolving Fund.

The Act provides $24.4 billion in funding for the Department of Housing and Urban Development, including full funding for my request to renew expiring Section 8 contracts, thus assuring continuation of HUD rental subsidies for low-income tenants in privately owned housing and 50,000 additional welfare-to-work housing vouchers to assist those welfare recipients for whom housing assistance is critical to getting or keeping a job. This Act provides increased funding to help revitalize communities through such programs as the HOME Investment Partnership; Community Development Block Grants; and HOPE VI, an initiative for severely distressed public housing and Brownfields redevelopment, which returns abandoned sites to productive uses. I am pleased that the bill continues to support States and cities through these vital economic development programs.

As I requested, the Act provides increased funding for Homeless Assistance Grants and Housing Opportunities for Persons with AIDS and for anti-discrimination efforts, including the Fair Housing Initiatives program. The Act also increases funds for the Office of Lead Hazard Control to reduce the risk of childhood lead poisoning and other health hazards.

I am encouraged by our efforts to work with the Congress to provide additional resources for a number of our priority programs in the FY 1999 Omnibus appropriations bill.

The Act includes my Administration's proposal to reform HUD's single-family property disposition program, which would produce substantial savings by improving the efficiency of the Federal Housing Administration's (FHA's) property disposition processes. In addition, H.R. 4194 furthers the Administration's goal to provide greater homeownership opportunities by increasing the FHA loan limit.

The Act also makes landmark housing reform a reality. This bipartisan bill will allow more economic integration and deconcentration in our Nation's public housing; encourage and reward work; provide protections for those most in need; and put the Nation back into the housing

business with the first new housing vouchers in 5 years.

I am also pleased that the Act includes $25 million for the Neighborhood Reinvestment Corporation to start my "Play-by the-Rules" homeownership initiative, which would make homeownership more accessible to 10,000 families who have good rental histories, but are not adequately served in the housing market.

Finally, the Act provides $17.3 billion for the medical care of our Nation's veterans.

WILLIAM J. CLINTON

The White House,
October 21, 1998.

NOTE: H.R. 4194, approved October 21, was assigned Public Law No. 105–276.

Message to the House of Representatives Returning Without Approval Foreign Affairs Reform and Restructuring Legislation
October 21, 1998

To the House of Representatives:

I am returning herewith without my approval H.R. 1757, the "Foreign Affairs Reform and Restructuring Act of 1998".

I take this action for several reasons, most importantly, because the Congress has included in this legislation unacceptable restrictions on international family planning programs and threatened our leadership in the world community by tying our payment of dues to the United Nations and other international organizations to these unrelated family planning issues.

Current law, with which Administration policy is fully consistent, already prohibits the use of Federal funds to pay for abortion abroad and for lobbying on abortion issues. This bill would go beyond those limits. One provision would deny U.S. Government funding for family planning programs carried out by foreign nongovernmental organizations (NGOs) that use their own funds to perform abortions even though the overall result of these NGO family planning programs is to reduce the incidence of abortion. Although the bill allows the President to waive this restriction, use of the waiver would also cripple many programs by limiting annual spending for international family planning to

$356 million, $44 million below the amount available for Fiscal Year 1998.

A second provision would attempt to restrict the free speech of foreign NGOs by prohibiting funding for those that use their own funds to engage in any activity intended to alter the laws of a foreign country either to promote or to deter abortion. The bill would even ban drafting and distributing material or public statements on abortion. The bill does not contain a waiver for this restriction.

These restrictions and the funding limit would severely jeopardize the ability of the United States to meet the growing demand for family planning and other critical health services in developing countries. By denying funding to organizations that offer a wide range of safe and effective family planning services, the bill would increase unwanted pregnancies and lead to more abortions than would otherwise be the case.

I am also deeply concerned that the Congress has effectively tied these unacceptable restrictions on international family planning to payment of legitimate U.S. arrears to the United Nations and other international organizations. A strong United Nations, with the United States playing a leadership role, is in our national interest. Payment of our dues to the United Nations is essential to our ability to lead. There are strongly held beliefs on both sides of the debate over international population policy. These issues ought to be considered separately on their own merits; they should not be permitted to hinder U.S. obligations to the world community.

The package authorizing arrears payments linked to UN reforms was the result of good-faith negotiations between my Administration and the Congress more than a year and a half ago. Unfortunately, due to the passage of time, some of these conditions are now outdated and are no longer achievable. In particular, the fact that the UN has concluded negotiations on assessment rates for the next 3 years has significantly decreased our ability to negotiate a limitation on the U.S. assessed share of the UN regular budget below 22 percent. Furthermore, the increase in contested arrears during this period requires that the United States have additional flexibility in obtaining a contested arrears account. While many of the UN reform bench-

marks in the package remain acceptable, significant revisions are required, and I look forward to working with the Congress next year to secure the payment of our arrears and an achievable package of UN reforms.

The Bill contains important and carefully negotiated authority to reorganize the foreign affairs agencies and other basic authorities for these agencies. Many of these provisions were supported by my Administration, and I am pleased that they have been included in the Omnibus Consolidated and Emergency Supplemental Appropriations Act for FY 1999.

For the foregoing reasons, I am compelled to return H.R. 1757 without my approval.

WILLIAM J. CLINTON

The White House,
October 21, 1998.

NOTE: H.R. 4328, the Omnibus Consolidated and Emergency Supplemental Appropriations Act, 1999, approved October 21, was assigned Public Law No. 105–277.

Letter to Congressional Leaders Reporting on the National Emergency With Respect to Significant Narcotics Traffickers Centered in Colombia
October 21, 1998

Dear Mr. Speaker: (Dear Mr. President:)

I hereby report to the Congress on the developments since my last report concerning the national emergency with respect to significant narcotics traffickers centered in Colombia that was declared in Executive Order 12978 of October 21, 1995. This report is submitted pursuant to section 401(c) of the National Emergencies Act, 50 U.S.C. 1641(c), and section 204(c) of the International Emergency Economic Powers Act (IEEPA), 50 U.S.C. 1703(c).

1. On October 21, 1995, I signed Executive Order 12978, "Blocking Assets and Prohibiting Transactions with Significant Narcotics Traffickers" (the "Order") (60 *Fed. Reg.* 54579, October 24, 1995). The Order blocks all property subject to U.S. jurisdiction in which there is any interest of four significant foreign narcotics traffickers, one of whom is now deceased, who were principals in the so-called Cali drug cartel centered in Colombia. These persons are listed

in the annex to the Order. The Order also blocks the property and interests in property of foreign persons determined by the Secretary of the Treasury, in consultation with the Attorney General and the Secretary of State, (a) to play a significant role in international narcotics trafficking centered in Colombia or (b) to materially assist in or provide financial or technological support for, or goods or services in support of, the narcotics trafficking activities of persons designated in or pursuant to the Order. In addition, the Order blocks all property and interests in property, subject to U.S. jurisdiction, of persons determined by the Secretary of the Treasury, in consultation with the Attorney General and the Secretary of State, to be owned or controlled by, or to act for or on behalf of, persons designated in or pursuant to the Order (collectively "Specially Designated Narcotics Traffickers" or "SDNTs").

The Order further prohibits any transaction or dealing by a United States person or within the United States in property or interests in property of SDNTs, and any transaction that evades or avoids, has the purpose of evading or avoiding, or attempts to violate, the prohibitions contained in the Order.

Designations of foreign persons blocked pursuant to the Order are effective upon the date of determination by the Director of the Department of the Treasury's Office of Foreign Assets Control (OFAC) acting under authority delegated by the Secretary of the Treasury. Public notice of blocking is effective upon the date of filing with the *Federal Register*, or upon prior actual notice.

2. On October 24, 1995, the Department of the Treasury issued a notice containing 76 additional names of persons determined to meet the criteria set forth in Executive Order 12978 (60 *Fed. Reg.* 54582, October 24, 1995). Additional notices expanding and updating the list of SDNTs were published on November 29, 1995 (60 *Fed. Reg.* 61288), March 8, 1996 (61 *Fed. Reg.* 9523), and January 21, 1997 (62 *Fed. Reg.* 2903).

Effective February 28, 1997, OFAC issued the Narcotics Trafficking Sanctions Regulations ("NTSR" or the "Regulations"), 31 C.F.R. Part 536, to further implement my declaration of a national emergency and imposition of sanctions against significant foreign narcotics traffickers centered in Colombia (62 *Fed. Reg.* 9959, March 5, 1997).

On April 17, 1997 (62 *Fed. Reg.* 19500, April 22, 1997), July 30, 1997 (62 *Fed. Reg.* 41850, August 4, 1997), September 9, 1997 (62 *Fed. Reg.* 48177, September 15, 1997), and June 1, 1998 (63 *Fed. Reg.* 29608, June 1, 1998), OFAC amended appendices A and B to 31 C.F.R. chapter V, revising information concerning individuals and entities who have been determined to play a significant role in international narcotics trafficking centered in Colombia or have been determined to be owned or controlled by, or to act for or on behalf of, or to be acting as fronts for the Cali cartel in Colombia.

On May 27, 1998 (63 *Fed. Reg.* 28896, May 27, 1998), OFAC amended appendices A and B to 31 C.F.R. chapter V, by expanding the list for the first time beyond the Cali cartel by adding the names of one of the leaders of Colombia's North Coast cartel, Julio Ceasar Nasser David, who has been determined to play a significant role in international narcotics trafficking centered in Colombia, and 14 associated businesses and 4 individuals acting as fronts for the North Coast cartel. Also added were six companies and one individual that have been determined to be owned or controlled by, or to act for or on behalf of, or to be acting as fronts for the Cali cartel in Colombia. These actions are part of the ongoing interagency implementation of Executive Order 12978 of October 21, 1995. These changes to the previous SDNT list brought it to a total of 451 businesses and individuals with whom financial and business dealings are prohibited and whose assets are blocked under the Order. A copy of the amendment is attached to this report.

3. OFAC has disseminated and routinely updated details of this program to the financial, securities, and international trade communities by both electronic and conventional media. In addition to bulletins to banking institutions via the Federal Reserve System and the Clearing House Interbank Payments System (CHIPS), individual notices were provided to all relevant State and Federal regulatory agencies, automated clearing houses, and State and independent banking associations across the country. OFAC contacted all major securities industry associations and regulators. It posted electronic notices on the Internet and over 10 computer bulletin boards and 2 fax-on-demand services, and provided the same material to the U.S. Embassy in Bogota for distribution to U.S. companies operating in Colombia.

4. As of September 4, 1998, OFAC had issued 11 specific licenses pursuant to Executive Order 12978. These licenses were issued in accordance with established Department of the Treasury policy authorizing the completion of presanctions transactions, the provision of legal services to and payment of fees for representation of SDNTs in proceedings within the United States arising from the imposition of sanctions, and certain administrative transactions. In addition, a license was issued to authorize a U.S. company in Colombia to make certain payments to two SDNT entities in Colombia (currently under the control of the Colombian government) for services provided to the U.S. company in connection with the U.S. company's occupation of office space and business activities in Colombia.

5. The narcotics trafficking sanctions have had a significant impact on the Colombian drug cartels. Of the 154 business entities designated as SDNTs as of September 4, 1998, 44, with an estimated aggregate income of more than $210 million, had been liquidated or were in the process of liquidation. As a result of OFAC designations, Colombian banks have closed nearly 400 SDNT accounts, affecting nearly 200 SDNTs. One of the largest SDNT commercial entities, a discount drugstore with an annual income exceeding $136 million, has been reduced to operating on a cash basis. These specific results augment the less quantifiable but significant impact of denying the designated individuals and entities of the Cartel access to U.S. financial and commercial facilities.

Various enforcement actions carried over from prior reporting periods are continuing and new reports of violations are being aggressively pursued. One criminal investigation is ongoing and a second, not presented for prosecution, was referred for civil penalty action, bringing the total of referrals since my last report to five.

6. The expenses incurred by the Federal Government in the 6-month period from April 21 through October 20, 1998, that are directly attributable to the exercise of powers and authorities conferred by the declaration of the national emergency with respect to Significant Narcotics Traffickers are estimated at approximately $600,000. Personnel costs were largely centered in the Department of the Treasury (particularly in the Office of Foreign Assets Control, the U.S. Customs Service, and the Office of the General Counsel), the Department of Justice,

and the Department of State. These data do not reflect certain costs of operations by the intelligence and law enforcement communities.

7. Executive Order 12978 provides this Administration with a tool for combatting the actions of significant foreign narcotics traffickers centered in Colombia and the violence, corruption, and harm that they cause in the United States and abroad. The Order is designed to deny these traffickers the benefit of any assets subject to the jurisdiction of the United States and to prevent United States persons from engaging in any commercial dealings with the traffickers, their front companies, or their agents. Executive Order 12978 demonstrates the United States commitment to end the damage that such traffickers inflict upon society in the United States and abroad.

The magnitude and scope of the problem in Colombia—perhaps the most pivotal country of all in terms of the world's cocaine trade—are extremely grave. I shall continue to exercise the powers at my disposal to apply economic sanctions against significant foreign narcotics traffickers as long as these measures are appropriate and will continue to report periodically to the Congress on significant developments pursuant to 50 U.S.C. 1703(c).

Sincerely,

WILLIAM J. CLINTON

NOTE: Identical letters were sent to Newt Gingrich, Speaker of the House of Representatives, and Albert Gore, Jr., President of the Senate. This letter was released by the Office of the Press Secretary on October 22.

Remarks on Adjournment of the Congress
October 22, 1998

Good morning. The closing gavel has come down now on the 105th Congress, and I want to take a moment to discuss what we've done and the unfinished, vital business that still remains.

Just a few moments ago, I was pleased to sign into law important legislation requested by my administration to encourage States and to help them to open more innovative, independent public charter schools and to hold these

schools strictly accountable for results. This will make sure that other public schools can actually learn from the best of these charter schools. That is the right way to strengthen our public schools.

When I took office in 1993, there was only one charter school actually operating in America. Now there are 1,000, many of them helped by previous administration-supported legislation.

This legislation puts us well on our way to creating 3,000 charter schools by the year 2000.

On charter schools, Congress did put progress over partisanship. But on too many other issues, Congress has left town and left the work of the American people behind. This Congress' failure to act in many areas has had real costs for our families. Partisanship killed my proposal to use tax cuts, fully paid for in the balanced budget, to build or modernize 5,000 schools. Partisanship killed the Patients' Bill of Rights, which would guarantee your right to see a specialist, to medical privacy, to the nearest emergency care, to keep your doctor during the course of treatment, to have medical decisions made by doctors, not insurance company accountants. Partisanship killed tough legislation to crack down on teen smoking, even as teen smoking continues to rise and is the number one public health problem our young people face. Partisanship killed an increase in the minimum wage, which would give a much needed pay raise to our hardest pressed working families. Partisanship killed our best chance in years for tough campaign finance reform. And partisanship blocked our efforts to make child care more affordable for working families.

The American people deserve better. I hope when the next Congress convenes, it will put progress ahead of partisanship in a way that this Congress has not done.

Wye River Middle East Peace Talks

Now I am returning to the Middle East talks on the Eastern Shore of Maryland. The hardest decisions now, at last, are on the table. Israel, the Palestinians, the region, and the world have very much at stake today. I hope the parties will seize this opportunity and not retreat from the clear moment to capture the momentum of peace and keep it moving forward.

NOTE: The President spoke at 8:55 a.m. on the South Lawn at the White House, prior to his departure for the Wye River Middle East peace talks. The 105th Congress adjourned *sine die* on October 21. H.R. 2616, the Charter School Expansion Act of 1998, approved October 22, was assigned Public Law No. 105–278.

Statement on Signing the Charter School Expansion Act of 1998
October 22, 1998

Today I am pleased to sign into law H.R. 2616, the "Charter School Expansion Act of 1998." This bill will help foster the development of high-quality charter schools, consistent with my goal of having 3,000 charter schools operating by early in the next century, and will help lead to improvements in public education more generally. I am particularly gratified by the bipartisan manner in which this bill passed the House and Senate.

I have long championed charter schools—public schools started by parents, teachers, and communities, open to all students regardless of background or ability, and given great flexibility in exchange for high levels of accountability. When I was elected President there was only one charter school in the Nation, and now there are more than 1,000 serving more than 200,000 students. This bill will help strengthen our efforts to support charter schools, providing parents and students with better schools, more choice, and higher levels of accountability in public education.

As the charter school movement spreads throughout the country, it is important that these schools have clear and measurable educational performance objectives and are held accountable to the same high standards expected of all public schools. To further this goal, H.R. 2616 requires the Department of Education to give priority in awarding grants to States in which the performance of every charter school is reviewed at least once every 5 years to ensure the school is fulfilling the terms of its charter and students are meeting achievement requirements and goals. It also will reward States that have made progress in increasing the number of high-quality, accountable charter schools. Finally, it makes clear that any charter school receiving funding under this program must be measured by the same State assessments as other public schools. These important quality-control measures will help charter schools fulfill their potential to become models of accountability for public education.

I am also pleased that H.R. 2616 provides new authority for successful charter schools to serve as models, not just for other charter schools, but for public schools generally. At a relatively low cost, such model schools will provide in-depth advice, materials, and other information on various aspects of their programs—helping to start up new public schools and helping existing schools learn from their successes. By drawing on the experience of high-performing charter schools throughout our Nation, this legislation will help bring the benefits of

innovation and creativity to hundreds of thousands of additional children.

I am confident that this legislation will augment the ability of parents, teachers, and others to strengthen public education in their communities. This bill represents an integral part of our effort to improve public schools and help all of our students get the high-quality public education they need and deserve.

WILLIAM J. CLINTON

The White House,
October 22, 1998.

NOTE: H.R. 2616, approved October 22, was assigned Public Law No. 105–278.

Statement on the National Rate of Homeownership
October 22, 1998

This morning the Census Bureau released fresh evidence that our strong economy continues to widen the circle of opportunity to more American families. Last quarter the national homeownership rate reached another record high. For the first time in history, more than two-thirds of American families own their own homes. Since I took office, 7.4 million families have become homeowners. I am especially pleased that these gains are being shared broadly, with African-American and Hispanic homeownership climbing even more rapidly than the overall rate.

Six years ago I put in place an economic strategy which helped produce a cycle of lower deficits, lower interest rates, stronger investment, higher incomes, and greater confidence. That virtuous cycle opened the door of homeownership to millions of Americans. Now the challenge is to keep our economy strong—which is why we must continue to maintain fiscal discipline, invest in our people, and lead the global economy. I will continue to work hard to take the steps necessary to make the dream of homeownership a reality for more Americans.

Letter to Congressional Leaders Reporting Budget Deferrals
October 22, 1998

Dear Mr. Speaker: (Dear Mr. President:)
In accordance with the Congressional Budget and Impoundment Control Act of 1974, I herewith report two deferrals of budgetary resources, totaling $167.6 million.

The deferrals affect programs of the Department of State and International Security Assistance.

Sincerely,

WILLIAM J. CLINTON

NOTE: Identical letters were sent to Newt Gingrich, Speaker of the House of Representatives, and Albert Gore, Jr., President of the Senate. This letter was released by the Office of the Press Secretary on October 23. The report detailing the deferrals was published in the *Federal Register* on November 17.

Remarks at the Wye River Memorandum Signing Ceremony
October 23, 1998

The President. Thank you. Thank you very much. Mr. Vice President, Madam Secretary. Your Majesty, Prime Minister Netanyahu, Chairman Arafat. To the Israeli and Palestinian delegations, the Members of Congress and the Cabinet, members of the diplomatic corps, my fellow Americans who are here, it's a great honor for me to welcome you here. I only wish the First Lady were here as well. She is in Chicago. We talked a few moments ago, and she sends her great happiness and best wishes, especially to Queen Noor and Mrs. Netanyahu.

After some very difficult negotiations—very long, dare I say, quite sleepless—the Israelis and Palestinians here have reached an agreement on issues over which they have been divided for more than 17 months. This agreement is designed to rebuild trust and renew hope for peace between the parties. Now both sides must build on that hope, carry out their commitments, begin the difficult, but urgent journey toward a permanent settlement.

Over the last 9 days I have witnessed extraordinary efforts on behalf of peace. I thank our team, beginning with its head, the Secretary of State, who showed remarkable creativity, strength, and patience. I thank the Vice President for his interventions. I thank my good friend Sandy Berger; our Director of Central Intelligence, George Tenet, who had an unusual, almost unprecedented role to play because of the security considerations; our Special Middle East Coordinator, Dennis Ross, who was a young man with no gray hair when all this began. [*Laughter*] I thank all the other outstanding members of our delegation.

I thank Prime Minister Netanyahu, who stood so firmly for the security of his citizens and of his country, and of the impressive members of his Cabinet and administration. I thank Chairman Arafat, who tenaciously defended the interests of his people, and the very impressive members of his team, as well. In the end, after all the twists and turns and ups and downs, all their late and ultimately sleepless nights, both reaffirmed their commitment to the path of peace. And for that, the world can be grateful.

And finally, let me thank His Majesty King Hussein, whose courage, commitment, wisdom,

and frankly, stern instruction at appropriate times were at the heart of this success. Your Majesty, we are all profoundly in your debt.

This agreement is good for Israel's security. The commitments made by the Palestinians were very strong, as strong as any we have ever seen. They include continuous security cooperation with Israel and a comprehensive plan against terrorism and its support infrastructure.

This agreement is good for the political and economic well-being of Palestinians. It significantly expands areas under Palestinian authority to some 40 percent of the West Bank. It also offers the Palestinian people new economic opportunities, with an airport, an industrial zone, soon safe passage between Gaza and the West Bank, and in time, a seaport. The Palestinian people will be able to breathe a little easier and benefit from the fruits of peace.

Most importantly, perhaps, this agreement is actually good for the peace process itself. For 18 months it has been paralyzed, a victim of mistrust, misunderstanding, and fear. Now ordinary Israelis and Palestinians once again can become partners for peace.

To bolster this effort, Chairman Arafat will invite members of the Palestinian National Council and other important political entities to reaffirm his prior commitments and their support for the peace process. I have agreed to address that meeting, several weeks hence, and to underscore the values of reconciliation, tolerance, and respect, and my support for those commitments and this process.

People around the world should be heartened by this achievement today. These leaders and those with whom they work have come a very long way. The Israeli and Palestinian peoples, whose bitter rivalry in this century has brought so much suffering to both sides, have moved yet another step closer toward fulfilling the promise of the Oslo accords, closer to the day when they can live peacefully as true neighbors, with security, prosperity, self-governance, cooperation, and eventually, God willing, genuine friendship.

No doubt, as peace gains momentum, forces of hate, no matter how isolated and disparate, will once again lash out. They know this, the leaders, and they are prepared to face it. Staying on the path of peace under these circumstances will demand even greater leadership and courage.

The work at Wye River shows what can happen when the will for peace is strong. But let me say once again to all the rest of you, everyone who is tempted to handicap every little twist and turn over the last 9 days, you need to know one overwhelming thing: The Prime Minister and the Chairman and the members of their delegation who supported this process, even when there were things about it they did not agree with, are quite well aware that the enemies of peace will seek to extract a price from both sides. They are quite well aware that in the short run, they themselves may have put themselves at greater risk. But by pledging themselves to the peaceful course for the future, to the same values and, ultimately, to the same enemies, they have given both Israelis and Palestinians a chance to have the future we all want for our children and our children's children.

Every effort will have to be exerted to ensure the faithful implementation of this agreement, not because the parties do not want to do so but because the agreement covers many things, was developed over many days, involved many discussions and sleepless nights. It will test whether the Palestinian people are prepared to live in peace, recognizing Israel's permanence, legitimacy, and a common interest in security. It will tell us whether Israelis want to help build a strong Palestinian entity that can fulfill the aspirations of its people and provide both real security and real partnership for Palestinians and Israelis.

The United States is determined to be of whatever help we can to both sides in their endeavors. I will consult with Congress to design a package of aid to help Israel meet the security costs of redeployment and help the Palestinian Authority meet the economic costs of development. I hope we will have support from Republicans and Democrats in that endeavor.

With respect to Mr. Pollard, I have agreed to review this matter seriously, at the Prime Minister's request. I have made no commitment as to the outcome of the review. Ultimately, the parties will have to translate the gains of Wye River into renewed efforts to secure a just and lasting peace. For as big a step as today is—and after 17 months, it is a very large step, indeed—it is just another step along the way. Therefore, perhaps as important as any other statement to be made today, let me say how grateful I am that the Prime Minister and the Chairman have agreed to begin permanent status talks upon ratification of this agreement.

I have agreed to convene the two leaders at an appropriate time to seek to complete these talks. We have all agreed to try to do it under circumstances which permit more sleep at night. [*Laughter*]

Let me say that no agreement can wipe away decades of distrust. But I think these last several days have helped each side to get a better understanding of the other's hopes and fears, a better feel for all they have in common, including on occasion, thank the Lord, a good sense of humor.

The future can be right for Israelis and Palestinians if they maintain the will for peace. If we continue to work together, the next generation will grow up without fear. Israel can have the genuine security and recognition it has sought for so long. The Palestinian people can, at long last, realize their aspirations to live free in safety, in charge of their own destiny.

So, on behalf of all the people of the United States, let me say to the Israeli and Palestinian peoples, *salaam, shalom,* peace be with you in the hard and hopeful days ahead. We value our friendship, and we thank you for your trust, for giving us the opportunity to walk this road with you.

Now it is my privilege to introduce Prime Minister Netanyahu. Let me say, I was, once again, extraordinarily impressed by the energy, the drive, the determination, the will, the complete grasp of every detailed aspect of every issue that this Prime Minister brought to these talks. He showed himself willing to take political risks for peace, but not to risk the security of his people. And as a result, this agreement embodies an enormous increase in the security of the people of Israel.

Mr. Prime Minister, the microphone is yours.

[*At this point, Prime Minister Binyamin Netanyahu of Israel made remarks.*]

The President. Let me say, I wish that all of you who care about this could have seen at least a portion of what I saw in the last 9 days in the interchanges between Prime Minister Netanyahu and Chairman Arafat. It was very interesting. They were so different. I can't imagine Mr. Netanyahu in a *kaffiyeh*. [*Laughter*] But they were very much alike in their tenacity and their astonishing intelligence and knowledge.

Just as I was able to say a thank you to Prime Minister Netanyahu, let me say to Chairman Arafat, I thank you. I thank you for turning away from violence toward peace. I thank you for embracing the idea that Palestinians and Israelis can actually share the land of our fathers together. I thank you for believing that the home of Islam and Judaism and Christianity can surely be the home of people who love one God and respect every life God has created. And I thank you for decades and decades and decades of tireless representation of the longing of the Palestinian people to be free, self-sufficient, and at home.

Mr. Chairman, the microphone is yours.

[*Chairman Yasser Arafat of the Palestinian Authority made remarks.*]

The President. Ladies and gentlemen, many kind things have been said about the efforts of the American delegation and the hours that I spent at Wye Plantation, every one of which I treasured. [*Laughter*] Some more than others. But in truth, all that was required of us was a listening ear and a helpful suggestion now and then, and a kind of a determination to keep us all moving forward.

It is a little too easy, I think, sometimes for people who are not directly, themselves, parties to a peace negotiation to believe they truly understand the judgments that the parties themselves must make, and how difficult they are, and what price they might carry. I think, as hard as we tried not to fall prey to that, from time to time we did. I know we did, because there are people on both sides smiling at me just now as I speak. So the lion's share of the credit belongs to Prime Minister Netanyahu and Chairman Arafat and their close aides.

But His Majesty King Hussein provided an element quite different from what the United States brought to these negotiations, for he reminded us of what rises above the facts, the arguments, the legitimate interests, even the painful sacrifices involved. He was the living embodiment of the best of our past and the brightest of our hopes for the future. And every time he was in the room, he made us all become a little closer to the people we all would like

to see ourselves as being. For that, we and the world are immeasurably in his debt.

Your Majesty.

[*King Hussein I of Jordan made remarks.*]

The President. Let me say—everyone sit down. We have to hurry because the hour is growing late, and it's almost Shabbat. I have to say one thing, very quickly. We have three men of peace here who have extraordinary military backgrounds. We have many others here; I want to mention two who came with Prime Minister Netanyahu: General Sharon and General Mordechai; we're glad to have you here. And I say that because I want you to understand a piece of history.

This table was brought to this house in 1869 by one of America's greatest military leaders, Ulysses Grant, who revolutionized infantry warfare in our Civil War. One hundred years ago this table was used to sign the peace treaty between the United States and Spain. And for 100 years, this table, brought here by one of our greatest warriors, has been the exclusive repository of our peace agreements, the one we signed with Your Majesty King Hussein on this table; President Kennedy's test ban treaty, signed on this table.

And so I think it is fitting that these three great leaders—two signers, one, His Majesty, observing—who know a great deal about war have come to make peace on this table, which, for our country, has come to embody it. And we thank them.

Thank you very much.

[*The memorandum was signed.*]

NOTE: The President spoke at 4 p.m. in the East Room at the White House. In his remarks, he referred to Queen Noor of Jordan; Prime Minister Netanyahu's wife, Sarah; former civilian U.S. Navy intelligence analyst Jonathan Pollard, convicted of treason and espionage in 1987; and Minister of Foreign Affairs Ariel Sharon and Minister of Defense Yitzhak Mordechai of Israel. The transcript released by the Office of the Press Secretary also included the remarks of Secretary of State Madeleine Albright, Vice President Al Gore, Prime Minister Netanyahu, Chairman Arafat, and King Hussein I.

The Wye River Memorandum
October 23, 1998

The following are steps to facilitate implementation of the Interim Agreement on the West Bank and Gaza Strip of September 28, 1995 (the "Interim Agreement") and other related agreements including the Note for the Record of January 17, 1997 (hereinafter referred to as "the prior agreements") so that the Israeli and Palestinian sides can more effectively carry out their reciprocal responsibilities, including those relating to further redeployments and security respectively. These steps are to be carried out in a parallel phased approach in accordance with this Memorandum and the attached time line. They are subject to the relevant terms and conditions of the prior agreements and do not supersede their other requirements.

I. Further Redeployments

A. *Phase One and Two Further Redeployments*

1. Pursuant to the Interim Agreement and subsequent agreements, the Israeli side's implementation of the first and second F.R.D. will consist of the transfer to the Palestinian side of 13% from Area C as follows:

1% to Area (A)

12% to Area (B)

The Palestinian side has informed that it will allocate an area/areas amounting to 3% from the above Area (B) to be designated as Green Areas and/or Nature Reserves. The Palestinian side has further informed that they will act according to the established scientific standards, and that therefore there will be no changes in the status of these areas, without prejudice to the rights of the existing inhabitants in these areas including Bedouins; while these standards do not allow new construction in these areas, existing roads and buildings may be maintained.

The Israeli side will retain in these Green Areas/Natural Reserves the overriding security responsibility for the purpose of protecting Israelis and confronting the threat of terrorism. Activities and movements of the Palestinian Police forces may be carried out after coordination and confirmation; the Israeli side will respond to such requests expeditiously.

2. As part of the foregoing implementation of the first and second F.R.D., 14.2% from Area (B) will become Area (A).

B. *Third Phase of Further Redeployments*

With regard to the terms of the Interim Agreement and of Secretary Christopher's letters to the two sides of January 17, 1997 relating to the further redeployment process, there will be a committee to address this question. The United States will be briefed regularly.

II. Security

In the provisions on security arrangements of the Interim Agreement, the Palestinian side agreed to take all measures necessary in order to prevent acts of terrorism, crime and hostilities directed against the Israeli side, against individuals falling under the Israeli side's authority and against their property, just as the Israeli side agreed to take all measures necessary in order to prevent acts of terrorism, crime and hostilities directed against the Palestinian side, against individuals falling under the Palestinian side's authority and against their property. The two sides also agreed to take legal measures against offenders within their jurisdiction and to prevent incitement against each other by any organizations, groups or individuals within their jurisdiction.

Both sides recognize that it is in their vital interests to combat terrorism and fight violence in accordance with Annex I of the Interim Agreement and the Note for the Record. They also recognize that the struggle against terror and violence must be comprehensive in that it deals with terrorists, the terror support structure, and the environment conducive to the support of terror. It must be continuous and constant over a long-term, in that there can be no pauses in the work against terrorists and their structure. It must be cooperative in that no effort can be fully effective without Israeli-Palestinian cooperation and the continuous exchange of information, concepts, and actions.

Pursuant to the prior agreements, the Palestinian side's implementation of its responsibilities for security, security cooperation, and other issues will be as detailed below during the time periods specified in the attached time line:

A. *Security Actions*

1. *Outlawing and Combating Terrorism Organizations*

(a) The Palestinian side will make known its policy of zero tolerance for terror and violence against both sides.

(b) A work plan developed by the Palestinian side will be shared with the U.S. and thereafter implementation will begin immediately to ensure the systematic and effective combat of terrorist organizations and their infrastructure.

(c) In addition to the bilateral Israeli-Palestinian security cooperation, a U.S.-Palestinian committee will meet biweekly to review the steps being taken to eliminate terrorist cells and the support structure that plans, finances, supplies and abets terror. In these meetings, the Palestinian side will inform the U.S. fully of the actions it has taken to outlaw all organizations (or wings of organizations, as appropriate) of a military, terrorist or violent character and their support structure and to prevent them from operating in areas under its jurisdiction.

(d) The Palestinian side will apprehend the specific individuals suspected of perpetrating acts of violence and terror for the purpose of further investigation, and prosecution and punishment of all persons involved in acts of violence and terror.

(e) A U.S.-Palestinian committee will meet to review and evaluate information pertinent to the decisions on prosecution, punishment or other legal measures which affect the status of individuals suspected of abetting or perpetrating acts of violence and terror.

2. *Prohibiting Illegal Weapons*

(a) The Palestinian side will ensure an effective legal framework is in place to criminalize, in conformity with the prior agreements, any importation, manufacturing or unlicensed sale, acquisition or possession of firearms, ammunition or weapons in areas under Palestinian jurisdiction.

(b) In addition, the Palestinian side will establish and vigorously and continuously implement a systematic program for the collection and appropriate handling of all such illegal items in accordance with the prior agreements. The U.S. has agreed to assist in carrying out this program.

(c) A U.S.-Palestinian-Israeli committee will be established to assist and enhance cooperation in preventing the smuggling or other unauthorized introduction of weapons or explosive materials into areas under Palestinian jurisdiction.

3. *Preventing Incitement*

(a) Drawing on relevant international practice and pursuant to Article XXII (1) of the Interim Agreement and the Note for the Record, the Palestinian side will issue a decree prohibiting all forms of incitement to violence or terror, and establishing mechanisms for acting systematically against all expressions or threats of violence or terror. This decree will be comparable to the existing Israeli legislation which deals with the same subject.

(b) A U.S.-Palestinian-Israeli committee will meet on a regular basis to monitor cases of possible incitement to violence or terror and to make recommendations and reports on how to prevent such incitement. The Israeli, Palestinian and U.S. sides will each appoint a media specialist, a law enforcement representative, an educational specialist and a current or former elected official to the committee.

B. *Security Cooperation*

The two sides agree that their security cooperation will be based on a spirit of partnership and will include, among other things, the following steps:

1. *Bilateral Cooperation*

There will be full bilateral security cooperation between the two sides which will be continuous intensive and comprehensive.

2. *Forensic Cooperation*

There will be an exchange of forensic expertise, training, and other assistance.

3. *Trilateral Committee*

In addition to the bilateral Israeli-Palestinian security cooperation, a high-ranking U.S.-Palestinian-Israeli committee will meet as required and not less than biweekly to assess current threats, deal with any impediments to effective security cooperation and coordination and address the steps being taken to combat terror and terrorist organizations. The committee will also serve as a forum to address the issue of external support for terror. In these meetings, the Palestinian side will fully inform the members of the committee of the results of its investigations concerning terrorist suspects already in custody and the participants will exchange additional relevant information. The committee will report regularly to the leaders of the two sides on the status of cooperation, the results of the meetings and its recommendations.

C. *Other Issues*

1. *Palestinian Police Force*

(a) The Palestinian side will provide a list of its policemen to the Israeli side in conformity with the prior agreements.

(b) Should the Palestinian side request technical assistance, the U.S. has indicated its willingness to help meet these needs in cooperation with other donors.

(c) The Monitoring and Steering Committee will, as part of its functions, monitor the implementation of this provision and brief the U.S.

2. *PLO Charter*

The Executive Committee of the Palestine Liberation Organization and the Palestinian Central Council will reaffirm the letter of 22 January 1998 from PLO Chairman Yasir Arafat to President Clinton concerning the nullification of the Palestinian National Charter provisions that are inconsistent with the letters exchanged between the PLO and the Government of Israel on 9/10 September 1993. PLO Chairman Arafat, the Speaker of the Palestine National Council, and the Speaker of the Palestinian Council will invite the members of the PNC, as well as the members of the Central Council, the Council, and the Palestinian Heads of Ministries to a meeting to be addressed by President Clinton to reaffirm their support for the peace process and the aforementioned decisions of the Executive Committee and the Central Council.

3. *Legal Assistance in Criminal Matters*

Among other forms of legal assistance in criminal matters, the requests for arrest and transfer of suspects and defendants pursuant to Article II(7) of Annex IV of the Interim Agreement will be submitted (or resubmitted) through the mechanism of the Joint Israeli-Palestinian Legal Committee and will be responded to in conformity with Article II(7)(f) of Annex IV of the Interim Agreement within the twelve week period. Requests submitted after the eighth week will be responded to in conformity with Article II(7)(f) within four weeks of their submission. The U.S. has been requested by the sides to report on a regular basis on the steps being taken to respond to the above requests.

4. *Human Rights and the Rule of Law*

Pursuant to Article XI(1) of Annex I of the Interim Agreement, and without derogating from the above, the Palestinian Police will exercise powers and responsibilities to implement this Memorandum with due regard to internationally accepted norms of human rights and the rule of law, and will be guided by the need to protect the public, respect human dignity, and avoid harassment.

III. Interim Committees and Economic Issues

1. The Israeli and Palestinian sides reaffirm their commitment to enhancing their relationship and agree on the need actively to promote economic development in the West Bank and Gaza. In this regard, the parties agree to continue or to reactivate all standing committees established by the Interim Agreement, including the Monitoring and Steering Committee, the Joint Economic Committee (JEC), the Civil Affairs Committee (CAC), the Legal Committee, and the Standing Cooperation Committee.

2. The Israeli and Palestinian sides have agreed on arrangements which will permit the timely opening of the Gaza Industrial Estate. They also have concluded a "Protocol Regarding the Establishment and Operation of the International Airport in the Gaza Strip During the Interim Period."

3. Both sides will renew negotiations on Safe Passage immediately. As regards the southern route, the sides will make best efforts to conclude the agreement within a week of the entry into force of this Memorandum. Operation of the southern route will start as soon as possible thereafter. As regards the northern route, negotiations will continue with the goal of reaching agreement as soon as possible. Implementation will take place expeditiously thereafter.

4. The Israeli and Palestinian sides acknowledge the great importance of the Port of Gaza for the development of the Palestinian economy, and the expansion of Palestinian trade. They commit themselves to proceeding without delay to conclude an agreement to allow the construction and operation of the port in accordance with the prior agreements. The Israeli-Palestinian Committee will reactivate its work immediately with a goal of concluding the protocol within sixty days, which will allow commencement of the construction of the port.

5. The two sides recognize that unresolved legal issues adversely affect the relationship between the two peoples. They therefore will accelerate efforts through the Legal Committee to address outstanding legal issues and to implement solutions to these issues in the shortest possible period. The Palestinian side will provide to the Israeli side copies of all of its laws in effect.

6. The Israeli and Palestinian sides also will launch a strategic economic dialogue to enhance their economic relationship. They will establish within the framework of the JEC an Ad Hoc Committee for this purpose. The committee will review the following four issues: (1) Israeli purchase taxes; (2) cooperation in combating vehicle theft; (3) dealing with unpaid Palestinian debts; and (4) the impact of Israeli standards as barriers to trade and the expansion of the A1 and A2 lists. The committee will submit an interim report within three weeks of the entry into force of this Memorandum, and within six weeks will submit its conclusions and recommendations to be implemented.

7. The two sides agree on the importance of continued international donor assistance to facilitate implementation by both sides of agreements reached. They also recognize the need for enhanced donor support for economic development in the West Bank and Gaza. They agree to jointly approach the donor community to recognize a Ministerial Conference before the end of 1998 to seek pledges for enhanced levels of assistance.

IV. Permanent Status Negotiations

The two sides will immediately resume permanent status negotiations on an accelerated basis and will make a determined effort to achieve the mutual goal of reaching an agreement by May 4, 1999. The negotiations will be continuous and without interruption. The U.S. has expressed its willingness to facilitate these negotiations

V. Unilateral Actions

Recognizing the necessity to create a positive environment for the negotiations, neither side shall initiate or take any step that will change the status of the West Bank and the Gaza Strip in accordance with the Interim Agreement.

This Memorandum will enter into force ten days from the date of signature.

Done at Washington, D.C this 23d day of October 1998.

B. Netanyahu	*Y. Arafat*
For the Government of the State of Israel	For the PLO

Witnessed by: William J. Clinton
The United States of America

NOTE: The joint memorandum, accompanied by a timeline attachment, was made available by the Office of the Press Secretary but was not issued as a White House press release. On October 28, a press release version of the memorandum was made available on the White House Internet site.

Statement on Signing the Federal Employees Health Care Protection Act of 1998
October 23, 1998

The Federal Employees Health Care Protection Act of 1998, H.R. 1836, that I have signed into law makes several critical improvements to the Federal Employees Health Benefits Program (FEHBP). For example, it gives the Office of Personnel Management's Inspector General critical new debarment authority to crack down on fraudulent providers and, when necessary, to debar those who defraud the program; it contains essential new provisions to maintain and improve consumer choice, the hallmark of FEHBP, by allowing fee-for-service plans to rejoin FEHBP; it makes health care more affordable for certain Federal employees and retirees of the Federal Deposit Insurance Corporation and the Federal Reserve Board by allowing them to participate in the FEHBP; and finally, it ensures that certain Federal physicians who provide high quality services will receive appropriate compensation for their services, which is critical to attracting and maintaining a high quality Federal physician work force.

I want to note, however, my objection to a provision in this legislation that appears to expand preemption of State law remedies for FEHBP enrollees who are injured as a result of wrongful benefit delay or denial by their plan. As I have consistently stated, I believe that a right without remedy is not a right at all. I strongly believe that Federal employees should have the right to legally enforceable remedies, including under State law, to protect them when health plans do not provide contractually obligated patient protections. I therefore want to clarify that my enactment of this legislation should in no way be construed to indicate my support for this preemption provision. I also would like to reiterate my disappointment that the Congress has adjourned without passing a Patients' Bill of Rights that would give new protections and remedies to all Americans, including Federal employees. Assuring that health plans provide needed patient protections and adequate remedies will be one of my top priorities for the next Congress.

WILLIAM J. CLINTON

The White House,
October 23, 1998.

NOTE: H.R. 1836, approved October 19, was assigned Public Law No. 105–266. An original was not available for verification of the content of this statement.

Statement on Signing the Omnibus Consolidated and Emergency Supplemental Appropriations Act, 1999
October 23, 1998

I have signed into law H.R. 4328, the "Omnibus Consolidated and Emergency Supplemental Appropriations Act, 1999."

This bill represents a significant step forward for America. It protects the surplus until we have saved Social Security for the 21st century, contains an agreement to fund the International Monetary Fund, and puts in place critical investments in education and training, from smaller class sizes to after-school care, and from summer jobs to college mentoring. I am pleased that this bill honors my commitment to maintain fiscal discipline by providing additional resources for essential new investments, which are fully financed within the limits of the Bipartisan Budget Agreement.

Specifically, the legislation provides needed funds for education and training, including a down payment on my plan to reduce class size in the early grades by hiring 100,000 new teachers. It provides added resources to protect the environment, to move people from welfare to work, to strengthen law enforcement, to enforce civil rights, and to further efforts that advance health, research, and development. And with this legislation, funds can be made available to farmers suffering through the worst farm emergency in a decade.

First, this legislation provides an additional $4.4 billion for education and training, furthering the goal of life-long education to help Americans acquire the skills they need to succeed in the new global economy. In addition to funding my class size initiative, this bill will help advance child literacy by meeting my full request for the America Reads program, and by increasing funding for Head Start. It also supports an important part of my child-care initiative: the focus on improving the quality of child-care programs and the funding provided for after-school programs should help approximately 1,600 21st Century Community Learning Centers, serving nearly a quarter of a million children, to provide extended learning activities and related services in safe and constructive environments with adult supervision.

I am pleased that included in this legislation are three other high-priority education initiatives—GEAR UP, Teacher Quality Enhancement Grants, and Learning Anytime, Anywhere Partnerships—that were recently authorized in the Higher Education Act. Charter School funding will provide start-up resources to about 1,400 schools, serving approximately 400,000 students; my Youth Opportunity Areas initiative will provide intensive training and related services to help 50,000 disadvantaged youth in very high poverty areas get good jobs; and more than a half-million young people will be able to participate in the Summer Jobs program.

College students will benefit from funding in this legislation, which provides the largest Pell Grant maximum award in history and expands the Work-Study program to help nearly one million students work their way through college. I am also very pleased that the Congress provided virtually all my requested increases for the Hispanic Education Action Plan funded in this bill.

My commitment to a clean and healthy environment is advanced significantly in this legislation. Additional resources will be used to combat water pollution through the Clean Water Action Plan, fight global warming, protect national parks and other precious lands, preserve wildlife, and develop clean energy technologies. There are also funds to support the Save America's Treasures Millennium Initiative, and for the purchase of sensitive and historic lands.

At the same time, we have been able to prevent the inclusion of harmful riders specific to the environment, including ones that would have delayed salmon restoration in the Northwest, built a road through designated wilderness areas in the Izembek National Wildlife Refuge, and forced overcutting of timber in national forests.

I am pleased that we are able to reach agreement with the bipartisan leadership to fulfill our commitment to fund and pay arrears to the Global Environmental Facility (GEF), established in 1991. This funding will help GEF in its fight against global warming, promotion of biodiversity, and reduction of energy consumption world-wide.

By providing $17.9 billion in funding for the International Monetary Fund, this legislation makes a significant contribution to protecting our domestic economy from global turmoil. In addition, I am pleased that the Congress has provided additional funding for key international programs. Some examples are assistance to the Newly Independent States (NIS), support for nonproliferation activities, such as the Korean Energy Development Organization and the Comprehensive Test Ban Treaty preparatory commission; and payments of assessed contributions to international organizations. However, I am deeply troubled that the United States remains unable to pay its arrears to the United Nations and other international organizations. Funding to meet our international commitments

should not be linked to unrelated family planning issues.

I am pleased that this legislation contains my proposal to streamline the executive branch's policy-making process in foreign affairs by putting matters of international arms control, sustainable development, and public diplomacy where they belong—at the heart of our foreign policy within a reinvented Department of State. Under the reorganization plan, first the Arms Control and Disarmament Agency, then the United States Information Agency will be integrated with the Department of State. The Agency for International Development will remain a distinct agency, but will share certain administrative functions with the Department of State and will report to and be under the direct authority and foreign policy guidance of the Secretary of State. I am also pleased that the bill includes the implementing legislation for the Chemical Weapons Convention, which the Senate approved in May 1997. It was critical to have legislation in this area before the Congress adjourned.

I appreciate the Congress approving the Administration's initiative to provide additional funding for military readiness and for ongoing operations in Bosnia. These funds will ensure that the U.S. military can sustain its high levels of preparedness and advance our efforts in Bosnia to implement the Dayton Accords.

For law enforcement, the bill provides $1.4 billion to ensure that my program to put 100,000 more police on the streets of America's communities by the year 2000 proceeds on schedule—17,000 additional officers will be funded. The bill also includes funding to support my Administration's efforts to both secure our borders and to provide immigration benefits to those seeking citizenship. Funding for 1,000 Border Patrol agents, border technology, and detention support has been provided to deter drug trafficking and illegal entry at the border. The funding level also provides an additional $171 million to address a backlog in citizenship applications, fix the naturalization program, and ensure that the benefit of citizenship is not delayed unnecessarily for those who have earned it. It funds the Indian Country law enforcement initiative that will increase the number of law enforcement officers on Indian lands, expand detention facilities, enhance juvenile crime prevention, and improve the effectiveness of tribal courts.

I am pleased that increased funding for the Legal Services Corporation (LSC) will enable the LSC to provide additional services to people with financial need. While it is regrettable that my full request for the LSC was not met this year, I intend to continue to press for additional funding to allow the expansion of services in the future.

Civil rights protection is enhanced on numerous fronts. There is an increase of funding to the Equal Employment Opportunity Commission to significantly expand the Commission's alternative dispute resolution program and reduce the backlog of discrimination complaints. There are also increases in funding to the Department of Education's Office of Civil Rights, the Department of Labor's Office of Federal Contract Compliance, and the Department of Justice's Office of Civil Rights and its Community Relations Service, which mediates and resolves racial and ethnic conflicts in communities.

This bill will also address the long-standing discrimination claims of many minority farmers by adopting my request to waive the statute of limitations on USDA discrimination complaints that date back to the early 1980s. This will finally provide these farmers the fair and expedited hearing—and where past discrimination is found, the fair compensation—they have long deserved.

In addition, funding for HUD's Fair Housing programs will increase significantly, and will provide resources for a new audit-based enforcement initiative.

I am pleased that this legislation contains a program of targeted grants to Empowerment Zones, providing communities with flexible funds to carry out local development strategies and to bring jobs and investment to disadvantaged areas. I look forward to working with the Congress next year to expand this program.

The District of Columbia receives a total of $620 million of Federal support, including $125 million of special one-time payments requested by my Administration for economic development, special education, and help for the District in addressing the Year 2000 computer problem. Funds for the District of Columbia will permit further implementation of my plan for revitalizing the Nation's Capital, and will be used to spur growth and for the public charter school program, among other programs.

While I am pleased that we were able to secure significant funding increases of AIDS services and prevention generally, I am nonetheless disappointed that the Congress has chosen to deny the people of the District of Columbia the right to save lives with a proven HIV prevention program of needle exchange. The Congress' action will deny Federal funding to any private agency in the District of Columbia that uses its own funds in this way, putting countless women and children at risk for AIDS and undermining the principle of home rule in the District.

There are significant advancements to improve the health of Americans by advancing research and by improving the safety of our food supply. The Food Safety Initiative will expand education, surveillance, import inspections, research, and risk assessment activities. The Congress also made a critical down payment on my proposed 21st Century Research Fund for America by adding $2 billion for biomedical research at the National Institutes of Health (NIH). This will enable NIH to pursue new methods of diagnosing, treating, preventing, and curing diseases such as cancer, diabetes, Alzheimer's, and HIV/AIDS. There are new increases in funding for disease prevention research at the Centers for Disease Control and for health outcomes research at the Agency for Health Care Policy Research. I am also pleased that this legislation provides $1.4 billion for Ryan White Care Act activities, including the AIDS Drug Assistance Program, which provides funds to States to help uninsured and underinsured people with HIV purchase life-saving pharmaceutical therapies. Finally, there is a new, critical $130 million investment to address the problem of HIV/AIDS in the minority community.

I am pleased that for the first time, this Act will require health plans that participate in the Federal Employees Health Benefits Program and provide prescription drug coverage to include contraceptives as part of that coverage. The section exempts from this requirement five specifically named religious plans and any other existing or future plan that objects to the requirement on the basis of religious beliefs.

I am also pleased that the Congress has agreed to fund several urgent needs on an emergency basis. The nearly $6 billion of funding in this bill for farm emergencies reflects my commitment to meet the needs of our Nation's farmers who are suffering through the worst agricultural crisis in more than a decade. The bill addresses my concerns over emergency farm assistance funding that prompted my veto of the Agricultural Appropriations bill earlier this month.

The Act also includes needed emergency funding to help parts of our country recover from recent natural disasters, including Hurricane Georges; address unanticipated requirements associated with year 2000 computer conversion activities; strengthen our diplomatic security, anti-terrorism, and counterterrorism efforts; support our troops in Bosnia; and enhance military readiness. While the Act provides many investments to help prepare America for the next century, there is still much work to do for the future.

Now that we have embarked on a path to adding 100,000 teachers to our school systems, we must make sure that they will be able to teach in new and modern schoolrooms, I will continue to fight for my school modernization program which, with fully paid for tax credits, would leverage nearly $22 billion in bonds to build and renovate schools.

While this bill provided important new funding to improve the quality of child care, more needs to be done. I will continue to push for additional critical investments, including subsidies and tax credits to make child care safer and more affordable for America's working families.

I believe strongly that a voluntary national test for our children's achievement is essential so that parents can know how well their children and their schools are performing on a basis that fairly compares them to others. This bill, unfortunately, includes language prohibiting any pilot testing or administration of voluntary national tests. We will continue work on test development, and we will continue to work with the Congress to eliminate this bar to national testing so that we can advance the hopes of all parents for their children's education.

I will continue to make it a top priority to urge the Congress to pass a strong, enforceable Patients' Bill of Rights that would assure Americans the quality health care they need. In a rapidly changing health care system, Americans need and deserve essential patient protections, such as access to specialists, an independent appeals process, and remedies to make these rights real. I also will urge the Congress to pass the bipartisan Work Incentives Improvement Act, which provides workers with disabilities the op-

tion to buy into Medicare and Medicaid, as well as other pro-work incentives. Finally, the Congress must pass needed tobacco legislation to reduce teen smoking.

The Act also contains provisions relating to preparations for the year 2000 Census. An accurate census is essential to our democracy and to basic fairness, and the Census Bureau is doing all it can to count each and every American in the 2000 Census. To count everyone, including nonrespondents, the Census Bureau must use proven scientific statistical techniques. Despite overwhelming support from impartial statistical experts for using such modern scientific methods, some in the Congress have opposed them. These opponents have proposed instead an approach that, even at vastly greater cost, will exclude millions of people—especially children and minorities. I am pleased that this Act contains sufficient funds to allow the Census Bureau to continue preparations for a decennial census using the most accurate methods.

This Act funds the Departments of Commerce, Justice, and State through June 15, 1999. By that time, we should have the benefit of the Supreme Court's decision whether we can use up-to-date scientific methods in the census for purposes of apportioning Congressional seats among the States. We are confident that the Court will not consign us to 18th century methods to deal with 21st century problems. It is imperative that the Congress, before June 15, 1999, fund these departments for the entire fiscal year without excluding millions of Americans from the census. I am committed to ensuring that the year 2000 is the most accurate census possible.

I am also disappointed that the Congress provided less funding than I requested for the Federal Aviation Administration to operate the Nation's air traffic control system. While safety of the flying public will not be compromised, these reductions will result in an enormous challenge to provide critical aviation services and keep pace with a growing aviation industry.

Unfortunately, the Act also includes language that would cap the award of plaintiffs' attorneys' fees in special education cases to a maximum of $50 per hour and $1,300 per case. While this language is less objectionable than the original proposal that sought to ban compensation for plaintiffs attorneys' fees for special education administrative proceedings, I still find this provision unacceptable. It will undoubtedly restrict poor families in the District of Columbia from having adequate access to the due process protections provided by the Individuals with Disabilities Education Act (IDEA). I pledge that next year I will work to eliminate this cap and ensure that the rights of disabled children and their families are protected.

It is unfortunate the bill does not lift the cap on transfers to Puerto Rico and the Virgin Islands of the excise tax on rum as I had proposed and many in the Congress supported. This measure was consistent with the basic laws regarding those jurisdictions and the Caribbean Basin Initiative. The objection that thwarted it will deny urgently needed fiscal assistance to the 4 million U.S. citizens who live on these islands.

I am disappointed that the Congress failed to enact either of my proposed trade initiatives, the African Growth and Opportunity Act or the Caribbean Basin Initiative. My plans to expand our trade relations with nations in Africa and the Caribbean would benefit the United States and the economies of these developing countries. I firmly believe that the free flow of goods and services is an essential part of our Nation's successful economic strategy and I will continue to pursue these initiatives so that economies in Africa and the Caribbean, as well as our own, can benefit from an expansion in free trade.

I am also disappointed that the Act includes a provision that could undermine the ability of Federal law enforcement to conduct large, multi-state investigations, such as those related to terrorist attacks, drug cartels, and interstate child exploitation. This provision was opposed by the law enforcement community, national victims groups, and many in the House and Senate. The effective date of the provision is 6 months from now. My Administration will work with the Congress over the next few months on potential legislative remedies to ensure that we can continue to enforce Federal laws and protect the public.

There are a number of provisions in the Act that may raise Constitutional issues. These provisions will be treated in a manner that is consistent with the Constitution.

I am concerned about section 117 of the Treasury/General Government appropriations section of the Act, which amends the Foreign Sovereign Immunities Act. If this section were to result in attachment and execution against foreign embassy properties, it would encroach on my authority under the Constitution to "receive Ambassadors and other public Ministers." Moreover, if applied to foreign diplomatic or consular property, section 117 would place the United States in breach of its international treaty obligations. It would put at risk the protection we enjoy at every embassy and consulate throughout the world by eroding the principle that diplomatic property must be protected regardless of bilateral relations. Absent my authority to waive section 117's attachment provision, it would also effectively eliminate use of blocked assets of terrorist states in the national security interests of the United States, including denying an important source of leverage. In addition, section 117 could seriously affect our ability to enter into global claims settlements that are fair to all U.S. claimants, and could result in U.S. taxpayer liability in the event of a contrary claims tribunal judgment. To the extent possible, I shall construe section 117 in a manner consistent with my constitutional authority and with U.S. international legal obligations, and for the above reasons, I have exercised the waiver authority in the national security interest of the United States.

Section 609 of the Commerce/Justice/State appropriations provision of the Act prohibits the use of funds to maintain diplomatic relations with Vietnam unless the President provides the Congress with a detailed certification that Vietnam has satisfied specific conditions. This provision unconstitutionally constrains the President's authority with respect to the conduct of diplomacy, and I will apply this provision consistent with my constitutional responsibilities.

Section 610 of the Commerce/Justice/State appropriations provision prohibits the use of appropriated funds for the participation of U.S. armed forces in a U.N. peacekeeping mission under foreign command unless the President's military advisers have recommended such involvement and the President has submitted such recommendations to the Congress. The "Contributions for International Peacekeeping Activities" provision requires a report to the Congress prior to voting for a U.N. peacekeeping mission. These provisions unconstitutionally constrain my diplomatic authority and my authority as Commander in Chief, and I will apply them consistent with my constitutional responsibilities.

Section 514 of the Foreign Operations/Export Financing appropriations section purports specifically to direct the Executive on how to proceed in negotiations with international organizations. These provisions could interfere with my constitutional authority in the area of foreign affairs. I shall treat all such provisions as advisory.

Section 625 of the Treasury/General Government appropriations section prohibits the use of appropriations to pay the salary of any employee who interferes with certain communications between Federal employees and Members of Congress. I do not interpret this provision to detract from my constitutional authority and that of my appointed heads of departments to supervise and control the operations and communications of the executive branch, including the control of privileged and national security information.

Section 722 of the Agriculture/Rural Development appropriations section specifies that funds may not be used to provide to any non-Department of Agriculture employee questions or responses to questions resulting from the appropriations hearing process. To the extent that this provision would interfere with my duty to "take Care that the Laws be faithfully executed," or impede my ability to act as the chief executive, it would violate the Constitution, and I will treat it as advisory.

Section 754 of the Agriculture/Rural Development appropriations section constrains my ability to make a particular type of budget recommendation to the Congress. This provision would interfere with my constitutional duty under the Recommendation Clause, and I will treat it as advisory.

Finally, several provisions in the Act purport to condition my authority or that of certain officers to use funds appropriated by the Act on the approval of congressional committees. My Administration will interpret such provisions to require notification only, since any other interpretation would contradict the Supreme Court ruling in *INS* v. *Chadha*.

The Omnibus Appropriations bill contains several emergency provisions that are contingent on a Presidential emergency designation.

I hereby designate the following amounts as emergency requirements pursuant to section 251(b)(2)(A) of the Balanced Budget and Emergency Deficit Control Act of 1985, as amended:

- Department of Defense: Military Construction, Army: $118,000,000;
- Department of Defense: Operation and Maintenance, Army: $104,602,000;
- Department of Defense: Operation and Maintenance, Air Force: $1,700,000;
- Legislative Branch: Architect of the Capitol, Capitol Visitor Center: $100,000,000;
- Legislative Branch: Capitol Police Board, Security Enhancements: $106,782,000;
- Legislative Branch: Senate, Contingent Expenses of the Senate, Sergeant at Arms and Doorkeeper of the Senate: $5,500,000;
- Legislative Branch: House of Representatives, Salaries and Expenses, Salaries, officers and employees: $6,373,000;
- Legislative Branch: General Accounting Office, Information Technology Systems and Related Expenses: $5,000,000;
- The Judiciary: Judicial Information Technology Fund: $13,044,000.

My Administration is undertaking a review of these issues and will make additional emergency designations in a timely manner.

WILLIAM J. CLINTON

The White House,
October 23, 1998.

NOTE: H.R. 4328, approved October 21, was assigned Public Law No. 105–277.

Statement on Emergency Assistance to Farmers and Ranchers
October 23, 1998

As provided for in the Omnibus bill I signed 2 days ago, I am pleased today to designate an additional $4.2 billion in emergency assistance to our nation's farmers and ranchers, to help them recover from the worst agricultural crisis in a decade. Coupled with the more then $1.6 billion in agricultural emergency funds released when I signed H.R. 4328, the Omnibus

Consolidated and Emergency Supplemental Appropriations Act, 1999, earlier this week, this brings the total to $5.9 billion. This amount is more than $1.6 billion greater than the amount included in the Agriculture Appropriations bill I vetoed on October 8 because it did not adequately address the farm crisis. I particularly want to thank Senator Daschle and my negotiating team for seeing to it that the final bill included the extra funds that will help a great many farmers stay in business.

There should be no confusion over the fact that these funds provide only a 1-year, temporary fix for the overall problems with the farm safety net. That is why I am equally pleased about other provisions in the bill that address the long-term need for farmers to get a fair income from the market and to help them better manage their variation in annual income. A major reason for the drop in prices for some major crops this year has been lower commodity exports, which account for a third of our farm output.

We fought long and hard to secure the nearly $18 billion in IMF funding included in the bill, which will especially help our customers in Asia and elsewhere so that they can continue to buy our farm products. The bill also makes permanent the ability of farmers to average their income across good years and bad to stabilize the farm family budget.

However, I also recognize that there are some fundamental shortcomings in the structure of the Federal farm income safety net. Therefore, I will review proposals for long-term improvements in the risk management and crop insurance programs to reduce the risk that next year farmers and ranchers will again suffer under such severe conditions.

I also want to thank Secretary of Agriculture Glickman for his tireless work on behalf of American agriculture. I know he and his staff are hard at work right now setting the process in place to deliver the assistance I am designating today. While it cannot happen overnight—in particular, we will not know the full extent of the 1998 crop losses and due compensation for some weeks to come—I know he will shortly begin delivering these funds to farmers and ranchers as quickly and as fairly as possible.

WILLIAM J. CLINTON

NOTE: H.R. 4328, approved October 21, was assigned Public Law No. 105–277. An original was not available for verification of the content of this statement.

Letter to Congressional Leaders Reporting on the National Emergency With Respect to Angola
October 23, 1998

Dear Mr. Speaker: (Dear Mr. President:)

I hereby report to the Congress on the developments since my last report of March 23, 1998, concerning the national emergency with respect to Angola that was declared in Executive Order 12865 of September 26, 1993. This report is submitted pursuant to section 401(c) of the National Emergencies Act, 50 U.S.C. 1641(c), and section 204(c) of the International Emergency Economic Powers Act, 50 U.S.C. 1703(c).

On September 26, 1993, I declared a national emergency with respect to the National Union for the Total Independence of Angola ("UNITA"), invoking the authority, *inter alia*, of the International Emergency Economic Powers Act (50 U.S.C. 1701 *et seq.*) and the United Nations Participation Act of 1945 (22 U.S.C. 287c). Consistent with United Nations Security Council Resolution ("UNSCR") 864, dated September 15, 1993, the order prohibited the sale or supply by United States persons or from the United States, or using U.S.-registered vessels or aircraft, of arms and related materiel of all types, including weapons and ammunition, military vehicles, equipment and spare parts, and petroleum and petroleum products to the territory of Angola other than through designated points of entry. The order also prohibited such sale or supply to UNITA. United States persons are prohibited from activities which promote or are calculated to promote such sales or supplies, or from attempted violations, or from evasion or avoidance, or transactions that have the purpose of evasion or avoidance, of the stated prohibitions. The order authorized the Secretary of the Treasury, in consultation with the Secretary of State, to take such actions, including the promulgation of rules and regulations, as might be necessary to carry out the purposes of the order.

1. On December 10, 1993, the Department of the Treasury's Office of Foreign Assets Control (OFAC) issued the UNITA (Angola) Sanctions Regulations (the "Regulations") (58 Fed. Reg. 64904) to implement the imposition of sanctions against UNITA. The Regulations prohibit the sale or supply by United States persons or from the United States, or using U.S.-registered vessels or aircraft, of arms and related materiel of all types, including weapons and ammunition, military vehicles, equipment and spare parts, and petroleum and petroleum products to UNITA or to the territory of Angola other than through designated points. United States persons are also prohibited from activities which promote or are calculated to promote such sales or supplies to UNITA or Angola, or from any transactions by any United States persons that evades or avoids, or has the purpose of evading or avoiding, or attempts to violate, any of the prohibitions set forth in the Executive order. Also prohibited are transactions by United States persons, or involving the use of U.S.-registered vessels or aircraft, relating to transportation to Angola or UNITA of goods the exportation of which is prohibited.

The Government of Angola has designated the following points of entry as points in Angola to which the articles otherwise prohibited by the Regulations may be shipped: *Airports*: Luanda and Katumbela, Benguela Province; *Ports*: Luanda and Lobito, Benguela Province; and Namibe, Namibe Province; and *Entry Points*: Malongo, Cabinda Province. Although no specific license is required by the Department of the Treasury for shipments to these designated points of entry (unless the item is destined for UNITA), any such exports remain subject to the licensing requirements of the Departments of State and/or Commerce.

2. On August 28, 1997, the United Nations Security Council adopted UNSCR 1127, expressing its grave concern at the serious difficulties in the peace process, demanding that the Government of Angola and in particular UNITA comply fully and completely with those obligations, and imposing additional sanctions against UNITA. Subsequently, the Security Council adopted UNSCR 1130 postponing the effective date of measures specified by UNSCR 1127 until 12:01 a.m., eastern standard time on October 30, 1997, at which time they went into effect.

On December 12, 1997, I issued Executive Order 13069 to implement in the United States the provisions of UNSCRs 1127 and 1130 (62 *Fed. Reg.* 65989, December 16, 1997). Executive Order 13069 prohibits (a) the sale, supply, or making available in any form, by United States persons or from the United States or using U.S.-registered vessels or aircraft, of any aircraft or aircraft components, regardless of origin, (i) to UNITA, or (ii) to the territory of Angola other than through a specified point of entry; (b) the insurance, engineering, or servicing by United States persons or from the United States of any aircraft owned or controlled by UNITA; (c) the granting of permission to any aircraft to take off from, land in, or overfly the United States if the aircraft, as part of the same flight or as a continuation of that flight, is destined to land in or has taken off from a place in the territory of Angola other than a specified point of entry; (d) the provision or making available by United States persons or from the United States of engineering and maintenance servicing, the certification of airworthiness, the payment of new claims against exiting insurance contracts, or the provision, renewal, or making available of direct insurance with respect to (i) any aircraft registered in Angola other than those specified by the Secretary of the Treasury, in consultation with the Secretary of State, and other appropriate agencies; (ii) any aircraft that entered the territory of Angola other than through a specified point of entry; (e) any transaction by any United States person or within the United States that evades or avoids, or has the purpose of evading or avoiding, or attempts to violate, any of the prohibitions set forth in this order. Executive Order 13069 became effective at 12:01 a.m., eastern standard time on December 15, 1997.

On June 12, 1998, the United Nations Security Council adopted UNSCR 1173, expressing its grave concern at the critical situation in the peace process and the failure of UNITA to implement its obligations under the Lusaka Protocol, and imposing additional sanctions against UNITA. Subsequently, the Security Council adopted UNSCR 1176 postponing the effective date of measures specified by UNSCR 1173 until 12:01 a.m., eastern daylight time on July 1, 1998, at which time they went into effect.

On August 18, 1998, I issued Executive Order 13098 to implement in the United States the provisions of UNSCRs 1173 and 1176 (63 *Fed. Reg.* 44771, August 20, 1998). Executive Order 13098 blocks all property and interests in property that are in the United States, that hereafter come within the United States, or that are or hereafter come within the possession or control of United States persons, of UNITA, or of those senior officials of UNITA, or adult members of their immediate families, who are designated pursuant to the order. In addition, the order prohibits the direct or indirect importation into the United States of all diamonds exported from Angola on or after the effective date of the order that are not controlled through the Certificate of Origin regime of the Angolan Government of Unity and National Reconciliation (the "GURN"). The order also prohibits the sale or supply by United States persons or from the United States or using U.S.-registered vessels or aircraft, of any equipment used in mining, or motorized vehicles or watercraft, and parts therefor, regardless of origin to the territory of Angola other than through a specified point of entry. Finally, the order prohibits any transaction by any United States person or within the United States that evades or avoids, or has the purpose of evading or avoiding, or attempts to violate, any of the prohibitions set forth in this order. Executive Order 13098 became effective at 12:01 a.m., eastern daylight time on August 19, 1998.

There have been no amendments to the Regulations since my report of March 23, 1998.

3. On December 31, 1997, OFAC issued an order to the Center for Democracy in Angola ("CEDA" or "CDA") to immediately close its offices in the United States as required by Executive Order 13069. CEDA responded that it had closed its only U.S. office, located in Washington, D.C., in compliance with Executive Order 13069.

The OFAC has worked closely with the U.S. financial and exporting communities to assure a heightened awareness of the sanctions against UNITA—through the dissemination of publications, seminars, and a variety of media, including via the Internet, fax-on-demand, special fliers, and computer bulletin board information initiated by OFAC and posted through the Department of Commerce and the Government Printing Office. There have been no license applications under the program since my last report. One investigation into an alleged violation has been initiated.

4. The expenses incurred by the Federal Government in the 6-month period from March 26 through September 25, 1998, that are directly attributable to the exercise of powers and authorities conferred by the declaration of a national emergency with respect to UNITA are about $160,000, most of which represent wage and salary costs for Federal personnel. Personnel costs were largely centered in the Department of the Treasury (particularly in the Office of Foreign Assets Control, the U.S. Customs Service, the Office of the Under Secretary for Enforcement, and the Office of the General Counsel) and the Departments of State (particularly the Office of Southern African Affairs) and Commerce.

I will continue to report periodically to the Congress on significant developments, pursuant to 50 U.S.C. 1703(c).

Sincerely,

WILLIAM J. CLINTON

NOTE: Identical letters were sent to Newt Gingrich, Speaker of the House of Representatives, and Albert Gore, Jr., President of the Senate.

Remarks Celebrating the 160th Anniversary of the Metropolitan African Methodist Episcopal Church
October 23, 1998

Thank you very much, "Reverend" Green. [*Laughter*] You know, Ernie was doing so well up here, it reminded me about what my grandmother used to say to me. She said, "Bill, I think you could have been a preacher if you'd been just a little better boy." [*Laughter*]

I want to thank Ernie Green for his lifetime of friendship. I thank my longtime friend Secretary Slater, who has done a magnificent job in our Cabinet. I am delighted to be here with Secretary Togo West and Mayor Barry, Congresswoman Norton, Johnnie Booker, Bishop Anderson, Reverend Harvey, Assistant HUD Secretary Cardell Cooper, many members of our White House staff. And I'm really glad to be here with Gwen Ifill. I told the Bishop on the way in—and Reverend Harvey—I said, you know, Gwen Ifill's daddy was an AME preacher. And we used to talk about the AME back in 1992 when I was—back when I had a life, when I was a real citizen, and I was running for President and she was covering me. And you know, when you get in the press corps in Washington, you tend to drift away. And I'm glad to see her back, getting close to the faith again tonight here, working with all of you. [*Laughter*] It's very good.

I wish you a happy 160th birthday. I thank you more than you will ever know for the prayers, the friendship to me and to my family over these last few months and, indeed, over these last many years. And I am honored to have been invited to be with you on this occasion. And believe you me, I am very happy that we wound up those Middle East peace talks today, so I could be here.

It is now 8:30, and I have been awake for 36 hours and 30 minutes. [*Laughter*] I think I can finish tonight. [*Laughter*] But in these last 9 days, when I have come home at 3 and 4 o'clock in the morning almost every night—and then last night, we had to work the whole night through—then it looked as if we were going to lose everything we had worked for. And then it came back together again. I felt so blessed to have had the opportunity to engage in these labors, to do this for our country, for the cause of peace, for the land of our faiths, the home of Christianity, Judaism, and Islam. I felt that it was a part of my job as President, my mission as a Christian, and my personal journey of atonement. And I am grateful that God gave me the chance to do this for the last 9 days.

The agreement that the Israelis and the Palestinians signed is a big step. It gives Israel genuine security, the cooperation of their neighbors among the Palestinians in fighting terrorism, the recognition that Israel has a right to be there, now and forever. It gives the Palestinian people at long last a chance to realize their aspirations to live free, in safety, in charge of their own destiny.

How tragic it is that two different groups of people, each who have known so much oppression in life, so much deprivation, so much downright abuse, because there is such a little bit of land there and so much accumulated insecurity, would be fighting with each other when they should be embracing one another. Now they have a chance to do that.

There's no way in 9 short days to wipe away decades of distrust. But you can do an awful lot in 9 days if you just lock people in a room and—[*laughter*]—see how well they get along. I believe if we can maintain the will and the momentum for peace, the future is bright there. But I also believe that we have to be realistic. There are enemies of peace. And in some ways, the very advance these people have made together will make them both more appealing targets to those who believe their lives only have meaning when they are hurting someone else, that they can only lift themselves up when someone else is being put down.

I say that to make a point about this church. I think the most moving thing to me about the last 9 days were the periodic visits to the peace talks of King Hussein of Jordan. Many of you know that he has been treated at the Mayo Clinic for several months for a serious illness. He's lost a lot of weight, and as he joked today, he's lost his hair, and what little he's got left, even in his mustache, has turned white. But even though he was the smallest person in the room, he was always the largest presence. Here was a man fighting for his own life, willing to take time to remind the people at the peace talks of what it was really all about.

I thought about today, when we were signing, that Mr. Netanyahu was in the Israeli commandos. Some of you may remember that his brother was the commander of the famous raid by the Israeli soldiers on Entebbe and Uganda, where they liberated their people who had been kidnapped, but his brother was killed. Mr. Arafat has been in battle after battle for decades. King Hussein, himself, was a jet fighter pilot; in the Israeli Cabinet now, two of the great generals in the history of Israel, Ariel Sharon and the Defense Minister, General Mordechai. And I think all these people have come to a common realization, that in life all of our victories over other people are ultimately hollow, and the only victories that really matter are those that we win for our common humanity.

And when King Hussein would walk in the room, people would see that he was frail, but strong of heart and voice. And he would admonish them to think of their children and grandchildren and to let go of some of their resentments and suspend some of their distrust and make one more reach. You could see, almost like a balm washing over the parties, how their attitudes would shift, and their hearts would open, and they would resolve to try again and try again.

That, after all, is the lesson of the church, isn't it? That is, children of God—the real victories in life are not the victories we win over other people. They are the victories we win for our common humanity as children of God. So this was a victory for the peace.

Exodus says that "If thou shalt do as God command thee, the people shall go to their place in peace." The Koran says, "They shall not hear therein any vain discourse, but only peace."

A couple of years ago, I almost gave a sermon at one of my State of the Unions because I took the theme from the 12th verse of the 58th chapter of Isaiah: "They that shall be of thee shall build up the old waste places. Thou shalt raise up the foundations of many generations. Thou shalt be called the repairer of the breach, the restorer of paths to dwell in." That is the work in which we have been involved.

But every good work is that kind of work. I thank God we have people like Eleanor Holmes Norton in the Congress of the United States to do that kind of work.

This church has received people, in these 160 years, from Frederick Douglass to Mary McCloud Bethune to Nelson Mandela to Jesse Jackson to Ernie Green. It's easy to forget when you see old Ernie and all of his prosperity—[*laughter*]—that he was just a scared, skinny kid 41 years ago at Little Rock Central High School, enduring the jeers, the waving fists, for the simple proposition that he ought to have the right to get the best education he could. Today, Central High School has become a place in our history as hallowed as Gettysburg. Earlier this week, Congress passed a bill to officially designate Little Rock Central High School as a national historic site. And thanks to our Senator

from Arkansas and others, the budget bill I signed authorizes me to give Congressional Gold Medals to each and every member of the Little Rock Nine.

The victory they won was not over the Governor who tried to keep them out, not over the angry racial epithets of those who hurled them. It was a victory for all of us, even those who opposed their entry into the school.

How did people keep on going? Rodney reminded me when back when I was Governor, and Rodney worked for me, and we had—he didn't have such a big, fancy office, and he wasn't so far away—[*laughter*]—we used to talk all the time about Bible verses and first one thing and another, and he knew that one of my favorite verses was the ninth verse of the sixth chapter of St. Paul's Letter to the Galatians. And he mentioned it to me tonight because of the Middle East peace talks: "Let us not grow weary in doing good, for in due season we shall reap if we do not lose heart." After about 30 hours, I was beginning to lose the admonition of the Scripture. [*Laughter*]

But what is it that gives people the power not to grow weary? What is the message emanating from this church, not only from this great pastor, whom I have had the privilege of sharing worship with, but for 160 years—that we walk by faith and not by sight? This is not a science course: faith in a loving and protective God; faith in the righteousness of worship; faith in a citizen's ability to be guided by respect for others and justice and equality and freedom; ultimately, faith not only in our God but in what our country is and what it can become. We walk by faith and not by sight, the assurance of things hoped for, the conviction of things unseen.

What a dreary world it would be if we had only to live with what was before us. If we could not imagine how things could be different, if there were no faith in the room I have occupied these last 9 days, I promise you there would be no agreement today.

So that is what I come to thank you for. When something really important happens like this agreement today, when we win a good struggle in Congress, as Eleanor and I and our colleagues did, and against all the odds we prevail in our battle to put 100,000 teachers out there to lower the class size in the early grades, we know it wouldn't have happened because it wasn't rational when we started; or when we are defeated, but we do not quit, even more importantly, we walk by faith, not by sight.

And so, I came here to thank you for 160 years of that gift of faith that, without regard to the color of our skin or the condition of our pocketbook or even the stain of our past sins, we are all children of God.

One of my favorite verses is the first verse in Isaiah 43 because it is the promise of faith: "Fear not, for I have redeemed thee. I have called thee by thy name. Thou art mine." When you believe that, there's nothing you can't do. And if you don't do what you want to do, then you know God may have another plan. But you can still live with vision and hope; you can always be a repairer of the breach, and you are never stupid enough to think that beating somebody else out of something is what life is really all about. That is a gift, to this Capital City and to this country, that this church has given.

I only want to say one other thing to you. For all the good things that have happened in our country—and I thank Ernie for mentioning them—for all the prosperity we enjoy, we still have many challenges. You know them well enough. You pick up the paper every day, and you know that there are still a lot of trouble spots in this old world. And as soon as we put out one fire, another one crops up. You know that for all of our prosperity, the world financial system is troubled, and you see it in other countries, the problems they're having. And we need to fix it, and I'm working on that.

You know that when all us baby boomers, like me, retire, there will only be two people working for every one person drawing Social Security. And that's why I didn't want to spend that surplus until we fix Social Security for the 21st century. And so I say to you that even though we don't have all the answers, we also have to have faith that we can be good citizens. And when we're citizens, we have to realize, number one, we have a moral responsibility to exercise our franchise on November 3d. But we should be voting not just to defeat the people we don't vote for but, in a far larger sense, to find ways to reaffirm our common humanity as children of God. And I want you to think about that.

President Franklin Roosevelt was a deeply religious man. On the day he died, he was working on a speech. And he would get these typewritten speeches that speechwriters would do, and then he'd get his ink pen, and he'd scratch through the words and write the words over and write a line here and a line there. This is the last line of the last speech the longest serving President in United States history, and certainly one of the greatest ones, ever wrote: "The only limit to our realization of tomorrow will be our doubts of today. Let us move forward with a strong and active faith."

So, your faith is strong. For 160 years, it has been active. You have taken me in and, on occasions, given me the chance to have my inaugural memorial service here in this church— some of the best music I ever heard, some from your choir, and some I brought to you. [*Laughter*] And every time when I left, I felt like I was 10 feet tall. But you do, too, don't you? And when the choir was singing, you felt taller, didn't you? And you felt stronger, and your heart was lighter, and so was the load you carried when you came to this dinner tonight.

So again I say to you, happy birthday. Thank you for 160 years of the gift of faith and the energy that flows from it. Be good citizens with your faith. Show up every chance you get. Don't grow weary in doing good. Don't be discouraged when it doesn't work out. And help me every day to convince America that the real victories we have to win are not our victories over one another, but the victories together we win for our common humanity as children of God.

Thank you, and God bless you.

NOTE: The President spoke at 8:28 p.m. in the International Ballroom Center at the Washington Hilton Hotel. In his remarks, he referred to event cochairs Ernest Green and Johnnie B. Booker, senior steward board members, and Rev. Dr. Louis-Charles Harvey, senior pastor, Metropolitan AME Church; Presiding Bishop Vinton Anderson, Second Episcopal District, AME Church; Mayor Marion S. Barry, Jr., of Washington, DC; Gwen Ifill, reporter, New York Times; King Hussein I of Jordan; Prime Minister Binyamin Netanyahu, Foreign Minister Ariel Sharon, and Defense Minister Yitzhak Mordechai of Israel; and Chairman Yasser Arafat of the Palestinian Authority. H.R. 4328, the Omnibus Consolidated and Emergency Supplemental Appropriations Act, 1999, approved October 21, was assigned Public Law No. 105–277.

The President's Radio Address
October 24, 1998

Good morning. Yesterday, after 9 days of difficult negotiations on Maryland's Eastern Shore, Israeli and Palestinian leaders signed an agreement that restores hope for peace in the Middle East. It strengthens security, increases cooperation against terrorism, and brings both sides closer to the day when they can live together as free people.

Keeping the peace process on track will require continued courage by Israelis and Palestinians in the months ahead. But this agreement shows what is possible when the will for peace is strong. And I'm proud that, together, we were able to make real progress. America will continue to work for a just and lasting peace in this land that is holy for so many people throughout the world.

Now I'd like to talk with you about an historic opportunity we face here at home. Ten days from now, the American people will head to the polls for one of the most important elections in recent years. You will help select a Congress that will determine whether we seize this moment of prosperity to save Social Security for the 21st century.

Earlier this month we celebrated America's first budget surplus in 29 years. But even before the black ink was dry, some in Congress were determined to squander our surplus on an unwise election-year tax plan. But we turned back these efforts. The balanced budget I signed this week protects our hard-won surplus until we save Social Security first. As a result, the new Congress will have the best chance ever to ensure that the baby boomers can retire in dignity, without imposing unfair burdens on our children.

As we begin the process of reform, I have proposed five core principles to guide our way: First, we have to reform Social Security in a way that strengthens and protects the system for the 21st century. We simply cannot abandon a program that represents one of our country's greatest successes. Second, we should maintain universality and fairness. Third, Social Security must provide a benefit people can count on, regardless of the ups and downs of the economy or the financial markets. Fourth, Social Security must continue to provide protection for disabled and low-income Americans. And finally, any reforms we adopt must maintain our fiscal discipline.

Today I'm proud to announce the next important step we'll take in putting these principles to work. On December 8th and 9th, we'll hold the first-ever White House Conference on Social Security to help pave the way toward a bipartisan solution early next year.

Unfortunately, some in Congress already may be backing away from this historic opportunity. Just last week the Senate majority leader said he may not be willing to join me in our efforts to save Social Security. That would be a grave mistake. As with so many other long-term challenges, if we act now, it will be far, far easier to resolve the problem than if we wait until a crisis is close at hand. I believe we must save Social Security and do it next year.

I pledge to work with anyone from any party who is serious about this task. We cannot let partisanship derail our best opportunity to strengthen Social Security for the 21st century.

For more than 60 years now, Social Security has formed the sacred bond between the generations. In the words of one elderly woman three generations ago, "It is a precious shield against the terror of penniless, helpless, old age."

If the Congress you elect in 10 days chooses progress, it can strengthen that shield for generations to come. But if it chooses partisanship, this historic opportunity will be lost. You have the power to shape a Congress that will keep our Social Security system as strong for our children as it was for our parents. You have the power to elect a Congress pledged to save Social Security first.

Thanks for listening.

NOTE: The address was recorded at approximately 6:30 p.m. on October 23 in the Oval Office at the White House for broadcast at 10:06 a.m. on October 24. The transcript was made available by the Office of the Press Secretary on October 23 but was embargoed for release until the broadcast.

Remarks at a Reception for Congressional Candidate Janice Hahn in Los Angeles, California
October 24, 1998

Thank you very much, Roz. I want to begin, I think, by thanking all of you for the raincheck. I'm sorry that I couldn't be here on time, but I'm glad the delay had a happy result.

I want you to see something. See these? Normally, when I give a speech, I do it from notes like this, which I can't even read now that my eyes are—[*laughter*]. And then, before I give a speech, they give me notes like this. And on the last day of the peace talks in Maryland— or however many days it was—until I went to bed last night, I was up for 39 hours, constantly. I didn't even do that in college. [*Laughter*] And so before I got off the plane, even though I did get a little nap before I came out and a decent night's sleep last night, my staff gave me these notes and they said, "Read this side. Read this side. We were so afraid you're so sleepy that you won't know what you're saying, and you might get up and say something you actually think and get us all in trouble." [*Laughter*]

And I might say, Roz, right before I got out of the car, I had a talk with Hillary, and she said to tell you hello, and she's sorry she's not here. And she told me to read these notes, too. [*Laughter*] But I don't think I will. [*Laughter*]

I want to begin by saying that the main reason I wanted to come here today is that Janice Hahn is a very important person. I've known Roz Wyman for years, long before I ever even thought of running for President, and this is the first time I've ever been invited to this house. [*Laughter*] So I'm delighted to be here. And if I had been here, I would have watched "The Godfather" the first time. [*Laughter*] But I also might have watched it the second and third time.

I want to thank Congresswoman Maxine Waters and her husband, Ambassador Sidney Williams, for being here; and Kathleen Connell, your State controller; and my longtime friend Nate Holden, thank you for coming. I want to say a special word of appreciation to Jane Harman for doing a great job in Congress. We've had 6 wonderful years together.

In many of the same ways, we represented what we hoped would be a new direction for our country and one that would bring our party to many years of majority in America. And she did a magnificent job for her congressional district. She destroyed a lot of gender stereotypes by becoming one of the great experts on defense in the United States Congress. She destroyed a lot of stereotypes about Democrats by proving that we could, first of all, reduce the deficit 93 percent without any help from the other party and then supporting our efforts which produced this marvelous balanced budget and surplus. And in so many other ways, she really embodied what I think is the best of public service, and I thank her for it very much.

I also want to thank Janice Hahn for simply making this race. The Congress needs more people who have been teachers, who have served the public in different ways, who have worked with gang alternative programs, and worked with groups like the Boys and Girls Clubs in Watts, who know all the faces of America.

I tell all the time that people in Congress, just because they may represent the dominant face at a moment in time, the thing that makes a democracy resilient and effective is when all of the faces of America are seen and all the voices are heard and all the needs are addressed.

And so I just appreciate the fact that she was willing to make this race. And when I couldn't get her on the phone the day the filing closed, I thought, well, there is one of two things going on: she's either out doing what it takes to file, or she's hiding from me and all the other people that are harassing her to run. [*Laughter*] And I'm glad it was the former.

I also want to thank her for giving the speech she gave here today and reminding you of what this election is all about. And I'd like to just take a couple of minutes to put this in some larger context.

What we saw in the last couple of days in this flowering of this peace process under the most difficult circumstances imaginable—the heroic periodic intervention by King Hussein, grappling with his own serious illness and reminding Prime Minister Netanyahu and Chairman Arafat and all the other people there, including a lot of people who have been involved in the wars that the Israelis and the Arab peoples of the Middle East have fought with each other, reminding them what the purpose of life is all about—represents in my view, in a larger sense, what ought to be the mission of America and the mission of public service.

And in 1992, when I ran for President, and California was undergoing such great economic turmoil, and you'd had the riots in L.A. and all the other things that were going on, I think the overriding reason I wanted to do it is that it seemed to me that Washington and the politics of Washington was nowhere near the politics that we saw unfold over the last week at the Middle East peace talks, that it was much more about winning victories over opponents than it was winning victories for the American people. It was much more about rhetoric than reality. It was much more about partisanship than progress.

And for 6 years I have labored to try to create a 21st century America in which every person would have an opportunity if he or she were willing to work for it, in which we would become reconciled to ourselves with all of our diversity as a stronger American community, and in which we would reassert after the cold war a positive role in the world for peace and freedom and prosperity for others as well as for ourselves. And I think we are well down that road.

I am grateful for the successes of the economy, for the healing of the social fabric, for the opportunities I have had to try to do these things. I am grateful that in this last session of Congress, because the Democrats, though in the minority, stood strong, stood together, we were able to win the fight to keep the surplus from being squandered on a tax cut and, instead, it will be saved to address the Social Security reform we have to make early next year; that we got the funding to put 100,000 teachers in our schools, which will enable us to bring class sizes in the early grades down to an average of 18; that we got funds that Senator Boxer fought so hard for for after-school programs for a quarter of a million more children in this country, to try to give them something good to do after school. I am grateful for all of that.

I am grateful that we beat off all the most serious assaults on the environment and passed our clean water initiative, which is designed to address the fact that for all of our progress, 40 percent of our rivers and lakes are still not fit for swimming or fishing. I am grateful for the fact the we passed our whole community empowerment initiative in housing and more empowerment zones, more facilities like the $400 million Community Development Bank that was established here in Los Angeles.

I am very grateful that in this last year, we have been a force for peace in Bosnia, with free elections in Kosovo, where I hope—it's too soon to say—but I hope we've headed off another Bosnia; the advances in Ireland, and of course, this great breakthrough in the Middle East. We're not out of the woods yet. The agreement still has to be implemented. And I hope that in Israel, the people and the members of his political coalition will support Prime Minister Netanyahu, who took significant risk, given the nature of his political support, to sign an agreement that will clearly increase the security of the people of Israel, even as it gives more land and more economic opportunity to the Palestinians.

To me, this is what politics is all about. And in a larger sense, that's what this election is all about. This is the 21st century Congress you're electing. And the real issue here is whether this election will be controlled by agenda or by apathy and financial advantage.

We have the agenda. I believe, in spite of the fact that the last Congress wouldn't do it, that most Americans believe we ought to have the National Government providing incentives to build or repair 5,000 schools. We've got more kids than we've ever had in school.

And you wouldn't believe the number of places I've been. I've been to a small town in Florida where one grade school had 12 trailers out behind it housing children. I've been in classrooms in magnificent old school buildings in our big cities on the East Coast, in Philadelphia, where the average school building is 65 years old. That's the bad news. The good news is you couldn't begin to afford to build a school like most of those schools are today. But it's wrong when the windows are broken, whole floors are shut down, spaces have to be boarded up, and the light doesn't come in because people can't afford to maintain them and repair them. This is a big issue.

You heard Janice tell her own story about the patient's problems with HMO's. I can say, I have what I think is a reasonable position on this. I believe when I became President that we need better management in the health care system because inflation was going up in health care at 3 times the overall rate of inflation. And eventually it was going to consume the whole economy, but no management technique can ever be permitted to overwhelm the purpose for which the enterprise was established in the first place. And I don't care whether you're selling food or automobiles or health care or whatever you're selling—management techniques are designed to enable the most efficient way of providing the quality of product or service that you're in business to do in the first place.

And I'm deeply disappointed that the HMO lobby essentially persuaded the members of the other party to defeat the Patients' Bill of Rights, which would have said, addressing just this, that every person in an HMO ought to have a right to have medical decisions made by a doctor, not by an accountant; that if your doctor says you should see a specialist, you should be able to see one; that if you get hurt, you ought to go to the nearest emergency room, not one all across town because it happens to be covered by your plan; that medical records ought to be kept private and that if your health care provider is changed by your employer while you're pregnant or while you're getting chemotherapy or while you're in the middle of any other treatment, you ought to be able to complete the treatment before you're forced to change your physician.

These are elemental, basic, fair things. It would be a modest, but a very modest, increase in cost in these plans, to give peace of mind and dignity and, in many cases, lifesaving care to Americans all across this country. I think these things are worth fighting for.

I think it's worth fighting for saving Social Security for the 21st century. The next Congress will have to do two things. It will have to, one more time, beat off a raid on the surplus. Just because we saved it once doesn't mean we won't have to deal with it again. Then it will have to decide how to reform Social Security so that we can still take care of the basic social mission. Today, one-half of the seniors in this country would be in poverty but for Social Security. And when all of us baby boomers retire, most

of them won't have the kind of pension I'll have.

Now, most people have sources of income other than Social Security, and I'm doing everything I can to try to make it easier for people to take out different kinds of retirement plans, do more saving on their own, and build up a decent lifestyle. But in the end, we still need that bedrock protection so that none of our seniors have to live in abject poverty.

And if we don't deal with it now, we'll have one of two choices. If we just sort of put it off, take this golden moment of prosperity where we have a surplus and just squander it, then a few years from now we'll have a few more economic hard times. There will always be some excuse not to do it. If we don't deal with it now, and we wait for the roof to cave in, then we'll have one of two choices: Either we will lower the standard of living of our seniors in a way that we'll be ashamed of, or we will lower the standard of living of our children and their ability to raise our grandchildren because it will take a whopping tax increase to maintain the system. Now is the time to deal with this.

So if you think about the great challenges of America, if you think about the health care challenge, if you think about the education challenge, if you think about the Social Security challenge, if you think about the need that this Congress passed up under pressure from the tobacco companies to pass legislation to protect our children from the dangers of tobacco, still the number one public health problem in the country—they passed up a chance to pass the campaign finance reform, even though we had a bill that had some Republican supporters as well; they've passed up a chance to raise the minimum wage, even though you can't raise a family on $5.15 an hour, and we'll never have an easier time when the unemployment rate and the inflation rate are both so low—there is a lot to do.

So again I say to you, what do we have to worry about? We have to worry about, first of all, getting this message out. That's why your presence here is important. Because in the last 2 weeks, according to what my staff tells me, our side will be outspent by their side roughly three to one, when you account for all the third party ads and the interest group ads and all these things that will come out there in all the races that are in play.

The second thing we have to do is to convince people that this election is as important as the Presidential election. No one questions this assertion. No one questions the fact that our party would do very, very well in these elections if it were a Presidential year, because we have the issues, because we have the momentum, because the country is doing well. Even with a financial disadvantage, we would do well.

But in off years, normally a lot of our folks don't vote—working women who have to deal with the hassles of child care and a job every day—so we vote on a workday still in America, so that's one more thing to worry about; minorities and low income people who live in cities that may not have adequate transportation, and it's enough trouble to get a bus to go to work, and then you've got to figure out how you're going to get to the polling place. There are objective reasons why these things happen. But if the people you know believe it matters, if they understand—I can tell you, every single vote in Congress matters, every single seat in the House, every single seat in the Senate— if the people know that, then Senator Boxer and Gray Davis and Janice Hahn will be elected on November 3d with strong margins.

So I just ask you to think about, when you leave here and you ask yourself, "Why did I go there?"—[*laughter*]—was it worth the money, hassling the traffic, whatever else you went through to get here, you just think about this: We're still around here after 220 years, as the greatest democracy in history, because most of the time most of the people make the right decision. So what's at stake in this election is your ability to persuade most of the people to show up.

So thank you for coming here, and thank you for giving your money, but you're not off the hook. [*Laughter*] Because every one of you, you have people you work with, people you socialize with, people you worship with, people you know, that you—if you ask them, will be more likely to be there.

And so, you were so kind when you stood and clapped when the references were made earlier to the work I did in this peace process. I don't need any applause. It was my obligation, and it was an honor, and it was a joy, even the meanest and toughest parts of it. But what you liked about it is what you should feel about public life and political work every day. What you liked about it was you knew that we were not there struggling so that Netanyahu could win a victory over Arafat, or Arafat could win a victory over Netanyahu, or they could win any victories over any of the other players there. They were there saying, we want to win a victory for the people we represent, for our common humanity. That's what that was all about.

And everybody knows it, which is why we feel elevated when something like this happens—that we—it gives us new energy and new hope, and it reminds us of what counts. And I'm telling you, it will be just as true on election day as it is now.

And there will be votes that Janice Hahn will count in Congress—cast in Congress—you will never know about because you just can't keep up with all of them. But more often than you can ever imagine, she will be called upon to reaffirm not a victory over some opponent, but a victory for the people she represents.

And she deserves, and you need, the voice of every person heard. That is true in Senator Boxer's race. It's true in Gray Davis' race. California has got to set a standard for America, and the best way to do it is with a record turnout on election day.

Thank you, and God bless you.

NOTE: The President spoke at 5:10 p.m. at a private residence. In his remarks, he referred to reception host Roz Wyman; Nate Holden, Los Angeles City Council member; King Hussein I of Jordan; Prime Minister Binyamin Netanyahu of Israel; Chairman Yasser Arafat of the Palestinian Authority; and California gubernatorial candidate Lt. Gov. Gray Davis. Janice Hahn was a candidate for California's 36th Congressional District.

Statement on the Murder of Dr. Barnett Slepian
October 24, 1998

I am outraged by the murder of Dr. Barnett Slepian in his home last night in Amherst, NY. The Department of Justice is working with State and local authorities to find the person or persons responsible and bring them to justice. While we do not have all the facts of this case, one thing is clear: this Nation cannot tolerate violence directed at those providing a constitutionally protected medical service.

No matter where we stand on the issue of abortion, all Americans must stand together in condemning this tragic and brutal act. We must protect the safety and freedom of all our citizens.

Hillary and I extend our thoughts and prayers to the family of Dr. Slepian.

Remarks at a Reception for Senator Barbara Boxer in Los Angeles
October 24, 1998

Thank you very much. Well, thank you for the wonderful welcome. Thanks for the raincheck. [*Laughter*] I want to thank Jim and Holly for having us here in this beautiful, beautiful setting tonight. I'd like to also acknowledge the presence in the audience of Congresswoman Jane Harman and Congressman Brad Sherman. I thank them for being here. Hello, Brad. There you are.

I just came from an event for Janice Hahn, who is running to succeed Jane Harman in the Congress. And I told the audience something I feel almost constrained to also say to you. This last week I had was a rather interesting one. [*Laughter*] I was home at 3 and 4 o'clock in the morning 4 or 5 times, and then on the last marathon day I was up for 39 hours. And I didn't even do that in college. [*Laughter*]

Now, when I go out, as we are tonight, to give a speech, it's always covered by the press. We feed these microphones into the press that is traveling with me, and there's a member of the press here tonight. And I always get these cards from my staff, these nice little cards that says Jim and Holly Brooks and all the reasons I'm for Barbara Boxer, as if I didn't know, and all that. [*Laughter*] And then what I did—it's too small a card, she said. [*Laughter*] And then what I do is I take these little cards, and I write on them, these things, you see? And no one can read my writing. And at my age, even I can't read it when it's this small. [*Laughter*]

So the last thing they said to me when I got off the plane was, "You went 39 hours without sleep; you've slept one night, last night, and got a little nap on the plane. Don't forget that. Read this card." [*Laughter*] "We're afraid of what you will say if you—read this card." [*Laughter*]

So I was on the way over here tonight, and I called Hillary, who wishes she could be here for this family event, to be with Barbara and Stu and Nicole and Doug and Tony and our nephew, Zach. And she said, "Read this card." [*Laughter*] So I think I'll read this card. [*Laughter*]

Let me say first of all, I'm very honored to be here because Barbara Boxer is not just my friend; she is really my colleague, and I believe in her. I believe in the depth of her passion and the purity of her heart and the determination of her service. You clapped when she said I helped to bring California back from the worst recession you've had in the long time. Don't forget that, apart from whatever we did specifically for this State, it all began with one vote in August of 1993 for the economic plan that reduced the deficit by 93 percent before the bipartisan balanced budget bill passed.

That's what brought the interest rates down, got the investment going, got the economy going again. And when that vote was cast, there was not a single member of the other party who voted for it. It passed by one vote in the Senate and one vote in the House, only. If she had changed her vote, we'd be here talking about something else tonight. I might not even be here as your President tonight.

And she could have said, "Hey, I had a tough race in '92. I didn't win by so much, and it's the first time I'd ever been on a statewide ticket." And she could have taken a dive. But she stood up, and on that night she was not a little adult; she was 10 feet tall in my mind. And so that vote, every Member who cast it can claim to have had an equal hand in the revitalization of our economy.

Barbara talked about the budget we passed and how we got the 100,000 teachers and the money for after-school programs. That's a quarter of a million children—a quarter of a million—who can stay after school, who wouldn't be able to do it otherwise.

She talked about a lot of other issues. I will tell you that her work for the environment has really been impressive, and one of the things we got in this budget, against all the odds, was a clean water initiative to help us deal with the fact that in spite of all of our environmental progress, 40 percent of our lakes and rivers are still not fit for swimming and fishing. And there was so much else. So I am for her because she has a good record. I'm also for her because we do have a lot to do.

If you just look at where we are now, in this budget, again, against all the odds, because my fellow Democrats stood with me, we beat off an unwise election-year tax cut scheme to save the surplus for Social Security until we reform that. We finally, after 8 months of imploring, got America's contribution to the International Monetary Fund so that I can try to organize the world to deal with this global financial turmoil we're all dealing with. So we got a lot done. But we have a lot to do.

If you look ahead—let me just mention some of the things that I think are terribly important. Number one, the next Congress will have to face the reform of Social Security for the baby boom generation. When all the baby boomers get in the Social Security system, we'll only have two people working for every one person drawing. Now, because we have the first surplus in 29 years, and because it's projected that over time—making allowances for recessions taking the money up and down—over time, we'll be able to stay on a balanced budget surplus pattern. We have the opportunity now to reform Social Security in a way that will secure its integrity for the baby boomers without putting undue financial burdens on our children and their ability to raise our grandchildren.

But if we don't do that—that is, if either we throw the money away on something else, or we just don't make the tough decisions—then when the time comes, we will be faced with one of two unpleasant alternatives. And keep in mind, not everybody in my age group is going to have as good a pension as I will. [*Laughter*] Today, you should know that half of the seniors in this country are living out of poverty because of Social Security. And if Social Security were taken away, they would be in poverty.

So if we don't do this, we'll have the following decisions that will affect every single person in this audience who is my age or younger, one way or the other. We will either have to say, "Well, I'm sorry, we spent the money on ourselves when we wanted it," or, "We just couldn't bear to make the tough decisions." And so when push comes to shove, we can say to the seniors, "I'm sorry, I hope you've saved enough for your own retirement." We've done a lot, by the way, to make that easier, and I thank Barbara for that. But what will happen is we'll see a lot of seniors in abject misery again. Or that will kill our consciences, and we'll say, "We can't do that; we have to maintain the system we have." And that will cause a whopping tax increase, which will lower the standard of living of our children and their ability to raise our grandchildren. Either side is wrong and unnecessary. But you need to think about that when you go to the polls. Who do you trust to make the complex but, ultimately, value-based decision to reform Social Security in a way that will care for the baby boom generation in a way that does not undermine our obligations to our children and grandchildren? It is a huge issue, very important.

The second thing this election is about, Barbara already talked about—we've got the first downpayment on 100,000 teachers. And we had to fight like crazy to get it. My ability to keep going until we do that, which will lower class size in the early grades to an average of 18 all across America, depends upon who's in the Congress.

The one thing we tried to do that we couldn't get done, that is so terribly important, is to pass a program that for the first time would have the National Government, through a paid-for tax incentive, help to build or repair 5,000 schools in this country. Where are the teachers going to teach? We've got the biggest group of schoolchildren in history. You have it here in this county. It's a big problem.

The next big issue we have to face is how we should reform the laws as they relate to HMO's and other managed care plans. Now, let me say, I feel a special responsibility here, because I've never been anti-HMO, per se. When I became President, health care costs were rising at 3 times the rate of inflation. It was totally unsustainable. It was going to bankrupt businesses, consume people's personal income, take away money we needed to be investing in education, in the environment, in medical research. It was a terrible problem. It was imperative that we manage our health care system better.

But no management tool should be allowed to consume the objective of the enterprise. I don't care what you're doing. I don't care whether you're running a school or a law office or a grocery store or a filling station or anything else. All management tools are designed to enhance the quality of the enterprise, not overcome it.

Now, we tried to pass a Patients' Bill of Rights, and we were defeated strictly on partisan lines. We had a handful of members of the other party who helped us, and I'm grateful for that, but not enough to overcome their opposition. And all our law says is—our Patients' Bill of Rights—is the medical decisions ought to be made by doctors, not accountants; if you get hurt in an accident, you ought to go to the nearest emergency room, not one clear across town because it's covered by your plan; if your doctor says you need a specialist, you should be able to see one; if your employer changes health care providers while you're in the middle of treatment, like you're pregnant, you're taking chemotherapy, whatever it is, you ought to be able to finish the treatment with the doctor you started with; and your medical records ought to be private. I think it's a good law, and I think we need it. And I think it's an important reason to reelect Barbara Boxer.

I'll tell you something else we're going to have to do; we may need help from Congress to do it. The global economy has benefitted us greatly. It has played a major role in the resurgence of California. I think all of you know that Asia, Latin America—you know what turmoil it's in now. Now, some of these things are growing pains; they were inevitable. Other developments are more harsh than they can safely be allowed to continue to be. And I need a Congress that will not wait 8 months just to make our elemental, fundamental investment, America's investment in stabilizing the global economy, because we're going to have more tough decisions. And if we want the benefits of the global economy—and no country in the world has benefitted as much as we have—we have to be willing to assume the responsibilities of leadership. That's a big issue in the next election.

Then there are some other things I'd just like to mention. We weren't able to overcome their majority last time in passing legislation to protect our children from the dangers of tobacco, the number one public health problem for kids in America. If we had a few more people like Barbara Boxer in the Congress, we could do that. We were not able to pass campaign finance reform. We were not able to raise the minimum wage. You know, you can't support a family on $5.15 an hour, and we have rarely had an economy with such low unemployment and such low inflation where there was so little risk to raising the minimum wage. And, you know, the people that we're arguing for will never be able to afford to come to an event like this, but they're Americans, too, and they deserve, if they're willing to work hard, their share of the future. And I feel strongly about that.

Now, let me just say one last thing. I thank you for coming here. I thank you for your contributions. I thank you for enabling Barbara to go up on television. But let me say, as you come here to the last 10 days or so of this election, most people know that we've got the right agenda for America, that we're pushing, that we have the ideas, that we're driving. On the other side, they have a lot more money than we do. Even after tonight, they will have more money than we do. [Laughter]

I saw some reports a couple of days ago that said that in these sort of independent expenditure committees, Democrats would be outspent better than three to one in the last 2 weeks of the election. There is something else they've got going for them, too, which is that this is not a Presidential election year. In Presidential elections, most people make an extra effort to vote. In the off-year elections they don't. And we are disproportionately, the Democrats, disadvantaged.

Why? Because we have a disproportionate number of the single working mothers, for example. Every day is big enough hassle. You've got to figure out what are you going to do with your kids, the child care, the school, go to work, get home. And now—ah, it's Tuesday, I've got to figure out how to vote, too?

We have a disproportionate share of people living in inner-city neighborhoods where it's all they can do to get on the bus and go to work, and now they've got to figure out, is the polling place on the bus line, or forking over the money for a taxi cab. These are not idle questions here. But we also have a lot of people who just don't think it's that big a deal. Now, I'm telling you, this is a big deal—a big deal.

And if you believe in this agenda, if you believe that we ought to do more on education, if you believe we ought to do more to stabilize the global economy, if you believe we ought to pass the Patients' Bill of Rights, if you want us to reform Social Security and do it in the right way, if you want these other things done, then between now and election day you've got to get everybody you know to show up.

And if you think about the people you work with, the people you socialize with, the people you worship with, the people you come in contact with—just in this crowd—there will be tens of thousands of people touched by you between now and November 3d who will never come to a political event like this—tens of thousands of people. And I want you to talk to them about this.

You know, you were so nice to give me such a nice reception over this Middle East peace breakthrough. And I thank you for that. But let me tell you something; I want you to know something about it. Number one, it's my job. [*Laughter*] Number two, I loved it, even the meanest, toughest moment. [*Laughter*] And number three, it was a profound honor. It was an honor.

But why did you do that? Why did you do that? Because it makes—when people who have been fighting and killing each other, when people who have their own political problems; when two leaders, who both will be in more danger, both political and physical, because they did this, do something like this, it just fills us up. It makes us feel good. It gives us hope. It gives us energy. It appeals to our better selves. When

people saw the heroic figure of King Hussein going back and forth, intervening—every time I called him, he showed up, and he went down there. And you know that he's dealt with these terrible health challenges, and still he labors on. It touches our common humanity.

Why? Because down deep inside we know that the most important victories in life are not the victories we win over other people; they're the victories we win for our common humanity. You know it, and I know it. And the older you get and the more times you win and the more times you lose, you know that in the end what counts are the victories you win for what you share in common with other people.

And if you think about the elation we felt over the Middle East peace process, the heartbreak we felt at the brutal beating and killing of young Matthew Shepard—why do we hate that? Because it violated our common humanity. Some people marked him out and said he didn't belong.

Now, when I came to California, running for President in 1992, I said I wanted to do three things to prepare our country for the new century: I wanted to restore opportunity for every American who would work for it; I wanted to bring this country together in a community across all the lines that divide us; and I wanted our country in a new era to still be the world's leader for peace and freedom and prosperity for everyone, not just ourselves.

We're further along than we were 6 years ago, but we have a great deal to do. And I'm telling you, there is a clear choice in this election. And if you really liked how you felt when you saw those two tough, grizzled enemies—[*laughter*]—that I kept up for 39 hours until they could hardly stand up—[*laughter*]—standing up there—and keep in mind, it was a lot harder for them than it was for me. All I had to do was to stay awake. [*Laughter*] All I had to do was stay awake. They have to go home and face the music. If you like how you felt when you saw them overcoming all their limitations, all their hatreds, all their scars, all the memories of their dead friends—in the Prime Minister of Israel's case, his dead brother—if you liked that, and you really believe that public life and citizenship is about the victories we win for our children, for our future, and our common humanity, then you get everybody you can to the polls November 3d.

Thank you, and God bless you.

NOTE: The President spoke at 6:53 p.m. at a private residence. In his remarks, he referred to reception hosts Jim and Holly Brooks; Senator Boxer's husband, Stuart, their son, Doug, their daughter, Nicole, and son-in-law, Tony Rodham, and their grandson, Zachary Rodham; Prime Minister Binyamin Netanyahu of Israel; Chairman Yasser Arafat of the Palestinian Authority; King Hussein I of Jordan; and murder victim Matthew Shepard.

Remarks at a Dinner for Senator Barbara Boxer in Los Angeles
October 24, 1998

You know, I only wish we knew how Barbra really feels about all of this. [Laughter] It's so hard when people hold back like that. [Laughter] Thank you. And thank you, Bob and Carole, for opening your beautiful home and leaving it open day after day after day—[laughter]—while I carried on at the Wye River. Thank you, Carole, for that wonderful set of songs. We were sitting there singing those songs with you, and I said, "You know, every time Carole King opens her mouth, you can make 30 years of my life vanish." [Laughter]

I am glad to be here with Senator Boxer and Stu and Doug and Nicole and Tony and my nephew, Zach. Hillary is very jealous of me being here tonight. I talked to her just before I came out. This is the third talk I've made, and I've started with the same story, but it's true, so I'm going to say it again. A true story you can tell more than once. [Laughter] So I want to tell another true story.

Every time I give a talk, my staff prepares a little card like this. At the top it says, "Barbra Streisand, Carole King, Bob Daly, Carole Bayer Sager." And it has little notes: "I'm glad to be here to support Senator Barbara Boxer for the Senate." [Laughter] And it says why I'm for her here. [Laughter] Barbara says the list is way too short. [Laughter] And then before I do it, I make out little notes like this in my handwriting. And at my age, in dilapidated condition, I can't read it anyway, so I have no idea what I said. [Laughter]

So before I got off the plane—I swear, before I got off the plane, my staff said, "When you were at this Middle East peace thing, every night you got home at 2 or 3 in the morning, and then the last night you didn't come home at all." I was up for 39 hours before I went to bed last night. I didn't even do that in college. [Laughter]

So they said, "Read this card—[laughter]—because the press is listening in, and Lord only knows what you'll say." [Laughter] So I talked to Hillary; she said, "Read the card; read the card." [Laughter] But I'm not going to read the card. [Laughter]

Anyway, I want to say just a couple of things about Barbara Boxer and then a couple of things about where we are right now and what's at stake. First of all, apart from our relationship by marriage and our deep friendship, I care a lot about her. And you should know that I see people in Washington in ways that their constituents often don't. I see Senators when they're mad—at me, sometimes. I see Senators when they call and want me to do things, and sometimes I can't do it. I see the tough votes and easy shots and just the whole thing.

This woman has a good mind, a good heart, a fierce spirit, and she would make you proud every day if you could see her as I do. And I'll also tell you that of all the members of the California delegation—this is no disrespect to the others—she has called me more than any other member of the California delegation on issues relating specifically to California. Sometimes it gets to the point where I hear she's calling me again, I just say, "Whatever she wants, just tell her, yes; I'm tired of dealing with her. Just tell her, yes; I'm tired of dealing with her." [Laughter]

So I think she has earned the right to be reelected. But she made a couple of points I'd like to reinforce. In August of '93, when I'd been through a rocky 8 months, a lot of controversy, and I knew our ability to really get this economy going again rested on the capacity of the Congress to vote for an economic plan I gave them to slash the deficit but keep investing in education and children and the environment and research; and that it would require a lot of controversial choices, but that if we didn't do it and it wasn't enough of a cut in the deficit, we'd never get the interest rates down; we'd never get the economy going again.

Now, at the time we did that, the stock market was at about 3200; interest rates were much higher; the unemployment rate was a whole lot higher; and the budget passed by a single vote in the Senate and in the House—one vote. So it is literally true that if in the last 6 years California had been represented by her opponent, we wouldn't have had the economic recovery to the extent we have, and I might not be here giving this talk tonight. [*Laughter*] So I think that's important to remember.

She voted to ban assault weapons. She voted for the Brady bill. She voted—which has kept a quarter of a million people with criminal histories and mental health problems from buying handguns. Lord knows how many lives we saved. Roughly 15 million Americans have taken advantage of the family and medical leave law, which says you can take some time off when a baby is born or a parent is sick without losing your job. I mean, she's done things that have made a difference to the life of the country. This last budget—you heard them talking about it— all those funds for after-school programs wouldn't be in that budget if it weren't for Barbara Boxer.

Let me just give you an example of what this means, just one. During all the years I served as Governor—I think most of you know Hillary is from Chicago, and we used to spend a lot of time in Illinois. And the Chicago school system had a reputation for being the worst big-city school system in the country. Every year it got shut down. They had a teacher strike in Chicago every year whether they wanted one or not, even whether the teachers wanted one. They—just sort of automatic—and they changed the whole way of governing the school system.

The teachers basically are a part of the governance of the school system now. There hasn't been a strike in years. And the schools all have parent councils and lots of other changes have been made. Chicago—big-city school system— ended social promotion. If you don't pass a test, you can't go on to the next grade. But they didn't declare children failures because the system failed them. Instead, they guaranteed summer school to all the kids that don't do well.

The summer school is now the sixth biggest school system in the United States—the summer school. And there are now in Chicago alone 40,000 children that eat 3 meals a day in the school system. Well, guess what's happened? Learning has gone way up. The dropout has gone way down. The juvenile crime rate has plummeted. That's what this after-school program means. And she did it, and she deserves the credit for it.

Now, let's talk a little bit about what the stakes are. First of all, in spite of the fact that the country is doing well economically, and that a lot of our social problems are abating, and we have, fortunately, been able to advance the cause of peace around the world and to become, I think, much more capable of dealing with the world as it's going to be, from Africa to China, to Bosnia and Kosovo, to Northern Ireland and the Middle East, we've got a lot of challenges at home and abroad. And this next Congress will have a lot to do with what 21st century America looks like for a long time.

I want to mention two or three things. Barbara mentioned the Patients' Bill of Rights. This is a huge deal. A hundred sixty million Americans are in managed care, and I support it. I always say this. You know, I was never against managed care in the beginning. A lot of people don't remember this, but in 1993, when I became President, the inflation rate in health care costs was 3 times the inflation rate in the economy as a whole. You have to manage any system that's taking that much money up. It's irresponsible to think otherwise. It will consume the economy.

On the other hand, no management technique or device can ever be allowed to consume the fundamental purpose of the endeavor, whatever it is. If you make movies or CD's, you want to do them as efficiently as possible; you don't want to do them in a way that you have a low quality CD or a lousy movie. If you run a grocery store, you want to run it as efficiently as possible, but you don't want to run it with bad milk or rotten fruit. You can save money a lot of ways; any endeavor that you're doing, you can save money. But if you undermine the purpose of the endeavor, you have thwarted the very reason you're trying to be more efficient.

That's what's going on here. You've got people who are out there dying, because their doctors say they need to have certain procedures or certain specialists, and it has to be approved by a managed care company, and the first person that gets it is a modestly paid accountant, a claims reviewer.

And put yourself in the position of the claims reviewer—we're talking about 160 million Americans now—suppose instead of being an Academy Award winning actor, you're a claims reviewer for an HMO. [*Laughter*] Now, wait a minute. What do you know? You know you're making a modest salary; you'd like a bonus at Christmastime; you'd like to have your job next year; you'd like to get a promotion someday. And all day long you're reviewing claims, and they're always the same thing, you know. The doctor says, "Well, so-and-so ought to see a specialist," or "so-and-so ought to have this procedure that may be experimental," and all this. What do you know about your job? You know one thing: You will never get in trouble for saying no.

I want you to understand this from a human point of view. You won't get in trouble if you say no. Why? Because if you make a mistake, they can always appeal the decision. And at the next level or maybe one more level removed, there will be a doctor there. And the doctor can ultimately, you say, make the right decision.

Some of the biggest damage being done to the quality of health care in America today is being done on the way up the appeals ladder, when ultimately a doctor will say, "Okay, yeah, this person should have the bone marrow transplant" or whatever, you name it, or should see the plastic surgeon instead of just a general surgeon. But by then it's too late to do the thing that was recommended in the first place. Now, this is how this really works out there.

Now, if we had to pay a modest amount more, all of us, just a modest—believe me, it's a modest amount; we're talking small bucks here—more, to have the benefits of a managed system, but a system where the purpose was protected so that if your doctor says you ought to be able to see a specialist or you ought to have a certain procedure or if you get in an accident, you ought to be able to go to the nearest emergency room, not one all the way across town because it's the one that's covered; or if you're pregnant or getting chemotherapy and your employer changes health care providers, you ought to be able to keep your doctor until you finish a treatment, and you ought to be able to keep your medical records private throughout—I think the American people would

like that kind of system. And we didn't do that this time because I didn't have enough people in the Congress who agreed with me and Barbara Boxer. This is a big deal, and it will only get bigger. This is huge.

On the education, we fought and we fought and we finally got the funds for the 100,000 teachers. And if we keep funding this, we'll get 100,000 teachers in the next few years, and that will enable us, because we're targeting them at the youngest children, to take average class size down to 18. Now, here's why this is a big deal. This is the first year—the last 2 years—the first time we've had more kids in school than the baby boom generation. But unlike the baby boomers, there is no arc where it ends after 18 years. It looks like it's going to keep on going, because so many of our young children are immigrants, and we continue to bring immigrants in, and they're younger people and have children.

Now, I was in a little town in Florida the other day—2 months ago—a little town that had a grade school with 12 trailers out back for classrooms. I've been in big cities all across this country with beautiful old school buildings where whole floors were shut down because they were in such disrepair. So what we didn't pass this time was a tax cut paid for in our budget that would have helped school districts to build or repair 5,000 schools. If you're going to hire the teachers, they have to have some place to teach. If you want a smaller classroom, there has to be more classrooms. I mean, this is not rocket science here. But it's a huge issue.

If you're going to say, "Okay, end social promotion, give the kids after-school, give the kids summer school, have smaller classes, bring excellence in education back"—then you send a huge signal to children—a huge signal—by the buildings that they attend school in. We have people—there are teachers in this country today conducting classes in broom closets. That's how bad it is. So we've got to win that. That's a big issue.

The next Congress—this year we saved off this ill-advised election-year tax cut with the first surplus we've had in 29 years so we could reform Social Security. Now, when all us baby boomers get in the retirement system, there will only be two people drawing for every one person—two people working for every one person drawing Social Security. To most of us, it won't make any difference. I've got a better pension than most Americans will have. Most Americans don't have a big pension. So we're trying to make it easier for them to save. But today, half the seniors in this country are living above the poverty line only because of Social Security.

Now, we've got to change the system. The system we have now will not support itself when there are only two people working for every one person drawing. It simply won't. Now, if we start now, we take this surplus and some portion of the surpluses we expect in the years ahead and make modest reforms, we can extend the life of Social Security so that the baby boomers can retire in dignity without bankrupting their kids. If we squander the money now or just avoid the tough decisions now, we'll have some really tough decisions to make in a few years. And there will only be two choices. We can either lower the standard of living of retirees, which will kill our consciences, or we can maintain the standard of living with a broken system by raising taxes on our kids in a way that undermines their ability to raise our grandkids. This is a huge issue.

And one reason you ought to vote for her is because she will vote, A, to change it, but she'll do it in a way that is humane and decent. And she won't throw all this money away that you've worked so hard to get us out of debt in—with.

One other issue—I'll just mention one other. There are lots of them, but one other—I've had two people at these events tonight come up and mention it to me. We have a lot at stake in America in the success of the global economy. No country has benefited more, and no State has done better in the last 6 years than California, because of our ability to trade with Asia, our ability to trade with Latin America. Now, you all know there are a lot of troubles out there. Some of it's just pure growing pains, and nobody has good times all the time. Some of it's just the cycle of things. But a lot of it is the direct result of the fact that in addition to global trade and global investment, the global flow of money has grown so rapidly and in such sweeping volumes. Now over one trillion dollars a day crosses national borders—over a trillion dollars a day—a lot of it in highly leveraged instruments where people only put up a small percentage of what it is they're investing. A vast amount of funds cross national borders every day just betting for and against national currencies.

This is all, frankly, necessary. If you want to have high volumes of investment, if you want to have high volumes of trade, if you want to have high volumes of travel, if you want all that, you've got to have some way of moving money around.

But the system that has—we have modified over the last 50 years is not adequate to keep the global economy growing and going without running the risk of the kind of boom/bust cycles that used to afflict countries before the Great Depression. After the Great Depression, the United States, Europe, Japan, every country figured out how to avoid it ever happening again. It's never happened. We have not had another Great Depression, have we? We had some stiff recessions. We had some bad times. But never did the wheel run off.

What we have to do is to devise a system for the global financial movement that will get the benefit of this money moving around without the risk of total collapse that you see affecting some of the countries in Asia and elsewhere. Now, it's not an easy thing. I think it's inconceivable we'll be able to do all that without having somebody help in Congress.

So these are just some things I want you to think about. These are big issues. There are some other things that are easier to understand. I tried to get the Congress this year to raise the minimum wage. Why? Because the minimum wage is 5 bucks and 15 cents an hour, and you can't raise a family on it. And when you've got low unemployment and low inflation and the rest of us are doing pretty well, that's the time when you ought to raise it.

I tried to pass legislation to protect children from the dangers of tobacco. Why? Because it's the biggest public health problem in the country for kids. And it's a huge issue. I tried to pass campaign finance reform so you wouldn't have to go to so many of these dinners every year. [*Laughter*] And, you know, there are a lot of things to be done.

Now, the last thing I want to say is this— what Barbra said. I want you to focus on this, just because—and I want to thank Barbra Streisand because she said she's going on the Internet to try to get people to vote. It is generally accepted now that our agenda this year is the winning agenda; that the American people support what we're trying to do; they believe in this; that they believe that we ought to be a force for peace and freedom around the world.

They support us stopping another Bosnia from happening in Kosovo. They support us being involved in the peace process in Ireland and in the Middle East. They support these domestic agenda items that—saving Social Security and more classrooms and the Patients' Bill of Rights.

The difficulty is that almost without exception when you have an election for Congress and you don't have an election for President, you get a big drop in the turnout. And a lot of our folks don't go—lower income working women that have a big enough hassle every day to figure out how to get the kids to child care, to school, and get to work; or inner-city residents who have to ride a bus to work every day, and the polling place is not on the bus route coming home. And just a lot of things happen. And a lot of people just don't think it's that big a deal. I'm telling you, this is a big deal. It is a big deal.

And so what I would like to ask you to do is to think about what you could do between now and a week from Tuesday. Is there an interview you could do? Is there—who do you come in contact with? Everybody you come in contact with at work or socializing or in any other way, that you could tell—this is a big deal, and they need to show up.

This election, in its potential significance, is like a Presidential election because these issues will shape the way we live for a long time to come. And we don't live in a dictatorship. So the President doesn't call all the shots. A lot of this has to be done by Congress and the President working together. Now, I just can't tell you how important it is.

But let me ask you to think about this when I close. The most heartbreaking thing that's happened in the last several days in America, I think, that's really seared the heart of the country, was the death of that young man out in Wyoming. And I called to talk to his parents and his brother—hard to think of what to say. And it moved us all because you see the picture of this fine looking young guy, this intelligent, vital young man with his whole life before him. And it appears that he was taken out by people who thought he didn't belong. So it offended our common sense of humanity.

You all stood up and clapped for me, and I appreciated that, over this Middle East peace thing. But, you know, I felt lucky to be doing that. I loved it, even the ugly parts, the tough parts, and the long nights. That's what I hired

on to do. That's why I ran for President. That's the kind of thing I wanted to do. I felt so fortunate to have been given the chance to do that.

And I might add, it's easier for the honest broker than it is for the parties. You see—I think Mr. Netanyahu has gotten some unfair criticism in this country for being too tough in the negotiating. If you've been watching the news today of what he's facing in Israel, you see that he has to bear the consequences of the commitments he made. Now, he made a good deal for his country. It will increase their security. It is a very good deal. But he's got a hill to climb to sell it to the people that are part of his coalition.

I think Mr. Arafat made a good deal for the Palestinians. It will help them with land. It will help them with the economy. But I'll guarantee you, there are people who don't want peace who will try to take him out over it.

But why did you like that so much? Why did you stand up and clap? I mean, think about it. Why did you do that? Because you know these folks have been fighting each other a long time. And you know Netanyahu and Arafat, they're both real strong-willed, hard-headed guys, right, and they're not supposed to get along.

And you think about the wreckage all of that estrangement has wrought. And you think, God, maybe it will be different now. And here are these people who reached across this divide and decided they'd hold hands and jump off this high dive together. And it makes you feel bigger, doesn't it? It makes you feel more alive. It gives you energy. It gives you hope. It sort of chips away all those layers of cynicism that we carry around encrusted on us all the time. Why? Because it's just the opposite of the murder of young Mr. Shepard. It reaffirms our common humanity. That's why we like it.

Now, what's that got to do with this election and Barbara Boxer? I'll tell you what. I made a decision to run for President in 1991 because I thought that we were not doing what we should do to prepare for this new century; because I wanted everybody to have an opportunity to live up to the fullest of their God-given abilities; because I wanted our country to be a better force for peace and freedom and prosperity for other people, as well ourselves; because I wanted America to be one community across all these various lines that divide us and all the crazy ways we're cut up; and because I thought Washington was a place where people were more interested in politics and power than in people and progress. And I thought the rhetoric coming out of there sounded like a broken record that gave me a headache. And I have done my best for 6 years to reconcile the American people to each other, to move this country forward, to bring it together, to make the world a better place.

In all that, I have succeeded more than I have succeeded in changing the dominant rhetoric and modus operandi of Washington. But Lord knows I have tried. And if we had a few more people like Barbara Boxer, then we could produce more days in Washington which would make you feel the way you did when you saw Prime Minister Netanyahu and Chairman Arafat up there saying, "Oh Lord, I don't know if I can do this, but I'm going to take a big leap and try."

I'm telling you, if you look at the people in this room, you will come in contact with tens of thousands of people, directly or indirectly, maybe millions if you do the Net, between now and election day. I thank you for your money. We'll put it up on the air. But you can have an even bigger impact if you don't let one person go without looking them in the eye and telling them their country needs them to show up on November 3d.

Thank you, and God bless you.

NOTE: The President spoke at 10 p.m. at a private residence. In his remarks, he referred to entertainer Barbra Streisand, who introduced the President; dinner hosts Robert A. Daly and Carole Bayer Sager; singer Carole King; Senator Boxer's husband, Stuart, their son, Doug, their daughter, Nicole, and son-in-law, Tony Rodham, and their grandson, Zachary Rodham; murder victim Matthew Shepard's parents, Dennis and Judy, and his brother, Logan; Prime Minister Binyamin Netanyahu of Israel; and Chairman Yasser Arafat of the Palestinian Authority.

Remarks at a Luncheon for Senator Barbara Boxer in San Francisco, California
October 25, 1998

Thank you very much, ladies and gentlemen. Thank you for your wonderful welcome, I'm delighted to be here with so many great supporters of Barbara Boxer. I want to thank Mark and Susie and my longtime friend Dick Fredericks, all the others who are responsible for this event today.

I am delighted to see Senator Cranston here, and thank you, sir. And I'm so glad that Gray Davis was able to come—another way station on his way to victory in a few days.

You know, I have had a great time at this event listening to other people speak, first of all because, believe it or not, I'm a little afraid to speak today because I still haven't had much sleep since the end of those peace talks. And I gave a couple speeches for Barbara yesterday in southern California, and I told everyone that before I got off the plane—my staff gives me these typewritten things, see, like this, and I always ignore them; I just stand up there and talk. So because I was up for 39 hours in a row at the end of the Middle East peace talks, and then had to come out here, and my system is a little—you know, I mean, I'm 52 years old. [*Laughter*] And I didn't even do that in college. So my staff said, "Please read the cards today." [*Laughter*]

And then Hillary called me to tell me to tell Barbara hello and to say how sorry she was she wasn't here. And she said, "Better read those cards today." [*Laughter*] So I've got these cards up here; I'll do my best to do it.

So the first thing is I'm tired. But secondly, you know the people who spoke before me, in image and in substance, to me represent the best of the party that I'm proud to belong to, the State that has been so good to me that I have seen come back from the doldrums once again to lead America and the world toward the future, and the country that we all love so much.

I want to thank Art Torres for his leadership of this party. I want to thank Dianne Feinstein for her strong leadership, for standing up for the assault weapons ban and helping us to protect the Mojave and doing a dozen other things of great value to this country. I want to thank Nancy Pelosi for her steadfast support for education and health care, for women's rights, for human rights around the world, and for her wonderful friendship to me. And then Barbara gave this marvelous speech. I mean, weren't you proud of all of them? Didn't you feel better just listening to them all speak? I mean, it was great, wasn't it? [*Applause*]

I sort of feel like that old saw that everything that needs to be said has already been said, but not everyone has said it yet. [*Laughter*] And so you have to endure one more speech. But I'd like to, if I might, put the stakes of this election into some larger perspective for you. That's one of my jobs as your President, to try to tell you where I think the big picture is.

When I came to California first in 1991 as a candidate and I asked the people here to support me, I did it because I felt that our country was not doing what we should to prepare for the 21st century. And I said, I want you to vote for me, even though I come from one of those little places Dianne Feinstein was talking about. I spent 12 years as a Governor trying to keep money from going to California, you know? [*Laughter*] And I spent 6 years as President trying to make it up to you, and I think you're net ahead on the deal, I think. [*Laughter*]

But anyway, I said, look, this is the America I dream of. I want us to go into this new era, where every person—every person—without regard to the circumstances of his or her birth, has a chance to live up to their God-given abilities. I want to live in a country that is still the world's strongest force for peace and freedom and prosperity, not just for ourselves but for others as well. I want America not just to become more diverse in the census statistics but in the daily lives of our people. I want us to relish the differences between us and still grow closer together as a genuine community.

And for 6 years, I've worked for this. And I believe we're closer to those goals than we were 6 years ago. And one of the reasons is that I have had people who would help pursue these goals, people like the three Members of Congress who spoke here today. If any one of them—any one of them—had been replaced in

Congress in 1993 by a member of the opposite party, if we'd had one less vote for our economic program, it would not have passed. That economic program reduced the deficit by 93 percent before the bipartisan balanced budget bill passed in 1997. It sparked a huge boom in investment, a big drop in interest rates. It also had more money for everything from education to the environment to research. And they were there.

Barbara Boxer was there. She had a tough race in '92; she could have taken a dive. But if she had taken a dive, then California would not have been able to rise. She didn't take a dive, and California ought to stick with her on November 3d.

We have worked to prove you can grow the economy and improve the environment. We've worked for cleaner air, cleaner water, safer food, fewer toxic waste dumps. Barbara worked especially for special safety standards for children. And it's worked. But every year it's a battle. We still, every year, have to fight people who believe that the only way to grow the economy is to, alas, damage the environment more, when all the evidence is that, with the new technologies available today, we can actually accelerate economic growth if we make an intelligent commitment to the preservation and improvement of the environment. That's a huge issue for California.

This is not some casual thing. If you want 33 million, 35 million, 40 million people to be able to live here, all different kinds of people elbow-to-elbow, with all the diversity you have, you want the people who serve this meal to have their children grow up without asthma, just as well as those who paid the full ticket price to come today, then California has to lead the way on the environment. Barbara Boxer has stood up for the environment and for the health of California's children, and California should stand up for Barbara Boxer on election day.

I could give you a lot of other examples, but let me just say, in this budget negotiation that we just went through, it is the time of maximum opportunity for the members of our party, because even though we're in the minority in the House and Senate now—I hope only for a few more days—and we have the White House, we don't have enough numbers to pass bills unless Republicans join with us.

And in a funny way, that's as it should be. We ought to have, basically, people in both parties who are willing to work with each other in good faith. We had a few who would work with us to protect our children from the dangers of tobacco, but they had enough to beat us. We had a few who would work with us to raise the minimum wage, but they had enough to beat us. We had a few who would work with us to reform the campaign finance reform laws, but they had enough to beat us. We had a handful, even, who stood up to the health insurance lobby and wanted to help us with the Patients' Bill of Rights, but they had enough to beat us.

But when we got to the budget, as long as they stood with me, then if they wanted a budget and they wanted the Government to go on and they wanted to be able go home and campaign and take advantage of the fact that they had defeated campaign finance reform, they defeated the effort to protect our kids from the dangers of tobacco and did what the health insurance companies wanted on the Patients' Bill of Rights, then they had to listen to us.

And so for the first time in history, in a Congress where the majority really did not want to do it, we got 100,000 teachers in the early grades to lower class size to an average of 18. We got that after-school money Barbara Boxer talked about, and she brought it to the Congress. She did it. And it will mean that 250,000 more kids who live on mean streets in tough neighborhoods with parents that don't get off work until 7 or 8 o'clock at night will be able to stay after school.

I have seen what this can do with my own eyes. In Chicago, where I was the other day, there are now 40,000 children who get 3 square meals a day in the schools. And guess what? Learning levels have gone up, and juvenile crime has done down. This is not rocket science. These children need support; they need something positive to do. And they can learn, and they can grow, and they can flourish.

And because of Barbara Boxer, that's a part of our budget. She stood up for the poorest of California's children, so they could make the richest contribution to California's future, and you ought to stand up for her on election day because of that as well.

We also had the best legislative session for the high-tech industry in California, I believe, ever in history. They had six or seven bills up there; we passed them all at the end. And she supported them, and they shouldn't forget it.

I could go on and on and on. She's talking about going to the Central Valley. Farmers have been hurt worse than anybody else in America so far by the Asian economic crisis. So we declared an emergency and went in to provide some help for people who don't deserve to go out of business because the financial system's gone haywire half a world away. And she helped me do that.

The Congress took 8 months to do it, but finally, when the budget time came, we finally got America's contribution to the International Monetary Fund, which is essential if you want me to help lead the world away from the financial crisis in Asia, if you don't want it to spread to Latin America, if you want America's economic growth to keep going.

So for all those reasons, she deserves to be reelected. But more important is what we're going to do in the future. What is our message in this election? Our message is that Washington ought to be about the business of America and its future and its children. Our message is, okay, we've got 100,000 teachers; now let's provide the tax incentives within our balanced budget to build or repair 5,000 schools so we'll have the classrooms for the teachers to teach in. Our message is, okay, we beat back the ill-advised election year tax cut to squander the surplus this year and for all years to come; but next year we have to actually save Social Security for the 21st century. And we have to do it in a way that protects the universal coverage of Social Security that has lifted half the seniors in this country out of poverty. But we have to do it in a way that does not overly burden our children and our grandchildren when the baby boomers retire. This is a huge decision. Voters should focus on this.

Why were we trying to save the surplus to save Social Security? Because we know, if we make modest changes now, we can preserve Social Security in the 21st century. And we know that we can do it in a way that brings our country together. Now, if we don't do it and we wait until people like me retire—and we know not everybody will have as good a pension as I do. [*Laughter*] You laugh about it; it's a serious thing. We've done a lot, by the way—and Barbara and Dianne and Nancy voted for every single initiative—we have done a lot to make it easier for people of modest means to save for their own retirement. It's very important. But half the seniors in the country today would be in poverty were it not for Social Security.

Now, when the baby boomers retire, there will be two people working for every one person drawing. We have basically three choices. We can deal with this now when we've got a projected surplus for many years to come, make some modest changes, not be afraid of the political heat, join together, and do what's right. Or we can wait until the wheel starts to run off, in which case we will have one of two choices, both bad. We can simply lower the standard of living of our seniors if they don't have good pensions and say, "I'm sorry." Or if that bothers our conscience too much, we can, by that time, have a whopping tax increase to maintain a system that is unsustainable in ways that lower the standard of living of our children and their ability to raise our grandchildren.

So Barbara Boxer stood up for me to save that surplus. And that's why we did it, because we waited 29 years to go from red ink to black, and we wanted to use the money first to take care of this enormous problem that defines who we are as a people. So she has voted to save Social Security first. She deserves a chance to be voting on how to save it. And we're going to do that next year, and that's another reason she should be elected.

So building the classrooms for the kids to be in smaller classes in, saving Social Security, the Patients' Bill of Rights—you've heard us talking about it, but let me remind you what it says. It says, if you're in an HMO, that's good. Care ought to be managed. But the doctor, not the accountant, ought to make the health care decision. You ought to be able to see a specialist if the doctor says you should. If you get hurt in an accident, you ought to go to the nearest emergency room, not one clear across town. If your employer changes health care providers while you're in the middle of a treatment, chemotherapy, or you're pregnant, or there is some other extended treatment, you should be able to finish the treatment before you have to be forced to change doctors. And your medical records ought to be kept private.

This is a big deal. I am telling you, we have tried for one year to pass this. And I need a few more folks like Barbara Boxer in the United States Congress, not fewer, if you want

the Patients' Bill of Rights, if you want the schoolrooms, and if you want Social Security saved.

We also have got to figure out what to do to deal with the challenges of the global financial system now, and I intend to spend—I've already been up working on that this morning. We need people, in short, who care about every individual citizen in every community, in every neighborhood in this State, but also understand we can only fulfill our responsibilities to them unless we do right in the larger world.

No State has benefited as much as California from our growing involvement in the global economy. No State should understand more clearly, with the diversity of your own population, how essential it is on the one hand to give every child a hand up and to reward the labor of every person, but also to reach out to the rest of the world.

And I'll leave you with this one final thought. I want you to ask yourself this question: Why did you clap so much when the speakers said the nice things they did about the Middle East peace accord? And my role in it was really your role in it, because I'm just your hired hand, your elected representative. Why did you feel so good? You may think it's self-evident. Ask yourself—what is your answer? Why?

Because you know how much trouble there has been there. You know how these people and their leaders have been at odds. You've read and seen the continuing tensions in the region. And after all the hope of peace in '93 and '94 and '95, the tragic killing of Prime Minister Rabin, the elections, the upheaval, then stalling, and there, in the middle of the place where the world's three great religions—Islam, Judaism and Christianity—believe in one God—were born, all of a sudden people were able to lay down their mistrust and lay down their hatred and grit their teeth and come together and say, "We're going to try again to reaffirm our commitment to peace. We're going to try together to live on this little piece of land. We're going to try to find a way to live together so that we, together, fight terrorists, who are the enemies of all of us. We're going to try to find a way to live together so that we don't have to put you down to lift ourselves up." And when something like that happens, we just feel big. It gives us energy. It gives us hope.

You know, I'm Irish. To have played a role in this Irish peace process is a great thing for me, to believe that the bedeviled land of my ancestors could finally be walking away from hundreds of years of absolute madness so that all the Irish writers and poets and musicians of the future will have to find some new subject to sing and write about—[*laughter*]—some new reason that justifies spending all night at the pub with a Guinness. [*Laughter*] You laugh, but it's a great joy. Why? Because in the end, we all know down deep inside that the things that make us happiest are those things which reaffirm our common humanity.

Now, what's the most troubling event that's happened in America in the last 2 weeks? I would argue that it's the tragic murder of that young man, Mr. Shepard, in Wyoming. You know, I saw his picture on television, and I talked to his parents and his brother. And I thought, that boy could have been my son. And I listened to his friends talk about him, how he always tried to help people and he was always trying to do things for people. And it looks like, pure and simple, someone took him out because he was gay, so they thought, well, he really is not a part of our deal here. But I think he is part of our deal here.

Now, what's all this got to do with this election? Because every fundamental decision in the end is about whether you have a unifying view of America and your own life and the future you want for your children; whether you really believe that there is such a thing as our common humanity and there is a way for us to advance it as citizens. And that has been America's mission from the beginning, since our Founding Fathers declared, when they knew it was not true in fact, that we were all created equal and that, in order to further our objectives of life, liberty, and the pursuit of happiness, we were going to bind together and try to form a more perfect Union.

Now, they said that, and they knew we weren't all equal in fact. And they knew we were a long way from the ideals we wanted. But they knew what we should be doing and the direction in which we should be going. Now, when you strip it all away, that's what's at stake in this election. And because these issues are so big—this is like an election for President in some ways. We have the message, we have the candidates, we have the unifying vision. Don't let the fact that this is a midterm election let the voter turnout be so low that we wind

up disappointing ourselves on the day after the election.

So I tell you all, I'm grateful for the money that we have given to Senator Boxer, and she'll spend it well. But you are not off the hook—[*laughter*]—because there are still several days between now and this election. You look at this crowd here. How many people do you believe that all of you will see, who never come to a political event like this, between now and Tuesday, November 3d? Tens of thousands? A hundred thousand? All the people you work with, the people you socialize with, the people you worship with, the people you bump into at a coffee shop—how many people will you see?

I'm telling you, we are about the business of defining our country and what it will be like. If you were heartbroken when that young man was killed, if you were elated by the fact that these two people—Prime Minister Netanyahu and Chairman Arafat—were able to reach across this great divide and say, hey, we don't exactly know what's out there, but we're going to jump off this high diving board together—and I might say, they deserve the credit, not me; it was an honor for me, every minute of it—but if you felt that, that means you know that we can't define our future by putting down people who are different from us, and we can't get ahead by pushing people behind. You know that.

You may think this is easy enough for me to say because I have no more elections in me. But I promise you, I believe this—the greatest victories we all win in life are not the victories we win over other people. It's the victories we win for our common humanity.

A day after this election, the great joy of Barbara Boxer's life will not be that she defeated Mr. Fong. He has been a worthy opponent. They have had a good race. The great joy will be that she's been given 6 more years by you to reaffirm our common humanity. And we have ample evidence that that is what our country desperately needs.

So don't you pass a person between now and November 3d—don't pass a one—and Barbara Boxer will go back to Washington.

Thank you, and God bless you.

NOTE: The President spoke at 3:58 p.m. in the Peacock Room at the Mark Hopkins Intercontinental Hotel. In his remarks, he referred to dinner hosts Mark Buell and his wife, Susie Thompkins

Buell; J. Richard Fredericks, senior managing director, NationsBanc Montgomery Securities, Inc.; former Senator Alan Cranston; gubernatorial candidate Lt. Gov. Gray Davis of California; Art Torres, State Democratic chair; murder victim Matthew Shepard's parents, Dennis and Judy, and his brother, Logan; Prime Minister Binyamin Netanyahu of Israel; Chairman Yasser Arafat of the Palestinian Authority; and Matt Fong, Republican senatorial candidate.

Statement on the Student Loan Default Rate
October 26, 1998

When I came into office, there was a student loan default crisis in this Nation. Nearly one out of every four students was failing to pay back his loan.

Today I am proud to announce that we have brought the default rate down below 10 percent, the lowest rate since these data have been collected. The student loan program is now a shining example of Government providing opportunity with accountability.

Some of those failing to pay back their loans were victims of fly-by-night schools that never followed through on their promises. I am proud that over the past 6 years, we have eliminated 1,065 schools from the student loan program, protecting students and taxpayers from fraud and abuse.

Other students had difficulty affording their loan payments, because they were just getting on their feet, or they had decided to take low-paying jobs serving their communities. I am pleased that the reforms for which I fought have given those borrowers a wide variety of options, including paying off their loans as a percentage of their income over time. And because of our economic strategy of reducing the deficit while investing in people's skills, there are jobs for those who finish college, so they can pay off their loans.

Unfortunately, there will always be some who just do not take their responsibilities seriously and then expect taxpayers to cover for them. Fortunately for the taxpayers, this Government has expanded the tools that it has to find these defaulters and arrange for payment. That has taught others that a student loan is not a free ride.

This success comes from the hard work of Government. It is a testament to the commitment of our Secretary of Education, to the policies that we have implemented, and to the people who have put them into practice.

Statement on the Ecuador-Peru Border Settlement Agreement
October 26, 1998

I want to congratulate Presidents Mahuad of Ecuador and Fujimori of Peru on the historic signing today in Brasilia of a border settlement agreement between Ecuador and Peru. This signing marks the end of the last and longest running source of armed international conflict in the Western Hemisphere.

I am proud of the role the United States has played, alongside the other Guarantors, Brazil, Argentina, and Chile, in bringing about the settlement. Mack McLarty, my former Special Envoy for the Americas, and Ambassador Luigi Einaudi, our Special Envoy for the Ecuador/Peru Process, have worked tirelessly over the past 3 years in cooperation with the parties and the other Guarantors to bring about this historic peace settlement. On October 9, I met with Presidents Mahuad and Fujimori at the White House to accept their joint request for the four Guarantors of the Rio Protocol to help them reach a final settlement.

U.S. military personnel, along with those of Brazil, Argentina, and Chile, have also made a vital contribution in manning the international observation force, which has monitored the cease-fire and helped maintain peace in the disputed area.

Remarks in a Roundtable Discussion on Women and Retirement Security
October 27, 1998

The President. Thank you, ladies and gentlemen. Welcome to the White House. I want to thank the Vice President, the members of the administration, Congressman Cardin, all the panelists who are here, the satellite audience at the 12 other sites across our country. I'd like to say a special word of appreciation and welcome to Betty Freidan, who has written with such insight and appreciation for the challenges women face as they grow older.

We're here to talk about the special impact of the challenge to Social Security on the women of the United States. I would like to put it in, if I might, a larger context. Six years ago, when the Vice President and I came here, we brought a new vision of Government against a backdrop of a $290 billion deficit and the kind of problem we're here to talk about today that we knew was looming in the future. We believed that we could give the American people a Government that would live within its means but at the same time invest in and empower our people.

It led to an array of new policies in education and the economy, the budget, the environment, in health care, in crime, in welfare reform. Indeed, it led to the very effort to reinvent Government, to use the Vice President's phrase, and the great effort that he made in that regard. But over the last 6 years, we have been more active, among other things, in family matters and health matters and a whole range of domestic areas, while giving the American people the smallest Federal establishment since President Kennedy was here.

And the results, I think, have been quite good for our people, in terms of prosperity. Opportunity is abundant; communities are stronger; families are more secure. This year, all year long, I have told the American people and done my best to persuade the Congress that it is terribly important to build on this prosperity and its newfound confidence to meet the remaining challenges this country faces on the edge of a new century, particularly, and perhaps most important, the need to save Social Security and to prepare for the retirement of the baby boomers.

On December 8th and 9th we will hold the first-ever White House Conference on Social Security, with a goal of paving the way toward a truly bipartisan national solution early next year. Social Security, as many of you know from your own experience and as all our panelists will be able to discuss in one way or the other, is more than a monthly check or an ID number. It represents a sacred trust among the generations. It represents a trust not only between grandparents, parents, and children, those in retirement and those that work, but also the able-bodied and those who are disabled. It is our obligation to one another, and it reflects our deepest values as Americans. And it must maintain a rock-solid guarantee.

We have a great opportunity to save Social Security. As all of you know, just this month we closed the books on our first balanced budget and surplus in 29 years. It is the product of hardworking Americans who drive the most powerful economic engine our country has had in a generation, the product of hard choices by lawmakers who put our Nation's long-term economic interest very often above their own short-term political interest. It is an achievement that all Americans can be proud of.

But we have to ask ourselves, to what end has this been done? Of course, balancing the budget is essential for our own prosperity in this time of intense global competition. But it also gives us a chance to do something meaningful for future generations by strengthening Social Security. And doing that will help to keep our economy sound and help to keep our budget balanced as we honor our duty to our parents and our children.

As the Vice President said, soon there will be many more older Americans. I hope that he and I will be among them—[*laughter*]—2 of the 75 million baby boomers who will be retiring over the next 30 years. By the year 2013, what Social Security takes in will no longer be enough to fund what it pays out. And then we'll have to dip into the Trust Fund as provided by law. But by 2032, as this chart on the left makes clear, the Trust Fund itself will be empty, and the money Social Security takes in will soon be only enough to pay 72 percent of benefits.

Now, that's the big reason I wanted to reserve the surplus until we decide what to do about Social Security. Every American must have retirement security in the sunset years. We plan for it, count on it, should be able to rely on it. That holds true for women as well as men. But in the case of women, Social Security is especially important. On average, women live longer than men; women make up 60 percent of all elderly recipients of Social Security, 72 percent of all recipients over the age of 85, as you can see here.

For elderly women, Social Security makes up more than half their income. And for many, it is literally all that stands between them and the ravages of poverty. You can see what the poverty rate is for elderly women. It's 13.1 percent with Social Security; without it, it would be over 50 percent. Study after study shows us that women face greater economic challenges in retirement than men do, for three reasons.

First, women live longer. A woman 65 years of age has a life expectancy of 85 years. A man 65 years of age has a life expectancy of 81 years. Second, for comparable hours of work, women still have lower lifetime earnings than men, although we're working on that. Third, women reach retirement with smaller pensions and other assets than men do.

Now, Social Security has a number of features to help women meet these challenges. And we have done a lot of work over the last 6 years to try to help make it easier for people to take out their own pensions and to make it more attractive for small businesses to help to provide pensions for their employees, which could have a disproportionate impact, positive impact, for women in the years ahead. But the hard fact remains that too many retired women, after providing for their families, are having trouble providing for themselves.

Now, we have worked these last 6 years to expand pension coverage, to make the pensions more secure, to simplify the management of pension plans. We've worked for the economic empowerment of women, to end wage discrimination, and strengthen enforcement of the Equal Pay Act. But we must do more until women earn one dollar for every dollar men earn for the same work, and today we're only three-quarters of the way there. We must work harder to give retired women the security they deserve that they could not get for themselves in the years they were working.

Today I am announcing two concrete steps we must take. First, I propose that workers who take time off under the Family and Medical Leave Act should be able to count that time toward retirement plan vesting and eligibility requirements. Sometimes the few months spent at home with a child mean the difference between pension benefits and no pension benefits. That is precisely the wrong message to send to people who are trying to balance work and family. Millions and millions of people have now taken advantage of the family leave act when a family member was desperately ill or a baby was born. None of them should have lost time for retirement vesting and eligibility benefits.

Second, I am proposing that families be given the choice to receive less of their pension when both spouses are living, leaving more for the surviving spouse if the breadwinner dies. That should help keep elderly widows out of poverty in their twilight years. And the poverty rate for single women, for elderly widows is much higher—almost—about 40 percent higher than that 13 percent figure there.

These proposals build on the work of Congressman David Price of North Carolina and Senator Barbara Boxer and Senator Carol Moseley-Braun. They will make a difference for our mothers, our wives, our sisters, and someday for our daughters. But let me emphasize again the most important thing we can do for future generations is to strengthen Social Security overall.

When I said in my State of the Union Address I would reject any attempt to spend any surplus until we save Social Security, I knew the congressional majority wanted to drain billions from the surplus even before it appeared on the books, much less having the ink dry, and not just this year but permanently. Now, I am not opposed to tax cuts; in my balanced budget we had tax cuts for education, for child care, for the environment, and for making it easier for people to get pensions. I'm just opposed to using the surplus to fund tax cuts until we have used all we need of it to save the Social Security system for the 21st century.

The threat of a veto put a stop to that effort in this last Congress. The next Congress will be the Congress I call upon actually to move to save Social Security for the 21st century. It should not be a partisan issue, and we should not have another partisan fight to save the surplus until we reform Social Security.

But recently, Republican leaders are still saying the surplus should go to fund tax cuts first, and the Senate majority leader has suggested that he may not even be willing to work with me to save Social Security. Well, I hope that's just election season rhetoric. After all, they were willing to work with the insurance lobbyists to kill the Patients' Bill of Rights. [*Laughter*] And then they worked with the tobacco companies to kill our teen smoking bill to protect our children from the dangers of tobacco. And they were happy to work with the special interests who were determined to kill campaign finance reform. I think the Senate majority leader will be able to find time to work with me to save Social Security. And I certainly hope so.

I say this partly with a smile on my face but in dead seriousness. This issue will not have the kind of money behind it that the tobacco interests can marshal or the health insurance companies could marshal against the Patients' Bill of Rights. And everybody here with an opinion is going to have to give up a little of it if we're going to make the right kind of decision to get there. This is the sort of decision that requires us to open our minds, open our eyes, open our ears, open our hearts, think about what America will be like 30 years from now, not just what it's like today, and imagine what it will be like when those of us who aren't retired will be retired and our children will be raising our grandchildren—increasingly, when those of us who are retired will be looking after our great-grandchildren, as the life expectancy goes up and up.

This requires imagination. And it will be hard enough under the best of circumstances. It would be foolish to take this projected structural surplus that has been built in through 6 hard years of effort and squander it, until we know what it will cost to have a system that all Americans, without regard to party, can be proud of.

Now, this is an issue that offers us that kind of choice, between progress and partisanship; moving forward, turning back; putting people over politics. In 11 days we will elect a Congress that will determine the future of Social Security. We need one that is 100 percent committed to saving Social Security first; to putting the long-term security of the American people, our parents and our children, ahead of the short-term politics.

Now let me say, I am eager to hear from our panelists. I think it's important to note on this day with this subject that one of America's first great advocates for Social Security was the Secretary of Labor, Frances Perkins. As Secretary Herman would tell you, Frances Perkins' name now graces the Department of Labor building, just down Pennsylvania Avenue. She was the first woman to hold that office or any other Cabinet office. Years later, on the 25th anniversary of Social Security, Frances Perkins looked ahead and said this: "We will go forward into the future a stronger Nation because of the fact that we have this basic rock of security under all our people."

That foundation, that rock, was laid by Frances Perkins and Franklin Roosevelt. It is up to all of us together, women and men, to make sure that rock will hold up all our people in the 21st century. Thank you very much.

Molly, why don't you go first? Tell us your story and your family's experience with Social Security.

[*Molly Lozoff described how Social Security had helped her family survive after her husband had a disabling stroke in 1955, in particular, the disability insurance for minor children of a disabled income provider. Ms. Lozoff said that as a senior citizen, she again depended on Social Security for basic living expenses.*]

The President. I'd just like to say, I think I speak for everyone in this room. I guess some bad things happen to everybody in life, and a lot of us were probably feeling nonetheless that we can't imagine how we would have dealt with what you have obviously dealt with so magnificently. And if Social Security helped, then I think we can all be grateful that it did. But we thank you very much.

[*Vice President Al Gore introduced Howard University student Tyra Brown, an AmeriCorps volunteer, who described how the Social Security survivors benefit had helped her following her mother's death when Tyra was 15 years old.*]

The President. We have heard from a student and a retiree. Now I'd like to call on someone who is working and planning for retirement. And I'd like to mention something that I mentioned in my opening remarks, to which the Vice President also referred, and that is that 60 percent of women workers, both part- and full-time, work at jobs that do not provide a pension. And as I said, we have worked very hard on this for the last 6 years, and we've tried to come up with all kinds of proposals that would facilitate more employers providing pensions. And we will do more on that.

But meanwhile, we are where we are. Most Americans, even on Social Security, have some other source of income. But as you see from the chart, over half the women in this country who are retired would be in poverty but for Social Security.

So I'd like for Bernice Myer to talk a little bit about the challenges that she's facing and how she's trying to deal with the prospect of retirement in the job that she's in.

Bernice.

[Bernice Myer, a home-care aide, explained that since she had a low-wage job with no pension, she planned to rely on Social Security when she retired.]

The President. One of the questions that we'll be asked to deal with, that most younger people who are interested in this will ask us to deal with, is the question of how much flexibility individual citizens should be given, and should there be alternative investment strategies for the Social Security fund. There will be a lot of these questions asked by young people, particularly.

And I think it is important to keep in mind that there is always a balance between greater flexibility with the prospects of greater return on the Trust Fund and rock solid certainty. And ironically, to people in Bernice's position, she'd actually be better off with both, because if you don't have a pension, you need a higher income out of Social Security; but if you don't have a pension, you have very little room for risk.

And there are—if you think about it, our society, for decades, by and large, made a bargain with our critical service workers, the people that pick up our trash every day or the police that patrol our streets or the teachers that teach our children. We say, "Okay, we'll get you the best pay we can, but even though you'll never get rich, at least you'll have a pension as well as Social Security."

Now, there's been an explosion, in the last 10 years especially, in America, of trying to provide more direct services to people in-home. And most everybody believes that's a good thing. It promotes more independence, a greater sense of security of the people receiving the services. But there are huge numbers of Americans like Bernice out there who are performing critical services and taking our country in a direction most people who study this believe we need to do more of. And one day, eventually, they'll all be covered by some kind of an organizational system that will give them a decent retirement plan. But meanwhile, you've got people like Bernice that are out there doing things that we should have been doing as a society long before, that are making this a better place, that don't yet either have the bargaining power, the political support, or whatever necessary to have the pensions that they need; either that or the economics of reimbursing for the service are not sufficient to support a pension. It is wrong to let people like her do all this work for us and not at least be able to rely on an adequate Social Security system in retirement.

This is not an isolated story. This is a person who represents a growing number of Americans, not a shrinking number of Americans, doing something that most experts believe is making us a better society.

I didn't want to take so much time, but I just think it's very important that you understand we picked these people—they're very compelling, I think, all of the panelists, but they're also representative, not isolated cases. And I think it's important to think about this when we make these plans for the future.

[Vice President Gore made brief remarks and introduced Wilma Haga, who described how she and her husband had worked hard to put their children through college. She said she had retired with a pension of $200 a month and an additional $300 a month from Social Security, but when her husband died, her Social Security payment rose an additional $600 a month at a time when it was really needed.]

The President. We asked Lucy Sanchez to come here to talk about the Family and Medical Leave Act and its effect on her life, because I think it's important to point out that while both men and women are equally eligible for the Family and Medical Leave Act, women are far more likely to take advantage of it. And they should not lose a year of eligibility, in terms of retirement vesting, when they do.

Keep in mind, if men and women all had retirement systems in addition to Social Security and they were more or less equal, then our task of dealing with handling the baby boomers in the retirement system would be much, much easier. And so anything we can do now to equalize the impact of retirement earnings among similarly situated people 20 years from now will change and make less difficult the changes we are going to have to make anyway in the Social Security system.

I think it's very important for everybody to kind of keep that in mind. So when I announced earlier today, a few moments ago, that we wanted people not to lose credit in retirement vesting when they access the Family and Medical Leave Act, I think it's important. We have an illustration of why it's important to have this law on the books and why it is inconsistent with being pro-work or pro-family to disallow retirement vesting just because people are taking advantage of the law.

Lucy?

[*Lucy Sanchez described how the Family and Medical Leave Act ensured her job stability throughout the previous year, when she had to take 90 days off to care for her husband and when her 85-year-old mother was hospitalized. Ms. Sanchez said she was concerned that her time off would affect her employee pension plan, and she expressed support for the President's proposal to count such time off toward retirement plan vesting and eligibility requirements.*]

The President. Well, thank you for sharing your story with us. We can all see how recent it has been and how difficult it has been for you, and you were very brave to come here and talk with us today. And we thank you for that very much.

We believe, the Vice President and I and our spouses, that the family leave law ought to be expanded some. We've tried in two Congresses to do that and haven't gotten very far. But we'll keep plugging away at it, because I think unless people have been in this situation where they're afraid they're going to lose their job or wreck their retirement because they're just doing what's necessary to hold their families together, they can't imagine it. And the law is

actually a great—it's actually good for businesses, too, because it doesn't put any employers at a competitive disadvantage if it applies to all employers equally. It tends to minimize the cost, the burden of risk, for that. And I thank you very much for what you said.

But I think if we can take this whole family leave issue out of the whole—just eliminate it in terms of whether your retirement vests or not, I think it would be a good thing to do, modest cost to the retirement systems, enormous benefit to the stability of families. So I thank you very, very much for that.

Well, I think our panelists have done a great job, and I want to thank them for that. Again, what we attempted to do today was to show that on the present facts, that women have a disproportionate interest in the stability of the Social Security system and in the adequacy of the benefit because they are disproportionately likely to need it and more likely to have other assets—or less likely to have other assets.

We also wanted to emphasize the disability and child survivor benefits, which our panelists have so eloquently done. None of this, however, is an excuse to avoid making the hard decisions we have to make because of the demographic changes that are occurring. It is just that we have to be mindful of it.

And what I'm hoping we did today was not to confuse anyone, that we've still got hard decisions to make, but to say we ought to be especially sensitive to how these decisions affect women, number one. And number two, we ought to be steely in our determination not to let the surplus go until we figure how much cost is involved and how we're going to balance all the difficult choices that have to be made and the risks that will have to be taken, because we've got to maintain the social cohesion that Social Security has given us.

Think about what we got out of Molly being able to live her life under the circumstances and raise her children. Think about what society got out of that. Think about what society is going to get out of Tyra Brown because she was not abandoned, when her mother suddenly passed away, at the age of 15. And we were all sitting there watching her talk, just feeling better being Americans, weren't we, every one of us. Don't you think it was worth it to take care of her, help her grandmother take care of her for 3 years? We all got something out of that, and she's got 60 years or more of giving back to society, that we're all going to benefit from that.

So I think as we—we identified, all of us, with each one of these panelists as they talked to us about their lives. And so I'll say again, none of this lets us off the hook for making the hard decisions, but it ought to make us determined to be more sensitive to how they affect women, number one, and determined not to let the surplus go, in case we need it to fill in the patches of the decisions to make sure

that we can have more stories like this 10, 20, 30, 40 years from now.

Thank you very much.

NOTE: The roundtable began at 2:30 p.m. in the East Room at the White House. The transcript released by the Office of the Press Secretary also included the opening remarks of Vice President Al Gore. In his remarks, the President referred to feminist Betty Freidan.

Remarks to Regional Federal Officials
October 27, 1998

Thank you very much and welcome. I know you have had a lot of briefings. I've been briefed on some of the briefings. [*Laughter*] I got a colorful briefing on Mr. Begala's exuberance when he was here. [*Laughter*]

Kosovo

I would like to, before I begin my remarks to you—it's my last opportunity to see the press today, and I'd like to say a few words about Kosovo and the recent developments there.

I'm very encouraged that NATO's persistence and resolve have compelled President Milosevic to pull back his forces and comply very substantially with the demands of the international community. Hopefully, now the climate of fear and intimidation can be lifted and Kosovar Albanians can return to their villages and, more importantly over the long run, that negotiations toward a durable and peaceful resolution can move forward.

From the outset, we have had three overriding objectives in Kosovo: first, to end the violence that threatens the fragile stability of the Balkans; second, to prevent a humanitarian crisis from becoming a catastrophe by stopping the repression of Kosovar Albanians; and third, to put Kosovo back into the hands of its people by giving them self-government again.

We've achieved real progress toward each of these objectives: The fighting has stopped; displaced people are beginning to return to their homes; humanitarian aid is flowing; and Mr. Milosevic has agreed to negotiate self-government for Kosovo with a timetable to achieve it.

It is not enough, however, for Mr. Milosevic to come into compliance. He must also stay in compliance. To verify that, the international community will continue to deploy an unprecedented international presence in Kosovo, on the ground and in the air, something Mr. Milosevic had resisted before for a decade.

As a result of the improving security climate, up to 40,000 displaced people already have been returned to their homes from the mountains, escaping the mortal jeopardy of a winter without shelter. As the cease-fire holds, more humanitarian relief workers and international verifiers move into Kosovo, Serb forces stay out, and roadblocks and checkpoints stay down. The confidence level of the remaining displaced people should now increase. And they, too, will be able to come in from the cold.

Over the long run, stability in Kosovo depends upon a durable political settlement, ultimately, on the establishment of democracy and civil society, including a free press throughout former Yugoslavia. Now Mr. Milosevic has agreed to internationally supervised democratic elections in Kosovo, substantial self-government, and a local police, in short, rights the Kosovars have been demanding since Mr. Milosevic stripped their autonomy a decade ago.

NATO's willingness to act, combined with determined diplomacy, created this chance to end the suffering and repression in Kosovo and to put its people on the path to peace. But this is a chance, not a guarantee. That is why NATO today agreed to retain the authority, the forces, and the readiness to act if Mr. Milosevic backslides on his commitments.

We are at a hopeful moment, but we should be under no illusion. There is still a lot of hard road to walk before hope can triumph over hatred in the Balkans. I feel much better today about this, but we've still got to stay on the case if we want to see hope, freedom, and peace prevail.

Again, I'd like to thank Mr. Solana, Secretary-General of NATO; General Clark, our Commanding General; and Mr. Holbrooke and Mr. Hill and others who have worked so hard on this.

Regional Issues

I'd also like to thank the people who helped to put together this day for you: Goody Marshall, Kris Balderston, Elisabeth Steele, Eric Dodds. I'm grateful that, at least once a year, you get to come here, and we get to tell you what we're doing, and you get to tell us what you're doing, more important, that we get to thank you for the essential role you play in making this administration work for the American people.

Here in Washington, we often come up with great sounding policies. You have to make them work in the real world. It's the GSA's Jay Pearson making our computers-in-school initiative work by donating hundreds of good computers to schools throughout the Pacific Northwest; or Elaine Guiney, creating the Nation's first one-stop capital shop in Boston to speed up small business loans; or John Pouland bringing together diverse groups to work to make the Rio Grande an economically vibrant and environmentally healthy American heritage river. All of you, in different ways, are the eyes and ears of this administration. You are the helping hands of our administration. And we are very, very appreciative of what you do.

And look at what, together, we have done with the American people: nearly 17 million new jobs, the lowest unemployment in 28 years, the smallest percentage of people on welfare in 29 years, more small businesses created in the past 5 years than in the previous 12 years combined, the highest homeownership in history. And last month, just a couple of days ago, we announced we reached a goal of two-thirds of the American people in their own homes, a goal we had set for the year 2000, almost 2 years ahead of time.

Now, these goals, plus the lowest crime rate in 25 years, the cleanest environment in a generation, and of course, the first balanced budget in 29 years, have been very, very encouraging to me. Just a couple of weeks ago we reached agreement with the Republican majority on a fiscally responsible balanced budget that seizes this moment of prosperity to invest more in our future. We fought for and won vital new investments for children: 100,000 new teachers; child literacy; continued funding for our goal to connect every classroom and library to the Internet by the year 2000; college mentoring programs so that we can go into middle schools and tell children that, number one, they can get the help they need now and, number two, we can tell them now exactly what kind of financial help they can get to go to college if they stay in school, learn their lessons, and look to the future.

We fought for and won full funding for the International Monetary Fund to help protect our own economy and to help to stabilize the financial turmoil around the world. We fought for and won emergency relief for hard-pressed farmers and ranchers. We fought for and won substantial increases for our clean water initiative, to head off the threat of global climate change, to protect more precious lands, to invest in science and medical research.

We can be particularly proud of the fact that we fought for and won the right to reserve every penny of the surplus until we save Social Security first. Despite efforts of some in the congressional majority to squander the surplus on election-year tax plans, we now are well positioned to save Social Security for the 21st century.

Although we should take pride in all this, and especially in the 8 days of progress that we had at the end of a long, long congressional session, 8 days of progress cannot make up for 8 months of partisanship. That killed our plan to build and modernize 5,000 more schools. The hundred thousand teachers will enable us to take class size down to an average of 18 in the early grades, but we can't do it if the teachers don't have classrooms in which to meet the children. It killed an increase in the minimum wage. It killed campaign finance reform. It killed the reform legislation to protect our children from the dangers of tobacco. It killed our chance to pass a real Patients' Bill of Rights.

So I am proud of the 100,000 teachers, saving the surplus for Social Security, protecting the environment, keeping our economy going strong. But we have so much more to do. I hope that every American will go out and vote in the election a week from today. I hope they will vote for Social Security first, for a Patients' Bill of Rights, for building and modernizing those 5,000 schools. I hope they will vote for progress over partisanship, for people over politics. You do that every day. And I thank you for it very much.

Thank you.

NOTE: The President spoke at 4:34 p.m. in Room 450 of the Old Executive Office Building. In his remarks, he referred to President Slobodan Milosevic of the Federal Republic of Yugoslavia

(Serbia and Montenegro); NATO Secretary General Javier Solana; Gen. Wesley K. Clark, USA, Supreme Allied Commander, Europe; Special Envoy Richard C. Holbrooke, the President's nominee to be United Nations Ambassador; Christopher R. Hill, U.S. Ambassador to the former Yugoslav Republic of Macedonia; event organizers Thurgood (Goody) Marshall, Jr., Assistant to the President and Cabinet Secretary, Kris M. Balderston, Deputy Assistant to the President and Deputy Cabinet Secretary, Elisabeth Steele, Special Assistant to the Cabinet Secretary, and Eric M. Dodds, Deputy Chief of Staff of the General Services Administration; and Elaine Guiney, Region I Advocate, Small Business Administration.

Statement on Signing the Community Opportunities, Accountability, and Training and Educational Services Act of 1998
October 27, 1998

Today I am pleased to sign into law S. 2206, the "Community Opportunities, Accountability, and Training and Educational Services Act of 1998." This legislation reauthorizes and amends Head Start, Community Services Block Grants (CSBGs), and the Low-Income Home Energy Assistance Program (LIHEAP). In addition, this bill effectively completes the community empowerment agenda I proposed in 1992 by establishing a new Individual Development Account (IDA) demonstration program to empower low-income individuals and families by helping them accumulate assets for their futures.

I particularly want to thank the chief sponsors of this legislation, Senators Coats, Jeffords, Kennedy, and Dodd and Representatives Goodling, Martinez, and Clay. Let me also thank Senator Harkin and Representative Tony Hall for their efforts to champion the IDA demonstration project.

More than 33 years have passed since President Johnson signed the legislation that began the historic experiment in child development called Head Start. I am proud that since I became President, we have raised Head Start funding by more than 50 percent; increased dramatically the number of children served; and improved the quality of the program significantly. I am particularly proud that we launched

Early Head Start to bring Head Start services to children through age three.

As we approach the 21st century, S. 2206 strengthens and expands Head Start—renewing our commitment to prepare our neediest children for school and helping parents to teach and support them. The legislation continues to build on the themes first expressed in the 1994 Report of the Advisory Committee on Head Start Quality and Expansion: improving program quality and accountability, responding to family needs, and strengthening partnerships with other community services. It raises qualifications for Head Start teachers; invests additional dollars in program quality improvement by increasing teacher salaries, benefits and training; and requires the Department of Health and Human Services to study the effects of these investments on children.

The bill also incorporates my recommendation to double the funding set-aside for the Early Head Start program. In light of new research on the significance of the earliest years, this expansion is an essential step to reach more of our most vulnerable infants and toddlers with critical services.

S. 2206 also includes a number of other important provisions to address the needs of low-income families. The IDA demonstration program provides incentives through Federal matching funds for low-income individuals and families to invest in their futures by saving for higher education, a first home, or to start a new small business. In addition, the bill's CSBG and LIHEAP provisions will help to address the need for critical urban and rural community development projects and heating and cooling assistance for vulnerable senior citizens, children, and persons with disabilities.

The Department of Justice advises, however, that the provision that allows religiously affiliated organizations to be providers under CSBG would be unconstitutional if and to the extent it were construed to permit governmental funding of "pervasively sectarian" organizations, as that term has been defined by the courts. Accordingly, I construe the Act as forbidding the funding of pervasively sectarian organizations

and as permitting Federal, State, and local governments involved in disbursing CSBG funds to take into account the structure and operations of a religious organization in determining whether such an organization is pervasively sectarian.

Overall, the bill is a fine example of the good that can be achieved when the Congress and the Administration join together to support programs that can break the cycle of poverty and despair and create economic opportunities for our Nation's neediest families. It is with great pleasure that I sign this legislation.

WILLIAM J. CLINTON

The White House,
October 27, 1998.

NOTE: S. 2206, approved October 27, was assigned Public Law No. 105–285.

Statement on Signing the International Religious Freedom Act of 1998
October 27, 1998

Today I have signed into law H.R. 2431, the "International Religious Freedom Act of 1998." My Administration is committed to promoting religious freedom worldwide, and I commend the Congress for passing legislation that will provide the executive branch with the flexibility needed to advance this effort.

The United States was founded on the right to worship freely and on respect for the right of others to worship as they believe. My Administration has made religious freedom a central element of U.S. foreign policy. When we promote religious freedom we also promote freedom of expression, conscience, and association, and other human rights. This Act is not directed against any one country or religious faith. Indeed, this Act will serve to promote the religious freedom of people of all backgrounds, whether Muslim, Christian, Jewish, Buddhist, Hindu, Taoist, or any other faith.

I intend to nominate Dr. Robert Seiple, the Special Representative of the Secretary of State for International Religious Freedom, for the position of Ambassador at Large created under the Act. It is my understanding that he will act as an ex-officio officer of the U.S. Commission on International Religious Freedom, an organization that is advisory in nature and does not have the authority to make specific findings concerning violations of religious freedom.

Section 401 of this Act calls for the President to take diplomatic and other appropriate action with respect to any country that engages in or tolerates violations of religious freedom. This is consistent with my Administration's policy of protecting and promoting religious freedom vigorously throughout the world. We frequently raise religious freedom issues with other governments at the highest levels. I understand that such actions taken as a matter of policy are among the types of actions envisioned by section 401.

I commend the Congress for incorporating flexibility in the several provisions concerning the imposition of economic measures. Although I am concerned that such measures could result in even greater pressures—and possibly reprisals—against minority religious communities that the bill is intended to help, I note that section 402 mandates these measures only in the most extreme and egregious cases of religious persecution. The imposition of economic measures or commensurate actions is required only when a country has engaged in systematic, ongoing, egregious violations of religious freedom accompanied by flagrant denials of the right to life, liberty, or the security of persons—such as torture, enforced and arbitrary disappearances, or arbitrary prolonged detention. I also note that section 405 allows me to choose from a range of measures, including some actions of limited duration.

The Act provides additional flexibility by allowing the President to waive the imposition of economic measures if violations cease, if a waiver would further the purpose of the Act, or if required by important national interests. Section 402(c) allows me to take into account other substantial measures that we have taken against a country, and which are still in effect, in determining whether additional measures should be imposed. I note, however, that a technical correction to section 402(c)(4) should be made to clarify the conditions applicable to this determination. My Administration has provided this technical correction to the Congress.

I regret, however, that certain other provisions of the Act lack this flexibility and infringe on the authority vested by the Constitution solely with the President. For example, section 403(b) directs the President to undertake negotiations with foreign governments for specified foreign policy purposes. It also requires certain communications between the President and the Congress concerning these negotiations. I shall treat the language of this provision as precatory and construe the provision in light of my constitutional responsibilities to conduct foreign affairs, including, where appropriate, the protection of diplomatic communications.

Section 107 requires that the Secretary of State grant U.S. citizens access to U.S. missions abroad for religious activities on a basis no less favorable than that for other nongovernmental activities unrelated to the conduct of the diplomatic mission. State Department policy already allows U.S. Government mission employees access to U.S. facilities for religious services in environments where such services are not available locally. The extension of this practice to U.S. citizens who generally enjoy no privileges and immunities in the host state has the potential to create conflicts with host country laws and to impair the ability of U.S. missions to function effectively. Care also must be taken to ensure that this provision is implemented consistent with the First Amendment. Accordingly, I have asked the Department of State to prepare guidance to clarify the scope of this provision and the grounds on which mission premises are generally available to nongovernmental organizations.

Finally, I will interpret the Act's exception in section 405(d) concerning the provision of medicines, food, or other humanitarian assistance to apply to any loans, loan guarantees, extensions of credit, issuance of letters of credit, or other financing measures necessary or incidental to the sale of such goods. Additionally, I will interpret the license requirements in section 423 regarding specified items to apply only to countries of particular concern.

WILLIAM J. CLINTON

The White House,
October 27, 1998.

NOTE: H.R. 2431, approved October 27, was assigned Public Law No. 105–292. An original was not available for verification of the content of this statement.

Statement on Signing the Curt Flood Act of 1998
October 27, 1998

Today I am pleased to have signed into law S. 53, the "Curt Flood Act of 1998." This legislation is the successful culmination of bipartisan efforts to treat employment matters with respect to Major League Baseball players under the antitrust laws in the same way such matters are treated for athletes in other professional sports.

It is especially fitting that this legislation honors a courageous baseball player and individual, the late Curt Flood, whose enormous talents on the baseball diamond were matched by his courage off the field. It was 29 years ago this month that Curt Flood refused a trade from the St. Louis Cardinals to the Philadelphia Phillies. His bold stand set in motion the events that culminate in the bill I have signed into law.

The Act appropriately limits baseball's special judicially created antitrust exemption by expressly applying the antitrust laws to certain conduct of Major League Baseball; the applicability of the antitrust laws with respect to all other conduct is unchanged. The Act in no way codifies or extends the baseball exemption and would not affect the applicability of those laws to certain matters that, it has been argued, the exemption would legitimately protect (including franchise relocation rules and the minor leagues).

The Act does not in any way limit the standing of the United States to bring an antitrust action. The antitrust laws protect the public's interest in the efficient operation of the free market system, thereby protecting consumers, and the United States has standing to sue to enjoin all violations.

It is sound policy to treat the employment matters of Major League Baseball players under the antitrust laws in the same way such matters are treated for athletes in other professional sports.

WILLIAM J. CLINTON

The White House,
October 27, 1998.

NOTE: S. 53, approved October 27, was assigned Public Law No. 105–297. An original was not available for verification of the content of this statement.

Statement on Signing Legislation Amending the Omnibus Crime Control and Safe Streets Act of 1968
October 27, 1998

Today I am pleased to approve S. 2235. This legislation amends the Omnibus Crime Control and Safe Streets Act of 1968, which makes grant funds available under the Justice Department's Community Oriented Policing Services (COPS) program, to encourage local school systems to enter into partnerships with local law enforcement agencies by employing "school resource officers" in and around elementary and secondary schools. A school resource officer will now be a sworn law enforcement officer and be deployed to work in collaboration with schools and community-based organizations. By helping to educate students in crime prevention techniques and peaceful conflict resolution and by identifying changes in a school's environment that might discourage crime and violence, the officer will address crime, disorder, gangs, and drug-related activities.

We have achieved almost 90 percent of our pledge to put 100,000 additional cops on the street in community policing activities, and this has helped drive down crime rates across the Nation. This bill will help bring those same successful community policing methods to our schools.

I want to thank the sponsors of this legislation for their leadership in securing enactment of this law: Senator Ben Nighthorse Campbell in the Senate, and Representative Jim Maloney of Connecticut who worked tirelessly to secure overwhelming bipartisan passage of this important safe schools measure in the House.

WILLIAM J. CLINTON

The White House,
October 27, 1998.

NOTE: S. 2235, approved October 27, was assigned Public Law No. 105–302. An original was not available for verification of the content of this statement.

Remarks at a Unity '98 Reception
October 27, 1998

Thank you very much. Just while he was speaking, Senator Rockefeller's trust fund earned enough interest to guarantee us five more congressional seats. [*Laughter*]

Let me say first, I want to thank Jay and Sharon for having us all here. I thank Steve Grossman and Bob Torricelli and Nancy Pelosi, all of whom are here, for their leadership in this Unity campaign. Senator Kerrey, thank you for your leadership on the Senate Campaign Committee. And my good friend and neighbor Congressman Bill Jefferson from New Orleans back there, where we hope we will get another Member of Congress from Louisiana in this election. I hope we can do that.

I want to say to Jay Rockefeller, we've been friends a long, long time. I used to say, Bob Kerrey and Jay Rockefeller and I were Governors together back when we had a life, before we all moved to Washington. And Jay Rockefeller could have done a lot of things with his life. His daughter is up there teaching in that school in New York because of the example that her father set and the example her mother set. And this is a better country because of you. And Hillary and I both love and admire you very much, and we thank you.

I want to say to all of you, you cannot imagine how important your contributions are in this, the 11th hour of this campaign. I think there is beginning to be a sense out there that this is not an ordinary election because it's not an ordinary time. What we have going for us are a lot of great candidates and the right message.

The American people want us not to spend this surplus until we save the Social Security system for the 21st century. They want us to put the education of our children first. And they understand that having smaller classes in the early grades, with the biggest group of students in history, is a laudable goal, and it's a great thing. We won the 100,000 teachers fight, but they know the majority in Congress kept us from passing an initiative to build or repair 5,000 schools. So if they have no place to sit, it will be hard for the teachers to teach the children.

They want us to pass a Patients' Bill of Rights, not because they're against managed care, but because they don't want the management to overcome the medical quality of care people get. They want us to do the things, in short, that we are trying to do in this election.

And I can tell you, I'm now spending a fair amount of time getting briefed every day. Hillary was in New York for Chuck Schumer today, and he has moved clearly ahead in the surveys up there. We have a remarkable young man running for the United States Senate in North Carolina, against an incumbent Republican, who moved decisively ahead today in the published opinion surveys.

We are doing the work of America's future. We have two things to contend with. One is an enormous disparity in financial resources. And the other is 150 years of history of midterm elections where it's normally a disadvantage for the party of the President, particularly in the sixth year. And the other is the natural advantage Republicans have when the voter turnout goes down because their electorate tends to be older and wealthier and more reliable even in off-year elections.

We are striving to overcome those disadvantages. You are helping us to do that. We do not have to have as much money as they do. But we have to have enough. We have a heroic Senate candidate in Kentucky, Scotty Baesler, a Congressman who is being outspent, I think, at least three to one there. It's unbelievable what's going on there. And today, again, he was 4 points ahead in the survey. And Senator Ford, who he's trying to replace, and the Governor assured me that they have all our forces out on the ground. They're going to do the best they can to win.

So I think it's very important that you understand that, in my view, this whole election still hangs in the balance, and it depends on whether the American people decide it's worth voting and whether they have some stake in the future. And that depends upon our ability to get the message out in all these individual races and across the country.

I feel good about it because I think we have a fighting chance. We're fighting history, money, and midterms, but we've got message; we've got candidates; and you've helped to propel them toward the finish line. I'm very proud of that, and I hope you are, too. And I hope Tuesday night we'll have a great celebration.

Thank you, and God bless you all.

NOTE: The President spoke at 7:35 p.m. at a private residence. In his remarks, he referred to dinner hosts Senator John D. Rockefeller IV, and his wife, Sharon, and their daughter, Valerie; Steve Grossman, national chair, Democratic National Committee; John Edwards, Democratic senatorial candidate for North Carolina; and Gov. Paul E. Patton of Kentucky.

Remarks at a Unity '98 Dinner
October 27, 1998

Thank you very much. Thank you so much. First of all, I'd like to join all those who have spoken in thanking the Cafaros for opening their wonderful alternative home to us—their non-Ohio home. [*Laughter*] This is a beautiful place. And I've already had a fascinating, if limited, tour. And I thank them for that and for their great friendship and support. I think it's been wonderful.

I also want to thank Steve Grossman for his heroic efforts these last couple of years to get our party out of debt and then to make our contribution to this congressional campaign and to the Governors races and the other things we've got going around the country, all of which look remarkably positive. And I can't say enough in appreciation of Senator Torricelli and Congresswoman Pelosi in the work they've done with Steve in this Unity campaign. They have been tireless, and they have seen to it that I would be tireless, even when I was tired. [*Laughter*] And I'm very grateful to them.

Let me say to all of you, normally when I go out to speak somewhere, I get these little cards that my staff does. You know, it says J.J. Cafaro, Janet, Renee, Capri, Senator Torricelli, Representative Pelosi, all the people who are going to be here. And then they—and everybody knows I don't pay any attention to them. [*Laughter*] But for the last several days, after we went through that marathon at the Wye Plantation in which, for several nights in a row, I came home at 2 or 3 o'clock in the morning, and then on the last day I was up for 39 hours straight, something I never did in college, when I had a much stronger constitution—[*laughter*]—my staff and my wife started saying, "Read the cards. You haven't had any sleep. We're

so afraid you're going to go to one of these events and mess up. Read the cards." [*Laughter*]

And so I went to California; Nancy and I had a great weekend in California for Senator Boxer. And I sort of didn't read the cards. And then I still haven't had any sleep, and so if I get nervous and grab the cards, you'll know what happened. [*Laughter*]

Let me—I'll be very brief. I am very grateful to have had the chance to spend those 8 days plus in the search for peace in the Middle East. There are a lot of you who have been particularly involved in that subject for a long time, and I would only say to you that it was an extraordinary experience. I think some of the tough, even grueling aspects of the negotiations based on the reports I've seen were, on occasion, exaggerated in terms of the conflicts but not in terms of the intensity and the effort. I mean, nobody slept for a week. I finally told—so by the end, my strategy was to be the last person standing. [*Laughter*] And I thought if I were the last person standing, we would eventually get a peace agreement.

But I have a great deal of admiration for Prime Minister Netanyahu and for Chairman Arafat. And all of us should know that just as we're always happy when the United States or the President can help bring peace, whether it's in the Middle East or in Ireland, it's important to remember that no matter how essential our role may seem to be, in the end we don't have to bear the consequences. They have to bear the consequences.

And there are consequences to both these leaders, but in particular, the political opposition that Prime Minister Netanyahu has been getting in Israel—even though about three-quarters of the people support it, critical chunks of his political constituency don't. There's a lot of intensity there. And I would just tell you that I am determined to do whatever I can to support them both, to help them implement the commitments they have made. And I hope that all Americans will feel the same way. This is a terribly important thing. Our future can be very different if there is no prospect of war in the Middle East. It can be very different, indeed.

That brings me to the next point I want to make, which is that I'm very grateful, in addition to that, that since I've seen most of you last, we passed a budget which had the decided imprint of this administration and our party in Congress. For 8 months we couldn't force the majority in Congress to do anything because they had more votes than we did. We could stop them from doing things we thought were wrong. But then the time came when there had to be a budget, or they couldn't go home and campaign.

And so because of people like Senator Torricelli and Congresswoman Pelosi, because they hung tough, because we were committed we got 100,000 new teachers and smaller class sizes in the early grades, we got after-school programs for children; we got a huge increase in scientific and medical research; we got a massive commitment to our clean water initiative; and we were able to kill most of the anti-environmental efforts of the congressional majority. There were a lot of good things that happened there.

But we have a lot to do. And I think the most important thing you need to know, from my point of view, is the reason I feel good about where we are in this election is not simply that our country is doing well, but that a clear majority of the American people know we can't afford to sit on our laurels. And we have an agenda.

We don't want to spend this surplus until we reform Social Security and secure it for the 21st century. There will be plenty of time, if there's any left over, to figure out what to do about it then. We know we can't have 100,000 teachers unless they have classrooms. I see Mr. Feinhold from Florida here; you know, I went to a grade school in a small town in Florida that had 12 housetrailers out back. So it's all very well for us to hire these teachers, but if they don't have classrooms, they won't be able to teach. And that's a big part of our initiative. And I can't say how strongly I feel that 70-something percent of the American people support us and not the members of the opposition party on the question of whether we should have a Patients' Bill of Rights that guarantees that medical decisions be made by doctors, not accountants. Those are just three of the issues.

Your contributing here tonight gives us a chance, even though we'll be badly outspent this last week—and I mean badly, breathtakingly in some cases—to get our message out and our voters out. We have good candidates; they're fighting good fights. We're doing much better than anybody thought they would be doing. But we have got to be able to be heard and to tell the American people this is not an ordinary election; this is not an ordinary time. These issues are clear cut; there is a clear difference. And if they understand that, we know that by huge margins they favor our position. All of that you have made possible, and for that I am very, very grateful.

Thank you very much.

NOTE: The President spoke at approximately 8:20 p.m. at a private residence. In his remarks, he referred to dinner hosts J.J. and Janet Cafaro and their daughters, Renee and Capri; Steve Grossman, national chair, Democratic National Committee; Prime Minister Binyamin Netanyahu of Israel; and Chairman Yasser Arafat of the Palestinian Authority.

Letter to Congressional Leaders on Continuation of the National Emergency With Respect to Sudan
October 27, 1998

Dear Mr. Speaker: (Dear Mr. President:)

Section 202(d) of the National Emergencies Act (50 U.S.C. 1622(d)) provides for the automatic termination of a national emergency unless, prior to the anniversary date of its declaration, the President publishes in the *Federal Register* and transmits to the Congress a notice stating that the emergency is to continue in effect beyond the anniversary date. In accordance with this provision, I have sent the enclosed notice to the *Federal Register* for publication, stating that the Sudanese emergency is to continue in effect beyond November 3, 1998.

The crisis between the United States and Sudan that led to the declaration on November 3, 1997, of a national emergency has not been resolved. The Government of Sudan continues to support international terrorism and engage in human rights violations, including the denial of religious freedom. Such Sudanese actions pose a continuing unusual and extraordinary threat to the national security and foreign policy of the United States. For these reasons, I have determined that it is necessary to maintain in force the broad authorities necessary to apply economic pressure on the Government of Sudan.

Sincerely,

WILLIAM J. CLINTON

NOTE: Identical letters were sent to Newt Gingrich, Speaker of the House of Representatives, and Albert Gore, Jr., President of the Senate. This letter was released by the Office of the Press Secretary on October 28. The notice of October 27 is listed in Appendix D at the end of this volume.

Remarks at the Welcoming Ceremony for President Andres Pastrana of Colombia
October 28, 1998

President Pastrana, Mrs. Pastrana, members of the Colombia delegation, I am proud to welcome you to the United States and to the White House.

Two months ago when Andres Pastrana stood in historic Bolívar Plaza, the people of Colombia inaugurated not just a new President but a new spirit of hope: hope for change; hope for reconciliation; hope for the fulfillment of his citizens' most profound dreams.

President Pastrana was inspired to public service by his father, who was Colombia's President a generation ago, and by the enduring spirit of the liberator, Bolívar. He was already working for the public good while still a teenager, backpacking across the country to collect money for the poor and raising funds for young burn victims.

Now, Mr. President, as Colombia's leader, you have made it your mission to renew your country for all your citizens; to revive the economy; to lead in the global fight against narcotics; to bring relief and progress to people caught in the crossfire of violence among rebels, paramilitaries, and drug traffickers; to bring peace.

Colombia is the last site of major civil strife in our hemisphere. In recent years, the violence and suffering have grown; the struggle has become intertwined with the deadly drug trade. The conflict has claimed the lives of many dedicated public servants. It has forced Colombians to flee their homes and made it difficult for others to run their businesses and farms.

Mr. President, we admire your courage and determination to end the violence, to heal the wounds of the past, to build a better future. We call on the insurgents and paramilitaries to respond to your bold initiative for peace by ending terrorism, hostage taking, and support for drug traffickers.

All around the world today, men and women who have suffered too long from the poison of hatred are choosing the path of peace: in Ireland, in Bosnia, in Southern Africa, and Central America, now with renewed hope in the Middle East, and just this week with the agreement to end their longstanding conflict in Peru and Ecuador. With your leadership, Mr. President, peace can come to Colombia, too.

As you embark on your mission to build an honorable and enduring peace, count on the United States as a friend and partner. Count on us, too, as you work to bring prosperity to all Colombians. We will work together to create jobs and improve opportunities for both our peoples. We already are your largest trading partner and foreign investor. But there is much more we can do together. And as part of the extraordinary process of integration now taking place all across our hemisphere, we will work together, and with our other friends throughout the Americas, to uphold human rights, root out corruption, fight crime, advance education and health care, overcome poverty, and protect our common environment. We will work together to combat illegal drugs. We have worked together, but we must do more, for both our peoples have suffered greatly from the drug trade and its brutality. The battle against drugs

is a common battle. It must unite our people, not divide them.

Colombians deserve normal lives. They deserve to live free in their homes with their families, to enjoy the phenomenal richness of their culture, the vallenato music, the paintings and sculptures of Botero, the fantastic writings of Gabriel Garcia Marquez.

Mr. President, we in the United States watched with pride as you took the oath of office in August, wearing the suit of clothes your father had worn when he was inaugurated President of Colombia 28 years ago. You said then, "This is not my day, but the day of all Colombians. Change begins today."

This is a new beginning for Colombia. It is also a new opportunity to strengthen the bonds between our peoples. So let us begin today. Again, Mr. President, welcome, and welcome back to the White House.

NOTE: President Clinton spoke at 9:50 a.m. on the South Lawn at the White House, where President Pastrana was accorded a formal welcome with full military honors. In his remarks, he referred to President Pastrana's wife, Nohra. The transcript released by the Office of the Press Secretary also included the remarks of President Pastrana.

The President's News Conference With President Andres Pastrana of Colombia
October 28, 1998

President Clinton. Good afternoon. Let me say again how very pleased I am to have President Pastrana, his wife, his children, and so many members of his government here with us. This is truly a new beginning for Colombia and a new opportunity for our nations to renew our bonds. We made a very good start today.

Our hemisphere is increasingly working together for democracy and opportunity, for justice and human rights, for the peaceful resolution of conflicts. For Colombia, the insurgency looms over all other challenges today. There is terror and assassination, kidnaping, including the kidnaping of United States citizens, and other affronts to human rights. The narcotics trade and the civil conflict have fed off each other

as rebels and paramilitaries do business with violent drug traffickers.

However, we know peace can come, even in the most difficult circumstances, if the will and the courage for peace is strong. President Pastrana has the will, the courage, and the support of his people to build peace. I welcome his efforts to open talks with insurgent groups. We stand ready to help. We hope the insurgents and paramilitaries will seize this opportunity the President has offered them by ending terrorism and hostage taking and involvement with drug traffickers.

The President and I have just signed a new alliance against drugs to intensify our joint efforts in education, in prevention and law enforcement, and extradition, eradication, economic development, and again, in efforts to end civil conflict. All are essential to this fight.

Also, we have reached an agreement on using the proceeds from assets forfeited by drug traffickers to bolster Colombia's counternarcotics enforcement efforts. As I said this morning, the fight against drugs is our joint responsibility. It must unite us, not divide us.

In that spirit, I am pleased to announce that we will provide more than $280 million in assistance to Colombia in the current fiscal year, not just for the frontline battle against drugs today but for development, to build a better future. The strong package of aid recently approved by Congress shows that there is bipartisan support here in America for Colombia's new leadership.

I appreciate the challenge Colombia faces in getting its fiscal house in order. I also appreciate the commitment President Pastrana has made to meeting that challenge. If our experience is any guide, Colombia's effort will be rewarded.

Today we learned, after decades of deficits, that this past year we had a surplus of exactly $70 billion. I'm very pleased that attempts to spend that surplus, rather than preserve it until we reform the Social Security system to meet the needs of the 21st century, were not successful in the last Congress. It is important that we maintain this position until we have saved Social Security. Hopefully, that will occur next year.

While we both work to improve our economies at home, we must do more together. The President and I have agreed to seek new ways to expand trade and to improve our financial stability. We will start consultations on a bilateral investment treaty and a trade and investment commission for the Andean region.

We will work together toward the creation of the Free Trade Area of the Americas. We agreed that developments must be carried out in ways that protect our natural environment and the public health. Toward that end, we have reached agreement for Colombia to become the 73d nation to join the GLOBE program for environmental education over the Internet.

We also reaffirmed our joint commitment to strengthening democracy, human rights, the rule of law. Our Agency for International Development has concluded an agreement to help the Colombian Government strengthen its judicial system to improve its ability to prosecute human rights abuses. And our Defense Department has established a working group with Colombia's Defense Ministry to improve military justice.

Finally, President Pastrana and I have asked Secretary of State Albright and Foreign Minister Fernandez to establish a joint consultative group to keep us in close contact and keep all this progress on track so that we can realize our common aspirations for greater democracy, prosperity, and peace in the new century.

Again, Mr. President, we take your election and your early actions as a very hopeful and positive sign for the people of Colombia and the opening of a new and strong chapter in our joint history together. Thank you for coming. The floor is yours.

President Pastrana. First of all, I'd like to express my thanks to President Clinton and to Mrs. Clinton for the splendid welcome that Nohra and I have been given. And I'd like to say to everyone that I've met in Washington, members of both political parties, both on this trip as well as on my earlier trip, that I am extremely impressed by your good wishes and by your will to work with us as we overcome past problems and enter a new era.

On behalf of our people, I would like to express our thanks to the people of the United States, and personally, I'd like to state that although I've only been President for 3 months now, it would be very difficult I think for Nohra and I to be welcomed so warmly anywhere else. I came here with the hope of forging an alliance with President Clinton and the United States, and I will leave having established a true friendship with the President, and I hope with his Nation.

We have made progress in all the areas placed before us: the environment, education, aviation, and economic cooperation. During this state visit, President Clinton and I have signed a new and historic alliance against drug trafficking in order to combat the growth, trafficking, and demand for drugs, which is a major achievement which reaffirms this new era in relations between Colombia and the United States.

I referred to all these areas earlier as items we have before us but not between us. These are matters of common interest. We are united on this, and united, there is much that we can achieve.

Finally, before answering your questions, allow me to say that my country and my compatriots feel deep respect for President Clinton and for his role as world leader. And as a rarity in history, he is one who forges world peace. President Clinton is a friend of Colombia, and in this visit we have solidified our friendship.

Thank you very much.

President Clinton. Now, what we will do is take a few questions. We will alternate between American and Colombian journalists. And we'll begin with Mr. Hunt [Terence Hunt, Associated Press].

Wye River Agreement

Q. Mr. President, less than a week after the Mideast agreement, Prime Minister Netanyahu has come under pressure from hardliners and says that he won't begin the pullback from the West Bank until he gets approval from his Cabinet, and he has delayed a Cabinet meeting indefinitely. Are you concerned about delays, the return of mistrust? And what can the United States do to prevent this agreement from unraveling?

President Clinton. Well, first of all, let me say that I believe it's a good agreement. It required principled compromise by both parties and extraordinary efforts.

Secondly, as you can see from the criticism both Prime Minister Netanyahu and Chairman Arafat have gotten, it took some courage for them to reach this agreement. I told everybody that I discussed this with before they came here that, if Prime Minister Netanyahu reached an agreement here, he would face a great deal of bitter criticism at home.

I personally think he did a good job at the Wye negotiations, a remarkable job, being strong, aggressive in defense of Israel's interests. The way I read the present state of things is that at the present moment, he knows there's a lot of opposition in the government and in his political base to this agreement, and he wants to be absolutely assured that the early steps will be taken on the other side. I believe that if we complete the security arrangements that were agreed to at Wye, that the Israeli Government will approve this and honor their commitment, and we'll go forward.

So I would urge all the onlookers here, including all of us in the press and in public life, not to over-react to every little bump and turn in the road. There was a lot of mistrust built up in this relationship. It wasn't going to evaporate even in 9 days. And a lot of the people who weren't there at Wye are going to be heard from in both camps now. I think the important thing is they all make commitments to do certain things on a certain timetable and no one should slip off of that. And it was pretty well synchronized so that there will be continual reaffirmations on both sides of the commitments made.

If we can just stay on that, I think we'll be fine. But all of this should only clarify to all the rest of us that they were both quite brave in doing what they did and that peace is a difficult business in the Middle East.

Colombian Domestic Peace Process

Q. President Clinton, how committed are you with bringing peace to Colombia? And will you personally take the lead in this effort?

President Clinton. Well, I would like to do anything that I can, but I think the President has taken the lead in a way that is, I think, innovative and very heartening to the rest of us. Again, I hope that those who have been involved in the turmoil in Colombia will take his offer in good faith.

From the point of view of the United States, I think we should be in a supporting role however we can be of help. One of the things that we would very much like is the United States citizens who have been kidnaped. If they are alive, we'd like them released. If they're not, we'd like them accounted for. That would help us a great deal.

But I personally have been struck with admiration for the way that President Pastrana has handled this so far. I don't know what else anybody could do, and I think that the path he is pursuing is the one most likely to bring results. If there is anything we can do to support that, of course, I would be happy to do so.

Helen [Helen Thomas, United Press International].

1998 Elections/Free Press in Colombia

Q. Mr. President, what is your take on the internal elections? How do you think the Democrats will fare? And do you think the impeachment process will impact on the election itself?

And for President Pastrana, do you have freedom of the press in your country? I understand that you have threatened to shut down a radio station.

President Clinton. Do you want to go first?
President Pastrana. Yes, please.
President Clinton. Yes, you want to go first—
or, yes, you want me to go first? [*Laughter*]
President Pastrana. You go first. [*Laughter*]
President Clinton. Let me say, I think that
these elections, first of all, are important. This
is an important time for our country, and therefore, this is a very important election. And I
hope there will be a big turnout. As to how
they will come out, it's very difficult to say.
There are an unusually large number of apparently quite close elections, which could be quite
good for the Democrats in a year when, by
150 years of history, we're not supposed to do
very well, especially since our side is being very
badly outspent.

But I think that the important thing is that
the choices are clear. We believe that none of
the surplus should be touched until we save
the Social Security program. The leadership of
the Republican Party apparently disagrees with
that. Mr. Kasich talked about it again yesterday.
We believe that it's important to pass a Patients'
Bill of Rights that lets medical decisions be
made by doctors, not accountants, that guarantees people can see a specialist, that their medical records are private, that they go to the nearest emergency room. They disagree with that.

We believe that it is very important that, now
that we're going to have 100,000 new teachers,
that we build or modernize 5,000 schools so
they'll have classrooms to teach in. They disagree with that. We think we ought to raise
the minimum wage; they disagree with that. We
think there ought to be tobacco legislation to
protect our children from the dangers of tobacco, that there ought to be campaign finance
reform. Even though some Republicans have
supported that, their leadership disagrees with
that.

So the choices in this election are very, very
clear. And all of these issues, plus my continuing
efforts to maintain financial stability, economic
stability around the world, and keep the economy going, make this a very important time.
And the only thing I can say is that every American should care about this and should go out
and vote, and I hope that every American will.

President Pastrana. Thank you very much for
your question.

First, I'd like to say that I am a colleague
of yours. I'm a journalist. And for that very
reason, I am one of the great defenders of free-

dom of the press. I think your question refers
to a fine or a sanction that was imposed by
the earlier administration. That's another one
of the legacies left us by the Samper administration. Two days before the end of the administration, the President fined a radio network in Colombia precisely because they violated the Colombian legal statute.

My administration now needs to wait for this
radio network. According to—Colombian law establishes the process necessary to appeal this
decision, and we as the Government have approximately one month to respond to whatever
appeal the network makes.

I think, in Colombia, we need to recover the
freedom of the press that was lost over the
last 4 years in great measure. And I would just
give you some examples. Families that were
owners of newspapers for over 100 years in Colombia had to close them down. TV licenses
that had complied with the law—as stated here
in the United States; even our Nobel Prize winner, Garcia Marquez, has stated this—these
things were taken away since these people were
not friends of that administration.

I think we're now in a new era where we
will recover freedom of the press in Colombia.
That is my commitment. I insist, as your colleague as a journalist, as a lover of democracy,
we will recover freedom of the press, which
I think to a great extent was lost over the last
few years in my country.

Colombian Domestic Peace Process

Q. President Clinton, does the U.S. believe
in the guerrillas' will for peace?
President Clinton. I can't say that because
I've never had any direct contact with them.
All I can say is, I've had quite a lot of experience now with this over the last 6 years. We
have worked to end a war in Bosnia. We have
worked to end three decades of conflict in
Northern Ireland. We have labored in the vine-
yards, as you know, of the complex Middle East
peace process. And we have worked in many
other areas, I and my partners here in our administration. And I have read a great deal about
the turmoil in Colombia and its roots. All the
parties share the same country. It cannot be
good for a nation over the long run to endure
the kind of fighting that Colombia has endured
and to have it all mixed in with the
narcotraffickers. It can't be good for the children
of the guerrillas. It can't be good for the areas

where they operate. It can't be good for the quality of life.

So now you have a President who is clearly independent of destructive forces, clearly committed to bringing people together, clearly committed to giving all the children of Colombia a better future. All I can do is hope and pray that the offer he has given—he has reached his hand out to these people, and I can only hope that they will shake his hand and take his offer.

Mr. McQuillan [Larry McQuillan, Reuters].

1998 Elections

Q. Mr. President, on the latest Republican campaign commercials, do you think it's fair for them to try to cast your personal life as a campaign issue? And do you think in broader terms, that it's fair that anyone should view next Tuesday's election as a referendum on you?

President Clinton. Well, first of all, I think the Republicans are free—in our country, they're free, and they should be free to make the election about whatever they want to make the election about. I hope the American people have seen in me over these last few weeks a real commitment to doing what I told them I would do from the beginning, to try to atone to them for what happened and to try to redouble my efforts to be a good President. And I hope they have sensed the inner changes that are going on and the manifestations and the efforts I've made to help the education of our children in the budget, to achieve peace in the Middle East talks.

But I believe that it's always best if the elections are about the American people and their families and their future. And that's why I believe that, with the choice so clear—we are for Social Security first; don't squander the surplus; we're for the Patients' Bill of Rights; doctors, not accountants, make decisions; we are for building those 5,000 schools so the teachers will have a place to teach and the kids will have a place to learn; we're for raising the minimum wage and for campaign finance reform and for legislation to protect our kids from tobacco. And they're against those things.

That's one of the reasons they have the enormous financial advantage they enjoy which is paying for a lot of those ads. And so to me, there's a clear choice. How can I object to them exercising their free speech rights in saying what they think the election is about? They also say,

I might add, apparently—I know what I've read; I've not seen these ads—they also say that the elections are about tax cuts and their plan on Social Security, which indicates to me that once again they are not committed to leaving this surplus alone until we reform Social Security. That, to me, is a very serious issue that will affect all the American people.

So I would hope that the American people will hear the differences between the two parties, see how far we've come in the last 6 years, and make their judgments. But in any case, I hope we'll have a big turnout. This is not an ordinary election because of the challenges facing our country, and we don't need an ordinary midterm turnout. We need people to show up. And I trust the American people. That's why we're still around here after over 200 years. I think they'll get it right.

Q. So, sir, does that mean——

President Clinton. I gave you my answer. The Republicans are free to say whatever they want to say. I told you what I believe the issues are that are most important facing the American people. I told you that I'm doing my best to be a good President and to evidence the commitment that I expressed to the American people over the last 2 months in what I do as President and how I do it.

But they have to decide whether to vote and on what to vote. I believe if the election is carried out on the issues affecting our children and our future, whether it's our financial stability or saving Social Security or the Patients' Bill of Rights or education, that the members of my party will do quite well, notwithstanding the enormous burden of history and the enormous financial disadvantage under which they labor. And so we're just going to go out there and keep reaching out to the American people and see what happens.

Colombia's Economic and Political Situation

Q. I'd like to know why you have been going down in the polls, and do you believe in those polls?

President Pastrana. I don't think life is about doing well in the polls or not. In our country we received a situation that all Colombians are very aware of, especially with regard to financial matters, where we have the highest fiscal deficit in Colombia's history. We were given a country with the highest rate of unemployment the country has had in the last few years. And clearly, I think that to a great extent this is due to the policies we've had to adopt and the policies we will continue to have to adopt to overcome the crisis.

What I've always repeated is that, as a leader, as a politician, a person has to be judged at the end of his or her term. Clearly, at least in my personal case, in spite of believing in polls, I think that logically we have to look at the mechanism; we have to see if we've talking about phone polls, personal polls, what kind of methodology has been used. But clearly, I think the important thing is that in 4 years we will know if these measures we've adopted were right or not.

We are committed to a peace process which is difficult, but we are committed to it, and we will forge ahead. We know the country we've received is in a financial situation worse than any in Colombia's history. We know we have to take harsh measures, and we will take them. We will protect the poorest sectors. Clearly, there are instructions to be given to ministers for all the social areas, those that have to do with social investment, with poverty, with health and education, with building houses; and matters of social interest are matters within the budget on which we are not going to try to reduce our expenses but try to keep them up and strengthen them. And we will have to make a major effort from the viewpoint of the administration, as we are doing, to cut our expenses, to cut a number of things.

And logically, within 4 years we will know if these measures we are taking today with the assistance I've asked President Clinton for from the United States, through their support at the World Bank and at the Inter-American Development Bank and at the International Monetary Fund, with the help that President Clinton's leadership can provide us in Europe, in Japan, so that we can overcome this crisis and obtain the resources necessary to again generate confidence in Colombia, and thus, as we see today, we will be able to overcome the kind of exchange pressure we're under.

If we manage to generate that trust again—you heard that yesterday from the Secretary of the Treasury; today you've heard it from the President of the United States—with their help, we will generate trust in the markets. We will take away the pressure on the exchange rate. We will lower our interest rates, and we will

reactivate our economy. And thus we will increase our employment. And at the end of my 4-year term, we will be able to say, although we had to take some tough measures, we know now that those were the right measures to lead Colombia forward.

President Clinton. I would like to make just a comment about that, because I am a totally disinterested observer in this sense. But the President has been in office 3 months, and I have now been here 6 years. For whatever it's worth, I think he's making the right decision. If you come into office and you face a difficult challenge—and keep in mind, he now faces two difficult challenges; he has a big economic challenge and he has the challenge of peace—it's always better to be high in the polls than low. We all run for office; everyone would rather be loved than hated. Everyone would rather be liked than disliked. But when you have a difficult economic situation, it's better to bite the bullet early and take the tough positions early so that people can get better. If you keep putting it off, the polls will slowly erode anyway, and in the end the people's lives won't change.

When we adopted our budget here in 1993, a lot of members of my party actually lost their seats because of it, and I've regretted it ever since for them. But when we celebrated the first balanced budget and surplus in 29 years, we invited all the ones who lost their seats to come back, and many did. And you'd be amazed how many told me that they did the right thing. They were proud of the fact that they got rid of the deficit of the country, and they gave us a new economy, a new lease on life.

This is the nature of things in the world today. Not all problems are easy. We'd all like it in life if everything we had to do was easy. But not everything we have to do is easy. And I think the President is doing the right thing. As a disinterested observer, I'll be very surprised if Colombia is not richly rewarded by much stronger economic success, more jobs, higher incomes, more success as a result of the decisions he is making today.

1998 Elections

Q. Mr. President, you said a moment ago that Republicans have a right to frame their ads in this election as they see fit. Two ways they've framed these latest ads—number one, they argue, in essence, that you are not trustworthy, and, therefore, you need a Republican

Congress to balance against your Presidency. And number two, they ask the question, what do you tell your kids about your relationship with Ms. Lewinsky. I wonder how you would answer those two questions, sir.

President Clinton. Well, first of all, I have answered the second question as far as I should. The decisions beyond that on the publicity were made by others, not me. I have answered that question. On whether I've been trustworthy, I think you can look at the record. Go back and look at what I said I would do in 1992, when I ran for President.

Yesterday I signed a bill, for example, which completed the agenda that I said I would try to achieve for poor people in America to give them a chance to get more jobs and to allow them to save more of their own money when they're moving off welfare. It was a very important bill. It also contained our increase in Head Start funds, another commitment I made. And Gene Sperling came in, and he handed me this statement we put out in September of '93. And everything I said I would do on that list has now been done.

A noted Presidential scholar said a couple of years ago before we had the success of the last 2 years that I had kept a higher percentage of my promises than the last five Presidents, in spite of the fact that I had made more detailed commitments to the American people when I ran.

And the consequences are good. We have an economic boom. We have declining social problems. We are a force for peace in the world. So I think that it's fair for a person to be judged on his whole record. I've never—I'm not trying to sugarcoat the fact that I made a mistake and that I didn't want anybody to know about it. I think I've talked about that. The American people have had quite a decent amount of exposure to that. I hope very much that they have seen that I'm doing my best to atone for it. I hope they can sense the rededication and the intensified efforts I'm making for the cause of peace around the world, for the cause of prosperity at home.

But if you look at what I said I'd do when I presented myself to the American people in 1991 and 1992, at the long list of things we've done we said we'd do, and at the good results that the American people have enjoyed—and it's a fact that the American people, I think, agree with us and not them. I think that's the

real issue here. Are we right or are they right? Should we save the surplus until we save Social Security? Should we pass a Patients' Bill of Rights, or not? Should we build classrooms for these teachers to teach in and classes so the kids can have smaller classes? Should we raise the minimum wage? Should we pass campaign finance reform? Should we protect our kids from the dangers of tobacco, or not? It's a clear choice. That will be the impact on people's lives in this election. That's what I believe.

But everyone else—that's why you have a vibrant democracy—everybody else gets to say whatever they want to say and debate it however they want to debate it. I can only tell you that I hope the American people will remember that, notwithstanding the best efforts of some to always take politics away from them and take decisions away from them and pretend that what happens to them and their lives is not important, it really is. And folks should show up and vote. And they should know that the decision not to vote is also a decision that will affect their lives.

That's all I can say. And I hope that many will go, and I trust them to make whatever decision is best for them and for our country.

Colombian Demilitarized Area

Q. Mr. President, a question on the demilitarization and the reservations in the United States with regard to those measures. President Clinton said that it would be good to face these subjects at the beginning. Did you talk about demilitarization in your meeting?

And I'd like to ask President Clinton what he thinks after his discussion with you this morning, what he thinks of that measure.

President Pastrana. I think that it's very important to be able to establish a dialog, a direct dialog with President Clinton, with the Secretary of State, with General McCaffrey, with the National Security Council Adviser, especially with this whole demilitarized area which, according to Colombian law, can be established so that the representatives of the guerrilla movement can come to that area so we can guarantee their life, so that the representatives of Government can go to that area and their lives will also be guaranteed. We can have international observers present in this demilitarized area, as well as journalists who will also be attending.

We had the opportunity today to explain to the President and to his Cabinet that this area will be established for 90 days. That was the commitment; that was the agreement. What we seek are 90 days after next November 7th. During that time we want the FARC to sit down at the negotiating table. They've already appointed three representatives. The Colombian administration will be naming a representative. We'll establish an agenda for those meetings.

But I think it's been very important to be able to share these ideas with President Clinton so that the U.S. Government can discuss it with us to allay their concerns. As I was saying to him this morning, sometimes there may be misinformation or lack of information with regard to this subject. But clearly we have had the opportunity to be able to share and discuss with him exactly what that demilitarized area is about, not just with the President but also with—we've had our Minister of Defense, our High Commissioner for Peace, all the members of our delegation to be able to answer any concern, allay any fear, any question they may have with regard to this process. And I think it's been very well expressed.

But I'd like to see if the President has any additional comment to make on it.

President Clinton. I agree. [*Laughter*]

Go ahead, Wolf [Wolf Blitzer, CNN].

1998 Elections

Q. Mr. President, the other theme that these new Republican ads say is this—I hate to beat a dead horse, but I'll just give you an opportunity to respond to it—they say the question of this election is this: Reward Bill Clinton or vote Republican. Larry asked you earlier if you think these elections are going to be a referendum on your behavior. Do you think they will be?

President Clinton. Well, I think they're running a great number of ads with a lot of issues. I'd like to go back—I'm not sure I answered your question exactly right. I was talking about—on the first question you asked, I think what people ought to say to their children is that when someone makes a mistake, they should admit it and try to rectify it and that this is an illustration of the fact that those rules should apply to everyone, but that when people do that, if they do it properly, they can be stronger in their personal lives and their family lives and in their work lives.

And many of us in life can cite examples where if we went through a period of assessing,

that we grew stronger from it, and we actually did better. With a humble spirit, with the grace of God, and with a lot of determination, I think that happens. And I think in that sense, the lesson is a good one, that it should apply to everyone, from the President on down.

But I believe, to go back to your point, since there has been a lot of talk about misleading, they have a right to say whatever they want to say; but in fairness, they're basically saying to the American people, "We want you to give up saving Social Security first. We want you to give up a Patients' Bill of Rights. We want you to give up modernizing or building 5,000 schools. We want you to give up a minimum wage increase. We want you to give up protecting your children from the dangers of tobacco, and we want you to give up campaign finance reform. We want you to give up all of that. We don't want you to think about yourself. We want you to, in effect, ratify the decisions we made for the tobacco companies, the health insurance companies, the special interests that didn't want campaign finance reform, all the people that gave us the money to put this ad on the air. We want you to give up everything that could help you. And if we can distract you and divert your attention, that will enable us to hold on to our jobs, even though we had 8 months of partisanship in the last Congress and didn't do much until we had to get a budget out. And then we agreed to go along with the President and the Democrats and let them do what they wanted to do for education."

So I would say it wouldn't be a very persuasive argument to me if I were a citizen out there, because I would always be trying to think, as a citizen, what is best for my family, for my children, for my community, and for my country. And I think that is always—always—got to be uppermost in all of our minds. I think it would be a more compelling debate if they would put whatever it is they want to do and explain why they were opposed to what we wanted to do here, and have a debate so people could evaluate how it affects their lives.

But again, it's not for me to tell them how to do it. All I can tell you is what we're for and what we think the issues are.

Colombian Domestic Peace Process/Immigration

[*A question was asked in Spanish, and the interpreter was unable to hear the question. Near* the end of the question, the following translation was given.]

Q. Just like you had Arafat in the United States, here in the White House, do you think at some point it would be possible to have one of our guerrilla leaders here?

President Clinton. Sorry, the interpreter did not hear, so could he repeat his question? If he could repeat his question in English, then you could answer in Spanish and the interpreter could hear you. [*Laughter*]

President Pastrana. Well, Colombia is not at war. Colombia has an internal conflict. I've been able to describe it to the President. For 36 years we've had an internal conflict in the country. And what we hope for is precisely to be able to achieve a peace process that will allow us to put an end to the violence that Colombia has lived through in the last few years.

As I was able to explain to the President and to the press, for the first time as well, we have an historic opportunity. The guerrillas have agreed to eradicate illicit crops. For the first time the FARC has made a commitment; in fact, they have set that forth in the document they've given to the government, which the public knows of. For the first time they're willing to work on eradicating illicit crops.

So I think it's an historic opportunity for the country. If we're able to make peace in Colombia, this is the first major battle in which we will defeat the narcotraffickers. The major enemy in Colombia is drug trafficking, drug traffickers. Therefore, we understand, and we know that we will win that battle. And by winning that battle, we will begin to do away with the global problems the entire world is suffering from today.

That's why I think it's a situation in which our country knows, we're already dealing with it. We've initiated our dialog with the ELN. And we hope after November 7th to begin the dialog with the FARC. And in this way we'll put an end to this process and, clearly, achieve the great wish of our people, which is to have a country at peace.

President Clinton. On the question you asked me about the immigration, the Colombians who are here, I don't know enough about the facts to answer the question. We did make—I tried to make good decisions regarding the Nicaraguans, the Salvadorans, and the Haitians. We have tried to be sensitive to the real facts of the individual's lives who are here—what were the circumstances under which they came to our country and under which they stayed—consistent with our other immigration laws, which are pretty open and broad, I think. But I would—before I could give you an answer, I would have to know more than I do now.

Thank you.

President Pastrana. Thank you.

President Clinton. Thank you very much.

NOTE: The President's 165th news conference began at 3:20 p.m. in the Rose Garden at the White House. In his remarks, he referred to President Pastrana's wife, Nohra; Foreign Minister Guillermo Fernandez of Colombia; Prime Minister Binyamin Netanyahu of Israel; Chairman Yasser Arafat of the Palestinian Authority. President Pastrana referred to the Fuerzas Armadas Revolucionarias de Colombia (FARC) and the Ejército de Liberación Nacional (ELN). President Pastrana spoke in Spanish, and his remarks were translated by an interpreter.

Joint Communique With President Andres Pastrana of Colombia
October 28, 1998

In their second meeting since President Pastrana's election last June, President Clinton and President Pastrana consolidated a comprehensive partnership between their two governments designed to promote democracy and economic growth, fight illicit drugs, strengthen respect for human rights, extend the rule of law, and help bring an end to Colombia's armed conflict. Toward these ends, President Clinton pledged over $280 million in new assistance to Colombia, to be made available in the course of the current fiscal year. President Clinton noted that the scope of this assistance, which is more than double that of last year, makes it by far the largest American assistance program for the hemisphere. This assistance is indicative of the strong bipartisan support, in the Congress as well as his Administration, for Colombia and its new leadership.

The two Presidents agreed on the importance of increased trade and investment in sustaining growth, reducing poverty, and permitting societies to meet the aspirations of their people. They expressed support for the establishment of a Free Trade Area of the Americas by 2005, while also noting the continuing importance of the Andean Trade Preferences in promoting economic growth throughout that region, and underpinning the viability of alternative development programs. They initiated consultations on a Bilateral Investment Treaty, and agreed to conclude with the other countries concerned the creation of a Trade and Investment Council for the Andean region. They welcomed the expanded activities of the Export Import Bank and the Overseas Private Investment Corporation in support of United States/Colombian trade and investment. President Clinton offered and President Pastrana accepted a program of technical assistance by the United States Treasury, with funding from United States Agency for International Development, for the financial sector. The Presidents agreed to work to create the fair and equitable conditions necessary to implement an Open Skies regime, and to conclude a new bilateral aviation agreement as soon as possible. President Pastrana welcomed the forthcoming visit of United States Commerce Secretary Daley to further expand cooperation in the fields of trade and investment.

The two Presidents signed an *Alliance Against Drugs* committing their nations to use all means at their disposal to stem narcotics production, trafficking, consumption and related crimes. They agreed that education, prevention, law enforcement, judicial action, extradition of narcotraffickers, aerial and other forms of eradication, alternative development and efforts to end armed conflict are all essential elements in an overall strategy to combat illegal drugs. They looked forward to the early completion of a customs mutual assistance agreement. They called for greater international efforts, and welcomed the work underway through the Organization of American States to forge a hemispheric alliance, and to establish a multilateral process to monitor and evaluate national as well as collective performance toward agreed goals.

President Clinton expressed admiration and support for President Pastrana's efforts, based upon democracy and the rule of law, to establish a dialogue with Colombia's insurgent groups, to initiate a peace process, and to seek an end to many decades of armed conflict. President Clinton pledged to work with other international donors to mobilize substantial additional resources to support implementation of the peace process, to promote programs for internally displaced persons, to give financial and technical support to a program of alternative development, and to thereby promote reconciliation within a democratic society of laws. The two Presidents agreed that concrete action on the part of insurgent groups to cease hostage taking and other forms of terrorism, to cut their ties to narcotrafficking, to respect international humanitarian law and to join the fight against illicit drugs will be the test of their sincerity and genuine interest in peace.

The two Presidents shared a commitment to a cleaner environment and sustainable development. They welcomed the signing of a "GLOBE" agreement to link schools and education together through the Internet for environmental work. President Pastrana expressed appreciation for the provision of Visiting Fellowships by the United States Environmental Protection Agency for the study of watershed management.

The two Presidents agreed that respect for human rights was at the core of their effort to promote peace, extend the rule of law, and strengthen democratic institutions. They welcomed the completion of a Memorandum of Understanding between the Government of Colombia and United States Agency for International Development establishing a program for the training and support for the Colombian judiciary. They welcomed the signing of a forfeited-assets sharing arrangement that will direct forfeitures to Colombian counternarcotics law enforcement efforts. They also attached special importance to the establishment between the two Defense Ministries of a Bilateral Working Group that will establish and oversee a program of support and training for the military justice system.

In order to manage and extend their comprehensive partnership, the two Presidents established a high-level Joint Consultative Group, led by the United States State Department and Colombian Foreign Ministry, with senior representation from all the other affected cabinet agencies, which will meet on a regular basis.

Acting Assistant Secretary Romero will lead a U.S. team to Colombia in early November to agree upon a work program for the Group, and to consult on the peace process.

NOTE: An original was not available for verification of the content of this joint communique.

Remarks Announcing the HIV/AIDS Initiative in Minority Communities
October 28, 1998

Thank you and welcome, every one of you. I'd like to begin by welcoming the Mayor of Baltimore, Kurt Schmoke, and the Mayor of East St. Louis, Gordon Bush. I'd like to thank the Members of Congress here behind me who are so responsible for the purpose for which we are called today.

I want to acknowledge Congresswoman Donna Christian-Green, Congressman Elijah Cummings, Congresswoman Eleanor Holmes Norton, Congressman Donald Payne. I will say more about Congresswoman Maxine Waters and Representative Lou Stokes in a moment. [*Laughter*] But I want to thank them and all the members of the Congressional Black Caucus, including all the House members and Senator Carol Moseley-Braun, for what they did. And then I would like to offer a special word of appreciation to Senator Arlen Specter and Congresswoman Nancy Pelosi, who helped us so much to get this done. Thank you very much.

I want to thank everyone in our administration who has worked so hard on the issue of HIV and AIDS, beginning with the Vice President, who couldn't be here today but who has worked very hard on all these issues; and Secretary Shalala; our wonderful Surgeon General, David Satcher; the Director of our AIDS Policy Office, Sandy Thurman, who has literally spent months sounding the alarm about the growing crisis in communities of color and working to help achieve these dramatic funding increases. There is no stronger or more effective advocate, and I think we ought to thank Sandy Thurman for what she's done.

Finally, I want to thank Denise Stokes for being here. As you will hear in a few moments, she has been living with HIV for 15 years and has been giving so much of herself to educate others. If we are to stop this cruel disease, we'll have to have brave people like Denise to reach out with candor and compassion to those at risk.

I really admire her very much. And you'll hear from her in a moment, but I think we ought to give her a hand for showing up today. [*Applause*]

We have good reason to feel encouraged that so many HIV-positive men and women are living longer and healthier lives. We should be proud that we've helped to speed the development of lifesaving therapies and nearly tripled funding to support those with HIV and AIDS.

But the AIDS epidemic is far from over in any community in our country. Today we're here to send out a word loud and clear: AIDS is a particularly severe and ongoing crisis in the African-American and Hispanic communities and in other communities of color. African-Americans represent only 13 percent of our population but account for almost half the new AIDS cases reported last year. Hispanics represent 10 percent of our population; they account for more than 20 percent of the new AIDS cases. And AIDS is becoming a critical concern in some Native-American and Asian-American communities, as well.

Like other epidemics before it, AIDS is now hitting hardest in areas where knowledge about the disease is scarce and poverty is high. In other words, as so often happens, it is picking on the most vulnerable among us.

The fact is HIV infection is one of the most deadly health disparities between African-Americans, Hispanics, and white Americans. And just as we have committed to help build one America by ending the racial and ethnic disparities in infant mortality and cancer and other diseases, we must use all our power to end the growing disparities in HIV and AIDS.

The AIDS crisis in our communities of color is a national one, and that is why we are greatly increasing our national response. Today I am proud to announce we are launching an unprecedented $156 million initiative to stem the AIDS crisis in minority communities.

It is one of the greatest victories in the balanced budget law I just signed. It never could have happened without the passionate and compassionate leadership of Maxine Waters, Lou Stokes, and the rest of the Congressional Black Caucus or the support of Senator Specter and Congresswoman Pelosi and so many others.

Now, this initiative will allow thousands of cities, churches, schools, and grassroots organizations to expand prevention efforts and target them to the specific needs of specific minority communities such as young men, students, pregnant mothers. It will allow minority communities to expand treatment for substance abuse. It will increase access to protease inhibitors and other new therapies, because lifesaving therapies cannot be a luxury reserved only for the rich.

It will increase access to skilled doctors and other health care providers. And finally, it will help us to assemble teams of public health experts from the Centers for Disease Control and other Federal agencies to visit individual communities and provide whatever technical assistance those communities need.

This new initiative will build on the other historic funding increases in HIV/AIDS funding we won in the new balanced budget, which Secretary Shalala will talk about in greater detail in a moment. I'm also pleased that it will build on our race and health initiative. Congress has taken a first step to fund this initiative, but we must do more. We are not one America

when some of our communities lag so far behind in health.

Of course, this room looks nothing like a house of worship except for a few collars I see. [*Laughter*] But I'd like to end my remarks today with what I think is quite an appropriate passage from the First Letter of Paul to the Corinthians: "The body is a unit, though it is made up of many parts. And though all its parts are many, they form one body. If one part suffers, every part suffers with it. If one part is honored, every part rejoices with it."

So it is with the body of Americans and a nation that strives to be one America. Every one of our communities is inextricably linked in suffering and rejoicing, in sickness and in health. And that is why we must work together in every community to stop this cruel disease. Black or white, gay or straight, rich or poor, you name it, we have to stop it.

Now I'd like to present America's Surgeon General, our Nation's family doctor, whose deep commitment to advancing our country's health is embodied in the 200-year-old guiding principle of our Public Health Service that you best protect the health of the entire Nation when you reach out to the most vulnerable people.

Dr. David Satcher.

NOTE: The President spoke at 5:16 p.m. in Room 450 of the Old Executive Office Building. In his remarks, the President referred to AIDS activist Denise Stokes, member, Presidential Advisory Council on HIV/AIDS.

Statement on Emergency Funding for the HIV/AIDS Initiative in Minority Communities
October 28, 1998

Today I am making available to the Department of Health and Human Services an additional $217 million in emergency funding. These funds were provided in P.L. 105–277, the Omnibus Consolidated and Emergency Supplemental Appropriations Act, 1999, which I signed into law on Wednesday, October 21st.

These funds will provide $50 million to the Secretary of Health and Human Services (HHS) to address the HIV/AIDS crisis facing the Afri-

can-American community and other racial and ethnic minority communities due to the changing demographics of the disease. These funds are available for HHS to transfer to other agencies for several important purposes:

- to expand and improve access to state-of-the-art HIV/AIDS therapies;
- to strengthen and expand targeted HIV/AIDS effective prevention and intervention activities;

- to support HIV/AIDS substance abuse activities;
- to provide critical technical assistance in high-risk communities; and
- to build and sustain HIV/AIDS infrastructure.

In addition, these emergency funds will provide HHS with $139 million to prepare for and manage the response to the medical and public health consequences of a chemical-biological weapons incident. Of the $139 million provided, the Centers for Disease Control and Prevention will use $127 million to establish a civilian pharmaceutical stockpile and to improve public health surveillance, communications, epidemiologic capabilities, and laboratory capacity to respond to a chemical-biological weapons incident.

HHS' Office of Emergency Preparedness will use $7 million to enhance medical response systems for a chemical-biological weapons incident, including funds to increase the number of local first responder teams. The remaining funds are for one-time projects initiated by Congress.

Finally, the Centers for Disease Control and Prevention will receive $28 million for global polio eradication and measles elimination efforts.

I am disappointed that Congress has chosen to earmark individual projects within the emergency funding provided by P.L. 105–277 for HHS' Public Health and Social Services Emergency Fund and has done so in such a way that I must request all of the funds provided or none at all.

Statement on Signing the Digital Millennium Copyright Act
October 28, 1998

Today I am pleased to sign into law H.R. 2281, the "Digital Millennium Copyright Act." This Act implements two landmark treaties that were successfully negotiated by my Administration in 1996 and to which the Senate gave its advice and consent to ratification on October 21, 1998. The Act also limits the liability of online service providers for copyright infringement under certain conditions.

The World Intellectual Property Organization (WIPO) Copyright Treaty and the WIPO Performances and Phonogram Treaty mark the most extensive revision of international copyright law in over 25 years. The treaties will grant writers, artists, and other creators of copyrighted material global protection from piracy in the digital age.

These treaties will become effective at a time when technological innovations present us with great opportunities for the global distribution of copyrighted works. These same technologies, however, make it possible to pirate copyrighted works on a global scale with a single keystroke. The WIPO treaties set clear and firm standards—obligating signatory countries to provide "adequate legal protection" and "effective legal remedies" against circumvention of certain technologies that copyright owners use to protect their works, and against violation of the integrity

of copyright management information. This Act implements those standards, carefully balancing the interests of both copyright owners and users.

I am advised by the Department of Justice that certain provisions of H.R. 2281 and the accompanying Conference Report regarding the Register of Copyrights raise serious constitutional concerns. Contrary to assertions in the Conference Report, the Copyright Office is, for constitutional purposes, an executive branch entity. Accordingly, the Congress may exercise its constitutionally legitimate oversight powers to require the Copyright Office to provide information relevant to the legislative process. However, to direct that Office's operations, the Congress must act in accord with the requirements of bicameralism and presentment prescribed in Article I of the Constitution. Further, the Congress may not require the Register to act in a manner that would impinge upon or undermine the President's discretion under Article II, section 3 of the Constitution to determine which, if any, executive branch recommendations to the Congress would be "necessary and expedient." Accordingly, I will construe sections 103(a), 104(b), 401(b), and 403(a) of H.R. 2281 to require the Register to perform duties only insofar as such requirements are consistent with these constitutional principles.

From the efforts of the Assistant Secretary of Commerce and Commissioner of Patents and Trademarks who acted as the lead negotiator for these treaties, to the agreement reached by interests affected by online service provider liability, to the improvements added by two House Committees and one Senate Committee, this Act reflects the diligence and talents of a great many people. Through enactment of the Digital Millennium Copyright Act, we have done our best to protect from digital piracy the copy-right industries that comprise the leading export of the United States.

WILLIAM J. CLINTON

The White House,
October 28, 1998.

NOTE: H.R. 2281, approved October 28, was assigned Public Law No. 105–304. An original was not available for verification of the content of this statement.

Statement on Signing the Next Generation Internet Research Act of 1998
October 28, 1998

I am pleased to sign into law H.R. 3332, the "Next Generation Internet Research Act of 1998." Building on the solid foundation of the High-Performance Computing Act of 1991, this bill authorizes an ambitious new research program in advanced communication technologies that will be critical for assuring American prosperity, national and economic security, and international competitiveness in the 21st century.

Federal investment in computer networking technology and related fields spurred technological developments that have created new businesses and jobs; given powerful new tools to the research community; made it easier for citizens to participate in their government; allowed small businesses, remote communities, and people with disabilities to participate in the world economy; and improved the Nation's quality of life. The work launched by this bill will lead to even greater achievements.

Specifically, H.R. 3332 authorizes the National Science Foundation, Department of Energy, National Institutes of Health, National Aeronautics and Space Administration, and National Institute of Standards and Technology to work with America's business and academic communities in an ambitious new research program. The role of the Department of Defense in this research has already been authorized in Public Law 105–261, which I signed on October 17, 1998. This research will lead to a new generation of Internet capabilities that will provide connections that are not only much faster, but also more reliable, secure, and high-quality. The next generation of the Internet will facilitate a range of unprecedented new services—such as the ability to support tele-surgery and other medical services—which require extremely high levels of reliability and protection.

The bill also authorizes an advanced "testbed" network that will link key Federal and university research centers. These testbeds will permit America's leading research teams to develop new Internet techniques and demonstrate how those techniques can advance a wide range of critical research initiatives.

This forward-looking legislation will help ensure that the Nation continues to support a balanced program of research in high-speed computers, communication systems, and the software necessary to put technology to practical use at work and at home.

Vice President Gore's vision and leadership led to the 1991 High-Performance Computing Act, and I want to thank him for the key role he has played in ensuring that research in this critical and fast-paced area is focused on the most important missions and is managed efficiently. This new legislation will build on that standard of excellence.

WILLIAM J. CLINTON

The White House,
October 28, 1998.

NOTE: H.R. 3332, approved October 28, was assigned Public Law No. 105–305. An original was not available for verification of the content of this statement.

Statement on Signing the Noncitizen Benefit Clarification and Other Technical Amendments Act of 1998
October 28, 1998

Today I have signed into law H.R. 4558, the "Noncitizen Benefit Clarification and Other Technical Amendments Act of 1998." This legislation will further the efforts that I have undertaken to reverse unduly harsh benefit restrictions on legal immigrants that have nothing to do with moving people from welfare to work. H.R. 4558 will ensure that thousands of elderly and disabled legal immigrants who are dependent on Supplemental Security Income (SSI) and Medicaid will continue to receive such benefits.

The Act also contains several warranted technical amendments. Most significantly, H.R. 4558 will clarify that (i) eligible children with life-threatening conditions may continue to receive limited cash awards from tax-exempt organizations without losing SSI benefits, and (ii) will amend implementation time-frames for certain Welfare-to-Work funds.

I applaud the bipartisan spirit of H.R. 4558 and am pleased to sign this important legislation.

WILLIAM J. CLINTON

The White House,
October 28, 1998.

NOTE: H.R. 4558, approved October 28, was assigned Public Law No. 105–306. An original was not available for verification of the content of this statement.

Statement on Emergency Funding for Antidrug Activities
October 28, 1998

I am making an additional $732 million in emergency funding available to support antidrug activities and drug interdiction. These funds were provided in the Omnibus Consolidated and Emergency Supplemental Appropriations Act, 1999, which I signed into law on Wednesday, October 21st.

Of the total amount I am making available, funds are distributed as follows:
- Department of Agriculture: $23,000,000
- Department of Defense: $42,000,000
- Department of Justice: $20,200,000
- Department of State: $232,600,000
- Department of Transportation: $133,700,000
- Department of the Treasury: $277,500,000
- Office of National Drug Control Policy: $1,200,000
- Federal Drug Control Programs: $2,000,000

NOTE: H.R. 4328, the Omnibus Consolidated and Emergency Supplemental Appropriations Act, 1999, was assigned Public Law No. 105–277.

Remarks at the State Dinner Honoring President Andres Pastrana of Colombia
October 28, 1998

Ladies and gentlemen, good evening. Mr. President, Mrs. Pastrana, members of the Colombian delegation, distinguished guests, it's a great pleasure to welcome all of you to the White House for this dinner in honor of the President and the First Lady of Colombia.

Today President Pastrana and I worked hard to advance the partnership between Colombia and the United States. Tonight we celebrate our friendship, among friends. It is a long friendship, indeed, going back to our struggles for independence, including, as President Pastrana discussed today, an alliance in war as well as peace.

After all these years, the United States remains captivated by Colombia, by the power of Colombian art, the force of Colombian literature, and I might add, the strength of Colombian coffee. [*Laughter*] Indeed, if ever a prize is given to any of the people who negotiated the peace treaty at Wye, something will have to be given to Colombia, for without the coffee it would not have occurred. [*Laughter*]

The United States is grateful for the many contributions Colombians make to our national life, as students, teachers, athletes, and every occupation between.

Mr. President, your election this summer marks the beginning of a new era in your country's history and in our long relationship. Bravely, you have placed Colombia on the path to peace. You have taken hard steps toward renewed prosperity. We look forward to walking with you into the 21st century. We still have much to learn from and to give to each other.

We live in a hemisphere on a planet growing ever smaller. In our independence, every day we grow more interdependent. If we would be strong, we must lift others. If we would fulfill our own promise, we must help others live their dreams. We must, in short, go forward together.

In the last phrase of what has famously become known in the United States as my favorite novel, "One Hundred Years of Solitude," our guest and friend tonight, Gabriel Garcia Marquez, says, "Races condemned to 100 years of solitude did not have a second opportunity on Earth." In the 21st century let us move away from isolation, solitude, loneliness, to build 100 years of an American family together.

Ladies and gentlemen, I ask you to join me in a toast to the President and First Lady of Colombia and to the people of their great land.

NOTE: The President spoke at 8:50 p.m. in the East Room at the White House. In his remarks, he referred to Nohra Pastrana, wife of President Pastrana. The transcript released by the Office of the Press Secretary also included the remarks of President Pastrana.

Interview With Walter Cronkite and Miles O'Brien of the Cable News Network in Cape Canaveral, Florida
October 29, 1998

John Glenn's Return to Space

Walter Cronkite. Good to see you, Mr. President.

The President. Good morning, Walter, and good morning, Miles—or good afternoon. I'm delighted to be here.

Mr. Cronkite. They say, Mr. President, that there are more visitors here than at any time since the Moon launchings, the Moon flights, and that includes the President of the United States. What's particularly appealing to you about this flight?

The President. Well, of course there is the John Glenn factor. Senator Glenn is a very good personal friend of Hillary's and mine, as well as an ally, a colleague. And like all Americans, I'm thrilled that he is going up today. But also this really is the last launch before we begin to put the international space station up. So

John Glenn began this first phase of our space program, and he's ending it just before we start on the space station.

So it's very exciting. It's important for the space program. But it's a great day for America, a great day for our senior citizens, and I hope that all Americans share the exuberance that I feel today.

Mr. Cronkite. You know, some naysayers say, Mr. President, that this flight of Glenn's is your reward to him for his stalwart support of you during his years in the Senate. Anything to that?

The President. No. I've always wanted John to be able to go back, as long as I've known he's wanted to. But if I had my druthers, he'd be home in Ohio running for reelection right now. [*Laughter*] And he said he was too old to serve another term in the Senate, but he wasn't too old to go into space.

And I think the American people should know that the decision to send him was made strictly by the book. I had no role in it. He had to pass the strenuous physical exams, and then, for each experiment he's going through, he had to prove that he was qualified and able to do that. I think this is very important.

One of the most important benefits that the American people derive from our space program is the whole rush of discoveries we get that help us here on Earth, environmental discoveries, health care discoveries of all kinds. We've got all kinds of medical scanning equipment today that we wouldn't have but for the space program. We've got protective clothing that people who are supersensitive to the Sun can wear, that we wouldn't have but for the space program.

So we're going to get a lot out of John Glenn going up there today, and I think the country is well served by doing it. And goodness knows, for a lifetime of service to us in the air and on the ground, he's earned this chance.

Mr. Cronkite. They say that President Kennedy grounded Glenn after his first flight because they didn't want to risk the death of a hero out there on a second flight. Would you have made that decision?

The President. Well, I don't know. I can't say because I wasn't there then, and it's easy to second-guess. But I'll say this, I think that John Glenn going up today is a very good thing for America. We're going to learn a lot from it, and we're all going to, I think, be thrilled by it. And I'm just glad he was brave enough to do it.

Russia-U.S. Space Station

Mr. Cronkite. You know, out there on Pad 39A, Mr. President, there to the right, to the south of 39B, from which this flight will take place, there's a shuttle scheduled to take into orbit in just a few months the first parts of the planned American-Russian joint international space station, almost a small city, permanently in space. Now that Russia has this desperate economic situation that endangered that schedule, it looks like we may have to put in a lot of money to try to keep that space station on schedule, the construction of it. Are we prepared to do that?

The President. Well, Walter, if it were required, I would be supportive of it, and I would be happy to talk to the congressional leaders in both parties. Our space program has been a great investment. It's had hardly any increase in funding since I became President, but we've gone from two launches to eight launches a year. We've dramatically cut costs. NASA is sort of the star, the poster child, of Vice President Gore's reinventing Government campaign, and we're getting a lot out of it.

If we were required now to help the Russians during this difficult period, which will not last forever, so that they could continue to participate, I would be in favor of that. I think that it's very important that we have the Europeans, the Japanese, the Canadians, and the Russians in the space station venture.

I've been here. I've been over the space station project many times in great detail in Houston; twice, I've been down there to look at that. And I think we're doing the right thing with this space station, and we need to stay with it.

Pre-Launch Excitement

Miles O'Brien. Mr. President, it's Miles O'Brien, I have a question for you. But first I want to check the countdown clock for our viewers for just a moment. We have now entered into a hold—a 10-minute hold. We are at T minus 20 minutes and holding. The hold began at 1:20 p.m. eastern standard time; it will end at 1:30 p.m. eastern time. And then we'll count down again to 9 minutes, another 10-minute hold at that point. Once again, to remind our viewers, this is simply a way of NASA keeping up with the important business at hand and making sure that everybody is doing their job on time.

Mr. President, I'm just curious, are you nervous?

The President. Oh, a little bit. I think that it's part of the excitement. I'm a little nervous, but I've got great confidence in these people. I've had a lot of great honors as President to meet people who serve our country, but meeting the people who are in the space program, the astronauts, those who work on the ground, those who plan these missions—they've done everything they can possibly do, and they would never compromise an iota of safety or reliability just because Hillary and I and all the rest of the world are here through the media—I feel good about this.

But yes, I'm nervous, and I'm excited. I feel like a kid at his first Christmas. I'm very excited about this.

Space Program Goals

Mr. Cronkite. Mr. President, President Bush in 1989 proclaimed a national goal to send humans to the planet Mars by the year 2019. That's the 50th anniversary of Neil Armstrong's first step onto the Moon. Do you affirm that goal for the Mars mission?

The President. Well, let me say, what we're doing now will help us once we get to the position of evaluating that. I don't want to either affirm or renounce it. What I think we should do is to recognize that what we have now is a set of very focused goals in our space program. We are working on the space station. We are working on the shuttle. We are working on space transportation. We are working on things that tell us about our environment on Earth. And then we're doing these special projects— the Hubble telescope, which is magnificent. And we did the *Mars Pathfinder* mission on, you remember, July 4th of last year.

And so we're going to see how we are. Let's get the space station up and going and evaluate what our long-term prospects are. I'll tell you this, I am for a continued, aggressive exploration of space in ways that are high quality, cost effective, and that will benefit us here on Earth. And I hope that we can have, as a result of this flight today, even more broadbased American support from all Americans and all parties and all walks of life for our mission in space. It's still very, very important.

1998 Elections

Mr. Cronkite. Mr. President, as a journalist, I think I'd be remiss at this moment in time if I didn't ask you what your advisers are telling you about the results of next Tuesday's election.

The President. The truth is they don't know. [*Laughter*] We've got an extraordinary number of very, very close elections. In this 2-year period the members of the other party have raised, I think, $100 million more than our folks did.

But we've got good candidates and an extremely good grassroots effort, I think, a good agenda.

The only thing I think I should say today to avoid being too political is that it's a very important election, and I would hope that every American who is eligible to vote would go and vote in that election.

If you look at this space launch today, this is a triumph of American democracy. It was made possible by the elected Representatives of the American people supporting the space program. And it is just one more example of why it's so important for citizens to stand up and be counted on election day. So if you feel patriotic when you see John Glenn and the others go up in space today, then keep that patriotic feeling until next Tuesday and go and vote for the candidate and the programs and the issues of your choice.

John Holliman

Mr. O'Brien. All right. Mr. President, thank you so much for being with us on CNN today.

The President. Thank you, Miles.

Mr. O'Brien. And we hope you enjoy the launch.

The President. Thank you, I will. I think I ought to say just one other thing because I'm talking to CNN. I know that I speak for a lot of people when I express my thanks to the late John Holliman for the work he did to advance our cause in space. And I know that all of you will be thinking about him and his family today. And I thank CNN for giving such a high profile to our space mission.

Thank you.

Mr. Cronkite. Thank you, Mr. President, for those words. Miles and I were going to dedicate this broadcast at an appropriate time to the memory of John Holliman, who was the space expert at CNN, as skilled as Miles—planned to be in this anchor chair and who was killed, unfortunately, in an automobile accident just a couple of weeks ago. This broadcast is dedicated to the memory of John Holliman.

NOTE: The interview began at 1:16 p.m. at the John F. Kennedy Space Center.

Remarks to the Staff of the Firing Room Prior to the Space Shuttle *Discovery* Launch in Cape Canaveral
October 29, 1998

Thank you very much. I have so many things to thank you for today. But among other things, I have to thank you for making the First Lady very happy, because about a year ago she said, "You know, we need to make a list of all the things we want to do before we leave office." I said, "Okay, what's on your list?" She said, "You have to take me to a space launch. I want to go."

We didn't have the courage to come here; we had confidence in you and pride in America and a conviction that our space program is good for the United States and good for the world. And I want to thank you today, because you made all of us terribly proud.

Let me also say that because of the intense interest in this, in the media and among ordinary citizens, the American people have had a unique opportunity today to see what you do, not just at the moment of launch but in the weeks and months and years that precede it,

all the hard work and all the preparation. And now they will learn over the next few days all the things that are being done in space that advance not only our mission in space but the quality of our life here on Earth. And all of that, too, has been made possible.

The last thing I would like to say is, it has been immensely impressive and important to me to have the chance to work with NASA over the last 6 years and see the revolution which has been undertaken, so that now you can, on virtually the same budget you had 6 years ago, do 8 launches a year instead of 2 and continue to explore the outer frontiers of space. I thank you for all of that. America is very, very proud of you today.

Thank you, and God bless you.

NOTE: The President spoke at 2:42 p.m. in the Launch Control Center at the John F. Kennedy Space Center.

Remarks to the Staff of the Launch Control Center Following the Space Shuttle *Discovery* Launch in Cape Canaveral
October 29, 1998

Thank you very much. I want to just add one little factual element to what Dan Goldin said about Hillary wanting to be an astronaut as a little girl. I just told a group up in the control room this. About a year ago we sat down and Hillary said, "You know, we're just going to be here 3 more years, and we need to make a list of every place we'd like to go and everything we'd like to do before we leave office." I said, "Okay, what's the first thing on your list?" She said, "I want to go to Cape Canaveral and see a launch." [*Laughter*]

I want to thank Dan Goldin and Roy Bridges, the Director of the Kennedy Space Center, all of you who work here. I want to thank Bob Cabana and Eileen Collins, two astronauts who accompanied us today, along with my Science Adviser, Dr. Neal Lane. I want to thank this

crew. And I'd like, with all the press here, one more time to call their names: Commander Brown; Pilot Steve Lindsey; Mission Specialists Stephen Robinson and Scott Parazynski; the two international astronauts, Dr. Mukai of Japan and Mr. Duque of the European Space Agency, the first Spanish citizen ever to fly in space.

I want to thank all of you who work on this, not just in that moment we all see on television or, in this case, we all saw from the rooftop, and we felt the ceiling rumble beneath our feet—[*laughter*]—because I know there are hours and weeks and months and years behind all this. I want to thank you. And of course I want to thank John Glenn, my good friend and a genuine American hero.

You know, a few days ago, I was in the White House working on something entirely different, and the phone rang and they said—no, no, no, that's not true—I was down at the Wye Plantation working on the Middle East peace talks. And we hadn't had a lot of sleep since then— [*laughter*]—but that's where I was. And one of my staff members came up and said, "John Glenn wants to talk to you." I thought, "Oh my goodness, something happened. He said he can't go."

We had a break, so I went and took the phone call. John said, "Mr. President." I said, "John," I said, "what's up?" He said, "I just called to make sure you're not going to chicken out on me. I want you down there when I go up." True story. [*Laughter*] He said, "I want you down there when I go up." So I said that wild horses couldn't keep Hillary or me away, and we would be there. And we just left Annie and John's family and the other family members of the crew, thanking them.

Let me say to all of you, I feel profoundly indebted to all of you who work at NASA because I know the changes through which this agency has gone in the last 5 years, I know the challenges this agency has faced, I know how, more than any other agency in Government, I believe you have embodied the ideal of the reinventing Government mission of our administration that the Vice President has headed. You have truly done more with less. We're now sending eight missions up a year as opposed to two before. We are doing it in much less time at much lower cost, all thanks to you. And I am profoundly grateful.

I also want to thank you for the next big mission and the opening of the next new chapter in our history in space when the international space station begins to go up, first in Kazakhstan and then here, in the first two installments.

And the last thing I'd like to say is, this mission is going to give America a chance to see what you do through new eyes, not only to experience the adventure, the spirit, but to understand the extent to which what we find out up there helps us live better lives down here. It has broadened the frontiers of medical research. It has helped us to understand how to cope with all kinds of physical conditions that otherwise were not manageable. It has helped us to learn about environmental trends and how to deal with them. It has helped us to see our future on Earth.

And these experiments in aging, which I'm getting more interested in with every passing day—[*laughter*]—in what happens to muscle and bone under the stress of space and in conditions of weightlessness; the sleeping disorder test, which I'd very much like to be a part of since I have suffered from one chronically for the last 30 years or so. [*Laughter*] This is very important. And the American people will now know this about what you do.

So I just want to say to all of you, I hope that the labors that you've made the last 5 years, culminating in the stunning excitement of this day, but also including the marvelous discoveries of the Hubble telescope, the breathtaking action of *Sojourner* on the *Mars Pathfinder* mission, all the other things that have been done, I hope that it will all crystallize here in your 40th anniversary year with this mission, with the intense public attention, with the ordinary citizen's interest at an all-time high, so that from now on into the future on every block in every street corner in every community large and small in America, there will be people from all races and all walks of life who will be proud to support as American citizens our space program as an integral part of our march into the 21st century.

Thank you, and God bless you all.

NOTE: The President spoke at 3:13 p.m. in the lobby of the Launch Control Center at the John F. Kennedy Space Center. In his remarks, he referred to Daniel S. Goldin, Administrator, National Aeronautics and Space Administration (NASA); Roy D. Bridges, Director, NASA's John F. Kennedy Space Center; Col. Robert D. Cabana, USMC, former Chief, NASA Astronaut Office; Lt. Col. Eileen M. Collins, USAF, scheduled to be the first female Mission Commander for an upcoming space shuttle *Columbia* mission. The President also referred to the following crew members of the space shuttle *Discovery*: Mission Commander Lt. Col. Curtis L. Brown, Jr., USAF; Mission Pilot Lt. Col. Steven W. Lindsey, USAF; Mission Specialists Stephen K. Robinson, Scott E. Parazynski, M.D., and Pedro Duque, European Space Agency; and Payload Specialists Chiaki Mukai, M.D., National Space Development Agency of Japan, and Senator John Glenn, who returned to space after 36 years.

Remarks on Arrival in West Palm Beach, Florida
October 29, 1998

Ladies and gentlemen, I am delighted to be here with Governor Chiles, Senator Graham, Commissioner Nelson, Congressman Deutsch, Congressman Wexler, my good friend Lieutenant Governor MacKay.

I know that along with all other Americans your hearts filled with pride today when you saw our space shuttle lift off with 77-year-old Senator John Glenn among the crew, going into the heavens for the second time—the first time over 36 years ago.

I'm here tonight in South Florida on behalf of our Democratic ticket and specifically for Lieutenant Governor MacKay. And I'd like to make two points. First of all, I hope the pride and the patriotism that the people of Florida and the United States felt this afternoon will carry over until Tuesday and that everyone will feel in their pride an obligation to go to the polls and vote, because this is no ordinary election. In profound ways we are shaping what America will look like and what this State will look like well into the 21st century.

In so many ways the challenges of Florida are the challenges of America. In terms of the education of our children in this last budget battle, thanks to the steadfast support of people like Bob Graham and Peter Deutsch and Rob Wexler, we were able to get a huge downpayment of my goal of putting 100,000 teachers in the early grades.

But it will be up to the Governor of Florida to determine whether we have a real commitment in this State, one of the fastest growing States in the country, for our children to have those smaller class sizes and classes for the children and the teachers to meet. That's a strong reason to support Buddy MacKay's bid for Governor.

And in the next session of Congress we will have to deal with the unfinished business of America in saving Social Security for the 21st century and protecting and reforming Medicare and finally passing a Patients' Bill of Rights.

But here in Florida, there will be a disproportionate impact on all these decisions because there are so many senior citizens. I've known Buddy MacKay a long time, and you know, I'm never surprised by what people do or say in the closing days of an election, but goodness, how anybody could claim that he had ever done anything other than be one of the strongest supporters the seniors of this State and this Nation ever had is a mystery to me, because he certainly has been.

And I will say again, to really do what we need to do for the seniors here, for the integrity of their health care and the security of their retirement and the stability of their lives, requires not only a President and a Congress but a Governor committed to them. That's another big reason to support Buddy MacKay for Governor on Tuesday.

And we're glad to be here. I wish him well. I wish the people of Florida well. And again I say, I hope everyone will be at the polls on Tuesday. If you felt good today, you can feel just that same way on Tuesday by being a good citizen and doing your part.

Thank you very much.

NOTE: The President spoke at 5:52 p.m. at the West Palm Beach International Airport. In his remarks, he referred to Governor Lawton Chiles of Florida; State Insurance Commissioner Bill Nelson; and gubernatorial candidate Lt. Gov. Buddy MacKay.

Letter to Congressional Leaders Transmitting the National Security Strategy Report
October 29, 1998

Dear Mr. Speaker: *(Dear Mr. President:)*

As required by section 603 of the Goldwater-Nichols Department of Defense Reorganization Act of 1986, I am transmitting a report on the National Security Strategy of the United States.

Sincerely,

WILLIAM J. CLINTON

NOTE: Identical letters were sent to Newt Gingrich, Speaker of the House of Representatives, and Albert Gore, Jr., President of the Senate. An original was not available for verification of the content of this letter.

Remarks at a Reception for Representative Peter Deutsch in Palm Beach
October 29, 1998

Thank you very much, Doctor. Thank you for your remarks—and Peter and Lori, and your families and your extended family here. Let me say at the outset that I had two thoughts when Peter was speaking—one sort of craven thought. I thought, I wish I had taped that, and the next time I really need a tough vote for him, I will play it back. [*Laughter*] My more noble thought was—[*laughter*]—was that, I was sitting there looking at Peter and thinking about the times we spent together, the times Lori used to go jogging with me before I hurt my leg. Now I use it as an excuse not to be humiliated. [*Laughter*] And I was thinking about the times we spent together, and I was thinking how fortunate our country is that people like him will do the work that he does. And we are very fortunate.

You know, this has been a pretty good 6 years for the economy, and if Peter Deutsch hadn't been in Congress, he would have made a lot of money in this economy. [*Laughter*] He would have done well in this economy. And our country is blessed by that.

Let me just be very brief here. Today I came to Florida with Hillary to see the space shuttle and to see a man who has been a very good personal friend of mine and of my wife's, John Glenn, go into space at the age of 77. It was a thrilling experience. I'm sure all of you who either saw it from a distance or saw it on television felt the same way. And a lot of people came up to me and said, "Gosh, you look tired."

And that's because I still haven't recovered from what I was doing last week at this time, which was finally announcing the end of 9 days of talks on the Middle East peace process, which culminated in a 30-something hour marathon. I was up 39 hours in a row, and I didn't even do that in college. [*Laughter*] I didn't know I had it in me at my old age and in my declining years. But anyway, I made it.

I say that because those two events, this space shuttle with John Glenn on it and that peace process, embody so much of what I've tried to do as President and so much about what I think is best in our country, the idea of giving everybody an opportunity to go as far as his or her dreams will carry them, the idea of being adventurous in all and daring to change and being willing to take a risk and always thinking about the future.

One of you who went through the line and had your picture taken with me tonight quoted back my 1992 campaign theme: Don't stop thinking about tomorrow. That's what that space program is all about. And then the peace process embodied not only the peace we would like to bring to the world but the peace we would like to bring to our own country, how strongly and earnestly we wish to reach across all the lines that divide us here to make one America and then to bring that spirit of reconciliation to the rest of the world in freedom, in democracy.

And when I became President I really set out to create a country for the 21st century where everyone who would work for it could have opportunity, where we would be one community across all our diversity, and where we would still be the world's leading force for peace and freedom and prosperity, not just for ourselves but for others as well.

None of the things that I have done that required any act from Congress would have been possible without people like Peter. And when things go well, the President gets the credit. But very often there are so many others whose work is utterly indispensable. And I think you should know that.

If we hadn't passed that economic plan in 1993, we wouldn't be here celebrating this today. If we hadn't passed the crime bill to give 100,000 police to our streets and to finally take on the Brady bill issues and the assault weapons ban, we wouldn't be here celebrating the lowest crime rate in a generation today. So there are lots of things that he and others deserve credit for.

In this last budget negotiation the reason we got, in a hostile Congress, the reason we got 100,000 teachers and after-school programs for kids in trouble and a big increase in our clean water plan and continued support to clean up the Florida Everglades and restore them was that the Congress stayed with me, the Democrats and our party, and we were reunited.

And I want to thank Peter for having this PAC and for being willing to not only help himself but help like-minded people throughout the country, because this election Tuesday is no ordinary election. This election will have a lot to do with 21st century America. And the differences between the parties are quite profound.

We don't believe that we—we waited 29 years for a surplus, and we do not believe we should spend it until we have saved Social Security for the 21st century. They disagree with that. Furthermore, I don't think we should do anything that gives the slightest signal of economic instability at a time when there's so much trouble in the rest of the world. And Florida depends upon trade, investment, and tourism to do well. You have a big interest in our doing the right thing by our economy and trying to stabilize the world economy.

So that's something we believe. The other—the leadership of the other party disagrees with that. We believe that it's a good thing to have properly managed health care but that the management of a system should not overcome its purpose; and that people who are in health plans ought to have a right to see a specialist if the doctor says they should see one; that they ought to—if they get in an accident, they ought to go to the nearest emergency room, not one that's 20 miles away because it's covered; if they're in the middle of a pregnancy or a chemotherapy treatment, they ought not lose their doctor just because their employer changes health plans during that period. That's what we believe. And they disagree with us on this Patients' Bill of Rights. It's something that would affect well over 100 million Americans. It's a huge issue.

We believe that our children should all have a chance to have a good education. That's why we fought for the 100,000 teachers. But we did not win the classrooms to teach them in. We also had a plan fully paid for in the balanced budget to help States build or repair 5,000 schools. No State in America needs that more than Florida. We disagree on that. They don't think we should be doing this in Washington. I think we should.

So I could go through lots of other issues. We tried to raise the minimum wage because unemployment and inflation are low, and they didn't think we should, and they stopped us. We believe that we should act to protect our children from the dangers of tobacco, the number one public health problem for kids in America, and they stopped us. We believe we should pass campaign finance reform, and they stopped us. There is a huge choice.

And you may have noticed in the press yesterday that in the last 2 years, not unrelated to the bills that they defeated, they were successful in raising $100 million more than we were in the last 2 years. But because of people like Peter and because of people like you, we are doing quite well in a blizzard of close races in which we're being outspent. So you have to understand that your being here, too, is an act of citizenship and that, if you weren't here doing this, that no matter how good our ideas are and no matter how big a majority there is in the country for our ideas, they wouldn't be heard by the voters.

The last thing I want to ask you to do is to do everything you can between now and Tuesday to ask everyone with whom you come in contact to go and vote. Everybody who felt patriotic when John Glenn went up in the spaceship today with his colleagues should carry that feeling through to Tuesday. Because the space program—that's the last thing I want to say— the space program is a product of a democratic system in which it was under complete assault when I became President. And the space program is exhibit A for the idea that Government can give you more at less cost. They're not spending much more money than they were the day I took office 6 years ago. Then, they were sending up two launches a year. Now they're sending eight launches a year at roughly half the cost per launch.

I know it's important to Florida. So I ask you—thank you for your money, thank you for Peter Deutsch. Keep him in Congress as long as he wants to stay. Give him a promotion some day. But you just remember what I said. There's a huge difference in a very clear way about what kind of 21st century America we're going to have. And you and everybody you touch between now and Tuesday needs to show up.

Thank you, and God bless you.

NOTE: The President spoke at 7:03 p.m. at a private residence. In his remarks, he referred to Dr. Edward Dauer, event cochair, who introduced the President; and Lori Deutsch, wife of Representative Peter Deutsch. A tape was not available for verification of the content of these remarks.

Remarks at a Florida Democratic Party Dinner in Palm Beach
October 29, 1998

The President. Thank you very much. The first thing I have to say is that Meyer Berman asked me to make a public service announcement—[*laughter*]—that in the interest of enlightened citizenship, he has for everyone here a copy of James Carville's latest book. [*Laughter*]

Let me, first of all, say to Danny and to Eva, thank you for bringing us into your beautiful home, for the wonderful dinner, for the music on the balcony. I thank all the people who served us tonight. I think they did a great job, and I think we ought to give them a round of applause.

I thank you and Meyer for cochairing this event. I thank all of you for coming, some of you my good friends from all around America. I'd like to say to all the public servants who are here a special word of appreciation. Florida has been, I think, particularly blessed to be well served. I want to thank Lawton Chiles for being a great United States Senator and a great Governor and a great partner for me and a great friend.

Congressman Alcee Hastings, thank you for your support and your friendship. Congressman Peter Deutsch and Lori; Congressman Rob Wexler and his wife, Laurie, thank you for being here. Senator Daryl Jones and State Representative Elaine Bloom, thank you for being here. This State needs good leadership.

I'd like to also say, back when I decided to run for President in 1991—I think I mentioned Senator Graham, did I? Where is he? He's here somewhere. I want to tell you, Senator Graham and I used to be seat mates. He taught me how to be a Governor. So I served with Bob Graham and Lawton Chiles, and I finally figured out how do the job. And that's really a big reason I got to be President.

But I want to come back to 1991, but I want to say that I think both of them would say that we really enjoyed being Governors. And I was so afraid that Bob Graham wouldn't run for reelection this year. And he's so desperately needed in the Senate, because when you get to be the Governor of a place like Florida, and there is so much to be done, and it's so exciting, and it's so vibrant, and things are changing so fast, and then you go to Washington, and you see there is so much to be done—[*laughter*]— and there are so many challenges, and it's so exciting, but nobody really wants to do it, or at least a lot of people would rather posture and position and sling words back and forth instead of actually rolling up their sleeves and doing it. That's why Lawton left the Senate and came back to Florida.

And yet I don't think it is wrong to say that that's really what America needs at every level, which brings me back to Buddy and Anne. When I wanted to run for President in 1991, really only my wife and my mother thought I had a chance to win—[laughter]—and apparently a few people in the Republican Party. [Laughter] But I came down here, and I knew—actually the first big test of a Presidential campaign is now in Florida. It's the straw poll conducted at the December State convention in Florida. Elaine remembers all the sort of traipsing around. And there were people in Florida who started with me in 1991 who have been my friends ever since.

But Buddy MacKay stood up for me and stood by me and was with me every step of the way. Now, one of the things I think you want in a Governor is somebody with a lot of foresight. And it looks to me like he qualifies just on that ground alone. [Laughter] He joined my mother and my wife in thinking I had a chance to win, and I think that's a big quality. [Laughter]

But let me say in all seriousness, I know this man very, very well. I admire him and his wife very much. And I made a—I sometimes—I guess because I'm not running again I can say things that are sort of impolitic, so I'll say something that's impolitic. It is not rational that he would be behind in the polls at all because he and Lawton Chiles have done a good job together as partners. And this is a better, stronger State than it was 8 years ago. The economy is stronger. The education initiatives are stronger. There's been an aggressive effort to grow the economy and preserve the environment. We're working together on the Everglades, trying to figure out what to do there to keep this thing going. And I can just go through issue after issue after issue.

And so I will ask everybody I talk to about Buddy's race, because—my staff makes fun of me because I've just been obsessed with this. I don't have any hard feelings about Mr. Bush. I just want him to be elected Governor because I think he's got the best program and the best record, and I think he'll be the best Governor for Florida. That's what I think. I have no negative feelings.

And as I get older, I'm sensitive to this. There's always going to be one candidate who will be younger and the other one will be a little older. And one candidate will have a little more money and the other one won't. And sometimes one candidate comes from a more famous family than the other one.

But let me ask you a question, all of you here that know Buddy MacKay. If he wins this election on Tuesday, do you have any doubt that he will be reelected 4 years from now? No, you don't, do you? Why? Because you know that he'd be a great Governor. Now, if you believe that, then you need to do what you can. You owe it to yourselves to go out and make sure he wins on Tuesday. You owe it to yourselves, to the future of this State. This is a very good man with an extraordinary record of service who will do this State proud. And you have big, big, big challenges here that require a serious, consistent, sustained response.

The education issue is one. Bob and Rob and Peter and I, we just worked like crazy, and we all stayed together, and we got enough money in this last budget to make a big downpayment on putting 100,000 more teachers in the schools, focused in the early grades so that when we get it all done we can take the average class size nationwide down to 18 in the first three grades. Very important.

But we can give you all that money in Florida, and you won't be able to take advantage of it. Why? Because in places as big as Tampa and as small as Jupiter and all places in between, everybody is in trailers already. So where are you going to put the teachers? We have to build more classrooms.

So no matter what we do, even if in this election I get enough help because the voters elect a few more Democrats to give a little more balance in the Congress, which I hope they will, and we pass our class size initiative, it will support what Florida has to do, but it won't supplant it, because you're growing so fast. So it's a huge deal. This is a big issue. If one candidate is committed to smaller classes and more classrooms and more teachers and building up the system, and the other isn't, that's a massive issue.

I'll just give you one other issue. We've got 160 million Americans in managed care plans. And we were talking around our table tonight about John Glenn being 77 and how we're all living longer. I certainly hope that's true. And I said that I was just reading that if a person lives to be 65 in America, then a man at 65 has a life expectancy of 81; a woman has a life expectancy of 85. And the fastest growing group of people in America, percentage-wise, as all Floridians probably know, are people over 85. And we were talking about Strom Thurmond, who is 96, who came to see me last week. And we were joking about that. He wanted to jog with me, but I couldn't keep up with him. [*Laughter*]

This is a huge issue. And more and more senior care will be in managed care. Now, I supported the managed care movement when I ran for President, and I did when I presented health care plans to the Congress, because when I became President—a lot of people have forgotten this; you talked about inflation being down—health care costs were going up at 3 times the rate of inflation. It was unsustainable. It was going to bankrupt every business, every State government, the Federal budget. Lawton and Bob and I, we talked about it a lot. It was unsustainable. We had to do something to manage the system better, but no system can be managed in a way that destroys the purpose for which it's set up in the first place.

And so we have this Patients' Bill of Rights in Washington. And you want to—Buddy wants to do a version of it here, which simply says some pretty basic things. If you're in a health care plan and your doctor says you need to see a specialist, you ought to be able to do it. If you're in a big city and you get in an accident, the ambulance ought to take you to the nearest emergency room, not one that's 20 miles away because it happens to be covered. If you're in the middle of a treatment, chemotherapy, or pregnancy, or any other sustained treatment, and your employer changes your health insurance provider, you ought to be able to keep that doctor until you finish your treatment. And, big issue, you should be able to keep your medical records private. That's all that does.

So if one party in Washington or in Florida is for it and the other is not, that's a huge difference that will affect the lives, the texture of life for millions and millions of people. This is not some casual passing thing. I could go on and on and on.

So I wanted to be here tonight because I am grateful to the Florida public servants who served with me, to Lawton Chiles and to Bob Graham, who I've known now for three decades, I guess, not for 30 years, but parts of three decades; to these two fine young Congressmen that I think have such a brilliant future; to my long-time friend, Congressman Hastings, who I'm trying to take dressing lessons from—[*laughter*]—I love that blue suit—and who has really been a champion for what is right in Washington in so many ways that I'm very grateful for. And I wanted to be here for Buddy MacKay.

I just want to say one last thing. So many of you have been very nice to me tonight. You've talked about what happened at the Wye Plantation, and then you said something me going without sleep. That's true. I was up for 39 hours at the end of those peace talks, and I never did that in college. [*Laughter*] And now I know why. [*Laughter*] Because I'm not over it yet.

But I would like to—a lot of you here have been heavily involved in Israel and many of you even with the Arabs and the Middle East, and you have a vested—you've got a real oar in the water. You have very sophisticated knowledge of this. But what I want to ask is, just as Americans, why did you and why did other people feel so good when that was announced? What was it about that that everybody feel so good?

Audience member. Hope.

The President. Hope, yes. You said, oh, my God, here are these two guys; they've been dumping all over each other. They all have got problems at home; they're going to get grief because they did this. Both of them are going to be in greater—everybody who understands it knows that they're both in greater physical danger because they made this deal. And here are these guys that can hardly bear to speak to each other, and they get up on this high dive, and they hold hands, and they jump off together. And it made us all feel more alive. We felt bigger—the possibility that things can change, and the possibility that people can be reconciled to one another after all the scars and all the injuries and all the wrongdoing and all the disappointments, that there can be both progress and community.

Why did we all love it when old John Glenn went up in the spaceship today? Because it was about possibility. It was about, oh, my God, the guy's 77 years old, and he still looks good in his clothes. [*Laughter*] He can lift weights, and he's sharp as a tack, and he's doing great. Gosh, maybe I can be like that. Maybe we can all change the way we are. Maybe we can push back the frontiers of possibility not just in space but here on Earth. And so it made us feel bigger.

What I'm trying to say to you is I've done nearly everything—or at least made real progress on nearly everything I told the American people I'd try to do when I ran in 1992. We haven't made health care available and affordable for all Americans yet. Every other major commitment I made, we've made real progress on. But the one thing I have not been able to do is to make Washington a less partisan, less negative place. I have—Lord knows, I have tried.

And one of the things that I hope will happen in this election season is that people will say, "Never mind who's got the most money on the ads and all this; I am going to choose a course for the future of my country that reflects the same aspirations and the same values that I felt when I was cheering for Netanyahu and Arafat, when I was cheering for John Glenn. But I believe that what that represents ought to be something that is a part of my everyday life as an American, as a Floridian, as a citizen, in my business, in my work, in my family, in everything, but especially in our public life." That is what I want. And I am trying so hard to make that argument to the American people.

And when you get right down to it, the investment you made tonight is going to give the people here in Florida who are working for our candidates and our causes and our issues the power to get more people to do that on Tuesday.

I told everybody, if you like what I did in the Middle East peace talks, keep in mind I am a hired hand. I was elected to do that by you. Everything that I did, if I had any role in it that was positive, I did through the direct authority of the people of the United States who voted on election day in 1996.

If you liked what happened when John Glenn went up in space, keep in mind that is the product of a democratic government. That shuttle could not have gone up today but for the votes in the Congress to keep the space program alive and to ratify its direction, which means that, in a profound sense, if you supported someone who supported the space program, your hand was on John Glenn's shoulder when he lifted off today.

If you voted for me and the direction I wanted to take in the Middle East peace, you were standing there when we announced the agreement at Wye. You have to see it this way.

I do not want to finish my term without knowing that we have not only helped the American people to become more reconciled to one another across racial and other lines that divide us but also without knowing that we have made our best efforts to have our political leaders in Washington behave the way most citizens behave in America every day. The only way you can get that done is to show up and elect people like Buddy MacKay next Tuesday.

Thank you, and God bless you.

NOTE: The President spoke at 8:55 p.m. at a private residence. In his remarks, he referred to Meyer Berman, sole proprietor, M.A. Berman & Co.; dinner hosts Danny and Eva Abraham; Gov. Lawton Chiles and State Senator Daryl L. Jones of Florida; Representative Peter Deutsch's wife, Lori; Democratic gubernatorial candidate Lt. Gov. Buddy MacKay of Florida and his wife, Anne; Republican gubernatorial candidate Jeb Bush; Prime Minister Binyamin Netanyahu of Israel; and Chairman Yasser Arafat of the Palestinian Authority.

Remarks on Strengthening the National and International Economy and an Exchange With Reporters
October 30, 1998

The President. Good morning. I want to say a few words today about the growth of our economy and important new steps we're taking to strengthen that growth as we move toward the new century. Six years ago, our economy lagged behind the rest of the world, so we changed course, with a new strategy for economic growth founded on fiscal discipline and lower interest rates. It has worked.

It has helped to produce an American economic renaissance with low inflation, low unemployment, low welfare rolls, rising wages, the highest rate of homeownership in history, the first balanced budget since Neil Armstrong walked on the Moon, and the smallest Federal Government since John Glenn orbited the Earth.

This morning's economic report shows that our economy is continuing to grow in a strong manner, at a solid 3.3 percent. It is continuing to expand opportunity, to create wealth, to lift the hopes of working families. In the face of worldwide economic turmoil, our economy remains the strongest in a generation. But to keep it going we must stay with the strategy that created the conditions of this enduring economic expansion, and we must address the challenges of the global economy. I'd like to say a word about both.

First, we must maintain our fiscal discipline. I have insisted we preserve our hard-won surplus until a plan is in place to strengthen Social Security. We stopped the Republican majority in the House from squandering the surplus in an election-year tax plan. They haven't given up, however. House Republican leaders have reaffirmed their desire to spend the surplus before we have a plan in place to save Social Security. And the Republican leader in the Senate now says he may not even work with me on saving Social Security.

On Tuesday the American people will choose a Congress that will decide whether and how to save Social Security for the 21st century. I believe the American people need a Congress that is 100 percent committed to preserving that surplus until we save Social Security first.

Second, to strengthen our economic growth, we must continue to invest in and improve the quality of our people's education. The budget I signed last week invests in after-school programs and makes a strong downpayment on 100,000 teachers to lower class size in the early grades to an average of 18. But the Congress refused to build or modernize 5,000 schools. I believe that was a mistake as well.

We need a new Congress to correct that error and modernize our schools. If we're going to have more teachers with more students in smaller classes, they have to have someplace to meet.

A stronger American economy also depends upon a stronger international economy. Growth at home increasingly depends upon growth abroad. Our economy increasingly depends upon exports, and many, many of our exports go to emerging markets. Those markets now are faltering. A full quarter of the world's markets, the world's population, now live in countries with declining or negative economic growth. This presents to us the biggest financial challenge in a half century.

Over the last year we have pursued a comprehensive strategy to fight the financial crisis and protect American jobs at home as well. Last month I outlined a set of specific actions to spur global growth. In the weeks since, we've been working with our G–7 partners and with those in the emerging markets to make significant progress toward that goal.

Think what's happened in the last month. Japan has committed substantial resources to repair its banking system. The European Union has joined the G–7 in recognizing that the balance of risk has shifted and that, above all, now, we must spur growth. The U.S., Japan, Canada, and several European nations have cut interest rates. America has met its obligations to the International Monetary Fund. This week Brazil announced a program to tackle its fiscal problems, and President Cardoso has assured me that he will implement the program swiftly.

To build on that progress, Prime Minister Blair of Great Britain and I have been working to rally support for several new measures to help strengthen the international community's ability to keep financial turmoil at bay. Secretary Rubin and Chairman Greenspan have been deeply engaged with their counterparts in the effort. And over the past week I've been speaking to other G–7 leaders about it.

Today I'm pleased to report that the world's leading economies have linked arms to contain the financial turmoil that threatened growth not only in emerging markets but in all markets of the world. The leaders of the major industrial economies have taken the following steps. This morning they've released a statement outlining our common agenda.

First, we have agreed to establish a new precautionary line of credit, anchored in the IMF, to help countries with sound economic policies ward off the global financial crisis in the first place. With substantial new resources at the IMF, this line of credit gives us a powerful new tool that can be used when it will do the most good at the lowest cost, before the trouble starts.

Second, we have also agreed to establish a new World Bank emergency fund to provide support in times of crisis to the most vulnerable members of society, and to encourage the World Bank to leverage private sector investments in countries now affected by the crisis.

And finally, even as we act to contain the crisis, we are building a modern framework for the global markets of the 21st century. Today we released detailed plans for greater openness and stronger standards for finance in the international marketplace. And we have agreed to ask our finance ministers to make new and very concrete recommendations to help to tame the excessive volatility in financial markets that can destroy hope and diminish wealth.

These steps are very, very important. Over the long run, if America's economy is to continue to grow, the economies of our trading partners must continue to grow. In a larger sense, if America's devotion to freedom and openness is to be met with success, we must put a human face on the global economy for the most vulnerable people in the emerging countries when they face hard times.

So I feel quite good about what my fellow G–7 leaders and others have done here. I thank them for their support. I thank especially Prime Minister Blair for his support.

Chief of Staff Erskine Bowles

Now, let me say, finally, for all of us here at the White House, this is not just a day of good economic news; it is personally a day of sad news because this is Erskine Bowles' last day as Chief of Staff. Sometime this afternoon, while I am in New York working, he is going home to North Carolina.

I want to say again how much I appreciate the indispensable role he has played in balancing the budget and developing sound economic policies, in improving our commitment to education in ways that will affect millions and millions of schoolchildren, and in his conviction that we were doing the right thing to pursue our race initiative.

Finally, he has been a marvelous role model for the young people who worked at the White House and for the not so young as well, putting us together into a team, getting everyone to work together, thinking every day about what good can come from our common efforts.

As all of you know, he is a very close personal friend of mine. I will miss him very much. But most of all today, I want to acknowledge his contributions to the people of the United States.

Thank you very much.

1998 Elections

Q. Mr. President, do you think voter turnout will be affected by the impeachment issue?

The President. The answer to your question is, I don't know. I know that this is no ordinary time, no ordinary election. What is at issue are big things that will affect every American and every American family's children. What is at issue is the future of Social Security, whether we will have a Patients' Bill of Rights for the over 160 million people in managed care plans, whether we will continue to advance the cause of education by building and modernizing our schools, whether we will continue the path of reform, raising the minimum wage, passing campaign finance reform, protecting our children from the dangers of tobacco. Those are the big issues.

I hope every American will go and vote and vote in good conscience and vote on what is important to this country and its future. All I can do is tell the American people, I know this is no ordinary time, no ordinary election, and they need to vote. I have no prediction about what the turnout will be, but I am confident that if people understand the stakes, it will be quite impressive.

Thank you.

NOTE: The President spoke at 11:16 a.m. at the South Portico at the White House, prior to his departure for New York City. In his remarks, he referred to President Fernando Henrique Cardoso of Brazil and Prime Minister Tony Blair of Great Britain.

Remarks at St. Sebastian's Parish Center in Queens, New York
October 30, 1998

Thank you very much for the warm welcome. Thank you, Monsignor Finnerty, for greeting me when I came through the door of St. Sebastian. Thank you, my longtime friend Claire Shulman, for being here. Thank you, Joe Crowley, for presenting yourself as a candidate for Congress.

He got good marks from Chuck Schumer as an athlete, and you must have noticed that he's quite a large man. I told him that next January I'd like him to be one of the whips in the Congress to get the votes gathered up, because I think people would be reluctant to say no to him.

I love coming to Queens. I never will forget the first time I came out here when I was running for President in 1992, and Harold Ickes was helping me. And he said, "We're going to go out to Queens, and we're going to meet with the Queens County Democratic Committee. And Congressman Tom Manton is the chairman of the committee." And he said, "I think we can get them to be for you."

I said, "Now, why in the world would they endorse me? Most of those people have probably never thought about Arkansas, much less been there." And he said, "Yes, but they're a lot like you out there in Queens. You'll be right at home. You'll like that." [*Laughter*]

So we got on the subway, and there was a television camera or two with me. And no one in New York knew who I was at the time, so they probably thought we were filming a commercial or something. We were on the subway banging everybody around, and then we got off and took a beautiful walk to the place where we had the committee meeting. And Tom had already convened the committee, and I walked up the stairs, and at length they introduced me.

And it was a setting sort of like this, and I was coming in from the back, and we walked down the middle of the aisle. And I got about halfway down the aisle, and there was this real tall African-American man standing there on the aisle, a member of the Democratic committee in this county. And he put his arm around me and he said, "Hey, Governor." He said, "Don't worry about this." He said, "I was born in Hope, Arkansas, too. You're going to be just fine." [*Laughter*]

Tom Manton has been taking care of me ever since. And I want you to know that he has done a wonderful job in Congress, and I appreciate what he did for you and for New York and for our country. And I will miss him very much. Thank you, friend.

You know, on the way out here we were standing out in the hall, and I first met Gert, and we started laughing about John Glenn going up in space yesterday. And she said she thought that was a fine thing for a young man like him to be doing. [*Laughter*] I want you to hold that thought, because I'm coming back to it. [*Laughter*] There's a real reason why we're here today.

And finally, let me thank Chuck and Iris Schumer for their friendship to me. I was in their home in 1992 over in Brooklyn. And I met their friends and relatives and the people with whom they worship. It was quite an exciting day for me. And I have been proud of the campaign that they have made together with their family and friends, starting out against overwhelming odds, bravely soldiering on, and, I'd say, doing right well on this eve of another election.

I'd like to ask all of you to think about something as New Yorkers, as well as Americans. New York at extraordinary times has given this country extraordinary leadership in the United States Senate. New York gave the American people Robert Wagner and Herbert Layman and Jacob Javits and Pat Moynihan in the United States Senate. New York gave the American people Robert Kennedy in the United States Senate.

And once, Robert Kennedy said, and I quote, "There is no basic inconsistency between ideals and realistic possibilities." I've worked with Chuck Schumer a lot. He's an idealist who is always struggling to get something done. And the longer I serve as your President, believe it or not, and in spite of everything, the more idealistic I am about America, what it stands for, what it means, and what it can do, but the more determined I am that every day should be used to turn ideals into action.

When it comes to education or Social Security or health care, when it comes to all those ideas, I can think of no person with whom I have worked in these last 6 years in the entire Congress who I think has more ability to turn ideals into action than Chuck Schumer. And that is one reason I am very proud to be here by his side and in support of him today.

Now, let me say also to all of you, this is not an ordinary election. I want you to go vote Tuesday, even if you are not going to cast your ballot the way I want you to. I hope you will, however. [Laughter] But I want you to go, because in this election we're going to choose the Congress of the 21st century. Really, the decisions that will be made, a lot of them in the next couple of years, will shape the way we as a people will live for far more than the next 2 years.

Now, for 6 years, since the people of New York gave the Vice President and me and Hillary and our whole team a chance to serve, we've turned the country's economic policy around. We've changed our social policy. We have essentially tried to make America work again so that we could take advantage of these incredible changes that are going on in the world and have a very strong economy but make sure we kept a human face on it, that we gave everybody a chance to benefit from his or her labors, and that we took care of those who through no fault of their own needed a little help to get by, and that we tried to bring the country together instead of driving it apart.

And after 6 years, we saw again today that our economy grew at 3.3 percent in the last quarter. We've had the lowest unemployment rate in 28 years; nearly 17 million new jobs; the lowest percentage of Americans on welfare in 29 years; the first balanced budget, as you heard Chuck say, in 29 years; and a surplus. For the first time in history, last week, thanks in part to the heroic efforts of New York's Secretary of Housing and Urban Development, Andrew Cuomo, we announced a year and a half ahead of time that we had met our goal. Now over two-thirds of the American people live in their own homes for the first time in the history of the United States. So we are moving in the right direction. That is a good thing.

And as I told somebody, we had also reduced the size of the Federal bureaucracy so that the Federal Government is now the smallest it was since the last time John Glenn went around the Earth. [Laughter]

Now, I thank Tom for what he said. Our administration has tried to be a force for peace and freedom around the world. We've worked hard to help the Irish reconcile with one another. We're working hard to promote peace in the Middle East, and we had a big breakthrough there last week on this day; we announced it on this day last week. If I seem a little slow of speech today, you'll have to forgive me, but on that last day I was up 39 hours without sleep. And the real way we made the agreement was I was the last one standing—[laughter]—and so they finally agreed so they could go to bed. [Laughter]

I say that because America has unique responsibilities and unique opportunities. Today I announced a program that I believe will help us to keep the world economy growing and to roll back some of the financial turmoil you read about that's engulfing the rest of the world. Now, that's a big deal because a quarter of our growth in the last 6 years has come from our ability to sell what we have to sell to other people, so that more and more, the success of every American business, even small businesses here in Queens, will be indirectly affected, at least, by the success of our friends and neighbors throughout the world.

Now, against that background, at this golden moment for our country, I think we have to look ahead to the future and say, "Well, what are we going to do with the first surplus in 29 years? What are we going to do with the lowest unemployment rate in 29 years? What are we going to do with this time when we seem to be doing pretty well, but a lot of our friends are in trouble around the world? What are we going to do with all those neighborhoods in New York City and elsewhere which haven't yet felt the economic recovery of the last 6 years? Shall we just sort of relax and enjoy it, which means that at midterm elections half the people just stay home? Or shall we instead look ahead to the future and say, you know, times like this don't come along very often."

Those of you out here who've seen a lot of years, how many periods in American history have we had like this? Not many in your lifetime. Not many. And nothing lasts forever. So that when you have these times like this, it is terribly important that we as Americans look to the future and take on our real challenges.

To me, that's the most important decision the American people have to make. Do you want to think big, think about what America should be like for your children, your grandchildren, your great-grandchildren? What can we do now when we are strong to give that kind of America to the Americans of the 21st century?

That's what this whole saving Social Security issue is about. When I heard Gert talking about it, I thought, you know, Social Security for us has become even more than a check in the mail, even though fully one-half the seniors in America would be in poverty today without it. Even though most people have some other source of income in addition to their Social Security check, nonetheless, if there were no Social Security, half the seniors in the country would be in poverty without it, instead of the 11 percent, which is the actual rate today. It's a huge deal. We're talking about untold millions of lives changed.

But in addition to the money, it is the symbol of our determination to honor family, to honor the contributions of those who went before us, to honor the proposition that in America we want to reward people who are good at what they're doing. We don't begrudge the athletes their success, the business people their success. But we know that a country is great because of the great mass of people who get up every day, work their hearts out, obey the law, pay their taxes, raise their kids, and build up neighborhoods. And they should be a part of our prosperity. We don't believe in leaving people behind who do their part for America. And Social Security symbolizes that.

Now, what's the issue here? Why is Social Security in trouble? First of all, if you're getting a check now, relax; you're going to be fine. That's not the issue. The issue is this: We are living longer. The baby boomers are coming up for retirement, and those of you who gave birth to baby boomers know that until this crowd started school last year, this crowd of children in school, the baby boomers were the largest American generation ever and larger than our children.

So that when we retire, the baby boomers, there will only be about two people working for every one person drawing Social Security. To give you an idea, today there are more than three people working—about three and a half people working for every one person drawing Social Security. In addition to that, there will be more and more and more women retiring and living on Social Security because women, on balance, have a longer life expectancy. And they are less likely to have pensions or personal

savings. For 25 percent of the women on Social Security, it's the only income they receive.

Now, when the 75 million baby boomers retire and when there are only two people on Social Security for every one person—two people working for every one person drawing, we will, in about 20 years, start having to pay out of the Social Security Trust Fund, as provided by law, benefits, because the annual income won't be enough to cover the annual outgo. Then in about 34 years, even the Trust Fund won't be enough to cover the benefit.

Now, here's what this is all about. If we start now and make some modest changes now that don't have to affect people on Social Security at all, and if we use this money that we have in the surplus which, I think I should add, was produced entirely by the Social Security tax itself, then we can make modest changes and preserve Social Security in the 21st century in a way that will accommodate the changing population patterns and still make sure it's there for the people who need it.

If we do not do that, if we say, "Well, heck, we waited 29 years for this surplus, let's take the money and run. Let's have a little fun. Give me a tax cut. Give me a new program. Give me this. Give me that, before we know whether we need this money to save Social Security"— and keep in mind it was produced by the Social Security tax—and we miss this opportunity, then what's going to happen? Sooner or later, within a few years—keep in mind, every year that goes by, the problem is only going to get tougher; it's not going to get easier, because you have less time to fix a big problem—then sooner or later we'll be forced with the choice of either saying, "Well, I'm sorry. We can't do this so we're just going to have to cut benefits 22 percent"—in which case a lot of seniors will be in deep trouble—or we'll say, "Our conscience won't let us live with ourselves, so we're going to raise the taxes 22 percent," and that's a whopping tax increase. And keep in mind, the payroll tax is paid by small businesses in years where they make money and years when they don't make any money; the payroll tax is paid by people on modest incomes as well as by wealthy people. .

And if we did that, we'd be saying, "Okay, we didn't fix this when we had a chance back in 1999, and because we didn't do it, now we're going to have to lower the standard of living of our children and their ability to raise our grandchildren because we didn't do the right thing."

Now, the generation that got us through World War II and built the greatest middle class in history and was educated by the G.I. bill knows that America should do right by the future. This is a huge issue.

For a long time I thought that this would be a completely bipartisan issue. All year long we had forums around the country, Democrats and Republicans together, talking about these ideas, honestly debating what the options were. But then the leadership in the House of the other party wanted to have a huge and permanent tax cut right before the election, disproportionately benefiting upper income people like me, before we did anything to fix Social Security and before we knew what it would cost.

Well, we beat that. Thanks to Chuck Schumer and Tom Manton and a lot of other people, we rolled that back. But just the other day, they reaffirmed their desire to do that, to deplete this surplus before we know how much we need for Social Security. And the majority leader in the Senate said that he might not even want to work with me next year on fixing Social Security.

So I say to you, I did not come here to trouble you about your Social Security. Your Social Security is okay. If we don't do anything, you'll be fine. But if you believe it's been a good thing, and if you want it there for the baby boomers, for your children, and if you want your children to be able to retire without having to undermine the incomes and the standard of living of your grandchildren, then I implore you to speak with a loud and clear voice and say, "Look, we have lived a long life, and sometimes you can't do the easy thing. We shouldn't take the money and run. We should save the money, save the surplus, and fix Social Security. If there's anything left over, then we can talk about what to do about it. But we cannot endanger this fundamental compact between the generations that has helped to make America what it is today. Save Social Security first."

That's the big reason I wanted to come here, the big reason I'm proud to stand with Chuck Schumer. There are other things. You heard—I think it was Tom who said we voted in this budget—we got one of our most important ideas in this budget: to hire 100,000 teachers to take class size down to an average of 18 in the early grades. But if you go around New York, you will see a lot of school buildings with rooms that can't be used. If you go to Florida, where I was yesterday—I went to a little town in Florida not very long ago, a small town. I went to one elementary school. There were 12 trailers out back; one school, 12 trailers to accommodate all the extra kids.

So one of the things we didn't succeed in doing in this election—and again I ask you to think about your grandchildren and your great-grandchildren—if we're going to have more teachers and smaller classes, they have to have someplace to teach. That means we have to build schools where we need them and we have to repair schools where we have them.

We have school buildings in the cities of this country, like New York and Philadelphia and Chicago, where I've been, that are priceless buildings. No one could afford to build such buildings today. They're great buildings, but they've been allowed to fall into such disrepair that they can't even be hooked up to the Internet. And all this work we're doing to bring our kids into the modern age is not possible. So that's another big issue that I think is important. And I thank Chuck Schumer and Tom Manton for their support for building and repairing 5,000 schools. And we need to do that next year.

We've tried to get a Patients' Bill of Rights passed for a year, and the health insurance companies persuaded the majority in Congress to beat us. But you know, Chuck talked about Medicare. We have the same challenges in Medicare, by the way, we do in Social Security. But one of the things that bothers me is more and more Americans are in managed care plans and HMO's. Now, that can be good if they just save money that would have otherwise have been wasted. Don't forget, 6 years ago inflation in health care costs was going up at 3 times the rate of inflation. And for elderly people that was a really troubling thing, since you use more health care. It was going to bankrupt the country. So to manage the system better is a good thing. But to manage the system only to save money without regard to whether it's good for health care is not a good thing. Doctors, not accountants, should ultimately make health care decisions.

We're trying to pass this Patients' Bill of Rights that simply says, look, we believe very strongly that we should have a law which says every person should have a right to see a specialist if his or her doctor recommends it; that every person in an accident should have a right to go to the nearest emergency room, not one halfway across New York City just because that's the one that's covered by the plan; that if a person is in a treatment, a chemotherapy treatment or a young woman being treated by an obstetrician, who's pregnant, and their employer changes health care plans, well, you ought to be able to keep the doctor you're dealing with until the treatment is over, until the baby is born; and that your medical records ought to be private.

Now, this is something that affects Americans of all ages, but disproportionately seniors who are in managed care plans. A lot of seniors want to go into managed care plans, Medicaid, Medicare, because they give prescription drugs which otherwise aren't covered. There are a lot of good things. But in the end, everybody ought to have those rights, those basic rights. And that's a big issue in this election that affects you and your children and your grandchildren.

So finally let me just say that there are a lot of things out here that you have to think about. And I've been urging the American people to vote and hoping we can get a little more balance in this Congress so that we can have people like Chuck Schumer who will put Social Security first, who will pass a Patients' Bill of Rights, who will make it possible for us to modernize and build our schools, in short, who will be thinking about the long term.

The temptation is great for people just to pass; they say, "Gosh, things are going so well, why is the President so agitated?" Because my job is to think for all the American people about next year and 5 years and 10 years and 20 years down the road. And I would argue that those of you who are senior citizens, your job is to think for all the American people about next year and 10 years and 20 years down the road.

We were sitting here talking about John Glenn going up 36 years ago, and Tom Manton said, "I remember when he went the first time,

and it seems like it was yesterday." Doesn't it to you, the ones that remember it? It seems like it was yesterday.

I remember once I met a man who is a friend of mine, who was 76 at the time, at an airport in Little Rock, and he looked terribly sad. And I said, "Why are you so sad?" He said, "Well, my sister just died, and I'm here to meet some family members." And he said, "When you came up to me, Bill," he said, "I was thinking about when we were 5 years old." He was 75. And he put his hand on my shoulder and he said, "Let me tell you something. It doesn't take long to live a life."

And all of you know that. We all are given our share of time here. We all try to make the best we can. We all try to build our families and build our lives, enjoy our friends, pursue our faiths. America is the greatest country in the world for giving us that chance.

All we all owe back to America is good citizenship. So I ask you, please, at this golden moment for our country, stand up for the proposition that we should save the Social Security system before we throw this money away that we've worked 6 years to build up; stand up for the proposition that every person ought to have decent integrity in their health care system; stand up for the proposition that children you and I may never know should have a world-class education in the 21st century.

I ask you for that and for your help for this good man, Chuck Schumer, and for all people who are always thinking about America's tomorrows.

Thank you, and God bless you.

NOTE: The President spoke at 1:43 p.m. In his remarks, he referred to Rev. D. Joseph Finnerty, pastor, St. Sebastian's Catholic Church; Claire Shulman, president, Borough of Queens; Joseph Crowley, candidate for New York's Seventh Congressional District; senatorial candidate Representative Charles E. Schumer and his wife, Iris; former Deputy Chief of Staff Harold Ickes; and Gertrude McDonald, senior citizen, Long Island City.

Remarks at a Reception for Senatorial Candidate Charles E. Schumer in Brooklyn, New York
October 30, 1998

Thank you. First, let me just thank Joe and Trina for welcoming all of us into this truly beautiful home. I've had a wonderful time. I want to—if I could say one thing, when we get close to an election like this, and Chuck and Iris and all the people that are working so hard for him, you are more and more nervous, and you don't get any sleep. And you're more or less on automatic, and it's so easy to forget why you've been doing all that. And then we come in here and see all of these huge families with the children and the grandchildren and the in-laws—*[laughter]*—I believe I could sort you all out now because I've got all the different cross currents here. [*Laughter*]

But let me tell you, I am thrilled. This is what America is all about. And I cannot thank you enough. I find myself for the second Friday in a row racing the Shabbat clock. [*Laughter*] Last week, we were at Wye. We had a deal; then we didn't have a deal. And we had a time to announce it, and then we didn't. I was up for 39 hours. That's really how—people say, "How did this get done?" It's simple. I was the last person standing. [*Laughter*] They were saying, "Please let us go to bed. Please let us." "No."

I don't want to race the clock again. I want to respect this very much. One of the reasons this country is around here after 220 years is that the first amendment to the Constitution guarantees to every person who comes here the absolute unrestricted practice of his or her faith. And there are people in this room who have given me a chance to help move people from Syria out and come here. And for giving me the chance to work with you, I thank you.

The work that I have been able to do with my own people in Ireland or for peace in the Middle East, where my faith was born as well, in all other parts of the world, in Bosnia, now in Kosovo, where I think we have averted another humanitarian disaster, is very important.

But we also need to remember what makes America the world's leader is our strength at home and our ability to live at home by what we say we believe. The power of our example is necessary for the power of our armies to make sense to anybody. Who else would the Israelis and the Palestinians say, "We would like your CIA to monitor part of our accords?" [*Laughter*] I mean if you think about it, it's an incredibly humbling thing, a great honor for a country to be trusted in that way.

And what I want to say to you, I can say very briefly. For 6 years I have worked to bring this country together, to move it forward, and to be a force for peace and freedom throughout the world. The country is better off today than it was 6 years ago, mostly because of people like you, but our policies clearly helped.

In the last year, I was deeply frustrated at all the things I tried to do that we couldn't do because of the increasing partisanship of the other party in Washington. And I can tell you that, especially for New York, to have someone like Chuck Schumer in the United States Senate, someone who could serve in the tradition of the greatest New York Senators and the greatest Senators in the history of this country, would be a great gift to America.

To have a few more Democrats like Chuck Schumer may mean the difference in whether we save Social Security or forget about our obligations to our parents and our children. It may make the difference in whether we can pass a Patients' Bill of Rights so all people, not just the well-to-do, can be guaranteed that they will get quality health care if they have health coverage. It may make the difference in whether we actually go out and build schools and hire teachers and provide excellence in education to all our people without regard to their incomes or their backgrounds or their family circumstances. In short, it can make a difference in whether America has more families that look like you do 10 years, 20 years from now.

You look at this room. If I could walk into any neighborhood in America and hold a meeting like this, we would have not 10 percent of the problems we have today. Look around here; look around. So I'm going to let you get on with the Shabbat, but remember, on Tuesday your responsibilities as citizens kick in.

And let me just ask you one more thing. Chuck said, you employ many thousands of people. Between now and Tuesday, you will come in contact with people with whom you worship, people with whom you work, people with whom you socialize, people with whom you may sit in a coffee shop. I implore you—usually in America—usually—we turn out in pretty good numbers for Presidential elections, and then half our people stay home in the off years.

This is not an ordinary time. These are big, big issues. And New York has a chance to give

a gift to itself and to the Nation in Chuck Schumer. And I want you to do everything you can between now and Tuesday, except when you're taking time off to worship, to ask people to show up. Will you do that?

Thank you, and God bless you.

NOTE: The President spoke at 3:35 p.m. at a private residence. In his remarks, he referred to Joe and Trina Cayre, dinner hosts; and Iris Schumer, wife of Representative Charles E. Schumer.

Remarks to the Clergy in Jamaica, New York
October 30, 1998

Thank you so much. Please be seated. Dr. Walker, Dr. Forbes, "Reverend" McCall—[*laughter*]—he was doing pretty good, wasn't he? Bishop Quick; Reverend Sharpton; my good friend Congressman Schumer and his wife, Iris, and their daughter, Jessica; I think Congressman Towns is here. President Fernando Ferrer, the Bronx Borough president; Virginia Fields, I think, may be here, the Manhattan Borough president; Judith Hope, our State chair. I'd like to thank the St. Paul Community Baptist Church Choir for singing Red Foley's old hymn for me. Thank you very much; it was quite wonderful.

When I was a little boy, I used to listen to Mahalia Jackson sing that song. And when I was a young man and living in England, I went to the Royal Albert Hall in London to hear Mahalia Jackson sing, not long before she died. It was 29 years ago, and it was an amazing thing. She was singing "Precious Lord." At the end of her concert, there were all these young people like me there—but most of them weren't like me, most of them were British; they didn't grow up listening to all this, you know. And these kids stormed the stage at the end, almost like she was a rock star. They were five and six deep, screaming for her to keep singing.

And you reminded me of all that just a moment ago, and I thank you for that. Weren't they wonderful? [*Applause*] They were great. Thank you.

Let me say to all of you, I thank Carl McCall for his leadership and for what he said. I have tried to be a friend to all Americans, without

regard to race or income or religion or standing in life. I am grateful that in an economy in which we have the lowest unemployment rate in 28 years that the African-American poverty rate is the lowest we have ever measured. I am grateful that the tax credit that Congressman Schumer helped me pass in 1993, the earned-income tax credit, cutting the taxes of lower income working people, when put with the minimum wage, has lifted over one million African-Americans out of poverty through their own efforts of work.

I am grateful to have had the chance to double the number of small-business loans to African-Americans and dramatically increase support for historically black colleges; to have had the largest number of African-Americans serving in the Cabinet in my 2 administrations, by far, than any President, and 54—54—Federal judges.

I say all that to make this point—maybe not as well as Dr. Forbes did. I don't seek any credit for that. It was an honor for me to do. It was something I wanted to do. It was a desire born of the life I have lived and the people I have known and the things I have seen that I like and the things I have seen that I deplored and the potential of people too long untapped that I was determined to do what I could to lift up. But it all happened because of the American system of democracy.

Yesterday, all over America, all kinds of people were watching John Glenn go up in space at 77 years old—kind of made us all think we had something to look forward to—[laughter]—77 years old. But you may not have thought of this if you were sitting in front of your television watching that: How did he get up in space? Oh yes, a rocket took him, all right. He got up in space because the Congress of the United States and the President of the United States, over time, but especially in these last 6 years when we had such budget problems, supported a mission for the United States in space and believed that mission ought to have benefits for us here on Earth, whether it's learning about the environmental challenges we face or making advances in health care and prevention of health problems. In other words, at bottom, it was a citizen's decision. So if you voted for a Member of Congress who supported the changes we made in the space program but didn't want to shut it down, wanted to keep it going, then you had your hand on John Glenn when he went up in space yesterday. Now, that's what I want you to think about.

A week ago today, I was in the White House with the Prime Minister of Israel and the Chairman of the Palestinian Authority announcing the next move forward in the Middle East peace process. And I'm very grateful for the nice things people said about the role that I played, but it was my job. It's what you hired me to do. And I wanted to do it because of what I know about what is going on, my heartbreak over the loss and my hope over the potential of the region which is the home to all three of the world's great monotheistic religions. But what I want you to know is that if you liked that last Friday and it made you feel good about your country, pushing for peace, if you supported me, then you were part of that peace process.

And today we announced we had another good quarter of economic growth, and I outlined what I was going to try to do to help these countries in trouble around the world, because they buy our things. We live in a world anymore where it is not just our neighbors that have to do well, down the block, if we want to do well. Our neighbors around the world need to do well. If we want to bring opportunity back into the neighborhoods of New York City where it hasn't happened yet, we have to have some place that would be matched up with us as partners. So if they do well in the Caribbean, if they do well in Latin America, if we have closer relations with Africa, it actually will help

us also to build up our own people—a lesson that those who study the Bible will not be surprised turned out to be true. But if you liked all that, if you supported me and my economic policies, you had a hand in it. It was your prosperity.

I think of all the things Carl McCall has done as comptroller that no comptroller ever did before, all the people he tried to help—loans to 300 New York businesses, thousands of new jobs, millions available to women- and minority-owned businesses. Nobody ever did that before. In a real sense, it wasn't just him doing that. You did that. He's your hired hand, just like I am. We have nothing that the people of New York and the United States don't give us under the constitutions under which we labor.

Mr. Schumer wants to be a Senator. New York has had some great Senators: Robert Wagner—so many years ago—the whole framework of our labor laws protecting the dignity of working people in the workplace; Herbert Lehman; Jacob Javits, a great Republican Senator; Senator Moynihan; Robert Kennedy. New York should have a Senator who can be very much in the mix of what needs to be done today and tomorrow, all the specific things, but also can help to lead the State and the Nation with a vision. He's that kind of person. I know him well, and I want you to help him.

And if you think about this election, it's about choices—clear choices. And if you vote and if the people you know and love vote, and the things you want to have happen, happen, then it's not just those of us whom you elect doing it. It's you doing it. It's being Americans in the best sense and being rewarded in the highest sense.

You know, we got some things done, some important things done, at the end of this last congressional session, but it's hard for 8 days of progress to overcome 8 months of partisanship. And if you look ahead, we've got the largest number of children in our schools we've ever had, for finally we've got more kids in school than when I was there in the baby boom generation—taking a big burden off our generation, I might add.

But as a result—and more and more of these children are immigrant children. They come from families whose first language is not English. And more and more they find themselves in these great big classrooms where the teachers can't give them the individual attention they need. And we know now that the most important factor in having enduring learning gains for children, particularly if they're poor children, is to be in a small class in the early grades with a good teacher who can individually help them get off to a good start. So we said, we want 100,000 teachers in the early grades to take class size down to an average of 18 in the early grades.

And then we've got all these wonderful old school buildings in New York with a lot of rooms and floors that aren't usable and that can't be hooked up to computers and things. And then we've got, in Florida and California, all these kids showing up and no buildings for them to be in. They're out in trailers out in the backyard somewhere, sometimes meeting in broom closets, literally. So we said we want to build or remodel 5,000 schools, because if you're going to hire the teachers and you've got the kids there anyway, they need someplace to meet. And this Congress said, "No, no, no, we don't believe in that." But we believe in that. If we had a little more balance, just a few more Democrats, we could get 5,000 more schools for America. That's what this issue is.

One hundred sixty million Americans are in managed care, and we may well have more in the future. A lot of seniors want to be in managed care programs for Medicare because then they get a prescription drug benefit. It's a big issue.

I have never been opposed to the managed care concept because when I became President, the inflation rate in health care costs was 3 times as high as the inflation rate in the economy, and it was bankrupting businesses and individual senior citizens, and it threatened to consume the country. So we had to have a better management of the money we were putting into health care.

But no management system should be allowed to swallow up the purpose of the endeavor. And today you've got people—heartbreaking people—who were denied the care they should have gotten because insurance company bureaucrats or accountants said, "No, you can't have it." You have people who get hurt in an accident, and instead of going to the nearest hospital emergency room, they're carted halfway across town through a bunch of red lights and waiting because that's the one covered in their plan. You have people in a plan, and their employer changes plans when it expires, but the worker

may be pregnant or the worker's spouse may be undergoing chemotherapy—to be told to change doctors in the middle of one of those streams.

You ever had anybody in your family on chemotherapy? I have. You know, it's a scary thing. And families try to pull together, and they want to make light of it. We made a lot of jokes in my family when my mother was on chemotherapy. Was she going to lose her hair or not? If she did, would the wig look better than her hair? You know, you try to make them laugh. But the truth is, you're scared to death. And you wonder if the person you love is going to get so sick they won't be able to eat anymore. And then in the middle of that, if somebody had told us, "I'm sorry. We changed carriers. Now you have to change doctors," I don't know what I would have done. But it happens. And I could give you a lot of other examples.

So we had this Patients' Bill of Rights. We said, look, we had 43 of these HMO's saying, "Mr. President, you're right." We had a national commission of all kinds of people recommending this Patients' Bill of Rights. And we tried to pass it into law because it's not fair for some HMO's to do it and others not, and then the people that aren't behaving well to get rewarded by getting more customers who are healthy with lower prices.

So we said, okay, everybody ought to—we're going to have a simple bill of rights for every patient. First of all, if your doctor tells you you ought to see a specialist, you can see one. Secondly, if you get hurt, you ought to go to the nearest emergency room. Thirdly, if you're having treatment that's serious, you ought to be able to finish it, even if your employer changes health care providers. Fourthly, your medical records ought to be kept private and not invaded. Finally, in essence, health care decisions ultimately should be made by health care professionals and patients, not by accountants. That's what we say.

Now—[*applause*]—you like that? If we had just a little more balance in the Congress, a few more Democrats, we wouldn't get beat on that Patients' Bill of Rights. If we had a few more people like Chuck Schumer in the House and in the Senate, we could give the American people a Patients' Bill of Rights.

And the same thing is true on Social Security. You've heard all this debate about saving Social

Security. Well, if you're on Social Security, relax, you're okay. What we're talking about is the baby boomers are moving to retirement. When they all retire, there will only be two people working for every one person drawing Social Security. The Trust Fund will be out of money in 2032, and we'll be into the Trust Fund in about 20 years. And if we make a few little changes now, modest changes, we can change and save this system in ways that we can all live with, and Social Security will be there.

That's why I say, look, we waited 29 years to balance the books. I've worked for 6 years on it. And before the ink is even dry, the black ink, the leaders in the other party, they want to give it back in a tax cut before we save Social Security. Now it may be popular, but it's not right. It's not right—it is not right. We owe it to the next generation to make sure the baby boom generation can retire in dignity without having to put a whopping tax increase on their children and undermine their children's ability to raise their grandchildren.

You know, I grew up with a bunch of people who were mostly middle class folks at home. A lot of them didn't go to college, out there working for a living. They could use any kind of tax cut they could get. They liked the ones we've provided already for child care and for education. And they'd like some more. But I don't know anybody my age that is not plagued with the notion that because we're such a large generation, our retirement will put unconscionable burdens on our children and our grandchildren.

Now, that's what this whole "save Social Security" thing is about. The pastors here who look after the flock and think about the generation, who work all the time at getting all of us, your sheep, to think about the long run and not just what's in front of our nose—this is an issue that you can feel deeply. And this election is not an ordinary election because this is a generational thing. We have a few more people like Congressman Schumer in the Senate and the House—give a little more balance to this thing—we can save Social Security for the 21st century.

So again I say to you, people like Carl McCall and Chuck Schumer, Ed Towns, our whole ticket, none of them get there by accident. And when they get there and do good things, we're not doing it alone. Every good thing I ever did, you had a hand in if you helped me be

President. The mistakes were my fault. The good stuff you had a hand in. Don't you forget about it. And that is true of Carl McCall; that is true of Chuck Schumer; that is true of every public official.

Somebody asked me the other day, "How did you ever get those folks to agree at the Wye Plantation after 8 days?" I said I was determined to be the last one standing. [Laughter] We were up for 39 hours. I didn't do that in college; I'm too old to do it now. [Laughter] I kept thinking of all those Scripture verses, you know, "Let us not grow weary in doing good, for in due season, we shall reap if we do not lose heart." I kept thinking, well, "They who wait upon the Lord will mount up with wings—[laughter]—run and not grow weary; walk and faint not." I almost got to the end of that verse before we got peace the other day. [Laughter]

Now, on Tuesday the people that we need to be there, a lot of them will be tired. A lot of them will be hassled. A lot of them don't make much money. A lot of them have enough trouble just figuring out how to get the kids to child care or school and get back and forth from work and get the kids home and ever have everybody in one piece by dinner time. And America is one of the countries—still—votes on a work day. It's a real hassle for them. A lot of them depend on mass transit to get back and forth to work, and the voting place is not on the same bus line or the same subway route. It's a hassle. Just remember, everybody that doesn't show can't gripe Wednesday morning. And everybody that does show is then a part of every good thing that flows from their decision if they're in the majority.

I want you to think about how you want to feel Wednesday morning. And I want you to think about it. If you felt good during the Middle East peace process, if you felt good when John Glenn went up into space, if you felt good when I was able to tell you we were going to get 100,000 new teachers, if you felt good when I talked about those 54 Federal judges, if you believe in your heart that you have been a part of my Presidency—and I tell you, you have; I wouldn't be here without you—then I ask you this one thing: Realize that this, too, is an important election; that it is not an ordinary time, it is therefore not an ordinary election; that what happens, all these people who will win races on Tuesday, will be a direct result not only of how you vote but, even more importantly, whether you vote.

You will come in contact with thousands of people between now and then. And when the Scripture said that we are all admonished to render unto Caesar those things which are Caesar's—well, I'm not Caesar, and we're not a dictatorship or an empire, but you know what the Bible means. It's more today. When that Scripture was written, all that meant was, pay your taxes. Nobody had a vote—nobody had a vote. Today you've got the vote. You can actually be in the driver's seat. There is no Caesar without you—[*laughter*]—unless you sit it out.

Our adversaries, they think a whole bunch of you will stay home. They know it's going to be a hassle. They know it will be an effort. But you just remember every good thing that you've felt good about in the last 6 years. And you think about how you want to feel Wednesday morning.

We need to reelect Carl McCall, and all America needs to know about Carl McCall, not just New York. All America needs to know about Carl. We need to send Chuck Schumer to the Senate because all America, and not just New York, needs that. We need to get that balance back in our Congress so we can do some of these things that we can't get done now. But it all depends on you. It all depends on you.

I am more grateful than you will ever know for the friendship and the support of the people of New York, to me, to my wife, to my Vice President, to our administration; for the friendship and support of the African-American community, and especially the clergy. But the thing about this kind of work is, you never get to stop—you never get to stop.

In the last week we've had a lot to celebrate. You had your hand on John Glenn's shoulder. You had your prayers answered about the continued process of peace. You can think about your children's future with 100,000 more teachers. But there are huge fights out there left to fight—huge. And we need you.

Thank you, and God bless you.

NOTE: The President spoke at 4:45 p.m. in Ballrooms B and C at the Ramada Plaza Hotel. In his remarks, he referred to human rights activist Rev. Wyatt Tee Walker, pastor, Canaan Baptist Church of Christ; Rev. James Forbes, pastor, Riverside Church; H. Carl McCall, New York State comptroller; Bishop Norman Quick, pastor, Childs Memorial Temple, Church of God in Christ; civil rights activist Rev. Al Sharpton; Prime Minister Binyamin Netanyahu of Israel; and Chairman Yasser Arafat of the Palestinian Authority.

Statement on Signing the Technology Administration Act of 1998
October 30, 1998

Today I am signing into law H.R. 1274, the "Technology Administration Act of 1998." The Act strengthens the technology programs of the Department of Commerce to meet the challenges of the 21st century.

The Act will enable the Commerce Department's National Institute of Standards and Technology (NIST) to better serve the Nation's more than 380,000 smaller manufacturers by eliminating the 6-year sunset provision for Federal co-funding of NIST Manufacturing Extension Partnership centers.

The Act also authorizes NIST to establish a program to help elementary and secondary school teachers to convey to their students important lessons in measurements, manufacturing,

technology transfer, and other areas in which NIST researchers possess world-class expertise.

I am especially pleased to sign this legislation because it includes an initiative that I have sought for the past 2 years: expansion of the Malcolm Baldrige National Quality Award to include education and health care organizations. The Foundation for the Malcolm Baldrige National Quality Award deserves special credit for its work to endow this expansion, as does NIST, which manages the program in close cooperation with the private sector. Now the Federal Government can do its share to foster performance excellence in schools, health care, and business.

The Act also officially establishes within the Department of Commerce an Office of Space

Commercialization and the Experimental Program to Stimulate Competitive Technology. These programs address two important components of our overall competitiveness strategy: our wise use of commercial space capabilities, consistent with public safety and national security requirements, and enhancement of technological opportunities for the States.

This Act furthers my Administration's commitment to ensure that technology remains the engine of economic growth. We have more work to do. My Administration will work with the 106th Congress on legislation to reauthorize the Commerce Department's Technology Administration and other NIST programs.

WILLIAM J. CLINTON

The White House,
October 30, 1998.

NOTE: H.R. 1274, approved October 30, was assigned Public Law No. 105–309.

Statement on Signing Wildlife and Wetlands Legislation
October 30, 1998

Today I am signing into law H.R. 2807, an omnibus measure that includes many provisions I supported to enhance fish and wildlife protection.

The Act reauthorizes the Rhinoceros and Tiger Conservation Act through FY 2002 and prohibits the sale, importation, and exportation of products labeled or advertised as derived from rhinoceroses or tigers. This will substantially eliminate the demand for products made from these endangered species. The Act also reauthorizes, through FY 2003, the North American Wetlands Conservation Act and the Partnerships for Wildlife Act, two of the most popular, cost-effective, and productive environmental conservation programs.

I note that section 304 of the Act amends the criteria for appointing individuals to the North American Wetlands Conservation Council. Specifically, this provision purportedly designates an officeholder of a named private organization as a Council member. This raises two issues. First, the Council is involved in the implementation of Federal wetlands conservation programs and, therefore, its members are considered officers of the United States. Pursuant to the Appointments Clause of the Constitution, the Congress may not appoint Federal officers. Consequently, I will instruct the Secretary of the Interior merely to consider the designated individual along with other appropriate candidates for appointment to the Council.

Second, if the Secretary ultimately selects the individual designated by the Act, that individual will be subject to executive branch standards of conduct and criminal conflict-of-interest statutes. The individual's ability to act fully as a Council member therefore may be somewhat curtailed by his or her affiliation with a private organization.

On balance, the Act provides a considerable benefit to the conservation of fish and wildlife, and I am pleased to sign it into law.

WILLIAM J. CLINTON

The White House,
October 30, 1998.

NOTE: H.R. 2807, approved October 30, was assigned Public Law No. 105–312.

Statement on Signing the Identity Theft and Assumption Deterrence Act of 1998
October 30, 1998

Today I signed into law H.R. 4151, the "Identity Theft and Assumption Deterrence Act of 1998." This legislation will make identity theft a Federal crime, with penalties generally of up to 3 years imprisonment and a maximum fine of $250,000.

Specifically, the legislation would penalize the theft of personal information with the intent to commit an unlawful act, such as obtaining fraudulent loans or credit cards, drug trafficking, or other illegal purposes. It would also direct the Federal Trade Commission to help victims deal with the consequences of this crime.

Tens of thousands of Americans have been victims of identity theft. Impostors often run up huge debts, file for bankruptcy, and commit serious crimes. It can take years for victims of identity theft to restore their credit ratings and their reputations. This legislation will enable the United States Secret Service, the Federal Bureau of Investigation, and other law enforcement agencies to combat this type of crime, which can financially devastate its victims.

I want to thank the Vice President for his leadership on this and other privacy issues. As we enter the Information Age, it is critical that our newest technologies support our oldest values.

WILLIAM J. CLINTON

The White House,
October 30, 1998.

NOTE: H.R. 4151, approved October 30, was assigned Public Law No. 105–318.

Statement on Signing the Torture Victims Relief Act of 1998
October 30, 1998

Today I am pleased to sign into law H.R. 4309, the "Torture Victims Relief Act of 1998." This Act authorizes continued and expanded U.S. contributions to treatment centers, both in the United States and around the world, for persons who suffer from the mental and physical anguish of having been tortured.

The United States has contributed to these centers for many years—directly to domestic centers through the Department of Health and Human Services and to overseas centers through the Agency for International Development, and indirectly, through Department of State contributions to the United Nations Voluntary Fund for the Victims of Torture. Contributions of this nature are a concrete and practical step that the U.S. Government takes to mitigate the effects of this serious, and far too pervasive, human rights violation.

I want to stress, however, that assisting torture victims does not end the curse of torture. The United States will continue its efforts to shine a spotlight on this horrible practice wherever it occurs, and we will do all we can to bring it to an end.

I want to take this opportunity to thank all those who have contributed to the successful passage of this legislation. I also salute those nongovernmental organizations active in the cause of human rights, who encouraged congressional passage of this Act and who work tirelessly to keep alive the spirit of human rights, in our hearts and in our domestic and foreign policy.

WILLIAM J. CLINTON

The White House,
October 30, 1998.

NOTE: H.R. 4309, approved October 30, was assigned Public Law No. 105–320.

Statement on the Council on Environmental Quality Chair Transition
October 30, 1998

Today, with regret, I accept the resignation of Kathleen McGinty as Chair of the Council on Environmental Quality.

As my principal environmental policy adviser for nearly 6 years, Katie has led this administration's efforts to protect and restore our environment. From the forests of the Pacific Northwest to Florida's Everglades and the red-rock canyons of Utah, she has helped preserve America's natural legacy for all time. And from our air to our water to our climate, she has worked tirelessly to ensure our children and grandchildren an environment both healthy and safe.

In all these endeavors, Katie has been guided by the firm belief that the environment truly is a common ground. She has strived to promote collaboration over conflict and to demonstrate that a healthy economy and a healthy environment not only are compatible but are inextricably linked. Indeed, today we enjoy the strongest economy and cleanest environment in a generation. I am deeply grateful for Katie's vision, dedication, and hard work.

I am pleased to announce that beginning November 7, upon Katie's departure, George T. Frampton, Jr., will become acting Chair of CEQ. I will formally announce my intent to nominate Mr. Frampton as Chair, and will submit nomination papers to the Senate, at the appropriate time.

Mr. Frampton comes to his position at CEQ with a wealth of experience in environmental matters. He served as Assistant Secretary of Interior for Fish and Wildlife and Parks from 1993 to 1997, and prior to that was president of the Wilderness Society. In addition, he has served as a law clerk for Supreme Court Justice Harry Blackmun, Deputy Director of the Nuclear Regulatory Commission's inquiry into the nuclear accident at Three Mile Island, and a visiting lecturer in constitutional law at Duke University Law School.

The President's Radio Address
October 31, 1998

Good morning. I'm speaking to you today from the Glen Forest Elementary School in Falls Church, Virginia, where I'm joined by students, parents, and teachers to talk about a problem they understand all too well: the urgent need in America for school construction. In fact, I'm speaking to you from one of nine trailer classrooms that sit outside the schoolhouse on what used to be a playground, because there's simply not enough room inside for all the students. And the 10th trailer goes up in a matter of days.

Falls Church is not the only place with this problem. Rundown schools and rising enrollments have made these trailers an increasingly common sight all over our country. Too many children are going to school every day in trailers like this one. In other schools, class is held in gymnasiums and cafeterias. I've even heard some stories of classes being held in closets. Crumbling walls and ceilings have forced still other schools to bus their students to neighboring facilities.

With a record number of school buildings in disrepair, especially in our larger cities, and school enrollments all over America at record highs and rising by the millions, the need to renew our Nation's public schools has never been more pressing. I've said many times that in this increasingly global world where what you earn depends upon what you learn, improving education must be our Nation's top priority for all our children.

For nearly 6 years now, I've done everything I could to meet that challenge. I'm especially proud of the victories for America's children our administration fought for and won in the balanced budget Congress passed just last week. We fought for and won new investments, from child literacy to college mentoring, from after-school programs to summer school programs, to opening the doors of college even wider by helping more people with financial aid. All these things will help all our children reach their highest potential no matter where they start out in life and where they go to school.

Perhaps even more important, we fought for and won an unprecedented commitment to put 100,000 new well-trained teachers in our Nation's classrooms, to reduce class size, decrease discipline problems, and increase student learning. But you don't have to be a math whiz to know that more teachers and smaller classes means we also need more classrooms. Unfortunately, the Republican leadership in Congress failed the simple test to pass my school construction initiative to help communities build, repair, and modernize 5,000 schools around our country.

I'm disappointed that Congress also blocked our efforts to raise academic standards and strengthen accountability in our schools. At a time when our children's education matters more than ever to our children's future and to our Nation's strength in the 21st century, there are still even some Republicans in Congress who would shut down the Department of Education.

Now, in just a few days Americans will go to the polls to elect the next Congress. And there's a lot at stake. Our children don't need another 2 years of partisanship; they need 2 years of progress, of putting people over politics. And we need a Congress that doesn't retreat from our commitment to hire 100,000 teachers; a Congress that makes a commitment to modern schools so those teachers can teach in classrooms, not in trailers; a Congress that puts aside partisanship and puts our children's future first.

The American people have the power to elect that kind of Congress. Our children are counting on us to do it. So this Tuesday, let me urge all of you, without regard to your party, please, go out and vote for a Congress that will strengthen education and strengthen our Nation for the 21st century.

Thanks for listening.

NOTE: The President spoke at 10:06 a.m. from Glen Forest Elementary School, Falls Church, VA.

Remarks to the Community at Glen Forest Elementary School in Falls Church, Virginia
October 31, 1998

The President. Good morning.

Audience members. Good morning.

The President. First, I would like to thank Susan Fitz, Fran Jackson; the teachers, Lori Kuzniewski—I was in her class—Ms. Kristen Mullen's class; Alan Leis, Paula Johnson, your superintendents; John Butterfield, from the education association; Jim and Molly Cameron, from the PTA; all the people who made me feel so welcome at this school today.

This is the best of our country's future. I look around this crowd today, and I see people whose roots are all over the world, whose languages are very different, whose cultures are different, whose religions are different, who have come together on this school ground in a common endeavor of learning with a promise that our country opens to all people who are willing to work hard and be good citizens and do their part. It is thrilling for me to be here and look at you. I have a much better view than you do today.

And I loved being with the children in the classroom. The best part of this morning so far, for me, has been answering the children's questions. They ask very good questions; some of them I didn't want to answer even, they were so good. [*Laughter*] And it gave me a great deal of hope for the future.

You just heard my weekly radio address, so you know that I am very concerned about the overcrowding in our Nation's classrooms. We have, almost suddenly, the largest group of schoolchildren in our Nation's history. I was part of the last large group, the baby boom generation; all of us are now between the ages of 34 and 52. This group in school today is the first group that is larger.

We have two huge problems: One is represented here, all the housetrailers; the other is represented by the dilemma in our largest cities, where we have huge numbers of students and wonderful old school buildings that were unoccupied for many years. They deteriorated. Many of them now can't even be hooked up to the Internet. And we must, as a nation, face this challenge.

In the last Congress, we were able to get a big downpayment on my plan for 100,000 more teachers in the early grades to take the average size of the classes down to 18 across America in the first 3 grades. But we have to have the school buildings, as well. And I did present a plan to the Congress, that I will present again early next year, that would enable us to build or modernize 5,000 schools. If you want the smaller classes, the teachers have to have some place to meet with the students.

And I ask all of you, based on your personal experience here and without regard to any political differences you may otherwise have, to please, please help me convince the Congress that it is the right thing for America's children to have the smaller classes, to have more teachers, and to have modern schools. Every single child in America deserves them, and the United States ought to be in the forefront of helping achieve that. And I thank you for that.

Let me also say to all of you, I learned when I came here today, because I received a little card from one of the students, that next week is the week you have student elections at the school here. Now, all the students are going to vote. And what I'd like to say is, I hope that all the parents will be just as good citizens as the students are. Because Tuesday is election day in America, as well.

For nearly 6 years, I have worked hard to bring our country together across all the lines that divide us, so that America would work the way this school works, so that we could all feel the way I think all of you feel today, coming from your different walks of life to this common ground. America ought to be a place of common ground, where we move forward together.

I am grateful for the fact that after 6 years we have nearly 17 million new jobs and the lowest unemployment in 28 years; the highest homeownership in history, over two-thirds of Americans in their own homes for the first time ever; the smallest percentage of our people on public assistance, welfare, in 29 years; lowest crime rate in 25 years. I am proud of that. I am also determined that we take this moment

of prosperity, which has given us the first balanced budget since 1969 and a surplus, to meet the long-term challenges of America.

We talked about education today. There are other long-term challenges. Those of you who come from the rest of the world and have come here as immigrants, who have relatives in other countries, know that there is a lot of financial turmoil in the rest of the world. I have done my best to try to help stabilize the global economy because America depends upon the success of other people in other countries and their being able to have good jobs and raise their children and do better.

I have done my best to see America stand on the forefront of world peace. A week ago yesterday, we announced the latest agreement between the Palestinians and the Israelis, and we hope it will be fully and faithfully implemented. And we will continue the work toward peace in the Middle East.

We have to look ahead to what happens when this huge generation of baby boomers retires, which is why I have said we should not spend this surplus on anything until we have reformed the Social Security system and reformed the Medicare system, to make sure that it can be preserved for the people who need it, especially when all the baby boomers retire.

We have to continue to work on the fact that many of our people, literally over half of our people, are in HMO's or other managed care plans. And this can be a good thing, because we have to save all the money we can. But it is wrong if a person is in a health care plan and the doctor says, "You need to see a specialist," and the plan says no. It is wrong if someone is in a car accident and they have to pass three hospitals that are closer on the way to an emergency room that happens to be covered by the plan. It is wrong if someone is pregnant and during the pregnancy, or someone is sick with cancer and has had chemotherapy and during that treatment, an employer changes health care providers and the person has to change doctors.

All of that is wrong. That's why we want a Patients' Bill of Rights, basically to say: Okay, let's manage the system, but let's put the health care of our people first and let medical decisions be made by medical professionals, not accountants. I think that is very important.

All these issues are out there, issues that will affect the long-term stability and strength of the

United States and our ability to do what should be done in the world.

So let me say that I've been very concerned periodically over the last 6 years, and I was especially concerned last year, that in Washington, DC, in National Government, there are not only different parties with different philosophies and different views—that is a good thing; we should have different parties, different philosophies, different views, different opinions—but there is a great deal of difference in constructive debate and extreme partisanship which keeps things from being done.

In the last year, for 8 months, we had extreme partisanship which kept things from being done. And what we need to do is to put the progress of all of our people over the partisanship; we need to put people over politics; we need to celebrate our differences, but work together.

That is what I am hoping will come out of this coming election. I hope that a Congress will be elected on Tuesday that will put the education of our children first and build or modernize these 5,000 schools.

I hope the election will produce a Congress that will not spend that surplus until we fix Social Security first, to stabilize our country, to stabilize our economy, and to avoid a situation where when we retire we will have to either lower our standard of living or lower the standard of living of our children because we refused to take this moment to fix the Social Security system.

I hope the next Congress will provide the American people with a Patients' Bill of Rights.

I hope the next Congress will provide the American people with a bill to protect our children from the dangers of tobacco, the number one public health problem in America today. It is wrong that 3,000 children start smoking every day; 1,000 will die sooner because of this.

I hope the next Congress will reach across partisan lines and raise the minimum wage for 12 million Americans. The unemployment rate is low; the inflation rate is low. You cannot support a family on $5.15 an hour. We can

afford to do it, and we should do it, and we ought to do it as Americans, across partisan lines.

I hope the next Congress will produce a genuine and bipartisan system of campaign finance reform, so that honest debate, instead of big money, controls elections.

All of these things are within your hands. So I say to all the adults who are here: Look at these children; look at how fortunate we are that they can come together and learn from each other and have the right kind of disagreements and go have an election next week in which they campaign and make their case and everybody votes. We should set a good example. This country is still around after 220 years, having undergone unbelievable changes in the makeup of our citizenry, because more than half the time, more than half the people have been right on the big issues.

This is no ordinary time. The world is changing very fast. It is, therefore, no ordinary election. The future of these children, the future of our country in the 21st century, is riding on it. So I implore all of you, if the education of our children is important to you, if the stability of our country and the stability and cause of peace in the world is important to you, please set a good example. Show up on Tuesday, vote, make your voice heard, and go home and talk to your children about what you did and how it is at the core of everything that makes our country worth living and fighting for.

Thank you, and God bless you all.

NOTE: The President spoke at 10:45 a.m. on the athletic field. In his remarks, he referred to principal Susan Fitz and teachers Fran Jackson, Lori Kuzniewski, and Kristen Mullen, Glen Forest Elementary School; Alan Leis, deputy superintendent of schools, and Paula Johnson, area superintendent, Fairfax County, VA; John Butterfield, president, Fairfax Education Association; and Jim and Molly Cameron, co-presidents, Parent Teacher Association.

Statement on Signing the Utah Schools and Land Exchange Act of 1998
October 31, 1998

Today I am very pleased to sign into law H.R. 3830, the "Utah Schools and Land Exchange Act of 1998."

This legislation is an occasion for celebration for the people of Utah and, indeed, all Americans who care about environmental protection and public land management.

This exchange of land, mineral rights, commercial properties, and natural treasures between the United States and the State of Utah is the largest such land exchange in the history of the lower 48 States. The exchange will help capitalize a long-neglected State school trust by putting it on solid footing and allowing it to pay rewards to the children of Utah for generations to come. The United States will obtain valuable land, thus allowing it to consolidate resources within the Grand Staircase-Escalante National Monument, the Goshute and Navajo Indian Reservations, and national parks and forests in Utah.

This Act brings to an end 6 decades of controversy surrounding State lands within Utah's national parks, forests, monuments, and reservations, and ushers in a new era of cooperation and progressive land management. We have shown that good faith, hard work, bipartisanship, and a commitment to protect both the environment and the taxpayer can result in a tremendous victory for all. I especially wish to thank Secretary of the Interior Bruce Babbitt and Kathleen McGinty, outgoing Chair of the Council on Environmental Quality, for their contribution to this major achievement.

The Grand Staircase-Escalante National Monument, a magnificent natural wonder and scientific treasure trove, was born 2 years ago. On that day, I made a promise to work to ensure that Utah's schoolchildren, the beneficiaries of the State trust holdings within the Monument, would in fact benefit from, and not be harmed by, the establishment of this national showcase.

I am proud to say we have kept our promise. We have delivered more, and in a shorter time, than perhaps anyone believed possible. In these 2 years, we have worked closely with citizens and elected officials alike to make America's newest National Monument a success of which we all can be proud.

This bipartisan legislation shows that we can work together for the common good, for our environment, for education, and for our shared legacy as stewards of the Nation's natural public land treasures.

WILLIAM J. CLINTON

The White House,
October 31, 1998.

NOTE: H.R. 3830, approved October 31, was assigned Public Law No. 105–335.

Statement on Signing the William F. Goodling Child Nutrition Reauthorization Act of 1998
October 31, 1998

Today I am signing into law H.R. 3874, the "William F. Goodling Child Nutrition Reauthorization Act of 1998." This legislation extends the authorization of appropriations for a number of child nutrition programs, including the Special Supplemental Nutrition Program for Women, Infants, and Children—more commonly known as WIC—and the Summer Food Service and Farmers Market Nutrition Programs. In addition, it makes various amendments to these programs to expand children's access to food assistance and improve the programs' operation, management, integrity, and safety. I am pleased that this Act includes many provisions that my Administration proposed.

The Act will help to improve the nutritional and health status of America's most needy children. In particular, H.R. 3874 permits schools and other nonprofit institutions providing after-school care to older, "at-risk" youth to receive meal supplements at no charge. In addition, it continues to allow children in the Even Start Family Literacy Program to be eligible for free school meals.

The Act makes a number of changes to improve the administration, efficiency, and integrity of the child nutrition programs while protecting health and safety standards. It removes barriers to the participation of private, nonprofit organizations in the Summer Food Service Program, especially in rural areas, and streamlines many National School Lunch Program procedures. In addition, it revises program licensing requirements to allow more child care providers to provide Federally funded snacks to needy children. Furthermore, it ensures health and safety inspections of school food service operations where they are currently not required.

The Act is tough on fraud and abuse. It allows the Department of Agriculture to permanently disqualify from the WIC program vendors convicted of trafficking food instruments—such as WIC vouchers or electronic benefit transfer cards—or selling firearms, ammunition, explosives, or controlled substances in exchange for them. In addition, it requires WIC applicants to appear in person to apply for benefits and document their income as a condition of receiving benefits.

It is well known that a strong relationship exists between children's nutritional status and their ability to learn, and I remain vitally concerned that all school children have what they need to succeed in school. In joining together to support H.R. 3874, my Administration and the Congress have forged a bipartisan opportunity to improve the nutrition, health, and well-being of our Nation's children. I am pleased to sign this legislation into law.

WILLIAM J. CLINTON

The White House,
October 31, 1998.

NOTE: H.R. 3874, approved October 31, was assigned Public Law No. 105–336.

Statement on Signing the Haskell Indian Nations University and Southwestern Indian Polytechnic Institute Administrative Systems Act of 1998
October 31, 1998

Today I am signing into law H.R. 4259, the "Haskell Indian Nations University and Southwestern Indian Polytechnic Institute Administrative Systems Act of 1998." Haskell Indian Nations University (Haskell) and Southwestern Indian Polytechnic Institute (SIPI) are the only Federally owned and operated schools in the United States dedicated to higher education for American Indians. Together they have provided thousands of American Indians valuable educational opportunities. This Act will broaden and increase those opportunities by assisting both institutions in their ongoing efforts to attract and retain highly qualified administrators, faculty, and staff.

The Act authorizes Haskell and SIPI each to conduct a 5-year demonstration project to test the feasibility and desirability of alternative personnel management systems designed to meet the special staffing circumstances in a college and university setting. Currently, Haskell and SIPI operate under the same civil service personnel system as most other Federal agencies. The demonstration projects authorized by H.R. 4259 will provide these schools flexibility to test personnel reforms in areas such as recruitment, hiring, compensation, training, discipline, promotion, and benefits. At the same time, the Act maintains continued adherence to applicable laws and regulations on matters such as equal employment opportunity, Indian preference, and veterans' preference. My expectation is that, at the conclusion of these demonstration projects, these schools will have tested alternative personnel systems that maintain important employee benefits and protections while promoting the flexibility necessary in a college and university setting.

In signing H.R. 4259, I recognize that the legislation raises several concerns. It allows Haskell and SIPI to conduct demonstration projects involving leave and other employee benefits, such as retirement, health benefits, and life insurance—something no other Federal agency has been permitted to do. We must be mindful that altering employees' benefits for even a brief portion of their careers can have a serious long-term effect. Should such modifications be applied to a large number of Federal employees through other demonstration projects they could have a damaging effect on the Federal retirement and insurance trust funds, which depend on spreading risk of loss over the largest possible group of individuals. These concerns are compounded by the fact that H.R. 4259 does not provide for the level of oversight by the Office of Personnel Management (OPM) that is typically required for personnel-related demonstration projects.

Because of these concerns, I am directing the Secretary of the Interior and the presidents of Haskell and SIPI to involve the OPM fully in the development and evaluation of the schools' demonstration projects. This involvement is only appropriate given the OPM's important role in managing and safeguarding Federal employee benefits programs and overseeing demonstration projects. Further, I strongly urge the Congress to await the outcome of the OPM's ongoing comprehensive review of the Government-wide benefits package for Federal employees before authorizing other demonstration projects outside the OPM's current statutory authority.

With these caveats, I trust that H.R. 4259 will prove helpful to Haskell and SIPI in attracting and retaining highly qualified employees, thereby enabling them to continue to fulfill their important mission of providing quality higher education opportunities to American Indians.

WILLIAM J. CLINTON

The White House,
October 31, 1998.

NOTE: H.R. 4259, approved October 31, was assigned Public Law No. 105–337.

Statement on Signing the Iraq Liberation Act of 1998
October 31, 1998

Today I am signing into law H.R. 4655, the "Iraq Liberation Act of 1998." This Act makes clear that it is the sense of the Congress that the United States should support those elements of the Iraqi opposition that advocate a very different future for Iraq than the bitter reality of internal repression and external aggression that the current regime in Baghdad now offers.

Let me be clear on what the U.S. objectives are:

The United States wants Iraq to rejoin the family of nations as a freedom-loving and law-abiding member. This is in our interest and that of our allies within the region.

The United States favors an Iraq that offers its people freedom at home. I categorically reject arguments that this is unattainable due to Iraq's history or its ethnic or sectarian make-up. Iraqis deserve and desire freedom like everyone else.

The United States looks forward to a democratically supported regime that would permit us to enter into a dialogue leading to the reintegration of Iraq into normal international life.

My Administration has pursued, and will continue to pursue, these objectives through active application of all relevant United Nations Security Council resolutions. The evidence is overwhelming that such changes will not happen under the current Iraq leadership.

In the meantime, while the United States continues to look to the Security Council's efforts to keep the current regime's behavior in check, we look forward to new leadership in Iraq that has the support of the Iraqi people. The United States is providing support to opposition groups from all sectors of the Iraqi community that could lead to a popularly supported government.

On October 21, 1998, I signed into law the Omnibus Consolidated and Emergency Supplemental Appropriations Act, 1999, which made $8 million available for assistance to the Iraqi democratic opposition. This assistance is intended to help the democratic opposition unify, work together more effectively, and articulate the aspirations of the Iraqi people for a pluralistic, participatory political system that will include all of Iraq's diverse ethnic and religious groups. As required by the Emergency Supplemental Appropriations Act for FY 1998 (Public Law 105–174), the Department of State submitted a report to the Congress on plans to establish a program to support the democratic opposition. My Administration, as required by that statute, has also begun to implement a program to compile information regarding allegations of genocide, crimes against humanity, and war crimes by Iraq's current leaders as a step towards bringing to justice those directly responsible for such acts.

The Iraq Liberation Act of 1998 provides additional, discretionary authorities under which my Administration can act to further the objectives I outlined above. There are, of course, other important elements of U.S. policy. These include the maintenance of U.N. Security Council support efforts to eliminate Iraq's prohibited weapons and missile programs and economic sanctions that continue to deny the regime the means to reconstitute those threats to international peace and security. United States support for the Iraqi opposition will be carried out consistent with those policy objectives as well. Similarly, U.S. support must be attuned to what the opposition can effectively make use of as it develops over time. With those observations, I sign H.R. 4655 into law.

WILLIAM J. CLINTON

The White House,
October 31, 1998.

NOTE: H.R. 4655, approved October 31, was assigned Public Law No. 105–338. H.R. 4328, the Omnibus Consolidated and Emergency Supplemental Appropriations Act, 1999, was assigned Public Law No. 105–277.

Statement on Signing the Women's Health Research and Prevention Amendments of 1998
October 31, 1998

Today I am pleased to sign into law S. 1722, the "Women's Health Research and Prevention Amendments of 1998," which will significantly advance women's health by strengthening national efforts to improve research and screening on diseases with particular impact on women, including osteoporosis, breast and ovarian cancer, and cardiovascular diseases.

This bill will authorize several women's health and research screening activities at the National Institutes of Health and the Centers for Disease Control for the next 5 years. It will expand coordinated Federal research into heart disease, strokes, and other cardiovascular diseases among women. In addition, life-saving screening for breast and cervical cancer will continue to be made available to thousands of low-income women.

I commend the sponsors of this bipartisan legislation, including Senator Bill Frist and cosponsors Senators Barbara Boxer, Barbara Mikulski, and Patty Murray, for their contributions that will help protect women from these deadly diseases and advance our scientific knowledge.

WILLIAM J. CLINTON

The White House,
October 31, 1998.

NOTE: S. 1722, approved October 31, was assigned Public Law No. 105–340.

Statement on Signing the Women's Progress Commemoration Act
October 31, 1998

Today I am pleased to sign into law S. 2285, the "Women's Progress Commemoration Act." This legislation establishes a 15-member Commission, appointed by the President and the

Congress to help commemorate, celebrate, and preserve women's history in America.

It is appropriate that we establish this Commission on the 150th anniversary of the Seneca Falls Convention, the first national congregation on the conditions and rights of women in the United States. It was there, at a time when women were denied many of the rights of citizenship, that 100 brave women and men proclaimed in their "Declaration of Sentiments" that "all men and women are created equal."

At Seneca Falls and throughout our history, women have braved enormous challenges and helped to build our Nation—from women patriots hiding General Washington's soldiers from the British, to Sojourner Truth and others leading slaves out of bondage, to suffragists risking imprisonment to secure for women the most basic rights of democracy. The Women's Progress Commemoration Commission will seek out the historical sites of such great moments in our Nation's history, and recommend the best way to preserve them for generations to come. The President's Commission on the Celebration of Women in American History, that I created by executive order in June of this year looks forward to working with the Commission created by S. 2285.

As we approach a new century and a new millennium, it is more important than ever that we honor these monuments to our enduring ideals. Therefore, it is with great pleasure that I sign this legislation.

WILLIAM J. CLINTON

The White House,
October 31, 1998.

NOTE: S. 2285, approved October 31, was assigned Public Law No. 105–341. Executive Order 13090 of June 29 on the President's Commission on the Celebration of Women in American History was published in the *Federal Register* at 63 FR 36151.

Joint Statement of the President of the United States and the Prime Minister of Israel
October 31, 1998

On October 31, 1998, President Clinton and Prime Minister Netanyahu concluded a Memorandum of Agreement on the potential threat to Israel posed by the proliferation of ballistic missiles and weapons of mass destruction in the region. This subject has been of great concern to both governments for some time, and the Memorandum of Agreement establishes a new mechanism for enhancing their cooperation in dealing with this potential threat. Pursuant to the Memorandum of Agreement, a joint strategic planning committee will be established to formulate recommendations on upgrading the framework of U.S.-Israeli strategic and military relationships, as well as technological cooperation.

NOTE: An original was not available for verification of the content of this joint statement.

Interview With Shlomo Raz and Jacob Eilon of Israeli Television Channel 2
October 31, 1998

Q. President Clinton, first of all, thank you very much for sitting down with us.

The President. Delighted to do it. Thank you.

Prime Minister Yitzhak Rabin's Legacy

Q. You know, it's exactly 3 years since the assassination of Prime Minister Yitzhak Rabin.

And Mrs. Rabin said she was rather disappointed that you failed to mention her husband during the East Room ceremony last Friday. How do you respond to that?

The President. Well, you know, the agreement is actually supposed to enter into force on the third anniversary of his passing, of his killing. And I think that if, in fact, it does do so, it is a fitting thing, because none of us would be here if it hadn't been for him. He really started all this in a profound way.

I know that the Madrid conference started before his election, but it was his conviction and his strength and security that he conveyed to the people of Israel, I think, that made this whole peace process possible. And I never do anything in the process that I don't think about him.

Prime Minister Binyamin Netanyahu

Q. Mr. President, from the tragic assassination to the current situation, Prime Minister Netanyahu might put himself at the same risk as Mr. Rabin. So perhaps it is unjustified to put pressure on him to follow the Oslo accord or the Oslo track.

The President. Well, I don't think there's any question that the Prime Minister has put himself at some physical risk in pursuing the peace process. But I believe that it's important that the people of Israel know that, at least in my opinion, it's a good agreement; that it strengthens Israel's security needs; that the agreements made with the Palestinians are fully consistent with Oslo.

And the Prime Minister worked very, very hard to advance Israel's security interests. Just for example, there was the whole issue of what should be done with the people whom Israel believes have committed acts of violence and terrorism against Israelis. And I am convinced that the Palestinians will now act against these people in a way that is consistent with the agreement and that will meet the Prime Minister's and Israel's needs. So that's an example of a whole array of security advances that were embedded in this agreement. And I think all Israelis who support the peace process should support the agreement because I think it furthers the cause of peace.

Palestinian National Council

Q. Mr. President, is it really the PNC, the Palestinian National Council, that is going to convene to revise the Palestinian covenant with your presence? Is it really the PNC?

The President. Well, it's the PNC plus a number of other groups. And some of these groups are embedded within the PNC; that is, they're dual membership for some of the people—in the Government, in the executive council, in the other councils involved. And some are outside the PNC.

But among other things at that meeting, we will seek a clear renunciation of the offending parts of the charter and a general endorsement of the agreement, this whole agreement, so that the process can be seen to be going forward with the support of those who represent grassroots Palestinian opinion.

The Prime Minister wanted me to support this provision, this effort, and he fought very, very hard for this, as did a number of members of his Cabinet who were there, because they thought that there needed to be a debate in a Palestinian forum, even if it was controversial and heated, which would give to the Palestinian people some evidence not only of a commitment to follow an agreement but of a changing of the heart, an opening of the heart of the Palestinians toward the Israelis.

And I thought that argument had a lot of appeal, even though it was not without its hazards for Mr. Arafat.

Q. Because——

The President. Because it's been 18 months since anything big has happened, and because there's a lot of—he has his problems, too, among them the fact that the standard of living for most Palestinians is lower today than it was when the peace process began, because the enemies of peace keep interrupting the flow of normal life.

So I agreed that if it was that important to Israel and Chairman Arafat were willing to try to accommodate that condition by the Israelis, that I would go to Gaza and address this group and ask them to support the peace and to renounce forever the idea of animosity toward and opposition to the existence of the state of Israel, and instead embrace the path not only of peace but of cooperation.

President's Upcoming Visit to Gaza

Q. I want to ask you about your visit to Gaza. Don't you think, Mr. President, that this trip may be seen as a first step in recognizing an independent Palestinian state?

The President. Well, if so it would be, I think, wrong, because I have tried strictly to adhere to the position of the United States that we would not take a position on any final status issue.

One of the reasons that I worked so hard at Wye to try to bring the parties together is, I thought it imperative to take this next big step along the peace process so that we could launch the final status talks and get them underway in good faith, so that neither side would seek to prejudge a final status issue. That is not what I'm doing in going there. The Prime Minister wanted me to go there and wanted us all to make this pitch.

I asked them if they would make some joint appearances and if they would both make the same speech to Palestinian and to Israeli audiences. And they said they would do that. I would like to see that happen; I think that would help. It would help the Palestinians to see Yasser Arafat saying the same thing to the Israelis he says to the Palestinians. It would help the Israelis, I think, also. And it would be a good thing for the Prime Minister to be able to give the same speech—whatever they decide to say, just say the same thing to both communities so that no one thinks that there's any evasion or shading or anything.

I think, just little things like this to open up a little awareness of the other's position and build a little confidence, I think would be quite good.

Jonathan Pollard

Q. Mr. President, why won't you release Jonathan Pollard?

The President. Well, I agreed to review his case and to take the initiative to review it. I have not released him in the past because since I've been President in the two previous normal reviews—that is, the ones that were initiated by his request for clemency—the recommendation of all my law enforcement and security agencies was unanimously opposed to it.

But the Prime Minister felt so strongly about it—and I might say, every Israeli Prime Minister I have dealt with on every occasion has asked me about Pollard. Yitzhak Rabin did, Shimon Peres did, and Prime Minister Netanyahu has.

Q. But you argued pretty—you had pretty harsh exchanges with Netanyahu, reportedly, about that?

The President. No. I thought then, I believe now, and I think the public opinion in Israel bears this out, that it was in Israel's interest to do this agreement on its own merits because it would advance the cause of Israeli security and keep the peace process going.

I think there's been a lot of reporting about this with which I don't necessarily agree. That's no criticism; I just want to tell you my perception. Bibi Netanyahu argued strongly for Pollard's release. He made the arguments that anyone who knows a lot about the case and thinks he should be released would make. But I took no offense at that. He was representing what he believes to be the interest of the State of Israel. And he did it in—you know, he doesn't make arguments halfway. You observe the Prime Minister, he's an aggressive person; he fights hard for what he believes. I took no offense at it at all.

And I would ask you all to remember, when evaluating reports that tempers were frayed or strong language was used—now, remember, the three of us, Mr. Arafat and Mr. Netanyahu and I, we were there for over 8 days. Most nights I was there, I went home at 2 and 3 o'clock in the morning. The last time we were there on this last day, I was up for 39 hours and so were they.

Now, I'm amazed that we didn't have more disruptive conduct and more harsh words, given how exhausted and frayed we were. But it shows you how hard the parties were trying, on the one hand, to make peace, but on the other hand, to protect their security interests. Particularly, I think, that was Mr. Netanyahu's concern. He was desperately trying to find a way to make peace or to advance the peace process that would enable him to go home and sell it to his Cabinet and his constituency. And this Pollard issue was very important to him. But I took no offense at that.

Q. But still, Mr. President, there were many reports that you were very upset with Mr. Netanyahu and were quoted saying that his behavior was despicable.

The President. That report is not true. That's just inaccurate. And this is the first opportunity I've had to say that. There was a moment in the negotiations when the two guys split apart, and there was an issue raised that I thought was wrong. And I said so in very graphic terms. But I never used the word "despicable" to describe the Prime Minister. I did not do that.

There was a moment where I thought—there were various moments in these negotiations when I thought—at least from my perspective, trying to be an honest broker—they were both wrong. You would expect this over 8 days.

But at that moment, the issue at stake had nothing to do with Pollard. It was an issue, a dispute between the Palestinians and the Israelis; it had nothing to do with Pollard. And it is true that there was a moment in which there was a heated exchange in which I said something rather graphic, but I did not adversely characterize the Prime Minister in the way that's reported.

Prime Minister Yitzhak Rabin

Q. I'd like to talk about the late Yitzhak Rabin. I think you know, Mr. President, that when you said the phrase, *shalom chaver*, "goodbye friend," I think you touched many many Israelis in a very, very special way. And we've been curious, how did you come up with this? I even noticed you have a pin that says *shalom chaver* on your desk right here in the Oval Office.

The President. Yes. I have many Jewish Americans working for me here, and they all knew how close I felt to Prime Minister Rabin. And they all knew how heartbroken I was when he was shot. And we were—everybody was sort of coming up with ideas. And Shimon Peres later told me that he had not seen those two words used together before because *chaver*, it's sort of a special word; it goes beyond normal friendship.

And one of my—I wish I could say that I knew enough Hebrew that I came up with it, but one of my staff members suggested that I say it. And they explained it to me, what it meant, and it seemed to be perfect for what I was trying to say. I must say, for me, that was more than a political loss. I felt very close to the Prime Minister, to Mrs. Rabin. I got to know their children, grandchildren. And I think always when I'm pushing the peace process forward that I'm doing it not just for myself but maybe also a little for him.

And I must say, in these last negotiations I was very pleased to see that Prime Minister Netanyahu—I saw in his eyes, I could almost see in his eyes the moment when he really made the decision that, well, maybe the Palestinians were going to make sufficiently specific security commitments that would be on a sufficiently

clear timetable that he could sell not just to the Israeli public at large but to a decisive portion of his own constituency, which is a very different thing, as all of you know better than I do. And he could see that, that he could personally believe that it would advance Israel's security. And I saw that look in his eyes. I felt from that point on that eventually we would get an agreement.

And that's the look that you want to see in a leader's eyes in a situation like that, because I still believe that the right formula is peace and security, and that you really can't have one without the other. But I also believe—I told Mr. Arafat once during these negotiations that we had to get to the point where Israel and the Palestinian Authority had the same enemies and that they felt that if they couldn't get to be friends, at least they could be comrades; and that if we could fulfill a role there, in the way this agreement was written, to build confidence between them on a daily basis, then that would be a good thing for us to do.

Q. Do you think, Mr. President, that things might have been different today if it wasn't for the assassination?

The President. Yes, of course they might have been. But it's hard to know and pointless to speculate. The main thing I think that is important for me, at least from my perspective as an American President and a friend of Israel, it's important for me that the people of Israel know that I watched these peace talks at Wye unfold, and that I believe that the Prime Minister and the members of his Cabinet who were there and his staff were trying their best to advance the cause of Israel's security. I believe that they would never have agreed to this, no matter how much I asked them to do so, if they were not absolutely convinced that it was a real advance for security; and that, therefore, if we can launch the final status talks, we can redeem the sacrifice of Rabin and all the other people who have died and given and given and given to secure Israel's place and future.

NOTE: The interview began at 8:25 p.m. in the Oval Office at the White House. In his remarks, the President referred to Prime Minister Binyamin Netanyahu of Israel; Chairman Yasser

Arafat of the Palestinian Authority; former civilian U.S. Navy intelligence analyst Jonathan Pollard, convicted of treason and espionage in 1987; and Leah Rabin, widow of Yitzhak Rabin. A tape was not available for verification of the content of this interview.

Remarks at the New Psalmist Baptist Church in Baltimore, Maryland
November 1, 1998

Thank you, "Reverend" Cummings. [*Laughter*] It's difficult enough to follow one sermon, much less two. [*Laughter*]

Let me say to Reverend Thomas, I never wanted your message to end. It was wonderful, thank you. I, too, join in wishing Mrs. Thomas a happy birthday. I thank all the wonderful staff and parishioners here at New Psalmist. I have to say that my staff especially appreciated the assistance from Dr. David Blow.

I thank Congressman Cummings for his welcome here. I tell you, I was here about 10 minutes, and I realized how Elijah got to Congress. [*Laughter*] And I thank all of his staff, Vernon Simmons and others. I thank Mayor Schmoke for all the help that your people gave us; thank you, sir. I thank your two wonderful Senators, Senator Sarbanes and Senator Mikulski. Senator Mikulski is running for reelection, but she's going to win by acclamation, so nobody remembers that she's on the ballot. But I think I should tell you that she is, and she would like it very much if you remembered that, as well.

I thank Governor Glendening and Lieutenant Governor Kathleen Kennedy Townsend for all they have done for Maryland, and I commend them to you. Congressman Cardin, thank you for being here. To Secretary of State John Willis, it's his birthday, too, today, by the way. I would like to thank Senator Blount, County Executive Ruppersberger, City Council President Bell, City Comptroller Joan Pratt. And I would like to say a special word of appreciation to a former Congressman and NAACP president and my wonderful, wonderful friend, Kweisi Mfume. Thank you for being here today. Thank you.

Now, it's been more than 40 years since Rosa Parks gave up her seat on a bus in Montgomery, Alabama, to change America forever. Dr. King said it is better to walk in dignity than to ride in shame. And ever since then, America has been on a long walk toward dignity. Some people who are not African-Americans don't know it yet, but we've all been on that walk—not just black Americans, all Americans—for none live in dignity when any are oppressed.

It is a journey this church knows well. Just think about it: 100 years ago, starting with 5 members, to come to this congregation of 6,000 men, women, and children in this magnificent house of worship. This is the day the Lord has made, and we can rejoice in it. You have all this high technology, and you are very modern, but you have not forgotten your mission: not only here, to hear the word of God, but to do it with a food bank, with scholarships for college, with health care, with a Boys Club, with the Girl Scouts, all the things this church is involved in. You have helped each other walk in dignity. You have fulfilled the admonition of the Scripture to be doers of the Word and not hearers only. And on Tuesday you will once again have the chance to be doers.

Now, the message today was from Matthew. So I just kind of rumbled through Matthew at the beginning of the service, not so as to distract my concentration from the message—[*laughter*]—and there are a few things from Matthew I'd like for us to remember. In Matthew, Jesus says to render unto Caesar the things which are Caesar's. Now, back then that didn't mean too much because Caesar was an emperor and all the people had to do to render unto Caesar was to pay their taxes and obey the law. But thank the Lord there is no Caesar in this country. And the good news is, there is no Caesar; the bad news is, the people who have to render have more to do, because you pick the people who make the decisions. You pick the people—or not—depending on what you do.

Elijah was so kind; he said those nice things to me. I'm proud of the fact that the American dream is closer to more Americans than it was 6 years ago, that more Americans can go to college, that we have the lowest poverty rate ever recorded among African-Americans, that we have the smallest welfare rolls in 29 years, and the lowest unemployment in 28 years. I'm proud of all that.

But let me tell you something. If you helped me get there, then you did that. You did that. You heard the pastor say today when he preaches the Word of God, it is God's gift, not his. You heard that, when he said that, didn't you? That's the way democracy works, except you're in the driver's seat. You're Caesar, not me—you—if you are a doer.

Remember when John Glenn went up in space a couple of days ago, didn't we all feel good? It gave all of us who aren't young anymore something to look forward to. [*Laughter*] I was so proud—proud because I know him to be a wonderful, good man; proud because of what he gave our country 36 years ago; but also proud because that was an act of democracy. That space program is paid for by you, voted for by your Congress, supported by your President. But in the end, therefore, if you supported me and those who supported that program, then you had your hand on John Glenn's shoulder when he went up in space. That's what this means. You had your hand on him.

In the last several days as I have traveled around America, so many people have come up to me and said, "Thank you for working for peace in the Middle East. Thank you for staying up for a week"—literally, 39 hours at the end—"Thank you for doing that." And I say to them, "It is my job and my honor. But because you put me there, if you felt good about that, you should feel good about yourself because you helped to make the peace in the Middle East."

Now, that's how this works. That's how this works, this march to dignity, a dignity that Rosa Parks talked about, the dignity that Martin Luther King died for, the dignity that Nelson Mandela spent 10,000 days in jail for. We had the President of Colombia here this week—a country ravaged by civil war, ravaged by drug traffickers—a man who himself was kidnaped, who just by the grace of God was not killed, with a wonderful wife who has had people in her whole family killed. I have worked with people in Colombia for 6 years now. Hundreds of law abiding people have been killed simply for trying to uphold the law. And we too often take this vote for granted and say, "Oh, it doesn't matter what we do."

If you think the things that Congressman Cummings said matter, don't pat me on the back, pat yourselves on the back. That's how this system works. If you think that the things that Senator Sarbanes votes for, that Senator Mikulski votes for, Congressman Cardin votes for; if you think it's a good thing that Lieutenant Governor Kathleen Kennedy Townsend made Maryland the first State in the country to say young children in school ought to serve their communities, it's a part of their education, it'll make them better citizens; if you think it's a good thing that Maryland, under Governor Glendening's leadership, has pioneered education reforms and environmental advances—if you like all that, you did that. You did that. You should feel that it is yours; it is part of your walk to dignity.

And that is what this is about. Tuesday there is no Caesar. Your vote counts as much as mine, counts as much as Speaker Gingrich. [*Laughter*] It does. It counts as much as anybody. It counts as much as people who can contribute vast fortunes to campaigns. Tuesday everything gets evened up again, if you show up.

Now, what I want to say to you is that this is not an ordinary time or an ordinary election. There is a lot at stake. This year, because the Members of Congress here present stood with me, we were able to stop a raid on the surplus before we saved Social Security, and we were able to get the funding for a big downpayment on our goal of 100,000 more teachers. And we did it, in the end, against the opposition of the members of the other party. But there is a lot more to be done.

We want to pass that Patients' Bill of Rights so medical decisions are made by doctors, not accountants. We want to pass that school construction proposal so all these teachers will have classrooms, not trailers, to teach our little children in. We want to raise the minimum wage because unemployment and inflation are low, but you still can't raise a family on $5.15 an hour. We want to pass a juvenile justice bill, yes, that punishes people who have to be, but remembers that the only real answer is to keep more of our children out of trouble in the first place and save our children, give them a chance to have a brighter future.

We want not just to save this surplus and save our economy; we want to reform the Social Security system so that it doesn't go broke when the baby boomers retire and our children will be able to continue to raise our grandchildren without having to take us on their backs. That's what we want to do.

Now, think of what was denied. We are fighting hard for the dignity of a living wage, in the face of partisanship that refused us last time; for a Patients' Bill of Rights, in the face of partisanship that listened to the health insurance companies the last time; for the dignity of sending our children to learn with good teachers and small classes in decent, modernized schools all hooked up to computers and the Internet, in the face of those who opposed us the last time; and we are fighting for the dignity of a secure retirement in old age way into the future, in the face of those who would squander this hard-won surplus on election-year promises.

Now, in this election we've had a tough time. Our friends in the other party have raised over $100 million more than we have. Now, you can do that if you take the positions they took: killing the Patients' Bill of Rights; killing campaign finance reform; refusing to raise the minimum wage; be willing to endanger the rights of mothers and their children and child support in changing the bankruptcy laws; refusing to pass legislation to protect our children from the dangers of tobacco, which still kills more people every year than any other public health problem.

Now, why would this happen? Why would people who live in a democracy vote against modern schools when most people are for them? Because they think most people won't vote. Why would they kill a tobacco reform bill most people support? Because they think most people won't vote. Why would they kill a raise in the minimum wage that most Americans of all incomes support? Because they think most Americans won't vote.

Now, just in case, of course, we got news yesterday that there's actually an effort to keep African-Americans and other minority voters from voting, in voter intimidation in Maryland and in six or seven other States. But you know what? On Tuesday you're in control of the arithmetic again, and you can vote.

I say that not in an angry spirit. You know all over America today there are people in other churches who have a different view, who believe that their principles require them to vote only for people at the extreme right wing of the Republican Party. But if you go back through all America, what is this about?

You know, I used to think because I was a young boy growing up in the South and I came from people that didn't have a lot of money, it used to break my heart when I would see my people, poor working people, be among the most hostile toward our black brothers and sisters. And finally I figured out that they did that, instead of joining hands with them to lift everybody together, because they thought they needed somebody to look down on.

And if you look around the whole world today from the Middle East to Ireland, where my people come from, to the tribal warfare in Africa, to the problems in Bosnia and Kosovo, you see all of this turmoil and human misery caused by people who believe that politics is about gaining power over somebody you can look down on. It's about dividing the country between us and them.

Now, that's why Elijah said the Pledge of Allegiance to you. That's why he said the Pledge of Allegiance. One Nation, indivisible. But make no mistake about it, in the 1950's, when I was a kid growing up, communism was a big problem and stayed so until the end of the cold war, so the dividers in our country would just try to paint their opponents as a little too pink, a little too close to the Communists. Then, we had race as an issue; now, immigrants—always some way to divide up the electorate so that there is us and them.

Now, why don't we have that view? Partly because you know what it's like to be treated like them. Partly because you read the whole Scripture. The Corinthians says, "Now we see through a glass, darkly." What does that mean? We just don't know everything. We don't have a right to look down on people and sort them out because we don't have the whole truth. The whole promise of the Scripture is that we will someday have it: "Now we see through a glass, darkly; but then face to face: now we know in part; but then we will know even as we are known. And now abideth faith, hope and love—charity—and the greatest of these is love." Why is love the greatest of these? Because we're all in this boat together. That's why.

Yes, you know, there's some divisions out there. But Matthew cautions us not to strain at a gnat and swallow a camel. And Matthew reminds us that a city and a house divided against itself cannot stand. What does the Bible say? What does the Bible tell us? One thing the Bible tells us hundreds of times—hundreds and hundreds of times about politics—the only thing it tells us hundreds and hundreds of times is to care for the poor, the weak, the needy. In Matthew, Jesus says, "Verily I say unto you, even as you have done this unto the least of these my brethren, you have also done it unto me." And then down the way a little bit, down the way a few verses it says, "And I say to you, even as you have not done it unto the least of these my brethren, you have not done it unto me."

So I say to you, we believe that our politics should be guided by what our Lord said was the first and most important commandment, and the second is like unto it. First we must try to love the Lord, our God, with all our heart. "And the second is like unto it, thou shalt love thy neighbor as thyself."

So I say, Tuesday is about whether we'll have a Patients' Bill of Rights, whether we'll have good schools for all our children, whether we will raise the minimum wage, whether we will save Social Security for the 21st century. But in a larger sense, it's about that march to dignity. It's about whether your hand is going to be on the shoulder of every person doing every good thing that will be done. It's about whether the people who believe they should divide America can leave you out because you stay home. It's about whether you believe that you have to be a doer.

I appreciate your applause. And I am more grateful by far for just having the chance to share this worship service with you, to be reminded of the truths that I need to hear, too, just like you. You remember that in this country there are only two places—only two, only two— where we have fulfilled both the admonition

of the Scriptures and the promise of the Founders that all of us are created equal—only two. One is when you come into your house of worship on Sunday, and the other is when you show up at the ballot box.

So I ask you: There are thousands here. You will see tens of thousands more between now and Tuesday. Be a doer. Tell them they should show up, too. Take them by the hand and bring them. Tell them about Rosa Parks. Ask them not to forget what Dr. King died for. Ask them not to forget what the issues in this election are.

But ultimately, it really is all about what Congressman Cummings said. I have done everything I could to bring this country together, to reconcile the American people to one another so we could go forward together. But in the end, that must be done by all of us together. And Tuesday, it's your turn. Take it.

Thank you, and God bless you.

NOTE: The President spoke at 1:58 p.m. In his remarks, he referred to Rev. Walter Scott Thomas, pastor, and David L. Blow, assistant pastor, New Psalmist Baptist Church; Reverend Thomas' wife, Patricia; Vernon Simms, district administrator for Representative Elijah E. Cummings; Mayor Kurt Schmoke of Baltimore; Gov. Parris N. Glendening of Maryland; State Senator Clarence W. Blount; Baltimore County Executive C.A. Dutch Ruppersberger; Baltimore City Council President Lawrence A. Bell; Baltimore City Comptroller Joan M. Pratt; civil rights activist Rosa Parks; President Nelson Mandela of South Africa; and President Andres Pastrana of Colombia and his wife, Nohra.

Interview With April Ryan of the American Urban Radio Networks in Baltimore
November 1, 1998

African-American Support/Voter Turnout

Ms. Ryan. Mr. President, thank you so much for joining us today. The focus: the African-American vote, getting African-Americans to the polls on November 3d. For so many weeks some members of the—some White House officials have been saying that you're trying to get every-

one—that there is, indeed, a definite effort to get the African vote; that's why you're at New Psalmist today, to talk to black congregations and blacks throughout the country. Is the African-American vote a make-it-or-break-it vote for this election?

The President. I think in many districts it will be, and perhaps in some of these close Senate seats. And I think it's important just to take a minute to explain why.

Traditionally in the United States, in Presidential elections the vote turnout is much bigger, and then it falls off in midterms. When times are good, as they are now, very often the falloff is even greater. And disproportionately, working people, lower income working people, or poor people are likely to be among those who fall off. Single mothers that have to worry about, on Tuesday, getting their children to school or to child care and then getting them home, going to work and getting back; people that live in cities, who have to take mass transit to work, and maybe the polling place is not on the bus line or the subway line coming home—they've got to go to a lot more trouble.

So we know that the American people as a whole agree with our program that's at stake in this election. They agree with our position on saving Social Security, on building modern schools, on passing the Patients' Bill of Rights, on raising the minimum wage. They agree with our position by 15 or 20 points when contrasted with a positive message from the Republicans. So the only way we won't do very well in this election is if our turnout is lower than theirs. So this is a big issue.

Ms. Ryan. Well, many people said when you first ran for the office that African-Americans brought you into office. Do you think that this African-American vote, if you reinvigorate it through this election, can help many Democrats in years to come, as well as this election?

The President. Oh, of course. And I think it can be something that we can sustain, that is, the idea that every election is important, that not just the Presidential elections but every election is important and helps to shape the future.

I think people understand, after this 8 months of partisan standoff we had in Congress this last year, when really nothing happened until the very end and they had to go through the congressional Democrats and me to get a budget, so they had to agree with us on some budget items for education and other things. I think the American people understand that these congressional elections are profoundly important. The Governors race and other races are profoundly important.

And as I said today in the church, election day is a day that everybody counts the same.

It's a real tragic thing, I think, when people pass the opportunity to be just as powerful as everyone else.

Republican Campaign Ads

Ms. Ryan. Well, as you said, these votes are important. You have people like Newt Gingrich who said—well, the Washington Post said that Newt Gingrich orchestrated attempts to make you look bad through Republican campaign ads. Do you think those ads are confusing to people? And do you also feel, like the Vice President, shocked that he did this?

The President. Well, I'm not—no, I don't feel shocked that he did it. It appeared to me that the message of the ad was, you know, you should be mad at the President; therefore you should punish someone else who had nothing to do with the mistake the President made; and in the end, you should punish yourself—you should deny yourself the Patients' Bill of Rights, deny your children a better education, deny people a rise in the minimum wage, deny the Democrats the votes they need to make sure we don't squander this surplus until we save Social Security.

I don't think it's a very persuasive message, once you tell people what the message is and give them a chance to think about it. And I hope it won't be successful. I don't think it will be.

Voter Turnout

Ms. Ryan. Well, President Clinton, I watched you in church today. You walked the walk, and you talked the talk. You quoted from Matthew. A lot of people called you "Reverend" Clinton. [*Laughter*] But what happens if you cannot generate the kind of support for the blacks to go to the polls like you want? What kind of answers will you have when the finger-pointing starts?

The President. Well, we've done everything we could to get the votes out, and I think we're going to do very well. If you look at the history of these midterm elections, particularly in the sixth year of a Presidency, almost everyone concedes, even the Republicans do, that we're going to outperform the historical average. And of course, it's unbelievable, since they have literally raised, through the Senate and House committees and the Republican National Committee, $110 million more than our people have.

So we're out here to work, and I don't worry about finger-pointing. I just do the best I can and work like crazy until the election is over and hope—you know, we've got a lot of good people out there who have done, I think, astonishing things, being outspent two, three to one in the last week, maybe four to one, or more, still hanging in there in these races. And I just want to make sure we light a fire under our voters and that they know what's at stake. And I think we're going to do pretty well on Tuesday.

African-American Support

Ms. Ryan. Did you see the response from the congregation when you came in? Did you see the people just jump up and shout and just—I mean, the faces were just brimming over with joy that you would come here to this church.

The President. I was very moved.

Ms. Ryan. Do you understand that African-Americans just love William Jefferson Clinton? And you know, it's gotten to the point where there are even some authors that are writing about you. Have you read the piece by Toni Morrison in the New Yorker magazine saying that President Clinton is a black man?

The President. No, but I take it as a compliment.

Ms. Ryan. Oh, do you?

The President. I mean just generally. I haven't read the piece; maybe there is some unflattering things Toni has to say in the piece. [*Laughter*]

Ms. Ryan. But do you understand that the African-American community just embraces you?

The President. Yes, I do. I do. And it has been a source of enormous—pride is the wrong word—but I have been very grateful for it.

A man came up to my wife the other day—a couple months ago and said to Hillary, he said, "You know"—an African-American man said—"the people who attack the President all the time say they don't understand why the African-American community supports him so strongly and why we like him so much." And he said, "It's not a very complicated thing. We support him, and we support you"—talking to Hillary—"because you like us, and we know it, and we can tell."

I don't know, I think it's more than just the policies I've supported and the African-Americans I've appointed to the Cabinet and to the Judiciary. I think people do understand that down deep inside I believe that we ought to

be one America and that we ought not to be fundamentally about race. I think that comes across. That's the only explanation I can give you, and I'm very grateful for it.

Reverend Thomas' Sermon

Ms. Ryan. So getting back to the church service today, the sermon from Reverend Thomas was on spiritual warfare. What did you get out of that?

The President. Well, first of all, I thought it was a very interesting sermon, theologically. He obviously has thought about this a lot; he's thought about what the nature of evil is. And he argued that evil is not embodied in any person or persons; evil infects everybody or threatens to. It's a force of life that is always there.

And then he argued that the church, the meaning of the church was to give redemption and give people who have flaws, who have been through difficulties, a chance to literally be reborn and to serve. And he had that great image of the open doors. The doors of death were only supposed to open one way. But if you believe in God and if you believe in the Christian faith, you believe that you can force the doors back open the other way, into eternal life, not just in death. I thought it was a very powerful sermon. It was both practical but extremely philosophical.

Ms. Ryan. Did it touch you?

The President. Oh, yes. I thought it was a magnificent message.

First Family

Ms. Ryan. President Clinton, you've been really great with me in granting me several interviews. And I want to ask you this, and you can say whatever you want to say. But the American public cares about you, one way or the other, and your personal life has been spread across the newspapers and in television. And your supporters and your detractors both want to know, how are you and the First Lady doing?

The President. Well, the thing that I want the country to know is that I'm doing my best, my dead-level-best, to heal my family—as well as my relationship with the American people—my wife and my daughter. And I love them very much, and I'm working on it. And I think that what the American people, I hope, will agree is that, beyond that, it ought to be private; the good times and the tough times, they ought to be private. I think most Americans want to know that I'm trying to do the right thing, and I can tell you, I am. But I think to talk about it would further degrade the privacy that I think has already been plundered too much in too many ways for too many people in America.

Ms. Ryan. Well, I just want to say this on that point, and that's the end of that, but a lot of—you're public; you are the leader of the free world, and Mrs. Clinton is the First Lady. And you recognize when you walk to the plane, when you have Buddy running around you or, you know, just together, people are looking at body language. You know, you are the President, and you've had something happen that many marriages have had happen. And people want to know, and they watch your body language. How does it make you feel, that you're literally under a microscope just for that right there?

The President. Well, on that, believe it or not—let me just say this. All the pain and humiliation and the anger and every other thing for me is behind me now, and I don't think much about that. What I think about is, how can I take care of my family? How can I take care of my country? I have always found that I should simply trust the American people. I don't agree with every decision they've made in every election. I wish they hadn't elected the Republican majority in 1994. But I've always found that if you give the American people enough time, they get it right. And we're still around here after 220 years because at every important time the American people have gotten it right. So they are free to think about whatever they wish to think, to say whatever they wish to say, to do whatever they wish to do. That's what makes this a great country. And I will continue to work on my family and on my country.

But I will say this to all the American people, without regard to what they think about that or any other issue, as I said to this church today: Tuesday is the only day of the year where every citizen counts the same. Everybody listen to me, everybody within the sound of our voice, yours and mine, on Tuesday they count just as much as I do; they count just as much as Mr. Gingrich does; they count just as much as any editor of any newspaper or any owner of any television network. They count just as much. And the only thing I would do is to implore them to remember that in the end, this country belongs to all the people. And the progress we make depends upon what they do

and, in the case of the voters, whether they do. My main goal for the next 48 hours is to get everybody there.

Iraq

Ms. Ryan. Okay, last question. There are some movements, or nonmovements, in Iraq now. What's the next step through the administration for Saddam Hussein?

The President. Well, we're examining that now. As a matter of fact, this afternoon my national security team is meeting. I've already had a couple of briefings about it. I think it's important to go back to the basics. First of all, let's look at the basics.

At the end of the Gulf war, as part of the conditions of peace, Saddam Hussein agreed to suspend his biological, chemical, and nuclear programs, to be subject to inspections to see that that was done and to see that all the materials were destroyed. We were actually making, I thought, quite a bit of progress in that inspection after the last little crisis we had. And we were moving toward a resolution of some of the issues when he first suspended the inspections and now, apparently, has decided to terminate his participation in the U.N. inspection system.

It's a clear violation of the commitments that he made, a clear violation of the U.N. Security Council resolutions. I, personally, am very pleased that the U.N. Security Council, including some people that I think have been a little tolerant with him in the past, strongly condemned what he did. From my point of view, we should keep all our options open, examine the nature of the action and where we are, and then do what's best for the integrity of the United Nations and the interests, the security interests, of the people of the United States.

I think that's all I should say about it now. I want to let my people meet, let them give me some advice, and see where we go from here.

Voter Turnout

Ms. Ryan. Mr. President, thank you so much. Do you have anything else you'd like to add?

The President. I just hope everybody who is listening to this will go and vote on Tuesday. It's no ordinary time and no ordinary election— big stakes. And when it's over, if you vote, even if you don't get your choice, you'll feel a lot better than if you pass.

Voter Intimidation

Ms. Ryan. Thank you so much.

Mr. President, we have a caveat to our interview. In the sermon—well, not the sermon, but when you spoke to the congregation, you talked about voter intimidation.

The President. Yes.

Ms. Ryan. Now, where is this coming from, and what's going on?

The President. Well, for the last several elections there have been examples in various States of Republicans either actually or threatening to try to intimidate or try to invalidate the votes of African-Americans in precincts that are overwhelmingly African-American, mostly in places where they think it might change the outcome of an election.

And we got some reports yesterday that some unusual steps were going to be taken, which I think you could only conclude would constitute voter intimidation, here in Maryland where we are, and perhaps in Michigan and Kentucky and Georgia and North Carolina and one or two other places. We have always fought it. We asked the Republicans to renounce it yesterday. The idea of having extra police officers just look at people when they go vote, or photographing them or doing videotapes when they go vote, or otherwise trying to scare people off from voting is totally abhorrent.

We don't try to keep anybody from voting for the Republicans. We think they have a perfect right to show up and do it. This is not American, this whole voter intimidation business. And if it's going on as has been reported, it ought to be stopped. I would challenge the Republican Party to stand up and stop it. They ought to be like me. I haven't discouraged any Republicans from voting on Tuesday. All I'm trying to do is get the Democrats to go vote. It would suit me if every registered voter in America would show up. And that ought to be their attitude, too.

Ms. Ryan. But you know what the Republicans are going to say. They're going to say you're coming up with this; you're making this whole thing up.

The President. Well, these reports were quite specific. So they can easily show that they're all wrong, factually. And if they are, then I will say, "Good, we've got both parties now in favor of everybody voting." Listen, nothing would please me more than to say this is something that the Republicans have renounced, and we're going to both be together from now on forever for everybody voting. I would love to say that. I don't take any pleasure in saying what I'm saying here.

NOTE: The interview began at 3:25 p.m. in the Pastor's Parlor at the New Psalmist Baptist Church. In his remarks, the President referred to Rev. Walter Scott Thomas, pastor, New Psalmist Baptist Church; author Toni Morrison; and President Saddam Hussein of Iraq. A tape was not available for verification of the content of this interview.

Telephone Interview With Tom Joyner, Sybil Wilkes, and Myra J. of the Tom Joyner Morning Show
November 2, 1998

Mr. Joyner. We go to Washington, DC, and on the line right now is the President of the United States, President Bill Clinton. Good morning, sir.

The President. Good morning, Tom.

Mr. Joyner. How are you this morning?

The President. I'm great. It's a beautiful day here, a little fall coolness in the air, but it's a beautiful day.

Ms. Wilkes. It's a great day before getting out the vote.

Myra J. Yes.

The President. It is. I hope tomorrow will be as good as today is—with the weather.

African-American Vote

Mr. Joyner. Now, we've been talking all along about how important it is for African-Americans to get out and vote. I want to go back, first of all, and let's talk about the times when black Americans didn't have the right to vote. Because I know that you came up in an era where you can remember the Little Rock Nine; you can remember Medgar Evers; you can remember the four little girls in Birmingham, where a lot of us only know about these events from recent movies.

The President. Absolutely.

Mr. Joyner. But you remember those times.

The President. I lived through all that. I lived through the churches being bombed and people being driven away from the polls. And then I lived through the poll tax era, where people would buy the poll taxes by the roll, and black people had to agree to vote the way they wanted and they—if they could get a certificate for the poll tax. I remembered all that——

Mr. Joyner. ——from Arkansas. And you probably heard a lot of hatred growing up in Arkansas, too.

The President. I did. Of course, I did. To me, the passage of the Civil Rights Act, the voting rights law, the open housing law, all those things, they were the pivotal events of my childhood as far as my citizenship goes—I mean, just the whole civil rights movement. Now I see that we do—at least on election day, we are all equal. As I said yesterday in Baltimore, tomorrow, whatever anybody thinks about all the challenges and problems we still have in America, every single person tomorrow is just as important as the President or the Speaker of the House or Mr. Gates at Microsoft or anybody else. Everybody shows up, and everybody's vote counts, unless you don't show up.

You know what kinds of debates we've had here in Washington over the last couple of years; you know what the big issues are. And the real challenge here is that if this were a Presidential year, then African-American voters, Hispanic voters, working people generally—single mothers who have to work for a living and figure out how to get their kids to child care or to school and work through how to get to the polling place—all these folks would be voting. And it's clear, if that were the case, that we would win the congressional races handily, and we could change the direction of this country. We could end this last 8 months of partisanship we went through and really start building on the successes of the last 6 years.

So what I've got to try to do is persuade enough people just to go out and vote, because this election is not an ordinary congressional election. This Congress will shape how the American people live in important ways for many years to come.

Mr. Joyner. The African-American vote is real important.

The President. Very important. It's important because in these midterm elections, normally, African-Americans do not vote in the same percentages as they do in Presidential elections. And normally the falloff is bigger than it is for hardcore Republican voters, who tend to be older, a little better off, have a little more free time, and more likely to vote. And of course, the so-called Christian Coalition, the very conservative right wing of the Republican Party, they always vote.

So if we want our voices heard and we want to continue the progress of the last 6 years, I need some support in Congress. We had a little more balance in Congress—if we had a few more Democrats in Congress, we could pass the Patients' Bill of Rights to make sure that health care decisions are made by doctors and not insurance company accountants. We could pass Senator Carol Moseley-Braun's school construction initiative to make sure that we have not only 100,000 teachers, but they're teaching our kids in modern schools and not classrooms that are all broken down buildings. We could pass an increase in the minimum wage. And we could stop this raid on the surplus until we save Social Security.

Those are huge issues. And that's really what this election is all about.

2000 Census

Ms. Wilkes. Mr. President, you were saying about African-Americans—and certainly there are a couple of things that are before the U.S. Government in the Congress, specifically, when you're looking at the U.S. census coming up and the importance of that, as well as representation in Congress, which the census obviously affecting that——

The President. Absolutely. Let me say to everyone here listening to us, the census is not just important because it's a way of telling us how many Americans there are and how we break down, what communities and States do we live in, what are our ages, what are our incomes, what are our racial backgrounds. The census also is used to draw the congressional maps and to determine the amount of assistance that comes in education aid and other things to various States and localities.

Now, all I have tried to do in this census is to guarantee that we have an accurate count. In the last census, we know we missed several million Americans, disproportionately Americans of color and Americans who live in urban areas. We know they were not counted. So all we've said is, let's take the most reliable way of doing that. The Republicans are adamantly opposed to the National Academy of Sciences' recommendations. They're opposed to the recommendations even of President Bush's own census taker. And the reason is, I think they don't want all Americans counted because if that happens we'll have a different distribution of the congressional district maps, and it will make a big difference for the long-term future of our country.

Now, this will happen in the year I leave office, 2000, my last year as President. But I just believe I owe it to the future as we grow ever more diverse. And this is not just an issue for African-Americans; this is an issue for Asian-Americans; this is an issue for Hispanic-Americans; this is an issue for new immigrants from even some of the Central European countries, countries of the former Soviet Union. All these people, if they're here, deserve to be counted. If they're citizens, they deserve to be counted and taken into account when we draw the congressional district maps. If they're legal immigrants, they should be counted so that we can give the appropriate distribution of Federal education and health care assistance and other things.

President's Motivation and Goals

Mr. Joyner. You know, Mr. President, I hear you talking about things like that and the fact that you'll be out of office soon, and I just read in the paper the other day about the millions of dollars that you have allocated for African-Americans and other minorities to fight AIDS. And I think that's a tribute to you and your dedication, and it makes me want to ask you what makes you keep pressing forward like this, knowing that you're going to be out of office soon? What makes you keep trying to do these kinds of things?

The President. Well, what would be the point of being President if you didn't use the power of the Presidency to try to solve the problems of the country, to meet the challenges of the country, to seize the opportunities of the country? When I ran for this job, I had a very

clear idea of what I wanted to do. I didn't know, obviously, every decision that would be presented to me or every challenge or crisis that would come up. But I knew that I wanted to turn the country. I wanted to change our economic policy. I wanted to change our education and our welfare policies. I wanted to give more young people the chance to serve their country in national service. But all of it together was designed to create a country that was ready for a new century and a new economy and a new world. And one of the critical things about getting ready is whether every person in this country believes that we're moving toward one America.

You mentioned that AIDS initiative. We got $156 million to try to do special things to reduce the dramatic increase in HIV and AIDS in the African-American community, in the Hispanic community, in other communities of color. That's where the growth is now. How can we be one America if a ravaging disease like this is being brought under control in part of our population but not in another?

So I think this is very important to me. I have—I can rest when I'm not President anymore. I need to work like crazy till the last minute of the last hour of the last day to try to make sure I have done everything I possibly could with this precious 8 years of time the American people gave me.

Mr. Joyner. So what do you want historians to write about you when it's all over?

The President. I want them to say that I helped to take America into a new era, that I really prepared America for a global economy, a global society, for increasing diversity at home, for responsibilities in a world where there was no cold war but we had a lot of challenges from terrorism, from racial and ethnic and religious wars. I want them to say that I did create an America of dramatically increased opportunity for all people, an America where we were coming together more in a spirit of unity, an America that was a leading force for peace and freedom and prosperity in the world. That's what I want them to say.

President's Advisory Board on Race

Ms. Wilkes. You know, Mr. President, when you were talking about the Little Rock Nine and how you lived through that, and also people have said that as you have promised—and you have carried through on that promise—to give us a reflection in your Cabinet and those around you of America, and one of the leading things that you brought to mind is the race relations panel. And I was just wondering what the status is on that.

The President. Well, we are preparing right now a final book on that. I got the report from Dr. John Hope Franklin and the other members of my panel on race, and we're going to do a book on it and get it out to the country. And then we're going to continue the work. We're going to take the recommendations of the panel and work with them on the next legislative program I present to the Congress, in the administrative policies of our Government, and in continuing to find things that are working at the local level and promoting them throughout the country.

I think this is very important. They did a terrific job. We've got literally hundreds of thousands of Americans involved all across America, and we're going to continue to work. I've got the report now, and we're going to be about the business of implementing it. I think it's very important.

Ms. Wilkes. And that's the importance of having the Congress that you can work with, that will get that out.

The President. That's right. That's right. And let me say this. The real problem now is that the Congress is basically dominated by not only the Republicans, but the right wing of the party is in the driver's seat. And if we get a big turnout here and we change the Congress, the composition of the Congress, you wouldn't have to change it all that much to get enough balance in there for us to be able to take some affirmative action.

If we had a few more Democrats we could do things positively instead of do what we had to do last year, which was to—this year—we fought a rear guard action for 9 months, and then at the very end they came in and had to deal with us on the budget. And because we all stuck together, we got 100,000 teachers; we did save the surplus for Social Security; we were able to get programs for children after school—hundreds of thousands—that was a good thing. But there is so much more we should do. And if the American people believe it's important to have modern schools and more teachers and to have the Patients' Bill of Rights, to have an increase in the minimum wage, to save Social Security, if they think these things

are important and they want us to keep coming together, not be driven apart, then it's important to show up tomorrow.

Voter Turnout

Myra J. Do you think the Republicans are counting on African-Americans not to come out tomorrow?

The President. Well, I think they are hoping that there will be a lower turnout among people who will vote for the Democrats, yes. They are hoping that there will be. And they are hoping there will be a higher turnout among people that they have tried to inflame, as they always do, in the various ways that they do it.

Republican Campaign Ads

Ms. Wilkes. And the Republican ads, certainly, have been flooding the airwaves.

The President. It's unbelievable. I think it's important that the people listening to us know that they raised over $100 million more than the Democrats did in their Senate and House committees and their national political committees—over $100 million. And they, over and above that, they have a lot of these so-called third-party expenditures where—just in the last 10 days they dropped another $750,000 against a congressional candidate in Michigan, a few hundred thousand dollars they dropped into a television ad campaign attacking one of our Democrats in rural Ohio. I've never seen this kind of money.

But we have the message; we have the issues. The country is in good shape, and we can do better. And the public agrees with us on our program, so it's basically their money and our issues and the question of who votes. And that's why this interview is so important to me.

Mr. Joyner. Radio stations, I told you I would be running long. I'm running right through the break with the President of the United States. Please hold with us.

Ms. Wilkes. Bigger name.

1998 Elections

Mr. Joyner. Yes, bigger name. [*Laughter*]

Mr. President, we've talked about what happens if African-Americans turn out to vote tomorrow. What if we don't turn out?

The President. Then they'll win a lot more seats than they otherwise would.

Mr. Joyner. So we're going to be to blame if it doesn't work out?

The President. Well, I wouldn't say that. I mean, who knows—President Kennedy once said, "Victory has a thousand fathers, and defeat is an orphan." I don't think it's worth thinking about that, but I think it's worth thinking about the difference between what—you know, Carol Moseley-Braun in Illinois has been behind this whole race. She has been badly outspent. She has run against someone with millions and millions of dollars who attacked her and basically refused to appear and tried to disguise his philosophical positions, which were far to the right of the voters of Illinois. She's made a huge comeback in the last week. It's amazing. One survey even had her leading by 2 points after being down by as much as 16. But it won't amount to anything unless the voters in Illinois who would vote for her show up.

Senator Hollings is in a tough fight in South Carolina. We have a chance to win a Senate seat in North Carolina. Chuck Schumer in New York, Barbara Boxer in California, these are huge, huge races, and there are many more. I just mention them. In Las Vegas, Nevada, where there's a substantial African-American population, we've got a congressional seat and a very important Senate seat in play. So the extent of the turnout all across America—and there are 30 or 35 congressional seats that could go one way or the other, and how they go will determine the shape of this next Congress and what their priorities will be.

Ms. Wilkes. And into the year 2000 and beyond.

The President. Yes.

Mr. Joyner. And you, personally, have a lot riding on this Congress, with all of the troubles that you're having.

The President. You know, I've just got 2 more years to be President, and I would like it—I'll be happy to fight, just like I did this last year, if that's the Congress I have to deal with, and at the end of the year we'll get something done, just like we did this year.

But it would be so much better—here we have the lowest unemployment rate in 28 years, the first budget surplus in 29 years, the lowest welfare rolls in 29 years, the highest home-ownership in history. The policies we've followed have been good for America, and it would be so much better now if we could just go to work and get rid of some of this bitter partisanship. The level of intense, angry partisan-ship that the Republicans have injected into Washington is really not good for America.

I want to work with all people here who have good ideas, to go forward. It is possible to do. But it's not possible to do as long as they think they can win with huge amounts of money and divisive attacks and negative campaigns. So if we can change the balance here a little bit, then we can get everybody to work together to move the country forward for the next 2 years. And yes, that's what I'd like to spend my time on. I think we ought to be working on people's problems out there in America and not just fighting with each other inside the beltway.

Ms. Wilkes. Mr. President, you talked about how good things are in the country and some people have said that they're too good and people have become too complacent to get out there and vote for any difference.

The President. Well, I have two things to say about that. First of all, they are good, but they can be a lot better. Yes, we have the lowest African-American poverty rate ever recorded. But is it low enough? Of course not. They can be a lot better. And I have offered to Congress initiatives to dramatically improve the schools, to dramatically improve the economic prospects of inner-city neighborhoods. I'd like to have a chance to pass them.

Think of the need we have for this Patients' Bill of Rights. Think of how many people are out there in HMO's that are having health care decisions made by accountants, not doctors. Think of the need we have, with the biggest school population in history, to build 5,000 modern schools that can be hooked up to the Internet and smaller classes for 100,000 teachers to teach in. Think of the need we have for a minimum wage increase. You know, even with low unemployment, you can't raise a family on $5.15 an hour. And think of the need we have to reform Social Security in the right way and to preserve the Medicare program and to meet these other challenges. So my first answer is that we have a lot to do.

The second thing I would say is that if everybody stays home and we have people in here who will be irresponsible and squander the surplus and risk our economic program and its stability as they did for the last 8 months here, if they tried to do that, then things could get worse in a hurry. So I believe that it would be a great mistake for anybody to stay home because times are good and to assume, "Well, the President is dealing with all these guys all right, and things are fine, and I don't really have to show up." That's a big risk that's not worth taking. We have too much to do.

Mr. Joyner. Well, that seems to be the mood.

The President. I don't know. I think a lot of people know this is a big election. I think they know what their priorities are, and you mentioned them. And I think they know what our priorities are. And I think they know that the Democrats are focused on the people out there in the country and not on some sort of a partisan power game here in Washington. That's what I want to get out there to the people, and if they understand that, I think they'll go. I certainly hope they will.

The American people, given enough time, virtually always make the right decision. But we need people to go, because otherwise this huge, vast amount of money that's been spent in this campaign is going to beat a lot of very, very

worthy people who would be very good in the Congress and the Senate.

Mr. Joyner. All right. Thank you, sir, for coming on the air and talking to us.

The President. Thank you.

Mr. Joyner. And we look for results tomorrow and a better day on Wednesday.

Ms. Wilkes. Are you going home to Little Rock to vote?

The President. No, I'm not. I voted absentee already. I've already cast my ballot.

Mr. Joyner. All right, Mr. President.

The President. Thank you. Goodbye.

NOTE: The interview began at 9:05 a.m. in Room 415 of the Old Executive Office Building. In his remarks, the President referred to Bill Gates, president, Microsoft; and Dr. John Hope Franklin, Chairman, President's Advisory Board on Race. Myra J. was the on-air name used by Myra Hughes.

Interview With Hispanic Journalists
November 2, 1998

Q. We will begin with a statement by President Bill Clinton.

1998 Elections

The President. Buenos dias. Good morning, everyone. And thank you for giving me this opportunity to address so many Hispanic-Americans and Latino media markets all across the United States, Puerto Rico, and in 18 other Latin American countries.

I'm glad to have the opportunity to discuss important issues with esteemed journalists from four major Latino radio networks: Radio Bilingue, MetroSource Network, CNN Radio Noticias, and Radio Unica.

Tomorrow is election day in America. It is no ordinary election. It is, instead, an election that will determine whether we as a nation focus on progress or partisanship for the next 2 years. It will determine which direction we take into the new millennium. It will be determined by who comes out to vote.

Our country is doing well now. I am very grateful to have had the opportunity to serve these last 6 years and grateful that we have

the lowest unemployment rate in 28 years, the smallest percentage of people on welfare in 29 years, the first surplus in 29 years. I'm grateful that poverty rates are dropping among all Americans and minority Americans. I'm very grateful that we have record numbers of new Hispanic-owned businesses, for example. But I think we all understand that a great deal of work still needs to be done in education, in health care, in child care.

We Democrats, we're running on an agenda of a Patients' Bill of Rights for all our Americans in health management organizations so they can have their health care decisions made by doctors, not accountants. We're running on an increase in the minimum wage. We're running on an aggressive program to improve our schools, with 100,000 more teachers and 5,000 new and rebuilt schools that are modern and good. We're running on a reform of the Social Security system so we can save it for the new century, and so much more. We also have run forthrightly on an open immigration policy and one America. And we have fought the Republicans on all these issues.

I hope very much that we'll have a good turnout on Tuesday. I'm looking forward to this interview. But I will say again, these races are very, very close. There are almost three dozen close House races that could go one way or the other. There are seven close Senate races that could go one way or the other. And we need a strong turnout.

Hurricane Mitch

Now, before I turn it over to the journalists to ask questions, I'd also like to say just one other word. Our prayers here at the White House go out to the citizens of Honduras, Nicaragua, Mexico, El Salvador, and Guatemala, who have suffered so much as a result of Hurricane Mitch and are trying to put their lives back together.

The United States is determined to help. We have provided over $2 million in funding for food, medicine, water, and other supplies. Two airlifts already have arrived with sheeting for shelter and food. Another airlift will take off today. In addition, foreign disaster assistance teams have been deployed to all the affected countries to coordinate our aid relief efforts, and we'll be looking at what else we can do. This is a terrible tragedy for the people of Central America, and we will do what we can to help them to recover.

Now I'd be happy to take your questions.

Q. Good morning, Mr. President.

The President. Good morning.

1998 Elections

Q. At least 30 million Hispanics in the United States are anxious to know if their hopes will be supported by the Government. When there is an election, we are accustomed to hear all kinds of promises, and the election passes, and we are already accustomed to all kinds of frustrations. Will there be any difference this time, Mr. President?

The President. Well, first of all, let me say that you have some evidence here. If you look at my record as compared with the record of the Republican Congress, you know what the issues are. We passed this year in our budget—because we refused to go home without it—a Hispanic education action plan to put more money into schools with high Latino populations, to reduce the dropout rate. There's a big difference in the dropout rate of Hispanic children in America as compared with all other groups. It was a huge victory for us.

We have continually fought for improved citizenship and naturalization activities to reduce the naturalization backlog. The Republicans have fought to delay naturalization and to complicate it. We have fought hard for a more accurate census, because millions of Latinos were not counted in 1990. The Republicans have fought for a system that will ensure that millions of Latinos will not be counted in 2000.

We have appointed a record number of Hispanic-Americans to positions in the Cabinet, in judgeships, in other places throughout the administration. We have fought to establish the North American Development Bank to help to deal with the economic and environmental challenges along our border with Mexico. We have fought to put more money into education to open the doors of college wider than ever before, to put police on our streets, where we have the lowest crime rate now in 25 years, to help our children deal with the challenges of crime and drugs, and to give them strong programs after school so that they can stay off the street and in school and learning.

So if you look at what we've done, if you just take this Hispanic education action plan, we have an increase of nearly $500 million targeted to help our Latino children stay in school, learn their lessons, and then go on to college. We have over $170 million committed to reducing the naturalization backlog.

So these are not just idle campaign promises. In the closing days of this last session of Congress, on October the 21st we confirmed a Hispanic-American to be United States Attorney for the District of Arizona, to be the Deputy Secretary of Housing and Urban Development, to be the Commissioner on Children and Youth in Families in the Department of Health and Human Services, to be on the Equal Employment Opportunity Commission, many other jobs, including a couple of ambassadorships.

So I'm not just talking something for the election here. There is a huge, huge difference in the positions of the Democratic and Republican Parties in the Congress on issues that are vital to Hispanics in America.

Q. Good morning, Mr. President.

The President. Good morning.

Republican Campaign Ads/Voter Turnout

Q. First of all, I was born in Honduras. I want to thank you very much for your words of encouragement to my Central American brothers. This is the worst tragedy in this century, and we're looking forward, all of you, to your support and your leadership in helping our countries build back. Thank you so much.

Now, sir, tomorrow, November 3d, is the sixth anniversary of your first election as President of the United States. According to the latest polls, there are some very closely contested elections tomorrow, as you said, especially in key States such as California, New York, Illinois, Florida, and Maryland, States which have large Hispanic populations.

The Hispanics backed you strongly in the Presidential elections of '92 and '96, and also in the midterm elections of '94. The Republicans have been running ads attacking you on the Monica Lewinsky issue. Do you feel these attacks on your personal conduct will cut down the attendance of Hispanic voters tomorrow or diminish their normal strong support for you and your party?

The President. I think it depends overwhelmingly on how people react to them. But just consider what the argument of those ads is. The argument of those ads is that voters, Hispanic voters and others, should punish completely innocent Democrats. In other words, they're saying punish someone else for this.

And ultimately, the argument is, they're telling the voters they should punish themselves. They should say, "Vote for us, even though everything we're doing is not good for you; and don't vote for them, even though they will vote for modernized schools and 100,000 teachers; they—the Democrats—they will vote for a Patients' Bill of Rights; they will vote to raise the minimum wage; they will vote to save Social Security; they will vote for a fair, complete, and accurate census."

Now, the argument of the Republican ads is you should forget about all that, all those things that are about you, and play our partisan political game here in Washington. And that's basically been what the Republicans are saying. I don't think the American people will buy that.

But what Hispanic voters need to understand is that the stakes are high here: the Senate seats in California and New York; any number of House seats in California; there are House seats up in Colorado, in New Mexico; a Senate seat and House seat up in Nevada; and the enormously important Senate race in Illinois, where Senator Carol Moseley-Braun has made a remarkable comeback in the last week; the elections in Florida; the elections in Maryland. And I could go on and on. There are about three dozen House of Representatives seats at issue here. Many, many of them have substantial Hispanic populations. There are seven or eight Senate seats at stake here, and several of them have substantial Hispanic populations; and then, of course, all these Governorships.

So I would say, this election ought to be about the American people and their children and their future and whether or not we have done a good job for them and whether or not our ideas are best for the future. They would like it, the Republicans, to use their $100 million financial advantage in contributions to get everyone to forget that they have killed the Patients' Bill of Rights, killed the minimum wage increase, that they have killed legislation to protect our children from the dangers of tobacco, that they killed the campaign finance reform, that they killed the school modernization initiative, and get people to buy into their Washington power games.

I think the American people know that my administration has been about people, not politics, about progress, not partisanship. And I think this election is very much worth voting in. But a decision not to vote is also a decision about what will go on here in Washington, DC, just as a decision to vote is.

California Proposition 10

Q. Good morning, Mr. President. It's quite an honor for me to take part in this conversation this morning. My question is as follows: The California children and families initiatives, which is known as Proposition 10, is to create programs for pregnant women and very young children, will be funded by cigarette smokers by paying a 50-cent tax per pack of cigarettes. Many in Los Angeles view this as another way to "attack" minorities as a proportion of people who smoke tend to be greater among minority groups.

In your view, what are the long-term benefits of passing this proposition, and how would you convince the Latino community that this measure will actually be working in their favor?

The President. Well, I think there are two things I would say about that. The only argument against raising the cigarette tax ever is that it disproportionately affects low-income people, because if all kinds of lower income people, working people, smoke, it will take a higher percentage of their income to pay a 50-cent-a-pack tax.

But consider the benefits. First of all, it will reduce smoking among young people, which will prevent more people starting. And we know now 3,000 young people a day start to smoke, even though it's illegal for them to do so, and 1,000 will have their lives shortened as a result of it.

Secondly, because the people are voting directly on this initiative in California, they are deciding, as they vote, how that money must be spent. So it would be illegal to divert the money to any other purpose. Therefore, you know that the health care of the people of California—and disproportionately the Hispanic population of California needs more money invested in health and education activities—you know that's where the money will go because that's what the initiative says. And under our law, if the people vote for it, they have a guarantee of how it will be spent. So you don't have to worry about what the legislature does, what the Governor does, what anybody does. You get to decide, okay, if I'm going to pay this, this is how I want it spent. And your vote will do that.

So those are the two arguments I think in favor of that initiative. I know that both my wife and I have worked with the people who put that initiative on the ballot and we trust them. We think that they're good people, and they certainly are trying to do something that will improve the health care and the future of the Hispanic children of California.

Immigration

Q. Mr. President, in this campaign, we haven't listened to any immigration agenda talks too much. Politicians don't talk too much about immigration. Is there any reason for that, or is there something going on that we don't know?

The President. Well, I'm very happy to talk about it. As you know, I have worked very hard to reverse anti-immigrant provisions of the law. We now have reversed almost all the anti-immigrant provisions of the welfare reform law, just as I said I would do. We have beat back anti-immigrant legislation in other areas here. And I am working very, very hard to reduce the backlog that we have in the naturalization and immigration process, which I think is very, very important. So from my point of view, the whole issue of how to deal with immigration is very important.

I have also tried to get changes in our law or changes in Justice Department policy to let immigrants stay here who came here under difficult circumstances many years ago and would otherwise have to now turn around and go back. So I want to see America continuing to have an open and fair and welcoming process for legal immigrants, and I believe that that's an important issue.

I also think that's an important issue that all the voters should consider in this election, because it would be hard to find an issue on which the parties have differed more than the Democrats and the Republicans on the issue of immigration for the last 4 years. And I would hope that everyone who cares about this issue would think that that issue alone is a justification to go out and support our Democratic candidates.

1998 Elections

Q. Thank you, Mr. President. Some closing thoughts about the importance of tomorrow's election?

The President. Well, again, let me just say that tomorrow the American people will decide on the Congress that will take us into the 21st century. They will decide whether it's a Congress that wants to represent all the American people and work for one America or a Congress that will continue to try to divide the American people in ways that undermine our ability to unite and to go forward. They will decide on whether they want a Congress that supports a Patients' Bill of Rights, that supports 100,000 teachers and smaller classes and modern schools, or a Congress that opposes those things; a Congress that supports an increase in the minimum wage, or one that opposes it; a Congress that supports protecting our surplus until we have saved Social Security for all the seniors in this country in the 21st century, or one that is still committed to squandering the surplus and endangering our economic strength in the long run so that we can't do what we should do on Social Security.

Now, these are big decisions. For Hispanic-Americans, you also have clear choices in terms of our commitment to a decent, fair, equitable, and accelerated process of immigration and naturalization, and their policy, which is to slow it down, make it more difficult, and do things which, in my view, are unfair to immigrants coming to this country.

So there are clear choices here, and I say again, a choice not to vote is just like a vote for someone you don't agree with. This is a very, very important election, and I would just urge all of you to talk about it today and to go and vote tomorrow. Your vote is your voice.

NOTE: The interview began at 9:40 a.m. in Room 415 of the Old Executive Office Building. Journalists participating in the interview were: Eduardo Carrasco, MetroSource Network; Jacobo Goldstein, CNN Radio Noticias; and William Restrepo, Radio Unica. A Radio Bilingue journalist did not participate in this interview but had a separate one in the evening.

Remarks on the Patients' Bill of Rights
November 2, 1998

Thank you so very much, Mrs. Jennings, for coming here with your son amidst your evident pain to share your experience with us. Thank you, Dr. Weinmann, for sharing your experiences with us. If you would do that every day until we pass a bill, you can drink my water every day. [*Laughter*] I loved it. [*Laughter*]

Thank you, Dr. Beverly Malone. Thank you, Secretary Herman, for the work you and Secretary Shalala did. Thank you, Deputy Secretary Gober; Director of OPM Janice Lachance. I'd also like to thank Linda Chavez-Thompson, the executive vice president of the AFL–CIO; Gerry McEntee, the president of AFSME; Bill Lucy, the secretary-treasurer of AFSME; John Sepulveda, the Deputy Director of OPM; and Rudy de Leon, the Under Secretary of Defense, for being here. And a special word of appreciation on this day before the election to Congressman Eliot Engel, one of the great supporters of the Patients' Bill of Rights from New York City. Thank you, sir, for being here.

Iraq

Let me say, before I begin, a few words about the situation in Iraq which has been dominating the news—and I haven't had a chance to talk to the American people through the press in the last couple of days.

Saddam Hussein's latest refusal to cooperate with the international weapons inspectors is completely unacceptable. Once again, though, it will backfire. Far from dividing the international community and achieving concessions, his obstructionism was immediately and unanimously condemned by the United Nations Security Council. It has only served to deepen the international community's resolve.

Just a short while ago, I met with my national security team to review the situation and discuss our next steps. Iraq must let the inspectors finish the job they started 7 years ago, a job Iraq promised to let them do repeatedly.

What is that job? Making sure Iraq accounts for and destroys all its chemical, biological, and nuclear weapons capability and the missiles to deliver such weapons. For Iraq, the only path to lifting sanctions is through complete cooperation with the weapons inspectors, without restrictions, runarounds, or roadblocks.

In the coming days, we will be consulting closely with our allies and our friends in the region. Until the inspectors are back on the job, no options are off the table.

Patients' Bill of Rights

Now let's talk about the Patients' Bill of Rights and what it means to the citizens of our country. A day from now, tomorrow, starting early in the morning, Americans from all walks of life will have a chance to exercise their right to vote. When citizens go to the polls tomorrow—and I hope very large numbers of them will—they will bring to bear their deepest hopes and concerns about their own families, their children, and our Nation. The choices Americans make tomorrow will have a profound effect on the future of our country.

This is not an ordinary time, and therefore it is not an ordinary election. We can have progress on health and a Patients' Bill of Rights, or more partisanship; progress in education and students in smaller, more modern classrooms rather than trailers, or more partisanship; progress towards saving Social Security for the 21st century, or more partisanship.

Perhaps there is no choice more stark than the one presented by the stories we have heard today, for we believe that a Patients' Bill of Rights offers protections every American deserves. We believe such a bill must be strong and enforceable and safeguard the security of patients and their families.

We need a bill of rights that says medical decisions should be made by informed doctors, not accountants; that specialists should be available whenever a doctor recommends them; that an emergency room coverage should be available wherever and whenever it is needed; that medical records should remain private; that no one can be forced to change doctors in the middle of treatment because an employer changes plans; that when people are harmed they have a right to hold the HMO accountable.

We have worked hard to extend these rights to as many people as we could through the use of executive authority. In February I asked all Federal agencies that administer health care—that's Medicare, Medicaid, the Federal employee plan, the Department of Defense, and the Veterans Administration—to do everything they could to provide these protections. Today the Vice President sent me a report on their progress. It is considerable. Through executive action we're doing everything we can to extend the protections of the bill of rights to Americans who get their health care through federally funded plans. As the report shows, we have done so while avoiding any excessive cost or burden on these plans. Still, the executive action alone cannot protect the millions and millions of Americans—160 million total—in managed care plans.

Now, these plans can save money. They can actually improve the delivery of care if the management is done properly. When I became President, I'd like to remind all of you—it was a long time ago now, 6 years; it's hard to remember sometimes—inflation in health care was increasing at about 3 times the national rate of inflation. It was becoming unsustainable for employers, for employees, for families. And so some management changes were in order.

But one of the things that we have learned—and I thought the doctor stated it very well—is that whenever any kind of management change or market-oriented change is instituted, if you're not careful, the technique itself, the management itself, or the bottom line, the money-saving itself completely swallows up the original purpose of the enterprise. The purpose of managed care is to deliver quality health care to everyone who needs it, in the most efficient way, at the lowest available cost, consistent with quality health care. The purpose of managed care is not to cut the costs as much as you can, as long as it still looks like you're giving health care, whether you are or not.

And that is the dilemma that I appointed this Commission on Consumer Rights in Health Care to consider, that Secretary Herman and Secretary Shalala cochaired. We had business people on it. We had medical people on it. We had Republicans and Democrats on it.

And let me say to you that—I want to say this as strongly as I can—the stories you heard from this doctor today, the heartbreaking story you heard from Mrs. Jennings today, they are not isolated stories. They are not, unfortunately, exceptional stories. There are stories like this all over the country. And I, frankly, have heard too many of them. I've heard too many doctors tearing their hair out. I've seen too many nurses literally crying, talking to me about the people they've been required to turn down care to. We have seen too many families that have lost a loved one either because of denial or delay, which as you heard in the case of Mrs. Jennings can be the same thing.

And I would also like to point out that there were 43 managed care organizations who supported our Patients' Bill of Rights, 43 companies who were up front enough to come forward and say, "Look, we either are doing this or we want to do it, but we don't think we should be put out of business for doing the right thing and people who are doing the wrong thing should be rewarded."

So, what are we to do? Unfortunately, insurance company accountants or bogus procedures are not the only thing delaying the Patients' Bill of Rights now. The Republican leadership in Congress delayed it all year long. For a full year we worked with lawmakers of both parties in good faith to try to craft a bill that would genuinely protect patient's rights. And to be fair, I want to make full disclosure on this eve of the election, we had a handful, a bare handful, but we did have a handful of Republicans who were willing to support it.

But in the House, they offered a bill, which I'll talk more about it in a minute, which didn't provide any of the protections, really, that the commission recommended and didn't cover 100 million people with what little it did provide. In the Senate, they brought the bill up, and the members in the other party that were in hotly contested races were, in effect, permitted to vote for the bill with us, and they still had enough votes to kill it. It was so cynical. And it's hard to be cynical once you hear the kind of stories we've heard today.

It was, to be sure, a profitable decision. The people who wanted the bill killed have spent vast sums of money attacking people like Congressman Engel. Now, he doesn't have a strong opponent and couldn't be defeated in his district, so he could be here with us today. But Congressman Frank Pallone from New Jersey, simply because he had the audacity to support this bill and say there should be no more Mrs. Jennings, a man representing a single congressional district found himself the target of ads run on New York television during the World Series. You know how expensive those are? [*Laughter*] The World Series—we're beaming it to you, New Jersey. We'll show these Congressmen, if they have the audacity to stand up and say we should be held accountable in the court of law like anybody else, that we ought to put the quality of health care first; we'll show them. Now, that's what this is about.

Now, let's look at the facts. Let's look at the facts. Look at this chart. I've shown this chart before, but this is a day before the election. I want the people of this country to see this chart. I don't want any smokescreen. I've seen some of these ads that members of the other party ran about how they're really for this Patients' Bill of Rights, and it made me think that ours wasn't strong enough. And I looked at the ad, and then I went back and looked at their bill. So I think we need to look at their bill one more time.

We say that medical decisions should be made by doctors, not accountants. Ours guarantees that; theirs doesn't. We say that there should be a guarantee of direct access to specialists if your primary doctor recommends it. Ours guarantees that; theirs doesn't. We say there should be real emergency room protections. Let

me stop and say what that means. That means if you get hit by a car and you're in an emergency, you ought to go to the nearest emergency room, not one halfway across town if you're in a big city because it happens to be covered. That may not seem like a big deal to you, but just imagine, have you ever been in New York City traffic or Los Angeles traffic? This is a big deal. This is a huge deal. This is not some idle talk here. This is not political rhetoric. This is a huge thing. Anybody that's ever been with a loved one in the back of an ambulance struggling to get to a hospital knows this is a huge deal.

We say you ought to keep your doctor through critical treatments. That's a guarantee of ours. What does that mean? It means if you're pregnant and your employer changes providers while you're pregnant, you can't be forced to get another obstetrician. Those of you who have had children, remember, how traumatic would that have been—seventh month of your pregnancy, say, "I'm sorry. Here's Dr. Smith. Get to know him." Even worse, chemotherapy—almost all of us have had somebody in our family now have chemotherapy treatment. Just think how traumatic it is—you sit there; you worry about the person that you love going through chemotherapy; you watch their hair fall out; you see the loss of appetite; you try to make jokes about it—and be told in the middle of the treatment you have to change doctors. It's a big issue. This is not just a word on a chart here. This is a big human issue.

Protecting patients from secret financial incentives—you heard the doctor, what he said. Certainly, there should be no money going to doctors in HMO's for making cost-cutting decisions. Protecting medical privacy laws, holding health plans accountable for harming patients, and covering all health plans—their bill, what little it did cover, didn't cover 100 million Americans.

Now, that's what is at issue here. This is a very practical bill. It is very important. And I will say, it should not be a partisan issue. Believe you me, this is not a partisan issue in any community in America, except Washington, DC. I have no idea what political party Mrs. Jennings belongs to. I don't know if the doctor has ever voted for a Democrat in his life. [*Laughter*] I don't know. I know nothing about that. This is not a political issue. When you haul into an emergency room, nobody asks you—and you fill out all those forms, there is not "Republican," "independent," "Democrat" on it. You don't check that. This has nothing to do, ordinarily, with partisan politics.

And I will say again, I believe we ought to save money. I worked for 6 years here to get this budget balanced, to get it in surplus. We eliminated hundreds of programs. But we didn't stop trying to invest in education and research or Head Start. I believe they ought to save all the money they can on the health care system. But you should not have a system where you get in trouble for taking care of people and where, in the first line of contact, you will never get in trouble for saying no.

That's the last point I want to make about this. And the doctor implied this; I want to make it explicit. Put yourself, every one of you, in a position—suppose you weren't a doctor. Suppose you were somebody with a BA in accounting, and you got a degree, and you're 25 or 28 years old; you get a degree, working for these health maintenance organizations, and you review these claims in the first position. What do you know? First of all, you'd like to keep your job. It's a nice place. You've got health benefits. [*Laughter*] You get 2 weeks—no, listen, think about that. You get 2 weeks' vacation. And you've never looked at Mrs. Jennings; you don't know her husband; you don't have to go home at night with their faces burned in your brain. What do you know? You know you will never get in trouble for saying no. That's the incentive. You won't lose your job if you say no every time. Why? Because eventually they'll kick it up to somebody who will eventually get it right, and if they're a doctor, they'll eventually get it right. The problem is, you just heard today one gripping example of what "eventually" can mean, in the life of the Jennings family.

That is why we need the roadmap. That's why we need the law. We shouldn't depend upon the roll of the dice about whether every person who reviews every one of these cases in every one of these plans all across America is willing to risk his or her job in the first instance, every time, to try to resolve doubt. And some of them don't even have enough knowledge to know what to do, trying to second-guess the doctors. This is a big deal, practically.

I've heard all these arguments about how, well, you don't want too many lawsuits, and all that. Now, I'm sympathetic to that; everybody is. But look, under the law today, one of our wits said on our side the other day, the only people in Washington who can't get sued anymore are foreign diplomats and HMO's. [*Laughter*] Now, nobody wants an unnecessary lawsuit. But people have to be held accountable in these cases so that we can change the incentives.

So I ask you all to think about this. And I ask the American people to think about it. Again, it should not be a partisan issue. It has been made a partisan issue not by us but by those who would not join us. There was a bipartisan makeup on this commission that came up with this recommendation. And I promise you, in every hospital in America today there is a bipartisan makeup in the hospital beds as you walk up and down the halls and in every nursing station.

This should be an American issue. Look folks, we've got to fix this. And this election, in no small measure, will be a referendum on whether we will put people over politics, the public interest over special interest, the health of our people over a very short-sighted definition of the bottom line.

Again I say, I hope the American people will go to the polls tomorrow in large numbers, and I hope they will vote in a way that sends a signal loud and clear that America needs a real Patients' Bill of Rights. I hope the Americans who see this will remember Frances Jennings, will remember Dr. Weinmann, will remember Beverly Malone, will remember the people who give care and the people who need it, and remember what this is all about.

Thank you very much.

NOTE: The President spoke at 2:07 p.m. in the East Room at the White House. In his remarks, he referred to Frances Jennings, who introduced the President and whose husband died as a result of a delayed health care decision; Dr. Robert Weinmann, Mr. Jennings' physician; Dr. Beverly Malone, president, American Nurses Association; Gerald W. McEntee, president, and William Lucy, international secretary-treasurer, American Federation of State, County, and Municipal Employees (AFL–CIO); and President Saddam Hussein of Iraq.

Statement on the Death of General James L. Day
November 2, 1998

Hillary and I were saddened to learn of the death of General James L. Day, USMC (Ret). Last January I awarded General Day our Nation's highest military honor, the Medal of Honor, for extraordinary heroism during the battle of Okinawa in 1945.

General Day's service did not end at Okinawa. He distinguished himself for courage and leadership in a career of service that spanned more than four decades. From World War II to Korea and Vietnam, he served his country with patriot-

ism, dedication, and unsurpassed bravery. General Day's lifetime of achievements embodied the words *Semper Fidelis*.

We will miss this true hero, whose selfless conduct as a Marine and citizen set a shining example for all Americans. We are grateful for all he did to preserve the freedom that is our most sacred gift. Our thoughts and prayers go to his wife, Sally, his son, Jim, and the entire Day family.

Telephone Interview With Samuel Orozco of Radio Bilingue
November 2, 1998

1998 Elections

Mr. Orozco. Is there any message you would like to send to our listeners in Radio Bilingue, Mr. President?

The President. Yes, Samuel, thank you very much. The first and most important message is to implore every person within the sound of my voice to vote on Tuesday, November 3d. November 3d is no ordinary election day, for on November 3d we will decide whether, as a nation, we focus on progress or partisanship for the next 2 years. We will decide the direction our country will take in the new century. And it will be determined, this election, not only by who votes but by who does not vote.

I have worked very, very hard to focus on matters of importance not only to Hispanics but to all Americans. When I came into office, we had a troubled economy, a big budget deficit, high crime, and deep partisanship. And over the last 6 years, the economy has improved; the crime rate is at a 25-year low; we had the first surplus in 29 years, the lowest percentage of people on welfare in 29 years, the lowest unemployment in 28 years. But we're still fighting these partisan battles.

I want very much to have the opportunity to do what America needs. I have a plan for 100,000 teachers and smaller classes and modern schools, a plan for a Patients' Bill of Rights that guarantees the right of people in HMO's

to see a specialist when they need one and to have the other medical protections they need, a plan to raise the minimum wage, a plan to save Social Security for the next century. We have to do these things and so much more.

And I think everyone within the sound of my voice understands that I and the Democrats have been fighting for this, that the Republicans have opposed us on these matters. So what I want to do is to make everyone understand that all the good things that we have done in the last couple of years, we have done in the face of intense opposition.

We got a big Hispanic education action plan passed at the end of this last Congress, because I wouldn't agree to a budget unless we put it in there—over $500 million to reduce the dropout rate and increase the college-going rate among Hispanics. We got a big initiative to reduce the naturalization backlog to make more citizens more quickly. We're moving forward in a whole range of areas.

But there is so much we will be able to do with a few more Democrats in Congress. And the kind of intense support that can come tomorrow from the Hispanic community can make a difference in California, in Illinois in the Senate race, in House races all across the United States, in New York in the very important race for the Senate there, many other places. So I believe that this election may well be riding on whether Hispanic-Americans vote.

Bilingual Education

Mr. Orozco. One issue very dear to Latino communities in our country, Mr. President, is bilingual education. Proposition 227, approved here in California, seeks to eliminate bilingual education. You have said that being able to speak more than one language is a gift that we all need. What role do you envision for the Spanish language in the U.S. in the next century, and how determined are you to stand by bilingual education?

The President. Well, as you know, I opposed Proposition 227 because I thought it was artificial. I do think all children, schoolchildren, whose native language is Spanish should become fluent in English and should be able to read, speak, and learn in English. But I believe that during that process, it's important to have effective bilingual programs.

I also believe that more and more children whose first language is not Spanish should learn to speak Spanish. I believe that more and more of our school districts, and perhaps even our States, should adopt a requirement that students, in order to get out of high school, should have 4 years of language and should demonstrate some proficiency in it. In a global economy, that would help us a lot. So I would like to see the bilingual education matter taken out of politics and put back into education.

The truth is that a lot of our children would not have to spend so long in bilingual programs if we had more well-trained bilingual education teachers who could teach the children the subjects they're learning and help them to learn English more quickly. And I think we ought to focus on the problem instead of turning it into a political football.

Immigration and Mexico-U.S. Border

Mr. Orozco. A final question, Mr. President. You have said that immigration is not only good for America, it is America. You have also enthusiastically supported the North American Free Trade Agreement, an agreement which is supposed to erase borders and bring friends together. However, the Mexico-U.S. border is becoming a costly, dangerous, and fortified wall. What are you doing to create a friendlier border with Mexico?

The President. Well, we're trying to work with the Mexican Government more on economic and environmental projects and on building up the economy on both sides of the border so there will be less danger of drug trafficking and more possibilities for commerce that benefit both sides. The Mexican Government has begun to work with us more closely to deal with narcotrafficking, because it's a big problem in Mexico as well as the U.S.

But we can't just have a negative approach. We also have to finance more economic projects and more environmental projects along the border and make sure the border operates more smoothly. And that's what I have worked hard to do.

I think that if we can keep this global financial crisis from reaching Mexico and the rest of Latin America, that we will see over the next 5 years a marked improvement in our relationships with Mexico, a marked improvement in the Mexican economy, a smaller problem with illegal immigration, and more joint action on drug trafficking. And that is my goal.

1998 Elections

Mr. Orozco. Mr. President, tomorrow is election day. Many Latinos will vote for the first time, and they make good voters. But many hesitate because they don't believe in *políticos*. They don't believe in the promises of the politicians. What message would you have as a final message for Latino voters?

The President. Well, first of all, I think you can look at the promises I have made to the American people, including Latinos, over the last 6 years, and you can look at how many jobs have been created, how much welfare has gone down, how much unemployment has gone down, how much crime has gone down. You can look at my record on immigration. You can look at my record on appointing Hispanics to key positions in my administration. You can look at my record in fighting AIDS in the Hispanic community and my record in trying to fight for this education initiative to improve the educational prospects of young Latinos. And you can look at my record in fighting for a fair census that counts all Americans. So I'm not just a politician making promises. I have a record. I have done what I said I would do, and it has been good for the Latino community in America.

And if you look ahead, basically if you want smaller classes, more teachers, and modern schools, and you want the National Government to help, then you only have one choice, because the Democrats and I are for it; the Republicans are opposed to our initiative. If you want a raise in the minimum wage, we're for it, and they're opposed to it. If you want to protect patients that are in managed care plans and give them the right they need to see specialists and to keep treatment going, we're for it, and they're opposed to it. If you want to see the surplus we have protected to save Social Security for the elderly, long term, and to protect the integrity of Medicare, then you should support us. If you want more done on child care to support working families with young children, we have an initiative; they're opposed to it.

So I would say, based on our record and the clear differences between parties, it is very much worth going out to vote. And if you don't vote, the consequences of not voting are that in the next 2 years the Congress will spend their time and money the same they have in the last year, which is basically fighting inside-Washington political games, trying to gain political advantage through investigations and other things, instead of doing the people's business.

So I would say there's a clear case for voting and a clear case for voting for the Democrats for Congress and Senate tomorrow. And I hope that everyone within the sound of my voice will do so.

Willie Velazquez spent his life at the Southwest Voter Education Project saying *"Su voto es su voz."* And it's really true, and more true now than ever before.

Mr. Orozco. Mr. President, on behalf of Radio Bilingue, thank you very much.

The President. Thank you very much, Samuel. Goodbye.

NOTE: The interview began at approximately 7 p.m. The President spoke by telephone from the Residence at the White House. A tape was not available for verification of the content of this interview.

Interview With Tavis Smiley of Black Entertainment Television
November 2, 1998

Mr. Smiley. Mr. President, it's nice to see you. Thanks again for sitting down, talking to us.

The President. Glad to be here.

1998 Elections

Mr. Smiley. Glad to have you. I have had the pleasure, as you know, to sit down with you one-on-one a few times in the past, and so I know that asking you to make a prediction is like wasting my time. So I'm not going to ask you to predict anything about tomorrow's elections, but let me ask you, on a scale of 1 to 10, if I can, 10 being confident, 1 being apprehensive, how do you feel about tomorrow on this election eve?

The President. I feel both confident and apprehensive. And I'll tell you why. If you look at it, first of all, in the House of Representatives, there are probably 36 elections that could go either way. And in my opinion, it will depend overwhelmingly on the turnout. Then there are in the Senate seven, perhaps eight, elections

that could go either way, depending on the turnout. Then in the Governorships, there are a huge number of Governorships—there are 36 up, but there are probably 10 of them still very much in play. So I think that it is really impossible to know.

It's clear to me that our message has resonated with the American people, though we have been at an enormous, enormous financial disadvantage, the largest in my lifetime. The Republican committees—the Senate committee, the House committee, and the national committee raised over $100 million more than their Democratic counterparts in these last 2 years. And there's been a breathtaking amount of money spent against some of our congressional candidates. So I just don't know. I feel good about it, but it depends upon who votes.

Mr. Smiley. You mentioned just a moment ago that this may be the election where the imbalance has been greatest with regard to fundraising in your lifetime, Republican and

Democrat, that you've been involved in. Speaking of your lifetime, let me ask you whether or not it would be fair for me or anyone else to suggest that this election is not just important to the country, it is not just important to African-Americans, but it is, in fact, quite important to William Jefferson Clinton. Would I be wrong in my assessment that this may be the most important election day of your entire political career?

The President. No, I don't agree with that. It's not the most——

Mr. Smiley. Not that much riding on it?

The President. No, no, it's not the most important election in my career. But it's very important to me because it will determine how much I can do for the American people in the next 2 years. We did very well here in this budget this year. We got a downpayment on our 100,000 teachers; we got programs for hundreds of thousands of kids after school; we fended off a Republican attempt to raid the surplus before we fixed Social Security.

But there was so much we did not do. And there is so much we still have to do that if we got a few more Democrats here, we could pass this Patients' Bill of Rights; we could have modernized schools and 100,000 more teachers; we could raise the minimum wage; we could secure Social Security; we could reform Medicare in the right way; we could do something for child care; we could do more for the areas of our country which still haven't felt the economic recovery.

And so the last 2 years of my Presidency, I think, would be far more focused on progress, as opposed to this Washington partisan politics. So I would like it very much. It's terribly important to me. But the most important elections were the election and reelection in '92 and '96.

Mr. Smiley. Let me follow up on that, and again I ask this respectfully, and I'll move on. I promise. The reason I asked that question in the first place is because you and I both know what you personally have at stake, what personally is riding on this election tomorrow. And you mentioned that the two most important elections were the one when you were elected in '92 and, of course, reelected in '96. And I would expect you to say that. But the reason why I asked whether or not you felt there was more riding on tomorrow is precisely because this election, depending on the outcome, could

be the beginning of the undoing, the unraveling of what those two elections were all about.

The President. Well, that depends upon who votes and what the message is. And I hope that the American people will turn out, and I hope that the electorate tomorrow will reflect what we know the electorate as a whole feels. The American people as a whole want us to put this partisanship behind us, want us to get back to their business. They think altogether too much time is spent in Washington on the considerations of the politics of Washington and altogether too little time spent on the real problems and the real opportunities of people out there in the country. So I agree with that, and I think that they can do a lot tomorrow to reduce partisanship and to increase progress if they all show up.

It's really a function of whether the people who show up tomorrow are fairly reflective of what all the research and all our instincts, mine and everybody else's, tell us where the American people as a whole are.

First Family

Mr. Smiley. We'll move on and ask a couple of questions that I admit at the outset I'm somewhat apprehensive in asking, but I ask them because they're things that you have spoken about in the past, and I want to give you a chance to expound and extrapolate, if you will. You've talked in the past a great deal about atonement, leading up to this election day tomorrow. It seems to me that you've talked about atonement in two regards: one, atoning as President, and secondly, atoning as a husband and a father.

With regard as atoning as President, you promised to work harder to be a better President. I don't know that anyone, Republican or Democrat—even your critics agree that you've been on a roll of late: the budget deal with Congress; the historic peace agreement between Israel and Palestine; I note last Friday the G–7 nations agreed on your proposal to put money into markets that are jittery at the moment. You're on a roll, domestically and internationally, with regard to that atonement issue and your being President.

What you've not talked about much lately—and I want to give you a chance to respond if you so choose—is how the atonement process is coming along with regard to your being a husband and a father. What's your assessment of how that atonement process is coming along?

The President. I haven't talked about it deliberately, because I think that it ought to be a private matter between me and my family. All I can tell you is I'm working at it very hard, and I think it's terribly important. It's more important than anything else in the world to me—more important than anything else in the world. But I think the less I say about it, the better.

I think one of the things that I hope will come out of the reassessment of this whole business is a conviction again, which I believe the American people already have, that even people in public life deserve some measure of private space within which to have their family lives and to deal with their—both the joys and the trials of their personal lives. So I don't think I should say more about it except that I'm working at it.

Whitewater

Mr. Smiley. I respect that.

As you know, there was not a single reference—not a single reference—to Whitewater, as your White House staff and the entire Clinton administration reminds us every day—not a single reference to Whitewater in the Starr report. On the eve of this election day, though, it occurs to me that you still, though, have not been, despite that reality, you still have not been officially exonerated with regard to the Whitewater matter. I'm wondering whether or not that frustrates you in any way, whether you're bothered by the fact that there wasn't anything in the report but you still have not been officially exonerated.

The President. Well, I think the American people should draw some comfort from the fact that after 4 years and $40 million, reviewing all my checks, contributions, and the pressure—the extraordinary pressure a lot of people were put under to say things damaging, that nothing has come out. That's because neither my wife or I did anything wrong. And eventually that will become clear to the American people. I hope it will become clear sooner rather than later, but I know that. I knew that in the beginning. I knew it from the start. And so I'm at peace about that, and I'll just have to let what others do be a matter for them to decide.

Rightwing Conspiracy

Mr. Smiley. "A vast rightwing conspiracy"—I'm sure you've heard those words somewhere before—"a vast rightwing conspiracy," of course, uttered by your wife on the "Today" show a few months ago. Since she uttered those words, three things have happened: Number one, as I just suggested, the Starr report has come out with embarrassing, lurid, salacious details, and no mention of Whitewater; we have since had a straight party-line partisan vote in the House to move forward with this impeachment inquiry; thirdly, the Washington Post tells us last week that the Speaker of the House, Mr. Gingrich himself, was behind these personal attack ads against you.

I'm wondering, in light of that, and a number of other things I'm sure you could list, but those are three things that come to my mind—I'm wondering whether now we can reassess the First Lady's comments and ask whether or not Hillary Rodham Clinton was right when she suggested that there is, in fact, a vast rightwing conspiracy.

The President. Well, I think the facts speak for themselves, and as more facts come out, they will speak for themselves. The only thing I would say is there's a sort of a permanent political class in Washington that tends to thrive on such matters because they're not affected by what I came here to do.

In other words, most of these people, it doesn't matter to them whether there's a Patients' Bill of Rights or not, to make sure doctors, instead of accountants, make health care decisions. It certainly doesn't matter to them whether there's a minimum wage increase. It doesn't matter to them whether we have 100,000 more teachers and modernized schools. It doesn't matter to them whether we save Social Security for the 21st century.

So there is a group in America where the acquisition of political power is more important than the purpose for which it's used. To me, I never came here to be part of that permanent political class. I didn't come—I'm not a Washington person, in that sense. I don't expect to be when I'm not President anymore. My whole goal was to use these precious years the American people have given me to deal with the challenges facing our country. I've done my best to do it, to move our country forward and to bring our country together.

And I have to say, I think I haven't really succeeded in reconciling the political parties in Washington. There is still too much partisanship here. But to me, that's what's going on here. This is a question of whether you've got politics or people as your top goal.

Politics of Hate

Mr. Smiley. That phrase, "a vast rightwing conspiracy," would seem to suggest on some level that there is a visceral hatred, if you will, of Bill and Hillary Clinton in this city by some folk. You buy that? Let me ask you, first of all, if you buy that, Mr. President. And number two, if you buy that, let me just ask you in a very point-blank and direct way—and I'm not so sure I've ever heard you asked this question before, so maybe I'm a revolutionary here, I don't know, maybe I'm not—why do they hate you so much?

The President. Again, I think that people whose whole life is whether or not they are in or out of power, rather than what they do with power when they get it, don't like it when they're out. And a lot of these people really never thought there would be another Democratic President in our lifetimes. They really didn't think so. And all the things they said about Democrats—that we couldn't run the economy, that we couldn't balance the budget, that we couldn't deal responsibly with welfare, that we couldn't be tough and smart on crime, that we couldn't be strong on foreign policy—all those things that they told the American people about Democrats generally over decades turned out not to be true. And we now have 6 years of evidence that it's not true.

So there are some, again, whose life is solely—they evaluate themselves solely on whether they're in or out, who are very angry about that. And I'm sorry for them. I'm not even angry at them anymore. I'm just sorry, because I believe that there are people in the Republican Party who are good people, who have honest differences of opinion with me, that I can work with, and we could have these debates and work through to have a good, positive result.

I think—but the ones that are consumed with personal animosity toward me or toward Hillary, I think, are just angry because they thought they and their crowd would always be able to drive up to the West Wing to work every day. To me, I just never thought of it that way. To me, every hour I serve here is an honor and a gift. But I never thought of myself as someone whose whole life was evaluated based on whether you were in or out. I think it's what you do when you're in that counts.

Politics of Race

Mr. Smiley. Speaking of what you do while you're in that counts, there are a significant number of African-Americans who feel that part of the reason why this hatred exists, part of the reason why this animosity exists, part of the reason why this friction exists between you and them is because you have been not just friendly to black folk and people of color—a lot of folk are friendly to black folk, and they speak and pat you on the back and stop by your fundraiser and your dinner—it's not just that you're friendly to black folk, it's that you appear downright comfortable with black folk and other people of color, and women, for that matter.

I'm wondering whether or not, with regard to the issues, you think that the reason why this hatred exists is because you have been so comfortable, so open, so accepting of diversity. Toni Morrison, as I'm sure you know, recently in the New Yorker magazine wrote that you are the first—Bill Clinton is the first black President. There are lot of black folk who feel that way about you. I'm wondering whether or not you think——

The President. [*Laughter*] I love that.

Mr. Smiley. ——might that be part of the reason why people don't like you, because you're just so friendly and so open to this concept of diversity?

The President. Well, it might be. I don't know. I honestly don't know the answer to that. I can tell you that I have watched over time, since I was a little boy, and we had all the racial troubles in the South when I was a kid—from that day to the present moment, where I'm trying to stop a disaster in Kosovo from occurring, and then we've dealt with Northern Ireland and the Middle East and tribal warfare in Africa and all these things—there are many different kinds of people in the world, but there are certainly two different kinds. There are those which draw their strength and identity from what they aren't and who they aren't, and they feel more secure when they know they're in a more dominant position over others. And then there are people who believe that they're more secure and stronger when they're unified with others, when they're connecting with people, when they're reaching across the lines that divide, and they don't feel threatened by the success of people who are totally different from them. And I was raised by my mother and by my grandparents to be in that latter group. And I don't claim any credit for it. That's just the way I am.

And this racial issue, to me, it goes way back before I was ever in politics. It's been a passion of a lifetime. I think my life is more interesting, more fun, more fulfilled because I have been able to reach out and have friends of different races and different backgrounds. And I just thank God that I was put in a position of political influence for a period of time where I could help more people to come into that mainstream of American life. I think this country is better off, and I think people individually are better off when they are connecting with people who are different from them. To me, that's one of the things that makes life interesting.

So it may be that that's a source of anger and animosity toward me. But if it is, I've gotten a lot more from this than I've paid for it. I can't imagine any more important job for the President right now than trying to unify this country across racial lines.

African-Americans and the Democratic Party

Mr. Smiley. As you know, the black community does not think or act monolithically. And while you have enjoyed a great deal of support—overwhelming, in fact—in the African-American community, there are some black folk who think that you have not been liberal enough. You are not the most liberal President, let's face it, that we've ever had. There are some folk who think that the black community still is taken for granted by the Democratic Party; that we are blindly loyal to the Democratic Party; that the Democratic Party wants black votes, but they don't put the resources they ought to put to secure those black votes, and then the weekend before election day everybody comes running to the black community begging for support.

What do you say to folk who think—black folk, particularly—who think that they're being taken advantage of, being taken for granted by the Democratic Party, and that too many of us, quite frankly, are blindly loyal, as black folk, to the Democratic Party?

The President. I would say a couple of things. First of all, I don't think the evidence supports that in my case. I mean, in these 6 years, whether you measure it by Cabinet members, by 54 Federal judges, by any other standard, I have tried to make black Americans an integral part of our national life and my administration.

Secondly, if you look at the record here—there are those who say I'm not liberal enough. Let's talk about that in two different ways. What is the standard? This economic policy I have pursued and the special efforts that we've made through empowerment zones and community development banks and other initiatives—housing initiatives in the inner city—has given us the highest homeownership in history, the highest African-American small-business ownership in history, the lowest African-American poverty ever recorded, more access to college than ever before. So I think that if you just look at that, I think the evidence is clear.

Now, there are those who say that I was wrong to sign the welfare bill that I signed. But I vetoed the welfare bills that would have taken food and medical guarantees away from poor children and families. The bill I signed simply says that every State has to make an effort to get able-bodied people in the workplace, and if able-bodied people can go into the workplace, they shouldn't be able to draw public assistance after a certain period of time. I think I was right about that.

The crime bill I signed puts 100,000 more police on the street, but it also gives young people programs and ways to stay off the street. Now—so I believe that.

Then there are some African-Americans who say that I'm not conservative enough because they favor—and they say they favor the Republicans on business grounds. It would be hard to argue that. We've done more to promote economic activity in the inner city and for African-Americans than anybody ever has.

So I actually would like it, believe it or not, someday if we could restore some balance in the party's appeal to the races. But as long as the Republicans follow the policies they're following, and if Democrats will follow the policies I've followed, I think that African-Americans are simply making the right decision based on what's right for their families and children.

I think most white Americans ought to be voting for us. Look at the economy. Look at the crime rate. Look at the welfare rolls. Look at the position of our country in the world. The truth is, I think you could make a compelling case that a lot of the non-African-Americans who vote for the Republicans are doing the irrational thing. They're voting against their self-interest and what's best for our country and what's good and strong for our country.

If you listen to what I say—the speech I gave in that Baltimore church yesterday, I could have made that speech in a white church. I could have made that speech to a white civic club. I believe that what I'm trying to do is to unify America, not divide it.

Mr. Smiley. I know that you are tight on time, and I appreciate your sitting down with me, and I'm getting some time cues here, so if I can squeeze out a couple of quick questions.

The President. Sure.

Apology for Slavery

Mr. Smiley. Far be it for me to rush the President off. I'd talk to you for another hour and a half. Let me squeeze out a couple more if I can.

When we last sat down—speaking of black folk—when we last sat down one-on-one, just a few months ago, you granted me an exclusive interview in Capetown, South Africa, as you recall. I thank you again for that. One of the questions I was pressing you on that particular day, as you were about to make a trip to Goree Island—I pressed you that day on whether or not when you got to Goree Island you were going to offer an apology for slavery. You made some rather provocative statements, but you didn't quite, in the minds of many, offer that apology for slavery. Your race commission, subsequently, has punted, if I could use that phrase, the question of the slavery apology. I'm wondering whether or not, since no one seems to want to apologize for slavery, whether or not in your mind that means that this country, America, is unapologetic about slavery.

The President. No, no. First of all, I think Dr. John Hope Franklin, who is the Chairman of my race commission, has enormous credibility with all African-Americans.

Mr. Smiley. Indeed he does—indeed.

The President. And I think what he decided was that he did not want—that, in effect, the country had been apologizing for it for over 100 years in the sense that it was abolished after the Civil War by, first, the Emancipation Proclamation of President Lincoln, and then by the passage of the constitutional amendment, the 13th amendment, and then that we had been on this long struggle, that it was self-evident that what we had done was wrong, and that we had been struggling to overcome it, and that all of us—at least virtually all thinking Americans and feeling Americans—were deeply sorry for what had happened and that we were still struggling to overcome it.

But I think that Dr. Franklin and the race commission concluded that it might be a diversion from our present task, which is to look at the problems we have today and to figure out how to overcome them, and to recognize, too, that the race issue in America is today and going forward even more complicated because it's not just about black and white Americans; it's about Hispanic-Americans; it's about Asian-Americans; it's about people from South Asia, people from the Middle East.

I gave a speech Saturday—a little talk—on my school modernization initiative over in Virginia at an elementary school, where there were children in just this elementary school from 23 different countries. And they said they were very sorry that they could not have simultaneous translation of my remarks in Spanish and Arabic.

So what I think the race commission wanted to do was to say, "Hey, the overwhelming majority of white Americans regret the whole episode of slavery, have been trying in various ways with fits and starts to overcome it for 100 years, have to continue to try to overcome it, but we should focus now on where we are and where we're going."

1998 Elections

Mr. Smiley. Last question. I asked you earlier how important you thought this election day was for you. I've tried in the few moments that I've had to ask you how important you think it is for black America, specifically. Let me close by asking you how important you think this election is for the entire country tomorrow.

The President. Well, that's the most important issue. And I think it's really a question of what the country wants us to do here. Do they want more of the last 8 months of partisanship, or would they like more progress? Do they want us to have more Washington politics as usual, or would they like the people of America to be the center of our focus?

When I say—we've got a mission here. We want to continue to prepare America for the new century. We want to finish the agenda that was unfinished in this last year. We want the Patients' Bill of Rights. We want modernized schools. We want an increase in the minimum wage. We want to save Social Security. We want to do more for child care for working people. We want to do more to spread economic opportunity where it hasn't been spread and to keep this economy going. We have a mission, an agenda. It's not about politics; it's about people.

And I can just tell you that this election will be determined by two groups of people: those who vote and those who don't. And if I were sitting out there in America, I'd say, I believe I'll be among those who vote.

Mr. Smiley. Mr. President, as always, a pleasure to sit down and talk to you, and I thank you for taking the time doing it and address us today.

The President. Thank you.

Mr. Smiley. Thank you, sir.

The President. Good to see you.

NOTE: The interview began at 11:13 a.m. in the Cabinet Room at the White House. The transcript was embargoed for release until 11:30 p.m. In his remarks, the President referred to Dr. John Hope Franklin, Chairman, President's Advisory Board on Race. A tape was not available for verification of the content of this interview.

Remarks Prior to a Meeting With the Economic Team and an Exchange With Reporters
November 3, 1998

Hurricane Mitch

The President. I'd like to begin by making a few comments about the tragedy that has been unfolding in Central America. Hurricane Mitch has already claimed thousands of lives in Honduras, Nicaragua, El Salvador, and Guatemala. Many thousands more are in urgent need of food and shelter. Across the region, communities have been devastated, bridges washed out, agriculture disrupted, schools and hospitals destroyed.

These nations are our neighbors. They all have people who are a part of our country now. They are both close to our shores and close to our hearts. We must do whatever we can to help, and we will.

Already, we have provided almost $3.5 million to airlift food, plastic sheeting, water containers, and blankets into the region. We've provided military aircraft and helicopters to get supplies to isolated areas, and deployed a disaster assistance response team to each affected country. We will be consulting with our friends in Central America and our people on the ground to see what more we can do in the days ahead.

International Economy

Now I am about to begin a meeting with my economic team to discuss a range of global economic issues. Over the long run, if our economy is to continue to grow, the economies of our trading partners must also continue to grow. Yet a full quarter of the world's population now lives in countries with declining or negative economic growth. This presents to us the biggest financial challenge in half a century.

Over the last year, we have pursued a comprehensive strategy to fight the financial crisis and to protect American jobs at home as well. Just last week, in an unprecedented step, leaders of the world's major economies agreed to create a precautionary line of credit to help countries with sound economic policies ward off crisis in the first place.

Japan recently committed substantial resources to repair its own banking system, an essential precondition to restoring growth there. The U.S., Japan, Canada, and several European nations have cut interest rates to spur global growth. And America, at last, made its contribution to the International Monetary Fund. Next week I will go to Asia, where we will continue to work with our Asian partners to spur growth, expand trade, and strengthen the social safety net, especially in the troubled countries.

In the face of worldwide economic turmoil, the American economy remains the strongest in a generation. We are grateful for that. But to keep it going we must stay with the strategy that created the conditions of growth in the first place, that helped us to build this enduring economic expansion, and we must address the challenges of the global economy to make sure it continues to endure.

1998 Elections

Q. Mr. President, since this is election day, what are your predictions for your own party?

The President. I don't know. As I said before, there are an unusual number of exceedingly close races. I can never remember a time when we had probably eight Senate seats within a few points one way or the other, and it appears to me almost three dozen House seats within a few points one way or the other.

So in large measure, it will depend upon who makes the effort to vote today. I voted. I presume everybody here has already voted or is about to. And my only message today is that every American who has not yet made the decision to go and vote, should do so.

We are going to elect a Congress that will deal with the challenges of Social Security and where it can be reformed and how, for the 21st century; that will deal with the Medicare challenge; that will deal with the challenge of providing an excellent educational opportunity for all of our people. I hope we will elect a Congress that will finally pass the Patients' Bill of Rights, that will raise the minimum wage, that will deal with a lot of our other big-time challenges, including campaign finance reform.

Q. How about your own survival? Is this a referendum on you?

The President. I think this election is a referendum on all the hopes of the American people for the future, and their assessment of the present condition, and how we get from here to a better tomorrow. I think that's what it will be. That's what all elections are, and none of us know what is going to happen. That's the honest truth. None of the pollsters know; nobody does.

Treasury Secretary Robert Rubin

Q. Mr. President, at this time of economic turmoil, what indication has Secretary Rubin given you regarding how long he intends to remain on the job? [*Laughter*]

The President. You ought to ask him. We haven't discussed it in quite a while. He knows that I want him to stay as long as he's comfortable sitting in that chair. And I think all of us know there are a lot of things going on in the world today, and the United States has a special responsibility. I'm very pleased at the work we've been able to do under Secretary Rubin's leadership to stabilize the financial conditions, especially in the last couple of months, the consensus we seem to be developing among the world's leading economies and many of the developing economies about some long-term reforms in the financial system that will enable us to continue to have growth without the kind of boom/bust cycle that has caused so much heartache in so many of the Asian economies and in Russia, and the work we've done to try to keep it from spreading to Latin America.

And he has played a critical role in all that, as well as in our own prosperity, the last several years. And I hope he'll stay as long as he feels that he can.

Hurricane Mitch

Q. Mr. President, the Central American countries that are affected are all democracies. They're all emerging markets. And it's not only a job of reconstruction, which is going to be very expensive; it's getting them back on their feet. You have shown a lot of interest in Latin America. Would you be willing to lead a movement of European countries or pan-Asian countries that would also help, because there is going to be a tremendous amount of reconstruction needed?

The President. We're going to be discussing that. I think there will be a lot of interest in the World Bank and elsewhere in trying to help put these countries back on their feet economically. But right now I think it's important that we focus on trying to help them with the present.

I mean, it's inconceivable to most Americans that a natural disaster would lead to the deaths of thousands and thousands of people. Keep in mind, all these countries are much smaller than we are. Imagine how we would feel in America if 7,000 people died in a natural disaster. And the combined population of these countries is so much smaller than ours. Virtually every family will be affected in some way or another.

And so I would say, first of all, let's help them deal with the present crisis and deal with it as rapidly and as well as possible. And then of course we will be looking at what we can do to help them rebuild and return to normal life.

President's Sixth Anniversary

Q. This is your sixth anniversary. Has it been 6 years——

The President. It is my sixth anniversary, isn't it? They have been 6 very good years, very good years for our country. And as I tell everybody around here, even the bad days are good. It's an honor to serve, and my gratitude today is immense to the American people for giving me two chances to do this and for the good things that have happened in our country over the last 6 years.

I think we can look back over 6 years and think, if you had known 6 years ago that our country would be in the position it is today, I think we would have all been almost incredulous, but we would have been full of energy and hope. I think it shows that if you just get a good team together and everybody works like crazy, and the American people do what they do, which is to get up every day and do their jobs, that good things can happen.

I'm just—I'm very grateful for these 6 years, and I'm grateful for the progress our country has made.

NOTE: The President spoke at 11:30 a.m. in the Cabinet Room at the White House. A tape was not available for verification of the content of these remarks. The related memorandum of November 6 on emergency disaster relief assistance for Honduras, Nicaragua, El Salvador, and Guatemala is listed in Appendix D at the end of this volume.

Statement on the Agreement on Fighting Sweatshop Practices
November 3, 1998

Today's agreement on fighting sweatshop practices is an historic step toward reducing sweatshop labor around the world and will give American consumers confidence that the clothes they buy are made under decent and humane working conditions. I applaud the apparel industry, labor unions, nongovernmental organizations, and consumer groups who answered the challenge I laid out 2 years ago to find cooperative ways to reduce sweatshop labor.

This agreement is only the beginning. We know that sweatshop labor will not vanish overnight. While this agreement is an historic step, we must measure our progress by how we change and improve the lives and livelihoods of apparel workers here in the United States and around the world. That is why I urge more companies to join this effort and follow these strict rules of conduct.

I want to thank all the parties who worked so hard to bring this agreement to a close, and especially Senator Tom Harkin, who first brought this issue to my attention a long time ago.

Statement on Signing the Securities Litigation Uniform Standards Act of 1998
November 3, 1998

Today I am pleased to sign into law S. 1260, the "Securities Litigation Uniform Standards Act of 1998," (Uniform Standards Act).

This country is blessed with strong and vibrant markets, and they function best when corporations can raise capital by providing investors with their best, good-faith future projections. This legislation will help stabilize the enforcement scheme of the Private Securities Litigation Reform Act of 1995 (the Reform Act) by ensuring that parties obtain the benefits of the protections that Federal law provides. The Uniform Standards Act reinforces our national capital markets by promoting uniform national standards for information generated for and used in national capital markets. If firms know that they can rely on the Reform Act's "safe harbor" for forward-looking information, they will provide the public with valuable information about their prospects, thus benefiting investors by enabling them to make wiser decisions.

The Reform Act substantially revised both substantive and procedural law governing private actions under Federal securities laws. It was designed to end litigation abuses and ensure that investors receive the best possible information by reducing the litigation risk to companies that make forward-looking statements. In addition to the safe harbor for forward-looking statements, the Reform Act created, among other things, a stay of discovery pending a defendant's motion to dismiss; limited the exposure of certain defendants by establishing proportionate liability, rather than joint and several liability, for parties not found to have "knowingly" committed violations; and required courts to assess whether all parties complied with Rule 11 of the Federal Rules of Civil Procedure, prohibiting frivolous legal filings.

Although I supported the Reform Act's goals, I vetoed the Act because I was concerned that it would erect procedural barriers and keep wrongly injured persons from having their day in court. In particular, I objected to certain statements in the 1995 Conference Report's Statement of Managers that created ambiguity with respect to whether the bill was adopting the pleading standard in private securities fraud cases of the U.S. Court of Appeals for the Second Circuit—the highest pleading standard of any Federal circuit court and a standard that I support. When the bill returned to the House and Senate floors after my veto, the bill's supporters made clear that they did in fact intend to codify the Second Circuit standard. After this important assurance, the bill passed over my veto.

Since passage of the Reform Act, there has been considerable concern that the goals of the Reform Act have not been realized. In particular, there was testimony that firms are not using the Federal safe harbor for forward-looking statements because they fear State court litigation over the same representations that are protected under Federal law. In addition, concerns have been raised that State actions are being used to achieve an "end run" around the Reform Act's stay of discovery.

In signing the Uniform Standards Act, I do so with the understanding, as reflected in the Statement of Managers for this legislation and numerous judicial decisions under the Reform Act adopting the pleading standard of the Second Circuit, that investors with legitimate complaints meeting the Second Circuit pleading standard will have access to our Nation's courts. This point was critical to my veto of the Reform Act in 1995; it was reaffirmed before ultimate passage of the 1995 Act over my veto; and its assurance was a prerequisite to my signing this legislation today, as indicated in the April 28, 1998, letter from my staff to Chairman D'Amato, Senator Gramm, and Senator Dodd. Since the uniform standards provided by this legislation state that class actions generally can be brought only in Federal court, where they will be governed by Federal law, clarity on the Federal law to be applied is particularly important. The Statement of Managers confirms that the Second Circuit pleading standard will be the uniform standard for pleading securities fraud. Thus, the uniform national standards contained in this bill will permit investors to continue to recover losses fairly attributable to reckless misconduct. I am aware of and agree with the expert views on this issue of the Securities and Exchange Commission (SEC), which, along with my staff, worked hard in shaping this legislation.

With these assurances in the Statement of Managers that reckless conduct will continue to be actionable and that complaints meeting the Second Circuit pleading standard will permit investors access to our Nation's courts, I believe that the uniform national standards created by this bill will generate meaningful information for investors and further reduce frivolous litigation without jeopardizing the critically important right of defrauded investors to obtain relief.

I do, however, object to one provision in this bill. Section 203 provides separate authority for job classification and pay of SEC economists. This provision was added to the bill at the last minute without any time for review or comment. There is no justification to treat SEC economists differently from other Federal employees. With that one exception, I am pleased to sign the Securities Litigation Uniform Standards Act of 1998 into law.

WILLIAM J. CLINTON

The White House,
November 3, 1998.

NOTE: S. 1260, approved November 3, was assigned Public Law No. 105–353.

Remarks on the Legislative Agenda and an Exchange With Reporters
November 4, 1998

The President. Good afternoon. Now that the election is over, it is time to put politics aside and once again focus clearly on the people's business. In yesterday's election, I think the message the American people sent was loud and clear: We want progress over partisanship and unity over division; we should address our country's great challenges; above all, now we must address the challenge to save Social Security for the 21st century.

We have work to do in other areas as well. We should move forward to pass a Patients' Bill of Rights. We should strengthen our schools by finishing the job of hiring 100,000 teachers and then passing the school modernization initiative, to give us 5,000 remodeled or new schools. We should increase the minimum wage. We should pass campaign finance reform. We must maintain our fiscal discipline to strengthen our own economy and maintain our efforts to stabilize the global economy.

But above all, now we have to seize this opportunity to save Social Security. And we're about to have another meeting here, one of many, in anticipation of the White House conference. I have spoken tonight and today with Senator Lott and Speaker Gingrich, with Senator Daschle and Mr. Gephardt, to ask them to join with me in this effort. On December 8th and 9th we will hold the first-ever White House Conference on Social Security, bringing together people from Congress and the administration, from the public and experts of all persuasions. We will only be able to do this if we reach across party lines, reach across generational lines, indeed, reach across philosophical lines to forge a true national consensus.

I believe we can do it. I believe we must do it. Yesterday's election makes it clear that the American people expect us to do it.

1998 Election Results

Q. To what do you attribute, Mr. President, the Democratic gains? I mean, was there one factor that you think was really the motivation?

The President. Well, let me say I'm very proud of what our party did yesterday in the face of the tide of history and an enormous financial disadvantage. I think it's clear what happened. I think that they stayed together; they had a message that was about the American people, their needs, their opportunities, and their future. I think that they won because they had a clear message that was about America, about saving Social Security, and improving education, and passing the Patients' Bill of Rights, and raising the minimum wage and those other things. I think that's why they won. And they were able to get an enormous outpouring of support in all quarters of the country. And I'm very proud of what they did. But I think they did it by putting progress over partisanship.

1998 Election Results and Impeachment Inquiry

Q. Mr. President, do you think the election results will have an impact, or should have an impact on the impeachment inquiry?

The President. That's in the hands of Congress and the American people. I've said that before; I'll say it again. I have nothing else to say about that.

Q. Mr. President, the Republicans have made no secret of the fact they intend to look at these elections and draw a lesson in terms of how they conduct an impeachment inquiry. What lesson would you hope they draw from these elections on that point?

The President. That's a decision for them to make. I'm not involved in that, and I'm not going to comment on it. I think that the lesson all people should draw is that the people who were rewarded were rewarded because they wanted to do something for the American people. They wanted to do something to pull this country together and to move this country forward.

If you look at all the results, they're clear and unambiguous. The American people want their business, their concerns, their children, their families, their future addressed here. That's what the message of the election was. And because the Democrats were able to do that in a unified fashion, even while being badly outspent and while running against a tide of history that goes back to, really to 1822, they were able to have an astonishing result. And I'm grateful for that.

But I think that people of both parties who care about these issues and want to pull the country together should now put the election behind us, put Social Security reform and education and health care reform before us, and go forward. That's what I want to do.

1998 Election Results

Q. [*Inaudible*]—the outcome is a vindication of your policies?

The President. I think it is a vindication of the policies and of the general policy of putting partisanship behind progress and of putting people before politics and of trying to find ways to bring people together instead of to divide them. It was clearly a vindication of the message that the Democrats put out there on education,

health care, Social Security and the minimum wage, campaign finance reform, the environment, a number of other things.

A lot of people worked very hard in this election—the Vice President did; the First Lady did; a lot of people did—but I think the American people basically said to all of us—all of us— "We sent you there to work for us, and we want you to find a way to do it, to address the challenges we face and to bring this country together and move this country forward." I think that was the loud, clear, completely unambiguous message of the election.

Governor-Elect Jesse Ventura of Minnesota

Q. [*Inaudible*]—the election of Ventura in Minnesota——

The President. I don't know. I think that you're going to have a lot of politicians spending time in gyms now. [*Laughter*]

NOTE: The President spoke at 1:15 p.m. in the Cabinet Room at the White House, prior to a meeting with the economic team.

Statement on the Russia-United States Agreement on Food Aid
November 4, 1998

I am pleased to announce that a U.S. team will begin today to finalize an agreement with the Government of Russia on a program to provide at least 3.1 million metric tons of food. This program will help sustain Russians through a serious food shortage this winter as well as their country's continuing economic distress. In addition, this agreement will bolster American farmers and ranchers who have been hit hard by an agricultural crisis here. We will be pre-

pared to consider additional assistance if necessary.

The program is being developed under the auspices of the binational commission chaired by Vice President Gore and Prime Minister Primakov. Our negotiating team will work with their Russian counterparts to ensure that our assistance is distributed properly and exempted from taxes and customs duties. These are key elements to a successful program.

Memorandum on a Guidebook for Victims of Domestic Violence
November 4, 1998

Memorandum for the Director of the Office of Personnel Management

Subject: Guidebook for Victims of Domestic Violence

Domestic violence is one of the most serious public health issues and criminal justice issues facing our Nation. About 30 percent of female murder victims are killed by intimates each year. Women aged 16–24 experience the highest rates of intimate violence. In 1996, women experienced an estimated 840,000 incidents of rape, sexual assault, robbery, and aggravated assault at the hands of intimates. While this number has declined from 1.1 million incidents in 1993, we must strive to eliminate domestic violence both for its effects on victims as well as on their children. Domestic violence does not discriminate—it affects individuals of every age, race, gender, class, and religion.

My Administration is committed to fighting the scourge of domestic violence. As part of the Violent Crime Control and Law Enforcement Act of 1994, I fought for and signed into law the historic Violence Against Women Act (VAWA), which provides a comprehensive approach to domestic violence, both through prosecuting offenders and providing assistance to victims. Through VAWA, my Administration has provided almost half a billion dollars through STOP (Services, Training, Officers, and Prosecutors) grants to the states for law enforcement prosecution, and victim services to prevent and respond to violence against women. The extension of the Brady Law prohibits anyone convicted of a domestic violence offense from owning a firearm. The Interstate Stalking Punishment and Prevention Act of 1996 makes it a Federal crime to cross State lines intending to injure or harass another person.

In 1995, I established the Violence Against Women Office at the Department of Justice, elevating the fight against domestic violence to the national level for the first time. Since 1996, the 24-hour National Domestic Violence Hotline (1–800–799–SAFE) has provided immediate crisis intervention, counseling, and referrals to those in need, responding to as many as 10,000 calls each month.

Domestic violence affects all aspects of our society—the family, the community, and the workplace. As the Nation's largest employer, the Federal Government has tried to set an example for private employers to protect and provide assistance to workers who are victims of domestic violence. In 1995, I signed an executive memorandum requiring all Federal departments to begin employee awareness efforts on domestic violence. Last year, the Vice President announced that the Office of Personnel Management had developed a guidebook for dealing with workplace violence that outlines a wide array of strategies for preventing violence at work and for helping supervisors, security, and employee assistance staff to recognize the signs of violence, including domestic violence.

Building upon these efforts, it is important to provide a resource guide to the thousands of Federal employees across the country, whether they are a victim of domestic violence or a family member, neighbor, friend, or co-worker of someone who is being abused. I accordingly direct you to prepare within 120 days a guidebook that will (1) assist Federal employees who are victims of domestic violence by providing up-to-date information about available resources and outline strategies to ensure safety; and (2) help those who know a Federal employee who is being abused to prevent and respond to the situation. This guidebook should list private as well as public resources such as counseling, law enforcement, workplace leave policies, and substance abuse programs. In developing this guidebook, you should consult with all interested parties, including the private sector and other Federal agencies and offices—particularly, the Department of Justice and the Department of Health and Human Services.

This guidebook, in conjunction with my Administration's continuing efforts to combat domestic violence, will help to promote the safety of all Federal workers and their families.

WILLIAM J. CLINTON

NOTE: The memorandum of October 2, 1995, on the Federal Employee Domestic Violence Awareness Campaign was published in the *Federal Register* at 60 FR 52821.

Remarks on the Legislative Agenda and an Exchange With Reporters
November 5, 1998

The President. Good morning. The Vice President and I have just finished a good meeting with Senator Daschle and Congressman Gephardt. We all agree that the message from the American people in the last election is clear—that they want us to pursue progress over partisanship and to find unity over division.

And we talked about how best to start that process. We believe the best way to start is by taking up the Patients' Bill of Rights, the legislation that would guarantee quality health care to Americans without regard to whether they are in managed care plans or not and would assure that medical decisions are made by doctors, not by accountants.

In the last session of Congress, that bill lost by only five votes in the House, and we now have five more Democrats coming to the House. It came very close to passing in the United States Senate. It need not be a partisan issue. Indeed, a cosponsor of the Patients' Bill of Rights in the House is Congressman Greg Ganske from Iowa, a Republican physician who has spoken very eloquently about the need for this legislation.

So what we want to do is to reach out to like-minded people in the other party to try to heed the admonition of the American people and the direction that we certainly agree we ought to take and get to work together. We're looking forward to it, and this is where we think we should begin.

1998 Election Results and Impeachment Inquiry

Q. Congressman Gephardt, what do you think this does to the impeachment hearings? Does it wipe them out, diminish them, slow them down, or what?

Representative Richard A. Gephardt. First, I want to agree with the President on the Patients' Bill of Rights. I feel very strongly that we can get this done. If you have a sick family member, you want it done now, so we're going to work very hard to see if we can get it done in the early part of this next year.

I don't know what is happening on Mr. Hyde's statement—if they are moving in our direction—we wanted them to some weeks ago, and they're going to get this over with in a fair and expeditious way. That's good.

Q. Mr. President, do you anticipate that your lawyers will vigorously attack the Starr report in the committee? And is there any testimony in that report, sir, that you dispute?

The President. I have nothing to say about that. I want these hearings to be constitutional, fair, and expeditious. At the appropriate time in the appropriate way, we will say whatever we intend to say. But I have nothing to say about it.

I think the important thing is that we've got to go back to doing the people's business. The American people sent us a message that would break the eardrums of anyone who was listening. They want their business tended to. They are tired of seeing Washington focused on politics and personalities. They want the people and their issues and their future taken care of, and that's what we're here to do.

The Vice President. If I could say a brief word. Before you all came in here, we had a long meeting. This subject never even came up. We heard what the American people said, and what they said was turn to the people's business. And that's what this whole meeting has been about.

Q. Mr. President, are you still in jeopardy, sir? Do you believe you're still in jeopardy?

The President. That's out of my hands. That's up to the American people and the Congress. All I know is I've got a day here, and I want to make the most of it.

Iraq

Q. Mr. President, are you concerned at all about the apparent lack of support among the Persian Gulf allies for a tougher action against Iraq at this point?

The President. Well, actually, my information is that Secretary Cohen had a good trip, and we believe we'll have the support that we need for whatever decisions we ultimately make.

Q. Including military action?

The President. We believe we'll have the support we need, and all options are on the table.

NOTE: The President spoke at 9:47 a.m. in the Oval Office at the White House, following a meeting with congressional leaders. A tape was not available for verification of the content of these remarks.

Remarks on Presenting the Arts and Humanities Awards
November 5, 1998

The President. Thank you, ladies and gentlemen, for the wonderful welcome. I just realized that at the moment of greatest unity for my political party in many years, my wife has told the president of the AFL–CIO that I crossed a picket line. [*Laughter*] But it's true. [*Laughter*]

Let me join Hillary in thanking the representatives of the NEA, the NEH, the Museum and Library Services for all they have done. I thank Senator Baucus, Senator Durbin, Congressman and Mrs. Engel, Congresswoman Morella for being here and for their support for the arts and humanities. There are many, many other supporters in both parties of the arts and humanities in the Congress who wanted to be here today, but in light of Tuesday's election results in Minnesota, they're in the gym working out. [*Laughter*]

I'd like to thank our USIA Director, Joe Duffey, for being here, and a special thanks to our wonderful Secretary of Education, Dick Riley, and his wife, Tunky. Thank you for being here. Secretary Riley's going to persuade them to try to work out their minds as well as their bodies. [*Laughter*]

Paul Klee once said, "Art does not reproduce the visible, rather it makes it visible." Today we honor an extraordinary group of Americans whose daring vision and indelible contributions to arts and humanities have opened all our eyes to the richness, diversity, and miracles of the human experience.

We are blessed to live in an era of breathtaking change and unlimited possibility: an economy that is the strongest in a generation; hopeful reductions in many of our social problems; around the world, a surging tide of democracy in lands where creativity and freedom once were viciously suppressed; an emerging global community united increasingly by the technological revolution, commercial ties, and greater interaction.

But we know that change also, always, brings new challenges and, perhaps even as important, can obstruct old, unresolved difficulties. Now more than ever, therefore, we need our artists and patrons, our historians and educators to help us make sense of the world in which we live, to remind us about what really matters in life, to embody the values we Americans hold most dear: freedom of expression, and tolerance and respect for diversity.

For more than 200 years, through dance and songs, in paint or on paper, Americans have expressed their individuality and their common humanity. This tradition of our shared culture is one we must nurture and take with us into the new millennium.

Today we proudly honor 19 men and women, a theater troupe, and one organization, all of whom have laid the foundation for a new century of greater American creativity.

First, the National Medal of the Arts. More than 50 years ago, a New York City mother, looking for a way to keep her 7-year-old son off the streets, decided to send him with his sister to her ballet class. From there, Jacques d'Amboise leapt to the pinnacle of the dance, thrilling audiences as principal dancers for the New York City Ballet, landing roles in Hollywood musicals, creating timeless ballets of his own. With his National Dance Institute, he has given thousands of children, like those we saw today, the same opportunity he had, to strive for excellence and expression through dance.

Those who know him know he would walk 1,000 miles for his kids. And this spring he will be doing just that, hiking the length of the Appalachian Trail to raise money for his institute.

Ladies and gentlemen, Jacques d'Amboise.

[*The President and the First Lady presented the medal and congratulated Mr. d'Amboise.*]

The President. From "Blueberry Hill" to Capitol Hill, and countless concert halls and honky-tonks in between, Fats Domino has brought musical joy to millions, including me. I was this morning trying to remember all the lyrics to all the songs that I could. I will spare you a recitation. [*Laughter*]

Antoine Domino grew up in New Orleans speaking French, English, and boogie-woogie. His talent was as big as his frame and his nickname. In a career spanning half a century, his rich voice and distinctive piano style helped to define rock and roll, the music that more than any other creative force in America has brought the races together. When I heard he couldn't make the ceremony, I thought, "Ain't That a Shame." [*Laughter*] But I'm thrilled that his daughter, Antoinette Domino Smith, is here to accept the medal on behalf of her remarkable father, Fats Domino.

[*The President and the First Lady presented the medal and congratulated Ms. Domino Smith.*]

The President. When the movie "Urban Cowboy" came out, Ramblin' Jack Elliot must have laughed, because even though he sings like he was raised on the range, he was actually born, as he puts it, "on a 45,000-acre ranch in the middle of Flatbush." [*Laughter*] He left home at 15 to join the rodeo, where he learned to sing cowboy songs. But it was hearing his first Woody Guthrie record that transformed him into the man Sam Shepard called a "wandering, true American minstrel."

Since then, he's traveled the world with his guitar and recorded more than 40 albums, winning a Grammy and fans from Bob Dylan to Mick Jagger. In giving new life to our most valuable musical traditions, Ramblin' Jack has, himself, become an American treasure. Ladies and gentlemen, Ramblin' Jack Elliot.

[*The President and the First Lady presented the medal and congratulated Mr. Elliot.*]

The President. From the industrial skyscrapers of Louis Sullivan to the prairie houses of Frank Lloyd Wright to the elegant geometry of I.M. Pei, Americans have defined the field of architecture in the 20th century. No architect better expresses the American spirit of our time than Frank Gehry. From concert halls to shopping malls, he has given the world buildings that are fearless and flamboyant, that trample the boundaries of convention. There are few architects whose works so stirs the imagination that people will cross oceans just to see it built. But his

Guggenheim Museum in Bilbao, Spain, has attracted architecture pilgrims for years.

When people ask what America aspired to on the eve of the 21st century, they will look to the work of this remarkable man, Frank Gehry.

[*The President and the First Lady presented the medal and congratulated Mr. Gehry.*]

The President. President Franklin Roosevelt once said that the conditions for art and democracy are one. Citizen activist and arts patron Barbara Handman has dedicated her entire life to ensure that those conditions are met. Her sustained support for the arts, fighting to keep some of New York's historic theaters from going dark, serving on the city's theater advisory board, and many other activities have enriched our Nation's cultural life. Her passionate advocacy of the first amendment has enlarged our vital freedoms.

When we celebrate the arts today, we also celebrate the commitment of Americans like Bobbie, whose activism and generosity are essential, and just as essential as our artists, to the flourishing of our arts and the preservation of our ideals.

Ladies and gentlemen, Barbara Handman.

[*The President and the First Lady presented the medal and congratulated Ms. Handman.*]

The President. The revered and visionary painter Agnes Martin once told a reporter that "everyone sees beauty, and art is a way to respond." Throughout a lifetime, she has responded to the beauty of her world with luminous graphite lines, fields of white, or bands of subtle color on canvas. For more than 40 years, her quiet, spare paintings have conveyed happiness and innocence to viewers and have earned the Saskatchewan native and naturalized American a place among America's foremost abstract artists. Her work is featured in the permanent collections of our finest galleries.

Today, even into her mideighties, she continues to paint every morning, finding inspiration in the solitude of her studio in Taos, New Mexico. Ladies and gentlemen, the remarkable Agnes Martin.

[*The President and the First Lady presented the medal and congratulated Ms. Martin.*]

The President. Sixty years ago, Gregory Peck abandoned pre-med studies for the sound stages of Hollywood. While he never practiced the healing art, his performances have helped to heal some of our countries deepest wounds. For many, he will always be Atticus Finch, the Alabama lawyer whose brave stand for justice and against racism in "To Kill a Mockingbird" stirred the conscience of a nation. He won an Oscar for that role and would star in 55 films: "Gentlemen's Agreement," "Roman Holiday," "The Guns of Navarone." He has been a tireless advocate for the arts, serving on the National Council on the Arts, as president of the Academy of Motion Picture Arts and Sciences.

Today, he tours America in a one-man show, sharing memories with fans who still consider him the handsomest man on Earth. It's a great honor for me to present this award as a genuine fan of Gregory Peck.

[*The President and the First Lady presented the medal and congratulated Mr. Peck.*]

The President. We've seen it so many times in movies and in real life, a star falls ill only to be replaced by a promising ingenue who then catapults to stardom. Fifty years ago, that stage was the Met; the opera was "Don Giovanni"; and the ingenue was a 19-year-old soprano from the Bronx, Roberta Peters. She went on to achieve international acclaim, giving voice to the great heroines of opera: Lucia, Gilda, the Queen of the Night. She is, you might say, for all of us coarser types, the Cal Ripken of opera—[*laughter*]—having performed as many as 30 times a season, achieved the longest tenure of any soprano in the Met's history, and appeared on the "Ed Sullivan Show" a record 65 times. She has sung for every President from President Eisenhower to President Bush. Now it is time for this President to honor her.

It is an honor to present our next winner with the Medal of Arts. Ladies and gentlemen, Roberta Peters.

[*The President and the First Lady presented the medal and congratulated Ms. Peters.*]

The President. What Dublin was to Joyce or Yoknapatawpha County was to Faulkner, Newark is to Philip Roth. [*Laughter*] Who would have though this melting pot of immigrant aspirations, of Jews, Italians, Irish, African-Americans, would have yielded a voice as distinct and powerfully American as Philip Roth? He and his many literary alter egos, from Nathan Zuckerman to, quote, Philip Roth, unquote,

have been among us now for four decades. He brought to the world's attention a generation of writers from what he calls "the other Europe," whose instinct for freedom matches his own. His last four books, "Patrimony," "Operation Shylock," "Sabbath's Theater," "American Pastoral," have each won a major literary award. Improbable as it may seem, this brash kid of Newark has become a grand old man of American letters.

Ladies and gentlemen, Philip Roth.

[*The President and the First Lady presented the medal and congratulated Mr. Roth.*]

The President. You know what he said when I gave him the award? He said, "I'm not so old as you think." [*Laughter*] And Hillary said, "It's just a literary expression." [*Laughter*]

To indulge his passion for art, something he needs, I might say, as an expatriate southerner who can never quite leave the romance of his roots, the chairman and CEO of Sara Lee, John Bryan, now just has to show up for work, for covering the walls of the Sara Lee's downtown Chicago headquarters is a vast collection of impressionist paintings by Monet, Matisse, Pissaro.

But a few months ago, Sara Lee announced that it would donate the entire collection to museums around the country. This generosity is not unusual. Under John's leadership, Sara Lee has supported the arts all across America; the Lyric Opera in Chicago, the Dixon Gallery and Gardens in Memphis are just two. From the cakes they bake to the paintings they share, Sara Lee does, indeed, nourish the world.

Thank you, John Bryan. Please accept this medal on behalf of Sara Lee and a grateful nation.

[*The President and the First Lady presented the medal and congratulated Mr. Bryan.*]

The President. The 1974 birth of Chicago's Steppenwolf Theatre in a church basement has been described as "a moment when the cosmos got lucky." Through a miraculous mix of talent and vision, Steppenwolf has reconciled the contradictions of modern theater. It stages edgy, experimental productions that still manage to attract mainstream audiences. It is an ensemble company that shuns the star system, and yet it has launched its fair share of stars: John Malkovich, Gary Sinise, Joan Allen. That those stars regularly skip movie roles to act in

Steppenwolf plays speaks volumes about the magic of this theater.

To the many Tony Awards Steppenwolf has won, it is now my privilege to add the National Medal of Arts. Dr. Martha Lavey, the artistic director, is here to accept the medal, along with an historic gathering of 32 members of her troupe. And if they're out there, I'd like to ask them to stand as she comes up, please.

[The President and the First Lady presented the medal and congratulated Dr. Lavey.]

The President. It's every performer's dream. In 1953 Gwen Verdon exited the stage after a brief solo in the Broadway musical "Can-Can," only to hear the crowd go wild, shouting, "We want Verdon." Quite literally, she stole the show. After that first Tony Award-winning performance, she just kept dancing. Her collaboration with the great choreographer, Bob Fosse, defined the art of jazz dance. She gave brilliant performances in shows from "Damn Yankees" to "Sweet Charity" to "Chicago," winning three more Tonys and fans all over the world. In movies ranging from "The Cotton Club" to the recent critically acclaimed film "Marvin's Room," this famous redhead is showing us all that she is still alive and kicking.

Ladies and gentlemen, Ms. Gwen Verdon.

[The President and the First Lady presented the medal and congratulated Ms. Verdon.]

The President. Now, the National Humanities Medals.

Ever since President Eisenhower asked the then 28-year-old Stephen Ambrose to edit his papers, he has animated history with stories of great leaders and average citizens whose common denominator is their uncommon heroism. With a storyteller's ear for narrative and a scholar's eye for detail, he puts us in the shoes of our most courageous Americans, from 19-year-old citizen soldiers storming the beaches of Normandy to Lewis and Clark as they opened the American West. His work has inspired Americans to make pilgrimages to long forgotten historic sites brought to life by his prose.

Ladies and gentlemen, Stephen Ambrose.

[The President and the First Lady presented the medal and congratulated Mr. Ambrose.]

The President. The son of a pianist and music store owner, E.L. Doctorow is perhaps the finest chronicler of the changing rhythms of American life. From "Ragtime" to "Billy Bathgate," to "The Waterworks," he has captured the cacophony of American life and turned it into melodies that resonate in readers' minds long after they turn the final page. His narratives are such compelling physic histories of a young nation, struggling with the divergent impulses of human nature, that they have earned him both critical acclaim and popular appeal. He's a true literary lion, a caring professor, a gentle soul. I am grateful that I have had the chance to learn a lot about my country from his work.

Ladies and gentlemen, E.L. Doctorow.

[The President and the First Lady presented the medal and congratulated Mr. Doctorow.]

The President. Ten years ago, Harvard's Diana Eck began to notice that her students weren't just choosing her class on Indian religions to learn about a foreign culture. They were enrolling to learn more about their own heritage. She was inspired to explore how America, founded by people in search of religious freedom, has changed and been changed by the religions of our recent immigrants.

She has found the religions of the world in America's own backyard: mosques in Massachusetts, Hindu temples in Houston, and even a century-old Buddhist temple in her native Montana. And through a new CD-ROM, "On Common Ground: World Religions in America," she is helping us to appreciate not only the richness of our diversity but the strength of our shared values.

Ladies and gentlemen, Diana Eck.

[The President and the First Lady presented the medal and congratulated Ms. Eck.]

The President. For 10 years an adult literacy teacher struggled to motivate her students. Then, when she became a mother, she realized that a parent will do for her child what she will not do for herself. "If you want to teach a person to read," Nancye Gaj thought, "teach her to read to her children." She brought this insight to her work with female inmates in a North Carolina prison, with dramatic results. The mothers not only learned to read; their children did better in schools, and their families grew stronger. Through her literacy program, MOTHEREAD, Gaj has unleashed the power of family reading in schools and homes all across

America. Today America honors a true revolutionary of literacy, Nancye Gaj, with the National Humanities Medal.

[*The President and the First Lady presented the medal and congratulated Ms. Gaj.*]

The President. Near the beginning of this century, W.E.B. Du Bois predicted a "black tomorrow" of African-American achievement. Thanks in large measure to Henry Louis Gates, that tomorrow has turned into today. For 20 years he has revitalized African-American studies. In his writing and teaching, through his leadership of the "dream team" of African-American scholars he brought together at Harvard, Gates has shed brilliant light on authors and traditions kept in the shadows for too long. From "Signifying Monkeys" to small-town West Virginia, from ancient Africa to the new New York, Skip Gates has described the American experience with force, with dignity and, most of all, with color.

Ladies and gentlemen, Henry Louis Gates, Jr.

[*The President and the First Lady presented the medal and congratulated Mr. Gates.*]

The President. In high school in Beirut, Vartan Gregorian was so brilliant his teachers called him "Professor." At the Carnegie Corporation of New York, now they call him "President." But at Brown University, where he just concluded 9 successful years at the helm, he's remembered simply and fondly as Vartan, the most approachable and engaging man on campus. Public education has been his faith and greatest enthusiasm—as an Armenian child in Iran, as a student in Lebanon and the United States, then as president of the New York Public Library, where he restored grandeur and purpose to one of America's great institutions.

President, philanthropist, friend, Vartan Gregorian is, as one magazine put it, "a phenomenon." And we're proud to honor him today.

[*The President and the First Lady presented the medal and congratulated Mr. Gregorian.*]

The President. Growing up in La Jolla, California, Ramon Eduardo Ruiz spent nights listening to his immigrant father's tales of the heroes and history of Mexico. After serving as a pilot in World War II, he took his passion for Mexico's past to the halls of academia, becoming one of America's premier and pioneering scholars of Latin American history.

He has dedicated his life to exploring what he calls "the saga of the Mexican people, a story of sporadic triumphs played out on a stage of tragic drama." His history of Mexico, "Triumphs and Tragedy," is taught in colleges and universities all across our country, shaping a new generation's understanding of the heritage and homeland of millions of our fellow Americans.

Ladies and gentlemen, Ramon Eduardo Ruiz.

[*The President and the First Lady presented the medal and congratulated Mr. Ruiz.*]

The President. For more than 50 years, Arthur Schlesinger has been at the vital center of our public life. He has not only chronicled American history, he has helped to define it, as the fighting intellectual of the Americans for Democratic Action, adviser to Adlai Stevenson, special assistant to President Kennedy. A renowned historian like his father, Schlesinger has steered Americans on a straight and sensible course through the changing tides of history, from "The Age of Jackson" to the multicultural Nation in which we live today.

As he has written of the leaders he served, Professor Schlesinger, throughout his life, has taken "the Promethean responsibility to affirm human freedom against the supposed inevitabilities of history." What a remarkable life he has lived; what wonderful books he has written.

Ladies and gentlemen, Arthur Schlesinger.

[*The President and the First Lady presented the medal and congratulated Mr. Schlesinger.*]

The President. I want to choose my words rather carefully now before honoring one of America's leading students of Presidential rhetoric. [*Laughter*] "Lincoln," Garry Wills has written, "knew the power of words to win a war, to change history, to shape a nation." Garry Wills, too, understands the power of words. And his own books and essays have given eloquent voice to our past and to our present.

In the Pulitzer Prize-winning "Lincoln at Gettysburg," he offered new perspectives on the most important speech in American history— the way it redefined our Constitution in the minds of our people and rededicated our Nation to our revolutionary ideals. Whatever his subject, politics or popular culture, the classics or even boxing, his insight is unsurpassed. I find that difficult to acknowledge from time to time.

[*Laughter*] Like his students at Northwestern, Hillary and I, and indeed, all America are grateful for his brilliant and iconoclastic scholarship.

Ladies and gentlemen, Garry Wills.

[*The President and the First Lady presented the medal and congratulated Mr. Wills.*]

The President. The late Dizzy Gillespie once said of his fellow jazz trumpeter, Louis Armstrong, who had blazed musical and professional trails before him, "No him, no me."

Today a grateful nation says to the 21 medalists in this room, "No you, no we." Thank you for opening doors of hope. Thank you for opening doors of artistic and intellectual possibility. Thank you for opening them for all Americans and lighting the way to our common future.

Thank you very much.

NOTE: The President spoke at 11:18 a.m. on the South Lawn at the White House. In his remarks, he referred to Patricia Engel, wife of Representative Eliot L. Engel; Ann (Tunky) Riley, wife of Secretary of Education Richard W. Riley; and actor/playwright Sam Shepard. The transcript released by the Office of the Press Secretary also included the remarks of the First Lady.

Statement Announcing a Presidential Mission to Central America To Assist in the Aftermath of Hurricane Mitch
November 5, 1998

The United States has close and longstanding ties with the people and governments of Central America, and many Americans have close family and cultural ties to these countries. In light of the devastation caused by Hurricane Mitch, I have asked Tipper Gore to lead a Presidential mission to Honduras and Nicaragua. Mrs. Gore will travel to the region November 10–11, 1998, to demonstrate our commitment to assist the people of Central America as they recover from this catastrophe.

Mrs. Gore will deliver supplies and participate in disaster relief efforts. She will be joined by U.S. Agency for International Development Administrator Brian Atwood and Members of Congress on the mission. I believe that this trip will expand awareness throughout the U.S. and the world of the devastation faced by the people of Central America in order to encourage a global relief effort.

Statement on Iraq's Noncompliance With United Nations Resolutions
November 5, 1998

Iraq's latest attempt to block the vital work of the international weapons inspectors is totally unacceptable. That is not just my belief or America's belief; it is the demand of the international community. A short while ago, the United Nations Security Council unanimously adopted a resolution condemning Iraq's intransigence and insisting it immediately resume full cooperation with the weapons inspectors—no ifs, no ands, no buts about it.

It is long past time for Iraq to meet its obligations to the world. After the Gulf war, the international community demanded and Iraq agreed to declare and destroy all of its chemical, biological, and nuclear weapons capability and the missiles to deliver them, and to meet other U.N. Security Council resolutions. We imposed these conditions to ensure that Iraq would no longer threaten the region or the world. We kept sanctions in place—exempting food, medicine, and other humanitarian supplies—to make sure that Iraq made good on its commitments.

Now, the better part of a decade later, Iraq continues to shirk its clear obligations. Iraq has no one to blame but itself—and the people of

Iraq have no one to blame but Saddam Hussein—for the position Iraq finds itself in today. Iraq could have ended its isolation long ago by simply complying with the will of the world. The burden is on Iraq to get back in compliance and meet its obligations—immediately.

Remarks at the Arts and Humanities Awards Dinner
November 5, 1998

Ladies and gentlemen, good evening. The good news is this is the only speech you have to listen to tonight. And I want to, first of all, welcome all of you back to the White House. To all of our honorees and their families and friends who are here today, let me say, for Hillary and me this is a day we look forward to every year, but today was an especially wonderful day. And as each of our honorees came through the line tonight, they all commented on how they felt that they were in quite good company today, being honored, and I agree with that.

As I see so often when it comes to maintaining stability in the global economy or working for peace in Bosnia or Kosovo or Northern Ireland or the Middle East, perhaps more than any other time in our over 220-year history, the entire world now looks to the United States to exert responsible leadership in technological innovation, preventing war, promoting peace, promoting prosperity and freedom and democracy.

I think it is worth asking ourselves tonight, when the historians and novelists, the poets and painters look back on America in the last years of the 20th century, on the verge of a new millennium, what will they say of that kind of work and that kind of leadership? For clearly the world does look to us for cultural leadership. The influence of our books, our movies, our music, our plays have never stopped at our borders. But now, thanks to technology, they reach more rapidly into even the remotest corners of the world. For example, in Bhutan, a Himalayan country so isolated just 5,000 people actually visit it every year, you can still find some of this year's most popular Hollywood blockbusters, for better or worse. [*Laughter*]

Hillary's book, "It Takes a Village," has been translated into a myriad of languages, not just French or Spanish or German but Bulgarian, even Kazakh. More than ever before, the world is listening to what America has to say. As our leading artists and intellectuals, you will have to answer. It is a tremendous opportunity and an enormous responsibility.

So tonight I challenge you to rise to this task and to relish it and, through your art, your music, your ideas, to make this time not simply a golden age for the United States but a time of greater understanding, enlightenment, and, yes, enjoyment for the entire world.

Thank you very much.

NOTE: The President spoke at 9:35 p.m. in the East Room at the White House.

Letter to Congressional Leaders Reporting on Iraq's Compliance With United Nations Security Council Resolutions
November 5, 1998

Dear Mr. Speaker: (*Dear Mr. President:*)

Consistent with the Authorization for Use of Military Force Against Iraq Resolution (Public Law 102–1) and as part of my effort to keep the Congress fully informed, I am reporting on the status of efforts to obtain Iraq's compliance with the resolutions adopted by the United Nations Security Council (UNSC). This report covers the period from September 3 to the present.

Introduction

On October 31, Iraq announced that it was ceasing all cooperation with the United Nations Special Commission (UNSCOM) including monitoring activity. This announcement represents a serious escalation of Iraq's August 5 decision to suspend cooperation with UNSCOM and the International Atomic Energy Agency (IAEA). On October 31, the UNSC issued a statement condemning Iraq's decision as a "flagrant violation of relevant Council resolutions and of the Memorandum of Understanding signed between the Secretary General and the Deputy Prime Minister of Iraq" last February. Iraq's action followed its receipt of a letter from the UK (as President of the Security Council) indicating a willingness to conduct a comprehensive review, but only after Iraq returned to full compliance. Since the October 31 statement, UNSCOM has been able to conduct only very limited monitoring activity.

Earlier, on September 9, the UNSC unanimously adopted Resolution 1194, which condemns Iraq's August 5 decision as a "totally unacceptable contravention of its obligations," demands that Iraq rescind its decision and resume cooperation, and suspends bimonthly sanctions reviews until UNSCOM and IAEA report that they are satisfied that Iraq has done so.

The resolution also notes the Council's willingness to hold a comprehensive review of "Iraq's compliance with its obligations under all relevant resolutions once Iraq has rescinded its . . . decision [to suspend cooperation] and demonstrated that it is prepared to fulfill all its obligations, including, in particular on disarmament issues, by resuming full cooperation with the Special Commission and the IAEA . . ."

On September 23, the P–5 Foreign Ministers issued a statement reiterating that Iraq's actions are "totally unacceptable," and confirmed that "Iraq must respond immediately to Security Council Resolution 1194 and resume full cooperation." The statement also noted that the prerequisite for a comprehensive review was Iraq's "unconditional resumption" of cooperation with UNSCOM and the IAEA.

Tariq Aziz spent several days at the United Nations in New York at the end of September discussing the comprehensive review with Security Council members and the Secretary General. The Secretary General's Special Representative Prakash Shah is engaged in discussions in Baghdad on the subject. Despite Iraq's lobbying efforts, the Secretary General and all Council members remain united in judging Iraq's actions unacceptable; all 15 Council members supported the Council President's letter to the Secretary General that said Iraq must rescind its August 5 decision and resume cooperation with UNSCOM and the IAEA. We continue to work with the Council to convince Iraq to reverse course, but we have not ruled out any option should the Council fail to reverse Iraq's decision.

We continue to support the international community's efforts to provide for the humanitarian needs of the Iraqi people through the "oil-for-food" program. On May 27, 1998, Iraq presented a distribution plan for the implementation of Resolution 1153, which had been adopted on February 20. Under phase three of the "oil-for-food" program, which ran from December 3, 1997, through June 2, 1998, $1.2 billion worth of humanitarian goods were approved for export to Iraq. Under the current phase, phase four, which began in June, the U.N. Sanctions Committee has approved the purchase of over $1.2 billion worth of humanitarian goods. United States companies can participate in the "oil-for-food" program, and over $185 million worth of direct contracts for U.S. firms have been approved since the program began.

Recent developments in northern Iraq demonstrate once again the power of persistent diplomacy. On September 17, leaders of the two main Iraqi Kurdish parties, Massoud Barzani and Jalal Talabani, met together for the first time in over 4 years to sign a forward-looking joint statement committing their parties to reconciliation. Their talks, held at the Department of State under U.S. auspices, followed 6 months of intensive discussions and close consultation with the Kurdish parties and with our Turkish and British allies. The statesmanlike achievement of the Iraqi Kurdish leaders signals a hopeful new chapter for all the people of northern Iraq.

On October 31, I signed into law the Iraq Liberation Act of 1998. Work also continues on the existing opposition program to help opposition groups unify politically, and the new Radio Free Iraq service began broadcasting in late October. These new programs will help us encourage the Iraqi people to build a pluralistic, peaceful Iraq that observes the international rule of law and respects basic human rights. Such an

Iraq would have little trouble regaining its rightful place in the region and in the international community.

U.S. and Coalition Force Levels in the Gulf Region

Saddam's record of aggressive behavior forces us to retain a highly capable force presence in the region in order to deter Iraq and deal with any threat it might pose to its neighbors. The United States and allied forces now in the theater are prepared to deal with all contingencies. We have the capability to respond rapidly to possible Iraqi aggression. We will continue to maintain a robust force posture and have established a rapid reinforcement capability to supplement our forces in the Gulf when needed. Our cruise missile force is twice the pre-October 1997 level and can be augmented significantly within days. Our contingency plans allow us the capability for swift, powerful strikes if that becomes necessary.

Our forces in the region include land and carrier-based aircraft, surface warships, a Marine expeditionary unit, a Patriot missile battalion, a mechanized battalion task force, and a mix of special operations forces deployed in support of U.S. Central Command operations. To enhance force protection throughout the region, additional military security personnel are also deployed.

Operation Northern Watch and Operation Southern Watch

The United States and coalition partners continue to enforce the no-fly zones over Iraq under Operation Northern Watch and Operation Southern Watch. There were no observed no-fly zone violations during the period covered by this report. We have made clear to Iraq and to all other relevant parties that the United States and coalition partners will continue to enforce both no-fly zones.

The Maritime Interception Force

The Maritime Interception Force (MIF), operating in accordance with Resolution 665 and other relevant resolutions, vigorously enforces U.N. sanctions in the Gulf. The U.S. Navy is the single largest component of this multinational force, but it is frequently augmented by ships, aircraft, and other support from Australia, Canada, Belgium, Kuwait, The Netherlands, New Zealand, the UAE, and the United Kingdom. Member states of the Gulf Cooperation Council also support the MIF by providing logistical support and shipriders and by accepting vessels diverted for violating U.N. sanctions against Iraq.

The MIF continues to intercept vessels involved in illegal smuggling into and out of Iraq. In late August, the MIF conducted stepped-up operations in the far northern Gulf in the shallow waters near the major Iraqi waterways. These operations severely disrupted smuggling operations in the region. A new round of stepped up activity took place in mid-October. Since the beginning of the year, over 40 vessels have been detained for violations of the embargo and sent to ports in the Gulf for enforcement actions. Kuwait and the UAE, two countries adjacent to the smuggling routes, have also stepped up their own enforcement efforts and have intercepted and detained vessels involved in sanctions violations. Although refined petroleum products leaving Iraq comprise most of the prohibited traffic, the MIF has also intercepted a growing number of ships in smuggling prohibited goods into Iraq in violation of U.N. sanctions resolutions and the "oil-for-food" program. Ships involved in smuggling frequently utilize the territorial seas of Iran to avoid MIF patrols. In September, Iran closed the Shatt Al Arab waterway to smugglers and we observed the lowest level of illegal gasoil smuggling in 2 years. Iran apparently reopened the waterway in October. Detailed reports of these smuggling activities have been provided to the U.N. Sanctions Committee in New York.

Chemical Weapons

Iraq continues to deny that it ever weaponized VX nerve agent or produced stabilized VX, despite UNSCOM's publicly stated confidence in the Edgewood Arsenal laboratory finding of stabilized VX components in fragments of Iraqi SCUD missile warheads. Tests by France and Switzerland on other warhead fragments have been conducted to help UNSCOM estimate the total number of warheads loaded with VX. On October 22 and 23, international experts from seven countries met to discuss all analytical results obtained in the course of UNSCOM's verification of Iraq's declarations related to VX activities. Ambassador Butler reported to the U.N. Security Council on October 26 that the international experts "unanimously concluded" that "all analytical data" provided by the United States, Swiss, and French laboratories involved were considered "conclusive and valid." Ambassador Butler continued, "the existence of VX degradation products conflicts with Iraqi declarations that the unilaterally destroyed special warheads had never been filled with CW agents." The experts recommended that UNSCOM ask Iraq to explain the origin and history of the fragments analyzed by all three laboratories and the presence of degradation products of nerve agents, and to explain the presence of a compound known as VX stabilizer and its degradation product.

Iraq still refuses to turn over the UNSCOM the Iraqi Air Force document found by UNSCOM inspectors that details chemical weapons expended during the Iran-Iraq war. We understand that UNSCOM believes the document indicates that Iraq's official declarations to UNSCOM have greatly overstated the quantities of chemical weapons expended, which means a greater number of chemical weapons are unaccounted for then previously estimated.

Biological Weapons

Iraq has failed to provide a credible explanation for UNSCOM tests that found anthrax in fragments of seven SCUD missile warheads. Iraq has been claiming since 1995 that it put anthrax in only five such warheads, and had previously denied weaponizing anthrax at all. Iraq's explanations to date are far from satisfactory, although it now acknowledges putting both anthrax and botulinum toxin into some number of warheads. Iraq's biological weapons (BW) program, including SCUD missile BW warheads, R–400 BW bombs, drop-tanks to be filled with BW, spray devices for BW, production of BW agents (anthrax, botulinum toxin, aflatoxin, and wheat cover smut), and BW agent growth media, remains the "black hole" described by Ambassador Butler. Iraq has consistently failed to provide a credible account of its efforts to produce and weaponize its BW agents.

In response to a U.S. proposal, the Security Council agreed on October 13 to seek clarification from Iraq of statements made by Iraqi officials on October 7 concerning the existence of additional information on biological weapons still in Iraq's hands, and about Iraq's refusal to turn over the Iraqi Air Force document on chemical weapons expended in the Iran-Iraq War.

Long-Range Missiles

While Iraq continued to allow UNSCOM to witness flight tests of nonprohibited Iraqi missiles with range under 150 km (this cooperation has not been tested since the October 31 decision), there has been no change in (1) Iraq's refusal to further discuss its system for concealment of long-range missiles and their components, (2) Iraq's refusal to provide credible evidence of its disposition of large quantities of the unique fuel required for the long-range SCUD missile, or (3) Iraq's continued test modifications to SA–2 VOLGA surface-to-air missile components, despite written objections by UNSCOM (reported to the Security Council). These areas contribute to an Iraqi capability to produce a surface-to-surface missile of range greater than its permitted range of 150 km.

While UNSCOM believes it can account for 817 of 819 imported Soviet-made SCUD missiles, Iraq has refused to give UNSCOM a credible accounting of the indigenous program that produced complete SCUD missiles that were both successfully test-flown and delivered to the Iraqi army.

Nuclear Weapons

The nuclear weapons situation remains as it was on August 11, 1998, when IAEA Director General El Baradei wrote to the President of the Security Council that Iraq's August 5 suspension of cooperation with UNSCOM and the IAEA allows only "limited implementation of its ongoing monitoring" and "makes it impossible . . . to investigate . . . remaining questions and concerns . . ." In its 6-month report to the U.N. Security Council on October 7, the IAEA stated that it had a "technically coherent" view of the Iraqi nuclear program. There are remaining questions, but IAEA believes they can be dealt with within IAEA's ongoing monitoring and verification effort.

But the report also stated that Iraq's current suspension of cooperation with the IAEA limits the IAEA's right to full and free access. The IAEA is currently unable to investigate further aspects of Iraq's clandestine program or to ensure that prohibited activities are not being carried out in Iraq, free from the risk of detection through direct measures.

Dual-Use Imports

Resolution 1051 established a joint UNSCOM/IAEA unit to monitor Iraq's imports of allowed dual-use items. Iraq must notify the unit before it imports specific items that can be used in both weapons of mass destruction and civilian applications. Similarly, U.N. members must provide timely notification of exports to Iraq of such dual-use items. Given Iraq's current decision to suspend cooperation with UNSCOM/IAEA, we remain constantly vigilant for evidence of smuggling of items usable in weapons of mass destruction.

The U.N.'s "Oil-for-Food" Program

We continue to support the international community's efforts to provide for the humanitarian needs of the Iraqi people through the "oil-for-food" program. Under the last phase of the "oil-for-food" program, which ran from December 3, 1997, through June 2, 1998, $1.2 billion worth of humanitarian goods were approved for export to Iraq. United States companies can participate in "oil-for-food," and $185 million worth of direct contracts for U.S. firms have been approved; millions of dollars more have been earned through subcontracts. Since the first deliveries under the "oil-for-food" program began in March 1997, 7 million tons of food worth over $2.25 billion and $336 million worth of medicine and health supplies have been delivered to Iraq.

Iraq is authorized to sell up to $5.2 billion worth of oil every 180 days, up from $2 billion in previous phases. Although Resolution 1153 was adopted on February 20, Iraq did not present an acceptable distribution plan for the implementation of Resolution 1153 until May 27, 1998; the plan was accepted by the U.N. Secretary General on May 29. The U.N. Office of the Iraq Programme (OIP) has recently released new estimates of the amount of oil revenues that will be available during this phase of the program. Citing declining world oil prices and the state of Iraq's oil industry, OIP now estimates that income for the 6-month period ending in December will be around $3.3 billion. Discussions are under way within the Sanctions Committee and OIP as to how best to meet the most immediate needs of the Iraqi people in light of this projected shortfall in income.

Under the current phase (four) of the "oil-for-food" program, 622 contracts for the purchase of humanitarian goods for the Iraqi people have been presented for approval; of these, 485 contracts worth over $1.2 billion have been approved and 80 are on hold pending clarification of questions about the proposed contracts. With regard to oil sales, 58 contracts with a total value of over $2 billion have been approved so far during this phase.

UNSC Resolution 1153 maintains a separate "oil-for-food" program for northern Iraq, administered directly by the United Nations in consultation with the local population. This program, which the United States strongly supports, receives 13 to 15 percent of the funds generated under the "oil-for-food" program. The separate northern program was established because of the Baghdad regime's proven disregard for the humanitarian needs of the Kurdish, Assyrian, and Turkomen minorities of northern Iraq and its readiness to apply the most brutal forms of repression against them. In northern Iraq, where Baghdad does not exercise control, the "oil-for-food" program has been able to operate relatively effectively. The Kurdish factions are setting aside their differences to work together so that Resolution 1153 is implemented as efficiently as possible.

The United Nations must carefully monitor implementation of Resolution 1153. As the current phase anticipates, infrastructure repairs in areas such as oil export capacity, generation of electricity, and water purification present increasing challenges to the U.N. monitoring regime.

The Iraqi government continues to insist on the need for rapid lifting of the sanctions regime, despite its clear record of noncompliance with its obligations under relevant UNSC resolutions. Although the Iraqi government maintains that sanctions cause widespread suffering among the Iraqi populace, the Iraqi government is still not prepared to comply with UNSC resolutions and thus create the conditions that would allow sanctions to be lifted. Even if sanctions were lifted and the Government of Iraq had complete control over oil revenues, it is doubtful that conditions would improve for the Iraqi people. The Iraqi government has for a number of years shown that meeting civilian needs is not among its priorities. Humanitarian programs such as "oil-for-food" have steadily improved the life of the average Iraqi (who, for example, now receives a ration basket providing 2,000 kilocalories per day; a significant improvement in nutrition since the program began) while denying Saddam Hussein control over oil revenues. We will continue to work with the U.N. Secretariat, the Security Council, and others in the international community to ensure that the humanitarian needs of the Iraqi people are met while denying any political or economic benefits to the Baghdad regime.

Northern Iraq: Kurdish Reconciliation

On September 16 and 17, Massoud Barzani, President of the Kurdistan Democratic Party (KDP), and Jalal Talabani, Chairman of the Patriotic Union of Kurdistan (PUK), met for the first time in more than 4 years in talks held at the Department of State. Secretary Albright, welcoming the two leaders, congratulated them on the courageous step they were taking on behalf of their people. She expressed the United States deep concern for the safety, security, and economic well-being of Iraqi Kurds, Shias, Sunnis, and others who have been subject to brutal attacks by the Baghdad regime. She also made it clear that the United States will decide how and when to respond to Baghdad's actions based on the threat they pose to Iraq's neighbors, to regional security, to vital U.S. interests, and to the Iraqi people, including those in the north.

While in Washington, Mr. Barzani and Mr. Talabani signed a joint statement committing themselves to a timeline to improve the regional administration of the three northern provinces in the context of the 1996 Ankara Accords. Over the next 9 months, they will seek to unify their administrations, share revenues, define the status of their major cities, and hold elections. A key component for the success of this program will be continued meetings between the two leaders. To make this possible, both parties have condemned internal fighting, pledged to refrain from violence in settling their differences, and resolved to eliminate terrorism by establishing stronger safeguards for Iraq's borders.

The Washington talks followed 6 months of intensive diplomatic efforts including a visit to northern Iraq by Principal Deputy Assistant Secretary of State David Welch and consultations in Ankara and London by both Kurdish parties. Since the Washington talks, we have continued to work closely on these issues with the Iraqi Kurds and with Turkey and Great Britain. Both leaders met with U.N. officials in New York and they were together hosted by members of the House of Representatives Committee on International Relations.

The United States firmly supports the unity and territorial integrity of Iraq. Supporting the rights and welfare of Iraqi Kurds within Iraq in no way contradicts this position. In their joint statement, the Kurdish leaders clearly enunciated this principle. The United States is committed to ensuring that international aid continues to reach the north, that the human rights of the Kurds and northern Iraq minority groups, such as the Turkomen, Assyrians, Yezedis, and others are respected, and that the no-fly zone enforced by Operation Northern Watch is observed.

The Human Rights Situation in Iraq

The human rights situation throughout Iraq continues to be a cause for grave concern. As I reported September 3, the regime increased its security presence in predominantly Shia southern Iraq after the assassinations of two distinguished Shia clerics—deaths widely attributed to regime agents. Since that time, the Iraqi army has conducted a series of repressive operations against the Shia in Nasiriya and Amara Provinces. In particular, the government continues to work toward the destruction of the Marsh Arabs' way of life and the unique ecology of the southern marshes. These events expose a callous disregard for human life and the free exercise of religion.

Summary, arbitrary, and extrajudicial executions also remain a primary concern. Baghdad still refuses to allow independent inspections of Iraqi prisons despite the conclusion of U.N. Special Rapporteur for Iraq, Max Van der Stoel, that "there is strong evidence that hundreds of prisoners (were) executed in Abu Gharaib and Radwaniyah prisons" late last year. The U.N. Human Rights Commission in April issued a strong condemnation of the "all-pervasive repression and oppression" of the Iraqi government. Nevertheless, sources inside Iraq report another wave of executions, with about 60 people summarily killed. Preliminary reports indicate that the killings continued into July and August.

In the north, outside the Kurdish-controlled areas, the government continues the forced expulsion of tens of thousands of ethnic Kurds and Turkomen from Kirkuk and other cities. In recent months, 545 more families were reportedly expelled from Kirkuk (al-Tamim province) with 7 new Arab settlements created on land seized from the Kurds. Reports from the Kurdish-controlled areas where the displaced persons are received indicate that they are forced to leave behind almost all of their personal property. Due to a shortage of housing, they are still living in temporary shelters as winter approaches.

The government also continues to stall and obfuscate attempts to account for more than 600 Kuwaitis and third-country nationals who disappeared at the hands of Iraqi authorities during or after the occupation of Kuwait. It shows no sign of complying with Resolution 688, which demands that Iraq cease the repression of its own people.

The Iraqi Opposition

It is the policy of the United States to support the Iraqi opposition by establishing unifying programs in which all of the opposition can participate. We are working to encourage and assist political opposition groups, nonpartisan opposition groups, and unaffiliated Iraqis concerned about their nation's future in peacefully espousing democracy, pluralism, human rights, and the rule of law for their country. These committed Iraqis hope to build a consensus on the transition from dictatorship to pluralism, convey to the United Nations their views on Iraqi noncompliance with U.N. resolutions, and compile information to support holding Iraqi officials criminally responsible for violations of international humanitarian law.

On October 31, I signed into law the Iraq Liberation Act of 1998. It provides new discretionary authorities to assist the opposition in their struggle against the regime. This Act makes clear the sense of the Congress that the United States should support efforts to achieve a very different future for Iraq than the bitter, current reality of internal repression and external aggression.

There are, of course, other important elements of U.S. policy. These include the maintenance of U.N. Security Council support efforts to eliminate Iraq's prohibited weapons and missile programs and economic sanctions that continue to deny the regime the means to reconstitute those threats to international peace and security. United States support for the Iraqi opposition will be carried out consistent with those policy objectives as well. Similarly, U.S. support must be attuned to what the opposition can effectively make use of as it develops over time.

The United Nations Compensation Commission

The United Nations Compensation Commission (UNCC), established pursuant to Resolution 687 and 692, continues to resolve claims against Iraq arising from Iraq's unlawful invasion and occupation of Kuwait. The UNCC has issued over 1.3 million awards worth approximately $7 billion. Thirty percent of the proceeds from the oil sales permitted by Resolutions 986, 1111, 1143, and 1153 have been allocated to the Compensation Fund to pay awards and to finance operations of the UNCC. To the extent that money is available in the Compensation Fund, initial payments to each claimant are authorized for awards in the order in which the UNCC has approved them, in installments of $2,500. To date, the United States Government has received funds from the UNCC for initial installment payments on approximately 1435 claims of U.S. claimants.

Conclusion

Iraq remains a serious threat to international peace and security. I remain determined to see Iraq comply fully with all of its obligations under U.N. Security Council resolutions. The United States looks forward to the day when Iraq rejoins the family of nations as a responsible and law-abiding member.

I appreciate the support of the Congress for our efforts and shall continue to keep the Congress informed about this important issue.

Sincerely,

WILLIAM J. CLINTON

NOTE: Identical letters were sent to Newt Gingrich, Speaker of the House of Representatives, and Strom Thurmond, President pro tempore of the Senate. This letter was released by the Office of the Press Secretary on November 6.

Remarks on Signing Legislation To Establish the Little Rock Central High School National Historic Site
November 6, 1998

Thank you very much. You know, when Ernie was up here introducing me, I remembered that he was the only senior among the Little Rock Nine. He graduated in the spring in 1958, and when they called him up to receive his diploma, the whole auditorium was quiet, not a single person clapped. But we're all clapping for you today, buddy.

I would like to thank all the members of the Little Rock Nine who are here, including Elizabeth Eckford, Carlotta LaNier, Jefferson Thomas, Minnijean Trickey, Terrence Roberts. Melba Pattillo Beals is not here. Gloria Ray Karlmark is not here. Thelma Mothershed-Wair is not here. I think we should give all of them another hand. [*Applause*]

I would like to thank Congressman Elijah Cummings, Congressman Gregory Meeks for coming; Mayor Woodrow Stanley of Flint, Michigan; Commissioner Edna Bell, the president of the National Association of Black County Officials, from Wayne County, Michigan. I'd like to thank and welcome the mayor-elect of Washington, DC, Anthony Williams. I told him I'd be for more Federal aid if he'd teach me how to tie a bow tie. I never learned how to do that.

I would like to thank Secretary of Transportation Rodney Slater and the Secretary of the Interior Bruce Babbitt for their presence and leadership. And I would like to say a special word of welcome, and profound appreciation for his historic role in Tuesday's historic turnout of voters, to Reverend Jesse Jackson. Welcome, sir, we're delighted to have you here.

I thank the United States Marine Band, as always, for their great performance, on the occasion of John Philip Sousa's birth anniversary. And let me say a special word of welcome again to the White House to the magnificent young people of the Eastern High School Choir from Washington, DC. Thank you.

Let me say, since we are here to talk about our reconciliation, I hope you will forgive me for taking just a moment—and I know I speak for all Americans who are here—to express my sympathy to the people of Israel, who this morning were once again the target of a vicious ter-

rorist attack. No nation should live under the threat of violence and terror that they live under every day.

When Prime Minister Netanyahu and Chairman Arafat signed the Wye River agreement, they knew they would face this moment. They knew when they went home both of them would be under more danger and the terrorists would target innocent civilians. They knew they would have to muster a lot of courage in their people to stick to the path of peace in the face of repeated acts of provocation.

There are some people, you know, who have a big stake in the continuing misery and hatred in the Middle East, and indeed everywhere else in this whole world, just like some people had a big stake in continuing it in Little Rock over 40 years ago.

I ask for your prayers and support today for the Israelis and the Palestinians who believe in this agreement and who are determined to carry out their responsibilities and who understand that the agreement is the best way to protect the safety of the Israeli people. It was tenaciously negotiated, hard fought, but it is the best way to safety for the Israelis, the best way to achieve the aspirations of the Palestinians, and in the end, the only answer to today's act of criminal terror. I hope you will all feel that in your heart.

Let me say, this is a very, very happy day for the people who were part of the Little Rock Nine experience, for the people of Little Rock, all the Arkansans who are here, African-Americans from throughout our country. There was an earlier reference made by Congressman Bennie Thompson—and I thank him for his outstanding leadership in this endeavor and for his fine remarks today—about the election.

Now, most of the publicity about the election has been the enormous turnout of African-American citizens in a midterm election that resulted in the victories that have been well publicized for non-African-American elected officials. And having been one of those on several occasions, I am immensely grateful. [*Laughter*]

But what has received less publicity that I would like to point out, because this too was a part of the road that the Little Rock Nine began to walk for us, is that on Tuesday in the State of Georgia, an African-American was elected the attorney general of the State, an African-American was elected the labor commissioner of the State. And in the South on Tuesday, African-American Congressmen were reelected in majority white districts, with large majority—large majority. That is a part of the road we have walked together, a part of what we celebrate today.

There are so many here who played a role in it. One more person I would be remiss if I did not recognize, that Hillary and I love so much and are so grateful to, is the wonderful Dr. Dorothy Height, chairman of the National Commission of Negro Women. Thank you for being here, Dorothy. Let's give her a big hand. [*Applause*] Thank you, and bless you.

Ladies and gentlemen, there is only one bittersweet element in this magnificent moment for Hillary and for me, and that is that we are celebrating the last piece of legislation passed by our good friend Dale Bumpers. We have walked a lot of steps together since I first met Dale Bumpers about 25 years ago when he was Governor. And we've had a lot of laughs at each other's expense. After I became President, just to make sure that I didn't get the big head, he went around Washington introducing me to people as the second-best Governor Arkansas ever had. [*Laughter*] Today I told him that I hadn't had much time to review my remarks and, therefore, hadn't had the opportunity to delete all the nice things that had been written for me to say about him. [*Laughter*]

But I do want to tell you that this is a truly astonishing public servant. Hillary and I admire him, admire his wife Betty, admire the things that he's stood for and she's stood for, and we will miss them. Last month, in a final and, as always, brilliant speech on the Senate floor, Dale mentioned an inspiring teacher who once stopped him when he was reading out loud and said to the whole class, "Doesn't he have a nice voice? Wouldn't it be tragic if he didn't use that talent?" I think it's fair to say that Dale Bumpers has done his teacher proud, because he used that eloquent, impassioned voice to make sure that all the children of his State and our Nation could make use of their God-given talents.

We owe him an enormous debt of gratitude for his nearly five decades of caring, often courageous public service, and I cannot thank him enough.

The bill that Senator Bumpers and Congressman Thompson have presented to me for signature today recognizes the courage of the Little Rock Nine and that of their parents, their leaders, their community leaders, especially our great friend Daisy Bates, who could not be here today.

Because of all of them, Central High has become a hallowed place, a place every bit as sacred as Gettysburg and Independence Hall. Interestingly enough, back in the 1920's, it was voted the most beautiful school in America. It is still a functioning school, very much so. There are some years when its students comprise 25 percent of our State's entire roster of National Merit Scholars. It's a place where children can still go and study Greek and Latin, something that's rare in all school districts throughout America. It is, I believe, about to become the only open, fully operating school that is a National Historic Site.

As Ernie said, Hillary and I welcomed the Little Rock Nine back to Little Rock on the 30th anniversary of the integration of Little Rock Central High School. Then I was profoundly honored to hold open the door of the school so they could walk through on the 40th anniversary. Today I was able to welcome them all to the White House to the Oval Office and now on the South Lawn.

On the fateful day they slipped into Central High School and were removed by the police, President Eisenhower was on vacation in Newport. When he learned what had happened to them, and that Governor Faubus had turned over the streets to the mob, he realized that— even as a conservative—the Federal Government had to act. The next day he flew back to the White House. His helicopter landed just a few steps from here. He had just ordered General Maxwell Taylor to put the might of the 101st Airborne Division behind their righteous march through the doors of Central High.

Now, thanks to Senators Bumpers and Congressman Thompson, and many others, as they said, our Nation has found two very fitting ways to honor that march to ensure that the memory of the Little Rock Nine and all they represent remains alive long after those of us with living memories are gone.

As part of the budget I signed 2 weeks ago, I was authorized to confer Congressional Gold Medals, the highest civilian honor the Congress can bestow, on each and every member of the Little Rock Nine. It was only a few months ago that we presented President Nelson Mandela with that same award, and he spoke so movingly of his long struggle to tear down the walls of apartheid. The Little Rock Nine broke through the doors of apartheid. I can't wait until the artists finish creating your medals and we can bestow them upon you, an honor you richly deserve.

And then, of course, the main reason we're here today is to make a living monument forever out of the setting of your struggle. Again, I thank Senator Bumpers and all the others. The bill will allow the National Park Service to work with the community to maintain and protect Central High's magnificent building. It will also allow the Park Service to start acquiring land in the surrounding neighborhood to create new facilities where people can learn about the origins and the aftermath of the 1957 crisis, topics that simply can't be fully explored in the existing visitor center's limited space.

Children will never fully understand what you experienced in 1957. Maybe that's not such a bad thing. But they need to know. And now, for all time to come, children will have an opportunity to walk the stairs you walked, to see the angry faces you braved, to learn of your sacrifice, and about what, as a result of your sacrifice, you, your fellow Arkansans, and your Nation have become. Perhaps they will even see what it was about the Little Rock confrontation that made racial equality a driving obsession for so many of us who were young at the time and seared by it.

Again, I want to thank you for staying together over these 40-plus years now, for being willing to show up and be counted and to remind us, for showing us the shining example of your lives so that we could never forget all those who went before you who never had the chance that you gave to all who came after.

Monuments and medals are important reminders of how far we have come, but it is not enough. The doors of our schools are open, but some of them are falling off their rusty hinges. And many of them are failing the students inside. The economy has never been stronger, but there are still striking disparities in jobs, in investments in neighborhoods, in edu-cation, and criminal justice. Still too many break down along what W.E.B. Du Bois first called the color line. And while the Little Rock Nine have enjoyed great success in business, in the media, in education, they can tell you that in spite of what we celebrated on Tuesday, there is still discrimination and hatred in the hearts of some Americans.

All of that we found in our Presidential initiative on race. And we must never forget that it is our continuing obligation to the Little Rock Nine and all others who brought us to this point to fight this battle.

The last point I want to make to you is that the face of America is changing and changing fast. I went to an elementary school last Saturday to talk about the need to build and modernize our schools. There were children from 24 nations there. The principal said, "Mr. President, we're so glad to have you here, and we've got all the parents here. I only wish that we could have translated your talk into Spanish and Arabic."

America is changing, and it is a good thing, if we remember to live by the ideals on which this country was founded, if we remember the sacrifices of the Little Rock Nine, if we listen to our teachers, like Dr. John Hope Franklin. We, in other words, have a whole new chapter in the Nation's march to equality to write.

Remember what Senator Bumpers' teacher said, "Wouldn't it be tragic if he didn't use that talent?" That's exactly what the struggle for one America is all about, because that is a question that should be asked of every single child in our country.

When we ask that question with the Little Rock Nine in mind, it helps us to keep our eyes on the prize, the prize of true equality and true freedom, that ever elusive, always worth seeking, more perfect Union.

These people that we honor today, in the school we save today for all time, have given us all a great and treasured gift. May God bless them and the United States.

Thank you very much.

NOTE: The President spoke at 11:43 a.m. in the South Lawn at the White House. In his remarks, he referred to Ernest Green, one of the Little Rock Nine; civil rights activists Rev. Jesse Jackson and Daisy Bates; Prime Minister Binyamin Netanyahu of Israel; and Chairman Yasser Arafat of the Palestinian Authority. S. 2232, approved

November 6, was assigned Public Law No. 105–356.

Remarks at the Northwest Arkansas Regional Airport Dedication Ceremony in Highfill, Arkansas
November 6, 1998

Thank you so much, Secretary Slater, for your support of this project and your terrific work. Thank you, Administrator Garvey, Senator Hutchinson, Congressman Hutchinson, Senator-elect Blanche Lambert Lincoln. Now, up here in northwest Arkansas, from my point of view, she's got the best of all worlds; she's a Democrat with a Republican last name. [*Laughter*] I want you to get to know her; you'll like her a lot.

Congressman Dickey, Congressman Hammer-schmidt, Mr. Green, thank you for your marvelous work here. Mr. Bowler, thank you for bringing American Eagle here. I want to thank the Springdale Band and the Fayetteville Choir. I thought they both did a superb job.

You know—I've got all these notes, but I don't really want to use them today. I was flying home today, and I have to begin by bringing you greetings from two people who were with me this morning who, for different reasons, wanted to come and couldn't. One is the First Lady, Hillary, who wanted me to tell her friends in northwest Arkansas hello and to say she wished she could be here. And the other is Senator Bumpers, who has a sinus condition and was told by his doctor not to get on the airplane, although I told him I thought it was a pretty nice plane I was trying to bring him down here in—[*laughter*]—and that we were trying to demonstrate that northwest Arkansas had a world-class airport. But he asked to be remembered to you.

I want to thank my good friend, former Chief of Staff, and our Envoy to Latin America, Mack McLarty, for being here. And all of you all out here—I've been looking out in this crowd at so many people I've known for 25 years, many more—I've been sort of reliving the last 25 years. I think I should begin by saying that in every project like this, there are always a lot of people who work on it. Rodney mentioned that many years ago, Senator Fulbright, who was my mentor, had the idea of there ought

to be an airport here. I know how long Congressman Hammerschmidt has worked on this. This project started in the planning stage under the Bush administration, and we completed it. We had bipartisan support, and as Senator Hutchinson said, invoking our friend Senator McCain, we had bipartisan opposition to it as well. [*Laughter*]

And I have found that there is in any project like this a certain squeaky wheel factor; there are people that just bother you so much that even if you didn't want to do it, you'd go on and do it anyway. And I would like to pay a certain special tribute to the people who were particular squeaky wheels to me, starting with Alice Walton, who wore me out—[*laughter*]—Uvalde and Carol Lindsey, who guilt-peddled me about every campaign they'd ever worked for me in; and Dale Bumpers, who made me relive every favor he'd ever done for me for 20 years. [*Laughter*] Now, there were others as well, but I want to especially thank them.

I want to say to all of you, I'm delighted to see Helen Walton here and members of the Walton family. I, too, wish Sam were here to see this day. I thank J.B. Hunt, who talked to me about this airport. George Billingsly once said, "You remember, I gave you the first contribution you ever got in Benton County; now build that airport." [*Laughter*] I have a lot of stories about this airport. I want you to understand how high public policy is made in Washington. [*Laughter*] And we're all laughing about this, but the truth is, this is a good thing, and it needed to be done.

You know, when I was a boy growing up in Arkansas—Tim talked about how we were all raised to believe you could build a wall around Arkansas—we thought in the beginning, for a long time, that roads would be our salvation. Forty-two years ago President Eisenhower signed the Federal Aid Highway Act into law, a bill sponsored by the Vice President's father,

Albert Gore, Sr., in the United States Senate. And it did a lot of good for America and a lot of good for Arkansas. And a lot of trucking companies in this State did a lot of good with it, and a lot of poultry companies, like Tyson's and others, made the most of those roads. And then we began to see that air traffic was important as well. And Secretary Slater talked a lot about that. And I got tickled when Senator Hutchinson was talking about transporting apples from Hiwassee by railroad in the twenties. I thought to myself, I wonder if I'm the first President who has ever known how to get to Hiwassee? [*Laughter*]

But I got to thinking about that and how now we move from interstates to highways, and the people—all these people I've mentioned today, Senator Hutchinson, Senator Bumpers, Senator Pryor, certainly Congressman Hammerschmidt, and Congressman Hutchinson now, and Secretary Slater, and before him, Secretary Peña, and all the people in Northwest Arkansas and their supporters—understand today if you can't fly, you can't compete. But if you can fly, you can soar to new heights. Today in a sentence, at long last, northwest Arkansas can fly.

And this means a lot to me. When I was landing here, I called all my Secret Service detail leaders together and I said, "I want you guys to look out the window. This is where I started my political career. I've been on every one of these roads." And we were sitting here, Congressman Hammerschmidt reached over and he said, "You know, your career, the career that led you to the Presidency, really started 24 years ago last Tuesday." What he didn't say was, comma, "when I beat you like a drum up here for Congress." [*Laughter*] But I learned a lot in that race. And ever since, driving into all the little towns and hamlets in this area, then as Governor, flying in and out of northwest Arkansas and all the airports that were up here, I have known for a long time that this could bring opportunity and empowerment, access to markets, a boom to tourism—all of this will happen.

And what I'd like to ask all of you to think about is to think of this airport—and it's not just going from here to Chicago but from here to tomorrow. I am glad to tell you that the FAA will release today a $5 million letter of intent for continued development of this airport.

I'm glad to say that we have not abandoned our bipartisan commitment, we Arkansans, to other kinds of transportation. When the Congress passed, with the vote of every Member of Congress here present, and I signed the Transportation Equity Act this year, it will mean $100 million more a year over the next 6 years to the State of Arkansas alone. And it, too, will do a lot of good to take us to the future.

We are committed also to modernizing the air traffic system. Our air traffic control system, with the new investments we're making in aviation service and infrastructure, will now be able to better handle the—listen to this—the 50 percent increase in global air travel we expect in just the next 7 years.

Our policy has helped our airlines and aerospace industries return to profitability. Now we're finalizing new means to promote more competition and lower fares at home. We've signed more than 60 agreements to expand air service with other nations, opening skies above as we open markets below.

We're also trying to do more to make sure those skies are safe and secure. Under the Vice President's leadership, with the joint efforts of the FAA and NASA and the airline industry, we're working to convert our air traffic control system to satellite technology, to change the way we inspect older aircraft, and most important over the long run, to combat terrorism with new equipment, new agents, new methods.

In the world of the future, we'll need great airports; we'll need wonderful airplanes; we'll need well-trained—well-trained pilots and people to maintain those airplanes. Our prosperity, more and more, will depend upon keeping the world's skies safe, secure, and open.

I've got to mention one other personal thing. I saw Lieutenant Governor Rockefeller here, and he probably has to hide it around election time, but when we were younger men we studied in Oxford, England, together—when people typically took a boat. Now, people our age then look at me when I tell them I took 6 days to get from here to England and they think I need my head examined. We are moving around very fast now.

And the last thing I'd like to ask you to think about is where we are going and how we're going to get there. We'll have better roads; we'll have better airports; we'll have safer air travel. But to me, as I have seen all the people before me speak, the people that really did the work—

all I had to do as President was to make sure my budget office didn't kill these requests and to make sure everybody I knew knew that I was personally supportive of this. But the Members of Congress and the others here present, the citizens, they did all the work. And all of you who worked on this—I saw the leaders stand up when their names were called—to me, this symbolizes America at its best: people working on a common objective, across party lines, putting people first, thinking about the future. It's a symbol of what I have tried to do in the 6 years I have been in Washington. And I learned most of what I know driving around on these backroads.

And I just want to tell all of you that I thank you for the role that you have played in helping to bring this country to the point where we not only have a surplus for the first time in 29 years but the lowest percentage of people on welfare in 29 years, the lowest unemployment in 28 years, the lowest crime rate in 25 years, the highest homeownership in history, with the smallest Government in Washington since the last time John Glenn orbited the Earth. And I am proud of that.

And what I ask you to think about is that we are—all of us—living in a smaller and smaller world, where our interdependence and our own power depends upon our constructive interdependence with our friends and neighbors beyond our borders, the borders of our region, our State, our Nation. If we're going to build a pathway to the future, we have to build it with air travel; we have to build it with the Internet; we have to build it with modern medical and scientific research; and we have to build it by giving every child—without regard to income, race, region, or background—a world-class education. We have to build it by recognizing that all the differences that exist in this increasingly diverse country—I know there are churches here in northwest Arkansas that now have service in Spanish on Sunday, which would have been unthinkable 24 years ago when I first started traipsing around on these roads. All of that is a great blessing, if we decide, when we soar into the future, we're all going to take the flight together.

You built this airport together. Take it into the future together. Thank you, and God bless you all.

NOTE: The President spoke at 3:05 p.m. In his remarks, he referred to former Representative John Paul Hammerschmidt; Stan Green, chairman, and George Billingsly, member, Northwest Arkansas Regional Airport Authority; Peter Bowler, president, American Eagle Airlines; Alice Walton, chair emeritus, Northwest Arkansas Council, and her mother, Helen, widow of Sam Walton, founder, Wal-Mart Stores, Inc.; Uvalde Lindsey, secretary-treasurer, and his wife, Carol, president, Ozark International Consultants; J.B. Hunt, founder and senior chairman, J.B. Hunt Transport, Inc.; former Senator David H. Pryor; and Lt. Gov. Winthrop P. Rockefeller of Arkansas.

Statement on Senator Daniel Patrick Moynihan's Decision Not To Seek Reelection
November 6, 1998

Senator Moynihan's decision to retire comes as sad news for all of us who have worked with him and learned from him during his long career of public service.

Pat Moynihan has been a larger-than-life figure in the Senate, ably filling the seat once held by Aaron Burr, Martin Van Buren, and Robert F. Kennedy. For the last 22 years, Senator Moynihan has been a prescient presence in the United States Senate, always prodding the country to face our toughest challenges. His experience and expertise in foreign policy, domestic policy, science, and the arts has guided the Senate and served the Nation. Senator Moynihan also served as U.S. Ambassador to India from 1973 to 1975, U.S. Representative to the United Nations from 1975 to 1976, and has the distinction of being the only person in

American history to serve in four successive Presidential administrations.

His personal story could have been written by Horatio Alger: His rise from a poor childhood in New York City's Hell's Kitchen to his place as the most popular statewide elected official in New York during four Senate terms is an inspirational life story that serves as a powerful rebuttal to the prevailing cynicism about politics and public service.

Hillary and I wish him and Elizabeth all the best. We will miss him. So will the Congress. So will America.

Statement on Representative Newt Gingrich's Decision Not To Seek Reelection as Speaker of the House of Representatives
November 6, 1998

Newt Gingrich has been a worthy adversary, leading the Republican Party to a majority in the House, and joining me in a great national debate over how best to prepare America for the 21st century.

Despite our profound differences, I appreciate those times we were able to work together in the national interest, especially Speaker Gingrich's strong support for America's continuing leadership for freedom, peace, and prosperity in the world.

Statement on Signing the Automobile National Heritage Area Act
November 6, 1998

Today I am pleased to sign into law H.R. 3910, the "Automobile National Heritage Area Act."

In 1896, when Charles and Frank Duryea built 13 identical horseless carriages with the idea of selling automobiles for a profit, Michigan was a rural State of dirt roads, with an economy fueled by agriculture and the timber industry. Trains, canals, and rivers were America's means of transporting commerce. People in rural communities had no easy means of traveling to surrounding towns and cities. The car ended this isolation and transformed Michigan into an industrial giant and America into a moving, working, modern economy. It is only appropriate that we now recognize and honor the cultural legacy of the automobile. The Automobile National Heritage Area—by bringing together a collection of historical facilities and assets and making them available for education, recreation, and tourism—will create something unique and lasting for both Michigan and America.

I am also pleased that H.R. 3910 will establish the Tuskegee Airmen National Historic Site to honor the African American World War II pilots who sacrificed so much during World War II. Fittingly, the Historic Site will be located at the Tuskegee Institute's Moton Field, the first and only training facility for African American pilots during the war. The successes of the Tuskegee Airmen, as they were known, paved the way to desegregation of the military. They proved to the American public that, when given the opportunity, African Americans would become effective leaders. The Historic Site will inspire present and future generations as they come to understand the contribution that these brave individuals made toward defending their Nation and advancing the subsequent civil rights movement.

In addition, H.R. 3910 will authorize a memorial to Benjamin Banneker to honor this Nation's first African American man of science. Mr. Banneker, a self-educated mathematician whose grasp of calculus and spherical trigonometry allowed him to publish his astronomical almanac from 1791 until 1796, is best remembered for his scientific and mechanical genius. It is appropriate to honor this great American by erecting a memorial here in the District of Columbia, where Mr. Banneker employed his celebrated talents to survey and establish the boundaries of the Federal City.

Clarification, however, is needed with respect to section 403(a)(2) of H.R. 3910, which provides that certain members of the Delaware and Lehigh National Heritage Corridor Commission shall "represent" specified State agencies. If this provision were construed to require the Secretary of the Interior to appoint employees of specified agencies to the Commission, it would violate the Appointments Clause of the Constitution. Accordingly, I will interpret this provision as merely requiring that the Secretary's appointees represent these agencies by endeavoring to understand and convey the agencies' concerns to the Commission. Under this construction, section 403 will not impermissibly restrict the Secretary's discretion to select and appoint the members of the Commission.

Much of H.R. 3910 was carefully crafted on a nonpartisan basis. I thank the Michigan delegation and others for their contribution, particularly Representative Joe Knollenberg and Representative John Dingell who, like his father before him, has tirelessly served the people of Michigan and provided the leadership necessary to make dreams such as the Automobile National Heritage Area a reality.

WILLIAM J. CLINTON

The White House,
November 6, 1998.

NOTE: H.R. 3910, approved November 6, was assigned Public Law No. 105–355.

Letter to Congressional Leaders Reporting on the National Emergency With Respect to Sudan
November 6, 1998

Dear Mr. Speaker: (Dear Mr. President:)

I hereby report to the Congress on developments concerning the national emergency with respect to Sudan that was declared in Executive Order 13067 of November 3, 1997, and matters relating to the measures in that order. This report is submitted pursuant to section 204(c) of the International Emergency Economic Powers Act, 50 U.S.C. 1703(c) (IEEPA), and section 401(c) of the National Emergencies Act, 50 U.S.C. 1641(c). This report discusses only matters concerning the national emergency with respect to Sudan that was declared in Executive Order 13067.

1. On November 3, 1997, I issued Executive Order 13067 (62 *Fed. Reg.* 59989, November 5, 1997—the "Order") to declare a national emergency with respect to Sudan pursuant to IEEPA. A copy of the Order was provided to the Congress by message dated November 3, 1997.

2. Executive Order 13067 became effective at 12:01 a.m., eastern standard time on November 4, 1997. On July 1, 1998, the Department of the Treasury's Office of Foreign Assets Control (OFAC) issued the Sudanese Sanctions Regulations (the "SSR" or the "Regulations" (63 *Fed. Reg.* 35809, July 1, 1998)). The Regulations block all property and interests in property of the Government of Sudan, its agencies, instrumentalities, and controlled entities, including the Central Bank of Sudan, that are in the United States, that hereafter come within the United States, or that are or hereafter come within the possession or control of United States persons, including their overseas branches. The SSR also prohibit: (1) the importation into the United States of any goods or services of Sudanese origin except for information or informational materials; (2) the exportation or reexportation of goods, technology, or services to Sudan or the Government of Sudan except for information or informational materials and donations of humanitarian aid; (3) the facilitation by a United States person of the exportation or reexportation of goods, technology, or services to or from Sudan; (4) the performance by any United States person of any contract, including a financing contract, in support of an industrial, commercial, public utility, or governmental project in Sudan; (5)

the grant or extension of credits or loans by any United States person to the Government of Sudan; and (6) transactions relating to the transportation of cargo. A copy of the Regulations is attached to this report.

3. Since the issuance of Executive Order 13067, OFAC has made numerous decisions with respect to applications for authorizations to engage in transactions under the Regulations. As of September 16, 1998, OFAC has issued 62 authorizations to nongovernmental organizations engaged in the delivery of humanitarian aid and 141 licenses to others. OFAC has denied many requests for licenses. The majority of denials were in response to requests to authorize commercial exports to Sudan—particularly of machinery and equipment for various industries—and the importation of Sudanese-origin goods. The majority of licenses issued permitted the unblocking of financial transactions for individual remitters who routed their funds through blocked Sudanese banks. Other licenses authorized the completion of diplomatic transfers, preeffective date trade transactions, intellectual property protection, the performance of certain legal services, and transactions relating to air and sea safety policy.

4. At the time of signing Executive Order 13067, I directed the Secretary of the Treasury to block all property and interests in property of persons determined, in consultation with the Secretary of State, to be owned or controlled by, or to act for or on behalf of, the Government of Sudan. On November 5, 1997, OFAC disseminated details of this program to the financial, securities, and international trade communities by both electronic and conventional media. This information included the names of 62 entities owned or controlled by the Government of Sudan. The list includes 12 financial institutions and 50 other enterprises. As of September 10, 1998, OFAC has blocked nearly $610,000 during this reporting period.

5. Since my last report, OFAC has collected one civil monetary penalty in the amount of $5,500 from a U.S. financial institution for its violation of IEEPA and the SSR relating to a funds transfer. Another 12 cases are undergoing penalty action. OFAC, in cooperation with the U.S. Customs Service, is closely monitoring potential violations of the import prohibitions of the Regulations by businesses and individuals. Various reports of violations are being aggressively pursued.

6. The expenses incurred by the Federal Government in the 6-month period from May 3 through November 2, 1998, that are directly attributable to the exercise of powers and authorities conferred by the declaration of a national emergency with respect to Sudan are reported to be approximately $375,000, most of which represent wage and salary costs for Federal personnel. Personnel costs were largely centered in the Department of the Treasury (particularly in the Office of Foreign Assets Control, the U.S. Customs Service, the Office of the Under Secretary for Enforcement, and the Office of the General Counsel), the Department of State (particularly the Bureaus of Economic and Business Affairs, African Affairs, Near Eastern Affairs, Consular Affairs, and the Office of the Legal Adviser), and the Department of Commerce (the Bureau of Export Administration and the General Counsel's Office).

7. The situation in Sudan continues to present an extraordinary and unusual threat to the national security and foreign policy of the United States. The declaration of the national emergency with respect to Sudan contained in Executive Order 13067 under-scores the United States Government's opposition to the actions and policies of the Government of Sudan, particularly its support of international terrorism and its failure to respect basic human rights, including freedom of religion. The prohibitions contained in Executive Order 13067 advance important objectives in promoting the antiterrorism and human rights policies of the United States. I shall exercise the powers at my disposal to deal with these problems and will continue to report periodically to the Congress on significant developments.

Sincerely,

WILLIAM J. CLINTON.

NOTE: Identical letters were sent to Newt Gingrich, Speaker of the House of Representatives, and Albert Gore, Jr., President of the Senate.

Memorandum on Preventing Firearms Sales to Prohibited Purchasers
November 6, 1998

Memorandum for the Secretary of the Treasury, the Attorney General

Subject: Preventing Firearms Sales to Prohibited Purchasers

Since 1993, my Administration has worked hand-in-hand with State and local law enforcement agencies and the communities they serve to rid our neighborhoods of gangs, guns, and drugs—and by doing so to reduce crime and the fear of crime throughout the country. Our strategy is working. Through the historic Violent Crime Control and Law Enforcement Act of 1994, we have given communities the tools and resources they need to help drive down the crime rate to its lowest point in a generation. Keeping guns out of the hands of criminals through the Brady Handgun Violence Prevention Act's background checks has also been a key part of this strategy. Over the past 5 years, Brady background checks have helped prevent a quarter of a million handgun sales to felons, fugitives, domestic violence abusers, and other prohibited purchasers—saving countless lives and preventing needless injuries.

On November 30, 1998, the permanent provisions of the Brady Law will take effect, and the Department of Justice will implement the National Instant Criminal Background Check System (NICS). The NICS will allow law enforcement officials access to a more inclusive set of records than is now available and will—for the first time—extend the Brady Law's background check requirement to long guns and firearms transfers at pawnshops. Under the NICS, the overall number of background checks con-

ducted before the purchase of a firearm will increase from an estimated 4 million annually to as many as 12 million.

We can, however, take additional steps to strengthen the Brady Law and help keep our streets safe from gun-carrying criminals. Under current law, firearms can be—and an untold number are—bought and sold entirely without background checks, at the estimated 5,000 private gun shows that take place across the country. This loophole makes gun shows prime targets for criminals and gun traffickers, and we have good reason to believe that firearms sold in this way have been used in serious crimes. In addition, the failure to maintain records at gun shows often thwarts needed law enforcement efforts to trace firearms. Just days ago, Florida voters overwhelmingly passed a ballot initiative designed to facilitate background checks at gun shows. It is now time for the Federal Government to take appropriate action, on a national basis, to close this loophole in the law.

Therefore, I request that, within 60 days, you recommend to me what actions our Administration can take—including proposed legislation—to ensure that firearms sales at gun shows are not exempt from Brady background checks or other provisions of our Federal gun laws.

WILLIAM J. CLINTON

NOTE: This memorandum was made available by the Office of the Press Secretary on November 6 but was embargoed for release until 10:06 a.m. on November 7.

The President's Radio Address
November 7, 1998

Good morning. This week the American people sent a clear message to Washington that we must put politics aside and take real action on the real challenges facing our Nation: saving Social Security for the 21st century, passing a Patients' Bill of Rights, strengthening our

schools by finishing the job of hiring 100,000 teachers, and passing my plan to build or modernize 5,000 schools across our country.

Over the past 6 years, we have taken real action to address another important challenge, making our communities safe for our families.

For too long it seemed that rising crime was a frightening fact of life in America. In too many communities, children could not play on the street or walk to school in safety, older Americans locked themselves in their homes with fear, and gangs armed with illegal guns boldly roamed our streets and schools. I took office determined to change this, committed to a comprehensive anticrime strategy based on more community policing, tougher penalties, and better prevention.

Today our strategy is showing remarkable results. We're ahead of schedule and under budget in meeting our goal of putting 100,000 police on the street. And all across America, crime rates have fallen to a 25-year low, respect for the law is on the rise, families are beginning to feel safe in their communities again.

Keeping guns out of the hands of criminals has been at the center of our strategy and an essential part of our success. Since I signed the Brady law, after a big debate in Congress which was led in the House of Representatives by now Senator-elect Charles Schumer of New York, background checks have put a stop to nearly a quarter of a million handgun purchases by fugitives or felons. Law enforcement officers from around the country have told us that fewer guns on the street have made a huge difference in the lives of families they serve.

At the end of this month, we will make the Brady law even stronger. For the first time ever, we will require background checks for the purchase of any firearm, whether purchased from a licensed gun dealer or a pawnshop. But under this new insta-check system, as it's called, we'll be able to run nearly twice as many background checks, and most of them in just a matter of minutes.

We've spent 5 years working with State and local law enforcement to put this system in place, but when it comes to our families' safety, we must take another important step. Every year, an untold number of firearms are bought and sold at an estimated 5,000 gun shows around our country. I come from a State where these shows are very popular. I have visited and enjoyed them over the years. They're often the first place parents teach their children how to handle firearms safely. I know most gun dealers and owners are dedicated to promoting safe and legal gun use. But at too many gun shows, a different, dangerous trend is emerging. Because the law permits some firearms to be sold without background checks, some of these gun shows have become illegal arms bazaars for criminals and gun traffickers looking to buy and sell guns on a cash-and-carry, no-questions-asked basis.

On Tuesday the people of Florida voted overwhelmingly to put a stop to these tainted transactions and make it harder for criminals to buy firearms. Under the new Florida law, communities now can take action to require background checks for the public sale of all guns. I believe this should be the law of the land: No background check, no gun, no exceptions.

Therefore, I am directing Secretary Rubin and Attorney General Reno to report back to me in 60 days with a plan to close the loophole in the law and prohibit any gun sale without a background check. We didn't fight as hard as we did to pass the Brady law only to let a handful of unscrupulous gun dealers disrespect the law, undermine our progress, put the safety of our families at risk. With this action, we are one step closer to shutting them down.

I look forward to working together with members of both parties in the new Congress to meet this challenge and all our challenges to build a safer and stronger America for the 21st century.

Thanks for listening.

NOTE: The address was recorded at approximately 9:30 a.m. on November 6 in the Oval Office at the White House for broadcast at 10:06 a.m. on November 7. The transcript was made available by the Office of the Press Secretary on November 6 but was embargoed for release until the broadcast.

Electronic Mail Message to John Glenn
November 7, 1998

Dear John,

Thanks for your message. Hillary and I had a great time at the launch. We are very proud of you and the entire crew, and a little jealous. We can't wait for you to get home so we can have a first hand report. Meanwhile back on earth, we're having a lot of fun with your adventure. At a camp rally in Queens, I asked an 83 year old lady what she thought of your trip. She replied that it seemed like a perfectly fine thing for a young man like you to do! I hope your last few hours go well. Give my best to the rest of the crew.

Sincerely,

BILL CLINTON

NOTE: The message was transmitted in the morning from the White House to John Glenn aboard the space shuttle *Discovery* orbiting the Earth. The transcript released by the Office of the Press Secretary also included the text of the message from John Glenn to the President, as follows:

Dear Mr. President,

This is certainly a first for me, writing to a President from space, and it may be a first for you in receiving an E mail direct from and orbiting spacecraft.

In any event, I want to personally thank you and Mrs. Clinton for coming to the Cape to d/see the launch. I hope you enjoyed it just half as much as we did on board. It is truly an awesome experience from a personal standpoint, and of even greater importance for all of the great research projects we have on Discovery. The whole crew was impressed that you would be the first President to personally see a shuttle launch and asked me to include their best regards to you Hillary. She has discussed her interest in the space program with Annie on several occasions, and I know she would like to be on a flight just like this one.

We have gone almost a third of the way around the world in the time it has taken me to write this letter, and the rest of the crew is waiting. Again, our thanks and best regards. Will try to give you a personal briefing after we return next Saturday.

Sincerely,

JOHN GLENN

Letter to Congressional Leaders on Continuation of the National Emergency With Respect to Iran
November 9, 1998

Dear Mr. Speaker: (Dear Mr. President:)

Section 202(d) of the National Emergencies Act (50 U.S.C. 1622(d)) provides for the automatic termination of a national emergency unless, prior to the anniversary date of its declaration, the President publishes in the *Federal Register* and transmits to the Congress a notice stating that the emergency is to continue in effect beyond the anniversary date. In accordance with this provision, I have sent the enclosed notice, stating that the Iran emergency declared in 1979 is to continue in effect beyond November 14, 1998, to the *Federal Register* for publication. Similar notices have been sent annually to the Congress and the *Federal Register* since Novem-

ber 12, 1980. The most recent notice appeared in the *Federal Register* on October 1, 1997. This emergency is separate from that declared with respect to Iran on March 15, 1995, in Executive Order 12957.

The crisis between the United States and Iran that began in 1979 has not been fully resolved. The international tribunal established to adjudicate claims of the United States and U.S. nationals against Iran and of the Iranian government and Iranian nationals against the United States continues to function, and normalization of commercial and diplomatic relations between the United States and Iran has not been achieved. On March 15, 1995, I declared a separate national emergency with respect to Iran pursuant to the International Emergency Economic Powers Act and imposed separate sanctions. By Executive Order 12959 of May 6, 1995, these sanctions were significantly augmented, and by Executive Order 13059 of August 19, 1997, the sanctions imposed in 1995 were further clarified. In these circumstances, I have determined that it is necessary to maintain in force the broad authorities that are in place by virtue of the November 14, 1979, declaration of emergency, including the authority

to block certain property of the government of Iran, and that are needed in the process of implementing the January 1981 agreements with Iran.

Sincerely,

WILLIAM J. CLINTON

NOTE: Identical letters were sent to Newt Gingrich, Speaker of the House of Representatives, and Albert Gore, Jr., President of the Senate. The notice is listed in Appendix D at the end of this volume.

Remarks to the 1998 NCAA Men's and Women's Basketball Champions
November 9, 1998

The President. Thank you. Please be seated. I want to welcome, in addition to the coaches and the university officials and the teams, Senator Ford from Kentucky; Senator Frist from Tennessee; Congressman Whitfield; Governor Patton; President Johnson; Coach Summitt; the team's captains, Chamique Holdsclaw and Kellie Jolly; Associate Athletic Director Larry Ivey; Coach Smith; your team captains, Allen Edwards, Cameron Mills, and Jeff Sheppard.

Before I begin, I have to turn the microphone over to someone who couldn't be here today, but who never misses an opportunity to remind me at this occasion that there is a team from Tennessee here always. [*Laughter*] Laura just said, the Vice President is supposed to call in, but he's a little late. I like it; I'll get to talk some more. Not yet? Give me the high sign, Laura.

So we'll go on with the program. [*Laughter*] I love November, not only because of Thanksgiving but because we get to start the college basketball season. It's the time of year also, lately, where I welcome the Lady Vols and the Kentucky Wildcats here. [*Laughter*] For Kentucky, it's been 2 out of the last 3 years. For the Vols—this reminds me, when I was Governor, there was this wonderful civics teacher in a little town in Arkansas. And every year, she was such a devoted teacher, she would always bring her class to the Governor's office. And every year, Pat Summitt brings her class to the White House. [*Laughter*] Just part of

a civics lesson that is unmatched in NCAA women's basketball history. [*Applause*] Thank you.

I want to congratulate Pat Summitt and Tubby Smith for knowing how to turn talent into victory. They are two different things, as we all know.

Let me begin by saluting the Lady Vols basketball team. There are few things in sports more thrilling than the way they roared off the bench in the first half of the championship in Indianapolis, scoring 55 points, tying an NCAA record—Tennessee's 61st NCAA win, the most by any school ever, at the end of a 39–0 season.

Not only that, they won each of these games by an average of 30 points. That's something that would not only make any coach jealous; it makes any politician drool. [*Laughter*] The Lady Vols have been called flawless, mega talents, without peer, merciless. Some say they are the best team ever to step on the floor, anytime, anywhere.

It was, of course, a victory for the team. But I think we should note that Chamique Holdsclaw led the Vols in scoring, was the Final Four MVP, swept Player of the Year honors—coincidentally, wearing number 23. And like Michael Jordan, she dominated every game of the season, averaging over 23.5 points a game; in the final victory, an impressive 25 points and 10 rebounds. I say that because young people in this country, especially young girls who are learning about women's basketball, will hear a lot more about her.

And let me also salute Coach Pat Summitt, Coach of the Year for the sixth time in 12 years, her third consecutive championship team. Only John Wooden has more collegiate basketball championships, and she's gaining on him every day. Thank you again for what you have done.

And now, is the Vice President on the phone?

The Vice President. Yes, I'm here, Mr. President. [*Laughter*]

The President. Okay, gloating time. [*Laughter*]

[*At this point, the Vice President made brief remarks by telephone from Carthage, TN.*]

The President. Thank you. I can't help noting that there's a little modest football game this weekend between Tennessee and Arkansas. [*Laughter*] And both teams are undefeated, but Tennessee is much higher ranked. And both the Vice President and Senator Frist refused to give me any points when we bet on this game. So I'm either going to have more barbecue than I can eat, or I'm going to have to take out a loan to finish Chelsea's college education after this. [*Laughter*] But I'm looking forward to it.

I'd like to say a few words about the Kentucky Wildcats. First of all, I think all of us who watched the tournament this year thought it was one of the best tournaments that any of us could remember. And the fact that Kentucky did come back by 10 points at halftime in the last game to defeat Utah—quite clearly a great, great team—the fact that we had so much competition in the final teams that made it certainly to the Final Four, but even the last 16—it was an unbelievable tournament. And Kentucky became the first team ever to come back from such a large deficit in the final game of the tournament—with heart, skill, and guts.

I want to congratulate the Final Four MVP, Jeff Sheppard, and all of his teammates. There were many solid scorers, no one who ran away. Kentucky had a team. They also did something that I think is very important for great teams. They got better and better and better as the season went on, winning their last 11 games by an average of 20 points.

Of course, Coach Tubby Smith faced a difficult task in his first year at Kentucky. People expected him to win all the time, and he had to start with that burden of expectation. I think the fact that he began his working life in tobacco fields with 16 brothers and sisters taught him something about teamwork. And he certainly brought what he knew about teamwork and family values and spirit to this work.

Jeff Sheppard said of Coach Smith that "he does a really good job of teaching us the game of basketball, but an even better job of teaching us how to be men." I think that says more than anything I could possibly say about this remarkable man and his remarkable team.

Now I'd like to introduce Dr. Joe Johnson, the president of the University of Tennessee.

[*University of Tennessee president Joseph E. Johnson and Lady Volunteers coach Pat Summitt each made brief remarks. Players Kellie Jolly and Chamique Holdsclaw then presented the President with gifts.*]

The President. I now have a whole wardrobe from them. [*Laughter*] It's great; I have all these matching workout clothes. Thank you very, very much.

Now I'd like to ask Larry Ivey, the University of Kentucky associate athletic director, to come up.

[*University of Kentucky associate athletic director Larry Ivey and Wildcats coach Tubby Smith each made brief remarks. Players Jeff Sheppard and Cameron Mills then presented the President with a Wildcats jersey, and Mr. Mills commented that the President never wore the jersey given to him after the Wildcats won their previous championship.*]

The President. Look how big it is. Cameron, for all you know, I slept in it. Look at this. [*Laughter*] Look, you are laughing about this, but I'll have you know that I was 6'8" before I got elected President. [*Laughter*]

Well, thank you very much. Let me say to both of you, I follow basketball quite closely, and I have had occasion to get to know Pat Summitt and her husband, R.B., and fine son, Tyler, who is kind of getting bored coming to see me every year. [*Laughter*] But it's nice for me because I've watched him grow up. [*Laughter*] He weighed about 15 pounds the first time I—and he came to see Buddy today, so my dog is eagerly awaiting his reunion there.

I also have very much admired Tubby Smith from afar. And I like it when teams can come back. Although I must say, I prefer to get ahead and stay ahead. [*Laughter*] But sometimes you just have to come back. [*Laughter*] So I think we've had the best of both worlds here today and a lot of what is best about our country.

Thank you, and God bless you all. Welcome.

NOTE: The President spoke at 6:10 p.m. in the East Room at the White House. In his remarks, he referred to Gov. Paul E. Patton of Kentucky; NBA Chicago Bulls player Michael Jordan; and UCLA head basketball coach emeritus John Wooden.

Remarks to the National Townhall Meeting on Trade
November 10, 1998

Thank you. Well, Lionel, you did a great job. The first thing I asked him today was whether or not his speech was going to be beamed into his school. [*Laughter*] I love Brooklyn. I've been to Senator-elect Schumer's home. I've spent a lot of time in Brooklyn. Neither Chuck Schumer nor I would have the courage to leave our electorate on election day. [*Laughter*] And you did, and for that reason alone I hope that you are rewarded. I'm glad you're with us.

I want to welcome the other student leaders and teachers, business people here today and those joining us by satellite and the Internet. I'd like to thank Mike Armstrong for his great leadership of the President's Export Council and all the other members of the Council who are here with us on the stage today for their service.

I want to thank Secretary Daley for doing a superb job as Commerce Secretary, not only in his responsibilities to promote America's exports and, generally, a free trading system throughout the world but for the many other good things he does for the American economy as the Secretary of Commerce.

I'm very glad to address this first-ever national townhall meeting on trade. When the President's Export Council was created 25 years ago to promote America's businesses and jobs—just think of it; people are joining us today via satellite and the Internet—25 years ago, communications satellites were largely tools of our military. Even 6 years ago, when I took office, the Internet was basically the private province of physicists. There were about 50 sites. Today, it's the fastest growing organ of communication in all of human history. Today, the Internet and communication satellites are not instruments of war but plowshares to help us to cultivate education and understanding, exports and the growth of our global economy.

I think I'd like to say that it's also fitting that this townhall be held in a building named in honor of President Reagan, because he believes deeply in our indispensable role in promoting freedom and free trade throughout the world. In 1982 he said this: "Great nations have responsibilities to lead. If we lower our profile, we might just wind up lowering our flag." Well, we still have a responsibility to lead—in the aftermath of the cold war, I would argue, a greater responsibility than ever before.

That is why, 6 years ago, we charted a new course for our country, designed to preserve both the American dream and the American community at home and America's leadership for peace and freedom and prosperity around the world. We had a three-word motto: opportunity, responsibility, and community. That meant, among other things, that we took a new direction with our economy, a new strategy that began first with fiscal discipline, because our deficit was $290 billion that year, slated to go to nearly $400 billion last year. No country can buy prosperity by spending itself into debt deeper and deeper every year.

In the years since, we have seen that the hard work of reducing the deficit and producing the first balanced budget in a generation has paid rich dividends: lower interest rates, higher investment, more growth, rising wages, a 28-year low in unemployment with a 32-year low in inflation. We have more to do. We must keep America fiscally sound. We must deal with the Social Security challenge that we face. We must expand the reach of enterprise into those neighborhoods and places in America that have not yet felt this economic recovery. But it is working.

The second thing we did in building this historic surplus was to make equally historic investments in our people, in education, in health care, in economic empowerment. In the new global economy, education and technology, research and development, health care and a clean environment—all these things will be increasingly valued, and without them it will be very difficult to prove that the global economy works for ordinary citizens. We have more to do, especially in education. And we have more potential in research, in medicine, and in economic and technological areas. But we are doing the right things.

The third thing that we did with our economy, after balancing the budget and increasing investment, was to try to make the global economy work more aggressively for our people. During the past 5 years, exports have helped to create more than 2 million jobs, high-skilled jobs that on average pay more than 15 percent above the average.

The free and open exchange of capital and ideas and goods across the globe has been vital to our prosperity throughout this century we're about to leave, but it will be far more important to our continued growth in the 21st century. That is why I have been so committed to opening markets to our goods and services throughout the world. During the past 5 years, we have completed 260 trade agreements to open global markets to areas from automobiles to telecommunications.

Now, as we meet here today, this global trading system is facing two great related challenges: first, the most serious financial challenge since World War II; and second, the continuing need to put a human face on the global economy, that is, to make sure that in every country increased trade and investment works to benefit ordinary citizens.

A full quarter of the world is now living in countries with declining or negative economic growth. Millions who were in the middle class in Asia or Russia, for example, have been devastated by economic problems in their own countries. Therefore, we see people, for the first time in a good while, beginning to question the premises of the free flow of goods and services and capital.

With the whole world increasingly linked together in a global marketplace, with global communications, clearly these shocks abroad also reverberate at home. We saw it most clearly in the last several months in the markets that our farmers no longer had in Asia, leading to steep drops in farm prices here at home. We see it most clearly today, perhaps, in the fact that America's economy has remained strong, and with other countries suffering from no growth or negative growth, the flooding of our markets by certain products, especially steel, which has become a big source of concern and about which I'll say more in a couple of minutes.

The point I want to make to all of you, especially to the students who are here, is that resolving the global crisis today is vitally important for the American people, from Brooklyn to North Dakota, in small towns and big cities. Why? Not only because it is in our interest to help our friends around the world to continue to enjoy the benefits of freedom and prosperity but because if we want to keep our own economy and social fabric strong, we have to do so in the context of a growing economy where people embrace the ideas of freedom and free exchange of goods and services. That is why America must continue to lead in building a strong financial and trading system for the 21st century.

Over the past year we have pursued a very aggressive strategy to combat the financial crisis and to protect our jobs here at home. In September I called for urgent action to spur growth and to aid those nations most in need. The nations of the world have rallied to this agenda. Japan has committed substantial resources to repair its troubled banking system. Brazil is moving forward to address its fiscal problems. The international community is working to support these efforts.

America, Japan, and others have cut interest rates. Our Congress agreed to fully fund our commitment to the International Monetary Fund. Through our Export-Import Bank and our Overseas Private Investment Council, we're providing credit and investment insurance to encourage the flow of capital to developing nations. The World Bank has announced that it will expand its spending to strengthen the social safety net in Asia, where so many people have been hurt by financial and economic collapse.

Just 10 days ago the Group of Seven major industrial nations announced additional steps: a new line of credit to help nations with sound economic policies fight off the financial contagion in the first place—it is always less expensive to keep something bad from happening than it is to fix it once it happens—and second, a new World Bank emergency fund to aid those who are suffering the most.

Now, these are very, very positive steps. But there is still much more to do to keep countries on the path to prosperity, to stop future crises before they start. I have called on the world community to act to adapt the architecture of the international financial system for the new realities of the 21st century, the 24-hour-a-day high-tech markets, with $1.5 trillion a day in currency exchanges.

Let me say that again. We set up a system—for all the students here—that would enable more and more trade to occur in goods and in services and more and more investment to occur. Now, obviously, if you're going to have more trade and more investment in other countries, and their money is different from yours, there has to be a system to ensure a fairly free flow of capital around the world because those things have to be purchased or invested in in other countries. But today, the financial markets, more than any other time, are operating as an independent economic force, and let me say again, $1.5 trillion a day is changing hands in international currency exchanges. That is many, many times the total value of goods and services traded in any given day.

And that is at the bottom of a lot of the challenges we're facing today: How do we continue to support the necessary free flow of capital so that we can have the trade, the investment we need, and avoid the enormous impact that a financial collapse can have when the money being traded on its own is so much greater than the total value of goods and services being traded or investments being made?

Later this week, leaders of the Asia-Pacific community of nations will gather in Asia to continue our efforts toward a more prosperous and secure future. We'll work on speeding the economic recovery in Asia, strengthening the social safety net, helping companies there to restructure their debt so they can emerge from the crushing burdens they face and once again employ people and pay them wages.

Now, in solving the current crisis in Asia, Japan is of particular importance. It is, after all, the second largest economy in the world. It has been a key engine of growth for the entire world over the last two decades. The restoration of growth in Japan, which has been stalled now for more than 5 years, is absolutely essential to the restoration of growth in the remainder of Asia. The rest of us look to Japan to move quickly to implement the good banking reforms which have been passed, to spur demand for goods and services in the home mar-

ket, to reduce unnecessary regulation, and to open its markets.

At the Asia-Pacific leaders summit, our nations will work together to bring down more barriers to trade. Last year we agreed to consider opening nine key sectors, worth more than $1.5 trillion a year in world trade. We need to deliver on that agreement.

We must also, here in the United States, move ahead on trade initiatives with Latin America, with Africa, with Europe. We must launch negotiations on agriculture and other areas within the World Trade Organization as we move toward next year's ministers meeting here at home in the United States. And here, on our domestic front, we need to find common ground on fast-track negotiating authority, so that I can continue to negotiate good trading agreements with other nations.

Now, as we deal with all these issues, we must remember that it's also important to keep in mind that there must be a human face on the global economy; we must be able to show that economic exchange benefits ordinary citizens. Therefore, we will continue to work for trade agreements that include important protections for workers, for health and safety, for the environment, and to work for a world trading system that is more open to all elements of society and more designed to lift the fortunes of all people in all trading countries. Expanded trade must not provoke the so-called race to the bottom.

We'll also work hard with our Congress to make our own sanctions policy more judicious, more fair, more cost-effective, something our business community has talked to us about quite a lot.

America must also continue to lead the world to have an open, rules-based trading system. If we expect the American people to support expanded trade, free trade must also be fair trade. I'm especially concerned, as I said earlier, about the impact of the international financial crisis on American steelworkers and our steel industry. We are committed to a full and timely enforcement of our trade laws to address unfair trade practices affecting this industry, and we will insist that our key trading partners play by the rules.

I am pleased that Secretary Daley earlier today released regulations to implement our laws against unfairly subsidized imports. This expedited action will greatly help our steel and other industries as they review the legal remedies available to them.

Our companies deserve fair treatment overseas as well. Earlier today I signed legislation approving an agreement with other industrial nations to crack down on bribery in international business transactions. This agreement requires the nations that sign it to enact laws barring their citizens from bribing foreign officials to win business in those countries.

We've had laws like that on the books for more than 20 years. I'm sorry to say, as many of the people up here on this platform can testify, it's cost us a lot of business over the last 20 years to do the right thing. But it is clearly the right thing. American companies deserve a level playing field, and now, with this legislation and this international agreement, we will have it.

Let me say one other thing. We believe the global economic system is strengthened by openness, so that people can judge whether governments, businesses, and international institutions like the WTO and the IMF act responsibly and honestly. And we will continue to push for greater openness.

Finally, as I have told audiences this year from Santiago to Shanghai, no matter what we do in the United States to try to restore growth, no matter how good our world trading and financial systems are, there are some things nations must do for themselves. Unless nations deepen their democracies, unless they provide good education, health care to the maximum ability according to their means, unless they have a fair legal system, unless the citizens of each nation feel they have an actual stake in their own economies and they've got a good chance to get a fair shake if they work hard and play by the rules—unless these things are present, then nations will resist; people will resist the reforms that a lot of these nations have to undertake now to recover and to grow over the long run. Unless people are empowered with the tools to master economic change, they will feel they are its victims, not its victors.

So I say again, we have heavy responsibilities here in the United States. We must continue with our efforts to generate greater economic growth, to seek freer and fairer trade, to see that trade and the global financial systems are modified to meet the needs of the 21st century, to roll back the present financial crisis, and to design efforts that will lift the lives of all people over the long run. We have to do this, but other countries must do their part as well.

All of you young people who are out here, if you look at where we are in the United States, with a population that is more diverse racially, ethnically, culturally than ever before in our history, we are well-positioned to do better in the 21st century than at any time in our glorious past. If you look at the efforts being made to overcome old problems, from Northern Ireland to the Middle East, to Bosnia and Kosovo, to tribal difficulties in Africa, and you look at the continuing troubles that are still out there, it is clear that if a unifying rather than a dividing vision of human life and human society is the dominant one the young people in this country and this world bring to the world of the 21st century, we have the chance to have the most peaceful, most prosperous, most healthy, most forward-looking period in all human existence for people throughout the globe.

But it is by no means certain. And this is a critical period. Everything we do for economics should be seen not as an economic matter alone but should be done because it also advances the texture and meaning and quality of life—the ability of families to raise their children, the ability of people to get better education, the ability of people to live in peace, the ability of people to look beyond their noses and the struggles of putting food on the table today to the need to reconcile our growing economy with our fragile environment around the globe.

That's what this is about. That's why your presence here is so important. And that's what I ask you to think of. Yes, America is blessed. Yes, we're doing well. Yes, we're making money from the global economy. Yes, we can make more money and have more jobs and enjoy more prosperity. But in the end, the purpose of all this is to improve the quality, the depth, the texture of life, not only for ourselves but for the cause of peace and freedom throughout the world.

I believe we can do it. I hope you will support that. And I hope very much that, once again in the coming year, we will make great advances here in the United States to that end.

Thank you very much.

NOTE: The President spoke at 1:35 p.m. in the Atrium at the Ronald Reagan Building and International Trade Center. In his remarks, he referred to Lionel Ogelsby, student, Washington Irving High School, New York City, who introduced the President; and C. Michael Armstrong, Chairman, President's Export Council, and chief executive officer, AT&T. S. 2375, the International Anti-Bribery and Fair Competition Act of 1998, approved November 10, was assigned Public Law No. 105–366.

Statement on Signing the International Anti-Bribery and Fair Competition Act of 1998
November 10, 1998

It is with great pleasure that I sign today S. 2375, the "International Anti-Bribery and Fair Competition Act of 1998." This Act makes certain changes in existing law to implement the Convention on Combating Bribery of Foreign Public Officials in International Business Transactions, which was negotiated under the auspices of the Organization for Economic Cooperation and Development (OECD). The Convention was signed on December 17, 1997, by the United States and 32 other nations. On July 31, 1998, the Senate gave its advice and consent to ratification of the Convention. With enactment of this bill, the United States is able to proceed with the deposit of its instrument of ratification, and it is my hope that the Convention will enter into force by the end of 1998, the target date established by OECD Ministers.

The United States has led the effort to curb international bribery. We have long believed bribery is inconsistent with democratic values, such as good governance and the rule of law. It is also contrary to basic principles of fair competition and harmful to efforts to promote economic development. Since the enactment in 1977 of the Foreign Corrupt Practices Act (FCPA), U.S. businesses have faced criminal penalties if they engaged in business-related bribery of foreign public officials. Foreign competitors, however, did not have similar restrictions and could engage in this corrupt activity without fear of penalty. Moreover, some of our major trading partners have subsidized such activity by permitting tax deductions for bribes paid to foreign public officials. As a result, U.S. companies have had to compete on an uneven playing field, resulting in losses of international contracts estimated at $30 billion per year.

The OECD Convention—which represents the culmination of many years of sustained diplomatic effort—is designed to change all that. Under the Convention, our major competitors will be obligated to criminalize the bribery of foreign public officials in international business transactions. The existing signatories already account for a large percentage of international contracting, but they also plan an active outreach program to encourage other nations to become parties to this important instrument. The United States intends to work diligently, through the monitoring process to be established under the OECD, to ensure that the Convention is widely ratified and fully implemented. We will continue our leadership in the international fight against corruption.

Section 5 of S. 2375 is unrelated to the Convention. However, it can be implemented in a manner that advances U.S. objectives for the privatization of the international satellite organizations, and does not put the United States in breach of its obligations under international agreements.

WILLIAM J. CLINTON

The White House,
November 10, 1998.

NOTE: S. 2375, approved November 10, was assigned Public Law No. 105–366.

Remarks in a Telephone Conversation With Tipper Gore on Hurricane Damage in Central America
November 10, 1998

The President. Hello?

Tipper Gore. Hello, Mr. President.

The President. Hi, Tipper.

Mrs. Gore. Hi, how are you? Thank you very much for the honor of leading the delegation. It's a privilege to bring the aid and the assistance to the people of Honduras. They need it. They have suffered an incredible amount of devastation, and they're very grateful for the $70 million and the additional $10 million that you authorized and that I was able to tell them about today.

The President. Well, what have you seen?

Mrs. Gore. Well, I took a helicopter tour along with the delegation of the area that had a great deal of devastation. We've seen communities and neighborhoods and entire areas wiped out. You can see that the base of their infrastructure is completely destroyed—farming, bridges knocked out. From the air I've seen dead animals, lots of vultures.

But I can tell you something else that's very important, and that is that in working in a neighborhood outside the capital with people that so have an inspirational spirit, they have learned how to reorganize, and we all worked to help them clean the mud out of a schoolhouse so it can be converted for medical facilities, first and foremost.

The President. That's really good. I wonder, what are your thoughts about how well we're doing in getting our aid down there, how we're going to handle extra volunteer help, all the other things you could do. What's the most important thing we could give next—that we should do next after the money that you brought down?

Mrs. Gore. I think the most important thing—and they are very, very appreciative of the money that you authorized and we brought—but the next most important thing would probably be if some of the FEMA—the Spanish-speaking FEMA people who have worked in Puerto Rico and have experience after Hurricane Georges be sent over here in order to help, again, with the acute relief effort. I think that would be a tremendous asset if that could be arranged.

The President. We'll arrange it.

Mrs. Gore. That's wonderful. That's wonderful.

The President. When you meet with the President and you finish your trip, I think when you come back, the thing that I think would be most helpful is if you could brief me and also brief Hillary before she goes down and be—let us know specifically what you really think we ought to do. I think everyone in the United States wants to do as much as we possible can to help, both in the immediate aftermath of this horrible tragedy and also for the long-term rebuilding.

And so one of the reasons I was hoping that you could go is to get a firsthand feel for what's going on that even the pictures don't give us here or the telephone calls, and just let me know exactly what you think we ought to do.

Mrs. Gore. Well, I will, and one thing I can tell you is this is a catastrophe of Biblical proportions. It's really unbelievable, and yet the spirit of the people is inspirational. And I will listen; I'm going into a meeting with the President. I've been with Mary Flores all day, working. And the delegation and I look forward to giving you a full report and telling you what we have learned and what we think will be the most helpful for you.

The President. That's great. Where are you going to spend the night tonight?

Mrs. Gore. I'm going to spend the night—we're pitching tents. We don't want to take any assets away from the relief effort, so we're pitching some tents, and we're going to sleep in those.

The President. That's good.

Mrs. Gore. And we're going to get up and go to Nicaragua tomorrow.

The President. That's great.

Mrs. Gore. Thank you again for allowing us to bring this and to work shoulder-to-shoulder with our neighbors who are in crisis right now.

The President. Well, thank you for going. I thank you and all the people on your delegation, all the congressional Members, I hope you'll thank them for me. And have a good night and have a good trip the rest of the way to

Nicaragua. And when you come back, let us know what we can do. And let them know that the people of the United States are pulling for them, and we want to be helpful today, tomorrow, and until everything is restored.

Mrs. Gore. Yes sir. I'll be happy to convey that message. Thank you very much.

The President. Goodbye, Tipper.

Mrs. Gore. Bye-bye.

NOTE: The President spoke at 7:05 p.m. from the Oval Office at the White House. In her remarks, Mrs. Gore referred to President Carlos Flores of Honduras and his wife, Mary.

Remarks at a Veterans Day Ceremony in Arlington, Virginia
November 11, 1998

Thank you very much, Secretary West, for those extraordinary remarks and your equally extraordinary service to our Nation. Commander Tanguma, General Ivany, Superintendent Metzler, Chaplain Maddry, Lee Thornton, thank you for being with us again.

To the distinguished leaders of our veteran organizations, General Ivany, Members of Congress, members of the Cabinet, Secretary Cohen and the Joint Chiefs, the clergy, the veterans, and their families, the members of the Armed Services here. We thank especially the Marine Band.

My fellow Americans, if you will let me begin on a point of personal privilege, I was especially proud to listen to Commander Tanguma's speech today. It was about 10 months, almost to the day, from this day that he and I were together in Mission, Texas, his hometown. He brought with him a distinguished group of Catholic war veterans, including a number from Texas, including a member of his post, the former chairman of the House Agriculture Committee, Congressman Kika de la Garza. We're glad to see you here, sir.

What I want you to know, that is in spite of all the incredible valor of Hispanic soldiers in our country's war, he is the very first Hispanic veteran ever to host this event. It is a great honor for all Americans that this has finally come to pass, and we thank you, sir, for being here.

Today, as a free nation, we come together to honor the men and women to whom we owe our freedom, to pay our own tribute here at this most sacred memorial to our Nation's past. Not only today but every day, some of us have the privilege to glance across the Potomac to see these silent white rows inscribed with their crosses and crescents and Stars of David to remind us that our achievements in peace are built on the sacrifices of our veterans in war and that we owe the most solemn debt to these brave Americans who knew their duty and did it so very well.

We come together today to acknowledge that duty to them, a duty to provide for our veterans and their families, to give them every possible opportunity to improve their education, to find a job, to buy a home, to protect their health. Just this morning I was proud to sign, in the presence of some of the veterans leaders here, the Veterans Programs Enhancement Act, which will increase compensation payments to veterans with disabilities as well as benefits to the survivors of Americans who died serving our country.

I have also directed the Secretaries of Defense, Veterans Administration, and Health and Human Services to establish a Military and Veterans Health Coordinating Board to improve health care for our Armed Forces, our veterans, and our families, and to make sure we know what the health risks are to our soldiers when we send them into harm's way.

We have a duty as well to remember the history that our veterans lived and to appreciate and honor the history they made. We cannot expect future generations to understand fully what those who came before saw, experienced, and felt in battle. But we can make sure that our children know enough to say "thank you." Those two simple words that can mean as much or even more than a medal. We can preserve their diaries and documents, their letters home, their stories of sorrow and pride. Neither the passage of time nor the comforts of peace should drive the memory and meaning of their sacrifice from the consciousness of our Nation.

We owe this to every American who fought in this century's wars. We owe it as well to the millions of Americans who served in our Armed Forces during the cold war. Because they stood ready, we live in a very different world. No longer is there a single overriding threat to our existence. Former adversaries are becoming our partners.

Still, this remains a dangerous world, and peace can never be a time for rest, for maintaining it requires constant vigilance. We can be proud that the United States has been a force for peace in Northern Ireland, in the Middle East, in Haiti, in Bosnia, in Kosovo. We have been able to secure peace because we have been willing to back up our diplomacy, where necessary, with military strength.

Nowhere is our vigilance more urgent than in the Persian Gulf, where Saddam Hussein's regime threatens the stability of one of the most vital regions of the world. Following the Gulf war, and as a condition for the cease-fire, the United Nations demanded, and Iraq agreed, to disclose and destroy its chemical, biological, and nuclear weapons capabilities.

This was no abstract concern. Saddam has fired Scuds at his neighbors, attacked Kuwait, and used chemical weapons in the war with Iran and even on his own people. To ensure that Iraq made good on its commitments, the United Nations kept in place tough economic sanctions while exempting food, medicine, and other humanitarian supplies to alleviate the suffering of the Iraqi people. The U.N. also established a group of highly professional weapons inspectors from dozens of countries, a group called UNSCOM, to oversee the destruction of Iraq's weapons capability and to monitor its ongoing compliance.

For 7 years now, Iraq has had within its power the ability to put itself on the path to ending the sanctions and its isolation simply by complying with obligations it agreed to undertake. Instead, it has worked to shirk those obligations, withholding evidence about its weapons capability; threatening, harassing, blocking the inspectors; massing troops on the Kuwaiti border in the South; attacking the Kurds in the North.

Our steadfast determination in maintaining sanctions, supporting the inspections system, enforcing a no-fly zone, and responding firmly to Iraqi provocations has stopped Iraq from re-

building its weapons of mass destruction arsenal or from threatening its neighbors seriously.

Now, over the past year Iraq has intensified its efforts to end the weapons inspection system, last fall threatening to overthrow—to throw American inspectors off the UNSCOM teams; then, in January, denying UNSCOM unfettered access to all the suspect weapon sites. Both times we built diplomatic pressure on Iraq, backed by overwhelming force, and Baghdad reversed course. Indeed, in March, again it gave a solemn commitment—this time to U.N. Secretary-General Kofi Annan—that it would reopen all of Iraq to international weapons inspectors, without conditions or restrictions.

In August, for the third time in only a year, again Iraq severely restricted the activities of the weapons inspectors. Again, we have gone the extra mile to obtain compliance by peaceful means, working through the U.N. Security Council and with our friends and allies to secure a unanimous Security Council resolution condemning Iraq's actions. We also supported, along with all the members of the Security Council, what Iraq says it wants, a comprehensive review of Iraq's compliance record, provided Saddam resumes full cooperation with the UNSCOM inspectors.

Now, if Saddam Hussein is really serious about wanting sanctions lifted, there is an easy way to demonstrate that: Let UNSCOM do its job without interference—fully comply. The international community is united that Saddam must not have it both ways, by keeping his weapons of mass destruction capability and still getting rid of the sanctions.

All of us agree that we prefer to resolve this crisis peacefully, for two reasons: first, because accomplishing goals through diplomacy is always preferable to using force; second, because reversing Iraq's decision and getting UNSCOM back on the job remains the most effective way to uncover, destroy, and prevent Iraq from reconstituting weapons of mass destruction and the missiles to deliver them.

But if the inspectors are not permitted to visit suspect sites or monitor compliance at known production facilities, they may as well be in Baltimore, not Baghdad. That would open a window of opportunity for Iraq to rebuild its arsenal of weapons and delivery systems in months—I say again, in months—not years. A failure to respond could embolden Saddam to act recklessly, signaling to him that he can, with impunity, develop these weapons of mass destruction or threaten his neighbors. And—this is very important, in an age when we look forward to weapons of mass destruction being a significant threat to civilized people everywhere. And it would permanently damage the credibility of the United Nations Security Council to act as a force for promoting international peace and security. We continue to hope—indeed, pray—that Saddam will comply, but we must be prepared to act if he does not.

Many American service men and women are serving in the Persian Gulf today, many others serving elsewhere around the world, keeping the peace in Bosnia, watching over the DMZ in Korea, working with our friends and allies to stop terror and drugs and deadly weapons.

Too often we forget that even in peacetime their work is hard and often very dangerous. Just 3 days ago, four brave, dedicated American flyers, Lieutenant Commander Kirk Barich, Lieutenant Brendan Duffy, Lieutenant Meredith Carol Loughran, and Lieutenant Charles Woodard—all four were lost in a crash aboard the U.S.S. *Enterprise.* Today our prayers are with their families.

When we give our Armed Forces a mission, there is a principle we must keep in mind. We should never ask them to do what they are not equipped to do, but always equip them to do what we ask them to do. The more we ask, the greater our responsibility to give our troops the support and training they require and the tools they need, from basic spare parts to the newest technology.

As Commander in Chief, I have no higher duty than this: to make certain our troops can do their job while maintaining their readiness to defend our country and defeat any adversary; to ensure they can deploy far from home, knowing their loved ones have the quality of life they deserve. For, as one sergeant recently said, "We enlist soldiers, but we reenlist families."

While our current state of readiness is sound, there are real concerns about the future. For that reason, I made a commitment to add resources to this year's budget to keep our readiness razor sharp and to improve recruitment. We asked the Congress to approve $1.1 billion in new funds for readiness, and it did. Today I am happy to announce that we are releasing those funds.

We have also obtained almost $2 billion in emergency funds to cover unanticipated oper- ations in Bosnia and shifted another $1 billion in our defense budget to meet readiness needs. We have approved pay raises that will significantly reduce the discrepancy between military and civilian pay.

In addition, I have ordered my administration to conduct a thorough review of our long-term readiness and have met with all of our service chiefs to discuss that. The process is now under way. I anticipate it will result in a set of budget and policy proposals for our year 2000 budget requests and for future years. My fellow Americans, this is a challenge we can and must meet. For while we certainly cannot solve all the world's problems, when our values and interests are at stake, we must be ready to act.

Let us always remember that our most profound duty to our Nation's veterans is to keep standing for the ideals for which they fought and for which too many died; to keep strengthening the alliances they forged, as we will next spring at NATO's 50th anniversary summit in Washington; to keep taking risks for peace; to keep faith with those who struggle for human rights, the rule of law, a better life.

We have a duty to seize, not shirk, the responsibilities of leadership, and we have an opportunity to create a world more peaceful, more free, more prosperous than any people have ever known. Therefore, we should look on leadership not as a burden but as a chance, a responsibility to give our children a world that reflects the hopes and enthusiasm that have inspired generation after generation of Americans to serve our country in uniform, from World War I hero Alvin York to World War II hero Waverly Wray, from General George Marshall to General Colin Powell, from John Glenn to John Glenn. [*Laughter*] I think we ought to give Senator Glenn a hand today, don't you? [*Applause*] Think of it, he's given us a whole new field of endeavor to look forward to in our old age. [*Laughter*]

We dedicate this day to all our veterans, to the retired schoolteacher who in his time helped liberate a death camp, to the hospital medic who learned to save lives in Vietnam, to the legionnaire who pins on his medals with pride, to the heroes buried in the Tomb of the Unknowns.To all of them and all they represent, we dedicate each and every day spent in service to our country and its ideals. May God bless them and their families. May God bless the United States of America.

Thank you.

NOTE: The President spoke at 11:45 a.m. in the Amphitheater at Arlington National Cemetery. In his remarks, he referred to Manuel Tanguma, Jr., commander, Catholic War Veterans of the U.S.A.; Maj. Gen. Robert R. Ivany, USA, commander, U.S. Army Military District of Washington; John C. Metzler, Jr., Superintendent, Arlington Na-

tional Cemetery; Hugh Maddry, Chief of Chaplains, Department of Veterans Affairs; Lee Thornton, master of ceremonies; and President Saddam Hussein of Iraq. A portion of these remarks could not be verified because the tape was incomplete. H.R. 4110, the Veterans Programs Enhancement Act of 1998, approved November 11, was assigned Public Law No. 105–368.

Statement on Funding for Military Readiness
November 11, 1998

Today, as part of the Omnibus Consolidated and Emergency Supplemental Appropriations Act, 1999, I am releasing $1.1 billion in military readiness funding that will enhance our Armed Forces' ability to maintain high standards of readiness throughout the coming year.

I consider military readiness—ensuring that our forces are always prepared to carry out their assigned mission in peace and in war—to be among America's highest priorities.

On September 15 I met with the Joint Chiefs of Staff and Unified Commanders in Chief, and they advised that, while our current state of readiness is sound, there are real concerns about the future. While our forces are now capable of meeting the security needs of the Nation, the chiefs raised several concerns about military readiness, especially regarding the future readiness of follow-on troops who would be deployed in a sustained conflict.

In response, I made a commitment to add resources to the current year's budget that will address emerging readiness concerns by reducing the backlog of equipment awaiting maintenance, buying additional spare parts for Air Force and Navy aircraft, and improving our recruiting efforts. In addition, I have ordered a thorough and complete readiness review, involv-

ing the Department of Defense, the National Security Council, and the Office of Management and Budget, as part of my administration's budget review process for fiscal year 2000.

The review process for fiscal year 2000 is already underway, and I anticipate a series of budget and policy proposals that will continue our effort to ensure that U.S. forces remain ready to meet the security needs of the Nation. Our challenge is to strike a balance between providing sufficient resources for military readiness while maintaining fiscal discipline and appropriate funding levels for other investments necessary to sustain our economy.

I look forward to working with the next Congress to ensure a viable defense budget that continues to guarantee that our forces are prepared, while investing wisely in modernization and supporting the overall policy goals of my administration. And I am pleased that this action today will address the most immediate readiness needs of the U.S. military.

NOTE: H.R. 4328, the Omnibus Consolidated and Emergency Supplemental Appropriations Act, 1999, approved October 21, was assigned Public Law No. 105–277.

Statement on Signing the Veterans Programs Enhancement Act of 1998
November 11, 1998

Today I am pleased to sign into law H.R. 4110, the "Veterans Programs Enhancement Act

of 1998." It is particularly appropriate on this Veterans Day to express the Nation's continued gratitude to our veterans by improving a wide range of veterans' benefits and programs. I am particularly pleased that H.R. 4110 includes so many Administration proposals.

Most important, the bill provides a 1.3 percent increase in compensation payments to veterans with service-connected disabilities and in dependency and indemnity compensation to the survivors of those whose deaths were service-related. This increase, effective December 1, 1998, reflects the same percentage increase in benefits that Social Security beneficiaries and veterans' pension recipients will receive. Approximately 2.3 million veterans and over 300,000 surviving spouses and children will benefit from this increase, which will ensure that the value of their well-deserved benefits is maintained.

The bill also furthers the Nation's commitment to veterans who served in the Persian Gulf War. In particular, it extends existing authority for providing priority health care to Gulf War veterans through December 31, 2001. In addition, the bill bolsters efforts by the Departments of Veterans Affairs (VA), Defense, and Health and Human Services, with the help of independent scientific organizations, to study and treat these veterans' illnesses in a scientifically sound and effective manner. Furthermore, this legislation enhances outreach efforts to Gulf War veterans and broadens the public's access to the findings of federally sponsored research on the health consequences of service in the Persian Gulf.

The bill contains a number of provisions to help veterans reach their educational and employment goals. For instance, the legislation expands veterans' options for entering on-the-job training programs and meeting requirements for Montgomery G.I. Bill benefits. In addition, the bill reinforces and expands an individual's right to return to a job after military service, as provided by the Uniformed Services Employment and Reemployment Rights Act.

Other provisions revise veterans' pension and insurance programs. For example, the legislation increases the special pension paid to recipients of the Medal of Honor, the Nation's highest military award. Additionally, the bill provides increased assistance to certain veterans with terminal illnesses by allowing them to receive a portion of their life insurance benefits as "living benefits," helping them to meet medical and living expenses during their time of special need.

The bill includes many other provisions to improve the quality and effectiveness of VA services to veterans. One provision permanently restructures and streamlines VA housing loan operations. Another provision contributes to high-quality VA health care by authorizing the Department to establish new educational benefits for certain categories of health care professionals to help attract and retain the best qualified employees.

This Nation owes no greater debt of gratitude than to our veterans, particularly those who have suffered disability or who made the supreme sacrifice while defending our freedoms. Each Veterans Day, the Nation makes a special effort to give thanks for and to honor the sacrifices of veterans and their families. This comprehensive legislation further expresses our gratitude to these brave men and women, not just on Veterans Day, but every day. For that reason, I am privileged to sign H.R. 4110 into law.

WILLIAM J. CLINTON

The White House,
November 11, 1998.

NOTE: H.R. 4110, approved November 11, was assigned Public Law No. 105–368.

Memorandum on the Creation of the Military and Veterans Health Coordinating Board
November 11, 1998

Memorandum for the Secretary of Defense, the Secretary of Veterans Affairs, the Secretary of Health and Human Services

Subject: Creation of Military and Veterans Health Coordinating Board

Our Nation is truly indebted to our active duty military, reservist, National Guard, and veterans for protecting America's interests around the globe. From small peacekeeping missions to large combat operations, these men and women put their lives on the line to ensure our peace and prosperity at home and abroad. We owe them and their families a great debt. We have an obligation to protect their health while they serve and to care for their service-connected injuries or illnesses for as long as they live.

Our experience with the Gulf War demonstrated that we were not adequately prepared to deal with the health consequences resulting from a large-scale combat deployment in the unique environment our soldiers faced. The aftermath of this conflict underscored the need to improve significantly our ability to address post-deployment health problems. Your extensive efforts to understand the causes and treat the illnesses experienced by Gulf War veterans have identified numerous deficiencies in the way we prepare for and deal with the health of our military, veterans, and their families. I am pleased that we are applying these lessons learned from the Gulf War and other recent military missions to current and future military deployments.

In its December 31, 1996, report, my Presidential Advisory Committee on Gulf War Veterans' Illnesses recommended that the National Science and Technology Council (NSTC) review existing Federal policies and programs and develop an interagency plan "to address health preparedness for and readjustment of veterans and families after future conflicts and peacekeeping missions." The NSTC's plan, developed by your departments, identifies numerous actions, including improved health protection for military forces, which must be taken to avoid the mistakes of the past. One of the key recommendations contained in the plan is to establish a Military and Veterans Health Coordinating Board to continue improving the coordination among your departments and to oversee the implementation of the NSTC's plan.

Therefore, I direct you to establish the Military and Veterans Health Coordinating Board and report annually to the Assistants to the President for National Security Affairs and for Science and Technology on its progress. Specifically, the Board should focus on issues associated with deployment health, research, and communications regarding health risks. In addition, the Board must ensure that record-keeping requirements linked to military and veterans health preparedness, health protection for military forces, disease prevention, and medical care are incorporated into your departments' relevant information technology and information management systems.

WILLIAM J. CLINTON

Remarks Announcing Grants for After-School Programs
November 12, 1998

The President. Thank you very much, Rose, for giving us a wonderful example of what these endeavors are all about. Hillary and I are delighted to have all of you—parents, administrators and teachers, child care advocates, grant recipients—here in the White House today. We especially thank Congressman Castle, Congresswoman Lowey, Senator Robb, Senator Specter, Congressmen Hoyer and Cardin and King and Levin and Quinn.

I thank Olivia Golden, our HHS Administrator for Children and Families, for being here, along with Mike Smith and Kent McGuire from the Education Department. We welcome Mayor Davis, Mayor Ganim, Mayor Schundler, and all of you.

I have enjoyed this day very much already because Hillary and I are, I think it's fair to say, virtually obsessed with the idea of expanding after-school programs and affordable child care. And to see this reaching across party lines to support our children, our families, and our communities is a deeply moving thing to me. But I'd like to begin my remarks, since I essentially can't add much to what has already been said—I want to ask you to think about a question that we have—all of us who are parents, at least, who have ever taken our children on trips when they were young—have heard them say, "Are we there yet? Are we there yet?" [*Laughter*]

So in spite of what we come to celebrate today, the truth is that when it comes to raising our children in this new era, we are not there yet. But when I look at the people on this podium and the faces out in this crowd, I realize that this is clearly an area where we can put the progress of our people ahead of our partisan differences and that, if we continue to do that, we might be able to give a different answer to our children.

Even though our economy is the strongest in a generation, all of you know that one of the principal struggles faced by real people out there in America was the one that Rose Bolz told us about today. Even with the lowest unemployment rate in 28 years, even with the fastest rising wage rates in over 20 years, how are people doing at balancing the work of parenting and the work of working? How do people fulfill their obligation to their children and to their workplace?

Well, first of all, it's not easy. In spite of the program that the First Lady described, in spite of the marvelous experience that Rose, as a parent, with her child have had, on any given day in America as many as 15 million school-age children are left to fend for themselves on the streets or alone at home. Half of all juvenile crime occurs in the few hours just after school lets out. And for families with children between the ages of 3 and 5, child care is the second or third greatest household expense.

Now, obviously, only parents can find the proper balance between work and child rearing, one that works for them or one that is imposed on them by their economic circumstances. What we have to do is to help them do the very best they can to meet their obligations at home and at work. That is the only responsible thing to do on the verge of this new century when the patterns of work and life are so very different.

As I have said many times, if you will indulge me I'd like to say once more, I know that all life is filled with choices and some of them are bound to be hard, but this is a choice we should not require our people to make, because if they have to choose, they lose, and we lose. If a person cannot function at work for worrying about the children at home, but economically they must work, then that weakens the fabric of the American economy. If in order to fulfill one's responsibility at work a parent has to neglect children, that is an even higher price, because in every society that is always the most important work that can be done.

That is why we have worked hard to help people reconcile these two obligations with the family and medical leave law, with policies designed to promote the idea that if people who work full-time and have children in the home should not be in poverty, the doubling of the earned-income tax credit, the $500-per-child tax credit that was a part of the bipartisan balanced budget bill passed last year, the raise in the minimum wage, the dramatic increase in tax credits and scholarships and loan program options for college education, the welfare reform that I believe did a great deal. Mike Castle and I were talking about this, because we've been working on this subject for more than 10 years together now, and we believe it makes a very good start at striking the proper balance between work and family, protecting the health care and the nutrition of children as a national guarantee, providing many more resources for child care and for transportation, giving States the flexibility to design programs that are more likely to move people more quickly from welfare to work without sacrificing their parental responsibilities. And since we have the smallest percentage of our people on welfare in 29 years, I'd say we're off to a pretty good start.

Now, since those initiatives, we have focused on two other major priorities: first, the after-school programs; and second, child care for lower income working families who may not have been on welfare and therefore are not eligible for the funds that were provided in welfare reform.

Last month, the bipartisan balanced budget bill, to which Senator Specter and others have referred, expanded Head Start and made new investments in improving the quality of child care. Thanks to that bill, and especially to the extra child care put in under the welfare reform law, I can tell you that there are nearly one and a quarter million low income children now receiving child care under the child care block grant program. That is up from one million the year before. That's a 25 percent increase in one year. And to all these Members of Congress who are here who supported this across party lines, I want to say a special thank-you for doing that.

Now, that is the good news. But if a child asks you, "Are we there yet?" here is the rest of the story. We've gone from a million to one and a quarter million in one year, a 25 percent increase; by income, under the law, another 8.75 million children in low income working families are eligible for child care assistance, but cannot receive it because we have not put sufficient funds into the program.

So this should continue to be a priority in the next Congress. Even though we were successful—and I appreciate what Senator Specter said about the nature of the budget process—Congress was very generous in the end in investing more money in education, we did not pass the child care proposal. I hope we can do better next time because of the large number of people out there.

Now I'd like to say just a little word about the after-school programs because I, too, think they're so important. The budget I signed last month included a fivefold increase in the number of children who will receive after-school programs. This program, this increase, was funded under the 21st century community learning center initiative initially sponsored by Senator Jeffords of Vermont. It was strongly supported by Senator Boxer, Senator Kennedy, Congresswoman Lowey, and others.

I want to tell you how fast and how far Congress has moved on this after-school program, again in a bipartisan fashion. In 1996 there was $1 million in this program. In 1997 there was $40 million in the program. In 1998, in this Congress—thank you, Mr. Appropriator—there was $200 million in the program. That's why

183 communities in 44 States and the District of Columbia today can receive $60 million to set up these academically enriched after-school programs. Roughly 75,000 more children will now have someplace to go other than the streets when school lets out. That's good news for America.

One of these recipients is Chicago's Lighthouse program, which the First Lady and I have both visited. Every day Lighthouse—listen to this—keeps 112,000 children in 248 Chicago schools off the street and out of trouble, while drilling them in math and reading, providing everything from computer instruction to supervised sports to a hot evening meal. Over 40,000 children in that school system now get 3 meals a day.

After-school programs like this honor our values and benefit our Nation. They offer opportunity and peace of mind to hard-working parents who can't always be at home when school lets out. They bolster responsibility and academic achievement among students. Math and reading scores have shot up in nearly every one of the 40 Chicago schools where the program began 2 years ago.

And I might add, parenthetically—I'll plug something I believe in—I am all for the proposition that in our most troubled inner-city schools we must raise academic standards, raise learning levels, and end social promotion, but it is wrong to brand a child a failure when the system has failed the child. So there have to be after-school programs and summer school programs. So Chicago has ended social promotion. But they've got 112,000 kids in after-school programs, and the summer school program is now the sixth largest school district in America.

So if we want our children to do well and if we believe our children can do well across racial and income lines, no matter where they were born, where they grow up—whether they're on the most distant rural Native American tribal reservation or in an absolutely abandoned inner-city neighborhood—and if we want to say, "Look, because we love you we're going to hold you to high standards," then we have to give them the tools they need to succeed.

So this is a terribly important thing to the strengthening of our community, to reducing juvenile crime, to doing the things that we all know we ought to do. Just think, in this huge budget of over $1.5 trillion, what started with

$1 million, then went to $40 million, then went to $200 million, has the potential to have a bigger impact on more children's lives, more families, and more communities' futures than virtually anything else we're doing around here—because it empowers people, like the people who work with Rose Bolz' daughter, to do more of that daily.

Now, again, are we there yet? When it comes to the end of the speech, the answer is "nearly." [*Laughter*] But back to the subject—are we there yet?

Audience members. No-o-o!

The President. A hundred and eighty-three new after-school grants, that's the good news. The rest of the news is, for every community that received a grant today, there were seven more which applied. Actually, that's also good news if you think about it. Everybody gets this now. But because they get it, we have to try harder. Like child care, the need for after-school programs simply outstrips our investment.

So when children ask from the back of the car, "Are we there yet?" it's always hard to give them a satisfactory answer. And how many of us as parents have explained how far we've come and that we've come further than we've

still got to go—all the answers that satisfy adults and never make it with kids. [*Laughter*]

On these issues, we should be as impatient as our children in the back seat of the car. We should be proud of what has been done. We should lift up the teachers, the community leaders, the parents, the child care workers who have done the right thing. But we should remember the impatience of our children. In the new economy, we can no longer think of high-quality child care and after-school programs as luxury items. In every period of economic and social change, what once was a luxury item becomes quickly standard equipment.

So are we there yet? No. But we'll get there together. Thank you very much.

NOTE: The President spoke at 2:54 p.m. in the East Room at the White House. In his remarks he referred to Rose Bolz, single working mother from Tucson, AZ, who introduced the President; Kent McGuire, Assistant Secretary, and Marshall S. Smith, Deputy Secretary, Department of Education; Mayor Ernest D. Davis of Mount Vernon, NY; Mayor Joseph P. Ganim of Bridgeport, CT; and Mayor Bret Schundler of Jersey City, NJ. A portion of these remarks could not be verified because the tape was incomplete.

Statement on the Retirement of Lewis Merletti as Director of the United States Secret Service
November 12, 1998

Lewis Merletti has done an outstanding job as Director of the United States Secret Service, and I am accepting his retirement with the deepest regret. I have great admiration for Lew and for what he has accomplished in service to our country.

From Lew's service in the United States Army with the Special Forces to his Secret Service assignments in Philadelphia, New York, and Washington, DC, and finally as Director, he has distinguished himself at every level.

I would like to thank Lew's wife, Patty, and their sons, Mike, Matt, and Chris, for accepting the pressures and difficulties that arise from being a part of the Secret Service family. Like many Secret Service families, they endured a number of moves from one city to another.

Their move to Cleveland and the Cleveland Browns organization will be one more challenge in Lew's accomplished career, one that he will undoubtedly meet with enthusiasm and great success. I also hope it will give Lew and Patty more time to spend with their children in the coming years.

On behalf of Hillary, Chelsea, the Vice President and his family, the former Presidents and their families—indeed, on behalf of everyone who has felt the reassurance of being in the care of Lew Merletti and the Secret Service agents he led—I want to thank this distinguished Director for his remarkable devotion to duty and country. I will miss him very much.

The U.S. Secret Service is a critical law enforcement agency. It provides a secure environment for the President, the Vice President, and their families, former Presidents and visiting heads of state while also playing a vital role in protecting our Nation from terrorism, counterfeiting, and other financial crimes.

Letter to Congressional Leaders on Continuation of the National Emergency Regarding Weapons of Mass Destruction
November 12, 1998

Dear Mr. Speaker: (Dear Mr. President:)

On November 14, 1994, in light of the dangers of the proliferation of nuclear, biological and chemical weapons ("weapons of mass destruction"—WMD) and of the means of delivering such weapons, I issued Executive Order 12938, and declared a national emergency under the International Emergency Economic Powers Act (50 U.S.C. 1701 *et seq.*). Under section 202(d) of the National Emergencies Act (50 U.S.C. 1622(d)), the national emergency terminates on the anniversary date of its declaration, unless I publish in the *Federal Register* and transmit to the Congress a notice of its continuation.

The proliferation of weapons of mass destruction and their means of delivery continues to pose an unusual and extraordinary threat to the national security, foreign policy, and economy of the United States. Indeed, on July 28, 1998, I issued Executive Order 13094 to strengthen Executive Order 12938 by, *inter alia*, broadening the types of proliferation activity that is subject to potential penalties. I am, therefore, advising the Congress that the national emergency declared on November 14, 1994, must continue in effect beyond November 14, 1998. Accordingly, I have extended the national emergency declared in Executive Order 12938, as amended, and have sent the attached notice of extension to the *Federal Register* for publication.

On July 28, 1998, I amended section 4 of Executive Order 12938 so that the United States Government could more effectively respond to the worldwide threat of weapons of mass destruction proliferation activities. The amendment to section 4 strengthens Executive Order 12938 in several significant ways. The amendment broadens the type of proliferation activity that subjects entities to potential penalties under the Executive order. The original Executive order provided for penalties for contributions to the efforts of any foreign country, project or entity to use, acquire, design, produce, or stockpile chemical or biological weapons; the amended Executive order also covers contributions to foreign programs for nuclear weapons and for missiles capable of delivering weapons of mass destruction. Moreover, the amendment expands the original Executive order to include attempts to contribute to foreign proliferation activities, as well as actual contributions, and broadens the range of potential penalties to expressly include the prohibition of United States Government assistance to foreign persons, as well as the prohibition of United States Government procurement and imports into the United States.

The following report, which covers activities on or before October 31, 1998, is made pursuant to section 204 of the International Emergency Economic Powers Act (50 U.S.C. 1703) and section 401(c) of the National Emergencies Act (50 U.S.C. 1641(c)), regarding activities taken and money spent pursuant to the emergency declaration. Additional information on nuclear, missile, and/or chemical and biological weapons (CBW) proliferation concerns and nonproliferation efforts is contained in the most recent annual Report on the Proliferation of Missiles and Essential Components of Nuclear, Biological and Chemical Weapons, provided to the Congress pursuant to section 1097 of the National Defense Authorization Act for Fiscal Years 1992 and 1993 (Public Law 102–190), also known as the "Nonproliferation Report," and the most recent annual report provided to the Congress pursuant to section 308 of the Chemical and Biological Weapons Control and Warfare Elimination Act of 1991 (Public Law 102–182), also known as the "CBW Report."

Nuclear Weapons

In May, India and Pakistan each conducted a series of nuclear tests. In response, I imposed sanctions on India and Pakistan as required by the Glenn Amendment. Beyond our unilateral response, world reaction was pronounced and included nearly universal condemnation across a broad range of international fora and a broad range of sanctions, including new restrictions on lending by international financial institutions unrelated to basic human needs and aid from the G–8 and other countries.

Since the mandatory imposition of U.S. sanctions, we have worked unilaterally, with other P–5 and G–8 members, and through the United Nations to dissuade India and Pakistan from taking further steps toward creating operational nuclear forces, to urge them to join multilateral arms control efforts, to persuade them to prevent an arms race and build confidence by practicing restraint, and to resume efforts to resolve their differences through dialogue. The P–5, G–8, and U.N. Security Council have called on India and Pakistan to take a broad range of concrete actions. The United States has over the past 5 months focused most intensely on several objectives that can be met over the short and medium term: an end to nuclear testing and prompt, unconditional adherence to the Comprehensive Nuclear Test Ban Treaty (CTBT); a moratorium on production of fissile material for nuclear weapons and other explosive devices, and engagement in productive negotiations on a fissile material cut-off treaty (FMCT); restraint in deployment of nuclear-capable missiles and aircraft; and adoption of controls meeting international standards on exports of sensitive materials and technology.

Against this backdrop of international pressure on India and Pakistan, U.S. high-level dialogue with Indian and Pakistani officials has yielded some progress. Both governments, having already declared testing moratoria, indicated publicly that they are prepared to adhere to the CTBT under certain conditions. Both withdrew their opposition to negotiations on an FMCT in Geneva at the end of the 1998 Conference on Disarmament session. They have also pledged to institute strict control of sensitive exports that meet internationally accepted standards. In addition, they have resumed bilateral dialogue on outstanding disputes, including Kashmir, at the Foreign Secretary level.

In recognition of these positive steps and to encourage further progress, I decided on November 3 to exercise my authority under the Brownback provision of the 1999 Omnibus Appropriations bill (Public Law 105–277) to waive some of the Glenn sanctions. Through this action, I have authorized the resumption of Export-Import Bank, Overseas Private Investment Corporation, Trade and Development Agency, and International Military Education and Training programs in India and Pakistan and have lifted restrictions on U.S. banks in these countries. We will continue discussions with both governments at the senior and expert levels, and our diplomatic efforts in concert with the P–5 and in international fora.

So far, 150 countries have signed and 21 have ratified the CTBT. During 1998, CTBT signatories conducted numerous meetings of the Preparatory Commission (PrepCom) in Vienna, seeking to promote rapid completion of the International Monitoring System (IMS) established by the Treaty.

On September 23, 1997, I transmitted the CTBT to the Senate, requesting prompt advice and consent to ratification. The CTBT will serve several U.S. national security interests by prohibiting all nuclear explosions. It will constrain the development and qualitative improvement of nuclear weapons; end the development of advanced new types; contribute to the prevention of nuclear proliferation and the process of nuclear disarmament; and strengthen international peace and security. The CTBT marks a historic milestone in our drive to reduce the nuclear threat and to build a safer world.

The Nuclear Suppliers Group (NSG) held its 1998 Plenary in Edinburgh, Scotland, March 30 to April 2, on the twentieth anniversary of the publication of the Nuclear Suppliers Guidelines. With 35 member states, the NSG is a mature, effective, and widely accepted export-control arrangement. Over the past 7 years the NSG has established a Dual-Use Regime (DUR), agreed to require full-scope safeguards as a condition of nuclear supply, created an effective Joint Information Exchange, and strengthened controls over technology and retransfers. The NSG is considering further activities to promote regime transparency, following the success of the 1997 Vienna transparency seminar, and is preparing for a transparency seminar in New York during the run-up to the 1999 NPT PrepCom.

The NSG is considering membership for Belarus, China, Cyprus, Kazakhstan and Turkey. China is the only major nuclear supplier that is not a member of the NSG, although China did join the Zangger Committee last year and recently has expressed an interest in learning more about the NSG.

The NPT Exporters (Zangger) Committee has demonstrated its continued relevance to the multilateral nonproliferation regime as the interpreter of Article III–2 of the NPT by the membership of China in October 1997 by recently agreeing to a statement deploring the Indian and Pakistani nuclear tests. This is the first time the Zangger Committee has ever issued a statement not directly related to publication of its Guidelines. Furthermore, the Zangger Committee is considering a U.S. proposal to add conversion technology to the Trigger List.

Chemical and Biological Weapons

The export control regulations issued under the Enhanced Proliferation Control Initiative (EPCI) remain fully in force and continue to be applied by the Department of Commerce in order to control the export of items with potential use in chemical or biological weapons or unmanned delivery systems for weapons of mass destruction.

Chemical weapons (CW) continue to pose a very serious threat to our security and that of our allies. On April 29, 1997, the Convention on the Prohibition of the Development, Production, Stockpiling and Use of Chemical Weapons and on Their Destruction (the Chemical Weapons Convention or CWC) entered into force with 87 of the CWC's 165 signatories as original States Parties. The United States was among their number, having deposited its instrument of ratification on April 25. Russia ratified the CWC on November 5, 1997, and became a State Party on December 5, 1997. As of October 31, 1998, 120 countries (including Iran, Pakistan, and Ukraine) have become States Parties.

The implementing body for the CWC—the Organization for the Prohibition of Chemical Weapons (OPCW)—was established at the entry into force (EIF) of the Convention on April 29, 1997. The OPCW, located in The Hague, has primary responsibility (along with States Parties) for implementing the CWC. It collects declarations, conducts inspections, and serves as a forum for consultation and cooperation among States Parties. It consists of the Conference of the States Parties, the Executive Council (EC), and the Technical Secretariat (TS).

The EC consists of 41 States Parties (including the United States) and acts as the governing body for the OPCW between annual meetings of the Conference of the States Parties. Since EIF, the EC has met numerous times to address issues such as scale of assessments, CW production facility conversion requests, facility and transitional verification arrangements, and staff regulations.

The TS carries out the verification provisions of the CWC, and presently has a staff of approximately 500, including about 200 inspectors trained and equipped to inspect military and industrial facilities throughout the world. The OPCW has conducted nearly 300 inspections in some 20 countries. It conducted nearly 100 such inspections in the United States. The OPCW maintains a permanent inspector presence at operational U.S. CW destruction facilities in Utah, Nevada, and Johnston Island.

The United States is determined to seek full implementation of the concrete measures in the CWC designed to raise the costs and risks for any state or terrorist attempting to engage in chemical weapons-related activities. The CWC's declaration requirements improve our knowledge of possible chemical weapons activities. Its inspection provisions provide for access to declared and undeclared facilities and locations, thus making clandestine chemical weapons production and stockpiling more difficult, more risky, and more expensive.

The Chemical Weapons Convention Implementation Act of 1998 was enacted into law in October 1998, as part of the Omnibus Consolidated and Emergency Supplemental Appropriation Act, 1999 (Public Law 105–277). Accordingly, we anticipate rapid promulgation of implementing regulations on submission of U.S. industrial declarations to the OPCW. Submission of these declarations will bring the United States into full compliance with the CWC. United States noncompliance to date has, among other things, undermined U.S. leadership in the organization as well as our ability to encourage other States Parties to make complete, accurate, and timely declarations.

Countries that refuse to join the CWC will be politically isolated and prohibited under the CWC from trading with States Parties in certain key chemicals. The relevant treaty provision is specifically designed to penalize in a concrete way countries that refuse to join the rest of the world in eliminating the threat of chemical weapons. We anticipate rapid promulgation of U.S. regulations implementing these CWC trade restrictions.

The United States also continues to play a leading role in the international effort to reduce the threat from biological weapons (BW). We are an active participant in the Ad Hoc Group (AHG) striving to complete a legally binding protocol to strengthen and enhance compliance with the 1972 Convention on the Prohibition of the Development, Production and Stockpiling of Bacteriological (Biological) and Toxin Weapons and on Their Destruction (the Biological Weapons Convention or BWC). This Ad Hoc Group was mandated by the September 1994 BWC Special Conference. The Fourth BWC Review Conference, held in November/December 1996, urged the AHG to complete the protocol as soon as possible but not later than the next Review Conference to be held in 2001. Work is progressing on a draft rolling text through insertion of national views and clarification of existing text. We held four AHG negotiating sessions in 1998, and five are scheduled for 1999.

On January 27, 1998, during the State of the Union Address, I announced that the United States would take a leading role in the effort to erect stronger international barriers against the proliferation and use of BW by strengthening the BWC with a new international system to detect and deter cheating. The United States will work closely with U.S. industry to develop U.S. negotiating positions and then to reach international agreement on: declarations, non-challenge clarifying visits, and challenge investigations. Other key issues to be resolved in the Ad Hoc Group in 1999 are details on mandatory declarations, placement of definitions related to declarations, and questions related to assistance and export controls.

On the margins of the 1998 U.N. General Assembly, senior United States Government representatives attended a Ministerial meeting hosted by the Government of New Zealand and sponsored by the Government of Australia to promote intensified work on the Compliance Protocol. I will continue to devote personal attention to this issue and encourage other heads of state to do the same.

The United States continued to be a leading participant in the 30-member Australia Group

(AG) CBW nonproliferation regime. The United States attended the most recent annual AG Plenary Session from October 12-15, 1998, during which the Group continued to focus on strengthening AG export controls and sharing information to address the threat of CBW terrorism. At the behest of the United States, the AG first began in-depth political-level discussion of CBW proliferation and terrorism during the 1995 Plenary Session following the Tokyo subway nerve gas attack earlier that year. At the 1998 plenary, at the behest of the United States, AG participants shared information on legal and regulatory efforts each member has taken to counter this threat. The AG also reaffirmed its commitment to continue its active outreach program of briefings for non-AG countries, and to promote regional consultations on export controls and nonproliferation to further awareness and understanding of national policies in these areas.

The Group also reaffirmed the participants' shared belief that full adherence to the CWC and the BWC is the best way to achieve permanent global elimination of CBW, and that all States adhering to these Conventions have an obligation to ensure that their national activities support this goal. The AG participants continue to seek to ensure that all relevant national measures promote the object and purposes of the BWC and CWC. The AG participants reaffirmed their belief that existing national export licensing policies on chemical weapons- and biological weapons-related items help to fulfill their obligations established under Article I of the CWC and Article III of the BWC that States Parties not assist, in any way, the acquisition, manufacture, or use of chemical or biological weapons. Given this understanding, the AG participants also reaffirmed their commitment to continuing the Group's activities, now that the CWC has entered into force.

During the last 6 months, we continued to examine closely intelligence and other reports of trade in CBW-related material and technology that might be relevant to sanctions provisions under the Chemical and Biological Weapons Control and Warfare Elimination Act of 1991. No new sanctions determinations were reached during this reporting period. The United States also continues to cooperate with its AG partners and other countries in stopping shipments of proliferation concern.

Missiles for Delivery of Weapons of Mass Destruction

The United States continues to carefully control exports that could contribute to unmanned delivery systems for weapons of mass destruction and to closely monitor activities of potential missile proliferation concern. We also continue to implement the U.S. missile sanctions law. In April 1998, we imposed Category I missile sanctions against North Korean and Pakistani entities for the transfer from North Korea to Pakistan of equipment and technology related to the Ghauri missile. Sanctions imposed against two North Korean entities in August 1997 for transfers involving Category II Missile Technology Control Regime (MTCR) Annex items also remain in effect.

During this reporting period, MTCR Partners continued to work with each other and with potential non-Partner supplier and transshipment states to curb proliferation. Partners emphasized the need for implementing effective export control systems and cooperated to interdict shipments intended for use in missile programs of concern.

The United States was an active participant in the MTCR's highly productive May 1998 Reinforced Point of Contact (RPOC) Meeting. At the RPOC, MTCR Partners engaged in an indepth discussion of regional missile proliferation concerns, focusing in particular on South Asia. They also discussed steps Partners could take to increase transparency and outreach to nonmembers, and reached consensus to admit the Czech Republic, Poland, and Ukraine to membership in the MTCR. (Reports on their membership have been submitted to the Congress pursuant to section 73A of the Arms Export Control Act.)

In May 1998, the United States was an active participant in the German-hosted MTCR workshop on brokering, catch-all controls, and other export control issues. In June, the United States played a leading role at the Swiss-hosted MTCR workshops on risk assessment in MTCR licensing decisions. The workshops involved the participation of MTCR Partners, as well as several non-MTCR members, and were successful in providing practical insights on export control and licensing issues. In particular, it helped participants identify risk factors and ways to assess them.

The MTCR held its Thirteenth Plenary Meeting in Budapest, Hungary on October 5–9. At the Plenary, the MTCR Partners shared information about activities and programs of missile proliferation concern and considered additional steps they can take, individually and collectively, to prevent the proliferation of delivery systems for weapons of mass destruction, focusing in particular on the threat posed by missile-related activities in South and North East Asia and the Middle East.

During their discussions, the Partners gave special attention to North Korean (DPRK) missile activities, expressing serious concern about the DPRK's missile export practices and its efforts to acquire increasingly long-range missiles. The MTCR Plenary Chairman issued a statement reflecting the Partners' concerns, noting in particular that the Partners urged the DPRK to refrain from further flight tests of WMD-capable missiles and to cease exports of equipment and technology for such missiles. The Partners also agreed to maintain special scrutiny over their missile-related exports in order not to support North Korean missile development in any way.

At Budapest, the Partners also discussed ways to further the MTCR's efforts to promote openness and outreach to nonmembers, including by sponsoring additional seminars and workshops for members and nonmembers. The Partners supported a U.S. proposal for an MTCR-sponsored workshop in 1999 on "intangible transfers of technology," in order to develop a greater understanding of how proliferators misuse the Internet, scientific conferences, plant visits, and student exchange programs to acquire sensitive technology and to identify steps countries can take to address this problem. They also agreed to give further consideration to a technical-level workshop for border guards and Customs authorities on export control enforcement. In addition, the Partners noted China's increased willingness to engage in meaningful dialogue on missile nonproliferation and export control issues, and renewed their previous invitation in principle to China to take the steps necessary to join the Regime.

The Partners also made additional progress at Budapest toward reformatting the MTCR Annex (the list of MTCR-controlled items) to improve clarity and uniformity of implementation while maintaining the coverage of the current Annex. They hope to complete this process in the near future.

During this reporting period, the United States also worked unilaterally and in coordination with its MTCR Partners to combat missile proliferation and to encourage nonmembers to export responsibly and to adhere to the MTCR Guidelines. Since my last report, we have continued missile nonproliferation discussions with China and North Korea and other countries in Central Europe, the Middle East, and Asia.

In October 1998, the United States and the DPRK held a third round of missile talks, aimed at constraining DPRK missile production, deployment, flight-testing, and exports. The United States expressed serious concerns about North Korea's missile exports and indigenous missile activities, and made clear that we regard as highly destabilizing the DPRK's attempt on August 31 to use a Taepo Dong 1 missile to orbit a small satellite. We voiced strong opposition to North Korea's missile exports to other countries and made clear that further launches of long-range missiles or further exports of such missiles or their related technology would have very negative consequences for efforts to improve U.S.-North Korean relations. The talks concluded with an agreement to hold another round at the earliest practical date.

In response to reports of continuing Iranian efforts to acquire sensitive items from Russian entities for use in Iran's missile development program, the United States continued its high-level dialogue with Russia aimed at finding ways the United States and Russia can work together to cut off the flow of sensitive goods to Iran's ballistic missile development program. This effort has netted some positive results. For example, during this reporting period, Russia began implementing "catch-all" provisions imposing controls over the export of any material destined for a WMD or missile program, and provided detailed implementing guidance on these controls for Russian entities. Russia also agreed to meet regularly with the United States to discuss export control issues. In addition, at the summit in September, President Yeltsin and I announced the formation of seven bilateral working groups—nuclear, missile, catch-all and internal compliance, conventional weapons, law enforcement, licensing, and customs—for the rapid exchange of information on the wide range of nonproliferation issues.

In July, Russia launched special investigations of nine entities suspected of cooperating with foreign programs to acquire WMD and missile delivery systems. Russia subsequently took steps to end exports to Iran by three of these entities and to pursue two of the cases as smuggling issues. Consistent with the Russian action, the United States took action against seven of the nine entities in July pursuant in part to Executive Order 12938, as amended. We suspended all United States Government assistance to these seven entities and banned all U.S. exports to them and all of their imports to the United States.

Expenses

Pursuant to section 401(c) of the National Emergencies Act (50 U.S.C. 1641(c)), I report that there were no expenses directly attributable to the exercise of authorities conferred by the declaration of the national emergency in Executive Order 12938 during the period from May 14, 1998, through October 31, 1998.

Sincerely,

WILLIAM J. CLINTON

NOTE: Identical letters were sent to Newt Gingrich, Speaker of the House of Representatives, and Albert Gore, Jr., President of the Senate. The notice is listed in Appendix D at the end of this volume.

Remarks on Signing Legislation on Educational Assistance for Families of Slain Officers and on Penalties for Criminals Using Guns
November 13, 1998

Situation in Iraq

Thank you very much, and good morning. Ladies and gentlemen, because this is the only time I'm going to be before the press today, at the outset of my remarks I'd like to say a few things about the situation in Iraq.

For more than 3 months, the United States and the international community have very patiently sought a diplomatic solution to Iraq's decision to end all its cooperation with the U.N. weapons inspectors. Iraq's continued refusal to embrace a diplomatic, peaceful solution, its continued defiance of even more United Nations resolutions, makes it plainer than ever that its real goal is to end the sanctions without giving up its weapons of mass destruction program.

The Security Council and the world have made it crystal clear now that this is unacceptable, that none of us can tolerate an Iraq free to develop weapons of mass destruction with impunity. Still, Saddam Hussein has it within his hands to end this crisis now by resuming full cooperation with UNSCOM. Just yesterday his own neighbors in the Arab world made it clear that this choice is his alone and the consequences, if he fails to comply, his alone in terms of responsibility.

Law Enforcement Legislation

Now, let me say to all of you, this is a very good day for the United States. I want to thank Officer Sandra Grace from New Bedford, Massachusetts, and Detective Gary McLhinney from Baltimore for their service, for sharing their stories, for representing their organizations so well, for reminding us why all of those here have worked so hard to pass the laws that in a few moments I will sign, laws to help us honor the memory of law enforcement officers by helping to prevent the kind of gun-related crimes that took their lives and by supporting the families they leave behind.

I'd also like to thank Secretary Rubin, Attorney General Reno, Director Magaw, the ATF, Assistant Secretary Johnson, and the others who are here from the Treasury and Justice Departments; Attorney General Curran from Maryland, who joined us today. And a special word of

thanks to my good friend Senator Biden, who had to leave; and to Congressman Stupak; Congressman King, who spoke so well and did so much. And thank you, Congressman Fox, for joining us here today in celebration of the work you did that I hope you'll be proud of all your life, sir. Thank you very much.

This is a special day for me personally because I was attorney general of my own State. I was Governor for a dozen years. I have spent a lot of hours riding around in State police cars with officers. I have been to altogether too many funerals of law enforcement officials killed in the line of duty. And because I come from a small State, very often I knew these people well. I knew their families, their children, their circumstances.

Just last weekend I went home to dedicate an airport, and the first people that came running up to me were the three State police officers who were assigned to work the event. And we stood there and relived a lot of old times.

So this issue is very, very vivid. And I think, again, we should thank, especially, the Members of Congress who are here; the police officers; Gil Gallegos and the FOP; Thomas Nee and the National Association of Police Officers; Jerry Flynn, the International Brotherhood of Police Officers; Rich Gallo, the Federal Law Enforcement Officers Association; Sam Cabral, the International Union of Police; and Debbie Geary from the Concerns of Police Survivors. I'd like to ask you all just to give them all another hand. [*Applause*]

Six years ago when I became President, one of my most urgent priorities was to put the Federal Government on the side of supporting our police officers and reducing the crime rate. At the time, the crime rate was on the rise; gangs, guns, and drugs were sweeping through our neighborhoods, terrorizing our families, cutting off the future of too many of our children. The thing that bothered me most when I was out around the country seeking the Presidency was that there were so many people who were full of hope and optimism for our country, but when it came to crime, they seemed almost to have given up, to have simply accepted the fact that a rising crime rate was a part of the price of the modern world. We were able to galvanize, all of us together, the energies of the American people to fight back.

I never met a law enforcement officer who believed that a rising crime rate was inevitable. Every law enforcement officer I met believed that if we did the right things—if we were tough, yes, but tough was not enough; we had to be smart, too—that if we both punished people who should be punished and did the intelligent things to prevent crime from happening in the first place, that the crime rate could go down.

And we passed in 1994 a historic crime bill, along with the Brady law, which among other things focused on community policing, aggressive prevention, and tougher penalties for violent repeat offenders. Now we're ahead of schedule and under budget in putting those 100,000 police on the street. We've gone after gangs and drugs with the full authority of Federal law. The Brady law has prevented about a quarter of a million felons, fugitives, and stalkers from buying firearms in the first place. Crime rates have fallen to a 25-year low. All across America, robbery is down; assault is down; murder is down. Respect for the law is on the rise. You can see it in little ways: fewer broken windows, less graffiti, cleaner streets in city after city after city.

We must never forget that this victory was won, however, at a very high price for some of our law enforcement officials. We must never forget that police officers put on their uniforms, their badges, go to work every day knowing that that day could be their last, just by doing their jobs.

Officer Bradley Arn served on the police force of St. Joseph, Missouri, for the last 7 years. He was a cop's cop. He patrolled the streets by day and worked his way through college by night. At 28, more than anything else, he wanted a better life for his wife and his 2-year-old twin daughters. On Tuesday, just a couple of days ago, he answered a distress call. A career criminal with a semiautomatic gun was terrorizing pedestrians. He responded to the call and was brutally gunned down. According to the police, the murderer had a deadly goal, quote, "He wanted to hurt people in black-and-white cars wearing dark blue uniforms." Only the bravery of a fellow officer stopped the shooting spree.

Every year there are too many police officers like Bradley Arn who make the ultimate sacrifice to keep us safe. Not very long ago, I went up to the Capitol to honor the two police officers who were killed there. But we have to do more than build monuments to honor these people. We have to take action to prevent more needless tragic deaths, to work for those who have given their lives, and we have to take action to help families they leave behind.

Two years ago we acted to provide college scholarships to the families of slain Federal law enforcement officers. Last year I pledged to make those same scholarships available to the families of State and local law enforcement officers and all public safety personnel. Today the legislation I sign honors that pledge. From now on, children and spouses of public safety officials who lose their lives in the line of duty will be able to apply for nearly $5,000 a year to pay for college tuition.

I should point out that because virtually 100 percent of these families will be people on very modest incomes, they will be eligible also for the $1,500-a-year HOPE tax credit in the first 2 years of college, tax credits for the junior and senior year, expanded work-study programs, student loan programs—a student loan program which in most places allows them to pay the loan back as a percentage of the income that they earn—and the IRA that can be withdrawn from without penalty if the money's used to educate children. Most of that was the product of the bipartisan Balanced Budget Act of 1997.

So we believe that if you look at this scholarship amount with the other things that have been passed in the last couple of years, as Peter King said, with overwhelming bipartisan support, Democrats and Republicans working together on these issues, we will be able to protect the families and the children in their education and, in so doing, to honor the families and the law enforcement officers. It's the least we can do, and we have to do it.

The bill I'm about to sign was enacted in memory of U.S. Deputy Marshal William Degan, the most decorated deputy marshal in our history, who lost his life in a brutal shootout. His son, Billy Degan, was the first young person to benefit from this program. He recently graduated from Boston College, and he's here with us today. I'd like to ask him to stand and be recognized. [*Applause*]

Now, let me say just a brief word about the other legislation that I'm going to sign; Mr. McLhinney talked about it. I'm very proud that we're announcing these scholarships, but I can't wait for the day when there is not a single person eligible for one. And I think that all of us should think about that.

We know from painful experience that the most serious threat to the safety of police officers is a criminal armed with a weapon. Most police officers who lose their lives die from gunshot wounds. That's why we fought hard to keep guns off the streets, out of the hands of criminals. Brady background checks, as I said earlier, have prevented nearly a quarter of a million felons, fugitives, and stalkers from buying guns. Last week I announced a new step to close a loophole in the law that makes it easier for gun traffickers and criminals to avoid those checks at private gun shows. Make no mistake, the insidious practice of sidestepping our guns laws is not an idle threat.

The city of Chicago recently concluded an undercover investigation of gun dealing. And as you saw, I hope, in the morning press, it has just filed suit alleging widespread practices by gun dealers in the Chicago area of selling guns illegally, counseling purchasers on how to evade firearms regulations, even selling guns to purchasers who say they intend to violate the law. We know legitimate gun dealers make every effort to comply with the law, but these charges in Chicago, if proven true, would demonstrate that at least some parts of the gun industry are helping to promote an illegal market in firearms. Such disrespect of our law endangers our people, and we will be watching the progress of this lawsuit closely.

The ATF already vigorously investigates gun dealers and other gun traffickers who violate Federal laws. We will continue to work closely with State and local police to trace the crime guns back to their source and prevent illegal gun sales, especially to criminals and juveniles.

But there is more we can do to protect our communities and police officers. You've heard a little bit of it from Detective McLhinney, but let me just say again, for several years now criminals who have used guns to commit their crimes have been subject to stiff mandatory penalties under Federal law and virtually every State law in the country. Today we go a step further. To protect our families and police officers, the bill I sign today will add 5 years of hard time to sentences of criminals who even possess firearms when they commit drug-related or violent crimes. Brandishing the firearm will draw an extra 7 years; firing it, another 10. A second conviction means a quarter century in jail. This is very important to try to reduce the threat of violent crime.

Just a couple of days ago on Veterans Day, as I have every year since I've been President, I laid a wreath on the tomb of the unknown servicemen who gave their lives in service to our country. Today it is with great pride that I stand here with many of our law enforcement officers who every day are prepared to make the same sacrifice. Together, we are working to make America stronger in the 21st century. And again, let me thank you all.

Now I'd like to ask the Members of Congress and Officers Grace and McLhinney and Mr. Degan, if you would come up here, I'd like for you to stand with us as we sign the bill, please.

NOTE: The President spoke at 12:17 p.m. in Room 450 of the Old Executive Office Building. In his remarks, he referred to President Saddam Hussein of Iraq; Attorney General J. Joseph Curran, Jr., of Maryland; Gil Gallegos, president, Fraternal Order of Police; Thomas Nee, president, Boston Police Patrolmen's Association; Jerry Flynn, national vice president, International Brotherhood of Police Officers; Richard J. Gallo, national president, Federal Law Enforcement Officers Association; Sam Cabral, president, International Union of Police Associations; and Debra J. Geary, national president, Concerns of Police Survivors. S. 191, An Act To Throttle Criminal Use of Guns, approved November 13, was assigned Public Law No. 105–386. S. 1525, the Police, Fire, and Emergency Officers Educational Assistance Act of 1998, approved November 13, was assigned Public Law No. 105–390.

Statement on International Economic Support for Brazil
November 13, 1998

Today's agreement between the International Monetary Fund and Brazil is an important step in our effort to deal effectively with the global financial crisis and protect American prosperity and jobs.

The United States has been working with our partners in the G–7 and the emerging markets on a set of specific actions to spur global growth. Last month the world's leading economies agreed to support new IMF tools to help countries with sound economic policies ward off global financial crisis. Today we are taking the first step to implement those ideas by putting Brazil in a position to confront the financial turmoil that threatens growth, not only in emerging markets but in economies around the world.

A strong Brazil is in America's interests, and President Cardoso has launched a solid program to tackle its fiscal problems that he has committed to implement swiftly. Under President Cardoso, Brazil has already embraced economic reform with the Real Plan and the support of the Brazilian people and the Brazilian Congress. Brazil has cut inflation from more than 2000 percent to single digits in less than 4 years, helped lift 13 million Brazilians above the poverty line, and achieved economic growth of 4 percent a year.

Brazil's prosperity is important for Americans. The United States is Brazil's largest single trading partner, and our exports to Brazil have more than doubled since 1992. A strong Brazil makes for a stronger United States, and today's announcement will help give both countries an opportunity to secure a brighter future.

Statement on Signing the Africa: Seeds of Hope Act of 1998
November 13, 1998

Today I am pleased to sign into law H.R. 4283, the "Africa: Seeds of Hope Act of 1998." This Act, which passed the Congress with broad bipartisan support, reaffirms the importance of helping Africans generate the food and income necessary to feed themselves. It is an important component of my Administration's efforts to expand our partnership with Africa and complements our efforts to expand trade and investment through the African Growth and Opportunity Act, which I hope will be passed by the next Congress.

During my trip to Africa last March, I pledged our continuing support to help reform-minded Africans help themselves. In the area of hunger and malnutrition, I announced the 1998 commencement of the Africa Food Security Initiative, a 10-year effort implemented through the U.S. Agency for International Development to help improve agricultural productivity, incomes, and nutrition for the rural poor.

The Africa: Seeds of Hope Act is another step in fulfilling that commitment and it demonstrates that both the Administration and the Congress are united in pursuit of a brighter future for the people of Africa.

Enactment of this bill comes at a critical time for Africa. At the 1996 World Food Summit, the United States pledged to help meet the goal of reducing malnutrition by half by the year 2015. Despite some recent progress, the percentage of malnourished people in Africa is the highest of any region in the world and U.S. help is greatly needed.

In signing H.R. 4283, I applaud the efforts that many African nations are making to improve the lives of their people. They are strengthening democracy and good governance, reforming economic policies to promote broad-based growth, and attacking diseases such as HIV/AIDS. They are doing a better job of educating their children, especially girls, and adopting improved farming practices. We need to do much more, however, to ensure that Africa and its rural poor are not left behind as we enter the next century. As demonstrated by the passage of the Africa:

Seeds of Hope Act, the United States remains ready to do its share.

WILLIAM J. CLINTON

The White House,

November 13, 1998.

NOTE: H.R. 4283, approved November 13, was assigned Public Law No. 105–385.

Statement on Signing the Centennial of Flight Commemoration Act
November 13, 1998

Today I have signed into law S. 1397, the "Centennial of Flight Commemoration Act."

On December 17, 1903, Orville and Wilbur Wright completed the first successful manned flight of a heavier-than-air machine. This historic moment marked the first step in a long journey through the skies that would ultimately take Americans beyond Earth's atmosphere and into space. This Act establishes a commission to coordinate the commemoration of this achievement, the benefits of which we are continuing to reap.

I am advised by the Department of Justice that section 9 of S. 1397, which authorizes the commission to devise a logo and regulate and license its use, is inconsistent with the Appointments Clause of the Constitution and that, accordingly, these functions may not be performed by the commission as it is currently organized. Similarly, although section 5(a)(3) directs the commission to "plan and develop" its own commemorative activities, the commission may not itself implement such activities because of Appointments Clause concerns. Finally, I also understand that the statute poses potential conflicts of interest problems. In contracting and in selecting an executive staff director and staff members (who will be considered Federal employees), the commission will need to take appropriate actions to avoid such conflicts. My Administration will work closely with the Congress to address these issues in future legislation.

WILLIAM J. CLINTON

The White House,
November 13, 1998.

NOTE: S. 1397, approved November 13, was assigned Public Law No. 105–389.

Statement on Signing the National Parks Omnibus Management Act of 1998
November 13, 1998

Today I am pleased to sign into law S. 1693, the "National Parks Omnibus Management Act of 1998."

The Act, which passed with bipartisan support in both Houses of Congress, is a major victory for all Americans who treasure and want to preserve the cultural and natural resources our parks have to offer. The Act contains a number of measures to assist National Park Service operations. This legislation is the first major overhaul of the way that the National Park Service awards concessions contracts in more than 3 decades. It ensures that all major contracts will be awarded through competitive bidding and makes concessions franchise fees available directly to the Park Service to improve the parks. These changes will result in better service to visitors and a better return to the taxpayers.

The Act requires the development of a training program that will allow Park Service employees the opportunity to gain the skills and experience they will need to protect parks. It also allows the Secretary of the Interior to lease park buildings consistent with other park legislation, and it lays out a clear process for the Park

Service to recommend areas to be studied for possible inclusion into the National Park System.

Finally, the Act establishes a park "passport," which includes a collectible stamp that provides an innovative way for the public to directly support parks. My Administration will work to minimize any confusion that may result between the introduction of this new parks-only passport and the continued use of the Golden Eagle Passport, which provides access to all public lands.

I commend retiring Senator Dale Bumpers, Senator Craig Thomas, and Representatives Don Young and George Miller for their outstanding work in forging a consensus to bring about the passage of S. 1693.

WILLIAM J. CLINTON

The White House,

November 13, 1998.

NOTE: S. 1693, approved November 13, was assigned Public Law No. 105–391.

Statement on Signing the Economic Development Administration and Appalachian Regional Development Reform Act of 1998
November 13, 1998

Today I have signed into law S. 2364, the "Economic Development Administration and Appalachian Regional Development Reform Act of 1998." This legislation reauthorizes the Economic Development Administration (EDA) and the Appalachian Regional Commission (ARC), which provide grant assistance to help rural and urban distressed areas create economic opportunity and job growth in their communities.

The EDA, a reinvented agency within the Department of Commerce, promotes economic development in distressed communities—communities with unemployment above the national average, low income, or special needs created by events such as natural disasters, military base closures, or defense industry downsizing. Title I of the Act reauthorizes the EDA and tightens eligibility criteria to ensure that the EDA can better serve the needs of distressed communities, simplifies application procedures, and streamlines statutory authorities by eliminating obsolete programs.

Title II of the Act reauthorizes the ARC. Established by the Congress in 1965, the ARC is a Federal-State partnership providing social and economic support for a 13-State region stretching from southern New York to northern Mississippi. The ARC targets its resources to the region's most distressed areas. Since the mid-1960s, the region's poverty rate has been cut in half; the percentage of adults with a high school education has doubled; and the infant mortality rate has been cut by two-thirds.

This Act recognizes that future growth requires improved physical infrastructure, a skilled workforce, an emphasis on creating entrepreneurial communities, the deployment of new technologies for business development, and a concerted effort to make the Nation more competitive in international markets. This legislation also maintains the critical role of local development districts in economic growth.

Reauthorization of the EDA and the ARC represents an important step in my Administration's efforts to ensure that all parts of America participate in the economic growth that this country has enjoyed over the past 6 years.

WILLIAM J. CLINTON

The White House,
November 13, 1998.

NOTE: S. 2364, approved November 13, was assigned Public Law No. 105–393.

The President's Radio Address
November 14, 1998

The President. Today I would like to talk about the hurricane that struck Central America 2 weeks ago and what we in the United States are doing to help. I'm joined by Tipper Gore, who will describe her trip leading our delegation to the region.

As Hurricane Mitch swept across the Caribbean, we were spared the brunt of the storm. But our neighbors in Honduras, Nicaragua, El Salvador, and Guatemala were not so lucky. We know the terrible death toll in those nations, more than 10,000 lives so far. But that figure only begins to convey the devastation. Hundreds of thousands are homeless. Mudslides and collapsed bridges have made it difficult to send help. In huge areas people have still almost no food and water. Roads, farms, schools, hospitals, all have been destroyed.

Tipper Gore led our Presidential mission to the region, and she just reported to me on the conditions there. I'd like to ask her now to tell what she saw.

Tipper Gore. Thank you, Mr. President.

In Honduras, we visited a neighborhood devastated by the storm. We joined the effort to clean up a school that will become a medical facility. That night J slept in a tent outside a shelter with homeless families, where I met a woman who was 6 months pregnant, a grandmother who was caring for four of her grandchildren, and a man who was alone and blind. They had all lost everything. They are now living together in one room, sleeping on mats.

In Nicaragua, I visited a refugee site for more than 1,000 men, women, and children whose homes along a riverbank are gone. The conditions are unimaginable. The Government has allocated a plot of land which is divided into parcels, one per family. Their shelter consists of sheets of plastic. Disease is rampant, and their biggest concerns right now are food, water, and medicine.

Yet everywhere, I was struck by the spirit of the people. They are not defeated. They're cleaning up, and they are rebuilding their lives. In Honduras, community leaders are working to help those most in need to get supplies to the outlying areas. In the makeshift shelters in Managua, many people were measuring foundations for new walls they will build when the materials are available.

You can see that this disaster has destroyed their homes but not their spirits. They will survive, and we will stand with them as they do so.

The President. Thanks, Tipper. Thank you for the trip and for your recommendations for what the United States should do next.

Next Monday the First Lady will also visit the region. We want to do everything we can to help, now and over the long run. To quickly address the catastrophe, I ordered $80 million in emergency aid. Over 1,300 American troops are assisting with relief efforts, providing food, water, and medicine. Engineers are rebuilding roads. Helicopters and planes are delivering vital supplies, 1.3 million tons to date. And more help is on the way.

In the wake of Mrs. Gore's trip, I am announcing today that we will offer $45 million in additional defense goods and services to provide the resources our troops need to continue their critical work toward recovery.

I've also asked Secretary of the Treasury Bob Rubin to find the best way to provide debt relief and emergency financial aid from the United States and the international community. We've already encouraged international institutions to provide more than $500 million in near-term financial aid, and we're working with them to secure sufficient money for reconstruction.

Finally, we intend to extend our stay of deportation through the holidays for citizens of the affected countries living in the United States, while examining on an urgent basis recommendations for further relief, consistent with the recommendation Mrs. Gore made to me.

A storm shows no respect for boundaries, and we should respond the same way. Many American citizens have relatives in Central America; our nations are related, too. They are our friends and our neighbors. We are going to share the future together. America is at its best when lending a helping hand to friends in need. Central Americans have taken great strides in the last decade in ending conflicts and strengthening democracies. We must not, and we will not, let a hurricane drown these aspirations.

The United States will spare no aid to people of Central America, our fellow Americans, as we all strive to build a better world in a new century.

Thanks for listening.

NOTE: The address was recorded at 1:59 p.m. on November 13 in the Roosevelt Room at the White House for broadcast at 10:06 a.m. on November 14. The transcript was made available by the Office of the Press Secretary on November 13 but was embargoed for release until the broadcast. The related memorandums of November 6 and 14 on emergency disaster relief assistance for Honduras, Nicaragua, El Salvador, and Guatemala are listed in Appendix D at the end of this volume.

Statement on the International Day of Prayer for the Persecuted Church
November 14, 1998

On this International Day of Prayer for the Persecuted Church, I want to reaffirm my administration's strong commitment to religious freedom around the world.

Today, in solidarity with millions of people at home and abroad, we pray for those who suffer for their beliefs—a suffering forewarned by Scripture: ". . . they shall lay their hands on you, and persecute you . . . [you will be] brought before kings and rulers for my name's sake." But with this warning comes the promise, "I will give you a mouth and wisdom, which none of your adversaries will be able to deny or resist." (Luke 21:12).

My administration worked closely with Members of Congress and the U.S. religious community to secure passage of the International Religious Freedom Act of 1998, which is an important addition to our ongoing efforts to make the promotion of religious freedom a national priority and an integral part of our foreign policy.

On this day, when we keep in our thoughts the noble struggle for religious freedom of people of all backgrounds, whether Muslim, Christian, Jewish, Buddhist, Hindu, Taoist, Baha'i, or of any other faith, we remember the words of the American Founding Father James Madison, who called religious liberty the "luster of our country." And we pray that our devotion to religious tolerance will serve as a beacon for all people everywhere who yearn for spiritual freedom.

NOTE: H.R. 2431, the International Religious Freedom Act of 1998, approved October 27, was assigned Public Law No. 105-292.

Remarks on the Situation in Iraq and an Exchange With Reporters
November 15, 1998

The President. Good morning. Last night Iraq agreed to meet the demands of the international community to cooperate fully with the United Nations weapons inspectors. Iraq committed to unconditional compliance. It rescinded its decisions of August and October to end cooperation with the inspectors. It withdrew its objectionable conditions. In short, Iraq accepted its obligation to permit all activities of the weapons inspectors, UNSCOM and the IAEA, to resume in accordance with the relevant resolutions of the U.N. Security Council.

The United States, together with Great Britain, and with the support of our friends and allies around the world, was poised to act militarily if Iraq had not reversed course. Our willingness to strike, together with the overwhelming weight of world opinion, produced the outcome we preferred: Saddam Hussein reversing course, letting the inspectors go back to work without restrictions or conditions.

As I have said since this crisis began, the return of the inspectors, if they can operate in an unfettered way, is the best outcome because they have been, and they remain, the most effective tool to uncover, destroy, and prevent Iraq from rebuilding its weapons of mass destruction and the missiles to deliver them.

Now, let me be clear: Iraq has backed down, but that is not enough. Now Iraq must live up to its obligations.

Iraq has committed to unconditionally resume cooperation with the weapons inspectors. What does that mean? First, Iraq must resolve all outstanding issues raised by UNSCOM and the IAEA. Second, it must give inspectors unfettered access to inspect and to monitor all sites they choose with no restrictions or qualifications, consistent with the memorandum of understanding Iraq itself signed with Secretary-General Annan in February. Third, it must turn over all relevant documents. Fourth, it must accept all weapons of mass destruction-related resolutions. Fifth, it must not interfere with the independence or the professional expertise of the weapons inspectors.

Last night, again, I confirmed with the U.N. Security-General, Kofi Annan, that he shares these understandings of Iraq's obligations.

In bringing on this crisis, Iraq isolated itself from world opinion and opinion in the region more than at any time since the Gulf war. The United Nations Security Council voted 15–0 to demand that Saddam Hussein reverse course. Eight Arab nations—Egypt, Syria, Saudi Arabia, five other Gulf states—warned Saddam that Iraq alone would bear responsibility for the consequences of defying the United Nations. The world spoke with one voice: Iraq must accept once and for all that the only path forward is complete compliance with its obligations to the world. Until we see complete compliance, we will remain vigilant; we will keep up the pressure; we will be ready to act.

This crisis also demonstrates, unfortunately, once again, that Saddam Hussein remains an impediment to the well-being of his people and a threat to the peace of his region and the security of the world. We will continue to contain the threat that he poses by working for the elimination of Iraq's weapons of mass destruction capability under UNSCOM, enforcing the sanctions and the no-fly zone, responding firmly to any Iraqi provocations.

However, over the long term, the best way to address that threat is through a government in Baghdad—a new government—that is committed to represent and respect its people, not repress them; that is committed to peace in the region. Over the past year we have deepened our engagement with the forces of change in Iraq, reconciling the two largest Kurdish opposition groups, beginning broadcasts of a Radio Free Iraq throughout the country. We will intensify that effort, working with Congress to implement the Iraq Liberation Act, which was recently passed, strengthening our political support to make sure the opposition—or to do what we can to make the opposition a more effective voice for the aspirations of the Iraqi people.

Let me say again, what we want and what we will work for is a government in Iraq that represents and respects its people, not represses them, and one committed to live in peace with its neighbors.

In the century we are leaving, America has often made the difference between tyranny and freedom, between chaos and community, between fear and hope. In this case, as so often in the past, the reason America can make this difference is the patriotism and professionalism of our military. Once again, its strength, its readiness, its capacity is advancing America's interest and the cause of world peace. We must remain vigilant, strong, and ready, here and wherever our interests and values are at stake. Thanks to our military, we will be able to do so.

Q. Mr. President, what you just said today sounds a lot less tough, sir, than what your National Security Adviser said yesterday. He called it, what Iraq said, "unconditionally unacceptable," and he said it had more holes than Swiss cheese.

The President. That's right, and look what they did after we said that. That's right—look what's happened since they said that. We decided to delay the attack when we were informed that Iraq was going to make a—offer us a statement—the world, committing to complete compliance. And you will recall, when that statement came in, there were members of the international community and members of the Security Council who said that they thought that the statement was sufficient to avoid a military conflict and to get UNSCOM back in. We did not agree, and the British did not agree. Mr. Berger and Prime Minister Blair both went out and made statements to that effect.

After that occurred, we received three subsequent letters from the Government of Iraq, going to the President of the Security Council, dealing with the three big holes we saw in the original Iraqi letter.

First of all, it became clear, and they made it clear, that the attachment to the letter was in no way a condition of their compliance, that their compliance was not conditional. Secondly, they explicitly revoked the decisions they made in August and October to suspend cooperation with UNSCOM. And thirdly, they made it clear that they would not just let the inspectors back in to wander around in a very large country but that their cooperation with them would be unconditional and complete.

Those were the things which occurred after Mr. Berger spoke and after Prime Minister Blair spoke. Those were the things which have caused us to conclude that world opinion unanimous and with the ability to actually—the prospect, at least—of getting this inspection system going until we can complete the work that we have been working on now since the end of the Gulf war—it was those three things that made us believe we should go forward. That is the difference between where we are now and where we were yesterday when the United States and Great Britain made its statements.

Q. Mr. President—[*inaudible*]——

Q. Mr. President—[*inaudible*]——

The President. Wait. Wait. Wait a minute.

Q. Why is there any reason to believe that Iraq will comply this time when it has failed to do so repeatedly in the past?

The President. Well, I think there are four things that I would say about it, with the beginning that no one can be sure. We're not—this is not a question of faith; this is a question of action. Let me remind you, the most important sentence in the statement I just read you was, "Iraq has backed down, but that's not enough. Now Iraq must live up to its obligations."

Now, let me just point out four things. Number one, we have an unprecedented consensus here. I do not believe that anyone can doubt that there was an unprecedented consensus condemning what Saddam Hussein had done in not cooperating with UNSCOM. Number two, we had a very credible threat of overwhelming force, which was imminent had we not received word that Iraq was prepared to make the commitments we had been asking for. Number three, the set of commitments we received, in the end, after making our position clear yesterday in refusing to negotiate or water down our position, is clear and unambiguous. And number four, we remained ready to act. So we don't have to rely on our feelings here, or whether we believe anything. The question is, have we made the proper judgment to suspend any military action in order to give Iraq a chance to fulfill its commitments, even though it has failed to do so, so many times in the past.

These four things are what you have to keep in mind. I believe—let me just say this—I believe we have made the right decision for a very specific reason, and I think it's very important that we keep hammering this home. If we take military action, we can significantly degrade the capability of Saddam Hussein to develop weapons of mass destruction and to deliver them, but that would also mark the end of UNSCOM. So we would delay it, but we would then have no oversight, no insight, no involvement in what is going on within Iraq.

If we can keep UNSCOM in there working and one more time give him a chance to become honorably reconciled by simply observing United Nations resolutions, we see that results can be obtained.

Look, what has happened this year? We had the VX testing, and this summer—I can't remember exactly when it was; I'm sure that when my team comes up here to answer the questions, they can—we uncovered a very important document giving us—giving the world community information about the quantity and nature of weapons stocks that had not been available before.

So I have to tell you, you have to understand where I'm coming from here. I really believe that if you have a professional UNSCOM, free and unfettered, able to do its job, it can do what it is supposed to do in Iraq. And given the fact that I believe that over the next 10 to 20 years, this whole issue of chemical and biological weaponry will be one of the major threats facing the world, having the experience, the record, and the success—if we can do it—of having a United Nations inspection regime in Iraq can have grave positive implications for the future—profound positive implications, if it works—and grave implications in a negative way if it doesn't.

So I believe we made the right decision, and I believe that the factors that I cited to you make it the right decision. Now, what I——

Q. Mr. President——

The President. Wait. Wait. Wait. What I'd like to do now—you, naturally enough, want to get into a lot of the specific questions here that I believe that Secretary Cohen and General Shelton and Mr. Berger can do a good job of answering. And none of us have had a great deal of sleep, but I think it would be appropriate for me to let them answer the rest of the questions.

Thank you.

NOTE: The President spoke at 11:30 a.m. in the Briefing Room at the White House. In his remarks, he referred to President Saddam Hussein of Iraq; United Nations Secretary-General Kofi Annan; and Prime Minister Tony Blair of the United Kingdom. The President also referred to the United Nations Special Commission (UNSCOM) and the International Atomic Energy Agency (IAEA). H.R. 4655, the Iraq Liberation Act of 1998, approved October 31, was assigned Public Law No. 105-338.

Remarks on the Tobacco Settlement
November 16, 1998

Thank you very much. To Attorney General Gregoire and all the others who are here, and the attorneys general of North Carolina and California who are not here but who are part of this initial group, I want to congratulate you. Bruce Reed, who spoke first and is my Domestic Policy Adviser, and I and the rest of us have been at this for quite a long time, and we are very pleased by your success.

Situation in Iraq

Because this is my only opportunity to appear before the press today, I'd like to begin by making a few comments about the situation in Iraq.

I am pleased that the weapons inspectors will return to Baghdad tomorrow to resume their work. As I've said from the start, the best outcome is to get the inspectors back on the job, provided they have unfettered access and full cooperation.

We know what the inspectors can accomplish. Since the system was created and the inspections began, Iraq has been forced to declare and destroy, among other things, nearly 40,000 chemical weapons, nearly 700 tons of chemical weapons agents, 48 operational missiles, 30 warheads especially fitted for chemical and biological weapons, and a massive biological weapons plant equipped to produce anthrax and other deadly agents.

The weapons inspectors, in short, have done a remarkable job. They must be permitted to finish their work. The burden of compliance is where it has always been—on Iraq. Baghdad has an affirmative obligation to comply with the U.N. resolutions that require it to disclose and destroy its weapons of mass destruction and the capability of delivering those weapons.

Governments all over the world today stand united in sharing the conviction that full compliance, and nothing short of full compliance, is needed from Iraq. The world is watching Saddam Hussein to see if he follows the words he uttered with deeds. Our forces remain strong and ready if he does not.

Tobacco Settlement

Now, let me join the others in once again saying that today is a milestone in the long struggle to protect our children from tobacco. This settlement between the State attorneys general and the tobacco companies is clearly an important step in the right direction for our country. It reflects the first time tobacco companies will be held financially accountable for the damage their product does to our Nation's health.

Again, let me thank Attorney General Gregoire, the others who are here, and those who are not. And I believe there were four States who previously signed individual settlements with the tobacco companies. All of them deserve the thanks of the country.

With this very large settlement which every other State has the opportunity to join, we are moving forward. But we have a lot more to do, for only the National Government can take the full range of steps needed to protect our children fully from the dangers of tobacco. So it is still up to Congress to act, to rise to its responsibility to pass national tobacco legislation.

Our administration began this effort nearly 4 years ago, with the strong leadership of Vice President Gore and the then-Commissioner of the Food and Drug Administration. The FDA then put in place a strong crackdown on tobacco advertising aimed at teenagers, the broadest and most significant effort to date to protect our children from the dangers of tobacco.

It has been challenged, as all of you know, in court by tobacco companies from the beginning. Today I want to report that the Solicitor General will ask the Supreme Court to resolve this matter. But let us be clear: When it comes to protecting our children from tobacco, ultimately, it is up to Congress to finish the job.

The past Congress began with strong momentum toward action, only to see national tobacco legislation derailed by partisanship and special pleading. In the new Congress, I am determined that all of us will choose progress over partisanship. I think that's what the voters were saying to us on election day.

Comprehensive national tobacco legislation must include many things, but especially it must clarify the jurisdiction of the FDA. And because of the cost inherent in this settlement and any further action by Congress, it should also include appropriate protections for tobacco farmers, as I have said from the beginning. It should

be, it must be, one of the top priorities for the new Congress. I will work hard to see that it becomes law.

We should always remember what the real stakes are. Let me say them one more time: Every day we fail to act, more than 3,000 children start to smoke, even though it is illegal to sell them cigarettes. More than 1,000 will die earlier than they would have as a result. Our children continue to be targeted by multi-million-dollar marketing campaigns designed to recruit what the industry has called in its confidential documents "replacement smokers." With strong legislation, working with what the attorneys general have already done, we can save a million lives in the first 5 years.

Our duty to our children, therefore, is clear. We should give them the future they deserve. We can do it.

This is a good day for our country, and I thank all of you who have helped to bring it about.

Thank you very much.

NOTE: The President spoke at 4:12 p.m. in the Roosevelt Room at the White House. In his remarks, he referred to State attorneys general Christine Gregoire of Washington, Daniel Lungren of California, and Mike Easley of North Carolina; President Saddam Hussein of Iraq; and former Commissioner of Food and Drugs David A. Kessler.

Joint Statement by President Clinton and Prime Minister Keizo Obuchi of Japan
November 16, 1998

Today we are pleased to announce a new multilateral initiative to revitalize private sector growth in Asia. Several of the countries hardest hit by the crisis have made great strides in recent months toward restoring stability. The major challenge they face today is restarting growth as quickly as possible. To support this effort, Japan and the United States, with the support of the World Bank and the Asian Development Bank, are launching the Asian Growth and Recovery Initiative.

This initiative has four main components:

First, accelerating the pace of bank and corporate restructuring by removing impediments to the return of growth. By mobilizing new financing to recapitalize banks, we aim to provide strong incentives to remove policy and institutional constraints that block rapid restructuring.

- The Asian Growth and Recovery Program, with the support of the World Bank, the ADB and bilateral contributors, will help catalyze significant private financing for countries in the region which have put comprehensive restructuring programs in place.

- The United States, Japan, the World Bank and the ADB are working together to establish this program and identify sources of funding. We will target mobilizing $5 billion in bilateral and multilateral support available initially, which we expect will leverage substantial new private financing.

Second, increased trade finance to give Asian companies greater access to funds they need to revive production and create jobs. Both the Japanese and the United States Export-Import Banks as well as Japan Export and Investment Insurance (EID/MITI) will contribute to this part of the initiative.

Third, efforts to mobilize new private sector capital to help Asian companies rebuild their balance sheets and move forward quickly with restructuring so they can make new investments and grow again. These efforts will be led by the International Finance Corporation (IFC), the Multilateral Investment Guarantee Agency (MIGA), the United States Overseas Private Investment Corporation (OPIC), and EID/MITI.

Fourth, enhanced technical assistance, to help equip countries with the expertise they need to overcome the complex financial and corporate restructuring issues they face.

To finalize the details of this initiative we will host a meeting in Tokyo shortly, bringing together senior officials and technical experts from the United States, Japan, and other Asian economies and the multilateral institutions. Japan and the United States welcome the participation of other economies in this initiative and encourage any interested economies to attend this meeting. The entire international community has a stake in restoring economic growth in Asia. By helping to accelerate the pace of restructuring and mobilizing renewed access to private financing, the Asian Growth and Recovery Initiative will make an important contribution toward that goal.

NOTE: An original was not available for verification of the content of this joint statement.

Letter to Congressional Leaders Reporting on the National Emergency With Respect to Iran
November 16, 1998

Dear Mr. Speaker: (*Dear Mr. President:*)

I hereby report to the Congress on developments since the last Presidential report of May 13, 1998, concerning the national emergency with respect to Iran that was declared in Executive Order 12170 of November 14, 1979. This report is submitted pursuant to section 204(c) of the International Emergency Economic Powers Act, 50 U.S.C. 1703(c)(IEEPA). This report covers events through September 30, 1998. My last report, dated May 13, 1998, covered events through March 31, 1998.

1. There have been no amendments to the Iranian Assets Control Regulations, 31 CFR Part 535 (the "IACR"), since my last report.

2. The Iran-United States Claims Tribunal (the "Tribunal"), established at The Hague pursuant to the Algiers Accords, continues to make progress in arbitrating the claims before it. Since the period covered in my last report, the Tribunal has rendered three awards. This brings the total number of awards rendered by the

Tribunal to 588, the majority of which have been in favor of U.S. claimants. As of September 30, 1998, the value of awards to successful U.S. claimants paid from the Security Account held by the NV Settlement Bank was $2,501,515,655.22.

Since my last report, Iran has failed to replenish the Security Account established by the Algiers Accords to ensure payment of awards to successful U.S. claimants. Thus, since November 5, 1992, the Security Account has continuously remained below the $500 million balance required by the Algiers Accords. As of September 30, 1998, the total amount in the Security Account was $107,563,705.15, and the total amount in the Interest Account was $26,226,833.16. Therefore, the United States continues to pursue Case No. A/28, filed in September 1993, to require Iran to meet its obligation under the Algiers Accords to replenish the Security Account.

The United States also continues to pursue Case No. A/29 to require Iran to meet its obligation of timely payment of its equal share of advances for Tribunal expenses when directed to do so by the Tribunal.

3. The Department of State continues to present other United States Government claims against Iran and to respond to claims brought against the United States by Iran, in coordination with concerned government agencies.

On April 20, 1998, the United States filed a major submission in Case No. B/1, a case in which Iran seeks repayment for alleged wrongful charges to Iran over the life of its Foreign Military Sales (FMS) program, including the costs of terminating the program. The April filing addressed liability for the costs arising out of termination of the FMS program.

Under the February 22, 1996, settlement agreement related to the Iran Air case before the International Court of Justice and Iran's bank-related claims against the United States before the Tribunal (see report of May 16, 1996), the Department of State has been processing payments. As of September 30, 1998, the Department has authorized payment to U.S. nationals totaling $17,521,261.89 for 55 claims against Iranian banks. The Department has also authorized payments to surviving family members of 228 Iranian victims of the aerial incident, totaling $56,550,000.

On June 5, 1998, the full Tribunal issued an award in Case No. A/27. The Tribunal held that, because of decisions of a United States District Court and Court of Appeals declining to enforce the Tribunal's July 1988 award to Iran in *Avco v. Iran*, the United States violated its obligation under the Algiers Accords to ensure that Tribunal awards be treated as binding.

On June 17, 1998, the Tribunal issued an order in Case No. B/61, in which Iran seeks compensation for the alleged non-transfer of certain military property. The order dismissed certain claims on grounds that they were duplicative of claims in other cases.

In Case No. A/30, a case in which Iran alleges that the United States has violated paragraphs 1 and 10 of the General Declaration of the Algiers Accords, based on an alleged covert action program aimed at Iran and U.S. sanctions, the United States and Iran filed submissions in response to Iran's request that the Tribunal require the United States to produce classified intelligence information.

4. U.S. nationals continue to pursue claims against Iran at the Tribunal. Since my last report, the Tribunal has issued awards in two private claims. On July 2, 1998, Chamber Two issued an award in *Kamran Hakim v.* Iran, AWD No. 587–953–2, ordering Iran to pay the claimant $691,611 plus interest as compensation for measures that deprived the claimant of his interest in a company he had established. The Tribunal dismissed claims regarding parcels of real property on grounds that, in certain instances, the claimant failed to prove expropriation or other measures affecting property rights, and failed in other instances to prove ownership.

On July 8, 1998, Chamber One issued an award in *Brown & Root, Inc. v. Iran*, AWD No. 588–432–1, giving effect to a settlement agreement between the parties, ordering Iran to pay the claimant $16,718,214.

5. The situation reviewed above continues to implicate important diplomatic, financial, and legal interests of the United States and its nationals and presents an unusual challenge to the national security and foreign policy of the United States. The Iranian Assets Control Regulations issued pursuant to Executive Order 12170 continue to play an important role in structuring our relationship with Iran and in enabling the United States to implement properly the Algiers Accords. I shall continue to exercise the powers at my disposal to deal with these problems and will continue to report periodically to the Congress on significant developments.

WILLIAM J. CLINTON

The White House,
November 16, 1998.

NOTE: Identical letters were sent to Newt Gingrich, Speaker of the House of Representatives, and Albert Gore, Jr., President of the Senate.

Statement on the Election of Representative James E. Clyburn To Chair the Congressional Black Caucus
November 17, 1998

I am pleased that Representative Jim Clyburn was elected by his colleagues to chair the Congressional Black Caucus. In January Representative Clyburn will begin his fourth term representing the people of the Sixth District of South Carolina. Throughout his career, he has been a tireless advocate for his constituents, and he has been a national leader on issues including rural economic development and affirmative action.

I commend outgoing CBC Chairwoman Maxine Waters for her outstanding leadership of the caucus, and I am confident that Representative Clyburn will be a most able successor. I look forward to working with Chairman Clyburn and the entire Congressional Black Caucus during the 106th Congress.

Statement on the Election of Representative Lucille Roybal-Allard To Chair the Congressional Hispanic Caucus
November 17, 1998

I am pleased that today the Congressional Hispanic Caucus (CHC) elected Representative Lucille Roybal-Allard as their new chair for the 106th Congress. Representative Roybal-Allard has already established a record of distinction, serving her constituents in the 33d District of California and as a national leader in the areas of education, financial services, homeownership, and women's and children's rights.

I commend outgoing CHC Chair Xavier Becerra for his outstanding leadership of the caucus, and I am confident that Representative Roybal-Allard will be an excellent advocate for the caucus and the entire Latino community. I look forward to working with Chairwoman Roybal-Allard and the entire Congressional Hispanic Caucus during the 106th Congress.

Remarks on Departure for Tokyo, Japan
November 18, 1998

Good morning. I wanted to say a few words before I depart about the goals for our trip to Japan and Korea. From the time our administration took office in 1993, we have believed it vital to the future of the United States to look not only to the west but, as a Pacific power, to the east as well and to forge a strong Asia-Pacific community for the 21st century. Central to that effort are the APEC leaders forum, which has just concluded, and the strengthening of our bonds with Japan and Korea, two of our strongest allies for promoting democracy, securing peace, building prosperity.

Our domestic economy remains very strong. Our strategy of fiscal discipline, investments in education and technology, and opening markets abroad has produced unprecedented gains for America's families. But our long-term prosperity requires a healthy global economy. American exports create jobs, and those jobs pay, on average, about 15 percent above normal other jobs in our economy.

If people overseas lose their jobs, therefore, they can't afford American products and our workers and farmers pay the price. We see that in the slight decline in our exports so far this year due to the global financial crisis in general and the problems in Asia in particular.

Clearly, in order to sustain progress at home, therefore, we have to exercise leadership abroad.

That is why we're pursuing a comprehensive plan to contain the global financial crisis, spur growth, and strengthen international financial systems for the 21st century.

We have met our obligation to the IMF, pressed the World Bank to more than double its investments to people who have suffered the most. We have helped to organize a new aid package to keep the contagion from spreading to our important trading partner Brazil—and Brazil, I might add, has also begun to take strong economic measures of its own—and we've established a program to keep the crisis from spreading to other countries which are vulnerable in spite of their own good economic policies. Now we're taking our efforts directly to Asia where the crisis began and where we must work to bring it to an end.

I have spoken with Vice President Gore, who represented the United States so ably at the Asia-Pacific Economic Conference. The situation in Iraq, as you know, prevented me from attending, but I followed the proceedings very closely, and I got a good report from the Vice President. The summit has just concluded, and I'm very pleased that the leaders there made progress on our efforts to make trade more free and more fair so that we can increase prosperity for the new century.

Prime Minister Obuchi and I also announced a new U.S.-Japan initiative to help Asian banks and businesses emerge from the crushing debt burdens they have and restore growth. This was another important objective in the program I announced at the Council on Foreign Relations in New York a few weeks ago.

Now, in Japan and Korea, I will work for further progress. Nothing is more important to restoring stability and growth in Asia than efforts to restart Japan's economy. It has long been Asia's engine of growth. It is, as all of us know, the second largest economy in the world, but it has been stalled for 5 years.

In meetings with Prime Minister Obuchi, a townhall with Japanese citizens, and other settings, I look forward to discussing how Japan can promptly and effectively implement its commitment to banking reform, stimulate consumer demand and growth, deregulate key economic sectors, and open its markets to fair trade. Just as the world looked to us in America 6 years ago to put our economic house in order, today nations look to Japan to take decisive steps to help the Japanese people to restore growth in Asia and around the world.

Now, in South Korea I will meet with President Kim Dae-jung. We all know he's a courageous leader who has devoted his life to strengthening Korean democracy. Now he and his fellow citizens face a difficult but necessary task of reforming their financial institutions, their corporate sector, and getting growth back on track there. It will be essential, in this regard, not only for the Government to act but for Korea's big business conglomerates to do their share for economic reform.

On this trip, we will also work to strengthen the security for our people. If Iraq's weapons of mass destruction have dominated recent headlines, we must be no less concerned by North Korea's weapons activities, including its provocative missile program and developments that could call into question its commitment to freeze and dismantle its nuclear weapons effort. This trip will give us an opportunity to address this critical issue where China has also played a very constructive role.

We also want to support President Kim's strategy of engagement on the Korean Peninsula and to ensure that our forces are strong and vigilant in Korea until there is a just and lasting peace there. And finally, on the way home, I'm looking very much forward to stopping in Guam and spending some time with our fellow citizens there.

Thank you very much.

NOTE: The President spoke at 8:52 a.m. on the South Lawn at the White House. In his remarks, he referred to Prime Minister Keizo Obuchi of Japan.

Letter to Congressional Leaders Transmitting a Report on Cyprus
November 18, 1998

Dear Mr. Speaker: (Dear Mr. Chairman:)

In accordance with Public Law 95–384 (22 U.S.C. 2373(c)), I submit to you this report on progress toward a negotiated settlement of the Cyprus question covering the period August 1 to September 30, 1998. The previous submission covered events during June and July 1998.

United States efforts to bring about a negotiated settlement of the Cyprus issue based on a bizonal, bicommunal federation remained steadfast. United States officials encouraged the Greek Cypriot and Turkish Cypriot leadership to focus on the core issues of the Cyprus dispute and encouraged all parties to prepare for even-

tual comprehensive negotiations. My Special Presidential Emissary for Cyprus, Richard C. Holbrooke, and the Special Cyprus Coordinator, Thomas J. Miller, underscored this message in a series of important meetings in September with Cypriot, Greek, and Turkish representatives attending the United Nations General Assembly.

Sincerely,

WILLIAM J. CLINTON

NOTE: Identical letters were sent to Newt Gingrich, Speaker of the House of Representatives, and Jesse Helms, chairman, Senate Committee on Foreign Relations.

Remarks in "A Conversation With President Clinton" With Tetsuya Chikushi in Tokyo
November 19, 1998

Opening Remarks

Tetsuya Chikushi. We have our special guest today who has the biggest influence and responsibility to the future of humankind. We have this most important bilateral relations, and he's the most responsible person in all of the United States. We are very happy to have him, to greet him with a large number of audience. Mr. Bill Clinton, the President of the United States.

Mr. President, welcome to our program, and I appreciate your choice to join us. It's really an honor. I will skip any more ceremonial remarks—*[inaudible]*. To begin with, you have something to say to the people.

The President. Yes. I will be very brief so that we can leave the most time possible for questions. But I would like to begin by thanking you and this station for making this program possible. I thank all of you for participating and also those in Osaka who are joining us.

I would like to open by just emphasizing some things I think we all know. First, the relationship between the United States and Japan is very, very important to both countries and to the world. We have a very broad partnership in

the security area, in the political area, in the economic area.

Over the years, there is sometimes greater emphasis on one issue than another. Over the years, sometimes America is having particular problems; sometimes Japan is. But the enduring nature of our democratic partnership across all the differences between our peoples is profoundly important. And on the edge of this new century and a new millennium, when there is so much change in the way people work and live and relate to each other, it will become more important.

That's why I'm here and why I wanted to be a part of this townhall meeting. And I thank you very much.

Mr. Chikushi. Thank you very much. There are about 100 people here and 30 people in Osaka, the second largest city, and everybody wants to discuss with you, to make some questions. And also, we gathered questions nationwide through Internet and facsimile. To start with, I would like to ask some casual questions, and I would like to expect a brief answer. From now on, I'd like to speak in Japanese.

We have many questions from children, many of them with—[*inaudible*]. I will pick one from the fifth grader of the primary school: "Did you have good grades at school when you were a kid?" [*Laughter*]

The President. Mostly. [*Laughter*]

Mr. Chikushi. Next question.

Chelsea Clinton

Q. [*Inaudible*]—when Chelsea, your daughter, was born, how much were you involved in baby raising, child raising?

The President. I'm sorry, would you read——

Q. How much were you involved in raising her?

The President. When my daughter was born, how involved was I with her? I was very involved with her from the time she was a very small baby, and always going to her events, working with her on her homework until it became too difficult for me—[*laughter*]—and trying to be a big part of her life. So, my wife and I both tried to be very involved in her life, and we still try to be, although she has reached an age where I don't think she thinks it's always such a good idea. [*Laughter*]

Public Speaking

Q. I am very bad in speaking in front of large number of people—and also the same question from the junior high school student—how can you speak so well in front of the large number of people? Could you give us some tip?

The President. My only advice is to imagine, no matter how many people are in your audience, that you're speaking to a few of your friends—because, look at the camera, the camera will take us to millions of people. I have been in crowds—the largest crowd I've been in was in Ghana in West Africa. We had maybe 400,000 or 500,000 people. But on the television, there are millions. And if you're in a big crowd, well, the microphone is your friend. You can speak normally because the sound will carry.

And I think many people have trouble speaking in public because they think they have to change. And you don't have to change. You just have to be yourself. Imagine you are at home, entertaining some friends, sharing something with your family, and speaking the way you would when your heart was engaged and your mind was engaged about something you cared about in your own life. That's my only advice.

Mr. Chikushi. Well, thank you. So, that being said, let's go into our Q&A session. So you spoke very well as President. Now talk about leadership and about your personality. I would like to welcome questions regarding leadership or his personality or the President as a person.

Pressures of the Presidency

Q. I'm involved in welfare. I am sure you feel a lot of pressure being President. Have you ever felt that you wanted to get away from these pressures? And also, how are you coping with these tremendous pressures as President?

The President. Well, of course, sometimes you want to get away from it. But I think the important thing is not to be overwhelmed by the work, that only people have these jobs and you have to take some time for family and some time for recreation. I spend a lot of time reading. I probably read more than I did before I became President. I exercise every day. I play a lot of golf, not as much as I wish but some, and certainly not as well as I wish. [*Laughter*] And I try to stay in touch with my family members beyond our home and also my friends around the country. And all these things help to keep balance in my life. I try to make sure on the weekends I spend time with my family. I take time to attend my church services. I do the things that remind me that I'm a normal person and I need a balanced life. And I think that's important.

President's Legacy

Q. I work for Kirin Beer Company. Thank you very much for this great opportunity. I really appreciate it. And I would like to congratulate you on the result of the midterm elections back in the United States. Now, my question: You're the 42d President of the United States. What would you like people in the future to remember you for?

The President. I would like to be remembered for having restored American confidence and opportunity, prepared America for the 21st century, and deepened America's partnership with people around the world to create a world more full of opportunities for ordinary citizens, more committed to preserving the environment, and more committed to working together for peace and prosperity.

I believe we're moving into a world where our interdependence with one another will be critical to maintaining our independence, as nations and as individuals. And I would like to be remembered as a President who prepared my country and the world for the 21st century. And I like your beer. [*Laughter*]

Japan's Leadership

Q. I'm—[*inaudible*]—from Sony Corporation—[*inaudible*]—in Japan the leadership is not as good as we would like it to be. What do you think—[*inaudible*]?

The President. Well, first of all, I think that, to be fair to the present leadership, Prime Minister Obuchi and his team, they have not had enough time for people to make a firm judgment. They just recently took office. That's the first point I would make, because the difficulties, the challenges Japan has today will not be solved overnight.

For example, when I became President in 1993, I had to make some very difficult decisions. And in the midterm elections in 1994, like the ones we just had, between the Presidential elections, my party suffered great losses. And people who voted for the tough decisions that I advocated, many of them were defeated because the people had not yet felt the benefits of the things which were done. So the first thing I would say is, do not judge too harshly too quickly.

The second thing I would say is, I think that the big things that have been done here are essentially moving in the right direction, the banking reform, stimulating the economy.

The third point I would make is that for leadership, you need first to know what is going on; you have to have a clear analysis of the present situation. Then you have to have a vision of the future you're trying to create. Without a vision, the rest of this doesn't matter. Then you have to have an action plan to achieve the vision. And then finally, in the world we're living in, where we do things like this, you must be able to have all kinds of ordinary citizens be able to buy into it, to support it, to say, "Yes, this will be good for me, good for my family, good for my future; I wish to be a part of this." And that, I think, is the great challenge of modern leadership: how to mobilize large numbers of people, even if unpopular things have to be done.

Monetary Rewards and Public Service

[*A participant commented that while many business leaders had amassed great wealth over the past 6 years, the President could not do so, given his income as President. He asked what kept the President motivated since he could not seek a third term.*]

The President. Well, first of all, you're right; I can't run for a third term under our laws. It's a good thing, because if I could, I would, I think. [*Laughter*] I like the work very much. But I think, first of all, people who get into public service must have a decision that they are not going to make as much money as they could make if they were doing something else. However, it is important that we pay them enough money so they can at least support their families, raise their children, pay their bills. Beyond that, I think that most people who are in public service should just be content, if they can raise their children and pay their bills, to think that when they get out of public service, they can do a little better.

And that's the way I've always looked at it. It never bothered me that I didn't make much money. That's not what was important to me in life. And I think that as long as there are rewards to public service in terms of being able to achieve what you wish to do—that is, help other people, help your country move forward—I think good people will wish to do it. I don't think that money will ever be able to attract quality people to public service. But if you expect people to starve, you can drive good people away.

Mr. Chikushi. Then we'll switch to Osaka. I guess they are waiting—[*inaudible*]—which is known for the shrine of the merchants—we have 30 people here; they are very vigorous Osakans. And 15 involved in retail business and 15 ladies that are present here, waiting for the opportunity to ask questions. We will start from a man.

First Family

Q. I'm involved in the metal business. Mr. President, out of the dishes that your wife cooks, what do you like best, and how much do you eat with your family a month? How many times do you eat with your family a month?

The President. Well, of course, our daughter has now gone to university, but my wife and I have dinner together every night when we're both home. That is, unless she has to go out to an engagement or I do, we always have dinner together. I would say probably 4 times a week we have dinner together, and maybe 3 times a week one of the two of us is out at night or out of town.

Over the last 20 years, of course, it's fairly well known in America that I like all different kinds of food. A lot of people make fun of me because of that. But I suppose my favorite dish is a Mexican dish, chicken enchiladas. That's what I really like the best, although I like sushi, too. [*Laughter*]

Q. Very nice to meet you. I have two children. I am a housewife. So nice to meet you, or talk to you. I have a question regarding Miss Monica Lewinsky. How did you apologize to Mrs. Clinton and Chelsea? And I'm sure I would never be able to forgive my husband for doing that, but did they really forgive you, Mr. President?

The President. Well, I did it in a direct and straightforward manner, and I believe they did, yes. [*Laughter*] But that's really a question you could ask them better than me.

Okinawa

Mr. Chikushi. Thank you very much. We'll go back to you, our viewers in Osaka. Let's change the topic now. Now our bilateral relationship is the most important of all bilateral relationships. Let's talk about U.S.-Japan relationship.

We collected about 4,000 questions from all over Japan, and the most popular questions were regarding Okinawa, American base issue of Okinawa. There are two independent countries, allies, but one country has the military presence in another country for a long time in such a large scale. Is it good for our relationship? Isn't it going to be a thorn of one side, so to speak? How do you feel about that, Mr. President?

The President. Well, first of all, I think there have been, obviously, some difficulties in the relationship in our military presence in Okinawa. Some of them, I think, are inevitable, and I'm very respectful of the challenges that our presence has caused the Government and the people on Okinawa.

On the other hand, both the Government of Japan and the Government of the United States agree that our security partnership is a good one and that we cannot say with confidence that there are no circumstances under which American forces would ever be called upon to defend Japan or our common allies. And if we were to move our forces back to Guam or to Hawaii, it would take them much, much longer to come anywhere in the northeast Asia area if there were difficulties.

So the question is, if we do need to be here for some period of years, how can we do it in the way that is least burdensome to the people of Okinawa? That has been my concern. I have worked now with Prime Minister Obuchi's government and with predecessor governments to try to be responsive to that. And I hope we can do that. I hope we can continue to ease the burden on the people of Okinawa but stay as long as both Japan and the United States agree that is wise for us to stay.

Military Conflicts

Q. Related to the previous question, the new guidelines have been developed, and Japan, of course, is not supposed to go into war. But once the United States gets into the war situation, I'm afraid that Japan might be sort of pulled into that, also, and I've been concerned. Can you comment on that?

The President. Yes. Of course, our strategy is to maintain a presence in the world so that there will be no war, so that there is a strong disincentive for anyone to drag anyone back into a war. There have been so many wars in Asia in this century, but in the last two to three decades, there has been an increased emphasis in the Asian countries on working on the economy, working on the society, working on the education of children, working on trade and other relations with people instead of military relations.

And my hope is that America's military strength will be used to deter any further military action so that we will have more peace, and in the decades ahead, war will become more and more unthinkable for everyone. That is what the whole defensive military strategy of our country is designed to do.

Japan-U.S. Trade

Q. I will ask about trade. Now, we are asked by the U.S. Government to further open our market. Do you have any Japanese-made product which you daily use, Mr. President?

The President. Yes, we have some Japanese televisions; we also have at least one European television, I think, in the White House complex.

And I have, over time, owned a number of them. When I was a Governor of my home State, we had a Sanyo plant in my home State that put together televisions that were mostly manufactured in Japan and the component parts sent there. So I'm quite well familiar with that, and I think it's very important.

Actually, we've worked hard on trying to keep our markets open during this period of economic difficulty, not only for Japan but for all of Asia. And you may know that our trade deficit has gone way up with Japan, with China, with others. Because of the Asian economic crisis, we're buying more exports, but no country can afford to keep buying imports from us if the economy is down.

And on the whole, the American people have supported this. It's our contribution to trying to stabilize Asia and bring it back. I have to say in all candor, there are some problems. Japanese imports into America of hot-rolled steel, for example, are up 500 percent in one year, and no one quite believes that that's just because of the economic problems. But by and large, there's a commitment in America to keeping open markets and purchasing Japanese products.

Let me also say, I believe that in addition to the financial reforms, which I think are very important to carry out aggressively, and the economic stimulus, domestically, I think Japan could get a lot of economic benefit in terms of new jobs, from greater openness. I'll just give you two examples.

In our country there was great controversy about deregulating and opening investment to international investors in airlines and in telecommunications. We did it. It was quite controversial. But we have created, as a result, far more jobs in both sectors because of the greater competition. Just since 1993, when we've been aggressive in telecommunications—and a lot of international firms have been a part of this— we have seen hundreds of thousands of jobs created in America because of the increased competition. So I think it would be good for the Japanese economy.

Let me say, I never consciously asked Japan or any other country to do something that is good only for the United States. My belief is that our country is strengthened if Japan is very strong, because if Japan is very strong, that brings back Asia. If Asia is strong, that's good for the American economy. It also means it's

good for stability, which means more prosperity and less likelihood of the military conflicts that I was asked about by the lady there.

Japanese Economic Policy

Q. This is relating to our economic relationship. In Japan, the certificate or consumption coupons will be issued to children and old people. Now, including this—and there are other measures to boost our economy—what do you think of what Japan is doing?

The President. Well, I know of no history with these coupons. It's a new idea. And so, obviously, I can't have an informed opinion. But I do believe that anything that can be done to increase consumption is a good thing, because I know the Japanese people are great savers, and that is also a good thing. And I know you worry about the population getting older and having to save more for retirement. But you need a balance between saving for your own retirement and growing the economy today, because as the population gets older, one of the things that will lift up the elderly population is a very strong economy. And so I think that anything that can be done to boost confidence of consumers and to boost consumption is a good thing.

Agricultural Trade

[*A participant explained that farming in Japan was a family-based operation which maintained cultural and social values, while farming in the United States was more efficient and enterprise-oriented. He stated that U.S. demands for agricultural trade liberalization were therefore unfair and then requested the President's views.*]

The President. Well, first of all, let me say, this is a subject about which I think I know something. Before I became President, I was the Governor of my home State, which produces 40 percent of all the rice grown in the United States. And in our State, most of the farms are still family farms.

But we see all over the world today family farmers having more trouble. For example, to show you the other side of this, in the northern part of the United States, in North Dakota, there was a huge drop in the number of family farmers this year because the Asian countries— not Japan—other Asian countries which had been buying their wheat could no longer afford to buy it. And a lot of them were threatened with going out of business.

In fairness, one of the reasons I believe we need this WTO process is so we can have a regular way of deciding how to open the markets that should be opened in agriculture and then give countries enough notice so they can figure how they're going to help the farmers if they have a policy of wanting family farmers to survive.

I can tell you, in my country we have tried to push for more open markets and a policy to keep family farmers in business by—and I can only say what the situation is in America. In America, the family farmers are as productive as the big enterprise farms, but the family farmers don't have a lot of money in the bank. And we all know that because of bad weather or bad prices or whatever, some years are good in farming; some years are bad in farming. The fundamental problem in the U.S. is that the family farmers need a system to help them through the bad years. The big enterprises have so much money, they take the bad years and wait for the good years. So we have tried to design a system that would address the needs of both, and we seem to be having some success there.

So I think there is a proper compromise here where you can open markets more gradually, open them to farming, particularly if there are different products. There are some products that Japan buys that can't be grown in Japan. And if you can open these markets, but do it in a way that preserves to the maximum extent possible the family farms, that I think is the best way to do it. And that is what we are trying to achieve in the U.S. I don't know if we'll succeed, but I think we're doing a pretty good job now.

Mr. Chikushi. Osaka is very interested in economic issues, so let's switch over to Osaka. Questions?

Financing for Small Business

Q. I'm in housing equipment and material. Osaka has a lot of small to medium-size businesses, and I boast ourselves for having supported the Japanese economy. But we are suffering right now. It's hard to get loans these days. And the first blow comes to us first. But in the United States, how are you helping these small to medium-size companies?

The President. We have, I think, three things that I would like to mention. First of all, for small businesses that are just getting started, we have a Small Business Administration in the Federal Government which can provide guarantees of the first loans. Now we have a pretty healthy banking system, quite healthy, that is pretty aggressive in making loans to businesses. In addition to that, we have something that many countries don't have: We have a very active system of venture capital, high risk capital, higher risk capital, people who will invest money in new areas or in small and medium-size businesses that are just trying to expand.

And having looked at the Japanese situation, I think it would be very helpful if, in addition to this bank reform, where the banks can get public money to protect depositors, and then they have to declare the bad loans and work through them—I think that will help because then the banks can start loaning money again, with the depositors protected. So it's very important to implement that.

But I would like to see some effort made at providing more of this venture capital, this risk capital, in Japan. And it may be that there is something we can do to encourage Japanese business people to set up these kind of ventures, because they have created millions of jobs in America, the venture capitalists have. And even though they lose money on ventures, on balance they make money over a period of years.

Japan-China-U.S. Relations

Q. I am also a merchant, selling kitchen material. Looking at the recent American diplomacy, you tend to go over the head of Japanese. You're interested in strengthening diplomatic relations with China. What we are afraid of is that in 2008 we would like to invite the Olympic Games to Osaka, and a very strong rival is Beijing of China, for the Olympics in 2008. So I would like to have your personal, private opinion about this. If Beijing and Osaka compete to get the Olympics, I am sure that you will support Osaka. I'd like to make sure of that. Or would you rather support Beijing? I certainly appreciate your support.

The President. Thank goodness I will no longer be President, and I don't have to make that decision.

Let me make two points. First of all, I did not intentionally go over the heads of the Japanese people in establishing better relations with

China. I think it is good for Japan if America has better relations with China. I think it is good for America if Japan has better relations with China. The Chinese President is coming here, I think, on a state visit in just the next couple of days. And it has now been quite a long time since the last World War, and I think whatever remaining misunderstandings there are should be resolved and that your two great countries should have a better relation. And I'm going to do my best to see a partnership involving all of us going into the future.

I'm not going to take a position on the Olympics. But let me say, before I became President, I spent a lot of time in Osaka because we had two companies in my State who were headquartered in Osaka. I even remember the last restaurant I ate at in Osaka, Steakhouse Ron, R–O–N. So if it's still there, maybe I got them some business tonight. [*Laughter*]

Balancing Work and Family in Japan

Q. I teach social studies in junior high school. We've been talking about expanding consumption. The Japanese junior high students spend so little time with their fathers at home. They have to go to—[*inaudible*]—school and fathers don't get home until very late. Talking about consumption, I think if they get fathers back, I think we will get a more stable society. Because if they get more free time, then they have more leisure time; they will spend more money that way. But in the male-oriented society of Japan, there is very little discussion regarding more holidays. What do you think about that?

The President. I think, first of all, the whole world admires both the excellent education system and the hard work ethic of the Japanese people, and admires the fact that you have been able to keep the family structure as strong as you have under the enormous pressures of work and education for the children, especially during this hard economic time. But I think that in all societies which are very busy and very competitive, the number one social question quickly becomes, how do you balance work and family?

I personally believe that the most important work of any society is raising children well. And if you have to sacrifice that to have a strong economy, then sooner or later your economy and your society won't be very strong. On the other hand, you don't want to sacrifice your economy in the service of raising children. There has to be a balance.

We are having that kind of debate in America. I don't have the answer for Japan; it would be wrong for me to suggest it. But I think you have asked the right question, and I hope maybe your being on this program tonight will spark a sort of national debate about it. It's worth asking that question, whether you could actually help the economy by providing people more free time with their children and their families. I never thought of it in this term before until you said it tonight. Thank you.

Disabled Americans

[*A participant asked the President what he planned to do for disadvantaged people in the United States.*]

The President. Thank you very much. First of all, you made a very important point. In 1992, we passed the Americans with Disabilities Act, which guarantees all Americans access to certain public facilities and other opportunities in our society. Previous to that we had tried to do the same thing with our schools, in educational facilities.

And all of you know, I'm sure, about all the fights we have in America between the Democratic Party and the Republican Party, and you see all that in the press here. But you should know that one of the things that we've had almost complete agreement on in the last 6 years since I've been President, is every year putting more money into education for Americans with disabilities.

In the last session of Congress, we came very close to passing a bill which would have dramatically expanded job opportunities to Americans with disabilities, over and above where we are now. So I think it's fair to say—and our administration has been very involved in this—our position is, every person should be looked at as a resource; every person should have all the opportunities necessary to live up to the fullest of his or her capabilities. And our policy is to do whatever we can to advance that goal. We believe it makes us a stronger country.

Q. Thank you, Mr. President.

American Visitors to Japan

Q. Every year many Japanese youth go to the United States for sightseeing or to study.

But compared with that, not too many Americans visit Japan. That's how I feel. I think it's important that the young generation understand each other, the American youth and the Japanese youth. Why do you think it's fewer American youth visit Japan?

The President. I think, first of all, it's because it's a long way away in the minds of most Americans. And secondly, because we have in America, as you know, people of every conceivable different racial and ethnic backgrounds, but relatively small number of Japanese-Americans—a significant number—we have several Japanese-Americans in our United States Congress, for example. But I think that the Americans, when they travel abroad, tend to go to places where either their own people came from or they know someone in the school who is from there, or something like that.

But there is an enormous interest in Japan in the United States, an enormous interest among the young people, wanting to understand the society, know more about it. And I think what we have to do is to try to facilitate more travel among older people, who have the means to travel, but more study groups among the younger people. Most young Americans could not afford to come here to study on their own. They would have to come as part of some scholarship program. And in the years since I've been President, we tried to find ways to increase the number of young Americans who could come here to study.

Our Ambassador here now, Tom Foley, who was formerly the Speaker of the House of Representatives, has been very active in this whole area of trying to build greater communications and travel for a long time. And I hope we can do a better job now, because I don't think we've done as much as we should have to bring Americans to Japan, to give them a chance to get to know the Japanese people, understand the Japanese system, and build long-term friendships for the future.

Mr. Chikushi. A very tough question to the President. [*Laughter*]

Landmines

Q. I work for a nongovernment organization. I'm a housewife. Mr. President, there is a book, "Give Us Not Land Mines, But Flowers." You autographed this. Do you remember it? Thank you. We have been engaged in the campaign to get rid of landmines, and we have signed the treaty to completely get rid of landmines. You have not signed that. Why is that? What is your policy on landmines?

The President. First of all, my policy is to support getting rid of them. And there is a reason that we have not signed the treaty. I would like to explain why.

Number one, the way the treaty is written, the mines that countries use to protect their soldiers against tanks, so-called antitank mines, not antipersonnel mines, are protected, except ours, because of the way the wording of the treaty is. And we pleaded with the people in Oslo not to do this, but they did. They basically wrote out—and they knew exactly what they were doing. Why they did it, I don't know. But they basically said that other countries, the way they designed their antitank mines was protected; the way we do it isn't.

The second issue is, the United States has, as all of you know very well, a United Nations responsibility in Korea. The border, the DMZ, is 18 miles from Seoul. So there is one place in the world where we have lots of landmines, because it's the only way to protect Seoul from all the North Korean Army, should they mass along the border. It is heavily marked. As far as we know, no civilian's ever been hurt there. All we asked for was the opportunity to find a substitute for the protection the landmines give the people of South Korea, and we would sign it.

Let me assure you all, I was the first world leader to call for a ban on landmines. We have destroyed almost 2 million landmines. We spend over half of the money the world spends helping other countries dig up their mines. So I strongly support the goals of the treaty, and I will continue to do so. I hope if we can resolve these two problems, we can sign the treaty, because I have spent a lot of my personal time on this landmine issue, and it's very important. And I thank you for what you're doing.

Thank you.

Nagasaki, Hiroshima, and Nuclear Weapons

Mr. Chikushi. Time is running short, so we turn our attention to the future. Something that is difficult for the people in the audience to ask, so I will do it. You have the button to destroy mankind 5 times over with your nuclear weapons. How much do you know about what really happened in Nagasaki and Hiroshima? Have you had any personal experience of getting in touch with the victims? And on that basis, you still continue to own, possess nuclear weapons.

The President. No, I have never had any personal contact with victims, but I have read a great deal about it. After I decided to run for President, I began to think about it much more than I ever had before.

Since I have been President, I have worked hard to reduce the number of weapons in our nuclear arsenal, along with the Russians, to extend the Nuclear Non-Proliferation Treaty. We were the first country to sign the Comprehensive Nuclear Test Ban Treaty. We are hoping that our friends in Russia will ratify the START II convention so we can immediately start on the next round of nuclear weapons reductions.

So I have done everything I could do to reduce the number of nuclear weapons and the threat of nuclear war. I have implored the people of India and Pakistan not to start a nuclear buildup with each other, because I never want to see another weapon dropped.

On the other hand, if you look at the last 50 years, nuclear weapons have not been used a second time, I think, because of the deterrent theory. And what I want to do is to reduce our weapons but always do it in a way that at least provides some disincentive from someone else using nuclear weapons, as well.

Mr. Chikushi. Well, unfortunately, I think the time is up. Or?

The President. I'll take a couple more.

Mr. Chikushi. There's two more questions regarding our future. How about a young person, how about over here?

Teenage Crime

Q. I want to ask you—I'm very sad these days that teenagers' crime is increasing—[*inaudible*]—what do you hope we can leave to our children?

The President. Let me ask you something. I have something to say about that, but why do you think the teenage crime is going up?

Q. Well, I think it is a little related to what the other guy asked you about, that no communication in the family, no father, and many times the mother does not work in the home. And this kind of no communication in the family— and also the area—we don't know other people, what they are doing.

The President. Well, I can tell you that in our country, one of the things that happened is that so many of our children were being let out of school, but they couldn't go home to their parents because there was no parent in the home. And so a lot of this crime was happening between the time school was over and the time the parents got home from work.

So what we have tried to do is to turn our schools into more community institutions. And so the children can stay there for longer hours, and they can do their homework, or they can get tutoring, or they can do other things. In some of our big cities, even, they're feeding the children there, if necessary. And what we're trying to do is to create, as much as we can, opportunities to overcome the fact that many of these children don't even have two parents in the homes in the U.S.

But I think the most important thing is, children have to believe that they are the most important people in the world to someone. They have to be—when you're young, you must know that you are the most important person in the world to someone. It gives you a root, an anchor in life. Of course, then all the work and the study and all that makes more sense. But·in the beginning you have to be valued just because you're alive and because you're in a family and because you're in a community and you matter, no matter what.

I think that is important. And I worry that in all of our societies we're working so hard, we're getting so busy, we're doing so many things that that sense of the innate, inherent worth of people can be lost. We can never afford to define ourselves solely in terms of how hard we work or how much money we have or what our grades are or anything else. Children have to believe that they matter just because they're alive. And I think that, all of our societies, if we're not careful, we lose that.

Mr. Chikushi. The last question; I can only accept one question. Would you like to point to somebody, Mr. President?

The President. If I'm late, the Prime Minister will stop speaking to me, and this whole thing will be—[*laughter*]—go ahead.

Situation in Iraq

Q. I have a question about—you decided not to attack Iraq—estimate by the Pentagon that more than 10,000 people would die—[*inaudible*].

The President. Well, first of all, the Pentagon estimate was not that high; but it's obvious that if we had conducted a comprehensive attack directed at their weapons of mass destruction program, the production capacity, the laboratories, all the supporting sites and the military infrastructure that supports it, that unless everyone knew in advance and left the premises, large numbers of people would be killed. And I believe the United States has a special responsibility, because of the unique position of our military might at this moment in history, to be very careful in that.

Now, that's why I always said if Saddam Hussein would comply with the United Nations resolutions, we would not attack. Shortly before the attack was about to begin, we received word that they were going to send a letter committing to compliance. Then we worked all day to try to clarify it, and I think it was a good thing to try to solve this peacefully. Peace is always better than war, if you can do it consistent with the long-term security and freedom of the people. So I feel good about that.

Secondly, I think that the inspection system offers us the best protection over the long run. But don't forget, you have suffered in Japan from the sarin gas attack. This is not an academic issue to you; this is a real issue to you. And Iraq is a nation that has actually used chemical weapons on its own people, on the Iranians, on others, had a biological weapons program of some significance, was attempting to develop a nuclear weapons program.

So this is a very important issue for the world, and I would hope that all the countries of the world would continue to support an aggressive stance. I hope it will not lead to military action, but we have to be prepared, I believe, to take military action because the issue is so great.

I think that young people like you—Japan lived in the shadow of the awful legacy of the atomic weapons, but the likelihood is that in your lifetime, your adult lifetime, and your children's lifetime, you will have to worry more about chemical and biological weapons put in the hands of terrorists as well as rogue states. You have seen this in Japan; you know this. But I think if we can do something to stop it now, we should do it even if it requires military action.

The gentleman behind you there.

International Finance in the 21st Century

Q. I'm a private banker for a European bank. In a few years, in many ways, we've come through a lot. We have increased investment in the United States. However, things are changing a little bit. Now you will be the first President of the 21st century, but what do you think you have to be most worried about as we go into the 21st century in terms of economics?

The President. I think the biggest challenge, long-term, is to adapt the international economic systems to the realities of the 21st century. The International Monetary Fund, the World Bank, all these institutions set up at the end of the Second World War have facilitated great trade and investment. But they weren't prepared for the fact that once you had trade and investment, you had to have money crossing national lines, and then that money would become a commodity traded in itself, and then it would be traded at great margins through the derivatives and the other mechanisms. Sometimes the money is traded, and you only put up 10 percent of the money you have at risk.

Today, $1.5 trillion crosses national borders every day in currency trading. And we don't have a system to avoid boom and bust, to keep recession from going to depression in the global financial markets. So, long-term, I think that's our big challenge. We are all working on it, and I think we'll have over the course of the coming year some very important things to do.

Meanwhile, we've come up with some short-term solutions, Japan and the U.S., with the Asia growth fund we announced—the Prime Minister and I announced a couple of days ago, a precautionary finance facility to keep the financial problems from reaching countries that are doing a good job, strengthening the IMF.

But over the long run, every country after the Great Depression that preceded World War II devised ways to stop those depressions from happening in their own countries. That's what you're doing here. You're just a question of whether you're doing enough to restore growth, right? But you've been able to stop things that happened all over the world in the 1920's and '30's.

Now what we have to do is to develop an international system that will achieve that goal, that will allow growth, free flow of money but won't have these radical swings of boom and bust that devastated the world in the 1930's. That, I think, is the biggest long-term economic challenge that we face.

Closing Remarks

Mr. Chikushi. Finally, you must have something to say to Japanese people.

The President. Well, first of all, I hope you have enjoyed this evening as much as I have. And I thank you again for your questions. I thank the people in Osaka for their questions. I thank you for your interest in your country and in our relationships with your country.

I would just like to say in closing that the United States views Japan as our friend, our ally for the future. We regret that you have the present economic challenges you have, but we don't think you should be too pessimistic about the future.

These things run in waves over time. Keep in mind, 10 years ago a lot of people said America's best days were behind it. And we looked to you, and we learned a lot of things from you. And we borrowed some things from you, and they helped us. And so now we're in a period of time where what we're doing is working pretty well for us and helping the rest of the world. But in the last 50 years, no country has demonstrated the capacity to change more than Japan and to lead and to emerge and to sort of redefine, continually redefine the mission of the nation. So I would first of all say, do not be discouraged by the present economic difficulties. They can be overcome.

The second thing I would say is, we had a big financial crisis in America, and it cost us 5 times more than it would have to fix because we delayed dealing with it. So now you have the laws on the books. I would urge you to support your Government in aggressively dealing with the financial institutions, aggressively moving to support greater consumption, aggressively moving for structural changes that will create more jobs, because a strong Japan is good for you but also essential to the rest of Asia emerging from its present difficulties. So don't be discouraged, but do be determined. That would be the advice of a friend. I say that because we have been through our tough times; we have learned so much from you.

And the last point I want to make is, the best days of Japan and the best days of America lay before us in the 21st century if we determine to go there together.

Thank you very much.

NOTE: The townhall meeting broadcast began at 5:37 p.m. in Studio A at the Tokyo Broadcasting System's studios during "News 23." In his remarks, the President referred to Prime Minister Keizo Obuchi of Japan; President Jiang Zemin of China; and President Saddam Hussein of Iraq. Mr. Chikushi and some of the other participants spoke in Japanese, and their remarks were translated by an interpreter.

Remarks at a Dinner Hosted by Prime Minister Keizo Obuchi of Japan in Tokyo
November 19, 1998

Prime Minister, Mrs. Obuchi, members of the Japanese delegation, and honored guests. First, let me say on behalf of the American delegation, I thank you for your warm hospitality.

It is a pleasure to look around this room tonight and see so many friendly faces from my previous trips to Japan: your distinguished predecessors, your Ambassador and former Ambassadors, distinguished business leaders. The relationship between our two countries has always been important, but never more important than now.

I, too, enjoyed our meeting in New York 2 months ago. Tonight I am delighted to be back

in the Akasaka Palace. I also—Prime Minister, I feel terrible about the schedule which we are on together, but since you mentioned it, perhaps we can make sure that we both stay awake at the dinner tonight. [*Laughter*]

Let me say, in all seriousness, too, I was deeply honored to be received by the Emperor and the Empress today, and very much appreciated the visit that we had and the good wishes they sent to my family.

Since my last visit here in the spring of 1996, strong winds have blown across the world, disrupting economies in every region. There have also been threats to peace and stability, from acts of terrorism to weapons of mass destruction. Yet, the world has made progress in the face of adversity. It is more peaceful today than it was 2 years ago when I was here. Hope has come to Northern Ireland. Peru and Ecuador have resolved their longstanding dispute. Bosnia is building a self-sustaining peace. A humanitarian disaster has been averted in Kosovo, and the people there have, now, hope for regaining their autonomy. The Middle East is back on the long road to peace.

All of these areas of progress have one thing in common: They represent the triumph of a wide circle of nations working together, not only the nations directly affected but a community of nations that brings adversaries to the table to settle their differences.

Year-in and year-out, Japan's generous contributions to peacekeeping efforts and your eloquent defense of the idea of global harmony have gone far to make this a safer world. In Central America, you have provided disaster relief in the wake of Hurricane Mitch. I should say, Mr. Prime Minister, that I wish my wife were with me tonight, but she is there, where they had the worst hurricane disaster in 200 years. And I thank you for helping people so far from your home.

In the Middle East, you have contributed substantial funds to aid the peace process. In recent months you have further advanced the cause of peace by taking your relations with Asian neighbors to a new and significantly higher level of cooperation. And despite economic difficulties at home, you have contributed to recovery efforts throughout Asia. That is true leadership.

Now, Mr. Prime Minister, you have made difficult decisions to overcome your own economic challenges. The path back to growth and stability will require your continued leadership, but we hope to work with you every step of the way.

In dealing with these difficulties, Japan can lead Asia into a remarkable new century, a century of global cooperation for greater peace and freedom, greater democracy and prosperity, greater protection of our environment, greater scientific discovery and space exploration.

At the center of all our efforts is the strong bond between the people of the United States and the people of Japan. Our security alliance is the cornerstone of Asia's stability. Our friendship demonstrates to Asia and to the world that very different societies can work together in a harmony that benefits everyone.

Two fine examples of our recent cooperation are the new Asia growth and recovery initiative that you and I recently announced, Prime Minister, and, as you mentioned, the space shuttle *Discovery*, which included your remarkable astronaut Chiaki Mukai. I understand that when Dr. Mukai spoke with you from space, Prime Minister, she offered the first three lines of a five-line poem, a tanka poem, and she invited the people of Japan to provide the final two lines. I want to try my hand at this.

As I understand it, her lines were:

Spinning somersaults;
Without gravity's limits
In space flight with Glenn.

I would add:

All is possible on Earth and in the heavens
When our countries join hands.

Ladies and gentlemen, I ask you to join me in a toast to the Prime Minister and Mrs. Obuchi and to the people of Japan.

NOTE: The President spoke at 7:50 p.m. in the Kacho No Ma Banquet Hall at Akasaka Palace. In his remarks, he referred to Prime Minister Obuchi's wife, Chizuko; Japanese Ambassador to the U.S. Kunihiko Saito; and Emperor Akihito and Empress Michiko of Japan. The transcript released by the Office of the Press Secretary also included the remarks of Prime Minister Obuchi.

Remarks to American and Japanese Business Leaders in Tokyo
November 20, 1998

Thank you very much. I have to practice saying "Mr. Ambassador" instead of "Mr. Speaker," but I want to say first to Tom Foley how very grateful I am for his willingness to undertake this service in Japan.

I think there could be no better evidence of the importance that the United States attaches to our relationship with Japan than the fact that in the last 6 years the United States has been blessed to be represented in Japan by former Vice President Walter Mondale and former Speaker of the House Ambassador Tom Foley.

I am very proud of Tom Foley, who has guided and advised me. And if I'd listened to him more, I'd even done better. [*Laughter*] And I'm very, very grateful to him for his service here.

I'm glad to see Glen Fukushima again, and I thank him for his welcome. And I thank him for his eagerness to get me to the platform. [*Laughter*] I wanted to come here today. I didn't intend to go anywhere, Glen. I was going to stay around. [*Laughter*]

I thank Patsy Mink for her distinguished service and her introduction, as well as Senator Max Baucus and Congressman Neil Abercrombie, Congressman Earl Pomeroy, and Delegate Robert Underwood, and all the members of the Cabinet and administration who are here. The United States Government is well represented in this distinguished group this morning. I thank you for inviting me to speak and for the work you do at the forefront of the new global economy, where so much of America's prosperity will reside in the 21st century.

Today I want to talk about the current international financial crisis, what we are doing about it, and the special role the United States and Japan must play to lead Asia and the world back to stability and growth.

Of course, in part, the present difficulties are the product of our own successes. The world financial system fashioned at the end of World War II has played a central role in dramatically expanding trade, promoting prosperity, reducing hunger and disease throughout the world. But today, the sheer volume of economic activity intensified by technological change has created new risks, risks which are not adequately being managed today by many national systems or by the current international arrangements.

The root of the problem lies in the sheer volume and speed of the movement of money, $1.5 trillion a day in international exchange transactions—far, far in excess of the total volume of trade in goods and services on any given day. In country after country we have seen rapid, large infusions of capital, often very highly leveraged, into banking systems and into cor-

porations, without adequate balance sheets or risk assessments necessary for appropriate loan rates. Then we have seen the equally rapid withdrawal of the money, too often leading to enormous debt, devaluation, and dislocation, and ultimately into political crisis and, in many countries, great personal suffering.

The collapse of communism, the rise of democracy, the information revolution, all these things have spurred people to seek the benefits of greater trade and investment. But in many places, institutions have not caught up with aspirations. Lack of openness, weak legal systems have bred irresponsibility and, on several occasions, corruption. They have fueled social unrest and, in turn, further economic instability.

Now, I know these challenges are quite complex. But I am convinced, with responsible leadership from Japan and the United States, from the European Union, and from many developing economies, we can restore hope and spur growth. We can build a trading system and a new financial architecture for a new century if we act promptly, responsibly, and creatively.

In September, after consulting with Japan and other partners, I called for specific and urgent steps to boost ailing economies, to halt the contagion, to restore growth and a long-term adaptation of the global financial institutions so that we can tame the cycles of boom and bust over the long run.

Nations around the world have rallied to this common agenda. America, Japan, and other nations have cut interest rates. We at home have met our obligations to the IMF. We're providing credit and investment insurance to encourage capital flows into developing nations. Brazil is taking strong measures to address its fiscal problems and ward off the contagion. The international community has come through with an aid package to help.

We have developed a precautionary finance facility designed to head off problems before they get started in countries that are vulnerable to economic unrest but have essentially sound economic policies. The World Bank and the Asian Development Bank will more than double their support to strengthen social safety nets across Asia to aid those who are suffering the most.

Just a few weeks ago, Japan announced the Miyazawa Plan to address the central challenge, helping viable Asian banks and businesses emerge from crushing debt burdens. And just this week, Prime Minister Obuchi and I announced a new U.S.-Japan initiative to extend this effort. Together, we will mobilize new financing to recapitalize banks and also increase funding for trade finance and technical assistance.

But nothing is so vital to world growth as ensuring that the United States and Japan, the world's two greatest economic powers, also do what is necessary to expand our own economies. For the United States, that means continuing the sound fiscal policies that have brought us to this point, investing more in our people and in our future, and continuing to work to open global markets.

For Japan, of course, the challenge is even greater today because of the economic difficulties of the present and the last few years. But no people have done more in the last 50 years to overcome obstacles, to exceed expectations, to prove that they can adapt to new economic realities than the Japanese. The people of Japan turned a closed society into an open democracy. They built from devastation a robust economy that became an engine of growth for all of Asia. They have created products and technologies that have improved the lives of people all around the world, including the United States. They have been leaders in development aid to help other nations build their own prosperity.

Even with current economic difficulties, Japan comprises 70 percent of Asia's economy. With others in the region still struggling, Japan—and only Japan—can lead Asia back to stability and growth by meeting its own economic challenges.

I want to be clear about something that I'm surprised there could be any doubt about: The United States wants a strong Japan, with a strong and growing economy. Japan's prosperity is vital to our own future. Already we have nearly $200 billion in annual trade and over $600 billion invested in each other's economies. We have a strong political and security partnership which is vital to the peace of this region and the peace of the world and which, I am convinced, cannot be maintained over the long run unless our economies are also strong.

Though the U.S. and Asia—indeed, all the world—will benefit from a revitalized Japanese economy, the greatest beneficiaries will be the Japanese people themselves, with new jobs, higher living standards, and a better capacity to deal with the looming issue of an aging population, a challenge that confronts virtually every advanced society in the world today.

The keys to Japan's recovery are easy to articulate but, of course, more difficult to achieve: reform of the banking system to clear up the balance sheets, protect depositors, get good lending going again; an increase in domestic demand for Japanese goods and services; greater deregulation, investment, and opening of Japanese economies to create more jobs through increased competitive activity.

Prime Minister Obuchi has announced a new package of tax cuts and funding increases to stimulate demand, and he has obtained passage of major legislation aimed at repairing Japan's banking system, legislation which must now be vigorously implemented.

As America learned with our own financial crisis, involving our savings and loans—and those of you who were in America in the eighties know that we wound up closing over 1,000 of them—delay in a crisis like this only makes matters worse. By waiting too long to act in America, we increased our eventual cleanup cost by over 500 percent. Rapid, vigorous implementation of bank reform legislation, therefore, will make the banks more open and accountable, prompt them to sell off bad loans, get them back into the business of lending to those who can create jobs and opportunities.

And rapid implementation of the economic stimulus plan is also important. Indeed, the people here may conclude that even more must be done to jolt the economy back into growth.

I think I should say, in light of the townhall meeting we did last night with Japanese citizens and the fascinating questions I was asked, that I was immensely impressed with the level of knowledge and interest of ordinary citizens in this country in the present conditions.

And one of the things that I hope our visit here will do is to at least convince the Japanese people that the leaders of the United States— all of the Cabinet members, all of the Congress Members, the high White House officials, all of us who are here—we have every confidence that Japan is fully capable of restoring growth to this country and all of Asia, fully capable of mastering this challenge just as it has the challenges of the last 50 years.

I think having that confidence in the mind of the Japanese citizens is absolutely key, over and above any Government program, any spending program, any tax cut program, any other kind of program, in convincing the citizens that they, too, have a critical role to play here in purchasing more goods and services in the domestic economy.

Now, a high savings rate is a very good thing, especially for a country that's going to have a rapidly aging population. But in order for the society to work, Japan needs both a good savings rate and a robust economy. And jobs cannot be created unless someone is buying what the people who are working are producing.

And so I hope that part of what has happened here will go beyond Government policy and that there will be a great debate among the citizens in this country about how they can have both the benefits of appropriate savings for their own retirement and the benefits of a growing economy by contributing in buying the products and services of the people who are going to work every day. Both will be required to deal with the challenges that Japan, the United States, Europe, other advanced countries face with an aging population.

I also believe that Japan will benefit by going forward with efforts to increase outside investment and to deregulate key economic sectors. Primarily, let me say, given the present state of things, I think this is important because it can make a major contribution to job growth here in Japan.

Just since 1993, when I took office and we began an aggressive effort on telecommunications which was culminated a few years ago by the passage of the Telecommunications Act, we have seen an enormous number of new jobs coming in to the American economy because of the telecommunications deregulation. Since we deregulated our domestic airline industry, we have seen tens of thousands of new jobs created. I am convinced the same thing would occur here. Yes, there would be some change and some disruption, but the net effect would be to create more jobs and better incomes and more stability for the people of Japan.

We made real progress on our enhanced deregulation initiative earlier this year at the G–8 summit, and I think it is crucial that we make further progress by the time the Prime Minister and I meet again next year.

We also have to do more on trade. Since 1993 the United States has been party to 260 trade agreements, opening global markets from agriculture to automobiles to create good jobs and lower prices for consumers. In 1994, at our APEC summit, the leaders resolved to create an Asia-Pacific free trade zone by 2020, and we have made good progress in some areas, especially with our information technology agreement to erase tariffs on computer and telecommunications equipment.

This week at APEC, we moved forward on the early voluntary sector liberalization initiative, to open trade in nine key sectors worth more than $1.5 trillion a year by referring the process to the World Trade Organization. As all of you know, I'm sure, we had some differences with our friends in Japan on those issues, and we wish that they had been more forthcoming on all nine areas. But the most important thing now is that Japan play a leadership role in getting a WTO agreement in all nine sectors. This is very, very important.

Again I say, restoring growth in Japan and restoring growth in Asia need to be seen as interlocking objectives. This year the Asian ailing economies' exports to Japan are down by $13 billion. In America they're up by $5 billion. We believe that this is something that we have to do together.

Let me say that I understand that every society has certain sectors which are especially sensitive to trade-opening initiatives. I also understand that even wealthy societies, and especially developing ones, face a constant conflict between the desire to get the aggregate benefit of an open economy and the gnawing fear that it will not be possible to maintain the social contract in the face of global economics and that this can undermine the solidity of communities and families and of society itself.

The key, as I said in a speech to the WTO in Geneva a few months ago, is to involve all sectors of society in the process of setting 21st century trade rules, to make a commitment up front that there ought to be due account taken of the need to preserve the social contract to advance the health and well-being of people as trade advances, to make sure ordinary citizens benefit from advanced trade, to make sure we're improving the global environment, not destroying it, as we expand trade.

We know that these things can be done. But the worst thing that can happen is if it appears that when times are tough, borders are closing up, other markets are being heavily penetrated in ways that can't be justified by economic forces, and then you're going to have, I'm afraid, a round of retaliatory protectionism. I'm quite worried about this now.

We had a meeting early on when it was obvious to us that this economic difficulty in Asia was going to be very, very severe. And I made a decision with the full support of my entire economic team that we would do everything we could to leave America's markets as open as possible, knowing full well that our trade deficit would increase dramatically for a year or two. I did it because I thought it was a major contribution we could make to stabilizing the global economy and the economies in Asia.

And so far, on balance, because our economy is continuing to grow, the American people and American political leadership have supported that. But if there is a perception of unfair trade, the consensus can disappear. You know this—I want this mostly to be a good news speech, but I have to say, in the United States now we have had this year, in one year, a 500 percent increase in the imports of hot-rolled steel from Japan and a 300 percent increase in the import of hot-rolled steel from Russia. No one seriously believes that this is solely because of changing economic conditions.

And if you put that against an inability to open more markets, to have more investment, to have more deregulation, to have more market access, it will create in our country the potential for a retrenchment here in a way that will not be good for Asia or Japan or for the United States over the long run. So I say again, we want to keep our markets open, but we need fair, rule-based, disciplined expansions, and we need to avoid market penetrations that have no relationship to market factors.

All of you in this room know a lot better than I do that it still remains extremely difficult for some non-Japanese businesses to succeed in the market here. We will continue to work for greater opening. But I will say again, I believe that what we're doing is not simply good for the United States; I think it's good for Japan as well. I would not come here and advocate any course of action that I believe was good for us but bad for Japan. That, in the end, is self-defeating.

We should follow these policies only if they are good for our countries, both our countries, over the long run, and not only good for those of us who are in positions of decisionmaking but good for the ordinary citizens of our country, good for their future prospects, good for

their ability to raise their children in a more secure and stable and prosperous world.

So I say, the last point I want to make is, let's not forget what this is all about. It's about more even than the success of your businesses, more than the profits that you might earn, more than the jobs you might have. It's about making it possible for citizens in free countries to pursue their chosen destinies, to live out their dreams, to give their children a chance to live out their dreams, to manage the tumult of the modern world in a way that seizes all the brilliant opportunities that are out there and deals with the challenges in a forthright and fair way. I believe that this is terribly, terribly important.

Let me also say I believe that it is very important that Japan and the United States, as two great democracies, continue our partnership for peace and freedom. There are those who say, "Well, all these global economic problems are inconsistent with democracy. Democracies can't deal with these issues. We need more authoritarian governments." Well, if you look at the evidence, it contradicts it—that assertion. Many more authoritarian governments have financial institutions and processes that are insufficiently open. One great democratically elected leader, the President of the Philippines, President Estrada, said the other day, noting—he was referring to calls for greater open processes and greater openness in institutions. He said, "Now, when Alan Greenspan and the common people have the same view, we should listen." [*Laughter*] I wish I'd thought of that line myself. [*Laughter*]

But if you look around the world, if you see the encouraging signs from Thailand to South Korea to eastern Europe to Mexico, you see that if people feel they have a stake in their societies, they are willing to sacrifice; they are willing to take responsibility; they are willing to give their governments leave to make decisions that are difficult today because they are right for tomorrow.

And so I say also, I hope that on this trip the United States and Japan will reaffirm what we have in common: our support for democracy, our support for openness, our support for the march of peace and freedom as well as the return of prosperity to Asia and the rest of the world.

In closing let me say, we have to have your help in all this. You know that. The private sector has a critical role to play if we're going to address the broad challenges of global change and the challenges of the financial crisis. All of this you understand, I'm quite sure, better than I. We need your creativity, your entrepreneurial strength. We need your sustained, direct investment in emerging markets, your support for training, health care, and good workplace conditions to ensure a strong work force and stable, broad-based support for open markets and global free enterprise.

Above all, right now, in every country, we need your leadership to support creativity and change. The world is different, and it is changing at a rapid rate. Inevitably, economics changes faster than politics. And yet, in the end, if we want stable societies and successful economics, we must have good politics. You can help us to achieve that.

President Franklin Roosevelt once said, "True wealth is not a static thing." How well we know that. It is a living thing, made out of the disposition of people to create and distribute the good things of life. We must find the right formulas to make this living thing grow stronger. Over

a generation of extraordinary progress, the people of Japan have shown what is possible.

Now it is the challenge of Japan and the United States, working at home and working together, to fulfill this promise, to restore stability to this region, growth to this country and to the world. I am absolutely convinced that the 21st century can be the best time humanity has ever known. I am more optimistic and idealistic today than I was the day I first took the oath of office as President in 1993. But I am also absolutely convinced, as my daughter's generation says, that denial is not simply a river in Egypt. [*Laughter*] We know what the challenges are, and we have to find the means to meet them. If we do, we will be richly rewarded.

Thank you very much, and God bless you.

NOTE: The President spoke at 10:25 a.m. at the Capitol Tokyo Hotel. In his remarks, he referred to Glen S. Fukushima, president, American Chamber of Commerce in Japan; Prime Minister Keizo Obuchi of Japan; and President Joseph Estrada of the Philippines.

Remarks Following Discussions With Prime Minister Keizo Obuchi of Japan and an Exchange With Reporters in Tokyo
November 20, 1998

Prime Minister Obuchi. Just now I have finished the meeting with President Clinton which lasted for about an hour and a half. Japan and the United States are allies bonded together with shared values. It is my pleasure to receive President Clinton in Japan less than 2 months after our first summit meeting in New York. And I regard it as testimony to the close cooperation and coordination between the two countries.

The President invited me to officially visit the U.S. during the Golden Week holidays next year, and I accepted it with great pleasure.

In today's summit meeting, the President and I exchanged views on a wide range of topics, including international situation and the world economy. Regarding North Korea, we had a substantive exchange of views on matters including KEDO, the suspected underground construction of nuclear facilities, and missile issues.

We confirmed that the two countries will maintain our close consultation with each other on various levels and will take a coordinated posture among Japan, South Korea, and the United States toward North Korea.

The President and I also consulted on major international issues, including Russia and China. We reaffirmed our two countries' contribution to the global peace and security which goes beyond our bilateral relations. And I told the President—and the President welcomed—that Japan would extend assistance to the Palestinians up to some $200 million in the next 2 years in order to accelerate the momentum for the Middle East peace process created by the Wye River agreement in which President Clinton took an instrumental role.

With regard to Central America, which was stricken by Hurricane Mitch, I explained to the

President about Japan's assistance to those countries. And the President and I also confirmed that the two countries will make closer cooperation toward the early realization of U.N. Security Council's reform.

The President and I welcomed the enhancement of the cooperation between Japan and the United States to stabilize the world economy. We are both pleased with the joint announcement of the Asian growth and recovery initiative, and we reaffirmed our cooperation in the area of strengthening the global financial system.

The President and I also agreed to continue the constructive dialog on the economic management of the two countries. In this context, I explained to the President that, recognizing the critical importance of Japan's economic recovery for the economic stability and prosperity in Asia, as well as in the world, Japan is simply implementing measures necessary for the revitalization and stabilization of its financial system and for its economic recovery. In particular, I finalized on November 16th the emergency economic package which aims to recover the economy. And we have also mentioned that the effort on the U.S. side is also to be welcomed, and we considered that the decision—we hope that these cooperative efforts by Japan and the United States will bear fruit and that the world economy will head for stability and recovery.

In today's summit meeting, the President and I confirmed the development in Japan-U.S. cooperation on various issues with global implications, and I would like you to refer to the distributed paper for the details.

It was a significant achievement of President Clinton's visit to Japan this time that the President and I could reconfirm the importance of Japan-U.S. relations and promote the cooperation and policy coordination between the two countries. As Japan and the U.S. face numerous issues which call for their joint effort, I would like to maintain close consultation and cooperation with the President.

President Clinton. Thank you very much. Let me begin by thanking Prime Minister Obuchi for welcoming me to Japan, for the warm hospitality, and for the good talks we have had yesterday and today.

The relationship between the United States and Japan is the cornerstone of stability and prosperity in the Asia-Pacific region. That is both a point of pride and a pledge that we will act together to promote stability and prosperity, especially now when so many nations in the region are facing economic difficulties and real distress.

To be the cornerstone of stability and prosperity, we must continue to carry our weight. We're going to meet our responsibilities first and foremost as allies. The Prime Minister and I had good discussions on important security issues, including our shared concerns about North Korea. The United States is reviewing our Korea policy to strengthen North Korea's compliance with its obligations, and of course, we will be consulting closely with Japan and others in the region as we move forward.

We are also going to meet our responsibilities as democracies with a common sense of purpose. Today we issue a joint statement on our support for democracy and human rights around the world. We've agreed to strengthen our cooperation on the environment. We both welcome Argentina's decision this week to become the very first developing country to accept binding limits on its greenhouse gas emissions, following up on the historic work done by Japan at the Kyoto conference last year. We recognize that there is and there must be no tradeoff between the human right to development and the human need to breathe clean air, drink safe water, live a healthy life.

We are also, I am confident, going to meet our responsibilities as the world's two largest economies. The United States will do its part with a determined policy to keep growth going, markets open to free and fair trade, and continued efforts to stabilize the global economy in the short and long term.

Japan has made important contributions to regional stabilization, efforts like the Miyazawa plan; the new Asia growth and recovery initiative the Prime Minister and I announced at APEC, to help banks and businesses in hard-hit countries emerge from debt; the precautionary finance facility to help the financial contagion not spread to countries with good policies; and of course, Japan has committed recently substantial resources to repair its banking system and announced new plans to stimulate the economy here.

I believe it is clearly not only in the interest of the world and the region but in the interest of the Japanese people for Japan to continue to move forward with Prime Minister Obuchi's strategy, with aggressive implementation of the significant bank reform legislation and taking the necessary steps to spur domestic demand and reignite economic growth. We in the United States learned a few years ago, often in painful fashion, that there is no substitute for decisive action to heal an ailing banking system so that growth can be restored.

We also believe that it is in Japan's interest to support open trade and more open, deregulated markets. An overwhelming consensus emerged from this week's APEC summit: Protectionism is a no-growth strategy that offers no way out of the current economic crisis. If coupled with actions which lead to an artificial explosion of exports in other countries, in fact, it can promote a protectionist reaction there, further slowing growth. The longer we wait to confront this reality, the harder it becomes to escape.

At APEC our nations agreed to pursue at the WTO market-opening measures in nine critical sectors covering $1.5 trillion in global trade. This is an important commitment, and we will count on Japan's support to see it through in 1999.

I know that there are painful choices going on throughout Asia and difficult challenges for Japan. I would just like to say as a friend that the United States wants, needs, and believes in a strong Japan; that in the last half century no nation has demonstrated its capacity for positive change more dramatically than Japan. Today, I believe Japan has, amidst all the difficulties, a win-win proposition. The steps necessary for the good of the Japanese people are also good for Asia and the rest of the world.

As Japan works to recover its growth and stability, it will lead all Asia into a more prosperous and peaceful 21st century. That is a goal I am proud to share with Prime Minister Obuchi, and one we will be working together to achieve in the months ahead.

Thank you very much.

Japanese Economic Recovery Efforts

Q. I'd like to ask you a question about economic matters. It was the economic recovery—Japanese Government has been resorting to various measures. However, we cannot say that we have seen any positive result. Mr. President, how do you assess the status quo and also the measures that have been taken by the Japanese Government? How do you assess them?

And also, Mr. Prime Minister, how have you been explaining to Mr. Clinton about the existing measures that have been taken by the Government and also the outlook of the recovery?

Prime Minister Obuchi. Let me respond first. During the Japan-U.S. summit, I have explained to Mr. Clinton the following: We are fully cognizant of the fact that it is extremely critical that Japanese economy makes a recovery in order to ensure the economic stability and prosperity of Asia and the world. To this end, we have been putting top priority and consider this to be an urgent matter in order to implement necessary measures for the recovery of the economy and the financial system.

And on the 16th of this month, we have presented the emergency economic stimulus package so that we will be able to state clearly for the fiscal 1999 that Japan has turned to the positive growth. And that means that the package includes 17 trillion yen on project basis and substantially—20 trillion yen, if the permanent tax reduction exceeding 6 trillion yen is included. And these are the measures necessary for us to create the bright 21st century and urgent matters for the economic—recovery—and also must take measures necessary to avoid the global economic risks and support Asia.

And the third supplementary budget has to be prepared as soon as possible. And this means that national and regional fiscal burden would be exceeding 10 trillion yen. So we are going to be moving toward the rapid and prompt preparation of the supplementary budget as soon as possible so that it can pass the extraordinary Diet.

And we believe that President Clinton has well received our efforts and has shown understanding and has expressed that he shall extend continued support towards such measures. We're very much appreciative of such a stand expressed by Mr. Clinton.

Number one economic power, the United States, and number two economic power, Japan, we must take initiatives in order to ensure the prosperity and stability in Asia and Asian economy as a whole. And we have confirmed mutually that we shall, together, exert efforts.

President Clinton. Let me, first of all, say I think it is unfair to have a negative judgment of the Government's efforts based on the fact that no one feels any results now. After all, Prime Minister Obuchi has not been in office very long. He has put together his government; he has passed this bank reform legislation; he has announced a plan to stimulate the economy with tax cuts and public investment.

You asked how I feel about it. I would make four points. Number one, I think the bank reform legislation is quite good because it puts up public money which financial institutions can get to protect depositors, but only if they recycle—or, if you will, write off their bad loans and clean up their balance sheets so they can start to loan money again. So I think that, if this legislation is vigorously implemented, it will be a big plus.

On the stimulus package, I think it is quite good. Whether it will be enough or not, I do not know, simply because the Prime Minister has had to change a policy that was not stimulating the economy, and sometimes when you have to turn a country around, it takes more than you think in the beginning. I don't know that.

The third thing I would say is we believe that greater trade and investment will actually generate more jobs and more growth in Japan. And therefore, we think it's important to continue with the market opening mechanisms, and we have suggested that perhaps deregulation in the areas of telecommunications and airlines would generate more jobs here only because they generated far more jobs for us in the United States when we did it than we could have known.

The last thing I'd like to say is I hope the Japanese people have great confidence in their country. And average citizens, the kind of people I talked to last night on that television show, they can help. This is not just for the Government alone. Average citizens, if they have confidence and they believe in the capacity of this country to meet its challenges, can help by purchasing more of the goods and services, more of the output of Japan to create more jobs and stabilize this economy. And I would hope that they would also do that.

North Korea

Q. Mr. President, you mentioned briefly your discussions on North Korea. I was wondering if you could tell us, in light of, first of all, a couple of reports this morning—one talks about new North Korean missile developments, another talks about the North Koreans requesting a sum of money in order for an inspection of that suspected complex—I'm wondering if you can give us an update on the report from

your representative who went to the region and what specific areas you two discussed as far as how to approach the situation, whether you need to be going more toward carrots, more toward sticks, more discussions, more direct negotiations. Thank you.

And I'd also like the Prime Minister, please, if he could give his input on that as well.

President Clinton. First of all, I think it is important to keep in mind the difference between the missile program, which we have always been quite concerned about but over which we have no agreement with the North Koreans, and the agreed framework for containing the nuclear program.

We're quite concerned by some of the news reports we have seen; not all of them, by the way, have been confirmed. But there are some disturbing signs there. It is true that when I sent a team into North Korea to talk about inspecting sites, there was some discussion of conditions which were completely unacceptable for such inspections. And I think it's fair to say that no one can be absolutely sure of whether the North Korean position is simply a product of economic difficulties, so they're attempting to get more money out of various countries for doing what they ought to be doing anyway, or whether they really are moving toward a more hostile posture.

We will evaluate that very carefully. I have appointed a former Defense Secretary, Bill Perry, to do a comprehensive review of our Korea policy and analyze all this and report back to me and to congressional leaders soon.

Now, the second thing I would say is, I still believe that we are doing the right thing to pursue the agreed framework because we know that if we had not been working on that these last several years, North Korea would have far more nuclear material for weapons productions than it has, because the agreed framework, in that sense, has worked.

And in that connection, I applaud what Prime Minister Obuchi has done in supporting the KEDO project. And we need to continue to work together with our friends in South Korea, hopefully with the support of the good wishes of the Chinese, to try to restrain hostile developments in North Korea and keep working in the spirit of the agreed framework and to avoid destabilizing things like this missile flight over Japan, which disturbed us greatly.

Prime Minister Obuchi. With respect to the North Korea issue, basically the United States, South Korea, and Japan should cooperate in trying to resolve the matter. And on this point, we have had discussions with the President, and I think that it has been confirmed that this kind of trilateral deliberations and consultations will continue.

The North Korean missile flew over our territory and landed in the Pacific Ocean, but it was a very shocking experience for us. And therefore, in that respect, Japan would like to try to see what kind of cooperation Japan can extend to North Korea to these consultations and consultative processes. However, there are some doubts about the underground nuclear facilities—should the North Koreans have—and therefore, we are looking forward to the surveys and investigations which will be conducted by the United States and hope that that kind of a doubt will be cleared very soon.

On the other hand, we have to cooperate on the KEDO project, and therefore, in that respect, we are trying to extend our cooperation as the President has just mentioned. And as Japan, we are going to be thinking of providing a billion dollars' worth of support; and therefore, in that respect, we hope that such underground nuclear facilities or facilities that are producing nuclear material is not there in reality because

if that happens, it will be very difficult for us to persuade the Japanese people about the kind of cooperation we would be able to extend to the North Koreans. And therefore, in that respect, we would like to ask for the understanding of the United States, and we're asking for the cooperation of the United States in this respect.

In any case, we do hope that we will be able to see that North Koreans will be able to coordinate their efforts together with the people that are involved. Although in the consultation tables we are not included ever, we hope that the United States and South Korea will provide us the needed information so that we will be able to pursue our policies in trying to stabilize this area and bring peace and stability into the region.

I'm sorry, the time is up. Thank you very much.

NOTE: The remarks began at 5 p.m. in the Asahi-No-Ma Room at the Akasaka Palace. In his remarks, the President referred to the Asia-Pacific Economic Cooperation forum (APEC), the World Trade Organization (WTO), and the Korean Peninsula Energy Development Organization (KEDO). Prime Minister Obuchi spoke in Japanese, and his remarks were translated by an interpreter.

Exchange With Reporters in Tokyo
November 20, 1998

Impeachment Inquiry

Q. Mr. President, we were told that you were briefed today on the Judiciary Committee hearings back in Washington. Can you tell us what was your impression about the hearings? What kind of guidance did you give your attorney David Kendall about his accusation that Kenneth Starr was guilty of prosecutorial misconduct? And what do you think about the subpoenas for Bruce Lindsey and Bennett?

The President. Well, first of all, I got only a cursory briefing. I didn't see any of the hearings, and I really can't comment on how they went. I only became aware recently, I think after I left, that Mr. Kendall was going to be able to ask some questions. So I don't know.

My understanding is that he essentially asked questions consistent with the letter he had written both to Mr. Starr and the Attorney General several weeks ago. But beyond that, I don't know. I really haven't talked to anybody back in Washington. I just got a general, cursory review of that.

Q. You didn't say anything to him about prosecutorial misconduct?

The President. I believe that—I don't know this because I haven't seen it, and I haven't talked to anybody—my understanding generally was that the issues he raised were issues he had raised months ago—at least several weeks ago. He wrote a letter to Mr. Starr and wrote a letter to the Attorney General. But I don't know very much about it. I've been here working on these economic and security issues, so I really can't say.

Q. And the subpoenas of Bennett and Lindsey?

The President. I'm not concerned about it, but I think Mr. Lindsey's subpoena was covered by previous decisions. But my understanding is that a subpoena for Mr. Bennett is without any precedent; that is, as far as I know, there has never been a case where a person's lawyer was asked to come and testify. But you will have to talk to them because I really—I haven't been there. I haven't been involved in it; I don't

know what they're saying. And we'll just have to see what happens.

I've got work to do here on the American economy and on these security issues, so that's all being handled by people back in Washington.

NOTE: The exchange began at 6:05 p.m. at Haneda Airport, prior to the President's departure for Seoul, South Korea. In his remarks, the President referred to his personal attorneys David E. Kendall and Robert F. Bennett; and Independent Counsel Kenneth Starr. A tape was not available for verification of the content of this exchange.

The President's News Conference With President Kim Dae-jung of South Korea in Seoul
November 21, 1998

President Kim. Good afternoon. I wholeheartedly welcome President Clinton's visit today, which marks his third visit during his term in office. The fact that in the first year of the new government in Korea we have had an exchange of summit meetings demonstrates to our peoples and the rest of the world the solidity of the alliance that binds our two countries.

We, the two heads of state, as we had agreed during the summit meeting in June in Washington, have decided to take the Korea-U.S. relationship to a higher level of partnership into the 21st century based on our shared treasured values of democracy and market economy.

Through my second summit meeting with President Clinton after my inauguration, I have had a broad and indepth consultation with President Clinton on the political situation on the Korean Peninsula and Northeast Asia, the East Asian economic crisis, and regional and global issues of common interest. In particular, our consultation focused primarily on the following four areas:

First, we agreed that the security alliance between the two countries must stand firm and solid. President Clinton reaffirmed the unwavering security commitment of the U.S. toward the Republic of Korea, and we, the two heads of state, agreed that his visit has provided an op-

portunity to further strengthen the close security alliance.

Second, President Clinton and I reviewed North Korea's recent attitudes towards the Republic of Korea and the United States, and we appreciated the present state of exchanges and cooperation between the North and the South. Given the current situation on the Korean Peninsula, we also agreed that the policy of engagement is the best policy from a realistic standpoint and that this ought to be pursued with consistency.

We also noted the contribution of the Geneva agreed framework, the contribution the framework is making toward peace and stability on the Korean Peninsula as well as the global efforts for nuclear nonproliferation. We affirmed that we will continue to work together to keep the light-water reactor construction going smoothly.

However, we, the two heads of state, we made it clear that we will not tolerate any possible attempt of North Korea to proliferate nuclear weapons, missiles, and other weapons of mass destruction, and decided to closely coordinate in talking with the North on a wide range of pending issues.

In particular, President Clinton and I had a full exchange of views regarding the suspicion surrounding underground construction activity within the North. I told President Clinton that the Korean Government considers this issue as a very serious one, given its implication for the security of the Peninsula, and we would continue to spare no efforts in supporting the U.S. endeavor to pursue its resolution. We have stressed that all necessary steps should be taken to clarify the purpose and character of the underground sites through full access. We have required North Korea to clear the suspicion and help implement the Geneva agreed framework smoothly.

We reaffirmed that the roles that the parties directly concerned, the South and the North, must play in resolving the problems on the Peninsula are important and agreed that the neighboring countries should spare no effort for the South and the North to make progress in dialog and play a leading role. We have noted the establishment of the subcommittees and other positive developments in the third plenary session of the four-party talks and decided to continue to work together to produce more substantive results in the future.

Third, we, the two heads of state, had an indepth consultation on how to promote economic cooperation between the two countries. President Clinton reiterated his firm support for Korea's efforts to move past the economic crisis. I explained the steps the Korean Government has taken to reform the economy, and President Clinton expressed the view that even though the Government reform measures might accompany short-term difficulties, they will eventually lead to an early resolution of the economic crisis. And he offered to lend as much support as possible.

I appreciated the leadership the United States has shown in the efforts to help Korea overcome the economic crisis and asked the President for further cooperation in this regard, emphasizing that greater foreign investment is what Korea needs to resolve the economic difficulties at an early date. President Clinton, for his part, said that he will send a trade and investment delegation, led by Commerce Secretary Daley, sometime early next year, and we decided to work together to ensure the early signing of a bilateral investment treaty.

I expressed my satisfaction with a smooth implementation of the economic measures that were agreed upon in the last summit meeting. In particular, I noted with gratitude that the U.S. Overseas Private Investment Corporation resumed investment guarantee programs in

Korea and welcomed the productive discussions held through the Korea-U.S. economic subcabinet consultation that resumed in early November, after a hiatus of 3 years.

President Clinton and I also decided to work together to resolve economic and trade issues in a mutually beneficial manner, as seen from the amicable resolution of the automobile talks. We also agreed to make concerted efforts on the basis of internationally agreed principles to expand electronic commerce and to resolve the Y2K problem. Through extra meetings and other means, our two countries will closely cooperate in these areas as well.

Fourth, President Clinton and I decided to work together towards a closer partnership in regional and global issues. As part of these efforts, we agreed to search for measures to simultaneously foster democracy and market economy in Asia. In this regard, we decided to create a democracy forum to bring together young leaders from the Asian region, led by the U.S. National Endowment for Democracy and the Korean Sejong Research Institute. The two institutions will continue to work out further details.

At the same time, President Clinton and I shared the view that coordination through the Asia-Pacific Economic Cooperation forum, APEC, and other multilateral institutions is needed, and agreed to work together closely to overcome the East Asian economic crisis.

Likewise, we found today that our views over a wide range of issues are in total accord. In this respect, I believe today's meeting was a valuable opportunity to deepen the close policy coordination and the mutual trust between the two countries.

Thank you.

President Clinton. First of all, I would like to thank President Kim for making the American delegation feel so welcome here in Korea. The importance of our relationship with Korea is evidenced by the fact that this is the second meeting President Kim and I have had in just a few months and that I am accompanied on this trip by a very distinguished delegation, including five Members of our United States Congress, who are here with me today, and many distinguished members of our administration. We all view President Kim as one of the world's great champions of democracy, an inspiration because of his longstanding faith, his firmness, his capacity for forgiveness, and his foresight, which I have seen again today.

We did a lot of work today to advance our common commitments and interests. Much of it has already been described by the President, but I would like to say a few words.

First, with regard to security, our goal is what it has always been, a peaceful Korea, part of a prosperous Asia. America stands by its unshakable alliance with the Republic of Korea. The alliance is based on a history of shared sacrifice and a future of united purpose, to defend freedom and to secure a stable and permanent peace on this Peninsula.

President Kim and I continue to support an approach that is a clear-eyed mix of diplomacy, through the four-party talks and President Kim's engagement policy; nonproliferation, through the agreed framework and the missile talks; and deterrence against North Korean aggression, through our defense cooperation.

I support President Kim's policy of gradual engagement with North Korea. The four-party peace talks offer the best avenue to a lasting settlement, but they demand tremendous patience and perseverance. Both President Kim and I, as you heard him say, are convinced that the agreed framework is the best way to prevent North Korea from developing nuclear weapons, provided Pyongyang abides by its commitments.

Now, North Korea's recent actions, including the Taepodong missile launch and the construction of a suspect underground facility, are cause for deep concern. We have made it clear to Pyongyang that it must satisfy our concerns and that further provocations will threaten the progress we have made.

The President and I, as he said, also addressed economics. Let me, first of all, say that the people of the United States extend their great support and understanding for all the pain and dislocation the people of Korea have endured in this economic crisis. But we admire the tough choices that President Kim's administration has made to address the financial crisis and to put Korea back on the path to economic growth. We also admire the support that average citizens here have given to making tough choices for a better tomorrow. It is encouraging to us that interest rates have fallen and Korea's currency has stabilized.

The U.S. has worked to support Korea's efforts with bilateral assistance and through the IMF and the multilateral development banks. To aid trade and investment, our Export-Import Bank, whose Director is here with us today, has offered an unprecedented $4 billion in credit, which over the next 2 years will support $8 billion in exports. The Overseas Private Investment Corporation has reopened its operations here to help the return of private investment. And we have just agreed to expand our agricultural export credits.

Earlier this week we joined with Japan to create the Asian growth and recovery initiative to help accelerating restructuring in the corporate and financial sectors, to help to work through the debt so that private sector growth can occur again here and throughout Asia.

And we particularly want to support President Kim's efforts to protect the most vulnerable members of Korean society. I know that Korea has endured much pain and still has a difficult road to travel, including reforming the financial sector, facilitating corporate restructuring, getting all the people back to work. The United States will support your efforts. It is very important that all segments of this society, including all the conglomerates, pay their part, as well. The President cannot do this alone. The Government cannot do this alone. The people, with all their good wishes, still need the help of all segments of this society.

The United States looks to Korea for its leadership in maintaining and expanding open markets during Asia's economic difficulties. We are especially grateful for Korea's leadership in APEC and supporting our sectoral liberalization initiative that we have in common.

At the same time, we also hope Korea will continue to open its markets, resist the temptation to protectionism. As President Kim said, we are very encouraged by the recent agreement to open Korea's automobile markets to American manufacturers. And I did ask the President to make sure we have special care to prevent unfair trade practices or subsidization in sensitive sectors like steel and semiconductors.

Let me finally say that President Kim is one of the world's most eloquent advocates for the proposition that democracy and prosperity must go hand in hand. Here in Asia, countries that are responding to the financial crisis by deepening their democracy, Korea, Thailand, for example, are faring better because the difficult solutions they propose have more legitimacy with their people. Over the long run, democracy and good governance will be vital to economic growth. The information-driven economies of the 21st century will be measuring the true wealth of their nations by the free flow of ideas and creativity.

Therefore, as President Kim has said, I welcome, too, the establishment here in Korea of a new forum on democracy and free markets to be led by the Korean Sejong Institute and our own NED.

I also want to thank President Kim for Korea's many contributions to peacekeeping, its defense of human rights and democracy in places like Burma, its growing support for the fight against global warming. We are proud of our strong alliance with Korea, proud that Korea has a visionary President willing to take on the challenges of today and the dreams of tomorrow. And we are committed to maintaining and improving our partnership in security, in economics, in the pursuit of freedom and democracy.

Thank you very much.

South Korean official. Thank you very much. And now your questions, please. First, a Korean reporter, and then a foreign reporter; we'll take turns. For the Korean reporters, I will be giving the speaking turns. For the foreign, American reporters, the White House spokesman will be giving the turns.

North Korea

Q. Regarding engagement vis-a-vis the North, both of you are actively supportive of engagement. There are positive and negative signs. The Kumgang Mountain tourism development is a positive sign. But on the other hand, we have suspicions about its underground construction site. President Kim, without the nature of the underground construction site having been ascertained, do you still plan to stay with engagement? How far can you go?

And President Clinton, I know there are hardliners in Congress vis-a-vis the North. The Congress has said that unless the suspicion is alleviated by May, it will be cutting its support for the heavy fuel oil to the North. Given the situation, do you think you will be able to ascertain the exact nature of the underground facilities?

President Kim. I will be answering first. North Korea, as you have said, is showing two sides, both negative and positive sides. Let us discuss the positive side first. As you know, the Kumgang Mountain tourism ship is in the North.

The tourism program is smoothly on track. This project was made possible because the

North Korean leader, Kim Jong-il, personally met with the honorary chairman of Hyundai to conclude the agreement on this project. This, to us, indicates a significant change in the North Korean attitude.

Secondly, the military armistice commission, which was halted during the past 7 years, has been revived under a different name. We now call it the general officers talks, but it carries out the same functions. So the military dialog has been resumed.

Thirdly, over the suspected underground construction site, the United States continues to engage the North in dialog.

And fourth, the North Korean Constitution has been amended to introduce elements of the market economy. And given the nature of the North Korean regime, a very stiff ideologue regime which rules by ideology, the changes in the Constitution is very significant.

And finally, in the four-party talks—in the third plenary of the four-party talks, the four sides reached agreement to establish two subcommittees to discuss peace on the Korean Peninsula. These are the positive developments.

But as you say, there are the negative signs. For example, the infiltration of North Korean submarines into our territorial waters. The suspected underground construction site is another negative indication. And of course, the Taepodong missile launching has raised tension not only on the Korean Peninsula but in Japan and the United States; it was a great shock. These are some of the negative developments.

Thus, for the positive signals, we should further encourage that; we should try to build upon those positive signs. But on the negative side, these are all serious issues, especially the construction site, the suspicion over the construction site. We must require full access and ways to ascertain the nature and the purposes of the construction site. If it is, in fact, proven that it is nuclear-related, we should demand immediate closedown.

On missiles, too, we must urge for solutions, for talks with the North toward resolving the issue. So we must be firm on these issues, and depending on how the North reacts, responds to these requirements, the United States, Korea, and Japan and the other countries can consult and come out with a common response.

Thank you.

President Clinton. I will be very brief. You asked about the feeling in our Congress. I do believe that next year when the time for review comes up, if there is a conviction in the United States Congress that North Korea has not kept its commitments under the agreed framework or has done other things which, in effect, make our efforts to resolve nuclear and other issues doomed to failure, then there will be great reluctance to continue to fund the American responsibilities under the agreed framework.

That's why it's so important that we get access to this site, this questionable site where, I want to make it clear, we have strong information that raises a suspicion, but no one yet knows for sure, at least in our camp, what the facility is and what its intended purpose is, specifically. But it raises a strong suspicion. We need access to it.

Now, let me back up one step and just make two points very quickly. First point: To date, the agreed framework has done its job. We are convinced that without the agreement to prevent the reprocessing of spent nuclear fuel rods, North Korea already would have produced a sizable amount of weapons-grade plutonium. Also, the agreement framework has given us a forum, if you will, a means to deal with other issues: the MIA remains, terrorism, the four-party talks, and the missile issue, which is very important as well.

So, could missile launches without notification, the construction of suspect facilities, other provocations undermine the policy we are pursuing? Of course, it could. I have appointed my former Defense Secretary, Bill Perry, as our Special Coordinator for Korea Policy to intensify our efforts to make sure we have the best possible policy. But if it does not work, it will be because of actions by the North Koreans.

I am absolutely convinced that President Kim has done the right thing. I am absolutely convinced that the policies we have followed together have been correct. And it would be a sad thing, indeed, if for no good end over the long run the North Koreans were to make it impossible for us to go forward, because this is the right way forward.

Situation in Iraq

Q. Mr. President, in another trouble spot, Iraq today balked at a U.N. request for documents relating to its weapons program and laid out conditions for the U.N. inspectors. Is this a breach of Iraq's promise for unconditional cooperation and what would be the consequences?

President Clinton. Well, first of all, I think it's important that we not overreact here on the first day. I want to make sure that I know exactly what the facts are. I believe that—the one thing that I would like to say, though, to Iraq and to the world, is that we think there are some affirmative obligations here. For most of the last several years, including the time when I've been President and the time before I was President, when most people would say that Iraq was cooperating with UNSCOM, their idea of cooperation was not to do anything affirmative to prevent UNSCOM from moving around a country that is a very large country. But for most of the time, they took no affirmative steps, as was their duty under the United Nations resolutions.

Now, I think that Mr. Butler is a professional person. They are testing Iraq's commitments. And I hope that Iraq will comply, as it said it would in the letters just a few days ago, with the letter and the spirit of the U.N. resolutions, and give them the information they seek. Now, if they have some independent grounds for objecting to some of this information—that is, if they think it's some effort to find out something having nothing to do with matters covered by the U.N. resolutions—they ought to say that, and then we should immediately resolve it.

But if they want the sanctions lifted because they have complied with all the U.N. resolutions on weapons, they have to give the information on the documents. And the longer they take to come up with the information on the documents and get to the bottom of this, the harder it's going to be to convince everyone else that they should get what they want.

So this documentation, this information issue, is quite important. I will get extensively briefed on it, and we'll see where the other folks are on it. But I think the important thing is, Mr. Butler is a professional, and he's clearly trying to get information that he believes is essential to do his job. And I think the rest of us should support that.

North Korea

Q. First of all, North Korea's long-range missiles development—a question to President Clinton. According to Washington Post, according to Madam Albright's comment, North Korea's long-range missile development is a cause of great concern. She says that relations with the North are at a critical point. It represented a rather hard-line stance. The American administration, in cooperation with our Government, has maintained engagement vis-a-vis the North, but in light of these comments, the recent comments, and in light of President Clinton's remark that the North must cooperate in the efforts to ascertain the nature of the suspected facilities to our satisfaction, does this in fact require a change in your stance vis-a-vis the North?

President Clinton. Is that a question for me or President Kim?

Q. That was a question to you, Mr. President.

President Clinton. I don't see this as a change. I see this as the potential for changed circumstances; that is, we have proceeded on the assumption that we would be making progress and that North Korea would honor the agreed framework as we have honored it and others have. We just had a very hopeful development in Japan, for example, where the Japanese Government agreed to put in a very large amount of money to support the KEDO project, again in furtherance of this agreement we made with North Korea.

So let me say again, I do not want to change policy. I support what President Kim is trying to do here. I think it is a wise policy, and I hope that the North Koreans will not do anything to force us to change policy.

Indonesia

Q. Mr. President, more than a dozen people have died in Indonesia in the last 10 days in clashes between protesters and Indonesian military forces. In your view, is President Habibie moving fast enough on political and economic reform? And are the Indonesian forces using excessive force in confronting the protesters?

President Clinton. On the second question, I think the candid answer is the best. I don't know that I have enough facts at this moment to give you the right answer.

On the first, all I can tell you is that there have been some hopeful signs over the last several months and some troubling signs coming out of Indonesia. I think if you look at the experience—I'll tell you what I hope will happen. If you look at the experience of Korea and the terrible difficulties the Korean people have endured, it is a profound argument in favor of having a government lead its people through tough times with the support of the people, not relying on power wielded in a military fash-

ion but relying on the spirit and the support of the people.

And so I think the important thing is that the United States hopes very much that there will be no backsliding as we come up into the election season in Indonesia, and that every effort will be made to minimize any harm to people who are exercising their voices to make their political views heard.

North Korea

Q. President Kim, during your visit to the U.S. in June, President Clinton and you, I believe, discussed the easing of economic sanctions to the North. Was this issue discussed during today's meeting?

President Kim. During our meeting today, there was no mention regarding the easing of sanctions, but there were some—in the discussion I think you can find answers to your question. As of now, North Korea, should it continue to engage in troublesome activities, we will deal with a firm, resolute attitude. If it responds to our calls for peace and cooperation, then we will return that with cooperative measures.

That was the extent to which our discussions went. The suspicion over the North Korean suspected underground site, on missiles—if the North responds in a cooperative fashion to our requirements in these regards, then, of course, we can respond with positive incentives, favorable responses. And I think the spirit of such an attitude is quite clear in the statement that the two of us made today.

President Clinton. I know you didn't ask me a question, but I would like to say something to support President Kim here.

Yesterday when we came here, our whole American delegation, including all the members of the press, a lot of us went into our rooms, and we turned on the television. And what was the picture? The picture was the tourist ship going into the North. Right? That's what the picture was. To us, this was amazing, and it was a very beautiful picture.

Now, what is the picture in our minds in this press conference? It is of some hole in the ground somewhere in North Korea where something might or might not be done, which might or might not be threatening to us in the future. Now, I ask you—I ask the North Koreans to think about this—they have a great opportunity here, an historic opportunity with the leadership of President Kim and the position that he has taken. We strongly support it. Never, nothing could ever be put into that hole in the ground—given our defense partnership here, nothing could ever be put in that hole in the ground that would give the North Koreans as much advantage, as much power, as much wealth, as much happiness as more of those ships going up there full of people from here. I think that is the most important message I would like to leave with you today.

Impeachment Inquiry

Q. Mr. President, you said before that it's up to Congress to decide your fate, but you have also said that you want to restore honor to your Presidency and bring closure to the Nation. Sir, do you personally believe that you should face some kind of punishment and that this requires some kind of punishment to bring closure to the Nation, like an apology before Congress?

President Clinton. Well, first of all, again I say, there has been a lot of suffering—that is different from punishment, although it's hard to see the difference sometimes as you're going through it. For me, this long ago ceased to be a political issue or a legal issue and became a personal one. And every day I do my best to put it right, personally.

It is simply not appropriate at this time, in my view, for me to comment on what the Congress should do. The American people and Congress can—I hope will do the right—I trust the American people, and I hope Congress will do the right thing in a nonpolitical way, if you will, to get beyond the partisanship and go on.

I do believe that the long-awaited acknowledgment that there is nothing on which to proceed in the travel issue and the file issue and Whitewater—which this matter was supposed to be about—is a positive thing. I think, surely, it will help us to get this over with. But my only concern, as I said, is that we get this behind us and go on with the business of the country. But I think the less I say about what should happen to me at this point, the better. To me it's—I need to focus on the work I came here to do, and others need to make that decision.

NOTE: The President's 166th news conference began at 1:53 p.m. in the Press Conference Hall at the Blue House. In his remarks, he referred to Richard Butler, executive chairman, United Nations Special Commission (UNSCOM); and President Bacharuddin Jusuf Habibie of Indonesia. President Kim referred to Chung Ju-yung, founder and honorary chairman, Hyundai Group conglomerate. President Kim spoke in Korean, and his remarks were translated by an interpreter.

Remarks in a Roundtable Discussion With Community Leaders in Seoul
November 21, 1998

The President. Thank you. First of all, I would like to thank all of you for coming here today to meet with us. I wanted to have an opportunity while I was in Korea to hear directly from some people who are living through these changes and who have different views and different experiences that I would hope you would share with me, because I want very much to understand how what is happening in Korea today and where you are going actually affects the lives of the people here in this country. And so that is why I wanted to do this. I thank you for being brave enough to come here and do this. Thank you for helping us.

And I want to thank Senator Baucus and Assistant Secretary Koh for joining me; he's coming home—[*laughter*]—and Senator Baucus and I feel at home here. And I want to thank my Ambassador. So maybe you guys could come around, and we could begin the meeting. I think we're through with the photos.

Ambassador Steven W. Bosworth. Mr. President, you spoke earlier of your admiration for the resolute spirit with which Korean people are responding to what President Kim Dae-jung has described as the most serious crisis in Korea since the Korean war. And I think we're fortunate to have a group of people around this table this afternoon who can give you some insight into how Korea is handling this crisis, what does the future look like here, and how individual

Koreans and individual Korean companies are responding to what is happening here.

And I don't have any particular order. If you care to say anything to begin, other than what you've already said, or if perhaps some of our guests would care to speak, then we can have what I hope will be a conversation.

The President. I would only like to make two points: first of all, that all over the world today, even where there is a good economy, in the places where this financial crisis has not hit, even there, there is a tension between getting the benefits of the global economy and the information revolution, and preserving, if you will, the social contract, the stability of life that honors work and family and community. And so one of the great challenges that we face is how to get the benefits of this emerging economy and still preserve an appropriate level of social cohesion and stability. And it's even an issue in the wealthiest countries of the world, you know, the ones that have not had any.

The second point I wish to make is that if you look at what has happened in Asia, in every case there are reasons which are unique to the country—that is, there are some problems that are particular to the country—but there are also common problems which cross the lines of country and which warn us very clearly that there must be, at least in my opinion, a global response not only to the present crisis but to the long-term need to adapt the financial system of the world to the realities of the 21st century, so that we do not have this kind of thing occurring again, sweeping across national lines. And I think there are some things that we have done and some things we can do to do that.

So what is important for me—of course, I want you to say whatever it is you would like to say to me, but what I am trying to do is to understand exactly what is happening here, your perspective on it, how it happened, why, and what you think either should be done further in Korea or what you believe the United States should do or advocate.

[*Ambassador Bosworth opened the discussion. Chang Ha Sung, chairman, Committee for Economic Democratization, said that although South Korea had accomplished economic growth, it was a relatively small nation, and in order to maintain an open and liberalized economy, it needed action from international institutions to stabilize the international financial market.*]

The President. I agree with that. Who would like to go next?

[*Park In-sang, president, Federation of Korean Trade Unions, agreed in acknowledging the internal causes of the South Korean economic and financial crisis but recognizing that the international financial market played a role as well. He emphasized that the United States must maintain a stable economy; discussed the importance of the steel industry to South Korea's economy; and urged the United States to be more patient concerning Korean steel exports.*]

The President. Maybe I could respond just for a minute. I would like to save my answer to Professor Chang until along toward the end because I want to talk more about the financial issues then. But I would like to just answer the steel question and the import question.

First of all, when Asia began to have such difficulties—about a year ago now, I remember, it was really getting bad. On our Thanksgiving holiday—which is next Thursday—last year, I spent 3 or 4 hours working on the problem in Indonesia. It became obvious to us that this problem would affect a lot of Asian countries and Russia. And so we made a decision, our Government did, that we would first try to stop the problem from spreading; second, we would try to help individual countries recover; and third, we would look at the long-term causes of this and the long-term changes in the world economic system that needed to be made.

Now, we made a deliberate decision that we would make every effort to keep our markets as open as possible, even though we knew our trade deficit would go way up. For example, in the case of Korea, Korean imports into the U.S. are up, and U.S. exports to Korea this year are about one-half what they were last year, about $12 billion or $13 billion less. But that's OK—that's understandable because of the economic problems.

I say that just to tell you, sir, that what we're trying to do is to help all the Asian economies and the Russian economy and others by keeping our own economic growth going, but also keeping our doors open so we can buy products in tough times and help our trading partners.

Now, here is the problem. If we have a big increase in our overall trade deficit and it's evenly spread, that's something we can live with for a year or two. But as a practical matter, if it's all concentrated in one or two areas, then our industries, which are in normal times quite productive, could be put out of business, and they could find a very hard time getting back in business when the economy improves, because of the cost of starting up.

We went through a big restructuring in our steel industry in the 1980's. We cut employment a lot. It was very painful for our union members and for our executives. And we have been doing pretty well. And you have to see the Korean experience, which is basically about a 140 percent increase, 120 percent increase in exports to America in steel this year, against the background of what's happening from other countries. In Japan there is a 500 percent increase in hot-rolled steel products; in Russia, 300 percent increase; a big increase from Brazil. So we have the American steel industry saying, "Okay, we want you to buy more products from other countries. We want you to help them in this tough time. But if it's all coming at our expense, when in normal times we are quite competitive, then what happens when normal times recover and we're not around anymore?"

So that's what I'm trying to—we're trying to balance that. So I guess what I'm saying, President Park, is, I agree with you. The United States should keep our markets open to the rest of the world and help our friends deal with this crisis. But we have to be sensitive if the price of doing that would be to basically erase a big part of our economy which then could not come back when normal times recovered. So we're trying to balance two difficult things.

[*Ambassador Bosworth called on Sohn Bong Sook, director, Center for Korean Women in Politics, who stated that women were the first to get laid off because they were not viewed as the breadwinners of the household, and that unemployment in general contributed to the erosion of traditional family values. She stressed that political corruption was one of the main causes of the economic problem and that further economic deterioration would act as a barrier to further democratic development. Park Yong-oh, chairman, Doosan Corp., described the 100-year-old firm's restructuring efforts, which began in 1995, and praised President Kim's commitment to restructuring to strengthen Korea's competitiveness.*]

The President. Can you tell us exactly what you did? In the restructuring, did you change the organization of your company; did you re-duce the layers of administration; did you reorganize the way the workers were working? How did you restructure your company? What were the two or three most important elements of your restructuring?

[*Chairman Park described selling off joint ventures and real estate holdings; reducing the work force through an early retirement program and strengthened pension programs; and merging nine separate companies into one. Park Byung Yeop, president, Pantech, said that as president of a small company, he thought the country's focus on big companies had contributed to the crisis, but that the Korean Government's restructuring program was on the right track. He stated that smaller companies would be the driving force for further growth of the Korean economy, noting that Motorola, one of the biggest telecommunications firms in Korea, had invested in his company. Yoo Seong-min, director, Korean Development Institute, stated that conglomerates were the unique characteristic of the Korean economy, contributing to development in the past as well as to the current crisis, and that while restructuring and reform efforts had been criticized for being too slow, he believed that moving too fast would have some bad effects. He then asked how the United States had harmonized economic development with political democratization.*]

The President. Well, first of all, I would like to say in response to the last comments that you made, that it is both my experience over the last 25 years and my observation of our history and global economic history that there is no economic model that succeeds forever, not in a business or in a country, because the very nature of the economy is the dynamic.

So I think that Korea should not, in effect, rewrite its own successful history. You have— this country has done some very great things in the last few decades since the end of the Korean war. And no economic model succeeds forever. I mean, keep in mind, today people come up to me and they say, all over the world, "Oh, America is doing so great." Well, you know, 10 years ago people were saying, "Oh, America is in decline, and they can't do anything right." Things change. So the trick is how to make the necessary changes and preserve the purpose of economic activity, which is to advance the quality of life, to lift people's lives.

So that's just a general observation. Now, I think Chairman Park made a very valuable point, which is that it takes time to change an organization if you wish to preserve the integrity of the organization and you want it to work and also if you don't want to hurt a lot of people. He cut the size of his operation by 50 percent, so if you want to do that, it takes time.

From my point of view, my impatience on the restructuring of the big five, I would say it should take time, and we should be patient, but they should begin. They should begin. That's what we're interested in. Are they going to begin?

From the point of view of President Park over here who was talking about his new business and his partnership with Motorola, I believe that one of the things that we should be very sensitive to in the United States, particularly dealing with Korea, since we have been through a lot of this, is if your big companies are going to restructure and reduce employment to increase profitability and their ability to compete, then I think it is very important that there be systems in this country that encourage the creation of more new companies. That's what you were talking about.

In the U.S., one of the most important parts of our economy is the so-called venture capital economy, where we have new companies being created all the time or smaller businesses being expanded all the time. And so I think it's important, even though there have been a lot of bad bank loans and people are worried about bad bank loans and everything, we have to realize, when all this is said and done, you must still have a good credit system here where people who have something to do should be able to borrow money to do it. I think that's very important.

The last point I would like to make is that—just about what all of you have said—is to go back to what Dr. Sohn said about the women. The more rapidly an economy or a society changes, whether it's going up or going down but especially if it's going down, the more strains will be put on family life.

Now, I believe at least, the most important work of any society is the raising of children. And in a funny way, we have opposite problems. Many people believe in America too many of our parents are in the work force, so nobody is home with the children. But in most Asian societies it's a good thing if you can have more opportunities—job opportunities for women so there can be some more balance and more income to raise the children.

So I think it would be a very good thing—I don't have the answers to this. What I have seen, though, in our own experience, is that there is no perfect answer, but there is a good process. And a good process is one that takes full account of the interests and feelings and ideas and opinions of the women of the society.

That is, what would be the best answer for Korea would not be the best answer for Thailand, would not be the best answer for the United States. But there is a good process. And in too many places in the world today, women are used economically when it's convenient and then discarded when it's not, and their voices aren't heard. And I think that's a mistake. So I think what you're doing is very important.

I wonder if Senator Baucus or Secretary Koh would like to say anything.

[Senator Max Baucus praised South Korea's accomplishments since the Korean war.]

The President. It's amazing. There's no other place in the world——

[Senator Baucus suggested that the Korean Government should not only be concerned about producers but also empower consumers to contribute to a dialog about how to address the economic crisis. Harold H. Koh, U.S. Assistant Secretary of State for Democracy, Human Rights, and Labor, then recalled his 1974 visit to South Korea, during a similar period of economic hardship in which people favored export-led growth controlled by an authoritarian government. He praised South Korea's new commitment to do it with democracy. Ambassador Bosworth asked for closing remarks, and labor leader Park In-sang stated that President Kim Dae-jung had broken away from the military and authoritarian approach of the past, and that from the labor perspective democracy was very important for economic growth. He then expressed concern that the U.S. military might cut 2,000 jobs in South Korea and asked for President Clinton's help on this issue. Dr. Sohn praised President Clinton's appointment of a female Secretary of State, saying it influenced other countries. She concluded that South Korea's nongovernmental organizations would play

an even more important role in such a transitional stage.]

The President. Thank you. She has done quite a wonderful job, our Secretary of State. And we have six women in the Cabinet now, including the Attorney General and the Secretary of Health and Social Services, the Secretary of Labor, the head of the Environmental Protection Agency, and the head of the Council of Economic Advisers, and our Trade Representative—seven women in the Cabinet—our Trade Representative. We're better for it. They're very good. Thank you.

Ambassador Bosworth. Mr. President, do you have any concluding remarks you would like to make?

The President. Does anyone else want to speak before we go?

[*A participant stated that the majority of South Koreans had confidence in the market economy and democracy, although the Korean family structure was suffering, and asked for the President's help in the areas of unemployment policy and corporate accountability regarding the work force.*]

The President. Anything else?

[*A participant said that Korea-U.S. trade was important to both economies and asked for continued support and assistance from the United States.*]

The President. You may be sure that we will do that. I think that we have to do more in many ways. We just announced a U.S.-Japan Asian economic initiative to try to work with the World Bank—I mean, the IMF—to help restructure some debt in countries where you have to restructure corporate and business debt, longer term repayments, do things that will keep employment up. We have more active presence of our Export-Import Bank and our Overseas Private Investment Corporation to try to facilitate economic activity in Korea. I think all this is important.

But I also believe it's quite important, if you're going to get into this restructuring of the conglomerates, you have to also say, where are the jobs going to come from? And part of what Senator Baucus was saying, that means you have to have a strong consumer ethic in the country, as well as a savings ethic.

But I believe some real attention needs to be given—and I would support this—toward

analyzing whether the banking system has adequate credit for businesses like yours for startups, for expansions, for going on, because the Korean people are so innovative, they work so hard, they're so gifted at economic things naturally, that if the system is open properly, I think you could have quite a quick recovery. So I think that ought to be looked at.

I just want to say one final thing about this. I haven't mentioned it, and we don't have time to talk about it now. But the rest of us—the United States and Europe, Japan, and Korea as an OECD member—we have responsibilities to deal with the problems that would be there if you solved all these issues. If there were none of these issues we just talked about, fast-growing countries would still be vulnerable to the kind of suffering you've seen because of the way money moves around the world today.

You talked to me about the trade issue in steel. Now, steel—let's just take steel, for example—any product. It's traded across the world under a set of rules governed by the WTO that basically readopted the last system in 1995—or '94, I guess, December of '94, the present WTO—in the United States, at least, we did. But it's essentially an outgrowth of a 50-year-old system. From the end of World War II, we established these institutions for trade in goods and services—the IMF, the World Bank, the trading rules—and to help countries that were struggling like that.

Money has to be able to move around the world if you're going to trade in goods and services. But one big problem is that now $1.5 trillion is traded every day in currency—trillion dollars—and money can move very rapidly. So if the Korean conglomerates or Korean banks, you know, well, they have a big demand for money, the money comes in. And there is a lot of enthusiasm because Korea has been growing for 30 years and no problem, you know. Then the problems come up, and boom, the money goes away. And if people lose money, then maybe they have to take money out of other countries, too, to cover their losses. To make matters more complex, a lot of this money is traded or moved on a very small margin, sometimes only 10 percent.

Now, there are no rules in the global economy comparable to the trading rules that govern our business in steel. Eventually—let's suppose we have this big argument about steel; eventually we have to go back to the rules. And whatever the deal is, it's limited; there's some limit on both sides so we can go on and do our business.

In this area, there aren't that many rules, and it has created a serious problem that makes every country, particularly the Asian countries because you've got so much money coming in, highly vulnerable to all the money going out. And what we have to do is to find a set of rules about, well, what do people have a right to know when they get loans, how are these loans going to be priced, should there be margin requirements on the derivatives and the hedge funds and all this sort of stuff, and all these things.

We don't have time to get into the details. The only point I want to make is, I would recommend that you focus very closely on what you should be doing in Korea, both within your own area and in the society at large. But don't be fooled; when $1.5 trillion is moving around the world every day, then the possibility for instability is great. And we need a set of rules that will enable the financial system to grow in the same way that the trading and investment system has grown, so you can have high levels of growth but still some limits to avoid a big

collapse. And that's one of the things we're trying to do. And you should not blame yourself for that, because the situation here is worse than it would have been because of the volatility and size of the financial crisis. The same thing is true everywhere. We have to keep the money flowing, but we have to figure out how to keep it from getting out of hand.

Ambassador Bosworth. Mr. President, I think you've just given us the subject for our next roundtable. [*Laughter*]

I want first of all to thank our Korean friends for joining us here this afternoon. I want to thank you, Mr. President, for giving us all the opportunity to have such a stimulating discussion. And I want to thank Senator Baucus and Secretary Koh for joining us as well. I want to thank you, Mr. President, in particular, for giving me the opportunity to serve as your representative in this country at this fascinating time. It is truly a life experience. Thank you all.

The President. I envy you. It's a good job. Thank you all very much.

NOTE: The President spoke at 3:40 p.m. at the National Folk Museum. The discussion participants spoke in Korean, and their remarks were translated by an interpreter.

Remarks at a Dinner Hosted by President Kim Dae-jung of South Korea in Seoul
November 21, 1998

Mr. President, thank you for your kind words and your kind welcome to Korea. I am very conscious that this visit, my third to Korea as President, comes at a pivotal time in the history of this great nation. In that regard, Mr. President, I would like to thank you for giving my fellow Americans and me the opportunity to have dinner tonight with such a broad range of people from every aspect of Korean society. And especially, thank you for having so many young people here, for it is their lives that will be most affected by the decisions we must make.

First, this is a moment of opportunity, on the 50th anniversary of your Republic, to complete what you, Mr. President, have called Ko-

rea's second nation building, securing in freedom the gains of your remarkable postwar transformation. It is also a challenging moment, for the Korean people have suffered from the whims of economic disruption and dislocation that have blown so strongly throughout all Asia. We in the United States have been heartened by the signs that your efforts at reform and recovery are beginning to succeed.

Mr. President, if Korea is on the right path— and I believe it is—it is not simply because economists have given good advice and leaders have made wise choices. More fundamentally, it is because a free people have given their leaders a mandate to confront problems with candor and the legitimacy to call for shared sacrifices.

Of course, there are still some who say that democracy is a luxury people can afford only when times are good. But Korea is proving that democracy can provide the necessary support for action when times are difficult.

At least one person in this room has known that truth for a long, long time. You, Mr. President, have committed a lifetime to the idea that liberty and prosperity can go hand in hand. For this, you were once treated as a dangerous criminal. But we all know that Kim Dae-jung was imprisoned not for crimes against his country but for his devotion to his country and his determination to put Korea's destiny into the hands of its people.

Now, Mr. President, look how your trust in the people has been rewarded. They have transferred you from a prison cell to the Blue House—although, if I might say, only partly in jest, on the hard days I imagine being in this job can feel like a form of solitary confinement. But this is a burden you have chosen to bear. What challenges you have embraced: protecting the security of your people while engaging their relatives in the North, restoring Korea's economy to growth while meeting human needs, and always maintaining the spirit of democracy.

Many years ago, President Kim said these words: "There are several paths to the mountaintop. During the course of climbing, the path we have chosen may seem to be the most treacherous, and the others may seem quite easy. There will be constant temptations to change course, but one should not succumb to them. Once on the mountaintop, there will be freedom to choose which path to follow on the descent."

All across Asia people once wondered which path Korea would choose. Now, Korea's answer—your answer, Mr. President—is helping to define what Asia's path will be in the 21st century. I believe Asia will emerge from this present crisis more prosperous, more stable, more democratic, thanks in no small measure to Korea's example.

Mr. President, we look forward to walking with you into the future, through hard times and good times, as allies, as friends, as pathfinders.

I ask now that all of you join me in a toast of appreciation to President Kim and to the people of Korea, and to the values and the future our nations will share.

NOTE: The President spoke at 7:50 p.m. in the State Banquet Room at the Blue House. The transcript released by the Office of the Press Secretary also included the remarks of President Kim. A tape was not available for verification of the content of these remarks.

The President's Radio Address
November 21, 1998

Good morning. Today I'm speaking to you from Korea. From the time our administration took office in 1993, we have believed it is vital to the future of the United States to look not only to the west but also, as a Pacific power, to the east. First in Tokyo, and now here in Seoul, I have reaffirmed America's commitment to our alliances with Japan and Korea and our resolve to build a safer, better world with our Asian allies.

My confidence that such a world is within our grasp springs in no small measure from my faith in the strength and skill of a remarkable group of Americans, the men and women who serve in our Armed Forces.

Last week, when Saddam Hussein agreed to let international weapons inspectors return to Iraq, he backed down because we backed our diplomacy with force. In Bosnia, where the peace brokered at Dayton is taking hold, American troops are helping to preserve stability. And here on the Korean Peninsula, the last fault line of the cold war, nearly 40,000 Americans are helping Korea defend its freedom.

Tomorrow I'll visit with U.S. troops and their Korean counterparts at the Osan and Yongsan Air Force Bases and the Korea Training Center. I always welcome the opportunity to meet with America's service men and women stationed overseas, especially around holiday time.

Back in Washington, we're working hard to make sure our forces have the resources they need to remain the best in the world. Every time we face a challenge, our Armed Forces deliver for America. It is imperative that we deliver for them by giving our military the support they need and deserve, from cutting-edge technology to the most basic parts, from the best training in the world to a good quality of life.

On Veterans Day I was pleased to release $1.1 billion in readiness funding authorized by Congress. With the support of Congress, we've also obtained nearly $2 billion to support peacekeeping and shifted another billion dollars within the Defense budget for additional readiness. Now, this money will help to ensure that we preserve a high state of readiness for our forward-deployed and first-to-fight forces, while we continue to fund other important initiatives such as quality of life, recruiting, and pay raises.

And we can't rest there. We must also plan for tomorrow's challenges as well as today's. That's why I've ordered a thorough review of our long-term readiness. It will generate budget and policy proposals to preserve readiness, to support our troops, to modernize our equipment well into the next century.

Next week Americans at home and around the world will give thanks for the countless blessings we enjoy today. I'd like to offer particular thanks to those of you serving our country overseas. Thanksgiving week is also Military Family Week. We must never forget that for every individual stationed abroad, an entire family is also serving our country.

On Thanksgiving I will be back in the United States. Like thousands of Americans, I will offer a prayer of gratitude for our troops at home and overseas and their indispensable contribution to freedom. Even when you are far from home, you are close to our hearts.

And especially here in Korea, let me thank our troops. I'm honored to be here representing the United States on a mission of peace and prosperity, with a strong congressional delegation representing many parts of our country. We all wish you the very best. And again, we thank you for your service to America.

Thanks for listening.

NOTE: The address was recorded at 10:10 p.m., local time, on November 20 in the Hyatt Hotel in Seoul, South Korea, for broadcast at 10:06 a.m., e.s.t., on November 21. (Due to the 14-hour time difference, the radio address was broadcast after completion of all other November 21 Presidential activities in South Korea.) The transcript was made available by the Office of the Press Secretary on November 21 but was embargoed for release until the broadcast. In his remarks, the President referred to President Saddam Hussein of Iraq.

Statement on the 1997 Uniform Crime Report
November 22, 1998

The 1997 Uniform Crime Report released by the FBI today shows that murder, rape, robbery, assault, and even juvenile crime fell across the board last year. Serious crime has now fallen for 6 years in a row. With the murder rate down by more than 25 percent since I took office and now at its lowest level in three decades, Americans are safer today than they have been in many years. Our strategy of putting more police on the beat and getting guns off the street is working. Americans have taken back their neighborhoods and shown that rising crime and deadly violence need not be tolerated. But in far too many communities, crime remains a serious problem, and our work is far from done. We must continue the job of putting 100,000 more police on our streets, tougher laws on our books, and more effective crime prevention in our schools. With these efforts, we can keep driving down the crime rates—and keep tipping the scales of justice in favor of law-abiding Americans.

NOTE: This statement was made available by the Office of the Press Secretary on November 21 but was embargoed for release until 9 a.m. on November 22.

Remarks to the Community at Osan Air Force Base, South Korea
November 22, 1998

I think the sergeant did a fine job under unusual circumstances. Let's give him another hand here. [*Applause*] He did tell Congressman Abercrombie not to make his introduction too short, but I think he was a little bit embarrassed by having the truth told.

Sergeant, we thank you for your heroism and your service. We thank two of your fellow airmen who helped you in that rescue mission, Staff Sergeant Thomas Metheny and Brian Stump. And we thank all of you for your service. And we thank all of you for your service.

I want to thank Congressman Abercrombie for his fine remarks. He's here with a delegation that includes Senator Max Baucus of Montana, Congresswoman Patsy Mink of Hawaii, Congressman Earl Pomeroy of North Dakota. Anybody here from North Dakota? There is one man up there with his hand up; another one. The reason I introduce them is it's very warm here, for them, compared to North Dakota. [*Laughter*] And Delegate Robert Underwood from Guam.

General Tilelli, General Hurd, General Dordal, General Dierker; members of the Republic of Korea Armed Forces; Ambassador and Mrs. Bosworth; our Secretary of Commerce, Bill Daley, and the National Security Adviser, Sandy Berger, and all the other members of our administration who are here; the family members and the men and women of the United States Armed Forces, I am honored to be here with you. I'm glad to see you out here in good spirits. I'm sorry you've had to wait awhile in the cold wind, and I'm glad we're starting early.

Let me say that I know that supply is an area of great expertise and importance, but just looking around the crowd today, it seems to me that the parkas are a little unevenly distributed. [*Laughter*] So I'll try to give a fairly brief speech.

What I have to say to you is simple. I am very proud of the work you do, U.S. Forces Korea, the 7th Air Force, the 51st Fighter Wing, all the 607th Group, the 631st Air Mobility Support Squadron, the soldiers and airmen, the sailors and marines, the Korean military personnel who are here, all of you. And I came, more than anything else, to say on behalf of all the American people, we thank you for your service to the United States.

As I also look at this vast sea of highly representative and diverse faces, I am reminded that it was 50 years ago this year, in 1948, when President Harry Truman courageously ordered the integration of America's Armed Forces. Now our Armed Forces are a model of unity and diversity for the entire world, people of different origins coming together, working together, for the common good.

I am proud of that, and so should you be, because though Harry Truman made the decision 50 years ago, it is you 50 years later who have fulfilled his vision and made it work. Osan Air Base is a community with stores and restaurants, homes and classrooms. In fact, back at the White House, we looked on the Internet and found the page of the Osan American High School. Listen to this; this is what the students modestly described their website as. They said it is "the most masterfully designed high school website of them all." I want to commend the designer for his or her extraordinary confidence. [*Laughter*]

I'd also like to commend the Department of Defense school system, one of the unsung heroes of our military service. I thank the teachers and the administrators here and throughout the world for your commitment to our children's future.

Osan Air Base is an important symbol of our commitment to liberty. It was just a few miles from here that United States soldiers first engaged enemy forces in the ground combat of the summer of 1950. And Americans gave their lives in the Korean war on the very grounds of this base. And Osan Air Base is a vital post in our ongoing determined effort to protect that liberty, shoulder to shoulder with our strong Korean allies.

No one should doubt today our joint commitment to freedom. It is stronger than ever. And Korea, under the leadership of President Kim Dae-jung, embodies that, for he as well as any person alive knows that the struggle for freedom requires strength, courage, and a lifetime of dedication. President Kim faced prison and persecution, death threats and death sentences, because he stood up for his belief in democracy and because he would not give up his hope that true democracy could flourish here in Korea. Now our countries work together more closely than ever before for peace and human rights around the world.

And none of that could happen without you, the American and Korean military forces. You have maintained the peace for 45 years. And let me say, again not so much to you because you know it, but through you and the media here to all of the American people back home, sometimes it's easy to forget that even in peacetime, military work is difficult and dangerous. Tensions have gone up and down on this peninsula over the years, but always there are risks.

I talked about, just a moment ago, the distinguished gentleman who introduced me and his fellow airmen who risked their lives to aid others. Just a few weeks ago, 50 miles from here, four Americans and one Korean soldier lost their lives returning from important training missions. Let me say their names: Private Joseph Biondo, Private First Class Joey Brantley, Specialist James Buis, Sergeant Brian Walsh, and Corporal Kim Yong Ku. We honor their service. We mourn their loss in the cause of peace and security. May the American people never forget this work is difficult and dangerous, and we owe you a lot for doing it.

America strongly supports President Kim's strategy of engagement with North Korea. In the 5 years since I last met with our troops along the DMZ, we have seen some hopeful signs. There have been peace talks, and over the summer, for the very first time, United States Command and the North Korean military began general officer talks aimed at preventing problems along the DMZ.

But unfortunately, not all has gone well. Lately, signs of danger have intensified, with incursions from the North, provocative missile tests, and the question of a suspect underground installation. So we must remain vigilant. And thanks to you, we are.

One of the greatest threats the world now faces is weapons of mass destruction. And though our attention lately has been focused on Iraq's efforts in that area, North Korea is also a major concern. Here at Osan, you are critical to this most dangerous battleground, deterring and, if necessary, defending against chemical and biological attacks.

Let me reaffirm the view of the United States: North Korea must maintain its freeze on and move ahead to dismantle its nuclear weapons program, as it has agreed to do. It must comply with its obligations under the Nuclear Non-Proliferation Treaty. It must halt its efforts to develop and proliferate chemical and biological weapons and ballistic missiles.

We will continue to press North Korea to take these steps for peace and security. But until it fully commits itself to a constructive role on this peninsula, we must remain ready. And thanks to you, we will. America will continue to do what it takes to promote the security of our citizens and our friends and allies, to be a force for peace as we have been in Haiti, in Northern Ireland, in Bosnia, in Kosovo, in the Middle East. Our ability to succeed in promoting peace is uniquely due to the fact that we can back up our diplomatic efforts, when necessary, with military strength. And that depends on you, the finest Armed Forces in the world.

We ask so much of you, to travel far from home, to work long hours, to risk your lives. We ask so much of your families, lengthy separations, career and school transitions. We owe an awful lot in return, at least the training and support you need, the tools to do your job—from high-tech equipment to the most basic spare parts—and the quality of life you deserve.

I spend a lot of time addressing these issues with Secretary of Defense Cohen, with General Shelton of the Joint Chiefs, with other leaders of our military. While our current state of readiness is sound, we have to ensure we're prepared for the future. To move us in the right direction, I asked the Congress to approve $1.1 billion in additional funds for readiness and recruitment in this year's budget. And I'm happy to say the Congress came through.

We obtained almost $2 billion in emergency funds to cover unanticipated operations in Bosnia. We shifted another $1 billion in existing defense funds to readiness needs. I've asked Secretary Cohen to prepare budget and policy proposals aimed at addressing these needs for the long term. And I've approved pay raises that will significantly reduce the gap between military and civilian pay. [*Applause*] I ought to quit while I'm ahead. [*Laughter*]

I want you to know that, working with Congress and the Joint Chiefs, we will continue to make our top priority your readiness: readiness for our first-to-fight forces like the soldiers I met earlier today from the 2d Infantry Division; readiness for our sailors in ships at sea, so vital to our efforts, particularly now, to contain the weapons of mass destruction threat of Saddam Hussein; readiness for our strategic and tactical air forces, crucial in meeting our security challenges in the Gulf, in Bosnia, here in Korea, indeed, all around the world.

Thursday is Thanksgiving. I know that your loved ones back home are thinking about you here, proud of your accomplishments, your service, your kindness, and your strength. I'm happy today to be bringing to you some prepaid phone cards generously provided by AT&T so you can call your families and friends across the ocean for free.

I hope that all Americans—all Americans, not just those who receive a call on Thanksgiving Day—as they sit down to their turkey and give thanks for all our blessings, will consider the debt of gratitude we all owe to our men and women in uniform. You have made the world a better place, and you will continue to do so. You have made us very proud, and we will continue to be very proud.

I thank you. I wish you well. God bless you, and God bless America.

NOTE: The President spoke at 3:46 p.m. at the U–2 hangar. In his remarks, he referred to M. Sgt. Tony Avalos, flight engineer, 31st Special Operations Squadron, who introduced the President and was credited with saving the lives of two aircraft crash victims in June; Gen. John H. Tilelli, Jr., USA, Commander in Chief, United Nations Command, United States Forces Korea, and Combined Forces Command Korea; Lt. Gen. Joseph E. Hurd, USAF, Commander, and Brig. Gen. Paul R. Dordal, USAF, Vice Commander, 7th Air Force; Brig. Gen. Robert Dierker, USAF, Commander, 51st Fighter Wing; and U.S. Ambassador to South Korea Steven W. Bosworth and his wife, Christine. A tape was not available for verification of the content of these remarks.

Remarks to Micronesian Island Leaders in Agaña Heights, Guam
November 23, 1998

Thank you very much, Governor and Geri. Ladies and gentlemen, I'm delighted to be here. I want to begin by thanking Dan and Ehlysa for their wonderful art work, and all the other children who gave me this. I will read this on the way home and treasure it always.

I'd like to thank Congressman Underwood for joining us, and for joining us on the long trip to Japan and Korea we have just taken, along with Senator Baucus and Congressman Pomeroy and Congressman Abercrombie. I'd like to thank the Lieutenant Governor, Lieutenant Governor Bordallo, who is, I believe, now the longest serving member of the Democratic National Committee. We thank her for her service.

Governor Gutierrez has been a good friend of mine and a great advocate for the people of Guam. He and Congressman Underwood I think clearly give this island the most forceful, clear, and detailed advocacy that it has probably ever had. And I thank him for inviting me here. I promised him I would come, and I'm only sorry it took me so long to keep my word. I can tell you now, just looking out at this view behind you, I don't want to leave. And I'm trying to think of some reason to stay. [*Laughter*]

I'd also like to say a particular word of appreciation to the leaders of so many islands who have joined us today: Governor and Mrs. Tenorio of the Northern Marianas; Governor Sunia of Samoa; the Presidents of the sovereign states of Micronesia who are freely associated with the United States, President Nakamura of the Republic of Palau, President Kabua of the Marshall Island Atolls, President Nena of the Federated States of Micronesia who is joined by the Governors of his States. Let's give them all a big hand. I am delighted that they are here today. [*Applause*]

As I said, I have been invited here several times by the Governor and the Congressman. Three years ago, Hillary had a chance to come here to see the beauty, to experience the hospitality, to learn about the culture. She told me, and has told me regularly for the last 3 years, that I needed to come to Guam. So now that I have satisfied all of my friends and my wife—[*laughter*]—I can only say that it obviously took me too long to make the decision. I am honored to be here.

I know why so many people call this part of the world paradise. You have some of the most important coral reef systems anywhere in the world. And I want to commend you for your stewardship of these reefs and for creating five new marine reserves. I want to invite Governor Gutierrez as well as Governors Sunia and Tenorio to serve on America's Coral Reef Task Force, part of our efforts to preserve the quality of the oceans, the marine biology, and the purity of the oceans. It's a big, big challenge throughout the world today. And I know these Governors will serve and serve with distinction. I will also ask the Congress to support your efforts to preserve these environmental treasures.

The world admired your remarkable recovery from the record-high winds of Typhoon Paka last December. I want to commend your courage and resilience. The world was also grateful for Guam's heroic response to the tragic crash of the Korean airliner in August of 1997. I'll never forget the conversations I had on the telephone with the Governor during that difficult period.

Later today I'm going to have a chance to speak about the important place Guam holds in American history, in America's family, and in America's future. I want to offer some more proposals to strengthen Guam and the people of this island for the 21st century. But since the other leaders of other Pacific islands are here with us today, I'd like to ask you to give me just a few minutes, before I come out into the crowd here and shake hands, to talk about the future of America's overall role in this part of the world.

I know Governor Tenorio; I have known him from the time we served as Governors. I know that we'll have a chance to talk about important issues in our relationship. The last time I saw Governor Sunia, he invited me to visit his island, our southernmost territory, in connection with the centennial of their relationship with the United States in the year 2000. Since that will be the first election year in a long time I won't

be on the ballot, I'm going to try to take him up on that invitation. I hope I can do so.

For years, our Nation has enjoyed a close, unique, and mutually beneficial partnership with the Freely Associated States. The compacts of free association have enabled us to work together to preserve peace, to foster economic development across more than a million square miles of the Pacific. It is a relationship the United States takes very seriously.

Recently, I signed Congressman Underwood's bills guaranteeing the eligibility of students from the Freely Associated States for Pell grants, and extended food aid to residents of the Marshall Islands who were harmed by U.S. nuclear testing during the cold war. I'm happy to announce that we will fulfill the final commitment made in our compact with Palau: We're allocating $150 million to build a 53-mile road to help you open your largest island, Babeldoab.

In less than 3 years, important provisions of our compacts with the Marshall Islands and the Federated States will expire. It's in our mutual interest to maintain and strengthen our ties in the new century. The United States hopes to begin formal negotiations soon so we can renew these provisions no later than next October.

Earlier this year I had a chance—[*applause*]—thank you, that's good. [*Laughter*] We have isolated applause here, depending on what I'm saying. [*Laughter*]

Earlier this year I had a chance to speak with President Nena at the opening of the U.N. General Assembly in New York. The First Lady met with President Nakamura in Washington. I understand the challenges that you're facing in building your economies. I want to encourage all the Presidents of the Freely Associated States to continue their effort to promote growth, reform, and good government. And the United States will remain a partner in all these efforts.

Again, I am proud to be in Guam at our westernmost boundary. There is an old Chamorro proverb, "Our heritage gives life to our spirit." I have learned from every person I have ever met from this part of the world that there is a proud and deep devotion to heritage. I have also sensed a very great spirit. We have much to give one another, much to learn from one another. Let us resolve to preserve all of our various heritages and our strong spirits, and walk together into the 21st century.

Thank you, and God bless you all.

NOTE: The President spoke at 1:56 p.m. at the Government House. In his remarks, he referred to Gov. Carl T.C. Gutierrez and his wife, Geraldine, and Lt. Gov. Madeleine Z. Bordallo of Guam; Dan Macaracy and Ehlysa Pablo, students who presented the President with gifts; Gov. Pedro P. Tenorio of the Northern Mariana Islands and his wife, Sophia; Gov. Tauese P.F. Sunia of American Samoa; and Presidents Kuniwo Nakamura of Palau, Imata Kabua of the Marshall Islands, and Jacob Nena of the Federated States of Micronesia.

Remarks to the Community in Hagatña, Guam
November 23, 1998

The President. Hafa adai [Hello].
Audience members. Hafa adai.
The President. What a wonderful day. What a wonderful welcome. I am delighted to be here. I want to thank Governor and Mrs. Gutierrez; Congressman Underwood; Lieutenant Governor Bordallo; Mayor McDonald; Speaker Unpingco and members of the legislature; Chief Justice; Toni Sanford, the visit host. I'd also like to acknowledge the young singers and one not-so-young singer who sang at the beginning. I thought they were quite wonderful, and I'm sure you did, too.

I want to say that I am joined today by three Members of Congress: Senator Max Baucus from Montana, Congressman Earl Pomeroy from North Dakota, Congressman Neil Abercrombie from Hawaii. And they're glad to be here as well.

Now, you heard Congressman Underwood say that he wished he could vote for me. [*Laughter*] And I was thinking, looking out at the ocean, looking at the bay, that I can't run for President again, and Governor Gutierrez can't run for Governor again, and maybe I could come here and give Congressman Underwood a chance to vote for me for Governor of Guam. Although, I think that after the speeches Mike and Roseanne gave, I'll have to run before they're old enough to oppose me, or I wouldn't have a chance. [*Laughter*]

I was sitting here thinking about all the things that you could say about Guam, but one of the things I didn't know—I heard—Bob Underwood gave his great speech, Governor Gutierrez gave his great speech, Mike and Roseanne got up and gave great speeches—one thing you should promote is that if people come to Guam, you will teach them how to give great speeches. You may have people coming from all over the world.

Let me begin my remarks with three simple words: My fellow Americans. Over the years of our administration, the First Lady and I have logged thousands of miles visiting many, many corners of America, trying to gain a greater understanding every day of the rich diversity of our Nation. No President, however, can ever claim to have seen the breadth of America without coming here to our westernmost boundary.

When the First Lady came here a couple of years ago, she came home and said, "You know, you need to go to Guam, but if you go, you might not want to come back." [*Laughter*] Every single time I have seen either your Governor or your Congressman in the last several years—every single time—they have asked me to come to Guam. Sometimes they have done more than ask. Sometimes they have insisted. Sometimes they have expected. We were about to get to the order stage before I cried "uncle" and said, "I'm dying to come, and I will be there." [*Laughter*] I thank you for making me feel so welcome today, where America's day begins.

I would also like to say a special word of appreciation to the members of America's Armed Forces who are here with us today and for the service they give our country every day. I'm proud to be here in the centennial year of the relationship between Guam and the United States. Though 15 times zones and a vast ocean separate you from the mainland, you have played an important role in the history of America and in humanity's fight for freedom.

A little over 50 years ago, Americans looked to Guam in our newspapers, on the radio, in the letters we received from our GI's. We knew then it was vital to the future of the world that the forces of freedom liberate this island.

I have just had the great honor of paying my respects at the Memorial to the People of Guam and to the American servicemen who lost their lives in the Second World War. I met there some Chamorro survivors and saw thousands of names etched on that very moving wall. I know behind each of those names, and in the history of so many families on this island, there is a tale of courage, sacrifice, patriotism, and honor.

The people of Guam, though they had not yet been granted American citizenship, risked all to hide American soldiers during the occupation, defiantly sang American songs at home, secretly sewed their own American flags. Many paid for their patriotism with their homes, their liberty, their lives.

Fifty years ago this island gave the world a precious and enduring gift, the chance for freedom and peace to triumph. And 50 years later I want to say, on behalf of every American, thank you.

Now I come here to ask you to look to the future, a very different future with new possibilities and new perils. I just came, as you may have noticed, from Japan and Korea, two countries with whom we have had very difficult relations over the last 50 years, both now our allies and partners for freedom, peace, and prosperity.

In the last year, the economic tides that once broadened prosperity all across the Pacific have blown cold winds into the economies of Japan and Korea. They have been felt all the way to Guam and Hawaii. We have to work together with our friends to restore economic growth and opportunity and to continue to stand up for freedom. And we will.

The challenges of this new century, the century in which the young people who introduced me will live most of their lives, will be different. There will be new risks and new opportunities here for you in Guam, as for all Americans. For the past 6 years, I've worked hard to prepare America for the 21st century, and together I want you to know that I am committed to make sure that we do everything we can to move forward into the new millennium with the people of Guam.

First, we must work together to ensure that Guam reaps all the benefits of the post-cold-war world, beginning with the timely return of lands no longer needed by our military. Four

years ago I was proud to sign Congressman Underwood's bill to return 3,200 acres of military land. I will see to it that the land is transferred to Guam as soon as possible. And I am happy to announce that we are also working to turn over another 7,300 acres, including the former naval air station and ship repair facility. When I return to Washington, I will ask the new Congress to simplify and expedite the process through which excess U.S. military land is transferred to Guam, and will form a White House-led task force to make sure the job gets done.

Second, we must work together to help Guam build a strong modern economy for the 21st century. In the global economy, Guam can be an important gateway to Asian markets. Today you face a dual economic challenge. The reduction of our military activities on this island has cost civilian jobs. At the same time, because of your close ties to your Pacific neighbors, like Hawaii, Guam has been more vulnerable than other parts of America to Asian financial woes. I am confident, however, that the people who weathered the high winds of Typhoon Paka with such courage and resilience can weather these economic storms as well.

The Federal Government will do our part to help. We will aid Guam in transforming the Navy ship repair facility into a viable commercial operation. The return of the naval air station will enable you to expand the airport named for the late, great Congressman Tony Won Pat and embark on new ventures to bring new jobs and new prosperity. And to further boost your economy, I will work with Congress to make it easier for products made here in Guam to enter the mainland market.

The third thing that we must do is to make sure every child here is prepared for the 21st century. The Congressman and I fought hard until we finally succeeded in the very last days of this year's budget negotiations with Congress to ensure that the children of Guam receive a fairer share in the new children's health insurance program. Now thousands of children will get the health care they deserve.

Fourth, we must work together to fulfill America's compact with the Freely Associated States. Thousands of Micronesians have come to Guam to live and work and build better lives for their families. In my next balanced budget, I will ask Congress to more than double funds to assist Guam in the task of meeting the education and health needs of these newcomers.

Finally, and most important, we must always honor Guam's special membership in the American family. Our administration has reviewed your commonwealth proposals. We have tried to offer viable alternatives. I want Congress to act to help the people of Guam meet their challenges and give you more effective self-government.

We will also respond seriously if the people of Guam seek a different political status. It is your decision to seek that. I will work to ensure that your voices are heard in Washington, that you are treated fairly and sensitively by the Federal Government, that you are consulted before policies are made that affect your lives.

I will establish a network of senior White House and Cabinet officials to develop and coordinate policy concerning the territories. The Defense Secretary, Bill Cohen, will also designate an aide in his personal office to see Guam's concerns in military matters carefully and appropriately considered.

In all of these efforts and in the progress that we can still make together, again I want to say, I am deeply indebted to Governor Gutierrez for his eloquent and persistent advocacy. I am deeply indebted to Congressman Underwood for his energetic presentation of your cause. Never has Guam been so forcefully, consistently, and helpfully represented as they are today. All of you should be very proud of both of these elected officials.

My fellow Americans, in just 403 days our country will awake, first here on Guam, to a new century and a whole new millennium. Now,

though we live on opposite sides of the Earth, in that new millennium still, with all of its changes, we will be bound together by our shared history, our shared values, our shared love of freedom. Whether our ancestors crossed the Atlantic on the *Mayflower,* whether they laid the ancient latte stones that still stand on this island, whether they came to Guam in recent decades seeking new opportunities, or came from all across the globe to the American mainland, now we are all Americans.

I ask you to always remember that as much as you have enjoyed this day, I have enjoyed it more. I hope you will know that when I go back to Washington, I will carry with me the rhythms, the energy, the smile, the realities of life here that I would never had understood so well had I not been able to come. And I hope you will look forward to walking hand in hand with your fellow Americans into that new millennium.

Thank you, and God bless you.

NOTE: The President spoke at 4:15 p.m. in the Ricardo J. Bordallo Office Complex at Adelup. In his remarks, he referred to Gov. Carl T.C. Gutierrez and his wife, Geraldine, and Lt. Gov. Madeleine Z. Bordallo of Guam; Mayor Paul M. McDonald of Agaña Heights; Speaker Antonio R. Unpingco of the 24th Guam Legislature; Chief Justice Peter Siguenza, Guam Supreme Court; event chair Antoinette D. Sanford, member, Guam Chamber of Commerce; and high school students Michael San Nicolas and Roseanne Apuran, who introduced the President. A tape was not available for verification of the content of these remarks.

Letter to Congressional Leaders Reporting on the National Emergency With Respect to Burma
November 23, 1998

Dear Mr. Speaker: (Dear Mr. President:)

I hereby report to the Congress on developments concerning the national emergency with respect to Burma that I declared in Executive Order 13047 of May 20, 1997, pursuant to section 570 of the Foreign Operations, Export Financing, and Related Programs Appropriations Act, 1997, Public Law 104–208 (the "Act"), and

the International Emergency Economic Powers Act (IEEPA). This report is submitted pursuant to section 204(c) of IEEPA, 50 U.S.C. 1703(c) and section 401(c) of the National Emergencies Act, 50 U.S.C. 1641(c). This report discusses only matters concerning the national emergency with respect to Burma that was declared in Executive Order 13047.

1. On May 20, 1997, I issued Executive Order 13047 (62 *Fed. Reg.* 28301, May 22, 1997), effective on May 21, 1997, to declare a national emergency with respect to Burma and to prohibit new investment in Burma by United States persons, except to the extent provided in regulations, orders, directives, or licenses that may be issued in conformity with section 570 of the Act. The order also prohibits any approval or other facilitation by a United States person, wherever located, of a transaction by a foreign person where the transaction would constitute new investment in Burma prohibited by the order if engaged in by a United States person or within the United States. This action was taken in response to the large-scale repression of the democratic opposition by the Government of Burma since September 30, 1996. A copy of the order was transmitted to the Congress on May 20, 1997.

By its terms, Executive Order 13047 does not prohibit the entry into, performance of, or financing of a contract to sell or purchase goods, services, or technology, except: (1) where the entry into such contract on or after May 21, 1997, is for the general supervision and guarantee of another person's performance of a contract for the economic development of resources located in Burma; or (2) where such contract provides for payment, in whole or in part, in (i) shares of ownership, including an equity interest, in the economic development of resources located in Burma; or (ii) participation in royalties, earnings, or profits in the economic development of resources located in Burma.

2. On May 21, 1998, the Department of the Treasury's Office of Foreign Assets Control (OFAC) issued the Burmese Sanctions Regulations (the "Regulations"), 31 C.F.R. Part 537, to implement the prohibitions of Executive Order 13047 (63 *Fed. Reg.* 27846, May 21, 1998). The Regulations apply to United States persons, defined to include U.S. citizens and permanent resident aliens wherever they are located, entities organized under U.S. law (including their foreign branches), and entities and individuals actually located in the United States. The sanctions do not apply directly to foreign subsidiaries of U.S. firms, although foreign firms' activities may be affected by the restriction on United States persons' facilitation of a foreign person's investment transactions in Burma. A copy of the Regulations is attached to this report.

The term "new investment" means any of the following activities, if such an activity is undertaken pursuant to an agreement, or pursuant to the exercise of rights under such an agreement, that is entered into with the Government of Burma, or a nongovernmental entity in Burma, on or after May 21, 1997: (a) the entry into a contract that includes the economic development of resources located in Burma; (b) the entry into a contract providing for the general supervision and guarantee of another person's performance of a contract that includes the economic development of resources located in Burma; (c) the purchase of a share of ownership, including an equity interest, in the economic development of resources located in Burma; or (d) the entry into a contract providing for the participation in royalties, earnings, or profits in the economic development of resources located in Burma, without regard to the form of participation.

3. Since the issuance of Executive Order 13047 on May 20, 1997, OFAC, acting under authority delegated by the Secretary of the Treasury, has implemented sanctions against Burma as imposed by the order. OFAC has issued several determinations with respect to transactions provided for by agreements and/or rights pursuant to contracts entered into by United States persons prior to May 21, 1997. One license was issued to authorize a United States person's disinvestment in Burma, since this transaction facilitated a foreign person's investment in Burma.

On May 21, 1997, OFAC disseminated details of this program to the financial, securities, and international trade communities by both electronic and conventional media. This included posting notices on the Internet and on ten computer bulletin boards and two fax-on-demand services, and providing the material to the U.S. Embassy in Rangoon for distribution to U.S. companies operating in Burma.

In addition, in early July 1997, OFAC sent notification letters to approximately 50 U.S. firms with operations in or ties to Burma informing them of the restrictions on new investment. The letters included copies of Executive Order 13047, provided clarification of several technical issues, and urged firms to contact OFAC if they had specific questions on the application of the Executive order to their particular circumstances.

4. The expenses incurred by the Federal Government in the 6-month period from May 20 through November 19, 1998, that are directly attributable to the exercise of powers and authorities conferred by the declaration of a national emergency with respect to Burma are estimated at approximately $300,000, most of which represent wage and salary costs for Federal personnel. Personnel costs were largely centered in the Department of the Treasury (particularly in the Office of Foreign Assets Control, the Office of the Under Secretary for Enforcement, and the Office of the General Counsel), and the Department of State (particularly the Bureau of Economic and Business Affairs, the Bureau of East Asian and Pacific Affairs, and the Office of the Legal Adviser).

5. The situation reviewed above continues to present an extraordinary and unusual threat to the national security and foreign policy of the United States. The declaration of the national emergency with respect to Burma contained in Executive Order 13047 in response to the large-scale repression of the democratic opposition by the Government of Burma since September 30, 1996, reflected the belief that it is in the national security and foreign policy interests of the United States to seek an end to abuses of human rights in Burma, to support efforts to achieve democratic reform that would promote regional peace and stability, and to urge effective counternarcotics policies.

In the past 6 months the State Law and Order Restoration Council (SLORC), recently renamed the State Peace and Development Council, has shown no sign of willingness to cede its hold on absolute power. Since refusing to recognize the results of the free and fair 1990 elections in which the National League for Democracy won a vast majority of both the popular vote and the parliamentary seats, the ruling junta has continued to refuse to negotiate with pro-democracy forces and ethnic groups for a genuine political settlement to allow a return to the rule of law and respect for basic human rights. Burma has taken limited but insufficient steps to counter narcotics production and trafficking.

The net effect of U.S. and international measures to pressure the SLORC to end its repression and move toward democratic government has been a further decline in investor confidence in Burma and deeper stagnation of the Burmese economy. Observers agree that the Burmese economy appears to be weakening further and the government has a serious shortage of foreign exchange reserves with which to pay for imports. While Burma's economic crisis is largely a result of the SLORC's own heavy-handed mismanagement, the SLORC is unlikely to find a way out of the crisis unless political developments permit an easing of international pressure. I shall continue to exercise the powers at my disposal to deal with these problems and will report periodically to the Congress on significant developments.

Sincerely,

WILLIAM J. CLINTON

NOTE: Identical letters were sent to Newt Gingrich, Speaker of the House of Representatives, and Albert Gore, Jr., President of the Senate.

Remarks at the Thanksgiving Turkey Presentation Ceremony
November 24, 1998

Good morning. Chairman Gessell, President Proctor, Walt Gislason, and all the children from the Greater Washington Boys and Girls Clubs, welcome to all of you. I want to thank you for joining us in the Rose Garden for our annual Thanksgiving Day celebration. I'd also like to thank the National Turkey Federation again for donating this year's tom turkey to the White House.

And of course, I want to acknowledge our special guest of honor, this good-looking turkey from the "Land of 10,000 Lakes," Minnesota. Minnesota is the second largest turkey producing State in our Nation. They have even more turkeys there than lakes. And I must say, of all the years I've been here, this is the most adventurous turkey we've ever had. [*Laughter*] Just ask him your questions. [*Laughter*] While the average turkey weighs about 15 pounds, they tell me our friend here weighs over 45 pounds.

As all of you know, Thanksgiving is a uniquely American holiday, dating back to the Pilgrims and Plymouth, Massachusetts. When the Pilgrims sat down for Thanksgiving dinner in 1621, of course, they didn't have the usual trimmings: no potatoes, no stuffing, no pumpkin pie. In fact, they didn't even have a turkey. They feasted on maize, squash, and venison.

A lot has changed in the last three and a half centuries in our country and not just the Thanksgiving dinner menu. But every year that I come here to do this ceremony, it seems we have more to be thankful for as Americans. Not only do we have turkey, mashed potatoes, and pie, but for this turkey and its owners, we have the Minnesota Vikings and their great season this year. [*Laughter*]

We're also fortunate this Thanksgiving to live in one of the most prosperous times in our history, with unemployment at its lowest level in 28 years, homeownership at its highest level ever. More Americans this Thanksgiving will spend this holiday in their own homes than ever before.

But we should never forget that there are still people in our Nation who need our concern and caring. The young people here today are interested in making the most of their own lives and in serving their own communities. They remind us that Thanksgiving is not simply a time for parades and a home-cooked meal but a time together with our friends, our families, our neighbors.

President Lincoln understood that when he issued the first official Proclamation of Thanksgiving during the Civil War. Although the American people then were engaged in a profound national struggle and, indeed, engaged with the very survival of our Nation, Mr. Lincoln reminded us that even in the darkest times, we all have something to be thankful for.

Therefore, I am honored to follow in the footsteps of President Lincoln, and President Truman who began this tradition 51 years ago of keeping at least one turkey off the Thanksgiving table. With this Presidential pardon, our friend here will retire to the petting zoo in Fairfax County, Virginia, to live out the remainder of his years surrounded by friends, not peas and sweet potatoes. [*Laughter*]

So let's bring the turkey up here, and I hope you all have a wonderful Thanksgiving.

NOTE: The President spoke at 12:47 p.m. in the Rose Garden at the White House. In his remarks, he referred to Frank Gessell, chairman, and Stuart Proctor, Jr., president, National Turkey Federation, and Mr. Gessell's friend Walter Gislason, charged with handling the turkey. The Thanksgiving Day proclamation of November 17 is listed in Appendix D at the end of this volume.

Remarks at a National Adoption Month Reception
November 24, 1998

Thank you very much. I asked Charday if she was happy about being here, and she said, "Yes, but I'm a little nervous." [*Laughter*] And I said, "Well, all these people are your friends, just remember that." And I thought she did a terrific job. Don't you think she did? I think she did. [*Applause*]

Governor and Mrs. Edgar, Senator Levin, Senator Landrieu, Congressman and Mrs. Oberstar, Mayor Barry, thank you all for joining us here today. I'd like to thank the previous participants on the program—Mayor-elect Williams, for the power of your example which speaks louder than our words. And Mrs. Williams, we're glad to have you here today, and we wish you well in your new endeavors. Judge Hamilton, thank you for your work and the power of your example. And Dave Thomas, he said some very nice things up here about Hillary and me, but the truth is that no other citizen in the United States today or ever has done as much as a private citizen to promote the cause of adoption as Dave Thomas. And we are very grateful to him. Thank you, sir.

I'd like to thank Secretary Shalala, the longest serving and, notwithstanding her voice today, the most effective Secretary of Health and Human Services in our history.

I want to congratulate all the families who are here today and thank them for coming. And I hope Judge Hamilton is right; I hope that the images of them that go across America today will inspire other parents to do the same. I want to also congratulate the Adoption 2002 award winners and thank them for the work they are doing in their States and communities.

I'd also like to say a special word today. Before we came in here, Dave Thomas said, "Well, you know, your administration has done more than any in history to promote adoption." And I told him that the real reason for that is because it has been a consuming passion of the First Lady for as long as I have known her. I remember when we were young and we hadn't been married long, when she had a client, a couple in Arkansas who were foster parents and who were in the foster system, and the rules then didn't permit them to adopt. And she waged a long and sometimes lonely legal battle through our courts to get that couple the right to adopt the child they loved very much and had already invested a great deal in. And it began to change things for a lot of families in our State.

I remember when she organized more than 25 years ago the Arkansas Advocates for Families and Children, and one of their missions was to improve the system of adoption, as well as the system of foster care in our State. And so I can tell you that while many people have played a role in what we have been able to do—especially in the remarkable bipartisan cooperation we've enjoyed in passing these two important adoption bills—no one deserves more credit than Hillary for what has happened in the last 6 years, and I'm very grateful to her.

As all the speakers have said, we are working hard on making good on our commitment to find our foster children the homes and the futures they deserve. We do want to double the number of adoptions by the year 2002. We want to reform our Nation's whole approach to this profoundly important issue, to make the system work better for the children and the families it should be serving. With pioneering efforts like those in the State of Illinois, we are getting closer to our goal of doubling the number of children adopted or permanently placed by 2002.

Between 1996 and 1997, the number of adoptions increased by 10 percent, from 28,000 to 31,000. We know, however, that that cannot be the sole measure of our progress. We also must ask ourselves whether our child welfare system always puts the health and safety of our children above all else; whether children have the chance to live out their dreams and fulfill their potential; whether families who open their arms can actually reach to embrace a child in need.

As we celebrate National Adoption Month, Americans can take pride in the progress we're making, but we know there is much more work to be done. We know geographic and other barriers to adoptions still exist. We know we have to do a better job in informing America's families about the many children who wait in the foster care system for adoption.

To give those children the permanent homes they need, to give our families the opportunity to give them those homes, we must make technology a partner and propel the public welfare system into the 21st century. Today, therefore, I am directing the Secretary of Health and Human Services to work with the States, the courts, the private agencies, to report to me within 60 days on a plan for a national Internet-based registry of children waiting to be adopted everywhere in the United States.

As Hillary said, there are 100,000 children, just like those whom we clapped for today, in foster care still waiting for permanent adoptive homes. The Internet holds the potential to shorten their wait, to make an on-line link between foster care centers and families looking to adopt. Some States and private partners already are forging these connections, bringing together families in Alaska and children as far away as Pennsylvania, for example.

We want to build on these efforts to the extent that it is possible and appropriate, working closely with the States, supporting their efforts, learning from them. We can use the Internet to promote adoptions while protecting the confidentiality of children and families. Technology has given us an important tool, and we should use it.

Again, Thanksgiving is approaching. Families across our Nation will come together to express their gratitude for all the things that matter most. We sometimes speak of the comforts of home as the small blessings. But when you look into the eyes of these children today, we remember that there are few greater blessings.

I'd like to encourage more families to follow the example of those we have honored here today, to open their arms, their hearts to children who need them very much, to give them the futures they deserve, and to make sure that in all of the Thanksgivings to come, we will all be blessed as a nation as more and more of our children come into loving homes.

A very happy Thanksgiving to all of you. And now let me invite all of you to join us to celebrate this special day with a reception in the State Dining Room.

Thank you very much.

NOTE: The President spoke at 2:26 p.m. in the East Room at the White House. In his remarks, he referred to adoptee Charday Mays, who introduced the President; Gov. Jim Edgar of Illinois and his wife, Brenda; Jean Oberstar, wife of Representative James L. Oberstar; Mayor Marion S. Barry, Jr., and Mayor-elect Anthony A. Williams of Washington, DC, and Mr. Williams' wife, Diane; Chief Judge Eugene N. Hamilton, Superior Court, Washington, DC; and Wendy's International, Inc., senior chairman Dave Thomas, founder, Dave Thomas Foundation for Adoption. The National Adoption Month proclamation of October 29 is listed in Appendix D at the end of this volume.

Memorandum on Using the Internet To Increase Adoptions
November 24, 1998

Memorandum for the Secretary of Health and Human Services

Subject: Using the Internet to Increase Adoptions

Technology will be an ever more important part of achieving our national goals as we approach the new millennium. New technological tools mean new opportunities for progress—helping us to strengthen the global economy, bolster public education, and improve the health of American families. Technology can also assist our continuing efforts to meet our national goal of doubling, by the year 2002, adoptions and other permanent placements from our Nation's foster care system.

As we celebrate National Adoption Month, it is fitting that we reflect on the important steps we have taken to strengthen our child welfare system and, specifically, to improve the process of adoption. Through the Family and Medical Leave Act and tax credits, we have made it easier for families to adopt children. We have worked to eliminate discrimination and delay based on race and ethnicity. And, last year, I was proud to sign into law the Adoption and Safe Families Act, tightening the time frame for decision-making and affirming that the health and safety of children in foster care must always come first.

We are making progress but there is more work to be done. Because geographic and other barriers to adoption still exist, we must do a better job of informing America's families about the many children that wait in foster care for permanent, adoptive homes. To give those children the future they deserve, to give our families the opportunity to provide them with happy, healthy homes, we must infuse the public child welfare system with the power of technology.

Therefore, I am directing you to work with the States, courts, private agencies, and others to develop a plan for expanding appropriate use of the Internet as a tool to find homes for children waiting to be adopted from the public child welfare system. There are approximately 100,000 children in our country waiting in foster care for permanent adoptive homes. Sharing information through a national Internet registry about children legally available for adoption could shorten the time needed to find adoptive families for such children. To take full advantage of the Internet's potential to promote adoptions while also ensuring appropriate confidentiality safeguards, close consultation with the States will be necessary.

You should report to me within 60 days with a plan to carry out this consultation; identify important issues and strategies to address them;

and build on promising existing efforts to create an effective, national registry.

WILLIAM J. CLINTON

NOTE: The National Adoption Month proclamation of October 29 is listed in Appendix D at the end of this volume.

Radio Remarks on Disaster Relief for Central America
November 25, 1998

Throughout this week, families in the United States are coming together to give thanks for the blessings we enjoy. As we celebrate, we must remember our neighbors, particularly the people in Central America whose lives were devastated by Hurricane Mitch a month ago.

The Americas are also a family, and many relatives of our own citizens live in the nations hardest hit by the hurricane: Honduras, Nicaragua, Guatemala, and El Salvador. The United States has already pledged $263 million to the relief effort, offering food, loans, and vital health services. Our Armed Forces are on the scene transporting supplies, rebuilding roads and communities. The First Lady and Tipper Gore visited the region and renewed our pledge to do all we can to help.

So this Thanksgiving I ask you to keep the hurricane victims in your thoughts and prayers and to continue your generous donation to relief organizations. In this season of need, we will not let down our fellow Americans.

NOTE: The President's remarks were recorded at approximately 5:40 p.m. on November 23 in the Oval Office at the White House for broadcast on November 25. The transcript was released by the Office of the Press Secretary on November 25.

Statement on the Murder of Russian Parliamentarian Galina Starovoytova
November 25, 1998

Americans everywhere join people across Russia in mourning the murder of Russian parliamentarian Galina Starovoytova. Through her work as a deputy in the State Duma, as an adviser to President Yeltsin, and as an early advocate of political change in Soviet times, Ms. Starovoytova made an immeasurable contribution to the development of democratic values and institutions throughout Russia. This tragic crime represents an assault on the Russian people's aspirations to build a society that is peaceful, tolerant, and governed by the rule of law. It is a terrible loss for friends of democracy around the world.

In recent days, the outpouring of grief in Ms. Starovoytova's beloved St. Petersburg and throughout Russia has testified to the enduring strength of the values she championed throughout her career. In mourning her loss, Russians and Americans are reminded of the importance of sustaining democracy and civility even at the most difficult times. Indeed, we are troubled by recent expressions of anti-Semitism and extremism in Russia, and we will continue to stand with those who, like Ms. Starovoytova, have been leading Russia toward a more pluralistic, more tolerant future. Our thoughts and prayers go to her family and friends.

The President's Radio Address
November 28, 1998

Good morning. This Thanksgiving weekend we gather in our homes with family and friends to share holiday meals and memories and to give thanks to God for our many blessings. But Thanksgiving is not only a day to give thanks; it is also a time when we renew our commitment to our deepest values and to the duty we owe to one another. Today I want to talk about an important step we're taking to help our neediest citizens.

This year Americans have much to be grateful for: grateful that our economy is the strongest in a generation, offering greater opportunity than ever before for every American; grateful that our communities are safer than they've been in 25 years, giving our families the security they need to thrive; grateful that our air and water are cleaner than they have been for decades, preserving the environment for our children; and grateful that America continues to shine as a beacon of peace, freedom, and democracy all around the world.

We're also grateful this Thanksgiving more Americans will spend this holiday in homes of their own than at any time of our history. But for millions of struggling senior citizens and people with disabilities, the peace and security of a decent home is a distant dream and the threat of homelessness an ever-present nightmare.

Too many of these hard-pressed Americans are warehoused in sterile nursing homes, not because they need to be but because they can't afford to live anywhere else. Too many are trapped in substandard housing, where broken plumbing, inadequate heat and hazardous hallways are a dangerous fact of life. And too many spend more than half of their very modest incomes on housing, often sacrificing basic needs like food and medical care just to pay the rent.

On Thanksgiving Day in 1933, at the height of the Great Depression, President Franklin Roosevelt entreated Americans to help the needy, recalling the steadfastness of those in every generation who fought to "hold clear the goal of mutual help in a time of prosperity as in a time of adversity." Today, at this moment of unparalleled prosperity, we must do no less.

Americans should never have to choose between putting a meal on the table or putting a roof over their heads. That's why I'm pleased that this month we're awarding nearly $700 million in Housing and Urban Development grants to make sure no one has to make that impossible choice. These grants will enable hundreds of nonprofit organizations, like the YMCA, Goodwill, and the Salvation Army, to build more than 8,000 new apartments for struggling senior citizens and people with disabilities and to subsidize their rents.

Today I'm also pleased to announce nearly $130 million for new housing vouchers to help people with disabilities in over 200 communities afford housing in the neighborhood of their choice. Together with our new housing grants, these steps will help nearly 30,000 Americans. And I thank HUD Secretary Cuomo for his tireless efforts to ensure that our neediest citizens have access to safe, affordable housing.

Let me give you just one example of the difference a home can make in the lives of Americans in need. Six years ago Helen Williams lost her husband to cancer and was losing her home. For 3 years she struggled to maintain her dignity and her health as she shuttled between friends' and families' houses, afraid to overstay her welcome but more frightened by the threat of homelessness. Fortunately, Mrs. Williams learned about one of the subsidized apartment buildings funded by HUD's housing program for the elderly.

Today, along with her dog, Mr. B, she's thriving there and giving back to her community. Just this week, at the age of 80, she's been busy working with her church to deliver Thanksgiving turkeys to families in need. That's the kind of Thanksgiving story we need to hear more of, all of us bound together across the generations in a cycle of mutual help, caring for one another, giving back to one another, thanking God for our blessings. With the steps we take today, we'll ensure the same spirit of Thanksgiving is alive every day of the year.

Hillary and I wish you and your loved ones a happy, healthy time of thanksgiving. Thanks for listening.

NOTE: The address was recorded at 4:10 p.m. on November 27 at Camp David, MD, for broadcast at 10:06 a.m. on November 28. The transcript was made available by the Office of the Press Sec-retary on November 27 but was embargoed for release until the broadcast.

Remarks at a Conference To Support Middle East Peace and Development
November 30, 1998

Thank you very much, Secretary Albright, and thank you for your work for peace in the Middle East. Chairman Arafat, welcome back to the United States. We're delighted to see you. I think it's fair to say that both of us have had more sleep than we had had the last time we met at the Wye Plantation, and I'm delighted to have a chance to meet with Chairman Arafat this morning.

I thank all the representatives who are here from Israel, the other countries of the Middle East—of course, the Norwegian delegation, the European Union, our friends from Asia, and Mr. Wolfensohn from the World Bank, and others.

Let me first of all say I had a good meeting with Chairman Arafat this morning. We reviewed both the progress made by both sides since the Wye memorandum was signed and the essential next steps on the road to peace, including the task of this conference, stimulating Palestinian economic growth. Chairman Arafat reaffirmed his pledge to uphold his side of the agreement and to work with Israeli authorities to promote Israel's security. I promised the continuing support of the United States as we move ahead in the next phase of the peace process. That phase begins today with this conference.

Today our purpose is to send a clear signal that this peace is more than a piece of paper, that the promise imagined at Oslo can become a concrete reality—a true peace, a growing peace, good for Palestinians, good for Israelis, good for the region and the world. There are roughly 50 international states and organizations represented here this morning. Most of you have traveled a great distance. I thank you for your persistence and for your generosity. We must convince those who have invested so much in this process that it was a sound investment.

We must look at Gaza and the West Bank in a new light, not as battlegrounds but as energetic places at the crossroads of the Middle East, endowed with well-educated populations, strongly supported by the Palestinian community around the world, ripe for further development once investors see that the peace agreement truly is taking hold.

For too long, too many young people have turned to terrorism and old hatreds, partly because they had nothing better to do. We must give them a different future to believe in. Every step toward opportunity is a step away from violence. Palestinians have a right to the same things all people aspire to: to be part of a normal, even happy, society where children receive a decent education, where there are jobs to go around and decent health care, where people's memories are reconciled with their hopes for the future and there is no fear.

Despite our best efforts since 1993, an honest assessment would lead us to the conclusion that we have not realized all our intentions. There has been too little tangible improvement in the lives of the Palestinian people. Per capita income is down. Unemployment is too high. Living conditions are extremely difficult.

At the outset of the next phase of the peace process, we must candidly acknowledge that we have to change these circumstances. No peace stands a chance of lasting if it does not deliver real results to ordinary people. Our challenge today, therefore, is to do more to deliver these results and to do it sooner rather than later.

I would like to make just a few more points before I let you move on to the business at hand. First, peace is built on compromise, and with any compromise, it is important to address the genuine needs of both parties. Both sides have made sacrifices to get where we are, including at the recent Wye summit. Both have taken steps since then to keep the process moving forward. There have been bumps in the road, to be sure, but the agreement is on track, and we must keep it on track. By our words and our actions, we must keep lending our support, anticipating problems before they arise, encouraging the parties to uphold their commitments, building confidence in both the Palestinian and Israeli people through sustained external support. These will be my goals when I visit the region in 2 weeks.

Second, we must persuade private organizations and individuals to join governments in deepening investments in the region. While public assistance can jump-start development, ultimately the private sector holds the key. There must be greater investment of private resources in Gaza and the West Bank. Each vote of confidence makes the infrastructure a little stronger. Each investment makes previous investments more likely to succeed. It is good economic policy, and it's the right thing to do.

Third, I am convinced for this peace to be real and lasting, it must be regional. Trade and investment must flourish throughout the Middle East, between the Arab world and Palestinians and also between the Arab world and Israelis. There can be no road different from this that leads to a just and lasting peace.

Many nations here have contributed significant resources already, including Norway, Saudi Arabia, Japan, the nations of the EU, and others. We saw a concrete result last week with the opening of the new airport in Gaza, built with international assistance, a powerful symbol of the Palestinian people's connection to the rest of the world. Institutions like the World Bank are helping, too, ensuring that donor pledges are matched with broad development strategies.

The United States has been proud to support these efforts and will continue to do so. The Middle East is profoundly important to our country, for all our citizens who love peace, stability, and the kindness of neighbor to neighbor. Virtues can be found in every faith that trace their roots to the Holy Land.

Today I want to announce that I intend to work closely with our Congress on developing a package to provide an additional $400 million to assist the Palestinian people, funds to help create jobs, improve basic education, enhance access to water, support the rule of law. This amount is in addition to the regular annual contribution provided by the United States, which will reach $100 million next year.

A great deal remains to be done, but I urge you to remember how much can be accomplished in just a year. At the beginning of 1998, Northern Ireland was dominated by its divisions, how they were drawn, and who was on what side. Today, the most important dividing line is whether one believes in the past or the future. Through courageous decision and a steady tide of investment, the people there are seeing peace grow from wish to fulfillment. Prosperity there, too, is the key to making it happen.

A breakthrough occurred at the Wye summit because the parties decided to look forward, not backward, to focus on the need for security and on tangible economic benefits like the Gaza airport, the future seaport, the safe passage between Gaza and the West Bank, the Gaza industrial estate, which may provide employment for up to 20,000 Palestinians. All these will enable the predictable movement of people and goods, crucial to building a healthy investment climate. Every economy needs a chance to breathe. These steps will provide good breathing room.

All of you here today know how important your work is. Too many lives have already been lost in the Middle East, from prime ministers to simple passers-by who became random victims of the burning hatred. Today you help again to change this dynamic. Today you know we have the best chance for peace there in our lifetimes.

By building prosperity in Gaza and in the West Bank, by promoting regional economic cooperation, by giving young Palestinians a chance to channel their dreams into positive opportunities, you lay the groundwork for a peace that will last not for a year or a lifetime but for generations to come. We are honored to have you in the United States, and we wish you well in this important endeavor.

Thank you very much.

NOTE: The President spoke at 10:48 a.m. in the Loy Henderson Conference Room at the State Department. In his remarks, he referred to Chairman Yasser Arafat of the Palestinian Authority.

Remarks on Electronic Commerce
November 30, 1998

Thank you very much. I feel like the fifth wheel here. [*Laughter*] Most of what needs to be said has certainly been said.

I want to thank the Vice President for his outstanding leadership. I thank Secretary Rubin and Ambassador Barshefsky and, in his absence, Secretary Daley; Administrator Alvarez, Mr. Podesta, and other members of the administration. I thank all the members of the high-tech community in various forms and permutations who are here in this audience today.

And I, too, want to thank the Members of Congress for their invaluable help. In spite of the ups and downs of partisan debate in Washington, this is one area where we've managed to really pull together a broad bipartisan coalition of Members of Congress to do a whole series of good things for America, through the Internet, over the long run.

I want to specifically thank Congressman Cox and Senator Wyden for sponsoring the Internet Tax Freedom Act. I want to thank Senator Hatch, who led the efforts on the copyright protection legislation. I thank Senator Burns, the cochair of the Internet caucus and who, along with Senators Rockefeller and Dorgan who are here, have played crucial roles on the Senate Commerce Committee in passing electronic commerce legislation; and Congressman Pickering, who has assisted us in the privatization of the domain name system and on many other issues. So I'd like to ask you to give these Members of Congress a round of applause. I thank them for what they are doing. [*Applause*]

I'm very grateful to John Chambers and Meg Whitman for being here today and for what they do with their own companies and what they represent for our country's future. I've been wondering what I was going to do in a couple years. I think I could be a successful trader on eBay, you know? [*Laughter*] At least I know where I can go and get my political memorabilia now. [*Laughter*]

I always liked John Chambers until I found out he had 70 vice presidents. [*Laughter*] I don't know what to make of that. He's more important than I am? He's less efficient than I am? [*Laughter*] Or one great Vice President is enough. How's that? [*Laughter*]

I also want to thank my friend of 30 years now, Ira Magaziner, who has been acknowledged, and who's here with his wonderful family, for years of work, including many months when this work did not get anything like this level of attention which it has today.

As all of you know, Thanksgiving weekend marked the beginning of the holiday shopping center and a new holiday tradition. Last year only 10 percent of those with home computers shopped for holiday gifts on-line; this year the figure is predicted to be over 40 percent. On-line shoppers are buying everything from the latest electronics to old-time Babe Ruth and Lou Gehrig baseball cards, thanks to eBay. This new era, therefore, will not only transform commerce, it will lift America's economy in the 21st century.

This Thanksgiving I had a chance again to give thanks for these good times in our country. Less than a decade ago, people were worrying that America could not keep up with global competition. Today, we have the strongest economy in a generation, about 17 million new jobs, the largest real wage growth in 20 years, the lowest unemployment in 28 years, the smallest percentage of people on welfare in 29 years. And we're leading the world in the technologies of the future, from telecommunications to biotechnology.

The qualities rewarded in this new economy—flexibility, innovation, creativity, enterprise—are qualities that have long been associated with Americans and our economy. We have to keep this momentum going. That's really what we're here to celebrate, ratify, and commit ourselves to today.

I think the first thing we have to do is to stay with the economic policies that have worked for the last 6 years: fiscal discipline, expanding trade, investing in education and research and development. I think we have to do more work here at home to expand the benefits of the economic recovery to areas and people who have not yet felt it, and I believe the Internet has an enormous potential role to play there.

I believe, to keep this going, we're going to have to do more to contain the economic crisis in the world, to reverse it in Asia, and to deal with the long-term challenges to global financial markets, which Secretary Rubin and I and others are working very hard on.

But finally, I think we have to clearly commit ourselves to making the most of what is clearly the engine of tomorrow's economy: technology. We have to make ourselves absolutely committed to the proposition that we will first do no harm, we will do nothing that undermines the capacity of emerging technologies to lift the lives of ordinary Americans; and secondly, that, insofar as we can, we will help to create an environment which will enhance the likelihood of success. That is what we are fundamentally celebrating today and committing ourselves to for tomorrow.

Information technology now accounts for more than a third of our economic growth. It has boosted our productivity and reduced inflation by a full percentage point. Obviously, few applications of this technology have more power than electronic commerce. If all the sales being conducted over the Internet were taking place at one shopping mall, that mall would have to be 30 times the size of the largest mall in the world, Minnesota's Mall of America. Five years from now we would need a facility 1,000 times the size of the Mall of America to handle the volume of sales.

Now, to fulfill this promise, we have to create the conditions for electronic entrepreneurs. You've heard that discussed. That's why I asked the Vice President to coordinate and Ira Magaziner to work on building a framework for global economic commerce back in late 1995. That's why we committed ourselves to the proposition that the Internet should be a free-trade zone with incentives for competition, protection for consumers and children, supervised not by governments but by people who use the Internet every day.

This year 132 nations followed the U.S. lead by signing a declaration to refrain from imposing customs duties on electronic commerce. We reached agreements supporting our market-driven approach with the European Union, Japan, and other nations. Today the Australian Prime Minister and I will issue a joint statement along these same lines. Working with Congress, industry, State and local officials, we passed a law to put a 3-year moratorium on new and discriminatory taxes on electronic commerce. And again, I thank Secretary Rubin and Deputy Secretary Summers for their work on that.

We ratified an international treaty to protect intellectual property on-line. We made it possible to conduct official transactions electronically. We secured the funds to challenge the Nation's research community to develop the next generation Internet. We passed a law to protect the privacy of our children on-line. We're working with companies representing a large share of the Internet traffic to help them meet our privacy guidelines. We have effectively privatized the Internet's domain name and routing systems. We have moved to improve the security and reliability of cyberspace by focusing attention on protecting critical infrastructures and solving the Y2K computer problem.

Now, that's a pretty impressive line of work for all concerned. But we see there are still challenges to overcome. Many people who surf the Web still don't shop there. They worry they won't get what they thought they were paying for; they'll have nowhere to go if they get cheated. We've already begun to address these fears, not with burdensome regulations that might stifle growth and innovation but with incentives for on-line companies to offer customers the protections they need.

We must do more. Our country has some of the strongest consumer protections in the world. Today I ask Secretary Daley to work with the FTC and other agencies, consumer advocates, industry, and our trading partners to develop new approaches to extend the proud tradition of consumer protection into cyberspace, to ensure truthful advertising and full disclosure of information are the foundations of global electronic commerce. People should get what they pay for on-line; it should be easy to get redress if they don't. We must give consumers the same protection in our virtual mall they now get at the shopping mall.

And if the virtual mall is to grow, we must help small businesses and families gain access to the same services at the same speeds that big business enjoys. For many people, connections are so slow that shopping at the virtual mall is filled with frustration. It is as if they had to drive over dirt roads to get to the mall, only to find an endless line of customers just waiting to get into the door. So today I'll also direct Secretary Daley and Ambassador Barshefsky to work with the FCC and our trading partners to promote greater competition to bring advanced high-speed connections into our homes and small businesses, to ensure that the

Internet continues to evolve in ways that will benefit all our people.

Our Nation was founded at the dawn of a period not so very unlike this one, a period of enormous economic upheaval when the world was beginning to move from an agrarian to an industrial economy. Alexander Hamilton, our first Secretary of the Treasury, understood these changes well. In his remarkable "Report on Manufactures" and other of his writings, Hamilton identified new ways to harness the changes then going on so that our Nation could advance.

Listen to this. He proposed what many thought were radical ideas at the time: a central bank, a common currency, a national system of roads and canals, a crackdown on fraud so that American products would be known all over the world for quality. He created the blueprint that made possible America's industrial age and, many of us believe, the preservation of the American Union.

Today, we are drawing up the blueprints for a new economic age, not for starting big institutions but for freeing small entrepreneurs. We have the honor of designing the architecture for a global economic marketplace, with stable laws, strong protections for consumers, serious incentives for competition, a marketplace to include all people and all nations.

Now, I may not know as much about cable modems and T–1 lines as the Vice President— [*laughter*]—I think we made a living of jokes out of that for 6 years. But I do know, thanks to his and others' work, that electronic commerce gives us an extraordinary opportunity to usher in the greatest age of prosperity not only Americans but people all over the world have ever known.

To me, the most moving thing said from this podium today involved the stories of people in Africa and Latin America lifting themselves from abject poverty through access to the Internet. That can happen to more than a billion other people in ways that benefit all of us, if we do this right.

We have made a good beginning. I am confident we will finish the job.

Thank you very much.

NOTE: The President spoke at 12:02 p.m. in Room 450 of the Old Executive Office Building. In his remarks, he referred to John Chambers, chief executive officer, Cisco Systems; Meg Whitman, chief executive officer, eBay; and Prime Minister John Howard of Australia. The transcript released by the Office of the Press Secretary also included the remarks of Vice President Al Gore.

Joint Statement From Australia and the United States on Electronic Commerce
November 30, 1998

Australia and the United States believe that the growth of the information economy is a significant and positive development for both countries and, generally, for society and global business. The benefits of e-commerce, in particular, include access to new markets, quality of service, encouragement of innovation, more efficient management of supply and distribution and better customer service. These benefits should accelerate economic growth in all sectors, and across all regions and communities.

I. *Purpose of Statement*

This joint statement is being made in order to accelerate the development of e-commerce in both countries and empowerment of individual citizens by: providing certainty and building confidence for government, business and consumers in key areas of e-commerce; facilitating progress in key areas, particularly a transparent and consistent legal framework; promoting a dialogue between Australia and the US on e-commerce issues which will benefit government, business and consumers.

II. *Policy Principles*

The growth of electronic commerce will be led by the private sector, and its continued development depends on leadership by the private sector in key areas both domestically and internationally.

Competitive market-based solutions to specific issues for the information economy will promote optimal growth and benefits. Governments should avoid imposing unnecessary regulations. When regulation is necessary, they should rely on a "light touch" regulatory environment. Where the market alone will not solve problems, self-regulation gives maximum control and responsibility to the individual and should be the preferred approach. In some cases this may need to be facilitated by legislation to ensure effective arrangements. In light of the global nature of e-commerce, government-based or industry-based approaches should be coordinated and harmonized domestically and internationally, as far as possible. Government should actively pursue excellence in the online delivery of government services and in its dealings with business.

III. Policy Issues

Australia and the United States agree on the following approaches to key areas of electronic commerce and the information economy:

1. Taxes and Tariffs

Rules for the taxation of the Internet and electronic commerce should be neutral, efficient, simple to understand and should promote certainty. Governments will cooperate closely to ensure effective and fair administration of their tax systems in relation to electronic commerce, including prevention of tax evasion and avoidance. In support of this the Australian and US national tax authorities should continue to consult and cooperate on the taxation issues associated with electronic commerce in international fora, such as the OECD and other bodies, and at a bilateral level in accordance with the exchange of information provisions of the 1982 Australia-US Double Tax Convention.

Australia and the US support the indefinite extension of the WTO declaration of May 1998 not to impose customs duties on electronic transmissions.

2. Developments in International Fora

A. World Trade Organization (WTO): The international trading system under the WTO should foster the growth of electronic commerce by reducing the scope for trade-distorting government intervention and to give enterprises greater access to the global marketplace. Australia and the United States are actively participating in the WTO work program on e-commerce, with the shared objective of undertaking

a comprehensive review of the implications of e-commerce for the application of WTO agreements and for mandated negotiations, taking into account the application of the established body of trade rules to electronic commerce and the importance of further expanding market access and trade liberalization commitments within the WTO framework. The program should also consider the potential contribution of e-commerce to development objectives, and means to promote greater access for enterprises in developing countries to the global digital network. The General Council should continue to coordinate the work program, avoiding duplication with work done elsewhere, focussing on workable outcomes, and keeping open the possibility of adding new issues to the work program.

B. Asia-Pacific Economic Cooperation (APEC): Both governments welcome the ongoing e-commerce work program in a range of APEC sub-fora, including agreement to the key themes and future work program outlined in the APEC Blueprint for Action on Electronic Commerce.

3. Business and Consumer Confidence

It is essential that business and consumers have confidence in transactions conducted electronically. This will be facilitated by action in the following areas:

A. Electronic Authentication: Governments should work towards a global framework that supports, domestically and internationally, the recognition and enforcement of electronic transactions and electronic authentication methods (including electronic signatures). At an international level this should include exploring the possibility of a convention or other arrangements to achieve a common legal approach that will support electronic transactions as well as a variety of authentication technologies and implementation models. This approach should:

a. Remove paper-based obstacles to electronic transactions by adopting relevant provisions from the UNCITRAL Model Law on Electronic Commerce; b. Permit parties to a transaction to determine the appropriate authentication technologies and implementation models for their transaction, with assurance that, to the maximum extent possible, those technologies and implementation models will be recognized and enforced; c. Permit parties to a transaction to have the opportunity to prove in court that their authentication technique and their transaction is valid; d. Take a non-discriminatory approach to electronic signatures and authentication methods from other countries.

B. Privacy: Ensuring the effective protection of privacy with regard to the processing of personal data on global information networks is necessary as is the need to continue the free flow of information. With regard to frameworks for personal data protection, governments and businesses should consider consumers' concern about their personal information. Governments should support industry in implementing effective privacy protection. Personal information should be collected and handled in a fair and reasonable manner consistent with generally accepted privacy principles. The OECD Privacy Guidelines provide an appropriate basis for policy development.

C. Critical Infrastructures: Protection of information, as well as the information systems and infrastructures themselves, is a key element in building user confidence. In some cases information infrastructures are critical to public safety and national economic well-being. The preferred approach to information security is through industry awareness and industry based solutions. The OECD Guidelines for the Security of Information Systems should be the basis for national approaches to information security. Governments should provide leadership and provide advice on threats, vulnerabilities and security responses to ensure that critical information infrastructures are protected.

D. Consumer Protection: Consumers should receive effective protection in the online environment which can be promoted through enforcement of existing consumer protection laws, modification of these laws as necessary to accommodate the unique characteristics of the online market, consumer education, and industry supported mechanisms to empower consumers, and resolve consumer complaints and concerns.

4. Content

The Internet is a medium for promoting, in a positive way, diffusion of knowledge, cultural diversity and social interaction, as well as a means of facilitating commerce. Governments should not prevent their citizens from accessing information simply because it is published online in another country. Empowerment of users, including parents in relation to material which may be unsuitable for children, should be achieved through information and education, as well as through the availability of filtering/blocking systems or other tools. Industry self-regulation will assist in the promotion of content labeling. Industry will need to deal appropriately with complaints about prohibited content. We encourage international cooperation between law enforcement authorities to prevent, investigate and prosecute illegal activities on the Internet and the illegal use of e-commerce by criminal and terrorist organizations.

5. Government Services and Information

Good administration is promoted by governments ensuring that they pursue excellence in delivery of government services and information online in a citizen-friendly way rather than reflecting bureaucratic structures. Governments can also contribute to the development of the information economy by acting as role models and market catalysts. Business and user confidence will be enhanced by effective government use of electronic payments systems.

Government led developments in public key and other authentication technologies should be encouraged to facilitate trade through the use of secure electronic exchange of permits and licenses.

Both countries recognize the value of, and will continue to support, international cooperation in electronic delivery of government services through bodies such as the International Council for Information Technology in Government Administration, and through collaborative work such as the G7 Government Online Project.

Governments consider the remediation of the Year 2000 computer date problem as a matter of critical importance to both countries and international communities. The exchange of appropriate information and expertise would provide significant assistance in addressing this issue.

6. Domain Name System (DNS)

Both countries agree on the following guiding principles:

Stability: The US Government should end its role in the Internet name and numbering system in a manner that ensures the stability of the Internet. The introduction of a new management system should not disrupt current operations or create competing root systems. During the transition and thereafter, the stability of the Internet should be the first priority of any DNS management system. Security and reliability of the DNS are important aspects of stability, and as a new DNS management system is introduced, a comprehensive security strategy should be developed with input from the private sector.

Competition: The Internet succeeds in great measure because it is a decentralized system that encourages innovation and maximizes individual freedom. Where possible, market mechanisms that support competition and consumer choice should drive the management of the Internet because they will lower costs, promote innovation, encourage diversity, and enhance user choice and satisfaction.

Coordination: Certain management functions require coordination. In these cases, responsible industry self-regulation is preferable to government control and is likely to be more flexible and responsive to the changing needs of the Internet and of Internet users. The self-regulatory process should, as far as possible, reflect the bottom-up governance that has characterized development of the Internet in this area to date.

Representation: Private sector mechanisms should be developed to ensure that domain name system management is responsive to Internet stakeholders worldwide.

7. Intellectual Property Rights

Adequate protection of intellectual property rights on a technology-neutral basis is essential for the development of e-commerce. The new WIPO Copyright Treaty and the Performances and Phonograms Treaty provide a sound basis in this regard. Further consideration of implementation of the measures in the treaties will be a positive step.

8. Infrastructure

The supporting infrastructure for online transactions must be technically and commercially suitable, particularly in terms of adequate bandwidth and competitive pricing. The optimal outcome will be achieved through competitive provision of infrastructure and telecommunication services within a pro-competitive regulatory framework.

IV. Work Program

Recognizing that bilateral cooperation can complement the development of essential multilateral frameworks, Australia and the United States will:

Work with the private sector and consumer groups in both countries to promote dialogue and cooperation on the issues contained in this statement, and facilitate the translation of such dialogue and cooperation into meaningful international frameworks.

Cooperate closely in relevant international fora to support the growth of and access to global e-commerce; these may include, for example, the WTO, WIPO, OECD, UNCITRAL, UNCTAD, and APEC.

Actively promote exchange of information and views at government level on all relevant e-commerce issues. This could include economic and trade issues such as how e-commerce affects small and medium sized enterprises, including their ability to develop markets and generate employment; and the broader economic and social impacts of e-commerce.

Work to ensure that the benefits of such exchanges are shared more broadly, particularly in the Asia Pacific region.

NOTE: An original was not available for verification of the content of this joint statement.

Memorandum on Electronic Commerce
November 30, 1998

Memorandum for the Heads of Executive Departments and Agencies

Subject: Successes and Further Work on Electronic Commerce

The Internet and electronic commerce have the potential to transform the world economy. The United States Government is committed to a market-driven policy architecture that will allow the new digital economy to flourish while at the same time protecting citizens' rights and freedoms.

Today my Administration has released a report that details the significant progress made on the implementation of my Directive on Electronic Commerce of July 1, 1997, and its accompanying policy statement, "A Framework for Global Electronic Commerce." The electronic commerce working group that has coordinated the United States Government's electronic commerce strategy has accomplished a great deal. I am proud of its significant achievements. Governments and private sector organizations around the world now recognize the importance of the Internet and electronic commerce and the viability of the approaches contained in the 1997 report as a means of ensuring future economic success. I am optimistic that the progress realized to date will be continued during the next year.

In order to complete implementation of my July 1, 1997, directive by January 1, 2000, I direct that work continue in the 13 areas listed therein.

In addition, new areas have emerged during the past year that deserve particular attention. To ensure progress in these areas, I hereby direct as follows:

Section 1. The Secretary of Commerce, in appropriate consultation with the Federal Communications Commission, shall encourage the deployment of advanced telecommunications capabilities for all Americans while preserving the vibrant and competitive free market that exists for the Internet and other interactive computer services. These agencies shall work with the Office of the United States Trade Representative to help ensure the elimination of foreign trade barriers to the deployment of advanced telecommunications capabilities.

Sec. 2. The Secretary of Commerce, in appropriate consultation with the Federal Trade Commission and other relevant agencies, shall foster consumer confidence in electronic commerce by working to ensure effective consumer protection online. This shall include exploring opportunities for global cooperation to enforce consumer protection laws and facilitating partnerships between industry and consumer advocates to develop redress mechanisms for online consumers. These agencies shall work with the Office of the United States Trade Representative to help avoid the creation of foreign trade barriers while protecting the interests of consumers.

Sec. 3. The Secretary of State, in appropriate cooperation with the Agency for International Development, the Secretary of Commerce, the Federal Communications Commission, the Overseas Private Investment Corporation, and other relevant agencies, shall initiate a program to help accelerate the spread of the Internet and electronic commerce to developing countries.

This shall include a demonstration of successful models for development in a small number of interested countries and should highlight and create incentives for public/private sector partnerships to serve as a catalyst for successful private action. The Secretary of State should seek the cooperation of the World Bank and other multilateral organizations in initiating this program.

Sec. 4. The Assistant to the President for Economic Policy, in appropriate consultation with the Secretaries of Commerce, the Treasury, Labor, and other relevant agency heads, shall analyze the economic impact of the Internet and electronic commerce in the United States and internationally. This shall include convening a conference of experts from the public and private sectors to assess the impact of investments in information technology and the influences of electronic commerce and related technologies on the economy. These experts shall consider new indicators for the information economy, new types of data collection, and new research that could be undertaken by organizations in the public and private sectors. To broaden public understanding of the impact of electronic commerce, the Department of Commerce shall publish a follow-up report to the "Emerging Digital Economy" report it issued this year.

Sec. 5. The Secretary of Commerce and the Administrator of the Small Business Administration shall develop strategies to help small businesses overcome barriers to the use of the Internet and electronic commerce. The initiative shall consider the need to train Federal Government employees who have contact with small businesses on the use of the Internet and electronic commerce; identify commonly used Government products and forms that should be moved to the Internet to enable small business to use the Internet to interact with the Government; and develop an outreach plan to enhance electronic access to information and services that can assist small businesses' development using the Internet and electronic commerce.

Sec. 6. The directives in sections 1–5 of this memorandum and my July 1, 1997, directive shall be conducted subject to the availability of appropriations and consistent with the agencies' priorities and my budget.

Sec. 7. The Vice President shall continue his leadership in coordinating the United States Government's electronic commerce strategy.

Further, I direct that heads of executive departments and agencies report to the Vice President and me through the Electronic Commerce Working Group in 1 year on their progress in meeting the goals of the July 1, 1997, directive as well as their accomplishments under this memorandum.

WILLIAM J. CLINTON

NOTE: The memorandum referred to the President's memorandum of July 1, 1997, on electronic commerce (*Public Papers of the Presidents: William J. Clinton, 1997 Book II* (Washington: U.S. Government Printing Office, 1999), p. 898).

Statement on the Death of Dante B. Fascell
November 30, 1998

Hillary and I were saddened to learn of the death of former Florida Congressman Dante Fascell. Just last month, I had the privilege to award Congressman Fascell with the Medal of Freedom for his 38 years of dedicated public service in the U.S. House of Representatives.

Dante Fascell contributed immeasurably to America's national security, to our leadership in the global economy, and to our quality of life. He demonstrated an unwavering commitment to civil rights, environmental protection, and

openness in Government. Dante served as the chairman of the House Foreign Affairs Committee for 9 years, supporting emerging democracies, pressing for arms control, and promoting fair trade and dialog among nations. His achievements are a testament to his vision and leadership. We will miss this true hero, whose selfless conduct as a public servant set a shining example for all Americans. Our thoughts and prayers go out to his wife, Jeanne-Marie, his two children, and the entire Fascell family.

Statement on the Death of John Stanford
November 30, 1998

Hillary and I are deeply saddened to learn of the death of General John Stanford. His life was marked by bravery and dedicated to the service of his country. From Vietnam to the Pentagon to the public school classrooms of Seattle, America is lucky to have been blessed by General Stanford's leadership, compassion, and vision. After 30 years of military service, the general brought his own infectious brand

of courage and optimism to a new battle. He streamlined and reinvigorated Seattle's schools, inspiring his students to strive for excellence and an entire community to believe once again in their public schools. Our thoughts and prayers go to his wife, Patricia, their sons, Steven and Scott, and the students, teachers, and schools of Seattle.

Remarks at WETA's "In Performance at the White House"
November 30, 1998

The President. Thank you. Ladies and gentlemen, the American musical is one of our Nation's most beloved art forms. It's also one of the most encompassing. What other country can

hum tunes from songwriters as varied as George Gershwin, Eubie Blake, Irving Berlin, Fats Waller, Cole Porter, Betty Comden, and Adolph Green?

And typical of our diverse Nation, the greatest excitement comes when America's various musical traditions intersect. When African-American, Jewish, and European classical traditions come together in the songs of George Gershwin, when Thomas "Fats" Waller and Andy Razaf mix the syncopation of jazz with the forms of popular musical theater, there is a new song in the world, a song that could only come from America.

Tonight we welcome to the East Room, from the musical theater, four artists who are at the top of their game. They have lent their voices to some of our most favorite American classics, and I'm sure they'll take American music to new heights in the next millennium, and hopefully in the next few minutes.

I think it's appropriate that we've gathered here in America's home because tonight we're going to hear what these terrific performers sing at home, with no one to please but themselves.

And now please join me in welcoming our emcee for the evening. I first met him after I saw his terrific performance in "City of Angels," for which he won a Tony. He won another Tony for his role in "Chicago" and sang at both my Inaugurations.

Ladies and gentlemen, Mr. James Naughton.

[*At this point, the program, entitled "The Singer and the Song," proceeded.*]

The President. Was this great or what? [*Applause*] Unbelievable. They were wonderful. Thank you all. Mr. Naughton, thank you. I think you have a whole new career, the "Righteous Father's Sons." [*Laughter*]

Well, it's been said that it's easier to understand a nation by listening to its music than by learning its language. Tonight we heard the energy, the excitement, the very soul of America.

I want to thank all of our wonderful performers, James Naughton, Brian Stokes Mitchell, Jennifer Holliday, and Patti LuPone, and all the great musicians and arrangers who accompanied them. This was a very special night. They have given us a great gift.

Thank you all, and good night.

NOTE: The President spoke at approximately 7:50 p.m. in the East Room at the White House. The program was recorded for later broadcast on public television.

Presidential Determination No. 99–6—Memorandum on Delegation of Authority Concerning Refugee Assistance
November 30, 1998

Memorandum for the Secretary of State

Subject: Delegation of Authority Under Section 2(b)(2) of the Migration and Refugee Assistance Act of 1962, as Amended

By virtue of the authority vested in me by the Constitution and laws of the United States of America, including section 301 of title 3 of the United States Code, I hereby delegate the functions and authorities conferred upon the President by section 2(b)(2) of the Migration and Refugee Assistance Act (MRAA) of 1962, as amended, 22 U.S.C. 2601(b)(2), to the Secretary of State, who is authorized to redelegate these functions and authorities consistent with applicable law. The Secretary of State, or his

or her delegate, is directed to provide notice to the President of any use of the functions and authorities delegated by this determination.

Any reference in this memorandum to section 2(b)(2) of the MRAA, as amended, shall be deemed to include references to any hereafter-enacted provision of law that is the same or substantially the same as such provision.

You are authorized and directed to publish this memorandum in the *Federal Register*.

WILLIAM J. CLINTON

NOTE: This memorandum was released by the Office of the Press Secretary on December 1. It was not received for publication in the *Federal Register*.

Remarks Announcing AIDS Initiatives
December 1, 1998

Thank you, Amy, for your magnificent remarks and the power of your example. Thank you, Cynthia, for coming to this big, scary crowd. [*Laughter*] She was nervous. I said, "Well, look at the bright side. At least you got out of school for a day." [*Laughter*]

I thank the other children who are here with us. And I want to thank all the members of our administration who have helped so much in this cause: Secretary Albright; Brian Atwood; Dr. Satcher; our AIDS Policy Director, Sandy Thurman; members of the Council on HIV and AIDS. We're glad to have Nafis Sadik here, the Director of the U.N. Population Fund. Richard Socarides from the White House, I thank you and all the other members of the administration. And I, too, want to join in expressing my appreciation to the Members of Congress who Brian mentioned for their support for AIDS funding.

But I especially want to thank Amy for being here and reminding us of what this is all about. When she was speaking, my mind wandered back to an incident that occurred when I was running for President in 1992. Some of you have heard me say this before, but I was in Cedar Rapids, Iowa, a place largely known for its enormous percentage of Czech and Slovak citizens. And there was in the crowd at this rally where I was speaking a woman who was either Czech or Slovak, probably, holding an African-American baby. And I said. "Whose baby is this?" She said, "This is my baby." And I said, "Where is this baby from?" She said, "Florida, I got her from Florida." [*Laughter*] And it was October in Cedar Rapids, and she should have been in Florida, probably. [*Laughter*] She said, "This baby was born with AIDS and abandoned, and no one would take this baby." This woman had—her marriage had dissolved; she was raising her own children alone. But because she heard about children like this wonderful little girl, she adopted this baby.

And every year since, about once a year, I see this young child. I've watched her grow up now, and I'm happy to tell you that 6 years later she's still alive and doing pretty well. She comes to the NIH for regular checkups, and she comes by the White House to see her friend. And every time I see Jimiya, I am reminded of what this whole thing is about.

And I think I should tell you one other thing. When Amy was standing up here with me and I was telling her what a fine job she did, she said, "I'm so glad that Cynthia could be here and that I could say Carla's name in your presence."

This is, I think, very important for people who have not been touched in some personal way—who have never been at the bedside of a dying friend, who have never looked into the eyes of a child orphaned by AIDS or infected with HIV—to understand. And I believe, always, that if somehow we could reach to the heart of people, we would always do better in dealing with problems, for our mind always conjures a million excuses in dealing with any great difficulty.

Let me begin, even in this traumatic moment, to say we have a lot to celebrate on this AIDS Day. We celebrate the example of Amy and Cynthia. Just think, a decade ago people really believed that AIDS was unstoppable. The diagnosis was a virtual death sentence. There was an enormous amount of ignorance and prejudice and fear about HIV transmission. Most of us knew people who couldn't get into apartment houses or were being kicked out or otherwise; their children couldn't be in school because of fears that people had about it. Every day, for people who had HIV or AIDS and their families, every day was a struggle a decade ago, a struggle for basic information, for treatment, for funding, and all too often, for simple compassion.

For 6 years, thanks to many of you, we have worked hard to change this picture, and so have tens of thousands of other people across our country and across the globe. We've worked hard to draw attention to AIDS and to better direct our resources by creating the office of National AIDS Policy and the President's Council on HIV and AIDS. We had the first-ever White House conference on AIDS. We helped to ensure that people with HIV and AIDS cannot be denied health benefits for preexisting conditions. We accelerated the approval of more than a dozen new AIDS drugs, helping hundreds of thousands of people with AIDS to live longer and more productive lives.

Working together with members of both parties in the Congress, we increased our investment in AIDS research to an historic $1.8 billion. This year we secured $262 million in new funding for the Ryan White CARE Act, providing medical treatment, medication, even transportation to families coping with AIDS. This October we declared that AIDS had reached crisis proportions in the African-American, Hispanic-American, and other minority communities, and fought for a $156 million initiative to address that. Today the Vice President is announcing $200 million in new grants for communities around the country to provide housing for people with AIDS.

The results of these and other efforts have been remarkable. For the first time since the epidemic began, the number of Americans diagnosed with AIDS has begun to decline. For the first time, deaths due to AIDS in the United States have declined. For the first time, therefore, there is hope that we can actually defeat AIDS.

But all around us there is, as we have heard from all the previous speakers, fresh evidence that the epidemic is far from over, our work is far from finished, that there are rising numbers of AIDS in countries like Zimbabwe, where 11 men, women, and children become infected every minute of every day. There are still too many children orphaned by AIDS, tens of thousands here in America, tens of millions in developing nations around the world.

And when so many people are suffering and with HIV transmission disproportionately high, still, among our own young people here in America, it's all right to celebrate our progress, but we cannot rest until we have actually put a stop to AIDS. I believe we can do it by developing a vaccine, by increasing our investment in other forms of research, by improving our care for those who are infected and our support for their families.

Last year at Morgan State University, I declared that we should redouble our efforts to develop an AIDS vaccine within a decade. Today I am pleased to announce a $200 million investment in cutting-edge research at the NIH to develop a vaccine. That's a 33-percent increase over last year. With this historic investment, we are one step closer to putting an end to the epidemic for all people.

I'm also pleased to say that there will be more than $160 million for other new research critical to fighting AIDS around the world, from new strategies to prevent and treat AIDS in children to new clinical trials to reduce transmission.

And as hard as we are working to stop the spread of AIDS, we cannot forget our profound obligation for the heartbreaking youngest victims of the disease, the orphaned children left in its wake. Around the world, as we have heard, millions of children have lost their parents. Their number is expected to rise to 40 million over the next 10 to 15 years. Some of them are free of AIDS; others are not. But sick or well, too many are left without parents to protect them, to teach them right from wrong, to guide them through life and make them believe that they can live their lives to the fullest.

We cannot restore to them all they have lost, but we can give them a future, a foster family, enough food to eat, medical care, a chance to make the most of their lives by helping them to stay in school. Today, through Mr. Atwood's agency, we are committing another $10 million in emergency relief that will, though seemingly a small amount, actually make a huge difference for many thousands of children in need around the world.

I'm also directing Sandy Thurman to lead a fact-finding mission to Africa, where 90 percent of the AIDS orphans live. Following the mission, she will report back to me with recommendations on what more we can do to help these children and give them something not only to live for but to hope for.

Eleven years ago, on the first World AIDS Day, we vowed to put an end to the AIDS epidemic. Eleven years from now, I hope we can say that the steps we took today made that end come about. If it happens, it will be in no small measure because of people like you in this room, by your unfailing, passionate devotion to this cause, a cause we see most clearly expressed in the two people sitting right behind me.

Thank you all, and God bless you.

NOTE: The President spoke at 1:15 p.m. in Room 450 of the Old Executive Office Building. In his remarks, he referred to HIV/AIDS activist Amy Slemmer, who introduced the President; Ms.

Slemmer's adopted daughter, Cynthia, and Carla Edwina Barrett, Cynthia's biological mother; and Laura Poisel and her adopted daughter, Jimiya, who was born with AIDS. The World AIDS Day proclamation of December 1 is listed in Appendix D at the end of this volume.

Radio Remarks Announcing Housing Grants for People With AIDS
December 1, 1998

For too many Americans living with AIDS, poverty is nearly as much a threat as the disease itself. People with AIDS face enormous medical bills and are often too sick to hold a job. Without our help, many would be forced to live in unfit housing or even to become homeless. We must not turn our backs on these Americans when they need us most. Today I am announcing $221 million in grants that will help meet the housing needs of the 85,000 Americans who have AIDS and those who live with a family member with the disease. These grants, administered by the Department of Housing and Urban Development, will mean that people fighting AIDS don't have to also fight to keep a roof over their heads.

NOTE: The President's remarks were recorded at approximately 5:47 p.m. on November 24 in the Oval Office at the White House for later broadcast. The transcript was released by the Office of the Press Secretary on December 1.

Presidential Determination No. 99–7—Memorandum on Pakistan and India
December 1, 1998

Memorandum for the Secretary of State

Subject: Pakistan and India

Pursuant to the authority vested in me as President of the United States, including under section 902 of the India-Pakistan Relief Act of 1998 (Public Law 105–277), to the extent provided in that section, I hereby waive until October 21, 1999, the sanctions and prohibitions contained in section 101 and 102 of the Arms Export Control Act, section 620E(e) of the Foreign Assistance Act of 1961, and section 2(b)(4) of the Export-Import Bank Act of 1945, insofar as such sanctions and prohibitions would otherwise apply to activities of the Export-Import Bank, the Overseas Private Investment Corporation, and the Trade and Development Agency with respect to Pakistan and India; assistance to Pakistan and India under the "International Military Education and Training" program; the making of any loan or the providing of any credit to the Government of India or the Government of Pakistan by any U.S. bank; and the extension of any loan or financial or technical assistance to Pakistan by any international financial institution in support of the assistance program that Pakistan is negotiating with the International Monetary Fund.

You are hereby authorized and directed to report this determination to the Congress and to arrange for its publication in the *Federal Register.*

WILLIAM J. CLINTON

NOTE: This memorandum was not received for publication in the *Federal Register.*

Remarks at a Democratic National Committee Dinner
December 1, 1998

Thank you very much. I'm delighted to see all of you. I think this is the first—virtually the first speech I've given since the election. I'm delighted to be here. I thank you for coming; I thank you for your support.

Thank you, Jeff and Andy and Charles and all the other cosponsors of tonight. I want to thank Governor Romer and Steve and Len Barrack and all the other people here from the DNC and the people who are here from the White House staff.

A great deal of what needs to be said has probably already been said, but I would like to just make a couple of remarks if I might. First of all, all of you who have been part of this administration, both formally and informally through your support, have helped us to make some real differences in the lives of Americans. I said today, at the World AIDS Day, that while there are alarming trends in the growth of AIDS around the world, we can take a lot of comfort in the fact that the rate of new infections is declining in America, that the death rate went down in America. And that is because, in no small part, I think, the efforts that you made which made it possible for us in the last 5½ to 6 years to have an increase in research of 65 percent and prevention of 34 percent and drug assistance up 640 percent—it's a big deal to me because I don't think we want medicine out there that ordinary people can't have access to—and the Ryan White Act funding of 240 percent.

You mentioned the minority initiative, which is very important. Today, on World AIDS Day, we announced that we would put $200 million in the next fiscal year into the NIH to develop an AIDS vaccine; another $160 million into NIH for other AIDS-related research; that we would invest several million dollars in trying to deal with the problems of AIDS orphans around the world; and that we would have $200 million, which the Vice President announced today, in housing assistance for people with HIV and AIDS. So we are moving in the right direction.

I'd like to ask you also to continue your support for the larger agenda of inclusion of this administration. The real mandate of this election was for the American people to pull together

and to go forward. We have a generation of baby boomers about to retire, and we've got to figure out how to save the Social Security system in a way that does not bankrupt our children and our grandchildren.

We have an enormously successful economy, but deeply disturbing trends that you may have seen on the front page of, I believe it was, the New York Times in the last couple of days, indications that we are now falling behind other countries in the rate of our children who are graduating from high school and the rate of our young people who are actually finishing college as opposed to those who are going. We have a big education agenda. Some of it was enacted in the last session of the Congress; some of it was not.

We have a huge health care agenda out there, including the Patients' Bill of Rights, which is very important for everybody who is covered by a managed care plan. And I feel especially driven on this issue because I have supported the expansion of managed care. I thought it was absolutely imperative to manage the health care expenditures of this country better when I became President. But I don't think it's wrong for people—right for people to be denied access to a specialist or otherwise to have enormous disadvantages simply because of the health care plan they happen to find themselves in.

We have enormous numbers of people between the ages of 55 and 65—most of you are younger than that, but if you're not that age, you'll be there before you know it. It doesn't take long to live a life, I've discovered. We have enormous numbers of people who can't get any health insurance. We proposed, at no cost to the taxpayers, to let them buy into the health plan of the Federal Government—I think, a very important initiative.

And so there's a whole broad agenda out there that helped to bring the American people together and to rally support to what we were trying to do in the last election. And Roy said he thought the inclusion message was important; I believe that. And I believe that what we have to continue to do is to demonstrate that we have more things in common than we have dividing us.

In the end, the American people are almost always called upon to make the same decision: Are you for progress or partisanship; are you for people or politics; are you for unity or division? And I think—I said this before; I hate to say it, and I wish it weren't true. But I think that—because I wish we never had to have these sober reminders—but sometimes when terrible tragedies strike us, they bring us to our senses in a way that would never otherwise be the case. And I think the horrible death of Matthew Shepard helped to sober the country up and think about what it is that is really essential, not just about our citizenship in this country but about our humanity.

So I ask you to continue to work with us, to continue to help push us forward, and to continue to help move this country forward, to continue to involve more people in the life of the administration and ultimately in the future of America.

I feel very grateful to be here serving, and I feel very grateful to have had the support of those of you around this table. And I look very much forward to 2 more years of significant progress.

Thank you very much.

NOTE: The President spoke at 7:10 p.m. in the Colonial Room at the Mayflower Hotel. In his remarks, he referred to dinner cohosts Jeff Soref, vice chair, Democratic National Committee Gay and Lesbian American Caucus, author Andy Tobias, and fashion designer Charles Nolan; Gov. Roy Romer of Colorado, general chair, Steve Grossman, national chair, and Leonard Barrack, national finance chair, Democratic National Committee; and murder victim Matthew Shepard.

Remarks at a Democratic National Committee Dinner
December 1, 1998

Thank you very much. Ladies and gentlemen, let me first of all say, when Steve Grossman was standing up here bragging on everyone else, I thought to myself: When he took over our party when we were $18 million in debt, it didn't seem like a very sound decision on his part—not a sound political decision, not a sound business decision because he had to stop doing other things, probably not a good thing for his family. And we wouldn't be here if he hadn't put in all those long hours and long days and long weeks and long months. He never got tired. People talk about how I don't; I do get tired. I plead guilty: I get tired. Steve Grossman never got tired. [Laughter] And I think we ought to tell him that we know that, and we thank him so much. [Applause] Thank you.

Let me say tonight is a special night for all of us because we're joined by three of our new Senators, and I'm very proud of all of them. Hillary and I have known Evan and Susan Bayh for a long time. They're both my golfing partners; they used to be my jogging partners back when I was young like they still are. And we served as Governors together. We've done a lot of things together for years. And I was abso-lutely thrilled to see the great success that they enjoy.

I met John Edwards in North Carolina when he and Elizabeth were down there. We went to a very hot rally one night, and I went away—and Erskine Bowles went down with me. It was the day we had the—we celebrated America's Heritage Rivers, and we did the New River in North Carolina. And then we went to this big event where John was the featured speaker. And we walked out, and Erskine and I had to go back to Washington. I said, "Erskine, I'll swear I believe that guy can be elected." This is months beforehand. [Laughter] And sure enough, he was, thanks to a magnificent effort in North Carolina.

And all of you know that Hillary and I virtually moved to New York State in the Schumer campaign. And I saw Chuck and Iris and their daughters up close on many occasions, campaigning. I thought I knew New York real well, but Chuck Schumer taught me a few things and showed me a few people and a few places and a few neighborhoods that I had not known before then.

And I really believe that these people embody not just the future of our party but the future of our country. And I am honored to serve with them, and I am very much looking forward to it.

Let me be very brief. All of you are here, this is sort of a yearend celebration, the last of a long series of efforts. I want to tell you also that it may be true, as Steve said—and as many of our friends in the Republican Party have said since the election in which they outspent us by more than $100 million—it may be true that money is trumped by message. And it must be true at some level, because they did outspend us by more than $100 million.

But I also think it's important to remember that the message has to get out. And if you hadn't been willing to come to so many of these events, hear me give the same speech over and over again, and be there for us in the bad times as well as the good, it wouldn't have been the same on election day. I have done this now for quite a long time, and I will never do it again on my own behalf, so I can tell you from a lifetime of experience that it is quite possible to win an election in which you are outspent, but only if you have enough to be heard. And so you gave our people a chance to be heard. And you gave our people a chance, as Steve never tires of saying, to be organized, to show up, to be counted. And I want you to know I am very grateful.

The last thing I want to say is we now have a heavier responsibility going into next year and the next year than we would otherwise have had because of the gains that were made, because of the elections that were won against all the odds, because the American people said so loudly, so clearly, so unmistakable, "We like the way we're changing. We like the path we're on. We want to keep on. We want to keep moving economically. We want to keep moving toward greater social harmony. We want to keep tackling our problems and solving them and getting them out of the way and going on. We want to keep reaching out to the rest of the world in a positive way."

Because they said that, because they did say, "We choose progress over partisanship and people over politics and unity over division," we have a higher responsibility. Elections are not simply the choices of people to sit in slots until the next election, they are a mandate for certain kinds of action or inaction, certain kinds of direction or changes of direction.

And so I say to you, we have a responsibility to lead and to try in good faith to work with the Republicans to save Social Security for the 21st century; to give every child in this country an excellent, world-class education; to deal with the challenges of the health care system, including the Patients' Bill of Rights; to do whatever it takes to maintain our leadership for peace and freedom around the world; and to stabilize the global financial system so that we can continue to have long-term prosperity and opportunity here at home and for our friends and neighbors in other countries.

And down deep, beneath it all, we have a responsibility to keep working to reconcile the American people to one another, to really stand up for the best kind of unity, to stand against the politics of division, to prove that we have more in common than what divides us.

That is what I believe the voters asked us to do a month ago, and that is what I intend to spend 2 years doing. And I am profoundly grateful that these three magnificent public servants are going to be in the United States Senate to carry their load and then some.

Thank you very much.

NOTE: The President spoke at 10:01 p.m. in the East Room at the Mayflower Hotel. In his remarks, he referred to Steve Grossman, national chair, Democratic National Committee; Senator-elect Evan Bayh and his wife, Susan; Senator-elect John Edwards and his wife, Elizabeth; and Senator-elect Representative Charles E. Schumer and his wife, Iris.

Remarks Following a Meeting With Congressional Leaders
December 2, 1998

Thank you very much, Senator. Ladies and gentlemen, first of all, I want to congratulate the new members of the leadership in the Democratic Senate caucus and thank the returning Members for their service.

I would like to acknowledge the presence and the leadership of one Senator who had to leave, Senator Patty Murray from Washington State, recently reelected. Patty Murray had to go home to a memorial service for General John Stanford, the superintendent of the Seattle schools. And on behalf of the First Lady and the Vice President and myself, I would like to say at the outset that we admire John Stanford. He was a patriot. He was a great educator. His loss is a loss to the children of Seattle and to the people of the United States, and our prayers are with his family. And we thank Senator Murray for going home to that service.

Now, let me say that we just had a good meeting, but it was a good meeting not about what happened last month but about what happened—what will happen in the months ahead and the mandate that we have received to move forward on the American people's agenda.

This is a remarkable moment for our country. We have the strongest economy in a generation. It gives us the opportunity and the obligation to move forward on the deepest concerns of the American people and the great challenges of our time, to move forward in education, to move forward in health care, to move forward on Social Security, to move forward in stabilizing the global economy so we can continue to grow the American economy.

The American people have made it clear that they expect us to focus on modern schools and world-class educations for their children, on a sound Social Security system for the 21st century, on strong patient protections in the area of managed care.

Senator Daschle, his colleagues, and we in the administration are determined to make pas-

sage of a comprehensive Patients' Bill of Rights a top priority in the next Congress. It is a decision that the Congress should be able to make in short order. We must give the American people the peace of mind that comes from knowing that when they fall ill, they will be treated as people, not dollar signs on a ledger.

I have taken many steps to do everything I could to strengthen patient protections. Just last week—or this week, our administration instructed hospitals all across America that waiting for approval from an insurance company cannot be a reason for denying a person emergency care.

We have also extended the protection of the Patients' Bill of Rights to people who are in federally funded health care coverage plans. We have gone to the Supreme Court to help clear the way for patients who have been harmed by health plans' decisions to seek justice under State law.

But now the time has come for Congress to do its part to give all Americans the protections of the Patients' Bill of Rights. With Senator Daschle and his colleagues leading the way, we will make this not a Democratic issue or a Republican issue but an American issue.

Thirty days ago the American people gave all of us our marching orders. They want us to work on their behalf. They want us to work on their business. They want us to go forward into the future with progress, not partisanship. We heard them, loud and clear. And all of us look forward to working with our colleagues, across party lines, to create a new season of achievement and progress for the American people.

Thank you very much.

NOTE: The President spoke at 11:10 a.m. at the South Portico at the White House.

Remarks Prior to Discussions With Prime Minister Nawaz Sharif of Pakistan and an Exchange With Reporters
December 2, 1998

President Clinton. Let me begin by saying I am delighted to welcome Prime Minister Sharif and his group here to the White House and to the Oval Office. The United States values its long friendship with Pakistan very, very much.

We have a very full agenda today. All of you know of my concern to do everything we can to end the nuclear competition in South Asia, which I believe is a threat to Pakistan and India and to the stability of the world. We also want to work with Pakistan to promote economic growth there, to continue our mutual concern to fight terrorism, and deal with some of the other regional issues.

So we have a great deal to discuss, and I'm very much looking forward to it.

Would you like to say anything?

Prime Minister Sharif. Thank you, Mr. President. I am also very delighted to meet you, and thank you for inviting me to America.

We've had meetings—also. I am sure that you are taking interest in the affairs of Pakistan, which of course also concern the United States of America, and we hope to work together. And you are doing your best and, of course, it is also my endeavor to remove all the misperceptions which are there in our bilateral relations.

And I look forward to working together with you and strengthening our relations with the United States of America.

F–16 Aircraft

Q. Mr. President, New Zealand has said that it has agreed to lease the 28 F–16's whose sale was blocked to Pakistan in 1990. Has that received the U.S. blessing?

And Mr. Prime Minister, would you accept or find acceptable such a deal which would only give you about $105 million, much, much less than you originally paid for the planes?

President Clinton. Let me say that I don't presume to answer for the Prime Minister, but we have—I have a report to make on this issue which is somewhat more extensive, and after we have a chance to discuss it, then we will make available, obviously, to the public where

we are on this. And so I'd like to have a chance to discuss it with him, and then we'll have a statement to make on it.

Impeachment Inquiry

Q. Mr. President, what about the direction of the Judiciary Committee's investigation, the expansion into campaign fundraising irregularities? What should you and the White House be doing to deal with that new turn in the investigation?

President Clinton. Well, you know, I have a group of lawyers handling that, and I presume they'll—we'll find some time to talk about that. But the Congress, in the end, has to make its own decisions about what it will do and how it will conduct itself. It's important for me to get on with the work of the country, and that's what I'm doing here, and that's what I intend to continue to do.

Q. Mr. President, why have you decided not to——

Future Visit to Pakistan and India

Q. [*Inaudible*]—on the signing of the Comprehensive Test Ban Treaty, and would you consider anything short of that that would allow you to go ahead with the visit to Pakistan and India next year?

President Clinton. I hope it will be possible for me to go next year. I've looked forward to it for a long time, and I hope I will be able to go. Obviously, I hope that the treaty will be signed.

Q. But is it a condition?

Pakistan-India Relations

Q. Mr. President, are you ready to bring both Prime Ministers from India and Pakistan here in Washington for further talks or to solve the problems of 50 years between the two countries?

Prime Minister Sharif. That is—[*inaudible*]. [*Laughter*]

President Clinton. You know, that's work that I always like to do. I've enjoyed my opportunities to work with the parties in the Middle East and in Northern Ireland, but it only works when both parties wish the United States to be involved. Otherwise we can't be effective.

Let me say that I have been very encouraged that the two Governments have resumed their direct conversations; I think it's very hopeful. And I think Prime Minister Sharif has been very forthcoming in this regard. And I think he deserves a lot of credit, and I hope the people of Pakistan support his decision to continue this dialog with India. I think it's very important.

At any time there's anything that I can do that both parties will agree to our doing, of course I will be happy to do it.

Mergers, Layoffs, and the Global Economy

Q. Sir, can I ask you a question on the—could I ask you an economic question, please? Could I ask you a question on the economy, please? Thousands of people are losing their jobs at Boeing plants. Kellogg today announced a similar move. The Exxon-Mobil merger is going to cause people to lose their jobs. What's your concern about the economic impact, and is there anything that the administration can do for these people?

President Clinton. Well, I think on the merger question—let's deal with that one first. Of course, you've heard what Exxon and Mobil have said; you know where the price of oil is; you know what the facts are. My position on mergers has always been that if they increase the competitiveness of the company and bring lower prices and higher quality service to the consumers of our country, then they're good. And if they don't, they aren't. And you know we've got the National Economic Council reviewing this whole merger issue.

On this specific one, I have to be very careful in what I say because of the way our law works and the judgment that might have to be made by independent people in the Federal Government about that.

On the Boeing and the economy generally, this is—particularly with Boeing, which I am very concerned about because I've worked so hard to help Boeing and our aerospace industry generally and to get employment up—I think it is clearly a result of the global financial crisis and in particular the economic problems in Asia. And that's why I have given such a high priority for the better part of a year now to trying to—actually slightly more than a year now—to trying to stabilize the situation there, limit the spread

of the financial contagion, and then reverse conditions in Asia and restore economic growth there.

I can't tell you how important it is from my point of view for the United States to be actively involved in trying to restore the conditions of growth in Asia. We can only maintain our leadership in the whole aerospace area if there are countries beyond our borders able to purchase the airplanes we produce. And this, I think, is purely and simply a function of the downturn in Asia. We saw it first in our farming communities, where the price of grain dropped because Asian purchases dropped so much. And if we can—that's why I went to Korea and Japan. And if we can make progress there and see some growth coming back in Asia, then you'll see these orders—the countries will be able to make good on these orders. They'll start buying the airplanes again, production lines will start up again, and they'll call the workers back.

And that's my goal, before it affects other industries, to try to get that growth going back in Asia. It's very, very important to the American people to do that.

[*At this point, one group of reporters left the room, and another group entered.*]

Discussions With Prime Minister Sharif

President Clinton. Let me say, if everyone is here, I would like to just make a brief remark. I am delighted to have the Prime Minister and members of his Government here in the Oval Office today. We value our friendship with Pakistan very much.

We have a very full agenda to discuss. All of you know of my concern to limit nuclear proliferation in South Asia. I don't believe it's good for the peace and stability and security of Pakistanis or Indians or the world. And I hope we can make some progress there. But I also want to be supportive in any way that we can to help the economy of Pakistan to grow, to benefit ordinary citizens of your country. And I hope we can discuss our common interest in fighting terrorism and a number of our other interests in the region.

So I am delighted to have the Prime Minister here, and I'm looking forward to our conversation.

Would you like to say something?

Prime Minister Sharif. I have already said, Mr. President, I am delighted to be here, too.

I thank you very much for extending this invitation to me. I'd like to work with you; Pakistan would like to work with the United States of America. And there are a lot of issues on which we have common interest, and we will be very happy to extend all the help and assistance as far as we are concerned, especially on the issue of terrorism. And we have been fighting terrorism, and you know that we've been cooperating with the United States of America also.

And all the other issues, as the President has mentioned, we have a full agenda today. We will discuss each and every thing that concerns America and Pakistan.

Nuclear Proliferation in South Asia

Q. Pakistan has been a victim of unilateral Pakistani-specific sanctions, whereas India, the—country of Pakistan has been let loose to tear up all their nuclear programs. India was the one who started the first proliferation there, but still Pakistan has been a victim of the U.S. sanctions. Don't you think it was unfair? And if it was unfair, what is your administration going to do to compensate for what Pakistan has already suffered?

President Clinton. Well, first of all, we have, as a part of our dialog on nonproliferation, we have actually lifted a large number of the sanctions that were applied against Pakistan to try to get economic activity going there again. And we will continue to discuss with the Prime Minister what we can do to make further progress.

In terms of the test, what we were required to do was mandated by an act of Congress. There was no discretion in the executive branch about it. I have worked very hard to put our relationships back on a more normal path, and we have lifted a number of these sanctions already. And I look forward to making further progress on that.

Kashmir

Q. Mr. President, that's not——

Q. [*Inaudible*]—you have been very effective in resolving the Palestine dispute in the Middle East, and would you also——

The President. That's a——

Q. I mean, to some extent. Would you also be using those good offices to resolving the Kashmir dispute which has festered and threatens a war in the subcontinent?

The President. Well, that is work that I think is important to do. I've worked, as you pointed out, in the Middle East and Northern Ireland. But the United States can be effective in that role only when both parties want us to do so. There is no case in which we have injected ourselves into a dispute in the absence of the agreement of both sides, because otherwise it doesn't work.

I will say this. I want to applaud the Prime Minister for supporting resumption of direct talks with the Indians. I think that is very important. I think if you look at, if you imagine what the world could be like in, let's say, 20 years if the dispute over Kashmir were resolved and South Asia—India and Pakistan were both reconciled to each other and focused on a positive future, I think the potential for increased prosperity among ordinary citizens and increased global influence that both have is virtually unlimited. I think this conflict is holding both nations back and diminishing the quality of life of ordinary citizens.

So I would do anything I could to help to resolve it. But the most important thing is that the leaders are discussing it again; they're working on it. And I think what they need, what both leaders need, is a little elbow room from the political forces in their country and from ordinary citizens, because we see in place after place after place, when people can resolve old differences, then they can look to new possibilities.

And if you look at the potential that Pakistan and India have for economic growth and for solving a lot of the personal problems that ordinary people have, it's absolutely staggering. There's no place on Earth with a greater potential for development in the next 30 years than South Asia, no place. And if this thorn can be taken from the sides of the people, that will occur. So I would support that in any way I could.

Q. Can I have a followup?

Q. Mr. President——

President Clinton. Yes, yes, one more.

Future Visit to Pakistan and India

Q. Will you renew your plan to visit the subcontinent, that you canceled last year?

President Clinton. Let me say two things before you go. First of all, on the question—I very much hope it will be possible for me to go next year. I have looked forward to going for many years. As I think you know, my wife had a wonderful trip not very long ago, and

I want to go, and I hope it will be possible for me to go.

One other thing, Prime Minister, if you'll indulge me before the Pakistani press leaves, I think I would like to say to the people of Pakistan, on behalf of not just myself personally but the United States, our country has been enormously enriched by the presence of Pakistani-American citizens and immigrants. And we are a stronger, better place today because of the people who have come from Pakistan to the United States, and that makes me all the more determined to try to be a positive force and a good friend and a good partner. And I hope we're going to make some progress today.

NOTE: The President spoke at 1:15 p.m. in the Oval Office at the White House. A tape was not available for verification of the content of these remarks.

Statement on the Resignation of Steve Grossman as National Chairman of the Democratic National Committee
December 2, 1998

While it is good news for his family, the resignation of DNC National Chairman Steve Grossman is a loss for the Democratic Party. Steve has been a leader, a party builder, a prolific fundraiser, and a wonderful friend to Hillary and me.

When Steve became national chairman in early 1997, the Democratic Party faced an enormous debt and the possibility that we would not have the financial resources to compete effectively in the midterm election. With Steve's energy and dedication, the party has nearly eliminated its debt, and we had the resources we needed to compete in November.

Steve and our general chairman, Governor Roy Romer, have made a remarkable team. The millions of voters mobilized under their leadership led to the extraordinary and historic successes of Democratic candidates nationwide.

Steve's life has been dedicated to public service, his community, and his faith. I will always be grateful to him for his service to our party and the Nation. Hillary and I wish the best to Steve, his wife, Barbara, and their sons, David, Benjamin, and Joshua.

Statement on the Acquittal of Former Secretary of Agriculture Mike Espy
December 2, 1998

I am pleased by the jury's verdict today acquitting former Secretary of Agriculture Mike Espy of all charges brought by the Independent Counsel. Mr. Espy served his country and my administration with distinction—first as a Congressman from Mississippi and then as Secretary of Agriculture.

As Secretary, Mike Espy worked hard and successfully to create a Department that now better serves the American people. He was a relentless champion for America's farmers and consumers. He reached out when lives and livelihoods were threatened by natural disasters in rural communities and offered relief. He was an advocate for those suffering from hunger, and he fought for the environment.

After what have been challenging times for Mr. Espy, both personally and professionally, I am heartened that he has, as he said, emerged from this ordeal stronger. I hope that, as he moves forward, he will continue his notable record of service to the country.

NOTE: The statement referred to Independent Counsel Donald C. Smaltz.

Remarks at a Democratic Leadership Council Dinner
December 2, 1998

Thank you very much. Ladies and gentlemen, I have to ask a couple of questions. The first question I want to ask is whether you can actually hear us. Can you hear? Some say yes; some say no. So-so. How's that? One of these mikes is working, but is that better? Okay. Still so-so. I'll do the best I can.

You know, this magnificent gallery may not be the best place for a speech, but most of you have heard my speech anyway. But it is a wonderful place, full of the rich history of Washington, full of the great culture of our country. It has special memories for me, because I once stood on a platform in this very same spot, a little over 3 years ago, with King Hussein, Shimon Peres, Yasser Arafat, and the late Prime Minister Rabin—the last time I ever saw him. So I have always very strong feelings, when I come to this place, about the importance of the public mission of citizens.

I was thinking on the way over here of the day, 7 years ago, when I spoke to the DLC in Cleveland, when our party was suffering, our Nation was struggling. The DLC was a very small group with very large ideas. And I said that we had to offer the American people a new choice rooted in old values, that offers opportunity, demands responsibility, gives citizens more say, provides them with responsive government, because we recognize that in fact we are a community. We are all in this together. We will go up or down together.

These words—opportunity, responsibility, community—came to identify and embody a new approach to government and politics, tying our oldest, most enduring values to the information age. We said we wouldn't seek to stop the currents of economic change, but we would not, as Americans and as Democrats, tell our people they had to sink or swim on their own. We said that the way to advance the spirit of FDR was not to preserve his programs in amber but to remember that he said, "New conditions impose new requirements." We said we were New Democrats, and we called our approach the Third Way.

I think it's fair to say that our ideas were not universally welcomed or even wholly understood by some of our own fellow partisans, by the Republicans, or by the press. But we believed America could work again and America could lead again, and we won the Presidency in 1992.

Then we made some tough and sometimes controversial decisions on the economy, on foreign policy, on crime, the environment, welfare, health care, but we got America moving again. And with our commitment to build a bridge to the 21st century, the American people gave our party the White House again in 1996, for the first time since 1936.

And in 1997 and 1998 we continued to push these new ideas, and I believe we have regained the trust of the American people in their Government. Last month, standing strong and united on a platform of fiscal responsibility, strengthening Social Security, renewing our public schools, protecting people in the new health care marketplace, dealing with the challenges of the global financial crisis, our party won an historic election victory.

I'm sure all of you know that it was the first time the President's party has gained seats in the House in the sixth year of the Presidency since 1822. Now, since I'm not a candidate anymore, I can say that the last time that happened, in 1822, the other party disappeared. [*Laughter*]

I don't believe that will happen this time, partly because those in the other party who had the greatest success in this election year were those who campaigned with language and often even policies strikingly similar to our own. When Republican Governors stand in front of banners that say "opportunity" and "responsibility," when they talk of community, it may not be the sincerest form of flattery, but it's flattery nonetheless. And even more, it's a sign that America is moving in the right direction, that the common sense and the uncommon dreams of the American people are being heard.

All of you know, I'm sure, that these same ideas are reviving center-left political parties throughout the industrialized world as people everywhere struggle to put a human face on the global economy, from Great Britain and Germany to Greece and The Netherlands.

Far from Europe, in Brazil, bold actions by like-minded President Cardoso have tamed that country's notorious inflation, pointed the way for a new model for emerging democracies. And it all started with the DLC, a political movement begun by people, many of whom were in rooms like this when we all began. Today, less than 15 years after we started, the ideas pushed by the DLC are literally sweeping the world, and you should be very, very proud.

I also think it is very important to point out that we have done more than fashion a politically appealing agenda that is well marketed. We have actually worked hard to find the right way to have a leading industrial nation thrive in the 21st century. We have worked hard to marry politics and policy, to build a new American consensus.

Now, having said that, here's the main point I want to make tonight: This is not a time for self-congratulation. I applaud the work being done by the DLC, bringing in people today to talk about tomorrow's ideas, working on finding and training people to run for public office who share those ideas. We have got America working again, but many of the difficult tasks of transforming our country for a new century and a new millennium still lie ahead. And we have to understand that there will be obstacles in the path. There are genuine problems out there in the global economy. We are beginning to feel them here, in energy, in aerospace, in steel, in agriculture. We have to face these challenges.

There are also many Americans who have not yet felt the benefit of the ideas we are pushing. There are many neighborhoods which still haven't seen the revitalization of enterprise that we're so proud of. There are many schools that still aren't working for their children. There are many challenges we have not met. Therefore, we have to move forward with a little humility, as well as with a great deal of determination.

I'd like to talk about how we got here and ask you to remember three things as you go forward. First, our ideas have met the most important test: They actually work in the real world. If we want our ideas for tomorrow and the next day to work, they have to meet that test as well.

There was a bestseller when I ran for President called "America: What Went Wrong?" In my first Inaugural Address, I said there is nothing wrong with America that can't be fixed by what is right with America. Today, the question is: America, what went right? What went right

was new ideas: welfare reform; community policing; doubling the earned-income tax credit; creating AmeriCorps, which now has its 100,000th member, and—they're doing a wonderful job around the country—and an economic plan that focused on reducing the deficit, expanding investment, and expanding trade.

By almost every measure, American families are better off. We have also met our responsibilities to promote peace, prosperity, and security around the world. And perhaps best of all, our country is regaining its legendary faith in itself. We actually believe that we can make tomorrow better than today for all Americans willing to work hard and be good citizens.

The second thing I think we ought to remember is that our ideas work because they're true to our values and our common sense. For too long, politics treated issues like education or crime or health care or welfare—you name it, any issue—as a battle over ideology, not a problem to be solved but a political matter to be exploited. The idea was to divide and conquer the electorate, to split blacks from whites, to split Hispanics and other immigrants from Americans who were born here, even though their parents or their grandparents or their great-grandparents weren't, to split the North from the South, the middle class from the working class.

If the American people said anything at all in the last election with a loud, resounding roar, it was, "No, thank you; we do not want to be split anymore. We choose progress over partisanship." The American people, out of the wreckage of Oklahoma City, out of the horror of the African-American citizen being brutally murdered in east Texas, out of the awful death of young Matthew Sheppard, out of the shooting of the doctor in New York, out of the arguments around the kitchen table, somehow they always get it right if they've got enough time. And they said, "In the world we're living in, our diversity is a blessing. It is a richness. It is our key to the future. We will not be divided. We are going forward together. There cannot be opportunity and responsibility unless there is community."

And we must never forget that lesson. It is our key, our heart and soul as a party.

And as we look ahead, we have to confront these difficult issues. I want to remind you that we did not say ever that all the choices would be easy but that, if we had to make hard choices, they ought to be the real choices. It is a false choice to say that we have to choose between work and help for the needy. It is a false choice to say people ought to have to choose between doing right by their children and being effective at their jobs. It is a false choice to say we have to choose between punishing people who commit violent crimes and trying to prevent kids from committing those crimes in the first place. It is a false choice to say you have to choose between cleaning up the environment and growing the economy. And it is a false choice to say you have to choose between being proud of your race, your religion, or any other special characteristic you have, and being most proud of being an American and a child of God. Those are false choices. We have enough hard, real choices to make, and we should make them.

The third thing I want to remind you of is that we made a decision that was profoundly important, that the way Government works matters, that we could not maintain the confidence of the American people and we could not have ideas that delivered unless the Government was functioning in a sensible, modern, and prudent way. Things that used to be boring, things you could never get people to stand still at a standup reception like that and listen to, became the Vice President's reinventing Government program. And we have worked at it very, very hard.

We didn't take a chainsaw to the Government, but we did slim it down, and we did change the programs. And we now have the smallest Federal Government since the first time John Glenn went into space. And it works better. The last time John Glenn went into space, a couple of weeks ago, just for example, in the last 6 years, NASA, with a smaller staff and a smaller budget, had gone from two space launches a year to six space launches a year. That matters to people.

It matters whether this thing works or not. And I know it will never get the headlines, and I know that it will not be in the reports of my speech tomorrow in the press, but it matters.

If you like the fact that the crime rate went down, remember there had to be a system for getting the 100,000 police out there. If you believe it's a good thing to have welfare reform, but people who are moved from welfare to work should have child care and health care for their children, there had to be a system to do that.

If you like the fact that we could cut the size of the deficit and increase our investment in education and transportation and many other areas, remember we had to reduce the size of Government by over 300,000 people to do that.

So I ask you, don't forget about the nuts and bolts. They matter. It really does matter whether people get up every day and go to work and worry more about what they're doing than what is said about what they're doing in the daily columns. It is very, very important that we remain serious about this.

The fourth thing that I want to say is that we have succeeded, in no small measure, because we understood that America's interests at home could no longer be divided from America's interests around the world; that America's values at home could no longer be protected unless we stood up for those values around the world. This is a very small globe.

It is a good thing that we work for peace in the Middle East, in Bosnia, in Kosovo, in Northern Ireland. It is a good thing that we worry about nuclear weapons on the Indian subcontinent. It is a good thing that we worry about whether people half a world away will have their children's legs blown off by landmines, or may be subject to chemical or biological weapons. It is a good thing that we worry about whether pollution is destroying the environment of people in Latin America, in Asia, in some other place, because it will all come home here.

We live in a world where our responsibilities to others are important and integral to our ability to do right by ourselves and our future. Those things we must remember.

And as we look ahead, let me say that I am very, very excited about the next 2 years. I'm looking forward to this State of the Union; I'm looking forward to working with this Congress. As we always do, we will do our best to work with members of both parties. We hope that the people in the other party will come forward and work with us, because we have a big agenda.

In the 20th century, we built a safety net to give dignity to our parents. In the 21st century, we have to prove that we can strengthen the Social Security system so we can take care of the baby boomers without bankrupting their children. We can do that.

In the 20th century, we built the first-ever mass middle class in the world, in no small measure through strong public schools. In the

21st century, with a much more diverse population, we have got to prove we can revolutionize those schools so they can prepare our children for the information age.

In the 20th century, we found a way to tackle the cycles of boom and bust, to prevent another Great Depression from occurring. In the 21st century, we have to prove we can do that with the global financial crisis so that we can be secure at home. I will say again what I said before: What you see here, when farm prices go down in the high plains because of the Asian financial crisis, when Boeing has to lay people off because people can't buy the airplanes they've ordered, when the steel industry is overwhelmed by imports from countries who can sell for nothing because their currencies have depleted—when you see these crises, they are simply symptoms of the larger reality that will govern our children and our grandchildren's lives.

We must be prepared to undertake the duty of leading the world toward a new resolution so that we can continue to grow the global economy without having another global collapse because we did not do our duty in our time, as our forebears did 50 years ago.

Now, there are a lot of other things to do, but you get the point. I am so grateful that I was given the chance to serve as President; that I was given a chance to implement so many of the ideas that many of us began, in the mid-eighties, to articulate. But it is just a beginning. It took a good while just to get America up and working again.

But when you reel off all the statistics—the lowest unemployment in 28 years, the smallest percentage of people on welfare in 29 years, the first balanced budget and surplus in 29 years, the fastest-rising wages in over two decades, the lowest crime rate in 25 years, the highest homeownership in history—I say to you, all that means is that America is working again, and that's a great tribute to the American people as well as to the ideas that we have helped to make real. But we have not completed the process of transforming this country for the 21st century, for the information age, and all of you know it.

So I say again, I ask you to leave here with renewed determination, with renewed energy, and with no little humility for the task ahead. When we met in Cleveland in 1991, no one there dreamed that we could have accomplished, either politically or substantively, for our country what has happened in the intervening years. No one but Al From; he knew it all along. [*Laughter*] No one else.

And you can be proud of that. This is the work worthy of a lifetime. I'm proud that I was fortunate enough to meet Al and Will Marshall and all the DLC people; I'm proud that I was able to work with people like Joe Lieberman and John Breaux. And I have to mention one other of our early DLC members who had a very good day today, former Secretary of Agriculture Mike Espy. I know we all wish him well, and we're happy for him.

But I leave you with this thought. The real test of our ideas is whether they outlive this Presidency; whether they are bigger than any candidate, any speech, any campaign, any debate. The real test is whether we can find a way to carry them on and on and on, and whether we can find a way to avoid self-satisfaction and self-congratulations, and always be searching for the new answers to the new challenges.

If we remember the basic things that got us here, if we remember how we were when we started, if we keep the fire for the future of not only our party but our children, our country, and our world, then 8 years from now, 80 years from now, the DLC will be here, doing its job in America's greatest days.

Thank you, and God bless you.

NOTE: The President spoke at 8:30 p.m. at the Corcoran Gallery of Art. In his remarks, he referred to King Hussein I of Jordan; former Prime Ministers Shimon Peres and Yitzhak Rabin of Israel; Chairman Yasser Arafat of the Palestinian Authority; President Fernando Henrique Cardoso of Brazil; Al From, president, Democratic Leadership Council; and William Marshall, president, Progressive Policy Institute.

Remarks to the Community in Newport, Rhode Island
December 3, 1998

Thank you. First of all, I want to thank Teri Sullivan for her introduction and for her work here for you. She's up here with all these politicians. I think she did a good job, don't you? Let's give her another hand. [*Applause*]

I'd like to thank Governor Almond, Senator Chafee, Senator Reed; Senator Pell, it's great to see you again; Congressman Kennedy, Congressman Weygand. I know that—and, Mr. Mayor, thank you for making me feel so welcome here today. I met you, members of the Newport City Council. I think former Governor Sundlun is here. John DeVillars is our EPA Regional Administrator. And your secretary of state, James Langevin, members of the legislature, I thank you all.

I'd also like to say that I have two staff members who are here from Rhode Island, and I brought them home today, Karen Tramontano and Marjorie Tarmey. I thank them for their service. Thank you all for being here.

You know, when Patrick Kennedy was up here speaking, he said that I had been to Rhode Island five times. President Eisenhower came right over there and stayed in that big yellow house and played golf. But only President Kennedy had been here more times. And I told the Governor, I said, "If you'll give me President Eisenhower's house and access to the golf course, I'll break the Kennedy record." [*Laughter*]

Actually, I feel compelled to admit, since we're here in this setting, that when I was a boy growing up, my greatest aspiration was to come to Rhode Island to play in the Newport Jazz Festival. And I always thought as a child, you know, when I was 16, I thought that would be the measure of my success. I couldn't have dreamed I'd become President. I thought, if I could just play one time in the Newport Jazz Festival, I would know I had arrived. It's not too late; in a couple of years maybe you'll let me come back when I get practiced up and play.

On the way in here, I thanked Senator Chafee in particular for his help in trying to sensitize the Congress to the great challenge of climate change and global warming. But on this magnificent December day in Rhode Island, it's hard

to see it as a threat, I must say. I appreciate this wonderful day. I'm glad to be in the "city by the sea," the once and future home of the America's Cup.

I thank you, too, for being such a vital center of our United States Navy. And I also thank you for the work done here to save the bay. I learned, in preparation for this trip, there's a documentary on the origin of the Star-Spangled Banner airing tonight, filmed right here at Fort Adams, overlooking this majestic sweep of the Narragansett Bay. The film, obviously, is about events which occurred during the War of 1812, in the battle surrounding Fort McHenry. Interestingly enough, it was shortly after that that the British came up the Potomac and burned the White House, completely gutting it inside, nearly destroying it totally. I think it's very interesting that that film was made here, and that's because the Narragansett Bay looks almost the same today as it did 200 years ago. You can be very, very proud of that, and I hope you are.

I came here today because I wanted to showcase your remarkable efforts to save this bay. I hope this picture will be broadcast all across the United States to people this afternoon and this evening. But I also wanted to talk about how your community and all communities across our Nation can protect our precious water resources, from the tap water to the rivers to the lakes to the ocean.

Last week, on Thanksgiving, all Americans had the opportunity—and I hope we took it—to give thanks for these good times in our country. This month our economy will achieve the longest peacetime expansion in American history. We have nearly 17 million new jobs, the lowest unemployment in 28 years, the lowest percentage of our people on welfare in 29 years, the first balanced budget and surplus in 29 years. For the first time in over 20 years the wages of all groups of Americans, all income groups, are on the rise. Homeownership is the highest in American history.

In Rhode Island, unemployment is down to 5 percent. There's a lot of new construction going on here in Newport. The Navy is building the Strategic Maritime Research Center. High-tech industries are flourishing. Our country has a lot to be thankful for.

But I think the question we should be asking ourselves now, particularly with all the financial turmoil going on in the rest of the world, is what are we to make of the success America has now? Should we just relax and enjoy it? Or should we instead say, this is a unique moment for us, and we need to use this moment of prosperity and confidence to look ahead to this new century, to the challenges our children will face, and do our best to use the resources we have now to meet the challenges of tomorrow? I think it is clearly what we should be doing, and I think most Americans agree.

So when you list those challenges—giving all of our children a world-class education so they compete in the global economy; making sure all of our people have access to quality health care and the protections in our Patients' Bill of Rights; making sure that we have made the changes in the global economy necessary to avert the kind of terrible financial crises we've seen engulfing Asia; saving Social Security for the 21st century in a way that does not bankrupt the children of the baby boomers; and finally, I will predict to you, the challenge of improving the environment, from global warming to cleaning up the oceans, to preserving our natural heritage, to preserving the cleanness of our water and air, to dealing with the problems of toxic waste—all of these issues, I predict to you—you look at all the children here—will dominate America's public debate for the next 30 years.

We now know something very important. We were talking about—your congressional delegation and I were talking about it when we got off the plane today. We know something very important. We know that for the last several years technological advances have made it possible for us to grow our economy while improving the environment. Most people who have control over decisions still believe that in order to grow the economy you have to destroy the environment, and they just want to destroy it as slowly as possible. That is simply not true anymore. And I came here to Rhode Island to say the American people need to lead the way into the 21st century in saving the environment.

Now, I also want to say that the only way we're ever going to make it is if we make this commitment as Americans, across party lines, across regional lines, and across all the lines of our various occupations and our different perspectives.

The first great environmental President of the United States was Theodore Roosevelt, a great progressive Republican. When he launched our Nation on the course of conservation at the dawn of our century, there were pessimists then who claimed that protecting the environment and expanding the economy were incompatible. The American people proved them wrong and Theodore Roosevelt right.

Then they said cutting pollution from cars would cause our economy to break down by the side of the road when we established air quality measures for automobiles. But we now have the most powerful automobile industry in the world again. America, in the last 3 years, has become number one in auto production again, because our people are doing a good job with cleaner cars that are more productive and more efficient. It didn't wreck our economy; it just helped our environment.

There were people who said if we banned deadly pesticides, it would cause American agriculture to wither and decline, but they were wrong. The more pure we have made the production of our food, the more our farmers have come to dominate worldwide competition in agriculture.

There were those who said if we acted in New England to curb acid rain, it would be the worst economic disaster since Noah's flood. Well, they were wrong. The last 6 years proved them wrong.

And I can give you example after example after example. Every time Americans have tried to clean the air, to clean the water, to look to the future, there have been those who said, "If you do this, it will wreck the economy."

Now, let's use our imagination. Every time you figure out how to make the water cleaner, someone has to discover something; someone has to make it; someone has to adapt all the machinery to use it. That creates a lot of jobs. Every time you figure out how to run a car on natural gas or on electricity, you create a whole new set of jobs for people. Every time you figure out how to advance the cause of clean water—when we have to deal with the challenges of cleaning up the ocean, which will be a huge challenge that will directly affect the lives and the quality of life of every child in this audience, it will create a lot of jobs.

We have got to get over this idea that protecting our environment and the quality of our lives is somehow bad for the economy. It will be one of the cheap generators of high-wage jobs in the 21st century, and I hope you here in Rhode Island will lead the way.

With the strong support of your congressional delegation, we have launched an historic plan to help communities clean up our rivers and streams, because every river in America should be healthy enough for our children to fish and swim. As I think at least one of your Members said earlier, the balanced budget I signed in October will allow us to protect dozens of more natural and historic sites around the country, including the Rhode Island National Wildlife Refuge Complex, the last remaining undeveloped coastal habitat in southern New England. And I thank all the officials here and the Vice President, who also lobbied very strongly for this.

Now, we are moving forward. We also had, as you heard, two Rhode Island rivers—and since you pronounced *cryptosporidium*, Senator Reed, I will try to pronounce the Woonasquatucket River—[*applause*]—and the Blackstone River as American Heritage Rivers. We're working with you to solve the problems that led to beach closings and to restore critical habitats damaged by the North Cape oil spill. We must restore your valuable lobster fishery and preserve forever the health of your cherished coast.

We also have to do more on the water we drink. As Senator Chafee said, with his great help and others, we strengthened the Safe Drinking Water Act 2 years ago with a virtually unanimous vote in Congress, to zero in on contaminants that posed the greatest threat, to help communities upgrade treatment plants like the fine one I just visited.

This past summer I announced a new rule requiring utilities across the country to provide their customers regular reports on the quality of their drinking water. When it comes to the water our children drink, Americans cannot be too vigilant.

Today I want to announce three other actions I am taking. First, we're escalating our attack on the invisible microbes that sometimes creep into the water supply. You heard Senator Reed refer to the tragic episode 5 years ago, early in my Presidency in Milwaukee, when *cryptosporidium* contaminated the city's drinking water, killing dozens of people, and literally making more than 400,000 people sick.

Today, the new standards we put in place will significantly reduce the risk from *cryptosporidium* and other microbes, to ensure that no community ever has to endure an outbreak like the one the people of Milwaukee suffered.

Second, we are taking steps to ensure that when we treat our water, we do it as safely as possible. One of the great health advances to the 20th century is the control of typhoid, cholera, and other diseases with disinfectants. Most of the children in this audience have never heard of typhoid or cholera, but their grandparents cowered in fear of it, and their great-grandparents took it as a fact of life that it would take away significant numbers of the young people of their generation.

But as with so many advances, there are tradeoffs. We now see that some of the disinfectants we use to protect our water can actually combine with natural substances to create harmful compounds. So today I'm announcing new standards to significantly reduce our exposure to these harmful byproducts, to give our families greater peace of mind with their water.

The third thing we are doing today is to help communities meet these higher standards, releasing almost $800 million to help communities in all 50 States to upgrade their drinking water systems, including more than $7 million for communities right here in Rhode Island, to give 140 million Americans safer drinking water.

Now, this is the sort of thing that we ought to be doing in America: tending to America's business, reaching across party lines, looking into the future, thinking about our children. I think it is a very important day.

Let me say that, as you think about the future, I hope you will think about how America will look in 10 or 20 or 30 years. I hope you will tell all your elected representatives, without regard to party: We're on the edge of a new century and a new millennium; we're in a period of unusual economic prosperity; we have the confidence; we have the resources; and we have the knowledge necessary to deal with these big challenges. You don't have every, every year in life when you can deal with the big challenges. How many times in your own lives have you had to worry about just how you were going to put the next meal on the table, how you were going to confront the next family emergency, how you were going to deal with the issue right in front of you?

Countries are like that, too. But now we have this chance, this precious chance to think about our children and our grandchildren and the big problems that they face. The environment is one of them. We ought to seize this chance, and do it for our children.

Thank you, and God bless you.

NOTE: The President spoke at 1:05 p.m. at the oceanfront at Fort Adams State Park. In his remarks, he referred to Teri S. Sullivan, microbiologist, City of Newport Water Department, who introduced the President; Gov. Lincoln Almond and former Gov. Bruce Sundlun of Rhode Island; former Senator Claiborne Pell; and Mayor David S. Gordon of Newport.

Statement on the Decision by Mayor Kurt Schmoke of Baltimore, Maryland, Not To Seek Reelection
December 3, 1998

Since becoming President in 1993, it has been my good fortune to work very closely with Mayor Kurt Schmoke on issues about which the residents of Baltimore and our Nation care. He has been a wonderful partner in our efforts to improve the quality of education for all children, increase the availability of health care and housing, enhance economic development in our inner cities, and revitalize our neighborhoods.

In addition, Mayor Schmoke has been a dependable ally in our efforts to make our streets free from drugs and guns.

I am grateful to the mayor for his public service to Baltimore and our Nation, and I look forward to making the most use of every day remaining in his current term of office to continue our work together.

Letter to Congressional Leaders Reporting on the National Emergency With Respect to the Federal Republic of Yugoslavia (Serbia and Montenegro)
December 3, 1998

Dear Mr. Speaker: (*Dear Mr. President:*)

On May 30, 1992, by Executive Order 12808, President Bush declared a national emergency to deal with the unusual and extraordinary threat to the national security, foreign policy, and economy of the United States constituted by the actions and policies of the Governments of Serbia and Montenegro, blocking all property and interests in property of those Governments. President Bush took additional measures to prohibit trade and other transactions with the Federal Republic of Yugoslavia (Serbia and Montenegro) by Executive Orders 12810 and 12831, issued on June 5, 1992, and January 15, 1993, respectively.

On April 25, 1993, I issued Executive Order 12846, blocking the property and interests in property of all commercial, industrial, or public utility undertakings or entities organized or located in the Federal Republic of Yugoslavia (Serbia and Montenegro) (the "FRY (S&M)"), and prohibiting trade-related transactions by United States persons involving those areas of the Republic of Bosnia and Herzegovina controlled by the Bosnian Serb forces and the United Nations Protected Areas in the Republic of Croatia. On October 25, 1994, because of the actions and policies of the Bosnian Serbs, I expanded the scope of the national emergency by issuance of Executive Order 12934 to block the property of the Bosnian Serb forces and the authorities in the territory that they controlled within the Republic of Bosnia and Herzegovina, as well as the property of any entity organized or located in, or controlled by any person in, or resident in, those areas.

On November 22, 1995, the United Nations Security Council passed Resolution 1022 ("Resolution 1022"), immediately and indefinitely suspending U.N. economic sanctions against the FRY (S&M). Sanctions were subsequently lifted by the United Nations Security Council pursuant to Resolution 1074 on October 1, 1996. Resolution 1022, however, continues to provide for the release of funds and assets previously blocked pursuant to sanctions against the FRY (S&M), provided that such funds and assets that are subject to claims and encumbrances, or that are the property of persons deemed insolvent, remain blocked until "released in accordance with applicable law." This provision was implemented in the United States on December 27, 1995, by Presidential Determination No. 96–7. The determination, in conformity with Resolution 1022, directed the Secretary of the Treasury, *inter alia,* to suspend the application of sanctions imposed on the FRY (S&M) pursuant to the above-referenced Executive orders and to continue to block property previously blocked until provision is made to address claims or encumbrances, including the claims of the other successor states of the former Yugoslavia. This sanctions relief was an essential factor motivating Serbia and Montenegro's acceptance of the General Framework Agreement for Peace in Bosnia and Herzegovina initialed by the parties in Dayton on November 21, 1995 (the "Peace Agreement") and signed in Paris on December 14, 1995. The sanctions imposed on the FRY (S&M) and on the United Nations Protected Areas in the Republic of Croatia were accordingly suspended prospectively, effective January 16, 1996. Sanctions imposed on the Bosnian Serb forces and authorities and on the territory that they controlled within the Republic of Bosnia and Herzegovina were subsequently suspended prospectively, effective May 10, 1996, in conformity with Resolution 1022. On October 1, 1996, the United Nations Security Council passed Resolution 1074, terminating U.N. sanctions against the FRY (S&M) and the Bosnian Serbs in light of the elections that took place in Bosnia and Herzegovina on September 14, 1996. Resolution 1074, however, reaffirms the provisions of Resolution 1022 with respect to the release of blocked assets, as set forth above.

The present report is submitted pursuant to 50 U.S.C. 1641(c) and 1703(c) and covers the period from May 30 through November 29, 1998. It discusses Administration actions and expenses directly related to the exercise of powers and authorities conferred by the declaration of a national emergency in Executive Order 12808 as expanded with respect to the Bosnian Serbs in Executive Order 12934, and against the FRY (S&M) contained in Executive Order 12810, Executive Order 12831, and Executive Order 12846.

1. The declaration of the national emergency on May 30, 1992, was made pursuant to the authority vested in the President by the Constitution and laws of the United States, including the International Emergency Economic Powers Act (50 U.S.C. 1701 *et seq.*), the National Emergencies Act (50 U.S.C. 1601 *et seq.*), and section 301 of title 3 of the United States Code. The emergency declaration was reported to the Congress on May 30, 1992, pursuant to section 204(b) of the International Emergency Economic Powers Act (50 U.S.C. 1703(b)) and the expansion of that national emergency under the same authorities was reported to the Congress on October 25, 1994. The additional sanctions set forth in related Executive orders were imposed pursuant to the authority vested in the President by the Constitution and laws of United States, including the statutes cited above, section 1114 of the Federal Aviation Act (49 U.S.C. App. 1514), and section 5 of the United Nations Participation Act (22 U.S.C. 287c).

2. The Office of Foreign Assets Control (OFAC), acting under authority delegated by the Secretary of the Treasury, implemented the sanctions imposed under the foregoing statutes in the Federal Republic of Yugoslavia (Serbia and Montenegro) and Bosnian Serb-Controlled Areas of the Republic of Bosnia and Herzegovina Sanctions Regulations, 31 C.F.R. Part 585 (the "Regulations"). To implement Presidential Determination No. 96–7, the Regulations were amended to authorize prospectively all transactions with respect to the FRY (S&M) otherwise prohibited (61 *Fed. Reg.* 1282, January 19, 1996). Property and interests in property of the FRY (S&M) previously blocked within the jurisdiction of the United States remain blocked, in conformity with the Peace Agreement and Resolution 1022, until provision is

made to address claims or encumbrances, including the claims of the other successor states of the former Yugoslavia.

On May 10, 1996, OFAC amended the Regulations to authorize prospectively all transactions with respect to the Bosnian Serbs otherwise prohibited, except with respect to property previously blocked (61 *Fed. Reg.* 24696, May 16, 1996). On December 4, 1996, OFAC amended Appendices A and B to 31 C.F.R. Chapter V, containing the names of entities and individuals in alphabetical order and by location that are subject to the various economic sanctions programs administered by OFAC, to remove the entries for individuals and entities that were determined to be acting for or on behalf of the Government of the Federal Republic of Yugoslavia (Serbia and Montenegro). These assets were blocked on the basis of these persons' activities in support of the FRY (S&M)—activities no longer prohibited—not because the Government of the FRY (S&M) or entities located in or controlled from the FRY (S&M) had any interest in those assets (61 *Fed. Reg.* 64289, December 4, 1996).

On April 18, 1997, the Regulations were amended by adding new section 585.528, to provide for the unblocking of the following five vessels: the M/V MOSLAVINA, M/V ZETA, M/V LOVCEN, M/V DURMITOR and M/V BAR (a/k/a M/V INVIKEN) after 30 days (62 *Fed. Reg.* 19672, April 23, 1997). Two previously blocked vessels, the M/V KAPETAN MARTINOVIC and the M/V BOR, were sold prior to August 18, 1997, pursuant to licenses and the proceeds of the sales placed in blocked interest-bearing accounts at U.S. financial institutions as substitute property for the blocked vessels.

On November 6, 1998, section 585.528 was amended to provide for the unblocking of these accounts, representing the two vessels, after 30 days (63 *Fed. Reg.* 59883, November 6, 1998). During this period, United States persons may negotiate settlements of their outstanding claims with respect to the vessels with the vessels' owners or agents. If claims remain unresolved by November 27, United States persons are generally licensed to seek and obtain judicial writs of attachment against the funds during the 10-day period prior to the accounts' unblocking. A copy of the amendment is attached to this report.

3. Over the past 2 years, the Departments of State and the Treasury have worked closely with European Union member states and other U.N. member nations to implement the provisions of Resolution 1022. In the United States, retention of blocking authority pursuant to the extension of a national emergency provides a framework for administration of an orderly claims settlement. This accords with past policy and practice with respect to the suspension of sanctions regimes.

4. During this reporting period, OFAC issued two specific licenses regarding transactions pertaining to the FRY (S&M) or property in which it has an interest. Specific licenses were issued (1) to authorize the payment from blocked funds of licensing fees due to the New York State Banking Department for one of the Serbian financial institutions blocked in 1992 and (2) to authorize the transfer of a blocked account from one financial institution into another.

During the past 6 months, OFAC has continued to oversee the maintenance of blocked FRY (S&M) accounts, and records with respect to: (1) liquidated tangible assets and personalty of the 15 blocked U.S. subsidiaries of entities organized in the FRY (S&M); (2) the blocked personalty, files, and records of the two Serbian banking institutions in New York previously placed in secure storage; and (3) remaining blocked FRY (S&M) tangible property, including real estate.

D.C. Precision, Inc. v. United States, et al., 97 Civ. 9123 CRLC, was filed in the Southern District of New York on December 10, 1997, alleging that the Government had improperly blocked Precision's funds held at one of the closed Serbia banking agencies in New York. This case is still pending.

5. Despite the prospective authorization of transactions with the FRY (S&M), OFAC has continued to work closely with the US. Customs Service and other cooperating agencies to investigate alleged violations that occurred while sanctions were in force. On February 13, 1997, a Federal grand jury in the Southern District of Florida, Miami, returned a 13-count indictment against one U.S. citizen and two nationals of the FRY (S&M). The indictment charges that the subjects participated and conspired to purchase three Cessna propeller aircraft, a Cessna jet aircraft, and various aircraft parts in the United States and to export them to the FRY (S&M) in violation of U.S. sanctions and the

Regulations. Timely interdiction action prevented the aircraft from being exported from the United States. On October 23, 1998, the defendants in the case entered guilty pleas. A sentencing date has not yet been scheduled.

Since my last report, OFAC has collected one civil monetary penalty totaling nearly $4,200 for violations of the sanctions. These violations involved prohibited importations into the United States of goods originating in Serbia.

6. The expenses incurred by the Federal Government in the 6-month period from May 30 through November 29, 1998, that are directly attributable to the declaration of a national emergency with respect to the FRY (S&M) and the Bosnian Serb forces and authorities are estimated at approximately $360,000, most of which represents wage and salary costs for Federal personnel. Personnel costs were largely centered in the Department of the Treasury (particularly in OFAC and its Chief Counsel's Office, and the U.S. Customs Service), the Department of State, the National Security Council, and the Department of Commerce.

7. In the last 2 years, substantial progress has been achieved to bring about a settlement of the conflict in Bosnia-Herzegovina acceptable to the parties. Resolution 1074 terminated sanctions in view of the first free and fair elections to occur in Bosnia and Herzegovina, as provided for in the Dayton Peace Agreement. In reaffirming Resolution 1022, however, Resolution 1074 contemplates the continued blocking of assets potentially subject to conflicting claims and encumbrances until provision is made to address them under applicable law, including claims of the other successor states of the former Yugoslavia.

The resolution of the crisis and conflict in the former Yugoslavia that has resulted from the actions and policies of the Government of the Federal Republic of Yugoslavia (Serbia and Montenegro), and of the Bosnian Serb forces and the authorities in the territory that they controlled, will not be complete until such time as the Peace Agreement is implemented and the terms of Resolution 1022 have been met. Therefore, on May 28, 1998, I continued for another year the national emergency declared on May 30, 1992, as expanded in scope on October 25, 1994, and will continue to enforce the measures adopted pursuant thereto. The importance of maintaining these sanctions is further reinforced by the unacceptable actions and policies of Belgrade authorities in Kosovo and in the areas of human rights, democratization, and war crimes investigations. These developments threaten to disrupt progress in implementation of Dayton and security in the region generally.

Accordingly, I shall continue to exercise the powers at my disposal with respect to the measures against the Government of the Federal Republic of Yugoslavia (Serbia and Montenegro), and the Bosnian Serb forces, civil authorities and entities, as long as these measures are appropriate, and will continue to report periodically to the Congress on significant developments pursuant to 50 U.S.C. 1703(c).

Sincerely,

WILLIAM J. CLINTON

NOTE: Identical letters were sent to Newt Gingrich, Speaker of the House of Representatives, and Albert Gore, Jr., President of the Senate.

Remarks on the Earned-Income Tax Credit
December 4, 1998

Amy's children are over there. And we also have Bernadette Hockaday and her children, and Rhonda Clarke and her children here. They're all here, and we thank them all for coming because they all have benefited from the earned-income tax credit.

I'd like to thank Gene Sperling, who believed passionately in this when I first met him, well over 6 years ago now; Janet Yellen, the Council of Economic Advisers; Secretary Herman, who was here in the White House helping us to implement the earned-income tax credit in '93. I thank Congressman John Lewis and Congressman Bob Matsui, who are here, who have been passionate advocates; and all the other advocates in the room here—Bob Greenstein, Justin Dart, the others who are here—we thank you for your support.

One of the main reasons that I ran for President in 1992 was that I believed that people like Amy could achieve real success if we could unstack the deck against them. I knew that when our Nation was taxing working families into poverty, that was wrong. I knew that when a mother rises at dawn, putting in an honest day's work, and still can't afford to buy the children's clothes, that's wrong. And I was determined to try to do something about it.

I also knew that there was a little-known provision in the Tax Code which had been in for several years called the earned-income tax credit that had the potential, if it were actually expanded at an appropriate level, to lift all working families out of poverty. And that's how all this started.

Again, let me say, I'm very grateful for everybody who has supported this. I think the important—one important thing I'd like to point out is that we have representatives here from the AFL–CIO, from AFSCME, from other unions, most of whose members do not get the earned-income tax credit, and they lobbied for it, too, because they thought it was right. And so, for all of you, I just say I'm very grateful.

What we tried to do in 1993 was two things. First of all, we had to get the economy moving again, and secondly, we had to focus on the special needs of people who were working hard at lower wage levels. But first things first—we had to get the whole economy moving again. Middle class incomes have been stagnant for 20 years, and we could never have given lower income working people the chance to raise their incomes if it hadn't been for a policy promoting overall economic growth.

Just this morning, we received more good news for America's families on our overall economic policies. Secretary Herman's Department reports that last month unemployment fell to 4.4 percent, while inflation remains low and stable. But for nearly a year and a half, the unemployment rate has remained below 5 percent, for the first time in 28 years. And in November the economy added more than a quarter of a million jobs, which means now America has created about 17.3 million jobs in the last 6 years. That is a very good record of which the American people can be very proud.

But let's go back to the main point. Even with all those new jobs, under the present circumstances, the way the economy works, millions and millions of those people would be working full-time and still be living in poverty. So what I wanted to do in 1993 was to create new incentives to help people climb the economic ladder and reach true independence, to enable people to succeed at work and at home, in raising their children.

So we got the dramatic increase in the earned-income tax credit into the budget in 1993. And 2 years ago we fought for and won a substantial increase in the minimum wage, which I still believe we ought to increase again. Unemployment and inflation are low, and it still has not recovered its levels of 20 or 25 years ago, in real-dollar terms.

Today we release a report prepared by the Council of Economic Advisers. It shows that the earned-income tax credit, as a family tax cut, has been a major factor in encouraging work among single mothers, which you heard Amy talk about. It has also been responsible for much of our strong progress in reducing child poverty. In fact, the report shows that of the 4.3 million people who have been lifted out of poverty since 1993 by the earned-income tax credit, over half of them—well over half of them—have been lifted out because we basically doubled the program in 1993.

And again, I want to say to Bob Matsui and John Lewis, we had—it was hard to raise the money to pay for that doubling. And there were a lot of people, even in our party, who were afraid to do it—and with some good reason, as it turned out. But it was the right thing to do, and I hope it is something that all of you will always be proud of.

Now, since 1993, families with two children and one parent working full-time at the minimum wage, therefore, have seen their incomes rise by more than $2,700 because of the increase in the minimum wage and the earned-income tax credit. This has strengthened families; it's strengthened communities. It's helped to restore our compact of mutual responsibility that people who work hard and play by the rules ought to have a chance to be rewarded for it. And again, it helps us to promote both the values of family and work.

So I feel very, very good about this. And I feel great about the overall economic news this morning. But let me also say to all of you, this is not a time for self-congratulation or a time to rest. We have more to do here at home and more to do to stabilize the global economy, if we expect economic growth to continue.

We all know about the economic troubles in Asia; we all see sectors of America's steel industry being overwhelmed by imports at firesale prices. We have all read the headlines about Boeing's layoffs because of the inability of Asian airlines to pay for planes which they have already ordered. We see other problems in the global economy as well. Now we're working hard to reverse the problems in Asia, to limit their reach, to stabilize the long-term system under which so many Americans and so many hundreds of millions of people around the world have benefited. But it is a sobering thought to remind us that we have to continue to work on this.

Finally, let me say, we have to continue to work on the conditions of working families here at home. Many people still cannot get affordable child care. The minimum wage should still be raised. We still have a great deal to do to stabilize the conditions of working families and to genuinely reward work in this country.

In the last session of Congress we passed an expansion of our empowerment agenda to try to bring more jobs, more incomes, more investments into poor inner-city and rural areas. We still have a great deal to do there.

So as you leave there today, and you think about Amy and these other two fine mothers and these beautiful children who are here, and the millions and millions of people whom they represent all across America, I hope you will always be proud of what you have done. But remember, this economy still is not working for everyone, and it is still living in a very turbulent international environment. So I ask you also to continue to support our efforts to deal with the challenges which still have to be met to keep the growth going, and to make sure that what we do here, so far from the lives of most Americans, actually helps them to make those lives better.

Thank you very much, and God bless you all. Thank you, Congressman Rangel. It's good to see you.

NOTE: The President spoke at 10:12 a.m. in the Roosevelt Room at the White House. In his remarks, he referred to Amy Hillen, a job counselor who introduced the President; working mothers Bernadette Hockaday and Rhonda Clarke; Robert Greenstein, executive director, Center on Budget and Policy Priorities; and Justin Dart, Jr., advocate for the rights of disabled persons.

Statement on the International Space Station
December 4, 1998

America has taken a bold and exciting step toward a permanent U.S. presence in space with today's launch of the first U.S.-built component of the International Space Station. A passion for discovery and a sense of adventure—both deeply rooted American qualities—spur our de-termination to explore new frontiers in space and spark our can-do spirit of technological determination. All Americans join me in congratulating the thousands of men and women in our space program that are transforming the dream of an orbiting space station into a reality.

Joint Statement From Pakistan and the United States
December 4, 1998

At the invitation of President Bill Clinton, the Prime Minister of Pakistan, Mohammad Nawaz Sharif, visited Washington on 1–4 De-cember 1998. The Prime Minister was accorded a warm welcome in Washington.

During a cordial and productive meeting and luncheon at the White House on December 2,

President Clinton and Prime Minister Sharif stressed the importance of the longstanding friendship and cooperative relations between Pakistan and the United States. They reaffirmed their commitment to further improve bilateral relations and addressed a number of issues of common concern.

The two leaders reviewed progress in the U.S.-Pakistan dialogue on security and non-proliferation. The President welcomed the Prime Minister's statement made at the UN General Assembly regarding adherence to the Comprehensive Test Ban Treaty and Pakistan's decision to participate constructively in the upcoming negotiations at Geneva on a Fissile Material Cut-off Treaty, consistent with its legitimate security interests.

The President emphasized the importance the U.S. attaches to further progress on non-proliferation and peace and security in South Asia. The Prime Minister affirmed Pakistan's desire to exercise mutual restraint with India consistent with Pakistan's security interests. Both sides welcomed progress made in the U.S.-Pakistani dialogue on security and nonproliferation. The President noted that further progress would facilitate the restoration of broad-based cooperation between the United States and Pakistan.

The President reaffirmed the United States' strong interest in a stable and prosperous Pakistan and reiterated the U.S. commitment to assist Pakistan through its current economic difficulties. Both leaders endorsed the efforts of the International Monetary Fund and multilateral development banks to assist Pakistan. They agreed that an effective, expeditiously approved, and fully implemented IMF program would be a major step to help Pakistan in maintaining sustained economic growth. They acknowledged the importance of reaching a settlement between the Pakistani government and foreign energy investors and expressed hope that such an agreement would help attract fresh foreign investment.

Prime Minister Nawaz Sharif appreciated President Clinton's decision to waive some of the sanctions which had been imposed on Pakistan. He expressed hope that further steps would be taken to remove all remaining sanctions. In this regard, the President emphasized the need for further progress in the ongoing U.S.-Pakistani dialogue on security and nonproliferation. The Prime Minister informed President Clinton about Pakistan's conventional defense requirements. He emphasized the need for an early and fair resolution of the F–16 issue. The President reaffirmed his commitment to such a resolution.

The two leaders reviewed the security situation in South Asia and emphasized the need to resolve all outstanding issues in the interest of peace and stability in the region. Prime Minister Sharif highlighted the centrality of the Jammu and Kashmir dispute to peace and security in South Asia and emphasized the need for an early resolution of this dispute in accordance with the relevant U.N. Security Council resolutions. The President emphasized the importance of the continuation of bilateral negotiations between Pakistan and India with a view to addressing the root causes of their disputes, including Kashmir, taking into account the wishes of the Kashmiri people. President Clinton reiterated his support for these negotiations and his expectation that they will bring results beneficial to both Pakistan and India. Prime Minister Nawaz Sharif welcomed the interest shown by the international community in addressing the Kashmir issue and emphasized his belief that the major powers, especially the United States, need to effectively engage in facilitating a just and lasting solution to the dispute. The President said the United States was willing to lend its assistance to the bilateral dialogue if both sides requested it.

The President and the Prime Minister reaffirmed their strong opposition to terrorism in all its forms and manifestations. They expressed their resolve to work closely to combat international terrorism and emphasized the need for prompt and effective action against international terrorists.

The two leaders agreed to work for an immediate end to the conflict in Afghanistan and the restoration of durable peace, stability and normalcy in the country based on the principals of sovereignty, territorial integrity and non-interference in internal affairs, as well as a political reconciliation and respect for the human rights of all Afghan citizens, including women and girls and ethnic minorities. In this context, they endorsed the efforts of the United Nations "Six Plus Two" group.

The President welcomed Pakistan's efforts to combat narcotics and offered additional funds for law enforcement training. The Prime Minister appreciated the offer, which would strengthen Pakistan's counternarcotics enforcement agencies and meet common goals, including interdiction, extraditions, and eradication.

The President and the Prime Minister agreed to remain in close contact and to continue efforts to build a strong and more broad-based relationship between the two countries. The

Prime Minister reiterated his cordial invitation already extended to President Clinton to visit Pakistan. The President said that he hoped it would be possible to visit Pakistan next year.

NOTE: An original was not available for verification of the content of this joint statement.

The President's Radio Address
December 5, 1998

Good morning. In 1993 I took office determined to get our country moving again, to provide opportunity for all responsible, hard-working citizens, and to create the conditions of a genuine community in our country.

First, we had to get the economy going. Yesterday we got the good news that unemployment is down to 4.4 percent, the lowest in 28 years, with 17.3 million new jobs. But America needs more than jobs to really work. Our country also has to be safer. And we've worked very hard to make our streets, our schools, our neighborhoods safer places to live, work, and raise families. We've put in place a comprehensive strategy of more prevention, strong enforcement, tougher punishment. We've taken more guns and criminals off the street and put more police on the beat. Crime has dropped for 6 years in a row now, to a 25-year low.

This week America launched a new effort to keep guns out of the hands of criminals and make our streets safer. For the first time ever, the Justice Department, working with the States, conducted computerized background checks on all firearm purchases. In its first 4 days, the new national instant check system reviewed more than 100,000 prospective gun sales to make sure only law-abiding citizens took home new guns. And in just 4 days, we stopped more than 400 felons, fugitives, stalkers, and other prohibited purchasers from walking away with new guns. That's more than 100 illegal gun sales blocked each day. Who knows how many lives were saved.

But within just 24 hours after the instant checks went into effect, the National Rifle Association went to court to stop the new system. The gun lobby's goal is plain. As the NRA's

executive director himself put it this week, they want to "scale back" the Brady law.

Five years ago, as the Brady bill was nearing passage in Congress, the gun lobby spent more than a million dollars in a desperate effort to kill it. Fortunately, the good sense of Congress and the will of the American people prevailed. The gun lobby lost. But the American people won. Unfortunately, as we saw this week, they'll stop at nothing to gut the Brady law and undermine our efforts to keep more guns from falling into the wrong hands, even though we now have 5 years of evidence that it works.

We can't turn back. In these last 5 years, Brady background checks have stopped nearly a quarter of a million illegal handgun sales. We can't go back to the days when dangerous criminals walked away from stores with new guns, no questions asked.

Police, prosecutors, and the American people they protect have made it clear they want to strengthen, not weaken, the Brady law. That's why, when the new Congress goes into session next month, one of my top priorities will be to pass legislation to require a minimum waiting period before a handgun sale becomes final. This "cooling off" period will help prevent rash acts of violence and give authorities more time to stop illegal gun purchases.

I also call on Congress to ban juveniles convicted of violent crimes from owning guns for life. There's no reason why young people convicted of violent crimes should be allowed to buy guns on their 21st birthday. And I want to thank Senator Bob Dole for his recent strong public support of this idea.

Finally, we must make sure that firearms sold at gun shows are not exempt from background checks, that gun shows do not circumvent our gun laws. Last month I asked Treasury Secretary Rubin and Attorney General Reno to find ways to close this loophole.

Reducing crime has been one of the American people's greatest achievements in recent years. A decade ago no one thought we could do it. But we did. We must not retreat on this hard-won progress. Instead, we must do even more to support the people and the laws that protect our children and families.

Thanks for listening.

NOTE: The address was recorded at 6:54 p.m. on December 4 in the Roosevelt Room at the White House for broadcast at 10:06 a.m. on December 5. The transcript was made available by the Office of the Press Secretary on December 4 but was embargoed for release until the broadcast.

Remarks at the Memorial Service for William Maurice Smith, Jr., in Wynne, Arkansas
December 5, 1998

Jane, Mark, Murray, Annette, all the members of the family and the friends of Maurice. I stayed up late last night and got up early this morning, and I was trying to think of what I should say. I told Maurice I'd be here, and I figured somebody might ask me to talk. So I thought, well, I ought to start with what he would say to me. Some of it is not repeatable in the church. [*Laughter*] But it would go something like this: Expletive deleted, don't say too much. [*Laughter*]

I think all of our lives we will remember a small man with a craggy face, a gravelly voice, a blunt manner, a keen mind, a kind heart, and powerful emotions; a man who was not always good to himself but was always good to others; a man who could say more with fewer words, or just a grunt or the tip of that crazy old hat of his, than anyone we ever knew.

Now, I collected stories the last 3 or 4 days, and this was the odds-on winner: Bill Clark reminded me that in 1984 we had our first meeting in the Governor's office about the '84 campaign. And we were sitting there, and I began the meeting by saying that I had been so impressed with Hillary's no-smoking policy at the Governor's Mansion I was going to apply it to the Governor's office. Maurice got his hat, put it on, stood up, and started walking. I said, "Where you going?" He said, "Birdeye." [*Laughter*] I said, "I am applying the no-smoking policy of the Governor's Mansion to the Governor's office the day after this next election." [*Laughter*]

He loved to help people. He loved a good fight. But he never sought to destroy his adversary. He loved political campaigns and legislative sessions. He never met a road or a bridge or a levee he didn't like. [*Laughter*] He loved the Fair Board and the University of Arkansas. He loved the land and the water and the people of this State. Most of all, he loved his family and his friends. He loved us. And how we loved him—often more than I think he knew.

Hillary was home a few weeks ago, and she went by to see Maurice in the hospital. And when she came back to Washington, she looked at me, she said, "I just love that man." And she said, "It seemed to me like everybody else in the hospital did, too."

I tried to call him over Thanksgiving, and then he called me back, and finally I got him back. We talked twice in the last week. The first time he said, "I wanted to talk to you one more time. I don't think I'm going to get out this time, and I just want you to know I'm proud of everything we did together, and I love you."

Well, all of you know that I owe him a lot. He was the finance chairman of all my campaigns, the master of ceremonies at my inaugurations—ensuring that they would be brief—my chief of staff. He served on the university board; he ran the highway department; and on the side, he always lobbied for Jane's causes for the disabled.

But when I was flying down here on Air Force One today, thinking I wouldn't be on this plane if it weren't for him, I thought of a day 18 years ago, when some of us here were standing on the backyard of the Governor's Mansion after the 1980 elections. And I had just become the youngest former Governor in the history of America—*[laughter]*—a man with limited future prospects. And that's pretty much the way I felt. And he put his hand on my shoulder, and he looked me in the eye, and he said, "It'll be all right; we'll be back."

I wrote this before I knew the pastor was going to read to us from Luke today. I was thinking of that day today, as we all say farewell to this small man who had such a large impact on all our lives. We say to him, as he said to me so many years ago: Maurice, it'll be all right; God has promised you mercy because you

were merciful to us; kindness because you were kind to us; forgiveness because you forgave us; love because you loved us with all your heart. So, farewell, old friend. I say to you what you said to me so many years ago: It'll be all right; you done good; we'll be together again before you know it.

May God bless his soul.

NOTE: The President spoke at 3:05 p.m. at Wynne Presbyterian Church. In his remarks, he referred to Mr. Smith's widow, Jane; his son, William Maurice (Mark) Smith III; his daughters, Murray Smith Johnson and Annette Smith Stacy; and William E. Clark, owner, CDI Contractors.

Exchange With Reporters Aboard Air Force One
December 5, 1998

[The President's remarks are joined in progress.]

Death of Former Senator Albert Gore, Sr.

The President. ——his father was—for people like me, growing up in our part of the country, Al Gore was the embodiment of the—Albert Gore, Sr., was the embodiment of everything public service ought to be. He was a teacher; he was a progressive; he helped to connect the South with the rest of America; he was progressive on race; he was courageous in standing up for what he believed in—Vietnam. You know, he might have been, himself, in national office if he hadn't been just a little too far ahead of his time.

He was a remarkable, remarkable man, and I'm very grateful that I had the chance to know him and his wife and spend some time with them as a result of our relationship with the Vice President. The country has lost a great patriot, a great public servant, a man who was truly a real role model for young people like me in the South in the 1960's.

Q. How far did you go back with him, sir? When did you first meet him?

The President. Oh, I don't know that I met him, except maybe to shake hands with him, until 1988. But I knew who he was in 1968—'66, when I was working as a young student in the Congress. And I knew who he was when I was in high school.

You know, keep in mind, he was talked about for national office from the fifties on. He and Estes Kefauver were both prominently mentioned. And Tennessee had these two very progressive, very articulate, and very effective voices in the Senate. It was a remarkable partnership. So I always knew who he was, from the time I became at all politically aware.

Q. How did people like Senator Gore, Sr., influence up-and-coming young Southern politicians like yourself?

The President. Well, first of all, they were progressive, and they cut against the grain and the image that the South had in the fifties and sixties of being, you know, anti-civil rights, discriminatory, undereducated, underdeveloped. He was progressive on education, progressive on civil rights, and sponsored the interstate highway bill. He wanted to connect the South to the rest of America, educate the children of the South, stand up for civil rights. He was a remarkable man. And he was brilliant, full of energy.

And the amazing thing was what a life he had after he left the Senate. When his son and I ran in 1992, he and Pauline—Mrs. Gore—they went all over the country, and he'd give these stemwinding stump speeches, you know. I remember once, in 1988, I spoke at the Oklahoma Democratic dinner, and he came to speak for his son. There were seven speakers that night. He gave by far the best speech, including mine, and everybody would have said that. So he was alert and active and contributing and remarkably free of bitterness or rancor even after he left the Senate and his elected life was terminated.

But his greatest impact may have been the inspiration that he provided to countless young people from the time he became a prominent figure in Tennessee.

Q. Did you speak to the Vice President tonight? How is he doing?

The President. I just found out a few minutes ago, so I'm going to go call him now.

NOTE: The President spoke at 6:55 p.m. en route to Washington, DC. These remarks follow the text as released by the Office of the Press Secretary. A tape was not available for verification of the content of this exchange. The related proclamation of December 7 on the death of Albert Gore, Sr., is listed in Appendix D at the end of this volume.

Remarks at the Kennedy Center Honors Reception
December 6, 1998

Thank you very much. The next time there will be three, and then four. [*Laughter*]

Hillary and I are honored to have you back again for another Kennedy Center honors. You know, the conviction that our land of liberty should also be a home for creativity in the performing arts goes all the way back to the very first President ever to live in this great house, John Adams. He wished for an America where, and I quote, "pomp and parade, shows and illuminations flourish from one end of this continent to another." Today, the illumination of our performing arts shines not only across the continent but, indeed, across the world as a life force of our free society.

Dostoyevski defined the mission of artists as "incessantly and eternally to make new roads, wherever they may lead." All the artists we honor tonight have traveled lifetimes across our stages, each in their own way, making those new roads. Their gifts of talent, heart, and spirit are joyous, indelible threads in the fabric of our national life. It is my honor to introduce them.

The "Tonight Show" has seen a lot of comedians come and go, but one night in 1963, a young man by the name of Bill Cosby took the stage and took the Nation by storm. His hilariously deadpan descriptions of Noah loading the ark with animals—[*laughter*]—I still remember it, too; it was pretty funny—launched his career. But it was his deeply personal, univer-

sally funny caricatures of his childhood friends—like Fat Albert and Weird Harold—that made him famous. One critic wrote, "No comic ever entered a child's mind with so much empathy and gusto."

Bill Cosby's remarkable gift is to be able to look inside the human experience and all its depth and diversity and hold it up to the universal light of laughter, and in so doing, to allow all of us to return to our child's mind. For more than 30 years, he has made the ordinary business of life extraordinarily funny business—in best selling books like "Fatherhood" and "Time Flies," blockbuster movies like "Uptown Saturday Night," eight gold records, and, of course, there were some minor successes in television along the way—[*laughter*]—"I Spy," "The Cosby Show," his new hit series.

Bill once said he wanted to make jokes about people's similarities, about what's universal in their experience, and in so doing, to bring us closer together. That is exactly what he has done. We thank him for the lessons and the laughter.

Ladies and gentlemen, Mr. Bill Cosby. [*Applause*]

The curtain parted, the painted face popped out, and "Cabaret" forever changed the musical theater. John Kander and Fred Ebb have given us dark and gleaming shows suffused with metallic melodies. Their musical left the happy days for the harder passages of our century—Germany at the decadent edge of the Nazi nightmare, a desperate dance marathon in the Depression era of Atlantic City, a jazz-age murder in Chicago, a jail cell in revolutionary South America. The New York Times wrote that they shook the ground under our feet—and they certainly set them tapping.

With "Cabaret," "Chicago," "Steel Pier," and "Kiss of the Spider Woman," Kander and Ebb took us a long way from "Oklahoma" and "South Pacific." It has been a relentlessly syncopated journey, with lyrical wit, musical drama, bold and lovely songs that infiltrate our minds and never leave. One of those songs, known to every American, has become the anthem of "New York, New York." [*Laughter*] After all, what good is sitting alone in a room when you can go out and see hit revivals of "Chicago" and "Cabaret"?

Fred Kander and John Ebb have entertained us, challenged us, and touched our consciences. Tonight we salute them for all the daring, all the shows, all the razzle-dazzle.

Ladies and gentlemen, John Kander and Fred Ebb. [*Applause*]

Willie Nelson's music has been a part of my life—like everybody from my part of the country—for a very long time now. After years of campaigning, we can always identify, Hillary and I, with what it's like to be "On the Road Again." [*Laughter*]

Willie Nelson is like America—always in the process of becoming. He changed all the rules about what country music was supposed to be. The granite-faced, long-haired man of the soil put down roots in folk, swing, pop, and rock and roll. And everywhere he went, he gave us something new. His songs are rugged and beautiful, raw and lilting; they're an individual, stubborn declaration of pride and hope amid a world of troubles. They're as restless as he is.

The American highway has been Willie Nelson's second home. In fact, I think that bus of his has gone more miles than Air Force One. [*Laughter*] When someone once asked him why he went into music, he replied, "I thought I could sing pretty good." Well, 200 albums and 5 Grammy Awards later, we know he was right.

A few years ago, the Texas Legislature declared July 4th to be Willie Nelson Day. Let me say that tonight is Willie Nelson's night all across America.

Ladies and gentlemen, Mr. Willie Nelson. [*Applause*]

Anyone who went to the movies in the 1950's knew the music of Andre Previn before they knew his name. From "Kismet" to "My Fair Lady" and 50 other films, his scores and orchestrations were the sounds of the silver screen, winning fans and Oscars.

For some musicians, this achievement might have been more than enough. But Andre Previn's hunger for great music could not be contained. The arc of his music is long, and he has soared across it. He has been called the greatest crossover artist since George Gershwin, and over the course of 50 years, quite literally, he has done it all. As a jazz musician, he has jammed with the best, from Charlie Parker to Ella Fitzgerald. As a conductor, his repertoire ranges from Bach to Stravinsky to Frank Zappa. As a composer, he has blazed a new trail in contemporary music. His new opera, "A Streetcar Named Desire," which opened in San Francisco, is simply the latest challenge in a fearless career.

Andre Previn was 9 years old when his family left Germany to find refuge here in America. Maestro Previn, I'm here to thank you for giving so much to those of us in your adopted country.

Ladies and gentlemen, Mr. Andre Previn. [*Applause*]

I'm happy to welcome Shirley Temple Black back to the White House. But I'm not the first President to do it. She was 7 years old when President Roosevelt asked to meet her, to thank her for the smiling face that helped America through the Great Depression. The price of movie tickets has gone up a little since then—[*laughter*]—but her smile hasn't changed, and Shirley Temple continues to be a household word for generations who weren't even born when she left the silver screen behind.

Let's face it, all little children are adorable, but how many can dance, sing, and act? She was the first child actor ever to carry a full-length A-list picture. She was the most sought-after star in Hollywood. Once, the New York Times hailed her as "the greatest trouper of all—greater than Garbo, Hepburn, and Ginger Rogers."

Shirley Temple had the greatest short career in movie history—[*laughter*]—and then gracefully retired to, as we all know, the far less strenuous life of public service. [*Laughter*] She did a masterful job as Ambassador, from Ghana to Czechoslovakia, where she made common cause with Václav Havel in the final, decisive days of the cold war. In fact, she has to be the only person who both saved an entire movie studio from failure and contributed to the fall of communism. [*Laughter*] From her childhood to the present day, Shirley has always been an ambassador for what is best about America.

Ladies and gentlemen, Miss Shirley Temple Black. [*Applause*]

Ladies and gentlemen, I just told Shirley's husband of 48 years, Charles, that I was watching one of her movies the other day, about the Civil War, and he said, "Yes, that's the one

where she met President Lincoln." And she told me, "I didn't just meet President Roosevelt; I sat on Abraham Lincoln's lap." [*Laughter*]

Ladies and gentlemen, this has been a wonderful night. I know we look forward to the honors. I thank you all for being here. And once again, let me thank our honorees for the great gifts they have given us. Thank you very much.

NOTE: The President spoke at 5:46 p.m. in the East Room at the White House. The transcript released by the Office of the Press Secretary also included the remarks of Hillary Clinton.

Letter to Congressional Leaders on Major Illicit Drug-Producing and Drug-Transit Countries
December 4, 1998

Dear _____:

In accordance with the provisions of section 490(h) of the Foreign Assistance Act of 1961, as amended, I have determined that the following countries are major illicit drug-producing or drug-transit countries: Afghanistan, Aruba, The Bahamas, Belize, Bolivia, Brazil, Burman, Cambodia, China, Colombia, Dominican Republic, Ecuador, Guatemala, Haiti, Hong Kong, India, Jamaica, Laos, Mexico, Nigeria, Pakistan, Panama, Paraguay, Peru, Taiwan, Thailand, Venezuela, and Vietnam.

This year I have removed Iran and Malaysia from the list of major drug producing countries and designated them as countries of concern.

Iran. On the list as a major drug producer since 1987, Iran has been a traditional opium producing country, with illicit poppy cultivation well beyond the statutory threshold limit of 1,000 hectares. A United States Government review in 1993 determined that there were at least 3,500 hectares of illicit opium poppy under cultivation in the country.

Over the past few years, the Government of Iran has reported success in eradicating illicit opium poppy cultivation. We were unable to test these claims until this year, when a United States Government review found no evidence of any significant poppy cultivation in the traditional growing areas. While we cannot rule out some cultivation in remote parts of the country,

it is unlikely that there would be enough to meet the threshold definition of a major drug producing country.

Although important quantities of opiates continue to transit Iran en route to Europe, the United States Government currently has no evidence to support a judgment that significant quantities of these drugs are headed to the United States. Therefore, Iran is not a major drug-transit country under section 481(e)(5) of the Foreign Assistance Act.

Malaysia. Although Malaysia's geographic location makes it a feasible transit route for heroin to the United States, as had been the case in the past, we have no indication that drugs significantly affecting the United States have transited the country in the past few years.

I have further determined that the following countries or regions are of concern for the purpose of U.S. counternarcotics efforts:

Netherlands Antilles. Though there is continuing drug activity taking place around the Netherlands Antilles, especially in the vicinity of St. Maarten, we have only anecdotal information that significant quantities of drugs bound for the United States are involved.

Turkey and Other Balkan Route Countries. I continue to be concerned about the large volume of Southwest Asian heroin moving through Turkey and neighboring countries (including

Bulgaria, Greece, the Federal Republic of Yugoslavia, Bosnia, Croatia, and the Former Yugoslavian Republic of Macedonia) to Western Europe along the Balkan Route. There is no clear evidence, however, that this heroin significantly affects the United States—as required for a country to be designated a major transit country.

Syria and Lebanon. I removed Syria and Lebanon from the list of major drug producers last year after the United States Government determined that there was no significant opium poppy cultivation in Lebanon's Biqa' Valley. A review again this year confirmed that there is still no evidence of significant replanting of opium poppy and no evidence that drugs transiting these countries significantly affect the United States. The relevant agencies continue, however, to monitor the situation.

Cuba. Cuba's geographical position astride one of the principal Caribbean trafficking routes to the United States makes the country a logical candidate for consideration for the majors list. Interdiction operations elsewhere in the region are driving drug smugglers increasingly to fly over Cuba to drop cocaine into Cuban and Bahamian waters. This trend makes it important for Cuba to take effective measures to stem the flow and to cooperate with others in doing so.

Major Cannabis Producers. While Kazakhstan, Kyrgyzstan, Morocco, the Philippines, and South Africa are important cannabis producers, they do not appear on this list because I have determined, pursuant to section 481(e)(2) of the Foreign Assistance Act, that in all cases the illicit cannabis is either consumed locally or exported to countries other than the United States, and thus such illicit cannabis production does not significantly affect the United States.

Central Asia. United States Government agencies this year again conducted reviews of potential cultivation sites in Tajikistan and Uzbekistan, traditional opium poppy growing areas of the former Soviet Union. These reviews indicated no evidence of significant opium poppy cultivation.

Finally, I would note that geography makes Central America a logical conduit and transshipment area for South American drugs bound for Mexico and the United States, and that there has been evidence of increased trafficking activity in this region over the past year. Its location between Colombia and Mexico, combined with thousands of miles of coastline, the availability of a number of container-handling ports in Costa Rica, Nicaragua, and Honduras, the presence of the Pan-American Highway, and limited law enforcement capability, have made the isthmus attractive to the drug trade. Hurricane Mitch has disrupted traffic flow through the region, but over the longer term resumption or even an increase in trafficking activity remains possible.

Consequently, I am concerned about drug trafficking through Costa Rica, El Salvador, Honduras, and Nicaragua. The appropriate agencies will continue to compile data on drug flows and their effect on the United States in order to determine whether any are major drug-transit countries. At the same time, I expressly reiterate my commitment to support the efforts of these governments to recover from the ravages of Hurricane Mitch, and to ensure that drug traffickers do not take advantage of this tragedy to make inroads into the region.

Sincerely,

WILLIAM J. CLINTON

NOTE: Identical letters were sent to Jesse Helms, chairman, and Joseph R. Biden, Jr., ranking member, Senate Committee on Foreign Relations; Ted Stevens, chairman, and Robert C. Byrd, ranking member, Senate Committee on Appropriations; Bob Livingston, chairman, and David R. Obey, ranking member, House Committee on Appropriations; and Benjamin A. Gilman, chairman, and Lee H. Hamilton, ranking member, House Committee on International Relations. This letter was released by the Office of the Press Secretary on December 7.

Remarks on Efforts To Combat Medicare Fraud
December 7, 1998

Thank you. I would like to welcome you all here today and thank Margaret Dixon for those fine remarks. I thank Deborah Briceland-Betts for representing the Older Women's League so well, and Nancy-Ann Min DeParle for the great job she does as our HCFA Administrator. I welcome our friend George Kourpias and representatives from the National Council of Senior Citizens.

And I want to say a special word of appreciation to Senator Tom Harkin, who has been on top of this issue for a very, very long time, and has long needed more support from administrations. And we certainly tried to give him ours, but he has been a real trailblazer, and we thank him.

I'd like to also thank, as others have, the HHS and especially June Gibbs Brown, the Inspector General, and Mike Mangano, the Deputy Inspector General, who is here today.

I'd also like to say one other word about Senator Gore, Sr., who was mentioned by Nancy-Ann. Al Gore, Sr., was a leader in the development and the passage of the original Medicare bill over 30 years ago. And that is one of the many, many things we remember him for at this time of his passing.

For more than 30 years now, Medicare has been more than a Government program. It has been a way that we could honor our obligations to our parents and our grandparents, an expression of the old profound American belief that the bonds of mutual love and support among the generations must remain strong. Any threat, therefore, to the integrity of Medicare is a threat to these bonds. And that is one of the main reasons that our administration has worked so hard to strengthen Medicare.

The balanced budget bill I signed last year extended the life of the Medicare Trust Fund for a decade. We also established a commission currently working to help Medicare meet the needs of the baby boom generation and the rising costs that inevitably come as we all live longer and longer and require more health care.

It is a troubling financial problem, but as a social matter it is a happy challenge. It is what I would call a high-class problem that we are all living longer and longer. But it does present

us with certain real challenges which we have to face. And I look forward to getting the report from Senator Breaux and the Medicare Commission and to working on a bipartisan basis with the next Congress to resolve this important matter.

Today I'm announcing additional steps to strengthen Medicare by fighting the threat of Medicare fraud. Every year, Medicare is cheated out of billions of dollars, money that translates into higher taxes on working Americans, higher copayments in premiums for elderly Medicare recipients. This has become, as I said, especially significant as we grow older and more and more of us become eligible for Medicare.

I'm proud of what we have already done to fight fraud and abuse and waste. Since 1993 we've assigned more Federal prosecutors and FBI agents to fight health care fraud. We've increased prosecutions by over 60 percent, convictions by 240 percent, saved $20 billion in health care claims. Money that would have lined the pockets of scam artists now is helping to preserve the Medicare Trust Fund and to provide high-quality, affordable health care.

But there is still more we can do. The private sector health care contractors that are responsible for fighting waste, fraud, and abuse too often are not living up to their responsibilities. We recently learned that one-fourth of those contractors have never reported a single case of fraud, even though the Inspector General is quite certain that fraud is pervasive in this area.

Therefore, we are using new authority we fought for to create new weapons in the fight against fraud. Beginning this spring we will empower new specialized contractors, Medicare fraud hunters, who will focus on waste, fraud, and abuse. These new fraud hunters, by tracking down scams and waste, can bring real savings to Medicare and strengthen the system for the 21st century.

I'm also requiring all Medicare contractors to notify the Government immediately when they learn of any evidence of fraud, so that we can detect patterns of fraud quickly and take swift action to stop them. And I'm asking HCFA to report back to me early next year with a comprehensive plan to fight waste, fraud, and abuse further in the Medicare program.

In the fight against Medicare fraud, Congress must also do its part. And I am encouraged by the bipartisan oversight hearings being held in Chicago this week by Senators Collins and Durbin. When it returns next year, I'll ask Congress to pass legislation that can save Medicare another $2 billion over the next 5 years: First, legislation that will allow us to empower our new fraud hunters to spot overpayments and keep crooked medical service providers from getting into the Medicare system to start with.

Second, the legislation will allow Medicare to pay much lower rates for prescription medications. Under current law, Medicare loses hundreds of millions of dollars each year by paying as much as 10 times more than the private sector does for certain drugs. It's just wrong.

Third, the legislation will force private insurers to pay claims that they are legally responsible for, so that Medicare does not get stuck with the bill. This happens more often than you would think.

Fourth, legislation will allow us to crack down on medical providers, particularly those claiming

to deliver mental health care, who bill for services they never, in fact, provide, a large and unfortunately, growing problem, according to our recent reports.

By passing these commonsense measures to fight Medicare waste and fraud, Congress can do more than help save taxpayers' money. It can demonstrate a bipartisan desire to preserve and strengthen Medicare for the future. If we take these actions now, we can help to assure that the system that has served our parents and grandparents so well will be there to serve our children and grandchildren well into the 21st century.

Thanks to the advocates who are here—Senator Harkin and others—I'm confident that is exactly what we will do next year.

Thank you very much, and happy holidays.

NOTE: The President spoke at 12:50 p.m. in Room 450 of the Old Executive Office Building. In his remarks, he referred to Margaret Dixon, immediate past president, American Association of Retired Persons; Deborah Briceland-Betts, executive director, Older Women's League; and George J. Kourpias, president, National Council of Senior Citizens.

Statement on International Maritime Organization Action To Protect the Northern Right Whale
December 7, 1998

Today's vote by the International Maritime Organization (IMO) to strengthen protections for the northern right whale is a vital step to ensure the survival of these majestic but endangered creatures.

Like many other marine mammals, the northern right whale once was hunted nearly to extinction. The 300 or so that survive spend much of the year in waters off Cape Cod and off the Georgia and Florida coasts. Biologists believe the greatest human threat they face today is collisions with large ships.

In April I instructed our representatives to the IMO to seek strong measures to address this threat. Under our proposal, approved unanimously today by the IMO, commercial ships entering the whale's calving and feeding grounds will be required to report by radio to the U.S. Coast Guard, which will relay back the latest information on the whales' locations and advice on avoiding collisions.

Today's action by the IMO demonstrates once again that through international cooperation we can restore and protect our precious oceans and the magnificent diversity of life they sustain.

Remarks at the White House Conference on Social Security
December 8, 1998

Good morning, ladies and gentlemen. Let me begin by welcoming all of you and acknowledging Senators Daschle and Santorum, Congressman Gephardt and Congressman Shaw, who will speak, and the very, very large delegation we have from the United States Congress, Members of both parties right out here to my left. I thank you all for coming.

I think the fact that we have such a large representation from the Congress, as well as leaders of various organizations of people throughout the United States and people concerned about the Social Security issue, is a testament to the profound importance of this issue and the commitment of the American people to do something about it.

I thank Secretary Rubin, Secretary Herman, Secretary Daley, and Gene Sperling, Jack Lew, Ken Apfel, and John Podesta, representing the administration, for their presence here.

This is the first-ever White House Conference on Social Security. There are all of you here in Washington, plus thousands of people watching at 60 satellite sites in all 50 States.

I'd also like to apologize for my early departure. I had hoped to be here for as much of this conference as I could, but, as all of you know, there is a service in Tennessee today for the father of our Vice President, former United States Senator Albert Gore, Sr., who was a true, great public servant. He and his generation built the entire postwar order, from Medicare to the Interstate Highway System, both of which he himself had a personal role in creating. They were civic institutions that have helped save our Nation and our world in the half-century since.

Now it is our turn to be builders, to renew the institutions that have made America strong. In this time, America faces no more important challenge than the need to save Social Security for the 21st century. Social Security is and must remain a rock-solid guarantee. It is a sacred trust among the generations, between parents and children, grandparents and grandchildren; between those in retirement and those at work; between the able-bodied and the disabled. It embodies our obligations to one another and our deepest values as Americans.

This year, I and a lot of people in this room, a lot of Members of the Congress, have spent a lot of time listening to the American people and speaking with them about Social Security. This White House conference, a gathering of lawmakers, experts, Americans from all walks of life, marks an important step in the direction of saving Social Security for the 21st century.

We'll hear a lot of ideas expressed about what course we should take. Let me shock you by saying I think there will be some differences of opinion expressed in this room. But we should begin this process on common ground, agreeing above all on the importance of acting and acting now, while we can, during prosperous and productive times that Americans have worked so hard to achieve.

Our economy is indeed a powerful engine of prosperity. In its wide wake, it creates something every bit as important as jobs and growth: the opportunity to do something meaningful for America's future and the confidence that we can actually do it, an opportunity to save Social Security for the 21st century. I hope history will record that we seized this opportunity.

Earlier this year I said we should reserve any surplus until we save Social Security first. We have done so. We should take the next step and act now. It is more than an opportunity; it is a solemn responsibility—to take the achievement of past generations, the Americans who, according to President Roosevelt, had a rendezvous with destiny, and to renew the social contract for a new era.

Through war and peace, from recession to expansion, our Nation has fulfilled its obligation to older Americans. It is hard, thankfully, to remember the time when growing old often meant growing poor. It seems impossible to believe, but in many cases, retirement meant being relegated to a rest home and the degradation of dependence. The normal aches and pains of aging were accompanied by the unbearable pain of becoming a burden to one's children.

That's why Social Security continues to offer much hope, much confidence, much peace of mind. It is one of the most important and ambitious undertakings in our Nation's entire lifetime.

President Roosevelt said there is no tragedy in growing old, but there is tragedy in growing old without means of support. Soon we will face a rising challenge in providing that support, as every one of you knows. Before too long, there will only be about two people working for every one person eligible to draw Social Security. As our panelists will discuss, we are actually going to have many, many older Americans.

Just last night Hillary and I were discussing a recent health report that infant mortality last year dropped to an all-time low, and the life expectancy of Americans rose to an all-time high, over 76 years. Some would argue that this problem we have with Social Security is, therefore, a high-class problem. I know that the older I get, the more high-class the problem looks to me.

It is, nonetheless, a significant challenge: 75 million baby boomers retiring during the next two decades. By 2013, what Social Security takes in will no longer be enough to fund what it pays out. That's just 15 years away. Then we'll have to use the proceeds from the Trust Fund. By 2032, just 34 years away, the money Social Security takes in will only be enough to pay 72 percent of benefits.

Now, there are many ways to deal with this, but there is only one way to get it done. Let me say to all the people on all sides of this debate, the only way we can save Social Security and avoid what I think is a result that none of us want, which is either a dramatic cut in the standard of living of retirees in America, a dramatic increase in the taxes on working Americans and the lowering of the standard of living of the children and grandchildren of the baby boomers—the only way we can avoid that is by working together, putting progress ahead of partisanship, placing the long-term interest of the Nation first.

Already, some are predicting that we are simply incapable of doing this in Washington. I am determined to prove them wrong. I hope every one of you are determined to do so, as well.

What does this mean? It means, first of all, not that we should forget about what we think is right. It means each of us should articulate what we think is right, and those who believe they disagree should listen to them. We should all listen to people who have different opinions; they might be right, and we might be wrong.

Secondly, it means that our differences cannot take the form of personal attacks. This is a complex issue, and I have found that on this issue most people believe what they really believe— we do not need to let our differences disintegrate into personal attacks.

Third, in the end, all of us in some sense will have to sacrifice our sense of the perfect to work together for the common good. There is in this process no room for rancor. The stakes are too high; the issues far too important. It's not about politics; it's about doing right by young Americans and older Americans and the future of America.

The whole point of this conference is to open honest debate and to build consensus, not to shoot down ideas or insist that one side or the other has to go first. Secretary Riley, our Secretary of Education, said that one of his greatest lessons from South Carolina politics was the old saying that "I'm for change, and you are, too; you go first." [*Laughter*]

I'm prepared to do whatever it takes to move us forward, but let's agree we have to march together. That's the only path to the finish line. Our ears, our minds must remain open to any good idea and to any person of good will.

In judging any proposal, I believe we should be guided by five principles. First, as I have said, we must strengthen and protect the guarantee of Social Security for the 21st century.

Second, we must maintain universality and fairness. Later, panelists will discuss the impact of reform on different groups. The First Lady was scheduled to discuss the special impact on women, who on average live longer than men, so depend on Social Security more. Now, keep in mind that only 4.6 percent of elderly married women are living in poverty. For elderly single women, the number is about 20 percent. Those who think we can wait should never forget that fact either. When we judge our plan to save Social Security, we need to ask whether it cuts the poverty rate among single elderly women and other groups in our population that are still at significant risk.

I must say, I have been quite impressed that proposals that span the conventional ideological spectrum have shown a sensitivity to this and to taking vulnerable people out of poverty and giving them the secure retirement they deserve.

Third, I believe we must construct a system where Social Security can be counted on regardless of the ups and downs of the economy or the markets.

Fourth, Social Security must continue to provide financial security for disabled and low income beneficiaries. One in three Social Security beneficiaries are not retirees, and we must never forget that.

And fifth, any proposal must maintain our hard-won fiscal discipline. It has helped to fuel the prosperity Americans enjoy today. That is, after all, what gives us the chance to do this in at least a less painful manner.

I look forward to transforming these ideas into action. Let us begin firm in our faith that Social Security can bind our people not only across generational divides but across party lines.

Let me say, too, in that regard, I am grateful for the presence here of Senator Santorum and Congressman Shaw from the Republican majority, and the minority leaders, Senator Daschle, and Congressman Gephardt. I thank you very

much for your presence here. And now I'd like to turn it over to them to make some opening remarks so we can get on with the work of this conference.

Let me say this before I sit down. You have to decide that we are going to do this. You have to tell these Members of Congress that you will support them if they act. If you come here representing a particular point of view and you know these Members of Congress agree with you, you should ask them to defend your point of view, but to be willing in the end to make a decision that will deal with the problem. This will only get harder, every single year we avoid resolving this, it will get harder and harder and harder. And everybody's favorite idea will have a less beneficial impact the longer we wait. Now is the time to do this.

Thank you very much.

NOTE: The President spoke at 8:50 a.m. in the Cotillion Ballroom at the Marriott Wardman Park Hotel.

Remarks at a Dinner Honoring Dale and Betty Bumpers
December 8, 1998

Ladies and gentlemen, Hillary began by saying this was a bittersweet moment for us, and indeed, it is. Nonetheless, I do want to thank all of you for making it possible. I thank Joan Baker, Deba Leach, and all the Peace Link folks. I thank our good friend Reverend Wogaman for praying over us. God knows we need it. I thank my friend Peter Duchin for being here and for playing.

And I thank Alan Simpson for destroying all the stereotypes that we Democrats like to have about Republicans. [*Laughter*] He's tall and funny. [*Laughter*] And you know, in his new career, he has finally destroyed the myth that Harvard is an elitist institution. [*Laughter*] And maybe even that it's an elite institution. [*Laughter*]

I thank Ann Bingaman for her wonderful remarks, and all the Members of the Senate, the diplomatic corps, and others who are here tonight; and our wonderful friends David and Barbara Pryor for being here.

You know, the six of us—we three couples—we've been together a long time. I met David Pryor when he was running for Congress in 1976. I voted for Dale Bumpers when he ran for Governor the first time, in 1970. We were all on the ballot in 1974, and I was the only one that lost. [*Laughter*] And—it's a good thing, I could have—if I had won, I'd have gone to Congress, been infected by people like Simpson, and never become President. [*Laughter*]

But over these last more than 20 years now, we've been together on countless occasions. When we were all in public office—when I was Governor and they were our Senators, we did all those parades that David talked about. We did countless toasts and roasts. We even crashed in a plane together once, nearly made every other politician in Arkansas ecstatic all at one time—we opened all the jobs at once. [*Laughter*] But we walked away from it.

We've borrowed each other's stories mercilessly. Then I became President, and they said it wasn't Presidential for me to tell jokes, so

I had to stop. I wish I had a nickel for every time Dale Bumpers has called me and said, "Now, tell me that joke one more time." [*Laughter*] And I'd get halfway through the joke, and he'd remember it and remember the punchline and start laughing. I could just hear the tears rolling down his cheeks, he'd laugh so much.

This would be a better place if we had more people who laugh like that. This would be a stronger National Capital if we had more people like Alan Simpson and Dale Bumpers and David Pryor that could tell these stories and reach across party lines.

You know, Betty and Dale were raised in a tradition in Arkansas—a little town in western Arkansas where, if you took yourself too seriously, you were deflated quickly. And people knew about you, all about you, and they loved you anyway. It's easy to get away from that, the more distance you get from real life and this business. So I have to tell you that one of the things that I am most grateful to both of them for is remaining real people in every way, throughout all these years—the laughter, the tears, the drama, the struggles; real flesh and blood, patriotic, wonderful human beings. It means a lot and more every passing day.

I thank Betty for her vision. We've made a lot of fun of all the things she's done with Peace Links, but if you think about it, it's a truly astonishing thing. It proves, really, that there is such a thing as citizen empowerment. And one person with vision and enough people, like Ann, ready to be dragooned into service, can change the course of history.

Think about what we're discussing today. Today, we're impatient because the Russians haven't ratified the START II treaty, so we can negotiate another treaty, so we can dramatically slash our nuclear arsenals further. And when we do, it still won't be enough to suit Betty, but it will be partly because she has been pushing us all this time, and all the other Peace Links members.

I want to thank Betty for something else, too, that she and Dale pioneered this whole business of immunizing our children. Last night we had a Christmas party at the White House, Betty, and I thought about you, because a young, handsome man came through the line and shook hands with Hillary and me, and he said—he looked at us, and he said, "I want you to know, for the last 3 years, I have run your immuniza-

tion program. And it's been the proudest experience of my life." He said, "We've gotten tens of thousands of volunteers all across America, and for the first time in our history we've got over 90 percent of our children immunized. And all these kids are going to live, that would not have lived; they'll be normal, that would not have had normal lives before." And you were the first person that sensitized me to that issue. And I thank you for that, and I hope you're proud of that achievement for your country.

I want to say just a word about Dale. I have to forgive him, for one thing—I'm in this sort of forgiveness mode. [*Laughter*] Dale Bumpers never fails to introduce me and David Pryor as the second-best Governors Arkansas ever had. [*Laughter*] And I forgive him, because it's probably true. He was an inspiration to David and me, as David said. And as I look back on his long public career, including his service as Governor and the 9,447 votes he cast in the United States Senate, votes for energy conservation, votes to preserve the ozone layer—people used to make fun of Dale Bumpers about the ozone layer, the way they used to make fun of Betty about Peace Links. Two days ago I got a report on the hole in the ozone over the South Pole; it's the biggest it has ever been, and its duration is longer than any we've ever measured. And we have at least made some progress on it, because he started griping about it so long ago.

He stood up for reform of our laws on natural resources, and he got some things done. And we didn't get everything we wanted to do done because there were too many people like Simpson stopping us, but—[*laughter*]—eventually we'll get it done.

He stood up for the Constitution of the United States, for the welfare of our children, for the future of America. In his own way, just as Betty did in Peace Links, he was always trying to build bridges to tomorrow over the fears and ignorance and conflicts of today, always trying to bring out the best.

And I was sitting here looking at David and Barbara and Betty and Dale, and I was thinking, it does not take long to live a life. Time passes quickly. And all we can do is make the most of every day God gives us. I think that my days have been richer, and I know that Hillary's have, and I believe our public service has been better because very early on we met, came to know, love, admire, and learn from Dale and Betty Bumpers. We will love them always.

On Dale Bumpers' last official visit to the White House, not very long ago, a couple of weeks ago, we had this huge gathering under a tent of every soul we could find in Washington connected to Arkansas. And I signed legislation making Little Rock Central High School an historic site, a companion to a bill that will award Congressional Gold Medals to all the Little Rock Nine who integrated that high school so long ago, a real milestone on America's long march towards justice and equality and reconciliation.

At this time, when the world needs so much from the Middle East to Northern Ireland to the Balkans to central Africa to our own meanest streets, a remembrance of what is basic and good and fundamental about our national life, when we need so badly to be reconciled one to another and to reach out to those around the world, the enduring legacy of Betty Bumpers and Peace Links, and Dale Bumpers' entire career as a public official, to me was somehow crystallized on that magic day when we celebrated a seminal event in all of our lives, and his commemorating it for all time to come.

We will remember them for all of our days with gratitude, thanks, and laughter. God bless you both, and congratulations on your award.

Please come on up.

This magnificent and beautiful award is richly deserved. It's also very heavy. [*Laughter*] But, what the heck. If John Glenn can go into space, they can hold this award.

God bless you. Congratulations.

NOTE: The President spoke at 8:36 p.m. in the ballroom at the Capitol Hilton Hotel. In his remarks, he referred to Joan Baker, chair, and Elisabeth (Deba) Leach, vice chair, Peace Links; Rev. J. Phillip Wogaman, who delivered the invocation; Peter Duchin, orchestra leader; Ann Bingaman, National Link and wife of Senator Jeff Bingaman; former Senator Alan K. Simpson, master of ceremonies; and former Senator David H. Pryor and his wife, Barbara. Peace Links, founded by Mrs. Bumpers in 1982 to help educate women on nuclear arms issues, presented Senator and Mrs. Bumpers with the Eleanor Roosevelt Living World Award at the 12th annual Peace on Earth gala for their combined years of public service.

Remarks on Receiving the W. Averell Harriman Democracy Award
December 8, 1998

Thank you for the wonderful welcome. My good and longtime friend Paul Kirk, thank you for your wise words and your kindness and for the award. Generally, I don't think Presidents should get awards, but I like this one awful well. [*Laughter*]

I am honored to be here with the NDI. I thank Ken Wollack, Jean Dunn, and all the others here who worked to make your work a success. I thank you for establishing a fellowship in Cecile Ledsky's name. I thank you for honoring our other honorees who richly deserve to be recognized.

I thank the members of our Government who have helped me to become involved in Ireland. I thank the Members of Congress who are here, whose support and interest and consistent commitment has been absolutely indispensable for the work that we have done in these last few years.

I thank our Ambassadors: Phil Lader, our Ambassador to Great Britain; and our new Ambassador to Ireland, my longtime friend Governor Mike Sullivan, I welcome him. Jim Lyons, thank you; Brian Atwood; all of our special guests from Northern Ireland and Ireland; my fellow Irish-Americans; and a special thanks to George Mitchell. I thank you all.

Let me also say I'm delighted to have an award named for Averell Harriman. Hillary and I had the great honor and real joy of getting to know Governor Harriman in his later years. We spent the night with him a time or two. We once stayed up half the night listening to him talk to us about how he was Roosevelt's envoy with Churchill and Stalin. It is a pretty hard act to follow.

But I think—I believe Governor Harriman and the men and women of his generation would be proud of America as it stands on the eve of a new century and a new millennium.

We can look ahead to the last year of this, the "American Century," with confidence that we have never been a stronger force for peace and for democracy.

Some of the most entrenched conflicts the world has known have given ground in the last few years to a new spirit of cooperation—countries dominated for centuries by strife, speaking a new language, talking about a shared future: in the Middle East, where religious hatred seemed as old as the region itself; in the Balkans, where I heard propagandists blame tensions on the battle of Kosovo in 1389; in Peru and Ecuador, where a border war had roots that went back centuries; and of course, in Northern Ireland, where the Troubles dragged on for nearly three decades, but the arguments went back for hundreds of years. Fortunately, the people of Northern Ireland today are looking forward to a shared 21st century in freedom, democracy, and peace.

So many people are making progress around the world, but we all know it's hard. It's hard right now in Northern Ireland. It's hard right now in the Middle East; Hillary and I and members of our administration are going to Israel and Gaza at the end of this week to do what we can to keep the process agreed to at Wye on track. It's hard in Kosovo, where American diplomacy under Dick Holbrooke's leadership and NATO's threat of military force averted a crisis, but where we still must have a political settlement and political reform in Serbia to have a lasting peace. It is hard.

One of the things that makes it so hard, and one of the things that makes democracy so essential, is that people have to be both free to be the best they can be, free to live their dreams and lift people according to their aspirations. They have to know that they count just as much as anyone else. But one of the things that makes democracy so essential is they have to know that there is some restraint, on themselves and on others, beyond which they cannot go.

For how many times have I seen, these last 6 years, leaders of opposition factions, in talks or at the edge of conflict or trying to get out of conflict, desperately, desperately want to reach across the lines that divide them to advance the cause of peace, but so frightened that, instead, they had to rub salt in their adversary's wounds so as not to lose the political support of their own folks at home. It is imperative that we push peace and democracy at the same time.

One thing I would like to say to the Irish here—both the Irish—Irish from the North and from the Republic, the American Irish—is that it is impossible for you to understand, perhaps, that even though all these issues may seem unrelated, a breakthrough in one area can dramatically increase the confidence and the passion of other peacemakers.

The Good Friday agreement and its overwhelming ratification by voters sent a strong signal around the world. It put a lot of extra pressure on me. Just a few days ago, I had a meeting with a group of Greek-Americans, and if I heard it once, I heard it 10 times, "Now, you did all that work in Ireland, and you sat there for 9 days and got that Wye agreement, and I do not understand why the Cyprus problem is beyond reach. I know that you can make some progress there."

That's good. Headache for me, probably, but it's good. It's good that when people do things in one part of the world, it makes other people believe that they're not stuck in this mindless rut of conflict.

So I thank you for this award. I'm very proud of my Irish heritage. I'm proud that I could play a role in the process so far. I'm proud of what the First Lady has done with the Vital Voices movement and other ways—for what she has done.

As I can't say too many times, I'm grateful to Senator Mitchell, to the Congress men and women in this room and beyond who have reached across party lines in America to work for peace across religious lines in Ireland. And I'm very proud of the Irish-American community.

But the people on the other side of the Atlantic still deserve the lion's share of the credit. Many of them are here: Gerry Adams, Lord John Alderdice, David Ervine, Monica McWilliams, Gary McMichael, Malachi Curran. There are others. I thank Tony Blair, Bertie Ahern; their predecessors John Bruton, Albert Reynolds, John Major; Mo Mowlam—one of a kind.

I'm sorry I didn't get here in time to see David Trimble and John Hume off to get the Peace Prize. But I've had some good and good-natured talks with them both. I told David Trimble—I know you noticed this tonight—ever since he won the Nobel Prize, he's dressing a lot better. [*Laughter*] Now, that's a very good sign for peace, you know. [*Laughter*] And my only complaint with the Nobel committee is that they should have given it to more people involved in this process as well, and we'd have had even a bigger, broader—[*inaudible*]—of enthusiasm. I thank you all.

I want you to think about this, because we're at a little bit of a tough spot in the road in Ireland right now. On the day that David and John get the Nobel Peace Prize, for their own work and as stand-ins for many of you, too, the world will also celebrate the 50th anniversary of one of the greatest documents of the 20th century, the Universal Declaration of Human Rights. The timing could not be better because, like democracy, the cause of human rights and peace are part and parcel of the same idea: the common claim to dignity of all humanity; the idea that self-respect and mutual respect are not exclusive, but two sides of the coin of peace and harmony.

In his Nobel speech a few years ago, Seamus Heaney said of Northern Ireland, "No place in the world prides itself more on its vigilance and realism. No place considers itself more qualified to censure any flourish of rhetoric or excess of aspiration." I think that is a dignified, Seamus way of saying, we don't like long speeches telling us what we have to do. So I will give you a short speech telling you what I think we have to do. [*Laughter*] I hope I can strike the right note between a celebration of how far we've come with a plea to keep the work going.

I hope the parties will move quickly to resolve the remaining differences, keeping an open mind, acting in good faith, remembering how much all have gained by the hard work that has already been done. Not only the letter but the spirit of the Good Friday accord must prevail.

I have closely followed recent efforts to hammer out agreements for the new executive political structures and the bodies to deal with cross-border issues. Bringing these institutions to life is absolutely essential to keep up the momentum for peace, and we urge a speedy resolution. I also applaud the tireless work of John de Chastelain toward achieving the vital goal of disposing of weapons now that the war is over.

Hillary just came back—[*applause*]—thank you—Hillary just came back from a profoundly moving trip to Central America, where our friends and neighbors are struggling in the after-math of Hurricane Mitch, the worst hurricane in 200 years—so devastating that we are concerned that if we don't do all we can to help them rebuild, that they could lose the democracy, the freedom, the peace for which they have fought so long and hard. But one reason we think that it will hold on in Guatemala and El Salvador is because, as a part of their peace process, they were vigorous in decommissioning, in giving up arms and moving toward peace.

Somehow or another, sooner or later, we all have to decide we can't shoot our way out of our differences and our difficulties.

We know the real prize still lies ahead, that day in the not-too-distant future when men, women, and children can walk all the streets of Belfast, Derry, Omagh without fear; when respect and trust has replaced suspicion; when machine guns and explosives are as irrelevant as suits of armor; when investors pour money into new ventures that spread opportunity to all; when the people of Ulster are known far and wide as the people who rose to this great challenge, proved they were bigger than their differences, and were able to go across the world, as I said the last time I was in Northern Ireland, and look at the people on Cyprus, look at the people in the Balkans, look at the people in Central Africa and say, "We did this, and we had troubles centuries old, not just 30 years. We did it. And you can, too."

We cannot afford to be complacent or frustrated or angry. We always knew there would be bumps in the road and that no matter what the referendum vote was, after the Good Friday agreement, there would be difficulties. The United States pledges again to be with you every step of the way, because all of us know that the Irish in America for more than 200 years have brought us to this day, as much as any group of people.

We all know, too, as I will say again, that we must have democracy and human rights in the end to have peace. As long as I am President, I will do everything I can to advance the cause of peace, democracy, and human rights; to do everything I can to anticipate conflicts before they occur; to listen to both sides when they do occur; to do my best to persuade parties that benefits lie just ahead if they stop living in the past and begin to imagine the future—yes, in Northern Ireland, in the Middle East, in Cambodia, Nigeria, Congo, Cyprus, the Balkans, everyplace where there are children who deserve a better future waiting to be born.

America will always stand with those who take risks for peace. I salute the NDI for keeping our democratic aspirations in sharp focus. I salute the honorees tonight, those of you whose names were called earlier. You really deserve these awards. I ask you to continue your efforts, to keep your spirits up, to keep your vision high, to remember how we felt when the Good Friday accord was ratified, to remember how you feel on the best days when the worst days come around, and to remember, no matter how tough it gets, it is always better for our children to reach across the lines that divide and build a future that they're all a part of together.

Thank you, and God bless you.

NOTE: The President spoke at 9:48 p.m. in the ballroom of the Shoreham Hotel, at a National Democratic Institute for International Affairs (NDI) dinner. In his remarks, he referred to Paul G. Kirk, Jr., chairman, Kenneth D. Wollack, president, and Jean Dunn, vice president for administration and development, NDI; James M. Lyons, Special Adviser to the President for Economic Initiatives for Ireland; former Senator George J. Mitchell, independent chairman of the multiparty talks in Northern Ireland; Special Envoy Richard C. Holbrooke; Sinn Fein leader Gerry Adams; Alliance Party leader Lord John Alderdice; Progressive Unionist Party spokesman David Ervine; Monica McWilliams of the Northern Ireland Women's Coalition; Ulster Democratic Party leader Gary McMichael; Northern Ireland Labour Party leader Malachi Curran; Prime Minister Tony Blair and former Prime Minister John Major of the United Kingdom; Prime Minister Bertie Ahern and former Prime Ministers John Bruton and Albert Reynolds of Ireland; United Kingdom Secretary of State for Northern Ireland Marjorie Mowlam; poet Seamus Heaney; and John de Chastelain, member and chair, Independent International Commission on Decommissioning. The President also referred to former State Department program officer Cecile W. Ledsky, who died December 2.

Remarks Honoring General Benjamin O. Davis, Jr., of the Tuskegee Airmen
December 9, 1998

Thank you. Well, Colonel McGee, I think this is one of those days where I'm supposed to take orders. [*Laughter*] I am delighted to see you. I thank you and Colonel Crockett for the jacket. I can't help saying as a point of personal pride that Colonel Crockett is a citizen of my home State, Arkansas. And we go back a ways, and we were together not all that long ago in Cambridge, England, when we celebrated the 50th anniversary of the D–Day invasion. And we were there together.

Colonel Campbell, I think you were picked to speak not because you were born in Tuskegee but because you give a good speech. [*Laughter*] I think you did a fine job. Thank you, sir.

Let me say to all the Tuskegee Airmen here, we are honored by your presence and grateful for your service. I'd like to ask all the Tuskegee Airmen who are here just to stand for a moment so we can express our appreciation. They are out in the audience as well as here. Please stand. [*Applause*] Thank you very much.

There are so many distinguished people here in the audience; let me begin by thanking Secretary Cohen for his outstanding leadership. Janet, we're glad to see you here, glad you did that interview with General Davis many years ago. I thank the people from the White House who are here, General Kerrick and others; the people from the Pentagon, Deputy Secretary Hamre, Secretary Caldera, Secretary Danzig, Acting Secretary Peters, General Shelton, all the Joint Chiefs are here today.

I'd like to say a special word of thanks to Senator John McCain, the driving force behind the legislation to authorize this promotion. Thank you, sir.

I also want to thank one of the finest supporters of our military and of this action in the United States Congress, Senator Chuck

Robb, for being here. Thank you, sir—and leaders of the veterans and service organization, members of the Armed Forces. There are many, many distinguished guests here, but I would like to mention two. First, a great American and former Secretary of Transportation, William Coleman, who is here. Thank you for coming, Mr. Secretary Coleman. And I might add, his son has served with great distinction in the Pentagon; we thank him for that.

And I'd like to recognize Governor Doug Wilder from Virginia, who has been very actively involved and wrote an introduction to a book about General Davis. Thank you for being here.

And we want to welcome Mrs. Elnora Davis McLendon and the family and friends of General Davis who are gathered here, and especially General Davis himself.

Much of the distinguished record of General Davis and the Tuskegee Airmen has been mentioned, but I would like, for the record of history, for you to bear with me and allow me to tell this story and the story of this remarkable family.

Today we advance to the rank of four-star general, Benjamin O. Davis, Jr., a hero in war, a leader in peace, a pioneer for freedom, opportunity, and basic human dignity. He earned this honor a long time ago.

Our Armed Forces today are a model for America and for the world of how people of different backgrounds working together for the common good can perform at a far more outstanding level than they ever could have divided. Perhaps no one is more responsible for that achievement than the person we honor today. When the doors were shut on him, he knocked again and again until finally they opened, until his sheer excellence and determination made it impossible to keep them closed. Once the doors were open, he made sure they stayed open for others to follow. Some who followed are in this audience today.

In 1899 General Davis' father, Benjamin Davis, Sr., a skilled National Guardsman, sought entry into West Point. He was told no blacks would be appointed. Undeterred, he enlisted in the Army and distinguished himself immediately. In less than 2 years, he was an officer. It takes longer if you go to West Point. [Laughter]

Twenty years later, Colonel Davis was teaching at the Tuskegee Institute. The Klu Klux Klan announced it would march through the Davises' neighborhood. The Institute instructed its staff to stay indoors, turn out their lights, to keep from provoking the marchers. But Colonel Davis refused. Instead, he put on his dress uniform, turned on the porch light, gathered his family. Theirs was the only light for miles. But they sat proudly and bravely outside as the hate marchers passed by. Benjamin Davis, Jr., never forgot about his father's shining porch light.

As a teenager, inspired by Charles Lindbergh's historic flight, he dreamed of becoming an aviator and a trailblazer. With hard work, he did gain admission to West Point, the very opportunity denied his father. The father saw that the son had the chance not only to serve his country but to inspire African-Americans all across America. "Remember," he wrote, "12 million people will be pulling for you with all we have."

But at West Point, as you have already heard today, Benjamin Davis was quite alone. For 4 years, fellow cadets refused to speak to him, hoping to drive him out. "What they didn't realize," he later recalled, "was that I was stubborn enough to put up with the treatment to reach the goal I had come to attain."

His request to join the Air Corps upon graduation was denied, because no units accepted blacks. Though he ranked 35th out of a class of 276, West Point's Superintendent advised him to pursue a career outside the Army. He refused. Arriving at Fort Benning to command an infantry company, he was again shunned from the Officers' Club, subject to segregation on and off the base.

But times were changing as World War II dawned. Just as President Roosevelt promoted Benjamin Davis, Sr., to Brigadier General, the first African-American general in our Nation's history, he ordered the Air Corps to create a black flying group. Benjamin Davis was named its leader, and in the spring of 1943, the 99th Fighter Squadron departed for North Africa and began combat missions. Their group commander soon recommended they be removed from combat, however, claiming—listen to this—that a black American did not have the desire or the proper reflexes to make a first-class fighter pilot.

Colonel Davis then proved he was just as skilled in the conference room as in the cockpit. His testimony, as you have so eloquently heard today, carried the day before a military panel, making the case for ability and bravery. The panel recommended that the 99th be reinstated and that more African-American squadrons be sent overseas.

Returned to the skies, as we all know, the Tuskegee Airmen proved themselves again and again. They destroyed far more planes than they lost; they disabled hundreds of enemy boxcars. They even sank an enemy destroyer, a unique achievement in the war. And as you have heard twice now, during 200 escort missions above the Third Reich, they never lost a single bomber to enemy fire.

The Tuskegee Airmen's extraordinary success and the invaluable contributions of other blacks and minorities in the war helped to turn the tide against official racism and to pave the way for President Truman's historic order 50 years ago mandating, and I quote, "equality of treatment and opportunity in the armed services." This led to an end of segregation in our forces.

For 25 years after the war, Benjamin Davis, Jr., rose to complex security challenges in Air Force postings at home and abroad. Wherever he went, he overcame bigotry through professionalism and performance. Following his retirement in 1970, he continued his distinguished public service, including at senior positions at the Department of Transportation.

I'd like to say something personal. A lot of these old-fashioned, almost amazing arguments against the capacity of black Americans were still very much in vogue during the civil rights movement in the 1950's and the 1960's. And for children like me who were taught that the civil rights movement was the right thing to do in the South, and who engaged in countless arguments against inane statements, you have to remember, we were raised in the generation right after World War II, and everyone recognized that everything about World War II in our minds was ideal and perfect and insurmountable and unsurpassable. The one stopper that any southerner had in a civil rights argument was the Tuskegee Airmen. They will never know how much it meant to us.

General Davis, through it all you have had the steadfast support of your wife, Agatha, whom I know is home today thinking of you. You struggled and succeeded together. I think you all should know that in 1973, Mrs. Davis wrote to a cadet who had been silenced by his classmates: "I think I know what your life at the Academy must have been. My best friend spent 4 years of silence at the Point. From 1936, when I married that best friend of mine, until

1949, I, too, was silenced by his classmates and their wives. There will always be those who will stand in your way. Don't resent them. Just feel sorry for them, and hold your head high."

Like so many military spouses past and present, this exceptional woman, an officer's wife who spent World War II toiling in a munitions factory, has worked and sacrificed to defend our freedom. And General, just as we salute you today, we salute her as well.

When Benjamin O. Davis, Jr., became an officer, he was the only black officer in our Air Corps. Now the Air Force has 4,000. Minorities and women remain underrepresented in our officer corps, but General Davis is here today as living proof that a person can overcome adversity and discrimination, achieve great things, turn skeptics into believers, and through example and perseverance, one person can bring truly extraordinary change.

So often today, America faces the challenge of helping to prevent conflicts overseas, fueled by these very divisions of race and ethnicity and religious differences. On Saturday I am going on a mission of peace to the Middle East, still embroiled in such conflicts. We cannot meet these challenges abroad unless we have healed our divisions at home.

To all of us, General Davis, you are the very embodiment of the principle that from diversity we can build an even stronger unity and that in diversity we can find the strength to prevail and advance. If we follow your example, America will always be strong, growing stronger. We will always be a leader for democracy, opportunity, and peace. We will be able to fulfill the promise of our Founders, to be a nation of equal rights and dignity for all, whose citizens pledge to each other our lives, our fortune, our sacred honor, in pursuit of that more perfect Union.

I am very, very proud, General Davis, of your service. On behalf of all Americans, I thank you. I thank you for everything you have done, for everything you have been, for what you have permitted the rest of us Americans to become.

Now I would like to ask the military aide to read the citation, after which, I invite General Davis' sister, Mrs. Elnora Davis McLendon, to join me in pinning on the General's fourth star.

Read the citation.

NOTE: The President spoke at 2:49 p.m. in Room 450 of the Old Executive Office Building. In his remarks, he referred to original Tuskegee Airmen Col. Charles McGee, USAF (Ret.), Lt. Col. Woodrow Crockett, USAF (Ret.), and Col. William A. Campbell, USAF (Ret.); Janet Langhart, wife of Defense Secretary William S. Cohen; former Secretary of Transportation William T. Coleman, Jr., and his son, William T. Coleman III, General Counsel, U.S. Army; and former Gov. Doug Wilder of Virginia.

Remarks on Lighting the National Christmas Tree
December 9, 1997

Thank you very much. Thank you, John. I want to thank you and all the people responsible, again, for this wonderful, wonderful evening. I'd like to thank our performers: Tony Bennett, Leona Mitchell, Jose Feliciano, the "Cats" crew, the Paul Hill choir, Al Roker, who has been a great Santa Claus tonight. I'd like to thank our Brownie and Cub Scout, Jessica Scott and Edgar Allen Sheppard. And of course, I'd like to thank Sammy Sosa and Mrs. Sosa for joining us tonight. We're delighted to see them all.

Hillary and I look forward to this every year, and this, as you may know, is the 75th anniversary of this Christmas tree lighting. For us, Christmas always starts with this Pageant of Peace. Tonight we celebrate the beginning of this season of peace and hope, of sharing and giving, of family and friends. We celebrate the birth of the child we know as the Prince of Peace, who came into the world with only a stable's roof to shelter him but grew to teach a lesson of love that has lasted two millennia. "Blessed are the peacemakers," he said, and his words still call us to action.

The lights we illuminate tonight are more than the flickering bulbs on a beautiful Colorado blue spruce. They represent millions of individual acts of courage and compassion that light our lives. Like the Star of Bethlehem, these lights shine the promise of hope and renewal.

Like the candles of Hanukkah, they stand for freedom against tyranny. Like the lamps that will soon light the mosques in the coming months of Ramadan, they evoke a call to community.

We light this tree in Washington, but all over the world we thank God that the light of peace is glowing as never before in Northern Ireland, in Bosnia, in the Middle East. In the coming year, let us rededicate ourselves to building the bonds of peace on Earth. Let those of us who are Americans express our appreciation to those who serve us in uniform, represented tonight by the United States Air Force Band, who help to preserve peace for us.

Now I'd like to ask Sammy and Jessica and Edgar to come up here and join me as we light the Christmas tree, our national tree. Let the spirit of the holidays, of peace and good will, be our beacon all year long. Merry Christmas. Happy New Year. May God bless you all.

Now put your hands on the switch, and I'll count down to one. Three, two, one. Light the tree!

NOTE: The President spoke at 5:50 p.m. on the Ellipse during the annual Christmas Pageant of Peace. In his remarks, he referred to John J. Betchkal, president, Christmas Pageant of Peace; and baseball player Sammy Sosa, National League Most Valuable Player, and his wife, Sonia.

Message on the Observance of Hanukkah, 1998
December 9, 1998

Warm greetings to all those celebrating Hanukkah.

For eight consecutive nights during this twilight of the year, in Jewish homes across America and around the world, the flames of the menorah will once again brighten steadfast spirits and gladden faithful hearts. Commemorating the rededication of the Holy Temple in Jerusalem more than two millennia ago, Hanukkah is a joyous celebration of the victory of the righteous over oppression and a reaffirmation of religious freedom as a fundamental right of people everywhere. This Festival of Lights is a reminder to all of us of the many blessings that brighten our lives: the love of God, the gift of freedom, the strength of family and community, and the hope of lasting peace.

As millions of families gather to kindle the flames of the menorah and to recite the special prayers of Hanukkah, Hillary and I extend our best wishes for a memorable celebration and for happiness and peace in the coming year.

BILL CLINTON

Memorandum on the Eleanor Roosevelt Award for Human Rights
December 9, 1998

Memorandum for the Secretary of State

Subject: The Eleanor Roosevelt Award for Human Rights

This month we mark the 50th anniversary of the Universal Declaration of Human Rights, the United Nations General Assembly declaration affirming a universal standard of human rights and fundamental freedoms. In so doing, we also honor the legacy of Eleanor Roosevelt, who served as the first Chairperson of the United Nations Commission on Human Rights and who was the driving force behind the Declaration.

To reaffirm our commitment to the principles of the Declaration and to honor the contributions of Eleanor Roosevelt, I hereby direct you to establish the Eleanor Roosevelt Award for Human Rights. You are authorized to take all necessary steps to establish an appropriate awards program under the auspices of your Department to recognize distinguished Americans who have made especially meritorious contributions to the promotion and protection of human rights within the United States or around the world.

These awards will be presented on or about December 10 of each year as part of the commemoration of the anniversary of the Universal Declaration of Human Rights. Prior to November 15 of each year, you shall present to me a list of nominees from which I will select up to five individuals or groups of individuals to receive this award. In preparing your list of nominees, you may consider the recommendations of appropriate individuals and groups and coordinate your nominations in consultation with other Federal agencies as appropriate. You may include recommendations for posthumous awards.

You are directed to publish this memorandum in the *Federal Register*.

WILLIAM J. CLINTON

NOTE: This memorandum was not received for publication in the *Federal Register*.

Remarks on Presenting the Eleanor Roosevelt Awards for Human Rights
December 10, 1998

Thank you very much. I want to welcome all of you here, the Members of Congress, the members of our foreign policy team who have worked on this, National Security Adviser Berger, Under Secretary Loy, Assistant Secretary Koh. I welcome Ambassador Nancy Rubin, the Ambassador to the U.N. Commission on Human Rights; Theresa Loar, the Senior Coordinator for International Women's Issues; members of the Roosevelt family; and other distinguished guests.

I would like to say also, before getting into my prepared remarks, that someday when I write the memoirs of these last several years, one of the proudest moments of our administration for me will be the work the First Lady has done to advance the cause of human rights. I remember the speech she gave in Beijing on a rainy day when people were struggling through the mud to get into that remote facility; the talk she gave just a few days ago at Gaston Hall at Georgetown University about Eleanor Roosevelt—I think one of the finest speeches she ever gave; but more important, the concrete work, the Vital Voices work in Northern Ireland and Latin America and all the little villages she visited in Latin America and Africa and Asia, on the Indian Subcontinent to try to advance the condition of women and children, especially young girls. And I think that every person who has ever been the parent of a daughter could identify strongly with the remarks she just made and the brave women who were just introduced.

You know, most of us, at least who have reached a certain age, we look forward to the holidays when our daughters come home from college, and they have the human right to decide whether they want to come home or not. [*Laughter*] When our daughters are married, and they have our grandchildren, we hope they'll find a way to come home. Imagine— I just wish there were some way for every American citizen to imagine how they would feel if the people Hillary just discussed were their daughters. I hope we can do more.

We are sponsoring these awards today and announcing them because, as all of you know so well, 50 years ago in Paris the U.N. General Assembly voted to approve the U.N. Universal Declaration of Human Rights. It was a watershed moment for what was then a very young United Nations; a new chapter, however, in a much, much older story, the unending striving of humanity to realize its potential in the life of every person.

For its time, the Universal Declaration was quite bold. If you look at the way the world is going today, it's still quite a bold document. Like all great breakthroughs, it was an act of imagination and courage, an opening of the heart and the mind with spare elegance. It served notice that for all our differences, we share a common birthright.

You know, it's easy for us to forget, but if you think back to 1948, it might not have been particularly easy to affirm faith in mankind's future. After all, it was just 3 years after a cataclysmic war and the Holocaust; the cold war was beginning to blight the postwar landscape; millions and millions more would die just in the Soviet Union under the terror of Stalin.

But this document did reaffirm faith in humankind. It is really the Magna Carta of our humanity. Article I states that: "All human beings are born free and equal in dignity and rights. They are endowed with reason and conscience and should act toward one another in a spirit of brotherhood." There are no commas or parentheses in this sentence, no qualifications or exceptions, just the power of affirmation.

Other articles assert the freedom to worship, to work, to assemble, to participate in a life of meaning and purpose. Those words have now been translated into every language of the United Nations. Though 50 years old, they still ring free, fresh, and powerful, don't they? They resonate today, because today human dignity is still under siege, not something that can be taken for granted anywhere.

We all know how much the Declaration owed to the remarkable leadership of Eleanor Roosevelt. She rose to every challenge. She defended American idealism. She honestly admitted our own imperfections. She always called on the best from each delegate, and she called on it again and again and again. Indeed, a delegate from Panama grew so exhausted by the pace that he had to remind Mrs. Roosevelt that the delegates had human rights, too. [*Laughter*]

Today we celebrate the life of this document and the lives it has saved and enhanced. Mrs. Roosevelt worried that it would be hard to translate ideas on paper into real places, into kitchens and factories and ghettos and prisons. But words have power. Ideas have power. And the march for human rights has steadily gained ground.

Since 1948, the United Nations has adopted legal instruments against torture, genocide, slavery, apartheid, and discrimination against women and children. As nations grow more interdependent, the idea of a unified standard of human rights becomes easier to define and more important than ever to maintain.

Obviously, all nations have more work to do, and the United States is no exception. We must improve our own record. We must correct our own mistakes, even as we fulfill our responsibility to insist on improvement in other nations—in totalitarian states, like North Korea; in military dictatorships, like Burma; in countries where leaders practice the politics of ethnic hatred, like Serbia and Iraq; in African nations where tribal differences have led to unimaginable slaughter; in nations where tolerance and faith must struggle against intolerant fundamentalism, like Afghanistan and Sudan; in Cuba, where persons who strive for peaceful democratic change still are repressed and imprisoned; in China, where change has come to people's daily lives, but where basic political rights are still denied to too many.

Some suggest today that it is sheer arrogance for the President or for the United States to discuss such matters in other countries. Some say it is because we are not perfect here at home. If we had to wait for perfection, none of us would ever advance in any way. Some say it is because there are Asian values or African values or Western values dividing the human race into various subcategories. Well, let's be honest: There are. There are genuine cultural differences which inevitably lead to different political and social structures. And that can be all to the good, because no one has a corner on the truth. It makes life more interesting.

The Universal Declaration of Human Rights does not say there are no differences among people. It says what we have in common is more fundamental than our differences, and therefore, all the differences must be expressed within certain limits beyond which we dare not go without violating our common humanity.

This is a phony attack on those of you who fight every day for human rights. None of us want everyone to be the same; none of us want to have all the same religious practices; none of us want to have all the same social and political structures; none of us say we know exactly how life should be organized everywhere under all circumstances and how every problem should be solved. We say we have a common humanity and whatever you think should be done differently must be done within the limits that respects our common humanity.

Now, that means a lot to us on the verge of a new century, where freedom and knowledge and flexibility will mean more to people than ever before, where people in the poorest villages on every continent on this Earth will have a chance to leapfrog years and years and years of the development process simply because of the communications revolution, if we respect universal human rights. The Vice President said so well recently, in Asia, that we believe the peaceful democratic process that we have

strongly endorsed will be even more essential to the world on the threshold of this new millennium.

Throughout 1998, old fears and hatreds crumbled before the healing power of honest communication, faith in the future, a strong will for a better future. Today in Oslo—I'm happy about this—today in Oslo, two leaders from Northern Ireland, John Hume and David Trimble, are receiving the Nobel Peace Prize for their efforts on the Good Friday accord. In the Middle East, where I will go in 2 days, Palestinians and Israelis are struggling to bridge mutual distrust to implement the Wye accords. In Kosovo, a serious humanitarian crisis has been averted, and the process toward reconciliation continues in Bosnia. All these breakthroughs were triumphs for human rights.

Today we recommit ourselves to the ideas of the Universal Declaration, to keep moving toward the promise outlined in Paris 50 years ago.

First, we're taking steps to respond quickly to genocidal conditions, through the International Coalition Against Genocide I announced during my visit to Africa and a new genocide early warning center sponsored by the Department of State and the CIA. We will provide additional support to the U.N. Torture Victims Fund and genocide survivors in Bosnia, Rwanda, and Cambodia. We will continue assistance to women suffering under the Taliban regime in Afghanistan. And USAID will provide up to $8 million to NGO's to enhance their ability to respond more rapidly to human rights emergencies.

Second, we must do more for children who have always been especially vulnerable to human rights violations. This year I sought and Congress provided dramatic new support for the fight against child labor with a tenfold increase in United States assistance to the International Labor Organization. Today the Immigration and Naturalization Service is issuing new guidelines for the evaluation of asylum claims by children, making the process better serve our youngest and most vulnerable asylum seekers.

Third, we must practice at home what we preach aboard. Just this morning I signed an Executive order that strengthens our ability to implement human rights treaties and creates an interagency group to hold us accountable for progress in honoring those commitments.

Fourth, I am concerned about aliens who suffer abuses at the hands of smugglers and sweatshop owners. These victims actually have a built-in disincentive—their unlawful status here—that discourages them from complaining to U.S. authorities. So I'm asking the Department of Justice to provide legislative options to address this problem. And I know the Deputy Attorney General, Eric Holder, and the Deputy Secretary of Labor, Kitty Higgins, are here, and I trust they will work on this, because I know they care as much about it as I do.

Finally, I'd like to repeat my support for two top legislative priorities, an employment non-discrimination act that would ban discrimination against gays and lesbians in the workplace, and a hate crimes prevention act. Last year, the entire Nation was outraged by the brutal killings of Matthew Shepard, a young gay student in Wyoming, and James Byrd, an African-American in Texas. All Americans are entitled to the same respect and legal protection, no matter their race, their gender, their sexual orientation. I agree with something President Truman once said, "When I say Americans, I mean all Americans."

We will never relinquish the fight to move forward in the continuing struggle for human rights. I am aware that much of the best work in human rights has been done by those outside government: students and activists, NGO's, brave religious leaders, people from all backgrounds who simply want a better, safer world for their children. Many have done so in the face of great adversity, the imprisoned members of the Internal Dissidents Working Group in Cuba, the political prisoners of the National League for Democracy in Burma, the imprisoned dissidents in China. We make common cause with them all.

That is why today we are presenting the first Eleanor Roosevelt Award for Human Rights to four outstanding Americans, not only for their own efforts but because we know that, by working together, we can do more. From different backgrounds and generations, they stand, all, in the great tradition of Eleanor Roosevelt, pioneers in the fight to expand the frontiers of freedom: Robert Bernstein, a pathbreaker for freedom of expression and the protection of rights at home and abroad; Bette Bao Lord, the head of Freedom House, a prolific author and campaigner; Dorothy Thomas, a champion of women's rights, the voice of a new generation

committed to human rights; and John Lewis, a veteran in the civil rights struggle, now serving his Congress with great distinction in the House of Representatives.

I would like to ask the military aide to read the citations.

[*At this point, Lt. Comdr. Wesley Huey, USN, Naval Aide to the President, read the citations, and the President presented the awards.*]

I'd like to ask the members of the Roosevelt family who are here to stand. [*Applause*] Thank you.

The day the U.N. delegates voted to approve the declaration, Eleanor Roosevelt wrote, "Long job over." [*Laughter*] One of the few mistakes she ever made. [*Laughter*] She left us and all our successors a big job that will never be over, for the Universal Declaration contains an eternal promise, one embraced by our Founders in 1776, one that has to be reaffirmed every day in every way.

In our country, each generation of Americans has had to do it: in the struggle against slavery led by President Lincoln, in FDR's Four Freedoms, in the unfinished work of Martin Luther King and Robert Kennedy, in the ongoing work here in this room.

I have learned in ways large and small in the last 6 years that there is within every person a scale of justice and that people can too easily be herded into hatred and extremism, often out of a belief that they have absolute truth and, therefore, are entitled to absolute power, that they can ignore any constitution, any laws, override any facts. There will always be work to be done. And again, I would say to you that this award we gave to these four richly deserving people is also for all of you who labor for human rights.

In the prolog of John Lewis's magnificent autobiography, "Walking With the Wind," he tells a stunning story that has become a metaphor for his life and is a metaphor for your work, about being a little boy with his brothers and sisters and cousins in the house of a relative, that was a very fragile house, when an enormous wind came up. And he said he was told that all the children had to hold hands, and one corner of the house would blow up in the wind and all the children would walk, holding hands, to the corner, and it would go down. And then another would come up, and all the children would hold hands again and go to the other corner until the house came down. And by walking with the wind, hand-in-hand, they saved the house and the family and the children.

John says that that walk is a struggle to find the beloved community. The Universal Declaration of Human Rights applies to individuals, but it can only be achieved by our common community.

Thank you, and God bless you all.

NOTE: The President spoke at 10:39 a.m. in Room 450 of the Old Executive Office Building. In his remarks, he referred to Ulster Unionist Party leader David Trimble and Social Democratic Party leader John Hume of Northern Ireland. The Executive order on implementation of human rights treaties and the Human Rights Day proclamation of December 10 are listed in Appendix D at the end of this volume.

Remarks on the Unveiling of a Portrait of Former Secretary of Agriculture Mike Espy
December 10, 1998

Oh, happy day. [*Laughter*] I'd like to begin by thanking Deputy Secretary Rominger, who has served so well both Secretary Espy and Secretary Glickman. I thank Dan Glickman and Rhoda for being a part of our administration's family.

Dan Glickman pointed out when I discussed this appointment with him that he would be in the proud tradition of my commitment to a Cabinet that looks like America and to diversity because there were even fewer Jewish farmers than black farmers. [*Laughter*]

I want to thank my friends Reverend Wintley Phipps, Reverend Walter Fauntroy, Reverend Beecher Hicks, and the Howard Gospel Choir here. They are wonderful. I thank the members of the Cabinet and former members of the Cabinet who are here, Secretary Herman, Secretary Richardson, Secretary O'Leary, EPA Administrator Browner, Ambassador Barshefsky. John Podesta and Bob Nash and a whole slew of people from the White House are here; Senator Leahy, Senator Carol Moseley-Braun, Congressmen Clyburn, Jefferson, Eddie Bernice Johnson, Stenholm, Congressman Thompson. We're glad to see former Congressmen Montgomery and Coelho and many other former Members of Congress here. And Reverend Jackson, thank you for coming; and to the Espy family and all the members of Mike Espy's extended family here.

Six years ago, on Christmas Eve, I announced that I would nominate, and I quote, "my neighbor, my friend, and my supporter, Mike Espy" to be Secretary of Agriculture. He was a young Congressman from Mississippi when I served

as Governor of Arkansas. We shared a passion for many issues, including rural development.

As a Congressman, Mike worked with my Senator, Dale Bumpers, to set up the Lower Mississippi Delta Development Commission, a commission I had the honor to chair. It brought jobs and growth to one of America's poorest, least developed regions. I came to know and respect Mike Espy in that endeavor.

I knew we also shared a vision for America, a new approach to government rooted in our most enduring values, changed and shaped to meet the challenges of the 21st century. The need for change was nowhere more evident than at the Department of Agriculture, which has, as Dan Glickman said, since the time of President Lincoln, nurtured the seeds of renewal for America.

On Christmas Eve I said, "The Department of Agriculture can't simply be a stolid representative of the interests of the past. It has to be a real force for family farmers in our country, for the agricultural issues of today and tomorrow." Mike understood that. As the first African-American to become the Secretary of Agriculture, he was the very embodiment of change not only here but in many other areas of administration policy—one of eight African-Americans who have now served in the President's Cabinet in the last 6 years. And I am very grateful for that.

And I'm grateful to Senator Leahy and Senator Carol Moseley-Braun for confirming them all.

In his 2 years at the helm Mike changed the Department of Agriculture as profoundly and beneficially as any Secretary in its history. It is fitting today we raise his portrait. He made history, and today we honor him for it.

I'd like to talk a little bit about his record as Secretary of Agriculture. His first great challenge came only a few days after he started on the job, when an outbreak of E. coli from tainted meat took the lives of three children in Washington State. Mike went to Washington, promised the victims' families strong action, and he delivered.

The new science-based inspection procedures developed during his tenure and put into place under Secretary Glickman have cut incidents of salmonella contamination in pork by a third, in poultry by nearly 50 percent, according to the preliminary data we have. The Department of Agriculture has no higher responsibility than ensuring the safety of America's food supply. Today it is fulfilling that responsibility, thanks in no small measure to Mike Espy's leadership.

Mike's second great challenge came in 1993 also. It was a challenging year, when floods of Biblical proportion struck the Midwest. In the past, the Federal Government had earned a reputation for slow and inadequate responses to natural disasters. But Mike Espy, along with James Lee Witt at FEMA, helped set a new, higher standard of Government service, providing thousands of communities and millions of Americans with the aid they needed swiftly and efficiently.

His third great challenge at USDA was to help our economy and our farm sector by expanding markets for America's agricultural bounty. When we negotiated the GATT accords in later 1993, some of the greatest obstacles were agricultural issues. Nobody worked harder, with greater success, to work through those issues and pave the way for the passage of GATT than Secretary Espy.

His fourth great challenge was to make USDA smaller, stronger, more responsive to farmers and consumers. In just 2 short years, Mike put in motion a process, which Secretary Glickman has carried through, that has reduced the work force by 18,000, closed and consolidated over 1,000 field offices, saved the taxpayers of our country $4.8 billion, all the while, thanks to the employees here, improving services to farmers, many of whom can now visit one location instead of driving from one USDA field office to another. I thank him, and I thank all of you who work here, for doing that.

The list of the good things he did for America goes on and on. He set higher nutritional standards for school lunches. He helped end the gridlock over logging on Federal lands in the Northwest. He spearheaded the Water 2000 effort to make sure that, by the end of the century, no American is without fresh, clean drinking water. Starting in Congress, continuing as Agriculture Secretary, Mike worked to win more resources for minority farmers and to fight discrimination in USDA programs, a fight that Secretary Glickman has energetically continued. I thank both of them for that. This year, finally, we fought for and won legislation to allow minority farmers' discrimination claims from almost the last two decades finally to be heard.

Mike left the USDA in 1994 to face a different kind of challenge, one no person could have chosen, but one he faced with characteristic resolve, integrity, and strength. I'd like to say—I don't know if this is appropriate or not, but I think we ought to give Mr. Weingarten and Mr. Wells a hand and ask them to stand. They did a heck of a job. [Applause] Thank you.

Mike drew inspiration from his family, his friends, the Holy Scripture. With his head held high, he persevered, and he triumphed. Often, Mike talks fondly of his late father Henry, who was a USDA Agricultural Extension Agent in Arkansas in the early 1940's, back in the days when black extension agents only served black farmers. The pride Henry Espy would feel if he could see this portrait of his son hanging in this room is something we can only imagine. But the pride that we can feel, for Mike, for the USDA, and for the progress of our Nation, is every bit as real.

I think all of us have been deeply moved to see this good man grow in mind, body, and spirit through this difficult ordeal. He often said he read the 27th Psalm. When I saw him outside the courtroom, I thought of the wonderful passage from Isaiah: "Be not afraid. I have redeemed you. I have called you by my name. You are mine." Well, Mike, the jury redeemed you, and you belong to the American people, and we are very proud of you.

Now I would like to ask Mike's children, Jamilla and Mike, to join me in unveiling this fine portrait by the Mississippi artist Jason Bouldin, who is also here. I would like to ask Mr. Bouldin to come up and stand on the stage with us, so we can appreciate his handiwork.

[*At this point, the portrait was unveiled.*]

Now, ladies and gentlemen, I think it's high time we heard from the man we came to honor, Secretary Mike Espy.

NOTE: The President spoke at 12:52 p.m. at the Department of Agriculture. In his remarks, he referred to Rhoda Glickman, wife of Agriculture Secretary Dan Glickman; civil rights activist Rev. Jesse Jackson; and attorneys Reid H. Weingarten and Ted Wells, Jr.

Statement on the National Education Goals Report
December 10, 1998

Today's release of the annual National Education Goals Report shows that America has made some progress toward achieving the National Education Goals but still has a long way to go. If we are going to reach these goals, we must strengthen accountability and raise standards for students, teachers, and schools. I will continue to press Congress to help give our students smaller classes, well-prepared teachers, and modernized school buildings. I will continue my efforts to expand access to early childhood programs, increase public school choice, make our schools safe, disciplined, and drug-free, open the doors of college education, and help Americans engage in lifelong learning.

I am pleased at the progress that the report shows in helping our young children arrive at school ready to learn, improving student achievement in math, and increasing the participation of women and minorities in math and science in higher education. Those responsible for such gains—parents and teachers, local and State education officials, colleges and universities, the business community, and students themselves—should be proud of what they have accomplished.

But we must do more. Education is a local function, a State responsibility, and a national priority. The National Education Goals define excellence in education, and Americans at all levels must redouble our efforts to meet them.

Remarks Following Discussions With Central American Leaders
December 11, 1998

President Clinton. Good morning. I have just concluded a very good meeting with the leaders of five Central American nations: President Rodriguez of Costa Rica, President Flores of Honduras, President Aleman of Nicaragua, President Calderon Sol of El Salvador, and Vice President Flores of Guatemala. We send our best wishes to President Arzu, who is in Guatemala recovering from a bout of pneumonia.

Over the past decade, Central Americans have transformed their countries. Nations where freedom once was denied, where there was once fear and violence, have now joined their neighbors as democracies in peace. Economic development has raised many from poverty. Now nature has put that progress at risk.

Central American nations face in varying degrees the formidable task of rebuilding from the region's deadliest storm in modern history: 9,000 confirmed dead, another 9,000 missing and feared dead, 3 million people homeless or displaced. The hurricane destroyed schools, hospitals, farms, utilities, roads, and bridges.

The governments and people of the region have made tremendous efforts to address this crisis, showing great courage and strength. But they are not, and they never will be, alone. I say to the leaders here and to the people of Central America, the United States will continue to do everything we can. *Ayudaremos a nuestros hermanos.* We will help our brothers and sisters. It is the right thing to do. And I say to my fellow Americans, it also serves our long-term interests in a stable, free, and prosperous hemisphere.

I'm very pleased that we have achieved an era of growing cooperation, respect, and friendship among the nations of the Americas. We stand together for democracy, opportunity, and peace. We stand together in good times and bad. The United States already has committed $283 million in assistance, and we will provide an additional $17 million through AID for food assistance.

Thousands of our troops and civilian officials are now in the region supporting relief efforts. With our help and with the help of others, the people of Central America have reopened roads, contained disease, restored drinking water in many areas. Both the First Lady and Tipper Gore have visited the region, and last month they led a conference of charitable organizations to coordinate aid.

Now we are shifting our focus to reconstruction. And the United States will do our share there as well. Working with Congress on a bipartisan basis, our effort will include funds for rebuilding, debt relief and new financing, trade and investment initiatives, and immigration relief.

Already, the United States has identified $125 million in additional funds for rebuilding. Right now, Senator Domenici, Housing Secretary Cuomo, and other American officials are in the region discussing reconstruction. With Congress and with other countries, we will provide funds to restore hope and growth.

Debt relief and new financing are essential to recovery. We and other creditor nations will relieve Honduras and Nicaragua, the hardest hit nations, from debt service obligations until 2001. We are working with international institutions for new financing, and we will work with Congress to help these countries meet their loan obligations. Together, these efforts could provide more than $1.5 billion in relief and new resources. For the longer term, we will support, and I am pleased other creditor nations have said they will support, substantial forgiveness of bilateral debt. We call on other creditors to join us.

Next week, Brian Atwood and USAID will convene a conference to encourage private sector aid and investment. Our Overseas Private Investment Corporation, under the leadership of George Muñoz, is working to spur U.S. business involvement, starting with an initiative to accelerate over $200 million in new projects for the region. We will continue to support Caribbean Basin enhancement legislation to make trade more free and more fair, and to help Central American nations restore their economies. I hope very much that it will pass in this coming Congress and quickly. We also plan to submit to the Senate our investment treaties with Nicaragua and Honduras.

Let me add that, after the hurricane struck, our immigration service stopped deportations to Honduras, Nicaragua, El Salvador, and Guatemala through early next year. We are considering further immigration measures, temporary and long-term, which will be announced shortly.

Finally, I want to say that the leaders have kindly invited me to visit their region, and I intend to travel to Central America early next year to consider how the United States can best help them and strengthen our partnership over the long run. I thank them for the invitation. It will be a chance to discuss moving beyond disaster recovery, to advance our shared agenda for the Americas: deepening democracy and good governance; improving education, health and the environment; expanding opportunity and trade.

I want to thank people all across the United States who have responded to this tragedy with generosity and hard work. And I want to thank these Central American leaders for their leadership and their friendship.

Now, I'd like to turn the podium over to President Flores, who will speak on behalf of the Central American leaders. Mr. President, the podium is yours.

President Flores. Mr. President, on behalf of the Presidents of Central America, I wish to express how very pleased we are with today's most fruitful and productive dialog with the President of the United States of America. That reaffirms our confidence in his strong leadership and superb ability to understand our people, both simply as human beings and in terms of their needs for the enormous task of rebuilding our devastated lands.

We also want to convey to the First Lady, Hillary Rodham Clinton, to Mrs. Tipper Gore, and the distinguished members of their delegations who made personal visits to our anguished communities following the tragic days of Hurricane Mitch, and to the very generous American people the deepest gratitude of Central America for the prompt and meaningful cooperation the

United States provided during our emergency, and in subsequent endeavors of relief and rehabilitation.

First, let us say that we come to Washington completely aware the potential and responsibility for rebuilding the Central American region lies in our own efforts. Inasmuch as we do appreciate and are grateful for the generous support that we have and are sure to receive from the United States and the international community, we also feel that it will not replace our own initiatives but will provide much-needed momentum.

The main concerns of our conversation with the President of the United States touched on the following issues: first, the leadership we expect and which we feel that the United States is exercising among the international community for the procurement of the financial resources that are needed in the process of rehabilitation and reconstruction of our devastated economies.

We have explained to President Clinton, and we surely think that he is convinced, that in order for Central America to rebuild, it is crucial that not only debt relief be granted but, more important, that new financial resources and concessionary credits are available in the magnitude that permits that we shall not reverse what we have so heartily fought for and accomplished in terms of economic growth, our political and institutional stability, peace, and a dignified life for our people.

Second, we touched on the negative effects that may result in the aftermath of this tragedy, where tens of thousands of people uprooted from their lands and their jobs, with no homes and no economic security for themselves and their families, if left with no hope or possibility of rapidly procuring their own means of a decent life in their own homeland. We do not wish to see repeated the unfortunate exodus that occurred in Central America in the past, when the cruel consequences of war and internal political problems robbed thousands of the security of their jobs and opportunities in their own countries.

For us, a rapid means of providing back to our people the possibilities which have been taken by the devastating effects of this hurricane, which, by the way, are much more graver than those inferred in the worst times of the Central American War, is by strengthening trade, open markets, and commerce opportunities. The enhancement of the Caribbean Basin Initiative, which originated as a bipartisan endeavor some years ago, would greatly increase these possibilities.

Third, we spoke about our profound concern, specially at this point where thousands have been left homeless and without jobs, that there be not only temporary measures but a definite solution to the immigration status of the many Central Americans now living and working in the United States.

We Central Americans have paid a very high price for upholding the principles of democracy and for insisting that our people live in freedom. We have made a commitment to ourselves and to the world to continue strengthening peace at home and to continue playing an important role in the stability and the security of the hemisphere, with a strength that surely comes from the most admirable determination of our people not to let themselves be defeated. We are committed to hard work and superior attitudes, so that this blow which we have had to endure is not a terminal one but a starting point for a more promising future for Central America.

Your hospitality, Mr. President, honors us and engages our commitments. We will be eagerly awaiting your visit to our Central American countries. We pray that God will continue to bless us all. And for you, Mr. President, on behalf of our people and our governments, we wish you the greatest success and strength as you lead your great and admirable country.

Thank you so much.

The President. Thank you so much. Thank you.

NOTE: The President spoke at 11:35 a.m. in the Rose Garden at the White House. In his remarks, he referred to President Miguel Rodriguez of Costa Rica; President Carlos Roberto Flores of Honduras; President Arnoldo Aleman of Nicaragua; President Armando Calderon of El Salvador; and Vice President Luis Flores and President Alvaro Arzu of Guatemala.

Remarks Prior to the House Judiciary Committee Vote on the First Article of Impeachment
December 11, 1998

Good afternoon. As anyone close to me knows, for months I have been grappling with how best to reconcile myself to the American people, to acknowledge my own wrongdoing, and still to maintain my focus on the work of the Presidency.

Others are presenting my defense on the facts, the law, and the Constitution. Nothing I can say now can add to that. What I want the American people to know, what I want the Congress to know, is that I am profoundly sorry for all I have done wrong in words and deeds. I never should have misled the country, the Congress, my friends, or my family. Quite simply, I gave in to my shame.

I have been condemned by my accusers with harsh words. And while it's hard to hear yourself called deceitful and manipulative, I remember Ben Franklin's admonition that our critics are our friends, for they do show us our faults.

Mere words cannot fully express the profound remorse I feel for what our country is going through and for what members of both parties in Congress are now forced to deal with.

These past months have been a tortuous process of coming to terms with what I did. I understand that accountability demands consequences, and I'm prepared to accept them. Painful though the condemnation of the Congress would be, it would pale in comparison to the consequences of the pain I have caused my family. There is no greater agony.

Like anyone who honestly faces the shame of wrongful conduct, I would give anything to go back and undo what I did. But one of the painful truths I have to live with is the reality

that that is simply not possible. An old and dear friend of mine recently sent me the wisdom of a poet, who wrote:

> The Moving Finger writes; and, having writ,
> Moves on: nor all your piety nor wit
> Shall lure it back to cancel half a line,
> Nor all your tears wash out a word of it.

So nothing, not piety, nor tears, nor wit, nor torment, can alter what I have done. I must make my peace with that. I must also be at peace with the fact that the public consequences of my actions are in the hands of the American people and their Representatives in the Congress. Should they determine that my errors of word and deed require their rebuke and censure, I am ready to accept that.

Meanwhile, I will continue to do all I can to reclaim the trust of the American people and to serve them well. We must all return to the work, the vital work, of strengthening our Nation for the new century. Our country has wonderful opportunities and daunting challenges ahead. I intend to seize those opportunities and meet those challenges with all the energy and ability and strength God has given me.

That is simply all I can do: the work of the American people.

Thank you very much.

NOTE: The President spoke at 4:10 p.m. in the Rose Garden at the White House. At approximately 4:25 p.m. the Committee on the Judiciary of the House of Representatives voted the first article of impeachment.

The President's Radio Address
December 12, 1998

Good morning. This month, as Americans begin to prepare for winter, our Nation's farmers begin to prepare for the spring planting ahead. But this year has been very hard on farmers—for some, the hardest in nearly two

decades—and many are strained to the breaking point. Today I want to talk about what we're doing to help America's farmers weather these hard times and to build a stronger safety net to protect them for years to come.

We're living in a remarkable time of prosperity and even greater promise for our future. Our economy is the strongest in a generation, with more than 17 million new jobs, family incomes rising, the lowest unemployment in nearly 30 years, the lowest inflation in more than 30 years, the smallest percentage of people on welfare in 29 years, and the highest homeownership in history.

America's farmers have helped to build this new prosperity, but far too many of our farming communities are not reaping its benefits. Flood and drought and crop disease have wiped out entire harvests in some parts of the country. Plummeting prices here at home and collapsing markets in Asia have threatened the livelihood of some farming communities.

Wherever we live and whatever work we do, every American has a stake in the strength of rural America. America's farmers are the backbone of our economy and the lifeblood of our land. Our farming families stand for the values that have kept our Nation strong for over 220 years: hard work, faith and family, perseverance, and patience. We can't afford to let them fail.

Last summer we took action to ease the immediate crisis on our farms. We began buying millions of tons of wheat and other food to ease the burden of dropping prices here at home and to feed hungry people in Africa, Russia, and all over the world. I signed legislation to speed farm program payments to farmers, who need the money now to start planting for next spring. And I called on the Congress to take action to help farmers survive this year's one-two punch from Mother Nature and the marketplace.

I am pleased to say that this October, as part of our balanced budget, I signed legislation that included a $6 billion plan for farmers in need. This November we started putting the plan into action, with nearly $3 billion in income assistance to farmers who have seen their profits wither as crop prices fell. Today I am pleased to announce the next major step to ease the crisis on our farms, nearly $2½ billion in emergency aid for farmers who have lost crops and livestock.

But with too many farm families still in danger of losing their land, and with crop prices still far too low, we know we must do more to strengthen the safety net for our Nation's farmers. Government has an important role to play in meeting this challenge, but it's not something Government can do alone. Ultimately, America's farmers will keep America's farms growing strong.

We know that no one can fully predict the changing weather or changing prices, but every farmer knows that crop insurance is one of the best ways to protect against the worst risks of farming. In good times, crop insurance gives farming families the security they need to thrive and grow. And in hard times, crop insurance can mean the difference between a spring planting and a spring sale of the family farm. But far too many farmers don't have crop insurance at all or only buy the bare minimum, not enough to withstand a really devastating year.

We need to do more to enable family farmers to fully protect themselves in hard times. That's why I am pleased to announce the funds we're releasing include $400 million in new incentives for farmers to buy crop insurance. We'll give farmers a one-time premium discount of up to 35 percent when they expand their crop insurance, and that will give our farming families greater security and more peace of mind.

Together, these steps will help thousands of farmers around our country to recover from this difficult time and plant a seed of hope for the future, not only for stronger farms but for a stronger America in the 21st century.

Thanks for listening.

NOTE: The address was recorded at 7:30 p.m. on December 11 in the Roosevelt Room at the White House for broadcast at 10:06 a.m. on December 12. The transcript was made available by the Office of the Press Secretary on December 11 but was embargoed for release until the broadcast.

Statement on the Death of Lawton Chiles
December 12, 1998

Hillary and I were deeply saddened to learn of the death of Governor Lawton Chiles. Lawton Chiles was a close friend of mine for many years. He served the people of Florida as an elected official for over 40 years, always putting the interests of ordinary people first with his unique political style. As a leader, he has been an indefatigable champion of Florida's children and families and a steadfast protector of the environment. He displayed courage time and time again, most recently challenging the Nation's top cigarette makers and emerging victorious.

Lawton was a statesman, a role model, and one of the most successful and respected public officials in the later half of the 20th century. He set a benchmark for how public servants will be judged and, I believe, created a legacy that will endure for generations.

Lawton never forgot the thousands of ordinary citizens he met as he walked the highways and backroads of his State, whom he served so well. And they will never forget him.

Remarks at the Arrival Ceremony in Tel Aviv, Israel
December 13, 1998

President and Mrs. Weizman, Prime Minister and Mrs. Netanyahu, first of all, on behalf of my family and our entire delegation, I would like to thank you for coming out here at this very late hour to welcome us. Hillary and Chelsea and I and all the Americans have been looking forward to this trip. I am delighted to be back in Israel.

As President Weizman said, this is the fourth time I have come here as President, to reaffirm America's unbreakable ties to Israel, to reaffirm our unshakable commitment to Israel's security, and this time, to fulfill the pledge I made at the Wye talks to speak with the people of Israel and the Palestinians about the benefits of peace and to stand by you as you take risks for a just, lasting, and secure peace. The United States will walk this road with Israel every step of the way.

Peacemaking has opened historic opportunities to Israel, but each step forward has been tempered with pain and understandable feelings of ambivalence when questions arise as to whether agreements are being implemented fully.

We share the conviction that without security, the peace process always will be clouded for the vast majority of Israelis who seek only to live normal lives as a free people in their own country, and we are determined that Israel's just requirements for security be met. At the same time, we believe that, for two peoples who are fated to share this land, peace is not simply an option among many but the only choice that can avert still more years of bloodshed, apprehension, and sorrow.

That is why I am here. In the past few weeks, the people of Israel, through their Government and Knesset, have endorsed the Wye River agreement, recognizing the promise it holds for putting the peace process on track and creating a positive environment for dealing with the complex and difficult final status talks.

I want to again, but for the first time in Israel, pay tribute to the Prime Minister and the representatives of his government for those long, arduous, difficult talks at Wye, often accompanied with sleepless nights. I believe it was the right thing to do. I believed it then. I believe it now. But both sides now must face the challenge of implementing Wye.

I will discuss that with the Prime Minister and his colleagues tomorrow and later in my meeting with Chairman Arafat. Then on Tuesday our family will have the chance to go to Bethlehem and Masada to explore more of this magnificent country and its sacred heritage.

Again, I thank you for welcoming us. I thank you for the struggles you have waged for freedom and for security. I thank you for the efforts you now make for peace. It is good to be back.

Thank you very much.

NOTE: The President spoke at 12 midnight at Ben-Gurion International Airport. In his remarks, he referred to President Ezer Weizman of Israel and his wife, Reuma; Prime Minister Binyamin Netanyahu of Israel and his wife, Sarah; and Chairman Yasser Arafat of the Palestinian Authority.

The President's News Conference With Prime Minister Binyamin Netanyahu of Israel in Jerusalem
December 13, 1998

Prime Minister Netanyahu. Mr. President, I want to welcome you and your entire delegation, the Secretary of State, the National Security Adviser, and your exceptional team, for coming here on this mission of peace and for your understanding of our concerns. We spent many hours in Wye River, and there and in our conversations this morning, I've come to appreciate and admire your extraordinary ability to empathize and the seriousness with which you examine every issue.

Your visit here is part of the implementation of the Wye River accords. Now, this was not an easy agreement for us, but we did our part. And we are prepared to do our part based on Palestinian compliance. When I say that we did our part, you know that within 2 weeks we withdrew from territory, released prisoners, and opened the Gaza airport, precisely as we undertook to do.

The Palestinians, in turn, were to live up to a series of obligations in the sphere of security, in ending incitement and violence, in the repeal of the Palestinian Charter, and in commitments to negotiate a final settlement in order to achieve permanent peace between us. I regret to say that none of these conditions have been met.

Palestinians proceeded to unilaterally declare what the final settlement would be. Coming out of Wye, they said again and again that regardless of what happens in the negotiations, on May 4th of 1999 they will unilaterally declare a state, divide Jerusalem, and make its eastern half the Palestinian capital. This is a gross violation of the Oslo and Wye accords, which commit the parties to negotiate a mutually agreed final settlement.

Mr. Arafat and the Palestinian Authority must officially and unequivocally renounce this attempt. I think no one can seriously expect Israel to hand over another inch of territory unless and until such an unambiguous correction is made.

I said that there are other violations. The Palestinians, I'm afraid, began a campaign of incitement. At Wye, as those who are here well know, we agreed to release Palestinian prisoners, but not terrorists with blood on their hands or members of Hamas who are waging war against us. No sooner did we release the agreed number of prisoners in the first installment that the Palestinian Authority refused to acknowledge what they agreed to at Wye. Falsely charging Israel with violating the prisoner release clause, Palestinian leaders openly incited for violence and riots, which culminated in a savage near-lynching of an Israeli soldier. And the Palestinian Authority organized other violent demonstrations. Therefore, the Palestinian Authority must stop incitement and violence at once, and they must do so fully and permanently.

There has also been some downgrading on parts of the security cooperation between us, and the Palestinian Authority must restore this cooperation again, fully and permanently. They must live up to their other obligations in the Wye agreement in the fields of weapons collections, illegal weapons collections, reducing the size of their armed forces, and the like.

Now, I stress that none of these are new conditions. All are integral parts of the Wye and Oslo agreements to which we are committed. We hope that tomorrow the Palestinian Authority will once and for all live up to at least one of their obligations. And if the PNC members will vote in sufficient numbers to annul the infamous Palestinian Charter, that will be a welcome development. And it's important; 5 years after the promise to do so at Oslo, to see this happen would be a welcome and positive development.

I think this is—it's just as important to see strict adherence to the other obligations in order to reinject confidence into the peace process and to get this process moving again, where Israel will also do its part.

Mr. President, I'm sure that we can achieve peace between Palestinians and Israelis if we stand firm on Palestinian compliance. I very much hope that you will be able to persuade the Palestinians what I know you deeply believe and I believe, that violence and peace are simply incompatible. Because, ultimately, what is required is not merely a checklist of correcting Palestinian violations but, I think, a real change of conduct by the Palestinian leadership. And they must demonstrate that they have abandoned the path of violence and adopted the path of peace. For us to move forward, they must scrupulously adhere to their commitments under the Wye agreement, on which we have all worked so hard.

And may I say, on a personal and national note and international note, that if there's anyone who can help bring the peace process to a satisfactory conclusion, it is you, President Clinton. Your devotion to this cause, your perseverance, your tireless energy, your commitment have been an inspiration to us all. May it help us restore peace and hope to our land and to our peoples.

President Clinton. Thank you very much, Prime Minister. I thank you for your statement and for your warm welcome. I would say to the people of Israel, I was told before I came here that no previous President had ever visited Israel more than once, and this is my fourth trip here. I may be subject to tax assessment if I come again in the next 2 years, but I am always pleased to be here.

I want to thank you, also, and the members of your team, for the exhausting effort which was made at Wye over those 9 days, the time we spent together, the sleepless nights, and the extraordinary effort to put together a very difficult, but I think sound, agreement.

Let me begin by talking about some of the things that we have discussed today. We've had two brief private meetings: one, a breakfast meeting with our wives this morning, and then a brief private meeting, and then our extended meeting with our two teams. I want to begin where I always do. America has an unshakable commitment to the security of the State and the people of Israel. We also have an unshakable commitment to be a partner in the pursuit of a lasting, comprehensive peace. I have told the Prime Minister that I will soon submit to the Congress a supplemental request for $1.2 billion to meet Israel's security needs related to implementing the Wye River agreement. Only if those needs are met can the peace process move forward.

At the same time, I am convinced, as I think we all are, everyone who has dealt with this problem over any period of time, that a lasting peace properly achieved is the best way to safeguard Israel's security over the long run.

Last month, at the conclusion of the Wye talks, Prime Minister and Chairman Arafat and I agreed that it would be useful for me to come to the region to help to maintain the momentum and to appear tomorrow before the PNC and the other Palestinian groups that will be assembled.

I also want to commend the Prime Minister for the steps he has taken to implement the Wye agreement which he just outlined. He has secured his government's support for significant troop withdrawal from the West Bank and begun the implementation of that withdrawal, reached an agreement that allowed for the opening of the Gaza airport, and he began the difficult process of prisoner releases.

The Palestinian Authority has taken some important steps with its commitments, a deepening security cooperation with Israel, acting against terrorism, issuing decrees for the confiscation of illegal weapons, and dealing with incitement, taking concrete steps to reaffirm the decision to amend the PLO Charter, which will occur tomorrow.

Have the Palestinians fulfilled all their commitments? They certainly could be doing better to preempt violent demonstrations in the street. This is a terribly important matter. I also agree that matters that have been referred, consistent with the Oslo agreement, for final status talks should be left there and should be subject to negotiations. But in other areas, there has been a forward progress on the meeting of the commitments.

Now, I know that each step forward can be excruciatingly difficult and that now real efforts have to be made on both sides to regain the momentum. We just had a good discussion about the specific things that the Israelis believe are necessary for the Palestinians to do to regain the momentum. And we talked a little bit about how we might get genuine communication going again so that the necessary steps can be taken to resume the structured implementation of the Wye River agreement, which is, I think, part of what makes it work; at least, it made it work in the minds of the people who negotiated it. And it can work in the lives of the people who will be affected by it if both sides meet all their commitments, and only if they do.

Each side has serious political constraints; I think we all understand that. Provocative pronouncements, unilateral actions can be counterproductive, given the constraints that each side has. But in the end, there has been a fundamental decision made to deal with this through honest discussion and negotiation. That is the only way it can be done. It cannot be done by resorting to other means when times get difficult. And again I say, the promise of Wye cannot be fulfilled by violence or by statements or actions which are inconsistent with the whole peace process. Both sides should adhere to that.

Let me also just say one other word about regional security. I think Israelis are properly concerned with the threat of weapons of mass destruction development, with the threat of missile delivery systems. We are working with Israel to help to defend itself against such threats, in particular, through the Arrow antiballistic missile program. We've also just established a joint strategic planning committee as a forum to discuss how we can continue to work together on security matters.

We're going to take a couple of questions, I know, but again I would like to say in closing, Mr. Prime Minister, I appreciate the courage you showed at Wye, your farsightedness in seeking peace and in taking personal and political risks for it, which should now be readily apparent to anyone who has followed the events of the last 6 weeks. Your determination, your tenacity to build an Israel that is both secure and at peace is something that I admire and support. And I think, if we keep working at it, we can keep making progress.

Thank you very much.

House Committee Impeachment Vote/ Palestinian Charter Vote

Q. Mr. President, what is your reaction to the decision of the Judiciary Committee of the House yesterday? Do you intend to resign, as did President Nixon? And with your permission, one question to Prime Minister Netanyahu in Hebrew.

[At this point, a question was asked in Hebrew and translated by an interpreter as follows.]

Interpreter. Mr. Prime Minister, you have, to some extent, appointed Mr. Clinton to act as a referee between the Israelis and the Palestinians. He will appear tomorrow in Gaza where the decision of the committee will be to revoke its objection to the existence of Israel. What will you do if this decision is taken, and how will you react to issues facing you with the Cabinet regarding a no-confidence vote?

President Clinton. My reaction to the committee vote is that I wasn't surprised. I think it's been obvious to anyone who is following it for weeks that the vote was foreordained. And now it is up to the Members of the House of Representatives to vote their conscience on the Constitution and the law, which I believe are clear. And I have no intention of resigning. It's never crossed my mind.

[Prime Minister Netanyahu then answered in Hebrew.]

Prime Minister Netanyahu. If you can translate all of that, you're a genius. *[Laughter]*

Interpreter. In essence, we expect to see the Palestinian side revoke the Palestinian Charter. We also expect the Palestinians to meet their commitment to stop incitement. If, in fact, tomorrow the Palestinian Charter is revoked, we will view it as a success of our policy. What we merely expect is the Palestinians honor their commitments. And that's our expectation.

Prime Minister Netanyahu. I would say that's a pretty good abbreviation of what I said. *[Laughter]* You have a great future as an editor. *[Laughter]*

The President. We all need one. *[Laughter]*

House Impeachment Vote

Q. Mr. President, how confident are you that you can avoid impeachment in the full House next week, and are you planning any particular kind of outreach—additional—to lawmakers or the public?

President Clinton. Well, I think it's up to—it's a question of whether each Member will simply vote his or her conscience based on the Constitution and the law. And I don't know what's going to happen. That's up to them. It's out of my hands. If any Member wishes to talk to me or someone on my staff, we would make ourselves available to them. But otherwise, I think it's important that they be free to make this decision and that they not be put under any undue pressure from any quarter.

Many of them have said they feel such pressure, but I can't comment on that because I haven't talked directly to many members of the House caucus, the Republican caucus. And I have talked to those—a few—who said they wanted to talk to me; otherwise, I have not. I don't think it's appropriate for me to be personally calling people; unless they send word to me that there is some question they want to ask or something they want to say, I don't think it's appropriate.

Middle East Peace Process

Q. Mr. President, you said that now it's up to the Members of the House to decide——

Prime Minister Netanyahu. May I ask a favor. You are free to ask any one of your questions, but I think the President has come here on a very clear message, on a very clear voyage of peace, and I believe that it would be appropriate also to ask one or two questions on the peace process. I would like to know the answers, too.

Q. This would be exactly my second question. The first one is about what will happen Thursday if the Members of the House will decide about impeachment, if in this case, whether you will consider resignation. And second question, about the peace process, after all what you see now, after you hear the Prime Minister, don't you think you were wrong in the Wye memorandum, that you figured you'd get an agreement which both sides cannot comply?

President Clinton. Well, the answer to both questions is no. And let me amplify on your second question. No, I don't think it was wrong. Look, if this were easy, it would have been done a long time ago. And we knew that in the Wye agreement it would be difficult for both sides to comply. Actually, the first 2 weeks were quite hopeful. In the first phase, I think there was quite good compliance on both sides.

And I think the Prime Minister feels that way as well.

A number of things happened with which you are very familiar which made the atmosphere more tense in the ensuing weeks. And one of the things that I hope to do while I'm here, in addition to going and meeting with the Palestinian groups, including the PNC, is to do what I did this morning, to listen very carefully to the Prime Minister and to his government about what specific concerns they have in terms of the agreement and compliance with it and then try to resolve those and listen to the Palestinians, as I will, so that we can get this process going again.

I find that when the parties are talking to each other and establish an atmosphere of understanding of the difficulty of each other's positions and deal with each other in good faith, we make pretty good progress. But there is a long history here. And 9 days at Wye, or 2 weeks of implementing, you know, it can't overcome all that history, plus which there are political constraints and imperatives in each position which make it more likely that tensions will arise.

But the fact that this has been hard to implement doesn't mean it was a mistake. It means it was real. Look, if we had made an agreement that was easy to implement, it would have dealt with no difficult circumstances, and so we'd be just where we are now, except worse off.

We have seen in the first phase of implementation that good things can happen on the security side from the point of view of the Israelis and on the development of the territory from the point of view of the Palestinians—and the airport—if there is genuine trust and actual compliance. And so what we have to do is to get more actual compliance and in the process rebuild some of that trust.

Perjury/Censure

Q. Mr. President, some Republicans want you to go further than a statement of contrition. They say that they want an admission of perjury. Are you willing to do that? And what do you think about Chairman Hyde and the Republican leadership opposing a vote in the full House on censure?

President Clinton. Well, on the second question, I think you ought to ask them whether they're opposed to it because they think that it might pass since, apparently, somewhere around three-quarters of the American people think that's the right thing to do.

On the first question, the answer is: No, I can't do that, because I did not commit perjury. If you go back to the hearing, we had four prosecutors—two Republicans, two Democrats—one the head of President Reagan's criminal justice division, who went through the law in great detail and explained that, that this is not a perjury case. And there was no credible argument on the other side. So I have no intention of doing that.

Now, was the testimony in the deposition difficult and ambiguous and unhelpful? Yes, it was. That's exactly what I said in the grand jury testimony, myself, and I agree with what Mr. Ruff said about it. Mr. Ruff answered questions, you know, for hours and hours and hours and tried to deal with some of the concerns the committee had on that. And I thought he did an admirable job in acknowledging the difficulty of the testimony.

But I could not admit to doing something that I am quite sure I did not do. And I think if you look at the law, if you look at the legal decisions, and if you look at what the Republican as well as the Democratic prosecutors said, I think that's entitled to great weight. And I have read or seen nothing that really overcomes the testimony that they gave on that question.

Jonathan Pollard

Q. What about Jonathan Pollard, Mr. President? What about Jonathan Pollard? Can you— [*inaudible*].

President Clinton. Yes, I can. I have instituted the review that I pledged to the Prime Minister. We've never done this on a case before, but I told him I would do it, and we did it. And my Counsel, Mr. Ruff, has invited the Justice Department and all the law enforcement agencies under it, and all the other security, intelligence, and law enforcement agencies in the Government and interested parties to say what they think about the Pollard case, to do so by sometime in January. And I will review all that, plus whatever arguments are presented to me on the other side for the reduction of the sen-

tence. And I will make a decision in a prompt way.

But we have instituted this review which as I said is unprecedented. We are giving everyone time to present their comments, and I will get comments on both sides of the issue, evaluate it, and make a decision.

Q. I would like to ask——

President Clinton. What did you say? They're demanding equal time, three and three?

Q. I just want to ask the Prime Minister——

President Clinton. Oh, he wants to ask you a question. That's good.

Q. Prime Minister, can you explain, perhaps to the American people, why you think Mr. Pollard is worthy of release at this point?

Prime Minister Netanyahu. Jonathan Pollard did something bad and inexcusable; he spied in the United States; he collected information on behalf of the Israeli Government. I was the first Prime Minister—and this is the first government—to openly admit it. We think that he should have served his time, and he did. He served for close to 13 years. And all that I appealed to President Clinton for is merely a humanitarian appeal. It is not based on exonerating Mr. Pollard. There is no exoneration for it. It is merely that he has been virtually in solitary confinement for 13 years. It's a very, very heavy sentence.

And since he was sent by us on a mistaken mission—not to work against the United States but, nevertheless, to break the laws of the United States—we hope that, on a purely humanitarian appeal, a way will be found to release him.

That is all I can tell you. It is not political. It is not to exonerate him. It is merely to end a very, very sorry case that has afflicted him and the people of Israel.

NOTE: The President's 167th news conference began at 1:50 p.m. in the Office of the Prime Minister. In his remarks, he referred to Chairman Yasser Arafat of the Palestinian Authority; and Edward S.G. Dennis, Jr., former Assistant Attorney General, Criminal Division. He also referred to the Palestine National Council (PNC).

Remarks at a Hanukkah Menorah Lighting Ceremony in Jerusalem
December 13, 1998

Thank you very much, Mr. President and Mrs. Weizman. Let me say a special word of welcome in greetings on behalf of Hillary and myself to all the children who are here, and my thanks to these wonderful voices we have just heard sing. And I congratulate this young man for holding the candle all that time and not burning himself. Congratulations! [*Laughter*]

It is our great honor, all of the American delegation here, the members of our administration and the Members of Congress, to celebrate the first day of Hanukkah with the President and some of Israel's finest young people. This is a joyous time of year for Jewish people everywhere, here in Israel, in America, around the world, a moment to cherish your extraordinary past, to strive for a future worthy of your history.

On this occasion, you celebrate not simply a long week of happiness but thousands of years of triumph over adversity. You thank God not only for miracles but for hard-earned achievement. May this menorah bring light through wisdom and illumination. May it bring warmth through faith and fellowship. May it kindle a divine spark of peace touching all the peoples and places of the Holy Land. May it bring hope that after 50 years of building, security finally will come to all the people of Israel. And may it bring more than hope; may it ignite in each of you the will and strength to bring these hopes to reality.

All of you in this way can serve as candles full of light. Let our descendants look back at Israel at the turn of this new century and say the words that every Jewish child knows from the letters on the dreidel: A great miracle happened here.

Happy Hanukkah.

NOTE: The President spoke at approximately 5:20 p.m. in the Foyer of Beit Hannassi, the residence of President Ezer Weizman of Israel. In his remarks, he referred to President Weizman's wife, Reuma; and Moshe Metbabo, who lit the first candle in the menorah. The transcript released by the Office of the Press Secretary also included the remarks of President Weizman.

Statement on Crime Rates
December 13, 1998

The preliminary crime data released by the FBI today confirm that crime rates in America are continuing to decline for the seventh straight year. During the first 6 months of 1998, serious crime fell by another 5 percent—with large reductions in murder and other violent crimes leading the way. If these trends hold for the remainder of the year, the number of murders will have been cut by nearly one-third since Vice President Gore and I took office. This is remarkable progress, and it shows that our strategy of more police, tougher gun laws, and better crime prevention is making a difference. But our work is far from done. In the coming year, as we finish the job of putting 100,000 more police on the streets, we must continue to do everything we can to make all of our communities safer.

NOTE: This statement was made available by the Office of the Press Secretary on December 12 but was embargoed for release until 6 p.m. on December 13.

Statement on the Death of Morris K. Udall
December 13, 1998

Hillary and I were saddened to learn of the death of Representative Morris Udall. Mo Udall was a leader whose uncommon wisdom, wit, and dedication won the love of his colleagues and the respect of all Americans. It was my pleasure to award him the Medal of Freedom, the highest civilian award a President can bestow.

Mo Udall represented the people of Arizona for more than three decades and guided the Nation forward on issues ranging from the reform of our election laws to improving the Postal Service. As a Presidential candidate and a leader of our party, his was an articulate voice

reminding us of what our Nation can achieve when we leave no one behind. Above all, he was a devoted steward of the land that God gave us and was responsible for the preservation of some of our most important wilderness areas. It is fitting that the easternmost point of the United States, in the Virgin Islands, and the westernmost point, in Guam, are both named "Udall Point." The Sun will never set on the legacy of Mo Udall.

Our thoughts and prayers go out to his wife Norma, their six children and many grandchildren, and the people of Arizona.

Remarks to the People of Israel in Jerusalem
December 13, 1998

Thank you very much. Let me begin by thanking the Prime Minister for his leadership for peace and his leadership of Israel; Mrs. Netanyahu, members of the Israeli Government; to the distinguished American delegation here. I want to say a special word of appreciation to the young man who spoke first, Ben Mayost. Didn't he do a good job? [*Applause*]

This is my third trip to Jerusalem as President, my third time in this magnificent hall, and the young woman who was with me here last time on the stage, Liad Modrik, is also here. Thank you; I'm really glad to see you. I'd like to also thank this magnificent choir, the Ankor Choir. Didn't they do a good job? They left, but they were great. I understand we have students here from Jerusalem, Tel Aviv, Haifa, Beer Sheva, Akko, and other cities; welcome to you all.

We come here today to speak about the future of Israel and the Middle East—your future. Six weeks ago Prime Minister Netanyahu came to the United States to seek a new understanding with the Palestinian Authority on the best way to achieve peace with security. Today I come to Israel to fulfill a pledge I made to the Prime Minister and to Chairman Arafat at Wye River, to speak to Israelis and Palestinians about the benefits of peace, and to reaffirm

America's determination to stand with you as you take risks for peace.

The United States will always stand with Israel, always remember that only a strong Israel can make peace. That is why we were, after all, your partners in security before we were partners for peace. Our commitment to your security is ironclad. It will not ever change.

The United States stood with Israel at the birth of your nation, at your darkest hour in 1973, through the long battle against terror, against Saddam Hussein's Scuds in 1991. And today, American marines and Patriot missiles are here in Israel exercising with the IDF. We have also stood with you as you reached out to your neighbors, always recognizing that only Israelis can make final decisions about your own future.

And as the Prime Minister said in his remarks about education for peace, we agree that peace must begin with a genuine transformation in attitudes. Despite all the difficulties, I believe that transformation has begun. Palestinians are recognizing that rejection of Israel will not bring them freedom, just as Israelis recognize that control over Palestinians will not bring you security.

As a result, in just the last few years you have achieved peace with Jordan, and the Arab world has accepted the idea of peace with Israel.

The boycotts of the past are giving way to a future in which goods move across frontiers while soldiers are able to stay at home. The pursuit of peace has withstood the gravest doubts. It has survived terrorist bombs and assassins' bullets.

Just a short while ago this afternoon, Hillary and I visited the gravesite of Prime Minister Rabin with Mrs. Rabin, her daughter and granddaughter. He was killed by one who hoped to kill the peace he worked so hard to advance. But the Wye memorandum is proof that peace is still alive, and it will live as long as the parties believe in it and work for it.

Of course, there have been setbacks, more misunderstandings, more disagreements, more provocations, more acts of violence. You feel Palestinians should prove in word and deed that their intentions have actually changed, as you redeploy from land on which tears and blood have been shed, and you are right to feel that.

Palestinians feel you should acknowledge they too have suffered and they, too, have legitimate expectations that should be met and, like Israel, internal political pressures that must be overcome. And they are right, too.

Because of all that has happened and the mountain of memories that has not yet been washed away, the road ahead will be hard. Already, every step forward has been tempered with pain. Each time the forces of reconciliation on each side have reached out, the forces of destruction have lashed out. The leaders at Wye knew that. The people of Israel know that.

Israel is full of good people today who do not hate but who have experienced too much sorrow and too much loss to embrace with joy each new agreement the peace process brings. As always, we must approach the task ahead without illusions but not without hope, for hope is not an illusion.

Every advance in human history, every victory for the human spirit, every victory in your own individual lives begins with hope, the capacity to imagine a better future and the conviction that it can be achieved. The people of Israel, after all, have beaten the most impossible odds, overcome the most terrible evils on the way to the Promised Land. The idea of the Promised Land kept hope alive. In the remaining work to be done, the idea of peace and security in the Promised Land must keep hope alive.

For all you young people today, under all the complexities and frustrations of this moment,

there lies a simple question: What is your vision for your future? There can be only two ways to answer that question. You could say that the only possible future for Israel is one of permanent siege, in which the ramparts hold and people stay alive, but the nation remains preoccupied with its very survival, subject to gnawing anxiety, limited in future achievement by the absence of real partnerships with your neighbors.

Perhaps you can live with that kind of future, but you should not accept it unless you are willing to say—and I will try to say properly— *ein breira,* there is no alternative. But if you are not willing to say that, not willing to give up on hope with no real gain in security, you must say, *yesh, breira,* there is an alternative.

If you are to build a future together, hard realities cannot be ignored. Reconciliation after all this trouble is not natural. The differences among you are not trivial. There is a history of heartbreak and loss. But the violent past and the difficult present do not have to be repeated forever.

In the historical relationship between Israelis and Palestinians, one thing and only one thing is predestined: You are bound to be neighbors. The question is not whether you will live side by side, but how you will live side by side.

Will both sides recognize there can be no security for either until both have security, that there will be no peace for either until both have peace? Will both sides seize this opportunity to build a future in which preoccupation with security, struggle, and survival can finally give way to a common commitment to keep all our young minds strong and unleash all your human potential?

Surely, the answer must be, yes. Israelis and Palestinians can reach that conclusion sooner, reducing the pain and violence they endure, or they can wait until later—more and more victims suffer more loss—and ultimately, the conclusion must be the same.

Your leaders came to an agreement at Wye because a majority of people on both sides have already said, "Now is the time to change."

I want to talk just a little bit about this agreement at Wye. It does not, by itself, resolve the fundamental problems that divide Israelis and Palestinians. It is a means to an end, not the end itself. But it does restore life to a process that was stalled for 18 months, and it will bring benefits that meet the requirements of both sides if both sides meet their obligations. Wye is an opportunity for both that must not be lost. Let me try to explain why.

Prime Minister Netanyahu went to Wye, rightly determined to ensure that the security of Israeli citizens is protected as the peace process moves forward. He fought hard, not to kill the peace but to make it real for all those Israelis who only want to live normal lives in their own country. And he succeeded in obtaining a set of systematic Palestinian security commitments and a structure for carrying them out.

The Palestinian Authority agreed to a comprehensive and continuous battle against terror. It pledged to combat terrorist organizations, to crack down on unlicensed weapons, to take action against incitement to terror. U.S.-Palestinian committees will be set up to review specific actions the Palestinians are taking in each of these areas and to recommend further steps. We also will submit to our Congress a $1.2 billion package to help Israel meet its future security needs, including those growing out of the redeployments agreed to at Wye.

The agreement can benefit Israel in another way. It offers the prospect of continuing a process that is changing how most Palestinians define their interests and their relationship with you. More and more, Palestinians have begun to see that they have done more to realize their aspirations in 5 years of making peace than in 45 years of making war. They are beginning to see that Israel's mortal enemies are, in fact, their enemies, too, and that is in their interests to help to defeat the forces of terror.

This transformation, however, is clearly unfinished. It will not happen overnight. There will be bumps in the road, and there have been some already. The Palestinian leaders must work harder to keep the agreement and avoid the impression that unilateral actions can replace agreed-upon negotiations. But it is vital that you, too, recognize the validity of this agreement and work to sustain it and all other aspects of the peace process.

Tomorrow I go to Gaza to address the members of the Palestinian National Council and other Palestinian organizations. I will witness the reaffirmation of their commitment to forswear, fully, finally, and forever, all the provisions in their Charter that called for the destruction of Israel.

I will also make it clear that with rights come responsibilities, reminding people there that violence never was and never can be a legitimate tool, that it would be wrong and utterly self-defeating to resume a struggle that has taken Palestinians from one tragedy to another. I will ask the Palestinian leaders to join me in reaffirming what the vast majority of Muslims the world over believe, that tolerance is an article of faith and terrorism a travesty of faith. And I will emphasize that this conviction should echo from every Palestinian schoolhouse and mosque and television tower.

I will point out, of course, all the ways in which this Wye agreement benefits Palestinians: It provides for the transfer of more territory, the redeployment of more Israeli troops, safe passage between Gaza and the West Bank, the opening of the airport in Gaza, other initiatives to lift their economic condition, and new commitments of international assistance to improve the lives of the Palestinian people.

In doing these things, this agreement benefits Israelis as well, for it is in Israel's interest to give the Palestinian economy space to breathe and the Palestinian people a chance to defeat the hopelessness that extremists exploit to unleash their terror. And it is surely in Israel's interest to deal with Palestinians in a way that permits them to feel a sense of dignity instead of despair.

The peace process will succeed if it comes with a recognition that the fulfillment of one side's aspirations must come with—not at the expense of—the fulfillment of the other side's dreams. It will succeed when we understand that it is not just about mutual obligations but mutual interest, mutual recognition, mutual respect; when all agree there is no sense in a tug-of-war over common ground.

It will succeed when we all recognize, as Prime Minister Netanyahu and Chairman Arafat did at Wye, that ultimately this can and must be a partnership between Israelis and Palestinians. It will succeed if both sides continue the work that Wye makes possible, if they face the hard decisions ahead so that the future continues to be shaped at the negotiating table, rather than by unilateral acts or declarations.

We cannot, of course, expect everyone to see that. There are still people in this region, indeed in every region, who believe that their unique cultures can thrive only behind walls that keep out those who are different, even if the price is mutual mistrust and hatred. There are some who still talk openly about the "threat" of peace because peacemaking requires making contact with the other side, recognizing the legitimacy of different faiths and different points of view, and openness to a world of competing ideas and values.

But I don't think that's the majority view in the Middle East any longer. What once was a conflict among mainstreams is evolving into a mainstream seeking peace. We must not let the conflict invade the mainstream of Israel or of the Palestinians or of any other group in this region again.

I believe you can not only imagine, you young people, but actually shape the kind of partnership that will give you the future you want. I think you can do it while protecting Israel's fundamental interests. To anyone who thinks that is impossible, I would ask you this: How many people thought Israel was possible when your grandparents were just people searching for a land? Who would have imagined the marvel Israel has become?

For decades, you lived in a neighborhood which rejected you. Yet, you not only survived and thrived but held fast to the traditions of tolerance and openness upon which this nation was founded. You were forced to become warriors, yet you never lost the thirst to make peace. You turned weakness into strength, and along the way, you built a partnership with the United States that is enduring and unassailable.

Now Israel enters its second half-century. You have nourished an ancient culture. You have built from the desert a modern nation. You stand on the edge of a new century prepared to make the very most of it. You have given your children a chance to grow up and learn who they are, not just from stories of wandering and martyrdom but from the happy memories of people living good lives in a natural way. You have proven again and again that you are powerful enough to defeat those who would destroy you, but strong and wise enough to make peace with those who are ready to accept you. You have given us every reason to believe that you can build a future on hope that is different from the past.

This morning the Prime Minister and Mrs. Netanyahu and Hillary and I had breakfast together, and he said something to me I'd like to repeat to you to make this point to all of you young people. He said: You know, there are three great ancient civilizations in the world—the Chinese civilization, the Indian civilization, and the Jewish civilization—all going back 4,000 years or more. The Chinese are 1.2 billion people; the Indians are nearly a billion people. To be sure, they have suffered invasion, loss in war; in the Indian case, colonization. But they have always had their land, and they have grown.

There are 12 million Jews in the world, driven from their homeland, subject to Holocaust, subject to centuries of prejudice. And yet, here you are. Here you are. If you can do this after 4,000 years, you can make this peace. Believe me, you can do this.

Years ago, before the foundation of Israel, Golda Meir said of her people, and I quote, "We only want that which is given naturally to all people of the world, to be masters of our own fate, only our fate, not the destiny of others; to live as a right and not on sufferance; to have the chance to bring the surviving Jewish children, of whom not so many are left in the world now, to this country, so that they may grow up like our youngsters who were born here, free of fear, with heads high."

This hope that all of us can live a life of dignity when respecting the dignity of others is part of the heritage of values Israel shares with the United States. On this, the first day of Hanukkah, may this hope be the candle that lights Israel's path into the new century, into a century of peace and security, with America always at your side.

Thank you, and God bless you.

NOTE: The President spoke at 6:38 p.m. in the Ussishkin Hall at the Jerusalem Convention Center. In this remarks, he referred to Prime Minister Binyamin Netanyahu of Israel and his wife, Sarah; Ben Mayost, chair, National Student Council; Liad Modrik, student council representative during the President's March 1996 visit to Israel; Chairman Yasser Arafat of the Palestinian Authority; President Saddam Hussein of Iraq; and Leah Rabin, widow of assassinated Israeli Prime Minister Yitzhak Rabin, her daughter, Dalia Rabin Filosof, and her granddaughter, Noa Ben Artzi.

Remarks at a Dinner Hosted by Prime Minister Binyamin Netanyahu of Israel in Jerusalem
December 13, 1998

Thank you very much. Mr. Prime Minister, Mrs. Netanyahu, leaders and citizens of Israel, my fellow Americans: Let me begin by thanking the Prime Minister, his family, and his administration for the warm welcome accorded to me and Hillary and Chelsea and our entire group. This is, as I have said many times today, my fourth visit to Israel since I became President. Perhaps that fact alone says something about the unique relationship between our two nations.

Last spring I walked out onto the South Lawn at the White House to lead my fellow Americans in our celebration of your 50th birthday as a nation. And as I did that, I thought about how that great old house—where every President since our second President has lived, for almost 200 years now—and how for the last 50 years it has been and now will forever be linked to Israel's destiny. It was in the White House that Harry Truman recognized the State of Israel only 11 minutes after you had declared your independence. And, I might add, he did so over the objection of some of his most senior advisers. It was in the White House a year later that President Truman wept when Israel's Chief Rabbi told him, "God put you in your mother's womb so you would be the instrument to bring the rebirth of Israel after 2,000 years."

Mr. Prime Minister, every President since Harry Truman has been strongly committed to the State of Israel and to Israel's security. No one should doubt that the United States will always stand with you.

Every President has also believed it is vital to Israel's security that together we seek peace between Israel and its Arab neighbors. Israel's own leaders again and again have said this, from Ben-Gurion to Golda Meir, Begin to Rabin and Peres. Now you, Mr. Prime Minister, have taken your own brave steps on the path to peace. This is the correct course because only through negotiated and implemented peace can Israelis live their dream of being both free and secure.

No one knows better the cost the enemies of peace can extract than you, Mr. Prime Minister. You have fought terrorism with your own hands. You have written powerfully about it. You lost your beloved brother to it. The citizens you now lead face the possibility of terrorism every day.

America knows something of this struggle, too. Hundreds of our citizens have perished in terrorist attacks over this generation, most recently at our Embassies in east Africa. We know we must stand strong against terrorism. We are determined to do so, just as we are determined to find just and peaceful solutions to conflicts and to overcome longstanding hatred and resentments. We know the closer we get, the more desperate the enemies of peace become. But we cannot let terrorists dictate our future. We will not let their bombs or their bullets destroy our path to peace.

Mr. Prime Minister, at Wye River you obtained commitments that will greatly strengthen Israel's security if they are honored. All of us who shared those 9 days and 9 long nights know you are a skilled and tenacious negotiator. Despite your long sojourn in America, there can be no doubt that you remain a *sabra* to the core, tough, the kind of leader with the potential to guide his people to a peaceful and secure future.

Many have pointed out that you are the first leader of Israel born after 1948, actually born in the State of Israel. But I know you never forget that the history of the Jewish people, as you have told us again tonight, is far, far longer, that the issues of today must be considered in light of events of a rich but often turbulent past, including 2,000 years of exile and persecution.

We honor your history, your struggles, your sacrifices. We pray for a permanent peace that will, once and for all, secure the rightful place of the people of Israel, living in peace, mutual respect, mutual recognition, and permanent security in this historic land, with the Palestinians and all your neighbors.

You mentioned, Mr. Prime Minister, the fact that my devotion to Israel had something to do with the instruction I received from my minister long ago. I will tell you, the real story is even more dramatic. I hesitate to tell it because then you will use it against me when it is helpful. [*Laughter*]

My pastor died in 1989. Before that, starting in 1937, he came here to the Holy Land more than 40 times. Once in the mid-1980's, we were sitting together—long before I had thought that a realistic prospect—and he looked at me and he said, "You might be President one day. You will make mistakes, and God will forgive you. But God will never forgive you if you forget the State of Israel." That's what he said.

When Hillary first came here with me 17 years ago this month, I was not in elected office. I came on a religious pilgrimage just after we celebrated Christmas. I saw Masada and Bethlehem for the first time, not through political eyes but through the eyes of a Christian. I can't wait to go back to Masada, and I can't wait to go back to Bethlehem.

You mentioned that the troubles and travails and triumphs of Jesus, a Jew, gave the world

the Christian religion, of which I am a part. In the Christian New Testament, we get a lot of instruction about what it takes to make peace and become reconciled to one another. We are instructed that we have to forgive others their sins against us if we expect to be forgiven our own. We are instructed that they who judge without mercy will be judged without mercy, but mercy triumphs over judgment. And we are told in no uncertain terms that the peacemakers are blessed, and they will inherit the Earth.

Please join me in a toast to Prime Minister and Mrs. Netanyahu, the people of Israel, and the promise of peace. *L'Chaim.*

NOTE: The President spoke at 9:16 p.m. at the Jerusalem Hilton. In his remarks, he referred to Prime Minister Netanyahu's wife, Sarah. The transcript released by the Office of the Press Secretary also included the remarks of Prime Minister Netanyahu.

Exchange With Reporters Prior to Discussions With Chairman Yasser Arafat of the Palestinian Authority in Gaza City, Gaza
December 14, 1998

Impeachment

Q. Mr. President, you say you haven't committed perjury. Can you say, sir, that you lied, as some people believe would help?

President Clinton. Sam [Sam Donaldson, ABC News], I've said what I have to say about that. Now, I'm here furthering America's interests, trying to make peace in the Middle East, to keep this peace process on track. I think it's important. I will say what I've said before: I don't believe it's in the interest of the United States or the American people to go through this impeachment process with a trial in the Senate. That's why I have offered to make every effort to make any reasonable compromise with the Congress. I still believe that, and I'm still willing to do that. That's all I know to do. Meanwhile, I'm going to keep working on my job.

Q. Do you think it's appropriate for the Republican leadership to call for your resignation while you are over here, overseas?

Q. President Clinton, how do you feel being in Gaza?

President Clinton. The boundaries of what's appropriate have been changed rather dramatically in the last several months, I think; you know, they'll have to be the judge of their own conduct. I'm just going to do my job as President.

President's Visit to Gaza

Q. President Clinton, how do you feel being in Gaza for the first time? And is there going to be a withdrawal on Friday?

President Clinton. Well, I want to talk to Chairman Arafat about all these issues related to the Wye agreement. But I'm delighted to be in Gaza for the first time. I'm delighted to be the first President to come on Palestinian territory. And I was very pleased to be at the dedication of the airport today. One of the important achievements of the Wye River agreement was the commitment to get this airport open and going, and I'm very, very pleased. It's quite beautiful. And I was pleased to be there, and I'm very glad to be here in Chairman

Arafat's headquarters, with his team. And we'll talk about all the other issues.

Q. And the withdrawal?

President Clinton. I'll have more to say about that later.

Implementation of the Wye Agreement

Q. Mr. President—[*inaudible*]—to be time—[*inaudible*]—on the implementation of the Wye agreement, as Israel has said to be asking?

President Clinton. Well, I would hope that we would continue to implement the Wye agreement on both sides. I would hope both sides would continue to implement every part of it. And I think it's important that both sides implement every part of it in good faith.

Keep in mind, Wye is not the end of this process. It's simply a means to an end. We also have to get the final status talks going and then get into them in earnest. But these confidence-building measures, which will enable the Palestinians not only to have an airport but to have more freedom of movement, more land, and more economic opportunity, and enable the Israelis to have a greater assurance of security cooperation, I think they're very important to the success of final status talks. So I'm committed to this agreement, and I hope that it will be implemented in a timely and aggressive manner by both sides.

Chairman Arafat. We consider the visit of President Clinton as a historic event for the Palestinian people and for the people in the Middle East. And we are grateful for his visit, and he honored us with this visit today.

We should never forget that under President Clinton's sponsorship, we signed a number of peace agreements at the White House. And through President Clinton, peace will prevail in the Middle East. And this is something that will not be forgotten by the Palestinian people or the Israeli people or the people in the Middle East. And once again, it is a great honor, and we are really proud to have President Clinton

among us here and among the Palestinian people.

I was hoping that logistically we would have been able to have a motorcade, because people are lined up waiting to greet President Clinton on both sides of the road. And I believe perhaps you took a glimpse of the people, flying in the chopper over Gaza, standing on both sides hoping that the motorcade would come by—from the airport, from the airport. [*Laughter*]

President Clinton. I would like to say just one other thing. There are two historic elements to this day. One is the opportunity that I have been given simply to come here and to have this meeting and to be a part of the airport dedication. The other is the truly historic meeting that the Chairman has convened of the PNC, the PCC, and the other Palestinian groups, and the opportunity that the Palestinian people, through their elected representatives, will have to make it clear and unequivocal that they are choosing the path of peace and partnership with Israel, and that we hope—I think all of us hope—that this will lead to a changing of hearts and minds throughout this region among all parties, so that it will be easier for everyone to implement the difficult commitments they have made at Wye and will have to make to get the final status talks completed.

This is a truly significant thing, and I, for one, very much appreciate it. It was a part of the Wye River agreements; it showed a lot of courage on Chairman Arafat's part; and I was delighted to be invited here. And so I just want to say how much I personally appreciate this and how much I think it will mean over the long run to the prospects for a successful peace agreement.

NOTE: The exchange began at 12 noon in Chairman Arafat's office. In his remarks, the President referred to the Palestine National Council (PNC) and the Palestinian Central Council (PCC). A tape was not available for verification of the content of this exchange.

Remarks at a Luncheon Hosted by Chairman Arafat of the Palestinian Authority in Gaza City
December 14, 1998

Chairman Arafat, Mrs. Arafat, distinguished leaders of the Palestinian community, colleagues, and friends: On behalf of my family and our entire delegation, we thank you for your warm and truly memorable welcome.

Mr. Chairman, as I promised you at Wye River, I have come to Gaza to speak about the benefits of peace based on mutual respect. I know that the circumstances you've faced since 1993 and the signing of the peace have remained difficult, but there are reasons for hope. For the first time in the history of the Palestinian movement, the Palestinian people and their elected representatives now have a chance to determine their own destiny on their own land.

I am proud to be the first American President to stand with the Palestinian people here as you shape your future. I want to emphasize that that future is possible because of the commitment you have made to live in peace and mutual respect with your neighbors, side by side.

All this would have been hard to imagine in the darkest years of struggle, when most people expected the Middle East would always be a separate set of armed camps. Sometimes it takes more courage and more strength to make peace than it does to continue war. I thank Chairman Arafat for having the strength, the courage, and the wisdom to make peace and then to persevere on the path of peace.

I thank the Chairman and, indeed, all Palestinians who embrace the idea that Palestinians and Israelis can share the land of their fathers together. I thank you for believing that the land which gave the world Islam and Judaism and Christianity can be the home of all people who love one God and respect every life our one God has created.

America wants you to succeed, and we will help you to create the society you deserve, a society based on respect for human rights, human dignity, the rule of law, a society that teaches tolerance, values education, and now, at last, has the chance to unleash the creative power of its people against the destructive pull of hopelessness and poverty.

I think of you at this hopeful moment as a family reuniting after too many years of dislocation and despair; a community of believers helping to build a Middle East in which people of all faiths can live in security and peace; a people known through the world, like the olive tree, for your attachment to this land and now to peace; a society that demands of yourselves what you rightly demand of others.

The way ahead may be hard and uncertain, but the way you have left behind is full of self-defeating violence and soul-withering hate. So we have no choice but the way ahead.

Tomorrow my family and I, along with Chairman and Mrs. Arafat, will have a chance to visit Bethlehem, to light the Christmas tree at the beginning of this season which is so important for those of us who are Christians. The next time people celebrate Christmas in Bethlehem, we will be on the edge of a new millennium, marking 2000 years since the birth of the Christ child, who became known to Christians as the Prince of Peace, who happened to be a Jew, who happens to be recognized by Islam.

Now, if all that can be true, surely we can figure out how to solve these problems and go into the future.

I close with these words of the poet Hafez Ibrahim:

People of a hopeful future, we are in need of leadership which builds and people who construct.

People of a hopeful future, we are in need of wisdom that counsels and a hand that liberates.

People of a hopeful future, we need you; fill the void, get to work.

People of a hopeful future, do not let tomorrow pass like yesterday, in dusty existence.

People of a hopeful future, your country implores you to think. God willing, we will think and feel and act as one.

Thank you. And thank you again.

NOTE: The President spoke at 2:15 p.m. at Zahrat Al Madian. In his remarks, he referred to Chairman Arafat's wife, Shua. The transcript released by the Office of Press Secretary also included the remarks of Chairman Arafat.

Remarks to the Palestine National Council and Other Palestinian Organizations in Gaza City
December 14, 1998

Thank you. Mr. Speaker—Mr. Za'anoun, Chairman Arafat, Mrs. Arafat; members of the Palestinian National Council, the Palestinian Central Council, the Palestinian Executive Committee, Palestinian Council heads of ministries; leaders of business and religion; to all members of the Palestinian community; and to my fellow Americans who come here from many walks of life, Arab-American, Jewish-American: This is a remarkable day. Today the eyes of the world are on you.

I am profoundly honored to be the first American President to address the Palestinian people in a city governed by Palestinians.

I have listened carefully to all that has been said. I have watched carefully the reactions of all of you to what has been said. I know that the Palestinian people stand at a crossroads: behind you a history of dispossession and dispersal, before you the opportunity to shape a new Palestinian future on your own land.

I know the way is often difficult and frustrating, but you have come to this point through a commitment to peace and negotiations. You reaffirmed that commitment today. I believe it is the only way to fulfill the aspirations of your people. And I am profoundly grateful to have had the opportunity to work with Chairman Arafat for the cause of peace, to come here as a friend of peace and a friend of your future, and to witness you raising your hands, standing up tall, standing up not only against what you believe is wrong but for what you believe is right in the future.

I was sitting here thinking that this moment would have been inconceivable a decade ago: no Palestinian Authority; no elections in Gaza and the West Bank; no relations between the United States and Palestinians; no Israeli troop redeployments from the West Bank and Gaza; no Palestinians in charge in Gaza, Ramallah, Bethlehem, Hebron, Tulkarem, Jenin, Nablus, Jericho, and so many other places; there was no Gaza International Airport.

Today I had the privilege of cutting the ribbon on the international airport. Hillary and I, along with Chairman and Mrs. Arafat, celebrated a place that will become a magnet for planes from throughout the Middle East and beyond, bringing you a future in which Palestinians can travel directly to the far corners of the world; a future in which it is easier and cheaper to bring materials, technology, and expertise in and out of Gaza; a future in which tourists and traders can flock here, to this beautiful place on the Mediterranean; a future, in short, in which the Palestinian people are connected to the world.

I am told that just a few months ago, at a time of profound pessimism in the peace process, your largest exporter of fruit and flowers was prepared to plow under a field of roses, convinced the airport would never open. But Israelis and Palestinians came to agreement at Wye River, the airport has opened, and now I am told that company plans to export roses and carnations to Europe and throughout the Gulf, a true flowering of Palestinian promise.

I come here today to talk about that promise, to ask you to rededicate yourselves to it, to ask you to think for a moment about how we can get beyond the present state of things where every step forward is like, as we say in America, pulling teeth. Where there is still, in spite of the agreement at Wye—achieved because we don't need much sleep, and we worked so hard, and Mr. Netanyahu worked with us, and we made this agreement. But I want to talk to you about how we can get beyond this moment, where there is still so much mistrust and misunderstanding and quite a few missteps.

You did a good thing today in raising your hands. You know why? It has nothing to do

2175

with the government in Israel. You will touch the people of Israel.

I want the people of Israel to know that for many Palestinians, 5 years after Oslo, the benefits of this process remain remote; that for too many Palestinians lives are hard, jobs are scarce, prospects are uncertain, and personal grief is great. I know that tremendous pain remains as a result of losses suffered from violence, the separation of families, the restrictions on the movement of people and goods. I understand your concerns about settlement activity, land confiscation, and home demolitions. I understand your concerns and theirs about unilateral statements that could prejudge the outcome of final status negotiations. I understand, in short, that there's still a good deal of misunderstanding 5 years after the beginning of this remarkable process.

It takes time to change things and still more time for change to benefit everyone. It takes determination and courage to make peace and sometimes even more to persevere for peace. But slowly but surely, the peace agreements are turning into concrete progress: the transfer of territories, the Gaza industrial estate, and the airport. These changes will make a difference in many Palestinian lives.

I thank you—I thank you, Mr. Chairman, for your leadership for peace and your perseverance, for enduring all the criticism from all sides, for being willing to change course, and for being strong enough to stay with what is right. You have done a remarkable thing for your people.

America is determined to do what we can to bring tangible benefits of peace. I am proud that the roads we traveled on to get here were paved, in part, with our assistance, as were hundreds of miles of roads that knit together towns and villages throughout the West Bank and Gaza.

Two weeks ago in Washington, we joined with other nations to pledge hundreds of millions of dollars toward your development, including health care and clean water, education for your children, rule of law projects that nurture democracy. Today I am pleased to announce we will also fund the training of Palestinian health care providers and airport administrators, increase our support to Palestinian refugees. And next year I will ask the Congress for another several hundred million dollars to support the development of the Palestinian people.

But make no mistake about it, all this was made possible because of what you did, because 5 years ago you made a choice for peace, and because through all the tough times since, when in your own mind you had a hundred good reasons to walk away, you didn't. Because you still harbor the wisdom that led to the Oslo accords, that led to the signing in Washington in September of '93, you still can raise your hand and stand and lift your voice for peace.

Mr. Chairman, you said some profound words today in embracing the idea that Israelis and Palestinians can live in peace as neighbors. Again I say, you have led the way, and we would not be here without you.

I say to all of you, I can come here and work; I can bring you to America, and we can work; but in the end, this is up to you—you and the Israelis—for you have to live with the consequences of what you do. I can help because I believe it is my job to do so; I believe it is my duty to do so; because America has Palestinian-Americans, Jewish-Americans, other Arab-Americans who desperately want us to be helpful. But in the end, you have to decide what the understanding will be, and you have to decide whether we can get beyond the present moment where there is still, for all the progress we have made, so much mistrust. And the people who are listening to us today in Israel, they have to make the same decisions.

Peace must mean many things: legitimate rights for Palestinians—[*applause*]—thank you—legitimate rights for Palestinians, real security for Israel. But it must begin with something even more basic: mutual recognition, seeing people who are different, with whom there have been profound differences, as people.

I've had two profoundly emotional experiences in the last less than 24 hours. I was with Chairman Arafat, and four little children came to see me whose fathers are in Israeli prisons. Last night, I met some little children whose fathers had been killed in conflict with Palestinians, at the dinner that Prime Minister Netanyahu had for me. Those children brought tears to my eyes. We have to find a way for both sets of children to get their lives back and to go forward.

Palestinians must recognize the right of Israel and its people to live safe and secure lives today, tomorrow, and forever. Israel must recognize the right of Palestinians to aspire to live free today, tomorrow, and forever.

And I ask you to remember these experiences I had with these two groups of children. If I had met them in reverse order, I would not have known which ones were Israeli and which Palestinian. If they had all been lined up in a row and I had seen their tears, I could not tell whose father was dead and whose father was in prison or what the story of their lives were, making up the grief that they bore. We must acknowledge that neither side has a monopoly on pain or virtue.

At the end of America's Civil War, in my home State, a man was elected Governor who had fought with President Lincoln's forces, even though most of the people in my home State fought with the secessionist forces. And he made his inaugural speech after 4 years of unbelievable bloodshed in America, in which he had been on the winning side but in the minority in our home. And everyone wondered what kind of leader he would be. His first sentence was, "We have all done wrong." I say that because I think the beginning of mutual respect, after so much pain, is to recognize not only the positive characteristics of people on both sides but the fact that there has been a lot—a lot—of hurt and harm.

The fulfillment of one side's aspirations must not come at the expense of the other. We must believe that everyone can win in the new Middle East. It does not hurt Israelis to hear Palestinians peacefully and pridefully asserting their identity, as we saw today. That is not a bad thing. And it does not hurt Palestinians to acknowledge the profound desire of Israelis to live without fear. It is in this spirit that I ask you to consider where we go from here.

I thank you for your rejection fully, finally, and forever of the passages in the Palestinian Charter calling for the destruction of Israel, for they were the ideological underpinnings of a struggle renounced at Oslo. By revoking them once and for all, you have sent, I say again, a powerful message not to the Government but to the people of Israel. You will touch people on the street there. You will reach their hearts there.

I know how profoundly important this is to Israelis. I have been there four times as President. I have spent a lot of time with people other than the political leaders, Israeli schoolchildren who heard about you only as someone who thought they should be driven into the sea. They did not know what their parents or grand-

parents did that you thought was so bad; they were just children, too. Is it surprising that all this has led to the hardening of hearts on both sides, that they refused to acknowledge your existence as a people and that led to a terrible reaction by you?

By turning this page on the past, you are taking the lead in writing a new story for the future. And you have issued a challenge to the Government and the leaders of Israel to walk down that path with you. I thank you for doing that. The children of all the Middle East thank you.

But declaring a change of heart still won't be enough. Let's be realistic here. First of all, there are real differences. And secondly, a lot of water has flowed under the bridge, as we used to say at home. An American poet has written, "Too long a sacrifice can make a stone of the heart." Palestinians and Israelis in their pasts both share a history of oppression and dispossession; both have felt their hearts turn to stone for living too long in fear and seeing loved ones die too young. You are two great people of strong talent and soaring ambition, sharing such a small piece of sacred land.

The time has come to sanctify your holy ground with genuine forgiveness and reconciliation. Every influential Palestinian, from teacher to journalist, from politician to community leader, must make this a mission to banish from the minds of children glorifying suicide bombers, to end the practice of speaking peace in one place and preaching hatred in another, to teach schoolchildren the value of peace and the waste of war, to break the cycle of violence. Our great American prophet Martin Luther King once said, "The old law of an eye for an eye leaves everybody blind."

I believe you have gained more in 5 years of peace than in 45 years of war. I believe that what we are doing today, working together for security, will lead to further gains and changes in the heart. I believe that our work against terrorism, if you stand strong, will be rewarded, for that must become a fact of the past. It must never be a part of your future.

Let me say this as clearly as I can: No matter how sharp a grievance or how deep a hurt, there is no justification for killing innocents.

Mr. Chairman, you said at the White House that no Israeli mother should have to worry if her son or daughter is late coming home. Your words touched many people. You said much the same thing today. We must invest those words with the weight of reality in the minds of every person in Israel and every Palestinian.

I feel this all the more strongly because the act of a few can falsify the image of the many. How many times have we seen it? How many times has it happened to us? We both know it is profoundly wrong to equate Palestinians, in particular, and Islam, in general, with terrorism or to see a fundamental conflict between Islam and the West. For the vast majority of the more than one billion Muslims in the world, tolerance is an article of faith and terrorism a travesty of faith.

I know that in my own country, where Islam is one of the fastest growing religions, we share the same devotion to family and hard work and community. When it comes to relations between the United States and Palestinians, we have come far to overcome our misperceptions of each other. Americans have come to appreciate the strength of your identity and the depth of your aspirations. And we have learned to listen to your grievances as well.

I hope you have begun to see America as your friend. I have tried to speak plainly to you about the need to reach out to the people of Israel, to understand the pain of their children, to understand the history of their fear and mistrust, their yearning, gnawing desire for security, because that is the only way friends can speak and the only way we can move forward.

I took the same liberty yesterday in Israel. I talked there about the need to see one's own mistakes, not just those of others; to recognize the steps others have taken for peace, not just one's own; to break out of the politics of absolutes; to treat one's neighbors with respect and dignity. I talked about the profound courage of both peoples and their leaders which must continue in order for a secure, just, and lasting peace to occur: the courage of Israelis to continue turning over territory for peace and security; the courage of Palestinians to take action against all those who resort to and support violence and terrorism; the courage of Israelis to guarantee safe passage between the West Bank and Gaza and allow for greater trade and development; the courage of Palestinians to confiscate illegal weapons of war and terror; the courage of Israelis to curtail closures and curfews that remain a daily hardship; the courage of Palestin-

ians to resolve all differences at the negotiating table; the courage of both peoples to abandon the rhetoric of hate that still poisons public discourse and limits the vision of your children; and the courage to move ahead to final status negotiations together, without either side taking unilateral steps or making unilateral statements that could prejudice the outcome, whether governing refugee settlements, borders, Jerusalem, or any other issues encompassed by the Oslo accord.

Now, it will take good faith, mutual respect, and compromise to forge a final agreement. I think there will be more breakdowns, frankly, but I think there will be more breakthroughs, as well. There will be more challenges to peace from its enemies. And so I ask you today never to lose sight of how far you have come. With Chairman Arafat's leadership, already you have accomplished what many said was impossible. The seemingly intractable problems of the past can clearly find practical solutions in the future. But it requires a consistent commitment and a genuine willingness to change heart.

As we approach this new century, think of this, think of all the conflicts in the 20th century that many people thought were permanent that have been healed or are healing: two great World Wars between the French and the Germans—they're best friends; the Americans and the Russians, the whole cold war—now we have a constructive partnership; the Irish Catholics and Protestants; the Chinese and the Japanese; the black and white South Africans; the Serbs, the Croats, and the Muslims in Bosnia—all have turned from conflict to cooperation. Yes, there is still some distrust; yes, there's still some difficulty; but they are walking down the right road together. And when they see each other's children, increasingly they only see children, together. When they see the children crying, they realize the pain is real, whatever the child's story. In each case there was a vision of greater peace and prosperity and security.

In Biblical times, Jews and Arabs lived side by side. They contributed to the flowering of Alexandria. During the Golden Age of Spain, Jews, Muslims, and Christians came together in an era of remarkable tolerance and learning. A third of the population laid down its tools on Friday, a third on Saturday, a third on Sunday. They were scholars and scientists, poets, musicians, merchants, and statesmen setting an example of peaceful coexistence that we can make a model for the future. There is no guarantee of success or failure today, but the challenge of this generation of Palestinians is to wage an historic and heroic struggle for peace.

Again I say this is an historic day. I thank you for coming. I thank you for raising your hands. I thank you for standing up. I thank you for your voices. I thank you for clapping every time I said what you were really doing was reaching deep into the heart of the people of Israel.

Chairman Arafat said he and Mrs. Arafat are taking Hillary and Chelsea and me—we're going to Bethlehem tomorrow. For a Christian family to light the Christmas tree in Bethlehem is a great honor. It is an interesting thing to contemplate that in this small place, the home of Islam, Judaism, and Christianity, the embodiment of my faith was born a Jew and is still recognized by Muslims as a prophet. He said a lot of very interesting things, but in the end, He was known as the Prince of Peace. And we celebrate at Christmastime the birth of the Prince of Peace. One reason He is known as the Prince of Peace is He knew something about what it takes to make peace. And one of the wisest things He ever said was, "We will be judged by the same standard by which we judge, but mercy triumphs over judgment."

In this Christmas season, in this Hanukkah season, on the edge of Ramadan, this is a time for mercy and vision and looking at all of our children together. You have reaffirmed the fact that you now intend to share this piece of land, without war, with your neighbors, forever. They have heard you. They have heard you.

Now, you and they must now determine what kind of peace you will have. Will it be grudging and mean-spirited and confining, or will it be generous and open? Will you begin to judge each other in the way you would like to be judged? Will you begin to see each other's children in the way you see your own? Will they feel your pain, and will you understand theirs?

Surely to goodness, after 5 years of this peace process and decades of suffering and after you have come here today and done what you have done, we can say, "Enough of this gnashing of teeth. Let us join hands and proudly go forward together."

Thank you very much.

NOTE: The President spoke at 5:30 p.m. in the Main Hall at the Shawwa Center. In his remarks, he referred to Speaker Salim Za'anoun of the Palestine National Council; Chairman Yasser Arafat of the Palestinian Authority, and his wife Shua; and Prime Minister Binyamin Netanyahu of Israel.

Statement on the Puerto Rico Status Referendum
December 14, 1998

I have advocated enabling the people of Puerto Rico to determine their future status among all the options—continuing the current governing arrangement, known as Commonwealth; nationhood, either independent from or in an association with the U.S.; and statehood. This year the House passed a bipartisan bill for this purpose, with my support, but the Senate majority leadership blocked it. In the end, the leadership simply recognized Puerto Ricans' right to choose and promised to review the results.

Yesterday Puerto Ricans voted on these issues under local law. A majority of the vote was not for any of the options. Among the rest, the overwhelming majority supported statehood.

I will, therefore, work with Members of Congress and the people of Puerto Rico and their leaders to enable Puerto Ricans to clarify their choice among the options. I remain committed to implementing a majority choice for Puerto Rico's future status.

Remarks Following Trilateral Discussions and an Exchange With Reporters at Erez Crossing, Israel
December 15, 1998

Good morning, everybody. I just had a very good meeting, a very frank meeting, with Prime Minister Netanyahu and Chairman Arafat. First, everyone agrees that yesterday's convening of all the Palestinian groups and the vote by the Palestinian National Council and the others to fully and forever reject the conflict with Israel and commit to a path to peace and cooperation was a truly historic day.

And what we focused on in our meeting is how to follow up on that. Where do we go from here; how can we vigorously implement the process that we agreed to at Wye? And I'd like to just—I have a few notes here from the meeting; I'd like to go over them with you.

The first thing that we agreed to do was to energize the permanent status talks. Keep in mind, the purpose of the Wye agreement was to resolve the matters that had to be resolved so we could get into permanent status talks and try to get back as close as possible to the timetable set out in 1993.

Secondly, we agreed to vigorously pursue the security issue through the appropriate committee. There is, I think, no space between the two sides in their understanding that maintaining security cooperation and minimizing security problems is the precondition to making all the rest of this work. It's what made Wye possible.

Thirdly, the prisoner issue, as you know, is a difficult one. But an informal channel has been agreed to for dealing with that, and it was agreed to—referred all the questions to that channel and to pursue that accordingly.

Fourthly, there is a so-called steering committee which is basically a clearinghouse for a lot of the other specific issues agreed to at Wye, questions of law enforcement, of weapons handling, of all the specifics there. They are going to meet today, and I anticipate that there will be agreement at the end of the day, at the end of this meeting, that a lot of the requirements of Wye for this next phase have, in fact, been met.

Then there are some other issues that I would like to mention, all of which we agreed to establish to deal with through established committee procedures: Education—I talked about this in my speech in Gaza yesterday, the importance of teaching children that a commitment has been made by these two people to be partners and to share this land together. It's a very important issue to the Israelis and one I think that the Palestinians recognize. Second, the economic committee, which is very important. And thirdly, one big issue that has been agreed to but the details haven't been worked out is the whole question of safe passage. And there is a committee on safe passage; and I expect it to meet, if not today, then very shortly, to continue to push forward on that.

So the message of this trip is that yesterday was a historic day. It was a very important day for both peoples. Again, I want to compliment and applaud Chairman Arafat and all the others who were at that meeting who made the decision, clear, public, and unambiguous, that we now have to decide practical means to go forward. And I think we are well on the way to doing that. So I have achieved what I came here to achieve, and I expect the Secretary of State to be back here in several weeks, and we'll just keep at it.

Israeli Troop Redeployment

Q. Mr. President, will the redeployment that is scheduled for Friday go ahead?

The President. Well, I think the proper way to answer that is that the Israeli Government in my meeting reaffirmed its commitment to the Wye process. And so we have to resolve a number of issues in order for the redeployment to go forward. I think it would be unfortunate if we got too far behind schedule, and I hope we can keep pretty much to the schedule that's there. But obviously, that remains to be worked out here.

We believe in keeping to these schedules as much as possible, and we worked very hard to put all this back on track here. I do think that we are back on track. We're going to see this through, and I feel good about where we are now.

Q. This clearinghouse you're speaking about——

Trilateral Discussions

Q. Are they talking again?

The President. Oh, yes, yes. We sat there for however long, an hour and 25 minutes today, with all the parties in the room, including the major members of each side's team, as well as the leaders, and everybody had their say. And there was some—we got beyond people stating their own positions to actual conversation, and I'm quite hopeful. I think the proof is always in what happens tomorrow, not what happens today, but I think at least we've got a process set up and we can go forward.

Middle East Peace Process

Q. Mr. President, have you been able to insulate the peace process from the domestic political problems affecting you and the Prime Minister?

The President. Oh, absolutely.

Q. How so?

The President. You show up for work every day. It's not a complicated thing.

Q. These clearinghouses, are these to clear those obstacles that stand in the way of Netanyahu going through with the next phase of the withdrawal? Is this to satisfy him that these various issues like unilateral declarations are being resolved so he can go ahead? I don't understand the clearinghouse.

The President. No, no. What I am saying is— no, there is a steering committee that we had set up at Wye that is supposed to deal with things like——

Q. Well, yes, prisoners, for instance.

The President. No, no, that's different. It's supposed to deal with things like—the steering committee deals with things like the weapons confiscation and destruction issue, the size of the police forces, all those specific issues that were set up at Wye not being dealt with in the security committee, not being dealt with in the informal channel on prisoners, not being dealt with in some other way.

And so what I would say, as I think you will get a report before the end of the day here, that these folks have gotten together, the reports have been made, and I think a determination will be made that a number of the requirements of the Wye agreement have been met so that we can go forward. But this is a complicated matter, obviously, and I hope we can stay as close to the schedule as possible.

Q. He set preconditions for going in. His latest one was unilateral declarations of statehood; he said that yesterday. Before that, it was the covenant. You got the covenant taken care of. What I am trying to determine is whether his preconditions have been swept away.

The President. Well, the meeting we did yesterday was part of the Wye agreement. The other question is one that I think both sides should observe, which is, it is okay to advocate how you want this to come out. That's okay. Neither side should try to stop the other from saying what their vision of the future is. That would be a terrible mistake. But it is not okay to imply that we're not going to resolve all the matters that were listed in the Oslo agreement for negotiations by negotiations. That is what we've got to do, and that's where I think the line ought to be drawn and the balance ought to be struck. If we stick with that, you know, we'll have fits and starts; it will be hard parts, but we'll get through this. We'll get through this just fine, and it will come out where it ought to.

Thank you.

NOTE: The President spoke at 10:35 a.m. in the Matak Headquarters. In his remarks, he referred to Prime Minister Binyamin Netanyahu of Israel and Chairman Yasser Arafat of the Palestinian Authority. A tape was not available for verification of the content of these remarks.

Statement on the Death of A. Leon Higginbotham, Jr.
December 15, 1998

Hillary and I were deeply saddened to learn of the death of Judge A. Leon Higginbotham, Jr. Throughout his life as a scholar, lawyer, and judge, Leon Higginbotham was one of our Nation's most passionate and steadfast advocates for civil rights.

When Leon Higginbotham was named to the Federal bench at the age of 36 by President Kennedy, he was the youngest Federal judge to be appointed in three decades. He served with distinction and eventually became judge of the Third Circuit Court of Appeals. He also found the time to write and speak with idealism and rigor on the great dilemmas of race and justice. And because of this remarkable service and his indelible spirit, I had the honor in 1995 to award Judge Higginbotham the Presidential Medal of Freedom, the highest honor given to citizens in the United States.

His retirement was spent remarkably—helping to draft the Constitution for a democratic South Africa and teaching a fresh generation of students at Harvard. Judge Higginbotham's life, as much as his scholarship, set an example of commitment, enlargement, and service to young minds at home and abroad.

Our thoughts and prayers are with his wife, Evelyn Brooks Higginbotham, and their four children.

Address to the Nation Announcing Military Strikes on Iraq
December 16, 1998

Good evening. Earlier today I ordered America's Armed Forces to strike military and security targets in Iraq. They are joined by British forces. Their mission is to attack Iraq's nuclear, chemical, and biological programs and its military capacity to threaten its neighbors. Their purpose is to protect the national interest of the United States and, indeed, the interest of people throughout the Middle East and around the world. Saddam Hussein must not be allowed to threaten his neighbors or the world with nuclear arms, poison gas, or biological weapons.

I want to explain why I have decided, with the unanimous recommendation of my national security team, to use force in Iraq; why we have acted now; and what we aim to accomplish.

Six weeks ago Saddam Hussein announced that he would no longer cooperate with the United Nations weapons inspectors, called UNSCOM. They are highly professional experts from dozens of countries. Their job is to oversee the elimination of Iraq's capability to retain, create, and use weapons of mass destruction and to verify that Iraq does not attempt to rebuild that capability. The inspectors undertook this mission, first, 7½ years ago at the end of the Gulf war, when Iraq agreed to declare and destroy its arsenal as a condition of the cease-fire.

The international community had good reason to set this requirement. Other countries possess weapons of mass destruction and ballistic missiles. With Saddam, there's one big difference: He has used them, not once but repeatedly, unleashing chemical weapons against Iranian troops during a decade-long war, not only against soldiers but against civilians; firing Scud missiles at the citizens of Israel, Saudi Arabia, Bahrain, and Iran, not only against a foreign enemy but even against his own people, gassing Kurdish civilians in northern Iraq.

The international community had little doubt then, and I have no doubt today, that left unchecked, Saddam Hussein will use these terrible weapons again.

The United States has patiently worked to preserve UNSCOM, as Iraq has sought to avoid its obligation to cooperate with the inspectors. On occasion, we've had to threaten military force, and Saddam has backed down. Faced with Saddam's latest act of defiance in late October, we built intensive diplomatic pressure on Iraq, backed by overwhelming military force in the region. The U.N. Security Council voted 15 to zero to condemn Saddam's actions and to demand that he immediately come into compliance. Eight Arab nations—Egypt, Syria, Saudi Arabia, Kuwait, Bahrain, Qatar, United Arab Emirates, and Oman—warned that Iraq alone would bear responsibility for the consequences of defying the U.N.

When Saddam still failed to comply, we prepared to act militarily. It was only then, at the last possible moment, that Iraq backed down. It pledged to the U.N. that it had made, and I quote, "a clear and unconditional decision to resume cooperation with the weapons inspectors." I decided then to call off the attack, with our airplanes already in the air, because Saddam had given in to our demands. I concluded then that the right thing to do was to use restraint and give Saddam one last chance to prove his willingness to cooperate.

I made it very clear at that time what "unconditional cooperation" meant, based on existing U.N. resolutions and Iraq's own commitments. And along with Prime Minister Blair of Great Britain, I made it equally clear that if Saddam failed to cooperate fully, we would be prepared to act without delay, diplomacy, or warning.

Now, over the past 3 weeks, the U.N. weapons inspectors have carried out their plan for testing Iraq's cooperation. The testing period ended this weekend, and last night, UNSCOM's Chairman, Richard Butler, reported the results to U.N. Secretary-General Annan. The conclusions are stark, sobering, and profoundly disturbing.

In four out of the five categories set forth, Iraq has failed to cooperate. Indeed, it actually has placed new restrictions on the inspectors. Here are some of the particulars:

Iraq repeatedly blocked UNSCOM from inspecting suspect sites. For example, it shut off access to the headquarters of its ruling party and said it will deny access to the party's other offices, even though U.N. resolutions make no exception for them and UNSCOM has inspected them in the past.

Iraq repeatedly restricted UNSCOM's ability to obtain necessary evidence. For example, Iraq obstructed UNSCOM's effort to photograph bombs related to its chemical weapons program. It tried to stop an UNSCOM biological weapons team from videotaping a site and photocopying documents and prevented Iraqi personnel from answering UNSCOM's questions. Prior to the inspection of another site, Iraq actually emptied out the building, removing not just documents but even the furniture and the equipment. Iraq has failed to turn over virtually all the documents requested by the inspectors; indeed, we know that Iraq ordered the destruction of weapons-related documents in anticipation of an UNSCOM inspection.

So Iraq has abused its final chance. As the UNSCOM report concludes, and again I quote, "Iraq's conduct ensured that no progress was able to be made in the fields of disarmament. In light of this experience and in the absence of full cooperation by Iraq, it must, regrettably, be recorded again that the Commission is not able to conduct the work mandated to it by the Security Council with respect to Iraq's prohibited weapons program."

In short, the inspectors are saying that, even if they could stay in Iraq, their work would be a sham. Saddam's deception has defeated their effectiveness. Instead of the inspectors disarming Saddam, Saddam has disarmed the inspectors.

This situation presents a clear and present danger to the stability of the Persian Gulf and the safety of people everywhere. The international community gave Saddam one last chance to resume cooperation with the weapons inspectors. Saddam has failed to seize the chance.

And so we had to act, and act now. Let me explain why.

First, without a strong inspections system, Iraq would be free to retain and begin to rebuild its chemical, biological, and nuclear weapons programs in months, not years.

Second, if Saddam can cripple the weapons inspections system and get away with it, he would conclude that the international community, led by the United States, has simply lost its will. He will surmise that he has free rein to rebuild his arsenal of destruction. And some day, make no mistake, he will use it again, as he has in the past.

Third, in halting our airstrikes in November, I gave Saddam a chance, not a license. If we turn our backs on his defiance, the credibility of U.S. power as a check against Saddam will be destroyed. We will not only have allowed Saddam to shatter the inspections system that controls his weapons of mass destruction program; we also will have fatally undercut the fear of force that stops Saddam from acting to gain domination in the region.

That is why, on the unanimous recommendation of my national security team, including the Vice President, Secretary of Defense, the Chairman of the Joint Chiefs of Staff, the Secretary of State, and the National Security Adviser, I have ordered a strong, sustained series of airstrikes against Iraq. They are designed to degrade Saddam's capacity to develop and deliver weapons of mass destruction, and to degrade his ability to threaten his neighbors. At the same time, we are delivering a powerful message to Saddam: If you act recklessly, you will pay a heavy price.

We acted today because, in the judgment of my military advisers, a swift response would provide the most surprise and the least opportunity for Saddam to prepare. If we had delayed for even a matter of days from Chairman Butler's report, we would have given Saddam more time to disperse his forces and protect his weapons.

Also, the Muslim holy month of Ramadan begins this weekend. For us to initiate military action during Ramadan would be profoundly offensive to the Muslim world and, therefore, would damage our relations with Arab countries and the progress we have made in the Middle East. That is something we wanted very much to avoid without giving Iraq a month's headstart to prepare for potential action against it.

Finally, our allies, including Prime Minister Tony Blair of Great Britain, concurred that now is the time to strike.

I hope Saddam will come into cooperation with the inspection system now and comply with the relevant U.N. Security Council resolutions. But we have to be prepared that he will not, and we must deal with the very real danger he poses. So we will pursue a long-term strategy to contain Iraq and its weapons of mass destruction and work toward the day when Iraq has a Government worthy of its people.

First, we must be prepared to use force again if Saddam takes threatening actions, such as trying to reconstitute his weapons of mass destruction or their delivery systems, threatening his neighbors, challenging allied aircraft over Iraq, or moving against his own Kurdish citizens. The credible threat to use force, and when necessary, the actual use of force, is the surest way to contain Saddam's weapons of mass destruction program, curtail his aggression, and prevent another Gulf war.

Second, so long as Iraq remains out of compliance, we will work with the international community to maintain and enforce economic sanctions. Sanctions have cost Saddam more than $120 billion, resources that would have been used to rebuild his military. The sanctions system allows Iraq to sell oil for food, for medicine, for other humanitarian supplies for the Iraqi people. We have no quarrel with them. But without the sanctions, we would see the oil-for-food program become oil-for-tanks, resulting in a greater threat to Iraq's neighbors and less food for its people.

The hard fact is that so long as Saddam remains in power, he threatens the well-being of his people, the peace of his region, the security of the world. The best way to end that threat once and for all is with a new Iraqi Government, a Government ready to live in peace with its neighbors, a Government that respects the rights of its people.

Bringing change in Baghdad will take time and effort. We will strengthen our engagement with the full range of Iraqi opposition forces and work with them effectively and prudently.

The decision to use force is never cost-free. Whenever American forces are placed in harm's way, we risk the loss of life. And while our strikes are focused on Iraq's military capabilities, there will be unintended Iraqi casualties. Indeed, in the past, Saddam has intentionally placed Iraqi civilians in harm's way in a cynical bid to sway international opinion. We must be prepared for these realities. At the same time, Saddam should have absolutely no doubt: If he lashes out at his neighbors, we will respond forcefully.

Heavy as they are, the costs of action must be weighed against the price of inaction. If Saddam defies the world and we fail to respond, we will face a far greater threat in the future. Saddam will strike again at his neighbors. He will make war on his own people. And mark my words, he will develop weapons of mass destruction. He will deploy them, and he will use them. Because we are acting today, it is less likely that we will face these dangers in the future.

Let me close by addressing one other issue. Saddam Hussein and the other enemies of peace may have thought that the serious debate currently before the House of Representatives would distract Americans or weaken our resolve to face him down. But once more, the United States has proven that, although we are never eager to use force, when we must act in America's vital interests, we will do so.

In the century we're leaving, America has often made the difference between chaos and community, fear and hope. Now, in a new century, we'll have a remarkable opportunity to shape a future more peaceful than the past but only if we stand strong against the enemies of peace. Tonight, the United States is doing just that.

May God bless and protect the brave men and women who are carrying out this vital mission, and their families. And may God bless America.

NOTE: The President spoke at 6 p.m. from the Oval Office at the White House. In his remarks, he referred to President Saddam Hussein of Iraq and United Nations Secretary-General Kofi Annan.

Remarks on the Military Strikes on Iraq and an Exchange With Reporters
December 17, 1998

The President. My national security team is about to update me and the Vice President on the status of our operation in Iraq. I'd like to begin by speaking for every American in expressing my gratitude to our men and women in uniform and also to our British allies, who are participating in this operation with us.

I am convinced the decision I made to order this military action, though difficult, was absolutely the right thing to do. It is in our interest and in the interest of people all around the world. Saddam Hussein has used weapons of mass destruction and ballistic missiles before; I have no doubt he would use them again if permitted to develop them.

When I halted military action against Saddam last November, after he had terminated the UNSCOM operations, I made it very clear that we were giving him a last chance to cooperate. Once again he promised in very explicit terms that he would fully cooperate. On Tuesday the inspectors concluded that they were no longer able to do their jobs and that, in fact, he had raised even new barriers to their doing their jobs.

Then yesterday morning I gave the order because I believe that we cannot allow Saddam Hussein to dismantle UNSCOM and resume the production of weapons of mass destruction with impunity. I also believe that to have done so would have, in effect, given him a green light for whatever he might want to do in his neighborhood. I think it would be a terrible, terrible mistake.

We acted yesterday because Secretary Cohen and General Shelton strongly urged that we act at the point where we could have maximum impact with minimum risk to our own people because of the surprise factor. We also wanted to avoid initiating any military action during the Muslim holy month of Ramadan, which is slated to begin in just a couple of days.

Our mission is clear: to degrade his capacity to develop and to use weapons of mass destruction or to threaten his neighbors. I believe we will achieve that mission, and I'm looking forward to getting this briefing.

Impeachment/Military Strikes on Iraq

Q. Mr. President, how are you going to stem the Republican drive to drive you out of office?

The President. Well, the Constitution has a procedure for that, and we will follow it.

Q. Mr. President, as you know, Senator Trent Lott and Dick Armey, the House majority leader, and other Republicans are questioning the timing, suggesting that this was simply a diversionary tactic to avoid an impeachment vote on the House floor. What do you say to those critics?

The President. That it's not true, that what I did was the right thing for the country. I don't think any serious person would believe that any President would do such a thing. And I don't believe any reasonably astute person in Washington would believe that Secretary Cohen and General Shelton and the whole rest of the National Security team would participate in such an action. This was the right thing for the country.

We have given Saddam Hussein chance after chance to cooperate with UNSCOM. We said in November that this was the last chance. We got the report from Mr. Butler saying that he was not cooperating and, in fact, raised new barriers to cooperation. And we acted just as we promised we would. We acted swiftly because we were ready, thanks to the very fine work of the Defense Department in leaving our assets properly deployed. We had the strong support of the British.

And I might add, I'm very gratified by the strong support we've gotten from people among both Democratic and Republican ranks in the Congress who are interested in national security, people like Senator Helms, Senator McCain,

Senator Warner, Senator Hagel, Senator Lugar, all have expressed support for this mission. So I feel good about where we are on that.

Q. Mr. President, will you confirm reports on ground troops in Kuwait?

Q. [*Inaudible*]—on the first day of the operation and would it undercut your authority if the House opened the impeachment debate during this operation?

The President. What was the first question, Terry [Terence Hunt, Associated Press]?

Q. Bomb damage assessment.

The President. I'm about to get it.

Q. You didn't get any from Mr. Berger?

The President. Obviously, I've kept up with it as best I could, but I have not gotten a full report.

Q. But you think it is a success?

The President. I'm about to get a—it's an ongoing mission. I want to wait——

Q. Because Joe Lockhart told us it was a success.

Q. And he undercut your authority, sir?

The President. No. First of all, I'm going to complete this mission—we're going to complete this mission. And the Republican leaders will have to decide how to do their job. That's not for me to comment on.

Kuwait

Q. Can you confirm reports of Saddam Hussein possibly advancing and invading Kuwait and the possible use of ground troops, sir?

The President. No, I have no comment on that. I think that surely he knows what a disastrous mistake that would be.

Civilian Casualties in Iraq

Q. Mr. President, the Iraqis are saying there's been heavy civilian casualties in this. Do you have any information so far that that's true?

The President. I do not. I can tell you what I said last night: We did everything we could to carefully target military and national security targets and to minimize civilian casualties. There is always a prospect that the missiles will miss, that they will be interrupted because of the missiles being fired at them, trying to deflect them from their intended targets. I am quite sure there will be, as I said last evening, unintended casualties, and I regret that very much.

That's one of the reasons that I have bent over backwards, not just in November but also on previous occasions to avoid using force in this case. I did not want to do it; I think all of you know it. But in November, we literally had planes in the air, and I said that it would be the last chance. I think it is very important that we not allow Saddam Hussein to destroy the UNSCOM system without any penalty whatever, to eventually get all these sanctions lifted and to go right on just as if he never made any commitments that were unfulfilled on this score. I think it would have been a disaster for us to do this.

And so, regrettably, I made this decision. There is, I believe, no way to avoid some unintended civilian casualties, and I regret it very much. But I believe far, far more people would have died eventually from this man's regime had we not taken this action.

NOTE: The President spoke at 10:45 a.m. in the Oval Office at the White House, prior to a meeting with the foreign policy team. In his remarks, he referred to President Saddam Hussein of Iraq; and Richard Butler, executive chairman, United Nations Special Commission (UNSCOM). A tape was not available for verification of the content of these remarks.

Remarks Honoring Eunice Kennedy Shriver at the Special Olympics Dinner
December 17, 1998

Thank you. Please be seated. Thank you. Pretty rowdy crowd tonight. [*Laughter*] I am delighted to join Hillary in welcoming all of you here. We're delighted to have you at this remarkable celebration of the 30th anniversary of the Special Olympics.

Let me say just for a moment, I am also thinking tonight about the brave American men and women in uniform who are carrying out our mission in Iraq with our British allies. I know that our thoughts and our prayers, indeed, those of all the American people, are with them tonight. And I wanted to say that what they are doing is important. It will make the world a safer, more peaceful place for our children in the 21st century.

I'd also like to say a word now about the Special Olympics. More than 30 years ago Eunice Kennedy Shriver had an idea as simple as it was revolutionary, to give young people with disabilities the chance to know the thrill of athletic competition, the joy of participation, the pride of accomplishment. Out of that powerful idea, dreamed up at a kitchen table and launched at a backyard in Rockville, Maryland, Special Olympics grew and grew and grew.

Just think of it, if you can remember back to the time before the Special Olympics, many people actually believed that people with disabilities were incapable of performing the most basic everyday activities, let alone competing in sports. But this year, 30 years later, there are more than one million Special Olympic athletes throwing the javelin, swimming the 500-meter butterfly, walking the balance beam—something most of the rest of us cannot do—[*laughter*]—and inspiring hope all over the world.

So tonight I ask all of you to stand and join me in toasting Eunice Kennedy Shriver; her wonderful family, who have supported her every step of the way; to all the people who work so hard year-in and year-out to make Special Olympics possible; and to the athletes who are an inspiration to us all—to Eunice Kennedy Shriver and the Special Olympics. Ladies and gentlemen, Eunice Shriver.

NOTE: The President spoke at approximately 8 p.m. in a pavilion on the South Lawn at the White House. In his remarks, he referred to Eunice Kennedy Shriver, founder, Special Olympics. The transcript released by the Office of the Press Secretary also included the remarks of First Lady Hillary Clinton.

Remarks at the Conclusion of the Special Olympics Dinner
December 17, 1998

Thank you. This has been a wonderful night. Hillary and I want to thank all the artists who have graced this stage. They have brought something special to this part of the White House lawn and this beautiful tent that we've never had before. They certainly have helped to put us all in the holiday spirit, including our good friend Whoopi, who I thought was terrific tonight, even in the breaks.

I feel very proud to be a part of this special evening to pay tribute to Special Olympics. Tonight we celebrate 30 years of breaking down barriers and building up hope, 30 years of widening the circle of opportunity, 30 years of helping Americans with disabilities to reach their highest potential. Tonight we celebrate the victory of the human spirit. We see the power of that spirit every single time an athlete like Loretta runs a race, every time a young person realizes the wonder that he can swim faster than almost anybody else in the pool, every time a parent's heart fills with pride as her child steps with confidence onto the winner's block, and every time a volunteer learns the joy of helping people with disabilities to make the most of their abilities.

As Special Olympics enters its fourth decade, this legacy is being passed from generation to generation, in a circle of hope, as the children of Special Olympics volunteers take their place in the dugouts and on the sidelines and as former competitors become coaches and mentors to new young athletes. The Special Olympics torch, which began as a small flicker of light in 1968 in Chicago, now burns brightly all around the world as a symbol of acceptance and pride.

Tonight, we thank all of you, every single one of you who have made this possible: the Shriver and Kennedy families, without whose vision there would be no Special Olympics; the thousands of supporters and volunteers whose dedication sustains that vision; the millions of athletes whose courage inspires and challenges all of us. And we salute the next generation of Special Olympics heroes who will keep that flame alive in the 21st century.

Now, I'd like to ask all the artists here with us tonight to come back on stage and sing just one more song for you, Eunice, and all the rest of us, and for Special Olympics.

Thank you very much.

NOTE: The President spoke at approximately 11:10 p.m. in a pavilion on the South Lawn at the White House. In his remarks, he referred to comedienne Whoopi Goldberg; Special Olympics athlete Loretta Clairborne; and Eunice Kennedy Shriver, founder, Special Olympics. The transcript released by the Office of the Press Secretary also included the remarks of First Lady Hillary Clinton.

Remarks at a Meeting With the President's Advisory Council on HIV/AIDS
December 18, 1998

[Office of National AIDS Policy Director Sandra Thurman made brief opening remarks and introduced the President.]

The President. Thank you very much. I want to get right to the subject of listening to all of you, but I would like to say that, as all of you know, we had a very good couple of days when we finally made the budget last year. We've had a lot of good increases, a lot of things that I know you care so much about, but we've got a lot of work to do, especially in prevention and in the vaccine development. I think we're going to—*[inaudible]*—pretty soon.

I would prefer, I think, because we've met before and I try to stay familiar with our concerns—I think we've done a good job of getting the money into the programs this time, but there's a lot more we can do—*[inaudible]*. However, you organized this. *[Laughter]*.

[At this point, Council Chair Dr. H. Scott Hitt introduced the cochair of the Council's Racial Ethnic Populations Subcommittee, Rev. Altagracia Perez, who led the participants in a prayer. Dr. Hitt then commended the President for his commitment to AIDS research.]

The President. Thank you.

[Dr. Hitt emphasized the need for better AIDS awareness efforts in ethnic communities, noting that many Americans infected with HIV were unaware of it. He stated that thousands of HIV-infected people could not get the Public Health Service recommended early treatment, but instead had to wait until they became disabled from the disease to become eligible. Council member Rabbi Joseph Edelheit remarked that the Council's duty was to ensure that help and

treatment, such as needle-exchange programs and drug therapies, for those living with HIV/AIDS continued into the next century. He presented the President with a dreidel, the traditional Hanukkah toy, and said the Council's hope was to revive the President's vision of a zero rate of transmission and equitable access to care. Council member B. Thomas Henderson, a person living with HIV, noted the progress made under the President's leadership, but pointed out the need for reform in Medicaid coverage for HIV/AIDS to enable patients to receive early treatment prior to disability. Citing a Health Care Financing Administration evaluation which concluded that could not be done in a budget-neutral manner, Mr. Henderson suggested that the administration needed to look for offset cost savings beyond Medicaid and consider a budget window longer than 5 years, rather than relying solely on demonstration-program legislation introduced by Senators Jeffords and Kennedy. He concluded that drug cost issues needed to be addressed at the same time.]

The President. Well, I'll see what I can do about that. You know, generally, this whole medical coverage problem is getting worse in America. It reminds me of that old joke that the Republicans used to tell on us; they told me, if I voted for Barry Goldwater, we'd get involved in Vietnam too much. And I did, and sure enough, it happened. *[Laughter]* And they said, when they attacked Hillary and me for our health care plan, they said that, if people supported it, things would get worse. And sure enough, they did. *[Laughter]*

We've had—these coverage problems have gotten quite profound, and as a consequence, with fewer and fewer people getting medical coverage at work, what you've got is more and more people trying to find a way to get into Medicare.

One of the things, for example, that I want to look at, as a result of this, is something we're doing with disabled people who get back into the workplace. I just started an initiative, not very long ago, to try and have people who have disabilities, which include some people with HIV and AIDS, and they get better—if you have disabilities and you go back to work, it used to be automatically you lose your Medicaid. And now, more and more people are working in small businesses where they don't have employer-based health insurance or they have small pools and they can't afford to take somebody with a preexisting condition. So we're trying to modify the rules so that when people are on disability, then they get off of it and they go back into the work force, they can keep their Medicaid for some period of time. And I want to go back and look and see exactly how we did that and what else we can do here.

Tom, I want to make sure what you said. You believe that there are savings in non-Medicaid areas that would come from keeping people off—help give people the drugs before they get sick in the first place.

Mr. Henderson. As you know, the process right now is for States to seek 1115 waivers. We've been working closely with a number of States who have been working on those waivers for submission at the present time. They believe that there are significant savings in SSI and SSDI, in other areas, that would result——

The President. [*Inaudible*]—all would be counted.

Mr. Henderson. Yes, sir. And current rules don't allow that.

The President. I've got to go back and look at that. Part of it is the way the law disaggregates money into mandatory and non-mandatory spending. I'll look at it and see if we can do something about that. I know it's very important.

[*At this point, Council member Bob Hattoy entered the meeting.*]

The President. I presume you still—hello, Bob.

Mr. Hattoy. Hello, Mr. President. [*Laughter*] Sorry I'm late.

The President. I'm glad you're here. [*Laughter*]

Mr. Hattoy. I'm glad you're here. [*Laughter*]

The President. [*Inaudible*]—notwithstanding what you said, you still think we ought to pass the Kennedy-Jeffords bill? They tell me it's a good bill.

Mr. Henderson. Yes, sir. Absolutely. We just think that there are some things that can be done in the near term, though, within the administration, that do not require legislation, that they would move this problem forward.

The President. I'll do some work on it—what you said.

[*H. Alexander Robinson, cochair of the Council's Prevention Subcommittee, said that prevention of new infections remained a problem. He proposed Federal funding for needle-exchange programs and a bold national media campaign by the White House Office of National AIDS Policy to promote voluntary HIV testing, which would be modeled on the national youth antidrug media campaign.*]

The President. It sounds like a good idea. I think Sandy is going to come up with a proposal, I think, about what we should do, but I think it's a good idea.

Ms. Thurman. We'll work with you and get one done.

The President. And it offers the promise of sort of getting by the divisive arguments of the past and actually doing something. I like it.

Participant. Proactive.

[*Council member Helen M. Miramontes stressed the need for continuing research both in vaccines and therapeutics. Praising the establishment of a 10-year goal for finding a vaccine, she pointed out the urgency of appointing a director for the vaccine center at the National Institutes of Health; following up on the preliminary vaccine meeting; placing a council-recommended vaccine effort coordinator within the Office of National AIDS Policy; and developing and implementing a comprehensive plan.*]

The President. Well, let me make a couple comments. First of all, I think the vaccine director is about to be appointed. I've been as impatient about that as you have. I've been—[*inaudible*].

Secondly, I do think Dr. Neal Nathanson, the new Director of the Office of AIDS Research, has been doing quite a good job. We got about a 33 percent increase in funds for vaccine research in the last budget, so that's good. And we're going to try to—I just had a brief meeting, before I came in here, with our folks, talking about how we can expand Sandy's office over here and introduce this kind of work and kind of ride her on this thing. I think that's important. It does make a difference just to have a sort of sustained White House involvement on any kind of project to keep cutting through the resistance.

[Council member Regina Aragón addressed the need for meaningful and substantial increases in HIV funding in the fiscal year 2000 budget. She thanked the President for his efforts in securing $156 million in funding for a Congressional Black Caucus initiative to address the AIDS crisis in the African-American and Latino communities but noted that conditions required a sustained and expanded Federal response. Ms. Aragón also underscored the importance of funding for a national testing awareness media campaign. Michael T. Isbell, cochair of the Council's Prevention Subcommittee, noted that more than 90 percent of HIV infections occur in the developing world. He commended the President for a $10 million program addressing the needs of AIDS-affected women and orphans and suggested making that funding a permanent part of the U.S. Agency for International Development. Saying that U.S. funding for global AIDS activities had declined in real dollars since 1993, he urged more funding in the upcoming budget and improved coordination of Federal international AIDS efforts.]

The President. Well, in general, let me say I think the budget should reflect better attention both to prevention at home and to the communities of color. And I've been trying to get more money for the USAID mission, and we'll put some more money in there. I think I'd like to make two points.

One is that this budget year will be more difficult than the last one because we got such big increases in everything last time. And because of the global economy kind of slowing down, we don't expect the same amount of revenues to come in this time, and we have to fund all the big increases we got last time again. But we'll do the best we can.

The second thing I would like to say is I think that it would be very helpful to have all of you using your—whatever influence you have

with Members of Congress in both parties to support more global efforts, because eventually all this is going to be a menace to the United States. So it's not only a moral imperative, it's also very practical over the long run.

One of the things that has kind of bothered me is that, in the aftermath of the cold war, we were able for several years to reduce our defense budget, and that was a good thing, and everyone—and even the Pentagon wanted to do it. There was just like about 300,000—the number of civilian employees—and they plan for further reductions there. But during that time, we actually needed to make a larger commitment on the diplomatic front or in the non-defense security areas, if you will. And with the exception of the special efforts we made in the former Soviet Union to dismantle and destroy nuclear weapons, basically there's been a wholesale effort to cut back on our diplomatic budget even though, contrary to popular wisdom, the United States spends a smaller percentage of our income on international affairs than any other major country.

And one of the things that I have seen—almost no one knows this, but it's true—one of the things I have—now, to be fair, we also spend more on defense, and a lot of our defense goes to protect other countries, as you see in the last couple of days. But still, for—the numbers are so much more modest, not only for 8 years; let's look at the USAID program, the health programs, the empowerment of women and children, especially young girls, initiatives, the small scale microeconomic development, all that stuff that doesn't cost much money and it has a huge impact, and especially a lot of the things we can do in public health—and, interestingly enough, a lot of the preventive activities that we would engage in with regard to AIDS, for example, would go quite well with other things we need to be doing out there with these large populations anyway in a lot of countries that have severe public health problems.

So we've been sitting here meeting in our—I've been having, each of the last 3 or 4 days, rather long, detailed budget sessions, trying to figure out how to get more blood out of that turnip. And one of the things that I'm trying to do is to figure out how to make the case to the Congress, in an effective way, that the United States has enormous interests, as well as obligations, in making these kinds of investments beyond our borders.

And I think anything you can do to help that, I would appreciate it. I mean, there is this sort of general awareness in Congress that the world is becoming more interdependent. There's a much more sophisticated understanding of the economics, for example. But it's not just economics. It's the environment; it's the public health; it's all these other things where we are becoming more and more caught up with each other.

Our major military mission in the last 6 months, before the operation in Iraq, has been to send several thousand of our uniformed personnel to Central America to help them rebuild after Hurricane Mitch. It's not only the right thing to do from a humanitarian point of view, it is in our national interest. Because if those countries don't rebuild, they will become highly vulnerable to all the drug traffickers. And if they don't rebuild, then all their people will have to come here and, if they can't get here legally, they will try to become illegal immigrants. So there's all these things that we need to begin to see our relationships beyond our borders as more of an extension of our relationships with one another rather than as something totally different and apart from our relations with one another.

And anyway, I don't mean to give you a speech on that; I know you believe that. But the point I want to make is most people who run for Congress never have to think about these things unless they have a large immigrant population within their district from a particular place. So it doesn't—this kind of discussion we're having, because you understand the HIV/AIDS issue—I'm preaching to the choir here. But anything you can do to sort of just sit down

and walk through this with congressional delegations or their chiefs of staff or whoever the appropriate people are from around the country, I would really appreciate, because I think there is a lot of support. For example, you can always get good support in Congress, bipartisan, for a big increase in the Ryan White Act. And now we've finally got pretty good support in Congress, this whopping increase we had to help people purchase the drugs, the medicines. But it drops off markedly when you try to talk about the connection between what we're doing here at home and beyond our borders. And I really think you could help, because this is one example of a more general challenge the country will have to face more every year for the next 20 years, maybe forever, but certainly for the next 20 years.

Dr. Hitt. Mr. President, we really have made—probably hundreds of recommendations in the past few years, I mean—[*laughter*]. We've tried our best to narrow down——

The President. This is the most energetic—[*laughter*].

Dr. Hitt. But we have narrowed down a few specific initiatives we brought to your attention today. And the reason is clear, that we've talked to many administration officials and this is where we feel that there's a logjam that you can really help and get involved in and take it to heart.

The President. I will.

Dr. Hitt. And thank you again for meeting with us.

The President. Thank you for the dreidel, the book, the letters. I came away so well, I might have to make the room again. [*Laughter*] Thank you very much.

NOTE: The meeting began at 5:45 p.m. in the Cabinet Room at the White House.

United States-European Union Joint Statement on Cooperation in the Western Balkans
December 18, 1998

Political, civil, and economic instability in some areas of the Western Balkans threatens peace and prosperity in all southeastern Europe and poses serious challenges across Europe and beyond. During the past six months, we have

achieved notable successes and are agreed on further cooperative steps in the Western Balkans.

Our envoys in Kosovo, Ambassadors Chris Hill and Wolfgang Petritsch, are working as a team to conclude successfully negotiations on an interim political settlement for Kosovo. In Kosovo, the U.S. and EU are collaborating to ensure implementation of the October 16 OSCE-FRY Agreement, notably in the OSCE's Kosovo Verification Mission (KVM). We are extremely concerned that recent acts of violence in Kosovo could spiral out of control, and call on all parties to preserve the cease fire and cooperate fully with KVM.

We remain committed to enhancing quickly confidence-building and to supporting civil society in Kosovo. The EU welcomes the U.S. initiative to begin quick impact efforts in Kosovo immediately. The U.S. welcomes the European Union's intention to play the leadership role in organizing the international community's response on reconstruction issues, and pledges its full support. The EU intends to organize an expert-level meeting in January 1999, following the conclusion of the ongoing damage assessment mission. Once a political agreement is in place, further concrete steps on assisting reconstruction and on democratization and civic development will be taken, including convening a donors' conference. We look to the international community to contribute substantially towards the speedy implementation of these endeavors. At present, humanitarian aid should continue, responding to the most urgent needs, in close cooperation between the U.S. and EU and under the coordination of UNHCR, which is the lead agency for humanitarian aid as well as for the return of Internally Displaced Persons (IDPs) and refugees.

We expect the Albanian, as well as the Bosnian, authorities to take primary responsibility for stabilizing their respective countries and leading them towards full democracy and economic development.

In Albania, we worked together to form the Friends of Albania, which the EU co-chairs with the OSCE; we are both making a substantial political and material commitment to stabilization, democratization and economic reform. We have taken note of the new Government's pledges at the Tirana Conference October 30 to move towards those goals. We welcome the

adoption of the new Constitution, which is a fundamental first step in that direction. We strongly urge all political parties to cooperate in the democratic process in the interest of all Albanian people.

We have furthered our cooperation in support of Dayton implementation in Bosnia and Herzegovina, and in Croatia. The Bosnian national elections in September further advanced democracy and pluralism in that country. The U.S. and EU continue to provide resources to assist Dayton implementation efforts. We call on the authorities in both Bosnia and Herzegovina and Croatia to consistently support Dayton implementation efforts and contribute to the process of stabilization and national reconciliation, including by supporting the return of refugees and displaced persons to their previous homes as a matter of priority. Job creation, through self-sustaining economic development, will help stabilize the political and social situation and will enhance the return to a multiethnic Bosnia and Herzegovina. Economic revitalization is essential for sustainable returns, especially in minority areas.

We call on all in the region to support efforts to establish security and economic stability. Without this support, resolving regional conflicts and advancing democratic, civic, and economic reform is only more difficult. We will use our political and economic resources to support those who support these efforts and, more generally, to advance an agenda of democracy, progress toward self-sustaining free market economics, and normal relations with their neighbors. We condemn steps taken by the government in Belgrade to suppress independent media and political opposition, and express strong support for emerging democracy and political pluralism in Montenegro. A Federal Republic of Yugoslavia that respects the democratic and human rights of its citizens and that upholds its international obligations is essential for regional peace and security and its own integration into Europe.

NOTE: An original was not available for verification of the content of this joint declaration.

United States-European Union Statement on Cooperation in the Global Economy
December 18, 1998

The U.S. and the EU are engines for global economic growth. We share a common vision of a market-based global economy and particular responsibilities for promoting stability, continued growth and prosperity. We must lead the way in keeping markets open. A rules-based international trade system and a strengthened international financial system are necessary to ensure transparency and predictability and to maintain public confidence in the benefits of open economies. We are concerned about the serious social and economic impact of the financial crisis on many countries, and we will work together with them in the face of their major economic difficulties.

We are committed to promoting open markets through further broad-based liberalization, including through strengthening the multilateral trading system, and through the Transatlantic Economic Partnership (TEP) on which we agreed in London in May. We have drawn up, and started to implement, a Joint Action Plan to pursue this Partnership. It will contribute to further market opening and strengthening of links between the U.S. and EU economies in ways that support and point the way for further multilateral liberalization, while benefiting our peoples. The TEP initiative will enable us to launch bilateral negotiations for the further reduction of trade barriers. We have now set in train a regular and comprehensive dialogue between us on multilateral trade issues and future World Trade Organization (WTO) negotiations. We attach high importance to the full respect of multilateral rules. We are determined to resolve trade disputes between us.

The Mutual Recognition Agreement, which entered into force December 1, is an example of how the U.S. and EU are striving to remove transatlantic barriers. The agreement covers six sectors and will save our private sectors as much as $1 billion annually. In reducing trade barriers, we re-affirm our commitment to preserving high levels of health, safety, consumer and environmental protection. We strongly support the current bilateral discussions aimed at achieving high standards of data privacy protection and avoiding transatlantic interruptions in exchanges of personal data. While continuing current efforts to avoid such interruptions, we would like to conclude the discussions successfully as soon as possible.

We intend to enhance our economic dialogue and cooperation, both bilaterally and in the context of international institutions and fora, to ensure that we act in a coherent and constructive manner.

We agree on the need to strengthen the international financial system and national financial sectors in order to capture the full benefits of international capital flows and global markets, minimize disruption and better protect the poorest and most vulnerable. It is important that all in the global economy play their part to promote sustainable growth and financial stability, by pursuing economic policies aimed at strengthening their national economy and enhancing their economic performance. We reiterate the importance of implementing the October 30 recommendations of G7 Leaders and G7 Finance Ministers and Central Bank Governors and look forward to additional proposals that they will develop, in consultation with other key countries, prior to the Cologne Summit.

We welcome the impending introduction of the Euro on January 1, 1999, which will be an event of historic significance. We look forward to a successful European Economic and Monetary Union that contributes to growth and to stability in the international monetary system.

We reaffirm our commitment to development cooperation, which has among its main objectives the fight against poverty, the creation of conditions favorable to economic growth and sustainable development, and the participation of the most vulnerable in this process. The prompt and generous U.S. and EU responses to the devastation caused by Hurricane Mitch in Central America are an example of our commitment. We will seek to ensure good coordination of international donor assistance to respond effectively to crises.

We call upon developing countries and economies in transition to continue the liberalization of trade and to develop clear, stable, and open regimes for investment. We urge the crisis-affected countries to promote sustainable recovery by pursuing full and proper economic restructuring. We support IMF conditionality as a means to promote sound macroeconomic policies. We welcome the fact that several governments have acted swiftly to minimize the negative impact of the crisis. We stress the importance of good governance and the respect for human rights, including core labor standards, efficient and transparent institutions, and more effective investment in education, training, and research. We will seek to ensure and support fuller participation of the developing countries

in the WTO and in future multilateral trade negotiations, with a view to better integrating them into the world economic system. In particular, we will seek to improve the trading opportunities for the least developed countries. We will each continue to support regional integration efforts.

Senior officials will report to the next U.S.-EU Summit on the practical implementation of this cooperation on the global economy.

NOTE: An original was not available for verification of the content of this joint statement.

United States-European Union Declaration on the Middle East Peace Process
December 18, 1998

The signature on October 23 of the Wye River Memorandum broke a dangerous deadlock in the Middle East and opened the perspective for new progress in the Peace Process. We welcome implementation of the first phase of the Memorandum by both sides. We call on the parties to implement fully the remaining obligations, and thereby contribute to rebuilding the confidence essential to the completion of the Peace Process begun at Madrid and Oslo.

We will work together, including through our respective envoys, in the political and economic area, to build on this achievement and to help the parties move the Peace Process forward to a successful conclusion. We will use our partnership to support the implementation of outstanding elements of the Interim Agreement. We will work for the early resumption of the Multilateral Track of the Process. We will also

seek ways to help the parties in the Lebanese and Syrian tracks to restart negotiations with the aim of reaching a comprehensive settlement.

Alongside other participants at the November 30 Washington Conference to Support Middle East Peace and Development, we made significant additional pledges of economic assistance to the West Bank and Gaza for the next five years. Against this background, the U.S. and the EU will continue their leading roles in the Palestinian donor effort in order to ensure that international assistance translates into tangible improvements in the living conditions of the Palestinians, starting at the coming meeting of the Ad Hoc Liaison Committee in February in Germany.

NOTE: An original was not available for verification of the content of this joint declaration.

Joint United States-European Union Statement on Chapter IV New Transatlantic Agenda Dialogues
December 18, 1998

The United States and European Union affirm their commitment to the process of strengthening and broadening public support on

both sides of the Atlantic for the U.S.-EU partnership by fostering "people-to-people" transatlantic links between non-governmental actors.

We applaud the steps taken during the Austrian EU Presidency to further the process of building bridges across the Atlantic, in particular, the establishment of the Transatlantic Consumer Dialogue and the on-going and constructive input we receive from the Transatlantic Business Dialogue. We have given encouragement to the Transatlantic Labor Dialogue to develop further its program of work. Building on work that began this year, we look forward to the formal launching of a Transatlantic Environmental Dialogue early next year. We welcome contacts that are taking place between development NGOs with a view to the possibility of establishing a Transatlantic Development Dialogue.

We look forward to these dialogues providing recommendations to us on an ongoing basis on issues of mutual concern, as they have done for today's Summit. We welcome input from these dialogues as well as other sectors of society to help shape our agenda.

We will work with all of the transatlantic dialogues to ensure that lines of communication to government are balanced and open. We will work with the dialogues to help ensure their sustainability. This process will require resources and support from outside of government, and we will encourage the development of links with the private sector, including foundations. We reaffirm our commitment to support initiatives to deepen the commercial, social, cultural, scientific and educational ties between our respective societies. We recognize that there is much that our transatlantic communities can learn from one another.

NOTE: An original was not available for verification of the content of this joint statement.

Message on the Observance of Ramadan
December 18, 1998

Warm greetings to all those observing the holy month of Ramadan.

Ramadan is a special time of reflection and renewal for Muslims around the world, including the 6 million Americans who are making Islam one of our nation's fastest-growing religions. Through fasting and devoted reading of the Koran, Muslims strengthen their faith in God and deepen the compassion that gives their faith such dignity and power in the eyes of Muslims and non-Muslims alike. It is a time for renewing our spirituality and for recognizing our common humanity. It is a time to remember all that we have done and all that we have yet to do to make this world worthy of its Creator.

As the crescent moon rises, and the ninth month begins, Hillary joins me in extending best wishes to you and your families for health, prosperity, and happiness. May our prayers for a better world soon be answered.

BILL CLINTON

Letter to Congressional Leaders on the Military Strikes Against Iraq
December 18, 1998

Dear Mr. Speaker: (Dear Mr. President:)

At approximately 5:00 p.m. eastern standard time on December 16, 1998, at my direction, U.S. military forces conducted missile and aircraft strikes in Iraq in response to Iraqi breaches of its obligations under resolutions of the United Nations Security Council. The strikes will degrade Iraq's ability to develop and deliver weapons of mass destruction (WMD) and its ability to threaten its neighbors. This action, carried out in concert with military forces of the United Kingdom, enjoys the support of many of our friends and allies. It is consistent with and has been taken in support of numerous U.N. Security Council resolutions, including Resolutions 678 and 687, which authorize U.N. Member States to use "all necessary means" to implement the Security Council resolutions and to restore peace and security in the region and establish the terms of the cease-fire mandated by the Council, including those related to the destruction of Iraq's WMD programs.

United States strikes are ongoing. United States forces have targeted facilities that are actively involved in WMD and ballistic missile activities, or pose a threat to Iraq's neighbors or to U.S. forces conducting this operation.

At the same time I ordered the strikes, I authorized the deployment of additional U.S. forces to Southwest Asia. These forces include U.S. Army, U.S. Navy, and U.S. Air Force units to reinforce those forces already present in the region. These forces will remain in the region as long as is necessary to protect the national security interests of the United States.

I directed these actions pursuant to my authority under the Constitution as Commander in Chief and as Chief Executive, and to conduct U.S. foreign relations, as well as under the Authorization for Use of Military Force Against Iraq Resolution (Public Law 102–1) enacted in January 1991.

I am providing this report as part of my efforts to keep the Congress fully informed, consistent with Public Law 102–1. I appreciate the support of the Congress as we continue to take all necessary steps to secure Iraqi compliance with U.N. Security Council resolutions.

Sincerely,

BILL CLINTON

NOTE: Identical letters were sent to Newt Gingrich, Speaker of the House of Representatives, and Strom Thurmond, President pro tempore of the Senate.

Address to Arab Nations
December 19, 1998

Thank you for this opportunity to address America's friends throughout the Arab and the entire Islamic world. I want to explain why we have taken military action against Saddam Hussein, and why we believe this action is in the interests of the Iraqi people and all the people of the Middle East.

Saddam has ruled through a reign of terror against his own people and disregard for the peace of the region. His war against Iran cost at least half a million lives over 10 years. He gassed Kurdish civilians in northern Iraq. In 1990 his troops invaded Kuwait, executing those who resisted, looting the country, spilling tens of millions of gallons of oil into the Gulf, firing missiles at Saudi Arabia, Bahrain, Israel, and Qatar. He massacred thousands of his own people in an uprising in 1991.

As a condition for the Gulf war cease-fire, Iraq agreed to disclose and to destroy its weapons of mass destruction and to demonstrate its willingness to live at peace with its neighbors. Iraq could have ended economic sanctions and isolation long ago by meeting these simple obligations. Instead, it has spent nearly 8 years defying them. Saddam has failed to disclose information about his weapons arsenal. He has threatened his neighbors and refused to account for hundreds of Kuwaitis still missing from 1991.

Each time Saddam has provoked a crisis, we've tried hard to find a peaceful solution, consulting our friends in the Arab world and working through the United Nations. A month ago we joined the other 14 members of the U.N. Security Council in demanding that Saddam come into compliance immediately. We supported what Iraq said it wanted: a comprehensive review of its compliance after it resumed full cooperation with the U.N. weapons inspectors. And we were gratified when eight Arab nations, Egypt, Syria, Saudi Arabia, Kuwait, Bahrain, Qatar, the UAE, and Oman, warned that Iraq would bear the blame—Iraq alone would bear the blame for the consequences of defying the U.N.

Now, I canceled a military strike when, at the last moment, Saddam promised to cooperate unconditionally with the inspectors. But this month he broke his promises again, and again defied the U.N. So, we had to act. Saddam simply must not be allowed to threaten his neighbors or the world with nuclear arms, poison gas, or biological weapons.

America understands that Saddam's first victims are his own people. That is why we exempted food and medicine when sanctions were imposed on Iraq. That is why, since 1991, we have offered to allow Iraq to sell its oil and use the proceeds to pay for humanitarian supplies. For 5 years, Saddam rejected that offer while building lavish palaces for himself and diverting resources to his military.

Finally, in 1996, Saddam allowed the oil-for-food program to take effect. Since then, the U.N. has delivered nearly $3 billion worth of food and medicine to the Iraqi people every year. Without the watchful eye of the U.N., we would soon see the oil-for-food program become oil-for-tanks, leading to less food for the Iraqi people and more danger for Iraq's neighbors.

No decision to use force is easy, especially at a time when I'm working so hard to build peace in the Middle East and to strengthen our own relations with the Arab world. My visit to Gaza last week reflected my deep commitment to the peace process. I will never forget the warm welcome I received from the Palestinian people, eager to shape their own future at last.

Let me also state my deep respect for the holy month of Ramadan. In the days ahead, I hope all Muslims will consider America's sincere desire to work with all people in the Middle East to build peace. We have the most profound admiration for Islam. Our dispute is with a leader who threatens Muslims and non-Muslims alike.

As the crescent moon rises, and the ninth month begins, Muslim-Americans and all Americans wish you the blessings of faith and friendship. May our prayers for a better world soon be answered.

Ramadan Kareem [Blessed Ramadan].

NOTE: This address was videotaped at approximately 12:20 p.m. in the Cabinet Room on December 18 for later broadcast on the U.S. Information Agency WORLDNET. In his address, the President referred to President Saddam Hussein of Iraq. The transcript was made available by the Office of the Press Secretary on December 18 but was embargoed for release until 7 a.m. on December 19. A tape was not available for verification of the content of this address.

The President's Radio Address
December 19, 1998

Good morning. As I speak to you, America's men and women in uniform and our British allies are fighting for security, peace, and freedom in the Persian Gulf. They're doing an outstanding job, showing bravery and skill, making our country proud. Our thoughts and prayers are with them.

Putting our troops in harm's way is the hardest decision any President faces. I believe our action in Iraq clearly is in America's interest. Never again can we allow Saddam Hussein to develop nuclear weapons, poison gas, biological weapons, or missiles to deliver them. He has used such terrible weapons before against soldiers, against his neighbors, against civilians. And if left unchecked, he'll use them again.

For 7½ years, United Nations weapons inspectors did a truly remarkable job in forcing Saddam to disclose and destroy weapons he insisted he did not have. But over the past year, Saddam repeatedly has blocked their efforts. Each time, with intensive diplomacy backed by the threat of force, we compelled him to back down.

Last month, when he agreed to fully cooperate, I canceled an American military action. But I, along with Prime Minister Tony Blair of Great Britain, made it absolutely clear that if he did not fully cooperate, we would have no choice but to act without further negotiation or warning.

For 3 weeks, the U.N. inspectors tested Saddam's commitment. He failed the test, hindering and preventing inspections, withholding and destroying documents. As their chairman concluded, the inspectors can no longer do their vital job. Under these circumstances, had we failed to respond, it would have given Saddam a green light to rebuild his arsenal and threaten his neighbors.

I acted quickly because, as my military advisors stressed, the longer we waited, the more time Saddam would have to disperse his forces and protect his arsenal. Our mission is clear: to degrade Saddam's capacity to develop and deliver weapons of mass destruction and threaten the region. Based on reports from the Secretary of Defense, the Chairman of the Joint Chiefs, and the CIA Director, I believe the mission is going well.

Now, where do we go from here? Our long-term strategy is clear: First, we stand ready to use force again if Saddam takes threatening action such as seeking to reconstitute his weapons of mass destruction, menacing his neighbors or his own Kurdish citizens, or challenging allied aircraft.

Second, so long as Iraq fails to live up to its obligations, we'll work with the international community to keep the sanctions in place. They have cost Saddam more than $120 billion, resources he would have devoted to rebuilding his weaponry. At the same time, we will continue to support the ongoing program to provide humanitarian supplies to the people of Iraq, so that Saddam uses his oil to buy food and medicine, not tanks and missiles.

Finally, we'll strengthen our engagement with Iraqis who want a new government, one that will respect its citizens and live in peace with its neighbors. We must not harbor illusions, however, that change will come easily or quickly. But we should go forward, and we will, with determination, working with opposition groups, strengthening the global consensus for bringing Iraq a government worthy of its people.

As our forces carry out their missions, I want to express my heartfelt thanks to all our soldiers, sailors, airmen, and marines in the Gulf and all around the world, who work every day to defend our freedom, promote stability and democracy, and bring hope. To those forces now engaged in the battle against Saddam Hussein, you have our appreciation for your courage, and our Nation's hopes for your safe and successful return.

To all those in our Armed Forces who will spend this holiday season away from home, away from your loved ones, we thank you for your service. You are helping to ensure a just and peaceful world.

As we enter the season of peace, we remain ever hopeful that one day all nations and all communities will actually live in peace, with tolerance, respect, and civility. There can be no greater gift for our children.

Thanks for listening.

NOTE: The President spoke at 10:06 a.m. from the Oval Office at the White House. In his remarks, he referred to President Saddam Hussein of Iraq and Richard Butler, executive chairman, United Nations Special Commission.

Remarks Following the House of Representatives Vote on Impeachment
December 19, 1998

Good afternoon. Let me begin by expressing my profound and heartfelt thanks to Congressman Gephardt and the leadership and all the members of the Democratic caucus for what they did today. I thank the few brave Republicans who withstood enormous pressure to stand with them for the plain meaning of the Constitution and for the proposition that we need to pull together, to move beyond partisanship, to get on with the business of our country.

I thank the millions upon millions of American citizens who have expressed their support and their friendship to Hillary, to me, to our family, and to our administration during these last several weeks.

The words of the Members here with me and others who were a part of their endeavor, in defense of our Constitution, were powerful and moving, and I will never forget them. The question is, what are we going to do now?

I have accepted responsibility for what I did wrong in my personal life. And I have invited Members of Congress to work with us to find a reasonable, bipartisan, and proportionate response. That approach was rejected today by Republicans in the House. But I hope it will be embraced by the Senate. I hope there will be a constitutional and fair means of resolving this matter in a prompt manner.

Meanwhile, I will continue to do the work of the American people. We still, after all, have to save Social Security and Medicare for the 21st century. We have to give all our children world-class schools. We have to pass a Patients' Bill of Rights. We have to make sure the economic turbulence around the world does not curb our economic opportunity here at home. We have to keep America the world's strongest force for peace and freedom. In short, we have a lot to do before we enter the 21st century.

And we still have to keep working to build that elusive one America I have talked so much about. For 6 years now, I have done everything I could to bring our country together, across the lines that divide us, including bringing Washington together across party lines. Out in the country, people are pulling together. But just as America is coming together, it must look—from the country's point of view—like Washington is coming apart.

I want to echo something Mr. Gephardt said. It is something I have felt strongly all my life. We must stop the politics of personal destruction. We must get rid of the poisonous venom of excessive partisanship, obsessive animosity, and uncontrolled anger. That is not what America deserves. That is not what America is about.

We are doing well now. We are a good and decent country. But we have significant challenges we have to face. In order to do it right, we have to have some atmosphere of decency and civility, some presumption of good faith, some sense of proportionality and balance in bringing judgment against those who are in different parties. We have important work to do. We need a constructive debate that has all the different voices in this country heard in the Halls of Congress.

I want the American people to know today that I am still committed to working with people of good faith and good will of both parties to do what's best for our country: to bring our Nation together, to lift our people up, to move us all forward together. It's what I've tried to do for 6 years; it's what I intend to do for 2 more, until the last hour of the last day of my term.

So, with profound gratitude for the defense of the Constitution and the best in America that was raised today by the Members here and those who joined them, I ask the American people to move with me to go on from here; to rise above the rancor; to overcome the pain and division; to be a repairer of the breach, all of us; to make this country, as one America, what it can and must be for our children in the new century about to dawn.

Thank you very much.

NOTE: The President spoke at 4:15 p.m. on the South Lawn at the White House. The transcript released by the Office of the Press Secretary also included the remarks of Chief of Staff John D. Podesta, House Minority Leader Richard A. Gephardt, and Vice President Al Gore.

Address to the Nation on Completion of Military Strikes in Iraq
December 19, 1998

On Wednesday I ordered our Armed Forces to strike military and strategic targets in Iraq. They were joined by British forces. That operation is now complete, in accordance with our 70-hour plan.

My national security team has just briefed me on the results. They are preliminary, but let me say just a few words about why we acted, what we have achieved, and where we want to go.

We began with this basic proposition: Saddam Hussein must not be allowed to develop nuclear arms, poison gas, biological weapons, or the means to deliver them. He has used such weapons before against soldiers and civilians, including his own people. We have no doubt that, if left unchecked, he would do so again.

Saddam must not be prepared to defy the will—be permitted—excuse me—to defy the will of the international community. Without a firm response, he would have been emboldened to do that again and again.

For 7½ years now, the United Nations weapons inspectors have done a truly remarkable job in forcing Saddam to disclose and destroy weapons and missiles he insisted he did not have. But over the past year, Saddam has repeatedly sought to cripple the inspection system. Each time, through intensive diplomatic efforts backed by the threat of military action, Saddam has backed down. When he did so last month, I made it absolutely clear that if he did not give UNSCOM full cooperation this time, we would act swiftly and without further delay.

For 3 weeks, the inspectors tested Saddam's commitment to cooperate. They repeatedly ran into roadblocks and restrictions, some of them new. As their chairman, Richard Butler, concluded in his report to the United Nations on Tuesday, the inspectors no longer were able to do their job. So far as I was concerned, Saddam's days of cheat and retreat were over.

Our objectives in this military action were clear: to degrade Saddam's weapons of mass destruction program and related delivery systems, as well as his capacity to attack his neighbors. It will take some time to make a detailed assessment of our operation, but based on the briefing I've just received, I am confident we have achieved our mission. We have inflicted significant damage on Saddam's weapons of mass destruction programs, on the command structures that direct and protect that capability, and on his military and security infrastructure. In a short while, Secretary Cohen and General Shelton will give you a more detailed analysis from the Pentagon.

So long as Saddam remains in power, he will remain a threat to his people, his region, and the world. With our allies, we must pursue a strategy to contain him and to constrain his weapons of mass destruction program, while working toward the day Iraq has a government willing to live at peace with its people and with its neighbors.

Let me describe the elements of that strategy going forward. First, we will maintain a strong military presence in the area, and we will remain ready to use it if Saddam tries to rebuild his weapons of mass destruction, strikes out at his neighbors, challenges allied aircraft, or moves against the Kurds. We also will continue to enforce no-fly zones in the north and from the

southern suburbs of Baghdad to the Kuwaiti border.

Second, we will sustain what have been among the most extensive sanctions in U.N. history. To date, they have cost Saddam more than $120 billion, resources that otherwise would have gone toward rebuilding his military. At the same time, we will support a continuation of the oil-for-food program, which generates more than $10 billion a year for food, medicine, and other critical humanitarian supplies for the Iraqi people. We will insist that Iraq's oil be used for food, not tanks.

Third, we would welcome the return of UNSCOM and the International Atomic Energy Agency back into Iraq to pursue their mandate from the United Nations, provided that Iraq first takes concrete, affirmative, and demonstrable actions to show that it will fully cooperate with the inspectors. But if UNSCOM is not allowed to resume its work on a regular basis, we will remain vigilant and prepared to use force if we see that Iraq is rebuilding its weapons programs.

Now, over the long-term, the best way to end the threat that Saddam poses to his own people in the region is for Iraq to have a different government. We will intensify our engagement with the Iraqi opposition groups, prudently and effectively. We will work with Radio Free Iraq to help news and information flow freely to the country. And we will stand ready to help a new leadership in Baghdad that abides by its international commitments and respects the rights of its own people. We hope it will return Iraq to its rightful place in the community of nations.

Let me say in closing, again, how terribly proud I am of our men and women in uniform. Once again they have done a difficult job with skill, dedication, and determination. I also want to say that I am very proud of our national security team. I want to thank Secretary Cohen and General Shelton; I want to thank Secretary Albright and Sandy Berger. The Vice President and I have relied on them very heavily; they have performed with extraordinary ability and restraint, as well as effectiveness. I am very, very grateful for the way this operation was planned and executed.

But again, foremost, I want to give my thanks to our men and women in uniform. We are waiting for the last planes to come home and praying that we'll be able to tell you tomorrow that every last one of them has returned home safely.

Thank you very much.

NOTE: The President spoke at 6 p.m. in the Roosevelt Room at the White House. In his address, he referred to President Saddam Hussein of Iraq; and Richard Butler, executive chairman, United Nations Special Commission (UNSCOM).

Remarks at D.C. Central Kitchen
December 21, 1998

Thank you. Good afternoon. I'm delighted to be here, delighted to see all of you. I want to thank Robert Egger and everybody here at the D.C. Central Kitchen for the magnificent job they do. Thank you, Harris Wofford, and all the wonderful AmeriCorps volunteers. Thank you, Secretary Glickman. Thank you, Tony Hall, for a lifetime of commitment to the cause embodied by this endeavor here.

I would like to thank Jill Muller, who worked with us, the young AmeriCorps volunteer. I'd like to thank Donna Simmons, the trainee who worked with us, who is very happy about the work she's doing. She has six children at home getting ready to celebrate Christmas. And this Christmas and the Christmases in the future, I think, will be brighter because of the work that has been done here.

I want to thank Susan Callahan for not only training Donna but for training Hillary and me to mass-produce lasagna today. [*Laughter*] We got—I think Jill said we got a reasonably good evaluation. We finished our task; we made enough lasagna for 500 people to eat in a timely and, I hope, edible fashion. But we enjoyed it very, very much.

There is another person, who is not here, I'd like to acknowledge who has been a great supporter of these causes, and that's Congresswoman Eleanor Holmes Norton. She is elsewhere in the city today, hosting an event for needy children.

I would like the members of the press and, through them, the public who are not here to know that since this remarkable organization began on January 20, 1989, D.C. Central Kitchen has taken 3½ million pounds of surplus donated food, turned them into 5.5 million meals for men in homeless shelters, women in battered women's shelters, children in after-school and child care programs. In the process, D.C. Central Kitchen has provided job skills and opportunities in training for a couple hundred Americans who needed it, with a very, very high percentage of people getting jobs and keeping them after 6 months.

You have found here an incredible, I think, an incredible social recipe to combine things that others may be working on but have never been quite put together in this same way. Every day, as much as we hate to admit it, there are people in America who get up hungry and who go to bed hungry. Yet every day, 25 percent of our food supply—25 percent—is wasted, from slightly bruised fruit at wholesale markets to unsold trays of lasagna at restaurants. While the food is going to waste, so are the abilities of millions of Americans who want to work but can't because they don't have skills for which there is a demand in today's economy.

The number of food-service jobs in our country is large and growing. Food-service wages are rising at twice the rate of inflation today. Therefore, the secret recipe is to take the wasted food and the wasted capacity, train people, put the food there, and solve the problem. It is a remarkable achievement. And as has already been said, the private sector has made major contributions to this endeavor.

I'd like to just acknowledge, if I might, the fact that—and this is something that I think is maybe most important of all—D.C. Central Kitchen has become a real model for others. And now there are similar efforts in 11 cities, from Chicago to Louisville, with 14 more slated to start by this time next year. So I think that is the ultimate test of your success when people copy you. That is the sincerest form of flattery, I think, and I know you're proud of that.

In 1996 I signed the Bill Emerson Good Samaritan Food Donation Act to try to have Government do more to help. It gives limited liability protection to companies that donate food and people like those who work here to process and redistribute the food. Secretary Glickman had a lot to do with the passage of that law, and I thank him. I'd also like to thank the Departments of Housing and Urban Development and Labor for providing food, training, and other resources. I know the Labor Department supports the training program here. So the Government can be a good partner.

And finally, as a matter of personal pride, I want to say again, I thank the AmeriCorps members. When we started AmeriCorps, I thought it would catch on. But to be frank, there's been even more interest in it and more commitment from more different kinds of people to serve their country in more different ways than even I could have imagined. And I thank all of you for being the best of America at this Christmas season. God bless you, and thank you very much.

Now, Hillary alluded to this, but I think I can't leave the microphone without saying that in 1993 in January, D.C. Central Kitchen baked 28,000 saxophone-shaped, butter-almond cookies for my first Inaugural. [*Laughter*] And it's about time I came here to pay them back—and also

cakes for the second Inaugural. I'm grateful for that.

I hope that everyone who sees the report on the news of all of our being here today will be inspired to follow suit at this Christmas season. The most important gifts we give are those that we give to those who need it the most, who may never know our names or remember our faces but who receive the gifts in the genuine spirit of the season.

And to all of you, those of you who are trainees, those of you who are volunteers, those of you who are AmeriCorps workers, all of you, I thank you. And most of all, Mr. Egger, I thank you and the people here at D.C. Central Kitchen. And I hope that as the news of this event beams across the country tonight, in the remaining days before Christmas and then in all the days of the new year, more people will want to make the kind of contribution to our common humanity that you have.

Thank you very much.

NOTE: The President spoke at 1:12 p.m. in the lunchroom. In his remarks, he referred to Robert Egger, director, Susan Callahan, executive chef, and Donna Simmons, trainee, D.C. Central Kitchen. He also referred to the Bill Emerson Good Samaritan Food Donation Act, Public Law 104–210.

Remarks at the Pan Am Flight 103 Bombing 10th Anniversary Observance in Arlington, Virginia
December 21, 1998

Lord Monro, Sir Christopher, chaplain, members of the Cabinet, Senator Kennedy, and most of all, the members of the families of Pan Am 103: I would like to begin by thanking all of you for giving Hillary and me the chance to be here today, and with a special word of appreciation to Jane Schultz for her efforts to bring us all together and to keep us all remembering and acting.

Even though it is painful today to remember what happened 10 years ago, it is necessary, necessary to remember that the people on that plane were students coming home for the holidays, tourists going on vacation in America, families looking forward to a long-awaited reunion,

business people on a routine flight. Their average age was just 27. Last week in the annual report on the condition of the health of the American people, the average life expectancy of Americans has now exceeded 76; their average age was 27. Beneath them, the people of Lockerbie were sitting down to supper on a quiet winter evening. And of course, we have already heard the names; those of you who loved them have relived their lives in that awful moment.

Now, for 10 years, you have cherished your memories, and you have lived with the thought, I'm sure, of what might have been. You have also, for 10 years, been steadfast in your determination to stand against terrorism and to demand justice. And people all around the world have stood with you, shared your outrage, admired your fellowship with one another, and watched with awed respect your determined campaign for justice. Although 10 years or 20 or 30 or 50 may never be long enough for the sorrow to fade, we pray it will not be too long now before the wait for justice and resolution is over.

We dedicate this day of the winter solstice to the memory of all who were lost, to the families who understand its meaning as no others can. We dedicate each day that follows—as the Sun rises higher and brighter in the morning sky and the daylight hours lengthen—to our common pursuit of truth and justice and to our common efforts to ensure that what happened 10 years ago to those of you here will not occur again.

I know I speak for every American citizen when I say a simple, humble, heartfelt thank-you for all you have done to keep the memory and spirit of your loved ones alive by the memorials you have built, the scholarships you have funded, the charities you have supported. We thank you for reaching out to one another, to the people of Lockerbie, to all others who have been victims of terrorism. We thank you for helping to strengthen the resolve of nations to defeat terror, to deny safe haven to terrorists, to isolate those who sponsor them. We thank you for working to improve security for air travelers and for all the lives your work has saved. We thank you for your determination to see that things that are good and meaningful and lasting come out of your overpowering tragedy. And we thank you for not letting the world forget that it is necessary and right to pursue the perpetrators of this crime, no matter how long it takes.

I thank you for what you have done to drive me to work harder on your behalf, not just the imperative of fighting terror but the passion and commitment and conviction of the families who have spoken to me and to the members of my administration, who all remind us this cannot be considered a mere misfortune; this was deliberate murder. And while all of us have to strive for reconciliation in our hearts, we must also pursue justice and accountability.

You know better than anyone else it is beyond your power to alter the past. There is no such thing as perfect justice. No trial or penalty or illumination of the facts can compensate you for the profound loss you have suffered. But as long as we can bring those responsible before the bar of justice and have a real trial, you have a right—and society has a need—to see that done.

We owe this not only to you but to all Americans who seek justice; for this was a tragedy felt by every American and, indeed, every man and woman of good will around the world. And none of us want to live in a world where such violence goes unpunished and people can kill with impunity. And none of us will be safe as long as there is a single place on our planet where terrorists can find sanctuary.

That is why our Nation has never given up the search for justice. For 10 years we have ensured that Libya cannot be a member of the international community until it turns over suspects in this case. That is why, in late August, after speaking with many of you, we put forward the initiative which has already been referred to: try the two suspects before a Scottish court sitting in The Netherlands.

Since then the Libyan leader, Mr. Qadhafi, has given us mixed signals. We believe there is still some possibility he will accept our offer. That would be the best outcome, for it would mean that finally there would be a trial. But let me be absolutely clear to all of you: Our policy is not to trust Mr. Qadhafi's claims; it is to test them. This is a take-it-or-leave-it offer. We will not negotiate its terms. If the suspects are convicted, they will serve their time in Scotland. And if the suspects are not turned over by the time of the next sanctions review, we will work at the United Nations with our allies and friends to seek yet stronger measures against Libya. In doing so, we will count on the support of all nations that counseled us to make this proposal in the first place. If the proposal fails, all should make clear that the responsibility falls on Mr. Qadhafi alone.

I make that commitment here, amidst the silent white rows and the heroes that rest beneath, at this place of remembrance where we come to pay tribute to those who lived bravely and often died too young for our Nation. This is a place where Americans come to gather the strength of memory to carry on into tomorrow. It is altogether fitting that this cairn was placed here in memory of your loved ones, for we have a duty to them no less profound than our duty to those who are buried here. Each stone in this monument is a memory, and each memory, a call to action.

The poet William Blake wrote: "To see a world in a grain of sand, and heaven in a wild flower, hold infinity in the palm of your hand, and eternity in an hour." That poem is inscribed at St. Paul's Cathedral in London. Ten years ago it was copied down by a young American who carried it on her final flight home, Pan Am 103. It reminds us of the dreams that terrible day left unfulfilled, but also of this eternal significance of all those lives that were lived fully, though too briefly, and of the infinite importance of each act of charity and faith committed in their memory.

Like the stones of this cairn, our memories of those we lost remain strong. And so must our determination be to complete on their behalf the unfinished business ahead. To that solemn task, I pledge you my best efforts. And I ask for your continued commitment, your continued involvement, your continued education of your fellow Americans, and your continued loving memories acted out to benefit those you may never know—for you are making a safer, fairer, more just world.

God bless you all, and God bless America.

NOTE: The President spoke at 2:23 p.m. at the Memorial Cairn to the victims of Pan Am 103 in Arlington National Cemetery. In his remarks, he referred to Lord Monro of Langholm (Hector Monro), who represented the Lockerbie area in the British House of Commons in 1988; British Ambassador to the U.S. Sir Christopher Meyer; Lt. Col. Ronald Wunsch, USA, chaplain, Fort McNair; Jane Schultz, mother of one of the victims and chief organizer of the memorial, who introduced the President; Pan Am 103 bombing suspects Lamen Khalifa Fhimah and Abdel Basset Ali al-Megrahi; and Libyan leader Col. Muammar Qadhafi.

Statement on Pay Raises for Armed Forces Personnel
December 21, 1998

In consultation with my Secretary of Defense, William Cohen, and the Joint Chiefs of Staff, I have decided to make significant improvements in pay and other compensation for our men and women in uniform. The defense budget I will submit to Congress for next year will include a pay raise of 4.4 percent for 2000, a restructuring of pay to reward performance as well as length of service, and an increase in retirement benefits.

These improvements will enhance the quality of life for our men and women in uniform, will encourage long-term service by the most talented service men and women, and will increase the Armed Forces' military readiness to engage fully, at any time, in order to protect the security and interests of the United States.

The sacrifices of our men and women in the Armed Forces are most vivid during the holidays while those of us at home are celebrating a time of peace with loved ones and family. As events in the Gulf showed us only days ago, our service men and women are asked by their Nation to travel far from home and to put their lives on the line to defend our interests.

I am proud of the men and women of our military, and I am pleased that they will receive the pay and retirement increases they richly deserve. Coupled with recent quality-of-life initiatives in housing, child care, and other areas, these improvements will continue to enhance the quality of life for American service men and women.

Message on the Observance of Christmas, 1998
December 22, 1998

Warm greetings to everyone celebrating Christmas.

Each year during this season of light and hope, of sharing and giving, we celebrate the birth of a Child. This Child came into the world with only a stable's roof to shelter Him; yet He grew to teach a lesson of love that continues to enrich our lives 2,000 years later.

That love is at the heart of Christmas. It is the love we give our children, who make our world radiant with joy and promise. It is the love of family and friends that inspires every gift and greeting we receive. It is the love that moves us to reject the prejudices that divide us. It is the love that calls us to ease the suffering of those touched by poverty, illness, injustice, or oppression. Above all, it is the love of God for each of us, revealed in the timeless gift of His Son.

Wherever Americans gather to celebrate the birth of Jesus, let us give thanks for the precious gift of love that graces our lives and lights our way toward a better future.

Hillary joins me in sending our warmest wishes for a memorable Christmas and a new year bright with the hope of joy and peace.

BILL CLINTON

Message on the Observance of Kwanzaa, 1998
December 22, 1998

Warm greetings to everyone observing Kwanzaa.

In millions of homes across America and around the world, the holiday of Kwanzaa is both a solemn and a joyous occasion. It is a time to honor God and to reaffirm a commitment to the values of love, community, and responsibility. It is a celebration of the diverse cultures within the African diaspora and a time to give thanks for the blessings of family and friendship. It is also an opportunity to reflect on the lessons and legacy of the past so that we might build a better future.

The seven principles of Kwanzaa—unity, self-determination, collective work and responsibility, cooperative economics, purpose, creativity, and faith—echo many of the same ideals that inspired our country's founders and shaped our nation's character. Crossing lines of religion, culture, and background, these common values help us to forge stronger families and communities and compel us to achieve our highest goals.

As families across our nation gather to celebrate this festive holiday, Hillary and I extend warmest wishes for a joyous Kwanzaa and a new year of peace and happiness.

BILL CLINTON

Christmas Greeting to the Nation
December 23, 1998

The President. On this joyous occasion, Hillary and I would like to wish all of you a very Merry Christmas. As we gather around our Christmas trees and dinner tables, let's take the time to give thanks for the blessings of the year just passed, to rejoice in our children, to enjoy the company of family and friends.

As we approach the feast of light, I'd like also to send a special greeting to all the brave men and women in uniform who are serving our country in lands far from home. You're in our hearts and our prayers. On behalf of all Americans, I thank you for the greatest gift of the season, for protecting our Nation and safeguarding the freedom we all hold dear.

The First Lady. Christmas reminds us that the values we share far outweigh whatever the differences there are between us. The twinkle of a child's eye, the joy of a grandmother's laughter, the love in the hearts of mothers and fathers for their children, all these blessings should be unwrapped on Christmas morning.

The President. May the spirit of the season be with you today and throughout the year. From our family to yours, Merry Christmas, Happy New Year, and God bless you all.

NOTE: The greeting was videotaped at approximately 11:30 a.m. on December 7 in the Diplomatic Reception Room for later broadcast. The transcript was released by the Office of the Press Secretary on December 23.

Remarks at a Housing and Urban Development Grant Announcement in Baltimore, Maryland
December 23, 1998

Thank you very much. Thank you. Well, if Christa Spangler hasn't put us in the spirit of the season, I don't know who could. Didn't she do a magnificent job? [*Applause*] Thank you very much. Thank you. Thank you, Secretary Cuomo, for your remarks and your remarkable work.

I want to say at this holiday season, the beginning of the Muslim holy month of Ramadan, the season of Hanukkah for Jewish-Americans, and Christmas for those of us who are Christians, when we are told we should count our blessings, one of the things that has been a great blessing for me in the last 6 years as President has been my proximity to and involvement with the city of Baltimore and the State of Maryland.

I have—as you heard Mayor Schmoke say, starting in 1992, I have visited the churches here; I have walked the streets here; I have seen the children here in their schools and their environmental projects and in other ways. I have loved this State. I have been to Annapolis and to Clinton, Maryland—[*laughter*]—and to Montgomery County—and Wayne—and to, obviously so many times, to Camp David and the environs there. And I feel very blessed.

But I was looking at your elected Representatives: Elijah Cummings, who is very well named; he sounds like a prophet about half the time; and I was thinking that there is no State in the country that has a pair of Senators with quite the combination of intelligence, compassion, and energy, and plain old pull that Mary-

land does. And I am so grateful for the work that Governor Glendening and Lieutenant Governor Kathleen Kennedy Townsend have done.

As all of you know, I've had also a special friendship with Mayor Schmoke, and I sort of regret the fact that both of us will be retiring before you know it. [*Laughter*] But he did a remarkable job. He has done and he has some more remarkable things to do for this city, and I thank him for that.

I'd also like to thank the other State legislators, county officials, city council members who are here. I'd like to thank the AmeriCorps members who are here for the wonderful work they do and the residents of Pleasant View Gardens.

You know, there's been a lot of talk today about this project as an embodiment of the community America can become. There's been a lot of talk today about the spirit of one America, as Secretary Cuomo said. But I think it's important, if you'll forgive me just one religious reference at Christmas time, that we remember what Christa Spangler said: Anybody can become homeless. What does that mean? That means: There, but for the grace of God, go I. And it means that in our minds, we should be going there.

Most people, most Christians at the Christian season read the Christmas story in Matthew or Luke. But at the end—along toward the end of the Book of Matthew, there is a great sermon where Jesus says—and I won't go through the whole thing, but basically: "Even as you have done it unto the least of these, you have done it unto me."

Now, what that really means is not what most people think. It doesn't really mean go out and give a bunch of money to poor people so you can feel righteous. That's not what it means. It means—what it really means is, whether you're tall or short, whether you're fat or thin, whether you're black, brown, or white, whether you look like a movie star or a person who had one boxing match too many—[*laughter*]—whatever the different circumstances of your life are, inside each of us there is a core that is the same and not one person is better than another. That's what it really means. That's what it really means.

So when I talk about one America, I don't mean that it makes me feel good to help people who are the least of these. What the real Biblical message is, is that there is no least of these. It is not an accident that the birth occurred in a manger. And it wasn't because I wanted to go out and get more votes because there's more poor people than rich people. Right?

So I just think it's important we think about that in this season, because every meaningful religion is trying to tell us the same thing. We organize our lives and our minds in categories; we have to do that. We want our kids to make good grades in school, not bad grades in school, so we tell them it's better to make good grades. We'd like to have a better job that pays more money so we can take better care of our families. We say, you know, it's better. It helped me to get reelected that we had a good economy instead of a bad economy. We all know that.

So we make judgments all the time, and we have to organize our lives so we are always putting people and conduct and things into categories, and that's good. It has to be done. But in order to have any meaning at all, underneath it all we have to know the real secret of life is that we have something that is no better than but, thank God, no worse than what anyone else has. And that is the gift we get from God; whatever our religious teaching and conviction and background, that is the gift we receive.

And our political conduct should at least—we can differ on a lot of things, about what's the best way to do this, the best way to do that or the other thing. But if we ever forget that what we have in common is far more fundamental than all these things that we differentiate

among ourselves, we have forgotten the most important thing.

The reason the American idea has worked for over 220 years is it rests on the premise that what we have in common is the most fundamental thing. And it recognized in the beginning—Thomas Jefferson: "I tremble, when I think of slavery, to believe that God is just." They knew that they were nowhere near living up to their ideals. And we accept today we are nowhere living up to our ideals. But we recognize that we have to move closer. That's really what we all came here to talk about here today. That's what we're all here to talk about today.

So we want America not only to be a rich country but one where everybody has a place at the table. That's what we come to celebrate.

I want to thank all of you and the American people for the work we have done in these last several years to make more room at the table for more people, to give people a chance to live as if they were what they in fact are: equal before the law and in the eyes of God.

Now, we have a lot to celebrate. Some of it's been mentioned: 17 million new jobs; the fastest wage growth in two decades; the lowest unemployment rate in 28 years; the smallest percentage of Americans on welfare in 29 years; the lowest African-American poverty rate ever recorded; the highest homeownership in history; crime, divorce, teen pregnancy, drug abuse rates falling. But I say, until we know that everybody has a chance to be a part of this, we have more to do. And I believe when times are good, we have a heavier responsibility to look at the long run, to meet the long-term challenges of the country, and to give everybody a chance to be a part of what it is we celebrate.

At the dawn of the 21st century, we have some big challenges. Not all our children have world-class educations, but all our children need them. You heard Elijah talking about the health care challenges. More and more people are having trouble finding health insurance. More and more people with health insurance are in managed care plans where they need a Patients' Bill of Rights. We have a huge looming challenge when all of us baby boomers retire and there will only be two people working for every one person drawing Social Security or on Medicare. And the young people of this country deserve—deserve—the right to live their lives, raise their children without their parents and grandparents bankrupting them. And so we have to save Social Security and Medicare for the 21st century without imposing on our children an unfair burden.

There's a lot of trouble in the world economy today, and we can't continue to grow unless we help our neighbors to get over that trouble and to stabilize the system. And again I say, underneath all that is our philosophy: Do we really believe that our ability to do well is connected to our neighbors' ability, and not only our neighbors down the street and across the town and across America but all of our neighbors on this increasingly small planet of ours? I think you believe that. That's one reason I enjoy coming here and being with you.

Now, I have watched—I came here to Baltimore the first time before some of you were born. I was an 18-year-old college student, and my best friend, later my college roommate, was from Baltimore. So I have seen this place change breathtakingly since I first came here in 1964. I see it in Camden Yards and the Inner Harbor, but I also see it in the communities throughout this city. And the changes you see here are just as profound as you see in your beautiful ballpark or your beautiful harbor and may have a longer lasting positive impact on the march of life in this city. You see it in west Baltimore, east Baltimore, Sandtown-Winchester, and of course, here in Pleasant View.

This is the model—the reason I came here today, among other things, besides the fact that I like to come here and be with all of you, is that I want people to understand what you have done. And I want people to understand that, if you can do this here, this can be done anywhere in America. And I want people to understand that the National Government is committed to being a partner, but all we can be is a partner. What makes the celebration of today possible is what you have done. You needed our help. That's what Senator Mikulski said. And you need more. That's why Senator Sarbanes talked about the budget. [Laughter] But it's very important to understand that all I have done here, all Secretary Cuomo has done here is to give you the tools to build a genuine community out of chaos and to give everybody a seat at the table.

And so I want to say again, we are committed to that. We want more empowerment zones like yours. We want more community development

banks. We want more comprehensive housing reform like we see here. What did you do with your empowerment zone? Would you like to know? Baltimore's empowerment zone has produced more than 2,800 new jobs; crime down 20 percent; $50 million in new private sector funding. It worked. So we're going to have, in the coming weeks, thanks to last year's budget, 20 new empowerment zones. Others can do it because you did it, and we want them to do it.

We have the best job market in a generation. But to really move people from welfare to work, we need more transportation, more child care, more housing vouchers to move people closer to the available jobs, and new commitments from civic, religious, business, and nonprofit groups. We will do that. We must build on the success of community policing, which prevents crime in the first place.

Already, we have helped to fund more than 92,000 of the 100,000 police officers promised by the crime bill of 1994. And here in Baltimore we're providing funding for another 100 officers, on top of the 450 you've already hired, specifically targeted to higher crime neighborhoods. If we want to build communities, our children have to feel safe on their streets.

One of the biggest things I am convinced we have to do is to do more to tap the potential of all our young people. We need more safe and more modern schools. We need desperately quality after-school programs for all the children, who otherwise will be on the street, not learning and getting in trouble. We need to give young people an opportunity to give something back to their community and to go on with their education.

I am very proud that Baltimore has one of the largest national service programs, AmeriCorps programs in the entire United States here. There are more than 300 young AmeriCorps members building new homes, removing lead paint, restoring parks. Nearly 500 more will join you in the coming year. So I want to thank the young AmeriCorps members who are here today for their service. Thank you very much. I appreciate that.

And we can do more to break the cycle of homelessness. We are serving many, many thousands, tens of thousands of more people than we were when I became President. I remember, when I first took office, and I used to run out of the White House in the morning on my morning jog, and I would go down 16th Street and 15th Street. And there were homeless people everywhere, and they would stop and talk to me. It was a great thing; the President could have a daily conversation with a homeless person. That was good for me but lousy for them because they were all spending the night on the street over the grates, waiting for the heat, even built fancy little tents so that the heat would blow up and keep their roof over their heads.

And there are fewer of them now. But we have a lot to do. The Continuum of Care strategy that Secretary Cuomo developed acknowledged that people who are homeless need more than a shelter. They are homeless for a reason. You heard that from Christa.

Today I am pleased to announce that we are awarding $850 million to communities in all 50 States to give homeless families a chance to rebuild their lives. Maryland will receive more than $17 million; grassroots organizations here in Baltimore more than $8 million. These grants will help you to reach out in innovative ways to homeless adults and children, to veterans and the disabled, to people with mental illness and with AIDS. They will help with emergency shelters and permanent housing, drug treatment and medication, job training and child care. They will help to give your fellow citizens a hand up. They will help you to give them the greatest benefit of all, the gift of self-sufficiency and hope.

Now, I am also pleased to announce that my next balanced budget will include a record $1.1 billion for homeless assistance. If enacted, if we can persuade the Congress to enact it, it will be the largest effort to combat homelessness in the history of America, and it will be done within the balanced budget.

Baltimore has always been known as the City of Neighborhoods. I want America to be known as the Country of Neighborhoods. And I want us to look at all people as our neighbors.

You know, not very long ago, Hillary and Chelsea and I took a brief trip to the Middle East to try to spur on the peace process there, to try to help the Palestinians and the Israelis become more reconciled to one another. And as a part of this trip, we were able to go to

Bethlehem, which ironically is now a predominantly Palestinian-Muslim city, where the Christians, in the birthplace of Christ, are in a minority but a respected minority. And we visited the Church of the Nativity, and we bent down and walked through that doorway that was built about 1500 years ago in that old church. And we went down into the crypt, where I'm sure some of you have been, where they believe the manger was where Jesus was born. And we were left there for a time, the three of us, by ourselves—something that almost never happens to us—to reflect on the meaning of that.

I say again, I came out of that, first of all, profoundly grateful for the opportunity to serve, for the many gifts in my life and my family's life but also determined again to remember what I think the fundamental lesson is, which is not that charity is the greatest virtue but that charity is an obligation because of our common humanity, because we are not better than those who, because of their circumstances, happen to need a hand up at any given moment in time.

So, as much as any place in our country, the State of Maryland and the city of Baltimore embodies that. You should be very proud and very grateful for what you have done and what you are. And it should make you more determined for what you can become.

I was sitting there looking at Christa Spangler, listening to her. She got a second chance, maybe a third or a fourth or a fifth chance. But here she is, sounding good, looking good, got a life, got a job, got a house, got a husband. Stand up; stand up here. This ought to be a country of neighbors, a country of equals, a country of people committed to a hand up.

God bless you, and happy holidays. Thank you.

NOTE: The President spoke at 12:07 p.m. in the gym at the Boys and Girls Club. In his remarks, he referred to Christa Spangler, former recipient of homeless assistance services, who introduced the President; Mayor Kurt Schmoke of Baltimore; Prince Georges County, MD, Executive Wayne K. Curry; and Gov. Parris N. Glendening of Maryland.

Statement on United Nations Efforts Toward a Political Settlement in Cyprus
December 23, 1998

The United States remains deeply committed to finding a viable solution to the Cyprus problem. A political settlement that would put an end to the tragic division of Cyprus has been and continues to be a high priority of my administration.

The United States strongly supports U.N. Secretary-General Annan's September 30, 1998, initiative to reduce tensions and promote progress toward a just and lasting settlement on Cyprus. The Security Council has adopted UNSCR 1218 endorsing Secretary-General Annan's initiative and requesting him to intensify his efforts to achieve specific objectives to reduce tensions and promote a comprehensive settlement to this longstanding dispute.

The United States wholeheartedly supports this resolution. We will take all necessary steps to support a sustained effort to implement UNSCR 1218.

I am encouraged by the cooperation and engagement demonstrated by the two sides thus far in working with the U.N. I believe 1999 can offer significant opportunities to achieve progress toward a Cyprus settlement that will meet the concerns of the parties involved. The Secretary-General's ongoing initiative is critically important to making those opportunities a reality.

Just as the international community is stepping up its efforts on Cyprus through the U.N., it is important for the Cypriots themselves to support those efforts. I urge all the parties to avoid taking any steps that could increase tensions on the island, including the expansion of military forces and armaments. This will make possible the significant efforts that I and others want to make in order to promote substantial progress toward a political settlement of the Cyprus problem in 1999.

Statement on the National Economy
December 24, 1998

Today we received more evidence that our economy remains solid and strong, more proof that the economic strategy we have had in place for 6 years is serving America's working families well. Last month personal income rose a strong 0.5 percent. That's good news in this holiday season and good news for our future. Over the past year, personal incomes have increased nearly 5 percent, far faster than the rate of inflation.

While we should be pleased with our strong economic progress, now is not a time to rest; it is a time to build. To ensure that America's economy continues to work for America's working families, we must maintain the three-part economic strategy that has helped produce these remarkable gains. We must maintain our fiscal discipline; continue to invest in our people through education, health care, and research and development; and continue to lead the global economy.

The President's Radio Address
December 26, 1998

Good morning. December is a month for families, a season of celebration and anticipation, especially for our children. But with alcohol flowing at parties and millions of families taking to the road to see friends and relatives, the holiday season can also be a season of tragedy.

Last December more than 1,300 Americans lost their lives in alcohol-related crashes. Who knows how many presents under the Christmas tree were left unopened, presents for a child killed by a drunk driver.

Today I want to talk about how we can work together to make our roads safer for our families. For a generation, drunk driving has been one of America's greatest public safety challenges. The sight of a car weaving through traffic is an all too familiar and frightening one for many Americans. Over the past decade, spurred to action by grassroots activists such as Mothers Against Drunk Driving, and with the leadership of the Department of Transportation and the National Highway Traffic Safety Administration, America has worked hard to keep drunk drivers off our roads with increased public awareness, stronger laws, and stricter enforcement.

My administration has made safety our number one transportation priority. In 1995 we helped States make it illegal for anyone under 21 to drive with any amount of alcohol in their system. We put young people on notice: just one drink before driving—one beer, one glass of wine, one shot—and you can lose your license.

There's good news to report. Last year the number of people killed in alcohol-related crashes dropped to an all-time low. For the first time since we started keeping track in 1975, alcohol-related deaths accounted for less than 40 percent of all traffic deaths and dropped by 5 percent among 15- to 20-year-olds. But we have much more to do.

In a report I'm releasing today, the Department of Health and Human Services estimates that in 1996 more than a quarter of all drivers—46.5 million—used drugs, alcohol, or both within 2 hours of driving. Ask any parent, any family, anyone who has lost a loved one to an alcohol related crash: One impaired driver is one too many.

So today I'm announcing that the Justice and Transportation Departments will strengthen their efforts in the new year, through grants to States and other incentives, to enforce underage drinking laws, to carry out alcohol impaired driving prevention programs, and to pass and enforce strong State highway safety legislation.

The most effective action we can take to make our roads even safer is to set the national impaired driving standard at .08 percent blood alcohol content. No one will ever doubt that a person with that much blood alcohol is unfit to drive after meeting Brenda Frazier. This spring at the White House she described the horror of watching a drunk driver run over her 9-year-old daughter at a school bus stop. The driver's blood alcohol content: .08 percent.

This year I worked with Members of Congress to make .08 the law of the land. Tragically, the special interests blocked this lifesaving measure. I am determined to succeed in setting a .08 standard in the new year. It's the right thing to do. In the meantime, I've asked Transportation Secretary Rodney Slater to work to make .08 the rule on Federal property. I commend the 16 States and the District of Columbia who have already adopted the stricter standard.

But every American family also must take responsibility for safer roads for all our families. Tell your neighbors and teach your own children about the dangers of drunk driving. And as we gather this week to ring in a new year, stop and think before getting behind the wheel. If you've had too much to drink, hand your keys to a designated driver. Together, we can make sure the new year is, indeed, a safe and happy one for all Americans.

Thanks for listening.

NOTE: The address was recorded at 11:04 a.m. on December 24 in the Roosevelt Room at the White House for broadcast at 10:06 a.m. on December 26. The transcript was made available by the Office of the Press Secretary on December 24 but was embargoed for release until the broadcast.

Statement on the 1997 National Crime Victimization Survey
December 27, 1998

The 1997 National Crime Victimization Survey released by the Department of Justice today shows that violent crime fell 7 percent last year and 21 percent since I took office. With the violent crime rate now its lowest level since 1973, Americans are safer today than they have been in many years. These new figures again show that our strategy of more police, stricter gun laws, and better crime prevention is work-ing. But we are not yet done. Working together, both in Washington and in communities across our Nation, we must redouble our efforts to make our streets, homes, and schools safer for all Americans.

NOTE: This statement was embargoed for release until 9 a.m.

Remarks Announcing Social Security System Compliance With Year 2000 Computer Problem Safeguards
December 28, 1998

Good morning. Let me say, one of the things that she might have told you is that before she volunteered for the National Council of Senior Citizens for 20 years, she was an employee until 1972, when she retired, of the Bureau of Engraving and Printing. Therefore, she worked for the Treasury Department. And on New Year's Eve, she will be 90 years old. [*Applause*] So we thank her.

Situation in Iraq

Ladies and gentlemen, before I get into my remarks, because this is the only opportunity I will have to appear before the press today, I think I should say a few words about an incident early this morning over the skies of Iraq, where American and British aircrews were enforcing a no-fly zone in northern Iraq. They were fired on by Iraq's surface-to-air missiles. They took evasive action, returned fire on the missile site, and returned safely to their base in Turkey.

We enforce two no-fly zones in Iraq: one in the north, established in 1991; another in the south, established in 1992, which now stretches from the southern suburbs of Baghdad down to the Kuwaiti border. The no-fly zones have been and will remain an important part of our containment policy. Because we effectively control the skies over much of Iraq, Saddam has been unable to use air power to repress his own people or to lash out again at his neighbors. Our pilots have the authority to protect themselves if they're threatened or attacked. They took appropriate action today in responding to Iraq's actions.

Once again, I want to tell you I am very proud of the work they do, the risks they take, the skill and the professionalism with which they do it. They attacked because they were attacked, and they did the appropriate thing. We will continue to enforce the no-fly zones.

Social Security and Year 2000 Computer Problem

Now, let me say, this is a very happy announcement today. And I want to thank Secretary Rubin, who most people associate with saving the economy, not saving Social Security, but that's an important part of his job, too. I want to thank Kathy Adams, who is one of those people in the Government that makes it go and never gets enough credit for it. So I'm delighted to see her up here and, through her, all the other people who work every day to make America work.

I've already told you about Pauline Johnson Jones. And I want to say, too, I have been very moved by how passionate Ken Apfel has been about making sure that this problem got solved. And today we saw that he has a vested interest in it: He doesn't want his father to cut him out of his will—[*laughter*]—and everybody always needs to be in better stead with their in-laws. [*Laughter*]

You know, this Y2K problem is a stunning problem—oh, one other thing: I want to acknowledge the presence here in the audience of the Member of Congress from Guam, Congressman Robert Underwood, his wife, and his five children. They're here; we're delighted to see all of them. We're delighted that they're here with us in this cold weather, instead of on warm and sunny Guam today.

We just heard that the new millennium is only 368 days away. And we want it to be a carefree celebration. The reason we're here today is to announce that on New Year's Day 2000, and on every day that follows, people like Pauline can rest easy because the millennium bug will not delay the payment of Social Security checks by a single day.

The Social Security system is now 100 percent compliant with our standards and safeguards for the year 2000. To make absolutely certain, the system has been tested and validated by a panel of independent experts. The system works; it is secure. And therefore, older Americans can feel more secure.

I thank all those who are responsible. This is a good day for America. Thank you very much.

The Social Security Administration and the Financial Management Service can be proud. The Social Security agency was the very first one to start work on the Y2K problem; it's been a leader and a model ever since. They couldn't have done it, these two agencies, if they hadn't worked as a team. Social Security generates the Social Security payments; the Financial Management Service issues those payments. They are in this together.

Indeed, we're all in this together. This involves not just Federal agencies but everyone who depends upon a computer, which is everyone, directly or indirectly. Federal and State governments and local governments, businesses large and small, the year 2000 problem reveals the connections between all of us.

We also, I want to point out, have been working very hard with other countries. Sally Katzen just told me that there was a meeting at the United Nations recently where we met with representatives of 120 other countries who are all now working together to solve this, because as all of you know, a lot of our economy is tied up with economic endeavors throughout the world, so even a problem a long way from our shores can have ramifications within our borders. And of course, we don't want any of our friends and neighbors hurt by this change either.

People are meeting this challenge, but I think a lot of people can still hardly imagine what caused this. I mean, computers, after all, are supposed to save us time, right? And I was describing this Y2K problem to Hillary, and she got so technophobic that I gave her a little digital alarm clock for Christmas, and she gave it back to me after I talked to her about it. And she said, "Why don't you just go get me one that winds up, that I can change in my hand?" [*Laughter*]

It happened, you know, because in the older computers the memory put on the chip was precious and much more limited than the phenomenal capacity of computer chips today, so that, in effect, they were all programmed, these older computers, just to change the last two digits on the four numbers of any date. And so what would happen is, when you get to the year 2000, it would show 1900 instead of 2000, because there is no provision for the 19 to go to 20, because of the limitations of memory in the older computer chips.

The problem is, obviously, that a lot of new computers are also interconnected with older computers, and a lot of people can't even be sure what chips are in what computers and what links are there. That's what makes this labor-saving device of the computer present the most labor-intensive problem imaginable. Retired people have had to come back—people with skills in working with the old computers have had to come back to help all kinds of businesses figure out how to unravel this problem. It sounds so simple, but it is so mammoth because you have to identify what computers and what chips are where and what the interconnections are.

And so it's an enormous, enormous effort. And we really, all of us, are so indebted to these people who have been recognized today with these two agencies, and to others all across the country who are working on this problem in the public and in the private sectors.

I say again, the American people don't know who—or didn't before today—know who Kathy Adams was. They don't know any of the people who are working with her. But when they get the checks for the first Social Security payment in the new millennium, it will be because of them. And I would just ask the American people today to be very sensitive, because there are people like Kathy Adams working in all these agencies, in State and local government and all these businesses throughout the country, and they need to be encouraged. And those who have not yet undertaken this task need to get on it and get on it now, because we just have a little more than a year to get the job done.

Now, we have made sure that Social Security checks will keep coming in the year 2000. I'd also like to say that after we've got the computer problem behind us, we have to continue to focus on the larger issue, the policy issue, which is to make sure that the Social Security checks keep coming throughout the 21st century. All of you know that at present rates of contribution and payment, present rates of retirement, present rates of aging and birth and immigration, we estimate that the Social Security Trust Fund will be exhausted in about 34 years. We have typically tried to keep the life of the Trust Fund at about 75 years to make sure it was absolutely stable. Thirty-four years seems like a long time away; I suppose the younger you are, the further away it seems. It doesn't seem so far to me now, because things that happened 34 years ago are implanted in my mind as if they occurred only yesterday.

But we are going to face early next year a great challenge of fashioning a bipartisan solution to save Social Security for the 21st century. I tell everybody it is a formidable problem, but it will only get worse if we delay it. And it is a high-class problem; we have this problem because we're living longer. The average life expectancy of the American people, as reported just a few weeks ago, exceeds 76 years. And that is a high-class problem. We should be grateful for this problem. When Social Security was established and there was no early retirement at 62 and you couldn't draw until 65, the average male life expectancy in America was 56—in the 1930's. So we've gone from 56 to over 76, and of course, for women, it's a couple of years higher. And as Pauline says, women are especially dependent on Social Security, for reasons that I think would be obvious to anyone, and therefore have a particularly large stake in our resolving this problem in a prompt and appropriate way.

Now, in the last year—in this year, 1998— I have gone around the country and held these bipartisan forums. Members of Congress in both Houses and both parties have taken a special interest and have been very good to attend these forums. Just a few days ago, we had a 2-day first White House Conference on Social Security. The second day, I went over to Blair House and met with nearly 50 Members of Congress, in both parties and both Houses. It was an astonishing outpouring of genuine interest.

Now, I don't want to minimize the problems—and they're different from the Y2K problem. The Y2K problem, you know what to do to fix it once you identify it. Here we've identified it, and there are obvious differences about what should be done to fix Social Security for the 21st century. But we all know that there are basically only three options: We can raise taxes again, which no one wants to do because the payroll tax is regressive. Over half the American people who are working pay more payroll tax than income tax today. We can cut benefits, and it might be all right for someone like me who has a good retirement plan, but it's not a very good idea for someone like Pauline. Or we can work together to try to find some way to increase the rate of return. And there are a number of options that we are discussing.

The point I want to make to all of you is that we have the same obligation to fix the system in policy terms for the 21st century that these fine people we honor today have discharged in fixing the Y2K problem. And if we approach it with the same can-do attitude and the same determination to reach a result, we can achieve that.

So today we celebrate, and I hope the celebration that we have today will steel our determination to make sure that people like Pauline can be making this speech 50 years from now.

Thank you very much, and Happy New Year.

NOTE: The President spoke at 10:35 a.m. in Room 450 of the Old Executive Office Building. In his remarks, he referred to Social Security recipient Pauline Johnson Jones, who introduced the President; President Saddam Hussein of Iraq; Kathleen M. Adams, Assistant Deputy Commissioner for Systems, Social Security Administration; and Delegate Robert A. Underwood of Guam and his wife, Lorraine.

Remarks Announcing the Children Exposed to Violence Initiative
December 29, 1998

Thank you very much, Eric Holder, for your leadership and your obvious intense commitment to this issue. Thank you, Chief, for your good work. When you were describing the initiatives in New Haven involving the Yale Child Study Center, it struck a particularly responsive chord because when I met my wife over 25 years ago at the law school, she was also working with the Yale Child Study Center. And it's a great institution.

We're delighted to be joined here by leaders of law enforcement and leaders of law enforcement organizations; Montgomery County Council member Marilyn Praisner. And I want to say a special word of welcome to Congressman Bud Cramer of Alabama, who has supported the 100,000 police program. We thank you, sir, for your presence here.

This is an important time for us to be making this announcement because the holiday season is always focused on our children, and properly so. I want our children to be at the center of our attention every day, every week, all year long.

Today we come here to talk about new actions to help millions of children who are exposed every year to violence, either as witnesses or victims. For many, many of them, it is very difficult to be a child because there is too much violence, too much cruelty, too much incivility. Children experience these things in our society at younger and younger ages. That is why we have worked hard—the Attorney General, the Deputy Attorney General, and others in our administration—to strengthen families, to bring safety and order to our schools, our communities, our streets.

We passed a crime bill with tougher penalties and more prevention. We've enforced zero tolerance for guns in schools, expelling more than 6,000 students in 1997 who brought weapons to schools. We've expanded and want to continue to expand after-school programs to keep children off the streets during the after-school hours when juvenile crime soars. We do have—the chief mentioned the 100,000 police program, the community policing program. We've now funded about 91,000 of those 100,000 police.

We're ahead of schedule and under budget, and I hope we can keep going.

With these efforts and with the efforts of countless parents and teachers, principals, judges, police officers, and others, real progress is being made, as you have heard. New crime statistics released by the Justice Department this past weekend show that overall crime has dropped to its lowest level in 25 years. Property and violent crime are down more than 20 percent since 1993, the murder rate down by nearly 30 percent. Juvenile crime rates finally have also started to fall. The juvenile murder rate has dropped 17 percent in one year, and juvenile arrest rates are now down 2 years in a row.

These are good signs. We should be pleased; we should be thankful. But we should not be complacent, for these rates are still very, very high—too high for any civilized society to tolerate. And there are still far too many children who are victims of violence; too many being abused and neglected; too many still witnessing serious violence with traumatic effects on them that, as you have already heard, will last a lifetime.

As the First Lady's Zero To Three conference last year showed, children's exposure to violence has tremendous negative consequences for them and for all the rest of us. A child who experiences serious violence is 50 percent—50 percent—more likely to be arrested as a juvenile and nearly 40 percent more likely to be arrested as an adult. If you want to keep the crime rates going down, you have to do more to break the cycle of violence to which children are exposed.

Today we launch a new Child Exposed to Violence Initiative, sponsored by the Justice Department, directed by Deputy Attorney General Holder. The aim of the initiative is to combat violence against children, to prevent children who are exposed to violence from being victimized a second time by the justice system.

As part of the initiative, I announce today four specific actions. First, I'm asking the Justice Department to send legislation to Congress to impose tougher penalties against those who expose children to violence. I believe it's time to send a message through the court that when a man assaults or kills someone in the presence of a child, he has committed not one horrendous act but two; time to ask why a bank robber who unintentionally kills an innocent bystander can be charged with felony murder, but a repeat child abuser who unintentionally kills a child cannot be.

Second, I'm directing the Justice Department to develop and distribute the critical information State and local law enforcement agencies need to do a better job of responding to the needs of children who have been victimized by a crime. Too often children are victimized anew by a criminal justice system that is designed by and for adults. With the help of the Justice Department's new training videos and in-the-field user guides, the first of which we are releasing today, criminal justice agencies all over our Nation can begin to provide children who have been exposed to violence with the healing they need and deserve.

Third, today we announce $10 million in Federal Safe Start grants to 12 cities to develop the kinds of comprehensive responses to children exposed to violence that New Haven has pioneered and that the chief so ably described just a few moments ago. The New Haven experience shows that trained law enforcement officers, paired with child psychologists, can provide the stability and comfort children need to overcome their feelings of fear and chaos that result from exposure to violence.

Fourth, I asked the Justice Department to hold a national summit on children exposed to violence next June, cohosted by the Department of Health and Human Services, local law enforcement agencies, media organizations, elected officials, the National Network of Children's Advocacy Centers, and other groups.

By working together, we have already made significant progress against crime and violence. We have made significant progress to make our children's lives safer. But if you look at the numbers of people who are still involved, the statistics are staggering and unacceptable. So I say, the fact that this progress has been made should give us courage, should give us hope, but should steel our determination to do the much, much greater work that lies ahead.

There is no excuse for us to lose any of our children. And if we keep working and we keep our children at the center of our concerns, we can make the 21st century a much, much safer, better, more wholesome place for them than the last three and a half decades of this century have been.

Thank you very much. Happy New Year.

NOTE: The President spoke at 10 a.m. in the Roosevelt Room at the White House. In his remarks, he referred to Melvin H. Wearing, chief of police, New Haven, CT; and Marilyn Praisner, president, Montgomery County Council, MD.

Letter to Congressional Leaders Transmitting a Report on the Emigration Policies and Trade Status of Certain Former Eastern Bloc States
December 29, 1998

Dear Mr. Speaker: *(Dear Mr. President:)*

On September 21, 1994, I determined and reported to the Congress that the Russian Federation was not in violation of paragraph (1), (2), or (3) of subsection 402(a) of the Trade Act of 1974, or paragraph (1), (2), or (3) of subsection 409(a) of that Act. On June 3, 1997, I determined and reported to the Congress that Armenia, Azerbaijan, Georgia, Moldova, and Ukraine were not in violation of the same provisions, and I made an identical determination on December 5, 1997, with respect to Kazakhstan, Kyrgyzstan, Tajikistan,

Turkmenistan, and Uzbekistan. These actions allowed for the continuation of most-favored-nation (MFN) status for these countries and certain other activities without the requirement of an annual waiver.

As required by law, I am submitting an updated report to the Congress concerning the emigration laws and policies of Armenia, Azerbaijan, Georgia, Kazakhstan, Kyrgyzstan, Moldova, the Russian Federation, Tajikistan, Turkmenistan, Ukraine, and Uzbekistan. The report indicates continued compliance of these countries with international standards concerning freedom of emigration.

Sincerely,

WILLIAM J. CLINTON

NOTE: Identical letters were sent to Newt Gingrich, Speaker of the House of Representatives, and Albert Gore, Jr., President of the Senate.

Letter to Congressional Leaders Transmitting a Plan and Report on Reorganization of the Foreign Affairs Agencies
December 29, 1998

Dear _____:

I hereby submit the reorganization plan and report required by section 1601 of the Foreign Affairs Reform and Restructuring Act of 1998 (Public Law 105–277, Division G). As required by the Act, the reorganization plan and report describe how the United States Arms Control and Disarmament Agency, the United States Information Agency, and portions of the United States Agency for International Development will be integrated into the Department of State.

Sincerely,

WILLIAM J. CLINTON

NOTE: Identical letters were sent to Jesse Helms, chairman, and Joseph R. Biden, Jr., ranking member, Senate Committee on Foreign Relations; Ted Stevens, chairman, and Robert C. Byrd, ranking member, Senate Committee on Appropriations; Benjamin A. Gilman, chairman, and Lee Hamilton, ranking member, House Committee on International Relations; and Robert L. Livingston, chairman, and David R. Obey, ranking member, House Committee on Appropriations. This letter was released by the Office of the Press Secretary on December 30.

Letter to Congressional Leaders on Continuation of the National Emergency With Respect to Libya
December 30, 1998

Dear Mr. Speaker: (Dear Mr. President:)

Section 202(d) of the National Emergencies Act (50 U.S.C. 1622(d)) provides for the automatic termination of a national emergency unless, prior to the anniversary date of its declaration, the President publishes in the *Federal Register* and transmits to the Congress a notice stating that the emergency is to continue in effect beyond the anniversary date. In accordance with this provision, I have sent the enclosed notice, stating that the Libyan emergency is to continue in effect beyond January 7, 1999, to the *Federal Register* for publication. Similar notices have been sent annually to the Congress and published in the *Federal Register*. The most recent notice was signed on January 2, 1998, and appeared in the *Federal Register* on January 6, 1998.

The crisis between the United States and Libya that led to the declaration of a national emergency on January 7, 1986, has not been resolved. The Government of Libya has continued its actions and policies in support of terrorism, despite the calls by the United Nations Security Council, in Resolutions 731 (1992), 748 (1992), and 883 (1993), that Libya demonstrate by concrete actions its renunciation of terrorism. Such Libyan actions and policies pose a continuing unusual and extraordinary threat to the national security and vital foreign policy interests of the United States. Furthermore, the Libyan government has not delivered the two Lockerbie bombing suspects for trial, even though the United States and United Kingdom accepted Libya's proposal to try the suspects in a Scottish court in a third country. Libya's stalling in handing over the suspects is yet another indication of Libya's continued support for terrorism and rejection of international norms. For these reasons, I have determined that it is necessary to maintain in force the broad authorities necessary to apply economic pressure to the Government of Libya to reduce its ability to support international terrorism.

Sincerely,

WILLIAM J. CLINTON

NOTE: Identical letters were sent to Newt Gingrich, Speaker of the House of Representatives, and Albert Gore, Jr., President of the Senate. The notice is listed in Appendix D at the end of this volume.

Letter to Congressional Leaders Reporting on the National Emergency With Respect to Libya
December 30, 1998

Dear Mr. Speaker: (*Dear Mr. President:*)

I hereby report to the Congress on the developments since my last report of July 6, 1998, concerning the national emergency with respect to Libya that was declared in Executive Order 12543 of January 7, 1986. This report is submitted pursuant to section 401(c) of the National Emergencies Act, 50 U.S.C. 1641(c); section 204(c) of the International Emergency Economic Powers Act (IEEPA), 50 U.S.C. 1703(c); and section 505(c) of the International Security and Development Cooperation Act of 1985, 22 U.S.C. 2349aa–9(c).

1. On December 30, 1998, I renewed for another year the national emergency with respect to Libya pursuant to IEEPA. This renewal extended the current comprehensive financial and trade embargo against Libya in effect since 1986. Under these sanctions, virtually all trade with Libya is prohibited, and all assets owned or controlled by the Government of Libya in the United States or in the possession or control of United States persons are blocked.

2. There have been no amendments to the Libyan Sanctions Regulations, 31 C.F.R. Part 550 (the "Regulations"), administered by the Office of Foreign Assets Control (OFAC) of the Department of the Treasury, since my last report of July 6, 1998.

3. During the reporting period, OFAC reviewed numerous applications for licenses to authorize transactions under the regulations. Consistent with OFAC's ongoing scrutiny of banking transactions, the largest category of license approvals (26) involved types of financial transactions that are consistent with U.S. policy. Most of these licenses authorized personal remittances not involving Libya between persons who are not blocked parties to flow through Libyan banks located outside Libya. Seven licenses were issued to U.S. firms to allow them to protect their intellectual property rights in Libya. One license was issued in connection with law enforcement activities and one authorized certain travel-related transactions. A total of 35 licenses were issued during the reporting period.

4. During the current 6-month period, OFAC continued to emphasize to the international banking community in the United States the importance of identifying and blocking payments made by or on behalf of Libya. The Office worked closely with the banks to assure the effectiveness of interdiction software systems used to identify such payments. During the reporting period, more than 87 transactions potentially involving Libya, totaling more than $7.9 million, were interdicted.

5. Since my last report, OFAC has collected 4 civil monetary penalties totaling more than $15,000 for violations of the U.S. sanctions against Libya. Three of the violations involved the failure of U.S. banks to block payments or letters of credit transactions relating to Libyan-owned or Libyan-controlled financial institutions. One U.S. individual paid an OFAC penalty for dealing in Government of Libya property.

On October 16, 1998, two Canadian corporations entered a guilty plea acknowledging IEEPA violations charged in a March 8, 1995, indictment. Pursuant to the plea agreement, the defendants each paid $65,000 in criminal fines and $10,000 in OFAC civil penalties.

Various enforcement actions carried over from previous reporting periods have continued to be aggressively pursued. Numerous investigations are ongoing and new reports of violations are being scrutinized.

6. The expenses incurred by the Federal Government in the 6-month period from July 7, 1998, through January 6, 1999, that are directly attributable to the exercise of powers and authorities conferred by the declaration of the Libyan national emergency are estimated at approximately $500,000. Personnel costs were largely centered in the Department of the Treasury (particularly in the Office of Foreign Assets Control, the Office of the General Counsel, and the U.S. Customs Service), the Department of State, and the Department of Commerce.

7. The policies and actions of the Government of Libya continue to pose an unusual and extraordinary threat to the national security and foreign policy of the United States. In adopting UNSCR 883 in November 1993, the United Nations Security Council determined that the continued failure of the Government of Libya to demonstrate by concrete actions its renunciation of terrorism, and in particular its continued failure to respond fully and effectively to the requests and decisions of the Security Council in

Resolutions 731 and 748, concerning the bombing of the Pan Am 103 and UTA 772 flights, constituted a threat to international peace and security. The United States will continue to coordinate its comprehensive sanctions enforcement efforts with those of other U.N. Member States. We remain determined to ensure that the perpetrators of the terrorist acts against Pan Am 103 and UTA 772 are brought to justice. The families of the victims in the murderous Lockerbie bombing and other acts of Libyan terrorism deserve nothing less. I shall continue to exercise the powers at my disposal to apply economic sanctions against Libya fully and effectively, so long as those measures are appropriate, and will continue to report periodically to the Congress on significant developments as required by law.

Sincerely,

WILLIAM J. CLINTON

NOTE: Identical letters were sent to Newt Gingrich, Speaker of the House of Representatives, and Albert Gore, Jr., President of the Senate. This letter was released by the Office of the Press Secretary on December 31.

Statement on Efforts To Increase Child Support Collections
December 31, 1998

Since I became President, my administration has waged an unprecedented campaign to make deadbeat parents pay the support their children need and deserve. Today we have new evidence that our efforts are working: child support collections have gone up a record 80 percent since I took office, from $8 billion in 1992 to an estimated $14.4 billion in 1998. But we must do more to ensure that each and every parent honors his obligation to his children. That is why my new budget will propose new funds

to help identify, investigate, and prosecute deadbeat parents. This effort will include new investigative teams in five regions of the country to identify, analyze, and investigate cases for criminal prosecution, and an eightfold increase in legal support personnel to help prosecute these new cases. With continued commitment and this new funding, we can do even more to support our Nation's children.

Appendix A—Digest of Other White House Announcements

The following list includes the President's public schedule and other items of general interest announced by the Office of the Press Secretary and not included elsewhere in this book.

July 1

In the morning, the President visited an Internet cafe in Shanghai, China. In the afternoon, he toured the Shanghai Stock Exchange and attended a luncheon for young entrepreneurs.

The President declared a major disaster in West Virginia and ordered Federal aid to supplement State and local recovery efforts in the area struck by severe storms, flooding, and tornadoes beginning on June 26 and continuing.

July 2

In the morning, the President and Hillary Clinton traveled from Shanghai to Guilin. In the afternoon, they took a cruise on the Li River, docking for a brief tour of Yucun village and then continuing the cruise to Yangshou. Later, they returned to Guilin.

In the evening, the President and Hillary Clinton traveled to Hong Kong. Later, the President met with Hong Kong Chief Executive C.H. Tung in the dining room of the Government House.

The President announced his intention to nominate Bert T. Edwards to be Chief Financial Officer at the State Department.

The President announced his intention to appoint Ann Lewis and Beth Newburger as Cochairs and the following individuals as members of the President's Commission on the Celebration of Women in American History:

Johnnetta B. Cole;
J. Michael Cook;
Barbara Goldsmith;
Ladonna Harris;
Gloria Johnson;
Elaine Kim;
Ellen Ochoa;
Frances Preston; and
Anna Roosevelt.

The President announced his intention to accord the personal rank of Ambassador to Ronald D. Godard in his capacity as Special Representative to the Inter-American Council of Integral Development at the General Assembly of the Organization of American States.

The President declared a major disaster in Maine and ordered Federal aid to supplement State and local recovery efforts in the area struck by severe storms and flooding beginning on June 13 and continuing.

The President declared a major disaster in New Mexico and ordered Federal aid to supplement State and local recovery efforts in the area threatened by extreme fire hazards on June 29 and continuing.

The Vice President announced that the President declared a major disaster in New Hampshire and ordered Federal aid to supplement State and local recovery efforts in the area struck by severe storms and flooding on June 12 and continuing.

The Vice President announced that the President declared a major disaster in Iowa and ordered Federal aid to supplement State and local recovery efforts in the area struck by severe storms, tornadoes, and flooding beginning on June 13 and continuing.

July 3

In the evening, the President and Hillary and Chelsea Clinton traveled to Elmendorf Air Force Base, AK, and then to Washington, DC, arriving early the next morning.

July 6

The President announced his intention to nominate Kathryn Dee Robinson to be Ambassador to Ghana.

The President announced his intention to nominate Ruby Butler DeMesme to be Assistant Secretary of the Air Force for Manpower, Reserve Affairs, Installations and Environment.

The President announced his intention to nominate Patrick T. Henry to be Assistant Secretary of the Army for Manpower and Reserve Affairs.

The President announced his intention to nominate Carolyn H. Becraft to be Assistant Secretary of the Navy for Manpower and Reserve Affairs.

The President announced his intention to nominate Charles F. Kartman for the rank of Ambassador during his tenure of service as Special Envoy for the Korean Peace Talks.

The President announced his intention to nominate Richard Henry Jones to be Ambassador to Kazakhstan.

The President announced his intention to appoint the following individuals as members of the President's Export Council:

Philip Condit;
Lodewijk J.R. de Vink;
Gary DiCamillo;
John P. Manning;
Ernest Micek; and
Jonathan Tisch.

The President announced that he has accepted an invitation from President Boris Yeltsin of Russia to meet in Russia in early September.

July 7

The President declared a major disaster in New York and ordered Federal aid to supplement State and local recovery efforts in the area struck by severe storms and flooding beginning on June 25 and continuing.

The President announced his intention to appoint Linda Chavez-Thompson as a member of the President's Committee on Employment of People with Disabilities.

The President announced his intention to appoint Thomas K. Thomas as a member of the Board of Trustees of the Christopher Columbus Fellowship Foundation.

The President announced his intention to nominate D. Bambi Kraus to be a member of the Board of Trustees of the Institute of American Indian and Alaska Native Culture and Arts Development.

July 8

In the afternoon, the President traveled to Arlington, VA. Later, he returned to Washington, DC.

The President announced the nomination of David Gordon Carpenter to be Assistant Secretary of State for Diplomatic Security and Director of the Office of Foreign Missions, with the Rank of Ambassador.

The President announced his intention to nominate Simon Ferro to be Ambassador to Panama.

The President announced his intention to nominate Eugene A. Conti, Jr., to be Assistant Secretary for Domestic Transportation Policy at the Department of Transportation.

July 9

In the morning, the President traveled to Atlanta, GA. In the afternoon, he traveled to Daytona, FL.

In the evening, the President traveled to Miami, FL, and later returned to Washington, DC, arriving after midnight.

The President announced his intention to nominate William B. Milam to be Ambassador to Pakistan.

The White House announced that the President has invited President Julio Maria Sanguinetti of Uruguay for a working visit on July 23.

July 10

In the afternoon, the President had a telephone conversation with President Boris Yeltsin of Russia, and he then met with Prime Minister Jerzy Buzek of Poland in the Oval Office. Later, the President and Hillary Clinton held an interview with Stars and Stripes in the Map Room at the White House.

The President announced his intention to appoint John Silberman, Jeff Valdez, and Ruth Whetstone Wagner as members of the Advisory Committee on the Arts of the John F. Kennedy Center for the Performing Arts.

July 11

In the evening, the President and Hillary Clinton attended a concert at the John F. Kennedy Center for the Performing Arts celebrating the 200th anniversary of the Marine Corps Band.

July 13

In the afternoon, the President had a luncheon with Senator Thomas A. Daschle and Representative Richard A. Gephardt in the Oval Office Dining Room.

The President announced his intention to nominate Karl J. Sandstrom to be a Commissioner of the Federal Election Commission.

The President announced his intention to nominate Christopher W.S. Ross for the rank of Ambassador during his tenure of service as Coordinator for Counterterrorism at the State Department.

July 14

The President announced his intention to nominate Charles R. Rawls to be General Counsel at the Department of Agriculture.

The President announced his intention to nominate Mike Walker to be Deputy Director of the Federal Emergency Management Agency.

The President announced his intention to nominate George M. Staples to be Ambassador to Rwanda.

July 15

The President announced his intention to nominate John J. Pikarski, Jr., to be a member of the Board of Directors of the Overseas Private Investment Corporation.

July 16

In the morning, the President met with President Emil Constantinescu of Romania in the Oval Office. Later, he attended a meeting with National Security Adviser Samuel Berger and NATO Secretary General Javier Solana in Mr. Berger's office at the White House. In the evening, he traveled to Chevy Chase, MD.

The President announced his intention to nominate John D. Hawke, Jr., to be Comptroller of the Currency at the Department of the Treasury.

The President announced his intention to nominate John Melvin Yates to be Ambassador to Cameroon.

July 17

In the morning, the President attended an American Legion Boys Nation reunion reception in the State Dining Room at the White House. In the afternoon, he traveled to Little Rock, AR.

The President announced his intention to nominate Romulo L. Diaz, Jr., to be Assistant Administrator for Administration and Resources Management at the Environmental Protection Agency.

The President announced his intention to nominate J. Charles Fox to be Assistant Administrator for Water at the Environmental Protection Agency.

The President announced his intention to nominate Patricia T. Montoya to be Commissioner of the Administration on Children, Youth, and Families at the Department of Health and Human Services.

July 19

In the afternoon, the President traveled to New Orleans, LA.

July 20

In the evening, the President returned to Washington, DC.

The President announced the appointment of Richard Davies, Susan Savage, and Thomas L. Strickland as members of the National Recreation Lakes Study Commission.

July 21

In the late afternoon, the President signed the National Underground Railroad Network to Freedom Act of 1998 in an Oval Office ceremony.

The President announced his intention to nominate Ritajean H. Butterworth to be a member of the Board of Directors of the Corporation for Public Broadcasting.

The President announced his intention to nominate Leigh A. Bradley to be General Counsel at the Department of Veterans Affairs.

The President announced his intention to nominate Bernard Rostker to be Under Secretary of the Army.

The President announced his intention to nominate John Melvin Yates to be Ambassador to Equatorial Guinea.

July 22

The President announced his intention to nominate James E. Newsome to be a Commissioner on the Commodity Futures Trading Commission.

The President announced his intention to nominate Harry J. Bowie to be a member of the Board of Directors of the National Consumer Cooperative Bank.

The President declared a major disaster in Indiana and ordered Federal aid to supplement State and local recovery efforts in the area struck by severe storms, tornadoes, and flooding on June 11–July 7.

July 23

In the afternoon, the President met with President Julio Maria Sanguinetti of Uruguay in the Oval Office.

The President declared a major disaster in Tennessee and ordered Federal aid to supplement State and local recovery efforts in the area struck by flooding and severe storms on July 13 and continuing.

The President announced the release to 11 States of $100 million in emergency Low Income Home Energy Assistance Program funds.

July 24

In the morning, the President met with University of Georgia gymnasts in the Oval Office. In the evening, he traveled to Camp David, MD.

The President announced his intention to appoint Robert L. Mallett as a member of the Board of Directors of the Overseas Private Investment Corporation.

The President announced his intention to appoint Robert Elliot Kahn as a member of the President's Information Technology Advisory Committee.

The President named Ambassador Richard L. Morningstar to be Special Adviser to the President and the Secretary of State for Caspian Basin Energy Diplomacy.

The President declared a major disaster in Wisconsin and ordered Federal aid to supplement State and local recovery efforts in the area struck by severe storms, straightline winds, tornadoes, heavy rain, and flooding on June 18–30.

July 25

In the morning, the President traveled to Norfolk, VA. In the afternoon, he traveled to Aspen, CO.

July 26

In the evening, the President traveled to Albuquerque, NM.

July 27

In the afternoon, the President departed for Washington, DC, arriving in the evening.

The President announced his intention to nominate Norine E. Noonan to be Assistant Administrator for Research and Development at the Environmental Protection Agency.

July 29

The President announced his intention to nominate James Bodner to be Principal Deputy Under Secretary of Defense for Policy.

The President announced his intention to nominate Gregory H. Friedman to be Inspector General of the Department of Energy.

The White House announced that the President will meet with Minister President Gerhard Schroeder of the German State of Lower Saxony at the White House on August 5.

July 30

In the morning, the President traveled to Ashe County, NC. In the afternoon, he traveled to Raleigh, NC, and in the evening, he returned to Washington, DC.

The President announced his intention to nominate Montie R. Deer to be Chair of the National Indian Gaming Commission.

The President announced his intention to nominate Charles G. Groat to be Director of the U.S. Geological Survey at the Department of the Interior.

July 31

In the afternoon, the President and Hillary Clinton traveled to East Hampton, NY.

The President announced the nomination of Harold Lucas to be Assistant Secretary for Public and Indian Housing at the Department of Housing and Urban Development.

The President announced the nomination of Cardell Cooper to be Assistant Secretary for Community Planning and Development at the Department of Housing and Urban Development.

The President announced the nomination of John U. Sepulveda to be Deputy Director of the Office of Personnel Management.

The President announced the nomination of Stephen W. Preston to be General Counsel of the Department of the Navy.

The President announced the nomination of David C. Williams to be Inspector General at the Department of the Treasury.

The President announced the nomination of Claiborne Pell to be an Alternate Representative of the United States of America to the 53d Session of the General Assembly of the United Nations.

The President announced the nomination of Michael M. Reyna to be a member of the Farm Credit Administration Board.

The President announced the nomination of Joseph E. Stevens, Jr., to the Board of Trustees of the Harry S. Truman Scholarship Foundation.

The President announced his intention to nominate Peter J. Basso, Jr., to be Assistant Secretary for Budget and Programs at the Department of Transportation.

The President announced his intention to nominate Terrence L. Bracy to be a trustee of the Morris K. Udall Scholarship and Excellence in National Environmental Policy Foundation.

The President announced his intention to appoint Mitchell Berger as Chair of the Board of Directors of the Student Loan Marketing Association (Sallie Mae).

August 2

In the morning, the President returned to Washington, DC.

August 3

In the morning, the President met with President-elect Andres Pastrana of Colombia in the Oval Office. Later, the President traveled to Cheverly, MD. In the afternoon, he returned to Washington, DC.

August 4

The President announced his intention to appoint Eugene Kinlow, Constance Newman, and Darius Mans as Chair, Vice Chair, and member, respectively, of the District of Columbia Financial Responsibility and Management Assistance Authority.

August 5

In the morning, the President spoke to the House Democratic caucus at the Cannon House Office Building.

In the evening, the President met with Deputy President Thabo Mbeki of South Africa in the Oval Office.

The President declared a major disaster in Michigan and ordered Federal aid to supplement State and local recovery efforts in the area struck by severe storms and high winds on July 21–22.

August 10

In the morning, the President traveled to Louisville, KY. In the afternoon, he traveled to Chicago, IL, and in the evening, he traveled to San Francisco, CA.

August 11

In the afternoon, the President traveled to Los Angeles, CA, and in the evening, he departed for Washington, DC, arriving early the next morning.

August 12

In the morning, the President met with members of the national security team and the foreign policy team concerning the Embassy bombings in Kenya and Tanzania. He also met with representatives from the National Economic Council and the National Security Council concerning the international economic situation and Russia.

The President announced the recess appointment of William Lacy Swing as Ambassador to the Democratic Republic of the Congo.

The President announced the recess appointment of David Gordon Carpenter as Assistant Secretary of State for Diplomatic Security and Director of the Office of Foreign Missions, with the rank of Ambassador.

The President declared a major disaster in Wisconsin and ordered Federal aid to supplement State and local recovery efforts in the area struck by severe storms and flooding beginning on August 5 and continuing.

August 13

In the morning, the President and Hillary Clinton traveled to Andrews Air Force Base, MD, where they met with family members of American victims of the Embassy bombing in Kenya. In the afternoon, the President and Hillary Clinton returned to Washington, DC.

August 14

The President announced his intention to appoint Birch Bayh, Allen H. Schechter, and Carolyn Matano Yang as members of the J. William Fulbright Foreign Scholarship Board.

August 16

In the evening, the President had a telephone conversation with Prime Minister Tony Blair of the

United Kingdom regarding the situation in Northern Ireland.

August 17

In the afternoon, the President testified before the Independent Counsel's grand jury by video hookup from the Map Room at the White House.

August 18

In the morning, the President met with foreign policy advisers to discuss Russia, Northern Ireland, east Africa, the Balkans, and Iraq.

In the afternoon, the President and Hillary and Chelsea Clinton traveled to Martha's Vineyard, MA, for a vacation.

August 19

The President had a telephone conversation with National Security Adviser Samuel Berger concerning foreign policy issues.

In the evening, the President and Hillary and Chelsea Clinton celebrated the President's birthday with the Vernon Jordan family at a private residence.

Later in the evening, the President had a telephone conversation with Vice President Al Gore.

August 20

In the morning, the President had telephone conversations with foreign policy advisers.

In the afternoon, the President returned to Washington, DC. While en route aboard Air Force One, he had a telephone conversation with House Speaker Newt Gingrich, Senate Majority Leader Trent Lott, and Senate Minority Leader Thomas A. Daschle.

August 21

In the morning, the President met with the national security team concerning the military action against terrorist sites in Afghanistan and Sudan and the overall effort to combat terrorism internationally. He also had telephone conversations with Prime Minister Nawaz Sharif of Pakistan and Prime Minister Binyamin Netanyahu of Israel concerning the military action.

In the evening, the President traveled to Martha's Vineyard, MA.

August 24

In the morning, the President was briefed by National Security Adviser Samuel Berger on developments in Russia, the President's upcoming visit to Russia, and the U.S. military action against terrorist sites in Afghanistan and Sudan.

August 25

In the morning, the President had a telephone conversation with President Boris Yeltsin of Russia concerning the Russian economic situation, the upcoming summit, and the U.S. military action against terrorist sites in Afghanistan and Sudan.

August 26

The President announced his intention to appoint Edward Schuh as Chair of the Board for International Food and Agricultural Development.

The President declared a major disaster in Texas and ordered Federal aid to supplement State and local recovery efforts in the area struck by Tropical Storm Charley beginning on August 22 and continuing.

August 27

In the morning, the President traveled from Martha's Vineyard to Worcester, MA. In the afternoon, he returned to Martha's Vineyard.

The President declared a major disaster in North Carolina and ordered Federal aid to supplement State and local recovery efforts in the area struck by Hurricane Bonnie on August 25 and continuing.

August 28

In the morning, the President participated in a conference call with Vice President Al Gore, the national security and economic teams, and Deputy Secretary of State Strobe Talbott concerning the President's upcoming visit to Russia.

The White House announced the President's intention to nominate Michael Sullivan to be Ambassador to Ireland.

August 30

In the morning, the President and Hillary Clinton departed for Washington, DC, arriving in the afternoon.

August 31

In the morning, the President traveled to Herndon, VA, and in the afternoon, he returned to Washington, DC. Later, the President and Hillary Clinton traveled to Moscow, Russia, arriving the following morning.

September 1

In the morning, the President participated in a wreath-laying ceremony at the Tomb of the Unknown Soldier at the Kremlin. Later, he presented the members of the U.S. delegation to President Boris Yeltsin of Russia in the Presidential Study at the Kremlin, after which the two Presidents had a separate meeting.

In the afternoon, the President had a working luncheon with President Yeltsin in the Presidential Living Room at the Kremlin. Later, the President and Hillary Clinton met with American business leaders at Moscow State University.

In the evening, the President and Hillary Clinton attended an official dinner hosted by President Yeltsin in Catherine Hall at the Kremlin.

The President announced his intention to appoint Roy A. Stein as Commissioner of the Great Lakes Fisheries Commission.

September 2

In the morning, the President met with President Yeltsin in the Presidential Study at the Kremlin.

September 3

In the morning, the President traveled to Belfast, Northern Ireland. Later, he met with First Minister David Trimble and Deputy First Minister Seamus Mallon of the Northern Ireland Assembly in Room 106 of the Parliament Building.

In the afternoon, the President and Hillary Clinton traveled to Omagh, Northern Ireland. In the evening, they participated in a wreath-laying ceremony on Market Street. Later, they traveled to Armagh, Northern Ireland, and then to Dublin, Ireland.

The President announced his intention to nominate Joseph Swerdzewski to be General Counsel at the Federal Labor Relations Authority.

The President announced his intention to nominate Anita K. Jones, Pamela A. Ferguson, and Robert C. Richardson to be members of the National Science Board, National Science Foundation.

September 4

In the evening, the President and Hillary Clinton traveled to Shannon, Ireland.

The President declared a major disaster in South Carolina and ordered Federal aid to supplement State and local recovery efforts in the area struck by Hurricane Bonnie on August 25–September 1.

The President declared a major disaster in Virginia and ordered Federal aid to supplement Commonwealth and local recovery efforts in the area struck by Hurricane Bonnie on August 25–September 1.

The President declared a major disaster in Florida and ordered Federal aid to supplement State and local recovery efforts in the area struck by Hurricane Earl on September 3.

September 5

In the morning, the President and Hillary Clinton traveled to Limerick, Ireland. In the evening, they returned to Shannon, Ireland, and then to Washington, DC.

September 8

In the afternoon, the President traveled to Silver Spring, MD, and later returned to Washington, DC.

In the evening, the President had a telephone conversation with St. Louis Cardinals first baseman Mark McGwire, to congratulate him on breaking the Major League Baseball single-season home run record with his 62d home run earlier in the evening.

September 9

In the morning, the President met with several Democratic Members of the House of Representatives in the Yellow Oval Room in the Residence. Later, the President traveled to Orlando, FL, where upon his arrival he met with Tim Forneris, the Busch Stadium groundskeeper who retrieved Mark McGwire's record-breaking home run ball.

In the evening, the President traveled to Miami, FL, and later returned to Washington, DC, arriving after midnight.

The President announced his intention to nominate T.J. Glauthier to be Deputy Secretary of Energy.

The President announced his intention to nominate Herbert Lee Buchanan III to be Assistant Secretary of the Navy for Research, Development, and Acquisition.

The President announced his intention to nominate Harold Hongju Koh to be Assistant Secretary of State for Democracy, Human Rights, and Labor.

The President announced his intention to nominate B. Lynn Pascoe to be Ambassador to Malaysia.

The White House announced that the President directed a drawdown of $20 million from the U.S. Emergency Refugee and Migration Assistance Fund to provide relief to refugees and displaced persons at risk due to the crisis in Kosovo.

September 10

In the morning, the President met with Democratic Members of the Senate in the Yellow Oval Room in the Residence.

In an afternoon ceremony in the Oval Office, the President received diplomatic credentials from Ambassadors James Bolger of New Zealand, Alexander Philon of Greece, Zalman Shoval of Israel, Vang Rattanagong of Laos, Arlette Conzemius-Paccoud of Luxembourg, Mario Lopes da Rosa of Guinea-Bissau, Sonia Merlyn Johnny of Saint Lucia, Philip Dimitrov of Bulgaria, Erato Kozakou-Marcoullis of Cyprus, William Howard Stixrud Herrera of Guatemala, Damodar Prasad Gautam of Nepal, and Alexis Reyn of Belgium.

In the evening, the President met with his Cabinet in the Yellow Oval Room in the Residence.

The President announced his intention to nominate Rand Beers to be Assistant Secretary of State for International Narcotics and Law Enforcement Affairs.

The President announced his intention to nominate Jeh Charles Johnson to be General Counsel for the Air Force.

The President announced his intention to nominate C. David Welch to be Assistant Secretary of State for International Organization Affairs.

The President announced his intention to designate Van B. Honeycutt as Chair of the President's National Security Telecommunications Advisory Committee.

The White House announced that the President appointed David Leavy as Special Assistant to the President, Deputy Press Secretary, and Senior Director for Public Affairs at the National Security Council.

The White House announced that the President invited President Andres Pastrana of Colombia for a state visit on October 28.

September 11

The President announced his intention to nominate Peter F. Romero to be Assistant Secretary of State for Inter-American Affairs.

The President announced his intention to nominate Craig Gordon Dunkerley for the rank of Ambassador during his tenure of service as Special Envoy for Conventional Forces in Europe.

The President announced his intention to nominate Richard Danzig to be Secretary of the Navy.

The President declared a major disaster in New York and ordered Federal aid to supplement State and local recovery efforts in the area struck by severe storms and high winds on September 7.

September 14

In the morning, the President and Hillary Clinton traveled to New York City. In an afternoon ceremony at the Waldorf Astoria Hotel, the President awarded the Presidential Medal of Freedom to Zachary Fisher for his philanthropic work for Armed Forces service members, veterans, and their families.

In the late evening, the President and Hillary Clinton returned to Washington, DC, arriving after midnight.

September 15

In the afternoon, the President had a telephone conversation with Chicago Cubs outfielder Sammy Sosa to congratulate him on his 62d home run, which tied the new Major League Baseball single-season home run record.

The White House announced that the President will travel to Illinois, California, and Texas on September 25–27.

September 16

In the morning, the President had meetings with President Václav Havel of the Czech Republic in the Oval Office and in the Cabinet Room.

The President announced his intention to nominate Gordon Davidson and Cleo Parker Robinson to be members of the National Council on the Arts.

September 17

In the morning, the President traveled to Cincinnati, OH. In the evening, he traveled to Boston, MA, and later returned to Washington, DC.

The President announced his intention to appoint Clarence V. Monin as a member of the Amtrak Reform Council.

September 18

The President announced his intention to nominate Bill Richardson to be U.S. Representative for the 42d Session of the International Atomic Energy Agency General Conference.

The President announced his intention to nominate Rose Eilene Gottemoeller to be Assistant Secretary for Nonproliferation and National Security at the Department of Energy.

The President announced his intention to nominate M. John Berry to be Assistant Secretary for Policy, Management, and Budget at the Department of the Interior.

The President announced his intention to appoint Richard N. Gardner and Dean R. O'Hare as members

of the Advisory Committee for Trade Policy and Negotiation.

September 20

In the morning, the President attended a brunch for Representative Donald M. Payne of New Jersey aboard the cruise ship *Spirit of Washington* at Pier 4 in Southwest Washington, DC.

In the early evening, the President and Hillary Clinton traveled to New York City, where the President met with Prime Minister Romano Prodi of Italy at the Waldorf Astoria Hotel.

September 21

The President announced his intention to nominate David Michaels to be Assistant Secretary for Environment, Safety, and Health at the Department of Energy.

The President announced his intention to nominate Eljay B. Bowron to be Inspector General of the Department of the Interior.

The President announced his intention to nominate William B. Bader to be Associate Director of Educational and Cultural Affairs at the U.S. Information Agency.

The President declared an emergency in the U.S. Virgin Islands and ordered Federal aid to supplement territory and local recovery efforts in the area struck by Hurricane Georges on September 21 and continuing.

The President declared an emergency in Puerto Rico and ordered Federal aid to supplement Commonwealth and local recovery efforts in the area struck by Hurricane Georges on September 21 and continuing.

The White House announced that Prime Minister Viktor Orban of Hungary will make a working visit to Washington on October 7.

September 22

In the afternoon, the President returned to Washington, DC.

September 23

In the morning, the President met with President Nelson Mandela of South Africa in the President's Study.

In the afternoon, the President had separate meetings with Head of State Abdulsalam Abubakar of Nigeria and Prime Minister Goh Chok Tong of Singapore in the Oval Office.

The President announced his intention to appoint Daniel L. Doctoroff as a member of the Board of Trustees of the Woodrow Wilson International Center for Scholars.

The President declared a major disaster in Texas and ordered Federal aid to supplement State and local recovery efforts in the area struck by severe storms and flooding associated with Tropical Storm Frances beginning on September 9 and continuing.

The President declared a major disaster in Louisiana and ordered Federal aid to supplement State and local recovery efforts in the area struck by Tropical Storm Frances beginning on September 9 and continuing.

September 24

In the afternoon, the President hosted a working luncheon for Crown Prince Abdullah of Saudi Arabia in the Old Family Dining Room. Following the luncheon, the President had telephone conversations with Chairman Yasser Arafat of the Palestinian Authority and Prime Minister Binyamin Netanyahu of Israel to discuss the Middle East peace process.

The White House announced that the President will meet at the White House with Prime Minister Netanyahu on September 28 and with Chairman Arafat later that week.

The President announced his intention to nominate William Clifford Smith to be a Commissioner on the Mississippi River Commission.

The President announced his intention to nominate C. Donald Johnson, Jr., for the rank of Ambassador during his tenure of service as Chief Textile Negotiator.

The President announced his intention to nominate the following individuals to be members of the National Science Board:

Luis Sequeira;
Chang-Lin Tien;
George Langford;
Maxine L. Savitz; and
Joseph Miller.

The President declared a major disaster in the U.S. Virgin Islands and ordered Federal aid to supplement territory and local recovery efforts in the area struck by Hurricane Georges on September 19–22.

The President declared a major disaster in Puerto Rico and ordered Federal aid to supplement Commonwealth and local recovery efforts in the area struck by Hurricane Georges on September 20–22.

September 25

In the morning, the President traveled to Chicago, IL. In the early evening, he traveled to San Jose, CA.

The President announced his intention to appoint Jack Quinn as a member of the Board of Directors of the Federal National Mortgage Association (Fannie Mae).

The President declared an emergency in Florida and ordered Federal aid to supplement State and local recovery efforts in the area struck by Hurricane Georges on September 22 and continuing.

The President announced the creation of the White House Task Force on the 2002 Olympic and Paralympic Games, an interagency effort to coordinate the extensive Federal activities involved in the planning and operation of the Salt Lake City winter games.

September 26

In the evening, the President traveled from San Jose, CA, to Los Angeles, CA.

September 27

In the morning, the President traveled to San Antonio, TX, and in the late afternoon, he traveled to Houston, TX. In the evening, he returned to Washington, DC, arriving after midnight.

September 28

The President declared a major disaster in Florida and ordered Federal aid to supplement State and local recovery efforts in the area struck by Hurricane Georges on September 25 and continuing.

The President declared an emergency in Alabama and ordered Federal aid to supplement State and local recovery efforts in the area struck by Hurricane Georges beginning on September 28 and continuing.

The President declared an emergency in Mississippi and ordered Federal aid to supplement State and local recovery efforts in the area struck by Hurricane Georges on September 28 and continuing.

The President announced that he authorized the Federal Emergency Management Agency to provide direct Federal assistance to Louisiana at 100 percent Federal funding for the first 72 hours for damage relating to Hurricane Georges.

September 29

In the morning, the President met with Chairman Yasser Arafat of the Palestinian Authority in the Oval Office. Later, he met with National Security Adviser Samuel Berger and Minister of Foreign Affairs Tang Jiaxuan of China in the Oval Office.

The President announced his intention to nominate Albert S. Jacquez to be Administrator of the Saint Lawrence Seaway Development Corporation at the Department of Transportation.

The President announced his intention to nominate Ashish Sen to be Director of the Bureau of Transportation Statistics at the Department of Transportation.

The President announced his intention to nominate Ira G. Peppercorn to be Director of the Office of Multifamily Housing Assistance Restructuring at the Department of Housing and Urban Development.

The President announced his intention to nominate Isadore Rosenthal to be a member of the Chemical Safety and Hazard Investigation Board.

The President announced his intention to nominate Jeffrey S. Merrifield to be a member of the Nuclear Regulatory Commission.

The President announced his intention to appoint F. Duane Ackerman to the President's Export Council.

September 30

In the morning, in the Oval Office, the President received the final report of the Assassination Records Review Board.

The President announced his intention to nominate Kenneth W. Kizer to be Under Secretary for Health at the Department of Veterans Affairs.

The President announced his intention to nominate Richard A. Grafmeyer and Gerald M. Shea to be members of the Social Security Advisory Board.

The President declared a major disaster in Alabama and ordered Federal aid to supplement State and local recovery efforts in the area struck by Hurricane Georges on September 25 and continuing.

The White House announced that the President will travel to Los Angeles, CA, and San Francisco, CA, on October 20–21, and that he will travel to Fayetteville, AR, to attend the dedication ceremony for the Northwest Regional Airport on November 6.

October 1

The President announced his intention to nominate Phyllis K. Fong to be Inspector General of the Small Business Administration.

The President declared a major disaster in Mississippi and ordered Federal aid to supplement State and local recovery efforts in the area struck by Hurricane Georges on September 25 and continuing.

October 2

In the morning, the President traveled to Cleveland, OH. In the afternoon, he traveled to Philadelphia, PA, and in the evening, he returned to Washington, DC.

The President announced his intention to nominate Maria Borrero to be Director of the Office for Victims of Crime at the Justice Department.

The President announced his intention to nominate Edward J. Gleiman to be Chair and Commissioner and Dana B. Covington to be Commissioner of the Postal Rate Commission.

The President announced his intention to appoint Eugene A. Ludwig as a member of the Advisory Council on Historic Preservation.

The White House announced that the President will meet with Chancellor-elect Gerhard Schroeder of Germany at the White House on October 9.

October 5

In the morning, the President had a telephone conversation with President Boris Yeltsin of Russia concerning the situation in Kosovo.

In the afternoon, the President met with Senate Minority Leader Thomas A. Daschle and House Minority Leader Richard A. Gephardt in the Oval Office.

The President announced his intention to nominate John Austin Moran to be a Commissioner of the Federal Maritime Commission.

The President announced his intention to nominate Stephen Hadley and Zalmay Khalilzad to be members of the Board of Directors of the U.S. Institute of Peace.

The President announced his intention to nominate John F. Walsh to be a member of the U.S. Postal Service Board of Governors.

The President announced his intention to nominate David M. Walker to be Comptroller of the United States at the General Accounting Office.

The President announced his intention to nominate Andrea Kidd Taylor to be a member of the Chemical Safety and Hazard Investigation Board.

The President announced his intention to appoint Lee R. Seeman to be a member of the Commission for the Preservation of America's Heritage Abroad.

The President declared a major disaster in Washington State and ordered Federal aid to supplement State and local recovery efforts in the area struck by severe storms and flooding on May 26–29.

October 6

In the morning, the President had a telephone conversation with Prime Minister Tony Blair of the United Kingdom concerning the situation in Kosovo and the international economic situation.

Later in the morning, the President met with President Carlos Menem of Argentina at the Marriott Wardman Park Hotel.

The President announced his intention to nominate Kay Kelley Arnold to be a member of the Board of Directors of the Inter-American Foundation.

The President announced his intention to nominate Timothy F. Geithner to be Under Secretary of the Treasury for International Affairs.

The President announced his intention to nominate Edwin M. Truman to be Assistant Secretary of the Treasury for International Affairs.

The President announced his intention to nominate Donnie R. Marshall to be Deputy Administrator of the Drug Enforcement Administration.

The President announced his intention to appoint Ralph B. Everett to the rank of Ambassador during his tenure of service as the Chair of the U.S. delegation to the 1998 International Telecommunication Union Plenipotentiary Conference.

October 7

In the afternoon, the President had a telephone conversation with President Fernando Cardoso of Brazil to congratulate Mr. Cardoso on his reelection and brief him on the October 6 economic meetings in Washington, DC. Later, the President met with Representative Vic Fazio, chairman of the House Democratic caucus, in the Oval Office.

The President announced his intention to nominate Harold J. Creel, Jr., to be a Commissioner on the Federal Maritime Commission.

October 8

The President announced his intention to nominate Gary L. Visscher to be a member of the Occupational Safety and Health Review Commission.

The President announced his intention to nominate Gary Gensler to be Under Secretary of the Treasury for Domestic Finance.

The President announced his intention to nominate Kenneth M. Bresnahan to be Chief Financial Officer at the Labor Department.

The President announced his intention to nominate Kathleen M. Gillespie to be a Commissioner on the Equal Employment Opportunity Commission.

October 9

In the afternoon, the President had a working luncheon with Chancellor-elect Gerhard Schroeder of Germany in the Old Family Dining Room.

Later, the President met with Presidents Alberto Fujimori of Peru and Jamil Mahuad Witt of Ecuador in the Oval Office, concerning settlement of the long-standing border dispute between the two countries.

The President announced the nomination of Timothy Fields, Jr., to be Assistant Administrator for Solid Waste at the Environmental Protection Agency.

The President announced his intention to nominate James M. Simon, Jr., to be Assistant Director for Administration at the Central Intelligence Agency.

The President announced his intention to nominate Arthur Naparstek to be a member of the Board of Directors of the Corporation for National and Community Service.

The White House announced that the President and Secretary of State Madeleine Albright will host Prime Minister Binyamin Netanyahu of Israel, Chairman Yasser Arafat of the Palestinian Authority, and their respective delegations at a summit opening on October 15 at the Wye River Conference Center in Maryland.

The White House announced that the President will travel to Guam, Malaysia, Japan, and Korea on November 13–22, to attend the annual Asia-Pacific Economic Cooperation Summit and then consult with two of the United States' closest allies in the region on the global economic situation, regional security, and other bilateral issues.

October 12

In the afternoon, the President traveled to New York City, and in the evening, he returned to Washington, DC, arriving after midnight.

October 13

In the afternoon, the President traveled to Silver Spring, MD, and later returned to Washington, DC.

October 14

The President announced his intention to nominate John C. Truesdale to be a member of the National Labor Relations Board.

The President declared a major disaster in Missouri and ordered Federal aid to supplement State and local recovery efforts in the area struck by severe storms and flooding on October 4–11.

The President declared a major disaster in Kansas and ordered Federal aid to supplement State and local recovery efforts in the area struck by severe storms, flooding, and tornadoes on October 1–8.

October 15

In the afternoon, the President traveled to Queenstown, MD. In the evening, he held separate meetings with Chairman Yasser Arafat of the Palestinian Authority and Prime Minister Binyamin Netanyahu of Israel in the Commons Room at the Aspen Institute Wye River Conference Center.

Later, the President hosted a dinner for the leaders and their delegations in the Carmichael House at the conference center. In the late evening, the President returned to Washington, DC.

October 16

In the morning, the President traveled to Chicago, IL, and in the evening, he returned to Washington, DC.

The President declared a major disaster in Washington State and ordered Federal aid to supplement State and local recovery efforts in the area struck by a landslide in Kelso on March 6 and continuing.

October 17

In the morning, the President traveled to Queenstown, MD.

In the afternoon, the President met with Chairman Yasser Arafat of the Palestinian Authority in Houghton House at the Aspen Institute Wye River Conference Center. Later, he had a telephone conversation with President Hosni Mubarak of Egypt concerning the Middle East peace process.

In the late afternoon, the President met with Prime Minister Binyamin Netanyahu of Israel in the River House at the conference center. In the evening, he returned to Washington, DC.

October 18

In the morning, the President traveled to Queenstown, MD.

In the afternoon, the President had a luncheon with Prime Minister Netanyahu at the Aspen Institute Wye River Conference Center. Later, he met twice with Chairman Arafat at the conference center.

After midnight, the President returned to Washington, DC.

October 19

In the afternoon, the President traveled to Queenstown, MD, where he met separately with Prime Minister Netanyahu and Chairman Arafat at the Aspen Institute Wye River Conference Center throughout the day. In the evening, he returned to Washington, DC, arriving after midnight.

The President announced his intention to appoint Marc B. Nathanson as Chair of the Broadcasting Board of Governors for the International Broadcasting Bureau.

The President announced his intention to appoint Eli Segal and Jose Villarreal as members of the Board of Directors of the Federal National Mortgage Association (Fannie Mae).

The President declared a major disaster in Missouri and ordered Federal aid to supplement State and local recovery efforts in the area struck by severe storms and flooding on July 10–31.

October 20

In the afternoon, the President traveled to Queenstown, MD, where he met with King Hussein I of Jordan at Carmichael Farm near the Aspen Institute Wye River Conference Center. He then returned to the conference center, where he had a telephone conversation with President Hosni Mubarak of Egypt, to update Mr. Mubarak on the peace process and to extend condolences concerning the train wreck near Alexandria, Egypt. Later, the President met with Chairman Arafat at the conference center.

In the evening, the President met with Prime Minister Netanyahu at the conference center until after midnight. The President then returned to Washington, DC.

The White House announced that the President will travel to Cape Canaveral, FL, to attend the launch of the space shuttle *Discovery* at the Kennedy Space Center on October 29.

The White House also announced that the President will travel to New York City on October 30.

October 21

The President announced his intention to nominate Douglas L. Miller to be a member of the Federal Housing Finance Board.

The President declared a major disaster in Texas and ordered Federal aid to supplement State and local recovery efforts in the area struck by severe storms, flooding, and tornadoes beginning on October 17 and continuing.

The White House announced that Prime Minister Janez Drnovsek of Slovenia will make a working visit to Washington, DC, on November 4.

October 22

In the morning, the President traveled to Queenstown, MD, where he met with Prime Minister Netanyahu and Chairman Arafat in the main dining room at the Aspen Institute Wye River Conference Center.

The President announced the recess appointment of Frederick L. Feinstein as General Counsel of the National Labor Relations Board.

October 23

In the afternoon, the President returned to Washington, DC.

The President announced his intention to appoint Zvi Kastenbaum as a member of the Commission for the Preservation of America's Heritage Abroad.

October 24

In the afternoon, the President traveled to Los Angeles, CA, and in the evening, he traveled to San Francisco, CA.

October 25

In the morning, the President had separate telephone conversations with King Hassan II of Morocco, President Hosni Mubarak of Egypt, Crown Prince Abdullah of Saudi Arabia, and Prime Minister Tony Blair of the United Kingdom on the Wye River Middle East peace talks.

In the afternoon, the President returned to Washington, DC, arriving after midnight.

October 27

In an afternoon ceremony in the Oval Office, the President received diplomatic credentials from Ambassadors Genaro Arriagada of Chile, Geza Jeszenszky of Hungary, Luis Alberto Moreno of Colombia, and Amilcar Spencer Lopes of Cape Verde.

October 29

In the morning, the President and Hillary Clinton traveled to Cape Canaveral, FL.

In the afternoon, the President awarded the Presidential Medal of Freedom to former Representative Dante B. Fascell in the Conference Room of the ATOM Building at the John F. Kennedy Space Center.

In the evening, the President traveled to West Palm Beach, FL, and later returned to Washington, DC.

The President announced his intention to appoint Anita Freedman as a member of the Commission for the Preservation of America's Heritage Abroad.

October 30

In the morning, the President traveled to New York City, and in the evening, he returned to Washington, DC.

The President announced his intention to appoint Myron M. Cherry as Arbitrator, International Center for the Settlement of Investment Disputes.

The President announced his intention to appoint James K. Huhta as a member of the Advisory Council on Historic Preservation.

The President announced his intention to appoint the following individuals as members of the Commission on Drug-Free Communities:

Marilyn Culp;
Thomas Dortch;
Ruby Hearn;
Jessica Hulsey;
Scott King;
Charles Larson;
Henry Lozano;
Claire McCaskill;
Mary Ann Solberg;
Carol Stone; and
Hope Taft.

October 31

In the morning, the President traveled to Falls Church, VA, and later returned to Washington, DC.

November 1

In the morning, the President traveled to Baltimore, MD, and in the afternoon, he returned to Washington, DC.

November 2

In the morning, the President participated in a radio conference call with African-American leaders and celebrities.

November 3

The President announced his intention to appoint Stephen J. Moses as a member of the Board of Trustees of the Christopher Columbus Fellowship Foundation.

November 4

In the morning, the President met with Prime Minister Janez Drnovsek of Slovenia in the Oval Office.

November 5

The President declared a major disaster in Kansas and ordered Federal aid to supplement State and local recovery efforts in the area struck by severe storms and flooding on October 30 and continuing.

The White House announced that President Joaquim Alberto Chissano of Mozambique will make a working visit to Washington, DC, on November 30.

November 6

In the afternoon, the President traveled to Highfill, AR, where he participated in the dedication ceremony for the Northwest Arkansas Regional Airport. In the evening, he returned to Washington, DC.

The President declared a major disaster in Florida and ordered Federal aid to supplement State and local recovery efforts in the area struck by Tropical Storm Mitch on November 4–5.

November 7

In the morning, the President and Hillary Clinton went to Camp David, MD. In the evening, the President had a telephone conversation with the crew of the space shuttle *Discovery* orbiting the Earth.

The White House announced that the President decided to ease sanctions against India and Pakistan in response to positive steps both countries have taken to address nonproliferation concerns following their nuclear tests in May.

November 9

In the morning, the President and Hillary Clinton returned to the White House.

The President announced his intention to appoint Leo Mullin to the President's Export Council.

The White House announced that the President asked former National Security Adviser Anthony Lake to return to the Horn of Africa to assist in talks concerning the border dispute between Ethiopia and Eritrea.

November 10

In the morning, the President met with House Minority Leader Richard A. Gephardt in the Oval Office.

In the afternoon, the President met with the Dalai Lama in the Map Room.

November 11

In the morning, the President traveled to Arlington, VA, and in the afternoon, he returned to Washington, DC.

November 13

The President announced his intention to appoint Irving J. Stolberg as a member of the Commission for the Preservation of America's Heritage Abroad.

The President announced the recess appointment of Montie R. Deer as Chair of the National Indian Gaming Commission.

November 14

In the afternoon, the President met with his national security team to discuss the situation in Iraq.

The White House announced that the President hopes to complete the Japan, South Korea, and Guam portions of his planned Asia trip, but that Vice President Al Gore will represent the United States at the APEC Summit in Malaysia.

November 17

The President announced his intention to nominate Gary S. Guzy to be General Counsel at the Environmental Protection Agency.

The President announced the following winners of the 1998 Malcolm Baldrige National Quality Award: Boeing Airlift and Tanker Programs, Long Beach, CA; Solar Turbines, Inc., San Diego, CA; and Texas Nameplate Co., Inc., Dallas, TX.

November 18

In the morning, the President traveled to Tokyo, Japan, arriving at approximately midnight.

The White House announced that the President will welcome His Holiness Pope John Paul II to the United States for a pastoral visit to St. Louis, MO, on January 26, 1999.

November 19

In the afternoon, the President met with Emperor Akihito and Empress Michiko of Japan at the Imperial Residence.

The President announced his intention to appoint Irene Rosenberg Wurtzel as a member of the President's Commission on the Celebration of Women in American History.

November 20

In the evening, the President traveled to Seoul, South Korea.

November 21

In the afternoon, the President toured the National Folk Museum in Seoul.

The President announced his intention to appoint Steven M. Hilton, Frank B. Moore, and William G. Simpson as members of the American Battle Monuments Commission.

The President announced his intention to appoint Jon S. Corzine and Donna Cochran McLarty to the Board of Trustees of the John F. Kennedy Center for the Performing Arts.

The President announced his intention to designate Maj. Gen. Roland Lajoie, USA (Ret.), as the Co-Chair of the U.S.-Russian Joint Commission on POW/MIA's, effective December 1.

November 22

In the morning, the President traveled to Yongsan, South Korea, where he attended church services at a U.S. military facility.

In the afternoon, the President visited the Korean Training Center, 25 miles northeast of Seoul, where he reviewed M–2 Bradley fighting vehicles and M–1 Abrams tanks with U.S. and South Korean troops. In a brief ceremony, he promoted Private First Class (E3) Matt E. Prickett to Specialist (E4).

Later, the President led troops in singing "Happy Birthday" to Command Sgt. Maj. Charles Thomas. He then had a "Meals-Ready-to-Eat" lunch with troops in the mess tent.

In the evening, the President returned to Seoul.

November 23

In the morning, the President traveled to Guam. After arriving in the afternoon, he visited the World War II memorial at the War in the Pacific National Historic Park.

Later, the President returned to Washington, DC, arriving the following evening.

November 25

In the morning, the President and Hillary Clinton went to Camp David, MD, for the Thanksgiving holiday.

The White House announced that the President asked Secretary of Health and Human Services Donna E. Shalala to visit Lebanon as his personal representative.

November 27

In the evening, the President and Hillary Clinton returned to the White House.

The White House announced that the President will travel to Israel, Gaza, and the West Bank on December 12–15.

November 30

In the morning, the President met with Chairman Yasser Arafat of the Palestinian Authority in the Oval Office at the White House.

The President appointed Jenny Luray as Deputy Assistant to the President and Director of Women's Initiatives and Outreach.

The President announced his intention to appoint Edgar M. Bronfman as Chair and the following individuals as members of the Advisory Commission on Holocaust Assets in the United States:

Roman Kent;
Ira Leesfield;
Jehuda Reinharz;
Margaret Richardson;
Patricia Schroeder;
William Singer;
Cecil Williams;
Stuart Eizenstat, Department of State;
Patrick Henry, Department of the Army;
James Robinson, Department of Justice; and
Neal Wolin, Department of the Treasury.

December 1

In the morning, the President met with President Joaquim Alberto Chissano of Mozambique in the Oval Office at the White House.

December 2

In the afternoon, the President hosted a working lunch for Prime Minister Nawaz Sharif of Pakistan in the Old Family Dining Room at the White House.

The President announced his intention to appoint Randy W. Deitering as Executive Director of the President's Foreign Intelligence Advisory Board.

The President announced his intention to appoint James H. Schiff as a member of the Advisory Committee of the John F. Kennedy Center for the Performing Arts.

The President announced his intention to appoint Angus S. King, Jr., as a member of the Advisory Council on Historic Preservation.

The President announced his intention to appoint Thomas S. Williamson, Jr., as a member of the District of Columbia Judicial Nomination Commission.

December 3

In the morning, the President traveled to Newport, RI. In the afternoon, he returned to Washington, DC.

The President announced his intention to appoint Bob Armstrong as Chair and W.F. (Rick) Cronk as a member of the National Recreation Lakes Study Commission.

The President announced his intention to appoint the following individuals as members of the U.S. Holocaust Memorial Council:

Roberta Bennett;
Michael Berenbaum;
Charles Kushner;
William Lerach;
Susan Bass Levin;
Arnold Lorber;
Jack Rosen;
Dennis Ross;

Gerald Sigal; and
Arnold Thaler.

December 4

The President announced his intention to appoint Lee Haney as a member of the President's Council on Physical Fitness and Sports.

The President announced his intention to appoint Frederick N. Frank and Ginger E. Lew as members of the Board of Directors of the Czech and Slovak American Enterprise Fund.

The President announced the recess appointment of G. Edward DeSeve as Deputy Director for Management in the Office of Management and Budget. Mr. DeSeve was nominated on March 13. The President intends to resubmit his nomination when the 106th Congress convenes.

The President announced the recess appointment of John C. Truesdale as Chair and member of the National Labor Relations Board. Mr. Truesdale was nominated on October 14. The President intends to resubmit his nomination when the 106th Congress convenes.

December 5

In the morning, the President traveled to Wynne, AR, and in the evening, he returned to Washington, DC.

December 7

In the evening, the President and Hillary Clinton hosted a congressional ball on the State Floor at the White House.

The President announced the recess appointment of Timothy F. Geithner as Under Secretary of the Treasury for International Affairs. Mr. Geithner was nominated on October 8. The President intends to resubmit his nomination when the 106th Congress convenes.

The President announced the recess appointment of Edwin M. Truman as Assistant Secretary of the Treasury for International Affairs. Mr. Truman was nominated on October 8. The President intends to resubmit his nomination when the 106th Congress convenes.

The President announced the recess appointment of John D. Hawke, Jr., as Comptroller of the Currency at the Department of the Treasury. Mr. Hawke was nominated on July 11. The President intends to resubmit his nomination when the 106th Congress convenes.

The White House announced that the President will host the White House Conference on Social Security on December 8 at the Marriott Wardman Park Hotel and December 9 at Blair House.

December 8

In the morning, the President and Hillary Clinton traveled to Nashville, TN, where they attended a memorial service for former Senator Albert Gore, Sr. In the afternoon, they returned to Washington, DC.

Later, the President met with Counsel to the President Charles F.C. Ruff to review Mr. Ruff's upcoming testimony before the House Judiciary Committee.

The President announced his intention to nominate John T. Spotila to be Administrator of the Office of Information and Regulatory Affairs in the Office of Management and Budget.

The President announced his intention to appoint the following individuals as members of the National Cancer Advisory Board:

Dr. Elmer Huerta;
Dr. Susan M. Love;
Mayor James McGreevey of Woodbridge Township, NJ;
Dr. Arthur Nienhuis;
Dr. Larry Norton; and
Dr. Amelie Ramirez.

The President announced the 1998 recipients of the Nation's highest science and technology honors:

National Medal of Science

Bruce N. Ames;
Don L. Anderson;
John N. Bahcall;
John W. Cahn;
Cathleen S. Morawetz;
Janet D. Rowley;
Eli Ruckenstein;
George M. Whitesides; and
William Julius Wilson.

National Medal of Technology

Denton A. Cooley, M.D.;
team award jointly to Kenneth L. Thompson and Dennis M. Ritchie (Lucent Technologies' Bell Laboratories);
team award jointly to Robert T. Fraley, Robert B. Horsch, Ernest G. Jaworski, and Stephen G. Rogers (Monsanto);
Biogen, Inc.; and
Bristol-Myers Squibb Co.

The White House announced that the President has invited President Carlos Menem of Argentina for a state visit on January 11, 1999.

December 9

In the afternoon, the President participated in the closing session of the White House Conference on Social Security with Members of Congress and senior administration officials at Blair House.

December 10

The White House announced that President Jacques Chirac of France has accepted the President's invitation for an official working visit on February 19, 1999.

December 12

In the morning, the President and Hillary and Chelsea Clinton traveled to Tel Aviv, Israel, arriving in the evening.

December 13

In the morning, the President and Hillary Clinton had breakfast with Prime Minister Binyamin Netanyahu of Israel and his wife, Sarah, in the Presidential Suite at the Jerusalem Hilton Hotel. Later, the President greeted U.S. Cabinet members and Members of Congress in the Aqua Restaurant at the hotel.

Later, the President met with Prime Minister Netanyahu in the Cabinet Room at Mr. Netanyahu's office complex.

In the afternoon, the President and Hillary Clinton visited the grave of assassinated Prime Minister Yitzhak Rabin at Mount Herzl in Jerusalem.

Later, the President met with President Ezer Weizman of Israel in the Jerusalem Room at Beit Hanassi, President Weizman's residence.

December 14

In the morning, the President and Hillary Clinton traveled to Gaza City, Gaza. Upon their arrival, they toured the main terminal of Gaza International Airport with Chairman Yasser Arafat of the Palestinian Authority and his wife, Shua.

In the afternoon, the President met with Chairman Arafat in the Cabinet Room at Mr. Arafat's office complex.

In the early evening, the President returned to Jerusalem, Israel.

December 15

In the morning, the President traveled to Bethlehem. Later, the President and Hillary Clinton toured the Church of the Nativity with Chairman Arafat and his wife, Shua.

In the afternoon, the President and Hillary and Chelsea Clinton participated in a Christmas tree lighting at the Church of the Nativity. Later, they traveled to Masada, where they toured the historic site.

In the late afternoon, the President and Hillary Clinton traveled to Tel Aviv. In the evening, they returned to Washington, DC.

December 16

In the morning, the President met with the national security team concerning the situation in Iraq.

In the afternoon, the President met with Representative Amo Houghton concerning the upcoming vote on the articles of impeachment.

The President announced his intention to appoint Anita Ray Arnold, Robert B. Barnett, Anita (Buffy) Cafritz, and Kenneth M. Duberstein to the Board of Trustees of the John F. Kennedy Center for the Performing Arts.

December 17

In the morning in the Oval Office, the President was briefed on the military operations in Iraq by Chairman of the Joint Chiefs of Staff Gen. Henry H. Shelton, Defense Secretary William S. Cohen, and the national security team. Later in the day, the President had separate telephone conversations concerning the ongoing operations in Iraq with Prime Minister Binyamin Netanyahu of Israel, President Hosni Mubarak of Egypt, King Hussein I of Jordan, and President Jacques Chirac of France, as well as Speaker of the House Newt Gingrich, House Majority Leader Bob Livingston, Senate Majority Leader Trent Lott, Senate Minority Leader Thomas A. Daschle, and House Minority Leader Richard A. Gephardt.

The White House announced that the President released $102.2 million of emergency supplemental funding included for the Army Corps of Engineers in the Omnibus Consolidated and Emergency Supplemental Appropriations Act, 1999, to carry out critical dredging activities and other repairs needed to maintain safe channels at navigation projects in Louisiana, Alabama, Mississippi, Florida, and Puerto Rico that were damaged by Hurricane Georges and other tropical storms.

December 18

In the morning, the President met with Representative Christopher Shays.

In the afternoon, in the Cabinet Room, the President met with Chancellor Viktor Klima of Austria, in his capacity as President of the European Council, and President Jacques Santer of the European Commission.

The President announced the recess appointment of William Clyburn, Jr., as a member of the Surface Transportation Board. Mr. Clyburn was nominated on September 2, 1997. The President intends to resubmit his nomination when the 106th Congress convenes.

The President announced the recess appointment of Albert S. Jacquez as Administrator of the Saint Lawrence Seaway Development Corporation at the Department of Transportation. Mr. Jacquez was nominated on September 29, 1998. The President intends to resubmit his nomination when the 106th Congress convenes.

December 20

In the afternoon and evening, the President and Hillary Clinton hosted holiday receptions in the Map Room.

December 21

In the morning, the President met with Senator Ted Kennedy in the Oval Office.

In the afternoon, the President traveled to Arlington, VA, and later returned to Washington, DC.

The President announced his intention to appoint Lawrence Rogers as Acting Inspector General for Tax Administration at the Department of the Treasury.

The President announced his intention to appoint Ellen Hart Peña as a member of the President's Council on Physical Fitness and Sports.

The President announced his intention to appoint Susan Weikers Volchok as a member of the U.S. Holocaust Memorial Council.

December 22

In the afternoon, the President and Hillary Clinton hosted a Christmas celebration for children in the East Room.

December 23

In the morning, the President traveled to Baltimore, MD, and in the afternoon, he returned to Washington, DC.

December 24

In the afternoon, the President had telephone conversations with U.S. military personnel to wish them a merry Christmas.

The President announced his intention to nominate J. Brian Atwood to be Ambassador to Brazil.

December 29

The White House announced that the President will travel to Mexico and Central America on February 10–15, 1999.

December 30

In the afternoon, the President and Hillary and Chelsea Clinton traveled to Hilton Head, SC, where they participated in the Renaissance Weekend retreat.

The President announced his intention to nominate Hassan Nemazee to be Ambassador to Argentina.

Appendix B—Nominations Submitted to the Senate

The following list does not include promotions of members of the Uniformed Services, nominations to the Service Academies, or nominations of Foreign Service officers.

Submitted July 7

Carolyn H. Becraft,
of Virginia, to be an Assistant Secretary of the Navy, vice Bernard Daniel Rostker.

Ruby Butler DeMesme,
of Virginia, to be an Assistant Secretary of the Air Force, vice Rodney A. Coleman, resigned.

Bert T. Edwards,
of Maryland, to be Chief Financial Officer, Department of State, vice Richard L. Greene, resigned.

Patrick T. Henry,
of Virginia, to be an Assistant Secretary of the Army, vice Sara E. Lister, resigned.

Joseph H. Melrose, Jr.,
of Pennsylvania, a career member of the Senior Foreign Service, class of Minister-Counselor, to be Ambassador Extraordinary and Plenipotentiary of the United States of America to the Republic of Sierra Leone.

John Shattuck,
of Massachusetts, to be Ambassador Extraordinary and Plenipotentiary of the United States of America to the Czech Republic.

David G. Carpenter,
of Virginia, to be an Assistant Secretary of State, vice Eric James Boswell, resigned.

David G. Carpenter,
of Virginia, to be Director of the Office of Foreign Missions, and to have the rank of Ambassador during his tenure of service, vice Eric James Boswell.

Robert Patrick Finn,
of New York, a career member of the Senior Foreign Service, class of Counselor, to be Ambassador Extraordinary and Plenipotentiary of the United States of America to the Republic of Tajikistan.

Richard Henry Jones,
of Nebraska, a career member of the Senior Foreign Service, class of Minister-Counselor, to be Ambassador Extraordinary and Plenipotentiary of the United States of America to the Republic of Kazakhstan.

Charles F. Kartman,
of Virginia, a career member of the Senior Foreign Service, class of Minister-Counselor, for the rank of Ambassador during his tenure of service as Special Envoy for the Korean Peace Talks.

Kathryn Dee Robinson,
of Tennessee, a career member of the Senior Foreign Service, class of Minister-Counselor, to be Ambassador Extraordinary and Plenipotentiary of the United States of America to the Republic of Ghana.

Submitted July 9

Simon Ferro,
of Florida, to be Ambassador Extraordinary and Plenipotentiary of the United States of America to the Republic of Panama.

D. Bambi Kraus,
of the District of Columbia, to be a member of the board of Trustees of the Institute of American Indian and Alaska Native Culture and Arts Development for a term expiring May 19, 2004, vice Marion G. Chambers.

William B. Milam,
of California, a career member of the Senior Foreign Service, class of Minister-Counselor, to be Ambassador Extraordinary and Plenipotentiary of the United States of America to the Islamic Republic of Pakistan.

Withdrawn July 9

Carlos Pascual,
of the District of Columbia, to be an Assistant Administrator of the Agency for International Development, vice Thomas A. Dine, resigned, which was sent to the Senate on June 11, 1998.

Submitted July 10

William B. Traxler, Jr.,
of South Carolina, to be United States Circuit Judge for the Fourth Circuit, vice Donald Stuart Russell, deceased.

Mary Beth West,
of the District of Columbia, a career member of the Senior Executive Service, for the rank of Ambassador during her tenure of service as Deputy Assistant Secretary of State for Oceans, Fisheries, and Space.

Withdrawn July 10

Mary Beth West,
of the District of Columbia, a career member of the Senior Executive Service, for the rank of Ambassador during her tenure of service as Deputy Assistant Secretary of State for Oceans and Space, which was sent to the Senate on February 24, 1998.

Submitted July 13

Christopher W.S. Ross,
of California, a career member of the Senior Foreign Service, class of Career Minister, for the rank of Ambassador during his tenure of service as Coordinator for Counterterrorism.

Karl J. Sandstrom,
of Washington, to be a member of the Federal Election Commission for a term expiring April 30, 2001, vice John Warren McGarry, term expired.

Submitted July 14

Bill Richardson,
of New Mexico, to be Secretary of Energy, vice Federico Peña, resigned.

Submitted July 15

Charles R. Rawls,
of North Carolina, to be General Counsel of the Department of Agriculture, vice James S. Gilliland, resigned.

George McDade Staples,
of Kentucky, a career member of the Senior Foreign Service, class of Counselor, to be Ambassador Extraordinary and Plenipotentiary of the United States of America to the Republic of Rwanda.

Robert M. Walker,
of Tennessee, to be Deputy Director of the Federal Emergency Management Agency, vice Harvey G. Ryland, resigned.

Submitted July 16

John D. Hawke, Jr.,
of the District of Columbia, to be Comptroller of the Currency for a term of 5 years, vice Eugene Allan Ludwig, resigned.

John Melvin Yates,
of Washington, a career member of the Senior Foreign Service, class of Minister-Counselor, to be Ambassador Extraordinary and Plenipotentiary of the United States of America to the Republic of Cameroon.

Submitted July 17

Romulo L. Diaz, Jr.,
of the District of Columbia, to be an Assistant Administrator of the Environmental Protection Agency, vice Jonathan Z. Cannon, resigned.

J. Charles Fox,
of Maryland, to be an Assistant Administrator of the Environmental Protection Agency, vice Mary Delores Nichols.

Paul Steven Miller,
of California, to be a member of the Equal Employment Opportunity Commission for the remainder of the term expiring July 1, 1999, vice Gilbert F. Casellas, resigned.

John J. Pikarski, Jr.,
of Illinois, to be a member of the Board of Directors of the Overseas Private Investment Corporation for the remainder of the term expiring December 17, 1998, vice Gerald S. McGowan.

John J. Pikarski, Jr.,
of Illinois, to be a member of the Board of Directors of the Overseas Private Investment Corporation for a term expiring December 17, 2001 (reappointment).

Submitted July 21

Leigh A. Bradley,
of Virginia, to be General Counsel, Department of Veterans Affairs, vice Mary Lou Keener, resigned.

Scott Richard Lassar,
of Illinois, to be U.S. Attorney for the Northern District of Illinois, vice James B. Burns, resigned.

Sylvia M. Mathews,
of West Virginia, to be Deputy Director of the Office of Management and Budget, vice Jacob Joseph Lew.

Robert C. Randolph,
of Washington, to be an Assistant Administrator of the Agency for International Development, vice Margaret V.W. Carpenter, resigned.

Bernard Daniel Rostker,
of Virginia, to be Under Secretary of the Army, vice Robert M. Walker.

James A. Tassone,
of Florida, to be U.S. Marshal for the Southern District of Florida for the term of 4 years, vice Daniel J. Horgan.

John Melvin Yates,
of Washington, a career member of the Senior Foreign Service, class of Minister-Counselor, to be Ambassador Extraordinary and Plenipotentiary of the United States of America to the Republic of Equatorial Guinea.

Ritajean Hartung Butterworth,
of Washington, to be a member of the Board of Directors of the Corporation for Public Broadcasting for a term expiring January 31, 2004 (reappointment).

Thomasina V. Rogers,
of Maryland, to be a member of the Occupational Safety and Health Review Commission for a term expiring April 27, 2003, vice Velma Montoya, term expired.

Withdrawn July 21

Thomasina V. Rogers,
of Maryland, to be a member of the Occupational Safety and Health Review Commission for the remainder of the term expiring April 27, 2001, vice Daniel Guttman, which was sent to the Senate on June 24, 1998.

Bernard Daniel Rostker,
of Virginia, to be an Assistant Secretary of Defense, vice Frederick F.Y. Pang, resigned, which was sent to the Senate on April 2, 1998.

Submitted July 22

James E. Newsome,
of Mississippi, to be a Commissioner of the Commodity Futures Trading Commission for the term expiring June 19, 2001, vice Joseph B. Dial, term expired.

Howard Hikaru Tagomori,
of Hawaii, to be U.S. Marshal for the District of Hawaii for the term of 4 years, vice Annette L. Kent, term expired.

Submitted July 29

James M. Bodner,
of Virginia, to be Deputy Under Secretary of Defense for Policy, vice Jan Lodal.

Eugene A. Conti, Jr.,
of Maryland, to be an Assistant Secretary of Transportation, vice Frank Eugene Kruesi, resigned.

Gregory H. Friedman,
of Colorado, to be Inspector General of the Department of Energy, vice John C. Layton, resigned.

Harry Litman,
of Pennsylvania, to be U.S. Attorney for the Western District of Pennsylvania, vice Frederick W. Thieman, resigned.

Paul M. Warner,
of Utah, to be U.S. Attorney for the District of Utah, vice Scott M. Matheson, resigned.

Patricia T. Montoya,
of New Mexico, to be Commissioner on Children, Youth, and Families, Department of Health and Human Services, vice Olivia A. Golden, resigned.

Norine E. Noonan,
of Florida, to be an Assistant Administrator of the Environmental Protection Agency, vice Robert James Huggett, resigned.

Submitted July 30

Francis M. Allegra,
of Virginia, to be a Judge of the U.S. Court of Federal Claims for a term of 15 years, vice Lawrence S. Margolis, term expired.

Legrome D. Davis,
of Pennsylvania, to be U.S. District Judge for the Eastern District of Pennsylvania, vice Edmund V. Ludwig, retired.

Harold Lucas,
of New Jersey, to be an Assistant Secretary of Housing and Urban Development, vice Kevin Emanuel Marchman.

Stephen W. Preston,
of the District of Columbia, to be General Counsel of the Department of the Navy, vice Steven S. Honigman.

Joseph R. Biden, Jr.,
of Delaware, to be a Representative of the United States of America to the 53d Session of the General Assembly of the United Nations.

Cardell Cooper,
of New Jersey, to be an Assistant Secretary of Housing and Urban Development, vice Saul N. Ramirez, Jr.

Montie R. Deer,
of Kansas, to be Chairman of the National Indian Gaming Commission for the term of 3 years, vice Tadd Johnson.

Rod Grams,
of Minnesota, to be a Representative of the United States of America to the 53d Session of the General Assembly of the United Nations.

Charles G. Groat,
of Texas, to be Director of the U.S. Geological Survey, vice Gordon P. Eaton, resigned.

Claiborne deB. Pell,
of Rhode Island, to be an Alternate Representative of the United States of America to the 53d Session of the General Assembly of the United Nations.

Michael M. Reyna,
of California, to be a member of the Farm Credit Administration Board, Farm Credit Administration, for

a term expiring May 21, 2004, vice Doyle Cook, term expired.

John U. Sepulveda,
of New York to be Deputy Director of the Office of Personnel Management, vice Janice R. Lachance.

Joseph E. Stevens, Jr.,
of Missouri, to be a member of the Board of Trustees of the Harry S. Truman Scholarship Foundation for a term expiring December 10, 2003 (reappointment).

David C. Williams,
of Maryland, to be Inspector General, Department of the Treasury, vice Valerie Lau, resigned.

Withdrawn July 30

Daryl L. Jones,
of Florida, to be Secretary of the Air Force, vice Sheila Widnall, resigned, which was sent to the Senate on October 22, 1997.

Tadd Johnson,
of Minnesota, to be Chair of the National Indian Gaming Commission for the term of 3 years, vice Harold A. Monteau, resigned, which was sent to the Senate on July 31, 1997, and September 2, 1997.

Cardell Cooper,
of New Jersey, to be Assistant Administrator, Office of Solid Waste, Environmental Protection Agency, vice Elliott Pearson Laws, resigned, which was sent to the Senate on September 2, 1997.

Submitted July 31

Terrence L. Bracy,
of Virginia, to be a member of the Board of Trustees of the Morris K. Udall Scholarship and Excellence in National Environmental Policy Foundation for a term expiring October 6, 2004 (reappointment).

Withdrawn July 31

Michael D. Schattman,
of Texas, to be U.S. District Judge for the Northern District of Texas, vice Harold Barefoot Sanders, Jr., retired, which was sent to the Senate on March 21, 1997.

Submitted August 31

Peter J. Basso, Jr.,
of Maryland, to be an Assistant Secretary of Transportation, vice Louise Frankel Stoll, resigned.

H. Dean Buttram, Jr.,
of Alabama, to be U.S. District Judge for the Northern District of Alabama, vice Robert B. Propst, retired.

Inge Prytz Johnson,
of Alabama, to be U.S. District Judge for the Northern District of Alabama, vice James H. Hancock, retired.

Submitted September 2

Robert Bruce Green,
of Oklahoma, to be U.S. Attorney for the Eastern District of Oklahoma for the term of 4 years, vice John W. Raley, Jr., retired.

Mary A. Ryan,
of Texas, a career member of the Senior Foreign Service, class of Career Minister, for the personal rank of Career Ambassador in recognition of especially distinguished service over a sustained period.

Submitted September 3

Pamela A. Ferguson,
of Iowa, to be a member of the National Science Board, National Science Foundation, for a term expiring May 10, 2004, vice Shirley Mahaley Malcom, term expired.

Anita K. Jones,
of Virginia, to be a member of the National Science Board, Nation Science Foundation, for a term expiring May 10, 2004, vice F. Albert Cotton, term expired.

Robert C. Richardson,
of New York, to be a member of the National Science Board, National Science Foundation, for a term expiring May 10, 2004, vice James L. Powell, term expired.

Joseph Swerdzewski,
of Colorado, to be General Counsel of the Federal Labor Relations Authority for a term of 5 years (reappointment).

Submitted September 9

David G. Carpenter,
of Virginia, to be Director of the Office of Foreign Missions, and to have the rank of Ambassador during his tenure of service, vice Eric James Boswell, to which position he was appointed during the last recess of the Senate.

David G. Carpenter,
of Virginia, to be an Assistant Secretary of State, vice Eric James Boswell, resigned, to which position he was appointed during the last recess of the Senate.

Margaret B. Seymour,
of South Carolina, to be U.S. District Judge for the District of South Carolina, vice William B. Traxler, Jr.

William Lacy Swing,
of North Carolina, a career member of the Senior Foreign Service, class of Career Minister, to be Ambassador Extraordinary and Plenipotentiary of the

United States of America to the Democratic Republic of the Congo, to which position he was appointed during the last recess of the Senate.

Submitted September 10

Herbert Lee Buchanan III,
of Virginia, to be an Assistant Secretary of the Navy, vice John Wade Douglass.

T.J. Glauthier,
of California, to be Deputy Secretary of Energy, vice Elizabeth Anne Moler.

Harold Hongju Koh,
of Connecticut, to be Assistant Secretary of State for Democracy, Human Rights, and Labor, vice John Shattuck.

B. Lynn Pascoe,
of Virginia, a career member of the Senior Foreign Service, class of Minister-Counselor, to be Ambassador Extraordinary and Plenipotentiary of the United States of America to Malaysia.

Submitted September 11

Craig Gordon Dunkerley,
of Massachusetts, a career member of the Senior Foreign Service, class of Minister-Counselor, for the rank of Ambassador during his tenure of Service as Special Envoy for Conventional Forces in Europe.

Submitted September 14

Richard Danzig,
of the District of Columbia, to be Secretary of the Navy, vice John H. Dalton, resigned.

Submitted September 16

William J. Hibbler,
of Illinois, to be U.S. District Judge for the Northern District of Illinois, vice James H. Alesia, retired.

Matthew F. Kennelly,
of Illinois, to be U.S. District Judge for the Northern District of Illinois, vice Paul E. Plunkett, retired.

Submitted September 18

Bill Richardson,
of New Mexico, to be the Representative of the United States of America to the Forty-second Session of the General Conference of the International Atomic Energy Agency.

Submitted September 22

William B. Bader,
of New Jersey, to be an Associate Director of the U.S. Information Agency, vice John P. Loiello.

Eljay B. Bowron,
of Michigan, to be Inspector General, Department of the Interior, vice Wilma A. Lewis, resigned.

Gordon Davidson,
of California, to be a member of the National Council on the Arts for a term expiring September 3, 2004, vice Kenneth Malerman Jarin, term expired.

Vivian Lowery Derryck,
an Assistant Administrator of the Agency for International Development, to be a member of the Board of Directors of the African Development Foundation for a term expiring September 27, 2003, vice John F. Hicks, Sr., term expired.

Rose Eilene Gottemoeller,
of Virginia, to be an Assistant Secretary of Energy (Non-Proliferation and National Security), vice Archer L. Durham, resigned.

David Michaels,
of New York, to be an Assistant Secretary of Energy (Environment, Safety, and Health), vice Tara Jeanne O'Toole, resigned.

Susan E. Rice,
an Assistant Secretary of State, to be a member of the Board of Directors of the African Development Foundation for a term expiring September 27, 2003, vice George Edward Moose, term expired.

Cleo Parker Robinson,
of Colorado, to be a member of the National Council on the Arts for a term expiring September 3, 2004, vice Ira Ronald Feldman, term expired.

Michael J. Sullivan,
of Wyoming, to be Ambassador Extraordinary and Plenipotentiary of the United States of America to Ireland.

Aleta A. Trauger,
of Tennessee, to be U.S. District Judge for the Middle District of Tennessee, vice John T. Nixon, retired.

Submitted September 23

Denise E. O'Donnell,
of New York, to be U.S. Attorney for the Western District of New York for the term of 4 years, vice Patrick H. NeMoyer, resigned.

Submitted September 24

C. Donald Johnson, Jr.,
of Georgia, for the rank of Ambassador during his tenure of service as Chief Textile Negotiator.

William Clifford Smith,
of Lousiana, to be a member of the Mississippi River Commission for a term expiring October 21, 2005, vice Frank H. Walk, term expired.

Submitted September 25

George M. Langford,
of New Hampshire, to be a member of the National
Science Board, National Science Foundation, for a
term expiring May 10, 2004, vice Charles Edward
Hess, term expired.

Joseph A. Miller, Jr.,
of Delaware, to be a member of the National Science
Board, National Science Foundation, for a term expiring May 10, 2004, vice John Hopcroft, term expired.

Maxine L. Savitz,
of California, to be a member of the National Science
Board, National Science Foundation, for a term expiring May 10, 2004, vice Frank H.T. Rhodes, term
expired.

Luis Sequeira,
of Wisconsin, to be a member of the National Science
Board, National Science Foundation, for a term expiring May 10, 2004, vice Ian M. Ross, term expired.

Chang-Lin Tien,
of California, to be a member of the National Science
Board, National Science Foundation, for a term expiring May 10, 2004, vice Richard Neil Zare, term expired.

Submitted September 28

Edward J. Damich,
of Virginia, to be a Judge of the U.S. Court of Federal
Claims for a term of 15 years, vice James F. Merow,
term expired.

Nancy B. Firestone,
of Virginia, to be a Judge of the U.S. Court of Federal
Claims for a term of 15 years, vice Moody R. Tidwell
III, term expired.

Emily Clark Hewitt,
of the District of Columbia, to be a Judge of the
U.S. Court of Federal Claims for a term of 15 years,
vice Robert J. Yock, term expired.

Alex R. Munson,
of the Northern Mariana Islands, to be Judge for
the District Court for the Northern Mariana Islands
for a term of 10 years (reappointment).

Submitted September 29

Albert S. Jacquez,
of California, to be Administrator of the Saint Lawrence Seaway Development Corporation for a term
of 7 years, vice Gail Clements McDonald, resigned.

Jeffrey S. Merrifield,
of New Hampshire, to be a member of the Nuclear
Regulatory Commission for the term expiring June
30, 2002, vice Kenneth C. Rogers, term expired.

Ira G. Peppercorn,
of Indiana, to be Director of the Office of Multifamily
Housing Assistance Restructuring (new position).

Ashish Sen,
of Illinois, to be Director of the Bureau of Transportation Statistics, Department of Transportation, for the
term of 4 years, vice Triruvarur R. Lakshmanan, resigned.

Isadore Rosenthal,
of Pennsylvania, to be a member of the Chemical
Safety and Hazard Investigation Board for a term of
5 years (new position).

Submitted September 30

Kenneth W. Kizer,
of California, to be Under Secretary for Health of
the Department of Veterans Affairs for a term of
4 years (reappointment).

Richard A. Grafmeyer,
of Maryland, to be a member of the Social Security
Advisory Board for the remainder of the term expiring
September 30, 2000, vice Harlan Matthews, resigned.

Gerald M. Shea,
of the District of Columbia, to be a member of the
Social Security Advisory Board for a term expiring
September 30, 2004 (reappointment).

Submitted October 1

Harry J. Bowie,
of Mississippi, to be a member of the Board of Directors of the National Consumer Cooperative Bank for
a term of 3 years, vice Tony Scallon, term expired.

Phyllis K. Fong,
of Maryland, to be Inspector General, Small Business
Administration, vice James F. Hoobler.

Submitted October 5

David M. Walker,
of Georgia, to be Comptroller General of the United
States for a term of 15 years, vice Charles A. Bowsher,
term expired.

Stephen Hadley,
of the District of Columbia, to be a member of the
Board of Directors of the U.S. Institute of Peace
for a term expiring January 19, 1999, vice Mary Louise
Smith, term expired.

Stephen Hadley,
of the District of Columbia, to be a member of the
Board of Directors of the U.S. Institute of Peace
for a term expiring January 19, 2003 (reappointment).

Zalmay Khalilzad,
of Maryland, to be a member of the Board of Directors of the U.S. Institute of Peace for a term expiring January 19, 2001, vice Christopher H. Phillips, resigned.

John A. Moran,
of Virginia, to be a Federal Maritime Commissioner for the term expiring June 30, 2001, vice Ming Hsu, term expired.

Norman A. Mordue,
of New York, to be U.S. District Judge for the Northern District of New York, vice Rosemary S. Pooler, elevated.

Andrea Kidd Taylor,
of Michigan, to be a member of the Chemical Safety and Hazard Investigation Board for a term of 5 years (new position).

John F. Walsh,
of Connecticut, to be a Governor of the U.S. Postal Service for a term expiring December 8, 2006, vice Bert H. Mackie, term expired.

Withdrawn October 5

Mari Carmen Aponte,
of Puerto Rico, to be Ambassador Extraordinary and Plenipotentiary of the United States of America to the Dominican Republic, which was submitted to the Senate on April 28, 1998.

Gus A. Owen,
of California, to be a member of the Surface Transportation Board for a term expiring December 31, 2002 (reappointment), which was sent to the Senate on February 2, 1998.

Submitted October 6

Kay Kelley Arnold,
of Arkansas, to be a member of the Board of Directors of the Inter-American Foundation for a term expiring October 6, 2004, vice Neil H. Offen, term expired.

Donnie R. Marshall,
of Texas, to be Deputy Administrator of Drug Enforcement, vice Stephen H. Greene.

Jose Antonio Perez,
of California, to be U.S. Marshal for the Southern District of California for the term of 4 years, vice Steven Simpson Gregg.

Submitted October 7

Harold J. Creel, Jr.,
of South Carolina, to be a Federal Maritime Commissioner for the term expiring June 30, 2004 (reappointment).

Robert W. Perciasepe,
of Maryland, to be an Assistant Administrator of the Environmental Protection Agency (reappointment).

Submitted October 8

John A. Moran,
of Virginia, to be a Federal Maritime Commissioner for the term expiring June 30, 2000, vice Joe Scroggins, Jr., term expired.

Timothy Fields, Jr.,
of Virginia, to be Assistant Administrator, Office of Solid Waste, Environmental Protection Agency, vice Elliott Pearson Laws, resigned.

Kenneth M. Bresnahan,
of Virginia, to be Chief Financial Officer, Department of Labor, vice Edmundo A. Gonzales, resigned.

Timothy F. Geithner,
of New York, to be an Under Secretary of the Treasury, vice David A. Lipton.

Gary Gensler,
of Maryland, to be an Under Secretary of the Treasury, vice John D. Hawke, Jr.

Edwin M. Truman,
of Maryland, to be a Deputy Under Secretary of the Treasury, vice Timothy F. Geithner.

Withdrawn October 8

John A. Moran,
of Virginia, to be a Federal Maritime Commissioner for the term expiring June 30, 2001, vice Ming Hsu, term expired, which was sent to the Senate on October 5, 1998.

Submitted October 9

Frank J. Guarini,
of New Jersey, to be a Representative of the United States of America to the 52d Session of the General Assembly of the United Nations.

Arthur J. Naparstek,
of Ohio, to be a member of the Board of Directors of the Corporation for National and Community Service for a term expiring October 6, 2003 (reappointment).

James M. Simon, Jr.,
of Alabama, to be Assistant Director of Central Intelligence for Administration (new position).

Jack J. Spitzer,
of Washington, to be Alternate Representative of the United States of America to the 52d Session of the General Assembly of the United Nations.

Submitted October 14

John C. Truesdale,
of Maryland, to be a member of the National Labor Relations Board for the term of 5 years expiring August 27, 2003, vice William B. Gould IV, resigned.

Submitted October 20

Douglas L. Miller,
of South Dakota, to be a Director of the Federal Housing Finance Board for a term expiring February 27, 2002, vice Lawrence U. Costiglio, term expired.

Appendix C—Checklist of White House Press Releases

The following list contains releases of the Office of the Press Secretary which are not included in this book.

Released July 1

Transcript of a press briefing by Press Secretary Mike McCurry and Deputy National Security Adviser Jim Steinberg on the President's visit to China

Released July 2

Transcript of a readout by Press Secretary Mike McCurry to the pool

Fact sheet: Environment Speech and Roundtable

Released July 3

Transcript of remarks to the pool by Press Secretary Mike McCurry and National Security Adviser Samuel Berger

Released July 6

Statement by the Press Secretary: President Clinton Announces Summit Meeting With Russian Federation President Boris Yeltsin

Transcript of a press briefing by National Security Council (NSC) Assistant Press Secretary for Foreign Affairs and Director of Public Affairs Col. P.J. Crowley, Deputy Press Secretary Joe Lockhart, and Deputy Assistant to the President for Health Policy Chris Jennings on Medicare and the President's upcoming visit to Russia

Released July 7

Transcript of a press briefing by Press Secretary Mike McCurry and Deputy Assistant to the President for Health Policy Chris Jennings on compliance with the Health Insurance Portability and Accountability Act

Released July 8

Transcript of a press briefing by Press Secretary Mike McCurry

Transcript of a press briefing by Assistant to the President for Domestic Policy Planning Bruce Reed on efforts to promote gun safety and responsibility

Released July 9

Statement by the Press Secretary: Working Visit With President Sanguinetti of Uruguay

Transcript of a press briefing by Office of National Drug Control Policy Director Barry McCaffrey, Chair-

man of the Partnership for a Drug Free America James Burke, and President of the Advertising Council Ruth Wooden of the national youth antidrug campaign

Released July 10

Transcript of a press briefing by Press Secretary Mike McCurry

Statement by the Press Secretary on the appointment of Carlos E. Pascual as Special Assistant to the President and Senior Director for Russian, Ukrainian, and Eurasian Affairs at the National Security Council

Announcement of nomination for a U.S. Court of Appeals Judge for the Fourth Circuit

Text of the citation read on the award of the Congressional Medal of Honor to Robert R. Ingram

Released July 11

Transcript of a press briefing by National Institute of Justice Director Jeremy Travis and Arrestee Drug Abuse Monitoring Program Director Jack Riley on initiatives on drug abuse and crime [1]

Released July 12

Statement by the Press Secretary: Violence in Northern Ireland

Released July 13

Transcript of a press briefing by Press Secretary Mike McCurry

Released July 14

Transcript of a press briefing by Press Secretary Mike McCurry

Transcript of remarks by Vice President Gore on the Year 2000 conversion computer problem

Transcript of a press briefing by President's Council on Year 2000 Conversion Chair John Koskinen on the Year 2000 conversion computer problem

Released July 15

Transcript of a press briefing by Press Secretary Mike McCurry

Statement by the Press Secretary on investigations by the Russian Government into export control violations

---

[1] This item was made available by the Office of the Press Secretary on July 10, but it was embargoed for release until 10:06 a.m. on July 11.

Statement by the Press Secretary: Congressional Consideration of Legislation to Increase the Number of H–1B Visas

Transcript of a press briefing by Health and Human Services Secretary Donna Shalala on the Patients' Bill of Rights

Released July 16

Transcript of a press briefing by Press Secretary Mike McCurry

Released July 17

Transcript of Press Secretary Mike McCurry's morning press gaggle

Statement by the Press Secretary: State Visit by President Havel of the Czech Republic

Released July 18

Transcript of a press briefing by Secretary of Agriculture Dan Glickman and Agency for International Development Administrator Brian Atwood on the President's radio address

Released July 20

Statement by the Press Secretary: President Clinton Will Visit Ireland and Northern Ireland

Statement by the Press Secretary: IMF Additional Financing for Russia

Announcement of nomination for U.S. Attorney for the Northern District of Illinois

Announcement of nomination for U.S. Marshal for the Southern District of Florida

Released July 21

Transcript of a press briefing by Press Secretary Mike McCurry

Transcript of a press briefing by Health and Human Services Secretary Donna Shalala and Health Care Financing Administrator Nancy-Ann Min DeParle on new nursing home regulations

Released July 22

Transcript of a press briefing by Press Secretary Mike McCurry

Announcement of nomination for U.S. Marshal for the District of Hawaii

Released July 23

Transcript of a press briefing by Press Secretary Mike McCurry

Statement by the Press Secretary: Visit of President Julio Maria Sanguinetti of Uruguay

Statement by the Press Secretary: Execution of Baha'i in Iran

Statement by the Press Secretary on proposed Senate legislation on nursing home care

Released July 24

Transcript of a press briefing by Press Secretary Mike McCurry

Statement by the Press Secretary: President Clinton Names Ambassador Richard L. Morningstar To Be Special Adviser to the President and the Secretary of State for Caspian Basin Energy Diplomacy

Fact sheet: Vital Voices of the Americas: Women in Democracy

Released July 27

Transcript of a press briefing by Deputy Press Secretary Barry Toiv

Released July 28

Transcript of a press briefing by Press Secretary Mike McCurry

Released July 29

Transcript of a press briefing by Press Secretary Mike McCurry

Statement by the Press Secretary: President To Meet With Gerhard Schroeder

Announcement of nomination for U.S. Attorney for the District of Utah

Announcement of nomination for U.S. Attorney for the Western District of Pennsylvania

Released July 30

Transcript of a press briefing by Dayton Duncan, Chairman of the American Heritage Rivers Initiative Advisory Committee, and Elliot Diringer, Assistant Director of Communications for the President's Council on Environmental Quality, on the designation of American Heritage Rivers

Statement by the Press Secretary: National Security Council Staff Realignment

Announcement of nominations for U.S. Court of Federal Claims Judge and U.S. District Judge for the Eastern District of Pennsylvania

Released July 31

Statement by the Press Secretary: Agreement To Protect New Mexico's Scenic Boca Ranch

Released August 3

Transcript of a press briefing by Deputy Press Secretary Barry Toiv

Transcript of a press briefing by NSC Senior Director for Inter-American Affairs Jim Dobbins on the President's meeting with President-elect Andres Pastrana of Colombia

Statement by the Press Secretary: On the Visit of President-Elect Andres Pastrana of Colombia

Released August 4

Transcript of a press briefing by Deputy Press Secretary Barry Toiv

Transcript of a press briefing by Assistant to the President for Domestic Policy Planning Bruce Reed and Labor Secretary Alexis Herman on the anniversary of the Personal Responsibility and Work Opportunity Reconciliation Act of 1996

Released August 5

Transcript of a press briefing by Deputy Press Secretary Barry Toiv and Assistant Press Secretary for Foreign Affairs Col. P.J. Crowley

Statement by the Press Secretary: President Clinton's Meeting with South African Deputy President Thabo Mbeki

Released August 6

Transcript of a press briefing by Deputy Press Secretary Barry Toiv and Assistant Press Secretary for Foreign Affairs Col. P.J. Crowley

Transcript of a press briefing by Assistant to the President for Domestic Policy Planning Bruce Reed and Special Assistant for Domestic Policy Jose Cerda on the proposed extension of the Brady Handgun Violence Prevention Act

Released August 7

Transcript of a press briefing by Deputy Press Secretary Barry Toiv and Assistant Press Secretary for Foreign Affairs Col. P.J. Crowley

Released August 10

Statement by the Press Secretary: Ceremony Marking Return of Remains for the American Citizens Who Lost Their Lives in Kenya

Announcement: President Clinton Welcomes Plan To Strengthen U.S. Leadership in Information Technology

Released August 12

Transcript of a press briefing by Deputy Press Secretary Joe Lockhart and Assistant Press Secretary for Foreign Affairs Col. P.J. Crowley

Released August 13

Transcript of a press briefing by Press Secretary Mike McCurry and Assistant Press Secretary for Foreign Affairs Col. P.J. Crowley

Released August 14

Transcript of a press briefing by Press Secretary Mike McCurry

Released August 17

Transcript of a press gaggle by Press Secretary Mike McCurry

Released August 18

Transcript of a press gaggle by Press Secretary Mike McCurry

Released August 19

Transcript of a press briefing by Press Secretary Mike McCurry

Released August 20

Transcripts of press briefings by Press Secretary Mike McCurry

Transcript of a press briefing by Secretary of State Madeleine Albright and National Security Adviser Samuel Berger on military action against terrorist sites in Afghanistan and Sudan

Released August 21

Transcript of a press briefing by National Security Adviser Samuel Berger and Press Secretary Mike McCurry

Statement by the Press Secretary on the appointment of Kenneth G. Lieberthal as Special Assistant to the President and Senior Director for Asian Affairs at the National Security Council

Released August 22

Transcript of a press briefing by Press Secretary Mike McCurry

Released August 24

Transcript of a press briefing by Press Secretary Mike McCurry

Released August 25

Transcript of a press briefing by Deputy Press Secretary Barry Toiv

Released August 26

Transcript of a press briefing by Deputy Press Secretary Barry Toiv

Statement by the Press Secretary on the appointment of Gregory L. Schulte as Special Assistant to the President and Director for Implementation of the Dayton Accords at the National Security Council

Statement by the Press Secretary: Federal Panel Orders Declassification of Selected Cold War Documents

Released August 28

Transcript of a press briefing by Deputy Press Secretary Barry Toiv

Transcript of a press briefing by National Security Adviser Samuel Berger, Deputy National Security Adviser Jim Steinberg, Deputy Treasury Secretary Larry Summers, and Ambassador at Large for the Newly Independent States Steve Sestanovich on the President's upcoming visit to Russia, Northern Ireland, and Ireland

Released August 29

Statement by the Press Secretary on the Northwest Airlines pilots strike

Announcement: Official Delegation to Russia

Announcement: Official Delegation to Northern Ireland and Ireland

Released August 31

Transcript of a press briefing by Press Secretary Mike McCurry, National Security Adviser Samuel Berger, and National Economic Council Director Gene Sperling on the President's upcoming visit to Russia

Announcement of nominations for U.S. District Judges for the Northern District of Alabama

Released September 1

Transcript of a press briefing by Special Assistant to the President for National Security Affairs Robert Bell, Assistant Secretary of Defense (Strategy and Threat Reduction) Ted Warner, NSC Senior Director for Nonproliferation Gary Samore, and Director of Policy and Regional Affairs for Russia and the New Independent States Debra Cagan on the President's visit to Russia

Transcript of a press briefing by Press Secretary Mike McCurry, Deputy Secretary of State Strobe Talbott, Deputy Treasury Secretary Larry Summers, National Economic Council Director Gene Sperling, and Senator Pete Domenici on the President's visit to Russia

Fact sheet: Plutonium Disposition Statement

Fact sheet: Joint Statement on the Exchange of Information on Missile Launches and Early Warning

Released September 2

Transcript of a press briefing by Deputy National Security Adviser Jim Steinberg and Press Secretary Mike McCurry on the President's visit to Russia

Fact sheet: U.S.-Russian Export Control Cooperation

Announcement of nomination for U.S. Attorney for the Eastern District of Oklahoma

Released September 3

Transcript of a press readout by Press Secretary Mike McCurry

Transcript of a press briefing by Deputy National Security Adviser Jim Steinberg on the President's visit to Northern Ireland

Text of the Plaque Presented to the People of Omagh

Statement by the Press Secretary: Rwanda Tribunal Verdict

Statement by the Press Secretary on the President's decision to send Special Middle East Coordinator Ambassador Dennis Ross back to the region

Released September 4

Transcript of a press briefing by Press Secretary Mike McCurry and Deputy National Security Adviser Jim Steinberg on the President's visit to Ireland

Released September 8

Transcript of a press briefing by Press Secretary Mike McCurry

Released September 9

Statement by the Press Secretary on assistance to Kosovo

Announcement of nomination for U.S. District Judge for the District of South Carolina

Released September 10

Transcript of a press briefing by Press Secretary Mike McCurry

Statement by the Press Secretary on the appointment of David C. Leavy as Special Assistant to the President, Deputy Press Secretary, and Senior Director for Public Affairs at the National Security Council

Statement by the Press Secretary: State Visit of President Pastrana of Colombia

Released September 11

Transcript of a press briefing by Press Secretary Mike McCurry

Transcript of a press briefing by attorney David Kendall and Counsel to the President Charles Ruff on the Independent Counsel's referral to the Congress

Released September 14

Transcript of a press briefing by Treasury Secretary Robert Rubin and National Economic Council Director Gene Sperling on global economic issues

Citation: Presidential Medal of Freedom to Zachary Fisher

Released September 15

Transcript of a press briefing by Press Secretary Mike McCurry

Released September 16

Transcript of a press briefing by Vice President Al Gore, Deputy Chief of Staff John Podesta, Principal Associate Deputy Attorney General Robert Litt, FBI Assistant Director Carolyn Morris, Under Secretary of Commerce William Reinsch, Deputy Secretary of Defense Jim Hamre, and Deputy National Security Adviser Jim Steinberg on updates in encryption policy

Statement by the Press Secretary: Administration Updates Encryption Policy

Fact sheet: Administration Updates Encryption Policy

Statement by the Press Secretary on the Africa trade bill

Announcement of nominations for U.S. District Judges for the Northern District of Illinois

Released September 18

Transcript of a press briefing by Deputy Press Secretary Barry Toiv and Assistant Press Secretary for Foreign Affairs Col. P.J. Crowley

Transcript of a press briefing by National Security Adviser Samuel Berger on the President's upcoming remarks to the United Nations General Assembly

Transcript of a press briefing by Deputy Chief of Staff Maria Echaveste, Small Business Administrator Aida Alvarez, and Rebecca Blank of the Council of Economic Advisers on the President's Initiative on Race

Announcement: Millennium Evening at the White House, "Jazz: An Expression of Democracy"

Released September 21

Transcript of a press briefing by Press Secretary Mike McCurry

Transcript of a press readout by Deputy Press Secretary Joe Lockhart

Transcript of a press briefing by National Security Adviser Samuel Berger on the President's visit to the United Nations

Statement by the Press Secretary on the release of materials relating to the Independent Counsel's investigation

Statement by the Press Secretary: Visit by Prime Minister Orban of Hungary

Announcement on emergency assistance to help farmers in crisis

Released September 22

Transcript of a press briefing by Press Secretary Mike McCurry

Transcript of a press briefing by U.S. Trade Representative Charlene Barshefsky, National Economic Council Director Gene Sperling, Deputy National Security Adviser Jim Steinberg, and Deputy Treasury Secretary Larry Summers on the President's meeting with Prime Minister Keizo Obuchi of Japan

Fact sheet: U.S.-Japan Y2K Cooperation Statement

Announcement of nomination for U.S. District Judge for the Middle District of Tennessee

Announcement of nomination for U.S. Attorney for the Western District of New York

Released September 23

Transcript of a press briefing by Press Secretary Mike McCurry

Statement by the Press Secretary: Meeting With Prime Minister Goh Chok Tong of Singapore

Statement of the Press Secretary: Meeting With Nigerian Head of State Abubakar

Released September 24

Transcript of a press briefing by Press Secretary Mike McCurry

Transcript of a press briefing by Council of Economic Advisers Chair Janet Yellen and National Economic Council Director Gene Sperling on the Census Bureau report on income and poverty

Statement by the Press Secretary: President and First Lady Extend Condolences to Victims of Hurricane Georges

Statement by the Press Secretary: President To Meet With Prime Minister Netanyahu and Chairman Arafat Next Week

Released September 25

Transcript of a press briefing by Deputy Press Secretary Barry Toiv

Statement by the Press Secretary: White House Task Force on 2002 Salt Lake City Olympic and Paralympic Games Established

Statement by James E. Kennedy, Special Adviser to the White House Counsel, on the House Judiciary Committee's decision to release materials relating to the Independent Counsel's investigation

Released September 28

Transcript of a press briefing by Press Secretary Mike McCurry

Transcript of a press briefing by Secretary of State Madeleine Albright on the President's meeting with Prime Minister Binyamin Netanyahu of Israel

Announcement of nominations for three U.S. Court of Federal Claims Judges

Announcement of nomination for U.S. District Judge for the District of the Northern Mariana Islands

Released September 29

Transcript of a press briefing by Press Secretary Mike McCurry

Transcript of a press briefing by Federal Emergency Management Agency Director James Lee Witt on Hurricane Georges

Statement by Treasury Secretary Robert Rubin and Council of Economic Advisers Chair Janet Yellen on the Federal Reserve Board's decisionmaking authority on the Nation's monetary policy and the national economy

Released September 30

Transcript of a press briefing by Press Secretary Mike McCurry

Photo release: The President Meets With the Assassination Records Review Board Members

Released October 1

Transcript of a press briefing by Press Secretary Mike McCurry

Released October 2

Statement by Press Secretary Mike McCurry on the upcoming visit of Chancellor-elect Gerhard Schroeder of Germany

Statement by the Press Secretary: Actions by Iran Against Baha'is

Transcript of remarks by Special Counsel Gregory Craig on the release of materials relating to the Independent Counsel's investigation

Released October 5

Transcript of a press briefing by Press Secretary Joe Lockhart

Transcript of a press briefing by National Economic Council Director Gene Sperling and Deputy Treasury Secretary Larry Summers on initiatives on the international economy

Announcement of nomination for U.S. District Judge for the Northern District of New York

Released October 6

Transcript of a press briefing by Press Secretary Joe Lockhart

Statement by the Press Secretary on the appointment of Robert Malley as Special Assistant to the President for Arab-Israeli Affairs and Director for Near East and South Asian Affairs at the National Security Council

Announcement of nomination for U.S. Marshal for the Southern District of California

Released October 7

Transcript of a press briefing by Press Secretary Joe Lockhart

Announcement of nomination for U.S. Attorney for the District of Minnesota

Announcement of nomination for U.S. Attorney for the District of Rhode Island

Released October 8

Transcript of a press briefing by Press Secretary Joe Lockhart

Statement by the Press Secretary on the appointment of D. Holly Hammonds as Special Assistant to the President for Economic Policy for both the National Economic Council and the National Security Council

Released October 9

Transcript of a press briefing by Press Secretary Joe Lockhart

Transcript of a press briefing by National Economic Council Director Gene Sperling and Assistant to the President for Domestic Policy Planning Bruce Reed on education funding in the budget

Transcript of a press briefing by NSC Senior Director for Inter-American Affairs Jim Dobbins on the President's meeting with President Alberto Fujimori of Peru and President Jamil Mahuad Witt of Ecuador

Statement by the Press Secretary: President Clinton's Meeting With Presidents Fujimori and Mahuad

Fact sheet: Ecuador-Peru Border Dispute

Statement by the Press Secretary: The Washington Summit at Wye River

Statement by the Press Secretary: President Clinton Will Attend APEC Summit

Statement by the Press Secretary announcing that the President will sign H.R. 4558, "Noncitizen Benefit Clarification and Other Technical Amendments Act of 1998"

Released October 10

Transcript of remarks by Chief of Staff Erskine Bowles on the budget

Released October 13

Transcript of a press briefing by Press Secretary Joe Lockhart

Transcript of a press briefing by National Security Adviser Samuel Berger on the situation in Kosovo

Released October 14

Transcript of a press briefing by Press Secretary Joe Lockhart

Transcript of a press briefing by Education Secretary Richard Riley and Associate Attorney General Ray Fisher on the White House Conference on School Safety: Causes and Prevention of Youth Violence

Released October 15

Transcript of a press briefing by Press Secretary Joe Lockhart and State Department Spokesman James Rubin on the Wye River Conference on the Middle East

Transcript of remarks by Prime Minister Binyamin Netanyahu of Israel

Transcript of remarks by Chairman Yasser Arafat of the Palestinian Authority

Transcript of a press briefing by Chief of Staff Erskine Bowles, Deputy Chief of Staff John Podesta, Office of Management and Budget Director Jack Lew, and National Economic Council Director Gene Sperling on the budget agreement

Released October 17

Transcript of a press readout by Press Secretary Joe Lockhart

Released October 19

Transcript of a press readout by Press Secretary Joe Lockhart

Released October 20

Transcript of a press gaggle by Press Secretary Joe Lockhart

Transcript of a press readout by Press Secretary Joe Lockhart

Released October 21

Transcript of a press briefing by Press Secretary Joe Lockhart

Transcript of a press briefing by Deputy U.S. Trade Representative Richard Fisher on the Korea-U.S. auto agreement

Statement by the Press Secretary on the waiver concerning blocked property of terrorist-list states

Statement by the Press Secretary on the upcoming visit of Prime Minister Janez Drnovsek of Slovenia

Statement by the Press Secretary condemning the information legislation passed by the Serbian Parliament in the Federal Republic of Yugoslavia

Released October 22

Transcript of a press readout by Press Secretary Joe Lockhart

Released October 23

Statement by the Press Secretary on congressional inaction on legislation to promote African growth and opportunity

Transcript of a press briefing by Secretary of State Madeleine Albright, National Security Adviser Sandy Berger, and Special Middle East Coordinator Dennis Ross on the Wye River Memorandum

Released October 26

Transcript of a press briefing by Press Secretary Joe Lockhart

Released October 27

Transcript of a press briefing by Press Secretary Joe Lockhart

Released October 29

Text of the citation for the Presidential Medal of Freedom awarded to Dante B. Fascell

Released October 30

Transcript of a press briefing by Press Secretary Joe Lockhart

Transcript of a press briefing by Treasury Secretary Robert Rubin, National Economic Council Director Gene Sperling, and Deputy Treasury Secretary Larry Summers on efforts to deal with the international financial crisis

Transcript of remarks by Special Counsel Gregory Craig on evidence of violations of grand jury secrecy by the Office of the Independent Counsel

Transcript of remarks by Vice President Al Gore on Republican attacks on the President

Advance text of remarks by National Security Adviser Samuel Berger at the National Press Club

Statement by the Press Secretary: 1998 National Security Strategy Report

Released November 2

Transcript of a press briefing by Press Secretary Joe Lockhart

Statement by the Press Secretary on the killing of Brian Service in Belfast, Northern Ireland

Released November 3

Transcript of a press briefing by Press Secretary Joe Lockhart

Released November 4

Transcript of remarks by Chief of Staff John Podesta on newly instituted personnel changes

Transcript of a press briefing by Press Secretary Joe Lockhart

Statement by the Press Secretary: Visit of Slovenian Prime Minister Drnovsek

Released November 5

Transcript of a press briefing by Press Secretary Joe Lockhart

Statement by the Press Secretary announcing emergency funding to support anti- and counter-terrorism activities and recovery from natural disasters

Statement by the Press Secretary: Visit of President Chissano of Mozambique

Transcript of a press briefing by Deputy Chief of Staff Maria Echaveste; NSC Senior Director of Multilateral Affairs Eric Schwartz; Agency for International Development Administrator J. Brian Atwood; Joint Chiefs of Staff Director for Operations Brig. Gen. Robert Wagner; and Deputy Under Secretary of Agriculture Jim Schroeder on the administration's response to Hurricane Mitch

Fact sheet: U.S. Government Response to Hurricane Mitch

Released November 6

Fact sheet: Stepped Up Disaster Assistance for Central America

Released November 7

Statement by the Press Secretary: Easing of Sanctions on India and Pakistan

Released November 9

Transcript of a press briefing by Press Secretary Joe Lockhart

Statement by the Press Secretary: Lake Mission to Ethiopia and Eritrea

Released November 10

Transcript of a press briefing by Press Secretary Joe Lockhart

Statement by the Press Secretary: Meeting With the Dalai Lama

Released November 11

Statement by the Press Secretary: Better Health Care for Our Military, Veterans, and Their Families

Released November 12

Transcript of a press briefing by Press Secretary Joe Lockhart

Transcript of a press briefing by National Economic Council Director Gene Sperling; Deputy National Security Adviser for International Economic Affairs Lael Brainard; NSC Senior Director for Russian, Ukrainian, and Eurasian Affairs Carlos Pascual; and NSC Senior Director for Asian Affairs Kenneth G. Lieberthal on the President's trip to the APEC Summit in Malaysia

Statement by the Press Secretary announcing the signing of the Kyoto Protocol on Climate Change

Fact sheet: President Clinton Announces New Grants for After-School Programs

Released November 13

Transcript of a press briefing by Press Secretary Joe Lockhart

Transcript of a press briefing by Treasury Secretary Robert Rubin and Deputy Treasury Secretary Larry Summers on international economic support for Brazil

Fact sheet: International Support for Brazil

Fact sheet: President Clinton: Honoring and Protecting Our Law Enforcement

Released November 14

Transcript of remarks by Press Secretary Joe Lockhart on the President's decision not to attend the APEC Summit due to the situation in Iraq

Transcript of a press briefing by National Security Adviser Samuel Berger on the situation in Iraq

Statement by the Press Secretary on the agreement in Buenos Aires to settle by the end of 2000 key issues arising from the Kyoto Protocol on Climate Change

Report to the President From Tipper Gore: Presidential Delegation to Central America [1]

Fact sheet: Administration Response to Hurricane Mitch [1]

Released November 15

Transcript of a press briefing by National Security Adviser Samuel Berger, Defense Secretary William Cohen, and Chairman of the Joint Chiefs of Staff Gen. Hugh Shelton on the situation in Iraq

Released November 16

Transcript of a press briefing by Press Secretary Joe Lockhart

Statement by the Press Secretary on the First Lady's announcement of expanded U.S. emergency disaster relief for Central American countries damaged by Hurricane Mitch

Released November 17

Transcript of a press briefing by Press Secretary Lockhart

Transcript of a press briefing by Deputy National Security Adviser Jim Steinberg, National Economic Council Director Gene Sperling, and Deputy Treasury Secretary Larry Summers on the President's upcoming visit to Japan, South Korea, and Guam

Released November 18

Transcript of remarks by Press Secretary Joe Lockhart on the impeachment inquiry

---

[1] These items were embargoed for release until 10:06 a.m.

Statement by the Press Secretary on the upcoming visit of His Holiness Pope John Paul II

Announcement: Official Delegation to Japan, Korea, and Guam

Released November 20

Transcript of a gaggle by Press Secretary Joe Lockhart

Transcript of a press briefing by Press Secretary Joe Lockhart

Transcript of a press briefing by National Economic Council Director Gene Sperling and NSC Senior Director for Asian Affairs Kenneth G. Lieberthal on the President's visit to Japan

Transcript of a press briefing by NSC Director for Asian Affairs Jack Pritchard and Deputy Treasury Secretary Larry Summers on the President's visit to Japan

Transcript of remarks by Special Counsel Gregory Craig on the impeachment inquiry

Released November 21

Transcript of a press briefing by Press Secretary Joe Lockhart

Transcript of a press briefing by National Security Adviser Samuel Berger on the President's visit to South Korea

Statement by the Press Secretary on the National Bioethics Advisory Commission's letter concerning hybrid embryonic stem cell research

Released November 24

Transcript of a press briefing by Press Secretary Joe Lockhart

Released November 25

Statement by the Press Secretary: Visit to Lebanon by the Secretary of Health and Human Services

Released November 27

Statement by the Press Secretary announcing the President's upcoming visit to the Middle East

Released November 30

Transcript of a press briefing by Press Secretary Joe Lockhart

Released December 1

Transcript of a press briefing by Press Secretary Joe Lockhart

Transcript of a press briefing by NSC Senior Director for African Affairs Gayle Smith on the President's discussions with President Joaquim Chissano of Mozambique

Transcript of a press briefing by National AIDS Policy Director Sandra Thurman on AIDS initiatives

Released December 2

Transcript of a press briefing by Press Secretary Joe Lockhart

Transcript of a press briefing by National Economic Council Director Gene Sperling on the upcoming White House Conference on Social Security

Transcript of a press briefing by NSC Senior Director for Near Eastern and South Asian Affairs Bruce Riedel and Assistant Secretary of State for South Asian Affairs Karl Inderfurth on the President's meeting with Prime Minister Nawaz of Pakistan

Released December 3

Statement by the Press Secretary on a letter from the House Judiciary Committee concerning the impeachment inquiry

Released December 4

Transcript of a press briefing by Press Secretary Joe Lockhart

Released December 7

Transcript of a press briefing by Press Secretary Joe Lockhart

Released December 8

Transcript of remarks by Vice President Al Gore at the funeral of his father, former Senator Albert Gore, Sr.

Advance text of remarks by National Security Adviser Samuel Berger at Stanford University

Statement by the Press Secretary: State Visit of President Menem of Argentina

Released December 9

Transcript of a press briefing by Press Secretary Joe Lockhart

Transcript of a press briefing by National Economic Council Director Gene Sperling on the White House Conference on Social Security

Released December 10

Transcript of a press briefing by Press Secretary Joe Lockhart

Transcript of remarks by Special Counsel Gregory Craig on the impeachment inquiry

Statement by the Press Secretary: Visit of French President Chirac

Fact sheet: Human Rights Day 1998 and Eleanor Roosevelt Human Rights Award

Fact sheet: U.S. Efforts To Promote Human Rights and Democracy

Released December 11

Transcript of a press briefing by Press Secretary Joe Lockhart

Transcript of a press briefing by Secretary of State Madeleine Albright and National Security Adviser Samuel Berger on the President's upcoming visit to the Middle East

List of official delegation to the Middle East

Statement by the Press Secretary on the formation of a private sector host committee for the 50th anniversary of NATO

Released December 12

Transcript of remarks by Special Counsel Gregory Craig on the House Judiciary Committee vote on impeachment

Released December 13

Transcript of a press briefing by Press Secretary Joe Lockhart

Transcript of a press briefing by Secretary of State Madeleine Albright and National Security Adviser Samuel Berger on the President's visit to the Middle East

Released December 14

Transcript of remarks by Vice President Al Gore on additional police officers and new technologies

Transcript of a press briefing by Press Secretary Joe Lockhart

Transcript of a press briefing by Secretary of State Madeleine Albright on the President's visit to the Middle East

Released December 15

Transcript of remarks by Vice President Al Gore at the All-American Cities Awards presentation

Transcript of a press briefing by National Security Adviser Samuel Berger on the President's visit to the Middle East

Released December 16

Transcript of remarks by Vice President Al Gore at the Business and Entrepreneurial Roundtable

Transcript of a press briefing by Press Secretary Joe Lockhart

Transcript of remarks by Press Secretary Joe Lockhart announcing the President's address to the Nation on military strikes on Iraq

Transcript of a press briefing by National Security Adviser Samuel Berger on military strikes on Iraq

Released December 17

Transcript of a press briefing by Press Secretary Joe Lockhart

Announcement of nomination for U.S. Attorney for the Central District of California

Released December 18

Transcript of a press briefing by Press Secretary Joe Lockhart

Transcript of a press briefing by Under Secretary of State for Economic, Business, and Agricultural Affairs Stuart Eizenstat and NSC Senior Director for European Affairs Don Bandler on the European Union-U.S. summit

Senior Level Group Report to the U.S.–EU Summit

Released December 19

Transcript of remarks by Press Secretary Joe Lockhart on Representative Bob Livingston's decision to resign

Released December 21

Transcript of remarks by Vice President Al Gore at the Plain Language Awards

Transcript of a press briefing by Press Secretary Joe Lockhart

Statement by the Press Secretary on the Pakistan-U.S. agreement on F–16 aircraft purchased by Pakistan

Released December 22

Transcript of a press briefing by Press Secretary Joe Lockhart

Released December 23

Advance text of remarks by National Security Adviser Samuel Berger at the National Press Club

Released December 29

Statement by the Press Secretary: Presidential Travel to Mexico and Central America

Released December 30

Transcript of a press briefing by Linda Lesourd Lader, Renaissance Institute president, on the President's participation in the Renaissance Weekend retreat in Hilton Head, SC

Fact sheet: Foreign Affairs Reorganization

Released December 31

Transcript of a press briefing by Deputy Press Secretary Amy Weiss

Appendix D—Presidential Documents Published in the Federal Register

This appendix lists Presidential documents released by the Office of the Press Secretary and published in the Federal Register. The texts of the documents are printed in the Federal Register (F.R.) at the citations listed below. The documents are also printed in title 3 of the Code of Federal Regulations and in the Weekly Compilation of Presidential Documents.

PROCLAMATIONS

OTHER PRESIDENTIAL DOCUMENTS

Subject Index

Name Index

Document Categories List